P9-DMD-765

ENCYCLOPAEDIA OF

Indian Cinema

ENCYCLOPAEDIA OF

Indian Cinema

ASHISH RAJADHYAKSHA / PAUL WILLEMEN

BRITISH FILM INSTITUTE

bfi

BFI PUBLISHING

OXFORD UNIVERSITY PRESS
New Delhi
1994

Produced in association with the
National Film Archive of India

First published in 1994 by the
British Film Institute
21 Stephen Street, London W1P 1PL
and
Oxford University Press
YMCA Library Building, Jai Singh Road
Post Box 43, New Delhi 110001

The British Film Institute exists to encourage the development of film, television and video in the United Kingdom, and to promote knowledge, understanding and enjoyment of the culture of the moving image.Its activities include the National Film and Television Archive; the National Film Theatre; the Museum of the Moving Image; the London Film Festival; the production and distribution of film and video; funding and support for regional activities; Library and Information Services; Stills, Posters and Design; Research, Publishing and Education; and the monthly *Sight and Sound* magazine.

Copyright © Ashish Rajadhyaksha and Paul Willemen 1994

All rights reserved

Cover: From the exhibition *Culture of the Streets* (1981) by M. F. Husain.
Reproduced, with grateful thanks, courtesy of M. F. Husain.
The authors respectfully dedicate this book to the memory of D. D. Kosambi.

British Library Cataloguing in Publication Data.
A catalogue record for this book is available from the British Library.

ISBN 0-85170-455-7 (UK)
019-563579-5 (India)

US Cataloguing data available from the Library of Congress.

Designed by Rashmi Chadha, London
Typeset in Great Britain by Method Ltd
Printed in India

CONTENTS

ACKNOWLEDGMENTS

We gratefully acknowledge the financial and institutional assistance of the UNESCO Participation Programme (1989); the Indian Council for Social Science Research, New Delhi; the Charles Wallace (India) Trust; and the Tata Institute of Social Sciences (Bombay).

A number of people have graciously and generously taken the time to give us advice and to comment on parts of the manuscript. Special thanks go to Nasreen Munni Kabir, M. S. S. Pandian, V. A. K. Ranga Rao, Geeta Kapur, Harish Raghuvanshi, P. K. Nair, Shivarama Padikkal and Roma Gibson.
Stills: Courtesy National Film Archive of India; BFI Stills, Posters and Designs; Kamat Foto Flash.

We would not have been able to complete the project without the contributions of the following consultants:
Assamese: Pradip Acharya (Guwahati)
Bengali: Moinak Biswas (Calcutta)
Bhojpuri and Rajasthani: Murlidhar Soni (Jaipur)
Gujarati: Amrit Gangar (Bombay)
Gujarati and Hindi: Harish Raghuvanshi (Surat)
Hindi: Nasreen Munni Kabir (London)
Kannada: Dr Vijaya (Bangalore)
Malayalam: P.K. Nair (Pune), R. Nandakumar (Trivandrum), Neelan (Trichur)
Oriya: Chandidas Mishra (Bombay/Bhubhaneshwar)
Punjabi: B.R. Garg (New Delhi), Anup Singh (London)
Silent Film: V.K. Dharamsey (Bombay)
Tamil: S. Theodore Baskaran (Bangalore)
Telugu: K.N.T. Sastry (Madras)

Research and editorial assistance were generously contributed by:
Bengali: Amitava Sen (Calcutta), Sanjit Choudhury (Calcutta)
Documentary Film: Subhash Chheda, Amrit Gangar (Bombay)
Hindi: Kavita Anand (Bombay), Ganga Mukhi (Bombay)
Kannada: Pushpamala N. (Mysore/Bombay), Sandhya Rao (Bangalore), Raghunandan (Mysore)
Malayalam: M.G. Radhakrishnan (Trivandrum), Koshy A.V. (Trivandrum), Sreekumar K. (Trivandrum) and Manambur Suresh (London)
Marathi: Vasudha Ambiye (Bombay)
Silent Film: Partha Datta (New Delhi)
Tamil: M. Ravi Kumar (Bombay)

This book, quite simply, would never have been realised without the assistance of a number of people within the British Film Institute (Richard Paterson, Bridget Kinally and Imdad Hussain), London, and the National Film Archive of India, Pune. In addition, we should like to thank the Nehru Centre in London, the London International Film Festival and Mr R. Advani of the Oxford University Press, Delhi, for their enthusiasm and support.

We are particularly grateful to Mr P.K. Nair who, in his former capacity as director of the NFAI, was a major supporter of the project and who later became one of its key contributors and authorities. His successor, Suresh Chabria, extended all the facilities of the NFAI for research and remained a source of encouragement and support. On several occasions the staff, especially the film and library staff, went beyond their official function to extend their belief in, and commitment to, this endeavour. Needless to say, none of this book's no doubt numerous shortcomings can be blamed on any of the contributors and advisers who have so generously and unselfishly given their time and expertise to this project.

A special thank you, at the end of a long journey, to all the contributors of this book. Most of them worked on it in their spare time, while holding down full-time jobs as bureaucrats, teachers, journalists or researchers in areas other than the cinema, which makes their involvement, their labour and their patience all the more valuable.

The already complicated problems of gathering information across the expanse of India, the absence of established networks and the, at times, bewildering logistics of simple communication systems, always and in every instance means that in India, people depend on other people, friends and colleagues, families, associates, relatives, acquaintances, to manage - even to set up - functioning systems in lieu of those that do not work. I could not even begin to list the many friends who extended their hospitality to me, those who sent me books and references or put me in touch with others who could help. Most heartfelt thanks must go especially to Geeta Kapur, Vivan Sundaram, Nasreen Munni Kabir, Prof. Mihir Bhattacharya, P. Govinda Pillai, Prof. Hiren Gohain and Dhiru Bhuyan, Tejaswini Niranjana, Anjali Monteiro at the TISS, Sudhir Nandgaonkar and the Prabhat Chitra Mandal, S. V. Rajendra Singh, Girish Kasaravalli, Satyamurthy Anandur, Sushant Mishra, and Subbalakshmi Iyer for her bibliography of Indian cinema. Gerhard Koch kindly advised us on the entry for Franz Osten. Randor Guy graciously reassured us about the accuracy of some of our information on Tamil cinema. Jyoti Bhatt gave us his kind permission to use and also provided the print for the picture illustrating the DMK Film entry. V. K. Dharamsey made available his encyclopaedic memory not only in his area of specialisation, but also to identify hundreds of film stills. Harish Raghuvanshi is largely responsible for whatever degree of accuracy we have achieved in our Hindi filmographies. K. P. R. Nair shot and S. B. Kanhere developed the prints in the NFAI collection for this book. The Films Division Commentary staff gave me access to every Indian language, a unique instance of the unique nature of many of our national institutions. Alaknanda Samarth's support at all times, and especially in that rainy February of 1992 in London at a particularly critical time for this project, as well as Mrs Ranu Biswas' hospitality in Calcutta and R. S. Amladi's for long stretches in Pune, are the kinds of support that, over time, became integral to the logistics of this programme. Above all, Kumar Shahani, Geeta Kapur, Susie Tharu and Parag Amladi provided not just a context for the work, but their own independent standards of achievement to which this book can only aspire.

Thanks also to the library staffs, too numerous to name, of the National Centre For Performing Arts, Mumbai Marathi Granthasangrahalaya, the Centre For Education and Documentation (Bombay), the Kerala Studies section of the Trivandrum University Library, the National Library, Gautam Chattopadhyay at Nandan, the libraries of Chitrabani, Cine Central and Cine Society (Calcutta), the Film and Television Institute of India (Pune), the Suchitra Film Society (Bangalore), the Nehru Memorial Museum and Library (New Delhi), the BFI's library and the India Office Library (London).Information about the careers of Indian directors in Malaysia was kindly supplied by Mr Dato' Haji Mohd Zain Haji Hamzah and Ms Shara Abdul Samad of the National Film Development Corporation Malaysia.

And, finally, Pushpamala, who shared with me every moment of the pain and the pleasure, the discoveries and the journeys of realisation we made together these last five years. The complexity these days of values like 'home' and 'belonging' and 'memory', the interrogation and enablement that is the very stuff of her work, makes her place in the world in which this book has been written perhaps the most special of all.

Ashish Rajadhyaksha
Bombay and London, May 1994

PREFACE

Producing a reference work about a national cinema is an uncomfortable project. Both Seamus Deane, an Irish intellectual, and Aijaz Ahmad, a subcontinental intellectual, have produced powerful critiques of the very attempts to provide a history of any particular art-form presented in terms of a nation-state's achievements. Deane's 'Critical Reflections' in *Artforum* of December 1993 argue the case in relation to the construction of national art histories. Ahmad's 'Indian Literature: Notes Towards the Definition of a Category', reprinted in his book *In Theory* (1992, pp. 243-85), examines the (im)possibility of there being a national Indian literary history. Ahmad points out that, even should the legitimacy of a category such as Indian literature be granted, it would have to encompass such diverse histories in so many languages tied to geographical terrains with constantly shifting boundaries that no single scholar can ever claim to practise the discipline of Indian literature. Furthermore, the territorial unity that can readily, though abusively, be imagined for German, French, US or Japanese cinemas and literatures, cannot be fantasised for India without restricting the terrain and the period to an absurdly small fragment of what should be addressed if we are to make any kind of sense of the cultural productions at issue. To restrict an account of Indian cinema to the geo-temporal frame constituted by the Indian nation-state since Independence or, more accurately, since Partition, would require us to ignore some of the most admirable cinematic achievements realised in Colonial India. More damagingly, it would also rule out any engagement with the longer-term dynamics which have shaped post-Partition Indian cinema.

Even if it were thought to be desirable, a rigorously 'nation-state' approach to Indian cinema, or to any other art-form, cannot be sustained. If we put the emphasis on 'nation' rather than on 'state', the problems only multiply. In other words, there is no sense of Indianness, nor of any other so-called national identity, that precedes the forms of historical and personal experience or expression given shape by particular, geographically and historically bounded institutions of government, by particular state forms providing and enforcing, and always necessarily falling short of doing so homogeneously, both geographical limits and social stratifications. Nations are retroactive, not retrospective constructions to which we are invited, often not very subtly, to adhere. Seamus Deane notes that 'the most essentialist figurings of history ... depend upon making an intersection between time and space, between chronology and territory. This is a feature of all writings that aim to provide a history of an art-form, of a literature, of a nation-state's achievement in the arts.' He goes on to ask:

> Is it possible to write a history of any form of 'Art', is it possible to locate it territorially, and at the same time to be free of any conception of art that is not at least implicitly essentialist and therefore subversive of the very idea and form of history - that is not in some sense either reactionary or ancestral in its longings, and, ultimately, impassive toward all forms of exposition or explanation?

In this respect, a reference work is no different from a historical account: both construct what they purport to address.

Deane's questions go to the heart of the matter. It may not be an accident that an Irish intellectual talking about 'Irish Art' should ask questions so pertinent to the very desire of producing a book about Indian cinema. As an intellectual marked by the history of the island of Ireland, including the experience of colonialism, post-colonialism and Partition, Deane's thought has a definite resonance for those who address notions of Indian art-forms.

A book purporting to be, however imperfectly, an encyclopaedia of Indian cinema(s) cannot but lay itself open to all the criticisms and strictures formulated by Deane and Ahmad. The very enterprise of compiling such an encyclopaedia is inevitably caught in the tensions, fantasies and, not to put too fine a point on it, the traps they describe. If the category of Indian cinema cannot be restricted to post-Partition India, neither can it be made to coincide with any definition of pre-Partition or of Colonial India. Any such definition would include all or part of Pakistan, Bangladesh, Sri Lanka and various bits and pieces of geography beyond the current borders of the Indian Republic. As even a cursory glance at the Chronicle in this book will make clear, the boundaries and composition of the Indian State have varied a great deal over the years. In addition, the cultural divisions between Indian cinema and other cinemas have been very flexible as well. To give but one example, and the editors of this book have debated the point, the beginnings of Iranian sound cinema could be seen as part of Indian cinema: Ardeshir Irani, the director of *Alam Ara*, also made the Persian film, *Dokhtar-e-Lor*, in 1933 in Bombay, commonly acknowledged as the first Iranian sound feature, a fact celebrated in Mohsen Makhmalbaf's *Nassereddin Shah Actor-e-Cinema* (*Once Upon a Time*, Cinema, 1992).

Any account of Indian cinema cannot but run the risk of essentialism as outlined by Deane, including its reactionary aspects and distasteful ancestral longings. To acknowledge, with Ahmad, that the art-form defined under such murky circumstances is always too diverse to fit neatly under any label that could be affixed to it, is small comfort, especially in the context of contemporary India where the risks to life and limb of ancestral longings and essentialism are so gruesomely made real. In such a context, it is not enough simply to point out that India is and always was plural and diverse and that any attempt to essentialise it, to force a coincidence between territory and chronology, or between nation, ethnicity, religion and state, is un-Indian (in the sense that it betrays the struggle which achieved an independent state in the first place) as well as murderous.

Deane tries to think his way through the problem of the 'national' art-form by invoking feminism: 'It is a crux of feminist theory that essentialism must be both accepted and confronted, cancelled, erased.' The present work on Indian cinema tries to learn this lesson from feminist theory, especially as formulated by, for example, Gayatri Chakravorty Spivak, who described the 'risk of essence' in terms of the need to acknowledge 'the dangerousness of something one cannot not use' (*Outside in the Teaching Machine*, London and New York: Routledge, 1993, p. 5).

On the one hand, essentialism is evoked and confronted in the attempt to offer a fairly comprehensive though no doubt seriously flawed introduction to an All-Indian cinematic history. It is All-Indian not in the sense of stressing a common denominator or in the negative acceptance of the term discussed in our entry on All-Indian Film, but in its attempt to engage with the film cultures that arose in all parts of India, rather than to privilege the Hindi cinema, and to give them space in accordance with their relative weight in Indian cinema as a whole. This strategy necessarily involves making judgments, and equally necessarily means getting some of the judgments wrong. So be it. Other books with similar aims will provide correctives and future, corrected and up-dated editions of this first effort will do likewise.

On the other hand, essentialism has been erased both in the critical methodology, which is consciously hybrid and 'impure', calling on knowledges, values and conceptual tools which are neither nativist nor rootlessly cosmopolitan, and in the scope of the book which unapologetically includes artists and films that could be claimed by Pakistan, Bangladesh, Malaysia, Singapore or even by Hollywood (Ellis Duncan) or Germany (Franz Osten, Paul Zils). The editors do not wish to suggest that these other national cinemas would be wrong to make such claims. It is just that Indian cinema is incomprehensible without the inclusion of these artists and films in the same way that Pakistani or Bangladeshi cinema cannot be understood without taking into account the work of artists commonly regarded as part of Indian cinema.

The editors have taken the risk, described by Deane, of 'going through essentialism, re-tracing the journey as much as possible against the grain of the received pattern while still accepting that pattern as the given, in order ultimately to replace it with something that is not essentialist, univocal, coercive'. In this task, we have been greatly helped by many scholars whose expertise in the many different Indian cinemas and cultures has made the editors acutely aware of the impossibility of mastering, unifying and essentialising Indian cinema as an artform coinciding with both a singular territory and chronology.

We have taken 'India', not as a fixed entity, but as a socio-cultural process, a changing and contested set of overlapping frameworks (always temporarily) stabilised by governmental institutions, be they the Colonial administration, the Indian government or the various institutions seeking to regulate (or deregulate, which is only a different type of regulation) the interface between culture and economy within, at any given time, specific territorial limits. In the end, our main guideline has been to focus on the works, the artists and the institutions which have addressed Indian cinema as a constituent part of 'India' as a socio-cultural process.

Paul Willemen
London, May 1994

INTRODUCTION

The sheer gigantomania of India's film factories in Bombay, Madras, Calcutta, Bangalore and Hyderabad, well known collectively as the world's largest national film industry, have attracted increasing, if sometimes bemused, attention from film scholars, not least because of the embarrassment of Indian cinema's near-chronic omission from most global film histories. However, for millions of Indians, wherever they live, a major part of 'India' derives from its movies. Here, the cinema has provided, for the better part of this century, the most readily accessible and sometimes the most inventive forms of mass entertainment. In its scale and pervasiveness, film has borne, often unconsciously, several large burdens, such as the provision of influential paradigms for notions of 'Indianness', 'collectivity' (in the generation of a unprecedented, nationwide, mass-audience), and key terms of reference for the prevailing cultural hegemony. In India, the cinema as apparatus and as industry has spearheaded the development of a culture of indigenous capitalism 'from below', and its achievement in doing so continues to influence and determine newer programming and publishing strategies with the proliferation of television channels and mass-circulation fan magazines.

So, at least, goes conventional wisdom about an admittedly complex, and at times bewilderingly vast, realm of cultural production. The prime example of a mass-entertainment industry operating in a nation-building context has clearly been, to date, Hollywood. Dozens of books have been devoted to speculation about, and a few to analyses of, the relationship between notions of 'America' and the 'America' constructed in the minds of people all over the world, including in the USA, by Hollywood's products. In the early decades of this century, the dime novel, popular journalism and then film provided not only the key narratives for that relationship, but also its most potent archives: a baggage of political fact and cultural revisionism that was accepted, in its entirety, by US television from the 1960s on.

The 'India' of its movies, like Hollywood's 'America', has spawned its own cinephilia, which at its most basic is animated by a distinctive 'insiderism', a buddy-culture of speech and body-language that has now expanded and replicated itself into idioms of popular literature with a dynamic of their own via reviews, gossip columns and magazines, publicity materials, novelisations, autobiographies, interviews and fan-club hagiographies. Unlike Hollywood, however, the dynamic of these idioms has not always intersected with that of official, 'national' India in any predictable fashion. To some extent, as Paul Willemen's *Preface* shows, this has to do with 'the national' itself, as ideology and as institution, as State and as imaginary motherland. India has changed dramatically, and more than once in this century. And, as can be imagined, the Indian state has required at different times different things from its popular culture to shore up, defend and/or perpetuate its realm of political and cultural control. To a much greater extent, and again unlike Hollywood, the 'Indian' in Indian cinema has all too often been a realm beyond what the State has been able to claim for itself: a complicit, if not always officially legitimate terrain of belonging, simultaneously envied and resented.

Most Indian readers of this book will be familiar with how, in the 1970s, cinephilia relating to mainstream Hindi cinema became an important source for celebrating 'indigenous' cultural populism while mounting a free-market attack on the Nehru-Indira Gandhi socialist model of state institutions, and how it influenced a great deal of state policy, especially, of course, policy addressing the Indian film industry itself. They will also recognise this cinephilia's role over the last two decades in the propagation of a sense of nostalgia, as glossy 'nostalgia films' and advertising campaigns invoke genres such as the classic 50s romances, even as political parties create an aggressive new frontier of right-wing 'Hindutva' for indigenous populism. Others may recognise the crucial part this and other kinds of nostalgia have played in the rhetoric of an Asian diaspora, which in turn further informed influential literary as well as cinematic fictions, along with, for instance, the Asian music-video industry and other kinds of actual or pretend political counter-cultures.

This reference book on Indian film has required of its editors and contributors some sensitivity to both the form and the history of this entire cluster of discourses, not least because an amalgam of them has, on several occasions, provided a stand-in for the history of Indian cinema itself, or at least for the kind of history mobilised by influential sectors of the film industry with its press and institutional support systems to perpetuate their economic and cultural claims and to record their achievements. Indeed, so influential is this amalgam of industrial, institutional and cinephiliac discourses, so thoroughly has it saturated the 'sources', that it has become virtually impossible consistently to ascertain historical 'facts' even as basic as filmographies or credits.

The problem is, of course, not new to India's historians. From the mid-19th century through to the late colonial period, India's history was virtually the plaything of an extraordinary variety of ideological movements, from Orientalists to Utilitarians, Evangelists, Reformers, Nationalists and religious revivalists, each presenting history as an idea of 'the past', choosing the one most suited to the kind of cultural mobilisation they were propagating in their present. Each of these in turn yielded simplified, uncritical but extraordinarily durable versions of their stand, which in turn not only influenced the popular art of its time but the actual process of history-writing itself. Many of the historians whose methods we adopted have been concerned with placing the 'fact' as a central question in their analysis, including, and crucially so, the forms and circumstances of the generation of 'records'. Referring, for instance , to Ranajit Guha's manifesto statement, 'On Some Aspects of the Historiography of Colonial India', and to the work of the Subaltern Studies Group, Edward Said (1988) pointed to the

> frequent reference to such things as gaps, absences, lapses, ellipses, all of them symbolic of the truths that historical writing is after all writing and not reality ... [which was controlled by] the Indian elite and the British colonizers who ran, as well as wrote the history of, India. In other words, subaltern history in literal fact is a narrative missing from the official story of India.

To supply the narrative requires 'a deeply engaged search for new documents, a ... re-deployment and re-interpretation of old documents, so ... that what emerges is a new knowledge'. One of the first historians to do so was D.D. Kosambi, to whom we dedicate this book. In his celebrated *Introduction to the Study of Indian History* (1956/80), Kosambi set out to 'reconstruct a history without episodes ... defined as the presentation, in chronological order, of successive developments in the means and relations of production', enjoining all historians of India to

> remember that no single mode [of production] prevailed uniformly over the whole country at any one time: so it is necessary to select for treatment that particular mode which, in any period, was the most vigorous, most likely to dominate production ... no matter how many of the older forms survived in outward appearance.

Clearly in India's 20th-century cultural arena, the mode of production at issue in cinema is capitalism, remembering that 'no single mode prevailed uniformly' and that 'older forms survived' at the same time. Even if those older forms survived only 'in appearance', that still means they must be taken into account since it is fatal to overlook appearances, especially in cinema. The lesson to be learned from D.D. Kosambi in this respect is that we must refuse to reduce a mode of production to either pure capitalism or to some older mode. In each case (film, studio, state) the particular mix of old and new will leave a particular imprint, with the capitalist mode of production in cinema providing a more (or less) dominant determination. When the cinema apparatus came into India, it was a technology and a mode of cultural manufacture and distribution without direct historical precedent in the country. On the other hand, from the earliest features of Phalke's work and ever since then, film presented its most critical value as being a neo-traditional cultural form *par excellence*, a gadget that worked at its best in suturing cultural difference and producing an easily consumable homogeneity for an increasingly undifferentiated mass audience. To aid this suturing, several film-makers, producers and institutions went some way in demonstrating the survival of older forms. Phalke himself attempted a theory of film that made it virtually a traditional Indian art in the context of Swadeshi. The studio-era film-makers commonly aspired to the respectability of the reform novel, just as 50s films were later to seek the 'high-art' credentials of a Satyajit Ray and other directors promoted as models by the Indian State. New Indian Cinema was born in the context of Indira Gandhi's developmentalist programmes culminating in the Emergency and the establishment of Doordarshan. Most influential of all, perhaps, was the way the Utopian 'India' of the pre-Independence period - the *tabula rasa* upon which were inscribed some of the most elaborate melodramas in Indian film history - gave way to the idea of regionalism, an idea of ethnic rootedness that effectively divided the nation into its constituent linguistic units.

All these areas inevitably came to be inscribed into the records of Indian cinema's history, as film-makers, using the technology uniquely equipped to celebrate, intervene in and record the rise of such epochal achievements as the emergence of an Indian working class and the birth of an independent nation, assimilated local political imperatives and the languages of the 'official' and the neo-traditional. From its earliest years, Indian film found its archive in the popular press and the publicity outlets of the industry. The problem of facts took an ideological turn when Indian cinema institutionalised itself, and, in the process, also institutionalised its several factions, their claims and their conflicts. Institutions representing the film industry and those managing the relations between state and industry, such as the various State Film Chambers of Commerce, the Film Federation of India, the various Film Development Corporations and the trade unions led by the Indian Motion Pictures Producers Association, have, over the years, expanded their ambit to include the authority to represent the 'official' history of whatever sector, region or special interest they represent politically. These histories, usually published on occasions commemorating the anniversaries of various cinema industries in India, accompanied by the felicitations of their pioneers and the valorisation of independent archivists and the private collections of individual cinephiles, are entirely susceptible to the critique Gyanendra Pandey (1991) mounts against contemporary historians' acceptance of the view that

> the 'centre' remains the recognised vantage point for a meaningful reconstruction of "Indian" history, and the 'official' archive ... the primary source for its construction. By attributing a 'natural' quality to a particular unity, such as 'India', and adopting its 'official' archive as the primary source of historical knowledge ... the history of India since the early 19th century has tended to become the biography of the emerging nation-state. It has also become the history in which the story of Partition, and the accompanying Hindu-Muslim and Muslim-Sikh riots ... is written up as a secondary story ... one that, for all its consequences, miraculously left the course of Indian history unaltered, [as] 'India' ... started firmly and 'naturally' on its secular, democratic, non-violent course.

Nevertheless, if today we accept that, far from being a straightforward move towards nationalism, secularism and democracy, India's history represents an extraordinarily chequered growth with its own share of conflicts and compromises, at least one reason for it would be the evidence provided by Indian cinema. When we started this encyclopaedic project, the aim was to provide a reference work on Indian film. In the process of its compilation, however, it developed a variety of more complex and less easily defined ambitions, a crucial one was to chronicle a sense of India that could move beyond its most obviously available nationalist construct, even as we chronicle the formation of that construct and its history through its cinematic product. Indian films are and always were read, and implicated in social transformations, in ways infinitely more complex than plot summaries or 'official' histories can claim or suggest. Attempts to 'locate' individual films or film-makers required constant cross-referencing between technological, economic, political and cultural chronologies, trying to read any one of these 'series' in terms of their intersections with all the others. The task was made all the harder by the simple, frustrating 'fact' that only a handful of India's silent films appear to have survived and that many of the key sound films are not readily available for consultation. This has meant that we have had to rely on contemporary (whenever possible) or subsequent accounts, surviving publicity materials and so on, all of them deeply enmeshed in the rhetorical amalgam of discourses mentioned earlier. Consequently, when approaching a film, the discourses 'placing' it would first have to be negotiated and 'placed' in their turn. Of course, that way madness lies as the critic-historian is relentlessly driven further and further away from the 'object', the 'source', the film. But it is a madness that must be faced, even risked, within limits which we have endeavoured not to overstep. For instance, many of the films have come to us via plot synopses which cry out (or was it the films that cried out?) for a psychoanalytic reading. Except in a few obvious instances, this is a temptation we have resisted. Similarly, we often had to contend with flagrantly partisan synopses presenting political and, most frequently, gender oppression as the 'natural' order of things. These we have tried to read against the grain in the hope that the partisan version, familiar to and internalised by most film publicists and their readers, will, when juxtaposed to our less familiar perspective, spark autonomous critical thought in our readers.

On the other hand, although it may seem that the actual film might get lost in this process, the amalgam of discourses surrounding a film, usually qualified as 'secondary', are not totally separate from the film either. They form part of the intertextual network that gave rise to and accompanied the film in its attempt to reshape parts of the very public sphere which engendered the film in the first place. It is true that nothing can substitute for a viewing of the 'original' film and that the scarcity of prints preserved in a decent condition (not to mention prints uncontaminated by censors or other vandals) is a severe drawback when attempting to describe and 'place' it. However, it is equally true that any encounter with a film is always already pre-structured, given that people are never utterly empty-headed when watching it. Reliance on the film alone is as misguided as an overestimation of the secondary discourses. As always, we have to see the one in terms of the other.

Most of the facts in this book are gleaned from available sources, representing the most reliable ones we could find for each of India's cinemas (the sources are listed below). Many of these are what we earlier called, somewhat dismissively, 'official'. Given the nature of the Indian film industry, however, there were compelling reasons for drawing on this material alongside other, not always less 'reliable' sources. The editors of this book, quite deliberately and as a matter of policy, have refused to accept any single 'authoritative' source on any of India's cinemas. On the contrary, we have endeavoured to produce a book providing the 'most likely' truth on the basis of often deeply conflicting sources. In this respect, what we offer here is not an authoritative source either (although these things are relative: we believe ours to be more authoritative than others simply because we were able to stand on the shoulders, so to speak, of the scholars who went before, even though none ever ventured to encompass as wide a field as we do in this project). Although this book will inevitably bear the scars inflicted by the unreliability of the sources used, we should like to believe that in consistently mapping India's film histories on to a national canvas, we also present several new discoveries, such as the sheer contiguity of historical processes nationwide that most Indian regions persist in viewing as unique, the influences of film-makers from one region onto another, or even the trajectories of individual careers that transgressed boundaries sometimes decades before these boundaries came to be asserted.

This book shares all the problems, and some of the credit, of any endeavour that is the 'first of its kind'. There are encouraging signs in India that several agencies, such as the National Film Archive of India, are gradually introducing sophisticated records, not only of their actual holdings but also of Indian cinema in general. Amrit Gangar and Subhash Chheda's recently completed computerised cross-indexing of the entire output of the Films Division means that the bulk of India's documentary cinema is now available for various kinds of research. India's Central Board of Film Censors may well take on board the need to compile their vast data in readily accessible form, a source that has not been available for this book except for the work of B.V. Dharap. Future editions of this Encyclopaedia will no doubt benefit substantially when that work becomes available.

To sum up: this book is very much designed as a research tool, a kind of baseline for others to amplify and correct, so that it may grow into a work of collective, constantly retuned scholarship.

Ashish Rajadhyaksha
Bombay, April 1994

FILMOGRAPHIES AND INDEX The biographical section of this volume addresses only some aspects of the film-making process: directors, actors, composers, scenarists and lyric writers, alongside brief entries on most of the major film studios, genres and art movements. Due to lack of space and the complexities involved, we were unable to include entries for producers, cinematographers, set designers, art directors, editors, choreographers, sound specialists, and so on. Filmographies have been provided for directors, actors and composers only. Although we generally used 1990 as the cut-off point, later extended to 1992, we have, whenever possible within the limits of our production schedule, updated the filmographies. Nevertheless, the filmographies of some South Indian actors and composers end in 1989. The filmographies, which have been listed by title and year of production (or release or censorship; often we could not be sure whether there was a difference), have to be checked against the Index for fuller information about individual titles. The Index lists titles alphabetically, providing the name of the director, the language and the year of production (release or censorship). A major effort has been made to provide also alternative and English titles whenever this seemed relevant, for example, commonly used translations and those used for other than local releases. Because of the extreme difficulties involved in the romanisation of Indian languages, readers may well experience problems locating a particular title (see below under 'spelling').

The Index, and several individual filmographies, have been compiled largely from the following sources:

1. B.V. Dharap's *Indian Film* annuals. Dharap's original project of compiling the entire record of the Central Board of Film Censors under the aegis of the National Film Archive of India, is now unevenly available in five different sets:

   1920-33: India's silent cinema, unpublished (available at the NFAI). This problematic volume lists titles by the year in which they were censored. This means that all films made before 1920 (the year from which Censor Board records were maintained) had to be separately dated.

   1931-50: In four volumes, unpublished (available at the NFAI).

   1972-78: Published annually as *Indian Films* by Motion Picture Enterprises, Pune.

   1979-82: Unpublished; although the work exists in manuscript, it was not made available to us. It is hoped that the NFAI will soon acquire this material from the author's heirs.

   1983-85: three volumes published by NFAI.This material represents the only publicly available record of the CBFC and is by and large the best filmographic source for the years covered. The periods 1920-1950, 1972-8, 1983-5 are referred to as the Dharap Years.

2. To cover the gaps in Dharap's work, we have used the following sources:

   Assamese cinema: T.M. Ramachandran (ed.), *70 Years of Indian Cinema* (1985: Assamese Cinema section) for the period 1935-83; Pradip Acharya provided us with information for the subsequent years.

   Bengali cinema: 'Filmography of Bengali Cinema (1897-1981)' in B. Jha (ed.), *Indian Motion Picture Almanac* (1986). Rathish Saha compiled the years 1984-90 for us. For the period 1942-52, Jha inexplicably eliminates all credits except the director's name. These have been collated with Kalish Mukhopadhyay's history (1962) until 1948, and for 1949-50 by the Dharap years. Actor and composer credits for the years 1951-2 and 1982 have been compiled from reviews and publicity material.

   Bhojpuri cinema: 1962-92 was compiled by M.D. Soni for this book, collated with listings in Har Mandir Singh (ed.), *Hindi Film Geet Kosh*, vols 1-4 (Hindi).

   Gujarati cinema: Manilal Gala and Amrit Gangar (eds), *Gujarati Chalachitron: 1982 Na Aare* (1982, Gujarati) provide information for 1932-82; thereafter we relied on Harish Raghuvanshi (ed.), *Gujarati Film Geet Kosh* (forthcoming, Gujarati).

   Hindi cinema: we consulted the pioneering work of Firoze Rangoonwala (ed.), *Indian Filmography, Silent and Hindi Film: 1897-1969* (1970) and its updated version, Rajendra Ojha (ed.), *75 Glorious Years of Indian Cinema: 1913-1988* (1988). For 1988-90, we used annual listings by *Film Information* (Bombay). This information was collated with Har Mandir Singh (ed.), *Hindi Film Geet Kosh*, vols 1-4, and Bishwanath Chatterjee (ed.), *Hindi Film Geet Kosh*, vol. 5. We also consulted annual listings by *Filmfare* (Bombay) 1953-71.

   Kannada cinema: 1934-84 is covered in Vijaya et. al. (eds), *Kannada Vakchitra Suvarna Mahotsava 1934-1984 Smarana Sanchike* (1984, Kannada), updated (1985-91) from the records of the Karnataka Film Chamber of Commerce, Bangalore.

   Malayalam cinema: 1938-70 is covered in the *Malayala Cinema Directory* (1970, Malayalam), which gives film credits and synopses, and in 'Malayalam Cinema from Vigathakumaran to Manjil Virinja Pookkal' in the journal *Nana* (Special Issue, 1982), which provides film titles and directors up to 1980. Titles only are listed in M. Saraswathy (ed.), *Malayala Cinema-Aranoottandu* (1987, Malayalam) and in M.G. Radhakrishnan (ed.), *Malayalam Cinema: 50 Years* (1989). Actor and composer credits for the years 1971, 1981 and 1986 (for the latter two, titles as well) are compiled from the records of the *Journal of the Film Chamber* (Madras).

   Marathi cinema: 1931-89 is covered in Vasant Sathe (ed.), *Chitrasampada* (1989, Marathi).

   Oriya cinema: 1934-84 is in Kartick Kumar Ghosh (ed.), *Oriya Chalachitrara Itihas* (1984, Oriya). Information after 1986 is likely to be incomplete.

   Punjabi cinema: 1935-92 was compiled by B.R. Garg (unpublished).

   Rajasthani cinema: 1942-92 is available in Murlidhar Soni (ed.), *Rajasthani Film Geet Kosh* (forthcoming) and in *Maruranjani: Rajasthani Film Mahotsav Smarika* (1993, Hindi).

   Tamil cinema: the only major Indian film industry whose filmography remains uncompiled. There is a list of Tamil titles from 1931 to 1985 in 'Filmnews' Anandan's *1931 Mudal 1985 Varai Veliyana Padamgal* (1985, Tamil), updated to 1990 in Randor Guy (ed.), *History of Tamil Cinema* (1991). This list has been collated with the monthly listings of the *Journal of the Film Chamber* (Madras) for the Index and directors' filmographies, supported by reviews, advertising and publicity pamphlets. Filmographies were built from available listings, such as the Manimekalai series on Tamil directors and stars. Wherever such listings were not available and filmographies have been compiled especially for this project, including the Tamil work of non-Tamil biographical entries, these are likely to be less comprehensive.

Telugu cinema: 1931-76 is covered in the *Andhra Film Chamber Journal* (December 1976, Telugu), and updated by K.N.T. Sastry for this book.

3. Documentaries. Until the mid-70s when independent Indian documentary cinema came of age, the genre was monopolised by the Films Division. Amrit Gangar and Subhash Chheda's computerised list and index updates with vital new information the *Films Division Catalogue of Films: 1949-1972* edited by V.N. Gulavani. Information about independent documentaries was in most cases compiled from information provided by the film-makers themselves or from the annual Indian Panorama catalogues (1977-92).

4. For all FTII student films, the *FTII Films 1964-1987* (1987) catalogue was used.

5. All-India quarterly listings of releases can be found in issues of Mangala Chandran (ed.), *Cinema in India* (April 1987-January/March 1990).

6. The above languages constitute all the major cinemas of India; minor cinemas such as Kashmiri, Tulu, Konkani, Haryanvi, Khasi and Maithili have been covered mainly through Dharap's listings and reviews. Under current conditions, no claim towards exhaustiveness can be made for these languages.

7. For non-Indian film titles we relied mostly on Markku Salmi's compilation published as the National Film Archive (London) *Catalogue of Stills, Posters and Designs*, London: British Film Institute, 1982.

BOLD Items in bold in the text indicate that there is a specific entry on the title or name (or institution, etc.) elsewhere in the volume.

DATES Indian sources (like many sources throughout the world) often do not specify which date is being used: the year when production was completed, when the director's cut was completed, when the film passed the Censor Board, when it was first screened to the trade or to the press or when it was first released to the public. Dates in Indian sources tend to be either the production date, the Censor Board date or the release date. We have given priority to the production date (when known); our second priority was the Censor Board date. When neither of these was available to us, we have relied on the release date. In most mainstream productions, these dates fall fairly close together. However, there can be significant differences for independent productions which may have received a delayed release, remain unreleased or even refused a Censor Board certificate (and therefore unrepresented in listings by industry sources). There are also several instances of productions being certified by the Censor Board several years after they were made. Dharap's compilations usually provide the censor year, while, for instance, Jha's *Almanac* in Bengal, Rangoonwala and Ojha or *Film Information* refer to release dates. We have attempted on all occasions (especially in entries on individual films) to provide dates closest to the completion of the first release print. However, the absence of reliable information on every title in the Index has prevented any uniform principle on dating, and we have adhered to the records listed above except in instances where more reliable information to the contrary was available.

FILMS the editors have endeavoured to provide individual entries on the most 'important' films in India's rich and varied film history; by 'important' we mean Indian films which have made a significant contribution to the development of Indian cinema from a number of points of view: economic, technological, aesthetic, intellectual, political and sociological (not necessarily in that order). Inevitably, many films which could legitimately have claimed an entry have been omitted, primarily because of lack of space. Other reasons for omissions include: the unavailability of the prints, which meant we were not able to check whether a particular film warranted inclusion or not; absence of relevant commentaries suggesting that particular film needed to be included; the editorial decision to end the film section in 1990, later extended to 1992 in view of the time required to compile this reference work; the editorial decision to concentrate on 'typical' items representative of an artist's work or of a genre rather than making vain attempts, in the light of space restrictions, to include all of an artist's good and significant work, and so on. The films have been organised according to their date and, within the production years, in alphabetical order.

GAUGE the gauge used is hardly ever recorded in any Indian filmographies and has therefore been omitted. Wherever possible, 'scope', has been used to indicate CinemaScope-type formats.

GENERAL ENTRIES in the Dictionary section of this book, the reader will find a number of entries referring to art movements (the Indian People's Theatre Association, the Kallol Group, the Progressive Artists Group, the Progressive Writers Association, the Navya Movement and others), techniques and art genres (Company School Painting, Photography, Sangeet Natak, Stage Backdrops, Pat Painting, Parsee Theatre and others), traditions (Art Schools, Music Schools) and political issues (Naxalite, Swadeshi). To some extent, these entries reflect the historical approach taken by the editors. Other items could have been added, such as Modernism, Reform Literature, various styles of poetry which have left their trace on film lyrics, and many others. Shortage of space and the need to concentrate on people, studios and films meant that we were able to include only a few such entries. Those selected for inclusion are intended to give readers a glimpse of the range of issues that must be taken into consideration when addressing Indian cinemas, as we attempt to make clear via elaborate cross-references to other, more directly 'cinematic' entries. While supplying basic information about such 'general' matters, we also intended signalling the need for cinema to be seen as a specific discursive form inextricably intertwined with a wide and complex network of industrial, institutional and cultural histories.

GENRES a great deal more work needs to be done on the problems of defining, analysing and periodising genres in Indian cinema. Given that many films deliberately combine, as in a menu, elements from what in the West would be regarded as different genres (comedy, thriller, horror, action, musical and so on), we have attempted to provide a rough outline of the main Indian genres in the full knowledge that any such attempt must at this stage be rudimentary and impressionistic. The genre entries will be found in the alphabetically arranged Dictionary section of the Encyclopaedia. There are entries for: All-India Film, Historicals, Melodrama, Mythologicals, New Indian Cinema, Saint Films and Social. The 'devotional' is in some respects a cross between the Saint Film and the Mythological, often closer to the former than to the latter. The 'Stunt Film' is a self-explanatory subcategory of the internationally known 'Action Film'. Neither of these two genres have been given separate treatment in this book.

HINDI-URDU the indication 'Hindi-Urdu' in the credits is meant to suggest that the we are dealing with a Hindi film making extensive use of Urdu, usually for the lyrics.

MULTILINGUALS in its most precise form, a bilingual or a trilingual was the kind of film made in the 1930s in the studio era, when different but identical takes were made of every shot in different languages, often with different leading stars but identical technical crew and music. The classic example would be V. Shantaram's *Kunku* (Marathi)/*Duniya Na Mane* (Hindi), 1937. However, it becomes extremely difficult to distinguish multilinguals in this original sense from dubbed versions, remakes, reissues or, in some cases, the same film listed with different titles, presented as separate versions in different languages. In this respect, Har Mandir Singh's work has substantially contained the problem in Hindi film, but it remains in most other languages. Wherever we found clear evidence that a title referred to a dubbed version, the secondary version has been dropped from the Index. When titles are divided by /, they are usually multilinguals in which each version counts as an original version. In all other instances, other versions are listed as 'aka' ('also known as'). Nevertheless, it will take years of scholarly work to establish definitive data in this respect.In some filmographies, a title may be followed, in brackets, by an indication of the language. This is to avoid confusion when films with identical titles were made in the same year in different languages.

PLOT SYNOPSES readers will notice very quickly that the plot outlines provided are extremely compressed, especially when we remember that most Indian films take many detours and mobilise multiple plot-lines in any given narrative. There may be two or three main plot-lines accompanied by a comedy plot and interspersed with song sequences which may or may not advance or impact upon any of the other plots, each of them intersecting with the others in ways not always easily integrated into a single, linear account of events. We have opted for an outline of the overall shape of the story, privileging a few narrative knots which we consider more important at this stage of Indian film scholarship. Such a procedure is risky, invites argument and should not be mistaken for an attempt to 'fix' what the film is about.

RUNNING TIMES running times are based on footage recorded by the censors. Sources for footage include Dharap's compilations; the *Madras Film Diary* (1957) for South Indian films 1951-6, thereafter the monthly and annual listings of the *Journal of the Film Chamber* (Madras); the *Journal of the Kerala Film Chamber* (Cochin) for post-1970 Malayalam films; the annual listings of 80s and 90s North Indian films in *Film Information* (Bombay); the collections of censorship data in the National Film Archive of India, and the prints struck from original negatives in the NFAI's holdings. Wherever these have not been available, the footage recorded on the Censor Certificate of available prints has been used. In instances where films with running times noticeably different from the original censored length have been in common circulation, these have been separately indicated in brackets. In several titles produced especially during WW2, Dharap's running times are either missing or have been given in round figures: in these cases, we have indicated that the running time is an approximate figure. For silent films, we have provided only the footage to allow for variable projection speeds.

SPELLING as indicated earlier, spelling problems have proved intractable. Given the general lack of standardisation in transliterations of Indian languages into English, as well as the extensive linguistic variations of languages like Tamil (e.g. the syllable 'zh') and Bengali (the syllable 'o') and complicated syllables like 'chch', the decision to include an all-India Index presented problems which a listing by language would have only partially overcome. In the end, we felt that an alphabetical Index would be of greater benefit to international users. Since most film-publicity outlets provide their own, often eccentric, transliterations, several films are already well known by a particular 'graphic image'. These titles have generally been retained, except where idiosyncratic diversions (e.g. Ramesh Sippy's recent *Akayla*, 1991) have forced a re-spelling in the more conventional form (*Akela*, aka *Akayla*). However, certain common proper nouns have been standardised for all languages, such as Seeta (not Sita or Seetha), Gauri (not Gowri), Ganga (not Gunga). In general, following the practice of popular film literature, 'common-sense' solutions have been used rather than any rigidly standardised notation, with extensive uses of the 'aka' and 'see' wherever alphabetical discrepancies are likely to cause serious difficulties in finding the title. In some cases, all we can suggest is that the reader make an imaginative effort and check other possible romanised spellings. For instance, the 'u' sound may be rendered as u or as oo; often a and u are used for the same sound, as in *Ganga Jumna* or *Gunga Jumna*; the sequence 'eni' at the beginning of a word may be rendered as 'ini'; a double aa may appear as a single a, g as k, and so on.

Square brackets around a letter or a word in a quote designate the omission of a portion of the text or the interpolation of text not in the original; elsewhere, their use is self-explanatory.

Finally, we should like to repeat that we would be extremely grateful if readers could send us their corrections together with an indication of their evidence. Only continuous collective scholarship can hope to establish a more solid basis for further work in chronicling the immensely rich but still grievously under-documented and under-analysed Indian cinemas.

Ashish Rajadhyaksha and Paul Willemen
Bombay and London, May 1994

ABBREVIATIONS

A	Assamese
act	actor/actress/acting
AIR	All India Radio
aka	also known as
anim	animation
a.o.	among others
AP	Andhra Pradesh
B	Bengal/Bengali
b&w	black and white
BBC	British Broadcasting Corporation
Bh	Bhojpuri
BJP	Bharatiya Janata Party
c	cinematography
c.	circa
cf	compare/see also
CFS	Children's Film Society
CIRCO	Cine Industries & Recording Company
Co.	Company
co-d/s	co-director/scenarist
col	colour
Corp.	Corporation
CP	Communist Party
CPI	Communist Party of India
CPI(M)	Communist Party of India (Marxist)
CPI(ML)	Communist Party of India (Marxist-Leninist)
d	director/directed
dial	dialogues/dialogue writer
Dist.	District
Distr.	distribution/distributors
DMK	Dravida Munnetra Kazhagam
Doc	documentary
E	English
e.g.	for instance
Ents	Enterprises
esp.	especially
Est:	established
et al.	and others
FFC	Film Finance Corporation
FTII	Film and Television Institute of India (Pune)
G	Gujarati
H	Hindi
ICC	*Report of the Indian Cinematograph Committee 1927-28.*
i.e.	that is to say
Int.	International
IPTA	Indian Peoples' Theatre Association
ISRO	Indian Space Research Organisation
K	Kannada
lp	leading players
lyr	lyrics/lyricist
Mal	Malayalam
Mar	Marathi
MGR	Ramachandran, Marudur Gopalamenon
MP	Member of Parliament/Madhya Pradesh
MPEAA	Motion Picture Export Association of America
MUKT	Marketing Union of Kinematograph Technicians
m	music
NFDC	National Film Development Corporation
NTR	Rama Rao, Nandamuri Taraka
O	Oriya
P	Punjabi
PAG	Progressive Artists Group
pc	production company
Pics	pictures
p	producer
pov	point of view
Prod.	production(s)
PWA	Progressive Writers' Association
R	Rajasthani
s	script and story
sc	script
Sh	short film
SITE	Satellite Instructional Television Experiment
St	Silent
st	story
Tam	Tamil
Tel	Telugu
TN	Tamil Nadu
tv	television
U	Urdu
UCLA	University of California at Los Angeles
UP	Uttar Pradesh
USC	University of Southern California
WW1/2	World War 1/2

1896
Plague in Bombay and Pune; national famine until 1897. E. B. Havell, one of the figureheads of the Bengal School of painting, is appointed Superintendent of the Government School of Art, Calcutta. Bankimchandra Chatterjee's *Vande Mataram* (Hail to the Mother), one of India's national anthems later appropriated by Hindu chauvinists, is recited for the very first time at the Indian National Congress. Bal Gangadhar Tilak inaugurates a festival around the figure of the 17th C. Maratha emperor Shivaji to generate nationalist sentiment. B. R. Rajam Aiyer publishes the social reform novel, *Kamalampal Charitram*, in Tamil. The singer Vishnu Digambar Paluskar leaves the Miraj court to popularise classical music.

First film screening at Watson's Hotel, Bombay, on 7 July, by the Lumière cameraman Maurice Sestier. The Madras Photographic Stores advertises imported 'animated photographs', reviewed in the *Journal of the Amateur Photographic Society* of Madras.

1897
Damodar Hari Chaphekar assassinates Charles Rand, the 'Plague Commissioner', and Ayres, the district magistrate, for their handling of plague relief measures; he is hanged with his two brothers in 1898.

First films shown in Calcutta and Madras. Clifton & Co. announce daily screenings at their Meadows Street photography studio, Bombay.

1898
The first gramophone record is released by Gramophone & Typewriter Ltd, Belgatchia. Bhai Vir Singh's Punjabi novel, *Sundri*.

Two Italians, Colorello and Cornaglia, organise film shows in tents at the Azad Maidan, Bombay. **Hiralal Sen** starts making films. Amritlal Bose screens a package of 'actualities' and 'fakes' at the Star Theatre, Calcutta, with plays and variety entertainments. The multinational Warwick Trading Co. commissions *Panorama of Calcutta* newsreel. Other films include *Poona Races* and *Train Arriving at the Churchgate Station* (by Andersonoscopograph).

1899
Calcutta receives electricity supply, although earlier that year the Maharaja of Bikaner had apparently been the first Indian to switch on an electric light bulb. Lord Curzon becomes Viceroy and Governor-General of India. Two seminal works of Urdu literature, Ruswa Mohammed Hadi Mirza's *Umrao Jaan Ada* and Abdul Halim Sharar's *Flora-Florinda*, are published. Performance of G. B. Deval's Marathi play, *Sangeet Sharada*, sometimes cited as the first reform 'social'.

H.S. Bhatavdekar films a wrestling match in Bombay's hanging gardens.

1900
Lord Curzon rejects the Congress Party's pleas for permanent land settlements, alleging that the weather, rather than excessive taxes, had caused the famine, but he later reduces salt tax and raises income tax thresholds. He also sets up a Railway Board, and opens 6100 miles of new rail track.

Major Warwick establishes a cinema in Madras. F. B. Thanawala's *Grand Kinetoscope* newsreels establish the genre's commercial possibilities. Footage of the Boer War is released at the Novelty Cinema, Bombay.

1901
The reformist leader Mahadev Govind Ranade dies. **Tagore** establishes the Brahmacharya Ashram, the nucleus of the Vishwabharati University of Shantiniketan. Fakir Mohan Senapati publishes his Oriya historical novel, *Lachama*. Vishnu Digambar Paluskar sets up the first music school, the Gandharva Mahavidyalaya, in Lahore. Edward VII is crowned following the death of Queen Victoria. The North West Frontier Province is created. Ramananda Sengupta starts editing *Prabasi*, a high-profile, extensively illustrated Bengali literary monthly which pioneers the popular mix of book excerpts, poetry and one-act plays alongside reviews and essays (occasionally on film); its serialised fiction includes several **Rabindranath Tagore** novels.

Hiralal Sen's Royal Bioscope establishes film exhibition alongside the commercial theatre in Calcutta, filming extracts from plays. **Bhatavdekar** films the landing of Sir M. M. Bhownuggree and the arrival (returning from Cambridge University) of Sir Wrangler Mr R. P. Paranjpye.

1902
Kakuzo Okakura, a Japanese artist and a militant proponent of a pan-Asian ideology, arrives in Calcutta as a guest of Surendranath Tagore. His ideas influence the Bengal School of painting and are given a nationalist gloss by Sister Nivedita. The first Indian to record a song on gramophone disc is Sashi Mukhi of Classic Theatres, Calcutta.

J. F. **Madan** launches his bioscope show in a tent on Calcutta's Maidan, the foundation of a massive exhibition and distribution empire which dominated silent Indian, Burmese and Sri Lankan cinemas.

1903
Bhatavdekar and American Biograph film Lord Curzon's Delhi Durbar, marking the enthronement of Edward VII.

1904
Madhav Prasad Mishra's short story, *Ladki Ki Bahaduri*, appears in the journal *Sudarshan*. It is sometimes cited as the first work of fiction in the still-evolving Hindustani language. Veer Savarkar, later associated with the right-wing Hindu Mahasabha, starts the Abhinav Bharat as a secret society of revolutionary terrorists. The Maharashtra Natak Mandali introduces naturalist prose theatre, later associated with the stage/film star **Keshavrao Date**.

Manek D. Sethna starts the Touring Cinema Co. in Bombay, showing *The Life of Christ* (two reels).

1905
Lord Curzon and the new Governor of Bengal, Andrew Fraser, announce the Partition of Bengal, ostensibly for the development of Assam. Partly in response, the Indian National Congress launches the **Swadeshi** Movement on 7 August, calling for the boycott of all foreign-manufactured goods. Lord Minto becomes Viceroy.

J. F. **Madan** turns producer with Jyotish Sarkar's film of a protest rally against Partition.

1906
Dadabhai Naoroji, President of the Congress, announces that the Party's aim is full 'self-government or Swaraj'. The artist **Raja Ravi Varma** dies.

Madan's Elphinstone Bioscope Co. dominates indigenous film production.

1907
The All-India Muslim League is formed in Dacca by a group of big landlords including the Aga Khan, the Nawab of Dacca and Nawab Mohsin-uk-Mulk, supporting the Partition of Bengal and calling for separate Muslim electorates and other safeguards for Muslims. Ramanand Chatterjee starts *The Modern Review* in Allahabad, discussing modernism in Indian art. It later published Tagore's debate with Gandhi about culture and ceased publication in 1920.

J. F. **Madan** opens the Elphinstone Picture Palace in Calcutta, the first of his cinema chain. Pathé establishes an Indian office.

1908
Establishment of The Tata Iron & Steel Co. India's largest private-sector corporation. Terrorist movements in Bengal, active since

1902, reach their peak with organisations such as the Anushilan Samiti of Calcutta and Dacca, the return of Hemchandra Kanungo from Paris and raids such as the Barrah dacoity by Pulin Das's group. The movement, often led by upper-caste men proclaiming a communal Hindu or casteist ideology, dominated the romantic imagination of Bengali nationalism for decades. Khudiram Bose, a former **Swadeshi** activist and member of the Revolutionary Party, is hanged on 11 August. Bal Gangadhar Tilak is convicted of sedition and deported to Mandalay. **Keshavrao Bhosle** starts the Sangeet Natak troupe, Lalitkaladarsh.

Abdulally Esoofally, a South Asian and Singaporean travelling showman, starts exhibiting in India.

1909
The Indian Councils Act 1909 (Morley-Minto Reforms) is announced, introducing elections while trying to split the nationalist movement along communal lines by introducing separate Muslim electorates. Ananda Coomaraswamy publishes *Essays in Nationalist Idealism*. The Amateur Dramatic Asociation is started in Bangalore, associated with playwright T. P. Kailasam and stage actor-director **Ballari Raghava**, bringing modernism to Kannada theatre. Performance in Bengal of Dwijendralal Roy's historical, *Shah Jehan*. Together with *Rana Pratapsingha* (1904), *Durgadas* (1906), *Noor Jehan* (1907) and *Mewar Patan* (1908), *Shah Jehan* anchors the stage historical in communal and nationalist politics.

1910
Rabindranath Tagore publishes *Geetanjali*. The All-India Hindu Mahasabha is launched at Allahabad, allegedly in response to the Muslim League, intensifying communal hostilities in Indian politics. **Dadasaheb Phalke** attends a screening of *The Life of Christ* at P. B. Mehta's America-India Cinema.

1911
George V visits Delhi. The grand Durbar is India's first extensively filmed public event, shot by **Hiralal Sen**, **Bourne & Shepherd**, Gaumont, Imperial Bioscope, **S. N. Patankar** and **Madan.** The Partition of Bengal is modified, followed in 1912 by the separation of Bihar and Orissa from Bengal. Tilak yokes Hindu chauvinism to the nationalist movement with his *Geeta Rahasya*. *Jana Gana Mana* is adopted as the second national anthem by the Congress Party.

Anadi Bose, Debi Ghosh and others start the Aurora Cinema Co. showing films in tents as part of a variety bill.

1912
British government transfers its Indian headquarters from Calcutta to Delhi. Ananda Coomaraswamy publishes his second text on an aesthetic theory for Indian nationalism, *Art and Swadeshi*.

Pundalik, probably the first Indian feature film.

1913
The first telephone service in India begins in Simla; the first carrier system is between Delhi and Agra in 1930. The militant Ghadar Movement, calling for the violent overthrow of British rule, is started by US-based Indians in San Francisco. Pherozeshah Mehta starts the *Bombay Chronicle*. Jaladhar Sen and Amulyacharan Bidyabhushan start the popular Bengali literary monthly *Bharatbarsha*; early essays on film include Pramathanath Bhattacharya's 'Bioscope' in the inaugural issue and Narendra Dev's 'Chhayay Mayay Bichitra Rahasya' on film-making techniques, later published as a book in 1934; the monthly also publishes Saradindu Bandyopadhyay's screenplay of *Kalidasa*. **Rabindranath Tagore** receives Nobel Prize for literature. **Bal Gandharva** starts the Gandharva Natak Mandali, the most famous of the Marathi Sangeet Natak repertories. The **Parsee Theatre** group, Khatau-Alfred, performs **Narayan Prasad Betaab**'s *Mahabharata* play.

Phalke's ***Raja Harishchandra*** opens on 2 April to a select audience; on 3 May it opens commercially in Bombay's Coronation Cinematograph.

1914
Start of WW1. Indian soldiers fight with British forces at Kut-al-Amara in Turkey and in Mesopotamia. Gandhi's agreement with General Smuts in South Africa on immigration and taxation laws for Indians is the first political success of his Satyagraha (non-violent) 'experiments with truth'. The *Komagata Maru* sails from Hong Kong to Vancouver carrying 376 passengers including several Sikh Ghadar activists, and is refused entry by Canadian authorities. The MacMahon Line fixes the border between India and China, leading to disputes erupting in the 1962 war.

Phalke shows his first three features, ***Raja Harishchandra***, *Mohini Bhasmasur* and *Satyavan Savitri*, in London. R. Venkaiah and **R. S. Prakash** build Madras's first permanent cinema, the Gaiety.

1915
The Defence of India Act. Gopal Krishna Gokhale dies. **Aga Hashr Kashmiri** writes his best-known and most often filmed play, *Yahudi Ki Ladki*. **Govindrao Tembe** starts the Shivraj Natak Mandali.

1916
Annie Besant and B. G. Tilak start their Home Rule Leagues on the lines of the Irish Home Rulers. Coomaraswamy's entire collection of South Asian art is moved to the Boston Museum of Fine Arts, and he becomes its curator: this move influences his subsequent opposition to progressive Indian nationalism and its modernising aspects. The South Indian Liberation Federation, aka Justice Party, is formed in Madras.

First South Indian feature: **R. Nataraja Mudaliar** *Keechaka Vadham*. Universal Pictures sets up Hollywood's first Indian agency.

1917
Gandhi's participation in the Champaran indigo planters' agitation against iniquitous local taxes by European thikadars, followed by the Kheda movement in 1918, introduces his philosophy of Satyagraha to India and again places revolutionary peasant movements at the forefront of Indian nationalism.

Baburao Painter starts the **Maharashtra Film Co.** at Kolhapur. **Patankar**-Friends & Co. is started, the predecessor of the **Kohinoor** Studio. J. F. **Madan**'s *Satyavadi Raja Harishchandra* is the first feature made in Calcutta. **Phalke** makes *How Films are Prepared*, a short film about film-making.

1918
WW1 ends. The first modern trade union, the Madras Labour Union, is founded.

The Indian Cinematograph Act, modelled on that of Britain, defines the terms of censorship and cinema licensing. The **Kohinoor Film** Co. and **Phalke**'s **Hindustan Cinema Films** Co. are established. **Patankar**'s *Ram Vanvas* is the first serial.

1919
The Government of India Act 1919 aka the Montagu-Chelmsford reforms, transfers selected areas of administration to Indian control. The Anarchical and Revolutionary Crimes Act, aka the Rowlatt Act, is designed to suppress all forms of nationalist protest. The massacre at Jallianwala Bagh, Amritsar, commanded by General R. E. H. Dyer on 13 April. **Rabindranath Tagore**, knighted in 1915, returns his knighthood in protest following Jallianwala Bagh. The All-India Khilafat Conference, uniting conservative Muslims in support of the defeated Caliph of Turkey, is supported by the Congress Party. It influences the non-co-operation movement the following year as well as the Moplah rebellion of 1921. Modern Indian shipping launched with the Scindia Steam Navigation Co. 's *Liberty*.

Release of the **Maharashtra Film** Co. 's début film, *Sairandhri*. *Bilwamangal* aka *Bhagat Surdas*, sometimes presented as the first Bengali feature, by Rustomji Dotiwala for **Madan** Theatres.

1920
Non-co-operation movement launched by Gandhi calling for the defiance of 'every single state-made law', and Muslim theologians announce that Muslims have only two alternatives before them: to declare a jihad (holy war) against the foreign infidels, or hijrat (emigration). M. N. Roy, who had formed the Communist Party in Mexico in 1919, the first outside the Soviet Union, starts the CP of India (CPI) in Tashkent on 17 October with six other members.

The Bengali film weekly *Bijoli* starts, edited throughout the 20s by Nalinikanta Sarkar, Barindrakumar Ghosh, Sachindranath Sengupta, Arun Sinha and writer-film-maker Dinesh Ranjan Das. Film censor boards set up in Bombay, Calcutta and Madras. The American-trained **Suchet Singh** releases ***Shakuntala*** with Dorothy Kingdom and other imported actors. **Ardeshir Irani** starts his first studio, Star Film Co. *Nala Damayanti* is the first international co-production (with Italy).

1921
The Moplah (or Mapilla) rebellion in Malabar, in which Muslim peasants kill or 'convert' Hindus, leads to bloody confrontations with the police and is a major setback to the non-co-operation movement's efforts to make a nationalist alliance between Hindus and Muslims. **Tagore**'s Vishwabharati University is officially recognised. The Bengali Theatrical Company stages Khirode Prasad Vidyavinode's *Alamgir*, introducing **Sisir Bhaduri**, and transforms the Bengali public theatre. Lalitkaladarsh stages its famous one-off production of *Sangeet Manapmaan*, featuring the reigning stars of Marathi theatre, **Bal Gandharva** and **Keshavrao Bhole**, to raise funds for Gandhi's Tilak Swarajya Fund. Abanindranath Tagore's seminal Calcutta lectures, the Bageshwari Shilpa Prabhandavali (loosely translated as *Some Notes on the Indian Artistic Anatomy and Sadanga, or The Six Limbs of Indian Painting*), defines an aesthetic theory for the 'New School' or the 'Bengal School' of Indian painting. The artist Jamini Roy abandons his Post-Impressionist landscapes in favour of a modernist, urban assimilation of popular and folk influences. His atelier of mass-produced paintings, opposing the dominant primitivist emphasis on tradition, becomes a major influence on contemporary Indian, especially Bengali, art. Vishnu Narayan Bhatkhande publishes *Hindustan Sangeet Paddhati*, making classical music compositions available to the public in the form of a textbook. Gandhi visits Gorakhpur campaigning for the non-co-operation movement. According to Shahid Amin (1984), the occasion marked the launch of the Messianic 'Mahatma' image. Novelist Premchand surrenders his government post to contribute pamphlets in support of the movement.
Kohinoor's *Bhakta Vidur*, banned in Madras and Sind, becomes Indian cinema's first censorship controversy. **Dhiren Ganguly**'s anti-Western satire, ***Bilet Pherat***, produced by the Indo-British Film Co. (Est: 1918). **R. S. Prakash** starts the Star of the East film company in Madras.

1922
The Chauri Chaura episode (5 February): a group of Congress and Khilafat protestors attack a police station and kill 22 policemen, causing Gandhi to call off the non-co-operation movement. The artist Nandalal Bose, later **Satyajit Ray**'s teacher, takes over the Kala Bhavan at Shantiniketan. Hemendraprasad Ghosh starts the Bengali literary monthly *Masik Basumati* (later the fortnightly *Basumati*) for the Basumati literary house, publishing literary fiction and theatre, book and film reviews; it also publishes essays on film by Hemendrakumar Roy and **Atorthy**'s seminal writings on silent Bengali cinema. Mama Warerkar's writes the play *Satteche Gulam*.

Entertainment tax on film exhibition is levied in Calcutta. **Sisir Bhaduri**, supported by a group of lawyers, starts the short-lived Taj Mahal Film Co. to adapt well-known literary works to film. The trend is later continued by other studios in Bengal. Rewashankar Pancholi starts Empire Film Distributors in Karachi and Lahore, importing American films.

1923
C. R. Das and Motilal Nehru start the Swaraj Party to enter legislative assemblies. It achieves wider Muslim and Hindu support than the Congress, but by 1928 the Party represents mainly conservative Hindu landlord interests in the communally charged Bengal. Aparesh Chandra Mukherjee's *Karnarjun* at Calcutta's Star Theatre confirms the commercial theatre's dominant language, influencing much of the early Bengali cinema. The *Hindustan Times* is launched. The Bengali literary journal ***Kallol***, edited by Dinesh Ranjan Das, is first published and becomes the foremost literary journal of its time, lending its name to the **Kallol Group**.

One of the early Bengali film weeklies, *Sachitra Sisir*, edited by Bijoyratna Majumdar, contains film and theatre reviews as well as production news. The élite literary journal *Bharati* (founded in 1877 and regarded as the journal of the **Tagore** clan) carries a serialised history of Bengali cinema. Entertainment tax of $12^1/_2$% is levied in Bombay. The **Saurashtra** Kinematograph is set up in Rajkot.

1924
First radio programme, broadcast privately with a 40w transmitter, by the Madras Presidency Club Radio. The station ran for three years.
Dhiren Ganguly exhibits **Nanubhai Desai** and **B. P. Mishra**'s *Razia Begum* in Hyderabad; the story of a Muslim princess falling in love with a Hindu leads to Ganguly's expulsion by the Nizam and the closure of his Lotus Film Co. Nanubhai Desai and others start **Saraswati Film**. Maneklal Patel starts **Krishna Film**. Kamala Movietone is started in Lahore. India's first periodical exclusively devoted to cinema, *Mouj Majah* (Gujarati), is launched in Bombay by J. K. Dwivedi. Hemendrakumar Roy and **Premankur Atorthy** start *Nachghar*, a weekly Bengali theatre and performing arts journal also publishing essays on film.

1925
In Amaravati, K. B. Hedgewar founds the Rashtriya Swayamsevak Sangh (RSS), a militant cadre-based civilian army, to establish a Hindu rashtra (state). One of its members later assassinated Gandhi and the group has been involved in communal confrontations ever since. A Puss Moth carrying mail from Karachi to Bombay inaugurates a civilian air service. The Gurdwara Law in Punjab vests the responsibility for the running of all major gurdwaras in the Shiromani Gurudwara Prabandhak Committee (SGPC) which, with the Akali Dal, has controlled Punjab politics ever since.

The first major film adaptation of the social reform novel: **Painter**'s ***Savkari Pash***; the Indo-German co-production ***Prem Sanyas*** aka *The Light Of Asia*. **Fatma Begum,** probably the first Indian woman producer and director, starts her production company and débuts as director with *Bulbul-e-Parastan*, released in 1926. **N. D. Sarpotdar** and Pandurang Talegiri start United Pictures Syndicate (formerly Deccan Pictures) in Pune; **Sharda Film** is started and formalises the stunt film genre. The Madurai Bala Shanmughananda Sabha, later known as the **TKS Brothers** troupe, is started, dominating pre-Independence Tamil theatre and film.

1926
The Arya Samaj leader Swami Shraddhanand is assassinated. Periyar E. V. Ramaswamy Naicker starts the Self-Respect Movement, propagating atheism to oppose caste discrimination. The Imperial Conference redefines Dominions as 'autonomous communities within the British Empire'. India is not offered Dominion Status until 1942, when the offer is rejected. The Conference also launches the notion of **Empire Films**. The Bengali literary monthly *Kalikalam*, edited by Murlidhar Basu, **Sailajananda Mukherjee** and **Premendra Mitra**, starts in the wake of **Kallol**'s success; indicted repeatedly by the conservative literary establishment for obscenity, it serialised Mitra's controversial *Pank*.

Foundation of the **Punjab Film** Corp. in Lahore, inaugurating the Punjabi film industry. **Ardeshir Irani** starts **Imperial Films**, eventually making India's first sound film. ***Vande Mataram Ashram***, the first Vande Mataram Film Co. production, is censored and briefly banned. The journal *Photoplay* starts in Calcutta.

1927

The Indian Trade Union Act comes into force on 1 June, defining the terms for union recognition and their frame of reference. Industrialists set up the Federation of Indian Chambers of Commerce and Industry (FICCI). The Indian Broadcasting Company starts operations in Bombay and Calcutta, inaugurating professional radio in India. **Modhu Bose** starts the Calcutta Amateur Players theatre group.

Indian Kinema Arts Studio starts in Calcutta, one of the predecessors of **New Theatres**. Film journals the *Movie Mirror* (Madras) and *Kinema* (Bombay) are started.

1928

Gandhi resumes Satyagraha, suspended after the Chauri Chaura violence, with the Bardoli peasant movement protesting against the 22% rise in land revenue collections. The movement also makes Vallabhbhai Patel a national leader. The Simon Commission, consisting of Sir John Simon and seven British MPs, arrives in India. It is boycotted by all major Indian Parties. Its 1930 report recommends abolition of diarchy and provincial autonomy, falling far short of Indian demands for autonomy. Lala Lajpat Rai is killed in a police charge on a demonstration in Lahore against the Simon Commission. Bhagat Singh and two other members of the Hindustan Socialist Republican Army retaliate by assassinating a British police officer. The first major textile strike in Bombay, led by the Girni Kamgar Union, lasts for six months and establishes the CPI as a political force.

The Indian Cinematograph Committee (1927-8) publishes its report. Appointed to counteract American imports with censorship regulations, the Report refused to give British films preferential treatment and recommended a series of measures to promote Indian films instead, with measures such as financial incentives to producers, the abolition of raw stock duty and the reduction of entertainment tax. The British administration ignores the report. **A. R. Kardar** starts the United Players Corporation in Lahore, the origin of Playart Phototone. **R. Padmanabhan** founds the Associated Films Studio in Madras, presiding over **K. Subrahmanyam**'s entry into the cinema and **Raja Sandow**'s directorial début. First Malayalam feature: J. C. Daniel's ***Vigathakumaran***.

1929

The defeat of the Public Safety Bill (1928), intended to deport socialist activists, leads to the Meerut Conspiracy when 31 CPI members, including three English CP representatives, are put on trial. The Devdasi Bill, combating prostitution in the name of religion and introduced by Muthulakshmi Reddy in the Madras legislature in 1926, is partially passed against conservative male opposition. It is passed in its full form only in 1947. The first commercial aviation service is offered by Imperial Airways, extending its weekly London-Cairo flight to Karachi.

Wall Street crashes, ending negotiations about a major Hollywood expansion into India. Several important studios are founded: **Prabhat Film** Co. in Kolhapur; **Ranjit Movietone** in Bombay; **British Dominion Films** Studio and **Aurora Film** Corp. in Calcutta; **General Pictures** Corp. in Madras. The influential Gujarati film periodical *Chitrapat*, edited by Naginlal Shah, and the *Moving Picture Monthly* are launched in Bombay. Universal's *Melody of Love* is the first sound feature released in India, at the Elphinstone Picture Palace. Bankimchandra Chattopadhyay (not the famous novelist) launches the Bengali monthly *Deepali* containing mainly film-news, reviews, memoirs and serialised fiction; the journal also produced an English weekly under the same title, edited by Manujendra Bhanja and addressing a 'highbrow' audience.

1930

The former Congress Party activist Surya Sen leads an Indian Republican Army raid on the police and auxiliary force armouries at Chittagong. The group launched a sustained guerrilla action against the British, triggering several terrorist movements in and around Midnapore, and brutal state reprisals against the entire nationalist movement. The poet Mohammed Iqbal suggests a merging of the North West Frontier Province, Punjab, Sind and Baluchistan into a single state, the ancestor of Pakistan. Gandhi inaugurates the civil disobedience movement with his epic march from Ahmedabad to Dandi to defy the Salt Act. The Department of Industries and Labour takes over radio operations and starts the Indian Broadcasting Service in Bombay and Calcutta. Physicist C. V. Raman wins the Nobel Prize for his theory of the 'Raman Effect' of scattered light. **Rabindranath Tagore**, who started painting aged 67, has his first exhibition at the Galerie Pigalle, Paris; the show travels through Europe and opens at the Town Hall, Calcutta, in 1931. Abanindranath Tagore paints his definitive work, the *Arabian Nights* series. Munshi Premchand publishes the first number of his journal *Hans*.

Sailajananda Mukherjee starts the Bengali film weekly *Bioscope* reporting the Hollywood, Bombay and Calcutta film industries and publishing reviews, pre-release synopses of films, industrial surveys and, occasionally, essays about technical and aesthetic issues. Ambalal Patel and Chimanlal Desai start **Sagar Film. Gubbi Veeranna** starts production with the Gubbi-Karnartaka Films Corp. at the Malleshwaram Studios in Bangalore.

1931

Bhagat Singh is hanged, after throwing a bomb at the Central Legislative Assembly 'to make the deaf hear'. He becomes India's first nationally renowned socialist martyr. The Gandhi-Lord Irwin Pact is signed, leading to the temporary suspension of the civil disobedience movement. It is resumed after the failure of the second Round Table Conference in London, where Winston Churchill refers to Gandhi as a 'half-naked seditious fakir'. New Delhi, designed by the Orientalist architect Edwin Lutyens, becomes India's capital.

Alam Ara is India's first sound film. ***Kalidas*** is the first Tamil sound feature; in Telugu it is *Bhakta Prahlada* and in Bengali *Jamai Sasthi*. B. N. Sircar founds **New Theatres**, a sound film expansion of International Filmcraft (Est: 1930). Pancholi's Empire Talkie Distributors acquires rights to RKO-Radio productions and RCA-Photophone sound equipment. The Bengali film weeklies *Batayan* (edited by Abinashchandra Ghoshal) and *Chitralekha* (edited by Bibhutibhushan Bannerjee) are launched. The Bengali literary quarterly *Parichay* (edited by Sudhindranath Datta) starts, arguably the most influential journal of cultural theory in pre-Independence Bengal.

1932

Within three days of the Congress Party's decision to resume the civil disobedience movement, the entire leadership is jailed and all civil liberties suspended. Over 80,000 non-violent protesters court arrest. Ramsay MacDonald's 'Communal Award', creating separate electorates in the provincial legislatures for Hindus, Muslims, Sikhs, Christians, Anglo-Indians, Europeans, Depressed Classes, Women, Marathas and 'Others', further emphasises British efforts to communalise the nationalist movement and gives a new lease of life to the Hindu Mahasabha, which becomes its most strident opponent.

First sound features in Gujarati (*Narasinh Mehta*) and Marathi (*Sant Tukaram*). The **East India Film** Co. starts in Calcutta, pioneering Bengali, Tamil and Telugu film-making. The Motion Picture Society of India is set up to represent the Indian film industry (in 1951, the Film Federation of India takes over). Hindi weekly *Cinema Sansar*, edited by Radhakrishna Sharma and featuring screenplays, lyrics, stories and film news, is launched in Bombay. In Bengal, the monthly *Chitrapanji* edited by Abani Basu includes serious essays by film-makers.

1933
The Indian Air Force is formed, named 'Royal' during WW2. The Indian Military Academy is started at Dehra Dun on the lines of the Sandhurst academy. The government of India nationalises radio broadcasting. Choudhury Rehmat Ali's note of 28 January is the first time the word 'Pakistan' (Land of the Pure) is used: it is also a loose acronym for 'Punjab, Afghanistan, Kashmir, Sind, Baluchistan'. In Calcutta, Bengal Lamps is India's first manufacturer of light bulbs and electrical equipment. Natyamanwantar stages its landmark Marathi stage production, *Andhalyanchi Shala*.

Prabhat Studio moves to Pune; its *Sairandhri*, processsed and printed in Germany, becomes India's first colour film. **Kolhapur Cinetone** is started. **Wadia Movietone** is founded, establishing the stunt film as a respectable, big-budget genre, with ***Hunterwali*** (1935). **Vijay Bhatt** and others start Prakash Pictures. **Vel Pictures** and Tamil Nadu Talkies are launched in Madras. **Himansu Rai**'s fourth international venture, ***Karma***, is premiered in London. The air-conditioned Regal Cinema opens in Bombay.

1934
The Congress Socialist Party is founded in Bombay, consisting of a group of Marxists, including Jayaprakash Narayan, Achyut Patwardhan and Yusuf Meherally; it later re-established links with the A. P. Kisan Sabhas and emphasised land reform as an integral part of the nationalist agenda. The CPI is banned. Jinnah returns from England to head the Muslim League. Major earthquake in Bihar, destroying the city of Monghyr. The Royal Indian Navy is set up. Bengal's 'establishment' literary weekly *Desh* starts.

Bombay Talkies is established. **Zubeida** and **Nanubhai Vakil** start Mahalaxmi Cinetone. First sound features in Oriya (***Seeta Bibaha***) and Kannada (***Bhakta Dhruva***). **Ch. Narasimha Rao**'s ***Seeta Kalyanam***, for **Vel Pictures**, is the first Telugu sound feature made in Madras. **Priyanath Ganguly** helps start Kali Films in Calcutta. The Hindi film periodical *Chitrapat*, edited by Hrishamcharan Jain, is launched in Delhi; it publishes scripts, fiction serials, poetry and news about international cinema. Bengali film weekly *Ruprekha*, edited by Jyotishchandra Ghosh, starts. The Urdu novelist Munshi Premchand is hired as a scenarist by Ajanta Cinetone at Rs 8000 per year.

1935
Buddhadev Bose and Samar Sen start the leading poetry quarterly *Kavita* in Bengal, introducing major writers such as Jibanananda Das and Bishnu Dey. The Indian Broadcasting Service starts its Delhi station. The Government of India Act (1935) provides provincial autonomy for elected ministers. Debates over participation in elections divide Congress. The Act defines an Anglo-Indian as a 'European with a male progenitor, but the female is a native Indian'. The Seventh Congress of the Communist International (1935) calls for united anti-Fascist fronts. The CPI, regrouped under P. C. Joshi, abandons its critique of the Congress as a 'party of the bourgeoisie' to make common cause with several left groups, including the Congress Socialists, the Royists and the All-India Kisan Sabha (founded in 1936). The broad socialist front is supported by Nehru.

India produces 228 features. In a booming South India, studios are started in Madras (**K. Subramanyam**'s Madras United Artists), Salem (Angel Films, 1934) and Coimbatore. The first All-India Motion Picture Convention is held. First films in Punjabi (*Sheila*) and Assamese (***Joymati***). ***Dhoop Chaon*** establishes playback singing as a standard practice. Launch of the seminal film monthly *Filmindia*; initially edited by D. K. Parker, it was later taken over by its proprietor Baburao Patel and lasted until 1961. The Quetta earthquake on 21 May; its after-effects are filmed by **P. V. Pathy**.

1936
The **Progressive Writers Association** conference, started in London in 1935, has its first all-India conference at Lucknow. The All-India Kisan Sabha, founded alongside the Congress session in Lucknow, publishes N. G. Ranga's Kisan Manifesto making a series of 'minimum demands' on behalf of small landowners, tenants and landless labourers. All-India Radio is started. Orissa and Bihar become independent states of India.

Amar Jyoti is shown in Venice. **Master Vinayak** and cameraman Pandurang Naik co-found Huns Pictures; the Telugu company Saraswati Talkies debuts with ***Draupadi Vastrapaharanam***. Sarathi Films, started the same year, presided over **Gudavalli Ramabrahmam**'s early work in the reform genre (e. g. ***Raitu Bidda***, 1939). **Raja Sandow**'s *Vasantsena* launches the prolific career of the Tamil comedy duo **N. S. Krishnan** and T. A. Mathuram. **Franz Osten** joins the Nazi Party. **Jaddanbai** starts Sangeet Film with films featuring her daughter **Nargis** as a child actress. **Sohrab Modi** and Rustom Modi start **Minerva Movietone**. The Bengal Motion Picture Association is founded in Calcutta. The second All-India Motion Picture Convention (Madras).

1937
Elections under the 1935 Act, when several political veterans contest for governmental office for the first time in their lives, leads to a Congress triumph in 8 of the 11 British-ruled provinces. C. P. Ramaswamy Aiyer, the dewan of Travancore, announces the Temple Entry proclamation and later concedes communal representation to keep the Christian, Ezhava and Muslim communities from becoming a joint opposition to Nair and caste-Hindu domination. Amrita Sher-Gil, who returned to India in 1934, visits the Ajanta and Mattancheri murals (1936-7), and paints her major works, *Brahmacharis* and *Bride's Toilet*.

First 'songless' film, **J. B. H. Wadia**'s ***Naujawan***. The first indigenously made colour film is **Gidwani**'s ***Kisan Kanya***, using the Cinecolor process acquired by **Imperial**. **T. R. Sundaram** starts **Modern Theatres** in Salem; Newtone Studio starts in Madras. The Indian Motion Picture Producers' Association (IMPPA) is formed in Bombay, the first and for several years the most influential trade union in the film industry. ***Sant Tukaram*** receives a special jury mention in Venice. The Amateur Cine Society of India is formed in Bombay by, a. o. , **P. V. Pathy**, Stanley Jepson and Rudi Van Leyden. Jogjiban Bandyopadhyay sets up the Bengali film weekly *Kheyali*.

1938
The Haripura Congress is marked by ideological rifts between the Right and the Left factions of Congress; it also exhibits Nandalal Bose's famous Haripura posters, showing India's working people and evoking Pat figurations and reliefs from Bengal's terracotta temples. The modernist sculptor Ram Kinker Baij makes his monumental *Santhal Family* cement sculpture at Shantiniketan. K. M. Munshi starts the Bhartiya Vidya Bhavan. Short-wave radio broadcasts are introduced. Veer Savarkar becomes president of the Hindu Mahasabha.

Duniya Na Mane is shown in Venice; none of the four Indian films shown in Venice in the 30s were bought for Western distribution. **Bombay Talkies** makes what is probably the first officially commissioned advertising film, for Lever's Dalda cooking oil, for the Lintas advertising agency (although **Niranjan Pal** is supposed to have made some ads in the early 30s). The South Indian Film Chamber of Commerce and the Indian Motion Picture Distributors' Association (IMPDA) are set up. The silver jubilee of the Indian film industry (usually dated from **Phalke**'s ***Raja Harishchandra***) is celebrated with 'official' versions of India's film history. The first Malayalam sound feature: *Balan*. The *Indian Screen Gazette* is started by **Wadia Movietone**, sponsored by the **Film Advisory Board**; **P. V. Pathy** films a three-reeler on the Haripura Congress for the *Gazette*.

1939
The British government declares war on Germany in the name of India. Nehru protests, declaring himself equally opposed to Fascism and imperialism, and pledges that an independent India, fighting Fascism alongside other free nations, would freely make its

resources available for the war. Congress minsters, elected in 1937, resign.

Vauhini Pictures is started by **B. N. Reddi** and **Gemini** by **S. S. Vasan**. Both companies expanded into studios in Madras in the 40s. *Film Industry*, a trade newspaper, is started in Bombay.

1940

The All-India Muslim League adopts the 'Pakistan resolution' at Lahore. The harmonium is banned from All-India Radio: its tempered scale, adapted from the organ, is considered antithetical to the shruti or the microtones that give Indian music its continuous scale. Only decades later would this commonly used musical instrument be allowed on radio again.

Film Advisory Board is set up by the government and is granted monopoly over raw stock. Intensification of censorship of films likely to support the independence movement with images or words. **P. K. Atre**, **Master Vinayak** and others start **Navyug Chitrapat** with public finance. **Mehboob** makes ***Aurat***, the original version of ***Mother India***. **Himansu Rai** dies, and **Devika Rani** takes over **Bombay Talkies**.

1941

Subhash Chandra Bose escapes from house arrest, travels to Berlin and meets Hitler (1942), who approves a plan to raise an army in South-East Asia. All-India Radio becomes part of the Ministry of Information & Broadcasting. **Rabindranath Tagore** dies. The first modern shipyard in India, at Vishakapatnam, comes on stream. Its first ship, Jala Usha, is commissioned in 1948. Churchill announces that the Atlantic Charter does not apply to India.

The Lahore-based film industry breaks into the national market with ***Khazanchi***. First Pushtu film: Sarhad Pictures' *Laila Majnu*. **Kadaru Nagabhushanam** and P. Kannamba start Rajarajeshwari Film. The Motion Picture Association is founded in Delhi, after similar regional bodies in Bengal and Madras.

1942

Sir Stafford Cripps arrives in India amid increasing fears that India might fall to Japan, which bombs the east coast and Calcutta. His proposals to frame a Dominion Constitution and a promise of independence after the war are rejected, especially since they imply Partition. Congress launches the 'Quit India' movement in August. Violent confrontations lead to massive reprisals as eight British brigades and 57 Indian battalions are used to quell what the viceroy describes as 'by far the most serious rebellion since that of 1857'. Matangini Hazra, a 72-year-old widow, leads a demonstration braving police bullets in Tamluk, Midnapore, becoming one of the icons of the August Kranti movement. The Japanese bomb Rangoon and Singapore. Representatives of Indian organisations from Japanese-occupied territories meet in Tokyo and Bangkok, and resolve to raise an Indian National army (aka Azad Hind Fauj) with Japanese support, consisting mainly of Indian prisoners of war. The CPI collaborates with the British following Hitler's invasion of the USSR and opposes the Quit India movement. It concentrates on organising the Telangana peasantry against the Nizam of Hyderabad and on the Travancore movement against Dewan Ramaswamy Aiyer's rule. Dr Dwarkanath Kotnis, head of a medical team sent to China, dies. Four years later, **V. Shantaram** films his story (***Dr Kotnis Ki Amar Kahani***) as a nationalist fable. Hindustan Motors is the first indigenous car-manufacturing company.

The Bombay Film Society is formed. Major shortages in raw stock; only recognised producers receive a maximum of 11,000 feet for features and 400 feet for publicity trailers. Priority is given to films supporting the war effort, leading to a rash of war movies. **Filmistan** is founded by a breakaway group from **Bombay Talkies** led by **S. Mukherjee** and **Ashok Kumar**. **A. R. Kardar** founds the Kardar Studio. First films in Sindhi (**Homi Wadia**'s *Ekta*) and Marwari (G. P. Kapoor's *Nazrana*). **V. Shantaram** starts the **Rajkamal Kalamandir** Studio on the former **Wadia Movietone** premises; **Homi Wadia** starts Basant Pictures. **Mehboob** starts his own production company (becoming a studio in 1952) with the hammer-and-sickle logo. **K. A. Abbas**, V. P. Sathe and others start the journal *Sound*, featuring politics, fiction, reviews and essays on Indian film.

1943

The Bengal famine (1943-4), a direct consequence of war profiteering and speculation, leaves five million dead. The best-known work of art dealing with the issues involved is Bijon Bhattacharya's play *Nabanna*, the inaugural production of the **Indian Peoples' Theatre Association**. Subhash Chandra Bose arrives in Singapore by submarine from Kiel and becomes Supreme Commander of the Indian National Army. He proclaims a 'Provisional Government of Azad Hind' (Free India). His government in exile is immediately recognised by Germany and Japan. The Muslim League amends the 'Quit India' resolution to 'Divide And Quit'. The Calcutta Group of painters, including Gopal Ghosh, Prodosh Dasgupta and Nirode Majumdar, has its first show.

Kismet, one of the biggest hits in Indian film history, is released. **Rajkamal Kalamandir**'s début feature, ***Shakuntala***, is a major hit. **Information Films of India** is started; the Defence of India Act is amended to force all distributors to pay for and to show the *Indian News Parade*. **K. Ramnoth** starts the Cine Technicians Association of South India. *Court Dancer*, the English version of ***Raj Nartaki***, is released in the USA in a few provincial theatres. Kalish Mukhopadhyay starts the seminal Bengali film monthly *Rupamancha*, with extensive film and performing arts reviews, committed to film education and to the reorganisation of the industry.

1944

The Indian National Army fights the British at Arakan, near Mandalay, and on Assam's north-east frontier. They 'liberate' 15,000 square miles including Japanese-occupied Andaman and Nicobar islands. The Dravidar Kazhagam Party is founded by Periyar E. V. Ramaswamy Naicker in Madras. The Bombay Plan, presented by a group of industrialists, commits the Indian private sector to nationalist responsibilities, envisaging the possibilities of a free-market economy coalescing into the socialist ideal of a planned economy. K. C. S. Panicker starts the Progressive Painters Association in Madras, later institutionalised into the Cholamandal artists' village (1966).

War profiteers increasingly launder their gains through the film industry, inflating star salaries and budgets, speeding up the shift away from studios towards independent production. The Navajyothi Studio is started in Mysore. The government appoints a Film Advisory Committee. Entertainment tax is increased in UP, Central Provinces, Bombay and Madras.

1945

The Indian National Army, hit by desertions and disease, surrenders, and several members are publicly tried. Bose is believed to have been killed in an air crash over Taipei. Central and provincial legislature elections: Congress wins majority but loses to the Muslim League in all Muslim-dominated provinces except the North West Frontier Province. A pact between Bhulabhai Desai of the Congress and Liaqat Ali of the Muslim League envisages joint control of an interim government, but both parties quickly repudiate any such understanding. Labour comes to power in Britain. C. R. Attlee sponsors a new initiative to break the Hindu-Muslim deadlock with the Simla Conference chaired by Lord Wavell. Jinnah rejects all compromise offers. The Tata Institute of Fundamental Research (TIFR) is inaugurated (it became operational only in 1954); it later pioneered India's nuclear and space research programmes. The best known Prithvi Theatres play, **Inder Raj Anand**'s *Deewar*, addresses the communal divide in the context of India's impending Partition.

M. K. Thyagaraja Bhagavathar and **N. S. Krishnan** are arrested on murder charges and imprisoned. Film trade representatives resign from the Film Advisory Committee. The government withdraws state control on raw stock distribution (imposed in July 1943).

1946
The Muslim League's call for a Direct Action Day (16 August) leads to the worst 20th C. communal riots in Bengal (Calcutta, Dacca, Noakhali and Tipperah). Riots in Bihar following the observance of 25 October as Noakhali Day. Nehru becomes vice-president of the Viceroy's Executive Council, heading the Interim Government of an undivided India. Jinnah declares the day (2 September) as a day of mourning for Muslims; the Muslim League joins the government on 13 October and Jinnah accompanies Lord Wavell, Nehru and others to London to try to break the political impasse over Partition. Mutiny by Royal Indian Navy ratings (18 February). The CPI-led Telangana peasant insurrection reaches its peak, fighting the feudal zamindar system and bonded labour, forced levies and illegal land seizures. In Travancore, a general strike against Dewan Ramaswamy Aiyer's insistence on continuing a despotic independence escalates into the CPI-led Punnapra-Vyalar uprising. India recalls its South African High Commission, repudiating the India-South Africa treaty of 1927. The privately owned Tata Airlines becomes the country's official international airline, Air India. Binode Behari Mukherjee paints his major mural, *Medieval Hindi Saints*, at the Hindi Bhavan, Shantiniketan (1946-8). Nehru publishes *The Discovery of India*.

IPTA's debut feature, ***Dharti Ke Lal***, with ***Neecha Nagar*** and ***Dr. Kotnis Ki Amar Kahani***, are made as war-effort films. ***Ranakdevi*** establishes the Gujarati cinema as a financially viable industry. MGM introduces commercial 16mm distribution, mainly for mobile cinemas. **Information Films of India** is dissolved; the Defence of India Rules on compulsory documentary screenings as well as footage restrictions are withdrawn.

1947
Lord Mountbatten becomes the last Viceroy and Governor General of India; he presents his plan for Partition (3 June), and announces the schedule for the transfer of power (14-15 August). The Indian Independence Bill is passed 15-16 July. Pakistan's Constituent Assembly meets (11 August) and elects Jinnah as its first President. Nehru becomes India's first Prime Minister (15 August), making his famous speech, 'A Tryst with Destiny', to the Constituent Assembly. In Punjab, the fall of Khizar Hayat Khan's Congress- and Sikh-supported ministry is followed by massive rioting in Lahore, Amritsar, Multan, Attock and Rawalpindi. Nearly 200,000 people are killed as six million Muslims from the East and over four million Hindus and Sikhs from the West become refugees in an exchange of populations. Communal attitudes merge with attitudes to sexual conquest and to property in a virtual war of extermination, as refugee trains carry more corpses than living people. The nizam of Hyderabad refuses to accede to the Indian Union and encourages the razakars, members of the Ittehad-ul-Muslimeen, to terrorise the peasantry. Pakistan attacks Kashmir; India signs a treaty of accession with Maharaja Hari Singh of Kashmir.

Udaya Studios, the first film studio in Kerala. The **AVM Film** Co. starts, adapting S. V. Sahasranamam's stage hit, ***Nam Iruvar***; **Master Bhagwan**'s Jagriti Studios is established near Bombay. **Paul Zils** and **Fali Bilimoria** start the Documentary Unit - India. **Satyajit Ray**, **Chidananda Das Gupta** and others start the Calcutta Film Society. Foundation of the Bengali film weekly *Rupanjali*, edited by Sudhangshu Basu.

1948
Gandhi is assassinated by an RSS member. Limited India-Pakistan war over Kashmir, as India complains to the UN Security Council. The Indian Army occupies Hyderabad, forcing the Nizam to surrender. The CPI, which had fought the Razakars, refuses to call off the Telangana insurrection, raising hopes of spearheading a nationwide revolution. The peasantry fights the army until the insurrection is called off in 1951. The Press Trust of India is formed as a news agency under an agreement with Reuter and the Indian & Eastern Newspaper Society. The **Progressive Artists Group**, formed in 1947 in Bombay, has its first show. **Sombhu Mitra** starts the theatre group Bohurupee. The Atomic Energy Act is passed.

Uday Shankar makes his nationalist dance spectacular ***Kalpana***; **S. S. Vasan**'s ***Chandralekha*** is the first Madras production to become an all-India hit; both films are made at the **Gemini** Studio. **Bhavnani**'s ***Ajit*** is made on 16mm Kodachrome and blown up to 35mm in the USA. *Nirmala* is the first Malayalam film made in Kerala. **Raj Kapoor** starts his R. K. Films, building his studio in 1950. Nehru announces a freeze on the construction of movie theatres. Gour Chattopadhyay initiates the Bengali film monthly *Chitrabani*, the most reliable record of 40s-50s Bengali cinema together with *Rupamancha*.

1949
The Indian constitution is drawn up, adopting the British model. Universal suffrage and equal rights for all are among its radical measures, but it also includes Articles 352-5, empowering the president to declare a State of Emergency and providing central government with virtually unlimited authority. Manipur becomes an Indian Territory. The State of Rajasthan is formed, merging the old state with the Rajput Princely States of Bikaner, Jaipur, Jodhpur and Jaisalmer. Ceasefire in Kashmir, as the Indian Constituent Assembly recognises Kashmir's independent status and its decision to become part of the Indian Union. This decision becomes a major rallying point for the Hindu Right which claims that Kashmiri Muslims have 'special status' in India. Ban on the RSS is withdrawn, after a pledge to eschew violence. Trade agreement to export jute, tea and castor oil to the USSR in return for wheat. The USSR becomes India's biggest trading partner and the only country to accept rupees as a currency for international trade. **Athreya**'s play, *N. G. O.* , pioneers realism on the Telugu stage.

Films Division is set up. The **DMK** (Dravida Munnetra Kazhagam) is founded by **C. N. Annadurai**. The Party launches its use of film as propaganda with ***Velaikkari*** and ***Nallathambi***. ***Dharti Ke Lal*** becomes the first Indian film to receive widespread distribution in the USSR. The Cinematograph Act of 1918 is amended; a new censorship classification is introduced. Entertainment tax for film is raised to 50% in the Central Provinces, going up to 75% in West Bengal. The Central Circuit Cine Conference, under Raibahadur Chunilal, protests at the increases and theatres go on strike. **Dev Anand** and **Chetan Anand** start Navketan Productions in Bombay, one of the independent producers through which **IPTA** members enter Hindi cinema. *Movie Times* is launched in Bombay, edited by B. K. Karanjia. *Indian Documentary* is launched by **Paul Zils** and others.

1950
India declares itself a sovereign democratic republic (26 January): population 350 million. The Republic is elected member of the UN Security Council for two years. The Assam earthquake (1 August). The Faculty of Fine Arts, Baroda, starts; ten years later, it becomes the pre-eminent centre for contemporary Indian art.

Jean Renoir and **Satyajit Ray** meet on the shoot of *The River* in Bengal. **Nemai Ghosh** makes ***Chinnamul*** in Calcutta. The celebrated Tamil film ***Ezhai Padum Padu*** establishes **Ramnoth**, **Nagaiah** and **Arudra**. **C. R. Subburaman**, **Samudrala Raghavacharya**, **Vedantam Raghavaiah** and others start the Vinoda Studio. **Vijaya Pictures** starts with ***Shavukaru***. The Pakistan government levies a tax of Re 1 per foot on all imported Indian films.

1951
The First Five-Year Plan is announced, with an outlay of Rs 2069 crore. Shyama Prasad Mukherjee starts the Bhartiya Jan Sangh on 2 October, an earlier version of the BJP, as the political wing of the RSS.

The S. K. Patil Film Enquiry Committee, appointed in 1949, reports on all aspects of cinema, noting the shift from the studio system to independent entrepreneurship. Its critique of the mass-cultural idiom, including black market money and the star system, is accompanied by recommendations for major state investment in film production, the setting up of a film finance corporation, a film institute and film archives. The report is ignored for a decade. Film Censorship is centralised under a Central Board located in Bombay. The Film Federation of India is formed, joining up all sectors of the industry, with **Chandulal Shah** as president. **Anjali Devi** and **Adi Narayana Rao** start the Anjali Pictures Studio. The success of ***Patala Bhairavi*** transforms Telugu cinema. **P. Subramanyam** starts the Merryland Studio in Kerala. The weekly newspaper *Screen* is set up by the Indian Express group. Pudovkin and Cherkassov tour India with a major Soviet film programme.

1952
Nehru forms a government in May after independent India's first general elections. Gopalakrishna Adiga's poetry anthology, *Nadedu Banda Dari*, is published; together with his *Bhumigita* (1959), these are considered the beginnings of the **Navya Movement**.

The first International Film Festival of India, held in Bombay, Madras and Calcutta, by **Films Division**. The films of De Sica make a tremendous impact. **Bimal Roy** moves to Bombay and sets up his production company. ***Parasakthi***, the most famous **DMK Film**, is released. The Indian Cinematograph Act 1952 is passed, replacing the 1918 Act, but makes few changes. The key section, banning films 'against the interests of the security of the State, friendly relations with other foreign states, public order, decency or morality', is retained. Film producers terminate their agreement with All-India Radio to broadcast film songs, when the radio refuses to credit producers or film titles. The radio starts its National Programme on music and its National Orchestra, conducted initially by Ravi Shankar. Colour films ***Aan*** and ***Jhansi Ki Rani*** (released in 1953) are made. **Bombay Talkies** ceases production. **Ritwik Ghatak** débuts with ***Nagarik***. The fortnightly journal *Filmfare* is launched, claiming to be the 'first serious effort in film journalism in India'. The Indore-based Hindi tabloid *Cinema*, edited by Manohar Prasad Gupta, starts publication. With the failure of protracted negotiations, West Pakistan finally bans the import of Indian films. An Indian film delegation visits Hollywood on invitation from the Motion Picture Association of America.

1953
The state of Andhra Pradesh, merging the former Central Provinces and Telangana, is formed, with the cessation of the CPI-led insurrection. Sheikh Abdullah, former Prime Minister of Kashmir, is arrested and imprisoned. Until 1975, Kashmir's politics are largely determined by the central government. The Sangeet Natak Akademi is launched to support and fund music and theatre; it is the first of the three autonomous institutions intended to channel government spending on the arts.

Do Bigha Zameen, showing the influence of Italian neo-realism, receives a special mention at Cannes (1954) and the Social Progress Award at Karlovy Vary. **Prabhat** Studio ceases production. ***Sharey Chuattar***, the first film starring **Uttam Kumar** and **Suchitra Sen**. The Cinematograph Act is amended, extending the powers of various authorities to suspend exhibition of certificated films. The Film Federation of India accepts an Advertisement Code. The trade weekly *Trade Guide* (edited B. K. Adarsh) is started; it remains the main Hindi film trade paper. *Filmfare* inaugurates its annual awards.

1954
Zhou Enlai visits India, and Nehru goes to Beijing where he signs the 'Five Principles of Peaceful Co-existence' with Mao Zedong. The National Gallery of Modern Art opens in New Delhi. The Lalit Kala (Fine Arts) Akademi and Sahitya (Literature) Akademi open.

The first national film awards go to ***Shyamchi Aai*** and Jagat Murari's short, *Mahabalipuram*. ***Awara*** is a major hit in the USSR. **Abbas**'s ***Munna*** is the second 'songless' film; it was shown at the Edinburgh Film Festival in 1955. Indian film delegations visit the Middle East and the USSR. Talks between the Film Federation of India and the government fail over All-India Radio's policy of broadcasting film songs without crediting sources, driving producers into using Radio Ceylon. The compulsory exhibition of 'approved films' (i. e. government propaganda films) in Madras is declared unlawful by the Supreme Court. The Premier Studio, Mysore's second studio premises, is started by M. N. Basavarajaiah.

1955
Nehru's celebrated speech at the Avadi Congress calls for a 'Socialistic Pattern of Society'. Khrushchev and Bulganin come to India. Nehru attends the Bandung Afro-Asian Conference, which inauguates the Non-Aligned Movement in a cold war context. The leaders of the movement, Nehru, Nasser and Tito, meet again at Briony in 1956. Cow slaughter is banned in Andhra Pradesh. The National Defence Academy is set up at Khadakvasla. The Hindu Marriage Act is amended, making the minimum marriageable age for women 15 and for men 18; it also provides for divorces and individual separations. Dharamvir Bharati writes his Hindi verse play, *Andha Yug*; staged by Satyadev Dubey for Theatre Unit in 1960, it is one of the inaugural productions of a modern, post-Independence Indian theatre.

Pather Panchali has its world première at the Museum of Modern Art, New York, coinciding with the official opening of the Textiles and Ornamental Arts of India Exhibition; in India, the film makes money for the West Bengal State Government, a significant factor in persuading the central government to set up the Film Finance Corporation in 1960, long after it had rejected the 1951 Enquiry Committee's recommendation as financially impracticable. Festivals of Indian cinema in Beijing and London. The **Children's Film Society** is set up. The South Indian Film Chamber of Commerce starts *the Journal of the Film Chamber*. The High Court at Andhra Pradesh grants an interim stay on the law of compulsory exhibition of 'approved' films and on the show tax.

1956
The Second Five-Year Plan, with a plan outlay of Rs 4800 crores. The government signs the controversial PL 480 agreement with the USA on foodgrain imports: India pays for the food in the form of loans to US multinationals in India and to private enterprises marketing American goods. The States Reorganisation Bill is passed; the State of Madhya Pradesh and the Union Territories of Delhi and Andaman and Nicobar Islands come into being. Language riots in Ahmedabad over the proposed division of Bombay into Maharashtra and Gujarat. Kerala State is formed, combining Malabar, Kasergod and most of Travancore-Cochin. Mysore State (later Karnataka) is formed, extending the old Mysore kingdom with parts of Madras and Bombay Presidencies and Hyderabad. On 14 October, Dr Babasaheb Ambedkar and 200,000 'scheduled caste' Hindus convert to Buddhism in Nagpur to overcome the iniquities of caste oppression. The first Indian newsprint factory at Nepanagar is started. APSARA, the first nuclear reactor in Asia outside the USSR, is commissioned at Turbhe, just outside Bombay city. The artist M. F. Husain paints his seminal works *Zameen* (1955) and *Between the Spider and the Lamp*, presenting an emblematic cultural amalgam for independent India. UNESCO gives a $20,000 grant to study the use of television as a medium for education and 'rural uplift'. The USA donates equipment and Philips sells a 500w transmitter at a nominal price.

Indian films are shown at Edinburgh, Karlovy Vary and Berlin. The government refuses to make its 'approved', compulsory propaganda films available free of charge to exhibitors. The freeze on construction of new cinemas in Bombay is lifted. The Kerala Film Chamber is started in Cochin. The *Andhra Film Chamber Journal* is launched in Vijaywada. Rossellini starts work on *India '57*. Despite major government support and funds, his visa is allowed to expire after a variety of controversies including allegations that he infringed local moral codes (by having an affair with a married Indian woman). The

Hindi journal *Film Sangeet*, published by the Sangeet Karyalaya, Hathras (which had earlier published Bhatkhande's pathbreaking textbook on North Indian classical music). Bhatkhande's influence is extended to written musical scores for film songs, in addition to essays on film music aesthetics and interviews with musicians.

1957
The first Communist ministry is formed in Kerala, led by E. M. S. Namboodiripad. Food prices increase by 50% since 1955, forcing the government to import wheat commercially from Australia and to accept aid under the controversial PL 480 agreement with the USA. The Indian Navy purchases the British aircraft carrier *Hercules*. All-India Radio starts its 'light entertainment' Vividh Bharati channel, later becoming its commercial channel, emphasising film-based entertainment.

Jagte Raho wins first prize in Karlovy Vary and ***Aparajito*** in Venice; ***Kabuliwala*** receives a special mention for music in Berlin. ***Mother India*** is released. ***Pardesi*** is the first Indo-Soviet co-production. Raw stock is declared an essential commodity and its import is centrally controlled. Dealers are forced to declare their stocks. The Cinematograph Bill, intended to start a national film board, production bureau and film institute, is withdrawn. **Chidananda Das Gupta**, **Satyajit Ray**, **Mrinal Sen** and others start the *Indian Film Quarterly*.

1958
The first phase of the Bhakra Nangal dam, the showpiece of Nehru's government, is completed. The dramatic deterioration in India's foreign exchange reserves, increased spending on imported arms and the need to double the envisaged foodgrain imports, force the government to adopt a radical development strategy emphasising agrarian reform, land ceilings and (following the Chinese model) the organisation of co-operatives. The Indian Copyright Act comes into force. Hindi playwright Mohan Rakesh writes his *Ashad Ka Ek Din*.

The first documentary film festival is held in Bombay. ***Ajantrik*** is shown in Cannes, out of competition. D. N. Sampat, founder of the **Kohinoor** Studio, dies.

1959
The government-sponsored steel plants at Rourkela and Bhilai are inaugurated; like the Bhakra Nangal dam, they exemplify Nehru's 'temples of the future'. In September, television arrives in India as a half-hour weekly service with a range of 40km around Delhi. C. Rajagopalachari starts the Right-wing pro-liberalisation Swatantra Party, combining the Forum of Free Enterprise and the All-India Agricultural Federation. China's suppression of the Tibetan revolt, violating the treaty signed by Nehru and Mao Zedong (1954), forces 14,000 Tibetan refugees, led by the Dalai Lama, to turn to India. One consequence is that the Chinese model of economic collectivisation is discredited. Most of the food imported under the subsidised PL 480 scheme from the USA is released in fair-price shops, inaugurating India's indebtedness to global lending organisations. The Communist ministry in Kerala is dismissed.

Six years after *The Robe*, **Guru Dutt** makes the first Indian CinemaScope film, ***Kaagaz Ke Phool***. ***Do Aankhen Bara Haath*** is shown in Berlin and wins the Hollywood Foreign Press Association and Samuel Goldwyn Awards for best foreign film. ***Pather Panchali***'s continuous 226-day run at the Fifth Avenue Playhouse, New York, apparently breaks a 30-year record for foreign releases in the USA. The Federation of Film Societies of India is founded, with **Satyajit Ray** as its president and Indira Gandhi as one of the vice-presidents. In Bombay, the Marathi weekly *Rasarang* (edited by A. D. Potnis), featuring sports and movies, is started; the Hindi monthly *Sushama*, an offshoot of the famous Urdu periodical *Shama* (edited by Yusuf Dehlvi in Delhi), features poetry, short stories, song lyrics and articles on Hindi films.

1960
Bombay State is divided into Maharashtra and Gujarat. Steel production starts at the Durgapur plant. Indian Navy's first aircraft carrier, the INS *Vikrant*, is commissioned in Belfast. The National Museum opens in New Delhi.

The government implements the 1951 Film Committee recommendation and starts the **Film Finance Corporation** to give low-interest loans to selected projects. In the late 60s, the FFC emphasises the financing of the independent sector. The Film Institute is started at Pune, on the former **Prabhat** Studio premises; the Institute for Film Technology is started in Madras. The Hindustan Photo Film Manufacturing Co. starts making b&w X-ray film. ***Mughal-e-Azam***, the most expensive feature to date, is completed. ***Ranadheera Kanteerava*** is the first big Kannada hit, establishing its star, **Rajkumar**. ***Shri Venkateshwara Mahatyam*** inaugurates **N. T. Rama Rao**'s political persona of the 'living god'. The weekly tabloid *Movieland* is launched in Madras. Gandhian Sarvodaya workers start a series of protests against indecent film posters and hoardings.

1961
India invades and annexes Goa, Daman, Diu and Nagar-Haveli, the remaining Portuguese colonies, which are now declared Union Territories, along with Nagaland. The All-India Census reveals India's population growth to be 2. 3% annually, considerably higher than the Central Statistical Organisation's projections. The Third Five-Year Plan introduces family planning programmes, which were later to prove controversial. School television project is launched in Delhi.

Ganga Jumna promotes the use of regional dialects in the mainstream Hindi film. First Rajasthani film: B. K. Adarsh's ***Babasa Ri Laadi***. Drastic cuts in the import of raw film stock. Second Film Festival of India in Delhi.

1962
The border war with China (20 October-21 November) in the North and North East. The ill-equipped Indian Army is routed. Nehru is violently attacked by the Congress right wing for the failure of his 'non-alignment' policies. In the general elections, Congress wins but the rise of the Jan Sangh and the Swatantra Parties signal a formidable merging of industrial pro-liberalisation forces with those of Hindu communalism in collective opposition to Nehru. The Bhakra-Nangal multipurpose river valley project on the river Sutlej, one of the biggest dams in the world, is complete. In 1954, Nehru had described this engineering feat as the 'greatest and holiest' of India's shrines.

Pakistan bans Indian films in the East (West Pakistan had banned them in 1952), hitting the Bengali cinema particularly hard. Radio Ceylon captures India's commercial radio audience by broadcasting film songs and film-based programmes, while All-India Radio concentrates on popularising classical music. First Bhojpuri film: ***Ganga Maiya Tohe Piyari Chadhaibo***. *Indian Film Culture*, the journal of the Federation of Film Societies of India, is launched in Calcutta.

1963
The 'Kamaraj Plan', initiated by K. Kamaraj, a senior Congress leader and Chief Minister of Madras, calls for the voluntary resignation of all senior Congress members from government posts in order to concentrate on revitalising the Party. Nehru uses the plan to purge the right wing from his ministry. Morarji Desai, one of the most vocal critics of Nehru's socialism, accuses him of preparing the rise to power of Indira Gandhi. Parliament approves the continued use of English as an official language beyond 1965. A 10kg 'toy rocket', launched into outer space from the Thumba Equatorial Rocket Launching Station near Trivandrum, is India's first space research success. The Group 1890, an art exhibition with J. Swaminathan's manifesto and an introduction by Octavio Paz, becomes the second major show, after the **Progressive Artists Group**, to redefine an indigenous modernism.

The Indian Motion Picture Export Corporation (IMPEC) is formed. The first Indian Merchant-Ivory film, *The Householder*. Barnouw and Krishnaswamy's *Indian Film* is published. The *Journal of the CTA of South*

India, a Madras-based monthly, is started; it is probably the first technical film journal in India, and reports on the work of major film technicians in the South.

1964

Nehru dies; Lal Bahadur Shastri becomes prime minister. The Communist Party of India splits, the majority of the rank and file going to the CPI (Marxist). The split is triggered by the India-China war, but the larger context is the CPSU's support for the Congress, regarded as an imperialist ally by the CPI's left wing. Following a split in the Congress and the imposition of president's rule in Kerala, 800 CPI(M) cadres are arrested, including A. K. Gopalan, the best known of Kerala's Marxist leaders. The indigenously manufactured Vaijayanta tank is the showpiece of the Indian Army's arsenal.

The **National Film Archive of India** is founded in Pune under the Information & Broadcasting Ministry. The Film Institute at Adyar, Madras, starts. *Report on Indian Cinema* for UNESCO by Jerzy Toeplitz, president of FIAF. He notes the Bombay cinema's impact on the Hindi language. First Kashmiri film: *Naizraat.*

1965

Second Indo-Pakistan War since Partition disputing the Kashmir borders. Pakistan invades Chhamb and the Rann of Kutch (1-23 September). Major language riots in South India over the adoption of Hindi as India's national 'link' language. Demonstrations in Madras exceed those of the 1942 Quit India movement. **M. Karunanidhi** is among the arrested DMK agitators. Kerala declares a strike on 18 February. The CPI(M) emerges as the dominant political party in Kerala's mid-term elections. However, its significant left wing concentrates increasingly on creating peasant organisations with an extra-parliamentary action programme. Charu Majumdar, leading the best known of these movements, declares: 'The real fight against revisionism can never be begun unless the peasant starts it through revolutionary practice'. Television becomes a daily service of one hour, restricted to Delhi.

The International Film Festival of India turns competitive. **R. Kariat**'s ***Chemmeen***.

1966

Indira Gandhi becomes prime minister, after the Tashkent peace talks followed by the death of Lal Bahadur Shastri. Punjab is divided into Punjab, Haryana and Himachal Pradesh. Devaluation of the rupee by 36. 5%. A growing number of political groups, both Left and Right, marginalise parliamentary politics and embark on violent protests. The Communists' emphasis on extra-parliamentary 'mass struggle' is emulated by a variety of regionalist, ethnic and communal groups. The FICCI considers a proposal to raise a large election fund to support a 'business party'.

Ghatak joins the **FTII** in Pune. Karnataka Chief Minister Veerendra Patil initates a scheme to subsidise all films made in the state. The initial subsidy is Rs 50,000 for b&w and Rs 1 lakh for a colour film. The Dolton Press, part of B. Nagi Reddy's publishing empire, starts the journal *Bommai* (edited by B. Vishwanatha Reddy) in Tamil. The **Dadasaheb Phalke** Lifetime-Achievement Awards are started. The first Dogri film is Kumar Kuldip's ***Gallan Hoyian Beetiyan***. The North Calcutta Film Society starts the quarterly *Chitravash* and publishes special issues on, e. g. , **Nemai Ghosh** and **Rajen Tarafdar**. The Cine Club in Calcutta starts the occasional journal *Kino* in English.

1967

Indira Gandhi leads her Party to victory in the National Elections. The Congress, hit by major defections and multi-party alliances cobbled together exclusively to oppose it, finds its popular support eroded and loses in eight of India's 17 states. Left United Fronts assume power in West Bengal and Kerala; the DMK wins in Madras on an anti-Hindi platform, and coalitions elsewhere include Hindu communalist factions, dissident ex-Congressmen and reincarnated pre-Independence royalty. The peasant uprising in the Naxalbari District of West Bengal, led by CPI(M) members, starts peacefully but turns into an armed insurrection against individual landowners. Chief Minister Ajoy Mukherjee, who leads the only major non-Marxist faction in Bengal's United Front, rigorously quells the rebellion, causing a split in the United Front and provoking the dismissal of the state government. '**Naxalite**' activity surfaces in Andhra Pradesh, at Srikakulam, where Girijan tribals take on local landlords and the police to create virtual soviets, redistributing land and establishing their own administrative machinery. The Srikakulam uprising is defeated only in 1969 by the Central Reserve Police Force. The Rohini RH75 rocket is launched from the Thumba base.

Bommai diversifies into the Telugu monthly, *Vijaychitra*. Start of the Bengali film monthly *Chitrabikshan* by Cine Central, Calcutta. Hindustan Photo Films makes India self-sufficient in b&w film and sound negative film. All colour stock is imported and locally perforated. The first 70mm wide-screen film screened in India. **M. G. Ramachandran** is shot and injured by co-star M. R. Radha. He also becomes a DMK Member of the Legislative Assembly and, in 1970, treasurer of the DMK. The Vividh Bharati channel on All-India Radio goes commercial in Bombay, Pune and Nagpur. Over the next decade, it becomes the dominant publicity medium for cinema, with, e. g. , sponsored serials and song compilation programmes.

1968

The All-India Co-ordination Committee of Communist Revolutionaries, the precursor of the CPI(ML), becomes the focus of the extra-parliamentary Left. The first Indian Triennale of International Art, organised by the Lalit Kala Akademi.

The G. D. Khosla Committee Report on Film Censorship criticises the censorship guidelines: 'If they are followed rigidly, not a single film, Indian or Western, is likely to be certified. ' **Abbas**'s independent short, ***Char Shaher Ek Kahani***, made in the context of the Khosla Committee's investigations, sparks a major censorship controversy by suggesting that censorship violates the constitutional right to free speech. Major reforms are instituted by the Hidaytullah judgment in the Supreme Court. A manifesto for a **New Indian Cinema** movement is issued by **Mrinal Sen** and Arun Kaul, advocating a state-sponsored author-cinema.

1969

Indira Gandhi splits the Congress, sacks her finance minister Morarji Desai, and announces the nationalisation of 14 of India's largest banks accounting for 52% of the national credit. She becomes the unquestioned leader of her Party. Her increasing use of radical socialist rhetoric attempts to neutralise both Left and Right opposition in the name of 'progressive forces'. The CPI(ML) is founded in Calcutta by Kanu Sanyal. The atomic power station at Tarapur becomes operational. The Bhabha Atomic Research Centre produces Uranium 235. The scientist Vikram Sarabhai, Chairman of the Atomic Energy Commission, presents his vision for Indian TV: to overcome simultaneously India's two major limitations, geographical distance and linguistic diversity.

Bhuvan Shome and ***Uski Roti***, financed by the **FFC**, inaugurate **New Indian Cinema**. ***Olavum Theeravum*** launches a second 'new wave' in Malayalam. ***Aradhana*** makes **Rajesh Khanna** a megastar in association with **Kishore Kumar**'s singing and **S. D.** and **R. D. Burman**'s scores. Publication of P. Parrain's *Regards sur le cinéma indien* in Paris. First **Satyajit Ray** retrospective at the Cinémathèque, Paris.

1970

The **Naxalite** Movement takes a new turn with student uprisings in Calcutta and other cities. Rebelling against corrupt and archaic education systems, problems of unemployment and the class divide separating Westernised urban life from the 'reality' of rural India, the student action becomes iconoclastic, defacing statues of Gandhi, Rammohun Roy, Ishwarchandra Vidyasagar, Vivekananda et al. Furious debates about the role of art and culture, the supportable and objectionable aspects of India's history, and the role of its petty bourgeoisie, end badly with brutal police and military crackdowns and indiscriminate killings. Anti-Naxalite hysteria grips the state machinery. The central government approves the West Bengal Prevention of Violent Activities Bill. Indira Gandhi's turn towards socialism is reflected in the new Industrial Licensing Policy, reversing the trend towards deregulation. This socialism is incarnated in the Fourth Five-Year Plan, with an outlay of Rs 15,902 crore. The government abolishes privy purses and all privileges to India's erstwhile royalty.

The English monthly *Stardust*, using 'Bombay English' and featuring movie star gossip and scandals, revolutionises the concept of the fanzine. *Journal of the Kerala Film Chamber* (Cochin) starts. *Close Up* (no. 5/6) publishes a special number on 'The Indian Film Scene'. ***Samskara*** inaugurates **New Indian Cinema** in Kannada. Firoze Rangoonwala publishes his *Indian Filmography: Silent and Hindi Films (1897-1969)*.

1971

The Pakistan government's crackdown on Sheikh Mujibur Rahman's Awami League leads to war with India and results in East Pakistan becoming Bangladesh. Indira Gandhi exploits India's success by announcing elections. Her Congress (R) wins a massive majority, which she uses to change the Constitution, giving greater powers to the parliamentary executive at the expense of the judiciary. President's Rule is declared in West Bengal and Union Minister Siddhartha Shankar Ray uses troops to quell what remains of the **Naxalite** Movement. A conservative estimate (quoted by Francine Frankel, 1978) is that 15,000 people were arrested, of whom 2000 were killed. By 1973, there are more than 30,000 political prisoners in Bengal, arrested under the Maintenance of Internal Security Act (MISA). India signs a 20-year Treaty of Peace and Friendship with the USSR, triggered by 'secret' talks between Kissinger and Zhou Enlai and the fear that both China and the USA would back Pakistan in the event of further conflict. This effectively ends the Nehruite non-alignment policy. The State of Himachal Pradesh is formed. **B. V. Karanth**'s theatre group, Benaka, stages **Karnad**'s *Hayavadana*, **Kambhar**'s *Jokumaraswamy* and **Lankesh**'s *Oedipus*, inaugurating a **Navya**-inspired avant-garde in Kannada theatre.

The agreement between the Indian government and the MPEAA is allowed to expire. From 114 foreign films censored in 1972, the number falls to 38 in 1973 and 26 in 1974. The directive to the **FFC** to sponsor independent film-making is written into its official objectives, enjoining it to turn film into 'an effective instrument for the promotion of national culture, education and healthy entertainment . . . by granting loans for modest but off-beat films of talented and promising persons in the field'. This directive was to last for only five years. India produces 433 feature films, making it the largest film producer in the world. The boom, started in the mid-60s, continues throughout the decade: in 1979, 714 Indian features were submitted to the censor. ***Pakeezah*** is released. ***Shantata! Court Chalu Aahe*** starts the **New Indian Cinema** movement in Marathi. Its original author, **Tendulkar**, writes the play *Sakharam Binder*.

1972

Government nationalises the coal-mining industry. Zulfiqar Ali Bhutto and Indira Gandhi reach agreement over Kashmir (the Simla Accord). **Amol Palekar**'s staging of Sadanand Rege's Marathi play *Gochee* starts the Chhabildas experimental theatre movement, deriving its name from a school in a lower-middle-class neighbourhood in Bombay, which the theatre group Aavishkar had earlier acquired to stage low-budget theatre experiments to a small audience. Television starts in Bombay (October). Stations are started the following year in Srinagar, Amritsar and Calcutta. Madras and Lucknow follow in 1975.

First art-house cinema opened by the **FFC**. First features in Manipuri (*Matamgi Manipur*) and Coorgi (*Nada Manne Nada Koolu*). The first film co-operative run by technicians, the Chitralekha Co-op, starts production with **Adoor Gopalakrishnan**'s début, ***Swayamvaram***. In Tamil Nadu, **M. G. Ramachandran** is expelled from the DMK and forms the Anna Dravida Munnetra Kazhagam. The Malayalam film weekly *Nana* starts, occasionally publishing filmographies and listings in between features on the Malayalam film industry. *Do Gaz Zameen Ke Neeche* establishes the **Ramsay Brothers** and the horror genre in Hindi.

1973

The former Mysore State becomes Karnataka. A Special Constitution Bench of the Supreme Court restricts Indira Gandhi's constitutional amendments of 1971, impeding her efforts to make parliament the supreme authority in the country's constitution. In retaliation, Mrs Gandhi selects and appoints a new chief justice, a 'blatant attempt . . . at undermining the independence of the judiciary', according to the Supreme Court Bar Association. Jayaprakash Narayan, the former socialist later associated with the Gandhian Sarvodaya Samaj, warns aginst the erosion of democracy. All private wholesale trading in wheat is banned; only the Food Corporation of India, and similar organisations, are authorised to purchase wheat. The fixing of procurement prices, coupled with the relative failure of the wheat crop, leads to large-scale hoarding and a major black market in food.

The **FFC** becomes the channelling agency for the import of raw stock, a role until then played by the State Trading Corporation of India. A 250% import duty on raw stock is imposed. First Haryanvi film: *Beera Shera*. ***Bobby*** reinvigorates the love story genre. ***Ankur*** is a commercial success, starting the 'middle-of-the-road' cinema of the independently financed, commercially designed art-house movie, a genre that soon dominates state-sponsored film and television. Launch of the Bombay-based weekly trade paper *Film Information*, providing the most reliable listings of Hindi cinema.

1974

The Nav Nirman student agitation in Gujarat, opposing a faction-ridden Congress, the corruption of Chief Minister Chimanbhai Patel and escalating prices of wheat and cooking oil, leads to President's Rule. The agitation spreads to Bihar as Jayaprakash Narayan announces his re-entry into political life to lead the movement, supported by the Jan Sangh, the Congress (O) and the CPI(M). A National Co-ordination Committee led by Narayan addresses a series of massive rallies, making Bihar the spearhead of the anti-Indira Gandhi campaign. **Anand Patwardhan**'s *Waves of Revolution* (1975) chronicles the movement towards what Narayan called 'sampoorna kranti' ('Total Revolution'). The strike of 1. 7 million railway workers continues for three weeks with wide support from the anti-Congress opposition. It is broken through the widespread use of preventive detention under the Maintenance of Internal Security Act (MISA). The 'peaceful' nuclear blast at Pokharan demonstrates India's acquisition of nuclear capability.

Hindstan Photo Films starts limited production of positive colour stock. The Film Festival of India becomes an annual event. The Film Institute of India is registered as an autonomous society, and is merged with the TV Training Centre to become the **Film & Television Institute of India**.

1975

Indira Gandhi is accused of 'corrupt practices' during her 1971 election campaign in the Rae Bareilly constituency. She is debarred from holding elective office for six years. This event, and the expansion of the Jayaprakash Narayan-led movement into Gujarat, the formation of a multi-party 'Janata Front' culminating in Narayan's major Delhi rally calling on the army and police to disobey 'illegal orders', lead to the declaration of Internal Emergency. All opposition leaders and thousands of intellectuals and political activists are jailed. Mrs Gandhi announces her Twenty-Point Economic Programme, using the unprecedented powers of her government to promise: the implementation of agricultural land ceilings, houses for landless labourers, the abolition of bonded labour, the liquidation of rural debt, cheaper prices, higher agricultural wages, increased production and employment, the socialisation of urban land, a crackdown on tax evasion, the confiscation of smuggled property and cheaper textbooks. Smallpox is eradicated from India. The Chasnala colliery disaster, in which 372 miners die. **Utpal Dutt** presents his play, *Dushwapner Nagari*. The USA loans its satellite ATS-6 for a one-year SITE project, while **Doordarshan** expands its number of terrestrial stations (Calcutta, Madras and Lucknow in 1975, Ahmedabad in 1976). The Aryabhata, a 360kg satellite, is made in India and launched from a Soviet cosmodrome.

A new agreement with the MPEAA means that US films can be imported again. ***Sholay*** and ***Jai Santoshi Maa*** are made. The Bengali film fortnightly *Anandalok* starts.

1976
Emergency attacks on civil liberties include the Prevention of Publication of Objectional Matter Act, effectively introducing pre-censorship of the press, and the 42nd Amendment, paving the way for a permanent dictatorship. A new National Population Policy is announced by Sanjay Gandhi, aiming to sterilise 23 million people over three years. Between April and September 1976, 3. 7 million Indians were sterilised, mostly among the lowest and most oppressed sections of the population, often forcibly in makeshift sterilisation camps. In the Turkman Gate and Jama Masjid neighbourhoods in Delhi, 700,000 people are made homeless by slum clearance and 'beautification' programmes. The Constitution's preamble is amended from 'Sovereign Democratic Republic' to 'Sovereign Socialist Secular Democratic Republic'. Food prices stabilise following a good monsoon; the number of days lost in industrial strikes goes down from 6 million between July and September 1974 to 1. 56 million between July and September 1975. **Doordarshan** TV is separated from All-India Radio and is allowed to take advertising.

During the Emergency, the Committee on Public Undertakings attacks the **FFC**'s 'art-film' policy because, from Rs 62. 5 lakhs disbursed since June 1969 for 30 features, Rs 38. 01 lakhs had not been recovered. From the 30 films financed, only 16 were completed and 10 of them 'have not proved successful at the box office'. The Committee ignores distribution and exhibition, exclusively blaming the films instead. It decrees a series of aesthetic criteria for future film funding, including 'human interest in theme', 'Indianness' and 'characters with whom the audience can identify'. Prefiguring the commercialised **Doordarshan** experiment, the Estimates Committee's 80th *Report* (1975-6), states that 'It should have been apparent to the [C]orporation that films are primarily a means of entertainment and unless the films financed provide good entertainment [t]hey would not be acceptable to the masses. ' The *Report* adds that in 1969-70, Indian films worth Rs 4. 35 crore were exported illegally. It also attacks the selection policy of Indian films entered in foreign festivals. The journal *Film Blaze* starts in Bombay. The YUKT co-op, a group of ex-students of the **FTII**, makes ***Ghashiram Kotwal***. The negative of Amrit Nahata's ***Kissa Kursi Ka*** (remade 1977), a satire on Emergency rule, is destroyed by Sanjay Gandhi's representatives.

1977
In the general election, Indira Gandhi is defeated and the Janata Party, a coalition of disparate opposition groups, takes power under Morarji Desai. The Emergency is withdrawn. In Tamil Nadu, the AIADMK comes to power with **M. G. Ramachandran** as chief minister. He introduces schemes to assist the Tamil film industry, including government subsidies.

Tamil film production leaps from 66 films in 1978 to 105 in 1979.

1978
Indira Gandhi starts the Congress (I) Party. The Janata Party's Foreign Exchange Regulation Act, and the founding of the Monopolies and Restrictive Trade Practices Commission, effectively terminate the licences to Coca Cola, IBM and other multinationals. The All-Assam Students Union (AASU) issues a 16-point Charter, including a demand to restrict the entry of foreigners, mainly Bangladeshi refugees, into Assam. The B. G. Verghese Working Group on Autonomy for Akashvani and **Doordarshan**, submits its report. The following year, the Prasar Bharati Bill cancels any possibility of real autonomy for TV.

The net Indian box-office take for 1978-9 is c. Rs 247 crore. Entertainment tax for the period is Rs 187 crore. On average, state governments collect 43% of the gross box office. The Orissa Film Development Corporation (Est: 1976) announces the financing of 'Janata cinema houses' in rural and semi-urban areas. The number of Oriya films reaches 15. Tamil Nadu and Andhra Pradesh adopt similar financing programmes while Punjab, UP and Kerala directly build state-owned theatres. Panorama of Indian cinema at the Carthage Film Festival. The Malayalam film journal *Chitrabhoomi* is started by the owners of the mainstream daily *Mathrubhoomi.*

1979
The Janata Party splits (e. g. because of the Jan Sangh's affiliations to the RSS), Morarji Desai resigns and Charan Singh becomes a caretaker prime minister as elections are announced. The Akali Dal General House defines the Anandpur Sahib Resolution, demanding that Chandigarh becomes the capital of Punjab and that the Supreme Court adjudicate disputes over the distribution of river water. The Congress (I) supports Jarnail Singh Bhindranwale for the Shiromani Gurudwara Prabandhak Committee elections. The film industry forms the National Party with a predominantly pro-industry, right-wing manifesto, denying that it is a version of the former Swatantra Party. This is the only occasion when the film industry attempted to start a political Party of its own, although several movie stars participated in parliamentary politics. Mass rallies in Assam, led by the AASU, on the issue of illegal immigrants, also generate anti-Muslim and regionalist anti-Bengali sentiment. The second satellite, Bhaskara-1, also built in India by ISRO, is launched from Bear's Lake, USSR. However, the first Satellite Launching Vehicle (SLV) at Sriharikota fails with a payload of 40kg.

Malayalam film production reaches 123 (54 in 1975), exceeding the Hindi cinema, partly because of the Kerala government's Chitranjali Film Studio and other subsidies, but mostly because of the influx of 'Gulf money' remitted by Malayalam workers in the Middle East. ***Shankarabharanam*** is a major Telugu musical hit.

1980
Indira Gandhi's Congress (I) returns to power, also winning Punjab with the support of Bhindranwale and other groups which unleash extreme Right terrorist attacks. As a result of the Foreign Exchange Regulation Act, the number of foreign companies in India falls from 510 in 1975 to 300 by 1980-1. The second rocket launch from Sriharikota, the satellite ROHINI, is successful. The first colour telecast from **Doordarshan**, an experiment on 18 July, announces the 1982 shift to colour and commercialisation. The Information & Broadcasting Minister makes colour TV one of the Congress (I)'s main election promises.

India has 6368 permanent and 4024 temporary 'touring' theatres. The Lotus Cinema, hired by the **FFC**, becomes Bombay's only venue for 'art' films, opening with Bimal Dutt's *Kasturi* (1978). The **FFC** merges with the Indian Motion Picture Export Corporation to become the **NFDC**. Independent film-makers start the Forum for Better Cinema and ask the government to invite **Satyajit Ray** to head the new organisation. **Ray** declines the offer, urging the Forum to exercise caution. The **NFDC**'s Board combines disparate interests and is unable to agree which kind of cinema to support. K. S. Karanth's *Report of the Working Group on National Film Policy* is published. It recommends, e. g. , the foundation of a Chalachitra Akademi for film in line with the academies for literature, theatre, dance and the visual arts. The academy would combine the Directorate of Film Festivals, the **National Film Archive of India**, a non-commercial import/export agency, a film museum and the means to fund film societies, education and research programmes. The government ignores the report. **Satyajit Ray** retrospective at the Indian International Film Festival; **Mrinal Sen** retrospective at the National Film Theatre, London. The journal *Cinema Vision (India)* starts in Bombay with an issue on silent cinema.

1981
Mrs Gandhi's government reverses its pre-Emergency commitment to socialist protectionism in the wake of its new space satellite programme. The shift to colour TV pioneers the liberalisation of import licences for unassembled TV kits, assembly and marketing initially being reserved for small businesses. India borrows $5 billion from the International Monetary Fund, the biggest such loan in history. The art exhibition *Place for People* (Bhupen Khakhar, Vivan Sundaram, Gulam Mohammed Sheikh, Nalini Malani, Sudhir Patwardhan) reconstitutes Indian modernism, drawing on popular arts and on figurative elements rather than abstraction. India's first geostationary telecommunications satellite, APPLE (Ariane Passenger Payload Experiment), weighing 670kg, is launched from French Guiana by the European Space Agency.

Celebration of Indian cinema's golden jubilee; formation of the short-lived Indian Academy of Motion Picture Arts & Sciences (IAMPAS). A three-part season tours the USA (billed as a pre-**Ray** package, a **Ray** retrospective and a **New Indian Cinema** programme). Special issue on Indian cinema by the *Journal for Asian Literature* (Washington). ***36 Chowringhee Lane*** achieves a commercially viable, English-speaking audience, enhanced by foreign sales.

1982
Continuing the Congress (I)'s liberalisation policies, Indian culture is marketed in a massive Festivals of India campaign starting in London, then in Paris and Moscow. India's finest traditional and contemporary artists are featured. The Bombay Textile strike, lasting almost a year. INSAT 1-A is launched from Cape Canaveral, inaugurating a national TV programme mobilising all prime time throughout the country for the New Delhi station. Colour TV starts on 25 April with the telecast of **Ray**'s ***Sadgati*** and ***Shatranj Ke Khiladi***. Regular colour telecasts through INSAT begin on 15 August. The Ninth Asian Games held in Delhi provide the first nationwide colour programmes, using the USSR's Stationary-5 satellite and 20 low-power transmitters.

N. T. Rama Rao starts the Telugu Desam Party. The failure of **Rawail**'s *Deedar-e-Yaar* is a major setback to the Hindi industry. The Tamil film weekly *Gemini Cinema* starts. First films in Brijbhasha (*Brij Bhoomi*) and Malvi (*Bhadwa Mata*).

1983
Violence erupts in Assam, led by the All-Assam Students Union (AASU) which boycotts the Assembly elections held with major military support, although none of the main Parties except the Congress (I) and some Left groups participate. Rampant terrorism in the Punjab countryside, briefly quelled by massive state intervention, gradually resurfaces. INSAT 1-B satellite is put into orbit from the US space shuttle *Challenger*, inaugurating the Special Plan for Expansion of the Television Network.

The Karnataka state subsidy to films is increased to Rs 1 lakh for b&w and Rs 1. 5 lakh for colour, provided the films are in Kannada and made entirely in the state. Producers are allowed to do post-production outside Karnataka until 1986, when several dubbing, mixing and re-recording studios (the Chamundeshwari and Vasant labs, followed by **Prasad** Studios and **Shankar Nag**'s Sanket Electronics) are established. Panorama of Indian Cinema at the Centre Pompidou, Paris. First film in Garhwali (*Jagwal*) and Khasi (*Ka Lawei Ha Ki Ktijong Ngi*).

1984
The Bhopal disaster, in which deadly emissions of methyl iso-cyanate from a Union Carbide (India) plant in Bhopal kill 3849 people (by official estimates) and maim 500,000 people in the countryside. The army attacks the Golden Temple, Amritsar, the most sacred of Sikh gurdwaras and the hideout of Jarnail Singh Bhindranwale. Over 2000 people die, including a third of the military contingent used. The Congress (I)'s former protégé, Bhindranwale, is killed. In retaliation, Indira Gandhi is assassinated by her security guards, triggering the Delhi riots in which 2717 people (official estimate), mostly Sikhs, are killed by mobs with alleged Congress (I) compliance. Rajiv Gandhi becomes prime minister. The P. C. Joshi Working Group on Software for **Doordarshan** is presented to parliament, with scathing criticism of TV's commercialism and 'Delhi-centrism'. The report is never officially published. **Doordarshan** starts a second channel from Delhi.

John Abraham starts the Odessa Collective in Cochin.

1985
The 52nd Amendment bill disqualifies Members of Parliament who defect from one Party to another. The Assam accord, after which the AASU-Asom Gana Parishad leadership takes over the state government. The Punjab accord is signed by Rajiv Gandhi and Harchand Singh Longowal, the most moderate of the Sikh leaders. Longowal is assassinated shortly afterwards.
Doordarshan becomes a fully commercial station selling prime time slots to private sponsors and manufacturers of TV soaps. Its first successful series, Kumar Vasudev's *Humlog* (1984-5), is modelled on the Mexican concept of the 'developmental' soap opera and is sponsored by Colgate-Palmolive and Nestlé. Several privately made serials follow as TV ownership jumps from 2. 7 million in 1984 to 12. 5 million in 1986.

Indian Cinema season at Pesaro Film Festival, Italy.

1986
The district judge of Faizabad orders the opening of the Babri Masjid mosque in Ayodhya to Hindu worshippers. According to fanatical Hindus, the mosque, built in 1528, stands on the spot where Ram, a Hindu god, was born. The Babri Masjid Action Committee (BMAC) is formed. G. M. Shah's ministry in Kashmir is dissolved and Kashmir is brought under President's rule. The Muslim Women (Protection of Rights on Divorce) Bill, better known as the Shah Bano Bill, follows the Supreme Court's judgment ordering Mohammed Ahmed Khan of Indore to pay alimony to his divorced wife Shah Bano. The Supreme Court is accused of violating the Shariat (the Koranic Commandments) by the Muslim Personal Law Board, and the government, to win conservative Muslim support, passes a Bill taking away all rights from divorced Muslim women. The assets of the top 574 companies identified by the Monopolies & Restrictive Trade Practices Act are, on average, Rs 70. 24 crore, almost double the value of Indian subsidiaries of foreign multinationals.

The actress **Smita Patil** dies, aged 31. The Calcutta-based journal *Splice* starts, edited by Samik Bandyopadhyay. It lasts for six issues.

1987
Institutionalised corruption and capital flight become dominant political issues. Arms deals (e. g. buying Bofors guns and HDW submarines) and the hiring of an American detective agency to trace illegal funds held by Indians abroad provoke a series of inquiry commissions. Finance Minister V. P. Singh is sacked and becomes a leading opponent of the Rajiv Gandhi regime. **Amitabh Bachchan** resigns as MP after allegations that his family is involved in the Bofors kickback scandal. In Deorala, Roop Kanwar is burnt alive on her husband's funeral pyre, reviving the ritual murder of widows which had been banned for a century. The Jharkhand agitation in Bihar strives for separate statehood. The government persecutes the *Indian Express*, a virulent anti-Rajiv Gandhi paper which relentlessly pursued the corruption scandals. 300,000 Muslims at a New Delhi rally demand the return of the Babri Mosque, while militant Hindus gather at Ayodhya to pledge the building of a temple. India sends troops to support the Sri Lankan government against the guerrilla movement launched by the

Liberation Tigers of Tamil Eelam. The Baroda art exhibition, *Questions and Dialogue*, signals the emergence of the Radical Painters & Sculptors Association dominated by artists from Kerala and takes a militant stand on the commercialisation of Indian art, emphasising a role for the radical avant-garde. The *Ramayana* TV serial (1986-8) becomes Indian TV's first major hit.

The **NFDC** starts the quarterly journal *Cinema in India*.

1988
Rajiv Gandhi's Defamation Bill, seeking to reimpose Emergency-type curbs on the press, is withdrawn following nationwide resistance. The National Front of opposition parties is launched in August; the Janata Dal, led by expelled Congress(I) member V. P. Singh, revives the centrist opposition unity of the Emergency, except for the BJP. The Bhartiya Kisan Union, led by Mahendra Singh Tikait, the most militant of the rich peasant organisations, organises a major rally at the Boat Club, New Delhi. The DMK wins the Tamil Nadu state assembly after **M. G. Ramachandran**'s death (1987) and the split in his AIADMK. IRS-1A, a remote sensing satellite, is launched from the Baikonur cosmodrome in the USSR. INSAT 1C, launched by the Ariane facility in Kourou, French Guiana, develops snags.

The journals *Cinemaya (A Quarterly on Asian Film)* and *Deep Focus* start.

1989
Satwant Singh and Kehar Singh, accused of assassinating Indira Gandhi, are hanged. Safdar Hashmi, a street theatre activist, is killed by thugs allegedly members of the Delhi Congress(I). Amid a nationwide outcry, the Safdar Hashmi Memorial Trust is formed, organising a series of Artists Against Communalism programmes featuring some of India's best-known musicians, dancers and artists. Agni, an intermediate-range ballistic missile, is fired, making India the fifth country to acquire IRBM capability. The Shilanyas ceremony is held at Ayodhya, as the foundation stone for a temple in the name of Ram is laid. Rajiv Gandhi, seeking Hindu support, allows the ceremony to take place. In the general elections (December), a coalition of the Janata Dal, supported by the right-wing BJP and the CPI(M), displace Rajiv Gandhi's government.

The Central Board of Film Censors allows 1268 video titles to be released, including 62 features, 213 shorts, 48 'long' films and 915 foreign shorts.

1990
The government's policy to increase quotas of jobs for 'scheduled castes' in public service is strongly attacked by upper-caste and middle-class sectors. **Karunanidhi**'s DMK government in Tamil Nadu is dismissed for allegedly supporting the Sri Lankan LTTE. A 'Rath-Yatra', evoking a medieval chariot procession, is led by L. K. Advani of the BJP from Somnath to Ayodhya, fomenting communal violence along its route. Advani is arrested by the Janata Dal; in retaliation, the BJP withdraws its support from the government, which falls. The second Shilanyas procession and the 'kar seva' at Ayodhya on 30 October in which several people are killed and injured in police action.

The first Bombay International Film Festival for Shorts and Documentaries, sponsored by **Films Division**.

1991
Rajiv Gandhi is assassinated by Tamil terrorists. A rising foreign debt and other dysfunctions inaugurate a policy of economic reform encouraging foreign investment. The USSR disintegrates. As the USSR leaves Afghanistan, the massive amount of weapons put into Pakistan by the USA and the CIA-trained Muslim terrorists heightens tension between India and Pakistan (eventually rebounding on the USA as ex-CIA protégés bomb the World Trade Centre in New York in 1993). The number of TV receivers increased from 12. 5 million in 1986 to 27. 8 million, with TV covering 82% of the population.

1992
India seeks closer ties with the USA. Violence in Kashmir spreads. BJP organises an attack on Ayodya and destroys the mosque, leading to major bloodbaths in Bombay and elsewhere.

INDIAN SOUND FEATURES 1931/1993

Year

Language	1931	1932	1933	1934	1935	1936	1937	1938	1939	1940	1941	1942	1943	1944	1945	1946	1947	1948	1949	1950	1951	1952	1953	1954	1955
Arabic	-	-	-	-	-	-	-	-	-	-	-	-	1	1	-	-	-	-	-	-	-	-	-	-	-
Assamese	-	-	-	-	1	-	-	-	1	-	1	-	-	-	-	-	2	-	2	-	-	-	1	1	2
Avadhi	-	-	-	-	-	-	-	-	-	-	-	-	-	-	-	-	-	-	-	-	-	-	-	-	-
Badaga	-	-	-	-	-	-	-	-	-	-	-	-	-	-	-	-	-	-	-	-	-	-	-	-	-
Bengali	4	5	9	10	19	20	16	19	16	16	19	18	21	14	9	15	33	37	62	42	39	43	50	48	52
Bhojpuri	-	-	-	-	-	-	-	-	-	-	-	-	-	-	-	-	-	-	-	-	-	-	-	-	-
Bodo	-	-	-	-	-	-	-	-	-	-	-	-	-	-	-	-	-	-	-	-	-	-	-	-	-
Brij Bhasha	-	-	-	-	-	-	-	-	-	-	-	-	-	-	-	-	-	-	-	-	-	-	-	-	-
Chhatisghari	-	-	-	-	-	-	-	-	-	-	-	-	-	-	-	-	-	-	-	-	-	-	-	-	-
Coorgi	-	-	-	-	-	-	-	-	-	-	-	-	-	-	-	-	-	-	-	-	-	-	-	-	-
Dogri	-	-	-	-	-	-	-	-	-	-	-	-	-	-	-	-	-	-	-	-	-	-	-	-	-
English	-	1	-	1	-	-	-	-	-	-	1	-	1	-	-	-	-	1	-	1	-	-	2	2	1
Garwhali	-	-	-	-	-	-	-	-	-	-	-	-	-	-	-	-	-	-	-	-	-	-	-	-	-
German	-	-	-	-	-	-	-	-	-	-	-	-	-	-	-	-	-	-	-	-	-	-	-	1	-
Gujarati	-	2	-	1	1	3	-	-	1	1	-	-	-	-	-	1	11	27	17	13	6	2	-	-	3
Gujjar	-	-	-	-	-	-	-	-	-	-	-	-	-	-	-	-	-	-	-	-	-	-	-	-	-
Haryanvi	-	-	-	-	-	-	-	-	-	-	-	-	-	-	-	-	-	-	-	-	-	-	-	-	-
Hindi	23	61	75	121	154	135	102	88	80	85	73	98	106	85	73	155	183	147	159	114	99	102	97	118	125
Iranian	-	-	-	-	-	-	-	-	-	-	-	-	-	-	-	-	1	-	-	-	-	-	-	-	-
Kannada	-	-	-	2	1	-	-	-	-	-	2	2	4	-	1	-	5	2	6	1	2	1	7	11	15
Karbi	-	-	-	-	-	-	-	-	-	-	-	-	-	-	-	-	-	-	-	-	-	-	-	-	-
Kashmiri	-	-	-	-	-	-	-	-	-	-	-	-	-	-	-	-	-	-	-	-	-	-	-	-	-
Khasi	-	-	-	-	-	-	-	-	-	-	-	-	-	-	-	-	-	-	-	-	-	-	-	-	-
Kodava	-	-	-	-	-	-	-	-	-	-	-	-	-	-	-	-	-	-	-	-	-	-	-	-	-
Kok Borok	-	-	-	-	-	-	-	-	-	-	-	-	-	-	-	-	-	-	-	-	-	-	-	-	-
Konkani	-	-	-	-	-	-	-	-	-	-	-	-	-	-	-	-	-	-	-	1	-	-	-	-	-
Kumaoni	-	-	-	-	-	-	-	-	-	-	-	-	-	-	-	-	-	-	-	-	-	-	-	-	-
Magdhi	-	-	-	-	-	-	-	-	-	-	-	-	-	-	-	-	-	-	-	-	-	-	-	-	-
Maithili	-	-	-	-	-	-	-	-	-	-	-	-	-	-	-	-	-	-	-	-	-	-	-	-	-
Malayalam	-	-	-	-	-	-	-	1	-	1	1	-	-	-	-	-	-	1	1	6	6	11	7	9	7
Malvi	-	-	-	-	-	-	-	-	-	-	-	-	-	-	-	-	-	-	-	-	-	-	-	-	-
Manipuri	-	-	-	-	-	-	-	-	-	-	-	-	-	-	-	-	-	-	-	-	-	-	-	-	-
Marathi	-	8	6	11	9	6	11	14	12	10	13	13	7	5	-	2	6	7	15	19	16	17	21	18	13
Marwari	-	-	-	-	-	-	-	-	-	-	-	1	-	-	-	-	-	-	-	-	-	-	-	-	-
Nagamese	-	-	-	-	-	-	-	-	-	-	-	-	-	-	-	-	-	-	-	-	-	-	-	-	-
Nagpuri	-	-	-	-	-	-	-	-	-	-	-	-	-	-	-	-	-	-	-	-	-	-	-	-	-
Nepali	-	-	-	-	-	-	-	-	-	-	-	-	-	-	-	-	-	-	-	-	1	-	-	-	-
Nimadi	-	-	-	-	-	-	-	-	-	-	-	-	-	-	-	-	-	-	-	-	-	-	-	-	-
Oriya	-	-	-	-	-	1	-	-	-	-	-	-	-	-	-	-	-	1	-	2	1	-	1	1	-
Persian	-	-	1	1	2	1	-	-	-	-	-	-	-	-	-	-	3	-	-	-	-	-	-	-	-
Pushtu	-	-	-	-	-	-	-	-	-	-	1	-	1	-	-	-	-	-	-	-	-	-	-	-	-
Punjabi	-	-	-	-	1	1	-	1	7	7	8	5	1	2	-	1	-	1	1	5	4	-	3	3	-
Rajasthani	-	-	-	-	-	-	-	-	-	-	-	-	-	-	-	-	-	-	-	-	-	-	-	-	-
Sanskrit	-	-	-	-	-	-	-	-	-	-	-	-	-	-	-	-	-	-	-	-	-	-	-	-	-
Sindhi	-	-	-	-	-	-	-	-	-	-	-	1	-	-	-	-	-	-	-	-	-	-	-	-	-
Sinhalese	-	-	-	-	-	-	-	-	-	-	-	-	-	-	-	-	1	-	-	-	-	-	-	-	-
Tamil	1	4	7	14	38	38	37	39	35	36	32	23	13	14	11	16	29	32	21	19	26	32	42	38	46
Telugu	-	3	5	3	7	12	10	10	12	14	15	12	6	6	5	9	6	7	7	18	21	25	29	28	24
Thai	-	-	-	-	-	-	-	-	-	-	-	-	-	-	-	-	-	-	-	-	-	-	-	-	-
Tulu	-	-	-	-	-	-	-	-	-	-	-	-	-	-	-	-	-	-	-	-	-	-	-	-	-
Urdu	-	-	-	-	-	-	-	-	-	-	-	-	-	-	-	-	-	-	-	-	-	-	-	-	-
Total	28	84	103	164	233	217	176	172	164	170	166	173	161	127	99	199	280	263	291	241	221	233	260	278	288

1956/1980

INDIAN SOUND FEATURES 1931/1993

Language	1956	1957	1958	1959	1960	1961	1962	1963	1964	1965	1966	1967	1968	1969	1970	1971	1972	1973	1974	1975	1976	1977	1978	1979	1980
Arabic	-	-	-	-	-	-	-	-	-	-	-	-	-	-	-	-	-	-	-	-	-	-	-	-	-
Assamese	3	3	2	5	-	2	1	3	1	-	2	2	1	2	3	5	7	9	3	6	5	7	6	10	7
Avadhi	-	-	-	-	-	-	-	-	1	-	-	-	-	-	-	-	-	-	-	-	-	-	-	-	-
Badaga	-	-	-	-	-	-	-	-	-	-	-	-	-	-	-	-	-	-	-	-	-	-	-	-	1
Bengali	54	55	45	38	36	35	42	39	38	29	30	25	29	29	36	30	25	35	35	35	32	29	37	37	37
Bhojpuri	-	-	-	-	-	-	1	2	7	5	2	-	1	-	-	1	-	-	-	-	-	2	1	2	3
Bodo	-	-	-	-	-	-	-	-	-	-	-	-	-	-	-	-	-	-	-	-	-	-	-	-	-
Brij Bhasha	-	-	-	-	-	-	-	-	-	-	-	-	-	-	-	-	-	-	-	-	-	-	-	-	-
Chhatisghari	-	-	-	-	-	-	-	-	-	1	-	-	-	-	-	1	-	-	-	-	-	-	-	-	-
Coorgi	-	-	-	-	-	-	-	-	-	-	-	-	-	-	-	-	1	-	-	-	-	-	-	-	-
Dogri	-	-	-	-	-	-	-	-	-	-	1	-	-	-	-	-	-	-	-	-	-	-	-	-	-
English	1	-	-	1	1	-	2	1	1	1	-	-	-	3	1	1	3	1	1	-	2	3	2	-	-
Garwhali	-	-	-	-	-	-	-	-	-	-	-	-	-	-	-	-	-	-	-	-	-	-	-	-	-
German	-	-	-	-	-	-	-	-	-	-	-	-	-	-	-	-	-	-	-	-	-	-	-	-	-
Gujarati	3	-	1	-	2	7	5	6	2	5	2	3	3	6	5	2	4	5	7	12	29	30	32	38	34
Gujjar	-	-	-	-	-	-	-	-	-	-	-	-	-	-	-	-	-	-	-	-	-	-	-	-	-
Haryanvi	-	-	-	-	-	-	-	-	-	-	-	-	-	-	-	-	-	1	1	-	-	-	-	-	-
Hindi	122	115	114	115	118	104	90	88	101	98	100	82	72	103	102	115	131	137	132	119	106	134	116	113	143
Iranian	-	-	-	-	-	-	-	-	-	-	-	-	-	-	-	-	-	-	-	-	-	-	-	-	-
Kannada	14	14	11	5	12	12	16	22	18	21	21	24	36	45	37	33	20	32	30	38	45	49	54	59	68
Karbi	-	-	-	-	-	-	-	-	-	-	-	-	-	-	-	-	-	-	-	-	-	-	-	-	-
Kashmiri	-	-	-	-	-	-	-	-	1	-	-	-	-	1	-	-	-	-	-	-	-	-	-	-	-
Khasi	-	-	-	-	-	-	-	-	-	-	-	-	-	-	-	-	-	-	-	-	-	-	-	-	-
Kodava	-	-	-	-	-	-	-	-	-	-	-	-	-	-	-	-	-	-	-	-	-	-	-	-	-
Kok Borok	-	-	-	-	-	-	-	-	-	-	-	-	-	-	-	-	-	-	-	-	-	-	-	-	-
Konkani	-	-	-	-	-	-	-	1	-	1	-	1	-	1	1	1	-	-	-	1	1	1	1	-	2
Kumaoni	-	-	-	-	-	-	-	-	-	-	-	-	-	-	-	-	-	-	-	-	-	-	-	-	-
Magdhi	-	-	-	-	-	-	-	-	1	1	-	-	-	-	-	-	-	-	-	-	-	-	-	-	-
Maithili	-	-	-	-	-	-	-	-	-	-	-	-	-	-	-	1	-	-	-	-	-	-	-	-	-
Malayalam	5	7	4	3	6	11	15	13	19	31	32	40	36	32	43	53	47	60	54	77	84	91	123	130	99
Malvi	-	-	-	-	-	-	-	-	-	-	-	-	-	-	-	-	-	-	-	-	-	-	-	-	-
Manipuri	-	-	-	-	-	-	-	-	-	-	-	-	-	-	-	-	2	-	2	-	1	-	-	3	-
Marathi	13	14	16	9	15	15	22	15	16	14	12	19	17	16	19	23	12	14	11	17	10	19	15	19	28
Marwari	-	-	-	-	-	-	-	-	-	-	-	-	-	-	-	-	-	-	-	-	-	-	-	-	-
Nagamese	-	-	-	-	-	-	-	-	-	-	-	-	-	-	-	-	-	-	-	-	-	-	-	-	-
Nagpuri	-	-	-	-	-	-	-	-	-	-	-	-	-	-	-	-	-	-	-	-	-	-	-	-	-
Nepali	-	-	-	-	-	-	-	-	-	-	1	-	1	-	1	-	-	-	-	-	-	-	1	1	-
Nimadi	-	-	-	-	-	-	-	-	-	-	-	-	-	-	-	-	-	-	-	-	-	-	-	-	-
Oriya	2	1	-	2	5	1	7	2	3	3	2	1	3	2	-	1	1	2	2	3	6	11	15	10	15
Persian	-	1	-	-	-	-	-	-	-	-	-	-	-	-	-	-	-	-	-	-	-	-	-	-	-
Pushtu	-	-	-	-	-	-	-	-	-	-	-	-	-	-	-	-	-	-	-	-	-	-	-	-	-
Punjabi	-	2	1	1	4	5	6	4	8	5	4	4	2	4	2	2	3	5	4	5	10	12	7	15	6
Rajasthani	-	-	-	-	-	1	-	3	3	1	-	-	-	1	-	-	-	1	-	-	-	-	-	-	-
Sanskrit	-	-	-	-	-	-	-	-	-	-	-	-	-	-	-	-	-	-	-	-	-	-	-	-	-
Sindhi	-	-	3	-	1	-	-	-	-	1	1	1	1	2	-	1	1	1	-	-	-	-	-	-	-
Sinhalese	-	-	-	-	-	-	-	-	-	-	-	-	-	-	-	-	-	-	-	-	-	-	-	-	-
Tamil	51	45	61	78	64	49	60	55	44	56	61	63	68	72	75	74	77	66	79	70	81	66	105	139	144
Telugu	27	36	36	47	54	55	48	46	41	50	41	62	77	60	72	85	73	74	69	88	93	99	94	131	152
Thai	-	-	-	-	-	-	-	-	-	-	-	-	-	-	-	-	1	-	-	-	-	-	-	-	-
Tulu	-	-	-	-	-	-	-	-	-	-	-	-	-	-	-	2	2	4	2	-	2	2	3	-	-
Urdu	-	-	-	-	-	-	-	-	-	-	-	-	-	-	-	-	-	-	-	-	-	-	-	-	-
Total	295	293	294	304	318	297	315	300	305	323	312	327	347	379	397	431	410	447	432	471	507	555	612	707	739

INDIAN SOUND FEATURES 1931/1993

Language	Year 1981	1982	1983	1984	1985	1986	1987	1988	1989	1990	1991	1992	1993
Arabic	-	-	-	-	-	-	-	-	-	-	-	-	-
Assamese	5	4	4	5	10	11	8	7	4	8	9	4	9
Avadhi	-	-	-	-	-	1	-	-	-	-	-	-	-
Badaga	-	-	-	-	-	-	-	-	-	-	-	-	-
Bengali	42	49	47	34	28	47	35	37	50	50	51	42	57
Bhojpuri	5	3	11	9	6	19	14	8	10	5	8	8	2
Bodo	-	-	-	-	-	2	-	-	-	1	-	-	-
Brij Bhasha	-	1	-	1	-	-	1	-	-	-	-	-	-
Chhatisghari	-	-	-	-	-	-	-	-	-	-	-	-	-
Coorgi	-	1	-	-	-	-	-	-	-	-	-	-	-
Dogri	-	-	-	-	1	-	-	-	-	-	-	-	-
English	2	1	1	2	1	-	1	5	3	4	1	5	2
Garwhali	-	-	1	1	-	1	3	-	-	1	-	1	1
German	-	-	-	-	-	-	-	-	-	-	-	-	-
Gujarati	34	39	27	30	22	13	11	6	9	14	16	5	3
Gujjar	-	-	-	-	-	-	-	-	-	-	-	-	1
Haryanvi	-	-	1	4	10	7	6	5	3	2	1	2	1
Hindi	148	155	133	163	185	159	150	182	176	200	215	189	183
Iranian	-	-	-	-	-	-	-	-	-	-	-	-	-
Kannada	65	50	71	80	69	59	88	67	75	81	92	92	78
Karbi	-	-	-	-	-	1	-	-	1	-	-	-	-
Kashmiri	-	-	1	-	-	-	-	-	-	1	-	-	-
Khasi	-	-	1	1	-	-	-	-	-	-	-	-	-
Kodava	-	-	-	-	-	-	-	-	-	-	-	-	1
Kok Borok	-	-	-	-	-	-	-	-	-	-	-	-	1
Konkani	-	1	-	-	-	-	-	-	-	-	-	-	-
Kumaoni	-	-	-	-	-	-	1	-	-	-	-	-	-
Magdhi	-	-	-	-	-	-	-	-	-	-	-	-	-
Maithili	-	1	-	-	-	-	-	-	-	-	-	-	-
Malayalam	113	118	111	121	136	130	103	83	96	126	94	90	71
Malvi	-	-	-	1	-	-	-	-	-	-	-	-	-
Manipuri	3	-	3	2	-	1	-	1	-	2	1	1	3
Marathi	27	24	20	25	16	17	27	23	30	25	29	25	35
Marwari	-	-	-	-	-	-	-	-	-	-	-	-	-
Nagamese	-	-	-	-	-	-	-	-	-	-	1	-	-
Nagpuri	-	-	-	-	-	-	-	-	-	-	-	1	-
Nepali	-	2	2	4	4	-	6	2	-	4	8	9	7
Nimadi	-	-	-	-	1	-	-	-	-	-	-	-	-
Oriya	10	9	12	14	17	17	9	16	13	13	11	11	20
Persian	-	-	-	-	-	-	-	-	-	-	-	-	-
Pushtu	-	-	-	-	-	-	-	-	-	-	-	-	-
Punjabi	8	6	19	9	8	7	8	6	2	7	9	12	14
Rajasthani	2	2	4	2	3	-	4	7	7	5	-	3	5
Sanskrit	-	-	1	-	-	-	-	-	-	-	-	1	-
Sindhi	-	-	-	1	-	1	-	-	-	-	-	1	-
Sinhalese	-	-	-	-	-	-	-	-	-	-	-	-	-
Tamil	138	140	127	148	190	154	167	152	148	194	186	180	168
Telugu	134	155	134	171	198	192	163	162	152	204	174	153	148
Thai	-	-	-	-	-	-	-	-	-	-	-	-	-
Tulu	1	-	1	1	-	-	1	1	1	1	-	-	1
Urdu	-	-	-	-	-	1	-	3	-	-	-	2	1
Total	737	761	732	829	905	840	806	773	780	948	906	837	812

INDIAN SILENT FILMS 1913/34

Year	No. of films
1913	3
1914	1
1915	-
1916	-
1917	3
1918	7
1919	8
1920	27
1921	44
1922	64
1923	52
1924	54
1925	86
1926	94
1927	90
1928	109
1929	140
1930	194
1931	200
1932	64
1933	41
1934	7
Total	1288

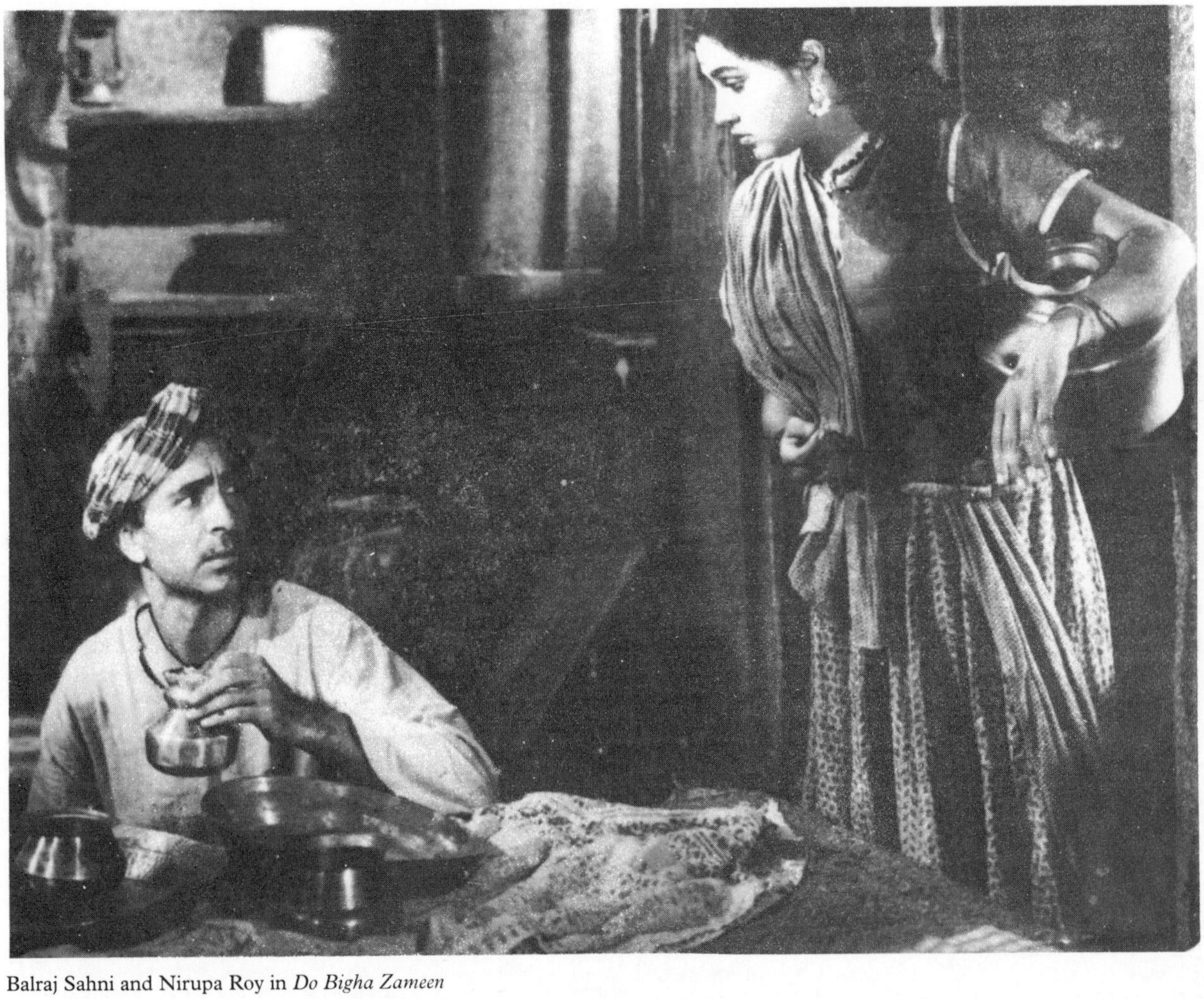

Balraj Sahni and Nirupa Roy in *Do Bigha Zameen*

LIST OF ENTRIES

Abbas, Khwaja Ahmad (1914-87)
Abraham, John (1937-87)
Acharya, N. R. (1909-56)
Advani, Jagatrai Pesumal (b. 1903)
Agarwala, Jyotiprasad (1903-51)
Agradoot
Ahluwalia, Sukhdev (b. 1932)
Akhtar, Javed [4msee[0m Salim-Javed
Akhtar, Sardar (1915-84)
Akhtar-ul-Iman (b. 1915)
Ali, Muzaffar (b. 1944)
All-India Film
Altekar, Parshwanath Yeshwant (1898-1957)
Aman, Zeenat (b. 1951)
Amarnath, Gelaram Khetarpal (1914-83)
Amrohi, Kamal (1918-93)
A. Na. Kru [4msee[0m Krishnarao, A. N.
Anand, Chetan (b. 1915)
Anand, Dev (b. 1923)
Anand, Inder Raj
Anand, Mukul Sudheswar (b. 1951)
Anand, Vijay (b. 1935)
Anjaneyalu, Chilakalapudi Seeta Rama (1907-63)
Annadurai, Canjeevaram Natarajan (1909-69)
Anthony, P. J. (1923-79)
Apte, Narayan Hari (1889-1971)
Apte, Shanta (1916-64)
Arathi (b. 1954)
Aravindan, Govindan (1935-91)
Art Schools
Arudra (b. 1925)
Arunaraje *or* Aruna-Vikas *see* Raje, Aruna
Ashwatamma, K. (1910-44)
Asif, Karimuddin (1924-71)
Athavale, Shantaram Govind (b. 1910)
Athreya, Acharya (1921-89)
Atma, K. P. [4msee[0m Pratyagatma, K.
Atma Ram (1930-94)
Atorthy, Premankur (1890-1964)
Atre, Pralhad Keshav (1898-1969)
Aurora Film Corporation
AVM Film Company
Azmi, Kaifi (b. 1925)
Azmi, Shabana (b. 1950)
Babu, Hanumappa Vishwanath (1903-68)
Baburaj, M. S. (b. 1921)
Bachchan, Amitabh (b. 1942)
Backer, P. A. (b. 1940-93)
Badami, Sarvottam (b. 1910)
Bagchi, Gurudas (b. 1926)
Bakshi, Anand (b. 1920)
Bakshi, Shanti Prakash (1925-88)
Balachander, Kailasam (b. 1930)
Balachander, Sundaram (1927-90)
Balaramaiah, Ghantasala (1906-53)
Balasaraswathi, R. (b. 1928)
Balasubramanyam, S. P. (b. 1945)
Bal Gandharva (1888-1967)
Bali, Geeta (1930-65)
Balkrishna, T. N. (b. 1913)
Baloch, Mohammed [4msee[0m Kumar, Mehul
Bannerjee, Bhanu (1920-83)
Bannerjee, Durgadas (1893-1943)
Bannerjee, Jyotish (b. 1887)
Bannerjee, Kali (1921-93)
Bannerjee, Kanu (1905-85)
Bapaiah, K.
Bapu (b. 1933)
Baran, Timir (1904-87)
Barua, Brojen (1925-72)
Barua, Jahnu (b. 1952)
Barua, Munin (b. 1948)
Barua, Nip (1925-92)
Barua, Padum (b. 1924)
Barua, Pramathesh Chandra (1903-51)
Barua, Ramen (b. 1938)
Bedekar, Vishram (b. 1906)
Bedi, Narendra (1937-82)
Bedi, Rajinder Singh (1915-84)
Benegal, Shyam (b. 1934)
Betaab, Narayan Prasad (1872-1945)
Bhaduri, Sisir Kumar (1889-1959)
Bhagavathar, C. Honappa (1914-92)
Bhagavathar, M. Krishnamurthy Thyagaraja (1909-59)
Bhagwan, Master (b. 1913)
Bhagyaraj, Krishnaswamy (b. 1953)
Bhanumathi, Paluvayi (b. 1924)
Bharathan, B. G. (b. 1946)
Bharatidasan (1891-1964)
Bharathirajaa (b. 1944)
Bhasi, Adoor (1929-90)
Bhasi, Thoppil (1925-92)
Bhaskara Das (1892-1952)
Bhaskaran, P. (b. 1924)
Bhatavdekar, Harishchandra Sakharam (b. 1868)
Bhatia, Vanraj (b. 1926)
Bhatt, Balwant N. (1909-65)
Bhatt, Mahesh (b. 1949)
Bhatt, Nanabhai N. (b. 1915)
Bhatt, Vijay Jagneshwar (1907-93)
Bhattacharya, Abhi (1922-93)
Bhattacharya, Ardhendu (1955-92)
Bhattacharya, Basu (b. 1934)
Bhattacharya, Bijon (1917-78)
Bhattacharya, Dhiraj (1905-59)
Bhavnani, Mohan Dayaram (1903-62)
Bhimsingh, A. (1924-78)
Bhole, Keshavrao Vaman (1896-1967)
Bhosle, Asha (b. 1933)
Bilimoria, Dinshaw (b. 1904)
Bilimoria, Fali (b. 1923)
Biswas, Anil (b. 1914)
Biswas, Sachindranath [Chhabi] (1900-62)
Bombay Talkies
Boral, Rai Chand (1903-81)
Bordoloi, Atul (b. 1938)
Bose, Debaki Kumar (1898-1971)
Bose, Modhu (1900-69)
Bose, Nitin (1897-1986)
Bose, Sadhona (1914-73)
Bose, Satyen (1916-93)
Bose, Tapan (b. 1946)
Bourne & Shepherd
British Dominion Films
Burma, Phani (b. 1897)
Burman, Rahul Dev (1939-94)
Burman, Sachin Dev (1906-75)
Calcutta Theatres
Chakraborty, Madhabi *see* Mukherjee, Madhabi
Chakraborty, Mithun (b. 1956)
Chakraborty, Tulsi (1899-1961)
Chakraborty, Utpalendu (b. 1948)
Chakrapani (?-1975)
Chakravarty, Amiya (1912-57)
Chanakya, Tapi (1925-73)
Chander, Krishan (1914-77)
Chandra, N. (b. 1952)
Chandrakant Gaur (b. 1929)
Chandrakant Sangani *see* Sangani, Chandrakant
Chandramohan (1905-49)
Chandrasekhar, Raja (1904-71)
Chatterjee, Anil (b. 1928)
Chatterjee, Basu (b. 1930)
Chatterjee, Dhritiman (b. 1946)
Chatterjee, Nabyendu (b. 1937)
Chatterjee, Pashupati (1906-91?)
Chatterjee, Sabitri (b. 1937)
Chatterjee, Soumitra (b. 1934)
Chattopadhyay, Kartick (1912-89)
Cherian, P. J. (1891-1981)
Chinappa, Pudukottai Ulaganathan (1915-51)
Children's Film Society
Chiranjeevi (b. 1955)
Chitnis, Leela (b. 1912)
Chopra, Baldev Raj (b. 1914)
Chopra, Yash (b. 1932)
Choudhury, Ahindra (1897-1974)
Choudhury, Basanta (b. 1928)
Choudhury, Kosaraju Raghavaiah [4msee[0m Kosaraju Raghavaiah Choudhury
Choudhury, Rama Shankar (1903-72)
Choudhury, Salil (b. 1925)
Choudhury, Santi P. (1929-82)
Choudhury, Supriya
Chughtai, Ismat (1915-91)
Chunder, Hemchandra (b. 1907)
Chunder, Krishan *see* Chander, Krishan (1914-77)
Company Natak
Company School Painting
Cooper, Patience (b. 1905?)
Dakshinamurthy, V. (b. 1919)
Damle, Vishnupant Govind (1892-1945)
Das, Jharana (b. 1945)
Dasgupta, Buddhadev (b. 1944)
Das Gupta, Chidananda
Dasgupta, Harisadhan (b. 1923)
Dasgupta, Kamal (?-1974)
Dasgupta, Protima (b. 1922)
Dasgupta, Sukumar (b. 1907)
Date, Keshavrao (1889-1971)
Datta Keshav Kulkarni (b. 1932)
Dave, Mohanlal G.
Dave, Ravindra (1919-92)
Debi, Suprabha (b. 1939)
Desai, Dhirubhai B. (1908-90)
Desai, Jayantilal Zinabhai (1909-76)
Desai, Manmohan (1936-94)
Desai, Nanubhai B. (1902-67)
Desai, Vasant (1912-75)
Devarajan, Paravur
Devare, Narayan Gopinath (1899-1954)
Devi, Anjali (b. 1927)
Devi, Arundhati (1923-90)
Devi, B. Saroja (b. 1945)
Devi, Chhaya (b. 1914)
Devi, Kanan (1916-92)
Devi, Saraswati (1912-80)
Devi, Seeta (b. 1912)
Devi, Sitara (b. 1919)
Devika Rani *see* Rani Choudhury, Devika
Dey, Krishna Chandra (1893-1962)
Dey, Nirmal (b. 1913)
Dhaiber, Keshavrao (1890-1978)
Dharmadhikari, Dattatreya Jagannath (1913-82)
Dharmaraj, Rabindra (1949-82)
Dharma Rao, Tapi (1887-1973)
Dharmendra Deol (b. 1935)
Dixit, Madhuri (b. 1968)
DMK Film
Doordarshan
Doshi, Chaturbhuj Anand (1894-1969)
Duncan, Ellis R. (b. 1908)
Durai
Dutt, Geeta (1930-72)
Dutt, Guru (1925-64)
Dutt, Sunil (b. 1930)

Dutt, Utpal (1929-93)
Dutta, J. P. (b. 1949)
East India Film Company
Ekalavya *see* Ghosh, Robi
Elangovan (1913-71)
Empire Films
Esoofally, Abdulally (1884-1957)
Fatma, Begum
Fattelal, Sheikh (1897-1964)
Fazil (b. 1953)
Film Advisory Board
Film and Television Institute of India
Film Finance Corporation *see* National Film Development Corporation
Filmistan
Films Division
Gadkar, Jayshree (b. 1942)
Gaggaiah, Vemuri (1895-1955)
Gandhi, Naval (b. 1897)
Ganesan, Sivaji (b. 1927)
Ganesh, Gemini
Ganguly, Dhirendranath (1893-1978)
Ganguly, Jahar (1904-69)
Ganguly, Jiban (1905-53)
Ganguly, Priyanath N. (1887-1956)
Gemini Pictures
General Pictures Corporation
George, Kulakkatil Geevarghese (b. 1945)
Ghai, Subhash (b. 1943)
Ghantasala Venkateswara Rao (1923-74)
Ghatak, Anupam (1911-47)
Ghatak, Ritwik Kumar (1925-76)
Ghosh, Gautam (b. 1950)
Ghosh, Kaliprasad (b. 1889)
Ghosh, Nachiketa (1924-76)
Ghosh, Nemai (1914-88)
Ghosh, Parbati (b. 1944)
Ghosh, Robi (b. 1931)
Gidwani, Moti B. (b. 1905)
Gohar, Kayoum Mamajiwala (1910-85)
Gopalakrishnan, Adoor (b. 1941)
Gopalakrishnan, K. S.
Gopi (b. 1937)
Gopichand, Tripuraneni (1910-62)
Gulzar, Sampooran Singh (b. 1936)
Gummadi *see* Venkateshwara Rao, Gummadi
Gupta, Dinen (b. 1932)
Gupta, Hemen (1914-67)
Haider, Ghulam (1908-53)
Haldar, Krishna *see* Atorthy, Premankur
Hamsalekha (b. 1951)
Hariharan, T.
Hazarika, Bhupen (b. 1926)
Heblikar, Suresh (b. 1945)
Hindustan Cinema Films Company
Historicals
Hublikar, Shanta (1914-92)
Husnlal-Bhagatram [Husnlal (?-1968), Bhagatram (?-1973)]
Hussain, Anwar (b. 1929)
Hussain, Nasir (b. 1931)
Ilaiyaraja
Ilangovan *see* Elangovan
Imperial Films Company
Indian Kinema Arts
Indian Peoples' Theatre Association
Information Films of India
Irani, Ardeshir Marwan (1886-1969)
Ishara, Babu Ram
Islam, Kazi Nazrul (1889-1976)
Iyer, Ganapathy Venkatramana (b. 1917)
Jaddanbai (b. 1908)
Jaffrey, Saeed (b. 1929)
Jaggaiah, Kongara (b. 1926)
Jagirdar, Gajanan (1907-88)
Jamuna, Nippani (b. 1937)
Janaki, S. (b. 1938)
Janaki, Sowcar (b. 1922)
Jaswantlal, Nandlal (b. 1906)
Jayalalitha Jayaram (b. 1948)
Jayamma, B. (1915-88)
Jayoo Nachiket *see* Jayoo and Nachiket Patwardhan
Jaywant, Nalini (b. 1926)
Jeetendra (b. 1942)
Jha, Prakash (b. 1952)
Joshi, Manilal (1893-1927)
Kale, Keshav Narayan (1904-74)
Kalingrao, P. (1914-81)
Kalki (1899-1954)
Kallol Group
Kalpana (?-1979)
Kalyanasundaram, Pattukotai (1930-59)
Kalyanji-Anandji [Kalyanji Veerji Shah & Anandji Virjee Shah]
Kamalabai, Surabhi (b. 1913)
Kamalahasan (b. 1954)
Kambadasan
Kambhar, Chandrasekhar (b. 1937)
Kameshwara Rao, Kamalakara *see* Rao, Kamalakara Kameshwara
Kanagal, Subraveshti Ramaswamy Puttanna (1933-85)
Kanam, E. J. (1926-87)
Kanchanmala (1923-81)
Kannadasan (1927-81)
Kannamba, Pasupuleti (1912-64)
Kapoor, Prithviraj (1906-72)
Kapoor, Raj (1924-88)
Kapoor, Shammi (b. 1931)
Kapoor, Shashi (b. 1938)
Kapur, Shekhar (b. 1945)
Kar, Ajoy (1914-85)
Karanth, B. V. (b. 1929)
Karanth, Prema (b. 1936)
Kardar, Abdul Rashid (1904-89)
Kariat, Ramu (1927-79)
Karnad, Girish Raghunath (b. 1938)
Karnataki, Vinayak *see* Vinayak, Master
Karun, Shaji N. (b. 1951)
Karunanidhi, Muthuvel (b. 1924)
Kasaravalli, Girish (b. 1949)
Kashmiri, Aga Hashr (1879-1935)
Kathavachak, Radheshyam (b. 1890)
Kaul, Mahesh (1911-72)
Kaul, Mani R. (b. 1942)
K.D. Brothers
Khandekar, Vishnu Sakharam (1898-1976)
Khanna, Rajesh (b. 1942)
Khayyam, Mohammed Zahur (b. 1927)
Khosla, Raj (1925-91)
Khote, Durga (1905-91)
Kohinoor Film Company
Kolhapur Cinetone
Komala, A. P. (b. 1934)
Kondke, Dada (b. 1932)
Kosaraju Raghavaiah Choudhury (1905-87)
Kottarakkara, Kuttan Pillai (b. 1924)
Kottarakkara Sridharan Nair *see* Nair, Kottarakkara Sridharan
Krishen, Pradeep (b. 1949)
Krishna Film Company
Krishna, Ghantamneni (b. 1943)
Krishnakant (b. 1922)
Krishnamurthy, Hunsur (b. 1914)
Krishnan, Nagerkoyil Sudalaimuthu (1905-57)
Krishnan-Panju [R. Krishnan (b. 1909), S. Panju (b. 1915)]
Krishnarao, Arakalagudu Narasinga Rao (1908-71)
Krishnarao Phulambrikar, Master (1891-1974)
Krishna Shastry, Devulapalli *see* Sastry, Devulapalli Krishna
Krishnaveni, C. (b. 1924)
Kulkarni, Datta Keshav *see* Datta Keshav Kulkarni
Kumar, Anup (b. 1932)
Kumar Ganguly, Ashok (b. 1911)
Kumar, Dilip (b. 1922)
Kumar, Hemant *see* Mukherjee, Hemanta
Kumar, Kalyana (b. 1936)
Kumar, Kishore (1929-87)
Kumar, Manoj (b. 1937)
Kumar, Mehul (b. 1949)
Kumar, Rajendra (b. 1929)
Kumar, Sampath *see* Kumar, Kalyana
Kumar, Udaya (1930-86)
Kumar, Uttam (1926-80)
Kumaran, K. P.
Kumari, Meena (1932-72)
Kumari, Usha *see* Vijayanirmala
Kunchako (1912-76)
Kurup, O. N. V. (b. 1931)
Lahiri, Bhappi
Lahiri, Nirendranath (1908-72)
Lajmi, Kalpana (b. 1954)
Lakshmirajyam (1922-87)
Lakshminarayan, N. (?-1991)
Lakshminarayan, Sattiraju *see* Bapu
Lankesh, P. (b. 1935)
Laxmikant-Pyarelal [Laxmikant Shantaram Kudalkar (b. 1937), Pyarelal Ramprasad Sharma (b. 1940)]
Leela, P. (b. 1933)
Leelavathi (b. 1938)
Ludhianvi, Sahir (1921-80)
Luhar, Chimanlal Muljibhoy (1901-48)
Madan Theatres
Madgulkar, Gajanan Digambar (1919-77)
Madhu
Madhubala (1933-69)
Mahapatra, Manmohan (b. 1951)
Mahapatra, Nirad
Maharashtra Film Company
Mahendra, Balu (b. 1946)
Mahendran, J. (b. 1939)
Majid, Abdul (b. 1932)
Majumdar, Nagendra (b. 1894)
Majumdar, Phani (1911-94)
Majumdar, Sushil (1906-88)
Majumdar, Tarun (b. 1932)
Malayil, Sibi
Malini, Hema (b. 1948)
Malvankar, Damuanna (1893-1975)
Mammootty (b. 1953)
Mane, Anant (b. 1915)
Mangeshkar, Lata (b. 1929)
Mani Rathnam *see* Rathnam, Mani
Manto, Sadat Hasan (1912-55)
Marudakasi, Ayyamperumal (1920-89)
Master, Homi (?-1949)
Mathur, Vishnu (b. 1944)
Mazumdar *see* Majumdar
Mehboob (1906-64)
Mehra, Prakash (b. 1939)
Mehta, Harshadrai Sakerlal
Mehta, Ketan (b. 1952)
Mehta, Vijaya (b. 1934)
Meiyappan Chettiar, A. V. *see* AVM Film Company
Melodrama
Menon, P. N. (b. 1928)
Menon, S. Balachandra (b. 1954)
Minerva Movietone
Mir, Ezra (1903-93)
Mirza, Saeed Akhtar (b. 1943)
Mishra, Bhagwati Prasad (1896-1932)
Mishra, Sisir (b. 1942)
Mistri, Babubhai (b. 1919)
Mitra, Kamal (1911-93)
Mitra, Naresh Chandra (1888-1968)
Mitra, Premendra (1904-88)
Mitra, Sombhu (b. 1916)
Modak, Shahu (1918-93)
Modern Theatres
Modi, Sohrab Merwanji (1897-1984)
Mohanan, K. R. (b. 1947)
Mohan Kohli, Madan (1924-75)

Mohanlal (b. 1962)
Mohapatra *see* Mahapatra
Motilal Rajvansh (1910-65)
Mudaliar, Pammal Vijayaranga Sambandham (1872-1964)
Mudaliar, R. Nataraja (1885-1972)
Mukherjee, Gyan (1909-59)
Mukherjee, Hemanta Kumar (1920-89)
Mukherjee, Hrishikesh (b. 1922)
Mukherjee, Madhabi (b. 1943)
Mukherjee, Sailajananda (1901-76)
Mukherjee, Subodh (b. 1921)
Mukkamala, Krishnamurthy (1920-87)
Mullick, Amar (1899-1972)
Mullick, Pankaj (1905-78)
Munshi, Kanhaiyalal Maneklal (1887-1971)
Murugadasa (b. 1900)
Music Schools
Muthuswamy, A. *see* Murugadasa
Muzumdar *see* Majumdar
Mythologicals
Nadia (b. 1910)
Nadkarni, Sundarrao
Nag, Anant (b. 1948)
Nag, Shankar (1954-90)
Nagabharana, T. S. (b. 1953)
Nagabhushanam, Kadaru (b. 1902)
Nagaiah, Chittor V. (1904-73)
Nagalingam, P. K. *see* Sandow, P. K. Raja
Nagarajan, A. P.
Nagendra Rao, Pingali *see* Rao, Pingali Nagendra
Nagendra Rao, R. *see* Rao, Nagendra R.
Nageshwara Rao, Akkineni *see* Rao, Akkineni Nageshwara
Nageshwara Rao, Pendyala *see* Pendyala Nageshwara Rao
Nageshwara Rao, Rajanala *see* Rao, Rajanala Nageshwara
Naik, Prabhakar *see* Nayak, Prabhakar
Nair, Kottarakkara Sridharan (1922-86)
Nair, Madathu Thekepattu Vasudevan (b. 1934)
Nair, Mira (b. 1957)
Nair, Thikkurisi Sukumaran (b. 1917)
Nanda, Prashanta (b. 1947)
Narasaraju, Datla Venkata (b. 1920)
Narasimha Rao, Bhimavarapu *see* Rao, Bhimavarapu Narashimha
Narasimha Rao, Chitrapu *see* Rao, Chitrapu Narasimha
Narasinga Rao, Bongu *see* Rao, Bongu Narasinga
Narayana Rao, Adi *see* Rao, Adi Narayana
Narayana Kavi, Udumalai (1899-1981)
Narayanamurthy, Chitrapu (1913-85)
Narayanan, A. (1900-39)
Narayana Rao, Adi *see* Rao, Adi Narayana
Narayana Rao, Dasari *see* Rao, Dasari Narayana
Narayan Kale, K. *see* Kale, K. Narayan
Narayan Rao, Balkrishna *see* Rao, Balkrishna Narayan
Nargis (1929-81)
National Film Development Corporation
Naushad Ali (b. 1919)
Navketan *see* Chetan Anand
Navya Movement
Navyug Chitrapat
Naxalite
Nayak, Prabhakar Manajirao (1920-86)
Nayyar, Omkar Prasad (b. 1926)
Nazir, Prem (1928-89)
Neelakantan, P. (b. 1916)
Neerja *see* Vijayanirmala
Nene, Raja (1912-75)
New Indian Cinema
New Theatres
Nihalani, Govind (b. 1940)
Nurjehan (b. 1929)
Nutan Samarth (1936-91)
Osten, Franz (1876-1956)
Pachajanya *see* Mahapatra, Nirad
Padmanabhan, R. (b. 1896)
Padmarajan, P. (1936-91)
Padmini, S. (b. 1934)
PAG *see* Progressive Artists Group
Pagnis, Vishnupant (1892-1943)
Painter, Baburao (1890-1954)
Pal, Niranjan (1889-1959)
Palekar, Amol (b. 1944)
Palit, Nitai (b. 1923)
Pancholi, Dalsukh M. (1906-59)
Pande, Vinod
Pandharibai (b. 1930)
Panthulu, Budugur Ramakrishnaiah (1911-74)
Paranjpe, Raja (1910-79)
Paranjpye, Sai (b. 1936)
Parsee Theatre
Patankar, Shri Nath (?-1941)
Patel, Jabbar (b. 1942)
Pathy, P. V. (1906-61)
Patil, Dinkar Dattajirao (b. 1915)
Patil, Smita (1955-86)
Pat Painting
Pattanayak, Kabichandra Kalicharan (b. 1900)
Patwardhan, Anand (b. 1950)
Patwardhan, Nachiket (b. 1948) and Patwardhan, Jayoo (b. 1949)
Pavithran, Vattaparambil Krishnan (b. 1950)
Pawar, Lalita (b. 1916)
Pendharkar, Baburao (1896-67)
Pendharkar, Bhalchandra Gopal [Bhalji] (b. 1898)
Pendyala Nageshwara Rao (1924-84)
Phadke, Sudhir Vinayak ((b. 1919)
Phalke, Dhundiraj Govind (1870-1944)
Phalke Films Company
Photography
Pillai, Muthukulam Raghavan (b. 1909)
Pothan, Prathap K. (b. 1952)
Prabhat Film Company
Prakash, Khemchand (1907-50)
Prakash, Raghupati Surya (1901-56)
Prakash Rao, Kovalapati Surya (b. 1914)
Prakash Rao, Tatineni (1924-92)
Prasad, L. V. (1908-94)
Pratyagatma, Kotayya (b. 1925)
Priyadarshan
Progressive Artists Group
Progressive Writers Association
Pullaiah, Chittajallu (1895-1967)
Pullaiah, P. (1911-85)
Punatar, Ratilal Hemchand (b. 1913)
Punjab Film Corporation
Puri, Om (b. 1950)
Puttanna, S. R. *see* Kanagal, S. R. Puttana
PWA *see* Progressive Writers Association
Qadir, Kozhikode Abdul
Rafi, Mohammed (1924-80)
Raghava, Ballari (1880-1946)
Raghavacharya, Samudrala (1902-68)
Raghavaiah, Kosaraju *see* Kosaraju Raghavaiah Choudhury
Raghavaiah, Vedantam (1919-71)
Raghavendra Rao, K.
Raghunath, T. R. (1912-90)
Raghuramaiah, Kalyanam (1915-68)
Rai, Himansu (1892-1940)
Rajalakshmi, T. P. (?-1964)
Rajamma, M. V. (b. 1923)
Rajanikant *see* Rajnikant
Rajan-Nagendra [Rajan (b. 1933), Nagendra (b. 1935)]
Rajarathnam, Bezawada (b. 1921)
Raja Sandow *see* Sandow, P. K. Raja
Rajdutt (b. 1932)
Raje, Aruna (b. 1946)
Rajendar, Thesingu (b. 1955)
Rajendran, Lenin (b. 1952)
Rajendra Singh, S. V. *see* Singh, S. V. Rajendra
Rajeswara Rao, Saluri *see* Rao, Saluri Rajeswara
Rajkamal Kalamandir
Rajkumar (b. 1929)
Rajnikant (b. 1950)
Raju, Thotakura Venkata (1921-73)
Ramabrahmam, Gudavalli (1902-46)
Ramachandran, Marudur Gopalamenon (1917-87)
Ramaiyadas, Thanjai (1914-69)
Ramakrishna Rao, P. S. *see* Rao, P. S. Ramakrishna
Raman, Mahalingam Venkat (b. 1913)
Rama Rao, Nandamuri Taraka (b. 1923)
Rama Rao, Tatineni (b. 1938)
Ramchandra, Narhar Chitalkar (1918-82)
Ramnoth, K. (1912-56)
Ramsay Brothers
Ranga, B. S. (b. 1918)
Ranga Rao, Samrla Venkata (1918-74)
Rani, Bulo C. (b. 1920)
Rani Choudhury, Devika (1907-94)
Ranjit Movietone
Rao, Adi Narayana (1915-91)
Rao, Akkineni Nageshwara (b. 1924)
Rao, A. Subba *see* Subba Rao, A.
Rao, Balkrishna Narayan (b. 1909)
Rao, Bhimavarapu Narasimha (?-1957)
Rao, Bongu Narasinga (b. 1946)
Rao, Chitrapu Narasimha (b. 1911)
Rao, Chittajalu Srinivasa (b. 1924)
Rao, Dasari Narayana (b. 1947)
Rao, Ghantasala Venkateshwara *see* Ghantasala Venkateshwara Rao
Rao, Kamalakara Kameshwara (b. 1911)
Rao, Pendyala Nageshwara *see* Pendyala Nageshwara Rao
Rao, Pingali Nagendra (1901-71)
Rao, Prakash *see* Prakash Rao, K. S.
Rao, Raghavendra *see* Raghavendra Rao, K.
Rao, R. Nagendra (1896-1977)
Rao, Rajanala Nageshwara (1926-59)
Rao, Rama *see* Rama Rao, N. T. [4mor[0m Rama Rao, Tatineni
Rao, P. S. Ramakrishna (1918-86)
Rao, Ranga *see* Ranga Rao, S. V.
Rao, Saluri Rajeswara (b. 1922)
Rao, Singeetham Srinivasa
Rao, T. Prakash *see* Prakash Rao, Tatineni
Rao, Yaragudipati Varada (1903-73)
Raskapur, Manhar (1922-80)
Rathnam, Mani (b. 1956)
Rathod, Kanjibhai J.
Rathod, Kantilal (1925-88)
Rawail, Harnam Singh (b. 1921)
Rawail, Rahul (b. 1951)
Ray, Satyajit (1921-92)
Reddi, Bommireddi Narasimha (1908-77)
Reddy, Hanumappa Muniappa (1882-1960)
Reddy, Kadri Venkata (1912-72)
Reddy, Pattabhi Rama (b. 1919)
Rehman, Waheeda (b. 1938)
Rekha (b. 1954)
Roy, Bimal (1909-66)
Roy, Charu (1890-1971)
Roy, Jahar (1929-77)
Roy, Nirupa (b. 1931)
Rupkonwar *see* Agarwala, Jyotiprasad
Sabhyasachi *see* Kar, Ajoy
Sadanandan, S. L. Puram (b. 1927)
Sagar, Ramanand (b. 1917)
Sagar Film Company
Sahni, Balraj (1913-73)
Sahu, Kishore (1915-80)
Saigal, Kundan Lal (1904-46)
Saikia, Bhabendranath (b. 1932)
Saint Films
Salim-Javed [Salim Khan, Javed Akhtar]
Samanta, Shakti (b. 1925)
Samarth, Nutan *see* Nutan Samarth
Samarth, Shobhana (b. 1916)

Sami, Arul Susai Anthony (b. 1917)
Sandow, P. K. Raja (1894-1942)
Sangani, Chandrakant (b. 1927)
Sangeet Natak
Sanyal, Pahadi (1906-74)
Saraiya, Govind (b. 1929)
Sardar Begum *see* Akhtar, Sardar
Sarhadi, Zia (b. 1914)
Sarma, Phani (1910-70)
Sarpotdar, Narayanrao Damodar (1896-1940)
Sasi, I. V. (b. 1948)
Sasikumar
Sastry, Bellave Narahari (1881-1961)
Sastry, Devulapalli Krishna (1897-1980)
Sathyan (1912-71)
Sathyu, Mysore Srinivasa (b. 1930)
Saurashtra Film Company
Save Dada *see* Bhatavdekar, H. S.
Savitri, Kommareddy (1937-81)
Segal, Mohan (b. 1921)
Sekhar, Raja C. *see* Chandrasekhar, Raja
Sen, Aparna (b. 1945)
Sen, Asit (b. 1922)
Sen, Hiralal (1866-1917)
Sen, Mrinal (b. 1923)
Sen, Satu (1902-72)
Sen, Suchitra (b. 1931?)
Sethumadhavan, K. S. (b. 1926)
Shah, Chandulal Jesangbhai (1898-1975)
Shah, Kundan (b. 1947)
Shah, Naseeruddin
Shahani, Kumar (b. 1940)
Shailendra (1923-66)
Shankar-Jaikishen [Shankarsinh Raghuwanshi (?-1987), Jaikishen Dayabhai Panchal (1929-71)]
Shantaram, Rajaram Vankudre (1901-90)
Sharada (b. 1945)
Sharda Film Company
Sharma, Aribam Syam (b. 1939)
Sharma, Kidar Nath (b. 1910)
Sharma, Ramesh
Sharmaji *see* Khayyam, Mohammed Zahur
Shobhana Samarth *see* Samarth, Shobhana
Shobhan Babu (b. 1936)
Shorey, Roshan Lal
Shorey, Roop Kishore (1914-73)
Simha, H. L. N. (1904-72)
Singh, Dara (b. 1928)
Singh, M. A.
Singh, Shankar V. Rajendra (b. 1948)
Singh, Suchet (?-1920)
Singh, Surinder (b. 1945)
Sinha, Mala (b. 1936)
Sinha, Tapan (b. 1924)
Sippy, Gopaldas Parmanand (b. 1915)
Sippy, Ramesh (b. 1947)
Sivan, Papanasam (1891-1973)
Social
Soundararajan, S. (?-1966)
Sridevi (b. 1960)
Sridhar, Chingelpet V.
Srinivasan, M. B. (1925-88)
Sriranjini Junior (1927-74)
Sriranjini Senior (1906-39)
Sri Sri (1910-83)
Stage Backdrops
Subbaiah Naidu, M. V. (1896-1962)
Subba Rao, Adurthi (1921-75)
Subburaman, C. R. (1921-52)
Subramanyam, Krishnaswamy (1904-71)
Subramanyam, P. (1910-78)
Suhasini
Sukhdev Singh Sandhu (1933-79)
Sulochana (1907-83)
Sultanpuri, Majrooh (b. 1924)
Sundaram, Tiruchengodu Ramalinga (1907-63)
Sundarrajan, S *see* Soundararajan, S.
Surabhi Theatres
Suraiya Jamal Sheikh (b. 1929)
Suryakant (b. 1925)
Suryakumari, Tantaguri (b. 1925)
Swadeshi
Swaminathan, Komal (b. 1935)
Tagore, Rabindranath (1861-1941)
Tagore, Sharmila (b. 1944)
Tarafdar, Rajen (1917-87)
Tembe, Govindrao (1881-1955)
Tendulkar, Vijay (b. 1925)
Thakur, Raja (1923-75)
Thakur, Ramchandra (1908-92)
Timirbaran *see* Baran, Timir
TKS Brothers
Torney, Ramchandra Gopal (1880-1960)
Trivedi, Upendra
Urs, D. Kemparaj (1918-82)
Vairamuthu
Vakil, Nanubhai B. (1904-80)
Vali
Vamsy (b. 1956)
Vanisree (b. 1951)
Varalakshmi, Garikipati (b. 1926)
Varalakshmi, S. (b. 1927)
Varkey, Mutatthu (b. 1918)
Varkey, Poonkunnam (b. 1908)
Varma, Raja Ravi (1848-1906)
Varma, Vyalar Rama (1929-75)
Vasan, S. S. (1903-69)
Vasudevan Nair, M. T. *see* Nair, Madathu Thekepattu Vasudevan
Vauhini Pictures
Veeranna, Gubbi (1890-1972)
Vel Pictures
Venkaiah, Raghupathi (?-1941)
Venkatesh, G. K. (1927-93)
Venkateshwara Rao, Ghantasala *see* Ghantasala Venkateshwara Rao
Venkateshwara Rao, Gummadi (b. 1927)
Venkatramaiah, Relangi (1910-75)
Venu, Master (1916-81)
Vijaya Pictures
Vijayabhaskar (b. 1931)
Vijayanirmala (b. 1945)
Vinayak Damodar Karnataki, Master (1906-47)
Vincent, Aloysius (b. 1928)
Vishnuvardhan (b. 1952)
Vishwanath, Kashinadhuri (b. 1930)
Vithal, Master (?-1969)
Vittalacharya, B. (b. 1920)
Vyas, Avinash (1912-84)
Vyas, Vishnukumar Maganlal (b. 1905)
Vyjayanthimala (b. 1936)
Wadia, Homi Boman (b. 1911)
Wadia, Jamshed Boman Homi (1901-86)
Wadia Movietone
Wadkar, Hansa (1923-72)
Walker, Johnny (b. 1925)
Yagnik, Indulal
Yatrik *see* Majumdar, Tarun
Yesudas, K. J. (b. 1940)
Yoganand, D. (b. 1922)
Yusufali, Abdulali *see* Esoofally, Abdulally
Zils, Paul (1915-79)
Zubeida (1911-90)

ABBAS, KHWAJA AHMAD (1914-87)

Hindi-Urdu director and scenarist mainly in the socialist-realist mode. Born in Panipat, Haryana; grandfather is the well-known poet Hali. Graduated from Aligarh Muslim University (1933). Journalist, novelist and short-story writer with prodigious output. Worked on *National Call*, a New Delhi paper (1933); started *Aligarh Opinion* when studying law (1934); obtained law degree in 1935; political correspondent and later film critic for nationalist *Bombay Chronicle*, Bombay (1935-47) praising Dieterle, Capra and esp. **Shantaram**. Wrote Indian journalism's longest-running weekly political column, *Last Page* (1941-86), in *Chronicle* and *Blitz*. Best-known fiction (*Zafran Ke Phool* situated in Kashmir, *Inquilab* on communal violence) places him in younger generation of Urdu and Hindi writers with Ali Sardar Jafri and **Ismat Chughtai**, whose work followed the **PWA** and drew sustenance from Nehruite socialism's pre-Independence, anti-Fascist and anti-communal commitments. Founder member of **IPTA**'s all-India front (1943), to which he contributed two seminal plays: *Yeh Amrit Hai* and *Zubeida*. Entered film as publicist for **Bombay Talkies** (1936) to whom he sold his first screenplay, ***Naya Sansar*** (1941). First film, ***Dharti Ke Lal***, made under IPTA's banner and drew on **Bijon Bhattacharya**'s classic play *Nabanna* (1944), dealing with the Bengal famine of 1943. Set up production company Naya Sansar (1951), providing India's most consistent representation of socialist-realist film (cf **Thoppil Bhasi** and **Utpal Dutt**). Best work is in the scripts for his own films and for those of **Raj Kapoor** (***Awara***, 1951; ***Shri 420***, 1955, both co-written with V.P. Sathe; ***Jagte Raho***, 1956; ***Bobby***, 1973) and Shantaram's ***Dr Kotnis Ki Amar Kahani*** (1946; adapted from his own book, *And One Did Not Come Back*), which combined aspects of Soviet cinema (Pudovkin) and of Hollywood (e.g. Capra and Upton Sinclair), influencing a new generation of Hindi cineastes (Kapoor, **Chetan Anand**) and sparking new realist performance idioms (**Balraj Sahni**). His ***Munna***, without songs or dances, and ***Shaher Aur Sapna***, cheaply made on location in slums, were described as being influenced by neo-realism. ***Pardesi*** is the first Indian-Soviet co-production, co-directed by Vassili M. Pronin. The landmark Supreme Court censorship judgement about his ***Char Shaher Ek Kahani*** (aka *A Tale Of Four Cities*) curtailed 'arbitrary' governmental pre-censorship powers on the grounds that the Indian Constitution guarantees the right to free speech. Published many books including *I Am Not An Island* and *Mad Mad World of Indian Films* (both 1977). Other important scripts: ***Neecha Nagar*** (1946); ***Mera Naam Joker*** (1970); *Zindagi Zindagi* (1972); *Henna* (1991). Abbas also brought a number of new talents into the film industry, such as **Amitabh Bachchan** in ***Saat Hindustani***.

FILMOGRAPHY: **1946**: ***Dharti Ke Lal***; **1947**: *Aaj Aur Kal*; **1952**: *Anhonee*; ***Rahi/Two Leaves And A Bud***; **1954**: ***Munna***; **1957**: ***Pardesi***; **1959**: ***Char Dil Char Raahein***; **1960**: *Id Mubarak* (Sh); **1961**: *Gir Game Sanctuary* (Doc); **1962**: ***Gyarah Hazaar Ladkiyan***; **1963**: ***Shaher Aur Sapna***, *Teen Gharaney*; **1964**: *Hamara Ghar*; **1965**: ***Aasmaan Mahal***; *Tomorrow Shall Be Better* (Sh); **1967**: *Dharti Ki Pukaar* (Sh); ***Bambai Raat Ki Bahon Mein***; **1968**: ***Char Shaher Ek Kahani*** (Doc); **1969**: ***Saat Hindustani***; **1971**: ***Do Boond Pani***; *Lav Kush* (Sh); **1972**: *Bharat Darshan* (Doc); **1973**: *Kal Ki Baat* (Sh); *Juhu* (TV-Sh); **1974**: *Faasla*; **1975**: *Papa Miyan of Aligarh* (Doc); **1976**: *Phir Bolo Aaye Sant Kabir* (Doc); **1978**: *Dr Iqbal* (Doc); **1979**: ***The Naxalites***; **1983**: *Hindustan Hamara* (Sh); **1984**: *Nanga Fakir* (TV); *Mr X* (unfinished).

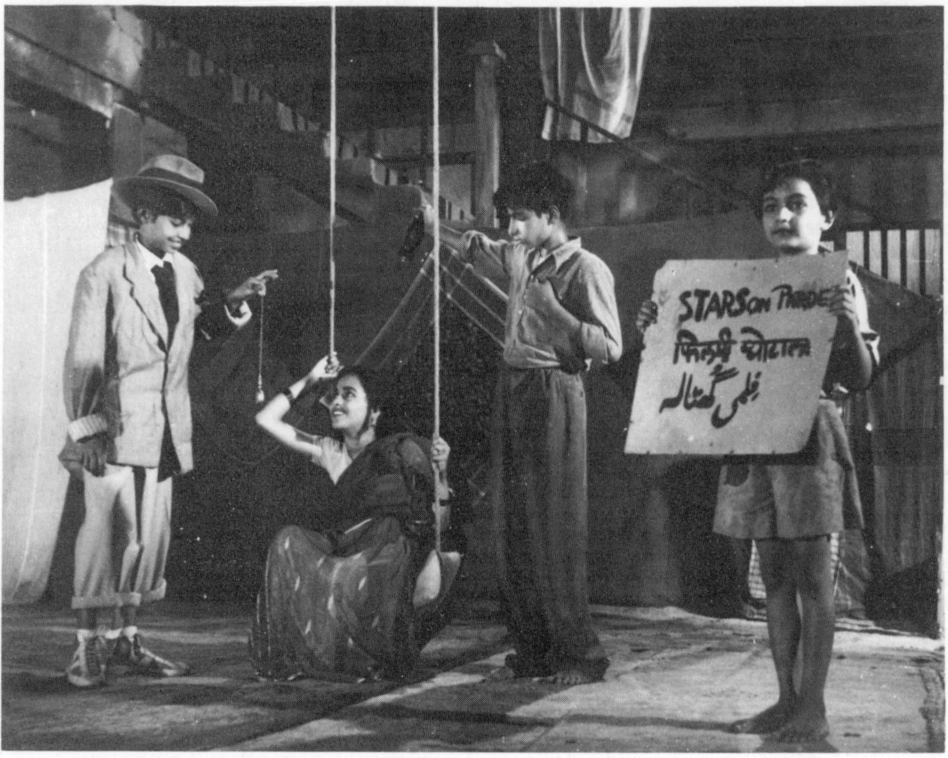

Romi (right) in K.A. Abbas' *Munna* (1954)

ABRAHAM, JOHN (1937-87)

Malayalam director born in Changanacherry, Kuttanad Dist., Kerala; studied economics at a college near Kottayam. Educated by grandfather who gave him his first camera. Worked as insurance salesman in Bellary; went to the **FTII** and studied under **Ghatak**. Assisted **Mani Kaul** on ***Uski Roti*** (1969) and worked on unreleased Hindi feature shot in Kerala, ***Trisandhya*** (1972). First films: ***Vidyarthikale Ithile Ithile***, made in Madras as group co-operative effort, and his internationally acclaimed ***Agraharathil Kazhuthai*** in Tamil. Lived a nomadic existence in the 70s, depending on support from friends and colleagues in Kerala, later the basis of the Odessa Collective (Est: 1984 in Calicut) launched with street play *Nayakali* staged in Fort Cochin (1984). Odessa funded ***Amma Ariyan*** through screening 16mm prints of e.g. Chaplin's *The Kid* (1921) and **Anand Patwardhan**'s ***Hamara Shaher*** (1985) in towns and villages throughout Kerala in return for small donations. After his accidental death, he is often portrayed as an example of the romantic artist who by-passed the tyranny of the market-place through a direct relationship with his people, raising money by travelling from village to village beating a drum and asking for contributions to a genuine 'people's cinema'. Others point to the probably Christian theme of infantile innocence in his work and place his marginal lifestyle in the cultural context of Kerala and the contentious history of authorial identity he inherited and lived out, exploring its alternatives. Suffered from alcoholism. Also wrote his own films.

FILMOGRAPHY: **1967**: *Koyna Nagar* (Doc); **1969**: *Priya* (Sh); *Hides And Strings* (Doc); **1971**: ***Vidyarthikale Ithile Ithile***; **1977**: ***Agraharathil Kazhuthai***; **1979**: ***Cheriyachente Kroora Krithyangal***; **1986**: ***Amma Ariyan***.

ACHARYA, N. R. (1909-56)

Hindi director born in Karachi. Was a government contractor when he joined **East India Film** in Calcutta (1934). Later worked as production manager at **Bombay Talkies**, where he directed the first examples of S. Mukherjee's new regime, e.g. ***Bandhan*** and the **Abbas** script ***Naya Sansar***. Became producer with **Sahu**'s ***Kunwara Baap*** (1942). Continued producing under the Acharya Arts Prod. banner until 1950. Also made Gujarati films, e.g. *Lagna Mandap*.

FILMOGRAPHY: **1940**: ***Bandhan***; ***Azad***; **1941**: ***Naya Sansar***; **1942**: *Uljhan*; **1943**: *Aage Kadam*; **1949**: *Parivartan*; *Shohrat* (with **K. Amarnath**); **1950**: *Lagna Mandap*; **1956**: *Dhola Maru*.

ADVANI, JAGATRAI PESUMAL (b. 1903)

Hindi director born in Hyderabad (now Pakistan). Studied film-making in Germany in the 20s and returned to become **Bhavnani**'s assistant. Directorial début at Krishnatone with *Heer Ranjha*, then at Saroj Movietone where he directed **Sardar Akhtar** (*Gafil Musafir*, *Johar-e-Shamsheer*, *Shah Behram*, *Tilasimi Talwar*). Made the Sardar Akhtar film *Farebi Duniya* at the Karachi-based Golden Eagle company; then directed e.g. Khursheed films (*Elaan-e-Jung*, *Shokh Dilruba*, *Sipahsalar*) and **Anil Biswas** musicals such as *Veena*, *Ladli* and *Lajawaab*. Apparently known as a director who could handle female stars to their advantage, his films starring Nimmi included *Wafaa* and a title probably produced by the star, *Danka*. His *Sassi Punnu* is a Hindi/Punjabi bilingual.

FILMOGRAPHY: **1931**: *Heer Ranjha*; **1933**: *Zehar-e-Ishq*; **1934**: *Afghan Abla*; *Dilara*; *Gafil Musafir*; *Johar-e-Shamsheer*; *Tilasmi Talwar*; *Vasantsena*; *Flashing Sword*; **1935**: *Bahar-e-Sulemani*; *Farebi Duniya*; *Shah Behram*; **1936**: *Elaan-e-Jung*; *Shokh Dilruba*; *Sipahsalaar*; **1937**: *Saqi*; *Insaaf*; **1939**: *Dekha Jayega*; **1940**: *Dharma Bandhan*; *Sneh Bandhan*; **1941**: *Shehzadi*; **1942**: *Suhagan*; **1943**: *Sahara*; **1946**: *Sassi Punnu*; **1948**: *Veena*; **1949**: *Laadli*; **1950**: *Wafaa*; *Lajawaab*; **1952**: *Saloni*; **1954**: *Danka*; **1955**: *Hasina*.

AGARWALA, JYOTIPRASAD (1903-51)

Aka Rupkonwar. First Assamese director. Born in Tezpur; radical playwright (e.g. *Sonitkonwari*, 1925; *Karengar-Ligari*, 1936; *Rupalim*, 1960). Stage director and songwriter who introduced traditional musical forms to contemporary Assamese stage. Graduate of Edinburgh University and Trinity College, Cambridge where he studied Western music (1926). Studied film-making at UFA, Germany (1930). Prominent political activist; jailed as member of Congress Party (1931-2); resigned from Tezpur Local Board protesting Assam government's compulsory financial contributions to WW2 and was involved in CP-led uprising of 1942. President of first **IPTA** conference in Assam at Silchar, following 1942 struggles. Briefly edited daily newspaper *Dainik Asamiya* (1944). First film, ***Joymati***, based on Sahityatri Bezbaruah's militant play, made in improvised studio adjoining his family's tea gardens near Tezpur, an event commemorated in **Bhupen Hazarika**'s film about the director, *Rupkonwar Jyotiprasad Aru Joymati* (1976).

FILMOGRAPHY: **1935**: ***Joymati***; **1939**: *Indramalati*.

AGRADOOT

Best-known instance of phenomenon unique to Bengali cinema: group of film technicians signing collectively as director. The Agradoot core unit, formed in 1946, consisted initially of Bibhuti Laha (cameraman born in 1915), Jatin Datta (sound), Sailen Ghosal (lab work), Nitai Bhattacharya (scenarist) and Bimal Ghosh (production). Bibhuti Laha was the driving force and after most of the other members had left the group, he continued directing under the Agradoot name while working as a cinematographer under his own name. They made several classic late 50s and 60s sentimental socials starring **Uttam Kumar**. Other film-makers who passed through the group include Saroj De, Salil Dutta and Aravind Mukherjee. Other well-known collectives include Sabhyasachi (cf **Ajoy Kar**), Agragami, **Yatrik**, Chitra Rath and Chitra Sathi.

FILMOGRAPHY: **1947**: *Swapna-o-Sadhana*; **1948**: *Samapika*; *Sabhyasachi/Pather Daabi*; **1949**: *Sankalpa*; **1951**: *Sahajatri*; ***Babla***; **1952**: *Aandhi*; **1954**: *Agni Pareeksha*; **1955**: *Anupama*; *Sabar Uparey*; **1956**: *Trijama*; **1957**: *Pathe Holo Deri*; **1958**: *Surya Toran*; **1959**: *Lalu Bhulu*; **1960**: *Kuhak*; *Khokha Babur Pratyabartan*; **1961**: *Agni Sanskar*; **1962**: *Bipasha*; *Nabadiganta*; **1963**: *Uttarayan*; *Badshah*; **1965**: *Antaral*; *Surya Tapa*; *Tapasi*; **1967**: *Nayika Sangbad*; **1968**: *Kokhono Megh*; **1969**: *Chiradiner*; **1970**: *Manjari Opera*; **1971**: *Chhadmabeshi*; **1973**: *Sonar Khancha*; **1974**: *Sedin Du-janay*; **1977**: *Din Amader*; **1981**: *Surya Sakhi*; **1989**: *Aparanher Alo*.

AHLUWALIA, SUKHDEV (b. 1932)

Mainstream Punjabi director who started as assistant cinematographer at the Modern Studios. Shot a number of Hindi films directed by Suraj Prakash before turning writer-director of ruralist melodramas (e.g. *Taakra* tells of a reformed black-marketeer accused of having killed his lover), often dealing with superstition. In *Jai Mata Sheran Wali*, daughter-in-law Radha overcomes oppression because of her belief in the mother goddess, but in the children's film *Sajre Phool* the superstitions of the oppressive landowner's wife are used to expose a crime. Currently works mainly in video. Also made *Kashmeera* about a lovable young tribal from Kashmir for the **CFS**.

FILMOGRAPHY: **1974**: *Do Sher*; **1975**: *Dharamjeet*; **1976**: *Taakra*; **1977**: *Do Sholay*; **1978**: *Jai Mata Sheran Wali*; **1979**: *Til Til Da Lekha*; *Kunwara Mama*; **1980**: *Ambe Maa Jagadambe Maa*; **1981**: *Sajre Phool*; **1983**: *Kashmeera*; **1984**: *Maanwan Thandian Chhanwan*; **1985**: *Takraar*; **1987**: *Maahi Mera Chann Varga*; **1990**: *Sounh Meno Punjab Di*.

Akhtar, Javed *see* **Salim-Javed**

AKHTAR, SARDAR (1915-84)

Aka Sardar Begum. Hindi-Urdu actress, born in Lahore. Started on the Urdu stage, which supplied the mainstream historical film with most of its acting talent. Joined films at Saroj Movietone. Early films with A.P. Kapur. Broke through in the role of the washerwoman opposite **Sohrab Modi** in ***Pukar***, where she also sang *Kaheko mohe chhede* in thumri style. Classic screen performance as the mother in **Mehboob**'s historical, ***Aurat***. With Mukhtar Begum and Naseem Banu, she is one of the few Urdu stage actresses to make a successful transition to cinema. Her weighty, languid histrionics and gravelly voice invested her style with an earthy quality lost to the cinema after Independence. Other films in which she sang include *Purnima* (the bhajan *Giridhar ke sangh*) and *Piya Ki Jogan*. She married Mehboob in 1942 and ran the Mehboob Studio after his death. Made a comeback with *Hulchul*.

FILMOGRAPHY: **1933**: *Id Ka Chand*; *Husn Ka Gulam*; *Malati Madhav*; *Naqsh-e-Sulemani*; *Roop Basant*; **1934**: *Ajamil*; *Dilara*; *Gafil Musafir*; *Hothal Padmini*; *Jan Nissar*; *Johar-e-Shamsheer*; *Tilasmi Talwar*; **1935**: *Delhi Express*; *Dharam Ki Devi*; ***Dhoop Chhaon***; *Farebi Duniya*; *Misar Ka Khazana*; *Shah Behram*; **1936**: *Karodpati*; *Piya Ki Jogan*; *Pratima*; *Prem Bandhan*; *Sangdil Samaj*; *Sher Ka Panja*; **1937**: *His Highness*; *Bismil Ki Arzoo*; *Khwab Ki Duniya*; **1938**: *Purnima*; ***State Express***; **1939**: ***Pukar***; **1940**: *Alibaba*; ***Aurat***; ***Bharosa***; ***Pooja***; **1941**: *Aasra*; *Nai Roshni*; **1942**: *Duniya Ek Tamasha*; *Ghar Sansar*; *Phir Milenge*; *Uljhan*; **1943**: *Fashion*; *Masterji*; **1945**: *Rahat*; **1971**: *Hulchul*; **1973**: *Bandhe Haath*; **1977**: *Jai Mata Di*.

AKHTAR-UL-IMAN (b. 1915)

Hindi-Urdu scenarist born in Bijnor Dist., UP. Joined **Filmistan** Studio as dialogue writer (1945). Major Urdu writer with seven poetry anthologies (e.g. *Yaadein*, 1961) and one verse play, *Sabrang* (1948). His Urdu poetry emphasises anti-romantic humanism, moving away from the traditional ghazal into new formal and symbolic articulations of modernity, as in the encounter between traditional metres and the rhythm of everyday prose in his major poem, *Ahd-e-Wafaa* [*Time of Promise*]. Directed one film, *Lahu Pukarega* (1980). Wrote Hindi scripts, dialogues or both for Najam Naqvi (*Actress*, 1948; *Nirdosh*, 1950), **B.R. Chopra** (***Kanoon***, 1960; ***Gumrah***, 1963; *Hamraaz*, 1967; *Dastaan*, 1972; ***Dhund***, 1973), **Raj Khosla** (*Mera Saaya*, 1966; *Chirag*, 1969), **Yash Chopra** (*Dharmaputra*, 1961; ***Waqt***, 1965; ***Ittefaq*** and *Admi Aur Insaan*, both 1969; ***Daag*** and *Joshila*, both 1973), Ramesh Sharma (*Flat No. 9*, 1961), **Nandlal Jaswantlal** (*Akeli Mat Jaiyo*, 1963), **A. Bhimsingh** (*Admi*, 1968; *Joru Ka Gulam*, 1972) and **Manmohan Desai**'s *Roti* (1974). Wrote **Sunil Dutt**'s monologue, ***Yaadein*** (1964) and Vimal Tewari's *Kunwara Badan* (1973). Further dialogue credits include: **Protima Dasgupta**'s *Jharna* (1948), Aspi's *Barood* (1960) and *Shabnam* (1964), Rakhan's *Kalpana* (1960), Ved-Madan's *Neeli Aankhen* (1962), Vasant Joglekar's *Aaj Aur Kal* (1963), Mehmood's *Bhoot Bangla* (1965), Chopra/**Hrishikesh Mukherjee**'s ***Gaban*** (1966), Raja Nawathe's *Patthar Ke Sanam* (1967), Deven Verma's *Bada Kabutar* and Hari Dutt's *Naya Nasha* (both 1973), Raj Tilak's *Chhattis Ghante* (1974), Ravi Chopra's **Bachchan** movie *Zameer* (1975), Sanjay Khan's *Chandi Sona* (1977), Devendra Goel's *Do Musafir* (1978) and actor Amjad Khan's *Chor Police* (1983).

ALI, MUZAFFAR (b. 1944)

Hindi-Urdu director born in Lucknow. Eldest son of the Raja Sajid Husain of Kotwara. Science graduate from Aligarh Muslim University (1966). Worked in advertising agencies Clarion-McCann (1966) and Advertising & Sales Promotion (1968), and in publicity division of Air India (1970-81). Amateur painter with exhibitions in Aligarh, Lucknow, Calcutta and Bombay. First film, ***Gaman***, about migrant labour in Bombay. ***Umrao Jaan*** returned to now rarely attempted (except in tv) genre of courtly melodrama set under Muslim rule. Worked with political themes with Subhashini Ali, a Kanpur-based trade unionist and one-time CPI(M) MP. Made and acted lead role of his tv serial *Jaan-e-Alam*, rehabilitating the Nawab Wajid Ali Shah, King of Avadh. The story was inspired by the *Indrasabha*, a nautanki ballet of the period (cf ***Indrasabha***, 1932). One of the founders of the MUKT (Marketing Union of Kinematograph Technicians) Co-operative. Last feature,

Zooni, remains unfinished. Now a fashion designer. Supports the UP-based Samajwadi (Socialist) Party of Mulayam Singh Yadav; unsuccessfully contested the state legislature elections in October 1993.

FILMOGRAPHY: 1978: ***Gaman***; **1981**: ***Umrao Jaan***; **1982**: *Vasiquedars: Pensioners of Avadh* (Doc); *Woodcraft of Sahranpur* (Doc); *Venue India* (Doc); *Laila Majnu Ki Nai Nautanki* (Doc); **1983**: *Sunehre Sapne* (Sh); *Wah! Maan Gaye Ustad* (Sh); *Agaman*; **1984**: *Vadakath: A Thervad In Kerala* (Doc); *Together Forever* (Sh); *Wapas Chalo* (TV-Sh); *Kue Yaar Mein* (Doc); **1985**: *Ganga Teri Shakti Apaar* (Doc); *India: An Unusual Environment for Meetings* (Doc); *Sheeshon Ka Masiha* (Doc); **1986**: ***Anjuman***; *Jaan-e-Alam* (TV); *Aaya Basant Sakhi*, *Kali Mohini*, *Semal Ki Darakht* (all Sh); **1991**: *Khizan* (Doc).

ALL-INDIA FILM

Generic term introduced and used most consistently by critic **Chidananda Das Gupta** to signify mass-produced film formula pioneered by post-WW2 Hindi cinema and duplicated by regional film industries predominantly in Tamil, Telugu, Malayalam and Bengali. As chronicled by the S.K. Patil Film Enquiry Committee Report (1951), following the withdrawal in 1946 of the licensing system imposed upon film-making during WW2 and the lifting of restrictions on raw stock: 'There was a sudden spurt in both production and exhibition. [T]heatre equipment imported in the two years 1946-47 and 1947-48 amounted in value to a crore of rupees. Studio equipment costing another crore of rupees was also imported and installed. [W]ithin three months of decontrol, over 100 new producers entered the field ... and new films released numbered over 200 in 1946 and 283 in 1947.' The All-India film appropriates aspects both from indigenous popular film and theatre genres and from Hollywood, subordinating them to an all-encompassing entertainment formula designed to overcome regional and linguistic boundaries. Das Gupta (1968) ascribes to this formula the function of a 'cultural leadership [that reinforces] some of the unifying tendencies in our social and economic changes [a]nd provides an inferior alternative [to a leadership that] has not emerged because of the hiatus between the intelligentsia, to which the leaders belong, and the masses'. The contention that the All-India film performs by default an integrating nationalist function similar to the consciously stated aim of AIR and more recently **Doordarshan**, has had a crucial influence on India's national film industry policies since the S.K. Patil Committee: the industry's inability to be financially self-sustaining is usually counterbalanced by its alleged ability to foster a unified contemporary 'indigenous' cultur.

ALTEKAR, PARSHWANATH YESHWANT (1898-1957)

Mainly Marathi director born in Kharepatan, Ratnagiri. Also worked in Hindi, Tamil and Kannada. Educated in Kolhapur and obtained arts degree from Wellington College in Sangli. Studied law in Bombay but turned to the theatre, acting in the first play he directed, *Rajsanyas*, in 1922. Marathi writer Mama Warerkar influenced Altekar's theatrical work as well as his shift to films, later providing songs and dialogues for the director's ***Geeta***. Film début in **Joshi**'s ***Prithvi Vallabh***. The following year (1925) he followed his mentor Warerkar into the United Pics Syndicate, where he played a series of major roles in Maratha historicals: Hansaji in **Sarpotdar**'s *Chandrarao More* and the title role in *Chhatrapati Sambhaji* (Altekar later remade the film in Marathi with **Master Vithal**). Acted in and was associated with the making of Sarpotdar's seminal realist experiment ***Maharachi Por***, conjoining film, journalism and the avant garde theatre movement, a mix that later culminated in the work of the Natyamanwantar group. Also played the role of Prithviraj in Deccan's *Prabhavati*. Joined the **Pendharkar** brothers' Vande Mataram Films, acting in and, according to some sources, helping to direct their controversial ***Vande Mataram Ashram***. Turned director at United Pics with the mythological *Jugari Dharma*, also playing the role of Bhim. In 1928, he went to **Imperial Film**, making four films, e.g. *Jagadguru Shrimad Shankaracharya*, which featured his future theatre associate **K. Narayan Kale** as actor, and *Gori Bala*, scripted by Warerkar. Worked for **Torney**'s Saraswati Cinetone (1933) while continuing his work in the theatre with Radio Stars and the Natyamanwantar group. Directed what is sometimes regarded as the first Kannada feature, ***Bhakta Dhruva***, from a Ratnavali Theatre play. After a stint at **Master Vinayak**'s Huns Pics (e.g. the **Khandekar** script *Sukhacha Shodh*) and CIRCO Films (*Geeta*, featuring **Chandramohan** in a double role; ***Mahatma Vidur*** with **Vishnupant Pagnis** and **Durga Khote**), he became an independent producer with his own Natraj Cinetone partnered by Durga Khote, **Govindrao Tembe**, Mubarak et al., making the important Tembe-Khote musical *Savangadi*. Made three Tamil films (*Parvati Kalyanam*, *Pati Bhakti*, *Bhishma Pratigna*, all 1936). Started a theatre training school (1938) and soon stopped making films, devoting his energies to theatre work. His films often continued his experiments with naturalist theatre for Natyamanwantar, Radio Stars and his repertory National Theatre Academy, for which he wrote several essays on the theory of stage performance in the Marathi journal *Yashwant* (e.g. *Rangabhoomichi Avashyakta Kay?* in December 1942; *Udyacha Nat* and *Udyachi Rangabhoomi* in November 1943).

FILMOGRAPHY (* only act/** also act): **1924**: ***Prithvi Vallabh****; **1925**: ***Maharachi Por****; *Chandrarao More**; *Chhatrapati Sambhaji**; *Kangal Qaidi**; *Mulraj Solanki**; *Prabhavati**; *Saurashtra Veer**; **1926**: ***Vande Mataram Ashram****; **1927**: *Jugari Dharma***; **1928**: *Jagadguru Shrimad Shankaracharya***; **1929**: *Vasal Ni Raat***; *Gori Bala*; **1931**: *Janma Haq* (all St); **1934**: ***Bhakta Dhruva***; *Vasavadatta*; *Chhatrapati Sambhaji*; **1936**: *Parvati Kalyanam*; *Pati Bhakti*; *Bhishma Pratigna*; **1938**: *Savangadi/Saathi*; **1939**: *Sukhacha Shodh/Mera Haq*; **1940**: ***Geeta***; **1943**: ***Mahatma Vidur***; **1952**: ***Chhatrapati Shivaji****.

AMAN, ZEENAT (b. 1951)

Actress. Former advertising model. First major role in ***Hare Rama Hare Krishna*** as emancipated 'hippie' sister of hero **Dev Anand**, heralding the 70s look of the Westernised, 'liberated' young woman in Hindi film. At its best, this attempt to represent 'modernity' redefined the love story (***Yaadon Ki Baraat***) by violating several moral codes advocated by earlier melodramas to control female sexuality. The image was adopted and negatively inflected, notably by Parveen Babi (the gangster's moll in ***Deewar***, 1975), in the context of **Amitabh Bachchan**'s vigilante themes. **Raj Kapoor** later used the image to stigmatise the obscenity of contemporary consumerist versions of religious symbolism in ***Satyam Shivam Sundaram***.

FILMOGRAPHY: 1971: *Hulchul*; ***Hare Rama Hare Krishna***; *Hangama*; **1973**: ***Dhund***; *Heera Panna*; ***Yaadon Ki Baraat***; **1974**: *Ajnabi*; *Ishq Ishq Ishq*; *Manoranjan*; *Prem Shastra*; *Roti Kapda Aur Makaan*; **1975**: *Chori Mera Kaam*; *Warrant*; **1976**: *Deewangee*; **1977**: *Ashiq Hoon Baharon Ka*; *Chhaila Babu*; *Darling Darling*; ***Dharam Veer***; *Hum Kisise Kum Nahin*; *Kalabaaz*; *Paapi*; **1978**: *Chor Ke Ghar Chor*; *Don*; *Heeralal Pannalal*; ***Satyam Shivam Sundaram***; *Shalimar*; **1979**: *The Great Gambler*; **1980**: *Abdullah*; *Alibaba Aur Chalis Chor*; *Bombay 405 Miles*; *Dostana*; ***Insaaf Ka Tarazu***; *Takkar*; *Ram Balram*; *Qurbani*; **1981**: *Qatilon Ke Qatil*; *Krodhi*; *Lawaris*; *Professor Pyarelal*; *Gopichand Jasoos*; *Vakil Babu*; *Daulat*; **1982**: *Ashanti*; *Samrat*; *Teesri Aankh*; *Jaanwar*; *Pyaas*; **1983**: *Bandhan Kachche Dhaagon Ka*; *Humse Hai Zamana*; *Mahaan*; *Namumkin*; *Pukar*; *Taqdeer*; **1984**: *Jagir/Teen Murti*; *Meri Adalat*; *Pakhandi*; *Sohni Mahiwal*; *Yeh Desh*; **1985**: *Amir Admi Gareeb Admi*; *Bhawani Junction*; *Yaar Kasam*; *Yaadon Ki Kasam*; *Haathon Ki Lakeeren*; **1986**: *Aurat*; *Baat Ban Jaye*; **1987**: *Daku Hasina*; **1989**: *Gawahi*; *Tujhe Nahin Chhodunga*.

AMARNATH, GELARAM KHETARPAL (1914-83)

Hindi and Tamil director born in Mianwali, now in Pakistan's Punjab province. Studied at the Rangmahal High School (1931) and at Craik Technical School, Lahore. Joined films as an extra in Lahore a year before moving to Calcutta (1932). Then went to Bombay (1933) and became assistant director until débuting as director in 1936, making many of his early films in Tamil, including ***Minnalkodi***. Known as a stunt film director associated with Mohan Pics, one of the major B-movie producers and filmed often with S. Nazir (*Chashmavali*, *Midnight Mail*, *Bandookwali*); made the Nazir-**Lalita Pawar** film *Captain Kishori*. Shifted to love stories in the late 40s with e.g. **Nurjehan**'s last big films in India (*Village Girl* and *Mirza Sahiban*, the first film he produced). In the early 50s he introduced **Shammi Kapoor** to films in romances such as *Laila Majnu* and *Mehbooba*. Started his own K. Amarnath Pics with *Alif Laila*. Directed Ajit's leading roles in *Baradari* (with **Geeta Bali**), *Bada Bhai* (with Kamini Kaushal), *Baraat* (with Shakila) and the colour film *Kabuli Khan* (with Helen).

FILMOGRAPHY: 1936: *Matwali Jogan*; *Madras Mail*; **1937**: *Danger Signal*; ***Minnalkodi***; *Pucca Rowdy*; **1938**: *Veer Ramani*; *Bhagya Leela*; **1939**: *Bahadur*

Ramesh; *Midnight Mail*; *Chashmawali*; *Jayakkodi*; **1940**: *Tatar Ka Chor*; *Captain Kishori*; **1941**: *Bulbul-e-Baghdad*; **1942**: *Zevar*; **1943**: *Chhed Chhaad*; **1944**: *Bandookwali*; **1945**: *Village Girl*; **1947**: *Mirza Sahiban*; *Roop Nagar*; **1949**: *Shohrat* (co-d **N.R. Acharya**); *Bazaar*; **1950**: *Beqasoor*; *Meharbani*; **1951**: *Sarkar*; **1953**: *Alif Laila*; *Laila Majnu*; **1954**: *Mehbooba*; **1955**: *Baradari*; **1956**: *Naya Andaz*; **1957**: *Bada Bhai*; **1960**: *Baraat*; **1963**: *Kabuli Khan*; **1964**: *Ishara*; **1971**: *Woh Din Yaad Karo*.

AMROHI, KAMAL (1918-93)

Originally Syed Amir Haider Kamal. Writer, poet (Hindi-Urdu) and director. Born in Amroha, UP. Early writing was within the Shakespearean contours of the Urdu **Parsee Theatre** (e.g. the script for Akhtar Hussain's *Romeo and Juliet*, 1947). Went to Bombay in 1938; worked as writer for **S. Modi** (***Jailor***, 1938; ***Pukar***, 1939; ***Bharosa***, 1940), **Kardar** (***Shahjehan***, 1946), and **K. Asif**'s spectacular ***Mughal-e-Azam*** (1960), reinvigorating the Urdu historical genre. Scenarist at **Bombay Talkies** (1938), which produced his feature debut, ***Mahal***. Established his own Kamal Pics (1953) and Kamalistan Studio in Bombay (1958), leasing the Mahal Studios mainly to make ***Pakeezah***, one of the most successful Indian films ever and a classic Urdu melodrama. Its star, **Meena Kumari**, was his third wife. They separated in 1964 but she nevertheless finished the film in 1971. Scripted his own films. Other scripts include Yusuf Naqvi's *Shankar Hussain* (1977), dialogues for **Jagirdar**'s *Main Hari* (1940), Zahur Raja's *Mazaaq* (1943) and K. Asif's *Phool* (1944). Also produced **Kishore Sahu**'s *Dil Apna Aur Preet Parayi*.

FILMOGRAPHY: 1949: ***Mahal***; **1953**: ***Daera***; **1971**: ***Pakeezah***; **1983**: *Razia Sultan*.

A. Na. Kru *see* **Krishnarao, A. N.**

ANAND, CHETAN (b. 1915)

Hindi director, scenarist and actor; elder brother of **Dev** and **Vijay Anand**. Born in Lahore. Worked for the BBC and taught at the Doon School, Dehradun. Went to Bombay to act in Hindi films. Played the lead in the **IPTA**'s stage production of **K.A. Abbas**'s *Zubeida* directed by **Balraj Sahni** (1943). First film ***Neecha Nagar*** made in parallel with Abbas's IPTA-backed ***Dharti Ke Lal*** (1946) and Uday Shankar's ***Kalpana*** (1948) under government licence (required during WW2). Together with Dev Anand started Navketan Prod. (1949). Directed (and co-wrote with his ex-wife Uma) their début film, ***Afsar***, adapted from Gogol's *The Government Inspector*. With composer **S.D. Burman** and lyricist **Sahir Ludhianvi**, Navketan marked an influential transition of IPTA's socialist realism into a brand of commercial Hindi cinema that drew from King Vidor, Capra, Huston and others to define a brief but crucial populist phase in Hindi films dealing with the working class (e.g. ***Taxi Driver***). Influenced several cineastes such as **Guru Dutt**, **Mohan Segal**, **Raj Khosla** and Vijay Anand. Started his own Himalaya Films (1960). After the war film ***Haqeeqat***, about the 1962 conflict with China, Anand remained the leading director associated with that genre, extending it into serial format for tv (*Param Veer Chakra*). His son, Ketan Anand, also became a director (*Toote Khilone*, 1978; *Hum Rahe Na Hum*, 1984).

FILMOGRAPHY (* also act): **1946**: ***Neecha Nagar***; **1950**: ***Afsar***; **1952**: ***Aandhiyan***; **1953**: *Humsafar* (act only); **1954**: ***Taxi Driver***; **1955**: *Joru Ka Bhai*; **1956**: *Funtoosh*; **1957**: *Anjali**; **1963**: *Kinare Kinare**; **1964**: ***Haqeeqat***; **1966**: ***Aakhri Khat***; **1967**: *Aman* (act only); **1970**: *Heer Ranjha*; **1973**: *Hindustan Ki Kasam**; *Hanste Zakhm*; **1976**: *Jaaneman*; **1977**: *Saheb Bahadur*; **1981**: *Kudrat*; **1985**: *Haathon Ki Lakeeren*; **1988**: *Param Veer Chakra* (TV).

ANAND, DEV (b. 1923)

Hindi star, producer and director. Born in Gurdaspur, Punjab, as Devdutt Pishorimal Anand. Arts degree from Punjabi University; went to Bombay to join elder brother **Chetan Anand** in the **IPTA**. Started acting at **Prabhat** (1945) where he met **Guru Dutt**. First hit, *Ziddi*, at **Bombay Talkies**. Launched Navketan (1949) with Chetan Anand, later (1953) joined by younger brother and star director **Vijay Anand** (e.g. ***Guide***). Produced Guru Dutt's directorial début, ***Baazi***. Navketan spawned much new talent: directors Guru Dutt, Vijay Anand, **Raj Khosla**, composers **S.D.** and **R.D. Burman**, Jaidev, lyricists **Sahir Ludhianvi** and Neeraj, cameramen Fali Mistry, V. Ratra and D.K. Prabhakar, actors **Johnny Walker**, **Zeenat Aman**, Ekta Sharma, Tina Munim. Top star at **Filmistan**; made several of his most famous hits with **Subodh Mukerjee** (***Munimji***, ***Paying Guest***) and other Filmistan-trained directors like **Nasir Hussain** and **Shakti Samanta**. Turned director in 1970. Directed, produced and starred in film launching his son, Suneil Anand (*Anand Aur Anand*). Now mainly produces and directs own starring vehicles deploying a more conventional heroic persona. Together with **Raj Kapoor** and **Dilip Kumar**, he ushered in the dominant acting idiom of post-Independence Hindi cinema. His style is demarcated from the naturalist method-acting modes of **Motilal**, **Balraj Sahni** and the **Ashok Kumar** of ***Kismet*** (1943). Amit Khanna noted: 'Dev Anand's forte was the boy next door, part lover, part clown and part do-gooder.' Although never the reviewers' favourite, he claimed that filming 'should be brought as close as possible to the making of a newspaper'. His deliberately awkward pastiches invoke various sources (e.g. Cary Grant, Gregory Peck). With directors Chetan and Vijay Anand, Guru Dutt and Subodh Mukherjee, along with playback singer **Kishore Kumar**, he satirised and reconstituted generic styles such as Capra's (***Nau Do Gyarah***), John Huston's (***Jaal***), the thriller (***Jewel Thief***, ***CID***), the love story (***Tere Ghar Ke Saamne***, *Paying Guest*) and the Hollywood epic in ***Guide***. Directorial concerns include the alleged aimlessness of today's youth contrasted with the civilisational glory of the freedom struggle (e.g. ***Hare Rama Hare Krishna***). Acted in the films he directed. Married actress Kalpana Kartik.

Dev Anand shooting *Loot Maar* (1980)

FILMOGRAPHY (* also d): **1946**: ***Hum Ek Hain***; **1947**: *Aage Badho*; *Mohan*; **1948**: *Hum Bhi Insaan Hain*; *Vidya*; *Ziddi*; **1949**: *Jeet*; *Namuna*; *Shayar*; *Udhaar*; **1950**: ***Afsar***; *Birha Ki Raat*; *Dilruba*; *Hindustan Hamara*; *Khel*; *Madhubala*; *Nili*; *Nirala*; **1951**: *Aaram*; ***Baazi***; *Do Sitare*; *Nadaan*; *Sanam*; *Sazaa*; *Stage*; **1952**: ***Aandhiyan***; ***Jaal***; *Tamasha*; *Zalzala*; ***Rahi/Two Leaves And A Bud***; **1953**: *Armaan*; *Humsafar*; *Patita*; **1954**: ***Baadbaan***; *Kashti*; ***Taxi Driver***; **1955**: *Faraar*; ***House Number 44***; ***Insaniyat***; *Milap*; ***Munimji***; **1956**: ***CID***; *Funtoosh*; *Pocketmaar*; **1957**: *Baarish*; *Dushman*; ***Nau Do Gyarah***; ***Paying Guest***; **1958**: *Amar Deep*; ***Kala Pani***; *Solva Saal*; **1959**: *Love Marriage*; **1960**: ***Bambai Ka Babu***; *Ek Ke Baad Ek*; ***Jaali Note***; ***Kala Bazaar***; *Manzil*; *Sarhad*; **1961**: ***Hum Dono***; ***Jab Pyar Kisise Hota Hai***; *Maya*; *Roop Ki Rani Choron Ka Raja*; **1962**: *Asli Naqli*; *Baat Ek Raat Ki*; **1963**: *Kinare Kinare*; ***Tere Ghar Ke Saamne***; **1964**: *Sharabi*; **1965**: ***Guide***; *Teen Deviyan*; **1966**: *Pyar Mohabbat*; **1967**: ***Jewel Thief***; **1968**: *Duniya*; *Kahin Aur Chal*; **1969**: *Mahal*; **1970**: ***Johnny Mera Naam***; ***Prem Pujari****; **1971**: ***Hare Rama Hare Krishna****; *Gambler*; ***Tere Mere Sapne***; **1972**: *Yeh Gulistan Hamara*; **1973**: *Chhupa Rustom*; *Joshila*; *Shareef Badmash*; *Banarasi Babu*; *Heera Panna**; **1974**: *Ishq Ishq Ishq**; *Amir Garib*; *Prem Shastra*; **1975**: *Warrant*; **1976**: *Bullet*; *Jaaneman*; **1977**: *Darling Darling*; *Kalabaaz*; *Saheb Bahadur*; **1978**: *Des Pardes**; **1980**: *Man Pasand*; *Lootmaar**; **1982**: *Swami Dada**; **1984**: *Anand Aur Anand**; **1985**: *Hum Naujawan**; **1989**: *Sachche Ka Bol Bala**; *Lashkar*; **1990**: *Awwal Number**; **1991**: *Sau Karod**; **1992**: *Pyar Ka Tarana* (only d).

ANAND, INDER RAJ

Scenarist and dialogue writer born in Miani (now Pakistan); uncle of **Mukul S. Anand**. Student years in Lahore and Hyderabad. Closely associated with the **IPTA**'s Bombay branch. Major contribution as playwright for **Prithviraj Kapoor**'s Prithvi Theatres: *Deewar* and *Ghaddar* mark its IPTA-influenced early 40s radical phase. Publicist for **Minerva** when **Raj Kapoor** hired him to write ***Aag*** (1948), leading to further collaborations: ***Aah*** (1953),

Chhalia (1960), ***Sangam*** (1964), *Sapnon Ka Saudagar* (1968). Also scripted **Mohan Segal**'s landmark satire ***New Delhi*** and the **Dev Anand** whodunit ***CID*** (both 1956). Since early 60s, worked mainly as a 'genre professional' for South Indian producers wishing to enter the Bombay-based mainstream: e.g. dialogues for the Hindi films of **L.V. Prasad**, **K. Balachander**, **Adurthi Subba Rao** and **Bharathirajaa**. Regular scenarist for 80s director Rajkumar Kohli. Wrote and directed one film, *Phoolon Ki Sej* (1964), influenced, he claimed, by James Jones's *From Here To Eternity* and Doris Lessing. Other script and/or dialogue credits include: *Phool Aur Kaante* (1948); *Birha Ki Raat* (1950); ***Anari***, ***Chhoti Bahen*** (both 1959); *Sasural* (1961); *Dil Tera Diwana* (1962); *Bahurani*, *Hamrahi* (both 1963); *Beti Bete*, *Dulha Dulhan* (both 1964); ***Aasmaan Mahal*** (1965); *Chhota Bhai* (1966); *Vaasna* (1968); *Bhai Bahen*, *Nannha Farishta* (both 1969); *Devi*, *Safar* (both 1970); *Jawani Diwani*, *Anokha Daan* (both 1972); *Gaai Aur Gori*, *Samjhauta*, *Insaaf* (all 1973); *Prem Nagar*, *Shubh Din*, *Faasla*, *Aaina* (all 1974); ***Julie***, *Raja*, *Sunehra Sansar* (all 1975); *Maa*, *Nagin* (both 1976); *Yahi Hai Zindagi* (1977); *Lovers*, *Yeh Ishq Nahin Asaan* (both 1983); *Ek Nai Paheli*, *Jeene Nahin Doonga*, *Raj Tilak* (all 1984).

ANAND, MUKUL SUDHESHWAR (b. 1951)

Hindi director associated with 90s **Bachchan** spectaculars (e.g. ***Hum***). Born in Bombay. Son of a chartered accountant and nephew of **Inder Raj Anand**. Former assistant of **Chetan Anand** and Ravi Tandon; later ghost-directed several films in Hindi, Punjabi and Gujarati. Early films are low-budget remakes of foreign hits (*Kanoon Kya Karega* is based on J. Lee Thompson's *Cape Fear*, 1961; *Aitbaar* on Hitchcock's *Dial M for Murder*, 1954). Big-budget extravaganzas since ***Sultanat*** place him in new generation of Hindi commercial film-makers. Makes advertising films in between features. First major hit, *Insaaf*, relaunched 70s stars Vinod Khanna and Dimple Kapadia. It created a fantasy world of sex, crime and sin despite its occasional references to the actual, widely reported death of a prostitute who 'fell' from a multi-storey block of flats belonging to a businessman suspected of criminal dealings. His films with **Bachchan** are also known for the star's efforts to adapt his heroic image to his advancing age (***Agneepath***, ***Hum***, ***Khuda Gawah***).

FILMOGRAPHY: 1984: *Kanoon Kya Karega*; **1985**: *Aitbaar*; **1986**: *Maa Ki Saugandh*; *Main Balwan*; ***Sultanat***; **1987**: *Insaaf*; **1988**: *Mahasangram*; **1990**: ***Agneepath***; **1991**: ***Hum***; *Khoon Ka Karz*; **1992**: ***Khuda Gawah***.

ANAND, VIJAY (b. 1935)

Accomplished Hindi actor, director and producer; younger brother of **Dev** and **Chetan Anand**, nicknamed Goldie. Born in Gurdaspur, Punjab. Arts degree from the University of Bombay. Scripted ***Taxi Driver*** (1954) and made some of Navketan's best films with Dev Anand, shaping Dev's screen personality. Made ***Guide***, the first Indo-American co-production (US version directed by Tad Danielewski). Made remarkable musical sequences using locations (e.g. the song inside the Qutub Minar in ***Tere Ghar Ke Saamne***) to achieve complex interactions between music, lyrics and story, at times evoking Western novelettes (Pearl Buck, A.J. Cronin) or Hollywood (Capra). Neo-realist overtones, inherited from brother Chetan, are used mainly as ballast to release the fantasy, a technique best exemplified by *Guide* and in the opening song of ***Kala Bazaar***. Wrote some of the films he directed and edited (*Kala Bazaar*, *Chhupa Rustom*, also co-lyricist for the latter) and returned to starring roles in e.g. *Chor Chor*, *Hum Rahe Na Hum*, *Double Cross*; also scenarist for ***Hum Dono*** (1961) and producer of *Jaan Hazir Hai* (1975).

FILMOGRAPHY (** also d/* only d): **1955**: *Joru Ka Bhai*; **1957**: *Agra Road*; ***Nau Do Gyarah****; **1960**: ***Kala Bazaar*****; **1963**: ***Tere Ghar Ke Saamne****; **1964**: ***Haqeeqat***; **1965**: ***Guide****; **1966**: ***Teesri Manzil****; **1967**: ***Jewel Thief****; **1968**: *Kahin Aur Chal**; **1970**: ***Johnny Mera Naam****; **1971**: ***Tere Mere Sapne*****; **1972**: *Double Cross*; **1973**: *Hindustan Ki Kasam*; *Chhupa Rustom***; *Blackmail***; **1974**: *Kora Kagaz*; *Chor Chor*; **1976**: *Bullet**; **1978**: *Main Tulsi Tere Aangan Ki*; **1980**: *Ram Balram**; **1981**: *Ghunghroo Ki Awaaz*; **1982**: *Rajput**; **1984**: *Hum Rahe Na Hum*; **1988**: *Main Tere Liye**.

ANJANEYALU, CHILAKALAPUDI SEETA RAMA (1907-63)

Born in Guntur Dist., AP. Actor and singer in stage mythologicals since early youth. Became one of the first major Telugu stars. Film début as Ram in **East India Film**'s *Ramadasu*. Early roles in Telugu mythologicals, esp. Krishna in ***Draupadi Vastrapaharanam*** and the title roles in *Tukaram* and in **P. Pullaiah**'s ***Shri Venkateshwara Mahatyam***. Changed to socials with **Raja Sandow**'s ***Choodamani***; became a comic villain in **L.V. Prasad**'s ***Grihapravesham***, repeating the character in e.g. ***Appu Chesi Pappu Koodu***. Other famous roles include the villainous farmer in ***Rojulu Marayi***, Ramappa Panthulu in *Kanyashulkam* and Kuchela in *Krishna Kuchela*. Best known for **K.V. Reddy**'s ***Maya Bazaar***, setting the standard for the image of the popular *Mahabharata* character, Shakuni.

FILMOGRAPHY: 1933: *Ramadasu*; **1936**: ***Draupadi Vastrapaharanam***; **1937**: *Tukaram*; **1939**: ***Shri Venkateshwara Mahatyam***; ***Jayapradha***; **1941**: ***Choodamani***; ***Talliprema***; **1942**: *Sumati*; **1945**: *Mayalokam*; *Paduka Pattabhishekham*; **1946**: ***Grihapravesham***; **1947**: ***Ratnamala***; **1948**: *Bhakta Siriyala*; **1949**: ***Laila Majnu***; **1950**: *Vali Sugriva*; ***Paramanandayya Shishyulu Katha***; **1951**: *Saudamini*; *Akasharaju*; ***Patala Bhairavi/Pataal Bhairavi***; ***Agni Pareeksha***; **1952**: *Dharmadevata*; *Manavati*; ***Prema/Kathal***; **1953**: ***Devadasu***; *Paropakaram*; *Vayyari Bhama*; ***Chandirani***; **1954**: ***Anta Manavalle***; *Iddaru Pellalu*; *Sati Sakkubai*; *Kanyadana/Kanyadanam*; ***Chakrapani***; **1955**: *Ante Kavali*; ***Rojulu Marayi***; *Kanyashulkam*; **1956**: *Bhale Ramudu/Prema Pasham*; *Bhakta Markandeya*; **1957**: *Repu Neede*; *Bhale Bhava*; *Bhale Ammayilu*; *Vaddante Pelli*; ***Maya Bazaar***; ***Suvarna Sundari***; **1958**: ***Ettuku Pai Ettu***; *Dongalunnaru Jagratha*; *Parvati Kalyanam*; ***Appu Chesi Pappu Koodu***; **1959**: *Pelli Sandadi*; *Rechukka Pragatichukka*; *Vachina Kodulu Nachindi*; **1960**: *Jagannathakam*; *Nityakalayanam Pachathoranam*; *Rani Ratnaprabha*; *Bhakta Raghunath*; *Annapurna*; *Runanubandham*; **1961**: ***Jagadeka Veeruni Katha/Jagathala Prathapan***; *Bava Maradallu*; *Bhakta Jayadeva*; *Pelli Pilupu*; *Krishna Kuchela*; *Bhikari Ramudu*; **1962**: *Kalimilemulu*; *Chitti Tamudu*; **1963**: *Irugu Porugu*; *Savati Koduku*; **1964**: *Peetalameeda Pelli*; *Babruvahana*; *Bobbili Yuddham*; **1967**: *Vasantsena*; **1968**: *Chellikosam*.

ANNADURAI, CANJEEVARAM NATARAJAN (1909-69)

Tamil scenarist, playwright and DMK Party politician who founded the **DMK Film** propaganda genre. Born into a Mudaliar weaver community in Kanjeevaram; studied at university while translating for the Justice Party and stood for them as a candidate in the Madras City elections (1936). Worked in labour unions and edited a trade union weekly, *Nava Yugam*. Became a disciple of Periyar E.V. Ramaswamy Naicker (1937) and was his lieutenant when Periyar started the Dravidar Kazhagam Party (1944). Wrote his first major play *Chandrodayam* (1943), in which both he and his later protégé **M. Karunanidhi** acted, as Party propaganda. Broke away from the DK to start his own Party, the Dravida Munnetra Kazhagam (1949), which he led to victory in the Tamil Nadu elections (1967). As Chief Minister, his only film-related action was to reduce entertainment tax. His leadership of the DMK, often considered the golden years of the Party, included diluting Periyar's anti-brahminism and anti-religious politics, while indulging in a nationalist Tamil rhetoric identifying Hindi, North India and the Congress Party collectively as the main enemy. The DMK's main ideologue, he wrote extensively on politics, dispensing his views (in e.g. *Kamba Rasam*, critiquing the *Ramayana* for glorifying Aryans) by way of propagandist short stories, novels and plays. Wrote the historical play *Shivaji Kanda Indhu Rajyam*, propelling **Sivaji Ganesan** into stardom as the Maratha emperor. Started the successful DMK Film genre, writing the scripts for ***Velaikkari*** (1949; based on his own stage play) and ***Nallathambi*** (1949), followed by *Ore Iravu* (1951), *Sorgavasal* (1954) and *Nallavan Vazhvan* (1961). His novel ***Rangoon Radha*** was adapted to the screen by **Karunanidhi** (1956). His début, *Velaikkari*, inaugurated via its lead character, Anandan (played by K.R. Ramaswamy), the enduring convention of subjecting a poor hero to many travails, often seeing his family destroyed, until he stridently denounces his oppressors, often equating the gods with the landlords as joint exploiters of the poor. Ramaswamy and **MGR**, 'discovered' by Annadurai because he was a major draw at the DMK's rallies, later became stellar figureheads of the DMK. Although Annadurai's political standing in Tamil Nadu remains unassailable, his scripts have been criticised for being modelled on Hollywood's approach: cf *Nallathambi* and Capra's *Mr Deeds Goes To Town* (1936), *Sorgavasal* and Rouben Mamoulian's *Queen Christina* (1933), *Rangoon Radha* and Cukor's *Gaslight* (1944).

ANTHONY, P. J. (1923-79)

Aka P.J. Antony, born in Ernakulam, Kerala. Malayalam actor whose career illustrates that the roots of Kerala's cinema are in the theatre. Major actor-playwright in the post-WW2 era with more than 90 plays, practising an Ibsen-derived naturalism; he acted in N. Krishna Pillai's seminal adaptation of *A Doll's House*: *Bhagnabhavanam* (1942). Drew on the **IPTA**'s radical nationalism. Ran the Pratibha Arts Club, an influential theatre group based in Ernakulam staging, e.g., Cherukadu's reformist plays. In cinema, famed for playing villains, except for his best-known performance in ***Nirmalayam*** as the priest torn between religious responsibilities and the amoral duplicity of those around him. Directed, scripted, acted in and provided lyrics for *Periyar*. Also wrote lyrics for *Suhruthu* (1952), the dialogues of *Kootukar* (1966) and *Virunnukari*, and the stories of *Chekuthante Kotta*, **A. Vincent**'s celebrated ***Nadhi*** and *Detective 909 Keralathil* (1970).

FILMOGRAPHY (* also d): **1958**: ***Randidangazhi***; **1961**: ***Mudiyanaya Puthran***; **1962**: *Kalpadukal*; **1963**: ***Ninamanninnya Kalapadakal***; *Ammeye Kannan*; **1964**: *Thacholi Othenan*; *Adya Kiranangal*; ***Bhargavi Nilayam***; *Kalanjukuttiya Thangam*; **1965**: ***Rosy***; *Rajamalli*; ***Murappennu***; **1966**: *Tharavatamma*; ***Kunjali Marakkar***; **1967**: ***Irutinte Atmavu***; *Sheelavati*; *Balyakalasakhi*; ***Anveshichu Kandatiyilla***; ***Ashwamedham***; *Nagarame Nandi*; *Pareeksha*; ***Kavalam Chundan***; *Chekuthante Kotta*; *Mulkireedam*; **1968**: *Karutha Pournami*; *Manaswini*; ***Asuravithu***; *Punnapra Vyalar*; *Lakshaprabhu*; *Kayalkarayil*; **1969**: *Anashchadanam*; *Veetu Mrugham*; *Almaram*; *Kattukurangu*; *Susie*; ***Nadhi***; *Virunnukari*; **1970**: *Pearl View*; *Kurukshetram*; *Cross Belt*; *Kakathampurati*; *Ambalapravu*; **1971**: *CID Nazir*; **1972**: *Manushya Bandhangal*; **1973**: *Periyar**; *Masappadi Mathupilla*; ***Nirmalayam***; *Dharma Yuddham*; **1974**: *Atithi*; **1975**: *Odakkuzhal*; *Priyamulla Sophia*; **1976**: *Muthu*; *Nurayum Pathayum*; **1978**: *Padasaram*; *Anayum Ambariyum*; **1979**: *Manninte Maril*.

APTE, NARAYAN HARI (1889-1971)

Marathi novelist and scenarist; key influence on the elaboration of the reformist social as a genre in the 20s and 30s. A product of 19th C. social reform movements in Maharashtra, Apte was self-taught and ran a publishing house, Apte & Co (Est: 1924) which brought out a literary-political journal, *Alhaad* (started in 1915). Author of novels and short-story anthologies within the conventions of the historical (e.g. *Manavi Asha*, *Rajputache Bhishma*), or of the social (*Na Patnari Goshta*, the source for ***Kunku/Duniya Na Mane***, 1937). Invented the social sub-genre of the *dainik kadambari* or 'daily life' novel, usually in a middle-class setting (*Paach Te Paach*, *Waiting Room*). Introduced to film by **Baburao Painter** writing ***Savkari Pash***, the historical *Rana Hamir* (both 1925) and ***Pratibha*** (1937). Best-known film writing for **Shantaram** at **Prabhat** Studio (***Amritmanthan***, 1934; *Kunku/Duniya Na Mane*, 1937). May have provided the story, uncredited, of **Phalke**'s ***Gangavataran*** (1937). Worked with **Dharmadhikari** (*Kunkvacha Dhani*, 1951) and **Dinkar D. Patil** (*Umaj Padel Tar*, 1960). Also wrote K.B. Bhave's *Dhruva Kumar* (1938), **Shantaram Athavale**'s *Bhagyarekha* (1948) and *Sansar Karaychay Mala* (1954).

APTE, SHANTA (1916-64)

Born in Dudhni, Maharashtra. Actress-singer trained at the Maharashtra Sangeet Vidyalaya music school in Pandharpur. One of the great singing stars in the pre-playback era (with **Kanan Devi**). Best known work at **Prabhat** Studio. In ***Amritmanthan***, as the hero's sister Sumitra, caused a box-office sensation with her songs, which became popular in the North (Amritsar and Lahore) leading to a distribution breakthrough for Prabhat. Although music director **Keshavrao Bhole** had doubted whether she could adapt to his light classical style (Bhole, 1964), her ability to counterpoint musical rhythm with gestural spontaneity proved a refreshing departure from the then prevalent ponderously stagey style. Best-known performance in ***Kunku/Duniya Na Mane***, opposite and contrasting with **Keshavrao Date**, ensuring the film's reputation as a progressive social still watchable today. Apart from her Prabhat films, also worked with **Bhalji Pendharkar** (who introduced her to films at the age of nine), **Phani Majumdar**, **Master Vinayak**, **Nandlal Jaswantlal**, **Moti Gidwani** and **Raja Paranjpe**. She featured in one Tamil film, *Savithri*, alongside the singing star (and Carnatic musician) M.S. Subbulakshmi. Wrote autobiography, *Jau Mi Cinemaat?* (1940). Went on a famous hunger strike at the gates of the Prabhat Studio in July 1939 in a protest over her contract.

FILMOGRAPHY (* also music d): **1932**: ***Shyam Sundar***; **1934**: ***Amritmanthan***; **1936**: ***Amar Jyoti***; ***Rajput Ramani***; **1937**: ***Kunku/Duniya Na Mane***; ***Wahan***; **1938**: ***Gopal Krishna***; **1941**: *Savithri*; **1942**: ***Apna Ghar/Aple Ghar***; ***Zamindar***; **1943**: ***Duhai***; ***Mohabbat***; **1944**: *Bhagya Lakshmi*; *Kadambari*; **1945**: *Sawan*; **1946**: *Panihari*; ***Subhadra***; *Uttara Abhimanyu*; *Valmiki*; **1948**: *Mandir*; *Bhagyarekha*; **1949**: *Main Abla Nahin Hoon**; *Swayamsiddha*; *Jaga Bhadyane Dene Aahe*; *Shilanganache Sone*; **1950**: *Jara Japoon*; **1951**: *Kunkvacha Dhani*; **1953**: *Tai Teleen*; **1955**: ***Mulu Manek***; **1957**: *Chandi Puja*.

ARATHI (b. 1954)

Kannada actress born in Aragal, Mysore, Karnataka. Star in 70s melodramas continuing **Kalpana**'s 60s films. Best work under **Puttanna Kanagal**'s direction in films built around her unique presence. Shot repeatedly and at length with an obsessive physical grossness, her body becomes the target of a destructive neurosis that **Kanagal** usually ascribes to the male lead. Her persona became an emblem elaborated over a series of films starting with ***Nagara Haavu*** and was later used by other film-makers. Her wooden acting coupled with a statuesque presence often adds a voyeurist dimension to long and complicated stories that end with the desecration of what she embodies and, sometimes, with her death (e.g. ***Ranganayaki***). Even her absence in Kanagal's *Manasa Sarovara* (1982) led to speculation about the 'real' meaning of the theme of a doctor who leaves his wife to cure a mentally deranged girl, falls in love with her, and goes insane when she falls for his nephew. Directed a tv series, *Namma Nammalli*. Briefly a member of the Karnataka State's legislative assembly representing the fanatic BJP.

FILMOGRAPHY: **1970**: ***Gejje Pooje***; *Takka! Bitre Sikka!!*; **1971**: *Kasturi Nivasa*; *Anugraha*; *Pratidhwani*; *Nyayave Devaru*; *Shri Krishna Rukmini Satyabhama*; **1972**: *Sipayi Ramu*; *Bhale Huchcha*; ***Nagara Haavu***; *Kulagaurava*; *Vooriki Upakari*; ***Bangarada Manushya***; **1973**: *Mane Belagida Sose*;

Shanta Apte (left) and Bipin Gupta (centre) in *Swayamsiddha* (1949)

Edakallu Guddada Mele; *Muruvare Vajragalu*; *Bangarada Panjara*; *Mannina Magalu*; **1974**: *Nanu Baalabeku*; *Upasane*; *Maha Thyaga*; *Bhale Bhatta*; **1975**: *Dari Tappida Maga*; *Shubhamangala*; *Bili Hendthi*; ***Katha Sangama***; *Devara Kannu*; *Hosilu Mettida Hennu*; **1976**: *Premada Kanike*; *Punaradatta*; *Bahadur Gandu*; *Raja Nanna Raja*; *Phalithamsha*; *Balu Jenu*; *Aparadhi*; **1977**: *Magiya Kanasu*; *Pavanaganga*; *Anurupa*; *Kudre Mukha*; **1978**: *Hombisilu*; *Matu Tappada Maga*; *Muyyige Muyi*; *Paduvarahalli Pandavaru*; *Anuragha Bandhana*; *Premayana*; *Vasanthalakshmi*; *Balu Aparupa Nam Jodi*; **1979**: *Dharmasere*; *Adalu Badalu*; *Na Niruvude Ninagangi*; *Manini*; *Nentaro Gantu Kallaro*; **1980**: *Bhakta Siriyala*; *Hanthakana Sanchu*; *Bangarada Jinke*; *Nyaya Nithi Dharma*; *Anurakthe*; **1981**: ***Ranganayaki***; *Thayiya Madilalli*; *Nari Swargakke Dari*; *Ganesha Mahime*; *Bhagyavantha*; *Chadurida Chitragalu*; *Bhagyada Belaku*; *Edeyuru Siddalingeshwara*; *Preetsi Nodu*; **1982**: *Pedda Gedda*; *Archana*; *Mullina Gulabi*; *Karmika Kallanalla*; *Mava Sose Saval*; *Parijata*; *Nyaya Yellide?*; *Kannu Terasida Hennu*; *Suvarna Sethuve*; *Hasyarathna Ramakrishna*; *Raja Maharaja*; **1983**: *Tirugu Bhana*; *Gedda Maga*; *Jaggu*; *Nyaya Gedditu*; *Kalluveene Nudiyitu*; *Thayiya Nudi*; *Sididedda Sahodara*; *Kranthiyogi Basavanna*; *Ananda Sagara*; *Muttaide Bhagya*; *Gandharvagiri*; *Akrosha*; *Chelisada Sagara*; *Samarpane*; *Premave Balina Belaku*; *Bekkina Kannu*; **1984**: *Kaliyuga*; *Khaidi*; *Poojaphala*; *Hennina Saubhagya*; *Avala Antaranga*; *Ramapurada Ravana*; *Pavitra Prema*; *Agnyathavasa*; *Preeti Vatsalya*; **1985**: *Nee Nakkaga*; *Sati Sakkubai*; *Lakshmi Kataksha*; *Kumkuma Thanda Saubhagya*; *Swabhimana*; *Shiva Kotta Saubhagya*; *Tulasi Dala*; *Haavu Eni Aata*; **1986**: *Bettada Thayi*; *Seelu Nakshatra*; **1987**: *Thaliye Ane*.

ARAVINDAN, GOVINDAN (1935-91)

Malayalam director, painter and cartoonist with an idiosyncratic style. Born in Kottayam, Kerala; son of the literary humourist, Govindan Nair. Worked as caricaturist for the *Mathrubhoomi* journal (1961-79), drawing the cartoon series *Small Man and Big World*, chronicling the adventures of Ramu, its corruptible proletarian hero, and Guruji; later did an occasional cartoon strip for the *Kala Kaumudi* journal, called *A Bird's Eye View*. His published cartoon collection (1978) highlights a change in drawing style in the early 70s, emphasising large blank spaces and characters almost disappearing below the frame. His films are known for their distinctive look, sparse naturalism, silences and long shots with darker shades of grey in b&w films. Film society activist in Kottayam and Calicut. Early work was the only consistent cinematic manifestation of late 60s Calicut-based modernism represented particularly by artist Devan, the playwright and satirist Thikkodiyan and the writer Pattathiruvila Karunakaran (who produced ***Uttarayanam***). A major influence on this group was the spiritualism of satirist and political activist Sanjayan. Later, like the visual artists associated with the Kerala Kalapeetam in Ernakulam, Aravindan combined this influence with the new, more mystical direction taken by K.C.S. Panicker's (1911-77) paintings (cf ***Kanchana Seeta***). His faithful producer and distributor, Ravindran of General Pics, ran a family business in cashew nuts. Worked at the Kerala Rubber Board throughout most of his film career. Also stage director, working in association with the playwright Srikantan Nair, after which he helped start the Navarangan (in Kottayam) and Sopanam theatre groups, staging e.g. *Kali* (1964) and *Avanavan Kadamba* (1976) using musical forms derived from the work of Kavalam Narayana Panicker, who later collaborated on the scripts of ***Kummatty*** and ***Estheppan***. Noted actors associated with this group were **Gopi** and Nedumudi Venu. Also trained in the Kirana-style Khayal. Occasionally music director for other film-makers: ***Yaro Oral*** (1978), ***Piravi*** and *Ore Thooval Pakshikal* (both 1988).

FILMOGRAPHY: 1974: ***Uttarayanam***; **1977**: ***Kanchana Seeta***; **1978**: ***Thampu***; **1979**: ***Kummatty***; ***Estheppan***; **1981**: ***Pokkuveyil***; **1985**: ***Chidambaram***; *Viti* (Doc); *The Brown Landscape* (Sh); **1986**: ***Oridathu***; *The Seer Who Walks Alone* (Doc); **1987**: *Contours of a Linear Rhythm* (Doc); **1988**: *Anandi Dhara* (Doc); ***Marattam*** (TV); *Sahaja* (Sh); **1989**: *Unni*; **1990**: ***Vasthuhara***.

ART SCHOOLS

The terms 'art school' or 'academic' aesthetic style in the visual arts refer to a series of art schools started in the mid-19th C. in Presidency cities, usually by Indian industrialists or entrepreneurs with support from the British government: the Calcutta School of Art (Est: 1854), the School of Industrial Arts in Madras (Est: 1854), the Sir Jamsetji Jeejibhoy School of Art in Bombay (Est: 1857) and the Mayo School of Arts in Lahore (Est: 1878). Set up to provide industrial craft training (e.g. weaving, metal and wood carving, gem cutting), they became fine arts institutions modelled on the Royal Academy to train artists in 'the whole paraphernalia of European art academies: the drawing-room copies, casts from "the antique", Gothic mouldings etc. [while] at the same time it has been held as totally unnecessary, if not demoralising, for them to study the principles and methods of Indian painting and sculpture' (E.B. Havell, Principal in early 20th C. of the Government School of Art, Calcutta, 1901). A valuable account of the art schools is given by T. Guha-Thakurta (1992), who points out that by the end of the 19th C. the art schools had managed to establish the idea that art could be a respectable vocation, in terms of the status of 'high art', as well as a career in terms of the middle-class employment opportunities offered by an 'applied arts' approach: '"Art", indicating painting and sculpture, and the "applied arts", indicating technical skills of draughtmanship, engraving, etching or lithography, were not considered two separate spheres, but two essential aspects of the same profession.' Extending the naturalist and neo-classical modes of British painting in India, the new academicism of the art schools, legitimated by, e.g., portrait commissions from the British and Indian ruling classes, also fed into the diversified conventions of the **Company School** as Indian artists formerly under feudal patronage started selling their wares in urban market-places. The academic style, both in genre and manner, had a function analogous to that of operatic style in the **Parsee Theatre**: it created a new hierarchy of taste in competition with classicist brahminical aspirations while maintaining an opposition to native popular arts which sought to assimilate industrial technology differently (cf **Pat Painting** and **Raja Ravi Varma** for alternative solutions). However, as Indian artists often found it difficult to incorporate the rules of monocular perspective, the art schools invented their own variations, reformulating the demand for verisimilitude in the painted or photographed image in terms of a naUve formalism, thereby creating a peculiar genre popular with the potentially democratic and culturally eclectic urban middle classes. This institutionalised aesthetic became a conduit for theatrical and cinematic naturalism, displaced though it was into various devices that substituted for illusionistic skills. These developments prefigure the painted **stage backdrops** and set design, e.g. in the work of artists and art directors such as M.R. Achrekar (in **Raj Kapoor** films) or Kanu Desai (in **Vijay Bhatt** and **Shantaram** mythologicals). Bansi Chandragupta's work for **S. Ray** is also relevant in this context, although other considerations come into play in his case as well. Later, the art school aesthetic influenced the posture of actors as they formed a frontal master-shot tableau within which the film-maker would insert close-ups or over-the-shoulder shots.

ARUDRA (b. 1925)

Telugu poet and film lyricist born in Vizag, AP, as Bhagavathula Shankara Sastry. Started publishing poetry as a teenager, e.g. *Loha Vihangalu*. Initially influenced by radical poet **Sri Sri**. After a brief stint in the army, he became a professional writer under the name Arudra. Early writing was romantic, but became more political under the influence of the Telangana anti-zamindari movements (cf *Twamevaham*). Major poetry anthologies include *Kunalamma Padyalu* (1964), *Enchina Padyalu* (1965) and *Intinti Padyalu* (1969). Also wrote patriotic songs during the India-China war (1962). Compiled an anthology of Telugu literature (*Samagrandhra Sahityam*). Film début in the Telugu version (*Beedala Patlu*) of **Ramnoth**'s classic ***Ezhai Padum Padu*** (1950). Made his reputation in films with *Premalekhalu* (1953), the Telugu dubbed version of **Raj Kapoor**'s ***Aah*** (1953). Described as the last of the pre-rock generation film lyricists. Recently worked for **Bapu** (*Pelli Pustakam*, 1991). Classic film lyrics anthologised by V.A.K. Ranga Rao in *Kondagali Tirigindi*.

Arunaraje *or* Aruna-Vikas *see* **Raje, Aruna**

ASHWATAMMA, K. (1910-44)

Star Kannada and Tamil actress-singer with brief but sensational film career. Launched on the stage (1934) and in film (1935) in title role of **Gubbi Veeranna**'s *Sadarame*, both with **Jayamma** as Draupadi. Adult stage career began with Mohammed Peer's Manolasini Nataka Sabha, which led to her career as a recording star and her biggest hit single, *Ha priya prashanta hridaya* (from the play *Mammatha Vijaya*). Her songs in *Sadarame* and her duet with **M.K.**

Thyagaraja Bhagavathar in **Y.V. Rao**'s *Chintamani* confirmed her as a South Indian film and recording star, although she did only one more film, **Sundarrao Nadkarni**'s *Sant Sakkubai*.

FILMOGRAPHY: **1935**: *Sadarame*; **1937**: *Chintamani*; **1939**: *Sant Sakkubai*.

ASIF, KARIMUDDIN (1924-71)

Urdu director born in Etawah, UP. Best known for expensive costume spectaculars centred around Muslim legend (cf **S. Modi**). Assistant to uncle film-maker and actor, S. Nazir (*Society*, 1942). Turned director in 1944 and producer in 1951 with S.K. Ojha's *Hulchul*. ***Mughal-e-Azam***, one of Indian cinema's biggest blockbusters, took 14 years to make, initially starring **Chandramohan**, who died and was replaced by **Dilip Kumar**. Left two big projects unfinished at his death: *Sasta Khoon Mahenga Paani* (which was to be shot in Jordan), and ***Love and God***, using the Sufi legend of Laila-Majnu, started with **Guru Dutt** but entirely re-shot after Dutt died. Eventually released in unfinished form by producer K.C. Bokadia, starring Sanjeev Kumar.

FILMOGRAPHY: **1944**: ***Phool***; **1960**: ***Mughal-e-Azam***; **1986**: ***Love and God***.

ATHAVALE, SHANTARAM GOVIND (b. 1910)

Marathi and Hindi director, better known as a Marathi lyricist; born in Pune, where he saw many classic **Sangeet Natak** performances in his childhood. Apprenticed to novelist **Narayan Hari Apte**, helping him to publish the journal *Madhukar* in Koregaon. When Apte was invited to script ***Amritmanthan*** (1934) for **Prabhat**, Athavale followed his mentor as a songwriter, and achieved instant success esp. with the song *Kiti sukhada*. Achieved even greater renown when he wrote the only new song for ***Sant Tukaram*** (1936), the others being the saint poet's original compositions. The song in question, *Adhi beej ekale*, convinced many Tukaram authorities that an unknown Tukaram composition had been discovered. He wrote most of the songs of Prabhat hits such as ***Kunku*** (1937), ***Mazha Mulga*** and ***Gopal Krishna*** (both 1938), ***Sant Dnyaneshwar*** (1940), ***Sant Sakhu*** and ***Shejari*** (both 1941), ***Daha Wajta*** (1942) and ***Ramshastri*** (1944), often in partnership with composer **Keshavrao Bhole**. Left Prabhat (1942) to write dialogues and lyrics for **Debaki Bose**'s ***Apna Ghar*** (1942) and lyrics for **Vijay Bhatt**'s ***Bharat Milap*** (1942). For his début as director with *Bhagya Rekha*, he hired his former teacher N.H. Apte together with the star associated with his songs, **Shanta Apte**. Athavale's *Main Abla Nahin Hoon* was one of Apte's better-known post-Prabhat performances. Made numerous educational shorts and documentaries, mostly in English. Wrote a history of Prabhat, *'Prabhat' Kaal* (1965).

FILMOGRAPHY: **1948**: *Bhagya Rekha*; **1949**: *Main Abla Nahin Hoon*; **1953**: *Vahinichya Bangdya*; **1954**: *Sansar Karaychay Mala*; **1955**: *Shevgyachya Shenga*; **1958**: *Padada*; **1960**: *Fix it Right* (Doc); *Write it Right* (Doc); **1961**: *How to Vote* (Doc); *Gift of Sight* (Doc); **1962**: *Citizens and Citizens* (Doc); *The Homecoming* (Doc); *Marriage and After* (Doc); **1963**: *Chatur Balak*; **1965**: *Vavtal*; **1968**: *Sankat Main Swasthya Aur Safai* (Doc); **1971**: *My Village My People* (Doc).

ATHREYA, ACHARYA (1921-89)

Telugu poet, scenarist, lyricist and noted playwright. Born near Sulurpetta, AP, as Kilambi Narasimhachari. Wrote several plays while a student at Nellore and Chittor and was associated with the Venkatagiri Amateurs stage group. Abandoned his studies to participate in the Quit India agitations and was imprisoned. Odd jobs including working as a clerk in a settlement office and assistant editor on the journal *Zamin Raitu*. Early plays in the historical genre (*Gautama Buddha*, 1946; *Ashoka Samrat*, 1947). Introduced a brand of realism on the stage, addressing contemporary political issues, e.g. *N.G.O.* (1949), later adapted to the screen as ***Gumasta*** (1953). Other major plays include *Ee Nadu* (1947), *Vishwashanti* (1953), *Bhayam* (1957). First film script was ***Samsaram*** (1950; uncredited), followed by **H.M. Reddy**'s ***Nirdoshi*** (1951). Wrote lyrics for more than 250 films, starting with *Deeksha* (1951). Secretary of the Andhra Screen Writers Guild (1955-6). Lyrics anthologised by the actor **K. Jaggaiah**. Directed one film: *Vagdanam* (1961).

Atma, K. P. *see* **Pratyagatma, K.**

ATMA RAM (1930-94)

Hindi director born in Bombay as Atmaram Padukone; younger brother of **Guru Dutt**. Did clerical work and joined the Socialist Party (1948-50); active trade unionist and secretary of the Press Workers' Union. Studied at the University of Bombay (1952); then assisted Guru Dutt. Worked for a while in London (1958-61) directing films produced by Stuart Legg and Arthur Elton for the Shell Film Unit; also scripted documentaries for James Beveridge for India's Shell Film Unit (1955-62). Turned to features, mostly musicals, after Guru Dutt's death (1964) and ran the company. Tried to go in a new direction with *Umang*, his first independent Atma Ram Films production, dispensing with major stars in favour of 'youth movie' ensemble play (with the then unknown **Subhash Ghai** as actor). His *Yeh Gulistan Hamara*, for Guru Dutt Films, is a nationalist movie in which **Dev Anand**, on behalf of the Indian government, quells the North Eastern frontier tribals with love to the tune of classic **S.D. Burman** numbers (*Kya yeh zindagi hai*, *Raina soyi soyi*). The Saira Banu and Vinod Khanna hit *Aarop* addressed corruption in journalism. Also made advertising films with his younger brother, Devi Dutt. Active in official institutions (e.g. at the **FTII** in the late 70s). Often worked for television.

FILMOGRAPHY: **1960**: *The Living Soil* (Doc); **1961**: *The Peaceful Revolution* (Doc); **1964**: *Kaise Kahun*; **1968**: *Shikar*; **1969**: *Chanda Aur Bijli*; **1970**: *Umang*; **1971**: *Memsaab*; *Yaar Mere*; **1972**: *Yeh Gulistan Hamara*; **1973**: *Aarop*; *Resham Ki Dori*; **1974**: *Imaan*; **1975**: *Qaid*; **1976**: *Ladusingh Taxiwala* (TV); **1977**: *Aafat*; *Ashanti Shantidas* (TV); **1978**: *Ramlal Shyamlal* (TV); **1979**: *Khanjar*; **1982**: *Pyar Ke Rahi*; **1988**: *JP* (Doc); *Yeh Sach Hai* (Doc); **1990**: *Beeswa Oonth* (TV); **1992**: *Tulsidas*; **1993**: *Vividha* (TV).

ATORTHY, PREMANKUR (1890-1964)

Bengali and Hindi director born in Faridpur (now Bangladesh). Noted novelist and playwright, author of many books including compilations of short stories, essays (e.g. on silent film, cf Atorthy, 1990) and plays. Best-known literary work: *Mahasthavir Jatak* (1922), a fictional autobiography in four volumes noted for its irreverent portrayal of Calcutta's early 20th C. élites. Associated with modernist literary journal *Bharati*; edited *Nachghar*, one of the first performing arts journals to take film seriously, with Hemendra Kumar Roy and film-maker **Pashupati Chatterjee**. Founded *Betar Jagat*, the journal of the AIR, Calcutta (1929). Started as scenarist and actor, using the pseudonym Krishna Haldar, at **Indian Kinema Arts** (*Punarjanma*, 1927; *Chasher Meye*, 1931). Remade *Punarjanma* in 1932. Joined B.N. Sircar's International Filmcraft as writer and assistant to Prafulla Roy (*Chasher Meye* is based on Atorthy's novel and script). Also scripted **Nitin Bose**'s *Buker Bojha* (1930). First film, *Dena Paona*, was **New Theatres**' first talkie, made in direct competition with **Madan Theatres**' *Jamai Sasthi* (1931). Made several Urdu films as part of New Theatres' effort to enter the North Indian market, including the classic film of **Aga Hashr Kashmiri**'s play ***Yahudi Ki Ladki***. His film versions of literary classics, e.g. from Saratchandra Chatterjee (*Dena Paona*), **Rabindranath Tagore** (*Chirakumar Sabha*) and Bankimchandra Chatterjee (*Kapal Kundala*), established the élite literary film genre intended to distinguish New Theatres' films from routine stage adaptations and remained important signifiers of high art in Bengali cinema. First Bengali film-maker to work in Western India, e.g. for **Kolhapur Cinetone** (1935) and for **Imperial** (1936). Credited with the supervision of H.K. Shivdasani's ***Yasmin*** (1935), made by the **Krishna** Studio.

FILMOGRAPHY: **1931**: *Dena Paona*; **1932**: *Mohabbat Ke Aansoo*; *Subah Ka Sitara*; *Zinda Lash*; *Punarjanma*; *Chirakumar Sabha*; **1933**: *Kapal Kundala*; ***Yahudi Ki Ladki***; **1935**: *Bharat Ki Beti*; ***Bhikharan***; ***Karwan-e-Hayat***; **1936**: *Hind Mahila*; ***Sarala***; **1937**: *Dhanwan*; **1938**: *Dulhan*; **1940**: *Kalyani*; **1941**: *Avatar*; **1942**: *Lajwanti*; **1943**: *Dikshul*; **1950**: *Sudhar Prem*.

ATRE, PRALHAD KESHAV (1898-1969)

Marathi-Hindi director and controversial literary figure in post-WW1 Maharashtra. Educated at the universities of Poona and London; studied experimental psychology under Cyril Burt and taught at Harrow before returning to India. Owner-editor of populist down-market *Maratha* newspaper; one-time Congress Party MLA. Author of 22 plays, 13 short-story collections, four books of poetry and a 4-volume autobiography (Atre, 1965-7). Teacher and producer of several school textbooks, often calling himself Principal Atre in his film credits. Aggressive polemicist

Vanamala in P.K. Atre's *Shyamchi Aai* (1953)

remembered for famous literary battles with N.S. Phadke and Mama Warerkar. Owned Chitramandir Studio/Atre Pictures (1940), the Atre Printing Press (1944) and Atre Arts (1968). Film career began adapting his own short stories for **Master Vinayak** (***Brahmachari***, 1938; ***Brandichi Batli***, 1939). Became a leading independent scenarist (e.g. ***Raja Rani***, 1942) and pioneered the entry of new literary modes emerging from non-fictional prose into post-Independence Marathi film. His chosen genre was political satire, usually directed against the realist conventions of pre-WW1 social reform novels with their caste biases and Anglophilia. However, his best-known film as director was the bitter-sweet melodrama ***Shyamchi Aai***. Wrote plays in many genres: thrillers (*To Mee Navhech*), tragedies (rewriting the reformist **Sangeet Natak** playwright Ram Ganesh Gadkari and his own *Udyacha Sansar*) and satire. Noted scripts: ***Dharmaveer***, *Premveer*, *Begunah* (all 1937), ***Ardhangi*/*Ghar Ki Rani***, ***Lapandav*** (both 1940). Preferred to hire directors rather than to direct. Produced and wrote his own movies, often starring his wife, Vanmala, through his Atre Pics, founded in 1940.

FILMOGRAPHY: 1944: *Dil Ki Baat*; **1945**: *Parinde*; **1948**: *Moruchi Mavshi*; **1949**: *Brahma Ghotala*; **1951**: *Hi Majhi Lakshmi*; **1953**: ***Shyamchi Aai***; **1954**: *Mahatma Phule*.

AURORA FILM CORPORATION

Studio in Calcutta initially named Aurora Cinema (Est: 1911) by founders Debi Ghosh, Anadi Bose and Charu Ghosh. It ran tent shows in Howrah and around Assam, showing Western films as part of a variety bill. Started making films in 1917, having won the contract to make shorts for the army during WW1 with cameras bought from **Hiralal Sen**. Early productions include shots of plays from Calcutta's Art Theatres (*Basabadatta*, *Chandrasekhar*) and Manmohan Theatres (*Bishabriksha*). Later known for major films like Surendra Narayan Roy's *Ratnakar* (1921) and *Bidyasundar* (aka *The Lover's Trance*, 1922) and *Aurora Tuki-taki* (*Aurora Tidbits*, compilations of clips). Converted into Aurora Film when Anadi Bose became sole proprietor, purchasing the studio premises of Barua Pics (1929). Made films in Bengali (e.g. by **Niranjan Pal** and **Naresh Mitra**), in Hindi and some in Telugu and Tamil (e.g. by **Sundarrao Nadkarni**). Niranjan Pal helped launch the pioneering *Aurora Screen News*, which shot the footage of **Rabindranath Tagore**'s funeral later used by **Satyajit Ray** in his documentary (1961). The only silent Bengali studio still operating in 1992.

AVM FILM COMPANY

One of the top South Indian studios set up in 1947 by film-maker, producer and mogul A.V. Meiyappan (1907-79). Born to a family of moneylenders, Meiyappan initially ran a shop named A.V. & Sons, later expanded to include the record label Saraswathi Stores. Début as producer with Saraswathi Sound (*Alli Arjuna*, 1935). His previous companies included Saraswathi Talkies and Pragati Pics, the latter known for comedy double bills written by A.T. Krishnaswamy (*Poli Panchali*, 1940; *Sabhapati*, 1941) and for the film of **R. Nagendra Rao**'s play, ***Bhukailasa*** (1940), directed by **Sundarrao Nadkarni**. Following his Tamil hit, *Shri Valli* (1945) starring singer-musician T.R. Mahalingam, Meiyappan established his AVM Studio adapting S.V. Sahasranamam's stage hit ***Nam Iruvar*** (1947). The film was a precursor of the classic **DMK Film** dramas made at this studio later, e.g. ***Parasakthi*** (1952). Developed a unique production infrastructure in four Indian languages, including Hindi films starting with ***Bahar*** (1951), starring **Vyjayanthimala** in a remake of her début, the hit *Vazhkai* (1949), directed by **M.V. Raman**. Main films such as ***Bedara Kannappa*** (1954) and *Sadarame* (1956) in Kannada, the **Raj Kapoor-Nargis** Hindi hit, ***Chori Chori*** (1956), the Tamil films *Andha Naal* (1954), ***Server Sundaram*** (1964). AVM also pioneered the practice of dubbing productions. Among the directors working in the four languages at AVM were M.V. Raman, **Krishnan-Panju**, **A. Bhimsingh**, A.C. Trilogchander and S.P. Muthuraman, who worked mainly in Tamil. Meiyappan published his autobiography, *Enadhu Vazhkai Anubhavangal/The Experiences of My Life* (1974). He is credited with the direction of *Sabhapati* (1941), *En Manaivi* (with S. Nadkarni, 1942), *Shri Valli* (1945), ***Nam Iruvar*** (1947) and *Vethala Ulagam* (1948).

AZMI, KAIFI (b. 1925)

Film lyricist and scenarist born in Azamgarh as Akhtar Husain Rizvi. Urdu poet in the tradition of Josh Mahilabadi and Faiz Ahmed Faiz (1911-84). Abandoned his studies of Persian and Urdu during the 1942 Quit India agitations, and shortly thereafter became a full-time Marxist activist. Went to Bombay (1945) and was for a while a trade union worker; closely involved with the **PWA** in Bombay. Published three anthologies of poetry (*Akhini-Shab*, *Jhankar* and *Awara Sajde*). Early work as story writer for **Nanubhai Vakil**'s films (*Yahudi Ki Beti*, 1956; *Parvin*, 1957; *Miss Punjab Mail*, 1958; *Id Ka Chand*, 1964). Wrote lyrics for numerous films, most notably for **Guru Dutt**'s ***Kaagaz Ke Phool*** (1959), **Chetan Anand**'s nationalist war movie ***Haqeeqat*** (1964) and **Kamal Amrohi**'s ***Pakeezah*** (1971). Established formidable reputation as perhaps the most charismatic writer in films, following the acclaim for his script, dialogue and lyrics for **M.S. Sathyu**'s ***Garam Hawa*** (1973), based on **Ismat Chughtai**'s story. Also wrote dialogues for Sathyu's *Kanneshwara Rama* (1977). Other contributions include dialogues for **Benegal**'s ***Manthan*** (1976), lyrics for **Hrishikesh Mukherjee**'s *Bawarchi* (1972) and for Kamal Amrohi's *Razia Sultan* (1983). Raman Kumar made a documentary, *Kaifi Azmi* (1979).

AZMI, SHABANA (b. 1950)

Actress. Daughter of **Kaifi Azmi** and celebrated **IPTA** actress Shaukat. Graduate of **FTII** acting course (1972); feature début in **Abbas**'s mediocre *Faasla*, released after her emergence in ***Ankur***. Became a regular presence in **Benegal** films (***Nishant***, ***Junoon***, ***Mandi***, ***Susman***, *Antarnaad*). Together with **Smita Patil**, Azmi is the most prominent star spawned by the New Indian Cinema, working with e.g. **Satyajit Ray** (***Shatranj Ke Khiladi***), **Mrinal Sen** (***Khandhar***, ***Genesis***, ***Ek Din Achanak***), **Saeed Mirza** (***Albert Pinto Ko Gussa Kyon Aata Hai***), **Gautam Ghosh** (***Paar***), **Sai Paranjpye** (***Sparsh***, ***Disha***), **Aparna Sen** (*Picnic*, ***Sati***), and **Mahesh Bhatt** films, including the notorious ***Arth***. Also worked with Western directors (John Schlesinger's *Madame Sousatzka*, 1988; Roland Joffe's *City of Joy*, 1992). Became a major mainstream Hindi star after *Fakira*, working in **Manmohan Desai**'s ***Amar Akbar Anthony***, *Parvarish* and **Prakash Mehra**'s *Jwalamukhi*. Initially practised, in her 'art' movies, a style of naturalist acting equated with the absence of make-up, an

Shabana Azmi in *Ankur* (1973)

emphasis on regional accents (e.g. the rural Andhra accent in *Ankur* and *Nishant* or the Parsee Hindi in ***Pestonjee***) and the theatre-derived technique of alternating the casual gesture and dramatic high points. Married scenarist **Javed Akhtar**. Also acted on the stage, including an acclaimed performance in the revived IPTA's 1980 Hindi version of *The Caucasian Chalk Circle* entitled *Safed Kundali* by M.S. Sathyu. First tv drama, *Picnic*, under Aparna Sen's direction. Briefly chairperson of the **CFS**. Known also as a courageous political activist associated with the Nivara Hakk Samrakshan Samiti, fighting the cause of Bombay's slum and pavement-dwellers, and with various anti-communal organisations, playing an effective, high-profile role in e.g. the 1993 communal riots in Bombay.

FILMOGRAPHY: 1973: *The December Evening* (Sh); *Munshiji* (Sh); ***Ankur***; **1974**: *Parinay*; *Ishq Ishq Ishq*; *Faasla*; **1975**: *Kadambari*; ***Nishant***; **1976**: *Fakira*; *Shaque*; *Vishwasghaat*; **1977**: *Adha Din Adhi Raat*; ***Amar Akbar Anthony***; *Chor Sipahi*; *Ek Hi Raasta*; *Hira Aur Patthar*; *Khel Khiladi Ka*; ***Kissa Kursi Ka***; *Parvarish*; ***Shatranj Ke Khiladi***; ***Swami***; *Kanneshwara Rama*; *Karm*; **1978**: *Atithi*; *Devata*; *Khoon Ki Pukar*; *Swarg Narak*; *Toote Khilone*; ***Junoon***; **1979**: *Amar Deep*; *Bagula Bhagat*; *Lahu Ke Do Rang*; ***Sparsh***; *Jeena Yahan*; **1980**: *Apne Paraye*; *Ek Baar Kaho*; *Jwalamukhi*; *Thodisi Bewafayi*; *Yeh Kaisa Insaaf*; ***Albert Pinto Ko Gussa Kyon Aata Hai***; ***Hum Paanch***; **1981**: *Ek Hi Bhool*; *Sameera*; *Shama*; *Raaste Pyar Ke*; **1982**: *Anokha Bandhan*; *Ashanti*; *Namkeen*; *Suraag*; *Yeh Nazdeekiyan*; ***Arth***; *Log Kya Kahenge*; ***Masoom***; **1983**: *Avatar*; *Doosri Dulhan*; ***Mandi***; *Sweekar Kiya Maine*; ***Khandhar***; *Pyaasi Aankhen*; **1984**: *Aaj Ka MLA Ramavatar*; *Bhavna*; *Gangvaa*; *Hum Rahe Na Hum*; *Kaamyaab*; *Yaadon KI Zanjeer*; *Kamla*; *Mr X*; *Lorie*; ***Paar***; *Ram Tera Desh*; **1985**: *Rahi Badal Gaye*; *Uttarayan*; *Khamosh*; *Shart*; **1986**: ***Anjuman***; ***Ek Pal***; *Samay Ki Dhara*; *Nasihat*; ***Susman***; ***Genesis***; **1987**: *Itihaas*; *Jallianwala Bagh*; ***Pestonjee***; **1988**: *Mardon Wali Baat*; ***Ek Din Achanak***; *Madame Sousatzka*; **1989**: *Oonch Neech Beech*; *Libaas*; *Jhoothi Sharm*; *Rakhwala*; *Main Azaad Hoon*; ***Sati***; **1990**: *Picnic* (TV); ***Disha***; *Amba*; *Muqaddar Ka Badshah*; *Ek Doctor Ki Maut*; **1991**: *Immaculate Conception*; *Dharavi*; **1992**: *Adharm*; *Jhoothi Shaan*; *City of Joy*; *Antarnaad*; **1993**: *In Custody*; *Patang*.

BABU, HANUMAPPA VISHWANATH (1903-68)

Major 30s Telugu director born in Bangalore. Studied medicine. Made mythologicals usually starring **Kannamba**, carrying on the genre's silent era version as practised in Bombay's studios where he began his career. Worked for **Kohinoor** as actor (1927), then at **Imperial** as actor and assistant to his brother-in-law, **H.M. Reddy** (1929-35). First and best-known film, ***Draupadi Vastrapaharanam***, made in competition with a Laxmi Films production starring **Ballari Raghava**. It also launched the pioneering Telugu production company, Saraswathi Talkies, which introduced **Gudavalli Ramabrahmam** to film-making.

FILMOGRAPHY: **1931**: *Bar Ke Pobar* (St; act only); **1936**: ***Draupadi Vastrapaharanam***; **1937**: *Kanakatara*; **1940**: *Bhoja Kalidasa*; **1941**: *Mandaravathi*; **1943**: ***Krishna Prema***; **1949**: *Dharmangada*; **1952**: *Adarsham*; **1955**: *Grihalakshmi*; **1963**: *Devasundari*.

BABURAJ, M. S. (b. 1921)

Malayalam music composer, born in Calicut, Kerala. First associated with Nilambur Balan's stage group, working mainly in the Malabar region of North Kerala. Based in Calicut, Baburaj was one of the first composers to introduce the North Indian classical influence into the otherwise Carnatic Malayalam film music. Until his work for **Kariat**'s films (cf ***Mudiyanaya Puthran***), the Northern influence had been restricted to e.g. **Kozhikode Abdul Qadir**'s imitations of **K.L. Saigal**. His compositions in e.g. **Vincent**'s ***Bhargavi Nilayam***, working outside the routine *madhya laya* (middle tempo) to create a slower beat using minimal orchestration, are still remembered for the early (and for some, the finest) songs of **Yesudas**. Associated most closely with **Bhaskaran**'s lyrics. Scored **P.N. Menon**'s independent film ***Olavum Theeravum*** and **Madhu**'s directorial début ***Priya***. Filmography unavailable after 1978.

FILMOGRAPHY: **1957**: ***Minnaminungu***; **1960**: *Umma*; **1961**: ***Kandam Bacha Coat***; ***Mudiyanaya Puthran***; **1962**: *Laila Majnu*; *Palattukoman*; *Bhagya Jatakam*; **1963**: ***Ninamanninnya Kalapadakal***; ***Moodupadam***; **1964**: *Thacholi Othenan*; *Kuttikkuppayam*; *Karutha Kayi*; ***Bhargavi Nilayam***; *Bharthavu*; **1965**: *Subaida*; *Kadatthukaran*; *Porter Kunjali*; *Kuppivala*; *Ammu*; *Thankakudam*; *Kattuthulasi*; *Mayavi*; *Chettathi*; *Thommente Makkal*; *Sarpakadu*; **1966**: *Manikya Kottaram*; *Pennmakkal*; *Kootukar*; *Kattumallika*; *Anarkali*; *Tharavatamma*; *Kanakachilanka*; **1967**: ***Irutinte Atmavu***; ***Agniputhri***; *Udyogastha*; *Balyakalasakhi*; *Karutharathrigal*; *Kadhija*; ***Anveshichu Kandatiyilla***; *Collector Malathi*; *Pareeksha*; **1968**: *Manaswini*; *Inspector*; *Karthika*; *Lakshaprabhu*; *Love In Kerala*; *Midumidukki*; *Anju Sundarigal*; **1969**: *Sandhya*; *Velliyazhcha*; *Virunnukari*; ***Olavum Theeravum***; **1970**: *Saraswathi*; *Anatha*; *Ambalapravu*; *Cross Belt*; *Bhikara Nimishinkal*; *Nizhalattam*; *Vivaham Swargathil*; ***Priya***; **1971**: *Neethi*; *Ernakulam Junction*; **1972**: *Sambhavami Yuge Yuge*; *Panimudakku*; *Pulliman*; *Azhimukham*; **1973**: *Bhadra Deepam*; *Aradhika*; *Ladies' Hostel*; *Soundarya Pooja*; *Manasu*; *Kamini*; *Chuzhi*; **1974**: *Nathoon*; *Swarna Malsiyam*; **1975**: *Gnan Ninne Premikkunu*; *Srishti*; *Criminals*; **1976**: *Allah-o-Akbar*; *Appooppan*; *Dweep*; *Pushpa Sarem*; **1977**: *Gandharvam*; *Yatheem*; **1978**: *Bhrashtu*; *Yagaswam*.

BACHCHAN, AMITABH (b. 1942)

Hindi cinema's biggest star actor. Born in Allahabad, son of noted Hindi poet Harivanshrai Bachchan. Former stage actor, radio announcer and freight company executive in Calcutta. Although he initially had difficulties being accepted as an actor, his productions eventually determined the health of the whole Hindi film industry. **Abbas** gave him his first small role in ***Saat Hindustani***; next came a voice-over for **Sen**'s ***Bhuvan Shome*** (1969). Later, he also did the voice-over for **Ray**'s ***Shatranj Ke Khiladi*** (1977). Eventually became the superstar of the mid-70s tv, radio and the press issued daily bulletins on his health when he suffered a near-fatal accident in 1982 while shooting ***Coolie***. In early **Gulzar**-scripted and **Hrishikesh Mukherjee**-directed films (***Anand***, ***Namak Haram***) and in *Saudagar*, based on Narendranath Mitra's story, Bachchan is presented as a brooding, melancholic anti-hero drawn from Bengali literary stereotypes traceable to novelist Saratchandra Chatterjee and introduced into Hindi film by **Nitin Bose**, **Bimal Roy** and **Asit Sen**. In this respect, he is in the tradition of **Dilip Kumar** (e.g. ***Deedar***, 1951), **Sunil Dutt** (***Sujata***, 1959; ***Gaban***, 1966) and **Dharmendra** (***Satyakam***, 1969). His persona of the angry youth was elaborated in directly political language in ***Zanjeer***, the first of his big vendetta films. Expanded in the films of **Prakash Mehra** and **Yash Chopra**, Bachchan's image reorganised the formulaic melodrama around the clash between the laws of kinship and the laws of the state, requiring the hero to become an outlaw governed by a higher code of conduct. In ***Deewar*** and ***Trishul*** this conflict still constituted the films' main theme but it quickly became a mere plot device, while a more directly political discourse began to insinuate itself into the films via the repeated references to the early 70s working class agitations (which culminated in the 1974 railway strike preceding the Emergency in 1975), as in e.g. ***Kala Patthar***. Other topical and politically loaded references invoked threats of national economic destabilisation in e.g. ***Trishul***, *Shakti* and *Mr Natwarlal*. The melodramatic plot structure also lent itself well to the enactment of the fantasy of the lumpen rebel-vigilante who achieves great personal success, at times turning the film into a gigantic masquerade (esp. with **Manmohan Desai**). In addition to his own charismatic presence and his sonorous voice, an important component in several Bachchan films is the **Salim-Javed** script. Bachchan's persona is often defined by two female figures: the melodramatic mother who symbolises the family and the 'liberated' woman as personified by Parveen Babi (***Deewar***), **Zeenat Aman** (*Don*), and their clones (e.g. Amrita Singh in ***Mard***). *Inquilab* was released as part of his election campaign: the climax showed him slaughtering a group of corrupt politicians. Elected MP for Allahabad supporting Rajiv Gandhi's Congress (I) in 1984, but he soon abandoned politics. After *Shahenshah* and his return to cinema, some of his films' unofficial budgets made them the most expensive Indian films ever. In the late 80s his popularity declined but revived with ***Hum*** (and other **Mukul Anand** films) showing the star coming to terms with the ageing process. His wife, the actress Jaya Bhaduri, stopped acting after their marriage, except for one noted appearance with her husband in ***Silsila***.

FILMOGRAPHY: **1969**: ***Saat Hindustani***; **1970**: ***Anand***; **1971**: *Parwana*; *Pyar Ki Kahani*; ***Reshma Aur Shera***; *Sanjog*; ***Guddi***; **1972**: *Bombay To Goa*; *Bansi Birju*; *Ek Nazar*; *Raaste Ka Patthar*; *Jaban*; **1973**: *Abhimaan*; *Bandhe Haath*; ***Namak Haram***; *Saudagar*; ***Zanjeer***; *Gehri Chaal*; **1974**: *Benaam*; *Kasauti*; *Kunwara Baap*; *Majboor*; *Roti Kapda Aur Makaan*; *Dost*; **1975**: *Chupke Chupke*; ***Deewar***; *Faraar*; *Mili*; ***Sholay***; *Zameer*; ***Chhotisi Baat***; **1976**: *Adalat*; *Do Anjaane*; *Hera Pheri*; ***Kabhie Kabhie***; **1977**: *Alaap*; ***Amar Akbar Anthony***; *Imaan Dharam*; *Khoon Pasina*; *Parvarish*; *Khatta Meetha*; *Charandas*; **1978**: *Besharam*; *Don*; *Ganga Ki Saugandh*; *Kasme Vaade*; ***Muqaddar Ka Sikandar***; ***Trishul***; **1979**: *Golmaal*; *Jurmana*; ***Kala Patthar***; *Manzil*; *Mr Natwarlal*; *Suhaag*; *The Great Gambler*; *Ahsaas*; **1980**: *Do Aur Do Paanch*; *Ram Balram*; *Shaan*; *Dostana*; **1981**: *Barsaat Ki Ek Raat/Anusandhan*; ***Chashme Buddoor***; *Kaliya*; *Lawaris*; ***Naseeb***; ***Silsila***; *Yaarana*; *Commander*; *Satte Pe Satta*; **1982**: *Bemisal*; *Desh Premi*; *Khuddar*; *Namak Halal*; *Shakti*; **1983**: *Andha Kanoon*; ***Coolie***; *Mahaan*; *Nastik*; *Pukar*; **1984**: *Inquilab*; *Pet Pyar Aur Paap*; *Sharabi*; **1985**: *Giraftaar*; ***Mard***; **1986**: *Aakhri Raasta*; *Jalwa*; **1987**: *Kaun Jeeta Kaun Hara*; **1988**: *Shahenshah*; *Soorma Bhopali*; *Ganga Jamuna Saraswati*; *Hero Hiralal*; **1989**: *Toofan*; *Jadugar*; *Main Azaad Hoon*; **1990**: ***Agneepath***; *Aaj Ka Arjun*; *Krodh*; **1991**: ***Hum***; *Ajooba*; *Indrajit*; *Akela*; **1992**: ***Khuda Gawah***.

BACKER, P. A. (b. 1940-93)

Malayalam director born in Trichur, Kerala. Started as journalist for *Kuttikal* and *Poomattukal*; then assistant to **Ramu Kariat** (1960), the focus of a renovatory wave in Malayalam cinema; broke away to produce **P.N. Menon**'s ***Olavum Theeravum*** (1969), launching a second renewal. His first film, ***Kabani Nadi Chuvannappol***, upset the censors during the Emergency. Claiming explicitly political but unaffiliated avant-gardism, his work constitutes a precedent for an independent Left cinema, e.g. of the Odessa Collective (Est: 1984 by **John Abraham**), Raveendran, T.V. Chandran et al. Much of Backer's cinema, like that of his successors, comes from an effort to elaborate the forms of discourse about 'independent' politics, seen as a transference of repression that is either sexual (*Kabani Nadi Chuvannappol*; ***Chuvanna Vithukal***), or religious (***Manimuzhakkum***), or the displacement of an infantile desire for salvation (***Sanghaganam***).

FILMOGRAPHY: **1975**: ***Kabani Nadi Chuvannappol***; **1976**: ***Manimuzhakkum***; ***Chuvanna Vithukal***; **1979**: ***Sanghaganam***; *Manninte Maril*; *Unarthupattu*; **1981**: *Charam*; **1982**: *Chappa*; **1985**: *Prema Lekhanam*; *Shri Narayana Guru*; **1987**: *Innaleyude Baaki*.

BADAMI, SARVOTTAM (b. 1910)

Hindi, Telugu and Tamil director born in Channapatna, Karnataka. Son of a revenue officer in Mysore. Worked as motor mechanic and handyman in garage owned by Ambalal Patel, then as a projectionist at Patel's Select Pictures cinema in Bangalore. When Patel partnered **Ardeshir Irani** and Chimanlal Desai in launching **Sagar Film** (1930), Badami, as the only available South Indian in the Bombay studio, was allowed to finish *Harishchandra* and *Galava Rishi* and went on to direct the Telugu *Paduka Pattabhishekham*. Made several socials at Sagar, usually starring Sabita Devi, including some of novelist **K.M. Munshi**'s best-known scripts, e.g. ***Dr Madhurika***, *Vengeance is Mine*. Also adapted Hollywood films, e.g. *Aap Ki Marzi*, based on E. Buzzell's *Paradise For Three* (1938). When Sagar closed down (1939), he followed mentor Patel to Sudama Pics. Worked in Famous Cine laboratory (1946-8). Chief producer (newsreel) at **Films Division** (1948-52) where he also made documentaries. Left Films Division in 1954 and became an industrialist based in Bangalore and was adviser to the Kamani industrial group.

FILMOGRAPHY: **1932**: *Harishchandra*; *Galava Rishi*; *Paduka Pattabhishekham*; *Shakuntala*; **1933**: *Chandrahasa*; **1934**: *Grihalakshmi*; **1935**: ***Dr Madhurika***; *Vengeance is Mine*; **1936**: *Jeevan Lata*; ***Grama Kanya***; **1937**: *Kokila*; *Kulavadhu*; **1938**: ***Three Hundred Days and After***; **1939**: *Aap Ki Marzi*; *Ladies Only*; **1940**: *Chingari*; *Sajani*; **1941**: *Holiday in Bombay*; **1942**: *Khilona*; **1943**: *Prarthana*; **1944**: *Bhagya Lakshmi*; **1945**: *Ramayani*; **1946**: *Uttara Abhimanyu*; **1947**: *Manmani*; **1951**: *Vinoba Bhave* (Doc); **1952**: *Roof Over the Head* (Doc).

BAGCHI, GURUDAS (b. 1926)

Bengali director born in Calcutta. Started as assistant to **Chhabi Biswas** on *Jar Jetha Ghar* (1949); then assisted Ardhendu Mukherjee and Chitta Bose (1954-60) before débuting as director in 1963.

FILMOGRAPHY: **1963**: *Dwiper Nam Tiya Rang*; **1964**: *Ta Holey*; **1969**: *Teer Bhoomi*; **1970**: *Samanaral*; **1972**: *Chhandapatan*; **1973**: *Bindur Chheley*; *Alo-o-Chhaya*; **1975**: *Srishtichhara*; **1976**: *Joi*; **1977**: *Ramer Sumati*; **1978**: *Tusi*; **1979**: *Chirantan*; *Jata Mat Tata Path*; **1981**: *Swami Stri*; **1983**: *Samarpita*; **1989**: *Mahapith Tarapith*.

BAKSHI, ANAND (b. 1920)

Prolific Hindi lyricist; wrote more than 2500 songs, averaging c.100 songs for c.20 films annually. Born in Rawalpindi (now Pakistan). Son of a bank manager; joined the army aged 18 as a field-telephone operator. Family migrated to India where he started as a scenarist for e.g. **Master Bhagwan**'s *Badla* (1943). Unable to obtain sufficient film assignments, rejoined the army until 1958. Broke through with Suraj Prakash's films, esp. with the songs *Kankaria more karke ishare* in *Mehndi Lagi Mere Haath* (1962), *Pardesiyon se na akhiyan milana* in *Jab Jab Phool Khile* (1965) and *Sawan ka mahina* in **Adurthi Subba Rao**'s *Milan* (1967). Confirmed his reputation for romantic songs with the **Rajesh Khanna** hit ***Aradhana*** (1969), writing most of Khanna's maudlin lyrics for several years thereafter, including *Amar Prem* (1971), which he considers to be his best work, esp. the song *Chingari koi bhadke*. One of the few songwriters of his generation to have no credentials as an independent poet. Consistently denies having any artistic pretensions. Recently wrote the **Bachchan** hit *Jumma chumma* in ***Hum*** (1991). Worked mainly with music directors **Laxmikant-Pyarelal**.

BAKSHI, SHANTI PRAKASH (1925-88)

Punjabi and Hindi director; started as scenarist and assistant to the major Punjabi cameraman-director Harcharan Singh Kwatra, scripting *Pilipili Saheb* (1954) and *Teesmar Khan* (1955). Kwatra produced Bakshi's first film *Kode Shah*, scored by Sardul Kwatra. Like Kwatra, Bakshi was basically a Bombay director making inexpensive Hindi films, often with Hindi stars. Also wrote **Amarnath**'s *Baradari* (1955) in Hindi. Directorial début in 1953 with Punjabi films. Made three Hindi features in the late 50s (*Mr Chakram*, *Pataal Pari* and *Sun To Le Hasina*).

FILMOGRAPHY: **1946**: *Kamli*; **1953**: *Kode Shah*; **1954**: *Ashtalli*; **1955**: *Mr Chakram*; **1957**: *Pataal Pari*; **1958**: *Sun To Le Hasina*; **1960**: *Heer Syal*; **1962**: *Pardesi Dhola*; **1965**: *Sassi Punnu*; **1986**: *Munda Naram Te Kudi Garam*.

BALACHANDER, KAILASAM (b. 1930)

Tamil, Telugu, Kannada and Hindi director and producer, born in Nannilam, Thanjavur. Graduated in science from Annamalai University, Madras (1951); employed as a civil servant in the Accountant General's office until 1964. Worked initially in the Tamil theatre as playwright and director. His best-known plays have been filmed: ***Server Sundaram*** by **Krishnan-Panju** (1964) and *Major Chandrakant* in Hindi by **Phani Majumdar** (***Oonche Log***, 1965) and by himself in Tamil. Film début as scenarist with the **MGR** film *Daivathai* (1964). Adapted his own play for his directorial début, *Neer Kumizhi*. Was employed by the Kalakendra Films unit for some years, before becoming an independent producer with his own company Kavithalaya. Known as the most consistent manufacturer of morality tales usually reinforcing middle-class conservatism, e.g. the joint-family structure (***Bhale Kodalu/Bhama Vijayam***), widow remarriage (*Aval Oru Thodarkathai*), the plight of divorced women (***Avargal***), the dowry problem (*Kalyana Agathigal*), Gandhian values (*Punnagai*), miscarriages of justice (*Major Chandrakant*). The TN government used his major hit *Arangetram* for its family-planning campaigns. His emphasis on the middle class, his sentimentalism and his practice of remaking his hits in other languages recall the **L.V. Prasad** style. Prasad produced his major Hindi hit, *Ek Duuje Ke Liye*, remaking his earlier Telugu success ***Maro Charithra***, both starring **Kamalahasan**. Like Prasad, he created several Tamil stars, e.g. Kamalahasan, **Rajnikant**, Sujata and S.V. Sekhar. Changed his idiom to make the political dramas ***Thanneer Thanneer***, based on **Komal Swaminathan**'s play, and based on his own story, ***Achamillai Achamillai***.

FILMOGRAPHY: **1965**: *Neer Kumizhi*; *Naanal*; **1966**: *Major Chandrakant*; **1967**: ***Bhama Vijayam/Bhale Kodalu***; *Anubavai Raja Anubavai*; **1968**: *Ethir Neechal*; *Thamarai Nenjam*; **1969**: *Poova Thalaiya*; *Iru Kodukal*; *Sattekalapu Sattaiah*; **1970**: *Pattam Pazhali*; *Ethiroli*; *Navagraham*; ***Kaviyath Thalaivi***; **1971**: *Bomma Borusa*; *Nanghu Suvarkal*; *Nootrukku Nooru*; *Punnagai*; **1972**: *Kanna Nalama*; *Velli Vizha*; **1973**: *Arangetram*; *Sollathen Ninaikiran*; **1974**: *Naan Avanillai*; *Aval Oru Thodarkathai/Aval Oru Thodarkatha/Aaina*; **1975**: ***Apoorva Ragangal***; **1976**: ***Manmatha Leelai***; *Moondru Mudichu*; *Anthuleni Katha*; **1977**: ***Avargal***; *Pattina Pravesham*; *Oka Talli Katha*; *Meethi Meethi Baatein*; **1978**: *Nizhal Nijamakirathu*; *Thappida Tala/Thappu Thalangal*; ***Maro Charithra***; **1979**: *Ninaithale Inikkum*; *Nool Veli*; *Andamaina Anubhavam*; *Idi Kathakadu*; *Edo Saritha*; *Gudippu Manasu*; **1980**: *Varumayin Niram Sigappu*; **1981**: *Akali Rajyam*; *Tholikodi Koosindhi*; *Enga Ooru Kannagi*; *Thillu Mullu*; *Ek Duuje Ke Liye*; ***Thanneer Thanneer***; *47 Natkal/47 Rojulu*; **1982**: *Agni Satchi*; *Pyara Tarana*; **1983**: *Benki Alli Aralida Hoovu*; *Kokilamma*; *Poikkal Kuthirai*; *Zara Si Zindagi*; **1984**: *Love Love Love*; ***Achamillai Achamillai***; *Ek Nai Paheli*; *Eradu Rekhagalu*; **1985**: *Mugila Mallige*; *Kalyana Agathigal*; ***Sindhu Bhairavi***; **1986**: *Punnagai Mannan*; *Sundara Swapnagalu*; **1987**: *Manadhil Urudhi Vendhum*; **1988**: *Rudraveena*; *Unnal Mudiyum Thambi*; **1989**: *Pudhu Pudhu Arthangal*; **1990**: *Oru Veedu Iru Vasal*; **1991**: *Azhagan*; **1992**: *Vaname Ellai*; *Jathi Malli*.

BALACHANDER, SUNDARAM (1927-90)

Tamil director born in Madras; son of a lawyer. Also a music composer, actor and producer, he is best known as a classical Carnatic musician and veena player. Child actor in **Prabhat**'s Tamil mythological *Seeta Kalyanam*. Employed briefly by the AIR. Early work as actor and composer in *Ithu Nijama* (playing twins), and *Rajambal* (in the popular role of a debonair villain). Directorial work includes the melodrama *En Kanavar* and the thriller *Kaidhi*. First major film was the war/spy drama, *Andha Naal*, influenced by *Rashomon* (1950). Another remarkable genre adaptation is ***Avan Amaran***, made for the Leftist Peoples' Films. His own productions were often adaptations, e.g. *Avana Evan* from George Stevens's *A Place in the Sun* (1951) and the Hitchcockian *Bommai*. His company, S.B. Creations (1960), was known for its thrillers, e.g. *Nadu Iravil* based on Agatha Christie's *Ten Little Niggers*. Scored the music of all the films he directed, where, in contrast to his classical musical reputation, he often provided a pastiche of jazz, Latin American music, Western and Indian classical styles. Left films to devote himself more to music.

FILMOGRAPHY (* only act/** also act): **1933**: *Seeta Kalyanam**; **1935**: *Radha Kalyanam**; **1936**: *Rukmini Kalyanam**; **1941**: *Kamadhenu**; ***Rishyashringar****; **1942**: *Nandanar**; **1948**: *Ithu Nijama**; *En Kanavar*; **1951**: *Rajambal**; *Devaki**; *Kaidhi***; **1952**: *Rani**; **1953**: *Inspector**; **1954**: *Penn**; *Andha Naal*; **1955**: *Dr Savithri**; **1958**: ***Avan Amaran***; **1962**: *Avana Evan*; **1964**: *Bommai*; **1970**: *Nadu Iravil***.

BALARAMAIAH, GHANTASALA (1906-53)

Telugu director born in Pottepalem village, AP. Well-known 20s Telugu stage actor, e.g. title role in *Ramadasu* directed by Radhakrishnaiah. Started Shri Rama Films, financed by rich landlords from Nellore, with **Chitrapu Narasimha Rao**'s *Sati Tulasi*, then set up Studio Kubera Pics with two **Chitrapu Narayanamurthy** films, *Markandeya* (1938) and *Mahiravana* (1940). Started directing after founding Pratibha Film with *Parvati Kalyanam*. His ***Garuda Garvabhangam***, starring **Bhanumathi** and **Gaggaiah**, instituted an influential variant of the mythological: a kind of heroic folklore loosely echoing forms like the Burrakatha. This trend, which he developed with the hit ***Swapna Sundari*** featuring **A. Nageshwara Rao** and **Anjali Devi**, was also continued by **K.V. Reddy** and provided in Gaggaiah an early model for the **NTR** persona.

FILMOGRAPHY (* only act): **1933**: *Ramadasu**; **1936**: *Sati Tulasi**; *Kabir**; **1941**: *Parvati Kalyanam*; **1942**: *Seeta Rama Jananam*; **1943**: ***Garuda Garvabhangam***; **1946**: *Mugguru Maratilu*; **1948**: *Balaraju*; **1950**: *Shri Lakshmamma Katha*; ***Swapna Sundari***; **1952**: *Chinnakodalu*.

BALASARASWATHI, R. (b. 1928)

Telugu and Tamil singer and actress, born in Madras. Daughter of musician K. Parthasarathy. Started recording when discovered as a 6-year-old by composer-lyricist Kopparapu Subba Rao. Début as actress in **C. Pullaiah**'s ***Ansuya*** (as Ganga); worked with **K. Subramanyam**, playing Krishna in *Bhakta Kuchela*, followed by the major role of Sarasa in his ***Balayogini***. Played several child roles before becoming a heroine in **Ramabrahmam**'s *Illalu*, acting and singing duets with **Saluri Rajeswara Rao**, who also composed popular non-film songs for her in the early 40s. Virtually retired from acting after she married the Rajah of Kolanka (1944), but continued as playback singer until the mid-50s. Her first playback number, *Tinne meedi chinnoda* for Kamala Kotnis in **P. Pullaiah**'s ***Bhagya Lakshmi*** (1943), was composed by **B. Narasimha Rao** and was one of the first film songs officially credited to the singer rather than the actor. Associated with some of the best compositions of music directors **C.R. Subburaman** (***Swapna Sundari***, 1950), G. Ashwathama (*Chinnakodalu*, 1952) and Ramesh Naidu (*Dampatyam*, 1957). Other classic songs include *Muntha perugandoyi* with comedians K. Subba Rao and **Relangi Venkatramaiah** in ***Prema*** (1952), *Tana panthame taniduvaru* in the unusual raga Rasili, written and scored by B. Rajnikanta Rao (*Manavati*, 1952). Came out of retirement to sing in the film directed by her niece **Vijayanirmala**, *Sangam Chekkina Silpalu* (1979). Also remembered as a dancer in e.g. *Suvarnamala*'s street scene.

FILMOGRAPHY: **1936**: ***Ansuya***; *Dhruva*; *Bhakta Kuchela*; ***Balayogini***; **1937**: *Tukaram*; **1939**: *Mahananda*; *Thiruneelakanthar*; **1940**: *Illalu*; **1941**: *Chandrahasa*; *Apavadu*; **1942**: *Thasippen*; **1947**: *Radhika*; **1948**: *Suvarnamala*; *Bilhana*; **1949**: ***Mana Desam***.

BALASUBRAMANYAM, S. P. (b. 1945)

Leading South Indian film singer, actor and composer. Born in Nellore, the son of a folk Harikatha performer. Studied engineering at Anantpur and Madras. First break as singer with composer Kothandapani. Sings in all four South Indian languages and in Hindi and Oriya. Broke through as singer in the **MGR** hit *Adimai Penn* (1969) and in **K. Vishwanath**'s musical megasuccess ***Shankarabharanam*** (1979). First Hindi hit was was **K. Balachander**'s *Ek Duuje Ke Liye* (1981), starring **Kamalahasan**.

BAL GANDHARVA (1888-1967)

Given name was Narayanrao Rajhans. Celebrated female impersonator on the stage, mainly in mythologicals (*Swayamvar*, *Saubhadra*) and occasionally in influential socials, e.g. the Gadkari musical *Ekach Pyala*. The plays had a massive impact in Maharashtra, Gujarat, Madhya Pradesh, Karnataka and in Thanjavur, TN. Also came to epitomise feminine beauty in the emerging fashion industry of these regions. His 'look' embodied the *tribhangi* posture from classical sculpture: a slightly inclined head and feet at an angle to the torso, also used in several **Ravi Varma** paintings (e.g. *Lady with a Mirror*). On stage, this became a tableau posture usually dividing the proscenium frame into three vertical areas offset by a gaze turned 3/4 towards the audience. Also top singing star of Marathi **Sangeet Natak**. Introduced by the Kirloskar Natak Mandali, but left to form his own Gandharva Natak Mandali (1913). **Prabhat** Studio gave great publicity to his recruitment to cinema (***Dharmatma***) but he left, feeling uncomfortable with film acting and with playing male roles, contrary to his public image. However, two of **Prabhat**'s top composers, **Govindrao Tembe** and **Master Krishnarao**, were products of Bal Gandharva's troupe, and his stage idiom, emphasising a flat proscenium layered with **stage backdrops**, as well as the conventions of feminine beauty he incarnated, had a major influence on early Marathi talkies. **Painter**'s *Sadhvi Mirabai* was a straight adaptation of a Gandharva Natak Mandali play.

FILMOGRAPHY: **1935**: ***Dharmatma***; **1937**: *Sadhvi Mirabai*; **1951**: *Vithal Rakhumai*.

BALI, GEETA (1930-65)

Hindi actress, dancer and singer, originally Harikirtan Kaur. Born in Amritsar, Punjab. Started in film aged 12 in a **Shorey** short (*The Cobbler*) followed by her feature début in Majnu's *Badnami*. Lively dancer, mainly in films by **Kidar Sharma** (***Suhaag Raat*** was her first major film), **Guru Dutt** (***Baazi***, *Baaz*, ***Jaal***, *Sailaab*) and **Master Bhagwan** (the hit musical ***Albela***). Also featured in whodunits by **Ravindra Dave** and **Shakti Samanta**. Only occasionally successful in dramatic roles, e.g. her famous portrayal of a blind girl in **Sohrab Modi**'s ***Jailor***. In **Sharma**'s ***Banwre Nain*** she used an eloquent gestural style to play the country girl betrayed by the hero, matched only by her contemporary, Nimmi. Co-starred with **Raj Kapoor**, **Dev Anand** and later with the man she would marry, **Shammi Kapoor**. Her death, from smallpox, caused the novelist **Rajinder Singh Bedi** to stop his directorial début based on his classic *Ek Chadar Maili Si* (completed by Sukhwant Dhadda, 1986).

FILMOGRAPHY: **1942**: *The Cobbler* (Sh); **1946**: *Badnami*; *Kahan Gaye*; **1948**: ***Suhaag Raat***; *Jalsa*; *Nai Reet*; *Patjhad*; **1949**: *Badi Bahen*; *Bansaria*; *Bholi*; *Dil Ki Duniya*; *Dulari*; *Garibi*; ***Girls' School***; *Jal Tarang*; *Kinara*; *Neki Aur Badi*; **1950**: ***Banwre Nain***; *Bhai Bahen*; *Gulenar*; *Nishana*; *Shaadi Ki Raat*; **1951**: ***Albela***; ***Baazi***; *Bedardi*; *Ek Tha Ladka*; *Ghayal*; *Johari*; *Lachak*; *Nakhre*; *Phoolon Ke Haar*; **1952**: ***Anandmath***; *Bahu Beti*; *Betaab*; ***Jaal***; *Jalpari*; *Najaria*; *Neelam Pari*; *Raag Rang*; *Usha Kiron*; *Zalzala*; **1953**: *Baaz*; *Firdaus*; *Gunah*; *Jhamela*; *Naina*; *Naya Ghar*; **1954**: *Ameer*; *Daku Ki Ladki*; *Kashti*; *Kavi*; *Suhagan*; **1955**: *Albeli*; *Baradari*; *Chhora Chhori*; *Faraar*; *Jawab*; *Milap*; *Miss Coca Cola*; *Sau Ka Note*; *Vachan*; **1956**: *Hotel*; *Inspector*; *Lalten*; *Pocketmaar*; *Rangeen Raatein*; *Sailaab*; *Zindagi*; **1957**: *Coffee House*; *Jalti Nishani*; **1958**: *Do Mastane*; *Aji Bas Shukriya*; ***Jailor***; *Ten o'Clock*; **1959**: *CID Girl*; *Mohar*; *Nai Raahein*; **1960**: *Bade Ghar Ki Bahu*; **1961**: *Mr India*; *Sapan Suhane*; **1963**: *Jabse Tumhe Dekha Hai*.

BALKRISHNA, T. N. (b. 1913)

Phenomenally successful Kannada comedian. Born in Arasikere, Karnataka. Was sold as a child to adoptive parents to pay his father's medical bills. Lost his hearing as a youth and dropped out of school. Acted in the play *Shri Rama Paduka Pattabhishekha* (1929); then apprenticed to painter of **stage backdrops** and later a professional sign painter. Returned to the stage as an actor in Harmonium Master Giri Gowda's group, the Lakshmasani Nataka company, and in Neelkantappa's Gowrishankar Nataka Mandali before joining **Gubbi Veeranna**'s theatre company. His presence was almost mandatory in Kannada films from the early 40s where, adapting the folk form Yakshagana, he formed a bumbling comedy duo with his constant sidekick Narasimhraju. Redefined the tone of 'comedy relief' by adding his own brand of ineffectual villainy. Also wrote some plays and scripts; started the Abhimana Studio in Bangalore (1968). Also starred in some Tamil films but did not succeed because of his difficulty with the language.

FILMOGRAPHY: **1943**: *Radha Ramana*; **1952**: *Dallali*; **1954**: *Devakannika*; *Kanyadana*; *Muttidella Chinna*; **1955**: *Ashadabhooti*; *Bhakta Mallikarjuna*; **1956**: *Daiva Sankalpa*; *Muttaide Bhagya*; *Pancharathna*; *Sadarame*; **1957**: *Mahiravana*; *Ratnagiri Rahasya*; *Shukradeshe*; ***Chintamani***; **1958**: *Anna Thangi*; *Mane Thumbida Hennu*; *Mangalya Yoga*; ***School Master***; **1959**: *Mangalsutra*; *Jagajyothi Basaveshwara*; **1960**: *Shivalinga Sakshi*; ***Ranadheera Kanteerava***; *Rani Honamma*; **1961**: *Intiki Deepam Illale*; *Kaivara Mahatme*; *Kantheredu Nodu*; ***Kittur Chanamma***; *Raja Satya Vrata*; *Shrishaila Mahatme*; **1962**: ***Bhoodana***; *Daiveleele*; *Tejaswini*; **1963**: *Kanya Ratna*; *Mana Mechhida Madadi*; *Sant Tukaram*; **1964**: *Chandavalliya Tota*; *Muriyada Mane*; *Mane Aliya*; ***Nandi***; **1965**: *Mahasati Ansuya*; ***Satya Harishchandra***; **1966**: *Mohini Bhasmasura*; **1967**: ***Bellimoda***; *Chakra Teertha*; *Immadi Pulakesi*; **1968**: *Arunodaya*; *Gandhinagara*; *Manku Dinne*; *Bhagya Devathe*; *Mysore Tonga*; *Bhagyada Bagilu*; *Rowdy Ranganna*; *Attegondukala Sosegondukala*; *Hoovu Mullu*; **1969**: *Margadarshi*; *Gandondu Hennaru*; *Mallammanna Pavada*; *Kappu Bilapu*; *Shiva Bhakta*; *Bhagirathi*; *Madhuve Madhuve Madhuve*; *Punarjanma*; *Kalpa Vruksha*; ***Uyyale***; *Chikamma*; *Manashanti*; **1970**: *Bhale Kiladi*; *Anirikshita*; *Aparajithe*; *Mrityu Panjaradalli Goodachari 555*; *Muru Muttugalu*; *Bhale Jodi*; *Sedige Sedu*; *Nanna Thamma*; *Sukha Samsara*; **1971**: *Signalman Siddappa*; *Hoo Bisilu*; *Kulagaurava*; *Namma Samsara*; *Amara Bharathi*; *Jatakarathna Gunda Joisa*; *Anugraha*; *Namma Baduku*; *Bhale Adrushtavo Adrushta*; *Pratidhwani*; *Sakshatkara*; *Mahadimane*; *Sothu Geddavalu*; **1972**: ***Bangarada Manushya***; *Nanda Gokula*; *Mareyada Deepavali*; **1973**: *Devaru Kotta Thangi*; *Sahadharmini*; *Swayamvara*; *Bharathada Rathna*; *Cowboy Kulla*; *Seetheyalla Savithri*; *Doorada Betta*; *Jaya Vijaya*; *Mane Belagida Sose*; *Gandhadagudi*; *Bangarada Panjara*; *Mannina Magalu*; *Bettada Bhairava*; **1974**: *Gruhini*; *Urvashi*; *Nanu Baalabeku*; *Boothayyana Maga Ayyu*; *Eradu Kanasu*; *Sampathige Saval*; *Bhakta Kumbhara*; *Professor Huchuraya*; *Anna Attige*; *Mahadeshwala Poojaphala*; *Namma Ura Devaru*; **1975**: *Jagruthi*; *Nanjuda Nakkaga*; *Kasturi Vijaya*; *Mane Belaku*; *Koodi Balona*; *Kaveri*; *Viplava Vanithe*; *Onderupa Eradu Guna*; *Hennu Samsarada Kannu*; *Trimurthi*; *Devaru Kotta Vara*; *Hosilu Mettida Hennu*; *Hoysala*; *Bangalore Bhootha*; **1976**: *Premada Kanike*; *Punaradatta*; *Bahadur Gandu*; *Mugiyada Kathe*; *Chiranjeevi*; *Raja Nanna Raja*; *Bayalu Dari*; *Na Ninna Mareyalare*; *Badavara Bandhu*; *Sutrada Bombe*; *Aparadhi*; *Devara Duddu*; **1977**: *Deepa*; *Bayasade Banda Bhagya*; *Bhagyavantharu*; *Lakshmi Nivasa*; *Pavanaganga*; *Manasinante Mangalya*; *Srimanthana Magalu*; *Sanadhi Appanna*; *Sahodarara Saval*; *Holavu Gelavu*; *Galate*

Geeta Bali in *Chhora Chhori* (1955)

Samsara; *Ganda Hendthi*; **1978**: *Halli Haidha*; *Shankar Guru*; *Vamsa Jyothi*; *Matu Tappada Maga*; *Sneha Sedu*; *Balu Aparupa Nam Jodi*; *Thayige Takka Maga*; **1979**: *Balina Guri*; *Na Ninna Bidalare*; *Asadhya Aliya*; *Na Niruvude Ninagangi*; **1980**: *Kulla Kulli*; *Auto Raja*; *Vajrada Jalapata*; *Mugana Sedu*; *Swamiji*; *Ondu Hennu Aaru Kannu*; *Biligiriya Bandalalli*; *Mayeya Musuku*; *Pattanakke Banda Patniyaru*; *Anveshane*; **1981**: *Tirada Bayake*; *Thayiya Madilalli*; *Anupama*; *Nee Nanna Gellalare*; *Bhagyavantha*; *Number Aidu Uyekka*; **1983**: *Devara Tirpu*; *Kavirathna Kalidasa*; *Benkiya Bale*; *Kamana Billu*; *Premave Balina Belaku*; **1984**: *Gajendra*; *Kaliyuga*; *Makkaliravva Mane Thumba*; *Ahuti*; **1985**: *Thayi Kanasu*; *Bettada Hoovu*; *Dhruva Tare*; *Bhagyada Lakshmi Baramma*; *Hosa Baalu*; **1986**: *Hennina Koogu*; *Henne Ninagenu Bandhana*; *Brahmastra*; *Satya Jyothi*; *Bete*; *Aparoopada Kathe*; **1987**: *Oluvina Udugore*; *Shruti Seridaga*; *Athiratha Maharatha*; *Thayikotta Thali*; **1988**: *Oorigittakolli*; *Dada*; **1989**: *Kalabhimani*; *Yuddhakanda*; *Hridaya Geethe*; *Avatara Purusha*; *Rudra*; *Samsara Nauka*; *Deva*; **1990**: *Tiger Gangu*; *Ashwamedha*; *Love Letter*; *Udbhava*; *Chakravarthi*; *Haliya Surasuraru*; **1991**: *Garuda Dhwaja*; *Kalyana Mantapa*.

Baloch, Mohammed *see* **Kumar, Mehul**

BANNERJEE, BHANU (1920-83)

Bengali comedian, born in Dhaka (now Bangladesh). Political activist associated with the terrorist group Anushilan in the Dhaka Dist., and after the Quit India movement with the Revolutionary Socialist Party. Later founded the Kranti Shilpi Sangha with writer (later film-maker) Salil Sen, staging the latter's landmark play ***Natun Yahudi*** (1951, filmed 1953) about East Bengal refugees for fund-raising and propaganda on their behalf in Calcutta. Briefly a government employee and then a film extra (*Jagran*). Broke through playing the voluble East Bengali businessman in **Nirmal Dey**'s ***Basu Parivar***, developing his trade mark: an idiosyncratic use of East Bengali dialect. One of Bengali film's most prolific comic actors, often partnering **Jahar Roy**. The duo were sometimes billed in the titles themselves (e.g. *Bhanu Pelo Lottery*, *Bhanu Goenda Jahar Assistant*). Continued as stage actor, e.g. ***Adarsha Hindu Hotel*** (1953) and esp. in Star Theatre productions (e.g. *Shamoli*, *Tapasi*, ***Parineeta***, *Dak Bungalow*). Directed the play *Jai Mahakali Boarding* (1979). Associated with folk Jatra companies Sushil Natya and Mukta Mancha.

FILMOGRAPHY: 1947: *Jagran*; **1949**: *Ja Hoy Na*; **1950**: *Mandanda*; ***Tathapi***; **1951**: *Sey Nilo Bidaya*; *Anuraag*; *Setu*; **1952**: *Chitta Banhiman*; ***Basu Parivar***; *Pasher Bari*; **1953**: ***Sharey Chuattar***; *Boudir Bone*; *Kajari*; ***Natun Yahudi***; *Keranir Jiban*; *Sabuj Pahar*; *Harilakshmi*; *Bana Hansi*; *Sosur Bari*; *Rami Chandidas*; *Lakh Taka*; *Bastab*; *Bou Thakuranir Haat*; *Adrishya Manush*; **1954**: *Atom Bomb*; *Moner Mayur*; *Ora Thake Odhare*; *Satir Dehatyaag*; *Vikram Urvashi*; *Kalyani*; *Ladies' Seat*; *Jagrihi*; *Mani-Aar-Manik*; *Sadanander Mela*; *Barbela*; *Chheley Kaar*; *Nilshari*; *Bhanga-Gara*; *Balay Gras*; **1955**: *Bratacharini*; ***Bandish***; *Nishiddha Phal*; *Sanjher Pradeep*; *Chatujye-Banrujye*; *Rani Rashmoni*; *Sajghar*; *Chhoto Bou*; *Aparadhi*; *Durlav Janma*; *Bir Hambir*; *Jyotishi*; *Joymakali Boarding*; *Dashyumohan*; *Bhalobasha*; *Ardhangini*; **1956**: *Mahanisha*; *Tonsil*; *Shubharatri*; *Savdhan*; *Ekti Raat*; *Asamapta*; *Mamlar Phal*; *Manraksha*; *Rajpath*; *Suryamukhi*; *Govindadas*; *Maa*; *Daner Maryada*; *Taka-Ana-Pai*; *Amar Bou*; **1957**: *Louha-Kapat*; *Andhare Alo*; *Natun Prabhat*; *Kancha-Mithey*; *Basanta Bahar*; *Ogo Sunchho*; *Jiban Trishna*; *Ek Gaon Ki Kahani*; **1958**: *Yamalaya Jibanta Manush*; *Manmoyee Girls' School*; *Nupur*; *Bhanu Pelo Lottery*; *Kalamati*; *Swarga Martya*; *Daktar Babu*; *Surya Toran*; **1959**: *Nauka Bilash*; *Pushpadhanu*; *Bhranti*; *Chhabi*; *Nirdharita Silpir Anupastithi Tey*; *Sonar Harin*; *Mriter Martye Agaman*; *Personal Assistant*; **1960**: *Sakher Chor*; ***Hospital***; **1961**: *Swayambara*; *Raibahadur*; *Mr & Mrs Choudhury*; *Bishkanya*; *Kanchanamulya*; *Kathin Maya*; *Kanamachi*; **1962**: *Atal Jaler Ahwan*; *Bodhu*; *Mayar Sansar*; *Abhisarika*; *Dada Thakur*; **1963**: *Dui Bari*; *Barnachora*; *Sat Bhai*; *High Heel*; *Bhranti Bilas*; *Dui Nari*; *Akash Pradeep*; *Hashi Sudhu Hashi Noy*; *Shreyasi*; **1964**: *Jiban Kahini*; *Deep Nebhey Noy*; *Binsati Janani*; **1965**: *Dolna*; *Alor Pipasa*; *Mahalagna*; *Ek Tuku Basa*; *Raj Kanya*; *Pati Sansodhini Samiti*; *Devatar Deep*; *Abhoya-o-Srikanta*; *Gulmohar*; *Mukhujey Paribar*; *Tapasi*; *Kal Tumi Aleya*; **1966**: *Galpa Holeo Satti*; *Mayabini Lane*; *Shesh Tin Din*; **1967**: *Ashite Ashio Na*; *Hathat Dekha*; *Kheya*; *Miss Priyambada*; **1968**: ***Apanjan***; *Baghini*; *Chowringhee*; *Garh Nasimpur*; *Pathe Holo Dekha*; *Rakta Rekha*; **1969**: *Shuk Sari*; *Dadu*; *Maa-o-Meye*; *Sabarmati*; **1970**: *Pratham Kadam Phool*; *Aleyar Alo*; *Sagina Mahato*; *Rajkumari*; **1971**: *Bhanu Goenda Jahar Assistant*; *Ekhane Pinjar*; *Malayadaan*; *Maha Biplabi Aurobindo*; *Pratham Basanta*; **1972**: *Stree*; **1973**: *Bindur Chheley*; *Nishi Kanya*; *Roudra Chhaya*; **1974**: *Sangini*; *Swikarokti*; **1975**: *Harmonium*; *Nishi Mrigaya*; *Priya Bandhabi*; *Swayamsiddha*; **1976**: *Nidhi Ram Sardar*; *Nandita*; *Asadharan*; *Ek Je Chhilo Desh*; **1977**: *Abirvab*; *Ramer Sumati*; **1979**: *Devdas*; **1980**: ***Bancharamer Bagan***; *Bhagya Chakra*; *Darpachurna*; *Priyatama*; *Sondhi*; **1981**: *Father*; *Kapal Kundala*; *Subarnalata*; *Shahar Theke Dooray*; **1982**: *Pipasa*; *Raj Bodhu*; *Amrita Kumbher Sandhaney*; *Matir Swarga*; *Prafulla*; **1984**: *Shorgol*.

BANNERJEE, DURGADAS (1893-1943)

Major Bengali actor in **Calcutta Theatres**. Born in Kalikapur, 24 Parganas District. Introduced to film by **Sisir Bhaduri** (Taj Mahal Film) in 1922. From his first major film, *Maanbhanjan*, until late 30s he was the definitive Bengali screen hero at **Madan** in **Jyotish Bannerjee**'s literary films, at Arya Films, at **Indian Kinema** and at **New Theatres**, where he played the lead in **Debaki Bose**'s epoch-making ***Chandidas*** and the king in ***Bidyapati***. His oft-mentioned aristocratic lineage - he was born in a zamindar (landlord) family - is said to be the key to his image of dignified, heroic reserve which massively influenced the next generation of Bengali actors (cf **Chhabi Biswas**). Remained major theatre star at the Star, Manmohan, Minerva and Rangmahal companies and in plays like *Karnarjun* (the landmark 1923 Art Theatre production of this play introduced him to the stage, and he later tackled the tough double role of both Karna and Arjun), *Iraner Rani*, *Rishir Meye*, *Chirakumar Sabha*. Many of these plays, later adapted to film, used performative idioms partly derived from his acting style.

FILMOGRAPHY: 1922: *Bishabriksha*; **1923**: *Maanbhanjan*; **1924**: *Chandranath*; *Premanjali*; *Mishar Rani*; **1925**: *Jaler Meye*; **1926**: *Dharmapatni*; *Krishnakanter Will*; **1927**: *Durgesh Nandini*; *Chandidas*; **1928**: *Bishabriksha*; *Sarala*; *Sasthi Ki Shanti*; **1929**: *Kapal Kundala*; *Rajani*; *Indira*; **1930**: *Radha Rani*; *Buker Bojha*; *Kanthahaar*; **1931**: *Swami* (all St); *Dena Paona*; **1932**: *Bhagya Lakshmi* (St); *Punarjanma*; *Chirakumar Sabha*; ***Chandidas***; **1933**: *Kapal Kundala*; ***Meerabai***; **1934**: *Mahua*; **1935**: ***Bhagya Chakra***; *Karodpati*; **1936**: *Paraparey*; **1937**: ***Didi***; ***Bidyapati***; **1938**: ***Desher Mati***; **1939**: *Parasmani*; **1940**: ***Thikadar***; **1941**: *Avatar*; **1943**: *Priya Bandhabi*.

BANNERJEE, JYOTISH (b. 1887)

Bengali and Hindi director born in Bihar. Started as a typist at **Madan Theatres**; later became the studio's main film-maker in silent era. Part of film-making team with **Priyanath Ganguly**, Jyotish Mukherjee, Amar Choudhury, B.J. Rajhans, Abdur Rehman Kabuli (later star of ***Indrasabha***, 1932) and cameramen Jyotish Sarkar and T. Marconi. Initially worked with Eugenio De Liguoro (*Dhruva Charitra*, *Nala Damayanti*, both 1921; *Ramayan*, 1922) and C. Legrand (*Vishnu Avatar*, 1921). Early films were mainly adaptations of stage spectaculars from the Elphinstone and Corinthian companies. His late 20s silents adapted several novels of Bankimchandra Chatterjee owned by Madan Theatres. Also filmed plays by Girish Ghosh and Rabindra Mohan Moitra and a novel by Romesh Chandra Dutt (*Madhabi Kankan*). These were early examples of the Bengali literary film genre later incarnated into a formula by **New Theatres**. Went on to make one of the most successful stage adaptations in the Bengali cinema, ***Manmoyee Girls' School***. Worked at Madan until 1933, then freelanced, notably at Radha Films, at Madan's successors Bharatlaxmi Pics and at the Indrapuri Studio.

FILMOGRAPHY (* uncertain attribution): **1920**: *Mahabharat**; **1921**: *Maa Durga**; **1922**: *Bhishma**; *Nartaki Tara**; *Bishabriksha**; *Matri Sneh**; **1924**: *Premanjali*; *Mishar Rani*; *Navin Bharat*; *Veer Bharat*; **1925**: *Sati Lakshmi*; *Jaler Meye*; **1926**: *Dharmapatni*; *Joydev*; *Prafulla*; **1927**: *Chandidas*; **1928**: *Bhranti*; *Sasthi Ki Shanti*; *Bishabriksha*; **1929**: *Indira*; *Rajani*; **1930**: *Radha Rani*; *Rajsingha*; *Jugalangriya*; *Manik Jorh*; *Bharat Ramani*; *Mrinalini*; **1931**: *Keranir Mas Kabar*; *Bibaha Bibhrat*; *Jore Barat*; *Rishir Prem*; **1932**: *Madhabi Kankan* (all St); *Vishnu Maya*; *Krishnakanter Will*; *Aankh Ka Tara*; **1933**: *Dhruva Charitra*; *Dhruva*; *Joydev*; **1934**: *Daksha Yagna*; *Nagan*; **1935**: ***Manmoyee Girls' School***; *Kanthahaar*; **1936**: *Ahalya*; *Rajani*; **1937**: *Ranga Bou*; **1938**: *Bekar Nashan*; *Rupor Jhumko*; *Khana*; *Ekalavya*; **1939**: *Nara Narayan*; *Rukmini*; **1941**: *Karnarjun*; *Shakuntala*; *Shri Radha*; **1942**: *Bhishma*; *Milan*; **1943**: *Devar*; **1945**: *Kalankini*; **1946**: *Prem Ki Duniya*; **1948**: *Banchita*; *Kalo Ghora*; **1949**: *Robin Master*; **1950**: *Sheshbesh*.

BANNERJEE, KALI (1921-93)

Bengali actor born in Calcutta. Professional stage actor from 1945 playing, e.g., in Mahendra Gupta's *Satabarsha Agey* and *Tipu Sultan*. Joined **IPTA** in the late 40s, acting in **Tagore**'s *Bisarjan*, staged as a riposte to the extreme Left attacks on the author. Returned to the commercial **Calcutta Theatres** with ***Adarsha Hindu Hotel*** (1953). Early and still best-known film roles in **Ghatak**'s ***Nagarik*** and ***Ajantrik***. Also played the Chinese trader in **Mrinal Sen**'s ***Neel Akasher Neechey***. Worked extensively with **Satyajit Ray** (***Parash Pathar***, ***Teen Kanya***), **Tapan Sinha** (*Louha-Kapat*, ***Hansuli Banker Upakatha***, ***Arohi***, *Harmonium*), **Dinen Gupta** and **Tarun Majumdar**. Made a mainstream comeback as an aged eccentric in Anjan Choudhury's ***Guru Dakshina***.

FILMOGRAPHY: 1947: *Burmar Pathey*; **1951**: ***Barjatri***; **1952**: ***Nagarik***; **1955**: *Rickshawala*; *Devimalini*; *Sabar Uparey*; *Kalindi*; **1956**: ***Aparajito***; *Tonsil*; *Shilpi*; **1957**: *Surer Parashey*; *Ogo Sunchho*; *Ami-Baro-Habo*; *Louha-Kapat*; ***Parash Pathar***; ***Ajantrik***; **1958**: *Dak Harkara*; *Nagini Kanyar Kahini*; *Surya Toran*; *Rajdhani Theke*; ***Neel Akasher Neechey***; **1959**: *Janmantar*; *Bari Theke Paliye*; *Agnisambhaba*; *Sonar Harin*; **1960**: *Dui Bechara*; *Prabesh Nishedh*; *Khudha*; *Shesh Paryanta*; *Natun Fasal*; **1961**: ***Teen Kanya***; *Pankatilak*; ***Punashcha***; **1962**: ***Hansuli Banker Upakatha***; *Shubha Drishti*; **1963**: *Ek Tukro Agun*; *Akash Pradeep*; *Tridhara*; *Badshah*; **1964**: *Saptarshi*; *Kinu Goyalar Gali*; *Kanta Taar*; ***Arohi***; *Dui Parba*; *Subah-o-Debatargrash*; **1965**: *Surer Agun*; *Dinanter Alo*; **1966**: *Joradighir Choudhury Paribar*; **1967**: *Seba*; **1968**: *Boudi*; *Hansamithun*; *Jiban Sangeet*; *Kokhono Megh*; *Rakta Rekha*; **1969**: *Protidan*; **1970**: *Shasti*; *Aleyar Alo*; *Muktisnan*; *Rupasi*; **1971**: *Attatar Din Pare*; *Janani*; *Nimantran*; **1972**: *Andha Atit*; *Ajker Nayak*; *Bighalita Karuna Janhabi Jamuna*; *Maa-o-Mati*; *Bawarchi*; *Subse Bada Sukh*; **1973**: *Agni Bhramar*; *Pranta Rekha*; **1974**: *Debi Choudhrani*; *Sangini*; *Natun Surya*; *Swikarokti*; *Umno-o-Jhumno*; **1975**: ***Sansar Simantey***; *Swayamsiddha*; *Hansaraj*; *Harmonium*; **1976**: *Dampati*; *Sandhya Surya*; *Yugo Manab Kabir*; *Ek Je Chhilo Desh*; **1977**: *Ae Prithibi Pantha Niwas*; *Ek Bindu Sukh*; *Pratima*; *Behula Lakhinder*; **1978**: *Joi Ma Tara*; **1979**: *Devdas*; *Nandan*; *Nauka Dubi*; *Sunayani*; **1980**: ***Dadar Kirti***; *Batasi*; *Bichar*; *Shesh Bichar*; **1981**: *Manikchand*; **1982**: *Simanta Raag*; *Preyasi*; *Matir Swarga*; *Chhoto Maa*; **1983**: *Agami Kal*; *Arpita*; *Indira*; *Jabanbandi*; *Nishi Bhor*; **1984**: *Sonar Sansar*; *Ahuti*; *Mukta Pran*; *Dada Moni*; **1985**: *Devika*; **1986**: *Urbashe*; *Parinati*; **1987**: ***Guru Dakshina***; **1988**: *Chhoto Bou*; *Parasmoni*; *Debibaran*; *Anjali*; **1989**: *Nayanmoni*; *Shatarupa*; *Mangaldip*; *Kari Diye Kinlam*; ***Sati***; **1990**: *Byabadhan*.

BANNERJEE, KANU (1905-85)

Bengali actor born in Jodhpur. Known primarily as the father, Harihar Rai, in **Satyajit Ray**'s Apu Trilogy. Early work in plays directed by **Sisir Bhaduri** (*Alamgir*, 1932; *Biraj Bou*, 1934). Mainly known as a stage comedian, also celebrated for his 'realist' performance, first on stage (1947) then in film, as the hapless Jamal, wrongly accused for stealing a bag of rice during the 1943 famine and tortured by police, in Tulsi Lahiri's *Dukhir Iman*. Introduced into films by **Phani Majumdar**. Early (pre-Ray) film work with writer-film-makers **Sailajananda Mukherjee** (***Shahar Theke Dooray***) and **Premendra Mitra** (*Kuasha*) (see **Kallol Group**).

FILMOGRAPHY: **1938**: ***Desher Mati***; **1940**: *Doctor*; **1941**: *Epar Opar*; *Pratishodh*; *Nandini*; **1942**: ***Garmil***; *Pashan Devata*; *Avayer Biye*; *Mahakavi Kalidas*; **1943**: *Sahadharmini*; *Swamir Ghar*; *Nilanguriya*; *Dampati*; ***Shahar Theke Dooray***; ***Jogajog***; **1944**: *Birinchi Baba*; *Bideshini*; *Pratikar*; **1945**: *Nandita*; *Kato Door*; *Abhinay Nay*; *Do Tana*; *Path Bendhe Dilo*; *Bhabhi-Kaal*; **1946**: *Natun Bou*; *Nivedita*; *Matrihara*; *Dukhe Jader Jiban Gara*; **1947**: *Ratri*; *Chorabali*; *Swapna-o-Sadhana*; *Abhijog*; *Dui Bandhu*; **1948**: *Mayer Dak*; *Sarbahara*; *Bish Bichar Agey*; *Priyatama*; **1949**: *Rangamati*; *Bamuner Meye*; *Kuasha*; *Parash Pathar*; **1950**: *Mandanda*; *Digbhranta*; **1951**: *Aparajito*; *Pandit Moshai*; **1952**: *Ratrir Tapasya*; *Prarthana*; *Siraj-ud-Dowla*; **1953**: *Haranath Pandit*; ***Natun Yahudi***; **1954**: *Moner Mayur*; *Dukhir Iman*; ***Champadangar Bou***; *Kalyani*; *Sadanander Mela*; *Sati*; *Bhanga-Gara*; *Mantra Shakti*; **1955**: *Sanjher Pradeep*; *Aparadhi*; *Bir Hambir*; *Jyotishi*; *Upahar*; ***Pather Panchali***; *Bhagwan Shri Shri Ramakrishna*; **1956**: *Govindadas*; *Daner Maryada*; ***Aparajito***; **1957**: *Punar Milan*; **1958**: *Sadhak Bama Kshyapa*; *Shri Shri Tarakeshwar*; *Marmabani*; **1959**: *Abhishap*; **1961**: *Pankatilak*; *Kathin Maya*; *Aaj Kal Parshu*; *Madhureno*; **1964**: *Ketumi*; **1967**: *Mahashweta*; **1969**: *Banajyotsna*; **1970**: *Ae Korechho Bhalo*; *Diba Ratrir Kabya*; **1972**: *Alo Amar Alo*; **1973**: *Agni Bhramar*; *Janmabhoomi*; **1978**: *Tushar Tirtha Amarnath*; **1980**: *Shodh*; **1981**: *Pahadi Phool*.

BAPAIAH, K.

Mainstream Telugu and Hindi director. Started as an editor at the **Vijaya** Studio in the mid-60s; then assistant director and début as solo director in 1970. Moved to low-budget Hindi remakes of Telugu hits, often starring **Jeetendra**, e.g. *Mawaali* and *Himmat Aur Mehnat*. Also directed **Mithun Chakraborty** in vendetta thrillers such as *Ghar Ek Mandir* and *Waqt Ki Awaaz*.

FILMOGRAPHY: **1970**: *Drohi*; **1973**: *Memu Manushulame*; **1974**: *Urvashi*; **1975**: *Soggadu*; *Vaikunthapali*; *Eduruleni Manishi*; **1977**: *Dildaar*; *Charitra Heenulu*; *Gadusu Pillodu*; *Indra Dhanushu*; **1978**: *Dil Aur Deewar*; *Sahasavanthudu*; *Yuga Purushudu*; **1979**: *Manade Gundalu*; **1980**: *Bandish*; *Takkar*; **1981**: *Sindoor Bane Jwala*; *Aggirava*; *Agni Poolu*; *Guru Shishyulu*; **1982**: *Kaliyuga Ramudu*; *Naa Desam*; **1983**: *Mawaali*; *Mundadugu*; **1984**: *Ghar Ek Mandir*; *Maqsad*; *Dandayatra*; *Intiguttu*; **1985**: *Aaj Ka Daur*; *Pataal Bhairavi*; *Chattamtho Poratam*; **1986**: *Aag Aur Shola*; *Ghar Sansar*; *Jayam Manade*; *Muddat*; *Swarg Se Sundar*; **1987**: *Himmat Aur Mehnat*; *Maavoori Maagadu*; *Majaal*; *Makutamleni Maharaju*; *Mard Ki Zabaan*; **1988**: *Charnon Ki Saugandh*; *Sone Pe Suhaaga*; *Waqt Ki Awaaz*; *Pyar Ka Mandir*; **1989**: *Sikka*; **1990**: *Pyar Ka Devata*; *Pyar Ka Karz*; *Izzatdar*; **1991**: *Pyar Hua Chori Chori*; **1992**: *Parda Hai Parda*; *Kasak*.

BAPU (B. 1933)

Telugu cartoonist, designer and director, also worked extensively in Hindi film. Born in Narsapur, Krishna Dist., AP, as Sattiraju Lakshminarayan. Graduated as a lawyer from Madras University (1955). Collaborated with comic writer Mullapoodi Venkataramana; political cartoonist for *Andhra Patrike* newspaper (1955) and illustrator. Worked in advertising in the early 60s. Début with ***Saakshi***, a rare instance of late 60s New Indian Cinema aestheticism in Telugu. Occasionally resorted to painterly imagery in his otherwise realist approach (e.g. ***Muthyala Muggu***). Transposed several mythological narratives into contemporary fables (*Manavoori Pandavalu*, remade in Hindi as ***Hum Paanch***). Some early work invoked rationalist ideology and *Hum Paanch* was strongly defended by populist independent Left. Later films are unashamedly revivalist: e.g. ***Thyagayya***, a remake of **Nagaiah**'s 1946 film. His Hindi films are usually remakes of Telugu ones: *Bezubaan* is based on S.P. Muthuraman's *Mayangurikal Oru Madhu* (1975) but with a modified role for **Naseeruddin Shah**; *Radha Kalyanam* is adapted from **Bhagyaraj**'s *Andha 7 Natkal* (1981); he remade his adaptation in Hindi as *Woh Saat Din*. Remade **B.R. Chopra**'s notorious rape movie, ***Insaaf Ka Tarazu*** (1980), as *Edi Nyayam Edi Dharmam*.

FILMOGRAPHY: **1967**: ***Saakshi***; **1968**: ***Bangaru Pichika***; **1969**: ***Buddhimanthudu***; **1970**: *Inti Gauravam*; *Balaraju Katha*; **1971**: *Sampoorna Ramayanam*; **1973**: *Andala Ramudu*; **1974**: ***Shri Ramanjaneya Yuddham***; **1975**: ***Muthyala Muggu***; **1976**: ***Seeta Kalyanam***; *Seeta Swayamvar*; *Shri Rajeshwari Vilas Coffee Club*; *Bhakta Kannappa*; **1977**: *Sneham*; **1978**: *Manavoori Pandavalu*; ***Gorantha Deepam***; *Anokha Shivbhakt*; **1979**: *Thoorpu Velle Rayulu*; *Rajadhi Raju*; **1980**: *Kaliyuga Ravana Surudu*; *Vamsha Vriksham*; ***Hum Paanch***; *Pandanti Jeevitham*; **1981**: *Bezubaan*; ***Thyagayya***; *Radha Kalyanam*; **1982**: *Edi Nyayam Edi Dharmam*; *Neethi Devan Mayakam*; *Pellidu Pillalu*; *Krishnavataram*; **1983**: *Woh Saat Din*; *Mantrigari Viyankudu*; **1984**: *Seetamma Pelli*; **1985**: *Mohabbat*; *Bullet*; *Jackie*; *Pyar Ka Sindoor*; **1986**: *Mera Dharam*; *Kalyana Tambulam*; **1987**: *Diljala*; **1989**: *Prem Pratigya*; **1990**: *Pelli Pustakam*; **1993**: *Mr Pellam*; *Shrinatha Kavi Sarvabhowma*.

BARAN, TIMIR (1904-87)

Aka Timirbaran Bhattacharya. Composer associated with the pioneering use of music for narrative purpose in early sound films. Born to a family of traditional Sanskrit scholars. Became a professional sarod player, studying first under Radhikaprasad Goswami and then, more extensively, with Ustad Allauddin Khan, continuing the latter's experiments with orchestral arrangements at Maihar when he joined Uday Shankar's dance troupe (1930), touring in Europe and the USA. Worked with **Modhu Bose**'s Calcutta Art Players (1934), enhancing Bose's Orientalist plays with an eclectic amalgam of symphonic structures for Indian instruments (*Alibaba*, *Bidyutparna*). Baran extended Bose's idiom after visits to Java and Bali whence he imported the xylophone. Continued working with Bose in film

(***Kumkum***, ***Raj Nartaki***). Best-known work at the **New Theatres**, starting with his classic score for **Barua**'s ***Devdas***. Moved briefly to Bombay (1939) working at **Sagar** and **Wadia** Studios. Took a break from films to work e.g. for AIR, creating an orchestral score to accompany **Tagore**'s ***Kshudista Pashan***, a symphony on non-violence to celebrate India's first Independence Day (1947), and a 75' programme on the *History of the Earth*. Joined the music faculty of Tagore's Shantiniketan in the 60s.

FILMOGRAPHY: **1935**: ***Devdas***; *Bijoya*; **1936**: ***Pujarin***; **1938**: ***Adhikar***; **1940**: ***Dharmapatni***; *Deepak*; *Lakshmi*; *Suhaag*; ***Kumkum/Kumkum The Dancer***; **1941**: ***Raj Nartaki/Court Dancer***; *Uttarayan*; **1944**: *Samaj*; **1945**: *Bondita*; **1949**: *Samapti*; **1954**: ***Baadbaan***; **1955**: *Amar Saigal*; **1959**: *Bicharak*; **1965**: *Thana Theke Aschhi*; **1970**: *Diba Ratrir Kabya*; **1978**: *Dak Diye Jai*.

BARUA, BROJEN (1925-72)

Assamese director, actor, stage director and singer. Former member of the Assamese **IPTA**. Elder brother of **Nip Barua** and **Ramen Barua**. Helped establish an Assamese film industry independent of theatrical techniques. First film ***Ito Sito Bohuto***, was Assam's first genuine comedy. His other famous film, *Dr Bezbarua*, although modelled on Hindi film formulas, was equally influential for successfully manufacturing a hit from purely local technical and performative resources, and for using outdoor locations.

FILMOGRAPHY: **1963**: ***Ito Sito Bohuto*** (also act); **1969**: *Dr Bezbarua*; **1970**: *Mukuta*; **1972**: *Opaja Sonor Mati*; *Lolita*.

BARUA, JAHNU (b. 1952)

Assamese director born in Lakowa. Graduated from Guwahati University and the **FTII** (1974). Joined ISRO; produced more than 100 children's science programmes for SITE in Ahmedabad (1975-6). Lives and works in Bombay, where he makes advertising and corporate films. Lectured at St Xavier's Institute of Communications. Films address the contemporary culture and politics of Assam. One of the most technically competent New Indian Cinema film-makers; deploys an almost expressionistic approach to regional reformism. ***Aparoopa*** is the first **NFDC**-financed Assamese film. Chairman of the Indian Film Directors' Association (1993).

FILMOGRAPHY: **1974**: *The F Cycle* (Sh); *Diary of a Racehorse* (Doc); **1976**: *One Hundred and Eighty Days of SITE* (Doc); **1982**: ***Aparoopa/Apeksha***; **1986**: ***Papori***; *Ek Kahani* (TV); **1987**: ***Halodiya Choraye Baodhan Khaye***; **1988**: *Adhikar* (TV); **1989**: ***Banani***; **1991**: *Firingoti*.

BARUA, MUNIN (b. 1948)

Assamese scenarist, musician and film-maker. Introduced as instrumentalist in Nalin Duara's *Mamata* (1973) but changed to become a scenarist. His scripts make him one of the main purveyors of middle-budget, deliberately middle-of-the-road and non-sensationalist socials of the 80s. Scripted, in addition to his own films, several productions by Siva Prasad (aka Siba) Thakur: *Bowari* (1982), *Ghar Sansar* (1983), *Son Moina* (1984) and *Mon Mandir* (1985). Also scripted *Ek Desh Mor Desh* (1986), Biju Phukan's *Bhai Bhai* (1988), and *Sewali* (1989).

FILMOGRAPHY: **1987**: *Pratima*; *Pita Putra*; **1991**: *Pahadi Kanya*.

BARUA, NIP (1925-92)

Best-known mainstream Assamese film-maker; younger brother of **Brojen Barua**. Started as cinematographer on Bengali and Assamese films. Directed the first big-budget multi-star Eastmancolor film in the language, ***Ajali Nabou***. Before his flamboyant film career, he was a musician and flautist, a footballer of some repute (playing for the Maharana AC and Assam state) and a cartoonist for the *Assam Tribune*. Mainly made family socials, often coming close to home-movie levels of intimacy; also made mythologicals (*Bhakta Prahlad*, *Narakasur*). Younger brother, **Ramen Barua**, is a noted composer.

FILMOGRAPHY: **1955**: *Smritir Parash*; **1957**: *Mak Aru Morom*; **1958**: ***Ranga Police***; *Bhakta Prahlad*; **1959**: *Amar Ghar*; **1961**: *Narakasur*; **1970**: *Baruar Sansar*; **1973**: *Sonetara*; **1975**: *Toramai*; **1977**: *Sonmai*; **1978**: *Manima* (also act); **1980**: ***Ajali Nabou***; **1983**: *Koka Deuta Nati Aru Hati*; **1984**: *Shakuntala Aru Shankar Joseph Ali*; **1985**: *Dadu Nati-o-Hati*; **1986**: *Antony Mor Naam*; **1988**: *Aai Mor Janame Janame*.

BARUA, PADUM (b. 1924)

Assamese director. His only film, ***Ganga Chiloner Pankhi*** (1975), took a decade to make. Hiren Gohain, one of the foremost commentators on contemporary Assamese culture, speaks of him as 'the first man to raise the standard of revolt against both the outworn theatrical mode and the slick Bombay style movie. [H]e is a director who can show us things.' Was musically inclined since childhood and an articulate cinephile since his student days at Benares Hindu University. Claims to have been influenced by John Ford, **P.C. Barua**, **V. Shantaram** and **Debaki Bose**.

BARUA, PRAMATHESH CHANDRA (1903-51)

Major, still undervalued Bengali-Hindi director of Assamese origin. Born into aristocratic family as the big game-hunting son of the Maharajah of Gauripur. Promising amateur sportsman and art-lover. Graduated from élite Presidency College, Calcutta (1924). Visited Europe and saw films (esp. René Clair and Lubitsch). Entered film as actor in silents; shareholder in **Dhiren Ganguly**'s **British Dominion Films** (1928). Spent a few months at Elstree to learn film-making and started Barua Pics in Calcutta (1929), producing e.g. **Debaki Bose**'s *Aparadhi* (1931) and *Nishir Dak* (1932). Joined Chittaranjan Das' Swarajya Party (1928) which represented Hindu zamindar interests after the Hindu-Muslim riots of 1926. Prominent member of Assam Legislative Assembly (1928-36) when his Party piloted the anti-tenant and anti-Muslim Tenancy Act through Bengal Legislative Council. Joined **New Theatres** (1932-39), freelanced thereafter. His ***Zindagi*** was remade in Bengali (1943). Making melancholic love stories set amid a nihilistically portrayed aristocracy, he evolved a unique melodramatic style, drawing from the literary traditions against which **Kallol** defined itself. The static stories and the mask-like actorial postures are counterpointed by the most mobile subjective camera in the Indian cinema of his time, the visual excess of his sweeping pans announcing the landscapes of later Bengal School painting. Wrote and starred in his productions, but remembered best for his Bengali version of ***Devdas*** (**Saigal** starred in the Hindi one), remade by **Bimal Roy** in 1955, and for his **Tagore** adaptation ***Mukti***. Died in Calcutta, leaving his last feature unfinished.

P.C. Barua (left) in *Rajat Jayanti* (1939)

FILMOGRAPHY (** also act/* only act): **1930**: *Panchasar**; **1931**: *Takay Ki Na Hay**; *Aparadhi**; **1932**: *Bhagya Lakshmi**; *Ekada* (all St); *Bengal 1983***; **1934**: *Rooplekha/Mohabbat Ki Kasauti***; **1935**: *Abasheshe**; ***Devdas*****; **1936**: ***Grihadah/Manzil*****; ***Maya***; **1937**: ***Mukti*****; **1938**: ***Adhikar*****; **1939**: ***Rajat Jayanti*****; **1940**: *Shapmukti***; ***Zindagi***; **1941**: *Mayer Pran***; *Uttarayan***; **1942**: ***Shesh Uttar/Jawab*****; **1943**: *Chandar Kalanka/Rani***; **1944**: *Subah Shyam*; **1945**: *Amiri*; **1946**: *Pehchan*; **1949**: *Iran Ki Ek Raat*; **1953**: *Maya Kanan***.

BARUA, RAMEN (b. 1938)

One of Assamese cinema's main music composers. Started as playback singer to his brother **Brojen Barua**'s music in his other brother **Nip Barua**'s *Smritir Parash* (1955). Turned composer in partnership with Brojen Barua, his own songs in *Amar Ghar* became major hits. Despite his popular and commercially successful work, he prefers the folk-derived music he composed for *Mukuta* and the classical compositions of *Sonmai*, extending his work as composer in the theatre and his experience with the **IPTA**. Also set some of **Jyotiprasad Agarwala**'s lyrics to music and re-released a series of Brojen Barua's old hits.

FILMOGRAPHY: 1959: *Amar Ghar*; **1969**: *Dr Bezbarua*; **1970**: *Mukuta*; **1971**: *Jog Biyog*; **1972**: *Lolita*; *Hridayar Proyojan*; *Opaja Sonor Mati*; **1973**: *Sonetara*; *Uttaran*; *Parinam*; **1975**: *Toramai*; **1977**: *Sonmai*; *Moromi*; **1978**: *Moram*; *Manima*; **1979**: *Ashray*; **1980**: ***Ajali Nabou***; *Raja Harishchandra*; **1981**: *Manashi*; *Uttar Sunya*; **1982**: *Raja*; **1983**: *Koka Deuta Nati Aru Hati*; **1984**: *Shakuntala Aru Shankar Joseph Ali*; **1985**: *Dada Nati-o-Hati*; *Deepjyoti*; **1986**: *Antony Mor Naam*.

BEDEKAR, VISHRAM (b. 1906)

Marathi and Hindi director, best known as a writer, born in Amravati, Eastern Maharashtra. Started with **Sangeet Natak** company Balwant Sangeet Mandali as playwright-lyricist. Moved to film-making when the theatre group expanded its box-office draw by producing *Krishnarjun Yuddha*, starring the group's writer-actor Chintamanrao Kolhatkar. Unlike other films produced by Sangeet Natak companies (e.g. Lalitkaladarsh), the film succeeded commercially and he co-directed three more with the group's owner-producer Vamanrao N. Bhatt. Scripted the mythological *Pundalik* (1936) and, according to his autobiography, co-d the film with V.N. Bhatt. Briefly studied film-making in the UK (1938); published his first novel, *Ranangan* (1938), on his return. Joined **Prabhat** briefly to write **Shantaram**'s ***Shejari/Padosi*** (1941), returning to the studio to script ***Ramshastri*** (1944, a re-edited version of which, credited to him, was later released as a children's film entitled *Ramshastri Ka Nyay*) and to direct **Guru Dutt**'s début, ***Lakhrani***. Made classic melodramas for **Baburao Pendharkar**'s New Huns, Baburao Pai's Famous Pics and **Minerva Movietone**. Wrote Shantaram's ***Amar Bhoopali*** (1951). Directed some of the **Ramsay Brothers**' pre-horror productions (***Rustom Sohrab***, *Ek Nannhi Munni Ladki Thi*). Works in modernist frame defined by **K. Narayan Kale**'s generation and G.B. Shaw; most of his literary and filmic work recasts stereotypes of pre-WW1 Marathi social reform novels into the declamatory style of prose melodrama with increasingly complex storylines. As playwright, works include *Brahmakumari*, *Vaje Paool Apule* and *Tilak Ani Agarkar* (1980). Also scripted his films. Published autobiography, *Ek Jhaad Ani Don Pakshi* (1985).

FILMOGRAPHY: 1934: *Krishnarjun Yuddha*; **1935**: *Satteche Prayog*; ***Thakicha Lagna***; **1936**: *Pundalik*; *Andheri Duniya*; **1938**: *Lakshmiche Khel*; **1942**: ***Pahila Palna***; **1943**: ***Paisa Bolto Aahe/Nagad Narayan***; **1945**: ***Lakhrani***; **1947**: *Chul Ani Mul*; **1948**: *Mera Munna*; **1950**: *Krantiveer Vasudev Balwant*; **1951**: *Lokmanya Bal Gangadhar Tilak* (Doc); *Bhola Shankar*; **1956**: *Ramshastri Ka Nyay*; **1957**: *Talash*; **1961**: *Do Bhai*; **1963**: *Vinobha Bhave: The Man* (Doc); ***Rustom Sohrab***; **1964**: *All God's Children* (Doc); **1968**: *At the Service of Small Industries* (Doc); **1970**: *Ek Nannhi Munni Ladki Thi*; **1971**: *Jai Jawan Jai Makan*; **1972**: *Bharat Ke Shaheed*.

BEDI, NARENDRA (1937-82)

Hindi director born in Bombay; son of **Rajinder Singh Bedi**. Arts degree from Bombay University and joined film industry as part of **G.P. Sippy**'s production team. Début film, produced by Sippy, is a **Rajesh Khanna** classic renovating the ruralist melodrama (cf ***Bangarada Manushya***, 1972). His second film, *Jawani Diwani*, a megahit, contained all-time **R.D. Burman** hits such as *Tum kahan*. Went on to make teenage musical romances in the 70s.

FILMOGRAPHY: 1969: ***Bandhan***; **1972**: *Jawani Diwani*; **1974**: *Benaam*; *Khote Sikkay*; *Dil Diwana*; **1975**: *Raffoo Chakkar*; **1976**: *Adalat*; *Maha Chor*; **1981**: *Kachche Heere*; **1982**: *Insaan*; *Sanam Teri Kasam*; *Taaqat*.

Bedi, Rajinder Singh (1915-84)

Director born in Sialkot Dist. (now Pakistan). Major short-story writer in Urdu, seen with **Krishan Chander** and **Sadat Hasan Manto** as constituting a new radical literary generation in the context of WW2, Independence and Partition, following Premchand, who introduced *khari boli* style of 'common man's prose' into the courtly idiom prevalent in Urdu literature. Focused on experience of being a cultural and political refugee (e.g. ***Garam Coat***, which he adapted to the screen in 1955) and peasant life (*Ek Chadar Maili Si*, his novel filmed by Sukhwant Dhadda with a Bedi script in 1986). Opposed notion of creative 'spontaneity' asssociated with Krishan Chander and Manto, strongly asserting craftmanship (Bedi, 1989). Stories often overlay the everyday with references to the mythological (e.g. ***Grahan***, 1972). Entered film as scenarist and dialogue writer in late 40s, working with **Sohrab Modi** (***Mirza Ghalib***, 1954), **Bimal Roy** (***Devdas***, 1955; ***Madhumati***, 1958) and **Hrishikesh Mukherjee** (***Anuradha***, 1960; *Memdidi*, 1961; ***Anupama***, 1966). Prolific scenario and dialogue writer, including **Raj Khosla**'s *Milap* (1955) and ***Bambai Ka Babu*** (1960), **Nitin Bose**'s *Dooj Ka Chand* (1964) and **Raj Kapoor**'s *Ab Dilli Door Nahin* (1957). Briefly director of the radio station Jammu and Kashmir Broadcasting Service. Directorial début in 1970 in the context of New Indian Cinema. His son, **Narendra Bedi**, had débuted as a director one year earlier.

FILMOGRAPHY: 1970: ***Dastak***; **1973**: *Phagun*; **1978**: *Aankhin Dekhi*; *Nawab Sahib*.

BENEGAL, SHYAM (b. 1934)

Hindi director born in Trimulgherry, AP; also worked in Telugu. Made first amateur film aged 12 with father's camera; cousin of **Guru Dutt**. Studied economics at Osmania University, Hyderabad; involved in student theatre. Founded Hyderabad Film Society. Moved to Bombay and worked for Lintas advertising agency (1959-63) and for Advertising & Sales Promotion Co. (1963-73). Made more than 900 advertisements and 11 corporate films (1959-73). Worked as documentarist; taught at the **FTII** (1969) and at Bhavan College (1966-73). Received Homi Bhabha fellowship (1969-72), allowing a stay in Britain and in the USA where he worked as associate producer for Boston WGBH TV and with the Children's Television Workshop in New York. First feature, ***Ankur***, with a 10-year-old script and independently financed, uses a quasi-realist style then considered antagonistic to the Hindi film industry. Its commercial success in the wake of ***Bhuvan Shome*** (1969) spawned a new sector of film-making later known as 'middle cinema' (cf **New Indian Cinema**). Early work sited in rural environment (*Ankur* and ***Nishant*** in AP, ***Manthan*** in Gujarat), using professional actors but with explicit references to the peasant unrest, initially CPI(ML)-led (see **Naxalite**) and acquiring a national dimension after the failure of the 1971-2 harvests. This work provided an early aesthetic articulation of what would soon become official government media policy towards the rural areas via the SITE programme. Later features are closer to the entertainment-led 'middle cinema'. Made several features (including fiction) on commission for clients, e.g. the National Dairy Development Board in Gujarat (*Manthan*), the CPI(M)-led Government of West Bengal (***Aarohan***), the Handloom Co-operatives (***Susman***), Indian Railways (*Yatra*), an Indo-Soviet government-sponsored feature-documentary (*Nehru*) and the 53-episode tv serial based on Nehru's book, *The Discovery of India* (*Bharat Ek Khoj*). Influential presence in national film policy organisations.

FILMOGRAPHY: 1962: *Gher Betha Ganga* (Sh); **1967**: *A Child of the Streets* (Doc); *Close to Nature* (Doc); **1968**: *Indian Youth: An Exploration* (Doc); *Sinhasta: Path to Immortality* (Doc); *Poovanam* (Sh); **1969**: *Flower Garden* (Sh); **1970**: *Quest for a Nation* (Doc); *Why Export?* (Doc); **1971**: *Pulsating Giant* (Doc); *Steel: A Whole New Way of Life* (Doc); **1972**: *Tala and Rhythm* (Doc); *Sruti and Graces in Indian Music* (Doc); *Raga and Melody* (Doc); *Notes on the Green Revolution* (Doc); *Foundations of Progress* (Doc); *Power to the People* (Doc); **1973**: ***Ankur***; *Suhani Sadak* (Doc); **1974**: *Violence: What Price? Who Pays?*

Shyam Benegal

(No. 5) (Doc); *You Can Prevent Burns* (Doc); **1975**: ***Charandas Chor***; ***Nishant***; *Epilepsy* (Doc); *Hero* (Sh); *The Quiet Revolution Pt 1* (Doc); **1976**: ***Manthan***; *Tomorrow Begins Today* (Doc); ***Bhumika***; **1977**: ***Kondura/Anugraham***; **1978**: ***Junoon***; **1979**: *The Quiet Revolution Pt 2* (Doc); *Reaching Out to People* (Doc); *Pashu Palan* (Doc); **1980**: ***Kalyug***; **1981**: *New Horizons in Steel* (Doc); **1982**: ***Aarohan***; *Growth for a Golden Future* (Doc); **1983**: ***Mandi***; *Sangathan* (Doc); *Vardan* (Doc); *Animal Reproduction and Artificial Insemination in Bovines* (Doc); *Tata Steel: Seventy Five Years of the Indian Steel Industry* (Doc); *Nehru* (Doc); **1984**: *Satyajit Ray* (Doc); **1985**: ***Trikaal***; *Festival of India* (Doc); **1986**: ***Susman***; *Yatra* (TV); *Katha Sagar* (TV); **1988**: *Bharat Ek Khoj* (TV); **1990**: *Nature Symphony* (Doc); *Abode of Kings: Rajasthan* (Doc); *A Quilt of Many Cultures: South India* (Doc); **1992**: *Antarnaad*; ***Suraj Ka Satwan Ghoda***.

BETAAB, NARAYAN PRASAD (1872-1945)

Playwright for Parsee theatre and scenarist mainly for the **Ranjit** Studio. Used the mythological genre (e.g. his best-known play, *Mahabharata*, for the Khatau-Alfred company, 1913) and inaugurated what the critic Agyaat called the Betaab Yug (c.1910-35), consolidating 19th C. efforts to define distinctively Hindi playwrighting practice. Whereas the 19th C. stage mythological mainly adapted familiar musical compositions interspersed with prose commentaries, the improvisational style of a traditional *kathakaar*, the Betaab style codified a more contemporary genre, determined politically by his explicitly brahminical adherences (underlined by his editorship of the journal *Brahma Bhatt Darpan*). His example greatly influenced the genre's cinematic form. Also created Hindi versions of original screenplays by e.g. **Chandulal Shah**. After working at **Ranjit**, Betaab wrote scripts for **Madan**, Ambika, **Sharda** and Saroj Studios. Definitive biography by Vidyavati Namra (1972). Story, dial and/or lyr credits include **Chandulal Shah**'s ***Devi Devayani*** (1931), ***Radha Rani***, ***Sati Savitri***, *Sheilbala* (all 1932), *Vishwamohini*, ***Miss 1933*** (both 1933), ***Barrister's Wife***, ***Keemti Aansoo*** (both 1935) and *Pardesi Pankhi* (1937); **Jayant Desai**'s *Krishna Sudama* (1933), *Nadira*, ***Sitamgarh***, ***Veer Babruwahan*** (all 1934), *College Girl*, *Noor-e-Watan* (both 1935), *Raj Ramani* (1936) and *Prithvi Putra* (1938); J.J. Madan's ***Zehari Saap*** (1933); **Nandlal Jaswantlal**'s *Pardesi Preetam* (1933) and *Kashmeera* (1934); **Raja Sandow**'s *Raat Ki Rani* (1935); Gunjal's *Ambarish* (1934); **Nanubhai Desai** and **J.P. Advani**'s *Shah Behram* (1935); **R.S. Choudhury**'s *Kal Ki Baat* (1937); Advani's *Sneh Bandhan* (1940) and *Parashuram* by Ramnik Desai (1947).

BHADURI, SISIR KUMAR (1889-1959)

Bengali director and actor born in Howrah, Bengal. Legendary figure in early 20th C. Bengali theatre embodying the transition from the 19th C. theatre dominated by Girishchandra Ghosh to a modernist sensibility that later assimilated aspects of Meyerhold, Reinhard and Brecht. Established reputation as actor while still at university, playing role of Kedar in **Rabindranath Tagore**'s play *Boikunter Khata* (1912). Lectured at Metropolitan Institute (later Bidyasagar College) 1914-21. First professional theatre appearance in title role of the landmark Bengali play, *Alamgir*, produced by Bengali Theatrical Co. controlled by **Madan** (1921). Established own theatre company, Natyamandir (1923), with Jogesh Choudhury's *Seeta*, a play redefining conventions of the mythological with greater emphasis on dramatically coherent performance idiom, elimination of stage wings and orchestra pit and a new type of background music (by Nripendra Nath Majumdar) in harmony with the songs of **K.C. Dey**. Best-known productions include re-edited 'traditional' plays by Girish Ghosh and D.L. Roy, the definitive stage interpretations of Tagore and, at the Srirangam theatre (1942-56), plays by a new generation of writers like Tulsi Lahiri (*Dukhir Iman*) and **Premankur Atorthy** (*Takht-e-Taus*). Several of Bengal's best-known actors, writers, musicians and technicians entered film via his theatre company and the Star Theatre. Participant in cultural anti-Fascist front and one of the very few commercial theatre personalities acknowledged by the **IPTA** as having influenced its own radical practice: his theatre hosted the IPTA's inaugural production, *Nabanna* (1943). Entered film as actor-director at Madan Theatres (1921). Founded and briefly ran his own Taj Mahal Studio (1922), returned to Madan and then worked at **New Theatres** and at **Priyanath Ganguly**'s Kali Films. Best-known films (*Seeta*, ***Talkie of Talkies*** and *Chanakya*) are adaptated from his stage plays. Acted in films he directed as well as in Satish Dasgupta's *Poshya Putra*, 1943.

FILMOGRAPHY: **1921**: *Mohini*; **1922**: ***Andhare Alo***; *Kamale Kamini*; **1929**: *Bicharak* (all St); **1932**: *Palli Samaj*; **1933**: *Seeta*; **1937**: ***Talkie of Talkies***; **1939**: *Chanakya*.

BHAGAVATHAR, C. HONAPPA (1914-92)

Kannada and Tamil actor and singer born in Choudasandra village, Karnataka. Trained in classical Carnatic music by Shamanna and Sambandhamurthy Bhagavathar. Acted in **Company Natak** plays in **Gubbi Veeranna**'s troupe, but his début was in the Tamil cinema, often acting in **Modern Theatres** films, e.g. **T.R. Sundaram**'s ***Burma Rani***, *Subhadra*. Introduced into Kannada via **Veeranna** productions directed by **H.L.N. Simha** (***Hemareddy Malamma***, ***Gunasagari***). Later played in remarkable Saint films (**P. Pullaiah**'s *Bhakta Gora Kumbhara*, K.R. Seetarama Sastry's *Mahakavi Kalidasa*), usually providing his own music. His music, performances and acting remain definitive of the genre in Kannada and Tamil. Also produced films, e.g. *Uzhavukkum Thozhilukkum Vandhanai Seivom*.

FILMOGRAPHY (* also music d): **1941**: *Subhadra*; *Krishna Kumar*; **1942**: *Sati Sukanya*; **1943**: *Arundhati*; *Devakanya*; **1944**: ***Burma Rani***; *Prabhavati*; *Rajarajeshwari*; **1945**: ***Hemareddy Mallamma***; *Bhakta Kalathi*; *Subhadra*; **1946**: *Kundalakesi*; *Shri Murugan*; *Valmiki*; **1948**: *Bhakta Jana*; *Gokula Dasi*; **1949**: *Devamanohari*; *Bhakta Gora Kumbhara**; **1953**: ***Gunasagari***; **1955**: *Mahakavi Kalidasa**; **1956**: *Pancharathna*; **1959**: *Uzhavukkum Thozhilukkum Vandhanai Seivom**; *Jagatjyoti Basaveshwara*; **1979**: *Sadananda*.

BHAGAVATHAR, M. KRISHNAMURTHY THYAGARAJA (1909-59)

One of the first major Tamil singing stars, introduced in **K. Subramanyam**'s mythological *Pavalakkodi* (as Arjuna). Born into a family of goldsmiths in Tiruchi; joined the theatre as a child in F.G. Natesa Iyer's troupe and went on to become the biggest Tamil stage star, sporting shoulder-length hair, diamond ear-rings and kohl around his eyes. After a successful film début, became briefly the highest-paid actor in South India, despite appearing in only 11 films, with classic performances in **Duncan**'s ***Ambikapathy***, **Y.V. Rao**'s *Chintamani* and **Raja Chandrasekhar**'s ***Ashok Kumar***, and the folk legend of the reformed saint *Haridas*, a major commercial hit. Helped launch the mainstream Newtone Studio (1937). As a musician, he adhered to the Tamizhasai movement, emphasising Tamil traditions as opposed to the Carnatic idiom dominated by Telugu, Kannada and Sanskrit. Arrested with **N.S. Krishnan** and jailed in 1945 for two years for the infamous Lakshmikantan murder (in which the two stars allegedly had a film gossip columnist, C.N. Lakshmikantan, killed). Made a high-profile comeback with Chandrasekhar's *Raja Mukthi*, but the film failed. Turned to direction with his last film *Pudhu Vazhvu*. Biography by Vindhan (1983).

FILMOGRAPHY (* also d): **1934**: *Pavalakkodi*; **1935**: *Sarangadhara*; **1936**: *Satya Seelan*; **1937**: ***Ambikapathy***; *Chintamani*; **1939**: *Thiruneelakantar*; **1941**: ***Ashok Kumar***; **1943**: *Sivakavi*; **1944**: *Haridas*; **1948**: *Raja Mukthi*; **1952**: *Amarakavi*; **1957**: *Pudhu Vazhvu**.

BHAGWAN, MASTER (b. 1913)

Hindi and Marathi actor and director; born Bhagwan Abhaji Palav in Bombay, the son of a mill worker. After devoting himself to body-building, he started in the silent era with his long-term partner, Chandrarao Kadam, in G.P. Pawar-directed stunt movies. Co-directed first feature with Pawar (1938), then producer (1942) with Jagriti Pics and Bhagwan Art Prod.; eventually owner of Jagriti Studios, Chembur (1947). Success of ***Albela*** established him briefly as a major post-Independence producer. Starred as a dancer and naUve simpleton in many stunt, adventure and ribald comedy movies. Acting style associated mainly with the elaboration of a minimalist dance movement which arguably became a major behavioural influence on Hindi film audiences (e.g. **Bachchan**'s dances, which today determine how people move on the streets in wedding or religious processions, bear the mark of Bhagwan's influence). **Balraj Sahni** wrote that while '**Raj Kapoor** and **Dilip Kumar** are [m]uch more popular than he is, they do not enjoy the popularity among the poorer classes that Bhagwan Dada does. [The working class] sees in him their own image and what endears him to them is that he, a fellow member of the proletariat, should make a beauty like **Geeta Bali** fall in love with him.' (Sahni, 1979). Since the early 70s, he has been largely relegated to cameo roles and comedy routines. Wrote the films he directed.

FILMOGRAPHY (* also d): **1931**: *Bewafa Ashq*; **1933**: *Daivi Khajina*; *Pyari Katar*; *Jalta Jigar*; (All St); **1935**: *Himmat-e-Mard*; **1936**: *Bharat Ka Lal*; **1937**: *Chevrolet 1936*; **1938**: *Bahadur Kisan**(co-d C. Kadam); **1939**: *Criminal**; **1941**: *Raja Gopichand**; *Vanamohini**; *Premabandhan*; **1942**: *Sukhi Jeevan**; **1943**: *Badla**; **1944**: *Bahadur**; **1945**: *Nagma-E-Sahra**; *Ji Haan*; **1946**: *Nargis*; *Dosti**; **1947**: *Matwale**; *Shake Hands**; *Bahadur Pratap**; *Madadgaar*; **1948**: *Jalan**; *Lalach**; *Matlabi**; *Tumhari Kasam*; **1949**: *Bachke Rehna**; *Bhedi Bungla**; *Bhole Bhale**; *Jigar**; *Bhole Piya*; *Bigde Dil*; *Jeete Raho*; *Joker*; *Khush Raho*; *Pyar Ki Raat*; *Roop Lekha*; *Shaukeen*; **1950**: *Achhaji*; *Aflatoon*; *Baksheesh*; *Dushmani*; *Jodidar*; *Babuji**; *Jungle Man*; *Rangile Musafir*; **1951**: ***Albela****; *Actor*; *Bade Saheb*; *Bhola Shankar*; *Damaad*; *Gazab*; *Ram Bharose*; **1952**: *Baghdad*; *Bhoole Bhatke*; *Daryai Lutera*; *Goonj*; *Sinbad the Sailor*; **1953**: *Char Chand*; *Rangila**; *Jhamela**; *Shamsheer*; **1954**: *Halla Gulla**; **1955**: *Deewar*; *Jhanak Jhanak Payal Baaje*; *Oonchi Haveli*; *Chhabila*; *Pyara Dushman**; **1956**: *Badshah Salamat*; *Char Minar*; ***Chori Chori***; *Mr Lambu*; *Sheikh Chilli*; *Passing Show**; *Bhagambhag**; *Kar Bhala**; **1957**: *Adhi Roti*; *Agra Road*; *Beti*; *Coffee House*; *Garma Garam*; *Gateway of India*; *Raja Vikram*; *Ustad*; *Uthavala Narad*; **1958**: *Don Ghadicha Dav*; *Chaalbaaz*; *Dulhan*; *Mr Q*; *Naya Kadam*; *Son Of Sinbad*; *Bhala Admi**; *Sachche Ka Bol Bala**; **1959**: *Chalis Din*; *Chacha Zindabad*; *Duniya Na Mane*; *Kangan*; *Lal Nishan*; *Madam XYZ*; *Mohar*; *O Tera Kya Kehana*; **1960**: *Diler Hasina*; *Nakhrewali*; *Rangila Raja*; *Road No. 303*; *Zimbo Comes To Town*; **1961**: *Salaam Memsaab*; *Sapan Suhane*; *Shola Jo Bhadke**; *Lucky Number*; *Stree*; *Teen Ustad*; *Zamana Badal Gaya*; **1962**: *Baghdad Ki Raatein*; *Madam Zapata*; *Rocket Girl*; *Tower House*; **1963**: *Awara Abdulla*; *Magic Box*; *Rustom-e-Baghdad*; *Dekha Pyar Tumhara*; **1964**: *Aandhi Aur Toofan*; *Magic Carpet*; *Hukum Ka Ekka*; *Main Bhi Ladki Hoon*; *Tarzan and Delilah*; **1965**: *Hum Diwane**; *Adventure Of Robin Hood and Bandits*; *Bekhabar*; *Flying Man*; *Khakaan*; *Sher Dil*; *Sinbad Alibaba and Alladdin*; *Tarzan and King Kong*; *Tarzan Comes To Delhi*; *Chor Darwaza*; **1966**: *Chale Hain Sasural*; *Duniya Hai Dilwalon Ki*; *Labela**; *Daku Mangal Singh*; *Ladka Ladki*; *Veer Bajrang*; **1967**: *Albela Mastana*; *Chhaila Babu*; *Duniya Nachegi*; *Gunehgaar*; *Hum Do Daku*; *Trip To The Moon*; *Arabian Nights*; **1968**: *Jhuk Gaya Aasmaan*; *Bai Mothi Bhagyachi*; **1969**: *Goonda*; *Inteqam*; *The Killers*; *Raat Ke Andhere Mein*; **1970**: *Geet*; *Mangu Dada*; *Choron Ka Chor*; *Night in Calcutta*; *Suhana Safar*; *Lakshman Resha*; **1971**: *Aag Aur Daag*; ***Guddi***; *Hangama*; *Joi Bangla Desh*; *Mera Gaon Mera Desh*; ***Tere Mere Sapne***; **1972**: *Putli Bai*; *Aan Baan*; *Tangewala*; *Sultana Daku*; *Gaon Hamara Shaher Tumhara*; *Do Chor*; *Raaste Ka Patthar*; **1973**: *Taxi Driver*; *Chhalia*; *Barkha Bahar*; *Banarasi Babu*; *Chori Chori*; *Shareef Badmash*; *Mahasati Savitri*; **1974**: *Badhti Ka Naam Daadhi*; *Balak Dhruv*; *Imaan*; *Tarzan Mera Saathi*; *Aarop*; *Badla*; *Paap Aur Punya*; *Aparadhi*; *Dulhan*; **1975**: *Faraar*; *Jaan Hazir Hai*; *Kala Sona*; *Maze Le Lo*; *Natak*; *Zindagi Aur Toofan*; *Daku Aur Bhagwan*; *Ek Gaon Ki Kahani*; *Jaggu*; *Mazaaq*; *Raffoo Chakkar*; *Zorro*; *Bhoola Bhatka*; *Shantata! Khoon Jhala Aahe*; **1976**: *Naag Champa*; *Sangram*; *Alibaba*; *Toofan Aur Bijli*; **1977**: *Banyabapu*; *Bhingri*; *Navara Mazha Brahmachari*; ***Ram Ram Gangaram***; *Chakkar Pe Chakkar*; *Jai Vijay*; *Khel Khiladi Ka*; *Agent Vinod*; *Mandir Masjid*; *Saheb Bahadur*; *Mukti*; **1978**: *Azad*; *Darwaza*; *Kasme Vade*; *Khoon Ka Badla Khoon*; *Main Tulsi Tere Aangan Ki*; *Sampoorna Sant Darshan*; *Ganga Sagar*; *Sawan Ke Geet*; *Bhairu Pahelwan Ki Jai*; **1979**: *Aitya Bilavar Nagoba*; *Apli Manse*; **1980**: *Asha*; *Karwa Chouth*; *Mera Salaam*; *Phatakadi*; *Hyoch Navara Pahije*; *Sharan Tula Bhagavanta*; **1981**: *Shitala Mata*; *Commander*; *Chhupa Chhupi*; *Govinda Ala Re Ala*; *Laath Marin Tithe Pani*; **1982**: *Honey*; *Ali Angavar*; *Preet Na Jaane Reet*; **1983**: *Dard-e-Dil*; *Bindiya Chamkegi*; *Aao Pyar Karen*; *Bekhabar*; *Jai Baba Amarnath*; *Kaise Kaise Log*; **1984**: *Bhatke Rahee*; *Bhool*; *Love Marriage*; *Mera Dost Mera Dushman*; *Meri Kahani*; *Jhootha Sach*; *Yaadgaar*; *Ali Lahar Kela Kahar*; *Bahurupi*; *Chorachya Manaat Chandani*; *Gulchhadi*; **1985**: *Pyari Bhabhi*; **1986**: *Andheri Raat Mein Diya Tere Haath Mein*; *Bijli*; *Dhondi Dhondi Pani De*; **1987**: *Bola Dajiba*; *Chhakke Panje*; *Prem Karuya Khullam Khulla*; *Diwana Tere Naam Ka*; *Tarzan and Cobra*; **1988**: *Halaal Ki Kamai*; *Khatarnak*; **1989**: *Ilaaka*; *Ina Mina Dika*; *Navara Baiko*; **1990**: *Naache Nagin Gali Gali*.

BHAGYARAJ, KRISHNASWAMY (b. 1953)

Top Tamil director once declared by **MGR** to be his cinematic heir. Dropped out of colleges in Coimbatore; was a rickshaw puller and a circus clown in Kakinada. In Madras, became assistant to G. Ramakrishna and **Bharathirajaa**, débuting in the latter's films as actor (first major role in ***Puthiya Varpugal***) and scenarist (*Kizhakke Pokum Rayil*, *Sigappu Rojakkal*, both 1978; *Niram Maratha Pookal*, 1979; *Oru Kaithiyin Diary*, 1985). Directorial début with the hit *Suvar Illatha Chitrangal* established a distinctive style, with the director usually playing the comic underdog in rural dramas voyeuristically presented and leavened with bawdy physical humour. Also scored many of his films. Several were remade in Hindi, often by **Bapu**: (e.g. *Andha 7 Natkal* remade as *Woh Saat Din*, 1983; *Thooral Ninnu Pochu* as *Mohabbat*, 1985). Other remakes include *Mundhanai Mudichu* as K. Raghavendra Rao's *Masterji* (1985) and *Enga Chinna Raja* as Indra Kumar's 90s hit *Beta* (1992). Bhagyaraj's big-budget Hindi **Bachchan** film, *Aakhri Raasta*, in which the star played both father and son, is a remake of *Oru Kaithiyin Diary*. Made an abortive effort to enter politics (1989).

FILMOGRAPHY (* only act): **1979**: ***Puthiya Varpugal****; *Kanni Paruvathinile**; *Suvar Illatha Chitrangal*; **1980**: *Bhama Rukmini*; *Kumari Pennin Ullathiley**; *Oru Kayi Osai*; **1981**: *Mouna Geethangal*; *Indru Poyi Nalai Vaa*; *Veediyum Varai Kathiru*; *Andha Ezhu Natkal*; **1982**: *Thooral Ninnu Pochu*; *Darling Darling Darling*; *Poyi Satchi*; **1983**: *Mundhanai Mudichu*; *Thavani Kanavukal*; **1984**: *Oomai Janangal**; *Mayadari Mogudu*; **1985**: *Chinna Veedu*; *Chithirame Chithirame*; *Aakhri Raasta*; **1987**: *Enga Chinna Rasa*; **1988**: *Vaddante Pelli*; ***Idu Namma Alu****; **1989**: *Aaro Ariraro*; **1990**: *Avasara Police 100*; *Sundara Kandam*; **1991**: *Pavunnu Pavanuthan*; **1992**: *Ammavandachu**; *Rasakutty*.

BHANUMATHI, PALUVAYI (b. 1924)

Aka Bhanumathi Ramakrishna. Born in Guntur Dist., AP. Actress-director and *grande dame* of the Telugu and Tamil cinemas. Her now legendary performances at the **Vauhini** and **Gemini** Studios were among their earliest post-WW2 bids for **All-India Film** industrial status. Major singing star of 40s/50s; later studio owner with her husband **P.S. Ramakrishna Rao** (Bharani Studios, 1947), scenarist, music composer, film-maker and popular author of 'mother-in-law' short stories (the *Attagari Kathalu* series). Film début as teenager in **C. Pullaiah**'s reformist melodrama ***Varavikrayam*** as Kalindi, a daughter who commits suicide because her parents cannot afford her wedding dowry. Her first major success came in the bizarre role of a village girl who grows into a 'society lady' in **B.N. Reddi**'s ***Swargaseema***. Mid-40s Telugu films, in addition to conventional mythologicals by **Balaramaiah** and **Babu** (***Krishna Prema***), often cast her in comedies dealing with anxieties about traditional (sometimes rural) cultures assimilating aspects of Western modernity, a subject central to much popular reform literature: in **Y.V. Rao**'s ***Tehsildar*** she wears high heels and attends a British tea party; **Prasad**'s 'feminist' ***Grihapravesham*** opens with her playing badminton and confronting the misogynist hero. This context, and her unique ability to function simultaneously in the reformist-social and the traditional mythological genres, was later used to remarkable effect in ***Nallathambi***, the seminal **DMK Film**, and in the Gemini trilingual adventure drama, ***Apoorva Sahodarargal***. Her incarnation of 'tradition', exemplified and stressed by her music, was later put to ideological use in the genre still most closely associated with her: 'damsel-in-distress' performances in **MGR**'s Robin Hood-derived vigilante films (***Malaikallan***, ***Alibabavum Narpathu Thirudargalum***, ***Madurai Veeran***). Her music drew on **C. Ramchandra**, Arabian folk (*Swargaseema*, ***Laila Majnu***) and even Pat Boone, but she is best remembered for her versions of Thyagaraja's kritis and Purandaradasa's bhajans, which led to her being nominated Principal of the Government College of Music in Madras in the mid-80s. Her songs and dances are featured in the compilation film, *Chitramala* (1985).

FILMOGRAPHY (* also d/** also music d): **1939**: ***Varavikrayam***; **1940**: *Malathi Madhavam*; ***Dharmapatni***; **1941**: ***Bhaktimala***; **1943**: ***Garuda Garvabhangam***; ***Krishna Prema***; **1944**: ***Tehsildar***; **1945**: ***Swargaseema***; **1946**: ***Grihapravesham***: **1947**: ***Ratnamala***; **1948**: *Rajamukthi*; **1949**: ***Laila Majnu***; ***Raksharekha***; *Ratnakumar*; ***Apoorva Sahodarargal/Nishan***; ***Nallathambi***; *Devamanohari*; **1950**: ***Apoorva Sahodaralu***; *Maya Rambha/Maya Rambai*; **1951**: ***Mangala***; ***Malleeshwari***; **1952**: ***Prema/Kathal***; *Rani*; **1953**: *Shamsheer*; ***Chandirani****; **1954**: ***Malaikallan***; *Aggiramudu*; ***Chakrapani*****; ***Vipranarayana*****; **1955**: *Kalvanin Kadhali*; ***Alibabavum Narpathu Thirudargalum***; **1956**: *Rambayin Kadhali*; *Sadaram*; *Thaikku Pinn Tharam*; ***Tenali Ramakrishna/Tenali Raman***; ***Madurai Veeran***; ***Rangoon Radha***; *Raja Rani*; ***Chintamani*****; **1957**: ***Ambikapathy***; *Makkalai Petra Maharasi*; *Nala Damayanti*; *Sarangadhara*; *Rani Lalithangi*; *Varudukavali/Manamagal Thevai***; **1958**: ***Nadodi Mannan***; **1959**: *Mani Mekalai*; *Bandaramudu/Adisaya Thirudan*; **1960**: *Raja Bhakti*; *Raja Desingu*; **1961**: *Batasari/Kanal Neer***; **1962**: *Annai/Penchina Prema*; *Rani Samuyktha*; *Vadivukku Valai Kappu*; *Vikramadithan*; **1963**: *Anuragham*; *Anubandhalu*; *Arivali*; *Kalai Arasi*; *Kanchi Thalaivan*; **1964**: *Bobbili Yuddham*; ***Vivahabandham*****; **1965**: *Sarasa BA*; *Todu Needa*; *Antastulu*; **1966**: *Palnati Yuddham*; **1967**: *Pattathu Rani*; *Grihalakshmi**; *Punyavati*; *Nai Roshni*; **1970**: *Kadhal Jyothi*; ***Vietnam Veedu***; **1971**: *Mattilo Manikyam*; **1972**: ***Anta Mana Manchike****/**; **1973**: *Vichitra Vivaham**; *Kattilla Thottilla*; **1974**: *Tatamma Kala*; *Mangalya Bhagyam*; *Ammayi Pelli**; *Pathumatha Bandham*; *Swathi Nakshatram*; *Thayi Pirandhal*; **1975**: *Melnattu Marumagal*; *Pandanti Samsaram*; *Eduppar Kayi Pillai*; *Ippadiyum Oru Penn**/**; **1976**: *Manamara Vazhthungal*; *Vanga Sambandhi Vanga**/**; *Manavadi Kosam**/**; **1980**: *Ranchayithri**/**; *Oke Naate Rathri**/**; **1982**: *Bhakta Dhruva Markandeya**/**; **1984**: *Mangammagari Manavudu*; **1985**: *Muddula Manavaralu*; **1986**: *Itni Jaldi Kya Hai**; *Attagaru Swagatham*; **1987**: *Mandala Dheesudu*; **1988**: *Attagaru Zindabad*; **1989**: *Bammamata Bangaru Pata*; **1992**: *Periamma**/**; *Samrat Ashok*.

BHARATHAN, B. G. (b. 1946)

Successful Malayalam and Tamil director with substantial art-house following. Born in Vadakkanacheri, Trichur Dist., Kerala. Graduate of Trichur School of Art; professional painter before he joined films as a set designer and publicist. Produced his début feature from his own story, later also composing the lyrics and the music for his own features. His films, often with few characters, address sexuality set in a bleak moral landscape that metes out primal justice (e.g. the snakebite and divine intervention in ***Rathi Nirvedham***). The format was extended into an indigenous version of the western with the big-budget CinemaScope film ***Thazhvaram***, in which a stranger (**Mohanlal**) appears in the frontier town to settle a long-standing feud. Changed his idiom for his major hit, ***Thevar Magan***, written and produced by **Kamalahasan** and devoted to the star's self-image.

FILMOGRAPHY: **1975**: *Prayanam*; **1977**: *Guruvayoor Kesavan*; *Aniyara*; **1978**: *Aravam*; ***Rathi Nirvedham***; **1979**: *Thakara*; *Chamaram*; **1980**: ***Lorry***; *Savithri*; **1981**: *Chatta*; *Nidra*; *Palangal*; *Parvathi*; *Parankimala*; *Rani*; **1982**: ***Ormakkayi***; ***Marmaram***; **1983**: *Eenum*; *Sandhya Mayungam Neram*; ***Kattathe Kilikoodu***; **1984**: *Ente Upasana*; *Ithiri Poove Chuvannapoove*; **1985**: *Kathodu Kathoram*; *Ozhivukalam*; *Unjaladum Uravugal*; **1986**: *Chilampu*; *Pranamam*; *Nilakurinhi Poothappol*; **1987**: *Oru Minnaminuginte Nurungu Vettam*; **1988**: *Oru Sayahnathinte Swapnam*; *Vaishali*; **1989**: ***Thazhvaram***; **1991**: *Amaram*; **1992**: ***Thevar Magan***; *Avarampu*; *Malootty*; *Vengalam*; **1993**: *Chamayam*; *Padhayam*.

BHARATIDASAN (1891-1964)

Major Tamil poet, playwright and scenarist. Seminal figure in the Tamil nationalist movement, prefiguring the regional political ideology of the Dravida Munnetra Kazhagam (cf **DMK Film**). Changed his name in 1908 from Kanaka Subburathnam to Bharatidasan, 'disciple of Bharati', in honour of his mentor, the poet Subramanya Bharati. Wrote religious poems and was briefly a follower of Gandhi; later became an atheist under the influence of Periyar E.V. Ramaswamy Naicker and joined the Dravidar Kazhagam. Published his first anthology, *Bharatidasan Kavitaikal* in 1938 (collected works published in 1977). Mounted several attacks on religious brahminism using a demotic Tamil; militantly affirmed a Tamil identity against Northern hegemony. Film début in P.V. Rao's *Balamani* (1937) as dialogue writer-lyricist. His dialogues for **Duncan**'s *Kalamegham* (1940) led to a long-term association with **Modern Theatres** where he wrote e.g. **T.R. Sundaram**'s *Subhadra* (1945) and *Sulochana* (1946), achieving mass popularity with Sundaram's *Apoorva Chintamani* (1947), followed by the story/dialogue/lyrics of Duncan's *Ponmudi* (1949). Also wrote **Sundaram**'s *Valayapathi* (1952). Poems have been used as lyrics in numerous Tamil films, notably **P. Neelakantan**'s *Ore Iravu* (1951).

BHARATHIRAJAA (b. 1944)

Real name Chinnaswamy. Successful Tamil director and scenarist; also worked extensively in Hindi and Telugu. Born in Allinagaram, Madurai, TN. Joined films having apparently been obsessed with **Sivaji Ganesan**'s movies during his childhood in a peasant family. Assisted **K.S. Sethumadhavan** (1968), **P. Pullaiah** and **Puttanna Kanagal** (whose influence he acknowledges). Début with ***Pathinaru Vayathinile***, scored by his childhood friend **Ilaiyaraja**, establishing both composer and lead star **Sridevi** in the Tamil cinema. It was remade in Hindi as *Solva Sawan*. Went on to translate the middle-class melodramas of **C.V. Sridhar** and **K. Balachander** into rural 'realist' romances and folk rituals (often featuring the local village deity as dramatic pivot, as in ***Vedham Pudithu***), while introducing technocentric fantasy elements. His signature sequence, until he disowned it, was an elaborately choreographed song with dancing women dressed in white, often shot with star-filters. His reliance on exotica heightens the **Kanagal**-inspired psychodrama, as at the end of *Kizhakke Pokum Rayil* when, in the nick of time, the hero saves the heroine from being sacrificed to placate the flooding river. Most of his non-Tamil films are remakes of Tamil hits (e.g. *Lovers* remakes *Alaigal Oyvathillai*; *Savere Wali Gadi* remakes *Kizhakke Pokum Rayil*). Best-known work, *Sigappu Rojakkal*, is a slasher film directed against women. It was remade with **Rajesh Khanna** in Hindi as *Red Rose* and triggered protests from feminists in Bombay and Delhi. Introduced several new actors in Tamil, e.g. Radha, Revathi, **Bhagyaraj** and Kartick.

FILMOGRAPHY: **1977**: ***Pathinaru Vayathinile***; **1978**: *Kizhakke Pokum Rayil*; *Sigappu Rojakkal*; *Solva Sawan*; **1979**: ***Puthiya Varpugal***; *Niram Maratha Pookal/Niram Maradha Pushpangal*; *Yar Gulabi*; **1980**: *Red Rose*; *Kallukkul Eram*; *Nizhalgal*; *Kotha Jeevithulu*; **1981**: *Alaigal Oyvathillai*; *Tik Tik Tik*; ***Seethakoka Chilaka***; **1982**: *Kathal Oviyam*; *Valibame Vaa*; **1983**: *Mann Vasanai*; *Lovers*; *Avemin Pudhumai Penn*; **1984**: *Oru Kaithiyin Diary*; **1985**: *Ee Tharam Illalu*; ***Muthal Mariyathai***; *Savere Wali Gadi*; *Yuvadharam Bilisindi*; **1986**: *Kadalora Kavathaikal*; **1987**: ***Vedham Pudithu***;

Aradhana; **1988**: *Jamadagni*; *Kodiparakkuthu*; **1990**: *En Uyir Thozhan*; **1991**: *Pudhu Nellu Pudhu Nathu*; **1992**: *Nadodi Thendral*; *Captain Magal*; **1993**: *Kizhakku Seemayile*.

BHASI, ADOOR (1929-90)

Malayalam cinema's best-known film star in the 60s and 70s after **Prem Nazir**. Until 1980, he starred in a third of all films made in Malayalam. Born in Adoor, originally named K. Bhaskaran Nair. A former textile technologist and stage performer, he went into films when he moved to Madras and worked briefly as production manager on Tamil films. A renowned comedian, he continued the slapstick style introduced into Malayalam cinema by S.P. Pillai. His first major role was as Anachal Krishna Pillai in **P. Bhaskaran**'s *Adya Kiranangal*. Later developed the persona of the wide-eyed, wooden-faced and sometimes unsmiling figure delivering lines in a staccato rhythm, which recalled the literary satires of his father, E.V. Krishna Pillai (1894-1938), especially in ***Kavya Mela***, where he plays a poet directly reminiscent of Krishna Pillai's *Kavitakkesu* (1929). His style evoked the major tradition of Malayalam farces pioneered by the plays of C.V. Raman Pillai, later used to parody the romantic poetry of the post-Vallathol era. As such, Bhasi functions as the satirical, even cynical, counter to Prem Nazir's extension of the romantic tradition as he mouths the lyrics of **Vyalar Rama Varma**. Bhasi's best-known performance outside Kerala is in **John Abraham**'s ***Cheriyachente Kroora Krithyangal***, masterfully cast as the cowering Cherian consumed by guilt. Also remembered for his out-of-character 'serious' role as the father in **Aravindan**'s ***Uttarayanam***, and for his triple role in *Padunna Puzha*. Also directed four films. Contested the Trivandrum Corp elections as an Independent candidate backed by the Left parties, but lost. The following filmography is incomplete for the years 1971 and 1979-82.

FILMOGRAPHY (* also d): **1961**: ***Mudiyanaya Puthran***; *Gnana Sundari*; **1962**: *Veluthampi Dalawa*; *Bhagya Jatakam*; *Viyarppinte Vila*; **1963**: ***Ninamanninnya Kalapadakal***; ***Moodupadam***; *Satyabhama*; *Chilampoli*; *Ammeye Kannan*; **1964**: *Devalayam*; *Thacholi Othenan*; *Kuttikkuppayam*; *School Master*; *Atom Bomb*; *Oralkoodi Kalanayi*; *Karutha Kayi*; *Adya Kiranangal*; ***Bhargavi Nilayam***; *Bharthavu*; *Kalanjukuttiya Thangam*; *Kudumbini*; *Althara*; **1965**: *Devatha*; *Shyamalachechi*; ***Odeyil Ninnu***; *Kadatthukaran*; *Porter Kunjali*; *Inapravugal*; *Muthalaly*; *Kalyanaphoto*; *Ammu*; *Thankakudam*; *Kattuthulasi*; *Mayavi*; *Jeevitha Yatra*; *Rajamalli*; *Kattupookal*; *Kathiruna Nikkah*; *Kochumon*; *Bhoomiyile Malakha*; *Shakuntala*; *Pattu Thoovala*; *Chettathi*; ***Kavya Mela***; ***Murappennu***; *Thommente Makkal*; *Sarpakadu*; **1966**: *Kalithozhen*; *Kusirthikuttan/Anni*; *Archana*; *Station Master*; *Pakal Kinavu*; *Rowdy*; *Pinchu Hridayam*; *Jail*; *Kootukar*; *Kalyana Rathriyil*; ***Kayamkulam Kochunni***; *Tharavatamma*; *Kanmanikal*; *Puchakanni*; *Kallipennu*; *Kanakachilanka*; *Karuna*; *Sthanarthi Saramma*; *Tilottama*; *Priyatama*; *Mayor Nair*; ***Kunjali Marakkar***; **1967**: ***Ashwamedham***; *Ramanan*; *Sahadharmini*; *Jeevikan Anuvadhikuka*; ***Irutinte Atmavu***; ***Agniputhri***; ***Kottayam Kola Case***; *Udyogastha*; *Postman*; *Kudumbam*; *Mainatharuvi Kola Case*; *Madatharuvi*; ***Aval***; *Bhagyamudra*; *Kannatha Veshankal*; ***Anveshichu Kandatiyilla***; ***Chitramela***; *Nagarame Nandi*; *Pavapettaval*; *Pareeksha*; *Cochin Express*; *N.G.O.*; ***Kavalam Chundan***; *Nadan Pennu*; *Kasavuthattam*; *Swapnabhoomi*; **1968**: ***Thirichadi***; *Viruthan Sanku*; *Manaswini*; *Inspector*; *Dial 2244*; ***Asuravithu***; *Vazhipizhacha Santhathi*; *Karthika*; *Padunna Puzha*; *Punnapra Vyalar*; *Lakshaprabhu*; *Love in Kerala*; *Kaliyalla Kalyanam*; *Yakshi*; ***Thulabharam***; *Midumidukki*; *Anju Sundarigal*; *Aparadhini*; *Kodungalluramma*; *Velutha Kathrina*; *Agni Pareeksha*; *Kayalkarayil*; *Bharyamar Sukshikuka*; **1969**: *Vila Kuranja Manushyar*; *Anashchadanam*; *Padicha Kallan*; *Veetu Mrugham*; *Almaram*; *Kattukurangu*; *Mr Kerala*; *Rahasyam*; *Susie*; ***Adimagal***; *Kannur Deluxe*; *Sandhya*; *Kadalpalam*; *Mooladanam*; *Jwala*; *Vilakkapetta Bandhangal*; ***Nadhi***; *Danger Biscuit*; *Kootu Kudumbam*; *Virunnukari*; *Rest House*; **1970**: *Ambalapravu*; *Kurukshetram*; *Moodalamanju*; *Pearl View*; *Saraswathi*; *Amma Enna Stree*; *Anatha*; *Palunku Pathram*; *Kalpana*; *Stree*; ***Vazhve Mayam***; *Cross Belt*; ***Ezhuthatha Katha***; *Bhikara Nimishankal*; *Dattuputhran*; *Rakta Pushpam*; *Vivaham Swargathil*; *Othenente Makan*; *Kuttavali*; *Vivahitha*; *Kakathampurati*; *A Chitrashalabham Paranotte*; ***Priya***; *Lottery Ticket*; *Triveni*; *Tara*; ***Aranazhikaneram***; **1971**: ***Abhijathyam***; *Line Bus*; *Achante Bharya*; *Neethi*; *CID Nazir*; *Moonnupukkal*; *Inquilab Zindabad*; *Marunattil Oru Malayali*; *Karakanakadal*; ***Ummachu***; *Vilakku Vangiya Veena*; *Shiksha*; ***Oru Penninte Katha***; *Lanka Dahanam*; ***Vidyarthikale Ithile Ithile***; *Vithukal*; **1972**: *Sambhavami Yuge Yuge*; *Nadan Premam*; *Aradi Manninte Janmi*; *Kandavarundo*; *Pushpanjali*; *Devi*; *Maya*; *Manthrakodi*; *Manushya Bandhangal*; *Aromalunni*; *Taxi Car*; *Mayiladum Kunnu*; *Omana*; *Kalippava*; *Ini Oru Janmam Tharu*; ***Chemparathi***; *Achannum Bappayum*; *Oru Sundariyude Katha*; *Miss Mary*; *Punarjanmam*; *Maraivil Thiruvu Sukshikuha*; *Gandharvakshetram*; *Nrithyasala*; *Azhimukham*; *Anveshanam*; *Snehadeepame Mizhi Thurakku*; *Brahmachari*; *Ananthasayanam*; *Putrakameshti*; *Shakti*; *Sathi*; *Postmane Kananilla*; *Chhayam*; *Teerthayatra*; ***Maram***; **1973**: *Police Ariyaruthu*; *Football Champion*; *Agnathavasam*; ***Enippadikal***; *Panchavati*; *Bhadra Deepam*; *Thiruvabharanam*; *Masappadi Mathupilla*; *Kalachakram*; *Udayam*; *Ponnapuram Kotta*; *Aradhika*; *Kavitha*; *Kaliyugam*; *Chenda*; *Veendum Prabhatam*; *Manushya Puthran*; *Rakkuyil*; *Thani Niram*; *Ladies' Hostel*; *Darshanam*; *Achani*; *Soundarya Pooja*; *Urvashi Bharathi*; *Thenaruvi*; *Pacha Nottukal*; *Pavangal Pennungal*; *Nakhangal*; *Kapalika*; *Dharma Yuddham*; *Prethangalude Thazhvara*; *Chukku*; *Driksakshi*; *Sastram Jayichu Manushyan Thottu*; *Interview*; *Poyi Mukhangal*; *Manasu*; *Thottavadi*; *Divya Darshanam*; *Ithu Manushiano?*; *Checkpost*; *Thekkan Kattu*; *Madhavikutty*; *Padmavyuham*; *Angathattu*; **1974**: *Manyashri Vishwamithran*; *Chanchala*; *Oru Pidi Ari*; *Pattabhishekham*; *Shapamoksham*; *Chandrakantham*; *Suprabhatam*; *Nathoon*; *Panchatanthram*; *Rahasya Rathri*; *Durga*; *Setu Bandhanam*; *Nellu*; *Alakal*; *Poonthenaruvi*; *Neela Kannukal*; *Chattakkari*; *Night Duty*; *Nagaram Sagaram*; *Aswathi*; *College Girl*; *Swarna Vigraham*; *Ayalathe Sundari*; *Kalyana Saugandhikam*; *Chakravakam*; *Thacholi Marumagan Chandu*; *Thumbolarcha*; *Nadhi Nadanmare Avasiamundu*; *Raja Hamsam*; *Sapta Swarangal*; ***Uttarayanam***; *Bhoomidevi Pushpiniyayi*; *Arakallan Mukkal Kallan*; *Chief Guest*; *Swarna Malsiyam*; **1975**: *Abhimanam*; *Alibaba and Forty-one Thieves*; *Aranyakandam*; *Babu Mon*; *Boy Friend*; *Cheenavala*; *Chumadu Thangi*; *Chuvanna Sandhyakal*; *Criminals*; *Dharmakshetre Kurukshetre*; *Hello Darling*; *Kottaram Vilakkanundu*; *Kuttichathan*; *Love*

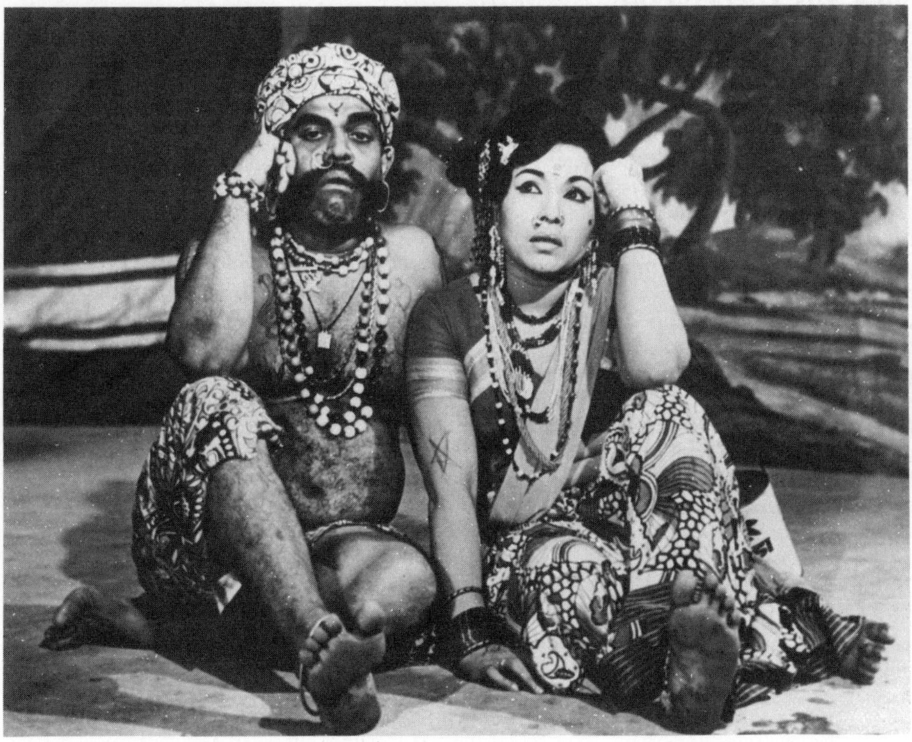

Adoor Bhasi and Manorama in *Vidyarthikale Ithile Ithile* (1971)

Marriage; *Madhura Pathinezhu*; *Makkal*; *Manishada*; *Mattoru Seeta*; *Mucheettu Kalikarante Magal*; *Neela Ponman*; *Omana Kunju*; *Padmaragam*; *Palazhi Madhanam*; *Pennpada*; *Picnic*; *Pravaham*; *Ragam*; *Sammanam*; *Surya Vamsam*; *Thamarathoni*; *Thiruvonam*; *Tourist Bungalow*; *Ullasa Yathra*; *Velicham Akale*; **1976**: *Abhinandanam*; *Ajayanum Vijayanum*; *Amma*; *Ammini Ammavan*; *Amritha Vahini*; *Anubhavam*; *Appooppan*; *Ayalakkari*; *Chennai Valarthiya Kutty*; *Chottanikara Amma*; *Dweep*; *Kamadhenu*; *Kanyadanam*; *Kayamkulam Kochunniyude Maghan*; *Light House*; *Manasa Veena*; *Mallanum Mathevanum*; *Mohini Attam*; *Muthu*; *Nee Ente Lahari*; *Neelasaree*; *Nurayum Pathayum*; *Ozhukkinethire*; *Panchami*; *Panchamrutham*; *Parijatham*; *Pickpocket*; *Ponn*; *Prasadam*; *Priyamvadha*; *Pushpa Sarem*; *Rathriyile Yathrakar*; *Rajayogam*; *Seemantha Puthran*; *Sexilla Stuntilla*; *Thuruppu Gulam*; *Vanadevatha*; *Vazhi Vilakku*; *Yakshaganam*; *Yuddha Bhoomi*; **1977**: *Suryakanthi*; *Acharam Ammini Osaram Omana**; *Adyapadam**; *Akale Akasam*; *Akshaya Pathram*; *Ammayi Amma*; *Anjali*; *Aparajitha*; *Bharya Vijayam*; *Chakravarthini*; *Chaturvedam*; *Gandharvam*; *Guruvayoor Kesavan*; *Itha Ivide Vare*; *Jalatarangam*; *Kaduvaye Pidicha Kiduva*; *Kannappanunni*; *Lakshmi*; *Madanolsavam*; *Makam Piranna Manka*; *Minimol*; *Mohamum Mukthiyum*; *Mutthate Mulla*; *Nalumani Pookkal*; *Nirakudam*; *Parivarthanam*; *Rathi Manmathan*; *Rendu Lokam*; *Samudram*; *Satyavan Savithri*; *Sneham*; *Sujatha*; *Sukradasa*; *Tholkkan Enikku Manassilla*; *Varadakshina*; *Veedu Oru Swargam*; *Vishukkani*; **1978**: *Anappachan*; *Aarum Anniyaralla*; *Adimakachavadam*; *Anubhoothikalude Nimisham*; *Ashokavanam*; *Aval Vishwasthayayirunnu*; *Balapareekshanam*; *Bharyayum Kamukiyum*; *Ee Ganam Marakkumo*; *Itha Oru Manushyan*; *Jayikkanai Janichavan*; *Kadathanattu Makam*; *Kalpa Vruksha*; *Kanalkkattakal*; *Kudumbam Namakku Sreekovil*; ***Mannu***; *Mattoru Karnan*; *Nakshatrangale Kaval*; *Nivedyam*; *Onappudava*; ***Rathi Nirvedham***; *Raghuvamsam**; *Shathru Samharam*; *Snehathinte Mukhangal*; *Thampuratti*; *Vadagaikku Oru Hridayam*; *Vyamoham*; *Yagaswam*; *Theerangal*; *Bandhanam*; **1979**: *Ward No. 7*; ***Cheriyachente Kroora Krithyangal***; **1981**: ***Ilakkangal***; **1983**: *Mahabali*; *Adhyathe Anuragam*; *Adhipathyam*; *Aroodam*; *Ashtapadi*; *Eenum*; *Ente Katha*; *Guru Dakshina*; *Himavahini*; *Justice Raja*; *Kuyiline Thedi*; *Maniyara*; *Nanayam*; *Onnu Chirikku*; *Oomakuyil*; *Pinninvalu*; *Sandhyakku Virinja Poovu*; *Sandhya Vandanam*; *Yangana Nee Marakkum*; **1984**: ***Alkoottathil Thaniye***; ***April 18***; *Athirathram*; *Ente Kalithozhen*; *Etha Ennumuthal*; *Jeevitham*; *Koottinilangili*; ***Lakshmana Rekha***; *Manithali*; *Muthodu Muthu*; *Onnanu Nammal*; *Pavam Poornima*; *Saundamevide? Bandamevide?*; *Thathamme Poocha Poocha*; *Vellom*; *Vepralam*; *Vettah*; **1985**: *Anakkorumma*; *Avidathepole Ivideyum*; *Eeran Sandhya*; *Ee Thalanil Ithirineram*; ***Kilippattu***; *Kochuthemmadi*; *Madhu Vidhurathri*; *Manya Mahajangale*; *Mulamoottil Adima*; *Nerariyum Nerathu*; *Orikkal Oridathu*; *Pachavelicham*; *Principal Olivil*; ***Yathra***; **1986**: *Vaiki Odunna Varathi*; **1987**: *Sarvakalasala*; *Manivathoorile Ayiram Sivarathrikal*; ***Purushartham***.

BHASI, THOPPIL (1925-92)

Malayalam director and prolific scenarist born in Vallikunnam, Alleppey. Often used the pseudonym Soman. Major literary and political figure in the Kerala CPI. Starting out as an activist for the state Congress, he became politicised and joined the CPI after being accused of murder and having to go underground for three years. Became a playwright, later adapting several of his best-known plays as film scripts: **Ramu Kariat**'s ***Mudiyanaya Puthran*** (1961), **A. Vincent**'s ***Ashwamedham*** (1967) and ***Thulabharam*** (1968), **P. Bhaskaran**'s *Mooladanam* (1969), and his own *Sarvekkalu*. His most famous play, and later his directorial début, ***Ningalenne Communistaki*** (*You Made Me a Communist*, 1952) launched the Kerala Peoples' Arts Club (see **IPTA**) and became emblematic of the influential literary socialist-realist tradition in post-Independence Kerala. The leading figure of Kerala's CPI(M) later described the play's lead character as the 'worst and most inane [i]n all of Kerala's radical theatre' (E.M.S. Namboodiripad, 1974). Bhasi also wrote many scripts for the Malayalam studio magnate, **Kunchako**, and for **Sethumadhavan**, Vincent and Bhaskaran. Was a member of the Travancore-Cochin State Legislature (1954) and, later (1956), of the Kerala State Legislature. His autobiography is one of the more detailed chronicles of the Party's late 40s movement against the erstwhile Travancore State ruled by Dewan C.P. Ramaswamy Aiyer. His son, Ajayan, made a promising début directing the critically acclaimed *Perumthachan* (1990).

FILMOGRAPHY: **1970**: ***Ningalenne Communistaki***; **1971**: *Sarasayya*; **1972**: *Oru Sundariyude Katha*; **1973**: ***Enippadikal***; *Madhavikutty*; **1974**: *Chakravakam*; **1975**: *Mucheettu Kalikarante Magal*; **1976**: *Sarvekkalu*; *Ponn*; *Missi*; **1977**: *Yuddha Kandam*; **1978**: *Ente Neela Akasham*; **1979**: *Mochanam*.

BHASKARA DAS (1892-1952)

Born in Madurai as Vellaisamy Thevar. First Tamil film lyricist, writing the songs for the first Tamil talkie, **H.M. Reddy**'s ***Kalidas*** (1931). Already known for several records of his lyrics sung by K.B. Sundarambal, M.S. Subbulakshmi, et al. Worked with the stage group Madurai Balaranjani Sangeeta Sabha, producing many successful **Company Natak** plays. Turned to politics with his Khilafat agitational songs (1919), later writing songs about e.g. the Jallianwala Bagh massacre (1919), many of which were banned by the British government. Wrote musical plays like *Usha Parinayam*, released as 78rpm disc sets by the Broadcast Gramophone Co. Wrote film songs, many addressing reformist themes like temperance and child marriage, for P.V. Rao's *Prahlada* and *Valli Thirumanam* (both 1933), **Raja Chandrasekhar**'s *Raja Desingu* (1936) and **A. Narayanan**'s *Rajasekharan* (1937).

BHASKARAN, P. (b. 1924)

Malayalam director, songwriter and poet. Born in Kodungallour, Kerala. Débuted with **Kariat** (***Neelakuyil***). Associated with 40s/50s cultural movements affiliated to the CPI in Kerala. Newspaper journalist for *Deshabhimani* and *Jayakeralam*. Producer at AIR in Calicut (1959) and briefly editor of Kottayam-based weekly, *Deepika*. Best known as a poet (c.20 books) and songwriter (more than 3000 lyrics in Malayalam) with strong roots in a 30s/40s literary tradition of romantic pastoralism exemplified by major 30s poet Changampuzha. First film as lyricist: *Chandrika* (1950). Acted in his first feature, co-d with Ramu Kariat. Early films attempted a hard-hitting realism but later work was mainly love stories and melodramas with social concerns. Made some revivalist mythologicals in the 70s (e.g. *Srimadh Bhagavad Geeta* and the Saint film, *Jagadguru Adi Shankaran*). Also made shorts, e.g. *Nattarangu*. Acted in and provided lyrics for *Manoratham* (1978). Currently associated with ASIANET, a privately owned satellite channel in Malayalam.

FILMOGRAPHY: **1954**: ***Neelakuyil***; **1956**: ***Rarichan Enna Pauran***; **1958**: *Nair Pidicha Pulivalu*; **1962**: *Laila Majnu*; *Bhagya Jatakam*; **1963**: *Ammeye Kannan*; **1964**: *Adya Kiranangal*; **1965**: *Shyamalachechi*; **1966**: *Tharavatamma*; **1967**: ***Irutinte Atmavu***; *Balyakalasakhi*; ***Anveshichu Kandatiyilla***; *Pareeksha*; **1968**: *Manaswini*; *Lakshaprabhu*; *Aparadhini*; *Kattukurangu*; **1969**: *Mooladanam*; *Kalli Chelamma*; **1970**: *Kurukshetram*; *Stree*; *Ambalapravu*; ***Thurakatha Vathil***; *Kakathampurati*; **1971**: *Moonnupukkal*; *Navavadhu*; *Vithukal*; *Muthassi*; ***Ummachu***; *Vilakku Vangiya Veena*; **1972**: *Aradi Manninte Janmi*; *Snehadeepame Mizhi Thurakku*; **1973**: *Udayam*; *Veendum Prabhatam*; *Rakkuyil*; **1974**: *Oru Pidi Ari*; *Arakallan Mukkal Kallan*; *Thacholi Marumagan Chandu*; **1975**: *Chumadu Thangi*; *Mattoru Seeta*; **1976**: *Appooppan*; *Vazhi Vilakku*; *Srimadh Bhagavad Geeta*; **1977**: *Jagadguru Adi Shankaran*; **1978**: *Vilakkum Velichavum*; **1983**: *Enikku Visakkunu*; **1984**: *Guruvayoor Mahatmiyam*; **1987**: *Nattarangu* (Doc); **1989**: *Vikasikkunna Chirakukal* (Sh); *Puthiya Chakravalangal* (Sh).

BHATAVDEKAR, HARISHCHANDRA SAKHARAM (b. 1868)

Aka Save Dada. Almost certainly the first Indian film-maker. Professional still photographer often portrayed as an amateur, but, in fact, a businessman trading in cameras and film equipment on a nationwide basis. Made several shorts, including one on a wrestling match and one on the antics of monkeys. Best-known footage shows the return from England of R.P. Paranjpye, Minister of Education in Bombay Presidency, which he exhibited with imported shorts in a tent bioscope in Bombay. Sold equipment to Karandikar of **S.N. Patankar**'s company and retired from cinema in 1907. Interviewed in *Screen*, Bombay (30 April 1954).

FILMOGRAPHY: **1899**: *The Wrestlers*; *Man and Monkey*; **1901**: *Landing of Sir M.M. Bhownuggree*; *Atash Behram*; **1902**: *Sir Wrangler Mr R.P. Paranjpye*; **1903**: *Delhi Durbar of Lord Curzon* (all St).

BHATIA, VANRAJ (b. 1926)

One of the few Hindi composers trained in classical Western music. Educated in Bombay. Studied at the Royal Academy of Music, London (1950). Travelled extensively in

Europe listening to opera. Tried to become a professional composer in Europe but eventually returned to Bombay. Provided music for documentaries and advertising films, and some incidental music for Merchant-Ivory's *The Householder* (with Jyotirindra Moitra). Made professional feature début for **Benegal**'s ***Ankur***. Best-known work for Benegal and **Kumar Shahani** (***Tarang***, ***Kasba***). One of the finest composers fusing Indian classical ragas with Western harmonics; his music for *Tarang* was performed as a concert by a chamber orchestra. Often expressed a desire to have his music played on every street corner of Bombay, but is also working on a full opera.

FILMOGRAPHY: **1963**: *The Householder*; **1973**: ***Ankur***; **1975**: ***Nishant***; **1976**: ***Manthan***; ***Bhumika***; **1977**: ***Kondura/Anugraham***; **1978**: ***Junoon***; **1980**: ***Kalyug***; **1981**: *Sazaaye Maut*; ***36 Chowringhee Lane***; **1983**: ***Mandi***; ***Jaane Bhi Do Yaaron***; ***Mohan Joshi Haazir Ho***; **1984**: ***Tarang***; *Hip Hip Hurray*; *Khandaan* (TV); **1985**: *Surkhiyaan*; *Aaghat*; ***Trikaal***; *Khamosh*; **1986**: *Yatra* (TV); ***Susman***; **1987**: ***Pestonjee***; ***Tamas*** (TV); *Mohre*; **1988**: *Bharat Ek Khoj* (TV); **1989**: *Khandaan* (TV); ***Percy***; **1990**: *Lifeline* (TV); ***Kasba***; **1992**: ***Suraj Ka Satwan Ghoda***; *Antarnaad*.

BHATT, BALWANT N. (1909-65)

Hindi director associated with stunt film genre; elder brother of **Nanabhai Bhatt** and uncle of **Mahesh Bhatt**. Born in Porbandar, Gujarat. Started as assistant to **Naval Gandhi** (1928-9) at **Imperial Films** and to **N.B. Vakil** at **Sagar** (1932). Then turned director during the last days of silent cinema at Royal Art, the predecessor of Prakash Pics. Moved to Royal Cinetone with the advent of sound and subsequently to Prakash Pics with *Actress*. Although working mostly in Hindi, made some Gujarati films as well (e.g. *Sansar Leela*, *Seth Sagalsha*, *Divadandi* and a version of *Snehlata*). Became a producer in 1942 (*Dillagi*).

FILMOGRAPHY: **1932**: *Chalta Purza*; **1933**: *Gunehgaar* (all St); *Alif Laila* (*co-d* Shanti Dave); **1934**: *Actress*; *Nai Duniya*; **1935**: *Sansar Leela*; **1936**: *Tope Ka Gola*; *Snehlata*; **1937**: *Challenge*; *His Highness*; **1938**: *Purnima*; **1939**: *Hero No. 1*; *Bijli*; **1940**: *Shamsheerbaaz*; *Suhaag*; **1941**: *Circus Ki Sundari*; *Mala*; *Madhusudhan*; **1942**: *Dillagi*; **1943**: *Aankh Ki Sharam*; **1944**: *Collegian*; **1946**: *Her Highness*; **1947**: *Seth Sagalsha*; **1949**: *Delhi Express*; *Joker*; **1950**: *Circuswale*; *Jodidar*; *Divadandi*; **1951**: *Hamari Shaan*; **1952**: *Mordhwaj*; **1953**: *Khoj*; **1955**: *Shahi Mehmaan*; **1957**: *Hazaar Pariyan*; **1966**: *Nagin Aur Sapera*.

BHATT, MAHESH (b. 1949)

Hindi director born and educated in Bombay. Son of film-maker **Nanabhai Bhatt** whose *Jeevan Rekha* (1974) he scripted. Dropped out of college in 1970. Former assistant to **Raj Khosla**. Along with **N. Chandra** and **J.P. Dutta**, one of an aggressive new generation of commercial Hindi film-makers whose early work was marked by psychological violence. Début film, ***Manzilein Aur Bhi Hain***, was banned for 14 months by the censors, allegedly for mocking the 'sacred institution of marriage'. His melodramas about illegitimacy and extra-marital affairs are more successful on video than as theatrical releases. Soap-opera sentimentalism is often given a voyeuristic edge by claiming autobiographical sources (notably his breakthrough film, ***Arth***). His successful 90s films are often love stories starring daughter Pooja Bhatt (*Dil Hai Ke Maanta Nahin*). Shifted increasingly to **Doordarshan** (e.g. *Daddy*) and made the first film production of STAR's Hindi channel Zee-TV, *Phir Teri Kahani Yaad Aayi*. Wrote a biography of U.G. Krishnamurthi. Currently editor of a video film magazine.

FILMOGRAPHY (* act only): **1973**: ***Manzilein Aur Bhi Hain***; **1976**: *Vishwasghaat*; **1978**: *Naya Daur*; **1979**: *Lahu Ke Do Rang*; **1980**: *Abhimanyu*; **1982**: ***Arth***; **1984**: ***Saaransh***; *Sheeshe Ka Ghar**; **1985**: *Janam*; **1986**: *Ashiana*; *Naam*; **1987**: *Kaash*; *Thikana*; *Aaj*; **1988**: *Kabzaa*; **1989**: *Daddy*; *Zameen*; **1990**: *Awaargi*; *Jurm*; *Aashiqui*; **1991**: *Haq**; *Deshwasi**; *Dil Hai Ke Maanta Nahin*; *Swayam*; *Saathi*; *Sadak*; **1992**: *Saatwan Asmaan*; *Junoon*; *Tadipaar;* **1993**: *Gumrah*; *Gunah*; *Sir*; *Phir Teri Kahani Yaad Aayi*; *Hum Hain Rahi Pyar Ke*.

BHATT, NANABHAI N. (b. 1915)

Hindi-Gujarati director; born as Yeshwant Bhatt in Porbandar, Gujarat. Seminal influence on the post-WW2 Hindi B-movie. Entered films as sound recordist at Prakash Pics where his elder brother **Balwant Bhatt** worked. First scripts under the name of Batuk Bhatt. Early career as director with stunt-movie producer Chandrarao Kadam. With **Babubhai Mistri**, was one of the founders of **Homi Wadia**'s Basant Pics (1945), then owned Deepak Pics in Bombay (1946). Début with the classic **Nadia** double-role crime movie ***Muqabala***. Films often based on cheaper variations of Prakash Pics megabudget mythologicals featuring tales from the *Ramayana* (*Ram Janma*). Also known for Arabian Nights fantasies (*Baghdad*, *Baghdad Ki Raatein*, *Arabian Nights*). Has often presented elaborate special effects, e.g. the famous scene of the sword fight between two invisible men in *Sinbad the Sailor*. Also made crime movies (*Kangan*, *Police Detective*). Appeared in the documentary about Nadia, *Fearless - The Hunterwali Story* (1993). Father of film-maker **Mahesh Bhatt**.

FILMOGRAPHY: **1942**: ***Muqabala***; **1945**: *Chalis Karod*; **1946**: *Maa Baap Ki Laaj*; **1947**: *Meerabai*; **1949**: *Shaukeen*; *Veer Ghatotkach*; **1950**: *Hamara Ghar*; *Janmashthami*; *Veer Babruwahan*; **1951**: *Lakshmi Narayan*; *Daman*; *Lav Kush*; *Ram Janma*; **1952**: *Apni Izzat*; *Baghdad*; *Sinbad the Sailor*; **1954**: *Toote Khilone*; *Watan*; **1956**: *Kismet*; **1957**: *Mr X*; *Ustad*; **1958**: *Chaalbaaz*; *Son of Sinbad*; **1959**: *Bazigar*; *Daaka*; *Kangan*; *Madam XYZ*; *Naya Sansar*; **1960**: *Lal Qila*; *Police Detective*; *Zimbo Comes to Town*; **1961**: *Teen Ustad*; **1962**: *Baghdad Ki Raatein*; *Rocket Girl*; **1963**: *Alapiranthavan*; *Bhootnath*; *Cobra Girl*; **1964**: *Samson*; **1965**: *Adhi Raat Ke Baad*; *Bekhabar*; **1966**: *Shankar Khan*; **1967**: *Arabian Nights*; **1968**: *Jung Aur Aman*; **1974**: *Jeevan Rekha*; **1975**: *Balak Aur Jaanwar*; **1976**: *Dharti Mata*; **1981**: *Gajara Maru*; **1982**: *Jaya Parvati Vrat*.

BHATT, VIJAY JAGNESHWAR (1907-93)

Hindi and Marathi director born in Palitana, Saurashtra, best known for classic *Ramayana* extravaganzas with **Shobhana Samarth**. Educated in Gujarat and Bombay. Studied electrical engineering. Started as playwright (e.g. successful Gujarati play *Lakho Phulani*) and writer in silent era. Provided stories for silent films, e.g. **Nagendra Majumdar**'s *Panima Aag*, *Fearless Phantom* and K.P. Bhave's *Vanthel Veshya* (all 1926), **R.S. Choudhury**'s *Heer Ranjha* (1929) and **Moti Gidwani**'s *Gulam* (1931). Partner with his elder brother Shankarbhai J. Bhatt in Royal Films (1928), later also distributor (Royal Pictures Corp). Founded Prakash Pics, later Prakash Studio (1933-71), also with his brother Shankarbhai as producer. Their younger brother Harsukh Jagneshwar Bhatt assisted Vijay for a while (1947-52) before co-directing three films with Bhalchandra Shukla and eventually going solo in 1957. Vijay started in stunt films (e.g. ***State Express*** and ***Leatherface***) and in socials (notably ***Samaj Ko Badal Dalo***). Launched his *Ramayana* series with the Samarth hit ***Bharat Milap***, consolidated with ***Ramrajya***, attempting a Hindu version of the costumed Urdu historical, rather than the more conventional special-effects mythological, although *Ramrajya*'s climax uses special effects in plenty. Followed this with *Rambaan*, *Ramayan* and a second *Ramrajya*. Made melodramas incorporating the legend of classical Indian music, e.g. the major hit ***Baiju Bawra*** and ***Goonj Uthi Shehnai***. Sometimes claimed that his interest in Hindu fantasy movies was a logical extension of his Gandhian sympathies. His autobiography was serialised in the journal *Janmabhoomi* (1968).

FILMOGRAPHY: **1937**: *Khwab Ki Duniya*; **1938**: ***State Express***; **1939**: ***Leatherface***; **1940**: *Ek Hi Bhool*; ***Narsi Bhagat***; **1942**: ***Bharat Milap/Bharat Bhet***; **1943**: ***Ramrajya***; **1945**: *Vikramaditya*; **1947**: ***Samaj Ko Badal Dalo***; **1948**: *Rambaan*; **1952**: ***Baiju Bawra***; **1953**: *Shri Chaitanya Mahaprabhu*; **1954**: *Ramayan*; **1956**: *Patrani*; **1959**: ***Goonj Uthi Shehnai***; **1960**: ***Angulimal***; **1962**: *Bapu Ne Kaha Tha* (Doc); ***Hariyali Aur Raasta***; **1965**: *Himalay Ki God Mein*; **1967**: *Ramrajya*; **1971**: *Banphool*; **1977**: *Heera Aur Pattha*.

BHATTACHARYA, ABHI (1922-93)

Lead actor in late 40s Bengali melodramas, débuting in Bengali version of **Nitin Bose**'s bilingual ***Nauka Dubi/Milan*** (**Dilip Kumar** took the role in Hindi). Worked at **New Theatres** (***Yatrik***) and in independent productions of former New Theatres directors Nitin Bose, **Debaki Bose** and **Bimal Roy** (***Biraj Bahu***). Often played the upright hero, evoking the Westernised liberal stereotype often used to characterise pre-WW2 Bengali urban upper middle class. Introduced this image into the Hindi cinema, notably in **Hrishikesh Mukherjee** films (e.g. ***Anuradha***), extending it into a tragic dimension (e.g. **Sohrab Modi**'s ***Jailor***). This image was later used to devastating effect by **Ghatak** in ***Subarnarekha***, where he played the upright Ishwar. Acted extensively with **Satyen Bose** as well as in **Shakti Samanta**'s ***Aradhana*** and his Hindi-Bengali bilinguals (e.g. ***Amanush***). Also featured regularly in mythologicals by **S. Fattelal** (*Jagadguru Shankaracharya*, ***Ayodhyapati***), **Babubhai Mistri** (*Mahabharat*, *Har Har Gange*) and Ashish Kumar devotionals.

FILMOGRAPHY: **1946**: ***Nauka Dubi/Milan***; **1948**: *Mayer Dak*; **1949**: *Bisher Dhoan*; **1950**: *Sheshbesh*; **1951**: *Bhairab Mantra*; *Paritran*; ***Ratnadeep/Ratnadeepam***; **1952**: *Chitta Banhiman*; ***Yatrik***; **1953**: *Naina*; *Rami Dhoban*; *Bhor Hoye Elo*; **1954**: *Ankush*; *Amar Prem*; ***Biraj Bahu***; *Jagriti*; *Parichay*; *Shobha*; **1955**: *Jagadguru Shankaracharya*; *Naata*; **1956**: ***Ayodhyapati***; *Gauri Puja*; *Keemat*; *Sailaab*; *Suryamukhi*; **1957**: *Aparadhi Kaun*; *Chhote Babu*; *Ek Gaon Ki Kahani*; *Madhu Malati*; **1958**: ***Jailor***; *Teesri Gali*; **1959**: *Deep Jalta Rahe*; *Fashionable Wife*; *Hum Bhi Insaan Hain*; *Love Marriage*; **1960**: ***Anuradha***; *Bade Ghar Ki Bahu*; *Trunk Call*; **1961**: *Do Bhai*; *Ramleela*; *Madhya Rater Tara*; *Shola Aur Shabnam*; **1962**: *Aashiq*; ***Subarnarekha***; *Vallah Kya Baat Hai*; **1964**: *Daal Mein Kala*; ***Dosti***; ***Kohraa***; **1965**: *Mahabharat*; **1966**: *Hum Kahan Ja Rahe Hain*; *Mere Lal*; *Netaji Subhashchandra Bose*; *Pinjre Ke Panchhi*; *Pari*; **1967**: *Badrinath Yatra*; *Ghar Ka Chirag*; *Jab Yaad Kisiki Aati Hai*; *Milan Ki Raat*; *Naunihal*; **1968**: ***Ashirwad***; *Har Har Gange*; *Jyot Jale*; **1969**: ***Aradhana***; *Balak*; *Dharti Kahe Pukar Ke*; *Ek Masoom*; *Jyoti*; *Mahal*; *Meri Bhabhi*; *Prarthana*; *Ram Bhakta Hanuman*; *Sambandh*; **1970**: *Aan Milo Sajna*; *Bhagwan Parashuram*; *Maa Ka Anchal*; *Pavitra Papi*; *Puraskaar*; *Sharafat*; **1971**: *Amar Prem*; ***Andaz***; *Door Ka Rahi*; ***Dushman***; *Hathi Mere Saathi*; *Kal Aaj Aur Kal*; *Mata Vaishno Devi*; *Memsaab*; *Parwana*; *Paraya Dhan*; ***Mere Apne***; *Maryada*; *Sansar*; *Seema*; *Tulasi Vivah*; **1972**: *Anuraag*; *Hari Darshan*; *Anokhi Pehchan*; *Savera*; *Seeta Aur Geeta*; *Anokha Milan*; *Bankelal*; *Samadhi*; **1973**: *Kahani Hum Sub Ki*; *Jhoom Utha Akash*; *Mera Desh Mera Dharam*; *Kahani Kismat Ki*; *Mehmaan*; **1974**: *Phir Kab Milogi*; *Ganga*; *Bhagat Dhanna Jat*; *Kasauti*; *Dost*; *Har Har Mahadev*; *Imtehan*; *Kisan Aur Bhagwan*; *Prem Shastra*; ***Amanush***; *Balak Dhruv*; **1975**: *Chaitali*; *Kehte Hain Mujhko Raja*; *Maya Machhindra*; *Pratigya*; *Badnaam*; *Phanda*; **1976**: *Bhagwan Samaye Sansar Mein*; *Do Anjaane*; *Dus Numbri*; *Meera Shyam*; *Sharafat Chhod Di Maine*; *Phool Aur Insaan*; **1977**: *Behula Lakhinder*, *Aankh Ka Tara*; *Anurodh*; *Gayatri Mahima*; *Hatyara*; *Khel Kismat Ka*; *Ooparwala Jaane*; *Solah Shukrawar*; **1978**: *Ganga Sagar*; *Dil Se Mile Dil*; *Mera Rakshak*; **1979**: *Dil Ka Heera*; *Raja Harishchandra*; **1980**: *Angar*; *Taxi Chor*; **1981**: *Ganga Maang Rahi Balidan*; *Barsaat Ki Ek Raat/Anusandhan*; **1983**: *Bekhabar*; *Gumnaam Hai Koi*; *Sant Ravidas Ki Amar Kahani*; *Dhat Tere Ki*; *Navratri*; **1984**: *Shravan Kumar*; *Sulagte Arman*; *Harishchandra Shaibya*; **1985**: *Mayuri* (H); **1986**: *Woh Din Aayega*; **1987**: *Daku Hasina*; *Sadak Chhaap*; *Khudgarz*; *Mera Karam Mera Dharam*; **1989**: *Sansar*; *Santosh*; *Swarna Trishna*.

BHATTACHARYA, ARDHENDU (1955-92)

Khasi-Assamese director born in Shillong. Postgraduate in philosophy at Shantiniketan; then joined **FTII**. Worked in Bombay, later in Gauhati. Made documentaries while lecturing in philosophy. His only feature, ***Manik Raitong*** (1984), is in Khasi, a North Eastern tribal language. Died before finishing a tv series based on Birendra Kumar Bhattacharya's novel, *Mrityunjaya*.

BHATTACHARYA, BASU (b. 1934)

Bengali director born in Murshidabad, West Bengal, into Brahmin family which provided hereditary priests to the Cossimbazar royal family. Educated in Behrampore. Moved to Calcutta to attend college, then to Bombay in the early 50s. Started as assistant to **Bimal Roy** (1958); married Roy's daughter Rinki, a noted critic. First film, the **Raj Kapoor** and **Waheeda Rehman** musical ***Teesri Kasam***, has several major 60s song hits. ***Anubhav*** and *Avishkar* represent stereotypical Hindi New Indian Cinema products of the 70s, a 'realist' emphasis being reduced to a concern with marital problems of upper-class couples. Served on several influential governmental committees concerning film policy, including the Working Group on National Film Policy (1980) and the board of the **NFDC**. Produced **Sai Paranjpye**'s ***Sparsh*** (1979). President of Indian Film Directors Association (1976-9). Father of director Aditya Bhattacharya (***Raakh***, 1988).

FILMOGRAPHY: **1966**: ***Teesri Kasam***; *Uski Kahani*; **1971**: ***Anubhav***; **1973**: *Avishkar*; **1975**: *Daku*; *Tumhara Kalloo*; *Sangat*; **1977**: *Known Yet Not Known* (Doc); **1978**: *Madhu Malati*; **1979**: *Grihapravesh*; **1982**: *Science India* (Doc); **1983**: *Horky Podzim S Vuni Manga* (co-d Jiri Sequens); **1985**: *Anveshan* (TV); **1986**: *Panchavati*; *Solar Energy* (Doc); **1991**: *Ek Saas Zindagi*.

BHATTACHARYA, BIJON (1917-78)

Actor, playwright, writer, scenarist, composer of stage music and theatre director. Born in Faridpur (now Bangladesh). Teenage years strongly influenced by Gandhi's Satyagraha agitations. Became a Marxist during WW2. Part of radical literary group, the Agami Chakra, and joined CPI in 1942. Founder member of **IPTA** for which he wrote *Aagun* (based on Binoy Ghosh's novel, *Laboratory*), *Jaban Bandi*, and one of modern Indian theatre's most influential plays, *Nabanna*. Dealing with the experience of the 1943 famine, the play as first staged by Bhattacharya and **Sombhu Mitra** (1943) tried to define post-WW2 documentary realism, which had a major impact later in theatre and cinema, in e.g. **Ghatak**, **Mrinal Sen** and **K.A. Abbas**'s ***Dharti Ke Lal*** (1946). Acted in **Nemai Ghosh**'s ***Chinnamul***. Left IPTA in 1948. Scenarist at **Filmistan** (1948-50). Wrote **Jaswantlal**'s mammoth hit ***Nagin*** (1954), loosely adapting his play *Jiyankanya*. Returned to Calcutta where he ran his Calcutta Theatres (1950-70) and the Kabach Kundal (1970-7). Did the classic scripts for **Nirmal Dey**'s **Uttam Kumar** movies (***Basu Parivar***, 1952; ***Sharey Chuattar***, 1953). Wrote the story of Binu Das Gupta's *Daktar Babu* (1958), dialogues for **Asit Sen**'s *Trishna*, in which he also acted, and story/dial. for Piyush Ganguly's *Debigarjan* (1984). Featured regularly in Ghatak's films, e.g. as father in ***Meghe Dhaka Tara***, Ishwar's friend Harprasad in ***Subarnarekha***, the Sanskrit scholar in ***Jukti Takko Aar Gappo***. His presence and performance in Sen's ***Padatik*** helped set the tone of the film's political address. His interest in religious motifs, which eventually turned into obscurantism, earned him criticism from former Marxist colleagues.

FILMOGRAPHY: **1950**: ***Tathapi***; ***Chinnamul***; **1954**: *Haan*; *Shoroshi*; **1959**: *Bari Theke Paliye*; **1960**: ***Meghe Dhaka Tara***; **1961**: ***Komal Gandhar***; **1962**: ***Subarnarekha***; **1964**: *Kashtipathar*; **1965**: *Trishna*; **1966**: *Swapnaniye*; **1969**: *Parineeta*; **1971**: *Nabaraag*; *Pratham Basanta*; *Sona Boudi*; **1972**: *Archana*; *Bohurupee*; **1973**: ***Padatik***; **1974**: ***Jukti Takko Aar Gappo***; **1975**: *Arjun*; **1977**: *Bhola Moira*; *Swati*; **1978**: ***Dooratwa***.

BHATTACHARYA, DHIRAJ (1905-59)

Actor born in Jessore (now Bangladesh). Degree in literature. Started as a policeman, then Bengali film star from the 20s to the 50s. Began at **Madan Theatres** in **Jyotish Bannerjee** silents. Worked with **Modhu Bose** in ***Giribala*** and with **Priyanath Ganguly** (*Kal Parinaya*, *Jamuna Puliney*). Developed his reputation as actor in films like **Charu Roy**'s seminal ***Bangalee***, Ardhendu Sen's ***Adarsha Hindu Hotel*** (having earlier done the role of Hajari Prasad on stage, at the Rungmahal Theatre, 1953), and several **Premendra Mitra** films, including ***Samadhan***, *Kuasha*, *Kankantala Light Railway*, *Moyla Kagaj*. Known later for his refined villain roles. One of the few Bengali stars not to emerge from the **Calcutta Theatres** stage, he turned to the theatre later as an established film star, acting in plays like *Sindhu Gaurab* (1932) and *Charitraheen* (1935). His autobiography was published in two volumes, one dealing with his life as a policeman, the other, on his film career, came out in 1956.

FILMOGRAPHY (* also d): **1925**: *Sati Lakshmi*; **1930**: ***Giribala***; *Kal Parinaya*; *Mrinalini*; **1932**: *Nauka Dubi* (all St); *Krishnakanter Will*; **1933**: *Jamuna Puliney/Radha Krishna*; *Annapurna* (St); **1934**: *Chand Saudagar*; *Daksha Yagna*; *Rajnati Basantsena*; *Seeta*; **1935**: *Kanthahaar*; *Satya Pathe*; *Basabdatta*; **1936**: *Krishna Sudama*; ***Bangalee***; ***Sonar Sansar***; *Bala Ki Raat*; *Joyar Bhanta**; *Chino Haar*; **1937**: *Rajgee*; *Mandir*; **1938**: ***Sarbajanin Bibahotsab***; *Abhinaya*; *Rupor Jhumko*; **1939**: *Pathik*; *Nara Narayan*; *Parasmani*; **1940**: ***Kumkum/Kumkum the Dancer***; *Byabadhan*; *Rajkumarer Nirbashan*; **1941**: *Epar Opar*; *Nandini*; *Banglar Meye*; **1942**: *Pashan Devata*; *Milan*; *Avayer Biye*; **1943**: *Sahadharmini*; *Swamir Ghar*; ***Samadhan***; *Dwanda*; *Shri Ramanuja*; *Nilanguriya*; *Daabi*; ***Shahar Theke Dooray***; ***Wapas***; **1944**: *Bideshini*; *Iraada*; **1945**: *Kato Door*; ***Mane Na Mana***; *Kalankini*; **1947**: *Natun Khabar*; *Giribala*; **1948**: *Pratibad*; *Jayjatra/Vijay Yatra*; *Kalo Chhaya*; *Sankha Sindoor*; *Taruner Swapna*; **1949**: *Kuasha*; **1950**: *Rakter Tan*; *Kankantala Light Railway*; *Eki Gramer Chhele*; *Kankal*; *Pattharar Kahini*; **1951**: *Chiner Putul*; *Niyati*; *Sparshamani*; *Setu*; **1952**: *Rani Bhabani*; **1953**: *Chirantani*; *Chikitsa Sankat*; *Dui Beyai*; **1954**: *Maa-o-Chhele*; *Moyla Kagaj*; *Ora Thake Odhare*; *Maraner Pare*; *Sati*; *Amar Prem*; **1955**: *Sanjher Pradeep*; *Dakinir Char*; **1956**: *Mahanisha*; *He Maha Manab*; *Manraksha*; *Amar Bou*; *Rajpath*; **1957**: *Bardidi*; ***Adarsha Hindu Hotel***; *Raat Ekta*;

Molina Devi and Dhiraj Bhattacharya in *Abhagin* (1938)

Neelachaley Mahaprabhu; *Shrimatir Sansar*; *Tamasha*; **1958**: *Manmoyee Girls' School*; *Bagha Jatin*; *Leela Kanka*; *Dhoomketu*; **1960**: *Gariber Meye*; *Aparadh*.

BHAVNANI, MOHAN DAYARAM (1903-62)

Hindi director born in Hyderabad, Sind. Studied at College of Technology, Manchester (1921-4), then studied film-making in Germany at UFA (1924). Contracted to **Kohinoor** (1925-6) where his **Sulochana** films were the earliest efforts in the Indian cinema to create a Hollywood-type movie star, e.g. ***Cinema Queen*** where she plays a famous actress with whom the painter hero falls in love, or ***Wildcat of Bombay*** where she played multiple roles. Joined **Imperial** (1927-9), where he interpreted Parsee Theatre-derived costume dramas, filming the first-ever version of **Kashmiri**'s *Khwab-e-Hasti*. *Vasantsena* was the first Kannada intertitled film. Returned to Germany to study sound film technique (1930-1); became independent producer with Indian Art Prod. (1931-2), Ajanta Cinetone (1933-4) and his own Bhavnani Prod. (1935-48). Sound début was a flop, but it introduced **Durga Khote**. Hired Premchand to script ***Mazdoor***, representing the author's only direct encounter with film, following it with the unemployment melodrama ***Jagran***. Produced and directed the first full-length colour film shot on 16mm Kodachrome and blown up to 35mm, ***Ajit***. Joined **Films Division** and became its first Chief Producer (1948-55). In 1958 Bhavnani followed up an invitation from Chou En-Lai to make a documentary on China and travelled extensively throughout the country shooting with cameramen Kishore Rege and S.K. Kulkarni. His wife Enakshi Rama Rao, who acted in some of his early films (e.g. *Vasantsena*), became a noted dancer and author of the book *The Dance of India* (1965).

FILMOGRAPHY: **1925**: ***Cinema Queen***; *Matri Prem*; *Veer Bala*; *Seth Sagalsha*; **1926**: *Pagal Premi*; *Diwan Bhamasha*; *Mena Kumari*; *Ra Kawat*; *Samrat Shiladitya*; *Bhamto Bhoot*; **1927**: *Naseeb Ni Lili*; *Daya Ni Devi*; *Trust Your Wife*; ***Wildcat of Bombay***; ***Gamdani Gori***; **1928**: *Pandav Patrani*; **1929**: *Hawai Swar*; *Khwab-e-Hasti*; *Mysore, Gem City of India* (Doc); *Khedda* (Doc); **1930**: *Vasantsena* (all St); **1931**: *Shakuntala*; *Farebi Jaal*; *Lafanga Langoor* (Sh); **1932**: *Veer Kunal*; **1933**: *Afzal*; *Rangila Rajput*; **1934**: *Dard-e-Dil*; ***Mazdoor***; *Sair-e-Paristan*; **1935**: *Jung Bahadur*; *Navjeevan*; *Shadi Ki Raat*; **1936**: *Dilawar*; *Garib Parwar*; ***Jagran***; *Wrestling* (Doc); **1937**: *Zambo the Ape Man*; **1938**: ***Double Cross***; *Himalay Ki Beti*; *Yangrilla*; **1939**: *Zambo Ka Beta*; **1940**: *Jhoothi Sharm*; *Prem Nagar*; **1945**: *Biswi Sadi*; **1946**: *Rang Bhoomi*; **1948**: ***Ajit***; **1949**: *Vale of Kashmir* (Doc); **1950**: *The Private Life of a Silkworm* (Doc); **1951**: *Lest We Forget* (Doc); **1952**: *Kumaon Hills* (Doc); **1953**: *Folk Dances of India* (Doc); *Republic Day Record* (Doc); **1955**: *Republic Day 1955* (Doc); **1956**: *Operation Khedda* (Doc); **1957**: *The Himalayan Tapestry* (Doc).

BHIMSINGH, A. (1924-78)

Tamil director; also worked in other South Indian languages and in Hindi. Born in Chittor, AP. Started as proofreader for the Telugu newspaper *Andhra Prabha*. Assistant to **Krishnan-Panju** in late 40s at **AVM**. First film, *Ammaiyappan*, was major Tamil hit. *Raja Rani*, scripted by **Karunanidhi**, consolidated the strong bid for a politically interventionist melodrama sponsored by the DMK movement (see **DMK Film**). Set up Buddha Pics (1956) with *Pati Bhakti* and introduced a commercially successful formula centred around family plots, usually with **Ganesan** and composers Vishwanathan-Ramamurthy. Later also helped found the Newtone Studio in Madras. From the early 60s, concentrated as much on Hindi films as on Tamil, often adapting his own and other directors' work, e.g. his best-known Hindi film *Admi*, which borrows from the Ganesan hit *Alayamani*. Made the bizarre comedy *Sadhu Aur Shaitan*, featuring the uninhibited duo of **Kishore Kumar** and Mehmood. Later films include the Jayakantan scripts ***Sila Nerangalil Sila Manithargal*** and ***Oru Nadigai Nadagam Parkiral*** representing Tamil actress Laxmi's best-known work. Many of his film titles, for superstitious reasons, begin with the Tamil syllable 'Pa' and show a statue of the Buddha.

FILMOGRAPHY: **1954**: *Ammaiyappan*; **1956**: *Raja Rani*; *Nane Raja*; **1958**: *Thirumanam*; *Pati Bhakti*; **1959**: *Bhagapirivinai*; *Ponnu Vilayum Bhoomi*; ***President Panchatcharam***; *Sahodari*; **1960**: *Padikkatha Methai*; *Kalathur Kannamma*; *Aai Phirse Bahar*; *Petra Manam*; **1961**: *Maavoori Ammayi*; *Pallum Pazhamum*; ***Pavamanippu***; ***Pasamalar***; **1962**: *Pavitra Prema*; *Parthal Pasi Theerum*; *Main Chup Rahungi*; *Raakhi*; *Senthamarai*; *Bandha Pasam*; *Padithal Mattu Pothuma*; **1963**: *Paar Magale Paar*; **1964**: *Pooja Ke Phool*; *Pachai Vilakku*; **1965**: *Khandaan*; *Pazhani*; **1966**: *Papa Pariharam*; **1967**: *Meharbaan*; *Paladai*; **1968**: *Admi*; *Gauri*; *Sadhu Aur Shaitan*; **1969**: *Bhai Bahen*; *Manishichina Maguva*; **1970**: *Oke Kutumbam*; *Gopi*; *Pathukappu*; **1972**: *Joru Ka Gulam*; *Malik*; *Sub Ka Saathi*; *Maa Inti Jyothi*; **1973**: *Loafer*; **1974**: *Naya Din Nayi Raat*; *Patha Poojai*; **1975**: *Bhagasthulu*; *Ragam*; *Amanat*; **1976**: *Bangaru Manishi*; *Chiranjeevi*; *Kanavan Manaivi*; ***Sila Nerangalil Sila Manithargal***; **1977**: *Evaru Devudu*; *Nee Vazhavendum*; *Yaaron Ka Yaar*; *Nirakudam*; *Sneham*; **1978**: *Vamsa Jyothi*; *Karunamayudu*; ***Oru Nadigai Nadagam Parkiral***; *Iraivan Kodutha Varam*; *Karunai Ullam*; *Kayi Pidithaval*; *Mattoli*.

BHOLE, KESHAVRAO VAMAN (1896-1967)

Music director born in Amravati, Maharashtra. Exposure to Western orchestras accompanying silent films prompted him to experiment successfully with orchestral compositions: 'The tones of the instruments, their timbre and how such diverse instruments could play together without sounding atonal, engaged my mind,' he wrote in his book *Mazhe Sangeet: Rachana Ani Digdarshan* (1964). First introduced piano, Hawaiian guitar and violin for Vartak's vanguard play *Andhalyanchi Shala*, staged by the Natyamanwantar group (1933). The music also performed the unusual function of tying the play to a fixed running time. Moved to **Prabhat** Studio (1933), replacing the more orthodox **Govindrao Tembe**, and scored some of the studio's best-known hits. For ***Amritmanthan***, the actors rehearsed to a score played live, tuning their performance rhythm to the music. The scales were also chosen to counterpoint the actors' speaking voices. Bhole's impact on performance idioms is most evident in ***Sant Tukaram***, where **Vishnupant Pagnis**'s outstanding achievement owes much to the score. Left Prabhat with **Raja Nene**, **Dharmadhikari** et al., working with them independently for some years.

FILMOGRAPHY: 1932: *Sant Sakhubai*; *Krishnavatar*; 1934: ***Amritmanthan***; 1935: ***Chandrasena***; 1936: ***Rajput Ramani***; ***Sant Tukaram***; 1937: ***Kunku/Duniya Na Mane***; 1938: ***Mazha Mulga/Mera Ladka***; 1940: ***Sant Dnyaneshwar***; 1941: ***Sant Sakhu***; 1942: ***Daha Wajta/Dus Baje***; 1944:

Ramshastri; **1945**: *Taramati*; **1947**: *Kuber*; **1948**: *Bhagyarekha*; **1951**: *Parijatak/Shri Krishna Satyabhama*.

BHOSLE, ASHA (b. 1933)

Singer born in Satara, Maharashtra. Trained by her father, Dinanath Mangeshkar. With her sister, **Lata Mangeshkar**, she dominated Indian film (playback) singing for more than three decades, releasing 20,000-plus songs in more than 14 languages. Introduced to film in **Ravindra Dave**'s *Chunaria* (1948). First solo number in Jagdish Sethi's *Raat Ki Rani* (1949). Best-known early work with music director **O.P. Nayyar**, continuing **Geeta Dutt**'s singing style and borrowing from Latin American dance music (e.g. the samba) as well as from North American big band pop featuring large brass sections. Two songs in 1957, *Mister John* (in Shankar Mukherjee's *Baarish*) and *Ina mina dika* (in **M.V. Raman**'s ***Aasha***) were landmarks in the Benny Goodman-style swing music pioneered by **C. Ramchandra**. The jazz influence was transformed into popular electronic music mainly through several 70s duets with **Kishore Kumar**, often composed by **R.D. Burman**.

BILIMORIA, DINSHAW (b. 1904)

Actor-director born in Kirkee. Usually described as the highest-paid silent star in India. Formed the celebrated lead couple with **Sulochana** esp. at **Imperial**. Introduced in stunt movie-derived historicals and mythologicals adapting Maratha legends at **N.D. Sarpotdar**'s United Pics. First two films at **Imperial**, **Bhavnani**'s ***Wildcat of Bombay*** and **Choudhury**'s *Anarkali*, were massive hits for him and Sulochana. His John Barrymore-style image was born in elaborate costume fantasies opposite Sulochana's Orientalised 'Queen of Romance', a reference elaborated later by some of the biggest directors of the silent era, e.g. **Choudhury**, **Chandulal Shah**, **Homi Master**, **Jaswantlal** and **Nanubhai Vakil**. Several of his silent hits were remade as sound films, notably ***Indira MA*** and *Anarkali*. Acted in some films at **Ranjit**.

FILMOGRAPHY (* also d): **1925**: *Chhatrapati Sambhaji*; **1926**: *Dha Cha Ma*; *Tai Teleen*; *Umaji Naik*; **1927**: ***Wildcat of Bombay***; **1928**: *Anarkali*; *Pandav Patrani*; *Qatil Kathiyani*; *Madhuri*; *Pita Ke Parmeshwar*; *Rajrang*; **1929**: *Khwab-e-Hasti*; *Mewad Nu Moti*; *Punjab Mail*; *Heer Ranjha*; *Rajputani*; *Hawai Swar*; **1930**: *Pahadi Kanya*; *Rasili Radha*; *Diwani Dilbar*; **1931**: *Azadi Nu Jung*; *Baghdad Nu Bulbul*; *Hoor-e-Roshan*; *Mojili Mashuq*; *Noor-e-Alam*; ***Prem Jogan*** (all St); ***Devi Devayani***; **1932**: *Sati Madalasa*; **1933**: *Daku Ki Ladki*; *Saubhagya Sundari*; *Sulochana*; **1934**: ***Gul Sanobar***; ***Indira MA***; *Khwab-e-Hasti*; ***Piya Pyare***; *Devaki*; **1935**: *Anarkali*; ***Do Ghadi Ki Mauj***; *Pujarini*; **1936**: ***Bambai Ki Billi***; *Jungle Queen*; *Shaan-e-Hind*; **1937**: *Jagat Kesari*; *New Searchlight*; *Wah Ri Duniya*; **1939**: *Prem Ki Jyot*; **1940**: *Azadi-e-Watan**; **1942**: ***Jawani Ki Pukar****.

BILIMORIA, FALI (b. 1923)

Born in Bombay; son of a lawyer. Abandoned medical studies (1946) and went into politics. Documentary director and producer since late 40s. Early career with **P.V. Pathy** and **Paul Zils**. Established Documentary Unit: India (1947) and later the Art Films of Asia (1952), both in partnership with Zils. When Zils returned to Germany, started his own Fali Bilimoria Prod. (1959). Best-known films on agricultural technology on behalf of US Technical Co-operation Missions in the context of the controversial Green Revolution promised by imported fertiliser, and also on American Public Law 480 aid to India. Also made films on co-operative movements in handloom, fisheries, housing, agriculture etc. supporting the 'Colombo Plan' foreign aid to India. Clients include Shell, British Transport, Deutsche Condor, the USIS and private American sponsors for whom, on one occasion, he filmed an interview with Jawaharlal Nehru to prove to the US State Department that Nehru was not a Communist (1958). Several noted films blur the distinction between documentary and fiction narrative by introducing professional actors (e.g. *A Tiny Thing Brings Death*, documentary on malaria starring **Sombhu Mitra**). Some titles in the filmography, all documentaries, were probably only produced by Bilimoria. Also made numerous advertising films. Retired in 1987.

FILMOGRAPHY (* co-d **Paul Zils**): **1947**: *Congress Session 1947*; **1948**: *Congress Session 1948*; *Mother/Child/Community**; **1949**: *White Magic**; *The Last Jewel**; *Flying Goods Wagon*; *General Motors in India**; *A Tiny Thing Brings Death**; **1954**: *Ujala**; **1956**: *Textiles*; *A Village in Travancore*; *Iron and Steel*; **1957**: *The Land of Bengal*; *Fifty Miles from Poona**; **1958**: *The Vanishing Tribe**; *Interview with Jawaharlal Nehru*; **1960**: *Four Families*; **1961**: *Rivers of Life/Jeevan Ki Nadiyan*; *Coir Worker*; *New Marketplace*; **1962**: *Comparative Religions*; **1965**: *The Weavers*; **1966**: *US Vice President Humphrey Visits India*; **1967**: *The House that Ananda Built*; **1968**: *Water*; **1972**: *Last Raja*; **1974**: *Look At Us Now*; **1975**: *Women of India*; **1976**: *A Small Family*; *There is Another Way*; **1980**: *Warning Signal*; **1982**: *The Ganga Bridge*; *People of India: The Anglo-Indians*.

BISWAS, ANIL (b. 1914)

Bengali and Hindi composer born in Barisal (now Bangladesh). A talented tabla player since infancy, he worked in amateur theatre as child singer. Became a political activist as a student and was associated with terrorist insurgency movements in Bengal. Repeatedly jailed in early 30s. Received early assignments as musician from **Kazi Nazrul Islam** at the Megaphone gramophone company; then scored and acted in several commercial **Calcutta Theatres** stage productions, notably in the Rangmahal theatre. Moved to Bombay (1934) where he was first employed by Ram Daryani's Eastern Art Syndicate, then by **Sagar** and its successor National Studio (1936-42) and finally by **Bombay Talkies** (1942-6) before turning freelance. Best-known compositions are among the most effective film adaptations of theatrical music, with 12-piece orchestras and full-blooded choral effects in e.g. the Amirbai Karnataki songs of **Gyan Mukherjee**'s ***Kismet*** and even more so in **Mehboob**'s early films. His recitative prose songs in ***Roti*** helped give the film its parable dimension and came close to an indigenous Brechtian mode. His work is a rare effort in popular Hindi film to define a cultural-political avant-garde. Later composed music for **K.A. Abbas**'s films (e.g. the famous 'songless' ***Munna***) and for **Mahesh Kaul**. Music co-d for *Begunah*, using the name Haribhai. Scored **Doordarshan**'s pioneering tv series *Humlog* (1984-5) and a number of **Films Division** documentaries (e.g. *Controlling Aphids in Mustard Crop*, 1979; *Development of Inland Fisheries*, 1988; *Modern Seeding and Planting Equipment*, 1991, etc.) .

FILMOGRAPHY (* also act): **1935**: *Bal Hatya*; *Bharat Ki Beti*; *Dharam Ki Devi**; **1936**: *Fida-e-Watan*; *Piya Ki Jogan*; *Pratima*; *Prem Bandhan*; *Sangdil Samaj*; *Sher Ka Panja*; *Shokh Dilruba*; **1937**: *Bulldog*; *Dukhiari*; *Gentleman Daku*; *Insaaf*; ***Jagirdar***; *Kokila*; *Mahageet*; **1938**: ***Three Hundred Days and After***; *Dynamite*; ***Gramophone Singer***; ***Hum Tum Aur Woh***; *Nirala Hindustan*; ***Abhilasha***; ***Watan***; **1939**: ***Jeevan Saathi***; ***Ek Hi Raasta***; **1940**: *Alibaba*; ***Aurat***; ***Pooja***; **1941**: *Aasra*; ***Bahen***; *Nai Roshni*; **1942**: *Apna Paraya*; ***Garib***; *Jawani*; ***Roti***; *Vijay*; **1943**: *Hamari Baat*; ***Kismet***; **1944**: *Char Aankhen*; ***Jwar Bhata***; *Lady Doctor*; **1945**: *Pehli Nazar*; **1946**: *Darban*; ***Nauka Dubi/Milan***; **1947**: *Bhookh*; *Manjdhar*; *Naiya*; **1948**: *Anokha Pyar*; *Gajre*; *Veena*; **1949**: ***Girls' School*** (with **C. Ramchandra**); *Jeet*; *Laadli*; *Begunah* (with **C. Ramchandra**); **1950**: *Arzoo*; *Beqasoor*; *Lajawaab*; **1951**: *Aaram*; *Badi Bahu*; *Do Sitare*; *Tarana*; *Saudagar* (with **C. Ramchandra**); **1952**: *Do Raha*; ***Rahi***; **1953**: *Akash*; *Faraib*; *Humdard*; *Jallianwala Bagh Ki Jyot*; *Mehmaan*; **1954**: *Maan*; *Mahatma Kabir*; ***Munna***; *Naaz*; ***Waris***; **1955**: *Faraar*; *Du-janay*; *Jasoos*; **1956**: *Heer*; *Paisa Hi Paisa*; **1957**: *Abhimaan*; *Jalti Nishani*; ***Pardesi***; **1958**: *Sanskar*; **1959**: ***Char Dil Char Raahein***; **1960**: ***Angulimal***; *Return of Mr Superman*; *Meera Ka Chitra*; **1961**: *Lucky Number*; *Savitri*; **1962**: *Hame Khelne Do*; ***Sautela Bhai***; **1964**: *Raju Aur Gangaram*; **1965**: *Chhoti Chhoti Baatein*.

BISWAS, SACHINDRANATH [CHHABI] (1900-62)

Actor born in Calcutta. Best-known outside Bengal for his two major performances in **Satyajit Ray**'s ***Jalsaghar*** and ***Kanchanjungha***. Epitomises the Bengali literary (and visual: cf **Company School Painting**) late 19th C. fascination with the colonial 'gentleman'. Used in a variety of ways to comment on the Westernising strand of 19th C. reform movements, or to parody Calcutta's urban élite (see **Dhiren Ganguly**, with whom Biswas acted in *Daabi*) in the form of the bhadralok stereotype elaborated at various times by all the major actors in 20th C. Bengal: **Sisir Bhaduri**, **Durgadas Bannerjee**, **Ahindra Choudhury**, **P.C. Barua**, **Pahadi Sanyal**. Before entering film, did amateur theatre while at Presidency College, Calcutta, in association with Bhaduri and **Naresh Mitra** (e.g. *Nemai Sanyas*), and Jatra performances. Turned professional at Natyaniketan (1938). Title roles in stage productions of *Devdas*, *Kashinath*, *Siraj-ud-Dowla* et al. are considered definitive performances in the era after Sisir Bhaduri and Ahindra Choudhury. Switched from early lead roles to successful 'character' roles, inevitably of the city-bred gentleman, culminating in Ray's *Kanchanjungha*. Other classic roles include the exploitative father-in-law in ***Devi*** and the title role of **Tapan Sinha**'s ***Kabuliwala***.

FILMOGRAPHY (* also d): **1936**: *Annapurnar Mandir*; **1937**: *Haranidhi*; **1938**: *Chokher Bali*; **1939**: *Sharmistha*; *Chanakya*; **1940**: *Swami Stri*; *Nimai Sanyasi*; ***Nartaki***; **1941**: *Epar Opar*; *Pratishodh*; *Pratisruti*; *Karnarjun*; *Banglar Meye*; **1942**: *Mahakavi Kalidas*; ***Garmil***; *Jiban Sangini*; *Milan*; *Ashok*; *Parineeta*; *Pativrata*; *Bondi*; *Avayer Biye*; *Shodhbodh*; *Nari*; *Saugandh*; *Pashan Devata*; **1943**: *Dampati*; *Aleya*; ***Samadhan***; *Dwanda*; *Nilanguriya*; *Daabi*; *Devar*; *Dikshul*; **1944**: *Pratikar**; *Matir Ghar*; *Chhadmabeshi*; **1945**: *Bondita*; *Raj Lakshmi*; *Path Bendhe Dilo*; *Stree Durga*; *Dui Purush*; **1946**: *Prem Ki Duniya*; *Sat Number Bari*; *Biraj Bou*; *Vande Mataram*; *Sangram*; *Nivedita*; *Tumi Aar Ami/Tum Aur Main*; **1947**: *Mandir*; *Pather Daabi*; *Abhijog*; *Nurse Sisi*; *Chandrasekhar*; **1948**: *Anirban*; *Nandaranir Sansar*; *Sadharan Meye*; *Sankha Sindoor*; *Shesh Nibedan*; *Umar Prem*(?); **1949**: *Jar Jetha Ghar**; *Manzoor*; *Bhuler Baluchare*; *Debi Choudhrani*; *Singhdwar*; **1950**: *Mandanda*; *Mahasampad*; *Garabini*; *Vidyasagar*; **1951**: *Durgesh Nandini*; *Maldar*; *Aparajito*; **1952**: *Krishnakanter Will*; *Ratrir Tapasya*; **1953**: *Sat Number Kayedi*; *Boudir Bone*; *Makarshar Jaal*; *Sabuj Pahar*; *Jog Biyog*; *Lakh Taka*; *Raja Krishna Chandra*; *Blind Lane*; *Sati Behula*; **1954**: *Shobha*; *Maa-o-Chhele*; *Ora Thake Odhare*; *Naa*; *Kalyani*; *Prafulla*; ***Dhuli***; *Banglar Nari*; *Sadanander Mela*; *Chheley Kaar*; *Shoroshi*; *Jadubhatta*; *Bhanga-Gara*; **1955**: *Sanjher Pradeep*; *Rani Rashmoni*; *Dattak*; *Pather Sheshey*; *Jharer Parey*; *Joymakali Boarding*; *Katha Kao*; *Prashna*; *Hrad*; *Upahar*; *Kalo Bou*; *Devimalini*; *Bratacharini*; *Drishti*; *Shribatsa-Chinta*; *Sabar Uparey*; **1956**: *Bhola Master*; *Kirti Garh*; *Asabarna*; *Saheb Bibi Golam*; *Shubharatri*; *Shankar Narayan Bank*; *Asamapta*; *Trijama*; *Mamlar Phal*; *Manraksha*; ***Ek Din Raatre***; *Rajpath*; *Chhaya Sangini*; *Suryamukhi*; *Govindadas*; *Madan Mohan*; *Putrabadhu*; *Falgu*; *Daner Maryada*; *Sinthir Sindoor*; *Raat Bhore*; ***Kabuliwala***; **1957**: *Shesh Parichaya*; *Bardidi*; *Ghoom*; *Bara Maa*; *Ektara*; *Tapasi*; ***Adarsha Hindu Hotel***; *Prithibi Amar Chay*; *Natun Prabhat*; *Neelachaley Mahaprabhu*; *Surer Parashey*; *Rastar Chhele*; *Kancha-Mithey*; *Chhaya Path*; *Abhishek*; *Sandhan*; *Abhoyer Biye*; *Mathur*; *Baksiddha*; *Antariksha*; *Garer Math*; *Kari-o-Komal*; *Madhabir Jonye*; *Pathe Holo Deri*; *Louha-Kapat*; ***Parash Pathar***; **1958**: *Yamalaya Jibanta Manush*; *Priya*; *Bandhu*; *Nupur*; *Daily Passenger*; *O Amar Desher Mati*; *Tansen*; *Nagini Kanyar Kahini*; *Sadhak Bama Kshyapa*; ***Jalsaghar***; *Indrani*; *Dhoomketu*; *Surya Toran*; *Marmabani*; **1959**: *Bicharak*; *Thakur Haridas*; *Derso Khokhar Kando*; *Shashi Babur Sansar*; *Bhranti*; *Gali Theke Rajpath*; *Chhabi*; *Amrapali*; *Nirdharita Silpir Anupastithi Tey*; *Khelaghar*; *Agnisambhaba*; *Nrityer Tale Tale*; *Headmaster*; *Rater Andhakare*; *Shubha Bibaha*; *Mriter Martye Agaman*; *Kshaniker Atithi*; **1960**: *Maya Mriga*; *Debarshi Narader Sansar*; *Raja-Saja*; ***Devi***; *Haat Baraley Bandhu*; ***Kshudista Pashan***; *Chupi Chupi Ashey*; *Sakher Chor*; *Gariber Meye*; ***Hospital***; *Smriti Tuku Thak*; *Shesh Paryanta*; *Ajana Kahini*; *Nader Nimai*; *Surer Pyasi*; *Suno Baro Nari*; **1961**: *Manik*; *Carey Shaheber Munshi*; *Bishkanya*; *Agni Sanskar*; *Madhya Rater Tara*; *Swayambara*; *Necklace*; *Kanchanmulya*; *Dainee*; *Ashay Bandhinu Ghar*; *Madhureno*; ***Saptapadi***; *Maa*; **1962**: *Sorry Madam*; *Bipasha*; *Kancher Swarga*; *Suryasnan*; *Shiulibari*; ***Kanchanjungha***; *Atal Jaler Ahwan*; *Agnisikha*; *Bodhu*; *Kajal*; *Mayar Sansar*; *Shubha Drishti*; *Dada Thakur*; *Dhoop Chhaya*; **1963**: *High Heel*; *Surya Sikha*; **1964**: *Kanta Taar*; **1976**: *Shri Shri Maa Lakshmi*.

Chhabi Biswas (left) in *Maa-o-Chhele* (1954)

BOMBAY TALKIES

Film studio set up by **Himansu Rai** in 1934. Among the biggest pre-WW2 talkie studios, it was the only major one launched as a fully fledged corporate body with a board of directors (including F.E. Dinshaw, Sir Chimanlal Setalvad, Sir Chunilal Mehta, Sir Pheroze Sethna and Sir Cowasji Jehangir as some of the 'dozen individuals who, by their control over banks, insurance companies and investment trusts, occupy commanding positions in the industrial life of Bombay' (A.R. Desai, 1948). It was one of the first studios with backing from major financial institutions, paying a regular dividend from the third year onwards. The resident star was **Devika Rani**. The scenarists were **Niranjan Pal** and J.S. Casshyap. The technical team was imported from Europe, including director **Franz Osten**, cameraman Josef Wirsching, set designer Carl von Spreti (later Count Carl von Spreti, the West German ambassador murdered in Guatemala in 1970) and soundman Len Hartley. The studio had three major phases. The first, the Rai-Osten era (***Achhut Kanya***, 1936; ***Kangan***, 1939) ended with Osten's arrest at the beginning of WW2 and, later, Rai's death (1940). The second saw Devika Rani, as production controller, split the studio into two production groups, one led by **Amiya Chakravarty** (best-known film of this period: ***Jwar Bhata***, 1944, introducing **Dilip Kumar**) and the other led by S. Mukherjee with Rai Bahadur Chunilal. The latter group broke away to start **Filmistan** (1942). The formal orthodoxy of Chakravarty's work (***Basant***, 1942) is clearly counterposed by a series of influential films, from **N.R. Acharya**'s ***Naya Sansar*** (1941) to ***Kismet*** (1943), all direct precedents of the Filmistan signature style. The third phase began when star **Ashok Kumar**, who had moved to Filmistan, and Savak Vacha returned and took over the studio (1946); it includes the early work of stars **Dev Anand** and Shyam, along with films by **Kamal Amrohi**, Shaheed Latif, **Bimal Roy**, **Nitin Bose** and **Phani Majumdar**. In the early 50s the studio declined despite efforts by the workers' association to save it, and it made only one more film, Majumdar's ***Baadbaan*** (1954).

BORAL, RAI CHAND (1903-81)

Music director aka Raichand Boral, born in Calcutta. Son of classical musician Lalchand Boral. Producer of Indian music programmes on Indian Broadcasting Co. in Calcutta (1927). Joined **New Theatres** during silent era, creating live score for **Charu Roy**'s *Chorekanta* (1931) and Prafulla Roy's *Chasher Meye* (1931), and remained the studio's top composer into the 40s. Although less associated with the dominant Rabindra Sangeet (**Tagore**'s lyrics) than e.g. **Pankaj Mullick**, his adaptations of the ghazal style into light classical, emotionally charged music were influential in the recording industry, esp. as interpreted by his famous protegé, actor-singer **Kundanlal Saigal**, in e.g. the Saigal-Umasashi duet *Prem nagar mein banaoongi ghar main* from **Nitin Bose**'s ***Chandidas***, *Balam aaye* and *Dukh ke* in **Barua**'s ***Devdas***, *Ek bangla bane nyaara* in ***President***, all remaining perennial hits. Other legendary compositions include **Phani Majumdar**'s ***Street Singer***, **Debaki Bose**'s ***Bidyapati***, and Nitin Bose's ***Lagan*** and ***Dhoop Chaon*** (claimed by some as the first use of playback in India), songs by **Pahadi Sanyal**, **Kanan Devi** and, in Hindi, by the ghazal exponent Talat Mahmood (e.g. *Swami Vivekananda*). Worked extensively with the early **Bimal Roy**, (***Udayer Pathey***, ***Anjangarh***, ***Maa***). His musical style rested heavily on songs with large string sections, with e.g. sitar and violins. In many of the songs he combined forms like Thumri, Keertan, Akhrai and the Kabigan, invoking a 19th C. Bengali tradition of cultural fusion in popular music associated with immigrants to Calcutta who brought musical forms from the North and the East. Also directed an animated short, *Pear Brothers*. Formed the independent MLB Prod. with actor Shyam Laha and **Amar Mullick**.

FILMOGRAPHY (* also d): **1931**: *Dena Paona*; **1932**: *Mohabbat Ke Aansoo*; *Chirakumar Sabha*; ***Chandidas***; *Subah Ka Sitara*; *Zinda Lash*; *Punarjanma*; *Palli Samaj*; **1933**: ***Puran Bhakt***; ***Meerabai/Rajrani Meera***; *Kapal Kundala*; *Mastuto Bhai*; **1934**: *Excuse Me, Sir*; *Rooplekha/Mohabbat Ki Kasauti*; ***Chandidas***; *Daku Mansoor*; *Pear Brothers** (Sh); **1935**: ***Devdas***; ***Dhoop Chhaon/Bhagya Chakra***; ***Inquilab***; **1936**: *Karodpati*; ***Grihadah/Manzil***; ***Maya***; **1937**: *Barababu*; ***Anath Ashram***; ***Didi/President***; ***Bidyapati/Vidyapati***; **1938**: ***Abhigyan/Abhagin***; ***Street Singer/Saathi***; **1939**: ***Sapurey/Sapera***; ***Jawani Ki Reet/Parajay***; ***Rajat Jayanti***; **1940**: ***Abhinetri/Haar Jeet***; **1941**: ***Parichay/Lagan***; *Pratisruti*; **1942**: *Nari*; *Saugandh*; **1943**: *Daɑbi*; ***Wapas***; **1944**: ***Udayer Pathey/Hamrahi***; **1945**: *Vasiyatnama*; **1946**: *Biraj Bou*; **1948**: ***Anjangarh***; **1949**: *Bishnupriya*; *Mantramughda*; *Swami*; **1950**: *Bara Bou*; *Pehla Admi*; **1951**: *Sparshamani*; *Paritran*; **1952**: *Maa*; **1953**: *Dard-e-Dil*; *Shri Chaitanya Mahaprabhu*; **1955**: *Amar Saigal*; *Swami Vivekananda*; **1957**: *Neelachaley Mahaprabhu*; **1959**: *Sagar Sangamey*; **1960**: *Natun Fasal.*

BORDOLOI, ATUL (b. 1938)

Assamese playwight and director born in Jorhat; initially a teacher after graduating from Gauhati University (1962). Author of 15 full-length and about 20 one-act plays in Assamese. Worked as journalist for the daily, *Natun Asomiya*. First film, ***Aparajeya***, was the unremarkable result of a remarkable film-making experiment sponsored by poet-playwright Phani Talukdar and made by a group, Chaturanga, including Gauri Burman and Munin Bayan. Bordoloi's films, set in deprived milieus, are known mainly for their multi-layered sense of reality achieved by suppressing narrative progression. Best-known film: ***Kallol***.

FILMOGRAPHY: **1970**: ***Aparajeya***; **1973**: *Banaria Phool*; *Anutaap*; **1978**: ***Kallol***; **1979**: *Megh*; **1990**: *Grahan*; *Drishti*; **1991**: *Sinyor.*

BOSE, DEBAKI KUMAR (1898-1971)

Bengali and Hindi director born in Akalpoush, Burdwan Dist., West Bengal; also worked in Tamil and in Marathi. Son of a noted solicitor, Madhusudhan Bose. Influenced by **Sisir Bhaduri**, his teacher at Bidyasagar College, Calcutta (1920). Left university to join non-co-operation movement after Calcutta Congress (1920). Edited journal, *Shakti*, from Burdwan (1927-8). Hired by **Dhiren Ganguly** as actor and scenarist for Dinesh Ranjan Das' *Kamaner Aagun* (1930). Devotee of Vaishnava evangelical movement. Joined **British Dominion Films** (1927) as scenarist, then director. Joined **P.C. Barua**'s Barua Pics (1930), then entered **New Theatres** (1932-4) together with Barua, directing the studio's first hit, ***Chandidas***. Its cinematic validation of a major stage genre - the quasi-legendary biographical - helped lessen Bengali cinema's dependence on the **Calcutta Theatres** for its themes as well as its literary, musical and acting talent. Early work known mainly for his free and inventive approach to established genres, esp. the mythological and the Saint film, creating a Bengali quality cinema (e.g. *Aparadhi* and *Chandidas*). Went to **East India Film** (1934-6) where he made the lyrical *Seeta* which launched **Prithviraj Kapoor** and **Durga Khote** as a star duo. Returned to New Theatres (1937-41), making the classic ***Bidyapati***. His independent Debaki Bose Prod. (1945) with stars from the Hindi and Marathi cinemas paved the way for other Calcutta cineastes after the decline of New Theatres in the early 40s. Made *Arghya*, a documentary on the caste system, based on four narrative poems by **Tagore** to celebrate the centenary of his birth.

FILMOGRAPHY: **1930**: *Kamaner Aagun* (only act); *Panchasar* (also act); **1931**: *Aparadhi*; *Shadows of the Dead*; **1932**: *Nishir Dak* (all St); ***Chandidas***; **1933**: ***Puran Bhakt***; ***Meerabai/Rajrani Meera***; *Dulari Bibi*; **1934**: *Seeta*; **1935**: ***Inquilab***; ***Jeevan Natak***; **1936**: ***Sonar Sansar/Sunehra Sansar***; **1937**: ***Bidyapati/Vidyapati***; **1939**: ***Sapurey/Sapera***; **1940**: ***Nartaki***; *Abhinav*; **1942**: ***Apna Ghar/Aple Ghar***; **1943**: *Shri Ramanuja*; **1945**: *Meghdoot*; *Swarg Se Sundar Desh Hamara*; **1946**: *Krishna Leela*; **1947**: *Chandrasekhar*; **1948**: *Sir Shankarnath*; **1949**: ***Kavi***; **1951**: ***Ratnadeep/Ratnadeepam***; **1953**: ***Pathik***; **1954**: *Kavi*; *Bhagwan Shri Krishna Chaitanya*; **1955**: *Bhalobasha*; **1956**: *Chirakumar Sabha*; *Nabajanma*; **1958**: *Sonar Kathi*; **1959**: *Sagar Sangamey*; **1961**: *Arghya.*

BOSE, MODHU (1900-69)

Bengali and Hindi director-scenarist born in Calcutta; grandson of the historian R.C. Dutt. Studied at Shantiniketan and Bidyasagar College, Calcutta, under **Sisir Bhaduri**. Entered film briefly as actor at **Madan Theatres** (1923). Assisted J.J. Madan on the making of *Turki Hoor* (1924); assisted and acted in **Himansu Rai**'s ***Prem Sanyas*** (1925). Went to London and assisted cameraman Baron Gaetano Ventigmilia on a Hitchcock film for Balcon/Gainsborough (1926; probably *The Mountain Eagle*) and worked briefly with Karl Freund at UFA (probably on Lang's *Metropolis*, 1925). Shot a Burmese film for the London Film Company, Rangoon, in 1927. Started the Calcutta Amateur Players (CAP) theatre group (1927). Production manager and actor in ***Prapancha Pash*** (1929). Married actress **Sadhona Bose**. Early films produced by Madan Theatres. Made *Khyber Falcon* for the **Punjab Film Corp.** in Lahore. Best-known work for Bombay-based **Wadia Movietone** and **Sagar**. Developed an influential generic hybrid from **Rabindranath Tagore**'s ballets (*Dahlia*) and Khirode Prasad Vidyavinode's ***Alibaba***, both starring his wife, **Sadhona Bose**. Made Orientalist song-dance-adventure spectaculars, indigenous variants of British 19th C. Ruritanian comedies (*Selima*, ***Kumkum***, ***Raj Nartaki***) and several Tagore adaptations. After 1936, when the CAP turned professional, concentrated mainly on stage work, e.g. **Niranjan Pal**'s *Zarina*, Manmatha Ray's *The Dreams of Omar Khayyam*. Also film biographicals of Girishchandra Ghosh, Michael Madhusudhan Dutt and Swami Vivekananda. Wrote autobiography: *Amar Jeeban* (1967).

FILMOGRAPHY: **1930**: ***Giribala***; *Dahlia*; **1932**: *Khyber Falcon* (all St); **1935**: *Selima*; **1936**: *Bala Ki Raat*; **1937**: ***Alibaba*** (also act); **1938**: *Abhinaya*; **1940**: ***Kumkum/Kumkum the Dancer***; **1941**: ***Raj Nartaki/Court Dancer***; **1942**: ***Meenakshi***; **1947**: *Giribala*; **1950**: ***Michael Madhusudhan***; **1953**: *Raakhi*; *Shesher Kabita*; **1954**: *Vikram Urvashi*; **1956**: *Mahakavi Girishchandra*; *Paradhin*; *Shubha Lagna*; **1964**: *Bireshwar Vivekananda.*

BOSE, NITIN (1897-1986)

Bengali and Hindi director, cameraman and producer; cousin of **Satyajit Ray**. Born in Calcutta. Learned still photography from his father, Hemendra Mohan Bose, owner of the famous Kuntalin Press and of Talking Machine Hall (distributor of Pathéphone recording systems). Acquired movie camera in his teens and became proficient in shooting home movies which he developed himself. Made newsreels in 1921-2 (the chariot festival at Puri, the elephant hunt of the Maharaja of Tripura) which he sold to the International Newsreel Corp. and to Fox Kinogram. First feature as cinematographer: Jaigopal Pillai's *Punarjanma* (1927). Cameraman on features for **Aurora**, **Indian Kinema Arts**, **Sisir Bhaduri** and International Filmcraft. Chief technical adviser and head of the camera department at **New Theatres** (1930). Shot many films for **Debaki Bose** (e.g. ***Chandidas***, 1932; ***Meerabai***, 1933) and **Atorthy** (e.g. *Dena Paona*, 1931; *Mohabbat Ke Aansoo*, *Subah Ka Sitara*, *Punarjanma*, all 1932); also shot *Shakuntala* for **Bhavnani** (1931). Directorial début when Debaki Bose left the studio in 1933. A key figure in the **New Theatres** organisation and maker of some of its most successful films. His early work continued in the vein of Debaki Bose (first feature was remake of Bose's ***Chandidas***). Later introduced a 'realist' element (***Didi/President***; ***Desher Mati/Dharti Mata***) foreshadowing the films of his own student and cameraman **Bimal Roy** (***Udayer Pathey***, 1944), and probably **Mrinal Sen**'s early films. His most successful films came after he left New Theatres in 1941 (e.g. ***Ganga Jumna*** in Hindi and Bhojpuri was one of the biggest hits of post-Independence cinema). Worked with major producers in Bombay: **Bombay Talkies** (***Nauka Dubi***) and **Minerva**. Started his own production company with *Dard-e-Dil* in 1953. When **A. Chakravarty** died, Bose finished ***Kathputli***. Set up Guwahati Studio in Assam.

FILMOGRAPHY: **1921**: *Belgian Emperor's Visit to India* (Doc); **1930**: *Buker Bojha* (all St); **1934**: ***Chandidas***; *Daku Mansoor*; **1935**: ***Dhoop Chhaon/Bhagya Chakra***; **1937**: ***Didi/President***; **1938**: ***Desher Mati/Dharti Mata***; ***Dushman/Jiban Maran***; **1941**: ***Parichay/Lagan***; **1943**: *Kashinath*; *Bichar/Paraya Dhan*; **1944**: *Mujrim*; **1945**: *Mazdoor*; **1946**: ***Nauka Dubi/Milan***; **1948**: *Drishtidaan*; **1950**: ***Mashaal/Samar***; **1951**:

Deedar; **1953**: *Dard-e-Dil*; **1954**: ***Waris***; **1955**: *Amar Saigal*; **1956**: *Char Dost*; **1957**: *Madhabir Jonye*; ***Kathputli***; **1958**: *Jogajog*; **1961**: ***Ganga Jumna***; **1962**: *Ummeed*; **1963**: *Nartaki*; **1964**: *Dooj Ka Chand*; **1966**: *Hum Kahan Ja Rahe Hain*; **1972**: *Samanata*.

BOSE, SADHONA (1914-73)

Actress born in Calcutta. Some sources give 1903 as year of birth. Granddaughter of 19th C. reformist leader Keshub Chunder Sen. Participated in her husband **Modhu Bose**'s dance spectaculars (***Kumkum***; ***Raj Nartaki***) which helped convert the late 19th/early 20th C. Parsee Theatre-influenced operatic mode into popular Bengali and Hindi films. A classically trained dancer (Kathak dance under Taraknath Bagchi and Manipuri under Guru Senarik Rajkumar) and musician (studied under Inayat Khan, **Timir Baran** and, briefly, **S.D. Burman**; piano with musician Franco Polo), her early work included ballets supervised by **Rabindranath Tagore** (one of which later became the film ***Dahlia***, 1930). In the 1929 stage version of *Alibaba*, met and briefly worked with Anna Pavlova. A classicist ideology was attributed to her work with Modhu Bose for the Calcutta Amateur Players and later in film. Her best-known play, ***Alibaba*** (1934; filmed 1937), helped translate the musical style of **Calcutta Theatres**, originating with Khirode Prasad Vidyavinode, into Broadway/Hollywood inspired Orientalist spectaculars. Introduced these into Hindi cinema, via directors like **Chaturbhuj Doshi** (***Shankar Parvati***) and **Kidar Sharma** (*Vish Kanya*). In her autobiography (Sadhona Bose, 1963), plays like *Theme Songs of Omar Khayyam* and *Hindu Dance Dramas*, *Birth of Freedom*, *Samarpan* and *Ajanta* are described as 'neo-classical ballets' while her later films are called 'film ballets', adhering to all the tenets of traditional art. Produced the show *Rhythm of Victory* as a political spectacular with more than 40 dancers. An English version of her best-known film, *Raj Nartaki*, was distributed in the USA as *Court Dancer*.

FILMOGRAPHY: **1937**: ***Alibaba***; **1938**: *Abhinaya*; **1940**: ***Kumkum/Kumkum the Dancer***; **1941**: ***Raj Nartaki/Court Dancer***; **1942**: ***Meenakshi***; **1943**: *Paigham*; ***Shankar Parvati***; *Vish Kanya*; **1945**: *Neelam*; **1946**: *Urvashi*; **1951**: *Bhola Shankar*; *For Ladies Only*; *Nand Kishore*; **1952**: ***Shin Shinaki Boobla Boo***; **1953**: *Shesher Kabita*; **1954**: *Maa-o-Chhele*; *Vikram Urvashi*.

BOSE, SATYEN (1916-93)

Bengali and Hindi director born in Purnea, Bihar. Commerce graduate from Bidyasagar College, Calcutta (1941). Worked on the railways and in a bank. Participant in amateur theatre as student. With friends set up National Progressive Pics (1948) and produced Hemen Gupta's *Bhuli Naai* in Bengali. Early films contextualised by post-Partition Bengal, addressing the fragmentation of the traditional middle class (e.g. *Bhor Hoye Elo*) under different social and political pressures, e.g. the schoolboy movie ***Paribartan***. Combined realism with comedy, esp. ***Barjatri***, which was praised by **S. Ray** for its typically Bengali spirit, humorous dialogue and spontaneous acting style. Moved to Bombay late in 1953 to make *Parichay*. Then worked mainly with the brothers **Kishore**, Anoop and **Ashok Kumar** in the sadly comic ***Bandi*** and the one slapstick classic of Hindi cinema, ***Chalti Ka Naam Gaadi***. Also directed **Nargis**'s last film, *Raat Aur Din*.

FILMOGRAPHY (* also act): **1949**: ***Paribartan****; **1951**: ***Barjatri****; **1953**: *Bhor Hoye Elo*; **1954**: *Jagriti*; *Parichay*; **1955**: *Rickshawala*; ***Bandish***; **1957**: ***Bandi***; **1958**: ***Chalti Ka Naam Gaadi***; *Savera*; *Sitaron Se Aage*; **1960**: *Masoom*; *Girl Friend*; **1964**: *Daal Mein Kala*; ***Dosti***; **1966**: *Aasra*; *Mere Lal*; **1967**: *Raat Aur Din*; **1968**: *Jyot Jale*; **1969**: *Wapas*; *Aansoo Ban Gaye Phool*; **1970**: *Jeevan Mrityu*; **1972**: *Sa Re Ga Ma Pa*; *Anokhi Pehchan*; *Mere Bhaiya*; **1977**: *Mastan Dada*; **1978**: *Anmol Tasveer*; **1979**: *Saanch Ko Aanch Nahin*; *Bin Maa Ke Bachche*; **1980**: *Payal Ki Jhankaar*; **1982**: *Tumhare Bina*; **1983**: *Kaya Palat*; **1986**: *Woh Din Aayega*.

BOSE, TAPAN (b. 1946)

Documentary director; part of Cinemart Foundation with actress Suhasini Mulay (***Bhuvan Shome***, 1969, ***Bhavni Bhavai***, 1980) and Salim Shaikh. Started as assistant to **Sukhdev**. Controversial cineaste, often hampered by officialdom. Independent début, *An Indian Story*, featured the infamous Bhagalpur incident in which prison inmates were blinded as part of police torture. Co-d his second film examining the consequences of the Bhopal gas disaster (1984). *From Behind the Barricade* attacks the central government's repression in Punjab. The film was banned for its overt support of separatist militants. An appellate tribunal revoked the ban, imposing other strictures such as the unprecedented requirement that 'In all interviews, so as to ensure the genuineness of the interviews and interviewees, except where the interviewee is a known public character, there shall, throughout the interview, be a subtitle ... depicting the name and address of the interviewee and the location where the interview was taken. In default, such interview to be deleted in its entirety' (see A.G. Noorani, 1993). Also works on video.

FILMOGRAPHY: **1981**: *An Indian Story*; **1986**: *Bhopal: Beyond Genocide*; **1991**: *The Vulnerable Road User*; **1993**: *From Behind The Barricade*; *Jharkhand*.

BOURNE & SHEPHERD

Calcutta-based company; oldest and most prominent still photography dealers in India, set up in 1840 as a studio by Samuel Bourne. Charles Shepherd and A. Robertson started a Photographic Artists Studio in Agra (1862) which became Howard & Bourne in Simla (1863) and finally Bourne & Shepherd in Calcutta (1868). Both were photographers, making portraits of political and arts personalities, urban scenes of Calcutta and royal Durbars and were dealers in equipment and stock. They produced photographic variants of **Company School painting** for the popular art market: **Hiralal Sen**'s career started when he won a Bourne & Shepherd photography competition in 1887. Their nationwide distribution and processing/printing network was one of the first to expand into film (by 1900) when, with the Bombay-based Clifton & Co., they started showing movies in their studios. Mainly sold

Sadhona Bose in *Raj Nartaki* (1941)

or hired out equipment by Pathé-Fr¤res, Gaumont and the Barker Motion Picture Co., aggressively marketing their services and making professional cameramen and crews available to shoot events of state or private importance on commission from the government, Indian royalty or business magnates (e.g. ***Pundalik***, 1912). Until the establishment of Pathé (India) in 1907, companies like Bourne & Shepherd occasionally worked as agents for the Pathé Exchange, the International Newsreel Corp. and Fox Films, purchasing locally made documentaries for them as 'News' films, or the cheaper 'Review' films. The first extensively filmed public event in India, the British Royal Family's visit in 1911 (shot by **Patankar**, **Hiralal Sen**, **Madan Theatres** and others) was also shot by the company: *Their Imperial Majesties in Delhi* (1911).

BRITISH DOMINION FILMS

Dhiren Ganguly's third and best-known silent studio, set up in 1929 in Dumdum, Calcutta. Board of directors comprised **P.C. Barua**, the Rajahs of Puri, Khadia and Patna, Tarubala Sen, N.N. Mukherjee and K.C. Roy Choudhury with Ganguly as managing director. Financially supported by royalty, it also sought colonial state support. Productions include first films by **Debaki Bose**, writer-film-maker Dinesh Ranjan Das and cameramen Sailen Bose and Dronacharya. Made only eight films. Closed down in 1930 as victim of the change to sound.

BURMA, PHANI (b. 1897)

Bengali director born in Calcutta. Started as actor (e.g. Nitish Mitra's ***Devdas***, 1928). Turned director while starring in *Shesh Path* on location in Burma. Concentrated on direction from 1936 onwards. Co-directed *Kamale Kamini* with Nirmal Goswami.

FILMOGRAPHY: **1930**: *Shesh Path* (St); **1936**: *Krishna Sudama*; *Jhinjhinyar Jer*; *Bishabriksha*; *Prabas Milan*; **1939**: *Janak Nandini*; *Debjani*; **1940**: *Kamale Kamini*; *Byabadhan*; *Nimai Sanyasi*; **1947**: *Mandir*; **1952**: *Prahlad*; *Vishwamitra*; **1954**: *Joydev*; **1955**: *Shribatsa Chinta*; **1957**: *Harishchandra*; *Onkarer Joy Jatra*; *Data Karna*.

BURMAN, RAHUL DEV (1939-94)

Hindi composer aka Pancham. Entered films as assistant to his father **S.D. Burman**, often playing the mouth organ in his father's orchestras. Trained under Ali Akbar Khan. Independent career coincided with the wave of early 70s **Rajesh Khanna** love stories (esp. *Kati Patang*, *Amar Prem*, *Apna Desh*) and the new lease of life they offered to singer **Kishore Kumar**. Informally assisted his father in composing the seminal Khanna-Kumar combination, **Shakti Samanta**'s ***Aradhana*** (1969). Breakthrough in **Nasir Hussain** musicals, starting with *Baharon Ke Sapne* and consolidated by the classic **Zeenat Aman** rock music teen-movie ***Yaadon Ki Baraat***, having earlier scored her début ***Hare Rama Hare Krishna***. Some of his best music is associated with **Gulzar**'s lyrics, e.g. ***Parichay*** and ***Aandhi***. Brought Hindi film music into the era of electronic rock with a series of enormously popular youth movies, e.g. **Narendra Bedi**'s *Jawani Diwani*. Worked mostly with singers **Asha Bhosle** and Kishore Kumar, providing much of the music that defines their reputations. Also produced independent albums, including one based on the samba and one with British pop star Boy George. Occasionally sings his own songs in a unique, grunting bass (e.g. the *Mehbooba mehbooba* number in ***Sholay***).

FILMOGRAPHY (* also act): **1961**: *Chhote Nawab*; **1965**: *Bhoot Bangla**; *Teesra Kaun*; **1966**: *Pati Patni*; ***Teesri Manzil***; **1967**: *Baharon Ke Sapne*; *Chandan Ka Palna*; **1968**: *Abhilasha*; ***Padosan***; **1969**: *Pyar Ka Mausam**; *Waris*; **1970**: *Rajkumari*; *Ehsan*; *Kati Patang*; *Puraskaar*; *Raaton Ka Raja*; *Saas Bhi Kabhi Bahu Thi*; *The Train*; **1971**: *Adhikar*; *Amar Prem*; *Buddha Mil Gaya*; *Caravan*; *Hangama*; ***Hare Rama Hare Krishna***; *Lakhon Mein Ek*; *Mela*; *Paraya Dhan*; *Pyar Ki Kahani*; *Hulchul*; *Sanjog*; **1972**: *Apna Desh*; *Bombay To Goa*; *Dil Ka Raja*; *Do Chor*; *Garam Masala*; *Gomti Ke Kinare*; *Jawani Diwani*; *Mere Jeevan Saathi*; ***Parichay***; *Parchaiyan*; *Raakhi Aur Hathkadi*; *Rampur Ka Lakshman*; *Rani Mera Naam*; *Samadhi*; *Savera*; *Seeta Aur Geeta*; *Shehzada*; *Double Cross*; **1973**: *Aa Gale Lag Jaa*; *Anamika*; *Bada Kabutar*; *Bandhe Haath*; *Chhalia*; *Do Phool*; *Heera Panna*; *Hifazat*; *Jaise Ko Taisa*; *Jheel Ke Us Paar*; *Joshila*; *Nafrat*; ***Namak Haram***; *Paanch Dushman*; *Raja Rani*; *Rickshawala*; *Shareef Badmash*; ***Yaadon Ki Baraat***; *Mr Romeo*; **1974**: *Aap Ki Kasam*; *Ajnabi*; *Benaam*; *Charitraheen*; *Dil Diwana*; *Doosri Seeta*; *Goonj*; *Humshakal*; *Imaan*; *Ishq Ishq Ishq*; *Khote Sikkay*; *Madhosh*; *Manoranjan*; *Phir Kab Milogi*; *Shaitan*; *Trimurti*; *Ujala Hi Ujala*; *Zehreela Insaan*; **1975**: ***Aandhi***; ***Deewar***; *Dharam Karam*; *Kala Sona*; *Khel Khel Mein*; *Khushboo*; *Mazaaq*; *Raja*; ***Sholay***; *Warrant*; *Kehte Hain Mujhko Raja*; **1976**: *Balika Badhu*; *Bandalbaaz*; *Bhanwar*; *Bullet*; *Khalifa*; *Maha Chor*; *Mehbooba*; *Nehle Pe Dehla*; *Vishwasghaat*; *Dhongee*; **1977**: *Chala Murari Hero Banne*; *Chalta Purza*; *Chandi Sona*; *Darling Darling*; *Hum Kisise Kum Nahin*; *Jeevanmukt*; *Karm*; *Kinara*; *Kitaab*; *Mukti*; **1978**: *Azad*; *Bhola Bhala*; *Chor Ho To Aisa*; *Devata*; *Ghar*; *Heeralal Pannalal*; *Naukri*; *Kasme Vade*; *Naya Daur*; *Phandebaaz*; *Shalimar*; **1979**: *Bhala Manus*; *Golmaal*; *The Great Gambler*; *Hamare Tumhare*; *Jhootha Kahin Ka*; *Jurmana*; *Manzil*; *Naukar*; *Ratnadeep*; *Salaam Memsaab*; **1980**: *Aanchal*; *Abdullah*; *Alibaba Aur Chalis Chor*; *The Burning Train*; *Dhan Daulat*; *Jal Mahal*; *Khubsoorat*; *Phir Wohi Raat*; *Red Rose*; *Shaan*; *Sitara*; *Takkar*; *Bulandi*; *Gunehgaar*; *Qatil Kaun*; **1981**: *Barsaat Ki Ek Raat/Anusandhan*; *Basera*; *Biwi-o-Biwi*; *Dhuaan*; *Gehra Zakhm*; *Ghunghroo Ki Awaaz*; *Harjaai*; *Jail Yatra*; *Kaliya*; *Kudrat*; *Love Story*; *Mangalsutra*; *Naram Garam*; *Raksha*; *Shaukeen*; *Rocky*; *Zamane Ko Dikhana Hai*; *Satte Pe Satta*; *Kachche Heere*; *Daulat*; *Angoor*; **1982**: *Aamne Samne*; *Ashanti*; *Bemisal*; *Ganga Meri Maa*; *Namkeen*; *Sanam Teri Kasam*; *Shakti*; *Swami Dada*; *Teri Kasam*; *Yeh To Kamaal Ho Gaya*; *Yeh Vaada Raha*; *Dard Ka Rishta*; ***Masoom***; **1983**: *Namumkin*; *Agar Tum Na Hote*; *Betaab*; *Chor Police*; *Jaan-e-Jaan*; *Kaun? Kaise?*; *Lovers*; *Mahaan*; *Main Awara Hoon*; *Mazdoor*; *Pukar*; *Qayamat*; *Rang Birangi*; *Romance*; *Shubh Kaamna*; *Farishta*; *Boxer*; *Bindiya Chamkegi*; *Bade Dil Wala*; *Aan Aur Shaan*; **1984**: *Anand Aur Anand*; *Andar Bahar*; *Awaaz*; *Bheema*; *Duniya*; *Hum Hain Lajawaab*; *Jagir/Teen Murti*; *Jawani*; *Sunny*; *Jhootha Sach*; *Karishma*; *Mati Mange Khoon*; *Manzil Manzil*; *Yeh Desh*; *Zameen Aasmaan*; *Hum Dono*; *Musafir*; **1985**: *Aar Paar/Anyay Abichar*; *Alag Alag*; *Amir Admi Gareeb Admi*; *Arjun*; *Awara Baap*; *Ek Se Bhale Do*; *Lava*; *Oonche Log*; *Rahi Badal Gaye*; *Ram Tere Kitne Naam*; *Joshilay*; *Sagar*; *Shiva Ka Insaaf*; *Sitamgarh*; *Zabardast*; *Savere Wali Gadi*; *Hum Naujawan*; *Rusvai*; **1986**: *Bond 303*; *Anokha Rishta*; *Ek Main Aur Ek Tu*; *Jeeva*; *Palay Khan*; *Samundar*; *Shatru*; *Zindagani*; **1987**: *Apne Apne*; *Dacait*; *Hifazat*; *Inaam Dus Hazaar*; *Itihaas*; *Jallianwala Bagh*; *Ekanto Apon*; *Ijaazat*; *Belagaam*; **1988**: *Agun*; *Mardon Wali Baat*; *Zalzala*; *Rama-o-Rama*; *Mil Gayi Manzil Mujhe*; *Chatran*; *Faisla*; *Libaas*; **1989**: *Aag Se Khelenge*; *Dost*; ***Parinda***; *Aakrosh*; *Jankar*; *Jurrat*; *Bahurani*; **1990**: *Ekhane Amar Swarga*; *Jeene Do*; *Dushman*; *Chor Pe Mor*; **1991**: *Gunehgaar Kaun*; *Indrajit*; **1992**: *Jhoothi Shaan*; *Sarphira*; *Siyasat*; *Drohi*; *Khule Aam*; **1993**: *Gurudev*; *Gardish*; *Tum Karo Vaada*.

BURMAN, SACHIN DEV (1906-75)

Music director born in Tripura. Classical training by his father, sitarist and Dhrupad singer Nabadwipchandra Dev Burman; later with Ustad Badal Khan and Bhishmadev Chatterjee. Early work for radio was based on East Bengali and North Eastern folk-music. In early 30s made a reputation in Bengal as singer of folk and light classical music, e.g. at the Allahabad Sangeet Sammelan (Music Conference) in 1935. Film début singing for **Pankaj Mullick** in **Atorthy**'s ***Yahudi Ki Ladki*** (1933) but the songs were scrapped and re-sung by **Pahadi Sanyal**. First film as singer: Tinkari Chakraborty's *Sanjher Pidim* (1935); also acted in **Dhiren Ganguli**'s *Bidrohi* (1935). Music director from 1939 onwards in Calcutta. Moved to Bombay (1944) and worked at **Filmistan** (***Eight Days***, ***Shabnam***), Navketan (***Afsar***, ***Taxi Driver***, ***Funtoosh***, ***Guide***) and for **Guru Dutt** (***Baazi***, ***Jaal***, ***Pyaasa***, ***Kaagaz Ke Phool***). Remained **Dev Anand**'s key composer for several years (***Paying Guest***, ***Tere Ghar Ke Saamne***, ***Jewel Thief***, ***Prem Pujari***). Also worked on films for **Bimal Roy** (***Devdas***, ***Sujata***, ***Bandini***). Film compositions often influenced by his huge repertory of folk-tunes from the Bengali Bhatiali, Sari and Dhamail traditions of the North East. As a singer, his thin but powerful, accented voice was often used as a bardic commentary: e.g. the *Wahan kaun hai tera musafir* number in ***Guide***, *Safal hogi teri aradhana* in the hit **Rajesh Khanna** movie ***Aradhana***. Wrote an autobiography: *Sargamer Nikhad*.

FILMOGRAPHY: **1937**: *Rajgee*; **1939**: *Jakher Dhan*; **1940**: *Amar Geeti*; *Rajkumarer Nirbashan*; **1941**: *Pratishodh*; **1942**: *Mahakavi Kalidas*; *Avayer Biye*; *Milan*; *Jiban Sangini*; *Ashok*; **1943**: *Jajsaheber Nathni*; **1944**: *Chhadmabeshi*; *Matir Ghar*; *Pratikar*; **1945**: *Kalankini*; **1946**: *Matrihara*; *Shikari*; ***Eight Days***; **1947**: *Chittor Vijay*; *Dil Ki Rani*; *Do Bhai*; **1948**: *Vidya*; **1949**: *Kamal*; ***Shabnam***; **1950**: ***Afsar***; ***Mashaal/Samar***; *Pyar*; **1951**:

Baazi; ***Bahar***; *Buzdil*; *Ek Nazar*; *Naujawan*; *Sazaa*; ***Babla***; **1952**: ***Jaal***; *Lal Kunwar*; **1953**: *Armaan*; *Jeevan Jyoti*; *Shahenshah*; **1954**: *Angarey*; *Chalis Baba Ek Chor*; *Radha Krishna*; ***Taxi Driver***; **1955**: ***Devdas***; ***House Number 44***; *Madh Bhare Nain*; ***Munimji***; *Society*; **1956**: *Funtoosh*; **1957**: *Miss India*; ***Nau Do Gyarah***; ***Paying Guest***; ***Pyaasa***; **1958**: ***Chalti Ka Naam Gaadi***; ***Kala Pani***; ***Lajwanti***; *Sitaron Se Aage*; *Solva Saal*; **1959**: *Insaan Jaag Utha*; ***Kaagaz Ke Phool***; ***Sujata***; **1960**: ***Apna Haath Jagannath***; ***Bambai Ka Babu***; *Bewaqoof*; *Ek Ke Baad Ek*; ***Kala Bazaar***; *Manzil*; *Miya Bibi Razi*; **1962**: *Baat Ek Raat Ki*; *Dr Vidya*; *Naughty Boy*; **1963**: ***Bandini***; *Meri Soorat Teri Aankhen*; ***Tere Ghar Ke Saamne***; **1964**: *Benazir*; *Kaise Kahun*; *Ziddi*; **1965**: ***Guide***; *Teen Deviyan*; **1967**: ***Jewel Thief***; **1969**: ***Aradhana***; *Jyoti*; *Talash*; **1970**: *Ishq Par Zor Nahin*; ***Prem Pujari***; **1971**: *Gambler*; *Naya Zamana*; *Sharmilee*; ***Tere Mere Sapne***; **1972**: *Anuraag*; *Yeh Gulistan Hamara*; *Zindagi Zindagi*; **1973**: *Abhimaan*; *Chhupa Rustom*; *Jugnu*; *Phagun*; **1974**: *Prem Nagar*; *Sagina*; *Us Paar*; **1975**: *Chupke Chupke*; *Mili*; **1976**: *Arjun Pandit*; *Barood*; *Deewangee*; *Tyaag*.

CALCUTTA THEATRES

Commercial theatre movement in late 19th and early 20th C. Calcutta, drawing on 18th C. British amateur theatricals, Gerasim Lebedeff's (1749-1817) influential Bengally Theatre (Est: 1795) and 'private' theatres from which emerged the first major Bengali playwright, Michael Madhusudhan Dutt (1824-73). Cultural and economic pinnacle coincided with the career of writer-actor Girishchandra Ghosh (1844-1912), first at National Theatre and later Minerva Theatre (1893-1912), including Ghosh's mythologicals, Dwijendralal Roy's historicals and Khirode Prasad Vidyavinode's musicals (notably *Alibaba*). Influenced by the Shakespearean Parsee Theatre, a realist current contemporaneous with the reformist Bengali novel (e.g. Dinabandhu Mitra's *Nildarpan*, staged by National in 1872, about the condition of peasants in Bengal's indigo plantations) and by operatic ballet experiments in the **Madan** repertories, later strongly mediated by **Rabindranath Tagore**'s dance dramas (e.g. by **Modhu Bose**'s Calcutta Amateur Players). Early 20th C. stage industry counted many very successful companies usually owned by rich financiers and run by manager-impresarios. They had a determinating impact on the early Bengali film industry (see **Hiralal Sen** and Madan Theatres). Conventionally, modern 20th C. Bengali theatre dates back to Star Theatres' 1923 production of *Karnarjun* (starring **Ahindra Choudhury**, **Naresh Mitra** and **Durgadas Bannerjee**). **Sisir Bhaduri**'s plays at Natyamandir later provided a generic backdrop to radical 'group' theatre movements launched in early 40s (see **Utpal Dutt**). The era of the great public theatres was later often evoked in films as pre-war nostalgia or as the nascent origin of Bengal's mass-culture industry (e.g. the **New Theatres'** ***Abhinetri/Haar Jeet***, 1940 and ***Meri Bahen***, 1944). Established several key genres, including the historical and mythological, for the cinema as much as for the popular Jatra theatre.Chakraborty, Madhabi *see* **Mukherjee, Madhabi**

CHAKRABORTY, MITHUN (b. 1956)

Bengali-Hindi actor. Major hits B. Subhash's *Disco Dancer* and *Dance Dance* earned him a major following in India and abroad, esp. in the USSR. Early work in realist 'political' films, e.g. ***Mrigaya***, ***The Naxalites*** and ***Hum Paanch***. Later achieved a brand image with gangland thrillers, indigenous Westerns and love stories for mid-level producers like Raveekant Nagaich, offering cheaper variants of what **Bachchan** was doing in the top bracket. Late 80s marketing strategies often cast him alongside **Bachchan**, playing second lead (**Manmohan Desai**'s *Ganga Jamuna Saraswati*, **Prakash Mehra**'s *Jadugar*, **Mukul Anand**'s ***Agneepath***). Regarded in the late 80s as the 'safest' investment in Hindi cinema, although he had no major hits until Vijay Sadanah's *Pyar Jhukta Nahin*, because he appealed to the semi-urban and rural audiences which sustained long-term distribution. Changed his image in **Buddhadev Dasgupta**'s *Tahader Katha* to win the national acting award.

FILMOGRAPHY: **1976**: *Do Anjaane*; ***Mrigaya***; **1977**: *Mukti*; **1978**: *Hamara Sansar*; *Mera Rakshak*; *Tere Pyar Mein*; *Kasturi*; *Phool Khile Hain Gulshan Gulshan*; *Nadi Theke Sagare*; **1979**: *Amar Deep*; *Bhayanak*; *Prem Vivah*; *Suraksha*; *Tarana*; ***The Naxalites***; *Chameli Memsaab*; **1980**: *Aakhri Insaaf*; *Bansari*; *Beshaque*; *Patita*; *Sitara*; *Taxi Chor*; *Unees Bees*; *Khwab*; *Kismet*; ***Hum Paanch***; *Ghamandi*; **1981**: *Dhuaan*; *Humse Badhkar Kaun*; *Jeene Ki Arzoo*; *Laparwah*; *Main Aur Mera Hathi*; *Sahas*; *Wardat*; *Kalankini Kankabati*; *Pahadi Phool*; *Upalabdhi*; *Sameera*; *Shaukeen*; **1982**: *Aadat Se Majboor*; *Aamne Samne*; *Ashanti*; *Disco Dancer*; *Heeron Ka Chor*; *Sun Sajna*; *Swami Dada*; *Taqdeer Ka Badshah*; *Ustadi Ustad Se*; **1983**: *Faraib*; *Humse Hai Zamana*; *Karate*; *Kaun? Kaise?*; *Mujhe Insaaf Chahiye*; *Marriage Bureau*; *Pasand Apni Apni*; *Taqdeer*; *Woh Jo Haseena*; *Boxer*; *Lal Chunaria*; *Wanted*; **1984**: *Baazi*; *Ghar Ek Mandir*; *Pyar Jhukta Nahin*; *Jhootha Sach*; *Jaag Utha Insaan*; *Jagir/Teen Murti*; *Kasam Paida Karne Wale Ki*; *Rakta Bandhan*; *Tarkeeb*; *Hanste Khelte*; *Sharara*; *Teri Baahon Mein*; **1985**: *Aandhi Toofan*; *Aar Paar/Anyay Abichar*; *Badal*; *Bepanah*; *Char Maharathi*; ***Ghulami***; *Karishma Kudrat Ka*; *Karm Yudh*; *Maa Kasam*; *Pyari Behna*; *Yaadon Ki Kasam*; *Ek Aur Sikandar*; **1986**: *Aisa Pyar Kahan*; *Amma*; *Avinash*; *Baat Ban Jaye*; *Dilwala*; *Jaal*; *Karamdata*; *Kismatwala*; *Main Balwan*; *Nasihat*; *Pyar Ke Do Pal*; *Sheesha*; *Swarg Se Sundar*; *Zindagani*; *Muddat*; **1987**: *Dance Dance*; *Diwana Tere Naam Ka*; *Hawalaat*; *Hirasat*; *Mera Yaar Mera Dushman*; *Param Dharam*; *Parivar*; *Watan Ke Rakhwale*; **1988**: *Charnon Ki Saugandh*; *Commando*; *Jeete Hain Shaan Se*; *Pyar Ka Mandir*; *Rukhsat*; *Waqt Ki Awaaz*; *Saazish*; *Sagar Sangam*; *Ganga Jamuna Saraswati*; *Agni*; *Bees Saal Baad*; *Mar Mitenge*; *Meri Zabaan*; *Mil Gayi Manzil Mujhe*; **1989**: *Guru*; *Hum Intezar Karenge*; *Ilaaka*; *Prem Pratigya*; *Garibon Ka Daata*; *Daata*; *Aakhri Gulam*; *Hisab Khoon Ka*; *Mujrim*; *Dost*; *Dana Pani*; *Ladaai*; *Bhrashtachar*; *Swarna Trishna*; *Galiyon Ka Badshah*; *Jadugar*; *Aakhri Badla*; **1990**: *Pyar Ke Naam Qurban*; ***Agneepath***; *Gunahon Ka Devta*; *Humse Na Takrana*; *Paap Ki Kamaai*; *Pati Patni Aur Tawaif*; *Roti Ke Keemat*; *Pyar Ka Karz*; *Pyar Ka Devata*; *Dushman*; *Shandaar*; **1991**: *Swarg Yahan Narak Yahan*; *Trinetra*; *Pratigyabadh*; *Pyar Hua Chori Chori*; *Shikari*; *Numbri Admi*; *Dil Ashna Hai*; **1992**: *Tahader Katha*; *Mere Sajna Saath Nibhana*; *Raju Dada*; *Jhoothi Shaan*; *Pitambar*; *Ghar Jamai*; **1993**: *Yugandhar*; *Phool Aur Angaar*; *Krishan Avatar*; *Meharbaan*; *Pardesi*; *Jeevan Ki Shatranj*; *Admi*; *Dalaal*; *Tadipaar*; *Shatranj*.

Mithun Chakraborty in *Mujrim* (1989)

CHAKRABORTY, TULSI (1899-1961)

Actor born in Calcutta. Acted the gormless fool in dozens of Bengali comedies in the 30s, an image used by **Satyajit Ray** in ***Parash Pathar*** casting him as Paresh Dutta, a middle-aged bank clerk who discovers the philosopher's stone. His image, characterised by his bald head and bulging eyes, is an enduring icon of early Bengali cinema. Known initially as a singer and dancer on the stage, e.g. in his major stage début for Star Theatres, *Jaidev*. Film début in **Atorthy**'s *Punarjanma*, also in a singing role. Acted in several **New Theatres** productions, e.g. by **Hemchandra Chunder** (***Wapas***, ***Meri Bahen***) and **Kartick Chattopadhyay** (***Ramer Sumati***, ***Mahaprasthaner Pathey***), **Bimal Roy** mobilised his earthy caricature of the Bengali middle class in a 'realist' context (***Udayer Pathey***, ***Anjangarh***, ***Naukri***). **Premendra Mitra** (*Moyla Kagaj*), **Tapan Sinha** and Ray (in ***Pather Panchali***, where he played the schoolteacher) extended this vein. He demonstrated his musical abilities only occasionally in his later career, e.g. in **Debaki Bose**'s ***Kavi***, singing his own compositions. Continued acting in theatre until 1961 (last play: *Shreyasi*) working with Star, Natyaniketan (e.g. *Maa*) and at Natyabharati and Rungmahal companies.

FILMOGRAPHY: 1932: *Punarjanma*; 1933: *Shri Gauranga*; 1934: *Dhruva*; *Sachidulal*; *Daksha Yagna*; *Rajnati Basantsena*; 1935: ***Manmoyee Girls' School***; *Kanthahaar*; 1936: *Krishna Sudama*; *Kritiman*; *Prabas Milan*; *Chino Haar*; 1938: *Halbangala*; *Bekar Nashan*; *Abhinaya*; *Ekalavya*; 1939: *Nara Narayan*; *Parasmani*; *Rikta*; *Vaman Avatar*; *Janak Nandini*; 1940: *Kamale Kamini*; *Nimai Sanyasi*; 1941: *Shri Radha*; *Uttarayan*; *Pratisruti*; 1942: ***Meenakshi***; ***Shesh Uttar/Jawab***; ***Garmil***; *Saugandh*; 1943: ***Jogajog/Hospital***; *Shri Ramanuja*; ***Wapas***; *Swamir Ghar*; *Aleya*; *Poshya Putra*; *Dampati*; *Dikshul*; 1944: *All-Star Tragedy*; ***Meri Bahen***; *Subah Shyam*; *Takraar*; ***Udayer Pathey/Hamrahi***; *Sondhi/Sandhi*; 1945: *Vasiyatnama*; *Path Bendhe Dilo*; ***Mane Na Mana***; *Bhabhi-Kaal*; *Dui Purush*; 1946: *Biraj Bou*; *Vande Mataram*; 1947: *Giribala*; *Jharer Parey*; *Alaknanda*; *Abhijog*; *Dui Bandhu*; *Gharoa*; ***Ramer Sumati/Chhota Bhai***; 1948: *Samapika*; ***Anjangarh***; *Anirban*; ***Bhuli Naai***; *Bankalekha*; *Priyatama*; *Sankha Sindoor*; *Taruner Swapna*; *Sir Shankarnath*; *Umar Prem*(?); *Mati-o-Manush*; 1949: *Satero Bachhar Pare*; ***Kavi***; *Bishnupriya*; *Swami*; *Manzoor*; 1950: *Radha Rani*; *Rupkatha/Roop Kahani*; *Mejdidi*; *Kuhelika*; 1951: *Biplabi Kshudiram*; ***Ratnadeep/Ratnadeepam***; ***Babla***; 1952: ***Mahaprasthaner Pathey/Yatrik***; *Patri Chai*; *Abu Hossain*; *Chhoti Maa*; 1953: *Bana Hansi*; *Nabin Yatra/Naya Safar*; ***Sharey Chuattar***; *Shri Shri Satyanarayan*; *Chirantani*; *Chikitsa Sankat*; *Jhakmari*; 1954: *Maa-o-Chhele*; *Atom Bomb*; *Moyla Kagaj*; *Moner Mayur*; *Ora Thake Odhare*; *Naramedh Yagna*; ***Champadangar Bou***; *Prafulla*; *Ladies' Seat*; *Jagrihi*; *Sadanander Mela*; *Annapurnar Mandir*; *Chheley Kaar*; *Bokul/Bakul*; *Shoroshi*; *Grihapravesh*; *Jadubhatta*; ***Naukri***; 1955: *Shribatsa-Chinta*; *Nishiddha Phal*; *Chhoto Bou*; *Aparadhi*; *Jharer Parey*; *Joymakali Boarding*; *Katha Kao*; *Upahar*; ***Pather Panchali***; *Godhuli*; *Devimalini*; *Paresh*; *Du-Janay*; *Sabar Uparey*; *Kalindi*; *Sanjher Pradeep*; 1956: *Shyamali*; *Saheb Bibi Golam*; *Savdhan*; *Chirakumar Sabha*; *Ekti Raat*; *Asamapta*; *Rajpath*; *Nagardola*; *Chore*; *Amar Bou*; *Nabajanma*; *Asha*; 1957: *Sindoor*; *Ektara*; ***Adarsha Hindu Hotel***; *Abhishek*; *Abhoyer Biye*; *Baksiddha*; *Madhabir Jonye*; *Tamasha*; *Janmatithi*; ***Parash Pathar***; ***Ajantrik***; *Kancha-Mithey*; *Ogo Sunchho*; *Chandranath*; 1958: *Meja Jamai*; *Yamalaya Jibanta Manush*; *Sonar Kathi*; *Rajalakshmi-o-Shrikanta*; *Nupur*; *Swarga Martya*; *Jonakir Alo*; *Sadhak Bama Kshyapa*; *Indrani*; *Joutuk*; *Surya Toran*; *Shri Shri Tarakeshwar*; *Rajdhani Theke*; 1959: *Chaowa-Pawa*; *Thakur Haridas*; *Derso Khokhar Kando*; ***Deep Jweley Jai***; *Gali Theke Rajpath*; *Nirdharita Silpir Anupastithi Tey*; *Abak Prithvi*; *Mriter Martye Agaman*; *Personal Assistant*; 1960: *Maya Mriga*; *Kuhak*; *Akash-Patal*; *Bhoy*; *Dui Bechara*; *Khokha Babur Pratyabartan*; *Khudha*; *Kono-Ek-Din*; *Shesh Paryanta*; *Ajana Kahini*; *Nader Nimai*; *Suno Baro Nari*; *Gariber Meye*; 1961: *Sandhya Raag*; *Manik*; *Sadhak Kamalakanta*; *Lakshmi Narayan*; *Mr & Mrs Choudhury*; *Bishkanya*; *Swayambara*; *Kanchanmulya*; *Aaj Kal Parshu*; *Madhureno*; ***Saptapadi***; *Dui Bhai*; *Kanamachi*; 1962: *Mon Dilona Bandhu*; *Suryasnan*; *Shasti*; *Agun*; *Kajal*; *Shesh Chinha*; *Banarasi*; 1963: *Dui Bari*; *High Heel*.

CHAKRABORTY, UTPALENDU (b. 1948)

Bengali director, musician and novelist. Born in Pabna Dist. (now Bangladesh). Was influenced in early youth by his uncle, Communist writer Swarnakamal Bhattacharya who wrote ***Chinnamul*** and ***Tathapi*** (both 1950). Master's degree in modern history from University of Calcutta (1967) and associated with CPI(ML)-led student agitations. Published emphatically emotive short stories in anthology *Prasab* under the name of Swaranamitra. Worked as informal teacher among the tribals of Bengal, Bihar and Orissa until ill health forced his return to Calcutta (1971). Taught at higher secondary school. First film was 16mm documentary ***Mukti Chai*** made during the Emergency, campaigning for the release of political prisoners. Subsequent features, made with reluctance given his often-declared mistrust of both state and private funding agencies, continue his emphatic discursive style. Made short tv series addressing the status of women and a documentary on **S. Ray**.

FILMOGRAPHY: 1977: ***Mukti Chai*** (Doc); 1980: *Moyna Tadanta*; 1982: ***Chokh***; 1983: *Debabrata Biswas* (Doc); 1984: *Music of Satyajit Ray* (Doc); 1985: ***Debshishu***; 1986: *Aparichita* (TV); *Rang* (TV); 1988: *Bikalpa* (TV); 1989: *Fansi*; *Janani* (TV); *Dwibachan* (TV); *Sonar Chheye Dami* (TV); ***Chhandaneer***.

CHAKRAPANI (?-1975)

Legendary Telugu scenarist, producer and journalist; co-owner of the **Vijaya** Studio with B. Nagi Reddy. Born as Aluri Venkata Subba Rao in Tenali, Guntur Dist., AP. Became a Hindi scholar and briefly started a Hindi school. Participated in Gandhi's salt agitations. Started a literary career translating Saratchandra Chatterjee into Telugu. First script: **P. Pullaiah**'s ***Dharmapatni*** (1940); first success with **B.N. Reddi**'s melodrama ***Swargaseema*** (1945) based on his story and dialogue. Joined Nagi Reddy as a partner at Vijaya, scripting all its influential early **L.V. Prasad** hits: ***Shavukaru*** (1950), ***Pelli Chesi Choodu*** (1952), ***Missiamma*** (1955), ***Appu Chesi Pappu Koodu*** (1958). Started, on behalf of Nagi Reddy's BNK Press, the children's monthly *Chandamama* (1947), now published in 14 languages. Also started the popular journal *Yuva*. Credited himself with the direction of two films: *Manithan Maravillai*, which is the Tamil version of **K. Kameshwara Rao**'s Chakrapani-scripted hit ***Gundamma Katha*** (1962), and *Arasa Kattali* (1967). He is satirised in the film ***Chakrapani*** (1954).

CHAKRAVARTY, AMIYA (1912-57)

Hindi director born in Bogra (now Bangladesh). Child actor-singer on stage. Full-time political activist in early 30s, arrested during the Salt Satyagraha (1930) and forced to leave Bengal in 1935. Joined **Bombay Talkies** apparently as Bengali tutor to **Niranjan Pal**'s son. Scenarist of Najam Naqvi's *Punar Milan* (1940, with **Gyan Mukherjee**) and **Sushil Majumdar**'s *Char Aankhen* (1944). Assigned by **Devika Rani** to direct her and **Ashok Kumar** (in ***Anjaan***) when she took over studio management following **Himansu Rai**'s death. The split that followed with the establishment of **Filmistan** (1942), and the success of ***Basant*** (introducing Mumtaz Shanti) and ***Jwar Bhata*** (**Dilip Kumar**'s début) made him the studio's top director in its most controversial period. With **N.R. Acharya** (***Naya Sansar***, 1941), pioneered a new generation of film-making at Bombay Talkies, but adhered more to the **Osten-Rai** orthodoxy, especially in scripts and performances. Formed production company Mars & Movies, e.g. the successful Dilip Kumar film ***Daag***. His last feature was completed by **Nitin Bose**.

FILMOGRAPHY: 1941: ***Anjaan***; 1942: ***Basant***; 1944: ***Jwar Bhata***; 1947: *Mera Suhaag*; 1949: ***Girls' School***; 1950: *Gauna*; 1951: ***Badal***; 1952: ***Daag***; 1953: *Patita*; *Shahenshah*; 1954: *Badshah*; 1955: *Seema*; 1957: ***Dekh Kabira Roya***; ***Kathputli***.

CHANAKYA, TAPI (1925-73)

Telugu director born in Vizianagaram, Andhra Pradesh. Son of scenarist/lyricist **Tapi Dharma Rao**. Early interests in Telugu theatre. Was a radio telegraphist, also in the Army. Assistant in the sound department at Shobhanachala Studios, Madras (1947). Début at the Sarathi Studios where his first film, ***Anta Manavalle***, was a hit. His next one, ***Rojulu Marayi***, was even bigger. It had an anti-feudal ruralist theme, **Waheeda Rehman**'s screen début as a dancer and a score that was widely imitated in 50s Telugu film music. Later worked at **Vijaya** Studios and also in Tamil (the **MGR** hit *Enga Veetu Pillai*), Hindi (e.g. ***Ram Aur Shyam***). His *Bangaru Talli* was a Telugu remake of ***Mother India*** (1957) starring **Jaggaiah**, **Jamuna** (in **Nargis**' role) and **Shobhan Babu**.

FILMOGRAPHY: 1954: ***Anta Manavalle***; 1955: ***Rojulu Marayi/Kalam Maripochu***; 1957: *Peddarikalu*; 1958: ***Ettuku Pai Ettu***; 1959: *Bhagya Devatha/Bhagya Devathai*; *Kalisivunte Kaladu Sukham*; 1960:

MGR (centre) in Tapi Chanakya's *Enga Veetu Pillai* (1965)

Kumkumarekha; *Jalsarayudu*; *Pudhiya Pathai*; **1962**: *Constable Koothuru*; **1964**: *Varasatwam*; *Ramudu Bheemudu*; **1965**: ***CID***; *Enga Veetu Pillai*; **1966**: *Adugu Jadalu*; *Naan Anaittal*; **1967**: ***Ram Aur Shyam***; **1968**: *Oli Vilakku*; ***Pudhiya Bhoomi***; **1969**: *Madhavi*; **1970**: *Vidhi Vilasam*; **1971**: *Bangaru Talli*; *Man Mandir*; *Bikhare Moti*; **1972**: *Jaanwar Aur Insaan*; *Bandhipotu Bhayankara*; *Manavata*; *Subah-o-Shyam*; **1973**: *Ganga Manga*.

CHANDER, KRISHAN (1914-77)

One of the main modern Urdu writers. Regarded, with **Sadat Hasan Manto** and **Rajinder Singh Bedi**, as the literary generation that revolutionised post-war fiction, esp. the short story. Author of c.30 short-story anthologies and 20 novels. Best-known early writing set in native Kashmir, often elaborating strong contrasts between social oppression and the fertility of surrounding nature (e.g. *Tilism-e-Khayal*). Short satire, *Annadata*, adopted multiple pov narrative to describe the 1943 Bengal famine and was an important source for **Abbas**'s ***Dharti Ke Lal*** (1946). His major novel, *Jab Khet Jaage*, situated in the 1949 Telangana peasant uprising, was adapted by **Gautam Ghosh**'s ***Maabhoomi*** (1979). Employed in early 40s as dialogue writer at Shalimar Cinetone, Pune, along with other noted Hindi/Urdu writers. Josh Mahilabadi records their collective experiences there in his book *Yaadon Ki Baraat* (published in Pakistan). Also worked at **Sagar**. Wrote scripts and dialogue, e.g. for K.B. Lall and **Kardar**. Adapted Minoo Masani's *Our India* to the screen for **Zils** (***Hindustan Hamara***, 1950); also scripted his *Zalzala* (1952). Directed one film he didn't write: *Private Secretary* (1962).

CHANDRA, N. (b. 1952)

Hindi director. Full name: Chandrasekhar Narvekar. Born in Bombay. One of the most commercially successful directors in late 80s Hindi cinema. Former film editor and assistant to **Gulzar**; also assisted **Bapu**. His Shiv Sena propaganda film ***Ankush*** and his first independent production ***Tezaab*** relied on violence and recognisably Bombay settings. Claims to have first-hand experience of his plot-lines in his own working-class antecedents. The dialogue and several visual references, evoking Bombay's encoded and highly communal inner-city speech forms, are a brutalised yet more complex version of **Manmohan Desai**'s style (e.g. *Tezaab*, which contained the megahit song *Ek Do Teen*). Scripts and edits his own films.

FILMOGRAPHY: **1985**: ***Ankush***; **1987**: *Pratighaat*; **1988**: ***Tezaab***; **1991**: ***Narasimha***; *Hamla*; **1993**: *Yugandhar*.

CHANDRAKANT GAUR (b. 1929)

Hindi B-movie director of action films and mythologicals. His work extends the **Babubhai Mistri** tradition, featuring **Dara Singh** (who also worked for Mistri) and Marathi star **Jayshree Gadkar**. Made Punjabi hits (e.g. *Bhagat Dhanna Jat*) reviving the Punjabi cinema. Also made Gujarati mythologicals.

FILMOGRAPHY: **1951**: *Riding Hero*; **1955**: *Ganga Maiya*; **1956**: *Delhi Durbar*; **1957**: *Adhi Raat*; *Sant Raghu*; **1958**: *Circus Sundari*; **1959**: *Jaggu Daku*; **1961**: *Ramleela*; **1962**: *Jadugar Daku*; **1963**: *Maya Mahal*; *Zingaro*; **1964**: *Badshah*; *Roop Sundari*; *Veer Bhimsen*; **1968**: *Balaram Shri Krishna*; **1970**: *Tarzan 303*; **1971**: *Tulasi Vivah*; *Kabhi Dhoop Kabhi Chhaon*; **1972**: *Hari Darshan*; **1973**: *Mahasati Savitri*; **1974**: *Kisan Aur Bhagwan*; *Har Har Mahadev*; *Bhagat Dhanna Jat*; **1976**: *Bajrang Bali*; **1977**: *Bolo He Chakradari*; *Shri Krishna Sharanam Mama*; **1979**: *Shankar Parvati*; **1984**: *Shravan Kumar*; **1986**: *Krishna Krishna*.

Chandrakant Sangani *see* **Sangani, Chandrakant**

CHANDRAMOHAN (1905-49)

Actor born in Narasingpur. Employed by **Prabhat**'s distributors, Famous Pics. Cast by **Shantaram** in ***Amritmanthan*** mainly for his one physical characteristic: unusually large grey eyes, used to advantage in the film's famous opening sequence. Subsequently cast as elaborately costumed villain in several films, e.g. the Macbeth figure in ***Jwala***, the evil Ravana in **Vijay Bhatt**'s mythological *Rambaan*. Mostly acted in mythologicals and historicals (the Emperor Jehangir in **Sohrab Modi**'s ***Pukar***, and Randhir Singh in **Mehboob**'s ***Humayun***) but best remembered as the rapacious industrialist Seth Dharamdas in **Mehboob**'s ***Roti***.

FILMOGRAPHY: **1934**: ***Amritmanthan***; **1935**: ***Dharmatma***; **1936**: ***Amar Jyoti***; **1937**: ***Wahan***; **1938**: ***Jwala***; **1939**: ***Pukar***; **1940**: ***Bharosa***; ***Geeta***; **1942**: ***Apna Ghar/Aple Ghar***; *Jhankar*; ***Roti***; **1943**: *Fashion*; ***Naukar***; ***Shakuntala***; ***Taqdeer***; **1944**: *Bade Nawab Saheb*; *Draupadi*; *Mumtaz Mahal*; *Raunaq*; *Us Paar*; **1945**: ***Humayun***; *Pannadai*; *Preet*; *Ramayani*; **1946**: *Magadhraj*; *Shalimar*; *Shravan Kumar*; **1948**: *Dukhiari*; *Rambaan*; *Shaheed*; **1950**: *Chocolate*; **1954**: *Ramayan*; **1955**: *Bal Ramayan*.

CHANDRASEKHAR, RAJA (1904-71)

Tamil and Kannada director born in Tiruchirapalli, TN; aka Raja C. Sekhar. Former textile engineer. Started in film in Bombay (1926). Assistant to **Fatma Begum** (1929). Later with **General Pics** and **East India Film**. First film adapted **Veeranna**'s stage hit *Sadarame*. Early practitioner of Tamil costume dramas derived from Bombay version of Douglas Fairbanks movies. Was the film-maker who (with **Duncan**) gave Tamil superstar **MGR** his breaks (*Dakshayagnam*, *Maya Machhindra*, ***Ashok Kumar***). May have co-directed **Badami**'s début, *Harishchandra* at **Sagar** Film, although some sources credit co-direction of the film to T.C. Vadivelu Naicker. Also sometimes credited with direction of **A. Narayanan**'s *Gnanasoundari* (1935).

FILMOGRAPHY: **1932**: *Harishchandra*; **1935**: *Sadarame*; **1936**: *Chandramohana*; *Raja Desingu*; **1937**: *Bhakta Tulsidas*; **1938**: *Dakshayagnam*; **1939**: *Maya Machhindra*; **1941**: ***Ashok Kumar***; **1943**: *Arundhati*; **1948**: *Raja Mukthi*.

CHATTERJEE, ANIL (B. 1928)

Actor born in Calcutta. Degree in literature and stage actor (e.g. in Eric Elliot's Shakespeare Group). Introduced in **Ritwik Ghatak** films and later, with **Bijon Bhattacharya** and **Kali Bannerjee**, featured in several roles (e.g. as Rishi in ***Komal Gandhar*** and singer Shankar in ***Meghe Dhaka Tara***). Central to Ghatak's integration of folk/popular and classical performance styles. Best-known early 60s films with **Satyajit Ray**: ***Teen Kanya*** (the postmaster), ***Kanchanjungha*** (flirtatious photographer Anil), ***Mahanagar*** (lead role of Subrata Majumdar). Became 'a somewhat shadowy figure ... only brought in to fill a place for the traditional, none-too-bright, middle-class individual' (Das Gupta, *Talking About Films*, 1981). Played numerous lead and supporting roles in Bengali films by **Tapan Sinha**, and in socials pioneered by the **Agradoot** and **Yatrik** units. Other major roles are that of the psychopath in *Agni Sanskar* and the title role in *Deshbandhu Chittaranjan*. Recent films include those of **Utpalendu Chakraborty** (***Chokh***), **Gautam Ghosh** (***Paar***) and **Aparna Sen** (***Paroma***). Music director for *Mayabini Lane* (1966); also worked as assistant director (e.g. *Jog Biyog*, ***Dhuli***, *Asabarna*).

FILMOGRAPHY: **1952**: ***Nagarik***; **1953**: *Jog Biyog*; **1954**: *Moyla Kagaj*; ***Dhuli***; **1955**: *Sajghar*; *Bidhilipi*; **1956**: *Asabarna*; **1957**: *Garer Math*; *Ulka*; *Abhishek*; ***Ajantrik***; **1958**: *Priya*; *Rajalakshmi-o-Shrikanta*; *Kalamati*; **1959**: *Marutirtha Hinglaj*; *Chaowa-Pawa*; *Shri Shri Nityananda Prabhu*; ***Deep Jweley Jai***; *Rater Andhakare*; *Kshaniker Atithi*; **1960**: *Akash-Patal*; *Dui Bechara*; ***Devi***; ***Meghe Dhaka Tara***; *Gariber Meye*; *Kono-Ek-Din*; *Smriti Tuku Thak*; *Aparadh*; **1961**: *Mr & Mrs Choudhury*; ***Komal Gandhar***; *Agni Sanskar*; *Swaralipi*; ***Teen Kanya***; *Megh*; *Kanchanmulya*; *Ahwan*; **1962**: *Kancher Swarga*; *Suryasnan*; ***Kanchanjungha***; *Agun*; *Bandhan*; *Shesh Chinha*; *Kumari Mon*; *Rakta Palash*; **1963**: *Dui Bari*; *Barnachora*; *Uttarayan*; *High Heel*; ***Nirjan Saikate***; ***Mahanagar***; **1964**: *Kaalsrote*; *Jotugriha*; *Sindoore Megh*; *Ashanta Ghoorni*; *Sandhya Deeper Sikha*; *Ketumi*; **1965**: *Faraar*; *Jaya*; *Ghoom Bhangar Gaan*; *Devatar Deep*; **1966**: *Ashru Diye Lekha*; *Nutan Jiban*; *Sannata*; **1967**: *Akash Chhoan*; *Mahashweta*; **1968**: *Baluchari*; *Boudi*; *Jiban Sangeet*; *Panchasar*; **1969**: *Protidan*; *Teer Bhoomi*; **1970**: *Samanaral*; *Muktisnan*; *Sagina Mahato*; *Deshbandhu Chittaranjan*; **1971**: *Khunje Berai*; *Pratham Basanta*; *Sona Boudi*; **1972**: *Bohurupee*; ***Bilet Pherat***; *Duranta Jay*; *Chhandapatan*; **1973**: *Andhar Periye*; ***Bon Palashir Padabali***; *Alo Andhare*; *Megher Pare Megh*; **1974**: *Alor Thikana*; *Sujata*; *Sagina*; ***Amanush***; *Phulu Thakurma*; *Raja*; **1975**: *Ami Sey-o-Sekha*; *Phool Sajya*; *Bandi Bidhata*; *Sabhyasachi*; *Harmonium*; **1976**: *Mom Batti*; *Ajasra Dhanyabad*; *Nayan*; *Aguner Phulki*; *Asomoy*; *Ek Je Chhilo Desh*; *Samrat*; **1977**: *Avatar*; *Kabita*; *Pratima*; *Shesh Raksha*; **1978**: *Dhanraj Tamang*; *Maan Abhiman*; *Singhdwar*; *Striker*; *Tusi*; *Chameli Memsaheb*; *Hirey Manik*; *Lattu*; *Parichay*; **1979**: *Dour*; *Jiban Je Rakam*; **1980**: *Byapika Biday*; *Kalo Chokher Tara*; **1981**: *Saheb*; *Upalabdhi*; **1982**: ***Chokh***; *Swarna Mahal*; *Prahari*; *Bandini Kamala*; **1983**: *Muktir Din*; *Aloye Phera*; *Sagar Balaka*; *Jay Parajay*; *Mohoner Dike*; **1984**: *Debigarjan*; *Didi*; *Anveshan*; ***Ankahee***; *Surya Trishna*; ***Andhi Gali***; ***Paar***; *Mukta Pran*; *Sonar Sansar*; *Ajantay*; *Jog Biyog*; **1985**: *Amar Prithibi*; ***Paroma/Parama***; *Putulghar*; **1986**: *Ashirwad*; *Atanka*; *Madhumoy*; **1987**: *Bandookbaj*; *Rudrabina*; *Mahamilan*; *Aaj Ka Robin Hood*; **1988**: *Boba Sanai*; *Apaman*; *Surer Sathi*; ***Ek Din Achanak***; **1989**: *Bandhobi*; *Chokher Aloye*; *Amar Shapath*; *Aghaton Ajo Ghatey*; *Swarna Trishna*; *Aakhri Badla*; **1990**: *Agnikanya*.

CHATTERJEE, BASU (b. 1930)

Hindi director born in Ajmer, Rajasthan. Arrived in Bombay in the 50s and worked for 18 years as cartoonist-illustrator for weekly tabloid *Blitz*. Helped found the Film Forum Society (1959). Assisted **Basu Bhattacharya** on ***Teesri Kasam*** (1966). Worked in western region of Federation of Film Societies of India and on editorial board of *Close Up*, published by Film Forum in the 70s. First film ***Sara Akash*** noted for award-winning work of cinematographer K.K. Mahajan. Second film, *Piya Ka Ghar*, adapted **Raja Thakur**'s Marathi melodrama *Mumbaicha Javai* (1970), set in a lower-class tenement in Bombay. Moved to low-budget middle class comedies starring **Amol Palekar** (***Rajanigandha***, ***Chhotisi Baat***), which he adapted into a formula of rapidly shot sentimental low budget films. Made 4 tv serials (1985-9), shooting and editing 30' episodes in two days each. Best known for *Rajani* (about consumer rights), *Darpan* (a dramatisation of well-known short stories) and *Kakkaji Kahin*, a satire about politicians. Like Hitchcock, the director appears in very minor parts in his own films.

FILMOGRAPHY: **1969**: ***Sara Akash***; **1971**: *Piya Ka Ghar*; **1974**: *Us Paar*; ***Rajnigandha***; **1975**: ***Chhotisi Baat***; **1976**: *Chit Chor*; **1977**: ***Swami***; *Safed Jhooth*; *Priyatama*; **1978**: *Khatta Meetha*; *Chakravyuha*; *Dillagi*; *Tumhare Liye*; *Do Ladke Dono Kadke*; **1979**: *Manzil*; *Baaton Baaton Mein*; *Prem Vivah*; *Ratnadeep*; *Jeena Yahan*; **1980**: *Man Pasand*; *Apne Paraye*; **1981**: *Shaukeen*; *Hamari Bahu Alka*; **1983**: *Pasand Apni Apni*; **1984**: *Lakhon Ki Baat*; **1985**: *Rajani* (TV); *Darpan* (TV); *Pyari Behna*; *Ek Ruka Hua Faisla* (TV); **1986**: *Sheesha*; *Chameli Ki Shaadi*; *Kirayedaar*; *Bhim Bhawani* (TV); **1987**: *Zevar*; **1988**: *Kakkaji Kahin* (TV); **1989**: *Kamala Ki Maut*; *Durga*; **1990**: *Hamari Shaadi*; **1993**: *Byomkesh Bakshi* (TV).

CHATTERJEE, DHRITIMAN (b. 1946)

Actor. Played the unemployed youth, Siddhartha, in **Ray**'s ***Pratidwandi*** and the **Naxalite** in **Sen**'s ***Padatik***, making him the icon of Calcutta's middle-class sense of uncertainty after the late 60s agitations of the CPI(ML), echoing Bikash Bhattacharya's paintings of aimless youths wandering through Calcutta and Mahashweta Devi's fictional descriptions of the time. Acted in **Aparna Sen**'s ***36 Chowringhee Lane*** and in Ray's ***Ganashatru*** and ***Agantuk***. Does films as amateur alongside a career in advertising.

FILMOGRAPHY: **1970**: ***Pratidwandi***; **1972**: *Picnic*; **1973**: ***Padatik***; **1974**: ***Jadu Bansha***; **1977**: *Abirvab*; **1980**: ***Akaler Sandhaney***; **1981**: ***36 Chowringhee Lane***; **1983**: *Tanaya*; *Ka Lawei Ha Ki Ktijong Ngi* (also d); **1989**: ***Ganashatru***; **1991**: ***Agantuk***.

CHATTERJEE, NABYENDU (b. 1937)

Bengali director who started out, unsuccessfully, as an actor. Then assistant to Aravind Mukherjee (1962-5). Directorial début with an experimental Hindi film, followed by a hit Bengali film and continued directing in that language, bemoaning the passing of his notion of village life in Bengal (*Aaj Kal Parshur Galpa*) and the Calcutta middle-class sense of disorientation which turns politically and economically weak men into violent oppressors of women (*Chopper*). The women in his films tend to stand for the values of a pre-modern patriarchal order. Unsuccessfully tried to extend **Mrinal Sen**'s early-70s approach in the 80s.

FILMOGRAPHY: **1967**: *Naya Raasta*; **1968**: *Adwitiya*; **1972**: *Chitthi*; *Ranur Pratham Bhaag*; **1981**: *Aaj Kal Parshur Galpa*; **1985**: *Chopper*; **1987**: *Sarisreep*; **1989**: *Parashuramer Kuthar*; **1990**: *Atmaya*; **1993**: *Shilpi*.

CHATTERJEE, PASHUPATI (1906-91?)

Bengali director born in Chandernagore, West Bengal. Graduated from Calcutta University and became a photo-journalist. Worked with **Premankur Atorthy** on the journal *Nachgar*. Assisted **Debaki Bose** (1934) on ***Inquilab***; then joined **New Theatres** (1935) where he worked with **Amar Mullick** (e.g. lyrics for ***Bardidi***, 1939; dialogues for ***Abhinetri***, 1940). Became an independent producer with *Swami* and was active in trade organisations. Early films based on Saratchandra's fiction. He edited a number of journals including the literary journal *Natun Lekha* and wrote extensively on film history, e.g. in the Calcutta Film Society journal *Chitravash*.

FILMOGRAPHY: **1942**: *Parineeta*; **1944**: *Shesh Raksha*; **1948**: *Priyatama*; *Arakshaniya*; **1949**: *Swami*; **1951**: *Nastaneer*; **1953**: *Niskriti*; **1954**: *Shoroshi*; **1955**: *Nishiddha Phal*; **1956**: *Mamlar Phal*; **1959**: *Mriter Martye Agaman*.

CHATTERJEE, SABITRI (b. 1937)

Bengali actress born in Comilla (now Bangladesh). Migrated to Calcutta at an early age; joined films as an extra, usually in dance sequences (e.g. *Anuraag*, *Alladdin-o-Ashcharya Pradeep*), while doing realistic theatre (e.g. Salil Sen's ***Natun Yahudi***, 1951, filmed in 1953). Début as lead actress in *Pasher Bari*. Following **Nirmal Dey**'s ***Basu Parivar*** and **Niren Lahiri**'s *Subhadra*, gained a reputation for comedy. Developed, along with actresses like Anubha Gupta and Manju Dey, an unorthodox style departing from the melodramatic mode of 40s Bengali film heroines. Also worked on stage, e.g. in *Adarsha Hindu Hotel* (with **Bhanu Bannerjee** and **Dhiraj Bhattacharya**) and in *Shyamali* (with **Uttam Kumar**). Acted in early **Mrinal Sen** films (*Raat Bhore*, *Abasheshe*) and produced his *Pratinidhi*.

FILMOGRAPHY: **1951**: *Anuraag*; **1952**: *Alladdin-o-Ashcharya Pradeep*; *Pasher Bari*; ***Basu Parivar***; *Subhadra*; **1953**: *Boudir Bone*; *Kajari*; ***Natun Yahudi***; *Keranir Jiban*; *Sosur Bari*; *Rami Chandidas*; *Lakh Taka*; *Sitar Patal Prabesh*; *Adrishya Manush*; *Blind Lane*; **1954**: *Atom Bomb*; *Moyla Kagaj*; ***Champadangar Bou***; *Bhanga-Gara*; *Kalyani*; *Annapurnar Mandir*; **1955**: *Pather Sheshey*; *Bidhilipi*; *Upahar*; *Godhuli*; *Dui Bone*; *Bratacharini*; *Paresh*; *Drishti*; *Kalindi*; *Ardhangini*; *Anupama*; *Raikamal*; **1956**: *Raat Bhore*; *Paradhin*; *Mamlar Phal*; *Chalachal*; *Govindadas*; *Maa*; *Daner Maryada*; *Sinthir Sindoor*; *Nabajanma*; *Savdhan*; **1957**: *Shesh Parichaya*; *Ektara*; *Natun Prabhat*; *Taser Ghar*; *Kancha-Mithey*; *Punar Milan*; *Basanta Bahar*; *Abhishek*; *Abhoyer Biye*; *Baksiddha*; ***Adarsha Hindu Hotel***; **1958**: *Priya*; *Megh Malhar*; *Dak Harkara*; *Nupur*; *Daktar Babu*; *Marmabani*; **1959**: *Nauka Bilash*; *Marutirtha Hinglaj*; *Shashi Babur Sansar*; *Gali Theke Rajpath*; *Abak Prithvi*; *Rater Andhakare*; **1960**: *Raja-Saja*; *Kuhak*; *Haat Baraley Bandhu*; *Khudha*; *Gariber Meye*; **1961**: *Dui Bhai*; *Kanamachi*; **1962**: *Khana*; *Nav Diganta*; *Abasheshe*; **1963**: *Uttarayan*; *Bhranti Bilas*; *Akash Pradeep*; *Shreyasi*; **1964**: *Pratinidhi*; *Marutrisha*; *Momer*

Alo; **1965**: *Antaral*; *Jaya*; *Pati Sansodhini Samiti*; *Dinanter Alo*; *Gulmohar*; *Kal Tumi Aleya*; **1966**: *Joradighir Choudhury Paribar*; *Susanta Sha*; **1967**: *Grihadah*; **1968**: *Baluchari*; *Pathe Holo Dekha*; **1970**: *Shasti*; *Aleyar Alo*; *Kalankita Nayak*; *Muktisnan*; *Sheela*; *Nala Damayanti*; *Nishipadma*; *Manjari Opera*; **1971**: *Dhanyi Meye*; *Pratham Pratisruti*; *Sansar*; *Sona Boudi*; **1972**: *Natun Diner Alo*; *Sapath Nilam*; *Shesh Parba*; **1973**: *Bhangan*; **1974**: *Umno-o-Jhumno*; *Mouchak*; *Swikarokti*; **1975**: *Phool Sajya*; *Sei Chokh*; **1976**: *Aguner Phulki*; **1977**: *Brajabuli*; *Mantramugdha*; *Shesh Raksha*; **1978**: *Hirey Manik*; **1980**: *Raj Nandini*; **1981**: *Pratishodh*; **1985**: *Hulusthul*; *Till Theke Tal*; **1986**: *Cheleta*; **1987**: *Nadiya Nagar*; *Tunibou*.

CHATTERJEE, SOUMITRA (b. 1934)

Bengali star. Started as radio announcer. Trained as actor under **Ahindra Choudhury** while still a student. Wrote, directed and acted in plays like *Rajkumar* and *Naam Jiban*. Also a poet and initiator of Bengal's best-known literary journal, *Ekshan* which he co-edited with Nirmal Acharya. With **Uttam Kumar** the major 60s and 70s star of Bengali film. Début with **Ray**'s ***Apur Sansar***; has thereafter remained associated with Ray, and was described by Pauline Kael as his 'one-man stock company'. **Chidananda Das Gupta** (*Talking About Films*, 1981) suggested Ray cast him so often because of a distinct physical resemblance to the young **Tagore**. Repeated aspects of his most famous Ray role in ***Charulata*** as a leitmotiv in ***Kapurush*** and ***Aranyer Din Ratri***, of the brash but insecure hero. Also played the detective Felu in children's films (***Sonar Kella***, ***Joi Baba Felunath***) and several 'character' roles, including the rough taxi driver in ***Abhijaan*** and the famine-stricken Brahmin in ***Ashani Sanket***. Other major roles in **Tapan Sinha**'s ***Kshudista Pashan***, **Mrinal Sen**'s ***Akash Kusum***, several **Ajoy Kar** films (***Saat Pake Bandha***, *Kanch Kata Hirey*) and **Majumdar**'s ***Sansar Simantey*** and ***Ganadevata***. Since ***Ghare Baire*** spent more time on the stage and doing poetry readings.

FILMOGRAPHY: 1959: ***Apur Sansar***; **1960**: ***Devi***; ***Kshudista Pashan***; **1961**: *Swaralipi*; ***Teen Kanya***; *Swayambara*; *Jhinder Bandi*; ***Punashcha***; **1962**: *Shasti*; *Atal Jaler Ahwan*; *Agun*; *Banarasi*; ***Abhijaan***; **1963**: ***Saat Pake Bandha***; *Shesh Prahar*; *Barnali*; **1964**: *Pratinidhi*; ***Charulata***; *Kinu Goyalar Gali*; *Ayananta*; **1965**: *Baksha Badal*; *Ek Tuku Basa*; *Raj Kanya*; ***Kapurush***; ***Akash Kusum***; *Eki Ange Eto Rup*; **1966**: *Joradighir Choudhury Paribar*; *Kanch Kata Hirey*; *Manihar*; **1967**: *Ajana Shapath*; *Hathat Dekha*; *Mahashweta*; *Prastar Swakshar*; **1968**: *Baghini*; *Parishodh*; **1969**: ***Aparichita***; *Chena Achena*; *Parineeta*; ***Teen Bhubhaner Parey***; ***Aranyer Din Ratri***; **1970**: *Aleyar Alo*; *Padmagolap*; *Pratham Kadam Phool*; **1971**: *Khunje Berai*; *Malayadaan*; *Sansar*; **1972**: *Jiban Saikate*; *Natun Diner Alo*; *Stree*; *Basanta Bilap*; ***Bilet Pherat***; **1973**: ***Ashani Sanket***; *Epar Opar*; *Nishi Kanya*; *Shesh Pristhay Dekhun*; *Agni Bhramar*; **1974**: *Asati*; *Jadi Jantem*; *Sangini*; ***Sonar Kella***; *Chhutir Phande*; **1975**: *Nishi Mrigaya*; ***Sansar Simantey***; *Sudur Niharika*; **1976**: *Datta*; *Nandita*; **1977**: *Babu Moshai*; *Mantramugdha*; *Pratima*; **1978**: *Nadi Theke Sagare*; ***Ganadevata***; *Job Charnaker Bibi*; ***Joi Baba Felunath***; *Pronoy Pasha*; **1979**: *Devdas*; *Nauka Dubi*; **1980**: *Darpachurna*; *Gharer Baire Ghar*; ***Hirak Rajar Deshe***; *Pankhiraj*; **1981**: *Father*; *Nyay Anyay*; *Khelar Putul*; **1982**: *Preyasi*; *Matir Swarga*; *Agradani*; *Simanta Raag*; **1983**: *Indira*; *Chena Achena*; *Amar Geeti*; **1984**: *Achena Mukh*; ***Kony***; *Lal Golap*; ***Ghare Baire***; *Vasundhara*; **1985**: *Baikunther Will*; *Tagori*; *Sandhya Pradeep*; **1986**: *Urbashe*; *Shyam Saheb*; *Atanka*; **1987**: *Raj Purush*; *Nyay Adhikar*; *Sukumar Ray*; **1988**: *Channachara*; *Agaman*; *Agni Sanket*; *Agun*; *Debibaran*; *Anjali*; *Pratik*; **1989**: *Maryada*; *Jankar*; *Amar Shapath*; ***Ganashatru***; **1990**: *Manasi*; *Ekhane Amar Swarga*; *Apon Amar Apon*; ***Shakha Proshakha***; **1991**: ***Mahaprithibi***; **1993**: *Uttoran*.

Sandhya Roy and Soumitra Chatterjee in *Ek Tuku Basa* (1965)

CHATTOPADHYAY, KARTICK (1912-89)

Bengali-Hindi director best known for late 40s **New Theatres** films e.g. ***Mahaprasthaner Pathey***. Début with *Rural Life in Bengal*. First feature, ***Ramer Sumati***, based on Saratchandra Chatterjee's story; launched K.C. Prod. (1954) with Arun Choudhury's *Ladies' Seat*. His *Saheb Bibi Golam*, adapted from Bimal Mitra's novel and starring **Uttam Kumar** was later re-adapted by **Guru Dutt**.

FILMOGRAPHY: 1947: *Rural Life in Bengal* (Doc); ***Ramer Sumati/Chhota Bhai***; **1952**: ***Mahaprasthaner Pathey/Yatrik***; **1953**: *Bana Hansi*; **1955**: *Godhuli*; **1956**: *Saheb Bibi Golam*; *Chore*; **1957**: *Neelachaley Mahaprabhu*; *Chandranath*; **1959**: *Jal-Jangal*; **1965**: *Gulmohar*.

CHERIAN, P. J. (1891-1981)

Actor-producer, born in Ernakulam Dist., Kerala. Produced P.V. Krishna Iyer's *Nirmala* (1948), the first Malayalam sound film made in Kerala. Regarded as the founder of the Malayalam film industry. Owned the Royal Dramatic Co. (later Royal Cinema & Dramatic Co.), the main professional stage company in 30s Kerala, known mainly for its staging of Christian themes (e.g. *Parudisa Nashtam*, adapting *Paradise Lost*). Known also as a painter in the **Raja Ravi Varma** tradition and was awarded the title of Artist Chevalier by the Pope. Acted in S.S. Rajan's ***Snehaseema*** (1954).

CHINAPPA, PUDUKOTTAI ULAGANATHAN (1915-51)

Major 40s Tamil star born in Pudukottai, the son of a stage actor. Joined the Madurai Original Boys' Co. aged 8; later known as actor and singer, releasing several records many of which (along with his subsequent film music) have remained popular. Trained in Carnatic music by Nannaya Bhagavathar and Karaikal Vedachala Bhagavathar; simultaneously trained in traditional martial arts (e.g. silabhum) and gymnastics. Début at Jupiter Pics in **Raja Sandow**'s *Chandrakantha*; broke through with a double role in **T.R. Sundaram**'s *Uthama Puthran* based on A. Dumas's *The Man in the Iron Mask*. Displayed his musical abilities as well as those of actor and stuntman in Sundaram's *Manonmani*; also remembered for his acting and clear diction as Kovalan in **T.R. Raghunath**'s ***Kannagi***.

FILMOGRAPHY: 1936: *Chandrakantha*; ***Iru Sahodarargal***; **1937**: ***Rajamohan***; **1938**: *Anadhai Penn*; *Punjab Kesari*; *Yayati*; **1939**: ***Mathru Bhoomi***; **1940**: *Uthama Puthran*; **1941**: *Kacha Devayani*; *Aryamala*; *Dharmaveeran*; *Dayalan*; **1942**: ***Kannagi***; *Prithvirajan*; *Harishchandra*; **1943**: *Kubera Kuchela*; *Manonmani*; **1944**: *Jagathala Prathapan*; ***Mahamaya***; **1945**: *Ardhanari*; **1946**: *Pankajavalli*; *Vikatakavi*; **1947**: *Tulasi Jalandhar*; **1948**: *Krishna Bhakti*; **1949**: *Mangayar Karasi*; *Ratnakumar*; **1951**: *Vanasundari*; *Sudarshan*.

CHILDREN'S FILM SOCIETY

Set up in 1955 as an autonomous body under the Central Government's Information & Broadcasting Ministry's control. Produced films by e.g. **Ezra Mir**, **Kidar Sharma**, **Tapan Sinha**, **Sai Paranjpye** and **Shyam Benegal**. Although it has no independent distribution, it makes 16mm prints of its own productions and of imported children's films available to educational institutions for nominal fees. Current annual production budget is c.Rs 5 million. Organises a biennial competitive international children's film festival. Renamed the National Centre of Films for Children and Young People in 1992. 1993 chairperson is Jaya Bhaduri-Bachchan, who presided over a fundamental reshaping of the organisation.

CHIRANJEEVI (b. 1955)

Macho 80s Telugu megastar. Born in Narasapuram taluk, AP, as Shivashankara Varaprasad. Student at the Madras Film Institute and amateur stage actor. First public performance in the Republic Day parade ballet of AP (1976). Early films with **Bapu** (*Manavoori Pandavalu*) and **K. Balachander** (*Idi Kathakadu*, *47 Rojulu*, and more recently, *Rudraveena*, produced by his brother-in-law and regular producer Allu Aravind). Routine career in late 70s films was transformed by the spectacular success of his negative role in Kodi Ramakrishna's *Intilo Ramayya Vidhilo Krishnayya*. Developed his main reputation in violent gangster thrillers, a genre pioneered by A. Kodandarami Reddy (*Khaidi*, *Goonda*, *Challenge*, *Vijeta*, *Marana Mridangam*, *Trinetrudu* etc.), Vijaya Bapineedu (*Khaidi No. 786*, *Gang Leader*) and more recently, Raviraja Pinisetty (*Jwala*, *Chakravarthi*). Much of his character impersonates the 'rowdysheeter', a legal term of colonial vintage, indicating a potentially violent person who's on a police list and gets rounded up when violence is anticipated. The term is referred to in titles like B. Gopal's *State Rowdy*. Hindi début with *Pratibandh*, followed by *Aaj Ka Goonda Raj*, both directed by Pinisetty (aka Ravi Raja), have established him as one of the highest-paid stars in the country in the early 90s.

FILMOGRAPHY: **1978**: *Punadhirallu*; *Pranam Khareedu*; *Manavoori Pandavalu*; *Thayaramma Bangaraiah*; *Priya*; **1979**: *Kukkakatuku Cheppu Debba*; *Idi Kathakadu*; *I Love You*; *Kotha Alludu*; *Shri Rama Bantu*; *Kotala Rayudu*; **1980**: *Kothapeda Rowdy*; *Chandi Priya*; *Arani Mantulu*; *Jatara*; *Punnani Mogudu*; *Nakili Manishi*; *Love in Singapore*; *Prema Tarangulu*; *Mogudu Kavali*; *Raktha Sambandham*; **1981**: *Adavallu Meeku Joharlu*; *Parvati Parameshwarulu*; *Todu Dongalu*; *Tiruguleni Manishi*; *Prema Natakam*; *Nyayam Kavali*; *Urikichina Mata*; *Rani Kasularangamma*; *47 Rojulu*; *Sirirasthu Subhamasthu*; *Chattaniki Kallulevu*; *Kirai Rowdylu*; *Intilo Ramayya Vidhilo Krishnayya*; **1982**: *Bandipotu Simham*; *Shubhalekha*; *Idi Pellantara*; *Seeta Devi*; *Radha My Darling*; *Tingu Rangadu*; *Patnam Vachina Pativrathalu*; *Billa Ranga*; *Yamakinkarudu*; *Mondighatam*; *Manchu Pallaki*; **1983**: *Bandhulu Anubandhulu*; *Prema Pichollu*; *Palletooru Monagallu*; *Abhilasha* (Tel); *Alayashikharam*; *Sivudu Sivudu Sivudu*; *Puli Bebbuli*; *Goodachari No. 1*; *Maha Maharaju*; *Rosha Gadu*; *Maa Inti Premayanam*; *Simhapuri Simham*; *Khaidi*; *Mantrigari Viyankudu*; *Sangharshana*; *Hero* (Tel); *Yuddha Bhoomi*; **1984**: *Allulostunnaru*; *Goonda*; *Devanthakudu*; *Mahanagaramlo Mayagadu*; *Challenge*; *Intiguttu*; *Naagu*; *Agni Gundam*; *Rustom*; **1985**: *Chattamtho Poratham*; *Donga*; *Chiranjeevi*; *Jwala*; *Puli*; *Raktha Sindooram*; *Adavi Donga*; *Vijeta*; *Kirathakudu*; **1986**: *Kondaveeti Raja*; *Mahadheerudu*; *Veta*; *Chantabbayi*; *Rakshasudu*; *Dhairyavanthudu*; *Chanakya Sapatham*; **1987**: *Donga Mogudu*; *Aradhana*; *Chakravarthi*; *Pasivadi Pranam*; *Swayamkrushi*; *Jebu Donga*; *Manchi Donga*; **1988**: *Rudraveena*; *Yamudiki Mogudu*; *Khaidi No. 786*; *Marana Mridangam*; *Trinetrudu*; **1989**: *Attaki Yamudu, Ammayiki Mugudu*; *State Rowdy*; *Lankeshwarudu*; *Kondaveeti Donga*; **1990**: *Jagadeka Veerudu Attilokasundari*; *Kodama Simham*; *Raja Vikramarka*; *Pratibandh*; **1991**: *Gang Leader*; *Rowdy Alludu*; *Aaj Ka Goonda Raj*; *Stuvartpuram Police Station*; **1992**: *Gharana Mogudu*; *Mutta Mestri*; **1993**: *Mechanic Alludu*.

Leela Chitnis and Bharat Bhushan in *Maa* (1952)

CHITNIS, LEELA (b. 1912)

Actress born in Dharwar, Karnataka. Best known for her mother roles in 60s/70s Hindi cinema. She brought to Hindi film a performative idiom developed in Marathi stage melodramas by the Natyamanwantar group's introduction of Ibsenite naturalism (see **K. Narayan Kale**). Early stage work in the Natyamanwantar group itself (e.g. the prose comedy *Usna Navra*, 1934) and with her theatre group Naytasadhana in **P.K. Atre**'s *Udyacha Sansar*. Wrote and directed the stage adaptation of Somerset Maugham's *Sacred Flame* (*Ek Ratra Ardha Diwas*, 1957). Entered films as extra at **Sagar**; later in B-grade mythologicals and Ram Daryani stunt pictures. In Daryani's *Gentleman Daku*, playing the elegant thief dressed in male costume, she was advertised in the *Times of India* (1938) as 'the first graduate society-lady on the screen from Maharashtra'. Worked at **Prabhat** (***Wahan***). First major role in **Ranjit**'s Saint film, ***Sant Tulsidas*** as **Vishnupant Pagnis**'s wife Ratnavali. Romantic lead opposite **Ashok Kumar** in major **Bombay Talkies** films ***Kangan***, ***Bandhan*** and ***Jhoola*** made her briefly one of the top stars of the early 40s. Played the mother (of hero **Dilip Kumar**) for the first time in *Shaheed* and consolidated her image in her famous portrayal of **Raj Kapoor**'s mother in ***Awara*** and, later, in the famous role of the mother of the warring brothers in ***Ganga Jumna***. Also acted key roles in **Master Vinayak** (***Chhaya***, ***Ardhangi***) and **Raja Paranjpe** (*Jara Japoon*, *Adhi Kalas Mag Paya*) films in Marathi. Produced *Kisise Na Kehna* (1942) and directed *Aaj Ki Baat*. Her autobiography was published in 1981.

FILMOGRAPHY (* also d): **1935**: *Dhuwandhaar*; *Shri Satyanarayan*; **1936**: *Berozgar*; ***Chhaya***; **1937**: *Insaaf*; *Gentleman Daku*; ***Wahan***; **1938**: *Chhote Sarkar*; ***Jailor***; *Ustad*; *Vijay Danka*; **1939**: *Chhotisi Duniya*; ***Sant Tulsidas***; ***Kangan***; **1940**: ***Azad***; ***Bandhan***; ***Ardhangi/Ghar Ki Rani***; **1941**: ***Jhoola***; *Kanchan*; **1942**: *Kisise Na Kehna*; **1943**: *Rekha*; **1944**: *Kiran*; *Char Aankhen*; *Manorama*; **1945**: *Ghazal*; **1946**: *Bhakta Prahlad*; *Devkanya*; *Shatranj*; **1947**: *Andhon Ki Duniya*; *Ghar Ghar Ki Kahani*; **1948**: *Lakhpati*; *Shaheed*; **1949**: *Namuna*; *Aakhri Paigham*; **1950**: *Saudamini*; *Jara Japoon*; **1951**: ***Awara***; *Saiyan*; **1952**: *Maa*; *Ek Hota Raja*; *Sangdil*; **1953**: *Rami Dhoban*; *Hari Darshan*;

Naya Ghar; 1954: ***Baadbaan***; 1955: *Aaj Ki Baat**; 1956: *Basant Bahar*; ***Awaaz***; 1957: ***Naya Daur***; 1958: ***Phir Subah Hogi***; ***Post Box 999***; *Sadhana*; 1959: *Barkha*; ***Dhool Ka Phool***; *Kal Hamara Hai*; *Main Nashe Mein Hoon*; *Ujala*; 1960: ***Apna Haath Jagannath***; *Ghunghat*; *Hum Hindustani*; *Kohinoor*; *Bewaqoof*; *Maa Baap*; *Parakh*; ***Kala Bazaar***; *Umaji Naik*; *Sakhya Savara Mala*; 1961: *Aas Ka Panchhi*; *Batwara*; *Kaanch Ki Gudiya*; *Char Diwari*; ***Ganga Jumna***; ***Hum Dono***; *Ramleela*; *Adhi Kalas Mag Paya*; 1962: *Aashiq*; *Prem Andhala Asta*; *Asli Naqli*; *Dr Vidya*; *Manmauji*; *Naag Devata*; 1963: *Dil Hi To Hai*; *Pahu Re Kiti Vaat!*; 1964: ***Dosti***; *Aap Ki Parchhaiyan*; *Pooja Ke Phool*; *Shehnai*; *Suhagan*; *Zindagi*; 1965: *Johar Mehmood In Goa*; *Mohabbat Isko Kehte Hain*; *Nai Umar Ki Nai Fasal*; ***Waqt***; ***Guide***; *Faraar*; 1966: *Dulhan Ek Raat Ki*; *Phool Aur Patthar*; 1967: *Gunahon Ka Devta*; *Aurat*; *Manjhli Didi*; 1969: *Inteqam*; *Prince*; *Badi Didi*; *The Killers*; *Ram Bhakta Hanuman*; 1970: *Man Ki Aankhen*; *Jeevan Mrityu*; *Bhai Bhai*; 1977: *Palkon Ki Chhaon Mein*; 1978: ***Satyam Shivam Sundaram***; 1979: *Janata Havaldar*; *Aangan Ki Kali*; *Bin Maa Ke Bachche*; 1980: *Takkar*; 1985: *Dil Tujhko Diya*.

CHOPRA, BALDEV RAJ (b. 1914)

Hindi director and producer born in Ludhiana, Punjab. He is the elder brother of **Yash Chopra**. Studied at the University of Lahore. Worked on fringe of Lahore-based film industry with **Pancholi** group and later as film journalist. Edited the *Cine Herald* (1937-47) at Lahore. After Partition moved to Delhi where he was briefly assistant editor of *The Listener* (1947), then to Bombay. Started as a producer for Shri Gopal Pics (*Karwat*, 1949, apparently also directing the film). The success of ***Chandni Chowk*** allowed him to found B.R. Films (1956). One of the most influential émigrés from Lahore (with **A.R. Kardar** and **Roop K. Shorey**) who imported their lumpenised versions of Hollywood suspense thrillers and melodrama. Since the mid-70s the Hindi film industry's senior spokesman and a regular contributor to *Screen* (Bombay) in late 60s and 70s, influencing the film-financing policy of the **NFDC**. Now concentrates on the business affairs of his company, leaving direction to his son Ravi who is credited as co-director on the 94 episodes of the tv serial *Mahabharat*, running on **Doordarshan** in 1988-90, with peak audience at 75% of the urban adult population and over Rs 10 million advertising revenue per episode. Also co-directed *Kal Ki Awaaz* with Ravi Chopra.

FILMOGRAPHY: 1949: *Karwat* (uncredited); 1951: ***Afsana***; 1953: *Sholay*; 1954: ***Chandni Chowk***; 1956: *Ek Hi Raasta*; 1957: ***Naya Daur***; 1958: *Sadhana*; 1960: ***Kanoon***; 1963: ***Gumrah***; 1967: *Hamraaz*; 1972: *Dastaan*; 1973: ***Dhund***; 1977: *Karm*; 1978: *Pati Patni Aur Woh*; 1980: ***Insaaf Ka Tarazu***; 1982: *Nikaah*; 1985: *Tawaif*; 1986: *Bahadur Shah Zafar* (TV); 1987: *Awaam*; 1988: *Mahabharat* (TV); 1992: *Kal Ki Awaaz*; *Sauda* (TV).

CHOPRA, YASH (b. 1932)

Hindi director and producer born in Jullundur, Punjab. Started as assistant to elder brother **B.R. Chopra** and then made several films for his company. Became independent producer with ***Daag***, working mostly with distributor Gulshan Rai. His B.R. Films are low-budget genre movies (e.g. suspense thrillers: ***Waqt***, ***Ittefaq***) but his own productions are plushy, soft-focus upper-class love stories (***Kabhi Kabhie***), battles over family honour (embodied by the mother: ***Deewar***, ***Trishul***) and the conflict between the laws of kinship and those of the State. **Amitabh Bachchan** made some of his best-known films with Chopra. In the 90s, he adapted his style to the image of Shah Rukh Khan for the hit *Darr*.

FILMOGRAPHY: 1959: ***Dhool Ka Phool***; 1961: *Dharmaputra*; 1965: ***Waqt***; 1969: *Admi Aur Insaan*; ***Ittefaq***; 1973: ***Daag***; *Joshila*; 1975: ***Deewar***; 1976: ***Kabhi Kabhie***; 1978: ***Trishul***; 1979: ***Kala Pathar***; 1981: ***Silsila***; 1984: *Mashaal*; 1985: *Faasle*; 1988: *Vijay*; 1989: ***Chandni***; 1991: *Lamhe*; 1992: *Parampara*; 1993: *Darr*.

CHOUDHURY, AHINDRA (1897-1974)

Actor born in Calcutta. Major **Calcutta Theatres** stage star launched with key role of Arjun in epochal production of *Karnarjun* at Star Theatre (1923). Stagework in e.g. *Iraner Rani*, *Bandini*, *Chirakumar Sabha*, *Mishar Rani* etc. had impact comparable to that of **Sisir Bhaduri**, who had a similar career. Early films at **Madan Theatres**, usually by **Jyotish Bannerjee** who continued to direct him into the talkie era, included stage successes like *Mishar Rani* and *Karnarjun*. At Madan also filmed scenes from his stage plays in early sound experiments. In 1928 attempted, unsuccessfully, to start the Ahindra Film Studio at Ultadanga, North Calcutta. Then directed some Telugu films for **Aurora** (*Ansuya*, *Vipranarayana*). Was a regular genre actor in Bengali cinema, notably in films by **Sailajananda Mukherjee**, **P.C. Barua** and **Modhu Bose**, until he retired in mid-50s. Wrote a two-volume autobiography, *Nijere Haraye Khunji* (1945).

FILMOGRAPHY (* also d): 1922: *Soul of a Slave*; *Bishabriksha*; 1924: *Premanjali*; *Mishar Rani*; 1926: *Krishna Sakha**; 1927: *Durgesh Nandini*; 1928: *Sasthi Ki Shanti*; *Bishabriksha*; 1930: *Rajsingha* (all St); 1931: *Rishir Prem*; *Prahlad*; 1932: *Vishnu Maya*; *Krishnakanter Will*; 1933: *Seeta*; 1934: *Chand Saudagar*; *Rooplekha/Mohabbat Ki Kasauti*; *Mahua*; *Daksha Yagna*; *Bhakta Ke Bhagwan*; 1935: *Ansuya**; *Devadasi*; *Prafulla*; *Kanthahaar*; *Balidan*; 1936: *Tarubala*; *Krishna Sudama*; *Paraparey*; *Rajani*; ***Sarala***; ***Sonar Sansar***; *Dalit Kusum*; *Prabas Milan*; *Chino Haar*; 1937: *Vipranarayana**; ***Talkie Of Talkies***; *Haranidhi*; *Indira*; *Samaj Patan*; 1938: *Abhinaya*; *Devifullara*; *Khana*; 1939: *Janak Nandini*; *Jakher Dhan*; *Nara Narayan*; *Rikta*; *Rukmini*; *Sharmistha*; *Chanakya*; *Vaman Avtar*; 1940: *Tatinir Bichar*; *Kamale Kamini*; *Suktara*; *Doctor*; *Amar Geeti*; *Rajkumarer Nirbashan*; 1941: ***Raj Nartaki/Court Dancer***; *Uttarayan*; ***Doctor***; *Avatar*; *Nandini*; *Karnarjun*; 1942: *Jiban Sangini*; *Ashok*; *Pativrata*; *Avayer Biye*; ***Shesh Uttar/Jawab***; ***Meenakshi***; 1943: ***Jogajog/Hospital***; *Janani*; *Dwanda*; *Devar*; 1944: *Matir Ghar*; *Sandhya*; *Sondhi/Sandhi*; *Shesh Raksha*; 1945: *Amiri*; *Banphool*; *Vasiyatnama*; *Abhinay Nay*; ***Mane Na Mana***; *Kalankini*; *Grihalakshmi*; *Bondita*; *Nandita*; *Dui Purush*; 1946: *Pehchan*; *Prem Ki Duniya*; *Pather Sathi*; *Natun Bou*; *Nivedita*; *Dukhe Jader Jiban Gara*; 1947: *Roy Choudhury*; *Mandir*; *Alaknanda*; *Giribala*; *Abhijog*; *Burmar Pathey*; 1948: *Jayjatra/Vijay Yatra*; *Bicharak*; *Ghumiye Ache Gram*; *Nandaranir Sansar*; *Priyatama*; *Sir Shankarnath*; *Swarnaseeta*; 1949: *Abhijatya*; *Bisher Dhoan*; *Niruddesh*; *Pratirodh*; *Nirdosh Abla*; 1950: *Kuhelika*; ***Michael Madhusudhan***; *Pattharar Kahini*; *Sanchali*; *Vidyasagar*; *Mahasampad*; 1953: *Mushkil Ashan*; *Chirantani*; 1954: *Maa-o-Chhele*; *Mantra Shakti*; 1955: *Devatra*; *Pratiksha*; *Bir Hambir*; *Kankabatir Ghat*; *Bratacharini*; 1956: *He Maha Manab*; *Chirakumar Sabha*; *Paradhin*; *Mahakavi Girishchandra*; *Shyamali*; *Rajpath*; *Bhola Master*; 1957: *Tapasi*; *Neelachaley Mahaprabhu*; 1973: *Shravan Sandhya*.

CHOUDHURY, BASANTA (b. 1928)

Aka Vasant Choudhury; Bengali actor born in Nagpur known for refined accent and romantic looks. Entered film at **New Theatres** with ***Mahaprasthaner Pathey***. Played the title role in **Debaki Bose**'s *Bhagwan Shri Krishna Chaitanya*. Was a romantic lead until **Uttam Kumar** overshadowed him. Shifted to character roles including villains (e.g. *Baidurya Rahasya*). Known best for his aristocratic rendition of characters, relying on his unique stage voice. In later films often played the villain. Known also as a radio star and stage actor with the best-known Jatra group, the Natya Company. Recent work mainly in **Dinen Gupta** and **Tapan Sinha** films; cameo appearance in **Gautam Ghosh**'s ***Antarjali Jatra***.

FILMOGRAPHY: 1952: ***Mahaprasthaner Pathey/Yatrik***; 1953: *Nabin Yatra/Naya Safar*; *Bhagwan Shri Krishna Chaitanya*; 1954: *Jadubhatta*; *Bokul/Bakul*; 1955: *Aparadhi*; *Pather Sheshey*; *Bhalobasha*; *Du-Janay*; *Devimalini*; 1956: *Shubharatri*; *Shankar Narayan Bank*; *Chhaya Sangini*; *Govindadas*; *Rajpath*; 1957: *Shesh Parichaya*; *Madhu Malati*; *Andhare Alo*; *Basanta Bahar*; *Haar Jeet*; *Khela Bhangar Khela*; 1958: *Jogajog*; 1959: ***Deep Jweley Jai***; *Shashi Babur Sansar*; 1960: *Khudha*; *Parakh*; 1962: *Sancharini*; *Agnisikha*; *Bodhu*; *Nabadiganta*; 1963: *Shreyasi*; 1964: *Kashtipathar*; *Anustup Chhanda*; 1965: *Alor Pipasa*; *Raja Rammohun*; *Abhoya-o-Srikanta*; *Eki Ange Eto Rup*; *Gulmohar*; 1966: *Sankha Bela*; *Susanta Sha*; *Uttar Purush*; 1970: *Diba Ratrir Kabya*; *Megh Kalo*; 1971: *Pratham Pratisruti*; *Sansar*; ***Grahan***; 1973: *Pranta Rekha*; 1974: *Debi Choudhrani*; *Jadi Jantem*; *Sangini*; 1975: *Nishi Mrigaya*; 1976: *Sankhabish*; 1977: *Babu Moshai*; 1978: *Parichay*; *Mayuri*; 1979: *Chirantan*; *Jiban Je Rakam*; 1980: *Bhagya Chakra*; 1981: *Kalankini*; 1983: *Indira*; *Deepar Prem*; 1985: *Baidurya Rahasya*; *Putulghar*; 1987: ***Antarjali Jatra/Mahayatra***; 1988: *Antarango*; *Sankhachur*; 1990: *Raktorin*; *Ek Doctor Ki Maut*; 1992: *Hirer Angti*.

Choudhury, Kosaraju Raghavaiah *see* **Kosaraju Raghavaiah Choudhury**

CHOUDHURY, RAMA SHANKAR (1903-72)

Hindi director born in Benares, UP. Graduated from J.J. School of Art (1922). Entered films as art director and designer of publicity pamphlets. Did remarkable covers for Gujarati film journal *Mouj Majah*. Joined Star Film and later assisted **Manilal Joshi** at Laxmi Film together with **Chandulal Shah**. First film at Laxmi is **Sandow**'s hit costume spectacular, ***Neera***. Best-known films at **Imperial** and **Sagar**, where he made several classics in historical genre, e.g. *Anarkali*, *Shirin Khushrau*, *Shaan-e-Hind*, often using the legendary epic as a nationalist allegory. Films often starred **Sulochana** and **Zubeida**. Regarded as teacher by **Mehboob** for whom he later scripted ***Roti*** (1942), ***Aan*** (1952) and *Son of India* (1962). Also scripted, in addition to his own films, e.g. **Kardar**'s *Pehle Aap* (1944), M. Sadiq's hit ***Rattan*** (1944) and several films for **Ravindra Dave**. Continued writing scripts until the 70s.

FILMOGRAPHY (* also act): **1926**: ***Neera***; *Asha*; **1927**: *Karmayili Kali*; **1928**: *Anarkali*; *Pita Ke Parmeshwar*; *Sarovar Ki Sundari**; *Madhuri*; **1929**: *Maurya Patan*; *Heer Ranjha*; *Indira BA*; *Punjab Mail*; *Shirin Khushrau*; *Talwar Ka Dhani*; **1930**: *Hamarun Hindustan*; **1931**: *Badmash*; ***Khuda Ki Shaan*** (all St); **1932**: ***Madhuri***; **1933**: *Sulochana*; **1934**: *Aaj Kal*; ***Piya Pyare***; **1935**: *Anarkali*; **1936**: ***Hamari Betiyan***; *Shaan-e-Hind*; **1937**: *Kal Ki Baat*; **1938**: *Rifle Girl*; **1939**: ***Sach Hai***; **1942**: *Aankh Micholi*; **1943**: *Adab Arz*; **1944**: ***Gaali***; **1946**: *Magadhraj*; **1953**: *Jallianwala Bagh Ki Jyot*.

CHOUDHURY, SALIL (b. 1925)

Self-trained composer and music director. Activist among peasantry in 24 Parganas Dist., Bengal. Did music for **IPTA** plays and musical squads performing in Bengali countryside, calling for cultural internationalism as opposed to an emphasis on regional folk traditions (cf **Bhupen Hazarika**; also Choudhury's *Modern Bengali Music in Crisis*, 1951). His influences in songs that have remained enduring favourites with Left cultural groups all over India include Mozart, Hanns Eisler and contemporary Latin American forms. **Ghatak**, in ***Komal Gandhar*** (1961), and **Mrinal Sen**, in ***Akaler Sandhaney***, used his music to typify the spirit of 40s Bengali agitational theatre movements, which he also extended to cover other genres, like **Zia Sarhadi**'s ***Awaaz*** and **Tarafdar**'s ***Ganga***. Entered films with **Satyen Bose**. First major hit was **Bimal Roy**'s ***Do Bigha Zameen***, based on his own story, with full-blooded choral compositions celebrating peasant vitality (monsoon song *Hariyala sawan*), a form still most associated with him. Went on to score the pathbreaking soundtrack of **Roy**'s ***Madhumati***. Also did notable work for **Hrishikesh Mukherjee** films, e.g. his début ***Musafir*** and the 70's hit ***Anand***. The only front-line Hindi composer to work in several languages: Assamese (the experimental ***Aparajeya*** by the Chaturanga collective), Kannada (A.M. Samiulla's films, including *Samshayaphala*, *Onderupe Eradu Guna* etc., and **Balu Mahendra**'s début *Kokila*), Tamil (***Doorathu Idhi Muzhakkam***) and Telugu (*Chairman Chalamayya*). Most spectacular work outside Bengali and Hindi is, however, for **Ramu Kariat**, scoring the several hits in his breakthrough ***Chemmeen***, followed by ***Ezhu Rathrikal***, *Abhayam*, *Nellu* etc.

FILMOGRAPHY (* also d/** also lyr): **1949**: ***Paribartan***; **1951**: ***Barjatri***; **1953**: ***Do Bigha Zameen***; *Banser Kella*; *Bhor Hoye Elo*; **1954**: *Aaj Sandhya*; *Mahila Mahal*; ***Biraj Bahu***; ***Naukri***; **1955**: *Amanat*; *Tangewali*; *Rickshawala*; **1956**: *Raat Bhore*; ***Awaaz***; *Parivar*; ***Jagte Raho/Ek Din Raatre***; **1957**: *Aparadhi Kaun*; *Gautama The Buddha* (Doc); *Ek Gaon Ki Kahani*; ***Lal Batti***; ***Musafir***; *Zamana*; **1958**: ***Madhumati***; **1959**: *Bari Theke Paliye*; **1960**: ***Ganga***; *Sunehri Raatein*; *Jawahar*; ***Kanoon***; *Parakh*; *Usne Kaha Tha*; **1961**: *Char Diwari*; *Chhaya*; ***Kabuliwala***; *Maya*; *Memdidi*; *Sapan Suhane*; *Raibahadur*; **1962**: ***Half Ticket***; *Jhoola*; *Prem Patra*; *Sunbai*; **1964**: *Kinu Goyalar Gali*; *Ayananta*; *Lal Patthar*; **1965**: *Chand Aur Suraj*; *Poonam Ki Raat*; ***Chemmeen***; **1966**: *Pinjre Ke Panchhi**; *Netaji Subhashchandra Bose*; *Pari***; **1968**: ***Ezhu Rathrikal***; *Jawab Ayega*; **1969**: ***Ittefaq***; ***Sara Akash***; **1970**: ***Anand***; *Abhayam*; ***Aparajeya***; **1971**: *Gehra Raaz*; ***Mere Apne***; *Samshayaphala*; **1972**: *Annadata*; *Anokha Daan*; *Anokha Milan*; *Mere Bhaiya*; *Subse Bada Sukh*; *Marjina Abdallah***; **1973**: *Swapnam*; **1974**: ***Rajanigandha***; *Nellu*; *Chairman Chalamayya*; **1975**: ***Chhotisi Baat***; *Sangat*; *Onderupa Eradu Guna*; *Neela Ponman*; *Ragam*; *Rasaleela*; *Thomasleeha*; **1976**: *Aparadhi*; *Thulavarsham*; *Jeevan Jyoti*; ***Mrigaya***; *Uranchoo*; **1977**: *Kabita***; *Sister***; *Minoo*; *Chinna Ninna Muddaduve*; *Kokila*; *Madanolsavam*; *Vishukkanni*; **1978**: *Paruvamazhai*; *Ee Ganam Marakkumo*; *Etho Oru Swapnam*; *Samayamayilla Polum*; *Naukri*; **1979**: *Jiban Je Rakam***; *Srikanter Will***; ***Kala Patthar***; *Jeena Yahan*; *Chuvanna Chirakukal*; **1980**: *Chehre Pe Chehra*; *Byapika Biday***; *Paribesh***; ***Akaler Sandhaney***; ***Doorathu Idhi Muzhakkam***; *Chirutha*; *Nani Maa*; **1981**: *Plot No. 5*; *Agni Pareeksha*; *Batasi Jhada*; **1982**: *Dil Ka Saathi Dil*; *Darpok Ki Dosti* (Sh); **1984**: *Kanoon Kya Karega*; **1985**: *Pratigya*; *Devika*; *Manas Kanya*; **1986**: *Jiban*; **1988**: *Trishagni*; **1989**: *Swarna Trishna*; *Jawahar*; *Kamala Ki Maut*; **1990**: *Triyartri*; ***Vasthuhara***; **1991**: *Netraheen Sakshi*.

CHOUDHURY, SANTI P. (1929-82)

Major independent documentary film-maker. Educated at Presidency College, Calcutta, and Glasgow University. Active participant in British film society movement (1954). Worked with **Satyajit Ray** (1955-7). Founded Little Cinema film unit in Calcutta (1958) which made over 100 shorts independent of government support, influencing the younger generation of documentarists. Also made children's films. Except for *Dakather Hatey Bulu* and *Heerer Prajapati*, all titles are documentaries.

FILMOGRAPHY: **1957**: *Songs of Bengal*; **1958**: *Virsa and the Magic Doll*; **1959**: *Their New Roots*; **1960**: *Rabindranath's Shantiniketan*; **1961**: *Lokeshilpay Terracottay Ramayan*; *Banglar Mandirey Terracotta*; **1962**: *Rabindranather Chitrakala*; **1963**: *Your Home Defence: Home Guards*; *They Met the Challenge*; *Science for Children*; *Dakather Hatey Bulu*; **1964**: *Handicrafts of Assam*; *To Light a Candle*; *Madhabir Biya*; **1965**: *Song of Punjab*; *Folk Instruments of Rajasthan*; **1966**: *A City in History*; *Calcutta*; *Electrocine*; **1967**: *To Share and to Learn*; *Handicrafts of Rajasthan*; **1968**: *Benarasi's Secret*; *Heerer Prajapati*; *Entertainers of Rajasthan*; **1969**: *Secularism*; **1971**: *Biju in Hyderabad*; *The Other Calcutta*; *Seeds of the Green Revolution*; *An Indian Journey*; *Working Together*; *Action for Calcutta*; **1972**: *Janasanstha*; *Indian Engineering*; *Dakshina Haryana*; *Mughal Gardens Pinjore*; *Green Horizon*; *ITC Tube: The Lifetimer*; **1973**: *An Environment*; *After Ten Years*; **1974**: *Asia '72*; *Silent Service*; *A Painter of Our Times*; **1975**: *Search for Self-Reliance*; **1976**: *We're Building an IOL Pipeline For You*; **1977**: *Parvati*; **1978**: *Banglar Kabigan*; *The Magic Hands*; **1980**: *Husain*; *Region of Harmony*; *Seven*; *Pahar Theke Shahar*; **1981**: *Subho Tagore*; **1982**: *Racing in India*.

CHOUDHURY, SUPRIYA

Actress. Bengali star of 60s socials best known as romantic lead opposite **Uttam Kumar** (with whom she apparently featured in 33 films). Spent some of her childhood in Rangoon; introduced into films by veteran Bengali actress Chandrabati Devi. Début in **Nirmal Dey**'s ***Basu Parivar***, after which she married and retired from films for some years. Incarnated the 'heroine' of reformist middle-class pulp fictions. Adhered more to melodramatic orthodoxy than her chief rival, **Suchitra Sen**, evoking e.g. Jamuna's acting in **P.C. Barua** productions and generating a sense of nostalgia for pre-Independence middle-class Bengali melodrama, thus providing a kind of cultural legitimation to the weepies of the **Agradoot**/Agragami/**Yatrik** units and film-makers like Piyush Bose. Known outside Bengal for her extraordinary performance as the heroine in **Ghatak**'s ***Meghe Dhaka Tara*** and ***Komal Gandhar***. These, and **Ajoy Kar**'s *Suno Baro Nari*, were rare instances in which she stepped out of her star image. Turned producer with the commercial flop *Uttar Meleni*.

FILMOGRAPHY: **1952**: ***Basu Parivar***; *Prarthana*; *Madhurati*; **1959**: *Amrapali*; *Ae Jahar Sey Jahar Noy*; *Sonar Harin*; *Shubha Bibaha*; **1960**: *Uttar Megh*; ***Meghe Dhaka Tara***; *Kono-Ek-Din*; *Ajana Kahini*; *Surer Pyasi*; *Natun Fasal*; *Suno Baro Nari*; **1961**: ***Komal Gandhar***; *Bishkanya*; *Agni Sanskar*; *Swaralipi*; *Swayambara*; **1962**: *Kajal*; *Abhisarika*; **1963**: *Begana*; *Nisithe*; *Uttarayan*; *Dui Nari*; *Surya Sikha*; **1964**: *Aap Ki Parchhaiyan*; ***Door Gagan Ki Chhaon Mein***; *Ayananta*; *Lal Patthar*; **1965**: *Kal Tumi Aleya*; **1966**: *Harano Prem*; *Sudhu Ekti Bachhar*; **1967**: *Akash Chhoan*; *Jiban Mrityu*; **1968**: *Teen Adhyay*; **1969**: *Chiradiner*; *Mon-Niye*; *Sabarmati*; **1970**: *Bilambita Lay*; **1971**: *Jiban Jignasa*; **1972**: *Andha Atit*; *Chinnapatra*; **1973**: ***Bon Palashir Padabali***; **1974**: *Jadi Jantem*; *Rakta Tilak*; **1975**: *Bagh Bandi Khela*; *Nagar Darpane*; *Sanyasi Raja*; *Sabhyasachi*; **1976**: *Samrat*; *Banhi Sikha*; *Mom Batti*; **1977**: *Bhola Moira*; *Sister*; **1978**: *Dui Purush*; **1979**: *Devdas*; **1980**: *Dui Prithibi*; **1981**: *Kalankini Kankabati*; **1982**: *Uttar Meleni*; *Iman Kalyan*; **1983**: *Raat Dastay*; **1984**: *Anveshan*; **1989**: *Kari Diye Kinlam*; **1992**: *Honeymoon*.

CHUGHTAI, ISMAT (1915-91)

Born in Badaun. The only major woman writer in 40s radical Urdu literary movements (see **Manto** and **Krishan Chander**). Her most famous stories are set in middle-class, often orthodox Muslim society and strongly imbued with sexual symbology informed by Freudian psychoanalysis (see Tahira Naqvi in Chughtai, 1990). Some of her writing caused major controversy for its violation of traditional morality codes: *Lihaaf* (1942) provoked obscenity trial in Lahore. Married to film-maker Shaheed Latif and was closely involved with the making of *Ziddi* (1948), **Dev Anand**'s first major hit. Worked as scenarist and occasionally as producer with Latif (*Arzoo*, 1950; *Darwaza*, 1954; *Society*, 1955; ***Sone Ki Chidiya***, 1958). Involved as dialogue writer and actress in **Benegal**'s ***Junoon*** (1978). Wrote the story for **Sathyu**'s ***Garam Hawa*** (1973) and the dialogues of Amar Kumar's films *Barkha Bahar* (1973) and *Mehfil* (1978). Wrote and co-directed *Faraib* (1953). Directed the children's film *Jawab Ayega* (1968) and the documentary *My Dreams* (1975).

CHUNDER, HEMCHANDRA (b. 1907)

Aka Hem Chunder. Hindi-Bengali director. Début in B.N. Sircar's International Filmcraft. Acted in Prafulla Roy's silent *Chasher Meye* (1931). Major films with **New Theatres**, where he was its principal Hindi director (1935-48) in its attempts to enter the Western Indian market. Second film, *Karodpati*, was one of **Saigal**'s best-known musicals. ***Anath Ashram***, starring **Prithviraj Kapoor** and scripted by novelist **Sailajananda Mukherjee**, made an influential intervention in the Bengali genre of the literary melodrama. Turned independent producer in collaboration with actress Meera Misra (H.M. Prod.).

FILMOGRAPHY: **1935**: ***Karwan-e-Hayat***; **1936**: *Karodpati*; **1937**: ***Anath Ashram***; **1939**: ***Jawani Ki Reet/Parajay***; **1941**: *Pratisruti*; **1942**: *Saugandh*; **1943**: ***Wapas***; **1944**: ***Meri Bahen***; **1948**: *Pratibad/Oonch Neech*; **1949**: *Bishnupriya*; **1952**: *Chhoti Maa*; **1954**: *Chitrangada*; **1955**: *Madh Bhare Nain*; *Teen Bhai*; **1956**: *Bandhan*; **1958**: *Manmoyee Girls' School*; **1960**: *Natun Fasal*.

Chunder, Krishan *see* **Chander, Krishan** (1914-77)

COMPANY NATAK

Popular theatre movement in late 19th C. Karnataka, predominantly around the Mysore court, contemporaneous with similar movements in Telugu (cf **Surabhi Theatres**) and Tamil (see **TKS Brothers**). Performed as night-long shows by travelling groups in tents, it evolved from the Yakshagana folk theatre and its variants, Dashavtara and Bailatta, and helped codify the mythological. **Gubbi Veeranna**'s company was its best-known exponent. The form assimilated aspects of Parsee theatre (e.g. versions of *Gul-e-Bakavali* and *Indrasabha*) and **Sangeet Natak**. As a folk-inspired genre, it allowed for a freewheeling, open-ended adaptation of speech and musical modes: Veeranna writes of using Urdu and pidgin Hindi phrases in Kannada texts while the numerous songs, using over 50 verses as bases for improvisation, could be accompanied by pedal-harmonium and claviolin as well as the traditional tabla, violin and sota. In the early 20th C., direct sponsorship from feudal élites helped imbue the form with a caste-conscious classicism usually signified by a recourse to translations of Sanskrit texts (e.g. Kalidasa) and Shakespeare, paralleling the increased emphasis on classical Bharat Natyam gestures in Yakshagana dance and dialogue-delivery, and on Carnatic music in the songs. In the late 30s some of the major groups moved into film, following Veeranna's Gubbi Co. which converted its stage hits into the first Kannada films. Mohammed Peer's Chandrakala Nataka Co. yielded two major 60s Kannada film-makers, **H.L.N. Simha** and **B.R. Panthulu**, while the Sahitya Samrajya Nataka Mandali run by film-maker **R. Nagendra Rao** and **M.V. Subbaiah Naidu** converted their hit plays *Yachhamanayika* and ***Bhukailasa*** (1938, 1940) into successful films. The Company Natak provided virtually all the major talent for the early Kannada film, e.g. **Honappa Bhagavathar**, megastar **Rajkumar**, **B. Jayamma** and **K. Ashwathamma** as well as scenarists **B.N. Sastry** and B. Puttaswamaiah. It defined the economic distribution infrastructure for a regional film industry and, crucially, paved the way for the political use of the mythological and the historical genres (see **A.N. Krishnarao**, Rajkumar and **G.V. Iyer**).

COMPANY SCHOOL PAINTING

An 18th and 19th C. painting style geared to the British presence. According to Mildred Archer, 'the favourite subjects were costumes, methods of transport and festivals, [H]indu deities and temples. Such subjects, arranged in sets, provided a conspectus of social life in India and, whether harsh and garish in the South or mild and soft as in the North East, the pictures recorded in pseudo-British terms the exotic environment in which [East India] Company officers and their successors lived. In these sets, each trade, craft or occupation was shown with identifying attributes - a bricklayer with measure and trowel, a shoemaker with awl and shoe, a cook with chicken and kettle' (Archer, 1977). Guha-Thakurta (1992) noted that with the dwindling of court patronage, court painters became reduced to the state of bazaar painters, 'a new colonial category that underlined their displacement and forced exposure and adjustment to Western demands in an open market. European paintings and engravings of Indian scenes began to be supplanted, more cheaply and abundantly, by the pictures produced by this pool of displaced artists. In commissioning pictures from these "bazaar" painters, the British preferred those with hereditary links with old painting ateliers. Yet the skills of these miniature artists were valued primarily for their adaptability to Western naturalistic conventions and the flair for precision and detail in the pictures and diagrams ordered of them.'From the middle of the 18th C., numerous British artists, both professional (the best known are William Hodges, Tilly Kettle, George Chinnery and John Zoffany) and sketch-book amateurs recorded scenes from India. Some of them were in the employ of Indian nobility and trained or otherwise influenced Indian artists, while numerous others simply imitated the style. The Company School mode, which usually functioned as a cheaper and barely legitimate version of European naturalism, established an influential visual lexicon of stereotypes used for a variety of purposes: parodies of the British and Indian gentry, local fashion primers, visual anthropology and some of the earliest examples of the mythological iconography later adopted by the cinema. Early documentaries in India, e.g. **Bourne & Shepherd**'s actuality and review films, F.B. Thanawala's *Splendid New Views of Bombay* (1899) and *Taboot Procession at Kalbadevi* (1900) as well as footage bought for c.10 cents to a dollar per foot by e.g. the Pathé Exchange, International Newsreel Corp. and Fox Films, inherited the disingenuous Orientalism of the Company School painters once Parsee businessmen, the Indian aristocracy and British multinationals like Warwick Trading in Calcutta (*Panorama of Calcutta*, 1898) shifted their patronage to film production.

COOPER, PATIENCE (b. 1905?)

Top star of silent cinema before **Sulochana**. Contracted to **Madan Theatres**. Started as a dancer in Bandmann's Musical Comedy, a Eurasian troupe; later employed by **Madan**'s Corinthian Stage Co. Played title roles in two major **Sisir Bhaduri** films, *Mohini* and *Kamale Kamini*. Dominant character in several films by **Jyotish Bannerjee** and **Priyanath Ganguly**: played Leelavati in ***Pati Bhakti***, Sushila in *Nartaki Tara*, the title role in *Noorjehan* and perhaps the earliest double roles in Indian film in *Patni Pratap* (where she played two sisters) and *Kashmiri Sundari* (as mother and daughter). Several scripts and adapted plays were prepared especially for her by **Aga Hashr Kashmiri**, e.g. *Turki Hoor* and *Hoor-e-Arab*. Often cast as the sexually troubled but innocent heroine at the centre of moral dilemmas represented by male protagonists, foreshadowing **Nargis**'s performances three decades later in **Mehboob**'s films (e.g. ***Humayun***, 1945). A major aspect of her star image was the successful achievement of the Hollywood look in spite of vastly different light and technical conditions. Her dark hair, sharp eyes and skin tone allowed technicians to experiment with the imported convention of eye-level lighting.

FILMOGRAPHY: **1920**: ***Nala Damayanti***; **1921**: *Behula*; *Vishnu Avatar*; *Mohini*; ***Dhruva Charitra***; **1922**: *Ratnavali*; *Nartaki Tara*; *Raja Bhoj*; *Sati*; *Bhagirathi Ganga*; ***Pati Bhakti***; *Matri Sneh*; *Laila Majnu*; *Ramayan*; *Kamale Kamani*; *Princess Budur*; **1923**: *Patni Pratap*; *Noorjehan*; **1924**: *Turki Hoor*; **1925**: *Kashmiri Sundari*; *Sati Lakshmi*; *Adooray Chheley*; *Sansar Chakra*; **1926**: *Dharmapatni*; *Prafulla*; *Joydev*; *Krishnakanter Will*; **1927**: *Chandidas*; *Jana*; *Durgesh Nandini*; **1928**: *Bhranti*; *Aankh Ka Nasha*; *Hoor-e-Arab*; **1929**: *Kapal Kundala*; **1930**: *Kal Parinaya*; *Rajsingha*; *Bharat Ramani*; *Ganesh Janma*; *Vaman Avatar*; **1931**: *Bibaha Bibhrat*; *Alladdin and the Wonderful Lamp* (all St); *Bharati Balak*; *Samaj Ka Shikar*; **1932**: *Bilwamangal*; *Chatra Bakavali*; *Hathili Dulhan*; *Alibaba and the Forty Thieves*; *Pati Bhakti*; *Educated Wife*; **1933**: *Madhur Murali*; *Naqli Doctor*; ***Zehari Saap***; **1934**: *Anokha Prem*; *Kanya Vikraya*; *Kismet Ka Shikar*; *Sakhi Lutera*; **1935**: *Asmat Ka Moti*; *Dil Ki Pyaas*; *Mera Pyara*; *Sulagto Sansar*; *Prem Ki Ragini*; *Khudadad*; **1936**: *Baghi Sipahi*; *Khyber Pass*; *Noor-e-Wahadat*; **1937**: *Fakhr-e-Islam*; **1943**: *Rani*; **1944**: *Iraada*.

DAKSHINAMURTHY, V. (b. 1919)

Malayalam film music director and composer, born in Alleppey, Kerala. Regarded as a 'classicist'. Concert singer in 50s/60s. Trained by Venkatachalam Potti; practised at the Vaikom temple. At their best, his Carnatic-inspired scores are deceptively simple (e.g. when putting G. Sankara Kurup's lyrics to music), trying to adapt the recitative rhythms to given raga patterns. Nearly all his work is raga-based, notably in *Khamboji*, *Sahana* (e.g. the musical leitmotif in ***Kavya Mela***), *Todi* and *Charukesi*. His compositions are a major influence on singers **P. Leela** and Vasanthakokila. Credits after 1978 and for films other than Malayalam are likely to be incomplete.

FILMOGRAPHY: 1950: *Chandrika* (with Govindarajulu Naidu); ***Nallathanka***; **1951**: ***Jeevitha Nauka***; ***Navalokam***; **1952**: *Amma*; **1953**: *Velaikkaran*; *Lokaneethi*; *Sario Thetto*; *Asha Deepam*; **1954**: *Avan Varunnu*; ***Snehaseema***; **1955**: *Kidappadam*; **1956**: *Atmarpanam*; **1959**: *Nadodikal*; **1960**: *Seeta*; **1961**: *Umminithanka*; *Gnana Sundari*; **1962**: *Veluthampi Dalawa*; *Sreekovil*; *Vidhithanna Vilakku*; *Viyarppinte Vila*; **1963**: *Satyabhama*; *Sushila*; *Chilampoli*; **1964**: *Devalayam*; *Shri Guruvayoorappan*; *Bharthavu*; (with **Baburaj**); **1965**: *Inapravugal*; ***Kavya Mela***; **1966**: *Pinchu Hridayam*; *Kadamattathachan*; **1967**: *Indulekha*; *Lady Doctor*; *Mainatharuvi Kola Case*; *Cochin Express*; **1968**: *Padunna Puzha*; ***Adhyapika***; *Bharyamar Sukshikuka*; **1969**: *Kannur Deluxe*; *Poojapushpam*; *Danger Biscuit*; **1970**: *Kalpana*; *Stree*; ***Ezhuthatha Katha***; *Kuttavali*; *Lottery Ticket*; *Sabarimala Shri Dharmasastha*; *Palunku Pathram*; **1971**: *Muthassi*; *Marunattil Oru Malayali*; *Achante Bharya*; **1972**: *Maya*; *Manushya Bandhangal*; *Nadan Premam*; *Shri Guruvayoorappan*; *Nrithyasala*; *Putrakameshti*; *Shakti*; *Sathi*; *Brahmachari*; **1973**: *Football Champion*; *Udayam*; *Veendum Prabhatam*; *Police Ariyaruthu*; *Urvashi Bharathi*; *Driksakshi*; *Sastram Jayichu Manushyan Thottu*; *Interview*; *Poyi Mukhangal*; **1974**: *Alakal*; *Night Duty*; *Aswathi*; *Bhugolam Thiriyunnu*; *Thacholi Marumagan Chandu*; *Sapta Swarangal*; *Arakallan Mukkal Kallan*; *Yauvanam*; **1975**: *Chumadu Thangi*; *Mattoru Seeta*; *Sammanam*; *Sathyathinde Nizhalil*; **1976**: *Neelasari*; *Prasadam*; *Priyamvadha*; *Sexilla Stuntilla*; *Srimadh Bhagavad Geeta*; *Thulavarsham* (with **Salil Choudhury**); *Thuruppu Gulam*; *Vazhi Vilakku*; *Oru Udhappu Kann Simittukirathu*; **1977**: *Nanda Enn Nilla*; *Jagadguru Adi Shankaran*; *Kaduvaye Pidicha Kiduva*; *Makam Piranna Manka*; *Muttathe Mulla*; *Niraparayum Nilavilakkum*; *Shri Chottanikkara Bhagavathi*; *Thalappoli*; **1978**: *Ashtamudikayal*; *Ashokavanam*; *Kalpa Vruksha*; *Kanalkkattakal*; *Kudumbam Namakku Sreekovil*; *Manoratham*; *Ninakku Gnanam Enikku Neeyum*; *Prarthana*; *Prema Shilpi*; **1984**: *Guruvayoor Mahatmiyam*; *Krishna Guruvayoorappa*; **1985**: *Madhu Vidhurathri*; *Navadakku Paniyedukku*; **1987**: *Idanazhiyil Oru Kalocha*; **1989**: *Season*.

DAMLE, VISHNUPANT GOVIND (1892-1945)

Marathi director and producer born in Pen, Raigad Dist., Maharashtra. Like his long-term collaborator, **Fattelal**, was apprenticed to Anandrao, the artist-technician cousin of **Baburao Painter**, helping to construct theatrical backdrops. Became expert set designer and cinematographer, making his own camera and processing film. Co-founded **Maharashtra Films** (1917) with Painter and Fattelal. With **Shantaram**, they broke away and established **Prabhat** in 1929. Damle took charge of the sound department and is credited with introducing the playback technique. Took over management of Prabhat after Shantaram left (1942) but without success. Best known for the classic ***Sant Tukaram*** and subsequent Saint films (co-d with Fattelal). Last film, ***Sant Sakhu***, co-d with **Raja Nene** and Fattelal.

FILMOGRAPHY (co-d with **S. Fattelal**): **1928**: *Maharathi Karna* (St); **1936**: ***Sant Tukaram***; **1938**: ***Gopal Krishna***; **1940**: ***Sant Dnyaneshwar***; **1941**: ***Sant Sakhu.***

DAS, JHARANA (b. 1945)

Major 60s Oriya actress in melodramas like ***Amada Bata***, *Abhinetri* and esp. the classic ***Malajanha.*** Born in a Christian family; a noted child artist on AIR, Cuttack. Learnt dance from Guru Kelucharan Mahapatra, the main dance teacher in the classical form of Odissi. Returned to radio work and achieved immense popularity in radio plays before joining films with *Amada Bata*. Appointed assistant station director for Cuttack **Doordarshan** and acted in tv programmes, e.g., *Ghare Bhada Diya Jiba* and *Manisha*, while continuing her film career. Directed a documentary on the Orissa politician H.K. Mahtab. Married Bengali cameraman Dipak Das.

FILMOGRAPHY: **1964**: ***Amada Bata***; *Nabajanma*; **1965**: *Abhinetri*; ***Malajanha***; **1970**: ***Adina Megha***; **1979**: *Shri Jagannath*; **1981**: *Tike Hasa Tike Luha*; **1982**: *Samaya Bada Balabaan*; *Hisab Nikas*; *Jwain Pua*; **1983**: *Mahasati Sabitri*; **1984**: *Ninad*; **1985**: *Pooja Phula*; **1987**: *Kasturi*; **1988**: *Lal Pan Bibi*; **1989**: *Topaye Sindoora Deepata Sankha*.

DASGUPTA, BUDDHADEV (b. 1944)

Bengali poet and director born in Anara, Purulia (Bengal). Former lecturer in economics at Calcutta University (1968-76) and Bengali poet since 1961, published in journals like *Kabita*, *Ekshan* and *Desh*; wrote many anthologies (*Govir Arieley*, 1963; *Coffin Kimba Suitcase*, 1972; *Him Jug*, 1977; *Chhata Kahini*, 1981; *Roboter Gaan*, 1985). Gave up academic post to extend poetic work into cinema. Early film-making (***Dooratwa***) attempted a didactic variation on **S. Ray**'s type of urban lyrical realism. With the thriller ***Grihajuddha*** and melodrama ***Andhi Gali***, both adapting novelist Dibyendu Palit, he tried new forms of addressing the contemporary situation in Bengal after the **Naxalite** movements, usually from the view of a guilt-ridden middle class. From this perspective, revisits established literary traditions, including the writings of Kamal Kumar Majumdar (***Neem Annapurna***), Narendranath Mitra (***Phera***) et al. Published a book of film essays, *Swapna Samay Cinema* (1991).

FILMOGRAPHY: **1968**: *Samayer Kache* (Sh); **1969**: *Continent of Love* (Doc); **1970**: *Fishermen Of Sundarban* (Doc); **1973**: *Dholer Raja Khirode Natta* (Doc); **1974**: *Saratchandra* (Doc); **1978**: ***Dooratwa***; **1979**: ***Neem Annapurna***; **1980**: *Vigyan O Tar Avishkar*; (Doc); **1981**: *Rhythm of Steel* (Doc); **1982**: ***Grihajuddha***; *Sheet Grishmer Smriti* (TV); **1984**: ***Andhi Gali***; *Indian Science Marches Ahead* (Doc); **1985**: *Story of Glass* (Doc); *India on the Move* (Doc); **1986**: *Ceramics* (Doc); ***Phera***; **1987**: *Contemporary Indian Sculpture* (Doc); **1989**: ***Bagh Bahadur***; **1990**: *History of Indian Jute* (Doc); **1992**: *Tahader Katha*; **1993**: *Charachar*.

DAS GUPTA, CHIDANANDA

Noted Indian film critic committed to a realist aesthetic and humanist philosophy best exemplified by **Satyajit Ray**. Founded with Ray et al. the Calcutta Film Society (1947) and the Federation of Film Societies of India (1960), functioning as its secretary until 1967. Editor of the *Indian Film Review* and *Indian Film Culture* and widely published film and arts journalist. Published *The Cinema Of Satyajit Ray* and the anthology *Film India: Satyajit Ray* (both 1981) in addition to numerous essays. Extended his argument for an organic film culture beyond Ray to cover mainstream Indian cinema, launching the notion of the **All-India Film** with a culturally integrative role in nationalist terms (see the essay 'The Cultural Basis of Indian Cinema', 1968). Recent essays collected in his *The Painted Face* (1991) describe the realist and the All-India Film as committed to, respectively, a cinema of fact and of myth. For some years editor of the journal *Span* published by the USIS. Also known as the director of the critically acclaimed feature ***Bilet Pherat*** (1972), and of the documentary about Ananda Coomaraswamy, *The Dance of Shiva* (1968). Other documentaries include *Portrait of a City* (1961), *The Stuff of Steel* (1969), *Birju Maharaj* (1972) and *Zaroorat Ki Purti* (1979). Father of Bengali star **Aparna Sen**, scored his daughter's film ***Sati*** (1989).

DASGUPTA, HARISADHAN (b. 1923)

Bengali documentary and fiction director born in Calcutta. Studied film-making first at USC and later at UCLA (1945). Apprenticed to Hollywood film-maker Irving Pichel and present during the making of RKO's *They Won't Believe Me* (1947) and Universal's *Mr Peabody and the Mermaid* (1948). Founder member with **S. Ray**, **C. Das Gupta**, **Asit Sen** et al. of the Calcutta Film Society (1947). Assisted Jean Renoir in making *The River* (1951) and shot best-known documentary *Konarak* (1949) with Renoir's brother Claude. The film was partly remade in a 'popular version' by his brother Bulu for **Films Division** (1958). Début, *A Perfect Day*, is a featurette promoting cigarettes sponsored by the National Tobacco Co. scripted by Ray, produced by C. Das Gupta and shot by **Ajoy Kar**. It combined a vérité style with a fictional script, announcing e.g. Ray's 50s realism. Later made the classic documentary *The Story of Steel* sponsored by Tata Steel, India's largest private sector corporation. It was scripted by Ray, shot by Claude Renoir and edited by **Hrishikesh Mukherjee** with music by Ravi Shankar. It became a model for the type of Nehruite nation-building socialist-realism later associated with Films Division. Best-known films with the Shell Film Unit. Dasgupta and Ray planned to film **Tagore**'s *Ghare Baire*, a project realised 30 years later by Ray in 1984. Made two features, *Kamallata* and the critically acclaimed *Eki Ange Eto Rup*. He is regarded as **Sukhdev**'s teacher, later contributing to ***Nine Months To Freedom*** (1972). His son Raja Dasgupta is now a documentary director. Also made several 30' films for USIS, the Ford Foundation, UNESCO etc. 1956-60 as well as for Hindustan Motors (1968).

FILMOGRAPHY: **1948**: *A Perfect Day*; **1949**: *Konarak: The Sun Temple*; **1953**: *Weavers of Maindargi*; *Shaher Ki Jhalak*; *Gaon Ki Kahani*; **1955**: *Panchthupi: A Village in West Bengal*; **1956**: *The Story of Steel*; **1960**: *Our Children Will Know Each Other Better*; **1961**: *Panorama of West Bengal*; *Acharya Prafulla Chandra Ray*; **1964**: *Bade Ghulam Ali Khan Saheb*; **1965**: *Baba*; *Malabar Story*; *Eki Ange Eto Rup*; *Glimpses of India*; *Quest for Health*; **1969**: *Kamallata*; *The Automobile Industry in India*; **1970**: *Terracotta Temples*; **1971**: *The Tale of Two Leaves and a Bud*; *Port of Calcutta*; **1973**: *Engineers (India) Limited*; **1976**: *Preservation of Ancient Monuments*; **1977**: *Bagha Jatin*; **1978**: *Haldia Dock Complex*; *The Brave Do Not Die*; **1981**: *The ITA Story*; **1982**: *This Land is Mine*; *Mizoram*; **1984**: *Acharya Nandalal*.

DASGUPTA, KAMAL (?-1974)

Bengali composer born in Dhaka (now Bangladesh). Début with the gramophone co. became widely known when his music was performed by the popular singer Juthika Roy and provided the definitive musical arrangements for some of **Kazi Nazrul Islam**'s compositions. Worked with **Barua** (e.g. ***Shesh Uttar/Jawab***, *Pehchan*) and extensively with **Niren Lahiri** (***Garmil***, *Jayjatra*). Compared with contemporaries such as **Anupam Ghatak** or Anil Bagchi, he is regarded as an orthodox composer with pre-**Tagore** 'puratani' elements, featuring Raagpradhan music and extensive use of Keertan, although he did score **Modhu Bose**'s Tagore-derived *Giribala*. Worked with **Sagar** directors **Luhar** (*Bindiya*) and **Badami** (*Manmani*) and, later in his career, with Pranab Roy, also producing Roy's *Prarthana*. Later years in Bangladesh.

FILMOGRAPHY: **1936**: *Pandit Moshai*; **1938**: ***Sarbajanin Bibahotsab***; **1939**: *Debjani*; **1942**: ***Shesh Uttar/Jawab***; ***Garmil***; **1943**: *Sahadharmini*; ***Jogajog/Hospital***; *Chandar Kalanka/Rani*; *Dampati*; **1944**: *Bideshini*; **1945**: *Nandita*; *Meghdoot*; *Bhabhi-Kaal*; **1946**: *Bindiya*; *Krishna Leela*; *Pehchan*; *Zameen Aasmaan*; **1947**: *Faisla*; *Giribala*; *Manmani*; *Chandrasekhar*; **1948**: *Jayjatra/Vijay Yatra*; **1949**: *Iran Ki Ek Raat*; *Rangamati*; *Anuradha*; **1951**: *Phulwari*; **1952**: *Prarthana*; **1953**: *Malancha*; **1954**: *Nababidhan*; *Bhagwan Shri Krishna Chaitanya*; **1955**: *Bratacharini*; **1956**: *Manraksha*; *Govindadas*; **1957**: *Madhu Malati*; *Sandhan*; **1967**: *Bodhu Baran*.

DASGUPTA, PROTIMA (b. 1922)

Hindi actress, producer and director born in Bhavnagar into wealthy family. Studied briefly in England; then at **Tagore**'s Shantiniketan where she was apparently a favoured student. Début in **Naresh Mitra**'s film of Tagore's *Gora*, her role apparently satisfying the author. Hindi début in **Modhu Bose**'s trilingual ***Raj Nartaki***. Acted in several **N.R. Acharya** productions directed by **Kishore Sahu.** Turned film-maker with *Chhamia* followed by the comedy *Pagle*, both with leading stars Begum Para and David. Her *Jharna* got into trouble when the Chief Minister of Maharashtra, Morarji Desai, banned it for what he felt were sexually explicit scenes. The film was a financial disaster and she retired from the cinema.

FILMOGRAPHY (* also d): **1938**: *Gora*; **1940**: *Path Bhoole*; *Suktara*; *Byabadhan*; **1941**: ***Raj Nartaki/Court Dancer***; **1942**: ***Kunwara Baap***; **1943**: *Namaste*; *Raja*; **1944**: *Shararat*; **1945**: *Chhamia**; **1948**: *Jharna**; **1950**: *Pagle**.

DASGUPTA, SUKUMAR (b. 1907)

Bengali director born in Calcutta. Started as scenarist for Prafulla Roy's *Abhishek* (1931) and **P.C. Barua**'s ***Maya*** (1936).
FILMOGRAPHY: **1936**: *Ashiana*; **1937**: *Rajgee*; **1940**: *Rajkumarer Nirbashan*; **1941**: *Epar Opar*; **1942**: *Pashan Devata*; **1945**: *Nandita*; **1946**: *Sat Number Bari*; **1949**: *Abhijatya*; **1950**: *Banprastha*; **1951**: *Pratyabartan*; **1952**: *Sanjibani*; **1953**: *Sat Number Kayedi*; **1954**: *Ora Thake Odhare*; *Sadanander Mela*; **1955**: *Parishodh*; **1956**: *Mahanisha*; **1957**: *Abhoyer Biye*; **1960**: *Haat Baraley Bandhu*; **1961**; *Sathi Hara*.

DATE, KESHAVRAO (1889-1971)

Major Marathi stage actor born in Adivare, Ratnagiri Dist., Maharashtra; one of the first practitioners of naturalist prose theatre at Maharashtra Natak Mandali (e.g. *Agryahun Sutka* and *Bebandshahi*) in an era dominated by **Sangeet Natak** musicals. Key participant, with writer-actor **K. Narayan Kale** and composer **Keshavrao Bhole,** of Natyamanwantar group's production of *Andhalyanchi Shala* (1933), a pinnacle of Stanislavsky (and Ibsen/Shaw) inspired naturalism in Marathi theatre, prompting **Shantaram** to hire all three for **Prabhat**. Kale suggests that Date's constant effort to reconcile reformist-social literature's stereotypes with European theatrical styles inevitably led to the expressionist technique of fragmenting characters into certain gestures and a speaking style, construed as an 'entry into the character's mind' (Kale, 1950). Best-known film work with Shantaram at Prabhat (e.g. the classic ***Kunku*** and ***Shejari***) and **Rajkamal** (***Dahej***, *Toofan Aur Diya*), where his declamatory speech and gesture fitted Shantaram's expressionist inclinations. Date's style remains a characteristic of Shantaram's influential variant of melodrama. Also directed some films at Rajkamal. Biography by V.V. Jog (1976).

FILMOGRAPHY (* also d): **1934**: ***Amritmanthan***; **1936**: *Savkari Pash*; **1937**: ***Kunku/Duniya Na Mane***; ***Pratibha***; **1938**: *Umaji Naik*; **1939**: ***Sant Tulsidas***; ***Adhuri Kahani***; **1940**: *Chingari*; *Diwali*; ***Holi***; **1941**: ***Shejari***; **1942**: *Kisise Na Kehna**; **1944**: *Bhakticha Mala/Mali**; **1946**: ***Dr Kotnis Ki Amar Kahani***; **1947**: *Andhon Ki Duniya**; **1948**: *Bhool*; **1949**: *Apna Desh/Nam Naadu*; **1950**: ***Dahej***; *Jara Japoon*; **1951**: *Kunkvacha Dhani*; *Sharada*; **1953**: *Teen Batti Char Raasta*; *Maisaheb*; *Surang*; **1955**: *Jhanak Jhanak Payal Baaje*; **1956**: *Toofan Aur Diya*; **1957**: ***Do Aankhen Barah Haath***; **1958**: *Mausi*; **1959**: *Navrang*; **1961**: *Stree*; **1963**: *Sehra*; **1964**: *Geet Gaya Pattharone*; **1965**: *Iye Marathyachi Nagari/Ladki Sahyadri Ki*.

DATTA KESHAV KULKARNI (b. 1932)

Marathi director and playwright born in Bombay. Assistant to **Dharmadhikari** (1952) before going to **Filmistan** as scenarist and director. Often also provided the lyrics for his own films.

Keshavrao Date in *Kunku* (1937)

FILMOGRAPHY: 1966: *Ati Shahana Tyacha*; **1968**: *Bai Mothi Bhagyachi*; *Yethe Shahane Rahataat*; **1970**: *Meech Tujhi Priya*; **1971**: *Dher Chalaki Jin Kara*; *Asel Mazha Hari*; **1973**: *Mala Dev Bhetla*; **1974**: *Bayano Navare Sambhala*; *Ovalite Bhauraya*; **1977**: *Badla*; *Bhingri*; *Navara Mazha Brahmachari*; **1980**: *Phatakadi*; *Savli Premachi*; *Jidda*; **1981**: *Mosambi Narangi*; **1982**: *Vishwas*; **1983**: *Kashala Udyachi Baat*; *Ranine Dav Jinkala*; **1985**: *Saubhagya Lene*; **1987**; *Porichi Dhamal Bapachi Kamal*; *Prema Saathi Vatelte*; *Sant Gajanan Shegavicha*; **1989**: *De Taali*; **1990**; *Dhamal Bablya Ganpyachi*; **1991**; *Yeda Ki Khula*.

DAVE, MOHANLAL G.

Top silent cinema scenarist; first scenarist to get his name above the title (see e.g. the publicity pamphlets of **Kohinoor Film** which often give no other credits). Started as an accountant; then publicist for Imperial Theatre in Bombay. Apparently honed his craft writing lively synopses in publicity handouts for Pathé's imports. Entered films with **S.N. Patankar** and moved to National Studio (where he was already paid Rs 10,000 a year to write a minimum of 15 stories) and Kohinoor, where he made his reputation and wrote about one screenplay a week. As a professional, he handled all genres, but his narrative style is related to the then emerging popular Gujarati fiction as introduced to the cinema by ex-novelists like Naranji Vassanji Thakkar, Gopalji Delwadekar, Shaida etc. His scripts are said to have included detailed camera movements, fades etc., as in **Rathod**'s complicated ***Gul-e-Bakavali*** (1924), written in 92 scenes. Major early scripts: the politically controversial ***Bhakta Vidur*** (1921), the Rathod hit ***Kala Naag*** (1924), **Chandulal Shah**'s début film *Panchdanda* (1925) and **Homi Master**'s ***Fankdo Fituri*** (1925). His sound films were often rewrites of his own silent hits with dialogue. His major successes were with **V.M. Vyas**, including the Gujarati film ***Ranakdevi*** (1946).

DAVE, RAVINDRA (1919-92)

Hindi and Gujarati director born in Karachi. Started as cinema manager in the **Pancholi** distribution empire. Later learnt editing under director Shaukat Hussain; also scenarist until 1941. Early films for Pancholi. 50s films were usually cop thrillers and murder mysteries (*Moti Mahal*, *CID Girl*, ***Guest House***). ***Post Box 999*** adapted plot of *Call Northside 777* (1947). Shifted to Gujarati cinema with the folk fantasy ***Jesal Toral***, a major hit. Thereafter worked mainly in the same genre and language. Also scripted **Mohan Segal**'s *Sajan* (1969).

FILMOGRAPHY: 1943: *Poonji*; **1945**: *Dhamki*; **1948**: *Chunaria*; *Patjhad*; **1949**: *Naach*; *Sawan Bhadon*; **1950**: *Meena Bazaar*; **1951**: *Nagina*; **1952**: *Lal Kunwar*; *Moti Mahal*; **1953**: *Naina*; **1954**: *Bhai Saheb*; **1955**: *Shikar*; *Lutera*; **1956**: *Char Minar*; **1957**: *Agra Road*; **1958**: *Farishta*; ***Post Box 999***; **1959**: *CID Girl*; *Ghar Ghar Ki Baat*; ***Guest House***; ***Satta Bazaar***; **1962**: *Aankh Micholi*; *Girls' Hostel*; **1963**: *Band Master*; **1964**: *Tere Dwar Khada Bhagwan*; *Dulha Dulhan*; *Punar Milan*; **1967**: *Raaz*; **1969**: *Road to Sikkim*; **1971**: ***Jesal Toral***; **1973**: *Raja Bhartrahari*; **1974**: *Hothal Padmini*; *Kunwarbainu Mameru*; **1975**: *Sant Surdas*; *Shetalne Kanthe*; *Bhadar Tara Vehta Pani*; **1976**: *Bhaibandhi*; *Malavpati Munj*; **1977**: *Jai Randalma*; *Maa Avret Jivrat*; *Paiso Bole Chhe*; *Son Kansari*; **1978**: *Chundadi Odhi Tara Namni*; *Patali Parmar*; *Bhagya Lakshmi*; **1979**: *Suraj Chandra Ni Sakhe*; *Preet Khandani Dhar*; **1980**: *Koino Ladakvayo*; *Virangana Nathibai*; **1981**: *Jagya Tyanthi Savar*; *Seth Jagadusha*; *Dukhda Khame Ee Dikri*; **1983**: *Palavade Bandhi Preet*; **1984**: *Nagmati Nagvalo*; **1985**: *Malo Naagde*.

DEBI, SUPRABHA (b. 1939)

Assamese writer, distributor and first woman director. Born into an established family from Golaghat, Upper Assam. Married the journalist and cineaste D.N. Debi. Involved in the films of Rajendra Chalachitra. After her husband's death, became distributor and producer, eventually directing as well.
FILMOGRAPHY: **1983**: ***Nayanmoni***; **1985**: *Sarbajan*.

DESAI, DHIRUBHAI B. (1908-90)

Hindi and Gujarati director born in Kaliawadi, near Navsari, Gujarat. Attended J.J. School of Art in Bombay. Started at **Sharda** Studio (1927); assisted A.P. Kapur. Completed *Maya Na Rang*, left unfinished by **Sarpotdar** when Bhogilal Dave took over his United Pics Syndicate in 1929. Early work marked by the Sharda genre of action films and later by **Indulal Yagnik**'s politically informed melodrama. Also worked for **Nanubhai Desai**'s Saroj Film. Set up own talkie studio, Vishnu Cinetone (with *Surya Kumari*, 1933), with Natwar Shyam Maniar and Chaturbhai Patel. Later also owned Chandrakala Pics. One of the few silent film-makers with a long career in Hindi and Gujarati B-movies. Post-40s films mainly cheap mythologicals, often remakes of silent hits.

FILMOGRAPHY: **1928**: *Maya Na Rang*; **1929**: *Kusum Lata*; *Nishan Danka*; *Mayavi Nagari*; *Bahadur Baharvatiyo*; **1930**: *Abad Veer*; *Chittor Ni Veerangana*; *Komalner Ni Kusum*; *Bhawani No Bhog*; **1931**: *Amar Yoddho*(?); *Lal Panjo*; *Aatishe Ishq*; *Jawahir-e-Hind*, *Kanak Kesari*; *Dariyai Devangana*; *Alakh Kishori*; **1932**: *Gurjar Veer*; *Sinh Santaan* (all St); **1933**: *Surya Kumari*; **1934**: *Bulbul-e-Paristan*; **1935**: *Dard-e-Ulfat*; *Delhi Ka Thug*; *Lal Chitta*; **1936**: *Hoor-e-Samundar*; **1937**: *Vanraj Kesari*; **1938**: *Fashionable Wife*; *Talwar Ka Dhani*; **1939**: *Baghi*; *Payame Haq*; **1940**: *Pyar*; *Rani Saheba*; **1941**: *Chandan*; **1942**: *Bolti Bulbul*; *Seva*; **1944**: *Maya Nagari*; **1946**: *Bhakta Prahlad*; *Devkanya*; **1947**: *Saat Samundaron Ki Mallika*; **1948**: *Satyavadi Harishchandra*; **1949**: *Bhakta Pundalik*; **1951**: *Jai Mahakali*; **1952**: *Bhakta Puran*; *Neelam Pari*; **1953**: *Shuk Rambha*; **1954**: *Durga Puja*; *Shiv Kanya*; **1955**: *Mastani*; *Oonchi Haveli*; **1956**: *Sati Ansuya*; **1957**: *Paristan*; *Raja Vikram*; **1958**: *Harishchandra*; **1959**: *Maa Ke Aansoo*; **1960**: *Saranga*; **1961**: *Jai Bhawani*; **1962**: *Kailashpati*; **1964**: *Bhakta Dhruvakumar*; **1965**: *Mahasati Ansuya*; **1967**: *Badrinath Yatra*; **1968**: *Mata Mahakali*; **1969**: *Pujarin*; **1970**: *Sampoorna Teerth Yatra*; **1972**: *Narad Leela*; **1975**: *Daku Aur Bhagwan*.

DESAI, JAYANTILAL ZINABHAI (1909-76)

Hindi director born in Surat, Gujarat. Entered films initially as Surat-based exhibitor, later scenarist for London Film, Rangoon, and for **Krishna** and **Sharda** Studios. Assisted **Chandulal Shah** (*Rajputani*, 1929). Turned director completing **Nandlal Jaswantlal**'s *Pahadi Kanya* (1930). Front-line **Ranjit** film-maker until 1943, then independent producer, owner of Jupiter Studio, Jayant Desai Prod. (1943) and Hemlata Pics. Also had exhibition interests with Hindmata Talkies and Star Theatres in Bombay and operated as a distributor in the 50s with his Jupiter Films. Directed **K.L. Saigal**'s last films. Desai's devotionals (e.g. ***Har Har Mahadev***) and historicals (***Tansen***) show how these genres were inflected towards neo-traditional melodrama (including his several Saint films and mythologicals) by a growing urban working-class audience and an economy determined by WW2.

FILMOGRAPHY: **1930**: *Pahadi Kanya* (uncredited); *Noor-e-Watan*; *Jawan Mard*; *Joban Nu Jadu*; **1931**: *Mukti Sangram*; *Banke Savaria*; *Vilasi Atma*; *Qatil Katari*; *Vijay Lakshmi*; *Fauladi Pahelwan*; **1932**: *Lal Swar*; *Sipahsalaar* (all St); *Bhutia Mahal*; *Char Chakram*; *Do Badmash*; **1933**: *Bhola Shikar*; *Bhool Bhulaiyan*; *Krishna Sudama*; **1934**: *Nadira*; ***Sitamgarh***; *Toofan Mail*; ***Veer Babruwahan***; **1935**: *College Girl*; *Noor-e-Watan*; **1936**: *Laheri Lala*; *Matlabi Duniya*; *Raj Ramani*; *Rangila Raja*; **1937**: *Toofani Toli*; *Mitti Ka Putla*; *Zameen Ka Chand*; **1938**: *Ban Ki Chidiya*; *Billi*; *Prithvi Putra*; **1939**: ***Sant Tulsidas***; **1940**: *Aaj Ka Hindustan*; *Diwali*; **1941**: *Beti*; *Shadi*; **1942**: *Chandni*; *Fariyad*; **1943**: *Bansari*; *Bhakta Raaj*; ***Tansen***; *Zabaan*; **1944**: *Lalkaar*; *Manorama*; **1945**: ***Samrat Chandragupta***; ***Tadbir***; **1946**: *Maharana Pratap*; **1950**: ***Har Har Mahadev***; *Shaan*; *Veer Bhimsen*; **1951**: *Dashavtar*; *Shri Ganesh Janma*; **1952**: *Amber*; *Nishan Danka*; *Shivashakti*; **1953**: *Hazaar Raatein*; *Manchala*; *Naya Raasta*; **1954**: *Miss Mala*; *Shiv Ratri*; **1955**: *Sati Madalasa*; **1956**: *Basant Panchami*; *Hamara Watan*; **1957**: *Lakshmi Pooja*; **1961**: *Zamana Badal Gaya*.

DESAI, MANMOHAN (1936-94)

Hindi director born in Bombay. Son of Kikubhai Desai, founder of the Paramount Studio which later housed Filmalaya (Est: 1958). Elder brother of the producer Subhash Desai. Started as assistant director to **Babubhai Mistri** in the late 50s; 60s work in line with **Shammi Kapoor**'s films at **Filmistan** (***Bluff Master***, *Badtameez*). Although the films rely on Hollywood models (esp. Elvis Presley) introduced into Hindi film by **Subodh Mukherjee** and **Nasir Hussain**, they also jettison some of the narrative ballast that e.g. Hussain puts into his romances. The narratives in the 70s films with **Rajesh Khanna** (***Sachcha Jhutha***) and **Jeetendra** (*Bhai Ho To Aisa*) develop a series of autonomously packaged sequences emotionally complete in themselves. Desai formula plots deploy good guy-bad guy dual roles or lost-and-found brother stories first elaborated by Tamil films (e.g. ***Parasakthi***, 1952), removing the political aspects from their populist approach and replacing them with a more diffuse, less targeted aggressiveness. Turned independent producer with ***Amar Akbar Anthony***, often financed by industrial family of Hindujas. Leading director in the 70s. Desai's best-known films, ***Naseeb*** and ***Coolie***, have **Bachchan** continuing the **MGR** mode of presenting himself in the guise of the oppressed subaltern. But Desai adds a celebration of lumpen power charged with communal references. Publicly announced his retirement as a director after *Ganga Jamuna Saraswati*. Recently, the resemblance between Desai's formula plots and the structure of US tv series caused his work to be associated with notions of postmodernism. His son Ketan Desai now makes films for MKD Films (e.g. *Allah Rakha*, 1986; *Toofan*, 1989).

FILMOGRAPHY: **1960**: ***Chhalia***; **1963**: ***Bluff Master***; **1966**: *Badtameez*; **1968**: *Kismet*; **1970**: ***Sachcha Jhutha***; **1972**: *Bhai Ho To Aisa*; *Rampur Ka Lakshman*; *Shararat*; **1973**: *Aa Gale Lag Jaa*; **1974**: *Roti*; **1977**: ***Amar Akbar Anthony***; *Chacha Bhatija*; ***Dharam Veer***; *Parvarish*; **1979**: *Suhaag*; **1981**: ***Naseeb***; **1982**: *Desh Premi*; **1983**: ***Coolie***; **1985**: ***Mard***; **1988**: *Ganga Jamuna Saraswati*.

DESAI, NANUBHAI B. (1902-67)

Born in Kaliawadi, near Navsari, Gujarat. Major producer and director of pioneering action and stunt films characteristic of the **Sharda** Studio style. Joined **Ardeshir Irani**'s Star Film; later partnered Dorabsha Kolha, Nowroji Pavri and his mentor Bhogilal Dave in Saraswati Film (Est: 1924), from which emerged the nucleus of Sharda started by Desai and Dave (1925). Founded Saroj Film (1929), later Saroj Movietone. Ran Amar Pics, which replaced the earlier **Sagar Film** when it split. Produced films by **R.S. Choudhury** et al. Ended up as production manager at the Pakshiraja Studio (e.g. for their Hindi film ***Azad***, 1955).

FILMOGRAPHY: **1923**: *Champraj Hado*; **1924**: *Razia Begum*; ***Sati Sardarba***; *Vikram Charitra*; **1925**: *Saurashtra Veer*; ***Bajirao Mastani***; *Bhadra Bhamini*; ***Mumbai Ni Mohini***; **1926**: *Vasant Bala*; *Dil Aram*; **1927**: *Bhedi Trishul*; *Gulzar*; *Kailash Kumari*; *Reshmi Sari*; *Asuri Lalsa*; *Jaan-e-Alam Anjuman Ara*; *Kala Pahad*; *Veer Garjana*; **1928**: *Maya Mahal* (all St).

DESAI, VASANT (1912-75)

Music director born in Kudal, Maharashtra. Employed at **Prabhat** as actor and studio-hand from 1929. Assistant to composers **Tembe**, **Krishnarao** and **Bhole** and actor-singer with successful solos in ***Ayodhyecha Raja*** and ***Amar Jyoti***. Music director at **Rajkamal**, where he was a regular in **Shantaram** films for over three decades starting with ***Shakuntala***. Best-known work mainly adapting traditional Maharashtrian musical modes of Powada and Lavni (e.g. in ***Lokshahir Ramjoshi*** and ***Amar Bhoopali***). Made several polemical statements calling for Marathi cinema's return to regional music traditions (e.g. Desai, 1950). Scored several mythologicals by **Vijay Bhatt** and **Babubhai Mistri** and two major **Sohrab Modi** films: ***Sheesh Mahal*** and ***Jhansi Ki Rani***. Later scored for **Hrishikesh Mukherjee** (***Ashirwad***, ***Guddi***) and **Gulzar** (*Achanak*).

FILMOGRAPHY (* act only): **1932**: ***Ayodhyecha Raja****; **1935**: ***Dharmatma****; **1936**: ***Amar Jyoti****; **1937**: ***Wahan****; **1940**: ***Sant Dnyaneshwar****; **1942**: *Shobha*; **1943**: *Aankh Ki Sharam*; *Mauj*; ***Shakuntala***; **1944**: *Parbat Pe Apna Dera*; **1946**: ***Dr Kotnis Ki Amar Kahani***; ***Jeevan Yatra***; ***Subhadra***; **1947**: *Andhon Ki Duniya*; ***Lokshahir Ramjoshi/Matwala Shayar Ramjoshi***; **1948**: *Mandir*; *Sona*; **1949**: *Narasinh Avatar*; *Udhaar*; *Sakharpuda*; *Nai Taleem*; **1950**: *Krantiveer Vasudev Balwant*; ***Dahej***; *Hindustan Hamara*; ***Sheesh Mahal***; **1951**: *Jeevan Tara*; ***Amar Bhoopali***; *Hi Majhi Lakshmi*; **1952**: *Hyderabad Ki Nazneen*; **1953**: *Anand Bhavan*; *Dhuaan*; ***Jhansi Ki Rani***; *Majhi Zameen*; ***Shyamchi Aai***; **1954**: *Kalakaar*; *Savdhan*; *Suhagan* (all 3 with **C. Ramchandra**); *Kanchanganga*; **1955**: *Ye Re Majhya Maglya*; *Jhanak Jhanak Payal Baaje*; **1956**: *Toofan Aur Diya*; **1957**: ***Do Aankhen Barah Haath***; **1958**: *Do Phool*; *Mausi*; **1959**: *Ardhangini*; *Do Behnen*; ***Goonj Uthi Shehnai***; *Samrat Prithviraj Chouhan*; **1960**: *Umaji Naik*; **1961**: *Pyar Ki Pyaas*; *Sampoorna Ramayan*; **1962**: *Baap Mazha Brahmachari*; **1963**: *Chhota Jawan*; *Molkarin*; **1964**: *Swayamvar Jhale Seeteche*; *Rahul*; ***Yaadein***; **1965**: *Amar Jyoti*; *Bharat Milap*; *Iye Marathyachi Nagari/Ladki Sahyadri Ki*; ***And Miles To Go...***; **1967**: *Ramrajya*; **1968**: *Dhanya Te Santaji Dhanaji*; ***Ashirwad***; **1970**: *Lakshman Resha*; **1971**: ***Guddi***; **1972**: ***Grahan***; **1973**: *Achanak*; **1974**: *Jai Radhe Krishna*; *Bayano Navre Sambhala*; *Raja Shivachhatrapati*; **1975**: *Rani Aur Lalpari*; **1976**: *Shaque*; *Tuch Majhi Rani*.

Shammi Kapoor (centre) in Manmohan Desai's *Bluff Master* (1963)

DEVARAJAN, PARAVUR

Prolific 60s and 70s Malayalam film composer. Established reputation with songs for plays of the left Kerala Peoples' Arts Club (see **IPTA**), esp. the **O.N.V. Kurup** lyric sung by K.S. George and Sulochana invoking the graves of the Communist rebels of Punnapra-Vyalar (1946), set to a militant rendition of the raga Hamsadhwani. Like **Dakshinamurthy**, was trained in classical Carnatic music but, unlike him, often borrowed extensively from folk influences. Early scores in **Puttanna Kanagal**'s Malayalam films (*School Master*, *Kalanjukuttiya Thangam*); broke through with **Sethumadhavan**'s 60s films, remaining his regular composer for several years (e.g. ***Odeyil Ninnu***, ***Daham***, ***Adimagal***, ***Aranazhikaneram***). Worked on several major **Vincent** films including ***Ashwamedham***, ***Thulabharam*** and ***Nadhi***. In the 70s, was associated with independent breakthroughs including **Menon**'s ***Kabani Nadi Chuvannappol*** and **Backer**'s work (e.g. *Charam*), while simultaneously working on **I.V. Sasi**'s mainstream productions. Composed **Aravindan**'s ***Chidambaram*** as well. Reputedly the first composer in Malayalam film to make sense of the non-verbal background score, with a bias for violin effects.

FILMOGRAPHY incomplete for 1978-82.

FILMOGRAPHY: **1955**: *Kalam Marunnu*; **1958**: *Chadurangam*; **1962**: *Bharya*; **1963**: *Nithya Kanyaka*; *Doctor*; *Kadalamma*; **1964**: *Anna*; *School Master*; *Manavatti*; *Omanakuttan*; *Kalanjukuttiya Thangam*; **1965**: ***Odeyil Ninnu***; *Kaliyodam*; *Kattupookal*; *Kathiruna Nikkah*; ***Daham***; *Shakuntala*; *Pattu Thoovala*; **1966**: *Kalithozhen*; *Rowdy*; *Jail*; *Kalyana Rathriyil*; *Kanmanikal*; *Karuna*; *Tilottama*; **1967**: *Swapnabhoomi*; *Sheelavati*; *Arakillam*; ***Aval***; ***Ashwamedham***; ***Chitramela***; *Pooja*; ***Kavalam Chundan***; *Nadan Pennu*; *Kasavuthattam*; **1968**: *Viplavakarikal*; *Thokkukal Katha Parayunnu*; *Hotel Highrange*; *Yakshi*; ***Thulabharam***; *Velutha Kathrina*; *Agni Pareeksha*; **1969**: *Anashchadanam*; *Padicha Kallan*; *Veetu Mrugham*; *Kattukurangu*; *Susie*; ***Adimagal***; *Urangatha Sundari*; *Kadalpalam*; *Mooladanam*; *Jwala*; ***Nadhi***; *Kootu Kudumbam*; *Kumara Sambhavam*; **1970**: *Mindapennu*; *Nishagandhi*; ***Vazhve Mayam***; *Dattuputhran*; *Othenente Makan*; *Abhayam* (with **Salil Choudhury**); ***Ningalenne Communistaki***; *Vivahitha*; *Nilakatha Chalanangal*; *Swapnangal*; *A Chitrashalabham Paranotte*; *Triveni*; *Tara*; ***Aranazhikaneram***; *Pearl View*; **1971**: *Shiksha*; ***Oru Penninte Katha***; *Thettu*; *Kalithozhi*; *Inquilab Zindabad*; *Sarasayya*; *Karakanakadal*; *Line Bus*; *Puthanveedu*; *Avalalppam Vaikippoi*; ***Sindoorachеppu***; ***Anubhavangal Palichakal***; **1972**: *Mayiladum Kunnu*; *Devi*; *Professor*; *Aromalunni*; *Omana*; ***Chemparathi***; *Achannum Bappayum*;

Akkarapacha; *Oru Sundariyude Katha*; *Punarjanmam*; *Maraivil Thiruvu Sukshikuha*; *Gandharvakshetram*; *Postmane Kananilla*; *Chhayam*; ***Maram***; **1973**: ***Enippadikal***; *Kalachakram*; *Ponnapuram Kotta*; *Gayatri*; *Manushya Puthran*; *Thani Niram*; *Darshanam*; *Achani*; *Thenaruvi*; *Pavangal Pennungal*; *Nakhangal*; *Dharma Yuddham*; *Prethangalude Thazhvara*; *Chukku*; *Madhavikutty*; *Swargaputhri*; *Angathattu*; *Masappadi Mathupilla*; *Kaliyugam*; *Chenda*; *Vijaya*; **1974**: *Chattakkari*; *Paruvakalam*; *Shapamoksham*; *Suprabhatam*; *Panchatanthram*; *Durga*; *Setu Bandhanam*; *Neela Kannukal*; *Nagaram Sagaram*; *Thumbolarcha*; *Devi Kanyakumari*; *Raja Hamsam*; *Vishnu Vijayam*; *Bhoomidevi Pushpiniyayi*; *Atithi*; *Mazhakkaru*; **1975**: *Alibaba and Forty-One Thieves*; *Ayodhya*; *Bharya Illatha Rathri*; *Boy Friend*; *Chalanam*; *Chuvanna Sandhyakal*; ***Kabani Nadi Chuvannappol***; *Kottaram Vilakkanundu*; *Makkal*; *Manishada*; *Mucheettu Kalikarante Magal*; *Palazhi Madhanam*; *Priyamulla Sophia*; *Swami Ayyappan*; *Antharangam*; **1976**: *Kumara Vijayam*; *Amba Ambika Ambalika*; *Ammini Ammavan*; *Anavaranam*; *Aruthu*; *Ayalakkari*; *Colonel and Collector*; *Hridayam Oru Kshetram*; ***Manimuzhakkum***; *Missi*; *Mohini Attam*; *Nee Ente Lahari*; *Nurayum Pathayum*; *Panchamrutham*; *Ponn*; *Rathriyile Yatrakar*; *Romeo*; *Sarvekkalu*; *Udyanalakshmi*; *Vanadevatha*; ***Chuvanna Vithukal***; **1977**: *A Nimisham*; *Acharam Ammini Osaram Omana*; *Agni Nakshatram*; *Akale Akasam*; *Anandam Paramanandam*; *Anjali*; *Chakravarthini*; *Chaturvedam*; *Guruvayoor Kesavan*; *Innale Innu*; *Itha Ivide Vare*; *Karnaparvam*; *Kavilamma*; *Lakshmi*; *Minimol*; *Nalumani Pookkal*; *Needhi Peedham*; *Oonjal*; *Pennpuli*; *Rajani*; *Rendu Lokam*; *Rowdy Rajamma*; *Saghakkale Munottu*; *Samudram*; *Satyavan Savithri*; *Shri Murugan*; *Sridevi*; *Varadakshina*; *Veedu Oru Swargam*; *Vidarunna Mottugal*; *Aniyara*; **1978**: *Nakshatrangale Kaval*; *Anappachan*; *Aazhi Alayazhi*; *Adimakachavadam*; *Amarsham*; *Ammuvinte Atinkutty*; *Avalakku Maranamilla*; *Avar Jeevikkunu*; *Ee Manohara Theeram*; *Gnan Gnan Mathram*; *Iniyum Puzha Ozhukum*; *Kadathanattu Maakkam*; *Mudra Mothiram*; *Nivedyam*; *Padasaram*; *Rappadigalude Gatha*; *Rajan Paranja Katha*; ***Rathi Nirvedham***; *Satrathil Oru Rathri*; *Snehikkan Oru Pennu*; *Thampuratti*; *Tharu Oru Janmam Koodi*; *Vadagaikku Oru Hridayam*; *Vayanadan Thampan*; *Vilakkum Velichavum*; *Yeetta*; **1979**: ***Sanghaganam***; **1981**: *Charam*; **1983**: *Eetapuli*; *Himavahini*; *Kattaruvi*; *Oru Madaupravinte Katha*; *Thimingalam*; *Kodugal Illatha Kolam*; *Pudhiya Varavu*; *Villainpur Matha*; **1984**: *Ningalil Oru Stree*; *Poomadathu Pennu*; *Vellom*; *Vikatakavi*; **1985**: *Ee Thalamura Inganna*; *Kochuthemmadi*; *Shri Narayana Guru*; ***Chidambaram***; **1987**: *Ivide Ellavarkkum Sukham*; ***Thoranam***; **1988**: *Innaleyude Baaki*; **1989**: *Utsavapittennu*; *Thangachi Kalyanam*.

DEVARE, NARAYAN GOPINATH (1899-1954)

Bombay-based cinematographer and director of the silent period; born in Bombay. Son of the court photographer and cameraman G.S. Devare. Studied photography and cinematography in Europe (1918-20); returned to India (1921) and worked briefly in his father's studio before joining **Kohinoor** as a technician in the early 20s, where he worked with his cousin Gajanan Shyamrao Devare, also a cameraman and director. N.G. Devare has been credited with directing films he shot for **Kanjibhai Rathod** and **Homi Master**. He also shot ***The Telephone Girl*** (1926), pioneering location shooting at the Grant Road Telephone Exchange in Bombay, and ***Bhaneli Bhamini*** and ***Gunsundari*** (both 1927). Turned director in 1927. Virtually ran Kohinoor when it became the employee-run Kohinoor U.A. (1928), establishing his own N.G. Devare Prod. in 1933, but the venture collapsed. Several film-makers were apprenticed to him, e.g. the then-cameraman **V.M. Vyas** for *Zakhmi Jigar* and **Jaswantlal** for *Ulfat-e-Mohammed*. Recorded his version of this controversial period in Kohinoor's history and of the silent studios in the film ***Daily Mail***. Co-directed a few Hindi and Marathi films in the late 30s and 40s with Homi Master (e.g. *Punjab Lancers*) and **Sarpotdar** (*Sant Janabai*). His cousin G.S. Devare had become a prominent cameraman with films such as ***Bhakta Vidur*** (1921), ***Kala Naag*** (1924), ***Fankdo Fituri*** and ***Lanka Ni Laadi*** (both 1925). As a director, G.S. Devare was associated with **J.B.H. Wadia** and later ran a film processing laboratory. The two Devares co-directed the Marathi film *Raigad*.

FILMOGRAPHY: **1927**: *Be Ghadi Mouj*; *Sati Madri*; **1928**: *Naag Padmini*; *Tajayali Taruni*; *Bharmayalo Bharthar*; *Princess Rajba*; **1929**: *Baghdad Nu Baharvatiyo*; *Zakhmi Jigar*; *Ulfat-e-Mohammed*; *Mumbaino Satodio*; *Nirdoshi Abla*; **1930**: ***Daily Mail***; *Baharvatiyo Ni Beti*; **1931**: *Afghan Abla* (all St); **1934**: *Sant Tulsidas*; *Neki Ka Taj*; **1935**: *Rang Bhoomi*; **1937**: *Punjab Lancers*; **1938**: *Sant Janabai*; **1939**: *Saguna Sarasa*; **1940**: *Raigad*; **1947**: *Ghar Ki Bahu*.

DEVI, ANJALI (b. 1927)

Telugu/Tamil/Hindi actress born in Peddapuram, Kakinada Dist. as Anjani Kumari. Started on the Telugu stage aged 10 under her future husband, composer **Adi Narayana Rao**, who instructed her in music and dance. Also stage actress with the Young Men's Happy Club. Performed in plays like *Srinivasa Kalyanam* and *Premavijayam* and gave live dance shows. Film début in **C. Pullaiah**'s *Gollabhama*. Early roles mainly as vamp (e.g. **Balaramaiah**'s *Balaraju*, ***Keeluguram***, **R. Padmanabhan**'s ***Raksharekha***, **T.R. Sundaram**'s *Sarvadhikari*). These directors, and **Raghavaiah**, were associated with her early career, and her best-known screen image, e.g. in the famous ***Swapna Sundari*** playing a heavenly damsel descending to earth, followed by hits like Raghavaiah's *Anarkali* (which ran for 100 weeks) and ***Suvarna Sundari***, **T.R. Raghunath**'s *Kanavane Kan Kanda Daivam* and **P. Neelakantan**'s *Chakravarthi Thirumagal*, which made her a top female Telugu and Tamil star for several years. Often acted with Telugu superstars **A. Nageshwara Rao** and **NTR** and, in Tamil, with **MGR** and **Gemini Ganesh.** Started her own Ashwini Pics which in 1951 became Anjali Pics Studio (aka Anjali Pixtures), in partnership with Adi Narayana Rao débuting with **Prasad**'s ***Poongothai/Paradesi***. In the 70s mainly played mother roles. Vice-president of the South Indian Film Chamber of Commerce (1950-51).

FILMOGRAPHY: **1947**: *Gollabhama*; *Mahatma Udhangar*; **1948**: *Balaraju*; *Madalasa*; *Adinathan Kanavu*; **1949**: ***Raksharekha***; ***Keeluguram/Maya Kudhirai***; *Kanniyin Kathali*; *Mangayar Karasi*; *Mayavathi*; **1950**: *Maya Rambha*; *Palletoori Pilla*; *Shri Lakshmamma Katha*; ***Swapna Sundari***; *Praja Rajyam*; **1951**: *Strisahasam*; *Mayalamari/Mayakkari*; ***Nirdoshi/Niraparadhi***; *Tilottama/Mayamalai*; *Sarvadhikari*; ***Marmayogi/Ek Tha Raja***; **1952**: ***Pedaraitu***; **1953**: ***Pakkinti Ammayi***; ***Poongothai/Pardesi***; *Ladki*; **1954**: *Annadata*; *Ponnavayal/Bangaru Bhoomi*; *Rechukka*; *Sangham*; **1955**: *Anarkali*; *Jayasimha/Jaisingh*; *Santosham/Naya Admi*; *Vadinagari Gajalu*; *Kanavane Kan Kanda Daivam*; ***Mudhal Thedi***; *Town Bus*; **1956**: *Naga Panchami*; *Jayam Manade*; *Ilavelpu*; *Mathurkula Manikyam/Charanadasi*; **1957**: *Peddarikalu*; *Allavudeenum Arputha Vilakkum/Allauddin Adbhuta Deepam/Alladdin Ka Chirag*; ***Suvarna Sundari/Manalane Mangayin Bhagyam***; *Sati Ansuya*; *Panduranga Mahatyam*; *Chakravarthi Thirumagal*; **1958**: ***Chenchulakshmi***; *Shobha*; *Raja Nandini*; *Aadapettanam*; **1959**: *Pelli Sandadi/Kalyana Penn*; *Jayabheri*; *Balanagamma*; *Naan Sollum Rahasiyam*; *Kalaivanan*; *Pachai Malai Kurathi*; **1960**: *Kuladaivam*; *Rani Ratnaprabha*; *Bhatti Vikramarka*; *Runanubandham*; *Adutha Veetu Penn*; *Advantha Daivam*; *Engal Selvi*; *Mannathai Mannan*; **1961**: *Shanta*; *Sati Sulochana*; *Bhakta Jayadeva*; *Saugandh*; *Pachani Samsaram*; *Pankalikal*; **1962**: *Bhishma*; *Swarnamanjari/Mangayir Ullam Mangada Selvam*; *Naag Devata*; **1963**: *Lavakusa*; *Paruvu Pratishthalu*; *Pareeksha*; *Raj Mahal*; **1964**: *Varasatwam*; *En Kadamai*; **1965**: *Sati Sakkubai*; **1966**: *Palnati Yuddham*; *Chilaka-Gorinka*; *Bhakta Potana*; *Hantakulostannuru Jagratha*; *Shri Krishna Tulabharam*; *Dr Anand*; ***Rangula Ratnam***; **1967**: *Bhakta Prahlada*; *Chadurangam*; *Kambojuraju Katha*; *Nirdoshi*; *Private Master*; *Rahasyam*; *Sati Sumati*; *Stree Janmam*; *Vasantsena*; **1968**: *Lakshminivasam*; *Challani Needa*; *Kumkumabharina*; *Mana Samsaram*; *Sati Arundhati*; *Veeranjaneya*; **1969**: *Adarsha Kutumbam*; *Shri Rama Katha*; *Bhale Mastaru*; *Bandhipotu Bhimanna*; **1970**: *Amma Kosam*; *Desamante Manasuloi*; *Agni Pareeksha*; *Raithe Raju*; **1971**: *Suputhrudu*; *Bangaru Kutumbam*; *Pagabattina Paduchu*; *Kalyana Mandapam*; *Vikramarka Vijayam*; *Raitu Kutumbam*; **1972**: *Mathru Murthi*; *Vamsodharakudu*; *Manchi Rojulu Vastai*; *Kodalu Pilla*; *Vichitra Bandham*; *Maa Inti Velugu*; *Badi Panthulu*; *Kalam Marindi*; *Vooriki Upakari*; ***Tata Manuvudu***; *Shanti Nilayam*; *Bava Diddina Kapuram*; *Akka Tammudu*; *Bala Bharatam*; **1973**: *Kanna Koduku*; *Talli Kodakulu*; *Nindu Kutumbam*; *Sreevaru Maavaru*; *Bhakta Tukaram*; *Minor Babu*; *Mayadari Malligadu*; *Abhimanavanthulu*; *Vakkuruthi*; **1974**: *Intinti Katha*; *Manchi Manushulu*; *Deeksha*; *Peddalu Marali*; *Manushulo Devudu*; *Uttama Illalu*; *Krishnaveni*; *Chakravakam*; *Palle Paduchu*; *Urmai Kural*; **1975**: *Gunavanthudu*; *Raktha Sambandhalu*; *Challani Talli*; *Gajula Kishtayya*; *Soggadu*; *Pichimaraju*; **1976**: *Monagadu*; *Vadhu Varulu*; *Mahakavi Kshetrayya*; *Magaadu*; *Devude Gelichadu*; *Raja*; **1977**: *Kurukshetramu*; *Sati Savitri*; *Seeta Rama Vanavasu*; *Ee Tharam Manishi*; *Bangaru Bommalu*; *Geetha Sangeetha*; **1978**: *Allari Bullodu*; *Anna Dammula Saval*; *Ramakrishnulu*; *Dudubasavanna*; *Simha Baludu*;

Anukunnadhi Sadhishta; *Angadi Bomma*; *K.D. No. 1*; *Kannavari Illu*; *Simha Garjana*; **1979**: *Shri Tirupati Venkateshwara Kalyanam*; *Amma Evarikaina Amma*; *Judagadu*; *Tiger*; *Sangam Chekkina Silpalu*; **1980**: *Bhale Krishnudu*; *Chandi Priya*; *Ram Robert Rahim*; *Shri Vasavi Kannika Parameshwari Mahatyam*; **1981**: *Guru Shishyulu*; *Puli Bidda*; *Jeevitha Radham*; **1983**: *Amayukudu Kadhu Asadhyudu*; *Lanke Bindelu*; *Poratham*; **1984**: *Pozhudu Vidinachu*; *Dongalu Baboi Dongalu*; **1985**: *Atmabalam*; *Kutumba Bandham*; *Shri Shirdi Saibaba Mahatyam*; *Surya Chandra*; *Mangalya Balam*; **1989**: *Krishnagari Abbayi*; *Chinnari Sneham*; *Ashoka Chakravarthi*.

DEVI, ARUNDHATI (1923-90)

Aka Arundhati Mukherjee (when married to film-maker Prabhat Mukherjee). Bengali actress, director and musician born in Barisal (now Bangladesh). Studied music at Shantiniketan, and acted as a child aged 6 in several **Tagore** plays directed by the poet himself (*Dakghar*, *Mayar Khela*, *Tasher Desh* et al.). Promising singer of the Rabindra Sangeet, trained by Sailaranjan Majumdar; also featured in the stage production of Tagore's *Balmiki Pratibha* (1943). Film début as actress in **Kartick Chattopadhyay**'s travelogue ***Mahaprasthaner Pathey/Yatrik.*** Major 50s star oozing a docile charm in contrast to contemporaries like **Suchitra Sen**, Manju Dey or Anubha Gupta (cf **Asit Sen**'s *Chalachal* and *Panchatapa*; Prabhat Mukherjee's *Bicharak*). Best-known screen role: *Bhagini Nivedita*, a nationalist biopic about Sister Nivedita. The film used the actress's middle-class image to convert its subject into a chaste Hinduised martyr. Turned director with ***Chhuti***; directed, scripted and scored films from well-known literary works. Her last film, *Gokul* was a tv featurette. Became an independent producer with her Anindiya Chitra (1969). Later married **Tapan Sinha** and acted in several of his films, e.g. ***Kshudista Pashan***, *Jhinder Bandi* and *Jotugriha*; also costume designer for Sinha's *Adalat-o-Ekti Meye*.

FILMOGRAPHY: (* only d/** also music d) **1952**: ***Mahaprasthaner Pathey/Yatrik***; **1954**: *Naad-o-Nadi*; *Sati*; *Bokul/Bakul*; *Shoroshi*; **1955**: *Prashna*; *Godhuli*; *Dashyumohan*; *Du-Janay*; **1956**: *Taka-Ana-Pai*; *Chalachal*; *Maa*; *Nabajanma*; **1957**: *Mamata*; *Panchatapa*; **1958**: *Shikar*; *Kalamati*; **1959**: *Janmantar*; *Bicharak*; *Shashi Babur Sansar*; *Pushpadhanu*; *Kichhukshan*; **1960**: *Akash-Patal*; ***Kshudista Pashan***; *Indradhanu*; **1961**: *Jhinder Bandi*; **1962**: *Bhagini Nivedita*; *Shiulibari***; **1963**: *Nyayadanda*; **1964**: *Jotugriha*; **1965**: *Surer Agun*; **1967**: ***Chhuti****; **1969**: ***Megh-o-Roudra****; **1972**: ***Padi Pishir Barmi Baksha****; **1975**: *Harmonium*; **1983**: *Deepar Prem**; **1985**: *Gokul**.

DEVI, B. SAROJA (b. 1945)

Top 60s star in Tamil, Telugu and Kannada cinemas. Associated mainly with sentimental melodrama. Also worked in several Hindi films. Early career in mythologicals after she was spotted by **Honappa Bhagavathar** who cast her in *Mahakavi Kalidasa*. Telugu début with **NTR** in the National Art Theatres' mythological, **K. Kameshwara Rao**'s *Panduranga Mahatyam*; later acted with NTR in several other Telugu films. Became a superstar with the Tamil hit ***Nadodi Mannan***, starring opposite **MGR**. Acted in over 160 films in four languages. Was Chairperson of the Karnataka Film Development Corp. and the Kanteerava Studios, Bangalore. Her main directors include **Panthulu** (***School Master***, *Ratnagiri Rahasya*, ***Kittur Chanamma***), **K. Subramanyam** (***Kacha Devayani***), **K.V. Reddy** and **A. Bhimsingh**.

FILMOGRAPHY: **1955**: *Mahakavi Kalidasa*; *Ashadabhooti*; *Shrirama Pooja*; **1956**: *Kacha Devyani*; *Kokilavani*; *Pancharathna*; **1957**: ***Chintamani***; *Ratnagiri Rahasya/Tangamalai Rahasyam*; ***Manalane Mangayin Bhagyam***; *Panduranga Mahatyam*; **1958**: *Illarame Nallaram*; *Manamulla Maratharam*; ***Nadodi Mannan***; *Shabash Meena*; *Sengottai Singam*; *Thedi Vantha Selvam*; *Thirumanam*; ***Bhukailasa***; *Bhuloka Rambha*; *Anna Thangi*; ***School Master/Badi Panthulu***; **1959**: *Jagajyothi Basaveshwara*; ***Paigham***; *Pelli Sandadi/Kalyana Penn*; *Bhagapirivanai*; ***Kalyana Parisu***; *Kudivazhanthal Kodi Nanmai*; *Ore Velaiyadu Papa*; ***President Panchatcharam***; *Vazha Vaitha Daivam*; **1960**: *Ellorum Innattu Mannar*; *Irumputhirai*; *Kairasi*; ***Parthiban Kanavu***; *Vidiveli*; *Yanai Pagan*; *Pelli Kanuka*; *Bhakti Mahima*; **1961**: *Seeta Rama Kalyanam*; *Intiki Deepam Illale*; ***Jagadeka Veeruni Katha/Jagathala Prathapan***; *Mahout*; *Opera House*; *Sasural*; ***Kittur Chanamma/Rani Chanamma***; *Vijayanagarada Veeraputra*; *Pallum Pazhamum*; *Panithirai*; *Thayi Sollai Thatthathe*; *Thirudathe*; *Krishna Kuchela*; **1962**: *Adiperaku*; *Alayamani*; *Kudumba Thalaivan*; *Madappura*; *Pasam*; *Parthal Pasi Theerum*; *Thayai Katha Thanayan*; *Valar Pirai*; *Devasundari*; *Hong Kong*; ***Shri Krishnarjuna Yuddham***; **1963**: *Pareeksha*; *Pyar Kiya To Darna Kya*; *Manchi Chedu*; ***Iruvar Ullam***; *Kalyanin Kanavan*; *Kulamangal Radhai*; *Needukkupin Pasam*; *Panathottam*; *Periya Idathu Penn*; **1964**: *Daivathai*; *En Kadamai*; *Padakottai*; *Panakara Kudumbam*; *Pasamum Nesamum*; *Pudhiya Paravai*; *Thayin Madiyil*; *Vazhkai Vazhvadarke*; *Atmabalam*; *Dagudu Moothulu*; *Beti Bete*; *Dooj Ka Chand*; ***Amarashilpi Jakanachari/Amarashilpi Jakanna***; **1965**: *Prameelarjuneyam*; *Beretha Jeeva*; *Todu Needa*; *Asai Mukham*; *Enga Veetu Pillai*; *Kalankari Vilakkam*; **1966**: *Anbe Vaa*; *Nadodi*; *Naan Anaittal*; *Parakkum Pavai*; *Petral Than Pillayya*; *Thali Bhagyam*; *Shakuntala*; *Preet Na Jane Reet*; **1967**: *Arasa Kattali*; *Penn Entral Penn*; **1968**: *En Thambi*; *Panama Pasama*; *Thamarai Nenjam*; *Umachandi Gauri Shankarula Katha*; *Arunodaya/Arunodhayam*; **1969**: *Mallammanna Pavada*; *Anbalipu*; *Thanga Malar*; *Odum Nadhi*; *Anjal Petty 520*; *Kulavilakku*; *Aindhu Laksham*; **1970**: *Kanmalar*; *Sinehithi*; *Malathi*; *Lakshmi Saraswati*; *Vijayam Manade*; *Mayani Mamata*; **1971**: *Purnima*; *Papa Punya*; *Thande Makkalu*; *Nyayave Devaru*; *Shri Krishna Rukmini Satyabhama*; *Thenum Palum*; *Uyir*; **1972**: *Shakti Leela*; *Hari Darshan*; ***Pandanti Kapuram***; *Mathru Murthi*; **1973**: *Sahadharmini*; **1974**: *Pathumatha Bandham*; *Chamundeshwari Mahime*; *Gruhini*; *Shri Srinivasa Kalyana*; *Manshulo Devadu*; ***Shri Ramanjaneya Yuddham***; **1975**: *Gunavanthudu*; *Bhagya Jyothi*; ***Katha Sangama***; **1976**: *Chiranjeevi*; **1977**: ***Daana Veera Shura Karna***; *Seetarama Vanavasu*; *Babruvahana*; *Bhagyavantharu*; *Shri Renukadevi Mahatme*; *Shani Prabhava*; **1978**: *Parsuraman*; **1980**: *Guru Sarvabhowma Shri Raghavendra Karune*; **1984**: *Guru Bhakti*; *Yarivanu?*; *Rudranaga*; **1985**: *Thayi Thande*; **1988**: *Poovukkul Pookambalam*; **1989**: *Ponmana Selvan*; *Ore Thayi Ore Kulam*; *Dharma Devan*; *Guru*; **1990**: *Bhale Chatura*; *Yamadharma Raju*; **1991**: *Alludu Diddina Kapuram*; *Apath Bandhavulu*; **1993**: *Paramparyam*.

B. Saroja Devi and Ajit in *Opera House* (1961)

DEVI, CHHAYA (b. 1914)

Bengali actress, born in Bhagalpur; her family was associated with the performing arts. Related to Hindi star **Ashok Kumar.** Early lessons in classical Hindustani music from Bundi Ustad and in Calcutta from **K.C. Dey** who introduced her in **Debaki Bose** films. First lead role in ***Sonar Sansar.*** Achieved a national reputation as Rani Lakshmibai in ***Bidyapati***. Performed on AIR as a singer. Her demure but seductive style managed to convey sexually charged messages through devotional gestures. Early films mainly with **Jyotish Bannerjee.** Later developed a formidable actorial presence, notably in **Tapan Sinha** films (***Nirjan Saikate***, *Hatey Bazarey*, ***Apanjan***) and **Arundhati Devi**'s ***Padi Pishir Barmi Baksha***. Acted in early **Mrinal Sen** (*Raat Bhore*, *Abasheshe*). Also sang in some films, e.g. *Rikta*, *Amar Geeti*.

FILMOGRAPHY: **1936**: *Pather Sheshey*; ***Sonar Sansar/Sunehra Sansar***; *Prabas Milan*; *Chino Haar*; **1937**: *Ranga Bou*; ***Bidyapati/Vidyapati***; **1938**: *Bekar Nashan*; *Halbangala*; *Khana*; **1939**: *Tumhari Jeet*; *Janak Nandini*; *Debjani*; *Rikta*; *Vaman Avatar*; *Jakher Dhan*; **1940**: ***Abhinetri/Haar Jeet***; *Swami Stri*; *Amar Geeti*; **1941**: *Banglar Meye*; **1942**: *Chowringhee*; *Pativrata*; *Avayer Biye*; *Mera Gaon*; **1943**: *Shri Ramanuja*; ***Samadhan***; **1944**: *Bideshini*; *Samaj*; **1945**: *Stree Durga*; *Bondita*; **1946**: *Uttara Abhimanyu*; **1947**: *Jharer Parey*; *Burmar Pathey*; **1948**: *Anirban*; *Bish Bichar Agey*; *Dhatri Debata*; *Mahakal*; **1949**: *Abhijatya*; *Abhimaan*; **1950**: *Indranath*; *Apabaad*; *Sati Simantini*; *Mahasampad*; **1951**: ***Ratnadeep/Ratnadeepam***; **1953**: *Chirantani*; **1954**: *Maa-o-Chhele*; **1955**: *Sanjher Pradeep*; *Bratacharini*; **1956**: *Raat Bhore*; *Saheb Bibi Golam*; *Sadhana*; *He Maha Manab*; *Shankar Narayan Bank*; *Trijama*; *Rajpath*; *Daner Maryada*; *Shubha Lagna*; ***Era Bator Sur***; **1957**: *Bardidi*; *Shesh Parichaya*; **1958**: *Bagha Jatin*; *Marmabani*; **1959**: *Shri Radha*; *Gali Theke Rajpath*; *Bhranti*; *Shubha Bibaha*; **1960**: *Saharer Itikatha*; **1961**: *Manik*; *Sadhak Kamalakanta*; *Agni Sanskar*; *Swayambara*; *Pankatilak*; ***Saptapadi***; **1962**: *Bipasha*; *Kancher Swarga*; *Atal Jaler Ahwan*; *Dada Thakur*; *Abasheshe*; **1963**: *Nisithe*; ***Saat Pake Bandha***; ***Nirjan Saikate***; *Shesh Prahar*; *Uttar Falguni*; *Deya Neya*; *Kanchan Kanya*; *Barnali*; **1964**: *Bibhas*; *Natun Tirtha*; ***Arohi***; **1965**: *Thana Theke Aschhi*; *Antaral*; *Raja Rammohun*; *Surya Tapa*; *Mukhujey Paribar*; *Eki Ange Eto Rup*; *Tu Hi Meri Zindagi*; **1966**: *Galpa Holeo Satti*; *Harano Prem*; *Kanch Kata Hirey*; *Manihar*; *Pagal Thakur*; *Mamata*; **1967**: *Akash Chhoan*; *Ajana Shapath*; ***Antony Firingee***; *Hatey Bazarey*; *Kedar Raja*; *Mahashweta*; **1968**: ***Apanjan***; *Baghini*; *Charan Kabi Mukundadas*; *Neel Kamal*; **1969**: *Andhar Surya*; *Arogyaniketan*; *Balak Gadadhar*; *Chena Achena*; *Maa-o-Meye*; *Mon-Niye*; *Parineeta*; *Pita Putra*; *Protidan*; *Sabarmati*; **1970**: *Kalankita Nayak*; *Muktisnan*; *Pratham Kadam Phool*; *Duti Mon*; *Megh Kalo*; *Rajkumari*; **1971**: *Kuheli*; **1972**: ***Padi Pishir Barmi Baksha***; *Shesh Parba*; *Zindagi Zindagi*; *Haar Mana Haar*; **1973**: *Roudra Chhaya*; *Shesh Pristhay Dekhun*; **1974**: *Alor Thikana*; *Debi Choudhrani*; *Sujata*; **1975**: *Chhoto Nayak*; *Harmonium*; *Kajal Lata*; *Nagar Darpane*; *Harano Prapti Niruddesh*; *Swayamsiddha*; *Sei Chokh*; *Phool Sajya*; **1976**: *Ek Je Chhilo Desh*; *Pratisruti*; *Rajbansha*; *Mom Batti*; **1977**: *Brajabuli*; *Babu Moshai*; *Ae Prithibi Pantha Niwas*; *Jaal Sanyasi*; *Pratima*; *Proxy*; *Alaap*; **1978**: *Dhanraj Tamang*; *Maan Abhiman*; *Nadi Theke Sagare*; *Singhdwar*; *Karunamayi*; *Pronoy Pasha*; **1979**: *Arun Barun-o-Kiranmala*; *Nabadiganta*; *Mother*; *Samadhan*; **1980**: *Aro Ekjan*; *Raj Nandini*; **1981**: *Manikchand*; *Nyay Anyay*; *Subarnalata*; *Kalankini*; **1982**: *Pipasa*; *Raj Bodhu*; *Bandini Kamala*; *Simanta Raag*; **1983**: *Chena Achena*; *Rang Birangi*; *Prayashchitta*; *Deepar Prem*; *Srinkhal*; **1984**: *Didi*; *Lal Golap*; *Rashifal*; **1985**: *Hulusthul*; *Kenaram Becharam*; **1987**: *Apan Ghare*; *Pratikar*; *Swarnamoir Thikana*; **1988**: *Boba Sanai*.

DEVI, KANAN (1916-92)

Actress and singer; started with the name Kananbala. Début as child actress in *Joydev*. Later contracted to Radha Films where she acted in **Jyotish Bannerjee** films (e.g. ***Manmoyee Girls' School***). **P.C. Barua** was unable to obtain her for the role of Paro in ***Devdas*** (1935) but she played the lead in his next film, ***Mukti***, which made her a star and launched her long association with **New Theatres**. The success of ***Bidyapati***, esp. her duets with **K.C. Dey**, made her the top star of this studio 1937-40. An untrained singer when she entered films, she later studied briefly with Ustad Allah Rakha at Lucknow. Employed as singer at Megaphone Gramophone receiving further training from Bhishmadev Chatterjee, possibly responsible for her distinctive Bengali style. Later learnt Rabindra Sangeet with Anadi Dastidar. She considered **Rai Chand Boral** to be her real teacher. One of the few New Theatres lead players not to have a stage background, her impact on Bengali film paralleled **Shanta Apte**'s on Marathi cinema, departing from proscenium frontality and privileging synchronous speech. Her singing style, usually in rapid tempo, is still identified with some of the biggest studio era hits (esp. *Bidyapati*, ***Street Singer***, ***Sapurey***). Resigned from New Theatres (1941) and freelanced in Bengali and Hindi films. Turned producer with Shrimati Pics (1949); later launched the Sabhyasachi collective with the film *Ananya* (cf **Ajoy Kar**). Wrote an autobiography, *Sabare Ami Nomi* (1973). The Marxist economist and noted columnist Ashok Mitra took her as an example to comment on the élitism of pre-Independence Calcutta society in his 'Calcutta Diary' (*Economic and Political Weekly*, 1-8 August 1992), describing her 'Eliza Doolittle' transformation from the illegitimate Kananbala into the glamorous Kanan Devi, stardom and her first marriage to the brother of the economist Prasanta Chandra Mahalanobis making her a member of Calcutta's cultural élite.

FILMOGRAPHY: **1926**: *Joydev* (St); **1931**: *Jore Barat*; *Rishir Prem*; **1932**: *Vishnu Maya*; **1933**: *Char Darvesh/Shri Gouranga*; **1934**: *Maa*; **1935**: *Basabdatta*; ***Manmoyee Girls' School***; *Kanthahaar*; **1936**: *Krishna Sudama*; *Khooni Kaun*; *Bishabriksha*; **1937**: ***Mukti***; ***Bidyapati/Vidyapati***; **1938**: ***Street Singer/Saathi***; **1939**: ***Sapurey/Sapera***; ***Jawani Ki Reet/Parajay***; **1940**: ***Abhinetri/Haar Jeet***; **1941**: ***Parichay/Lagan***; **1942**: ***Shesh Uttar/Jawab***; **1943**: ***Jogajog/Hospital***; **1944**: *Bideshini*; **1945**: *Banphool*; *Raj Lakshmi*; *Path Bendhe Dilo*; **1946**: *Arabian Nights*; *Krishna Leela*; *Tumi Aar Ami/Tum Aur Main*; **1947**: *Faisla*; *Chandrasekhar*; **1948**: *Anirban*; *Bankalekha*; **1949**: *Ananya*; *Anuradha*; **1950**: *Mejdidi*; **1951**: *Darpachurna*; **1954**: *Nababidhan*; **1955**: *Devatra*; **1956**: *Asha*; **1959**: *Indranath Srikanta-o-Annadadidi*.

DEVI, SARASWATI (1912-80)

Music director born as Khursheed Manchershah Minocher-Homji. Student of V.N. Bhatkhande's music school, Sharada Sangeet Vidyalaya. Specialised in Dhrupad and Dhamar music. Ran popular late 20s orchestra group, Homji Sisters, performing on Indian Broadcasting Company, Bombay, where she sang to the accompaniment of sitar, mandolin, dilruba and organ. These instruments also feature prominently in her film compositions. Associated mainly with **Bombay Talkies.** In her first film she refused to appear as a singer, dubbing her elder sister Manek instead. Her major achievement was probably to persuade star **Devika Rani** to sing. Several of her best-known songs, rendered in film by amateur singers **Ashok Kumar** and Rani, succeeded because of their nursery rhyme simplicity (e.g. *Main ban ka panchi* in ***Achhut Kanya***, *Chali re meri nao* in ***Jhoola***). Worked briefly with **Sohrab Modi** after leaving Bombay Talkies. Also scored **Jaswantlal**'s hit musical *Amrapali*. Collaborated at times with Ramchandra Pal on music.

FILMOGRAPHY: **1935**: ***Jawani Ki Hawa***; **1936**: ***Achhut Kanya***; ***Janmabhoomi***; ***Jeevan Naiya***; *Mamata*; *Miya Bibi*; **1937**: *Izzat*; ***Jeevan Prabhat***; *Prem Kahani*; ***Savitri***; *Nirmala*; **1938**: *Bhabhi*; *Vachan*; **1939**: ***Durga***; ***Kangan***; ***Navjeevan***; **1940**: ***Azad***; ***Bandhan***; *Punar Milan*; **1941**: ***Jhoola***; ***Naya Sansar***; **1943**: *Bhakta Raidas*; *Prarthana*; ***Prithvi Vallabh***; **1944**: *Dr Kumar*; ***Parakh***; **1945**: *Amrapali*; **1946**: *Maharani Meenal Devi*; **1947**: *Khandani*; **1948**: *Naqli Heera*; **1949**: *Usha Haran*; **1950**: *Kunwara Pati*; **1961**: ***Babasa Ri Laadi***.

DEVI, SEETA (b. 1912)

Stage name of actress Renee Smith. Star at **Madan Theatres**' Elphinstone Theatre. Début with **Dhiren Ganguly**; thereafter acted in **Priyanath Ganguly**'s 20s Madan films. Became a star as the exotic Oriental in **Himansu Rai**'s ***Prem Sanyas.*** Played the 'other woman' in ***Shiraz*** and the heroine in ***Prapancha Pash***. Also worked with **Niranjan Pal** and **Naval Gandhi.** The silent cinema scholar V.K. Dharamsey suggests that both Renee Smith and her sister Percy Smith may have appeared as 'Seeta Devi'.
FILMOGRAPHY: **1922**: *Indrajit*; *Bimata*; **1925**: ***Prem Sanyas***; **1926**: *Krishnakanter Will*; **1927**: *Durgesh Nandini*; **1928**: *Sarala*; ***Shiraz***; ***The Loves of a Mughal Prince***; **1929**: *Kapal Kundala*; ***Prapancha Pash***; **1930**: *Naseeb Ni Balihari*; *Kal Parinaya*; *Bharat Ramani*; **1931**: *Kashmir Nu Gulab* (all St); **1932**: *Shikari*.

DEVI, SITARA (b. 1919)

Actress born in Calcutta. One of the foremost exponents of classical *Kathak* dance, with notable appearances as a dancer in early

Sitara Devi in *Hulchul* (1951)

Mehboob films. Daughter of Sukhdev Maharaj of Benares, former court musician at Nepal, she was trained by her father and by Achan Maharaj at the palace of the Rajah of Mymensingh and later by Kathak maestros Shambhu and Lachhu Maharaj. Entered films as a child actress at **Sagar** where she first worked with Mehboob, with whom she later did her best-known films. Turned lead player with his ***Watan***. Salaried artist at **Ranjit** Studio, working with **Chandulal Shah** (***Achhut***) and on some famous films by **Kardar** (***Holi***, ***Pagal***, ***Pooja***). Her amazingly lively performance as a 'tribal' practising primitive communism and **Anil Biswas**' music were responsible for the successful use of the parable form in ***Roti***. Married **K. Asif**, and featured in his ***Phool*** and ***Mughal-e-Azam***.

FILMOGRAPHY: **1931**: *Digvijay* (St); **1933**: *Aurat Ka Dil*; **1934**: *Anokhi Mohabbat*; ***Shaher Ka Jadoo***; *Vasantsena*; **1935**: *Azad Abla*; ***Judgement of Allah***; *Vengeance is Mine*; *Registan Ki Rani*; **1936**: ***Grihadah/Manzil***; *Prem Bandhan*; *Zan Mureed*; **1937**: *Begunah*; *Calcutta after Midnight*; *Jeevan Swapna*; *Kokila*; *Mahageet*; **1938**: ***Baghban***; *Professor Waman M.Sc.*; ***Watan***; **1939**: *Meri Aankhen*; *Nadi Kinare*; *Pati Patni*; **1940**: ***Achhut***; *Aaj Ka Hindustan*; *Haiwan*; ***Holi***; ***Pooja***; ***Pagal***; ***Zindagi***; **1941**: ***Swami***; **1942**: *Dhiraj*; *Dukh Sukh*; *Kalyug*; ***Roti***; *Society*; **1943**: *Aabroo*; *Andhera*; *Bhalai*; *Chhed Chhad*; ***Najma***; *Salma*; **1944**: *Chand*; *Dr Kumar*; ***Phool***; **1945**: ***Badi Maa***; *Parinde*; **1947**: *Amar Asha*; **1949**: *Lekh*; **1950**: *Bijli*; **1951**: *Hulchul*; **1957**: *Anjali*; **1960**: ***Mughal-E-Azam***.

Devika Rani *see* **Rani Choudhury, Devika**

DEY, KRISHNA CHANDRA (1893-1962)

Music director and actor born in Calcutta, mostly credited as K.C. Dey. Blind from age of 14. Taking advantage of e.g. the 19th C. playwright Girish Ghosh's use of blind and mad characters as a kind of chorus, following a convention in Bengali Jatra theatre, Dey often played an itinerant blind singer in **New Theatres** films (e.g. ***Chandidas***, ***Bidyapati***, ***Devdas***). His deep voice at times evoked the Baul style, but his music was mainly a light classical variant of the bhajan or keertan. Major stage reputation with **Sisir Bhaduri**, with whom he first appeared in 1924 in *Basanta Leela* (role of Basant-doot or the Herald of Spring) and *Seeta* (as Baitalik). Partner in Rungmahal Theatre with actor Rabindra Mohan Roy (1931-41) where he scored several plays such as **Bhaduri**'s *Shri Shri Vishnupriya* (1932). Early films include **A.R. Kardar**'s productions at **East India Film**. Worked in several Hindi films in Bombay as actor and music composer. Hit solos in *Devdas*, *Bidyapati* and ***Dhoop Chhaon*** rank as all-time favourites. Nephew is playback singer Manna Dey.

FILMOGRAPHY (* act only/** also act): **1932**: ***Chandidas****; **1933**: *Nala Damayanti**; ***Puran Bhakt****; *Sabitri**; *Abe Hayat*; **1934**: *Kismet Ki Kasauti***; *Seeta***; *Chandragupta*; ***Shaher Ka Jadoo*****; *Grihalakshmi**; **1935**: ***Inquilab****; ***Devdas****; ***Dhoop Chhaon/Bhagya Chakra****; *Bijoya**; *Biraha*; *Bidrohi*; *Bidyasundar*; *Prafulla*; **1936**: ***Sonar Sansar/Sunehra Sansar***; *Paraparey*; ***Maya****; ***Pujarin****; ***Grihadah/Manzil****; **1937**: ***Ambikapathy***; ***Bidyapati/Vidyapati****; *Milap*; *Ranga Bou*; **1938**: ***Desher Mati/Dharti Mata****; **1939**: ***Saporey/Sapera****; *Sharmistha*; *Chanakya***; **1940**: *Alochhaya/Aandhi***; **1942**: *Mera Gaon***; *Tamanna*; ***Meenakshi****; *Nari**; **1943**: *Andhera**; ***Mohabbat****; *Badalti Duniya***; **1944**: *Suno Sunata Hoon***; *Insaan**; **1945**: *Devadasi***; **1946**: *Insaaf**; *Shravan Kumar**; *Door Chalein***; **1948**: *Anirban**; **1953**: *Raakhi***; **1957**: *Madhu Malati**; *Ektara**.

DEY, NIRMAL (b. 1913)

Bengali director born in Mymensingh (now Bangladesh). Graduate in fine arts. Published short fiction in the 30s. Assisted **Bimal Roy** at **New Theatres** as cameraman, later sharing joint screenplay credit with him for ***Udayer Pathey*** (1944). Turned director when Murlidhar Chatterjee of MP Prod. persuaded him to give up his self-imposed retirement at Shantiniketan to make ***Basu Parivar***. Débuted with the unfinished but important *Bedeni* based on a Tarashankar Bannerjee story (**Ghatak** took it over for a while before it was abandoned). His ***Sharey Chuattar*** launched the screen duo of **Uttam Kumar** and **Suchitra Sen**, followed by ***Champadangar Bou*** and a string of successes. **Satyajit Ray** rated them among the most important early Bengali sound films, regarding the director as the first genuine purveyor of Bengali social comedies. His formal training in the visual arts, literature and photography often yielded dexterous combinations of witty dialogue, inventive acting and a fluid narrative style that rarely resorted to middle-class sentimentalism while evoking, with a sense of self-mockery, its manners and conversational culture. Despite their success, Dey made only a few more films, scripting other film-makers's work instead, including Gurudas Bagchi's *Samanaral* (1970).

FILMOGRAPHY: **1952**: *Bedeni* (incomplete); ***Basu Parivar***; **1953**: ***Sharey Chuattar***; **1954**: ***Champadangar Bou***; **1955**: *Du-Janay*; **1959**: *Nirdharita Silpir Anupastithi Tey*.

DHAIBER, KESHAVRAO (1890-1978)

Marathi and Hindi director, cameraman and actor born in Kurukali, Kolhapur. After a brief military career as a Lancer and employment as a tax inspector, befriended **Baburao Painter** and joined **Maharashtra Films** as a technician, also acting in Painter's ***Sinhagad*** (1923). Apprenticed to **Damle**, co-directed **Shantaram**'s directorial début *Netaji Palkar* (1927) and was cameraman for many Shantaram classics. Joined the breakaway **Prabhat Film** in 1928 as cameraman, e.g. ***Sinhagad***, in which he also acted, and, also in 1933, a colour version of *Sairandhri*. His best-known Prabhat film is ***Rajput Ramani***, although he remained the least successful of the studio's regular film-makers. Married the actress Nalini Tarkhad and briefly had his own Jayshri Films (1935) before joining **Minerva Movietone** as a director (e.g. *Akrava Avatar*, *Ulti Ganga*) before rejoining Prabhat as production supervisor (1943-6). Then worked at Famous Studios (1946-7). Tried to start a new independent company at Lucknow, but the business soon collapsed. Made some documentaries, e.g. of the coronation of the Maharaja of Baroda (1940) and assignments for the Maharashtra and Gujarati state governments. Published an autobiography, *Eka Zindagichi Patkatha* (1967).

FILMOGRAPHY (* act only/** also act): **1923**: ***Sinhagad****; **1927**: *Netaji Palkar* (co-d with **V. Shantaram**); **1928**: *Maharathi Karna**; **1929**: *Baji Prabhu Deshpande**; **1930**: *Khooni Khanjar*; *Rani Saheba*** (co-d with **V. Shantaram**); **1931**: *Zulm* (all St); **1933**: ***Sinhagad****; **1936**: ***Rajput Ramani***; **1938**: *Nandakumar*; **1939**: *Akrava Avatar***; **1942**: *Ulti Ganga*; **1943**: *Bhakta Raidas*; **1949**: *Ahimsapath*; **1958**: *Sudamyache Pohe*.

DHARMADHIKARI, DATTATREYA JAGANNATH (1913-82)

Marathi and Hindi director born in Kolhapur. Doorkeeper at **Prabhat** (1934), then bit player (1936) and assistant to **K. Narayan Kale** (***Mazha Mulga***, 1938), **Damle** and **Fattelal**, and **V. Shantaram**. One of the younger cineastes (e.g. **Raja Nene**, editor **Anant Mane**, scenarist **Shantaram Athavale** and musician **Keshavrao Bhole**) who left **Prabhat** (1944) to work collectively in Bombay. Assisted Raja Nene at Mohan Studios, then at Balasaheb Pathak's Manik Studios. Made first film for Raja Nene's company, probably co-directed by Nene. Launched Alhaad Chitra (1951-4) which revitalised the Marathi cinema converting the social into very successful stage-inspired weepies (e.g. ***Chimni Pakhare/Nannhe Munne***, *Stree Janma Hi Tujhi Kahani*), often ending with funerals. This style was continued by e.g. Anant Mane, Datta Mane and **Datta Keshav** (all from Alhaad Chitra), grafting Hindi **All-India film** norms on to Marathi cinema. Also worked in Hindi for **Homi Wadia**'s Basant Studio and at **Filmistan**. Appeared as actor in ***Sant Dnyaneshwar*** (1940). His son Alhaad Dattatreya Dharmadikari (b. 1947) became a noted child actor in Hindi and Marathi films.

FILMOGRAPHY: **1947**: *Shadi Se Pehle*; **1949**: *Maya Bazaar*; *Bala Jo Jo Re*; **1951**: *Kunkvacha Dhani*; **1952**: *Akher Jamla*; ***Chimni Pakhare/Nannhe Munne***; *Stree Janma Hi Tujhi Kahani*; **1953**: ***Bhagyavaan***; *Saubhagya*; *Mahatma*; **1954**: *Savdhan*; **1956**: *Sudarshan Chakra*; **1957**: *Aliya Bhogasi*; **1959**: *Deep Jalta Rahe*; *Pativrata*; **1961**: *Ek Dhaga Sukhacha*; *Kalanka Shobha*; **1962**: *Kshan Aala Bhagyacha*; ***Saptapadi***; *Vithu Mazha Lekurvala*; **1963**: *Subhadra Haran*; **1964**: *Vaishakh Vanava*; **1967**: *Thamb Lakshmi Kunku Lavte*; **1969**: *Saticha Vaan*; *Mujhe Seene Se Laga Lo*; **1973**: *Nasti Uthathev*; **1975**: *Bhakta Pundalik*; **1978**: *Dhakti Mehuni*; **1980**: *Satichi Punyayi*.

DHARMARAJ, RABINDRA (1949-82)

Documentarist and Hindi director. Former journalist (e.g. Vietnam War from US perspective) and radio newsreader whose 'BBC voice' was later used extensively for strident commentaries by **Films Division** productions. Joined Pentecostal Church. Moved to Bombay (1971) and assisted **Fali Bilimoria, Benegal** et al. Did short course in film and video in California. Bombay-based executive in advertising agencies Lintas and Hindustan Thompson (as film-maker). Died soon after the first screening of his only feature, ***Chakra***.

FILMOGRAPHY: **1971**: *Crisis on the Campus* (Sh); **1974**: *No Tree Grows* (Sh); **1976**: *Indian Airlines ... Pride of India* (Sh); **1980**: ***Chakra.***

DHARMA RAO, TAPI (1887-1973)

Telugu scenarist-lyricist, poet, journalist and literary critic born in Behrampur. Influenced as a student by the historian Gidugu Ramamurthy Panthulu, who advocated a *vyavaharika* (or demotic) Telugu. Was personal secretary to the Rajah of Bobbili, a Justice Party ideologue for the interests of the zamindar class. Pursued the notion of a people's language in his poetry (esp. in *Dyayonam*, *Bhikshapatram*, *Andhra Tejam*) and in plays like *Vilasarjunam*, *Taptashrukanam* and *Avanni Kannellena*. Wrote essays on historical and cultural issues, e.g. in journals like *Samadarshini* and *Janavani*, later collected in his *Kottapali Onamalu Sahitya Mormaralu*. Worked on films by **Ramabrahmam** (***Malapilla***, 1938; ***Raitu Bidda***, 1939). Wrote scripts and lyrics for, e.g., **L.V. Prasad**'s ***Drohi*** (1948), B.A. Subba Rao's *Palletoori Pilla* (1950) and **K.S. Prakash Rao**'s *Deeksha* (1951). A major advocate of a separate state for Telugu-speaking people prior to the formation of Andhra Pradesh. Wrote c.40 scripts and several very popular lyrics. Father of film director **Tapi Chanakya.**

DHARMENDRA DEOL (b. 1935)

Actor born in Phagwara, Punjab. Former mechanic in a factory. Top Hindi star for three decades. Created an influential image as a markedly North Indian, even specifically Punjabi macho man devoted to his mother and committed to upholding the honour of the family or of the village. Since the mid-70s, after **Bachchan**'s impact, mainly in action films, occasionally using complicated gadgetry but always emphasising peasant simplicity and beating the villain in physical combat. Since mid-80s, notably in **T. Rama Rao**'s films but also in other Madras-based Hindi productions, his presence is used mainly to ensure a film's nationwide distribution in a respectable economic category. His early 60s films, in sharp contrast to his current post-***Sholay*** image, presented a secularised Hindustani version of Bengali literary stereotypes, launched by **Bimal Roy**'s ***Bandini*** and continued in **Hrishikesh Mukherjee**'s 60s socials (***Anupama***, *Manjhli Didi*, ***Satyakam***) and in **Phani Majumdar**'s *Akashdeep*. Early 70s work transposed this image into tales of existential suffering (**Mohan Segal**'s *Raja Jani*) and into Mukherjee's whimsical comedies (***Guddi***, *Chupke Chupke*) made alongside Pramod Chakravarty and Arjun Hingorani thrillers and films like **Vijay Anand**'s *Blackmail*. Currently promoting his son Sunny Deol (e.g. *Sunny*; ***Ghayal***, 1990); best-known performances of the 90s in **J.P. Dutta** films.

FILMOGRAPHY: **1955**: ***Railway Platform***; **1960**: *Dil Bhi Tera Hum Bhi Tere*; **1961**: *Boy Friend*; *Shola Aur Shabnam*; **1962**: *Anpadh*; *Shadi*; **1963**: *Soorat Aur Seerat*; ***Bandini***; *Begana*; **1964**: *Aap Ki Parchhaiyan*; *Aayi Milan Ki Bela*; *Ganga Ki Lehren*; ***Haqeeqat***; *Main Bhi Ladki Hoon*; *Mera Kasoor Kya Hai*; *Pooja Ke Phool*; **1965**: *Akashdeep*; *Chand Aur Suraj*; *Kajal*; *Neela Akash*; *Purnima*; **1966**: ***Anupama***; *Aaye Din Bahar Ke*; *Baharen Phir Bhi Aayengi*; *Devar*; *Dil Ne Phir Yaad Kiya*; *Dulhan Ek Raat Ki*; *Mamata*; *Pari*; *Mohabbat Zindagi Hai*; *Phool Aur Patthar*; **1967**: *Ghar Ka Chirag*; *Chandan Ka Palna*; *Jab Yaad Kisiki Aati Hai*; *Manjhli Didi*; **1968**: *Aankhen*; *Baazi*; *Baharon Ki Manzil*; *Izzat*; *Mere Humdum Mere Dost*; *Shikar*; **1969**: *Soldier*; *Admi Aur Insaan*; *Aaya Sawan Jhoom Ke*; *Pyar Hi Pyar*; ***Satyakam***; *Yakeen*; ***Khamoshi***; **1970**: *Ishq Par Zor Nahin*; *Jeevan Mrityu*; *Kab Kyon Aur Kahan*; *Man Ki Aankhen*; ***Mera Naam Joker***; *Sharafat*; *Tum Haseen Main Jawan*; **1971**: ***Guddi***; *Mera Gaon Mera Desh*; *Naya Zamana*; *Rakhwala*; **1972**: *Do Chor*; *Lalkaar*; *Raja Jani*; *Seeta Aur Geeta*; *Samadhi*; *Jiban*; *Anokha Milan*; **1973**: *Blackmail*; *Jheel Ke Us Paar*; *Jugnu*; *Jwar Bhata*; *Kahani Kismat Ki*; *Keemat*; *Loafer*; *Phagun*; ***Yaadon Ki Baraat***; **1974**: *Dost*; *International Crook*; *Kunwara Baap*; *Patthar Aur Payal*; *Pocketmaar*; *Resham Ki Dori*; *Do Sher*; **1975**: *Teri Meri Ik Jindri*; *Apne Dushman*; *Chaitali*; *Chupke Chupke*; *Dhoti Lota Aur Chowpatti*; *Ek Mahal Ho Sapnon Ka*; *Kehte Hain Mujhko Raja*; *Pratigya*; *Saazish*; ***Sholay***; **1976**: *Charas*; *Maa*; **1977**: *Chacha Bhatija*; *Do Sholay*; *Dream Girl*; *Khel Khiladi Ka*; *Chala Murari Hero Banne*; ***Dharam Veer***; *Do Chehre*; *Tinku*; *Charandas*; *Kinara*; ***Swami***; **1978**: *Azad*; *Dillagi*; *Phandebaaz*; *Shalimar*; **1979**: *Dil Ka Heera*; *The Gold Medal*; *Kartavya*; *Chunauti*; **1980**: *Alibaba Aur Chalis Chor*; *Ram Balram*; *The Burning Train*; *Aas Paas*; **1981**: *Qatilon Ke Qatil*; *Krodhi*; *Professor Pyarelal*; *Khuda Kasam*; ***Naseeb***; **1982**: *Badle Ki Aag*; *Baghavat*; *Do Dishayen*; *Ghazab*; *Main Inteqam Loonga*; *Meharbani*; *Rajput*; *Samrat*; *Teesri Aankh*; **1983**: *Naukar Biwi Ka*; *Andha Kanoon*; *Putt Jattan De*; *Jaani Dost*; *Qayamat*; *Razia Sultan*; **1984**: *Dharam Aur Kanoon*; *Jagir/Teen Murti*; *Jeene Nahin Doonga*; *Jhootha Sach*; *Raj*

Meena Kumari and Dharmendra in *Purnima* (1965)

Tilak; *Sunny*; *Baazi*; **1985**: ***Ghulami***; *Karishma Kudrat Ka*; *Sitamgarh*; **1986**: *Begana*; *Main Balwan*; *Mohabbat Ki Kasam*; *Savere Wali Gadi*; ***Sultanat***; *Insaniyat Ke Dushman*; *Loha*; **1987**: *Aag Hi Aag*; *Dadagiri*; *Hukumat*; *Insaaf Kaun Karega*; *Insaaf Ki Pukar*; *Jaan Hatheli Pe*; *Mard Ki Zabaan*; *Mera Karam Mera Dharam*; *Watan Ke Rakhwale*; **1988**: *Khatron Ke Khiladi*; *Mardon Wali Baat*; *Soorma Bhopali*; *Zalzala*; *Mahaveera*; *Paap Ko Jalakar Raakh Kar Doonga*; *Ganga Tere Desh Mein*; *Sone Pe Suhaaga*; *Vardi*; *Aakhri Muqabala*; ***Yateem***; **1989**: *Kasam Suhaag Ki*; *Nafrat Ki Aandhi*; *Sachaai Ki Taaqat*; ***Batwara***; *Elaan-e-Jung*; *Sikka*; *Shehzade*; ***Hathyar***; *Ilaaka*; **1990**: *Pyar Ka Karz*; *Nakabandi*; *Humse Na Takrana*; *Veeru Dada*; *Sher Dil*; *Kanoon Ki Zanjeer*; *Paap Ki Aandhi*; **1991**: *Kaun Kare Qurbani*; *Mast Kalandar*; *Dushman Devata*; *Farishte*; *Trinetra*; *Hamla*; *Kohraa*; **1992**: *Virodhi*; *Zulm Ki Hukumat*; *Tahalka*; *Kal Ki Awaaz*; *Khule Aam*; *Kshatriya*; **1993**: *Superman*; *Kundan*; *Aag Ka Toofan*.

DIXIT, MADHURI (b. 1968)

Hindi actress born in Ratnagiri. The youngest of a Bombay engineer's four children. Mother was trained in classical music. As a biology student at the Parle College, Madhuri agreed to act in the Hindi film *Abodh*, which flopped. Her breakthrough came with **N. Chandra**'s ***Tezaab***, in which she introduced a novel kind of sensuality, mainly via the song 'Ek do teen', choreographed by Saroj Khan. Her sensual dances, often exuding sexuality more overtly than had been the convention in Hindi films, guaranteed mass appeal. Performed the suggestive 'Dhak dhak' song in *Beta* and her reputation culminated with the controversial 'Choli ke peeche' in **S. Ghai**'s *Khalnayak*, which included the piquant question: 'What's behind the blouse?' Considered by many as the leading female star of the 90s.

FILMOGRAPHY: **1984**: *Abodh*; **1986**: ***Swati***; **1987**: *Hifazat*; *Uttar Dakshin*; *Mohre*; **1988**: *Dayavan*; *Mahasangram*; *Khatron Ke Khiladi*; *Vardi*; ***Tezaab***; **1989**: *Ilaka*; *Mujrim*; *Paap Ka Ant*; ***Parinda***; *Prem Pratigya*; *Tridev*; ***Ram Lakhan***; *Kanoon Apna Apna*; **1990**: *Diwana Mujhsa Nahin*; ***Dil***; *Jamai Raja*; *Jeevan Ek Sangharsh*; *Izzatdar*; *Kishan Kanhaiya*; *Sailaab*; *Thanedar*; *Khilaaf*; *Pyar Ka Devata*; **1991**: *100 Days*; ***Prahaar***; *Pratikar*; *Dharavi*; *Saajan*; **1992**: *Beta*; *Sangeet*; *Zindagi Ek Jua*; *Prem Diwani*; *Khel*; **1993**: *Khalnayak*; *Phool*; *Prem Pooja*; *Sahiban*; *Dil Tera Aashiq*; *Aansoo Bane Angarey*.

DMK FILM

Unique and extraordinarily influential type of propaganda cinema pioneered in Tamil Nadu by the Dravida Munnetra Kazhagam (DMK). Histories of the DMK trace the party's ancestry to 19th C. reform literature in the erstwhile Madras Presidency, where writers like Subramanya Bharati (1882-1921; sometimes considered the greatest modern Tamil poet) extended their reformist politics to advocate a specifically Tamil nationalism. After the establishment of the Justice Party aka the South Indian Liberation Federation (Est: 1917), this nationalism retained a strongly anti-Aryan thrust in its claim to represent the indigenous cultures of South India, attempting e.g. to rewrite Indian history to trace the Tamil influence back to the Indus Valley civilisation. The Justice Party had a strategic alliance with the pro-imperialist landed élite but also advocated bourgeois-democratic reformism opposing e.g. caste oppression. The party broadened its base in Kerala and Andhra Pradesh, esp. when contesting the provincial elections after the Montagu-Chelmsford reforms (1919) on an anti-Brahmin platform. The Party was transformed in the post-WW2 era by one of the most influential politicians in 20th C. Tamil Nadu, Periyar E.V. Ramaswamy Naicker (1879-1973), a former Congress Party member who founded the Self-Respect Movement (1926), a social action group aimed at eradicating Untouchability and caste and advocating an atheist politics. According to Charles Ryerson, at that time the movement deployed five principles: no God, no religion, no Gandhi, no Congress and no Brahmins. In 1944, Periyar transformed the Justice Party into the seperatist Dravidar Kazhagam (DK) and later called for India's first Independence Day in 1947 to be declared a day of mourning, since his demand for an independent Dravida Nadu or Tamil state remained unrealised. In 1949, his chief disciple, the playwright and scenarist **C.N. Annadurai** broke away to found the DMK. The DMK was elected to the TN state assembly in 1967, mainly on an anti-Hindi platform, repeating their victory in 1971 through a conditional alliance with Indira Gandhi's Congress. The DMK split once again when its most famous member, film star **MGR**, was expelled for indiscipline and launched the Anna-DMK (ADMK) in 1972, which later became the All-India Anna Dravida Munnetra Kazhagam (AIADMK), winning power along with the Congress in 1977 and making MGR the Chief Minister. The DMK under **Karunanidhi** returned to power in 1988 after MGR died, but was dismissed by the Congress (I)-backed minority government in 1990 and then decimated in the 1991 elections following Rajiv Gandhi's assassination which brought into power MGR's former heroine **Jayalalitha** as the new AIADMK leader and Chief Minister.The DMK Film genre is the most spectacular of the party's propaganda fronts and helped make five film personalities Chief Ministers (Annadurai, Karunanidhi, MGR, his wife and former star V.N. Janaki, and Jayalalitha) since 1967. Annadurai launched the genre adapting his own play ***Velaikkari*** to the screen, followed by his script for ***Nallathambi*** (both 1949). The films, esp. *Nallathambi*, were major hits and spawned many more as the party decided to use film as its main propaganda medium with writers like A.V.P. Asaithambi (dialogue for **T.R. Sundaram**'s *Sarvadhikari*, 1951), A.K. Velan and the DMK poet **Kannadasan** who also produced the propaganda hit ***Sivagangai Seemai*** (1959). Karunanidhi scripted ***Manthiri Kumari*** (1950) as MGR's first folk legend for directly political purposes. He also wrote and contributed lyrics for the most famous DMK film, ***Parasakthi*** (1952), **Sivaji Ganesan**'s début. A string of hits followed, often starring MGR or Ganesan: ***Marmayogi*** and *Sarvadhikari* (both 1951), *Sorgavasal* (1954), and the MGR-directed ***Nadodi Mannan*** (1958). Annadurai had codified an elaborately plotted and highly charged melodramatic idiom promoting an iconoclastic 'rationalism' and an anti-Brahmin, Tamil-nationalist ideology. The films incorporated numerous references to Party symbols and colours, anagrams of Party leaders' names and characters reciting whole passages from Annadurai's speeches (cf **Pandharibai** in *Parasakthi*). These devices are part of a very rhetorical visual and literary style as the hero, usually in the courtroom at the end of the film, presents his (and his Party's) case in a speech that could last up to 30'. The success of the DMK Film idiom has been linked (see Bhaskaran and Sivathamby) to the fact that the cinema was an important social equaliser in Tamil Nadu, where the other performing arts traditions were rigidly demarcated along class/caste lines. The old Congress Party's attempt (e.g. by C. Rajagopalachari) to continue that élitism in the cinema allowed its DMK opponents to present cinema as a people's art. Numerous studies have been devoted to the DMK Film: K. Sivathamby's *The Tamil Film as a Medium of Political Communication* (1981); Robert Hardgrave's *When Stars Displace the Gods: The Folk Culture of Cinema in Tamil Nadu* (1975); Hardgrave and Anthony Neidhart, *Film and Political Consciousness in Tamil Nadu* (1975); S. Theodore Baskaran's *The Message Bearers* (1981) which deals with the pre-DMK history of political film; Ka. Thiranavukarasu's *Dravidar Iyakkamum Thiraipada Ulagamum* (1990); M.S.S. Pandian's *The Image Trap: M.G. Ramachandran in Film and Politics* (1992). For histories of the DMK Party and Tamil politics, see Margaret Ross-Barnett's *The Politics of Cultural Nationalism in South India* (1976) and Charles Ryerson's *Regionalism and Religion: The Tamil Renaissance and Popular Hinduism* (1988).

DOORDARSHAN

Official title for state-owned Indian television, after it was delinked from the AIR and established as an independent corporation under the Ministry of Information & Broadcasting (1976). TV was introduced experimentally in 1959, supported by UNESCO, the US government and Philips, with a weekly half-hour service covering a radius of 40km cenred on Delhi. With Indira Gandhi as the new Information & Broadcasting Minister, this became a daily service (1965). In 1972, a station was established in Bombay, then in Srinagar (1973) followed by Calcutta and Madras, with 39 more centres set up in the 80s. In 1975, the Satellite Instructional Television Experiment (SITE) was launched with support from NASA using Delhi and Ahmedabad as ground stations to broadcast 'instructional programmes' to 2500 villages in six states (Bihar, MP, Orissa, Rajasthan, AP and Karnataka). The programme was briefly accompanied by a much smaller but arguably more significant experiment at Pij, in Gujarat, where a 1-kV transmitter addressed 750 community sets in 350 villages: several major film-makers produced programmes and discussed them with the villagers. Colour programmes were introduced, controversially, in 1982, to telecast the Asian Games in New Delhi with imported outside broadcast and electronic news-gathering units using Soviet satellite services while setting up 20 low-power transmitters. The first Indian telecommunications satellite assembled at the ISRO failed; the second, INSAT 1B, launched in 1983, also inaugurated the Special Plan for the Expansion of the Television Network. The Plan claimed to be unique in the history of tv expansion, eventually installing 13 high-power and 113 low-power transmitters, linking them up to make terrestrial broadcasts available to 70% of the population within a period of 18 months (1983-4). The Seventh Five-Year plan doubled its communications media investment to Rs 150 billion, 49% of this sum going to Doordarshan alone.Although advertising had been allowed since 1977, Doordarshan went commercial only in 1982, also making New Delhi the centre of a daily 'national programme' dominating peak-hour viewing. Initially, its commercial shows were predominantly film-based, such as the *Chitrahaar* series (stringing together song sequences from Indian movies) and the weekend feature films. Started selling 30' slots for independently made tv serials sponsored by advertisers with the serial *Hum Log* (*We, the People*, 1984-5), a 'developmental' soap opera sponsored by Colgate-Palmolive and Nestlé. In 1987, advertising revenue topped Rs 10 billion with 65% coming from only six multinational corporations. Best-known serials were the Hindu epics, *Ramayan* (by **Ramanand Sagar**, 1986-8) and *Mahabharat* (by **B.R. Chopra**, 1988-90). Doordarshan's monopoly over both advertising and news and its role as the ruling government's most effective propaganda platform was often criticised. The Janata Party's 1977 election manifesto promised to make Doordarshan fully autonomous and set up the B. G. Verghese Working Group on Autonomy for Akashvani and Doordarshan (1978) to work out the logistics of such a move. However, the Prasar Bharati bill presented in 1979 offered a vastly watered-down version of the promised autonomy. The report of the government-appointed Working Group on Software for Indian tv, aka the P.C. Joshi Committee Report (1984), was extremely critical of Doordarshan's 'Delhi-centrism', its mode of introducing consumerism in the countryside and its dependence on foreign networks for programme ideas. The report appeared only in excerpts in independent journals. Doordarshan started collaborating with the **NFDC** (1988), producing films by e.g. **Aravindan, Adoor Gopalakrishnan, Girish Kasaravalli, Mira Nair** and **Mani Kaul**, initially to reduce its massive dependence on the film industry. The results were mostly telecast in late-night film slots. In 1992-3, the Hong Kong-based STAR-TV cable network challenged Doordarshan's monopoly. In response, Doordarshan introduced the commercial Metro Channel (1993) and announced three entertainment satellite channels (news, sport and imported soap opera).

DOSHI, CHATURBHUJ ANAND (1894-1969)

Hindi and Gujarati director born in Kathiawar, Gujarat. Journalist for progressive daily *Hindustan* (1926) under editor **Indulal Yagnik**. Silent era scenarist (1930) for **Jayant Desai, Nandlal Jaswantlal, Nanubhai Vakil** etc. Wrote several **Ranjit** films. One of the top Gujarati scenarists; scripted the key **Punatar** productions that launched a Gujarati film industry (*Gunsundari, Nanand Bhojai*, both 1948) and **Raskapur**'s ***Mehndi Rang Lagyo*** (1960); at times considered a successor to scenarist **Mohanlal Dave**. As film-maker, he is known for devising a more rationalist interpretation of the mythological.

FILMOGRAPHY: **1938**: *Gorakh Aya*; *Secretary*; **1939**: ***Adhuri Kahani***; **1940**: *Musafir*; **1941**: *Pardesi*; *Sasural*; **1942**: *Bhakta Surdas*; *Dhiraj*; *Mehmaan*; **1943**: *Chhoti Maa*; ***Shankar Parvati***; **1944**: *Bhartrahari*; **1945**: *Murti*; **1946**: *Phulwari*; **1947**: *Bela*; *Kaun Hamara*; **1948**: *Jesal Toral*; *Karaiyavar*; *Sati Sone*; **1949**: *Bhakta Puran*; *Vevishal*; **1950**: *Akhand Saubhagya*; *Kisi Ki Yaad*; **1954**: *Aurat Teri Yahi Kahani*; **1956**: *Aabroo*; *Dassehra*; **1957**: *Khuda Ka Banda*; *Shesh Naag*; **1958**: *Sanskar*.

DUNCAN, ELLIS R. (b. 1908)

Tamil director and American cinematographer born in Ohio; graduate of UCLA and the American Institute of Cinematography and worked in Hollywood as a cameraman (1927). Came to India (1935) to sell camera equipment and stayed for 17 years making several major Tamil films, starting with *Sati Leelavathi*, based on **S.S. Vasan**'s novel and introducing **MGR**. Some accounts suggest M.L. Tandon, who probably met Duncan at UCLA, got him to direct films. ***Iru Sahodarargal***, also with MGR, made him the top director of a nascent Tamil film industry, also editing his own work and integrating music and comedy routines into the plot, which was perhaps his most influential contribution. A series of hits followed: ***Ambikapathy*** with **M.K. Thyagaraja Bhagavathar** at Salem Shankar Films; *Shakuntalai* and the memorable ***Meera*** with the singer M.S. Subbulakshmi at Chandraprabha Cinetone. Best-known work at **Modern Theatres**: *Ponmudi* and, with **T.R. Sundaram**, the seminal MGR hit ***Manthiri Kumari***. Although Duncan did not know Tamil (his interpreters were known as ' rush directors'), his work is remembered for its emphasis on Tamil dialogue: the famed scenarist **Elangovan** débuted in his *Ambikapathy* while *Ponmudi* remains one of the poet **Bharatidasan**'s best-known scripts; *Manthiri Kumari* was **Karunanidhi**'s first major literary contribution to cinema. Duncan worked with well-known actor-singers such as G.N. Balasubramanyam, M.S. Subbulakshmi and Rajarathnam Pillai. Credited with co-direction of an Indo-US co-prod., *The Jungle* (William Berke, 1952), starring Rod Cameron, Marie Windsor and Caesar Romero, later dubbed into Tamil as *Kaadu*. During WW2 made propaganda shorts (e.g. *Returning Soldier* with T.S. Balaiah), and after Independence was commissioned by the government to film the transfer of power ritual. In the 50s returned to live in Wheeler city, West Virginia, occasionally working in India, e.g. as a 2nd unit photographer for Hugo Fregonese's *Harry Black* (1958) and John Guillermin's *Tarzan Mera Saathi* (1962).

FILMOGRAPHY: **1936**: *Sati Leelavathi*; *Simantini*; ***Iru Sahodarargal***; **1937**: ***Ambikapathy***; **1940**: *Shakuntalai*; *Suryaputri*; *Kalamegham*; **1943**: *Daasi Penn*; **1945**: *Valmiki*; ***Meera***; *Returning Soldier*; **1949**: *Ponmudi*; **1950**: ***Manthiri Kumari***; **1952**: *Kaadu*.

DURAI

Prominent 70s independent Tamil director. Former assistant to **Yoganand** and **G.V. Iyer** (***Hamsa Geethe***, 1975). First film, ***Avalum Penn Thaane***, is a tragic portrayal of an orphaned woman saved from a vice den who sacrifices her life to protect another woman from being trapped into prostitution. It attracted some critical attention as one of the better mid-70s commercial films engaging with the feminist movement. However, he went on to make a formula of this theme, featuring a series of florid female characters such as the tragic heroine who marries her lover's son in ***Oru Veedu Oru Ulagam***. Best-known film is ***Pasi***, which redeems its sentimentalism through a realistic usage of dialect and a number of well-sketched characterisations. Worked in Hindi, Kannada, Telugu and Malayalam. Also scripted his films.

FILMOGRAPHY: **1974**: ***Avalum Penn Thaane***; **1975**: *Oru Kudumbathin Kathai*; **1976**: *Mugiyada Kathe*; *Asai Arubathu Naal*; **1977**: *Raghupati Raghava Rajaram*; **1978**: *Aval Thantha Uravu*; *Chadurangam*; *Pavathin Sambalam*; *Ayiram Janmangal*; ***Oru Veedu Oru Ulagam***; **1979**: *Kadamai Nenjam*; ***Pasi***; *Neeya*; *Needhikku Mun Neeya Nana*; *Malligai Mohini*; *Priya Bandhavi*; *Pathai Marinal*; **1980**: *Kaadu*; *Maria My Darling*; *Pennukku Yar Kaval*; *Enga Vathiar*; *Porkalam*; *Thani Maram*; *Oli Pirandathu*; **1981**: *Aval Oru Kaviyam*; *Vadagai Veedu*; *Mayil*; *Kilinjalgal*; **1982**: *Ruby My Darling*; *Velicham Vitharunna Pennkutty*; *Nalanthana*; *Thunai*; *Theerpugal Thirutha Padalam*; **1983**: *Do Gulab*; **1984**: *Pet Pyar Aur Paap*; **1985**: *Veli*; **1986**: *Oru Manithan Oru Manaivi*; **1987**: *Veera Pandian*; **1988**: *Palaivanathil Pattampoochi*; **1990**: *Pudhiya Athiyayam*.

DUTT, GEETA (1930-72)

Aka Geeta Roy. Singer born in Faridpur (now Bangladesh). Trained under composer Hanuman Prasad who launched her in *Bhakta Prahlad* (1946). First major hit in **Filmistan** production *Do Bhai* (1947) where, to **S.D. Burman**'s music, she sang *Mera sundar sapna*. Although an orthodox rendition compared with her later work, it pioneered a move away from the ghazal-inflected folk style inherited from the studio era represented by e.g. Amirbai Karnataki or by Shamshad Begum's **Pancholi** songs. She had hits in ***Jogan*** (1950), composed by **Bulo C. Rani** (e.g. *Ghunghat ke pat khole re*) and ***Anarkali*** (1953), but is best remembered for her **Guru Dutt** films (she was married to the director) ***Mr and Mrs '55*** (1955), ***Pyaasa*** (1957), ***Kaagaz Ke Phool*** (1959) and ***Sahib Bibi Aur Ghulam*** (1962). The songs of these films remain among the biggest successes in post-Independence Hindi cinema.

DUTT, GURU (1925-64)

Hindi film director and actor. Born in Bangalore as Gurudatta Padukone. Educated in Calcutta. Studied dance at Uday Shankar's dance academy in Almora (1942-4). Telephone operator in Calcutta before joining **Prabhat** Studio (1944) as actor, then choreographer and assistant director (***Hum Ek Hain***, 1946). Met **Dev Anand** and was part of an informal group of ex-**IPTA** members at Navketan, the company that produced his first film, ***Baazi***. Set up own production house with *Baaz*. Introduced **Waheeda Rehman** in ***CID*** (1956), propelling her to stardom through his films. Made adventure films, comedies (also starring in *Twelve O'Clock*) and love stories. Films often referred to social issues and exploitation, partly following **Chetan Anand**'s version of John Huston-type realism but imbuing them with thematic layers amid complex, richly stylised imagery (courtesy of cinematographer V.K. Murthy) and exquisite songs. Made India's first CinemaScope film, ***Kaagaz Ke Phool***, which flopped. Refused to sign his films after that but continued as producer and actor. ***Sahib Bibi Aur Ghulam*** was credited to his co-scenarist Abrar Alvi but is attributable to Dutt. His premature death by suicide was foreshadowed in the autobiographical *Kaagaz Ke Phool*. His last film, *Baharen Phir Bhi Aayengi*, was finished by his brother Atma Ram in 1966, with **Dharmendra** in the role Dutt had played. A 2nd film left unfinished, **K. Asif**'s ***Love and God***, was eventually released in 1986 in a completely reshot and recast version. As producer, launched the career of his assistant **Raj Khosla** with *CID*. With the darkly romantic ***Pyaasa***, inspired by Saratchandra's novel *Srikanta*, muted social critique suddenly veers to tragedy as Dutt launched a cycle of films that have remained India's most spectacular achievement in melodrama. His work encapsulates with great intensity the emotional and social complexities affecting the artist when the reformism associated with Nehruite nationalism disintegrated under the pressures of industrialism and urbanisation, creating the space for Indian modernism but also generating immense social dislocation. Dutt's work, like his life, is located on the faultline of those conflicting forces and his supreme achievement is to have succeeded, at times, in both using and modifying available aesthetic modes to represent a profoundly contradictory experience, often via a focus on his extraordinary female figures (e.g. Waheeda Rehman) who are made to represent the conflictual dynamics of history. Book-length analysis of his films by Arun Khopkar (1985).

FILMOGRAPHY (* also act/** act only): **1945**: ***Lakhrani*****; **1951**: ***Baazi***; **1952**: ***Jaal***; **1953**: *Baaz**; **1954**: ***Aar Paar****; **1955**: ***Mr and Mrs '55****; **1956**: *Sailaab*; **1957**: ***Pyaasa****; **1958**: *Twelve O'Clock***; **1959**: ***Kaagaz Ke Phool****; **1960**: ***Chaudhvin Ka Chand*****; **1962**: ***Sahib Bibi Aur Ghulam*****; ***Sautela Bhai*****; **1963**: *Bahurani***; *Bharosa***; **1964**: *Sanjh Aur Savera***; *Suhagan***.

DUTT, SUNIL (b. 1930)

Hindi star and director born in Khurd, Jhelum Dist. (now Pakistan) as Balraj Dutt. Former announcer on Radio Ceylon. Best known in his early career as the outlaw hero of ***Mother India***, playing the son of his future wife **Nargis**. Then shifted to the image of the clean-cut modern youth in late 50s socials (**Bimal Roy**'s ***Sujata***). Continued with both images throughout his career. Also played remarkable comedy roles, e.g. the bumbling lover in ***Padosan***. Best work with **B.R. Chopra**. Recently, like **Dilip Kumar**, specialises in larger-than-life roles (*Shaan*). Directorial début, ***Yaadein***, is an overtly experimental one-man show. Launched his son Sanjay Dutt to Hindi stardom with *Rocky*. Became MP representing Congress (I) in North Bombay constituency in 1979, playing a heroic role in the 1993 communal riots in Bombay.

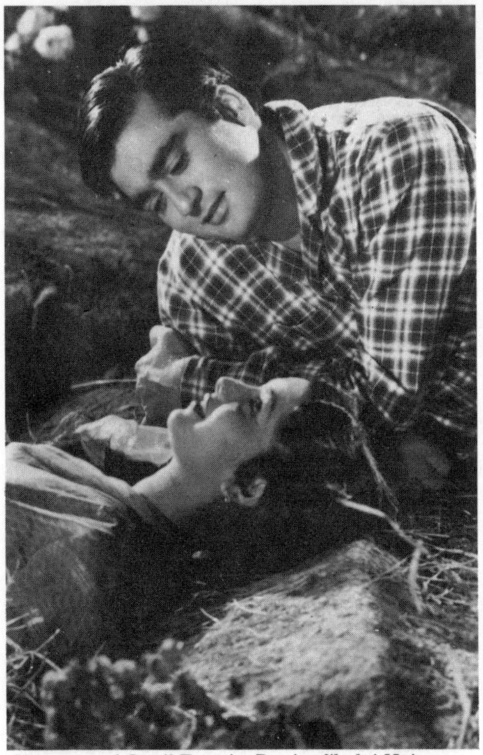

Shyama and Sunil Dutt in *Duniya Jhukti Hai* (1960)

FILMOGRAPHY (* also d): **1955**: *Kundan*; ***Railway Platform***; **1956**: *Ek Hi Raasta*; *Kismet Ka Khel*; *Rajdhani*; **1957**: ***Mother India***; *Payal*; **1958**: ***Post Box 999***; *Sadhana*; **1959**: *Didi*; *Insaan Jaag Utha*; ***Sujata***; **1960**: *Duniya Jhukti Hai*; *Ek Phool Char Kaante*; *Hum Hindustani*; *Usne Kaha Tha*; **1961**: *Chhaya*; **1962**: *Jhoola*; *Main Chup Rahungi*; **1963**: *Aaj Aur Kal*; ***Gumrah***; *Mujhe Jeene Do*; *Yeh Raaste Hain Pyar Ke*; *Nartaki*; **1964**: *Beti Bete*; *Ghazal*; ***Yaadein****; **1965**: *Khandaan*; ***Waqt***; **1966**: *Amrapali*; ***Gaban***; *Mera Saaya*; **1967**: *Hamraaz*; *Meharbaan*; *Milan*; **1968**: *Gauri*; ***Padosan***; *Sadhu Aur Shaitan*; **1969**: *Bhai Bahen*; *Chirag*; *Meri Bhabhi*; *Pyaasi Shyam*; **1970**: *Darpan*; *Bhai Bhai*; *Jwala*; **1971**: ***Reshma Aur Shera****; **1972**: *Jai Jwala*; *Zameen Aasmaan*; *Zindagi Zindagi*; **1973**: *Heera*; *Pran Jaye Par Vachan Na Jaye*; *Man Jeete Jag Jeet*; **1974**: *Chhattis Ghante*; *Geeta Mera Naam*; *Kora Badan*; **1975**: *Himalay Se Ooncha*; *Neelima*; *Umar Qaid*; *Zakhmi*; **1976**: *Nagin*; *Nehle Pe Dehla*; **1977**: *Sat Shri Akal*; *Ladki Jawan Ho Gayi*; *Aakhri Goli*; *Darinda*; *Gyaniji*; *Paapi*; *Charandas*; **1978**: *Jindri Yar Di*; *Kala Admi*; *Ram Kasam*; *Daku Aur Jawan**; **1979**: *Ahimsa*; *Jaani Dushman*; *Muqabala*; **1980**: *Ek Gunah Aur Sahi*; *Ganga Aur Suraj*; *Lahu Pukarega*; *Shaan*; *Yari Dushmani*; **1981**: *Rocky* (d. only); **1982**: *Badle Ki Aag*; *Dard Ka Rishta**; **1984**: *Laila*; *Raj Tilak*; *Yaadon Ki Zanjeer*; **1985**: *Faasle*; **1986**: *Kala Dhandha Goray Log*; *Mangal Dada*; **1987**: *Watan Ke Rakhwale*; **1988**: *Dharamyudh*; **1991**: *Yeh Aag Kab Bujhegi**; *Qurban*; *Pratigyabadh*; *Hai Meri Jaan*; **1992**: *Virodhi*; *Kshatriya*; *Parampara*; **1993**: *Phool*.

DUTT, UTPAL (1929-93)

Prolific Bengali and Hindi actor born in Shillong, Assam; also director and a major Marxist theatre personality in Bengal later associated with the CPI(M). Started career in early 40s with Geoffrey Kendall's theatre group performing Shakespeare, later directing Shakespeare for the Little Theatre Group. Formed his own group in 1949, then joined the Bengal unit of **IPTA** (1950-1) doing agitational plays staged on street corners and occasionally during political rallies to massive audiences, such as *Chargesheet* (1950), written overnight following the arrest of CP members and performed next day at Hazra Park. *The Special Train* was performed on behalf of striking workers of the Hindustan Automobile Factory, Uttarpara (1961). Also did theatrical spectaculars: *Angar* (1959), *Kallol* (1965; a play about the Royal Indian Navy mutiny of 1946, sparking off political rallies), *Din Badaler Pala* (1967, written for the CPI(M)'s electoral campaign) and *Tiner Talwar* (1970). *Barricade* (1972) and *Dushwapner Nagari* (1975) were staged in the context of the Emergency. Also made major interventions in the Jatra form (e.g. *Rifle*, *Sanyasir Tarabari*). Claims influence of Erwin Piscator to ' create proletarian myths of revolution' (cf Dutt, 1984). His work, comprising mostly historical reconstructions, was criticised by the Left for its determinism and the recourse to the ' great man' theory of history. Prolific film actor with a spectacular début as ***Michael Madhusudhan***, a legendary 19th C. Bengali theatre personality, repeating the role several times on the stage. After **Mrinal Sen**'s ***Bhuvan Shome***, shifted to Hindi films, often playing retired soldiers or tearful fathers in melodramas. Also important comedy roles in Bengali, e.g. *Mohan Baganer Meye*, *Shriman Prithviraj* et al. Claimed to act in films mainly to finance his theatrical work. Played key roles in recent **Satyajit Ray** films, e.g. the king in ***Hirak Rajar Deshe*** and the stranger in ***Agantuk***. Directorial work extends his theatrical work. Autobiography, including his views on theatre, published in 1982.

FILMOGRAPHY (* also d): **1950**: ***Michael Madhusudhan***; *Vidyasagar*; *Jaan Pehchan*; **1952**: *Siraj-ud-Dowla*; **1953**: *Maharaj Nandakumar*; **1954**: *Vikram Urvashi*; *Chitrangada*; **1955**: *Rani Rashmoni*; **1956**: *Kirti Garh*; *Shubha Lagna*; **1958**: *Jogajog*; *Rajdhani Theke*; **1960**: *Uttar Megh*; **1961**: *Megh**; *Pankatilak*; *Dilli Theke Kolkata*; **1962**: *Kancher Swarga*; *Abasheshe*; **1963**: *Shesh-Anka*; **1964**: *Momer Alo*; **1965**: *Ghoom Bhangar Gaan**; *Shakespeare Wallah*; **1967**: *Mahashweta*; **1968**: *Chowringhee*; **1969**: ***Aparichita***; *Bibaha Bibhrat*; ***Bhuvan Shome***; ***Saat Hindustani***; *The Guru*; **1970**: *Bombay Talkie*; *Kalankita Nayak*; **1971**: *Fariyad*; *Khunje Berai*; *Kuheli*; ***Ek Adhuri Kahani***; ***Guddi***; **1972**: ***Calcutta '71***; *Shesh Parba*; *Mere Jeevan Saathi*; *Sabse Bada Sukh*; *Marjina Abdallah*; *Shriman Prithviraj*; *Parivartan*; **1973**: *Mr Romeo*; *Agni Bhramar*; *Honeymoon*; *Shravan Sandhya*; *Rodon Bhora Basanta*; **1974**: ***Amanush***; *Asati*; *Charitraheen*; *Bisarjan*; *Bikele Bhorer Phool*; ***Chorus***; *Phuleshwari*; *Sadhu Judhishthirer Karcha*; *My Friend*; *Thagini*; *Alor Thikana*; *Sedin Du-janay*; ***Jukti Takko Aar Gappo***; *Chhutir Phande*; *Swikarokti*; **1975**: ***Palanka***; ***Sansar Simantey***; *Swayamsiddha*; *Salaam Memsaab*; *Nishi Mrigaya*; ***Julie***; *Anari*;

Aparajito; *Sei Chokh*; *Ek Hans Ka Joda*; ***Jana Aranya***; *Mohan Baganer Meye*; **1976**: *Ananda Mela*; *Dampati*; *Sandhya Surya*; *Datta*; *Kitne Paas Kitne Door*; *Raees*; *Yugo Manab Kabir*; *Nidhi Ram Sardar*; *Do Anjaane*; *Shaque*; *Santan*; *Asadharan*; *Pratisruti*; *Jatayu*; **1977**: *Anand Ashram*; *Anurodh*; *Farishta Ya Qatil*; *Ek Hi Raasta*; *Babu Moshai*; *Mantramugdha*; *Sister*; *Swati*; *Imaan Dharam*; ***Kissa Kursi Ka***; *Kotwal Saab*; *Priyatama*; *Lal Kothi*; *Safed Hathi*; ***Swami***; *Yahi Hai Zindagi*; *Sanai*; **1978**: *Moyna*; *Tilottama*; *Dhanraj Tamang*; *Bandi*; *Atithi*; *Toote Khilone*; *Striker*; ***Joi Baba Felunath***; **1979**: ***Jhor****; *Nauka Dubi*; *Golmaal*; *Kartavya*; *Prem Vivah*; *The Great Gambler*; **1980**: *Bandhan*; *Gharer Baire Ghar*; ***Hirak Rajar Deshe***; *Paka Dekha*; *Pankhiraj*; *Shesh Bichar*; *Agreement*; *Apne Paraye*; *Khwab*; *Nishana*; *Ram Balram*; **1981**: *Baisakhi Megh**; *Kalankini*; *Subarna Golak*; *Saheb*; *Barsaat Ki Ek Raat/Anusandhan*; *Naram Garam*; *Shaukeen*; *Meghmukti*; *Angoor*; *Raaste Pyar Ke*; ***Chaalchitra***; **1982**: *Raj Bodhu*; *Matir Swarga*; *Hamari Bahu Alka*; **1983**: *Rang Birangi*; *Maa**; *Achha Bura*; *Kisise Na Kehna*; *Pasand Apni Apni*; *Shubh Kaamna*; *Agami Kal*; *Indira*; *Jay Parajay*; *Duti Pata*; *Srinkhal*; **1984**: *Ahuti*; *Harishchandra Shaibya*; *Madhuban*; *Pujarini*; *Rashifal*; *Inquilab*; *John Jani Janardan*; *Lakhon Ki Baat*; ***Paar***; *Bandh Honth*; *Yeh Desh*; *Love Marriage*; *Inquilab Ke Baad**; **1985**: *Ulta Seedha*; *Aar Paar/Anyay Abichar*; *Bhalobasha Bhalobasha*; *Pratigya*; *Putulghar*; *Tagori*; *Bandhan Anjana*; *Saheb*; **1986**: *Uttar Lipi*; *Jiban*; *Pathbhola*; *Aap Ke Saath*; *Baat Ban Jaye*; *Kirayedaar*; *Main Balwan*; *Sada Suhagan*; **1987**: *Aaj Ka Robin Hood*; *Pyar Ke Kabil*; *Sukumar Ray* (Sh); *Samrat-o-Sundari*; *Pratikar*; *Jar Je Priyo*; **1988**: *Prati Paksha*; *Agun*; *Agaman*; *Mahaveera*; *Sagar Sangam*; *Pratik*; **1989**: *Asha-o-Bhalobasha*; *Biday*; *Gili Gili Ge*; *Bahurani*; *Judge Saheb*; *Aakrosh*; *Angar*; *Kari Diye Kinlam*; *Libaas*; **1990**: *Mera Pati Sirf Mera Hai*; *Raktorin*; *Agnikanya*; *Triyatri*; *Jawani Zindabad*; **1991**: ***Agantuk***; **1992**: ***Padma Nadir Majhi***.

DUTTA, J. P. (b. 1949)

Hindi director born in Bombay. Son of cineaste O.P. Dutta. Belongs to late 80s generation of Hindi commercial film-makers (e.g. Vinod Chopra, **N. Chandra**) aiming for a realist surplus through the sensory intensification of established film genres, as in 70s Hollywood films (e.g. Scorsese). Locates all his scripts in feudal Rajasthan, among conflicts featuring the Jat and the immensely powerful Thakur zamindars. His début, *Sarhad* (1978) was to star Vinod Khanna but remained unfinished. Faced major controversy when his next film, ***Ghulami***, sparked off communal violence in Rajasthan. Best-known film ***Hathyar*** extended the ancestral conflict into Bombay's gang wars.

FILMOGRAPHY: **1985**: ***Ghulami***; **1988**: ***Yateem***; **1989**: ***Hathyar***; ***Batwara***; **1992**: *Kshatriya*.

EAST INDIA FILM COMPANY

Est: 1932 in Calcutta. One of the first sound studios in Bengal, set up with RCA-Photophone equipment and Mitchell cameras. Owned by B.L. Khemkar. Bengali productions include films by Tulsi Lahiri (*Jamuna Puliney*, 1933), **Naresh Mitra**'s *Sabitri* (1933), **Dhiren Ganguly** (*Bidrohi*, 1935) and **Debaki Bose** (***Sonar Sansar***, 1936). Most prominent in-house director was Hindi film-maker **A.R. Kardar** (1933-6). The studio branched out into Tamil (e.g. **K. Subramanyam**'s *Bhakta Kuchela*, 1936) and Telugu films (e.g. **Pullaiah**'s ***Savithri***, 1933). Until the mid-40s it was the only fully equipped sound studio available to Tamil film-makers and was a major reason for numerous Bengali film technicians, particularly cameramen (best known: Jiten Bannerjee) working in the South, a tradition later continued by **Gemini** Studios.

Ekalavya *see* **Ghosh, Robi**

ELANGOVAN (1913-71)

Tamil script and dialogue writer in the 40s, originally named T.K. Thanikachalam. Début with **Duncan**'s seminal ***Ambikapathy*** (1937), followed by several story and script credits for films which established a new style in film melodrama: **Raja Chandrasekhar**'s ***Ashok Kumar*** (1941), **T.R. Raghunath**'s ***Kannagi*** (1942), Central Studios' *Sivakavi* (1943), R.S. Mani's ***Mahamaya*** (1944: some accounts credit him with direction as well), **K. Subramanyam**'s *Gokula Dasi* (1948), S.M. Sreeramulu Naidu's *Pavalakkodi* (1949), and especially **Ramnoth**'s epic ***Ezhai Padum Padu*** (1950). Formerly associated with the journal *Manikodi* whose literary idiom he transferred to cinema (cf **Kannamba**'s monologues in *Kannagi*). Critic and film-maker K. Hariharan writes: ' He breathed new fire into film dialogues [with] a passion quite removed from the standard mythologicals' and quotes popular scenarist A.L. Narayanan as saying that Elangovan and **P. Neelakantan**, ' were the first real screen writers in Tamil'. The literary scripting style was adopted later by e.g. V.V. Somayajulu in *Chintamani* (1937); T.V. Chari in *Manonmani* (1942); **A.S.A. Samy** in *Valmiki* (1946) and S.D. Sundaram in *Kanniyin Kathali* (1949). it was also an important precursor of **Annadurai**'s later declamatory scripts. Wrote **Raja Sandow**'s *Thiruneelakantar* (1939), Raja Chandrasekhar's *Arundhati* (1943), S. Nottani's *Inbavalli* (1949), K.S. Gopalakrishnan's *Parijatham* (1950) and many others.

EMPIRE FILMS

The Imperial Conference (1926) resolved to reserve 7.5% of screen time in the British Empire for films made within the Empire. This measure was intended to privilege the British film industry as opposed to the US industry in the Indian market, helping to revitalise the post-WW1 British cinema in the process. However, although the idea was initially welcomed by organisations like the Bombay Cinema and Theatres Association and the Indian Motion Picture Producers Association, such organisations soon raised the demand, that as the Empire's main film industry, 50% of the quota should be reserved for Indian cinema. Whereas the first result of the Conference was to limit Hollywood's access to the Indian market, the Indian demands effectively ended up regulating British access to the Indian market as well, favouring indigenous production. In the context of the **Swadeshi** polemic, the Indian Merchants Chamber led by Seth Walchand Hirachand argued that the only answer to combat Hollywood (and, implicitly, Britain) in India was a combination of tax incentives and the tenfold escalation of customs duty on imported films. Many of these debates informed the Indian Cinematograph Committee's work (1928), published in 5 volumes.

ESOOFALLY, ABDULALLY (1884-1957)

Exhibitor born in Surat, Gujarat. Travelled 1908-14 with tent bioscope through large parts of the Far East, including Burma, Singapore and Indonesia, introducing the cinema to these regions. In 1914 he settled in Bombay where he partnered **Ardeshir Irani** in an exhibition concern based on the acquisition of the Alexandra Theatre and later of the Majestic. Remained **Irani**'s partner for over 40 years. Active member of the Cinema Exhibitors Association of India since 1946.

FATMA, BEGUM

Probably first woman director in India. Married the Nawab of Sachin and mother of silent superstars Sultana and **Zubeida** as well as of Shahzadi. Career on Urdu stage, then film actress in **Irani**'s Star Film (***Veer Abhimanyu***); set up Fatma Film (1926), later Victoria-Fatma Film (1928). Actress at **Kohinoor** and **Imperial** Studios while producing, writing and directing (often also acting in) her own films at the Fatma Co. Continued acting in the 30s, e.g. for **Nanubhai Vakil** and **Homi Master**.

FILMOGRAPHY (* also d): **1922**: ***Veer Abhimanyu***; **1924**: ***Prithvi Vallabh***; ***Gul-e-Bakavali***; ***Kala Naag***; ***Sati Sardarba***; **1925**: *Naharsinh Daku*; *Devadasi*; ***Mumbai Ni Mohini***; *Gaud Bangal*; **1926**: *Khubsoorat Bala*; *Indrajal*; *Panna Ratna*; ***Bulbul-e-Paristan****; **1927**: *Goddess of Love*(?); **1928**: *Chandravali**; *Heer Ranjha**; *Sarojini*; *Bharmayalo Bharthar*; *Naag Padmini*; **1929**: *Kanakatara**; *Milan Dinar**; *Naseeb Ni Devi**; *Shakuntala**; *Shahi Chor**; *Lanka Lakshmi*; *Mahasundar*; *Punya Prabhav*; *Pardesi Saiyan*; **1930**: *Baharvatiyo Ni Beti*; *Zalim Zulekha*; *Ranchandi*; **1931**: *Afghan Abla*; *Aflatoon Abla*; *Lutaru*; *Sorathi Yoddho*; *Veer Bahadur* (all St); **1934**: *Neki Ka Taj*; *Sant Tulsidas*; *Seva Sadan*; **1935**: *Rang Bhoomi*; **1937**: *Punjab Lancers*; **1938**: ***Duniya Kya Hai***.

FATTELAL, SHEIKH (1897-1964)

Marathi director and technician. Real name: Yashin Mistri, aka Sahebmama Fattelal also spelt Fatehlal. Born in Kagal, Kolhapur. Belonged to hereditary artisanal caste (Mistri means ' carpenter', although his father was a stonemason). Apprenticed to the Kolhapur artist Abalal Rehman. Lifelong partner of **Vishnupant Damle**. Co-disciple with Damle of Baburao's technician-artist cousin, Anandrao Painter. Co-founder of and all-round technician at **Maharashtra Film**. Partner and head of art department at **Prabhat** where he organised spectacular sets (e.g. ***Amritmanthan***, 1934). Co-directed Saint films with Damle, including ***Sant***

Tukaram (1936) (for filmography, see Damle). Also major achievements as art director: e.g. ***Ayodhyecha Raja/Ayodhya Ka Raja***, ***Maya Machhindra*** (both 1932), ***Amar Jyoti*** (1936), ***Kunku/Duniya Na Mane*** (1937), ***Mazha Mulga/Mera Ladka*** (1938), ***Manoos/Admi*** (1939), ***Shejari/Padosi*** (1941) and ***Ramshastri*** (1944). Produced a film after Damle's death (1945) for Prabhat; then solo direction of two features.

FILMOGRAPHY: **1955**: *Jagadguru Shankaracharya*; **1956**: ***Ayodhyapati***.

FAZIL (b. 1953)

Successful Malayalam director who shifted to big-budget Tamil films in the mid-80s. Born in Alleppey, Kerala; theatre director and actor while at university. Degree in literature; later worked with Kavalam Narayana Panicker's theatre group Thiruvarung. Film début assisting **A. Vincent**. Directorial début: the musical *Manjil Virinja Pookkal* which he also scripted and produced. Since then has been associated with the urban middle-class family musical melodrama, displacing **K. Balachander**'s domination of the genre in the 70s Tamil cinema. Film-maker and critic K Hariharan writes: ' His forte lies in the amount of narration that he manages to pack into his compositions, and the art of telling stories through song situations,' claiming that with better actors his work could come close to that of **Guru Dutt** or **Bimal Roy**. His Tamil films are sometimes adapted from his own Malayalam hits (e.g. the melodrama ***Ente Mamattukuttiamma*** remakes *En Bommu Kutti Ammavukku*), although the incisiveness of the original (says Hariharan) is usually diluted to suit the populist tastes of Tamil distributors.

FILMOGRAPHY: **1980**: *Manjil Virinja Pookkal*; **1981**: *Dhanya*; **1983**: *Eettillam*; *Marakkailo Rikalum*; ***Ente Mamattukuttiamma***; **1984**: ***Nokketha Dhoorathu Kannum Nattu***; **1985**: *Poove Poo Chooda Va*; **1986**: *Ennum Kannettante*; *Poovinnu Puthiya Poonthennal*; **1987**: *Poovizhi Vasalile*; *Manivathoorile Ayiram Sivarathrikal*; **1988**: *En Bommu Kutti Ammavukku*; **1989**: *Varusham 16*; **1990**: *Arangetra Velai*; **1991**: *Ente Suryaputhrikku*; *Karpura Mullai*; **1992**: *Killer*; *Papayude Sontham Appoose*; **1993**: *Kilipetchu Ketkava*.

FILM ADVISORY BOARD

Est: 1940. First instance of direct state production of documentary film in India. Started as part of the Dept of Information to advise on the making of propaganda shorts during WW2 under chairmanship of Alexander Shaw (formerly associated with John Grierson in the Empire Marketing Board and later producer with Crown Film Unit). **J.B.H. Wadia**, **V. Shantaram** and **Ezra Mir** worked briefly as chief producers (1942). The FAB was intended to collaborate with independent producers/financiers, co-ordinating and overseeing the distribution of indigenous and imported war propaganda films. Initial productions included documentaries and newsreels made at **Wadia Movietone** (e.g. early work of documentarist **P.V. Pathy**), films commissioned from the advertising agency D.J. Keymer and localised versions of newsreels by 20th Century-Fox. Replaced in 1943 by **Information Films of India**.

FILM AND TELEVISION INSTITUTE OF INDIA

India's premier training institute for film-making, cinematography, editing and sound-recording. Founded in 1960, a decade after the S.K. Patil Film Enquiry Committee's recommendations, as the Film Institute of India. It was established in Pune using the premises of the former **Prabhat** Film. Became an autonomous organisation funded by the Ministry of Information & Broadcasting in 1974, simultaneously expanding to include a tv section in the context of **Doordarshan**'s development plans. The FTII's history is most closely associated with **Ritwik Ghatak** who joined as Professor of Film and Vice-Principal (1966-7) and formed several of the New Indian Cinema pioneers, such as **Kumar Shahani**, **Mani Kaul**, **Adoor Gopalakrishnan** et al., as well as numerous key technicians, e.g. cinematographer K.K. Mahajan.

Film Finance Corporation *see* **National Film Development Corporation**

FILMISTAN

Bombay-based studio; Est: 1942. Launched by major breakaway group from **Bombay Talkies** led by their production controller Rai Bahadur Chunilal and producer Shashadhar Mukherjee. Their first film was **Gyan Mukherjee**'s ***Chal Chal Re Naujawan*** (1944, with **Ashok Kumar**). The studio continued more or less from S. Mukherjee's two influential Bombay Talkies productions: ***Naya Sansar*** (1941) and the colossal hit ***Kismet*** (1943). Both introduced into Hindi film a Hollywood notion of genre. The studio's subsequent output elaborated this into the first consistent generic codification and regulation of a post-Independence All-India Film market-place. By the early 50s, the ' film factory' (as **B.R. Chopra**, who worked there briefly, called it) had revolutionised distribution with mid-budget genre productions selling mainly on their star value and their music. The approach was exemplified by Gyan Mukherjee himself and extended by **Subodh Mukherjee**, **Nasir Hussain** and Najam Naqvi, with stars Ashok Kumar, **Dev Anand**, **Dilip Kumar**, **Shammi Kapoor** and **Nalini Jaywant**, and music directors **C. Ramchandra** and **S.D. Burman**. Filmistan's style arguably had the largest impact of any studio on later independent commercial film-making in Hindi. This is evident, e.g., in **Manmohan Desai**'s cinema. Other notable Filmistan cineastes are **Nitin Bose**, **Nandlal Jaswantlal** and **Kishore Sahu**. The studio yielded yet another mutation when Shashadhar Mukherjee moved out to start Filmalaya (1958).

FILMS DIVISION

Est: 1949. A ' mass-media unit' run by the Ministry of Information & Broadcasting, it is ' the central film-producing organisation responsible for the production and distribution of newsreels, documentaries and other films required by the the Government of India for public information, education and for instructional and cultural purposes' (Unesco report, 1973; quoted in Jag Mohan, 1990). Until the post-Emergency period which saw, for the first time, the independently made documentary (cf **Anand Patwardhan**), the Films Division had the monopoly on documentary cinema in India, making upwards of 200 shorts/documentaries and weekly newsreels (*Indian News Review*). Each film had over 9000 prints and was dubbed into 18 Indian languages and exhibited through compulsory block booking in every permanent cinema in the country. Its early work used imagery today considered typical of the iconography of the Nehru era, such as N.S. Thapa's documentary on the Bhakra Nangal dam (1958), and connects via the war propaganda productions of the **Film Advisory Board** with the British documentary tradition pioneered by John Grierson, a link further strengthened by film producers Jean Bhownagry, James Beveridge (Shell Film Unit) and, briefly in the late 60s, film-maker Basil Wright working at Films Division on loan from UNESCO. Best-known 70s work was by **Sukhdev**. Recent productions include **Shyam Benegal**'s feature-length documentaries *Nehru* and *Satyajit Ray* (both 1984) and **Mani Kaul's** ***Siddheshwari*** (1989). However the bulk of the Films Division's enormous output is by in-house film-makers.

GADKAR, JAYSHREE (b. 1942)

Actress born in Karwar Dist., Karnataka. Introduced into films by **Raja Paranjpe** as child actress. Major 60s and 70s star in Marathi film, imaged repeatedly as innocent and tearful daughter-in-law in some of the longest and most sentimental Marathi socials/melodramas (e.g. **Bhalji Pendharkar**'s *Mohityanchi Manjula*). Early work strongly influenced by **Hansa Wadkar** who played her foster-mother in her first major hit, ***Sangtye Aika***. Played Tamasha dancing-girl in several **Anant Mane** and **Dinkar D. Patil** rural melodramas in the 60s, when **Dhirubhai**

Jayashree Gadkar in *Patlachi Soon* (1966)

Desai and **Babubhai Mistri** also cast her in Hindi mythologicals. Now associated with roles opposite stunt star **Dara Singh** in **Chandrakant** films (*Har Har Mahadev*, *Kisan Aur Bhagwan*). Published autobiography in 1986.

FILMOGRAPHY: **1956**: *Dista Tasa Nasta*; *Gaath Padli Thaka Thaka*; **1957**: *Aliya Bhogasi*; *Aai Mala Kshama Kar*; *Pahila Prem*; *Devagharcha Lena*; *Utavala Narad*; **1958**: *Sanskar*; *Padada*; **1959**: ***Sangtye Aika***; *Yala Jeevan Aise Nav*; *Pativrata*; *Ek Armaan Mera*; *Madari*; *Do Gunde*; *Charnon Ki Dasi*; **1960**: *Avaghachi Sansar*; *Lagnala Jato Mi*; *Saranga*; *Paishyacha Paoos*; *Pancharati*; *Bindiya*; *Police Detective*; **1961**: *Kalanka Shobha*; ***Manini***; *Rangapanchami*; *Shahir Parashuram*; *Vyjayanti*; *Jai Bhawani*; *Ramleela*; *Sasural*; **1962**: *Baap Mazha Brahmachari*; *Bhagya Lakshmi*; *Preeti Vivah*; *Sukh Ale Majhya Daari*; *Private Secretary*; **1963**: *Mohityanchi Manjula*; *Naar Nirmite Nara*; *Subhadra Haran*; *Sukhachi Savli*; *Yeh Dil Kisko Doon*; *Mere Arman Mere Sapne*; **1964**: *Ek Don Teen*; *Kai Ho Chamatkar*; *Saval Mazha Aika*; *Sundara Manamadhye Bharli*; *Vaishakh Vanava*; *Sati Savitri*; *Seeta Maiya*; **1965**: *Gopal Krishna*; *Mahasati Ansuya*; *Aai Kuna Mhanu Mi*; *Malhari Martand*; ***Sadhi Manse***; *Yugo Yugo Mi Vat Pahili*; *Kadhi Karishi Lagna Mazhe*; **1966**: *Toofan Mein Pyar Kahan*; *Hi Naar Rupasundari*; *Hirva Chuda*; *Patlachi Soon*; *Pavanakathcha Dhondi*; *Veer Bajrang*; **1967**: *Poonam Ka Chand*; *Baharon Ke Sapne*; *Bai Mi Bholi*; *Sangu Kashi Mi*; *Shrimant Mehuna Pahije*; *Thamb Lakshmi Kunku Lavte*; *Suranga Mhantyat Mala*; *Lav Kush*; **1968**: *Balaram Shri Krishna*; *Har Har Gange*; *Mata Mahakali*; *Ek Gao Bara Bhangadi*; *Jivhala*; **1969**: *Dongarchi Maina*; *Gan Gaulan*; *Murali Malhari Rayachi*; *Tila Lavite Mi Raktacha*; *Ram Bhakta Hanuman*; **1970**: *Bhagwan Parashuram*; *Dagabaaz*; *Shri Krishna Leela*; *Gharkul*; *Veer Ghatotkach*; *Meech Tujhi Priya*; **1971**: *Maya Bazaar*; *Tulasi Vivah*; *Aai Ude Ga Ambabai*; *Lakhat Ashi Dekhani*; *Ashich Ek Ratra Hoti*; *Mata Vaishno Devi*; **1972**: *Naag Panchami*; *Hari Darshan*; *Kasa Kai Patil Bara Hai Ka?*; *Kunku Mazha Bhagyacha!*; *Pathrakhin*; *Soon Ladki Hya Gharchi*; *Shiv Bhakt Baba Balak Nath*; **1973**: *Mi Tuzha Pati Nahi*; *Mahasati Savitri*; **1974**: *Har Har Mahadev*; *Dawat*; *Balak Dhruv*; *Kisan Aur Bhagwan*; *Soon Majhi Savitri*; *Sugandhi Katta*; *Bhagat Dhanna Jat*; **1975**: *Paach Rangachi Paach Pakhare*; *Ek Gaon Ki Kahani*; *Alakh Niranjan*; *Ghar Gangechya Kathi*; **1976**: *Mazha Mulga*; *Bajrang Bali*; **1977**: *Gayatri Mahima*; *Bolo He Chakradhari*; **1978**: *Chandoba Chandoba Bhaglas Ka?*; **1979**: *Har Har Gange*; *Lagebandhe*; **1980**: *Savat*; *Jidda*; *Kadaklakshmi*; *Saubhagyavan*; *Shiv Shakti*; *Nishana*; **1981**: *Jiyo To Aise Jiyo*; *Soon Majhi Lakshmi*; *Baine Kela Sarpanch Khula*; *Jai Tulaja Bhawani*; **1982**: *Avhaan*; *Farz Aur Kanoon*; *Sati Naag Kanya*; **1983**: *He Daan Kunkvache*; *Thorli Jau*; **1984**: *Attaracha Phaya*; *Gangavatarana*; *Rath Jagannathacha*; *Jakhmi Vaghin*; *Naya Kadam*; *Sulagte Arman*; *Shravan Kumar*; *Sindoor Ka Daan*; *Maya Bazaar*; **1985**: *Masterji*; *Veer Bhimsen*; *Khichadi*; *Devashapath Khara Sangen*; **1986**: *Bijali*; *Krishna Krishna*; *Patton Ki Baazi*; *Ramayan* (TV); **1987**: *Bhatak Bhawani*; *Poorna Satya*; *Sher Shivaji*; *Nazrana*; **1988**: *Mar Mitenge*; *Eeshwar*; *Pandharichi Vari*; *Shiv Ganga*; **1989**: *Mal Masala*; *Kanoon Apna Apna*; **1990**: *Amiri Garibi*.

GAGGAIAH, VEMURI (1895-1955)

Noted Telugu stage and film actor of the 40s. Legendary stage star with an imposing presence and loud voice, which suited demonic roles in mythologicals, e.g. Yama and Kans. Film début with **East India Film**'s production of ***Savithri*** playing Yama, god of death. Known mainly as one of the first actors to define a performative idiom tailored to the mythological.

FILMOGRAPHY: **1933**: ***Savithri***; **1935**: ***Shri Krishna Leelalu***; **1936**: ***Draupadi Vastrapaharanam***; *Sati Tulasi*; **1937**: ***Mohini Rugmangada***; **1938**: *Markandeya*; **1940**: ***Chandika***; *Mahiravana*; **1941**: ***Dakshayagnam***; **1942**: *Bhakta Prahlada*; **1943**: ***Garuda Garvabhangam***; **1948**: *Bhakta Siriyala*.

GANDHI, NAVAL (b. 1897)

Hindi director born in Karachi. Graduated in Ahmedabad (1919) and went on European study tour. Joined **Irani**'s Majestic (1923). Later worked at Orient Pics where he made one of the most discussed quality films of the silent era, ***Balidan***, adapted from **Tagore**. Went on to direct its star, **Zubeida**, at Orient and at **Kohinoor**. Worked at the Directorate of Services Kinematography, the film wing of the armed forces during WW2, where he produced **P.V. Pathy**'s documentaries. Went into radio in the early 50s.

FILMOGRAPHY: **1924**: *Chandan Malayagiri*; *Mumbai Ni Sethani*; *Paap No Pashchatap*; *Shahjehan*; ***Paap No Fej***; *Sanyasi*; **1926**: *Yauvan Chakra*; **1927**: ***Balidan***; **1930**: *Devadasi*; *Veer Rajput*; **1931**: *Nadira*; *Diwani Duniya* (all St); **1932**: *Shikari*.

GANESAN, SIVAJI (b. 1927)

Tamil superstar, originally Viluppuram Chinnaiahpillai Ganesan but best known as Sivaji. Born in Sirkali, TN, into the peasant Kallar caste although his father worked on the railways. According to the official biography, the day he was born his father was jailed for participating in the Independence movement in Nellikuppam. Enjoyed a fitful education and joined theatre groups. Made his reputation as actor in **C.N. Annadurai**'s play *Sivaji Kanda Indhu Rajyam*, a historical on the Maratha Emperor Shivaji which also gave him his screen name. He followed Annadurai when the latter started the DMK (1949), and his début, in the wordy role of Gunasekharan in ***Parasakthi***, made him the official icon of the Party for some years (cf **DMK Film**). He started distancing himself from the DMK in the mid-50s, joining E.V.K. Sampath's Tamil Nationalist Party (1961), then joined Congress and wound up supporting the opposition Janata Dal. Moving away from the early DMK's atheistic politics, he acted in several mythologicals, esp. *Sampoorna Ramayanam* and *Thiruvillaiyadal*, in nationalist historicals (his most famous film ***Veerapandiya Kattaboman***) and in biographicals (***Kappalotiya Thamizhan***, a film on V.O. Chidambaram Pillai, a 19th C. anti-imperialist who defied the British to start the Steam Navigation Co.). According to K. Sivathamby (1981), Ganesan and his main rival, **MGR** (with whom he acted in one film, *Kundukkili*), dominated the Tamil cinema to such an extent that the two automatically demanded Madras distribution rights in their contracts and could bankrupt a producer by causing production delays, a power the stars used to further their political ambitions. Their power base is buttressed by several fan clubs and the Ganesan Rasikar Manram. Rajya Sabha Member of Parliament (1982-8). His younger brother ran Sivaji Prod. and his son Prabhu was propelled to stardom in the 80s in films like *Vetri Vizha* (1989, adapting Robert Ludlum's *The Bourne Identity*).

FILMOGRAPHY: **1952**: ***Parasakthi***; *Panam*; **1953**: ***Poongothai/Pardesi***; *Anbu*; *Kangal*; *Thirumbi Paar*; *Manithanum Mrigamum*; ***Pempudu Koduku***; **1954**: *Andha Naal*; *Illara Jyothi*; *Ethirparadathu*; *Kalyanam Panniyum Brahmachari*; *Kundukkili*; *Thuli Visham*; *Thooku Thooki*; ***Manohara/Manohar***; **1955**: *Ulagam Palavitham*; *Kalvanin Kadhali*; *Kaveri*; *Koteshwaran*; *Mangayar Thilakam*; ***Mudhal Thedi/Modalatedi***; ***Pennin Perumai***; **1956**:

Sivaji Ganesan and Helen in *Sitamgarh* (1958)

Amara Deepam; ***Tenali Raman***; *Naney Raja*; *Nalla Veedu*; *Raja Rani*; *Naan Petra Selvam*; ***Rangoon Radha***; *Vazhvile Oru Naal*; **1957**: *Pudhuvayal*; *Tangamalai Rahasyam*; *Makkalai Petra Maharasi*; *Manamagal Thevai*; *Bhagyavati*; *Vanangamudi*; *Rani Lalithangi*; ***Ambikapathy***; *Sarangadhara*; **1958**: *Annaiyin Aanai*; *Uthama Puthran*; *Kathavarayan*; *Shabash Meena*; *Sampoorna Ramayanam*; *Pati Bhakti*; *Bommalapelli/Bommai Kalyanam*; *Suhaag*; ***School Master***; *Sitamgarh*; **1959**: *Aval Yar*; *Thangapathumai*; *Naan Sollum Rahasiyam*; *Bhagapirivinai*; *Maragatham*; ***Veerapandiya Kattaboman/Amar Shaheed***; **1960**: *Daiva Piravi*; *Kurvanji*; *Irumputhirai*; *Padikkatha Methai*; *Petra Manam*; *Pavai Vilakku*; *Raja Bhakti*; *Makkala Rajya/Kuzhandaigal Kanda Kudiyarasu*; *Vidiveli*; **1961**: *Ellam Unnakkaga*; ***Kappalotiya Thamizhan***; ***Pasamalar***; *Punarjanmam*; ***Pavamanippu***; *Marudu Nattu Veeran*; *Pallum Pazhamum*; *Shri Valli*; **1962**: *Alayamani*; *Senthamarai*; *Nishchaya Thambulam*; *Padithal Mattu Pothuma*; *Bale Pandian*; *Bandha Pasam*; *Parthal Pasi Theerum*; *Vadivukku Valai Kappu*; *Valar Pirai*; **1963**: *Arivali*; *Annai Illam*; ***Iruvar Ullam***; ***Raktha Tilakam***; *Kulamagal Radhai*; *Chittor Rani Padmini*; *Kumkumam*; *Paar Magale Paar*; *Naan Vanangum Daivam*; *Kalyanin Kanavan*; *Mamakaram*; **1964**: ***Karnan***; *Pachai Vilakku*; *Andavan Kathali*; *Kaikodutha Daivam*; *Pudhiya Paravai*; *Muradhan Muthu*; *Navarathri*; *School Master*; **1965**: *Pazhani*; *Anbukkarangal*; *Shanti*; *Thiruvillaiyadal*; *Neelavanam*; **1966**: ***Motor Sundaram Pillai***; *Mahakavi Kalidas*; *Saraswathi Sabatham*; *Selvam*; *Thaye Unakkaga*; **1967**: ***Kandan Karunai***; *Nenjirukumvarai*; *Pesum Daivam*; ***Thangai***; *Paladai*; *Thiruvarut Selvar*; *Iru Malargal*; *Ootivarai Uravu*; **1968**: *Thirumal Perumai*; *Harishchandra*; *Enga Ooru Raja*; *Galatta Kalyanam*; *En Thambi*; ***Thillana Mohanambal***; *Lakshmi Kalyanam*; *Uyarntha Manithan*; *Arunodhayam*; **1969**: *Anbalipu*; *Thanga Surangam*; ***Kaval Daivam***; *Gurudakshinai*; *Anjal Petty 520*; *Nirai Kudam*; *Daivamagan*; *Thirudan*; *Sivantha Mann*; **1970**: *Enga Mama*; *Vilayattu Pillai*; ***Vietnam Veedu***; *Ethiroli*; *Raman Ethanai Ramanadi*; *Dharti*; *Sorgam*; *Engiruthu Vandhal*; *Pathukappu*; **1971**: *Iru Thuruvam*; *Thangaikkaga*; *Kulama Kunama*; *Sumathi En Sundari*; *Praptham*; *Savale Samali*; *Thenum Palum*; *Moondru Daivangal*; *Babu*; **1972**: *Raja*; ***Gnana Oli***; *Pattikada Pattanama*; *Dharmam Engay*; *Thavaputhalvan*; *Vasantha Maligai*; *Neethi*; *Maa Inti Jyothi*; **1973**: *Bharatha Vilas*; *Raja Raja Chozhan*; *Ponnunnjal*; *Engal Thanga Raja*; *Gauravam*; *Manithiral Manikam*; *Raja Part Rangadurai*; *Ranganna Sabatham*; **1974**: *Sivakamyin Selvan*; *Thayi*; *Vani Rani*; *Thanga Padakkam*; *En Magan*; *Anbai Thedi*; *Gauravam*; **1975**: *Manithanum Daivamagalam*; *Avanthan Manithan*; *Mannavan Vandanadi*; *Anbe Aruyere*; *Vaira Nenjam*; *Doctor Siva*; *Pattam Bharathamum*; **1976**: *Unakkaga Naan*; *Grihapravesham*; *Sathyam*; *Uthaman*; *Chitra Pournami*; *Rojavin Raja*; *Avan Oru Charitram*; *Ilaya Thalaimurai*; *Ennai Pol Oruvan*; **1977**: *Deepam*; *Naam Pirandha Maan*; *Annan Oru Koyil*; *Andaman Kathali*; *Chanakya Chandragupta*; *Jeevana Theeralu*; **1978**: *Thyagam*; *Punya Bhoomi*; *General Chakravarthi*; *Thacholi Ambu*; *Pilot Premnath*; *Justice Gopinath*; **1979**: *Thirisulam*; *Emayam*; *Kavariman*; *Nallathoru Kudumbam*; *Naan Vazhavippen*; *Pattakathi Bhairavan*; *Vetrikku Oruvan*; **1980**: *Dharma Raja*; *Yamanukku Yaman*; *Ratha Pasam*; *Rishi Moolam*; *Vishwa Roopam*; **1981**: *Amarakaviyam*; *Sathyam Sundaram*; *Mohana Ponnagai*; *Kalthoon*; *Lorry Driver Rajakannu*; *Madi Veetu Ezhai*; *Kizhvanam Sivakkam*; **1982**: *Hitler Umanath*; *Oorukku Oru Pillai*; *Vaa Kanna Vaa*; *Garuda Sowkiyama*; *Sangili*; *Vasanthathil Oru Naal*; *Theerpu*; *Thyagi*; *Paritchaikku Neramchu*; *Oorum Uravum*; *Nenjangal*; *Nivurigappina Nippu*; *Thunai*; **1983**: *Neethipathi*; *Imaigal*; *Sandhippu*; *Mridanga Chakravarthi*; *Sumangali*; *Vellai Roja*; *Uruvavugal Maralam*; *Bezwada Bebbuli*; **1984**: *Thiruppam*; *Chiranjeevi*; *Tharasu*; *Vazhkai*; *Charitra Nayakan*; *Simma Soppanam*; *Ezhuthantha Sattangal*; *Iru Methaigal*; *Vamsa Vilakku*; *Thavani Kanavukal*; **1985**: *Bandham*; *Nam Iruvar*; *Padikkatha Panayar*; *Neethiyin Nizhal*; *Nermai*; ***Muthal Mariyathai***; *Raja Rishi*; *Padikkadhavan*; **1986**: *Sadhanai*; *Marumagal*; *Ananda Kannir*; *Viduthalai*; *Thaikku Oru Thalattu*; *Maaveeran*; *Lakshmi Vandhachu*; **1987**: *Veerapandian*; *Mutukkal Moonru*; *Anbulla Appa*; *Thambathiyam*; *Vishwanatha Nayakudu*; *Agni Putrudu*; **1988**: *En Thamil En Makkal*; *Marmagal*; *Pudhiya Vanam*; **1991**: *Gnana Paravai*; **1992**: *Muthal Kural*; ***Thevar Magan***; *Nangal*; *Chinna Marumagal*; **1993**: *Paramparyam*.

GANESH, GEMINI

Aka Ramaswamy Ganesan. Tamil star also known for performances in Telugu, Malayalam and Hindi. Graduated in chemistry and worked at the Madras Christian College. Joined the **Gemini** Studio in 1946 as actor and casting assistant. Became a star with his double role in *Manampola Mangalyam*, during the making of which he met Telugu and Tamil star Savitri, whom he married. Known mainly for soft romantic roles (e.g. ***Kalyana Parisu***). Later played in mythologicals, e.g. **A.P. Nagarajan**'s ***Kandan Karunai*** and several **P. Subramanyam** films in Malayalam such as *Kumara Sambhavam*; the melodramatic lead with **Sowcar Janaki** in **Panthulu**'s Tamil remake of ***School Master***. Father of Hindi star **Rekha**.

FILMOGRAPHY 1979-82 and after 1986 probably incomplete.

FILMOGRAPHY (* also d): **1947**: *Miss Malini*; **1952**: ***Kalyanam Panni Paar***; *Thayi Ullam*; **1953**: ***Avvaiyyar***; *Manampola Mangalyam*; **1954**: *Penn*; **1955**: *Maheshwari*; *Valliyin Selvam*; *Maman Magal*; *Kanavane Kan Kanda Daivam*; ***Kalam Maripochu***; ***Pennin Perumai***; ***Missiamma***; **1956**: *Prema Pasham*; *Asai*; *Devata*; *Mathurkula Manikyam*; *Sadaram*; **1957**: *Miss Mary*; ***Manalane Mangayin Bhagyam***; *Mallika*; ***Maya Bazaar***; *Yar Paiyan*; *Saubhagyavati*; *Karpurakarasi*; *Kutumba Gauravam*; **1958**: *Thirumanam*; *Vanjikottai Valiban*; ***Raj Tilak***; *Suhaag*; *Pati Bhakti*; ***Kadam Vangi Kalyanam***; ***School Master/Badi Panthulu***; **1959**: ***Kalyana Parisu***; ***Veerapandiya Kattaboman/Amar Shaheed***; *Vazha Vaitha Daivam*; *Nalla Theerpu*; *Adisaya Thirudan*; *Bhagya Devatha/Bhagya Devathai*; *Ponnu Vilayum Bhoomi*; **1960**: *Kalathur Kannamma*; ***Parthiban Kanavu***; *Pudhiya Pathai*; *Meenda Sorgam*; *Ellorum Innattu Mannar*; *Kairasi*; **1961**: ***Kappalotiya Thamizhan***; ***Pasamalar***; *Nazrana*; *Saugandh*; *Bhagya Lakshmi*; *Thennilavu*; ***Pavamanippu***; *Panithirai*; **1962**: *Kathirunda Kankal*; *Konjum Salangai*; *Adiperaku*; *Parthal Pasi Theerum*; *Sumaithangal*; ***Manithan Maravillai***; *Patha Kannikkai*; *Swarnamanjari/Mangaiyar Ullam Mangada Selvam*; **1963**: *Pareeksha*; *Lavakusa*; *Idayathil Nee*; *Karpagam*; *Ezhai Pangalan*; **1964**: *Oralkoodi Kalanayi*; *Pasamum Nesamum*; *Vazhkai Vazhvadarke*; **1965**: *Hello Mister Zamindar*; **1966**: *Ramu*; *Chinnachiru Ulagam*; *Thene Mazhai*; **1967**: ***Kandan Karunai***; *Pattathu Rani*; *Seeta*; *Padhyam*; *Penn Entral Penn*; **1968**: *Balaram Shri Krishna*; *Panama Pasama*; *Thamarai Nenjam*; **1969**: *Kumara Sambhavam*; *Avare En Daivam*; *Iru Kodukal*; *Kuzhandai Ullam*; *Thanga Malar*; *Porsilai*; *Aindhu Laksham*; *Manaivi*; *Shanti Nilayam*; *Kulavilakku*; **1970**: *Ethirkalam*; *Tapalkaran Thangai*; *Sorgam*; *Sinehithi*; *Kanmalar*; ***Kaviyath Thalaivi***; *Malathi*; **1971**: *Punnagai*; **1972**: *Kanna Nalama*; *Enna Mudalali Sowkiyama*; *Appa Tata*; *Kurathi Magan*; *Ellai Kodu*; *Velli Vizha*; *Daivam*; *Shakti Leela*; *Professor*; *Shri Guruvayoorappan*; **1973**: *Ganga Gauri*; *Nalla Mudivu*; *School Master*; *Thirumalai Daivam*; *Malai Nattu Mangai*; *Kattilla Thottilla*; *Jesus*; **1974**: *Manikka Thothil*; *Nan Avanillai*; *Devi Shri Karumariamman*; *Devi Kanyakumari*; **1975**: *Swami Ayyappan*; *Uravukku Kayi Koduppam*; **1976**: *Dashavatharam*; *Idaya Malar**; *Lalitha*; *Unakkaga Naan*; **1977**: *Naam Pirandha Maan*; *Shri Murugan*; *Oka Thalli Katha*; **1978**: *Shri Kanchi Kamakshi*; *Bhrashthu*; **1983**: *Soorakottai Singhakutty*; **1988**: *Rudraveena*; *Unnal Mudiyum Thambi*; *Ponmana Selvan*.

GANGULY, DHIRENDRANATH (1893-1978)

Bengali director, painter and actor born in Calcutta. Studied in Shantiniketan, graduated from the Government School of Art, Calcutta (1915); art teacher in the Nizam's Art College, Hyderabad. Successful portrait painter and sought to extend his oil painting techniques into photography. Published 2 collections of photographic self-portraits, *Bhaber Abhiyakti* and *Biye* (1922), as photomontages with Ganguly himself modelling all the characters. Set up Indo-British Film (1918) in Calcutta with Nitish Lahiri. First film, ***Bilet Pherat***, was probably ready in 1919. Returned to Hyderabad and set up Lotus Film (1922-4) on the Nizam's invitation. Went back to Calcutta, after a short stay in Bombay, and started **British Dominion Films** Studio (1929) together with **P.C. Barua**. Remained ardent supporter of **Empire Films** concept. Unable to sustain his studio into the sound era, he went freelance in 1934, including two separate periods at **New Theatres**. With *Bilet Pherat* introduced a type of satire into film (continued in *The Marriage Tonic*, *Takay Ki Na Hay*) analogous to 19th C. tradition of Naksha satirical literature, drawing on **Pat painting** and the musical satires of **Calcutta Theatres**. Among his later films were adaptations of **Premendra Mitra**'s novels (e.g. *Ahuti*, *Daabi*).

FILMOGRAPHY (* act only): **1921**: ***Bilet Pherat****; *Shri Radha Krishna**; **1922**: *Sadhu Aur Shaitan**; *Indrajit*; *Lady Teacher*; *Hara Gauri*; *Chintamani*; *Bimata*; **1923**: *The Marriage Tonic*; *Yayati*; **1924**: *Sati Simantini*; **1927**: *Shankaracharya**; **1930**: *Panchasar**; *Kamaner Aagun**; *Alik Babu*; **1931**: *Takay Ki Na Hay*;

Charitraheen; *Maraner Pare** (all St); **1933**: *Mastuto Bhai*; **1934**: *Excuse Me, Sir*; *Night Bird*; *Halkatha*; **1935**: *Bidrohi*; **1936**: *Country Girl*; *Dwipantar*; **1938**: *Halbangala*; *Achin Priya*; *Abhisarika*; **1940**: *Path Bhoole*; *Karmakhali*; **1941**: *Pratishodh**; *Ahuti*; **1943**: *Daabi*; **1947**: *Srinkhal*; **1948**: *Shesh Nibedan*; **1949**: *Cartoon*; **1962**: *Abhisarika**; *Rakta Palash**.

GANGULY, JAHAR (1904-69)

Actor born in 24 Parganas Dist., Bengal. Major stage actor, dancer and singer in **Calcutta Theatres** (e.g. as Bhola Moira in *Anthony Kabial* and as Fatikchand in *Poshyaputra* (1932). Broke through in film with **Premankur Atorthy**'s *Dena Paona*. Cast in almost 1/3 of Bengali films in 40s and 50s as a character actor in comedy counterparts to the dramatic lead. A crucial mediator between the Calcutta Theatres style and popular cinema (e.g. his **Jyotish Bannerjee** and **Naresh Mitra** films). Best-remembered lead role as Manas opposite **Kanan Devi**'s Niharika in ***Manmoyee Girls' School***, a part reprised from his 1932 Art Theatres production. Also major role in ***Shahar Theke Dooray***. Continued as stage actor until the 60s.

FILMOGRAPHY: **1931**: *Geeta* (St); *Dena Paona*; **1934**: *Tulsidas*; **1935**: ***Manmoyee Girls' School***; *Mantra Shakti*; *Payer Dhulo*; *Kanthahaar*; **1936**: *Pather Sheshey*; *Kal Parinaya*; *Mahanisha*; *Bishabriksha*; **1937**: ***Talkie of Talkies***; **1938**: ***Sarbajanin Bibahotsab***; *Bekar Nashan*; *Ekalavya*; **1939**: *Janak Nandini*; *Jakher Dhan*; *Nara Narayan*; *Sharmistha*; *Vaman Avatar*; **1941**: *Kavi Joydev*; *Bijoyini*; *Pratishodh*; *Shri Radha*; *Nandini*; *Pratisruti*; *Karnarjun*; **1942**: *Nari*; *Bhishma*; ***Garmil***; *Milan*; *Bondi*; *Pashan Devata*; ***Shesh Uttar/Jawab***; **1943**: ***Shahar Theke Dooray***; *Sahadharmini*; ***Jogajog/Hospital***; *Dwanda*; *Poshya Putra*; *Nilanguriya*; *Jajsaheber Nathni*; *Paper Pathey*; *Dampati*; *Rani*; *Priya Bandhabi*; **1944**: *Matir Ghar*; *Samaj*; *Shesh Raksha*; *Chhadmabeshi*; *Sandhya*; **1945**: *Bondita*; *Kato Door*; *Do Tana*; *Path Bendhe Dilo*; ***Mane Na Mana***; *Kalankini*; *Grihalakshmi*; *Dui Purush*; *Raj Lakshmi*; **1946**: *Pather Sathi*; *Sat Number Bari*; *Ae To Jiban*; *Natun Bou*; *Bande Mataram*; *Matrihara*; *Tumi Aar Ami*; *Dukhe Jader Jiban Gara*; **1947**: *Pather Daabi*; *Abhiyatri*; *Srinkhal*; *Ratri*; *Jharer Parey*; *Mandir*; *Swapna-o-Sadhana*; *Tapobhanga*; **1948**: *Anirban*; *Bankalekha*; *Nandaranir Sansar*; *Narir Rup*; *Sadharan Meye*; *Samapika*; **1949**: *Rangamati*; *Sankalpa*; *Anuradha*; *Abhijatya*; *Abhimaan*; *Kamana*; *Mahadan*; *Niruddesh*; *Singhdwar*; **1950**: *Biresh Lahiri*; *Indranath*; *Mahasampad*; *Kankantala Light Railway*; *Eki Gramer Chhele*; *Banprastha*; *Garabini*; *Gipsy Meye*; *Mejdidi*; *Sahodar*; **1951**: *Kulhara*; ***Babla***; **1952**: *Meghmukti*; **1953**: *Sat Number Kayedi*; *Makarshar Jaal*; *Keranir Jiban*; *Harilakshmi*; *Sitar Patal Prabesh*; *Niskriti*; **1954**: *Maa-o-Chhele*; *Nababidhan*; *Naa*; *Kalyani*; *Mani-Aar-Manik*; *Sati*; *Barbela*; *Agni Pareeksha*; *Nilshari*; *Shivashakti*; *Grihapravesh*; *Mantra Shakti*; **1955**: *Nishiddha Phal*; *Devatra*; *Parishodh*; *Bidhilipi*; *Kalo Bou*; *Godhuli*; *Dui Bone*; *Mejo Bou*; *Bhagwan Shri Shri Ramakrishna*; *Bhalobasha*(?); **1956**: ***Sagarika***; *Asabarna*; *Saheb Bibi Golam*; *He Maha Manab*; *Chirakumar Sabha*; *Paradhin*; *Asamapta*; *Trijama*; *Mamlar Phal*; *Rajpath*; *Nabajanma*; *Bandhan*; *Chhaya Sangini*(?); *Asha*; **1957**: *Bara Maa*(?); *Tapasi*; *Madhu Malati*; *Ghoom*; *Baksiddha*; ***Adarsha Hindu Hotel***; *Chhaya Path*; *Parer Chheley*; *Punar Milan*; *Ogo Sunchho*; *Abhoyer Biye*; *Ami-Baro-Habo*; *Madhabir Jonye*; *Chandranath*; ***Parash Pathar***; **1958**: *Shri Shri Maa*; *Bandhu*; *Manmoyee Girls' School*; *Kangsa*; *Dak Harkara*; *Jogajog*; *O Amar Desher Mati*; *Purir Mandir*; **1959**: *Janmantar*; **1960**: *Khokha Babur Pratyabartan*; *Chhupi Chhupi Ashey*; *Gariber Meye*; *Ajana Kahini*; *Nader Nimai*; *Biyer Khata*; **1961**: *Manik*; *Raibahadur*; *Kathin Maya*; **1962**: *Bandhan*; *Nabadiganta*; **1963**: *Dui Bari*; *Barnachora*; *Sat Bhai*; ***Nirjan Saikate***; *Palatak*; *Tridhara*; *Nyayadanda*; *Uttar Falguni*; **1964**: *Jiban Kahini*; *Bireshwar Vivekananda*; *Kanta Taar*; *Natun Tirtha*; *Dui Parba*; **1965**: *Dinanter Alo*; *Raja Rammohun*; *Mukhujey Paribar*; **1966**: *Ramdhakka*; *Shesh Tin Din*; *Sudhu Ekti Bachhar*; **1967**: *Mahashweta*; **1968**: *Charan Kabi Mukundadas*; *Hansamithun*; **1969**: *Arogyaniketan*; *Pita Putra*; *Protidan*.

GANGULY, JIBAN (1905-53)

Calcutta Theatres stage star, e.g. as Lav in **Sisir Bhaduri**'s Natyamandir production of *Seeta* (1924). Lead role in the film of **Atorthy**'s novel *Chasher Meye* made a substantial impact on **New Theatres**' early style of ' following the path of literature' (B.N. Sircar, 1952; cf B. Jha, 1990). Played several literary roles, e.g. in **Sailajananda Mukherjee**'s novel *Pataal Puri* filmed by **Priyanath Ganguly** and in **Tagore**'s *Gora* filmed by **Naresh Mitra**.

FILMOGRAPHY: **1927**: *Shankaracharya*; **1930**: *Bigraha*; **1931**: *Chasher Meye*; *Abhishek*; **1932**: *Sandigdha* (all St); **1933**: *Sabitri*; **1934**: *Taruni*; **1935**: *Pataal Puri*; *Swayambara*; **1936**: *Kal Parinaya*; ***Sonar Sansar***; **1937**: *Ranga Bou*; *Muktisnan*; **1938**: ***Sarbajanin Bibahotsab***; ***Abhigyan***; *Gora*; **1939**: *Parasmani*; ***Parajay***; **1940**: *Tatinir Bichar*; *Shapmukti*; ***Thikadar***; **1941**: *Mayer Pran*; **1943**: *Paper Pathey*; **1949**: *Samarpan*; *Pratirodh*; **1950**: *Krishan*; *Panchayat*; **1951**: *Kulhara*; **1954**: *Vikram Urvashi*; *Naramedh Yagna*; *Chitrangada*.

GANGULY, PRIYANATH N. (1887-1956)

One of **Madan**'s top silent directors together with **Jyotish Bannerjee**. Started working for Madan in 1904. Directorial début with experimental comedy short *Bear-scare in the Rajah's Garden Party*. Embarked on a series of documentaries, Swadeshi Films, for Madan's Elphinstone Bioscope, made with Kumar Gupta and covering, e.g., the Prince of Wales's visit (1905), the Grand Masonic Procession (1906), etc. Started Asiatic Cinematograph Co. in Calcutta, a production and distribution concern that built two theatres in the city and shot Indian visit of George V in direct competition with the Madan unit and **Hiralal Sen** (1911). Early features at Madan included versions of Bankimchandra Chatterjee's novels (*Krishnakanter Will*, *Durgesh Nandini* and *Debi Choudhrani*). Manager of Madan's Elphinstone Picture Palace in the early 30s. Joined **East India Film** and took over Kali Films/India Film Industry (1935) where he hired **Sisir Bhaduri, Satu Sen, Sushil Majumdar**, Tulsi Lahiri and encouraged the post-***Kallol*** generation of film-makers (esp. novelist-film-maker **Sailajananda Mukherjee**, filming his novel *Pataal Puri*). Kali Films also produced the first film in Oriya, the mythological ***Seeta Bibaha*** (1934).

FILMOGRAPHY: **1926**: *Krishnakanter Will*; **1927**: *Jana*; *Durgesh Nandini*; **1928**: *Sarala*; **1929**: *Kapal Kundala*; **1930**: *Kal Parinaya*; **1931**: *Debi Choudhrani* (all St); *Prahlad*; **1933**: *Jamuna Puliney/Radha Krishna*; **1934**: *Taruni*; **1935**: *Pataal Puri*; *Bidyasundar*; **1936**: *Kal Parinaya*.

GEMINI PICTURES

Aka Gemini Studios. Best-known Madras studio in the 40s for redefining the concept of mass entertainment with ***Chandralekha*** (1948), the first Madras film to break successfully into the Hindi cinema. **S.S. Vasan** started Gemini as a distribution agency, the Gemini Pics Circuit, distributing and partly financing films by **K. Subramanyam**'s Motion Pics Producers Combine. When the Combine went bankrupt, Vasan bought the studio in 1939 at public auction for a mere Rs 86,427-11 (Annas)-9 (Paise) (according to Randor Guy). The studio's début feature was probably **Balkrishna Narayan Rao**'s *Madanakamarajan* (1941), but it only took off when cameraman-scenarist **K. Ramnoth** joined it along with his **Vauhini** partner, art-director A.K. Sekhar. This team made most of Gemini's early features: *Mangamma Sapatham* (1943), *Kannamma En Kadhali* (1945) and *Miss Malini* (1947) before the *Chandralekha* blitz catapulted it on to the national stage. In the early days, the most important event in the studio was Uday Shankar's dance extravaganza ***Kalpana*** (released 1948) which also provided training for most of Gemini's technicians. A few minor hits followed *Chandralekha* before the studio's second major onslaught on the national box office with ***Apoorva Sahodarargal*** (1949), a trilingual that established the studio's dominance in the genre of the costumed adventure movie. Although its Hindi version ***Nishan*** was not a major success, Vasan continued making Hindi films, often signing them himself: e.g. the **Dilip Kumar** and **Dev Anand** film ***Insaniyat*** (1955), **Vyjayanthimala**'s ***Raj Tilak*** (1958) and ***Paigham*** (1959) starring Dilip Kumar, Raaj Kumar and Vyjayanthimala. They also made the megabudget Tamil classic ***Avvaiyyar*** (1953). In 1958 the studio expanded into the Gemini Colour lab, licensed by Eastmancolor Kodak film. Gemini's productions declined in the 70s, although it remained successful as a studio and equipment rental business.

GENERAL PICTURES CORPORATION

First professional film studio in Madras; Est: 1929 at Tondiarpet by film-maker **A. Narayanan** after visiting Universal City in Hollywood. It was linked to a distribution-exhibition network extending into Burma and Singapore. Prominent film-makers included **R.S. Prakash, C. Pullaiah** (as cameraman) and **V.Y. Rao** (initially as actor). General Pics consolidated the pioneering work of **R. Venkaiah** and Prakash with Star of the East Film and made 18 features and a number of shorts commissioned by, e.g., the Health Department and by Imperial Chemical

Industries (*Burma Oil Company Fire, The Spirit of Agriculture*, etc.). It closed in 1933, being replaced by the Srinivasa Cinetone sound studio in 1934.

GEORGE, KULAKKATIL GEEVARGHESE (b. 1945)

Malayalam director born in Changanacherry, Kerala, into Syrian Christian family; son of a signboard painter. Graduate in political science from University of Kerala (1968). Diploma from **FTII** (1971), then for three years assistant to **Kariat**, for whom he co-wrote *Nellu* (1974). Films often use contemporary political or social issues as a pivot for thriller-like plots (e.g. ***Yavanika***). Controversial film ***Lekhayude Maranam Oru Flashback*** (*Lekha's Death* is a shorter version by c.40') faced legal controversy for allegedly exploiting the suicide of actress Shobha. Commercially successful films also enjoy a large art-house following in Kerala.

FILMOGRAPHY: **1971**: *Faces (Sh)*; *Health in the Village* (Doc); **1973**: *Manavallakurchi: My Village* (Doc); **1975**: ***Swapnadanam***; **1977**: *Vyamoham*; **1978**: *Onappudava*; *Rappadigalude Gatha*; ***Mannu***; *Ini Aval Urangatte*; **1979**: *Ulkadal*; **1980**: *Mela*; ***Kolangal***; **1982**: ***Yavanika***; **1983**: ***Lekhayude Maranam Oru Flashback***; ***Adaminte Variyellu***; **1984**: ***Panchavadippalam***; **1985**: ***Irakal***; **1987**: *Kathakku Pinnil*; **1988**: *Mattoral*; *Yathrayude Anthyam* (TV); **1990**: *Ee Kanni Koodi*.

GHAI, SUBHASH (b. 1943)

Hindi director born in Nagpur. Along with **Manmohan Desai** and **Ramesh Sippy**, one of the top producer-directors of 80s Hindi cinema. Graduated as actor from the **FTII** (1968), then actor and scenarist, collaborating with B.B. Bhalla (e.g. *Khan Dost*, 1976). Directorial début produced by N.N. Sippy. Broke through with ***Karz***. Lavish song picturisations underline his commitment to big-screen spectaculars. Claims independence from the star system but relies on it for his extravagant marketing campaigns, regularly using **Dilip Kumar**, Anil Kapoor and Jackie Shroff. Also acted in a number of films (***Aradhana***, 1969; *Umang*, 1970; *Bharat Ke Shaheed* and *Do Bachche Dus Haath*, 1972; ***Grahan***, 1972; *Dhamki*, 1973; *Natak*, 1975). Became independent producer with his own Mukta Arts (1983). His most recent feature, *Khalnayak*, attracted censorship problems because of **Madhuri Dixit**'s performance of the provocative song *Choli ke peeche*. The film also featured Sanjay Dutt who was arrested shortly before its release charged with being implicated in the bomb explosions in Bombay in March 1993.

FILMOGRAPHY: **1976**: *Kalicharan*; **1978**: *Vishwanath*; **1979**: *Gautam Govinda*; **1980**: ***Karz***; **1981**: *Krodhi*; **1982**: *Vidhata*; *Meri Jung*; **1983**: ***Hero***; **1986**: ***Karma***; **1989**: ***Ram Lakhan***; **1991**: ***Saudagar***; **1993**: *Khalnayak*.

GHANTASALA VENKATESWARA RAO (1923-74)

Telugu and Tamil composer and also singer. Legendary name in popular Telugu music who sang over 10,000 songs in his career, and composed, apparently, for over 125 films. Born in Chautapelle, Gudivada Taluk, AP, the son of a musician. Orphaned as a child. Child actor, in near slavery conditions, in plays like *Chintamani* and *Sant Sakkubai*. Apprenticed to the school of Susarlu Krishna Brahma Sastry; graduated from the music school at Vijayanagar while earning a living as an itinerant singer and beggar. Received the title of Vidwan in 1941. Was arrested and imprisoned in the Alipore jail for singing patriotic songs during Gandhi's Satyagraha agitations (1942). Went to Madras (1945); cast in small film roles, e.g. **Balaramaiah**'s *Seeta Rama Jananam* (1942) and ***Thyagayya*** (1946), while occasionally recording for AIR. Broke through in ***Swargaseema*** (1945), singing duets with **Bhanumati** to **Nagaiah**'s score. Turned composer for **L.V. Prasad**'s ***Mana Desam***. Known mainly for love duets (recently released on cassette by HMV, titled *Divyaprema*). Combined native idioms with classical Carnatic styles, e.g. in compositions for *Chiranjeevulu* and *Rahasyam*, set to the lyrics of Malladi Ramakrishna Sastry. His work in these two films was, to V.A.K. Ranga Rao, his best film work although both films flopped. Also produced *Paropakaram* (1953). Made a rare screen appearance in the hit ***Shri Venkateshwara Mahatyam*** (1960).

FILMOGRAPHY (* act only): **1949**: ***Mana Desam***; ***Keeluguram/Maya Kudhirai***; **1950**: ***Shavukaru***; *Lakshmamma*; **1951**: ***Nirdoshi/Niraparadhi***; ***Patala Bhairavi***; **1952**: ***Palletooru***; ***Pelli Chesi Choodu***; **1953**: ***Chandraharam***; *Paropakaram*; *Bratuku Theruvu*; **1955**: *Kalvanin Kadhali*; **1956**: *Chiranjeevulu*; **1957**: ***Maya Bazaar***; *Thodi Kodallu*; *Vinayaka Chaviti*; **1958**: *Manchi Manushuku Manchi Roju*; **1959**: *Shabash Ramudu*; **1960**: *Shantinivasam*; ***Shri Venkateshwara Mahatyam****; **1961**: *Raktha Sambandham*; **1962**: ***Gundamma Katha***; **1963**: *Lavakusa*; ***Veera Kesari/Bandhipotu***; *Valmiki*; *Paruvu Pratishthalu*; *Anuragham*; **1964**: *Satyanarayana Mahatyam*; **1965**: *Simhachala Kshetram*; ***Pandava Vanavasam***; *Madhuve Madi Nodu*; ***CID***; **1966**: *Paramanandayya Sishyulu Katha*; **1967**: *Peddakayya*; *Rahasyam*; *Punyavati*; *Nirdoshi*; **1968**: *Veerapooja*; *Govula Gopanna*; *Pantalu Pattimpulu*; **1969**: *Jarigina Katha*; **1970**: *Nanna Thamma*; **1971**: *Ramalayam*; **1972**: *Menakodalu*; *Vamsodharakudu*; **1973**: *Poola Mala*; **1974**: *Ammayi Pelli*; *Tulasi*; **1977**: *Sati Savitri*; *Vasthade Maa Bava*.

GHATAK, ANUPAM (1911-47)

Second-generation Bengali-Hindi composer (after **Rai Chand Boral** and **Pankaj Mullick**) born in Mymensingh (now Bangladesh). Studied music under his father Atul Ghatak and later under Keshab Ganesh Dhekan, becoming a noted flautist. Sang on radio (1930). Assisted composer Bishen Chand Boral in Hiren Bose's *Mahua* (1934) at **New Theatres**, and then Rai Chand Boral for the classic ***Bidyapati/Vidyapati*** (1937). First independent film score: *Payer Dhulo*. Later worked at **Sagar Film** in Bombay, composing **Zia Sarhadi**'s *Bhole Bhale* and a series of films for **Badami**, **Luhar** et al. (1939). Returned to Calcutta, notably for **Barua**'s *Shapmukti*; thereafter had assignments in both Calcutta and Lahore. Known for his wide range, from the sentimental *Ekti paisa dao go babu* in *Shapmukti* to the experimental *Gane more kon indradhanu* in *Agni Pareeksha*.

FILMOGRAPHY (* act only): **1934**: *Mahua**; **1935**: *Payer Dhulo*; *Bidrohi**; **1936**: ***Grihadah****; **1939**: *Bhole Bhale*; *Ladies Only*; *Sadhana*; ***Seva Samaj***; *Uski Tamanna*; **1940**: *Shapmukti*; *Civil Marriage*; **1941**: *Karnarjun*; *Mayer Pran*; **1942**: *Pashan Devata*; **1943**: *Shri Ramanuja*; **1945**: *Champa*; **1946**: *Ayi Bahar*; *Badnami*; *Khush Naseeb*; *Shalimar*; **1947**: *Aisa Kyon*; *Faisla*; **1948**: *Banjare*; **1949**: *Abhishapta*; **1950**: *Shri Tulsidas*; **1953**: *Shamsheer*; **1954**: *Kalyani*; *Agni Pareeksha*; **1955**: *Anupama*; *Devimalini*; *Paresh*; *Drishti*; **1956**: *Kirti Garh*; *Ekti Raat*; *Shankar Narayan Bank*; *Asamapta*; *Nagardola*; **1957**: *Madhabir Jonye*; *Ektara*; *Surer Parashey*; *Parer Chheley*.

GHATAK, RITWIK KUMAR (1925-76)

Bengali director born in Dhaka. Left East Bengal (now Bangladesh) in early youth when family migrated to Calcutta. Became politically active (1946) and joined the **IPTA** as playwright, director and actor (1948-54), including **Bijon Bhattacharya**'s production of *Nabanna* (1948) and his *Jwala* (1950) and *Officer* (1952). Set up Natyachakra Theatre Group, then broke away to work with **Sombhu Mitra**'s Bohurupee Group (1949). Entered film as assistant to Manoj Bhattacharya (***Tathapi***, 1950). Acted and was generally involved in the making of ***Chinnamul***, helping to transform documentary film into committed fiction cinema, an effort extended into ***Nagarik*** (1952, released in 1977). Continued street theatre work and was voted best theatre actor and director at all-India IPTA conference, Bombay (1953). Forced out of IPTA because of ideological differences and set up Group Theatre (1954) animated by his interpretation of Stanislavski's approach. Purged from CPI (1955). Joined **Filmistan** in Bombay as scenarist; scripted **Bimal Roy**'s ***Madhumati*** (1958) and collaborated with **Hrishikesh Mukherjee** on ***Musafir*** (1957). Professor of Film Direction and Vice-Principal of the **FTII** (1966-7). Wrote the play *Sei Meye* while in a mental asylum and staged it there with doctors and patients (1969). Suffered increasingly from alcoholism. Active in cine technicians' unions throughout his career.

Ritwik Ghatak in his *Jukti Takko Aar Gappo* (1974)

Authored numerous short stories, at least eight plays including Bengali adaptations of Gogol and Brecht. Among his published writings on film are *Chalachitra Manash Ebam Aro Kichhu* (1975) and *Cinema and I* (1987, the first volume of a collected works project by the Ritwik Memorial Trust). Anthologies of critical writings on Ghatak by Shampa Bannerjee (1982), Haimanti Bannerjee (1985) and Rajat Roy (1979, 1983). Also scripted *Swaralipi* (1961), *Kumari Mon* (1962), *Dwiper Nam Tiya Rang* (1963) and *Raj Kanya* (1965). Within the political framework of WW2, the 1943 famine and Partition, Ghatak launched with ***Ajantrik*** a new investigation into film form, expanding the refugee experience into a universalised leitmotiv of cultural dismemberment and exile evoking an epic tradition drawing on tribal, folk and classical forms (Buddhist sculpture, Baul music, the khayal). As a film-maker investigating cinema's image-sound dialectic in epic constructs, Ghatak has no precedents in Indian cinema but aesthetically his work can be placed alongside that of Bengali novelist Manik Bandyopadhyay (1908-56) and the teachings of his musical forbear Ustad Allauddin Khan. His influence has been most fundamental on his FTII students (1964-5), e.g. **Kumar Shahani**, **Mani Kaul** and **John Abraham**.

FILMOGRAPHY (* act only): **1950**: ***Tathapi*****; ***Chinnamul*****; **1952**: *Bedeni* (incomplete); ***Nagarik***; **1954**: *Naramedh Yagya*; **1955**: *Adivasiyon Ka Jeevan Srot* (Doc); *Bihar Ke Darshaniya Sthan* (Doc); **1957**: ***Ajantrik***; **1959**: *Bari Theke Paliye*; *Kata Ajanare* (incomplete); **1960**: ***Meghe Dhaka Tara***; **1961**: ***Komal Gandhar***; **1962**: ***Subarnarekha***; *Scissors* (Sh); **1963**: *Ustad Allauddin Khan* (Doc) (uncredited); **1964**: *Bagalar Bangadarshan* (incomplete); **1965**: *Fear* (Sh); *Rendezvous* (Sh); **1967**: *Scientists of Tomorrow* (Doc); **1968**: *Raunger Gholam* (incomplete); **1970**: *Puruliar Chhou Nritya* (Doc); *Amar Lenin* (Sh); *Yeh Kyun?* (Sh); **1971**: *Durbargati Padma* (Sh); **1972**: *Indira Gandhi* (Doc) (incomplete); **1973**: ***Titash Ekti Nadir Naam***; **1974**: ***Jukti Takko Aar Gappo***; **1975**: *Ramkinker* (Doc) (incomplete).

GHOSH, GAUTAM (b. 1950)

Bengali director born in Faridpur, East Bengal (now Bangladesh). Father was a professor of English literature. Active in student politics in Calcutta. Freelance journalist and fringe theatre director. Made early documentaries as extension of his photojournalism. Influenced in this early practice by documentarist **Sukhdev**, who inspired him to do his own screenplays, camerawork, music and editing (in his early films). First feature, ***Maabhoomi***, based on the Telangana uprising of 1941, imbues fiction with semi-documentary mode influenced by Solanas/Getino films of the 60s and by the folk Burrakatha form. Later moved to more conventional forms. Often places his stories in conditions of extreme social marginality, presented through his actors as physical, primitive and elemental battles of survival (***Dakhal***, ***Paar***). Worked with the writings of Bengali novelist Kamal Kumar Majumdar (e.g. ***Antarjali Jatra***). Most recent film ***Padma Nadir Majhi*** is an ambitious and expensive Indo-Bangladesh co-production adapting a classic novel by Manik Bandyopadhyay. Also directed a tv series adapting famous Bengali short stories (1986).

FILMOGRAPHY: **1973**: *New Earth* (Doc); **1976**: ***Hungry Autumn*** (Doc); *Chains of Bondage* (Doc); **1979**: ***Maabhoomi***; **1981**: ***Dakhal***; *Development in Irrigation* (Doc); **1984**: ***Paar***; **1985**: *Parampara* (Doc); **1986**: *The Land of Sand Dunes* (Doc); *A Tribute to Odissi* (Doc); **1987**: *Ek Ghat Ki Kahani* (Doc); ***Antarjali Jatra/Mahayatra***; **1989**: *Sange Meel Se Mulaqat* (Doc); **1990**: *Mohor* (Doc); **1991**: *The Bird of Time* (Doc); **1992**: ***Padma Nadir Majhi***; **1993**: *Patang*.

GHOSH, KALIPRASAD (b. 1889)

Bengali director educated at Calcutta University. Started as theatre director with **Calcutta Theatres**' Minerva Company. Established **Indian Kinema Arts** (1927) with Minerva proprietor Ghanshyamdas Chokhani. Joined **East India Film** in 1932 and Bombay's **Sagar** Movietone in 1934 before returning to Calcutta (1936).

FILMOGRAPHY: **1927**: *Shankaracharya*; **1928**: *Nishiddha Phal*; **1929**: *Apahrita*; **1930**: *Kanthahaar*; **1932**: *Bhagya Lakshmi* (all St); **1934**: ***Shaher Ka Jadoo***; **1936**: ***Lagna Bandhan***; **1943**: *Jajsaheber Nathni*; **1948**: *Dhatri Debata*; **1950**: *Vidyasagar*; **1952**: *Kar Papey*; **1955**: *Rani Rashmoni*; **1958**: *Shri Shri Maa*.

GHOSH, NACHIKETA (1924-76)

Bengali and Hindi composer. A doctor by training; also known as an accomplished tabla player. Trained in music by Anathnath Basu and Latafat Hussain. Worked briefly in radio. His compositions recall **Hemanta Mukherjee**'s work in defining a typically post-Independence ' adhunik' (modern/contemporary) popular idiom characterised by eclecticism and its sentimental address to an urban middle class. Popular compositions in *Joydev* and in 70s films like *Bilambita Lay*, *Nishipadma*, *Dhanyi Meye* and *Stree*. Also set nursery rhymes to music which remained popular.

FILMOGRAPHY: **1953**: *Boudir Bone*; **1954**: *Joydev*; **1955**: *Nishiddha Phal*; *Pather Sheshey*; *Jharer Parey*; *Bhalobasha*; *Ardhangini*; **1956**: *Trijama*; *Nabajanma*; **1957**: *Tapasi*; *Prithibi Amar Chai*; *Harishchandra*; *Natun Prabhat*; *Rastar Chhele*; **1958**: *Bandhu*; *Bhanu Pelo Lottery*; *Indrani*; *Rajdhani Theke*; *Jonakir Alo*; **1959**: *Chaowa-Pawa*; *Swapna Puri*; *Derso Khokhar Kando*; *Kichhukshan*; *Nirdharita Silpir Anupastithi Tey*; *Personal Assistant*; **1960**: *Akash-patal*; *Haat Baraley Bandhu*; *Khudha*; *Biyer Khata*; **1961**: *Kanamachi*; **1964**: *Kanta Taar*; **1968**: *Chhoto Jignasa*; *Rakta Rekha*; **1969**: *Chiradiner*; *Shesh Theke Shuru*; **1970**: *Nishipadma*; *Bilambita Lay*; **1971**: *Fariyad*; *Dhanyi Meye*; **1972**: *Chinnapatra*; *Natun Diner Alo*; *Stree*; *Sabari*; **1973**: *Agni Bhramar*; ***Bon Palashir Padabali***; *Nakal Sona*; *Nani Gopaler Biye*; *Shravan Sandhya*; **1974**: *Alor Thikana*; *Asati*; *Sujata*; *Mouchak*; **1975**: *Chhutir Phande*; *Kajal Lata*; *Nagar Darpane*; *Priya Bandhabi*; *Sanyasi Raja*; *Swayamsiddha*; *Sei Chokh*; **1976**: *Mom Batti*; *Ananda Mela*; *Hotel Snow Fox*; **1976**: *Asadharan*; **1977**: *Brajabuli*; **1984**: *Abhishek*.

GHOSH, NEMAI (1914-88)

Bengali and Tamil director/cameraman. Born in Calcutta. Assistant to Bibhuti Das at the **Aurora** Studio (1932); resigned following a trade union dispute. For several years involved with a cine-technicians' union. Member of the Calcutta Film Society from the outset (1943) and was considered by **Ray** as his first-choice cameraman for ***Pather Panchali*** (1955). Member of the **IPTA**, acting in its seminal play *Nabanna*. First film: ***Chinnamul***, a classic of IPTA-inspired socialist realism, admiringly reviewed by Pudovkin in *Pravda* (1951). Moved to Madras (1951) where he worked as cameraman on Tamil and Kannada films, e.g. **G.V. Iyer**'s ***Hamsa Geethe*** (1975). Key member of a Marxist collective, the Kumari Films Co-op, which produced ***Padhai Theriyudu Paar***. Also made documentaries, e.g. *Light and Candle* and *Mysore University*. Vice-President of the Federation of Film Societies for several years and a **Naxalite** sympathiser in the 70s.

FILMOGRAPHY: **1950**: ***Chinnamul***; **1960**: ***Padhai Theriyudu Paar***; **1981**: *Sooravalli*.

GHOSH, PARBATI (b. 1944)

Oriya actress and director. Started as actress aged 6. Known mainly as producer, with husband Gaura Ghosh, producing seminal films in the early history of the Oriya cinema, e.g. *Bhai Bhai* (1956); *Lakhmi* (1962); ***Kaa*** (1966). Turned to direction with *Sansar* (with her husband), and then adapted Fakir Mohan Senapati's classic 19th C. novel, *Chamana Atha Guntha* for directorial comeback.

FILMOGRAPHY: **1971**: *Sansar*; **1986**: *Chamana Atha Guntha*.

GHOSH, ROBI (b. 1931)

Major Bengali comedian. Best known in the role of Bagha in **Satyajit Ray**'s fantasy, ***Goopy Gyne Bagha Byne***, repeating the character in ***Hirak Rajar Deshe*** and in Sandeep Ray's sequel *Goopy Bagha Phere Elo*. Stage actor with **Utpal Dutt**'s Little Theatre Group (1953-60), e.g. *Chhayanat* and *Angar*. 60s films continued in the line of Bengali film comedians (e.g. Tinkari Chakraborty, Indu Mukherjee, **Amar Mullick**, etc.). Ghosh regarded **Tulsi Chakraborty**, along with Harold Lloyd and Harry Langdon, as his main influence. Also acted in other Ray films (***Abhijaan***, ***Mahapurush***, ***Aranyer Din Ratri***, ***Jana Aranya***), for **Tapan Sinha** (***Apanjan***, *Sabuj Dwiper Raja*) and **Mrinal Sen** (*Abasheshe*, ***Chorus***). Also acted in almost all **Dinen Gupta** films between 1972-85. His small body, mobile face and extraordinary timing was acclaimed by his stage mentor, Utpal Dutt, for its Brechtian ability to slip in and out of the characters and stereotypes (used subversively in the role of Mr Mitter in *Jana Aranya*). Ghosh regards the comedian as uniquely able to communicate with diverse audiences, having assimilated both the boisterous folk comedy and the urbane comedy of manners. Ran the amateur stage group, Chalachal, which closed in 1970. Returned to the professional stage with, e.g., *Bibar* (1973), *Shrimati Bhayankari* (1980), *Kane Bibhrat* (1983) and *Sabash Peto Panchu* (1988). Also directed two films, one (1974) under the pseudonym Ekalavya.

FILMOGRAPHY (* also d): **1959**: *Kichhukshan*; **1961**: *Megh*; **1962**: ***Hansuli Banker Upakatha***; ***Abhijaan***; *Agun*; *Abasheshe*; **1963**: ***Nirjan Saikate***; *Palatak*; *Shesh Prahar*; *Chhaya Surya*; *Binimoy*; *Nyayadanda*; **1964**: *Saptarshi*; *Kashtipathar*; *Natun Tirtha*; *Momer Alo*; *Lal Patthar*; *Subah-o-Debatargrash*; ***Mahapurush***; **1965**: *Ek Tuku Basa*; *Surer Agun*; *Kal Tumi Aleya*; **1966**: *Dolgobinder Karcha*; *Galpa Holeo Satti*; *Griha Sandhaney*; *Manihar*; *Swapnaniye*; *Uttar Purush*; **1967**: *Ashite Ashio Na*; **1968**: ***Apanjan***; *Baghini*; *Baluchari*; *Hansa Mithun*; *Panchasar*; ***Goopy Gyne Bagha Byne***; **1969**: *Arogyaniketan*; *Bibaha Bibhrat*; ***Teen Bhubhaner Parey***; ***Satyakam***; ***Aranyer Din Ratri***; *Teer Bhoomi*; **1970**: *Sheela*; *Ae Korechho Bhalo*; *Rupasi*; **1971**: *Dhanyi Meye*; *Kuheli*; *Pratibad*; **1972**: *Ajker Nayak*; *Chhayatir*; ***Padi Pishir Barmi Baksha***; *Shesh Parba*; *Basanta Bilap*; *Chitthi*; *Marjina Abdallah*; *Shriman Prithviraj*; *Alo Amar Alo*; *Maa-o-Mati*; *Subse Bada Sukh*; ***Calcutta '71***; **1973**: *Megher Pare Megh*; *Achena Atithi*; *Daabi*; *Pranta Rekha*; **1974**: *Sadhu Judhishthirer Karcha**; *Bikele Bhorer Phool*; ***Chorus***; ***Jadu Bansha***; *Phuleshwari*; *Rakta Tilak*; *Sangini*; *Thagini*; *Chhutir Phande*; *Mouchak*; *Premer Phande*; **1975**: *Raag Anuraag*; ***Sansar Simantey***; *Salaam Memsaab*; ***Jana Aranya***; *Mohan Baganer Meye*; *Sudur Niharika*; *Harano Prapti Niruddesh*; **1976**: *Nidhi Ram Sardar**; *Ek Je Chhilo Desh*; *Ananda Mela*; *Dampati*; *Era-Ek-Jug*; *Jatayu*; *Samrat*; *Sankhabish*; **1977**: *Abirvab*; *Brajabuli*; *Mantramugdha*; *Pratima*; *Proxy*; *Bar Bodhu*; **1978**: *Nadi Theke Sagare*; ***Ganadevata***; *Lattu*; *Charmurti*; *Tilottama*; **1979**: ***Jhor***; *Chirantan*; *Nauka Dubi*; *Ghatkali*; *Sabuj Dwiper Raja*; *Samadhan*; **1980**: *Bandhan*; ***Bancharamer Bagan***; *Ae To Sansar*; *Gopal Bhanar*; ***Hirak Rajar Deshe***; *Paka Dekha*; *Priyatama*; *Batasi*; **1981**: *Baisakhi Megh*; *Kalankini*; *Pahari Phool*; *Satma*; *Subarna Golak*; *Meghmukti*; *Shahar Theke Dooray*; *Swami Stri*; *Sonay Suhaga*; **1982**: *Malancha*; *Matir Swarga*; *Simanta Raag*; **1983**: *Aparoopa*; *Ae Chhilo Mone*; *Amar Geeti*; *Din Jay*; *Indira*; *Jay Parajay*; *Jiban Maran*; *Robi Shom*; *Kauke Bolo Na*; *Aloye Phera*; *Samarpita*; *Srinkhal*; **1984**: *Prarthana*; *Rashifal*; *Shorgol*; *Uncle*; *Vasundhara*; *Inquilab Ke Baad*; **1985**: *Abasheshe*; *Hulusthul*; *Kenaram Becharam*; *Pratigya*; *Tagori*; **1986**: *Abhishap*; **1987**: *Aaj Ka Robin Hood*; *Bidrohi*; ***Antarjali Jatra/Mahayatra***; *Raj Purush*; *Samrat-o-Sundari*; *Amor Sangi*; **1988**: *Agni Sanket*; *Koroti*; **1989**: *Amar Tumi*; **1991**: *Goopy Bagha Phere Elo*; ***Agantuk***; **1992**: ***Padma Nadir Majhi***.

GIDWANI, MOTI B. (b. 1905)

Hindi director born in Karachi. Studied film-making in Britain (1926-7) and returned to make his first feature, which failed and helped close down **Maharashtra Film**. Went on to direct for **Imperial** and **Sagar** and made a name as a ' safe' freelance director. Evidence suggests he co-operated with **Irani** on making of ***Alam Ara*** (1931). Major successes in collaboration with **Dalsukh Pancholi**: the Punjabi film *Yamla Jat*, the musical thriller ***Khazanchi*** that lifted Lahore's local film industry into national prominence, and ***Zamindar***. His ***Kisan Kanya*** was India's first colour production using Cinecolour process (*Sairandhri*, 1933, was processed in Germany).

FILMOGRAPHY: **1929**: *Nisha Sundari*; **1930**: *Bachha-i-Sakka*; *Veer Na Ver*; *Dav Pech*; **1931**: *Gulam* (all St); *Anangsena*; **1932**: *Niti Vijay*; **1933**: *Daku Ki Ladki*; *Insaan Ya Shaitan*; **1934**: *Manjari*; *Noor Mahal*; **1936**: *Gulam Daku*; **1937**: ***Kisan Kanya***; *Do Auratein*; **1940**: *Yamla Jat*; **1941**: ***Khazanchi***; **1942**: ***Zamindar***; **1945**: *Kaise Kahun*; **1946**: *Khamosh Nigahen*.

GOHAR, KAYOUM MAMAJIWALA (1910-85)

Mainly silent Hindi actress often billed as the Glorious Gohar. Born in Lahore. Daughter of actress; started on the stage as a child. Major star at **Kohinoor**. Left with **Chandulal Shah** to form Jagdish Film and then **Ranjit**. Her first hit was **Homi Master**'s ***Lanka Ni Laadi***. Acted in several Master films in roles especially scripted for her by **Mohanlal Dave** with strong roots in popular Gujarati serial novels. Shah later used her screen persona for his famous satires on Gujarat's urban business communities in Gohar's best-known silents, *Typist Girl*/*Why I Became a Christian* and ***Gunsundari/Why Husbands Go Astray***. Some later films, esp. those alongside **Raja Sandow**, developed mythological associations, e.g. **Betaab**'s scripts (***Sati Savitri***, *Vishwamohini*). Other films, in which she plays the upper-class socialite opposite the suave heroics of the brothers **Bilimoria** (*Toofani Taruni*, ***Barrister's Wife***) were important items in Ranjit's popular film-novelettes.

FILMOGRAPHY: **1925**: ***Baap Kamai***; *Ghar Jamai*; ***Lanka Ni Laadi***; **1926**: *Briefless Barrister*; *Lakho Vanjaro*; *Mumtaz Mahal*; *Prithvi Putra*; *Ra Kawat*; *Samrat Shiladitya*; *Sati Jasma*; *Shirin Farhad*; ***The Telephone Girl***; *Delhi No Thug*; *Typist Girl*; *Mena Kumari*; **1927**: ***Bhaneli Bhamini***; ***Gunsundari***; *Sati Madri*; *Sindh Ni Sumari*; **1928**: *Grihalakshmi*; *Vishwamohini*; **1929**: *Bhikharan*; *Chandramukhi*; *Pati Patni*; *Rajputani*; **1930**: *Pahadi Kanya*; *Raj Lakshmi*; *Diwani Dilbar* (all St); **1931**: ***Devi Devayani***; **1932**: ***Radha Rani***; ***Sati Savitri***; *Sheilbala*; **1933**: ***Miss 1933***; *Vishwamohini*; **1934**: *Mera Imaan*; *Tara Sundari*; *Toofani Taruni*; ***Gunsundari***; **1935**: ***Barrister's Wife***; ***Desh Dasi***; ***Keemti Aansoo***; **1936**: ***Prabhu Ka Pyara***; ***Sipahi Ki Sajni/Sipahini Sajni***; *Raj Ramani*; **1937**: *Pardesi Pankhi*; **1940**: ***Achhut***; **1948**: *Nadiya Ke Paar*.

GOPALAKRISHNAN, ADOOR (b. 1941)

Malayalam director born in Adoor, Kerala, in family of patrons of Kathakali theatre. Stage début as actor aged 8. Graduated from Gandhigram Rural University (1960) having produced over 20 plays, including ones he wrote himself. Resigned from government job and graduated from the **FTII** (1965). Founder and president of the Chitralekha Film Co-op in Trivandrum (1965), the first of its kind in India, set up by FTII graduates as a production-distribution centre for personal films outside the commercial sector. In the mid-70s, a laboratory was added to the Trivandrum studio. Writes his own scripts, two of which (***Elippathayam*** and ***Mukha Mukham***) were published in English by Seagull Books in Calcutta (1985). Films show an emphasis on psychology depicted through gesture, making him the only Indian film-maker to adhere consistently to S. Ray's norms. Theorised his approach in *Cinemayude Lokam* (1983). The reformist dimension of his work achieves an extra edge given the relative absence of that tradition in Travancore's literature. Travancore's delayed entry into the nationalist mainstream and its sudden transformation from a feudal state ruled by Dewan C.P. Ramaswamy Aiyer into one run by a CPI government, created a break in Kerala's history which animates his films: e.g. his portrayal of the Nair community of former rent collectors in *Elippathayam* and of the Communist movement itself in *Mukha Mukham* and ***Mathilukal***.

FILMOGRAPHY: **1965**: *A Great Day* (Sh); **1968**: *And Man Created* (Doc); *Danger At Your Doorstep* (Doc); **1969**: *Towards National STD* (Doc); **1972**: ***Swayamvaram***; **1974**: *Guru Chengannur* (Doc); **1975**: *Past in Perspective* (Doc); **1977**: *The Myth* (Doc); ***Kodiyettam***; **1979**: *Yakshagana* (Doc); **1980**: *The Chola Heritage* (Doc); **1981**: ***Elippathayam***; **1982**: *Krishnattam* (Doc); **1984**: ***Mukha Mukham***; **1987**: ***Anantaram***; **1989**: ***Mathilukal***; **1993**: *Vidheyan*.

GOPALA KRISHNAN, K. S.

Tamil director. Originally a playwright, joined films when he scripted **Bhimsingh**'s *Padikkatha Methai* (1960) and later **Krishnan-Panju**'s *Annai* (1962). Commercially successful middle-budget director in 60s/70s Tamil cinema, initially making theatrical melodramas (début feature, *Sharada*, is about a man with sexual problems) often set in proscenium-like interiors. Shifted to mythologicals with the hit *Adi Parasakthi* after **A.P. Nagarajan** revived the genre. *Adi Parasakthi* is sometimes seen as the first mythological hit to revive the famous ' little' tradition of 50s Tamil cinema: films featuring local deities rather than stories from pan-Indian epics. Launched his own studio after the success of *Karpagam*, naming it after the film. He is not to be confused either with an earlier Tamil director who worked at the **Gemini** Studios in the 40s, or with the more recent Malayalam director with the same name.

FILMOGRAPHY: **1962**: *Sharada*; *Daivathin Daivam*; **1963**: *Karpagam*; **1964**: *Ayiram Roopai*; *Kaikodutha Daivam*; *Suhagan*; **1965**: *Rishte Naate*; **1966**: *Chinnachiru Ulagam*; ***Chitthi***; *Selvam*; **1967**: *Kan Kanda Daivam*; *Pesum Daivam*; **1968**: *Panama Pasama*; *Uyira Manama*; **1969**: *Kulavilakku*; **1970**: *Malathi*; *Tapalkaran Thangai*; **1971**: *Adi Parasakthi*; *Kulama Kunama*; **1972**: *Kurathi Magan*; *Vazhai Yadi Vazhai*; **1973**: *Nathayil Muthu*; *Vandhale Magarasi*; **1974**: *Swathi Nakshatram*; **1976**: *Dashavatharam*; *Vayilla Poochi*; **1977**: *Palabhisekham*; *Punniyam Seithaval*; *Rowdy Rakkamma*; **1978**: *Shri Kanchi Kamakshi*; *Ullathil Kuzhanthayadi*; **1979**: *Adukku Malli*; **1980**: *Nandri Kalangal*; *Neer Nilam Neruppu*; **1981**: *Magarantham*; **1982**: *Daiviyin Thiruvilaiyadal*; *Nayakarin Magal*; **1983**: *Yuga Dharmam*; **1985**: *Padikkatha Panayar*; **1986**: *Mahashakti Mariamman*; **1988**: *Parthal Pasu*; **1989**: *Athaimadi Methaiyadi*; **1992**: *Kaviyath Thalaivan*.

GOPI (b. 1937)

Aka Bharath Gopi. Malayalam actor and more recently director, born in Chirayankil near Trivandrum. Full name: V. Gopinathan Nair. Known mainly as stage actor before joining films. Discovered by noted playwright and director of the Trichur School of Drama, G. Shankara Pillai; then lead actor of the Prasadhana Little Theatre. Achieved a major reputation on the stage, before **Adoor Gopalakrishnan** cast him in ***Swayamvaram*** and ***Kodiyettam***, in folk-dominated plays of Kavalam Narayana Panicker's Thiruvarung (e.g. *Avanevan Kadamba*). His theatrical experience of stylised choreography, Kalaripayattu-derived footwork, complex incantatory speech and folk percussion patterns, provided him with unique skills to internalise the rhythm of a shot (cf the raising of the circus tent scene in ***Thampu***, or the tea-stall scene in **Mani Kaul**'s ***Satah Se Uthata Admi***). Played several straight dramatic roles, e.g. as the government co-ordinator Mamachen in **George**'s ***Adaminte Variyellu***, the drunk in *Neram Pularumbol* and the corrupt trade union leader in **Nihalani**'s *Aaghat*. Suffered a partial paralysis in the late 80s forcing him to abandon his acting career. He turned to direction having débuted earlier with *Njattadi*, a jaundiced view of Leftist activists deploring the blind adventurism besetting the movement. Recently also worked as a theatre director (e.g. Kavalam Narayana Panicker's *Thirumudi*).

FILMOGRAPHY (* d only): **1972**: ***Swayamvaram***; **1974**: *Thumbolarcha*; **1976**: *Choondakari*; **1977**: ***Kodiyettam***; **1978**: *Aaru Manikkur*; ***Thampu***; **1979**: ***Peruvazhiyampalam***; *Njattadi* (also d); **1980**: ***Satah Se Uthata Admi***; ***Greeshamam***; **1981**: *Kallan Pavithran*; **1982**: ***Ormakkayi***; ***Yavanika***; ***Marmaram***; **1983**: ***Adaminte Variyellu***; ***Akkare***; *Asthram*; ***Lekhayude Maranam Oru Flashback***; *Nizhal Moodia Nirangal*; ***Rachana***; *Ashtapadi*; ***Kattathe Kilikoodu***; ***Ente Mamattukuttiamma***; *Sandhya Mayungam Neram*; **1984**: *Aduthaduthu*; *Appunni*; ***April 18***; *Arorumariyathe*; *Oru Painkillikatha*; ***Panchavadippalam***; *Swantham Sarika*; **1985**: ***Chidambaram***; *Aaghat*; *Archana Aradhana*; *Kanathaya Pennkutty*; *Karimbin Poovinakkare*; *Kayyum Thalayum Purathidaruthu*; *Neram Pularumbol*; *Onathumbikorunjai*; *Punnaram Cholli Cholli*; *Scene No. 7*; ***Irakal***; ***Meenamasathile Sooryan***; **1986**: *Nilavinte Nattil*; **1989**: *Ulsavapittennu**; **1991**: *Yamanam**; **1994**: *Swaham*.

GOPICHAND, TRIPURANENI (1910-62)

Telugu director born in Telangana, AP. Wrote c.300 Telugu short stories, two major novels (*Parivartana*, 1942; *Asamarthuni Jiva Yatra*, 1945) and essays on political theory, e.g. *Marxism Ante Emiti?* (1954). Was briefly the Secretary of the Andhra Radical Democratic Party (1954). Arguments for ideology of rational reformism were presented in his literary column ' Ubhaya Kushalopari' for **Ramabrahmam**'s journal *Prajamitra*. Wrote scripts for **L.V. Prasad**, **P. Pullaiah** and **Adurthi Subba Rao**. First film as director, *Lakshmamma*, made in direct competition to a **Balaramaiah** film on a satirical Telugu folk story. Made only two more films, both based on his own literary fiction.

FILMOGRAPHY: **1950**: *Lakshmamma*; **1951**: *Perantalu*; **1952**: *Priyuralu*.

Gopi in *Kodiyettam* (1977)

GULZAR, SAMPOORAN SINGH (b. 1936)

Mainstream Hindi-Urdu director and writer born in Deena, Jhelum Dist. (now Pakistan). Started as a poet associated with the **PWA**; became **Bimal Roy**'s lyricist (*Mora gora ang lai* in ***Bandini***, 1963), then his full-time assistant. Wrote scripts and lyrics for several film-makers (**Hrishikesh Mukherjee**, **Asit Sen**, **Basu Chatterjee**, **Buddhadev Dasgupta**, **Kumar Shahani** etc). First film: ***Mere Apne***, a remake of **Tapan Sinha**'s ***Apanjan*** (1968). Though himself an Urdu writer, claims strong influence of Bengali literature. Made one film based on a Saratchandra Chatterjee novel (*Khushboo*) and two on Samaresh Basu's writing (*Kitaab*, *Namkeen*). Finished **S. Sukhdev**'s last film, *Sahira*. He describes his cinema as a ' study of human beings ... interesting human relationships in different aspects, different situations' (Vasudev and Lenglet, 1983). Has published three anthologies of poetry (*Janam*, *Ek Boond Chand*, *Kuch Aur Nazme*) and several books for children including verse tales from the Panchtantra in Hindi. Writes his own scripts and prolific dialogue writer as well as lyricist (e.g. ***Ashirwad***, 1968; ***Khamoshi***, 1969; *Safar*, 1970; *Gharonda* and *Khatta Meetha*, both 1977; ***Masoom***, 1982).

FILMOGRAPHY: **1971**: ***Mere Apne***; **1972**: ***Koshish***; ***Parichay***; **1973**: *Achanak*; **1975**: *Khushboo*; ***Mausam***; ***Aandhi***; **1977**: *Kinara*; *Kitaab*; **1979**: *Meera*; **1980**: *Sahira*; **1981**: *Angoor*; **1982**: *Namkeen*; **1984**: *Suniye/Aika* (Sh); **1985**: *Ek Akar* (Doc); **1987**: *Ijaazat*; **1988**: *Mirza Ghalib* (TV); *Libaas*; **1990**: ***Lekin ...***; *Ustad Amjad Ali Khan* (Doc); **1992**: *Pandit Bhimsen Joshi* (Doc).

Gummadi *see* **Venkateshwara Rao, Gummadi**

GUPTA, DINEN (b. 1932)

Bengali director and cameraman born in Calcutta into a family in the film business. Member of the 50s generation of Calcutta cineastes (**Ghatak**, **Sen** et al.) influenced by the **IPTA**, the Calcutta Film Society (Est: 1941) and Italian neo-realism (screened in India at the International Film Festival in 1952). Early work as assistant to cameraman Ramananda Sengupta: shot some of Ghatak's early films (e.g. ***Ajantrik***, 1957; *Bari Theke Paliye*, 1959), **Tarafdar**'s ***Ganga*** (1960) and **Harisadhan Dasgupta**'s work. Directorial début with ***Natun Pata*** locates him, somewhat belatedly, in the post-***Pather Panchali*** (1955) tradition of rustic lyricism. *Pratham Pratisruti* was based on Ashapurna Devi's famous novel. *Ajker Nayak* belonged to the ' lumpen rebel' genre that emerged in 70s Bengali cinema after the **Naxalite** uprising, but it stuck closer to, e.g., **Sinha**'s version of events rather than the better-known M. Sen iconography. Later made some comic melodramas (e.g. *Basanta Bilap*, *Raag Anuraag*, etc.). Shoots his own films as well as those of other film-makers.

FILMOGRAPHY: **1969**: *Banajyotsna*; ***Natun Pata***; **1971**: *Pratham Pratisruti*; **1972**: *Ajker Nayak*; *Basanta Bilap*; *Marjina Abdallah*; **1973**: *Pranta Rekha*; **1974**: *Debi Choudhrani*; *Sangini*; **1975**: *Raag Anuraag*; *Nishi Mrigaya*; **1977**: *Rajani*; *Sanai*; *Proxy*; **1978**: *Tilottama*; **1979**: *Srikanter Will*; **1980**: *Priyatama*; **1981**:

Kalankini; **1982**: *Sathe Satyam*; *Jwain Pua*; **1983**: *Indira*; *Sagar Balaka*; **1984**: *Rashifal*; **1985**: *Abasheshe*; **1987**: *Mahamilan*; *Sargam*; **1988**: *Antaranga*; **1990**: *Bakulbasar* (TV); *Tero Sandhyar Galpo* (TV); **1991**: *Kato Bhalobasha*.

GUPTA, HEMEN (1914-67)

Bengali-Hindi director born in Rajasthan. Degree in literature from Calcutta University. Private secretary of Subhashchandra Bose; full-time radical activist in 1930-2 Civil Disobedience movement and in terrorism around Midnapore Dist., Bengal. Arrested, jailed (1932-8) and allegedly sentenced to death. This period is commemorated in two of his best-known films, ***Bhuli Naai*** and ***'42***. His film project on the Bengal famine (1945) was banned by the British government. Moved to Bombay in 1951 and made several Hindi films for **Filmistan** and for **Bimal Roy**, e.g. the classic adaptation of **Tagore**'s ***Kabuliwala***. His *Insaaf Kahan Hai* was never released. *Raj Kamal* was left incomplete (1957), as was his last film, *Anamika* (1967).

FILMOGRAPHY: **1943**: *Dwanda*; **1944**: *Takraar*; **1947**: *Abhiyatri*; **1948**: ***Bhuli Naai***; **1949**: ***'42***; **1952**: ***Anandmath***; **1954**: *Kashti*; *Meenar*; **1956**: ***Taksaal***; **1959**: *Insaaf Kahan Hai*; **1960**: *Babar*; **1961**: ***Kabuliwala***; **1966**: *Netaji Subhashchandra Bose*.

HAIDER, GHULAM (1908-53)

Music composer born in Hyderabad (Sind, Pakistan). Studied dentistry. Leading composer from the Lahore group with e.g. Shyam Sundar, Khurshid Anwar and S.D. Batish. With **Naushad** initiated a musical revolution helping to institutionalise an **All-India Film** aesthetic in the 40s. Learnt music from Babu Ganeshlal, with whom he worked in theatre playing harmonium in Calcutta. Briefly composer for the Jenaphone recording label. Broke into films in Lahore with directors **Shorey** and **Kardar**; then worked for **Pancholi** starting with the Punjabi film *Gul-e-Bakavali* featuring **Nurjehan** as a child actress. Regular composer for Pancholi until *Poonji*. His score for ***Khazanchi*** led to a series of Pancholi hits pioneering new marketing strategies. Best-known compositions, often sung by Shamshad Begum, invoke Punjabi folk rhythms and extensively feature percussion instruments like the dholak. Moved to Bombay in 1944 where he worked in **Filmistan** (***Chal Chal Re Naujawan***) and **Minerva**. Composed one successful **Mehboob** film (***Humayun***) and gave **Lata Mangeshkar** her first big break in playback singing (*Majboor*, in duets with **Geeta Dutt** and Mukesh). Returned to Lahore after Partition, where he started Filmsaz with director S. Nazir Ajmeri and actor S. Gul, making *Beqaraar*. Also scored *Akeli*, *Bheegi Palkein* and the two Nurjehan films *Gulenar* (1953) and *Laila*.

FILMOGRAPHY: **1934**: *Thief of Iraq*; **1935**: *Majnu 1935*; *Swarg Ki Sidhi*; **1939**: *Gul-e-Bakavali*; **1940**: *Yamla Jat*; **1941**: *Choudhury*; ***Khazanchi***; **1942**: ***Khandaan***; ***Zamindar***; **1943**: *Poonji*; **1944**: *Bhai*; ***Chal Chal Re Naujawan***; ***Phool***; **1945**: ***Humayun***; **1946**: *Behram Khan*; *Jag Biti*; *Shama*; **1947**: *But Tarash*; *Manjdhar*; *Mehndi*; **1948**: *Barsaat Ki Ek Raat*; *Majboor*; *Padmini*; *Patjhad*; *Shaheed*; **1949**: ***Kaneez***; **1950**: *Do Saudagar*; *Putli*; **1953**: *Aabshar*. Haldar, Krishna *see* **Atorthy, Premankur**

HAMSALEKHA (b. 1951)

Star Kannada music composer; also in Tamil and Telugu films. Born in Bangalore. Former stage actor; writer and director with his own theatre company, Viveka Ranga. Film career as scenarist, dialogue writer and composer (1986). Broke through with second film, Ravichandran's rock musical, ***Premaloka***. Was part of the Kannada film boom in the late 80s. Scored c.100 films in six years. Mostly writes the dialogues and the lyrics for his Kannada films.

FILMOGRAPHY (* also lyr): **1986**: *Henne Ninagenu Bandhana**; **1987**: ***Premaloka****; *Mr Raja**; *Antima Theerpu**; *Digvijaya**; *Bedi**; *Sangrama**; *Daiva Shakti**; **1988**: *Avale Nanna Hendthi**; *Ranadheera**; *Prema Tapaswi**; *Vijaya Khadga*; *SP Sangliana**; *Matrudevobhava*; *Anjada Gandu**; *Balondu Bhavageethe**; *Jadiketha Moodi*; *Ranaranga**; *Dharmapatni*; *Pelli Chesi Choodu*; *Kodiparakkuthu*; *Pudhiya Vanam*; *Kirataka**; **1989**: *Mutyamanta Muddu*; *Anantana Avanthara*; *Yuddhakanda**; *Idhu Ungal Kudumbam*; *Avane Nanna Ganda**; *Amanusha**; *Yuga Purusha**; *Sura Sundaranga**; *Indrajit**; *Arthanadam*; *CID Shankar**; *Kindara Jogi**; *Singari Bangari*; *Onti Salaga**; *Neram Nadhi Kadhu*; *Agni*; *Narasimha**; *Parashurama**; *Poli Huduga**; *Premagni**; **1990**: *Kaliyuga Abhimanyudu*; *Nammoora Hemmira**; *SP Sangliana II**; *Kempu Gulabi**; *Trinetra**; *Avesha**; *Velai Kidaichiruchu*; *Bannada Gejje**; *Prema Yuddham*; *Hosa Jeevana**; ***Muthina Hara****; *Sididedda Gandu**; *Abhimanyu**; *Rani Maharani**; *Pratap**; *Aata Bombata**; *Ananta Prema**; *Challenge Gopalakrishna**; *Nighooda Rahasya**; *College Hero**; **1991**: *Bhujangayana Dashavatara**; *Hatyakanda*; *Ajagajanthara**; *Punda Prachanda**; *Neenu Nakkare Haalu Sakkare*; *Ide Police Belt**; *Garuda Dhwaja**; *Navatare**; *SP Bhargavi**; *Ramachari**; *Shanti Kranti*.

HARIHARAN, T.

Malayalam director born in Calicut. Arts teacher in Kerala and film critic; also associated with the theatre. Became assistant to M.S. Mani in Madras (1960) and to M. Krishnan Nair. Continued as assistant until successful directorial début in 1973 with a hit about a wealthy young woman who returns from Singapore and is sought after for her money. Films often written by M.T. Vasudevan Nair. Made one Hindi film, *Anjaam*.

FILMOGRAPHY: **1973**: *Ladies' Hostel*; **1974**: *College Girl*; *Raja Hamsam*; *Ayalathe Sundari*; *Bhoomidevi Pushpiniyayi*; **1975**: *Babu Mon*; *Love Marriage*; *Madhura Pathinezhu*; **1976**: *Panchami*; *Rajayogam*; *Themmadi Velappan*; *Kanyadanam*; *Ammini Ammavan*; **1977**: *Ivanente Priyaputhran*; *Sujatha*; *Sangamam*; *Tholkkan Enikku Manassilla*; **1978**: *Adimakachavadam*; *Kudumbam Namakku Sreekovil*; *Snehathinte Mukhangal*; *Yagaswam*; **1979**: *Edavazhiyile Pucha Mindappucha*; *Sharapanjaram*; **1980**: *Muthichippikal*; *Lava*; **1981**: ***Valarthu Mrugangal***; *Pucha Sanyasi*; **1982**: *Anuraga Kodathi*; **1983**: *Varanmare Avashyamundu*; *Evedayo Oru Sathru*; **1984**: *Poomadathu Pennu*; *Vikatakavi*; *Vellom*; **1986**: ***Panchagni***; *Nakshatrangal*; *Anjaam*; **1987**: *Amritam Gamaya*; **1988**: *Aranyakam*; **1989**: ***Oru Vadakkan Veeragatha***; *Charan Data*; **1990**: *Oliyambugal*; **1992**: *Sargam*.

HAZARIKA, BHUPEN (B. 1926)

Born in Sadiya, Arunachal Pradesh. Most important Assamese singer and composer in post-Independence period. Deeply influenced by Paul Robeson. Child actor in **Agarwala**'s second film, *Indramalati* (1939). Degree from Benares University (1946); doctorate at Columbia University with a thesis on the role of mass communication in India's adult education (1952). Returned to lecture at Gauhati University, but resigned (1955) in favour of film-making and music. Member of Assam's first **IPTA** provincial committee (with Agarwala, Bishnu Rabha and **Phani Sarma**, 1946). Released first record, *Mahatmer Mahaprayam*, in 1948. Major intervention in musical forms like Bihu (spring festival music), Ban-geet and Bar-geet (devotionals written by medieval Saint poets Shankara Deb and Madhab Deb), and plantation workers' music. Toured Assam's riot-affected areas with Hemango Biswas and their musical troupe (1960). Early films as music director were part of continuing collaboration with IPTA colleagues Rabha and Sarma, as was his directorial début, ***Era Bator Sur***, starring **Balraj Sahni**. His *Shakuntala* starred the popular singer Khagan Mahato. His films are noted for tremendously popular music, often with singers from Bombay, e.g. **Lata Mangeshkar** in *Era Bator Sur*, Talat Mahmood in *Pratidhwani* and **Asha Bhosle**, **Kishore Kumar** and Mukesh in *Chik Mik Bijuli*. Member of Assamese State Legislative Assembly (1967-72). Edited art journal *Gati* (1964-7), columnist on *Amar Pratinidhi* (1963-80). Published several books of essays and anthologies of songs. Wrote and scored his own films, music director only on the others. Equally popular as a Bengali singer.

FILMOGRAPHY (* also d): **1948**: ***Siraj***; **1953**: *Sati Behula*; **1955**: ***Pioli Phukan***; **1956**: ***Era Bator Sur****; **1957**: *Dhumuha*; *Kari-o-Komal*; *Jiban Trishna*; **1958**: *Jonakir Alo*; **1959**: *Mahut Bandhu Re**; *Kecha Sone*; *Puwati Nishar Sapon*; **1960**: *Dui Bechara*; **1961**: *Shakuntala**; **1963**: *Maniram Dewan*; **1964**: *Pratidhwani/Ka Swarati**; **1966**: *Lati Ghati**; **1969**: *Chik Mik Bijuli**; **1971**: *Ekhane Pinjar*; **1973**: ***27 Down***; **1974**: *Aarop*; ***Bristi***; *For Whom the Sun Shines** (Doc); **1975**: *Chameli Memsaab*; *Khoj*; **1976**: *Dampati*; *Mera Dharam Meri Maa**; *Rupkonwar Jyotiprasad Aru Joymati**; *Palasor Rong*; **1977**: *Banahansa*; *Through Melody and Rhythm** (Doc); **1978**: *Banjoi*; **1979**: *Chameli Memsaab*; *Mon Prajapati**; **1980**: *Akan*; **1981**: *Nagpash*; **1982**: ***Aparoopa/Apeksha***; **1985**: *Angikar*; **1986**: *Sankalpa*; ***Ek Pal***; *Swikarokti** (Sh); **1988**: *Siraj**; *Lohit Kinare* (TV); **1992**: *Rudali*.

HEBLIKAR, SURESH (b. 1945)

Kannada director and actor born in Dharwar. Studied economics at Karnatak University and advertising in Bombay. Worked in a bank and performed on the amateur stage in English and in Kannada. Hired to play the lead in *Kankana* (1975) and continued as a screen actor, appearing in ***Rushya Shringa*** (1976), *Khandavideko Mamsavideko* (1979), *Vatsalya Patha* (1980), *Alemane* (1981), *Amara Madhura Prema* and *Jyoti* (1982), *Matte Vasantha* (1983) and *Kanoonige Saval* (1984). Turned director in 1983.

FILMOGRAPHY: **1983**: *Antarala*; **1984**: *Ecology of the Western Ghats* (Doc); *Energy* (Doc); *Smoking Tuna* (Doc); **1985**: *Agantuka*; **1988**: *Kadina Benki*; **1990**: *Prathama Usha Kirana*; **1992**: *Chamatkar*.

HINDUSTAN CINEMA FILMS COMPANY

Est: 1918 in Nasik, Maharashtra. First purely indigenous film studio with corporate shareholding. Started by **Phalke** to replace the ailing **Phalke Films** with partners Waman Shridhar Apte, Mayashankar Bhatt (later financier for **Sharda** Studio), Gokuldas Damodar and Madhavji Jessing. Phalke resigned from the Board (1919) but returned to become its chief producer and technical adviser (1923) as well as its main film-maker, directing 43 of its 96 films. 35 of the films were directed by G.V. Sane, 11 by Shinde (including *Tukaram*, 1921); other directors include V.S. Nirantar (4), Kashinath Bharadi, Munshi Abbas and Abhaychand Lahiri who each made one film there. The first studio to have its own distribution operation (run briefly by Bhogilal Dave) with offices in Bombay and Madras. Started offshoot Bharat Film (1919). Its last film, Phalke's *Setu Bandhan* (1932), was post-synchronised for sound but the studio failed in 1933.

HISTORICALS

Like the reformist social, the historical genre derived from late 19th C. novel and theatre writing. Used mainly to glorify epochs of regional (usually military) power, it incorporated ' Tipu Sultan in Kannada, Shivaji in Marathi, Pratapaditya or Siraj-ud-Dowla in Bengali - although Maratha and Rajput history transcended all bounds to gain an all-India popularity' (Meenakshi Mukherjee, 1985). Often the language of the most spectacular historicals (see **K. Asif**, **Sohrab Modi** and **Kamal Amrohi**) was Urdu and the favourite settings were the Caliphates, the Delhi Sultanate (13th-16th C.) or the Mughal empire (16th C.). As Mukherjee points out via novelist Abdul Halim Sharar, the ' Muslim evocation of a glorious past could hark back to the days of Moorish domination of Spain and other Mediterranean lands'. Generally, the genre was invented to represent the ' moment of departure' for Indian nationalism (Partha Chatterjee, 1986), resurrecting national or regional glory to create allegories for communal and regional difference and to consolidate the reform movements' new historiography. The specific functions of the genre varied from region to region: in conditions where royalty had been reduced to a largely ceremonial role (e.g. South India), it was a specific response to imperialist domination: e.g. in Travancore where the first major novel by C.V. Raman Pillai (1858-1922), ***Martanda Varma*** (1891; filmed in 1931) resurrected the 18th C. emperor; in the old Mysore province several **Company Natak** plays returned to the glory of the Vijayanagar Empire (14th C.). The early cinema takes off directly from the stage historical (cf **Baburao Painter**). The most evident influence was the Parsee theatre, where the genre was interpreted entirely as a play about feudal power and therefore a crucial mediation of kinship relations (see **Aga Hashr Kashmiri**, **Mehboob**). Influential regional imitations of this mode included the Bengali plays of Dwijendralal Roy (*Mewar Patan*, 1909), interpreted by Parthasarathy Gupta in the context of **Swadeshi** (cf Gupta, 1988), and the famous *Shahjehan* (1909) or those of Khirode Prasad Vidyavinode (e.g. *Alamgir*, 1921, staged by **Sisir Bhaduri**). **Imperial** Studio re-coded the genre along Cecil B. DeMille lines. **Bhalji Pendharkar** and **G.V. Iyer** (in his **Rajkumar** films) used the genre for directly ideological ends. In most instances where the cinema took off from folk or popular theatre (as in Telugu), early historicals are usually blurred into other genres like the mythological or the Saint film (e.g. **Vel Pics**) and are conventionally referred to as ' costume' dramas, a tradition later continued by **Gemini**'s adventure films and politicised as an imaginary pseudo-history by **MGR**.

HUBLIKAR, SHANTA (1914-92)

Actress born in Hubli, Karnataka. Entered films at Kolhapur, where she worked with **Torney**, **Bhalji Pendharkar** and probably in **Phalke**'s ***Gangavataran***. Became an icon in Marathi cinema with her popular role as the prostitute Maina in **Shantaram**'s ***Manoos/Admi*** and esp. with the song *Ab kis liye kal ki baat*, one of the biggest hits in the **Prabhat** repertoire. Its Marathi version, *Kashalya Udyachi Baat* (Why speak of tomorrow?) became the title of her autobiography (1990). Also played the rich Nalini who discovers higher moral principles through meeting the poor but honest Diwakar (**Shahu Modak**) in **K. Narayan Kale**'s ***Mazha Mulga/Mera Ladka*** at Prabhat. Later acted in Hindi films (e.g. by **V.M. Vyas**), one Kannada film opposite **Kemparaj Urs** (***Jeevana Nataka***) and did some stage roles in **Sangeet Natak** musicals.

FILMOGRAPHY: **1934**: *Bhedi Rajkumar/Thaksen Rajputra*; **1937**: ***Kanhopatra***; ***Gangavataran***; **1938**: ***Mazha Mulga/Mera Ladka***; **1939**: ***Manoos/Admi***; **1941**: *Ghar Ki Laaj*; *Prabhat*; **1942**: *Malan*; ***Pahila Palna***; ***Jeevana Nataka***; **1945**: *Kul Kalank*; **1958**: *Ghar Grihasthi*; *Saubhagyavati Bhava*.

HUSNLAL-BHAGATRAM (HUSNLAL: ?-1968; BHAGATRAM: ?-1973)

Music composer duo. First instance of two composers working together and signing all their work jointly. Popular in Hindi film in late 40s/50s, esp. *Pyar Ki Jeet* (e.g. the **Mohammed Rafi** hit *Ik dil ke tukde*), *Badi Bahen*, *Adhi Raat*, ***Afsana***, *Sanam*. **Suraiya** sang several of their compositions and some of their hits were popularised over Radio Ceylon. Later became members of **Laxmikant-Pyarelal**'s orchestra. Har Mandir Singh's *Geet Kosh* credits them with the music of *Bambi* in the 40s, but gives no further information.

FILMOGRAPHY: **1944**: *Chand*; **1946**: ***Hum Ek Hain***; *Nargis*; **1947**: *Heera*; *Mirza Sahiban*; *Mohan*; *Romeo and Juliet*; **1948**: *Aaj Ki Raat*; *Lakhpati*; *Pyar Ki Jeet*; **1949**: *Amar Kahani*; *Balam*; *Badi Bahen*; *Bansaria*; *Hamari Manzil*; *Jal Tarang*; *Naach*; *Raakhi*; *Sawan Bhadon*; **1950**: *Adhi Raat*; *Apni Chhaya*; *Birha Ki Raat*; *Chhoti Bhabhi*; *Gauna*; *Meena Bazaar*; *Pyar Ki Manzil*; *Sartaj*; *Surajmukhi*; **1951**: ***Afsana***; *Sanam*; *Shagun*; *Stage*; **1952**: *Kafila*; *Raja Harishchandra*; **1953**: *Aansoo*; *Farmaish*; **1954**: *Shama Parwana*; **1955**: *Adl-e-Jehangir*; *Kanchan*; *Mr Chakram*; **1956**: *Aan Baan*; **1957**: *Dushman*; *Jannat*; *Krishna Sudama*; **1958**: *Trolley Driver*; **1961**: *Apsara*; **1963**: *Shaheed Bhagat Singh*; **1965**: *Tarzan And The Circus*; **1966**: *Sher Afghan*.

Shahu Modak and Shanta Hublikar in *Mazha Mulga* (1938)

HUSSAIN, ANWAR (b. 1929)

Assamese director. Completed first film, the formally and ideologically orthodox *Sarapat*, aged 26: a resigned tale of human failure and family disaster. Later work is an early use in Assamese cinema of the language of mythology, both secular and religious, seen most notably in *Tejimola*.

FILMOGRAPHY: **1955**: *Sarapat*; **1958**: *Natun Prithibi*; **1963**: *Tejimola*; **1977**: *Paap Aru Prayashchitta*; **1983**: *Shri Shri Maa Kamakhya*.

HUSSAIN, NASIR (b. 1931)

Hindi director born in Bhopal, MP. Briefly worked for **A.R. Kardar**, then joined **Filmistan** as scenarist (1948); wrote some of **Subodh Mukherjee**'s films starring **Dev Anand**: ***Munimji*** (1955), ***Paying Guest*** (1957). First film, ***Tumsa Nahin Dekha***, was **Shammi Kapoor**'s first big hit and inaugurated a new type of 60s musicals with **Mohammed Rafi**'s singing clearly influenced by rock and roll. Independent producer with his own Nasir Hussain Films (1960). Made some of the most popular and frequently imitated love stories: ***Jab Pyar Kisise Hota Hai***, the **Zeenat Aman** hit ***Yaadon Ki Baraat***, *Hum Kisise Kum Nahin* starring Rishi Kapoor, and ***Qayamat Se Qayamat Tak*** (1988), produced and scripted by him, directed by his son Mansoor, which launched his nephew and 90s star Aamir Khan. The film spearheaded the return of the teenage love theme. Since then produces his son's films.

FILMOGRAPHY: **1957**: ***Tumsa Nahin Dekha***; **1959**: ***Dil Deke Dekho***; **1961**: ***Jab Pyar Kisise Hota Hai***; **1963**: *Phir Wohi Dil Laya Hoon*; **1967**: *Baharon Ke Sapne*; **1969**: *Pyar Ka Mausam*; **1971**: *Caravan*; **1973**: *Aangan*; ***Yaadon Ki Baraat***; **1977**: *Hum Kisise Kum Nahin*; **1981**: *Zamane Ko Dikhana Hai*; **1984**: *Manzil Manzil*; **1985**: *Zabardast*.

ILAIYARAJA

Prolific Tamil composer with a legendary reputation. Born as Rajayya, the 8th son of an estate supervisor in Pannaipuram, TN. Joined his stepbrother Varadarajan, a CP member, to form a music group, Pavalar Brothers, staging live concerts often as election propaganda for Left groups. Went to Madras as a teenager, where he learnt Western classical music and the Western technique of writing musical scores. Learnt Carnatic music from singer and mridangam performer T.V. Gopalakrishnan. Joined films as a member of various film orchestras. Sensational début as composer in ***Annakkili***, using rural folk melodies. Introduced fusion effects into Tamil cinema combining Carnatic, Western classical and pop (cf ***Raja Parvai***). Early hits for the films of his childhood friend **Bharathirajaa** (***Pathinaru Vayathinile***). Extensively associated with playback singer **S.P. Balasubramanyam** and, for a while, lyricist **Vairamuthu**. Recent music hits notably in **Mani Rathnam**'s films, e.g. *Raja rajadhirajan indha raja* in ***Agni Nakshatram***, followed by the songs of ***Anjali***, etc. Currently commands fees equalling those of the highest-paid actors in Tamil and is an independent star attraction. Made two independent music albums, *How to Name It* and *Nothing but Wind*, both continuing his fusion experiments, as in the composition *I Love You, Mozart* in which he has flautist Hariprasad Chaurasia playing the raga *Kalyani* with a violin evocation of Mozart's *40th Symphony*. Occasionally provided lyrics and sang his compositions. Composed music apparently for c.450 films in five languages (the exhaustive filmography is virtually impossible to compile). Published two books, the European travelogue *Sangeetha Kanavugal*, and *Vettaveliyil Kotti Kidakkudhu*, addressing his philosophical preoccupations.

FILMOGRAPHY: **1976**: ***Annakkili***; *Bhadrakali*; *Paluti Valartha Kili*; *Uravadum Nenjam*; **1977**: *Alukkoru Asai*; *Avar Enakke Sontham*; *Bhuvana Oru Kelvi Kuri*; *Deepam*; *Durga Devi*; *Gayatri*; *Kavikuyil*; *Odi Vilayadu Thatha*; *Penn Janmam*; *Sainthadamma Sainthadu*; ***Pathinaru Vayathinile***; *Thunai Eruppal Meenakshi*; **1978**: *Achani*; ***Aval Appadithan***; *Aval Oru Pachchai Kuzhandhai*; *Bhairavi*; *Chattam En Kaiyil*; *Chittu Kuruvi*; *Elamai Vunjaladugiradhu*; *Ithu Eppadi Irukku*; *Kannan Oru Kayi Kuzhanthai*; *Katrinile Varum Geetham*; *Kizhakke Pokum Rayil*; *Mariamman Thiruvizha*; ***Mullum Malarum***; *Sigappu Rojakkal*; *Sondhadu Needana*; *Thirukalyanam*; *Thyagam*; *Vattathukkul Chaduram*; *Vazha Ninaithal Vazhalam*; *Matu Tappada Maga*; *Aaru Manikkur*; *Vyamoham*; *Vayasu Pilichindi*; *Priya*; **1979**: *Urvashi Neenu Nanna Preyasi/Urvashi Nive Naa Preyasi*; ***Yugandhar***; *Azhage Unnai Aradikiran*; *Akal Vilakku*; *Annai Oru Alayam*; *Azhiyada Kolangal*; *Aarilirunthu Arubathu Varai*; *Udhiri Pookal*; *Kalyanaraman*; *Kavariman*; *Kuppathu Raja*; *Chella Kili*; *Dharma Yuddham*; *Thayillamal Nannilai*; *Naan Vazhavippen*; *Niram Maratha Pookal/Niram Maradha Pushpangal*; *Pagalil Oru Iravu*; ***Puthiya Varpugal***; *Poonthalir*; *Ponnu Urukku Puthusu*; *Mudhal Iravu*; **1980**: *Janma Janmada Anubandha*; *Anbukku Naan Adimai*; *Ilamaikolam*; *Ullasa Paravaigal*; *Enga Oor Rasathi*; *Kallukkul Eram*; *Kannil Theriyum Kathaigal*; *Kali*; *Gramathu Adhiyayam*; *Guru*; *Samanthi Poo*; *Savithri*; *Soolam*; *Sundarime Varuga Varuga*; *Thayi Pongal*; *Nadhiyai Thedi Vandha Kadal*; *Nizhalgal*; *Nenjathai Killathey*; *Poottadha Poothukkal*; *Ponnagaram*; *Murattu Kalai*; *Moodupani*; *Rishi Moolam*; *Rusi Kanda Poonai*; *Johnny*; *Sridevi*; **1981**: ***Raja Parvai***; *Geetha*; *Nee Nanna Gellalare*; *Bhari Bharjari Bete*; *Shikari*; *Do Dil Diwane*; *Alaigal Oyvathillai*; *Aradhanai*; *Ellam Inbamayam*; *Idru Poyi Nalai Vaa*; *Enakkaga Kathiru*; *Garjanai/Garjanam/Garjane*; *Kadal Meengal*; *Karaiyellam Shenbagappu*; *Kalthoon*; *Kazhagu*; *Koyil Pura*; *Shankaral*; *Tik Tik Tik*; *Nandu*; *Netrikkan*; *Panneer Pushpangal*; *Balanagamma*; *Pennin Vazhkai*; *Madhumalar*; *Meendum Kokila*; *Rajangam*; *Ram Lakshman*; *Ranuva Veeran*; *Veediyum Varai Kathiru*; ***Seethakoka Chilaka***; **1982**: *Kanya Dweep*; *Azhagiya Kanney*; *Archanai Pookkal*; *Ilanjodigal*; *Echil Iravugal*; *Engeyo Ketta Kural*; *Kalyana Kalam*; *Kanne Radha*; *Kathal Oviyam*; *Kozhi Kuvutthu*; *Sahalakala Vallavan*; *Sangili*; *Thanikatu Raja*; *Thayi Moogambikai*; *Marumagaley Varuga*; *Thyagi*; *Theerpu*; *Thooral Ninnu Pochu*; *Nalanthana*; *Nizhal Thedum Nenjalgal*; *Nenaivellam Nithya*; *Nenjalgal*; *Payanangal Mudivathillai*; *Pakkathu Veetu Roja*; *Paritchaikku Neramchu*; *Pannaipurathu Pandavargal*; *Puthu Kavithai*; *Boom Boom Madu*; *Pookkari Raja*; *Magane Magane*; ***Moondram Pirai***; *Metti*; *Ranga*; *Rani Theni*; *Lottery Ticket*; *Valibame Vaa*; *Vaa Kanna Vaa*; *Hitler Umanath*; **1983**: *Adutha Varisu*; *Anandakummi*; *Andha Sila Natkal*; *Anney Anney*; *Ayiram Nilave Vaa*; *Bhagavathipuram Railway Gate*; *Devi Sridevi*; *Ennaipar En Azhagai Paar*; *Ethanai Konam Ethanai Parvai*; *Ilamai Kalangal*; *Indru Nee Nalai Naan*; *Inimai Idho Idho*; *Jyothi*; *Kan Sivanthal Man Sivakkum*; *Kokkarako*; *Malaiyur Mambattiyan*; *Manaivi Solle Mandiram*; *Mann Vasanai*; *Mellappesungal*; *Mundhanai Mudichu*; *Muthu Engal Sotthu*; *Oru Odai Nadhiyagiradhu*; *Payum Puli*; *Ragangal Maruvathillai*; *Sattai Illatha Pambaram*; *Soorakottai Singhakutty*; *Thanga Magan*; *Thoongathe Thambi Thoongathe*; *Urangatha Ninaivugal*; *Veetile Raman Veliyele Krishnan*; *Vellai Roja*; *Yuga Dharmam*; *Pallavi Anupallavi*; *Nyaya Gedditu*; *Aa Rathri*; *Oomakuyil*; *Pinninvalu*; *Sandhyakku Virinja Poovu*; *Sadma*; *Abhilasha* (Tel); *Mantrigari Viyankudu*; *Rajakumar*; ***Sagara Sangamam***; **1984**: *Alaya Deepam*; *Ambigai Neril Vandhal*; *Anbe Odi Vaa*; *Anbulla Malare*; *Anbulla Rajnikant*; *Avemin Pudhumai Penn*; *Dhavani Kanavugal*; *Enakkul Oruvan*; *Ezhuthantha Sattangal*; *Ingeyum Oru Gangai*; *January 1*; *Kayi Kodukkum Kayi*; *Kairasikaran*; *Komberi Mookan*; *Kuva Kuva Vathukal*; *Magudi*; *Meendum Oru Kadhal Kadai*; *Mudivalla Arambham*; *Nalai Onadu Naal*; *Naan Mahaan Alla*; *Naan Padum Padal*; *Nalla Naal*; *Nallavanukku Nallavan*; *Neengal Kettavai*; *Nee Thodum Pothu*; *Neram Nalla Neram*; *Nilavu Suduvathillai*; *Nyayam*; ***Nooravathunaal***; *O Mani Mane*; *Poovilangu*; *Pozhudu Vidinachu*; *Sanganatham*; *Thalaiyana Mandiram*; *Thambikku Entha Ooru*; *Thangamdi Thangam*; *24 Mani Neram/24 Hours*; *Unnai Naan Santhithan*; *Vaidehi Kathirunthal*; *Vazhkai*; *Vellai Pura Ondru*; *Nagara Mahime*; ***Accident***; *Mangalam Nerunne*; ***My Dear Kuttichathan/Chhota Chetan***; *Onnanu Nammal*; *Unaroo*; *Challenge*; *Gadusu Pindam*; *Ithe Naa Saval*; *Jalsarayudu*; *Mayadari Mogudu*; *Merupu Dadi*; *Noorava Roju*; *Nuvva Nena/Neeya Nanna*; *Prema Sangamam*; *Sahasame Jeevitham*; ***Sitara***; *Takkaridonga*; *Tiger Rajani*; *Veerabhadrulu*; *Etho Mogam*; *Kalyana Kanavugal*; *Thavani Kanavukal*; **1985**: *Aan Pavam*; *Aduthathu Albert*; *Alai Osai*; *Amudha Ganam*; *Anbin Mukavari*; *Andha Oru Nimidam*; *Annai Bhoomi*; *Chinna Veedu*; *Eetti*; *En Selvame*; *Hello Yaar Pesarathu*; *Idaya Koyil*; *Japanil Kalyanaraman*; *Kakki Chattai*; *Kanni Rasi*; *Ketti Malam*; *Kumkuma Chimizh*; *Malargal Naniginrana*; ***Muthal Mariyathai***; *Nane Raja Nane Mandiri*; *Naan Sigappu Manithan*; *Nallathambi*; *Neethiyin Marupakkam*; *Oru Kaithiyin Diary*; *Padikkadhavan*; *Padikkatha Panayar*; *Pagal Nilavu*; *Pillai Nila*; *Pudhiya Theerpu*; *Raja Rishi*; *Selvi*; ***Sindhu Bhairavi***; *Shri Raghavendrar*; *Thanga Mana*; *Thendrale Ennai Thodu*; *Udaya Geetham*; *Unnai Thedi Varuven*; *Un Kannil Neer Vazhindal*; *Urimai*; *Uyarntha Ullam*; *Ajeya*; *Namma Bhoomi*; *Mera Inteqam*; *Anveshana*; *Illali Sapadham*; *Jalsa Bullodu*; *Khooni*; *Kirathakudu*; *Mangalya Bandham*; *Monagadu Mosagadu*; *Muthyala Jallu*; *Jwala*; *Praja Poratam*; *Preminchu Pelladu*; *Rahasya Hanthakudu*; *Shivabhakta Naga Shakti*; *Shri Shirdi Saibaba Mahatyam*; *Geetanjali*; *Poove Poo Chooda Va*; ***Yathra***; **1986**: *Satya Jyothi*; *Jadu Nagari*; *Amman Koil Kizhakkale*; *Aruvadainal*; *Ananda Kannir*; *Iravu Pookkal*; *Isai Padum Thendrai*; *Unakkagave Vazhkiran*;

Enakku Nane Needipathi; *Engal Thaikulame Varuga*; *Kannukku Mai Ezhuthu*; *Karimedi Karivayan*; *Kalamellam Un Mediyil*; *Kodai Malai*; *Sadhanai*; *December Pookkal*; *Dharmapatni*; *Thaluvatha Kaikal*; *Thaikku Oru Thalattu*; *Nam Ooru Nalla Ooru*; *Natpu*; *Nanum Oru Thozhilali*; *Neethana Anda Kuyil*; *Punnagai Mannan*; *Paru Paru Pattinam Paru*; *Palaivana Rojakkal*; *Maragatha Veenai*; *Mandhira Punnagai*; *Maaveeran*; *Mr Bharat* (Ta); *Mudhal Vasantham*; *Murattu Karangal*; *Mella Thirandathu Kathavu*; ***Mouna Ragam***; *Yaro Ezhuthia Kavithai*; *Vikram*; *Vidunja Kalyanam*; **1987**: *Poovizhi Vasalile*; *Ninaikka Therindha Maname*; *Ullam Kavarntha Kalvan*; *Teertha Karayanile*; *Vazhgai Valarga*; ***Nayakan***; *Puyal Padum Pattu*; *Kalyana Kacheri*; *Anand*; *Iniya Uravu Poothathu*; *Manadhil Urudhi Vendhum*; *Sankeerthana*; *Aradhana*; *Khaidi*; *Andarikante Ghanudu*; *Rendu Thokala Titta*; *Kamagni*; ***Ore Oru Gramathile***; ***Veedu***; *Idhu Oru Thodarkathai*; *Enga Ooru Pattukaran*; *Kadamai Kanniyam Kattupadu*; *Kadhal Parisu*; *Krishnan Vandhan*; *Sirai Paravai*; *Chinna Kuyil Padhutthu*; *Ninaive Oru Sangeetham*; *Thoorathu Pachai*; *Padu Nilave*; *Persollum Pillai*; *Mangai Oru Gangai*; *Irattaival Kuruvi*; *Velaikkaran*; *Jalli Kattu*; **1988**: *Shenbagame Shenbagame*; *En Uyir Kannamma*; *Rasave Unnai Nambi*; *Satya*; *Irandil Onru*; *Oruvar Vazhum Alayam*; *Solla Thudikuthu Manasu*; *En Jeevan Paduthu*; *En Bommu Kutti Ammavukku*; *Guru Shishyan*; ***Agni Nakshatram***; *Therkkithi Kallan*; *Pasaparaivaigal*; *Parthal Pasu*; *Poonthotha Kavalkaran*; *Soora Samharam*; *Ennai Veetu Pogathe*; *Naan Sonnadhe Sattam*; *Unnal Mudiyum Thambi*; *Illam*; *Enga Ooru Kavalkaran*; *Idhu Engal Needhi*; *Manamagale Vaa*; *Dharmathin Thalaivan*; *Padatha Thenikkal*; *Thayam Onnu*; *Moonnam Pakkam*; *Maharshi*; *Rudraveena*; *Abhinandana*; *Shri Kanakamahalaxmi Recording Dance Troupe*; *Jamadagni*; *Swarna Kamalam*; *Varasoduchadu*; *Rakthabhisekham*; *En Vazhi Thani Vazhi*; **1989**: *Ennai Petha Rasa*; *En Purushanthan Enakkum Mattumthan*; *Varusham 16*; *Rajadhi Raja*; *Thenral Sudum*; *Pongivarum Kaveri*; *Pattukoru Thalaivan*; *Pandinattu Thangam*; *Apoorva Sahodarargal/Appu Raja*; *Ninaivu Chinnam*; *Shiva* (Ta); *Enga Ooru Mappillai*; *Poruthanthu Potham*; *Annanukkey Jey*; *Raja Rajathan*; *Kadhal Oyvathillai*; *Pickpocket*; *Chinnappadas*; *Karagatta Karan*; *Ponmana Selvan*; *Dharmam Vellum*; *Vadhiyar Veetu Pillai*; *Mappillai*; *Pasa Mazhai*; *Anbu Kattalai*; *Padicha Pullai*; *Kaiveesu Amma Kaiveesu*; *Pudhu Pudhu Arthangal*; *Thiruppumunai*; *Vetri Vizha*; *Thangamana Rasa*; *Mahadev*; *Garijinchina Ganga*; *Prema*; *Chettukinda Pleader*; ***Geetanjali***; *Rudra Neta*; *Gopalraogari Abbayi*; *Ashoka Chakravarthi*; *Indrudu Chandrudu*; **1990**: ***Anjali***; *Arangetra Velai*; *Adisaya Piravi*; *Urudhimozhi*; *Ooru Vittu Oru Vandhu*; *Engatta Modathe*; *En Oyir Tholan*; *Oru Pudhiya Kadhai*; *Kavalukku Kettikaran*; *Kizhakku Vasal*; *Kiladi Kanmani*; *Kshatriyan*; *Thalattu Padava*; *Nadigan*; *Nilapennay*; *Panakkaran*; *Pudhu Pattu*; *Pattukku Naan Adimai*; *Pulan Visaranai*; *Periaveetu Pannaikaran*; *Pondatti Thevai*; *Michael Madana Kamarajan*; *My Dear Marthandan*; *Mounam Sammadham*; *Raja Kaiye Vacha*; *Vellaya Thevan*; *Velai Kidaichiruchu*; **1992**: ***Thevar Magan***.

Ilangovan *see* **Elangovan**

IMPERIAL FILMS COMPANY

Est: 1926. Successor to the Majestic and Royal Art Film companies set up by **Ardeshir Irani** as a diversification of his exhibition interests in partnership with **Esoofally**, Mohammed Ali and Dawoodji Rangwala. Organised as a vertically integrated combine with its own exhibition infrastructure. Started following the decline of **Kohinoor**, it continued many of the latter's **Mohanlal Dave**-inspired genres, often with the same stars and film-makers. Imperial became closely associated with the costumed historical genre launched with *Anarkali* (1928), shot and released almost overnight in direct competition to **Charu Roy**'s ***The Loves of a Mughal Prince*** (1928). Irani also rushed out ***Alam Ara*** (1931), released as India's first full talkie narrowly beating **Madan Theatres**' ***Shirin Farhad*** (1931). Imperial was the first studio to shoot scenes at night (in *Khwab-e-Hasti*, 1929) using incandescent lamps. It owned India's top silent star, **Sulochana**, and promoted her along with **Zubeida**, Jilloo and, for a while, the young **Prithviraj Kapoor**. This was perhaps the first major instance of a deliberate manufacturing of a star-cult as a marketing strategy. Top Imperial film-makers include **R.S. Choudhury**, **B.P. Mishra** and **Mohan Bhavnani**, whose film-making set the house style, as did **Nandlal Jaswantlal**'s sound films. A fair number of the studio's talkies were remakes of its own silent hits with Sulochana (*Anarkali*, 1928 & 1935), *Indira BA* (1929) became ***Indira MA*** (1934), ***Wildcat of Bombay*** (1927) became ***Bambai Ki Billi*** (1936), etc. It made films in at least nine languages: Hindi, Gujarati, Marathi, Tamil, Telugu, Burmese, Malay, Pushtu and Urdu. The first Iranian sound film, *Dukhtar-e-Lur* (aka *Dokhtare Lor Ya Irane Diruz Va Emruz*, 1932) was also made here. ***Kisan Kanya*** (1937) by **Gidwani** was India's first indigenously manufactured colour film, made with the Cinecolour process. When it closed in 1938, its economic and generic inheritance was continued by **Sagar** Movietone.

INDIAN KINEMA ARTS

Silent studio; Est: 1927 in Calcutta by exhibitor Ghanshyamdas Chokhani. First film was the influential *Punarjanma* (1927) scripted by **Premankur Atorthy** and shot by **Nitin Bose**, the début of a combination that later launched International Filmcraft with *Chasher Meye* (1931). With **P.C. Barua**'s Barua Pics and **Dhiren Ganguly**'s **British Dominion Films**, this studio is a direct predecessor of the **New Theatres**. Following the advent of New Theatres (1931), it was taken over by B.D. Rawal and converted into a studio facility for hire.

INDIAN PEOPLES' THEATRE ASSOCIATION

Theatre movement informally affiliated to the CPI; launched as an All-India front in Bombay (1943) with a manifesto calling for a ' defence of culture against Imperialism and Fascism'. While its immediate antecedents were in the **PWA** (1936) and thus in the European anti-Fascist movements of the 30s, the front found its identity with **Sombhu Mitra**'s staging of **Bijon Bhattacharya**'s play *Nabanna* (1943) and with Jyotindra Moitra's song series *Nabajibaner Gaan* (1944). Both works were based on the Bengal famine of 1943. Subsequent work included travelling musical and theatre groups, predominantly in context of 40s CPI-led struggles in Bengal, Andhra (Telangana) and Kerala. Through the 40s and early 50s, it grew into the only instance of a cultural avant-garde in contemporary Indian history. It was active also in Punjab, Assam (see **Jyotiprasad Agarwala** and **Bhupen Hazarika**), Orissa (see **K. Pattanayak**) and AP (the Praja Natya Mandali, which also made one film, Raja Rao's ***Puttillu***, 1953), despite a near-programmatic emphasis on reclaiming the popular vernacular by using local folk and occasionally popular modes of performance. The strategy's major strength lay in enabling several regional movements to forge new links and to reinvent their own local traditions, e.g. in Kerala, where the Kerala Peoples' Arts Club (KPAC) played a key role in the CP's organisation of the peasantry in Malabar and North Travancore leading to the insurrection against the erstwhile Travancore State (1946-50). Radical theatre movements around e.g. **Thoppil Bhasi**'s plays also traced an ancestry via the Young Namboodiri movements of the 30s (with V.T. Bhattathirippad) to the Yogakshema Sabha (Est: 1908) and to the major early 20th C. poet Kumaran Asan. The less activist but equally influential aspect of the front was in the major urban centres with e.g. the work of playwright-film-maker **K.A. Abbas** and dancer Uday Shankar. For a brief period following WW2 and in the early years of Independence, virtually the entire cultural intelligentsia was associated with or influenced by IPTA/PWA initiatives, possibly because it was seen as the ' only cultural organisation engaged in serious creative activity' (Sudhi Pradhan, 1979). The IPTA's impact on cinema includes the collective effort of ***Dharti Ke Lal*** (1946) mobilising actors **Balraj Sahni** and Sombhu Mitra, musician Ravi Shankar and writer-scenarist **Krishan Chander**; ***Neecha Nagar*** (1946: cf **Chetan Anand**); the plays of **Inder Raj Anand** staged by **Prithviraj Kapoor** which led to **Raj Kapoor**'s film team with, e.g., scenarist Abbas and music directors **Shankar-Jaikishen**. The IPTA also supported some independently made films: e.g. **Shantaram**'s ***Dr Kotnis Ki Amar Kahani*** (1946). In Bengal, its influence on film was mediated throuh Manoj Bhattacharya's ***Tathapi*** and **Nemai Ghosh**'s ***Chinnamul*** (both 1950), which represent **Ghatak**'s and Bijon Bhattacharya's first encounters with film. Other Bengali films connected with the IPTA include **Bimal Roy**'s ***Udayer Pathey/Hamrahi*** (1944); **Satyen Bose**'s *Bhor Hoye Elo* (1953) and *Rickshawalla* (1955) and **Sushil Majumdar**'s *Dukhir Iman* (1954). In Kerala, the key event for the IPTA style's transition to film was ***Neelakuyil*** (1954) by **Ramu Kariat** and **P. Bhaskaran** though the KPAC tradition itself was best exemplified by Thoppil Bhasi's films and scripts.

INFORMATION FILMS OF INDIA

Est: 1943 as a successor to the **Film Advisory Board**. Launched as producer of war propaganda documentaries, shorts and the *Indian News Parade* (ancestor to **Films Division**'s current *Indian News Review*).

Started by the British-Indian government, it required all exhibitors to include up to 2000 ft of ' Government-approved film' in each screening. This law was incorporated as an amendment to the Defence of India Act (Rule 44A). In the four years when the IFI was in force (i.e. before it yielded to the **Films Division**), its chief producer was **Ezra Mir** and the producer of the *Indian News Parade* was William J. Moylan. It produced c.170 shorts in addition to the newsreels before it closed in 1946.

IRANI, ARDESHIR MARWAN (1886-1969)

Director and producer in several languages; born in Pune. Studied at the J.J. School of Art in Bombay; teacher and kerosene inspector before joining his father in the phonograph and musical instruments trade in Bombay. Entered film as exhibitor representing Western Indian interests of Universal Film. Partnered **Abdulally Esoofally** in exhibition interests launched with acquisition of Alexandra and Majestic theatres (1914). The partnership lasted 55 years. Initially went into film production to keep distribution outlets supplied. Launched Star Film (1920) in partnership with Bhogilal K.M. Dave, releasing their first film, **Manilal Joshi**'s ***Veer Abhimanyu*** in 1922. They became Majestic Film (1923), then Royal Art Studio (1926) and finally the major silent era studio, **Imperial Film** (1926). A ' mogul' in the mould of the big Hollywood studio bosses; credited with between 225 and 250 productions in his lifetime, about half in the silent era, and talkies in nine languages including Farsi (*Dukhtar-e-Lur*, the first Iranian sound film). Early screen directions often jointly credited to **Naval Gandhi** but took rare solo directorial credit for India's first full sound feature, ***Alam Ara***, for which, having imported a sound technician from Hollywood (Wilford Deming), he finally recorded most of the sound himself. Bought rights to Cinecolour process and set up colour laboratory, producing India's first indigenously processed colour film ***Kisan Kanya*** (1937). Produced only one film after **Imperial** went into liquidation in 1938 (*Pujari*, 1946) but remained active member of the Indian Motion Picture Producers Association (IMPPA) of which he had been, in 1933, its first president. In 1974, Kennedy Bridge in Bombay was renamed Ardeshir Bridge and his Jyoti Studios (Est: 1939) passed to his son, Shapur A. Irani.

FILMOGRAPHY: **1924**: *Mumbai Ni Sethani*; *Shahjehan*; ***Paap No Fej***; **1925**: *Navalsha Hirji* (all St); **1931**: ***Alam Ara***; **1933**: *Dukhtar-e-Lur*.

ISHARA, BABU RAM

Hindi director born in Una, Himachal Pradesh, as Roshanlal Sharma. Went to Bombay aged 16 to enter the film industry. Late 60s scenarist and dialogue writer in Hindi for Dulal Guha, B.K. Adarsh, etc. Early 70s films (*Chetna*, *Charitra*) sparked major censorship debates over nudity and ' artistic licence' of exploitation cineastes, particularly because of their art-house claims (cf **New Indian Cinema**). His work indirectly led to the governmental guidelines addressed to the Censor Board (1979) directing the deletion of ' scenes which have the effect of justifying or glorifying drinking [and of] vulgarity, obscenity and depravity'. Prolific scenarist; also wrote his own films.

FILMOGRAPHY: **1969**: *Insaaf Ka Mandir*; **1970**: *Chetna*; *Gunah Aur Kanoon*; **1971**: *Man Tera Tan Mera*; **1972**: *Ek Nazar*; *Maan Jaiye*; *Milap*; *Zaroorat*; **1973**: *Charitra*; *Dil Ki Raahein*; *Ek Nao Do Kinare*; *Hathi Ke Daant*; *Nai Duniya Naye Log*; **1974**: *Bazaar Band Karo*; *Dawat*; *Prem Shastra*; **1975**: *Kaagaz Ki Nao*; **1978**: *Pal Do Pal Ka Saath*; *Rahu Ketu*; **1979**: *Ghar Ki Laaj*; **1980**: *Kaaran*; **1981**: *Khara Khota*; **1982**: *Log Kya Kahenge*; **1983**: *Jai Baba Amarnath*; **1984**: *Hum Do Hamare Do*; *Aurat Ka Inteqam*; **1985**: *Sautela Pati*; **1986**: *Aurat*; **1987**: *Besahara*; *Sila*; **1988**: *Woh Phir Aayegi*.

ISLAM, KAZI NAZRUL (1889-1976)

Composer and songwriter born in Burdwan Dist., Bengal. With **Tagore** he was the major influence on popular Bengali music in the 20th C. Known as the Bidrohi Kavi or Rebel Poet and directly associated with radical nationalist movements (e.g. through the journal *Dhoomketu* which he edited in 1922, leading to his imprisonment on a charge of sedition), his poetry constitutes the first radical intervention into Hindu and Muslim devotional music, e.g. his famous addresses to the goddess Kali, his ghazal compilations (*Chokher Chatak*, 1929) and Islamic devotionals (*Zulfikar*, 1932). Also offered militant interpretation of Bengal's Baul music. Much of his music, continued by the **IPTA**'s Bengali song repertoire, was polemically seen as a radical-romantic use of the ' tradition' (see, e.g., **Salil Choudhury**, 1955). One of the first composer-writers to sign contracts with major record companies in Bengal (for Megaphone and Senola and later HMV) and with the Indian Broadcasting Corp., opening up new employment opportunities to a generation of younger composers such as **Anil Biswas** and **S.D. Burman**. Created an urban variation of tribal *jhumur* music for **Sailajananda Mukherjee**'s *Pataal Puri* and wrote the songs for *Nandini* (1941) and *Dikshul* (1943). Some sources credit him as director for *Dhruva*, in which he played the Hindu god Narad. Started Bengal Tiger Pics with Abbasuddin Ahmed. Their film of Islam's novel *Madina* remained unfinished.

FILMOGRAPHY (* also act): **1934**: *Dhruva**; **1935**: *Pataal Puri*; **1936**: *Graher Pher*; **1938**: *Gora*; **1942**: *Chowringhee*.

IYER, GANAPATHY VENKATRAMANA (b. 1917)

Kannada director born in Nanjangud, Karnataka. Also major lyricist, scenarist, producer and actor, nicknamed ' the barefoot director'. Belongs to family of temple priests in old Mysore. Started in theatre in 1928. Career in two phases: actor-playwright for **Gubbi Veeranna**, scenarist for several key historicals starring **Rajkumar**, film-maker (usually with co-director T.V. Singh Thakore) and sought-after lyricist-scenarist for c.65 Kannada films; then, after **Reddy**'s ***Samskara*** (1970), promoter of art-house cinema. Produced **Karnad** and **Karanth**'s ***Vamsha Vriksha*** (1971); directed ***Hamsa Geethe*** and first Sanskrit feature, ***Adi Shankaracharya***. Later made another, *Bhagavad Geeta*. Culturally the two periods are closely linked: his recent Saint films argue for a revival of brahminical orthodoxy and Advaita philosophy to recover ' ancient truths', thus returning to themes inherent in mythologicals derived from feudal-brahminical literature, music and theatre under royal patronage around the turn of the century. Early scripts for Rajkumar (e.g. ***Ranadheera Kanteerava***, 1960) were part of a populist effort to reposition South India's feudalism in terms of Karnataka's regional-chauvinist movements from mid-40s onwards. His wordy prose socials, e.g. ***Bhoodana***, and the use of classical Carnatic music in *Hamsa*

Rajkumar (right) in G.V. Iyer's *Kiladi Ranga* (1966)

Geethe are part of an effort to update old Mysore's brahminical art forms seen as the pinnacle of achievement in conservative views of Karnataka's cultural history. Also acted in, e.g., *Radha Ramana* (1943), ***Bedara Kannappa*** (1954), *Bhakta Mallikarjuna*, *Mahakavi Kalidasa*, *Sodari* (all 1955), *Sadarame/Sadarama* (1956), *Kantheredu Nodu* (1961), and *Hemavathi* (1977). Published *Mooru Chitra Mooru Daari* (1984).

FILMOGRAPHY: **1962**: ***Bhoodana***; *Thayi Karulu/Thayin Karunai*; **1963**: *Lawyara Magalu*; *Bangari*; **1964**: *Post Master*; **1966**: *Kiladi Ranga*; **1967**: *Rajashekhara*; **1968**: *Mysore Tonga*; *Nane Bhagyavati*; **1969**: *Chowkada Deepa*; **1975**: ***Hamsa Geethe/Aakhri Geet***; **1976**: *Nalegalannu Maduvavaru*; **1977**: *Kudre Motte*; **1983**: ***Adi Shankaracharya***; **1986**: *Madhavacharya*; **1989**: *Shri Ramanujacharya*; *Wall Poster*; **1992**: *Bhagavad Geeta*.

JADDANBAI (b. 1908)

Hindi-Urdu director, singer, composer and actress born in Allahabad, UP. Joined Playart Phototone in Lahore (1932); later set up Sangeet Films (1936), writing, scoring and directing its films. Sang in Hindi and in Punjabi films such as *Insaan Ya Shaitan*, *Seva Sadan*, *Talash-e-Haq* and *Raja Gopichand*, also scoring the last two films. Scripted *Anjuman* (1948). Mother of 50s/60s Hindi superstar **Nargis**.

FILMOGRAPHY (* act only): **1933**: *Raja Gopichand**; *Insaan Ya Shaitan**; **1934**: *Prem Pareeksha**; *Seva Sadan**; *Naachwali**; **1935**: *Talash-e-Haq**; **1936**: *Hridaya Manthan*; *Madam Fashion*; **1937**: *Jeevan Swapna*; *Moti Ka Haar*.

JAFFREY, SAEED (b. 1929)

Internationaly successful actor born in Maler Kotla in Punjab. His father worked in the Indian Medical service. Degree in history in Allahabad; worked for AIR (1951-6); formed English theatre company, the Unity Theatre, in New Delhi (1951). Worked for tv in India (1955-6). Studied at RADA in London (1956) and at the Catholic University of America. Worked for United Nations Radio and at the India Tourist Office in the USA (1958-60). Toured Shakespeare across the USA and joined the Actors' Studio in New York. Extensive stage career in the USA and in Great Britain (1966). Cartoonist for *New York Mirror*. Wrote, produced and narrated *Reflections of India* for WQXR radio (1961-2). Made a recording of his poetry readings, *Adventures in Appreciation*. Hindi début in **Ray**'s ***Shatranj Ke Khiladi***. Acts in many commercial Hindi films often using the Lucknowi dialect. Narrated early Merchant-Ivory shorts and appeared in their features. Numerous tv appearances in Britain, including his own series *Tandoori Nights* (1985-7). Made a big impact in the innovative tv series *Gangsters* and in the British tv film, *My Beautiful Launderette*.

FILMOGRAPHY: **1969**: *Callan: The Worst Soldier I Ever Saw* (TV); *The Guru*; *View from the Window* (TV); *The Perfumed Garden*; **1971**: *The Horsemen*; **1972**: *The Sun Rises in the East* (TV); **1974**: *The Wilby Conspiracy*; **1975**: *The Man Who Would Be King*; **1976**: *Gangsters* (TV); **1977**: ***Shatranj Ke Khiladi***; **1978**: *Hullabaloo over Georgie and Bonnie's Pictures*; *The Last Giraffe*; *Destiny* (TV); **1979**: *Tales of the Unexpected: Poison* (TV); *Minder: The Bengal Tiger* (TV); *Ek Baar Phir*; **1980**: *We Think the World of You* (TV); *Staying On* (TV); **1981**: ***Chashme Buddoor***; *Sphinx*; **1982**: *Star*; *Gandhi*; *Courtesans of Bombay*; ***Masoom***; **1983**: *The Jewel in the Crown* (TV); *Kisise Na Kehna*; *Romance, Romance*; *Agaman*; *Ek Din Bahu Ka*; ***Mandi***; *Cricketer*; **1984**: *A Passage to India*; *The Far Pavilions* (TV); *Mashaal*; *Bhavna*; *The Razor's Edge*; *Le Soleil se l¤ve ß l' est*; **1985**: *Sagar*; *Phir Aayi Barsaat*; *My Beautiful Laundrette* (TV); *Far from the Kama Sutra* (TV); *White Lies* (TV); *Down With Oswald Pick* (TV); *Far from the Ganges* (TV); *Film Fare* (TV); *Ram Teri Ganga Maili*; *Jaanoo*; *Karishma Kudrat Ka*; *Tandoori Nights* (TV); **1986**: *Mohammed's Daughter* (Sh); *Qatl*; *Jalwa*; *Kala Dhandha Goray Log*; **1987**: *Awaam*; *Khudgarz*; *Aulad*; *Adalat*; *Isi Bahane* (TV); ***Tamas*** (TV); *Killing on the Exchange* (TV); **1988**: *Vijay*; *Khoon Bhari Maang*; *Just Ask for Diamond*; *Eeshwar*; *Kab Tak Chup Rahungi*; *Hero Hiralal*; *The Deceivers*; *Partition* (TV); **1989**: ***Ram Lakhan***; *Daata*; *Aakhri Gulam*; *Hisab Khoon Ka*; *Chaalbaaz*; *Hard Cases* (TV); *Manika, Une vie plus tard*; *Romancing the Taj* (TV); **1990**: *Aandhiyan*; *Yaadon Ka Mausam*; *Sindoor Ki Awaaz*; *Solah Satra*; *Diwana Mujhsa Nahin*; ***Dil***; *Naya Khoon*; *Shaandaar*; *After Midnight*; *Ghar Ho To Asia*; *Patthar Ke Insaan*; **1991**: *Ajooba*; *Masala*; *Harum Scarum* (TV); *Rumpole and the Quacks* (TV); *Gunehgaar Kaun*; *Henna*; *Indrajit*; *Yaara Dildara*; **1992**: *Vartmaan*; *Suryavanshi*; *Laatsaab*; *Nishchay*; **1993**: *Balma*; *Guddu*; *Anmol*; *Chalte Chalte* (TV); *Aashiq Awara*; *Aaina*; *15th August*; *Ek Hi Raasta*; *Aulad Ke Dushman*; *Little Napoleons* (TV).

JAGGAIAH, KONGARA (b. 1926)

Telugu actor born in Morampudi, Tenali taluk, AP. Graduated from Andhra Christian College, Vijaywada, where he staged amateur plays with **NTR**. Schoolteacher in Duggirala while working with NTR's National Art Theatre, e.g. his best-known play, *Chesina Papam* (1946). Sanskrit scholar and student of Jampala Venkata Narasimham. Activist with the Navya Sahitya Parishat (1942) and the **PWA** (until 1949). Telugu newsreader at AIR, New Delhi. Début in **H.V. Babu**'s *Adarsham*. Lead role in **Gopichand**'s *Priyuralu*. Appeared regularly in Telugu films mainly playing the second lead to heroes like **A. Nageshwara Rao** (***Ardhangi***, *Dr Chakravarthi*) until the 70s. Known for his classically accented oratory. Character actor in 80s melodrama, often in heavily made up grandfather roles. Also known for translations of Rabindra Sangeet into Telugu and for his compilation of **Acharya Athreya**'s work. Member of Parliament representing the Congress (O) from the Ongole constituency, AP, in 1967.

FILMOGRAPHY: **1952**: *Adarsham*; *Priyuralu*; **1954**: ***Bangaru Papa***; **1955**: *Ante Kavali*; *Beedala Asti*; ***Ardhangi/Pennin Perumai***; *Pasupu Kumkuma*; *Santosham/Naya Admi*; ***Donga Ramudu***; **1956**: *Muddubidda*; *Melukolupu*; *Balasanyasamma Katha*; **1957**: *Repu Neede*; *Aalu Magalu*; *Peddarikalu*; *Veera Kankanam*; *Bhale Bhava*; *Varudukavali/Manamagal Thevai*; *Bhale Ammayilu*; *MLA*; **1958**: *Anna Thamudu*; *Atta Okinti Kodale*; *Shri Krishna Garudi*; *Dongalunnaru Jagratha*; *Mundadugu*; ***Appu Chesi Pappu Koodu/Kadam Vangi Kalyanam***; **1959**: *Koothuru Kapuram*; *Bhagya Devatha*; **1960**: *Renukadevi Mahatyam*; *Kuladaivam*; *Dharmane Jayam*; *Pelli Kanuka*; *Kumkumarekha*; *Jalsarayudu*; *Annapurna*; *Samajam*; **1961**: *Velugu Needulu*; *Kanna Koduku*; *Taxi Ramudu*; *Intiki Deepam Illale*; *Pellikani Pillalu*; **1962**: *Padandi Munduku*; *Gali Medalu*; ***Aradhana***; *Appagintalu*; *Chitti Tamudu*; *Constable Koothuru*; **1963**: *Eedu Jodu*; *Anubandhalu*; *Manchi Rojulu Vastai*; *Thobuttuvulu*; **1964**: ***Poojapalam***; *Atmabalam*; *Gudigantalu*; *Peetalameeda Pelli*; *Dr Chakravarthi*; **1965**: *Uyyala Jampala*; *Chaduvukonna Bharya*; *Keelu Bommalu*; *Antastulu*; *Preminchi Choodu*; *Manushulu Mamathalu*; *Veelunama*; **1966**: *Manase Mandiram*; *Ame Evaru*; *Astiparulu*; **1967**: ***Pranamithrulu***; **1968**: *Bandhipotu Dongalu*; *Chinnari Papalu*; *Chuttarikalu*; *Gramadevathulu*; *Kalasina Manushulu*; *Papakosam*; *Veeranjaneya*; **1969**: *Ardha Rathri*; *Dharmapatni*; *Jarigina Katha*; *Sepoy Chinnaiah*; **1970**: *Talli Tandrulu*; *Yamalokapu Goodachari*; *Kodalu Diddina Kapuram*; *Drohi*; *Manasu Mangalyam*; ***Maro Prapancham***; **1971**: *Jeevitha Chakram*; *Vintha Samsaram*; *Suputhrudu*; *Patindalla Bangaram*; *Raitu Bidda*; *Bangaru Talli*; *Naa Thammudu*; *Chinnanati Snehitulu*; *Ramalayam*; *Talli Kuthulu*; *Kalyana Mandapam*; *Bharya Biddalu*; **1972**: *Collector Janaki*; *Shabash Papanna*; *Prajanayakudu*; *Shabash Baby*, *Badi Panthulu*; *Koduku Kodalu*; *Balamithrula Katha*; *Bangaru Babu*; **1973**: *Ramrajyam*; *Nindu Kutumbam*; *Devudu Chesina Manushulu*; *Ramude Devudu*; *Vintha Katha*; *Memu Manushulame*; *Kaidi Baba*; *Marapurani Manishi*; *Meena*; **1974**: *Mangalya Bhagyam*; ***Bhoomikosam***; *Manchi Manushulu*; *Devadasu*, *Deeksha*; *Gali Patalu*; *Kode Naagu*; *Peddalu Marali*; ***Alluri Seetaramaraju***; *Tulasi*; *Manushulu Matti Bommalu*; *Harathi*; *Dora Babu*; **1975**: *Eduruleni Manishi*; *Kavitha*; *Pellikani Thandri*; *Ramuni Minchina Ramudu*; *Samsaram*; *Manasakshi*; **1976**: *Aradhana*; *Rama Rajyamlo Raktha Pasam*; *Oka Deepam Veligindhi*; *Devude Gelichadu*; *Raja*; *Peddanayya*; *Muthyala Pallaki*; *Shri Rajeshwari Vilas Coffee Club*; *Uttamuralu*; **1977**: *Bangaru Bommalu*; *Adavi Ramudu*; *Raja Ramesh*; *Jeevana Theeralu*; *Panchayathi*; *Premalekhalu*; *Edureetha*; *Gadusu Ammayi*; *Jeevithamlo Vasantham*; **1978**: *Dongala Veta*; *KD No.1*; *Karunamayudu*; *Lambadolla Ramadasu*; *Sahasavanthudu*; *Vichitra Jeevitham*; *Ramakrishnulu*; *Yuga Purushudu*; *Shri Rama Raksha*; *Moodu Puvvulu Aaru Kayalu*; **1979**: *Ramabanam*; *Maavari Manchithanam*; *Judagadu*; ***Yugandhar***; *Samajaniki Saval*; *Mangala Toranalu*; **1980**: *Edantastulameda*; *Bhale Krishnudu*; *Kalyana Chakravarthi*; *Ram Robert Rahim*; *Shri Vasavi Kannika Parameshwari Mahatyam*; *Sandhya*; *Ragile Jwala*; *Srishti Rahasyulu*; *Manavude Mahaniyudu*; **1981**: *Talli Kodakala Anubandham*; *Guru Shishyulu*; *Tiruguleni Manishi*; *Nyayam Kavali*; *Jeevitha Radham*; *Rani Kasularangamma*; ***Seethakoka Chilaka***; **1982**: ***Megha Sandesam***; *Gopala Krishnudu*; **1983**: *Agni Samadhi*; *Chanda Sasanudu*; *Dharma Poratam*; *Koteeshwarudu*; *Poratham*; *Rama Rajyamlo Bheemaraju*; *Sivudu Sivudu Sivudu*; *Yuddha Bhoomi*; **1984**: *Kanchu Kagada*; *Suvarna Sundari*; *Anubandham*; *Babulugadi*

Debba; *Disco King*; *Grihalakshmi*; *Jagan*; *Mr Vijay*; *Naagu*; *Palnati Puli*; *Raaraju*; *Ramayanamlo Bhagavatham*; *Sahasame Jeevitham*; ***Swati***; *Udanthudu*; *Alaya Deepam*; **1985**: *Kirathakudu*; *Krishnagaradi*; *Uriki Soggadu*; *Palnati Simham*; *Thirugubatu*; *Agni Parvatham*; *Nyayam Meere Cheppali*; *Maha Sangramam*; *Lanchavatharam*; *Rechukka*; *Bharya Bharthala Bandham*; *Maharaju*; *Pachani Kapuram*; *Illale Devata*; *Adavi Donga*; *Vijeta*; *Mahamanishi*; *Edadugula Bandham*; **1988**: *Inspector Pratap*; *Tiraga Bidda Telugu Bidda*; *Prema Kiritam*; *Ashwathama*; *Jeevana Ganga*; *Ramudu Bheemudu*; *Rakthabhisekham*; *Dharma Teja*; **1989**: *Mamatala Kovela*; *Bala Gopaludu*; *Adarshavanthudu*; *Ajatashatru*.

JAGIRDAR, GAJANAN (1907-88)

First major freelance director-character actor in Marathi and Hindi cinema. Born in Amravati. Child actor on amateur stage. Started Arun Players in Pune and staged Chekov's *Cherry Orchard* and Harindranath Chattopadhyay's *Returned from Abroad*. Claimed Ernst Lubitsch's *The Patriot* (1928) as a major influence. Started in films as writer of English intertitles at **Prabhat**; then bit actor. Apprenticed to **Bhalji Pendharkar**. Made films for **Master Vinayak**'s Huns Pictures, briefly at **Minerva Movietone** as scenarist for **Sohrab Modi** (*Meetha Zaher*, ***Talaaq***, etc.) and at **P.K. Atre**'s company. Best-known film: ***Ramshastri*** (at Prabhat), taking over the direction from **Raja Nene** and **Bedekar** as well as playing the lead role. Main performance was as the Muslim patriarch in **Shantaram**'s ***Shejari***. Appointed first director of the **FTII** (1960) and became well-known pedagogue applying, e.g., Stanislavski's theories to local conditions in a book about acting (1983). Published two autobiographies (1971 & 1986). Made a tv serial, *Swami*, on the life of Madhavrao Peshwa, celebrating Marathi chauvinism.

FILMOGRAPHY (* also d/** only d): **1932**: ***Jalti Nishani/Agnikankan***; **1934**: *Sinhasan***; **1936**: *Honhar**; *Aseer-e-Hawas*; **1937**: *Begunah***; **1938**: *Umaji Naik***; *Meetha Zaher*; ***Talaaq***; **1940**: *Main Hari***; **1941**: ***Payachi Dasi/Charnon Ki Dasi****; ***Shejari/Padosi***; **1942**: ***Vasantsena****; **1943**: *Kanoon*; **1944**: ***Ramshastri****; *Kiran**; *Anban*; **1945**: *Kaise Kahun*; **1946**: *Jhumke*; *Shatranj*; *Behram Khan**; **1947**: *Jail Yatra**; **1948**: *Dhanyavaad**; **1950**: *Birha Ki Raat**; *Sabak*; *Pagle*; **1952**: ***Chhatrapati Shivaji***; **1953**: *Armaan*; *Mahatma*; **1954**: *Maan*; *Mallika-e-Alam Nurjehan*; ***Oon Paoos***; *Angarey*; *Mahatma Kabir***; **1955**: *Ghar Ghar Mein Diwali**; **1956**: *Chhoo Mantar*; *Zindagi Ke Mele*; *Dassehra*; **1957**: ***Paying Guest***; *Aparadhi Kaun*; *Talash*; *Yahudi Ki Ladki*; *Zamana*; **1958**: *Taxi Stand***; *Trolley Driver**; *Dulhan*; *Karigar*; ***Raj Tilak***; **1959**: *Qaidi No. 911*; *Chacha Zindabad*; **1960**: *Babar*; *Hum Hindustani*; *Umaji Naik***; **1961**: *Shahir Parashuram*; *Vaijayanti**; ***Hum Dono***; *Tanhaai*; **1962**: *Main Chup Rahungi*; *Aarti*; **1963**: *Chhota Jawan*; *Sukhachi Savli**; *Grihasthi*; **1964**: *Ek Don Teen*; *Sarfarosh*; **1965**: *Yugo Yugo Mi Vaat Pahili*; *Ek Saal Pahele*; ***Guide***; *Kajal*; *Main Hoon Alladdin*; *Tu Hi Meri Zindagi*; **1966**: *Dillagi*; *Suraj*; *Amrapali*; *Chhota Bhai*; *Hum Kahan Ja Rahe Hain*; *Shankar Khan*; *Bandar Mera Saathi*; **1967**: *Mera Munna*; **1968**: *Farishta*; *Dil Aur Mohabbat*; *Humsaya*; *Mangalsutra*; *Jhuk Gaya Aasmaan*; **1969**: *Admi Aur Insaan*; *Beti Tumhare Jaisi*; *Saajan*; *Anmol Moti*; ***Ittefaq***; *Nai Zindagi*; *Paisa Ya Pyar*; **1970**: *Insaan Aur Shaitan*; *Poraki*; *Ti Mi Navhech*; *Dr X*; *Devi*; *Ghar Ghar Ki Kahani*; *Jeevan Mrityu*; *Raaton Ka Raja*; *Jwala*; **1971**: *Nate Jadle Don Jivache*; *Donhi Gharcha Pahuna**; *Hulchul*; **1972**: *Sub Ka Saathi*; *Aai Mi Kuthe Jau?*; *Zindagi Zindagi*; **1973**: *Aa Gale Lag Jaa*; *Bandhe Haath*; *Chori Chori*; *Garibi Hatao*; *Naina*; *Sonal*; **1974**: *Raja Shivachhatrapati*; *Ashiana*; *Badi Maa*; *Hamrahi*; *Woh Main Nahin*; *Mera Vachan Gita Ki Kasam*; **1975**: *Badnaam*; *Mutthi Bhar Chawal*; **1976**: *Aaj Ka Yeh Ghar*; *Gumrah*; *Meera Shyam*; *Raksha Bandhan*; **1977**: *Admi Sadak Ka*; *Aankh Ka Tara*; *Paradh*; *Imaan Dharam*; *Ram Bharose*; *Chhota Baap*; *Dhoop Chhaon*; *Do Dilwale*; *Mandir Masjid*; *Naami Chor*; *Shankar Hussain*; **1978**: *Anjaam*; *Des Pardes*; *Karmayogi*; *Dost Asava Tar Asa*; **1979**: *Maan Apmaan*; **1980**: *Deva Pudhe Manoos*; *Mantryanchi Soon*; *Paij*; **1981**: ***Umrao Jaan***; **1983**: *Rishta Kaagaz Ka*; *Lal Chunaria*; *Love In Goa*; **1984**: *Bhool*; **1986**: *Aap Ke Saath*; *Yeh Preet Na Hogi Kam*; *Sutradhar*; **1988**: *Swami*** (TV).

Gajanan Jagirdar in *Ramshastri* (1944)

JAMUNA, NIPPANI (b. 1937)

Telugu actress, also worked in Hindi, Tamil and Kannada. Born in Hampi, Karnataka; educated in Duggirala. Associated with the stage group Praja Natya Mandali, e.g. the play *Maabhoomi*. Screen début in her colleague Rajarao's film, ***Puttillu***. Early films with Tilak and **Chanakya** (e.g. ***Anta Manavalle***). Famous role in *Bangaru Talli*, the Telugu remake of **Mehboob**'s opus ***Mother India*** (1957). First Hindi starring role in **Prasad**'s comedy, *Miss Mary*.

FILMOGRAPHY: **1953**: ***Puttillu***; **1954**: ***Anta Manavalle***; *Iddaru Pellalu*; *Maa Gopi*; *Menarikam*; ***Nirupedalu***; *Vaddante Dabbu*; ***Bangaru Papa***; **1955**: *Santosham/Naya Admi*; *Vadinagari Gajalu*; ***Donga Ramudu***; ***Missamma/Missiamma***; **1956**: ***Tenali Ramakrishna***; ***Chintamani***; *Nagula Chaviti/Adarshasati*; **1957**: ***Bhagya Rekha***; *Veera Kankanam*; *Dongalo Dora*; *Vinayaka Chaviti*; *Sati Ansuya*; *Miss Mary*; **1958**: ***Bhukailasa***; *Bommalapelli/Bommai Kalyanam*; *Pellinati Pramanalu*; *Shri Krishnamaya*; ***Appu Chesi Pappu Koodu***; **1959**: *Koothuru Kapuram*; *Maa Inti Mahalakshmi/Enga Veetu Mahalakshmi*; *Sipayi Kooturu*; *Vachina Kodulu Nachindi*; *Vazhkai Oppantham*; *Nalla Theerpu*; *Naradhar Kalyanam*; *Kanniraindha Kanavan*; *Thayi Magalukku Kattiya Thali*; **1960**: *Kadavunin Kuzhandai*; *Dharmane Jayam*; *Mahakavi Kalidasa*; *Annapurna*; *Jalsarayudu*; **1961**: *Usha Parinayam*; *Krishna Prema*; *Pellikani Pillalu*; **1962**: *Gul-e-Bakavali Katha*; *Pelli Thambulam/Nishchaya Thambulam*; ***Gundamma Katha/Manidan Maravalli***; **1963**: *Thobuttuvulu*; *Nadi Aada Janma*; ***Moogamanushulu***; **1964**: ***Murali Krishna***; *Manchi Manishi*; *Bobbili Yuddham*; ***Poojapalam***; **1965**: ***CID***; *Dorikite Dongalu*; *Mangamma Sapatham*; *Keelu Bommalu*; *Todu Needa*; **1966**: *Shri Krishna Pandaviyam*; *Palnati Yuddham*; *Navarathri*; *Srikakula Andhra Mahavishnu Katha*; *Sangeetalakshmi*; *Shri Krishna Tulabharam*; *Letamanushulu*; *Adugu Jadalu*; *Ramu*; **1967**: *Chadurangam*; *Poolarangudu*; *Upayamlo Apayam*; **1968**: *Paala Manushulu*; *Sati Arundhati*; *Amayukudu*; *Chinnari Papalu*; *Challani Needa*; *Bangaru Sankellu*; *Pelliroju*; *Bandhipotu Dongalu*; **1969**: *Ekaveera*; *Muhurtabalam*; **1970**: *Aada Janma*; *Manasu Mangalyam*; ***Maro Prapancham***; **1971**: *Bangaru Talli*; *Mattilo Manikyam*; *Pavitra Hridayalu*; *Ramalayam*; *Sati Ansuya*; *Shrimanthudu*; **1972**: *Atthanu Diddina Kodalu*; *Collector Janaki*; *Maa Inti Kodalu*; *Vintha Dampathulu*; *Sampoorna Ramayanam*; *Menakodalu*; ***Pandanti Kapuram***; **1973**: *Pasi Hridayalu*; *Mamatha*; *Dabbuku Lokam Dasoham*; *Bangaru Manushulu*; *Dhanama? Daivama?*; *Inti Dongalu*; *Memu Manushulame*;

Nindu Kutumbam; *Snehabandham*; **1974**: *Peddalu Marali*; *Manushulu Matti Bommalu*; *Deergha Sumangali*; *Deeksha*; *Gauri*; ***Bhoomikosam***; **1975**: *Vanaja Girija*; *Moguda Pellamma*; *Yashoda Krishna*; *Parivarthana*; *Bharati*; *Anuragalu*; *Samsaram*; *Ee Kalam Dampathulu*; **1976**: *America Ammayi*; *Manishi Mrugham*; ***Seeta Kalyanam***; **1977**: *Chanakya Chandragupta*; *Gadusu Pillodu*; *Sati Savitri*; *Seeta Rama Vanavasu*; **1978**: ***Akbar Saleem Anarkali***; ***Shri Rama Pattabhishekham***; *Katakatala Rudraiah*; **1979**: *Bangaru Chellalu*; *Shrimad Virata Parvam*; **1980**: *Shri Vinayaka Vijayam*; **1987**: *Mandala Dheesudu*.

JANAKI, S. (b. 1938)

South Indian singer born in Pallapatla, Guntur Dist., AP. Made her reputation with an AIR prize (1956) and became a staff artist at **AVM** (1957). Broke through in Tamil cinema under T. Chalapathi Rao and in Telugu via a duet with singer **Ghantasala** performing under the musical direction of **Pendyala**. Has sung over 13,000 songs in 12 languages.

JANAKI, SOWCAR (b. 1922)

Telugu, Tamil, Kannada and Hindi actress, originally Shankaramanchi Janaki. Born in the 24 Parganas Dist., Bengal. Acted in several radio plays when a child. Married aged 15; separated soon after and sought a career in films as a single parent. Discovered by **L.V. Prasad**, whom she considers her mentor, and made her début in ***Shavukaru***. Although the film wasn't a hit, she appended its title to her name ever since. Made her Tamil début at **Modern Theatres**, in the **Bharatidasan** scripted *Valayapathi*. Often paired in 50s Tamil films with M.R. Radha (e.g. *Nalla Idathu Sambandham*). Also acted in Tamil plays, e.g. by **K. Balachander**. Produced and acted in Balachander's melodrama ***Kaviyath Thalaivi***, followed by **Krishnan-Panju**'s *Ranga Rathnam*. Her sister, Krishnakumari, was also a noted Tamil, Kannada and Telugu star, and granddaughter Vaishnavi joined films in the late 80s.

FILMOGRAPHY: **1950**: ***Shavukaru***; **1952**: *Adarsham*; *Valayapathi*; **1953**: *Prapancham*; *Pichhipullaiah*; **1954**: *Vaddante Dabbu*; *Devakannika*; **1955**: *Cherupukura Chedevu*; *Kanyadanam*; *Pasupu Kumkuma*; ***Rojulu Marayi/Kalam Maripochu***; *Kanyashulkam*; **1956**: *Nagula Chaviti/Adarshasati*; *Bhagya Chakra*; *Bhagyodaya*; *Sadarame/Sadarama*; **1957**: *Aalu Magalu*; *Bhale Bhava*; *Ratnagiri Rahasya/Tangamalai Rahasyam*; ***Bhagya Rekha***; **1958**: *Nalla Idathu Sambandham*; ***School Master/Badi Panthulu***; *Anna Thamudu*; *Ganga Gauri Samvadam*; **1959**: *Abalai Anjugam*; ***Mahishasura Mardini/Durga Mata***; **1960**: *Naan Kanda Sorgam*; *Kodeduddulu Ekaramnela*; *Mohabbat Ki Jeet*; ***Shri Venkateshwara Mahatyam***; **1961**: *Batasari/Kanal Neer*; **1962**: *Manchi Manushulu/Penn Manam*; *Daivaleele*; *Parthal Pasi Theerum*; **1963**: *Kanya Ratna*; *Gauri*; *Malli Madhuve*; *Sati Shakthi*; *Paar Magale Paar*; *Saaku Magalu/Pempudu Koothuru*; *Savati Koduku*; *Devasundari*; **1964**: *Deshadrohulu*; *Peetalameeda Pelli*; *Dr Chakravarthi*; *Navakoti Narayana*; **1965**: *Naanal*; **1966**: ***Motor Sundaram Pillai***; *Mahakavi Kalidas*; **1967**: ***Thaikku Thalaimagan***; ***Bhama Vijayam/Bhale Kodalu***; **1968**: *Manchi Kutumbam*; *Teen Bahuraniyan*; *Chinnari Papalu*; *Undamma Bottupeduta*; *Ethir Neechal*; *Lakshmi Kalyanam*; *Uyarntha Manithan*; *Chakram*; **1969**: ***Kaval Daivam***; *Thunaivan*; *Iru Kodukal*; **1970**: *Rendu Kutumbala Katha*; *Nadu Iravil*; *Kasturi Tilakam*; ***Kaviyath Thalaivi***; **1971**: *Ranga Rathnam*; **1972**: *Prajanayakudu*; *Appa Tata*; *Thiruneelakantar*; *Daivam*; *Thanga Thurai*; *Neethi*; **1973**: *Prarthanai*; *School Master*; *Engal Thanga Raja*; *Khaidi Baba*; *Padmavyuham*; **1974**: *Sorgathil Thirumanam*; *Kaliyuga Kannan*; **1975**: *Cinema Paithiyam*; *Manithanum Daivamagalam*; *Nalla Marumagal*; *Uravukku Kayi Koduppam*; *Balipeetam*; *Devudulanti Manishi*; *Naaku Swatantram Vachindi*; *Vemulavada Bhimakavi*; **1976**: *Manasakshi*; *Premabandham*; *Athirishtam Azhaikkirathu*; *Dashavatharam*; *Idaya Malar*; *Nalla Penmani*; *Perum Pukazhum*; **1977**: *Olimayamana Ethirkalam*; *Adrushtavanthuralu*; *Oka Talli Katha*; **1978**: *Anbin Alaigal*; *Kannan Oru Kayi Kuzhanthai*; **1983**: *Rajakumar*; *Engalamum Mudiyum*; **1984**: *Chiranjeevi*; *Kayi Kodukkum Kayi*; **1987**: *Brahma Nayudu*; *Sardar Krishnama Nayudu*; *Gauthami*; *Vairagyam*; **1988**: *Murali Krishnudu*; *Adade Adharam*; **1989**: ***Geetanjal***.

JASWANTLAL, NANDLAL (b. 1906)

Hindi director born in Bardoli, Surat. Son of Jaswantlal Mehta, administrative officer at **Kohinoor**. Started career as Kohinoor Studio employee (1924). Assisted **Chandulal Shah** (1926-9) and directed films for **Ranjit** Studio (1929-33). Silent star scenarist **Mohanlal Dave** apparently joined Ranjit solely to be able to work with Jaswantlal. Left to make a tour of Europe (1934); then joined **Imperial** (1934-6) where he directed **Sulochana** in several remakes of her own **R.S. Choudhury** and **Bhavnani** silent hits. Worked briefly in Madras running a film laboratory (1937), then returned to direction. Silent work influenced by Gandhian nationalism. Best known for his later **Filmistan** musicals: ***Anarkali*** (with Bina Rai and music by **C. Ramchandra**) and ***Nagin*** (with **Vyjayanthimala**), one of the biggest post-Independence musical hits. Admired for his sophisticated lighting (with cameraman Pandurang Naik). Used extreme close-ups and unusual angles creating disjointed but dramatic and sensual spaces (e.g. the beginning of *Anarkali*).

FILMOGRAPHY: **1929**: *Jawani Diwani*; *Pardesi Saiyan*; **1930**: *Pahadi Kanya*; **1931**: ***Prem Jogan***; *Ghunghatwali* (all St); **1933**: *Pardesi Preetam*; **1934**: ***Indira MA***; *Kashmeera*; **1935**: *Pujarini*; **1936**: ***Bambai Ki Billi***; *Jungle Queen*; **1939**: ***Jeevan Saathi***; **1941**: *Kamadhenu*; **1943**: *Pratigya*; **1944**: *Kadambari*; **1945**: *Amrapali*; **1947**: *Sati Toral*; *Veerangana*; **1951**: *Sanam*; **1953**: ***Anarkali***; **1954**: ***Nagin***; **1956**: *Taj*; **1957**: *Champakali*; **1963**: *Akeli Mat Jaiy*.

JAYALALITHA JAYARAM (b. 1948)

Tamil, Telugu and Kannada star, now better known as a politician. Born in Mysore, the daughter of screen star Sandhya. Learnt the Bharat Natyam aged 4. Claims that she wanted to study law, but dropped out of school to follow her aunt Vidyavati (who acted in, e.g., ***En Veedu/Naa Illu***, 1953) into films to support her family. Début in Shankar V. Giri's unreleased English film *Epistle*. Early career in Kannada where her second film, *Chinnada Gombe*, was a major hit. Introduced to Tamil by **C.V. Sridhar** (*Vennira Adai*). Telugu début in *Manushulu Mamathalu*, but became a star in that language playing the vampish lead in **G. Krishna**'s James Bond-type hit *Goodachari 116*. First film with **MGR**, the star most closely associated with both her cinematic and political careers, is **Panthulu's** *Ayirathil Oruvan*, followed by M.A. Thirumugham's *Kannithai*. She is a crucial element in MGR's films, esp. 1968-70 when she was at the pinnacle of her career and featured in almost every MGR film, usually to allow the proletarian hero to move across class barriers (e.g. ***Nam Naadu***, ***Mattukkara Velan***). Left films about the same time as MGR, after which she wrote for Cho's fortnightly *Tughlaq* until MGR made her an important member of his All-India Anna Dravida Munnetra Kazhagam (1981). After MGR's death became embroiled in a bitter rivalry with MGR's wife V.N. Janaki over the leadership of the party, which she eventually led to victory, becoming Chief Minister (1991). Made a comeback in films playing ' herself' (as a politician/Chief Minister) in *Neenga Nalla Erukkanum*, delivering a message on prohibition.

FILMOGRAPHY: **1961**: *Epistle*; *Shrishaila Mahatme*; **1964**: *Chinnada Gombe*; *Mane Aliya*; ***Amarashilpi Jakanachari***; **1965**: *Vennira Adai*; *Nanna Kartavya*; *Ayirathil Oruvan*; *Nee*; *Manushulu Mamathalu*; *Kannithai*; *Mavana Magalu*; **1966**: ***Motor Sundaram Pillai***; *Muharassi*; *Yar Nee*; ***Kumari Penn***; *Chandrodyam*; *Thanipiravi*; *Major Chandrakant*; *Gauri Kalyanam*; *Mani Makudam*; *Badukuva Daari*; *Goodachari 116*; *Ame Evaru*; *Astiparulu*; *Navarathri*; *Kanni Pilla*(?); **1967**: ***Thaikku Thalaimagan***; ***Kandan Karunai***; *Arasa Kattali*; *Madi Veetu Mappilai*; *Raja Veetu Pillai*; *Kavalkaran*; *Naan*; *Gopaludu Bhoopaludu*; *Chikkadu Dorakudu*; **1968**: *Rahasiya Police 115*; *Andru Kanda Mukham*; *There Thiruvizha*; *Kudiruntha Koil*; *Galatta Kalyanam*; *Panakara Pillai*; *Kannan En Kathalan*; *Moonrezuthu*; *Bommalattam*; ***Pudhiya Bhoomi***; ***Kanavan***; *Muthu Chippi*; *Enga Ooru Raja*; *Kadhal Vaghanam*; *Oli Vilakku*; *Sukha Dukhalu*; *Niluvu Dopidi*; *Brahmachari*; *Tikka Shankaraiah*; *Baghdad Gajadonga*; *Izzat*; *Attagaru Kottakodalu*; **1969**: *Adimai Penn*; *Gurudakshinai*; *Daivamagan*; ***Nam Naadu***; *Shri Rama Katha*; *Adrushtavanthalu*; *Katha Nayakudu*; *Gandikota Rahasyam*; *Adarsha Kutumbam*; *Kadaladu Vadaladu*; ***Mattukkara Velan***; **1970**: *Enga Mama*; *En Annan*; ***Engal Thangam***; *Engiruthu Vandhal*; *Thedi Vantha Mappillai*; *Anadhai Anandan*; *Pathukappu*; *Akkachellelu*; *Alibaba 40 Dongalu*; *Shri Krishna Vijayam*; *Dharmadatha*; **1971**: *Kumari Kottam*; *Sumathi En Sundari*; *Savale Samali*; *Thanga Gopuram*; *Annai Velanganni*; *Adi Parasakthi*; *Neerum Neruppum*; *Oru Thai Makkal*; *Bharya Biddalu*; *Shri Krishna Satya*; **1972**: *Raja*; *Thikkutheriyatha Kattil*; *Raman Thediya Seethai*; *Pattikada Pattanama*; *Dharmam Engay*; *Annamitta Kai*; *Shakti Leela*; *Neethi*; *Akka Tammudu*; *Devudamma*; **1973**: *Ganga Gauri*; *Vandhale Magarasi*; *Suryakanthi*; *Pattikatu Ponnaiah*; *Baghdad Perazhagi*; *Devudu Chesina Manushulu*; *Dr Babu*; *Jesus*; **1974**: *Thirumangalyam*; *Thayi*; *Vairam*; *Anbu*

Thangai; *Anbai Thedi*; *Premalu Pellilu*; **1975**: *Avalukku Ayiram Kangal*; *Avanthan Manithan*; *Pattam Bharathamum*; *Yarukkum Vetkamillai*; **1976**: *Chitra Pournami*; *Kanavan Manaivi*; **1977**: *Shri Krishna Leela*; *Unnai Chutrumugalam*; **1980**: *Nadhiyai Thedi Vandha Kadal*; **1992**: *Neenga Nalla Erukkanu*.

JAYAMMA, B. (1915-88)

First star of Kannada cinema and singer with classical training. Born in Chikmagalur, Karnataka. Started aged 7 on the **Company Natak** stage in **Gubbi Veeranna**'s theatre troupe, where she worked with her niece, B. Sundaramma, the group's star actress. Became lead actress in 1928 and played Draupadi on stage in their big-budget spectacular, *Kurukshetra* (1934). Entered films in Veeranna-produced films directed by Belgian Raphael Algoet, **Y.V. Rao**, **S. Soundarrajan** and **H.L.N. Simha**, mostly in adaptations of the Gubbi Co. stage mythologicals. Also played major roles in 40s **Vauhini** films in Telugu. Made a late 60s comeback, playing e.g. the haughty queen mother of hero **Rajkumar** in *Immadi Pulakesi*.

FILMOGRAPHY: **1931**: *His Love Affair*; **1932**: *Hari Maya* (both St); **1935**: *Sadarame*; **1938**: *Gul-e-Bakavali*; **1941**: *Subhadra*; **1942**: ***Bhakta Potana***; ***Jeevana Nataka***; **1944**: *Bhartrahari* (Ta); **1945**: ***Hemareddy Mallamma***; ***Swargaseema***; **1946**: *Lavangi*; ***Thyagayya***; **1947**: *Brahma Ratham*; **1949**: *Natya Rani*; *Mangayar Karasi*; **1950**: *Raja Vikrama*; **1951**: *Mantradandam*; **1953**: ***Gunasagari/Sathya Shodhanai***; ***Gumasta***; *Jaladurga/Karkottai*; **1958**: *Anna Thangi*; **1965**: *Mavana Magalu*; **1966**: *Prema Mayi*; **1967**: *Immadi Pulakesi*; **1968**: *Anna Thamma*; *Bedi Bandhavalu*; **1970**: ***Mukti***; **1971**: *Sakshatkara*.

Jayoo Nachiket *see* **Jayoo** and **Nachiket Patwardhan**

JAYWANT, NALINI (b. 1926)

Actress born in Bombay; cousin of **Shobhana Samarth**. Début aged 13; started as singer in *Radhika*. In **Mehboob**'s ***Bahen*** she sang the Wajahat Mirza duet, *Nahin khate hain bhaiyya mere paan*, with Sheikh Mukhtar, central to the film's incest theme. A *Filmfare* cameramen's poll voted her the most photogenic Indian actress ever. In her best-known work she usually functioned as the one who embraces life in counterpoint to the otherwise ' realistic' melodrama of **R.S. Choudhury**, **Mehboob**, **Paul Zils** and **Mahesh Kaul** (e.g. *Naujawan*). Later she developed a curiously autonomous, guilt-free performative style (e.g. the Navketan thriller ***Kala Pani***). Her association with realism was extended by Ramesh Saigal, **Bimal Roy** and most notably **Zia Sarhadi**'s ***Awaaz***, while films with **Kardar** and **Gyan Mukherjee** developed the alternate musical persona exemplified by the 50s **Filmistan** musicals with **Dev Anand** (e.g. ***Munimji***). Often partnered **Ashok Kumar** in 1950-2 after their success in Filmistan's ***Samadhi*** and ***Sangram*** at **Bombay Talkies**.

FILMOGRAPHY: **1941**: *Radhika*; *Nirdosh*; ***Bahen***; **1942**: *Aankh Micholi*; **1943**: *Adab Arz*; **1946**: *Phir Bhi Apna Hai*; **1948**: *Anokha Pyar*; *Gunjan*; *Varasdar*; **1949**: *Chakori*; **1950**: *Aankhen*; ***Hindustan Hamara***; *Muqaddar*; ***Samadhi***; ***Sangram***; **1951**: *Ek Nazar*; *Jadu*; *Nand Kishore*; *Naujawan*; **1952**: *Do Raha*; *Kafila*; *Naubahar*; *Saloni*; *Jalpari*; ***Rahi***; **1953**: *Shikast*; **1954**: *Baap Beti*; *Kavi*; *Lakeeren*; *Mehbooba*; *Naaz*; *Nastik*; **1955**: *Chingari*; *Jai Mahadev*; *Lagan*; ***Munimji***; ***Railway Platform***; *Raj Kanya*; **1956**: *Aan Baan*; ***Awaaz***; *Durgesh Nandini*; *Fifty-Fifty*; *Hum Sub Chor Hain*; *Insaaf*; *Twenty-Sixth January*; *Sudarshan Chakra*; **1957**: *Kitna Badal Gaya Insaan*; *Miss Bombay*; *Mr X*; *Neel Mani*; *Sheroo*; **1958**: ***Kala Pani***; *Milan*; **1959**: *Maa Ke Aansoo*; **1960**: *Mukti*; **1961**: *Amar Rahe Yeh Pyar*; *Senapati*; **1962**: *Girls' Hostel*; *Zindagi Aur Hum*; **1965**: *Bombay Race Course*; **1983**: *Nastik*.

JEETENDRA (b. 1942)

Major 70s Hindi star with **Rajesh Khanna** in an era dominated by love stories preceding **Bachchan**. Original name Ravi Kapoor. Introduced in **Shantaram**'s late 50s/60s musicals, his early work was in mid-budget B-productions, often dancing in white, patent-leather shoes. He made a serious attempt to change his image by sticking on a moustache in 70s **Gulzar** films (e.g. *Kinara* and *Khushboo*) and playing a male Julie Andrews in the *Sound of Music* adaptation, ***Parichay***. Later work pioneered a more financially efficient but formally impoverished industrial cinema in Madras, e.g. films by **K. Raghavendra Rao** (*Himmatwala*, *Jaani Dost*), **K. Bapaiah** (*Mawaali*, *Maqsad*) and **Dasari Narayana Rao** (*Justice Choudhury*, *Prem Tapasya*).

FILMOGRAPHY: **1959**: *Navrang*; **1963**: *Sehra*; **1964**: *Dulha Dulhan*; *Geet Gaya Pattharone*; **1966**: *Dillagi*; **1967**: *Boond Jo Ban Gaye Moti*; *Farz*; *Gunahon Ka Devta*; *Parivar*; **1968**: *Aulad*; *Mere Huzoor*; *Suhaag Raat*; **1969**: *Anmol Moti*; *Badi Didi*; *Dharti Kahe Pukar Ke*; *Do Bhai*; *Jeene Ki Raah*; *Jigri Dost*; *Vishwas*; *Waris*; **1970**: *Himmat*; *Humjoli*; *Maa Aur Mamta*; *Naya Raasta*; *Mere Humsafar*; *Khilona*; *Jawab*; **1971**: *Chahat*; *Kathputli*; *Banphool*; *Bikhare Moti*; *Caravan*; *Ek Nari Ek Brahmachari*; *Yaar Mere*; **1972**: *Bhai Ho To Aisa*; *Ek Bechara*; *Ek Hasina Do Diwane*; ***Parichay***; *Roop Tera Mastana*; *Shadi Ke Baad*; *Sazaa*; **1973**: *Anokhi Ada*; *Chori Chori*; *Gehri Chaal*; *Jaise Ko Taisa*; **1974**: *Bidaai*; *Dulhan*; *Roti*; **1975**: *Aakhri Dao*; *Khushboo*; *Rani Aur*

Ashok Kumar and Nalini Jaywant in *Kafila* (1952)

Lalpari; *Umar Qaid*; **1976**: *Sankoch*; *Santan*; *Udhaar Ka Sindoor*; *Nagin*; **1977**: *Palkon Ki Chhaon Mein*; *Apnapan*; ***Dharam Veer***; *Ek Hi Raasta*; *Dildaar*; *Jai Vijay*; *Kasam Khoon Ki*; *Kinara*; *Priyatama*; *Zamanat*; **1978**: *Badalte Rishte*; *Chowki No. 11*; *Dil Aur Deewar*; *Karmayogi*; *Swarg Narak*; *Tumhari Kasam*; *Nalayak*; **1979**: *Love In Canada*; *Aatish*; *Hum Tere Aashiq Hain*; *Jaani Dushman*; *Khandaan*; *Lok Parlok*; *Jaandaar*; *Naya Bakra*; *The Gold Medal*; **1980**: *Aap Ke Diwane*; *Asha*; *Jal Mahal*; *Judaai*; *Jyoti Bane Jwala*; *Maang Bharo Sajana*; *Neeyat*; *Nishana*; *Waqt Ki Deewar*; *Takkar*; *The Burning Train*; **1981**: *Ek Hi Bhool*; *Jyoti*; *Khoon Aur Pani*; *Khoon Ka Rishta*; *Raaste Pyar Ke*; *Meri Awaaz Suno*; *Pyaasa Sawan*; *Raksha*; *Shaaka*; *Sharada*; *Chorni*; *Mosambi Narangi*; **1982**: *Jeevan Dhara*; *Anokha Bandhan*; *Apna Bana Lo*; *Badle Ki Aag*; *Deedar-e-Yaar*; *Farz Aur Kanoon*; *Dharam Kanta*; *Insaan*; *Jiyo Aur Jeene Do*; *Mehndi Rang Layegi*; *Samrat*; *Justice Choudhury*; **1983**: *Arpan*; *Himmatwala*; *Jaani Dost*; *Mawaali*; *Nishan*; *Prem Tapasya*; **1984**: *Akalmand*; *Haisiyat*; *Kaamyaab*; *Maqsad*; *Qaidi*; *Tohfa*; *Yeh Desh*; *Zakhmi Sher*; **1985**: *Balidan*; *Haqeeqat*; *Hoshiyar*; *Locket*; *Mera Saathi*; *Pataal Bhairavi*; *Sanjog*; *Sarfarosh*; **1986**: *Aag Aur Shola*; *Aisa Pyar Kahan*; *Bond 303*; *Dosti Dushmani*; *Dharam Adhikari*; *Ghar Sansar*; *Jaal*; *Sada Suhagan*; *Sinhasan*; *Suhagan*; *Swarg Se Sundar*; **1987**: *Apne Apne*; *Aulad*; *Himmat Aur Mehnat*; *Insaaf Ki Pukar*; *Jaan Hatheli Pe*; *Khudgarz*; *Madadgaar*; *Majaal*; *Sindoor*; *New Delhi*; **1988**: *Mulzim*; *Tamacha*; *Kanwarlal*; *Sone Pe Suhaaga*; *Mar Mitenge*; **1989**: *Aag Se Khelenge*; *Nafrat Ki Aandhi*; *Aasmaan Se Ooncha*; *Dav Pech*; *Kasam Vardi Ki*; *Souten Ki Beti*; *Majboor*; **1990**: *Taqdeer Ka Tamasha*; *Zehreelay*; *Amiri Garibi*; *Hatimtai*; *Mera Pati Sirf Mera Hai*; *Shesh Naag*; *Nyay Anyay*; *Agnikaal*; *Aaj Ka Shahenshah*; *Thanedar*; **1991**: *Shiv-Ram*; *Ranabhoomi*; *Sapnon Ka Mandir*; *Maa*; *Dil Ashna Hai*; **1992**: *Insaaf Ki Devi*; *Sone Ki Lanka*; *Yeh Raat Phir Na Aayegi*; **1993**: *Aaj Ki Aurat*; *Prateeksha*; *Geetanjali* (H); *Bhookamp*; *Rang*; *Admi Khilona Hai*; *Tahqiqaat*; *Aansoo Bane Angarey*.

JHA, PRAKASH (b. 1952)

Hindi director born in Champaran, Bihar. Briefly trained as editor at the **FTII** (1976), dropped out and made documentaries. *Faces after the Storm*, on Biharsharif riots, was unofficially banned. First feature *Hip Hip Hurray* within 60s Hollywood schoolboy-cheerleader genre. Sees himself as a political film-maker. Briefly married to the actress Deepti Naval (1984).

FILMOGRAPHY: **1976**: *Rhythms of a Land and its People* (Doc); **1977**: *Darpok Ki Dosti* (Sh); **1978**: *Friends Together* (Doc); **1979**: *Ode to the Child* (Sh); **1981**: *Pas de deux* (Doc); **1982**: *Faces after the Storm* (Doc); **1983**: *Shri Vatsa* (Sh); *May I Think Sir?* (Doc); **1984**: *Hip Hip Hurray*; ***Damul***; **1986**: **1987**: *Ek Aur Itihas* (Doc); *Looking Back* (Doc); *Parinati*; **1988**: *An Expression* (Sh); **1989**: *Katha Madhopur Ki* (Sh); **1990**: *Mungerilal Ke Haseen Sapne* (TV); *Tribal Festival* (Doc).

JOSHI, MANILAL (1893-1927)

Major silent director and one of the first to stand up for authorial rights of film directors. Also initiated the convention of giving on-screen credit to cast and crew. Former schoolteacher in Bombay, joined **Kohinoor** Studio under cameraman V.B. Joshi (1920). Turned film-maker at **Ardeshir Irani**'s Star Film (1922) with *Veer Abhimanyu*, apparently containing Indian cinema's first flashbacks. His first independent production house (Swastika Film; Est: 1923) failed; then set up Ashoka Pics (1924) and made ***Prithvi Vallabh***. Its success encouraged others to go independent as well. Worked for Kohinoor and took over production of its sister company, Laxmi Films (1925), where he hired **R.S. Choudhury**, **B.P. Mishra** and **Chandulal Shah**. Later work includes ***Mojili Mumbai***, about the decadence of the urban Westernised bourgeoisie, one of the first films in a contemporary setting. Also worked briefly at **Sharda** Studio and at Vazir Haji's Excelsior Film (1927). Films distinguished by careful cinematography. His last film, interrupted by his death, was completed by **Nagendra Majundar** and released in 1930.

FILMOGRAPHY: **1922**: ***Veer Abhimanyu***; *Raja Parikshit*; *Ratnavali*; **1923**: *Sati No Sraap*; *Kirat Arjun*; **1924**: ***Prithvi Vallabh***; **1925**: *Indrasabha*; *Raj Yogi*; *Desh Na Dushman*; ***Veer Kunal***; ***Mojili Mumbai***; *Devadasi*; *Suvarna*; *Khandani Khavis*; *Kala Chor*; *Sati Simantini*; **1926**: *Abola Rani*; *Jungle Ni Jadibuti*; *Ajabkumari*; *Ratan Manjari*; *Dulari*; *Kashmeera*; **1927**: ***Nanand Bhojai***; *Parsa Eblis*; *Shrimati Nalini*; *Laila Majnu*; *Lohika Lilam*; *Prem Ni Pratima*; *Khada Na Khel* (all St).

KALE, KESHAV NARAYAN (1904-74)

Marathi and Hindi director born in Dayal, Ratnagiri Dist., Maharashtra. Started as a journalist. Noted Marathi literary and theatre critic associated with radical journals *Ratnakar*, *Yashwant* and *Pratibha*. Co-founded vanguard theatre group Natyamanwantar (cf **Date** and **Bhole**) in 1933, claiming influence of Ibsen, Shaw and Stanislavski (whose theoretical writings he translated into Marathi). As the group's ideologue, actor and playwright, emphasised the absence of a performance theory in Marathi theatre and sought to rewrite its history in terms of acting and emotionality. Joined cinema as actor (1926) with **S.N. Patankar**, later worked at **Imperial** and **Ranjit** Studios. Left cinema to study law (1931-4). Hired as scenarist for **Prabhat** (1934). Wrote dialogue and lyrics for ***Dharmatma***, giving this Saint film a political thrust by drawing analogies between Sant Eknath and Gandhi and by deflecting the mandatory miracle scenes towards more social concerns. Provided the lyrics for ***Chandrasena*** and the script for ***Amar Jyoti***. Turned director at Prabhat in 1937 and made best-known film ***Mazha Mulga*** as fictional autobiography about the struggles of a young radical writer. Worked with humourist **P.K. Atre** and filmed two of his screenplays (***Lapandav***, *Baeelweda*). Devoted himself to the theatre (1943-53) before making more films. Published a number of books, e.g. several essays on film theory and a volume of poetry, *Sahakarmanjari* (1932). First Professor of Film Appreciation at the **FTII** in early 60s. Worked on the Marathi journal, *Sahitya Patrika*.

FILMOGRAPHY (* act only): **1926**: *Satyavijaya**; **1928**: *Pataal Ketu**; *Jagadguru Shrimad Shankaracharya**; **1929**: *Bhikharan**; *Jai Somnath**; *Pati Patni** (all St); **1932**: *Marathyatil Dulhi/Amar Shaheed**; **1935**: ***Dharmatma****; **1936**: ***Amar Jyoti****; **1937**: ***Wahan***; **1938**: ***Mazha Mulga/Mera Ladka***; **1940**: ***Lapandav***; **1943**: *Baeelweda*; **1953**: ***Ammaldar***; *Bolavita Dhani**; **1959**: *Didi*.

KALINGRAO, P. (1914-81)

Singer and music director. Major influence on the introduction of bhava geet (light classical music) into popular Kannada music with several HMV and Columbia singles using the medieval Saint poetry of Purandaradasa and contemporary poetry including Masti Venkatesha Iyengar, Ku.Vem.Pu. and D.R. Bendre. The son of Yakshagana performer Pandaveshwara Puttaiah, he worked since childhood on the **Company Natak** stage with the Ambikaprasada Natak Mandali. Composed film music for **H.L.N. Simha** (***Abba! A Hudgi***, 1959), **Kemparaj Urs** (*Bhakta Ramadas*, 1948), and C.V. Raju (*Krishnaleele*, 1947; *Shri Krishna*, 1953; ***Natashekhara***, 1954). Also acted in the Kannada film *Vasantsena* (1941) and scored the Malayalam one, *Sasidharan* (1950).

KALKI (1899-1954)

Pen name of the noted Tamil novelist R. Krishnamurthy. Left school to join Gandhi's non-co-operation agitations (1921) and was jailed several times by the British. Journalist for *Navashakti*, then for the famous *Ananda Vikatan* owned by **S.S. Vasan**, where he published some of his best-known stories. Scripted **K. Subramanyam**'s seminal ***Thyagabhoomi*** (1939), publishing a novelised version in *Ananda Vikatan* with stills of the film and a racy text about ' a thwarted woman dishing it back to her husband in later years' (C.S. Lakshmi, 1984). His many contributions to the journal and to his own periodical, *Kalki*, are mainly reformist stories and Walter Scott-type historicals, largely determining the iconography of **Gemini**'s historicals. Apparently, M.S. Subbulakshmi used her earnings from *Savithri* (1941) to finance *Kalki*. Several of his novels were filmed, e.g. *Kalvanin Kadhali* (1955), *Ponvayal* (1954) and ***Parthiban Kanavu*** (1960). As a popular lyricist, he wrote songs for M.S. Subbulakshmi in **Duncan**'s ***Meera*** (1945), including the song *Katrinile varum geetham*. Together with writers of the famous Manikodi group (e.g. B.S. Ramaiah) and with director K. Subramanyam, Kalki is one of the pro-Congress film people in the pre-**DMK Film** period to call for a more responsible attitude to film and to draw attention to the medium's political potential. His reviews of early Tamil films are collected in his book *Kalaichelvam* (1956).

KALLOL GROUP

The first literary collective to influence cinema in Bengal was the group around the journal *Bharati* (Est: 1877). Founded by Dwijendranath Tagore and others as the Tagore clan's house journal, it published a history of the Bengali cinema in 1923. The journal's writers **Premankur Atorthy**, Hemendra Kumar Roy, Narendra Dev and Sourindramohan Mukherjee were the first to write seriously for and about cinema, eventually becoming film-makers. The second group, launched in 1923 by the Bengali journal *Kallol*, came to be known as the Kallol Group. Its immediate predecessor was the Four Arts Club which published *Jharer Dola* (1922) with stories by Dinesh Ranjan Das, Gokulchandra Nag, Suniti Devi and Manindralal Basu. *Kallol*, edited by Dinesh Ranjan Das, was followed by other journals, notably *Kalikalam* (1926) and *Pragati* (1927). Collectively they defined a literary realism contextualised by 20s peasant agitations and urban unemployment, self-consciously transgressive of the middle-class norms exemplified by **Tagore** and Saratchandra Chatterjee, e.g. through their interest in popular industrialised fictional forms. Malini Bhattacharya wrote (1988) that their ' sound and fury [d]id not produce anything like a formal breakthrough leading to a fictional discourse [other than] demanding a greater representation in fiction of problems pertaining to [p]easants, workers and women'. However the movement signified an era that also saw the first Bengali translations of Thomas Mann, Tolstoy, Proust, Romain Rolland, Gorky and Knut Hamsun, and the emergence of writers like Jibananda Das, Bishnu Dey and Buddhadev Bose together with lyricist **Kazi Nazrul Islam**. The movement directly touched the cinema when Dinesh Ranjan Das became a film-maker at **British Dominion** (*Kamaner Aagun*, 1930) and later at **New Theatres** (*Abasheshe*, 1935), followed by writers **Premendra Mitra** and **Sailajananda Mukherjee**, first as scenarists and then as successful directors. The realist emphasis in some of their films has been seen as a precedent for **IPTA**-inspired films in 50s Bengal. The modernist tendency in *Kallol*'s work was later consolidated by the journals *Parichay* (1931) and *Kavita* (1935).

KALPANA (?-1979)

60s Kannada star who formed the top screen duo with **Rajkumar** in Kannada film history. Born in Mangalore. Trained in classical dance by Shri Vittal Shetty; stage actress while at university in Mangalore with the Ballari Lalithamma Nataka Mandali. Started under **Panthulu**'s direction (*Saaku Magalu*, *Chinnada Gombe*) but **Puttanna Kanagal** moulded her career after her breakthrough in his ***Bellimoda***. In several key roles she embodied the ' woman' as imaged in the Kannada author Triveni's romantic fictions. Her tragic roles (***Gejje Pooje***, ***Sharapanjara***, in **Lakshminarayan**/Chaduranga socials) helped define a cinema derived from popular literature (cf **Navya Movement**) and pulp fiction. Also acted in mythologicals by **Hunsur Krishnamurthy** where her distinctive tragic style, (e.g. *Shri Kannika Parameshwari Kathe*) departs from the norms set by her predecessor, **Leelavathi**. Committed suicide in a lonely traveller's bungalow in Gotur, Karnataka.

FILMOGRAPHY: **1963**: *Saaku Magalu*; **1964**: *Chinnada Gombe*; ***Nandi***; **1965**: *Kavaleradu Kulavondu*; **1966**: *Mantralaya Mahatme*; *Shri Kannika Parameshwari Kathe*; *Sadhu Mirandal*; *Madras To Pondicherry*; *Mayor Nair*; **1967**: *Pattathu Rani*; *Padavidhara*; ***Bellimoda***; *Bangarada Hoovu*; *Dhanapishachi*; *Immadi Pulakesi*; *Premakku Permitte*; **1968**: *Gandhinagara*; *Mahasati Arundhati*; *Sarvamangala*; ***Hannele Chiguridaga***; *Anandakanda*; *Anna Thamma*; *Hoovu Mullu*; *Manninamaga*; **1969**: *Odahuttidavaru*; *Kappu Bilapu*; ***Uyyale***; *Mathru Bhoomi*; *Kaanike*; *Mukunda Chandra*; *Brindavana*; **1970**: ***Gejje Pooje***; *Arishina Kumkuma*; *Anirikshita*; *Pratikara*; *Karulina Kare*; *Lakshmi Saraswathi*; *Vagdhana*; *Namma Mane*; *Seeta*; *Devara Makkalu*; ***Mukti***; **1971**: *Ondekula Ondedaiva*; ***Sharapanjara***; *Bhale Adrushtavo Adrushta*; *Sothu Geddavalu*; *Kulagaurava*; **1972**: *Nari Munidare Mari*; *Subhadra Kalyanam*; *Uttara Dakshina*; *Yavajanmada Maitri*; *Na Mechida Huduga*; *Jeevana Jokaali*; *Goodu Putani*; *Menakodalu*; *Mareyada Deepavali*; **1973**: *Bidugade*; *Triveni*; *Gandhadagudi*; *Kesarina Kamala*; *Andala Ramudu*; **1974**: *Tulasi*; *Eradu Kanasu*; *Idu Namma Desha*; **1975**: *Dari Tappida Maga*; *Beluvalada Madilalli*; *Nireekshe*; *Asthi Kosam*; *Kotalo Paga*; *Maya Machhindra* (Tel); *Ramuni Minchina Ramudu*; **1976**: *Bayalu Dari*; *Vijayavani*; *Rajanarthakiya Rahasya*; **1978**: *Sandarbha*; *Vamsa Jyothi*; *Maleya Makkalu*.

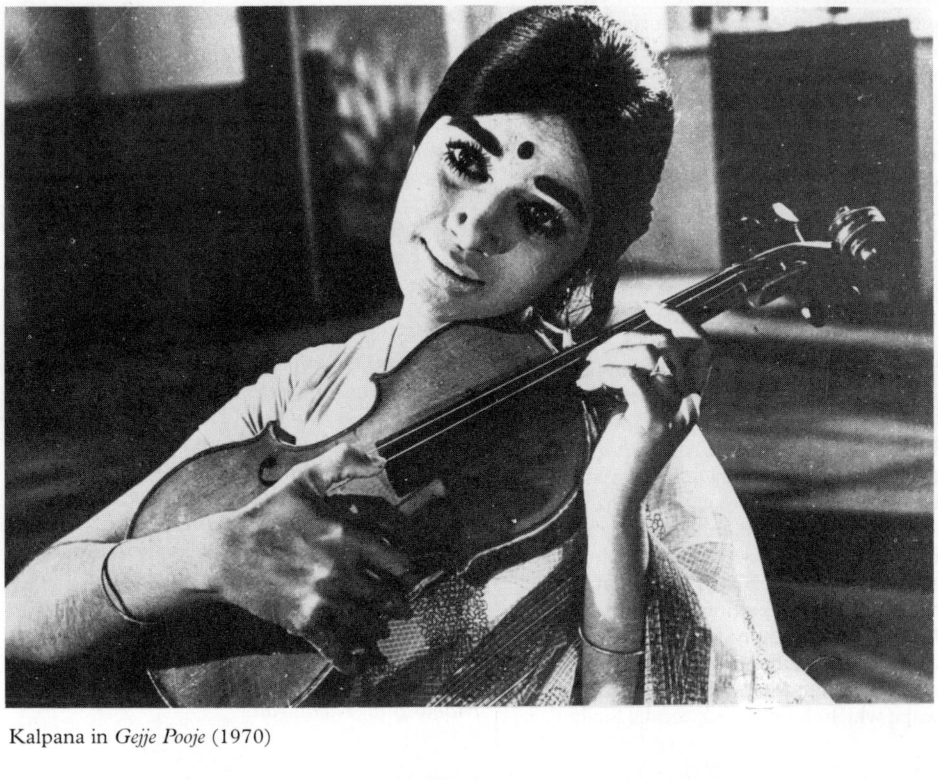

Kalpana in *Gejje Pooje* (1970)

KALYANASUNDARAM, PATTUKOTAI (1930-59)

Tamil lyricist, born in Pattukotai village, TN. Son of folk composer Arunachalam Pillai. Worked as farmer and labourer in salt flats, later as organiser of the peasantry in the Thanjavur delta. One of his early poems was used in a play, *Kannin Manigal*, staged at the Tamil Nadu Farmers' Conference, Dindigul (1954). Film début with A.L. Narayanan's *Paditha Penn* (1956). His best-known work was in **T.R. Raghunath**'s *Maheshwari* (1955) and **A.S. Nagarajan**'s *Pasavalai* (1956). His last film was A. Kasilingam's *Kalai Arasi* (1963). Wrote 196 often propagandist songs in over 55 films in a brief 9-year career, many of them for **MGR**'s films. Although his lyrics bore the stamp of Pa. Jeevanandan's brand of Marxism, they also showed the vitality of the folk idiom and the reformist ardour derived from poets like Subramanya Bharati and **Bharatidasan**. Published his poetry extensively in journals like *Janasakthi*. His biography is by P.E. Balakrishnan (1965).

KALYANJI-ANANDJI

(aka **Kalyanji Veerji Shah** and **Anandji Veerjee Shah**) Music composers; started career as musicians in film orchestras and conductors of live bands. The elder brother, Kalyanji, a former assistant to **Shankar-Jaikishen**, pioneered a virtual revolution in film music when he imported a claviolin and first played it to get the sinuous snake music composed by **Hemanta Mukherjee** in ***Nagin*** (1954), the first instance of electronic instrumentation in Hindi film. He started as music director for **Babubhai Mistri** and **Ravindra Dave**. Subsequent electronics-dominated music for films by Dave, **Manmohan Desai** and **Prakash Mehra** was central to musicals with **Shammi Kapoor** (*Bluff Master*), **Rajesh Khanna** (***Sachcha Jhutha***, ***Bandhan***) and **Bachchan** (*Don*, ***Muqaddar Ka Sikandar***, ***Zanjeer***), preceding, e.g., **Bhappi Lahiri** and **Ilaiyaraja**. Their music for **Saraiya**'s ***Saraswatichandra*** was a big hit. Currently known more for their live concerts in India, at Madison Square Garden in New York, the Wembley Arena in London and in South Africa, often featuring Bachchan in stage extravaganzas. Had a major recent success with Rajiv Rai's *Tridev*, its song *Oye oye* becoming one of the most popular in 80s Hindi cinema.

FILMOGRAPHIES: **Kalyanji**: **1958**: *Samrat Chandragupta*; ***Post Box 999***; **1959**: *Bedard Zamana Kya Jaane*; *Chandrasena*; *Ghar Ghar Ki Baat*; *O Tera Kya Kehana*. **Kalyanji-Anandji**: **1959**: *Madari*; ***Satta Bazaar***; **1960**: ***Chhalia***; *Delhi Junction*; *Dil Bhi Tera Hum Bhi Tere*; **1961**: *Passport*; *Pyaase Panchhi*; **1962**: *Gangu*; *Mehndi Lagi Mere Haath*; **1963**: ***Bluff Master***; *Kahin Pyar Na Ho Jaye*; *Phool Bane Angarey*; *Sunehri Nagin*; **1964**: *Birju Ustad*; *Dulha Dulhan*; *Ishara*; *Ji Chahta Hai*; *Majboor*; **1965**: *Himalay Ki God Mein*; *Jab Jab Phool Khile*; *Johar Mehmood In Goa*; *Purnima*; *Saheli*; **1966**: *Johar In Kashmir*; *Preet Na Jane Reet*; **1967**: *Aamne Samne*; *Dil Ne Pukara*; *Mera Munna*; *Parivar*; *Raaz*; ***Upkaar***; **1968**: *Baazi*; ***Hasina Maan Jayegi***; *Juari*; ***Saraswatichandra***; *Suhaag Raat*; *Teen Bahuraniyan*; **1969**: ***Bandhan***; *Ek Shriman Ek Shrimati*; *Mahal*; *Nannha Farishta*; *Raja Saab*; *Tamanna*; *Vishwas*; **1970**: *Aansoo Aur Muskaan*; *Geet*; *Ghar Ghar Ki Kahani*; *Gopi*; *Holi Aayee Re*; ***Johnny Mera Naam***; *Kab Kyon Aur Kahan*; *Mere Humsafar*; *Priya*; *Purab Aur Paschim*; ***Sachcha Jhutha***; *Safar*; *Yaadgaar*; **1971**: *Chhoti Bahu*; *Hum Tum Aur Woh*; *Joi Bangla Desh*; *Johar Mehmood In Hong Kong*; *Kathputli*; *Maryada*; *Paras*; *Preet Ki Dori*; *Rakhwala*; *Upaasna*; *Kangan*; **1972**: *Anokhi Pehchan*; *Aparadh*; *Ek Hasina Do Diwane*; *Hari Darshan*; *Jaanwar Aur Insaan*; *Joru Ka Gulam*; *Lalkaar*; *Malik*; *Manavata*; *Sub Ka Saathi*; *Victoria No 203*; **1973**: *Agni Rekha*; *Banarasi Babu*; *Blackmail*; *Ek Kunwari Ek Kunwara*; *Gulam Begum Badshah*; *Heera*; *Kahani Kismat Ki*; *Kashmakash*; *Samjhauta*; ***Zanjeer***; *Raja Kaka*; **1974**: *Albeli*; *Anjaan Raahein*; *Chattan Singh*; *Five Rifles*; *Haath Ki Safai*; *Har Har Mahadev*; *Hamrahi*; *Jeevan Sangram*; *Kasauti*; *Kora Kagaz*; *Paap Aur Punya*; *Patthar Aur Payal*; *Shubh Din*; *Vardan*; *Vachan*; **1975**: *Anokha*; *Apne Dushman*; *Bhoola Bhatka*; *Chori Mera Kaam*; *Dharmatma*; *Do Thug*; *Faraar*; *Himalay Se Ooncha*; *Mounto*; *Raffoo Chakkar*; *Uljhan*; *Zorro*; **1976**: *Adalat* (H); *Bairaag*; *Do Anjaane*; *Do Shatru*; *Bajrang Bali*; *Ek Se Badkhar Ek*; *Hera Pheri*; *Kabeela*; *Kalicharan*; *Khan Dost*; *Lagaam*; *Rangila Ratan*; *Sankoch*; *Shankar Shambhu*; **1977**: *Aakhri Goli*; *Chakkar Pe Chakkar*; *Chalu Mera Naam*; *Darinda*; *Farishta Ya Qatil*; *Hatyara*; *Hira Aur Patthar*; *Kalabaaz*; *Kasam Khoon Ki*; *Khel Khiladi Ka*; *Khel Kismat Ka*; *Khoon Pasina*; ***Kulavadhu***; *Naami Chor*; *Yaaron Ka Yaar*; **1978**: *Aakhri Daku*; *Anjaam*; *Anjane Mein*; *Atithi*; *Besharam*; *Chor Ke Ghar Chor*; *Do Musafir*; *Don*; *Ganga Ki Saugandh*; *Karmayogi*; ***Muqaddar Ka Sikandar***; *Nasbandi*; *Rahu Ketu*; *Trishna*; *Nalayak*; **1979**: *Ahimsa*; *Bagula Bhagat*; *Guru Ho Jaa Shuru*; *Jaandaar*; **1980**: *Qurbani*; *Desh Drohi*; *Bombay 405 Miles*; *Jwalamukhi*; *Kashish*; *Neeyat*; *Sau Din Saas Ke*; **1981**: *Aakhri Mujra*; *Commander*; *Haqdaar*; *Itni Si Baat*; *Qatilon Ke Qatil*; *Khoon Ka Rishta*; *Krodhi*; *Lawaris*; *Main Aur Mera Hathi*; *Professor Pyarelal*; *Yeh Rishta Na Toote*; **1982**: *Khush Naseeb*; *Raj Mahal*; *Rustom*; *Vidhata*; *Log Kya Kahenge*; **1983**: *Ghunghroo*; *Haadsa*; *Kalakaar*; *Nastik*; *Taqdeer*; **1984**: *Dharam Aur Kanoon*; *Raj Tilak*; *Yahan Wahan*; *Bandh Honth*; *Ek Chitthi Pyar Bhari*; **1985**: *Karishma Kudrat Ka*; *Pighalta Aasmaan*; *Yudh*; *Pahunche Huye Log*; **1986**: *Baat Ban Jaye*; *Chameli Ki Shaadi*; *Jaanbaaz*; *Mangal Dada*; *Nasihat*; ***Sultanat***; *Jhanjhar*; *Imaandar*; **1987**: *Hirasat*; *Kalyug Aur Ramayan*; *Thikana*; **1988**: *Falak*; *Sherni*; *Mohabbat Ke Dushman*; *Rukhsat*; *Mahaveera*; *Saazish*; **1989**: *Izhaar*; *Daata*; *Tridev*; *Jadugar*; **1990**: *Pyar Ka Toofan*; *CID*; *Naache Nagin Gali Gali*; *Ghar Parivar*; *Iraada*; **1991**: *Kaun Kare Qurbani*; *Pratigyabadh*; *Dharam-Sankat*.

KAMALABAI, SURABHI (b. 1913)

Telugu actress born in the famed **Surabhi Theatres** troupe of AP: her mother developed labour pains during a show, absented herself briefly and then the troupe presented the newly born infant to the audience. Kamalabai became a top actress with Surabhi; film début when **H.M. Reddy** hired the troupe for Telugu cinema's first sound film, ***Bhakta Prahlada***. Worked in the Telugu films of the **Sagar** Studio (Bombay) and **East India Film** (Calcutta). Also in the film version of **Ballari Raghava**'s stage classic ***Draupadi Manasamrakshanam***. Starred alongside **C.S.R. Anjaneyalu** in the Saint film, *Tukaram*. Later acted middle-aged women in Telugu and Tamil films.

FILMOGRAPHY: **1931**: ***Bhakta Prahlada***; **1932**: *Paduka Pattabhishekham*; *Shakuntala*; **1933**: ***Savithri***; ***Prithvi Putra***; **1936**: ***Draupadi Manasamrakshanam***; **1937**: *Tukaram*; **1938**: ***Bhakta Jayadeva***; **1942**: ***Patni***; **1949**: ***Keeluguram/Maya Kudhirai***; **1951**: ***Patala Bhairavi/Pataal Bhairavi***; ***Mangala***; **1952**: *Manavati*; ***Prema/Kathal***; **1953**: *Rohini*; *Vayyari Bhama*; ***Ammalakulu/Marumagal***; **1955**: *Vijayagauri*; **1959**: *Shabash Ramudu*; **1961**: *Velugu Needulu*; **1968**: *Umachandi Gauri Shankarula Katha*.

KAMALAHASAN (b. 1954)

Tamil star and a major figure in Malayalam, Telugu and briefly in Hindi cinemas. Born in Paramakudi near Madurai Dist., TN. Joined films aged 6 in **Bhimsingh**'s Tamil films (*Kalathur Kannamma*, *Parthal Pasi Theerum*) and in **Sethumadhavan**'s Malayalam *Kannum Karalum*. Rediscovered as an adult by **K. Balachander** (*Arangetram*), featuring regularly in the director's 70s films, in his Telugu hit ***Maro Charithra***, and in its equally successful Hindi remake (Kamalahasan's Hindi début) *Ek Duuje Ke Liye*. Tried to shift to Hindi cinema, playing the Chaplinesque hero in **Ramesh Sippy**'s love triangle *Sagar*, but was not successful. Acted in some of **I.V. Sasi**'s Malayalam films but broke away from his established image in **K. Vishwanath**'s ***Sagara Sangamam***, astounding viewers with his dancing skills in the difficult Bharat Natyam style (he was trained as a dancer by K.J. Sarasa and had worked as a choreographer in films). Following the ribald, wordless comedy ***Pushpak***, he imposed yet another image with the Brando-inspired starring role in ***Nayakan***. Since then performed, like De Niro, major physical transformations (e.g. the dwarf in *Apoorva Sahodarargal*), combining a light ' heroic' style with a heavier naturalism for older characters. Acted with **Sivaji Ganesan** in another *Godfather* adaptation, ***Thevar Magan***, which he scripted and produced as well. The film allowed Kamalahasan to return to the theme of feudal landlords in his native Madurai landscape which, he claimed, recalls Sicily.

FILMOGRAPHY: **1960**: *Kalathur Kannamma*; **1962**: *Parthal Pasi Theerum*; *Patha Kannikkai*; *Kannum Karalum*; **1963**: *Vanambadi*; *Ananda Jyoti*; **1973**: *Arangetram*; *Sollathen Ninaikiran*; **1974**: *Paruvakalam*; *Gumastavin Magal*; *Nan Avanillai*; *Panathukkaga*; *Aval Oru Thodarkathai*; *Kanyakumari*; *Vishnu Vijayam*; **1975**: *Ayirathil Oruthi*; *Antharangam*; ***Apoorva Ragangal***; *Cinema Paithiyam*; *Malai Sooda Va*; *Melnattu Marumagal*; *Pattam Poochi*; *Pattikatu Raja*; *Thangathile Vairam*; *Then Sindhuthe Vanam*; *Gnan Ninne Premikkunu*; *Thiruvonam*; *Mattoru Seeta*; *Raasleela*; **1976**: *Idaya Malar*; *Kumara Vijayam*; *Lalitha*; ***Manmatha Leelai***; *Moham Muppathu Varusham*; *Moondru Mudichu*; *Oru Udhappu Kann Simittukirathu*; *Sathyam*; *Unarchikal*; *Agnipushpan*; *Appooppan*; *Aruthu*; *Samasya*; *Swimming Pool*; *Ponn*; *Nee Ente Lahari*; *Sivathandavam*; *Ashirvadam*; *Madhura Swapnam*; *Kuttavum Sitshayum*; *Anthuleni Katha*; **1977**: *Aadu Puli Atham*; ***Avargal***; *Naam Pirandha Maan*; ***Pathinaru Vayathinile***; *Uyarnthavargal*; *Unnai Chutrumugalam*; *Sridevi*; *Ashtamangalyam*; *Nirakudam*; *Ormakal Marikkumo*; *Anandam Paramanandam*; *Satyavan Savithri*; *Adyapadam*; *Madanolsavam*; *Kokila*; *Kabita*; **1978**: ***Aval Appadithan***; *Chattam En Kaiyil*; *Elamai Vunjaladugiradhu*; *Manitharil Ithanai Nirangala*; *Nizhal Nijamkirathu*; *Paruvamazhai*; *Sigappu Rojakkal*; ***Maro Charithra***; *Vayasu Pilichindi*; *Sommokadidhi Sokokadidhi*; *Kathrina Nimisham*; *Anumodhanam*; *Vayanadan Thampan*; *Yeetta*; *Padakkudhira*; **1979**: *Neeya*; *Sigappukkal Mookuthi*; *Ninaithale Inikkum*; *Thayillamal Nannilai*; *Kalyanaraman*; *Mangala Vadyam*; *Neela Malargal*; *Allavudeenum Albutha Velakkum/Allavudeenum Arputha Vilakkum*; *Andamaina Anubhavam*; *Idi Kathakadu*; **1980**: *Ullasa Paravaigal*; *Guru*; *Varumayin Niram Sigappu*; *Maria My Darling*; *Kalyana Jyothi*; **1981**: *Meendum Kokila*; *Rama Lakshman*; ***Raja Parvai***; *Kadal Meengal*; *Ellam Inbamayam*; *Tik Tik Tik*; *Saval*; *Akali Rajyam*; *Ek Duuje Ke Liye*; *Do Dil Diwane*; *Prema Pichhi*; *Shankarlal*; **1982**: *Simla Special*; *Pagadai Pannirendu*; *Vazhve Mayam*; ***Moondram Pirai***; *Sahalakala Vallavan*; *Sanam Teri Kasam*; *Yeh To Kamaal Ho Gaya*; *Dil Ka Sathi Dil*; *Pyara Tarana*; *Andhiveyilille Ponnu*; *Ezham Rathri*; *Afsana Do Dilon Ka*; **1983**: *Thoongathe Thambi Thoongathe*; *Uruvavugal Maralam*; *Chattam*; ***Sagara Sangamam***; *Snehabandham*; *Zara Si Zindagi*; *Sadma*; *Snehabhishekham*; **1984**: *Ek Nai Paheli*; *Enakkul Oruvan*; *Yeh Desh*; *Yaadgaar*; *Raj Tilak*; *Karishma*; *Jalsarayudu*; *Sahasa Simham*; **1985**: *Oru Kaithiyin Diary*; *Andha Oru Nimidam*; *Japanil Kalyanaraman*; *Kakki Chattai*; *Mangamma Sapatham*; *Meendum Parasakthi*; *Uyarntha Ullam*; *Sagar*; *Giraftaar*; *Swati Muthyam*; *Jalsa Bullodu*; **1986**: *Manakanakku*; *Vikram* (Tam); *Punnagai Mannan*; *Oka Radha Idduru Krishnulu*; *Nanum Oru Thozhilali*; **1987**: *Persollum Pillai*; ***Nayakan***; *Pesum Padum*; *Vrutham*; ***Pushpak/Pushpak Vimana***; **1988**: *Sathya*; *Soora Samharam*; *Unnal Mudiyum Thambi*; **1989**: *Apoorva Sahodarargal/Appu Raja*; *Vetri Vizha*; *Indrudu Chandrudu*; *Chanakyam/Chanakyan*; **1990**: *Michael Madana Kamarajan*; **1991**: *Guna*; *Singaravelan*; **1992**: ***Thevar Magan***; **1993**: *Maharasan*; *Kalaingan*.

KAMBADASAN

Tamil lyricist; born as C.S. Rajappa in Villayanur near Pondicherry. Stage actor, musician and lyric writer introduced to the theatre by **P. Sambandam Mudaliar**. Film début in Fram Sethna's *Vamana Avataram* (1939), and wrote dialogue/lyrics for **Balkrishna Narayan Rao**'s *Salivahanan* (1944). Became a leading lyricist with the success of *Arul tharum deva mathave* in Nagoor/Taliath's *Gnanasoundari* (1948) and with Jiten Bannerjee's *Mangayar Karasi* (1949), esp. the song *Parthal pasi theerum* sung by **P.U. Chinappa**. These and other songs were among the early musical hits to achieve an independent popularity on disc. Also wrote the hits of *Vanaratham* (1956), a dubbed Tamil version of S.U. Sunny's ***Udan Khatola*** (1955) with **Naushad**'s music.

KAMBHAR, CHANDRASEKHAR

(b. 1937) Kannada director born in Belgaum Dist., Karnataka. Noted Kannada poet, folklorist and playwright (*Jokumaraswamy*, 1972; *Sambhasiva*, 1985; *Siri Sampige*, 1986, written in the Yakshagana idiom); author of a dictionary of Kannada folklore (1984). Fulbright Scholar (1968) and lecturer at the Universities of Chicago and Bangalore. Vice-Chancellor of the newly established university at Hampi, Karnataka. Advocate of a depoliticised folk revivalism particularly strong in Karnataka theatre (cf **B.V. Karanth**) and literature since the early 70s. Extended his views into features and documentaries when, with other Kannada writers and theatre directors, he turned to film in the late 70s (cf **Navya Movement**).

FILMOGRAPHY (* also act/** only music): **1977**: *Udugore***; **1978**: *Sandarbha***; ***Kaadu Kudure****; **1981**: *Sangeetha**; **1989**: *Kote Udugore***; **1990**: *Hasiru Kaibisi Karedavo*.

Kameshwara Rao, Kamalakara *see* **Rao, Kamalakara Kameshwara**

KANAGAL,SUBRAVESHTI RAMASWAMY PUTTANNA (1933-85)

Kannada director born in Kanagal, Karnataka; also worked in Malayalam (signing S.R. Puttanna) and in Hindi. Graduated in Mysore. Younger brother of noted Kannada theatre personality Kanagal Prabhakara Sastry. Later employed as an actor in Soorat Ashwath's Kala Sangha stage company. Also worked as still photographer in Mysore. Joined **Panthulu** as assistant (*Ratnagiri Rahasya*, 1957). Successful Kannada cineaste in the late 60s and 70s, and the first to achieve a mass audience among the urban middle class. Sometimes hailed as predecessor to 70s **Navya Movement**-inspired cinema that followed ***Samskara*** (1970). Early work in Malayalam elaborated Panthulu's definition of the progressive social (e.g. the remake of ***School Master***). After the first Kannada film, ***Bellimoda***, this was modulated into a variant of reformist fiction drawn from sentimental novellas and short stories: writers like M.K. Indira (***Gejje Pooje***) Ta Ra Su, Triveni, etc. Classic formula usually privileges family unit shown coping with traumatic crises, often focusing on women characters. Later work, in colour and post-***Nagara Haavu*** (remade in Hindi as *Zehreela Insaan*) developed hallucinatory psychodrama, psychological realism being replaced by a destructive passion often characterised as a sense of being ' possessed' from within. The sheer duration of his films (averaging over 3 hrs) reinforces the sense of heightened emotionality, juxtaposed with very mobile, often highly subjective camera movements. Noted for authoritarian directorial style and for introducing new acting talent (**Kalpana**, **Arathi**, Shivaram, etc). Set up his own company in 1977.

FILMOGRAPHY: **1964**: *School Master*; *Kalanjukuttiya Thangam*; **1965**: *Chettathi*; *Pakkalo Bellem*; **1966**: *Puchakanni*; *Mayor Nair*; **1967**: *Swapnabhoomi*; ***Bellimoda***; **1968**: *Teacheramma*; **1969**: *Mallammana Pavada*; *Kappu Bilapu*; **1970**: ***Gejje Pooje***; *Karulina Kare*; *Iddaru Ammayilu*; **1971**: ***Sharapanjara***; *Sakshatkara*; *Sudurum Sudavalliyum*; *Irulum Valiyum*; **1972**: ***Nagara Haavu***; **1973**: *Edakallu Guddada Mele*; **1974**: *Upasane*; *Zehreela Insaan*; **1975**: *Shubhamangala*; *Bili Hendthi*; ***Katha Sangama***; **1976**: *Collegeranga*; *Phalithamsha*; **1978**: *Paduvarahalli Pandavaru*; **1979**: *Dharmasere*; **1981**: ***Ranganayaki***; **1982**: *Manasa Sarovara*; **1983**: *Dharanimandala Madhyadolage*; **1984**: *Amrutha Galige*; *Runamukthalu*; **1985**: *Manasada Hoovu*.

KANAM, E. J. (1926-87)

Malayalam writer born in Kottayam, Kerala. Schoolteacher; later journalist; known mainly for introducing sentimental middle-class pulp fiction known as paingili into Malayalam, which became a staple source for the work of, e.g., **Kunchako**, **P. Subramanyam**, M. Krishnan Nair and P.A. Thomas. Film début at Kunchako's Udaya Studios with the story for *Bharya* (1962). Other notable films include Kunchako's ***Thirichadi*** (1968) and *Dattuputhran* (1970); P. Subramanyam's *Kaliyodam* (1965), *Puthri*, *Kattumallika* and *Priyatama* (all 1966), ***Adhyapika*** (1968) and *Swargaputhri* (1973). Worked for P.G. Vishwambaran in the early 80s: *Himavahini* (1983), *Sandhyakenthinu Sindhuram* and ***Thirakkil Alpa Samayam*** (both 1984).

KANCHANMALA (1923-81)

Telugu actress born in coastal AP. Stage star in Telugu; then entered cinema at **Sagar** Studio, Bombay, with a minor role in *Veer Abhimanyu*. After her 2nd film, at Calcutta's **Aurora**, **Ahindra Choudhury**'s *Vipranarayana*, broke through in **H.M. Reddy**'s ***Grihalakshmi***, where her sexually charged performance as the dancer Madhuri next to **Kannamba**'s role as the suffering wife solicited a kind of male voyeurism later exploited in **Vauhini**'s 40s socials. Played the victimised wife in **B.N. Reddi**'s nationalist ***Vande Mataram***; also appeared in reformist socials by, e.g., **Ramabrahmam** (***Malapilla***, *Illalu*) and sang duets with composer Ogirala in **Y.V. Rao**'s ***Malli Pelli***. Played the title role in **Gemini**'s ***Balangamma***, after which a legal dispute with the studio boss **S.S. Vasan** effectively put her career in limbo for almost a decade. Her acting style was later extended by stars like Kamala Kotnis and **Bhanumati**.

FILMOGRAPHY: **1935**: *Shri Krishna Tulabharam*; **1936**: *Veer Abhimanyu*; **1937**: *Vipranarayana*; **1938**: ***Grihalakshmi***; ***Malapilla***; **1939**: ***Vande Mataram***; ***Malli Pelli***; **1940**: *Mahiravana*; *Illalu*; **1942**: ***Balanagamma***; **1951**: *Chandravanka*; *Mayapilla*; **1955**: *Aadabidda*; **1963**: *Nartanasala*.

KANNADASAN (1927-81)

Prodigious Tamil poet, lyricist (over 5000 film songs) and producer. Key figure in the early **DMK Film** propaganda genre, often credited with reintroducing a classical Tamil literary ' tradition' to contemporary film audiences. Born as A.S. Muthaiah in Amaravatipudur, TN. Joined the journal *Tirumakal* (1944) which published his first poems. Published his own journals, the weekly *Tenral*, the monthly *Mullai* and the film journal *Tenral Tirai*; also edited the monthly *Kannadasan* and newspaper *Katitam*. Joined **Modern Theatres**' story department (1947). Début as lyricist for **Ramnoth**'s *Kanniyin Kathali* (1949) but worked mainly as a dialogue writer until G.R. Rao's *Illara Jyothi* (1954). Joined the DMK (1947-64); responsible for some of their main propaganda lyrics in, e.g., **N.S. Krishnan**'s *Panam* (1952), **T.R. Sundaram**'s *Thirumbi Paar* (1953) and **Yoganand**'s **MGR** classic ***Madurai Veeran*** (1956). Founded Kannadasan Pics producing *Malai Itta Mangai* (1958), ***Sivagangai Seemai*** (1959), *Kavalai Illatha Manithan* (1960), *Vanambadi* (1963), etc. Became an independent star attraction after his successful lyrics in **Bhimsingh**'s early films, usually set to music by the Vishwanathan-Ramamurthy team (e.g. *Ponal pokattum poda* in *Pallum Pazhamum*, 1961). Left the DMK after an argument with **Karunanidhi**, an incident often cited to indicate the degree to which personal rivalries between film people affected the DMK Party structure. Kannadasan later became a member of the Tamil Nadu Congress Committee. One of his last films is **Balu Mahendra**'s ***Moondram Pirai*** (1982). Credited with the direction of *Vaa Arugil Vaa* (1991). Other writings include 21 novels, 10 volumes of religious discourses and over 4000 poems.

KANNAMBA, PASUPULETI (1912-64)

Telugu and Tamil actress and singer. Started on the stage at the Rajarajeshwari Natya Mandali and was largely responsible for the group's initial popularity along with her mentor (and later husband), stage and film director **Kadaru Nagabhushanam**. Film début in the screen version of their play *Harishchandra*, initially filmed by Prafulla Ghosh and remade by Nagabhushanam himself in 1943. Continued in film versions of their plays with acclaimed music scores: **H.V. Babu**'s ***Draupadi Vastrapaharanam*** and *Kanakatara*, **C. Pullaiah**'s *Sarangadhara*. Played the destitute wife in **H.M. Reddy**'s ***Grihalakshmi***, incarnating its rational reformism with her passionate denunciation of God and religious notions of truth. Later associated with emphatic acting in, e.g., ***Talliprema*** and *Mayalokam*, also playing **Sivaji Ganesan**'s mother in ***Manohara*** and **MGR**'s mother in *Thaikupinn Tharam*. Best known for the title role in ***Kannagi***. Some of her still popular music has been reissued by the musicologist V.A.K. Ranga Rao.

FILMOGRAPHY: **1935**: *Harishchandra*; **1936**: ***Draupadi Vastrapaharanam***; **1937**: *Kanakatara*; *Sarangadhara*; **1938**: ***Grihalakshmi***; **1940**: ***Chandika***; *Bhoja Kalidasa*; *Krishnan Thoothu*; **1941**: ***Ashok Kumar***; ***Talliprema***; **1942**: ***Kannagi***; *Sumati*; **1943**: *Harishchandra*; **1944**: ***Mahamaya***; **1945**: *Mayalokam*; *Maya Machhindra*; *Paduka Pattabhishekham*; **1947**: *Daiva Neethi*; *Tulasi Jalandhar*; ***Palnati Yuddham***; **1949**: *Mangayar Karasi*; ***Navajeevan***; **1950**: *Laila Majnu*; **1952**: ***Pedaraitu***; *Moonru Pillaigal/Mooguru Kodukalu*; **1954**: ***Manohara***; *Sati Sakkubai*; **1955**: *Anarkali*; *Vadina*; **1956**: *Naga Panchami*; *Thaikku Pinn Tharam*; **1957**: *Makkalai Petra Maharasi*; *Kutumba Gauravam*; **1958**: *Aadapettanam*; ***Avan Amaran***; **1959**: *Pelli Meeda Pelli*; *Uzhavukkum Thozhilukkum Vandhanai Seivom*; *Vazha Vaitha Daivam*; *Raja Sevai*; ***Raja Mukutam***; **1960**: *Dharmane Jayam*; *Jalsarayudu*; *Abhimanam*; **1961**: *Usha Parinayam*; *Intiki Deepam Illale*; *Pelli Pilupu*; *Krishna Kuchela*; ***Jagadeka Veeruni Katha/Jagathala Prathapan***; **1962**: *Pelli Thambulam*; *Dakshayagnam*; *Swarnamanjari*; *Nuvva Nena*; *Atmabandhuvu*; **1963**: *Paruvu Pratishthalu*; *Apta Mithrulu*; **1964**: *Bangaru Timmaraju*; *Ramadasu*; **1965**: *Keelu Bommalu*.

KAPOOR, PRITHVIRAJ (1906-72)

Revered actor born in Peshawar (now Pakistan) as Prithvinath Kapoor. Son of a police officer. Earned a major reputation on the amateur stage in Lyallpur and Peshawar. Interrupted law studies to join **Imperial** (1929). Acted in several **B.P. Mishra** adventure and love stories (e.g. ***Cinema Girl***, opposite Ermeline, India's version of Clara Bow). Starred in India's first sound film, ***Alam Ara***. He impressed with a perfect speaking voice (he never sang). Then joined the Grant Anderson theatre company and performed Shakespeare in English, with special acclaim for his Laertes in *Hamlet*. Worked in **New Theatres** (1933-9), playing the hero in Hindi versions (**Durgadas Bannerjee** often playing the same role in Bengali) of its hit bilinguals. Broke through with **Debaki Bose**'s ***Rajrani Meera*** and as Rama in *Seeta* opposite **Durga Khote**. ***Vidyapati*** was his crowning achievement in Calcutta. **Chandulal Shah** hired him for the **Ranjit** Studio (1938-40) in Bombay, where he acted in some remarkable melodramas with **Kardar** (e.g. ***Pagal***) and **Chaturbhuj Doshi** (***Adhuri Kahani***). Best-known performance as freelance actor was in the title role of Alexander the Great in **Sohrab Modi**'s military epic ***Sikandar***. The film heightened his enduring reputation, enhanced by the role of Emperor Akbar in ***Mughal-e-Azam***, as the embodiment of Mughal royalty in Hindi-Urdu cinema (spoofed by K. Shankar's ***Rajkumar***). Invested his earnings in the Hindi theatre, setting up Prithvi Theatres (1944) where he produced plays while shooting films at night. Mounted a major play against Partition, **Inder Raj Anand**'s *Deewar* (1945) which earned him death threats from Islamic fundamentalists. He persisted with anti-sectarian politics, producing the technically and artistically masterful plays *Gaddar* (1947) and *Pathan* (1948). Launched many new talents through Prithvi Theatres, including **Ramanand Sagar** (*Kalakaar*, 1951), music directors **Shankar-Jaikishen** and assistant Ramesh Saigal (who later made ***Phir Subah Hogi***, 1958), all of whom were later key members of **Raj Kapoor** film units, as well as launching his sons Raj, **Shammi** and **Shashi**. His main performances of the 50s: in **Shantaram**'s ***Dahej*** and in his son's ***Awara***, which ended on a dramatic confrontation between the fictional father and son played by a real father and son. *Kal Aaj Aur Kal* featured three generations of Kapoors in a celebration of feudal patriarchy. While directing *Paisa*, adapted from a Prithvi Theatres play, he lost his voice, which never regained its full sonorousness. Had to close his theatre and reduce his film work. In the late 60s and 70s acted in several Hindi and some Punjabi mythologicals. Played the patriarchal lead in the Saint film ***Nanak Naam Jahaaz Hai***, credited with the revival of the Punjabi film industry. Died of cancer in 1972.

FILMOGRAPHY (* also d): **1929**: *Be Dhari Talwar*; **1930**: ***Cinema Girl***; *Prince Vijaykumar*; *Sher-e-Arab*; **1931**: *Namak Haram Kon*; *Bar Ke Pobar*; *Golibar*; *Toofan* (all St); ***Alam Ara***; ***Draupadi***; **1932**: *Dagabaaz Ashiq*; **1933**: ***Rajrani Meera***; **1934**: *Daku Mansoor*; *Ramayan*; *Seeta*; **1935**: ***Inquilab***; *Josh-e-Inteqam*; *Swarg Ki Sidhi*; **1936**: ***Grihadah/Manzil***; **1937**: *Milap*; ***President***; ***Vidyapati***; ***Jeevan Prabhat***; ***Anath Ashram***; **1938**: ***Abhagin***; ***Dushman***; **1939**: ***Adhuri Kahani***; ***Sapera***; **1940**: *Aaj Ka Hindustan*; *Deepak*; *Chingari*; ***Pagal***; *Sajani*; **1941**: ***Raj Nartaki/Court Dancer***; ***Sikandar***; **1942**: *Ujala*; *Ek Raat*; **1943**: *Aankh Ki Sharam*; *Bhalai*; *Gauri*; *Ishara*; *Vish Kanya*; **1944**: *Maharathi Karna*; ***Phool***; **1945**: *Devadasi*; *Nala Damayanti*; *Shri Krishnarjun Yuddha*; *Vikramaditya*; **1946**: *Prithviraj Samyukta*; *Valmiki*; **1947**: *Parashuram*; **1948**: *Azadi Ki Raah Par*; **1950**: ***Dahej***; ***Hindustan Hamara***; **1951**: ***Awara***; *Deepak*; **1952**: ***Anandmath***; ***Chhatrapati Shivaji***; *Insaan*; **1953**: *Aag Ka Dariya*; **1954**: *Ehsan*; **1957**: *Paisa**; ***Pardesi***; **1958**: ***Lajwanti***; **1960**: ***Mughal-e-Azam***; **1961**: *Senapati*; **1963**: *Harishchandra Taramati*; *Pyar Kiya To Darna Kya*; ***Rustom Sohrab***; *Gujree*; **1964**: *Ghazal*; *Jahan Ara*; ***Rajkumar***; *Zindagi*; **1965**: ***Aasmaan Mahal***; *Jaanwar*; *Jahan Sati Wahan Bhagwan*; *Khakaan*; *Lutera*; *Shri Ram Bharat Milap*; *Sikandar-e-Azam*; **1966**: *Daku Mangal Singh*; *Insaaf*; *Lal Bangla*; *Love And Murder*; *Shankar Khan*; *Sher Afghan*; *Yeh Raat Phir Na Aayegi*; **1967**: *Shamsheer*; **1968**: *Balaram Shri Krishna*; *Teen Bahuraniyan*; **1969**: *Insaaf Ka Mandir*; *Nai Zindagi*; *Sati Sulochana*; ***Nanak Naam Jahaaz Hai***; **1970**: *Ek Nannhi Munni Ladki Thi*; *Gunah Aur Kanoon*; *Heer Ranjha*; **1971**: *Kal Aaj Aur Kal*; *Padosi*; *Sakshatkara*; *Nanak Dukhiya Sab Sansar*; **1972**: *Mele Mitran De*; *Bankelal*; *Naag Panchami*; **1973**: *Naya Nasha*; **1976**: *Bombay By Nite*.

KAPOOR, RAJ (1924-88)

Hindi megastar, producer, director and all-round showman. Born in Peshawar (now Pakistan) as Ranbirraj Kapoor; son of actor **Prithviraj Kapoor**. Worked with his father as stage actor, prod. manager and art director. First film role aged 11. Started as clapper-boy at **Bombay Talkies**; then assistant director there and at **Ranjit** (1946). Set up R.K. Films (1948) to make ***Aag***. Expanded into a full-

Raj Kapoor in *Main Nashe Mein Hoon* (1959)

scale studio at Chembur in Bombay (1950), continuing with **Mehboob**, **Kardar** and **Sohrab Modi** the studio tradition into the post-Independence period. Screen persona makes repeated references to Chaplin's tramp, but Kapoor also asserted his debt to Capra (their first meeting is recorded in Capra's autobiography) and to De Sica (esp. *Miracolo a Milano*, 1950). The earlier films, esp. ***Awara*** and ***Shri 420*** scripted by **K.A. Abbas**, evince a sentimental approach to social reform, presenting political Independence as a loss of innocence in exchange for stability, condensed into the persona of the mother/lover as played by **Nargis**. With their elaborate sets, fine camerawork and music (usually composed by **Shankar-Jaikishen** and written by **Shailendra** and Hasrat Jaipuri), the films achieved immense popularity throughout India, in the USSR and in the Middle East. Although ***Boot Polish*** was credited to Prakash Arora, one of his assistants, most of the film's final version was attributable to Kapoor. Also produced his classic performance in ***Jagte Raho/Ek Din Raatre***. ***Sangam***, his first colour film, used locations in exotic Europe. Became more sexually explicit in the 70s after the box-office failure of his ambitious ***Mera Naam Joker***, a maudlin epic inspired by *Limelight* (1951) which took 6 years to make. ***Bobby*** introduced Dimple Kapadia as star opposite Rishi Kapoor. The combination of sentimentalism with lush stylisation and steamy sexuality (presented with moral indignation) in his later work recalls Cecil B. DeMille. **Kidar Sharma** (1952) described Raj Kapoor as an example of 'The director with the Cave Man conception of love.' **Mahesh Bhatt** (1993) described him as 'An audacious film-maker who displayed the feverish carnality of a schoolboy in most of his films.' Produced his own directions.

FILMOGRAPHY (* also d/** only d): **1935**: ***Inquilab***; **1943**: *Hamari Baat*; *Gauri*; **1946**: *Valmiki* (H); **1947**: ***Neel Kamal***; *Dil Ki Rani*; *Chittor Vijay*; *Jail Yatra*; **1948**: ***Gopinath***; *Amar Prem*; ***Aag****; **1949**: ***Barsaat****; ***Andaz***; *Sunehre Din*; *Parivartan*; **1950**: *Banwra*; ***Banwre Nain***; ***Dastaan***; *Jaan Pehchan*; *Pyar*;

Sargam; 1951: ***Awara****; 1952: *Amber*; *Ashiana*; *Anhonee*; *Bewafa*; 1953: *Dhun*; *Paapi*; ***Aah***; 1954: ***Boot Polish***; 1955: ***Shri 420****; 1956: ***Jagte Raho/Ek Din Raatre***; ***Chori Chori***; 1957: *Sharada*; 1958: *Parvarish*; ***Phir Subah Hogi***; 1959: ***Anari***; ***Char Dil Char Raahein***; *Do Ustad*; *Kanhaiya*; *Main Nashe Mein Hoon*; 1960: ***Jis Desh Mein Ganga Behti Hai***; ***Chhalia***; *Shriman Satyavadi*; 1961: *Nazrana*; 1962: *Aashiq*; 1963: *Dil Hi To Hai*; *Ek Dil Sau Afsane*; 1964: ***Sangam****; *Dulha Dulhan*; 1966: ***Teesri Kasam***; 1967: *Around the World*; *Diwana*; 1968: *Sapnon Ka Saudagar*; 1970: ***Mera Naam Joker****; 1971: *Kal Aaj Aur Kal*; 1973: ***Bobby*****; *Mera Desh Mera Dharam*; 1975: *Do Jasoos*; *Dharam Karam*; 1976: *Khan Dost*; 1977: *Chandi Sona*; 1978: ***Satyam Shivam Sundaram*****; *Naukri*; 1980: *Abdullah*; 1981: ***Naseeb***; *Gopichand Jasoos*; *Vakil Babu*; 1982: *Chor Mandli*; *Prem Rog***; 1985: *Ram Teri Ganga Maili***.

KAPOOR, SHAMMI (b. 1931)

Actor born in Bombay. Younger brother of **Raj Kapoor**. Introduced in mildly successful swashbuckling imitations of Errol Flynn. With ***Tumsa Nahin Dekha*** he shaved his pencil moustache and started evoking James Dean and Elvis Presley (e.g. *Baar baar dekho* in ***China Town***) following the more freewheeling approach elaborated by **Dev Anand**. This style set the tone for **Filmistan**'s late 50s films, e.g. **Shakti Samanta**'s b&w whodunits and colour romances, laying the foundations for **Manmohan Desai**'s later appeal to an urban lumpen culture in, e.g., ***Bluff Master***. Kapoor often played a spoiled, rich lad who wins over the girl but also gets embroiled in gang rackets or family feuds, all of which are solved by beating up the villain. Most remarkable performance in ***Junglee***. Presided over the Hindi cinema's first consistent attempts to address a Westernised teenage audience with songs invoking Western rock, often picturised in discotheques. These were the prototypes of a 60s consumerist cinema that, in Manmohan Desai's words, consisted entirely of 'highlights', i.e. loosely strung together, dramatically self-contained episodes. His 70s directorial efforts include a Hindi remake of *Irma La Douce*, 1963 (*Manoranjan*). Married **Geeta Bali**. Remarried after her death. Since the mid-70s has often appeared in bearded, middle-aged character parts.

FILMOGRAPHY (* also d): 1953: *Gul Sanobar*; *Jeevan Jyoti*; *Laila Majnu*; *Rail Ka Dibba*; *Thokar*; 1954: *Chor Bazaar*; *Ehsan*; *Mehbooba*; *Shama Parwana*; 1955: *Daku*; *Miss Coca Cola*; *Naqab*; *Tangewali*; 1956: *Hum Sub Chor Hain*; *Mem Sahib*; *Rangeen Raatein*; *Sipahsalaar*; 1957: *Coffee House*; *Mirza Sahiban*; *Maharani*; ***Tumsa Nahin Dekha***; 1958: *Mujrim*; 1959: ***Dil Deke Dekho***; *Mohar*; *Raat Ke Rahi*; *Ujala*; ***Char Dil Char Raahein***; *Sahil*; 1960: *Basant*; *College Girl*; *Singapore*; 1961: *Boy Friend*; ***Junglee***; 1962: ***China Town***; *Dil Tera Diwana*; *Professor*; *Vallah Kya Baat Hai*; 1963: ***Bluff Master***; *Pyar Kiya To Darna Kya*; *Shaheed Bhagat Singh*; 1964: ***Kashmir Ki Kali***; ***Rajkumar***; 1965: *Jaanwar*; 1966: *Badtameez*; ***Teesri Manzil***; *Preet Na Jane Reet*; 1967: *An Evening in Paris*; *Laat Saheb*; 1968: *Brahmachari*; 1969: *Prince*; *Sachaai*; *Tumse Achha Kaun Hai*; 1970: *Pagla Kahin Ka*; 1971: ***Andaz***; *Jaane Anjane*; *Preetam*; *Jawan Mohabbat*; 1974: *Manoranjan**; *Chhote Sarkar*; 1975: *Salaakhen*; *Zameer*; 1976: *Bandalbaaz**; 1977: *Mama Bhanja*; *Parvarish*; 1978: *Shalimar*; 1979: *Ahsaas*; *Meera*; 1981: *Ahista Ahista*; *Armaan*; *Harjaai*; *Professor Pyarelal*; ***Naseeb***; 1982: *Yeh Vaada Raha*; *Desh Premi*; *Prem Rog*; *Vidhata*; 1983: *Betaab*; *Ek Jaan Hain Hum*; ***Hero***; *Romance*; *Aan Aur Shaan*; *Wanted*; 1984: *Sohni Mahiwal* (H); 1985: *Badal*; *Balidan*; *Ek Se Bhale Do*; *Ram Tere Kitne Naam*; 1986: *Allah Rakha*; *Kala Dhandha Goray Log*; *Karamdaata*; *Ghar Sansar*; 1987: *Himmat Aur Mehnat*; *Hukumat*; 1989: *Daata*; *Bade Ghar Ki Beti*; *Mohabbat Ka Paigam*; ***Batwara***; 1991: *Ajooba*; *Mast Kalandar*; *Lakshmanrekha*; 1992: *Nishchay*; *Humshakal*; *Tahalka*; *Chamatkar* (H); *Heer Ranjha*; *Khule Aam*; 1993: *Gardish*; *Aaja Meri Jaan*; *Dosti Ki Saugandh*; *Tum Karo Vaada*.

KAPOOR, SHASHI (b. 1938)

Hindi star, producer and director; son of **Prithviraj Kapoor** and younger brother of **Raj** and **Shammi Kapoor**. Started on the stage aged 6 in his father's production of *Shakuntala* (1944). Also acted the child, Raj, in ***Aag*** and in ***Awara***. Abandoned studies and worked for Prithvi Theatres; then met Joseph Kendall's touring theatrical group (1957) and joined them in Bangalore, playing Shakespeare in English and eventually marrying actress Jennifer Kendall. Turned to film in 1960. Started working with Merchant-Ivory prod. with *The Householder* (1963). Achieved a reputation in the West (which peaked as he played the title role in Conrad Rooks's *Siddhartha*) and stardom in Indian love stories after *Jab Jab Phool Khile*, often starring opposite Asha Parekh and **Sharmila Tagore**. Increasingly caught up in dramatically undemanding films and later played the second principal role in a series of **Bachchan** films following the success of their ***Deewar*** (***Kabhi Kabhie***, ***Trishul***, ***Kala Patthar***, *Shaan*). Set up his own company, Film-Valas, to distribute Merchant-Ivory's *Bombay Talkie*, branching into production in 1978 with **Benegal**'s ***Junoon*** and ***Kalyug*** as well as **Aparna Sen**'s ***36 Chowringhee Lane*** (1981) and **Girish Karnad**'s ***Utsav***. Regularly acted in British productions. As an actor he was not often given the chance to stretch himself and his image remains that of a lighthearted, slightly cynical seducer. His major cultural achievements are the works he produced and the revival of the Prithvi Theatre in Bombay in honour of his father. Directed one film, *Ajooba*, an Indo-Soviet production starring Bachchan in an Arabian Nights spectacular. Returned from semi-retirement to play the ageing Urdu poet in Ismail Merchant's *In Custody*. Not to be confused with the older Hindi actor, Shashi Kapoor, who acted mostly in mythologicals.

FILMOGRAPHY (* also d): 1948: ***Aag***; 1950: ***Sangram***; 1951: ***Awara***; 1961: *Char Diwari*; *Dharmaputra*; 1962: *Prem Patra*; *Mehndi Lagi Mere Haath*; 1963: *Holiday In Bombay*; *The Householder*; *Yeh Dil Kisko Doon*; 1964: *Benazir*; 1965: *Jab Jab Phool Khile*; *Mohabbat Isko Kehte Hain*; ***Waqt***; *Shakespeare Wallah*; 1966: *Biradari*; *Neend Hamari Khwab Tumhare*; *Pyar Kiye Jaa*; 1967: *Pretty Polly*; *Aamne Samne*; *Dil Ne Pukara*; 1968: ***Hasina Maan Jayegi***; *Juari*; *Kanyadaan*; 1969: *Ek Shriman Ek Shrimati*; *Jahan Pyar Mile*; *Pyar Ka Mausam*; *Raja Saab*; 1970: *Bombay Talkie*; *Abhinetri*; *My Love*; *Rootha Na Karo*; *Suhana Safar*; 1971: *Patanga*; *Sharmilee*; 1972: *Jaanwar Aur Insaan*; 1973: *Aa Gale Lag Jaa*; *Chori Chori*; *Naina*; *Mr Romeo*; 1974: *Chor Machaye Shor*; *Insaniyat*; *Jeevan Sangram*; *Paap Aur Punya*; *Vachan*; *Roti Kapda Aur Makaan*; 1975: *Anari*; *Chori Mera Kaam*; ***Deewar***; *Prem Kahani*; *Salaakhen*; 1976: *Aap Beeti*; *Deewangee*; *Fakira*; *Koi Jeeta Koi Haara*; *Shankar Dada*; *Naach Utha Sansar*; ***Kabhi Kabhie***; 1977: *Chakkar Pe Chakkar*; *Chor Sipahi*; *Doosra Admi*; *Farishta Ya Qatil*; *Heera Aur Patthar*; *Imaan Dharam*; *Mukti* (H); 1978: *Ahuti*; *Amar Shakti*; *Apna Khoon*; *Atithi*; *Do Musafir*; *Heeralal Pannalal*; *Muqaddar*; *Phaansi*; *Rahu Ketu*; ***Satyam Shivam Sundaram***; *Trishna*; ***Trishul***; ***Junoon***; *Siddhartha*; 1979: *Ahsaas*; *Kali Ghata*; *Duniya Meri Jeb Mein*; *Gautam Govinda*; ***Kala Patthar***; *Suhaag*; 1980: *Do Aur Do Paanch*; *Ganga Aur Suraj*; *Kala Pani*; *Neeyat*; *Shaan*; *Swayamvar*; ***Kalyug***; 1981: *Basera*; *Ek Aur Ek Gyarah*; *Kranti* (H); *Krodhi*; *Maan Gaye Ustad*; ***Silsila***; *Vakil Babu*; 1982: *Bezubaan*; *Namak Halal*; *Saval* (H); *Vijeta*; 1983: *Bandhan Kachche Dhaagon Ka*; *Ghunghroo*; *Heat And Dust*; 1984: *Pakhandi*; *Ghar Ek Mandir*; *Zameen Aasmaan*; *Swati* (H); *Yaadon Ki Zanjeer*; ***Utsav***; *Bandh Honth*; 1985: *Aandhi Toofan*; *Alag Alag*; *Bepanah*; *Bhawani Junction*; *Pighalta Aasmaan*; ***New Delhi Times***; 1986: *Anjaam*; *Aurat*; *Door Desh*; *Pyar Ki Jeet*; *Karamdata*; *Ek Main Aur Ek Tu*; *Ilzaam*; 1987: *Maa Beti*; *Ijaazat*; *Naam-o-Nishan*; *Sindoor*; *Ghar Ka Sukh*; *Sammy And Rosie Get Laid*; *Chakma*; 1988: *Commando*; *Hum To Chale Pardes*; *Farz Ki Jung*; *The Deceivers*; *Meri Zabaan*; *Aakhri Muqabala*; 1989: *Bandook Dahej Ke Seene Par*; *Apna Ghar*; *Desh Ke Dushman*; *Mera Muqaddar*; *Mera Farz*; *Tauheen*; *Oonch Neech Beech*; *Gair Kanooni*; *Clerk*; 1991: *Ajooba**; *Raeeszada*; *Akela*; 1993: *In Custody/Muhafiz*.

KAPUR, SHEKHAR (b. 1945)

Aka Chandrasekhar Kapur; actor and director born in Lahore. Educated in New Delhi. Chartered accountant and management consultant in London. Entered Hindi films as actor. Directorial début with ***Masoom***, a low-budget, Hollywood-inspired melodrama using techniques derived from advertising films. Also directed the 'curry' western, *Joshilay* (resigning before it was complete; final version, released in 1989, was credited to the producer, Sibte Hasan Rizvi) and the special-effects-laden ***Mr India***. Reputedly a fine director of children. Currently concentrates on acting in tv serials. Compered a controversial Channel 4 (UK) tv discussion programme, *On The Other Hand*. Made many advertising films and is a noted fashion model. Several of his big Hindi productions have been delayed, leading to a reputation for an expansive, slow-working style. However, has recently completed a fiction film, *Bandit Queen*, on the life of the bandit Phoolan Devi for Channel 4 in London based on Mala Sen's book.

FILMOGRAPHY (* only d): 1974: *Ishq Ishq Ishq*; 1975: *Jaan Hazir Hai*; 1978: *Pal Do Pal Ka Saath*; *Toote Khilone*; 1979: *Jeena Yahan*; 1980: *Bhula Na Dena*; 1982: ***Masoom****; *Bindiya Chamkegi*; 1985: *Joshilay**; *Khandaan*

(TV); **1987**: ***Mr India****; **1988**: *Swayamsiddha* (TV); *Falak*; **1989**: *Gawahi*; *Udaan* (TV); *Mahanagar* (TV); **1989**: ***Nazar***; **1990**: ***Drishti***; **1992**: *Saatwan Asmaan*; **1994**: *Bandit Queen**.

KAR, AJOY (1914-85)

Bengali director and cameraman born in Calcutta. Left college to become a professional photographer (1931); assistant cameraman to Jatin Das at **East India Film** (1935) and cinematographer at Indrapuri Studios, Calcutta (1938). Shot over 80 features. Became director in the Sabhyasachi collective with Binoy Chatterjee (scripts), Jatin Datta (sound), Kamal Ganguly (editor), Bishnu Chakraborty (art d), Bimal Ghosh (prod. controller) and actress **Kanan Devi**. Signed first 3 films as Sabhyasachi. Made several films based on **Rabindranath Tagore** and Saratchandra Chatterjee novels. Crucial figure in reformist Bengali prose cinema of late 50s and 60s surrounding **Uttam Kumar** (cf the classic ***Saptapadi***). Founded India Film Laboratory in Calcutta (1957). Studied colour film technology in the USA (1976). Work often located on the cusp between literary respectability and broad melodrama (e.g. *Malayadaan*, adapting Tagore to tell the story of a dull orphan girl growing into womanhood).

FILMOGRAPHY: **1949**: *Ananya*; *Bamuner Meye*; **1950**: *Mejdidi*; **1951**: *Jighansa*; **1954**: *Grihapravesh*; **1955**: *Sajghar*; *Paresh*; **1956**: *Shyamali*; **1957**: *Bardidi*; *Harano Sur*; **1959**: *Khelaghar*; **1960**: *Suno Baro Nari*; **1961**: ***Saptapadi***; **1962**: *Atal Jaler Ahwan*; **1963**: ***Saat Pake Bandha***; *Barnali*; **1964**: *Prabhater Rang*; **1966**: *Kanch Kata Hirey*; **1969**: *Parineeta*; **1971**: *Malayadaan*; **1973**: *Kaya Hiner Kahini*; **1976**: *Datta*; **1979**: *Nauka Dubi*; **1984**: *Bishabriksha*; *Madhuban*.

KARANTH, B. V. (b. 1929)

Kannada director born in Bangalore. Apprenticed as child to **Gubbi Veeranna**'s theatre company and sent to Benares to learn Hindi and North Indian classical music. Stage productions in Kannada of *Oedipus* (adapted by **P. Lankesh**), **Girish Karnad**'s *Hayavadana* and **Kambhar**'s *Jokumaraswamy* (all in 1971) for his own theatre group Benaka. Introduced folk idioms borrowed from the Yakshagana to the stage, pioneering a trend later associated with cultural indigenism. Director of the National School of Drama (1978-81), and of Repertory at Bharat Bhavan, Bhopal (1981-6). He had to leave following allegations of having tried to burn alive one of the company's actresses. Returned to his native Karnataka where he runs the state's repertory company, Rangayana. Most of his film-making was partnered by Karnad, except for ***Chomana Dudi***. Scored several films, e.g. **G.V. Iyer**'s ***Hamsa Geethe*** (1975), **Mrinal Sen**'s ***Parashuram*** (1978), ***Ek Din Pratidin*** (1979) and ***Kharij*** (1982), **M.S. Sathyu**'s *Kanneshwara Rama* (1977, also act), **Girish Kasaravalli**'s ***Ghattashraddha*** (1977), *Akramana* (1980), *Mooru Darigalu* (1981), ***Tabarana Kathe*** (1986) and ***Bannada Vesha*** (1988), the children's film *Hangama Bombay Ishtyle* (1978) and his wife **Prema Karanth**'s ***Phaniyamma*** (1982).

FILMOGRAPHY (* also act): **1971**: ***Vamsha Vriksha****; **1975**: ***Chomana Dudi***; *Kalla Kalla Bachitko/Chor Chor Chhupja*; **1977**: *Tabbaliyu Neenade Magane/Godhuli*.

KARANTH, PREMA (b. 1936)

Kannada director born in Bangalore. Brought up by grandparents in a small Karnataka village in Kolar District. Wrote stories and articles for children's magazine, *Chandamama*. Well-known director on Kannada stage noted particularly for children's theatre (e.g. **Kambhar**'s *Alibaba and the Forty Thieves*, 1978). Studied at Benares University and graduated in direction at National School of Drama (1971), worked in Delhi-based theatre groups Yatrik and Dishantar, and in husband **B.V. Karanth**'s Benaka in Bangalore (1975). Did costumes for over 120 plays in English, Hindi and Kannada. Assisted **Karnad** and Karanth on *Tabbaliyu Neenade Magane/Godhuli* (1977), **G.V. Iyer** on *Kudre Motte*, in which she also acted. Worked at the Adarsh Film Institute with **Kasaravalli**.

FILMOGRAPHY (* only act): **1977**: *Kudre Motte**; **1982**: *Amara Madhura Prema**; ***Phaniyamma***; **1983**: *Simhasana**; **1985**: *The Jewel of Manipur: Part 1* (Doc); **1986**: *The Jewel of Manipur: Part 2* (Doc); **1988**: *Appiko* (Doc); **1989**: *Nakkala Rajkumari*; **1990**: *Sapne Huye Sakaar* (Doc).

KARDAR, ABDUL RASHID (1904-89)

Hindi-Urdu director born into Lahore's landed gentry; affectionately known as 'Miyanji'. Considered a promising painter and still photographer. Moved to Bombay (1922) to work at **Kohinoor**. Did poster-paintings at **Sharda** Studio. Acted in a few films but, unable to get directorial assignment, returned to Lahore. Joined B.R. Oberai's Pioneer Prod. as actor. Started United Players Corp. (1928), which, with partners Kardar and Hakim Ramprashad, grew into Playart Phototone. Made genre quickies derived from the commercial stage and Hollywood B films imported into North India in bulk by **Pancholi**'s Empire Film Distributors. Despite their influence on the Lahore film industry, Kardar's Playart talkies were not commercial hits. Moved to Calcutta (1933) and became top director for **East India Film** (1933-6); then to Bombay (**Ranjit** and National Studios). Bought CIRCO Studio to launch the Kardar Studios with *Sharada*. It closed in 1968 despite an all-industry rescue effort. Started Musical Pics (1950). Launched directors **Nasir Hussain**, M. Sadiq (who later directed **Guru Dutt** in ***Chaudhvin Ka Chand***, 1960) and S.U. Sunny. Made his best-known films in 1940, a series of psychodramas attempting to match the realism of Urdu literature (***Pagal***, ***Holi***, ***Pooja***). Then moved to portmanteau musicals featuring his regular composer **Naushad**, including comedy spoofs with **Kishore Kumar** (*Baap Re Baap*). Apparently ***Dastaan*** was based on the US film *Enchantment* (1948), *Jadu* on Raoul Walsh's *The Loves of Carmen* (1927) and *Baghi Sipahi* on R.V. Lee's *Cardinal Richlieu* (1935). His comeback with ***Dil Diya Dard Liya*** went wrong and **Dilip Kumar** ended up directing the movie credited to Kardar.

FILMOGRAPHY (* also act/** act only): **1929**: *Husn Ka Daku**; *Heer Ranjha***; **1930**: *Sarfarosh*; *Safdar Jung*; *Farebi Shahzada*; **1931**: *Khooni Katar**; *Bhatakta Joban*; *Life After Death*** (all St); **1932**: *Heer Ranjha*; **1933**: *Aurat Ka Pyar*; *Abe Hayat***; **1934**: *Seeta***; *Chandragupta*; *Sultana*; **1935**: *Swarg Ki Sidhi*; **1936**: *Baghi Sipahi*; **1937**: *Mandir*; *Milap*; **1938**: ***Baghban***; **1939**: ***Thokar***; **1940**: ***Holi***; ***Pagal***; ***Pooja***; **1941**: ***Swami***; **1942**: *Nai Duniya*; *Sharada*; **1943**: *Kanoon*; ***Sanjog***; **1944**: *Pehle Aap*; **1945**: *Sanyasi*; **1946**: ***Shahjehan***; **1947**: *Dard*; **1949**: *Dillagi*; *Dulari*; **1950**: ***Dastaan***; **1951**: *Jadu*; **1952**: *Diwana*; **1953**: *Dil-e-Nadaan*; **1955**: *Baap Re Baap*; *Yasmin*; **1958**: *Do Phool*; **1966**: ***Dil Diya Dard Liya***; **1975**: *Mere Sartaj*.

KARIAT, RAMU (1927-79)

Malayalam director born in Engandiyur, Trichur Dist., Kerala, into a farming family. Started writing poetry and prose as a teenager for the weekly *Mathrubhoomi*. Assisted Vimal Kumar and P.R.S. Pillai on ***Thiramala*** (1953). First film, ***Neelakuyil*** (co-d with **P. Bhaskaran**), started independent cinema in Kerala. An unaffiliated Marxist, early work is in context of the broad cultural renaissance spearheaded by the Kerala Peoples' Arts Club (see **IPTA**), indebted to the 40s CPI-led uprising against Travancore State. Several major writers entered film through Kariat, e.g. Thakazhy Shivashankar Pillai (author of ***Chemmeen***), Uroob (who scripted *Neelakuyil*), playwrights **Thoppil Bhasi**, K.T. Mohammed and **S.L. Puram Sadanandan**. Opened up new areas in Malayalam film with work strongly imbued with lyrical, even mystical feelings about a newly discovered sense of community through subjects often placed among fisherfolk and villagers. Briefly a Kerala MP. Finished shooting the Telugu film *Kondagali* before his death, but it remained unedited. His *Chemmeen* was later re-released in a Hindi-dubbed version called *Chemmeen Lahren* (1980). Acted in Bhaskaran's ***Rarichan Enna Pauran*** (1956). Also produced M. Lakshmanan's Tamil film *Kannamma* (1972). His last film, *Karimbu*, was completed later by K. Vijayan and released in 1984.

FILMOGRAPHY: **1954**: ***Neelakuyil***; **1956**: *Bharata Natyam* (Doc); **1957**: ***Minnaminungu***; **1961**: ***Mudiyanaya Puthran***; **1963**: ***Moodupadam***; **1965**: ***Chemmeen***; **1968**: ***Ezhu Rathrikal***; **1970**: *Abhayam*; **1972**: *Maya*; **1974**: *Nellu*; **1976**: *Dweep*; **1978**: *Ammuvinte Attinkutty*; *Kondagali*; **1979**: *Karimbu*.

KARNAD, GIRISH RAGHUNATH (b. 1938)

Kannada and Hindi actor and director. Born in Matheran, Maharashtra, into medical family. Educated in English and Marathi but wrote in Kannada. Graduated in mathematics and statistics (1958). Rhodes Scholar, Oxford University (1960-3), later President of the Oxford Union Society (1963). Wrote first play *Yayati* (1961) in England. Manager of Oxford University Press in Madras (1963-70). Known mainly as playwright (also wrote: *Tughlaq*, 1964; *Hayavadana*, 1971; *Anjumallige*, 1977; *Hittina Hunja*, 1980; *Nagamandala*, 1986), where he is often considered part of a new post-Independence theatre movement with Badal Sircar, Mohan Rakesh and **Vijay Tendulkar**. Unlike the others, his plays are generally mythologicals informed by psychoanalytic symbology (*Hayavadana*, *Nagamandala*). Homi Bhabha fellowship for creative work in folk theatre (1970-2). Joined film as scenarist and lead actor for ***Samskara***. First film as director, ***Vamsha Vriksha*** (with **B.V. Karanth**, the director of his stage plays), in the wake of *Samskara*'s success. Moved to Hindi film to work with **Benegal** as actor and scenarist (***Nishant***, 1975; ***Manthan***, 1976, and the script of ***Kalyug***, 1980). Since then has been a prolific actor in Hindi film and on television. Made one big-budget Hindi film for **Shashi Kapoor**, ***Utsav***. First director of autonomous **FTII** (1974-5). President of the Karnataka State Nataka Akademi (1976-8) and of the Sangeet Natak Akademi (1988-93). His best-known film, ***Kaadu***, placed him, with Benegal, squarely within New Indian Cinema's ruralism, although he also made the martial-arts adventure movie ***Ondanondu Kaladalli*** inspired by Kurosawa. Scripted his own films.

FILMOGRAPHY (* only d/** also d)): **1970**: ***Samskara***; **1971**: ***Vamsha Vriksha*****; **1973**: *D.R. Bendre** (Doc); ***Kaadu****; *Jadu Ka Shankh*; **1975**: ***Nishant***; **1976**: ***Manthan***; *Kanakambara*; **1977**: ***Swami***; *Jeevanmukt*; *Tabbaliyu Neenade Magane/Godhuli**; **1978**: ***Ondanondu Kaladalli****; **1979**: *Ratnadeep*; **1980**: *Anveshane*; *Asha*; *Apne Paraye*; *Man Pasand*; **1981**: *Paanch Qaidi*; *Shama*; ***Umbartha/Subah***; **1982**: *Teri Kasam*; ***Aparoopa/Apeksha***; **1983**: *Ananda Bhairavi*; *Ek Baar Chale Aao*; *Sampark*; *Divorce*; **1984**: ***Utsav****; ***Tarang***; *Woh Ghar** (TV); *Khoon Aur Sazaa*; **1985**: *Meri Jung*; *Sur Sangam*; *Nee Thanda Kanike*; *Khandaan* (TV); *Pyari Bhabhi*; **1986**: *Nilakurinhi Poothappol*; *Naan Adimai Illai*; *Sutradhar*; **1987**: *Swami*; **1988**: *Akarshan*; *Kadina Benki*; *Kanaka Purandaradasa** (Doc); *Mil Gayi Manzil Mujhe*; **1989**: *Lamp in the Niche** (Parts 1&2) (Doc); **1990**: *Santha Shishunala Shareefa*; *Sara Jahan Hamara* (TV); **1991**: *Swami and Friends* (TV); *Mysore Mallige*; *Jawahar*; **1992**: ***Cheluvi*****.

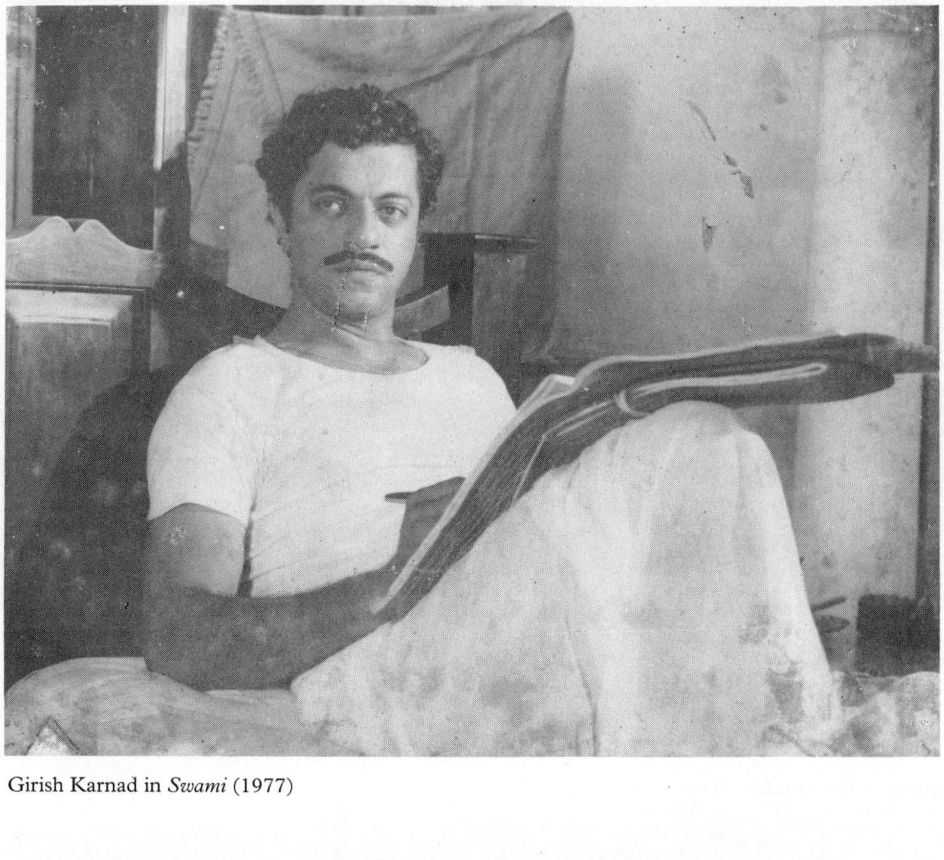

Girish Karnad in *Swami* (1977)

Karnataki, Vinayak *see* **Vinayak, Master**

KARUN, SHAJI N. (b. 1951)

Malayalam director born in Trivandrum. Well-known cameraman, notably for **Aravindan**'s films but also for **K.G. George** and **M.T. Vasudevan Nair**. Graduate from the **FTII**'s cinematography course (1974). Directorial début, ***Piravi***, was widely discussed in India and abroad. His camerawork (e.g. for Aravindan) virtually defines the look of Kerala's New Indian Cinema with its soft, half-light effects that, in the black and white period, played a role reminiscent of Subrata Mitra's work in 60s Bengali film. Colour work tends to suppress primary colours, their harsh introduction symbolising degeneracy or corruption.

FILMOGRAPHY: **1974**: *Lady of the Landing* (Sh); **1988**: ***Piravi***; **1994**: *Swaham*.

KARUNANIDHI, MUTHUVEL (b. 1924)

Tamil scenarist and DMK politician born in Tirukkuvalai, Tanjore Dist., TN. Political activist with the Dravidar Kazhagam (DK) from the age of 14; left school to become **C.N. Annadurai**'s assistant and worked on Periyar E.V. Ramaswamy Naicker's paper, *Kudiarasu*. Led the 1953 Kallakkudi riots in which the DMK protested against the renaming of a railway station after a North Indian industrialist. Elected to the Tamil Nadu State Assembly in 1957 on a DMK ticket. Key figure in the anti-Hindi agitation of 1965, for which he was imprisoned. Minister for Public Works and Transport under Annadurai when the DMK was elected in 1967. Chief Minister in 1969 following Annadurai's death; defeated by his former protégé **MGR** in 1977. Returned to power (1988), but was dismissed by the Congress (I)-backed minority government in 1990; in the 1991 election his party lost every seat in the state assembly except his own. Film début at the Jupiter Studio, co-scripting A. Kasilingam's *Abhimanyu* (1948) with **A.S.A. Sami**. First **DMK film**: MGR's ***Manthiri Kumari*** for **T.R. Sundaram** (1950). Wrote Kasilingam's *Maruthanattu Ilavarasi* (1950), three films for **L.V. Prasad** (***Manohara***, 1954; *Thayilla Pillai*, 1961; ***Iruvar Ullam***, 1963) and his best-known film, **Krishnan-Panju**'s ***Parasakthi*** (1952). According to Ka. Thiranavukarasu (1990), he scripted 57 films, e.g. S.M. Sreeramulu Naidu's MGR hit ***Malaikallan*** (1954), Kasilingam's **Sivaji Ganesan** film ***Rangoon Radha*** (1956) based on Annadurai's novel, and **P. Neelakantan**'s *Poompuhar* (1964) and *Poomalai* (1965). Also wrote c.50 short stories (e.g. *Kuppai Thothi/Dustbin*), many speeches, commentaries on Tamil literature and a speculative archaeology of the Tamil language tracing it to the Sangam poets and the Indus Valley. Turned producer with Mekala Pics, initially with MGR, MGR's wife V.N. Janaki and P.S. Veerappa (*Naam*, 1953); the partnership soon broke up leaving Karunanidhi sole proprietor.

KASARAVALLI, GIRISH (b. 1949)

Kannada director born in Kasaravalli village, Karnataka. Degree in pharmacology (1971). Even before graduating from the **FTII** (1975) had virtually taken over direction of **Nagabharana**'s ***Grahana*** (1978). First feature, ***Ghattashraddha***, in the wake of ***Samskara*** (1970) and based on U.R. Ananthamurthy's writing, extended the anti-brahminism of the literary **Navya Movement**. Principal of Adarsh Film Institute, Bangalore; edited a Kannada anthology on film theory with essays by Eisenstein, Kracauer, Bazin, Metz, Wollen et al (1983).

FILMOGRAPHY: **1975**: *Avashesh* (Sh); *Anya* (Sh); **1977**: ***Ghattashraddha***; **1980**: *Akramana*; **1981**: *Mooru Darigalu*; **1986**: ***Tabarana Kathe***; *Glowing Embers* (Doc); **1988**: ***Bannada Vesha*** (TV); **1990**: ***Mane/Ek Ghar***.

KASHMIRI, AGA HASHR (1879-1935)

Scenarist and best-known early 20th C. Urdu-Hindi playwright of enormously influential Parsee theatre plays. On contract to the Alfred Theatre in Bombay (1901-5) and then to the **Madan Theatres**' Elphinstone and Corinthian companies in Calcutta, providing adaptations of Shakespeare (*A Winter's Tale* became *Mureed-e-Kash*, 1899; *Measure for Measure* became *Shaheed-e-Naaz* aka *Achhuta Daman* in Hindi, 1902; *King John* became *Saeed-e-Havas*, 1907; *Macbeth* was *Khwab-e-Hasti*). Made a big impact with his linguistic transpositions of Shakespearean tragedy's feudal elements of blood ties and blood feuds, honour, sacrifice and destiny into Farsi, Arabic (he knew both languages) and Moorish legends, simultaneously taking on board the European baroque's Orientalist treatment of such sources. He extended his Shakespearean matrix to several partially original plays like *Meethi Churi* (1902), *Safed Khoon* (influenced by *King Lear*, 1907) and his best-known play, *Yahudi Ki Ladki* (1915), all of which were repeatedly filmed in the silent and early sound periods. His initial writing style followed the post-*Indrasabha* convention of mixing Urdu prose and poetry with Hindustani music. Later, with plays like *Pehla Pyar* (1911) and *Van Devi* (1916), he started writing in Hindustani, shifting away from historicals into socials and Pauranic mythologicals treated in the social genre: *Bhishma* (1925), *Seeta Banwas* (1927). This linguistic and generic convergence helped, through his scripts, shape the films of Madan Theatres (***Pati Bhakti***, 1922; *Paper Parinam*, 1924; *Dharmapatni*, 1926; *Aankh Ka Nasha*, 1928 and *Bharati Balak*, 1931, which he also directed) and formed the persona of **New Theatres**' famed tragedian, **K.L. Saigal**, scripting his influential ***Chandidas*** (1934), ***Yahudi Ki Ladki*** (1933) and writing his lyrics (e.g. *Prem nagar mein banaoongi ghar main* and *Dukh ab din beetat nain*).

KATHAVACHAK, RADHESHYAM (b. 1890)

Writer born in Bareilly. Major 1920s Parsee theatre playwright, e.g. for New Alfred Co. In plays like *Shri Krishnavtar* (1926), *Rukmini Mangal* (1927) and *Shravan Kumar* (1928) he more or less invented the mythological in its familiar Hindi film version, still practised in, e.g., **Sagar**'s tv serial, *Ramayan* (1986-8). He drew upon his strong familial roots in the performative traditions of the Ramleela and pioneered the mediation of Northern and Central Indian folk performances into the later mass cultural manifestation of the genre in Hindi cinema. Unlike, e.g., **Betaab**, he made few claims for classicism beyond that of writing in 'pure' Hindi (as distinct from Urdu). He attempted to link up with the devotional rather than with the spectacular and addressed a proletarian audience through the publications of his Radheshyam Press in Bareilly. Worked briefly for **Madan Theatres** as scenarist and songwriter and freelanced often for former New Alfred colleagues. His autobiography (1957) is considered a classic description of the early 20th C. commercial theatre and also gives a first-hand description of the Madan film factory. Also scripted or wrote lyrics for **Bhavnani**'s *Shakuntala* (1931), Dhrupad Rai's *Shri Satyanarayan* (1935), Varma's *Usha Haran* (1940), **Sohrab Modi**'s ***Jhansi Ki Rani*** (1953) and Sharad Desai's *Shravan Kumar* (1960).

KAUL, MAHESH (1911-72)

Hindi director born in Lahore. Educated at Moni College, Nagpur, and worked as a journalist and as branch manager of a bank. Entered films as lyricist and dialogue writer. Début as actor in **Abbas**-scripted ***Naya Sansar***. Played Dronacharya in **Altekar**'s mythological, ***Mahatma Vidur***. Also produced his third film as director, ***Gopinath***, featuring **Raj Kapoor** in one of his first major roles alongside **IPTA** actress Tripti Mitra. The film presents an influential version of a starkly realist acting idiom in 40s Hindi political melodrama. Worked briefly in **Filmistan** in mid-50s. Directed **Guru Dutt** in ***Sautela Bhai*** and played the crusty colonial father-in-law in ***Kaagaz Ke Phool***. Scripted Daryani's *Dukh Sukh* (1974). Uncle of **Mani Kaul**.

FILMOGRAPHY (* act only): **1941**: ***Naya Sansar****; **1942**: ***Apna Ghar/Aple Ghar****; **1943**: ***Mahatma Vidur****; *Angoori*; **1944**: *Paristan*; **1948**: ***Gopinath***; **1951**: *Naujawan*; **1953**: *Jeevan Jyoti*; **1957**: *Abhimaan*; **1958**: *Aakhri Dao*; *Talaaq*; **1959**: ***Kaagaz Ke Phool****; **1961**: *Pyar Ki Pyaas*; **1962**: ***Sautela Bhai***; **1967**: *Diwana*; *Palki*; **1968**: *Sapnon Ka Saudagar*; **1969**: *Raakhi Raakhi*; **1971**: ***Tere Mere Sapne****; **1973**: *Agni Rekha*.

KAUL, MANI R. (b. 1942)

Director born in Jodhpur, Rajasthan. Graduate from University of Jaipur (1963) and from the **FTII** (1966) where he was taught by **Ghatak**. Nephew of **Mahesh Kaul**. Often acted in Film Institute student films in the mid-60s, and appeared as actor in **Basu Chatterjee**'s ***Sara Akash*** (1969). Received Jawaharlal Nehru Fellowship (1974-6). Part of the YUKT Collective that made ***Ghashiram Kotwal***. Prominent cultural activist and organiser, often making common cause with **Shahani** in efforts to extend the range of Indian film cultures, and significant teacher of a new generation of **FTII** graduates, some of whom became key members of his film unit. First film, ***Uski Roti***, is a cinematic exploration of narrative space and volume, defining much of New Indian Cinema's formal vocabulary. Since ***Satah Se Uthata Admi***, based on Hindi poet G.M. Muktibodh, made features on, e.g., Dhrupad music and on terracotta artisans, emphasising improvised reconstruction of available material. Edits his colour films first in b&w, having printed every single take. Later work strongly influenced by his study of Dhrupad music with Ustad Zia Mohiyuddin Dagar and of Anandvardhan's *Dhwanyaloka*, a 9th C. Sanskrit text on aesthetics exploring states of conscious perception while positing language as possessing a specific, suggestive dimension beyond its denotative or metaphoric faculties. Developing aspects of classical music theories, particularly the *Sangeet Samay Saar* (14th C.), Kaul emphasises the value of what is absent - the varjit, the forbidden - as perennially in 'argument' (*vivadi*) with what is narratively present. The evanescent moment of creation is posed at the point where human action simultaneously registers what exists and in the process, produces something unprecedented. His elaborate theory of contemporary aesthetic practice, 'Seen From Nowhere', was presented in the cultural historian Kapila Vatsyayan's seminar *Inner Space, Outer Space* (Indira Gandhi National Centre For Art) and published in the book *Concepts of Space: Ancient and Modern*. Among various non-Indian sources, has drawn from haiku poetry, the *nouveau roman*, mannerist painting, Bresson and Ozu. Recent return to fiction cinema draws mainly from Dostoevsky (***Nazar***, ***Idiot***). Refused to sign the documentary *Historical Sketch of Indian Women* during the Emergency when its producers, **Films Division**, required him to change the last shot and the commentary.

FILMOGRAPHY: **1967**: *Yatrik* (Sh); *6.40 p.m.* (Sh); *Homage to the Teacher* (Sh); **1968**: *Forms and Design* (Doc); **1969**: ***Uski Roti***; **1970**: *During and after Air Raid* (Doc); **1971**: ***Ashad Ka Ek Din***; **1973**: ***Duvidha***; **1974**: *The Nomad Puppeteers* (Doc); **1975**: *Historical Sketch of Indian Women* (Doc; uncredited); **1976**: *Chitrakathi* (Doc); ***Ghashiram Kotwal***; **1979**: *Arrival* (Doc); **1980**: ***Satah Se Uthata Admi***; **1981**: *Desert of a Thousand Lines* (Sh); **1982**: ***Dhrupad***; **1984**: ***Mati Manas***; **1988**: *Before My Eyes* (Doc); **1989**: ***Siddheshwari***; ***Nazar***; **1991**: ***Idiot***.

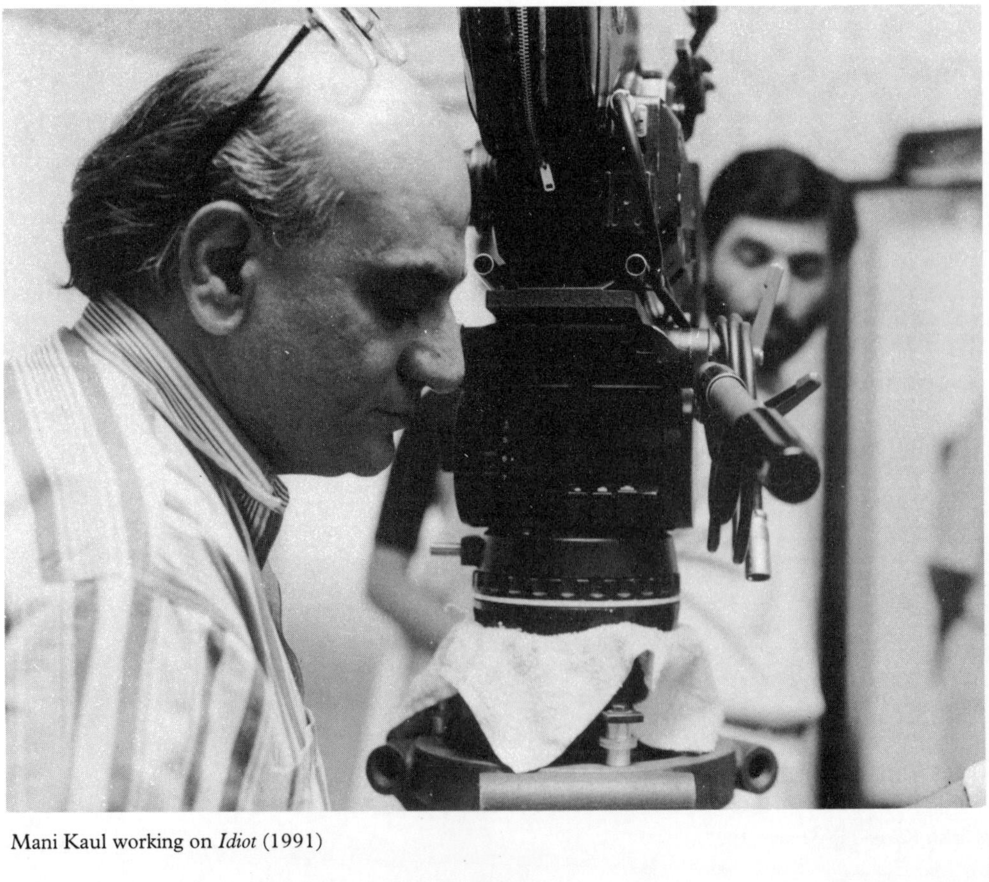

Mani Kaul working on *Idiot* (1991)

K.D. BROTHERS

Often described as India's largest film importers in the early silent era, the company, not well documented because of its early closure, was apparently owned by Krishnadas Dwarkadas. Its advertised imports in the *Bombay Chronicle* include William Fox's *A Wife's Sacrifice* (1919), the *Gaumont Gazette* and, in 1921, independently made newsreels showing events connected with the **Swadeshi** agitations: e.g. *Collecting Foreign Clothes in the Streets of Bombay*, *Enthusiasts on their way to the Bonfire near the Elphinstone Mills* and several shots of Gandhi and Maulana Shaukat Ali. By the early 20s, K.D. Brothers mainly dealt with newsreels such as Chimanlal **Luhar**'s early work. Probably starting with tent bioscopes, by the early 20s their interests expanded to include two of Bombay's front-line theatres, the Globe and the West End. An advertisement saying that the West End would release 'no serial and no Indian film' while the Globe would show the 'best of serial chapter plays and the pick of Indian productions', clearly reveals their twin distribution interests. Among the Indian films they distributed, within India and abroad (foreign distribution was for a while controlled by **A. Narayanan**) were **Hindustan Cinema** and Bharat films, the first two **Dhiren Ganguly** films and **Suchet Singh**'s *Narasinh Mehta* (1920).

KHANDEKAR, VISHNU SAKHARAM (1898-1976)

Influential Marathi writer and essayist born in Sangli, Maharashtra. Closely associated with the progressive, secular tradition of the reformist G.G. Agarkar. A former schoolteacher, his best-known novels (*Ulka*, 1934; *Hirva Chafa*, 1938; *Pandhre Dhag*, 1939) are often deliberately pedagogical, with characters presented as social 'types' in situations devised as guides to morally correct behaviour. Wrote several original scripts, e.g. for **Master Vinayak** (***Jwala***, 1938; ***Amrit*** and Junnarkar's *Sangam*, both 1941) some of which he later novelised (*Rikama Devhara* based on ***Devata***, 1939; *Sukhacha Shodh*, 1939, etc.). His literary world is 'peopled on the one side by ambitious men who have lost their humanity and, on the other, by the poor [w]ho suffer but never lose their humaneness; poverty is always perceived as a social consequence of crippling ambition' (Mordekar, Aug 1941). His stories are high melodrama full of sacrifices bravely borne, passionate revenge and holy sin in extraordinarily convoluted plots (***Chhaya***, 1936; ***Mazhe Bal***, 1943), exerting a strong influence in Marathi cinema, e.g. on **Raja Paranjpe/G.D. Madgulkar**. Based scripts on C.V. Joshi's popular political satires featuring the bumbling duo Gundyabhau and Chimanrao: ***Lagna Pahave Karun*** (1940) and ***Sarkari Pahune*** (1942). Scripted C. Raghuvir's *Soneri Savli* (1953), Madhav Shinde's *Antaricha Diva* (1960), *Mansala Pankh Astaat* (1961) and *Sunbai* (1962; also providing the lyrics together with Shanta Shelke).

KHANNA, RAJESH (b. 1942)

Originally Jatin Khanna. The first of the late 60s/early 70s Hindi superstars with a big impact on the industry, later equalled only by **Bachchan**. His late 60s roles were often low-budget genre films (e.g. **Yash Chopra**'s thriller ***Ittefaq***). Broke through in two popular love stories made and released simultaneously: ***Aradhana*** and ***Do Raaste***, which shaped his film persona, later elaborated by **Shakti Samanta**. His image is traceable to Gulshan Nanda's novelettes generated in the context of the industrialisation of 60s Hindi publishing pioneered by Mitra Prakashan's best-selling journal, *Manohar Kahaniyan*, in Allahabad, and its numerous imitations aiming serials at less-educated readers. In the 70s, he often played a social orphan (*Hathi Mere Saathi*) deprived of maternal love and stricken by some existential malaise (*Amar Prem*) driving him to depravity (***Dushman***, *Kati Patang*) from which the heroine and foster-mother rescue him, usually by naming him as their protector. Often partnered by **Sharmila Tagore** or Mumtaz in his best-known films. His image of the innocent in a big bad world extended also to famous roles as a man who laughs to cover up some internal tragedy (***Anand***, ***Andaz***). This approach influenced film-makers like Yash Chopra, but it was quickly overtaken in the mid-70s by Bachchan, making Khanna's style an anachronism in the 80s. Stood for election as a Congress (I) candidate in Delhi, almost defeating the right-wing BJP leader, L.K. Advani. In a by-election he defeated the film star Shatrughan Sinha (who now represented the BJP) and became an MP.

FILMOGRAPHY: **1966**: ***Aakhri Khat***; **1967**: *Baharon Ke Sapne*; *Raaz*; *Aurat*; **1969**: ***Aradhana***; ***Bandhan***; ***Do Raaste***; *Doli*; ***Ittefaq***; ***Khamoshi***; **1970**: *Aan Milo Sajna*; ***Anand***; *Kati Patang*; ***Sachcha Jhutha***; *Safar*; *The Train*; **1971**: *Amar Prem*; ***Andaz***; *Badnaam Farishte*; *Chhoti Bahu*; ***Dushman***; *Hathi Mere Saathi*; *Maryada*; *Mehboob Ki Mehndi*; **1972**: *Apna Desh*; *Anuraag*; *Bawarchi*; *Dil Daulat Duniya*; *Joru Ka Gulam*; *Malik*; *Mere Jeevan Saathi*; *Shehzada*; **1973**: *Avishkar*; ***Daag***; ***Namak Haram***; *Raja Rani*; **1974**: *Aaina*; *Aap Ki Kasam*; *Ajnabi*; *Humshakal*; *Prem Nagar*; *Roti*; **1975**: *Akraman*; *Prem Kahani*; **1976**: *Bandalbaaz*; *Maha Chor*; *Mehbooba*; *Tyaag*; *Ginny Aur Johnny*; **1977**: *Anurodh*; *Chalta Purza*; *Chhaila Babu*; *Karm*; *Palkon Ki Chhaon Mein*; *Tinku*; *Aashiq Hoon Baharon Ka*; **1978**: *Bhola Bhala*; *Prem Bandhan*; *Chakravyuha*; *Naukri*; **1979**: *Amar Deep*; *Janata Havaldar*; *Muqabala*; **1980**: *Bandish*; *Phir Wohi Raat*; *Red Rose*; *Thodisi Bewafayi*; *Aanchal*; **1981**: *Dard*; *Dhanwan*; *Fifty-Fifty*; *Kudrat*; *Dil-e-Nadaan*; **1982**: *Ashanti*; *Dharam Kanta*; *Rajput*; *Suraag*; *Jaanwar*; **1983**: *Agar Tum Na Hote*; *Avatar*; *Nishan*; *Souten*; *Babu*; **1984**: *Aaj Ka MLA Ramavatar*; *Asha Jyoti*; *Awaaz*; *Maqsad*; *Naya Kadam*; *Paapi Pet Ka Sawaal Hai*; *Durga*; *Hum Dono*; *Dharam Aur Kanoon*; **1985**: *Alag Alag*; *Aakhir Kyon*; *Awara Baap*; *Bewafai*; *Insaaf Main Karoonga*; *Masterji*; *Oonche Log*; *Zamana*; **1986**: *Adhikar*; *Amrit*; *Angarey*; *Anokha Rishta*; *Mohabbat Ki Kasam*; *Nasihat*; *Shatru*; **1987**: *Gora*; *Awaam*; *Nazrana*; *Seetapur Ki Geeta*; **1988**: *Vijay*; *Woh Phir Aayegi*; **1989**: *Paap Ka Ant*; *Mamata Ki Chhaon Mein*; *Main Tera Dushman*; *Ghar Ka Chirag*; **1990**: *Ghar Parivar*; *Swarg*; **1991**: *Rupaye Dus Karod*.

KHAYYAM, MOHAMMED ZAHUR (b. 1927)

Hindi music director born in Jullundur. Studied for a while with Pandit Amarnath and with music directors **Husnlal-Bhagatram**. Went to Bombay to become a film actor, then worked in Lahore. Early films composed in association with Aziz Khan, **Bulo C. Rani** et al. Worked at **Ranjit** Studio. Sang a duet in Akhtar Hussein's *Romeo and Juliet* (1947) and acted in S.D. Narang's *Yeh Hai Zindagi* (1947). First independent composing assignment, **Zia Sarhadi**'s ***Footpath***, including the hit *Shyam-e-gam ki kasam* sung by Talat Mahmood. Worked extensively in the traditional ghazal format. His collaboration with **Sahir Ludhianvi** on songs satirising Nehruite politics in ***Phir Subah Hogi*** (*Chin-o-Arab hamara* and *Woh subah kabhi to aayegi*) are definitive of 50s Hindi cinema's engagement with existential realism. Made a comeback with the hit love songs of **Yash Chopra**'s ***Kabhi Kabhie*** and **Muzaffar Ali**'s Urdu period movie, ***Umrao Jaan***. Also did music for Esmayeel Shroff's love stories in the 80s. Credited as 'Sharmaji' on his first 4 films. Har Mandir Singh's *Geet Kosh* suggests he also scored *Hum Hain Rahi Pyar Ke* in the 60s.

FILMOGRAPHY: **1948**: *Heer Ranjha*; **1949**: *Parda*; **1950**: *Biwi*; **1951**: *Pyar Ki Baatein*; **1953**: ***Footpath***; **1954**: *Dhobi Doctor*; *Gul Bahar*; **1955**: *Tatar Ka Chor*; **1958**: *Lala Rukh*; ***Phir Subah Hogi***; **1960**: *Barood*; ***Bambai Ki Billi***; **1961**: *Shola Aur Shabnam*; **1964**: *Shagun*; **1965**: *Mohabbat Isko Kehte Hain*; **1966**: ***Aakhri Khat***; **1967**: *Mera Bhai Mera Dushman*; **1974**: *Pyaase Dil*; *Sankalp*; **1975**: *Sandhya*; *Mutthi Bhar Chawal*; **1976**: ***Kabhi Kabhie***; **1977**: *Shankar Hussain*; **1978**: ***Trishul***; **1979**: *Meena Kumari Ki Amar Kahani*; *Noorie*; *Khandaan*; *Chambal Ki Kasam*; **1980**: *Thodisi Bewafayi*; **1981**: *Ahista Ahista*; *Dard*; *Nakhuda*; ***Umrao Jaan***; *Dil-e-Nadaan*; **1982**: *Bazaar*; *Banwri*; *Dil Aakhir Dil Hai*; *Saval* (H); **1983**: *Mehndi*; *Razia Sultan*; **1984**: *Lorie*; **1985**: *Bepanah*; *Tere Shaher Mein*; **1986**: ***Anjuman***; **1988**: *Parbat Ke Us Paar*; *Ek Naya Rishta*; **1989**: *Jaan-e-Wafaa*; **1990**: *Jawani Zindabad*.

KHOSLA, RAJ (1925-91)

Hindi director born in Ludhiana, Punjab. Family moved to Bombay (1934). Studied music from an early age and learned singing under Pandit Jagannath Prasad. Graduated in history and economics from Elphinstone College; arts degree from Bombay University. Joined AIR as singer (1946). **Dev Anand** made him assistant to **Guru Dutt** who gave him first major directorial assignment, ***CID***. Acted a small role in Dutt's ***Jaal*** (1952). Worked for Navketan and Filmalaya. Production partnership with cameraman Jal Mistry, Naya Films (e.g. ***Bambai Ka Babu***, about incest). Then solo with Raj Khosla Films (1967). His ***Do Raaste*** helped make **Rajesh Khanna** a superstar. Returned in late 70s to the themes of bravely borne suffering, mainly addressing female audiences, which is unusual in recent Hindi cinema (*Main Tulsi Tere Aangan Ki*; *Teri Maang Sitaron Se Bhar Doon*, etc.). Known for inventive song picturisations, a skill he learnt from Guru Dutt. Also producer (e.g. *Do Chor*, 1972).

FILMOGRAPHY: **1955**: *Milap*; **1956**: ***CID***; **1958**: ***Kala Pani***; *Solva Saal*; **1960**: ***Bambai Ka Babu***; **1962**: *Ek Musafir Ek Hasina*; **1964**: ***Woh Kaun Thi***; **1966**: *Do Badan*; *Mera Saaya*; **1967**: *Anita*; **1969**: *Chirag*; ***Do Raaste***; **1971**: *Mera Gaon Mera Desh*; **1973**: *Kachche Dhaage*; *Shareef Badmash*; **1975**: *Prem Kahani*; **1976**: *Nehle Pe Dehla*; **1978**: *Main Tulsi Tere Aangan Ki*; **1980**: *Do Premi*; *Dostana*; **1981**: *Daasi*; **1982**: *Teri Maang Sitaron Se Bhar Doon*; **1984**: *Mera Dost Mera Dushman*; *Sunny*; *Mati Mange Khoon*; **1988**: *Naqab*.

KHOTE, DURGA (1905-91)

The first Marathi star to catapult to **All-India film** popularity. Born into an élite Maharashtra family in Bombay; educated in Cathedral School and influenced by Avantikabai Gokhale who helped put feminist issues on to the nationalist agenda. Her class background, unusual for an actress, allowed her to assume different images from the conventional **Sangeet Natak** stereotypes. Acted in **Bhavnani**'s *Farebi Jaal* but effectively introduced in **Prabhat**'s first sound film, ***Ayodhyecha Raja/Ayodhya Ka Raja***. She then shifted to **New Theatres** to work with **Debaki Bose**, being the only actress featuring simultaneously in the two leading studios. As the queen in **Shantaram**'s ***Maya Machindra***, with the Cheetah at her feet or in her most famous early role as the pirate in ***Amar Jyoti***, she recalled the Talmadge sisters or Mary Pickford. Following her role in **Atre**'s ***Payachi Dasi***, she settled down to a long career as character actress (e.g. as queen mother in ***Mughal-e-Azam***) and did some theatre, being associated for a while with the **IPTA** (she acted in their production of *Andolan* to replenish the Gandhi Fund). Also acted in and directed some Marathi plays, starting with *Bhaubandhaki*. Started Durga Khote Prod. for advertising and short films, run by her daughter-in-law, Tina Khote. Wrote an autobiography, *Mee Durga Khote* (1982).

FILMOGRAPHY: **1931**: *Farebi Jaal*; **1932**: ***Ayodhyecha Raja/Ayodhya Ka Raja***; ***Maya Machhindra***; **1933**: *Patit Pawan*; ***Rajrani Meera***; **1934**: *Seeta*; **1935**: ***Jeevan Natak***; ***Inquilab***; **1936**: ***Amar Jyoti***; **1937**: ***Pratibha***; *Kal Ki Baat*; **1938**: ***Nandakumar*** (Mar); *Savangadi/Saathi*; **1939**: ***Adhuri Kahani***; **1940**: ***Narsi Bhagat***; ***Geeta***; *Raigad*; **1941**: ***Payachi Dasi/Charnon Ki Dasi***; **1942**: ***Bharat Milap/Bharat Bhet***; *Vijay*; **1943**: *Qurbani*; *Mahasati Ansuya*; ***Prithvi Vallabh***; ***Tasveer***; *Zameen*; ***Mahatma Vidur***; **1944**: *Dil Ki Baat*; *Maharathi Karna*; ***Phool***; **1945**: ***Lakhrani***; *Pannadai*; *Veer Kunal*; *Village Girl*; **1946**: *Rukmini Swayamvar*; *Daasi Ya Maa*; ***Hum Ek Hain***; *Maharani Meenal Devi*; **1948**: *Anjuman*; *Moruchi Mavshi*; *Seeta Swayamvar*; **1949**: *Maya Bazaar*; *Jeet*; *Singaar*; **1950**: *Alakh Niranjan*; *Hamara Ghar*; *Magroor*; *Mi Daru Sodli*; *Shri Krishna Darshan*; *Surajmukhi*; ***Har Har Mahadev***; ***Hindustan Hamara***; *Nishana*; *Veer Bhimsen*; *Beqasoor*; *Kalyan Khajina*; **1951**: *Jashaas Tase*; *Aaram*; *Hamari Shaan*; ***Humlog***; *Malati Madhav*; *Muraliwala*; *Nai Zindagi*; *Nand Kishore*; *Sagar*; *Sazaa*; **1952**: ***Aandhiyan***; *Hyderabad Ki Nazneen*; *Lal Kunwar*; *Indrasan*; *Mordhwaj*; *Sandesh*; *Narveer Tanaji*; **1953**: *Anand Bhavan*; *Chacha Choudhury*; *Dharmapatni*; *Mashuqa*; *Naulakha Haar*; *Shikast*; *Naag Panchami*; *Shri Chaitanya Mahaprabhu*; *Malkin*; **1954**: *Laila*; *Ramayan*; *Lakeeren*; ***Mirza Ghalib***; *Khel Chalala Nashibacha*; *Jhanjavaat*; **1955**: *Hasina*; *Adl-e-Jehangir*; *Madh Bhare Nain*; *Shri Ganesh Vivah*; *Jagadguru Shankaracharya*; **1956**: *Dwarkadheesh*; *Insaaf*; *Parivar*; *Patrani*; *Harihar Bhakti*; *Rajdhani*; **1957**: *Bade Sarkar*; *Bhabhi*; *Mera Salaam*; ***Musafir***; *Ram Hanuman Yuddha*; *Talash*; **1958**: *Gopichand*; ***Raj Tilak***; **1959**: *Ardhangini*; *Maine Jeena Seekh Liya*; *Ghar Ghar Ki Baat*; **1960**: *Love in Simla*; ***Mughal-e-Azam***; *Parakh*; *Usne Kaha Tha*; *Umaj Padel Tar*; **1961**: ***Bhabhi Ki Chudiyan***; *Do Bhai*; *Ek Ladki Saat Ladke*; *Senapati*; *Kismat Palat Ke Dekh*; **1962**: *Main Shaadi Karne Chala*; *Manmauji*; *Rangoli*; **1963**: *Mujhe Jeene Do*; *The Householder*; **1964**: *Benazir*; *Door Ki Awaz*; *Kaise Kahun*; *Tere Dwar Khada Bhagwan*; *Masterji* (also d); **1965**: *Do Dil*; *Raigadacha Rajbandi*; *Kajal*; *Purnima*; *Janam Janam Ke Saathi*; **1966**: ***Anupama***; *Dadi Maa*; *Devar*; *Pyar Mohabbat*; *Sagaai*; **1967**: *Chandan Ka Palna*; **1968**: *Jhuk Gaya Aasmaan*; ***Sangharsh***; *Sapnon Ka Saudagar*; **1969**: *Dharti Kahe Pukar Ke*; *Jeene Ki Raah*; *Mera Dost*; *Pyar Ka Sapna*; *Ek Phool Do Mali*; **1970**: *Dhartichi Lekre*; *Gopi*; *Dev Manoos*; *Khilona*; *Umang*; **1971**: *Banphool*; *Dharti Ki God Mein*; *Ek Nari Ek Brahmachari*; **1972**: *Bawarchi*; *Mangetar*; *Mere Bhaiya*; *Shararat*; *Raja Jani*; **1973**: *Abhimaan*; *Agni Rekha*; ***Bobby***; *Door Nahin Manzil*; ***Namak Haram***; *Sone Ke Haath*; *Paanch Dushman*; **1974**: *Insaniyat*; *Bidaai*; *Dil Diwana*; **1975**: *Biwi Kiraye Ki*; *Chaitali*; *Do Thug*; *Kala Sona*; *Khushboo*; *Vandana*; **1976**: *Bajrang Bali*; *Jaaneman*; *Rangila Ratan*; *Shaque*; **1977**: *Chacha Bhatija*; *Chor Sipahi*; *Darling Darling*; *Do Chehre*; *Naami Chor*; *Paheli*; *Paapi*; *Saheb Bahadur*; **1980**: ***Karz***.

Durga Khote in *Bharat Bhet* (1942)

KOHINOOR FILM COMPANY

Est: 1918. India's largest and most influential silent studio. Preceded by **S.N. Patankar**'s Patankar Friends & Co., where Kohinoor proprietor D.N. Sampat (1884-1958) entered film production, and followed by the **Imperial**, **Krishna** and **Sharda** Studios, it was until 1928 the place where Indian cinema turned professional. Launched in partnership with Maneklal Patel, then an Ahmedabad exhibitor, some of the studio's first films were documentaries informed mainly by Sampat's Gandhian adherences, e.g. the film of the Ali brothers' arrival (1919) and Horniman's return to Bombay after release from prison (1925). Early **Kanjibhai Rathod** films were restricted to Bombay and Western Indian exhibition outlets but the studio made a national impact in the wake of the notoriety generated by the banning of the nationalist ***Bhakta Vidur*** (1921), followed by the success of ***Gul-e-Bakavali*** and ***Kala Naag*** (both 1924), all aimed at a pan-Indian audience. The big breakthrough was the appointment of independent distribution agents, Bachubhai Bhagubhai, who bought rights to all their films. By 1925 the studio's monthly booking revenue exceeded Rs 50,000. The idea of the Hollywood-style film factory with several simultaneous productions, of story sessions and the building of star careers, transformed the production practices of the till then **Phalke**-dominated notion of a studio as a family-based cottage industry. Although Kohinoor's surviving publicity pamphlets indicate only one overdetermining authorial presence, writer **Mohanlal Dave** (until **Manilal Joshi** shifted the practice by writing his own screenplays and giving a full list of credits, even the actors were rarely mentioned and almost never the director), it was nevertheless the place where the star system was born with Moti and Jamna and where the silent cinema's most successful film-maker, **Homi Master**, did his best-known films. Tara, Khalil, **Raja Sandow** and **Zubeida** started there, as did **Sulochana** in **Bhavnani**'s *Veer Bala* (1925). Other major Kohinoor figures include **Chimanlal Luhar**, **Harshadrai Mehta**, cameraman Pandurang Naik, **Gohar**, **V.M. Vyas**, Haribhai Desai (later of Surya Film) and **Ranjit** proprietor **Chandulal Shah**. Virtually the entire Imperial stable of directors, including **R.S. Choudhury**, Bhavnani and **Nandlal Jaswantlal**, came from Kohinoor. After a fire virtually destroyed the studio in 1923, Maneklal Patel pulled out to start Krishna, and after 1928 Devare was mostly responsible for the studio's new incarnation as the employee-run co-operative venture Kohinoor United Artists. A key figure in the studio's later years was cameraman-director **N.G. Devare**. It closed in 1932.

KOLHAPUR CINETONE

A rare instance of a film studio funded directly by feudal royalty. Amid the popular cultural renaissance in the first decades of the 20th C. around the court of the Shahu Maharaj at Kolhapur, **Baburao Painter**'s **Maharashtra Film** was already a showpiece. When **V. Shantaram**, **Damle-Fattelal** and **Baburao Pendharkar** left to start **Prabhat** in 1929, and later when Painter himself resigned to seal the fate of Maharashtra Film, numerous efforts were made by the Shahu Maharaj himself to continue the tradition that had earned Kolhapur the title of the 'Hollywood of Marathi film'. The family started the Shalini Cinetone exclusively to keep Painter employed. In 1933, when Prabhat moved to Pune, they launched Kolhapur Cinetone as its rival, enticing Baburao Pendharkar, **Bhalji Pendharkar** and **Master Vinayak** to quit Prabhat and to take over this new venture. Apart from Bhalji Pendharkar's mythological, ***Akashwani*** (1934) and Vinayak's début feature ***Vilasi Ishwar*** (1935), the other notable production before the studio closed is **Dadasaheb Phalke**'s only sound film, his intended *magnum opus*, ***Gangavataran*** (1937).

KOMALA, A. P. (b. 1934)

One of the most popular singers in Telugu, Tamil, Malayalam and Kannada film. Classically trained in the Carnatic style. Début with **Chittor V. Nagaiah**'s film, ***Thyagayya*** (1946).

KONDKE, DADA (b. 1932)

Marathi and Hindi director-actor born in Bombay. Employed as a millworker. Started in Vidushaka roles ('the fool') in Marathi *lok natya*, a bawdy working-class adaptation of Tamasha, e.g. his classic performance in the most famous play of the genre, Vasant Sabnis's *Vichha Majhi Puri Kara* (1965). The Tamasha was first adapted to film in 40s Marathi cinema (***Lokshahir Ramjoshi***, 1947; ***Sangtye Aika***, 1959) but Kondke took it to extremes. His film titles and dialogues are famous for their vulgarity and inventiveness. Often cast Usha Chavan as his leading lady. Début with **Bhalji Pendharkar** in *Tambdi Mati*. Started producing films with Govind Kulkarni's ***Songadya*** (1971). Turned director in 1975. Had censorship trouble during the Emergency with ***Ram Ram Gangaram*** (originally called *Gangaram Veeskalmi*), intended as a spoof of the Twenty-point Economic Programme. It was remade by **Mehul Kumar** in Gujarati as *Ram Ram Amtharam*, as was ***Pandu Havaldar***, which became *Chandu Jamadar*. Currently a vocal supporter of the Hindu communalist party based in Bombay, Shiv Sena. Acted in his own directions.

FILMOGRAPHY (* act only): **1969**: *Tambdi Mati**; **1971**: ***Songadya****; **1972**: *Ekta Jeev Sadashiv**; **1973**: *Andhala Marto Dola**; **1975**: ***Pandu Havaldar***; **1976**: *Tumcha Amcha Jamla*; **1977**: ***Ram Ram Gangaram***; *Chandu Jamadar**; **1978**: *Bot Lavin Tithe Gudgudlya*; **1980**: *Hyoch Navara Pahije*; **1981**: *Ram Ram Amtharam**; *Ganimi Kava**; **1982**: *Ali Angavar*; **1984**: *Tere Mere Beech Mein*; **1986**: *Andheri Raat Mein Diya Tere Haath Mein*; **1987**: *Muka Ghya Muka*; **1988**: *Mala Gheoon Chala*; *Aage Ki Soch*; **1989**: *Khol De Meri Zabaan*; **1990**: *Palva Palvi*; **1992**: *Yevu Ka Gharat*.

KOSARAJU RAGHAVAIAH CHOUDHURY (1905-87)

Prolific Telugu lyricist born in Appikatla, Guntur Dist., AP. Influenced by Kondamudi Narasimham Panthulu, in whose play based on the *Ramayana* he acted when still in his teens. Worked as a journalist in the *Raitu Patrika* where he met the composer **Samudrala Raghavacharya** and the director **Ramabrahmam**. Published his first poetry anthology, *Kadagandlu*. Turned to film lyrics with ***Raitu Bidda*** (1939), including the song *Nidramelkonara tammuda*. Returned to films with humorous lyrics for **K.V. Reddy**'s ***Pedda Manushulu*** (1954), followed by one of his most famous songs, *Jebulu bumma je jela bomma* (in B.A. Subba Rao's *Raju Peda*, 1954). Known for his earthy poetry, often referring to popular morality tales. Wrote lyrics for c.350 films.

KOTTARAKKARA, KUTTAN PILLAI (b. 1924)

Scenarist, dialogue writer and one of the most successful producers in 70s Malayalam cinema. Born in Kottarakkara, Kerala. Stage actor aged 8. Début in 1950 as film actor (*Atmasakhi*, 1950; *Ponkathir, 1953*; *Avakashi*, 1954). Dialogues for *Ponkathir* were followed with scripts for over 25 films, after which he débuted as producer with the Tamil film *Parisu* (1963), directed by **Yoganand** and starring **MGR**. Concentrated on producing films which he scripts himself, making c.50 films in three languages (Malayalam, Kannada and Tamil), mainly love stories and suspense dramas. Noted scripts include the **Sivaji Ganesan** hit ***Pasamalar*** (1961). Kottarakkara Sridharan Nair *see* **Nair, Kottarakkara Sridharan**

KRISHEN, PRADEEP (b. 1949)

Hindi and English director born in New Delhi. Educated at Mayo College and St. Stephen's College (1966-9), then at Balliol, Oxford (1969-71). Taught history at Ramjas College, New Delhi (1971-6). Started his film career when he bought a Bell & Howell 16mm camera (1973); briefly apprenticed to **Shyam Benegal** (1973). Assisted Georges Luneau (*Ballade de Babuji*, 1975); then worked with the private Delhi-based TVNF company producing 81 popular sci-fi films of 15' each, shooting and directing some of them himself. Freelance documentarist with Grapevine Media. Début feature in Hindi, ***Massey Sahib***, which was four years in the making; next two films were in English, sponsored by tv and aimed at an international market. Edited a special issue of the *India International Centre Quarterly* (March 1980) on cinema. *Electric Moon* is a UK production, mainly for Channel 4 in London.

FILMOGRAPHY: 1977: *The Social Life of the Honey Bee*; *Medicinal Drugs*; *Reinventing the Wheel*; *King Coal*; *Reading the Moon Rocks*; **1978**: *The Birth of the Himalayas*; *The Silicone Chip*; *Lovesongs*; *Nestmates*; **1979**: *Glass*; *Why Birds Sing*; *The Age of the Earth*; **1981**: *By Word of Mouth* (all Sh); **1985**: ***Massey Sahib***; **1988**: ***In Which Annie Gives It Those Ones*** (TV); **1991**: *Electric Moon* (TV).

KRISHNA FILM COMPANY

Silent studio; Est: 1924 as a diversification of the Krishna Film Laboratory in Bombay by Maneklal Patel, a former exhibitor in Ahmedabad, scenarist (usually under name of Krishna Kumar), film-maker and partner in the **Kohinoor** Studio. Among the most successful of Kohinoor's offshoots, they made 44 films 1925-31, including works by **Luhar**'s partner **Harshadrai Mehta**, **Kanjibhai Rathod**, Mohanlal Shah, A.P. Kapur and Prafulla Ghosh, cameramen Gordhanbhai Patel and Ambalal Patel and actors such as Gulab, Ermeline, Nandram and Rampiary. Its most famous silent productions were Prafulla Ghosh's mammoth 4-part serial, ***Hatimtai*** (1929) and the much-discussed (e.g. by the 1928 Cinematograph Committee) ***Janjirne Jankare*** (1927). The studio made a major financial investment in sound as Krishnatone, making 5 talkies in 1931 (4 by **Rathod**), but it closed in 1935 following major litigation concerning their last film, ***Fashionable India*** (1935), with financiers Kapurchand & Co and the agency supplying imported film stock. In the silent days, Krishna hired some of the best-known Gujarati novelists as scenarists: Narayanji Vassanji Thakker, Gopalji Delwadakar, Shaida, **K.M. Munshi** and Ramanlal Desai.

KRISHNA, GHANTAMNENI (b. 1943)

Telugu actor, producer and director born in Tenali taluk, Guntur, AP. Educated in Tenali; graduated from the Eluru C.R. Reddy College. Stage actor before joining films. First break in **Adurthi Subba Rao**'s all-new-faces film ***Thene Manushulu***, playing the second lead. Achieved critical acclaim in **Bapu**'s ***Saakshi***, working for the first time with his future wife, actress-film-maker **Vijayanirmala**. Became a top Telugu star with the influential hit,

Goodachari 116 (remade in Hindi as *Farz*, 1967), a James Bond-type thriller. Known mainly for thrillers and police dramas, including remakes of Hollywood films. In the 70s he starred in over a dozen films annually. Established the Padmalaya Films prod. co. which grew into the famous Padmalaya Studio in Hyderabad, one of the largest and most elaborately equipped studios in the country. With *Mosagalluku Mosagadu*, he introduced aspects of the Italian western into Telugu cinema. Ventured successfully into Hindi with the **Jeetendra** and **Sridevi** film *Himmatwala* (1983), but could not repeat the success with *Sinhasan/Simhasanam*, a big-budget flop starring Jeetedra in the Hindi and himself in the Telugu versions. Elected MP in 1989 for the Congress (I), but lost his seat in 1991. Made *Praja Pratinidhi* and *Sahasame Naa Upiri* as campaign films, attacking his former colleague **NTR**'s rule in AP.

FILMOGRAPHY (* also d): **1965**: ***Thene Manushulu***; **1966**: *Kanne Manushulu*; *Goodachari 116*; **1967**: *Iddaru Monagallu*; ***Saakshi***; *Marupurani Katha*; *Stree Janmam*; *Upayamlo Apayam*; *Private Master*; *Ave Kallu*; **1968**: *Asadhyulu*; *Niluvu Dopidi*; *Manchi Kutumbam*; *Sircar Express*; *Amayukudu*; *Attagaru Kottakodalu*; *Lakshminivasam*; *Nenante Nene*; *Undamma Bottupeduta*; *Chellikosam*; *Vintha Kapuram*; **1969**: *Manchi Mithrulu*; *Love in Andhra*; *Bhale Abbayilu*; *Bommalu Cheppina Katha*; *Mahabaludu*; *Shabash Satyam*; *Astulu Antastulu*; *Takkaridonga Chakkanichukka*; *Vichitra Kutumbam*; *Muhurtabalam*; *Jarigina Katha*; *Jagath Kiladilu*; *Anna Damulu*; *Karpura Arathi*; *Bandhipotu Bhimanna*; **1970**: *Akkachellelu*; *Maa Nanna Nirdoshi*; *Malli Pelli*; *Vidhi Vilasam*; *Amma Kosam*; *Talli Bottu*; *Pelli Sambandham*; *Pelli Koothuru*; *Maa Manchi Akkaiah*; *Pagasadhishta*; *Agni Pareeksha*; *Akhantudu*; *Pachani Samsaram*; *Rendu Kutumbala Katha*; *Alludu Menalludu*; **1971**: *Andariki Monagadu*; *Prema Jeevalu*; *Master Kiladi*; *Attalu Kodallu*; *Pattu Kunte Laksha*; *Nammaka Drohulu*; *Anuradha*; *Bangaru Kutumbam*; *Mosagalluku Mosagadu*; *Nenu Manishine*; *Chalaki Rani Kiladi Raja*; *James Bond 777*; **1972**: *Monagadosthunnadu Jagratha*; *Raj Mahal*; ***Anta Mana Manchike***; *Maavoori Monagallu*; *Goodu Putani*; *Hanthakulu Devanthakulu*; *Kodalu Pilla*; *Menakodalu*; *Bhale Mosagadu*; ***Pandanti Kapuram***; *Nijam Nirupishta*; *Abbaigaru Ammaigaru*; *Kathula Rathaiah*; *Maa Inti Velugu*; *Prajanayakudu*; *Marapurani Talli*; *Illu Illalu*; *Manchivallaku Manchivadu*; **1973**: *Malamma Katha*; *Talli Kodakulu*; *Nindu Kutumbam*; *Sreevaru Maavaru*; *Puttinillu Mettinillu*; *Snehabandham*; *Neramu Siksha*; *Devudu Chesina Manushulu*; *Mamatha*; *Mayadari Malligadu*; *Pasi Hridayalu*; *Vintha Katha*; *Ganga Manga*; *Meena*; **1974**: *Gali Patalu*; *Peddalu Marali*; *Uttama Illalu*; ***Alluri Seetaramaraju***; *Manushulu Matti Bommalu*; *Radhamma Pelli*; *Adambaralu Anubandhalu*; *Gauri*; *Deergha Sumangali*; *Intinti Katha*; *Dhanavanthulu Gunavanthulu*; *Satyaniki Sankellu*; *Devadasu*; **1975**: *Raktha Sambandhalu*; *Santhanam Saubhagyam*; *Abhimanavathi*; *Kotha Kapuram*; *Saubhagyavati*; *Chikati Velugulu*; *Gajula Kishtayya*; *Devudulanti Manishi*; *Padi Panthulu*; **1976**: *Shri Rajeshwari Vilas Coffee Club*; *Manavoori Katha*; *Rama Rajyamlo Raktha Pasam*; *Kolleti Kapuram*; *Bhale Dongalu*; *Devude Gelichadu*; *Manasakshi*; **1977**: *Kurukshetramu*; *Savasagallu*; *Eenati Bandham Yenatido*; *Janma Janmala Bandham*; *Panchayathi*; *Dongalaku Donga*; *Manushulu Chesina Dongalu*; *Indra Dhanushu*; **1978**: *Patnavasam*; *Allari Bullodu*; *Anna Dammula Saval*; *Agent Gopi*; *Dongala Dopidi*; *Mugguru Muggure*; *Chal Mohanaranga*; *Dongala Veta*; *Simha Garjana*; *Cheppindi Cheshta*; *Kumara Raja*; *Atanikante Ghanudu*; *Moodu Puvvulu Aaru Kayalu*; **1979**: *Viyalavari Kayalu*; *Hema Hemeelu*; *Dongalaku Saval*; *Kotha Alludu*; *Evadabba Somu*; *Manade Gundalu*; *Mutthaiduva*; *Sankhu Teertham*; *Buripalem Bullodu*; *Captain Krishna*; *Samajaniki Saval*; **1980**: *Bhale Krishnudu*; *Devudichina Koduku*; *Kothapeda Rowdy*; *Gharana Donga*; *Mama Allula Saval*; *Adrushtavanthudu*; *Ram Robert Rahim*; *Sirimalle Navvindi*; *Chuttalunnaru Jagratha*; *Ragile Hrudayalu*; *Kiladi Krishnudu*; *Bandodu Gundamma*; *Hare Krishna Hello Radha*; *Maa Inti Devatha*; *Ammayi Mogadu Mamaku Yamadu*; *Allari Bhava*; *Bangaru Bhava*; *Raktha Sambandham*; **1981**: *Urinki Monagadu*; *Todu Dongalu*; *Guru Shishyulu*; *Bhogimanthulu*; *Boga Bhagyalu*; *Gadasari Attaha Sosagari Kodalu*; *Jatagadu*; *Antham Kadidi Arambham*; *Mayadari Alludu*; *Nayadugarabbai*; **1982**: *Bangaru Bhoomi*; *Bangaru Koduku*; *Krishnarajunulu*; *Doctor Cineactor*; *Nivurigappina Nippu*; *Prema Nakshatram*; *Vayyari Bhamulu Vagalamari Bharthulu*; *Jagannatha Rathachakralu*; *Pagabattina Simham*; *Krishnavataram*; *Ekalavya*; *Shamsher Shankar*; *Kalavari Samsaram*; *Ee Nadu* (Tel); *Kannodu Kann**; **1983**: *Bezwada Bebbuli*; *Urantha Sankranthi*; *Mundadugu*; *Kirai Kotigadu*; *Chattaniki Veyi Kallu*; *Adavi Simhalu*; *Siripuram Monagadu*; *Amayakudu Kadhu Asadhyudu*; *Rama Rajyamlo Bheemaraju*; *Shakti*; *Praja Rajyam*; *Lanke Bindelu*; *Poratham*; **1984**: *Iddaru Dongalu*; *Yuddham*; *Pulijudam*; *Mukhya Mantri*; *Nayakulaku Saval*; *Kirai Alludu*; *Bangaru Kapuram*; *Udanthudu*; *Kanchu Kagada*; *Dongalu Baboi Dongalu*; **1985**: *Agni Parvatham*; *Maha Sangramam*; *Andarikante Monagadu*; *Palnati Simham*; *Vajrayudham*; *Pachani Kapuram*; *Surya Chandra*; *Krishnagaradi*; *Devalayam**; *Mahamanishi*; *Vande Mataram**; **1986**: *Brahmastham*; *Sinhasan/Simhasanam**; *Khaidi Rudraiah*; *Krishna Paramatma*; *Pratibhavanthudu*; *Jayam Manade*; *Parasuramudu*; *Naa Pilupe Prabhanjanam**; *Shantinivasam*; **1987**: *Sardar Krishnama Nayudu*; *Muddayi*; *Dongoduchhadu*; *Makutamleni Maharaju*; *Dongagaru Swagatham*; *Muddubidda*; *Maavoori Maagadu*; *Thene Manushulu*; *Vishwanatha Nayakudu*; *Savkharavam**; **1988**: *Dorakani Donga*; *Kaliyuga Karnudu**; *Chuttalabbai*; *Rowdy No. 1*; *Jamadagni*; *Ashwathama*; *Agni Keratalu*; *Maharajashri Mayagadu*; *Praja Pratinidhi*; *Mugguru Kodakulu**; **1989**: *Prajala Manishi**; *Rajakiya Chadurangam*; *Atta Mechina Alludu*; *Manchi Kutumbam*; *Goodachari 117*; *Sahasame Naa Upiri*; *Ajatashatru*; *Sarvabhowmudu*; *Rickshawala**; *Goonda Rajyam*; *Parthudu*; *Koduku Diddina Kapuram**; **1990**: *Inspector Rudra**; **1991**: *Paramashivudu**; *Naa Ille Naa Swargam*; *Nagastharam**; *Indra Bhavanam**; *Anna Thamudu**; *Alludu Diddina Kapuram**; **1992**: *Pachani Samsaram*.

KRISHNAKANT (b. 1922)

Gujarati and Hindi actor and director born in Howrah, Bengal, as Maganlal Atmaram Bukhanwala. Son of a textile engineer; educated in Surat and in Bombay. Obtained a diploma in radio and electrical engineering (1940); then joined the Rooptara Studio in Bombay, working in the sound department. Assisted **Nitin Bose** for five years, then worked with Aravind Sen on *Muqaddar* (also acting in it) and with **Subodh Mukherjee** (***Paying Guest***, 1957). First major acting role in **Phani Majumdar**'s ***Andolan***; other notable roles are a paralytic in **Amiya Chakravarty**'s *Patita* and the villain in **Shakti Samanta**'s *Detective*. Left films in the late 50s to concentrate on Gujarati theatre work (e.g. Pravin Joshi's *Manas Name Karigar*) mainly with Harkrishen Mehta's group. Returned to cinema in the early 70s; turned to direction with *Dakurani Ganga*, adapting Mehta's novel *Pravaha Paltavyo*. Directed a series of Gujarati films based on plays or films from other languages: e.g. *Visamo* based on Harkrishen Mehta's play, in which he acted the role of an old teacher, recalling **Paranjpe**'s ***Oon Paoos*** (1954) and **Panthulu**'s ***School Master*** (1958). Also adapted **Anant Mane**'s ***Manini*** (1961) as *Maa Dikri*. With these films he introduced a novel style of urban entertainment to Gujarati cinema, although relying on conventional reformist melodrama plots about the joint family, the generation gap and the exploitation of women.

FILMOGRAPHY (* also d): **1950**: *Chor*, *Muqaddar*; ***Mashaal***; **1951**: ***Andolan***; **1952**: ***Daag***; *Tamasha*; *Zalzala*; **1953**: *Patita*; **1954**: ***Baadbaan***; *Dhobi Doctor*; ***Naukri***; **1955**: *Faraar*; *Subse Bada Rupaiya*; *Ghar Ghar Mein Diwali*; *Seema*; **1956**: *Sailaab*; ***Jagte Raho***; *Patrani*; *Sudarshan Chakra*; *Dhola Maru*; **1957**: *Agra Road*; ***Bandi***; *Begunah*; *Hum Panchhi Ek Dal Ke*; *Yahudi Ki Ladki*; **1958**: *Ghar Sansar*; *Detective*; ***Howrah Bridge***; *Mehndi*; *Parvarish*; ***Post Box 999***; **1959**: *Insaan Jaag Utha*; ***Satta Bazaar***; **1961**: *Tanhaai*; **1969**: ***Do Raaste***; **1971**: *Duniya Kya Jaane*; *Hathi Mere Saathi*; *Pyar Ki Kahani*; *Sharmilee*; *Paraya Dhan*; **1972**: *Mere Jeevan Saathi*; *Do Chor*; *Annadata*; **1973**: *Gaai Aur Gori*; *Suraj Aur Chanda*; *Mr Romeo*; *Manchali*; **1974**: *Parinay*; *Ajnabi*; *Trimurti*; *Vardan*; *Aarop*; **1975**: *Anari*; *Kala Sona*; **1976**: *Deewangee*; *Koi Jeeta Koi Haara*; *Sajjo Rani*; *Dakurani Ganga**; **1977**: *Jagriti*; ***Kulavadhu****; **1978**: *Khoon Ki Pukar*; *Visamo**; *Maa Dikri**; *Ghar Sansar**; **1979**: *Sonba Ane Rupba**; **1980**: *Maniyaro**; *Meru Mulande**; *Jog Sanjog**; **1982**: *Prem Lagna**; *Dharmo**; *Jawabdaar**; **1983**: *Main Awara Hoon*; **1986**: *Teesra Kinara**; *Chhota Admi**.

KRISHNAMURTHY, HUNSUR (b. 1914)

Born in Hunsur, Karnataka. Kannada and Telugu director of stage-inspired mythologicals, often starring **Rajkumar**. While writing **Company Natak** plays (e.g. *Swarga Samrajya*) for Bangalore-based Bharat Natak, also worked as scenarist, esp. for **Vijaya** Studio, remaking **L.V. Prasad**'s hit ***Pelli Chesi Choodu*** (1952) in Kannada as *Madhuve Madi Nodu*. Began as bit actor at **Bombay Talkies**; briefly with **Bal Gandharva**'s theatre troupe, then with **Veeranna** and Mohammed Peer's Chandrakala Natak where, with **Panthulu**, he assisted **Simha** on ***Samsara Nauka*** (1936). Like Panthulu, from 1958 directed mid-budget morality plays. Claimed that mythological genre commanded better budgets, allowed greater emotional freedom and called for more directorial inventiveness than the socials. Helped redefine the Rajkumar persona from his earlier historicals into narratively freer near mythic fantasies ruled by destiny and the individual quest for eternal goodness. Script credits include: ***Hemareddy Malamma*** (1945; also act); *Krishnaleele* (1947); *Jagan Mohini* (1951); *Nala Damayanti* (1957); ***Bangarada Manushya*** (1972) and *Boothayyana Maga Ayyu* (1974). Also acted in *Muttaide Bhagya* (1956). His biography was written by Shyama Sundar Kulkarni (1988).

FILMOGRAPHY: 1958: *Shri Krishna Garudi*; **1960**: *Ashasundari/Ramasundari*; **1961**: *Mera Suhaag*; **1962**: *Ratnamanjari*; **1964**: *Veera Sankalpa*; **1965**: ***Satya Harishchandra***; *Madhuve Madi Nodu*; **1966**: *Shri Kannika Parameshwari Kathe*; **1967**: *Devuni Gelichina Manavudu/Devara Gedda Manava*; **1968**: *Addadari*; **1971**: *Vishakanya*; **1972**: *Jaga Mechida Maga*; **1974**: *Bhakta Kumbhara*; **1975**: *Mantra Shakti*; **1977**: *Babruvahana*; *Veera Sindhoora Lakshmana*; **1980**: *Bhakta Siriyala*; *Guru Sarvabhowma Shri Raghavendra Karune*; **1981**: *Edeyuru Siddhalingeshwara/Siddhalingeshwara Mahima*; *Kurubara Lakka*(?); *Shiva Mahima*; **1982**: *Bhakta Dnyanadeva*; **1984**: *Shivakanya/Shivakanye*; **1985**: *Shiva Kotta Saubhagya*.

KRISHNAN, NAGERKOYIL SUDALAIMUTHU (1905-57)

Legendary Tamil film comedian, stage actor and political activist. Born in Nagerkoyil, in former Travancore. Joined the **TKS Brothers** drama troupe aged 17, replacing the comedian and film star M.R. Swaminathan (seen in, e.g., *1000 Thalaivangi Apoorva Chintamani*, 1947). Was already a noted stage star when débuting in the TKS Brothers production of **Raja Sandow**'s *Menaka*. Early films with Sandow (*Vasantsena*, *Chandrakantha*) where he met his wife and long-term comedy partner T.A. Mathuram (1918-1974). Played the lead role in *Alibabavum 40 Thirudargalum*, establishing his distinctive brand of comedy. Classic screen image developed Kattiyakaran folk theatre conventions with a separate sub-plot and spoken dialect as opposed to the high-flown **Elangovan**-type language (e.g. playing fishermen with T.S. Dorairaj in *Shakuntalai*; ***Mudhal Thedi***). In this style, the comedian can address the audience directly and allude to topical events (e.g. his funny song in *Paithiakaran*, referring to his jail sentence; his lines in the costumed period movie *Amarakavi* referring to a recent visit to the USSR). The style is enhanced by the comic but politically strident lyrics of **Udumalai Narayana Kavi**, written specially for Krishnan (e.g. ***Nallathambi***). Initially a Marxist sympathiser and a friend of Pa. Jeevanandan (whom he sheltered when the CP was banned), Krishnan became first a nationalist and then a DMK supporter, producing **C.N. Annadurai**'s **DMK Film** *Nallathambi*, directing *Panam* and acting in the **Karunanidhi**-scripted *Raja Rani* and ***Rangoon Radha***. Together with **M.K. Thyagaraja Bhagavathar**, he was convicted of murdering the gossip columnist Lakshmikantan although he proclaimed his innocence all his life. His wife started the N.S.K. Nataka (aka Eneskay Nataka Sabha) staging plays mainly directed by and featuring the star S.V. Sahasranamam. Their best-known play is **P. Neelakantan**'s nationalistic ***Nam Iruvar***, later filmed (1947) by the **AVM** Studio. The company débuted in film production with *Paithiakaran*; their best-known productions are *Nallathambi* and the Krishnan-directed *Manamagal* and *Panam*. *Panam*, a major DMK film, featured the ***Parasakthi*** (1952) combination of writer Karunanidhi and star **Ganesan** while Krishnan sang a pro-DMK song. It also featured documentary footage of a DMK Party conference. Died during the shooting of **MGR**'s ***Madurai Veeran***, an event recorded in an obituary integrated into the film's plot. Biography by Aranthai Narayanan (1992).

FILMOGRAPHY (* also d): **1935**: *Menaka*; **1936**: *Vasantsena*; *Chandrakantha*; *Sati Leelavathi*; **1937**: ***Ambikapathy***; *Balamani*; **1938**: *Dakshayagnam*; **1939**: *Thiruneelakantar*; *Maya Machhindra*; *Manikavasagar*; *Ramalinga Swamigal*; *Rambayin Kadhal*; *Sirikathe*; *Ananda Ashramam*; *Prahlada*; **1940**: *Bhakta Tulsidas*; *Naveena Tenali Raman*; *Parasuramar*; *Naveena Vikramadithan*; *Budhiman Balwan Ivan*; *Kalamegham*; *Mani Mekalai*; *Bhuloka Rambha*; *Shakuntalai*; *Uthama Puthran*; **1941**: *Alibabavum 40 Thirudargalum*; *Ezhanda Kadal*; ***Ashok Kumar***; *Vedavathi*; *Aryamala*; *Krishnapidaran*; *Chandrahari*; **1942**: ***Kannagi***; *Prithvirajan*; *Sivalinga Satchi*; *Manonmani*; **1943**: *Arundhati*; *Sivakavi*; *Mangamma Sapatham*; ***Bhagya Lakshmi***; **1944**: ***Burma Rani***; ***Mahamaya***; *Bhartrahari* (Tam); *Jagathala Prathapan*; *Prabhavati*; *Poompavai*; *Raja Rajeshwari*; *Haridas*; *Salivahanan*; *Kalikala Minor*; *Palli Natakam*; *Soora Puli*; **1945**: *Paranjoti*; *Bhakta Kalathi*; *Shri Valli*; **1946**: *Pankajavalli*; **1947**: *Paithiakaran*; *Kannika*; **1948**: *Devadasi*; ***Chandralekha***; *Krishna Bhakti*; **1949**: ***Nallathambi***; *Ratnakumar*; *Mangayar Karasi*; *Inbavalli*; *Pavalakkodi*; **1950**: *Laila Majnu*; *Parijatham*; **1951**: *Manamagal/Pelli Koothuru**; *Vanasundari*; **1952**: *Panam**; *Amarakavi*; **1954**: *Nallakalam*; **1955**: ***Mudhal Thedi***; *Kaveri*; *Nam Kuzhandai*; *Dr Savithri*; *Stree Ratna*; **1956**: *Raja Rani*; *Nannambikkai*; *Asai*; ***Madurai Veeran***; *Kannin Manigal*; *Kudumba Vilakku*; ***Rangoon Radha***; **1957**: *Chakravarthi Thirumagal*; *Pudhu Vazhvu*; *Yar Paiyan*; ***Ambikapathy***; **1959**: *Thangapathumai*; **1960**: *Raja Desingu*; *Thozhan*; **1961**: *Arasilankumari*.

KRISHNAN-PANJU: R. KRISHNAN (B. 1909) AND S. PANJU (b. 1915)

Duo of Tamil melodrama directors and producers. Krishnan was born in Madras, Panju in Umayalapuram, Thanjavur. Krishnan began as a laboratory assistant in 1934 while Panju assisted **Duncan** on *Sati Leelavathi* (1936). Both left Duncan for Premier Cinetone in Coimbatore, where Panju also worked independently as an editor. They made their joint début in Coimbatore (*Poompavai*). Their third film was for **N.S. Krishnan** with S.V. Sahasranamam's script (*Paithiakaran*), followed by Krishnan's major **DMK Film**, ***Nallathambi***, and the even more significant ***Parasakthi***. Later associated with the **AVM** Studio, directing some of its main Hindi hits, e.g. *Bhabhi*, *Barkha*, *Bindiya*, *Shadi* etc. Also worked in Telugu.

FILMOGRAPHY: 1944: *Poompavai*; **1946**: *Pankajavalli*; **1947**: *Paithiakaran*; **1949**: ***Nallathambi***; *Ratnakumar*; **1952**: ***Parasakthi***; **1953**: *Kangal*; **1954**: *Ratha Kanneer*; **1955**: *Sant Sakhu*; **1956**: *Kiladaivam*; **1957**: *Bhabhi*; *Pudhuvayal*; **1959**: *Barkha*; *Mamiyar Meetriya Marumagal*; **1960**: *Bindiya*; *Daiva Piravi*; *Thilakam*; **1961**: *Suhaag Sindoor*; **1962**: *Manmauji*; *Shadi*; *Annai/Penchina Prema*; **1963**: *Kumkumam*; **1964**: *Mera Kasoor Kya Hai*; ***Server Sundaram***; *Vazhkai Vazhvadarke*; **1965**: *Kuzhanthiyum Daviamum*; **1966**: *Laadla*; *Letamanushulu*; *Petral Than Pillayya*; **1968**: *Do Kaliyan*; *Uyarntha Manithan*; **1969**: *Annaiyum Pithavum*; **1970**: *Anadhai Anandan*; ***Engal Thangam***; **1971**: *Main Sundar Hoon*; *Ranga Rathnam*; **1972**: *Akka Tammudu*; *Idaya Veenai*; *Pillaiyo Pillai*; **1973**: *Pookkari*; **1974**: *Shandaar*; *Kaliyuga Kannan*; *Pathumatha Bandham*; **1975**: *Kashmir Bullodu*; *Anaya Vilakku*; *Vazhanthu Kattukiran*; **1976**: *Enna Thavam Saithen*; *Ilaya Thalaimurai*; *Vazhvu En Pakkam*; **1977**: *Chakravarthi*; *Sonnathai Seivan*; **1978**: *Annapoorni*; *Pare Solla Oru Pillai*; **1979**: *Nadagame Ulagam*; *Neela Malargal*; *Velli Ratham*; **1980**: *Mangala Nayaki*; **1985**: *Malarum Ninaivugal*.

KRISHNARAO, ARAKALAGUDU NARASINGA RAO (1908-71)

Aka A.Na.Kru; scenarist and prolific Kannada novelist, playwright and essayist with c.250 published titles. A major regional chauvinist ideologue in Karnataka. Initially associated with the professional **Company Natak**. After books like *Udayaraga* (1924), a thinly disguised fictional biography of Bengal School painter Nandalal Bose, and several others featuring anxiety-ridden artists as central protagonists, he tended more towards the 'modern' within the anglophile Amateur Dramatic Association and the literary Pragatisila movement derived from the **PWA**. Used influential cultural platforms such as the Madhol conference (1945) of the Kannada Ekikaran Parishat (the Kannada unification movement) to deflect most debates about progressivism and modernism towards discussions of Karnatakatva ('Kannada-ness'), usually by appealing to 'the masses' whose 'point of view' was said to be ignored by writers speaking about and addressing an urban middle class (Krishnarao, 1944). This equation of political regionalism with cultural populism was later developed most notably by the films of **Rajkumar**. Wrote a major **Veeranna** film, ***Jeevana Nataka*** (1942), the original book on which the Kannada film *Sandhya Raga* (1966) is based, and the script of **B.R. Panthulu**'s historical ***Shri Krishnadevaraya*** (1970). Wrote a novel about his experiences in the film industry, *Chitra Vichitra* (1952) and a critical study of **Ravi Varma** (1932). Also scripted *Stree Ratna* for **K. Subramanyam** (1955).

KRISHNARAO PHULAMBRIKAR, MASTER (1891-1974)

Music composer and actor born in Alandi, Maharashtra. Trained by Bhaskarbua Bakhle in music school Bharat Gayan Samaj. Employed by **Bal Gandharva**'s Gandharva Natak Mandali as male lead and composer. With **Govindrao Tembe**, he helped shape Bal Gandharva's enormously influential populist versions of North Indian classical music.

Entered film at **Prabhat** Studio with Bal Gandharva in **Shantaram**'s ***Dharmatma*** and stayed on to do several films, developing a reputation as an orthodox **Sangeet Natak** classicist, distinguishing him from his Prabhat contemporary, **Keshavrao Bhole**. His songs for ***Manoos/Admi*** (esp. **Hublikar**'s seduction number, *Ab kis liye kal ki baat*) and the musical spoofs of **Bombay Talkies** and **New Theatres** were among the few original compositions when, particularly at Prabhat, most songs drew on the repertoire of traditional gharanas (notably the Jaipur gharana). His only success after the studio era was at **Rajkamal** in *Mali*, also playing the lead role.

FILMOGRAPHY (* also act): **1935**: ***Dharmatma***; **1936**: ***Amar Jyoti***; **1937**: *Sadhvi Meerabai*; ***Wahan***; **1938**: ***Gopal Krishna***; **1939**: ***Manoos/Admi***; **1941**: ***Shejari/Padosi***; **1942**: ***Vasantsena***; **1944**: *Bhakticha Mala/Mali**; **1945**: ***Lakhrani***; **1947**: *Meri Amanat* (act only); **1949**: *Sant Ramdas*; **1953**: *Tai Teleen*; **1959**: *Keechaka Vadha*; **1962**: *Vithu Mazha Lekurvala*.

Krishna Shastry, Devulapalli *see* **Sastry, Devulapalli Krishna**

KRISHNAVENI, C. (b. 1924)

Telugu/Tamil actress and producer born in Rajahmundhry, AP. Child actress in stage plays. Débuted in the title role of **C. Pullaiah**'s children's film, ***Ansuya***. Acted in Telugu and Tamil films, but it was again Pullaiah who launched her in her adult career with *Gollabhama*. Actorial reputation based mainly on roles in *Lakshmamma*, ***Mana Desam*** and *Perantalu*. Married the Rajah of Mirzapur (1941), founder of the Jaya Films Studio (1940) in Teynampet, Madras. This later became the famous Shobhanachala Studio, launched with **L.V. Prasad**'s political melodrama *Mana Desam*. Turned producer with MRA Prod. Only Tamil film is *Kamavalli*. Introduced composers **Ghantasala Venkateshwara Rao** (*Mana Desam*) and Ramesh Naidu (*Dampatyam*, 1957). Sang classic songs in *Gollabhama* (*Bhoopati jampitiyin, Ravoyi jeevanajyoti*) and a hit duet with M.S. Rama Rao in *Mana Desam* (*Emito ee anubandham*). Sang playback in ***Keeluguram***, 1949, directed by her husband. Produced several films, e.g. *Lakshmamma, Perantalu, Dampatyam* and *Yamanukku Yaman* (1980). Returned to the stage in the late 50s.

FILMOGRAPHY: 1936: ***Ansuya***; *Dhruva*; **1937**: ***Mohini Rugmangada***; **1938**: *Kacha Devayani*; **1939**: *Mahananda*; **1940**: *Jeevana Jyoti*; **1941**: ***Dakshayagnam***; **1944**: *Bhishma*; **1947**: *Gollabhama*; **1948**: *Madalasa*; *Kamavalli*; **1949**: *Dharmangada*; ***Mana Desam***; **1950**: *Lakshmamma*; **1951**: *Perantalu*; **1952**: *Savasam*; **1953**: ***Pakkinti Ammayi***.

Kulkarni, Datta Keshav *see* **Datta Keshav Kulkarni**

KUMAR, ANUP (b. 1932)

Bengali actor born in Calcutta; son of singer and stage composer Dhirendranath Das. Début as child actor in **Dhiren Ganguly**'s unreleased *Halkatha*. First major role in **Kaliprasad Ghosh**'s *Dhatri Debata*. A prolific genre performer, often as the hero's comic counterpart. Belongs to the second generation of Bengali comedians with **Bhanu Bannerjee, Robi Ghosh** and **Jahar Roy**. Acted with **Tapan Sinha** (*Tonsil, Kalamati, Ek Je Chhilo Desh*) in early **Mrinal Sen** films (*Abasheshe, Pratinidhi*), and for **Tarafdar** (*Agnisikha, Jiban Kahini*). A regular member of the **Tarun Majumdar** and **Dinen Gupta** film units. Routine career occasionally enlivened by critically acclaimed roles, e.g. in Yatrik's *Palatak*. Stage début at Star Theatres (1949) in *Bejoynagar* and *Samudragupta*. Acted with **Sisir Bhaduri** in the play *Takht-e-Taus* (1951). Later worked at the Bishwaroopa theatre. Also directed plays, e.g. *Aghatan* (1978). Not to be confused with the popular Hindi comedian Anup Kumar, the brother of Ashok and **Kishore Kumar**.

FILMOGRAPHY: 1934: *Halkatha*; **1946**: *Sangram*; **1948**: *Dhatri Debata*; *Bankalekha*; **1949**: *Sankalpa*; *Krishna Kaveri*; *Sakshigopal*; **1950**: *Vidyasagar*; *Maryada*; **1951**: *Bhakta Raghunath*; ***Barjatri***; **1952**: *Pasher Bari*; *Rani*; **1953**: *Banser Kella*; *Sosur Bari*; *Rami Chandidas*; *Adrishya Manush*; **1954**: *Aaj Sandhya*; *Mahila Mahal*; *Ae Satyi*; *Annapurnar Mandir*; *Agni Pareeksha*; *Nilshari*; **1955**: *Rani Rashmoni*; *Bidhilipi*; *Joymakali Boarding*; *Kankabatir Ghat*; *Mejo Bou*; *Anupama*; **1956**: *Sinthir Sindoor*; ***Sagarika***; *Tonsil*; *Ekti Raat*; *Asamapta*; *Shyamali*; *Madan Mohan*; *Nagardola*; **1957**: *Ulka*; *Ratri Sheshey*; ***Adarsha Hindu Hotel***; *Prithibi Amar Chai*; *Surer Parashey*; *Rastar Chhele*; *Kancha-Mithey*; *Punar Milan*; *Ogo Sunchho*; *Garer Math*; *Pathe Holo Deri*; *Janmatithi*; **1958**: *Priya* (B); *Kalamati*; *Daktar Babu*; *Leela Kanka*; *Marmabani*; **1959**: *Nauka Bilash*; *Derso Khokhar Kando*; *Shashi Babur Sansar*; *Gali Theke Rajpath*; **1960**: *Dui Bechara*; *Prabesh Nishedh*; *Biyer Khata*; *Natun Fasal*; **1961**: *Mr & Mrs Choudhury*; *Bishkanya*; *Arghya*; *Kanchanmulya*; *Kathin Maya*; *Aaj Kal Parshu*; *Ahwan*; *Maa*; *Kanamachi*; **1962**: *Agnisikha*; *Shesh Chinha*; *Abhisarika*; *Banarasi*; *Shubha Drishti*; *Abasheshe*; **1963**: *Barnachora*; *Sat Bhai*; *High Heel*; *Palatak*; *Dui Nari*; *Kanchan Kanya*; *Shreyasi*; **1964**: *Pratinidhi*; *Ta Holey*; *Jiban Kahini*; *Kashtipathar*; *Binsati Janani*; **1965**: *Alor Pipasa*; *Mahalagna*; *Antaral*; *Jaya*; *Ek Tuku Basa*; *Dinanter Alo*; *Dolna*; *Mukhujey Paribar*; *Tapasi*; **1966**: *Kalanki Raat*; *Nutan Jiban*; *Shesh Tin Din*; *Uttar Purush*; *Rajdrohi*; *Mayabini Lane*; **1967**: *Hathat Dekha*; *Kheya*; **1968**: *Baluchari*; *Boudi*; *Chhoto Jignasa*; *Garh Nasimpur*; *Jiban Sangeet*; *Teen Adhyay*; **1969**: *Bibaha Bibhrat*; *Dadu*; *Duranta Charai*; *Panna Hirey Chunni*; *Pita Putra*; **1970**: *Samanaral*; *Aleyar Alo*; *Kalankita Nayak*; *Ae Korechho Bhalo*; *Nishipadma*; *Manjari Opera*; **1971**: *Anya Mati Anya Rang*; *Nimantran*; *Pratham Basanta*; *Attatar Din Pare*; **1972**: *Jiban Sangram*; *Basanta Bilap*; *Biraj Bou*; *Naya Michhil*; *Shesh Parba*; *Natun Diner Alo*; *Sabari*; **1973**: *Pranta Rekha*; *Daabi*; *Ek Je Chhilo Bagh*; **1974**: *Phuleshwari*; *Sangini*; *Thagini*; *Mouchak*; *Phulu Thakurma*; *Swikarokti*; **1975**: *Nishi Mrigaya*; *Raag Anuraag*; *Sei Chokh*; *Phool Sajya*; *Tin Pari Chhoy Premik*; *Harano Prapti Niruddesh*; **1976**: *Chander Kachhakachhi*; *Ajasra Dhanyabad*; *Ek Je Chhilo Desh*; *Pratisruti*; *Ananda Mela*; **1977**: ***Baba Taraknath***; *Babu Moshai*; *Bhola Moira*; *Ae Prithibi Pantha Niwas*; *Pratima*; *Sanai*; *Proxy*; *Golap Bou*; **1978**: *Dak Diye Jai*; *Nadi Theke Sagare*; *Tusi*; *Niskriti*; *Tilottama*; **1979**: *Devdas*; *Chirantan*; *Ghatkali*; **1980**: ***Dadar Kirti***; **1981**: *Pratishodh*; *Swami Stri*; *Sei Sur*; *Subarnalata*; *Shahar Theke Dooray*; *Meghmukti*; *Khelar Putul*; **1982**: *Pipasa*; *Sathe Satyam*; *Bodhan*; *Preyasi*; *Mayer Ashirbad*; *Amrita Kumbher Sandhaney*; **1983**: *Abhinay Nay*; *Ae Chhilo Mone*; *Amar Geeti*; *Arpita*; *Indira*; *Jiban Maran*; *Jyotsna Ratri*; *Nishi Bhor*; *Prayashchitta*; *Samapti*; *Srinkhal*; **1984**: *Harishchandra Shaibya*; *Lal Golap*; *Rashifal*; *Shatru*; *Shorgol*; *Agni Shuddhi*; *Ahuti*; *Surya Trishna*; **1985**: *Amar Prithibi*; *Baikunther Will*; *Bhalobasha Bhalobasha*; *Neelkantha*; *Putulghar*; *Sandhya Pradeep*; *Till Theke Tal*; **1986**: *Swarga Sukh*; *Anurager Choa*; *Urbashe*; *Ashirwad*; *Daktar Bou*; *Abhishap*; **1987**: *Bidrohi*; *Raj Purush*; *Swarnamoir Thikana*; *Radha Rani*; *Sargam*; *Abir*; *Dabar Chal*; **1988**: *Kalankini Nayika*; *Channachara*; *Boba Sanai*; *Kidnap*; *Antarango*; *Tumi Koto Sundar*; *Debibaran*; *Agaman*; **1989**: *Shatarupa*; *Mangaldip*; *Aparanher Alo*; *Asha*; *Abhisar*; *Jankar*; *Amar Shapath*; *Aghaton Ajo Ghatey*; ***Chhandaneer***; **1990**: *Anuraag*; *Apon Amar Apon*; *Raktorin*.

KUMAR GANGULY, ASHOK (b. 1911)

Hindi star and producer; nicknamed Dadamoni. Born in Bhagalpur, Bihar; the son of a lawyer and deputy magistrate. Originally called Kumudlal Kunjilal Ganguly. Grew up in Khandwa. Briefly studied law in Calcutta, then joined his mentor and future brother-in-law, Shashadhar Mukherji, at **Bombay Talkies**, first as laboratory assistant. He was cast in the lead opposite **Devika Rani** in ***Jeevan Naiya*** and ***Achhut Kanya*** but she was dissatisfied and had him relegated to the editing room as a trainee. After **Himansu Rai**'s death (1940), he enjoyed the protection of Mukherji, who co-managed the studio with Devika Rani. He was allowed to act in films opposite **Leela Chitnis**. Broke through as the Bogartian journalist in the **Abbas**-scripted ***Naya Sansar***. Other classic roles include the title role in **Mehboob**'s ***Humayun*** and the double role of magistrate and playboy in ***Afsana***. His most famous role was in ***Kismet*** as the gracefully cigarette-smoking anti-hero, showing that Hindi cinema had quickly assimilated Hollywood's film noir style. Set up **Filmistan** (1943) with S. Mukherji, **Gyan Mukherjee** and Rai Bahadur Chunilal. He later returned to Bombay Talkies as production chief. Directed some of their films (e.g. ***Eight Days***) but never took the official credit. Joined with his brothers **Kishore** and Anup Kumar in the comedies ***Chalti Ka Naam Gaadi*** and *Chalti Ka Naam Zindagi*. In the 60s freelanced as character actor, often playing a sympathetic parent (e.g. *Mili*). According to **Tapan Sinha**, with whom he first acted in *Hatey Bazarey*, 'he was the first to apply "normal" acting in our industry; until Ashok Kumar we had jatra-style acting or screen acting that followed theatrical trends. [H]e is the man who showed that film acting is something else. He began to speak and to behave normally.' He excelled in Robin Hood-type roles with sparse dialogues and his way of holding a cigarette in *Kismet* became a trade-mark. He anchored the tv soap *Humlog* and appeared in many tv serials. His image is a generic icon virtually autonomous from the plot, at first representing Bombay Talkies' version of Indian modernity and then underpinning Filmistan's commitment to the mass entertainment formula.

FILMOGRAPHY: 1936: ***Jeevan Naiya***; ***Achhut Kanya***; ***Janmabhoomi***; 1937: *Izzat*; *Prem Kahani*; ***Savitri***; 1938: *Nirmala*; *Vachan*; 1939: ***Kangan***; 1940: ***Azad***; ***Bandhan***; 1941: ***Anjaan***; ***Jhoola***; ***Naya Sansar***; 1943: *Angoothi*; ***Kismet***; ***Najma***; 1944: ***Chal Chal Re Naujawan***; *Kiran*; 1945: *Begum*; ***Humayun***; 1946: ***Eight Days***; *Shikari*; 1947: *Saajan*; *Chandrasekhar*; 1948: *Padmini*; 1949: ***Mahal***; 1950: *Adhi Raat*; *Khiladi*; ***Mashaal***; *Nishana*; ***Samadhi***; ***Sangram***; 1951: ***Afsana***; ***Deedar***; 1952: *Betaab*; *Bewafa*; *Jalpari*; *Kafila*; *Naubahar*; *Poonam*; *Raag Rang*; *Saloni*; *Tamasha*; 1953: *Nagma*; ***Parineeta***; *Shamsheer*; *Sholay*; 1954: ***Baadbaan***; *Lakeeren*; *Naaz*; *Samaj*; 1955: ***Bandish***; *Sardar*; 1956: *Bhai Bhai*; *Ek Hi Raasta*; *Inspector*; *Shatranj*; *Jaldeep*; 1957: ***Bandi***; *Ek Saal*; *Jeevan Saathi*; *Mr X*; *Sheroo*; *Talaash*; *Ustad*; 1958: ***Chalti Ka Naam Gaadi***; *Farishta*; ***Howrah Bridge***; *Karigar*; *Night Club*; *Ragini*; *Savera*; *Sitaron Se Aage*; 1959: *Baap Bete*; *Bedard Zamana Kya Jaane*; *Daaka*; ***Dhool Ka Phool***; *Kangan*; *Naach Ghar*; *Nai Raahein*; 1960: *Aanchal*; *Kala Admi*; *Kalpana*; ***Kanoon***; *Masoom*; ***Hospital***; 1961: *Dark Street*; *Flat No. 9*; *Warrant*; 1962: *Aarti*; *Bezubaan*; *Burma Road*; *Hong Kong*; *Isi Ka Naam Duniya Hai*; *Mehndi Lagi Mere Haath*; *Naqli Nawab*; *Private Secretary*; *Raakhi*; *Ummeed*; 1963: *Aaj Aur Kal*; ***Bandini***; *Grihasthi*; ***Gumrah***; ***Mere Mehboob***; *Meri Soorat Teri Aankhen*; *Ustadonke Ustad*; *Yeh Raaste Hain Pyar Ke*; 1964: *Benazir*; ***Chitralekha***; *Dooj Ka Chand*; *Phoolon Ki Sej*; *Pooja Ke Phool*; 1965: ***Shevatcha Malusara***; *Adhi Raat Ke Baad*; *Akashdeep*; *Bahu Beti*; *Bheegi Raat*; *Chand Aur Suraj*; *Naya Kanoon*; ***Oonche Log***; 1966: *Afsana*; *Dadi Maa*; *Mamata*; *Yeh Zindagi Kitni Haseen Hai*; *Toofan Mein Pyar Kahan*; 1967: ***Jewel Thief***; *Meharbaan*; *Bahu Begum*; *Nai Roshni*; *Hatey Bazarey*; 1968: *Aabroo*; ***Ashirwad***; *Dil Aur Mohabbat*; *Ek Kali Muskayi*; *Sadhu Aur Shaitan*; 1969: ***Aradhana***; *Aansoo Ban Gaye Phool*; *Bhai Bahen*; *Do Bhai*; *Inteqam*; *Paisa Ya Pyar*; *Pyar Ka Sapna*; ***Satyakam***; 1970: *Jawab*; *Maa Aur Mamta*; *Purab Aur Paschim*; *Safar*; *Sharafat*; 1971: *Adhikar*; *Door Ka Rahi*; *Naya Zamana*; *Ganga Tera Pani Amrit*; *Hum Tum Aur Woh*; *Kangan*; ***Pakeezah***; ***Guddi***; 1972: *Rani Mera Naam*; *Anuraag*; *Dil Daulat Duniya*; *Malik*; *Raakhi Aur Hathkadi*; *Sa Re Ga Ma Pa*; *Sazaa*; *Victoria No. 203*; *Zameen Aasmaan*; *Zindagi Zindagi*; 1973: *Bada Kabutar*; ***Dhund***; *Do Phool*; *Hifazat*; *Taxi Driver*; 1974: *Do Aankhen*; *Dulhan*; *Khoon Ki Keemat*; *Paise Ki Gudiya*; *Prem Nagar*; *Ujala Hi Ujala*; *Badhti Ka Naam Daadhi*; 1975: *Love in Bombay*; *Akraman*; ***Chhotisi Baat***; *Chori Mera Kaam*; *Dafaa 302*; *Ek Mahal Ho Sapnon Ka*; *Mili*; *Uljhan*; 1976: *Aap Beeti*; *Arjun Pandit*; *Barood*; *Bhanwar*; *Ek Se Badkhar Ek*; *Harfan Maula*; *Mazdoor Zindabad*; *Rangila Ratan*; *Shankar Dada*; *Santan*; 1977: *Anand Ashram*; *Anurodh*; *Chala Murari Hero Banne*; *Dream Girl*; *Hira Aur Patthar*; *Jadu Tona*; *Khatta Meetha*; *Mastan Dada*; *Prayashchit*; *Safed Jhooth*; *Premi Gangaram*; 1978: *Anmol Tasveer*; *Anpadh*; *Apna Khoon*; *Chor Ke Ghar Chor*; *Dil Aur Deewar*; *Do Musafir*; *Mehfil*; *Phool Khile Hain Gulshan Gulshan*; *Tumhare Liye*; 1979: *Bagula Bhagat*; *Guru Ho Jaa Shuru*; *Janata Havaldar*; *Amar Deep*; *Salaam Memsaab*; 1980: *Khwab*; *Aakhri Insaaf*; *Aap Ke Diwane*; *Judaai*; *Khubsoorat*; *Nazrana Pyar Ka*; *Sau Din Saas Ke*; *Saajan Mere Main Saajan Ki*; *Takkar*; *Jyoti Bane Jwala*; 1981: *Chalti Ka Naam Zindagi*; *Jyoti*; *Jail Yatra*; *Maan Gaye Ustad*; *Yeh Kaisa Nasha Hai*; *Shaukeen*; 1982: *Sambandh*; *Anokha Bandhan*; *Chor Mandli*; *Dial 100*; *Dushmani*; *Heeron Ka Chor*; *Mehndi Rang Layegi*; *Patthar Ki Lakeer*; *Dard Ka Rishta*; *Shakti*; 1983: *Haadsa*; *Bekaraar*; *Farishta*; *Raja Aur Rana*; *Love In Goa*; *Farz Ki Keemat*; *Mahaan*; *Chor Police*; *Prem Tapasya*; *Shilalipi*; *Kaya Palat*; *Pasand Apni Apni*; 1984: *Hum Rahe Na Hum*; *Akalmand*; *Duniya*; *Grihasthi*; *Durga*; *Humlog* (TV); *Ram Tera Desh*; 1985: *Bhago Bhoot Aaya*; *Ek Daku Shaher Mein*; *Tawaif*; *Phir Aayi Barsaat*; 1986: *Amma*; *Inteqam Ki Aag*; *Pyar Kiya Hai Pyar Karenge*; *Shatru*; *Qatl*; *Dada Dadi Ki Kahaniyan* (TV); *Pyar Ki Jeet*; *Woh Din Aayega*; *Bhim Bhawani* (TV); 1987: *Awaam*; *Hifazat*; ***Mr India***; *Watan Ke Rakhwale*; *Jawab Hum Denge*; 1988: *Inteqam*; 1989: *Clerk*; *Sachaai Ki Taaqat*; *Mamata Ki Chhaon Mein*; *Maut Ki Sazaa*; *Dana Pani*; *Majboor*.

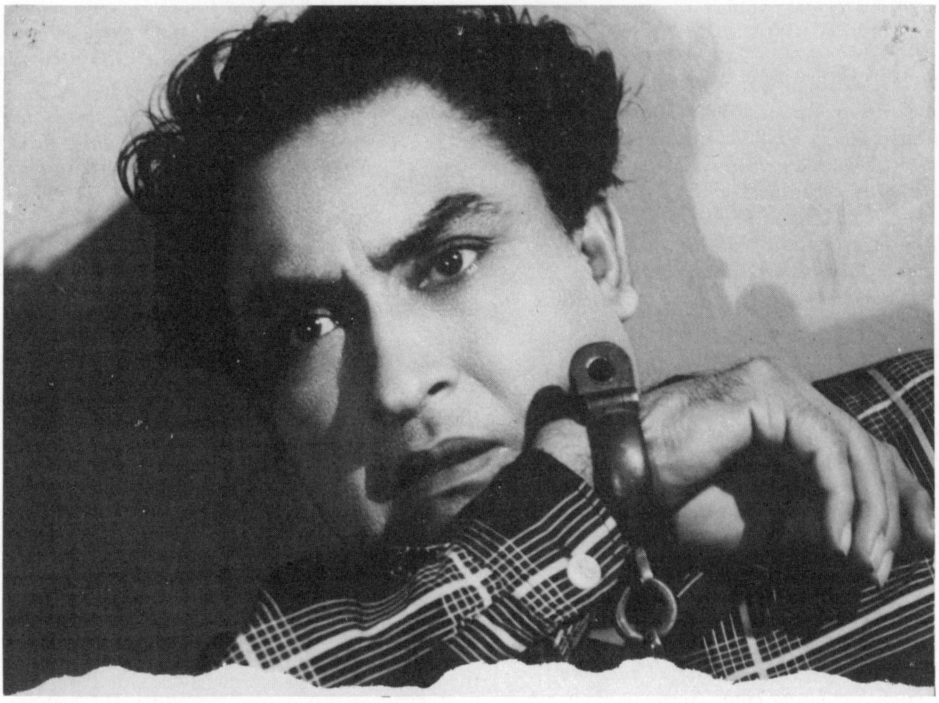

Ashok Kumar in *Isi Ka Naam Duniya Hai* (1962)

KUMAR, DILIP (b. 1922)

Hindi-Urdu cinema's top 50s and 60s star. Born in Peshawar (now Pakistan) as Yusuf Khan in a Pathan family of 12 children. They moved to Maharashtra as fruit merchants. Worked in a British army canteen in Bombay (1940). **Devika Rani** claimed to have recruited him for **Bombay Talkies**. A noted Hindi novelist, Bhagwati Charan Varma, renamed him Dilip Kumar. Attained stardom with *Jugnu*. Achieved an enduring reputation for naturalist acting although he claims to have followed in the footsteps of **Motilal**. ***Andaz*** brought him superstardom and he acted again with **Nargis** in ***Jogan***. Presented, e.g. in ***Footpath***, as an exponent of indigenous neo-realism. His style developed tragic dimensions, e.g. in the Oedipal drama ***Deedar***, where he blinds himself, and in ***Devdas***, as the lovesick aristocrat. Eventually decided to change to a more swashbuckling image with ***Aan***, ***Azad***, ***Insaniyat***, *Kohinoor*, etc., apparently on advice of his psychoanalyst, athough he kept his romantic image going as well. Like his contemporary **Raj Kapoor**, his filmic identity offered a complex cultural/psychological terrain displaying the anxieties of Independence and the nostalgias of a pre-Partition childhood. Unlike Kapoor, Dilip Kumar's naturalist underplaying often presented him as an innocent loner caught in and destroyed by conflicting social pressures, as in the only film he did with Raj Kapoor, *Andaz*, a classic drama of male guilt paid for by the woman. His acting was used mainly to address issues of identity in the Hindi films of Bengali directors: **Nitin Bose**'s ***Deedar*** and ***Ganga Jumna***, **Bimal Roy**'s ***Madhumati*** and **Tapan Sinha**'s *Sagina Mahato*, after which he stopped acting for 8 years. Married actress Saira Banu of ***Junglee*** (1961) fame. Made a comeback with *Kranti* and esp. with *Shakti*, starring opposite **Bachchan** in a larger-than-life role confirming his legendary star status. Recent films with **Subhash Ghai** (***Karma***, ***Saudagar***). Although he virtually directed some of his films (e.g. ***Ganga Jumna***, ***Dil Diya Dard Liya***) his first official directorial credit is for *Kalinga* (in prod.).

FILMOGRAPHY: 1944: ***Jwar Bhata***; 1945: *Pratima*; 1946: ***Milan***; 1947: *Jugnu*; 1948: *Anokha Pyar*; ***Ghar Ki Izzat***; *Nadiya Ke Paar*; *Mela*; *Shaheed*; 1949: ***Andaz***; ***Shabnam***; 1950: *Arzoo*; ***Babul***; ***Jogan***; 1951: *Hulchul*; *Tarana*; ***Deedar***; 1952: ***Aan***; ***Daag***; *Sangdil*; 1953: ***Footpath***; *Shikast*; 1954: ***Amar***; 1955: ***Azad***; ***Devdas***; ***Insaniyat***; ***Udan Khatola***; 1957: ***Musafir***; ***Naya Daur***; 1958: ***Madhumati***; ***Yahudi***; 1959: ***Paigham***; 1960: *Kohinoor*; ***Mughal-e-Azam***; 1961: ***Ganga Jumna***; 1964: *Leader*; 1966: ***Dil Diya Dard Liya***; *Pari*; 1967: ***Ram Aur Shyam***; 1968: *Sadhu Aur Shaitan*; *Admi*; ***Sangharsh***; 1970: *Gopi*; *Sagina Mahato*; 1972: *Anokha Milan*; *Dastaan*; 1974: *Sagina*; *Phir Kab Milogi*; 1976: *Bairaag*; 1981: *Kranti*; 1982: *Shakti*; *Vidhata*; 1983: *Mazdoor*; 1984: *Duniya*; *Mashaal*; 1986: *Dharam Adhikari*; ***Karma***; 1989: *Kanoon Apna Apna*; 1990: *Izzatdar*; 1991: ***Saudagar***.

Kumar, Hemant *see* **Mukherjee, Hemanta**

KUMAR, KALYANA (b. 1936)

Kannada star; also acted in Telugu and Tamil films. Original name: Chokkanna. Born in Bangalore. Achieved stardom with his first film, ***Natashekhara***. Hero in 60s Kannada-Telugu bilinguals by **B. Vittalacharya**, **Nagendra Rao** and **Panthulu**. Regular actor in early **G.V. Iyer** films (***Bhoodana***, *Thayi Karulu*, *Lawyara Magalu*, *Bangari*). Most famous Kannada roles in ***Amarashilpi Jakanachari*** and ***Bellimoda***; best-known Tamil role: *Nenjil Ore Alayam*. Turned director in the late 60s; also produced and directed stage plays (e.g. *Ramu Nanna Thamma*, *Chikamma*), often written by his wife, Revathi. Directed *Love in Bangalore* under the pseudonym Sampath Kumar.

FILMOGRAPHY (* also d): **1954**: ***Natashekhara***; **1956**: *Bhagya Chakra*; *Muttaide Bhagya*; *Ohileshwara*; *Sadarame*; **1957**: *Bettada Kalla*; *Premada Putri*; *Rayara Sose*; **1958**: ***Bhukailasa***; **1959**: *Manegebanda Mahalakshmi*; **1960**: *Kadavunin Kuzhandai*; **1961**: ***Thayilla Pillai***; **1962**: *Nenjil Ore Alayam*; ***Bhoodana***; *Daivaleele*; *Devasundari*; *Galigopura/Gali Medalu*; *Thayi Karulu/Thayin Karunai*; *Thendral Veesum*; *Shriman Petra Selvangal*; *Azhagu Nila*; *Pasam*; **1963**: *Lawyara Magalu*; *Bangari*; *Kaduvulai Kandan*; *Mani Osai*; *Nenjam Marappathillai*; *Neenkada Ninaivu*; *Yarukku Sontham*; **1964**: ***Amarashilpi Jakanachari/Amarashilpi Jakanna***; *Chinnada Gombe*; *Mane Aliya*; **1965**: *Beretha Jeeva*; *Nanna Kartavya*; *Balarajana Kathe*; *Mavana Magalu*; **1966**: *Endu Ninnavane**; *Love in Bangalore**; *Badukuva Daari*; *Subba Sastry*; **1967**: ***Bellimoda***; *Muddu Meena*; *Premakku Permitte*; *Kallu Sakkare**; **1968**: *Pravasi Mandira**; *Arunodaya*; *Manku Dinne*; *Mysore Tonga*; *Mammathe*; *Bedi Bandhavalu*; *Anandakanda*; *Anna Thamma*; *Nane Bhagyavati*; *Attegondukala Sosegondukala*; **1969**: *Odahuttidavaru*; *Niraparadhi*; *Kannu Muchale*; *Mukunda Chandra*; **1970**: *Arishina Kumkuma*; *Aparajithe*; **1971**: *Papa Punya*; *Sedina Kidi*; *Amara Bharathi*; **1974**: *Avalukku Nihar Avale*; **1975**: ***Katha Sangama***; **1976**: *Collegeranga*; *Tulasi*; **1977**: *Mugdha Manava*; *Banashankari*; *Subhashaya*; *Udugore*; **1978**: *Anuragha Bandhana*; **1979**: *Maralu Sarapani*; **1980**: *Mother*; **1983**: *Thayiya Nudi*; *Chinnadanta Maga*; *Simha Garajane*; **1984**: *Nagabekamma Nagabeku*; *Shubha Muhurta*; *Guru Bhakti*; *Police Papanna*; *Avala Antaranga*; *Marali Goodige*; **1985**: *Pudhu Yugam*; *Thayi Thande*; *Kiladi Aliya*; **1986**: *Thavaru Mane*; *Usha*; **1987**: *Thaliya Aane*; **1988**: *Sarkarai Pandal*; *Oorigittakolli*; **1989**: *Thaligagi*; **1990**: *Bannada Gejje*.

KUMAR, KISHORE (1929-87)

Actor, singer, director, music director and producer born in Khandwa, MP. Moved to Bombay and featured occasionally in **Saraswati Devi**'s chorus at **Bombay Talkies** where elder brother **Ashok Kumar** was the top star. Imitated his hero, **K.L. Saigal**, e.g. in the **Khemchand Prakash** song in ***Rimjhim*** (1949). Early reputation as an actor who sang his own songs mostly in slapstick comedies, often playing the unemployed youth (***Musafir***, ***Naukri***). After ***New Delhi*** and ***Chalti Ka Naam Gaadi***, gained recognition for off-beat humour and for providing a new musical sound. His career as India's most famous male playback singer was effectively launched when he became **Dev Anand**'s singing voice with *Ziddi* (*Marne ki duaayen*) and ***Munimji*** (1955: *Jeevan ke safar*). Formally untrained, he assimilated jazz-scat fragmented musical notes into a rhythmic sequence and, once its beat was established, departed from the pattern and combined notes and words/syllables into new kinds of musical harmony in the 50s (largely restricted to melody with the singer following the instrumentation). Composer **Kalyanji**, with whom Kishore Kumar pioneered the use of electronic music, said that his riyaz (practice) lay more in his skills as a mimic rather than in technique. His songs spanned many genres: *Ina mina dika* was the pinnacle of a US-derived popular song introduced by **C. Ramchandra** in the 50s; he sang several 'sad' numbers, esp. in films he directed and which, contrary to his image, were often tragedies (e.g. the song *A chal ke tujhe* in ***Door Gagan Ki Chhaon Mein***); practised yodelling in the title song of ***Jhumroo*** and continued in later films; sang about his income-tax harassment during the Emergency and once, the legend goes, he set the Malthusian theory of population to music. The unpredictability of his musical sequencing was translated into his performances where the slapstick comedy of *Baap Re Baap*, ***Half Ticket***, *New Delhi* and *Chalti Ka Naam Gaadi* have been seen as one of the Hindi cinema's precedents of postmodernism: the apparently 'tribal' music of *Jhumroo* is a pastiche of *Tequila*; in *Half Ticket*, the classic chase sequence has hero and villain dancing in Nautanki garb and in a freewheeling Slavic harvest number. His approach echoes the Tashlin/Jerry Lewis style of comedy, but the performative idiom is largely original although he refused to claim auteur status. The songs, however, fall into two fairly distinct periods: one as Dev Anand's singing voice, the other as **Rajesh Khanna**'s playback voice after ***Aradhana*** (1969), leading to classic **Bachchan** numbers including the *Don* (1978) song, *Khaike pan banarasvala*. In the 80s gave huge public concerts in India and abroad. His Madison Square Garden concert became a best seller on cassette. His son, Amit Kumar, is currently a top singer in Hindi films.

FILMOGRAPHY (* also d & music d/** also music d): **1946**: *Shikari*; **1947**: ***Shehnai***; **1948**: *Sati Vijaya*; *Ziddi*; **1950**: *Muqaddar*; **1951**: ***Andolan***; **1952**: *Cham Chama Cham*; *Tamasha*; **1953**: *Faraib*; *Ladki*; *Lehren*; **1954**: *Adhikar*; *Dhobi Doctor*; *Ilzaam*; *Miss Mala*; ***Naukri***; *Pehli Jhalak*; **1955**: *Baap Re Baap*; *Char Paise*; *Madh Bhare Nain*; *Rukhsana*; **1956**: *Aabroo*; *Bhagambhag*; *Bhai Bhai*; *Dhake Ki Malmal*; *Mem Sahib*; *Naya Andaz*; ***New Delhi***; *Parivar*; *Paisa Hi Paisa*; **1957**: *Miss Mary*; ***Aasha***; ***Bandi***; *Begunah*; ***Musafir***; **1958**: ***Chalti Ka Naam Gaadi***; *Chandan*; *Delhi Ka Thug*; *Kabhi Andhera Kabhi Ujala*; *Ragini*; *Lookochuri*; **1959**: *Chacha Zindabad*; *Jaalsaaz*; *Shararat*; **1960**: ***Apna Haath Jagannath***; *Bewaqoof*; *Girl Friend*; *Mehlon Ke Khwab*; **1961**: ***Jhumroo*****; *Karodpati*; *Madhya Rater Tara*; **1962**: *Bambai Ka Chor*; ***Half Ticket***; *Manmauji*; *Naughty Boy*; *Rangoli*; **1963**: *Ek Raaz*; **1964**: ***Door Gagan Ki Chhaon Mein****; *Baghi Shahzada*; *Mr X In Bombay*; *Daal Mein Kala*; *Ganga Ki Lehren*; **1965**: *Hum Sub Ustad Hain*; *Shriman Funtoosh*; *Ek Tuku Chhoya Lage*; **1966**: *Akalmand*; *Ladka Ladki*; *Pyar Kiye Jaa*; **1967**: *Hum Do Daku**; *Dustu Prajapati*; *Albela Mastana*; *Duniya Nachegi*; **1968**: *Do Dooni Char*; *Hai Mera Dil*; ***Padosan***; *Sadhu Aur Shaitan*; *Shrimanji*; *Payal Ki Jhankaar*; **1970**: *Aansoo Aur Muskaan*; **1971**: *Door Ka Rahi**; *Hangama*; **1972**: *Pyar Diwana*; *Bombay To Goa*; *Zameen Aasmaan***; **1974**: *Badhti Ka Naam Daadhi**; **1978**: *Ek Baap Chhe Bete*; *Shabash Daddy**; **1981**: *Chalti Ka Naam Zindagi**; **1982**: *Door Wadiyon Mein Kahin**; **1989**: *Mamata Ki Chhaon Mein* (d only, completed by Amit Kumar).

KUMAR, MANOJ (b. 1937)

Hindi actor, director and producer born in Abbotabad, North West Frontier Province (now Pakistan) as Hari Krishna Goswami. Went to India on Partition and lived in a refugee camp near Delhi. Début as actor in his cousin Lekhraj Bhakri's films. Broke through with *Kaanch Ki Gudiya* and ***Hariyali Aur Raasta***. Well-known hero in 60s commercial Hindi socials, e.g. as Bhagat Singh in the biopic *Shaheed*. Worked as a ghost director before his official début. Described his directorial début, ***Upkaar***, as a '16000-foot-long celluloid flag of India'. Indulges in national chauvinism, contrasting son-of-the-soil goodness with Western evil, providing moral lessons together with the commercially attractive scenes of the abhorred debauchery (e.g. *Purab Aur Paschim*). Prominent campaigner for the fanatic Hindu communalist Bhartiya Janata Party in 1991 elections. Also acted in his productions.

FILMOGRAPHY (* also d): **1957**: *Fashion*; **1958**: *Panchayat*; *Sahara*; **1959**: *Chand*; **1960**: *Sunehri Raatein*; **1961**: *Kaanch Ki Gudiya*; *Piya Milan Ki Aas*; *Reshmi Rumal*; *Suhaag Sindoor*; **1962**: *Apna Banake Dekho*; *Banarasi Thug*; *Dr Vidya*; ***Hariyali Aur Raasta***; *Maa Beta*; *Naqli Nawab*; *Shadi*; **1963**: *Ghar Basake Dekho*; *Grihasthi*; **1964**: *Apne Huye Paraye*; *Phoolon Ki Sej*; ***Woh Kaun Thi***; **1965**: *Bedaag*; *Gumnaam*; *Himalay Ki God Mein*; *Poonam Ki Raat*; *Shaheed*; **1966**: *Picnic*; *Do Badan*; *Sawan Ki Ghata*; **1967**: ***Upkaar****; *Anita*; *Patthar Ke Sanam*; **1968**: *Admi*; *Neel Kamal*; **1969**: *Saajan*; **1970**: *Purab Aur Paschim**; ***Mera Naam Joker***; *Pehchan*; *Yaadgaar*; **1971**: *Balidan*; **1972**: *Shor**; *Beimaan*; **1974**: *Roti Kapda Aur Makaan**; **1975**: *Sanyasi*; *Amanat*; **1976**: *Das Numbri*; **1977**: *Shirdi Ke Sai Baba*; **1981**: *Kranti**; **1987**: *Kalyug Aur Ramayan*; **1989**: *Clerk**; *Santosh*; *Deshwasi*.

KUMAR, MEHUL (b. 1949)

Gujarati and Hindi director, aka Mohammed Baloch. Born in Jamnagar; graduated from Bombay University and worked as a journalist, including film reviews in the magazine *Chitarang*. Involved in Gujarati theatre (1974-5), then assistant to **Chandrakant Sangani** (1975-6) and to Tahir Hussain. His début is a Gujarati remake of **Dada Kondke**'s spectacularly successful lowbrow Marathi comedy, ***Pandu Havaldar*** (1975). 80s work mainly in mid-budget Hindi masala films, introducing this formula into Gujarati and achieving a broader acceptance and larger budgets. *Marte Dam Tak*, featuring the senior star Raaj Kumar alongside B-movie hero Govinda, made him one of the best-known vendetta action directors. He then yoked this genre successfully to a highly rhetorical story about nationalism to make the biggest Hindi hit of 1992, *Tiranga*, getting Raaj Kumar to act with the younger character actor, Nana Patekar.

FILMOGRAPHY: **1977**: *Chandu Jamadar*; *Janam Janamna Saathi/Phir Janam Lenge Hum*; **1978**: *Kanchan Ane Ganga*; **1979**: *Rajputani*; **1981**: *Ranchandi*; *Garvi Naar Gujaratni*; *Gamdani Gori*; *Kanchan Aur Ganga*; **1982**: *Maa Vina Suno Sansar*; *Dholi*; *Anokha Bandhan*; *Naseeb No Khel*; **1983**: *Dhola Maru*; *Maradno Mandvo*; **1984**: *Hiranne Kanthe*; *Love Marriage*; **1985**: *Meru Malan*; *Preet Na Karsho Koi*; *Bhauji Maay*; **1986**: *Sayba Mora*; *Ujali Meraman*; **1987**: *Marte Dam Tak*; **1989**: *Na Insaafi*; *Nafrat Ki Aandhi*; *Jungbaaz*; *Aasmaan Se Ooncha*; **1990**: *Paap Ki Aandhi*; **1991**: *Meet Mere Man Ke*; **1992**: *Tiranga*; **1993**: *Aansoo Bane Angarey*.

KUMAR, RAJENDRA (b. 1929)

60s Hindi film star, esp. in musical romances. Born R.K. Tuli in Sialkot, West Punjab. Film début as assistant to director **H.S. Rawail** and played a small role in his *Patanga*. Introduced by **Kidar Sharma** in ***Jogan***, followed by a leading part in ***Awaaz***; first major starring role in the **V. Shantaram** production *Toofan Aur Diya*. Early films capitalised on his resemblance to **Dilip Kumar**. In his early films, he is remembered as the straight man who throws into relief the histrionics of the other actors: e.g. **Mala Sinha** as the betrayed woman in ***Dhool Ka Phool***; the rebellious **Sunil Dutt** contesting familial authority along with feudal oppression in ***Mother India***; **Ashok Kumar** as the court judge suspected of murder in ***Kanoon***; the other man in the **Raj Kapoor** love triangle, ***Sangam***; the doctor who treats the cancer-affected husband (Raaj Kumar) of his former lover **Meena Kumari** in **Sridhar**'s *Dil Ek Mandir*. However, his musicals in the 60s were more popular and he was often called 'the Jubilee hero' because his films would have a 'jubilee' run. In the 80s he launched his son Kumar Gaurav, effectively directing his début feature, *Love Story* (1981).

FILMOGRAPHY: **1949**: *Patanga*; **1950**: ***Jogan***; **1955**: *Vachan*; **1956**: ***Awaaz***; *Toofan Aur Diya*; **1957**: *Duniya Rang Rangili*; ***Mother India***; *Ek Jhalak*; **1958**: *Devar Bhabhi*; *Ghar Sansar*; *Khazanchi*; *Talaaq*; **1959**: *Chirag Kahan Roshni Kahan*; *Do Behnen*; ***Dhool Ka Phool***; ***Goonj Uthi Shehnai***; *Santan*; **1960**: ***Kanoon***; *Maa Baap*; *Patang*; ***Mehndi Rang Lagyo***; **1961**: *Aas Ka Panchhi*; *Amar Rahe Yeh Pyar*; *Gharana*; *Pyar Ka Sagar*; *Sasural*; *Zindagi Aur Khwab*; **1963**: *Akeli Mat Jaiyo*; *Dil Ek Mandir*; *Gehra Daag*; *Hamrahi*; ***Mere Mehboob***; **1964**: *Aayi Milan Ki Bela*; ***Sangam***; *Zindagi*; **1965**: *Arzoo*; **1966**: *Suraj*; **1967**: *Aman*; *Palki*; **1968**: *Jhuk Gaya Aasmaan*; *Saathi*; **1969**: *Anjaana*; *Shatranj*; *Talash*; **1970**: *Dharti*; *Ganwaar*; *Geet*; ***Mera Naam Joker***; **1971**: *Aap Aye Bahar Ayi*; **1972**: *Aan Baan*; *Gaon Hamara Shaher Tumhara*; *Gora Aur Kala*; *Lalkaar*; *Tangewala*; **1975**: *Do Jasoos*; *Rani Aur Lalpari*; *Sunehra Sansar*; **1976**: *Mazdoor Zindabad*; **1977**: *Shirdi Ke Sai Baba*; *Daku Aur Mahatma*; *Do Sholay*; **1978**: *Ahuti*; *Saajan Bina Suhagan*; *Sone Ka Dil Lohe Ke Haath*; **1979**: *Bin Phere Hum Tere*; **1980**: *Badla Aur Balidan*; *Dhan Daulat*; *O Bewafa*; *Gunehgaar*; *Saajan Ki Saheli*; **1981**: *Love Story*; *Yeh Rishta Na Toote*; **1982**: *Rustom*; **1983**: *Lovers*; **1988**: *Main Tere Liye*; **1989**: *Clerk*; **1993**: *Phool*. Kumar, Sampath *see* **Kumar, Kalyana**

KUMAR, UDAYA (1930-86)

Kannada actor, originally named Suryanarayana, born in Palkad, Salem. Worked for several years in the Gandhian Bharat Seva Dal. Employed as a physical training teacher. Joined **Gubbi Veeranna**'s stage company. Early heroic roles in Kannada films later became more nuanced villainous characters, often counterpointing **Rajkumar**'s heroic persona in historicals and mythologicals. Produced *Ide Mahasudina* and scripted **C.S. Rao**'s *Shri Renukadevi Mahatme*. Also known as playwright (e.g. *Bhakta Kanakadasa*, *Tapasvi Ravana*, *Inspector Taranath*, etc.), novelist and essayist with 8 prose anthologies (e.g. *Akshara Brahma*, *Kavi Charithre*). Started the Udaya Kala Niketan acting school (1983).

FILMOGRAPHY: **1956**: *Bhagyodaya*; *Daiva Sankalpa*; *Panchrathna*; **1957**: *Bettada Kalla*; *Premada Putri/Preme Daivam*; *Ratnagiri Rahasya*; *Varadakshine*; **1958**: ***Bhakta Prahlada***; *Mane Thumbida Hennu*; ***School Master/Badi Panthulu***; **1959**: ***Mahishasura Mardini***; *Veer Bhaskaradu*; **1960**: *Shivalinga Sakshi*; *Bhakta Kanakadasa*; *Dashavatara*; *Ivan Avanethan*; *Yanai Pagan*; **1961**: *Raja Satya Vrata*; *Vijayanagarada Veeraputra*; *Mahout*; **1962**: ***Bhoodana***; *Ratnamanjari*; *Thayi Karulu*; *Vidhi Vilasa*; **1963**: *Nanda Deepa*; *Malli Madhuve*; *Bevu Bella*; ***Veera Kesari/Bandhipotu***; *Mana Mechhida Madadi*; *Chandrakumara*; *Sant Tukaram*; *Shri Ramanjaneya Yuddha*; **1964**: *Chandavalliya Tota*; *Kalavati*; ***Amarashilpi Jakanachari/Amarashilpi Jakanna***; **1965**: *Kavaleradu Kulavondu*; *Chandrahasa*; *Vatsalya*; ***Satya Harishchandra***; *Veera Vikrama*; *Ide Mahasudina*; *Bettada Huli*; *Sati Savitri*; *Miss Leelavathi*; *Madhuve Madi Nodu*; *Pativrata*; **1966**: *Mane Katti Nodu*; *Mantralaya Mahatme*; *Kathari Veera*; *Badukuva Daari*; *Deva Manava*; *Madhu Malathi*; *Mohini Bhasmasura* (K); *Sandhya Raga*; **1967**: *Padavidhara*; *Parvathi Kalyana*; *Sati Sukanya*; *Rajashekhara*; *Rajadurgada Rahasya*; *Bangarada Hoovu*; *Chakra Teertha*; *Immadi Pulakesi*; **1968**: *Jedara Bale*; *Matheye Maha Mandira*; *Arunodaya*; *Mahasati Arundhati*; *Mysore Tonga*; *Anna Thamma*; *Namma Ooru*; *Nane Bhagyavati*; *Dhumketu*; *Simha Swapna*; *Hoovu Mullu*; **1969**: *Odahuttidavaru*; *Madhura Milana*; *Shiva Bhakta*; *Bhagirathi*; *Makkale Manege Manikya*; *Madhuve! Madhuve!! Madhuve!!!*; *Kalpa Vruksha*; *Ade Hridaya Ade Mamathe*; *Mathru Bhoomi*; *Chaduranga*; *Mukunda Chandra*; *Bhale Basava*; **1970**: ***Mukti***; *Rangamahal Rahasya*; *Pratikara*; *Kallara Kala*; *Hasiru Thorana*; *Takka! Bitre Sikka!!*; *Mrityu Panjaradalli Goodachari 555*; *Modala Rathri*; *Sedige Sedu*; *Aaru Mooru Ombattu*; **1971**: *Sidila Mari*; *Purnima*; *Signalman Siddappa*; *Samshayaphala*; *Jatakarathna Gunda Joisa*; *Kasidre Kailasa*; *Bhale Bhaskar*; *Mahadimane*; *Bhale Rani*; **1972**: *Nari Munidare Mari*; *Kulla Agent 000*; *Kaanch Aur Heera*; **1973**: *Triveni*; *Bharathada Rathna*; *Cowboy Kulla*; *Mannina Magalu*; *Premapasha*; *Bettada Bhairava*; **1974**: *Chamundeshwari Mahime*; *Nanu Baalabeku*; **1975**: *Jagruthi*; *Sarpa Kavalu*; *Mantra Shakti*; *Ashirwada*; *Bili Hendthi*; **1976**: *Sutrada Bombe*; *Rajanarthakiya Rahasya*; **1977**: *Shri Renukadevi Mahatme*; *Girikanye*; *Srimanthana Magalu*; *Hemavathi*; *Shani Prabhava*; *Banashankari*; **1978**: *Devadasi*; *Matu Tappada Maga*; *Bhale Huduga*; *Madhura Sangama*; *Parasuraman*; **1979**: *Putani Agents 1-2-3/Agent 1-2-3*; **1980**: *Maria My Darling*; *Vajrada Jalapata*; *Mugana Sedu*; **1981**: *Thayiya Madilalli*; *Kulaputra*; *Garjane*; **1982**: *Kempu Hori*; *Sahasa Simha*; *Mava Sose Saval*; **1983**: *Devara Tirpu*; *Kalluveene Nudiyitu*; *Nodi*

Mala Sinha and Rajendra Kumar in *Dhool Ka Phool* (1959)

Swamy Navirodu Hige; *Maha Maharaju*; *Bhayankara Bhasmasura*; **1984**: *Maryade Mahalu*; *Agni Gundam*; *Bharyamani*; **1985**: *Pitamah*; *Vish Kanya*.

KUMAR, UTTAM (1926-80)

Bengali superstar who at times was the Tollygunge-based Bengali film industry. Real name: Arun Kumar Chatterjee. Employed as a clerk in the port commissioner's office, Calcutta, before joining films. Briefly stage actor at the Star Theatre (e.g. in *Shyamali*, 1953, filmed in 1956). Début as extra in uncompleted *Mayadore*. Broke with the prevailing theatrical acting styles and achieved stardom with **Nirmal Dey**'s ***Sharey Chuattar***, which also initiated his famed co-starring films with **Suchitra Sen**: they featured in some of the most spectacular Bengali melodramas made by **Naresh Mitra**, **Sushil Majumdar**, **Ajoy Kar** and the **Agradoot** and Agragami units, epitomising the genre of the soft-focus musical romance (with **Hemanta Mukherjee** as his regular playback voice). Melodramas of suffering, betrayal and the struggle for truth (cf ***Sagarika***, ***Saptapadi***) made an embattled literary tradition (with a Bhadralok middle-class identity and an apolitical humanist philosophy) popular again after a long history of radical attacks on the Bengali novel. In e.g. **Kartick Chattopadhyay**'s *Saheb Bibi Golam* and in the Ajoy Kar and **Tapan Sinha** films, the Uttam Kumar persona abandoned many conservative tenets of this tradition while receiving an unprecedented degree of mass adulation. **S. Ray** presented his version of the phenomenon in ***Nayak***, which many saw as the star's autobiography. The two also worked together in ***Chidiakhana***. His biographer Gourangaprasad Ghosh claimed that when his effort to go 'national' with the Hindi film *Chotisi Mulaqat* proved a failure, he finally turned into an actor of mass-produced romances. Except for ***Amanush***, his Hindi films were mostly unsuccessful. His last film, *Ogo Bodhu Sundari*, a version of *My Fair Lady*, was completed with another actor. Wrote his autobiography (1979).

FILMOGRAPHY (* also d/** also music d): **1948**: *Drishtidaan*; **1949**: *Mayadore* (incomplete); *Kamana*; **1950**: *Maryada*; **1951**: *Ore Jatri*; *Sahajatri*; *Nastaneer*; **1952**: *Sanjibani*; ***Basu Parivar***; *Kar Papey*; **1953**: ***Sharey Chuattar***; *Lakh Taka*; *Nabin Yatra*; *Bou Thakuranir Haat*; **1954**: *Moner Mayur*; *Ora Thake Odhare*; ***Champadangar Bou***; *Kalyani*; *Maraner Pare*; *Sadanander Mela*; *Annapurnar Mandir*; *Agni Pareeksha*; *Bokul*; *Grihapravesh*; *Mantra Shakti*; **1955**: *Sanjher Pradeep*; *Anupama*; *Raikamal*; *Devatra*; *Shap Mochan*; *Bidhilipi*; *Hrad*; *Upahar*; *Kankabatir Ghat*; *Bratacharini*; *Sabar Uparey*; **1956**: *Raat Bhore*; ***Sagarika***; *Saheb Bibi Golam*; *Laksha-Hira*; *Chirakumar Sabha*; *Ekti Raat*; *Shankar Narayan Bank*; *Shyamali*; *Trijama*; *Putrabadhu*; *Shilpi*; *Nabajanma*; **1957**: *Haar Jeet*; *Bardidi*; *Yatra Holo Suru*; *Prithibi Amar Chai*; *Taser Ghar*; *Surer Parashey*; *Punar Milan*; *Harano Sur*; *Abhoyer Biye*; *Chandranath*; *Pathe Holo Deri*; *Jiban Trishna*; **1958**: *Rajalakshmi-o-Shrikanta*; *Bandhu*; *Manmoyee Girls' School*; *Daktar Babu*; *Shikar*; *Indrani*; *Joutuk*; *Surya Toran*; **1959**: *Marutirtha Hinglaj*; *Chaowa-Pawa*; *Bicharak*; *Pushpadhanu*; *Gali Theke Rajpath*; *Khelaghar*; *Sonar Harin*; *Abak Prithvi*; **1960**: *Maya Mriga*; *Raja-Saja*; *Kuhak*; *Uttar Megh*; *Haat Baraley Bandhu*; *Khokha Babur Pratyabartan*; *Sakher Chor*; *Saharer Itikatha*; *Suno Baro Nari*; **1961**: *Sathi Hara*; *Agni Sanskar*; *Jhinder Bandi*; *Necklace*; ***Saptapadi***; *Dui Bhai*; **1962**: *Bipasha*; *Shiulibari*; *Kanna*; **1963**: *Shesh-Anka*; *Nisithe*; *Uttarayan*; *Bhranti Bilas*; *Surya Sikha*; *Deya Neya*; **1964**: *Bibhas*; *Jotugriha*; *Natun Tirtha*; *Momer Alo*; *Lal Patthar*; **1965**: *Thana Theke Aschhi*; *Raj Kanya*; *Surya Tapa*; *Kal Tumi Aleya***; **1966**: *Sudhu Ekti Bachhar**; ***Nayak***; *Rajdrohi*; *Sankha Bela*; **1967**: ***Antony Firingee***; ***Chidiakhana***; *Grihadah*; *Jiban Mrityu*; *Nayika Sangbad*; *Chhotisi Mulaqat*; **1968**: *Chowringhee*; *Kokhono Megh*; *Teen Adhyay*; *Garh Nasimpur*; **1969**: ***Aparichita***; *Chiradiner*; *Kamallata*; *Mon-Niye*; *Sabarmati*; *Shuk Sari*; **1970**: *Kalankita Nayak*; *Bilambita Lay*; *Duti Mon*; *Nishipadma*; *Manjari Opera*; *Rajkumari*; **1971**: *Chhadmabeshi*; *Dhanyi Meye*; *Ekhane Pinjar*; *Jay Jayanti*; *Jiban Jignasa*; *Nabaraag*; **1972**: *Alo Amar Alo*; *Andha Atit*; *Biraj Bou*; *Chinnapatra*; *Haar Mana Haar*; *Memsahib*; *Stree*; **1973**: *Kaya Hiner Kahini*; *Rater Rajanigandha*; *Roudra Chhaya*; *Sonar Khancha*; ***Bon Palashir Padabali****; *Rodon Bhora Basanta*; **1974**: *Alor Thikana*; ***Amanush***; *Bikele Bhorer Phool*; ***Jadu Bansha***; *Jadi Jantem*; *Rakta Tilak*; *Mouchak*; **1975**: *Ami Sey-o-Sekha*; *Agniswar*; *Bagh Bandi Khela*; *Kajal Lata*; *Nagar Darpane*; *Priya Bandhabi*; *Sanyasi Raja*; *Sei Chokh*; *Sabhyasachi***; **1976**: *Banhi Sikha*; *Chander Kachhakachhi*; *Mom Batti*; *Nidhi Ram Sardar*; *Rajbansha*; *Hotel Snow Fox*; *Ananda Mela*; *Asadharan*; **1977**: *Bhola Moira*; *Jaal Sanyasi*; *Sister*; *Anand Ashram*; *Kitaab*; *Brajabuli*; **1978**: *Bandi*; *Dhanraj Tamang*; *Dui Purush*; *Nishan*; **1979**: *Dooriyan*; *Devdas*; *Nabadiganta*; *Samadhan*; *Srikanter Will*; *Sunayani*; **1980**: *Aro Ekjan*; *Darpachurna*; *Dui Prithibi*; *Pankhiraj*; *Raja Saheb*; *Raj Nandini*; **1981**: *Plot No 5*; *Kalankini Kankabati**; *Khana Baraha*; *Pratishodh*; *Ogo Bodhu Sundari*; *Surya Sakhi*; **1982**: *Desh Premi*; *Iman Kalyan*; **1987**: *Mera Karam Mera Dharam*.

KUMARAN, K. P.

Malayalam director born in Kutkupuramba, North Kerala. Actively associated with the experimental theatre movements of the early 60s; helped found the Chitralekha Film Society. Film début with an experimental 100-second short, *Rock*. Co-scripted **Adoor Gopalakrishnan**'s ***Swayamvaram*** (1972). Feature début *Atithi* adapted his own play. Also made several documentaries (*Oru Chuvadu Munnottu*, *Kerala Thanimayude Thalam*, *Oru Thuli Velicham* and the video film *An Unmistakable Identity*) and tv programmes for PTI-TV (New Delhi).

FILMOGRAPHY: 1974: *Atithi*; **1976**: *Lakshmi Vijayam*; **1979**: *Thanthulli*; *Adipapam*; **1982**: *Kattile Pattu*; **1985**: *Neram Pularumbol*; **1988**: *Rukmini*.

KUMARI, MEENA (1933-72)

Hindi-Urdu star born in Bombay; daughter of the Parsee theatre actor, singer and music teacher Ali Bux and the dancer Iqbal Begum. Having hit upon hard times and living near the Roopatra Studios, Ali Bux sought to get his three daughters into films. The middle daughter, Mahajabeen, was hired aged 6, re-named Baby Meena and cast by **Vijay Bhatt** in ***Leatherface***. Later, for Bhatt's big musical ***Baiju Bawra***, she was named Meena Kumari. Acted in mythologicals by, e.g., **Homi Wadia** and **Nanabhai Bhatt**. Best known in the 50s for comedies (*Miss Mary*) and socials (***Parineeta***), even appearing in ***Do Bigha Zameen***. Her main persona was constructed via **Kamal Amrohi**'s ***Daera***, **Bimal Roy**'s ***Yahudi*** and **Guru Dutt**' ***Sahib Bibi Aur Ghulam***, culminating in her most famous film, ***Pakeezah***. Deploying the image of the 'innocent' courtesan first developed by **Zubeida**, her arched body, limpid eyes and tremulous voice combined with the lavish sets and costumes to create the classic image of the exotic Oriental, an icon achieved by mixing

Master Aziz and Meena Kumari in *Bhabhi Ki Chudiyan* (1961)

the Urdu stage historical with European neo-classical ornamentation (cf **Aga Hashr Kashmiri**), e.g. in the *mise en sc¤ne* of the *Na jao saiyan* song in ***Sahib Bibi Aur Ghulam***. Married **Amrohi**, director of her best work, but then broke with him in 1964. The couple eventually completed the film they had jointly conceived, ***Pakeezah***, in 1971 just before her death. Her off-screen life extended her image as the lovelorn woman who drowns her passion in drink. Wrote poems in Urdu using the pen-name Naaz, a collection of which, *Tanha Chand* [The Solitary Moon], compiled by **Gulzar**, was published after her death. In their *Women Writing in India* (vol. 2, 1993), which includes one of the star's poems, Susie Tharu and K. Lalitha describe her as 'an exceptionally beautiful and talented actress, always dressed in white', and they quote Afeefa Banu's comment that she is 'an object of fantasy and a motif of melancholy'.

FILMOGRAPHY: 1939: ***Leatherface***; **1940**: *Ek Hi Bhool*; ***Pooja***; **1941**: *Kasauti*; ***Bahen***; *Nai Roshni*; **1942**: ***Garib***; **1943**: *Pratigya*; **1944**: *Lal Haveli*; **1946**: *Bachchon Ka Khel*; *Duniya Ek Sarai*; **1947**: *Piya Ghar Aaja*; **1948**: *Bichhade Balam*; **1949**: *Veer Ghatotkach*; **1950**: *Magroor*; *Shri Ganesh Mahima*; *Hamara Ghar*; **1951**: *Hanuman Pataal Vijay*; *Lakshmi Narayan*; *Madhosh*; *Sanam*; **1952**: *Alladdin And The Wonderful Lamp*; ***Baiju Bawra***; *Tamasha*; **1953**: ***Daera***; *Dana Pani*; ***Do Bigha Zameen***; ***Footpath***; *Naulakha Haar*; ***Parineeta***; **1954**: ***Baadbaan***; ***Chandni Chowk***; *Ilzaam*; **1955**: *Adl-e-Jehangir*; ***Azad***; ***Bandish***; *Rukhsana*; **1956**: *Bandhan*; *Ek Hi Raasta*; *Halaku*; *Mem Sahib*; *Naya Andaz*; *Shatranj*; **1957**: *Miss Mary*; *Sharada*; **1958**: *Farishta*; *Sahara*; *Savera*; ***Yahudi***; **1959**: *Ardhangini*; *Chand*; ***Char Dil Char Raahein***; *Chirag Kahan Roshni Kahan*; *Jagir*; *Madhu*; ***Satta Bazaar***; *Shararat*; **1960**: *Bahana*; *Dil Apna Aur Preet Parayi*; *Kohinoor*; **1961**: ***Bhabhi Ki Chudiyan***; *Pyar Ka Sagar*; *Zindagi Aur Khwab*; **1962**: *Aarti*; *Main Chup Rahungi*; ***Sahib Bibi Aur Ghulam***; **1963**: *Akeli Mat Jaiyo*; *Dil Ek Mandir*; *Kinare Kinare*; **1964**: *Benazir*; ***Chitralekha***; *Ghazal*; *Main Bhi Ladki Hoon*; *Sanjh Aur Savera*; **1965**: *Bheegi Raat*; *Kajal*; *Purnima*; **1966**: *Phool Aur Patthar*; *Pinjre Ke Panchhi*; **1967**: *Bahu Begum*; *Chandan Ka Palna*; *Manjhli Didi*; *Noorjehan*; **1968**: *Abhilasha*; *Baharon Ki Manzil*; **1970**: *Jawab*; *Saat Phere*; **1971**: ***Dushman***; ***Mere Apne***; ***Pakeezah***; **1972**: *Gomti Ke Kinare*.

Kumari, Usha *see* **Vijayanirmala**

KUNCHAKO (1912-76)

Malayalam director and major producer born in Alleppey. One of the founders of the Kerala film industry when he set up his Udaya Studio (1947) in Alleppey and made *Vellinakshatram* (1949). Scripted M.R.S. Mani's *Kidappadam* (1954). Long-time partner K.V. Koshy (they ran K & K Prod.) claimed in his autobiography (1968) to have followed the Telugu film-maker **B.N. Reddi**'s example and brought respectability to Malayalam cinema mainly by distancing themselves from Tamil film's dominant genre conventions. Collaborated closely with scenarists **Muthukulam Raghavan Pillai** and **K.P. Kottarakkara**. This period provided the first Malayalam film stars, including Augustine Joseph and Sebastian Kunju Kunju Bhagavar (actor-singers from the professional theatre), **Thikkurissi Sukumaran Nair** and **Kottarakkara Sridharan Nair**. In the 60s the earlier stage-inspired cinema was replaced by megastar **Prem Nazir**'s work. Films directed ranged across genres such as thrillers with barely concealed references to major scandals (*Mainatharuvi Kola Case*), political films (*Pazhassi Raja*, *Jail*, *Punnapra Vyalar*) and S.P. Pillai comedies (*Neelisally* et al., forerunners of the **Adoor Bhasi** style). Later films referred to literary melodrama tradition known in local parlance as the paingili novel. Also made and produced mythologicals.

FILMOGRAPHY: 1960: *Umma*; *Seeta*; *Neelisally*; **1961**: ***Unniyarcha***; *Krishna Kuchela*; **1962**: *Palattukoman*; *Bharya*; **1963**: *Kadalamma*; *Rebecca*; **1964**: *Pazhassi Raja*; *Ayesha*; **1965**: *Inapravugal*; *Shakuntala*; **1966**: *Jail*; *Anarkali*; *Tilottama*; **1967**: *Mainatharuvi Kola Case*; *Kasavuthattam*; **1968**: ***Thirichadi***; *Punnapra Vyalar*; *Kodungalluramma*; **1969**: *Susie*; **1970**: *Pearl View*; *Dattuputhran*; *Othenente Makan*; **1971**: *Panchavan Kadu*; **1972**: *Aromalunni*; *Postmane Kananilla*; **1973**: *Ponnapuram Kotta*; *Thenaruvi*; *Pavangal Pennungal*; **1974**: *Durga*; *Thumbolarcha*; **1975**: *Neela Ponman*; *Cheenavala*; *Dharmakshetre Kurukshetre*; *Manishada*; **1976**: *Chennai Valarthiya Kutty*; *Mallanum Mathevanum*; **1977**: *Kannappanunni*.

KURUP, O. N. V. (b. 1931)

Songwriter. With **Vyalar Rama Varma** and **P. Bhaskaran**, he formed the troika ruling Malayalam film song since the early 50s. Like the others, he was rooted in the Kerala Peoples Arts Club's radical theatre, for which he wrote some of its most famous songs: *Balikutterangale*, *Aa malar poikayil* (both scored by **Devarajan**) and *Madala poopoloru* (scored by **Salil Choudhury**). Although he shares the pervasive influence of post-Changampuzha 'romantic' poetry, his best-known early work in both his independent poetry (e.g. the anthologies *Samarattinte Santatikal/Offspring of the Revolution*, 1951; *Mattuvin Chattangale/Change the Laws*, 1955) and in his film writing, is more militant than that of his 2 colleagues.

LAHIRI, BHAPPI

Extremely prolific music composer sometimes referred to as the **R.D. Burman** of B movies. Early work in Bengali cinema. Had a major success with **Mithun Chakraborty**'s disco films directed by B. Subhash (*Disco Dancer*, *Dance Dance*). His scores, including for all the **Ramsay** horror films (***Aur Kaun***, ***Saboot***) rely on electronic instrumentation and display an open rejection of originality. His work, often made on a shoestring for South Indian directors, is cited as the emblem of bad taste in mass culture. In some Bengali films, notably Anjan Choudhury's ***Guru Dakshina***, he caused a sensation with compositions based on classical Indian music.

FILMOGRAPHY: 1969: *Dadu*; **1972**: *Janatar Adalat*; **1973**: *Nannha Shikari*; *Charitra*; **1974**: *Bazaar Band Karo*; **1975**: *Zakhmi*; **1976**: *Chalte Chalte*; *Sangram*; **1977**: *Aap Ki Khatir*; *Haiwan*; *Paapi*; *Phir Janam Lenge Hum*; *Pratima Aur Payal*; **1978**: *College Girl*; *Dil Se Mile Dil*; *Khoon Ki Pukar*; *Toote Khilone*; *Tere Pyar Mein*; **1979**: *Shiksha*; *Aangan Ki Kali*; *Ahsaas*; ***Aur Kaun***; *Do Hawaldar*; *Iqraar*; *Jaan-e-Bahar*; *Lahu Ke Do Rang*; *Suraksha*; *Manokamna*; **1980**: *Apne Paraye*; *Agreement*; *Ek Baar Kaho*; *Humkadam*; *Kismet*; *Morcha*; *Patita*; *Pyara Dushman*; *Saboot*; *Taxi Chor*; *Bhula Na Dena*; *Guest House*; **1981**: *Armaan*; *Dahshat*; *Jeene Ki Arzoo*; *Jyoti*; *Laparwah*; *Paanch Qaidi*; *Sahas*; *Wardat*; *Maa Bipat Tarini Chandi*; *Ogo Bodhu Sundari*; *Nai Imarat*; *Josh*; *Hathkadi*; *Dulha Bikta Hai*; **1982**: *Gumsum*; *Dial 100*; *Disco Dancer*; *Do Ustad*; *Namak Halal*; *Sambandh*; *Saugandh*; *Suraag*; *Taqdeer Ka Badshah*; *Farz Aur Kanoon*; *Pyaas*; *Justice Choudhury*; *Shiv Charan*; **1983**: *Do Gulab*; *Doosri Dulhan*; *Faraib*; *Film Hi Film*; *Himmatwala*; *Humse Na Jeeta Koi*; *Jaani Dost*; *Jeet Hamari*; *Karate*; *Kisise Na Kehna*; *Lalach*; *Love in Goa*; *Mawaali*; *Naukar Biwi Ka*; *Pasand Apni Apni*; *Wanted*; *Raja Aur Rana*; *Ek Din Bahu Ka*; *Du-Janay*; *Protidan*; *Apoorva Sahodarigal*; **1984**: *Tarkeeb*; *Aaj Ka MLA Ramavatar*; *Bhavna*; *Gangvaa*; *Haisiyat*; *Hum Rahe Na Hum*; *Kaamyaab*; *Kasam Paida Karne Wale Ki*; *Maqsad*; *Meri Adalat*; *Naya Kadam*; *Pet Pyar Aur Paap*; *Qaidi*; *Shapath*; *Sharabi*; *Tohfa*; *Yaadgaar*; *Waqt Ki Pukar*; *Kamla*; *Teri Baahon Mein*; *Shravan Kumar*; *Sheeshe Ka Ghar*; **1985**: *Thavam*; *Uttarayan*; *Aaj Ka Daur*; *Aandhi Toofan*; *Aitbaar*; *Badal*; *Balidan*; *Bandhan Anjana*; *Bewafai*; *Bhawani Junction*; *Giraftaar*; *Haqeeqat*; *Haveli*; *Hoshiyar*; *Insaaf Main Karoonga*; *Karm Yudh*; *Lover Boy*; *Maa Kasam*; *Maha Shaktiman/Maharudra*; *Mahaguru*; *Masterji*; *Mera Saathi*; *Mohabbat*; *Pataal Bhairavi*; *Pyari Behna*; *Saamri*; *Saheb*; *Salma*; *Tarzan*; *Wafadaar*; *Antaraley*; *Shart*; *Locket*; *Kala Suraj*; **1986**: *Urbashe*; *Jhoothi*; *Adhikar*; *Avinash*; *Dharam Adhikari*; *Dilwala*; *Ilzaam*; *Insaaf Ki Awaaz*; *Kirayedaar*; *Kismatwala*; *Main Balwan*; *Mera Dharam*; *Muddat*; *Sheesha*; *Sinhasan*; *Suhagan*; **1987**: *Thene Manushulu*; *Savkharavam*; *Samrat*; *Pratikar*; *Amor Sangi*; ***Guru Dakshina***; *Aag Hi Aag*; *Dak Bangla*; *Dance Dance*; *Diljala*; *Himmat Aur Mehnat*; *Majaal*; *Mera Yaar Mera Dushman*; *Param Dharam*; *Pyar Karke Dekho*; *Pyar Ke Kabil*; *Sadak Chhaap*; *Satyamev Jayate*; *Sheela*; *Muqaddar Ka Faisla*; *Collector Vijaya*; **1988**: *Manmadha Samrajyam*; *Antarango*; *Debibaran*; *Pratik*; *Aaj Ke Angarey*; *Ghar Ghar Ki Kahani*; *Hatya*; *Kab Tak Chup Rahungi*; *Kasam*; *Mulzim*; *Paap Ki Duniya*; *Tamacha*; *Veerana*; *Waqt Ki Awaaz*; *Commando*; *Kanwarlal*; *Halaal Ki Kamai*; *Mardangi*; *Sone Pe Suhaaga*; *Gunahon Ka Faisla*; *Sagar Sangam*; *Zakhmi Aurat*; *Mera Shikar*; *Farz Ki Jung*; **1989**: *Sachche Ka Bol Bala*; *Guru* (H); *Gair Kanooni*; *Hum Intezar Karenge*; *Kahan Hai Kanoon*; *Paanch Paapi*; *Prem Pratigya*; *Garibon Ka Daata*; *Hum Bhi Insaan Hain*; *Na-Insaafi*; *Aakhri Gulam*; *Mitti Aur Sona*; *Gentleman*; *Love Love Love*; *Mohabbat Ka Paigam*; *Sikka*; *Gola Barood*; *Khoj*; *Kasam Vardi Ki*; *Kanoon Apna Apna*; *Zakhm*; *Paap Ka Ant*; *Nafrat Ki Aandhi*; *Asha-o-Bhalobasha*; *Sansar*; *Amar Tumi*; *Agni Trishna*; *Mangaldip*; *Amor Prem*; *Pronami Tomai*; *Ghar Ka Chirag*; *Aag Ka Gola*; *Khooni Murda*; *Kali Ganga*; *Saaya*; *Tauheen*; **1990**: *Aandhiyan*; *Pyar Ke Naam Qurban*; *Shandaar*; *Shaitani Ilaaka*; *Awaragardi*; *Ghar Ho To Aisa*; *Nakabandi*; *Awwal Number*; *Shera Shamshera*; ***Ghayal***; *Haar Jeet*; *Aaj Ka Arjun*; *Sailaab*; *Roti Ki Keemat*; *Aaj Ka Shahenshah*; *Karishma Kali Ka*; *Thanedar*; *Din Dahade*; *Raktorin*; *Mandira*; *Badnaam*; *Patthar Ke Insaan*; *Raeeszada*; **1991**:

Dushman Devata; Hafta Bandh; Naachnewale Ganewale; Phool Bane Angarey; Pratikaar; Pratigyabadh; Farishte; Yodha; Numbri Admi; First Love Letter; Vishkanya; Kohraa; Hai Meri Jaan; Jungle Beauty; Rupaye Dus Karod; Swarg Jaisa Ghar; Sau Karod; **1992**: *Insaaf Ki Devi; Shola Aur Shabnam; Sanam Tere Hain Hum; Naseebwala; Zindagi Ek Jua; Tyaagi; Police Aur Mujrim; Isi Ka Naam Zindagi; Kisme Kitna Hai Dum; Geet;* **1993**: *Kundan; Aaj Ki Aurat; Aankhen; Aaj Ki Taaqat; Bomb Blast; Geetanjali* (H); *Izzat Ki Roti; Policewala; Veerta; Aag Ka Toofan; Dalaal.*

LAHIRI, NIRENDRANATH (1908-72)

Bengali and Hindi director born in Calcutta. Started as actor in **P.C. Barua**'s studio (*Ekada*, 1932); assisted **Barua** at **New Theatres**. Music director for *Ashiana, Tarubala* and *Annapurnar Mandir* (all 1936), and acted in **Debaki Bose**'s *Abhinav* (1940) before turning director. Best-known films based on writers associated with progressive **Kallol** literature (e.g. *Bhabhi-Kaal* by **Premendra Mitra**). Themes often invoke nationalist idealism (***Garmil***, *Bhabi-Kaal*). Also filmed Saratchandra Chatterjee's novels (e.g. *Palli Samaj, Subhadra*).

FILMOGRAPHY (* also music d): **1942**: *Mahakavi Kalidas;* ***Garmil***; **1943**: *Sahadharmini; Dampati;* **1944**: *Anban;* **1945**: *Bhabhi-Kaal; Banphool;* **1946**: *Arabian Nights;* **1948**: *Sadharan Meye; Jayjatra/Vijay Yatra;* **1949**: *Niruddesh; Singhdwar;* **1950**: *Garabini;* **1952**: *Palli Samaj; Subhadra;* **1953**: *Kajari**; *Lakh Taka**; **1954**: *Shobha; Kalyani; Jadubhatta;* **1955**: *Devimalini;* **1956**: *Bhola Master; Shankar Narayan Bank;* **1957**: *Madhu Malati; Bara Maa; Prithibi Amar Chai;* **1958**: *Tansen; Indrani;* **1959**: *Chhabi;* **1966**: *Rajdrohi;* **1983**: *Raat Dastay.*

LAJMI, KALPANA (b. 1954)

Hindi director based in Bombay; niece of **Guru Dutt**. Assistant to **Benegal** (1974-82). Started assisting **Bhupen Hazarika** (1977) and has consistently collaborated with him since then, managing his career from 1982 onwards. Directorial début with a portrait of **Dhiren Ganguly**; made several documentaries and promotionals before her feature début with ***Ek Pal***. Directed the 13-episode tv series *Lohit Kinare*, adapting Assamese short stories.

FILMOGRAPHY: 1978: *D.G. Movie Pioneer* (Doc); **1979**: *A Work Study in Tea Plucking* (Doc); **1981**: *Along the Brahmaputra* (Doc); **1986**: ***Ek Pal***; **1988**: *Lohit Kinare* (TV); **1992**: *Rudaali.*

Lakshmikant-Pyarelal *see* **Laxmikant-Pyarelal**

LAKSHMIRAJYAM (1922-87)

Telugu actress and producer born near Vijaywada, AP, into a family of stage performers. Joined the Ramatilakam-Pulipati stage company in Vijaywada. Studied music, including the folk Harikatha style, from composer **Saluri Rajeswara Rao**. First break in Calcutta in **C. Pullaiah**'s *Shri Krishna Tulabharam*. Acted in mythologicals, e.g. Radha in ***Shri Krishna Leelalu***, *Maya Bazaar*, etc. After *Illalu*, was associated prominently in melodramas by **Ramabrahmam** in e.g. *Apavadu* and *Panthulamma*, **L.V. Prasad** and **K.V. Reddy**. Turned producer with Rajyam Prod. (1952) and made films like ***Daasi***, *Nartanasala, Shakuntala* and *Rangeli Raja.*

FILMOGRAPHY: 1935: *Shri Krishna Tulabharam;* ***Shri Krishna Leelalu***; **1936**: *Maya Bazaar;* **1939**: *Amma;* **1940**: *Illalu;* **1941**: *Apavadu;* **1943**: *Panthulamma;* **1946**: *Mangalsutram; Narada Naradi;* **1948**: ***Drohi***; **1949**: ***Gunsundari Katha***; **1950**: ***Paramanandayya Sishyulu Katha; Samsaram***; **1951**: ***Agni Pareeksha***; *Akasharaju; Mayalamari; Mayapilla;* **1952**: ***Daasi***; *Prajaseva;* **1954**: *Raju Peda;* **1956**: *Harishchandra;* **1958**: ***Ettuku Pai Ettu***; **1960**: *Vimala;* **1963**: *Nartanasala;* ***Iruvar Ullam***; **1966**: *Shakuntala;* **1968**: *Govula Gopanna;* **1971**: *Rangeli Raja.*

LAKSHMINARAYAN, N. (?-1991)

Kannada director born in Srirangapatna, Karnataka. First explicitly experimental film-maker in Kannada with wordless short *Bliss*. Studied cinematography in Bangalore. Early career as apprentice to his uncle, B.R. Krishnamurthy; then to **R. Nagendra Rao**. Claimed influence of De Sica and **Satyajit Ray** in first attempts at art cinema in Kannada, prior to the **Navya Movement**-inspired notion of film as an extension of literature. His melodramatically inclined work claims roots in psychological realism. His ***Nandi*** was a big success and launched **Kalpana** as a star.

FILMOGRAPHY: 1961: *Bliss* (Sh); **1964**: ***Nandi***; **1969**: ***Uyyale***; **1970**: ***Mukti***; **1973**: ***Abachurina Post Office***; **1979**: *Muyyi;* **1985**: *Bettada Hoovu;* **1987**: *Belaku.*

Lakshminarayan, Sattiraju *see* **Bapu**

LANKESH, P. (b. 1935)

Kannada director born in Shimoga Dist., Karnataka. Also major Kannada novelist, poet and playwright. His novel, *Biruku* (1967), ranks with Ananthamurthy's *Samskara* (1966) as the pinnacle of the **Navya Movement**. Acted in film version of ***Samskara*** (1970). Other noted works: *Kereya Niranu Kerege Chelli* (short stories, 1964), *Bitchhu* (poems, 1967), *Sankranthi* (play, 1973). Films continue his literary enterprise. Co-scripted **Kambhar**'s *Sangeetha* (1981). Vociferous political commentator and owner-editor of the down-market weekly tabloid *Lankesh Patrike* (Est: 1980). Established his own political party to fight the general elections of 1989.

FILMOGRAPHY (* also act): **1976**: ***Pallavi****; **1977**: *Anurupa;* **1979**: *Khandavideko Mamsavideko;* **1980**: *Ellindalo Bandavaru.*

LAXMIKANT-PYARELAL (LAXMIKANT SHANTARAM KUDALKAR, b. 1937, AND PYARELAL RAMPRASAD SHARMA, b. 1940)

Music composers at the top of their profession in the 70s and 80s. Composed the two biggest hit songs of the late 80s, *Ek do teen* (from ***Tezaab***) and the **Bachchan** number *Jumma chumma* (from ***Hum***). Both musicians started as performers in orchestras, becoming arrangers for Hindi film music, which often included ghosting for composers. Laxmikant learnt the violin with **Husnlal** while Pyarelal learnt music from the Goan music teacher, Anthony Gonsalves (a memory celebrated in his score for ***Amar Akbar Anthony***). Pyarelal assisted **Bulo C. Rani** at **Ranjit**; both assisted **Naushad, C. Ramchandra** and **Kalyanji-Anandji**. Their first film as music directors, ***Parasmani***, yielded a major hit, *Hansta hua nurani chehra*. Broke through with *Milan* and the **Lata Mangeshkar**/Mukesh hit, *Sawan ka mahina*. Real success came in the 70s with their **Rajesh Khanna** films (***Dushman***, *Hathi Mere Saathi*, ***Do Raaste***) and with **Raj Kapoor**'s ***Bobby***. Since then they have worked on many **Manmohan Desai** films (***Dharam Veer, Naseeb***), **Shekhar Kapur**'s ***Mr India*** and the film that breathed new life into their career, *Tezaab*, followed by *Hum*. They tend to ascribe their success to their integration of classical Indian and folk rhythms with electronic synthesisers. The lyrics of their songs are frequently written by **Anand Bakshi**.

FILMOGRAPHY: 1963: ***Parasmani***; *Harishchandra Taramati;* **1964**: *Aaya Toofan;* ***Dosti***; *Mr X in Bombay; Sant Dnyaneshwar; Sati Savitri;* **1965**: *Boxer; Hum Sub Ustad Hain; Lutera; Shriman Funtoosh;* **1966**: *Aasra; Aaye Din Bahar Ke; Chhota Bhai; Daku Mangal Singh; Dillagi; Laadla; Mere Lal; Naag Mandir; Pyar Kiye Jaa; Sau Saal Baad;* **1967**: *Anita; Milan Ki Raat; Chhaila Babu; Duniya Nachegi; Farz; Jaal; Milan; Night in London; Patthar Ke Sanam; Shagird;* ***Taqdeer***; **1968**: *Baharon Ki Manzil; Izzat; Mere Humdum Mere Dost; Raja Aur Runk; Sadhu Aur Shaitan; Spy in Rome;* **1969**: *Aansoo Ban Gaye Phool; Anjaana; Aaya Sawan Jhoom Ke; Dharti Kahe Pukar Ke; Do Bhai;* ***Do Raaste***; *Inteqam; Jeene Ki Raah; Jigri Dost; Madhavi; Mera Dost; Meri Bhabhi; Pyaasi Shyam; Saajan;* ***Satyakam***; *Shart; Wapas;* **1970**: *Aan Milo Sajna; Abhinetri; Bachpan; Darpan; Devi; Himmat; Humjoli; Jawab; Jeevan Mrityu; Khilona; Maa Aur Mamta; Man Ki Aankhen; Mastana; Pushpanjali; Sharafat; Suhana Safar;* **1971**: *Aap Aye Bahar Ayi; Banphool; Bikhare Moti; Chahat;* ***Dushman***; *Hathi Mere Saathi; Haseenon Ka Devta; Jal Bin Machhli Nritya Bin Bijli; Lagan; Man Mandir; Mehboob Ke Mehndi; Mera Gaon Mera Desh; Uphaar; Woh Din Yaad Karo;* **1972**: *Buniyaad; Dastaan; Ek Bechara; Ek Nazar; Gaon Hamara Shaher Tumhara; Gora Aur Kala; Haar Jeet; Jeet; Mom Ki Gudiya; Piya Ka Ghar; Raaste Ka Patthar; Raja Jani; Shadi Ke Baad; Shor; Subah-o-Shyam; Wafaa; Roop Tera Mastana;* **1973**: *Anhonee; Anokhi Ada; Barkha Bahar;* ***Bobby; Daag***; *Gaddar; Gaai Aur Gori; Gehri Chaal; Insaaf; Jalte Badan; Jwar Bhata; Kachche Dhaage; Kahani Hum Sub Ki; Loafer; Manchali; Nirdosh; Keemat; Suraj Aur Chanda; Sweekar;* **1974**: *Amir Garib; Badla; Bidaai; The Cheat; Dost; Dulhan; Duniya Ka Mela; Free Love; Geeta Mera Naam; Imtehan; Jurm Aur Sazaa; Majboor; Naya Din Nayi Raat; Nirmaan; Pagli; Paise Ki Gudiya; Prem Shastra; Roti; Roti Kapda Aur Makaan; Shandaar; Vaada Tera Vaada; Pocketmaar; Sauda;* **1975**: *Aakhri Dao; Akraman; Anari; Apne Rang Hazaar; Chaitali; Dafaa 302; Lafange; Mere Sajna; Ponga Pandit; Pratigya; Prem Kahani; Sewak; Zinda Dil; Zindagi Aur Toofan; Natak;* **1976**: *Aaj Ka*

Mahatma; *Aap Beeti*; *Charas*; *Do Ladkiyan*; *Das Numbri*; *Jaaneman*; *Koi Jeeta Koi Haara*; *Maa*; *Nagin*; *Santan*; *Naach Utha Sansar*; **1977**: *Adha Din Adhi Raat*; *Aashiq Hoon Baharon Ka*; ***Amar Akbar Anthony***; *Anurodh*; *Apnapan*; *Chacha Bhatija*; *Chhaila Babu*; *Chhota Baap*; *Chor Sipahi*; ***Dharam Veer***; *Dildaar*; *Dream Girl*; *Imaan Dharam*; *Jagriti*; *Kachcha Chor*; *Kali Raat*; *Mastan Dada*; *Ooparwala Jaane*; *Palkon Ki Chhaon Mein*; *Parvarish*; *Thief of Baghdad*; *Tinku*; *Prayashchit*; **1978**: *Ahuti*; *Amar Shakti*; *Badalte Rishte*; *Daku Aur Jawan*; *Dil Aur Deewar*; *Kala Admi*; *Main Tulsi Tere Aangan Ki*; *Phansi*; *Phool Khile Hain Gulshan Gulshan*; *Prem Bandhan*; ***Satyam Shivam Sundaram***; *Sawan Ke Geet*; *Chakravyuha*; **1979**: *Amar Deep*; *Dil Ka Heera*; *Gautam Govinda*; *Jaani Dushman*; *Kartavya*; *Lok Parlok*; *Maan Apmaan*; *Magroor*; *Muqabala*; *Prem Vivah*; *Sargam*; *Suhaag*; *Yuvraaj*; *Zalim*; *Kali Ghata*; *Chunauti*; **1980**: *Asha*; *Bandish*; *Berahem*; *Choron Ki Baraat*; *Do Premi*; *Dostana*; *Ganga Aur Suraj*; ***Gehrayee***; *Judaai*; *Jyoti Bane Jwala*; *Kala Pani*; ***Karz***; *Maang Bharo Sajana*; *Nishana*; *Patthar Se Takkar*; *Ram Balram*; *Yari Dushmani*; ***Hum Paanch***; *Waqt Ki Deewar*; *Aas Paas*; **1981**: *Ek Aur Ek Gyarah*; *Ek Duuje Ke Liye*; *Ek Hi Bhool*; *Fifty-Fifty*; *Khoon Aur Pani*; *Khuda Kasam*; *Kranti*; *Krodhi*; *Ladies' Tailor*; *Meri Awaaz Suno*; ***Naseeb***; *Pyaasa Sawan*; *Sharada*; *Vakil Babu*; *Raaste Pyar Ke*; **1982**: *Apna Bana Lo*; *Badle Ki Aag*; *Baghavat*; *Deedar-e-Yaar*; *Do Dishayen*; *Desh Premi*; *Ghazab*; *Insaan*; *Jeevan Dhara*; *Jiyo Aur Jeene Do*; *Main Inteqam Loonga*; *Mehndi Rang Layegi*; *Prem Rog*; *Rajput*; *Samrat*; *Taaqat*; *Teesri Aankh*; *Teri Maang Sitaron Se Bhar Doon*; *Davedar*; *Farz Aur Kanoon*; *Jaanwar*; **1983**: *Andha Kanoon*; *Arpan*; *Avatar*; *Bekaraar*; ***Coolie***; ***Hero***; *Mujhe Insaaf Chahiye*; *Prem Tapasya*; *Woh Saat Din*; *Yeh Ishq Nahin Asaan*; *Zara Si Zindagi*; *Agami Kal*; **1984**: *Asha Jyoti*; *Akalmand*; *All Rounder*; *Baazi*; *Ek Nai Paheli*; *Ghar Ek Mandir*; *Inquilab*; *Jeene Nahin Doonga*; *John Jani Janardhan*; *Bad Aur Badnaam*; *Do Dilon Ki Dastaan*; *Mera Faisla*; *Sharara*; *Zakhmi Sher*; ***Utsav***; *Pyar Jhukta Nahin*; *Mera Dost Mera Dushman*; *Khazana*; *Pakhandi*; *Kahan Tak Aasmaan Hai*; **1985**: *Dekha Pyar Tumhara*; ***Ghulami***; *Jaanoo*; *Jawab*; *Kali Basti*; *Mera Ghar Mere Bachche*; *Mera Jawab*; *Meri Jung*; *Patthar Dil*; *Sanjog*; *Sarfarosh*; *Sur Sangam*; *Teri Meherbaniyan*; *Yaadon Ki Kasam*; *Triveni*; **1986**: *Swati*; *Aag Aur Shola*; *Aakhri Raasta*; *Aap Ke Saath*; *Aisa Pyar Kahan*; *Amrit*; *Anjaam*; *Asli Naqli*; *Dosti Dushmani*; *Kala Dhandha Goray Log*; *Love 86*; *Mazloom*; *Naache Mayuri*; *Naam*; *Nagina*; *Naseeb Apna Apna*; *Pyar Kiya Hai Pyar Karenge*; *Qatl*; *Sada Suhagan*; *Swarg Se Sundar*; ***Karma***; *Loha*; **1987**: *Sansar*; *Aulad*; *Hukumat*; *Insaaf*; *Insaaf Kaun Karega*; *Insaaf Ki Pukar*; *Jaan Hatheli Pe*; *Jawab Hum Denge*; *Kudrat Ka Kanoon*; *Madadgaar*; *Mard Ki Zabaan*; *Mera Karam Mera Dharam*; ***Mr India***; *Nazrana*; *Parivar*; *Sindoor*; *Uttar Dakshin*; *Watan Ke Rakhwale*; **1988**: *Charnon Ki Saugandh*; *Khatron Ke Khiladi*; *Pyar Ka Mandir*; *Pyar Mohabbat*; *Ram Avatar*; *Shoorveer*; *Hamara Khandaan*; *Biwi Ho To Aisi*; *Dayavan*; *Ganga Tere Desh Mein*; ***Tezaab***; *Janam Janam*; *Mar Mitenge*; *Agni*; *Do Waqt Ki Roti*; *Inteqam*; *Qatil*; *Bees Saal Baad*; *Eeshwar*; ***Yateem***; **1989**: *Gharana*; *Oonch Neech Beech*; *Elaan-e-Jung*; *Nigahen*; *Santosh*; *Shehzade*; *Bhrashtachar*; *Chaalbaaz*; *Do Qaidi*; ***Hathyar***; *Main Tera Dushman*; *Suryaa*; *Dost Garibon Ka*; ***Ram Lakhan***; *Kasam Suhaag Ki*; *Pati Parmeshwar*; *Bade Ghar Ki Beti*; *Paraya Ghar*; *Sachaai Ki Taaqat*; ***Batwara***; *Naag Nagin*; *Majboor*; *Sahebzade*; *Deshwasi*; **1990**: *Paap Ki Aandhi*; *Krodh*; *Pratibandh*; *Pyar Ka Devata*; *Pyar Ka Karz*; *Pyar Ka Toofan*; *Sanam Bewafa*; *Sher Dil*; *Shesh Naag*; *Azad Desh Ke Gulam*; *Hatimtai*; *Jeevan Ek Sangharsh*; *Izzatdar*; *Krodh*; *Amiri Garibi*; *Atishbaaz*; ***Agneepath***; *Pati Patni Aur Tawaif*; *Humse Na Takrana*; *Veeru Dada*; *Amba*; *Jamai Raja*; *Qayamat Ki Raat*; *Khilaaf*; *Kanoon Ki Zanjeer*; **1991**: *Ajooba*; *Benaam Badshah*; *Do Matwale*; *Pyar Hua Chori Chori*; *Qurban*; ***Hum***; ***Narasimha***; *Khoon Ka Karz*; *Mast Kalandar*; *Ranabhoomi*; *Shankara*; *Akela*; *Banjaran*; *Sapnon Ka Mandir*; *Lakshmanrekha*; **1992**: *Prem Diwani*; *Humshakal*; *Heer Ranjha*; *Angar*; *Aparadhi*; *Tirangaa*; *Kshatriya*; **1993**: *Dil Hi To Hai*; *Yugandhar*; *Roop Ki Rani Choron Ka Raja*; *Aashiq Awara*; *Badi Bahen*; *Khalnayak*; *Dil Hai Betaab*; *Gumrah*; *Chahoonga Main Tujhe*; *Bedardi*.

LEELA, P. (b. 1933)

Together with P. Susheela, Leela is one of the main South Indian singers, with many hits since the late 40s in Tamil, Malayalam, Telugu and Kannada. Born in Chittor, North Kerala. Film début in *Kankanam* (1947); broke through with songs in ***Gunsundari Katha*** (1949). Playback singer in more than 400 films. Has been on a long-term contract with Columbia Gramophone, releasing over 250 records for their label. Made numerous radio appearances in Madras.

LEELAVATHI (b. 1938)

Versatile Kannada actress born in Mangalore, Karnataka. Joined **M.V. Subbaiah Naidu**'s stage group aged 3. Was a well-known Kannada stage actress when she débuted in film as the comedienne in ***Bhakta Prahlada***. Her first lead role was in *Mangalya Yoga*. Achieved stardom as *Rani Honamma*, her first film with **Rajkumar**, going on to do c.20 more films with him, dominating Kannada cinema for over a decade. Acted in melodramas for **Kanagal** (***Gejje Pooje***, ***Sharapanjara***) and developed into a dramatically intense actress, often cast as a mother; also known for light comedy.

FILMOGRAPHY: 1958: ***Bhakta Prahlada***; *Mangalya Yoga*; **1959**: *Dharma Vijaya*; *Raja Malaya Simhan*; *Jagajyothi Basaveshwara*; ***Abba! A Hudgi***; **1960**: ***Ranadheera Kanteerava***; *Dashavtara*; *Rani Honamma*; **1961**: *Kaivara Mahatme*; *Kantheredu Nodu*; ***Kittur Chanamma***; **1962**: ***Bhoodana***; *Galigopura*; *Karuneye Kutumbada Kannu*; *Ratnamanjari*; *Vidhi Vilasa*; *Valar Pirai*; *Sumaithangal*; **1963**: *Nanda Deepa*; *Kanya Ratna*; *Jeevana Taranga*; *Malli Madhuve*; *Kulavadhu*; *Kalitharu Henne*; *Bevu Bella*; ***Veera Kesari/Bandhipotu***; *Valmiki*; *Mana Mechhida Madadi*; *Sant Tukaram*; **1964**: *Marmayogi*; *Shivarathri Mahatme*; *Tumbidakoda*; **1965**: *Naga Pooja*; *Chandrahasa*; *Vatsalya*; *Veera Vikrama*; *Ide Mahasudina*; *Madhuve Madi Nodu*; **1966**: *Thoogu Deepa*; *Prema Mayi*; *Paduka Pattabhishekham*; *Mohini Bhasmasura*; **1967**: *Gange Gauri*; **1968**: *Bhagya Devathe*; *Mammathe*; *Anna Thamma*; *Attegondukala Sosegondukala*; **1969**: *Kalpa Vruksha*; *Brindavana*; **1970**: ***Gejje Pooje***; *Aparajite*; *Boregowda Bangaloruge Banda*; *Sukha Samsara*; *Aaru Mooru Ombattu*; **1971**: ***Sharapanjara***; *Signalman Siddappa*; *Sothu Geddavalu*; *Sipayi Ramu*; **1972**: *Naa Mechida Huduga*; ***Nagara Haavu***; *Dharmapatni*; **1973**: *Sahadharmini*; *Muruvare Vajragalu*; *Premapasha*; **1974**: *Upasane*; *Maha Thyaga*; *Bhakta Kumbhara*; *Professor Huchuraya*; *Maga Mommaga*; *Naan Avanillai*; *Aval Oru Thodarkathai/Aval Oru Thodarkatha*; *Devara Gudi*; *Idu Namma Desha*; **1975**: *Koodi Balona*; *Kalla Kulla*; *Bhagya Jyothi*; *Bili Hendthi*; *Hennu Samsarada Kannu*; ***Katha Sangama***; *Hosilu Mettida Hennu*; **1976**: *Makkala Bhagya*; *Bangarada Gudi*; *Collegeranga*; *Na Ninna Mareyalare*; *Phalithamsha*; **1977**: *Deepa*; *Dhanalakshmi*; *Mugdha Manava*; *Kumkuma Rakshe*; *Veera Sindhoora Lakshmana*; ***Avargal***; **1978**: *Devadasi*; *Kiladi Kittu*; *Matu Tappada Maga*; *Kiladi Jodi*; *Gammathu Goodacharulu*; *Vasanthalakshmi*; **1979**: *Karthika Deepam*; *Idi Kathakadu*; *Na Ninna Bidalare*; *Pakka Kalla*; *Vijaya Vikram*; *Savathiya Neralu*; **1980**: *Nanna Rosha Nooru Varusha*; *Kulla Kulli*; *Auto Raja*; *Subbi Subakka Suvvalali*; *Namma Mane Sose*; *Simha Jodi*; *Vasantha Geethe*; *Nyaya Neethi Dharma*; *Jatara*; **1981**: *Thayiya Madilalli*; *Kulaputra*; *Hana Balavo Jana Balavo*; *Edeyuru Siddhalingeshwara/Siddalingeshwara Mahima*; **1983**: *Sidededda Sahodara*; *Mududida Tavare Aralitu*; *Samarpane*; **1984**: *Shravana Bantu*; *Endina Ramayana*; *Chanakya*; *Olavu Moodidaga*; **1985**: *Balondu Uyyale*; *Ajeya*; *Nanu Nanna Hendthi*; *Pudhir*; *Hosa Baalu*; **1986**: *Bettada Thayi*; *Katha Nayaka*; *KD No 1*; *Mrigalaya*; *Seelu Nakshatra*; **1987**: ***Premaloka***; *Olavina Udugore*; *Huli Hebbuli*; **1989**: *Yuga Purusha*; *Gagana*; *Abhimana*; *Doctor Krishna*; **1990**: *Golmaal Radhakrishna*; *Tiger Gangu*; **1991**: *Golmaal Bhaga II*.

LUDHIANVI, SAHIR (1921-80)

Urdu lyricist and major poet born in Ludhiana. Originally called Abdul Hayee. Author of two anthologies (*Talkhian*, 1945, and *Parchaiyan*) and several books, including *Ao Koi Khawab Banen* and *Gaata Jaye Banjara*. Member of the **PWA**. Worked extensively as a journalist, editing the journal *Adab-e-Latif*, and briefly *Pritlari* and *Shahrab* in Delhi. Moved to Bombay (1949) and débuted in films with **Mahesh Kaul**'s *Naujawan* (1951). First major success was with **Guru Dutt**'s ***Baazi*** (1951). Worked with Navketan productions and formed a team with composer **S.D. Burman** (e.g. ***Taxi Driver***, 1954). Transferred the progressive Urdu literature exemplified by poet Faiz Ahmed Faiz to the Hindi film lyric, e.g. the songs in ***Naya Daur*** (1957, esp. *Saathi haath badhana*), ***Phir Subah Hogi*** (1958, esp. *Woh subah kabhi to aayegi*) and all the classic songs of ***Pyaasa*** (1957). Also claimed the influence of Mayakovsky and Neruda. His songs continue to influence all forms of radical music (e.g. that of street theatre groups) while remaining popular favourites.

LUHAR, CHIMANLAL MULJIBHOY (1901-48)

Hindi director. Chemistry graduate from Bombay University. Noted author and critic in early 1920s, e.g. in journals like *Vismi Sadi*, *Navchetan* and *Bombay Chronicle*. Started career as laboratory assistant at **Kohinoor** Studio in the 20s. Became noted cameraman working, e.g., for several documentaries with Bombay-based production unit **K.D. Brothers**, apparently under tutelage of an English cameraman affiliated to the Prince of Wales's official entourage during his tour of India. Following brief stints at **Krishna** Studio and **Saurashtra Film** in Rajkot (1926), joined **Sharda** (1928-31), where his camerawork was central to the studio's **Master Vithal** stunt movies. Turned producer (1932) with long-term partner Harshadrai Mehta (Mehta-Luhar Prod.) continuing in the Master Vithal vein of stunt and adventure thrillers starring Navinchandra. Then a partner in Sharda (1933) and a director at **Sagar** (1934-40), where he began signing his name to his films and introduced the stunt genre. Later directed Prakash Pics (1941-6).

FILMOGRAPHY: 1932: *Sassi Punnu*; 1935: ***Silver King***; *Talash-e-Haq*; **1936: *Do Diwane/Be Kharab Jan***; **1937**: *Captain Kirti Kumar*; **1938**: *Dynamite*; **1939**: *Kaun Kisika*; ***Seva Samaj***; **1940**: *Saubhagya*; **1941**: *Darshan*; **1942**: ***Station Master***; **1943**: *School Master*; **1944**: *Us Paar*; **1946**: *Bindiya*.

MADAN THEATRES

Giant distribution corporation and studio which dominated India's silent cinema. Built by Jamshedji Framji Madan (1856-1923) into one of the country's premier Parsee theatre companies. J.F. Madan came from a middle-class Bombay Parsee family of theatre enthusiasts: his brother Khurshedji was a partner in the Original Victoria Theatrical Club while Jamshedji and another brother, Pestonji, started as actors. In the 1890s, J.F. Madan bought two prominent theatre companies, the Elphinstone and the Khatau-Alfred, including their creative staff and the rights to their repertoire. Shifted his base to Calcutta in 1902, establishing J.F. Madan & Sons (maintaining his other interests like pharmaceuticals). By 1919, J.F. Madan & Sons had become the joint stock company Madan Theatres, running the Elphinstone Theatrical Co. (expanding from the Elphinstone Picture Palace and the ancestor of the Elphinstone Bioscope) and its flagship organisation, the Corinthian Theatre. They employed several of the leading Urdu-Hindi playwrights (**Kashmiri, Betaab**) and stars (**Patience Cooper, Seeta Devi**). Some historians claim that J.F. Madan started showing films in a tent bioscope in 1902 on the Calcutta maidan, but it is more likely that the Madans did not seriously get into film until 1905, financing some of Jyotish Sarkar's documentaries (e.g. *Great Bengal Partition Movement*, 1905) which they presented at the Elphinstone. In 1907 the Elphinstone followed the Minerva and Star theatres (see **Hiralal Sen**) and went into exhibition and distribution, winning the agency rights for Pathé, who also represented First National. They expanded by buying or leasing theatres located in urban areas with European residents, commanding higher ticket prices and catering to the British armed forces before and during WW1. On J.F. Madan's death, the third of his five sons, Jeejeebhoy Jamshedji Madan, took over and expanded the empire, continuing to direct some of the company's films. By 1927 the Madan distribution chain controlled c.1/2 of India's permanent cinemas. At their peak they owned 172 theatres and earned half the national box office. Up to WW1 they showed mainly British films supplied by the Rangoon-based London Film, but after the war they imported Metro and United Artists product, mostly bought 'blind' with rights for the entire subcontinent. By the mid-20s they were the first of the five major importers of Hollywood films, followed by Pathé, Universal, Globe and **Pancholi**'s Empire distributors. In the silent era, their exhibition and distribution were more important than their production work, mainly making shorts for export until *Satyavadi Raja Harishchandra* (1917) and Dotiwala's *Bilwamangal* (1919; the first Bengali feature) both proved successful. Their early features were mainly filmed plays, converting their playwrights into scenarists and their actors into stars. Many were directed by C. Legrand, formerly a Pathé man, and later by **Jyotish Bannerjee**. Claimed to have done international co-productions, although ***Savitri*** (1923) made by Giorgio Mannini for Cines in Rome and starring Rina De Liguoro opposite Angelo Ferrari, probably was not co-produced but only released by Madan. However, he did work with the Italian cineaste E.D. Liguoro and cameraman T. Marconi. In the early 20s, the Madans also acquired the rights to the major 19th C. Bengali novelist Bankimchandra Chatterjee's writings, forming the basis of their 'literary film' genre which came to dominate Bengali cinema for several decades. By the end of the silent era the group had become too large for its managerial structure. It invested heavily into sound afer it premiered Universal's *Melody of Love* at the Elphinstone Bioscope (1928) and made the expensive ***Shirin Farhad*** (1931, narrowly beaten by ***Alam Ara*** as India's first sound film), Amar Choudhury's *Jamai Sasthi* (1931, the first Bengali sound feature) and ***Indrasabha*** (1932). Their closure in the late 30s is usually blamed on a failed deal with Columbia but this may only have put the final seal on a decline caused by crippling sound conversion costs, the stabilisation of film imports and the spread of the more efficient managing-agency system able to attract more speculative financing.

MADGULKAR, GAJANAN DIGAMBAR (1919-77)

Marathi scenarist, songwriter, actor and poet. First film as lyric writer: **Bedekar**'s ***Pahila Palna*** (1942), which was also his acting début. Achieved prominence in the 50s via his popular film songs on the radio and on discs which, following the spread of playback, evolved the bhava geet: orchestrated songs of about three minutes duration using simple emotive lyrics. His texts were mainly sung and orchestrated by **Sudhir Phadke**, their *Geet Ramayan* record series of 1957 remaining very popular with the Marathi middle class and a precursor of the 70s *bhajan* craze. Often wrote for **Raja Paranjpe** (*Jivacha Sakha*, 1948; ***Pudhcha Paool***, 1950; ***Lakhachi Goshta*** and ***Pedgaonche Shahane***, both 1952; ***Oon Paoos***, 1954; *Ganget Ghoda Nhala*, 1955; *Andhala Magto Ek Dola* and *Deoghar*, both 1956; ***Pathlaag***, 1964). This work dominated the Marathi cinema in the 50s and 60s and is associated with the shift, on the formation of the state of Maharashtra, to a concern with Marathi identity accompanied by the creation of industrial infrastructures (and audiences) based on regional capital. First script, **Shantaram**'s ***Lokshahir Ramjoshi/Matwala Shayar Ramjoshi*** (1947; also act), launched the gramin chitrapat genre of 'rural' film typically using dialect, located in a village and telling of a power struggle between a good peasant lad and an evil sarpanch (village elder). Also wrote scripts for **Dinkar D. Patil**, the best-known Marathi director in the genre (*Baap Mazha Brahmachari* and *Prem Andhala Asta*, both 1962). However, where Patil used the genre as an indigenous version of the western, Madgulkar's scripts conveyed a sense of political awareness in line with, e.g., Vyankatesh Madgulkar's stories about rural characters. Wrote prose melodramas, e.g. for **Dharmadhikari** (e.g. *Bala Jo Jo Re*, 1951; *Stree Janma Hi Tujhi Kahani*, 1952). Also adapted mythologicals and historicals to the studios' industrial requirements (e.g. *Maya Bazaar*, 1949; *Shri Krishna Darshan*, 1950; *Narveer Tanaji*, 1952). Acted in, e.g., *Pedgaonche Shahane*, *Jeet Kiski* (both 1952), *Banwasi*, *Adalat* (both 1948).

MADHU

Malayalam actor and director introduced by **Kariat** and **Bhaskaran** in the early 1960s. Originally Madhavan Nair, born in Trivandrum, Kerala. Graduate of the Benares Hindu University, later diploma in acting from the National School of Drama. Together with **Sathyan** and **Prem Nazir**, he defined Malayali machismo in commercial productions, often playing the sad and suffering lover. After ***Chemmeen***, which gave him a reputation as a character actor, acted regularly in independent productions (e.g. **P.N. Menon**'s ***Olavum Theeravum***, **Adoor Gopalakrishnan**'s ***Swayamvaram***). In recent films like ***Ottayadi Paathakal*** he became better known for his emphatic playing than for his more numerous conventional starring roles. His 'offbeat' reputation was enhanced by his first directorial effort, ***Priya***, featuring Bengali actress Lili Chakraborty, which received much critical attention in Kerala. An admirer of Bengali culture, he chose to play the Bengali commando in **Abbas**' national integration war movie ***Saat Hindustani***. Founded the Uma Studio, Trivandrum.

FILMOGRAPHY (* also d): **1963**: ***Moodupadam***; ***Ninamanninnya Kalapadakal***; *Ammeye Kannan*; **1964**: *Thacholi Othenan*; *Kuttikkuppayam*; *Manavatti*; *Adya Kiranangal*; ***Bhargavi Nilayam***; **1965**: *Subaida*; *Kaliyodam*; *Kalyanaphoto*; *Ammu*; *Mayavi*; *Jeevitha Yatra*; *Kattupookal*; *Pattu Thoovala*; ***Murappennu***; *Thommente Makkal*; *Sarpakadu*; ***Chemmeen***; **1966**: *Manikya Kottaram*; *Puthri*; *Archana*; *Karuna*; *Tilottama*; **1967**: *Ramanan*; *Udyogastha*; *Lady Doctor*; *Karutharathrigal*; ***Aval***; *Kadhija*; ***Anveshichu Kandatiyilla***; ***Ashwamedham***; *Nagarame Nandi*; *Chekuthante Kotta*; *Ollathu Mathi*; **1968**: *Viplavakarikal*; *Karutha Pournami*; *Manaswini*; *Vazhipizhacha Santhathi*; *Kadal*; ***Thulabharam***; *Ragini*; ***Adhyapika***; **1969**: *Vila Kuranja Manushyar*; *Veetu Mrugham*;

Almaram; ***Janmabhoomi***; *Kuruthikalam*; ***Nadhi***; *Velliyazhcha*; *Virunnukari*; ***Saat Hindustani***; ***Olavum Theeravum***; **1970**: *Ambalapravu*; *Palunku Pathram*; *Stree*; *Bhikara Nimishankal*; ***Thurakatha Vathil***; *Abhayam*; *Nilakatha Chalanangal*; *Swapnangal*; *Kakathampurati*; ***Priya****; **1971**: *Karakanakadal*; *Line Bus*; ***Ummanchu***; ***Sindooracheppu****; *Vilakku Vangiya Veena*; *Kochaniyathi*; *Vithukal*; *Moonnupukkal*; ***Abhijathyam***; *Inquilab Zindabad*; *Sarasayya*; **1972**: *Preethi*; ***Chemparathi***; *Aradi Manninte Janmi*; *Panimudakku*; *Devi*; *Manushya Bandhangal*; *Nadan Premam*; *Pulliman*; *Ini Oru Janmam Tharu*; *Gandharvakshetram*; *Azhimukham*; *Snehadeepame Mizhi Thurakku*; ***Swayamvaram***; *Putrakameshti*; *Lakshyam*; *Teerthayatra*; *Sathi**; **1973**: ***Enippadikal***; *Thiruvabharanam*; *Udayam*; *Chenda*; *Manushya Puthran*; *Police Ariyaruthu*; *Swapnam*; *Soundarya Pooja*; *Kaadu* (Mal); *Nakhangal*; *Chukku*; *Yamini*; *Divya Darshanam*; *Thekkan Kattu*; *Madhavikutty*; *Swargaputhri*; **1974**: *Oru Pidi Ari*; *Yauvanam*; *Bhoomidevi Pushpiniyayi*; *Swarna Malsiyam*; *Manyashri Vishwamithran**; *Neela Kannukal**; *Mazhakkaru*; **1975**: *Sammanam*; *Sindhu*; *Akkaldama**; *Kamam Krodham Moham**; *Omana Kunju*; **1976**: *Dheere Sameere Yamuna Theere**; *Theekkanal**; *Amma*; *Aparadhi*; *Hridayam Oru Kshetram*; *Kanyadanam*; *Manasa Veena*; *Muthu*; *Nurayum Pathayum*; *Samasya*; *Themmadi Velappan*; *Yakshaganam*; **1977**: *A Nimisham*; *Akale Akasam*; *Itha Ivide Vare*; *Jalatarangam*; *Kaithapoova*; *Kavilamma*; *Nalumani Pookkal*; *Needhi Peedham*; *Poojakkedukatha Pookkal*; *Rowdy Rajamma*; *Santha Oru Devatha*; *Saritha*; *Vidarunna Mottugal*; *Yuddha Kandam*; *Aradhana**; **1978**: ***Agni***; *Asthamayam*; *Avar Jeevikkunu*; *Beena*; *Ee Manohara Theeram*; *Gnan Gnan Mathram*; *Ithanende Vazhi*; *Itha Oru Manushyan*; *Kanyaka*; *Randu Penkuttikal*; *Rowdy Ramu*; *Simantini*; *Snehathinte Mukhangal*; *Snehikkan Samayamilla*; *Society Lady*; *Uthrada Rathri*; *Vadagaikku Oru Hridayam*; *Yeetta*; **1979**: *Ward No. 7*; *Kaliyankattu Nili*; *Sudhikalasham*; *Edavazhiyile Pucha Mindappucha*; *Enikku Gnan Swantham*; *Hridayathinte Nirangal*; *Kayalum Kayarum*; *Krishna Parunthu*; *Simhachanam*; *Oru Ragam Pala Thalam*; *Jeevitham Oru Ganam*; *Pratiksha*; **1980**: *Pratishodh*; *Muthichippikal*; *Ambala Vilakku*; *Akalangalil Abhayam*; *Rajnigandhi*; *Ithile Vannavar*; *Meen*; *Swantham Enna Padam*; *Deepam*; *Theeram Thedunnavar*; *Vaiki Vanna Vasantham*; **1981**: *Pinneyum Pookunna Kadu*; *Arikkari Ammu*; *Dhandha Gopuram*; *Thusharam*; *Archana Teacher*; **1982**: *Kartavyam*; *Gnan Ekananu*; **1983**: *Bandham*; *Ana*; *Adhipathyam*; *Angam*; *Arabikadal*; *Kodungattu*; *Mortuary*; *Nanayam*; *Paalam*; *Passport*; *Pinninvalu*; *Rathi Layam*; *Samrambham*; *Yuddham*; **1984**: *Alakadalinakkare*; *Ariyatha Veethigal*; *Attuvanchi Ulanjappol*; *Chakkarauma*; *Edavellakku Sesham*; *Ithiri Poove Chuvannapoove*; *Jeevitham*; *Kurisuyuddham*; *Manase Ninakku Mangalam*; *Oru Painkillikatha*; ***Thirakkil Alpa Samayam***; *Vellom*; **1985**: *Ayanam*; *Chorakku Chora*; *Evide Ee Theerath*; *Guruji Oru Vakku*; *Janakeeya Kodathi*; *Kannaram Pothi Pothi*; *Katha Ithuvare*; *Orikkal Oridathu*; *Pachavelicham*; **1986**: *Oru Yuga Sandhya**; *Udayam Padinjaru**; **1988**: *Simon Peter Ninakku Vendi*; ***Aparan***; *Oozham*; *Witness*; *Athirthigal*; *Oru Sayahnathinte Swapnam*; *Unnikrishnante Adyathe Christmas**; ***Ayarthi Thollayirathi Irupathonnu***; **1989**: *Mudra*; *Devdas*; *Jathakam*; *Naduvazhigal*; *Adikkurippu**; **1990**: ***Ottayadi Paathakal***; *Mounam Sammadham**; **1991**: *Kadalora Kattu*; **1993**: *Ekalaivan*.

MADHUBALA (1933-69)

Screen name of the Hindi-Urdu actress Begum Mumtaz Jehan. Born in Delhi, she started as Baby Mumtaz at **Bombay Talkies** (***Basant***). Her first major hit was in **Kidar Sharma**'s ***Neel Kamal***, starring opposite **Raj Kapoor**, but her distinct persona was concretised in *Lal Dupatta* and in **Kamal Amrohi**'s ghost story, ***Mahal***, playing the gardener's daughter. Often acted with **Dilip Kumar**, e.g. ***Amar*** and her most famous performance as Anarkali, 'the living creation of Mughal sculptors', in ***Mughal-e-Azam***. Her most durable reputation rested on musical comedies, esp. with her husband **Kishore Kumar** (***Chalti Ka Naam Gaadi***, *Dhake Ki Malmal*, ***Half Ticket***, ***Jhumroo***) and in **Guru Dutt**'s ***Mr and Mrs '55***. Also played in **Shakti Samanta** (***Howrah Bridge***) and **Dev Anand** (***Kala Pani***) whodunits. Produced D.N. Madhok's *Naata* through her own Madhubala Co. Often nostalgically considered the greatest and most glamorous star of the 50s Hindi musical, probably because she died before she was relegated to supporting roles like **Nutan** and **Waheeda Rehman**. Had started directing *Farz Aur Ishq* just before she died.

FILMOGRAPHY: **1942**: ***Basant***; **1944**: *Mumtaz Mahal*; **1945**: *Dhanna Bhagat*; **1946**: *Phulwari*; *Pujari*; **1947**: *Khubsoorat Duniya*; ***Neel Kamal***; *Chittor Vijay*; *Dil Ki Rani*; *Mere Bhagwan*; **1948**: *Amar Prem*; *Lal Dupatta*; *Parai Aag*; **1949**: *Daulat*; *Dulari*; *Imtehan*; *Aparadhi*; ***Mahal***; *Paras*; *Neki Aur Badi*; *Singaar*; *Sipahiya*; **1950**: *Beqasoor*; *Hanste Aansoo*; *Madhubala*; *Nirala*; *Nishana*; *Pardes*; **1951**: *Aaram*; ***Badal***; *Khazana*; *Nadaan*; *Nazneen*; *Saiyan*; *Tarana*; **1952**: *Sangdil*; *Saqi*; **1953**: *Armaan*; *Rail Ka Dibba*; **1954**: ***Amar***; *Bahut Din Huye*; **1955**: ***Mr and Mrs '55***; *Naata*; *Naqab*; *Tirandaz*; **1956**: *Dhake Ki Malmal*; *Rajhaath*; *Shirin Farhad*; **1957**: *Ek Saal*; *Yahudi Ki Ladki*; *Gateway of India*; **1958**: *Baghi Sipahi*; ***Chalti Ka Naam Gaadi***; ***Howrah Bridge***; ***Kala Pani***; *Phagun*; *Police*; **1959**: *Do Ustad*; *Insaan Jaag Utha*; *Kal Hamara Hai*; **1960**: *Barsaat Ki Raat*; ***Jaali Note***; *Mehlon Ke Khwab*; ***Mughal-e-Azam***; **1961**: *Boy Friend*; ***Jhumroo***; *Passport*; **1962**: ***Half Ticket***; **1964**: *Sharabi*; **1970**: *Jwala*.

MAHAPATRA, MANMOHAN (b. 1951)

First Oriya art-house director; later made ruralist melodramas. Graduate from Utkal University, then from the **FTII** (1975). Début feature was a critical success, establishing the landscape of feudal Orissa as the setting for most of his films. His most acclaimed films are ***Neerab Jhada*** and ***Klanta Aparanha***. Early films present a bleak and cynically tragic view which, according to the director, emanates from local conditions, although the cinematic idiom deployed is similar to that of the Assamese director **Bhabendranath Saikia**.

FILMOGRAPHY: **1975**: *Anti-Memoirs* (Sh); **1982**: ***Seeta Raati***; *Voices of Silence* (Sh); **1983**: *Konarak: The Sun Temple* (Sh); **1984**: ***Neerab Jhada***; **1985**: ***Klanta Aparanha***; **1986**: *Trisandhya*; *Kuhuri*; **1987**: *Majib Pahacha*; **1988**: *Kichu Smriti Kichu Anubhooti*; **1989**: *Andha Diganta*.

Madhubala and Raj Kapoor in *Do Ustad* (1959)

MAHAPATRA, NIRAD

Oriya director born in Bhadrak. Educated in Bhubaneshwar. Interrupted his studies in political science to attend the **FTII**. Graduated (1971) and returned to Orissa but found no opportunity to make films. Lectured at the FTII (1972-4). Writer and film society organiser in Pune, Bombay and Orissa. Editor of Oriya film journal, *Mana Phasal*. Returned to live in Bhubaneshwar. The tv film *Tamasa Tire* (1989), although supervised in every respect by Nirad Mahapatra, was credited to his brother Sampad who used the pseudonym Pachajanya.

FILMOGRAPHY: **1971**: *Sunmica* (Sh); *Confrontation* (Doc); **1975**: *Dhauligiri Shantistupa* (Sh); **1978**: *The Story of Cement* (Doc); **1983**: ***Maya Miriga***; **1986**: *Chhau Dances of Mayurbhanj* (Doc); **1987**: *Pat Paintings of Orissa* (Doc).

MAHARASHTRA FILM COMPANY

Set up in 1917 by **Baburao Painter** in Kolhapur with a home-made camera, initial capital of Rs 15,000 from Tanibai Kagalkar and a dedicated team of disciples. Their first successful production was ***Sairandhri*** (1919), eliciting praise from B.G. Tilak. Sardar Nesrikar persuaded the Shahu Maharaj to give him land, an electric generator and equipment. A contemporary of **Phalke**'s **Hindustan Film**, Maharashtra Film made a greater impact on the Marathi cinema with the first films of **V. Shantaram** (*Netaji Palkar*, 1927), **Damle-Fattelal** (*Maharathi Karna*, 1928) and **Bhalji Pendharkar** (*Rani Rupmati*, 1931). After 26 films, the studio lost Shantaram, Damle, Fattelal and **Baburao Pendharkar** who set up **Prabhat** in 1929. Painter left in 1930 and joined Shalini Cinetone, set up for him by the Kolhapur royal family. The company closed in 1932 after some expensive disasters: **Moti Gidwani**'s *Nisha Sundari* (1929) and Baburao Patel's *Kismet* (1932).

MAHENDRA, BALU (b. 1946)

Tamil cameraman and director, born in Sri Lanka as Benjamin Mahendra. Son of a college professor. Voracious film viewer; developed an early interest in photography. Graduated from London University and from the **FTII** (1969) as cinematographer, going on to shoot *Nellu* (1974) for **Kariat**. Pioneered innovative camera style in South India. Worked mainly in the Malayalam avant-garde shooting films for **Sethumadhavan** and **P.N. Menon**, Telugu directors **Bapu** and **K. Vishwanath** and Tamil director **J. Mahendran**. Made his first film in Kannada (*Kokila*); later work mainly in Malayalam and Tamil. Regards his Malayalam films, made with greater freedom in a less demanding economic system, as his personal work. Pioneered a new brand of Tamil art cinema. Films have a strong literary base but rely on sharply defined visuals, sparse dialogue and few characters. His moral tales are often concerned with the status of women (*Kokila*), the aged (***Sandhya Ragam***), sexual violence (his most famous film, ***Moondram Pirai***) or bureaucracy (***Veedu***). Although he claims an affiliation with the realism of De Sica and **Satyajit Ray**, film-maker and critic K. Hariharan points to similarities with the French New Wave's fascination with the American cinema from which Mahendra borrowed themes and stylistic devices: *Moodupani* was based on *Psycho* (1960); *Olangal* borrows from Dick Richards' *Man, Woman and Child* (1982); *Irattaival Kuruvi* is based partly on Blake Edwards's *Micki and Maude* (1984) and *Azhiyada Kolangal* borrows from *Summer of '42* (1971). The emphasis on psychological realism at times combines with popular elements such as calendar art and novelettes (e.g. the climactic scene of *Moondram Pirai*). Writes, edits and shoots own films as well as closely controlling make-up, costumes, etc.

FILMOGRAPHY: **1977**: *Kokila*; **1979**: *Azhiyada Kolangal*; **1980**: *Moodupani*; *Manju Moodal Manju*; **1982**: ***Moondram Pirai***; *Nireekshana*; *Olangal*; **1983**: *Sadma*; *Oomakuyil*; **1984**: *Neengal Kettavai*; **1985**: *Un Kannil Neer Vazhindal*; ***Yathra***; **1987**: *Rendu Thokala Titta*; *Irattaival Kuruvi*; ***Veedu***; **1989**: ***Sandhya Ragam***; **1991**: *Vanna Vanna Pookkal*; **1992**: *Chakravyuham*; **1993**: *Marupadiyam*.

MAHENDRAN, J. (b. 1939)

Popular 80s Tamil playwright and director, originally J. Alexander; born in Madras. Graduated from Madras University. Assistant editor of Cho Ramaswamy's political fortnightly *Tughlaq*; author of stage hits *Thanga Padakkam* and *Rishimoolam* (1978). His story *Sivakamyin Selvan* was filmed by C.V. Rajendran (1974). Script début adapting *Thanga Padakkam*, filmed by P. Madhavan (1974). Assisted director A. Kasilingam. First film: ***Mullum Malarum***, shot by **Balu Mahendra** from a story by Umachandran in which hero **Rajnikant** exerts an infantile domination over his sister's life. Early work, including adaptations from Tamil literature (e.g. *Udhiri Pookal* is based on Pudumaipithan's story *Citrannai*), often portrayed women facing loveless marriages (cf *Puttadha Poothukkal*, in which a married woman has an affair and gets pregnant, her child being accepted by her impotent husband).

FILMOGRAPHY: **1978**: ***Mullum Malarum***; **1979**: *Udhiri Pookal*; *Puttadha Poothukkal*; **1980**: *Nenjathai Killathey*; *Johnny*; **1981**: *Nandu*; **1982**: *Azhagiya Kanney*; *Metti*; **1984**: *Kayi Kodukkum Kayi*; **1986**: *Kannukku Mai Ezhuthu*; **1992**: *Oor Panjayathu*.

MAJID, ABDUL (b. 1932)

Assamese director. Started as playwright with *Banchita*, *Dhuli Makoti*, *Char*, *Sihat Ahise*, *Chor* et al. Entered films as actor in **Nip Barua**'s ***Ranga Police*** (1958). Produced, wrote and directed his films, acting in c.25. Best-known film: *Chameli Memsaab*, deploying a staid narrative progression weaving romance into clearly defined themes.

FILMOGRAPHY: **1968**: *Maram Trishna*; **1975**: *Chameli Memsaab*; **1977**: *Banahansa*; **1978**: *Banjui*; **1981**: *Ponakan*; **1990**: *Uttarkaal*.

MAJUMDAR, NAGENDRA (b. 1894)

Hindi director and actor born and educated in Baroda, Gujarat. Employed as a policeman in Baroda, he became involved in the amateur theatre (1923-5) and directed Gujarati plays. Made his début at the Royal Art Studio, then joined Laxmi Films, completing *Khada Na Khel* when **Manilal Joshi** died. Directed some **Indulal Yagnik** productions (*Kalina Ekka*, *Rasili Rani*), worked at **Imperial** directing *Qatil Kathiyani* and at the Kaiser-e-Hind Studio. Made several love stories at **Ranjit** with the studio's leading stars E. Bilimoria and Madhuri. His sound films are mainly in the stunt genre, adapting *Arabian Nights*-type adventures, but he also made some Marathi films such as the historical *Shatakarta Shivaji*. Set up Pratima Pics (1933) and Honey Talkies (1934). Scripted K.B. Athavale's *Sant Tukaram* at **Sharda Movietone** (1932). Illness forced him to retire. His son Ninu Majumdar became a film composer.

FILMOGRAPHY: **1925**: *Ra Navghan*; *Yashodevi*; **1926**: *Panima Aag*; **1927**: *Khada Na Khel*; **1928**: *Amrit Ki Zaher*; *Goddess Mahakali*; *Punarlagnani Patni*; *Qatil Kathiyani*; *Vasavadatta*; **1929**: *Jayant*; **1930**: *Albelo Sawar*; *Jagmagti Jawani*; *Kalina Ekka*; *Khandana Khel*; *Rasili Rani*; **1931**: *Diwano*; *Gwalan*; *Kashmir Nu Gulab*; *Premi Pankhida*; **1932**: *Bahuroopi Bazaar*; *Khubsoorat Khawasan*; *Matrubhoomi*; *Rangilo Rajput* (all St); *Raas Vilas*; **1933**: *Mirza Sahiban*; *Patit Pawan*; **1934**: *Kala Wagh*; *Mera Imaan*; *Shatakarta Shivaji*; **1935**: *Alladdin-II*; *Rangila Nawab*; **1936**: *Kimiagar*; **1937**: *Laheri Lutera*; **1946**: *Swadesh Seva*; *Talwarwala*.

MAJUMDAR, PHANI (1911-94)

Hindi and Bengali director born in Faridpur (now Bangladesh). Also worked in other languages. Graduated from Carmichael College (1930); worked as a typist. Employed by **P.C. Barua** (1931-7) as stenographer and later as assistant director and scenarist for ***Mukti*** (1937). Also scripted Prafulla Roy's ***Abhigyan*** (1938). First film: ***Street Singer***, a big **New Theatres** hit which added a new dimension to the **K.L. Saigal** persona initially moulded by Barua. **Kanan Devi** is the female lead and **Rai Chand Boral**'s music included Saigal's biggest hit song, *Babul Mora*. *Doctor* is based on a **Sailajananda Mukherjee** story and scored by **Pankaj Mullick**. Moved to Bombay (1941) and worked at Laxmi Prod. making musicals with **Suraiya** (*Tamanna*), **Shanta Apte** (***Mohabbat***) and his regular collaborator, **K.C. Dey**. Associated with New Maharashtra Film as producer; also made films at **Bombay Talkies**, at **Ranjit** and as a freelancer. Late 40s work became more 'socially conscious'(*Insaaf*, *Hum Bhi Insaan Hain*, ***Andolan***). ***Baadbaan*** is the last film of Bombay Talkies, financed by the studio's employees in an attempt to stave off bankruptcy. Like **Balkrishna Narayan Rao**, he made several features for Shaws Malay Film Prod. (1956-9) in Singapore, starring e.g. the singer P. Ramlee in *Hang Tuah*, one of the earliest Malay colour features, and in *Kaseh Sayang*, a successful war movie about the Japanese invasion; also made *Long House/Rumah Panjang*, an English-Malay bilingual about Borneo headhunters shot on location, and his last film before returning to India, *Circus*, a Chinese-Malay bilingual. The prominent Malaysian film-maker Jamil Sulong assisted Majumdar on 6 of the 8 films. Later wrote the travelogue *Borneo Ke Naramund Shikari* (1983). Also made films in less familiar Indian languages: Magadhi (*Bhaiya*) and Maithili (*Kanyadaan*), having already made a Punjabi film (*Chambe Di Kali*) while still in Calcutta. Also made several documentaries and children's shorts, such as *Saral Biswas* based on a **Tagore** poem, *Veer Purush* and tv series such as *Bulbul* and the 52-episode *Our India* (1993). Best-known films include *Tamasha* and *Baadbaan*, starring **Ashok Kumar**. Script credits include Sharan Agarwal's *Pratima Aur Payal* (1977) and Raghunath Jhalani's *Badalte Rishte* (1978).

FILMOGRAPHY: **1938**: ***Street Singer/Saathi***; **1939**: *Kapal Kundala*; **1940**: *Doctor*; **1941**: *Chambe Di Kali*; **1942**: *Aparadh*; *Tamanna*; **1943**: ***Mohabbat***; **1944**: *Meena*; **1945**: *Devadasi*; **1946**: *Door Chalein*; *Insaaf*; **1948**: *Hum Bhi Insaan Hain*; **1951**: ***Andolan***; **1952**: *Goonj*; *Tamasha*; **1954**: ***Baadbaan***; *Dhobi Doctor*; *Two Worlds* (Doc); **1955**: *Faraar*; **1955**: *Hang Tuah*; **1956**: *Anakku Sazali*; **1957**: *Kaseh Sayang*; *Long House/Rumah Panjang*; **1958**: *Masyarakat Pincang*; *Sri Menanti*; *Doctor*; **1959**: *Circus*; *Saral Biswas*; **1960**: *Veer Purush*; **1961**: *Bhaiya*; *Savitri*; **1962**: *Aarti*; **1965**: *Birthday*; *Akashdeep*; ***Oonche Log***; *Kanyadaan*; *Mamata*; **1966**: *Toofan Mein Pyar Kahan*; **1968**: *Apna Ghar Apni Kahani*; **1969**: *Munna*; **1975**: *Shri Aurobindo*: *Glimpses of His Life* (Doc/3 parts); **1989**: *Babul*; **1990**: *Fire* (Sh); *Common Accidents* (Doc).

MAJUMDAR, SUSHIL (1906-88)

Bengali and Hindi director born in Komilla, Tripura (now Bangladesh). Educated at Shantiniketan (1911-21) and at Kashi Vidyapeeth, Benares, and studied engineering at Jadavpur. Participated in non-co-operation agitations (1922). Actor for the amateur University Institute theatre group, then in the **Calcutta Theatres** stage company Manmohan Theatres (1927). Manager of touring company in Chittagong and actor in the silent Bengali film *Komilla*. Joined Bengal Movie & Talkie Film (e.g. *Jeevan Prabhat*), and then **P.C. Barua**'s studio (1930). Acted in Barua's short comedy *Ekada*, for which he is sometimes credited with co-direction, and **Debaki Bose**'s *Aparadhi* and *Nishir Dak*. Early work strongly influenced by Calcutta theatres' stage conventions (e.g. *Tarubala*), but also moved into new directions, e.g. *Muktisnan*'s depiction of political corruption. Later work, esp. Tulsi Lahiri's scripts, moved closer to **IPTA**-influenced film (*Dukhir Iman*). The only Bengali director from the 30s to retain his popularity for over 40 years, e.g. with the **Ashok Kumar** starrer, ***Hospital***, and one of **Uttam Kumar**'s best-known performances in *Lal Patthar*. His *Rikta* was re-edited and reissued in 1960. Turned producer with *Digbhranta*.

FILMOGRAPHY (* also act/** act only): **1929**: *Komilla***; **1931**: *Jeevan Prabhat***; *Aparadhi***; **1932**: *Nishir Dak***; *Ekada** (all St); *Bengal 1983***; **1936**: *Tarubala*; **1937**: *Muktisnan*; *Basanti Purnima*; **1939**: *Rikta**; **1940**: *Tatinir Bichar*; *Abhinav***; **1941**: *Pratishodh*; **1942**: *Avayer Biye*; **1943**: ***Jogajog/Hospital***; **1944**: *Char Aankhen*; **1945**: *Begum*; **1947**: *Abhijog**; **1948**: *Soldier's Dream*; *Sarbahara*; **1950**: *Digbhranta**; **1952**: *Ratrir Tapasya*; **1954**: *Moner Mayur*; *Dukhir Iman**; *Bhangagara*; **1955**: *Aparadhi*; **1956**: *Shubharatri*; *Daner Maryada*; **1957**: *Shesh Parichaya*; **1958**: *Marmabani*; **1959**: *Pushpadhanu*; *Agnisambhaba*; **1960**: ***Hospital****; **1961**: *Kathin Maya*; **1962**: *Sancharini*; **1964**: *Kaalsrote*; *Lal Patthar**; **1966**: *Dolgobinder Karcha***; **1969**: *Shuk Sari*; **1971**: *Lal Patthar**.

MAJUMDAR, TARUN (b. 1932)

Bengali director born in Bogra, now Bangladesh. Moved to Calcutta in 1946. Trained as a scientist. Assistant director at Rupasree Studio (1952-9), then made advertising films. Début with **Kanan Devi**'s film unit. Formed the Yatrik Film collective with Dilip Mukherjee and Sachin Mukherjee (1959-63, including his first four films). His *Palatak*, credited to Yatrik and produced by **V. Shantaram**, marked the comedian **Anup Kumar**'s change to a heroic image. The film was remade in Hindi as *Rahgir*. With his best-known film, the romantic musical *Balika Bodhu*, revitalised the genre of the rustic lyrical melodrama assisted by **Hemanta Mukherjee**'s music. Made some 70s hits such as *Nimantran*, *Phuleshwari* and a Hindi remake of *Balika Bodhu*, causing a renewed 80s interest in the theme of the country-city divide as representing a conflict of morality, with ***Dadar Kirti***. It has, however, proved unsuccessful with later films, e.g. *Parasmoni*, *Agaman* et al. Changed genre for the **Rajen Tarafdar**-scripted ***Sansar Simantey***. One of the last commercial Bengali directors to trace his ancestry to **Debaki Bose**, **P.C. Barua**, **Bimal Roy** and 50s art-house cinema (cf **Tapan Sinha**) rooted in popular Bengali literature: e.g. ***Ganadevata***, based on a Tarashankar Bannerjee novel.

FILMOGRAPHY: **1959**: *Chaowa-Pawa*; **1960**: *Smriti Tuku Thak*; **1962**: *Kancher Swarga*; **1963**: *Palatak*; **1965**: *Alor Pipasa*; *Ek Tuku Basa*; **1967**: *Balika Bodhu*; **1969**: *Rahgir*; **1971**: *Nimantran*; **1972**: *Shriman Prithviraj*; **1974**: *Phuleshwari*; *Thagini*; **1975**: ***Sansar Simantey***; **1976**: *Balika Badhu*; **1978**: ***Ganadevata***; **1980**: ***Dadar Kirti***; **1981**: *Shahar Theke Dooray*; *Meghmukti*; *Khelar Putul*; **1983**: *Amar Geeti*; **1985**: *Bhalobasha Bhalobasha*; *Aranya Amar* (Doc); **1986**: *Pathbhola*; **1988**: *Parasmoni*; *Agaman*; **1990**: *Apon Amar Apon*; **1991**: *Path-o-Prasad*; *Sajani Go Sajani*.

MALAYIL, SIBI

Successful Malayalam director. Started as assistant in Appachan's Navodaya Studio and became a director in 1985.

FILMOGRAPHY: **1985**: *Mutharamkunnu P.O.*; **1986**: *Chekkaran Oru Chilla*; *Doore Doore Koodu Kottam*; **1987**: *Ezhuthapurangal*; *Thaniyavartanam*; **1988**: *August 1*; *Mudra*; *Vicharana*; **1989**: *Dasharatham*; *Kireedam*; **1990**: *His Highness Abdullah*; *Radha Madhavan*; *Kshanakathu*; *Parampara*; *Adhipathi*; **1991**: *Bharatam*; *Dhanam*; **1992**: *Sadayam*; *Kamalathalam*; *Valayam*; **1993**: *Maya Mayuram*; *Akshadhoodu*.

MALINI, HEMA (b. 1948)

Hindi star born in Madras. After **Vyjayanthimala**, Hema Malini is only the second major South Indian actress to become successful in Hindi films. Like her predecessor, she was trained in Bharat Natyam dance. Starring début with **Raj Kapoor** in *Sapnon Ka Saudagar*. Received top billing for her double role in **Ramesh Sippy**'s *Seeta Aur Geeta*. Established herself mainly in Pramod Chakravarty films (e.g. *Naya Zamana*) which promoted her as a 70s 'dream girl' (cf the title of Chakravarty's 1977 film with her). Associated in this period mainly with crime thrillers and love stories starring opposite **Dev Anand** (e.g. the hit ***Johnny Mera Naam*** followed by ***Tere Mere Sapne***, *Chhupa Rustom*, *Amir Garib*) and **Dharmendra** (*Tum Haseen Main Jawan*, the epic ***Sholay***). Tried to change her glamorous image via **Gulzar**'s lyrically realist films (*Kinara*, *Khushboo* and in the title role of the saint film *Meera*) and then in **Basu Chatterjee**'s art-house movie which she produced, ***Swami***. Cast opposite **Bachchan** in the late 70s (***Trishul***, ***Naseeb***, *Satte Pe Satta*). Then concentrated on 'character' roles, often with feminist undertones (e.g. ***Rihaee***). The tv series *Noopur*, which she directed, was designed to re-establish her as a classical dancer, playing a female star who abandons her career to return to her guru in Tanjore. Also directed *Dil Ashna Hai*. Married to Dharmendra.

FILMOGRAPHY (* also d): **1968**: *Sapnon Ka Saudagar*; **1969**: *Jahan Pyar Mile*; *Waris*; **1970**: *Abhinetri*; *Aansoo Aur Muskaan*; ***Johnny Mera Naam***; *Sharafat*; *Tum Haseen Main Jawan*; **1971**: ***Andaz***; *Lal Patthar*; *Naya Zamana*; *Paraya Dhan*; ***Tere Mere Sapne***; **1972**: *Babul Ki Galiyan*; *Bhai Ho To Aisa*; *Gora Aur Kala*; *Raja Jani*; *Seeta Aur Geeta*; **1973**: *Chhupa Rustom*; *Gehri Chaal*; *Joshila*; *Jugnu*; *Shareef Badmash*; **1974**: *Amir Garib*; *Dost*; *Dulhan*; *Haath Ki Safai*; *Kasauti*; *Kunwara Baap*; *Patthar Aur Payal*; *Prem Nagar*; **1975**: *Dharmatma*; *Do Thug*; *Kehte Hain Mujhko Raja*; *Khushboo*; *Mrig Trishna*; *Pratigya*; *Sanyasi*; ***Sholay***; *Sunehra Sansar*; **1976**: *Aap Beeti*; *Charas*; *Das Numbri*; *Ginny Aur Johnny*; *Jaaneman*; *Maa*; *Mehbooba*; *Naach Utha Sansar*; *Sharafat Chhod Di Maine*; **1977**: *Chacha Bhatija*; *Chala Murari Hero Banne*; *Dhoop Chhaon*; *Dream Girl*; *Kinara*; *Palkon Ki Chhaon Mein*; *Shirdi Ke Sai Baba*; ***Swami***; *Tinku*; **1978**: *Azad*; *Apna Khoon*; *Cinema Cinema*; *Dillagi*; ***Trishul***; **1979**: *Dil Ka Heera*; *Hum Tere Aashiq Hain*; *Janata Havaldar*; *Meera*; *Ratnadeep*; **1980**: *Aas Paas*; *Alibaba Aur Chalis Chor*; *Bandish*; *Do Aur Do Paanch*; *The Burning Train*; **1981**: *Dard*; *Jyoti*; *Kranti*; *Krodhi*; *Kudrat*; *Maan Gaye Ustad*; *Meri Awaaz Suno*; ***Naseeb***; *Satte Pe Satta*; **1982**: *Baghavat*; *Desh Premi*; *Do Dishayen*; *Justice Choudhury*; *Farz Aur Kanoon*; *Meharbani*; *Rajput*; *Samrat*; *Suraag*; **1983**: *Andha Kanoon*; *Babu*; *Ek Naya Itihaas*; *Nastik*; *Razia Sultan*; *Taqdeer*; **1984**: *Durga*; *Ek Nai Paheli*; *Hum Dono*; *Phaansi Ke Baad*; *Qaidi*; *Raj Tilak*; *Ram Tera Desh*; *Sharara*; **1985**: *Aandhi Toofan*; *Ramkali*; *Yudh*; **1986**: *Anjaam*; *Ek Chadar Maili Si*; **1987**: *Apne Apne*; *Hirasat*; *Jaan Hatheli Pe*; *Kudrat Ka Kanoon*; *Seetapur Ki Geeta*; **1988**: *Mohabbat Ke Dushman*; *Mulzim*; ***Rihaee***; *Tohfa Mohabbat Ka*; *Vijay*; **1989**: *Desh Ke Dushman*;

Deshwasi; *Galiyon Ka Badshah*; *Paap Ka Ant*; *Sachche Ka Bol Bala*; *Santosh*; **1990**: *Jamai Raja*; ***Lekin ...***; *Shadayantra*; *Noopur** (TV); **1991**: *Dil Ashna Hai**; *Hai Meri Jaan*; *Indira*; **1992**: *Aman Ke Farishte*; *Marg*.

MALVANKAR, DAMUANNA (1893-1975)

Portly Marathi comedian with a squint. Started in **Keshavrao Date**'s 'naturalist' Maharashtra Natak Mandali. Worked with the **Sangeet Natak** group, Balwant Sangeet Mandali, and entered cinema when they moved into film with **Bedekar**. His major films were with **Vinayak** and **Atre**, playing the caricature of a Marathi gentleman (***Brandichi Batli/Brandy Ki Botal, Brahmachari***). His image became identified with the part of Chimanrao, the middle-aged householder of C.V. Joshi's political satires, partnered by Vishnupant Jog's Gundyabhau (***Lagna Pahave Karun, Sarkari Pahune***). They remained partners for many years. Other directors filmed Joshi stories with them (e.g. **Raja Thakur**'s *Gharcha Jhala Thoda*) but never with **Vinayak**'s incisiveness. Malvankar went on to play many stereotyped character parts, usually as the foil to the lead actor, and one major 'serious' role, the lead character of *Gajabhau*.

FILMOGRAPHY: 1934: *Krishnarjun Yuddha*; **1935**: ***Thakicha Lagna***; *Satteche Prayog*; **1936**: *Pundalik*; *Andheri Duniya*; **1938**: ***Brahmachari***; *Lakshmiche Khel*; **1939**: ***Brandichi Batli/Brandy Ki Botal***; ***Devata***; *Sukhacha Shodh/Mera Haq*; **1940**: ***Ardhangi/Ghar Ki Rani***; ***Lagna Pahave Karun***; **1941**: ***Amrit***; *Gharjavai*; *Sangam*; **1942**: *Tuzhach*; ***Pahili Mangalagaur***; ***Sarkari Pahune***; **1943**: *Chimukla Sansar*; ***Mazhe Bal***; **1944**: *Gajabhau*; **1945**: ***Badi Maa***; **1946**: ***Jeevan Yatra***; ***Subhadra***; **1947**: *Chul Ani Mul*; *Main Tera Hoon*; **1948**: *Moruchi Mavshi*; **1949**: *Brahma Ghotala*; *Galyachi Shapath*; *Sakharpuda*; **1950**: *Baiko Pahije*; *Chalitil Shejari*; *Dev Pavla*; ***Ram Ram Pahuna***; **1952**: *Devacha Kaul*; **1954**: *Purshachi Jaat*; *Taraka*; **1955**: *Varaat*; *Ye Re Majhya Maglya*; **1956**: *Vakda Paool*; **1957**: *Pahila Prem*; *Gharcha Jhala Thoda*; *Jhakli Mooth*; **1958**: *Choravar Mor*; *Dhakti Jau*; *Don Ghadicha Dav*; *Guruchi Vidya Gurula?*; *Raja Gosavichi Goshta*; **1959**: *Satajanmacha Sobti*; *Pativrata*; *Rajmanya Rajashri*; *Yala Jeevan Aise Nav*; **1960**: *Avaghachi Sansar*; *Lagnala Jato Mi*; *Paishyacha Paoos*; *Sangat Jadli Tujhi An Majhi*; *Duniya Jhukti Hai*; *Vanakesari*; **1961**: *Ek Dhaga Sukhacha*; *Matlabi Duniya*; **1962**: *Baap Mazha Brahmachari*; *Bhagya Lakshmi*; *Char Divas Sasuche Char Divas Suneche*; *Drishti Jagachi Aahe Nirali*; *Gariba Gharchi Lek*; *Nandadeep*; *Preeti Vivah*; *Saptapadi*; *Sonyachi Paoole*; *Varadakshina*; **1963**: *Pahu Re Kiti Vaat!*; *Vaibhav*; **1964**: *Vaat Chuklele Navre*; **1965**: *Kama Purta Mama*; *Sudharlelya Baika*; **1966**: *Chala Utha Lagna Kara*; **1967**: *Chimukla Pahuna*; *Daiva Janile Kuni*; *Shrimant Mehuna Pahije*; *Sukhi Sansar*; **1968**: *Bai Mothi Bhagyachi*; *Mangalsutra*; **1970**: *Ti Mi Navhech*; **1971**: *Bahaklela Brahmachari*; *Bhagyavati Mi Hya Sansari*; *Mihi Manoosach Aahe*.

MAMMOOTTY (b. 1953)

Malayalam star of the 80s. Born Mohammed Kutty in Chembu. Former lawyer practising in Manjiri. Discovered by the writer-director **M.T. Vasudevan Nair**, who cast him in a small role in the unfinished *Devalokam*. Formal début in *Vilkannudu Swapnangal* and *Mela*. Was associated in the early 80s mainly with low-budget art-house films, e.g. ***Akkare, Koodevide?, Lekhayude Maranam Oru Flashback***. Together with a new generation of directors like **I.V. Sasi** (***America America***; ***Alkoottathil Thaniye***; ***Angadikkapurathu***; ***Ayarthi Thollayirathi Irupathonnu***), Jesey (***Akalathe Ambili***), P.G. Vishwambaran (***Sagaram Shantham***) et al., he signalled a new era in Malayalam cinema after **Sathyan** and **Prem Nazir**'s work of the 70s. The 80s in Kerala are marked by the 'Gulf money' remitted by expatriate workers, spawning a 'newly rich' consumerist sector and fostering a lumpenised urban mass culture. Mammootty's films, like those of the other main star in Kerala, **Mohanlal**, were often financed by 'Gulf money' and played to the new audience of Gulf migrants. His best-known films repeatedly feature the hero as victim in violent vendetta stories (often with explicit caste overtones), evoking political and economic corruption and condemning the good hero either to cultural exile or to a violent death while defending his and his kinfolk's honour. Dislocations within Kerala's culture give new, local meanings to vigilante figures modelled on e.g. Bronson or Eastwood. Unlike **Bachchan**'s vigilante roles of the early 70s, Mammooty's films stress religion and caste (he often plays a Christian or a Muslim, while his oppressors are often from the Nair community) and have a tragic ending. Classic roles include the forest conservator in ***Yathra***, the misunderstood Kalaripayattu martial-arts exponent in ***Oru Vadakkan Veeragatha***, the Moplah freedom fighter in *Ayarthi Thollayirathi Irupathonnu* and his cop roles in ***Oru CBI Diary Kuruppu*** and ***Avanazhi***. His reputation spread beyond Kerala with **Adoor Gopalakrishnan**'s ***Anantaram*** and ***Mathilukal*** (playing the Malayalam writer Vaikom Mohammed Basheer in the latter film). Published his autobiography: *Chamayangalillathe*.

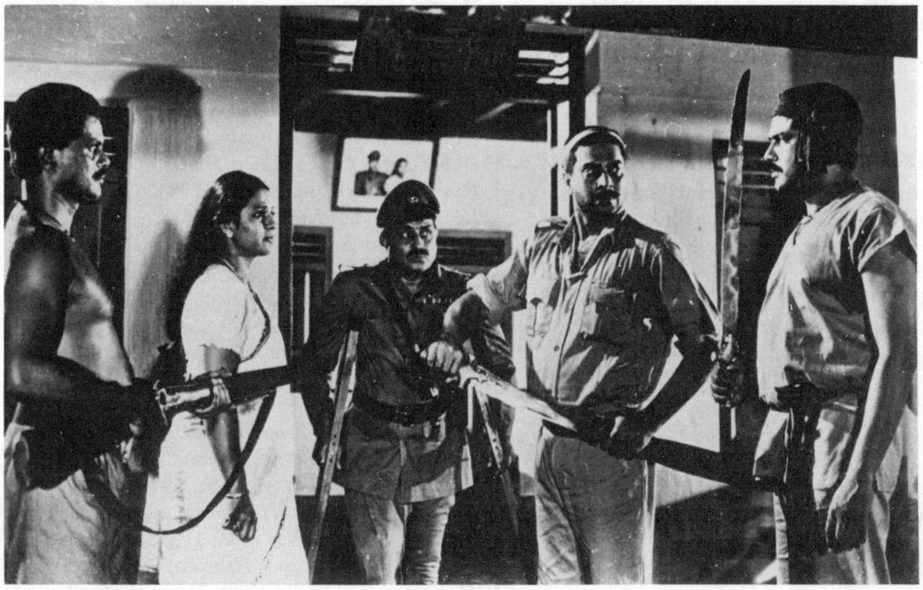
Mammootty (2nd from right) in *Ayarthi Thollayirathi Irupathonnu* (1988)

FILMOGRAPHY: 1980: *Vilkannudu Swapnangal*; *Mela*; **1981**: *Trishna*; **1982**: ***Ee Nadu***; *Thadagam*; *Pooviriyum Pulari*; ***Yavanika***; **1983**: ***Adaminte Variyellu***; *A Rathri*; ***Akkare***; ***America America***; *Asthram*; *Chakravalam Chuvannapol*; ***Chengathem***; ***Coolie*** (Mal); *Eettillam*; *Ente Katha*; *Guru Dakshina*; *Himavahini*; ***Iniyenkilum***; *Kattaruvi*; *Kodungattu*; ***Koodevide?***; ***Lekhayude Maranam Oru Flashback***; *Manasi Oru Mahasamudram*; *Maniyara*; *Nadhi Muthal Nadhi Vare*; *Nanayam*; *Onnu Chirikku*; *Oru Madaupravinte Katha*; *Oru Mugham Pala Mugham*; *Oru Swakariam*; *Pinninvalu*; *Pratigna*; ***Rachana***; *Rukma*; ***Sagaram Shantham***; *Sandhyakku Virinja Poovu*; *Sesham Kazhchayil*; *Theeram Thedunna Thira*; *Visa*; **1984**: ***Alkoottathil Thaniye***; *Ayiram Abhilashangal*; *Adiyozhukkukal*; *Aksharangal*; *Alakadalinakkare*; *Anthi Chuvappu*; *Ariyatha Veethigal*; *Arorumariyathe*; *Athirathnam*; *Attuvanchi Ulanjappol*; *Chakkarauma*; *Edavellakku Sesham*; *Enganeundasane*; *Ente Upasana*; *Etha Ennumuthal*; *Ethirpukkal*; *Ithiri Poove Chuvannapoove*; ***Kaanamarayathu***; *Kodathi*; *Koottinilangili*; ***Lakshmana Rekha***; *Mangalam Nerunne*; *Manithali*; *Onnanu Nammal*; *Onnum Mindatha Bharya*; *Oru Kochu Katha Arum Parayatha Katha*; *Pavam Poornima*; *Sandhyakenthinu Sindhuram*; *Sannarbham*; ***Thirakkil Alpa Samayam***; *Veendum Chalikunna Chakram*; *Vettah*; *Vikatakavi*; **1985**: *A Neram Alpa Dooram*; ***Akalathe Ambili***; ***Angadikkapurathu***; *Anubandham*; *Arappatta Kettiya Gramathil*; *Avidathepole Ivideyum*; *Ayanam*; *Ee Lokam Ivide Kure Manushyar*; *Eeran Sandhya*; *Ee Shabdam Ennathe Shabdam*; *Ee Thalanil Ithirineram*; *Ente Kannakuyil*; *Ida Nilangal*; *Iniyum Katha Thudarum*; *Kanathaya Pennkutty*; *Kandu Kandarinju*; *Karimbin Poovinakkare*; *Katha Ithuvare*; *Kathodu Kathoram*; *Kochuthemmadi*; *Makan Ente Makan*; *Manya Mahajanangale*; ***Muhurtam At 11.30***; *Neram Pularumbol*; *Nirakkootte*; *Oduvil Kittiya Vartha*; *Onningu Vannengil*; *Oru Nokku Kannan*; *Oru Sandesha Koodi*; *Parayanumvayya Parayathirikkanumvayya*; *Puli Varunne Puli*; *Puzhayozhukum Vazhi*; *Thammil Thammil*; ***Thinkalazhcha Nalla Divasam***; *Upaharam*; *Vilichu Vilikettu*; ***Yathra***; **1986**: ***Avanazhi***; *Oru Katha Oru Nunakkatha*; *Ithile Iniyum Varum*; *Pranamam*; *Shyama*; *Alorungi Arangorungi*; ***Vartha***; *Kariyila Kattu Pole*; *Malarum Kiliyum*; *Padayani*; *Poovinnu Puthiya Poonthennal*; ***Gandhinagar 2nd Street***;

Prathyekam Sradhikkuka; *Shaminchu Ennoruvakku*; *Poomugappadiyil Ninneyum Kathu*; *Rakkuyilin Rajassadasil*; *Alorungi Arangorungi*; **1987**: *Kathakku Pinnil*; *Nombarathi Poovu*; *Adimagal Udumagal*; *Athinumappuram*; *New Delhi*; *Thaniyavartanam*; *Manivathoorile Ayiram Sivarathrikal*; *Ankiliyude Tharattu*; ***Anantaram***; *Nalkawala*; **1988**: *Vicharana*; *Dinarathrangal*; ***Oru CBI Diary Kuruppu***; *Manu Uncle*; *Abkari*; *Sangham*; *Mattoral*; *August 1*; ***Ayarthi Thollayirathi Irupathonnu***; *Thanthram*; *Mukti*; *Shankhanadam*; **1989**: *Charithram*; *Mudra*; *Adikkurippu*; *Uttaram*; ***Oru Vadakkan Veeragatha***; *Jagratha*; *Artham*; *Carnival*; *Nair Saab*; *Mahayanam*; ***Mathilukal***; **1990**: *Triyatri*; *Mounam Sammadham*; *Adhipathi*; **1991**: *Swati Kiranam*; *Dalapathi*; *Amaram*; *Nayam Vethamakkunnu*; *Inspector Balram*; *Adhayalam*; *Kanal Katru*; *Anaswaram*; *Neelagiri*; **1992**: *Gauravar*; *Johnny Walker*; *Suryamanasam*; *Papayude Sontham Appoose*; *Kizhakkan Pathrose*; *Dhruvam*; *Ayirappara*; **1993**: *Vatsalyam*; *Jackpot*; *Sarovaram*; *Kilipetchu Ketkava*; *Dhartiputra*; *Padhayam*.

MANE, ANANT (b. 1915)

Marathi and Hindi director born in Kolhapur. Started as editor at **Prabhat** (1930-44) on films like ***Ramshastri*** (1944); left with **Raja Nene**, **Datta Dharmadhikari**, **Bhole**, etc. to work independently. Editor of Nene-Dharmadhikari films, including (uncredited) ***Daha Wajta*** (1942). In his autobiography, *'Anant' Athvani* (1987), claims to have ghost-directed several Nene hits (e.g. ***Patthe Bapurao***, 1950) and Dharmadhikari productions. Early work continues Dharmadhikari-style melodrama scripted by **G.D. Madgulkar**, occasionally abandoning literary sources for original screenplays (e.g. *Paidali Padleli Phule*). Helped graft **All-India Film** commercial formulas on to Marathi cinema. Set up Chetana Chitra (1956) for production. Pioneered the producer-director's move into distribution with Chandravilas Films (1968). Best known for musical Tamasha films, e.g. the classic ***Sangtye Aika***, one of Marathi cinema's biggest successes. Introduced several new actors (Raja Gosavi, Nilu Phule, Sharad Talwalkar) and developed Loknatya-style ribald comedy genre. Among his script credits are Dharmadhikari's ***Chimni Pakhare/Nannhe Munne*** (1952), **Shantaram**'s ***Pinjra*** (1972) and Kulkarni's *Tamasgeer* (1981).

FILMOGRAPHY: 1949: *Jai Bhim*; **1950**: *Ketakichya Banaat*; **1953**: *Aboli*; **1954**: *Kalakaar*; *Ovalani*; *Shubhamangal*; *Suhagan*; **1955**: *Punavechi Raat*; **1956**: *Paidali Padleli Phule*; **1957**: *Jhakli Mooth*; *Preetisangam*; **1958**: *Dhakti Jau*; *Don Ghadicha Dav*; **1959**: ***Sangtye Aika***; *Satajanmacha Sobti*; **1960**: *Avaghachi Sansar*; *Paishyacha Paoos*; **1961**: ***Manini***; *Rangapanchami*; *Shahir Parashuram*; **1962**: *Bhagya Lakshmi*; *Chimnyanchi Shala*; *Preeti Vivah*; **1963**: *Mazha Hoshil Ka?*; *Naar Nirmite Nara*; **1964**: *Kai Ho Chamatkar*; *Saval Mazha Aika*; **1965**: ***Kela Ishara Jata Jata***; **1967**: *Sangu Kashi Mi*; **1968**: *Ek Gao Bara Bhangadi*; **1969**: *Dongarchi Maina*; *Gan Gaulan*; **1971**: *Aai Ude Ga Ambabai*; *Ashich Ek Ratra Hoti*; **1973**: *Mi Tuzha Pati Nahi*; **1975**: *Paach Rangachi Paach Pakhare*; **1976**: *Pahuni*; **1977**: *Asla Navara Nako Ga Bai*; **1978**: *Kalavanteen*; *Lakshmi*; *Sushila*; **1979**: *Duniya Kari Salaam*; *Haldi Kunku*; **1980**: *Savaj*; **1981**: *Aai*; *Pori Jara Japoon*; *Totaya Amdaar*; **1982**: *Don Baika Phajiti Aika*; *Galli Te Dilli*; **1983**: *Sansar Pakharancha*; **1984**: *Jagavegali Prem Kahani*; *Kulaswamini Ambabai*; **1985**: *Gao Tasa Changla Pan Veshila Tangla*; **1991**: *Bandhan*; *ZP*.

MANGESHKAR, LATA (b. 1929)

Prolific megastar playback singer central to Hindi film music for the past four decades. Allegedly recorded over 25000 songs in 14 Indian languages, although Nerurkar's compilation (1989) lists a total of 5066 Hindi songs between 1946 and 1989, which should be the bulk of her output. Born in Indore, MP. Daughter of noted **Sangeet Natak** actor-singer, Dinanath Mangeshkar, started as a child actress in **Master Vinayak** films. Sang her first song in Vasant Joglekar's Marathi film *Kiti Hasaal* (1942), but the song was dropped, making her real début with Joglekar's *Aap Ki Sewa Mein* (1947). Came to prominence with **Ghulam Haider**'s score in *Majboor* (1948). Worked with all leading music directors, including **Anil Biswas, Naushad, Shankar-Jaikishen** and **C. Ramchandra**. Occasionaly composed for Marathi films, starting with **Dinkar D. Patil**'s ***Ram Ram Pahuna*** (1950) and then, under the pseudonym Anandadhan, only for **Bhalji Pendharkar** (*Mohityanchi Manjula*, 1963; *Maratha Tituka Melavava*, 1964; ***Sadhi Manse***, 1965; *Tambdi Mati*, 1969). Turned producer with the Marathi films *Vadal* and *Jhanjhar* (both 1953), *Kanchan* (1955) and ***Lekin ...*** (1990). Since the 50s, possibly following *Bhai Bhai* (1956), she perfected her apparently effortless, high-pitched voice projection, usually in C sharp, a technique said to overcome the crude sound reproduction on rickety gramophones and in suburban and rural cinemas. Until the late 80s, recorded about 2 songs a day, featuring in almost every Hindi and most other language films. The major Khayal performer, Neela Bhagwat, commented that Mangeshkar's performances regrettably became the norm for the Indian middle-class notion of feminine beauty in music. **Kumar Shahani** suggested that only she could have sung the difficult Ektaal-based song, *Sangh so javo* in his ***Tarang*** (1984). She appeared as actress in ***Pahili Mangalagaur*** (1942), ***Mazhe Bal*** and *Chimukla Sansar* (1943), *Gajabhau* (1944), ***Badi Maa*** (1945), ***Jeevan Yatra*** and ***Subhadra*** (both 1946), *Mandir* (1948) and ***Chhatrapati Shivaji*** (1952).

Mani Rathnam *see* **Rathnam, Mani**

MANTO, SADAT HASAN (1912-55)

Major Urdu writer and scenarist whose work has defined the literary and the filmic iconography of Partition (e.g. in his most famous story, *Toba Tek Singh*, cf Manto, 1987), of the urban dispossessed and of the post-Independence political and bureaucratic ruling class. Often wrote diary or travelogue-type fictions with himself as observer or in conversation with his protagonist. A journalist in Aligarh, he went to Bombay to edit the film weekly *Mussawar* (1936). Joined **Imperial** as storywriter; in 1943 joined **Filmistan**, injecting some contemporary consciousness into its largely apolitical productions (e.g. Dattaram Pai's ***Eight Days***, 1946). Later, with **Ashok Kumar**, rejoined **Bombay Talkies** and in 1948 migrated to Lahore to get away from the persecution of Muslims in Bombay. His published writings include 15 short-story anthologies, one novel (*Baghair Unwan Ke*, 1940), a play (*Teen Auratein*, 1942), essays (*Manto Ke Mazamin*, 1942) and a famous autobiographical account of his years in films, *Meena Bazaar* (1962/1984). His work was the basis of the British tv film *Partition* (1987), followed by the publication of his *Kingdom's End and Other Stories*; acclaimed by Salman Rushdie as the 'master of the modern Indian short story'. Among the main films he scripted are **Gidwani**'s ***Kisan Kanya*** (1937), Dada Gunjal's ***Apni Nagariya*** (1940), Shaukat Hussain's ***Naukar*** (1943), **Gyan Mukherjee**'s ***Chal Chal Re Naujawan*** (dial), **Harshadrai Mehta** & Ramesh Saigal's *Ghar Ki Shobha* (both 1944), *Eight Days*, J.K. Nanda's *Jhumke* (st), Savak Vacha's *Shikari* (dial; all 1946) and **Sohrab Modi**'s ***Mirza Ghalib*** (st; 1954).

MARUDAKASI, AYYAMPERUMAL (1920-89)

Tamil film lyricist born in Melakudikadu, TN; farmer's son. Influenced by musician Rajagopala Iyer, brother of composer **Papanasam Sivan**. Worked as a village official; left his government job to join the famous Tamil theatre troupe **TKS Brothers**. Also worked in Nawab Rajamanikkam's theatre group and for Devi Drama, for which he wrote his first songs. Film début as songwriter in **T.R. Sundaram**'s *Mayavathi* (1949). First hit number is *Varai ... varai* in ***Manthiri Kumari*** (1950). Wrote over 3000 songs in c.300 Tamil films, reaching the pinnacle of his career in the 50s and 60s. At this time, his lyrics were often sung by playback singer T.M. Soundarrajan and composed by M.S. Vishwanathan. A compilation of his film songs was published in 1988.

MASTER, HOMI (?-1949)

Top **Kohinoor** director in the 20s, esp. 1924-6: ***Lanka Ni Laadi***, ***Fankdo Fituri***, ***The Telephone Girl*** were big silent hits. Joined leading Parsee theatre company Baliwala aged 13; became very popular stage actor, notably in *Pakzaad Parveen*. Employed briefly at **Hindustan Film** and was by some accounts sent abroad to market **Phalke**'s films in Europe. Joined Kohinoor as actor (he played Duryodhan in ***Bhakta Vidur***, 1921; the lead in ***Kala Naag***, 1924) and as assistant to **Kanjibhai Rathod**. As director created one of the most successful teams of 20s Indian film with scenarist **Mohanlal Dave** and cameraman D.D. Dabke. Described by silent star **Gohar** as perhaps the most 'dramatic' film-maker she worked with, contrasting with, e.g., the 'realism' of **Bhavnani** and **Chandulal Shah**. Made several B films in Hindi and in Gujarati. Ended his career as production manager at **Kardar**'s Studio in Bombay.

FILMOGRAPHY (* also act): **1924**: ***Bismi Sadi***; *Kanya Vikraya Ni Kahani*; *Manorama*; *Raja Harishchandra**; *Ra Mandlik*; *Sati Sone*; *Veer Ahir*; **1925**: *Ghar Jamai*; *Kunj Vihari*; ***Lanka Ni Laadi***; *Sansar Swapna*; ***Fankdo***

*Fituri**; *Hirji Kamdar*; ***Kulin Kanta***; *Mari Dhaniyani*; *Rambha Of Rajnagar*; **1926**: ***The Telephone Girl***; *Briefless Barrister*; *Lakho Vanjaro*; *Mumtaz Mahal*; *Sati Jasma*; *Shirin Farhad*; *Delhi No Thug*; **1927**: *Rangmahal Ni Ramani*; *Return Of Kala Naag**; *The Mission Girl*; ***Bhaneli Bhamini***; *Surat No Sahukar*; **1928**: *Lekh Par Mekh*; *Gul Sanobar*; *Veerangana*; **1929**: *Bilwamangal*; *Lanka Lakshmi*; *Punjab Kesari*; *Punya Prabhav*; *Sinh Ka Bachha Sinh*; *Lutaru Lalna*; **1930**: *Mast Fakir*; *Shoorveer Sharada*; *Ranchandi*; *Patan Ni Paniari*; **1931**: *Rao Saheb*; *Shahi Firman*; *Dushman-e-Iman*; **1932**: *Ranadevata*; *Mahiari*; *Hind Kesari*; *Vanarsena*; *Prabhu Na Chor* (all St); *Hoor-e-Misar*; **1933**: *Jagat Mohini* (St); *Misar Nu Moti* (St); *Saubhagya Sundari*; **1934**: ***Samaj Ki Bhool***; ***Gul Sanobar***; *Khwab-e-Hasti*; **1935**: ***Do Ghadi Ki Mauj***; ***Ghar Jamai***; *Naya Zamana*; **1936**: *Akkal Na Bardan*; *Zaat-e-Sharif*; **1937**: *Jagat Kesari*; *New Searchlight*; *Punjab Lancers*; **1938**: *Chhote Sarkar*; **1939**: *Fankdo Fituri*; **1940**: *Neelamalai Kaidhi*; **1946**: *Chamakti Bijli*; **1948**: *Bhaneli Vahu*; *Gharwali*; *Jai Ranchhod*; *Lagan Na Umedvar*; **1949**: *Shethno Salo*.

MATHUR, VISHNU (b. 1944)

Hindi director born in Ahmedabad. Graduated from the **FTII** (1970). Assisted **Mani Kaul** and **Mrinal Sen**. Employed by **Films Division** (1975-8) but resigned over directorial freedom. Feature début, ***Pehla Adhyay***, pioneered a complex and innovative approach to cinematic space and rhythm, also in evidence in his unconventional portrait of the Carnatic veena-player Savithri Rajan (***Flying Bird***). Works in collaboration with noted Tamil writer and feminist intellectual C.S. Lakshmi (aka Ambai).

FILMOGRAPHY: 1969: *Wardrobe* (Sh); **1970**: *In Panchgani* (Sh); *Film Gaze* (Doc); **1973**: *This Our Only Earth* (Doc); *Small-Scale Industries of India* (Doc); *Drought in Maharashtra* (Doc); *President Nyerere's Visit to India* (Doc); **1975**: *Discipline on the Road* (Doc); **1976**: *Sharing Experience* (Doc); *Sixth International Film Festival of India* (Doc); **1977**: *Communication Security/Sanchar Suraksha* (Doc); **1978**: *Surdas* (Sh); **1981**: ***Pehla Adhyay***; **1983**: *Towards Zero Population Growth in Kerala* (Doc); **1985**: *Through the Looking Glass* (Doc); **1989**: ***The Flying Bird*** (Doc).

Mazumdar *see* **Majumdar**

MEHBOOB (1906-64)

Aka Mehboob Khan. Hindi-Urdu director regarded as one of the most important influences on post-50s cinema. Born as Ramjan Khan in Bilimoria, Gujarat. Ran away to Bombay to join film industry. Started as extra and factotum in **Imperial** Studio where he met director **R.S. Choudhury** (later scenarist for ***Roti*** and ***Aan***) and cameraman Faredoon A. Irani. Acted as one of the thieves in *Alibaba and the Forty Thieves*. Directorial début at **Sagar** (1935). Worked in National Studios (1940-2) along with **Kardar**. Founded Mehboob Prod. in 1942 (established as studio in 1952) using a hammer and sickle emblem even though formally unassociated with the CP. Acclaimed first as heir to Imperial's historicals (***Judgement of Allah***, ***Humayun***); he continued its trend of merging DeMille with the conventions of the Urdu stage but brought to the formula a greater self reflexiveness (*Roti*). His ***Mother India*** (a subcontinental equivalent of *Gone with the Wind* which has been declared India's most successful film ever) also evoked Dovzhenko's lyricised socialist-realist imagery. Immensely successful on an international scale, Mehboob's films often derive from a clash between pre-capitalist ruralism (with its blood feuds, debts of honour, kinship laws etc.) and an increasingly modernised state with its commercial-industrial practices and values. His elaboration of political themes within popular generic conventions provides the bridge between the pre-Independence cinema of, e.g., **Bhavnani** (***Mazdoor***, 1934) and the social critiques attempted by **Raj Kapoor** in the post-1947 industrial mainstream. With ***Andaz*** he made what was regarded as the first Indian film set in 'modern times' among an affluent middle class, exerting an enormous influence on later films (e.g. ***Awara***, 1951).

FILMOGRAPHY (* only act): **1927**: *Alibaba and the Forty Thieves**; *Allah Ka Pyara**; **1929**: *Shirin Khushrau**; **1930**: *Mewad No Mawali**; **1931**: *Raj Tilak**; *Dilawar** (all St); *Meri Jaan**; *Veer Abhimanyu**; **1932**: *Bulbul-e-Baghdad**; **1933**: *Chandrahasa**; *Pandav Kaurav**; *Mirza Sahiban**; *Premi Pagal**; **1934**: *Grihalakshmi**; *Naachwali**; *Sati Anjani**; **1935**: *Vengeance Is Mine**; ***Judgement of Allah***; **1936**: ***Deccan Queen***; ***Manmohan***; **1937**: ***Jagirdar***; **1938**: ***Hum Tum Aur Woh***; ***Watan***; **1939**: ***Ek Hi Raasta***; **1940**: *Alibaba*; ***Aurat***; **1941**: ***Bahen***; **1942**: ***Roti***; **1943**: ***Najma***; ***Taqdeer***; **1945**: ***Humayun***; **1946**: ***Anmol Ghadi***; **1947**: ***Elaan***; **1948**: ***Anokhi Ada***; **1949**: ***Andaz***; **1952**: ***Aan***; **1954**: ***Amar***; **1957**: ***Mother India***; **1962**: *Son of India*.

MEHRA, PRAKASH (b. 1939)

Hindi director and producer born in Bijnaur, UP. Assistant to **Dhirubhai Desai** at Vishnu Cinetone (1958-9). Worked as a lyricist in the 60s, then director. Made **Bachchan**'s first major hit, ***Zanjeer*** and launched the star's image as a lumpen-vigilante hero, an orphaned (*Zanjeer*) or illegitimate (***Muqaddar Ka Sikandar***) outsider. Also made some of Bachchan's best-known buddy films, usually co-starring Vinod Khanna (*Muqaddar Ka Sikandar*, *Hera Pheri*).

FILMOGRAPHY: 1968: ***Hasina Maan Jayegi***; **1971**: *Mela*; **1972**: *Aan Baan*; *Samadhi*; **1973**: *Ek Kunwari Ek Kunwara*; ***Zanjeer***; **1974**: *Haath Ki Safai*; **1976**: *Hera Pheri*; *Khalifa*; **1978**: *Aakhri Daku*; ***Muqaddar Ka Sikandar***; **1980**: *Desh Drohi*; *Jwalamukhi*; **1981**: *Lawaris*; **1982**: *Namak Halal*; **1984**: *Sharabi*; **1987**: *Muqaddar Ka Faisla*; **1988**: *Mohabbat Ke Dushman*; **1989**: *Jadugar*; **1992**: *Zindagi Ek Jua*.

MEHTA, HARSHADRAI SAKERLAL

Pioneer Hindi and Tamil director born in Mota, Bardoli Dist., Gujarat. Started as a painter, editor and cameraman at **Kohinoor** (1919), but made his début for **Irani**'s Majestic Film (*Ver Ni Vasulat*). Joined **Krishna Films** where he became a prolific director in 1925. At Krishna he met his long-time partner and cameraman **Luhar** (e.g. *Be Din Ni Badshahi*, *Amar Asha*) making melodramas often starring the Anglo-Indian star Ermeline. Best-known film of this period is ***Janjirne Jankare***, the much-acclaimed Rajput romance written and shot by Luhar. Made his most influential films with the famous Mehta-Luhar Prod. set up with Babubhai Desai and the informal support of the **Sharda** Studio (1932). Made several Sharda-type stunt movies featuring, e.g., Navinchandra. Moved to Coimbatore's Premier Cinetone (1937) and made a number of Tamil films. His last film appears to have been co-directed by Ramesh Saigal.

FILMOGRAPHY: 1925: *Swapna Sundari*; *Ver Ni Vasulat*; *Chandrakant*; *Hothal Padmini*; *Jal Kumari*; *Krishna Kumar*; **1926**: *Be Din Ni Badshahi*; *Amar Asha*; *Panna Ratna*; *Ram Bharose*; *Bhool No Bhog*; *Panch Kalyani*; **1927**: ***Janjirne Jankare***; *Swadesh Seva*; *Keemti Ansoo*; *Roop Sundari*; *Sharad Purnima*; *Keshavkant BA*; *Naqli Rani*; *Vadia Dhor*; **1928**: *Gul Badan*; *Karuna Kumari*; *Raj Tarang*; *Saundarya Sura*; *Sassi Punnu*; **1929**: *Dilruba*; *Miss Dolly*; *Jai Somnath*; *Satta No Mad*; *Pataal Padmini*; *Ranagarjana*; **1930**: *Talwar Ka Pati*; *Daku Ke Dilbar*; *Soneri Khanjar*; **1931**: *Kala Wagh*; *Raj Bhakta*; *Priyatama*; *Ronak Mahal*; *Tirandaz*; *Solanki Shamsher*; *Dharti Kaamp*; *Dard-e-Jigar*; *Hridaya Veena*; *Jadu-e-Mohabbat*; *Pardes Ni Preet*; **1932**: *Kalo Sawar*; *Hoor-e-Hind*; *Vanraj Kesari*; *Bharat Veer*; *Bhedi Rajkumar*; **1933**: *Jasal*; *Jallad* (all St); *Sohni Mahiwal*; *Vikram Charitra*; *Rambha Rani*; **1934**: *Veerangana Panna*; **1935**: *Meethi Nazar*; **1936**: *Pahadi Kanya*; **1938**: *Eknath*; *Shri Kanda Leela*; **1939**: *Shakti Maya*; **1940**: *Parasuramer*; **1942**: *Alli Vijaam*; **1944**: *Ghar Ki Shobha*.

MEHTA, KETAN (b. 1952)

Gujarati and Hindi director born in Navsari, Gujarat. Educated in New Delhi where he graduated in economics. Extensive theatre work: acted for Dishantar group, New Delhi, directed English plays *Zoo Story* and *The Lesson* for Motley, Bombay (1976-7), and staged *Channas*, a Gujarati adaptation of *One Flew over the Cuckoo's Nest*, for Indian National Theatres, Bombay (1983); also did stage lighting for dancers Birju Maharaj and Kumudini Lakhia. Graduated from the **FTII** (1975). Worked in Space Application Centre, Ahmedabad (1975-6). Made controversial tv serial on Ahmedabad TV, *Wat Tamari*, on landless labourers and Untouchables in Gujarat. First feature ***Bhavni Bhavai***, dedicated to Brecht, comic-strip authors Goscinny and Uderzo and to Asait Thakore, pioneer of the Bhavai form, is a rare successful filmic adaptation of folk theatre. Work thereafter has increasingly concentrated on adapting popular art conventions rather than folk, occasionally evoking the action and stunt genres of 50s Hindi film. Opposed to earlier notions of self-conscious art-cinema, he believes in the creative potential of explicitly lumpen cultures while also chronicling their power to destroy (***Holi***). Recent films include adaptation of *Madame Bovary* (*Maya Memsaab*) and a biographical on Sardar Vallabhbhai Patel (*Sardar*). Married to *Maya Memsaab*'s lead actress Deepa Sahi.

FILMOGRAPHY: 1975: *Madhsurya* (Sh); *Coolies at Bombay Central* (Doc); **1977-8**: *Wat Tamari* (TV); **1977**: *Experience India* (Doc); **1980**: ***Bhavni***

Bhavai/Andher Nagari; 1982: *Fair Folk at Tarnetar* (Doc); 1983: ***Holi***; 1985: ***Mirch Masala***; *Ba Ki Yaad Mein* (Doc); *Kisi Ek Phool Ka Naam Lo* (TV); 1987: *Bandhani* (Doc); 1988: *Hero Hiralal*; *Pehla Kadam* (Sh); 1989: *Mr Yogi* (TV); 1992: *All in the Family* (Doc); *Maya Memsaab*; 1993: *Sardar*.

MEHTA, VIJAYA (b. 1934)

Actress and director born in Baroda, Gujarat. Graduated from Bombay University; studied theatre with E. Alkazi in Delhi and with Adi Marzban. Was **Durga Khote**'s daughter-in-law, then widowed at 27 and re-married Farrokh Mehta who was active on the English amateur stage. Became a major figure in 60s Marathi experimental theatre. Founder member of Rangayan (Est: 1960) with playwright **Vijay Tendulkar**, Arvind Deshpande and Shreeram Lagoo. Stage production of C.T. Khanolkar's *Ek Shoonya Bajirao* (1966) is a landmark in contemporary Indian theatre. Claims to have introduced Brecht into Marathi theatre with adaptation of *Caucasian Chalk Circle* (*Ajab Nyay Vartulacha*), and Ionesco with *Chairs* (1962). Helped launch the 70s Chhabildas theatre movement with her Mahesh Elkunchwar plays *Sultan*, *Yatanaghar* and *Holi* (all 1970). Collaborated on Indo-German theatre projects with German director Fritz Bennewitz including a traditional performance of Bhasa's *Mudrarakshasa* with German actors. Except ***Pestonjee***, most of her work consists of film and tv adaptations of her stage plays: *Haveli Bulund Thi* adapted Mahesh Elkunchwar's play *Wada Chirebandi*, and *Rao Saheb* is from Jaywant Dalvi's play *Barrister* (1977).

FILMOGRAPHY (* also d): 1980: ***Kalyug***; 1983: ***Smritichitre**** (TV); 1984: ***Party***; 1986: ***Rao Saheb****; *Shakuntala** (TV); 1987: ***Pestonjee*** (d only); *Sher Shivaji*; *Hamidabai Ki Kothi** (TV); *Haveli Bulund Thi** (TV); 1990: *Lifeline* (TV).

Meiyappan Chettiar, A. V. *see* **AVM Film Company**.

MELODRAMA

Defined in the Indian context mainly as a 'musical dramatic' narrative in accordance with its original generic meaning. From c.1912, when the Indian cinema first attempted cinematic fiction as an indigenous economic enterprise, it relied on the melodramatic mode to narrativise the moving image and to give a sequential logic to the convention of frontal address central to India's performative and visual art traditions. Melodrama drew from the same sources as, e.g., the mythological but functioned as the aesthetic regime accompanying the socio-economic transition from feudal-artisanal practices to industrial ones, both formally and in its content matter (e.g. **Painter**'s ***Savkari Pash***, 1925 & 1936). It recomposed traditional performative idioms and themes, drawing on Western narrative forms and similarly negotiating modernisation tensions. Often aligned with the reformism of the literary social reform movement, esp. in the inter-war period when it was mobilised to recast modernisation in nationalist terms by e.g. **V. Shantaram** and **B.N. Reddi**, continuing into the work of **B.R. Panthulu** and **Puttanna Kanagal**. The classic example of this development was the **DMK Film** which provided Indian cinema with some of its most spectacular melodramas. After Independence, the genre received a new, intense and conflict-ridden inflection in the work of **Raj Kapoor** and **Guru Dutt** in the 50s, generating a social-critical type of melodrama. In their work, the negative sides of capitalist modernisation propel a darkly romantic narrative isolating the tragic hero as an individual. Ravi Vasudevan (1989) noted that this period of Hindi melodrama was overdetermined by the Oedipal triangle of the fearsome father, the nurturing mother and the traumatised son who could deal with these tensions either through renunciation or lawlessness. After WW2, the reformist melodramatic current was deployed to elaborate a pan-Indian narrative regime (see **All-India Film**) culminating in **Mehboob**'s influential *Mother India* (1957), restating the priority of kinship relations and parental/state authority. This later yielded **Amitabh Bachchan**'s or **Uttam Kumar**'s hero-as-outlaw, upholding an imaginary past's 'traditional' values in the face of a degenerated modernity. In Maharashtra, melodrama was used to legitimate a growing regional market (**Bhalji Pendharkar**, scenarist **G.D. Madgulkar**). In Bengal, where a cinema had developed which was economically strong but culturally subservient to the novel, melodrama acquired an oppositional force, e.g. in **Barua**'s work which subverted the literary, and in the **Kallol** film-makers where it later found new alignments with the **IPTA**'s formal emphasis on the folk theatre. Bengal also saw the only instance in Indian film where melodrama became the site where popular and classical idioms of performance merged with a Brechtian aesthetic, yielding a unique authorial practice: the work of **Ritwik Ghatak**, massively influential on the films of, e.g., **Kumar Shahani** and the early **Mani Kaul**. Classic melodramas include: ***Savkari Pash*** (1925), ***Devdas*** (1935), ***Kunku/Duniya Na Mane*** (1937), ***Swargaseema*** (1945), ***Andaz*** (1949), ***Ezhai Padum Padu*** (1950), ***Awara*** (1951), ***Parasakthi*** (1952), ***Mother India*** and ***Pyaasa*** (both 1957), ***Kaagaz Ke Phool*** (1959), ***Meghe Dhaka Tara*** (1960), ***Nagara Haavu*** (1972), ***Muqaddar Ka Sikandar*** (1978), ***Tarang*** (1984). See also **Social**.

MENON, P. N. (b. 1928)

Malayalam director born in Malchad, Trichur. Studied at Trichur School of Art. Went to Madras (1957), worked at **Vauhini** Studio as painter of sets; later at Salem-based studios. Freelance visual artist in theatre (1960); made publicity posters and hand-outs for Tamil, Telugu and Malayalam cinema. First major film ***Olavum Theeravum*** launched the loose collective headed by the film's producer **Backer**, breaking with Kerala cinema's studio and stagebound conventions. This helped pave the way for, e.g., **Adoor Gopalakrishnan**'s early films. Later cloaked his anti-feudal politics in existential mysticism (e.g. ***Malamukalile Daivam***).

FILMOGRAPHY: 1965: ***Rosy***; 1969: ***Olavum Theeravum***; 1971: *Kuttiyedathi*; *Mappusakshi*; 1972: *Panimudakku*; ***Chemparathi***; *Chhayam*; 1973: *Darshanam*; *Gayatri*; 1974: *Mazhakkaru*; 1975: *Odakkuzhal*; 1976: *Udhayam Kizhakku Thanne*; 1977: *Taxi Driver*; 1979: *Devathai*; 1981: *Archana Teacher*; 1982: *Anu*; *Kadamba*; 1983: *Asthram*; *Glimpses of Kerala* (Doc); ***Malamukalile Daivam***; 1988: *Padippura*; 1990: *Money Order* (TV).

MENON, S. BALACHANDRA (b. 1954)

Malayalam director and actor born in Ernakulam, Kerala. Journalist for the magazine *Nana*. Failing admission at the **FTII**, started as an independent low-budget film-maker. Début *Uthradha Rathri* was a dark comedy about a hypochondriac doctor who commits suicide after making love to a colleague dying of cancer. Acts in all his films, but started playing the lead following his successful ***April 18***.

FILMOGRAPHY: 1978: *Uthradha Rathri*; 1979: *Radha Enna Pennkutti*; 1980: *Aniyatha Valakkal*; *Ishtamanu Pakshe*; *Kalika*; *Vaiki Vanna Vasantham*; 1981: *Maniyan Pillai Athava Maniyan Pillai*; *Prema Geethangal*; *Tharattu*; 1982: *Chiriyo Chiri*; *Ithiri Neram Othiri Karyam*; *Kelkatha Shabdam*; *Kilukilukkam*; 1983: *Kariyam Nisaram*; *Prashnam Orutharam*; *Sesham Kazhchayil*; 1984: ***April 18***; *Arante Mulla Kochu Mulla*; *Oru Painkilli Katha*; 1985: *Ente Ammu Ninte Thulasi Avarude Chakki*; *Menechippu Thurannapol*; *Parvathi*; 1986: *Thaikku Oru Thalattu*; *Vivahitare Itihile*; 1987: *Achuvettante Veedu*; ***Ruthubhedam*** (act only); ***Oru Maymasappularayil*** (act only); *Vilambaram*; 1988: *Kandatham Kettatham*; 1991: *Nayam Vethamakkunnu*; 1993: *Ammayana Sathyam*.

MINERVA MOVIETONE

Est: 1936 by **Sohrab Modi** and his brother Rustom. It emerged from Stage Films, set up in 1935 to film the stage repertoire of Rustom's group, Arya Subodh Natak Mandali. Renowned for big-budget historicals, the studio benefited from the Modi family's existing distribution interests in Gwalior, expanded by the third brother, Keki Modi, into Western India Theatres, owning a chain of 27 theatres in 10 cities. Used the Central Studios owned by Keki Modi, reducing its overheads. Set up the first Technicolor laboratory (1952) with Film Group and made ***Jhansi Ki Rani*** (1953).

MIR, EZRA (1903-93)

Hindi director born as Edwin Myers in Calcutta. Actor on the **Madan** stage (played Khusro in *Noorjehan* and later filmed the play) and in two silent Madan films (1922-3). Sailed to New York in 1924 and worked as extra in Rudolph Valentino's *A Sainted Devil* (1924). Worked in editing and story departments of Universal (1925-7) and moved to United Artists (1927-9). Made short film, *The Symbolesque*. Returned in 1930 to **Imperial** and made *Noorjehan* (he had acted in a 1923 version). Moved to **Sagar** (1932-4) where he made, e.g., the **Zubeida** film *Zarina*, adapting **Niranjan Pal**'s play, before returning to Madan (1935). Their Kajjan starrers helped delay the studio's demise. After a European voyage, he went to Bombay to make the **Kidar Sharma**-scripted *Rickshawala* for **Ranjit** Studio. Set up Everest Pics in 1939 (***Sitara***). During the war, inspired by the *March of Time* series, turned to documentary: *Road to Victory* used newsreel material lent by Universal and 20th Century-Fox. Joined the **Film Advisory Board** (1940-1) and produced over 175 films for its successor **Information Films of India** 1942-6. Took over **Films Division** in 1956 and was chief producer until 1961, moulding that institution into its current shape. Also ran the **CFS** (1962-4).

FILMOGRAPHY: **1929**: *The Symbolesque* (Sh) (St); **1931**: *Noorjehan*; **1932**: *Zarina*; **1933**: *Premi Pagal*; **1934**: *Farzande Hind*; **1935**: *Mera Pyara*; *Rashida*; **1936**: *Parivartan*; *Shaitan Ka Pash*; *Jeevan Sangram*; **1938**: *Rickshawala*; **1939**: ***Sitara***; *Road to Victory* (Doc); **1941**: *Voice of Satan* (Sh); **1942**: *Whispering Legend* (Doc); **1947**: *Beete Din*; **1954**: *Pamposh*; **1958**: *Do You Know?* (Doc); **1964**: *Raju Aur Gangaram*.

MIRZA, SAEED AKHTAR (b. 1943)

Hindi-Urdu director born in Bombay. Son of noted scenarist Akhtar Mirza. Worked in advertising before joining the **FTII** (1973-6). Co-founder of Yukt Film Co-op with K. Hariharan, **Mani Kaul**, Kamal Swaroop et al., where he made ***Arvind Desai Ki Ajeeb Dastaan***. Early films attempt a free-flowing narrative style claiming partial influence of Brazilian Cinema Novo, using vérité shots usually of Bombay's working class. Started Iskra in collaboration with **Kundan Shah**, producing major tv series with each episode directed in turn by Mirza, Shah and colleagues like Raman Kumar and brother Aziz Mirza. Directed 17 of *Nukkad*'s 39 episodes, a drama series set on a Bombay street corner. Made 11 of *Intezaar*'s 26 episodes, a drama series about life in Kamalpura, a very small town. The group faced censorship trouble when Kundan Shah's serial *Police Station* was denied telecast permission by **Doordarshan**. Stated that his tv work was aimed at 14-year-olds 'because the medium is geared to that age level.'

FILMOGRAPHY: **1976**: *Corpses* (Doc); *An Actor Prepares* (Doc); **1977**: *The Problem of Urban Housing* (Doc); **1978**: *Slum Eviction* (Doc); ***Arvind Desai Ki Ajeeb Dastaan***; **1980**: ***Albert Pinto Ko Gussa Kyon Aata Hai***; **1982**: *Piparsod* (Sh); **1983**: ***Mohan Joshi Haazir Ho***; **1984**: *Rickshaw Pullers of Jabalpur* (Doc); **1986**: *Nukkad* (TV); **1987**: *Is Anybody Listening* (Doc); **1988**: *We Shall Overcome* (Doc); *Intezaar* (TV); **1989**: ***Salim Langde Pe Mat Ro***; **1992**: *Ajanta and Ellora* (Doc).

MISHRA, BHAGWATI PRASAD (1896-1932)

Hindi director, actor and producer born and educated in Benares. Achieved some renown as photographer and painter; apprenticed to painter Hussain Bux (1916-21). Worked in theatre group Vyakul Bharat Natak Mandali in Meerut. Joined Star Film as poster designer (1921). Directorial début: *Razia Begum*, causing communal controversy in Hyderabad (see **Dhiren Ganguly**). Worked with **Ardeshir Irani**'s Majestic, Royal and **Imperial** Studios as actor-director, making some of the latter's big-budget sequels to ***Alam Ara*** (1931). Promoted independent companies Indian Pic. Corp. and Zarina Pics. Then worked in **Sharda** and **Sagar** Studios until his death. His films, with those of colleague **R.S. Choudhury**, are often cited among the first silent productions to stress the visual rather than the plot. Did several covers and illustrations for press books, including the striking designs for *Naharsinh Daku*.

FILMOGRAPHY (* also act/** act only): **1924**: *Razia Begum*; *Veer Durgadas**; ***Paap No Fej****; *Mumbai Ni Sethani***; *Shahjehan***; *Vijaya*; **1925**: *Kangal Qaidi***; *Naharsinh Daku*; *Noor-e-Deccan*; *Devi Ahalyabai*; *Rana Pratap*; *Amarsinh Daggar*; *Paisa Ni Khumari*; **1926**: *Indrajal*; *Slaves of Custom*; *Pahadi Pindharo*; *Sheesh Mahal*; *Pyari Mamta*; *Pagal Premi***; *Dorangi Duniya***; **1927**: *Alladdin and the Wonderful Lamp*; *Gutter Nu Gulab*; *Poonam No Chand*; *Alibaba and the Forty Thieves*; **1928**: *Hoor-e-Baghdad*; *Ek Abla*; *Haiyan No Haar*; *Kamala Kumari*; *Rajrang*; *Samrat Ashok*; **1929**: *Anarbala*; *Mirza Sahiban*; *Jai Bharati*; *Be Dhari Talwar*; *Mewad Nu Moti*; *Raj Ramani*; **1930**: ***Cinema Girl***; *Nai Roshni*; *Sher-e-Arab*; *Arunodaya*; **1931**: *Golibar*; *Toofani Taruni*; *Toofan* (all St); ***Draupadi***; **1932**: ***Zalim Jawani***; *Sati Madalasa*.

MISHRA, SISIR (b. 1942)

Oriya and Hindi director; lecturer in physics at Bhadrak College, Orissa. Went to Bombay to make films (1965) and after a decade of assisting various directors, made his début with the melodrama *Sindura Bindu*, a melancholic tale of childhood lovers who reunite only when the hero's wife dies of cancer. Best-known Hindi film is *Bheegi Palkein*, an art-house film with **Smita Patil** and Raj Babbar. His *Samay Ki Dhara* is a remake of his own *Samaya Bada Balabaan*.

FILMOGRAPHY: **1976**: *Sundura Bindu*; **1978**: *Suna Sansar*; **1982**: *Bheegi Palkein*; *Samaya Bada Balabaan*; **1983**: *Subarna Seeta*; **1986**: *Samay Ki Dhara*; *Ei Aama Sansar*; **1989**: *Billoo Badshah*; **1991**: *Bastra Haran*.

MISTRI, BABUBHAI (b. 1919)

Hindi and Gujarati director and cameraman born in Surat, Gujarat; also worked in Telugu film. India's first and most influential special-effects expert. Early career in Prakash Pics (1933-7) and Filmco (1938-45). Then went to Madras to work on **Ellis Duncan**'s ***Meera*** (1945). Returned to Bombay and, as director and art director, helped establish **Homi Wadia**'s Basant Studio (1942). Made a crucial contribution to the iconography of the post-war B-movie mythological, e.g. the miracle sequences of **Nanabhai Bhatt** and **Wadia** films (*Jungle Princess*, 1942; *Husn Ka Chor*, 1953; ***Hatimtai***, 1956). Pioneering special effects include the invisible man in **Vijay Bhatt**'s *Khwab Ki Duniya* (1937) and the travelling matte shots showing the genie lifting the palace and flying through the air in **Nanubhai Vakil**'s *Alladdin* (1945). These sequences were admired by Pudovkin when he visited the studio. Also worked as art director at CIRCO. Directed several mythologicals and the stunt classic ***King Kong***. Later films often feature wrestler **Dara Singh**. Continued working as a special-effects consultant for many productions, including the mammoth tv serial *Ramayan* (1986-8).

FILMOGRAPHY: **1942**: ***Muqabala***; **1943**: *Mauj*; **1945**: *Ji Haan*; **1953**: *Nav Durga*; **1954**: *Tilottama*; **1955**: *Shri Krishna Bhakti*; **1956**: *Sati Naagkanya*; **1957**: *Naag Lok*; *Pawan Putra Hanuman*; **1958**: ***Maya Bazaar***; *Samrat Chandragupta*; **1959**: *Bedard Zamana Kya Jaane*; *Chandrasena*; *Madari*; *Veer Ghatotkajan*; **1960**: *Hanuman Pathal Vijayan*; *Maya Machhindra*; **1961**: *Sampoorna Ramayan*; **1962**: ***King Kong***; *Maya Jaal*; **1963**: *Kan Kan Mein Bhagwan*; ***Parasmani***; *Sunehri Nagin*; **1964**: *Magic Carpet*; **1965**: *Bharat Milap*; *Mahabharat*; *Sangram*; **1967**: *Sardar*; *Shamsheer*; **1968**: *Har Har Gange*; **1969**: *Anjaan Hai Koi*; *Sansar Leela*; **1970**: *Bhagwan Parashuram*; *Naag Lok*; **1971**: *Brahma Vishnu Mahesh*; *Saat Sawaal*; *Shri Krishna Arjun Yudh*; *Daku Mansingh*; **1972**: *Naag Panchami*; **1973**: *Ranakdevi*; **1974**: *Hanuman Vijay*; *Harishchandra Taramati*; **1975**: *Alakh Niranjan*; *Maya Machhindra*; **1976**: *Veer Mangdavalo*; **1978**: *Jai Mahakali*; *Amar Suhagin*; **1979**: *Pati Parmeshwar*; *Har Har Gange*; *Amarsinh Rathod*; **1980**: *Mahabali Hanuman*; **1982**: *Sati Naagkanya*; **1983**: *Sant Ravidas Ki Amar Kahani*; *Kurukshetra*; *Sampoorna Mahabharat*; **1984**: *Maya Bazaar*; *Gangavatarana*; **1987**: *Kalyug Aur Ramayan*; **1990**: *Hatimtai*; **1991**: *Mahamayi*.

MITRA, KAMAL (1911-93)

Bengali actor born in Burdwan. Started in amateur theatre. Film début with Gunamoy Bannerjee and in **Debaki Bose**'s Hindi films. First major hit: *Sat Number Bari*, coinciding with his successes on the professional Calcutta stage (*Seetaram*, *Tipu Sultan*, etc). Acted with Minerva, Star and Srirangam theatres and in jatra groups. His tall stature and deep voice made him a natural for aristocratic patriarchal roles, e.g. already in his early career he continued the stereotype of the pipe-smoking father established by **Chhabi Biswas**. Later played several roles as screen villain but acted heroic roles in mythologicals (e.g. *Kangsa*, *Mahishasur Badh*). Retired in 1981. Autobiography: *Flashback* (1989).

FILMOGRAPHY: **1943**: *Nilanguriya*; *Shri Ramanuja*; **1945**: *Swarg Se Sundar Desh Hamara*; *Banphool*; **1946**: *Sat Number Bari*; *Sangram*; *Dukhe Jader Jiban Gara*; *Nivedita*; *Tumi Aar Ami*; **1947**: *Tapobhanga*; *Ratri*; *Abhiyatri*; *Roy Choudhury*; *Purbaraag*; **1948**: *Samapika*; *Bankalekha*; *Sabhyasachi/Pather Daabi*; **1949**: *Samarpan*; *Pratirodh*; *Sankalpa*; *Krishna Kaveri*; *Abhijatya*; *Ananya*; **1950**: *Indira*; *Jagrata Bharat*; *Apabaad*; *Banprastha*; *Vidyasagar*; *Roopkatha*; *Maryada*; *Sahodar*; *Panchayat*; **1951**: *Kulhara*; *Aparajito*; *Abhishapta*; *Sahajatri*; *Ananda Math*; *Minoti*; ***Ratnadeep***; **1952**: *Alladdin-o-Ashcharya Pradeep*; ***Mahaprasthaner Pathey/Yatrik***; *Madhurati*; *Bhuler Sheshe*; *Mahishasur Badh*; **1953**: *Rami Chandidas*; *Shri Shri Satyanarayan*; **1954**: *Maa-o-Chhele*; *Atom Bomb*; *Satir Dehatyaag*; *Maa Annapurna*; *Nababidhan*; *Prafulla*; *Mani-Aar-Manik*; *Sati*; *Amar Prem*; *Agni Pareeksha*; *Shoroshi*; **1955**:

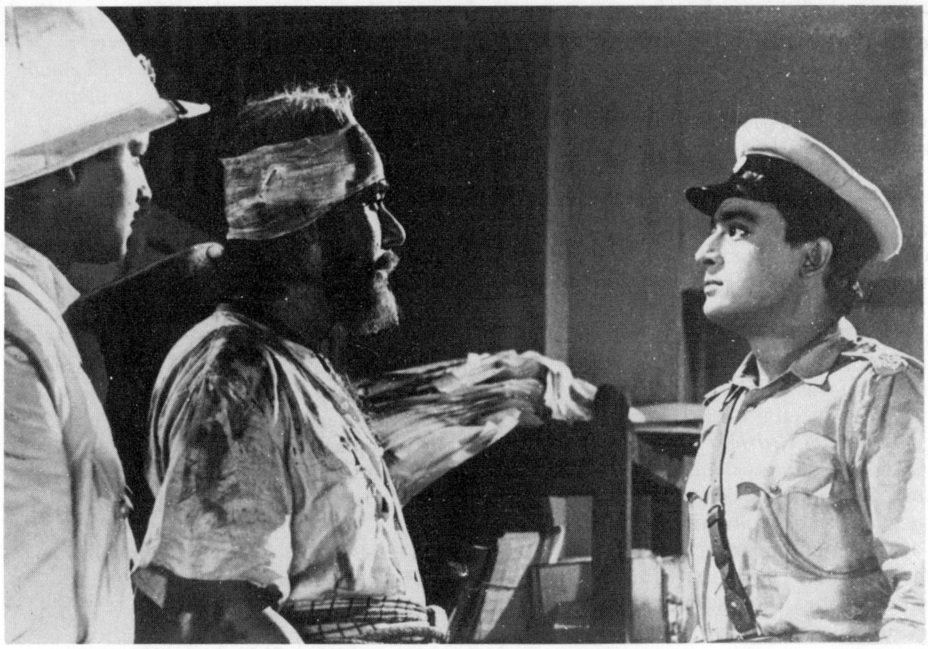

Kamal Mitra (centre) and Nirmal Kumar (right) in *Louha-Kapat* (1957)

Sajghar; *Pratiksha*; *Shap Mochan*; *Bir Hambir*; *Bidhilipi*; *Kankabatir Ghat*; *Devimalini*; *Bhalobasha*; *Paresh*; *Drishti*; *Shribatsa Chinta*; *Sabar Uparey*; *Atmadarshan*; *Kalindi*; **1956**: ***Sagarika***; *Kirti Garh*; *Laksha-Hira*; *Ekti Raat*; *Asamapta*; *Trijama*; *Rajpath*; *Shilpi*; *Sinthir Sindoor*; *Amar Bou*; *Asha*; **1957**: ***Parash Pathar***; *Haar Jeet*; *Shesh Parichaya*; *Sindoor*; *Ulka*; *Tapasi*; *Panchatapa*; *Yatra Holo Suru*; *Punar Milan*; *Chandranath*; *Data-Karna*; *Louha-Kapat*; **1958**: *Yamalaya Jibanta Manush*; *Nupur*; *Daily Passenger*; *Bhanu Pelo Lottery*; *Daktar Babu*; *Purir Mandir*; *Joutuk*; *Surya Toran*; *Shri Shri Tarakeshwar*; *Kangsa*; **1959**: *Derso Khokhar Kando*; *Amrapali*; *Ae Jahar Sey Jahar Noy*; **1960**: *Uttar Megh*; *Dui Bechara*; *Sakher Chor*; *Kono-Ek-Din*; ***Hospital***; *Surer Pyasi*; **1961**: *Lakshmi Narayan*; *Kanchanmulya*; *Mithun Lagna*; *Ashay Bandhinu Ghar*; **1962**: *Bipasha*; *Bodhu*; *Khana*; *Mayar Sansar*; *Shesh Chinha*; *Rakta Palash*; *Dhoop Chhaya*; **1963**: *Shesh-Anka*; *High Heel*; *Deya Neya*; *Barnali*; *Shreyasi*; **1964**: *Bibhas*; *Agni Banya*; *Kashtipathar*; *Sandhya Deeper Sikha*; **1965**: *Thana Theke Aschhi*; *O'Kay?*; *Raja Rammohun*; *Mukhujey Paribar*; *Tapasi*; *Kal Tumi Aleya*; **1966**: *Angikar*; *Firey Chalo*; *Joradighir Choudhury Paribar*; *Manihar*; *Rajdrohi*; *Ramdhakka*; *Susanta Sha*; **1967**: *Ashite Ashio Na*; *Jiban Mrityu*; **1968**: *Boudi*; *Chowringhee*; *Garh Nasimpur*; **1969**: *Andhar Surya*; *Chiradiner*; *Parineeta*; *Pita Putra*; *Sabarmati*; ***Teen Bhubhaner Parey***; **1970**: *Samanaral*; *Muktisnan*; **1971**: *Trinayani Maa*; **1972**: *Biraj Bou*; *Chinnapatra*; **1973**: *Agni Bhramar*; *Roudra Chhaya*; *Alo Andhare*; *Jiban Rahasya*; **1974**: *Jadi Jantem*; *Phulu Thakurma*; **1975**: *Amriter Swad*; **1976**: *Yugo Manab Kabir*; *Asadharan*; *Shri Shri Maa Lakshmi*; **1977**: *Din Amader*; *Jaal Sanyasi*; **1979**: *Jata Mat Tata Path*; **1980**: *Aro Ekjan*; *Bhagya Chakra*; *Daksha Yagna*; *Kalo Chokher Tara*; **1981**: *Pahadi Phool*; *Khelar Putul*.

MITRA, NARESH CHANDRA (1888-1968)

Bengali actor and director born in Agartala, Tripura. Law graduate from Calcutta University but became a major stage star, starting at Minerva Theatre (1922) with *Chandragupta*; joined Star Theatre with *Karnarjun* (1923). Acted in several plays for different companies, mostly playing villains. Entered film to complete ***Andhare Alo***, begun by **Sisir Bhaduri**. Then actor-director, first at the Taj Mahal company, later at **East India Film** and **Priyanath Ganguly**'s Kali Films. Style dominated by **Calcutta Theatres** conventions in themes commonly drawn from plays/novels based on **Rabindranath Tagore** (e.g. *Nauka Dubi* and *Gora*), Saratchandra Chatterjee (***Devdas***), Anuroopa Devi and on his own stage hits (e.g. *Mahanisha*, *Banglar Meye*, *Pather Sathi* etc). Later films starring **Uttam Kumar** (e.g. *Bou Thakuranir Haat*, *Annapurnar Mandir*) provide rare examples of a 30s stage style translated into post-Independence Bengali film. Acted in several films, such as those by younger **Kallol** directors like **Sailajananda Mukherjee** (e.g. ***Shahar Theke Dooray***, *Roy Choudhury*). Towards the end of his life, was most closely associated with the folk Jatra.

FILMOGRAPHY (* also d): **1922**: ***Andhare Alo****; **1923**: *Maanbhanjan**; **1924**: *Chandranath**; **1927**: *Durgesh Nandini*; **1928**: ***Devdas***; **1929**: *Kapal Kundala*; **1930**: ***Giribala***; *Kal Parinaya*; **1931**: *Debi Choudhrani*; *Bibaha Bibhrat*; **1932**: *Nauka Dubi** (all St); **1933**: *Sabitri**; **1935**: *Prafulla*; **1936**: *Mahanisha**; *Pather Sheshey*; *Chino Haar*; **1938**: *Gora**; **1939**: *Sharmishtha**; *Chanakya*; **1941**: *Kavi Joydev*; *Pratishodh*; *Banglar Meye**; **1942**: *Pativrata*; *Bondi*; ***Meenakshi***; **1943**: *Swamir Ghar*; ***Shahar Theke Dooray***; **1944**: *Samaj*; **1945**: *Bondita*; **1946**: *Nivedita*; *Pather Sathi**; **1947**: *Swayamsiddha**; *Roy Choudhury*; *Swapna-o-Sadhana*; **1949**: *Bidushi Bharya**; **1950**: *Kankal**; **1951**: *Niyati**; *Pandit Moshai**; **1953**: *Bou Thakuranir Haat**; **1954**: *Annapurnar Mandir**; **1955**: *Kalindi**; **1957**: *Ulka**; **1960**: *Khudha*; **1961**: *Maa*; **1968**: *Parishodh*.

MITRA, PREMENDRA (1904-88)

Bengali director and writer born in Benares, UP. Major novelist of **Kallol** era, associated with journal *Kalikalam* (Est: 1926). One of the main Bengali literary figures to move to film, first as scenarist, then as director (others were **Sailajananda Mukherjee** and Dinesh Ranjan Das). Studied briefly at Shantiniketan and later at Dhaka. Worked as journalist on *Banglar Katha*; later edited the children's journal, *Rangmashal* (1933), and worked on *Nabashakti* (1936). First major novel, *Pank* (*Mud*, 1924), published by journal *Kallol* in 1926 and criticised by **Rabindranath Tagore** for obscenity, was an important event in articulating the journal's anti-romantic stance. Wrote c.150 books, including novels, essay collections, short stories and poems. Entered film as scenarist, writing the dialogue for **Charu Roy**'s *Graher Pher* (1936). Best-known work for **Dhiren Ganguly**, **Niren Lahiri** and **Sushil Majumdar**. Considered his film scripts sentimental and not representative of his best writing, and later disowned his cinema entirely. His own films, introducing a literary realism to the traditional social, combined aspects of pre-WW2 Bengali modernist fiction, **IPTA** influences (*Moyla Kagaj*) and the post-WW2 assimilation of melodramatic Italian neo-realism. Wrote all his own films; provided scripts and at times dialogues and lyrics for e.g. **Ganguly**'s *Ahuti* (1941) and *Daabi* (1943), **Sushil Majumdar**'s *Rikta* (1939), *Pratishodh* (1941), *Avayer Biye* (1942), ***Jogajog*** (1943) and *Digbhranta* (1950), **Phani Burma**'s *Byabadhan* (1940) and **Debaki Bose**'s *Sagar Sangamey* (1959). Also dialogues for Prafulla Roy's *Nari* (1942) lyrics for **Jyotish Bannerjee**'s *Milan* (1942). Many of his stories have been filmed, e.g. **Mrinal Sen**'s ***Khandhar*** (1983). An English anthology of short stories was published in 1990.

FILMOGRAPHY: **1943**: ***Samadhan***; **1944**: *Bideshini*; **1945**: *Path Bendhe Dilo*; *Raj Lakshmi*; **1947**: *Natun Khabar*; **1948**: *Kalo Chhaya*; **1949**: *Kuasha*; **1950**: *Kankantala Light Railway*; **1951**: *Setu*; **1952**: *Hanabari*; **1953**: *Dui Beyai*; **1954**: *Moyla Kagaj*; **1955**: *Dakinir Char*; **1960**: *Chhupi Chhupi Ashey*.

MITRA, SOMBHU (b. 1916)

Bengali-Hindi actor and director born in Hooghly Dist., Bengal. One of the most significant figures of 20th C. Indian theatre. The first play he staged, **Bijon Bhattacharya**'s *Nabanna* (1943), based on the 1943 Calcutta famine, was seminal to realist political theatre and a reference-point for the **IPTA**. He made his film début in **K.A. Abbas**'s IPTA-sponsored film version of the play ***Dharti Ke Lal***. Set up his own theatre group, Bohurupee (1948), pioneering indigenous variations of Ibsen's naturalist idiom in tandem with **Rabindranath Tagore**'s *Char Adhyay* and *Raktakarabi*. Later theatre work includes exploration of Greek tragedy (*Oedipus*) and Brecht (*Galileo*). Invited by **Raj Kapoor** to direct ***Jagte Raho***. Considered the greatest Bengali actor after **Sisir Bhaduri**.

FILMOGRAPHY (* only d/** also d): **1946**: ***Dharti Ke Lal***; **1947**: *Abhiyatri*; **1949**: *Abarta*; **1950**: *Hindustan Hamara*; **1953**: *Maharaj Nandakumar*; ***Pathik***; *Bou Thakuranir Haat*; **1954**: *Maraner Pare*; *Shivashakti*; **1955**: *Durlav Janma*; **1956**: ***Jagte Raho/Ek Din Raatre*****; **1959**: *Shubha Bibaha**; **1961**: *Manik*; **1962**: *Suryasnan*; **1967**: *Panna*; **1969**: ***Natun Pata***; **1971**: *Nishachar*.

MODAK, SHAHU (1918-93)

Marathi-Hindi star born in Ahmednagar, Maharashtra, in Christian family. Introduced by **Bhalji Pendharkar** together with **Shanta Apte**, as child star (***Shyam Sundar***). Double role in second film *Aut Ghatkecha Raja*. Top Marathi star following his role as the upright policeman Ganpat in **Shantaram**'s ***Manoos/Admi***. Earlier reputation in contemporary socials (e.g. ***Mazha Mulga***) was later superseded by ***Sant Dnyaneshwar*** after which, for several decades, he played mainly Saint films and mythologicals by e.g. **V.M. Vyas, Dhirubhai Desai** and **Vijay Bhatt**. Apparently played Krishna in 29 mythologicals, in Marathi, Hindi and Bhojpuri films.

FILMOGRAPHY: **1932**: ***Shyam Sundar***; **1933**: *Awara Shehzada/Aut Ghatkecha Raja; Bulbul-e-Punjab*; **1934**: *Radha Mohan/Nand Ke Lala; Seva Sadan*; **1936**: *Honhar; Hind Mahila*; **1937**: *Begunah*; **1938**: ***Mazha Mulga/Mera Ladka***; **1939**: ***Manoos/Admi***; **1940**: ***Sant Dnyaneshwar***; **1942**: ***Bharat Milap/Bharat Bhet***; *Apna Paraya*; ***Pahili Mangalagaur***; *Shobha*; ***Vasantsena***; **1943**: *Dulhan; Kanoon; Ladaai Ke Baad; Mahasati Ansuya*; **1944**: *Geet; Maharathi Karna*; **1945**: *Meghdoot; Shri Krishnarjun Yuddha*; **1946**: *Daasi Ya Maa; Uttara Abhimanyu*; **1947**: *Seedha Raasta*; **1948**: *Mandir*; **1949**: *Nara Narayan; Maya Bazaar; Veer Ghatotkach; Sant Namdev*; **1950**: *Bhagwan Shri Krishna; Bhishma Pratigya; Shri Ram Avatar*; **1951**: *Jai Mahakali; Hi Majhi Lakshmi; Parijatak/Shri Krishna Satyabhama; Vithal Rakhumai*; **1952**: *Bhakta Puran; Draupadi Vastraharan*; **1954**: *Durga Puja; Chakradhari; Ramayan; Amar Keertan*; **1955**: *Mastani; Shiv Bhakta; Mi Tulas Tujhya Angani; Bal Ramayan*; **1956**: *Aastik; Dassehra; Dwarkadheesh; Harihar Bhakti; Sudarshan Chakra*; **1957**: *Uthavala Narad; Bhakta Dhruva; Lakshmi Puja; Mohini; Naag Lok; Narsi Bhagat; Raja Vikram; Ram Lakshman; Shyam Ki Jogan; Shesh Naag*; **1958**: *Sudamyache Pohe; Gopichand; Harishchandra; Ram Bhakta Vibhishan; Gaja Gauri*; **1959**: *Grihalakshmi*; **1960**: *Bhakta Raaj*; **1962**: *Rangalya Ratri Asha; Sunbai; Vithu Mazha Lekurvala*; **1963**: *Subhadra Haran*; **1964**: *Bhakta Dhruvakumar; Sant Dnyaneshwar; Tere Dwar Khada Bhagwan; Veer Bhimsen*; **1965**: *Mahasati Ansuya* (H); *Shankar Seeta Ansuya; Sant Tukaram*; **1968**: *Balaram Shri Krishna; Jyot Jale; Mata Mahakali*; **1970**: *Sampoorna Teerth Yatra; Jhala Mahar Pandharinath*; **1972**: *Sant Tulsidas; Hari Darshan; Narad Leela*; **1973**: *Shri Krishna Bhakti; Vishnu Puran*; **1974**: *Har Har Mahadev*; **1975**: *Daku Aur Bhagwan; Mahapavan Teerth Yatra; Shri Satyanarayan Ki Mahapooja*; **1976**: *Bajrang Bali*; **1977**: *Jai Ambe Maa*; **1978**: *Ashapura Matani Chundadi*; **1979**: *Ashta Vinayak*; **1980**: *Bhalu*; **1983**: *Razia Sultan*.

MODERN THEATRES

Angel Films, started in 1934 by **T.R. Sundaram** in partnership with S.S. Velayudham Pillai, became the Modern Theatres Studio in 1937, soon one of South India's most influential and busiest studios before the WW2 period, at its peak making films in Tamil, Telugu, Kannada, Hindi, Sinhalese and Malayalam. Located in Salem, over 300km from Madras, it related to the vast Southern hinterland largely ignored by Madras and Bombay. It created a Malayalam film industry, producing its first sound film, Nottani's ***Balan*** (1938) and Sundaram's ***Kandam Bacha Coat*** (1961), the first Malayalam colour film. The studio did the same for Telugu productions in the 40s, introducing megastars **Anjali Devi** and **S.V. Ranga Rao** (in B.V. Ramanandam's *Varudini*, 1946). Film-makers working in Tamil, the studio's native language, include **Ellis R. Duncan**, C.V. Raman, **K. Ramnoth, T.R. Raghunath** etc., while among the Tamil stars introduced there was M.R. Radha (in *Santhanathevam*, 1939). Also sponsored the early **DMK Films** mainly because of their financial success. The poet and scenarist **Bharatidasan** was employed here, and the studio later produced the **Karunanidhi**-scripted ***Manthiri Kumari*** (1950). Nevertheless, the studio claimed ideological neutrality, unlike the major Madras studios led by, e.g., **K. Subramanyam** and later **S.S. Vasan**. Its commitment to pure entertainment allowed for tighter budgets and the Modern formula was later replicated by several studios in Salem itself as well as in nearby Coimbatore, making these regions into Southern production centres rivalling Madras.

MODI, SOHRAB MERWANJI (1897-1984)

Hindi-Urdu director, actor and producer; born in Bombay. Son of a civil servant; after education in Rampur, UP, and in Bombay, started as a travelling exhibitor in Gwalior (1914) with brother K.M. Modi. Elder brother Rustom Modi, together with Ittefaq, set up Arya Subodh Natya Mandali theatre group (1923). Sohrab played Jehangir (Hamlet) opposite Naseem Banu (Ophelia) in *Khoon Ka Khoon*, one of the biggest Urdu stage hits of the 20s. Rustom Modi started Stage Films (1935) mainly to adapt their plays to the cinema. The film version of ***Khoon Ka Khoon*** was followed by **Aga Hashr Kashmiri**'s Shakespeare adaptation, *Saeed-e-Havas*. Broke away to found **Minerva Movietone** (1936). Although Modi went beyond the Parsee theatre for his choice of themes, his formal approach remained tied to it and evokes the way Parsee theatre looked and sounded, using frontal composition and staging the narrative in spatial layers. Also copious use of Urdu dialogues. Regarded as the man who brought Shakespeare to the Indian screen. Best-known for his spectacular costumed historicals (together with **Asif** and **Amrohi**), which, after ***Pukar***, he alternated with contemporary psychodramas that often dealt with marital problems from a misogynist viewpoint (e.g. ***Jailor, Talaaq, Bharosa***). Acted in all the films he directed and wrote most of them. Started acting for other directors after **Bimal Roy**'s ***Yahudi***.

FILMOGRAPHY (* only act): **1935**: ***Khoon Ka Khoon***; **1936**: *Saeed-e-Havas*; **1937**: *Atma Tarang; Khan Bahadur*; **1938**: ***Jailor; Talaaq***; *Meetha Zaher*; **1939**: ***Pukar***; **1940**: ***Bharosa***; **1941**: ***Sikandar***; **1942**: *Phir Milenge*; **1943**: ***Prithvi Vallabh***; **1944**: ***Parakh***; **1945**: *Ek Din Ka Sultan*; **1947**: *Manjdhar*; **1949**: *Daulat; Narasinh Avatar*; **1950**: ***Sheesh Mahal***; **1953**: ***Jhansi Ki Rani***; **1954**: ***Mirza Ghalib***; **1955**: *Kundan*; **1956**: *Rajhaath*; **1957**: *Nausherwan-e-Adil*; **1958**: ***Jailor***; *Farishta**; ***Yahudi****; **1959**: *Minister**; *Pehli Raat**; **1960**: *Ghar Ki Laaj**; *Mera Ghar Mere Bachche*; **1965**: *Bharat Milap**; **1967**: *Woh Koi Aur Hoga**; **1969**: *Samay Bada Balwan*; **1970**: *Jwala**; **1971**: *Ek Nari Ek Brahmachari**; **1975**: ***Tanariri****; **1979**: *Ghar Ki Laaj**; *Meena Kumari Ki Amar Kahani*; **1981**: *Ganga Maang Rahi Balidan**; **1982**: *Rustom**; **1983**: *Razia Sultan**.

MOHANAN, K. R. (b. 1947)

Malayalam director born in Trichur Dist., Kerala. Graduated in zoology; then diploma in direction at the **FTII**. Known mainly as director of shorts and documentaries, often for the Kerala State Film Development Corp. where he worked for several years. Feature début: ***Ashwathama***, updating the *Mahabharata* legend into the present, is based on the lead player Madampu Kunjukuttan's novel and was widely acclaimed. However, a decade elapsed before his second film.

FILMOGRAPHY: **1978**: ***Ashwathama***; **1987**: ***Purushartham***; **1992**: *Swaroopam*.

MOHAN KOHLI, MADAN (1924-75)

Hindi film composer born in Baghdad. Son of Rai Bahadur Chunilal, the production controller of **Bombay Talkies** and founder of **Filmistan**. Joined the army in WW2. Employed in the Lucknow station of AIR (1946) where he received his only musical education in the company of singers like Faiyaz Khan, Bade Ghulam Ali Khan and Begum Akhtar. First film: Devendra Goel's *Aankhen*, where singer **Lata Mangeshkar** apparently refused to sing for him, considering him an untrained newcomer. However, they became close friends and his second film, **J.B.H. Wadia**'s *Madhosh*, features both Mangeshkar and Talat Mahmood, the latter singer being most closely associated with his compositions. *Madhosh* included the hit Talat song *Meri yaad mein*. Wrote some of Hindi cinema's most famous compositions, such as **Geeta Dutt**'s *Ai dil mujhe bata de* in M.V. Raman's *Bhai Bhai*, Mangeshkar's *Lag ja gale* and *Naina barase* in ***Woh Kaun Thi*** and several ghazals, like *Aapki nazaron ne samjha* in Mohan Kumar's *Anpadh*. Was **Chetan Anand**'s regular composer following the popularity achieved by the songs from ***Haqeeqat***. In the 70s worked with **Hrishikesh Mukherjee** (*Bawarchi*) and **Gulzar** (***Koshish, Mausam***). Apparently also scored the following films which remained uncensored: *Jahan Mile Dharti Akash, Jahan Tum Wahan Hum, Ummeed Pe Duniya Jeete Hain, Maine To Mohabbat Ki Hai, Naya Janam Phir Wohi Shyam, Rehnuma* and *Salma*.

FILMOGRAPHY: **1950**: *Aankhen*; **1951**: *Ada; Madhosh; Shabistan*; **1952**: *Anjaam; Ashiana; Khubsoorat; Nirmohi*; **1953**: *Baghi; Chacha Choudhury; Dhun; Dana Pani*; **1954**: *Ehsan; Ilzaam; Mastana*; **1955**: ***Railway Platform***; *Santosham/Naya Admi*; **1956**: *Bhai Bhai; Fifty Fifty; Mem Sahib; Pocketmaar*; **1957**: *Beti; Chhote Babu*; ***Dekh Kabira Roya***; *Gateway of India; Samundar; Sheroo*; **1958**: *Aakhri Dao; Adalat; Chandan; Ek Shola*; ***Jailor***; *Khazanchi; Khota Paisa; Night Club*; **1959**: *Baap Bete; Bank Manager; Chacha Zindabad; Duniya Na Mane; Jagir; Minister; Mohar*; **1960**: *Bahana*; **1961**: *Sanjog; Senapati*; **1962**: *Anpadh; Manmauji*; **1963**: *Akeli Mat Jaiyo*; **1964**: *Aap Ki Parchhaiyan; Ghazal*; ***Haqeeqat***; *Jahan Ara; Pooja Ke Phool; Sharabi*; ***Woh Kaun Thi***; *Suhagan*; **1965**: *Bombay Race Course; Naya*

Kanoon; *Neela Akash*; *Rishte Naate*; *Dak Ghar*; **1966**: *Dulhan Ek Raat Ki*; *Ladka Ladki*; *Mera Saaya*; *Neend Hamari Khwab Tumhare*; **1967**: *Ghar Ka Chirag*; *Jab Yaad Kisiki Aati Hai*; *Naunihal*; *Nawab Siraj-ud-Dowla*; **1968**: *Ek Kali Muskayi*; **1969**: *Chirag*; **1970**: ***Dastak***; *Heer Ranjha*; *Maa Ka Aanchal*; *Maharaja*; **1971**: *Parwana*; **1972**: *Bawarchi*; ***Koshish***; *Sultana Daku*; **1973**: *Dil Ki Raahein*; *Ek Mutthi Aasmaan*; *Hanste Zakhm*; *Hindustan Ki Kasam*; *Prabhat*; **1974**: *Asliyat*; *Chowkidar*; **1975**: ***Mausam***; **1976**: *Laila Majnu*; *Sharafat Chhod Di Maine*; **1977**: *Saheb Bahadur*; **1978**: *Jalan*; *Inspector Eagle*; **1980**: *Chaalbaaz*.

MOHANLAL (b. 1962)

Malayalam star born in Trivandrum, Kerala. Unlike his contemporary **Mammootty**, with whom he dominated Kerala's cinema in the 80s, his bulky physique makes for an unusual heroic figure. Moved to Madras where he acted in *Thiranottam*, an amateur production by actors and directors trying to get a break into films. Started professional acting career at Navodaya Studio. A villain in his early work (cf *Attakkalasam* starring **Prem Nazir**). Shifted to his best-known 80s genre, musical comedy, with *Engane Nee Marakkum*. Was later associated closely with the foremost director of this genre, **Priyadarshan** (cf their hits ***Chithram*** and *Kilukkam*). His films privilege comic routines, a Trivandrum-Malayalam accent and dances where the star often shows amazing agility. Director Priyadarshan says that in a Mohanlal dance, 'I do not go in for well-rehearsed and conducted steps of dancing, but instead make the camera move according to the music.' Mohanlal's slightly spoofy, satirical musicals and romance dramas (which often end tragically) are sometimes contrasted with Mammootty's grim, songless vendetta thrillers (*New Delhi*, 1987; ***Oru CBI Diary Kuruppu***, 1988). Both stars often acted together, e.g. the hit ***Gandhinagar 2nd Street*** and **I.V. Sasi**'s political drama ***Vartha***. Shifted his style to play an Eastwood-Leone figure in **Bharathan**'s ***Thazhvaram*** and a very unheroic officer in the rehabilitation ministry in **Aravindan**'s ***Vasthuhara***.

FILMOGRAPHY: 1980: *Manjil Virinja Pookkal*; **1982**: *Padayottam*; **1983**: *Engane Nee Marakkum*; *Attakkalasam*; *Adhipathyam*; ***Akkare***; *Arabikadal*; *Asthram*; *Bhukambam*; *Chakravalam Chuvannappol*; *Ente Katha*; ***Ente Mamattukuttiamma***; *Guru Dakshina*; *Hello Madras Girl*; *Himavahini*; ***Iniyenkilum***; ***Kattathe Kilikoodu***; *Kola Komban*; *Kuyiline Thedi*; *Marakkailo Rikalum*; *Naseema*; *Nanayam*; *Oru Mugham Pala Mugham*; *Pinninvalu*; *Sesham Kazhchayil*; *Visa*; *Yangana Nee Marakkum*; **1984**: *Vanitha Police*; ***Alkoottathil Thaniye***; *Adiyozhukkukal*; *Aduthaduthu*; *Appunni*; *Ariyatha Veethigal*; *Athirathnam*; *Etha Ennumuthal*; *Ivide Thodangannu*; *Kaliyil Alpan Karyam*; *Kilikonchal*; *Kurisuyuddham*; ***Lakshmana Rekha***; *Manasariyathe*; *Nayakan*; ***Nokketha Dhoorathu Kannum Nattu***; *Onnanu Nammal*; *Oru Kochu Swapnam*; *Pavam Poornima*; *Poochakkoru Mookuthi*; *Saundamevide? Bandamevide?*; *Shri Krishnaparunthu*; *Thirakal*; *Unaroo*; *Uyyarangalil*; *Vettah*; **1985**: *Adhiyayam Odhu Mudhal*; ***Angadikkapurathu***; *Anubandham*; *Aram Aram = Kinnaram*; *Avidathepole Ivideyum*; *Azhiyatha Bandhangal*; *Boeing Boeing*; *Ezhamuthal Onpathuvare*; *Guruji Oru Vakku*; *Ida Nilangal*; *Jeevante Jeevan*; *Kandu Kandarinju*; *Karimbin Poovinakkare*; *Koodum Thedi*; *Mulammoottil Adima*; *Neram Pularumbol*; *Gnan Piranna Natil*; *Omanikkan Ormavaikkan*; *Onnanam Kunnil Oradi Kunnil*; *Pathamudayam*; *Parayanumvayya Parayathirikkanumvayya*; *Rangam*; *Uyaram Gnan Nadake*; *Vasantsena*; **1986**: ***Vartha***; *Pappan Priyapetta Pappan*; *Oppom Oppathinoppam*; *Mazha Peyyunnu Maddalam Kottunnu*; ***Panchagni***; *Abhayam Thedi*; *Desadanakkili Karayilla*; *Ninnishtam Ennishtam*; *Kunjatta Kiligal*; *Revathikkoru Pavakkutty*; *Hello My Dear-Wrong Number*; *Iniyum Kurukshetrám*; *Kaveri*; ***Gandhinagar 2nd Street***; *Doore Doore Koodu Kootam*; ***Thalavattam***; *Sanmanassu Illavakkaru Samadhanam*; **1987**: *Abhimanyu*; *January Oru Orma*; *Amritam Gamaya*; *Adimagal Udumagal*; *Sarvakalasala*; *Unnikale Oru Katha Parayam*; *Thoovana Thumbigal*; *Vazhiyora Kazhchagal*; *Ivide Ellavarkkum Sukham*; *Cheppu*; *Nadodikattu*; **1988**: *Kilukkam*; *Mukunthetta Sumitra Vilikkunnu*; *Ayitham*; *Orkapurathu*; *Padamudra*; *Pattana Praveshanam*; *Anuragi*; *Aryan*; *Moonnam Mura*; ***Chithram***; **1989**: *Utsavapittennu*; *Lal Americayil*; *Dauthiyam*; *Season*; *Varavelpu*; *Naduvazhigal*; *Kireedam*; *Vandanam*; *Dasharatham*; *Adipan*; ***Thazhvaram***; **1990**: ***Vasthuhara***; *Indrajalam*; *His Highness Abdullah*; **1991**: *Dhanam*; *Vishnulokam*; *Ulladakkam*; *Kizhakkunarum Pakshi*; *Advaitham*; *Rajashilpi*; **1992**: *Sadayam*; *Kamalathalam*; *Agam*; *Yoddha*; *Nadodi*; *Vietnam Colony*; **1993**: *Midhunam*; *Devasuram*; *Butterflies*; *Maya Mayuram*; *Gandharvam*.

Mohapatra *see* **Mahapatra**

MOTILAL RAJVANSH (1910-65)

Hindi actor born in Simla; best known as the gentleman crook in **Gemini**'s ***Mr Sampat***, based on R.K. Narayan's famous novel, and as the tragic hero's city friend in **Bimal Roy**'s 1955 version of ***Devdas***. Played several roles as the urbane city-bred sophisticate, e.g. in **Mehboob**'s ***Taqdeer***, and most notably in **Hrishikesh Mukherjee**'s ***Anari***, where his suave performance as a business magnate counterpoints **Raj Kapoor**'s awkward Oedipal rebellion. Also played a spectacular antipathetic role in **Kardar**'s ***Holi***. Together with Sabita Devi, he formed a top 30s screen couple in **Sagar**'s socials, e.g. **Badami**'s **K.M. Munshi**-scripted ***Dr Madhurika***. Later worked at **Ranjit** in **Chandulal Shah**'s ***Achhut***, in **Jayant Desai**'s *Diwali* and *Shadi* and in **Chaturbhuj Doshi**'s *Pardesi* and *Sasural*, usually with Madhuri. Elaborated a realistic acting style relying on casual dialogue delivery, often hailed as the first example of naturalistic film acting in India. His style marked the early work of Mehboob (***Jagirdar***, ***Hum Tum Aur Woh***, *Taqdeer*) and **Kidar Sharma** (***Armaan***, *Kaliyan*) and was acknowledged by **Dilip Kumar** as a significant predecessor. Cousin of playback singer Mukesh.

FILMOGRAPHY (* also d): **1934**: ***Shaher Ka Jadoo***; **1935**: ***Silver King***; ***Dr Madhurika***; **1936**: *Jeevan Lata*; ***Lagna Bandhan***; ***Do Diwane***; **1937**: *Captain Kirti Kumar*; ***Jagirdar***; *Kokila*; *Kulavadhu*; **1938**: ***Three Hundred Days And After***; ***Hum Tum Aur Woh***; **1939**: *Aap Ki Marzi*; ***Sach Hai***; **1940**: ***Achhut***; *Diwali*; ***Holi***; **1941**: *Pardesi*; *Sasural*; *Shadi*; **1942**: ***Armaan***; *Iqraar*; **1943**: *Muskurahat*; *Prarthana*; *Pratigya*;

Mohanlal in *Rachana* (1983)

Taqdeer; ***Tasveer***; *Vijay Lakshmi*; *Aage Kadam*; **1944**: *Dost*; *Kaliyan*; *Mujrim*; *Pagli Duniya*; *Raunaq*; *Umang*; **1945**: *Biswi Sadi*; *Murti*; *Pehli Nazar*; *Piya Milan*; *Sawan*; **1946**: *Phulwari*; **1947**: *Beete Din*; *Do Dil*; **1948**: *Aaj Ki Raat*; *Gajre*; *Mera Munna*; **1949**: ***Ek Thi Ladki***; *Lekh*; *Parivartan*; **1950**: *Hanste Aansoo*; *Hamari Beti*; *Sartaj*; **1952**: *Apni Izzat*; *Betaab*; *Kafila*; ***Mr Sampat***; **1953**: *Dhuan*; *Ek Do Teen*; *Jhanjhar*; *Pehli Shaadi*; **1954**: *Khushboo*; *Mastana*; *Savdhan*; **1955**: ***Devdas***; *Shri Naqad Narayan*; **1956**: *Bandhan*; *Guru Ghantal*; ***Jagte Raho***; *Lalten*; **1957**: *Ab Dilli Door Nahin*; **1958**: *Hathkadi*; *Do Mastane*; **1959**: ***Anari***; ***Paigham***; **1960**: *Mukti*; *Parakh*; *Zameen Ke Tare*; **1963**: *Yeh Raaste Hain Pyar Ke*; **1964**: *Leader*; *Ji Chahta Hai*; **1965**: *Chhoti Chhoti Baatein**; ***Waqt***; **1966**: *Duniya Hai Dilwalon Ki*; *Yeh Zindagi Kitni Haseen Hai*.

MUDALIAR, PAMMAL VIJAYARANGA SAMBANDHAM (1872-1964)

Influential Tamil director; former lawyer and dramatist. Founded the amateur theatre group Suguna Vilas Sabha (1904), staging, e.g., Shakespeare and Sanskrit classics in the Victoria Public Hall, Madras. Wrote c.68 plays staged for the city's political and cultural élite. Many of his plays were filmed, often directly from the stage: e.g. **Sarvottam Badami**'s *Galava Rishi* (1932), the second Tamil sound feature, and Mudaliar's own directions *Sati Sulochana* and *Manohara*. Other films based on his plays, setting the norms for an élite, 'apolitical' entertainment, include Prafulla Ghosh's *Ratnavali* (1935), M.L. Tandon's *Yayati* (1938), **T.R. Raghunath**'s *Ramalinga Swamigal* (1939), K.S. Mani's *Chandrahari* (1941), **Murugadasa**'s *Urvashi Sahasam* (1940), **Duncan**'s *Daasi Penn* (1943), **A.V. Meiyappan**'s *Sabhapati* (1941) and *Vethala Ulagam* (1948). Published two books on Tamil film in 1937.

FILMOGRAPHY (* also act): **1934**: *Sati Sulochana*; **1936**: *Manohara**.

MUDALIAR, R. NATARAJA (1885-1972)

Pioneer cineaste of South India born in Vellore. Initially in the cycle business (1906), then the car trade (1911). Apprenticed in 1912 to a Mr Stewart, the official cinematographer of Lord Curzon's 1903 durbar. Inspired by **Phalke**'s work, set up India Film in Madras (1916) with a second-hand Williamson camera and finance from businessman S.M. Dharmalingam. The studio was set up in a makeshift space on Miller's Road where he made *Keechaka Vadham*, intertitled in Tamil, Hindi and English. His second film, *Draupadi Vastrapaharanam*, featured an Anglo-Indian actress, Marian Hill, as Draupadi. Made his other features, all mythologicals, around his home town of Vellore. In 1923, his studio burnt down and his son died, prompting him to retire.

FILMOGRAPHY: 1916: *Keechaka Vadham*; **1917**: *Draupadi Vastrapaharanam*; **1918**: *Mayil Ravana*; **1919**: *Lavakusa*; **1920**: *Kalinga Mardanam*; **1921**: *Rukmini Kalyanam*; **1923**: *Markandeya*.

MUKHERJEE, GYAN (1909-59)

Hindi director born in Benares. Graduated as a scientist; editor of journal *Science and Culture*. Joined **Bombay Talkies** as a supervising technician. Wrote script for ***Bandhan*** (1940) and collaborated with **Abbas** on script of ***Naya Sansar*** (1941). Directed **Ashok Kumar** at **Bombay Talkies** (***Jhoola***, ***Kismet***) and **Filmistan**, creating a new image for him with a big impact on later Hindi film (e.g. on the image of **Dilip Kumar**). His ***Chal Chal Re Naujawan*** launched Filmistan. Style drawn largely from 30s Warner Bros with naturalist underplaying for greater psychological complexity (e.g. the seminal *Kismet*). **Guru Dutt** dedicated ***Pyaasa*** (1957) to him.

FILMOGRAPHY: 1941: ***Jhoola***; **1943**: ***Kismet***; **1944**: ***Chal Chal Re Naujawan***; **1950**: ***Sangram***; **1953**: *Shamsheer*; **1955**: *Sardar*; **1956**: *Shatranj*; **1959**: *Madhu*.

MUKHERJEE, HEMANTA KUMAR (1920-89)

Aka Hemant Kumar. Bengali-Hindi composer and singer. Born in Varanasi. Left school to become a professional singer. Studied under Phani Bannerjee and Shailendraprasad Gupta. Early songs for radio. Released his first record in 1937, with the still-popular numbers *Janite jadi go* and *Balogo more*. Considered the foremost Rabindra Sangeet singer of his time, starting under the tutelage of Anadi Dastidar and then singing mainly in the tradition of **Pankaj Mullick**. Changed his style in context of a brief but fruitful collaboration with composer **Salil Choudhury** (1949-52) associated with the **IPTA**. Début as singer in Bengali film with **Phani Burma**'s *Nimai Sanyasi* (1940) and in Hindi with *Iraada* (1944). Early compositions for **Hemen Gupta** (***Bhuli Naai***, ***'42***, ***Anandmath***, *Kashti*). Established himself as a Bengali composer with **Ajoy Kar**'s *Jighansa*. Although he went on to become one of the most popular Bengali film composers, his main fame derives from playback singing for **Uttam Kumar**, his baritone becoming a key ingredient of the star's romantic dramas: e.g. classic hits *Jher utteche* in Sudhir Mukherjee's *Shap Mochan*; *Nir chhoto khati nei* in **Niren Lahiri**'s *Indrani* (1958); *Ei path jadi na shesh hoi* in Ajoy Kar's ***Saptapadi***, etc. From the 50s onwards his voice incarnated Bengali middle-class romanticism, having an enduring influence on all male playback singers in the language ever since. Became a star singer in Hindi with the classic *Yeh raat yeh chandni* in **Guru Dutt**'s ***Jaal*** (1952), picturised on **Dev Anand** on the beach among the fishing nets. Collaborated extensively with Dutt, e.g. *Jaane who kaise log the* in ***Pyaasa*** (1957) and scored the hauntingly beautiful numbers of ***Sahib Bibi Aur Ghulam***. First Hindi hit as composer is ***Nagin***, adapting a tune from **Bijon Bhattacharya**'s play *Jiyankanya* for the sinuous snake dance number *Man dole*, a landmark in the introduction of electronics into Hindi film music. Composed regularly for **Tarun Majumdar** and for the early **Mrinal Sen**, producing Sen's ***Neel Akasher Neechey***. As producer he often worked with set designer turned director Biren Nag, showing a penchant for thrillers like ***Bees Saal Baad*** (adapting *The Hound of the Baskervilles*), and ***Kohraa***, borrowed from Daphne du Maurier's (and Hitchcock's) *Rebecca*. Also produced Pinaki Mukherjee's *Faraar*, **Hrishikesh Mukherjee**'s *Biwi Aur Makaan*, Tarun Majumdar's *Rahgir* and **Asit Sen**'s **Rajesh Khanna** psychodrama ***Khamoshi***. Autobiography *Amar Ganer Swaralipi* (1988).

FILMOGRAPHY (* also d): **1947**: *Purbaraag*; *Abhiyatri*; **1948**: ***Bhuli Naai***; *Padma Paramatti Nadi*; *Priyatama*; **1949**: *Diner Par Din*; ***'42***; *Sandipan Pathshala*; *Swami*; **1951**: *Jighansa*; **1952**: ***Anandmath***; **1954**: *Daku Ki Ladki*; *Kashti*; *Jagriti*; ***Nagin***; *Samrat*; *Shart*; **1955**: *Bahu*; ***Bandish***; *Bhagwat Mahima*; *Lagan*; *Shap Mochan*; **1956**: *Suryamukhi*; *Anjaan*; *Arab Ka Saudagar*; *Bandhan*; *Durgesh Nandini*; *Ek Hi Raasta*; *Hamara Watan*; *Inspector*; *Lalten*; *Taj*; **1957**: ***Bandi***; *Champakali*; *Ek Jhalak*; *Fashion*; *Hill Station*; *Kitna Badal Gaya Insaan*; *Miss Mary*; *Payal*; *Yahudi Ki Ladki*; *Shesh Parichaya*; *Taser Ghar*; *Harano Sur*; *Naikinichi Sajja*; **1958**: *Lookochuri*; *Shikar*; *Joutuk*; *Surya Toran*; *Do Mastane*; *Police*; *Sahara*; ***Neel Akasher Neechey***; **1959**: *Chand*; *Hum Bhi Insaan Hain*; *Marutirtha Hinglaj*; ***Deep Jweley Jai***; *Khelaghar*; *Sonar Harin*; *Kshaniker Atithi*; **1960**: *Kuhak*; *Khokha Babur Pratyabartan*; ***Baishey Shravan***; *Gariber Meye*; *Shesh Paryanta*; *Duniya Jhukti Hai*; *Girl Friend*; **1961**: *Sathi Hara*; *Agni Sanskar*; *Swaralipi*; *Madhya Rater Tara*; ***Saptapadi***; *Dui Bhai*; ***Punashcha***; **1962**: ***Hansuli Banker Upakatha***; *Atal Jaler Ahwan*; *Agun*; *Dada Thakur*; *Nabadiganta*; ***Bees Saal Baad***; *Maa Beta*; ***Sahib Bibi Aur Ghulam***; **1963**: *Bin Badal Barsaat*; *Ek Tukro Agun*; *Barnachora*; ***Saat Pake Bandha***; *High Heel*; *Palatak*; *Shesh Prahar*; *Tridhara*; *Badshah*; **1964**: ***Kohraa***; *Pratinidhi*; *Bibhas*; *Swarga Hotey Biday*; *Sindoore Megh*; *Prabhater Rang*; *Natun Tirtha*; ***Arohi***; **1965**: *Alor Pipasa*; *Ek Tuku Basa*; *Surya Tapa*; *Ek Tuku Chhoya Lage*; *Do Dil*; *Faraar*; **1966**: ***Anupama***; *Biwi Aur Makaan*; *Sannata*; *Kanch Kata Hirey*; *Manihar*; **1967**: *Balika Bodhu*; *Dustu Prajapati*; *Nayika Sangbad*; *Manjhli Didi*; *Ajana Shapath*; **1968**: *Do Dooni Char*; *Adwitiya*; *Baghini*; *Hansamithun*; *Jiban Sangeet*; *Panchasar*; *Parishodh*; **1969**: *Chena Achena*; *Mon-Niye*; *Parineeta*; *Shuk Sari*; ***Khamoshi***; *Rahgir*; **1970**: *Deshbandhu Chittaranjan*; *Us Raat Ke Baad*; *Duti Mon*; **1971**: *Kuheli*; *Malayadaan*; *Nabaraag*; *Nimantran*; *Sansar*; **1972**: *Bees Saal Pehle*; *Anindita**; *Shriman Prithviraj*; **1974**: *Bikele Bhorer Phool*; *Thagini*; *Phuleshwari*; **1975**: *Agniswar*; *Nishi Mrigaya*; *Raag Anuraag*; ***Sansar Simantey***; *Mohan Baganer Meye*; **1976**: *Banhi Sikha*; *Datta*; *Sankhabish*; *Pratisruti*; **1977**: *Rajani*; *Din Amader*; *Hatey Roilo Tin*; *Mantramugdha*; *Pratima*; *Sanai*; *Shesh Raksha*; *Swati*; *Proxy*; **1978**: *Nadi Theke Sagare*; ***Ganadevata***; *Pronoy Pasha*; *Do Ladke Dono Kadke*; **1979**: *Love in Canada*; **1980**: *Bandhan*; ***Dadar Kirti***; *Paka Dekha*; *Pankhiraj*; *Shesh Bichar*; **1981**: *Subarna Golak*; *Kapal Kundala*; *Meghmukti*; *Khelar Putul*; *Shahar Theke Dooray*; **1982**: *Chhoto Maa*; **1983**: *Amar Geeti*; *Rajeshwari*; **1984**: *Agni Shuddhi*; *Ajantay*; *Bishabriksha*; *Didi*; *Madhuban*; **1985**: *Bhalobasha Bhalobasha*; *Tagori*; **1986**: *Pathbhola*; **1987**: *Pratibha*; *Tunibou*; **1988**: *Boba Sanai*; *Parasmoni*; *Surer Sathi*; *Agaman*.

MUKHERJEE, HRISHIKESH (b. 1922)

Hindi director and editor born in Calcutta. Studied science at Calcutta University; then a teacher and a freelance artist at AIR. Joined **New Theatres** (1945) as laboratory assistant, then editor. First full editing assignment: ***Tathapi*** (1950). Worked as assistant director and editor for **Bimal Roy**; later also edited films by **R. Kariat** and **R. Tarafdar**. Renowned for introducing editing conventions basic to Hindi film: e.g. insertion of close-up as bridge between incompatible shots. Acquired reputation of being able to salvage films that went out of control during shooting (e.g. Kariat's ***Chemmeen***, 1965). First film as director in collaboration with **Ritwik Ghatak** and **Salil Choudhury** (***Musafir***). 60s films continue in the vein of Bimal Roy's socials. Introduced 'cancer films' with ***Anand***, a very popular type of melodrama with terminally ill characters, which featured the reigning 70s superstars **Rajesh Khanna** and **Bachchan**. Repeated the duo in ***Namak Haram***. Later films often produced by N.C. Sippy are low-budget family melodramas. Chairman of Central Board of Film Censors and of the **NFDC**.

FILMOGRAPHY: **1957**: ***Musafir***; **1959**: ***Anari***; **1960**: ***Anuradha***; **1961**: *Chhaya*; *Memdidi*; **1962**: *Aashiq*; *Asli Naqli*; **1964**: *Sanjh Aur Savera*; **1965**: *Do Dil*; **1966**: ***Anupama***; *Biwi Aur Makaan*; ***Gaban***; **1967**: *Manjhli Didi*; **1968**: ***Ashirwad***; **1969**: *Pyar Ka Sapna*; ***Satyakam***; **1970**: ***Anand***; **1971**: *Buddha Mil Gaya*; ***Guddi***; **1972**: *Bawarchi*; *Subse Bada Sukh*; **1973**: *Abhimaan*; ***Namak Haram***; **1974**: *Phir Kab Milogi*; **1975**: *Chaitali*; *Chupke Chupke*; *Mili*; **1976**: *Arjun Pandit*; **1977**: *Alaap*; *Kotwal Saab*; **1978**: *Naukri*; **1979**: *Jurmana*; *Golmaal*; **1980**: *Khubsoorat*; **1981**: *Naram Garam*; **1982**: *Bemisal*; **1983**: *Namumkin*; *Achha Bura*; *Kisise Na Kehna*; *Rang Birangi*; **1986**: *Jhoothi*; *Hum Hindustani* (TV); **1988**: *Lathi*; **1992**: *Talash* (TV).

MUKHERJEE, MADHABI (b. 1943)

Bengali actress, worked on stage with, e.g., **Sisir Bhaduri**, **Ahindra Choudhury**, Nirmalendu Lahiri and **Chhabi Biswas**. Acted in plays like *Naa* (at the Kashi Vishwanath Manch) and *Kalarab* (at the Netaji Manch) before débuting as child actress in films with **Premendra Mitra**'s *Kankantala Light Railway*. Exemplifies the filmic incarnation of **Rabindranath Tagore**'s literary heroines. Achieved an exemplary Tagore characterisation in **Satyajit Ray**'s ***Charulata***. When Ray later returned to Tagore with ***Ghare Baire*** (1984), his heroine, Swatilekha Chatterjee, bears a striking resemblance to Madhabi. **Ritwik Ghatak** also extensively alludes to her way of performing literary figures, e.g. in ***Subarnarekha***: the way Seeta flicks her long hair dry or sits on the runway or by the river after eloping with Abhiram. Her first major film was **Mrinal Sen**'s ***Baishey Shravan***. For Ray she played the housewife who becomes a saleswoman in ***Mahanagar***. Also acted in **Harisadhan Dasgupta**'s first foray into fiction, *Eki Ange Eto Rup*. Later work includes Purendu Pattrea's *Swapnaniye* and 70s Tagore adaptation *Streer Patra*.

Madhabi Mukherjee in *Streer Patra* (1972)

FILMOGRAPHY: **1950**: *Kankantala Light Railway*; **1952**: *Prarthana*; **1956**: *Tonsil*; **1960**: ***Baishey Shravan***; **1961**: *Aaj Kal Parshu*; **1962**: ***Subarnarekha***; **1963**: ***Mahanagar***; **1964**: *Swarga Hotey Biday*; *Godhuli Belaye*; ***Charulata***; *Sindoore Megh*; *Binsati Janani*; **1965**: *Thana Theke Aschhi*; *Ghoom Bhangar Gaan*; ***Kapurush***; *Eki Ange Eto Rup*; *Devatar Deep*; **1966**: *Joradighir Choudhury Paribar*; *Sankha Bela*; *Swapnaniye*; **1967**: *Ajana Shapath*; *Kheya*; **1968**: *Adwitiya*; *Chhoto Jignasa*; *Garh Nasimpur*; *Parishodh*; **1969**: *Agni Yuger Kahini*; *Duranta Charai*; *Teer Bhoomi*; **1970**: *Swarna Sikhar Pranganey*; *Samanaral*; *Diba Ratrir Kabya*; **1971**: *Chhadmabeshi*; **1972**: *Biraj Bou*; ***Calcutta '71***; *Chinnapatra*; *Archana*; *Chhayatir*; *Streer Patra*; **1973**: *Andhar Periye*; *Bindur Chheley*; ***Bon Palashir Padabali***; *Haraye Khunji*; *Jiban Rahasya*; **1974**: *Chhutir Ghanta*; *Natun Surya*; **1975**: *Agniswar*; *Phool Sajya*; *Amriter Swad*; **1976**: *Yugo Manab Kabir*; **1977**: *Avatar*; *Ramer Sumati*; **1978**: ***Ganadevata***; **1980**: *Moyna Tadanta*; ***Bancharamer Bagan***; **1981**: *Manikchand*; *Subarnalata*; *Saheb*; **1982**: *Malancha*; *Matir Swarga*; *Prafulla*; *Chhoto Maa*; *Bandini Kamala*; ***Chokh***; **1983**: *Kauke Bolo Na*; *Shuparna*; *Samapti*; **1984**: *Jog Biyog*; **1985**: *Bhalobasha Bhalobasha*; *Jiban Sathi*; *Antaraley*; *Dadu Nati-o-Hati*; *Putulghar*; **1986**: *Anurager Choa*; *Artanad*; *Uttar Lipi*; *Madhumoy*; **1987**: *Bandookbaj*; *Rudrabina*; *Pratikar*; **1988**: *Hirer Shikal*; *Maa Ek Mandir*; *Anjali*; **1989**: *Kari Diye Kinlam*; *Aghaton Ajo Ghatey*; ***Chhandaneer***; **1990**: *Manasi*.

MUKHERJEE, SAILAJANANDA (1901-76)

Bengali director born in Andal, Burdwan District. Noted Bengali novelist and contemporary of **Kallol Group**. Closely associated in early youth with writer-musician **Kazi Nazrul Islam**. Worked in Raniganj collieries, the location of his first major literary work, *Koila Kuthi*, published in the journal *Basumati* (1922). The story later gave its name to a sub-genre of literary realism: a starkly realist manner, relying on personal experience and dialects (commonly those of the Dhanbad and Raniganj collieries and of Birbhum) violating the novelistic tradition that valued linguistic purity. Early writings include *Atmaghatir Diary* (*Diary of a Suicide*) published in *Bansari* journal, viewed as a violation of the prevailing norms of literary decency. Went to Calcutta where he met **Premendra Mitra**, Probodh Kumar Sanyal, Achintyakumar Sengupta and Kallol writer and film-maker Dinesh Ranjan Das. Briefly edited the *Kalikalam* journal. Later also edited the journals *Shahana* and *Bioscope*. Started in films as scenarist for **Hemchandra Chunder** (***Anath Ashram***, 1937). Also wrote scripts, in collaboration with Binoy Chatterjee, for **New Theatres** while assisting **Nitin Bose** (e.g. ***Dushman/Jiban Maran***, 1938). Directed works are early instances of a commercially successful cinema set among peasantry and urban working class, mostly based on his own writings (e.g. ***Mane Na Mana***). During shooting, he would often close his eyes, only listening to the dialogues in the long, static takes, permitting no deviation from the script. Published autobiography, *Je Katha Bola Hoy Ni* (1968). Scripted his own films as well as contributing stories or scripts to *Ae To Jiban* and *Santi* (1946), the Oriya film *Lakhmi* (1962), *Rup Sanatan* (1965) and *Anand Ashram* (1977).

FILMOGRAPHY: **1941**: *Nandini*; **1942**: *Bondi*; **1943**: ***Shahar Theke Dooray***; **1945**: *Abhinay Nay*; ***Mane Na Mana***; *Stree Durga*; **1947**: *Roy Choudhury*; **1948**: *Ghumiye Ache Gram*; *Rang Berang*; **1950**: *Sandhya-Belar Rupkatha*; *Eki Gramer Chhele*; **1953**: *Blind Lane*; **1954**: *Banglar Nari*; *Mani-Aar-Manik*; **1955**: *Katha Kao*; **1957**: *Ami-Baro-Habo*.

MUKHERJEE, SUBODH (b. 1921)

Hindi director and producer born in Jhansi, UP. Younger brother of **Filmistan** boss Shashadhar Mukherjee. Assistant to **Gyan Mukherjee** for ***Chal Chal Re Naujawan*** (1944). Début film ***Munimji*** is best illustration of **Dev Anand**'s use of the masquerade, continued in ***Paying Guest*** (one of Anand's most spectacular hits of the 50s). Continued and sharpened the Gyan Mukherjee-**Ashok Kumar** strategy of making blatant (male) star performance vehicles (e.g. ***Junglee***, starring **Shammi Kapoor**). Continued by **Nasir Hussain**'s films, they can be seen as precedents for **Manmohan Desai**'s films with Shammi Kapoor (***Bluff Master***, 1963) and **Bachchan** (***Amar Akbar Anthony***, 1977). Also wrote Vrajendra Gaud's *Kasturi* (1954).

FILMOGRAPHY: **1955**: ***Munimji***; **1957**: ***Paying Guest***; **1959**: *Love Marriage*; **1961**: ***Junglee***; **1964**: *April Fool*; **1966**: *Saaz Aur Awaz*; **1970**: *Abhinetri*; **1982**: *Teesri Aankh*; **1984**: *Ulta Seedha*.

MUKKAMALA, KRISHNAMURTHY (1920-87)

Telugu actor, producer and film-maker born in Guntur Dist., AP, where he was educated at Andhra Christian College. Worked with the theatre group run by **NTR**, **K. Jaggaiah**, etc., appearing in, e.g., Shakespeare plays. Wrote plays while a student at the Law College, Madras. Joined films as assistant to **C. Pullaiah** in *Maya Machhindra*, in which he also played the role of Gorakhnath. Turned full-time actor thereafter. Started his own M.K.M. Prod. (1951), and produced/directed *Maradalu Pelli*. In the 70s, often appeared in **Bapu**'s films, e.g. ***Shri Ramanjaneya Yuddham***, ***Seeta Kalyanam***, *Sneham*.

FILMOGRAPHY (* also d): **1945**: *Maya Machhindra*; **1949**: ***Laila Majnu***; **1950**: *Adrushta Deepudu*; ***Swapna Sundari***; **1951**: ***Nirdoshi/Niraparadhi***;

Mayalamari/Mayakkari; *Perantalu*; **1952**: *Dharmadevata*; ***Prema/Kathal***; *Maradalu Pelli**; **1953**: *Paropakaram*; **1954**: *Aggiramudu*; *Rechukka*; *Palle Paduchu*; **1956**: ***Tenali Ramakrishna/Tenali Raman***; **1957**: ***Maya Bazaar***; *Nala Damayanti*; **1958**: *Shobha*; *Shri Ramanjaneya Yuddham*; *Karthavarayan Katha*; **1959**: *Jayavijaya*; **1960**: *Jalsarayudu*; *Annapurna*; **1961**: *Rushyashrunga/Rishyashringar**; *Varalakshmi Vratam*; ***Jagadeka Veeruni Katha/Jagathala Prathapan***; **1962**: *Gul-e-Bakavali Katha*; *Mohini Rugmangada*; ***Mahamantri Timmarasu***; **1963**: *Guruvuniminchina Shishyudu*; **1964**: *Navagraha Pooja Mahima*; *Aggipidugu*; *Babruvahana*; *Bobbili Yuddham*; **1965**: *Jwaladeepa Rahasyam*; ***Pandava Vanavasam***; ***Satya Harishchandra***; **1966**: *Shakuntala*; *Potti Pleader*; *Vijayasankalam*; *Goodachari 116*; *Adugu Jadalu*; **1967**: *Satyame Jayam*; ***Bhama Vijayam/Bhale Kodalu***; ***Shri Krishnavataram***; **1968**: *Mana Samsaram*; *Umachandi Gauri Shankarula Katha*; *Chellikosam*; **1970**: *Janmabhoomi*; *Marina Manishi*; *Vijayam Manade*; **1971**: *Katha Nayakuralu*; **1972**: *Hanthakulu Devanthakulu*; *Kiladi Bullodu*; *Korada Rani*; *Maa Inti Kodalu*; ***Anta Mana Manchike***; *Goodu Putani*; *Shri Krishnanjaneya Yuddham*; *Manavudu Daanavudu*; *Shanti Nilayam*; *Vintha Dampathulu*; *Neethi*; **1974**: *Kode Naagu*; *Andaru Dongale*; *Vijaya Ramudu*; *Manchi Manushulu*; *Theerpu*; ***Shri Ramanjaneya Yuddham***; **1975**: *Jeevana Jyoti*; *Pandanti Samsaram*; *Amma Nana*; *Pichimaraju*; ***Muthyala Muggu***; **1976**: *Kolleti Kapuram*; *Neram Nadhikadu Akalidi*; ***Seeta Kalyanam***; **1977**: ***Daana Veera Shura Karna***; *Edureetha*; *Jeevitha Nauka*; *Kurukshetramu*; *Maa Iddari Katha*; *Sneham* (Tel); **1978**: ***Jagan Mohini***; *Karunamayudu*.

MULLICK, AMAR (1899-1972)

Bengali actor and director born in Calcutta. Actor and film-maker associated with **New Theatres** style. Civil engineer by profession, he started as actor at International Filmcraft, encouraged by B.N. Sircar. With **Atorthy**, **Nitin Bose** and I.A. Hafiz, was one of the first to join New Theatres (1932) where he acted in the Bengali versions of several classic bilinguals, usually playing the 'lighter' roles, as well as being production chief. Formed his own A.M. Prods. Known as director of literary adaptations from Saratchandra (***Bardidi***, *Biraj Bou*) and as character actor.

FILMOGRAPHY (* also d): **1931**: *Chorekanta*; *Swami*; *Chasher Meye* (all St); *Dena Paona*; **1932**: *Sandigdha* (St); *Punarjanma*, *Chirakumar Sabha*; ***Chandidas***; **1933**: ***Meerabai***; *Kapal Kundala*; **1935**: ***Devdas***; *Abasheshe*; ***Bhagya Chakra***; *Bijoya*; **1936**: *Karodpati*; ***Grihadah***; **1937**: ***Didi***; ***Mukti***; ***Bidyapati***; **1938**: ***Desher Mati***; ***Saathi***; **1939**: ***Bardidi/Badi Didi****; ***Parajay***; **1940**: ***Abhinetri/Haar Jeet****; *Doctor*; **1941**: ***Doctor***; **1943**: *Kashinath*; **1944**: *Sandhya*; *Shesh Raksha*; **1945**: *Bhabhi Kaal*; *Nandita*; **1946**: *Biraj Bou**; **1947**: *Ratri*; *Mandir*; *Chandrasekhar*; *Natun Khabar*; **1949**: *Swami**; *Samapti**; **1951**: *Durgesh Nandini**; **1952**: *Bhuler Sheshe**; **1954**: *Sati**; *Naad-o-Nadi*; *Chheley Kaar*; **1955**: *Shap Mochan*; *Ardhangini*; *Swami Vivekananda**; **1956**: *Mahanisha*; **1957**: *Louha-Kapat*; ***Parash Pathar***; **1958**: *Sonar Kathi*; *Jogajog*; *Purir Mandir*; *Rajdhani Theke*; **1959**: *Chaowa-Pawa*; *Shashi Babur Sansar*; *Pushpadhanu*; *Agnisambhaba*; *Rater Andhakare*; *Mriter Martye Agaman*; *Personal Assistant*; **1960**: *Prabesh Nishedh*; *Ajana Kahini*; *Biyer Khata*; *Natun Fasal*; **1961**: *Kathin Maya*; **1962**: *Kancher Swarga*; *Abhisarika*; **1963**: ***Nirjan Saikate***; **1966**: *Sudhu Ekti Bachhar*; *Susanta Sha*; *Uttar Purush*; **1967**: *Seba*; **1968**: *Pathe Holo Dekha*; **1969**: *Chena Achena*; *Shuk Sari*.

MULLICK, PANKAJ (1905-78)

Bengali composer, singer and actor born in Calcutta. Left college to concentrate on music; trained by Durgadas Bannerjee and then by Dinendranath Tagore. Released his first record for Vielophone (1926) and made his début on radio at the Indian Broadcasting Co. in its inaugural year (1927). Associated for several years with radio as producer, musician and educator e.g. in the popular programme *Sangeet Shikshar Asar* (from Sept. 1929) and the annual *Mahishamardini* broadcast. Film début conducting the live orchestra for International Filmcraft's silents *Chasher Meye* and *Chorekanta* (both 1931). Joined **New Theatres**, composing **Atorthy**'s epic ***Yahudi Ki Ladki***. Scored several films with **R.C. Boral**, e.g. **Barua**'s ***Devdas***, ***Grihadah*** and ***Maya***, **Chunder**'s *Karodpati* and **Nitin Bose**'s ***Didi/President***. Achieved fame through his Rabindra Sangeet for ***Mukti***, popularising **Tagore**'s lyrics with the poet's endorsement. After *Mukti*'s success he concentrated for some years on playback singing (e.g. ***Anjangarh***, 1948) and on acting. Returned to composition for **Kartick Chattopadhyay**'s films and **Paul Zils**'s *Zalzala*. Released a record singing the songs he composed for **Saigal** in ***Meri Bahen***, e.g. *Chupo na*, *Do naina matwale* et al. Published his memoirs, *Ganer Surer Asanakhani*, in a special issue of *Desh* (1973) and his autobiography under the title *Amar Jug Amar Gaan* (1980).

FILMOGRAPHY (* also act/** act only): **1933**: ***Yahudi Ki Ladki***; **1935**: ***Bhagya Chakra***; ***Devdas***; **1936**: *Karodpati*; ***Maya***; ***Grihadah***; **1937**: ***Didi/President***; ***Mukti****; **1938**: ***Adhikar*****; ***Abhigyan*****; ***Desher Mati****/***Dharti Mata***; ***Dushman/Jiban Maran***; **1939**: ***Bardidi/Badi Didi***; *Kapal Kundala**; **1940**: ***Zindagi***; ***Nartaki****; *Alochhaya/Aandhi***; *Doctor**; **1941**: ***Doctor****; **1942**: ***Meenakshi***; **1943**: *Kashinath*; *Dikshul*; **1944**: ***Meri Bahen***; **1945**: *Dui Purush*; **1947**: *Nurse Sisi*; ***Ramer Sumati/Chhota Bhai***; **1948**: *Pratibad/Oonch Neech*; **1949**: *Manzoor*; **1950**: *Roopkatha/Roop Kahani*; **1952**: ***Mahaprasthaner Pathey/Yatrik***; *Chhoti Maa*; *Zalzala*; **1953**: *Bana Hansi*; *Nabin Yatra/Naya Safar*; **1954**: *Chitrangada*; **1955**: *Amar Saigal*; *Raikamal*; **1957**: *Louha-Kapat*; **1961**: *Ahwan*; **1972**: *Bighalita Karuna Janhabi Jamuna*.

MUNSHI, KANHAIYALAL MANEKLAL (1887-1971)

Major Gujarati novelist, playwright, essayist and social reformer. Worked briefly at **Sagar** where his scripts were a seminal generic influence on its reformist socials, esp. ***Dr Madhurika*** and *Vengeance is Mine* (both 1935, the latter based on his story *Ver Ni Vasulat*), feeding into **Mehboob**'s historicals. Early writings were reformist socials following in the wake of the most significant novelist in modern Gujarati, Govardhanram Tripathi (1855-1907). Became popular with historicals and period fables often set in the Solanki period (AD961-1242): e.g. *Patanant Prabhuta* (1916), *Gujarat No Natha* (1917), *Rajadhi Raja* (1922). Author of the spectacularly successful historical ***Prithvi Vallabh*** (1920), filmed in the silent era by **Manilal Joshi** (1924) and later by **Sohrab Modi** (1943). In later years better known as a lawyer and politician, co-founding the right-wing Swatantra Party and briefly as a cabinet minister in the Congress.

MURUGADASA (b. 1900)

Pioneering Tamil director and producer, originally A. Muthuswamy Iyer. Graduate from St Joseph's College, Tiruchi; journalist for *The Mail*, Madras; edited the film journal *Sound and Shadow*, one of South India's first English film journals. Assisted **Baburao Pendharkar** in **Prabhat**'s Tamil film *Seeta Kalyanam* (1933), making his début with cameraman **Ramnoth** and set designer A.K. Sekhar. The trio then started the influential **Vel Pics** in Adyar, Madras: e.g. *Markandeya* and later *Paduka Pattabhishekham* (co-d Ramnoth), which introduced the major lyricist **Papanasam Sivan** and actor, musician and director **S. Balachander** who played a magician in the film. Started the Karthikeya Films Studio (1937) but returned to journalism when it burnt down. His best-known film is *Nandanar*, a reform drama addressing Untouchability and featuring the Carnatic musician Dandapani Desigar. Worked with the Cine Technicians' Association, editing their journal, apparently living on Union premises.

FILMOGRAPHY: 1935: *Bhakta Ramadasa*; *Markandeya*; **1936**: *Paduka Pattabhishekham*; *Pattinathar*; **1937**: *Sundaramurthy Nayanar*; **1940**: *Urvashi Sahasam*; *Bhakti*; **1941**: ***Venuganam***; **1942**: *Nandanar*; **1948**: *Gnanasoundari*.

MUSIC SCHOOLS

In 1896, Vishnu Digambar Paluskar ran away from his teacher Pandit Balkrishnabua Ichalkaranjikar, a court musician at Miraj. Like his contemporary, **Ravi Varma**, in the visual arts, Paluskar wanted to move away from feudal patronage and address the market-places of growing urban centres. He started a music school, the Gandharva Mahavidyalaya, at Lahore in 1901. Over the next thirty years, dozens of similar schools spread throughout Northern and Western India, e.g. the Saraswati Sangeet Vidyalaya in Karachi (1916), the Gopal Gayan Samaj in Pune (1918), the Gandharva Mahavidyalaya in Kolhapur (1920) and the School of Indian Music in Bombay (1925). Paluskar's action stemmed from a nationalistic disaffection from the feudal *gharana* system which was then sponsored and owned by the nobility who kept its repertory available only to the Guru's kinsmen. His colleague, V.N. Bhatkhande, compiled and published all the available classical musical compositions in an accessible textbook, *Hindustani Sangeet Paddhati* (1921). Equally influential was the simultaneous effort to define a primitive notation system capable of recording the complex performance codes. Barring a few notable exceptions, the bulk of the students in the new system lacked the rigour of the traditional discipline, but they were also free from the conservatism of *gharana* ideology. They usually found their way into the recording industries of Lahore, Karachi and Calcutta, into the **Sangeet Natak** and **Company Natak** troupes and, after 1932, into film. **Master Krishnarao** was trained at the Bharat Gayan Samaj, actress **Shanta Apte** at the Maharashtra Sangeet Vidyalaya, Pandharpur. The parent school in Lahore also produced several musicians and composers central to the Lahore-based film industry: Rafiq Ghaznavi, an extremely popular ghazal singer with best-selling records in Karachi and an actor-music director in films like *Prithviraj Sanyogita* (1933), *Bahen Ka Prem* (1935) and later in some **Mehboob** and **Sohrab Modi** films. Prof. B.R. Deodhar, disciple of Paluskar and key ideologue for the music school aesthetic, stated in 1933 a position closely analogous to that prevalent in the art schools. In his opinion, the major issues facing classical Indian music were those of voice production and the antithetical relationship between Indian music and Western principles of notation, which made it difficult to arrive at indigenous systems of orchestration as well as to find equivalents for perceiving pure sound effects (like thunder or rain sounds). His polemical view was that these could only be solved through borrowing from Western classical musical systems (Deodhar, 1933).Muthuswamy, A. *see* **Murugadasa**Muzumdar *see* **Majumdar**

MYTHOLOGICALS

The Malayalam cinema has a tradition of Biblical mythologicals traceable to **P.J. Cherian**'s stage work (e.g. *Snapaka Yohannan*, 1963; P.A. Thomas' *Jesus*, 1973; the biblical epic shot in 1991 for tv by Appachan), but the genre effectively refers to the Hindu mythological and is also known as the Pauranic genre. 'Puranas' or 'ancient stories' have become mere religious fables and cant, whatever historical content they once possessed having become encrusted with myth and diluted with semi-religious legends. The stories were collected and elaborated into the *Mahabharata*, a text going back to 400 BC and undergoing a series of mutations until c.AD400. This process, which saw the rise of a caste system in India, also evolved a textual hierarchy with the 'official' Sanskritised text repeatedly rewritten to justify the accumulation of agrarian surplus by the Brahmins (priest caste). There are several popular versions presented for the benefit of the lower classes but these also continued the oral and pictorial traditions of the 'heroic lays of ancient war' (Kosambi, 1962). Major historical interventions include the Buddhist revolution and the regional linguistic proliferation leading to the medieval Bhakti and Sufi movements. Industrial genres immediately preceding film are evidenced in the visual arts (see **Pat Painting** and **Ravi Varma**) and in the theatre (see **Radheshyam Kathavachak** and **Betaab**). An economically developed commercial stage in most urban centres often adapted modes of folk performance to the European proscenium, creating technical precedents for several of the earliest conventions of film shooting and editing (see **Phalke**). The most famous traditions are the Ramleela and Raasleela (later assimilated into Parsee theatre; cf ***Indrasabha***, 1932), the Yakshagana, Nautanki, Bhavai, Burrakatha and Jatra. The form has been and continues to be used for explicitly ideological ends. Among its first industrialised manifestations were Ravi Varma's self-conscious appropriation of Brahmical 'classicism' for the benefit of his royal patron and the Mysore court (cf **G.V. Iyer**). The stories were also used as encoded messages of nationalist patriotism (e.g. **Phalke**'s work, or ***Bhakta Vidur***, 1921), as a way of conveying 'Gandhian' national chauvinism in **Vijay Bhatt**'s films, to bolster regionalist separatism in **Rajkumar**'s Kannada films or simply to shore up temple cults with a mass following (e.g. the films on the Guruvayoor and Sabarimalai icons in Kerala). Recently, mythologicals have been used to propagate Hindu chauvinism, e.g. in **Ramanand Sagar**'s tv *Ramayan* (1986-8). The genre can also be seen in terms of its performative traditions shading into the melodramatic idiom, condensing complex contemporary tensions and codes in its figures. **Ritwik Ghatak** mobilises this dimension as do **Raj Kapoor** and several others, e.g. in their references to the goddess Seeta when wives and mothers are at issue. In spite of the pervasive references to the myths in Indian cinema, mythologicals cannot be regarded as a matrix or a master text for Indian narrative art in general, but rather as a nationally familiar and flexible stock of figures and topoi which can be used as shorthand to register more immediate historical issues (cf *Bhakta Vidur*, 1921). The invocation of myths is less important than the way the stories are treated as a genre, modified as narratives or formally deployed as allegorical relays within a conservatively constructed notion of the **social** as a cinematic genre.

NADIA (b. 1910)

Aka 'Fearless' Nadia. Indian cinema's most famous stunt actress was born Mary Evans in Perth, Australia. She worked in Zacko's Russian circus before touring the Asian subcontinent with Madame Astrova's ballet group, doing live shows in between silent films for British and Indian troops. She joined **Wadia Movietone** as chorus girl for ***Lal-e-Yaman***. ***Hunterwali***, the first of her highly successful films usually directed by her husband **Homi Wadia**, launched her as 'India's Pearl White' in action films set in an unspecified period or in Tarzan-land (*Jungle Princess*) or in a fantasy version of Hollywood gangster movies. She was always accompanied by her horse, Punjab Ka Beta, except when swinging from one building to another or through high-domed halls via chandeliers (*Hunterwali*), fighting the villain atop a rolling carriage (***Diamond Queen***) and, most popular of all, jumping from roof to roof on a moving train. She made several 'train' films, esp. ***Miss Frontier Mail***, to show off this talent. The villain was always the devious Sayani and her (usually masked) hero was initially Boman Shroff who started the Wadia stunt tradition in silent films playing Fairbanks roles. After *Punjab Mail*, John Cawas replaced him as her leading man. Riyad Vinci Wadia, **J.B.H. Wadia**'s grandson and the current owner of Wadia Movietone, made a documentary about the star, *Fearless: The Hunterwali Story* (1993).

FILMOGRAPHY: 1933: ***Lal-e-Yaman***; **1935**: ***Desh Deepak***; *Noor-e-Yaman*; ***Hunterwali***; **1936**: ***Miss Frontier Mail***; *Pahadi Kanya*; **1937**: ***Hurricane Hansa***; **1938**: *Lutaru Lalna*; **1939**: *Punjab Mail*; **1940**: ***Diamond Queen***; **1941**: *Bambaiwali*; **1942**: *Jungle Princess*; ***Muqabala***; **1943**: *Hunterwali Ki Beti*; *Mauj*; **1946**: *Flying Prince*; *Lady Robin Hood*; *Sher-e-Baghdad*; *Toofan Queen*; **1947**: *Himmatwali*; *Stunt Queen*; *Toofani Tirandaz*; *Chabuk Sawar*; **1948**: *Eleven O'Clock*; *Jungle Goddess*; *Tigress*; **1949**: *Delhi Express*; *Dhoomketu*; *Maya Mahal*; *Billi*; **1950**: *Circuswale*; **1952**: *Jungle Ka Jawahar*; **1953**: *Shamsheerbaaz*; **1954**: *Sher Dil*; **1955**: ***Carnival Queen***; **1956**: *Baghdad Ka Jadu*; *Fighting Queen*; *Jungle Queen*; **1957**: ***Diler Daku***; **1959**: *Circus Queen*; **1968**: *Khiladi*; **1993**: *Fearless: The Hunterwali Story* (Doc).

Habib and Fearless Nadia in *Jungle Queen* (1956)

NADKARNI, SUNDARRAO

Tamil director; also worked in Telugu and Kannada. Drawn to cinema apparently by watching Eddie Polo silents in his native Shimoga, Karnataka. Started as actor with **Sarpotdar** at Deccan Pics, United Pics and Aryan. Début as director was left unfinished when Sarpotdar sold United Pics; the film was completed by **Dhirubhai Desai**. Became the top director of Surya Film (1930), set up in Bangalore to replicate the **Sharda** Studio's **Master Vithal** stunt films with Ganpat Bakre and Zunzharrao Pawar. Turned to Tamil cinema with sound, mostly making mythologicals. Briefly worked as cameraman for Fazalbhoy's Film City (1934); then went to the Sundaram Sound Studio where he made his first Tamil films (*Raja Bhakti*, *Bhasmasur Mohini*, ***Bhukailasa***). Later worked at Jupiter Studio (*Valmiki*, *Krishna Vijayam*). Started his own Shri Ganesh Prasad Movies (1955) with *Koteshwaran* starring **Sivaji Ganesan**. Best known for his Telugu and Tamil film of **R. Nagendra Rao**'s hit play *Bhukailasa*. His last films were in Kannada.

FILMOGRAPHY (* act only): **1924**: ***Poona Raided****; **1925**: *Chandrarao More**; *Chhatrapati Sambhaji**; **1928**: *Maya Na Rang*; **1929**: *Julia Dalia**; *Mard Ki Zabaan**; *Kodandhari Ram**; *Raktacha Sood**; **1930**: *Dhoomketu*; *Randhir*; *Kalika No Kop*; **1931**: *Baaz Bahadur*; *Ishq No Anjam*; *Zindagi Nu Jugar*; *Qurbani*; *Taj Ke Talwar*; *Teer-e-Qatil* (all St); **1934**: *Sakkubai*; **1936**: *Raja Bhakti*; **1937**: *Bhasmasur Mohini*; **1938**: ***Bhukailasa***; **1939**: *Sant Sakkubai*; **1940**: ***Bhukailasa***; **1942**: *En Manaivi*; **1944**: *Haridas*; **1946**: *Valmiki*; **1949**: *Krishna Vijayam*; **1951**: *Sudarshan*; **1952**: *Krishna Kanhaiya*; **1953**: *Azhagi*; **1955**: *Koteshwaran*; **1957**: *Mahadevi*; **1963**: *Sant Tukaram*; **1968**: *Gauri Ganda*.

NAG, ANANT (b. 1948)

Actor born in Bombay as Anant Nagarkatti. One of the better-known New Indian Cinema actors committed to psychological characterisation. Bank employee while doing amateur theatre in Marathi and Kannada. Introduced by **Shyam Benegal**'s début feature, ***Ankur***, in Hindi and by **G.V. Iyer**'s revivalist musical ***Hamsa Geethe*** in Kannada cinema. Became a major Kannada star although, unlike his younger brother **Shankar Nag**, he tended to restrict himself to 'complex' character roles. Acted regularly for Benegal in the 70s. Other roles include the legendary Kannada brigand *Kanneshwara Rama* and the 19th C. Travancore musician-king, ***Swathi Thirunal***. Also acted in most films and tv serials directed by Shankar Nag. Member of the Karnataka Legislative Council for the Janata Dal.

FILMOGRAPHY: 1972: *Sankalpa*; **1973**: ***Ankur***; **1975**: ***Hamsa Geethe***; ***Nishant***; *Devara Kannu*; **1976**: *Bayalu Dari*; ***Manthan***; ***Bhumika***; **1977**: *Kanneshwara Rama*; *Anurupa*; *Premalekhalu*; ***Kondura/Anugraham***; *Kudre Mukha*; **1978**: *Sandarbha*; *Matu Tappada Maga*; *Premayana*; *Madhura Sangama*; **1979**: *Na Ninna Bidalare*; *Chandanada Gombe*; *Muttu Ondu Muttu*; *Dhairyalakshmi*; **1980**: ***Minchina Ota***; *Ondu Hennu Aaru Kannu*; *Narada Vijaya*; *Janma Janmada Anubandha*; *Premajwale*; ***Gehrayee***; ***Kalyug***; ***Bara/Sookha***; *Anveshane*; **1981**: *Mangalsutra* (K); *Anupama*; *Mareyada Haadu*; *Jivakke Jiva*; *Shriman*; **1982**: *Anandada Aramane*; *Bhadada Hoo*; *Mullina Gulabi*; *Nanna Devaru*; *Hasyarathna Ramakrishna*; *Bettale Seve*; ***Phaniyamma***; **1983**: *Lalach*; *Simhasana*; *Benkiya Bale*; *Hosa Teerpu*; *Kamana Billu*; *Bhakta Prahlada*; *Ebbani Karagitu*; *Mududida Tavare Aralitu*; *Gayatri Madhuve*; *Makkale Devaru*; *Chelisada Sagara*; *Nodi Swamy Navirodu Hige*; *Premave Balina Belaku*; **1984**: *Sukha Samsarakke Hanneradu Sutragalu*; *Premasakshi*; *Ramapurada Ravana*; *Olave Bedaku*; ***Accident***; *Olavu Moodidaga*; *Makkaliralavva Mane Thumba*; **1985**: *Bidugadeya Bedi*; *Haavu Eni Aata*; *Sedina Hakki*; *Koogu*; *Hosa Neeru*; **1986**: *Nenapina Doni*; *Maneye Manthralaya*; **1987**: *Thayi*; *Agni Parva*; *Avasthe*; *Kurukshetra*; *Athiratha Maharatha*; *Daiva Shakti*; ***Swathi Thirunal***; *Antima Ghatta*; **1988**: *Ranadheera*; *Shanti Nivasa*; *Varna Chakra*; *Shri Venkateshwara Mahime*; *Balondu Bhavageethe*; *Muttaide*; *Dharmatma* (K); **1989**: *Amanusha*; *Hendthige Helabedi*; *Idu Saadhya*; *Gagana*; **1990**: *Jurm*; *Golmaal Radhakrishna*; *Ramrajyadalli Rakshasaru*; *Swarna Samsara*; *Challenge Gopalakrishna*; *Udbhava*; *Mathe Hadithu Kogile*; *Ganeshana Madhuve*; **1991**: *Golmaal Bhaga II*; *Rollcall Ramakrishna*; *Gauri Ganesha*; *Shanti Kranti*; *Ratri/Raat*; **1992**: *Undu Roda Konda Hoda*; *Vajrayudha*; *Ganesha Subramanya*; *Ondu Cinema Kathe*; *Shakti Yukti*; *Atanka*; **1993**: *Mangalya Bandhana*; *Kadambari*.

NAG, SHANKAR (1954-90)

Kannada actor and director born in Udupi, Karnataka, as Shankar Nagarkatti. Educated in Bombay. Encouraged by his brother, **Anant Nag**, to work in Bombay on Marathi experimental stage where he directed, e.g., Sartre's *No Exit* and **Vijay Tendulkar**'s *Ashi Pakhare Yeti*. Also active on Hindi, English and Gujarati stage. Assistant of **Sai Paranjpye** (1976-7). Entered film as hero of **Girish Karnad**'s martial-arts film ***Ondanondu Kaladalli***. Best known as actor in action thrillers and rogue cop films. Karnad provided the script for his début feature as director, ***Minchina Ota***, produced by Sanket Films, which he helped set up (1980). Known for his tv adaptation of R.K. Narayan's novels (e.g. *Malgudi Days*). Ran amateur theatre group Sanket. Starred with his brother in many Kannada films, often playing brothers in family dramas (e.g. *Ramrajyadalli Rakshasaru*). Died in a road accident.

FILMOGRAPHY (* also d/** only d): **1978**: ***Ondanondu Kaladalli***; ***Sarvasakshi***; **1979**: *Seeta Ramudaithe*; *I Love You*; *Preeti Madu Tamashe Nodu*; *Madhuchandra*; **1980**: *Auto Raja*; *Haddina Kannu*; *Mugana Sedu*; *Ondu Hennu Aaru Kannu*; *Arada Gaya*; *Rustom Jodi*; ***Minchina Ota****; *Janma Janmada Anubandha**; **1981**: *Geetha***; *Karinaga*; *Thayiya Madilalli*; *Kulaputra*; *Hana Balavo Jana Balavo*; *Devara Aata*; *Bhari Bharjari Bete*; *Muniyana Madari*; *Jivakke Jiva*; **1982**: *Archana*; *Benki Chendu*; *Karmika Kallanalla*; *Dharma Dari Tappitu*; *Nyaya Yellide?*; **1983**: *Gedda Maga*; *Nyaya Gedditu*; *Chandi Chamundi* (K); *Keralida Hennu*; *Akrosha*; *Rakta Tilaka*; *Nagabekamma Nagabeku*; *Hosa Teerpu***; *Nodi Swamy Navirodu Hige**; *Lalach***; **1984**: ***Accident****; *Thaliya Bhagya*; *Ganda Bherunda*; *Benki Birugali*; *Kalinga Sarpa*; *Indina Bharatha*; *Bedaru Bombe*; *Shapatha*; *Pavitra Prema*; *Makkaliralavva Mane Thumba*; ***Utsav***; *Asha Kirana*; *Apoorva Sangama*; **1985**: *Thayi Kanasu*; *Manava Danava*; *Thayiye Nanna Devaru*; *Kiladi Aliya*; *Vajra Mushti*; *Parameshi Prema Prasanga*; **1986**: *Bettada Thayi*; *Na Ninna Preetisuve*; *Raste Raja*; *Samsarada Guttu*; **1987**: *Ondu Muthina Kathe**; *Swami*** (TV); *Malgudi Days** (TV); *Thayi*; *Ee Bandha Anubandha*; *Huli Hebbuli*; *Antima Ghatta*; *Digvijaya*; *Lorry Driver*; **1988**: *Shakti*; *Navabharata*; *SP Sangliana*; *Thayi Karulu*; *Dharmatma* (K); **1989**: *Tarka*; *Maha Yuddha*; *Antinta Gandu Naanalla*; *CID Shankar*; *Rajasimha*; *Narasimha*; *Idu Saadhya*; **1990**: *Pundara Ganda*; *Maheshwara*; *Hosa Jeevana*; *Bhale Chatura*; *Aata Bombata*; *Nighooda Rahasya*; *Ramrajyadalli Rakshasaru*; *S.P. Sangliana II*; **1991**: *Punda Prachanda*; *Sundara Kanda*; *Nagini*; **1993**: *Prana Snehitha*.

NAGABHARANA, T. S. (b. 1953)

Kannada director born in Bangalore. Started in theatre in 1969 as apprentice to noted Kannada playwright and director Adya Rangacharya. Directed several short plays for **B.V. Karanth**'s theatre group Benaka (1970-5) and participated in their major productions of *Hayavadana*, *Oedipus* and *Jokumaraswamy*. Assisted **Karanth** and **Karnad** in their early films (cf ***Kaadu***, 1973). Début ***Grahana*** in the context of the 70s art film movement in Kannada adapted from literary and theatre movements (see **Navya Movement**). Was the only film-maker from the group to make a successful transition to the commercial mainstream. Continues as theatre director and actor with the Benaka and Rangasampada theatre groups. Made several documentaries and promotional shorts.

FILMOGRAPHY: 1978: ***Grahana***; **1980**: *Anveshane*; *Bangarada Jinke*; **1982**: *Praya Praya Praya*; **1983**: ***Banker Margayya***; *Onti Dhwani*; *Prema Yuddha*; **1984**: *Makkaliralavva Mane Thumba*; *Ahuti*; *Sedina Sanchu*; *Hoysala and Chalukyan Architecture of Karnataka* (Doc); **1985**: *Netra Pallavi*; **1986**: *Nenapina Doni*; *Nammana Mali* (TV); **1986-1987**: *Shriman Shrimanya* (TV); **1987**: *Ravana Rajya*; **1988**: *Aasphota*; **1989**: *Premagni*; *Sura Sundaranga*; **1990**: *Santha Shishunala Shareefa*; *Tenali Raman* (TV); **1991**: *Mysore Mallige*; *Stone Boy* (TV); **1992**: *Thirugubana* (TV); **1993**: *Akasmika*; *Chinnari Mutha* (TV).

NAGABHUSHANAM, KADARU (b. 1902)

Telugu and Tamil director born in Kistna Dist., AP. Prominent theatre personality with Rajarajeshwari Nataka Mandali. Married its lead star **Kannamba**. Together they expanded it into Rajarajeshwari Film (1941), initially filming their own stage hits. Produced and directed 35 films under this banner, mainly mythologicals. Probably starred in E. Nagabhushanam's ***Sampoorna Ramayanam*** (1936).

FILMOGRAPHY: 1942: *Sumati*; **1943**: *Harishchandra*; **1945**: *Paduka Pattabhishekham*; **1947**: *Tulasi Jalandhar*; **1949**: ***Navajeevan/Navajeevanam***; **1951**: *Saudamini*; **1952**: ***Pedaraitu***; *Enzhai*

Vazhavan; **1953**: *Lakshmi*; **1954**: *Sati Sakkubai*; **1955**: *Shri Krishna Tulabharam*; **1956**: *Naga Panchami*; **1957**: *Sati Savitri*; *Sati Ansuya*; **1959**: *Veer Bhaskaradu*; **1960**: *Dharmane Jayam*; **1961**: *Usha Parinayam*; **1962**: *Dakshayagnam*; **1963**: *Apta Mithrulu*; **1965**: *Chaduvukonna Bharya*; **1966**: *Thali Bhagyam*; *Usha Kalyanam*.

NAGAIAH, CHITTOR V. (1904-73)

Actor, singer and composer born in Repalle, Guntur, AP; later settled at Chittor. One of the first major stars of the Telugu and, after ***Ashok Kumar***, Tamil cinemas. Renowned stage actor and recording star in Telugu, launched as a youth in the **Surabhi theatre** group. Later associated with **Ballari Raghava** (playing Kabir in *Ramadasu*), the Madras-based Suguna Vilas Sabha and Chennapuri Andhra Mahasabha. Staged the mythological *Shri Krishna Leelalu* as an independent production. Early screen career mainly in **B.N. Reddi** films at **Vauhini** Studios where his 'humanist' performances - e.g. in ***Sumangali***, partly based on the life of the reformer Kandakuri Veerashaligram Panthulu (1848-1919) - were central to the studio's revivalist nationalist melodrama contrasting 'ancient' civilisation with decadent modernity. His later and most successful work was in the Saint film genre with ***Thyagayya*** and ***Bhakta Potana***, two of the biggest South Indian hits in the 40s associating a revivalist Hindu ascetism with 'Gandhian' moralism as in **Ramnoth**'s mammoth ***Ezhai Padum Padu***, an adaptation of *Les Misérables*. In early films at Vauhini he composed the music of ***Vande Mataram***, *Sumangali*, ***Devatha*** and ***Bhakta Potana*** as well as acting in them. These compositions are still remarkable for their extreme simplicity and the ease with which they are integrated into the narrative. From the mid-50s on he appeared in smaller roles in Telugu and Tamil films, also directing one last Saint film, *Ramadasu*. Ran Renuka Films in Madras. Published his autobiography, *Swiya Charitra* in 1983.

FILMOGRAPHY (* also d & music d/** also music d): **1938**: ***Grihalakshmi***; **1939**: ***Vande Mataram*****; **1940**: ***Sumangali*****; ***Vishwamohini***; **1941**: ***Devatha*****; ***Ashok Kumar***; **1942**: ***Bhakta Potana*****; **1943**: ***Bhagya Lakshmi***; ***Chenchulakshmi***; **1945**: ***Swargaseema*****; ***Meera***; ***Hemareddy Mallamma*** (music d only); **1946**: ***Thyagayya****; **1947**: ***Yogi Vemana*****; **1948**: *Bhakta Jana*; *Chakradhari*; **1949**: ***Mana Desam***; ***Navajeevan/Navajeevanam***; **1950**: ***Ezhai Padum Padu****/Beedala Patlu*; **1951**: *Sarvadhikari*; **1952**: *Thayi Ullam*; **1953**: *Inspector*; *Jataka Phala/Jatakapalam/Jatakam*; *Panakkari*; *Ulagam*; ***En Veedu/Naa Illu****; ***Gumasta***; *Penn/Ladki*; *Prapancham*; **1954**: *Maa Gopi*; *Sangham*; *Thuli Visham*; *Ethirparadathu*; *Nanban*; ***Viduthalai***; *Rihaee*; **1955**: *Kanavane Kan Kanda Daivam*; *Nam Kuzhandai*; *Anarkali*; ***Ardhangi/Pennin Perumai***; **1956**: *Bhakta Markandeya*; *Muddubidda*; ***Tenali Ramakrishna/Tenali Raman***; *Naga Panchami* (Tel); ***Amara Deepam***; *Asai*; *Marmaveeran*; **1957**: *Vanagamudi/Tala Vanchani Veerudu*; ***Ambikapathy***; *Nala Damayanti*; *Sati Savitri*; *Panduranga Mahatyam*; **1958**: *Bommalapelli/Bommai Kalyanam*; ***Ettuku Pai Ettu***; *Ganga Gauri Samvadam*; *Shri Ramanjaneya Yuddham*; *Parvati Kalyanam*; *Manamalai*; *Naan Valartha Thangai*; *Pati Bhakti*; *Sampoorna Ramayanam*; *Thirumanam*; *Piya Milan*; **1959**: *Kalaivanan*; *Mala Oru Mangala Vilakku*; *Manaiviye Manithanin Manikkam*; *Nalla Theerpu*; *Sahodari*; *Jayabheri*; ***Veerapandiya Kattaboman***; *Sipayi Kooturu*; *Bandaramudu*; ***Mahishasura Mardini***; ***Raja Mukutam***; **1960**: *Abhimanam*; *Bhakta Raghunath*; *Bhakta Shabari*; *Maa Babu*; *Samajam*; *Shantinivasam*; ***Shri Ventakeshwara Mahatyam***; *Thangarathinam*; *Ramayan*; **1961**: *Anbu Magan*; *Ellam Unnakkaga*; *Manappandanal*; ***Pavamanippu***; *Thirudathe*; *Bhakta Jayadeva*; *Intiki Deepam Illale*; *Seeta Rama Kalyanam*; *Vagdanam*; *Pelli Pilupu*; *Nagarjuna*; **1962**: *Dakshayagnam*; ***Aradhana***; *Swarnamanjari*; *Alayamani*; *Nagamalai Azhgai*; *Valar Pirai*; *Constable Koothuru*; ***Siri Sampadalu***; **1963**: *Mani Osai*; ***Veera Kesari/Bandhipotu***; *Anuragham*; *Lavakusa*; *Idu Sathiyam*; *Karpagam*; *Nanum Oru Penn*; *Naan Vanangum Daivam*; *Kubera Theevu*; **1964**: *Atmabalam*; *Kaikodutha Daivam*; *Vengai Nattu Veeran*(?); *Pachai Vilakku*; *Ramadasu**; *Aggipidugu*; ***Vivahabandham***; ***Amarashilpi Jakanachari/Amarashilpi Jakanna***; *Gudigantalu*; *Dagudu Moothulu*; **1965**: *Prachanda Bhairavi*; *Chaduvukonna Bharya*; *Devatha*; *Simhachala Kshetram*; *Vishala Hridayalu*; ***Satya Harishchandra***; ***Pandava Vanavasam***; *Todu Needa*; *Shanti*; ***Enga Veetu Penn***; **1966**: ***Motor Sundaram Pillai***; *Ramu*; *Sadhu Mirandal*; *Saraswathi Sabatham*; *Selvam*; *Parakkum Pavai*; *Astiparulu*; *Adugu Jadalu*; *Navarathri*; *Paramanandayya Sishyulu Katha*; *Shakuntala*; *Shrimati*; ***Kumari Penn***; **1967**: *Private Master*; *Kanchukota*; *Punyavati*; *Maa Vadina*; *Stree Janmam*; *Bhakta Prahlada*; ***Thangai***; *Iru Malargal*; *Poolarangudu*; ***Shri Krishnavataram***; **1968**: *Sati Arundhati*; *Tikka Shankaraiah*; *Bharya*; *Mana Samsaram*; *Nindu Samsaram*; *Undamma Bottupeduta*; **1969**: *Ardha Rathri*; *Muhurtabalam*; *Bandhipotu Bhimanna*; *Jarigina Katha*; *Mooganomu*; *Prema Kanuka*; *Annaiyum Pithavum*; *Manasakshi*; *Ulagam Ivvalavuthan*; **1970**: *Tapalkaran Thangai*; *Pattam Pazhali*; *Daiva Penn*; *Aada Janma*; *Amma Kosam*; *Kodalu Diddina Kapuram*; *Malli Pelli*; **1971**: *Maa Ilavelupu*; *Jeevitha Chakram*; *CID Raju*; *Vintha Samsaram*; *Shri Krishna Satya*; *Anuradha*; *Iru Thuruvam*; *Mayakkum Mohini*; *Kulagaurava/Kulagauravam*; **1972**: *Ganga*; *Mohammed-bin-Tughlaq*; *Raja* (Ta/Te); *Shri Krishnanjaneya Yuddham*; ***Anta Mana Manchike***; *Maa Inti Kodalu*; *Maa Inti Velugu*; *Neethi Nijayathi*; *Nijam Nirupistha*; *Shabash Baby*; *Vichitra Bandham*; *Vintha Dampathulu*; *Vooriki Upakari*; *Goodu Putani*; *Jakkamma*; *Neethi*; *Amma Mata*; *Rocket Rani*; *Pedda Koduku*; *Monagadosthunnadu Jagratha*; *Beedala Patlu*; *Sampoorna Ramayanam*; *Shabash Papanna*; *Papam Pasivadu*; *Shakti Leela*; **1973**: *Pattikatu Ponnaiah*; *Pennai Nambungal*; *Malamma Katha*; *Vishali*; *Panjaramlo Pasipapa*; *Jeevitham*; *Deshoddharakulu*; *Puttinillu Mettinillu*; *Jagame Maya*; *Mahishasura Mardini*; **1974**: *Inti Kodalu*; *Anaganaga Oka Thandri*; **1976**: *Ennai Pol Oruvan*; **1977**: *Evaru Devudu*.

Shankar Nag and Sujatha in *Akrosha* (1983)

Nagalingam, P. K. *see* **Sandow, P. K. Raja**

NAGARAJAN, A. P.

Tamil director and scenarist. Considered one of the pioneering new generation of scenarists in the mid-50s in context of the anti-religious thrust of the **DMK Film**. Playwright and actor associated with the **TKS Brothers**; début in film adapting the play *Nalvar* into a script (1953; he also acted in the film). Like the DMK writers and directors, he tried to go beyond what film-maker and critic K. Hariharan calls the 'Therukoothu vaudeville', but he rejected their politics and was mainly responsible for the revival of the discredited mythological genre when he wrote K. Somu's hit *Sampoorna Ramayanam* (1958). The film had a major impact on **Sivaji Ganesan**'s political career, helping the star to overcome his earlier association with the atheist DMK. Nagarajan then started his own production company with actor V.K. Ramaswamy, scripting and producing Somu's *Nalla Idathu Sambandham* (1958). His early films as director are melodramas often bewailing, like the DMK films, the loss of 'tradition' and the 'decadence' of modern times. e.g. in *Navarathri*, a woman runs away from home and meets nine different men on nine consecutive nights, apparently experiencing each of the nine rasas of Indian aesthetic theory in the process; in ***Vaa Raja Vaa***, a boy ekes out a living as a tourist guide in Mahabalipuram; ***Thillana Mohanambal***, one of his bigger hits, is set in Thanjavur and features a dancer and musician. Best known for a series of 60s mythologicals: *Thiruvillaiyadal*, *Saraswathi Sabatham*, ***Kandan Karunai***, *Thirumal Perumai*, etc., reinvoking the stage-derived conventions he had earlier opposed, mobilising their kitschy inventiveness as in *Saraswathi Sabatham* where Shiva is dressed as a Greek general, and hiring retired stage actors from the 50s. His films often starred Ganesan. Had a brief political career with Sivagangam's Thamizharasu Party, editing its journal *Sattai*, from where he attacked the DMK.

FILMOGRAPHY: 1962: *Vadivukku Valai Kappu*; **1963**: *Kulamagal Radhai*; **1964**: *Navarathri*; **1965**: *Thiruvillaiyadal*; **1966**: *Saraswathi Sabatham*; **1967**: ***Kandan Karunai***; *Seeta*; *Thiruvarut Selvar*; **1968**: ***Thillana Mohanambal***; *Thirumal Perumai*; **1969**: *Gurudakshinai*; ***Vaa Raja Vaa***; **1970**: *Thirumalai Thenkumari*; *Vilayattu Pillai*; **1971**: *Kankatchi*; **1972**: *Agathiar*; *Tirupati Kanyakumari Yatra*; **1973**: *Karaikkal Ammaiyar*; *Raja Raja Chozhan*; *Thirumalai Daivam*; **1974**: *Gumastavin Magal*; **1975**: *Melnattu Marumagal*; **1977**: *Navarathnam*; *Shri Krishna Leela*.

Nagendra Rao, Pingali *see* **Rao, Pingali Nagendra**
Nagendra Rao, R. *see* **Rao, Nagendra R.**
Nageshwara Rao, Akkineni *see* **Rao, Akkineni Nageshwara**
Nageshwara Rao, Pendyala *see* **Pendyala Nageshwara Rao**
Nageshwara Rao, Rajanala *see* **Rao, Rajanala Nageshwara**
Naik, Prabhakar *see* **Nayak, Prabhakar**

NAIR, KOTTARAKKARA SRIDHARAN (1922-86)

Malayalam theatre star born in Kottarakkara, Cochin, Kerala. Major actor over four decades in Malayalam cinema. His single most famous role was that of the father in **Kariat**'s ***Chemmeen***. Tended to play a tradition-bound villain but his main impact was in shaping the iconography of the extreme right-wing Nair Service Society (NSS), the political voice of the formerly dominant Nair caste which later joined with Christian groups to create the militant Vimochana Samara to oppose the Communist government of Kerala by appealing to the military glories of this once-ruling warrior caste. Gave a high-flown, declamatory performance as *Veluthampi Dalawa*, the legendary Nair diwan who fought the British and later defied his own king. This figure became the subject of several stage and literary historicals (e.g. a play by Kainikkara Padmanabha Pillai) and was integrated into Kerala Congress rhetoric. This role and others like that of ***Kunjali Marakkar***, a Muslim nationalist who joined the Zamorins in fighting the Portuguese in Malabar, defined the Rajapaat, i.e. the image of the royal costumed hero in Malayalam cinema. Another famous Kottarakkara role is that of the old and lonely man who feels death to be 'half an hour away' in **K.S. Sethumadhavan**'s ***Aranazhikaneram***.

FILMOGRAPHY: 1950: *Sasidharan*; *Chechi*; *Prasanna*; **1951**: *Yachakan*; **1952**: *Atmashanti*; **1953**: *Lokaneethi*; **1954**: *Avakashi*; *Avan Varunnu*; *Manasakashi*; ***Snehaseema***; *Kidappadam*; **1955**: *Kalam Marunnu*; *CID*; **1956**: *Atmarpanam*; *Manthravadi*; **1957**: ***Padatha Paingili***; *Jailpully*; **1958**: *Thaskara Veeran*; ***Randidangazhi***; **1959**: *Nadodikal*; *Minnal Padayali*; **1960**: *Poothali*; **1961**: *Christmas Rathri*; ***Bhakta Kuchela***; *Umminithanka*; *Shri Sabarimalai Shri Ayyappan*; **1962**: *Veluthampi Dalawa*; *Sneha Deepam*; *Sreekovil*; *Puthiya Aksham Puthiya Bhoomi*; *Shri Rama Pattabhishekham*; *Bhagya Jatakam*; **1963**: *Nithya Kanyaka*; *Snapaka Yohannan*; *Satyabhama*; *Kadalamma*; *Rebecca*; **1964**: *Anna*; *Pazhassi Raja*; *Althara*; *Devalayam*; **1965**: *Shyamalachechi*; *Inapravugal*; *Thommente Makkal*; *Kalyanaphoto*; *Kattuthulasi*; *Mayavi*; *Shakuntala*; *Pattu Thoovala*; *Sarpakadu*; ***Chemmeen***; **1966**: *Rowdy*; *Jail*; *Pennmakkal*; *Kootukar*; *Kalyana Rathriyil*; *Anarkali*; *Kanmanikal*; *Tilottama*; *Mayor Nair*; ***Kunjali Marakkar***; **1967**: *Jeevikan Anuvadhikuka*; ***Kottayam Kola Case***; *Balyakalasakhi*; *Lady Doctor*; *Mainatharuvi Kola Case*; *Collector Malathi*; *Cochin Express*; *Pooja*; *Kasavuthattam*; *Ollathu Mathi*; **1968**: ***Thirichadi***; *Viruthan Sanku*; *Hotel Highrange*; *Punnapra Vyalar*; *Midumidukki*; ***Adhyapika***; *Kodungalluramma*; **1969**: *Vila Kuranja Manushyar*; *Almaram*; ***Janmabhoomi***; *Nurse*; *Susie*; *Jwala*; *Kootu Kudumbam*; *Kumara Sambhavam*; **1970**: *Pearl View*; *Kurukshetram*; *Cross Belt*; *Kakathampurati*; *Sabarimala Shri Dharmasastha*; *Detective 909 Keralathil*; ***Aranazhikaneram***; **1972**: *Puthanveedu*; *Ananthasayanam*; *Chhayam*; *Panimudakku*; *Professor*; ***Chemparathi***; *Achannum Bappayum*; *Thottilla*; *Shri Guruvayoorappan*; **1973**: ***Enippadikal***; ***Nirmalayam***; *Gayatri*; *Swapnam*; *Darshanam*; *Achani*; *Kaadu* (Mal); *Driksakshi*; *Thottavadi*; *Yamini*; *Chuzhi*; *Checkpost*; *Thekkan Kattu*; *Swargaputhri*; *Padmavyuham*; **1974**: *Chanchala*; *Nellu*; *Devi Kanyakumari*; *Atithi*; *Mazhakkaru*; **1975**: *Akkaldama*; *Kamam Krodham Moham*; *Palkadal*; *Prayanam*; **1976**: *Amba Ambika Ambalika*; *Colonel and Collector*; **1977**: *Shri Murugan*; *Vezhambal*; **1978**: *Padasaram*; *Priyadarshini*; **1984**: ***My Dear Kuttichathan/Chhota Chetan***; **1985**: *Daivathe Orthu*.

NAIR, MADATHU THEKEPATTU VASUDEVAN (b. 1934)

Malayalam director born in Malappuram, Kerala. Major Malayalam novelist and scenarist. His first novel, *Nalukettu* (1958), contributed to the renewal of a literary tradition initiated by Thakazhy Shivashankar Pillai, Basheer and Uroob in the 50s. Sub-editor of the influential literary journal *Mathrubhoomi* (1956); later its editor (1968-81). Best-known writing addresses the tensions, incarnated by a central character, between traditional family structures in a declining feudal system and economic development (e.g. Appunni in *Nalukettu*, 1958, Govindakutty in *Asuravithu*, 1962, or Sethu in *Kalam*, 1969). The melodrama of feudal nostalgia, ambivalently presented, had a major influence on 70s Malayalam cinema (e.g. **Vincent** and **Sethumadhavan**) and was one of the major forces behind the **P.N. Menon/P.A. Backer** breakthrough into realist cinema with ***Olavum Theeravum*** (1969). First film as director, ***Nirmalayam***, is an influential contribution to the 'literary' version of 70s New Indian Cinema. He directed only four more films, all based on his own stories. Currently top Malayalam scenarist with independent star status. Script credits include ***Murappennu*** (1965), *Nagarame Nandi* (1967) and *Asuravithu* (1968) for Vincent; S.S. Rajan's *Pagal Kinavu* (1966); **Bhaskaran**'s ***Irutinte Atmavu*** (1967); P.N. Menon's *Kuttiyedathi* (1971); Sethumadhavan's *Kanyakumari* (1974) and ***Oppol*** (1980). Scripted **Hariharan**'s *Edavazhiyile Pucha Mindappucha* (1979), ***Valarthu Mrugangal*** (1981), *Evedayo Oru Sathru* (1983), *Vellom* (1984), ***Panchagni*** (1986), *Nakshatrangal* (1986), *Amritam Gamaya* (1987) and ***Oru Vadakkan Veeragatha*** (1989). Also wrote several films for **I.V. Sasi** including *Aroodam* (1983), ***Alkoottathil Thaniye*** (1984), *Adiyozhukkukal* (1984), *Uyyarangalil* (1984); and **Prathap Pothan**'s ***Ruthubhedam*** (1987), Recently returned to directing with *Kadavu*. Aravindan Vallachira (1991) has a book-length analysis of his films.

FILMOGRAPHY: 1973: ***Nirmalayam***; **1977**: *Mohini Attam* (Doc); **1978**: *Bandhanam*; **1982**: *Manju*; *Varikkuzhi*; **1991**: *Kadavu*.

NAIR, MIRA (b. 1957)

English and Hindi director born in Bhubaneshwar, Orissa; daughter of a civil servant. Educated at the Irish Catholic School in Simla and at the University of New Delhi. Active as an actress in repertory theatre in India. Went to Harvard (1976) where she graduated in sociology (1979). Started making films in the USA for R. Leacock and D.A. Pennebaker. Produced her own documentaries and short films. Achieved major international success with *India Cabaret* and *Salaam Bombay*. Works mainly in the USA. Made a cameo appearance as a gossip in her *Mississippi Masala*.

FILMOGRAPHY: 1979: *Jama Masjid Street Journal* (Sh); **1982**: *So Far from India* (Doc); **1985**: *India Cabaret* (TV); **1987**: *Children of Desired Sex* (TV); **1988**: *Salaam Bombay*; **1991**: *Mississippi Masala*.

NAIR, THIKKURISI SUKUMARAN (b. 1917)

Actor, scenarist, novelist, poet, playwright and director born in Thikkurisi, Kerala. Major Malayalam star since 1950. Known more recently for elderly 'character' roles. Wrote five plays 1944-9, the best known being *Stree*, the film version of which was also his acting début. His early work helped the Malayalam stage and cinema move away from the pervasive influence of the Tamil stage by eliminating the musical conventions of the Tamil Bhagavathars' (actor-singers) hour-long invocations, their emphasis on the high scale and the use of the pedal-organ. He kept his accompanyists behind the stage curtain and recited his own Malayalam compositions in metrical structures closer to lyric poetry than to Carnatic forms. Extended this style in his early films, e.g. ***Jeevitha Nauka***, the Koshy-**Kunchako** production that tried to establish an indigenous Kerala film culture. Directed many remakes of Tamil hits, rewritten and reperformed to address a local milieu: e.g. *Palunku Pathram* remade **K.S. Gopalakrishnan**'s *Kaikodutha Daivam* (1964). One of the three stars (with **Prem Nazir** and comedian **Adoor Bhasi**) who dominated Malayalam films in the 60s and 70s. In addition to his big Udaya Studio films, famous roles include key films by **Kariat** (e.g. *Maya*), **Bhaskaran** (***Irutinte Atmavu***) and **Vincent** (***Abhijathyam***). Also wrote dialogues and lyrics for *Devasundari* (1957), dialogues for *Sabarimalai Shri Ayyappan* (1962) and *Muthalaly* (1965), and st/dial for **P. Subramanyam**'s *Ana Valarthiya Vanampadi* (1971).

FILMOGRAPHY (* also d): **1950**: *Stree*; *Chandrika*; **1951**: ***Jeevitha Nauka***; ***Navalokam***; **1952**: *Amma*; *Visappinte Vili*; *Achan*; ***Andaman Kaithi***; **1953**: *Sario Thetto** (also music d); **1954**: *Puthradharmam*; *Kidappadam*; **1955**: *Harishchandra*; *Kalam Marunnu*; **1956**: *Atmarpanam*; **1957**: *Achannum Maganam*; **1958**: *Thaskara Veeran*; *Mariakutty*; ***Randidangazhi***; **1960**: *Umma*; *Seeta*; *Poothali*; **1961**: *Christmas Rathri*; ***Kandam Bacha Coat***; ***Unniyarcha***; *Shri Sabarimalai Shri Ayyappan*; ***Bhakta Kuchela***; *Gnana Sundari*; **1962**: *Laila Majnu*; *Veluthampi Dalawa*; *Sneha Deepam*; *Sreekovil*; *Shri Rama Pattabhishekham*; *Viyarppinte Vila*; **1963**: *Nithya Kanyaka*; *Doctor*; *Snapaka Yohannan*; *Satyabhama*; *Chilampoli*; *Kaleyum Kaminiyum*; **1964**: *Devalayam*; *School Master*; *Atom Bomb*; *Karutha Kayi*; *Shri Guruvayoorappan*; *Omanakuttan*; *Kalanjukuttiya Thangam*; *Kudumbini*; **1965**: ***Odeyil Ninnu***; *Inapravugal*; *Kaliyodam*; *Muthalaly*; ***Rosy***; *Mayavi*; *Jeevitha Yatra*; *Kattupookal*; *Kathiruna Nikkah*; *Kochumon*; *Bhoomiyile Malakha*; *Shakuntala*; *Chettathi*; **1966**: *Kusirthikuttan/Anni*; *Kadamattathachan*; *Jail*; *Kootukar*; ***Kayamkulam Kochunni***; *Puthri*; *Anarkali*; *Tharavatamma*; *Kanmanikal*; *Puchakanni*; *Kallipennu*; *Kanakachilanka*; *Karuna*; *Tilottama*; *Priyatama*; *Mayor Nair*; **1967**: ***Irutinte Atmavu***; *Postman*; *Madatharuvi*; ***Anveshichu Kandatiyilla***; ***Chitramela***; *Pareeksha*; *Nadan Pennu*; **1968**: *Vidyarthi*; *Viruthan Sanku*; *Manaswini*; *Inspector*; *Vazhipizhacha Santhathi*; *Kadal*; *Hotel Highrange*; *Punnapra Vyalar*; ***Thulabharam***; ***Adhyapika***; *Aparadhini*; *Kodungalluramma*; **1969**: *Ballathapahayan*; *Chattambi Kavala*; ***Nadhi***; *Kumara Sambhavam*; *Nurse**; *Poojapushpam**; **1970**: *Amma Enna Stree*; *Cross Belt*; ***Ezhuthatha Katha***; *Nizhalattam*; *Vivaham Swargathil*; *Triveni*; *Tara*; *Saraswathi**; *Palunku Pathram**; **1971**: ***Abhijathyam***; *Achante Bharya**; *Puthanveedu*; **1972**: *Maya*; *Thavaputhalvan*; *Professor*; *Aromalunni*; *Shri Guruvayoorappan*; *Maraivil Thiruvu Sukshikuha*; ***Swayamvaram***; *Shakti*; **1973**: *Thiruvabharanam*; *Ponnapuram Kotta*; *Kavitha*; *Chenda*; *Thani Niram*; *Kattu Vithachavan*; *Kaadu* (Mal); *Nakhangal*; *Prethangalude Thazhvara*; *Sastram Jayichu Manushyan Thottu*; *Divya Darshanam*; *Checkpost*; *Swargaputhri*; *Asha Chakram*; *Jesus*; *Angathattu*; *Urvashi Bharathi**; *Pacha Nottukal*; **1974**: *Suprabhatam*; *Nathoon*; *Yauvanam*; *Nellu*; *Nagaram Sagaram*; *Swarna Vigraham*; *Ivide Thodangannu*; *Kalyana Saugandhikam*; *Thumbolarcha*; *Devi Kanyakumari*; *Nadhi Nadanmare Avasiamundu*; *Vishnu Vijayam*; *Sapta Swarangal*; *Swarna Malsiyam*; **1975**: *Abhimanam*; *Alibaba and Forty-One Thieves*; *Aranyakandam*; *Bharya Illatha Rathri*; *Cheenavala*; *Dharmakshetre Kurukshetre*; *Manishada*; *Padmaragam*; *Sammanam*; *Surya Vamsam*; *Swami Ayyappan*; *Thomasleeha*; *Sathyathinde Nizhalil*; *Neela Ponman*; **1976**: *Ammini Ammavan*; *Amritha Vahini*; *Appooppan*; *Chennai Valarthiya Kutty*; *Chirikuduka*; *Dheere Sameere Yamuna Theere*; *Kayamkulam Kochunniyude Maghan*; *Mallanum Mathevanum*; *Romeo*; *Sarvekkalu*; *Srimadh Bhagavad Geeta*; *Swimming Pool*; *Thuruppu Gulam*; *Vazhi Vilakku*; *Yakshaganam*; **1977**: *Aparajitha*; *Chaturvedam*; *Harsha Bhashpam*; *Kannappanunni*; *Kavilamma*; ***Kodiyettam***; *Madanolsavam*; *Manas Oru Mayil*; *Minimol*; *Niraparayum Nilavilakkum*; *Parivarthanam*; *Rathi Manmathan*; *Saghakkale Munottu*; *Satyavan Savithri*; *Vishukkani*; *Yatheem*; *Suryakanthi*; **1978**: *Kanyaka*; *Ashtamudikayal*; *Asthamayam*; *Avar Jeevikkunu*; *Chakrayudham*; *Jayikkanai Janichavan*; *Kadathanattu Maakkam*; *Kalpa Vruksha*; *Kanalkkattakal*; *Madhurikuna Rathri*; *Manoratham*; *Snehikkan Oru Pennu*; *Society Lady*; *Sundari Marudde Swapnangal*; *Thacholi Ambu*; **1983**: *Ahankaram*; **1984**: *Attahasam*; *Oodarathuammava Alariyum*; *Oru Sumangaliyuda Katha*; **1985**: *Azhiyatha Bandhangal*; *Ee Thalamura Inganna*; **1986**: ***Avanazhi***; **1988**: *Mukunthetta Sumitra Vilikkunnu*; *Oru Muthassi Katha*; *Aryan*; **1990**: *His Highness Abdullah*.

Thikkurisi Sukumaran Nair (centre) and Adoor Bhasi (right) in *Almaram* (1969)

NANDA, PRASHANTA (b. 1947)

Major Oriya actor, director and producer. Acting début in Prabhat Mukherjee's Oriya films (*Dasyu Ratnakara*). Became a star with **Mrinal Sen**'s ***Matir Manisha***. Studied arts and law while pursuing acting career in Orissa. Made some major films with **Nitai Palit** (*Bandhan*, *Dharitri*, *Mana Akasha*) before turning producer with Byomkesh Tripathi's seminal hit ***Mamata*** (also contributing the story). Turned director the following year with the tragic melodrama ***Shesha Shrabana***; since then acted only in his own films. Made three films in Hindi and the Oriya-Bengali bilingual, *Jaa Devi Sarva Bhuteshu/Nyaya Chakra*.

FILMOGRAPHY (* also d): **1962**: *Dasyu Ratnakara*; *Nua Bou*; **1964**: *Jeevana Sathi*; *Nabajanma*; **1966**: ***Matir Manisha***; **1969**: *Bandhan*; **1970**: ***Adina Megha***; **1972**: *Dharitri*; **1973**: *Ghara Sansara*; **1974**: *Mana Akasha*; **1975**: *Samaya*; ***Mamata***; **1976**: *Krishna Sudama*; *Sindura Bindu*; ***Shesha Shrabana****; **1977**: *Naga Phasha*; *Paheli**; **1978**: *Taapoi*; *Balidan**; **1979**: *Gauri*; *Naiya**; **1980**: *Maa-o-Mamata**; **1981**: *Pooja**; **1982**: *Hisab Nikas**; **1983**: *Swapna Sagara**; **1984**: *Dora**; *Jaga Balia**; *Grihasthi**; **1986**: *Bagula Baguli**; *Pakal Kambal Pot Chhota**; **1987**: *Golamgiri**; **1988**: *Lal Pan Bibi**; **1989**: *Jaa Devi Sarva Bhuteshu/Nyaya Chakra**; **1992**: *Maa**.

NARASARAJU, DATLA VENKATA (b. 1920)

Telugu screenwriter born in Talluri village, AP. Educated in Guntur, Vijaywada and Madras. Started a drama troupe for which he wrote plays and often acted. First play was *Antarvani*; achieved a reputation as humorist with his hit play, *Natakam* (1951), based on P.G. Wodehouse's *The Play's the Thing*. Best-known plays are situated in the everyday, e.g. *Yee Illu Ammabadunu*. Film début scripting ***Pedda Manushulu*** (1954) based on Ibsen's *Pillars of Society*. Wrote over 100 scripts, including ***Donga Ramudu*** (1955), ***Gundamma Katha*** (1962) and *Nirdoshi* (1967).

Narasimha Rao, Bhimavarapu *see* **Rao, Bhimavarapu Narashimha**
Narasimha Rao, Chitrapu *see* **Rao, Chitrapu Narasimha**
Narasinga Rao, Bongu *see* **Rao, Bongu Narasinga**
Narayana Rao, Adi *see* **Rao, Adi Narayana**

NARAYANA KAVI, UDUMALAI (1899-1981)

Tamil lyric writer. Born in a merchant (Chettiar) family; learnt music from theatre songwriter Udumalai Sarabam Muthusami Kavi. Adopted part of his teacher's name as a tribute. Early work for gramophone companies like Tasophone, Odeon and HMV, often writing comic songs. Employed as lyric writer by theatre groups, e.g. Arya Gana Sabha, where he also occasionally acted. Film début in *Krishna Leela* (1934). Worked at Angel Films, Salem (*Draupadi Vastrapaharanam*, 1934; *Thooku Thooki*, 1935). Campaigned in 1937 for the Congress Party and wrote several nationalistic songs for films like *Maya Jyothi* (1941), elaborating his characteristic type of humorous propaganda songs. A Dravidar Kazhagam ideologue and early follower of Periyar. Best-known work in the propaganda genre with the comedian **N.S. Krishnan**, adopting a rationalist atheism also found in the **DMK Film**. Wrote several propaganda songs for DK films, starting with *Ezhanda Kadal* (1941). The most famous one was ***Nallathambi*** (1949), scripted by **C.N. Annadurai** and starring Krishnan. Also wrote classic verse opposing the brahminical clergy in *Sorgavasal* (1954). Songs were often in the old popular **Company Natak** style, with simple rhymes. His lyrics and poetry were compiled by the Dravidar Kazhagam (1986, edited by Sanghai Velavam).

NARAYANAMURTHY, CHITRAPU (1913-85)

Telugu director born in Masulipatnam, AP. Early work on Telugu stage in National Theatres troupe which staged mythologicals, including *Bhakta Markandeya*, the subject of his first film. Introduced to films by Pinapala Venkatadasu, founder of **Vel Pics** Studio. Worked as assistant and later as film editor in brother **Chitrapu Narasimha Rao**'s films. First break with **G. Balaramaiah**'s Kubera Studio (1938), but made best-known films at Shobhanachala Studio until mid-40s as the studio's top director of Burrakatha-inspired folklore movies. Attempted independent production with Venkatramana Pics (1944). By early 50s had moved largely into the more lucrative Tamil industry where, in addition to freelancing for smaller producers, he worked at **AVM** which produced his last film, a Telugu-Tamil remake of his 1942 hit *Bhakta Prahlada*.

FILMOGRAPHY: **1938**: *Markandeya*; **1940**: *Mahiravana*; **1941**: ***Dakshayagnam***; **1942**: *Bhakta Prahlada*; **1944**: *Bhakta Kabir*; *Bhishma*; *Samsara Naradi*; **1947**: *Brahma Ratham*; **1948**: *Madalasa*; **1949**: *Brahma Ratham*; **1952**: *En Thangai*; **1953**: *Naa Chellelu*; **1954**: *Ethirparadathu*; **1956**: *Nagula Chaviti/Adarshasati*; *Naga Panchami*; **1957**: *Pathni Daivam*; **1958**: *Manamalai*; *Annaiyin Aanai*; *Naan Valartha Thangai*; **1959**: *Daivame Thunai*; **1960**: *Bhakta Shabari*; **1961**: *Krishna Kuchela*; *Tallichina Ajna*; **1963**: *Chittor Rani Padmini*; **1964**: *Pativrata*; **1967**: *Bhakta Prahlada*

NARAYANAN, A. (1900-39)

Director, producer and exhibitor in Tamil film. Former insurance agent; worked for the distribution wing of **K.D. Brothers**. Manager of Queen's Cinema, Calcutta (1922) and started Popular Cinema in Triplicane, Madras. Started Exhibition Film Services (1927), later with branches in Bombay, Delhi, Rangoon and Singapore, and made extensive efforts to find an American market for Indian films, including a USA visit with a print of **Naval Gandhi**'s ***Balidan*** (1927) and **Imperial**'s *Anarkali* (1928), during which he befriended Carl Laemmle and Douglas Fairbanks Sr. Started influential **General Pics** in Madras (1929) with film-makers such as **R.S. Prakash**, **Y.V. Rao** and **C. Pullaiah**. Its sound version, Srinivasa Cinetone (1934), is claimed as South India's first sound studio. Nationalist activist, committed participant in **Swadeshi** agitations; influenced by writer Va.Ra. of the militant Tamil Manikodi writers group; associated with leaders of the freedom struggle in Madras such as C.R. Rajagopalachari, the chief minister, and S. Satyamurthy, the right-wing Congress leader. Also made several documentaries, e.g. *Maternity and Child Welfare*, *Venereal Diseases* (both for health dept. and the govt); *Unfurling the National Flag*; *Burma Oil Company Fire*; *The Spirit of Agriculture* (for Imperial Chemical Industries), etc.

FILMOGRAPHY: **1927**: *Indian National Congress at Gauhati* (Doc); **1928**: *Kovalan*; **1929**: *Dharmapatni*; *Garuda Garvabhangam*; *Gnana Sundari*; *Nandanar* (all St); **1934**: *Draupadi Vastrapaharanam*; *Srinivasa Kalyanam*; **1935**: *Krishna Arjuna*; *Gnanasoundari*; *Rajambal*; **1936**: *Indrasabha*; *Mahatma Kabirdas*; *Mandayarkal Sandhippu*; *Meerabai*; *Tara Sasankam*; *Vishwamitra*; **1937**: *Krishna Tulabharam*; *Rajasekharan*; *Vipranarayana*; *Virata Parvam*; **1938**: *Mada Sambrani*; *Tenali Raman*; *Tulasi Brinda*.

Narayana Rao, Adi *see* **Rao, Adi Narayana**
Narayana Rao, Dasari *see* **Rao, Dasari Narayana**
Narayan Kale, K. *see* **Kale, K. Narayan**
Narayan Rao, Balkrishna *see* **Rao, Balkrishna Narayan**

NARGIS (1929-81)

Hindi-Urdu megastar born in Allahabad as Fatima A. Rashid. Daughter of actress, singer and film-maker **Jaddanbai** who introduced her to films aged 5 as Baby Rani in Sangeet Films' *Talash-e-Haq*. Early films with **Mehboob** including her first lead role in ***Taqdeer*** and as Hamida Bano in ***Humayun***. Best known as **Raj Kapoor**'s romantic lead in some of Indian cinema's most enduring melodramas: ***Barsaat***, ***Andaz***, ***Awara***, ***Shri 420***, and *Anhonee* in which she played a double role. Kapoor used a suggestive image from their *Barsaat* as the emblem for his R.K. Films. Both Kapoor and Mehboob in their later films built upon her early screen image in historicals and indigenised Shakespearean love tragedies (e.g. the **Kamal Amrohi**-scripted *Romeo and Juliet*) where she was often presented as the *femme fatale* doomed to destruction by her beauty, an updated version of a stereotype from Islamic literature and music. Her performances in, e.g., ***Babul*** and ***Jogan*** also remained the model for that stereotype. From the beginning, Nargis's performances were authentic to a degree unprecedented in Indian cinema, giving the **Imperial** and **Sagar** Studios' *Arabian Nights* fantasies new layers of meaning. Mehboob used her as the pivotal figure in his attempts to merge the symbologies of feudal patriarchy into those of capitalism (*Andaz*) while Raj Kapoor injected Oedipal impulses into his encounters with 'tradition'. The pinnacle of her career was ***Mother India***, an epic pot-pourri of psychoanalytic, historic and technological symbols condensing the All-India Film's post-WW2 nationalist sentiment. Turned producer with Nargis Art, producing films directed by Akhtar Hussain. Married actor **Sunil Dutt** (1959) who played her son in *Mother India*. Then virtually retired but remained an important public figure, becoming a Congress (I) MP in the early 80s, at one time using that platform for a scathing attack on **Satyajit Ray**'s films for exporting images of India's poverty. She was much honoured by the Indian and Soviet governments. Died of cancer shortly after seeing her and Sunil Dutt's son, Sanjay, in his screen début in *Rocky* (1981).

FILMOGRAPHY (* as Baby Rani): **1934**: *Naachwali**; **1935**: *Talash-e-Haq**; **1936**: *Hridaya Manthan**; *Madam Fashion**; **1937**: *Moti Ka Haar**; **1942**: *Tamanna*; *Pardanasheen*; **1943**: ***Taqdeer***; **1944**: *Anban*; *Ismat*; **1945**: *Biswi Sadi*; ***Humayun***; *Ramayani*; **1946**: *Nargis*; **1947**: *Mehndi*; *Romeo and Juliet*; **1948**: ***Aag***; *Anjuman*; *Anokha Pyar*; *Mela*; **1949**: ***Andaz***; ***Barsaat***; *Darogaji*; *Lahore*; *Rumal*; **1950**: *Adhi Raat*; ***Babul***; *Bhishma Pratigya*; *Birha Ki Raat*; *Chhoti Bhabhi*; *Jaan Pehchan*; ***Jogan***; *Khel*; *Meena Bazaar*; *Pyar*; **1951**: ***Awara***; ***Deedar***; *Hulchul*; *Pyar Ki Baatein*; *Sagar*; **1952**: *Amber*; *Anhonee*; *Ashiana*; *Bewafa*; *Sheesha*; **1953**: ***Aah***; *Dhun*; *Pehli Shaadi*; *Paapi*; **1954**: *Angarey*; **1955**: ***Shri 420***; **1956**: ***Chori Chori***; ***Jagte Raho/Ek Din Raatre***; **1957**: *Miss India*; ***Mother India***; ***Pardesi***; **1958**: *Adalat*; *Ghar Sansar*; ***Lajwanti***; **1967**: *Raat Aur Din*.

NATIONAL FILM DEVELOPMENT CORPORATION

The Film Finance Corporation was set up in 1960 on the recommendation of the S.K. Patil Film Enquiry Committee Report (1951). Initially controlled by the Ministry of Finance, it was transferred to the Ministry of Information & Broadcasting in 1964. Its original objective was to promote and assist the mainstream film industry by 'providing, affording or procuring finance or other facilities for the production of films of good standard'. In its first six years, it extended production loans for c.50 films, notably **Ray**'s ***Charulata*** (1964), ***Nayak*** (1966) and ***Goopy Gyne Bagha Byne*** (1968). Under the direct influence of Prime Minister Indira Gandhi, the FFC initiated the **New Indian Cinema** with **Mrinal Sen**'s ***Bhuvan Shome*** and **Mani Kaul**'s ***Uski Roti*** (both 1969). In 1971, the I & B Ministry laid down, as part of the FFC's obligations, the directive that it 'develop the film in India into an effective instrument for the promotion of national culture, education and healthy entertainment [b]y granting loans for modest but off-beat films of talented and promising people in the field'. The new policy yielded instant results as a whole generation of new film-makers was allowed to emerge. However, both the terms on which loans were granted (usually requiring collateral from producers) and the limited distribution outlets, exacerbated by the FFC/NFDC's apparent inability to build its own exhibition network, gave their films a reputation for lacking 'financial viability'. In 1968 the FFC's remit was extended to include distribution and export. In 1973 it became the channelling agency for imported raw stock, and in 1974 (after the withdrawal of the MPEAA from the Indian market) it started importing foreign films for local distribution. These activities soon became the FFC's major profit centres leading to an increasing marginalisation of its film production/financing responsibilities. By 1976, the FFC's independent cinema policy came under withering attack from various quarters. The Committee on Public Undertakings issued a Report (79th Report, 1976) on the FFC arguing that 'there is no inherent contradiction between artistic films of good standard and films successful at the box office [and] the Corporation should [s]atisfy itself in all possible ways that the films [h]ave a reasonable prospect of being commercially successful'. In 1980 the current NFDC was established by amalgamating the FFC with the partially state-owned Indian Motion Pictures Export Corporation (IMPEC), making it the sole canalising agent for the import of all foreign films, with incentives to non-resident Indians to buy, import and distribute foreign films in India. Between 1981 and 1988 the NFDC was also the parent organisation for the Directorate of Film Festivals. With the haphazard extensions of its remit and the repeated policy shifts imposed on it, the absence of a clear definition of the NFDC's responsibilities to the Indian cinema has remained a persistent problem. In spite of its monopolistic privileges in the 80s the NFDC continued to describe itself as a victim of state policies on, e.g., taxation. The 1983-4 chairman, **Hrishikesh Mukherjee**, stated in the 1984 report that 'Unhealthy and underhand dealings particularly in the big cities are a part of the national distribution and exhibition system. Unless and until one becomes a part of this racket, it is practically impossible to operate in this area.' Consequently, the NFDC sought to institutionalise a confused desire for 'good' cinema, measured mainly in terms of national film awards and international film festival exposure, that should be able to make a profit in a market where it could not compete with the industrial cinema's levels of expenditure on exhibition, production and promotion. In the early 90s the NFDC changed again, its co-production policy with **Doordarshan** effectively shielding it from most industrial pressures. In 1993 the NFDC took over Doordarshan's private Metro Channel.

NAUSHAD ALI (b. 1919)

Hindi-Urdu composer born in Lucknow. One of the most spectacular products of the 40s Hindi cinema, he was one of the first to introduce sound mixing and the separate recording of voice and music tracks in playback singing. Also known for using a mammoth orchestra with over 100 musicians for **Mehboob**'s ***Aan***. Since early childhood he was an avid listener to the live orchestras accompanying silent films. Studied under Ustad Ghurbat Ali, Ustad Yusuf Ali and Ustad Babban Saheb. Before moving to Bombay in 1937, he composed for amateur theatricals such as the Windsor Music Entertainers, a group he helped set up. In Bombay, he worked as a pianist in composer Mushtaq Hussain's orchestra; later assisted **Khemchand Prakash** (whom he considers his teacher) at **Ranjit** Studio. Employed by **Kardar** as in-house composer at Kardar Studio after *Nai Duniya*; composed some of his most memorable music for Kardar and his disciple, M. Sadiq (e.g. ***Rattan***, Naushad's breakthrough film). Scored Mehboob's films after ***Anmol Ghadi***, including ***Anokhi Ada***, ***Andaz*** and ***Mother India***. Partner in Sunny Art Prod., producing e.g. ***Udan Khatola***. Other classic compositions include ***Baiju Bawra*** (using the eminent Khayal singer Amir Khan along with D.V. Paluskar), **Asif**'s epic ***Mughal-e-Azam*** (where Ustad Bade Ghulam Ali Khan sang), **Nitin Bose**'s ***Ganga Jumna***. The music for **Kamal Amrohi**'s ***Pakeezah*** is credited to Ghulam Mohammed but Naushad also contributed to it.

FILMOGRAPHY: **1940**: *Prem Nagar*; **1941**: *Kanchan*; *Darshan*; *Mala*; **1942**: *Nai Duniya*; *Sharada*; ***Station Master***; **1943**: *Kanoon*; *Namaste*; ***Sanjog***; **1944**: *Geet*; *Jeevan*; *Pehle Aap*; ***Rattan***; **1945**: *Sanyasi*; **1946**: ***Anmol Ghadi***; *Keemat*; ***Shahjehan***; **1947**: *Dard*; ***Elaan***; *Natak*; **1948**: ***Anokhi Ada***; *Mela*; **1949**: ***Andaz***; *Chandni Raat*; *Dillagi*; *Dulari*; **1950**: ***Babul***; ***Dastaan***; **1951**: ***Deedar***; *Jadu*; **1952**: ***Aan***; ***Baiju Bawra***; *Diwana*; **1953**: *Char Chand*; **1954**: ***Amar***; *Shabab*; **1955**: ***Udan Khatola***; **1957**: ***Mother India***; **1958**: *Sohni Mahiwal*; **1960**: *Kohinoor*; ***Mughal-e-Azam***; **1961**: ***Ganga Jumna***; **1962**: *Son of India*; **1963**: ***Mere Mehboob***; **1964**: *Leader*; **1966**: ***Dil Diya Dard Liya***; *Saaz Aur Awaz*; **1967**: *Palki*; ***Ram Aur Shyam***; **1968**: *Admi*; *Saathi*; ***Sangharsh***; **1970**: *Ganwaar*; **1971**: ***Pakeezah***; **1972**: *Tangewala*; **1974**: *My Friend*; *Aaina*; **1975**: *Sunehra Sansar*; **1979**: *Chambal Ki Rani*; **1982**: *Dharam Kanta*; **1986**: ***Love and God***; **1989**: *Dhwani*; **1990**: *Awaaz De Kahan Hai*; **1993**: *Teri Payal Mere Geet*.

Navketan *see* **Chetan Anand**

NAVYA MOVEMENT

Influential modernist literary movement in Kannada initiated by Gopalakrishna Adiga's two poetry collections, *Nadedu Banda Dari* (1952) and *Bhumigita* (1959). The movement is described in G.B. Joshi and Kirtinath Kurthakoti's major rewriting of Kannada literary history in a 3-volume book with the same title as Adiga's anthology, *Nadedu Banda Dari* (1959). Navya represented a departure from Navodaya's transcendental romanticism, emphasising instead a more limited protagonist placed within contemporary mass-culture and consumerism. It acknowledged the influence of Kafka, Camus, Sartre and Freud. The movement reached its creative pinnacle in the late 60s with U.R. Ananthamurthy's fiction (*Samskara*, 1966) and developed an uncompromising political opposition to the hegemonic Brahmin élite. It extended directly into the cinema with **Pattabhi Rama Reddy**'s film of ***Samskara*** (1970), encouraging modernist writers, playwrights and stage directors to turn to the cinema (e.g. **P. Lankesh**, **Girish Karnad**, **Chandrasekhar Kambhar**, **B.V. Karanth**, Baraguru Ramchandrappa, actor C.R. Simha et al.). The shift into cinema perpetuated the belief that film is an extension of literature, spawning many adaptations of the writings of, e.g., Masti Venkatesha Iyengar, Chaduranga, Triveni, T.R. Subba Rao and S.L. Bhairappa. In retrospect, only three films - *Samskara*, Lankesh's ***Pallavi*** (1976) and **Girish Kasaravalli**'s ***Ghattashraddha*** (1977) - have direct political and formal links with Navya. Later, many 'kalatmaka' (artistic) or 'Prayogika' (experimental) films claimed to derive e.g. from Chaduranga's novels (the writer filmed his own novel *Sarvamangala*,

Nargis in *Jogan* (1950)

1968), while directors like **N. Lakshminarayan**, **G.V. Iyer** and **Puttanna Kanagal** went on to formulate an art-house aesthetic quickly enshrined in Karnataka film and tv policies.

NAVYUG CHITRAPAT

The first film production company to market its shares directly to the public. Started in 1940 by **P.K. Atre** with a 'Managing Agency' comprising **Master Vinayak**, **Baburao Pendharkar** and cameraman Pandurang Naik. The business was based on the assets of Huns Pics, enhanced by Rs 100 shares sold via advertisements in English and Marathi papers and journals. **Atre** also toured large parts of Maharashtra hawking the shares. Worries about the risks of investing in the film industry were partially offset by Huns' previous successes and by Atre and Vinayak's reputations. Enough finance was raised to make two of Vinayak/**Khandekar**'s classic films: ***Lagna Pahave Karun*** (1940) and ***Sarkari Pahune*** (1942). When Pendharkar and Naik resigned and Vinayak formed Prafulla Pics, Navyug closed down (1942).

NAXALITE

Term used to refer to members of the extreme Left CPI(ML) launched by Charu Majumdar in 1969. The word refers to the site of the party's first major political action (1967), the village of Naxalbari in Bengal. Following the split in the CPI (1964), several members of the breakaway CPI(M) turned to a Maoist, cadre-based mass-action programme among the peasantry leading to the nationwide crackdown on the CPI(ML) ordered by prime minister Lal Bahadur Shastri. The schisms between Left and Right within the CPI(M), the latter insisting on the parliamentary road, were aggravated by the victory of United Fronts in Kerala and West Bengal in the 1967 State Assembly elections. Although the Naxalbari insurrection itself, in which peasant groups seized land, held people's courts and dispensed 'justice' to landlords and hoarders, was rapidly quelled, it had widespread and long-term consequences. The CPI(M)'s withdrawal of support in protest against Chief Minister Ajoy Mukherjee's use of the police against their members eventually brought down the United Front government. In August 1967, two months after Naxalbari, Girijan tribals led a similar insurrection in Srikakulam, evoking the CPI-led Telangana uprising (1946-51). The All India Co-ordination Committee of Communist Revolutionaries (AICCCR) was established as the apex body for all extra-parliamentary Left activity. Organisations affiliated to it, as well as several others, launched armed movements in parts of Uttar Pradesh, Bihar, Punjab, Kerala and Tamil Nadu. In 1969 the AICCCR was replaced by the CPI(ML), immediately recognised by the Chinese government. In 1970, actions sympathetic to the Naxalites were initiated by student groups in Calcutta and spawned major debates about revolutionary cultural aesthetics, often emphasising an anarchist iconoclasm (e.g. Saroj Dutta's essay 'In Defence of Iconoclasm', 1970: cf Samar Sen, 1978). In November 1970 the West Bengal Prevention of Violent Activities Bill gave the central government complete control over law and order in West Bengal, and the student movements in Calcutta as well as the peasant actions in, e.g., Debra and Gopiballavpur were brutally suppressed by the police and the army. This suppression, coupled with the splintering of the movement itself, effectively ended Naxalite activity as an all-India phenomenon by 1972. The CPI(ML) survived mainly in Andhra Pradesh with the activities of the Peoples' War Group. Culturally, however, its critique of the parliamentary system as well as the ideological and moral divides it caused within the Left movement as a whole, found an echo among independent film-makers, as in **Mrinal Sen**'s Calcutta Trilogy (see esp. ***Calcutta '71***, 1972), in **Satyajit Ray**'s Calcutta Trilogy, **Tapan Sinha**'s ***Apanjan*** (1968), **Ghatak**'s ***Jukti Takko Aar Gappo*** (1974), **Benegal**'s ***Nishant*** (1975), **Nihalani**'s ***Aakrosh*** (1980) and **Shahani**'s ***Tarang*** (1984). The Naxalite movement's emphasis on agitation around civil liberties opened up a major space for independent documentary film-making (cf **Anand Patwardhan, Tapan Bose**) and for Left political and aesthetic discourses. Other film-makers influenced by these currents include **John Abraham**, the musical, theatre and poetic sources of **B. Narasinga Rao**, and **Utpalendu Chakraborty**'s rhetoric about acceptable and unacceptable capital resources for film-making. In Andhra Pradesh, where the movement is currently the strongest, campaign films featuring exaggerated plotlines and emphatic performances, an idiom associated in that state with Naxalite aesthetics, were financially backed by media baron and producer Ramoji Rao in the mid-80s, continuing into, e.g., Narayamurthy's *Lal Salaam* (1992).

NAYAK, PRABHAKAR MANAJIRAO (1920-86)

Marathi director born in Nanded Dist. Joined **Navyug** in Bombay in the 30s as a projectionist. Assisted Naqvi (1942-5), **Pendharkar** and **Raja Paranjpe**, débuting as director in 1958. Made melodramas and comedies adapting the style of the ribald urban Tamasha. His best-known films include *Pathrakhin*, a classic **Jayashree Gadkar** weepie, and *Thapadya*, a parable about honesty in which a chronic liar reforms and claims the sexy Tamasha dancer. Often cast stars from the Loknatya tradition, e.g. Usha Chavan, Sarla Yevlekar, Nilu Phule and Ram Nagarkar. Occasionally acted, e.g. in Y. Pethkar's *Keechaka Vadha* (1959) and in many of his own films. Produced his own last film. Also lyricist.

FILMOGRAPHY: 1958: *Punarjanma*; **1960**: *Sangat Jadli Tujhi An Majhi*; **1965**: *Sudharlelya Baika*; *Chala Utha Lagna Kara*; **1966**: *Hi Naar Rupasundari*; **1968**: *Khandobachi Aan*; **1970**: *Aai Aahe Shetat*; **1971**: *Dam Kari Kaam*; **1972**: *Pathrakhin*; **1973**: *Patla Tar Vhay Mhana*; *Thapadya*; **1974**: *Tevdha Sodun Bola*; **1975**: *Pandoba Porgi Phasli*; *Varaat*; **1977**: *Manasa Paris Mendhre Bari*; *Padarachya Savleet*; **1978**: *Chandal Chaukadi*; **1979**: *Baeelweda*; **1981**: *Laath Marin Tithe Pani*.

NAYYAR, OMKAR PRASAD (b. 1926)

Composer born in Patiala, Punjab. Employed by AIR, Jullundur. Début scoring the background music for ***Kaneez***. First break as composer for **Pancholi** films (*Aasmaan*). Scored very popular music for many 50s films such as early **Guru Dutt** (*Baaz*, ***Aar Paar***, ***Mr and Mrs '55***) and **Kishore Kumar** films (P.L. Santoshi's *Cham Chama Cham* and **Kardar**'s *Baap Re Baap*). Late 50s films include ***Tumsa Nahin Dekha***, the film in which **Shammi Kapoor** changed into his Presley image, and ***Howrah Bridge***, with the most famous song, *Mera naam Chin Chin Choo*. Also scored the biggest film in Kapoor's 'Yahoo' image, ***Kashmir Ki Kali***. A characteristic scene of his b&w films is a cabaret dancer performing - often to a Rhumba rhythm - in front of the Boss in a nightclub (*Twelve O'Clock*, ***Aar Paar***). Introduced several Punjabi rhythms, esp. from the Bhangra folk dances, into Hindi film as well as producing 'light' popular music with rock overtones for **Geeta Dutt** and **Asha Bhosle**'s early hits. Returned to score a Telugu film, *Neerajanam*, after a decade out of work.

FILMOGRAPHY: 1949: ***Kaneez***; **1952**: *Aasmaan*; *Cham Chama Cham*; **1953**: *Baaz*; **1954**: ***Aar Paar***; *Mangu*; *Mehbooba*; **1955**: *Baap Re Baap* (with **C. Ramchandra**); *Miss Coca Cola*; ***Mr And Mrs '55***; *Musafirkhana*; *Subse Bada Rupaiya*; **1956**: *Bhagambhag*; ***CID***; *Chhoo Mantar*; *Dhake Ki Malmal*; *Hum Sub Chor Hain*; *Mr Lambu*; *Naya Andaz*; *Shrimati 420*; **1957**: *Bade Sarkar*; *Duniya Rang Rangili*; *Johnny Walker*; *Mai Baap*; ***Naya Daur***; *Qaidi*; ***Tumsa Nahin Dekha***; *Ustad*; **1958**: *Farishta*; ***Howrah Bridge***; *Kabhi Andhera Kabhi Ujala*; *Mr Qartoon MA*; *Mujrim*; *Phagun*; *Ragini*; ***Sone Ki Chidiya***; *Twelve O'Clock*; **1959**: *Do Ustad*; **1960**: *Basant*; ***Jaali Note***; *Kalpana*; *Mitti Mein Sona*; **1962**: *Ek Musafir Ek Hasina*; *Hong Kong*; **1963**: *Phir Wohi Dil Laya Hoon*; **1964**: ***Kashmir Ki Kali***; **1965**: *Mere Sanam*; **1966**: *Akalmand*; *Baharen Phir Bhi Aayengi*; *Do Dilon Ki Dastaan*; *Love and Murder*; *Mohabbat Zindagi Hai*; *Sawan Ki Ghata*; *Yeh Raat Phir Na Aayegi*; **1967**: *CID 909*; *Nasihat*; **1968**: *Dil Aur Mohabbat*; *Humsaya*; *Kahin Din Kahin Raat*; *Kismet*; *Shrimanji*; **1969**: *The Killers*; *Sambandh*; **1971**: *Aisa Bhi Hota Hai*; **1972**: *Ek Baar Muskurado*; **1973**: *Taxi Driver*; *Pran Jaye Par Vachan Na Jaye*; **1978**: *Khoon Ka Badla Khoon*; **1979**: *Heera Moti*; *Bin Maa Ke Bachche*; **1989**: *Neerajanam*; **1992**: *Nishchay*.

NAZIR, PREM (1928-89)

Aka Chiriyinkil Abdul Kader. Actor born in Chiriyinkil, South Kerala, and graduated from St Berchman's College, Changanassery. Biggest star in Malayalam film history. Started in **Kunchako**'s Excel company. The bulk of his prodigious output was for the Udaya and Merryland Studios where he was the first of a new generation of stars manufactured to bolster specifically Malayalam film genres. Nazir, the oldest of the generation (cf **Sathyan** and **Madhu**), resembles **Gemini**'s version of the Tamil hero, e.g. **Gemini Ganesh**. His image merged with what Ayyappa Panicker (1987) called 'the second generation of romantics', poets working within a tradition framed largely by Vallathol (1878-1958) and exemplified by 'pastoral' poets Changampuzha and G. Sankara Kurup. Most famous Malayalam film lyricists emerged from that tradition (**Vyalar Rama Varma**, **O.N.V. Kurup**, **P. Bhaskaran**) and Nazir's acting is a performative counterpart to their imagery. His embodiment of the ideal male is usually seen as more accessible than, e.g., **Sathyan**'s remoteness, and at its best it drew attention to exploitative aspects of social and religious systems (***Padatha Paingili***), the breakdown of the joint family (e.g. **Kariat**'s *Maya*) and the modern engagement with folk narratives (e.g. ***Unniyarcha***). With the new generation of 60s film-makers such as **Vincent** (the ghost story ***Bhargavi Nilayam***) and K.T. Mohammed (Nazir's classic village simpleton in ***Thurakatha Vathil***), the films tend to elaborate a strangely intermediate world between fantasy and the contemporary, culminating in his consecration as a totally self-contained icon, a development evoked in **Lenin Rajendran**'s *Prem Nazirine Kanmanilla* with Nazir, playing himself, kidnapped by tribals and 'forgotten' by the outside world as he matches his unreality with that of tribals living outside his definitions of the world. Wrote a book on the film characters he played, *Enne Thediyetha Kathapatrangal*.

FILMOGRAPHY: 1952: *Marumagal*; *Visappinte Vili*; *Achan*; **1954**: *Avakashi*; *Avan Varunnu*; *Manasakshi*; *Balya Sakhi*; *Kidappadam*; **1955**: *Anujathi*; *CID*; **1956**: *Atmarpanam*; *Manthravadi*; *Avarunarunnu*; **1957**: *Devasundari*; ***Padatha Paingili***; *Jailpully*; **1958**: *Lily*; *Mariakutty*; *Chadurangam*; **1960**: *Seeta*; **1961**: *Krishna Kuchela*; *Gnana Sundari*; ***Unniyarcha***; **1962**: *Laila Majnu*; *Kalpadukal*; *Shri Rama Pattabhishekham*; **1963**: ***Ninamanninnya Kalapadakal***; *Snapaka Yohannan*; *Kattu Maina*; *Chilampoli*; *Kaleyum Kaminiyum*; *Satyabhama*; **1964**: *Kuttikkuppayam*; *Devalayam*; *School Master*; *Oralkoodi Kalanayi*; *Pazhassi Raja*; *Ayesha*; *Kudumbini*; *Althara*; *Karutha Kayi*; ***Bhargavi Nilayam***; **1965**: *Devatha*; ***Odeyil Ninnu***; *Porter Kunjali*; *Inapravugal*; *Kaliyodam*; *Muthalaly*; *Kuppivala*; *Thankakudam*; ***Rosy***; *Mayavi*; *Jeevitha Yatra*; *Rajamalli*; *Kathiruna Nikkah*; *Kochumon*; *Bhoomiyile Malakha*; *Shakuntala*; *Chettathi*; ***Kavya Mela***; ***Murappennu***; **1966**: *Kalithozhen*; *Station Master*; *Pinchu Hridayam*; *Pennmakkal*; *Kootukar*; *Kalyana Rathriyil*; *Anarkali*; *Kanmanikal*; *Puchakanni*; *Kanakachilanka*; *Sthanarthi Saramma*; *Tilottama*; *Priyatama*; ***Kunjali Marakkar***; **1967**: *Ramanan*; *Jeevikan Anuvadhikuka*; ***Irutinte Atmavu***; ***Agniputhri***; ***Kottayam Kola Case***; *Uayogastha*; *Balyakalasakhi*; *Kudumbam*; *Bhagyamudra*; *Kannatha Veshankal*; *Collector Malathi*; ***Ashwamedham***; ***Chitramela***; *Nagarame Nandi*; *Pareeksha*; *Cochin Express*; *Pooja*; *NGO*; *Nadan Pennu*; *Kasavuthattam*; *Ollathu Mathi*; *Swapnabhoomi*; *Pathirapattu*; **1968**: ***Thirichadi***; *Vidyarthi*; *Thokkukal Katha Parayunnu*; *Inspector*; *Dial 2244*; ***Asuravithu***; *Padunna Puzha*; *Punnapra Vyalar*; *Lakshaprabhu*; *Love In Kerala*; ***Thulabharam***; *Anju Sundarigal*; *Kodungalluramma*; *Velutha Kathrina*; *Agni Pareeksha*; *Kayalkarayil*; *Bharyamar Sukshikuka*; **1969**: *Anashchadanam*; *Padicha Kallan*; *Vila Kuranja Manushyar*; *Almaram*; *Ballathapahayan*; *Mr Kerala*; *Rahasyam*; *Susie*; ***Adimagal***; *Kannur Deluxe*; *Poojapushpam*; *Kadalpalam*; *Mooladanam*; *Jwala*; *Vilakkapetta Bandhangal*; ***Nadhi***; *Danger Biscuit*; *Kootu Kudumbam*; *Virunnukari*; *Rest House*; **1970**: ***Aranazhikaneram***; *Moodalamanju*; *Mindapennu*; *Pearl View*; *Amma Enna Stree*; *Anatha*; *Palunku Pathram*; *Kalpana*; *Nazhikakallu*; ***Ezhuthatha Katha***; *Dattuputhran*; *Rakta Pushpam*; *Nizhalattam*; *Vivaham Swargathil*; ***Thurakatha Vathil***; *Othenente Makan*; ***Ningalenne Communistaki***; *Vivahitha*; *Kakathampurati*; *A Chitrashalabham Paranotte*; *Lottery Ticket*; *Triveni*; *Tara*; *Saraswathi*; **1971**: ***Anubhavangal Palichakal***; *CID Nazir*; *Lanka Dahanam*; *Muthassi*; *Neethi*; *Shiksha*; *Moonnupukkal*; *Kalithozhi*; *Marunattil Oru Malayali*; *Puthanveedu*; *Ernakulam Junction*; *Vilakku Vangiya Veena*; **1972**: *Sambhavami Yuge Yuge*; *Aradi Manninte Janmi*; *Pushpanjali*; *Devi*; *Maya*; *Manthrakodi*; *Manushya Bandhangal*; *Aromalunni*; *Taxi Car*; *Mayiladum Kunnu*; *Omana*; *Oru Sundariyude Katha*; *Miss Mary*; *Punarjanmam*; *Maraivil Thiruvu Sukshikuha*; *Gandharvakshetram*; *Nrithyasala*; *Adhyathe Katha*; *Anveshanam*; *Brahmachari*; *Postmane Kananilla*; *Pani Teertha Veedu*; ***Maram***; **1973**: *Police Ariyaruthu*; *Football Champion*; *Agnathavasam*; *Panchavati*; *Bhadra Deepam*; *Thiruvabharanam*; *Kalachakram*; *Ponnapuram Kotta*; *Veendum Prabhatam*; *Thani Niram*; *Ladies' Hostel*; *Achani*; *Urvashi Bharathi*; *Thenaruvi*; *Pacha Nottukal*; *Pavangal Pennungal*; *Dharma Yuddham*; *Sastram Jayichu Manushyan Thottu*; *Interview*; *Azhakulla Saleena*; *Poyi Mukhangal*; *Manasu*; *Thottavadi*; *Padmavyuham* (Mal); *Angathattu*; **1974**: *Chanchala*; *Pattabhishekham*; *Chandrakantham*; *Suprabhatam*; *Panchatanthram*; *Rahasya Rathri*; *Pathiravum Pakalvelichavum*; *Durga*; *Setu Bandhanam*; *Nellu*; *Poonthenaruvi*; *Night Duty*; *College Girl*; *Ayalathe Sundari*; *Chakravakam*; *Thacholi Marumagan Chandu*; *Thumbolarcha*; *Raja Hamsam*; *Honeymoon*; *Bhoomidevi Pushpiniyayi*; *Arakallan Mukkal Kallan*; *Chief Guest*; **1975**: *Abhimanam*; *Alibaba and Forty-One Thieves*; *Aranyakandam*; *Ashtami Rohini*; *Ayodhya*; *Babu Mon*; *Cheenavala*; *Chumadu Thangi*; *Dharmakshetre Kurukshetre*; *Hello Darling*; *Kottaram Vilakkanundu*; *Love Marriage*; *Manishada*; *Neela Ponman*; *Padmaragam*; *Palazhi Madhanam*; *Picnic*; *Pravaham*; *Priyamulla Sophia*; *Pulival*; *Sammanam*; *Sindhu*; *Surya Vamsam*; *Thamarathoni*; *Thiruvonam*; *Tourist Bungalow*; **1976**: *Ayiram Janmangal*; *Ajayanum Vijayanum*; *Ammini Ammavan*; *Amritha Vahini*; *Aparadhi*; *Chennai Valarthiya Kutty*; *Chirikuduka*; *Kamadhenu*; *Kanyadanam*; *Kayamkulam Kochunniyude Maghan*; *Light House*; *Mallanum Mathevanum*; *Ozhukkinethire*; *Panchami*; *Panchamrutham*; *Parijatham*; *Pickpocket*; *Prasadam*; *Pushpa Sarem*; *Rajayogam*; *Seemantha Puthran*; *Themmadi Velappan*; *Thulavarsham*; *Thuruppu Gulam*; *Vanadevatha*; *Vazhi Vilakku*; **1977**: *Suryakanthi*; *Acharam Ammini Osaram Omana*; *Akshaya Pathram*; *Anjali*; *Anugraham*; *Aparajitha*; *Aval Oru Devalayam*; *Chaturvedam*; *Gandharvam*; *Haridhayame Sakshi*; *Innale Innu*; *Ivanente Priyaputhran*; *Kaduvaye Pidicha Kiduva*; *Kannappanunni*; *Lakshmi*; *Minimol*; *Mohamum Mukthiyum*; *Muttathe Mulla*; *Parivarthanam*; *Rathi Manmathan*; *Rendu Lokam*; *Saghakkale Munottu*; *Samudram*; *Sujatha*; *Tholkkan Enikku Manassilla*; *Varadakshina*; *Veedu Oru Swargam*; *Vishukkani*; **1978**: *Anappachan*;

Prem Nazir in *Lottery Ticket* (1970)

Amarsham; *Ashtamudikayal*; *Bharyayum Kamukiyum*; *Ee Ganam Marakkumo*; *Jayikkanai Janichavan*; *Kadathanattu Maakkam*; *Kalpa Vruksha*; *Kanalkkattakal*; *Kudumbam Namakku Sreekovil*; *Liza*; *Mudra Mothiram*; *Ninakku Gnanam Enikku Neeyum*; *Nivedyam*; *Prarthana*; *Raju Rahim*; *Shathru Samharam*; *Snehathinte Mukhangal*; *Sundari Marudde Swapnangal*; *Thacholi Ambu*; *Tharu Oru Janmam Koodi*; *Vilakkum Velichavum*; *Yagaswam*; **1979**: *Ward No. 7*; *Kalam Kathu Ninilla*; *Irumpazhigal*; *Vijayanum Veeranum*; *Mamankam*; *Prabhu*; *Pamparam*; *Tharangam*; *Thirayum Thiravum*; **1980**: *Air Hostess*; *Kari Puranda Jeevithangal*; *Agni Kshetram*; *Ithikkara Pakki*; *Theekadal*; *Mr Michael*; *Digvijayam*; *Chandrahasam*; *Palattu Kunjikannan*; *Lava*; *Pralayam*; *Anthappuram*; *Nayattu*; **1981**: *Charam*; *Areyappedatha Rahasyam*; *Thadavara*; *Thalam Manasinte Thalam*; *Theekali*; *Sanchari*; *Choothatham*; *Kodumudikal*; *Ellam Ninakku Vendi*; *Kilungatha Changalakal*; *Pathiya Suryan*; *Sangharsham*; *Attamari*; *Raktham*; *Vida Parayum Munpe*; *Itihasam*; *Parvathi*; *Dhruva Sangamam*; *Adimachangala*; *Kadathu*; **1982**: *Idiyum Minnalum*; *Ivan Oru Simham*; *Angachamayam*; *Mayilanji*; *Jambulingam*; *Oru Thira Pinneyum Thira*; *Maruppacha*; *Panchajanyam*; *Champalakadu*; *Padayottam*; *Arambham*; *Akrosham*; *Shri Ayyappanum Vavarum*; *Raktha Sakshi*; **1983**: *Bandham*; *Adhyathe Anuragam*; *Attakkalasam*; *Adhipathyam*; *Angam*; *Ashrayam*; *Bhukambam*; *Chakravalam Chuvannappol*; *Deeparadhana*; *Ee Yugam*; *Ente Katha*; *Himam*; *Justice Raja*; *Kariyam Nisaram*; *Kodungattu*; *Mahabali*; *Marakkailo Rikalum*; *Mortuary*; *Oru Madaupravinte Katha*; *Passport*; *Prashnam Orutharam*; *Pratigna*; *Prem Nazirine Kanmanilla*; *Theeram Thedunna Thira*; *Yuddham*; **1984**: *Makale Maapu Tharu*; *Alakadalinakkare*; *Amme Narayana*; *Ende Nandini Kutty*; *Inakkilli*; *Kadamattathachan*; *Krishna Guruvaroorappa*; *Kurisuyuddham*; *Madhu Vidhu Theerum Munpe*; *Manase Ninakku Mangalam*; *Manithali*; *Ningalil Oru Stree*; *Oru Thettinde Katha*; *Piriyilla Naam*; *Poomadathu Pennu*; *Vanitha Police*; *Vellom*; *Vikatakavi*; **1985**: *Daivathe Orthu*; *Manya Mahajanangale*; *Mukhya Manthri*; *Nerariyum Nerathu*;; *Orikkal Oridathu*; *Orunal Innorunal*;

Ozhivukalam; *Sannaham*; *Snehicha Kuttathinu*; *Uyirthezhunnelppu*; *Shatru*; **1986**: *Ayalvasi Oru Dharithavasi*; **1988**: *Dhwani*; **1989**: *Lal Americayil*.

NEELAKANTAN, P. (b. 1916)

Tamil director associated mainly with **MGR**'s persona; also worked in Sinhalese (*Suneetha* and *Sujake Rahase*) and Kannada. Born in Villuppuram. Congress Party worker aged 15. Former journalist (with *Jeevamani* in 1935, *Vijayan* in 1936, *Indira* in 1940 and established his own journal *Kalaivani* in 1940) and radio playwright. Broke through with two famous plays, *Mullil Roja*, performed by the **TKS Brothers** and attacking the infamous Devadasi system, and *Nam Iruvar*, staged by **N.S. Krishnan**'s theatre troupe (Krishnan was in jail at the time and the play was done by T.A. Mathuram and S.V. Sahasranamam). ***Nam Iruvar*** was later filmed by **A.V. Meiyappan** (1947) as a stridently nationalist drama with Neelakantan's script (he was also asst. d). Its success established **AVM** and was followed by other scripts for Meiyappan, including the hits *Vethala Ulagam* (1948) and *Vazhkai* (1949). Directorial début: *Ore Iravu*, based on a noted play by the DMK's founder, **C.N. Annadurai**, who also scripted the film. Shifted briefly to Kannada to direct two films produced by and starring **B.R. Panthulu** (***Modalatedi*** and *Shivasharane Nambekka*), before returning to the **DMK film** idiom with Tamil hits like ***Ambikapathy*** with **Sivaji Ganesan**. Directed two films with **Karunanidhi** scripts, *Poompuhar* and *Poomalai*. Was a partner in Panthulu's Padmini Pics before starting his own Arasu Prod. (1957). Most of his films star MGR. According to M.S.S. Pandian (1992), the hit *Thirudathe* inaugurated the MGR persona of a subaltern in the service of society. This trend continued in ***Mattukkara Velan*** with MGR playing the double role of the cowherd and the lawyer, and in *Ninaithathai Mudippavan* with MGR demonstratively consuming proletarian food and displaying an inability to eat peas with a fork.

FILMOGRAPHY: 1951: *Ore Iravu*; **1954**: *Kalyanam Panniyum Brahmachari*; **1955**: *Gomathiyin Kathali*; ***Modalatedi*/*Mudhal Thedi***; *Shivasharane Nambekka*; **1957**: ***Ambikapathy***; *Chakravarthi Thirumagal*; **1958**: *Thedi Vantha Selvam*; **1960**: *Advantha Daivam*; **1961**: *Nallavan Vazhvan*; *Thirudathe*; **1962**: *Ethayum Thangam Idayam*; **1963**: *Koduthu Vaithaval*; *Raj Mahal*; **1964**: *Poompuhar*; **1965**: *Anandi*; *Poomalai*; **1966**: *Avan Pithana*; **1967**: *Kavalkaran*; **1968**: ***Kanavan***; *Kannan En Kathalan*; **1969**: ***Mattukkara Velan***; **1970**: *En Annan*; **1971**: *Neerum Neruppum*; *Oru Thai Makkal*; **1972**: *Raman Thediya Seethai*; *Sangey Muzhangu*; **1974**: *Netru Indru Nalai*; **1975**: *Ninaithathai Mudippavan*; **1976**: *Needhikku Thalai Vanangu*; **1981**: *Daiva Thirumanangal*.

Neerja *see* **Vijayanirmala**

NENE, RAJA (1912-75)

Hindi and Marathi director, actor and producer originally called Gajanan Hari Nene. Nephew of **Vishnupant Damle** who got him a job at **Prabhat** Studio as assistant director. Assisted **Shantaram** on ***Chandrasena*** (1935) and ***Amar Jyoti*** (1936); he was a key figure in the making of ***Sant Tukaram*** (1936) and of the subsequent Damle-**Fattelal** films, receiving co-d credit for ***Sant Sakhu***. Played the part of the boorish Pandit, son of Kakasaheb, in Shantaram's classic ***Kunku*/*Duniya Na Mane***. Directed the successful ***Daha Wajta*** at Prabhat. Together with **Athavale**, **Datta Dharmadhikari** and **Keshavrao Bhole**, he walked out of the studio shortly afterwards, leaving the studio's magnum opus ***Ramshastri*** (1944) incomplete. The group joined Mohan Studio to make *Taramati*. Started his own Raja Nene Prod. (1947) co-directing Dharmadhikari's first film, *Shadi Se Pehle*. After **Rajkamal Kalamandir**, Nene Prod. was the second major production house to emerge from the Prabhat Studio and was followed by Dharmadhikari's Alhaad Chitra. Nene's next production was the classic Tamasha musical ***Patthe Bapurao***, reserving the lead part for himself. **Anant Mane** later claimed to have ghost-directed this hit as well as *Ketakichya Banaat*. ***Pehli Tareekh***, Nene's most successful Hindi film, was remade in Kannada and Tamil by **P. Neelakantan** as ***Modalatedi*** (1955).

FILMOGRAPHY (* also act/** act only): **1937**: ***Kunku*/*Duniya Na Mane*****; **1941**: ***Sant Sakhu***; **1942**: ***Daha Wajta*/*Das Baje***; **1944**: ***Ramshastri***; **1945**: *Taramati*; **1946**: *Bachchon Ka Khel*; *Phir Bhi Apna Hai*; **1947**: *Lalat*; *Shadi Se Pehle**; **1949**: *Sant Ramdas**; **1950**: *Ketakichya Banaat**; ***Patthe Bapurao****; **1951**: *Shri Vishnu Bhagwan*; **1952**: *Indrasan*; *Lanka Dahan*; *Rajrani Damayanti*; **1954**: *Hanuman Janma*; ***Pehli Tareekh***; *Radha Krishna*; **1957**: *Pahila Prem**; **1958**: *Gauri Shankar*; **1959**: *Yala Jeevan Aise Nav*; **1964**: *Tuka Jhalase Kalasa*.

NEW INDIAN CINEMA

Promotional label for a sector of state sponsored film-making said to have originated either with **Mrinal Sen**'s ***Bhuvan Shome*** (1969) or **Mani Kaul**'s ***Uski Roti*** (1969). Associated in the late 60s/early 70s with financial support from the FFC (see **NFDC**), making it the first major result of governmental support for feature-film production outside the industrial mainstream. Among its beneficiaries were **FTII** graduates like **Kumar Shahani**, **Mani Kaul**, **Saeed Mirza** and **Ketan Mehta**. It also generated technicians who pioneered aesthetic and technological innovations which had a substantial impact on the technical standards of the film industry itself: the camerawork of K.K. Mahajan in Hindi, Venu in Malayalam and Ramchandra in Kannada cinemas, the sound recording of Kuldeep Sud and later Hitendra Ghosh and P.C. Padmanabhan. Described by the popular press as a 'new wave' in a facile comparison with the French *nouvelle vague*, prompting **Satyajit Ray** to issue a somewhat dismissive response to the sector, 'An Indian New Wave?' (1971: cf Ray, 1976)). What shaped the new cinema most decisively was the cultural and political dynamic sparked by the mainstream industry's massive opposition to it. While attacking 'financially unviable' films, the industry also sought to exploit its aura of cultural value for its own purposes (cf **B.R. Ishara**). The films that articulated an 'official' agenda were **Pattabhi Rama Reddy**'s ***Samskara*** (1970) and **Shyam Benegal**'s ***Ankur*** (1973). Both, like *Bhuvan Shome* and **M.S. Sathyu**'s ***Garam Hawa*** (1973), were low-budget box-office successes. *Samskara* gave a new dimension to the predominantly literary movements in Kannada (see **Navya Movement**) and encouraged the notion of 'regional realism', claiming Satyajit Ray as its major progenitor (a role Ray was happy to play) although **Tendulkar**'s theatre work offered a more credible source. This development was extended into the Malayalam cinema by **Adoor Gopalakrishnan** and **Aravindan**. In its later, post-Benegal phase, New Indian Cinema often drew on advertising capital and aesthetics for art-house film-making, legitimating a new definition enshrined in, e.g., the parliamentary committee's instructions, during the Emergency, to the FFC to grant loans on the following criteria: '1. Human interest in the story; 2. Indianness in theme and approach; 3. Characters with whom the audience can identify; 4. Dramatic content and 5. Background and capability of the applicant' (*Committee On Public Undertakings Report*, 1976). This ideology became official cultural policy in the 7th Five-Year Plan and had a decisive impact on **Doordarshan** as well as shaping the NFDC's and the Directorate of Film Festivals' institutional priorities.

NEW THEATRES

Main Bengali studio and one of the élite banners in pre-Independence Indian cinema. Set up by Birendra Nath Sircar (1901-80) in 1931 as a sound studio in Tollygunge, Calcutta, following on from Sircar's silent International Filmcraft (Est: 1930 in association with **Charu Roy** and Prafulla Roy). New Theatres acquired Tanar equipment and the services of Wilford Deming, a Hollywood sound technician imported by **Ardeshir Irani**. The studio attracted major technical and creative talent from several smaller silent studios then on the verge of collapse: **Indian Kinema** provided **Nitin Bose**, the writer, scenarist and film-maker **Premankur Atorthy**, the stars **Durgadas Bannerjee**, **Amar Mullick**, **Jiban Ganguly**, etc.; from Barua Pics came **P.C. Barua** himself and **Sushil Majumdar**; **British Dominion Films** supplied **Dhiren Ganguly**. Sircar aimed for a cinematic equivalent of literature: 'Immediately after the establishment of New Theatres, the first film I made was Saratchandra [Chatterjee]'s *Dena Paona* (1931). The first director of New Theatres was Premankur Atorthy, the famed litterateur. The film was not a success. Yet, I could perceive that following the path of literature would lead to the discovery of the right path. Seven subsequent films met with the same fate but each film pointed to the ultimate way' (1961, in Jha, 1990). This formula had been launched at **Madan Theatres** when they purchased exclusive film rights to all of Bankimchandra Chatterjee's prose and was followed by New Theatres, leading to such cinematic oddities as the big-budget ***Natir Puja*** (1932), credited with **Rabindranath Tagore**'s direction. New Theatres then opted for a more melodramatic mode with **Debaki Bose**'s ***Chandidas*** (1932). The most famous New Theatres productions were the P.C. Barua and Nitin Bose films and its major star was **K.L. Saigal**. The studio had many directors on its payroll (most studios managed with one in-house director, using B-films made by assistants or other employees to keep the production flow going) and invested massively in technological innovation (e.g. the work of sound recordist Mukul Bose). The decline of the studio is usually linked to the resignation in 1941 of Nitin Bose, one of their top directors and head of the technical units. Its fall is also connected with the rise of the Western and Southern Indian markets during and immediately after WW2, as the studio had never established its own outlets and was increasingly at the mercy of professional distributors charging crippling commissions. There are several accounts of the studio's outright sale of film rights to groups like the Kapurchands, often at a loss. The studio finally closed in 1955, although Sircar remained closely involved with film industry organisations, being on the board of the **FFC** for some years.

NIHALANI, GOVIND (b. 1940)

Hindi director born in Karachi (now Pakistan) into a merchant family. During Partition, his family fled to Udaipur (1947) and then to Delhi. Studied cinematography at S.J. Polytechnic, Bangalore (1959-62). Assisted cameraman V.K. Murthy in Bombay (1962-71). An early and influential colleague was Bombay-based playwright and theatre director Satyadev Dubey, whose ***Shantata! Court Chalu Aahe*** (1971) was Nihalani's first feature as cameraman. Shot over 200 advertising films and documentaries, directing 100 more for Krishna Movies in Bombay. Also shot **Benegal**'s early films. Turned director in 1980. Made **Tendulkar**-scripted political films dealing with urban crime and official corruption. Did 2nd unit work for Attenborough's *Gandhi* (1982). His box-office hit ***Ardh Satya***, used a *Dirty Harry* plot which was familiar in Hindi and regional commercial cinemas (e.g. **Prakash Mehra**'s ***Zanjeer***, 1973, in Hindi, and **S.V. Rajendra Singh**'s ***Antha***, 1981, in Kannada). *Ardh Satya* itself was adapted into Tamil by K. Vijayan (*Kaval*, 1985). Takes politically sensational topics and turns them into individual moral dilemmas, usually enacted by **Om Puri**. His tv serial ***Tamas***, set during Partition, proved controversial and resulted in a court ruling asserting the right to freedom of expression on tv. Recent work mainly adaptations of stage plays to tv (Ibsen, Strindberg and Lorca). A book-length interview with Nihalani was published in 1992 (ed. Samik Bandyopadhyay).

FILMOGRAPHY: **1980**: ***Aakrosh***; **1982**: *Vijeta*; **1983**: ***Ardh Satya***; **1984**: ***Party***; **1985**: *Aaghat*; **1986**: ***Tamas*** (TV); **1989**: *Jazeerey* (TV); **1990**: ***Drishti***; **1991**: *Pita*; *Rukmavati Ki Haveli*.

NURJEHAN (b. 1929)

Hindi-Urdu and Punjabi actress and singer born in Kasur village, Punjab. Studied music under Ghulam Mohammed Khan. Stage actress in Calcutta as a child, and introduced to films apparently by Sukhlal Karnani of Indra Movietone. Joined films when still a child in Punjabi productions of K.D. Mehra and featured prominently in **Pancholi**'s hit musical *Gul-e-Bakavali*. Married film-maker Shaukat Hussain and acted in many of his films, including ***Khandaan***, ***Naukar*** and *Jugnu*, the latter co-starring **Dilip Kumar** and produced by their own Shaukat Art Prod. **V.M. Vyas** brought her to Bombay (1942) to act in ***Duhai***. She returned to Lahore after Partition, acting in, e.g., Imtiaz Ali Taj's *Gulenar* and Shaukat Hussain's *Laila*, both scored by **Ghulam Haider**; she also produced *Chanway*. Known as the Melody Queen, almost all her Bombay films were hits with extremely popular music, and she remained a leading playback singer in Pakistan, notably in Punjabi productions. Best remembered for her songs *Awaaz de* and *Jawan hai mohabbat* in **Mehboob**'s ***Anmol Ghadi*** and for *Yahan badala wafa ka* in *Jugnu*. As a singer, she is often considered **Lata Mangeshkar**'s predecessor. Recorded two parts of the musical series 'Taranum' in the 1980s/90s in Pakistan.

FILMOGRAPHY: **1935**: *Gaibi Gola*; *Misar Ka Sitara*; *Azadi*; **1936**: *Sheila*; *Nariraj*; **1937**: *Mr 420*; *Taranhar*; *Fakhr-e-Islam*; *Kiski Pyari*; **1938**: *Heer Syal*; **1939**: *Gul-e-Bakavali*; *Sassi Punnu*; **1940**: *Yamla Jat*; **1941**: *Choudhury*; **1942**: ***Khandaan***; **1943**: ***Naukar***; ***Duhai***; ***Nadaan***; **1944**: *Dost*; *Lal Haveli*; **1945**: ***Badi Maa***; *Bhaijan*; *Village Girl*; *Zeenat*; **1946**: ***Anmol Ghadi***; *Dil*; *Humjoli*; **1947**: *Jugnu*; *Mirza Sahiban*; **1951**: *Chanway*; **1952**: *Dupatta*; **1953**: *Gulenar*; **1955**: *Patey Khan*; **1956**: *Lakht-e-Jigar*; *Intezaar*; **1957**: *Nooran*; **1958**: *Chhoo Mantar*; *Anarkali*; **1959**: *Pardesan*; *Neend*; *Koel*; **1961**: *Ghalib*; **1963**: *Baji*.

NUTAN SAMARTH (1936-91)

Top Hindi 60s star, introduced to films by her mother, **Shobhana Samarth**, in *Hamari Beti*. Her screen image was moulded by **Bimal Roy** (***Sujata***, ***Bandini***) and by those who continued in the Roy tradition: **Hrishikesh Mukherjee** (***Anari***), Bimal Dutt (*Kasturi*) and Sudhendu Roy (*Saudagar*). Her persona, confirmed in, e.g., **Saraiya**'s ***Saraswatichandra*** and in **Raj Khosla**'s melodramas (*Teri Maang Sitaron Se Bhar Doon*), developed a naturalism borrowed from reformist Bengali and Gujarati novels, constituting an indigenised variant of neo-realism. This aspect of her acting, anticipating **Smita Patil**'s image, became crucial to, e.g., the iconography of the New Indian Cinema's notion of 'Indianness'. In her best-known films she performed with a frothy uninhibitedness comparable to **Madhubala**: the **Filmistan** musical ***Paying Guest*** and Navketan's **Vijay Anand** hit ***Tere Ghar Ke Saamne*** are fine examples of the romantic duo she formed with **Dev Anand**. In later years she acted mother roles.

FILMOGRAPHY: **1945**: *Nala Damayanti*; **1950**: *Hamari Beti*; **1951**: ***Humlog***; *Nagina*; **1952**: *Hangama*; *Nirmohi*; *Parbat*; *Shisham*; **1953**: *Aaghosh*; *Laila Majnu*; *Malkin*; **1954**: *Shabab*; **1955**: *Seema*; **1956**: *Heer*; *Jaldeep*; **1957**: *Baarish*; ***Paying Guest***; **1958**: *Aakhri Dao*; *Chandan*; *Delhi Ka Thug*; *Kabhi Andhera Kabhi Ujala*; ***Sone Ki Chidiya***; *Zindagi Ya Toofan*; **1959**: ***Anari***; *Kanhaiya*; ***Sujata***; **1960**: *Basant*; *Chhabili*; ***Chhalia***; *Manzil*; **1963**: *Soorat Aur Seerat*; ***Bandini***; *Dil Hi To Hai*; ***Tere Ghar Ke Saamne***; **1964**: *Chandi Ki Deewar*; **1965**: *Khandaan*; *Rishte Naate*; **1966**: *Chhota Bhai*; *Dil Ne Phir Yaad Kiya*; *Dulhan Ek Raat Ki*; **1967**: *Laat Saheb*; *Meharbaan*; *Mera Munna*; *Milan*; **1968**: *Gauri*; ***Saraswatichandra***; **1969**: *Bhai Bahen*; **1970**: *Devi*; *Maa Aur Mamta*; *Maharaja*; *Yaadgaar*; **1971**: *Lagan*; **1972**: *Anuraag*; *Mangetar*; ***Grahan***; **1973**: *Saudagar*; **1976**: *Zid*; *Ginny Aur Johnny*; **1977**: *Duniyadari*; *Jagriti*; *Mandir Masjid*; *Paradh*; **1978**: *Anjaam*; *Ek Baap Chhe Bete*; *Hamara Sansar*; *Main Tulsi Tere Aangan Ki*; *Saajan Bina Suhagan*; *Kasturi*; **1980**: *Saajan Ki Saheli*; *Sanjh Ki Bela*; **1982**: *Jiyo Aur Jeene Do*; *Teri Maang Sitaron Se Bhar Doon*; **1983**: *Rishta Kaagaz Ka*; **1984**: *Yeh Kaisa Farz*; **1985**: *Aar Paar/Anyay Abichar*; *Meri Jung*; *Paisa Yeh Paisa*; *Yudh*; *Mayuri* (H); *Mujrim Hazir* (TV); *Pyari Bhabhi*; *Ricky*; **1986**: ***Karma***; *Naam*; **1987**: *Hifazat*; **1988**: *Sone Pe Suhaaga*; **1989**: *Guru* (H); *Mujrim*; *Kanoon Apna Apna*; *Aulad Ki Khatir*; **1992**: *Naseebwala*.

Nutan (centre) in *Bandini* (1963)

OSTEN, FRANZ (1876-1956)

Hindi director born in Munich as Franz Ostermayer, the elder brother of successful producer Peter Ostermayer. They set up a travelling cinema, Original Physograph (1907) and founded Mnnchner Kunstfilm (1909) after Osten had been making shorts for Pathé, Gaumont and Eclair. Their first feature: *Die Wahrheit* (1910). Osten's début as director: *Erna Valeska* (1911). War correspondent in 1915. Joined Peter's company Emelka (later Bavaria Film) in 1918. Made *Der Ochsenkrieg* (1920) with young cameraman Frank Planer of later Hollywood fame, one of Osten's several contributions to a budding genre that after WW2 became known as the Heimatfilm. In fact, the Ostermayr/Osten brothers claimed to be the originators of the genre. When **Himansu Rai** and Emelka made a deal to produce ***Prem Sanyas*** aka *Light of Asia*, Osten was assigned to direct. Continued directing **Rai**'s productions, often shooting in India as well as in Europe, in addition to directing for numerous companies in Berlin. Moved with cameraman Josef Wirsching and set designer Karl von Spreti to India to work at **Himansu Rai**'s **Bombay Talkies** (1934). While in Bombay, became a member of the Nazi Party (1936). Interned by the British at the outbreak of WW2 while shooting his last film there, ***Kangan***. Released and allowed to return to Germany (1940). Employed by Bavaria Film until 1945, for casting and setting up its film archive. In addition to Indian films, directed 33 silent features and 10 sound films. After WW2 became manager of a Bavarian spa. His Indian films, following UFA tradition, were huge Orientalist spectacles with elephants, camels and expansive vistas often shot in deep focus. Effective authorship shared by producer Rai and scenarist **Niranjan Pal**. Adopted European conventions to introduce main actors, e.g. backlit mid-shots in soft focus gradually becoming more contrasted; also used mobile outdoor shots as in the railway-crossing sequence of ***Achhut Kanya***. Strongly influenced younger Bombay Talkies film-makers **Amiya Chakravarty** and **Gyan Mukherjee**, though they used his techniques for very different purposes.

FILMOGRAPHY (Indian films): **1925**: ***Prem Sanyas***; **1928**: ***Shiraz***; **1929**: ***Prapancha Pash*** (all St); **1935**: ***Jawani Ki Hawa***; **1936**: ***Achhut Kanya***; ***Janmabhoomi***; ***Jeevan Naiya***; *Mamata*; *Miya Bibi*; **1937**: *Izzat*; ***Jeevan Prabhat***; *Prem Kahani*; ***Savitri***; **1938**: *Bhabhi*; *Nirmala*; *Vachan*; **1939**: ***Navjeevan***; ***Durga***; ***Kangan***.

Pachajanya *see* **Mahapatra, Nirad**

PADMANABHAN, R. (b. 1896)

One of the pioneer Tamil producer-directors. Son of a Sivagangai-based lawyer, entered films as distributor (1926) of Indian and imported films and retailer of cinema equipment. Set up the Madras-based Associated Films Studio (1928) with financial support from K.S. Venkatramani Iyer (father-in-law of **K. Subramanyam**). The studio's early work includes **Raja Sandow**'s first films. In the silent era, run by technicians imported from Bombay, it was the biggest South Indian production centre after **General Pics**. With the coming of sound, Padmanabhan first returned to distribution; then director for Oriental Films, a partnership involving Ramalinga Mudaliar.

FILMOGRAPHY: **1935**: *Maya Bazaar*; *Dhruva*; *Nalla Thangal*; *Subhadra Haran*; **1936**: *Nalayini*; *Garuda Garvabhangam*; **1937**: *Setu Bandhanam*; *Asai*; **1940**: *Meenakshi Kalyanam*; **1941**: *Maya Jyothi*; *Appothi Adigal*; **1943**: *Devakanya*; **1945**: *Bhakta Kalathi*; **1946**: *Setu Bandhanam*; *Sakata Yogam*; **1949**: ***Raksharekha***; **1952**: *Kumari*; *Rajeshwari*; **1955**: *Ellam Inbamayam*; **1962**: *Indra En Selvam*.

PADMARAJAN, P. (1936-91)

Malayalam director, writer and scenarist. Studied chemistry in Trivandrum, where he also worked as an AIR announcer. Author of 15 novels and scenarist before becoming a director. His naturalist novels about people on the margins, crime and sexual jealousy were the sources for, e.g., **Bharatan**'s and **I.V. Sasi**'s films. As director often adapted his own novels, e.g. ***Peruvazhiyampalam***, *Kallan Pavithran*. Best-known film is ***Koodevide?***, a psychological drama about the violence simmering underneath polite discourse. His folk parable ***Oridathoru Phayalwan*** is about the rise and fall of a childishly simple wrestler who makes a success of his sport, marries the prettiest woman in the village but finds himself a loser in life. Script credits include: **Bharathan**'s *Prayanam* (1975), ***Rathi Nirvedham*** (1978), *Thakara* (1979), *Lorry* (1980) and *Eenum* (1983); **I.V. Sasi**'s *Itha Ivide Vare* (1977), *Vadagaikku Oru Hridayam* (1978), *Kaikeyi* (1983) and ***Kaanamarayathu*** (1984); **K.S. Sethumadhavan**'s *Nakshatrangale Kaval* (1978); **K.G. George**'s *Rappadigalude Gatha* (1978); Mohan's *Salini Ente Kuttukari* (1980).

FILMOGRAPHY: **1979**: ***Peruvazhiyampalam***; **1981**: ***Oridathoru Phayalwan***; *Kallan Pavithran*; **1982**: *Novemberinte Nashtam*; **1983**: ***Koodevide?***; **1984**: *Parannu Parannu Parannu*; **1985**: ***Thinkalazhcha Nalla Divasam***; *Arappatta Kettiya Gramathil*; **1986**: *Desadanakkili Karayilla*; *Namukku Parkkan Munthiri Thoppukal*; *Kariyila Kattu Pole*; **1987**: *Nombarathi Poovu*; *Thoovana Thumbigal*; **1988**: ***Aparan***; *Moonnam Pakkam*; **1989**: *Innale*; **1991**: *Gnan Gandharvan*.

PADMINI, S. (b. 1934)

Malayalam, Tamil, Hindi and Telugu star and classical dancer born in Trivandrum. Second, and best-known, of the 3 famed Travancore sisters (Ragini and Lalitha). Dance training under Guru Gopinath. Début in Uday Shankar's dance spectacular ***Kalpana***, followed by roles in S.M. Sreeramulu Naidu and **Sundarrao Nadkarni**'s productions. Then acted in several Tamil films, with both **MGR** (***Manthiri Kumari***, *Maruthanattu Ilavarasi*) and **Sivaji Ganesan** (***Verapandiya Kattaboman***, ***Thillana Mohanambal***, ***Vietnam Veedu***). First major Hindi role in **Gemini**'s ***Mr Sampat*** but mainly associated with **Raj Kapoor** (***Jis Desh Mein Ganga Behti Hai***, ***Mera Naam Joker***). Known mainly as a Bharat Natyam dancer (cf *Thillana Mohanambal*) and actress in sentimental melodramas (typically ***Adhyapika***). Left films briefly in the late 70s when she moved to the USA, making her comeback in 1984. Thereafter known for her **Fazil** films. Probably made more Tamil films than are listed in her filmography.

FILMOGRAPHY: **1948**: ***Kalpana***; *Bhakta Jana*; *Gnanasoundari*; *Mahabali*; **1949**: ***Velaikkari***; *Devamanohari*; *Geetha Gandhi*; *Krishna Vijayam*; *Vinodini*; *Mayavathi*; *Natya Rani*; *Pavalakkodi*; *Ponmudi*; ***Laila Majnu***; **1950**: ***Ezhai Padum Padu/Beedala Patlu***; *Laila Majnu*; ***Manthiri Kumari***; *Maruthanattu Ilavarasi*; *Parijatham*; *Prasanna*; **1951**: ***Bahar***; *Jeevan Tara*; *Navvitte Navarathrulu*; *Singari*; **1952**: *Krishna Kanhaiya*; ***Mr Sampat***; *Kanchana*; *Velaikkaran*; **1953**: *Asha Deepam*; ***Ammalakulu/Marumagal***; *Oka Talli Pillalu*; **1954**: *Ethirparadathu*; ***Snehaseema***; *Illara Jyothi*; **1955**: *Rajkumari*; *Shiv Bhakta*; *Mangayar Thilakam*; *Vijayagauri*; *Kathanayaki*; *Kaveri*; *Koteshwaran*; **1956**: ***Madurai Veeran***; ***Amara Deepam***; *Raja Rani*; *Kannin Manigal*; *Verum Pechalla*; **1957**: *Payal*; ***Pardesi***; *Qaidi*; **1958**: *Amar Deep*; *Ragini*; ***Raj Tilak***; *Sitamgarh*; *Chadurangam*; **1959**: ***Veerapandiya Kattaboman/Amar Shaheed***; *Thangapathumai*; *Maragatham*; *Daivame Thunai*; *Ponnu Vilayum Bhoomi*; *Minnal Padayali*; **1960**: *Bindiya*; ***Jis Desh Mein Ganga Behti Hai***; *Kalpana*; *Maya Machhindra*; *Ramayan*; *Singapore*; *Daiva Piravi*; *Meenda Sorgam*; *Raja Desingu*; *Mannathai Mannan*; **1961**: *Umminithanka*; *Apsara*; *Sampoorna Ramayan*; *Shri Sabarimalai Shri Ayyappan*; **1962**: *Aashiq*; *Meri Bahen*; *Rani Samyuktha*; *Senthamarai*; *Vikramadithan*; **1963**: *Kattu Roja*; *Naan Vanangum Daivam*; *Veera Dalapathi Veluthambi*; ***Iruvar Ullam***; **1964**: *Shri Guruvayoorappan*; **1965**: *Kalyanaphoto*; *Kajal*; *Mahabharat*; **1966**: *Afsana*; *Kanakachilanka*; ***Chitthi***; *Thaye Unakkaga*; **1967**: *Aurat*; ***Irutinte Atmavu***; *Pareeksha*; *Pooja*; *Pesum Daivam*; *Engalukam Kalamvaryam*; *Kan Kanda Daivam*; *Iru Malargal*; **1968**: *Love in Kerala*; ***Adhyapika***; *Aparadhini*; *Vaasna*; ***Thillana Mohanambal***; *Thirumal Perumai*; *Kuzhandaikaka*; **1969**: *Kumara Sambhavam*; *Chanda Aur Bijli*; *Madhavi*; *Nannha Farishta*; *Bhai Bahen*; *Gurudakshinai*; *Mr Kerala(?)*; ***Adimagal***; **1970**: ***Penn Daivam***; ***Vietnam Veedu***; *Aansoo Aur Muskaan*; *Mastana*; ***Mera Naam Joker***; *Vivahitha*; *Vilayattu Pillai*; *Ethirkalam*; **1972**: *Appa Tata*; *Vasantha Maligai*; *Maa Inti Jyothi*; **1973**: *Veetu Mappillai*; *Pillai Selvam*; **1974**: *Kadavul Mama*; *Thayi*; *Thirudi*; *Roshakkari*; *Devi Shri Karumariamman*; **1975**: *Engalukkum Kathal Varum*; *Oru Kudumbathin Kathai*; **1976**: *Ungalil Oruthi*; *Uzhaikum Karangal*; **1977**: *Navarathnam*; **1978**: *Padakkudhira*; **1984**: ***Nokketha Dhoorathu Kannum Nattu***; **1985**: *Poove Poo Chooda Va*; **1986**: *Thaikku Oru Thalattu*; **1990**: ***Vasthuhara***.

PAG *see* **Progressive Artists Group**

PAGNIS, VISHNUPANT (1892-1943)

Professional actor on the Marathi **Sangeet Natak** from the age of 10; part of Kolhapur's Swadeshi Hitchantak Natak Mandali where he played the female roles of Sharada and Shakuntala in command performances for the Shahu Maharaj. Appeared in some silent **Maharashtra Film** movies but became known for his female roles in Mama Warerkar's

Vishnupant Pagnis in *Sant Tukaram*

first play, *Kunjvihari* (1908), and in **Tembe**'s Shivraj Natak where he played the heroine in the Hindi version of *Siddhasansar*. His style is said to have been strongly influenced by the Gujarati actor of female roles, Jaishankar Sundari. He became a music teacher in a municipal school when his stage career flagged and was a last-minute casting decision in the lead of ***Sant Tukaram*** (1936). Apparently remained under the spell of the great saint-poet whom he played. Was thereafter in some demand as a keertan singer. He did four more films, all in the Saint films genre, with **Jayant Desai** and **Vjay Bhatt**. Functioned as music director for *Sant Janabai* (1938). His performance as Tukaram has become a major reference-point in debates about Indian performance idioms: e.g. **Kumar Shahani**'s essay *The Saint Poets of Prabhat*, 1980 (cf Ramachandran, 1985); Geeta Kapur's *Mythical Material in Indian Cinema*, 1987.

FILMOGRAPHY (* also music d): **1921**: *Surekha Haran*; **1924**: ***Poona Raided***; **1936**: ***Sant Tukaram***; **1938**: *Sant Janabai* (music d only); **1939**: ***Sant Tulsidas****; **1940**: ***Narsi Bhagat***; **1943**: ***Mahatma Vidur***; *Bhakta Raaj*.

PAINTER, BABURAO (1890-1954)

Marathi-Hindi director born Baburao Krishnarao Mestri in Kolhapur, into family of traditional craftsmen. Taught himself to paint (hence his name) and sculpt in academic art-school style. He and his artist cousin Anandrao Painter were, between 1910 and 1916, the leading painters of **stage backdrops** in Western India, doing several famous curtains for **Sangeet Natak** troupes (esp. **Bal Gandharva** and **Tembe**'s companies) but also for Gujarati Parsee theatre. Became avid filmgoers after seeing ***Raja Harishchandra*** (1913). Perceiving its theatrical limitations, they turned to cinema, first as exhibitors (Shivaji theatre, Kolhapur) while trying to assemble their own camera. Anandrao died in 1916. Baburao and his main disciple, **Damle**, eventually put together a working camera in 1918. With financial support from local nobility, started **Maharashtra Film** with *Seeta Swayamvar*. Remained head of studio until 1932, launching many talented cineastes, including the group that later left to set up **Prabhat**: Damle, **Fattelal** and **Shantaram**. Following closure of Maharashtra Film (1932) ran Shalini Cinetone (1932-8). Then occasional freelance director (e.g. ***Lokshahir Ramjoshi*** on Shantaram's invitation, although Shantaram finished the film himself). Added a Marathi soundtrack to his *Prem Sangam* and re-released it in 1934 as his first sound film. Practised cinema as a continuation of earlier craft traditions, seen as a contribution to **Swadeshi**, legitimated by nationalist leader B.G. Tilak's public commendation of his achievements (1918). Developed sophisticated art direction and shooting techniques, e.g. the use of backdrops in red and yellow to register the right shades of grey on film, the manufacture of primitive filters with tinted glass, the first use of indoor electric lighting with generators, use of fades, etc. Also used costume design and art direction to relate to characters' spaces, reserving elaborate sets and design for fantasy films. Helped codify the mythological and founded the social (***Savkari Pash***) and the historical (***Sinhagad***, *Baji Prabhu Deshpande*) as film genres.

FILMOGRAPHY: 1918: *Seeta Swayamvar*; **1919**: *Congress Session in Bombay* (Doc); ***Sairandhri***; **1921**: *Surekha Haran*; **1922**: *Bhagwata Bhakta Damaji*; **1923**: *Markandeya*; ***Sinhagad***; *Shri Krishna Aavtar*; **1924**: ***Sati Padmini***; ***Kalyan Khajina***; **1925**: *Shahala Shah*; *Rana Hamir*; *Maya Bazaar*; ***Savkari Pash***; **1926**: *Gaja Gauri*; ***Bhakta Prahlad***; **1927**: *Muraliwala*; *Sati Savitri*; **1929**: *Baji Prabhu Deshpande*; **1930**: *Lanka*; **1932**: *Prem Sangam* (all St); **1935**: ***Usha***; **1936**: *Savkari Pash*; **1937**: ***Pratibha***; *Sadhvi Meerabai*; **1946**: *Rukmini Swayamvar*; **1947**: ***Lokshahir Ramjoshi/Matwala Shayar Ramjoshi***; **1952**: *Vishwamitra*; **1953**: *Mahajan*.

PAL, NIRANJAN (1889-1959)

Director and scenarist born in Calcutta. Son of nationalist leader Bipin Chandra Pal. Participated marginally in early youth in terrorist action around Calcutta (1908). Sent to Marseilles and to London where he lived until 1929. Met Veer Savarkar, leader of the extreme right-wing Hindu Mahasabha, and was linked with the assassination of William Hutt Curzon Wyllie (achieved at the Imperial Institute in London on 1 July 1909). In London, worked with the Natural Color Kinematograph Co. (1913); wrote short stories, plays and sold several scripts such as *Faith of a Child* (F. Martin Thornton, 1915) and *A Gentleman of Paris* (Sinclair Hill, 1931), based on his own novel *His Honour the Judge*. Started Indian Players group and staged plays like *Bluebottle* and *The Goddess*. Met **Himansu Rai**, an actor in *The Goddess*, and discussed making ***Prem Sanyas*** (1925). Pal claims in his unpublished memoirs, *Such is Life*, that the film was his idea as well as his script. Collaborated as scenarist on all Himansu Rai's silent productions (***Shiraz***, 1928; ***Prapancha Pash***, 1929). Revived Indian Players and *The Goddess* on stage in Calcutta with participation of **Premankur Atorthy**, **Modhu Bose** and **Charu Roy**. His play *Zarina*, staged by Bose's Calcutta Amateur Players, was later filmed by **Ezra Mir** (1932). Made promotional films for a French motor car company and Imperial Tobacco, exhibited with Chaplin films in tent shows around Calcutta (1930-3). Made newsreels for **Aurora** called *Aurora Screen News* (1938-42) and occasional features for Aurora, including the children's film *Hatekhari*. Rejoined Rai at **Bombay Talkies** (1934-7) as chief scenarist and wrote some of the studio's biggest hits (***Jeevan Naiya*** and ***Achhut Kanya***, both 1936; *Izzat* and ***Savitri***, both 1937). Made documentaries for Punjab government and worked in the **Film Advisory Board** as chief scriptwriter (1942). Also wrote the story of Modhu Bose's *Khyber Falcon* (1932) and **Jayant Desai**'s *Qatil Katari* (1931).

FILMOGRAPHY: 1930: *Naseeb Ni Balihari*; **1931**: *Sui Ka Naka*; *Pardesia*; *Pujari*; **1932**: *Dardi* (all St); **1939**: *Hatekhari*; *Amma*; **1940**: *Suktara*; *Ditiya Path*; **1941**: *Rashpurnima*; *Chitthi*; *Brahman Kanya*; **1951**: *Bodhodaya*.

PALEKAR, AMOL (b. 1944)

Actor and director born in Bombay, where he attented the J. J. School of Art (1965). Noted director on Marathi experimental stage with Satyadev Dubey (1968-72) and with his own Aniket group set up in 1972, e.g. Sadanand Rege's *Gochee* (1972) and Badal Sircar's *Juloos* (1975). Introduced theatre of the absurd in Maharashtra and a street theatre-inspired practice of performing plays in the round. Employed as bank clerk in Bombay when he was cast as actor by **Basu Chatterjee** in ***Rajanigandha*** (1974), which led to many parts in middle-class comedies, usually as the blundering lover. Also known for his remarkable performance as the scheming Rahul in **Kumar Shahani**'s epic melodrama ***Tarang***. Was a well-known Bengali star after he did Narayan Chakraborty's *Mother*, followed by Dinen Gupta's *Kalankini* and *Abasheshe* and Pinaki Choudhury's *Chena Achena*. Also starred in one Malayalam film, **Balu Mahendra**'s *Kolangal*. Became director with Marathi film ***Aakriet***, casting himself as a psychotic serial killer. Directed two more films, ***Ankahee*** and ***Thodasa Rumani Ho Jaye***, and several tv serials.

FILMOGRAPHY (* also d/** only d): **1971**: ***Shantata! Court Chalu Aahe***; *Bajiravacha Beta*; **1974**: ***Rajanigandha***; **1975**: ***Chhotisi Baat***; **1976**: *Chit Chor*; *Tuch Majhi Rani*; ***Bhumika***; **1977**: *Kanneshwara Rama*; *Agar*; *Taxi Taxi*; *Safed Jhooth*; *Gharonda*; **1978**: *Damaad*; *Do Ladke Dono Kadke*; *Solva Sawan*; **1979**: ***22 June 1897***; *Baaton Baaton Mein*; *Golmaal*; *Meri Biwi Ki Shaadi*; *Mother*; **1980**: *Apne Paraye*; *Chehre Pe Chehra*; *Aanchal*; **1981**: ***Aakriet****; *Naram Garam*; *Plot No. 5*; *Sameera*; *Kalankini*; *Agni Pareeksha*; **1982**: *Jeevan Dhara*; *Ramnagari*; *Shriman Shrimati*; *Olangal* **1983**: *Rang Birangi*; *Chena Achena*; *Pyaasi Aankhen*; *Nirvana*; **1984**: *Prarthana*; ***Ankahee****; *Ashray*; ***Tarang***; ***Admi Aur Aurat***; *Mr X*; *Saleysaab* (TV); **1985**: *Abashashe*; *Khamosh*; **1986**: *Baat Ban Jaye*; *Jhoothi*; **1987**: *Kachhi Dhoop*** (TV); **1988**: *Naqab*** (TV); **1989**: *Fitness for Fun, Fitness for Everyone*** (Doc); **1990**: ***Thodasa Rumani Ho Jaye****; **1991**: *Mrignayani*** (TV); **1993**: *Paoolkhuna*** (TV).

PALIT, NITAI (b. 1923)

Best-known Oriya director, born in Cuttack. Playwright and theatrical producer; vice-president of the **IPTA**'s Utkal branch. Started in film as actor (Vinay Bannerjee's *Amari Gaan Jhua*, 1953), then directed *Kedar Gouri*, a tragic love story. Broke through with ***Malajanha***, based on Upendra Das's novel, featuring the Oriya star **Jharana Das**. Admires the Bengali masters **Ray**, **Ghatak** and **Sen**.

FILMOGRAPHY: 1954: *Kedar Gouri* (also act); **1956**: *Bhai Bhai*; **1959**: *Maa*; **1965**: ***Malajanha***; **1968**: *Kie Kahara*; **1969**: *Bandhan* (O); **1972**: *Dharitri*; **1974**: *Mana Akasha*; **1976**: *Krishna Sudama*; **1977**: *Bandhu Mohanty*; **1980**: *Anuraag*; **1981**: *Kiye Jite Kiye Hare*.

PANCHOLI, DALSUKH M. (1906-59)

Hindi director. Exhibitor and Punjabi-Hindi producer born in Karachi. Studied scriptwriting and cinematography in New York. Inherited cinema network built by Rewashankar Pancholi during WW1. Expanded Empire Film Distributors (1922) into Empire Talkie Distributors (1931), established in Lahore and the largest importer of American films in Northern and Western India (approx 24 films annually). Exclusive contract with RKO gave them access to Photophone sound equipment. Made some documentaries, including footage on the Karachi Congress session (1931). Entered film production relatively late (1941), but early productions in Punjabi (*Gul-e-Bakavali*, 1939, *Yamla Jat*, 1940) and Hindi (***Khazanchi***, 1941) were instrumental in bringing Lahore's film industry into the national mainstream. Built his studio Pancholi Art Pics in Lahore with five floors but abandoned everything to migrate to Bombay following Partition (1946), apparently taking only the negative of his unfinished film, *Patjhad* (1948). For some years his team of film-makers (e.g. **Gidwani** and **Ravindra Dave**), actors (Ramola, **Nurjehan**, Smriti Biswas, Om Prakash, etc.) and composers (**Ghulam Haider**, **O.P. Nayyar**) were very influential in shaping a hybrid mass cultural film formula for a growing migrant working class in North India. Usually credited himself for his productions' stories and scripts.

FILMOGRAPHY: 1952: *Aasmaan*.

PANDE, VINOD

Hindi director. Worked in London where he had an advertising agency, Image Enterprises, for which he made two documentaries, several commercials and the first Hindi film made entirely in the UK, *Ek Baar Phir*. Also worked for AIR and as newsreader for the BBC. Made *Star*, an attempt to work in the Barbra Streisand-style musical.

FILMOGRAPHY: 1979: *Ek Baar Phir*; **1982**: *Yeh Nazdeekiyan*; *Star*; **1988**: *Ek Naya Rishta*; **1989**: *Sach*.

PANDHARIBAI (b. 1930)

Kannada cinema's first film heroine. Her early work was mainly in **Company Natak**-derived mythologicals by **Simha** and **Kemparaj Urs**. Also on the Tamil stage with S.V. Sahasranamam (e.g. *Seva Samaj*). Became a front-line star when she featured opposite **Rajkumar** in ***Bedara Kannappa***, one of Kannada cinema's earliest successes. *Sant Sakhu*, the first film of her own Shri Panduranga Prod., emphasised her 'progressive' image as a woman assuming the burdens of a feudal patriarchy, an image continued by, e.g., *Rayara Sose* and by her films with **G.V. Iyer** and T.V. Singh Thakore. It is exemplified by the seminal **DMK Film *Parasakthi***, where she became the voice of **C.N. Annadurai**'s political philosophy. ***Bellimoda*** was a key moment for her later mother image: most unusually for the stereotype, she gives birth to a male heir in the story, triggering an inheritance crisis for the heroine. Her later films establish her as South Indian cinema's counterpart to **Nirupa Roy**'s many mother roles (e.g. *Ramrajyadalli Rakshasaru*), although after 1985 her roles began diminishing.

FILMOGRAPHY: 1943: *Vani*; **1947**: *Bhakta Gora Kumbhara*; **1951**: *Raja Vikrama*; **1952**: ***Parasakthi***; **1953**: ***Gunasagari***; ***Gumasta***; ***Poongothai/Pardesi***; **1954**: ***Bedara Kannappa***; ***Manohara***; **1955**: *Bhakta Mallikarjuna*; *Sant Sakhu*; *Sodari*; *Vadina*; **1956**: *Bhakta Vijaya*; *Hari Bhakta*; *Renuka Mahatme*; **1957**: *Rayara Sose*; *Sati Nalayini*; *Bhabhi*; **1958**: *Panchayat*; *Anbu Engay*; **1959**: *Chand*; *Pathirai Matru Thangam*; *Nattukoru Nallaval*; *Alli Petra Pillai*; *Naalu Veli Neelam*; *Aval Yar*; *Engal Kula Daivi*; ***Abba! A Hudgi***; *Grihalakshmi*; ***Paigham***; **1960**: *Bhakta Shabari*; *Thanthaikupin Thamayan*; *Anbukkor Anni*; *Kurvanji*; *Ivan Avanethan*; *Raja Bhakti*; *Pavai Vilakku*; **1962**: *Tejaswini*; *Indra En Selvam*; *Punithavathi*(?); **1963**: *Shri Ramanjaneya Yuddha*; **1964**: *Navajeevana*; *Annapurna*; *Muriyada Mane*; *Pratigne*; *Pathiye Daiva*; *Shri Guruvayoorappan*; **1965**: ***Satya Harishchandra***; *Mahasati Ansuya*; *Bettada Huli*; *Chandrahasa*; ***CID***; **1966**: *Shri Kannika Parameshwari Kathe*; *Sandhya Raga*; *Laadla*; ***Motor Sundaram Pillai***; **1967**: *Anuradha*; ***Bellimoda***; *Shri Purandaradasaru*; *Premalopramadam*; *Punyavati*; **1968**: *Amma*; *Paala Manushulu*; **1969**: *Suvarnabhoomi*; *Odahuttidavaru*; *Madhura Milana*; *Namma Makkalu*; *Bhagirathi*; *Manashanti*; *Chowkada Deepa*; *Nannha Farishta*; ***Nam Naadu***; **1970**: *Aparajithe*; *Mooru Muttugalu*; *Bhale Jodi*; *Namma Mane*; ***Gejje Pooje***; **1971**: *Anugraha*; *Namma Baduku*; *Pratidhwani*; *Mahadimane*; *Rakhwala*; *Ganga Tera Pani Amrit*; *Bhale Rani*; *Bandhavya*; **1972**: *Janma Rahasya*; *Hridayasangama*; *Bandagi*; *Rivaaj*; *Shehzada*; *Sampoorna Ramayanam*; *Ranganna Sabatham*; *Nijam Nirupistha*; *Kodalu Pilla*; ***Pandanti Kapuram***; *Mathru Murthi*; *Marapurani Talli*; *Daiva Sankalpam*; *Thavaputhalvan*; *Aval*; *Annamitta Kai*; *Vasantha Maligai*; ***Dhakam***; **1973**: *Nee Ulla Varai*; *Gauravam*; *Neramu Siksha*; *Vaade Veedu*; *Stree Gauravam*; *Palletoori Chinnodu*; *Hemareddy Mallamma*; **1974**: *Peddalu Marali*; *Ramaiah Thandri*; *Devadasu*; *Krishnaveni*; *Thirumangalyam*; *Gumastavin Magal*; *Onne Onnu Kanne Kannu*; *Netru Indru Nalai*; *Patha Poojai*; *Thayi Pirandhal*; ***Avalum Penn Thaane***; ***Alluri Seetaramaraju***; **1975**: *Doctor Siva*; *Idhayakkani*; *Pallandhu Vazhga*; *Pattikatu Raja*; *Padmaragam*; *Asthi Kosam*; *Anna Dammula Katha*; *Katha Nayakuni Katha*; *Moguda Pellamma*; *Puttinti Gauravam*; *Raktha Sambandhalu*; *Ramuni Minchina Ramudu*; *Santhanam Saubhagyam*; *Thota Ramudu*; **1976**: *America Ammayi*; *Bangaru Manishi*; *Maa Daivam*; *Manavadi Kosam*; *Muthyala Pallaki*; *Neram Nadhikadu Akalidi*; *Raju Vedale*; *Seetamma Santhanam*; *Swami Drohulu*; *Mugiyada Kathe*; *Colonel and Collector*; *Athirishtam Azhaikkirathu*; *Avan Oru Charitram*; *Etharkum Thuninthavan*; *Lalitha*; *Muthana Muthallava*; *Perum Pukazhum*; *Uthaman*; *Uzhaikum Karangal*; *Bhadrakali*; **1977**: *Aaru Pushpangal*; *Indru Pol Endrum Vazhga*; *Palabhisekham*; *Punitha Anthoniar*; *Punniyam Seithaval*; *Thaliya Salangaiya*; *Thani Kudithanam*; *Uyarnthavargal*; *Dongalaku Donga*; *Eenati Bandham Yenatido*; *Geetha Sangeetha*; *Janma Janmala Bandham*; *Maa Iddari Katha*; *Oke Raktham*; *Seeta Rama Vanavasu*; **1978**: *Devadasi*; *Bandhipotu Mutha*; *Dongala Veta*; *Dudubasavanna*; *Kalanthakulu*; *Lambadolla Ramadasu*; *Lawyer Vishwanath*; *Moodu Puvvulu Aaru Kayalu*; *Nindu Manishi*; *Prema Chesina Pelli*; *Sahasavanthudu*; *Sommokadidhi Sokokadidhi*; *Swargaseema*; *Kamatchiyin Karunai*; *Kumkumam Kadhai Solgiradhu*; *Makkal Kural*; ***Oru Veedu Oru Ulagam***; *Chadurangam*; *Taxi Driver*; *Unakkum Vazhvu Varum*; *Vazhthungal*; **1979**: ***Vetagadu***; **1981**: *Chhaya*; *Keralida Simha*; **1983**: *Adadani Saval*; *Amarajeevi*; *Amayakudu Kadhu Asadhyudu*; *Dharma Poratam*; *Kaliyuga Daivam*; *Koteeshwarudu*; *Lalitha*; *Mayagadu*; *Palletoori Pidugu*; *Pralaya Garjanai*; *Raghu Ramudu*; *Shri Ranganeethulu*; *Ennaipar En Azhagai Paar*; *Malargalile Aval Malligal*; *Ragangal Maruvathillai*; *Saatchi*; *Sasthi Viratam*; *Vellai Roja*; **1984**: *Vetri*; *Amayakudu Kadu Aggi Bharothalu*; *Ithe Naa Saval*; *Naga Bhairava*; *Vasantha Geetam*; **1985**: *Ragile Gundelu*; *Andha Oru Nimidam*; *Arthamulla Asaigal*; *Jhansi Rani*; *Ketti Malam*; *Mel Maruvathur Adi Parasakthi*; *Pudhu Yugam*; *Shri Raghavendrar*; **1990**: *Ramrajyadalli Rakshasaru*.

PANTHULU, BUDUGUR RAMAKRISHNAIAH (1911-74)

Kannada director and actor also associated with Tamil and Telugu theatre. Born in Budugur, AP. Studied in Madras. Worked as schoolteacher, apparently using this experience to make his best-known film, the social ***School Master***. Simultaneously acted in several plays, eventually turning professional actor with the Chandrakala Nataka Sabha (1932) in productions including *Samsara Nauka*, *Sadarame*, *Gul-e-Bakavali*, etc. Worked with **Veeranna** in plays *Asha Pasha* and *Shri Krishna Garudi*. Then started his own stage company, Kala Seva Mandali, in partnership with stage (later film) actor Dikki Madhava Rao. Joined films when Devi Films, Madras, commissioned **H.L.N. Simha** to adapt Chandrakala's stage hit ***Samsara Nauka***. Partnered music maestro T.R. Mahalingam in a stage company that later became Sukumar Prod. with **P. Pullaiah**'s *Macharekhai*. Started Padmini Pics with writer-publisher **P. Neelakantan** (first film: *Kalyanam Panniyum Brahmchari*); later became the company's sole proprietor. First film as director, *Ratnagiri Rahasya*, was a hit. Films usually continued the Chandrakala Sabha's anti-mythological emphasis on social relevance. Made some spectacular period films with **Sivaji Ganesan**, e.g. ***Veerapandiya Kattaboman***, ***Kappalotiya Thamizhan***, ***Karnan***. The Kurukshetra battle scenes of *Karnan* were shot at Jaipur with troops of the 61st Cavalry regiment, using 80 elephants, 400 horses and three camera units. Made 12 Tamil films, some featuring **MGR** (e.g. the hit *Nadodi*). Best-known films are lower-budget socials claiming realist values inspired by **B.N. Reddi**. Panthulu remade *School Master* in Tamil; **Puttanna Kanagal** then remade it again in Malayalam. Kanagal, who was his assistant, developed this genre into a brand of psychological melodrama. Panthulu's films often starred **M.V. Rajamma**.

FILMOGRAPHY (** also act/* act only): **1936**: ***Samsara Nauka****; *Raja Bhakti**; **1940**: *Daana Shura Karna**; *Tilottama**; **1941**: ***Bhaktimala****; **1943**: *Radha Ramana**; **1944**: ***Tehsildar****; **1946**: *Vijayalakshmi**; *Lavangi**; **1947**: ***Nam Iruvar****; **1948**: *Bhakta Jana**; *Samsara Nauka**; **1950**: *Macharekhai**; **1953**: ***Ammalakulu/Marumagal****; **1954**: *Kalyanam Panniyum Brahmachari**; **1955**: ***Modalatedi/Mudhal Thedi****; *Shivasharane Nambekka**; *Vadina**; **1957**: *Ratnagiri Rahasya/Tangamalai Rahasyam***; **1958**: ***School Master/Badi Panthulu*****; *Suhaag*; *Engal Kudumbam Parisu*; *Shabash Meena*; **1959**: ***Veerapandiya Kattaboman/Amar Shaheed***; ***Abba! A Hudgi****; *Shabash Pilla*; **1960**: *Sangaili Thevan*; *Makkala Rajya/Pillalu Techina Chalana Rajyam/Kuzhadaigal Kanda Kudiyarasu*; **1961**: ***Kappalotiya Thamizhan***; ***Kittur Chanamma/Rani Chanamma***; **1962**: *Galigopura/Gali Medalu***; *Dil Tera Diwana*; *Bhale Pandian*; **1963**: *Saaku Magalu/Pempudu Koothuru*; **1964**: *Chinnada Gombe/Muradhan Muthu***; ***Karnan/Karna/Daanveer Karna***; **1965**: *Ayirathil Oruvan*; *Katha Nayakudu Katha*; **1966**: *Enga Papa*; *Nadodi*; *Nammaveeti Lakshmi*; *Dudde Doddappa***; *Emme Thammanna*; **1967**: *Gange Gauri*; *Beedhi Basavanna*; **1968**: *Chinnari Puttana***; *Amma***; *Rahasiya Police 115*; **1969**: *Gandondu Hennaru***; **1970**: ***Shri Krishnadevaraya*****; *Thedi Vantha Mappillai*; **1971**: *Aliya Geleya*; *Malathi Madhava***; **1972**: *Ondu Hennina Kathe*; **1973**: *Ganga Gauri*; *School Master*.

PARANJPE, RAJA (1910-79)

Prolific Marathi actor and genre director born in Miraj, Maharashtra. Started as organ player and bit actor in Natyamanwantar productions *Andhalyanchi Shala* (1933) and *Lapandav*. A protégé of **Keshavrao Date**, obtained an acting role in **Painter**'s remake of ***Savkari Pash***. Became known as comedy actor. Assisted and acted in films by **Bhalji Pendharkar** (***Kanhopatra***, *Gorakhnath*, *Sunbai*) and **Master Vinayak** productions. Directorial début in 1948. Strongly influenced by Vinayak's screenplay-dominated prose melodrama and socials. Regular collaborators on his films were scenarist-lyricist **Madgulkar** and music director **Sudhir Phadke**. Claimed that the bulk of his work was vinodi, not vidushaki (based on literate humour rather than folk clowning), a claim exemplified by the comedy ***Lakhachi Goshta***. The rest were kautumbik, i.e. morality tales of everyday life: demonstratred by films like ***Oon Paoos*** and ***Pedgaonche Shahane***. Unlike **Datta Dharmadhikari** cathartic weepies, Paranjpe shared **Khandekar**'s strong commitment to a social morality and to the use of cinematic plotting as a means of creating exemplary characters. By the mid-60s, the Tamasha-derived musical comedies of, e.g., **Anant Mane** and **Kondke** had displaced both idioms by addressing larger audiences than the urban middle class to which Paranjpe restricted himself. Though he resisted pressures to blur the distinctions, his disciple **Rajdutt** managed to do so successfully. Autobiography excerpted in *Rudravani* (1975).

FILMOGRAPHY (* also d/** only d): **1936**: *Savkari Pash*; **1937**: ***Kanhopatra***; ***Pratibha***; **1938**: *Dhruva Kumar*; **1940**: *Gorakhnath/Alakh Niranjan*; **1942**: *Sunbai*; *Tuzhach*; **1943**: *Ladaai Ke Baad*; *Naya Tarana*; **1944**: *Swarna Bhoomi*; *Panna*; *Pundalik*; **1945**: *Din Raat*; **1946**: *Room Number Nine*; *Sasurvas*; **1947**: *Karasthan*; **1948**: *Balidan/Do Kaliyan***; *Jivacha Sakha**; **1949**: *Jaga Bhadyane Dene Aahe*; *Main Abla Nahin Hoon*; **1950**: *Jara Japoon**; ***Pudhcha Paool****; *Var Pahije*; **1951**: *Jashaas Tase*; *Parijatak/Shri Krishna Satyabhama***; **1952**: ***Lakhachi Goshta*****; ***Pedgaonche Shahane****; *Akher Jamla*; *Stree Janma Hi Tujhi Kahani*; **1953**: *Bolavita Dhani*; *Chacha Choudhury**; **1954**: ***Oon Paoos****; *Een Meen Sadeteen*; *Ovalani*; *Purshachi Jaat*; **1955**: *Ratnaghar*; *Ganget Ghoda Nhala***; **1956**: *Andhala Magto Ek Dola***; *Deoghar***; *Gaath Padli Thaka Thaka***; *Pasant Aahe Mulgi***; **1958**: *Punarjanma*; **1959**: *Baap Bete***; **1960**: ***Jagachya Pathivar****; **1961**: *Adhi Kalas Mag Paya**; *Suvasini**; **1962**: *Sonyachi Paoole***; *Baikocha Bhau*; *Kshan Aala Bhagyacha*; **1963**: ***Bandini***; *Te Mazhe Ghar*; *Baiko Maheri Jaate**; *Ha Mazha Marg Ekala**; **1964**: ***Pathlaag*****; **1965**: *Padchaya***; **1966**: *Gurukilli**; *Love And Murder***; **1967**: *Kaka Mala Vachva**; ***Madhuchandra***; *Santha Vahate Krishnamai*; **1968**: *Yethe Shahane Rahataat*; *Preet Shikva Mala*; **1969**: *Adhaar**; *Aparadh*; **1971**: *Jal Bin Machhli Nritya Bin Bijli*; *Tithe Nandate Lakshmi*; **1972**: *Piya Ka Ghar*; **1973**: *Nasti Uthathev*; *Varhadi Ani Vajantri*; **1974**: *Us Paar*; **1975**: *Preet Tujhi Majhi*; *Shantata! Khoon Jhala Aahe*; *Ya Sukhano Ya*.

PARANJPYE, SAI (b. 1936)

Hindi director born to Russian/Marathi parents in Lucknow into an illustrious family associated with social reform movements (cf Shakuntala Paranjpye's role in **Shantaram**'s ***Kunku/Duniya Na Mane***, 1937). Educated in Australia where her father was High Commissioner. Published collection of fairy tales in Marathi when 8 years old. Well-known Marathi playwright and stage director, famous for spoofs on middle-class Maharashtrian conservatism, and for her children's plays. Introduced the stage revue form (e.g. *Nanda Saukhya Bhare*, *Sakkhe Shejari*) into Marathi theatre. Started directing for tv (1965), then in charge of **CFS** productions (1974-5). Producer for **Doordarshan** in early 70s. Films offer moral tales (***Katha***, situated in Bombay's middle class, is based on the story of the hare and the tortoise) spiced with comedy routines. Translated the tv script of ***Sparsh*** into a film released in 1984. With the commercialisation of Doordarshan in the mid-80s, has concentrated mainly on independent tv serials, e.g. *Ados Pados*.

FILMOGRAPHY: **1972**: *The Little Tea Shop* (TV); **1973**: *Jadu Ka Shankh*; **1975**: *Begaar* (Sh); **1976**: *Sikandar*; *Dabcherry Milk Project* (Doc); **1977**: *Captain Laxmi* (Sh); **1978**: *Freedom from Fear* (Doc); **1979**: ***Sparsh***; **1981**: ***Chashme Buddoor***; *Books that Talk* (Doc); **1982**: ***Katha***; **1985**: *Ados Pados* (TV serial); *Chhote Bade* (TV); **1988**: *Angootha Chhaap* (Sh); **1990**: ***Disha***; **1993**: *Chudiyan*; *Papeeha*.

PARSEE THEATRE

Commercial theatre movement sponsored by the Parsees, Zoroastrians of Persian origin who settled largely on India's Western coast. Traditionally involved in shipbuilding and shipping, by the early 19th C. they were the dominant mercantile community in the Bombay Presidency in collaboration with the British Free Traders (cf A. Guha, 1970). By the mid-19th C. they had become India's first commercial bourgeoisie, going into banking and setting up the Bombay Chamber of Commerce (1836). The Bombay Theatre, built in 1776 as a copy of London's Drury Lane and performing English plays mainly for British soldiers and East India Co. bureaucrats, was bought in 1835 by Sir Jamshedjee Jeejeebhoy who also set up the Sir J. J. School of Art in 1857. In 1846, the Grant Road Theatre came to prominence under the Parsee magnate Jagannath Shankarshet, staging plays in English, then in Marathi, Gujarati and Hindi, performed mainly by Parsee amateur troupes. By the 90s the troupes employed full-time writers; copyright legalities began to be established and groups started publishing plays as well as building their own theatres, almost all of which later switched to film. Parsee mercantile capital underpinned India's entertainment industry until the 1930s and substantially founded the early film distribution infrastructure (see **Madan Theatres**) together with at least three major silent and sound studios: **Imperial Film**, **Minerva Movietone** and **Wadia Movietone**. Major theatre groups included the Parsee Stage Players (Est: 1853) with Dadabhai Naoroji as chief patron; the Victoria Co. (Est: 1867, which built the Victoria Theatre in 1868 later bought by Madan); the Elphinstone Dramatic Club (Est:

1863); the Zoroastrian Theatrical Club (Est: 1866); the Empress Victoria Natak Mandali (1876) with major shareholding by Lalsingh Dulhasingh of Delhi; the Alfred Co. (1871) which split into the Parsee Alfred and New Alfred companies and built the Tivoli Theatre in Bombay. Calcutta was dominated by Madan Theatres with the Corinthian Theatre as the showpiece and the Parsee Imperial and Elphinstone companies. By the turn of the century, there were groups in Karachi (e.g. New Shining Star), Jodhpur, Agra, Aligarh, Hyderabad, Meerut, Lucknow and Lahore. Major playwrights include **Aga Hashr Kashmiri, Narayan Prasad Betaab** and **Radheshyam Kathavachak**. The dominant genres of the Parsee theatre were the historical, the romantic melodrama and the mythological, with a major influence being the 17th C. Elizabethan theatre, esp. via translations and adaptations of Shakespeare, a tradition that fed into film through Kashmiri's scripts and **Sohrab Modi** and **Prithviraj Kapoor**'s films. The first original plays, written mainly in Gujarati by Vamanji Cawasji, Jehangir Nosherwanji Patel etc., drew on Persian lyric poetry like Firdausi's *Shah Nama*, deploying themes of heroism (featuring characters like Rustom and Sohrab) and love legends (*Shirin Farhad*). Its dominant language became Urdu, mixing a rhetorical prose with musical forms such as Thumri, Dadra and Jhinjhoti sung in Brijbhasha, a hybrid form with roots in the play *Indrasabha* by Syed Aga Hasan 'Amanat' (1852) at Wajid Ali Shah's court in Lucknow (see ***Indrasabha***, 1932). Another big influence which migrated via the Parsee theatre into regional stage traditions like the **Sangeet Natak**, the Kannada/Tamil **Company Natak** and the Bengali **Calcutta Theatres** was the European opera. The Anglophile Parsee repertoire's 'classicism', comparable to 'academic' naturalism in the visual arts, substantially determined the transformation of classical and popular music into urban stage (and later recording) modes, a transition assimilated into the early sound cinema.

PATANKAR, SHRI NATH (?-1941)

Pioneer producer-director-cameraman with an impact on early Indian film equivalent to **Phalke**'s. Fragments of biographical information suggest that he was born in the early 1880s and became a still photographer who bought a film camera from **Bhatavdekar** and filmed the great Delhi Durbar (1911) also shot by **Hiralal Sen**, **Madan Theatres** and others. Started Patankar Union in partnership with V.P. Divekar and A.P. Karandikar (1913) and made some films mainly to raise funds. They were helped by nationalist leader Lokmanya Tilak, who persuaded financiers Bhagwandas Chaturbhuj and Dharamdas Narayandas to invest in the company. His second feature, *Narayanrao Peshwa*, is almost certainly India's first historical. The company only took off in 1917 with the entry of Dwarkadas Sampat into Patankar-Friends & Co. Films made 1918-20, usually scripted by **Mohanlal Dave**, prepared the emergence of the **Kohinoor** Studio. Following Sampat's exit (1920), Patankar started a third studio, National Film (1922), financed by Thakurdas Vakil and Harilal, and then a fourth, Pioneer Film financed by Vazir Haji, which was also the parent company of the Excelsior Studio. His historicals and mythologicals were among the most professionally made films before the studio era (pre-1925). With the transformation of Pioneer into the Excelsior Studio, freelanced for a while as cameraman and art director in Bombay. Shot all the films he directed.

FILMOGRAPHY: 1912: *Savitri*; **1915**: *The Death of Narayanrao Peshwa*; **1917**: *Bhakta Prahlad*; **1918**: *Jaimini*; *King Shriyal*; *Ram Vanvas*; **1919**: *Kacha Devayani*; *Kabir Kamal*; **1920**: *Sati Madalasa*; *Narasinh Avatar*; *Shakuntala*; *Seeta Swayamvar*; *Vichitra Gutika*; *Katorabhar Khoon*; **1922**: *Bhakta Bodana*; *Jadunath*; *Karna*; *King Bhartrahari*; *Mahashweta Kadambari*; *Kalidas*; *Sati Anjani*; *Shri Markandeya Avatar*; **1923**: *Durvas Shaap*; *Guru Machhindranath*; *Krishna Satyabhama*; *Ranakdevi*; *Sati Veermati*; *Shri Dnyaneshwar*; *Shri Krishna Bhakta Peepaji*; *Vanraj Chavdo*; *Videhi Janak*; *Vaman Avatar*; **1924**: *Karan Ghelo*; **1926**: *Chatra Bakavali*; *Dorangi Duniya*; *Kacha Devayani*; *Manovijaya*; *Paanch Mahabhoot*; *Satyavijaya* (all St).

PATEL, JABBAR (b. 1942)

Marathi film director and paediatrician. Born in Pandharpur, Maharashtra. Together with his wife, a gynaecologist, runs a clinic in Daund near Pune. Founded the best-known Marathi experimental theatre group, Theatre Academy. Landmark stage production of **Vijay Tendulkar**'s play *Ghashiram Kotwal* (1972). Also adapted Brecht's *Threepenny Opera* (*Teen Paishacha Tamasha*, 1974) to the stage in Marathi, using rock music and conventions from Hindi commercial cinema. His films, often scripted by Tendulkar (e.g. ***Saamna***, ***Sinhasan***), rely on topical political references and theatrical acting styles. Best-known feature is ***Umbartha***, representing **Smita Patil**'s most renowned screen performance.

FILMOGRAPHY: 1975: ***Saamna***; **1977**: *Jait Re Jait*; **1979**: ***Sinhasan***; **1981**: ***Umbartha/Subah***; **1986**: *Musafir*; *Maharashtra* (Doc); **1987**: *Mi SM* (Doc); **1988**: *Indian Theatre* (Doc); *Pathik* (Doc); **1989**: *Lakshman Joshi* (Doc); **1990**: *Sea Forts* (Doc); **1991**: *Dr Babasaheb Ambedkar* (Doc); **1992**: *Ek Hota Vidushak*.

PATHY, P. V. (1906-61)

Born in Madras as Pithamandalam Venkatachalapathy. Major documentarist; originator of ethnographic film-making which developed into a politically relevant mode of pseudo-historical films associated with **Films Division**. Wrote thesis on *The Contemporary Theatre of the Andhras* (1927). Studied at the Sorbonne (1933) where he met Indologists Sylvain Lévy and Louis Renou. Later, at the école Technique de Photographie et Cinématographie (ETPC) in Paris, he made some shorts apparently influenced by Cavalcanti. Travelled in North Africa with American explorer Horace Ashton. Indian correspondent for *Universal News* and *British Paramount News*, filming, e.g., the Quetta Earthquake (1935). Collaborated with **Wadia Movietone** on India's first newsreel series sponsored by the **Film Advisory Board**, the *Indian Screen Gazette* (1938), including a 3-reeler on the historic Haripura Congress. Set up Motion Picture Society of India with K.S. Hirlekar and D.G. Tendulkar. War effort films for **Information Films of India** and **Naval Gandhi**'s Directorate of Services Kinematography. Assisted and did camerawork for **Paul Zils** in several documentaries. He was one of the two film-makers who filmed the transfer of power to the Indian government at midnight, 15 August 1947; later worked with his own production unit. All his films are shorts and/or documentaries. Biography by Jag Mohan (1972).

FILMOGRAPHY: 1934: *Paris by Night*; *Colonial Exposition: Paris*; **1938**: *Indian Screen Gazette*; **1940**: *Mahatma Gandhi Vazhkai*; *He's in the Navy Now*; *The Planes of Hindustan*; **1941**: *In Self Defence*; **1942**: *The Golden Grain of Bharatkhand*; **1943**: *Home Front*; **1946**: *Along the Jumna*; **1948**: *Mahatma Gandhi*; **1954**: *The Golden River*; **1956**: *The Etawah Story*; *Earth and Water*; **1957**: *Shipyards to Seaways*; *Look to the Sky*; **1958**: *Bases of Progress*; **1960**: *Pen to People*.

PATIL, DINKAR DATTAJIRAO (b. 1915)

Successful Marathi director-producer born in Belgaum near Kolhapur, Maharashtra. Assistant to **Master Vinayak** (1941-8). Started as director by completing *Mandir* following Vinayak's death. Set up Surel Chitra (1952) with **Lata Mangeshkar** and Shinde; then founded his own Dinkar Chitra (1953). Famous for work in the gramin chitrapat genre, rural blood and gore dramas with vendetta motifs, evil moneylenders or zamindars, poor peasant heroes, demure housewives, Tamasha dancing-girls, etc. Written usually by himself or with scenarist-lyricist **G.D. Madgulkar**, the films mark both an economic and a cultural shift in addressing a specifically Marathi audience, and in constructing an imaginary Marathi countryside which appears to resemble the Vidarbha region in the state. Prolific writer for other film-makers (e.g. Madhav Shinde, **Datta Keshav**). Wrote several plays, a biography of **Master Vinayak** (1971) and an autobiography, *Patlacha Por* (1986). Script credits include, in addition to most of his own films: *Jai Malhar* (1947); *Mayecha Pazhar* (1952); *Vadal* (1953); *Shikleli Baiko* (1959); *Pancharati* (1960); *Bhintila Kan Astaat* (1962); *Sudharlelya Baika* (1965); *Patlachi Soon* (1966); *Pathcha Bhau* (1967); *Janaki* (1969); *Murali Malhari Rayachi* (1969); *Pathrakhin* (1972); *Soon Ladki Hya Gharchi* (1972); *Kartiki* (1974); *Jyotibacha Navas* (1975); *Netaji Palkar* (1978); *Darodekhor* (1980); *Patleen* (1981); *Mosambi Narangi* (1981); *Chorachya Manaat Chandana* (1984).

FILMOGRAPHY: 1948: *Mandir*; **1950**: ***Ram Ram Pahuna***; **1951**: *Sharada*; *Patlacha Por*; **1952**: *May Bahini*; **1953**: *Gharbar*; **1954**: *Taraka*; **1955**: *Muthbhar Chane*; *Kuladaivat*; **1956**: *Dista Tasa Nasta*; **1957**: *Dev Jaga Aahe*; *Navara Mhanu Naye Aapla*; **1960**: *Bhairavi*; *Umaj Padel Tar*; **1961**: *Majhi Aai*; **1962**: *Varadakshina*; *Baap Mazha Brahmachari*; *Prem Andhala Asta*; **1965**: *Kama Purta Mama*; *Malhari Martand*; **1967**: *Suranga Mhantyat Mala*; **1968**: *Dhanya Te Santaji Dhanaji*; **1970**: *Kali Baiko*; *Kortachi Pairi*; **1971**: *Adhikar*; *Mihi Manoosach Aahe*; **1972**: *Kunku Mazha*

Bhagyacha!; **1979**: *Sunbai Oti Bharun Ja*; **1980**: *Mantryanchi Soon*; *Savat*; *Sulavarchi Poli*; **1981**: *Kunkvacha Tila*; **1982**: *Bhamta*; **1985**: *Sulakshana*; **1987**: *Bhatak Bhawani*; **1992**: *Sona Ani Mona*; **1993**: *Shivarayachi Soon Tararani.*

PATIL, SMITA (1955-86)

Powerful yet subtle actress in many languages as well as on the stage. Born in Pune, the daughter of a government minister of Maharashtra. Studied literature at Bombay University. Worked briefly as a tv announcer. First role in Arun Khopkar's student film at the **FTII**; then in **Benegal**'s children's film, ***Charandas Chor***. First major role in ***Manthan*** as the Harijan woman who leads the revolt of the milk co-operative, earning her an international reputation. Major performances in ***Bhumika*** (the fictionalised life story of actress **Hansa Wadkar**) and as the uninhibited tribal in **Ketan Mehta**'s ***Bhavni Bhavai***. Acquired a unique status as an actress equally at home in the 'realistic' New Indian Cinema (***Chakra***, ***Sadgati***) and in cinephile fantasies (***Mandi***, Mehta's Gujarati fables and many B-films, e.g. *Dance Dance*, *Badle Ki Aag*). Trained largely in Pune's experimental theatre (the source of **Jabbar Patel**'s early cinema, in which she also acted, e.g. ***Saamna***). Her amazingly versatile performances developed alongside and in rivalry with those of **Shabana Azmi**, the only other Hindi actress of her generation with a similar range. Notable performances in **Kumar Shahani**'s ***Tarang***, as the social worker Sulabha in Patel's ***Umbartha/Subah*** and the legendary Sonbai who single-handedly defies the authoritarian subedar in ***Mirch Masala***. Also acted in Bengali (**Mrinal Sen**'s ***Akaler Sandhaney***), Malayalam (**Aravindan**'s ***Chidambaram***), and Kannada (**T.S. Nagabharana**'s *Anveshane*). Her work has been celebrated at the festival of La Rochelle and by the French cinémath¤que (1984). An activist on behalf of women and a member of the feminist Women's Centre in Bombay. She died shortly after giving birth to a son. Developed a posthumous reputation as a photographer (cf the 1992 exhibition of her photographic portraits, *Through the Eyes of Smita*, at the National Centre For Performing Arts, Bombay).

FILMOGRAPHY: 1974: *Teevra Madhyam* (Sh); *Raja Shivachhatrapati*; **1975**: ***Saamna***; ***Charandas Chor***; ***Nishant***; **1976**: ***Manthan***; ***Bhumika***; **1977**: ***Kondura/Anugraham***; *Jait Re Jait*; **1978**: ***Sarvasakshi***; ***Gaman***; **1979**: ***The Naxalites***; **1980**: ***Bhavni Bhavai/Andher Nagari***; *Ashwamedher Ghora*; ***Akaler Sandhaney***; ***Aakrosh***; ***Albert Pinto Ko Gussa Kyon Aata Hai***; ***Chakra***; *Anveshane*; **1981**: ***Sadgati*** (TV); *Tajurba*; ***Umbartha/Subah***; *Dil-e-Nadaan*; **1982**: *Badle Ki Aag*; *Bazaar*; *Bheegi Palkein*; *Namak Halal*; *Shakti*; *Sitam*; ***Arth***; *Chatpatee*; *Dard Ka Risha*; **1983**: ***Ardh Satya***; *Ghunghroo*; *Qayamat*; *Haadsa*; ***Mandi***; *Farishta*; **1984**: *Aaj Ki Awaaz*; *Anand Aur Anand*; *Giddh*; *Kanoon Meri Mutthi Mein*; *Kasam Paida Karne Wale Ki*; *Mera Dost Mera Dushman*; *Pet Pyar Aur Paap*; *Ravan*; *Shapath*; ***Tarang***; *Hum Do Hamare Do*; **1985**: *Aakhir Kyon*; ***Ghulami***; *Jawab*; *Kabhi Ajnabi The*; *Mera Ghar Mere Bachche*; ***Chidambaram***; ***Mirch Masala***; ***Debshishu***; *Abhinetri* (TV); *Tere Shaher Mein*; **1986**: *Dehleez*; *Oont*; *Rahi*; *Aap Ke Saath*; *Amrit*; *Angarey*; *Anokha Rishta*; *Dilwala*; *Kaanch Ki Deewar*; *Teesra Kinara*; *Insaniyat Ke Dushman*; *Sutradhar*; **1987**: *Awaam*; *Dance Dance*; *Nazrana*; *Sher Shivaji*; *Thikana*; *Aaj*; **1988**: *Akarshan*; *Hum Farishte Nahin*; *Waris*; **1989**: *Oonch Neech Beech*; *Galiyon Ka Badshah*.

Smita Patil in *Tarang* (1984)

PAT PAINTING

'Chitra-pat', the Hindi term for 'cinema', actually means 'mural' and refers to several traditions of folk painting practised in Bengal, Orissa, Rajasthan, Maharashtra and Gujarat. The Pat is the surface as well as the material support of a painting, e.g. a cloth or paper scroll depicting a fable or myth, unrolled while a singer shaman pointed out the images accompanying his narration (e.g. the bhopa in the Rajasthani Pabuji-no-pad or the badvo in the Chhota Udaipur Pithoro form). This combination of performance and narrative imagery had been preceded by a variety of mural traditions. Towards the end of the 19th C., many painters moved to the cities and invented variants of the Pat styles adapted to mass-production, such as catchpenny prints to compete with lithography, photography and the printed news-sheet in the urban bazaar. The most famous manifestation of this practice was around the Kalighat temple in Calcutta. Though now contested, it was maintained for a long time that the bazaar pictures of Kalighat were the result of British influence: 'In place of tempera, the British medium of water-colour was adopted as more suitable to flowing brush strokes. The use of blank background, as in British natural history paintings, economised time. Folio-sized sheets [w]ere convenient for a popular market. Shading, as used by the British, emphasised volume' (W.G. Archer, 1962). It has been pointed out that visual techniques to produce volume and rhythm for voluptuous figuration had long been part of the interaction between classical and folk traditions in India. However, a narrative shift did occur as the voice and the performance of the narrator/storyteller was inscribed into a serial production process, prefiguring the practices of mechanical reproduction (photography, silent cinema).

PATTANAYAK, KABICHANDRA KALICHARAN (B. 1900)

Noted Oriya poet, composer and writer, born in the former Baramba State of Orissa. Major stage personality associated with the Utkal Natya Sangh and the Orissa wing of the Bhartiya Natya Sangh; pioneering scenarist and producer of early Oriya cinema. Proprietor of Suralekha Record Prod. for which he made several short films. Made notable contributions to Kalyan Gupta's early films as the scenarist of *Lalita* (1949), the Oriya cinema's second film, and writing the story of *Rolls-28* (1951). Also wrote the lyrics for **Nitai Palit**'s *Kedar Gouri* (1954), the script of Shiba Bhattacharya's *Jayadeb* (1963) and provided the music for Trilochan's *Nari* (1963). Also associated with AIR, Cuttack.

PATWARDHAN, ANAND (b. 1950)

Documentarist born in Bombay. Worked on a voluntary rural education and development project in MP (1972-3) where he made a tape-slide show on tuberculosis treatment. Graduate of Brandeis University, Boston, where he made his first film *Business as Usual.* Worked for JP Movement in Bihar (1974) and made Super-8 film about the period. Postgraduate sociology thesis at McGill University, Montreal, on *Guerilla Cinema: Underground and in Exile* (1982). Made clandestine documentary during Emergency, ***Prisoners of Conscience***, shown 3 years later. Co-d a film about Indian farm workers' strike in Canada. Returned to Bombay (1982) and continued making courageous, cinematically challenging films about key social-political issues. Set up a mobile cinema group, Samvad (Dialogue) taking films into squares and villages in context of political action. Recent work displays great mastery of documentary form, without sloganising, allowing the complexities of social situations, people's behaviour, film-making and political action to inform the filming as well as the presentation of issues. Currently addressing communal questions in different parts of India. The respect for the people he films extends to his heterogeneous soundtracks: ***Unda Mitterandi Yaad Pyari*** has a soundtrack spoken in English, Punjabi and Hindi; ***Hamara Shaher*** uses Hindi, Marathi, Tamil and English.

FILMOGRAPHY: **1972**: *Business as Usual*; **1975**: ***Waves of Revolution***; **1978**: ***Prisoners of Conscience***; **1981**: *A Time to Rise*; **1985**: ***Hamara Shaher***; **1989**: ***Unda Mitterandi Yaad Pyari***; **1992**: ***Ram Ke Naam***; **1993**: *The Other Side* (Sh); *Nahi Amhi Vanar Bannar* (Sh).

PATWARDHAN, NACHIKET (b. 1948)/ PATWARDHAN, JAYOO (b. 1949)

Husband and wife team of directors, architects and art directors. Graduated together from M.S. University, Baroda, in architecture. Started with art direction and costumes for ***Ghashiram Kotwal*** (1976). Have worked with **Saeed Mirza**, **Girish Karnad** (e.g. art direction for ***Utsav***, 1984, ***Cheluvi***, 1992).

FILMOGRAPHY: **1979**: *22 June 1897*; **1985**: *Anantyatra.*

PAVITHRAN, VATTAPARAMBIL KRISHNAN (b. 1950)

Malayalam director and musician. Born in Kandanassery, Trichur Dist., Kerala. Studied at Christ College, Iranjalakuda, and at Maharaja's College, Cochin. Tried to enter the **FTII** but failed, enrolled in nearby Law College, Pune, instead, spending his time at the FTII. During Emergency produced **P.A. Backer**'s acclaimed film ***Kabani Nadi Chuvannappol*** (1975); Indira Gandhi's followers tried to destroy it. Made the experimental ***Yaro Oral*** with music by **Aravindan**. Scored T.V. Chandran's Malayalam film *Krishnankutty* (1980). With Chandran, represents a continuation of Backer's style of independently made tragic melodramas.

FILMOGRAPHY: **1978**: ***Yaro Oral***; **1986**: ***Uppu***; **1989**: *Uttaram*; **1990**: *Kallinde Katha* (Doc); **1991**: *Bali.*

PAWAR, LALITA (b. 1916)

Hindi and Marathi actress born in Indore as Lalitabai Hanuman Prasad. Early career as child star at **Sarpotdar**'s Aryan Film. Used stage name Ambu. Married stunt film-maker G.P. Pawar who directed most of her later silents and early sound films. One of those silents, ***Diler Jigar***, still exists. Pawar's partner Chandrarao Kadam usually played the hero (e.g. *Daivi Khajina*, *Jalta Jigar*, *Nek Dost*, *Pyari Katar*, *Himmat-e-Mard*), producing through his Chandra Arts Co. She briefly turned producer (***Duniya Kya Hai***). Played lead roles in early 40s films opposite Nazir (*Rajkumari*, *Captain Kishori*), E. Bilimoria (*Nirali Duniya*), Trilok Kapoor (*Nari*). Developed her best-known persona of the vamp-like, scheming mother in ***Ramshastri***, turning her slightly defective left eye into a trademark (e.g. as **Madhubala**'s guardian in ***Mr and Mrs '55***). She apparently developed her slight squint in an accident on the set of an early stunt movie. Remembered also as a compassionate foster-mother in several **Raj Kapoor** films, e.g. the banana seller in ***Shri 420*** and the landlady Mrs D'Sa in ***Anari***.

Lalita Pawar in *Mahatma Kabir* (1954)

FILMOGRAPHY: **1928**: *Patitoddhar*; *Ganimi Kava*; *Raja Harishchandra*; *Arya Mahila*; **1929**: *Dasharathi Ram*; *Parijatak*; *Prem Pash*; *Prince Thaksen*; *Prithviraj Sanyogita*; *Shri Balaji*; *Subhadra Haran*; **1930**: *Chatur Sundari*; *Shamsher Bahadur*; *Song of Life*; *Subramanyam*; **1931**: ***Diler Jigar***; *Shri Krishna Maya*; **1932**: *Bhawani Talwar*; *Kailash*; *Mastikhor Mashuq*; **1933**: *Daivi Khajina*; *Jalta Jigar*; *Nek Dost*; *Pyari Katar* (all St); **1935**: *Himmat-e-Mard*; *Qatil Katar*; **1937**: *Chevrolet 1936*; **1938**: ***Duniya Kya Hai***; *Rajkumari*; **1939**: ***Netaji Palkar***; **1940**: *Captain Kishori*; *Nirali Duniya*; **1941**: ***Amrit***; **1942**: *Bhakta Damaji*; *Gora Kumbhar*; *Kirti*; *Mamaji*; *Nari* (H); **1943**: *Ashirwad*; *Bhakta Raidas*; **1944**: ***Ramshastri***; **1945**: *Yateem*; **1946**: *Behram Khan*; *Santan*; *Jhumke*; **1947**: *Jai Malhar*; *Janata*; *Woh Zamana*; **1948**: *Dhanyavaad*; *Grihasthi*; *Phool Aur Kaante*; *Rang Mahal*; **1949**: *Dil Ki Basti*; *Sant Namdev*; *Manacha Pan*; **1950**: *Bahurani*; *Banwra*; ***Dahej***; **1951**: *Jai Mahakali*; *Nand Kishore*; *Sazaa*; ***Amar Bhoopali***; **1952**: ***Chhatrapati Shivaji***; *Mayecha Pazhar*; *Aasmaan*; *Bhakta Puran*; ***Daag***; *Parchain*; *Raja Harishchandra*; *Sandesh*; *Usha Kiron*; **1953**: *Sant Bahinabai*; *Aabshar*; *Faraib*; *Patita*; *Firdaus*; *Shuk Rambha*; *Thokar*; **1954**: *Bahut Din Huye*; *Mahatma Kabir*; *Shiv Kanya*; **1955**: *Khandaan*; *Do Dulhe*; *Miss Coca Cola*; ***Mr and Mrs '55***; *Navratri*; *Oonchi Haveli*; *Patit Pawan*; ***Shri 420***; *Shri Krishna Bhakti*; *Ratnaghar*; *Kalagi Tura*; **1956**: *Gauri Puja*; *Heer*; *Jayashree*; *Pocketmaar*; *Rajrani Meera*; *Sajani*; *Zindagi Ke Mele*; *Paidali Padleli Phule*; **1957**: ***Aasha***; *Alladdin Laila*; *Baarish*; *Ek Gaon Ki Kahani*; *Ek Jhalak*; ***Nau Do Gyarah***; *Neel Mani*; *Paristan*; *Ram Lakshman*; *Sant Raghu*; *Devagharcha Lena*; **1958**: *Balyogi Upamanyu*; *Kabhi Andhera Kabhi Ujala*; *Karigar*; *Malik*; *Mehndi*; *Naag Champa*; *Naya Kadam*; *Parvarish*; ***Raj Tilak***; *Taxi 555*; *Samrat Chandragupta*; *Sukhache Sobti*; **1959**: ***Anari***; *Baap Bete*; *Didi*; *Grihalakshmi*; ***Guest House***; *Kanhaiya*; *Maa Ke Aansoo*; *Mohar*; *Mr John*; *Pehli Raat*; *Sati Vaishalini*; ***Sujata***; **1960**: ***Jis Desh Mein Ganga Behti Hai***; *Aanchal*; *Bhakta Raaj*; *Bindiya*; *Chand Mere Aaja*; *Sarhad*; *Qatil*; **1961**: *Chhaya*; *Gharana*; ***Hum Dono***; ***Jhumroo***; ***Junglee***; *Main Aur Mera Bhai*; *Maya*; *Memdidi*; *Opera House*; *Sampoorna Ramayan*; *Sasural*; **1962**: *Banarasi Thug*; *Maa Beta*; *Professor*; *Raakhi*; **1963**: *Akela*; *Bahurani*; *Band Master*; *Bharosa*; ***Bluff Master***; *Ek Dil Sau Afsane*; *Ek Raaz*; *Gehra Daag*; *Ghar Basake Dekho*; *Grihasthi*; *Hamrahi*; *Mummy Daddy*; *Sehra*; **1964**: *Apne Huye Paraye*; ***Kohraa***; *Mahasati Behula*; *Majboor*; *Phoolon Ki Sej*; ***Sangam***; *Sharabi*; *Tere Dwar Khada Bhagwan*; *Sundara Manamadhye Bharli*; **1965**: *Bedaag*; *Janam Janam Ke Saathi*; *Khandaan*; **1966**: *Biradari*; *Chhota Bhai*; *Insaaf*; *Love In Tokyo*; *Phool Aur Patthar*; *Suraj*; *Tasveer*; **1967**: *Patthar Ke Sanam*; *Aurat*; *Bahu Begum*; *Boond Jo Ban Gaye Moti*; *Diwana*; *Hare Kaanch Ki Chudiyan*; *Laat Saheb*; *Manjhli Didi*; *Noorjehan*; **1968**: *Aabroo*; *Aankhen*; *Duniya*; *Ek Kali Muskayi*; *Izzat*; *Neel Kamal*; *Teen Bahuraniyan*; **1969**: *Chirag*; *Hum Ek Hain*; ***Khamoshi***; *Meri Bhabhi*; *Road To Sikkim*; *Tumse Achha Kaun Hai*; *Saticha Vaan*; *Tambdi Mati*; **1970**: ***Anand***; *Darpan*; *Devi*; *Gopi*; *Man Ki Aankhen*; *Naya Raasta*; *Pushpanjali*; *Saas Bhi Kabhi Bahu Thi*; *Suhana Safar*; *Jwala*; **1971**: *Buddha Mil Gaya*; *Jaane Anjane*; *Lakhon Mein Ek*; *Mela*; *Naya Zamana*; *Parwana*; *Preet Ki Dori*; **1972**: *Bombay To Goa*; *Bees Saal Pehle*; *Gaon Hamara Shaher Tumhara*; *Yeh Gulistan Hamara*; **1973**: *Hifazat*; *Jugnu*; *Do Phool*; *Ek Mutthi Aasmaan*; *Kahani Hum Sub Ki*; **1974**: *Goonj*; *Hamrahi*; *Naya Din Nayi Raat*; *Doosri Seeta*; *Kunwara Baap*; *Aaina*; **1975**: *Khel Khel Mein*; *Tapasya*; **1976**: *Aaj Ka Yeh Ghar*; *Alibaba*; *Bandalbaaz*; *Do Anjaane*; *Khalifa*; *Raksha Bandhan*; *Sangram*; *Shankar Shambhu*; *Choricha Mamla*; **1977**: *Chakkar Pe Chakkar*; *Dream Girl*; *Jai Vijay*; *Kali Raat*; *Mama Bhanja*; *Mandir Masjid*; *Niyaz Aur Namaaz*; *Prayashchit*; *Taxi Taxi*; **1978**: *Dil Se Mile Dil*; *Ganga Sagar*; *Prem Bandhan*; *Tumhari Kasam*; *Vishwanath*; *Sasurvasheen*; **1979**: *Naukar*; *Raja Harishchandra*; *Duniya Meri Jeb Mein*; *Jaan-e-Bahar*; *Janata Havaldar*; *Manzil*; **1980**: *Badrinath Dham*; *Do Aur Do Paanch*; *Phir Wohi Raat*; *Sau Din Saas Ke*; **1981**: ***Naseeb***; *Sannata*; **1982**: *Chatak Chandani*; **1983**: *Ek Din Bahu Ka*; *Kaise Kaise Log*; *Nastik*; **1984**: *Apna Bhi Koi Hota*; *Jhootha Sach*; *Gharcha Bhedi*; *Kulaswamini Ambabai*; *Ram Tera Desh*; **1985**: *Ram Tere Kitne Naam*; *Pyari Bhabhi*; **1986**: *Ghar Sansar*; ***Love and God***; *Pyar Ke Do Pal*; *Ram Milai Jodi*; **1987**: *Madadgaar*; *Hifazat*; *Watan Ke Rakhwale*; *Uttar Dakshin*; **1988**: ***Bai Chali Sasariye***; *Kali Ganga*; *Zalzala*; *Sherni*;

Bhatakti Jawani; *Pyaasi Atma*; **1989**: *Garibon Ka Daata*; **1990**: *Hatyare*; **1993**: *Shiv Teri Mahima Nyari*.

PENDHARKAR, BABURAO (1896-67)

Pioneer Marathi actor and producer born in Kolhapur. Actor-manager of **Maharashtra Film** (1919); then a partner in **Prabhat** (1929); manager and main star at **Kolhapur Cinetone** (1933) and for several years associated with **Master Vinayak** at Huns Pics (1936) and **Navyug Chitrapat**; then producer with Navhans (1943). Best-known work after the mid-40s was with **V. Shantaram** at **Rajkamal Kalamandir**, including the classic role of the Chinese general in ***Dr Kotnis Ki Amar Kahani***, and with his brother, the director **Bhalji Pendharkar**. Noted actor as a villain in mythologicals (e.g. in Shantaram's ***Ayodhyecha Raja/Ayodhya Ka Raja***, Kans in Vasant Joglekar's *Nand Kishore*, and Keechaka in Pethkar's *Keechaka Vadha*) and for character roles in socials by **Atre** (the crotchety grandfather in ***Shyamchi Aai***; the title role of *Mahatma Phule*). Directed Prabhat's only major Tamil film, *Seeta Kalyanam*, a landmark in Tamil cinema. Also a noted stage actor. His autobiography (1961/1983) is also an important record of Marathi film history .

FILMOGRAPHY (* also d): **1919**: ***Sairandhri***; **1921**: *Surekha Haran*; **1922**: *Bhagwata Bhakta Damaji*; **1926**: ***Vande Mataram Ashram***; **1930**: *Rani Saheba*; ***Udaykal***; **1931**: *Zulm* (all St); **1932**: ***Ayodhyecha Raja/Ayodhya Ka Raja***; ***Jalti Nishani/Agnikankan***; ***Maya Machhindra***; **1933**: *Seeta Kalyanam**; ***Sinhagad***; **1934**: ***Akashwani***; **1935**: ***Vilasi Ishwar/Nigah-e-Nafrat***; **1936**: ***Chhaya***; **1937**: ***Dharmaveer***; *Begunah*; **1939**: ***Devata***; *Sukhacha Shodh/Mera Haq*; **1940**: ***Ardhangi/Ghar Ki Rani***; ***Lapandav***; **1941**: ***Amrit***; **1942**: *Bhakta Damaji*; ***Pahila Palna***; **1943**: ***Paisa Bolto Aahe/Nagad Narayan***; **1945**: *Pehli Nazar*; *Vikramaditya*; *Parinde*; **1946**: ***Dr Kotnis Ki Amar Kahani***; ***Jeevan Yatra***; *Valmiki*; *Jeena Seekho*; *Magadhraj*; *Rukmini Swayamvar*; **1947**: *Jai Malhar*; **1948**: *Adalat*; *Bhagyarekha*; **1949**: ***Meeth Bhakar***; *Shilanganache Sone*; *Sakharpuda*; *Nara Narayan*; *Manacha Pan*; *Mazha Ram*; **1950**: *Mi Daru Sodli*; *Kalyan Khajina*; *Sant Kanhopatra*; *Chalitil Shejari*; **1951**: *Jashaas Tase*; *Nand Kishore*; **1952**: ***Chhatrapati Shivaji***; *May Bahini*; *Devyani*; *Jeet Kiski*; **1953**: ***Shyamchi Aai***; **1954**: *Mahatma Phule*; **1955**: *Kalagi Tura*; *Ye Re Majhya Maglya*; *Punavechi Raat*; **1956**: *Pavankhind*; *Pasant Aahe Mulgi*; *Jagavegali Goshta*; *Gaath Padli Thaka Thaka*; *Deoghar*; *Paidali Padleli Phule*; **1957**: *Preetisangam*; *Dev Jaga Aahe*; *Naikinichi Sajja*; ***Do Aankhen Barah Haath***; *Devagharcha Lena*; **1958**: *Mausi*; **1959**: *Navrang*; *Keechaka Vadha*; *Baap Bete*; **1961**: *Stree*; **1963**: *Baiko Maheri Jaate*; *Te Mazhe Ghar*; *Thoratanchi Kamala*; *Sehra*; **1966**: *Amrapali*.

PENDHARKAR, BHALCHANDRA GOPAL [BHALJI] (b. 1898)

Marathi and Hindi director, producer, scenarist and lyricist born in Kolhapur, the son of King Shahu's court physician. Committed from early years to Hindu and Marathi regional chauvinism. Younger brother of cineaste **Baburao Pendharkar** and **V. Shantaram**'s cousin. Disciple of Veer Savarkar and founder of Kolhapur branch of Hindu Mahasabha, functioning as its regional director for a while. Worked for Lokmanya Tilak's political journal *Kesari*; started film journal *Cinema Samachar*. Started in theatre; wrote six plays, notably *Sangeet Kaydebhang*, and acted in *Krantikarak*. As film-maker, found support among local nobility and sought to achieve an economically autonomous Marathi cinema. Wrote and acted in **Manilal Joshi**'s ***Prithvi Vallabh*** (1924), then made his directorial début at **Sharda**. Wrote **Baburao Painter**'s *Markandeya* (1923), and all the early Shantaram films: ***Udaykal***, *Rani Saheba* and *Khooni Khanjar* (all 1930), and *Zulm* (1931). Scenarist for **Prabhat** (1932-3), before he moved to **Kolhapur Cinetone** (***Akashwani***). Started his own studios, Arun Pics (1939) in Pune, later the Famous-Arun Studio in partnership with Shiraz Ali Hakim. Also helped start the Jayaprabha Studio in Kolhapur. His historicals, usually starring the brothers Chandrakant and **Suryakant**, often exploit the 17th C. Marathi empire of Shivaji, the figurehead of the Hindu chauvinist Shiv Sena party in Maharashtra. His ***Vande Mataram Ashram*** was banned by the British and triggered a major censorship case in 1927-8. Also made ruralist socials. Tamasha star **Dada Kondke** made his début in *Tambdi Mati*. Nearly always wrote his own scripts, dialogues and lyrics. Other script credits include Shantaram's *Sairandhri* (1933), Nimbalkar's *Swarajya Seemevar* (1937), Jaishankar Danve's *Jai Bhawani* (1947), **Master Vithal**'s *Swarajyacha Shiledar* (1951: using the pseudonym Shyam Sundar), **Dinkar D. Patil**'s *May Bahini* (1952), **Raja Paranjpe**'s *Gaath Padli Thaka Thaka* (1956), **Rajdutt**'s *Gharchi Rani* (1968), Govind Kulkarni's *Sakhya Sajana* (1972); and his son Prabhakar Pendharkar's films *Bal Shivaji* (1981) and *Shabas Sunbai* (1986). Autobiography *Sadha Manoos* (1993).

FILMOGRAPHY: 1925: ***Bajirao Mastani***; **1926**: ***Vande Mataram Ashram***; **1931**: *Rani Rupmati* (all St); **1932**: ***Shyam Sundar***; **1934**: ***Akashwani***; *Parthakumar*; **1935**: *Kaliya Mardan/Muraliwala*; **1936**: *Savitri*; *Rukmini Kalyanam*; **1937**: ***Kanhopatra***; **1938**: *Raja Gopichand*; **1939**: ***Netaji Palkar***; **1940**: *Gorakhnath/Alakh Niranjan*; **1941**: ***Thoratanchi Kamala***; **1942**: *Sunbai*; *Bhakta Damaji*; **1943**: *Bahirji Naik*; **1944**: *Maharathi Karna*; *Swarna Bhoomi*; **1946**: *Sasurvas*; *Valmiki*; **1949**: ***Meeth Bhakar***; *Shilanganache Sone*; **1950**: *Mi Daru Sodli*; **1952**: ***Chhatrapati Shivaji***; **1953**: *Majhi Zameen*; **1954**: *Maharani Yesubai*; **1955**: *Ye Re Majhya Maglya*; **1956**: *Pavankhind*; **1957**: *Naikinichi Sajja*; **1959**: *Akashganga*; **1963**: *Mohityanchi Manjula*; **1964**: *Maratha Tituka Melavava*; **1965**: ***Sadhi Manse***; **1969**: *Tambdi Mati*; **1981**: *Ganimi Kava*.

PENDYALA NAGESHWARA RAO (1924-84)

Telugu composer born in Kattur, coastal AP. Son of a music teacher. Harmonium accompanist in the theatre; joined films as a musician, playing the harmonium in Jyotish Sinha's ***Talliprema*** (1941). First break as composer in **L.V. Prasad**'s ***Drohi***. Early films mainly with **K.S. Prakash Rao**. Best-known work associated with the lyrics of **Arudra**, e.g. in K.B. Tilak's and **K.V. Reddy**'s films. Regarded as the one who introduced rural folk music into the Telugu film song, influencing contemporaries like **Ghantasala**. Singers P. Susheela and **S. Janaki** both débuted with him. Scored most of **NTR**'s big 70s mythologicals (***Daana Veera Shura Karna***, *Chanakya Chandragupta*, ***Shri Rama Pattabhishekham***).

FILMOGRAPHY: 1948: ***Drohi***; **1950**: *Modathi Rathri*; **1951**: *Deeksha*; **1953**: ***Kanna Talli/Petrathai***; **1954**: *Balanandam*; *Jyoti/Illara Jyoti*; *Menarikam*; **1955**: ***Donga Ramudu***; **1956**: *Muddubidda*; *Melukolupu*; *Penki Pellam*; **1957**: ***Bhagya Rekha***; *MLA*; *Saubhagyavati*; **1958**: *Shri Krishna Garudi*; **1959**: *Jayabheri*; **1960**: ***Shri Venkateshwara Mahatyam***; *Mahakavi Kalidasa*; *Nityakalayanam Pachathoranam*; *Bhatti Vikramarka*; *Kadedullu Ekaram Nela*; *Bhakta Shabari*; **1961**: *Velugu Needulu*; *Krishna Prema*; ***Jagadeka Veeruni Katha/Jagathala Prathapan***; *Vagdanam*; *Bava Maradallu*; **1962**: ***Mahamantri Timmarasu***; *Chitti Tamudu*; ***Shri Krishnarjuna Yuddham***; **1963**: *Paruvu Pratishthalu*; *Eedu Jodu*; *Anuragham*; **1964**: *Ramudu Bheemudu*; *Raktha Tilakam*; *Shabash Soori*; **1965**: *Uyyala Jampala*; ***Satya Harishchandra***; *Prameelarjuneyam*; *Prachanda Bhairavi*; **1966**: *Srikakula Andhra Mahavishnu Katha*; *Shri Krishna Tulabharam*; **1968**: *Bandhipotu Dongalu*; *Bhagya Chakram*; *Gramadevathulu*; *Pantalu Pattimpulu*; *Papakosam*; *Umachandi Gauri Shankarula Katha*; **1970**: *Maa Nanna Nirdoshi*; *Pelli Sambandham*; *Shri Krishna Vijayam*; *Manasu Mangalyam*; **1971**: *Naa Thammudu*; *Shri Krishna Satya*; **1972**: *Mathru Murthi*; **1974**: *Kode Naagu*; *Dhanavanthulu Gunavanthulu*; ***Bhoomikosam***; *Deeksha*; **1975**: *Vemulavuda Bhimakavi*; **1976**: *Kolleti Kapuram*; *Shri Rajeshwari Vilas Coffee Club*; *Suprabhatam*; **1977**: *Koilamma Koosindi*; ***Daana Veera Shura Karna***; *Chanakya Chandragupta*; *Sati Savitri*; **1978**: ***Shri Rama Pattabhishekham***; **1979**: *Shri Tirupati Venkateshwara Kalyanam*; *Galivana*; *Priya Bandhavi*; **1984**: *Kala Ranjani*; **1985**: *Kondi Kshetrayya*; **1987**: *Prema Deepalu*.

PHADKE, SUDHIR VINAYAK (b. 1919)

Marathi-Hindi singer and composer born in Kolhapur, Maharashtra. Started at **Prabhat** (Pethkar's *Aage Badho*); later associated mainly with the lyrics of **G.D. Madgulkar**, which he set to music in numerous films, esp. by **Raja Paranjpe**. Also recorded Madgulkar's rewritten version of the *Ramayana* in simple Marathi verse, one of the most enduringly popular pieces of Marathi devotional music. Hindi compositions include **Kishore Kumar**'s hit number *Pehli tareekh hai yeh paheli tareekh hai* from ***Pehli Tareekh***.

FILMOGRAPHY: 1946: *Gokul*; *Rukmini Swayamvar*; **1947**: *Aage Badho*; **1948**: *Seeta Swayamvar*; *Jivacha Sakha*; *Vande Mataram*; **1949**: *Aparadhi*; *Jai Bhim*; *Maya Bazaar*; *Ram Pratigya*; *Sant Janabai*; **1950**: *Shri Krishna Darshan*; *Johar Maibaap*; ***Pudhcha Paool***; **1951**: *Malati Madhav*; *Muraliwala*; *Jashaas Tase*; **1952**: ***Lakhachi Goshta***; *May Bahini*; *Narveer Tanaji*; *Pratapgad*; **1953**: *Bolavita Dhani*; *Kon Kunacha*; *Kuberache Dhan*;

Saubhagya; *Vahinichya Bangdya*; **1954**: ***Pehli Tareekh***; *Een Meen Sadeteen*; *Maharani Yesubai*; ***Oon Paoos***; *Ovalani*; *Postatil Mulgi*; *Reshmachya Gaathi*; **1955**: *Ratnaghar*; *Ganget Ghoda Nhala*; *Mi Tulas Tujhya Angani*; *Shevgyachya Shenga*; **1956**: *Sajani*; *Andhala Magto Ek Dola*; *Deoghar*; *Mazhe Ghar Majhi Manse*; **1957**: *Devagharcha Lena*; *Gharcha Jhala Thoda*; **1958**: *Gaja Gauri*; **1959**: *Gokul Ka Chor*; **1960**: ***Jagachya Pathivar***; *Umaj Padel Tar*; **1961**: *Adhi Kalas Mag Paya*; *Kalanka Shobha*; *Majhi Aai*; *Nirupama Ani Parirani*; ***Prapancha***; *Suvasini*; ***Bhabhi Ki Chudiyan***; **1962**: *Bhintila Kan Astaat*; *Char Divas Sasuche Char Divas Suneche*; *Chimnyanchi Shala*; *Gariba Gharchi Lek*; *Sonyachi Paoole*; **1963**: *Baiko Maheri Jaate*; *Ha Mazha Marg Ekala*; *Te Mazhe Ghar*; **1964**: *Daivacha Khel*; **1966**: *Gurukilli*; **1967**: *Sant Gora Kumbhar*; **1968**: *Amhi Jato Amuchya Gava*; *Ekati*; **1969**: *Adhaar*; **1970**: *Dev Manoos*; *Dhakti Bahin*; *Mumbaicha Javai*; *Jhala Mahar Pandharinath*; **1971**: *Bajiravacha Beta*; *Jhep*; *Lakhat Ashi Dekhani*; *Mihi Manoosach Aahe*; **1972**: *Daraar*; **1973**: *Anolkhi*; *Javai Vikat Ghene Aahe*; **1974**: *Kartiki*; **1975**: *Jyotibacha Navas*; **1976**: *Aram Haram Aahe*; **1978**: *Chandra Hota Sakshila*; *Dost Asava Tar Asa*; **1982**: *Aplech Daat Aplech Oth*; *Shapit*; **1983**: *Thorli Jau*; **1984**: *Chorachya Manaat Chandana*; *Maherchi Manse*; **1986**: *Dhakti Soon*; *Pudhcha Paool*; **1987**: *Sher Shivaji*; **1988**: *Reshim Gaathi*.

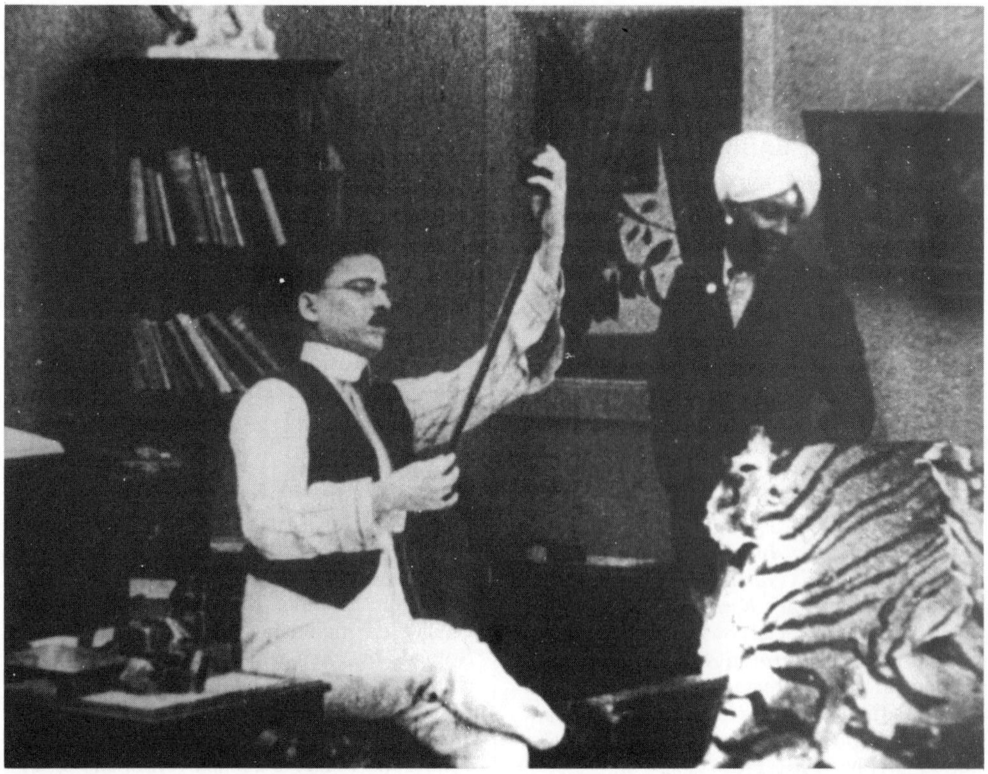

D.G. Phalke in *How Films Are Made* (1917)

PHALKE, DHUNDIRAJ GOVIND (1870-1944)

Pioneering director aka Dadasaheb Phalke. Born in Trymbakeshwar, Nasik. Claimed to have started the film industry in India with ***Raja Harishchandra***. Saw his cinema as a direct contribution to **Swadeshi**. Son of Sanskrit scholar. Studied at J.J. School of Art (1885) and at Kala Bhavana, Baroda (see **art schools**). Then studied architecture. Became proficient as landscape painter of academic nature studies. Worked in photographic studio and learnt to develop and print negative film. At Ratlam studied three-colour blockmaking, photolithography and ceramics (1890). Worked as portrait photographer, stage make-up man, assistant to a German illusionist and as a magician (as Professor Kelpha). Started Phalke's Art Printing & Engraving Works at Lonavala (1908), later Laxmi Art Printing Works. Did photolitho transfers of **Ravi Varma** oleographs. Sailed to Germany to obtain three-colour printing equipment (1909).Saw *The Life of Christ* around Christmas 1910 in a Bombay cinema, an event he describes with great passion although contemporary notices suggest it must have been around Easter 1911. Strongly moved by the 'magic' of cinema, also dedicated himself to bringing Indian images to the screen. Raised finance from Yeshwant Nadkarni, a photographic equipment dealer, with short trick film, *Birth of a Pea Plant*, shooting one frame a day to show a plant growing. Went to London in February 1912 to familiarise himself with film technology and to acquire equipment. Bought a Williamson camera, Kodak negative and a perforator. Cecil Hepworth tutored him at Walton Studios. Returned to establish **Phalke Films** on Dadar Main Road in Bombay (1912) for which he made five films, starting with *Raja Harishchandra*. Went to England again in 1914 to organise trade shows and received many offers to remain in Europe. Returned to India with new equipment, closed Phalke Films and set up the **Hindustan Cinema Films** (1918). Made c.44 silent features, several shorts and one talkie, ***Gangavataran***. The films introduced the mythological genre to Indian cinema, allowing him to merge his notion of Swadeshi with an industrial practice and a politico-cultural aesthetic. Satish Bahadur compiled the film *D.G. Phalke, the First Indian Film Director* for the **FTII** (1964); the film contains the only existing footage of *How Films Are Made*, footage of himself directing *Raja Harishchandra*, and *Setu Bandhan*, and is a tribute not only to the founder of the Indian film industry but also to a daring experimenter with animation techniques (including match-sticks), inventor of promotional films and of documentaries, creator of special effects and codifier of a new generic form, the mythological film. Essays on film, 'Bharatiya Chitrapat', were published in *Navyug* (1917-8).

FILMOGRAPHY 1913: *Birth of a Pea Plant* (Sh); ***Raja Harishchandra***; **1914**: *Pithache Panje* (Sh); *Scenes of the River Godavari* (Sh); *Mohini Bhasmasur*; *Satyavan Savitri*; **1915**: *Glass Factory at Talegaon* (Sh); **1916**: *Dhumrapan Leela* (Sh); *Lakshmicha Galicha* (Sh); *Sanlagna Ras* (Sh); *Swapna Vihar* (Sh); *Professor Kelpha's Magic* (Sh); *Kartiki Purnima Utsav* (Sh); **1917**: *Aagkadyancha Mauja* (Sh); *Dhandhal Bhatjiche Gangasnaan* (Sh); *How Films Are Made* (Sh); *Satyavadi Raja Harishchandra*; ***Shri Krishna Janma***; ***Lanka Dahan***; **1919**: *Sinhastha Parvani* (Sh); ***Kaliya Mardan***; **1922**: *Gajandravache Bhagya* (Sh); *Ahmedabad Congress*(?) (Doc); *Patwardhan's Royal Circus* (Sh); *Rajrishi Ambarish*; *Sant Namdev*; **1923**: *The Thirty-Seventh Gaya Congress*(?) (Doc); *Unusual Scenes from Bodhgaya*(?) (Doc); *Jarasandha Vadha*; *Mahananda*; *Babruwahan*; *Buddhadev*; *Ashwathama*; *Guru Dronacharya*; **1924**: *Shivajichi Agryahun Sutaka*; *Municipal Elections* (Doc); *Vinchavacha Dansh*; **1925**: *Ganesh Utsav*(?) (Sh); *Ellora Caves* (Sh); *Vichitra Shilpa* (Sh); *Khod Modali* (Sh); *Vachanbhang* (Sh); *Khandalyacha Ghat* (Sh); *Simantak Mani*; *Hidimb Bakasur Vadha*; *Kakasahebanchya Dolyat Jhanjhanit Anjan*; *Chaturthicha Chandra*; *Satyabhama*; **1926**: *Nashikcha Panjarpol* (Sh); *Sant Eknath*; *Janaki Swayamvar*; ***Bhakta Prahlad***; *Balaji Nimbalkar*; **1927**: *Rugmangad Mohini*; *Nala Damayanti*; *Hanuman Janma*; *Draupadi Vastraharan*; *Bhakta Sudama*; *Rukmini Haran*; **1928**: *Kumari Millche Shuddhikaran* (Sh); *Shri Krishna Shishtai*; *Parashuram*; *Bhakta Damaji*; **1929**: *Malavikagnimitra*; *Chandrahasa*; *Vasantsena*; *Bolki Tapeli*; *Sant Meerabai*; *Kacha Devayani*; *Malati Madhav*; **1932**: *Setu Bandhan* (all St); **1937**: ***Gangavataran***.

PHALKE FILMS COMPANY

One of the founding institutions of Indian cinema. Set up by **Dadasaheb Phalke** and his family at Dadar Main Road, Bombay (1912). Initial capital came from a loan against his insurance policy and the main equipment was imported from London. Staffed by Phalke's family and friends, e.g. Trymbak B. Telang, whom he trained to use the Williamson camera. Mrs Phalke (Saraswati aka Kaki) was an essential partner who took upon herself the managerial and technical tasks, included perforating raw Kodak stock. The family kitchen was turned into a laboratory. The first production, ***Raja Harishchandra*** (1913), was a success released at the Coronation Cinematograph and Variety Hall in Bombay as part of a programme with Miss Irene Del Mar in a duet and dance number, a comical sketch by the McClements, Alexandroff the Wonderful Foot Juggler and Tip-Top Comics. In 1913 the company moved to Nasik for easier access to locations Phalke deemed essential for cinema: rivers, mountains, and several famous shrines (locations where popular superstition placed some of the *Ramayana* stories). After four films, it became evident that a familial-artisanal set-up could not cope with the administration for production, processing, distribution and exhibition. In 1918 the company folded and was replaced by the more professional partnership enterprise **Hindustan Cinema Films**.

PHOTOGRAPHY

Established as an industry in India c.1840 when Thacker & Co. advertised the sale of imported daguerreotypes in Calcutta. In the 1850s, several photography studios sold equipment and took portraits on commission (e.g. **Bourne & Shepherd**), providing an infrastructure later extended into film. Earliest British uses of photography include journalism (e.g. the Robertson and Beato partnership which covered the last days of the 1857 Mutiny), military expeditions, surveys and, after 1861, the Central Directorate of Archaeology's records for the preservation of ancient monuments. Encouraged as an amateur practice by the founding of the Photographic Societies of Bombay (1854), Calcutta and Madras (1856). Although there were Indian photographers in the 1850s (e.g. Narayan Dajee, the Merwanjee and Bomanjee company in Bombay) and some Indian aristocrats sponsored the practice (esp. Maharaja Sawai Ram Singh II of Jaipur), the technology became popular among Indians only after the 1880s with the introduction of dry-plate printing. It developed into a popular bazaar art alongside lithographs and woodcut prints, becoming the main medium through which the conflict was played out between traditional Indian aesthetic practices and the Western representational conventions deploying a renaissance 'vanishing-point' perspective. Indian usage almost uniformly emphasised surface rather than depth, working mainly through flattened planar effects. The best-known Indian photography pioneer was Lala Deen Dayal (1844-1905), employed by Tukoji Rao II, the Maharaja of Indore and, after 1885, the court photographer of the Nizam of Hyderabad. He had studios in Secunderabad and Indore, a 'zenana' studio for women in Hyderabad and a major workshop in Bombay. His numerous still photographs attempt several innovations vis-a-vis the portraiture conventions of easel paintings, often suppressing perspective lines and temporal moulding while reintroducing narrative devices from earlier pictorial techniques. This was further emphasised in most bazaar photographs by tinting, painting or sticking things on to the photographic print, often adding theatrical backdrops and three-dimensional objects to give contextualised 'grandeur' to the sitter who commissioned the portrait photograph. Several techniques as well as modes of signification were invented in the process, such as, e.g., **stage backdrops** which sometimes duplicated photographs on massive stage curtains to anchor the enacted fiction in a sense of reality. Like the urban **Pat Painting** and **Company School painting** genres, the illusion of photographic verisimilitude was used to suggest an 'objective' reproduction transcending human fallibility, offering a promise of immortality to the photographed/painted subject. One of the most famous forms of hybrid photography-painting combinations developed as the Manoratha in the temples of Nathdwara, where, as a record of their presence and devotion, photographs of devotees would be glued on to the lower part of a painting of Krishna in the place where formerly small figures of devotees would be painted. Several of these forms later influenced the framing and editing conventions adopted in the early silent cinema (see **Phalke** and **Ravi Varma**).

PILLAI, MUTHUKULAM RAGHAVAN (b. 1909)

Malayalam playwright, actor and one of Kerala's first scenarists and lyricists (***Balan***, 1938). Scripted, e.g., Krishna Iyer's ***Nallathanka*** (1950), K. Vembu's ***Jeevitha Nauka*** (1951), E.R. Cooper's *Velaikkaran* and Velappan's *Lokaneethi* (both 1953). Wrote the dialogues for **K.S. Sethumadhavan**'s ***Daham*** (1965). Turned actor with *Jeevitha Nauka*, later playing small roles in, e.g., ***Navalokam*** (1951) and ***Snehaseema*** (1954). Author of 127 plays, including *Manushyan* on which **K. Ramnoth**'s *Manithan* (1953) is based.

POTHAN, PRATHAP K. (b. 1952)

Malayalam and Tamil director and actor; educated in Madras. Started as actor in **Bharathan**'s *Aravam* and broke through in **Balu Mahendra**'s *Azhiyada Kolangal*, often playing obsessive characters. Turned to direction in 1984 while continuing his acting career (acting credits are incomplete).

FILMOGRAPHY (* act only): **1978**: *Aravam**; **1979**: *Thakara**; *Chamaram**; *Azhiyada Kolangal**; **1980**: ***Lorry****; **1980**: *Varumayin Niram Sigappu**; *Nenjathai Killathey**; *Moodupani**; **1981**: ***Aparna****; **1984**: *Meendum Oru Kadhal Kadai*; **1985**: ***Sindhu Bhairavi****; **1987**: ***Ruthubhedam***; **1988**: *Daisy*; *Jeeva*; **1989**: *Vetri Vizha*; **1991**: *Chaitanya*; **1992**: *Magudam*; **1993**: *Atma*.

PRABHAT FILM COMPANY

Est: 1929 in Kolhapur as partnership by four key figures from **Maharashtra Film**: **V. Shantaram**, **Vishnupant Damle**, **Fattelal** and **Baburao Pendharkar**. Moved to Pune in 1933 where it became Western India's élite studio with a national reputation comparable only to Calcutta's **New Theatres**. It had the largest stage floor in India and an art department under Fattelal regarded as the country's finest. Like New Theatres, Prabhat had many stars on the payroll, well-equipped sound and editing departments and its own laboratory. Early films were mainly remakes of Maharashtra Film productions. Their first major hit was Shantaram's ***Amritmanthan*** (1934). The studio's success benefited from astute distribution arrangements, first with Baburao Pai's Famous Pics and long-term contracts with exhibitors, later taking on distribution itself through its Central Film Exchange and building theatres in Bombay, Pune and Madras. This made them fairly independent from managing-agency financiers for production capital. The studio also benefited from its cultural policies in the wake of significant developments in popular theatre, music and literature. Apart from its Maharashtra Film inheritances, the studio's repertoire was crucially shaped by two major stage phenomena: **Sangeet Natak** superstar **Bal Gandharva**, whose Gandharva Natak Mandali provided its two most famous music composers **Govindrao Tembe** and **Master Krishnarao**, and the vanguard Natyamanwantar group whose *Andhalyanchi Shala* (1933) led to **K. Narayan Kale**, composer **Keshavrao Bhole** and star **Keshavrao Date** joining the studio. Untroubled by New Theatres' type of classical aspirations, Prabhat pioneered new popular forms such as the Bhakti biographicals or Saint films by Damle-Fattelal and socials by Shantaram. Other major Prabhat film-makers include K. Narayan Kale, **Raja Nene**, **Keshavrao Dhaiber**, **Vishram Bedekar** and **Gajanan Jagirdar**. **Master Vinayak** started at Prabhat as an actor, and an influential post-Independence generation of Marathi film-makers led by **Anant Mane** and **Datta Dharmadhikari** began their careers as technical assistants there. The studio closed in 1953. A.V. Damle is presently constructing a video collection of the classic Prabhat films. **Shantaram Athavale** wrote a history of the company, *Prabhat Kaal* (1965).

PRAKASH, KHEMCHAND (1907-50)

Composer associated mainly with the **Ranjit** Studio which he joined in 1940 and where he scored music for **Kardar** (***Holi***, ***Pagal***), **Jayant Desai**'s **Saigal** film ***Tansen*** and some **Kidar Sharma** films (*Gauri*, *Vish Kanya*, *Bhanwara*). Born in Jaipur. Son of Pandit Govardhan Prasad, court singer at the Jaipur palace. Learnt kathak for a while. Aged 19, was appointed court singer by the Maharaja of Bikaner, and later also served under the Nepal royalty. Radio artist in Calcutta; later worked with **Timir Baran** at **New Theatres**. Scored the classic soundtrack of **Amrohi**'s ***Mahal*** at **Bombay Talkies**, with his most memorable song *Ayega anevala* sung by **Lata Mangeshkar**. Introduced **Kishore Kumar** as playback for **Dev Anand** in Shaheed Latif's *Ziddi*. His last film, *Tamasha*, was the studio's last production.

FILMOGRAPHY: 1939: *Gazi Salauddin*; *Meri Aankhen*; **1940**: *Aaj Ka Hindustan*; *Diwali*; ***Holi***; ***Pagal***; **1941**: *Holiday in Bombay*; *Pardesi*; *Pyaas*; *Shadi*; *Ummeed*; **1942**: *Baraat*; *Chandni*; *Dukh Sukh*; *Fariyad*; *Iqraar*; *Khilona*; *Mehmaan*; **1943**: *Chirag*; *Gauri*; *Qurbani*; ***Tansen***; *Vish Kanya*; **1944**: *Bhanwara*; *Bhartrahari*; *Mumtaz Mahal*; *Shahenshah Babar*; **1945**: *Dhanna Bhagat*; *Prabhu Ka Ghar*; **1947**: *Chalte Chalte*; *Gaon*; *Mera Suhaag*; *Mulaqat*; ***Samaj Ko Badal Dalo***; *Sindoor*; **1948**: *Asha*; *Ziddi*; **1949**: ***Mahal***; ***Rimjhim***; *Sawan Aya Re*; **1950**: *Bijli*; *Jaan Pehchan*; *Muqaddar*; *Sati Narmada*; **1951**: *Jai Shankar*; *Shri Ganesh Janma*; **1952**: *Tamasha*.

PRAKASH, RAGHUPATI SURYA (1901-56)

Full name: Raghupati Surya Prakasha Rao. South Indian pioneer director and cinematographer. Worked in Tamil and Telugu. Born in Madras, son of **Raghupathi Venkaiah**, a wealthy Andhra businessman and photographer who started film exhibition in South India around 1910 and built the first cinema in Madras (1914). Educated by Christian missionaries in Vepery. Sent overseas to learn film-making, he went to London and joined Barkers Motion Photography in Ealing (1918), then went to Germany (where he saw Murnau at work) and to Hollywood. He travelled to various European countries, bringing a 35mm camera home to Madras (1920). The faulty camera ruined his first feature, *Meenakshi Kalyanam*. Set up Star of the East Studio, known as the Glass Studio, in Purasawalkam, Madras (1921), where he made *Bhishma Pratigya*. **A. Narayanan, C. Pullaiah** and other pioneers worked with him there. The films were distributed throughout the subcontinent with intertitles in various languages. Bad management ruined the studio. Probably directed the Catholic propaganda film, ***The Catechist of Kil-Arni***, produced and written by the Irish priest Thomas Gavin Duffy together with Bruce Gordon as a fund-raiser for the Paris Foreign Mission Society in Pondicherry. Operated as distributor (1924-5) and founded Guarantee Pics (1926) with backing from the merchant-landlord Moti Narayana Rao, but it also went bankrupt. Helped Narayanan to set up the famous **General Pics** (for which he made the hit *Leila the Star of Mingrelia*) and Srinivasa Cinetone Studio (1928-39). Started a laboratory (1930). Separated from Narayanan in the mid-30s and joined Sundaram Sound Studio. Worked with Govardhan Film Distributors, owning 3 cinemas in Madras. Shot, developed and edited all his early films. Known as a brilliant technician: in *Draupadi Vastrapaharanam* he managed to make one actor appear in 5 places within one image, apparently without resorting to optical effects. Freelance director from mid-30s. Influenced **Y.V. Rao** who acted in his *Gajendra Moksham*. Associated mostly with mythologicals, often shot at the Gingee Fort in Madras. His Tamil reformist social, *Anadhai Penn*, is an early instance of nationalist propaganda just before WW2. There is contradictory evidence about some of Prakash's early Tamil sound films, which some sources ascribe to Prakash and others to his collaborator Narayanan; e.g. *Draupadi Vastrapaharanam*, *Krishna Arjuna*, *Indrasabha* and *Rajasekharan*. We have credited them to both film-makers. Also, the Telugu film *Bondam Pelli* (1940), made at the Madras United Artists and officially credited to **H.M. Reddy**, is at times credited to Prakash.

FILMOGRAPHY: **1921**: *Bhishma Pratigya*; **1923**: ***The Catechist of Kil-Arni***; *Gajendra Moksham*; *Bhakta Nandan*; **1924**: *Samudra Madanam*; *Draupadi Bhagya*; *Usha Swapna*; **1925**: *Mahatma Kabirdas*; **1926**: *Mohini Avatar*; **1927**: *Dashavtar*; **1929**: *Stage Girl*; *Shri Kannika Parameshwari*; **1930**: *Gajendra Moksham*; *Lanka Dahana*; *Gandhariyin Pulambal*; **1931**: *Pavalakkodi*; *Leila the Star of Mingrelia*; *Nara Narayana*; *Rose of Rajasthan*; **1932**: *Vishnu Leela* (all St); **1934**: *Draupadi Vastrapaharanam*; **1935**: *Lanka Dahanam*; *Thooku Thooki*; *Krishna Arjuna*; **1936**: *Krishna Naradi*; *Nalayini*; *Indrasabha*; **1937**: *Andal Thirukalyanam*; *Soldier's Wife*; *Rajasekharan*; **1938**: *Anadhai Penn*; *Porveeran Manaivi*; **1939**: *Sirikathe*; **1940**: ***Chandika***; **1941**: *Tara Sasankam*; **1942**: *Babruvahana*; **1951**: *Mayapilla*; **1956**: *Moondru Penngal*.

PRAKASH RAO, KOVALAPATI SURYA (b. 1914)

Telugu director, also worked in Tamil. Born in Kistna Dist., AP. Associated with the Praja Natya Mandali, the Telugu wing of the **IPTA**. Started in films as lead actor in **Ramabrahmam**'s *Apavadu* (1941) and ***Patni*** (made in 1940, released in 1942); acted in **R.S. Prakash**'s *Babruvahana* (1942); produced and acted in **L.V. Prasad**'s ***Drohi*** (1948) for Swatantra Pics, which he replaced by his own Prakash Prod. (1949), producing and directing *Modathi Rathri* and *Deeksha*. Expanded this company into the Prakash Studio. 50s films were melodramas which later became psychological fantasies: e.g. *Prem Nagar*, a story of unrequited love drowned in liquor written by Kousalya Devi, and *Kode Naagu*, a remake of **Kanagal**'s demented love story ***Nagara Haavu*** (1972). Made Kannada films in the late 70s. His son **K. Raghavendra Rao** is a mainstream Telugu director of action fantasies.

FILMOGRAPHY: **1950**: *Modathi Rathri*; **1951**: *Deeksha/Anni*; **1953**: ***Kanna Talli/Petrathai***; **1954**: *Balanandam*; **1955**: *Ante Kavali*; **1956**: *Melukolupu*; *Marumalarchi*; **1960**: *Renukadevi Mahatyam*; **1961**: *Gullopelli*; **1962**: *Mohini Rugmangada*; **1966**: *Badukuva Daari*; **1967**: *Stree Janmam*; **1968**: *Bharya*; *Harishchandra*; *Bandhipotu Dongalu*; **1969**: *Vichitra Kutumbam*; **1971**: *Naa Thammudu*; *Bhale Papa*; *Prem Nagar*; *Tehsildarugari Ammayi*; **1972**: *Pedda Koduku*; *Vasantha Maligai*; **1973**: *Jeevitham*; *Ida Lokam*; **1974**: *Kode Naagu*; *Satyaniki Sankellu*; *Prem Nagar*; **1975**: *Chikati Velugulu*; **1976**: *Secretary*; *Suprabhatam*; *Avan Oru Charitram*; **1977**: *Ganda Hendthi*; **1979**: *Balina Guri*; **1982**: *Garuda Sowkiyama*; *Kotha Neeru*; **1983**: *Muddula Mogadu*.

PRAKASH RAO, TATINENI (1924-92)

Telugu, Tamil and Hindi director born in Kapileshwaram village, Krishna Dist., AP. Member of the CPI before Independence and associated with the radical theatre movements in Telugu. Joined **L.V. Prasad** as assistant director (1947-51). Début ***Palletooru***, starring **NTR**, a strident but influential ruralist melodrama in which the hero represents the grandeur of the Andhra people when he confronts the village moneylender. Later work continues the Prasad tradition of the mid-budget family drama and musical, often remade from other languages: e.g. *Illarikam*, produced by Prasad, adapted **Ch. Narayanamurthy**'s Tamil film *Ethirparadathu* (1954) and starred Telugu cinema's leading star duo of the 50s, **A. Nageshwara Rao** and **Anjali Devi**, as stepson and stepmother. The film was remade again, by L.V. Prasad, in Hindi as *Sharada* (1957). Prakash Rao took over Prasad Art Pics, running it with **Pratyagatma**. Made several Hindi films, e.g. the **Rajendra Kumar** and **B. Saroja Devi** hit *Sasural*, which included the calendar art Garden of Eden hit song *Teri pyari pyari soorat ko* sung by **Mohammed Rafi**. Directed **Sivaji Ganesan** (*Uthama Puthran*) and **MGR** (*Padakottai*). In the 70s also made children's films (*Ganga Bhawani*, *Engalamum Mudiyum*).

FILMOGRAPHY: **1952**: ***Palletooru***; **1953**: *Pichhipullaiah*; **1954**: ***Nirupedalu***; *Parivarthana*; **1956**: *Jayam Manade*; *Mathurkula Manikyam/Charanadasi*; ***Amara Deepam***; **1958**: *Amar Deep*; *Sitamgarh*; *Uthama Puthran*; **1959**: *Kanniraindha Kanavan*; *Nalla Theerpu*; *Illarikam*; **1960**: *College Girl*; *Maa Babu*; *Ellorum Innattu Mannar*; **1961**: *Anbu Magan*; *Sasural*; **1962**: *Kathirunda Kankal*; **1963**: *Bahurani*; *Hamrahi*; **1964**: *Padakottai*; **1965**: *Bahu Beti*; **1966**: *Suraj*; **1968**: *Duniya*; *Izzat*; *Vaasna*; **1969**: *Nannha Farishta*; **1970**: *Ghar Ghar Ki Kahani*; **1972**: *Rivaaj*; **1973**: *Minor Babu*; **1974**: *Gali Patalu*; **1975**: *Samsaram*; **1976**: *Pogarubottu*; **1977**: *Chiranjeevi Rambabu*; **1978**: *Ganga Bhawani*; *Hamara Sansar*; **1981**: *Asha Jyoti*; **1983**: *Engalamum Mudiyum*; **1987**: *Bharatamlo Arjundu*; **1988**: *Kab Tak Chup Rahungi*.

PRASAD, L. V. (1908-94)

Full name Akkineni Lakshmana Vara Prasad Rao. Telugu, Tamil and Hindi producer and director born in Elluru, TN. Actor and studio hand in Bombay-based studios (1930), including a small role in **Imperial**'s ***Alam Ara*** (1931). Assisted and acted for **H.M. Reddy** in the first Telugu sound film, ***Bhakta Prahlada*** (1931) and in the Tamil ***Kalidas*** (1931). Starred in several other Reddy films. Occasionally acted in Prithvi Theatres plays. Directorial début for the Sarathi Studio with a **Tripuraneni Gopichand** script, ***Grihapravesham***, stressing comic routines instead of the story's reformism. ***Palnati Yuddham*** completed **Ramabrahamam**'s dream project: a big-budget historical with allusions to India's Independence struggle. Made his mark at the **Vijaya** Studio with ***Shavukaru*** and ***Samsaram***, remaining the studio's top director for five years with successful domestic melodramas consistently featuring the urban middle class, a new departure for Telugu cinema. Elaborated this genre into a distinctive set of mid-budget soap-operas produced and distributed by Prasad Art Pics (1956), which assigned a group of younger directors to these multilinguals, often remaking hits from other languages. In the Prasad school of film-makers are his former assistants **T. Prakash Rao** and **K. Pratyagatma** who, together, briefly ran Prasad Art Pics in the early 60s; **Yoganand**, K.B. Tilak, **Adurthi Subba Rao**, Ranganath Das and Rajanikant. Shifted to Tamil in the late 50s and 60s, directing films scripted, surprisingly, by the DMK politician **Karunanidhi** (***Manohara***, ***Thayilla Pillai*** and ***Iruvar Ullam***). Hindi début in 1957 with the melodrama *Sharada*, a remake of the Tamil *Ethirparadathu* (1954) and the Telugu *Ilavelpu* (1956), in which **Raj Kapoor** finds that he has become the stepson of his beloved, **Meena Kumari**. The comedy *Miss Mary* is the Hindi version of two previous hits: ***Missiamma*** (Tamil) and ***Missamma*** (Telugu). His third Hindi film, ***Chhoti Bahen***, remade the Tamil film *En Thangai* (1952). Launched the Prasad Studio (1965) and the Prasad Film laboratory (1976), currently considered India's finest lab. After *Beti Bete*, signed only his Hindi films. Scripted *Udhaar Ka Sindoor* (1976). Persuaded by **Kamalahasan** to return to acting, aged 73, for ***Raja Parvai***. Biography by K.N.T. Sastry (1993).

FILMOGRAPHY (* also act/** only act): **1931**: ***Alam Ara*****; ***Kalidas*****; ***Bhakta***

Sivaji Ganesan (centre) in L.V. Prasad's *Manohara* (1954)

Prahlada**; **1933**: *Seeta Swayamvar***; **1940**: *Barrister Parvatisham***; *Bondam Pelli***; *Chaduvukonna Bharya***; **1941**: ***Tenali Ramakrishna*****; **1942**: ***Gharana Donga*****; **1946**: ***Grihapravesham****; **1947**: ***Palnati Yuddham****; **1948**: ***Drohi****; **1949**: ***Mana Desam***; **1950**: ***Shavukaru***; ***Samsaram***; **1952**: ***Pelli Chesi Choodu/Kalyanam Panni Paar***; *Rani*; **1953**: ***Poongothai/Pardesi***; ***Pempudu Koduku****; **1954**: ***Manohara/Manohar***; **1955**: ***Missamma/Missiamma***; *Mangayar Thilakam*; **1957**: *Bhagyavati*; *Miss Mary*; *Sharada*; **1958**: ***Appu Chesi Pappu Koodu/Kadam Vangi Kalyanam***; **1959**: ***Chhoti Bahen***; **1961**: ***Thayilla Pillai***; **1963**: ***Iruvar Ullam***; **1964**: *Beti Bete*; **1966**: *Dadi Maa*; **1969**: *Jeene Ki Raah*; **1972**: *Shadi Ke Baad*; **1974**: *Bidaai*; **1977**: *Jai Vijay*; **1981**: ***Raja Parvai*****.

PRATYAGATMA, KOTAYYA (b. 1925)

Aka K.P. Atma. Telugu and Hindi director born in Gudivada, AP. Political activist in the Congress-affiliated Andhra Youth Federation (1946-8) and later editor and publisher of Madras-based film journal *Jwala* (Est: 1951). Early work in films as scenarist in **L.V. Prasad**'s Prasad Art Prod, e.g. for **T. Prakash Rao** with whom he later took over the company. Best known as manufacturer of L.V. Prasad-derived family melodramas, often remade in Hindi. Started independent production company Atma Arts (1966) signing as K.P. Atma. Wrote his own films as well as ***Nirupedalu*** (1954), *Maa Inti Mahalakshmi* (1959) and *Tandrulu Kodukulu* (1961).

FILMOGRAPHY (* as K.P. Atma): **1961**: *Bharya Bartulu*; **1962**: ***Kulagothralu***; **1963**: ***Punarjanma***; **1964**: *Manchi Manishi*; **1965**: *Manushulu Mamathalu*; **1966**: *Chilaka-Gorinka*; *Chhota Bhai**; **1967**: *Maa Vadina*; **1968**: *Raja Aur Runk**; **1969**: *Tamanna**; *Adarsha Kutumbam*; **1970**: *Bachpan**; *Manasu Mangalyam*; **1971**: *Shrimanthudu*; *Ek Nari Ek Brahmchari**; **1973**: *Mehmaan**; *Palletoori Bhava*; *Stree*; **1974**: *Deeksha*; *Mugguru Ammayilu*; **1976**: *Do Ladkiyan**; *Alludochadu*; *Attavarillu*; **1977**: *Gadusu Ammayi*; **1978**: *Kannavari Illu*; *Manchi Manasu*; **1979**: *Kamalamma Kamatam*; **1980**: *Nayakudu Vinayakudu*.

PRIYADARSHAN

Malayalam director trained at Appachan's Navodaya Studio in Kerala. Started as scenarist (e.g. M. Mani's *Kuyiline Thedi*, 1983). Directorial début in 1984. Makes musicals mainly with Malayalam megastar **Mohanlal**; the pair started working together with Priyadarshan's second film *Puchakkoru Mookuthi*, but hit their most successful formula with a string of late 80s hits ***Thalavattam***, ***Chithram*** and *Kilukkam*. Made a high-profile entry into Hindi films with the Jackie Shroff movie *Gardish*.

FILMOGRAPHY: 1984: *Oodarathuammava Alariyum*; *Puchakkoru Mookuthi*; **1985**: *Parayanumvayya Parayathirikkanumvayya*; *Boeing Boeing*; *Aram Aram = Kinnaram*; *Onnanam Kunnil Oradi Kunnil*; *Punnaram Cholli Cholli*; **1986**: *Ayalvasi Oru Dharithavasi*; *Dheem Tharikita Thom*; *Hello My Dear-Wrong Number*; *Mazha Peyyunnu Maddalam Kottunnu*; *Ninnishtam Ennishtam*; *Rakkuyilin Rajassadasil*; ***Thalavattam***; **1987**: *Cheppu*; *Abhimanyu*; **1988**: *Aryan*; ***Chithram***; *Kilukkam*; *Mukunthetta Sumitra Vilikkunnu*; *Oru Muthassi Katha*; **1989**: *Vandanam*; **1991**: *Nirnayam*; *Gopura Vasalile*; *Advaitham*; **1992**: *Muskurahat*; **1993**: *Gardish*; *Midhunam*.

PROGRESSIVE ARTISTS GROUP

Movement in the visual arts launched in Bombay in 1947 by the painter Francis Newton Souza (b. 1924). Visual art precedents include the pro-CPI Calcutta Group (Prodosh Dasgupta, Nirode Majumdar, Gopal Ghosh, Gobardhan Ash and Rathin Maitra) formed in 1943, and the Progressive Painters Association initiated in Madras by K.C.S. Panicker in 1944, although the title referred to the **PWA**. Souza, briefly a CPI member, had been expelled by the British Principal of the J.J. School of Art for his nationalist demonstrations. The first PAG show (1947), featuring S.H. Raza, M.F. Husain, K.H. Ara, H.A. Gade and Bakre, published an exhibition manifesto attempting to define a socially responsive aesthetics for the visual arts. However, the very next year the group distanced itself from these aims, with Souza claiming to have 'changed all the chauvinist ideas and the Leftist fanaticism which we had incorporated in our manifesto at the inception of the group. [T]he gulf between the so-called people and the artists cannot be bridged' (cf Kapur, 1978). The PAG broke up shortly thereafter, most of the artists migrating to Paris or London except Husain. A second phase of the Bombay Progressives included Akbar Padamsee, Krishen Khanna and Tyeb Mehta as affiliates. Subsequently, a series of Progressive groups were started in Kashmir, Andhra Pradesh and Karnataka. More than in its political thrust, the Bombay group's major impact lay in Souza's oft-repeated claim that the PAG introduced modernism into Indian art. Although this claim is partially belied by subsequent art-historical revaluations of **Tagore**, Binode Behari Mukherjee and Amrita Sher-Gil as formidable antecedents, the PAG's work certainly adheres to the Western modernist canon in presenting an ideology of high art as opposed to the popular. Their consciously stated disaffiliation after Independence from nationalism informed the first significant expressionist current in India (although expressionism had been used sporadically in, e.g., Ram Kinker Baij's work). The group made an existential as well as a more painterly alliance with expressionism, foregrounding figural motifs through pigment and brushwork as well as through the use of a compact figure-ground Gestalt.

PROGRESSIVE WRITERS ASSOCIATION

Movement of Indian writers launched in London (1935) in the wake of the meeting in Paris of the International Association of Writers for the Defence of Culture against Fascism led by Gorky, Gide, Malraux et al. It became a broadly based cultural movement after the first All-India Congress in Lucknow (1936) with Munshi Premchand as President. As the first major cultural initiative involving the independent Left and the CPI, the PWA made a formidable impact, introducing a politically aware realism into the predominantly feudal and reformist traditions of Urdu, Punjabi, Hindi, Bengali, Marathi, Telugu and Malayalam literatures. However, it was overshadowed by its theatrical successor, the **IPTA**. The PWA's influence on film was both formal, signifying a populist vanguardism for the commercial industry (e.g. **Bhavnani**'s ***Mazdoor***, 1934, scripted by Premchand) and economic, giving virtually all the progressive Hindi-Urdu writers employment as scenarists in Bombay: **Krishan Chander**, **Rajinder**

Singh Bedi, **Sadat Hasan Manto**, **Ismat Chughtai**, Amritlal Nagar and Josh Mahilabadi, poets-songwriters **Kaifi Azmi**, **Sahir Ludhianvi** et al.

PULLAIAH, CHITTAJALLU (1895-1967)

Telugu director born in Kakinada, AP. Started in 1913 as camera apprentice at **R. Venkaiah**'s Star of the East (Madras), and at **Kohinoor** (Bombay). Toured Kakinada exhibiting films and later ran the permanent Minerva theatre. **East India Film** in Calcutta, then attempting to enter the South Indian market, invited him (1933) to make Telugu films. Directed the hit ***Savithri*** and four more films for the Calcutta studio. Made double bill ***Ansuya*** and *Dhruva* starring his son **C. Srinvasa Rao** for its rival studio, **Aurora**. Best-known work at **Gemini**, including the highly successful ***Balanagamma***, virtually redefining the Telugu mythological (being codified then by **Balaramaiah**) and the adventure saga ***Apoorva Sahodharalu*** adapting Dumas's *The Corsican Brothers*. The latter was remade into successful Tamil and Hindi versions in the same year. Known as Star-Brahma (God of the Stars) for having introduced several of Telugu's best-known actors to film, such as **Bhanumati** (***Varavikrayam***), **Anjali Devi** (*Gollabhama*) and Pushpavalli (*Chal Mohanaranga*). His last *Lavakusa* was an elaborate **NTR**-Anjali Devi remake of the 1934 film made at East India, co-d with his son C. Srinivasa Rao.

FILMOGRAPHY: 1933: ***Savithri***; **1934**: ***Lavakusa***; **1935**: *Shri Krishna Tulabharam*; **1936**: ***Ansuya***; *Dhruva*; **1937**: *Dasavataramulu*; **1938**: *Satyanarayana Vratam*; *Kasulaperu*; *Chal Mohanaranga*; ***Mohini Bhasmasura***; **1939**: ***Varavikrayam***; **1940**: *Malathi Madhavam*; **1941**: *Subhadra*; **1942**: ***Balanagamma***; **1945**: *Maya Machhindra*; **1946**: *Narada Naradi*; **1947**: *Gollabhama*; **1948**: *Vindhyarani*; **1950**: ***Apoorva Sahodharalu***; **1952**: ***Sankranti***; **1953**: ***Pakkinti Ammayi***; **1960**: *Devanthakudu*; **1963**: *Lavakusa*; **1966**: *Paramanandayya Sishyulu Katha*; **1967**: *Bhama Vijayam*; *Bhuvana Sundari Katha*.

PULLAIAH, P. (1911-85)

Telugu and Tamil director born in Nellore, AP. Actor and singer on stage. Graduate from Madras University. Had several successful song and recitation records released by Gramophone Company and worked for them as a talent scout. Assistant to **Baburao Painter** at Shalini Cinetone (1934), leading to a long-standing engagement with Marathi cinema: cf ***Dharmapatni***, shot in Kolhapur and based on a **V.S. Khandekar** story; or *Jayabheri*, adapted from **V. Shantaram**'s Tamasha classic ***Lokshahir Ramjoshi*** (1947). Turned producer investing in Star Combines (launched with the **Kannamba** film *Harishchandra*). Set up the successful mid-budget Tamil company Ragini Films (Est: 1948) in partnership with Bhimavarapu Narasimha Rao (first film: *Bhakta Jana*). Started Padmasree Films. Made the very successful **NTR** mythological ***Shri Venkateshwara Mahatyam***, sometimes seen as launching NTR's political career. Many of his films starred Shantakumari, whom he married.

FILMOGRAPHY: 1935: *Harishchandra*; **1937**: *Sarangadhara*; **1939**: ***Shri Venkateshwara Mahatyam***; **1940**: ***Dharmapatni***; **1941**: *Premabandhan*; **1943**: ***Bhagya Lakshmi***; **1948**: *Bhakta Jana*; **1949**: *Bhakta Gora Kumbhara*; **1950**: *Macharekhai*; *Veetukkari*; *Thirugubatu*; **1952**: *Dharmadevata*; **1953**: *Manampola Mangalyam*; **1954**: *Rechukka*; **1955**: ***Ardhangi/Pennin Perumai***; *Kanyashulkam*; **1956**: *Umasundari*; **1957**: *Vanangamudi/Tala Vanchani Veerudu*; **1958**: *Illarame Nallaram*; **1959**: *Kalaivanan*; *Jayabheri*; *Bandaramudu/Adisaya Thirudan*; **1960**: ***Shri Venkateshwara Mahatyam***; *Naan Kanda Sorgam*; **1961**: *Pachani Samsaram*; **1962**: ***Siri Sampadalu***; **1964**: ***Murali Krishna***; **1965**: *Preminchi Choodu*; *Asai Mukham*; **1966**: *Thaye Unakkaga*; **1967**: ***Pranamithrulu***; **1970**: *Alludu Menalludu*; **1972**: *Koduku Kodalu*; **1975**: *Andaru Bagundali*.

PUNATAR, RATILAL HEMCHAND (b. 1913)

Gujarati-Hindi director aka Ratibhai Punatar. Born in Jamnagar, Gujarat. Production manager at **Ranjit**. Directorial début when, following the spectacular success of ***Ranakdevi*** (1946), Ranjit started subsidiary Ajit Pics to exploit the interest in Gujarati films. First major film, *Gunsundari*, remade **Chandulal Shah**'s pathbreaking silent film and remains, with ***Mehndi Rang Lagyo*** (1960) and ***Jesal Toral*** (1971), one of the Gujarati cinema's biggest hits, the first one to tap a substantial urban audience for a Gujarati cinema until then restricted to semi-urban B film circuits. Third film ***Mangalfera*** was also very successful, and continued the *Gunsundari* and *Nanand Bhojai* theme of a crumbling joint-family system faced with the values of a mercantile economy. Also made films based on Prabhulal Dwivedi's folk theatre (***Gadano Bel***) and on, e.g., D.N. Madhok's popular novels.

FILMOGRAPHY: 1948: *Gunsundari*; *Nanand Bhojai*; **1949**: ***Mangalfera***; **1950**: *Man Ka Meet*; *Nili*; ***Gadano Bel***; **1953**: *Bahadur*; **1961**: *Chundadi Chokha*.

PUNJAB FILM CORPORATION

Est: 1926 as fully equipped studio in Lahore under the technical supervision of **R.L. Shorey**, marking the beginning of a Punjabi film industry. Ironically, the pioneers of the Lahore-based industry (**Shorey**, **Kardar**, **Pancholi**) started with a reputation for making educational films even though they were adapting Universal's 'epics' and RKO's Westerns imported by Pancholi's Empire distributors. The educational films were mainly sponsored documentaries by, e.g., the Rural Community Board, the Peninsular Railway Board and the Punjab Directorate of Industries. In the silent era, these were the only agencies sponsoring film production in a region where finance was concentrated in the exhibition sector. The Punjab Film Corp. was intended as a co-operative organisation supported by the government providing facilities for the nearly 40 registered production companies in Punjab. Its objective was to further the 'educational' film in the region. With the coming of sound and the establishment of independent studios like Kardar's Playart Phototone, Shorey's Kamla Movietone effectively took over Punjab Film; the 'educational' notions faded away but the facilities remained crucial to the growing industry until Partition (1946) shifted the Punjabi industry to Bombay.

PURI, OM (b. 1950)

Character actor, born in Ambala, Punjab, who shot to stardom in **Govind Nihalani**'s ***Aakrosh*** followed by his best-known screen role, the police officer in ***Ardh Satya***. A former student of the National School of Drama (1970-3) in Delhi and the **FTII** (1974-6), Pune. Taught at Roshan Taneja's Actors' Studio, Bombay (1976-8). Formed the Majma Theatre group which staged its opening play, *Udhwastha Dharmashala*, at **Shashi Kapoor**'s Prithvi Theatre. This was followed by *Bichhoo* (*The Scorpion*). Feature début in **B.V. Karanth**'s *Chor Chor Chhupja* followed by **Benegal**'s ***Bhumika***. His gaunt, pockmarked face and deep-set eyes tended to be used as a demotic archetype even before his Nihalani films and Benegal's ***Aarohan***, e.g. in **Saeed Mirza**'s rhetorical student documentary, *An Actor Prepares*. This image, one of the icons of the New Indian Cinema, was also mobilised in Attenborough's *Gandhi* where he played an angry slum-dweller. His main departures from this persona, **Ketan Mehta**'s ***Bhavni Bhavai*** and ***Mirch Masala***, recall his earlier stage work mixing Ibsenite naturalism (*An Enemy of the People*, *Udhwastha Dharmashala*) with folk musicals (*Bichhoo*, *Jasma Odan*), both styles rendered with equal elan. Was a member of the Yukt Film Co-operative, playing the difficult title role in the experimental film ***Ghashiram Kotwal***. Played a major role in the Punjabi hit ***Chann Pardesi***. Late 80s/90s films in Hindi (main villain in **N. Chandra**'s ***Narasimha***) and Telugu (Ramgopal Varma's *Ratri*, and Uma Maheshwara Rao's *Darshana* and *Ankuram*).

FILMOGRAPHY: 1975: *Kalla Kalla Bachitko/Chor Chor Chhupja*; **1976**: *Amrita* (Sh); *Corpses* (Sh); *An Elusive Dream* (Sh); *Khukhari* (Sh); *Lokayat* (Sh); *Navjatak* (Sh); *An Actor Prepares* (Doc); *Duniya Chalti Hai* (Sh); ***Ghashiram Kotwal***; ***Bhumika***; **1977**: *Tabbaliyu Neenade Magane/Godhuli*; **1978**: ***Arvind Desai Ki Ajeeb Dastaan***; **1979**: ***Sparsh***; *Shayad*; **1980**: ***Albert Pinto Ko Gussa Kyon Aata Hai***; ***Aakrosh***; ***Bhavni Bhavai/Andher Nagari***; ***Kalyug***; ***Chann Pardesi***; *Shodh*; **1981**: ***Sadgati*** (TV); *Raaste Pyar Ke*; **1982**: ***Aarohan***; *Gandhi*; ***Chokh***; *Disco Dancer*; *Waqt Waqt Ki Baat*; *Vijeta*; *Shrant*; **1983**: ***Ardh Satya***; ***Jaane Bhi Do Yaaron***; ***Mandi***; *The Jewel in the Crown* (TV); ***Holi***; *Long Da Lishkara*; **1984**: *Ashray*; *Giddh*; *Mati Mange Khoon*; ***Party***; *Ram Ki Ganga*; *Ravan*; ***Tarang***; *Yeh Desh*; *Sanjhi*; ***Paar***; *Duniya*; *Sheeshe Ka Ghar*; **1985**: *Aaghat*; *Nasoor*; *Patthar*; ***Mirch Masala***; *Bahu Ki Awaaz*; ***Debshishu***; *Zamana*; ***New Delhi Times***; *Khandaan* (TV); **1986**: *Halaat*; ***Susman***; *Yatra* (TV); ***Genesis***; *Raag Darbari* (TV); **1987**: ***Tamas*** (TV); *Marte Dam Tak*; **1988**: *Hum Farishte Nahin*; *Puravrutham*; *Ek Hi Maqsad*; *Sam and Me*; **1988-89**: *Bharat Ek Khoj* (TV); **1989**: *Ilaaka*; *Kakkaji Kahin* (TV); *Mr Yogi* (TV); *Darshana*; *Sava Ser Gehnu*; **1990**: ***Disha***; ***Ghayal***; *Halaat*; *Iraada*; **1991**: ***Narasimha***; *Dharavi*; *Current*; *Ratri/Raat*;

Om Puri (right) in *Dharavi* (1991)

Meena Bazaar; **1992**: *City of Joy*; *Antarnaad*; *Angar*; *Ankuram*; *Karamyoddha*; *Purush*; **1993**: *In Custody*; *Patang*; *Woh Chokri*.

Puttanna, S. R. *see* **Kanagal, S. R. Puttana**
PWA *see* **Progressive Writers Association**

QADIR, KOZHIKODE ABDUL

Major Malayalam singer and popular music figure before **Yesudas**. Worked in Nilambur Balan's theatre group where his political songs earned him the title 'prophet of the peace movement'. Came from North Kerala's Malabar region and his songs, strongly reminiscent of **K.L. Saigal**, were among the first examples of popular music from that region assimilating non-Carnatic influences, a practice later influencing composer **Baburaj**'s work. Sang first for ***Navalokam*** (1951) and for 7 more films, including the hits of **Kariat**'s and **Bhaskaran**'s first film, ***Neelakuyil*** (1954).

RAFI, MOHAMMED (1924-80)

One of the three most popular Hindi playback singers ever, with **Kishore Kumar** and Mukesh. Born in Kotta Sultansingh village, Punjab (now Pakistan). Moved to Lahore aged 14, where he was a student of the musicians Khan Abdul Waheed Khan, Jeevanlal Matto and Ghulam Ali Khan. The composer Feroz Nizami introduced him to Radio Lahore. Film début for the music director Shyam Sundar in the Punjabi film *Gul Baloch* (1944). Moved to Bombay in 1944, where he was given his break by **Naushad** (*Pehle Aap*, 1944). Found musical stardom with **Mehboob**'s ***Anmol Ghadi*** (1946). Sang the classic duet with the legendary **K.L. Saigal**, *Meri sapnon ki rani* in ***Shahjehan*** (1946). First big hits were in duets with **Nurjehan** in *Jugnu* (1947: he appeared briefly in the film as a student singing in the college dormitory), *Saajan* (1947) and *Mela* (1948). Remained popular until he died. His earlier work was associated with **S.D. Burman**'s and **Shankar-Jaikishen**'s music but esp. with that of **Naushad** (***Deedar***, 1951; ***Aan***, 1952; ***Baiju Bawra***, 1952; ***Udan Khatola***, 1955; ***Mughal-e-Azam***, 1960), doing his best playback singing for **Dilip Kumar** and in **Guru Dutt**'s ***Pyaasa*** (1957) and ***Kaagaz Ke Phool*** (1959). In the early 60s made a remarkable transition to **Shammi Kapoor**'s 'Yahoo' films (***Junglee***, 1961; ***Kashmir Ki Kali***, 1964) and became the unchallenged monarch of Indian film music until the late 60s when he was partially displaced by Kishore Kumar's **Rajesh Khanna** wave.

RAGHAVA, BALLARI (1880-1946)

Major Telugu and Kannada stage and screen actor with a big impact on the early Telugu cinema. Key figure in the Amateur Dramatic Association which demarcated itself from the **Sastry**-style **Company Natak** through its anglophile modernism. Visited London (1928), befriended G.B. Shaw and theatre director Forbes-Robertson, returning with new ideas for rehearsing and 'blocking' stage movement, calling for a socially relevant theatre to help 'nation building' and arguing for the professionalisation of theatres and training schools. Stressed naturalistic prose rather than music and often individuated characters by heightening the sense of moral dilemma, e.g. his traitor Pathan Rustom in Kolachalam Srinivasa Rao's play, *Sultana Chand Bibi* and his Chanakya in *Chandragupta* as adapted from Dwijendralal Roy's Bengali play. Entered films with ***Draupadi Manasamrakshanam***, a megabudget adaptation of his own play, upstaged by **H.V. Babu**'s more modest inaugural production (1936). Best film role as Narsi Reddy in **Ramabrahmam**'s seminal ***Raitu Bidda***, confirming his reputation for realism. Uneasy with the film medium, he returned to the stage and did the social *Teerada Samasya*. Essays on theatre published in 1976, and biography by Doddanegowda (1972).

FILMOGRAPHY: 1936: ***Draupadi Manasamrakshanam***; **1939**: ***Raitu Bidda***; **1940**: ***Chandika***; **1955**: *Kanyashulkam*.

RAGHAVACHARYA, SAMUDRALA (1902-68)

Telugu director and scenarist born in Repalle taluk, AP. in a family of Sanskrit scholars. A popular versifier in the Avadhanam tradition in his teens. Participated in Gandhi's salt Satyagraha. Employed as a writer by **Ramabrahmam**'s theatre group, Bharatamuni Brundam, and stayed with the group for several years, jointly publishing the influential journal *Prajamitra* (1934) with them. Started as scenarist with **H.V. Babu**'s *Kanakatara* (1937). Employed by **H.M. Reddy** to script ***Grihalakshmi*** (1938). Scripted and wrote lyrics for several of **Vauhini**'s best-known films, e.g. ***Vande Mataram*** (1939), ***Sumangali*** (1940), ***Devatha*** (1941), ***Bhakta Potana*** (1942), ***Yogi Vemana*** (1947). Also wrote **P. Pullaiah**'s ***Bhagya Lakshmi*** (1943), **Nagaiah**'s Saint film classic, ***Thyagayya*** (1946), Ramabrahmam's *Panthulamma* (1943) and several films for **Vedantam Raghavaiah** (e.g. *Strisahasam*, 1951; *Shanti*, 1952; *Anarkali*, 1955; *Sarangadhara*, 1957; ***Suvarna Sundari***, 1957; *Swarnamanjari*, 1962). Also worked with directors like **B.S. Ranga**, **C.S. Rao** and **B.R. Panthulu**. Became a partner in Vinoda Studios (1950). His son, Samudrala Ramanujacharyulu, also became a noted screenwriter, often referred to as Samudrala Junior. Also directed some mythologicals.

FILMOGRAPHY: 1957: *Vinayaka Chaviti*; **1960**: *Bhakta Raghunath*; **1964**: *Babruvahana*.

Raghavaiah, Kosaraju *see* **Kosaraju Raghavaiah Choudhury**

RAGHAVAIAH, VEDANTAM (1919-71)

Telugu director born in Kistna Dist., AP. Trained in classical Kuchipudi dance. Started as choreographer for **Ramabrahmam**'s ***Raitu Bidda*** (1939) and for several 40s and 50s Telugu films (***Vande Mataram***, 1939; ***Swargaseema***, 1945; ***Raksharekha***, 1949; ***Vipranarayana***, 1954), acting in some of them. Third film as director was ***Devadasu***, starring **A. Nageshwara Rao**, in an adaptation of Saratchandra Chatterjee's often-filmed novel, *Devdas*. The hit inaugurated the well-known Vinoda Pics Studio started by distributor G.K. Manga Rao. Subsequent films include Telugu versions of hits in other languages, e.g. **Jaswantlal**'s ***Anarkali*** (1953), *Bhale Ramudu* (adapted from ***Kismet***, 1943, and using **Ghantasala**'s music). These films opened up new directions for Telugu cinema displacing its dominant mythological genre. Made the **Anjali Devi** hit ***Suvarna Sundari***, but its big-budget sequel *Swarnamanjari* failed.

FILMOGRAPHY (* act only): **1943**: ***Garuda Garvabhangam****; **1945**: ***Swargaseema****; **1949**: ***Raksharekha****; **1951**: *Strisahasam*; **1952**: *Shanti*; **1953**: ***Devadasu***; **1954**: ***Vipranarayana****; *Annadata*; **1955**: *Anarkali*; **1956**: *Bhale Ramudu/Prema Pasham*; *Chiranjeevulu*; **1957**: ***Suvarna Sundari/Manalane Mangayin Bhagyam***; *Bhale Ammayilu/Iru Sahodarargal*; **1958**: *Raja Nandini*; *Intiguttu*; **1959**: *Balanagamma*; *Jai Bhawani*; **1960**: *Adutha Veetu Penn*; *Runanubandham*; *Mamaku Tagga Alludu*; **1962**: *Swarnamanjari/Mangayir Ullam Mangada Selvam*; **1965**: *Nanna Kartavya*; *Sati*

Sakkubai; *Aadabrathuku*; **1967**: *Rahasyam*; *Sati Sumati*; **1968**: *Kumkumabharina*; **1969**: *Saptaswarulu*; *Ulagam Ivvalavuthan*; **1970**: *Bhale Ethu Chivaraku Chittu*.

RAGHAVENDRA RAO, K.

Successful mainstream Telugu director, son of **K.S. Prakash Rao**. Makes action fantasies and romances; broke through in the 80s. Announced his intentions with the **NTR** and **Sridevi** cop movie ***Vetagadu***. Known mainly for his megahit *Himmatwala*, marking Sridevi's transition into the Hindi cinema opposite **Jeetendra**. He repeated both stars in several heavily melodramatic romance movies (*Tohfa*; *Dharam Adhikari* with **Dilip Kumar**), usually adapting into Hindi the plots of established Telugu hits. The father-and-son double role in *Justice Choudhury* was played by **Nageshwara Rao** in the Telugu and Jeetendra in Hindi version. Made the extremely succesful **Chiranjeevi** and Sridevi film *Jagadeka Veerudu Attilokasundari* (which was a hit even in dubbed Hindi version), and NTR's comeback movie as the florid Telugu nationalist *Major Chandrakant*.

FILMOGRAPHY: 1975: *Babu*; **1976**: *Jyoti*; *Raja*; **1977**: *Amara Deepam*; *Ame Katha*; *Adavi Ramudu*; *Kalpana*; *Premalekhalu*; **1978**: *Radha Krishna*; *Simha Baladu*; *KD No 1*; **1979**: *Driver Ramudu*; *Nindu Noorellu*; ***Vetagadu***; **1980**: *Gajadonga*; *Gharana Donga*; *Bhale Krishnudu*; *Nippulanti Nijam*; *Prema Kanuka*; *Ragile Jwala*; *Rowdy Ramudu Konte Krishnudu*; *Nishana*; **1981**: *Tiruguleni Manishi*; *Urinki Monagadu*; *Satyabhama*; *Satyam Shivam*; *Kondaveeti Simham*; **1982**: *Thirisoolam*; *Justice Choudhury*; *Devatha*; *Farz Aur Kanoon*; *Madhura Swapnam*; **1983**: *Himmatwala*; *Jaani Dost*; *Shakti*; *Adavi Simhalu*; *Yuddha Bhoomi*; **1984**: *Kaamyaab*; *Naya Kadam*; *Tohfa*; *Bobbili Brahmana*; *Iddaru Dongalu*; **1985**: *Hoshiyar*; *Masterji*; *Mera Saathi*; *Adavi Donga*; *Agni Parvatham*; *Pattabhishekham*; *Vajrayudham*; **1986**: *Dharam Adhikari*; *Suhagan*; *Chanakya Sapatham*; *Kondaveeti Raja*; *Ravana Brahma*; *Apoorva Sahodaralu*; **1987**: *Manchi Donga*; *Agni Putrudu*; *Bharatamlo Arjundu*; *Sahasa Samrat*; **1988**: *Dil Lagake Dekho*; *Akhani Poratam*; *Janaki Ramudu*; *Donga Ramudu*; **1989**: *Rudra Neta*; *Vontari Poratham*; *Agni*; **1990**: *Jagadeka Veerudu Attilokasundari*; *Alludugaru*; **1991**: *Rowdy Alludu*; *Coolie No 1*; **1992**: *Allari Mogadu*; *Sundara Kanda*; *Ashwamedham*; **1993**: *Allari Priyudu*; *Major Chandrakant*.

RAGHUNATH, T. R. (1912-90)

Tamil director born in Trivandrum, Kerala. Assisted **Raja Chandrasekhar** and **A. Narayanan** on *Gnanasoundari* (1935); sound recordist with Narayanan at Srinivasa Cinetone (e.g. *Tara Sasankam*, 1936). Directorial début: the 3-reeler *Kizhattu Mappillai*, followed by *Ramalinga Swamigal*, made in Calcutta. Third film ***Kannagi*** adapted a Tamil literary epic and was one of **Kannamba**'s best-known screen performances. **MGR** appeared, mainly in minor roles, in his 40s films: *Vedavathi*, *Thasippen*. Later made *Raja Desingu* with MGR, adapting Raja Chandrasekhar's 1936 version. Best-known work in the 60s with all-star adventure films packed with sword fights, songs and dances, e.g. *Kanavane Kan Kanda Daivam*. Later technical adviser at Karpagam Studios, Madras. Appointed President of the **Films Division**, Madras, by his former protégé, MGR.

FILMOGRAPHY: 1936: *Kizhattu Mappillai*; **1939**: *Ramalinga Swamigal*; **1941**: *Vedavathi*; **1942**: ***Kannagi***; *Thamizhariyum Perumal*; *Thasippen*; **1944**: ***Mahamaya***; *Prabhavati*; **1945**: *Ardhanari*; *Paranjoti*; **1946**: *Udayanan Vasavadattha*; **1951**: *Singari*; *Vanasundari*; **1952**: *Mappillai*; **1954**: *Vilayattu Bommai*; **1955**: *Kanavane Kan Kanda Daivam*; *Maheshwari*; *Rajkumari*; **1956**: *Marmaveeran*; **1957**: *Rani Lalithangi*; *Yar Paiyan*; *Allavudeenum Arputha Vilakkum/Allauddin Adbhuta Deepam/Alladdin Ka Chirag*; **1958**: *Kanniyin Sabatham*; *Mangalya Bhagyam*; *Piya Milan*; **1959**: *Vannakkili*; **1960**: *Anbukkor Anni*; *Raja Desingu*; **1961**: *Marudu Nattu Veeran*; *Naga Nandini*; **1962**: *Kavitha*; *Vikramadithan*; **1971**: *Lora Nee Evide*; **1972**: *Mappillai Azhaippu*; **1973**: *Angathattu*.

RAGHURAMAIAH, KALYANAM (1915-68)

Telugu singing star, born in Guntur, AP. Original name: Venkatasubbaiah. Developed a characteristic singing style combining it with whistling (later even whistling classical Carnatic tunes). Joined Telugu theatre aged 8, playing Raghurama in the mythological play *Bhakta Ramadas*. In 1928 he acted the female role of Shakuntala in front of **Rabindranath Tagore**, who called him Andhra Nataka Kokila. With his second film, *Kuchela*, became known for acting Krishna, later adding the role of Narada to his repertoire.

FILMOGRAPHY: 1933: ***Prithvi Putra***; **1935**: *Kuchela*; **1936**: *Lanka Dahanam*; **1937**: *Rukmini Kalyanam*; **1939**: *Pasupatastrama*; **1941**: *Apavadu*; ***Talliprema***; **1947**: *Gollabhama*; *Brahma Rathnam*; *Radhika*; **1948**: *Madalasa*; **1950**: *Maya Rambha*; **1951**: ***Agni Pareeksha***; *Chandravanka*; *Mayapilla*; **1952**: *Aadabrathuku*; **1953**: *Prapancham*; **1954**: *Sati Sakkubai*; **1955**: *Shri Krishna Tulabharam*; **1956**: *Bhakta Markandeya*; ***Chintamani***; *Nagula Chaviti*; **1958**: *Shri Ramanjaneya Yuddham*; *Shri Krishna Maya*; **1959**: *Bhakta Ambarish*; **1960**: *Devanthakudu*; **1961**: *Usha Parinayam*; *Nagarjuna*; *Rushyashrunga/Rishyashringar*; *Krishna Kuchela*; **1963**: *Valmiki*; *Somavara Vratham*; *Vishnu Maya*; **1966**: *Mohini Bhasmasura*.

RAI, HIMANSU (1892-1940)

Film producer and actor; founder and chief of **Bombay Talkies**. Born into a wealthy Bengali family with a private theatre. Law degree from the University of Calcutta and studied with **Rabindranath Tagore**. Trained as a lawyer in London in the early 20s where he also acted in the theatre and worked as a consultant for films with an Oriental theme. Acted in the London run of **Niranjan Pal**'s play *The Goddess*. With Pal's script adapted from Edwin Arnold's poem *The Light of Asia*, went into partnership with the major German producer Peter Ostermayer whose brother (**Franz Osten**) directed the film (***Prem Sanyas***) co-financed by the Delhi-based Great Eastern Film Corp. owned by Sir Moti Sagar and Prem Sagar. Rai played the lead: the Buddha. To overcome distribution problems in Britain, he screened the film for the Anglo-German Royal family at Windsor Castle. The film was fairly successful in Central Europe and launched Rai on a series of international co-productions on Orientalist themes. His next film, ***Shiraz***, was pre-sold to UFA and to British Instructional Films. ***Prapancha Pash*** was co-financed by UFA and Harry Bruce Woolfe in London and introduced **Devika Rani**, married to Rai in 1929. Osten directed all the Pal scripts as Orientalist exotica, claiming *Prem Sanyas* to be the 'first authentically Indian film'. British support for the films made it seem that Rai and Pal were working within the terms of the objectives of **Empire Films** as established at the 1926 Imperial Conference. Since the films

Himansu Rai (right) in *Prem Sanyas* (1925)

were pre-sold, Rai made no money from their success. His next production, ***Karma*** (1933), was in English, directed by J.L. Freer Hunt and wholly produced by Rai. Although critically acclaimed, it flopped. The introduction of sound and the Nazi's seizure of power in Germany persuaded Rai to abandon international co-productions and to concentrate on the domestic market. With Devika Rani, he set up Bombay Talkies (1934) relying on his European collaborators and on the support of wealthy financiers such as Sir Cowasji Jehangir and Sir Chunilal Mehta. After 3 years, Rai was able to pay dividends to his backers. His main artistic achievement is the story and production of ***Achhut Kanya*** (1936), starring Devika Rani as an Untouchable. The outbreak of WW2 meant that the German technicians and director were interned by the British, crippling the studio. Rai died in 1940. After his death, Devika Rani took over the studio.

FILMOGRAPHY: **1925**: ***Prem Sanyas***; **1928**: ***Shiraz***; **1929**: ***Prapancha Pash***; **1933**: ***Karma/Nagan Ki Ragini***.

RAJALAKSHMI, T. P. (?-1964)

Actress, producer and first Tamil woman director. Born in Salaimangalam near Thanjavur; married and separated when aged 7. Learnt dance and music, and made her stage début under the tutelage of the famous Sankaradas Swamigal, considered the father of the modern Tamil theatre. Film début in the first Tamil feature, **H.M. Reddy**'s ***Kalidas***, where she also sang a nationalist song in praise of Gandhi. Major star with **R. Prakash**'s *Anadhai Penn*. Became a novelist (*Kamalavalli* and *Vimala*), then a director adapting her first novel as *Miss Kamala*.
FILMOGRAPHY (* also d): **1931**: ***Kalidas***; **1935**: *Gul-e-Bakavali*; *Lalithangi*; *Poornachandra*; **1936**: *Bhakta Kuchela*; *Bhama Parinayam*; *Miss Kamala**; *Simantini*; **1937**: *Kausalya Parinayam*; **1938**: *Madurai Veeran**; ***Nandakumar***; *Anadhai Penn*; **1939**: *Bhakta Kumaran*; *Saguna Sarasa*; *Tamil Thayi*; **1943**: *Uthami*; **1945**: *Paranjoti*; **1947**: *Jeevajyoti*; **1950**: *Idhaya Geetham*.

RAJAMMA, M. V. (b. 1923)

Kannada, Tamil and Telugu actress born in Agandanahalli, TN. Associated mostly with **B.R. Panthulu**'s films, with whom she started her stage career at Chandrakala Natak Mandali. First film: the lead role in Simha's ***Samara Nauka***. Established her own production company, Vijaya Films, for *Radha Ramana* (1943), later merged into Panthulu's Padmini Pics. Her acting remains the most distinctive element of Panthulu's influential brand of melodrama, both in its reformist-realist aspect (***School Master***) and in its historical-spectacular avatar (***Kittur Chanamma***, ***Shri Krishnadevaraya***). Acted in **K. Subramanyam**'s films *Ananthasayanam*, *Bhaka Prahlada* and *Gokula Dasi* amd in the seminal **DMK Film *Velaikkari***. She was a star in 3 languages and made over 100 films.

FILMOGRAPHY: **1936**: ***Samsara Nauka***; **1938**: *Krishna Jarasandha*; *Yayati*; **1940**: *Uthama Puthran*; **1941**: ***Gumastavin Penn***; *Madanakamarajan*; **1942**: *Ananthasayanam*; *Bhakta Prahlada* (K); **1943**: *Radha Ramana*; **1945**: *Mayalokam*; *Ardhanari*; **1946**: *Vijayalakshmi*; **1947**: ***Yogi Vemana***; **1948**: *En Kanavar*; *Gnanasoundari*; *Gokula Dasi*; **1949**: *Kanakangi*; ***Laila Majnu***; ***Velaikkari***; **1950**: *Parijatham*; *Raja Vikrama*; **1952**: *Puiyal*; *Penn Manam*; *Thayi Ullam*; **1954**: *Iddaru Pellalu*; **1955**: ***Modalatedi***; *Shivasharane Nambiyakka*; **1956**: *Kudumba Vilakku*; *Kannin Manigal*; **1957**: ***Manalane Mangayin Bhagyam***; *Ratnagiri Rahasya/Tangamalai Rahasyam*; **1958**: ***School Master/Badi Panthulu***; *Suhaag*; **1959**: ***Abba! A Hudgi***; **1960**: *Makkala Rajya/Pillalu Techina Chalana Rajyam/Kuzhandaigal Kanda Kudiyarasu*; **1961**: ***Pavamanippu***; ***Thayilla Pillai***; ***Kittur Chanamma***; **1962**: *Galigopura/Gali Medalu*; *Thayi Karulu/Thayin Karunai*; **1963**: *Sati Shakthi*; **1964**: *Chinnada Gombe/Muradhan Muthu*; ***Karnan/Karna/Daanveer Karna***; **1965**: *Aadabrathuku*; **1966**: *Dudde Doddappa*; *Emme Thammanna*; **1968**: *Amma*; **1970**: *Thedi Vantha Mappillai*; ***Shri Krishnadevaraya***; **1971**: *Thayi Devaru*; *Malathi Madhava*; **1972**: *Ondu Hennina Kathe*; **1973**: *Bangarada Panjara*; **1974**: *Sampathige Saval*; **1975**: *Dari Tappida Maga*; **1976**: *Besuge*; *Vijayavani*.

Rajanikant *see* **Rajnikant**

RAJAN-NAGENDRA (RAJAN, b. 1933; NAGENDRA, b. 1935)

Composer duo mainly in Kannada cinema; dominated popular music since the early 50s (with **G.K. Venkatesh**). They are brothers, both born in Mysore, taught by their father, Rajappa, a classical musician who also worked in live orchestras for silent films. Rajan was trained as a violinist, Nagendra, who also sang, on jaltarang. Learned classical Carnatic music under Bidaram Krishnappa. They went to Madras and worked under Tamil film composer H.R. Padmanabha Sastry. Returned to Mysore to record with singer **P. Kalingrao** for AIR. Nagendra first sang in *Shri Srinivasa Kalyana* (1952) by **B. Vittalacharya**, who then gave them their first break as composers in *Chanchala Kumari*. The bulk of their music used traditional instruments and evoked diluted versions of Carnatic music. They claim their more recent work introduced sophisticated recording devices and instruments in Kannada, including stereophony in *Singaporenalli Raja Kulla*, recorded in Singapore. Important predecessors of a former assistant, **Ilaiyaraja**.

FILMOGRAPHY: **1953**: *Saubhagya Lakshmi*; *Chanchala Kumari*; **1954**: *Kanyadana*; *Rajalakshmi*; **1956**: *Muttaide Bhagya*; **1958**: *Mane Thumbida Hennu*; *Mangalya Yoga*; **1959**: *Manegebanda Mahalakshmi*; **1961**: *Nagarjuna*; **1962**: *Ratnamanjari*; **1964**: *Mangala Muhurta*; *Veera Sankalpa*; *Navajeevana*; *Annapurna*; **1965**: *Patala Mohini*; **1966**: *Endu Ninnavane*; *Mantralaya Mahatme*; *Shri Kannika Parameshwari Kathe*; **1967**: *Anuradha*; *Sati Sukanya*; *Devara Gedda Manava*; *Bangarada Hoovu*; **1968**: *Addadari*; *Pravasi Mandira*; **1969**: *Mayor Muthanna*; **1970**: *Kanneeru*; *Aparajithe*; *Mooru Muttugalu*; *Boregowda Bangaloruge Banda*; **1971**: *Ondekula Ondedaiva*; *Bethaala Gudda*; *Anugraha*; *Nyayave Devaru*; *Vishakanya*; *Darde Budedi*; **1972**: *Nari Munidare Mari*; *Kulla Agent 000*; *Bhale Huchcha*; *Dharmapatni*; *Pagetha Puge*; **1973**: *Premapasha*; *Beesida Bale*; *Swayamvara*; *Cowboy Kulla*; *Gandhadagudi*; **1974**: *Eradu Kanasu*; *Maha Thyaga*; *Professor Huchuraya*; *Shri Srinivasa Kalyana*; *Devara Gudi*; **1975**: *Kalla Kulla*; *Mantra Shakti*; *Beluvalada Madilalli*; *Pooja*; **1976**: *Mugiyada Kathe*; *Bayalu Dari*; *Vijayavani*; *Na Ninna Mareyalare*; *Mangalya Bhagya*; *Devara Duddu*; *Phoenix*; **1977**: *Bayasade Banda Bhagya*; *Bhagyavantharu*; *Pavanaganga*; *Girikanye*; *Thayiginte Devarilla*; *Kittu Puttu*; *Panthulamma*; **1978**: *Hombisilu*; *Anuragha Bandhana*; *Parasangada Gendethimma*; *Kiladi Jodi*; *Madhura Sangama*; *Singaporenalli Raja Kulla*; *Sommokadidhi Sokokadidhi*; **1979**: *Na Ninna Bidalare*; *Putani Agents 1-2-3*; *Preeti Madu Tamashe Nodu*; *Na Niruvude Ninagangi*; *Chandanada Gombe*; *Dangeyedda Makkalu*; *Nanobba Kalla*; *Maralu Sarapani*; *Intinti Ramayanam*; **1980**: *Point Parimala*; *Rama Parashurama*; *Kulla Kulli*; *Auto Raja*; *Rama Lakshmana*; *Biligiriya Bandalalli*; *Mankuthimma*; **1981**: *Galimathu*; *Kudi Balidare Swargasukha*; *Yava Hoovu Yara Mudigo*; *Premanu Bandha*; *Muniyana Madari*; *Chadurida Chitragalu*; *Jivakke Jiva*; *Prema Pallavi*; *Avala Hejje*; **1982**: *Archana*; *Parijata*; *Tony*; *Nanna Devaru*; *Chelisuva Modagalu*; *Bettale Seve*; *Nagalu Stambalata*; **1983**: *Onde Guri*; *Jaggu*; *Benkiya Bale*; *Prema Parva*; *Ibbani Karagitu*; *Gayatri Madhuve*; *Kotikokkadu*; *Lanke Bindelu*; *Moodu Mullu*; *Puli Bebbuli*; *Raju Rani Jackie*; **1984**: *Mareyade Mahalu*; *Premasakshi*; *Kalinga Sarpa*; *Mooru Janma*; *Yarivanu?*; *Rampurada Ravana*; *Premigala Saval*; *Onde Raktha*; *Preeti Vatsalya*; *Marali Goodige*; *Olavu Moodidaga*; **1985**: *Anuragabandham*; *Bidugadeya Bedi*; *Bettada Hoovu*; *Kadina Raja*; *Giri Bale*; *Sedina Hakki*; *Shabdagalu*; *Jeevana Chakra*; **1986**: *Usha*; *Prema Gange*; *Mrigalaya*; *Guri*; *Mathondu Charithre*; **1987**: *Karunamayi*; *Inspector Krantikumar*; *Apath Bandhava*; *Raga Leela*; **1988**: *Sambhavame Yuge Yuge*; *Nammoora Raja*; *Jana Nayaka*; *Suprabhata*; *Dharmatma* (K); **1989**: *Hridaya Geethe*; *Gagana*; *Doctor Krishna*; **1990**: *Chappala Channigaraya*; *Kempu Soorya*; *Shiva Shankar*; *Mathe Hadithu Kogile*; *Bare Nanna Muddina Rani*; *Ganeshana Maduve*; **1991**: *Gandanige Thakka Hendthi*; *Modada Mareyalli*; *Gauri Ganesha*; *Nagunagutha Nali*; *Jagadeka Veera*.

RAJARATHNAM, BEZAWADA (b. 1921)

Actress and singer in Telugu film. Born in Tenali, AP. Studied music under Tenali Saraswathi and Jonavittula Sheshgiri Rao. Started recording through Lanka Kameshwara Rao and became a known recording star, esp. for the number *Sabha gopala*, set to lyrics by actor-singer Kopparapu Subba Rao. Also known for her music in plays like *Rukmini Kalyanam* (in the role of Rukmini), *Pundarika* (as the courtesan), *Radha Krishna* (as Radha), the title role of *Meera*, etc. Film star after ***Malli Pelli***, with hit singles like *Eepoo podarinta* (from ***Vishwamohini***), *Rade cheli* (from ***Devatha***). Playback singer in the late 40s in, e.g., ***Bhakta Potana*** (1942) and *Mohini* (1948). After a major performance in **Balaramaiah**'s *Mugguru Maratilu*, then returned to film singing after a gap of 22 years with ***Jagadeka Veeruni Katha*** (1961).

FILMOGRAPHY: 1934: ***Seeta Kalyanam***; 1939: ***Malli Pelli***; 1940: ***Vishwamohini***; 1941: ***Devatha***; ***Dakshayagnam***; 1942: *Jeevana Mukti*; **1946**: *Mugguru Maratilu*; **1947**: ***Yogi Vemana***; *Shanbagavalli*.Raja Sandow *see* **Sandow, P. K. Raja**

RAJDUTT (b. 1932)

Aka Rajdutt Mayalu. Marathi director and actor born in Dhamangaon, Vardha District. Studied commerce, then worked as theatre reviewer and sub-editor of the Nagpur daily *Tarun Bharat*. Assistant of **Raja Paranjpe** for 12 years, acting in some of his films; later remade Paranjpe's *Pudhcha Paool*. Continued the tradition of Marathi prose melodrama, flavoured, after 1970, with notions of social relevance as promoted by the New Indian Cinema (e.g. *Shapit*, based on a novel by Marathi writer Arun Sadhu. The film was originally started by the noted experimental theatre director Arvind Deshpande, and completed by Rajdutt when he died). Regarded, with **Raja Thakur**, as part of the 'decent' middle-class 60s orthodoxy preceding the trend exemplified by **Dada Kondke** and the Mahesh Kothare-Lakshmikant Berde comedies (e.g. *Thartharaat*, 1989). Divorced from the literary and theatrical moorings of the Paranjpe and **Madgulkar** films, his work tends to present the exhaustion of established Marathi genres like the Saint film (*Devaki Nandan Gopala*) or his revisiting of the traditional genre of the urban-rural divide in the comedy *Mumbaicha Fauzdar*.

FILMOGRAPHY (* act only): **1960**: ***Jagachya Pathivar****; **1961**: *Suvasini**; **1966**: *Gurukilli**; **1967**: ***Madhuchandra***; **1968**: *Gharchi Rani*; **1969**: *Aparadh*; *Adhaar**; **1970**: *Dev Manoos*; *Dhakti Bahin*; **1971**: *Jhep*; **1973**: *Bholi Bhabdi*; *Varhadi Ani Vajantri*; **1975**: *Ya Sukhano Ya*; **1977**: *Devaki Nandan Gopala*; **1978**: *Chandra Hota Sakshila*; **1979**: *Ashta Vinayak*; **1980**: *Bhalu*; **1981**: *Are Sansar Sansar*; **1982**: *Aplech Daat Aplech Oth*; *Shapit*; **1983**: *Raghumaina*; *Sasu Varchad Javai*; **1984**: *Hech Mazha Maher*; *Mumbaicha Fauzdar*; **1985**: *Ardhangi*; **1986**: *Aaj Jhale Mukt Mi*; *Mazhe Ghar Mazha Sansar*; *Pudhcha Paool*; *Maphicha Sakshidar*; **1987**: *Anandi Anand*; *Sarja*; **1990**: *Phaansi Ka Phanda*.

RAJE, ARUNA (b. 1946)

Hindi director born in Pune. Graduated as editor from the **FTII** (1969). Early features co-d. with Vikas Desai, jointly signed Arunavikas. First solo feature, ***Rihaee***, was a commercial hit. Also makes ads, promotional films and tv serials (most recently, the documentary series *Shadi Ya ...* for the cable channel Zee-TV).

FILMOGRAPHY: **1976**: *Shaque*; **1980**: ***Gehrayee***; **1982**: *Sitam*; **1988**: ***Rihaee***; **1993**: *Shadi Ya ...* (TV).

RAJENDAR, THESINGU (b. 1955)

Successful Tamil director and star who claims to be the writer, composer, director, cameraman, lead star, publicist and distributor of all his films. Born in Mayavaram, Tanjore Dist. in a family of musicians; entered films as uncredited scenarist and lyricist of E.M. Ibrahim's *Oru Thalai Ragam* (1980). Director-critic K. Hariharan writes about his 6th successive hit, *En Thangai Kalyani*: 'Everything he does is against all reasonable and accepted methods of presentation. From the casting of himself as the hero, to the indiscriminate use of trolleys and cranes, from his bizarre, opulent sets to the cacophonic background scores, his cinema defies logic ... yet, almost the entire population of Tamil Nadu must have seen his films.' Hariharan suggests their strong counter-cultural thrust is due mainly to the overturning of the **DMK Film**'s conventions: women cause the problems in his films, his use of rhyming dialogue and puns contrasts with the DMK film's emphasis on rhetoric, and he eliminates all location shooting while using psychedelic lighting patterns. He publicly rebuffed megastar and chief minister **MGR** in a dispute over the distribution rights of *Uravai Katha Kili*, using the rival DMK platform. Introduced several young actors such as Amala and Anand Babu. Became a DMK supporter in 1984, but then started his own Party for the Resurgence of the Motherland, contesting and losing the state assembly elections to the star and future chief minister, **Jayalalitha** (1991).

FILMOGRAPHY: **1980**: *Vasantha Azhaippukkal*; **1981**: *Rail Payanangalil*; **1982**: *Ragam Thedum Pallavi*; *Nenjil Oru Ragam*; **1983**: *Uyir Ulla Varai Usha*; *Thangaikor Geetham*; **1984**: *Uravai Katha Kili*; *Prema Prema Prema*; **1986**: *Maithili Ennai Kathali*; **1987**: *Oru Thayin Sabhatham*; **1988**: *En Thangai Kalyani*; **1989**: *Samsara Sangeetham*; **1991**: *Shanti Enathu Shanti*; **1992**: *Enga Veetu Velan*; **1993**: *Shabash Babu* (act only).

RAJENDRAN, LENIN (b. 1952)

Malayalam director born in Trivandrum, Kerala. Started as **P.A. Backer**'s assistant. Worked in several genres including love stories and the elaborately mounted period film ***Swathi Thirunal***. Best-known work tries to rewrite Kerala's political history informed by CPI(M) positions, e.g. on the 19th C. feudal history of Travancore and the agrarian reform struggles in the 40s (see ***Meenamasathile Sooryan***). Contested 1989 and 1991 General Elections as CPI(M)-sponsored independent candidate. Also made documentaries, e.g. *Uppukattu*, *Nervazhi* and *Badratha*. Employed in the Kerala State Film Development Corp.

FILMOGRAPHY: **1981**: *Venal*; **1982**: *Chillu*; **1983**: *Prem Nazirine Kanmanilla*; **1985**: ***Meenamasathile Sooryan***; **1987**: ***Swathi Thirunal***; **1988**: *Puravrutham*; **1989**: *Vachanam*; **1992**: *Daivathinte Vikrithikal*.

Rajendra Singh, S. V. *see* **Singh, S. V. Rajendra**
Rajeswara Rao, Saluri *see* **Rao, Saluri Rajeswara**

RAJKAMAL KALAMANDIR

Studio started by **V. Shantaram** in the former **Wadia Movietone** buildings in Bombay (1942). Début feature was ***Shakuntala*** (1943), and the fourth film here was ***Dr Kotnis Ki Amar Kahani*** (1946). With **Mehboob** and **Raj Kapoor**, he was one of the few to sustain a studio infrastructure into the post-WW2 and post-Independence era. Rajkamal's productions were directed by Shantaram and former colleagues like **Vinayak** (who made ***Jeevan Yatra***, 1946, here), **Keshavrao Date**, his brother cameraman V. Avadhoot and his son Kiran Shantaram. Overall they adhered to **Prabhat**'s generic formulas but departures include the virtual launch of the successful Marathi Tamasha genre with ***Lokshahir Ramjoshi*** (1947). The shift into the industrialised All-India Film, after *Jhanak Jhanak Payal Baaje* (1955) and especially with colour (*Navrang*, 1959), went with the decline of the popular into a lumpenised mass culture. Rajkamal is now mainly rented for tv serials and audio facilities.

RAJKUMAR (b. 1929)

Kannada superstar born in Gajanur, Karnataka; made over 200 films (25% of the industry) since the mid-50s. Child actor for **Veeranna** playing Arjuna in the stage spectacular *Kurukshetra* (1924). Broke through in **R. Nagendra Rao** and **Subbaiah Naidu**'s theatre company, playing Narada in *Bhukailasa* (repeating the role in K. Shankar's 1958 film version) and Ramakant in *Ambarish*. Film début in **H.L.N. Simha**'s Gubbi-Karnataka production based on **G.V. Iyer**'s play, ***Bedara Kannappa***, which established him as a mythological hero overcoming the severest tests of conscience to prove his devotion to his ideals. Formed a loose collective with G.V. Iyer, T.V. Singh Thakore, **Balkrishna**, Narasimhraju, etc., the Kannada Film Artists' Association, which produced one film, ***Ranadheera Kanteerava***. Although the group did not survive, it became the nucleus for a Kannada film industry. His image, mainly moulded by Iyer, was politicised into a quest for Karnataka's cultural glory. The bulk of his historicals (*Ranadheera Kanteerava*, *Immadi Pulakesi*) and mythologicals were geared to a populist, regional-chauvinist version of Karnataka's history in terms of a return to the Southern Kingdoms from the 7th C. Pallava period and to the 14th C. Vijayanagara Empire, focusing on Dravidian feudalism's resistance to the North Indian agrarian systems. In his films, Rajkumar often absents himself as he weaves through the bewilderingly complex narrative and kinship structures towards the final assertion of truth, unfailingly built around soliloquies expressing moral dilemmas redolent with political wish-fulfilment. Expanded the idiom from the early mythologicals into the contemporary with ***Bangarada Manushya***. His persona takes upon itself all the burdens which in Tamil **DMK Films** would be distributed across several figures. His effectiveness is illustrated by the way he modulates his performances from the historical to the mythological (*Shri Kannika Parameshwari Kathe*), from contemporary melodrama (*Karulina Kare*) to James Bond thrillers (*Goadalli CID 999* and his Dorairaj-Bhagavan films). Retired after making 200 films to become a producer promoting his sons, Shivraj Kumar (introduced as hero in **Singeetham Srinivasa Rao**'s *Ananda*, 1986) and Raghavendra Rajkumar. Shyamasundar Kulkarni published a monograph, *Dr Rajkumar* (1988), and **P. Lankesh** edited a special issue of *Lankesh Patrike*, 'Innuru Chitragala Raj'(July 1988), devoted to the star.

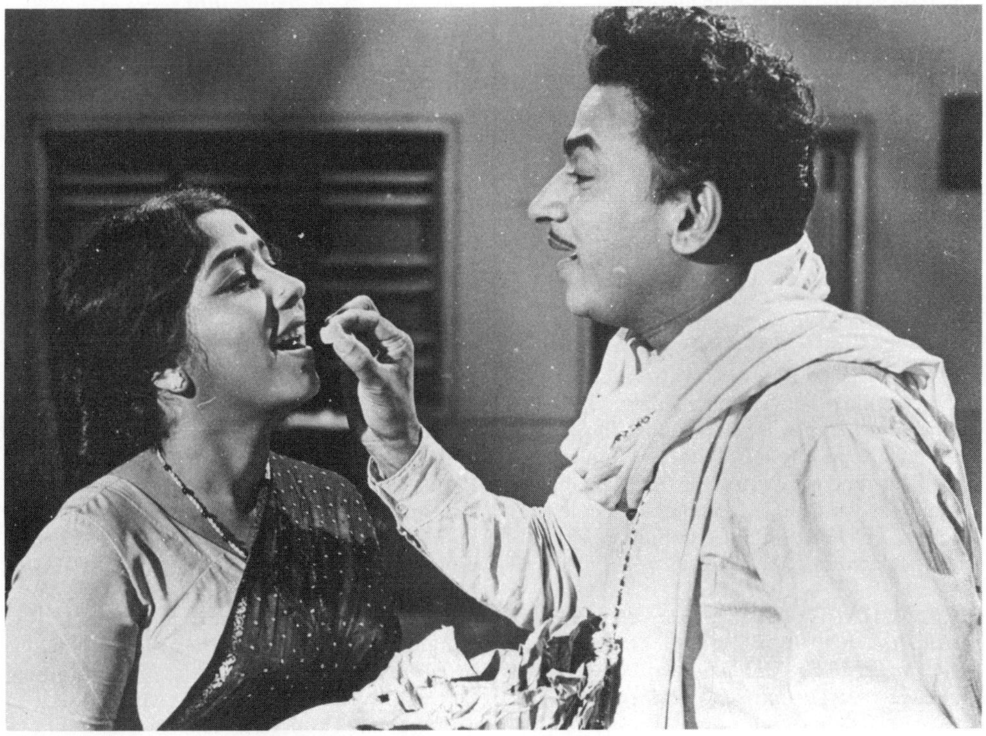

Jayanthi and Rajkumar in *Chakra Teertha* (1967)

FILMOGRAPHY: 1954: ***Bedara Kannappa***; **1955**: *Sodari*; **1956**: *Bhakta Vijaya*; *Hari Bhakta*; *Ohileshwara*; ***Tenali Raman***; **1957**: *Rayara Sose*; *Sati Nalayini*; **1958**: *Anna Thangi*; ***Bhukailasa***; *Shri Krishna Garudi*; **1959**: ***Abba! A Hudgi***; *Dharma Vijaya*; *Jagajyothi Basaveshwara*; ***Mahishasura Mardini***; **1960**: ***Ranadheera Kanteerava***; *Ashasundari*; *Bhakta Kanakadasa*; *Dashavtara*; *Rani Honamma*; **1961**: *Bhakta Cheta*; *Kaivara Mahatme*; *Kantheredu Nodu*; ***Kittur Chanamma***; *Nagarjuna*; *Shrishaila Mahatme*; **1962**: ***Bhoodana***; *Devasundari*; *Galigopura*; *Karuneye Kutumbada Kannu*; *Mahatma Kabir*; *Swarna Gauri*; *Tejaswini*; *Vidhi Vilasa*; **1963**: *Nanda Deepa*; *Saaku Magalu*; *Kanya Ratna*; *Gauri*; *Jeevana Taranga*; *Malli Madhuve*; *Kulavadhu*; *Kalitharu Henne*; ***Veera Kesari***; *Valmiki*; *Mana Mechhida Madadi*; *Chandrakumara*; *Sant Tukaram*; *Shri Ramanjaneya Yuddha*; *Sati Shakthi*; **1964**: *Navakoti Narayana*; *Chandavalliya Tota*; *Shivarathri Mahatme*; *Annapurna*; *Tumbidakoda*; *Shivagange Mahatme*; *Muriyada Mane*; *Pratigne*; ***Nandi***; **1965**: *Naga Pooja*; *Chandrahasa*; *Sarvagna Murthy*; *Vatsalya*; ***Satya Harishchandra***; *Mahasati Ansuya*; *Ide Mahasudina*; *Bettada Huli*; *Sati Savitri*; *Madhuve Madi Nodu*; *Pativrata*; **1966**: *Mantralaya Mahatme*; *Kathari Veera*; *Balanagamma*; *Thoogu Deepa*; *Prema Mayi*; *Kiladi Ranga*; *Madhu Malathi*; *Emme Thammanna*; *Mohini Bhasmasura* (K); *Shri Kannika Parameshwari Kathe*; *Sandhya Raga*; **1967**: *Parvathi Kalyana*; *Sati Sukanya*; *Gange Gauri*; *Rajashekhara*; *Lagna Patrike*; *Rajadurgada Rahasya*; *Devara Gedda Manava*; *Beedhi Basavanna*; *Manasiddare Marga*; *Bangarada Hoovu*; *Chakra Teertha*; *Immadi Pulakesi*; **1968**: *Jedara Bale*; *Gandhinagara*; *Mahasati Arundhati*; *Manasakshi*; *Sarvamangala*; *Bhagya Devathe*; *Bangalore Mail*; ***Hannele Chiguridaga***; *Bhagyada Bagilu*; *Natasarva Bhowma*; *Rowdy Ranganna*; *Dhumketu*; *Amma*; *Simha Swapna*; *Goadalli CID 999*; *Manninamaga*; **1969**: *Margadarshi*; *Gandondu Hennaru*; *Mallammana Pavada*; *Punarjanma*; *Bhale Raja*; ***Uyyale***; *Churi Chikanna*; *Mayor Muthanna*; *Operation Jackpot*; *Chikamma*; **1970**: ***Shri Krishnadevaraya***; *Karulina Kare*; *Nadina Bhagya*; *Hasiru Thorana*; *Bhoopathiranga*; *Mr Rajkumar*; *Bhale Jodi*; *CID Rajanna*; *Nanna Thamma*; *Balu Belagithu*; *Devara Makkalu*; *Paropakari*; **1971**: *Kasturi Nivasa*; *Bala Bandhana*; *Kulagaurava*; *Namma Samsara*; *Kasidre Kailasa*; *Thayi Devaru*; *Pratidhwani*; *Sakshatkara*; *Nyayave Devaru*; *Shri Krishna Rukmini Satyabhama*; *Sipayi Ramu*; **1972**: *Janma Rahasya*; ***Bangarada Manushya***; *Hridayasangama*; *Krantiveera*; *Bhale Huchcha*; *Nanda Gokula*; *Jaga Mechida Maga*; **1973**: *Devaru Kotta Thangi*; *Bidugade*; *Swayamvara*; *Doorada Betta*; *Gandhadagudi*; *Muruvare Vajragalu*; *Bangarada Panjara*; **1974**: *Eradu Kanasu*; *Sampathige Saval*; *Bhakta Kumbhara*; *Shri Srinivasa Kalyana*; **1975**: *Dari Tappida Maga*; *Mayura*; *Trimurthi*; **1976**: *Premada Kanike*; *Bahadur Gandu*; *Raja Nanna Raja*; *Na Ninna Mareyalare*; *Badavara Bandhu*; **1977**: *Babruvahana*; *Bhagyavantharu*; *Sanadhi Appanna*; *Holavu Gelavu*; *Girikanye*; **1978**: *Shankar Guru*; *Operation Diamond Rocket*; *Thayige Takka Maga*; **1979**: *Huliya Halina Mevu*; *Nanobba Kalla*; **1980**: *Ravichandra*; *Vasantha Geethe*; **1981**: *Havina Hedde*; *Nee Nanna Gellalare*; *Bhagyavantha*; *Keralida Simha*; **1982**: *Hosa Belaku*; *Halu Jenu*; *Chelisuva Modagalu*; **1983**: *Kavirathna Kalidasa*; *Kamana Billu*; *Bhakta Prahlada*; *Eradu Nakshatragalu*; **1984**: *Samayada Gombe*; *Shravana Bantu*; *Yarivanu?*; *Apoorva Sangama*; **1985**: *Ade Kannu*; *Jwalamukhi*; *Dhruva Tare*; *Bhagyada Lakshmi Baramma*; **1986**: *Anuragha Aralitu*; *Guri*; **1987**: *Ondu Muthina Kathe*; *Shruti Seridaga*; **1988**: *Shiva Mechida Kannappa*; *Devatha Manushya*; **1992**: *Jeevana Chitra*; **1993**: *Akasmika*.

RAJNIKANT (b. 1950)

80s-90s Tamil megastar; also worked in Hindi, Telugu and Kannada films. Born as Shivajirao Gaekwad in Bangalore, the son of a police constable; employed as a bus-conductor in the city before he joined the Madras Film Institute. Début in a brief role in **Puttanna Kanagal**'s ***Katha Sangama***, in the *Munithayi* episode; broke through in **K. Balachander**'s ***Apoorva Ragangal***. A fanatic film viewer since childhood, his unique acting style is characterised by a trade-mark gesture: flipping a cigarette in the air before he catches it with his mouth. Claims to 'explode like a tiger on screen'. First Hindi success: *Andha Kanoon*, trying to out-swagger **Bachchan** (they acted together again in *Giraftaar* and in ***Hum***). With make-up covering his dark skin, making it look slightly purple, heavy-lidded eyes affecting a 'macho' gaze and a manic, infantile energy, his acting can appear embarassing but is much appreciated by teenagers. A trade paper described him as prey to 'faulty diction, unconventional looks and flashy overacting'. The style, evoking a childish delight in film acting, is aptly mobilised in **Mani Rathnam**'s *Dalapathi*. Played the Hoskins role in *Raja Chinna Roja*, the Tamil version of Spielberg's *Who Framed Roger Rabbit?* (1988).

FILMOGRAPHY: 1975: ***Katha Sangama***; ***Apoorva Ragangal***; **1976**: *Moondru Mudichu*; *Katha*; **1977**: *Aadu Puli Atham*; *Aaru Pushpangal*; ***Avargal***; *Bhuvana Oru Kelvi Kuri*; *Gayatri*; *Kavikuyil*; *Raghupati Raghava Rajaram*; ***Pathinaru Vayathinile***; ***Chilakamma Cheppindi***; *Ame Katha*; *Sahodarara Saval*; *Kumkuma Rakshe*; *Galate Samsara*; *Tholireyi Gadichindi*; **1978**: *Ayiram Janmangal*; ***Aval Appadithan***; *Bhairavi*; *En Kelvikku Enna Bathil*; *Iraivan Kodutha Varam*; *Elamai Vunjaladugiradhu*; *Justice Gopinath*; *Mangudi Minor*; ***Mullum Malarum***; *Pavathin Sambalam*; *Chadurangam*; *Shankar Saleem Simon*; *Thayi Meethu Sathyam*; *Thappida Tala/Thappu Thalangal*; *Vanakathukuria Kathaliye*; *Priya*; *Anna Dammula Saval*; *Kiladi Kittu*; *Matu Tappada Maga*; **1979**: *Kuppathu Raja*; *Ninaithale Inikkum*; *Thayillamal Nannilai*; *Dharma Yuddham*; *Arulirundhu Arupadhu Varai*; *Amma Evarikaina Amma*; *Naan Vazhavippen*; *Annai Oru Alayam*; *Allavudeenum Albutha Velakkum/Allavudeenum Arputha Vilakkum*; *Tiger*; **1980**: *Billa*; *Anbukku Naan Adimai*; *Ram Robert Rahim*; *Naan Potta Saval*; *Kali*; *Johnny*; *Ellam En Kairasi*; *Polladhavan*; *Muharattu Kalai*; *Mayadari Krishnudu*; *Mr Rajnikant*; *Kurinchi Malar*(?); **1981**: *Thee*; *Thillu Mullu*; *Kazhugu*; *Netrikkan*; *Garjanai*; *Ranuva Veeran*; **1982**: *Pookkari Raja*; *Puthu Kavithai*; *Ranga*; *Thanikatu Raja*; *Engeyo Ketta Kural*; **1983**: *Payum Puli*; *Adutha Varisu*; *Sasthi Viratam*; *Sigappu Suryan*; *Thayi Veedu*; *Thanga Magan*; *Thudikkum Karangal*; *Uruvavugal Malaram*; *Moondru Mugam*; *Prema Pariksha*; *Andha Kanoon*; *Jeet Hamari*; **1984**: *Anbulla Rajanikant*; *Kayi Kodukkum Kayi*; *Naan Mahaan Alla*; *Nallavanukku Nallavan*; *Thambikku Entha Ooru*; *Tiger Rajani*; *Takkaridonga*; *Rowdycaku Saval*; *Nuvva Nena*; *Ithe Naa Saval*; *Meri Adalat*; *Gangvaa*; *John Jani Janardan*; *Aakhri Sangram*; *Zulm Ki Zanjeer*; **1985**: *Chithirame Chithirame*; *Padikkadhavan*; *Shri Raghavendrar*; *Naan Sigappu Manithan*; *Un Kannil Neer Vazhindal*; *Mahaguru*; *Wafadaar*; *Bewafai*; *Giraftaar*; *Aaj*

Ka Dada; *Mera Inteqam*; *Nyayam Meere Cheppali*; **1986**: *Naan Adimai Illai*; *Viduthalai*; *Maaveeran*; *Jeevana Poratam*; *Mr Bharat*; *Bhagwan Dada*; *Asli Naqli*; *Dosti Dushmani*; **1987**: *Velaikkaran*; *Insaaf Kaun Karega*; *Uttar Dakshin*; *Oor Kavalan*; *Manithan*; *Sattam Oru Vilayattu*; *Daku Hasina*; **1988**: *Guru Shishyan*; *Dharmathin Thalaivan*; *Kodiparakkuthu*; *Tamacha*; **1989**: *Rajadhi Raja*; *Shiva* (Ta); *Raja Chinna Roja*; *Mappillai*; *Bhrashtachar*; *Chaalbaaz*; *Gair Kanooni*; *En Purushanthan Enakkum Mattumthan*; **1990**: *Panakkaran*; *Dharmadurai*; **1991**: *Dalapathi*; *Mannan*; ***Hum***; *Phool Bane Angarey*; *Shanti Kranti*; *Nattukoru Nallavan*; *Farishte*; *Khoon Ka Karz*; **1992**: *Annamalai*; *Pandian*; *Tyaagi*; **1993**: *Yajaman*; *Uzhaippali*; *Valli*; *Insaniyat Ka Devata*.

RAJU, THOTAKURA VENKATA (1921-73)

Telugu-Tamil composer; also worked on Kannada films. Originally called T. Venkataraju. Born in Rajahmundhry taluk, AP. Learnt music in his native village from Nallan Chakravarthula Krishnamacharyulu. Stage actor in Madras under the name Master Venkataraju. Harmonium accompanyist for **Anjali Devi**'s dance performances. Assisted **Adi Narayana Rao** on *Palletoori Pilla* (1950). His first film was B.A. Subba Rao's *Tinguranga*. Also scored films by **Yoganand**, **Raghavaiah**, **K. Kameshwara Rao**, **NTR** and **K. Vishwanath**'s early 70s films.

FILMOGRAPHY: **1952**: *Tinguranga*; **1953**: *Pichhipullaiah*; **1954**: ***Todu Dongalu***; ***Nirupedalu***; **1955**: *Jayasimha*; *Aadabidda*; **1957**: *Panduranga Mahatyam*; **1958**: *Raja Nandini*; *Shri Krishna Maya*; **1959**: *Balanagamma*; **1961**: *Taxi Ramudu*; **1963**: *Savati Koduku*; **1965**: *Vishala Hridayalu*; *Simhachala Kshetram*; *Mangamma Sapatham*; **1966**: *Shri Krishna Pandaviyam*; *Bhimanjaneya Yuddham*; **1967**: *Ummadi Kutumbam*; ***Shri Krishnavataram***; *Chadurangam*; ***Bhama Vijayam/Bhale Kodalu***; *Nindu Manushulu*; *Kambojuraju Katha*; **1968**: *Tikka Shankaraiah*; *Baghdad Gajadonga*; *Devakanya*; *Kalisochina Adrushtam*; ***Varakatnam***; **1969**: *Tara Sasankam*; *Katha Nayakudu*; *Bhale Mastaru*; *Vichitra Kutumbam*; *Karpura Arathi*; *Bandhipotu Bhimanna*; *Gandikota Rahasyam*; *Saptaswarulu*; *Kadaladu Vadaladu*; *Bhale Tammudu*; ***Nindu Hridayalu***; **1970**: *Marina Manishi*; *Kodalu Diddina Kapuram*; *Talla Pellama*; **1971**: *Chinnanati Snehitulu*; *Nindu Dampatulu*; **1972**: *Raj Mahal*; *Shri Krishnanjaneya Yuddham*; *Rani Yar Kulandai?*; *Kanimuthu Papa*; **1973**: *Dhanama? Daivama?*; **1977**: *Ella Hanakkagi*.

RAMABRAHMAM, GUDAVALLI (1902-46)

Telugu director born in Nandamuru, AP. Educated at National College, Masulipatnam (1918). Early films were seminal influences on the political preoccupations of 40s Telugu film. Started in literature and theatre, influenced by the Telugu poet Vishwanath Satyanarayana. Theatre critic for nationalist journal *Swarajya*. Established his own theatre group, Bharatamuni Brundam, in Masulipatnam (1929), employing, e.g., **S. Raghavacharya** as a writer; then went into politics, first with the Justice Party and later Congress (1931). Editor of *Samadarshini* (1930) and helped start the Madras-based journal *Prajamitra* (1932). Publicity adviser to **Vel Pics**. Joined Saraswathi Cinetone as production manager and supervised **H.V. Babu**'s ***Draupadi Vastrapaharanam*** (1936). Early work at Sarathy Films (Est: 1936) includes ***Malapilla*** and ***Raitu Bidda***, directly alluding to topical politics. Both films show how Telugu folk performance idioms (cf Burrakatha) were adapted into film, combining their political usage by the Kisan Sabhas with Basavaraj Apparao's Bengali Baul-inspired music. The films also provided a start for **V. Raghavaiah**'s career as a choreographer. Films influenced by the politics of the Telugu reformists Kandakuri Veerashaligram (1848-1919) and Kaviraj Ramaswamy Choudhury, and by Gandhi's anti-Untouchability campaign. *Malapilla*, his best-known film, faced major opposition from the Andhra landed élite and is dedicated to the Maharaja of Travancore, who opened temples to people of all castes. His last, and most ambitious, film was completed by **L.V. Prasad**.

FILMOGRAPHY: **1938**: ***Malapilla***; **1939**: ***Raitu Bidda***; **1940**: *Illalu*; **1941**: *Apavadu*; **1942**: ***Patni***; **1943**: *Panthulamma*; **1945**: *Mayalokam*; **1947**: ***Palnati Yuddham***.

RAMACHANDRAN, MARUDUR GOPALAMENON (1917-87)

Aka MGR. Tamil megastar since 1950 and populist politician; one of the most controversial figures in Indian cinema. Born in Kandy, Sri Lanka (possibly in 1912). Legend has it that his birth coincided with his father's death, and the family moved to Tamil Nadu where they lived poorly. Three siblings died as well. Aged 6, joined a theatre group, the Madurai Original Boys, where he learned dancing, acting and swordplay. Screen début for **Ellis R. Duncan** (1936); first major starring role in **A.S.A. Sami**'s *Rajakumari* (1947). Joined the DMK Party (1953), having featured in the **Karunanidhi** scripted ***Manthiri Kumari***. Apparently modelled on Douglas Fairbanks, his 50s screen persona in adventure films directed by **T.R. Sundaram**, Ramanna, **Yoganand** and **P. Neelakantan** constructed an image of political as well as physical invincibility (vanquishing tigers with his bare hands in *Gul-e-Bakavali* and righting all wrongs) identified with 'the people' and promoting his political programme. In the 60s, esp. after *Thirudathe*, he turned to more 'realistic' fantasies in a contemporary setting, often playing a saintly member of an oppressed class: e.g. a peasant, fisherman, rickshaw-puller, gardener and taxi driver. Member of the DMK (1953-72), including a brief stint in the Madras Legislative Council (1962-4); member of the Legislative Assembly (1967) when the Party won the state elections. DMK Party Treasurer (1970); fell out with the DMK's boss, Karunanidhi, and used the **DMK Film**'s propaganda idiom against the DMK itself in ***Nam Naadu***. Set up the rival Anna-DMK (1972), claiming allegiance to the DMK's founder, **Annadurai**, who had died in 1969. In 1977, his party, renamed the All-India Anna Dravida Munnetra Kazhagam (AIADMK), won the state elections in alliance with Indira Gandhi's Congress; became chief minister and was re-elected for three consecutive terms, organising a totalitarian crackdown on all political dissent while introducing populist schemes like the Chief Minister's Nutritious Meal Programme and taxing the poor to subsidise the rural rich. Having survived a bullet wound when he was shot by fellow actor M.R. Radha in 1967 (affecting his speech), he achieved demi-god status following a paralytic stroke in 1984 which he survived for three years, acquiring the label 'thrice-born' in the process. Last film released in 1978. Thousands

MGR in *Nadodi Mannan* (1958)

of fan clubs provide a political and promotional support structure with a constant stream of, e.g., lithographs depicting the star as a godlike figure. **Ganesan**, who acted with MGR in *Kundukkili*, became an opposition MP. MGR developed a fantasy land via his movies, borrowing as much from stage historicals as from pamphleteering rhetoric. The economist M.S.S. Pandian's *The Image Trap: M.G. Ramachandran in Film and Politics* (1992) noted: 'The social universe of the MGR films is a universe of assymetrical power. [T]hus we have landlords who try to grab peasants' land (*Vivasayee*), rural rich who wield whips on farm hands (*Enga Veetu Pillai*), moneylenders who bleed the poor (*Padakottai*), industrialists who dismiss workers at their whim (*Thozhilali*), avaricious men who desire others' property (*Muharassi*, *Madappura*, *Ayirathil Oruvan*), city slickers who leave poor rural girls pregnant (*There Thiruvizha*), married men who desire other women (*Genova*, *Asai Mukham*, *Mahadevi*). The conflict between these upper caste/class oppressors and MGR as a subaltern, and its resolution, form the core of his films. MGR, in the course of the conflict, appropriates several signs or symbols of authority or power from those who dominate. Three such symbols that repeatedly and prominently appear are the authority to dispense justice and exercise violence, access to literacy/education and access to women. [T]he hero's invincibility on the screen acquires a certain authenticity and appears credible not merely because of the dreamlike experience of film-watching but equally because the subaltern consciousness most often dwells between the impossible religious myth and possible history.' To construct this impossible myth, MGR used food (***Mattukkara Velan***, *Ninaithathai Mudippavan*), colour patterns (black and red, symbols of the DMK), masquerades (often through double roles of oppressor and oppressed), etc. Viewing an MGR film has been promoted as a ritual, with stories of poor people selling their blood to get money to see his films on first release. His funeral procession was attended by over 2 million people. A temple has been built in Madras with MGR as the deity.

FILMOGRAPHY (* also d): **1936**: *Sati Leelavathi*; ***Iru Sahodarargal***; **1938**: *Dakshayagnam*; *Veer Jagdish*; **1939**: *Maya Machhindra*; *Prahlada*; **1941**: ***Ashok Kumar***; *Vedavathi*; **1942**: *Thasippen*; *Thamizhariyum Perumal*; **1943**: *Harishchandra*; **1944**: *Salivahanan*; **1945**: ***Meera***; **1946**: *Shri Murugan*; **1947**: *Paithiakaran*; *Rajakumari*; **1948**: *Abhimanyu*; *Mohini*; *Raja Mukthi*; **1949**: *Ratnakumar*; **1950**: *Maruthanattu Ilavarasi*; ***Manthiri Kumari***; **1951**: ***Marmayogi/Ek Tha Raja***; *Sarvadhikari*; **1952**: ***Andaman Kaithi***; *Kumari*; *En Thangai*; **1953**: *Genova*; *Naam*; *Panakkari*; **1954**: ***Malaikallan***; *Kundukkili*; **1955**: *Gul-e-Bakavali*; ***Alibabavum Narpathu Thirudargalum***; **1956**: ***Madurai Veeran***; *Thaikku Pinn Tharam*; **1957**: *Chakravarthi Thirumagal*; *Mahadevi*; *Pudumaipithan*; *Rajarajan*; **1958**: ***Nadodi Mannan****; **1959**: *Thayi Magalukku Kattiya Thali*; **1960**: *Baghdad Thirudan*; *Mannathai Mannan*; *Raja Desingu*; **1961**: *Arasilankumari*; *Nallavan Vazhvan*; *Shabhash Mappillai*; *Thayi Sollai Thattathe*; *Thirudathe*; **1962**: *Kudumba Thalaivan*; *Madappura*; *Pasam*; *Rani Samyuktha*; *Thayai Katha Thanayan*; *Vikramadithan*; **1963**: *Ananda Jyoti*; *Dharmam Thalai Kakum*; *Kalai Arasi*; *Kanchi Thalaivan*; *Koduthu Vaithaval*; *Needhikkupin Pasam*; *Panathottam*; *Parisu*; *Periya Idathu Penn*; *Raj Mahal*; **1964**: *Daivathai*; *En Kadamai*; *Padakottai*; *Panakara Kudumbam*; *Thayin Madiyil*; *Thozhilali*; *Vettaikaran*; **1965**: *Asai Mukham*; *Ayirathil Oruvan*; *Enga Veetu Pillai*; *Kalankari Vilakkam*; *Kannithai*; *Panam Padaithavan*; *Thazampoo*; **1966**: *Anbe Vaa*; *Naan Anaittal*; *Muharassi*; *Nadodi*; *Chandrodyam*; *Parakkum Pavai*; *Petral Than Pillayya*; *Thali Bhagyam*; *Thani Piravi*; **1967**: *Arasa Kattali*; *Kavalkaran*; ***Thaikku Thalaimagan***; *Vivasayee*; **1968**: *Rahasiya Police 115*; *There Thiruvizha*; *Kudiruntha Koil*; *Kannan En Kathalan*; ***Pudhiya Bhoomi***; ***Kanavan***; *Oli Vilakku*; *Kathal Vaghanam*; **1969**: *Adimai Penn*; ***Nam Naadu***; ***Mattukkara Velan***; **1970**: *En Annan*; *Thalaivan*; *Thedi Vantha Mappillai*; ***Engal Thangam***; **1971**: *Kumari Kottam*; *Rickshawkaran*; *Neerum Neruppum*; *Oru Thai Makkal*; **1972**: *Sangey Muzhangu*; *Nalla Neram*; *Raman Thediya Seethai*; *Annamitta Kai*; *Naan En Pirandein*; *Idaya Veenai*; **1973**: ***Ulagam Sudurum Valiban****; *Pattikatu Ponnaiah*; **1974**: *Netru Indru Nalai*; *Urimai Kural*; *Sirithu Vazha Vendum*; **1975**: *Ninaithathai Mudippavan*; *Nalai Namadhe*; *Idayakkani*; *Pallandhu Vazhga*; **1976**: *Needhikku Thalai Vanangu*; *Uzhaikum Karangal*; *Oorukku Uzhaippavan*; **1977**: *Navarathnam*; *Indru Pol Endrum Vazhga*; *Meenava Nanban*; *Maduraiyai Meeta Sundara Pandian**.

RAMAIYADAS, THANJAI (1914-69)

Popular 50s Tamil lyricist. Former schoolteacher in Thanjavur, resigned when his pro-Congress affiliations prevented him from working, and joined the theatre. Music teacher with the Sudarshana Gana Sabha; later started his own stage company, the Jayalakshmi Gana Sabha (e.g. *Macharekhai*). Film début in **T.R. Sundaram**'s *1000 Thalaivangi Apoorva Chintamani* (1947). Became known for his Tamil dialogues for the **Vijaya** Studio's hit ***Patala Bhairavi*** (1951); went on to write songs (and sometimes dialogue) for several Vijaya productions (e.g. the song *Varayo vennilave* for ***Missiamma***, 1955). Also wrote lyrics for R.M. Krishnaswamy's *Thooku Thooki* (1954) and acted in Jambulingam's ***Nam Naadu*** (1969).

Ramakrishna Rao, P. S. *see* **Rao, P. S. Ramakrishna**

RAMAN, MAHALINGAM VENKAT (b. 1913)

Tamil, Telugu and Hindi director born on Tiruchirapalli, TN. Graduated as an accountant but became cameraman, sound recorder and editor at Srinivas Studio in Madras (1936). Directorial début in 1945, breaking through with *Vazhkai* and his Hindi remake ***Bahar***. These films established the **AVM** Studio, and also introduced the future Hindi star **Vyjayanthimala**. Founded his own Raman Prod. in the 50s, making, e.g., the **Kishore Kumar** and Vijayanthimala hit, ***Aasha***, scored by **C. Ramchandra** and featuring **Asha Bhosle**'s hit song, *Ina mina dika*, a landmark in the introduction of Benny Goodman-style jazz into Indian music.

FILMOGRAPHY: 1945: *Parvati Kalyanam*; **1949**: *Vazhkai/Jeevitham*; **1951**: ***Bahar***; **1953**: *Penn/Ladki*; **1954**: *Pehli Jhalak*; *Sangham*; **1955**: *Chellapillai*; *Vadina*; **1956**: *Bhai Bhai*; **1957**: ***Aasha***; **1958**: *Chandan*; **1959**: *Athisaya Penn*; **1962**: *Konjum Salangai*; **1967**: *Pattanathil Bhootham*; **1968**: *Payal Ki Jhankaar*; **1970**: *Jwala*.

RAMA RAO, NANDAMURI TARAKA (b. 1923)

Aka NTR. Telugu megastar, producer, director and politician. Born into farming family in Gudivada Dist., AP. Studied in Vijaywada, where he started acting in and directing college plays, often playing female roles. Attracted attention for his role as Prince Salim in Muddu Krishna's *Anarkali*. Staged plays with **K. Jaggaiah** at the Andhra Christian College (e.g. *Chesina Papam*, 1946) and at the amateur National Art Theatre group, which he set up (1946). It was also an effective fund-raiser for drought and famine relief in AP in the early 50s. With ***Todu Dongalu*** (1954), it became N.A.T. Film run by Rama Rao's brother, Trivikrama Rao. Worked briefly as a clerk in the Registrar's office at Guntur (1947). Film début with **L.V. Prasad** (***Mana Desam***). First heroic lead in B.A. Subba Rao's *Palletoori Pilla*. Broke through with Prasad's ***Shavukaru*** and had a two-year contract with the **Vijaya** Studio (hits include ***Patala Bhairavi***, ***Malleeshwari*** and ***Pelli Chesi Choodu***), making him the top star of Telugu cinema along with **Akkineni Nageshwara Rao**. First mythological is Vijaya's ***Maya Bazaar***, playing Krishna, a role he played in 17 films (typically in those by **K. Kameshwara Rao**) and often invoked in his political career. His 'living god' persona took off with **P. Pullaiah**'s hit, ***Shri Venkateshwara Mahatyam***, playing the deity of the Tirupati temple. He cultivated this identification, even publicly receiving devotees from Tirumala in front of his Madras house. Often directed himself in mythologicals playing multiple roles, e.g. ***Daana Veera Shura Karna*** (triple role) and ***Shri Rama Pattabhisekham***. Started in melodrama (e.g. ***Palletooru***) and folk fantasies, later modulated, often via younger actresses like **Sridevi**, into vigilante characters facing a corrupt society, adapting, e.g., the **Prakash Mehra**-type movie into Telugu (***Yugandhar***, ***Vetagadu***, *Bobbili Puli*, etc.). Set up the populist regional Telugu Desam Party in 1982 which unseated Congress in AP for the first time since Independence. Chief minister of the state until 1989 when his party was defeated. His reign as chief minister has been extensively analysed by civil liberties activist K. Balagopal (1988), linking his films with his populist politics representing a Telugu regional bourgeoisie. Returned to film-making in 1990 to direct and act as *Brahmarishi Vishwamitra*, an unsuccessful campaign film for the 1991 General elections. Biography by S. Venkatnarayan (1983).

FILMOGRAPHY (* also d): **1949**: ***Mana Desam***; **1950**: *Palletoori Pilla*; ***Shavukaru***; ***Samsaram***; *Maya Rambha*; **1951**: ***Patala Bhairavi/Pataal Bhairavi***; ***Malleeshwari***; **1952**: ***Pelli Chesi Choodu/Kalyanam Panni Paar***; ***Palletooru***; ***Daasi***; **1953**: *Pichhipullaiah*; ***Chandirani***;

Ammalakulu/Marumagal; ***Chandraharam***; **1954**: ***Todu Dongalu***; *Aggiramudu*; *Vaddante Dabbu*; *Sangham*; *Rechukka*; *Raju Peda*; *Iddaru Pellalu*; *Parivarthana*; **1955**: ***Missamma***; *Jayasimha/Jaisingh*; *Santosham/Naya Admi*; *Vijayagauri*; *Cherupukura Chedevu*; *Kanyashulkam*; **1956**: ***Chintamani***; *Jayam Manade*; *Charanadasi*; *Umasundari*; *Chiranjeevulu*; *Shri Gauri Mahatyam*; *Sontavooru*; ***Tenali Ramakrishna/Tenali Raman***; *Penki Pellam*; **1957**: *Panduranga Mahatyam*; ***Bhagya Rekha***; *Sarangadhara*; *Bhale Ammayilu*; *Veera Kankanam*; *Kutumba Gauravam*; *Vinayaka Chaviti*; *Sati Ansuya*; *Sankalpam*; ***Maya Bazaar***; **1958**: *Anna Thamudu*; *Shobha*; ***Bhukailasa***; *Raja Nandini*; *Karthavarayan Katha*; *Manchi Manushuku Manchi Roju*; *Intiguttu*; *Sampoorna Ramayanam*; ***Appu Chesi Pappu Koodu***; **1959**: *Rechukka Pragatichukka*; *Vachina Kodulu Nachindi*; *Shabash Ramudu*; *Daivabalam*; *Bandaramudu*; *Balanagamma*; *Kalasivunte Kaladu Sukham*; *Raja Sevai*; ***Raja Mukutam***; **1960**: ***Shri Venkateshwara Mahatyam***; *Devanthakudu*; *Deepavali*; *Rani Ratnaprabha*; *Bhatti Vikramarka*; *Kadedullu Ekaram Nela*; *Vimala*; *Bhakta Raghunath*; **1961**: *Seeta Rama Kalyanam**; *Intiki Deepam Illale*; ***Jagadeka Veeruni Katha***; *Shanta*; *Taxi Ramudu*; *Pelli Pilupu*; *Sati Sulochana*; *Raktha Sambandham*; **1962**: *Gul-e-Bakavali Katha*; *Gali Medalu*; *Tiger Ramudu*; *Bhishma*; *Dakshayagnam*; ***Gundamma Katha***; ***Mahamantri Timmarasu***; *Swarnamanjari*; *Atmabandhuvu*; ***Shri Krishnarjuna Yuddham***; ***Siri Sampadalu***; **1963**: *Irugu Porugu*; *Pempudu Koothuru*; *Valmiki*; *Savati Koduku*; *Lavakusa*; *Paruvu Pratishthalu*; *Apta Mithrulu*; ***Bandhipotu***; *Lakshadhikari*; *Tirupathamma Katha*; *Nartanasala*; *Manchi Chedu*; *Somavara Vratham*; *Nadi Aada Janma*; **1964**: *Gudigantalu*; *Marmayogi*; *Kalavari Kodulu*; *Deshadrohulu*; *Ramudu Bheemudu*; *Satyanarayana Mahatyam*; *Aggipidugu*; *Dagudu Moothulu*; *Shabash Soori*; *Babruvahana*; ***Vivahabandham***; *Manchi Manishi*; *Varasatwam*; *Bobbili Yuddham*; ***Karna***; **1965**: ***Pandava Vanavasam***; *Dorikite Dongalu*; *Mangamma Sapatham*; ***Satya Harishchandra***; *Todu Needa*; *Prameelarjuneyam*; *Devatha*; *Veer Abhimanyu*; *Vishala Hridayalu*; ***CID***; *Aadabrathuku*; **1966**: *Shri Krishna Pandaviyam**; *Palnati Yuddham*; *Shakuntala*; *Srikakula Andhra Mahavishnu Katha*; *Paramanandayya Sishyulu Katha*; *Mangalsutram*; *Aggibarata*; *Sangeetalakshmi*; *Piduguramudu*; *Adugu Jadalu*; *Dr Anand*; *Shri Krishna Tulabharam*; *Ramu*; **1967**: *Gopaludu Bhoopaludu*; *Nirdoshi*; *Kanchukota*; *Bhuvana Sundari Katha*; *Ummadi Kutumbam*; ***Bhama Vijayam/Bhale Kodalu***; *Nindu Manushulu*; *Stree Janmam*; ***Shri Krishnavataram***; *Punyavati*; ***Aada Paduchu***; *Chikkadu Dorakudu*; *Pinni*; **1968**: *Umachandi Gauri Shankarula Katha*; *Niluvu Dopidi*; *Talliprema*; *Tikka Shankaraiah*; *Kalisochina Adrushtam*; *Ninne Pelladuta*; *Bhagya Chakram*; *Nene Monaganni*; *Baghdad Gajadonga*; *Nindu Samsaram*; ***Varakatnam****; **1969**: *Katha Nayakudu*; *Bhale Mastaru*; *Gandikota Rahasyam*; *Vichitra Kutumbam*; *Kadaladu Vadaladu*; ***Nindu Hridayalu***; *Bhale Tammudu*; *Aggiveerudu*; *Mathrudevata*; *Ekaveera*; **1970**: *Talla Pellamma**; *Lakshmi Kataksham*; *Alibaba 40 Dongalu*; *Pettandarulu*; *Vijayam Manade*; *Chitti Chellalu*; *Mayani Mamata*; *Marina Manishi*; *Kodalu Diddina Kapuram*; *Oke Kutumbam*; *Shri Krishna Vijayam*; *Kannan Varuvan*; **1971**: *Nindu Dampatulu*; *Jeevitha Chakram*; *Rajakota Rahasyam*; *Raitu Bidda*; *Adrushta Jathakudu*; *Pavitra Hridayalu*; *Chinnanati Snehitulu*; *Shri Krishna Satya*; *Kulagauravam*; **1972**: *Shri Krishnanjaneya Yuddham*; *Badi Panthulu*; *Shanti Nilayam*; **1973**: *Dabbuku Lokam Dasoham*; *Deshoddharakulu*; *Dhanama? Daivama?*; *Devudu Chesina Manushulu*; *Vaade Veedu*; *Errakota Veerudu*; *Palletoori Chinnodu*; **1974**: *Tatamma Kala**; *Ammayi Pelli*; *Manushulo Devadu*; *Nippulanti Manishi*; *Deeksha*; ***Shri Ramanjaneya Yuddham***; *Theerpu*; **1975**: *Katha Nayakuni Katha*; *Maya Machhindra* (Te); *Samsaram*; *Ramuni Minchina Ramudu*; *Anna Dammula Anubandham*; *Eduruleni Manishi*; *Vemulavada Bhimakavi*; **1976**: *Aradhana*; *Manushulanta Okkate*; *Magaadu*; *Neram Nadhikadu Akalidi*; *Bangaru Manishi*; *Maa Daivam*; *Manchiki Maro Peru*; **1977**: *Adavi Ramudu*; *Edureetha*; *Sati Savitri*; *Evaru Devudu*; *Maa Iddari Katha*; *Yama Gola*; *Chanakya Chandragupta**; ***Daana Veera Shura Karna****; **1978**: ***Akbar Saleem Anarkali****; ***Shri Rama Pattabhishekham****; *Melukolupu*; *Ramakrishnulu*; *Yuga Purushudu*; *Rajaputra Rahasyam*; *Simha Baladu*; *Sahasavanthudu*; *Lawyer Vishwanath*; *K.D. No. 1*; **1979**: *Shrimad Virata Parvam**; *Shri Tirupati Venkateshwara Kalyanam**; *Driver Ramudu*; *Maavari Manchithanam*; ***Vetagadu***; *Tiger*; *Shringara Ramudu*; ***Yugandhar***; **1980**: *Attagadu*; *Gajadonga*; *Challenge Ramudu*; *Circus Ramudu*; *Superman*; *Rowdy Ramudu Konte Krishnudu*; *Sardar Paparayudu*; *Sharada Ramudu*; *Subhodayam*; **1981**: *Prema Simhasanam*; *Tiruguleni Manishi*; *Satyam Shivam*; *Vishwa Roopam*; *Aggirava*; *Kondaveeti Simham*; *Maha Purushudu*; **1982**: *Kaliyuga Ramudu*; *Anuraga Devatha*; *Justice Choudhury*; *Bobbili Puli*; *Vayyari Bhamulu Vagalamari Bharthulu*; *Naa Desam*; **1983**: *Simham Navindi*; *Chanda Sasanudu**; **1984**: *Shrimad Virat Veerabrahmendra Swami Charitra**; **1991**: *Brahmarishi Vishwamitra**; **1992**: *Samrat Ashok**; **1993**: *Major Chandrakant*; *Shrinatha Kavi Sarvabhowma*.

RAMA RAO, TATINENI (b. 1938)

Telugu and Hindi director born in Kapileshwaram, AP. Assisted his cousin **T. Prakash Rao** and later **K. Pratyagatma** at Prasad Art Prod. Début remade the **Sivaji Ganesan** hit *Navarathri* (1964) into Telugu with **A. Nageshwara Rao**, and **Jayalalitha** in a small role. Became a major Telugu director with his crude variations upon **L.V. Prasad**-Pratyagatma's family drama theme, relying on dialogue, rapid cutting and spectacle. Introduced the genre into Hindi with his **Jeetendra** films. First Hindi feature *Lok Parlok* was a hit, and he repeated the formula with *Judaai* and *Maang Bharo Sajana*, along with violent **Bachchan** movies *Andha Kanoon* and *Inquilab*. A virtually uninterrupted run of success, establishing a distinct trend of the 'Madras movie' - replicating successful plots and cheaper shooting styles from South Indian films into Hindi - came to an end with the failure of the **Dharmendra** movie *Sachaai Ki Taaqat*, followed by *Pratikar*.

FILMOGRAPHY: 1966: *Navarathri*; **1968**: *Brahmachari*; *Challani Needa*; *Nadimantrapu Siri*; **1969**: *Manchi Mithrulu*; *Bhale Rangudu*; **1971**: *Suputhrudu*; *Bharya Biddalu*; *Raitu Kutumbam*; **1973**: *Jeevana Tarangulu*; *Marapurani Manishi*; **1974**: *Dora Babu*; *Devudu Chesina Pelli*; **1976**: *Raju Vedale*; **1977**: *Aalu Magalu*; *Athmiyudu*; *Yama Gola*; **1978**: *Amara Prema*; *Shri Rama Raksha*; **1979**: *Lok Parlok*; **1980**: *Judaai*; *Maang Bharo Sajana*; *Attagadu*; **1981**: *Ek Hi Bhool*; *Illalu*; **1982**: *Anuraga Devatha*; *Jeevan Dhara*; *Main Inteqam Loonga*; *Yeh To Kamaal Ho Gaya*; **1983**: *Andha Kanoon*; *Mugguru Monagallu*; *Mujhe Insaaf Chahiye*; **1984**: *Inquilab*; *John Jani Janardan*; *Yeh Desh*; **1985**: *Pachani Kapuram*; *Haqeeqat*; **1986**: *Dosti Dushmani*; *Naache Mayuri*; *Naseeb Apna Apna*; *Sada Suhagan*; **1987**: *Presidentgari Abbayi*; *Insaaf Ki Pukar*; *Sansar*; *Watan Ke Rakhwale*; **1988**: *Khatron Ke Khiladi*; *Nyayakini Siksha*; *Agni Keratalu*; **1989**: *Sachaai Ki Taaqat*; *Majboor*; *Laila*; **1990**: *Muqaddar Ka Badshah*; **1991**: *Pratikar*; *Talli Tandrulu*; **1992**: *Golmaal Govindan*; *Muqabala*.

RAMCHANDRA, NARHAR CHITALKAR (1918-82)

Composer born in Punatambe, Maharashtra. Best known as C. Ramchandra but also signed his name as Annasaheb (*Bahadur Pratap*, *Matwale*, *Madadgaar*), Ram Chitalkar (*Sukhi Jeevan*, *Badla*, *Mr Jhatpat*, *Bahadur*, *Dosti*), Shyamoo (*Yeh Hai Duniya*, *Begunah*). Often sang and acted in Marathi films under the name R.N. Chitalkar. Music student under Vinayakbua Patwardhan at Gandharva Mahavidyalaya music school. Joined films playing the lead in **Y.V. Rao**'s flop, *Naganand*. Then bit roles at **Minerva Movietone** (*Saeed-e-Havas*, *Atma Tarang*). Became harmonium accompanyist for Minerva composers Bundu Khan and Habib Khan. Début as music director in Tamil films with *Jayakkodi* and *Vanamohini*. Broke through as composer in **Master Bhagwan**'s *Sukhi Jeevan*, establishing a long-term association that culminated with the musical megahit ***Albela***. Influenced by Benny Goodman, he introduced, e.g., the alto sax in combination with guitar and harmonica, also whistling in one of his most famous songs, *Aana meri jaan Sunday ke Sunday* in ***Shehnai***. Used a bongo, oboe, trumpet, clarinet and sax combination for *Shola jo bhadke* in *Albela*. ***Shin Shinaki Boobla Boo*** featured him singing the title song with **Lata Mangeshkar** assimilating some rock rhythms. Introduced scat singing for *Ina mina dika* in ***Aasha***. Also used the traditional Qawali in ***Azad***. Worked on Telugu and Bhojpuri films. Briefly turned producer with New Sai Prod. in 1953 (*Jhanjhar*, *Lehren*, *Duniya Gol Hai*). To overcome a fallow period in the late 60s, he relaunched himself as music director, producer and actor in successful Marathi films: *Dhananjay*, *Gharkul*. Autobiography published in 1977.

FILMOGRAPHY (* also act/** act only): **1935**: *Naganand***; **1936**: *Saeed-e-Havas***; **1937**: *Atma Tarang***; **1939**: *Jayakkodi*; **1941**: *Vanamohini*; *Narad Naradi*; **1942**: *Hanso Hanso Ai Duniyawalon*; *Sukhi Jeevan*; **1943**: *Badla*; *Bhakta Raaj*; *Mr Jhatpat*; *Muskurahat*; *Zabaan*; **1944**: *Bahadur*; *Dil Ki Baat*; *Lalkaar*; *Lal Haveli* (with Mir Saheb); *Manorama*; *Raunaq*; **1945**: *Nagma-e-Sahra*; ***Samrat Chandragupta***; *Sawan*; **1946**: *Bachchon Ka Khel*; *Dosti*; *Safar*; **1947**: *Ahimsa*; *Bahadur Pratap*; *Leela*; *Madadgaar*; *Matwale*; *Saajan*; *Shadi Se Pehle* (with Pandit

Ramakant/**Karnad**); ***Shehnai***; *Chul Ani Mul**; **1948**: *Jalan*; *Khidki*; *Lalach*; *Matlabi*; *Mera Munna*; *Nadiya Ke Paar*; *Tumhari Kasam*; *Yeh Hai Duniya* (with Payami); **1949**: *Bachke Rehna*; *Bhedi Bungla*; *Bhole Bhale*; *Duniya*; ***Girls' School*** (with **Anil Biswas**); *Jigar*; *Namuna*; *Patanga*; *Roshni*; *Sanwaria*; *Sipahiya*; *Begunah* (with **Anil Biswas**); **1950**: *Babuji*; *Baksheesh*; *Nirala*; *Rupaiya*; ***Samadhi***; *Sangeeta*; ***Sangram***; *Sargam*; **1951**: ***Albela***; *Khazana*; *Sagaai*; *Shabistan*; *Saudagar* (with **Anil Biswas**); *Ustad Pedro*; *Nadaan* (uncredited); **1952**: ***Chhatrapati Shivaji***; *Ghunghroo*; *Hangama*; *Parchain*; ***Shin Shinaki Boobla Boo***; *Saqi*; *Rangili* (uncredited); *Zamindar*; **1953**: ***Anarkali*** (with Basant Prakash); *Jhamela*; *Jhanjhar*; *Ladki* (with Dhaniram/R. Sudarshan); *Lehren*; *Shagufa*; **1954**: *Kalakaar*; *Suhagan*; *Savdhan* (all 3 with **Vasant Desai**); *Kavi*; *Meenar*; *Nastik*; *Pehli Jhalak*; *Subah Ka Tara*; **1955**: ***Azad***; *Baap Re Baap* (with **O.P. Nayyar**); *Duniya Gol Hai*; ***Insaniyat***; *Lutera*; *Tirandaz*; *Yasmin*; **1956**: *Twenty-Sixth January*; *Devata*; *Shatranj*; **1957**: ***Aasha***; *Baarish*; *Naushermwan-e-Adil*; *Sharada*; *Talash*; **1958**: ***Raj Tilak***; *Amar Deep*; *Karigar*; *Talaaq*; **1959**: *Navrang*; ***Paigham***; **1960**: *Aanchal*; *Sarhad*; **1961**: *Amar Rahe Yeh Pyar*; *Stree*; **1963**: *Bahurani*; **1964**: *Sant Nivrutti Dnyandev*; *Daal Mein Kala*; *Veer Bhimsen*; **1965**: *Hum Diwane*; *Sher Dil*; *Zindagi Aur Maut*; **1966**: *Dhananjay**; *Labela*; *Tasveer*; *Mitwa*; **1967**: *Wahan Ke Log*; **1968**: *Balaram Shri Krishna*; *Dharmapatni**; *Payal Ki Jhankaar*; **1970**: *Rootha Na Karo*; *Gharkul*; **1971**: *Patondru Ketten*; *Tulasi Vivah*; **1973**: *Nijam Cheppithe Nammaru*; **1978**: ***Akbar Saleem Anarkali***; *Toofani Takkar*.

RAMNOTH, K. (1912-56)

Tamil director and cameraman born in Trivandrum. Key technician in pre-50s Tamil and Telugu film. Started as apprentice at Kodak (Madras) in 1930. Part of *Sound and Shadow*'s editorial team. First film as cameraman is **Prabhat**'s Tamil *Seeta Kalyanam* (1933), assisting cinematographer V. Avadhoot. Helped set up **Vel** Studio (1933) with **Murugadasa**, the co-director of his earliest films, and set designer A.K. Sekhar. Then joined the newly established **Vauhini** launched by **B.N. Reddi**, where became he key scenarist and cameraman. Scripted and shot Reddi's early films ***Vande Mataram*** (1939), ***Sumangali*** (1940) and ***Devatha*** (1941). Joined **Gemini** as production chief (1942-8). Believed to have worked closely with Uday Shankar on ***Kalpana*** (1948); shot the famed drum dance in ***Chandralekha*** (1948) inspired by *Kalpana*'s choreography. Apparently directed Gemini's *Mangamma Sapatham* (1943) credited to **Raghavacharya**, *Miss Malini* (1947) credited to Kothamangalam Subbu, and *Mohini* (1948) at Jupiter Studio credited to Lanka Sathyam. Best-known films as director are the epic melodrama ***Ezhai Padum Padu*** at the Pakshiraja Studio, based on Victor Hugo's *Les Misérables*, and the seminal **MGR** hit ***Marmayogi***, a key **DMK Film**. Founded the Cine Technicians Association in Madras (1943). Made one film in Hindi, *Rihaee*, unreleased.

FILMOGRAPHY: **1935**: *Markandeya*; **1936**: *Paduka Pattabhishekham*; **1949**: *Kanniyin Kathali*; **1950**: ***Ezhai Padum Padu/Beedala Patlu***; **1951**: ***Marmayogi/Ek Tha Raja***; **1952**: *Thayi Ullam*; **1953**: *Manithan*; **1954**: *Rihaee*; *Sugam Engay*; ***Viduthalai***; **1955**: *Kathanayaki*.

RAMSAY BROTHERS

Family of film-makers, until recently the only makers of horror films in India. After producing a Sindhi film, *Nakuli Shaan*, and **Vishram Bedekar**'s later, unremarkable genre films, ***Rustom Sohrab*** (1963) and *Ek Nannhi Munni Ladki Thi* (1970), the family hit gold with *Do Gaz Zameen Ke Neeche*, starting an extraordinary B film formula with minimal budgets, no stars and mixing conventional horror plots with mythological overtones and various other genres (e.g. adventure films, action thrillers and romances). Their films exude a sense of delight in cinema itself which, combined with the obsessive energies which animate the fantasy genre, lends a fascination to their work often missing from both commercial and 'quality' cinema. They have built up committed small-town and rural audiences. The family consists of father F.U. Ramsay (1917-1989), a radio manufacturer and producer, and his seven sons, of which Kumar, Shyam, Keshu, Tulsi and Gangu Ramsay are actively associated with film. Most of the films have been directed by Tulsi (b. 1944) and Shyam (b. 1952) as a team, both having been Bedekar's assistants. Keshu, who branched out as a solo director, does not make horror films. Kumar, the eldest, produced, e.g., Raj Sippy's *Kali Ganga* (1989). Kiran, the youngest, traditionally in charge of the crucial (for the genre) department of sound recording, débuted as director with *Shaitani Ilaaka*. The Tulsi/Shyam duo moved to tv with the best-selling late-night serial, the *Zee Horror Show*, on the Zee cable channel.

FILMOGRAPHY: **1971**: *Nakuli Shaan*; **1972**: *Do Gaz Zameen Ke Neeche*; **1975**: *Andhera*; **1978**: *Darwaza*; **1979**: ***Aur Kaun***; **1980**: *Saboot*; *Guest House*; **1981**: *Sannata*; *Dahshat*; *Hotel*; *Ghunghroo Ki Awaaz*; **1984**: *Purana Mandir* (Tulsi); **1985**: *Saamri*; *Haveli* (Keshu); *Telephone*; *Veerana*; **1986**: *Tahkhana*; **1987**: *Dak Bangla* (Keshu); **1988**: *Mera Shikar* (Keshu); **1989**: *Purani Haveli*; *Anokha Darr*; *Saaya* (Keshu); *Khoj* (Keshu); *Mahal* (Keshu); **1990**: *Shaitani Ilaaka* (Kiran); *Bandh Darwaza*; *Aakhri Cheekh*; **1991**: *Ajooba Kudrat Ka*; *Inspector Dhanush/Police Mattu Dada*; **1993**: *Mahakaal*; *The Zee Horror Show* (TV); *Ashant* (Keshu).

RANGA, B. S. (b. 1918)

Tamil, Telugu and Kannada director and cameraman born in Madras, TN. Started as assistant to Krishna Gopal (1937); then went to **Gemini** (1941) as cameraman and lab technician. Shortly after directing his first Tamil feature, *Bhakta Tulsidas* (which he remade a few years later), his first assignment as cinematographer was **Soundararajan**'s Tamil film, *Bhakta Nandanar* (1942). Often worked with the Bombay-based **Balkrishna Narayan Rao**. Broke through with the bilingual ***Tenali Ramakrishna/Tenali Raman***, following this with a trilingual. Set up the Vikram Studios in Madras and, later, the Vasanth Colour Laboratories in Bangalore, enabling him to make the first colour film in Kannada, the hit ***Amarashilpi Jakanachari***.

FILMOGRAPHY: **1940**: *Bhakta Tulsidas*; **1947**: *Bhakta Tulsidas*; **1954**: *Maa Gopi*; **1955**: *Jaya Gopi*; **1956**: ***Tenali Ramakrishna/Tenali Raman***; *Bhakta Markandeya*; **1957**: *Kutumba Gauravam*; **1959**: *Raja Malaya Simhan*; ***Mahishasura Mardini/Durga Mata***; **1960**: *Mohabbat Ki Jeet*; *Gunavathi*; **1961**: *Pelli Thambulam/Nishchaya Thambulam*; **1962**: *Ashajeevulu*; *Thendral Veesum*; **1963**: *Pyar Kiya To Darna Kya*; **1964**: ***Amarshilpi Jakanachari/Amarshilpi Jakanna***; *Pratigne*; **1965**: *Mahasati Ansuya*; *Chandrahasa*; **1967**: *Parvathi Kalyanam*; *Vasantsena*; **1969**: *Bhale Basava*; **1970**: *Mr Rajkumar*; **1971**: *Sidila Mari*; **1973**: *Mannina Magalu*; *Pattikatu Ponnaiah*; **1975**: *Ganga Ki Kasam*; **1978**: *Suli*; **1981**: *Bhagyavantha*; **1982**: *Hasyarathna Ramakrishna*; **1984**: *Huliyada Kala*.

RANGA RAO, SAMRLA VENKATA (1918-74)

Telugu actor born in Nuzivadu, AP. Educated in Madras, in Vishakapatnam and Kakinada. Played several Shakespearean characters in plays staged by the Kakinada Young Men's Happy Club. Was a fire inspector until he broke through in the role of Pravaraka in *Varudini*. After ***Shavukaru***, he regularly acted in **Vijaya** Studio productions, whose bilinguals introduced him to the Tamil film industry (***Patala Bhairavi***). Known for emotion-charged roles like Keechaka in *Nartanasala* and Koliah, the criminal who undergoes a spiritual transformation in ***Bangaru Papa***.

FILMOGRAPHY (* also d): **1946**: *Varudini*; **1949**: ***Mana Desam***; **1950**: *Palletoori Pilla*; *Thirugubatu*; ***Shavukaru***; **1951**: ***Patala Bhairavi/Pataal Bhairavi***; *Akasharaju*; **1952**: ***Pelli Chesi Choodu/Kalyanam Panni Paar***; ***Daasi***; ***Palletooru***; **1953**: *Bratuku Theruvu*; ***Chandirani***; ***Devadasu***; ***Poongothai/Pardesi***; *Rohini*; *Jataka Phala/Jatakapalam/Jatakam*; ***Pempudu Koduku***; ***Chandraharam***; **1954**: *Annadata*; ***Anta Manavalle***; *Raju Peda*; *Sangham*; *Raji En Kanmani/Raji Naa Pranam*; ***Bangaru Papa***; *Thuli Visham*; *Rajguru*; **1955**: *Anarkali*; *Jayasimha/Jaisingh*; ***Missamma/Missiamma***; ***Santhanam***; *Gunsundari*; ***Ardhangi/Pennin Perumai***; ***Donga Ramudu***; **1956**: *Harishchandra*; ***Chintamani***; *Kanakatara*; *Naan Petra Selvam*; *Mathurkula Manikyam/Charanadasi*; **1957**: *Saubhagyavati*; *Repu Neede*; *Sati Savitri*; *Pathni Daivam*; ***Maya Bazaar***; *Sarangadhara*; *Thodi Kodallu*; *Allavudeenum Arputha Vilakkum/Allauddin Adbhuta Deepam/Alladdin Ka Chirag*; **1958**: *Anbu Engay*; *Annaiyin Aanai*; *Shabash Meena*; *Thirumanam*; ***Bhukailasa***; *Bommalapelli/Bommai Kalyanam*; ***Chenchulakshmi***; *Pellinati Pramanulu*; ***Appu Chesi Pappu Koodu/Kadam Vangi Kalyanam***; **1959**: *Mangalya Balam/Manjal Magimai*; *Balanagamma*; *Bhakta Ambarish*; *Krishna Leelalu*; *Rechukka Pragatichukka*; *Jayabheri*; *Kalasivunte Kaladu Sukham*; *Maa Inti Mahalakshmi/Enga Veetu Mahalakshmi*; *Vazhkai Oppantham*; *Kalaivanan*; *Aval Yar*; *Raja Sevai*; **1960**: *Namminabantu/Pattayilin Vetri*; *Bhatti Vikramarka*; *Mamaku Tagga Alludu*; *Mahakavi Kalidasa*; *Deepavali*; *Devanthakudu*; *Irumputhirai*; *Padikkatha Methai*; ***Parthiban Kanavu***; *Petra Manam*;

Naan Kanda Sorgam; *Vidiveli*; **1961**: *Velugu Needulu/Thooya Ullam*; *Krishna Prema*; *Sati Sulochana*; *Usha Parinayam*; *Ellam Unnakkaga*; ***Kappalotiya Thamizhan***; *Pankalikal*; *Kumudam*; **1962**: *Pelli Thambulam/Nishchaya Thambulam*; *Tiger Ramudu*; *Gali Medalu*; *Padandi Munduku*; *Atmabandhuvu*; *Manchi Manushulu/Penn Manam*; ***Gundamma Katha****/Manidan Maravalli*; *Dakshayagnam*; *Kathirunda Kankal*; *Padithal Mattu Pothuma*; *Kavitha*; *Sharada*; *Muthu Mandapam*; *Annai/Penchina Prema*; *Daivathin Daivam*; **1963**: *Thobuttuvulu*; *Nartanasala*; ***Iruvar Ullam***; *Kalyanin Kanavan*; *Kumkumam*; *Needhikkupin Pasam*; *Annai Illam*; *Karpagam*; **1964**: *Ramudu Bheemudu*; ***Murali Krishna***; *Bobbili Yuddham*; *Kaikodutha Daivam*; *Pachai Vilakku*; **1965**: *Paditha Manaivi*; *Naanum Oru Penn/Nadi Aada Janma*; ***Pandava Vanavasam***; **1966**: *Atabommalu*; *Monagalluku Monagadu*; *Srikakula Andhra Mahavishnu Katha*; *Bhakta Potana*; *Mohini Bhasmasura*; ***Kumari Penn***; *Ramu*; **1967**: ***Thaikku Thalaimagan***; *Kan Kanda Daivam*; *Bhakta Prahlada*; *Maa Vadina*; *Chadurangam*; *Vasantsena*; *Rahasyam*; *Madi Veetu Mappillai*; *Punyavati*; ***Bhale Kodalu***; **1968**: *Bandhavyulu**; *Sukha Dukhalu*; *Chinnari Papalu*; *Lakshminivasam*; *Kumkumabharina*; *Veeranjaneya*; *Amayukudu*; **1969**: ***Nam Naadu***; *Mamaku Tagga Kodalu*; *Jagath Kiladilu*; *Bandhipotu Bhimanna*; **1970**: *Desamante Manasuloi*; *Iddaru Ammayilu*; *Shri Krishna Vijayam*; *Basti Kiladilu*; **1971**: *Kiladi Singanna*; *Vikramarka Vijayam*; *Rowdy Rangadu*; *Dasara Bullodu*; *Jagath Jentreelu*; *Bhale Papa*; *Debakku Thha Dongala Muttha*; *Shri Krishna Satya*; ***Vidyarthikale Ithile Ithile***; **1972**: *Mohammed-bin-Tughlaq*; *Bala Bharatam*; *Shri Krishnanjaneya Yuddham*; *Shanti Nilayam*; ***Tata Manuvudu***; *Kathula Rathaiah*; *Vamsodharakudu*; *Vazhai Yadi Vazhai*; *Vasantha Maligai*; *Sampoorna Ramayanam*; ***Pandanti Kapuram***; *Bava Diddina Kapuram*; *Papam Pasivadu*; *Vichitra Bandham*; *Kalam Marindi*; *Bangaru Babu*; *Koduku Kodalu*; **1973**: *Anbu Sahodarargal*; *Pillai Selvam*; *Devudu Chesina Manushulu*; *Marapurani Manishi*; *Samsaram Sagaram*; *Ramrajyam*; *Dabbuku Lokam Dasoham*; *Abhimanavanthulu*; *Dr Babu*; *Nija Roopalu*; *Palletoori Chinnodu*; *Ramude Devudu*; *Varasuralu*; **1974**: *Jeevithasayam*; *Sivakamyin Selvan*; *Premalu Pellilu*; *Jeevitha Rangamu*; *Gali Patalu*; *Andaru Dongale*; *Bangaru Kalalu*; *Inti Kodalu*; *Chakravakam* (Te); **1975**: *Bharati*; *Challani Talli*; *Mallela Manushulu*; *Yashoda Krishna*; *Kotha Kapuram*; **1976**: *Vadhu Varulu*.

RANI, BULO C. (B. 1920)

Composer and singer in Hindi films called Bulo Chandiram Ramchandani, born in Hyderabad (Sind), now Pakistan. Joined **Ranjit** Studio (1939) as assistant to **Khemchand Prakash**, making his début as a singer in Prakash's compositions for **Chaturbhuj Doshi**'s *Mehmaan* (1942) with the popular number *Rootha pyar mein*. Later assisted and sang for Gyan Dutt (***Shankar Parvati***, 1943). Composed a series of popular hits in the 40s, e.g. his second film *Murti* with *Badaria baras gayi* sung by Khursheed, Hamida Bano and Mukesh. Best-known and most successful film is **Kidar Sharma**'s ***Jogan***, where he set several Meera bhajans to new scores, esp. *Sundarata ke sabhi shikari* adapting Pandit Indra's lyric. Worked with Ranjit Studio throughout his career which lasted until the studio's closure. Last films were often stunt B movies directed by, e.g., Aakkoo. Occasionally participated in AIR programmes in the 70s.

FILMOGRAPHY: 1943: *Paigham* (with Gyan Dutt); ***Tansen*** (with **Khemchand Prakash**); **1944**: *Pagli Duniya*; *Caravan*; **1945**: *Chand Chakori*; *Murti*; *Prabhu Ka Ghar* (with **Khemchand Prakash**); *Preet*; **1946**: *Dharti*; *Magadhraj*; *Rajputani*; *Salgirah*; *Shravan Kumar*; **1947**: *Bela*; *Kaun Hamara*; *Lakhon Mein Ek* (with Hansraj Behl); *Pehli Pehchaan* (with Hansraj Behl); *Piya Ghar Aaja*; *Woh Zamana*; **1948**: *Anjuman*; *Bichhade Balam*; *Gunsundari* (with Hansraj Behl); *Jai Hanuman*; *Mitti Ke Khilone* (with Hansraj Behl); *Nanand Bhojai*; **1949**: *Bhool Bhulaiyan*; *Darogaji*; *Garibi*; *Narad Muni*; *Nazare*; **1950**: ***Jogan***; *Lavangi* (with C.S. Ram); *Magroor* (with Sajjad/Ram Punjwani); *Wafaa* (with Vinod); **1951**: *Pyar Ki Baatein* (with **Khayyam**); **1952**: *Baghdad*; *Izzat*; *Nirmal*; **1953**: *Gul Sanobar* (with **Sharmaji**); *Husn Ka Chor*; **1954**: *Aurat Teri Yahi Kahani*; *Bilwamangal*; **1955**: *Hasina*; *Madhur Milan*; *Shikar*; *Veer Rajputani*; **1956**: *Aabroo*; *Badshah Salamat*; *Noor-e-Yaman* (with **J.B.H. Wadia**); *Ram Navami*; **1957**: *Jahazi Lutera*; *Jeevan Saathi*; **1958**: *Al Hilal*; **1959**: *Tin Tin Tin*; **1960**: *Abdullah*; *Black Tiger*; *Pedro*; **1961**: *Anarbala*; *Room No. 17*; **1962**: *Jadu Mahal*; *Madam Zorro*; *Shri Ganesh*; **1963**: *Magic Box*; **1964**: *Haqdaar*; **1965**: *Chhupa Rustom*; *Shahi Lutera*; *Son of Hatimtai*; **1966**: *Jadu*; *Sunehre Kadam*.

RANI CHOUDHURY, DEVIKA (1907-94)

Star and later manager of **Bombay Talkies**, from where she dominated the first decade of the Indian sound film and set the standard for the post-1950 Hindi film heroine. Daughter of Col. Choudhury who later became surgeon-general of Madras. Grandniece of **Tagore**; studied at the Royal Academy of Dramatic Arts and at the Royal Academy of Music (London); degree in architecture and successful designer of Paisley textiles. Met **Himansu Rai** in London and married him in 1929. Her first film, produced by Rai and directed by **Osten**, was as costume designer (and probably as an extra) for ***Prapancha Pash*** (1929). In Germany, where the film was edited, Rani was able to see Fritz Lang, G.W. Pabst and Sternberg at work and assisted Marlene Deitrich on the set of *Der blaue Engel* (1930). Also worked briefly with Max Reinhardt. One of the early BBC broadcasts to India featured a Devika Rani recital (15 May 1933). When European co-production, especially with Germany, became difficult after 1933, the couple returned to India. Starred in Rai's first sound film, ***Karma***, made in English and sold as 'the first Indian talkie with English dialogue'. The couple started Bombay Talkies in Bombay (1934). In ***Achhut Kanya***, her arched eyebrows, beads and the vaguely Rajasthani-style, knee-length dress of the Untouchable, defined the 'village belle' for the Hindi cinema. She and **Ashok Kumar** remained the studio's stars until Rai died (1940) and she took over its management until she retired in 1945 and married the Russian émigré painter Svetoslav Roerich.

FILMOGRAPHY: 1933: ***Karma/Nagan Ki Ragini***; **1935**: ***Jawani Ki Hawa***; **1936**: ***Achhut Kanya***; ***Janmabhoomi***; ***Jeevan Naiya***; *Mamata*; *Miya Bibi*; **1937**: *Izzat*; ***Jeevan Prabhat***; *Prem Kahani*; ***Savitri***; **1938**: *Nirmala*; *Vachan*; **1939**: ***Durga***; **1941**: ***Anjaan***; **1943**: *Hamari Baat*.

RANJIT MOVIETONE

Aka Ranjit Film Company. Long-running Bombay studio set up in 1929 and active until the late 60s. Started by **Chandulal Shah** and his leading star **Gohar**, with financial support from Vithaldas Master and from the Jamnagar royalty which supplied subsidised facilities in and around Jamnagar city. Best known in early

Devika Rani in *Karma* (1933)

years for mid-budget socials, satires and stunt-derived mythologicals reworked into an allegory of the family drama (e.g. in **Raja Sandow** films). Their story department included Gunwantrai Acharya, scenarist-film-maker **Chaturbhuj Doshi** and playwright **Betaab**. They also drew on Dayaram Shah, the author of ***Gunsundari*** (1927, remade 1934 and 1948). The studio flourished in the early sound era with an assembly-line approach to production and was India's biggest producer until the 50s. Their early 30s films directed by **Jayant Desai**, by Shah himself, by **Nandlal Jaswantlal** and later by **A.R. Kardar** and **Kidar Sharma**, suggest the solid entrenchment of genres associated with the post-WW2 Hindi cinema, ranging from films around **Nirupa Roy**'s mythological mother figure to those with **Prithviraj Kapoor**, **Motilal** and **K.L. Saigal** (***Tansen***, 1943). Their subsidiary, Ajit Pics (1948), produced, e.g., **Ratibhai Punatar**'s regionalised Gujarati remakes of early Ranjit hits.

RAO, ADI NARAYANA (1915-91)

Telugu-Tamil music composer born in the Godavari Dist., AP. Studied music and dance as a child under Saluru Seetarama Sastry. Aged 13, joined the theatre group Jaganmohini Vilasa Sabha in Kakinada. Earliest compositions for plays like *Only Daughter*, *Classmates*, etc. Ran his own theatre group featuring **S.V. Ranga Rao** and introduced Telugu star **Anjali Devi** as a child actress. Started composing for films with B.V. Ramanandam's *Varudini* (1946) but his first fully realised assignment as music director and lyric writer was **C. Pullaiah**'s *Gollabhama*, which was also **Anjali Devi**'s screen début. They later married and set up Anjali Pixtures (Est: 1951). Wrote classic film scores, e.g. *Palletoori Pilla*, *Tilottama*, *Mayalamari*, ***Pardesi*** and *Anarkali*, sometimes revealing an unusual for AP influence of North Indian classical music. Was the regular composer for **Vedantam Raghavaiah** films. The musicologist V.A.K. Ranga Rao considered him to have introduced **C. Ramchandra**'s style into Telugu music.

FILMOGRAPHY: **1947**: *Gollabhama*; **1950**: *Palletoori Pilla*; **1951**: *Tilottama/Mayamalai*; *Mayalamari/Mayakkari*; **1953**: ***Poongothai/Pardesi***; **1954**: *Annadata*; **1955**: *Anarkali*; **1957**: ***Suvarna Sundari/Manalane Mangayin Bhagyam***; **1960**: *Runanubandham*; *Adutha Veetu Penn*; **1962**: *Swarnamanjari/Mangayir Ullam Mangada Selvam*; **1964**: *Phoolon Ki Sej*; **1965**: *Sati Sakkubai*; **1970**: *Amma Kosam*; *Agni Pareeksha*; **1971**: *Kalyana Mandapam*; **1972**: *Pedda Koduku*; **1973**: *Bhakta Tukaram*; **1974**: ***Alluri Seetaramaraju***; **1976**: *Mahakavi Kshetrayya*; **1978**: *Kannavari Illu*.

RAO, AKKINENI NAGESHWARA (b. 1924)

Telugu megastar with **NTR** since 1950s. Born in Venkatraghavapuram, Krishna Dist., AP. Child stage actor playing, e.g., the female lead in *Harishchandra* aged 12. Later played several female roles with Excelsior Dramatic Assoc. in Gudivada, establishing a substantial reputation. His second film, playing the male lead, Rama, in **Balaramaiah**'s *Seeta Rama Jananam*, launched his career in mythologicals, which required him to unlearn several of his (female) stage mannerisms. Top hero of 40s Telugu film fantasies, often playing folk heroes (e.g. *Balaraju*, ***Keeluguram***). Following the success of ***Laila Majnu***, was often paired with **Bhanumati** in Bharani Studio productions. Changed his persona with ***Samsaram*** followed by a series of melodramas, culminating in his highly successful rendition of Saratchandra's Devdas (***Devadasu***). Acted in several **Adurthi Subba Rao** films, and set up Annapurna Pics (1957) where Subba Rao and later **K. Vishwanath** made some of their art-house socials. The company diversified, e.g. into agriculture and insecticide manufacture, and became a full-scale film studio in 1976. Continued the melodramatic style into the films of **T. Rama Rao** and **Dasari Narayana Rao**, notably the latter's ***Megha Sandesam***. His son, Nagarjuna, became a major Telugu star in the 80s (e.g. *Shiva*, 1989). Biography by Krishnakumari (1984/1992).

FILMOGRAPHY: **1940**: ***Dharmapatni***; **1942**: *Seeta Rama Jananam*; **1945**: *Mayalokam*; **1947**: ***Palnati Yuddham***; ***Ratnamala***; **1948**: *Balaraju*; *Vindhyarani*; **1949**: ***Keeluguram/Maya Kudhirai***; ***Laila Majnu***; ***Raksharekha***; **1950**: *Palletoori Pilla*; *Shri Lakshmamma Katha*; ***Swapna Sundari***; ***Samsaram***; ***Paramanandayya Sishyulu Katha***; **1951**: *Mantradandam*; *Mayalamari/Mayakkari*; *Saudamini*; *Strisahasam*; *Tilottama/Mayamalai*; *Ore Iravu*; **1952**: ***Prema/Kathal***; **1953**: *Bratuku Theruvu*; ***Devadasu***; ***Kanna Talli/Petrathai***; ***Poongothai/Pardesi***; *Pratigna*; *Vayyari Bhama*; **1954**: ***Chakrapani***; *Annadata*; ***Nirupedalu***; *Parivarthana*; ***Vipranarayana***; **1955**: *Anarkali*; ***Ardhangi/Pennin Perumai***; ***Missamma/Missiamma***; ***Rojulu Marayi/Kalam Maripochu***; ***Santhanam***; *Vadina*; ***Donga Ramudu***; **1956**: ***Tenali Ramakrishna***; *Bhale Ramudu*; *Ilavelpu*; *Mathurkula Manikyam/Charanadasi*; **1957**: *Thodi Kodallu*; *Sati Savitri*; ***Maya Bazaar***; *Allavudeenum Arputha Vilakkum/Allauddin Adbhuta Deepam/Alladdin Ka Chirag*; ***Suvarna Sundari***; *Dongalo Dora*; **1958**: ***Bhukailasa***; ***Chenchulakshmi***; *Shri Krishnamaya*; *Aadapettanam*; *Pellinati Pramanulu*; **1959**: *Mangalya Balam/Manjal Magimai*; *Pelli Sandadi/Kalyana Penn*; *Athisaya Penn*; *Jayabheri*; ***Kalyana Parisu***; *Illarikam*; *Kalaivanan*; *Vazhkai Oppantham*; *Daivame Thunai*; *Naradhar Kalyanam*; *Kanniraindha Kanavan*; *Maa Inti Mahalakshmi/Enga Veetu Mahalakshmi*; **1960**: *Shantinivasam*; *Namminabantu/Pattayilin Vetri*; *Mahakavi Kalidasa*; *Pelli Kanuka*; *Engal Selvi*; *Abhimanam*; *Runanubandham*; *Maa Babu*; **1961**: *Velugu Needulu/Thooya Ullam*; *Anbu Magan*; *Bharya Bartulu*; *Bhakta Jayadeva*; *Batasari/Kanal Neer*; *Vagdanam*; *Shabash Raja*; *Iddaru Mithralu*; **1962**: ***Aradhana***; *Manchi Manushulu/Penn Manam*; ***Gundamma Katha****/Manidan Maravalli*; *Kalimilemulu*; ***Kulagothralu***; ***Siri Sampadalu***; ***Shri Krishnarjuna Yuddham***; **1963**: *Chaduvukonna Ammayilu*; ***Punarjanma***; ***Moogamanushulu***; **1964**: ***Poojapalam***; *Atmabalam*; ***Murali Krishna***; ***Amarashilpi Jakanna***; *Dr Chakravarthi*; **1965**: *Sumangali*; *Antastulu*; *Preminchi Choodu*; *Manushulu Mamathalu*; **1966**: *Zamindar*; *Atmagauravam*; *Navarathri*; *Manase Mandiram*; *Astiparulu*; **1967**: *Grihalakshmi*; ***Pranamithrulu***; *Vasantsena*; *Rahasyam*; *Poolarangudu*; *Sudigundalu*; **1968**: *Brahmachari*; *Manchi Kutumbam*; *Govula Gopanna*; *Bandhipotu Dongalu*; *Bangaru Gajulu*; **1969**: *Adrushtavanthalu*; *Mooganomu*; *Adarsha Kutumbam*; *Atmiyulu*; *Bhale Rangudu*; ***Buddhimanthudu***; *Sepoy Chinnaiah*; **1970**: *Akkachellelu*; *Jai Jawan*; ***Maro Prapancham***; *Dharmadatha*; *Manasu Mangalyam*; *Iddaru Ammayilu*; **1971**: *Dasara Bullodu*; *Pavitra Bandham*; *Rangeli Raja*; *Suputhrudu*; *Amayakuralu*; *Shrimanthudu*; *Prem Nagar*; *Bharya Biddalu*; *Raitu Kutumbam*; **1972**: *Beedala Patlu*; *Manchi Rojulu Vachai*; *Dattaputhrudu*; *Vichitra Bandham*; *Koduku Kodalu*; *Bangaru Babu*; **1973**: *Kanna Koduku*; *Bhakta Tukaram*; *Palletoori Bhava*; *Andala Ramudu*; *Marapurani Manishi*; *Manchi Vadu*; **1974**: *Premalu Pellilu*; *Bangaru Kalalu*; *Dora Babu*; **1976**: *Mahakavi Kshetrayya*; *Secretary*; *Mahatmudu*; **1977**: ***Chakradhari***; *Aalu Magalu*; *Bangaru Bommalu*; *Raja Ramesh*; *Chanakya Chandragupta*; *Athmiyudu*; **1978**: *Chilipi Krishnudu*; *Devadasu Malli Puttadu*; *Vichitra Jeevitham*; *Ramakrishnulu*; *Shri Rama Raksha*; **1979**: *Ravanude Ramudaithe*; *Hema Hemeelu*; *Muddula Koduku*; *Andaman Ammayi*; **1980**: *Edantastulameda*; *Nayakudu Vinayakudu*; *Buchi Babu*; *Pilla Zamindar*; *Prema Kanuka*; *Pratibimbalu*; *Sreevari Muchatlu*; *Premabhishekham*; *Manavude Mahaniyudu*; **1981**: *Guru Shishyulu*; *Satyam Shivam*; *Prema Mandiram*; *Prema Simhasanam*; **1982**: *Raga Deepam*; *Bangaru Kanuka*; *Gopala Krishnudu*; ***Megha Sandesam***; *Yuvaraju*; **1983**: *Muddula Mogadu*; *Urantha Sankranthi*; *Ramudu Kadu Krishnudu*; *Bahudoorapu Batasari*; *Amarajeevi*; *Shri Ranganeethulu*; *Koteeshwarudu*; **1984**: *Tandava Krishnudu*; *Anubandham*; *S.P. Bhayankar*; *Vasantha Geetam*; *Justice Chakravarthy*; *Sangeetha Samrat*; **1985**: *Bharya Bharthala Bandham*; *Dampatyam*; *Illale Devatha*; **1986**: *Aadi Dampathulu*; *Brahma Rudrulu*; *Captain Nagarjuna*; *Guru Brahma*; **1987**: *Collectorgari Abbayi*; *Agni Putrudu*; *Atma Bandhavulu*; **1988**: *Ravugarillu*; **1989**: *Rajakiya Chadurangam*; *Bhale Dampathulu*; *Sutradharulu*; *Adarshavanthudu*; **1990**: *Iddaru Iddare*; **1991**: *Ragulatunna Bharatamu*; *Seeta Ramaigari Manavarulu*; *Pranadata*; **1992**: *College Bullodu*; *Rajeshwari Kalyanam*; **1993**: *Radhasarathi*; *Mechanic Alludu*.

Rao, A. Subba *see* **Subba Rao, A.**

RAO, BALKRISHNA NARAYAN (b. 1909)

Tamil director and actor born in Tellicherry, Kerala. Also worked in Hindi and in Telugu. Started acting at **Imperial** (1926); assisted **R.S. Choudhury** and the cameramen Adi and Rustom Irani. Went to **East India Co.** (1933) and later to **Madan** in Calcutta, where he débuted as director with Hindi films. In 1937, moved to the Central Studios in Coimbatore; then to **Gemini** in Madras (1940) where he directed what is taken to be the studio's début feature, *Madanakamarajan*. Established himself as a successful director in the late 40s; then left to work for Shaws Malay Film Prod. (1953-6) making films starring P. Ramlee, and for Cathay Keris Film Studio (1957-64) in Singapore, directing e.g. Maria Menado, Nordin Ahmad and Latifah Omar. Returned to India for one more feature and retired in Madras.

FILMOGRAPHY: **1935**: *Veer Kumari*; *Keemti Qurbani*; **1938**: *Tukaram*; **1939**: *Rambayin Kadhal*; *Prahlada*; **1940**: *Bhuloka Rambha*; *Sati Murali*; **1941**: ***Gumastavin Penn***; *Madanakamarajan*; **1944**: *Daasi*; *Salivahanan*; **1947**: *Ekambavanan*; **1948**: *Bilhana*; **1949**: *Natya Rani*; **1953**: *Putus Harapan*; *Hujan Panas*; *Siapa Salah*; **1954**: *Gelora Hidup*; *Perjodohan*; *Merana*; **1955**: *Abu Hassan Pencuri*; *Roh Membela*; **1956**: *Adikku*; **1957**: *Pontianak*; *Dendam Pontianak*; **1958**: *Sumpah Pontianak*; *Mahsuri*; **1959**: *Jula Juli Bintang Tiga*; **1960**: *Yatim Mustafa*; **1961**: *Siti Zubaidah*; **1962**: *Laila Majnun*; **1963**: *Gul Bakawali*; *Putri Cempaka Biru*; **1964**: *Pontianak Gua Musang*; **1974**: *Nitya Sumangali*.

RAO, BHIMAVARAPU NARASIMHA (?-1957)

Composer in Telugu cinema. Regarded as the first composer in the current sense (previous ones were mostly conductors of orchestrations of popular stage and folk music). He used the independently composed lyrics of Basavaraju Appa Rao for ***Malapilla***, achieving an unprecedented success in Telugu film. Some of the songs (*Nallavade gollapilivade*, *Aa Mabbu eemabbu*) have remained popular hits. Also did music for **Ramabrahmam**'s ***Raitu Bidda*** and for **P. Pullaiah**'s 50s films.

FILMOGRAPHY (* also d): **1936**: *Sati Tulasi*; ***Draupadi Vastrapaharanam***; **1937**: ***Mohini Rugmangada***; *Kanakatara*; **1938**: ***Malapilla***; **1939**: ***Raitu Bidda***; **1940**: *Meerabai**; **1941**: *Apavadu*; **1943**: ***Bhagya Lakshmi***; **1946**: *Bhakta Tulsidas*; **1950**: *Thirugubatu*; **1955**: ***Ardhangi/Pennin Perumai***; *Kanyashulkam*; **1958**: *Dongalunnaru Jagratha/Thiudargal Jagrathi**.

RAO, BONGU NARASINGA (b. 1946)

Telugu director, writer, painter and musician born in Pragnapur, Medak Dist., AP. Arts graduate studies in Hyderabad. Photographer and theatre activist associated with cultural front of **Naxalite** peasant agitations in North Andhra in mid-70s. Produced **Gautam Ghosh**'s début ***Maabhoomi*** (1979), one of the first full-length fiction films in India made and shown in the Solanas-Getino sense of Third Cinema. First film was a fictionalised autobiography chronicling the politicisation of a young painter (played by himself) racked by moral doubt: ***Rangula Kala***. All his features and documentaries are contextualised by the radical political traditions of Andhra: e.g. ***Daasi*** is located within the oppressive feudal conditions opposed by the historic Telangana movement of 1946-51. Mostly scripts and composes the music for his films. Published four volumes of poetry and researcher in Andhra folk art and music.

FILMOGRAPHY: **1983**: ***Rangula Kala*** (also act); **1984**: *The Carnival* (Doc); **1985**: *The City* (Doc); **1987**: *Maa Ooru* (Doc); **1988**: ***Daasi*** (TV); **1990**: ***Matti Manushulu***.

RAO, CHITRAPU NARASIMHA (b. 1911)

Telugu director born in Masulipatnam, AP. Owner of a family printing press in Masulipatnam printing a.o. cheap calendar art and film publicity leaflets. Pioneer director of mythologicals codifying the genre at **Vel Pics**. Assisted **H.M. Reddy** on Telugu film's first talkie, ***Bhakta Pralhada*** (1931), and then **Baburao Pendharkar** in **Prabhat** Studio's only but influential foray into Tamil cinema, *Seeta Kalyanam* (1933), remaking it the following year in Telugu. His version was Vel's inaugural production. After working with Prabhat's technical units, he stressed the importance of sound technology, influencing Vel Studio's pioneering shift to sound production. Younger brother **Chitrapu Narayanamurthy** also became a film director.

FILMOGRAPHY: **1934**: ***Seeta Kalyanam***; 1935: ***Shri Krishna Leelalu***; **1936**: *Sati Tulasi*; **1937**: ***Mohini Rugmangada***; **1938**: *Jarasandha*; **1939**: ***Jayapradha***.

RAO, CHITTAJALU SRINIVASA (b. 1924)

Born in Kakinada, AP. Mainstream Telugu film-maker of sentimental dramas, mythologicals and contemporary socials. Also worked in Kannada. Son of **C. Pullaiah**, in whose children's films *Dhruva* and ***Ansuya*** (both 1936) he acted. Sponsored commercial Telugu theatre group Navagraha Kootam. Joined **Gemini** as assistant director (1946) and worked with **Pullaiah**, **Ramnoth**, A.K. Sekhar and on Uday Shankar's ***Kalpana*** (1948). A major figure in perpetuating the cultural orthodoxy of, e.g., **Vel Pics** and the early Gemini in combining values of entertainment with sentimental moralism, a trend continued by his assistants A. Sheshgiri Rao, Ramchandra Rao, etc. Married actress Rajasulochana, a consistent presence in his work since the late 50s.

FILMOGRAPHY: **1953**: *Ponni*; **1954**: *Pona Vachan Thirumbi Vandhan*; **1955**: *Shri Krishna Tulabharam*; **1958**: *Anna Thamudu*; *Manchi Manushuku Manchi Rojulu*; *Shri Krishna Maya*; **1959**: *Shabash Ramudu/Shabash Ramu*; *Naradhar Kalyanam*; **1960**: *Abhimanam*; *Shantinivasam*; **1961**: *Pellikani Pillalu*; **1962**: *Tiger Ramudu*; **1963**: *Lavakusa*; *Valmiki*; **1965**: *Keelu Bommalu*; *Prachanda Bhairavi*; *Pratignapalana*; **1967**: *Kanchukota/Pallava Sevangal*; **1968**: *Niluvu Dopidi*; *Govula Gopanna*; *Mana Samsaram*; *Bangaru Gajulu*; *Nindu Samsaram*; *Gramadevathulu*; **1969**: *Mamaku Tagga Kodalu*; *Ekaveera*; **1970**: *Desamante Manasuloi*; *Malli Pelli*; *Pettandarulu*; *Marina Manishi*; *Rendu Kutumbala Katha*; **1971**: *Rangeli Raja*; *Jeevitha Chakram*; *Bhagyavanthudu*; **1972**: *Shri Krishnanjaneya Yuddham*; **1973**: *Deshoddharakulu*; *Dhanama? Daivama?*; **1974**: *Bandhulu Anubandhulu*; *Anaganaga Oka Thandri*; *Adambaralu Anubandhalu*; **1975**: *Yashoda Krishna*; *Devudulanti Manishi*; **1976**: *Mahakavi Kshetrayya*; *Manchiki Maro Peru*; *Punardatta*; **1977**: *Shri Renukadevi Mahatme*; **1978**: *Allari Pillalu*; *Parasuraman*; **1982**: *Radhamma Mogadu*; **1983**: *Maro Maya Bazaar*; *Bhayankara Bhasmasura*; **1984**: *Satya Harishchandra/Raja Harishchandra*; **1985**: *Grihalakshmi*; **1988**: *Yogi Vemana*.

RAO, DASARI NARAYANA (b. 1947)

Telugu and Hindi director, writer and actor; born in Palakollu, AP. Started as a child actor on the stage. Graduated from Andhra University, then theatre director, playwright and actor. Went to Madras and joined the film industry as assistant to Bhavanarayana and **Padmarajan** in the 60s. Assisted scenarist Palagummi Padmaraju in Madras in late 60s; then became a successful freelance scenarist writing for, e.g., K. Raghava and Bhavnarayana. Directorial début in 1972. Best known for late 80s Hindi **Jeetendra** potboilers. Early films (e.g. ***Tata Manuvudu***) were notoriously sentimental weepies, later extended (*Devadasu Malli Puttadu*, *Premabhishekham*) into a ***Devdas***-like love-triangle formula. Made several classical music-based melodramas (***Megha Sandesam***). Comedies often feature himself (e.g. *Peddillu Chinnillu*) and are also presented as political satires; mid-budget quickies often star Krishnamraju and Mohan Babu. Filmed his autobiography in *Addala Meda* (1981), playing himself. One-time owner of the mainstream 3-edition Telugu newspaper, *Udayam* (1984). In 1988, directed Congress(I) supporter **G. Krishna** in *Praja Pratinidhi*, explicitly critiquing the political rule of **NTR**.

FILMOGRAPHY (* also act/** act only): **1972**: ***Tata Manuvudu***; **1973**: *Samsaram Sagaram*; **1974**: *Banthrotu Bharya*; *Radhamma Pelli*; *Tirapathi*; *Evariki Vare Yamuna Theere*; **1975**: *Balipeetam*; *Devude Digivaste*; *Bharatamlo Oka Ammayi*; *Swargam Narakam**; **1976**: *Yavanam Katesindi*; *Manushulanta Okkate*; *Muddabanthi Puvvu*; *Padavoyi Bharatheeyuda*; *Thoorpu Padamara*; *O Manishi Thirigi Chudu*; **1977**: ***Chilakamma Cheppindi****; *Kanya Kumari**; *Bangarakka*; *Idekaddi Nyayam*; *Chillarakottu Chittamma*; *Jeevithame Oka Natakam*; **1978**: *Sivaranjani*; *Katakatala Rudraiah*; *Swarg Narak*; *Devadasu Malli Puttadu*; **1979**: *Korikile Gurralaite*; *Ravanude Ramudaithe*; *Peddillu Chinnillu**; *Kalyani*; *Needa*; *Rangoon Rowdy*; *Gorintaku*; **1980**: *Natchatiram*; *Edantastulameda*; *Circus Ramudu*; *Buchi Babu*; *Seeta Ramulu*; *Ketugadu*; *Bandodu Gundamma*; *Sardar Paparayudu*; *Swapna*; *Premabhishekham*; *Deeparadhana*; *Paalu Neelu*; *Jyoti Bane Jwala*; *Yeh Kaisa Insaaf*; *Sreevari Muchatlu*; *Bhola Shankarudu**; **1981**: *Pyaasa Sawan*; *Prema Mandiram*; *Addala Meda*; *Vishwa Roopam*; *Adavallu Meeku Joharlu*; *Prema Simhasanam*; **1982**: *Yuvaraju*; *Jagannatha Rathachakralu*; *Krishnarajunulu*; *Bobbili Puli*; *Golkonda Abbulu*; *Swayamvaram*; *Jayasudha***; *Raga Deepam*; *Mehndi Rang Layegi*; *Sivamettina Satyam*; ***Megha Sandesam***; *O Adadi O Magadu*; **1983**: *Prem Tapasya*; *Bahudoorapu Batasari**; *MLA Yedukondalu**; *Urantha Sankranthi**; *Police Venkataswamy**; *Ramudu Kadu Krishnudu*; *Rudrakali*; **1984**: *Abhimanyudu*; *Justice Chakravarthy*; *Aaj Ka MLA Ramavatar*; *Asha Jyoti*; *Haisiyat*; *Yaadgaar*; *Zakhmi Sher*; *Police Papanna*; *Jagan*; *Yuddham*; **1985**: *Lanchavatharam**; *Pelli Meeku Akshintalu Naaku**; *Brahma Mudi*; *Thirugubatu*; *Edadugula Bandham*; *Sarfarosh*; *Wafadaar*; *Paari Poyina Kaidilu***; **1986**: *Aadi Dampathulu*; *Dharma Peetam Daddarillindi*; *Ugranarasimham*; *Tandra Paparayudu*; **1987**: *Majnu*; *Nene Raju Nene Manthri*; *Brahma Nayudu*; *Vishwanatha Nayakudu*; *Atma Bandhavulu**; *Rotation Chakravarthi***; **1988**: *Kanchana Seeta*; *Praja Pratinidhi*; *Brahma Puthrudu*; *Intinti Bhagavatham*; **1989**: *Naa Mogadu Nanke Sontham*; *Black Tiger*; *Lankeshwarudu*; *Two Town Rowdy*; **1990**: *Mama*

Alludu; **1991**: *Ramudu Kadu Rakshasudu*; *Mamagaru***; *Niyantha*; **1992**: *Ahankari*; *Venkanna Babu**; *Soori Gadu*; *Parvathalu Pangallu***; *Pellam Chattu Mogudu***; **1993**: *Santan*; *Mama Kodalu**; *Akka Peddadanam Chelleli Kapuram*.

Rao, Ghantasala Venkateshwara *see* **Ghantasala Venkateshwara Rao**

RAO, KAMALAKARA KAMESHWARA (b. 1911)

Telugu director born in Masulipatnam, AP. Former film critic, writing under pseudonym Cine Fan for journal *Krishna Patrika*. Scripted **H.M. Reddy**'s ***Grihalakshmi*** (1938) and assistant director to **B.N. Reddi** (***Devatha***, 1941) and **K.V. Reddy** (***Bhakta Potana***, 1942). Wrote scripts for **Vauhini** films, influencing their verbose reformist dramas. Director at the **Vijaya** Studio. Début film, ***Chandraharam***, designed as big-budget successor to **Vasan**'s ***Chandralekha*** (1948), defined Vijaya's 50s economic ambitions. Best known as maker of mythologicals (only four films in other genres) emphasising the heroic, often derived from folk legends. Responsible for introducing many of the genre's political references later used by his main star **NTR**.

FILMOGRAPHY: 1953: ***Chandraharam***; **1955**: *Gunsundari*; **1956**: *Penki Pellam*; **1957**: *Panduranga Mahatyam*; **1958**: *Shobha*; **1959**: *Rechukka Pragatichukka*; *Pachai Malai Kurathi*; *Raja Sevai*; **1960**: *Mahakavi Kalidasa*; **1962**: ***Mahamantri Timmarasu***; ***Gundamma Katha***/*Manidan Maravallai*; *Gul-e-Bakavali Katha*; **1963**: *Nartanasala*; **1965**: ***Pandava Vanavasam***; **1966**: *Shakuntala*; *Shri Krishna Tulabharam*; **1967**: ***Shri Krishnavataram***; *Kambojuraju Katha*; **1968**: *Veeranjaneya*; *Kalasina Manushulu*; **1969**: *Shri Seeta Rama Hanuman*; **1970**: *Shri Krishna Vijayam*; *Mayani Mamata*; **1972**: *Bala Bharatam*; **1974**: *Jeevithasayam*; **1977**: *Kurukshetramu*; *Seeta Rama Vanavasu*; **1979**: *Gnana Kuzhandhai*; **1980**: *Shri Vinayaka Vijayam*; *Shri Vasavi Kannika Parameshwari Mahatyam*; **1981**: *Daiva Thirumanangal*; **1982**: *Ekalavya*; **1983**: *Santoshi Mata Vratha Mahatyam*; **1985**: *Shri Datta Darshanam*; *Badarinatha Darshanam*; **1986**: *Devi Navagraha Nayaki*; *Ashtalakshmi Vaibhavamu*; **1991**: *Edu Kondalaswamy*.

Rao, Pendyala Nageshwara *see* **Pendyala Nageshwara Rao**

RAO, PINGALI NAGENDRA (1901-71)

Telugu scenarist-lyricist, born in Rajolu, AP. Educated and railway clerk in Bunder; also active in a trade union. Influenced as writer by the poet Tirupati Venkatakavi. Congress Party worker during freedom struggle and wrote several nationalist poems, e.g. *Janmabhoomi* (1940), which got him imprisoned by the British. Worked on Kauta Shrirama Sastry's journal, *Sharada*, while translating Hindi plays into Telugu. Following the success of his play *Vindhyarani* (filmed by **C. Pullaiah** in 1948), turned scenarist with *Bhale Pelli* (1941). Employed by **Vauhini** and **Vijaya** Studio where he scripted several **K.V. Reddy** films (***Gunsundari Katha***, 1949; ***Patala Bhairavi***, 1951; ***Maya Bazaar***, 1957, etc). Also wrote popular lyrics for classic **L.V. Prasad** films e.g. ***Pelli Chesi Choodu*** (1952), ***Missamma*** (1955). Considered a major stylist in his use of popular Telugu speech forms.

Rao, Prakash *see* **Prakash Rao, K. S.**
Rao, Raghavendra *see* **Raghavendra Rao, K.**

RAO, R. NAGENDRA (1896-1977)

Born in Holalkere, Karnataka. Kannada actor, singer, playwright and director. Worked in Kannada **Company Natak**, first with A.V. Varadacharya's Ratnavali Nataka Mandali and later with Mysore-based Chamundeshwari Company. Worked briefly in Bombay making Tamil and Telugu films at **Imperial**, then went back to the stage to start the Shri Sahitya Samrajya Nataka Mandali with **M.V. Subbaiah Naidu**, which had a major impact on Kannada cinema: its first talkie, **Y.V. Rao**'s ***Sati Sulochana***, was drawn from their stage repertoire and Nagendra Rao acted in and scored the film. His mythological play ***Bhukailasa***, a perennial hit on the Kannada stage, was filmed repeatedly, by **Sundarrao Nadkarni** (1938, 1940) and as a trilingual by K. Shankar (1958). His play *Yachhamanayika* also became a film hit. Joined **Gemini** (1947) as actor and director. Left to form his own company R.N.R. Prod. (1951-64). Then continued as character actor playing roles of the good but confused father facing moral dilemmas posed by unconventional offspring (*Shri Kannika Parameshwari Kathe*, *Karulina Kare*, etc.). Has three sons in the film business: the actor-singer R. Sudarshanam, the lyricist, director and actor R.N. Jayagopal, and cameraman R.N.K. Prasad. Published his autobiography as told to C. Sitharam, *Idu Nanna Kathe* (1974). Acted in films he directed.

FILMOGRAPHY (* also d): **1932**: *Ramadasu*; *Parijata Pushpaharanam*; **1933**: *Kovalan*; **1934**: ***Sati Sulochana*** (also music d); **1935**: *Naveena Sadarame*; **1940**: ***Bhukailasa***; **1941**: *Vasantsena*; **1943**: *Satya Harishchandra**; **1947**: *Mahatma Kabir**; **1949**: ***Apoorva Sahodarargal/Nishan***; **1950**: ***Apoorva Sahodaralu***; **1952**: *Moonru Pillaigal/Mooguru Kodukalu**; **1953**: ***Chandirani***; *Jataka Phala/Jatakapalam/Jatakam**; **1955**: *Santosham/Naya Admi*; **1956**: *Nagula Chaviti/Adarshasati*; *Renuka Mahatme*; *Bhakta Markandeya*; **1957**: *Bettada Kalla*; *Mahiravana*; *Premada Putri/Preme Daivam/Anbe Daivam**; **1959**: *Amudhavalli*; **1960**: ***Ranadheera Kanteerava***; **1961**: *Vijayanagarada Veeraputra**; **1962**: *Galigopura/Gali Medalu*; **1963**: ***Veera Kesari/Bandhipotu***; *Ananda Bashpa**; **1964**: *Pathiye Daiva**; **1965**: *Nanna Kartavya*; *Balarajana Kathe*; *Madhuve Madi Nodu*; **1966**: *Thoogu Deepa*; **1967**: *Shri Kannika Parameshwari Kathe*; *Premakku Permitte**; *Nakkare Ade Swarga*; *Shri Purandaradasaru*; *Janara Jana*; **1968**: ***Hannele Chiguridaga***; *Attegondukala Sosegondukala*; **1969**: *Kannu Muchale*; *Grihalakshmi*; *Namma Makkalu**; *Makkale Manege Manikya*; **1970**: *Nadina Bhagya**; ***Shri Krishnadevaraya***; *Lakshmi Saraswathi*; *Karulina Kare*; **1971**: *Aliya Geleya*; *Sakshatkara*; *Kulagaurava*; **1972**: *Kalavari Kutumbam*; *Na Mechida Huduga*; **1973**: *Mannina Magalu*; *Premapasha*; **1974**: *Professor Huchuraya*.

RAO, RAJANALA NAGESHWARA (1926-59)

Telugu actor, known mainly for villain roles in 50s films. Born in coastal AP. Graduate of the Aligarh Muslim University. Joined films as employee of distribution co. Premium Distr. Centre and later worked as manager of Paramount theatre, Secundrabad. Début with **P. Pullaiah**. Established reputation in B.A. Subba Rao's *Raju Peda* in the role of Vikram. Often acted alongside **A. Nageshwara Rao** in the 50s.

R. Nagendra Rao (centre) in his film *Premada Putri* (1957)

FILMOGRAPHY: **1952**: ***Sankranti***; **1953**: ***Kanna Talli***; *Paropakaram*; ***Devadasu***; **1954**: *Raju Peda*; *Aggiramudu*; *Rechukka*; **1955**: *Cherupukura Chedevu*; ***Donga Ramudu***; *Santosham/Naya Admi*; **1957**: ***Maya Bazaar***; *Sankalpam*; *Dongalo Dora*; *Vinayaka Chaviti*; **1958**: *Pellinati Pramanulu*; *Anna Thamudu*; *Raja Nandini*; *Mundadugu*; *Intiguttu*; *Shri Ramanjaneya Yuddham*; *Bhuloka Rambha*; ***Appu Chesi Pappu Koodu***; **1959**: *Shabash Ramudu*; **1960**: *Jagannathakam*; *Bhakta Shabari*; *Anna Chellalu*; *Pillalu Techina Chalana Rajyam*; ***Shri Venkateshwara Mahatyam***.

Rao, Rama *see* **Rama Rao, N. T.** *or* **Rama Rao, T.**

RAO, P. S. RAMAKRISHNA (1918-86)

Telugu and Tamil director and producer born in Kurnool, AP. Entered films as assistant editor at **Vel Pics** (1936); later worked with **H.V. Babu** at Star Combines. Married actress and director **Bhanumathi** (1943). They set up Bharani Pics to produce their own films, later expanding the enterprise into Bharani Studios (1952-7) where he produced her trilingual film ***Chandirani*** (1953). Co-directed her hit *Grihalakshmi* (1967) and is often assumed to have co-directed the films which he produced and she directed.

FILMOGRAPHY: **1947**: ***Ratnamala***; **1948**: *Bhakta Siriyala*; **1949**: ***Laila Majnu***; **1952**: ***Prema/Kathal***; **1953**: *Bratuku Theruvu*; **1954**: ***Chakrapani***; ***Vipranarayana***; **1956**: ***Chintamani***; **1957**: *Varudukavali/Manamagal Thevai*; **1961**: *Batasari/Kanal Neer*; *Shabash Raja*; **1962**: *Atma Bandhuvu*; **1963**: *Anubandhalu*; **1964**: ***Vivahabandham***; **1967**: *Grihalakshmi*; **1987**: *Gandhinagar Rendava Veedhi*.Rao, Ranga *see* **Ranga Rao, S. V.**

RAO, SALURI RAJESWARA (b. 1922)

Composer; son of Sanyasiraju, a music teacher at the maharaja's court in Vijayanagaram. Achieved some success as a child performer of the folk Harikatha at festivals and was recorded by a gramophone company. Introduced into Telugu films as child actor in **Vel Pics**' ***Shri Krishna Leelalu*** for his ability to sing and play harmonium and tabla. First composed music for ***Jayapradha*** and, according to music historian V.A.K. Ranga Rao, was the first Telugu composer to use a Western conception of orchestral harmony. His second film, **Ramabrahmam**'s *Illalu*, aimed for a sense of modernity, e.g. assimilating styles associated with **R.C. Boral** and **Timir Baran**. However the music was not a commercial success. Ranga Rao described their compositions for **R. Balasaraswathi**, released on disc in the 40s, as 'more sophisticated music [which didn't] find its way into films but established [h]ow the Telugu lyric could be coupled with Western craft'. This approach made a big impact, including the epochal ***Chandralekha***, helping the studio's aim to conquer the All-India film market. His major hit song: *Koyalokasarochi koosi poyindi* (in *Apavadu*), with Basavaraj Apparao's lyrics. Scored the music for **B.S. Ranga**'s Kannada and Telugu films in the 60s, and was associated with **Adurthi Subba Rao** and **K. Vishwanath**'s art-house musicals. His brother Saluri Hanumantha Rao is also a noted Telugu film composer. His son Koti also scored Telugu films in the late 80s.

FILMOGRAPHY (* also act/** act only): **1935**: ***Shri Krishna Leelalu*****; **1936**: *Maya Bazaar***; **1939**: ***Jayapradha****; **1940**: *Illalu**; **1941**: *Apavadu*; **1942**: ***Balanagamma***; *Jeevana Mukti*; **1943**: *Mangamma Sapatham*; **1944**: *Bhishma*; *Daasi*; **1945**: *Kannamma En Kadhali*; *Paduka Pattabhishekham*; **1948**: ***Chandralekha***; **1949**: ***Apoorva Sahodharargal/Nishan***; **1950**: *Vali Sugriva*; *Mangala*; **1951**: ***Malleeshwari***; **1952**: *Priyuralu*; ***Mr Sampat***; **1953**: *Vayyari Bhama*; *Bratuku Theruvu*; ***Pempudu Koduku***; **1954**: *Raju Peda*; ***Vipranarayana***; **1955**: ***Missamma/Missiamma***; **1956**: *Bhale Ramudu*; **1957**: *Allavudeenum Arputha Vilakkum/Allauddin Adbhuta Deepam/Alladdin Ka Chirag*; *Bhale Ammayilu/Iru Sahodarargal*; *Sati Savitri*; **1958**: ***Chenchulakshmi***; *Aadapettanam*; ***Appu Chesi Pappu Koodu/Kadam Vangi Kalyanam***; **1959**: *Rechukka Pragatichukka*; **1960**: *Rani Ratnaprabha*; **1961**: *Iddaru Mithralu*; *Bhakta Jayadeva*; **1962**: ***Kulagothralu***; ***Aradhana***; *Manchi Manushulu/Penn Manam*; **1963**: *Chaduvukonna Ammayilu*; **1964**: ***Amarashilpi Jakanachari/Amarashilpi Jakanna***; *Dr Chakravarthi*; *Bobbili Yuddham*; *Mahiravana*; ***Poojapalam***; **1965**: *Dorikite Dongalu*; ***Bangaru Panjaram***; **1966**: *Palnati Yuddham*; *Chilaka-Gorinka*; *Sangeetalakshmi*; *Bhakta Potana*; *Mohini Bhasmasura*; ***Rangula Ratnam***; **1967**: *Bhakta Prahlada*; *Raktha Sindooram*; *Poolarangudu*; *Vasantasena*; **1968**: *Veeranjaneya*; **1969**: *Mamaku Tagga Kodalu*; *Adarsha Kutumbam*; *Atmiyulu*; *Dharmapatni*; **1970**: *Desamante Manasuloi*; *Jai Jawan*; *Chitti Chellalu*; *Mr Rajkumar*; **1971**: *Amayukuralu*; *Bangaru Talli*; *Pavitra Bandham*; *Shri Venkateshwara Vaibhavam*; **1972**: *Bala Bharatam*; *Kalam Marindi*; *Neethi Nijayathi*; **1973**: *Deshoddharakulu*; *Mannina Magalu*; *Neramu Siksha*; *Nindu Kutumbam*; **1974**: *Ram Rahim*; *Jeevithasayam*; *Jeevitha Rangamu*; *Bangaru Kalalu*; *Tatamma Kala*; *Palle Paduchu*; *Nitya Sumangali*; **1975**: *Challani Talli*; *Anna Dammula Katha*; *Bharatamlo Oka Ammayi*; *Yashoda Krishna*; **1976**: *Manchiki Maro Peru*; *Manushulanta Okkate*; *Dashavataram*; **1977**: *Idekaddi Nyayam*; *Eenati Bandham Yenatido*; *Kurukshetramu*; **1978**: *Prema Paga*; *Devadasu Malli Puttadu*; *Lambadolla Ramadasu*; *Radha Krishna*; *Sneha Sedu*; **1980**: *Ondu Hennu Aaru Kannu*; *Manavude Mahaniyudu*; **1983**: *Muddula Mogadu*.

RAO, SINGEETHAM SRINIVASA

Successful Telugu director; born in Nellore Dist., AP. Worked extensively in Tamil, Kannada, Malayalam and Hindi. Studied physics in Madras. Amateur playwright and theatre director. Started as unpaid assistant to **K.V. Reddy** (1955-7). Early work in Telugu in **Pattabhi Rama Reddy** and K.V. Reddy's Jayanthi Pics. Best-known films, following ***Raja Parvai***, extend the work of Tamil megastar **Kamalahasan**: in ***Pushpak***, he plays an unemployed man dreaming of wealth. The film has no dialogue and opened up a new dimension in art-house entertainment, consolidated later by *Apoorva Sahodarargal* (released in a Hindi dubbed version as *Appu Raja*). Made most of his Kannada films with **Rajkumar** (notably *Halu Jenu*, *Eradu Nakshatragalu* and *Bhagyada Lakshmi Baramma*). Has a characteristic shooting style of rapid and rough-edged pans, extensive use of zoom lenses, and extremely brief shots that eliminate virtually everything except the plot from his films. Also composer for K.N. Chandrasekhar Sharma's *Samyukta* (1988). Biography by Satyamurthy Anandur (1988).

FILMOGRAPHY: **1972**: *Neethi Nijayathi*; **1973**: *Dikkatra Parvathi*; **1975**: *Zamindarugari Ammayi*; **1976**: *America Ammayi*; *Oka Deepam Veligindhi*; **1977**: *Niraparayum Nilavilakkum*; *Andame Anandam*; *Panthulamma*; ***Tharam Marindi***; **1978**: *Gammathu Goodacharulu*; *Ramachilaka*; *Sommokadidhi Sokokadidhi*; **1979**: *Mangala Toranalu*; **1980**: *Triloka Sundari/Trilok Sundari*; *Pilla Zamindar*; *Gandhara Golam*; **1981**: *Jai Gantalu*; ***Raja Parvai***; **1982**: *Halu Jenu*; *Chelisuva Modagalu*; **1983**: *Eradu Nakshatragalu*; *Raju Rani Jackie*; **1984**: *Shravana Bantu*; *Sangeetha Samrat*; *Vasantha Geetam*; **1985**: *Bhagyada Lakshmi Baramma*; *Jwalamukhi*; ***Mayuri***; **1986**: *Ananda*; **1987**: ***Pushpak/Pushpaka Vimana***; *America Abbayi*; *Pesum Padum*; **1988**: *Chiranjeevi Sudhakara*; *Devatha Manushya*; **1989**: *Apoorva Sahodarargal/Appu Raja*; **1990**: *Michael Madana Kamarajan*; **1991**: *Aditya 369*; **1992**: *Brindavanamu*; *Ksheera Sagara*; **1993**: *Phool*.

Rao, T. Prakash *see* **Prakash Rao, Tatineni**

RAO, YARAGUDIPATI VARADA (1903-73)

Tamil and Telugu director born in Nellore, AP. Medical student at Madras University. Went to Bombay and acted in **Manilal Joshi**'s Laxmi Pics (1925) and **Ardeshir Irani**'s Royal Art Studio before joining **General Pics** (Madras) as art director and actor, notably in **R.S. Prakash**'s silents. Directorial dèbut in 1929 and started his own Chintamani Pics (1939) and Shri Varuna Films (early 50s). The only film-maker to work in all major West and South Indian film centres (Bombay, Kolhapur, Madras and Mysore) and to make films in seven languages including Marathi, Kannada and Konkani (one film, *Jeevit Amche Ashe*). Best-known films were a major influence upon filmic conversion of stage **Company Natak** traditions, e.g. *Hari Maya* (for **Gubbi Veeranna**), ***Sati Sulochana*** (first Kannada talkie starring **M.V. Subbaiah Naidu** and **R. Nagendra Rao**) and *Chintamani* (made in Calcutta but based on a hit Tamil stage mythological). His multilingual talkies pioneered a cultural hybrid, e.g. in cross-breeding regional conventions of language, gesture and costume, crucial to the economic amalgamation of a unified South Indian film industry. His wife, Rukmini, was a noted star, as is their daughter Laxmi in Tamil and Telugu films, and their granddaughter Aishwarya.

FILMOGRAPHY (* also act/** act only): **1929**: *Garuda Garvabhangam***; **1930**: *Gajendra Moksham***; *Gandhariyin Pulambal***; *Pandava Agyathavas*; *Sarangadhara*; *King Bhoj**; **1931**: *Rose of Rajasthan***; *Nara Narayana***; **1932**: *Hari Maya* (all St); **1934**: ***Sati Sulochana****; **1935**: *Naganand*; **1936**: *Bhama Parinayam*; **1937**: *Chintamani**; **1938**: *Bhakta Meera**; *Swarnalatha**; **1939**: ***Malli Pelli****; **1940**: ***Vishwamohini****; **1941**: *Savithri**; **1942**: ***Satyabhama****; **1944**:

Tehsildar*; **1946**: *Lavangi**; **1948**: *Ramadas**; **1950**: *Lavangi**; *Jeevit Amche Ashe*; **1952**: *Manavati*; **1953**: *Manjari*; **1956**: *Bhagya Chakra*; **1958**: *Shri Krishna Garudi*; **1961**: *Nagarjuna*; **1963**: *Hennina Balu Kanneru**.

RASKAPUR, MANHAR (1922-80)

Major Gujarati director; born in Surat. Insisted on using the language in the late 40s during the post-WW2 boom in Hindi films. For several years, Raskapur and producer Champsibhai Nagda were the only team consistently making Gujarati films with their Roop Chhaya company (1947). Following the success of his début feature, *Jogidas Khuman*, he remade the film twice and was planning a third remake when he died. Best-known film: ***Mehndi Rang Lagyo***, a perennial hit. Introduced **Shanta Apte** in Gujarati with ***Mulu Manek***. Made the Rajput war sagas into anti-imperialist fables (***Kadu Makrani***, *Mulu Manek*), and fantasies of Gujarat's history and traditions (*Mehndi Rang Lagyo*). Filmed major novels (e.g. Pannalal Patel's ***Malela Jiv***) and made a biopic of the popular early 20th C. Gujarati poet ***Kalapi***. A strongly committed genre cineaste, he made socials (*Santu Rangili*), dacoit and children's films (*Miya Fuski 007*).

FILMOGRAPHY: **1948**: *Jogidas Khuman*; **1950**: *Kahyagaro Kanth*; **1951**: *Kanyadaan*; **1955**: ***Mulu Manek***; **1956**: ***Malela Jeev***; **1960**: ***Kadu Makrani***; ***Mehndi Rang Lagyo***; **1962**: *Jogidas Khuman*; **1963**: *Akhand Saubhagyavati*; **1966**: ***Kalapi***; **1971**: *Upar Gagan Vishal*; **1973**: *Vala Taro Deshma Danko*; **1975**: *Jai Ranchhod*; *Jogidas Khuman*; **1976**: *Santu Rangili*; **1977**: *Bhrashtachar Murdabad*; *Mari Hel Utaro Raj*; **1978**: *Miya Fuski 007*; *Nari Tu Narayani*; **1980**: *Saurashtrano Sinh-Chhelbhai*.

RATHNAM, MANI (b. 1956)

Major commercial Tamil director; born in Madras, the son of the producer 'Venus' Rathnam. Studied at Madras University and then received a management degree at the Bajaj Institute, Bombay. Worked as a management consultant. Started his career with a Kannada film (*Pallavi Anupallavi*), then a Malayalam one (*Unaroo*). Invested heavily in the acquisition of technologically sophisticated equipment. His initial, heavily melodramatic style (cf ***Mouna Ragam***) together with an unusual awareness of Hollywood's generic conventions culminated in his breakthrough film, ***Nayakan***, relocating *The Godfather* (1972) in Bombay's Tamil underclass. Went on to make India's first music video-inspired feature, ***Agni Nakshatram***, using extensive soft focus, flare filters, back-lighting, seductive camera movement and extensive dissolves. The music tv style also marks his Telugu film ***Geetanjali***, mostly shot in the misty landscape of Ooty, and ***Anjali***, in which a group of street children perform several elaborately choreographed breakdance numbers. Works with major stars (e.g. **Kamalahasan** in *Nayakan*; the Tamil star **Rajnikant** and his Malayalam counterpart **Mammootty** in *Dalapathi*), but transforms their images with a style involving, according to critic and director K. Hariharan, 'a strong violation of tonal, focal and colour continuity ... intercutting between sharply focused and soft images and a total denial (in the later musicals) of any image which could remotely call itself "natural"'. Received a nationwide release for ***Roja*** unprecedented in recent Tamil cinema, and also sparked off a major political controversy. Represented by G.V. Films, a public limited company owned by his brother G. Venkateswaran, the films are apparently sold against sealed tenders invited from distributors. In addition to MTV and Coppola, with whom he shares a tendency to celebrate the machinic aspects of cinema, the director acknowledges the influence of **Ramesh Sippy**. Married Tamil star **Suhasini**.

FILMOGRAPHY: **1983**: *Pallavi Anupallavi*; **1984**: *Unaroo*; **1985**: *Idaya Koyil*; *Pagal Nilavu*; **1986**: ***Mouna Ragam***; **1987**: ***Nayakan***; **1988**: ***Agni Nakshatram***; **1989**: ***Geetanjali***; **1990**: ***Anjali***; **1991**: *Dalapathi*; **1992**: ***Roja***; **1993**: *Thiruda Thiruda*.

RATHOD, KANJIBHAI J.

Often considered the first professional director in Bombay cinema. Former still photographer, he joined **Suchet Singh** as an actor (1918), appearing in *Mrichhakatik* and playing the lead in *Narasinh Mehta*; probably completed the unfinished films of Singh's Oriental Film with G.S. Devare. Joined **Kohinoor** (1920) and remained top director with the 20s hit ***Gul-e-Bakavali*** and the celebrated ***Bhakta Vidur***, banned for political reasons. Then worked in **Saurashtra Film** in Rajkot (1924-6). Returned to Bombay and became the force behind **Krishna** Studio (1926-9) and Krishna Movietone, making five sound-films in 1931. His ***Kono Vak?***, from a story by **Munshi**, was a radical social for its time and confirmed his authorial signature. Briefly worked in talkies at **Sagar**, then made a few inexpensive films in Hindi and Gujarati as freelancer. Towards the end of his career was employed as production manager in **Dhirubhai Desai**'s Chandrakala Pics, even as the latter remade several Rathod silents, including *Bolti Bulbul* (1942), *Devkanya* and *Bhakta Prahlad* (both 1946). He may not have directed films marked (?).

FILMOGRAPHY (* act only): **1920**: *Mrichhakatik**; *Narasinh Mehta**; *Vikram Urvashi*; **1921**: *Meerabai*; *Pundalik*; ***Mahasati Ansuya***; *Subhadra Haran*; ***Bhakta Vidur***; *Vishwamitra Menaka*; *Krishna Maya*; *Rukmini Haran*; *Chandrahasa*; **1922**: *Bhakta Ambarish*; *Malati Madhav*; *Sati Toral*; *Shri Satyanarayan*; *Ajamil*; *Devi Todi*; *Parashuram*; *Sukanya Savitri*; *Surya Kumari*; **1923**: *Sati Narmada*; *Karmadevi*; *Minal Devi*; *Vratasur Vadha*; *Veer Bhimsen*; *Goswami Tulsidas*; *Shri Balkrishna*(?); *Shuk Rambha*(?); **1924**: ***Gul-e-Bakavali***; ***Kala Naag***; ***Sadguni Sushila***(?); *Shareef Badmash*; **1925**: ***Baap Kamai***; *Kamallata*; *Anath Abala*; *Swapna Sundari*; **1926**: *Raja Ne Gami Te Rani*; *Khubsoorat Bala*; *Veer Kesari*; *Burkhawali*; *Bolti Bulbul*; **1927**: *Kuldeepak*; *Mardna Gha*; *Mahasati Ansuya*; **1928**: *Chandrahasa*; *Neelam Manek*; *Swarga Vihar*; *Devkanya*; *Bodku Mathu*; *Kal Ratrinu Khuni Khanjar*; **1929**: *Veer Rathod*; *Raj Hansa*; ***Kono Vak?***; **1930**: *Math No Sadhu*; *Nirbhagi Nirmala*; *Rajkumari Ni Ranagarjana*; *Tati Talwar* (all St); **1931**: *Chintamani*; *Ghar Ki Lakshmi*; *Harishchandra*; *Laila Majnu*; *Pak Daman*; **1932**: *Bhakta Prahlad*; *Bhasmasur Mohini*; **1933**: *Lanka Dahan*; **1934**: *Hothal Padmini*; *Jan Nissar*; *Sati Anjani*; *Thief Of Iraq*; **1936**: *Punjab Ka Sinh*; **1937**: *Gul Badan*; **1938**: *Ghunghatwali*; **1939**: *Sairandhri*; **1940**: *Anjaam*; **1949**: *Shethno Salo*.

RATHOD, KANTILAL (1925-88)

Gujarati and Hindi director and animator born in Raipur. Trained as a painter in Calcutta and at the Art Institute of Chicago, where he made a short film about a child's paintings, *Cloven Horizon*, distributed by the Encyclopaedia Britannica. Worked with Norman MacLaren at the National Film Board of Canada. Set up animation unit for Hunnar Films and authored celebrated animated films like *Adventures of a Sugar Doll* and *Business is People*. His ***Kanku*** inaugurated a Gujarati art cinema although he went on to make films in Hindi. Made shorts and features for his own Akar Films, also making films on commission from **Films Division**, the **CFS** and the US Information Agency.

FILMOGRAPHY: **1956**: *Mr and Mrs Peacock* (Sh); **1959**: *Buddha Aur DCM* (Doc); **1960**: *Withering Flowers* (Sh); **1965**: *Cloven Horizon* (Doc); *Adventures of a Sugar Doll* (Animation); **1966**: *The Parts that Build the Auto* (Doc); **1967**: *Peace-Time Armada* (Sh); **1968**: *Pinjra* (Sh); **1969**: *Strife to Stability* (Doc); ***Kanku***; **1971**: *Freedom Freedom* (Doc); **1973**: *Tested Berries* (Sh); *Short Cut* (Sh); **1974**: *Parinay*; **1975**: *Business is People* (Sh); **1976**: *Sardar Vallabhbhai Patel* (Doc); **1977**: *Zangbo and the Zing Zing Bar*; **1982**: *Ramnagari*; *The Choice is Yours* (Doc); **1985**: *Doongar Ro Bhed*; **1989**: *Save Energy through Efficient Motors* (Doc).

RAWAIL, HARNAM SINGH (b. 1921)

Hindi-Urdu director born in Lyallpur (now Pakistan). Went to Bombay in his teens to join films. Slept on the streets and in the Madhav Baug temple precincts. These experiences were later retold in quasi-autobiographical *Pocketmaar*. Left for Calcutta where he became assistant to **Kidar Sharma**. His first script is *Banke Sipahi* (1937), a version of *The Three Musketeers*. Wrote several scripts, usually in stunt genre, at Indrapuri Studios where he also received his first break as director. Turned producer in Calcutta (1948), then returned to Bombay (1949) and later established Roshni Pics (1955) and Rahul Theatres (1960). Made comedies (best known is **Kishore Kumar**'s slapstick *Shararat*) and love stories. ***Sangharsh*** was based on major Bengali novelist Mahashweta Devi's *Laila Aasmaner Aaina*. After ***Mere Mehboob***, made period romances and love legends. Last film *Deedar-e-Yaar*, written by his son **Rahul Rawail**, was one of the biggest financial disasters of 80s Hindi film. Since then has produced films for his son.

FILMOGRAPHY: **1940**: *Dorangia Daku*; **1944**: *Shukriya*; **1945**: *Zid*; **1948**: *Jhoothi Kasmein*; **1949**: *Do Baatein*; *Patanga*; **1951**: *Sagaai*; *Jawani Ki Aag*; **1952**: *Saqi*; **1953**: *Lehren*; *Shagufa*; **1954**: *Mastana*; **1955**: *Tirandaz*; **1956**: *Pocketmaar*; **1959**: *Shararat*; **1961**: *Kaanch Ki Gudiya*; *Roop Ki Rani Choron Ka Raja*; **1963**: ***Mere Mehboob***; **1968**: ***Sangharsh***; **1971**: *Mehboob Ki Mehndi*; **1976**: *Laila Majnu*; **1982**: *Deedar-e-Yaar*.

RAWAIL, RAHUL (B. 1951)

Hindi director born in Bombay. Son of **H.S. Rawail**, who also produced some of his films. Classmate of Rishi Kapoor, which allowed him to become assistant to **Raj Kapoor** for seven years. Directorial début with the hit *Love Story* (1981), produced by **Rajendra Kumar** to launch his son Kumar Gaurav, but the film was delayed and he eventually refused the directorial credit. Known for launching new faces, incl. **Dharmendra**'s son and 80s star Sunny Deol in *Betaab* and Kajol in *Bekhudi*. Wrote his father's megaflop *Deedar-e-Yaar* (1982). Involved in the video serial, *Dharamyudh*; also did tv series, *Honee Anhonee*.

FILMOGRAPHY: 1980: *Gunehgaar*; **1981**: *Love Story* (uncredited); *Biwi-o-Biwi*; **1983**: *Betaab*; **1985**: *Arjun*; **1986**: *Samundar*; **1987**: *Dacait*; **1988**: *Honee Anhonee* (TV); *Dharam Yuddh* (TV); **1990**: *Jeevan Ek Sangharsh*; **1991**: *Yodha*; *Mast Kalandar*; **1992**: *Bekhudi*.

Satyajit Ray directing *Goopy Gyne Bagha Byne* (1968)

RAY, SATYAJIT (1921-92)

Bengali director born in Calcutta. Grandson of Upendra Kishore Ray-Choudhury, publisher, musician, author and creator of children's fiction characters Goopy and Bagha (see ***Goopy Gyne Bagha Byne*** and ***Hirak Rajar Deshe***). Son of noted satirist and writer of limericks and nonsense rhymes, Sukumar Ray, about whom he made a documentary. Family counted prominent members of the secular reformist Sadharan Brahmo Samaj. Student at Kala Bhavan, Shantiniketan (1940-2) under the painter Nandlal Bose. Left without completing the course but maintained long-standing loyalties to its notions of Oriental discourse, later invoked in, e.g., his appreciation of Kurosawa and Japanese film. Started the Calcutta Film Society (1947) with **Chidananda Das Gupta** et al., which introduced him to European and Soviet cinemas. Met and assisted Jean Renoir (*The River*, 1951). First film: ***Pather Panchali***, receiving major acclaim on the Euro-American festival and art-house circuits making him India's first internationally recognised film-maker. Films mostly seen as relating to the ideological liberalism of Nehru and, particularly, to Ray's artistic and intellectual mentor, **Rabindranath Tagore**, whose writings he filmed (***Teen Kanya***, ***Charulata***, ***Ghare Baire***) and about whom he also made a documentary. Early films often associated with the chronicling of India's transition from feudal decadence and agrarian economic systems to capitalist modernity. Their slow rhythm and finely tuned evocation of emotional mid-ranges also derives substantially from cameraman Subrata Mitra's expertise (he shot the films up to ***Devi***, then also ***Kanchanjungha*** and *Charulata*). Likewise, his celebrated attention to realist detail, notably in his period films situated in 19th C. Bengal and in Wajid Ali Shah's court at Avadh (***Shatranj Ke Khiladi***) draws from set designer Bansi Chandragupta's explorations into the habits and customs of Colonial India through 19th C. academic and popular painting. Late 60s films invoke a sharper critique of urban culture (***Nayak***) and acknowledge an increasingly irreconcilable split between the rootless urban and the economically oppressed rural conditions (***Aranyer Din Ratri***, ***Ashani Sanket***) and prefigure his major 70s shift towards contemporary Calcutta (***Pratidwandi***, ***Seemabaddha***, ***Jana Aranya***). After *Shatranj Ke Khiladi*, his only non-Bengali feature, Ray focused exclusively on his native state, sometimes revisiting his earlier genres of the children's movie and Tagore adaptations, but also attempting new directions in chronicling Bengal's history through original screenplays. Published numerous short stories (some of which were filmed by his son Sandeep Ray in two tv series called *Satyajit Ray Presents*) for annual Puja numbers of Bengali literary journals and for the children's journal he used to edit, *Sandesh*. Extensively chronicled biography: Seton (1971), Das Gupta (1980) and Robinson (1989; including bibliography). Wrote autobiography encompassing his childhood years, *Jakhan Choto Chilam* (*When I Was Small*, 1982) and essays on film: *Our Films, Their Films* (1976), *Bisoy Chalachchitra* (*On Cinema*) (1976), *Ekei Bole Shooting* (*We Call it Shooting*) (1979). Most of Ray's novels and stories have been published as books by Ananda Publishing, Calcutta. English translations of his fiction include *Phatikchand* (1983), *The Adventures of Feluda* (1985), *Bravo! Professor Shonku* (1986), *Stories* (1987). Most of the screenplays are published in Bengali in the *Eksan* journal. Also worked, mainly as composer or writer, on **H. Dasgupta**'s *The Story of Steel* (1956) and *Quest for Health* (1967); Bansi Chandragupta's *Darjeeling-Himalayan Fantasy*, *Glimpses of West Bengal* and *Ganga Sagar Mela*; Tony Mayer's *House that Never Dies* and John Thiele's *Max Mueller*. Also did music for *Shakespeare Wallah* (1965), Nityananda Dutta's *Baksha Badal* (1965) and worked on all his son's films (*Phatikchand*, 1983, *Goopy Bagha Phere Elo*, 1991). Received an Oscar for his 'lifetime achievement' in 1992. Also the subject of a number of documentaries (e.g. by **Benegal** and K. Bikram Singh's *Satyajit Ray: An Introspection* (1990).

FILMOGRAPHY: 1955: ***Pather Panchali***; **1956**: ***Aparajito***; **1957**: ***Parash Pathar***; **1958**: ***Jalsaghar***; **1959**: ***Apur Sansar***; **1960**: ***Devi***; **1961**: ***Teen Kanya***; ***Rabindranath Tagore*** (Doc); **1962**: ***Kanchanjungha***; ***Abhijaan***; **1963**: ***Mahanagar***; **1964**: ***Charulata***; *Two* (Sh); ***Mahapurush***; **1965**: ***Kapurush***; **1966**: ***Nayak***; **1967**: ***Chidiakhana***; **1968**: ***Goopy Gyne Bagha Byne***; **1969**: ***Aranyer Din Ratri***; **1970**: ***Pratidwandi***; **1971**: ***Seemabaddha***; *Sikkim* (Doc); **1972**: ***The Inner Eye*** (Doc); **1973**: ***Ashani Sanket***; **1974**: ***Sonar Kella***; **1975**: ***Jana Aranya***; **1976**: *Bala*; **1977**: ***Shatranj Ke Khiladi***; **1978**: ***Joi Baba Felunath***; **1980**: ***Hirak Rajar Deshe***; ***Pikoo*** (TV); **1981**: ***Sadgati*** (TV); **1984**: ***Ghare Baire***; **1987**: *Sukumar Ray* (Doc); **1989**: ***Ganashatru***; **1990**: ***Shakha Proshakha***; **1991**: ***Agantuk***.

REDDI, BOMMIREDDI NARASIMHA (1908-77)

Telugu director and producer born in Kothapalli, Cuddappah Dist., AP. Professional accountant and amateur theatre actor with Madras-based group Chennapuri Andhra Mahasabha, where he also worked with **Ballari Raghava**. Set up the BNK Printing Press (1936). Entered films as associate financier of **H.M. Reddy**'s Rohini Pics and as scenarist for ***Grihalakshmi*** (1938). At Rohini he met **K. Ramnoth, Chittor V. Nagaiah, K.V. Reddy** and art director A.K. Sekhar, the nucleus of what was to be one of the largest studios of South India, **Vauhini** (prod. co. 1939; studio 1946). Best-known Vauhini films in 40s are among the most elaborate melodramas ever made in Telugu (possibly in India). Set in a rural family situation, they usually contrast a nostalgic past with contemporary big city values, industrialism, unemployment and 'loose women'. The form itself was politically legitimated through **Ramabrahmam**'s claim that it was in line with Gandhian progressivism. The genre was continued in the early **Vijaya** films, made by disciples K.V. Reddy, **K. Kameshwara Rao** and most notably by the **L.V. Prasad** school of film-makers. Monograph on Reddi by Randor Guy (1985).

FILMOGRAPHY: 1939: ***Vande Mataram***; 1940: ***Sumangali***; 1941: ***Devatha***; 1945: ***Swargaseema***; 1951: ***Malleeshwari***; 1954: ***Bangaru Papa***; 1957: ***Bhagya Rekha***; 1959: ***Raja Mukutam***; 1964: ***Poojapalam***; 1965: ***Bangaru Panjaram***; 1966: ***Rangula Ratnam***.

REDDY, HANUMAPPA MUNIAPPA (1882-1960)

Pioneering Telugu and Tamil director born and educated in Bangalore, Karnataka. Made the first talkies in Tamil (***Kalidas***) and Telugu (***Bhakta Prahlada***). Policeman in Bangalore; resigned and followed his brother-in-law, **H.V. Babu**, to Bombay. Assistant to **B.P. Mishra** (1927) before turning film-maker at **Imperial** with **Prithviraj Kapoor** adventure fantasies, *Vijaykumar* and *Bar Ke Pobar/A Wager in Love*. Also directed **L.V. Prasad** in many features, including *Bhakta Prahlada* and *Kalidas* for Imperial subsidiaries. Both were strongly influenced by the **Surabhi Theatres** tradition of the stage mythological and featured extensive musical sequences with members of the group. Enjoyed the reputation of being an actors' director, usually for **Anjali Devi**'s first lead performance in ***Nirdoshi*** and for the hit ***Grihalakshmi*** which provided the breakthrough for **Chittor V. Nagaiah** (making his début), **Kannamba** and **Kanchanmala**. Freelance work 1932-7 including Hindi, Tamil and Telugu films in Bombay, Madras and Kolhapur. Launched Rohini Pics (1937) with finance from M/S Reddi & Co. representing **B.N. Reddi**'s first association with film production, making it the origins of the **Vauhini** Studio monolith. The Rohini unit also introduced **K.V. Reddy** and Y.R. Swamy to film-making. Wrote Swamy's *Pratigna* (1953). Associated with launching of the Navajyothi Studio in Mysore (1944).

FILMOGRAPHY: 1930: *Vijaykumar*; 1931: *Bar Ke Pobar* (all St); ***Bhakta Prahlada***; ***Kalidas***; 1932: *Jazz of Life* (St); 1933: *Seeta Swayamvar*; *Savitri*; 1938: ***Grihalakshmi***; 1939: ***Mathru Bhoomi***; 1940: *Barrister Parvatisham*; *Bondam Pelli*; *Chaduvukonna Bharya*; 1941: ***Tenali Ramakrishna***; 1942: ***Gharana Donga***; 1946: *Sati Seeta*; 1951: ***Nirdoshi/Niraparadhi***.

REDDY, KADRI VENKATA (1912-72)

Telugu director born in Tadpatri, AP. Degree in science. Former assistant to **H.M. Reddy**. Production executive at **Vauhini** (1938) and key participant in all of **B.N. Reddi**'s 40s melodramas. First two films, ***Bhakta Potana*** and ***Yogi Vemana***, contributed to **Chittor V. Nagaiah**'s image as South Indian cinema's most famous actor in the Saint film genre. Continued his spectacular success with ***Patala Bhairavi***, whose 100-day run in 28 cinemas in 1951 effectively established Vauhini's successor, **Vijaya** Pics He attributed his success in the early 50s to his ability to get the sequence of 'introduction, commentarial exposition, conflicts, resolution, sub-climax, climax and message' in the correct order. Telugu cinema's best-known exponent of its most successful 50s genre: the action fantasy locally dubbed the 'folklore' film. Other famous films include ***Gunsundari Katha***, an apparent assimilation of *King Lear*, and ***Pedda Manushulu***, which borrowed the story of Ibsen's *Pillars of Society*.

FILMOGRAPHY: 1942: ***Bhakta Potana***; 1947: ***Yogi Vemana***; 1949: ***Gunsundari Katha***; 1951: ***Patala Bhairavi/Pataal Bhairavi***; 1954: ***Pedda Manushulu***; 1955: ***Donga Ramudu***; 1957: ***Maya Bazaar***; 1958: *Pellinati Pramanulu*; 1959: *Vazhkai Oppantham*; 1961: ***Jagadeka Veeruni Katha/Jagathala Prathapan***; 1962: ***Shri Krishnarjuna Yuddham***; 1965: ***Satya Harishchandra***; 1968: *Umachandi Gauri Shankarula Katha*; *Bhagyachakram*; 1971: *Shri Krishna Satya*.

REDDY, PATTABHI RAMA (b. 1919)

Kannada director born in Nellore, AP. One of the first free-verse poets in Telugu. Studied English at Calcutta University and mathematics at Columbia, New York (1940-3). Joined the Madras Players amateur theatre. Participant in the opposition to Indira Gandhi's 1975-7 regime with his wife Snehlata Reddy, who died in police custody (1977) for want of medical assistance. Founded Jayanti Pics with **K.V. Reddy**, producing some early work of the box-office director **Singeetham Srinivasa Rao**. Made ***Samskara***, a milestone of South Indian film (see **Navya Movement**).

FILMOGRAPHY: 1970: ***Samskara***; 1977: *Chanda Marutha*; 1984: *Sringara Masa*.

REHMAN, WAHEEDA (b. 1938)

Hindi-Urdu star of the 50s and 60s who came to prominence after an extraordinary performance as the prostitute in **Guru Dutt**'s ***Pyaasa***. Born into a traditional Muslim family in Hyderabad, AP. A student of Bharat Natyam, she débuted in **Yoganand**'s Telugu film *Jayasimha*; her second film, **Chanakya**'s ***Rojulu Marayi***, was a massive hit, partly due to her dancing. Guru Dutt cast her in **Raj Khosla**'s ***CID*** with **Dev Anand**. Classic scenes in *CID* like the song *Kahin pe nigahen* (sung by **Geeta Dutt**), where she tries to seduce the villain and allow the hero to escape, reveal her extraordinary facial mobility and dancer's grace, both repeatedly used in Dutt's song sequences (as in *Jaane kya tune kahi* in *Pyaasa* as she leads Vijay through alleys and beneath bridges or in *Bhawra bada nadaan* in ***Sahib Bibi Aur Ghulam***). Her physical presence was used by Dutt to convey an intense sense of life, often counterposed to another female role associated with death (e.g. **Meena Kumari** in *Sahib Bibi*). Aspects of this image continued into **Vijay Anand**'s ***Guide*** and **Asit Sen**'s ***Khamoshi***, where she is a nurse in an institution for the mentally deranged replacing sick hero **Rajesh Khanna** as victim. Also acted in **Satyajit Ray**'s ***Abhijaan***. Currently plays white-haired mothers, including **Amitabh Bachchan**'s violated mother in ***Trishul***.

FILMOGRAPHY: 1955: *Jayasimha/Jaisingh*; ***Rojulu Marayi/Kalam Maripochu***; ***Alibabavum Narpathu Thirudargalum***; 1956: ***CID***; 1957: ***Pyaasa***; 1958: *Solva Saal*; *Twelve O'clock*; 1959: ***Kaagaz Ke Phool***; 1960: ***Chaudhvin Ka Chand***; *Ek Phool Char Kaante*; *Girl Friend*; ***Kala Bazaar***; 1961: *Roop Ki Rani Choron Ka Raja*; 1962: *Baat Ek Raat Ki*; ***Bees Saal Baad***; *Raakhi*; ***Sahib Bibi Aur Ghulam***; ***Abhijaan***; 1963: *Ek Dil Sau Afsane*; *Kaun Apna Kaun Paraya*; *Mujhe Jeene Do*; 1964: ***Kohraa***; *Majboor*; *Shagun*; 1965: ***Guide***; 1966: ***Dil Diya Dard Liya***; ***Teesri Kasam***; 1967: *Palki*; *Patthar Ke Sanam*; ***Ram Aur Shyam***; *Ghar Ka Chirag*; 1968: *Admi*; *Baazi*; *Neel Kamal*; 1969: ***Khamoshi***; *Meri Bhabhi*; *Shatranj*; 1970: *Dharti*; *Man Ki Aankhen*; ***Prem Pujari***; *Darpan*; 1971: *Man Mandir*; ***Reshma Aur Shera***; 1972: *Dil Ka Raja*; *Subah-o-Shyam*; *Zindagi Zindagi*; ***Trisandhya***; 1973: *Insaaf*; *Phagun*; 1975: *Love in Bombay*; 1976: *Adalat*; ***Kabhi Kabhie***; 1977: *Aaj Ki Dhara*; 1978: ***Trishul***; 1979: *Jiban Je Rakam*; 1980: *Jwalamukhi*; *Jyoti Bane Jwala*; 1981: ***Naseeb***; 1982: *Dharam Kanta*; *Namak Halal*; *Namkeen*; *Saval* (H); 1983: ***Coolie***; *Ghunghroo*; *Himmatwala*; *Mahaan*; *Pyaasi Aankhen*; 1984: *Maqsad*; *Mashaal*; *Sunny*; 1986: *Allah Rakha*; *Sinhasan*; 1989: ***Chandni***; 1991: *Lamhe*.

Waheeda Rehman in *Bees Saal Baad* (1962)

REKHA (b. 1954)

Originally Bhanurekha. One of the few contemporary Indian film stars with a legendary status far outstripping her screen roles. The daughter of Tamil-Telugu stars **Gemini Ganesh** and Pushpavalli. Début as Baby Bhanurekha in **B.N. Reddi**'s ***Rangula Ratnam***. Eventually became a star via **Mohan Segal**'s hit, *Sawan Bhadon*. Overweight and gawky in her initial years, she made a spectacular physical change which was later marketed through, e.g., tips for body beautification and Jane Fonda-style aerobics. Her image, often as a rural belle, became that of a vulnerable yet sexually driven woman following the role of the prostitute Zohra in ***Muqaddar Ka Sikandar***. She made a bid for actorial respectability by appearing in New Indian Cinema-type films: **Muzaffar Ali**'s ***Umrao Jaan***, **Benegal**'s ***Kalyug*** and **Girish Karnad**'s ***Utsav***. Her personal life as reflected in gossip magazines and in the media was the subject of ***Silsila*** in which she is said to have played herself. Married the industrialist Mukesh Aggarwal who committed suicide shortly afterwards, triggering a new wave of public gossip invoking her *femme fatale* image.

FILMOGRAPHY: 1966: ***Rangula Ratnam***; **1970**: *Sawan Bhadon*; **1971**: *Dost Aur Dushman*; *Elaan*; *Haseenon Ka Devta*; *Saaz Aur Sanam*; **1972**: *Rampur Ka Lakshman*; *Ek Bechara*; *Sazaa*; *Zameen Aasmaan*; *Gaon Hamara Shaher Tumhara*; *Do Yaar*; *Gora Aur Kala*; *Double-Cross*; **1973**: ***Namak Haram***; *Kashmakash*; *Pran Jaye Par Vachan Na Jaye*; *Anokhi Ada*; *Dharma*; *Barkha Bahar*; *Keemat*; *Khoon Khoon*; *Mehmaan*; *Kahani Kismat Ki*; **1974**: *Do Aankhen*; *Duniya Ka Mela*; *Woh Main Nahin*; *Hawas*; **1975**: *Dafaa 302*; *Dharam Karam*; *Dharmatma*; *Kehte Hain Mujhko Raja*; *Zorro*; *Akraman*; **1976**: *Aaj Ka Mahatma*; *Do Anjaane*; *Kabeela*; *Nagin*; *Santan*; *Khalifa*; **1977**: *Aap Ki Khatir*; *Alaap*; *Chakkar Pe Chakkar*; *Dildaar*; *Farishta Ya Qatil*; *Imaan Dharam*; *Kachcha Chor*; *Khoon Pasina*; *Palkon Ki Chhaon Mein*; *Ram Bharose*; **1978**: *Bhola Bhala*; *Ganga Ki Saugandh*; *Ghar*; *Karmayogi*; *Muqaddar*; ***Muqaddar Ka Sikandar***; *Parmatma*; *Prem Bandhan*; *Rahu Ketu*; *Ram Kasam*; *Sawan Ke Geet*; *Aakhri Daku*; *Do Musafir*; *Kasme Vade*; *Do Shikari*; **1979**: *Gautam Govinda*; *Muqabala*; *Ahimsa*; *Jaani Dushman*; *Kartavya*; *Mr Natwarlal*; *Suhaag*; *Kali Ghata*; *Naya Bakra*; **1980**: *Aanchal*; *Agreement*; *Chehre Pe Chehra*; *Jal Mahal*; *Judaai*; *Khubsoorat*; *Maang Bharo Sajana*; *Ram Balram*; *Neeyat*; *Jyoti Bane Jwala*; ***Kalyug***; *Saajan Ki Saheli*; **1981**: *Basera*; ***Chashme Buddoor***; *Khoon Aur Pani*; *Daasi*; *Ek Hi Bhool*; *Ghunghroo Ki Awaaz*; *Mangalsutra*; ***Silsila***; ***Umrao Jaan***; *Raaste Pyar Ke*; **1982**: *Mehndi Rang Layegi*; *Apna Bana Lo*; *Deedar-e-Yaar*; *Ghazab*; *Jeevan Dhara*; *Vijeta*; **1983**: *Agar Tum Na Hote*; *Mujhe Insaaf Chahiye*; *Nishan*; *Prem Tapasya*; *Bindiya Chamkegi*; **1984**: ***Utsav***; *Asha Jyoti*; *Baazi*; *Jhootha Sach*; *Kaamyaab*; *Mati Maange Khoon*; *Khazana*; *Zameen Aasmaan*; *Musafir*; **1985**: *Ram Tere Kitne Naam*; *Faasle*; *Locket*; **1986**: *Insaaf Ki Awaaz*; *Jaal*; *Jaanbaaz*; *Sada Suhagan*; *Jhoothi*; *Pyar Ki Jeet*; **1987**: *Apne Apne*; *Jaan Hatheli Pe*; *Sansar*; *Ijaazat*; **1988**: *Soorma Bhopali*; *Biwi Ho To Aisi*; *Khoon Bhari Maang*; *Ek Naya Rishta*; *Akarshan*; *Jism Ka Rishta*; **1989**: *Kasam Suhaag Ki*; *Clerk*; *Ladaai*; *Bhrashtachar*; *Souten Ki Beti*; *Bahurani*; **1990**: *Amiri Garibi*; *Azad Desh Ke Gulam*; *Mera Pati Sirf Mera Hai*; *Shesh Naag*; **1991**: *Phool Bane Angarey*; *Yeh Aag Kab Bujhegi*; **1992**: *Insaaf Ki Devi*; **1993**: *Geetanjali* (H); *Madam X*.

ROY, BIMAL (1909-66)

Director regarded as one of Hindi cinema's top cineastes in the 50s. Born in Dhaka (now Bangladesh) into a landholding family. Studied in Calcutta. Hired as camera assistant by **Nitin Bose** for **New Theatres**. Shot many films, such as **P.C. Barua**'s ***Devdas*** (1935), ***Grihadah***, ***Maya*** (both 1936) and ***Mukti*** (1937) and **Amar Mullick**'s ***Bardidi*** (1939) and ***Abhinetri*** (1940). Remade Barua's *Devdas* and Mullick's *Biraj Bou* (as ***Biraj Bahu***). Directorial début at New Theatres with ***Udayer Pathey***, introducing a new era of post-WW2 romantic-realist melodrama that was to pioneer the integration of the Bengal School style with that of De Sica. Made the classic of the radical-popular **IPTA**-supported cinema: ***Do Bigha Zameen***. Wrote Manoj Bhattacharya's ***Tathapi*** (1950). Left New Theatres (1950), worked briefly at **Bombay Talkies** and set up Bimal Roy Prod. in Bombay (1952) making 13 films in 11 years, including some of his best-known socials in Hindi (esp. ***Sujata*** and ***Bandini***). ***Madhumati*** (with story, script and apparently directorial input by **Ritwik Ghatak**) was one of the biggest Hindi hits of 50s, with a popular soundtrack by **Salil Choudhury**. Supported younger Bengali film-makers who followed him to Bombay, producing films by **Hemen Gupta** (***Kabuliwala***, 1961) and **Asit Sen** (*Parivar*, 1956; *Aparadhi Kaun*, 1957). Roy's film-making team contained many talents who went on to become major film-makers themselves, e.g. **Hrishikesh Mukherjee**, **Gulzar** and Bimal Dutt. Monograph on him by his daughter Rinki Bhattacharya (1989).

FILMOGRAPHY: 1943: *Bengal Famine* (Doc); **1944**: ***Udayer Pathey/Hamrahi***; **1948**: ***Anjangarh***; **1949**: *Mantramugdha*; **1950**: *Pehla Admi*; **1952**: *Maa*; **1953**: ***Do Bigha Zameen***; ***Parineeta***; **1954**: ***Naukri***; ***Biraj Bahu***; *Baap Beti*; **1955**: ***Devdas***; **1958**: ***Madhumati***; ***Yahudi***; **1959**: ***Sujata***; **1960**: *Parakh*; **1961**: *Immortal Stupa* (Doc); **1962**: *Prem Patra*; **1963**: ***Bandini***; **1964**: *Life and Message of Swami Vivekananda* (Doc); **1967**: *Gautama the Buddha* (Doc).

ROY, CHARU (1890-1971)

Bengali painter and director born in Behrampore, West Bengal. Graduated in geology from Presidency College, Calcutta (1918). As a painter, he considered the Bengal School's Abanindranath Tagore to be his teacher. Associated with Indian Society for Oriental Art; paintings reproduced in journals *Bharat Varsha* and *Prabashini* (1913). Cartoonist for daily *Ananda Bazar Patrika* and other journals like *Prabashi*, *Modern Review*, etc. (1922-7). Worked on the first Bengali film journal, *Bioscope* (1930); later edited *Rangmahal* journal. Became a renowned set designer, e.g. for **Sisir Bhaduri**'s *Seeta*, where he pioneered naturalist, three-dimensional stage design and perspectival lighting. Entered film as art director for **Himansu Rai** (e.g. ***Prem Sanyas***, 1925). Also acted in some of the **Osten** films (e.g. ***Shiraz***, 1928; ***Prapancha Pash***, 1929). First film as director was a megabudget Great Eastern production in Orientalist spectacular genre, ***Loves of a Mughal Prince***, but was upstaged by **R.S. Choudhury**'s quickly made *Anarkali* (1928). Also continued as art director, e.g. for **Modhu Bose**'s ***Michael Madhusudhan*** (1950) and Prafulla Roy's *Malancha* (1953). His ***Bangalee*** was praised by **Satyajit Ray** for its avoidance of Hollywood influences and for its accurate depiction of the Bengali middle-class lifestyle. Roy acknowledged his debt to Osten (in particular to cinematographer Wirsching) for his use of source lighting and for overcoming theatrical acting styles.

FILMOGRAPHY: 1928: ***The Loves of a Mughal Prince***; **1930**: *Bigraha*; **1931**: *Chorekanta*; *Swami* (all St); **1934**: *Rajnati Basantsena*; **1935**: *Daku Ka Ladka*; *Diljani*; **1936**: *Kuhu-o-Keka* (Sh); ***Bangalee***; ***Sarala***; *Graher Pher*; **1939**: *Pathik*.

ROY, JAHAR (1929-77)

Some sources give 1919 as his birth year. Born in Barisal, now Bangladesh, the son of the early film comedian Satu Roy. Became one of the top comedians of the Bengali cinema, remembered as a fat actor with a squint prone to boisterous performances, and for his trade-mark giggle. Broke through with **Bimal Roy**'s ***Anjangarh***. Teamed up with **Bhanu Bannerjee**, several of their films featuring the names of either or both stars in the title: e.g. *Ae Jahar Sey Jahar Noy*, *Bhanu Goenda Jahar Assistant*. Remembered as the foreman in **Ghatak**'s ***Subarnarekha*** and the villainous prime minister in **Ray**'s ***Goopy Gyne Bagha Byne***. A major stage actor and director, from 1953 (when he first appeared as Nakul in *Durabhashi*) he was the driving force of the main Calcutta Theatres company, Rungmahal, until 1977, when he played Bhujanga Roy in ***Aparichita***.

FILMOGRAPHY: 1947: *Purbaraag*; **1948**: ***Anjangarh***; **1950**: *Pehla Admi*; *Roopkatha/Roop Kahini*; *Vidyasagar*; **1952**: *Chhoti Maa*; ***Basu Parivar***; **1953**: *Adrishya Manush*; *Jog Biyog*; ***Sharey Chuattar***; **1954**: ***Dhuli***; *Nababidhan*; *Chitrangada*; *Agni Pareeksha*; *Bhakta Bilwamangal*; *Moner Mayur*; *Ankush*; *Naramedh Yagna*; *Sada-Kalo*; *Kalyani*; *Ladies' Seat*; *Jagrihi*; *Sadanander Mela*; *Sati*; *Barbela*; *Chheley Kaar*; **1955**: *Nishiddha Phal*; *Chatujye-Banrujye*; *Dakinir Char*; *Anupama*; *Devatra*; *Chhoto Bou*; *Aparadhi*; *Jharer Parey*; *Dashyumohan*; *Mejo Bou*; *Bhalobasha*(?); *Upahar*; *Shribatsa Chinta*; *Hrad*; *Paresh*; **1956**: *Asabarna*; *Savdhan*; *Chirakumar Sabha*; *Ekti Raat*; *Chalachal*; *Rajpath*; *Govindadas*; *Nagardola*; *Chore*; *Amar Bou*; *Chhaya Sangini*(?); **1957**: *Bara Maa*(?); *Tapasi*(?); *Chhaya Path*; *Ulka*; ***Adarsha Hindu Hotel***; *Kancha-Mithey*; *Punar Milan*; *Mamata*; *Ogo Sunchho*; *Tamasha*; ***Parash Pathar***; *Gharer Math*; **1958**: *Yamalaya Jibanta Manush*; *Rajalakshmi-o-Shrikanta*; *Manmoyee Girls' School*; *Dak Harkara*; *Nupur*;

Bhanu Pelo Lottery; *Jonakir Alo*; *Nagini Kanyar Kahini*; *Shri Shri Tarakeshwar*; *Rajdhani Theke*; *Kalamati*; *Surya Toran*; **1959**: *Shri Shri Nityananda Prabhu*; *Sagar Sangamey*; *Derso Khokhar Kando*; *Jal-Jangal*; *Abhishap*; *Mahut Bandhu Re*; *Gali Theke Rajpath*; *Bari Theke Paliye*; *Ae Jahar Sey Jahar Noy*; *Rater Andhakare*; *Mriter Martye Agaman*; **1960**: *Maya Mriga*; *Debarshi Narader Sansar*; *Akash-Patal*; *Haat Baraley Bandhu*; *Prabesh Nishedh*; *Kono-Ek-Din*; *Shaharer Itikatha*; *Nader Nimai*; *Biyer Khata*; *Suno Baro Nari*; *Dui Bechara*; *Gariber Meye*; **1961**: *Raibahadur*; *Sathi Hara*; *Mr and Mrs Choudhury*; *Bishkanya*; *Megh*; *Pankatilak*; *Dilli Theke Kolkata*; *Aaj Kal Parshu*; *Madhureno*; *Kanamachi*; **1962**: *Mon Dilona Bandhu*; *Sorry Madam*; *Atal Jaler Ahwan*; *Bandhan*; *Kajal*; *Abhisarika*; ***Subarnarekha***; **1963**: *Dui Bari*; *Barnachora*; *Sat Bhai*; *High Heel*; *Palatak*; *Dui Nari*; *Hashi Sudhu Hashi Noy*; *Surya Sikha*; *Shreyasi*; **1964**: *Pratinidhi*; *Swarga Hotey Biday*; *Kinu Goyalar Gali*; *Kashtipathar*; *Kanta Taar*; *Binsati Janani*; *Ketumi*; *Marutrisha*; **1965**: *Roop Sanatan*; *Alor Pipasa*; *Mahalagna*; *Ek Tuku Basa*; *Ghoom Bhangar Gaan*; *Pati Sansodhini Samiti*; *Devatar Deep*; *Dinanter Alo*; *Abhoya-o-Srikanta*; *Dolna*; *Mukhujey Paribar*; *Kal Tumi Aleya*; **1966**: *Firey Chalo*; *Kanch Kata Hirey*; *Nutan Jiban*; *Ramdhakka*; *Shesh Tin Din*; *Mamata*; *Ashru Diye Lekha*; **1967**: *Abhishapta Chambal*; *Balika Bodhu*; *Wohi Ladki*; *Ajana Shapath*; ***Antony Firingee***; *Ashite Ashio Na*; *Bodhu Baran*; *Hathat Dekha*; *Miss Priyambada*; *Mahashweta*; *Nayika Sangbad*; *Prastar Swakshar*; **1968**: *Adyashakti Mahamaya*; *Baghini*; *Baluchari*; *Boudi*; *Chowringhee*; *Kokhono Megh*; *Panchasar*; *Parishodh*; *Pathe Holo Dekha*; *Rakta Rekha*; *Hansamithun*; ***Goopy Gyne Bagha Byne***; **1969**: *Agni Yuger Kahini*; *Chena Achena*; *Dadu*; *Duranta Charai*; *Kamallata*; ***Natun Pata***; *Pita Putra*; *Shuk Sari*; *Rahgir*; **1970**: *Muktisnan*; *Ae Korechho Bhalo*; *Nala Damayanti*; *Rajkumari*; *Nishipadma*; *Rupasi*; **1971**: *Anya Mati Anya Rang*; *Bhanu Goenda Jahar Assistant*; *Chhadmabeshi*; *Dhanyi Meye*; *Ekhane Pinjar*; *Nabaraag*; *Nimantran*; *Pratham Pratisruti*; *Sachimar Sansar*; **1972**: *Biraj Bou*; *Chhayatir*; *Chinnapatra*; *Memsahib*; *Haar Mana Haar*; *Nayikar Bhumikay*; ***Padi Pishir Barmi Baksha***; *Shesh Parba*; *Stree*; *Chitthi*; *Chhandapatan*; *Duranta Jay*; *Jiban Sangram*; *Marjina Abdallah*; **1973**: *Ek Je Chhilo Bagh*; ***Bon Palashir Padabali***; *Nakal Sona*; *Shesh Pristhay Dekhun*; *Daabi*; *Pranta Rekha*; *Shravan Sandhya*; **1974**: *Debi Choudhrani*; *Sangini*; *Sujata*; *Chhutir Phande*; *Umno-o-Jhumno*; *Phulu Thakurma*; *Biley Naren*; **1975**: *Chhoto Nayak*; *Mohan Baganer Meye*; *Agniswar*; *Kajal Lata*; *Hansaraj*; *Sei Chokh*; *Amriter Swad*; *Tin Pari Chhoy Premik*; *Arjun*; *Bandi Bidhata*; **1976**: *Asadharan*; *Ek Je Chhilo Desh*; *Nana Ranger Dinguli*; *Balak Saratchandra*; *Ananda Mela*; *Laila Majnu* (B); **1977**: *Babu Moshai*; *Din Amader*; *Hatey Roilo Tin*; *Ami Ratan*; **1979**: *Jata Mat Tata Path*; **1981**: *Sonay Suhaga*.

ROY, NIRUPA (b. 1931)

Hindi and Gujarati actress, originally called Kokila Kishorechandra Balsara. Born in Valsad, Gujarat. She is the most famous screen mother in Indian cinema. Début in **V.M. Vyas**'s successful Gujarati feature, ***Ranakdevi***. Broke through with *Gunsundari*. Best-known for roles as a mother goddess, e.g. Seeta thrice, Parvati thrice and Lakshmi, Taramati, Draupadi and Damayanti once. Also played *Rani Rupmati*, elaborating this persona in other period movies like *Amarsinh Rathod*, *Veer Durgadas* and *Jai Chittor*. Worked extensively at **Ranjit** following the success of ***Har Har Mahadev***, often in mythologicals opposite male lead Trilok Kapoor. First played the mother in **Dev Anand**'s ***Munimji***. Also acted in realist tragedies, often with **Balraj Sahni** (***Do Bigha Zameen***, ***Garam Coat***). Developed a new dimension to her image playing **Bachchan**'s mother in **Manmohan Desai**'s ***Amar Akbar Anthony*** and in **Yash Chopra** films. She is the pivot of ***Deewar*** and triggered the line addressed by the 'good' brother, **Shashi Kapoor**, to the bad one, Bachchan: 'Mere paas maa hai' (I have mother on my side). She plays to perfection the role of the mother as victim, so that Bachchan or **Dharmendra** may engage in vendettas to restore the family honour.

FILMOGRAPHY: 1946: *Amar Raj*; ***Ranakdevi***; **1947**: *Bhanwar*; *Lakhon Mein Ek*; *Meerabai*; **1948**: *Jeevan Palto*; *Gunsundari*; *Hip Hip Hurray*; *Jai Hanuman*; *Mitti Ke Khilone*; *Satyavan Savitri*; *Nanand Bhojai*; **1949**: *Garibi*; *Hamari Manzil*; *Udhaar*; ***Mangalfera***; *Sati Sukanya*; **1950**: *Jawabdari*; *Alakh Niranjan*; *Bhai Bahen*; ***Har Har Mahadev***; *Veer Bhimsen*; ***Gadano Bel***; **1951**: *Bade Bhaiya*; *Dashavtar*; *Ishwar Bhakti*; *Jai Mahakali*; *Kashmir*; *Lav Kush*; *Maya Machhindra/Gorakhnath*; *Nai Zindagi*; *Ram Janma*; *Shri Ganesh Janma*; *Shri Vishnu Bhagwan*; *Parnetar*; **1952**: *Bhakta Puran*; *Izzat*; *Rajrani Damayanti*; *Shivashakti*; *Sinbad the Sailor*; *Veer Arjun*; **1953**: ***Bhagyavaan***; *Dharmapatni*; ***Do Bigha Zameen***; *Madmust*; *Manchala*; *Naag Panchami*; *Naulakha Haar*; *Naya Raasta*; *Raj Ratan*; *Shuk Rambha*; *Teen Batti Char Raasta*; **1954**: *Aulad*; *Aurat Teri Yahi Kahani*; *Bilwamangal*; *Chakradhari*; *Durga Puja*; *Hukumat*; ***Pehli Tareekh***; *Shiv Kanya*; *Shiv Ratri*; *Watan*; **1955**: ***Garam Coat***; *Mahasati Savitri*; ***Munimji***; *Navratri*; *Oonchi Haveli*; *Sati Madalasa*; *Shri Ganesh Vivah*; *Tangewali*; *Teen Bhai*; *Vaman Avatar*; *Raj Durbar*; **1956**: *Bajrang Bali*; *Basant Panchami*; *Bhai Bhai*; *Dassehra*; *Gauri Puja*; *Lalkaar*; *Ram Navami*; *Sati Naagkanya*; ***Taksaal***; *Amarsinh Rathod*; **1957**: *Chandi Puja*; *Do Roti*; *Ek Gaon Ki Kahani*; *Janam Janam Ke Phere*; *Krishna Sudama*; *Lakshmi Pooja*; *Mohini*; ***Musafir***; *Naag Lok*; *Naag Mani*; *Narsi Bhagat*; *Ram Hanuman Yuddha*; *Sant Raghu*; *Shesh Naag*; *Blackmailer*; **1958**: *Chaalbaaz*; *Dulhan*; *Karigar*; *Naag Champa*; *Pati Parmeshwar*; *Raj Pratigya*; *Ram Bhakta Vibhishan*; *Samrat Chandragupta*; **1959**: *Bazigar*; *Bedard Zamana Kya Jaane*; *Charnon Ki Dasi*; *Daaka*; *Dr Z*; *Heera Moti*; *Kangan*; *Kavi Kalidas*; *Pakshiraj*; *Rani Rupmati*; **1960**: *Aanchal*; *Ghar Ki Laaj*; *Lal Qila*; *Maya Machhindra*; *Superman*; *Veer Durgadas*; **1961**: *Apsara*; *Batwara*; *Chhaya*; *Dharmaputra*; *Jai Chittor*; *Razia Sultana*; *Chundadi Chokha*; **1962**: *Aalha Udal*; *Bezubaan*; *Bijli Chamke Jamna Paar*; *Maa Beta*; **1963**: *Chandrasekhar Azad*; *Grihasthi*; ***Gumrah***; *Kaun Apna Kaun Paraya*; *Mujhe Jeene Do*; **1964**: *Benazir*; *Bhakta Dhruvakumar*; *Hameer Hath*; *Phoolon Ki Sej*; *Shehnai*; **1965**: *Chand Aur Suraj*; *Shaheed*; *Shankar Seeta Ansuya*; *Shri Ram Bharat Milap*; **1966**: *Aasra*; *Laadla*; *Neend Hamari Khwab Tumhare*; **1967**: *Badrinath Yatra*; *Jaal*; ***Ram Aur Shyam***; **1968**: *Ek Kali Muskayi*; *Jyot Jale*; *Raja Aur Runk*; *Aabroo*; **1969**: *Surya Devata*; *Anjaana*; *Aansoo Ban Gaye Phool*; *Aaya Sawan Jhoom Ke*; *Hum Ek Hain*; *Jigri Dost*; *Pyar Ka Mausam*; *Rahgir*; **1970**: *Maharaja*; *Aan Milo Sajna*; *Abhinetri*; *Ghar Ghar Ki Kahani*; *Gopi*; *Maa Aur Mamta*; *My Love*; *Purab Aur Paschim*; **1971**: *Chhoti Bahu*; *Ganga Tera Pani Amrit*; *Jawan Mohabbat*; *Nadaan*; *Sansar* (H); **1972**: *Anokhi Pehchan*; *Ek Hasina Do Diwane*; *Jaanwar Aur Insaan*; *Jawani Diwani*; **1973**: *Kachche Dhaage*; *Manchali*; *Pyar Ka Rishta*; *Taxi Driver*; **1974**: *Aaina*; *Badla*; *Roti*; *The Cheat*; *Zehreela Insaan*; **1975**: ***Deewar***; *Mounto*; *Ponga Pandit*; **1976**: *Aap Beeti*; *Maa*; *Santan*; *Dharti Mata*; **1977**: *Saubhagya Sindoor*; *Aakhri Goli*; *Aankh Ka Tara*; ***Amar Akbar Anthony***; *Anurodh*; *Hatyara*; *Kasam Khoon Ki*; *Khoon Pasina*; **1978**: *Anjane Mein*; *Besharam*; *Dil Aur Deewar*; *Ram Kasam*; *Nalayak*; ***Muqaddar Ka Sikandar***; **1979**: *Ahimsa*; *Jaandaar*; *Kartavya*; *Khandaan*; *Suhaag*; *Chambal Ki Kasam*; *Zalim*; **1980**: *Lootmaar*; *Aas Paas*; **1981**: *Jail Yatra*; *Qatilon Ke Qatil*; *Khoon Aur Pani*; *Kranti*; *Professor Pyarelal*; **1982**: *Ganga Meri Maa*; **1983**: *Betaab*; *Mawaali*; *Aan Aur Shaan*; *Chor Police*; **1984**: *Pavitra Ganga*; *Mera Faisla*; *Ram Tera Desh*; **1985**: *Aaj Ka Daur*; *Giraftaar*; ***Mard***; *Pataal Bhairavi*; *Ramkali*; *Maanu Mangalsutra*; *Locket*; *Dharam Shatru*; **1987**: *Naam-o-Nishan*; *Pyar Karke Dekho*; **1988**: *Pyar Ka Mandir*; *Charnon Ki Saugandh*; *Sone Pe Suhaaga*; *Aurat Teri Yahi Kahani*; *Ganga Tere Desh Mein*; *Inteqam*; *Ganga Jamuna Saraswati*; **1989**: *Dana Pani*; *Santosh*; **1990**: *Karnama*; **1991**: *Pratikar*; *Hai Meri Jaan*; **1992**: *Mere Sajna Saath Nibhana*; *Humshakal*.

Nirupa Roy in *Navratri* (1955)

Rupkonwar *see* **Agarwala, Jyotiprasad**
Sabhyasachi *see* **Kar, Ajoy**

SADANANDAN, S. L. PURAM (b. 1927)

Prolific Malayalam scenarist and major playwright. Film début adapting his best-known play, *Oralkoodi Kalanayi*, on the theme of unemployment, for the film by P.A. Thomas (1964). Scenarist mainly with M. Krishnan Nair (e.g. ***Kavya Mela***, 1965; *Pinchu Hridayam* and *Kalyana Rathriyil*, 1966; ***Agniputhri*** and *Collector Malathi*, 1967). Also wrote for **Sethumadhavan** (e.g. *Sthanarthi Saramma*, 1966; ***Kottayam Kola Case***, 1967). Adapted Thakazhy Shivashankar Pillai's landmark novel for the equally epochal film ***Chemmeen*** (1965); later wrote *Nellu* (1974) for its director, **Kariat**. Wrote the dialogues for **George**'s ***Lekhayude Maranam Oru Flashback*** (1983). Provided script and/or dialogues for c.150 Malayalam films since 1964.

SAGAR, RAMANAND (b. 1917)

Hindi director, producer and writer born in Lahore as Ramanand Shankardas Chopra. Journalist for the *Daily Milap* and the *Daily Pratap* (1936-42). Assisted, e.g., H.S. Thakur (*Raiders of the Railroad*, 1936) and obtained a degree in Sanskrit (1942). Migrated to Bombay on Partition, recording the communal holocaust in his classic Hindi novel, *Aur Insaan Mar Gaya* (1948). Using the names Ramanand Chopra and Ramanand Bedi, published prose stories (*Diary of a TB Patient*, 1942; *Jawar Bhata*, 1943; *Aine*, 1944; *Jab Pahle Roz Barf Giri*, 1944; *Mera Hamdam Mere Dost*, 1945; *Phool Aur Kaante*, 1949) and plays (e.g. *Gaura*, part of which was staged by **Prithviraj Kapoor**'s Prithvi Theatres as *Kalakaar*, 1951). Broke through in cinema writing **Raj Kapoor**'s epochal ***Barsaat*** (1949). Wrote scripts and dialogues for **S.S. Vasan**'s Hindi films (***Insaniyat***, 1955; ***Raj Tilak***, 1958; ***Paigham***, 1959) and directed two films (*Ghunghat*, *Zindagi*) for Vasan's **Gemini** Studio. Produced most of his own films via his Sagar Art (1953). Notable recent work includes the 91-episode tv serial *Ramayan*, **Doordarshan**'s first major success with peak Sunday morning viewing of c.78% of the audience. Continued with a sequel derived from the *Mahabharata* (released on video). Addressing communally charged ideals of Hindu glory, with a tacit glorification of sati, the serial claims to be founded on Tulsidas's 16th C. *Ramcharitamanas*, but formally it remains within the ambit of, e.g., **Radheshyam Kathavachak**'s popular playwrighting style.

FILMOGRAPHY: 1953: *Mehmaan*; **1954**: *Bazooband*; **1960**: *Ghunghat*; **1964**: *Zindagi*; **1965**: *Arzoo*; **1968**: *Aankhen*; **1970**: *Geet*; **1972**: *Lalkaar*; **1973**: *Jalte Badan*; **1976**: *Charas*; **1978**: *Prem Bandhan*; **1982**: *Baghavat*; **1983**: *Romance*; **1985**: *Salma*; **1986-8**: *Ramayan* (TV); **1989**: *Krishna* (TV).

SAGAR FILM COMPANY

Bombay studio started in 1930 by Chimanlal Desai and Ambalal Patel, Southern distributors of Select Pics, **Imperial** and **Ardeshir Irani** (who withdrew in 1931). Its major early film-maker was **Sarvottam Badami** (e.g. ***Dr Madhurika***, 1935); **Ezra Mir** contributed some seminal Parsee theatre-derived films and novelist **K.M. Munshi** helped formulate the codes that were to shape **Mehboob**'s early work. Others who started their careers in the studio, and in the same genre, were **Zia Sarhadi** and **Ramchandra Thakur**. When **Chimanlal Luhar** joined, they made some stunt movies, including Mehboob's ***Deccan Queen*** (1936). The studio also made nationalist documentaries, on Nehru and Shubash Bose, with the active collaboration of their subjects. In 1939 Ambalal Patel withdrew to start Sudama Pics and Fazalbhoy took over, possibly with investment from the Tatas, and it became National Film. One of their earliest films was Mehboob's classic ***Aurat*** (1940), made at Sagar but released by National.

SAHNI, BALRAJ (1913-73)

Born in Rawalpindi (now Pakistan), and the best-known film actor to emerge from the post-WW2 Left cultural movements. Studied at the Government College of Lahore, graduating in literature. Started writing poetry in English and involved in 'realist' theatre, absorbing the then prevalent desire for both nationalism and Westernisation. Married Damayanti who was a noted theatre actress. Taught Hindi and English at Shantiniketan. Wrote his first compilation of Hindi fiction, *Shahzadonka Drink* (1936). Worked as a journalist and briefly as radio announcer for the BBC's Hindi service. Started the *Monday Morning* journal in Delhi. Went to Bombay (1947) and became a key figure in **IPTA** plays; also director and lead actor in *Zubeida* (by **Abbas**) and *The Inspector General* (both 1944). Ran the Juhu Art Theatre group in the 1960s. After a walk-on part in **Phani Majumdar**'s *Insaaf*, starred in Abbas's first film, ***Dharti Ke Lal***. Damayanti died in the late 40s and Sahni later married Santosh. Made his reputation as the displaced rickshaw-puller in **Bimal Roy**'s ***Do Bigha Zameen***, continuing the neo-realist style he had adopted for *Dharti Ke Lal*. In ***Garam Coat*** he gave the classic performance of the displaced person as represented in the writings of **Rajinder Singh Bedi** and **Krishan Chander**. He embodied the tragedy of the people of Punjab (partitioned during Independence) and the ethnic groups of the North West Frontier (e.g. the Pathans) so effectively that his very presence came to signify a host of historical connotations, as in ***Kabuliwala***, in ***Sone Ki Chidiya*** where he plays a radical poet and defender of the rights of film extras, or in the war movie ***Haqeeqat*** where his acting inflected the film's nationalist chauvinism, and in the Lucknow-based story ***Garam Hawa***. Wrote the story and dialogues of **Guru Dutt**'s ***Baazi*** (1951). Wrote extensively on many issues, including novels and an autobiography (1971). Remained a Left activist throughout his life and was part of cultural delegations to the Soviet Union and to China. Communist leader P.C. Joshi compiled the book *Balraj Sahni: An Intimate Portrait* (1974) with Sahni's writings and speeches in addition to Joshi's own recollections of the radical theatre movement.

FILMOGRAPHY (* also d): **1946**: ***Dharti Ke Lal***; *Insaaf*; **1947**: *Gudiya*; **1948**: *Gunjan*; **1951**: ***Humlog***; *Maldar*; **1952**: *Badnaam*; ***Rahi***; **1953**: *Akash*; ***Do Bigha Zameen***; **1954**: *Aulad*; *Bazooband*; *Chalis Baba Ek Chor*; *Majboori*; **1955**: ***Garam Coat***; *Jawab*; *Joru Ka Bhai*; *Seema*; *Tangewali*; *Vachan*; **1956**: ***Taksaal***; ***Era Bator Sur***; **1957**: ***Lal Batti****; ***Pardesi***; *Bhabhi*; *Do Roti*; ***Kathputli***; *Krishna Sudama*; *Mai Baap*; *Mamata*; **1958**: *Devar Bhabhi*; *Ghar Grihasthi*; *Ghar Sansar*; *Khazanchi*; ***Lajwanti***; *Naya Kadam*; ***Sone Ki Chidiya***; **1959**: *Black Cat*; *Chand*; ***Chhoti Bahen***; *CID Girl*; *Heera Moti*; ***Satta Bazaar***; **1960**: ***Anuradha***; *Bindiya*; *Dil Bhi Tera Hum Bhi Tere*; *Nai Maa*; **1961**: ***Bhabhi Ki Chudiyan***; ***Kabuliwala***; *Sapan Suhane*; *Suhaag Sindoor*; **1962**: *Anpadh*; *Shadi*; **1963**: *Akela*; **1964**: *Punar Milan*; ***Haqeeqat***; *Main Bhi Ladki Hoon*; **1965**: *Faraar*; ***Waqt***; *Dak Ghar*; **1966**: *Aaye Din Bahar Ke*; *Aasra*; *Laadla*; *Neend Hamari Khwab Tumhare*; *Pinjre Ke Panchhi*; **1967**: *Aman*; *Hamraaz*; *Naunihal*; **1968**: *Aabroo*; *Duniya*; *Izzat*; *Neel Kamal*; ***Sangharsh***; **1969**: ***Do Raaste***; *Ek Phool Do Mali*; *Hum Ek Hain*; *Nannha Farishta*; *Talash*; **1970**: *Dharti*; *Ghar Ghar Ki Kahani*; *Holi Aayee Re*; *Mere Humsafar*; *Naya Raasta*; *Pavitra Papi*; *Pehchan*; **1971**: *Jawan Mohabbat*; *Paraya Dhan*; **1972**: *Jungle Mein Mangal*; *Jawani Diwani*; ***Shayar-e-Kashmir Mahjoor***; **1973**: *Chimni Ka Dhuan*; *Daman Aur Aag*; ***Garam Hawa***; *Hanste Zakhm*; *Hindustan Ki Kasam*; *Pyar Ka Rishta*; **1975**: *Amanat*.

SAHU, KISHORE (1915-80)

Hindi actor, writer, director and producer born in Durg, MP. Son of the Raja of Raigarh's chief minister. Degree in literature from the University of Nagpur (1937). Wrote many short stories. Started as actor in **Bombay Talkies** playing a **Barua**-like ineffectual lover opposite **Devika Rani** in ***Jeevan Prabhat***. Prominent early instance of a total author: an actor-director of mid-budget socials usually scripted by and starring himself. Films often claimed classic European sources (e.g. Olivier's *Hamlet*, 1948). Started Kishore Sahu Prod. (1940) and Hindustan Chitra (1944). Part of late 40s **Filmistan** stable. Wrote *Insaan* (1944)

Kishore Sahu in his film *Hamlet* (1954)

and *Apnapan* (1977); wrote dialogues for **Vasan**'s *Aurat* (1967) and *Teen Bahuraniyan* (1968). Villainous figure in several **Dev Anand** films, e.g. ***Kala Pani***, ***Guide***, ***Hare Rama Hare Krishna***.

FILMOGRAPHY (* also d/** only d): **1937**: ***Jeevan Prabhat***; **1940**: *Bahurani*; *Punar Milan*; **1942**: ***Kunwara Baap****; **1943**: *Raja***; **1944**: *Shararat**; *Insaan*; **1945**: *Veer Kunal**; **1947**: *Saajan***; *Sindoor**; **1948**: *Nadiya Ke Paar***; **1949**: *Sawan Aya Re**; *Namuna*; ***Rimjhim***; **1951**: *Buzdil*; *Kali Ghata**; **1952**: *Zalzala*; *Hamari Duniya*; *Sapna*; **1954**: *Hamlet**; ***Mayurpankh****; **1956**: *Kismet Ka Khel***; **1957**: *Bade Sarkar**; **1958**: ***Kala Pani***; **1960**: ***Kala Bazaar***; *Love in Simla*; *Dil Apna Aur Preet Parayi***; **1963**: *Grihasthi***; *Ghar Basake Dekho***; **1965**: *Poonam Ki Raat***; ***Guide***; **1967**: *Hare Kaanch Ki Chudiyan***; **1969**: *Beti*; **1970**: *Pushpanjali**; **1971**: *Gambler*; ***Hare Rama Hare Krishna***; **1974**: *Dhuen Ki Lakeer***.

SAIGAL, KUNDAN LAL (1904-46)

Legendary actor and singer whose performance in the lead role of **Barua**'s ***Devdas*** set the standard for musical melodrama acting. Born in Jammu. As a child, he occasionally played Seeta in the Ramlila of Jammu. His only formal training apparently came from a little-known Sufi peer, Salman Yussuf. The singing tradition he assimilated, sometimes described as the Kotha (where the courtesans performed), had little classical rigour, but emphasised the poetic 'bending' of syllables into musical curves in forms like the thumri and the ghazal. His renditions of Mirza Ghalib's poetry and his identification with its tragic iconography formed the famous Saigal persona. Worked as a typewriter salesman when B.N. Sircar recruited him for his singing ability. His style was substantially shaped at **New Theatres** by **Rai Chand Boral** who, with **Timir Baran** and **Pankaj Mullick**, composed most of the songs which remain among the most popular hits in Indian film history. Acted in a Bengali film for the first time when he did a small role, including two songs, in the Bengali version of *Devdas* (having first had to satisfy Saratchandra Chatterjee that he could do it). Later proved very popular in Bengali films, e.g. ***Didi***, ***Desher Mati***. At New Theatres, the films of **Nitin Bose** (***President***, ***Jiban Maran***) and **Phani Majumdar** (***Street Singer***) allowed his music to develop its own autonomy. Inspired a whole generation of musicians such as Mukesh, Talat Mahmood, **Kishore Kumar** and **Kozhikode Abdul Qadir**. Worked at **Ranjit** in the 40s (e.g. the classic ***Tansen***). Biography by Menon (1989).

FILMOGRAPHY: 1932: *Mohabbat Ke Aansoo*; *Zinda Lash*; *Subah Ka Sitara*; **1933**: ***Puran Bhakt***; ***Rajrani Meera***; ***Yahudi Ki Ladki***; *Dulari Bibi*; **1934**: ***Chandidas***; *Daku Mansoor*; *Mohabbat Ki Kasauti*; **1935**: ***Karwan-e-Hayat***; ***Devdas***; *Bijoya*; **1936**: *Karodpati*; ***Pujarin***; **1937**: ***Didi/President***; **1938**: ***Desher Mati/Dharti Mata***; ***Street Singer/Saathi***; ***Dushman/Jiban Maran***; **1940**: ***Zindagi***; **1941**: ***Parichay/Lagan***; **1942**: *Bhakta Surdas*; **1943**: ***Tansen***; **1944**: *Bhanwara*; ***Meri Bahen***; **1945**: *Kurukshetra*; ***Tadbir***; **1946**: *Omar Khayyam*; ***Shahjehan***; **1947**: *Parwana*.

SAIKIA, BHABENDRANATH (b. 1932)

Assamese director born in Nowgong. Physicist with doctorate from Imperial College of Science and Technology, London (1960). Lecturer at Gauhati University (1962-81). Major Assamese short-story writer (e.g. the anthologies *Sindoor*, 1973; *Shrinkhal*, 1976). Prolific radio playwright. Currently edits fortnightly *Prantik* and children's monthly *Safura*. Writes his own films, which he believes to be the most important of his creative output, occasionally based on his fiction: e.g. ***Kolahal***, his best-known film, based on his radio play, and ***Agnisnan***, based on his own novel. Directorial début in 1977. Makes art-house films with a strongly melodramatic literary tendency combined with an ethnographic realism (e.g. the truck scenes of *Kolahal*).

FILMOGRAPHY: 1977: ***Sandhya Raag***; **1981**: *Anirban*; **1985**: ***Aginsnan***; **1988**: ***Kolahal***; **1991**: *Sarothi*; **1993**: *Abartan*.

SAINT FILMS

Genre of film biographicals of the medieval Saint-poets. This Bhakti tradition emerged from the proliferation of regional and lower-caste cultures after the 7th C. when the Pauranic texts and portions of the *Mahabharata* were rendered in the Prakrit or demotic languages spoken by the lowest castes of Shudra or Atishudra. Starting with Shankara (8th C.) and Ramanuja (12th C.), the movement expanded into several sects: e.g. the Jaina, the Shaiva, the Natha, the Lingayata, the Mahanubhav. It was strongest in the South and the West, creating the first major literatures in Tamil, Telugu, Kannada and Marathi. Directly addressing the peasantry and the artisans, the Bhakti tradition was revived in several currents of 19th C. nationalist and egalitarian reformism, e.g. by Mahadev Govind Ranade (1842-1901) who opposed a Vedantic revivalism by modelling his own sermons on the verses of the 17th C. Marathi poet, Sant Tukaram. In Telugu and Kannada the movement is traced to the spread of the Veerasaiva cult, pioneered by Mallikarjuna Pandit and Basvanna respectively, leading to the earliest reform movements which, as e.g. with the educational activities of the Lingayat Viratka monks in 19th C. Karnataka, fed into the social reform movement under British occupation (see **Social**). Used for the first time to create a political language in the banned film ***Bhakta Vidur*** (1921), a tradition continued by, e.g., **Prabhat**'s famous Saint films: ***Dharmatma*** (1935) drew parallels between Gandhi and the 16th C. poet Eknath; ***Sant Dnyaneshwar*** (1940) made a call for peace in the context of WW2. The theatrical version of the genre emphasised miracle sequences in narratives culminating in intense devotional emotions. This approach found a natural extension into filmic spectacle beyond the means of the conventional mythological, best exemplified by **S.S. Vasan**'s big budget ***Avvaiyyar*** (1953). In Telugu the form is uniquely associated with the star **Chittor V. Nagaiah** (***Bhakta Potana***, 1942; ***Thyagayya***, 1946; ***Yogi Vemana***, 1947 et al.). Other classic Saint films are ***Chandidas*** (Bengali, 1934), ***Sant Tukaram*** (Marathi, 1936), *Bhakta Cheta* (Tamil, 1940), *Bhakta Kabir* (Hindi, 1942), ***Meera*** (Hindi/Tamil 1945), *Bhakta Gora Kumbhara* (Kannada, 1949), etc. The last major film in the genre is the Punjabi classic ***Nanak Naam Jahaz Hai*** (1969) although this is not strictly a biographical.

SALIM-JAVED (SALIM KHAN, JAVED AKHTAR)

The most successful scenarists of 70s Indian cinema. Javed Akhtar, born in 1945 in Gwalior, started his career in the late 60s writing the dialogues of, e.g., S.M. Sagar's *Sarhadi Lutera* (1966). Salim Khan established himself as a scenarist with 70s megastar **Rajesh Khanna**'s hit *Hathi Mere Saathi* (1971). The two teamed up to write, e.g., dialogues for **Ramesh Sippy**'s *Seeta Aur Geeta* (1972) and the script for **Nasir Hussein**'s hit teen-picture, ***Yaadon Ki Baraat*** (1973). They broke through as a team in 1973 mainly with the rise of **Amitabh Bachchan**, writing his first vigilante movie, **Prakash Mehra**'s ***Zanjeer*** (1973). Established themselves in the wake of Bachchan's success, with ***Deewar*** and ***Sholay*** (both 1975), followed by *Don* and ***Trishul*** (both 1978), later claiming the authorship of the star's screen persona. Became independent attractions with equal billing as the stars while inaugurating a new era in professional screenplay writing. They separated around 1980, after which Akhtar wrote several hit films such as ***Mr India*** (1989) and the massively successful song *Ek do teen* of **N. Chandra**'s ***Tezaab*** (1988). Salim Khan returned to top-billing status with Shashilal Nair's *Falak* (1988) although he remained less successful than his former partner. Together with his wife **Shabana Azmi**, Akhtar participates in civil rights and communal harmony campaigns. Khan's son Salman Khan became a star with ***Maine Pyar Kiya*** (1989).

SAMANTA, SHAKTI (b. 1925)

Hindi director and producer born in Burdwan District. Science student; then assistant director on **Raj Kapoor**'s *Sunehre Din* (1949). Assisted and wrote scripts for **Phani Majumdar** (***Baadbaan***, *Dhobi Doctor*, both 1954). Early films include successful crime thrillers (1953-63) in the **Filmistan** mould (***Howrah Bridge***, *Detective*, ***Jaali Note***) and classic **Shammi Kapoor** hits (***China Town***, *Singapore*), switching abruptly to love stories (1964-74) when he started working in colour (***Kashmir Ki Kali***). Best-known film: ***Aradhana***, launching 70s superstar **Rajesh Khanna** and initiating a new version of the tragic love story formula, continued with *Amar Prem* and *Anuraag*. Has made Hindi-Bengali bilinguals (roughly 1975-85), starring Bengali star **Uttam Kumar**. ***Amanush*** introduced the Hindi melodrama genre into 80s Bengali cinema, and its success led to a series of Bengali hits, e.g. Kanak Mukherjee's *Lal Kothi* (1977), some made by non-Bengali directors, e.g. Batra Mohinder's *Prahari* (1982) and Pramod Chakravarty's *Teen Murti* (1984). Wrote **Bhimsingh**'s *Ragam* (1975). Currently produces films made by son Ashim Samanta (*Main Awara Hoon*, 1983; *Palay Khan*, 1986).

Appointed chairman of the Central Board of Film Censorship (1990).

FILMOGRAPHY: 1955: *Bahu*; 1956: *Inspector*; 1957: *Hill Station*; *Sheroo*; 1958: ***Howrah Bridge***; *Detective*; 1959: *Insaan Jaag Utha*; 1960: ***Jaali Note***; *Singapore*; 1962: ***China Town***; *Isi Ka Naam Duniya Hai*; *Naughty Boy*; 1963: *Ek Raaz*; *Aayel Basant Bahar*; 1964: ***Kashmir Ki Kali***; 1966: *Sawan Ki Ghata*; 1967: *An Evening in Paris*; 1969: ***Aradhana***; 1970: *Kati Patang*; *Pagla Kahin Ka*; 1971: *Amar Prem*; *Jaane Anjane*; 1972: *Anuraag*; 1974: *Ajnabi*; *Charitraheen*; ***Amanush***; 1976: *Mehbooba*; 1977: *Anand Ashram*; *Anurodh*; 1979: *The Great Gambler*; 1980: *Khwab*; 1981: *Barsaat Ki Ek Raat/Anusandhan*; 1982: *Ayaash*; 1984: *Awaaz*; 1985: *Aar Paar/Anyay Abichar*; *Alag Alag*; 1990: *Dushman*; 1993: *Geetanjali*.

Samarth, Nutan *see* **Nutan Samarth**

SAMARTH, SHOBHANA (b. 1916)

Hindi film actress born in Bombay. Started with **Master Vinayak** at **Kolhapur Cinetone**. Acted in **Sagar** films (1936-41), often with **Motilal**. Established her definitive screen image in her first **Vijay Bhatt** film, ***Bharat Milap/Bharat Bhet***, playing Seeta, repeating the role in ***Ramrajya***, one of the most successful mythologicals in Indian cinema. She repeated the role several more times (*Rambaan*, *Ram Vivah*) opposite Prem Adib as Ram. This duo's image fundamentally shaped the contemporary iconography of the *Ramayana* legend in comic books, calendar paintings and, recently, in tv as well as in Vishwa Hindu Parishad posters in the context of the Hindu Ram Janmabhoomi movement. Although associated almost solely with the Seeta figure, she also appeared in other mythologicals: esp. *Nala Damayanti* (with **Prithviraj Kapoor**) and **Kishore Sahu**'s *Veer Kunal*, as well as in melodramas like Shaukat Hussein Rizvi's ***Naukar***. Turned producer and director with *Hamari Beti*, launching her daughter **Nutan**. Her other daughter, Tanuja, is also a Hindi star featuring in many comedies.

FILMOGRAPHY (* also d): 1935: ***Vilasi Ishwar/Nigah-e-Nafrat***; 1936: ***Do Diwane/Be Kharab Jan***; 1937: *Kokila*; 1938: *Nirala Hindustan*; 1939: *Kaun Kisika*; *Pati Patni*; *Sadhana*; 1940: ***Apni Nagariya***; *Saubhagya*; 1941: *Darpan*; *Holiday in Bombay*; *Gharjavai*; 1942: *Baraat*; ***Bharat Milap/Bharat Bhet***; *Mata*; *Nai Duniya*; *Savera*; *Shobha*; *Swaminath*; 1943: *Mahasati Ansuya*; ***Naukar***; ***Ramrajya***; *Vijay Lakshmi*; 1944: *Anban*; *Insaan*; 1945: *Taramati*; *Nala Damayanti*; *Veer Kunal*; *Shri Krishnarjun Yuddha*; 1946: *Urvashi*; 1947: *Mallika*; *Sati Toral*; *Shahkar*; *Veerangana*; 1948: *Rambaan*; 1949: *Narasinh Avatar*; *Ram Vivah*; 1950: *Hamari Beti**; *Janmashthami*; 1951: *Jai Mahalakshmi*; *Ram Janma*; 1954: *Prisoner of Golconda*; 1955: ***Insaniyat***; 1959: *Keechaka Vadha*; 1960: ***Chhalia***; 1965: *Nai Umar Ki Nai Fasal*; 1972: *Do Chor*; *Ek Baar Muskurado*.

SAMI, ARUL SUSAI ANTHONY (b. 1917)

Tamil director born and educated in Colombo, Sri Lanka; son of a theatre contractor. Quit his job as university lecturer in Colombo to move to Madras, where his play *Bilhana*, originally written for the radio and later performed with great success by **M.K. Thyagaraja Bhagavathar** and by the **TKS Brothers**, went on to become a major film hit produced by TKS (1948). Sami, who scripted the film, got a job at Jupiter Studio, Coimbatore, where he wrote, e.g., **Sundarrao Nadkarni**'s *Valmiki* (1946), A. Kasilingam's *Abhimanyu* (1948, with **Karunanidhi**) and the story of Lanka Sathyam's *Mohini* (1948). His début as director, *Rajakumari*, an Arabian Nights movie he also scripted, is **MGR**'s first hit in a lead role and put Sami in the front-line of Tamil directors. His second film, ***Velaikkari***, is a **DMK Film** propaganda classic written by **Annadurai**. His sole Hindi film, *Maya Sundari*, is largely dubbed from the Tamil hit *Karpurakarasi*, but includes a new dance number sung by **Geeta Dutt** with music by **Bulo C. Rani** (uncredited).

FILMOGRAPHY: 1947: *Rajakumari*; 1949: ***Velaikkari***; 1950: *Vijayakumari*; 1951: *Sudarshan*; 1953: *Ponni*; 1954: *Thuli Visham*; 1955: *Neethipathi*; 1957: *Karpurakarasi*; 1959: *Kalyanikku Kalyanam*; *Thangapathumai*; 1960: *Kaidhi Kanniyiram*; 1961: *Arasilankumari*; 1962: *Meri Bahen*; *Muthu Mandapam*; 1963: *Ananda Jyoti*; *Asai Alaigal*; *Kaduvulai Kandan*; 1964: *Vazhi Piranthudu*; 1967: *Maya Sundari*; 1971: *Thirumagal*.

SANDOW, P. K. RAJA (1894-1942)

Aka P.K. Nagalingam. Silent star, Hindi actor and Tamil director born in Pudukottai, TN. A passionate gymnast, he started his career as a stunt actor in **S.N. Patankar**'s National Film (1922). Top star at **Kohinoor** (1922-8) under **Manilal Joshi** (***Mojili Mumbai***), **R.S. Choudhury** and **Homi Master**. Achieved fame when he formed a trio with director **Chandulal Shah** and heroine **Gohar**, starting Jagdish Film with them (1928) and its successor, **Ranjit Film** (1929-36). Sandow's star image in reformist melodramas, playing complex psychological characters opposite Gohar, was launched with ***Gunsundari*** and extended in several classic 'negative' roles in Shah-Gohar sound films, esp. ***Indira MA*** where he plays Kishore, ***Barrister's Wife*** in the role of the public prosecutor, and love triangles like ***Desh Dasi*** and ***Prabhu Ka Pyara*** with E. Bilimoria and Gohar. Directed his first film with **R. Padmanabhan**'s Madras-based Associated Films (*Anadhai Penn*), embarking on a series of reformist socials. *Anadhai Penn*, *Nandanar* (the story of an Untouchable Hindu saint, subtitled *The Elevation of the Downtrodden*), *Peyum Pennum* and *Taranhaar* were followed by sound films *Vasantsena* and *Chandrakantha*, all influential predecessors to **K. Subramanyam**'s nationalist melodramas (e.g. ***Thyagabhoomi***, 1939). *Menaka*, produced by the **TKS Brothers**, introduced the star **N.S. Krishnan**. Continued a freelance career as actor at **Imperial**, with **Jaswantlal**'s *Kashmeera*, **Homi Wadia**'s *Dhoomketu*, and **Babubhai Mistri**. Some films with footage of Sandow were released after his death. Early memoirs excerpted in the *Movie Mirror* in 1928.

FILMOGRAPHY (* also d/** only d): 1922: *Bhakta Bodana*; *Surya Kumari*; 1923: *Vratrasur Vadha*; *Veer Bhimsen*; 1924: *Ra Mandlik*; ***Bismi Sadi***; *Razia Begum*; *Sati Sone*; 1925: *Indrasabha*; *Suvarna*; *Kala Chor*; *Devadasi*; *Panchdanda*; *Desh Na Dushman*; ***Mojili Mumbai***; ***Veer Kunal***; *Vimala*; *Khandani Khavis*; *Matri Prem*; 1926: *Madhav Kam Kundala*; *Mena Kumari*; *Mumtaz Mahal*; ***Neera***; *Bhasmasur Vadha*; *Ra Kawat*; *Samrat Shiladitya*; *Typist Girl*; ***The Telephone Girl***; 1927: ***Bhaneli Bhamini***; ***Gunsundari***; *Sati Madri*; *Sindh Ni Sumari*; *The Mission Girl*; ***Gamdani Gori***; 1928: *Grihalakshmi*; *Naag Padmini*; *Vishwamohini*; *Sneh Jyoti***; 1929: *Anadhai Penn***; *Chandramukhi*; *Pati Patni*; *Punjab Kesari*; *Rangilo Rajavi*; *Nandanar***; *Mother India*; 1930: *Raj Lakshmi*; *Sati Usha Sundari***; *Rajeshwari***; *Peyum Pennum**;

Sulochana and Raja Sandow in *Indira MA* (1934)

1931: *Bhaktavatsala**; *Taranhaar***; *Signet Ring*** (all St); **1932**: *Parijata Pushpaharanam***; **1933**: *Noor-e-Imaan*; *Pardesi Preetam*; **1934**: ***Indira MA***; *Kashmeera*; *Toofani Taruni*; *Devaki*; **1935**: *College Girl*; ***Desh Dasi***; *Ratan Manjari*; *Raat Ki Rani**; *Menaka***; ***Barrister's Wife***; **1936**: *Dil Ka Daku*; *Matlabi Duniya*; ***Prabhu Ka Pyara***; *Chandrakantha***; *Chalak Chor**; *Vasantsena**; **1937**: *Minor Rajamani***; **1938**: *Vishnu Leela**; **1939**: *Thiruneelakantar***; **1941**: ***Choodamani*****; **1942**: *Araichi Mani***; **1949**: *Dhoomketu*; **1952**: *Alladdin and the Wonderful Lamp*; **1953**: *Nav Durga*; *Husn Ka Chor*.

SANGANI, CHANDRAKANT (b. 1927)

Gujarati director, writer and actor, born in Saurashtra, Gujarat. Started as a radio performer. Journalist for the Gujarati paper *Prajatantra* (1957-63). Active playwright, stage actor and director as well as author of five novels in the 50s and 60s. Turned to cinema in 1968 and directs mostly Gujarati films.

FILMOGRAPHY: 1968: *Mare Javun Pele Paar*; **1970**: *Jigar Ane Ami*; **1975**: ***Tanariri***; **1976**: *Sati Jasma Odan*; **1977**: *Vanjari Vav*; *Saubhagya Sindoor*; **1978**: *Tamere Champone Ame Kel*; **1979**: *Garvo Garasiyo*; **1980**: *Parayana To Pyara Ladi*; **1981**: *Vansdi Vagi Valamni*; **1982**: *Prem Diwani*; **1983**: *Raakhna Ramakada*; **1985**: *Sorathno Savaj*; **1988**: *Gunahon Ke Shatranj*; *Ghar Ek Mandir* (TV); **1992**: *Mayavi Jaal* (TV); **1993**: *Geetanjali*.

SANGEET NATAK

Marathi musical theatre tradition believed to have been launched by Vishnudas Bhave's *Seeta Swayamvar* (1853). The play adapted the coastal folk form of Dashavtara to the proscenium, merging it with visual art and theatrical forms from Tanjore while retaining elements like the use of a mobile curtain to signify spaces and to frame actors. It emerged as a popular urban art form alongside the **art schools** (practising the academic visual art style on the elaborate **stage backdrops**) and the **music schools** of the late 19th/early 20th C. The best-known initial groups were Annasaheb Kirloskar's Kirloskar Natak Mandali (Est: 1880), **Keshavrao Bhole**'s Lalitkaladarsh (1908), **Bal Gandharva**'s Gandharva Natak Mandali (1913) and **Govindrao Tembe**'s Shivraj Natak Mandali (1915). Their initial theatrical repertoire adapted Sanskrit classics and Shakespeare: e.g. the famous playwright G.B. Deval wrote five major plays, three adapting Kalidasa and one Shakespeare (*Othello*, as *Zunzharrao*, 1890) with only one original (*Sangeet Sharada*, 1898). The music usually created popular vernacular versions of classical North Indian music, adapted by singers like Ramakrishnabua Vaze and Bhaskarbua Bakhle (who taught **Master Krishnarao**). The form increasingly came under the influence of the operatic **Parsee theatre**, creating an influential local version of classical art, contemporaneous with (and sometimes formally similar to) **Ravi Varma**'s paintings. The first feature film in India, ***Pundalik*** (1912), is based on a Sangeet Natak play by the Shripad Sangeet Mandali, Nasik. Later, **Baburao Painter** - a noted painter of stage backdrops - translated its conventions into cinematic *mise en sc¤ne*. The form greatly influenced the early **Prabhat** Studio via, e.g., the noted composers Tembe and Krishnarao and the stage stars Bal Gandharva and **Vishnupant Pagnis**, as well as many other theatre actors who turned to the cinema. Sangeet Natak troupes, travelling through Maharashtra, Gujarat, Karnataka and Madhya Pradesh, also set in place much of the distribution infrastructure of the early Kolhapur- and Pune-based Marathi cinema.

SANYAL, PAHADI (1906-74)

Aka Narendranath Sanyal born in Darjeeling. Joined **New Theatres** (1931) and became one of its main stars. A trained musician with a diploma from Morris College, Lucknow. Worked as private secretary of the Raja of Avadh. Started mainly as a singing star in early **Atorthy**, **Barua** and **Debaki Bose** films, often accompanying **K.L. Saigal** (e.g. ***Devdas***). His most famous music of this period was in ***Adhikar***: the song *Suhag ki raat* set to **Baran**'s music. Featured in several romantic hero roles, but later found his métier in classic biographicals (e.g. **Modhu Bose**'s *Mahakavi Girishchandra*) drawn from literary melodrama and creating a new, more lasting 'character' image in Bengali films for 40 years. The crucial transition took place in Bombay, where he moved in 1942, in films like **Jaswantlal**'s *Kadambari* and **Nitin Bose**'s ***Milan***. Acted in **Satyajit Ray**'s ***Kanchanjungha*** as Jagdish, the man interested more in watching birds than in the material machinations of the family, and in ***Aranyer Din Ratri*** as the old retired singer Sadasib Tripathi.

FILMOGRAPHY: 1933: ***Meerabai/Rajrani Meera***; ***Yahudi Ki Ladki***; **1934**: ***Chandidas***; *Rooplekha/Mohabbat Ki Kasauti*; *Daku Mansoor*; **1935**: ***Karwan-e-Hayat***; ***Devdas***; ***Dhoop Chhaon/Bhagya Chakra***; *Bijoya*; **1936**: *Karodpati*; ***Pujarin***; ***Maya***; **1937**: ***Mukti***; ***Bidyapati/Vidyapati***; **1938**: ***Adhikar***; **1939**: ***Bardidi/Badi Didi***; ***Sapurey/Sapera***; ***Rajat Jayanti***; **1940**: ***Abhinetri/Haar Jeet***; ***Zindagi***; **1941**: *Pratisruti*; **1942**: *Kisise Na Kehna*; *Saheli*; *Saugandh*; **1943**: *Inkaar*; *Mazaaq*; ***Mohabbat***; *Mauj*; *Sharafat*; **1944**: *Anban*; *Bade Nawab Saheb*; *Insaan*; *Mahakavi Kalidas*; *Paristan*; *Kadambari*; **1945**: *Main Kya Karun*; *Preet*; *Ramayani*; **1946**: *Shravan Kumar*; ***Nauka Dubi/Milan***; **1948**: *Priyatama*; *Rang Berang*; *Sadharan Meye*; **1949**: *Bamuner Meye*; *Jar Jetha Ghar*; *Ultorath*; *Bishnupriya*; *Swami*; **1950**: *Pehla Admi*; *Kashmir Hamara Hai*; *Maryada*; *Indrajal*; *Panchayat*; *Sandhya Belar Rupkatha*; *Vidyasagar*; **1951**: *Rupantar*; *Aparajito*; ***Ratnadeep/Ratnadeepam***; *Darpachurna*; *Pratyabartan*; *Setu*; ***Babla***; **1952**: *Rani Bhabani*; *Chhoti Maa*; ***Basu Parivar***; **1953**: *Malancha*; *Raja Krishna Chandra*; *Blind Lane*; *Bou Thakuranir Haat*; **1954**: *Maa-o-Chhele*; *Sada-Kalo*; ***Dhuli***; *Sadanander Mela*; *Shivashakti*; *Grihapravesh*; *Kavi*; *Joydev*; *Balay Gras*; **1955**: *Amar Saigal*; *Sajghar*; *Parishodh*; *Shap Mochan*; *Bir Hambir*; *Prashna*; *Kalo Bou*; *Devimalini*; *Mejo Bou*; *Sabar Uparey*; *Paresh*; *Du-Janay*; *Drishti*; *Ardhangini*; *Teen Bhai*; **1956**: *Mahanisha*; ***Sagarika***; *Bhaduri Mashai*; *Sadhana*; *Ekti Raat*; *Mahakavi Girishchandra*; *Asamapta*; *Chalachal*; *Manraksha*; ***Jagte Raho/Ek Din Raatre***; *Rajpath*; *Suryamukhi*; *Govindadas*; *Madan Mohan*; *Shilpi*; *Sinthir Sindoor*; *Dhular Dharani*; **1957**: *Haar Jeet*; *Shesh Parichaya*; *Bardidi*; *Sindoor*; *Ratri Sheshey*; *Tapasi*; *Panchatapa*; *Yatra Holo Suru*; *Prithibi Amar Chai*; *Raat Ekta*; *Natun Prabhat*; *Surer Parashey*; *Basanta Bahar*; *Harano Sur*; *Mathur*; *Kari-o-Komal*; *Tamasha*; *Pathe Holo Deri*; *Janmatithi*; *Jiban Trishna*; ***Parash Pathar***; **1958**: *O Amar Desher Mati*; *Yamalaya Jibanta Manush*; *Megh Malhar*; *Shri Shri Maa*; *Tansen*; *Jonakir Alo*; *Indrani*; *Leela Kanka*; *Dhoomketu*; **1959**: *Janmantar*; *Marutirtha Hinglaj*; *Bicharak*; *Shri Shri Nityananda Prabhu*; ***Deep Jweley Jai***; *Shashi Babur Sansar*; *Bhranti*; *Ae Jahar Sey Jahar Noy*; *Nrityer Tale Tale*; *Shubha Bibaha*; *Personal Assistant*; **1960**: *Akash-Patal*; *Haat Baraley Bandhu*; *Sakher Chor*; ***Hospital***; *Shaharer Itikatha*; *Ajana Kahini*; **1961**: *Manik*; *Carey Shaheber Munshi*; *Lakshmi Narayan*; *Agni Sanskar*; *Swayambara*; *Necklace*; *Kathin Maya*; *Mithun Lagna*; ***Punashcha***; *Kanamachi*; **1962**: *Bipasha*; *Kancher Swarga*; *Suryasnan*; *Sancharini*; ***Kanchanjungha***; *Agnisikha*; *Agun*; *Kajal*; *Abhisarika*; *Nabadiganta*; *Abasheshe*; **1963**: *Ek Tukro Agun*; *Shesh-Anka*; *Dui Bari*; ***Saat Pake Bandha***; *Uttarayan*; ***Nirjan Saikate***; *Dui Nari*; *Akash Pradeep*; *Shesh Prahar*; *Chhaya Surya*; *Uttar Falguni*; *Deya Neya*; *Kanchan Kanya*; *Barnali*; *Shreyasi*; *The Householder*; **1964**: *Kaalsrote*; *Ta Holey*; *Bibhas*; *Swarga Hotey Biday*; *Kinu Goyalar Gali*; *Deep Nebhey Noy*; *Ketumi*; **1965**: *Alor Pipasa*; *Mahalagna*; *Antaral*; *Jaya*; *Ek Tuku Basa*; *Dolna*; *Surya Tapa*; *Tapasi*; **1966**: *Manihar*; *Mayabini Lane*; *Nutan Jiban*; *Sankha Bela*; *Mamata*; **1967**: *Ajana Shapath*; *Grihadah*; *Hathat Dekha*; *Kedar Raja*; *Nayika Sangbad*; *Nai Roshni*; **1968**: *Baluchari*; *Boudi*; *Saathi*; **1969**: *Rahgir*; *Kamallata*; *Mon-Niye*; ***Aradhana***; *Sabarmati*; ***Aranyer Din Ratri***; **1970**: *Dharti*; *Muktisnan*; *Rajkumari*; **1971**: *Bhanu Goenda Jahar Assistant*; *Nimantran*; *Pratham Basanta*; **1972**: *Haar Mana Haar*; *Shesh Parba*; **1973**: *Agni Bhramar*; *Ami Sirajer Begum*; *Kaya Hiner Kahini*; *Rater Rajanigandha*; *Rodon Bhora Basanta*; *Sajarur Kanta*; **1975**: *Kajal Lata*; *Chhoto Nayak*.

SARAIYA, GOVIND (b. 1929)

Gujarati and Hindi director born in Nadiad, Gujarat. Graduated from Bombay University. Studied animation on UNESCO fellowship at Walt Disney Studios and at the National Film Board of Canada where he was briefly apprenticed to Norman MacLaren. Employed at **Films Division**, where he set up the animation lab before becoming independent film-maker. Feature films noted for their literary sources in Gujarati classics. Best-known film is his feature début ***Saraswatichandra*** which, along with its sequel *Gunsundari No Ghar Sansar*, is based on the epic novel of Govardhanram Tripathi. *Saraswatichandra* became a commercial hit helped by **Kalyanji-Anandji**'s music. *Mansai Na Diva*, written by Zaverchand Meghani, is a biographical based on a cult figure in Gujarat, Ravishankar Maharaj, who worked among the 'criminal' tribes of Patanwadia and Baraiya, and later participated in Gandhi's Bardoli Satyagraha.

FILMOGRAPHY: 1956: *Electricity in the Service Of Man* (Doc); *Growing Wings* (Doc); **1957**: *All About Teeth* (Doc); *Freedom on Wheels* (Doc); *Operation Sky* (Doc); **1958**: *The Metric System* (Doc); *You and the Railways: Footboard Travel* (Doc); **1959**: *Banyan Deer*

(Doc); *Notes that Matter* (Doc); *On Stamps and Stamping* (Doc); **1960**: *A Great Problem* (Doc); *When Dreams Come True* (Doc); **1961**: *Portrait of a Postman* (Doc); *Romance of the Indian Coin* (Doc); **1962**: *Dust the Killer* (Doc); *Metric Measures* (Doc); **1963**: *A Man of Valour* (Doc); *Quickfire Plan* (Doc); **1964**: *It Happened on a Saturday* (Doc); *Sterilisation of The Female* (Doc); **1965**: *My Wise Daddy* (Doc); **1967**: *The Dreams of Mouji Ram* (Doc); **1968**: ***Saraswatichandra***; **1969**: *Leela* (Doc); **1970**: *Priya*; **1971**: *Chain Reaction* (Doc); *The Cheats* (Doc); **1972**: *Gunsundari No Ghar Sansar*; **1975**: *Angarey*; **1976**: *Sajjo Rani*; **1977**: *Mansai Na Diva*; **1980**: *Karo Kankuna*; *Four Faces* (Doc); **1982**: *Tran Treniya Chha Chhabila Baharvatiya/Bachche Teen Aur Daku Chhe*; **1984**: *Waqt Se Pehle*; **1991**: *Saiyan Ke Gaon Mein* (Doc).

Sardar Begum *see* **Akhtar, Sardar**

SARHADI, ZIA (b. 1914)

Hindi-Urdu director and scenarist born in Peshawar (now Pakistan). Entered film in 1933 at **East India Film**, Calcutta; then joined **Sagar** (1934) where he met **Mehboob**, who later produced his best-known film, ***Awaaz***. Played the lead in Mehboob's ***Manmohan*** as well as writing the script and the lyrics. Also scripted Mehboob's ***Bahen*** (1941) and was also a noted scenarist and writer at **Ranjit**. Sarhadi's cinema drew inspiration from and gave sustenance to the **IPTA** style of film-making. Although himself an unaffiliated Marxist, ***Humlog***, ***Footpath*** and *Awaaz* were very influential when the IPTA's film efforts were at their peak between the end of WW2 and Independence. Migrated to Pakistan after Independence, remaining there except for a brief period in the mid-70s. Apart from his own films, other writing credits include ***Jagirdar***, *Kal Ki Baat* (both 1937), ***Jeevan Saathi*** (1939), *Sajani* (1940), ***Garib*** (1942), ***Badi Maa*** (1945), ***Elaan*** (1947), *Anokha Pyar* (1948), *Dil Ki Duniya* (1949) and *Khel* (1950); also wrote the dialogue for ***Baiju Bawra*** (1952).
FILMOGRAPHY (* act only): **1936**: ***Manmohan****; **1937**: ***Jagirdar****; **1938**: ***Abhilasha***; *Afsana*; **1939**: *Bhole Bhale*; ***Seva Samaj****; **1942**: *Swapna*; **1943**: ***Nadaan***; **1945**: *Yateem*; **1951**: ***Humlog***; **1953**: ***Footpath***; **1956**: ***Awaaz***.

SARMA, PHANI (1910-70)

Assamese actor and director. One of the most enigmatic figures in Assamese film. Stage enthusiast, footballer, bohemian, actor, playwright and film-maker. Worked initially as a trader with his comrade-in-arms Bishnu Rabha; then became a stage actor and achieved a major reputation in the 30s. Became a key member of **Jyotiprasad Agarwala**'s Tezpur-based film unit in the 30s, playing the cruel Gaathi in Agarwala's ***Joymati***, and also acted in his second film, *Indramalati*. Continued working in the touring theatre groups of Assam, including an adaptation of Gogol's *The Government Inspector*, and in the original plays *Kiya*, *Kolabazar*. etc. Together with Agarwala and **Bhupen Hazarika**, he was a key figure in the provincial committees of the Assamese **IPTA** (1946). Adapted ***Siraj***, a plea for Hindu-Muslim unity, from a story by Lakhidar Sarma, filming it in 1948 (apparently co-directed by Bishnu Rabha and with Hazarika débuting as composer) and staging it in 1962. After 1963, known mainly as film actor following a tremendously successful comic performance in **Brojen Barua**'s ***Ito Sito Bohuto***.

FILMOGRAPHY (* also d): **1935**: ***Joymati***; **1939**: *Indramalati*; **1948**: ***Siraj****; **1955**: ***Pioli Phukan****; *Sarapat*; **1956**: ***Era Bator Sur***; **1957**: *Dhumuha**; **1958**: *Bhakta Prahlad*; **1959**: *Amar Ghar*; *Kecha Sone**; *Puwati Nishar Sapon**; **1960**: *Lachit Barphukan*; **1961**: *Shakuntala*; *Narakasur*; **1963**: ***Ito Sito Bohuto***; *Maniram Dewan*; **1964**: *Pratidhwani/Ka Swariti*.

SARPOTDAR, NARAYANRAO DAMODAR (1896-1940)

Marathi and Hindi director, scenarist and producer; born in Ratnagiri Dist., Maharashtra. Short-story writer and playwright (*Unad Pendya*, *Chandrarao More*, which later turned into his first film). One of the first and most significant studio producer-directors in the Pune-based Marathi cinema outside **Prabhat**. Early career in **Maharashtra Film**, Kolhapur (1919). Acted in **Baburao Painter**'s *Bhagwata Bhakta Damaji* (1922). First film started for Deccan Pics (1924) which he bought and ran, with Pandurang Talegiri, as United Pics Syndicate (1925-7) in Pune. Started Aryan Film (1927-32) and, in addition to his own films, wrote the scripts for *Raja Harishchandra* (1928), *Shri Balaji*, *Dasharathi Ram* (both 1929), *Subrahmanyam* and *Shamsher Bahadur* (both 1930, some directed by Y.D. Sarpotdar). Worked briefly at **Imperial** (1932-6) before joining Master Prod. Wrote film criticism under the name Charudatta and published a poetry volume, *Mudrikar*. Also managed a hotel in Pune. Films continue the historical mode introduced by Baburao Painter, conventionally based on Maratha history, chiefly the rule of Shivaji and the subsequent Peshwai. In specifically addressing a Maharashtrian audience, they also initiated a strand later taken up by **Bhalji Pendharkar** (who remade *Thoratanchi Kamala* in 1941).

FILMOGRAPHY: **1925**: *Chandrarao More*; ***Maharachi Por***; *Chhatrapati Sambhaji*; *Prabhavati*(?); **1926**: *Totayache Bund*; *Dha Cha Ma*; *Tai Teleen*; *Umaji Naik*; *Babanchi Bayko*; **1927**: *Thoratanchi Kamala*; *Krishna Sambhav*; **1928**: *Ganimi Kava*; *Arya Mahila*; *Namak Haram*; *The Daughter of the Maharattas*; *Patitoddhar*; *Udantappu*; **1929**: *Subhadra Haran*; *Parijatak*; *Prithviraj Sanyogita*; **1930**: *Jai Vijay*; *Bhimsen the Mighty*; *Chatur Sundari*; **1931**: *Nakoga Bai Lagna*; *Chandbibi*; **1932**: *Bhawani Talwar* (all St); **1933**: *Prithviraj Sanyogita*; *Rukmini Haran*; **1934**: *Devaki*; **1935**: *Chalta Putla*; **1938**: *Sant Janabai*; ***Nandakumar***; **1939**: *Bhagwa Jhenda*.

SASI, I. V. (b. 1948)

Prolific trendsetting Malayalam director; born in Calicut, Kerala. Also worked in Hindi, Tamil and Telugu. Received diploma at the Madras School of Fine Art. Joined films as art-director for A.B. Raj's *Kaliyalla Kalyanam* (1968); worked as cameraman in the early 70s. Associated mainly with the expansion of the Malayalam film industry in the 70s in the wake of the 'Gulf boom' produced by remittances from émigré labour. Working in the context of the infamous 'Blade companies' (investing in Malayalam films often at usurious interest rates), he dealt with issues of Malayalam identity, often featuring **Mammootty**. Makes 7 or 8 films annually, often drawing on the work of the Marxist writer Damodaran, in which the hero fights an oppressive contemporary reality by turning vigilante. Broke through with *Avalude Ravukal*, originally a poignant if sexually explicit love story featuring an orphan brother and sister, notorious in a dubbed version titled *Her Nights*. His fantasies about the nexus between crime, politics and the law-enforcement machinery grew in the 70s to grandiose dramas, e.g. ***America America*** (largely set in Florida) or ***Iniyenkilum***, which contrasts Kerala's economic and cultural conditions to those in Japan. Typical hits are, e.g., ***Avanazhi***, apparently based on a notorious Emergency scandal in which a student was tortured and killed in jail (also the subject of **Shaji Karun**'s ***Piravi***, 1988), featuring mainly a violent policeman (Mammootty) who uses illegal means to capture people otherwise beyond the law; or ***Vartha*** in which a newspaper editor hires his own men to bring political criminals to book. Shifted his style for the big-budget historical ***Ayarthi Thollayirathi Irupathonnu*** aka *1921*, recreating the famous Moplah (aka Mapilla) rebellion in the former Malabar.

FILMOGRAPHY: **1975**: *Ulsavam*; **1976**: *Abhinandanam*; *Alinganam*; *Anubhavam*; *Ashirvadam*; *Ayalakkari*; **1977**: *A Nimisham*; *Abhinivesam*; *Akale Akasam*; *Anandam Paramanandam*; *Angikaram*; *Anjali*; *Antardhanam*; *Hridayame Sakshi*; *Innale Innu*; *Itha Ivide Vare*; *Oonjal*; **1978**: *Amarsham*; *Anumodhanam*; *Avalude Ravukal*; *Ee Manohara Theeram*; *Gnan Gnan Mathram*; *Iniyum Puzha Ozhukum*; *Itha Oru Manushyan*; *Vadagaikku Oru Hridayam*; *Yeetta*; **1979**: *Allavudeenum Albutha Velakkum/Allavudeenum Arputha Vilakkum/Alladdin And The Wonderful Lamp*; *Anubhavangale Nandi*; *Arattu*; *Ezham Kadalinakkare*; *Man Ka Aangan*; *Manasa Vacha Karmana*; *Ore Vanam Ore Bhoomi*; *Pagalil Oru Iravu*; **1980**: *Angadi*; *Ashwaratham*; *Evar*; *Guru*; *Kali*; *Kanthavalayam*; *Karimbana*; *Meen*; *Patita*; *Pratishodh*; **1981**: *Ahimsa*; *Orikkalkoodi*; *Trishna*; *Hamsa Geetham*; **1982**: ***Ee Nadu***; *Ina*; *Innalenkil Nale*; *John Jaffer Janardhan*; *Sindoora Sandhyakku Mounam*; *Thadagam*; **1983**: *Ahankaram*; ***America America***; *Aroodam*; ***Iniyenkilum***; *Kaikeyi*; *Nanayam*; **1984**: *Adiyozhukkukal*; *Aksharangal*; ***Alkoottathil Thaniye***; *Athirathnam*; ***Kaanamarayathu***; *Karishma*; ***Lakshmana Rekha***; *Minimol Vathikanil*; *Uyyarangalil*; *Disco Disco*; **1985**: ***Angadikkapurathu***; *Anubandham*; *Ida Nilangal*; *Karimbin Poovinakkare*; *Rangam*; **1986**: *Abhayam Thedi*; *Anokha Rishta*; ***Avanazhi***; ***Vartha***; **1987**: *Adimagal Udumagal*; *Nalkawala*; *Vrutham*; **1988**: ***Ayarthi Thollayirathi Irupathonnu***; *Anuragi*; *Illam*; *Mukti*; *Abkari*; **1989**: *Aksharathettu*; *Avedana*; *Manchivaru Maavaru*; **1991**: *Inspector Balram*; *Miss Stella*; *Neelagiri*; **1992**: *Aparadha*; *Kallanum Polisum*; **1993**: *Devasuram*.

SASIKUMAR

Prolific Malayalam director born in Alleppey, Kerala. Started in **Kunchako**'s Udaya Studio in Trivandrum. Acted a small part in P.R.S. Pillai's ***Thiramala*** (1953). His first feature was co-directed by P.A. Thomas. Best known for sex comedies and titillation melodramas. One of the latter, *Interview*, is not to be confused with **Mrinal Sen**'s film of 1970.

FILMOGRAPHY: 1964: *Porter Kunjali*; **1965**: *Jeevitha Yatra*; *Thommente Makkal*; **1966**: *Kanmanikal*; *Pennmakkal*; *Kootukar*; **1967**: ***Kavalam Chundan***; **1968**: *Velutha Kathrina*; *Vidyarthi*; *Love in Kerala*; **1969**: *Rest House*; *Rahasyam*; **1970**: *Rakta Pushpam*; **1971**: *Bobanum Molyum*; *Lanka Dahanam*; **1972**: *Anveshanam*; *Brahmachari*; *Pushpanjali*; *Maravil Thiruvu Sukshikuha*; **1973**: *Divya Darshanam*; *Interview*; *Padmavyuham*; *Panchavati*; *Thani Niram*; *Thekkan Kattu*; *Thiruvabharanam*; **1974**: *Setu Bandhanam*; *Night Duty*; *Panchatanthram*; *Poonthenaruvi*; **1975**: *Abhimanam*; *Aranyakadam*; *Alibaba and Forty-One Thieves*; *Chattambi Kalyani*; *Padmaragam*; *Palazhi Madhanam*; *Picnic*; *Pravaham*; *Sindhu*; *Sammanam*; *Pulival*; **1976**: *Ajayanum Vijayanum*; *Amritha Vahini*; *Kamadhenu*; *Kayamkulam Kochunniyude Maghan*; *Pickpocket*; *Pushpa Sarem*; *Swimming Pool*; *Panchamrutham/Pachamirutham*; *Thuruppu Gulam*; **1977**: *Minimol*; *Mohamum Mukthiyum*; *Lakshmi*; *Aparajitha*; *Chaturvedam*; *Rathi Manmathan*; *Rendu Lokam*; *Parivarthanam*; *Muttathe Mulla*; *Saghakkale Munottu*; *Vishukkani*; *Varadakshina*; *Akshaya Pathram*; **1978**: *Bharyayum Kamukiyum*; *Kalpa Vruksha*; *Kanyaka*; *Jayikkanai Janichavan*; *Mattoru Karnan*; *Mudra Mothiram*; *Mukkuvane Snehicha Bhootham*; *Ninakku Gnanam Enikku Neeyum*; *Nivedyam*; *Shathru Samharam*; **1979**: *Ormayil Nee Mathram*; *Manavadharmam*; *Nithiyavasatham*; *Vellayani Paramu*; *Chula*; **1980**: *Ithikkara Pakki*; *Theenalagal*; *Oru Varsham Oru Masam*; *Kari Puranda Jeevithangal*; *Prakatanam*; **1981**: *Kodumudikal*; *Ellam Ninakku Vendi*; *Dhruva Sangamam*; *Attamari*; *Theekali*; **1982**: *Post Mortem*; *Thuranna Jail*; *Jambulingam*; *Koritharicha Naal*; *Madrasille Mohan*; *Sooryan*; **1983**: *Arabikadal*; *Kattaruvi*; *Mahabali*; *Chakravalam Chuvannappol*; *Yuddham*; *Sandhya Vandanam*; *Attakkalasam*; *Kola Komban*; **1984**: *Ivide Thodangannu*; *Saundamevide? Bandamevide?*; *Makale Maapu Tharu*; **1985**: *Azhiyatha Bandhangal*; *Ezhamuthal Onpathuvare*; *Ente Kannakuyil*; *Makan Ente Makan*; *Mouna Nombaram*; *Shri Vamanavatharam*; *Pathamudayam*; **1986**: *Akalangalil*; *Iniyum Kurukshetram*; *Kunjatta Kiligal*.

SASTRY, BELLAVE NARAHARI (1881-1961)

Kannada cinema's first scenarist-lyricist. Foremost author of **Company Natak** mythologicals with c.40 plays, nearly all for **Veeranna**, including the hit *Sadarame* (1935). Key figure in the translation of Yakshagana folk forms into proscenium stagecraft and films, incorporating many ritual forms such as the initial invocation of the gods in his *Krishna Leela*. Renowned for plays with miracle scenes like the *Kaliya Mardana* (Krishna killing the demon Kaliya) and *Vishwaroopa Darshan* (the world seen in Krishna's mouth). Historian Marulasiddappa (1983) commented that Sastry's idealisation of the divine and the heroic were the kind of formal anachronism castigated by the 'modernist' Amateur Dramatic Assoc. but his more casual scenes of e.g. village life were remarkable for their use of popular dialect. Also successful lyricist with hits like *Aseye neerase yaadude* in **H.L.N. Simha**'s ***Hemareddy Mallamma*** (1945). Other scripts: **Y.V. Rao**'s ***Sati Sulochana*** (1934), Chavan's *Bhakta Purandaradasa* (1937), **C. Pullaiah**'s *Subhadra* (1941), **Ch. Nayaranamurthy**'s *Bhakta Prahlada* (1942) and **K. Subramanyam**'s *Krishna Sudama* (1943).

SASTRY, DEVULAPALLI KRISHNA (1897-1980)

Telugu lyric writer and noted poet, born in Pithapuram, AP. Born in a family of traditional literary scholars in the employ of the Rajah of Pithapuram. Associated with the rationalist and social reformer Raghupati Venkataratnam Naidu. Published his first anthology of poetry, *Krishna Paksham* (1925), initiating a new age of romantic literature described as the Bhava kavitam. Also known for devotional poems, published under the name Mahati, and prose compilations (*Bahukala Darshanam*, *Pushpa Lavikulu*). A popular figure on early radio, broadcasting several plays and lectures. Film début with **B.N. Reddi**'s ***Malleeshwari*** (1951) as songwriter. Wrote several film lyrics and his poetry has been extensively used in films.

SATHYAN (1912-71)

Top star, with **Prem Nazir**, in Malayalam cinema, providing the embodiment of Malayali machismo. Former Malayalam teacher when aged 16. Joined the army (1941) becoming the Viceroy's commissioned officer, seeing action in Imphal, Burma and (former) Indochina against the Japanese. Later, a clerk at the Trivandrum secretariat and a police sub-inspector. Stage actor with **Thikkurisi Sukumaran Nair**; entered cinema at Merryland Studio (*Atmasakhi*). His classic screen persona of the brooding, remote and unreachable outlaw was shaped mainly by **Kariat**'s ***Mudiyanaya Puthran*** (where he spurns love with a Byronic disregard for merely human emotion) and ***Chemmeen*** (as an orphan battling with the forces of nature). In his many films with Nazir, he acquired the image of a loser (e.g. ***Odeyil Ninnu***). Partner in Manjilas Films, with director **Sethumadhavan** and M.O. Joseph.

FILMOGRAPHY: 1952: *Atmasakhi/Priyasakhi*; **1953**: ***Thiramala***; *Lokaneethi*; *Asha Deepam*; **1954**: ***Neelakuyil***; ***Snehaseema***; **1955**: *Kalam Marunnu*; **1956**: *Avarunarunnu*; **1957**: *Achannum Maganam*; *Minnunnathellan Ponnalla*; *Devasundari*; **1958**: *Thaskara Veeran*; *Lily*; *Nair Pidicha Pulivalu*; **1959**: *Minnal Padayali*; **1961**: ***Unniyarcha***; ***Arappavan***; *Krishna Kuchela*; ***Mudiyanaya Puthran***; **1962**: *Laila Majnu*; *Sreekovil*; *Palattukoman*; *Kannum Karalum*; *Vidhithanna Vilakku*; *Bhagya Jatakam*; *Viyarppinte Vila*; *Bharya*; **1963**: *Nithya Kanyaka*; *Doctor*; ***Moodupadam***; *Kadalamma*; *Ammeye Kannan*; *Rebecca*; **1964**: *Manavatti*; *Pazhassi Raja*; *Adya Kiranangal*; *Omanakuttan*; *Kalanjukuttiya Thangam*; *Ayesha*; *Thacholi Othenan*; *Anna*; **1965**: *Devatha*; *Shyamalachechi*; ***Odeyil Ninnu***; *Kadatthukaran*; *Inapravugal*; *Ammu*; *Kattu Thulasi*; ***Daham***; *Shakuntala*; *Chettathi*; *Thommente Makkal*; ***Chemmeen***; **1966**: *Station Master*; *Pagal Kinavu*; *Rowdy*; *Jail*; *Kootukar*; ***Kayamkulam Kochunni***; *Anarkali*; *Tharavatamma*; *Kallipennu*; *Tilottama*; **1967**: *Thallirukal*; *Sahadharmini*; *Sheelavati*; *Udyogastha*; *Arakillam*; *Postman*; *Kudumbam*; *Mainatharuvi Kola Case*; *Kadhija*; ***Anveshichu Kandatiyilla***; ***Ashwamedham***; *Pavapettaval*; *NGO*; ***Kavalam Chundan***; *Nadan Pennu*; *Chekuthante Kotta*; *Swapnabhoomi*; *Mulkireedam*; *Ollathu Mathi*; **1968**: *Thokkukal Katha Parayunnu*; *Manaswini*; *Vazhipizhacha Santhathi*; *Karthika*; *Kaliyalla Kalyanam*; *Yakshi*; *Midumidukki*; *Pengal*; *Aparadhini*; *Velutha Kathrina*; *Agni Pareeksha*; **1969**: *Veetu Mrugham*; *Kattukurangu*; *Kuruthikalam*; *Urangatha Sundari*; *Sandhya*; *Kadalpalam*;

Sathyan (holding rifle) in *Adya Kiranangal* (1964)

Vilakkapetta Bandhangal; *Chattambi Kavala*; *Velliyazhcha*; *Kootu Kudumbam*; ***Adimagal***; *Mooladanam*; **1970**: *Amma Enna Stree*; *Kurukshetram*; *Kalpana*; *Stree*; ***Vazhve Mayam***; *Cross Belt*; *Bhikara Nimishankal*; *Dattuputhran*; *Othenente Makan*; *Kuttavali*; ***Ningalenne Communistaki***; *Vivahitha*; *Nilakatha Chalanangal*; *Triveni*; *Tara*; ***Aranazhikaneram***; **1971**: *Shiksha*; *Moonnupukkal*; *Thettu*; ***Oru Penninte Katha***; *Kalithozhi*; *Inquilab Zindabad*; *Sarasayya*; *Karakanakadal*; *Vimochana Samaram*; ***Anubhavangal Palichakal***; **1972**: *Kalippava*; *Akkarapacha*; *Lakshyam*; **1973**: *Checkpost*; *Asha Chakram*.

SATHYU, MYSORE SRINIVASA (b. 1930)

Hindi, Urdu and Kannada director born in Mysore, Karnataka; noted theatre director and set designer. Graduated from Central College, Bangalore; moved to Bombay in 1952. Directed plays in Bombay and Delhi while freelancing as set designer and lighting director for, e.g., Parvati Kumar ballets (*Dekh Teri Bambai*, *Discovery of India*). Associated with **IPTA**, Bombay, and with its various offshoots: e.g. the Left organisation Bombay Youth (which published a journal edited by theatre director Habib Tanvir) and **Balraj Sahni**'s Juhu Art Theatre. Staged *Aakhri Shama* (1969), a biographical play on the poet Mirza Ghalib, along with writer **Kaifi Azmi** and Sahni in the role of Ghalib. Both later contributed to his début feature, and best-known film, ***Garam Hawa***. Other noted plays for IPTA include Sarveshwar Dayal Saksena's *Bakri*, *Sufaid Kundali* (from Brecht's *Causasian Chalk Circle*) and *Moteram Ka Satyagrah* (adapting Premchand). Also directed the play *Sookshma Roop* written by Sahni for the latter's Juhu Art Theatre. Joined films assisting **Chetan Anand** (e.g. ***Haqeeqat***, 1964) and documentarists Homi Sethna and Zul Velani. Also collaborated on the children's film *Chernaya Gora* (aka *Black Mountain*, 1971), an Indo-Soviet co-production by Alexander Zguridi based on a story by **K.A. Abbas**. Made c.20 shorts and 12 documentaries; now works mainly for tv, e.g. the 13-part series, *Choli Daman*, and adaptating Masti Venkatesha Iyengar's Kannada short stories into Tamil and Kannada (e.g. *Pratidhwani*). His wife, Shama Zaidi, wrote scripts for **S. Benegal**.

FILMOGRAPHY: **1967**: *Ek Tha Chhotu Ek Tha Motu*; **1969**: *Ghalib* (Doc); *Irshad Panjatan* (Doc); **1970**: *Kala Parvat*; **1971**: *Chernaya Gora*; **1973**: ***Garam Hawa***; **1977**: *Kanneshwara Rama*; **1978**: ***Chithegu Chinthe***; **1980**: ***Bara*/*Sookha***; **1981**: *Your Enemy: TB* (Doc); **1986**: *Kahan Kahan Se Guzar Gaye*; **1988**: *Choli Daman* (TV); **1991**: *Kayar* (TV).

SAURASHTRA FILM COMPANY

Est: 1923 as the Saurashtra Kinematograph in Rajkot, making it the first fully equipped studio in Gujarat. Founded by Vajeshankar Kanji Pattani (1889-1957) and Champakraj Kanji Pattani (1897-1958) with financial support from Sir Prabhashankar Pattani, Diwan of Bhavnagar. Major films include **Kanjibhai Rathod**'s *Anath Abala* (1925) and V.K. Pattani's *Baliyagna* (1924). Among the other talent employed was **Chimanlal Luhar**, actors Madanrai Vakil and Miss Ermeline and the comedian (later cameraman) Gatubhai Vaidya. Shiraz Ali started his career at the studio before establishing the Famous Cine Lab. The studio, which also made newsreels, closed in 1929.

Save Dada *see* **Bhatavdekar, H. S.**

SAVITRI, KOMMAREDDY (1937-81)

Telugu-Tamil actress and director born in Chirravuru, Krishna Dist., AP, into a wealthy family. She learnt music and dance under Sista Purnayya Sastry and gave some public performances as a child in Vijaywada. Worked in the theatre company run by **NTR**, **K. Jaggaiah** et al. Started her own group, the Navabharata Natya Mandali. Also acted in the play *Atma Vachana* by Buchi Babu. Début at the **Vijaya** Studio with **L.V. Prasad**'s ***Samsaram***, then **K.V. Reddy**'s ***Patala Bhairavi***. Minor film roles until ***Pelli Chesi Choodu*** made her a star, although she had to wait until ***Ardhangi*** to establish her acting credentials. Played the lead role of Mary in Prasad's comedy ***Missamma***. Acted in several films by the choreographer-director **Raghavaiah**, e.g. ***Devadasu***. Turned director and producer (1968-71) without much commercial success. Married to **Gemini Ganesh**.

FILMOGRAPHY (* also d): **1950**: ***Samsaram***; **1951**: ***Patala Bhairavi*/*Pataal Bhairavi***; *Roopavati*; **1952**: *Adarsham*; *Priyuralu*; ***Pelli Chesi Choodu*/*Kalyanam Panni Paar***; ***Palletooru***; *Shanti*; ***Sankranti***; **1953**: ***Chandraharam***; *Bratuku Theruvu*; ***Devadasu***; *Kodarikam*; *Paropakaram*; ***Pempudu Koduku***; *Pratigna*; **1954**: *Jyoti*/*Illara Jyoti*; *Menarikam*; *Parivarthana*; *Bahut Din Huye*; **1955**: ***Ardhangi*/*Pennin Perumai***; *Vijayagauri*; ***Missamma*/*Missiamma***; ***Santhanam***; *Vadina*; ***Donga Ramudu***; *Kanyashulkam*; **1956**: *Bhale Ramudu*/*Prema Pasham*; *Mathurkula Manikyam*/*Charanadasi*; ***Amara Deepam***; **1957**: *Thodi Kodallu*; ***Maya Bazaar***; *Bhale Ammayilu*/*Iru Sahodarargal*; *MLA*; *Kutumba Gauravam*; *Karpurakarasi*; *Mahadevi*; *Saubhagyavati*; **1958**: *Intiguttu*; *Karthavarayan Katha*; ***Appu Chesi Pappu Koodu*/*Kadam Vangi Kalyanam***; **1959**: *Mangalya Balam*/*Manjal Magimai*; *Bandaramudu*/*Adisaya Thirudan*; *Bhagya Devatha*/*Bhagya Devathai*; *Kalasivunte Kaladu Sukham*; *Illarikam*; **1960**: *Namminabantu*/*Pattayilin Vetri*; ***Shri Venkateshwara Mahatyam***; *Kumkumarekha*; *Deepavali*; *Chiviraku Migiledi*; *Abhimanam*; *Vimala*; *Mamaku Tagga Alludu*; *Maa Babu*; *Kalathur Kannamma*; *Pudhiya Pathai*; **1961**: *Maavoori Ammayi*; *Tallichina Ajna*; *Pasamalar*/*Raktha Sambandham*; ***Kappalotiya Thamizhan***; ***Pasamalar***; ***Pavamanippu***; **1962**: ***Aradhana***; *Manchi Manushulu*/*Penn Manam*; ***Gundamma Katha***/*Manidan Maravalli*; ***Siri Sampadalu***; *Kathirunda Kankal*; *Atmabandhuvu*; *Pavitra Prema*; *Parthal Pasi Theerum*; *Konjum Salangai*; *Padithal Mattu Pothuma*; *Vadivukku Valai Kappu*; **1963**: ***Raktha Tilakam***; *Karpagam*; *Parisu*; *Chaduvukonna Ammayilu*; *Nartanasala*; *Thobuttuvulu*; *Mamakaram*; ***Moogamanushulu***; *Naanum Oru Penn*/*Nadi Aada Janma*; **1964**: ***Karnan*/*Karna***; ***Poojapalam***; *Raktha Tilakam*; *Pativrata*; *Dr Chakravarthi*; *Kaikodutha Daivam*; *Ganga Ki Lehren*; *Vettaikaran*; *Navarathri*; **1965**: *Sumangali*; ***Pandava Vanavasam***; *Devatha*; *Manushulu Mamathalu*; **1966**: *Monagalluku Monagadu*; *Papa Pariharam*; *Navarathri*; *Bhakta Potana*; *Manase Mandiram*; *Saraswathi Sabatham*; **1967**: *Seeta*; *Kanchukota*; *Nirdoshi*; *Ummadi Kutumbam*; ***Pranamithrulu***; ***Kandan Karunai***; **1968**: *Bandhavyulu*; *Moogajeevulu*; *Talliprema*; *Chinnari Papalu**; ***Varakatnam***; **1969**: *Chiranjeevi**; *Mathrudevata**; *Manishichina Maguva*; *Vichitra Kutumbam*; *Kuzhandai Ullam**; **1970**: ***Maro Prapancham***; *Pettandarulu*; *Talli Tandrulu*; *Kodalu Diddina Kapuram*; **1971**: *Vintha Samsaram**; *Suputhrudu*; *Talli Kuthulu*; *Nindu Dampatulu*; *Praptham**; **1972**: *Jakkamma*; *Thaikku Oru Pillai*; *Kanna Talli*; *Amma Mata*; *Shabash Baby*; *Shabash Papanna*; **1973**: *Deshoddharakulu*; *Ramrajyam*; *Puttinillu Mettinillu*; *Jyoti Lakshmi*; *Poola Mala*; *Chuzhi*; *Veetu Mappillai*; *Suryakanthi*; *Engal Thayi*; *Baghdad Perazhagi*; **1974**: *Akkarai Pachai*; *Jeevitha Rangamu*; *Gali Patalu*; *Uttama Illalu*; *Tulasi*; *Manushulu Matti Bommalu*; *Anaganaga Oka Thandri*; *Adambaralu Anubandhalu*; *Bandhulu Anubandhulu*; *Mugguru Ammayilu*; **1975**: *Bharatamlo Oka Ammayi*; *Kavitha*; *Maa Inti Devudu*; *Pooja*; *Santhanam Saubhagyam*; *Pellikani Thandri*; *Puthu Vellam*; *Chillara Devullu*; **1977**: *Punitha Anthoniar*; *Rambha Urvashi Menaka*; *Panchayathi*; **1978**: *Rowdy Rangamma*; *Amara Prema*; *Prema Paga*; *Allari Pillalu*; *Devadasu Malli Puttadu*; *Vattathukkul Chaduram*; ***Jagan Mohini***; *Mugguru Muggure*; **1979**: *Rangoon Rowdy*; *Gorintaku*; **1980**: *Circus Ramudu*; *Prema Tarangalu*; **1981**: *Puli Bidda*; **1985**: *Andarikante Monagadu*.

SEGAL, MOHAN (b. 1921)

Hindi director born in Jullundur, Punjab. Degree in literature. Studied dance at Uday Shankar's India Culture Centre, Almora. Member of theatre group invited by the **IPTA** and the **PWA** to tour their *Shadow Play* in working-class areas throughout Bombay to raise funds for Bengal famine relief (1944). Worked at **Prithviraj Kapoor**'s Prithvi Theatres as actor (e.g. *Deewar* and *Shakuntala*, 1945) and choreographer. Remained closely involved with the IPTA in Bombay. Wrote and directed the play *Desh Bhakt*; also directed **Balraj Sahni**'s play *Jadu Ki Kursi*. Joined films as actor and assistant director to **Chetan Anand** (***Neecha Nagar***). Choreographed **Nanabhai Bhatt**'s *Chalis Karod*, and the first two films he directed. His best-known films are the freewheeling **Kishore Kumar** satires of the late 50s: ***New Delhi***, ***Apna Haath Jagannath*** and *Karodpati*. His spectacular hit, *Sawan Bhadon*, introduced the 70s/80s star **Rekha**.

FILMOGRAPHY (* act only): **1945**: *Chalis Karod**; **1946**: ***Neecha Nagar****; **1948**: *Phool Aur Kaante**; **1949**: *Raaz**; **1950**: ***Afsar****; **1953**: *Humsafar**; **1954**: *Aulad*; *Adhikar*; **1956**: ***New Delhi***; **1960**: ***Apna Haath Jagannath***; **1961**: *Karodpati*; **1966**: *Devar*; **1968**: *Kanyadaan*; **1969**: *Saajan*; **1970**: *Sawan Bhadon*; **1972**: *Raja Jani*; **1974**: *Woh Main Nahin*; **1976**: *Santan*; **1977**: *Ek Hi Raasta*; **1979**: *Kartavya*; **1981**: *Daulat*; **1982**: *Samrat*; **1984**: *Hum Hain Lajawaab*; **1989**: *Kasam Suhaag Ki*.

Sekhar, Raja C. *see* **Chandrasekhar, Raja**

SEN, APARNA (b. 1945)

Bengali actress and director born in Calcutta, daughter of critic and cineaste **Chidananda Das Gupta**. Grew up watching European art films. Graduated in English. Stage actress in **Utpal Dutt**'s Little Theatre Group and made film début as a teenager in the *Samapti* episode of **S. Ray**'s ***Teen Kanya***. Went on to star in many mainstream melodramatic plays and films. Directorial début with the English-language film, ***36 Chowringhee Lane***, produced by **Shashi Kapoor** as explicitly apolitical cinema. As director she deploys psychological realism familiar from Western art films but concentrates on female characters, often imbued with a strong sense of nostalgia. Edits a women's fashion glossy, *Sananda*. Directed **Shabana Azmi**'s first tv drama, *Picnic*. Recently returned to the commercial stage with *Pannabai* (1989) and *Bhalo Kharap Meye* (1991).

FILMOGRAPHY (* only d): **1961**: ***Teen Kanya***; **1965**: ***Akash Kusum***; **1968**: *Hansamithun*; **1969**: ***Aparichita***; *Vishwas*; *The Guru*; ***Aranyer Din Ratri***; **1970**: *Kalankita Nayak*; *Padmagolap*; *Bombay Talkie*; **1971**: *Ekhani*; *Ekhane Pinjar*; *Jay Jayanti*; *Khunje Berai*; **1972**: *Jiban Saikate*; *Mem Sahib*; *Nayikar Bhumikay*; *Basanta Bilap*; ***Bilet Pherat***; **1973**: *Epar Opar*; *Kaya Hiner Kahini*; *Rater Rajanigandha*; *Shesh Pristhay Dekhun*; *Sonar Khancha*; **1974**: *Alor Thikana*; *Asati*; ***Jadu Bansha***; *Sujata*; *Chhutir Phande*; **1975**: ***Jana Aranya***; *Kajal Lata*; *Nishi Mrigaya*; *Raag Anuraag*; **1976**: *Nidhi Ram Sardar*; *Ajasra Dhanyabad*; *Asomoy*; **1977**: *Proxy*; *Imaan Dharam*; *Kotwal Saab*; **1978**: *Hullabaloo over Georgie and Bonnie's Pictures*; **1979**: *Nauka Dubi*; **1980**: ***Pikoo*** (TV-Sh); **1981**: *Abichar*; *Bandi Balaka*; ***36 Chowringhee Lane****; **1982**: *Amrita Kumbher Sandhaney*; *Bijoyini*; **1983**: *Abhinay Nay*; *Indira*; *Mohaney Dike*; **1984**: *Bishabriksha*; **1985**: ***Paroma/Parama****; *Devika*; *Neelkantha*; **1986**: *Shyam Saheb*; **1987**: *Ekanto Apon*; *Jar Je Priyo*; **1988**: ***Ek Din Achanak***; **1989**: *Kari Diye Kinlam*; ***Sati****; **1990**: *Picnic** (TV); **1991**: ***Mahaprithibi***.

SEN, ASIT (b. 1922)

Bengali and Hindi director born in Dhaka (now Bangladesh). Early interest in photography. Joined films as camera assistant to D.K. Mehta at Bharatlaxmi Prod. (1946); then assisted his uncle, the noted cameraman Ramananda Sengupta, on Ardhendu Mukherjee's *Purbaraag* (1947). Made an independent 16mm documentary on Gandhi's tour of Noakhali and Patna, joining Gandhi's entourage for a month. Début in Assamese film (***Biplabi***), went uncredited following a dispute with the producers over its ending. Ran a photography studio (1949) while seeing Hitchcock and Danny Kaye and other Hollywood films which, he says, he studied extensively, often persuading the manager of the New Empire and Light House theatres in Calcutta to run selected reels specially for him. His Bengali début, *Chalachal*, was a major **Arundhati Devi** hit; it was followed by *Panchatapa* with the same star. The **Suchitra Sen** hits ***Deep Jweley Jai*** and *Uttar Falguni* established a new generation of post-war and post-Independence (and in Bengali film, post-**New Theatres**) brand of romantic love story, using several new lyrical-expressionist devices such as the mobile camera of *Deep Jweley Jai* and the dramatic montage of *Uttar Falguni*. Much of his style is comparable to **Bimal Roy**'s in its simultaneous assimilation of romantic Bengali literature, Hollywood and neo-realism. Roy produced Sen's third film, his first in Hindi, *Parivar*, and later also *Anokhi Raat*. Remade *Uttar Falguni* in Hindi as *Mamata*. In the late 1960s/70s, he directed Hindi star **Rajesh Khanna** in two big romances, ***Khamoshi*** (remaking *Deep Jweley Jai*) and *Safar*, both strongly imbued with the Bengali romantic lyricism of his early work.

FILMOGRAPHY: 1948: ***Biplabi***; **1956**: *Chalachal*; *Parivar*; **1957**: *Aparadhi Kaun*; *Panchatapa*; *Jiban Trishna*; **1958**: *Jonakir Alo*; **1959**: ***Deep Jweley Jai***; **1961**: *Swaralipi*; *Swayambara*; **1962**: *Agun*; **1963**: *Uttar Falguni*; **1965**: *Trishna*; **1966**: *Mamata*; **1968**: *Anokhi Raat*; **1969**: ***Khamoshi***; **1970**: *Maa Aur Mamta*; *Safar*; *Sharafat*; **1972**: *Annadata*; *Anokha Daan*; **1975**: *Anari*; **1976**: *Bairaag*; **1981**: *Vakil Babu*; **1983**: *Mehndi*; **1984**: *Prarthana*; **1985**: *Pratigya*.

SEN, HIRALAL (1866-1917)

Bengali film pioneer born in Bakjuri village, Munshiganj (now Bangladesh). India's first film-maker with **Bhatavdekar**. The son of a lawyer, he started as photographer and achieved considerable renown. Almost definitely saw first-ever film show, at Star Theatres, featuring Prof. Stevenson's shorts on double-bill with Star's stage hit, *The Flower of Persia* (1898). His first film, made with equipment and guidance from Stevenson, was based on scenes from *The Flower of Persia* and shown at Star, with Stevenson's package, in repeated shows that year. Acquired camera from London, a projector from Warwick Trading and set up Royal Bioscope (1899) with his brother, Motilal Sen. His best-known outlet was Amar Dutta's Classic Theatre in Calcutta, where Royal initially exhibited imported footage (e.g. *Transvaal War Pictures*, *Splendid Magical Exhibitions*, *A Few Marvellous Scenes of a Well-known Circus Played at Paris Exhibition*) in intervals between stage shows. Best-known work in collaboration with Classic, filming scenes from its stage repertoire (1901-4). The partnership culminated in what was perhaps Sen's only feature-length film, *Alibaba and the Forty Thieves* (the film's length is disputed). Also did many request shows in private houses of landed gentry, command performances at the court of local maharajas, etc. Made some advertising films. Increasing competition from **Madan Theatres** in partnership with Pathé and the rise of several newer bioscope companies in Calcutta are among the reasons for Royal Bioscope's decline. Apparently all its films were destroyed in a fire shortly before the studio closed down.Sen's filmography is still a controversial issue among film historians. This one combines titles given by various sources. Further research will have to establish the definitive filmography.

FILMOGRAPHY: 1898: *Dancing Scenes from* The Flower of Persia; **1899**: *Moving Pictures of Natural Scenes and Religious Rituals*; **1901**: *Scenes from* Bhramar; *Scenes from* Seetaram; *Scenes from* Sarala; *Scenes from* Alibaba; *Scenes from* Buddhadev; *Scenes from* Hariraj; *Scenes from* Dol Leela; **1903**: *Scenes from* Sonar Swapan; *Scenes from* Maner Matan; *Dances from* Alibaba; *Alibaba and the Forty Thieves*; *Indian Life and Scenes*; *Coronation Ceremony and Durbar*; **1904**: *The Bengali Fisherman*; *The Fisherman's Boy*; **1905**: *The Bengal Partition Film*; *Edward's Anti-malarial Specific*; *C.K. Sen's Jaba Kusum Oil*; *Sarsaparilla of W. Major Company*; **1906**: *Tilak Bathing at the Ganges with Thousands, The Panoramic View of the Ghat, The Grand Procession of Memorable Day Headed by Well-known Heroes of Bengal*; **1912**: *Grand Delhi Coronation Durbar and Royal Visit to Calcutta Including Their Majesties' Arrival at Amphitheatre, Arrival at Howrah, Princep's Ghat, Procession, Visit to Bombay and Exhibition*; **1913**: *Hindu Bathing Festival at Allahabad*.

SEN, MRINAL (b. 1923)

Leading Bengali director; also worked in Oriya, Telugu and in Hindi. Born in Faridpur (now Bangladesh). Studied science in Calcutta; worked as apprentice in sound recording studio, as journalist and medical representative. Joined the CPI. Read voraciously about cinema

Mrinal Sen's *Matir Manisha* (1966)

and aesthetics; also reviewed films. Associated with the **IPTA** (1943-7) and remained active in Left politics. Early influences include Arnheim's writings. Authored book on Chaplin (1951) and Bengali translation of Karl Capek's *The Cheat* (1946). Directorial début in 1956 and his 2nd film was banned for two months by the government, but didn't break through until ***Akash Kusum***, which generated a passionate debate with **S. Ray**. His ***Bhuvan Shome***, made in Hindi, was a commercial success in Bombay and is said to have pioneered the New Indian Cinema, generating the 70s debates about low-budget alternatives to commercial cinema. In his films Sen has consistently and unambiguously downgraded notions of artistic 'originality' and deployed a wide array of influences from Glauber Rocha's early work to Truffaut (*Akash Kusum*) and from Augusto Boal's *Theatre of the Oppressed* to Solanas and Getino (the Calcutta trilogy: ***Interview***, ***Calcutta '71*** and ***Padatik***), Fellini (***Akaler Sandhaney***) and most recently Bresson (***Khandhar***). Best-known 70s work evoked Brecht transformed through the prism of **Ghatak** and the radical currents of Bengali theatre and folk forms, achieving a freewheeling style Sen later described as 'playing around with tools as often as I could, as a child plays with building blocks. Partly out of sheer playfulness, partly out of necessity, also partly to shock a section of our audiences [to violate the] outrageously conformist ... mainstream of our cinema.' His political films, drawing also from the IPTA and from **Utpal Dutt**'s 70s theatre group, culminated in the Calcutta trilogy made in the wake of the dismantling of the United Front Ministry in Bengal, with massive anti-Left reprisals, esp. against **Naxalite** factions. The films became a *cause cél¤bre* as their screenings became meeting-points for Left activists (with Sen's encouragement) and were raided regularly by the police. This period was later commemorated by Reinhard Hauff in his documentary *Ten Days In Calcutta: A Portrait of Mrinal Sen* (1984). 80s work, introduced by ***Ek Din Pratidin***, returns to a storytelling style he presents as a more contemplative way of advocating 'a greater awareness of reality'. In addition to scripting his own films, also wrote Ajit Lahiri's *Joradighir Choudhury Paribar* and **Ajoy Kar**'s *Kanch Kata Hirey* (both 1966). Published books on cinema, *Chalachitra Bhut Bartaman Bhabhishya* and *Views on Cinema* (both 1977) and *Cinema, Adhunikata* (1992).

FILMOGRAPHY: 1956: *Raat Bhore*; **1958**: ***Neel Akasher Neechey***; **1960**: ***Baishey Shravan***; **1961**: ***Punashcha***; **1962**: *Abasheshe*; **1964**: *Pratinidhi*; **1965**: ***Akash Kusum***; **1966**: ***Matir Manisha***; **1967**: *Moving Perspective* (Doc); **1969**: *Ichhapuran*; ***Bhuvan Shome***; **1970**: ***Interview***; **1971**: ***Ek Adhuri Kahani***; **1972**: ***Calcutta '71***; **1973**: ***Padatik***; **1974**: ***Chorus***; **1976**: ***Mrigaya***; **1977**: ***Oka Oorie Katha***; **1978**: ***Parashuram***; **1979**: ***Ek Din Pratidin***; **1980**: ***Akaler Sandhaney***; **1981**: ***Chaalchitra***; **1982**: ***Kharij***; **1983**: ***Khandhar***; **1984**: ***Tasveer Apni Apni*** (TV); **1986**: ***Genesis***; **1987**: *Kabhi Door Kabhi Paas* (TV); **1988**: ***Ek Din Achanak***; **1990**: *Calcutta My Eldorado* (Doc); **1991**: ***Mahaprithibi***; **1993**: *Antareen*.

SEN, SATU (1902-72)

Bengali director; pioneering art director on commercial Bengali stage before entering films; considered to have influenced later masters such as Bansi Chandragupta and Tapas Sen, the lighting technician for several **IPTA** plays and for **Utpal Dutt**. Early training in Europe and USA. Saw Meyerhold's work in Moscow; apprenticed to Stanislavski's student Richard Boleslawski at Laboratory Theatre, New York (1926). Also saw Max Reinhard perform in Berlin, Gordon Craig in London and Sarah Bernhardt on Broadway. Technical director of Laboratory Theatre; then mainly responsible for building Woodstock Theatre (1929). Returned to Calcutta (1930) where he worked for major **Calcutta Theatre** companies: Rangmahal (1931), Natya Niketan (1931-42) and **Sisir Bhaduri**'s Srirangam (1942-56). Best-known plays co-directed with **Naresh Mitra**, often starring major Bengali film actors: **Dhiraj Bhattacharya, Jahar Ganguly**, Shanti Gupta, etc. Also introduced the revolving stage, mood (or 'psychological') lighting, etc. Freelanced as film-maker, e.g. Sachindranath Sengupta's well-known comedy produced by **Priyanath Ganguly**, ***Sarbajanin Bibahotsab***. Wrote autobiography (1976), including theoretical essays on colour and light.

FILMOGRAPHY: 1935: *Mantra Shakti*; **1936**: *Abartan*; *Pandit Moshai*; *Impostor*; **1938**: ***Sarbajanin Bibahotsab***; *Chokher Bali*; **1940**: *Swami Stri*.

SEN, SUCHITRA (b. 1931?)

Bengali star; originally called Roma Sen. Born in Patna, Bihar. Début in unreleased *Shesh Kothai*. First role opposite **Uttam Kumar** in ***Sharey Chuattar***. They lasted as a screen duo in Bengali romantic melodramas for more than 20 years, becoming almost a genre unto themselves. Her career peaked in the late 50s with films like *Shap Mochan*, ***Sagarika***, *Harano Sur* and ***Saptapadi***, creating a new image in Bengali film of the articulate and assertive heroine. First Hindi film was **Bimal Roy**'s ***Devdas***. Did some films with **Dev Anand** in the 60s (e.g. ***Bambai Ka Babu***) and later returned again to the Hindi cinema to star in **Gulzar**'s ***Aandhi***, in a role apparently modelled on Indira Gandhi. The announcement of her early retirement triggered a wave of nostalgia for her romantic films. Mother of current Bengali-Hindi star Moon Moon Sen. Her assertiveness on screen was coupled with a personal anxiety over the way she was photographed while her rigid gestures and mask-like make-up at times contradicted her strong screen persona, dividing the star from the stereotype (e.g. ***Hospital***).

FILMOGRAPHY: 1952: *Sesh Kothai*; **1953**: *Sat Number Kayedi*; ***Sharey Chuattar***; *Kajari*; **1954**: *Atom Bomb*; *Ora Thake Odhare*; ***Dhuli***; *Maraner Pare*; *Sadanander Mela*; *Annapurnar Mandir*; *Agni Pareeksha*; *Grihapravesh*; *Balay Gras*; *Bhagwan Shri Krishna Chaitanya*; **1955**: *Sanjher Pradeep*; ***Devdas***; *Sajghar*; *Shap Mochan*; *Mejo Bou*; *Bhalobasha*; *Sabar Uparey*; **1956**: ***Sagarika***; *Shubharatri*; *Ekti Raat*; *Trijama*; *Shilpi*; *Amar Bou*; **1957**: *Harano Sur*; *Chandranath*; *Pathe Holo Deri*; *Jiban Trishna*; ***Musafir***; *Champakali*; **1958**: *Rajalakshmi-o-Shrikanta*; *Indrani*; *Surya Toran*; **1959**: *Chaowa-Pawa*; ***Deep Jweley Jai***; **1960**: ***Hospital***; *Sarhad*; ***Bambai Ka Babu***; *Smriti Tuku Thak*; **1961**: ***Saptapadi***; **1962**: *Bipasha*; **1963**: ***Saat Pake Bandha***; *Uttar Falguni*; **1964**: *Sandhya Deeper Sikha*; **1966**: *Mamata*; **1967**: *Grihadah*; **1969**: *Kamallata*; **1970**: *Megh Kalo*; **1971**: *Fariyad*; *Nabaraag*; **1972**: *Alo Amar Alo*; *Haar Mana Haar*; **1973**: *Shravan Sandhya*; **1974**: *Debi Choudhrani*; **1975**: *Priya Bandhabi*; ***Aandhi***; **1976**: *Datta*; **1978**: *Pronoy Pasha*.

SETHUMADHAVAN, K. S. (b. 1926)

Prolific Malayalam director; also worked in Tamil, Hindi and made one film (*Manini*) in Kannada. Born in Palghat. Science graduate from Madras University. Assistant to **K. Ramnoth** (1952), later worked briefly with **L.V. Prasad** (1954) and more extensively with **T.R. Sundaram** (1957). First major hit: *Kannum Karalum*. Early films produced by Manjilas, a collaboration between Sethumadhavan, star **Sathyan** and M.O. Joseph. Adapted novels by Kesavadev (***Odeyil Ninnu***, *Adhyathe Katha*), Thakazhy Shivashankar Pillai (*Omanakuttan*, *Chukku*, both scripted by **Thoppil Bhasi**), Uroob (*Mindapennu*) etc., often with playwright-scenarist K.T. Mohammed. Together with **Vincent**'s films, his work exemplifies a cinema promoted after 1970 by official institutions as 'good' films (see **New Indian Cinema**). Best-known films claimed to address social justice issues mainly through bizarre portrayals of deviant sex, seen from the 'tragic' viewpoint of decaying but good tradition (*Odeyil Ninnu*, ***Adimagal***, *Chattakkari*, and his best-known film outside Kerala and Tamil Nadu, ***Oppol***). Remade **Nasir Hussain**'s teen movie ***Yaadon Ki Baraat*** (1973) as *Nalai Namadhe* with **MGR**.

FILMOGRAPHY: 1961: *Gnana Sundari*; **1962**: *Kannum Karalum*; **1963**: *Nithya Kanyaka*; *Sushila*; **1964**: *Anna*; *Manavatti*; *Omanakuttan*; **1965**: ***Odeyil Ninnu***; ***Daham***; **1966**: *Rowdy*; *Archana*; *Sthanarthi Saramma*; **1967**: ***Kottayam Kola Case***; *Nadan Pennu*; *Ollathu Mathi*; **1968**: *Thokkukal Katha Parayunnu*; *Yakshi*; *Bharyamar Sukshikuka*; *Paal Manam*; **1969**: ***Adimagal***; *Kadalpalam*; *Kootu Kudumbam*; **1970**: *Mindapennu*; *Amma Enna Stree*; *Kalpana*; ***Vazhve Mayam***; *Kuttavali*; ***Aranazhikaneram***; *Kalyana Urvalam*; **1971**: ***Oru Penninte Katha***; *Thettu*; ***Anubhavangal Palichakal***; *Karakanakadal*; *Inquilab Zindabad*; *Line Bus*; **1972**: *Devi*; *Achannum Bappayum*; *Punarjanmam*; *Adhyathe Kadha*; *Pani Teertha Veedu*; **1973**: *Kaliyugam*; *Chukku*; *Azhakulla Saleena*; **1974**: *Jeevikkan Marnupoya Sthree*; *Chattakkari*; *Kanyakumari*; **1975**: *Chuvanna Sandhyakal*; *Makkal*; ***Julie***; *Nalai Namadhe*; **1976**: *Priyamvadha*; **1977**: *Amme Anupame*; *Ormakal Marikkumo*; *Yahi Hai Zindagi*; **1978**: *Nakshatrangale Kaval*; **1979**: *Manini*; **1980**: ***Oppol***; **1982**: *Afsana Do Dilon Ka*; *Nijangal*; **1984**: *Zindagi Jeene Ke Liye*; *Ariyatha Veethigal*; *Arorumariyathe*; **1985**: *Avidathepole Ivideyum*; **1986**: *Sunil Vayasu 20*; **1990**: *Marupakkam*; **1991**: *Venal Kinavukal*.

SHAH, CHANDULAL JESANGBHAI (1898-1975)

Hindi director born in Jamnagar, Gujarat. Attended Bombay University (1924) and trained as a stockbroker. Among the biggest moguls in Indian cinema with his studio, **Ranjit**. Introduced to films by his brother, Dayaram J. Shah, the publicity manager of **Irani**'s Majestic theatre and later scenarist at Ranjit. Assistant to **Manilal Joshi** for whose Laxmi Film he made his directorial début (1925); left to work at **Kohinoor** (1926-7). His third film *Typist Girl/Why I Became a Christian* featured **Sulochana** and **Gohar**. Founded Jagdish Film where the nucleus of his Ranjit Movietone in Bombay (Est: 1929) was gathered: Gohar (his actress and common law wife), **Raja Sandow** and cameraman Pandurang Naik. By 1950, Ranjit had produced over 160 films, the largest number under any single banner in Indian cinema (e.g. work by **Nanubhai Vakil** and **Jayant Desai**). Their films largely adhered to the genres inherited from the Kohinoor scenarist **Mohanlal Dave**, including social melodramas addressing the joint-family system, occasionally with mythological overtones based on original scripts by **Narayan Prasad Betaab**, Gunwantrai Acharya, **Chaturbhuj Doshi** et al. The breakthrough film founding the genre was ***Gunsundari***. The films were distributed by his elder brother, Dayaram Shah. A leading spokesman for the industry in his later years (first president of the Film Federation of India, 1951). He died in poverty.

FILMOGRAPHY: **1925**: *Panchdanda*; *Vimala*; **1926**: *Typist Girl*; *Madhav Kam Kundala*; **1927**: ***Gunsundari***; *Sati Madri*; *Sindh Ni Sumari*; **1928**: *Grihalakshmi*; *Vishwamohini*; **1929**: *Bhikharan*; *Chandramukhi*; *Pati Patni*; *Rajputani*; **1930**: *Diwani Dilbar*; *Raj Lakshmi* (all St); **1931**: ***Devi Devayani***; **1932**: ***Sati Savitri***; *Sheilbala*; ***Radha Rani***; **1933**: ***Miss 1933***; *Vishwamohini*; **1934**: *Toofani Taruni*; ***Gunsundari***; *Tara Sundari*; **1935**: ***Barrister's Wife***; ***Desh Dasi***; ***Keemti Aansoo***; **1936**: ***Prabhu Ka Pyara***; ***Sipahi Ki Sajni/Sipahini Sajni***; **1937**: *Pardesi Pankhi*; **1940**: ***Achhut***; **1953**: *Paapi*; **1955**: *Ootpatang*; **1960**: *Zameen Ke Tare*.

SHAH, KUNDAN (b. 1947)

Hindi director. Studied commerce at Sydenham College, Bombay (1968). Employed in educational publishing at Popular Prakashan. Spent time in London but returned to join the **FTII** where he took a special interest in silent comedy. Graduated (1976) and did some documentaries for the Municipal Corp. of Hyderabad as part of a film collective. Returned to Bombay to work with **Dharmaraj**. Début feature ***Jaane Bhi Do Yaaron*** introduced to the New Indian Cinema the genre of ribald comedy. The tv series *Yeh Jo Hai Zindagi* inaugurated the era of sponsored serials on **Doordarshan**. Partner in Iskra, a company founded with **Saeed Mirza**, Aziz Mirza, Sudhir Mishra et al., directing alternate episodes of *Nukkad*. His *Police Station* started as a serial but ran into censorship problems over its depiction of police brutality; it was broadcast as a tv film using footage from the three episodes that had been shot. The serial *Circus* discovered 1990s superstar Shah Rukh Khan, with whom Shah made the love story *Kabhi Haan Kabhi Naa*, returning to mainstream features.

FILMOGRAPHY: **1976**: *Bonga* (Sh); *Posters-Neons* (Doc); **1981**: *Vision Of The Blind* (Doc); **1983**: ***Jaane Bhi Do Yaaron***; **1985**: *Yeh Jo Hai Zindagi* (TV); **1987**: *Nukkad* (TV); *Police Station* (TV); **1988**: *Intezaar* (TV); **1989**: *Wagle Ki Duniya* (TV); **1993**: *Kabhi Haan Kabhi Naa*.

SHAH, NASEERUDDIN (b. 1950)

One of the icons of New Indian Cinema with **Smita Patil**, **Shabana Azmi** and **Om Puri**. Born in Barabanki, student at the National School of Drama in Delhi and the **FTII**. First roles in **Benegal**'s ***Nishant***, ***Manthan*** and ***Bhumika***, followed by the lead role in **Saeed Mirza**'s ***Albert Pinto Ko Gussa Kyon Aata Hai*** and as the lawyer in **Nihalani**'s ***Aakrosh***. His use of hesitant speech and casual gesture to signify psychological complexity has been widely adopted as the norm for 'realist' characterisation, e.g. by **Mrinal Sen** in ***Khandhar***, **Girish Kasaravalli** in ***Mane*** and **Sai Paranjpye** in ***Sparsh***. He also reveals a talent for comedy, e.g. in **Ketan Mehta**'s films (in comics and catchpenny print-inspired roles in ***Bhavni Bhavai*** and ***Mirch Masala***), the corrupt, smooth-talking lawyer in ***Mohan Joshi Hazir Ho!***, and in ***Mandi***. Shah also works in commercial cinema, where he is best-known for his Tirchi Topiwala role in Rajiv Rai's big-budget hit, *Tridev*. Also actor and director in English and Hindi plays. Often cast as an innovative actor in demand by commercial directors for character roles, e.g. ***Karma***, where he was pitted against **Dilip Kumar**.

FILMOGRAPHY: **1975**: *Hand Held* (Sh); *Hero* (Sh); ***Nishant***; **1976**: ***Manthan***; *A Proposal* (Sh); ***Bhumika***; **1977**: *Tabbaliyu Neenade Magane/Godhuli*; **1978**: ***Junoon***; **1979**: *Shayad*; *Sunayana*; ***Sparsh***; **1980**: *Khwab*; ***Aakrosh***; ***Albert Pinto Ko Gussa Kyon Aata Hai***; ***Bhavni Bhavai/Andher Nagari***; ***Chakra***; ***Hum Paanch***; **1981**: *Kanhaiya*; *Sazaaye Maut*; *Tajurba*; ***Umrao Jaan***; ***Adharshila***; **1982**: *Bezubaan*; *Bazaar*; *Dil Aakhir Dil Hai*; *Pyara Dost*; ***Masoom***; *Sitam*; *Swami Dada*; ***Katha***; **1983**: ***Ardh Satya***; *Haadsa*; *Nirvana*; ***Mandi***; *Woh Saat Din*; ***Jaane Bhi Do Yaaron***; ***Khandhar***; ***Mohan Joshi Haazir Ho!***; ***Holi***; *Protidan*; **1984**: ***Party***; ***Paar***; *Lorie*; **1985**: *Bahu Ki Awaaz*; ***Ghulami***; *Misaal*; *Surkhiyaan*; ***Mirch Masala***; ***Trikaal***; *Khamosh*; *Shart*; *Maan Maryada*; **1986**: ***Ek Pal***; ***Karma***; *Jalwa*; *Yeh Woh Manzil To Nahin*; **1987**: ***Pestonjee***; *Ijaazat*; **1988**: *The Perfect Murder*; *Zulm Ko Jala Doonga*; *Hero Hiralal*; *Malamaal*; ***Rihaee***; **1989**: *Anjaam Khuda Jaane*; *Tridev*; *Khoj*; **1990**: ***Mane***; *Police Public*; *Chor Pe Mor*; **1991**: *Shikari*; *Libaas*; *Electric Moon*; *Lakshmanrekha*; **1992**: *Vishwatma*; *Panaah*; *Tahalka*; *Chamatkar*; **1993**: *Game*; *Lutere*; *Hasti*; *Sir*; *Bedardi*; *Kabhi Haan Kabhi Naa*.

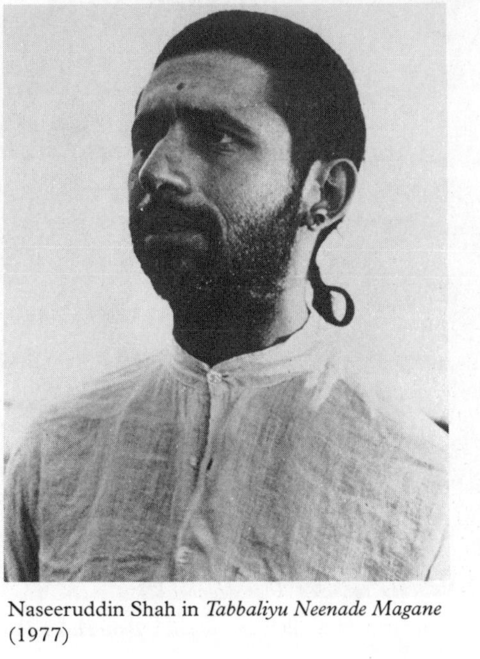

Naseeruddin Shah in *Tabbaliyu Neenade Magane* (1977)

SHAHANI, KUMAR (b. 1940)

Director born in Larkana, Sind (now Pakistan). Early life marked by Partition. Graduated from the University of Bombay (1962) and from the **FTII** (1966) where he was one of **Ghatak**'s students. Also student of the historian and anthropologist D.D. Kosambi. Further film studies in France (1967-68) where he assisted Bresson on *Une Femme Douce* (1969). Was an enthusiastic participant in the May 1968 movements in France. After the intense and innovative ***Maya Darpan***, he obtained no support from the **NFDC** for 12 years. Homi Bhabha fellowship (1976-8) to study the epic tradition as represented by the *Mahabharata*, Buddhist iconography, classical Indian music and the Bhakti movement, leading to the production of ***Tarang***. Made two more features subsequently, adapting a Chekhov story for ***Kasba***, and investigating the North Indian classical Khayal music for ***Khayal Gatha***. Taught and lectured extensively, including at the FTII, presented the film appreciation programme on Bombay TV, *Montage* (1974-6) and wrote numerous essays and lectures on cinematic aesthetics, defining the terrain of an independent cinema movement in India.Early work contextualised by the political events of the 60s/70s (the **Naxalite** insurgency culminating in the Emergency) and the definitive shifts in the Nehruite nationalist model caused by the Indira Gandhi regime. Developed from the iconographies of revolt and repression characterising this period, and evident in, e.g., his documentary *Fire in the Belly*, his contemporary terms of reference for the epic in cinema. Developed his key formulation of the narrative sequence (as against the shot or the frame) from theories of performance and visual representation in Indian art, to define what he sees to be the two crucial needs of an oppositional art practice: the need 'to innovate [and] to individuate'. Has addressed, from this vantage point, questions of nationalism, indigenous modernism, the forms of capitalist commodification and their impact on both feudal/patriarchal systems and on the Left movement. Recent work, such as *Khayal Gatha* and ***Bhavantarana*** (on Odissi dancer Guru Kelucharan Mahapatra), investigates more specifically the process of cultural classicisation in India, where the epic often comes to be the most precise representation for history itself. Writings on cinema published by *Framework* (No. 30/31, *Dossier on Kumar Shahani*). Major essays include 'Film as a Contemporary Art' (In *Social Scientist*, March, 1990) and the Rita Ray Memorial Lectures, 'The Self as an Objective Entity', 'Narrativity' and 'Figures of Film' (unpublished, 1987). Directed actress Alaknanda Samarth in two stage plays *La Voix humaine* and *Kunti*.

FILMOGRAPHY: **1966**: *The Glass Pane* (Sh); **1967**: *Manmad Passenger* (Sh); **1969**: *A Certain Childhood* (Sh); **1970**: *Rails for the World* (Sh); **1971**: *Object* (Sh); **1972**: ***Maya Darpan***; **1973**: *Fire in the Belly* (Doc); **1976**: *Our Universe* (Sh); **1984**: ***Tarang***; **1987**: *Var Var Vari* (Sh); **1988**: ***Khayal Gatha***; **1989**: *A Ship Aground* (Sh); **1990**: ***Kasba***; **1991**: ***Bhavantarana***.

SHAILENDRA (1923-66)

Hindi and Urdu lyric writer often associated with **Raj Kapoor**'s films. Part of a long-lasting team with composers **Shankar-Jaikishen** and Urdu lyricist Hasrat Jaipuri. Worked in **IPTA** plays in Bombay. Employed in a railway yard when he was offered a job by Kapoor (***Barsaat***, 1949). Wrote many of the best-known songs of Kapoor's 50s and 60s output, including the title numbers of *Barsaat* and ***Awara*** (1951) and ***Mera Naam Joker*** (1970). He also produced ***Teesri Kasam*** (1966), based on the novel by Phaneshwar Nath 'Renu', and starring Raj Kapoor and **Waheeda Rehman**. Wrote songs for c.170 films, working with several music directors.

SHANKAR-JAIKISHEN, aka SHANKARSINH RAGHUWANSHI (?-1987) and JAIKISHEN DAYABHAI PANCHAL (1929-71).

Composers who started as orchestra musicians in **Prithviraj Kapoor**'s Prithvi Theatres where they first met **Raj Kapoor**. Jaikishen was born in Bulsar, Gujarat, and migrated to Bombay in 1945. Shankar was born in Hyderabad. They assisted composer Ram Ganguly in Kapoor's inaugural production, ***Aag*** (1948). Scored ***Barsaat*** and continued working with Kapoor and his favourite playback singer, Mukesh, for the next two decades, including ***Awara*** and ***Shri 420***. Their extraordinary popularity was enhanced by numerous films, e.g. **Amiya Chakravarty**'s ***Daag***, *Patita* (using the ghazal singer Talat Mahmood), *Seema* and ***Kathputli***, **Vijay Bhatt**'s *Patrani* and ***Hariyali Aur Raasta***, **Mohan Segal**'s ***New Delhi***, **Bimal Roy**'s ***Yahudi***. Also did the Hindi films at **AVM**. Changed in early 60s to rock music in the **Shammi Kapoor** era: **Nasir Hussain**'s ***Jab Pyar Kisise Hota Hai***, **Subodh Mukherjee**'s ***Junglee*** (with the famous Shammi Kapoor 'Yahoo' number) and *April Fool*; ***Rajkumar***, *An Evening in Paris* etc. Composed for all leading playback singers, but also worked with unknown singers like Subir Sen and Sharada. After Jaikishen died, Shankar carried on scoring films signing their joint names. For Chandrasekhar's *Street Singer*, Shankar used the name Suraj.

FILMOGRAPHY: **1949**: ***Barsaat***; **1951**: ***Awara***; ***Badal***; *Kali Ghata*; *Nagina*; **1952**: ***Daag***; *Parbat*; *Poonam*; **1953**: ***Aah***; *Aas*; *Aurat*; *Naya Ghar*; *Shikast*; *Patita*; **1954**: *Badshah*; ***Boot Polish***; ***Mayurpankh***; *Pooja*; **1955**: *Seema*; ***Shri 420***; **1956**: *Basant Bahar*; ***Chori Chori***; *Halaku*; *Kismet Ka Khel*; ***New Delhi***; *Patrani*; *Rajhaath*; **1957**: *Begunah*; ***Kathputli***; **1958**: *Baghi Sipahi*; ***Yahudi***; **1959**: ***Anari***; ***Chhoti Bahen***; *Kanhaiya*; *Love Marriage*; *Main Nashe Mein Hoon*; *Shararat*; *Ujala*; **1960**: *College Girl*; *Dil Apna Aur Preet Parayi*; *Ek Phool Char Kaante*; ***Jis Desh Mein Ganga Behti Hai***; *Singapore*; **1961**: *Aas Ka Panchhi*; *Boy Friend*; ***Jab Pyar Kisise Hota Hai***; ***Junglee***; *Karodpati*; *Roop Ki Rani Choron Ka Raja*; *Sasural*; **1962**: *Aashiq*; *Asli Naqli*; *Dil Tera Diwana*; ***Hariyali Aur Raasta***; *Professor*; *Rangoli*; **1963**: *Dil Ek Mandir*; *Ek Dil Sau Afsane*; *Hamrahi*; **1964**: *Apne Huye Paraye*; *April Fool*; *Aayi Milan Ki Bela*; *Beti Bete*; ***Rajkumar***; *Sanjh Aur Savera*; ***Sangam***; *Zindagi*; **1965**: *Arzoo*; *Gumnaam*; *Jaanwar*; **1966**: *Amrapali*; *Badtameez*; ***Gaban***; *Love in Tokyo*; *Pyar Mohabbat*; *Suraj*; ***Teesri Kasam***; *Street Singer* (only Shankar); **1967**: *Aman*; *An Evening in Paris*; *Around the World*; *Chhotisi Mulaqat*; *Diwana*; *Gunahon Ka Devta*; *Hare Kaanch Ki Chudiyan*; *Laat Saheb*; *Raat Aur Din*; **1968**: *Brahmachari*; *Duniya*; *Jhuk Gaya Aasmaan*; *Kahin Aur Chal*; *Kanyadaan*; *Mere Huzoor*; *Sapnon Ka Saudagar*; *Shikar*; **1969**: *Bhai Bahen*; *Chanda Aur Bijli*; *Jahan Pyar Mile*; *Prince*; *Pyar Hi Pyar*; *Sachaai*; *Shatranj*; *Tumse Achha Kaun Hai*; *Yakeen*; **1970**: *Bhai Bhai*; *Dharti*; ***Mera Naam Joker***; *Pagla Kahin Ka*; *Pehchan*; *Tum Haseen Main Jawan*; *Umang*; *Jwala*; *Bombay Talkie*; **1971**: *Albela*; ***Andaz***; *Balidan*; *Duniya Kya Jaane*; *Ek Nari Ek Brahmachari*; *Elaan*; *Jaane Anjane*; *Jawan Mohabbat*; *Kal Aaj Aur Kal*; *Lal Patthar*; *Main Sundar Hoon*; *Nadaan*; *Parde Ke Peechhe*; *Patanga*; *Preetam*; *Seema*; *Yaar Mere*; *Jeevitha Chakram*; **1972**: *Aan Baan*; *Aankh Micholi*; *Aankhon Aankhon Mein*; *Bandagi*; *Beimaan*; *Dil Daulat Duniya*; *Jungle Mein Mangal*; *Rivaaj*; **1973**: *Aaj Ki Taaza Khabar*; *Chori Chori*; *Daman Aur Aag*; *Door Nahin Manzil*; *Naina*; *Pyar Ka Rishta*; *Archana*; **1974**: *Chhote Sarkar*; *Insaniyat*; *International Crook*; *Resham Ki Dori*; *Tarzan Mera Saathi*; *Vachan*; *Mera Vachan Geeta Ki Kasam*; **1975**: *Do Jhooth*; *Love in Bombay*; *Neelima*; *Saazish*; *Sanyasi*; **1977**: *Dhoop Chhaon*; *Duniyadari*; **1978**: *Mehfil*; **1979**: *Atmaram*; *The Gold Medal*; **1980**: *Garam Khoon*; **1981**: *Nari*; *Chorni*; **1982**: *Eent Ka Jawab Patthar*; **1984**: *Paapi Pet Ka Sawaal Hai*; **1986**: *Inteqam Ki Aag*; *Kaanch Ki Deewar*; *Krishna Krishna*.

SHANTARAM, RAJARAM VANKUDRE (1901-90)

Hindi and Marathi director, producer and actor aka V. Shantaram. Born in Kolhapur. Worked on the railways as a teenager; apprentice in **Bal Gandharva**'s Gandharva Natak Mandali (1914-15) where he was trained by people he later employed (e.g. **Govindrao Tembe**, the tabla master Tirakhwan); then odd-job man at a local cinema (1917). Became assistant photographer, then joined **Painter**'s **Maharashtra Film** (1920) learning all production skills, including acting (*Surekha Haran*, ***Sinhagad***, ***Savkari Pash***) and eventually directing *Netaji Palkar*. Left together with **Damle**, **Fattelal**, **Keshavrao Dhaiber** and S.B. Kulkarni to start **Prabhat** in Kolhapur (1929), directing all the studio's silent films. Released 3 sound films in 1932 launching **Durga Khote** (e.g. ***Ayodhyecha Raja***). Established Prabhat Studio in Pune (1933). Prabhat's films made him one of the most celebrated Indian directors of the 30s. The spectacular ***Amritmanthan*** consecrated **Shanta Apte** as a major star. Married one of his stars, Jayshree (***Shakuntala***) and launched their daughter, Rajshree in *Geet Gaya Pattharone*. Later teamed up with the dancer and actress Sandhya (*Jhanak Jhanak Payal Baaje*). Chief Producer of Government **Film Advisory Board** during WW2 (producing documentaries, e.g. *Sangeet Bharat*, *Song of Maharashtra*, both 1956; *Important People*, *Magic Touch* and *Symphony of Life*, all 1957). Established his own studio **Rajkamal Kalamandir** in Parel, Bombay (1942). Founded V. Shantaram Prod., 1962. Published autobiography, *Shantarama* (1986). Up to 1933, followed the Painter mould of mythologicals and historicals, occasionally with political overtones (***Udaykal***). After 1933, following long visit to Germany's UFA Studios, his films show the influence of the expressionist *Kammerspiel* film. Perceived by Shantaram himself as 'classical' art, the films arguably mobilise a 19th C. German Orientalism to

V. Shantaram in his film *Do Aankhen Bara Haath* (1957)

achieve a modernist return to classic Sanskrit Indian cultural values. His later Rajkamal films ended up offering degraded versions of the classical arts (e.g. India's first Technicolor film, the musical extravaganza *Jhanak Jhanak Payal Baaje* - later re-released in 70mm - or *Jal Bin Machhli Nritya Bin Bijli*). Early reformist socials (***Kunku*/*Duniya Na Mane***) were exemplary of the genre in pre-Independence India and led to, e.g., ***Dr Kotnis Ki Amar Kahani*** (which pleased the British, the nationalists and the Communists all at the same time) and ***Do Aankhen Barah Haath***. ***Lokshahir Ramjoshi*** (co-d. Painter) helped originate the Tamasha musical in Marathi cinema. His critical approach to feudal traditions in melodramas and socials, together with determined efforts to break into US and European markets (e.g. with ***Shakuntala***) earned him the reputation of being influenced by foreign (read German and Hollywood) elements. Many, including **K.A. Abbas**, regard ***Manoos*/*Admi*** as his finest film.

FILMOGRAPHY (* also act/** act only): **1921**: *Surekha Haran***; **1923**: ***Sinhagad*****; *Shri Krishnavatar***; **1924**: ***Sati Padmini*****; **1925**: *Shahala Shah***; ***Savkari Pash*****; *Rana Hamir***; *Maya Bazaar***; **1926**: *Gaja Gauri***; *Bhakta Prahlad***; **1927**: *Muraliwala***; *Sati Savitri***; *Netaji Palkar* (with **K. Dhaiber**); **1928**: *Maharathi Karna***; **1929**: *Baji Prabhu Deshpande***; *Nisha Sundari***; ***Gopal Krishna***; **1930**: *Rani Saheba**; *Khooni Khanjar*; ***Udaykal****; **1931**: *Chandrasena* (all St); **1932**: ***Ayodhyecha Raja*/*Ayodhya Ka Raja***; ***Jalti Nishani*/*Agnikankan***; ***Maya Machhindra***; **1933**: ***Sinhagad***; *Sairandhri*; **1934**: ***Amritmanthan***; **1935**: ***Chandrasena***; ***Dharmatma***; **1936**: ***Amar Jyoti***; **1937**: ***Kunku*/*Duniya Na Mane***; **1939**: ***Manoos*/*Admi***; **1941**: ***Shejari*/*Padosi***; **1943**: ***Shakuntala***; **1944**: *Parbat Pe Apna Dera**; **1946**: ***Dr Kotnis Ki Amar Kahani****; **1947**: ***Lokshahir Ramjoshi*/*Matwala Shayar Ramjoshi***; **1949**: *Apna Desh*/*Nam Naadu*; **1950**: ***Dahej***; **1951**: ***Amar Bhoopali***; **1952**: *Parchain*; **1953**: *Surang*; *Teen Batti Char Raasta*; **1954**: *Subah Ka Tara*; **1955**: ***Jhanak Jhanak Payal Baaje***; **1957**: ***Do Aankhen Barah Haath****; **1959**: *Navrang*; **1961**: *Stree**; **1963**: *Sehra*; **1964**: *Geet Gaya Pattharone*; **1965**: *Iye Marathyachi Nagari*/*Ladki Sahyadri Ki*; **1967**: *Boond Jo Ban Gaye Moti*; **1971**: *Jal Bin Machhli Nritya Bin Bijli*; **1972**: ***Pinjra***; **1977**: ***Chaani***; **1986**: *Jhanjhar*.

SHARADA (b. 1945)

Aka Saraswati, aka 'Urvashi' Sharada. Malayalam, Telugu, Tamil and Hindi star born in Tenali, AP. Studied Bharat Natyam dance as a child. Early youth in Burma. Spotted by **L.V. Prasad** in a Telugu play, *Rakthakanni*. Married Chellam, the co-star of her début film, *Tandrulu Kodukulu*. Second film, *Iddaru Mithralu*, a hit made by **Adurthi Subba Rao** for **A. Nageshwara Rao**'s Annapurna Studio, established her in mid-budget Telugu melodramas in secondary roles and as a comedy actress. **Sivaji Ganesan** noticed her in **Athreya**'s play *Thirupati* which led to her first Tamil film, *Kumkumam*. Achieved major stardom in Malayalam with **Kunchako**'s *Inapravugal*. Best film work is in Malayalam, e.g. for **Sethumadhavan**, **A. Vincent** and **Kariat**, with intensely emotional performances chronicling the decline of matriarchal power. Cast in **Adoor Gopalakrishnan**'s début ***Swayamvaram*** and in his ***Elippathayam***, in **K.G. George**'s ***Lekhayude Maranam Oru Flashback*** and in **P.N. Menon**'s films. Returned to Telugu cinema when her award-winning Malayalam film by Vincent, ***Thulabharam***, was remade in Telugu as *Manushulu Marali* and in Hindi as ***Samaj Ko Badal Dalo***, featuring her in all three versions.

FILMOGRAPHY: 1961: *Tandrulu Kodukulu*; *Iddaru Mithralu*; **1962**: *Atmabandhuvu*; **1963**: *Valmiki*; *Thobuttuvulu*; *Kumkumam*; **1964**: *Vazhkai Vazhvadarke*; *Arunagiri Nathar*; ***Murali Krishna***; *Dagudu Moothulu*; **1965**: *Chaduvukonna Bharya*; *Inapravugal*; *Kattuthulasi*; *Rajamalli*; *Kathiruna Nikkah*; ***Murappennu***; **1966**: *Manikya Kottaram*; *Archana*; *Pagal Kinavu*; *Jail*; *Kanmanikal*; *Karuna*; *Tilottama*; *Bhakta Potana*; *Shakuntala*; *Shrimati*; **1967**: *Thallirukal*; ***Irutinte Atmavu***; *Udyogastha*; *Arakillam*; ***Anveshichu Kandatiyilla***; ***Chitramela***; *Pareeksha*; ***Kavalam Chundan***; *Kasavuthattam*; *Mulkireedam*; **1968**: *Karutha Pournami*; *Manaswini*; ***Asuravithu***; *Karthika*; *Kadal*; *Hotel Highrange*; *Punnapra Vyalar*; *Kaliyalla Kalyanam*; *Yakshi*; ***Thulabharam***; *Midumidukki*; *Aparadhini*; *Agni Pareeksha*; *Mana Samsaram*; **1969**: *Shri Rama Katha*; *Manushulu Marali*; *Vila Kuranja Manushyar*; *Veetu Mrugham*; *Kattukurangu*; *Susie*; ***Adimagal***; *Sandhya*; *Mooladanam*; *Jwala*; *Vilakkapetta Bandhangal*; ***Nadhi***; *Velliyazhcha*; *Kootu Kudumbam*; **1970**: *Mindapennu*; *Pearl View*; *Stree*; *Cross Belt*; *Kuttavali*; *Kakathampurati*; *Triveni*; *Tara*; ***Samaj Ko Badal Dalo***; *Sambarala Rambabu*; *Pasidi Manushulu*; *Ambalapravu*; **1971**: ***Abhijathyam***; *Vilakku Vangiya Veena*; *Amayakuralu*; *Jeevitha Chakram*; *Pagabattina Paduchu*; *Sati Ansuya*; *Sisindri Chittibabu*; **1972**: *Kalam Marindi*; *Manavudu Danavudu*; *Maya*; *Professor*; *Shri Guruvayoorappan*; *Gandharvakshetram*; *Anveshanam*; *Brahmachari*; ***Swayamvaram***; ***Gnana Oli***; *Snehadeepame Mizhi Thurakku*; **1973**: ***Enippadikal***; *Udayam*; *Veendum Prabhatam*; *Thekkan Kattu*; *Agni Rekha*; *Abhimanavanthulu*; *Ida Lokam*; *Jeevitham*; *Mallamma Katha*; ***Sharada***; *Vishali*; *Mayadari Malligadu*; *Devudu Chesina Manushulu*; **1974**: *Harathi*; *Urvashi* (Te); *Premalu Pellilu*; *Thulabharam*; *Radhamma Pelli*; *Adambaralu Anubandhalu*; *Palle Paduchu*; *Devudu Chesina Pelli*; *Oru Pidi Ari*; *Thayi Pirandhal*; **1975**: *Ninaithathai Mudippavan*; *Ragam*; *Abhimanam*; *Palkadal*; *Thiruvonam*; *Saubhagyavati*; *Vaikunthapali*; *Bharati*; *Zamindarugari Ammayi*; *Balipeetam*; **1976**: *Mahatmudu*; *Suprabhatam*; *Amritha Vahini*; *Chennai Valarthiya Kutty*; *Kanyadanam*; *Nurayum Pathayum*; *Ennai Pol Oruvan*; *Mazhai Megam*; **1977**: *Aradhana*; *Amme Anupame*; *Anjali*; *Aparajitha*; *Hridayame Sakshi*; *Itha Ivide Vare*; *Rendu Lokam*; *Sridevi*; *Taxi Driver*; *Vishukkani*; *Indra Dhanushu*; *Swarganiki Nitchenalu*; *Bhale Alludu*; ***Daana Veera Shura Karna***; **1978**: *Navodayam*; *Anubhootikalude Nimisham*; *Asthamayam*; *Ithanende Vazhi*; ***Mannu***; *Onappudava*; *Raghuvamsam*; *Rowdy Ramu*; *Society Lady*; *Sundari Marudde Swapnangal*; *Mattoli*; *Manoratham*; **1979**: *Ente Sneham Ninakku Mathram*; *Ward No. 7*; *Karthika Deepam*; *Captain Krishna*; *Rajadhi Raju*; *Gorintaku*; *Shivamettina Satyam*; **1980**: *Alayam*; *Alludu Pattina Bharatham*; *Dharma Chakram*; *Pratishodh*; *Adhikaram*; *Akalangalil Abhayam*; *Mangala Gauri*; *Sannayi Appanna*; *Sardar Paparayudu*; *Ramudu Parashuramudu*; **1981**: ***Elippathayam***; *Prema Natakam*; *O Amma Katha*; *Sindoor Bane Jwala*; **1982**: *Nipputho Chelagatam*; *Jagannatha Rathachakralu*; *Pratikaram*; **1983**: ***Lekhayude Maranam Oru Flashback***; *Nizhal Moodiya Nirangal*; *Apath Bandhavulu*; *Durga Devi*; *Kala Yamudu*; *Kaliyuga Daivam*; *Poratham*; *Bandhipotu Rudramma*; *Bahudoorapu Batasari*; *Kumkuma Tilakam*; *Raghu Ramudu*; *Alaya Shikharam*; *Kurukshetramlo Seeta*; *Swarajyam*; **1984**: *Raaraju*; *Apanindalu Adavallakena*; *Bobbili Brahmana*; *Iddaru Dongalu*; *Katha Nayakudu*; *Marchandi Mana Chattalu*; *Rowdy*; *Sardar*; *Ugra Roopam*; *Bharatamlo Sankharavam*; *Justice Chakravarthy*; ***Swati***; *Chadurangam*; *Bharyamani*; *Nimaijanam*; *Charitra Nayakan*; *Alaya Deepam*; **1985**: *Bhale Tammudu*; *Agni Parvatham*; *Illaliko Pariksha*; *Maha Sangramam*; *Palnati Simham*; *Devalayam*; *Raktha Sindooram*; *Ee Samajam Maakodu*; *Adavi Donga*; *Bebbuli Veta*; *Vijeta*; *Pattabhishekham*; *Krishnagaradi*; *Intiko Rudramma*; **1986**: *Kondaveeti Raja*; *Muddula Krishnaiah*; *Mr Bharat*; *Manavudu Danavudu*; *Khaidi Rudraiah*; *Ravana Brahma*; *Ansuyammagari Alludu*; *Deshoddharakulu*; *Apoorva Sahodaharalu*; *Jailupakshi*; **1987**: *Rotation Chakravarthi*; *Repati Swarajyam*; *Muddayi*; *Agni Putrudu*; *Sharadamba*; *Bhargava Ramudu*; *Samrat*; *Lawyer Bharti Devi*; *Presidentgari Abbayi*; *Sankharavam*; *Kulala Kurukshetram*; *Ramu*; *Oru Minnaminuginte Nurungu Vettam*; **1988**: *Prajaswamyam*; *Samsaram*; *Raktha Tilakam*; *Ashwathama*; *Illu Illalu Priyuralu*; *Donga Ramudu*; *Rowdy No. 1*; *Brahma Puthrudu*; *Maa Telugu Talli*; *Dharma Teja*; *August 15 Rathri*; *Rakthabhisekham*; **1989**: *Manchi Kutumbam*; *Goonda Rajyam*; *Pardhudu*; *Raktha Kanneeru*; *Dhruvanakshatram*; *Nari Nari Naduma Murari*; *Dr Bhawani*; **1990**: *Lorry Driver*; *Kadapa Redamma*; *Prema Kaidi*; **1991**: *Jagannathakam*; *Nayakuralu*; *Coolie No. 1*; *Killer*; **1992**: *Mother India*; **1993**: *Major Chandrakant*; *Pelli Gola*.

SHARDA FILM COMPANY

Studio set up by Bhogilal K.M. Dave and **Nanubhai Desai** under direct control of financier Mayashankar Bhatt (formerly of **Hindustan Cinema Film**) in 1925. The most famous of the silent era's stunt film producers, Sharda's output was marked by its biggest star, **Master Vithal**. Around his image they developed a style combining special effects, *Arabian Nights* exotica and tales from the *Ramayana*. Their fast editing has remained part of the genre ever since (cf **Dara Singh**). Dave's Suvarna Pics extended this approach, as did the Surya Studio, launched by former Sharda distributor Haribhai Desai and where **Dhirubhai Desai** made his directing début. Nanubhai Desai went on to found Saroj Movietone. Actors like Ganpatrao Bakre and Zunzharrao Pawar, working under **Sundarrao Nadkarni**'s direction, also continued the Sharda signature.

SHARMA, ARIBAM SYAM (b. 1939)

Manipuri director born in Imphal. Graduated in philosophy and music from Shantiniketan. Lecturer in philosophy and worked in the

Aryan Theatre in Imphal in the late 60s. Well-known singer with classical training. Films often written with Manipuri author Maharajkumari Binodini Debi and usually feature mystical versions of traditional cultures contrasted with economic modernity. Manipur's marginalised and colonised relations with the Indian mainstream, leading to insurrectionist movements (70s and 80s), are referenced obliquely, e.g. the toy guns in *Paokhum Ama*, the child playing Krishna in a folk performance in ***Imagi Ningthem*** or the Meitei rituals in ***Ishanou***. Acted in and scored the first Manipuri film, Deb Kumar Bose's *Matamgi Manipur* (1972).

FILMOGRAPHY: **1974**: *Lamja Parashuram*; **1976**: *Saphabee*; **1979**: *Olangthagee Wangmadasoo*; **1981**: ***Imagi Ningthem***; **1982**: *Paokhum Ama*; **1983**: *Sagol Sanabi*; **1986**: *Tales of Courage* (Doc); **1988**: *Sangai Dancing Deer of Manipur* (Doc); *Keibul Lamjao National Park* (Doc); *Koro Kosii* (Doc); **1989**: *The Deer on the Lake* (TV); **1990**: ***Ishanou***; **1991**: *Indigenous Games of Manipur* (Doc); **1992**: *Lai Haraoba* (Sh).

SHARMA, KIDAR NATH (b. 1910)

Hindi director and scenarist born in Narowal, Sialkot (now Pakistan). Signboard painter at **New Theatres**; promoted to dialogue writer-lyricist for the studio's Hindi versions, including **Barua**'s ***Devdas*** (1935) and ***Mukti*** (1937), **Debaki Bose**'s ***Vidyapati*** (1937) and ***Sapera*** (1939). Author of classic **Saigal** numbers such as *Balam aayo baso more man mein* (*Devdas*). Moved to Bombay (1941). His ***Chitralekha*** was a major musical hit. Noted for having introduced several famous Hindi actors to their best-known image: e.g. Mehtab (in *Chitralekha*), Ramola (*Dil Hi To Hai*), Shamim (***Armaan***), **Raj Kapoor** and **Madhubala** (***Neel Kamal***), **Geeta Bali** (***Suhaag Raat***). Acted the lead in his own *Neki Aur Badi*. Made several films at **Ranjit** Studio in mid-40s. In recent years made children's films (e.g. *Jagdeep*). Wrote his own scripts, which were the films' most saleable aspects. In an essay in *Filmfare* (1952), Sharma distanced himself from the dominant ways sensuality was portrayed in films, criticising 'The director with the Cave Man conception of Love. This is the technique made vivid on the Indian screen mostly by Raj Kapoor and other film artistes graduating from the Prithvi Theatres.' His own favoured technique was to evoke the passionate imagery of Urdu poetry in tragic romances (***Jogan***, ***Banwre Nain***) with wide-angle shots of nature in the form of rain or howling wind playing a major commentative role. Made several shorts for the **Children's Film Society**.

FILMOGRAPHY (* only act/** act also): **1935**: ***Inquilab****; ***Devdas****; ***Dhoop Chhaon****; **1936**: *Karodpati**; **1937**: ***Vidyapati****; **1939**: ***Badi Didi****; *Dil Hi To Hai*; **1941**: ***Chitralekha***; **1942**: ***Armaan***; **1943**: *Gauri*; *Vish Kanya*; **1944**: *Bhanwara*; *Kaliyan*; *Mumtaz Mahal*; **1945**: *Chand Chakori*; *Dhanna Bhagat*; **1946**: *Duniya Ek Sarai*; **1947**: ***Neel Kamal***; **1948**: ***Suhaag Raat***; **1949**: *Neki Aur Badi***; *Thes*; **1950**: ***Banwre Nain***; ***Jogan***; **1951**: *Bedardi*; *Shokhiyan*; **1952**: *Sapna*; **1953**: *Gunah*; *Jhanjhar*; **1955**: *Chhora Chhori*; **1956**: *Jaldeep*; *Rangeen Raatein*; **1957**: *Bachchon se Baatein* (Doc); *Ganga Ki Lehren* (Sh); **1958**: *Scout Camp*; *Gulab Ka Phool* (Sh); **1959**: *Ekta* (Sh); **1960**: *Chetak*; *Meera Ka Chitra* (Sh); **1961**: *Hamari Yaad Ayegi*; *Mahateerth* (Sh); **1964**: ***Chitralekha***; *Fariyad*; **1967**: *Maikhana*; **1972**: *Kavi Sammelan* (Doc); **1981**: *Pehla Kadam*; **1983**: *Khuda Hafiz*.

SHARMA, RAMESH

Hindi director born in Kalimpong near Darjeeling, where he attended university. Postgraduate studies in Montreal at McGill University. Returned to India (1974) and joined a media company in Calcutta. Made ads for the Sikkim Government. Went independent in 1979. Through his own company, Rigsum Prod., published the book *Images of Sikkim*. Feature début in 1985. Produces current affairs series for tv, *Focus*.

FILMOGRAPHY: **1979**: *Rumtek: A Monastery Wreathed in a Thousand Rainbows* (Sh); **1981**: *Drikung: A Faith in Exile* (Sh); **1985**: ***New Delhi Times***.

Sharmaji *see* **Khayyam, Mohammed Zahur**
Shobhana Samarth *see* **Samarth, Shobhana**

SHOBHAN BABU (b. 1936)

Telugu star born in Tallidevarapalli, Krishna Dist., AP. Studied science and law; broke into films playing Lakshmana in **NTR**'s mythological *Seeta Rama Kalyanam*; also played Abhimanyu in *Nartanasala* and *Veer Abhimanyu* (his first solo hit). Early films extended the classic **Vijaya** Studio-NTR idiom, e.g. third film, **K. Kameshwara Rao**'s ***Mahamantri Timmarasu***. Departed from mythologicals and aristocratic roles with *Loguttu Perumallukeruka*, achieving great success with *Manushulu Marali*. Made the hit cop movie *Goodachari 116* with main rival, **G. Krishna**. Although known mainly for macho roles in action melodramas and musicals e.g. by V. Madhusudana Rao, returned to mythologicals with, e.g., **Bapu**'s *Sampoorna Ramayanam* and Kameshwara Rao's *Kurukshetramu*.

FILMOGRAPHY: **1960**: *Bhakta Shabari*; **1961**: *Seeta Rama Kalyanam*; **1962**: ***Mahamantri Timmarasu***; **1963**: *Somavara Vratham*; *Irugu Porugu*; *Chaduvukonna Ammayilu*; *Nartanasala*; **1964**: *Navagraha Pooja Mahima*; *Mahiravana*; *Deshadrohulu*; **1965**: *Prameelarjuneyam*; *Veer Abhimanyu*; ***Bangaru Panjaram***; **1966**: *Loguttu Perumallukeruka*; *Potti Pleader*; *Kanne Manushulu*; *Goodachari 116*; **1967**: *Pinni*; *Satyame Jayam*; *Private Master*; ***Shri Krishnavataram***; *Poolarangudu*; ***Aada Paduchu***; *Raktha Sindooram*; *Kambojuraju Katha*; *Punyavati*; *Pattu Kunte Padivelu*; **1968**: *Bharya*; *Chuttarikalu*; *Lakshminivasam*; *Pantalu Pattimpulu*; *Jeevitha Bandham*; *Kalasina Manushulu*; *Kumkumabharina*; *Mana Samsaram*; **1969**: *Manchi Mithrulu*; *Mooganomu*; *Vichitra Kutumbam*; *Sattekalapu Sattaiah*; *Mamaku Tagga Kodalu*; ***Nindu Hridayalu***; ***Buddhimanthudu***; *Manushulu Marali*; *Mathrudevata*; *Kannulapanduga*; *Tara Sasankam*; *Pratikaram*; **1970**: *Bhale Goodachari*; *Desamante Manasuloi*; *Iddaru Ammayilu*; *Maa Manchi Akkaiah*; *Mayani Mamata*; *Pasidi Manushulu*; *Inti Gauravam*; *Pettandarulu*; *Talli Tandrulu*; *Jagath Jettelu*; **1971**: *Mooga Prema*; *Jagath Jentreelu*; *Bangaru Talli*; *Chelleli Kapuram*; *Chinnanati Snehitulu*; *Dabukku Thha Dongala Muttha*; *Katha Nayakuralu*; *Koothuru Kodalu*; *Naa Thammudu*; *Sati Ansuya*; *Sisindri Chittibabu*; *Talli Kuthulu*; *Tehsildarugari Ammayi*; *Vichitra Dampathyam*; *Kalyana Mandapam*; *Ramalayam*; **1972**: *Kalam Marindi*; *Kiladi Bullodu*; *Manavudu Danavudu*; *Pedda Koduku*; *Sampoorna Ramayanam*; *Shanti Nilayam*; *Vamsodharakudu*; *Amma Mata*; *Kanna Talli*; *Bangaru Babu*; **1973**: *Dr Babu*; *Ganga Manga*; *Puttinillu Mettinillu*; *Ida Lokam*; *Jeevana Tarangulu*; *Jeevitham*; *Kannavari Kalalu*; *Khaidi Baba*; ***Sharada***; *Minor Babu*; **1974**: *Chakravakam* (Te); *Kode Naagu*; *Andaru Dongale*; *Manchi Manushulu*; *Devudu Chesina Pelli*; **1975**: *Soggadu*; *Andharu Manchivare*; *Babu*; *Jeevana Jyoti*; *Balipeetam*; *Jebu Donga*; *Pichimaraju*; *Gunavanthudu*; **1976**: *Iddaru Iddare*; *Monagadu*; *Premabandham*; *Raja*; *Raju Vedale*; *Pogarubottu*; **1977**: *Khaidi Kalidas*; *Ee Tharam Manishi*; *Gadusu Pillodu*; *Jeevitha Nauka*; *Kurukshetramu*; **1978**: *Enki Nayudu Bava*; *Naidu Bava*; *Nindu Manishi*; *Mallepoovu*; *Radha Krishna*; *Manchi Babai*; *Kalanthakulu*; **1979**: *Manade Gundalu*; *Karthika Deepam*; *Bangaru Chellalu*; *Judagadu*; **1980**: *Chandi Priya*; *Sannayi Appanna*; *Chesina Basalu*; *Dharma Chakram*; *Ramudu Parashuramudu*; *Manavude Mahaniyudu*; *Pandanti Jeevitham*; *Deeparadhana*; *Kaksha*; *Ketugadu*; *Kodalu Vastunaru Jagratha*; **1981**: *Jeevitha Ratham*; *Gharana Gangulu*; *Devudu Mamayya*; *Illalu*; *Jagamondi*; *Samsaram Santhanam*; **1982**: *Pratikaram*; *Swayamvaram*; *Illali Korikalu*; *Balidanam*; *Krishnarajunulu*; *Iddaru Kodakulu*; *Korukunna Mogadu*; *Prema Moorthalu*; *Devatha*; *Vamsagauravam*; **1983**: *Bandhulu Anubandhulu*; *Mugguru Monagallu*; *Mundadugu*; *Raghu Ramudu*; *Rajakumar*, *Todu Needa*; **1984**: *Danavudu*; *Iddaru Dongalu*; *Kodetharachu*; *Mr Vijay*; *Bava Maradallu*; *Punyam Kodi Purushudu*; *Jagan*; *Abhimanyudu*; *Sampoorna Premayanam*; *Dandayatra*; *Illalu Priyuralu*; *Bharyamani*; **1985**: *Maha Sangramam*; *Kongumudi*; *Devalayam*; *Jackie*; *Maharaju*; *Mugguru Mithrulu*; *Mangalya Balam*; *Sreevaru*; *Uriki Soggadu*; **1986**: *Shravana Sandhya*; *Mr Bharat* (Te); *Jeevana Poratam*; *Jailupakshi*; *Driver Babu*; *Jeevana Rangam*; *Bandham*; **1987**: *Ummadi Mogudu*; *Karthika Pournami*; *Punya Dampathulu*; **1988**: *Samsaram*; *Chattamtho Chadarangam*; *Donga Pelli*; *Bharya Bartulu*; **1989**: *Dorikite Dongalu*; **1990**: *Doshi Nirdoshi*; **1991**: *Sarpayagam*; **1993**: *Evandi Avide Ochindi*.

SHOREY, ROSHAN LAL

Pioneer Punjabi cineaste. Started in photolitho dept. of the Military Staff College in Quetta. Specialised in photography in the USA and returned to Lahore where he founded Kamala Movietone (1924), later to house the **Punjab Film** Corp. set up in 1926 with R.L. as its technical director and facilities provided by Shorey Studios. Began film career with government-sponsored instructional films but sound prompted the move into features (the mythological *Radhe Shyam*). From 1942, Shorey Pics grew into a major financier and distributor of post-Independence Hindi film. His son **Roop K. Shorey** was the in-house director.

FILMOGRAPHY: **1932**: *Radhe Shyam*; **1940**: *Ik Musafir*.

SHOREY, ROOP KISHORE (1914-73)

Hindi and Punjabi director and producer born in Quetta (now Pakistan). Son of **R.L. Shorey**. Cinematographer, lab assistant, editor and producer in Kamala Movietone. Produced and directed more than fifty shorts in Lahore. Turned feature director with the coming of sound, pioneering cheap versions of Bombay films: e.g. mythologicals, Laila-Majnu love stories and Tarzan movies. Although preceded in this by B.R. Oberoi and **Kardar**, Shorey was the first to demonstrate the financial viability of this formula, esp. in partnership with distributor **Dalsukh M. Pancholi** (1938). Worked with **Information Films of India** in WW2. Migrated to Bombay following Partition. Established Shorey Films in Bombay (1948). His last film, *Ek Thi Rita*, is an English bilingual (*A Girl Named Rita*) intended to tap the US market. His wife Meena Shorey (1920-87) acted in several of his films and, after her hit song in ***Ek Thi Ladki***, became known as the 'La-ra-lappa' girl.

FILMOGRAPHY: 1935: *Majnu 1935*; **1938**: *Tarzan Ki Beti*; **1939**: *Khooni Jadugar*; **1940**: *Dulla Bhatti*; *Ik Musafir*; **1941**: *Himmat*; **1942**: *Nishani*; *Mangti*; **1943**: *Koel*; **1945**: *Din Raat*; **1946**: *Shalimar*; **1947**: *Paro*; **1948**: *Chaman*; **1949**: ***Ek Thi Ladki***; **1951**: *Dholak*; *Mukhda*; **1953**: *Aag Ka Dariya*; *Ek Do Teen*; **1955**: *Jalwa*; **1961**: *Ek Ladki Saat Ladke*; *Aplam Chaplam*; **1962**: *Main Shaadi Karne Chala*; **1966**: *Akalmand*; **1971**: *Ek Thi Rita/A Girl Named Rita*.

SIMHA, H. L. N. (1904-72)

Kannada director; also well-known Kannada **Company Natak** actor and stage director. Worked in several theatre companies such as Bharata Manolasini Co. (Mysore) and **Gubbi Veeranna**'s. Best stage work, including his own landmark play, ***Samsara Nauka***, for Mohammed Peer's Chandrakala Nataka which he filmed twice, in Kannada (1936) and Tamil (1948). Started his own Select Artists in the mid 30s. Started in film as assistant to Belgian director Raphael Algoet's Veeranna-produced silent film, *His Love Affair* (1931). With theatre colleagues B. Puttaswamaiah and **B.R. Panthulu**, he abandoned the conventions of the mythological as practised by **B.N. Sastry** and the Gubbi Co., in favour of a more 'contemporary' approach, derived from the Amateur Dramatic Assoc.'s (Est: 1909) socials and historicals and from G.B. Shaw. In this respect, modernist Kannada cineastes paralleled the Marathi avant-garde of the 30s (see **K. Narayan Kale**). His films transposed his own plays and those of the Gubbi repertoire. Best-known: ***Bedara Kannappa***, introducing Kannada superstar **Rajkumar** to the screen.

FILMOGRAPHY: 1936: ***Samsara Nauka***; **1938**: *Muthal Mappillai*; **1940**: *Tilottama*; **1948**: *Samsara Nauka*; **1953**: ***Gunasagari/Sathya Shodhanai***; **1954**: ***Bedara Kannappa***; **1955**: *Shiv Bhakta*; **1959**: ***Abba! A Hudgi***; **1962**: *Tejaswini*; **1971**: *Anugraha*.

SINGH, DARA (b. 1928)

Dara Singh in *Veer Bajrang* (1966)

The best known of the B-grade stunt actors in the **Master Vithal** tradition. Born in Dharmuchak near Amritsar, Punjab. Started as a professional wrestler and later self-proclaimed world champion in live bouts usually with masked foreign challengers. **Babubhai Mistri**'s version of ***King Kong*** launched him in a stunt movie series often playing Tarzan. His early career extended the Mistri-**Nanabhai Bhatt** tradition of the **Wadia Movietone** and Prakash Pics stunt movie, in films like *Samson* and *Shankar Khan*. Set up his own Dara Films (1970) and turned to direction with a hit Punjabi devotional, *Bhagat Dhanna Jat*, made in the wake of ***Nanak Naam Jahaz Hai***'s 1969 success. Later work in quasi-mythologicals playing the *Ramayana* characters Balram or Hanuman. Often worked with director **Chandrakant**. Obtained a substantial urban working-class and semi-urban following. His most famous recent role as Hanuman, the monkey god revered by traditional village wrestlers in North India, was in **Sagar**'s television epic *Ramayan*. Also acted sentimental roles of the strong man with a tender heart in, e.g., ***Anand***, and the commando trainer in ***Karma***. Kedar Kapoor paid tribute to the star with a feature called *Dara Singh* (1964). In the early 90s, promoted his son Vindoo in action films.

FILMOGRAPHY (* also d): **1954**: *Pehli Jhalak*; **1962**: ***King Kong***; **1963**: *Awara Abdulla*; *Ek Tha Alibaba*; *Faulad*; *Rustom-e-Baghdad*; *King of Carnival*; **1964**: *Aandhi Aur Toofan*; *Aaya Toofan*; *Badshah*; *Dara Singh*; *Hercules*; *Rustom-e-Rome*; *Samson*; *Veer Bhimsen*; **1965**: *Bekhabar*; *Boxer*; *Hum Sub Ustad Hain*; *Khakaan*; *Lutera*; *Mahabharat*; *Raaka*; *Rustom-e-Hind*; *Saat Samandar Paar*; *Sangram*; *Sher Dil*; *Sikandar-e-Azam*; *Tarzan and King Kong*; *Tarzan Comes to Delhi*; **1966**: *Dada*; *Daku Mangal Singh*; *Insaaf*; *Jawan Mard*; *Khoon Ka Khoon*; *Naujawan*; *Shankar Khan*; *Thakur Jarnail Singh*; *Bahadur Daku*; *Husn Ka Gulam*; **1967**: *Do Dushman*; *Nasihat*; *Sangdil*; *Sardar*; *Trip to the Moon*; **1968**: *Balaram Shri Krishna*; *Jung Aur Aman*; *Thief of Baghdad*; *Watan Se Door*; **1969**: *Apna Khoon Apna Dushman*; *Beqasoor*; *Chaalbaaz*; *Danka*; *Hum Ek Hain*; *Jaalsaaz*; *The Killers*; *Toofan*; **1970**: ***Anand***; *Choron Ka Chor*; *Gunahon Ke Raaste*; ***Mera Naam Joker***; *Ilzaam*; *Nanak Dukhiya Sab Sansar**; **1971**: *Tulasi Vivah*; *Sher-e-Watan*; *Daku Mansingh*; *Kabhi Dhoop Kabhi Chhaon*; *Maya Bazaar*; **1972**: *Dukh Bhanjan Tera Naam*; *Mele Mitran De*; *Lalkaar*; *Sultana Daku*; *Hari Darshan*; *Aankhon Aankhon Mein*; **1973**: *Mera Desh Mera Dharam**; *Phir Aya Toofan*; *The Criminals*; **1974**: *Kunwara Baap*; *Bhagat Dhanna Jat**; *Har Har Mahadev*; *Kisan Aur Bhagwan*; *Zehreela Insaan*; *Shaheed-e-Azam Sardar Bhagat Singh*; **1975**: *Dharmatma*; *Dharam Karam*; *Warrant*; **1976**: *Alibaba*; *Bajrang Bali*; *Raakhi Aur Rifle*; *Sawa Lakh Se Ek Ladaun**; **1977**: *Jai Mata Di*; *Bolo He Chakradhari*; *Ram Bharose*; **1978**: *Bhakti Mein Shakti/Dhyanoo Bhagat**; *Sone Ka Dil Lohe Ke Haath*; *Nalayak*; **1979**: *Chambal Ki Rani*; *Banmanush*; **1980**: *Shiv Shakti*; *Guru Suleman Chela Pahelwan*; *Khel Muqaddar Ka*; **1982**: *Rustom**; *Main Inteqam Loonga*; **1983**: *Aan Aur Shaan*; *Bhulekha*; *Unkhili Muttiar**; **1984**: *Shravan Kumar*; **1985**: *Veer Bhimsen*; ***Mard***; *Babul Da Vedha*; **1986**: ***Karma***; *Krishna Krishna*; **1988**: *Mahaveera*; *Mardangi*; *Paanch Fauladi*; *Shiv Ganga*; **1989**: *Elaan-e-Jung*; *Shehzade*; *Maut Ki Sazaa*; **1990**: *Nakabandi*; *Triyatri*; **1991**: *Ajooba*; *Dharam-Sankat*; **1992**: *Prem Diwani*; *Main Hoon Sherni*; **1993**: *Bechain*; *Anmol*.

SINGH, M. A.

Manipuri director. Graduated from Shantiniketan University in Bengal; obtained **FTII** diploma (1973) and moved to Bombay. Worked for tv, then returned to Manipur and made newsreels and documentaries. Shot his first feature, Manipur's first colour film, on 16mm.

FILMOGRAPHY: 1983: ***Sanakeithel***; **1984**: *Langlen Thadoi*.

SINGH, SHANKAR V. RAJENDRA (b. 1948)

Kannada director; also worked extensively in Telugu and Hindi. Born in Mysore, Karnataka. Son of director Shankar Singh, itinerant exhibitor with Mahatma and Nehru Talkies; owner of the influential Kannada company, Mahatma Pics, started with **Kemparaj Urs** in 1947. Rajendra Singh entered films as child actor in 50s in his father's Mahatma productions. Assisted **Hunsur Krishnamurthy**. Started Rohini Pics (1974), expanding it with a distribution wing (1976). ***Nagarhole*** is a children's thriller modelled on disaster movies. Best-known film, ***Antha***, remade in Hindi as *Meri Awaaz Suno*, introduced a Kannada version of the **Bachchan**-type vigilante, with publicity slogans enjoining audiences to 'see it before it is banned'. *Ganda Bherunda* was strongly influenced by *Mackenna's Gold* (1968). His war film, ***Muthina Hara***, had one of the biggest-ever Kannada film budgets.

FILMOGRAPHY: 1975: *Naga Kanye*; **1977**: ***Nagarhole***; **1978**: *Kiladi Jodi*; **1980**: **1981**: ***Antha***; *Simhada Mari Sainya*; *Bhari Bharjari Bete*; *Meri Awaaz Suno*; **1984**: *Ganda Bherunda*; *Bandhana*; *Sharara*; *Mera Faisla*; *Aaj Ke Sholay*; **1985**: *Ek Se Bhale Do*; *Prem Yuddham/Prem Yudh*; *Elam Singam*; **1987**: *Thene Manushulu*; **1990**: *Bannada Gejje*; ***Muthina Hara***.

SINGH, SUCHET (?-1920)

Pioneer of the pre-studio era comparable to **Dadasaheb Phalke** and **S.N. Patankar**. Studied film-making in USA at Vitagraph. Returned to India (1917) and, with assistance from Haji Alla Rakhia (editor of the prominent Gujarati journal, *Vismi Sadi*), started Oriental Film (1918) in partnership between Abu Hasan (who later financed **Irani**), Chunilal Munim (later manager of Universal's Bombay office), Mangaldas Parekh and H.M. Mehta. Went back to USA (1919); returned with actress Dorothy Kingdom and cameraman Baron Van Rayvon (probably Hollywood cameraman Roy N. Vaughan). Died in a car crash. His unfinished productions were apparently finished by his assistant and actor, **Kanjibhai Rathod**.

FILMOGRAPHY: 1920: ***Shakuntala***; *Rama Or Maya*; *Mrichhakatik*; *Narasinh Mehta*; *Doctor Pagal* (all St).

SINGH, SURINDER (b. 1945)

Punjabi director born in Jullunder. Obtained degrees in the arts (1965) and in English (1969), then graduated from the **FTII** (1973). Films often address questions of Punjabi ethnicity: *Sachcha Mera Roop Hai/Khalsa Mera Roop He*, co-d by B.S. Shaad, dealt with the politically contentious concept of 'Khalsa', the term used by Guru Gobind Singh to define Sikhs as the chosen people and later inflected into a territorial Sikh nationalism, in a story where the heroine returns from abroad and learns about the history of her native Punjab. Other stories feature fratricidal conflicts within the Punjabi joint family, blood ties (in *Dharti Sadi Maa* two men are close friends until the wife of one is suspected of having an affair with the other) and feuds over agrarian property. His best-known film ***Marhi Da Deeva*** is based on a popular novel also adapted to the stage by Gurdial Singh (1964). Teaches at the FTII.

FILMOGRAPHY: 1976: *Sachcha Mera Roop Hai*; *Dharti Saddi Ma*; 1977: *Saal Solvan Chadiya*; 1979: *Mutiyar*; 1982: *Reshma*; 1989: ***Marhi Da Deeva/Deep***; 1992: *Udikan Saun Diyan*.

SINHA, MALA (b. 1936)

Hindi and Bengali star of Nepali origin born in Calcutta. Introduced in Bengali films by Pinaki Mukherjee, acting in his classic ***Dhuli***. Made her Hindi début under the direction of **Amiya Chakravarty** in *Badshah*. Became one of the leading stars in 50s melodramas with a series of tragic roles often featuring marital discord. Played **Guru Dutt**'s former girlfriend in ***Pyaasa***, the single mother in **Yash Chopra**'s ***Dhool Ka Phool*** and **Ashok Kumar**'s estranged wife in **B.R. Chopra**'s ***Gumrah***. Her best-known performance was as the self-sacrificing Shobhana in **Vijay Bhatt**'s ***Hariyali Aur Raasta***; she also did his next film *Himalay Ki God Mein*. Acted in the hit *Maryada* with the rising star **Rajesh Khanna**, but then receded into supporting roles. Currently promoting her daughter Pratibha Sinha as a star.

FILMOGRAPHY: 1953: *Jog Biyog*; *Shri Krishna Leela*; *Roshanara*; 1954: *Bhakta Bilwamangal*; ***Dhuli***; *Chitrangada*; *Badshah*; *Hamlet*; 1955: *Ekadashi*; *Riyasat*; 1956: *Putrabadhu*; *Paisa Hi Paisa*; *Rangeen Raatein*; 1957: *Surer Parashey*; *Prithibi Amar Chai*; *Louha Kapat*; *Aparadhi Kaun*; *Ek Gaon Ki Kahani*; *Fashion*; ***Lal Batti***; *Nausherwan-e-Adil*; *Naya Zamana*; ***Pyaasa***; 1958: *Bandhu*; *Lookochuri*; *Chandan*; *Detective*; *Devar Bhabhi*; *Ek Shola*; *Parvarish*; ***Phir Subah Hogi***; 1959: *Chhabi*; *Khelaghar*, ***Dhool Ka Phool***; *Duniya Na Mane*; *Jaalsaaz*; *Love Marriage*; *Main Nashe Mein Hoon*; *Ujala*; 1960: *Shaharer Itikatha*; *Bewaqoof*; *Mitti Mein Sona*; *Patang*; 1961: *Raibahadur*; *Sathi Hara*; *Dharmaputra*; *Maya*; *Suhaag Sindoor*; 1962: *Aankh Micholi*; *Anpadh*; *Bombay Ka Chor*; *Dil Tera Diwana*; ***Gyarah Hazaar Ladkiyan***; ***Hariyali Aur Raasta***; 1963: *Bahurani*; *Gehra Daag*; ***Gumrah***; *Phool Bane Angarey*; 1964: *Apne Huye Paraye*; *Jahan Ara*; *Main Suhagan Hoon*; *Pooja Ke Phool*; *Suhagan*; 1965: *Abhoya-o-Shrikanta*; *Bahu Beti*; *Himalay Ki God Mein*; 1966: *Aasra*; *Baharen Phir Bhi Aayengi*; *Dillagi*; 1967: *Jaal*; *Jab Yaad Kisiki Aati Hai*; *Nai Roshni*; *Night in London*; 1968: *Aankhen*; *Do Kaliyan*; *Humsaya*; *Mere Huzoor*; 1969: *Do Bhai*; *Paisa Ya Pyar*; *Pyar Ka Sapna*; *Tamanna*; 1970: *Geet*; *Holi Aayee Re*; 1971: *Chahat*; *Maryada*; *Kangan*; *Sanjog*; 1972: *Lalkaar*; *Rivaaj*; 1973: *Archana*; *Kahani Hum Sub Ki*; *Rickshawala*; 1974: *Chhattis Ghante*; *Kora Badan*; *Phir Kab Milogi*; 1975: *Sunehra Sansar*; 1976: *Do Ladkiyan*; *Mazdoor Zindabad*; *Zindagi*; 1977: *Kabita*; *Prayashchit*; 1978: *Karmayogi*; 1980: *Berahem*; *Dhan Daulat*; 1981: *Harjaai*; *Yeh Rishta Na Toote*; 1982: *Nek Perveen*; 1983: *Babu*; 1984: *Aasmaan*; 1985: *Dil Tujhko Diya*; 1992: *Khel*; *Radha Ka Sangam*.

SINHA, TAPAN (b. 1924)

Bengali director born in Calcutta. Studied in Bihar, where his family owned much land. Science graduate at Calcutta University (1945). Worked as sound engineer at **New Theatres** (1945-9) where he observed **Nitin Bose** and **Bimal Roy**. Did the sound for **Satyen Bose**'s ***Paribartan*** (1949). Invited to the London Film Festival, he stayed and spent a few months at Pinewood Studios (1950-1). Committed to making mid-budget 'honest entertainment'. Worked in many genres including comedies and children's films. Best-known work is derived from literature: e.g. **Tagore** (*Atithi*, ***Kabuliwala***, ***Kshudista Pashan***), Narayan Ganguly's story *Sainik* (*Ankush*), **Sailajananda Mukherjee**'s *Krishna* (*Upahar*), Jarasandha (*Louha-Kapat*), Ramapada Sengupta (*Kalamati*, *Ekhani*), Samaresh Bose's travelogue (***Nirjan Saikate***), Shankar (*Ek Je Chhilo Desh*), Sunil Ganguly (the chldren's film *Sabuj Dwiper Raja*). Films usually focus on literary rather than cinematic qualities. Occasionally made more expensive melodramas with major stars from Bengali (**Uttam Kumar**) or Hindi film (**Ashok Kumar** in *Hatey Bazarey*; **Dilip Kumar** in *Sagina Mahato*). Introduced a brand of political cinema with ***Apanjan***, later continued in *Raja* and *Adalat-o-Ekti Meye*, addressing the contemporary in the wake of the **Naxalite** uprising, revealing a greater sense of social critique when dealing with women's oppression. *Raja* and *Adalat-o-Ekti Meye* were accused by Provas Phadikar, West Bengal's Minister of Information & Cultural Affairs, of having incited political violence. Writes and scores many of his own films.

FILMOGRAPHY: 1954: *Ankush*; 1955: *Upahar*; 1956: *Tonsil*; ***Kabuliwala***; 1957: *Louha-Kapat*; 1958: *Kalamati*; 1959: *Kshaniker Atithi*; 1960: ***Kshudista Pashan***; 1961: *Jhinder Bandi*; 1962: ***Hansuli Banker Upakatha***; 1963: ***Nirjan Saikate***; 1964: *Jotugriha*; ***Arohi***; 1965: *Atithi*; 1966: *Galpa Holeo Satti*; 1967: *Hatey Bazarey*; 1968: ***Apanjan***; 1970: *Sagina Mahato*; 1971: *Ekhani*; 1972: *Zindagi Zindagi*; 1973: *Andhar Periye*; 1974: *Sagina*; *Raja*; 1975: *Harmonium*; 1976: *Ek Je Chhilo Desh*; 1977: *Safed Hathi*; 1979: *Sabuj Dwiper Raja*; 1980: ***Bancharamer Bagan***; 1981: *Adalat-o-Ekti Meye*; 1983: *Abhimanyu*; 1984: ***Admi Aur Aurat***; 1985: *Baidurya Rahasya*; 1986: *Atanka*; 1987: *Aaj Ka Robin Hood*; 1990: *Ek Doctor Ki Maut*; 1991: *Antardhan*.

SIPPY, GOPALDAS PARMANAND (b. 1915)

Director born in Hyderabad (Sind). Jailed as a student for participation in the Independence Movement (1930-42). Became a lawyer and

G.P. Sippy in his film *Blackmailer* (1957)

ran a restaurant in Karachi. Moved to Bombay following Partition. Floated G.P. Prod. with *Sazaa* (1951). Financed other productions like **Amiya Chakravarty**'s *Shahenshah* (1953) and **Raja Nene**'s *Radha Krishna* (1954). Started Sippy Films, now one of the biggest Hindi producers and distributors, with *Marine Drive*. Concentrated on production and distribution in the 60s; since the early 70s a leading industry representative involved in government policy. Produced blockbusters such as ***Sholay*** (1975), *Shaan* (1980) and *Sagar* (1985) by his son **Ramesh Sippy**, a major box-office director. Currently heads the industry's initiatives against video piracy.
FILMOGRAPHY (* also act): **1955**: *Marine Drive*; *Adl-e-Jehangir*; **1956**: *Chandrakant*; *Shrimati 420*; **1957**: *Blackmailer**; **1958**: *Light House*; **1959**: *Bhai Bahen*; **1961**: *Mr India*.

SIPPY, RAMESH (b. 1947)

Hindi director born in Karachi. Son of producer **G.P. Sippy** under whose banner he made most of his films. Graduated from Bombay University. Début, ***Andaz***, is a love story featuring **Rajesh Khanna** at the peak of his popularity, **Hema Malini** and **Shammi Kapoor**. Known for big-budget multi-starrers. One of the few accomplished genre directors in India, he made a remarkable sci-fi espionage thriller (*Shaan*), a love story (*Sagar*) and virtually redefined the Hindi version of the western with ***Sholay***, a hit of legendary proportions. His regular scenarists, **Salim-Javed** (more recently only Javed), helped define his story patterns enhanced by carefully choreographed, technically accomplished action sequences: *Sholay*'s opening chase sequence, based on *How the West Was Won* (1962), was made with the technical assistance of the British technician Jim Allen, as were the helicopter shots of **Sunil Dutt**'s kidnapping in *Shaan*, shot in Somerset. Made the first major tv serial, *Buniyaad*, planned as a film drama shot on 16mm but deadlines forced him to shoot mainly on video.

FILMOGRAPHY: **1971**: ***Andaz***; **1972**: *Seeta Aur Geeta*; **1975**: ***Sholay***; **1980**: *Shaan*; **1982**: *Shakti*; **1985**: *Sagar*; **1987-88**: *Buniyaad* (TV); **1989**: *Bhrashtachar*; **1991**: *Akela*.

SIVAN, PAPANASAM (1891-1973)

Tamil songwriter and composer. Originally called P.R. Ramaiyyer. Trained in music at the Maharaja's Sanskrit College, Trivandrum. Became known as a classical musician in the Carnatic style at the royal court, where he was also a disciple of the musicians Mahadeva Bhagavathar and Samba Bhagavathar. Lived as an itinerant singer of devotional songs. Taught music to the members of a drama company at Papanasam village, TN, also acting in some plays. Moved to Madras (1930) and published his first book of devotional lyrics (1934). Film début for **Prabhat** Studio's Tamil film *Seeta Kalyanam* (1933) as songwriter and composer. Had a big impact, esp. through the films in which M.S. Subbulakshmi and G.N. Balasubramanyam sang his compositions, on the induction of the Carnatic style into film music (e.g. ***Seva Sadan***, 1938; *Shakuntalai*, 1940). Best-known work for **K. Subramanyam**: e.g. music and lyrics for *Seva Sadan*, and major roles in *Bhakta Kuchela* (1936) and ***Thyagabhoomi*** (1939). Also worked with **Duncan**, writing lyrics/music for ***Ambikapathy*** (1937) and *Shakuntalai*.

SOCIAL

See also **Melodrama.** The social is a loosely defined generic label for melodrama with a 20th C. setting, rehearsing a variety of 'social' issues. It overlaps with melodrama when these issues are elaborated in terms of family problems and sexuality. It also extends beyond melodrama by giving the social issues relating to tensions of modernisation a broader canvas than just the family. It would be possible to see the Social as an umbrella genre encompassing all stories with a 20th C. setting relying on an orchestration of affect at the expense of narrative propulsion. In this sense, the Social becomes a hegemonic genre absorbing melodrama.It is also possible to argue that the more a reformist story is treated cinematically, departing from the literariness of its model, the more melodramatic the result. In that sense, a Social is a film which is still insufficiently cinematic and a Melodrama would be a genuinely cinematic treatment of the issues addressed by reform literature.A narrower usage refers specifically to the films that emerged from the social reform movement initiated in British-controlled India towards the beginning of the 19th C. The reform movement in this sense was initiated by Christian missions (e.g. the Society for the Propagation of the Gospel, the London Missionary Society, the Church Missionary Society, the Wesleyan Mission, the Free Church Mission of Scotland) when they established institutionalised education (later extended by the British government). The impact was notable particularly in Bengal, Maharashtra, AP and Malabar (North Kerala). Among the first to redefine this reformism in line with the requirements of an Indian middle class was Raja Rammohun Roy (1772-1833) who established the Brahmo Samaj (1828). His focus on the social oppression of women and the lower castes went together with his efforts to displace established religiosity by appealing to the Vedas and the Upanishads as embodying the 'real' tradition. The numerous texts of the movement, including journalism, archaeology and its privileged art form, the reform novel, repeatedly negotiate a 'traditional' idiom and symbology to find a way of representing modernity. Key novelists were the Bengali writers Bankimchandra Chatterjee, whose work, despite important differences, is extended by **Rabindranath Tagore** and the early 20th C. writers Bibhutibhushan and Tarashankar Bannerjee; the seminal Telugu playwright Gurzada Appa Rao (*Kanyashulkam*, 1892); the Malayalam writer O. Chandu Menon (*Indulekha*, 1889), the Marathi novelist Hari Narayan Apte and others. The form provided some of the key stereotypes for the early cinema: e.g. 'More than half of Saratchandra [Chatterjee]'s 20 novels and about as many short stories deal either centrally or partially with the situation of a widow' (Meenakshi Mukherjee, 1985). Elsewhere, e.g. in Karnataka, reformism produced key literary works (e.g. Masti Venkatesha Iyenagar, K.V. Puttappa) formulating a cultural universalism within the nationalist-regionalist experience, a strategy later adopted in many films. From the silent era onwards, Socials based on classic novels sought to transfer literature's respectibility to the cinema. At times (e.g. in Maharashtra), reform novelists were hired as scenarists (**Narayan Hari Apte**, **V.S. Khandekar**). **Bhavnani** persuaded the best-known 20th C. Hindi-Urdu novelist, Premchand, to write a film script: ***Mazdoor*** (1934).

SOUNDARARAJAN, S. (?-1966)

Tamil director and producer, born in Kottacheri, TN. Worked with the Cummaiah theatre group and started Tamil Nadu Talkies (1933), débuting as director with the mythological *Lavakusa*. Introduced through his films actors like Vasundhara Devi, R. Ranjan, Krishna Kumari, Rama Shankar, **Gummadi Venkateshwara Rao**, the musician and director **S. Balachander**, etc. His first Telugu film, the hit ***Chenchulakshmi***, is composer **C.R. Subburaman**'s début. Films included early colour experiments, e.g. *Mohini Rugmangada* used hand-tinting for a sequence; *Miss Sundari* is printed in sepia, advertised as Trucolor. Best-known film: *Rajadrohi*, featuring an autocratic diwan from a princely state, a thinly disguised reference to C.P. Ramaswamy Aiyer, Diwan of Travancore, who banned the film in his state, thus ensuring its success everywhere else. Directed the seminal **Gubbi Veeranna** Kannada stage adaption ***Hemareddy Malamma***. Also credited with having set up the first processing lab in South India.

FILMOGRAPHY: **1934**: *Lavakusa*; **1935**: *Gul-e-Bakavali*; *Mohini Rugmangada*; **1936**: *Mahabharatam*; **1937**: *Miss Sundari*; **1938**: *Rajadrohi*; **1940**: *Thirumangai Alwar*; **1941**: ***Rishyashringar***; **1942**: *Bhakta Nandanar*; *Naradar*; **1943**: ***Chenchulakshmi***; **1945**: ***Hemareddy Malamma***; **1950**: *Adrushta Deepudu*; **1951**: *Navvitte Navarathrulu*; **1952**: *Penn Manam*.

SRIDEVI (b. 1960)

Major star mainly known until the mid-80s for Tamil and Telugu films, then for big-budget Hindi films. Started as a child actress aged 5 with **Sivaji Ganesan** (***Kandan Karunai***); also with **MGR** (***Nam Naadu***). Became a major star with **Bharathirajaa**'s début ***Pathinaru Vayathinile***, its Hindi remake *Solva Sawan* being her first Hindi film. Played in key **NTR** vigilante films (***Vetagadu***, *Bobbili Puli*) and opposite the Telugu star **Krishna**. Made Hindi B-movies with **Dasari Narayana Rao**, **K. Raghavendra Rao** and **K. Bapaiah**, including dubbed versions of her Telugu films. Broke through in Hindi with K. Raghavendra Rao's *Himmatwala*, and made several more films with its male lead **Jeetendra**. **Shekhar Kapur**'s ***Mr India*** was her first solo success, her famous song in this film, *Hawa hawaii*, being quoted in **Mira Nair**'s *Salaam Bombay* (1988). Of another song in *Mr India* Ravi Vasudevan writes: 'In the most sexual of her performances, [s]he is sensualised by the lovemaking of an invisible man. It could be argued that this empty space invites the insertion of the male spectator, [b]ut it is somehow still consistent with the narcissistic, auto-erotic regime of sexuality implied in the persona of this female star.' With her 'sequined dress and feathers look' (as choreographer Chinni Prakash put it) and inch-long false eyelashes, Sridevi is the latest in a line of buxom South Indian stars (**Vyjayanthimala**, **Rekha**, Jayapradha). *Nashilee Jawani* was promoted as her first 'sex film'. Currently the highest-paid actress in India, and the main sales asset of India's most expensive film to date, *Roop Ki Rani Choron Ka Raja*.

FILMOGRAPHY: **1967**: ***Kandan Karunai***; **1969**: ***Nam Naadu***; *Kumara Sambhavam*; **1970**: *Swapnangal*; *Agni Pareeksha*; *Maa Nanna Nirdoshi*; **1971**: *Poombatta*; *Bharya Biddalu*; *Naa Thammudu*; *Nenu Manishine*; *Shrimanthudu*; **1972**: *Bala Bharatam*; *Kanimuthu Papa*; *Amma Mata*; *Raj Mahal*; *Badi Panthulu*; *Teerthayatra*; **1973**: *Prarthanai*; *Mallamma Katha*; *Marapurani Manishi*; *Bhakta Tukaram*; **1974**: *Avalukku Nihar Avale*; **1975**: *Anuragalu*; *Devudulanti Manishi*; *Ee Kalapu Pillalu*; *Yashoda Krishna*; ***Julie***; **1976**: *Moondru Mudichu*; *Padavoyi Bharatheeyuda*; *Abhinandanam*; *Alinganam*; *Ashirvadam*; *Kuttavum Sitshayum*; *Thulavarsham*; **1977**: *Gayatri*; *Kavikuyil*; *Sainthadamma Sainthadu*; ***Pathinaru Vayathinile***; *Bangarakka*; *Vezhambal*; *A Nimisham*; *Amme Anupame*; *Angikaram*; *Antardhanam*; *Nalumani Pookkal*; *Nirakudam*; *Oonjal*; *Satyavan Savithri*; **1978**: *Priya*; *Ayiram Janmangal*; *Elaya Rani Rajalakshmi*; *Ganga Yamuna Kaveri*; *Ithu Eppadi Irukku*; *Machanai Parthingala*; *Manitharil Ithanai Nirangala*; *Mudichooda Mannan*; *Pilot Premnath*; *Rajavukku Etha Rani*; *Sigappu Rojakkal*; *Taxi Driver*; *Vanakathukuria Kathaliye*; *Kannan Oru Kayi Kuzhanthai*; *Radhai Ketra Kannan*; *Sakka Podu Podu Raja*; *Solva Sawan*; *Padaharella Vayasu*; *Avalude Ravukal*; **1979**: *Sigappukkal Mookuthi*; *Dharma Yuddham*; *Kalyanaraman*; *Kavariman*; *Neela Malargal*; *Thayi Illamal Nanillai*; ***Vetagadu***; *Buripalem Bullodu*; *Naan Oru Kayi Parkiren*; *Lakshmi*; *Pagalil Oru Iravu*; *Arumbugal*; **1980**: *Guru*; *Johnny*; *Varumayin Niram Sigappu*; *Vishwa Roopam*; *Kaksha*; *Sardar Paparayudu*; *Sandhya*; *Bangaru Bhava*; *Prema Kanuka*; *Devudichina Koduku*; *Gharana Donga*; *Mama Allula Saval*; *Attagadu*; *Adrushtavanthudu*; *Chuttalunnaru Jagratha*; *Rowdy Ramudu Konte Krishnudu*; **1981**: *Balanagamma*; *Daiva Thirumanangal*; *Meendum Kokila*; *Ranuva Veeran*; *Shankarlal*; *Bhoga Bhagyalu*; *Gadasari Attaha Sosagari Kodalu*; *Rani Kasularangamma*; *Akali Rajyam*; *Prema Simhasanam*; *Puli Bidda*; *Aggirava*; *Gharana Gangulu*; *Kondaveeti Simham*; **1982**: ***Moondram Pirai***; *Pookkari Raja*; *Thanikatu Raja*; *Vazhve Mayam*; *Bangaru Koduku*; *Devatha*; *Bangaru Kanuka*; *Bangaru Bhoomi*; *Andagadu*; *Anuraga Devatha*; *Krishnarajunulu*; *Vayyari Bhamulu Vagalamari Bharthulu*; *Krishnavataram*; *Shamsher Shankar*; *Bobbili Puli*; *Justice Choudhury*; *Aadi Vishnulu*; *Kalavari Samsaram*; *Daiviyin Thiruvilaiyadal*; **1983**: *Adutha Varisu*; *Mundadugu*; *Adavi Simhalu*; *Muddula Mogadu*; *Urantha Sankranthi*; *Rama Rajyamlo Bheemaraju*; *Kirai Kotigadu*; *Ramudu Kadu Krishnudu*; *Himmatwala*, *Jaani Dost*; *Kalakaar*; *Mawaali*; *Sadma*; *Shri Ranganeethulu*; *Devi Sridevi*; *Lanke Bindelu*; *Simham Navindi*; **1984**: *Akalmand*; *Amme Narayana*; *Aakhri Sangram*; *Jaag Utha Insaan*; *Maqsad*; *Naya Kadam*; *Tohfa*; *Zulm Ki Zanjeer*; *Inquilab*; *Tandava Krishnudu*; *Kodetharachu*; *Kanchu Kagada*; **1985**: *Vajrayudham*; *Aaj Ka Dada*; *Balidan*; *Masterji*; *Sarfarosh*; *Pachani Kapuram*; *Santham Bheekaram*; *Joshilay*; **1986**: ***Karma***; *Aag Aur Shola*; *Aakhri Raasta*; *Bhagwan Dada*; *Dharam Adhikari*; *Ghar Sansar*; *Jadu Nagari*; *Jaanbaaz*; *Nagina*; *Suhagan*; ***Sultanat***; *Naan Adimai Illai*; *Jayam Manade*; *Khaidi Rudraiah*; **1987**: *Aulad*; *Himmat Aur Mehnat*; *Jawab Hum Denge*; *Majaal*; ***Mr India***; *Nazrana*; *Watan Ke Rakhwale*; **1988**: *Ram Avatar*; *Sherni*; *Waqt Ki Awaaz*; *Sone Pe Suhaaga*; *Akhani Poratam*; *Halla Gulla*; **1989**: *Gair Kanooni*; *Guru*; *Main Tera Dushman*; *Nigahen*; ***Chandni***; *Chaalbaaz*; *Mera Farz*; **1990**: *Jagadeka Veerudu Attilokasundari*; *Nakabandi*; *Patthar Ke Insaan*; **1991**: ***Kshana Kshanam***; *Lamhe*; *Farishte*; *Aasman Se Gira*; *Banjaran*; **1992**: ***Khuda Gawah***; *Laila Majnu*; *Roop Ki Rani Choron Ka Raja*; *Heer Ranjha*; **1993**: *Gurudev*; *Gumrah*; *Chandramukhi*.

SRIDHAR, CHINGELPET V.

Major Tamil director of melodramas; also worked extensively in Telugu, Hindi and Kannada. Playwright while employed in a government office in his native Chingelpet. Became a scenarist after adapting his best-known play, *Raktha Pasam*, staged by the **TKS Brothers**, for R.S. Mani's film (1954). Scripted e.g. Ch. Narayamurthy's *Ethirparadathu* (1954), **T. Prakash Rao**'s ***Amara Deepam***, *Mathurkula Manikyam* (both 1956; the latter based on **Tagore**'s *Nauka Dubi*) and *Uthama Puthran* (1958). Partner in Venus Pics (1956). Directorial début with ***Kalyana Parisu*** for the producers of ***Amara Deepam***. It is a grisly but successful love triangle presenting a brutally neurotic man as a tragic hero and starred **Gemini Ganesh** and **B. Saroja Devi**. For his own Chithralaya Pics (1961), he scripted and directed, e.g., *Nenjil Ore Alayam*, a story about three people in a hospital enhanced by the popular songs of A.M. Raja. It was remade as *Dil Ek Mandir*, **Rajendra Kumar** playing a doctor who has to cure the terminally ill husband (Raaj Kumar) of his former lover **Meena Kumari**. K. Hariharan suggests that Sridhar's type of 'intense emotional drama confined to just two or three characters and with a strong emphasis on composition and gesture' was inherited by the Malayalam and Tamil director **Fazil**. His best-known Hindi film, *Pyar Kiye Jaa*, is a slapstick comedy featuring one of Mehmood's most famous performances. Remade **Chanakya**'s Telugu film *Constable Koothuru* (1962) in Tamil as *Policekaran Magal*. Briefly partnered cameraman and Malayalam director **A. Vincent** in business in the 60s; his early work often featured the composer duo Vishwanathan and Ramamurthy. Launched **Jayalalitha** (in *Vennira Adai*), Ravichandran and Kanchana as lead characters.

FILMOGRAPHY: **1959**: ***Kalyana Parisu***; **1960**: *Meenda Sorgam*; *Pelli Kanuka*; *Vidiveli*; **1961**: *Nazrana*; *Punarjanmam*; *Thennilavu*; **1962**: *Nenjil Ore Alayam*; *Policekaran Magal*; *Sumaithangal*; **1963**: *Dil Ek Mandir*; *Nenjam Marappathillai*; **1964**: *Kadalikka Neramillai*; *Kalai Kovil*; **1965**: *Vennira Adai*; **1966**: *Kodimalar*; *Manase Mandiram*; *Pyar Kiye Jaa*; **1967**: *Nai Roshni*; *Nenjirukumvarai*; *Ootivarai Uravu*; **1968**: *Saathi*; **1969**: *Sivantha Mann*; **1970**: *Dharti*; **1971**: *Avalukendu Ore Manam*; *Duniya Kya Jaane*; **1973**: *Alaigal*; *Gehri Chaal*; **1974**: *Urimai Kural*; **1975**: *Jagruthi*; *Lakshmi Nirdoshi*; *Ninagagi Nanu*; *Vaira Nenjam*; **1976**: *Oh Manju*; **1977**: *Meenava Nanban*; ***Seeta Geeta Datithe***; **1978**: *Elamai Vunjaladugiradhu*; *Vayasu Pilichindi*; **1979**: *Azhage Unnai Aradikiran*; *Urvashi Neenu Nanna Preyasi/Urvashi Nive Naa Preyasi*; **1980**: *Hare Krishna Hello Radha*; *Sundarime Varuga Varuga*; **1981**: *Mohana Ponnagai*; **1982**: *Dil-e-Nadaan*; *Nenaivellam Nithya*; **1983**: *Oru Odai Nadhiyagiradhu*; *Thudikkum Karangal*; **1984**: *Alaya Deepam*; *Prema Sangamam*; *Rowdicaku Saval*; **1985**: *Thendrale Ennai Thodu*; *Unnai Thedi Varuven*; **1986**: *Nanum Oru Thozhilali*; *Yaro Ezhuthai Kavithai*; **1987**: *Andarikante Ghanudu*; *Iniya Uravu Poothathu*; **1988**: *Premayanam*; **1991**: *Thanduvitten Ennai*.

SRINIVASAN, M. B. (1925-88)

One of the more enigmatic figures in Malayalam and Tamil film music. Born in Chittor, AP; nephew of the CPI leader M.R. Venkatraman and himself a CPI member and organiser of the trade union movement in the Tamil film industry. Together with director **Nemai Ghosh**, he is a key figure in the brief career of the Leftist Kumari Films. Its best-known film, ***Padhai Theriyudu Paar***, included the popular song written by Jayakantan and set to the xylophone, *Thennan keethu oonjalile*. His political allegiances hampered his Tamil career and he did his best-known work in Malayalam, initially for **P. Subramanyam** and **K.S. Sethumadhavan**, then for **Adoor Gopalakrishnan** (his use of the raga *Chakrabhagam* in ***Swayamvaram*** is a cinematic innovation), **K.G. George** (***Adaminte Variyellu***) and **Lenin Rajendran** (***Swathi Thirunal***). Best remembered for playing the lead in and scoring **John Abraham**'s ***Agraharathil Kazhuthai***, where he used the melancholic Carnatic raga *Neelambiri*, usually sung by women, in the cow-milking scene. Composed choral songs like *Vanam Namadhu thandai* and *Bharatha samudayam* in ***Dhakam***.

FILMOGRAPHY: **1960**: ***Padhai Theriyudu Paar***; **1962**: *Sneha Deepam*; *Puthiya Aksham Puthiya Bhoomi*; *Kalpadukal*; *Kannum Karalum*; *Swargarajyam*; **1963**: *Kaleyum Kaminiyum*; **1964**: *Althara*; ***Vivahabandham***; **1966**: *Puthri*; **1968**: *Kadal*; *Aparadhini*; **1969**: *Nurse*; **1970**: *Madhuvidhu*; **1971**: ***Vidyarthikale Ithile Ithile***; *Vimochana Samaram*; **1972**: ***Dhakam***; *Ini Oru Janmam Tharu*; ***Swayamvaram***; **1974**: *Kanyakumari*; ***Uttarayanam*** (with Raghavan); *Pathiravum Pakalvelichavum*; *Swarna Vigraham*; **1975**: *Eduppar Kayi Pillai*; *Puthu Vellam*; *Prayanam*; **1976**: *Sivathandavam*; *Voorummadi Brathukulu*; *Madana Malligai*; **1977**: ***Agraharathil Kazhuthai*** (also act); **1978**: *Onappudava*; *Bandhanam*; **1980**: ***Greeshamam***; ***Kolangal***; ***Oppol***; **1981**: ***Elippathayam***; ***Valarthu Mrugangal***; ***Ilakkangal***; **1982**: ***Yavanika***; **1983**: ***Adaminte Variyellu***; ***Akkare***; *Evedayo Oru Sathru*; *Katthi*; ***Lekhayude Maranam Oru Flashback***; *Omana Thingal*; *Parasparam*; *Prem Nazirine Kanmanilla*; ***Rachana***; *Rukma*; ***Sagaram Shantham***; *Oru Swakariam*; **1984**: ***Mukha Mukham***; *Oru Kochu Swapnam*; ***Panchavadippalam***; *Thathamme Poocha Poocha*; **1985**: *Ayanam*; ***Irakal***; ***Kilippattu***; ***Meenamasathile Sooryan***; **1987**: ***Purushartham***; ***Swathi Thirunal***; *Manivathoorile Ayiram Sivarathrikal*; ***Anantaram***; **1988**: *Mattoral*.

SRIRANJINI (Junior) (1927-74)

Telugu and Tamil actress; younger sister of **Sriranjini (Senior)**. Born in Narasaraopet, AP. Known mainly for her roles as the long-suffering wife. In her Tamil film ***Parasakthi*** she epitomises the male ideal of virtuous Hindu womanhood. Joined films in Telugu with **L.V. Prasad**'s ***Grihapravesham*** as Lalita, the ill-reputed girlfriend of **C.S.R. Anjaneyalu**. Acted in films by **K. Kameshwara Rao, K.V. Reddy** and **P.S. Ramakrishna Rao**. Retired from films in 1960, returning to play a few guest roles after 1969.

FILMOGRAPHY: **1944**: *Bhishma*; **1946**: ***Grihapravesham***; **1948**: *Madalasa*; **1949**: ***Gunsundari Katha***; ***Laila Majnu***; *Brahma Ratham*; **1950**: *Vali Sugriva*; **1951**: *Mantradandam*; **1952**: ***Prema/Kathal***; *Aadabrathuku*; *Manavati*; *Rajeshwari*; ***Sankranti***; ***Parasakthi***; **1953**: *Bratuku Theruvu*; ***Chandraharam***; **1954**: ***Pedda Manushulu***; *Raji En Kanmani/Raji Naa Pranam*; *Amara Sandesham*; **1955**: ***Santhanam***; **1956**: *Shri Gauri Mahatyam*; **1957**: *Swayamprabha*; *Premada Putri/Preme Daivam/Anbe Daivam*; *Vaddante Pelli*; **1958**: *Shri Ramanjaneya Yuddham*; **1959**: *Bhakta Ambarish*; *Ore Vazhi*; **1960**: *Thilakam*; *Mahakavi Kalidasa*; **1962**: ***Shri Krishnarjuna Yuddham***; **1965**: ***Bangaru Panjaram***; **1969**: *Bhale Tammudu*; **1973**: *Bangaru Manushulu*; *Jeevana Tarangulu*; *Bhakta Tukaram*; *Snehabandham*; *Vishali*; *Pookkari*; **1974**: *Kode Naagu*; *Inti Kodalu*.

SRIRANJINI (Senior) (1906-39)

Actress known as 'Senior' to distinguish her from her younger sister, the Telugu and Tamil star **Sriranjini** (Junior). Born in Narasaraopet taluk, AP. A major singing star of the 30s; became known through her record albums and audio releases of plays by the Gramophone Company of India. Stage actress (often playing male roles, e.g. *Abhimanyu*, *Satyavan*, *Krishna*) in Krishna Vilas Nataka Samajam-produced mythologicals. Débuted in **C. Pullaiah**'s ***Lavakusa***. Thereafter with **Vel Pics** in ***Shri Krishna Leelalu*** and *Maya Bazaar*. She died 4 years later from cancer.

FILMOGRAPHY: **1934**: ***Lavakusa***; **1935**: ***Shri Krishna Leelalu***; *Nala Damayanti*; **1936**: *Maya Bazaar*; *Sati Tulasi*; **1938**: *Chitranaliyam*; **1939**: ***Vande Mataram***; ***Varavikrayam***.

SRI SRI (1910-83)

Telugu lyricist for over 150 films. Originally called Srirangam Srinivasa Rao; born in Vishakapatnam, AP. Major radical Telugu poet (e.g. *Prabhava*) and novelist (e.g. *Veerasimha Vijayasimhulu*). Introduced free verse into his socially concerned poetry (*Maha Prasthanam*). Known for the original songs for *Ahuti* (1950), a Telugu dubbed version of an unspecified, possibly Tamil, film credited to 'Naveena'. Some of the songs, *Hamsavale o padava*, *Oogisaladenayya*, *Premaye janana marana leela*, scored by **Saluri Rajeshwara Rao**, were major hits. Also did some strident songs like *Padavoyi bharatiyudu* in *Velugu Needulu* (1961). Biography and compilation of his writings by Chalasani Prasad (1990).

STAGE BACKDROPS

One of the earliest recorded uses of stage backdrops in the popular theatre was Vishnudas Bhave's Marathi play *Seeta Swayamvar* (1853). The practice derived from the Sanskrit theatre where a mobile curtain called the yavanika or pati would be held by two men to modulate acting spaces: to mark different styles of entry of the gods and rakshasas (demons), to introduce the sutradhara (chorus) and vidushaka (jester-commentator), the women's sanctum, etc. This device remains in use in Kathakali and related performance modes. The form developed in the **Parsee theatre** as a means of giving spectacular dimensions to the proceedings. Haji Abdullah's *Sakhawat Khodadost Badshah*, staged by the Indian Imperial Co., used 14 curtains. The Zoroastrian Club's famous backdrop for *Badshah Ustaspa* showed the angel Zarathustra with a ball of fire in his hands. Initially the curtains in the Parsee theatre were painted by Europeans (Italians, in particular), later by painters trained in Indian **art schools**. The scenes depicted became increasingly elaborate showing streets, gardens, industrial and urban locations. In the Lalitkaladarsh production of Mama Warerkar's *Satteche Gulam* (1922), the painter P.S. Kale took the next logical step and duplicated a photograph of a Bombay street intersection on to the backdrop. **Baburao Painter** and his brother Anandrao were among the most famous backdrop painters in Western India. The back curtain had a double function: it presented a locale to match the one evoked in the fiction through dialogue and song, but it also provided a fantasy space beyond the physical, contiguous acting space on the stage where actors would constitute realistic tableaux. Both functions were crucial to early Indian cinema from **Phalke** and **Hiralal Sen** onwards. The pictorial paradoxes potentially set up by the relations between the backdrop space and the stage space helped determine the concept of the shot in early fiction films. The technique of spatial juxtaposition to ground the narrative in effect substituted spatial contiguity for temporal continuity, relaying the viewer's gaze from one spatially fixed tableau to another.

SUBBAIAH NAIDU, M. V. (1896-1962)

Kannada actor-singer, best known for heroic roles in **Company Natak**. Started as child actor in Bailatta folk theatre. Played female roles in the Seeta Manohar Natak and worked with **Simha** in the Manolasini Co.; eventually joined **Veeranna**'s troupe (1925) where he achieved stardom. With **R. Nagendra Rao**, he staged *Bhakta Ambarisha*, *Bhukailasa* and *Yachhamanayika* (all were later filmed), introducing cinematic techniques to the Kannada stage and thus to early Kannda cinema: elaborate scene changes and backdrops, stage dimmers, spotlights, cycloramas and trick scenes such as the severing of Ravana's head in ***Bhukailasa***. Naidu established the pattern for the heroic look in his incarnation of Indrajit in the first Kannada talkie, **Y.V. Rao**'s ***Sati Sulochana***, and as Charudatta in *Vasantsena*. Also composed the music for *Bettada Kalla* (1957).

FILMOGRAPHY (* also d): **1931**: *His Love Affair* (St); **1934**: ***Sati Sulochana***; **1940**: ***Bhukailasa***; **1941**: *Vasantsena*; **1943**: *Satya Harishchandra*; **1947**: *Mahatma Kabir*; **1958**: ***Bhakta Prahlada****.

SUBBA RAO, ADURTHI (1921-75)

Mainstream Telugu director born in Rajamundhri, AP. Still photographer; assistant cameraman in **Vijay Bhatt**'s Prakash Studio (Bombay), editor (including parts of Uday Shankar's ***Kalpana***, 1948), occasional lyricist (*Okaroju Raju*, 1944; *Mangalsutram*, 1946) and assistant to **T. Prakash Rao**. Also worked for Radha Films, Calcutta (1937). Best-known films at Annapurna provided art-house variation on melodrama, backed by Telugu megastar **A. Nageshwara Rao**. Early work acclaimed for its heightened realism (e.g. the bullock-cart race in *Namminabantu*). The experimental aspect, which in, e.g., ***Thene Manushulu*** simply meant working with new faces such as the future star **Krishna**, became a strategy when Subba Rao combined with **Nageshwara Rao** to found Chakravarthi Chitra (*Sudigundalu*). Its commercial failure and that of ***Maro Prapancham***, the company's only other film, ended their experimental aspirations. Hindi début *Milan* remade *Moogamanushulu* with **Sunil Dutt** and **Nutan**. Made several Hindi and Tamil films.

FILMOGRAPHY: **1954**: *Amara Sandesham*; **1957**: *Thodi Kodallu*; **1958**: *Aadapettanam*; **1959**: *Mangalya Balam/Manjal Magimai*; *Engal Kula Daivi*; **1960**: *Namminabantu/Pattayilin Vetri*; **1961**: *Velugu Needulu/Thooya Ullam*; *Krishna Prema*; *Iddaru Mithralu*; *Kumudam*; **1962**: *Manchi Manushulu/Penn Manam*; **1963**: *Chaduvukonna Ammayilu*; *Mamakaram*; *Kattu Roja*; *Neenkada Ninaivu*; ***Moogamanushulu***; **1964**: *Thayin Madiyil*; *Dr Chakravarthi*; *Dagudu Moothulu*; **1965**: *Sumangali*; ***Thene Manushulu***; *Todu Needa*; **1966**: *Kanne Manushulu*; **1967**: *Poolarangudu*; *Milan*; *Sudigundalu*; **1968**: *Man Ka Meet*; **1969**: *Doli*; **1970**: *Darpan*; *Mastana*; ***Maro Prapancham***; **1971**: *Rakhwala*; **1972**: *Jeet*; *Vichitra Bandham*; **1973**: *Mayadari Malligadu*; *Insaaf*; *Jwar Bhata*; **1974**: *Bangaru Kalalu*; **1975**: *Gunavanthudu*; *Gajula Kishtayya*; *Sunehra Sansar*; **1976**: *Mahakavi Kshetrayya*.

SUBBURAMAN, C. R. (1921-52)

Telugu composer and singer born in Chintamani, Tirunel Dist., AP. Employed as harmonium accompanist and later composer at HMV, Madras, where he worked until 1945. Performed occasionally in film orchestras. First film as composer, uncredited, is ***Chenchulakshmi***, after **S. Rajeswara Rao** and R.N. Chinnaiah had already worked on the film. His contribution is a major departure from established norms in its use of Latin American rhythms in the title music and for a tribal dance sequence. His first full assignment is for ***Ratnamala*** at the Bharani Studios, becoming a top Telugu film composer with the success of ***Laila Majnu***. Regular composer for the Jupiter Studio. Established the Vinoda Studio (1950) in partnership with the writer **Samudrala Raghavacharya** and the director **Vedantam Raghavaiah**. The group made one of the most memorable musicals of the 50s,

Devadasu, shortly before Subburaman died. Music historian V.A.K. Ranga Rao describes his compositions with M.L. Vasanthakumari in Tamil and with **R. Balasaraswathi** in Telugu as the norm for the 1943-53 period when playback was coming into South Indian film. Also occasionally sang in films, e.g. in **N.S. Krishnan**'s *Manamagal/Pelli Koothuru* (1951).

FILMOGRAPHY: **1943**: ***Chenchulakshmi***; **1947**: ***Ratnamala***; **1948**: *Abhimanyu*; *Mohini*; **1949**: ***Laila Majnu***; *Kanniyin Kathali*; *Pavalakkodi*; *Ratnakumar*; ***Velaikkari***; **1950**: *Parijatham*; ***Swapna Sundari***; *Vijayakumari*; **1951**: *Roopavati*; ***Marmayogi/Ek Tha Raja***; *Manamagal/Pelli Koothuru*; **1952**: *Dharmadevata*; *Shanti*; ***Prema***; ***Daasi***; **1953**: ***Ammalakulu/Marumagal***; ***Chandirani***; ***Devadasu***.

SUBRAMANYAM, KRISHNASWAMY (1904-71)

Tamil director, scenarist and producer; key figure in the establishment of a Madras-based Tamil film industry. Born in Papanasam, TN. Started film career as scenarist and producer at **R. Padmanabhan**'s Associated Films, working e.g. on **Raja Sandow**'s silent film *Peyum Pennum/The Devil and the Damsel* (1930). Then started Meenakshi Cinetone with Alagappa Chettiar, directing his first film, *Pavalakkodi*, the film début of the legendary stage star **M.K. Thyagaraja Bhagavathar**. Early work derived mainly from Tamil stage conventions. He made a remarkable shift with the politically emphatic ***Balayogini***, attacking the caste system. His best-known work, displaying a stridently nationalistic reformism, is contemporaneous with **V. Shantaram**'s and **B.N. Reddi**'s melodramas and culminates in ***Thyagabhoomi***. Other classics in the genre are ***Seva Sadan***, advocating a better deal for women, the Saint film *Bhakta Cheta*, critiquing Untouchability, and the war-effort film *Manasamrakshanam*. Established Madras United Artists (1935) with S.D. Subbulakshmi, but shot his films (*Naveena Sadarame*, *Balayogini*, *Mr Ammanji*) at **East India Films** in Calcutta. Expanded his company into the Motion Picture Producers Combines Studio, which later became **Gemini** when **S.S. Vasan** bought it. Made some Kannada mythologicals 1942-3 (*Bhakta Prahlada*, *Krishna Sudama*) and 1955-6 (*Stree Ratna* and *Kacha Devayani*). Some accounts suggest he supervised the direction of ***Andaman Kaithi*** (1952). Participated in the setting up of the South Indian Film Chamber of Commerce, the South Indian Artists Association and the Film Producers Guild of South India. Produced documentaries for **Information Films of India**, and was an adviser on Indian affairs for UNESCO's International Film and Television Committee in the 50s. Ironically, the credit due to Subramanyam for establishing the political link between cinematic and institutional reformism was later claimed by the commercially populist Vasan at Gemini and by the political populism of the **DMK Film** which redirected the reformist conventions into their own very different programmes. His son, Subramanyam Krishnaswamy, wrote, with Eric Barnouw, the classic book, *Indian Film* (1963, updated 1980). May have directed a Sinhalese film, *Kapatrika Rakshakayam*.

FILMOGRAPHY: **1934**: *Pavalakkodi*; **1935**: *Naveena Sadarame*; *Naveena Sarangadhara*; **1936**: ***Balayogini***; *Bhakta Kuchela*; *Usha Kalyanam*; **1937**: *Kausalya Parinayam*; *Mr Ammanji*; **1938**: ***Seva Sadan***; **1939**: ***Thyagabhoomi***; **194O**: *Mani Mekalai*; *Bhakta Cheta*; **1941**: ***Prahladan***; *Kacha Devayani*; **1942**: *Bhakta Prahlada*; *Ananthasayanam*; **1943**: *Krishna Sudama*; **1944**: *Manasamrakshanam*; *Bhartrahari*; **1946**: *Vikatakavi*; **1947**: *Vichitra Vanitha*; **1948**: *Gokula Dasi*; **1949**: *Geetha Gandhi*; **1955**: *Stree Ratna*; **1956**: *Kacha Devayani*; **1959**: *Pandithevan*.

SUBRAMANYAM, P. (1910-78)

Malayalam director and producer born in Nagercoil, TN. Owner of Merryland Studio (Est: 1951), the second studio in Kerala after **Kunchako**'s Udaya and a major influence in the establishment of Kerala's Malayalam film industry. Started as exhibitor with the first permanent sound cinema in Kerala, the New Theatres in Trivandrum. A large part of his own films, produced with the studio-affiliated Neela Pics, were mid-budget melodramas often based on **Kanam** and **Mutatthu Varkey**'s stories. Made ***Randidangazhi***, a rare script by Malayalam novelist Thakazhy Shivashankar Pillai. His mythologicals had bigger budgets and often dealt with religious cults surrounding the temples of Guruvayoor and Sabarimalai. Some of them featured Tamil star **Gemini Ganesh** (e.g. *Kumara Sambhavam*).

FILMOGRAPHY: **1956**: *Manthravadi*; **1957**: ***Padatha Paingili***; *Jailpully*; **1958**: *Mariakutty*; ***Randidangazhi***; **1959**: *Yanai Valartha Vanampadi*; **1960**: *Petraval Kanda Peru Vazhvu*; *Poothali*; **1961**: *Christmas Rathri*; ***Bhakta Kuchela***; *Yar Manamagam*; **1962**: *Shri Rama Pattabhishekham*; *Sneha Deepam*; **1963**: *Snapaka Yohannan*; *Kaleyum Kaminiyum*; **1964**: *Atom Bomb*; *Althara*; **1965**: *Kaliyodam*; *Pattu Thoovala*; **1966**: *Puthri*; *Kattumallika/Kattu Malligai*; *Priyatama*; **1968**: *Kadal*; *Hotel Highrange*; ***Adhyapika***; **1969**: *Urangatha Sundari*; *Kumara Sambhavam*; **1970**: *Swapnangal*; **1971**: *Kochaniyathi*; *Yanai Valartha Vanampadi Magan*; *Adavi Veerulu*; *Dabukku Thha Dongala Muttha*; **1972**: *Professor*; *Shri Guruvayoorappan*; **1973**: *Hum Jungli Hain*; *Malai Nattu Mangai*; *Kaadu* (Mal); *Swargaputhri*; **1974**: *Vandikkari*; *Devi Kanyakumari*; **1975**: *Swami Ayyappan*; **1976**: *Amba Ambika Ambalika*; *Hridayam Oru Kshetram*; **1977**: *Shri Murugan*; *Vidarunna Mottugal*; *Khaidi Kalidas*; *Manishilo Manishi*; *Rowdy Rajamma*; **1979**: *Kanchika Cheerani Katha*; *Hridayathinte Nirangal*.

SUHASINI

South Indian actress born in Parmakudi, TN. Daughter of actor Charuhasan and niece of the Tamil star **Kamalahasan**. Known for performances in Malayalam, Telugu and Kannada films. Trained as a cinematographer at the Madras Film Institute. Assistant to **J. Mahendran**, who introduced her as an actress (*Nenjathai Killathey*). Often cast in feminist roles (e.g. ***Swati***, *Lawyer Suhasini*) developing a mature performance style best used in her Malayalam films (e.g. **K.G. George**'s ***Adaminte Variyellu***, **Padmarajan**'s ***Koodevide?***). Directed the tv series *Penn*. Married to Tamil director **Mani Rathnam**.

FILMOGRAPHY: **1980**: *Nenjathai Killathey*; **1981**: *Palaivana Solai*; *Kudumbam Oru*

Prathap and Suhasini in *Nenjathai Killathey* (1980)

Kadambam; *Kotha Jeevithulu*; **1982**: *Kalyana Kalam*; *Lottery Ticket*; *Manchu Pallaki*; *Marumagaley Varuga*; *Nandri Meendum Varuga*; *Thottalsudum*; *Gopurangal Saivathillai*; *Azhagiya Kanney*; **1983**: *Benki Alli Aralida Hoovu*; ***Koodevide?***; *Maa Intiki Randi*; *Maha Maharaju*; *Mukku Pudaka*; ***Oru Indhiya Kanavu***; *Thayi Veedu*; *Uruvavugal Maralam*; *Veetile Raman Veliyele Krishnan*; *Shubha Muhurtam* (Tam); ***Adaminte Variyellu***; *Pudhiya Sangamam*; *Muddula Mogudu*; **1984**: *Illalu Priyuralu*; *Arorumariyathe*; *Adhiko Alladiko*; *Aksharangal*; *Aparadhi*; *Bandhana*; *Challenge*; *Gudigantalu Mrogayi*; *Mangammagari Manavudu*; *Nirdoshi*; *Santhanam*; ***Swati***; *Thathamme Poocha Poocha*; *Unni Vanna Divasam*; *Bava Maradallu*; *Intiguttu*; *Justice Chakravarthy*; *Ente Upasana*; **1985**: *Bullet*; ***Sindhu Bhairavi***; *Kirathakudu*; *Kongumudi*; *Mangalya Bandham*; *Jackie*; *Shiksha*; *Mugguru Mithrulu*; *Muddula Manavaralu*; *Brahma Mudi*; *Dampatyam*; *Maharaju*; *Sagar* (Te); *Katha Ithuvare*; *Mazhakkala Megham*; **1986**: *Patnam Pilla Palletoori*; *Mr Bharat*; *Karpura Deepam*; *Shrivenella*; **1987**: *Lawyer Suhasini*; *Aradhana*; *Thene Manushulu*; *Punya Dampathulu*; *Presidentgari Abbayi*; *Brahma Nayudu*; *Sardar Krishnama Nayudu*; *Gauthami*; *Manivathoorile Ayiram Sivarathrikal*; *Ezhuthapurangal*; *Samsaram Oka Chadarangam*; *Manadhil Urudhi Vendhum*; *Manchi Donga*; **1988**: *Chuttalabbai*; *Chattamtho Chadarangam*; *En Bommu Kutti Ammavukku*; *Bharya Bartulu*; *Marana Mridangam*; *Suprabhata*; *Dharmathin Thalaivan*; *Ramudu Bheemudu*; *Oru Sayahnathinte Swapnam*; *Oohakachavadam*; **1989**: *En Purushanthan Enakkum Mattumthan*; *Bala Gopaludu*; *Mamatala Kovela*; **1990**: ***Muthina Hara***; **1993**: *Radhasarathi*.

SUKHDEV SINGH SANDHU (1933-79)

India's leading Griersonian documentarist. Born in Dehra Dun; son of a Sikh farmer from Ludhiana. Educated in Bombay. Assistant to the German émigré cineaste **Paul Zils** (1955). Directorial début with film on handmade paper industry produced by Zils. When Zils left India, set up own company, United Film Arts (1958). First major work: ***And Miles To Go ...*** (though censors imposed a hectoring soundtrack). Worked mostly for **Films Division** where he made several industrial and instructional films. Best-known film, ***India 67*** (released as *An Indian Day*; later shortened and released as *India Today*), used documentary montage technique and rhythmic association of images. Also mixed documentary with enacted footage, casting himself (e.g. *No Sad Tomorrow*) and his family (*After the Eclipse*). Intense sympathiser with the Mukti Bahini's Bangladeshi independence struggle. Extended the Griersonian aesthetic with a combination of highly stylised yet bluntly propagandistic movies (e.g. ***Nine Months To Freedom***). Made one feature, starring **Shashi Kapoor** and **Sharmila Tagore**: *My Love*, shot in Kenya. Major propagandist for Indira Gandhi's Emergency rule. Suffered from alcoholism and died of a heart attack in Delhi. His last film, *Sahira*, was finished by **S.S. Gulzar**. Published work includes talks on documentary practice as well as poems in English and in Urdu. Acted in **Abbas**'s ***Saat Hindustani*** (1969), in a Punjabi feature by **Dara Singh** and in Merchant-Ivory's *Bombay Talkie* (1970). Left an unfinished film, *Four Directors*, with footage of Kurosawa, Antonioni, Kazan and **S. Ray** at the Delhi Film Festival (1977). A friend and colleague, Jag Mohan, published a commemorative monograph on Sukhdev (1984).

FILMOGRAPHY: 1958: *Wazir the Kazhgi*; **1960**: *The Saint and the Peasant*; **1961**: *The Evolution and Races of Man*; **1962**: *Man the Creator*; *Castor*; **1964**: *After the Eclipse*; *Frontiers of Freedom*; **1965**: ***And Miles To Go...***; *Kal Udaas Na Hogi/No Sad Tomorrow*; **1967**: ***India 67***; *Homage to Lal Bahadur Shastri*; **1968**: *Thoughts in a Museum*; **1970**: *Tomorrow may be Too Late*; *Kathak*; *My Love*; **1971**: *A Village Smiles*; *Khilonewala*; **1972**: ***Nine Months to Freedom: The Story of Bangladesh***; **1973**: *Co-operation is Success*; *You Must Be Your Own Policemen*; *Science-4*; **1974**: ***Behind the Breadline***; *Violence: What Price? Who Pays?* No. 4; *Wild Life Sanctuaries of India*; *Voice of the People*; *A Few More Questions*; **1975**: *For a Happier Tomorrow*; *The Food Front*; *Maa Ki Pukar*; **1976**: ***Thunder of Freedom***; **1977**: *After the Silence*; *New World of Power*; **1978**: *Maha Kumbh*; **1980**: *Sahira*.

SULOCHANA (1907-83)

Born in Pune as Ruby Myers, one of the many Eurasian actresses to become silent stars (cf **Seeta Devi**, **Patience Cooper** and Ermeline). A former telephone operator (1925), she became a star under **Bhavnani**'s direction at **Kohinoor**. Début in films as a stunt actress. Reputedly the highest-paid star in the film industry at **Imperial**. She was billed as the Queen of Romance or the Jungle Queen in DeMille-type costume epics, often co-starring with **D. Bilimoria** under her favourite director, **R.S. Choudhury**. A fair portion of Imperial's sound films were remakes of their silent Sulochana hits. e.g. *Anarkali* (1928 and 1935), *Indira BA* (1929, remade as ***Indira MA*** in 1934), ***Wildcat of Bombay*** (1927, remade as ***Bambai Ki Billi*** in 1936), *Khwab-e-Hasti/Magic Flute* (1929 and 1934) and ***Madhuri*** (1928 and 1932). In *Wildcat of Bombay*, she played eight roles including a gardener, a policeman, a Hyderabadi gentleman, a street urchin, a banana seller and a European blonde. Also known for costumed period movies, e.g. *Alibaba* and her favourite role of Anarkali. **Jaswantlal** pays tribute to her association with the Anarkali figure in his 1953 version of the legend. Started her own Rubi Pics in the mid-30s, continuing production after she retired as actress. From the 60s, she had to accept cameo roles in Hindi films. Ismail Merchant's short, *Mahatma and the Mad Boy* (1974), contains a passing tribute to her.

FILMOGRAPHY: 1925: *Veer Bala*; ***Cinema Queen***; **1926**: ***The Telephone Girl***; *Pagal Premi*; *Mumtaz Mahal*; *Ra Kawat*; *Samrat Shiladitya*; *Typist Girl*; *Bhamto Bhoot*; **1927**: *Alibaba and the Forty Thieves*; *Naseeb Ni Lili*; ***Balidan***; *Gutter Nu Gulab*; *The Mission Girl*; *Daya Ni Devi*; ***Gamdani Gori***; ***Wildcat of Bombay***; **1928**: *Anarkali*; *Madhuri*; *Rajrang*; *Pita Ke Parmeshwar*; **1929**: *Heer Ranjha*; *Indira BA*; *Mewad Nu Moti*; *Khwab-e-Hasti*; *Punjab Mail*; *Talwar Ka Dhani*; **1930**: *Sood*; *Hamarun Hindustan*; *Raat Ki Baat*; **1931**: *Rani Rupmati*; *Noor-e-Alam*; *Pujari*; ***Khuda Ki Shaan*** (all St); **1932**: ***Madhuri***; **1933**: *Daku Ki Ladki*; *Saubhagya Sundari*; *Sulochana*; **1934**: ***Gul Sanobar***; ***Indira MA***; *Khwab-e-Hasti*; ***Piya Pyare***; *Devaki*; **1935**: *Anarkali*; ***Do Ghadi Ki Mauj***; *Pujarini*; **1936**: ***Bambai Ki Billi***; *Jungle Queen*; *Shaan-e-Hind*; **1937**: *Jagat Kesari*; *New Searchlight*; *Wah Ri Duniya*; **1939**: *Prem Ki Jyot*; **1942**: *Aankh Micholi*; **1946**: *Chamakti Bijli*; **1947**: *Jugnu*; **1949**: *Shayar*; **1953**: ***Anarkali***; **1957**: ***Lal Batti***; **1959**: ***Anari***; **1960**: ***Kadu Makrani***; **1962**: *Son of India*; **1963**: *Soorat Aur Seerat*; *Akeli Mat Jaiyo*; **1964**: ***Haqeeqat***; **1973**: *Honeymoon*; **1975**: ***Julie***; **1977**: *Khatta Meetha*; **1978**: *Akhiyon Ke Jharokhon Se*.

SULTANPURI, MAJROOH (b. 1924)

Prolific Hindi-Urdu songwriter originally called Asrar Hussain Khan; born in Sultanpur, UP, the son of a police constable. Studied Persian at Aligarh; moved to Bombay to practise his poetry. His early and best-known independent poetry, inspired by Jigar Muradabadi, is in the ghazal form, and was criticised by writers associated with the **PWA** for its feudal decadence. Film début with **Kardar**'s ***Shahjehan*** (1946), which included **Saigal**'s classic song *Jab dil hi toot gaya*. Early hits: e.g. ***Andaz*** (1949) and songs for **Shammi Kapoor** (*Miss Coca Cola*, 1955; ***Tumsa Nahin Dekha***, 1957). Worked at **Filmistan** for many **Dev Anand** films (***Paying Guest***, 1957; ***Kala Pani***, 1958; ***Bambai Ka Babu***, 1960) and with **Guru Dutt** (***Aar Paar***, 1954; ***Mr and Mrs '55***, 1955). Wrote songs for ***CID*** (1956). His songs are often set to music by **O.P. Nayyar** or **S.D. Burman**. Also worked with **Bimal Roy** (***Sujata***, 1959). Attempted pop lyrics like *Aja aja* in ***Teesri Manzil*** (1966), in ***Yaadon Ki Baraat*** (1973) and in ***Qayamat Se Qayamat Tak*** (1988).

SUNDARAM, TIRUCHENGODU RAMALINGA (1907-63)

Tamil director and producer born in Tiruchengode, TN. Studied textile engineering at Leeds University. Worked at Angel Films (1933), later taking it over to start the **Modern Theatres** Studio (1937) in Salem. Apparently produced 98 films, including work by **Duncan**, **C.V. Raman**, M.L. Tandon, **K. Ramnoth** and **T.R. Raghunath**. Approached film-making in South India in a businesslike manner, importing foreign technicians for his début, *Sati Ahalya*, made in two versions, one for Modern Theatres and one for Chandra Bharathi Cinetone. Produced the first Malayalam sound film, ***Balan*** (1938) as well as the first colour films in Tamil (***Alibabavum Narpathu Thirudargalum***) and in Malayalam (***Kandam Bacha Coat***). Worked in several genres, most notably the swashbuckling adventure movies of **P.U. Chinappa** (e.g. *Uthama Puthran*, adapting Dumas's *The Man in the Iron Mask*) that later developed into the **MGR** filmic and political signature: e.g. the **Karunanidhi** script ***Manthiri Kumari***, and the Alibaba film *Alibabavum Narpathu Thirudargalum*. Also adapted Tamil epics (*Manonmani*, *Valyapathi*) and made the war movie ***Burma Rani***.

FILMOGRAPHY: 1937: *Sati Ahalya*; *Padma Jyothi*; **1938**: *Thayumanavar*; **1939**: *Manikavasagar*; **1940**: *Harihara Maya*;

Rajayogam; *Uthama Puthran*; *Vikrama Urvashi*; **1942**: *Manonmani*; *Sati Sukanya*; **1943**: *Diwan Bahadur*; **1944**: ***Burma Rani***; *Kalikala Minor*; *Palli Natakam*; *Soora Puli*; *Chow Chow*; **1945**: *Subhadra*; **1946**: *Sulochana*; **1947**: *1000 Thalaivangi Apoorva Chintamani*; **1948**: *Adinathan Kanavu*; *Ahimsa Yuddham* (Doc); **1949**: *Mayavathi*; **1950**: *Digambara Swamiyar*; ***Manthiri Kumari***; *Maya Rambha/Maya Rambai*; **1951**: *Sarvadhikari*; **1952**: *Valayapathi*; *Savithri Poru*; **1953**: *Mangala Gauri*; *Thirumbi Paar*; **1955**: ***Alibabavum Narpathu Thirudargalum***; **1956**: *Rani Rangamma*; **1959**: *Thalai Koduthan Thambi*; **1960**: *Baghdad Thirudan/Baghdad*; **1961**: ***Kandam Bacha Coat***.

Sundarrajan, S. *see* **Soundararajan, S.**

SURABHI THEATRES

Popular 19th C. theatre tradition in AP with a fundamental impact on early Telugu cinema, passing on its definition of the mythological and supplying a large number of its actor-singers. The name came from the large family that pioneered this industry: a family of Maharashtrian warriors which fought on the side of the British in the 1857 mutiny and later settled in the Surabhi village in Rayalseema. Initially, narrative forms were borrowed from the Andhra leather puppet tradition as used by the brothers Vanarasa Ramayya, Venkoji and Krishnajirao in the mid-19th C. It involved complex conventions: colours to show different rasas, the gods always entering from the right and the demons from the left (*Thodu Bommalatu*: a folk tradition performed with leather puppets). The most famous theatrical form was due to Venkoji's adopted son, Vanarasa Govindarao, who staged the mythological *Keechaka Vadha*, one of the most frequently staged and filmed episodes from the *Mahabharata*. He subsequently established the Sarada Vinodini Nataka Sabha (1895) and became the most successful touring theatre in the state, virtually inventing a theatrical style drawn partly from the folk Harikatha mode and partly from the leather puppets (e.g. in the chalk, yellow, red ochre and lampblack used for make-up). The plays and lyrics were either written by the family itself or by well-known Harikatha performers commissioned to adapt *Ramayana* or *Mahabharata* scenes. By 1910 the group split into three. Each was assigned a territory to prevent competition. Over the next 50 years, thirty companies grew up, all claiming the same ancestry. The most famous ones were the Govindaraya Surabhi Natya Mandali, the Sarada Vijaya Nataka Mandali and the Venkateswara Natya Mandali. **H.M. Reddy**'s first two sound films, ***Kalidas*** (1931) and ***Bhakta Prahlada*** (1931), the first talkies in Tamil and Telugu respectively, used the Surabhi repertoire and featured the theatre family's most famous film star, Surabhi Kamala aka **Kamalabai**.

SURAIYA JAMAL SHEIKH (b. 1929)

Major singing star of 50s Hindi-Urdu film born in Lahore. Débuted as child actress in 1941 (*Taj Mahal*). Later did playback singing for Mehtab (*Sharada*, 1942). Effectively launched as a singing and dancing star in the **Bombay Talkies** film *Hamari Baat*. Acted with **Saigal** in some of his last Hindi films: *Omar Khayyam*, ***Tadbir*** and *Parwana*. With **Nurjehan** (with whom she acted in ***Anmol Ghadi***) and Khurshid (*Mumtaz Mahal*, 1944), she introduced an acting style strongly nostalgic for the *adakari* (manners) of North Indian Muslim feudalism (e.g. her Urdu historicals like ***Mirza Ghalib*** and melodramas like **K. Asif**'s ***Phool***). That style was often used, most notably by **Mehboob** in his classic *Anmol Ghadi* and **Kardar** in ***Dastaan***, to endow modernity with an aura of tradition. It served this function even in her otherwise radically different **Dev Anand** films (***Afsar***, *Shayar*, *Jeet*). Like **Shanta Apte**, the other major singing star of the time, her performance expertly integrated gesture, music and speech.

FILMOGRAPHY: **1941**: *Taj Mahal*; **1942**: ***Station Master***; *Tamanna*; **1943**: *Ishara*; *Hamari Baat*; **1944**: ***Phool***; **1945**: *Main Kya Karun*; ***Tadbir***; *Yateem*; ***Samrat Chandragupta***; **1946**: *Chehra*; *Eighteen Fifty-Seven*; *Hasrat*; *Jag Biti*; *Omar Khayyam*; *Urvashi*; ***Anmol Ghadi***; **1947**: *Dak Bangla*; *Dard*; *Do Dil*; *Do Naina*; *Natak*; *Parwana*; **1948**: *Aaj Ki Raat*; *Gajre*; *Kajal*; *Pyar Ki Jeet*; *Rang Mahal*; *Shakti*; *Vidya*; **1949**: *Amar Kahani*; *Badi Bahen*; *Balam*; *Char Din*; *Dillagi*; *Duniya*; *Jeet*; *Lekh*; *Naach*; *Shayar*; *Singaar*; **1950**: ***Afsar***; ***Dastaan***; *Kamal Ke Phool*; *Khiladi*; *Nili*; *Shaan*; **1951**: *Do Sitare*; *Rajput*; *Sanam*; *Shokhiyan*; **1952**: *Diwana*; *Goonj*; *Khoobsurat*; *Lal Kunwar*; *Moti Mahal*; *Resham*; **1953**: *Mashuqa*; **1954**: *Bilwamangal*; ***Mirza Ghalib***; *Shama Parwana*; ***Waris***; **1955**: *Inaam*; *Kanchan*; **1956**: *Mr Lambu*; **1958**: *Malik*; *Miss 1958*; *Trolley Driver*; **1961**: *Shama*; **1963**: ***Rustom Sohrab***.

SURYAKANT (b. 1925)

Marathi actor born in Kolhapur. With elder brother Chandrakant, was one of the first major stars of the Marathi cinema. Début aged 12 in D.K. Kale's mythological *Dhruva* made in Kolhapur, playing the child god Vishnu. **Pendharkar** fashioned him as the archetypal Maratha Emperor Shivaji in *Bahirji Naik*, later in *Pavankhind* and then towards the end of his career in *Ganimi Kava*. The classic Shivaji role in Marathi film, ***Chhatrapati Shivaji*** (1952), was, however, played by his brother. Suryakant repeated the role also in *Jai Bhawani* and several times on the stage (*Agryahun Sutka*, *Bebandshahi*). Also known for films in the ruralist 'gramin chitrapat' genre with **Mane** (e.g. the genre's classic ***Sangtye Aika***) and **Dinkar D. Patil** (e.g. *Malhari Martand*); also in **Dharmadhikari**'s melodramas (e.g. *Bala Jo Jo Re*, *Akher Jamla*, *Pativrata*). Wrote his autobiography (1986).

FILMOGRAPHY (* also d): **1938**: *Dhruva*; **1943**: *Bahirji Naik*; **1946**: *Sasurvas*; **1947**: *Jai Bhawani*; **1949**: ***Meeth Bhakar***; *Shilanganache Sone*; **1950**: *Ketakichya Banaat*; **1951**: *Bala Jo Jo Re*; *Swarajyacha Shiledar*; **1952**: *Akher Jamla*; *Stree Janma Hi Tujhi Kahani*; **1953**: *Aukshavanta Ho Bala*; *Muka Lekru*; *Majhi Zameen*; **1954**: *Kanchanganga*; *Maharani Yesubai*; *Purshachi Jaat*; *Sasar Maher*; *Shubhamangal*; **1955**: *Bal Mazha Navasacha*; *Bhaubeej*; *Kuladaivat*; *Punavechi Raat*; *Ratnaghar*; **1956**: *Kar Bhala*; *Jagavegali Goshta*; *Pavankhind*; *Gaath Padli Thaka Thaka*; *Ranpakhare*; **1957**: *Grihadevata*; *Pahila Prem*; *Preetisangam*; **1958**: *Sant Changdev*; **1959**: *Akashganga*; *Pativrata*; ***Sangtye Aika***; *Shikleli Baiko*; **1960**: *Antaricha Diva*; *Kanyadaan*; *Lagnala Jato Mi*; *Pancharati*; *Salami*; *Sakhya Savara Mala*; **1961**: *Bhav Tethe Dev*; *Kalanka Shobha*; *Mansala Pankh Astaat*; *Rangapanchami*; *Shola Jo Bhadke*; *Vaijayanti*; **1962**: *Baikocha Bhau*; *Bhintila Kan Astaat*; *Gariba Gharchi Lek*; *Gavachi Izzat*; **1963**: *Fakira*; *Mohityanchi Manjula*; *Subhadra Haran*; *Thoratanchi Kamala*; *Tu Sukhi Raha*; **1964**: *Sant Nivrutti-Dnyandev*; **1965**: *Malhari Martand*; ***Sadhi Manse***; **1966**: *Hi Naar Rupasundari*; *Patlachi Soon*; *Pavanakathcha Dhondi*; *Tochi Sadhu Olakhava*; **1967**: *Bara Varshe Saha Mahine Teen Divas*; *Pathcha Bhau*; *Sangu Kashi Mi*; **1968**: *Amhi Jato Amuchya Gava*; *Angai*; *Dhanya Te Santaji Dhanaji*; **1969**: *Murali Malhari Rayachi*; *Tila Lavite Mi Raktacha*; **1970**: *Ashi Rangali Ratra*; *Kortachi Pairi*; *Mala Tumchi Mhana*; *Varanecha Vagh*; **1971**: *Aai Ude Ga Ambabai*; *Asel Mazha Hari*; *Lakhat Ashi Dekhani*; **1972**: *Kaul De Re Khanderaya*; *Kunku Mazha Bhagyacha!*; *Soon Ladki Hya Gharchi*; **1973**: *Mi Tuzha Pati Nahi*; **1974**: *Soon Majhi Savitri*; **1975**: *Jyotibacha Navas*; **1978**: *Irsha**; *Netaji Palkar*; **1979**: *Aitya Bilavar Nagoba*; *Ashta Vinayak*; **1980**: *Savat*; **1981**: *Baine Kela Sarpanch Khula*; *Ganimi Kava*; *Manacha Kunku*; *Tamasgeer*; **1982**: *Daivat*; *Don Baika Phajiti Aika*; *Rakhandar*; **1983**: *Sasu Varchad Javai*; **1989**: *Auntie Na Vajavili Ghanti*.

SURYAKUMARI, TANTAGURI (b. 1925)

Major Telugu and Tamil actress and singer born in Vijaywada, AP. Studied at Cambridge University; trained in dance and music. Elected Miss India. First major female singing star in Telugu with hits in *Vipranarayana* and ***Jayapradha***. Played the hero's sister in **B.N. Reddi**'s reformist ***Devatha***. Established herself in the bigger, more influential Tamil industry with e.g. *Katakam* and *Samsara Nauka*. Hindi début in *Watan*; her big Hindi hit is ***Udan Khatola*** (although she didn't sing in it). Sang in *Nam Naadu*, **Shantaram**'s Telugu version of *Apna Desh* (1949). Performed in nationalist political rallies. Recorded songs on the Odeon label, including nationalist numbers, devotionals and romantic *bhavageetham* with composers like B. Rajnikanta Rao and Manchala Jagannatha Rao, often singing the poetry of Basavaraja Apparao and **D. Krishna Sastry**.

FILMOGRAPHY: **1937**: *Vipranarayana*; **1939**: ***Jayapradha***; ***Raitu Bidda***; **1941**: *Chandrahasa*; ***Devatha***; **1942**: *Dinabandhu*; **1943**: ***Bhagya Lakshmi***; ***Krishna Prema***; **1947**: *Katakam*; **1948**: *Geetanjali*; *Samsara Nauka*; **1949**: *Bharati*; **1954**: *Watan*; **1955**: ***Udan Khatola***; **1964**: *Ramadasu*.

SWADESHI

Nationalist programme for the boycott of all foreign manufactures and, by extension, a spur to self-reliance and 'Indianness' in education, the arts, technology, etc. Originated in the 1895 agitations against the British government's discriminatory cotton tariffs. Formally adopted as a political programme by Indian National Congress (1905). By 1912, following the enormous pressure from a growing sector of Indian entrepreneurs to define Swadeshi as a simple transfer of control into Indian hands, questions of Indianness became controversial. Gandhi's emphasis on village crafts as urban forms of popular art was accompanied by positions on 'high' art by Bengal School theoreticians E.B. Havell (Havell, 1901) and Ananda Coomaraswamy (Coomaraswamy, 1911, 1918/1977), opposing, e.g., the **Company School**'s assimilation of imported technology with a call for a more fundamental restatement of the Indian tradition. This debate influenced perceptions of a 'borrowed' technology such as cinema and determined both the rhetoric and the formal choices of film-makers like **Phalke**, **Painter**, **Barua**, **K. Subramanyam** et al.

SWAMINATHAN, KOMAL (b. 1935)

Tamil director, playwright and scenarist, and noted Marxist intellectual born in Chettinad, TN. Associated in his youth with the theatre personality S.V. Sahsaranamam, whose group he joined (1957) apparently to learn playwriting. Later worked with director **K.S. Gopalakrishnan** while writing hit political plays like *Puthiya Pathai* (1960) and his best-known work, ***Thanneer Thanneer***, originally staged by his own theatre group, Stage Friends, and filmed by **K. Balachander** (1981). Wrote the melodrama about inheritance and legitimacy filmed by Devaraj-Mohan as *Paluti Valartha Kili* (1976). Turned to direction in 1983, making three films all released in one year before returning to his writing. His best-known film is ***Oru Indhiya Kanavu***, a political thriller in which **Suhasini** is a fearless crusader who comes up against corrupt and sadistic ministers. Now edits the journal *Subamangala*.

FILMOGRAPHY: **1983**: *Anal Katru*; ***Oru Indhiya Kanavu***; *Yuddha Kandam*.

TAGORE, RABINDRANATH (1861-1941)

Poet, playwright, essayist, painter and significant figure in 20th C. India's cultural history. Born in Calcutta into the numerous family of Debendranath Tagore, the leading Brahmo Samaj intellectual. Privately educated, Rabindranath started writing at an early age and first visited Europe in 1878. His creative output and institutional interventions largely set the terms for India's cultural modernity. His writings and political contributions are still highly topical and contentious. Some of the more actively discussed areas include his influence on cultural nationalism, the recasting of European neo-classicism in, e.g., his literary assimilation of Goethe and Heine and his influence on education, esp. through the arts university, Shantiniketan (Est: 1901) and its industrial-agrarian counterpart, Sriniketan. In addition, Tagore exerted a formidable influence through his poetry: a whole musical industry was generated by his Rabindra Sangeet, with over 2000 lyrics which he set to music and seminal experiments with orchestration. His dance ballets were assimilated into the commercial Calcutta Theatres repertories. In the 20s, the nascent Bengali cinema often borrowed from the music, literature and theatre industries, following Tagore's example of trying to elaborate an industrially valid synthesis of diverse cultural traditions. The Bengali cinema drew heavily on Tagore's stories and music (e.g. films by **Naresh Mitra**, **Modhu Bose**, **Satyajit Ray**, **Ajoy Kar**, **Tapan Sinha**, etc.). However, Tagore's personal involvement with cinema was more significant than conventional film histories allow. His one major, extensively quoted statement on cinema came in a letter to Murari Bhaduri (1929): 'The principal element of a motion picture is the "flux of image". The beauty and grandeur of this form in motion has to be developed in such a way that it becomes self-sufficient without the use of words. If some other language is needed to explain its own, it amounts to incompetence. If music can achieve profundity without the words of the cadence of a melody, then why should not this "motive form" be considered as a distinct aesthetic experience?' In addition, Arunkumar Roy (1986) noted that, in 1907, a dance ballet that he had directed was filmed in his presence. Ajit Sheth (1981) quoted **Nitin Bose** saying that, in 1917, Tagore had directly requested him to film a dance recital of his songs and 'showed a great deal of interest in the technique of filming'. His letters of 1920-3 contain references to cinema (apparently Douglas Fairbanks visited him at the time) including his responses to **Naresh Mitra**'s filming of his *Maanbhanjan* (1923). In 1925, sailing to Europe, he saw a film and refers in *Paschim Jatrir Diary* (1925), to its 'speed of motion', suggesting that it could be addictive to young people; later he described Western society as 'one huge cinema'. Closely involved in Modhu Bose's ***Giribala*** (1930), apparently writing the intertitles himself. Scripted parts of *Dahlia* (1930), adapting his short story of the same name. Later (1936) wrote a screenplay subtitled 'a play fit to be filmed' merging parts of *Dahlia* with a novel, *Rajorshi*. In Germany he wrote an English script for Ufa, *The Child* (1930), later adapting it into Bengali as *Shishu Tirth*. It was inspired by seeing a German passion play. Also in 1930, on a visit to the USSR, he asked to see *Bronenosets Potemkin* (1925). Later, in Germany, he met Eisenstein along with Stefan Zweig, Lion Feuchtwanger and Pirandello. In 1932, in a much touted production, **New Theatres** announced that he would direct a film for them, which he may have done with two stationary cameras: ***Natir Puja*** (1932). According to Roy, he was 'disappointed with the result'. Finally, he worked closely with **Pankaj Mullick** on the songs and the music of **Barua**'s ***Mukti*** (1937), the first film extensively featuring Rabindra Sangeet.

TAGORE, SHARMILA (b. 1944)

Bengali actress introduced in **Satyajit Ray**'s ***Apur Sansar*** as the wife of the adult Apu. Also cast by **Ray** in ***Devi***, ***Nayak***, ***Aranyer Din Ratri*** and ***Seemabaddha***. Worked for other Bengali film-makers like **Ajoy Kar** (*Barnali*, *Prabhater Rang*), **Tapan Sinha** (***Nirjan Saikate***), Partha Prathim Choudhury (***Jadu Bansha***), etc. Became a Hindi star in **Shakti Samanta**'s ***Kashmir Ki Kali*** opposite **Shammi Kapoor**, acquiring a reputation as a sex symbol. Caused a sensation in Samanta's *Sawan Ki Ghata*, posing in a bikini; consolidated her image playing a cabaret dancer in *An Evening in Paris*, once again with Shammi Kapoor. She changed her persona for ***Aradhana***, playing both **Rajesh Khanna**'s wife and his mother, and went on to form with him the most successful duo in 70s Hindi films: e.g. *Safar*, *Amar Prem*. Alternated between Khanna and **Shashi Kapoor** love stories like *Suhana Safar* and *Aa Gale Lag Jaa*; also did tragic romances for **Hrishikesh Mukherjee** (***Anupama***, ***Satyakam***), **Basu Bhattacharya** (*Avishkar*, *Grihapravesh*) and Samanta's Hindi-Bengali bilinguals with **Uttam Kumar** (***Amanush***, *Anand Ashram*). Her reputation was consolidated in **Gulzar**'s ***Mausam***, playing a prostitute. Also gave a notable performance in **Ramesh Sharma**'s ***New Delhi Times***.

FILMOGRAPHY: **1959**: ***Apur Sansar***; **1960**: ***Devi***; **1963**: ***Nirjan Saikate***; *Shesh Prahar*; *Chhaya Surya*; *Barnali*; *Shesh-Anka*; **1964**: *Kinu Goyalar Gali*; *Prabhater Rang*; ***Kashmir Ki Kali***; **1965**: ***Waqt***; *Dak Ghar*; **1966**: ***Anupama***; *Devar*; *Sawan Ki Ghata*; *Yeh Raat Phir Na Aayegi*; ***Nayak***; **1967**: *Aamne Samne*; *An Evening in Paris*; *Milan Ki Raat*; **1968**: *Dil Aur Mohabbat*; *Humsaya*; *Mere Humdum Mere Dost*; **1969**: ***Aranyer Din Ratri***; ***Aradhana***; *Pyaasi Shyam*; ***Satyakam***; *Talash*; *Yakeen*; **1970**: *Mere Humsafar*; *My Love*; *Safar*; *Suhana Safar*; **1971**: ***Seemabaddha***; *Amar Prem*; *Badnaam Farishte*; *Chhoti Bahu*; **1972**: *Dastaan*; *Malik*; *Yeh Gulistan Hamara*; **1973**: *Aa Gale Lag Jaa*; *Avishkar*; ***Daag***; *Raja Rani*; **1974**: ***Jadu Bansha***; *Charitraheen*; *Paap Aur Punya*; *Shaitan*; *Shandaar*; ***Amanush***; **1975**: *Khushboo*; *Anari*; *Chupke Chupke*; *Ek Mahal Ho Sapnon Ka*; *Faraar*; ***Mausam***; **1976**: *Ek Se Badhkar Ek*; *Tyaag*; *Do Shatru*; **1977**: *Anand Ashram*; **1978**: *Besharam*; **1979**: *Chuvanna Chirakukal*; *Dooriyan*; *Mother*; **1980**: *Grihapravesh*; **1981**: ***Naseeb***; *Kalankini Kankabati*; **1982**: *Desh Premi*; *Namkeen*; *Divorce*; **1983**: *Protidan*; *Tanaya*; *Doosri Dulhan*; **1984**: *Jawani*; *Sunny*; *Swati*; **1985**: *Bandhan Anjana*; *Ek Se Bhale Do*; *Uttarayan*; ***New Delhi Times***; *Ricky*; **1986**: *Door Desh*; *Mera Dharam*; **1987**: *Anurodh*; *Zindagi* (TV); *Maa Beti*; *Saat Saal Baad*; **1988**: *Hum To Chale Pardes*; **1989**: *Doorie*; **1991**: *Dastoor*; *Mississippi Masala*; **1993**: *Aashiq Awara*.

TARAFDAR, RAJEN (1917-87)

Bengali director born in Rajsahi (now Bangladesh). Arts degree in Calcutta (1940). Trained as commercial designer and worked for J. Walter Thompson (1944-58). Active in amateur theatre. Introduced to cinema via Renoir's presence in India to shoot *The River* (1951), the Calcutta Film Society and exposure to Italian neo-realism (***Ganga*** can be seen as a variant on *La terra trema*, 1947). Best-known films try to integrate fiction and ethnographic realism into quasi-documentary regime: *Ganga* and *Nagpash* were shot in the Sundarbans region in a fishing community. Claimed influence of vérité film-makers Jacques Rozier, Fran†ôis Reichenbach and Chris Marker. Innovative use of crane shots, long takes and diffused lighting, which, **Chidananda Das Gupta** suggests, contradicts the otherwise realist intention by evoking romanticised notions of a Sonar Bangla (Golden Bengal). Also scripted his own *Akash Chhoan* and ***Palanka*** in addition to e.g. ***Sansar Simantey*** (1975) and ***Ganadevata*** (1978). Acted in **Mrinal Sen**'s ***Akaler Sandhaney*** (1980) and in **S. Benegal**'s ***Aarohan*** **(1981)**.

FILMOGRAPHY: 1957: *Antariksha*; **1960**: ***Ganga***; **1962**: *Agnisikha*; **1964**: *Jiban Kahini*; **1967**: *Akash Chhoan*; **1975**: ***Palanka***; **1981**: *Nagpash.*

TEMBE, GOVINDRAO (1881-1955)

Musician, actor, playwright, theatrical personality and compulsive theorist. Composed the music for **Painter**'s films and some early **Prabhat** movies. Born in Kolhapur when it was at the forefront of a major cultural renaissance: the Khayal was adapted to concerts and recording techniques; the music schools and **Sangeet Natak** were recasting the classical-popular musical idiom. Tembe mentions the enormous impact on him of singers like Ustad Alladiya Khan of the Jaipur gharana (then living under the patronage of the Shahu Maharaj), Bhaskarbua Bakhle (later with **Bal Gandharva**) and Ramakrishnabua Vaze, crucial figures in the evolution of the Sangeet Natak. Became the chief music director of Bal Gandharva's group (1913-15), then set up his own stage group the Shivraj Natak Mandali, employing the Painters for his **stage backdrops**. Joined Prabhat and was responsible for some of the first hit singles of Marathi film (e.g. *Bala ka jhop yeyina* in ***Ayodhyecha Raja***). However, in the words of his successor, **Bhole** (1964): 'He was never to know the difference between stage and film music.' Wrote extensively about aesthetic problems, e.g. on attempts to create post-Sangeet Natak classical Khayal in Marathi; on problems of notating Indian music; on the harmonium, his favourite instrument (banned by AIR for being antithetical to the system of classical music). He also argued that cinema should be understood as an experience between reading and visualising what is read. Publications include *Jeevan Vihar* (1948) and *Mazha Sangeet Vyasanga* (1939).

FILMOGRAPHY (* act only/** also act): **1932**: ***Ayodhyecha Raja/Ayodhya Ka Raja*****; ***Jalti Nishani/Agnikankan***; ***Maya Machhindra*****; **1933**: *Sairandhri*; *Sati Mahananda*; **1934**: *Manjari***; *Seeta**; **1935**: *Raj Mukut*** (also d); ***Usha*****; **1936**: *Savkari Pash*; *Aseer-e-Hawas*; *Vish Vaman*; **1937**: ***Pratibha***; **1938**: *Savangadi/Sathi*; *Vasanti*; *Nandakumar** (M/H); **1941**: *Nirdosh*; **1943**: *Bahirji Naik.*

TENDULKAR, VIJAY (b. 1925)

Scenarist and Marathi playwright born in Kolhapur. Regarded with **Karnad**, Mohan Rakesh and Badal Sircar as a new generation of literary and theatrical realists. One of the founders of the vanguard theatre group Rangayan, launched with **Vijaya Mehta**'s performance of his play *Bali* (1960). 70s stage work (e.g. *Sakharam Binder*, 1971, causing a notorious censorship debacle; ***Ghashiram Kotwal***, 1972, the film version of which in 1976 he scripted but disowned) offered a psychological exploration of physical violence with an overtly political dimension, a concern later reflected in his scripts for **Benegal** (***Nishant***, 1975; ***Manthan***, 1976), **Nihalani** (***Aakrosh***, 1980; ***Ardh Satya***, 1983) and **Jabbar Patel** (***Saamna***, 1975; ***Sinhasan***, 1979; ***Umbartha/Subah***, 1981). Stories featured political vendettas often in rural situations, with fights between feudal rulers and oppressed castes shading into statements about the inevitability of the oppressed themselves turning into oppressors. Co-scripted **Saeed Mirza**'s début, ***Arvind Desai Ki Ajeeb Dastaan*** (1978).

THAKUR, RAJA (1923-75)

Marathi director born in Phonda, Goa, as Rajaram Dattatray Thakur. Assistant to **Vinayak** (later continuing Vinayak's series of **Malvankar**-Jog comedies with *Gharcha Jhala Thoda*) and to **Raja Paranjpe**. With **Rajdutt**, he is regarded as part of the 60s middle-class orthodoxy in Maharashtra prior to the earthier comedies of, e.g., **Dada Kondke**. Turned producer with his own Nava Chitra company. Made one film in English, *Birbal My Brother*, and his *Mumbaicha Javai* was adapted in Bengali by **Basu Chatterjee** as *Piya Ka Ghar* (1971).

FILMOGRAPHY: **1953**: *Bolavita Dhani*; **1954**: *Reshamchya Gaathi*; **1955**: *Mi Tulas Tujhya Angani*; **1956**: *Mazhe Ghar Majhi Manse*; **1957**: *Gharcha Jhala Thoda*; *Uthavala Narad*; **1958**: *Gaja Gauri*; **1959**: *Rajmanya Rajashri*; **1961**: *Putra Vhava Aisa*; **1962**: *Rangalya Ratri Asha*; **1963**: *Pahure Kiti Vaat!*; **1965**: *Raigadacha Rajbandi*; **1966**: *Dhananjay*; **1967**: *Sant Gora Kumbhar*; **1968**: *Ekati*; **1970**: *Gharkul*; *Mumbaicha Javai*; **1971**: *Ajab Tujhe Sarkar*; *Bajiravacha Beta*; **1972**: *Birbal My Brother*; **1973**: *Javai Vikat Ghene Aahe*; **1975**: *Zakhmi*; **1976**: *Raeeszada.*

THAKUR, RAMCHANDRA (1908-92)

Hindi and Gujarati director. Born in Chitroda, North Gujarat. A polyglot who spoke eleven languages, he was also a Pali scholar and a journalist at *Mouj Majah* (1928). Publicity officer at **Sagar**, later assisted **C.M. Luhar** and Hiren Bose. First film, ***Gramophone Singer***, is said to have introduced back projection without recourse to optical superimposition (with cameraman Keki Mistry). *Civil Marriage* was hailed by **Abbas** as a precursor to his own 40s cinema. Worked at Sagar and its successor National Film in collaboration with progressives around **R.S. Choudhury**, including **Mehboob** and **Zia Sarhadi**. With the decline of National, worked with **Ranjit** writing scripts in Gujarati for **Punatar** (*Nanand Bhojai*, 1948; ***Mangalfera***, 1949; ***Gadano Bel***, 1950). Later work mainly as freelancer. Known for his ability to work within very tight budgets to help independent producers in financial trouble. Wrote two novels and several short stories, one of which, *Amrapali*, was the basis of **Nandlal Jaswantlal**'s hit in 1945. Scripted his own films, as well as, e.g., *Dynamite* (1938), *Narad Muni* (1949), ***Baiju Bawra*** (1952), *Tulsi Vivah* (1971), *Hari Darshan* (1972). Apparently directed ***Kaa*** and *Stree* (both 1966) in Oriya under the name Siddharth. As a scenarist, he used the name Sarangapani.

FILMOGRAPHY: **1938**: ***Gramophone Singer***; **1940**: *Civil Marriage*; **1941**: *Kasauti*; **1942**: ***Garib***; *Apna Paraya*; **1943**: *Ashirwad*; **1945**: *Aarti*; *Sharbati Aankhen*; **1947**: *Geet Govind*; **1948**: ***Vadilona Vanke***; *Jai Hanuman*; **1949**: *Garibi*; *Rumal*; **1951**: *Ghayal*; **1952**: *Veer Arjun*; **1953**: *Dharmapatni*; **1955**: *Jai Mahadev*; **1956**: *Sheikh Chilli*; *Makheechoos*; **1960**: *Chandramukhi*; *Veer Durgadas*; **1961**: ***Hiro Salaat***; **1967**: *Nawab Siraj-ud-Dowla*; **1969**: *Jyoti* (Doc).

Timirbaran *see* **Baran, Timir**

TKS BROTHERS

Best-known early 20th C. commercial Tamil theatre company. It was run by the four sons of the actor T.S. Kannuswamy Pillai. Shankaran, Muthuswamy, Shanmugham and Bhagavathi were apprenticed in 1918 to the noted playwright Sankaradas Swamigal. They later joined the group run by T.K. Krishnaswamy Palavar, then producing plays with nationalist themes (cf *Kadarin Vetri*), and then the playwright Sarabam Muthuswamy Kavirayar's group. As established actors, they launched their own company, the Madurai Bala Shanmughananda Sabha (1925), best

Durga Khote (centre) and Govindrao Tembe (right) in *Nandakumar* (1938)

known by the initials of the most famous brother, T.K. Shanmugham. They débuted with the play *Kovalan*. Although the group was considered to be the legitimate heir to the 19th C. tradition of their mentor Sankaradas Swamigal, during the course of staging 32 original plays they gradually shifted to reform melodrama and evolved a new writing and acting style which had a big influence on early Tamil sound films. In 1935, T.K. Shanmugham started Shanmugham Talkies, co-producing **Raja Sandow**'s *Menaka* (1935) which featured the brothers along with **N.S. Krishnan** in an adaptation of one of their plays. This was followed by *Balamani* (1937) and the seminal reformist film ***Gumastavin Penn*** (1941). Their other noted productions adapted to film include ***Andaman Kaithi*** (1952) and *Ratha Pasam* (1954). Their theatre includes the earliest writings of a new generation of playwrights (and **DMK Film** directors) like **A.S.A. Sami** (*Bilhana*, filmed by TKS in 1948), **P. Neelakantan** (the play *Mullil Roja*) and former actor-writer **A.P. Nagarajan**. More significantly perhaps, the group nurtured a whole generation of film actors such as the legendary N.S. Krishnan, S.S. Rajendran, S.V. Sahasranamam, M.N. Rajam and, more recently, **Kamalahasan**. They also worked in other languages, e.g. the Malayalam play *Manithan*, later adapted by **Ramnoth** (1953).

TORNEY, RAMCHANDRA GOPAL (1880-1960)

Hindi and Marathi director; born in Sukulwadi and educated in Malwan, coastal Maharashtra. Employed by Greaves Cotton Electrical in Bombay (1896); then transferred as a branch manager to Karachi. Resigned and returned to Bombay (1920). He is often cited as **Phalke**'s rival for having apparently made the feature ***Pundalik*** (1912) a year before ***Raja Harishchandra*** (1913). Recent research suggests that it was probably made by N.G. Chitre, the owner of Coronation Cinematograph (which released *Raja Harishchandra*) with P.R. Tipnis, Coronation's manager and later noted exhibitor in Delhi. Torney is best-known as a distributor, initially representing Laxmi Film (1924-6) and **Imperial** (1927-31). Début film, as co-director, was the commercial hit ***Neera*** (1926). Started the Movie Camera Co. (1922), later the distributors of Audio-Camex 'Tanar' sound equipment, a joint venture with Baburao Pai of Famous Pics (1929). Provided the sound equipment for **Irani**'s ***Alam Ara*** (1931) and other talkies. Took over Saraswathi Film in Pune (1932), started as a technicians' enterprise by **Nanubhai Desai**, Bhogilal Dave, Dorabsha Kolha and others in 1926. Saraswathi Cinetone closed down in 1942 after an unsuccesful move into Hindi cinema. Torney made Marathi comedies in late 30s and early 40s, often starring comedian Dinkar Kamanna. Made films for his own studios, Imperial, **Sagar** and Sikandar; also art direction and sound recording for some early Marathi talkies. Scripted Madanrai Vakil's *Mewad No Mawali* (1930).

FILMOGRAPHY: 1926: ***Neera***; **1930**: *Sinbad Khalashi*; **1931**: *Dilawar* (all St); **1933**: *Bhakta Prahlad*; **1934**: *Bhedi Rajkumar/Thaksen Rajputra*; **1935**: *Pyara Dushman*; **1939**: *Majhi Ladki*; **1941**: *Bahaklela Brahmachari*; *Narad Naradi*; *Navardev*.

TRIVEDI, UPENDRA

Major Gujarati film star and producer, known also in Gujarat for his stage productions. Introduced to films by **Raskapur**; début in ***Kadu Makrani*** and ***Mehndi Rang Lagyo***, films usually cited as the renaissance of Gujarati cinema. Reappeared in an equally epochal production, **Dave**'s ***Jesal Toral***, playing the outlaw lover. Associated prominently with Dave's films: e.g. *Shetalne Kanthe*, *Malavpati Munj* (which retells the extensively filmed **K.M. Munshi** story, ***Prithvi Vallabh***) and *Paiso Bole Chhe*. His brother Arvind Trivedi is also a noted stage and film star in Gujarati who shot to fame playing Ravana in **Sagar**'s *Ramayan* tv series (1986-8).

FILMOGRAPHY (* also d): **1960**: ***Kadu Makrani***; ***Mehndi Rang Lagyo***; **1961**: ***Hiro Salaat***; *Veer Ramwalo*; **1962**: *Jogidas Khuman*; **1963**: *Vanraj Chavdo*; **1971**: ***Jesal Toral***; *Parde Ke Peeche*; **1972**: ***Zer To Pidhan Jani Jani****; *Jungle Mein Mangal*; **1973**: *Kadu Makrani*; *Raja Bhartrahari*; *Ranakdevi*; *Mahasati Savitri*; *Blackmail*; **1974**: *Ghunghat*; *Harishchandra Taramati*; *Hothal Padmini*; **1975**: *Jai Ranchhod*; *Jogidas Khuman*; *Shetalne Kanthe*; *Bhadar Tara Vehta Pani*; **1976**: *Chundadino Rang*; *Malavpati Munj*; *Ra Navghan*; *Santu Rangili*; *Veer Mangdavalo*; **1977**: *Bhrashtachar Murdabad*; *Halaman Jethvo*; *Manno Manigar*; *Paiso Bole Chhe*; *Sadavant Savlinga*; *Son Kansari*; *Kali Raat*; *Khel Khiladi Ka*; **1978**: *Chundadi Odhi Tara Namni*; *Dada Khetrapal*; *Manekthamb*; *Patali Parmar*; *Ver Ni Vasulat*; **1979**: *Amarsinh Rathod*; *Garvo Garasiyo*; *Kunwari Satino Kesariyo Kanth*; *Lakwadi Phoolwadi*; *Navrang Chundadi*; *Preet Khandani Dhar*; *Rang Rasiya*; *Sona Indhoni Roopa Bedlun*; *Suraj Chandra Ni Sakhe*; *Vahue Vagovya Mota Khorda*; *Veer Pasali*; **1980**: *Chitadano Chor*; *Jivi Rabaran*; *Kesar Kathiyani*; *Koino Ladakvayo*; *Namni Nagarvel*; *Sorathni Padmini*; **1981**: *Amar Devidas*; *Bhav Bhavna Bheru*; *Mehulo Luhar*; *Seth Jagadusha*; *Vansdi Vagi Valamni*; **1982**: *Retina Ratan*; **1983**: *Vachda Dadani Dikri*; **1984**: *Dhartina Ami*; *Mali Methan*; *Mansaina Diva*; *Machhu Tara Vehta Pani*; *Nagmati Nagvalo*; *Sajan Sonalde*; **1985**: *Malo Naagde*; **1988**: *Sole Somwar*.

URS, D. KEMPARAJ (1918-82)

Kannada director, actor and producer; also worked in Tamil and Telugu. Born in Hunsur, Mysore Dist., into the aristocratic Arasu family. Studied medicine for three years while doing amateur theatre. Film début as actor in **Veeranna**'s ***Jeevana Nataka***. Also small role in **Prabhat**'s ***Ramshastri***. Pioneer producer-director of Kannada cinema with *Raja Vikrama* and key influence on its historicals. *Jaladurga*, shot simultaneously in Tamil as *Karkottai*, was based on *The Count of Monte Cristo*. Was actively involved in Congress politics when brother Devaraj Urs was Karnataka Chief Minister and campaigned for Indira Gandhi when she fought the controversial Chikmagalur elections (1980). Later chairman of Karnataka Film Development Corp. Wrote two autobiographical books, *Naanu* (1979) and *Alvat Varshalu*.

FILMOGRAPHY (* also act/** act only): **1942**: ***Jeevana Nataka*****; **1944**: ***Ramshastri*****; **1947**: *Krishnaleele***; *Mahananda***; **1948**: *Bhakta Ramadas**; **1950**: *Shiva Parvati***; *Raja Vikrama**; **1953**: *Jaladurga/Karkottai**; *Shri Krishna***; **1957**: *Nala Damayanti**; **1959**: *Azhagarmalai Kalvan**; **1964**: *Navajeevana***.

VAIRAMUTHU

Poet and noted Tamil lyricist in 70s/80s, sometimes considered a successor to **Kannadasan**. Born in Thamaraikulam near Madurai; graduated in Madras; employed by the government as a translator. His early poetry is often broadcast on the radio; published his first anthology in 1972. Film début in **Bharathirajaa**'s *Nizhalgal* (1980), remaining associated with this director and with composer **Ilaiyaraja** until his highly publicised break with the latter. Wrote the songs for **Balachander**'s ***Thanneer Thanneer*** (1981).

VAKIL, NANUBHAI B. (1904-80)

Hindi director born in Valsad, Gujarat. Educated in Bombay, where he graduated as a lawyer (1926). Started as a scenarist at **Sharda** Film, then at **Chandulal Shah**'s Jagdish Film. Prolific director at **Ranjit** (silent) and **Sagar** (sound). Directed the first Gujarati sound feature, ***Narasinh Mehta***. Definitive films were with **Zubeida** in Mahalakshmi Cinetone, co-founded with her (1934-5). Helped found Jayashree Cinetone in Calcutta, but returned to Bombay (1938) and joined Kikubhai Desai's Paramount Film. Until late 60s, he mainly remade silent adventure movies derived from Parsee theatre's versions of legends from Firdausi's 10th C. *Shah Nama* and from the *Arabian Nights*. His films helped define the B-movie production in post-WW2 period. 50s films (*Yahudi Ki Beti*, *Parvin*, *Flying Rani*) are also the first scripts by the Marxist poet **Kaifi Azmi**. Adapted Premchand's novel for *Seva Sadan*, but the author distanced himself from the film, thus enabling **Subramanyam**'s definitive 1938 version to be made.

FILMOGRAPHY: 1929: *Tit For Tat*; *Veer Pujan*; *Mrignayani*; *Kumud Kumari*; *Sinhaldweep Ki Sundari*; **1930**: *Sheikh Chilli*; *Madhbhar Mohini*; *Sorathi Baharvatiyo*; *Desh Deepak*; *Ranakdevi*; *Rasili Radha*; *Vifreli Waghan*; *Vanraj*; **1931**: *Albeli Mumbai*; *Azadi Nu Jung*; *Mojili Mashuq*; *Hoor-e-Roshan*; *Noor-e-Alam*; *Baghdad Nu Bulbul*; **1932**: *Nakhreli Nar*; *Baghdad Ka Badmash* (all St); *Bulbul-e-Baghdad*; ***Narasinh Mehta***; *Maya Bazaar*; **1933**: *Bulbul-e-Punjab*; *Pandav Kaurav*; **1934**: *Nanand Bhojai*; *Radha Mohan/Nand Ke Lala*; ***Rashk-e-Laila***; *Seva Sadan*; **1935**: *Birbal Ki Beti*; *Gulshan-e-Alam*; **1936**: *Mr and Mrs Bombay*; *Nariraj*; **1937**: *Fakhr-e-Islam*; **1938**: *Alladdin and the Wonderful Lamp*; *Banke Savaria*; **1939**: *Son of Alladdin*; *Madhu Bansari*; *Sansar Naiya*; **1940**: *Deepak Mahal*; *Golibar*; *Hatimtai Ki Beti*; *Jadui Kangan*; **1941**: *Jadui Bandhan*; *Taj Mahal*; **1942**: *Firman*; **1943**: *Naya Zamana*; **1944**: *Kismatwala*; **1945**: *Alladdin*; *Kul Kalank*; *Hatimtai Ki Beti*; **1946**: *Alibaba*; *Arab Ka Sitara*; *Baghdad Ka Chor*; *Sinbad the Sailor*; *Mohabbat Ki Duniya*; **1947**: *Flying Man*; *Kismet Ka Sitara*; **1948**: *Azad Hindustan*; *Desh Seva*; *Hind Mail*; *Jadui Bansari*; *Ratan Manjari*; **1949**:

Flying Express; *Alladdin Ki Beti*; **1950**: *Raj Mukut*; **1951**: *Jai Mahalakshmi*; **1953**: *Raj Mahal*; **1954**: *Gul Bahar*; *Noor Mahal*; **1955**: *Darbar*; *Hatimtai Ki Beti*; *Sakhi Hatim*; *Shah Behram*; **1956**: *Alam Ara*; *Indrasabha*; *Khul Jaa Sim Sim*; *Lal-e-Yaman*; *Lalkaar*; *Yahudi Ki Beti*; **1957**: *Bansari Bala*; *Parvin*; *Sati Pariksha*; **1958**: *Miss Punjab Mail*; *Shaan-e-Hatim*; *Pehla Pehla Pyar*; **1959**: *Flying Rani*; *Kya Yeh Bambai Hai*; **1960**: *Alam Ara Ki Beti*; **1964**: *Id Ka Chand*; **1971**: *Shaan-e-Khuda*; **1973**: *Alam Ara*.

VALI

Prolific Tamil lyricist with c.6500 songs, prominently associated with composer M.S. Vishwanathan and with films starring **MGR**. Born as Rangarajan, in Tiruchi, TN. Started as visual artist in the College of Art, Madras. Started an independent journal in Tiruchi, writing under the name Netaji. **Kalki** got him a job at the AIR. Early reputation as writer of theatre dialogue. Breakthrough in film with *Azhagarmalai Kalvan* (1959), consolidated by the success of **P. Neelakantan**'s *Nallavan Vazhvan* (1961). Major hits in **Chanakya**'s *Enga Veetu Pillai* (1965), esp. the number *Nan anaiyital* (*If I could command*), contributed to star MGR's screen image. Top lyric writer of 80s Tamil film, e.g. **Mani Rathnam**'s musical hit ***Agni Nakshatram*** (1988).

VAMSY (b. 1956)

Telugu and Kannada art-house director. Born in Karnataka. Prolific novelist including novelisations of films, e.g. **K. Vishwanath**'s ***Shankarabharanam*** (1979). Joined films as assistant to K. Vishwanath, whom he regards as his teacher along with **Bharathirajaa**. Films feature extensive music (usually by **Ilaiyaraja**) and dance. Best-known film: ***Sitara***.

FILMOGRAPHY: **1982**: *Manchu Pallaki*; **1984**: ***Sitara***; **1985**: *Anveshana*; *Preminchu Pelladu*; **1986**: *Ladies' Tailor*; *Alabhama*; **1987**: *Lawyer Suhasini*; **1988**: *Maharshi*; **1989**: *Chettukinda Pleader*; *Amrutha Bindu*; **1991**: *April 1 Vidudala*; **1993**: *Joker*.

VANISREE (b. 1951)

Telugu and (briefly) Kannada star born in Nellore, AP. Educated in Andhra Mahila Sabha, Madras, where she learnt the Bharat Natyam dance. Début in B.A. Subba Rao's *Bhishma*; first lead role in Tamil: Joseph Taliath's *Kathal Paduthum Padu*. Known as a star in Kannada cinema while playing comedienne roles in her early Telugu films. Broke through in Telugu with *Marupurani Katha*, going on to star opposite, e.g., **NTR**, **A. Nageshwara Rao** and **Shobhan Babu**. Financed and acted in **Shyam Benegal**'s only Telugu film, ***Anugraham***.

Vanisree in *Bangaru Panjaram* (1965)

FILMOGRAPHY: **1962**: *Bhishma*; **1964**: *Thotalopilla Kotalo Rani*; *Mane Aliya*; **1965**: *Sati Sakkubai*; *Pakkalo Bellem*; ***Pandava Vanavasam***; ***Satya Harishchandra***; *Chandrahasa*; ***Bangaru Panjaram***; *Mangamma Sapatham*; *Prameelarjuneyam*; *Patala Mohini*; **1966**: *Potti Pleader*; *Aggibarata*; *Kanne Manushulu*; *Shri Krishna Tulabharam*; *Bhoolokamlo Yamalokam*; *Kathari Veera*; *Logattu Perumallukeruka*; *Kathal Paduthum Padu*; *Nammaveeti Lakshmi*; ***Rangula Ratnam***; **1967**: ***Thanga Thambi***; *Marupurani Katha*; *Gopaludu Bhoopaludu*; *Kanchukota*; *Bhuvana Sundari Katha*; *Devuni Gelichina Manavudu/Devara Gedda Manava*; *Nindu Manushulu*; *Stree Janmam*; ***Aada Paduchu***; *Janara Jana*; **1968**: *Sukha Dukhalu*; *Lakshminivasam*; *Asadhyudu*; *Ranabheri*; *Veerapooja*; *Bharya*; *Pantalu Pattimpulu*; *Kalasina Manushulu*; *Uyarntha Manithan*; **1969**: *Mahabaludu*; *Shabash Satyam*; *Astulu Antastulu*; *Atmiyulu*; *Jagath Kiladilu*; *Bhale Rangudu*; ***Nindu Hridayalu***; *Anna Damulu*; *Karpura Arathi*; *Rajasimha*; *Kuzhandai Ullam*; *Ayiram Poyi*; *Nirai Kudam*; *Kanni Penn*; *Annaiyum Pithavum*; *Manasakshi*; *Athai Magal*; **1970**: *Tapalkaran Thangai*; *Thalaivan*; *Pelli Sambandham*; *Kodalu Diddina Kapuram*; *Chitti Chellalu*; *Drohi*; *Iddaru Ammayilu*; *Jagath Jettelu*; *Katha Nayika Molla*; *Pachani Samsaram*; **1971**: *Dasara Bullodu*; *Kiladi Singanna*; *Mooga Prema*; *Ananda Nilayam*; *Raitu Bidda*; *Adrushta Jathakudu*; *Chinnanati Snehitulu*; *Dabukku Thha Dongala Muttha*; *Jagath Jentreelu*; *Jeevitha Chakram*; *Katha Nayakuralu*; *Pavitra Bandham*; *Prem Nagar*; *Attalu Kodallu*; *Chelleli Kapuram*; *Kasidre Kailasa*; **1972**: *Amma Mata*; *Dattaputhrudu*; *Vichitra Bandham*; *Bangaru Babu*; *Abbaigaru Ammaigaru*; *Illu Illalu*; *Maa Inti Kodalu*; *Marapurani Talli*; *Shri Krishnanjaneya Yuddham*; *Koduku Kodalu*; *Avasara Kalyanam*; *Velli Vizha*; *Vasantha Maligai*; **1973**: *Deshoddharakulu*; *Ganga Manga*; *Minor Babu*; *Ramudu Devudu*; *Sreevaru Maavaru*; *Vintha Katha*; *Manchi Vadu*; *Khaidi Baba*; *Kanne Vayasu*; *Kannavari Kalalu*; *Jeevana Tarangulu*; **1974**: *Chaduvu Samskaram*; *Manushulo Devadu*; *Satyaniki Sankellu*; *Krishnaveni*; *Chakravakam*; *Sivakamyin Selvan*; *Vani Rani*; **1975**: *Eduruleni Manishi*; *Katha Nayakuni Katha*; *Abhimanavathi*; *Babu*; *Maya Machhindra* (Te); *Jeevana Jyoti*; *Ramuni Minchina Ramudu*; *Chikati Velugulu*; *Pooja*; **1976**: *Secretary*; *Doralu Dongalu*; *Premabandham*; *Aradhana*; *Bhakta Kannappa*; *Pogarubottu*; *Suprabhatam*; *Ilaya Thalaimurai*; *Oorukku Uzhaippavan*; *Rojavin Raja*; **1977**: *Thaliya Salangaiya*; *Edureetha*; ***Chakradhari***; *Raja Ramesh*; ***Kondura/Anugraham***; *Aalu Magalu*; *Janma Janmala Bandham*; *Jeevana Theeralu*; *Sati Savitri*; **1978**: *Chilipi Krishnudu*; ***Gorantha Deepam***; *Devadasu Malli Puttadu*; *Enki Nayudu Bava*; *Ramachilaka*; *Vichitra Jeevitham*; *Simha Baludu*; *Sahasavanthudu*; *Shri Rama Raksha*; *Punya Bhoomi*; **1979**: *Kamalamma Kamatam*; *Nallathoru Kudumbam*; *Andaman Ammayi*; **1980**: *Shri Vinayaka Vijayam*; **1981**: *Devudu Mamayya*; **1989**: *Swati Chinukulu*; *Attaki Yamudu Ammayiki Mugudu*; *Poolarangudu*; **1990**: *Bobbili Raja*; **1992**: *Pellam Chattu Mogudu*; **1993**: *Evandi Avide Ochindi*; *Bhavya Bharata*; *Preme Naa Pranam*; *Rowdygari Teacher*.

VARALAKSHMI, GARIKIPATI (b. 1926)

Telugu and Tamil actress, singer and producer born in Ongole, AP. Aged 11, she ran away to Vijaywada to join the theatre. Worked in Tungala Chalapathi's and in Kotirathnam's troupes, playing, e.g., Radha in *Sakkubai* and Prabhavati in *Rangoon Rowdy*. Film début in **H.M. Reddy**'s *Barrister Parvatisham*, where she acted opposite **L.V. Prasad**. After a brief spell at the Shobhanachala Studio, she was relaunched by Prasad in ***Drohi*** and ***Pelli Chesi Choodu***. Acted in several films by her husband, **K.S. Prakash Rao** (whom she married in 1943). Known in her early films as a stunt and action film actress; played the vamp in *Vindhyarani*. Acted lead and character roles in several Tamil and Telugu films; then acted with stars like **MGR** (*Gul-e-Bakavali*) and **Sivaji Ganesan** (*Naan Petra Selvam*). Produced, wrote, directed and starred in the film *Moogajeevulu*.

FILMOGRAPHY (* also d): **1940**: *Barrister Parvatisham*; *Bondam Pelli*; **1941**: ***Dakshayagnam***; **1942**: *Bhakta Prahlada*; **1946**: *Vanarani*; **1948**: ***Drohi***; *Vindhyarani*; **1950**: *Modathi Rathri*; *Vali Sugriva*; *Lakshmamma*; ***Swapna Sundari***; *Maya Rambha/Maya Rambai*; **1951**: *Deeksha/Anni*;

Nirdoshi/Niraparadhi; **1952**: *Manavati*; ***Pelli Chesi Choodu/Kalyanam Panni Paar***; **1953**: ***Kanna Talli/Petrathai***; *Prapancham*; *Paropakaram*; *Rohini*; *Naa Chellelu*; *Ulagam*; **1954**: *Jyoti/Illara Jyoti*; *Maa Gopi*; *Menarikam*; *Palle Paduchu*; *Kutumbam*; **1955**: *Ante Kavali*; *Pasupu Kumkuma*; *Porter Kandhan*; *Gul-e-Bakavali*; *Nalla Thangai*; **1956**: *Balasanyasamma Katha*; *Marumalarchi*; *Naan Petra Selvam*; *Melukolupu*; **1957**: *Dampatyam*; *Dongalo Dora*; *Pathni Daivam*; **1958**: *Raja Nandini*; *Dongalunnaru Jagratha*; **1959**: *Mamiyar Meetriya Marumagal*; **1960**: *Sivagami*; *Renukadevi Mahatyam*; **1961**: *Iddaru Mithralu*; *Nagarjuna*; **1962**: *Bhishma*; *Kalimilemulu*; ***Kulagothralu***; *Padandi Munduku*; **1963**: *Anuragham*; **1966**: *Atabommalu*; *Shri Krishna Tulabharam*; *Letamanushulu*; *Astiparulu*; **1967**: *Rahasyam*; **1968**: *Moogajeevulu**; *Veerapooja*; *Amayukudu*; *Bangaru Sankellu*; *Attagaru Kottakodalu*; *Harishchandra*; **1969**: ***Nindu Hridayalu***; **1970**: *Jai Jawan*; **1971**: *Mooga Prema*; *Bhale Papa*; *Pavitra Bandham*; **1972**: *Abbaigaru Ammaigaru*; *Vazhai Yadi Vazhai*; **1973**: *Veetukku Vandha Marumagal*; *Dr Babu*; *Ganga Manga*; *Neramu Siksha*; *Ramrajyam*; *Geetha*; *Vishali*; **1974**: *Premalu Pellilu*; *Chakravakam* (Te); *Tulasi*; *Vani Rani*; **1975**: *Thota Ramudu*; *Katha Nayakuni Katha*; *Ee Kalapu Pillalu*; *Vayasochina Pilla*; *Rajyamlo Rabandulu*; **1976**: *Attavarillu*; *Manchiki Maro Peru*; *Swami Drohulu*; *Mahatmudu*; **1977**: *Talle Challani Daivam*; **1978**: ***Gorantha Deepam***; *Nindu Manishi*.

VARALAKSHMI, S. (b. 1927)

Telugu and Tamil actress and singer. Born in Jaggampetah, AP. Début as child actress in **K. Subramanyam**'s ***Balayogini*** and ***Seva Sadan***. First adult role in **Ramabrahmam**'s *Mayalokam*. Top 50s Tamil star with several musical hits. Turned producer with Varalakshmi Films (1957).

FILMOGRAPHY: 1936: ***Balayogini***; **1938**: ***Seva Sadan***; **1939**: ***Raitu Bidda***; *Prem Sagar*; **1940**: *Illalu*; **1945**: *Mayalokam*; **1947**: ***Palnati Yuddham***; *Apoorva Chintamani*; **1948**: *Balaraju*; *Bhojan*; *Chakradhari*; **1949**: ***Navajeevan/Navajeevanam***; *Jeevitham*; **1950**: *Macharekhai*; **1951**: *Saudamini*; *Mohanasundaram*; **1952**: *Tinguranga*; *Chinnadurai*; *Velaikkaran*; *Shyamala*; **1953**: *Kodarikam*; *Vayyari Bhama*; **1954**: *Sati Sakkubai*; **1955**: *Shri Krishna Tulabharam*; **1956**: *Naga Panchami*; *Kanakatara*; **1957**: *Sati Savitri*; *Chakravarthi Thirumagal*; **1959**: *Sati Tulasi*; *Veer Bhaskaradu*; *Rechukka Pragatichukka*; ***Veerapandiya Kattaboman***; *Jai Bhawani*; ***Sivagangai Seemai***; **1960**: ***Shri Venkateshwara Mahatyam***; *Abhimanam*; **1961**: *Krishna Prema*; **1962**: ***Mahamantri Timmarasu***; ***Shri Krishnarjuna Yuddham***; **1964**: *Babruvahana*; **1965**: *Vijayasimha*; ***Satya Harishchandra***; **1966**: *Bhimanjaneya Yuddham*; *Shri Krishna Tulabharam*; **1967**: *Gopaludu Bhoopaludu*; ***Bhama Vijayam/Bhale Kodalu***; ***Shri Krishnavataram***; **1968**: *Nindu Samsaram*; **1969**: *Adarsha Kutumbam*; *Sattekalapu Sattaiah*; ***Mattukkara Velan***; **1970**: *Drohi*; **1971**: *Bhagyavanthudu*; *Bomma Borusa*; *Naa Thammudu*; *Shri Krishna Satya*; **1972**: *Bullet Bullodu*; *Pedda Koduku*; *Atthanu Diddina Kodalu*; *Bangaru Babu*; *Bala Bharatam*; *Delhi To Madras*; *Daiva Sankalpam*; *Velli Vizha*; **1973**: *Valli Daivanai*; *Raja Raja Chozhan*; *Thirumalai Daivam*; *Nathayil Muthu*; *Sreevaru Maavaru*; *Devudu Chesina Manushulu*; *Meena*; **1974**: *Inti Kodalu*; *Thayi*; *Devi Shri Karumariamman*; **1975**: *Cinema Paithiyam*; *Abhimanavathi*; *Ee Kalam Dampathulu*; *Pichimaraju*; *Ramuni Minchina Ramudu*; *Yashoda Krishna*; **1976**: *Doralu Dongalu*; *Dashavatharam*; *Needhikku Thalai Vanangu*; **1977**: *Navarathnam*; *Swarganiki Nitchenalu*; *Chanakya Chandragupta*; ***Daana Veera Shura Karna***; *Oka Talli Katha*; **1978**: *Ananda Bhairavi*; **1983**: *Muddula Mogadu*; *Neti Bharatham*; *Shri Ranganeethulu*; *Adutha Varisu*; *Thungatha Kanniru Onru*; *Shubha Muhurtam*; **1984**: *Tharasu*; *Premagola*; *Punyam Kodi Purushudu*; *Takkaridonga*; *Bangaru Kapuram*; *Devanthakudu*; **1985**: *Aggiraju*; *Uriki Soggadu*; *Sreevaru*; *Bullet*; **1991**: *Guna*.

VARKEY, MUTATTHU (b. 1918)

Writer, born in Chanagnassery, Kerala. One of the most famous purveyors of a Malayalam literature known as 'paingili' fiction: romances pioneered in the serials of the Malayalam magazine, *Malayala Manorama*, with weekly instalments of formulaic love stories often dealing with extramarital sex, people going away to work or the attractive returnee from the city or abroad causing emotional turmoil. These fictions were a major influence on Malayalam melodrama and on star personae such as **Prem Nazir** and **Sharada**. Joined films as scenarist for **P. Subramanyam**. Wrote, e.g., ***Padatha Paingili***, *Jailpully*, (both 1957); *Mariakutty* (1958); *Poothali* (1960); *Sneha Deepam* (1962), *Snapaka Yohannan* (1963). Also wrote for **Kunchako** (*Inapravugal*, 1965) and for **K.S. Sethumadhavan** (e.g. *Gnana Sundari*, 1961; *Sthanarthi Saramma*, 1966). Varkey's style has been perpetuated by the writer and scenarist **Kanam**, his successor in the paingili genre.

VARKEY, POONKUNNAM (b. 1908)

Influential Malayalam writer turned scenarist. Prominent member of a new generation of radical Malayalam short-story writers with, e.g., P. Kesavadev, Vaikom Mohammed Basheer and Thakazhy Shivashankar Pillai. According to the literary critic and poet Ayyappa Panicker (1987), many of his stories are 'open attacks on the Church' and 'attempt to bring to light the hidden motivations for outwardly pious actions' (1987). Dialogue writer in the 50s and 60s, e.g. for V. Krishnan's ***Navalokam*** (1951), G.R. Rao's *Asha Deepam* (1953), S.S. Rajan's ***Snehaseema*** (1954), M. Krishnan Nair's *Viyarppinte Vila* (1962), **Kunchako**'s *Bharya* (1962: from a **Kanam** story), **K.S. Sethumadhavan**'s *Nithya Kanyaka* and *Susheela* (both 1963). Adapted **Panthulu**'s original Kannada version of ***School Master*** (1958) into Malayalam, directed by **Puttanna Kanagal** (1964).

VARMA, RAJA RAVI (1848-1906)

Painter who greatly influenced the iconography of early Indian popular painting, theatre and mass-produced lithographs and oleographs. Born in a feudal family with blood ties to the royal house of Travancore, Kerala. Apprenticed to the Travancore court painter Ramaswamy Naicker and probably studied under the Dutch painter Theodore Jensen. Quickly became known as a portraitist in demand by the Indian nobility and the top British administrators. Then changed direction in a way that left an extraordinary and lasting imprint on popular Indian art forms: he started painting Indian gods and goddesses and famous scenes from the *Puranas* in a naturalist, 'academic' style, extending this practice into mass-produced oleographs manufactured at a press near Lonavala (1894), an unprecedented development at the time. The 'surrogate realism' (Geeta Kapur, 1989) of his oils and the way they evolved into the first industrialised visual art genre, the mythological, was partly overdetermined by the political aspirations of his royal patrons in Travancore. Varma was part of a current which was explicitly elaborated by the poet and novelist Kerala Varma (1845-1914) and included 'Chambu poets, composers of Kathakali literature, Manipravala poets, anagrammatists, riddle-mongers, instant rhymsters and Shakuntala translators' (R. Nandakumar, 1989). Its political role was to match the cultural credentials of the ruling élite with those of brahminical 'tradition' and Victorian race and class consciousness. This period in 19th C. Travancore was typical of a phenomenon in many feudal South Indian areas (e.g. Mysore), where a reinvented 'classicism' substituted for a social reform movement. Varma's early paintings reinterpret the tenets of academic boudoir painting: e.g. his adaptation of Tanjore glass paintings to create his full-bosomed figures. Combining traditional performative discourses and myth with the requirements of industrial production, he achieved, in G. Kapur's words, 'the allegorical transfer of the heroic ages into the current cultural resurgence'. Its impact was not limited to painting. His *mise en scène* in spatial tableaux was directly appropriated by the **Sangeet Natak** and by the early cinema: e.g. the way Varma painted his historical/mythological figures in the foreground and signified their actions through a layered background was adopted by **stage backdrop** painters. Kapur suggested that the oleographs could have emerged directly from his oils, its colours brightened in consonance with Indian light, making the pictures float to the surface:'The technique of the oleograph captures this up-floated image, the depthless printing inks and high varnish of the technique, making the image all surface'. This flattening effect became a formal convention for middle-class drawing-room painting, for religious expression (e.g. the sewing of gilded sequins around the image of the gods) and for the low-technology cottage industries of label and poster printing, magazine illustrations and greetings cards. J. Sasikumar made a documentary, *Raja Ravi Varma* (1990), about the artist.

VARMA, VYALAR RAMA (1929-75)

The top lyricist of Malayalam cinema from the 1950s. Born in Vyalar. As a noted poet, he was one of the few members of the erstwhile Travancore aristocracy to join the CP-led cultural resurgence in the late 40s in Kerala. His poems continued the 30s Changampuzha (1911-48) tradition of romantic verse but often shift their rampant idealism into strongly materialist concerns:

e.g. his poem *Sagara Sangeetham*, evoking the cosmic moment of creation replacing God with material reality. According to the historian V.A.K. Ranga Rao (1991), 'He brought the essence of Marxism, Darwin's theory of evolution [the song *Itihasangal janikkum munbe* in *Chuvanna Sandhyakal*, 1975], the parables from the Bible, all into Malayalam film song,' adding that Vyalar is never afraid to be explicitly erotic in the tradition of Kalidasa and Jayadeva. Ranga Rao also points out that **M.T. Vasudevan Nair** consciously models his prose dialogues on Vyalar's lyrical iconography, e.g. in **K.S. Sethumadhavan**'s films.

VASAN, S. S. (1903-69)

Original name: Thiruthiraipoondi Subramanya Srinivasan Iyer. Director and best-known Madras producer; owner of **Gemini** Studio. Born in Thiruthiraipoondi, Thanjavur Dist., TN. Started in advertising; later published the journal *Ananda Vikatan* (still a best-selling weekly), pioneering a trend of serialised fiction that also introduced writers who later became scenarists (e.g. **Kalki**). His own novel *Sati Leelavathi* was filmed by **Duncan** in 1936: the film was **MGR**'s début. Turned distributor with **Subramanyam**'s ***Thyagabhoomi*** (1939) and financier investing in the Motion Pics Producers Combine; then bought the studio in a government auction to establish Gemini Pics, named after his star sign. Their first film, *Madanakamarajan* (1941), a major hit, signalled a big shift in the Madras entertainment industry, exemplified by his most famous film, ***Chandralekha***, and by his manifesto in defence of cinematic populism, *Pageants for our Peasants*. The Gemini signature was equated with multi-starrers and megabudget spectaculars, involving songs, sword fights, massive sets and huge battle scenes, in part derived from Hollywood but more from popular fairy-tale variants of Indian epics mediated by adventure fiction inspired as much by Alexandre Dumas as by Douglas Fairbanks. The formula called for direct control over distribution, which included a publishing empire, a star stable, a studio and, after 1958, a full-scale Eastmancolor laboratory. His unrepentant populism and commercial acumen, which at his peak virtually established Madras as a direct rival to Bombay, can be seen in part as a consequence of the nationalist mobilisation of popular culture (cf K. Subramanyam) and the first real bid by Madras-based capital for the national All-India film market. As director, he concentrated on the Hindi versions of his studio's productions, often simply putting his name as director of bilingual versions.

FILMOGRAPHY: **1948**: ***Chandralekha***; **1949**: *Nishan*; **1950**: *Mangala*; **1951**: *Sansar*; **1952**: ***Mr Sampat***; **1954**: *Bahut Din Huye*; **1955**: ***Insaniyat***; **1958**: *Vanjikottai Valiban*; ***Raj Tilak***; **1959**: ***Paigham***; **1960**: *Irumputhirai*; **1961**: *Gharana*; **1967**: *Aurat*; **1968**: *Teen Bahuraniyan*; **1969**: *Shatranj*.

Vasudevan Nair, M. T. *see* **Nair, Madathu Thekepattu Vasudevan**

VAUHINI PICTURES

Telugu production company in Madras set up by **B.N. Reddi** (1939) following on from **H.M. Reddy**'s Rohini Pics, which first assembled the team of **K. Ramnoth**, A.K. Sekhar and **K.V. Reddy**, later key contributors to Vauhini's 40s film output. Known mainly for B.N. Reddi's elaborate nationalist melodramas (e.g. ***Vande Mataram***, 1939; ***Sumangali***, 1940; ***Swargaseema***, 1945) and for K.V. Reddy's early mythologicals. In 1948 Vauhini Pics became the studio Vauhini Prod., launched in partnership with Moola Narayanswamy. Ranked with **Gemini** as pioneering South Indian film institution. It changed hands the following year as B. Nagi Reddy took over and made it a sister concern of his **Vijaya** Pics.

VEERANNA, GUBBI (1890-1972)

Theatre and film actor, producer and entrepreneur born in Gubbi village, Mysore. Regarded as the founder of the Kannada stage and film industries. The most prominent practitioner of early 20th C. Kannada **Company Natak**. Aged 11, joined the Gubbi Shri Channabasaveshwara Swami Krupa Poshita Nataka Mandali, better known as the Gubbi Co., a travelling theatre group set up in 1884. Took charge of the group in 1917, performing almost only mythologicals with spectacular stage effects, rapid scene changes and the use of live animals. Set up a theatre school (1924) in Bangalore. At his peak, he ran three repertories, including one for children, with 250 salaried staff. Started film production (1927) partnered by Devudu Narasimha Sastry and Srinivasa Murthy of the Oriental Bank who later set up the Karnataka Films Corp. (1930) with studios in Malleshwaram. A Belgian cameraman and ethnographic film-maker, Raphael Algoet, helped direct Veeranna's second feature, *His Love Affair*. The studio became Gubbi-Karnataka Prod. with support from **A.V. Meiyappan**. For its early productions Veeranna hired famous directors from other languages to make Kannada films: **Y.V. Rao** for *Hari Maya*, **Raja Chandrasekhar** for *Sadarame* (this film, based on the group's most famous stage production, was also the studio's first success). **C. Pullaiah** made *Subhadra* and **S. Soundararajan** made ***Hemareddy Malamma***. Real success came, however, with entirely local talent: ***Bedara Kannappa*** (1954), based on **G.V. Iyer**'s play for the Gubbi Co., directed by **H.L.N. Simha**. It was also Kannada megastar **Rajkumar**'s first film. Veeranna set up Karnataka Film Distributors (1942), the Sagar Talkies Cinema in Bangalore with money borrowed from diwan Sir Mirza Ismail and later expanded his distribution interests by renting other cinemas. Co-founder of the Shri Kanteerava Studios in Bangalore (1966). Member of the Karnataka State Legislature. Wrote his autobiography, *Kaleye Kayaka* (1969).

FILMOGRAPHY: **1930**: *Song of Life*; **1931**: *His Love Affair*; **1932**: *Hari Maya*; **1935**: *Sadarame*; **1941**: *Subhadra*; **1942**: ***Jeevana Nataka***; **1945**: ***Hemareddy Malamma***; **1953**: ***Gunasagari/Satya Shodhanai***; **1956**: *Sadarame/Sadarama*.

VEL PICTURES

Pioneer sound studio of Telugu cinema set up (1933) by exhibitor Pinapala Venkatadasu (aka P.V. Dasu) in Madras in collaboration with M.T. Rajan, C.D. Sami, C.P. Sarathi and Jayantilal Thakare. Launched with **Chitrapu Narasimha Rao**'s 1934 Telugu remake of **Prabhat**'s Tamil film, *Seeta Kalyanam* (1933), involving the Prabhat team that later effectively ran the studio: directors **K. Ramnoth** and **Murugadasa** and art director A.K. Sekhar. It used RCA equipment apparently installed with assistance from Prabhat technicians. South India's most famous sound recordist, C.E. Biggs (who later worked for three decades with **Gemini**) started here with **Sarpotdar**'s *Nandakumar* (1938). With **General Pics**, Vel represents the first efforts to establish a production infrastructure in Madras (away from Calcutta). The studio lasted only four years. P.V. Dasu died (1936) leaving his most ambitious film, *Maya Bazaar* (1936), incomplete. The impetus to local production it gave later provided precedents for the Karthikeya Studio (set up as a workers' co-operative in Madras), for **Vauhini**'s output and for **Ramabrahmam**'s films at Sarathi. The Vel premises later became the Narasu Studios.

VENKAIAH, RAGHUPATHI (?-1941)

Popular photographer with a studio on Mount Road, Madras; as exhibitor he is sometimes credited with introducing cinema to South India. Imported the Chrono-Megaphone system through John Dickinson & Co., Madras, with an attached gramophone player which presented the illusion of synchronised sound. Screened films like *Raja's Casket* and *Pearl Fish* in the Victoria Public Hall. Many of his screenings were limited to c.500 ft of film in order to match the duration of the record disc. Some sources claim he travelled through Burma and Sri Lanka in 1912, before building the Gaiety, the first permanent cinema in Madras (1914). Also built the Crown and the Globe theatres in that city, showing mainly British and American films. Father of **Raghupati Prakash**.

VENKATESH, G. K. (1927-93)

Prolific Kannada composer. Entered film as a child actor. Assistant to music director S. Venkatraman. Early film scores in collaboration with Padmanabha Sastry, e.g. T.V. Singh Thakore's *Sodari*. This film was followed by a series of Thakore and **G.V. Iyer** productions, often starring **Rajkumar**. Set several of Iyer's lyrics to music and scored almost all Rajkumar's major musical hits. Known for emphatic scores which remain identified with the emotional intensity of Kannada mythologicals and melodramas. Also worked successfully on Kannada variations of the James Bond sub-genre (*Goadalli CID 999*; *Operation Diamond Rocket*), **Sathyu**'s offbeat fantasy, ***Chithegu Chinthe***, and **Rajendra Singh**'s vendetta thriller, ***Antha***. He sang in e.g. **Karanth**'s ***Chomana Dudi*** (1975). Superstar composer **Ilaiyaraja** started as his assistant.

FILMOGRAPHY: **1950**: *Chechi*; **1955**: *Sodari*; **1956**: *Hari Bhakta*; *Ohileshwara*; **1958**: *Anna Thangi*; **1959**: *Dharma Vijaya*; *Jagajyothi Basaveshwara*; ***Mahishasura Mardini***; **1960**:

Ranadheera Kanteerava; *Dashavtara*; **1961**: *Kaivara Mahatme*; *Kantheredu Nodu*; ***Arappavan***; **1962**: ***Bhoodana***; *Karuneye Kutumbada Kannu*; *Thayi Karulu/Thayin Karunai*; **1963**: *Lawyara Magalu*; *Kanya Ratna*; *Gauri*; *Malli Madhuve*; *Kulavadhu*; *Kalitharu Henne*; *Ananda Bashpa*; *Bangari*; **1964**: *Kalavati*; *Tumbidakoda*; **1965**: *Kavaleradu Kulavondu*; *Sarvagna Murthy*; *Nanna Kartavya*; *Sati Savitri*; **1966**: *Kiladi Ranga*; *Madhu Malathi*; *Sandhya Raga*; **1967**: *Parvathi Kalyana*; *Rajashekhara*; *Rajadurgada Rahasya*; *Immadi Pulakesi*; **1968**: *Jedara Bale*; *Manasakshi*; *Goadalli CID 999*; *Dial 2244*; **1969**: *Bhagirathi*; *Kannu Muchale*; *Mukunda Chandra*; *Operation Jackpot*; **1970**: *Devara Makkalu*; **1971**: *Kasturi Nivasa*; *Bala Bandhana*; *Naguva Hoovu*; *Thayi Devaru*; *Pratidhwani*; *Thande Makkalu*; **1972**: *Yara Sakshi*; ***Bangarada Manushya***; *Somari Pothu*; *Kodalu Pilla*; **1973**: *Doorada Betta*; *Devi Lalithamba*; *Talli Kodakulu*; *Sreevaru Maavaru*; *Pasi Hridayalu*; *Ponnukku Thanga Manasu*; *Kartavyada Kare*; **1974**: *Murugan Kattiya Vazhi*; *Boothayyana Maga Ayyu*; *Sampathige Saval*; *Bhakta Kumbhara*; *Anna Attige*; **1975**: *Dari Tappida Maga*; *Koodi Balona*; *Mayura*; *Nireekshe*; *Trimurthi*; *Zamindarugari Ammayi*; *Piriya Vidhai*; *Thennankeetru*; *Yarukkum Vetkamillai*; **1976**: *Adavallu Apanindalu*; *America Ammayi*; *Raja Nanna Raja*; *Bangarada Gudi*; *Balu Jenu*; **1977**: ***Chakradhari***; ***Tharam Marindi***; *Vedantha*; *Sose Thanda Saubhagya*; *Srimanthana Magalu*; *Sanadhi Appanna*; *Holavu Gelavu*; *Galate Samsara*; **1978**: *Devadasi*; *Vamsa Jyothi*; *Operation Diamond Rocket*; *Bhale Huduga*; ***Chithegu Chinthe***; **1979**: *Na Ninna Bedenu*; *Asadhya Aliya*; *Huliya Halina Mevu*; *Kamala*; *Nentaro Gantu Kallaro*; *Dhairyalakshmi*; **1980**: *Usha Swayamvara*; *Rustom Jodi*; **1981**: *Havina Hedde*; ***Antha***; *Hana Balavo Jana Balavo*; *Bhoomige Banda Bhagavanta*; *Minchina Belakalli*; *Mareyada Haadu*; **1982**: *Rudri*; *Shankar Sundar*; *Bhakta Dnyanadeva*; *Halu Jenu*; *Karmika Kallanalla*; *Bhoodi Muchida Kenda*; *Snehada Sankole*; **1983**: *Asha*; *Hosa Teerpu*; *Eradu Nakshatragalu*; *Nodi Swamy Navirodu Hige*; *Kashmir Kathali*; *Urumulu Merupulu*; **1984**: *Prachanda Kulla*; *Gajendra*; *Guru Bhakti*; *Kaliyuga*; *Jiddu*; *Male Bantu Male*; *Raakasi Nagu*; *Makkaliralavva Mane Thumba*; *Muthondu Muthu*; **1985**: *Parameshi Prema Prasanga*; *Guru Jagadguru*; *Ade Kannu*; *Shabash Vikrama*; *Chaduranga*; *Yauvanada Suliyalli*; *Bhayankar Bakasarudu*; *Hosa Baalu*; *Hosa Neeru*; **1986**: *Preeti* (K); **1987**: *Jaganmatha*; *Poornachandra*; **1989**: *Gandandre Gandu*.

Venkateshwara Rao, Ghantasala *see* **Ghantasala Venkateshwara Rao**

VENKATESHWARA RAO, GUMMADI (b. 1927)

Telugu actor born in Tenali, AP. Owned a shop selling electrical goods and started in amateur theatre aged 16. Professional stage career mainly 1947-50, playing roles like Duryodhana, acting often along with Madhavapalli Venkatramaiah. Film début in Tamil Nadu Theatres' production *Adrushta Deepudu*. Lead role in ***Mahamantri Timmarasu***. Broke through with **NTR**'s National Art Theatre Films: the estate manager in *Pichhipullaiah*, and ***Todu Dongalu*** in which he played the corrupt millowner. Starred in some 50s mythologicals. Better known for supporting roles (e.g. the henpecked husband in ***Ardhangi***). Known in later films for his numerous elderly characters in Telugu films.

FILMOGRAPHY: 1950: *Adrushta Deepudu*; **1953**: *Pichhipullaiah*; **1954**: ***Todu Dongalu***; **1955**: ***Ardhangi/Pennin Perumai***; **1957**: *Dampatyam*; *MLA*; *Sati Ansuya*; *Sarangadhara*; *Premada Putri/Preme Daivam*; ***Maya Bazaar***; ***Suvarna Sundari***; **1958**: *Dongalunnaru Jagratha*; *Aadapettanam*; ***Ettuku Pai Ettu***; *Intiguttu*; **1959**: *Sati Tulasi*; *Pelli Sandadi*; *Illarikam*; *Shabash Ramudu*; *Sipayi Kooturu*; ***Raja Mukutam***; **1960**: ***Shri Venkateshwara Mahatyam***; *Renukadevi Mahatyam*; *Kuladaivam*; *Pelli Kanuka*; *Sahasrachirasedha Chintamani*; *Rani Ratnaprabha*; *Jalsarayudu*; *Bhatti Vikramarka*; *Dharmane Jayam*; *Annapurna*; *Vimala*; **1961**: *Seeta Rama Kalyanam*; *Bharya Bartulu*; *Rushyashrunga/Rishyashringar*; *Iddaru Mithralu*; *Shanta*; *Tandrulu Kodukulu*; **1962**: *Bhishma*; *Khaidi Kannayya*; *Kalimilemulu*; ***Mahamantri Timmarasu***; ***Siri Sampadalu***; ***Kulagothralu***; *Constable Koothuru*; ***Aradhana***; ***Shri Krishnarjuna Yuddham***; **1963**: *Irugu Porugu*; *Savati Koduku*; *Chaduvukonna Ammayilu*; *Paruvu Pratishthalu*; *Eedu Jodu*; *Anuragham*; ***Bandhipotu***; *Lakshadhikari*; *Tirupathamma Katha*; ***Punarjanma***; ***Moogamanushulu***; *Naanum Oru Penn/Nadi Aada Janma*; **1964**: ***Murali Krishna***; *Peetalameeda Pelli*; *Dr Chakravarthi*; *Dagadu Moothulu*; *Varasatwam*; *Ramadasu*; ***Poojapalam***; **1965**: ***Pandava Vanavasam***; *Chandrahasa*; *Preminchi Choodu*; *Vishala Hridayalu*; ***CID***; **1966**: *Zamindar*; *Loguttu Perumallukeruka*; *Palnati Yuddham*; *Atmagauravam*; *Kanne Manushulu*; *Bhakta Potana*; *Hantakulostannuru Jagratha*; *Manase Mandiram*; **1967**: *Pattu Kunte Padivelu*; *Satyame Jayam*; *Upayamlo Apayam*; *Rahasyam*; *Peddakayya*; *Kambojuraju Katha*; ***Pranamithrulu***; **1968**: *Paala Manushulu*; *Sati Arundhati*; *Sircar Express*; *Govula Gopanna*; *Chuttarikalu*; *Mana Samsaram*; *Pantalu Pattimpulu*; *Aggimada Guggilam*; *Bangaru Sankellu*; *Bandhipotu Dongalu*; **1969**: *Jagath Kiladilu*; *Bhale Rangudu*; ***Buddhimanthudu***; *Shri Rama Katha*; *Tara Sasankam*; *Bhale Abbayilu*; *Adarsha Kutumbam*; **1970**: ***Maro Prapancham***; *Agni Pareeksha*; *Amma Kosam*; *Jai Jawan*; *Katha Nayika Molla*; *Pachani Samsaram*; **1971**: *Dasara Bullodu*; *Amayakuralu*; *Bangaru Kutumbam*; *Bhagyavanthudu*; *Bharya Biddalu*; *Nenu Manishine*; *Nindu Dampatulu*; *Pavitra Hridayalu*; *Prem Nagar*; *Sisindri Chittibabu*; *Suputhrudu*; **1972**: *Abbaigaru Ammaigaru*; *Atthanu Diddina Kodalu*; *Beedala Patlu*; *Kalam Marindi*; *Koduku Kodalu*; *Maa Inti Kodalu*; *Manchi Roluju Vastai*; *Marapurani Talli*; *Kalavari Kutumbam*; *Neethi Nijayathi*; *Collector Janaki*; *Sampoorna Ramayanam*; *Menakodalu*; ***Pandanti Kapuram***; *Vichitra Bandham*; *Vooriki Upakari*; *Illu Illalu*; *Bangaru Babu*; *Balamithrula Katha*; ***Tata Manuvudu***; **1973**: *Ramrajyam*; *Kanna Koduku*; *Kanne Vayasu*; *Snehabandham* (Te); *Marapurani Manishi*; *Samsaram Sagaram*; *Meena*; *Dr Babu*; *Jeevana Tarangulu*; *Khaidi Baba*; *Mallamma Katha*; *Minor Babu*; *Vichitra Vivaham*; *Vintha Katha*; *Kannavari Kalalu*; **1974**: *Gali Patalu*; *Intinti Katha*; *Chaduvu Samskaram*; *Manushulo Devadu*; *Anaganaga Oka Thandri*; *Tulasi*; *Jeevitha Rangamu*; *Mangalya Bhagyam*; *Ammayi Pelli*; *Peddalu Marali*; ***Alluri Seetaramaraju***; *Manushulu Matti Bommalu*; *Krishnaveni*; *Inti Kodalu*; *Dhanavanthulu Gunavanthulu*; ***Bhoomikosam***; *Dora Babu*; *Devadasu*; *Chinnanati Kalalu*; **1975**: *Kotha Kapuram*; *Lakshmana Rekha*; *Moguda Pellamma*; *Naaku Swatantram Vachindi*; *Pichodi Pelli*; *Soggadu*; *Saubhagyavati*; *Yashoda Krishna*; *Pandanti Samsaram*; *Babu*; *Zamindarugari Ammayi*; *Vaikunthapali*; *Chikati Velugulu*; **1976**: *Jyothi*; *Aradhana*; ***Seeta Kalyanam***; *Neram Nadhikadu Akalidi*; *Pogarubottu*; *America Ammayi*; *Adavallu Apanindalu*; *Bangaru Manishi*; *Devude Gelichadu*; *Mangalyaniki Maro Peru*; *Oka Deepam Veligindhi*; *Padavoyi Bharatheeyuda*; *Rama Rajyamlo Raktha Pasam*; *Secretary*; *Uttamuralu*; *Yavanam Katesindi*; **1977**: *Aalu Magalu*; ***Chakradhari***; *Ee Tharam Manishi*; *Geetha Sangeetha*; *Indra Dhanushu*; *Janma Janmala Bandham*; *Kalpana*; *Kurukshetramu*; *Savasagallu*; *Sati Savitri*; *Seeta Rama Vanavasu*; *Jeevana Theeralu*; *Jeevitha Nauka*; **1978**: *Sahasavanthudu*; *Manchi Babai*; *Kalanthakulu*; *Enki Nayudu Bava*; ***Akbar Saleem Anarkali***; *Allari Bullodu*; *Chal Mohanaranga*; *Devadasu Malli Puttadu*; *Dudubasavanna*; *Nindu Manishi*; *Prema Chesina Pelli*; *Simha Garajana*; *Vichitra Jeevitham*; *Ganga Bhawani*; **1979**: *Captain Krishna*; *Maa Inti Lakshmi*; *Manade Gundalu*; *Karthika Deepam*; *Bangaru Chellalu*; **1980**: *Premabhishekham*; *Sreevari Muchatlu*; *Kiladi Krishnudu*; **1981**: *Asha Jyoti*; *Jeevitha Ratnam*; **1982**: *Jagannatha Rathachakralu*; *Gopala Krishnudu*; *Kaliyuga Ramudu*; **1983**: *Dharma Poratam*; *Dharmathmudu*; *Ee Pillaku Pellavuthunda*; *Ekanaina Marindi*; *Koteeshwarudu*; *MLA Yedukondalu*; *Mundadugu*; *Police Venkataswamy*; *Prema Pichollu*; *Rojulu Marayi*; *Rudrakali*; *Sangharshana*; *Shubha Muhurtam*; *Todu Needa*; **1985**: *Kongumudi*; *O Thandri Teerpu*; **1987**: *Thene Manushulu*; **1991**: *Talli Tandrulu*; **1992**: *Brindavanamu*.

VENKATRAMAIAH, RELANGI (1910-75)

Telugu actor born in Ravulapadu, AP. Educated in Kakinada. Professional folk Harikatha performer. Also did folk theatre and acted female roles in stage musicals. Expert

Relangi Venkatramaiah in *Varakatnam* (1968)

harmonium player. Joined films playing the Vidushaka (jester) in **C. Pullaiah**'s *Shri Krishna Tulabharam*. Assisted Pullaiah as production manager for several years before returning to acting. Became a star with *Gollabhama*. First major comedy role in *Vindhyarani*, continuing his reputation as a comedy actor in ***Missamma***, *Bhale Ramudu* and *Iddaru Mithralu*. Played minor roles until the late 50s, becoming a regular face in **Vijaya** Studio films. Often paired with Suryakantam (e.g. ***Samsaram***), and formed a trio with Girija and Ramana Reddy.

FILMOGRAPHY: **1935**: *Shri Krishna Tulabharam*; **1939**: ***Varavikrayam***; **1940**: *Malathi Madhavam*; **1942**: ***Balanagamma***; **1947**: *Gollabhama*; **1948**: *Madalasa*; *Vindhyarani*; **1949**: ***Gunsundari Katha***; ***Keeluguram/Maya Kudhirai***; ***Mana Desam***; **1950**: *Maya Rambha*; ***Samsaram***; ***Shavukaru***; *Vali Sugriva*; ***Paramanandayya Shishyulu Katha***; **1951**: ***Patala Bhairavi/Pataal Bhairavi***; *Perantalu*; ***Agni Pareeksha***; **1952**: ***Daasi***; *Dharmadevata*; *Manavati*; ***Pelli Chesi Choodu/Kalyanam Panni Paar***; ***Pedaraitu***; ***Prema/Kathal***; *Priyuralu*; *Tinguranga*; **1953**: *Bratuku Theruvu*; ***Chandirani***; ***Pakkinti Ammayi***; *Paropakaram*; ***Ammalakulu/Marumagal***; ***Chandraharam***; ***Pardesi***; **1954**: ***Pedda Manushulu***; *Aggiramudu*; *Amara Sandesham*; *Balanandam*; *Maa Gopi*; *Raju Peda*; *Sati Sakkubai*; ***Vipranarayana***; **1955**: *Cherupukura Chedevu*; *Jayasimha/Jaisingh*; *Shri Krishna Tulabharam*; ***Missamma/Missiamma***; ***Rojulu Marayi/Kalam Maripochu***; ***Santhanam***; *Santosham/Naya Admi*; *Vadina*; *Vijayagauri*; ***Donga Ramudu***; *Aadabidda*; **1956**: ***Chintamani***; *Harishchandra*; *Ilavelpu*; *Bhale Ramudu/Prema Pasham*; *Jayam Manade*; *Shri Gauri Mahatyam*; *Umasundari*; *Mathurkula Manikyam/Charanadasi*; *Penki Pellam*; **1957**: *Dongalo Dora*; *Sarangadhara*; *Sati Savitri*; *Nala Damayanti*; *Repu Neede*; ***Maya Bazaar***; *Dampatyam*; *Peddarikalu*; *Allavudeenum Arputha Vilakkum/Allauddin Adbhuta Deepam/Alladdin Ka Chirag*; ***Suvarna Sundari/Manalane Mangayin Bhagyam***; *Veera Kankanam*; *Bhale Bhava*; *Sankalpam*; *Bhale Ammayilu/Iru Sahodarargal*; *Sati Ansuya*; *Thodi Kodallu*; ***Bhagya Rekha***; **1958**: ***Ettuku Pai Ettu***; *Anna Thamudu*; ***Chenchulakshmi***; *Raja Nandini*; *Shobha*; *Aadapettanam*; *Manchi Manushuku Manchi Rojulu*; *Bhuloka Rambha*; ***Appu Chesi Pappu Koodu/Kadam Vangi Kalyanam***; **1959**: *Mangalya Balam/Manjal Magimai*; *Jayabheri*; *Veer Bhaskaradu*; *Illarikam*; *Rechukka Pragatichukka*; *Shabash Ramudu*; *Daivabalam*; *Vachina Kodulu Nachindi*; *Bandaramudu/Adisaya Thirudan*; *Balanagamma*; *Bhagya Devatha*; *Kalasivunte Kaladu Sukham*; **1960**: *Shantinivasam*; ***Shri Venkateshwara Mahatyam***; *Kuladaivam*; *Rani Ratnaprabha*; *Dharmane Jayam*; *Pelli Kanuka*; *Mahakavi Kalidasa*; *Kumkumarekha*; *Bhakta Raghunath*; *Kodeduddulu Ekaramnela*; *Annapurna*; *Runanubandham*; *Abhimanam*; *Samajam*; *Vimala*; **1961**: *Velugu Needulu*; *Usha Parinayam*; *Intiki Deepam Illale*; *Bhakta Jayadeva*; *Bharya Bartulu*; *Pelli Pilupu*; *Krishna Prema*; *Rushyashrunga/Rishyashringar*; *Taxi Ramudu*; *Vagdanam*; ***Jagadeka Veeruni Katha***; *Iddaru Mithralu*; *Raktha Sambandham*; **1962**: *Mohini Rugmangada*; *Khaidi Kannayya*; ***Aradhana***; *Tiger Ramudu*; *Pelli Thambulam*; *Bhishma*; ***Gundamma Katha***; ***Mahamantri Timmarasu***; ***Kulagothralu***; ***Siri Sampadalu***; *Ashajeevulu*; *Atmabandhuvu*; **1963**: *Irugu Porugu*; *Edureetha*; *Pempudu Koothuru*; *Chaduvukonna Ammayilu*; *Paruvu Pratishthalu*; *Anuragham*; ***Bandhipotu***; *Lakshadhikari*; *Savati Koduku*; **1964**: *Mahiravana*; *Atmabalam*; *Gudigantalu*; ***Amarashilpi Jakanna***; *Deshadrohulu*; *Ramudu Bheemudu*; *Babruvahana*; *Varasatwam*; ***Poojapalam***; **1965**: *Sumangali*; *Mangamma Sapatham*; ***Satya Harishchandra***; *Prameelarjuneyam*; *Preminchi Choodu*; *Vishala Hridayalu*; *Sati Sakkubai*; *Aadabrathuku*; *Simhachala Kshetram*; **1966**: *Zamindar*; *Atmagauravam*; *Navarathri*; *Srikakula Andhra Mahavishnu Katha*; *Vijayasankalam*; *Goodachari 116*; *Letamanushulu*; *Adugu Jadalu*; *Manase Mandiram*; *Astiparulu*; *Ramu*; **1967**: *Bhakta Prahlada*; *Pinni*; *Sati Sumati*; ***Pranamithrulu***; ***Bhale Kodalu***; *Vasantsena*; *Private Master*; *Rahasyam*; ***Aada Paduchu***; **1968**: ***Varakatnam***; *Veerapooja*; *Talliprema*; *Tikka Shankaraiah*; *Govula Gopanna*; *Amayukudu*; *Chinnari Papalu*; *Chuttarikalu*; *Challani Needa*; *Bangaru Gajulu*; *Umachandi Gauri Shankarula Katha*; *Kalasina Manushulu*; *Pelliroju*; *Baghdad Gajadonga*; *Nindu Samsaram*; **1969**: *Shri Rama Katha*; *Bhale Abbayilu*; ***Nindu Hridayalu***; *Bhale Tammudu*; *Mathrudevata*; *Karpura Arathi*; **1970**: *Dharmadatha*; *Pettandarulu*; *Vidhi Vilasam*; *Yamalokapu Goodachari*; *Kodalu Diddina Kapuram*; **1971**: *Jeevitha Chakram*; *Patindalla Bangaram*; **1972**: *Kalavari Kutumbam*; *Shabash Papanna*; **1973**: *Dabbuku Lokam Dasoham*; *Geetha*; *Dr Babu*; *Ganga Manga*; *Manavu Manasu*; *Palletoori Bhava*; **1974**: *Mugguru Ammayilu*; *Manushulo Devadu*; *Radhamma Pelli*; *Ram Rahim*; **1975**: *Pooja*; **1976**: *Vadhu Varulu*.

VENU, MASTER (1916-81)

Telugu music composer born in Bandar, AP. Learnt music from a relative, Ramaiah Naidu, and later Chebrolu Venkatarathnam. Concert vocalist as a teenager. Introduced by Dr Giri of the Giri Museum in Madras to music director **B. Narasimha Rao** (1938), whom he assisted on ***Raitu Bidda*** (1939) and *Meerabai* (1940). Also worked in **Vasant Desai**'s orchestra. Employed as chief conductor of the **Vijaya** Studio orchestra, pioneering the use of electronic synthesisers in Telugu films. First film as composer, ***Anta Manavalle***, at Sarathi Studio. Became a star with ***Rojulu Marayi***, esp. with the folk number *Eruvaaka sagaloi*. The song, enacted by **Waheeda Rehman** in her screen début, caused major debates regarding its origins. It was adapted into Tamil and **S.D. Burman** made its Hindi version for ***Bambai Ka Babu*** (1960).

FILMOGRAPHY: **1950**: *Vali Sugriva*; **1954**: ***Anta Manavalle***; **1955**: ***Rojulu Marayi/Kalam Maripochu***; **1956**: *Melukolupu*; **1957**: *Sati Savitri*; *Peddarikalu*; **1958**: ***Ettuku Pai Ettu***; **1959**: *Mangalya Balam/Manjal Magimai*; *Bhagya Devatha*; ***Raja Mukutam***; *Kalasivunte Kaladu Sukham*; **1960**: *Shantinivasam*; *Kuladaivam*; *Kumkumarekha*; *Jalsarayudu*; **1961**: *Batasari/Kanal Neer*; **1962**: ***Siri Sampadalu***; **1963**: *Irugu Porugu*; *Somavara Vratham*; **1964**: ***Murali Krishna***; **1965**: *Preminchi Choodu*; **1966**: *Adugu Jadalu*; **1968**: *Kalasina Manushulu*; *Vintha Kapuram*; *Nindu Samsaram*; *Bharya*; *Baghdad Gajadonga*; **1969**: *Bommalu Cheppina Katha*; *Ardha Rathri*; **1970**: *Aada Janma*; *Vidhi Vilasam*; **1972**: *Atthanu Diddina Kodalu*; **1974**: *Uttama Illalu*; **1975**: *Andaru Bagundali*; **1976**: *Vadhu Varulu*; **1978**: *Melukolupu*; **1980**: *Maa Inti Devatha*.

VIJAYA PICTURES

Production company established in partnership between erstwhile publishers (and owners of BNK Press) B. Nagi Reddy and **Chakrapani**. They started with **L.V. Prasad**'s first film, ***Shavukaru*** (1950). Nagi Reddy had invested in **Vauhini** (1949) and became its studio manager, while Chakrapani was mainly a scenarist. With the production wing of Vauhini still run by its founder, **B.N. Reddi**, the Nagi Reddy-Chakrapani duo started their own production unit, Vijaya Pics, which gradually took over the studio's entire production section. Known as the Vijaya-Vauhini Studio complex, it is considered one of South India's most elaborately equipped studio floors. Invented the folklore genre with ***Maya Bazaar*** (1957), ***Patala Bhairavi*** (1958), ***Jagadeka Veeruni Katha*** (1961) et al., in part derived from the children's fiction published in the 14-edition children's journal *Chandamama* published by the BNK Press. Since the landmark hit *Shavukaru*, Vijaya's productions are known mainly for relatively low-budget family films, a genre pioneered by L.V. Prasad (***Pelli Chesi Choodu***, 1952; ***Missamma***, 1955; ***Appu Chesi Pappu Koodu***, 1958) and expanded by Vijaya in Tamil and Hindi. The films were directed by e.g., **K.V. Reddy**, **K. Kameshwara Rao**, **Chanakya**, **T. Prakash Rao** (who made their Hindi film *Ghar Ghar Ki Kahani*, 1970) and **K.S. Sethumadhavan** (***Julie***, 1975).

VIJAYABHASKAR (b. 1931)

Kannada music director since 1955; worked in 6 languages. Best known for **Puttanna Kanagal**'s films. Work includes classic songs from ***Bellimoda***, ***Nagara Haavu*** and *Manasa Sarovara*. Also worked with **Lakshminarayan** and **Nagabharana** (e.g. ***Grahana***, with music drawn from tribal folk rituals). Formally trained in both Carnatic and North Indian classical music (the latter under G.K. Bhave) and worked as assistant to **Naushad** and Madhavlal Master before becoming an independent composer. His second assignment, **Y.V. Rao**'s *Bhagya Chakra*, was based on his own script and dialogues as well.

FILMOGRAPHY: **1955**: *Shrirama Pooja*; **1956**: *Bhagya Chakra*; **1957**: *Premada Putri/Preme Daivam/Anbe Daivam*; **1960**: *Rani Honamma*; **1963**: *Mana Mechhida Madadi*; *Sant Tukaram*; **1964**: *Post Master*; *Pathiye Daiva*; ***Nandi***; **1965**: *Beretha Jeeva*; *Amarajeevi*; **1966**: *Thoogu Deepa*; *Kusirthikuttan/Anni*; **1967**: *Jeevikan Anuvadhikuka*; ***Bellimoda***; *Lagna Patrike*; *Premakku Permitte*; *Pathirapattu*; **1968**: *Kayalkarayil*; *Manku Dinne*; *Mysore Tonga*; *Bhagyada Bagilu*; *Anandakanda*; *Anna Thamma*; *Natasarva Bhowma*; *Manninamaga*; **1969**: *Suvarnabhoomi*; *Namma Makkalu*; *Mallammana Pavada*; *Eradu Mukha*; *Makkale Manege Manikya*; ***Uyyale***; *Brindavana*; **1970**: ***Gejje Pooje***; *Arishina Kumkuma*; *Anirikshita*; *Bhoopathiranga*; *Takka! Bitre Sikka!!*; *Lakshmi Saraswathi*; *Balu Belagithu*; *Aaru Mooru Ombattu*; *Seeta*; ***Mukti***; *Balapanjara*; **1971**:

Sharapanjara; *Signalman Siddappa*; *Kalyani*; *Bhale Adrushtavo Adrushta*; **1972**: *Yavajanmada Maitri*; *Hridayasangama*; *Naa Mechida Huduga*; *Nanda Gokula*; *Mareyada Deepavali*; *Jeevana Jokaali*; ***Nagara Haavu***; **1973**: *Devaru Kotta Thangi*; *CID 72*; *Sankalpa*; *Seetheyalla Savithri*; *Jaya Vijaya*; *Mane Belagida Sose*; *Kesarina Kamala*; ***Abachurina Post Office***; **1974**: *Upasane*; *Krishnaveni*; *Kalyanamam Kalyanam*; *Ungal Virupam*; *Unnaithan Thambi*; *Engamma Sabatham*; **1975**: *Aan Pillai Singam*; *Engalukkum Kathal Varum*; *Malai Sooda Va*; *Mayangurikal Oru Madhu*; *Thottathellam Ponnagum*; *Unga Veetu Kalyanam*; *Uravu Solla Oruvan*; *Yarukku Mappillai Yaro*; *Ammayila Sabatham*; *Shubhamangala*; *Kasturi Vijaya*; *Bhagya Jyothi*; *Ninagagi Nanu*; *Bili Hendthi*; *Hennu Samsarada Kannu*; ***Katha Sangama***; **1976**: *Makkala Bhagya*; *Besuge*; *Chiranjeevi*; *Tulasi*; *Maya Manushya*; *Phalithamsha*; *Kalangalil Aval Vasantham*; *Moham Muppathu Varusham*; *Kalamadi Kalam*; *Sangharsha*; **1977**: *Aadu Puli Atham*; *Aval Oru Athisayam*; *Mamiyar Veedu*; *Olimayamana Ethirkalam*; *Harake*; *Deepa*; *Magiya Kanasu*; *Mugdha Manava*; *Kumkuma Rakshe*; *Banashankari*; *Devare Dikku*; *Ganda Hendthi*; **1978**: *Havina Hejje*; *Siritanakke Saval*; *Paduvarahalli Pandavaru*; *Premayana*; *Thappida Tala/Thappu Thalangal*; *Vasanthalakshmi*; *Aluku*; *Amarnath*; *Pare Solla Oru Pillai*; *Rajavukku Etha Rani*; ***Grahana***; **1979**: *Adalu Badalu*; *Sadananda*; *Muyyi*; *Mallige Sampige*; *Dangeyedda Makkalu*; **1980**: *Akhanda Brahmacharigalu*; *Hanthakana Sanchu*; *Kappu Kola*; *Ellindalo Bandavaru*; *Subbi Subakka Suvvalali*; *Namma Mane Sose*; *Mother*; *Bangarada Jinke*; *Mithuna*; *Driver Hanumanthu*; *Hare Krishna Hello Radha*; *Sundarime Varuga Varuga*; *Anveshane*; **1981**: *Sooravalli*; *Leader Vishwanath*; *Tirada Bayake*; *Chalagara*; *Nari Swargakke Dari*; *Balu Bangara*; *Bangarada Mane*; *Preetisi Nodu*; **1982**: *Jodi Jeeva*; *Jimmygallu*; *Manasa Sarovara*; *Suvarna Sethuve*; **1983**: *Devara Tirpu*; *Dharanimandala Madhyadolage*; ***Banker Margayya***; *Matte Vasantha*; *Ananda Sagara*; *Muttaide Bhagya*; *Amayaka Chakravarthi*; *Oru Kayi Paapam*; **1984**: *Rajahmundhry Romeo*; *Amrutha Galige*; *Shubha Muhurta*; *Huli Hejje*; *Pavitra Prema*; *Runamukthalu*; **1985**: *Haavu Eni Aata*; *Mavano Aliyano*; *Manasada Hoovu*; *Bhayankara Bakasarudu*; **1986**: *Thavaru Mane*; *Nenapina Doni*; *Sundara Swapnagalu*; ***Malaya Marutha***; **1987**: *Huli Hebbuli*; *Thaliya Aane*; *Aaseya Bale*; *Avasthe*; *Bandha Mukti*; *Surya*; *Antima Ghatta*; **1988**: *Thayiya Aase*; *Bhoomi Thayane*; *Gudugu Sidilu*; *Thayigobba Karna*; *Mithileya Seetheyaru*; *Kadina Benki*; **1989**: *Thaligagi*; *Madhu Maasa*; ***Mathilukal***; *Amrutha Bindu*; **1990**: *Yeduru Mane Meena*; *Prathama Usha Kirana*.

VIJAYANIRMALA (b. 1945)

Telugu actress and director. Started acting aged 5 under **P. Pullaiah** (*Macharekhai*), in male role. Début in adult roles in Tamil and Malayalam: B. Nagi Reddy's ***Enga Veetu Penn*** (a remake of ***Shavukaru***, 1950) for the **Vijaya** Studio, whence her screen name. Cast in **A. Vincent**'s début, ***Bhargavi Nilayam*** (Malayalam) playing the ghost. May have acted in 60s Malayalam films under the pseudonyms Neerja and Usha Kumari. First Telugu film was **Bapu**'s ***Saakshi***, after which she married its star, **Krishna**, working with his Padmalaya Studio since then. Appeared in over 130 films in Telugu, Kannada and Malayalam.

Vijayanirmala in *Pulliman* (1972)

Directorial début with *Kavitha* in Malayalam, later remade in Telugu. Together with her husband, set up own production company and directed most of their films, at times starring her son, Naresh, but mostly featuring Krishna himself, one of **NTR**'s main rivals. Her film *Sahasame Naa Upiri* was a campaign film on behalf of the Congress(I), attacking NTR's government. Made many box-office hits but is said to prefer her flop, *Devadasu*, which starred Krishna in her version of the classic Saratchandra love story featuring her as Paro opposite Krishna's Devdas.

FILMOGRAPHY (* also d/** only d): **1950**: *Macharekhai*; **1957**: *Panduranga Mahatyam*; **1958**: ***Bhukailasa***; **1964**: ***Bhargavi Nilayam***; **1965**: ***Enga Veetu Penn***; **1966**: *Kalyana Rathriyil*; *Puchakanni*; ***Chitthi***; ***Rangula Ratnam***; **1967**: *Padhyam*; ***Anveshichu Kandatiyilla***; *Udyogastha*; *Pooja*; *Pinni*; ***Saakshi***; *Upayamlo Apayam*; ***Bhale Kodalu***; *Poolarangudu*; **1968**: *Sircar Express*; *Attagaru Kottakodalu*; ***Bangaru Pichika***; *Nilagiri Express*; *Soppu Seppu Kannadi*; *Uyira Manama*; *Sathyam Thavarathe*; *Karutha Pournami*; **1969**: *Love in Andhra*; *Manchi Mithrulu*; *Bommalu Cheppina Katha*; *Takkaridonga Chakkanichukka*; *Vichitra Kutumbam*; *Muhurtabalam*; *Mamaku Tagga Kodalu*; *Anna Damulu*; ***Buddhimanthudu***; *Prema Kanuka*; *Bandhipotu Bhimanna*; **1970**: *Agni Pareeksha*; *Amma Kosam*; *Alludu Menalludu*; *Akkachellelu*; *Maa Nanna Nirdoshi*; *Malli Pelli*; *Marina Manishi*; *Pagasadhishta*; *Pettandarulu*; *Rendu Kutumbala Katha*; *Pelli Sambandham*; *Talli Bottu*; *Vidhi Vilasam*; **1971**: *Adavi Veerulu*; *Anuradha*; *Rowdy Rangadu*; *Ramalayam*; *Bangaru Kutumbam*; *Bangaru Talli*; *Bomma Borusa*; *Master Kiladi*; *Mosagalluku Mosagadu*; *Nindu Dampatulu*; *Vichitra Dampathyam*; *Bullemma Bullodu*; **1972**: *Kalippava*; ***Gnana Oli***; *Pulliman*; *Postmane Kananilla*; *Manchivallaku Manchivadu*; *Shabash Papanna*; ***Tata Manuvudu***; *Bhale Mosagadu*; ***Pandanti Kapuram***; *Kathula Rathaiah*; *Maa Inti Velugu*; **1973**: *Nija Roopalu*; *Varasuralu*; *Nenu Naa Desam*; *Devudu Chesina Manushulu*; *Kavitha**; *Meena**; *Ponnapuram Kotta*; *Kattu Vithachavan*; *Thenaruvi*; *Pavangal Pennungal*; **1974**: *Durga*; *Devadasu**; *Gali Patalu*; *Banthrotu Bharya*; *Dhanavanthulu Gunavanthulu*; *Jeevithasayam*; ***Alluri Seetaramaraju***; *Nitya Sumangali*; *Ram Rahim*; **1975**: *Mallela Manushulu*; *Santhanam Saubhagyam*; *Pichodi Pelli*; *Padi Panthulu*; *Kavitha**; **1976**: *Devude Gelichadu**; *Rama Rajyamlo Raktha Pasam*; *Colonel and Collector*; **1977**: *Ardhangi*; *Kurukshetramu*; *Morotudu*; *Maarpu*; ***Chakradhari***; *Chillarakottu Chittamma*; *Panchayathi**; **1978**: *Moodu Puvvulu Aaru Kayalu**; *Rowdy Rangamma**; *Prema Chesina Pelli**; *Devadasu Malli Puttadu*; *Manavoori Pandavalu*; *Patnavasam*; **1979**: *Bangaru Chellalu*; *Korikile Gurralaite*; *Sangam Chekkina Silpalu**; *Hema Hemeelu**; *Sankhu Teertham**; **1980**: *Ram Robert Rahim**; *Kiladi Krishnudu**; *Sirimalle Navvindi**; *Raktha Sambandham***; **1981**: *Antham Kadidi Arambham**; *Bhogimanthulu**; **1982**: *Doctor Cineactor**; *Prema Sankellu**; **1983**: *Todu Needa*; *Amayakudu Kadhu Asadhyudu***; *Bezwada Bebbuli**; *Chattaniki Veyi Kallu***; *Lanke Bindelu***; **1984**: *Mukhya Mantri***; *Mukkopi**; *Sumangali Kolam**; **1985**: *Vijeta*; *Hasyabhishekham*; *Surya Chandra***; **1986**: *Shantinivasam**; *Naa Pilupe Prabhanjanam*; *Krishna Paramatma**; *Parasuramudu**; **1987**: *Sankharavam**; *Pagasadhishta**; *Mandala Dheesudu*; *Collector Vijaya**; **1988**: *Rowdy No. 1*; *Praja Pratinidhi*; **1989**: *Prajala Manishi*; *Gandipeta Rahasyam*; *Pinni**; *Sahasame Naa Upiri**; *Ajatashatru**; **1991**: *Vadina Mata**.

VINAYAK DAMODAR KARNATAKI, MASTER (1906-47)

Marathi and Hindi actor-director known as Master Vinayak. Born and educated in Kolhapur. Son of the cinematographer Vasudev Karnataki and cousin of **Baburao Pendharkar**. Started as a teacher while acting on the Marathi stage, then actor in **Shantaram**'s films, making his mark in the early **Prabhat** films with his powerful singing and acrobatic acting style. Moved to **Kolhapur Cinetone** (1933) where he made his first film, ***Vilasi Ishwar***. Launched the famous Huns Pics (1936), later **Navyug Chitrapat** (1940), and then Prafulla Pics (1943-7). Used remarkable scripts by Mama Warerkar, **P.K. Atre** and **V.S. Khandekar**, members of a new literary generation aggressively seeking to go beyond the then dominant social reform conventions. Scripts engaged with contemporary politics, transforming melodrama into satire, deploying slang and journalistic techniques. Often played the gullible fool, in ***Brahmachari***, ***Ardhangi***, ***Dharmaveer***. Also did some inspired casting, e.g. the Gundyabhau-Chimanrao duo reminiscent of Laurel and Hardy played by **Malvankar** and Vishnupant Jog, based on C.V. Joshi's celebrated political satires (***Lagna Pahave Karun*** and ***Sarkari Pahune***, both scripted by Khandekar). Huns Pics commissioned scripts from writer-director teams, e.g. V.V. Bokil and R.S. Junnarkar (***Pahili Mangalagaur***, 1942) or Bokil and Vasant Joglekar (*Chimukla Sansar*, 1943). This system was continued by Atre's productions and by, e.g., P.L. Deshpande and Ram Gabale (*Doodh Bhaat*, *Ghardhani*, both 1952) and **G.D. Madgulkar** and **Raja Paranjpe**. His biography was written by his chief disciple **Dinkar D. Patil** (1971), who finished Vinayak's last feature, *Mandir*.

FILMOGRAPHY (* also d/** only d): 1932: ***Ayodhyecha Raja/Ayodhya Ka Raja***; ***Jalti Nishani/Agnikankan***; ***Maya Machhindra***; **1933**: *Sairandhri*; ***Sinhagad***; **1934**: ***Akashwani***; **1935**: ***Bhikharan***; ***Vilasi Ishwar/Nigah-e-Nafrat****; **1936**: ***Chhaya****; **1937**: ***Dharmaveer****; *Premveer**; **1938**: ***Jwala****; ***Brahmachari****; **1939**: ***Brandichi Batli/Brandy Ki Botal*****; ***Devata*****; **1940**: ***Ardhangi/Ghar Ki Rani****; ***Lagna Pahave Karun*****; ***Lapandav***; **1941**: *Sangam*; ***Amrit****; **1942**: ***Sarkari Pahune*****; **1943**: ***Mazhe Bal****; *Chimukla Sansar*; **1944**: *Gajabhau***; **1945**: ***Badi Maa*****; **1946**: ***Subhadra*****; ***Jeevan Yatra*****; ***Dr Kotnis Ki Amar Kahani***; **1948**: *Mandir***.

VINCENT, ALOYSIUS (b. 1928)

Malayalam director and noted cameraman born in Calicut, Kerala, in a Syrian Christian family. Apprentice cameraman at the **Gemini** Studio (1947) where he assisted Kamal Ghosh and N. Natarajan. Key technician on **Kariat**'s ***Neelakuyil*** (1954) and later on ***Mudiyanaya Puthran*** (1961); also worked for Venus Pics, Madras: e.g. **T. Prakash Rao**'s ***Amara Deepam*** (1956), **Sridhar**'s ***Kalyana Parisu*** (1959). Début as director with landmark Malayalam film ***Bhargavi Nilayam***, a fantasy derived from Vaikom Mohammed Basheer's writing. Became a noted reformist director together with, e.g., **Sethumadhavan**, often using scripts by the novelist and scenarist **M.T. Vasudevan Nair** (e.g. ***Murappennu***, *Nagarame Nandi*, ***Asuravithu***). He does not usually photograph his own films.

FILMOGRAPHY: 1964: ***Bhargavi Nilayam***; **1965**: ***Murappennu***; **1967**: ***Ashwamedham***; *Nagarame Nandi*; *Engalukam Kalamvaryam*; **1968**: ***Asuravithu***; ***Thulabharam***; **1969**: *Almaram*; ***Nadhi***; **1970**: *Nizhalattam*; *Triveni*; **1971**: ***Abhijathyam***; **1972**: *Gandharvakshetram*; *Teerthayatra*; **1973**: *Chenda*; *Achani*; *Nakhangal*; *Dharma Yuddham*; **1974**: *Thirumangalyam*; **1975**: *Nalla Marumagal*; *Priyamulla Sophia*; **1976**: *Anavaranam*; **1977**: *Agni Nakshatram*; *Naam Pirandha Maan*; **1978**: *Vayanadan Thampan*; *Anappachan*; **1982**: *Ponnu Poovam*; **1983**: *Theeram Thedunna Thira*; **1984**: *Shri Krishnaparunthu*; **1985**: *Pournami Ravil*; *Kochuthemmadi*.

VISHNUVARDHAN (b. 1952)

With Ambarish, the top male star in 70s/80s Kannada film. Début in **Karnad/Karanth**'s ***Vamsha Vriksha***. Made a major impression as the misguided rebel in **Kanagal**'s ***Nagara Haavu***: with hunched shoulders and stunted, reptilian moves he gave perhaps the one classic Kanagal performance replete with overtly phallic symbology and dramatic fatalism transcending psychological naturalism. The film showed he was capable of more than the star turns in discotheques and elaborate song picturisations which constitute the bulk of his work (esp. ***Premaloka***). Acted often with **S.V. Rajendra Singh**, notably the army officer in ***Muthina Hara***. Début in Hindi cinema with **Ramsay**'s *Inspector Dhanush*.

FILMOGRAPHY: 1971: ***Vamsha Vriksha***; **1972**: ***Nagara Haavu***; **1973**: *Seetheyalla Savithri*; *Mane Belagida Sose*; *Gandhadagudi*; *Alaigal*; **1974**: *Boothayyana Maga Ayyu*; *Professor Huchuraya*; *Anna Attige*; *Devara Gudi*; **1975**: *Koodi Balona*; *Kalla Kulla*; *Bhagya Jyothi*; *Naga Kanye*; *Onderupa Eradu Guna*; *Lakshmi Nirdoshi*; *Devaru Kotta Vara*; *Hosilu Mettida Hennu*; **1976**: *Pellade Bomma*; *Makkala Bhagya*; *Bangarada Gudi*; **1977**: *Bayasade Banda Bhagya*; *Sose Thanda Saubhagya*; ***Nagarhole***; *Chinna Ninna Muddaduve*; *Shrimanthana Magalu*; *Sahodarara Saval*; *Shani Prabhava*; *Galate Samsara*; *Kittu Puttu*; **1978**: *Hombisilu*; *Sandarbha*; *Kiladi Kittu*; *Vamsa Jyothi*; *Muyyige Muyyi*; *Siritanakke Saval*; *Pratima*; *Nanna Prayashchitta*; *Sneha Sedu*; *Kiladi Jodi*; *Vasanthalakshmi*; *Amarnath*; *Bhale Huduga*; *Madhura Sangama*; *Singaporenalli Raja Kulla*; **1979**: *Asadhya Aliya*; *Vijaya Vikram*; *Na Niruvude Ninagangi*; *Manini*; *Nentaro Gantu Kalloro*; **1980**: *Nanna Rosha Nooru Varusha*; *Rama Parashurama*; *Kalinga*; *Hanthakana Sanchu*; *Makkala Sainya*; *Biligiriya Bandalalli*; *Simha Jodi*; *Rahasya Rathri*; *Bangarada Jinke*; *Driver Hanumanthu*; *Mazhalai Pattalam*; **1981**: *Mane Mane Kathe*; *Naga Kala Bhairava*; *Maha Prachandaru*; *Guru Shishyaru*; *Snehitara Saval*; *Avala Hejje*; *Preetisi Nodu*; *Adimachangala*; **1982**: *Pedda Gedda*; *Sahasa Simha*; *Karmika Kallanalla*; *Urige Upakari*; *Jimmygallu*; *Suvarna Sethuve*; **1983**: *Onde Guri*; *Kalluveene Nudiyitu*; *Sididedda Sahodara*; *Gandharvagiri*; *Gandugalli Rama*; *Chinnadanta Maga*; *Simha Garjane*; **1984**: *Purnandayya Shishyulu Katha*; *Sardar Ramudu*; *Prachanda Kulla*; *Rudranaga*; *Khaidi*; *Benki Birugali*; *Endina Ramayana*; *Huli Hejje*; *Bandhana*; *Chanakya*; *Aradhane*; *Madhuve Madu Tamashe Nodu*; **1985**: *Kartavya*; *Mahapurusha*; *Veeradhi Veera*; *Nee Bareda Kadambari*; *Kiladi Aliya*; *Mareyada Manikya*; *Nanna Prathigne*; *Jeevana Chakra*; *Nee Thanda Kanike*; *Eetti*; *Mazhakkala Megham*; **1986**: *Karna*; *Ee Jeeva Ninagagi*; *Katha Nayaka*; *Satya Jyothi*; *Krishna Nee Begane Baaro*; ***Malaya Marutha***; *Viduthalai*; **1987**: ***Premaloka***; *Saubhagya Lakshmi*; *Karunamayi*; *Jayasimha*; *Aaseya Bale*; *Jeevana Jyothi*; *Shubha Milana*; *Satyam Shivam Sundaram*; **1988**: *December 31st*; *Olavina Asare*; *Nammoora Raja*; *Jana Nayaka*; *Suprabhata*; *Krishna Rukmini*; *Mithileya Seetheyaru*; *Dada*; **1989**: *Ondagi Baalu*; *Hridaya Geethe*; *Rudra*; *Deva*; *Doctor Krishna*; **1990**: *Shiva Shankar*; ***Muthina Hara***; *Mathe Hadithu Kogile*; **1991**: *Lion Jagapathy Rao*; *Neenu Nakkare Haalu Sakkare*; *Jagadeka Veera*; *Inspector Dhanush/Police Mattu Dada*; **1992**: *Rajadhi Raja*; *Ravi Varma*; **1993**: *Sangharsha*; *Vaishakada Dinagalu*; *Nanendu Nimmavane*; *Rayara Bandharu Mavana Manege*; *Vishnu Vijaya*; *Ashant*.

VISHWANATH, KASHINADHURI (b. 1930)

Telugu and Hindi director born in Vijaywada, AP, where his father worked for **Vauhini** distribution. Science degree (1948) and started as sound engineer at Vauhini Studio. Assisted **Adurthi Subba Rao** at Annapurna and scripted, e.g., the **A. Nageshwara Rao** production *Sudigundalu* (1967). Made his début in Telugu with Nageshwara Rao's support, continuing the Annapurna brand of art-house melodrama. Broke through with ***Nindu Hridayalu***, followed by the major success of ***Shankarabharanam***, which led to a series of films on classical music and dance. Tends to advocate a vulgarised classicism passed off as traditionalism, even Hindu revivalism in the arts and moderate liberalism in social customs. Hindi début, *Sargam*, remade ***Siri Siri Muvva***. Has adapted several of his Telugu hits into Hindi, e.g. *Sur Sangam*, which remade *Shankarabharanam* with **Girish Karnad**. Writes his own Telugu films and prefers location shooting.

FILMOGRAPHY: 1965: *Atmagauravam*; **1967**: *Private Master*; **1968**: *Kalisochina Adrushtam*; *Undamma Bottupeduta*; **1969**: ***Nindu Hridayalu***; **1971**: *Nindu Dampatulu*; *Chinnanati Snehitulu*; *Chelleli Kapuram*; **1972**: *Kalam Marindi*; **1973**: ***Sharada***; *Neramu Siksha*; **1974**: *O Seeta Katha*; *Amma Manasu*; **1975**: *Jeevana Jyoti*; **1976**: *Mangalyaniki Maro Peru*; ***Siri Siri Muvva***; *Premabandham*; **1977**: *Jeevitha Nauka*; **1978**: *Kalanthakulu*; *Seetamalakshmi*; **1979**: *Sargam*; ***Shankarabharanam***; *President Peramma*; **1980**: *Alludu Pattina Bharatham*; *Subhodayam*; **1981**: *Saptapadi*; **1982**: *Shubhalekha*; *Kaamchor*; **1983**: ***Sagara Sangamam***; *Shubh Kaamna*; **1984**: *Jaag Utha Insaan*; *Janani Janma Bhoomi*; *Allulostunnaru*; **1985**: *Swati Muthyam*; *Sanjog*; *Sur Sangam*; **1986**: *Shrivenella*; **1987**: *Srutilayalu*; *Swayamkrushi*; **1988**: *Swarna Kamalam*; **1989**: *Eeshwar*; *Sutradharulu*; **1990**: *Sirimuvvala Simhanadamu*; **1991**: *Swati Kiranam*; **1992**: *Sangeet*; *Apath Bandhavulu*; **1993**: *Dhanwan*.

VITHAL, MASTER (?-1969)

Best-known Marathi and Hindi stunt star. Stage début as a child at the Rajapurkar Natak Mandali. Worked as editor at **Maharashtra Film**, a studio with a reputation for stunts in their mythologicals, e.g. by legendary actors Zunzharrao Pawar (1891-1982) or Ganpat Bakre (1901-1983). Vithal started playing a dancing-girl in ***Kalyan Khajina***. Acted in **Bhalji Pendharkar** silents before breaking through at the **Sharda** Studio. He was its top star for several years, usually playing Douglas Fairbanks-type roles grafted on to indigenous Rajput and Maratha legends. Bhogilal Dave's special effects accompanied his work, along with the rapid editing of directors like A.P. Kapur, **Nanubhai Desai**, **Harshadrai Mehta**, **Luhar**, etc. The style Vithal helped shape had a tremendous impact, making the Sharda Studio synonymous with low-budget stunt films in the silent era. **Wadia Movietone** later tried to redefine the stunt genre with direct reference to the Niblo/Fairbanks figure of Zorro to distance the genre from Vithal. Vithal also starred in India's first talkie, ***Alam Ara***, and in **Sagar** and Saraswathi Studio productions, ending his career in the 60s playing minor parts in Marathi films.

FILMOGRAPHY (* also d): **1924**: ***Kalyan Khajina***; **1925**: ***Bajirao Mastani***; **1926**: ***Vande Mataram Ashram***; *Vasant Bala*; *Ratan Manjari*; ***Suvarna Kamal***; *Madan Kala*; *Gunial Gulab*; **1927**: *Bansari Bala*; *Kala Pahad*; *Mahasati Ansuya*; *Swadesh Seva*; *Asuri Lalsa*; ***Balidan***; *Bhedi Trishul*; *Jaan-e-Alam Anjuman Ara*; *Shiraz-ud-Dowla*; *Veer Garjana*; **1928**: *Gul Badan*; *Hira Sundari*; *Kanak Kanta*; *Raj Tarang*; *Sassi Punnu*; *Sohni Mahiwal*; *Saundarya Sura*; *Karuna Kumari*; **1929**: *Nishan Danka*; *Chirag-e-Kohistan*; *Bhedi Sawar*; *Shiraz-ud-Dowla*; *Rank Nu Ratan*; *Veer Garjana*; *Rangilo Rajput*; *Mirza Sahiban*; **1930**: *Bachha-i-Sakka*; *Veer Na Ver*; *Arunodaya*; *Dav Pech*; **1931**: *Dilawar*; *Gulam*; *Meethi Churi*; *Hoor-e-Misar* (all St); ***Alam Ara***; *Anangsena*; *Daulat Ka Nasha*; *Meri Jaan*; **1932**: ***Zalim Jawani***; *Kalo Bhoot* (St); *Burkhewala* (St); **1933**: *Awara Shehzada/Aut Ghatkecha Raja**; **1934**: *Bhedi Rajkumar/Thaksen Rajputra*; *Chhatrapati Sambhaji*; **1935**: *Rangila Nawab*; *Jaan-e-Alam Anjuman Ara*; *Raj Tarang*; **1936**: *Hind Mahila*; **1937**: *Asiai Sitara*; **1939**: ***Netaji Palkar***; **1940**: *Jagat Mohini*; *Mohini*; **1941**: ***Amrit***; **1942**: *Sunbai*; **1943**: *Bahirji Naik*; **1944**: ***Ramshastri***; **1945**: *Nagma-e-Sahra*; *Pannadai*; **1946**: *Jadugar*; *Kashmir Ki Kali*; *Rukmini Swayamvar*; *Sasurvas*; **1947**: *Jai Bhawani*; **1948**: *Garibanche Rajya*; **1949**: *Vikram Shashikala*; ***Meeth Bhakar***; *Shilanganache Sone*; **1951**: *Swarajyacha Shiledar**; *Mard Maratha*; **1952**: ***Chhatrapati Shivaji***; *Mayecha Pazhar*; *Narveer Tanaji*; **1953**: *Tai Teleen*; *Vadal*; **1956**: *Pavankhind*; **1957**: *Naikinichi Sajja*; **1958**: *Matevin Bal*; **1959**: *Akashganga*; **1960**: *Vanakesari*; **1963**: *Mohityanchi Manjula*; **1965**: ***Sadhi Manse***; *Vavtal*; **1966**: *Sheras Savasher*; *Shodha Mhanje Sapdel*.

VITTALACHARYA, B. (b. 1920)

Telugu and Kannada director born in Udupi, Karnataka, in a region exceptionally rich in traditional performing arts. Professes an interest in stage mythologicals, magicians and the fantastic tales of Harikatha performers. Film début in the pioneering Kannada Mahatma Pics, in the tradition exemplified by the company's best-known film ***Nagakannika*** (1949). Shifted to Telugu films (1953), launching his own Vittal Prod. His work is characterised by fantasy, the evocation of legends, the use of special effects and of performing monkeys and dogs.

FILMOGRAPHY: 1952: *Shri Srinivasa Kalyana*; **1953**: *Saubhagya Lakshmi*; **1954**: *Kanyadana/Kanyadanam*; *Rajalakshmi*; **1956**: *Muttaide Bhagya*; **1957**: *Vaddante Pelli*; **1958**: *Mane Thumbida Hennu*; *Nabegebaboa Hennu*; **1959**: *Jayaveeran/Jayavijaya*; *Pelli Meeda Pelli*; **1960**: *Anna Chellalu*; *Kanakadurga Puja*; **1961**: *Varalakshmi Vratam*; **1962**: *Madana Kamaraju Katha*; *Khaidi Kannayya*; **1963**: ***Veera Kesari/Bandhipotu***; *Guruvuniminchina Shishyudu*; *Manthiri Kumaran*; **1964**: *Veera Pandian*; *Aggipidugu*; *Navagraha Pooja Mahima*; **1965**: *Vijayasimha*; *Mangamma Sapatham*; *Jwaladeepa Rahasyam*; **1966**: *Aggibarata*; *Piduguramudu*; *Madurai Manuvan*; **1967**: *Yar Vallavan*; *Aggidora*; *Iddaru Monagallu*; *Chikkadu Dorakudu*; **1968**: *Bhale Monagadu*; *Ninne Pelladuta*; **1969**: *Aggiveerudu*; *Gandikota Rahasyam*; *Kadaladu Vadaladu*; *Rani Dongala Rani*; **1970**: *Lakshmi Kataksham*; *Alibaba 40 Dongalu*; *Vijayam Manade*; **1971**: *Mosagalluku Mosagadu*; *Rajakota Rahasyam*; *Baghavat*; **1972**: *Beedala Patlu*; *Pilla? Piduga?*; **1973**: *Palletoori Chinnodu*; **1975**: *Kotalo Paga*; **1978**: ***Jagan Mohini***; **1979**: *Gandharva Kanya*; **1980**: *Madana Manjiri*; **1981**: *Shri Raghavendra Vaibhavam*; **1982**: *Lakshmi Pooja*; **1984**: *Nava Mohini*; **1986**: *Mohini Sapatham*; **1988**: *Sridevi Kamakshi Kataksham*; **1991**: *Shrishaila Bhamarambika Katakshyam*; **1992**: *Karuninchina Kanakdurga*.

VYAS, AVINASH (1912-84)

Foremost music director in Gujarati cinema with music for **Punatar**'s *Gunsundari* and ***Mangalfera***. Début with **V.M. Vyas**, but established himself at the **Ranjit** Studio. Also contributed to Ranjit film-makers **Chaturbhuj Doshi** and **Jayant Desai**'s efforts to establish a Gujarati film industry. His music was a key component of **Raskapur**'s films. Vyas pioneered a music industry in Gujarati before he entered films, composing songs for National Gramophone. Was a well-known AIR name in the 40s. Vyas's musical adaptations from the Hindi merged with popular Raas-Garba and Bhavai music from Gujarat, tailoring All-India Film formulas and 'national' genres to regional requirements, e.g. his semi-classical ballets choreographed by Yogendra Desai, such as *Chauladevi*, featuring Hindi star Asha Parekh.

FILMOGRAPHY: 1943: *Mahasati Ansuya*; **1944**: *Krishna Bhakta Bodana*; *Laheri Badmash*; **1947**: *Hothal Padmini*; *Janeta*; *Krishna Sudama*; *Seth Sagalsha*; **1948**: *Gunsundari*; *Jeevan Palto*; *Jesal Toral*; *Nanand Bhojai*; *Sati Sone*; *Radhe Shyam*; *Varasdar*; **1949**: *Gorakh Dhandha*; ***Mangalfera***; *Narad Muni*; *Sati Sukanya*; *Vargheli*; **1950**: *Akhand Saubhagya*; ***Gadano Bel***; ***Har Har Mahadev***; *Ramtaram*; **1951**: *Bhakta Tulsidas*; *Lagna Bandhan*; *Mangalsutra*; *Parnetar*; *Vadilono Varso*; *Dashavtar*; *Jai Mahalakshmi*; *Ram Janma*; *Shri Vishnu Bhagwan*; **1952**: *Rajrani Damayanti*; *Shivashakti*; *Veer Arjun*; *Manuni Masi*; **1953**: ***Bhagyavaan***; **1954**: *Maha Pooja*; *Mallika-e-Alam Nurjehan*; *Adhikar*; *Chakradhari*; **1955**: *Andher Nagari Choupat Raja*; *Ekadashi*; *Jagadguru Shankaracharya*; *Riyasat*; *Naag Devata*; *Vaman Avatar*; **1956**: *Dwarkadheesh*; *Sudarshan Chakra*; ***Malela Jeev***; *Sati Analde*; **1957**: *Adhi Roti*; *Bhakta Dhruva*; *Lakshmi*; *Sant Raghu*; **1958**: *Gopichand*; *Great Show of India*; *Jung Bahadur*; *Pati Parmeshwar*; *Ram Bhakti*; **1959**: *Charnon Ki Dasi*; *Grihalakshmi*; **1960**: *Bhakta Raaj*; ***Kadu Makrani***; ***Mehndi Rang Lagyo***; **1961**: *Chundadi Chokha*; *Ghar Divdi*; ***Hiro Salaat***; *Narasaiyani Hundi*; *Ra Mandlik*; *Nandanvan*; *Veer Ramwalo*; **1962**: *Bapu Ne Kaha Tha*; *Hawa Mahal*; *Kailashpati*; *Jai Bhadrakali*; *Janam Janamna Saathi*; *Jogidas Khuman*; *Kanku Ane Kanya*; **1963**: *Royal Mail*; *Gharni Shobha*; *Vanraj Chavdo*; **1964**: *Ramat Ramade Ram*; **1965**: *Chhogala Chhaganlalno Varghodo*; *Jamairaj*; **1966**: ***Kalapi***; **1967**: *Samayvarte Savdhan*; **1968**: *Mare Javun Pele Paar*; *Mata Mahakali*; **1969**: *Badmash*; *Beti Tumhare Jaisi*; *Surya Devata*; *Hastamelap*; *Majiyara Haiya*; *Sansar Leela*; **1970**: *Takht Aur Talwar*; **1971**: ***Jesal Toral***; **1972**: ***Zer To Pidhan Jani Jani***; **1973**: *Mahasati Savitri*; *Kadu Makrani*; *Raja Bhartrahari*; *Vala Taro Deshma Danko*; **1974**: *Ghunghat*; *Harishchandra Taramati*; *Hothal Padmini*; *Kunwarbainu Mameru*; **1975**: *Daku Aur Bhagwan*; *Jai Ranchhod*; *Jogidas Khuman*; *Ra Mandlik*; *Sant Surdas*; *Seth Sagalsha*; *Shetalne Kanthe*; *Veer Champrajvalo*; *Bhadar Tara Vehta Pani*; **1976**: *Bhabhi*; *Bhaibandhi*; *Chundadino Rang*; *Dharti Mata*; *Malavpati Munj*; *Ra Navghan*; *Santu Rangili*; *Sorathi Sinh*; *Veer Ebhalvalo*; *Veer Ramwalo*; *Verno Varas*; *Veer Mangdavalo*; *Shamalshano Vivah*; ***Sonbaini Chundadi***; **1977**: *Bhrashtachar Murdabad*; *Dada Ho Dikri*; *Maa Baap*; *Manno Manigar*; *Paiso Bole Chhe*; *Rupande Malde*; *Son Kansari*; **1978**: *Ashapura Matani Chundadi*; *Bhakta Gora Kumbhar*; *Chandan Malayagiri*; *Chundadi Odhi Tara Namni*; *Dada Khetrapal*; *Jai Mahakali*; *Jantarwalo Jeevan*; *Maa Dikri*; *Mota Gharni Vahu*; *Nari Tu Narayani*; *Patali Parmar*; *Sansar Chakra*; *Sati Ansuya* (G); *Sati Sorath*; *Visamo*; **1979**: *Apyo Jadro*; *Amarsinh Rathod*; *Ashadhi Beej*; *Chudi Chandlo*; *Jai Bhadrakali*; *Koinu Mindhal Koina Hathe*; *Kunwari Satino Kesariyo Kanth*; *Lalwadi Phoolwadi*; *Maa Te Maa*; *Navrang Chundadi*; *Pithino Rang*; *Preet Khandani Dhar*; *Rang Rasiya*; *Roopli Daatanwali*; *Shankar Parvati*; *Sonba Ane Rupba*; *Suraj Chandra Ni Sakhe*; *Veer Pasali*; **1980**: *Abhan Lakshmi*; *Bhakta Prahlad*; *Chitadno Chor*; *Jivi Rabaran*; *Karo Kankuna*; *Kesar Kathiyani*; *Khordani Khandani*; *Koino Ladakvayo*; *Lahini Sagar*; *Mari Bena*; *Parayana To Pyari Ladi*; *Sachun Sagapan*; *Sachun Sukh Sasaryiaman*; *So Dahada Sasuna To Ek Dahado Vahuno*; *Sukhma Sau Dukhma Vahu*; *Vaya Viramgam*; **1981**: *Albeli Naar*; *Amar Devidas*; *Bhav Bhavna Bheru*; *Chhel Chhabili Sonal*; *Hiro Ghoghe Jai Avyo*; *Mehndino Rang*; *Naag Panchami*; *Ranchandi*; *Seth Jagadusha*; *Vansdi Vagi Valamni*; *Vaheta Ansu Vahuna*; **1982**: *Bhakta Muldas*; *Di Vaale Ee Dikra*; *Jamuna Bani Jagadamba*; *Jawabdaar*; *Khabardar*; *Maa Kali Pavavali*; *Nala Damayanti*; *Naseeb No Khel*; *Prem Diwani*; *Retina Ratan*; *Sherne Mathe Savasher*; *Tran Treniya Chha Chhabila Baharvatiya/Bachche Teen Aur Daku Chhe*; **1983**: *Chhel Chhabilo Gujarati*; *Ghar Gharni Vaat*; *Jithro Bhabho*; *Kankuni Kimat*; *Khara*

Kharino Khel; *Kurukshetra*; *Maa Koini Marsho Nahin*; *Raakhna Ramakada*; **1984**: *Maya Bazaar*; *Bhakta Narasinh Mehta*; *Bhagwan Shri Krishna*; *Dhartina Ami*; *Maana Aansoo*; *Sonani Jaal*; *Tejal Garasani*; *Vavazodun*; **1985**: *Maanu Mangalsutra*; *Sagan Sahu Swarthana*; *Vali Bharawadan*.

VYAS, VISHNUKUMAR MAGANLAL (b. 1905)

Hindi and Gujarati director born and educated in Ahmedabad, Gujarat. Credited with launching a Gujarati film industry with ***Ranakdevi***, adapted by scenarist **Mohanlal Dave** from his own script initially filmed by **Patankar** at National (1923) and later by **Vakil** at **Ranjit** (1930). Throughout his long career consistently made mid-budget melodramas scripted by Dave. Started as a tabla accompanyist for live musical scores at **Kohinoor** where he also became assistant cameraman; shot films for **Homi Master** and **N.G. Devare** when Kohinoor became Kohinoor United Artists. Continued as cinematographer in Bombay and Lahore until his directorial début at Kohinoor with *Dukhiari*. His melodramas and devotionals were derived from popular Gujarati fiction serials later popularised by the journal *Chitralekha*, addressing a middle-class and often explicitly female audience. His *Ranakdevi* led to major shifts in the production priorities: e.g. Ranjit started a subsidiary, Ajit Pics, mainly for Gujarati films of this genre.

FILMOGRAPHY: **1930**: *Dukhiari*; *Veer Vijaysingh*; **1931**: *Veer Bahadur* (all St); **1934**: *Saubhagya Lakshmi*; **1939**: *Daughters of India*; *Garib Ka Lal*; **1940**: *Kanyadaan*; *Nirali Duniya*; **1941**: *Ghar Ki Laaj*; *Prabhat*; **1942**: *Ghar Sansar*; *Malan*; **1943**: ***Duhai***; *Mahasati Ansuya*; **1944**: *Maa Baap*; **1945**: *Ghar*; **1946**: *Dhanwan*; ***Ranakdevi***; **1947**: *Baharvatiyo*; *Kunwarbainu Mameru*; *Sati Jasma*; *Amar Asha*; *Bhakta Ke Bhagwan*; **1948**: *Bhabhina Het*; *Bhai Bahen*; *Shamalshano Vivah*; **1949**: *Gunial Gujaratan*; *Veenaveli*; **1950**: *Pyar*; **1952**: *Sanskar*; **1953**: *Dana Pani*; **1955**: *Naag Devata*; **1958**: *Bharatni Vani*; *Dulhan*; *Ghar Sansar*; **1959**: *Do Gunde*; **1960**: *Bhakta Raaj*; *Ghar Ki Laaj*; *Maa Baap*; **1961**: *Apsara*; *Narsaiyani Hundi*.

VYJAYANTHIMALA (b. 1936)

South Indian actress born in Madras. Trained as a classical dancer in the Bharat Natyam style. With **Padmini**, she is one of the first Southern actresses in post-Independence All-India film to become a national star. Started in Tamil films under **M.V. Raman**'s direction at **AVM**; Raman also cast her in her first Hindi film, AVM's hit ***Bahar***. A bigger success still was ***Nagin***, esp. her sinuous snake dance to the smash hit *Man dole mera tan dole*. Since then, almost always has a mandatory dance sequence evoking 'classical art' associations: ***Devdas***; **Kishore Kumar**'s elaborate spoof ***New Delhi*** where she performs Bharat Natyam to his Fred Astaire imitation in the song *Nakhrewali*; ***Ganga Jumna*** (the song *Dhoondo dhoondo re sajna*) and *Amrapali*. This pseudo-classical style (also practised by, e.g., **Hema Malini** and Jayapradha) is a filmic equivalent of calendar-art's version of Ajanta murals and Tanjore glass paintings, taking over the icon of the large-hipped, full-bosomed beauty developed, e.g., by **Ravi Varma**. In ***Sangam***, **Raj Kapoor** used this image for his post-60s exploration of links between voyeurism and decadent classicism. Other film-makers who used Vyjayanthimala's calendar-art style include **B.R. Chopra** (***Naya Daur***, *Sadhana*), **S.S. Vasan** (***Raj Tilak***) and **T. Prakash Rao** (Amar Deep/***Amara Deepam***). Best cinematic performance in the title role of ***Madhumati***. Elected MP for Congress(I) in Madras (1984).

Vyjayanthimala in *Naya Kanoon* (1965)

FILMOGRAPHY: **1949**: *Vazhkai/Jeevitham*; **1951**: ***Bahar***; **1952**: *Anjaam*; **1953**: *Penn/Ladki*; **1954**: *Miss Mala*; ***Nagin***; *Pehli Jhalak*; **1955**: ***Devdas***; *Jashan*; *Sitara*; *Yasmin*; **1956**: *Devata*; *Kismet Ka Khel*; ***New Delhi***; *Patrani*; *Taj*; *Anjaan*; **1957**: ***Aasha***; *Ek Jhalak*; ***Kathputli***; ***Naya Daur***; **1958**: *Amar Deep*; ***Madhumati***; *Piya Milan*; ***Raj Tilak***; *Sadhana*; *Sitaron Se Aage*; **1959**: *Jawani Ki Hawa*; ***Paigham***; **1960**: *College Girl*; *Baghdad Thirudan/Baghdad*; *Irumputhirai*; *Raja Bhakti*; ***Parthiban Kanavu***; **1961**: *Aas Ka Panchhi*; ***Ganga Jumna***; *Nazrana*; **1962**: *Dr Vidya*; *Jhoola*; *Rangoli*; **1964**: *Ishara*; *Leader*; *Phoolon Ki Sej*; ***Sangam***; *Zindagi*; **1965**: *Naya Kanoon*; **1966**: *Amrapali*; *Do Dilon Ki Dastaan*; *Suraj*; **1967**: *Hatey Bazarey*; *Chhotisi Mulaqat*; ***Jewel Thief***; **1968**: *Duniya*; *Saathi*; ***Sangharsh***; **1969**: *Prince*; *Pyar Hi Pyar*; **1970**: *Ganwaar*.

WADIA, HOMI BOMAN (b. 1911)

Hindi director and producer born in Surat. Younger brother of **J.B.H Wadia**. Entered films as a laboratory worker at Vivekananda Film Laboratory (1929); then cameraman and colleague of his brother, whom he joined as director at the Young United Players, remaking Fairbanks-Niblo's *Mark of Zorro* (*Diler Daku*). H.B. and J.B.H. co-founded **Wadia Movietone** (1933). Operated as studio's main director and editor, responsible for successful **Fearless Nadia** action films co-starring John Cawas. Also made the stunt film *Ekta* in Sindhi. Left to start Basant Pics in 1942 (it became a studio in 1947), carrying on the Wadia stunt-action trade-mark. Later work includes several Pauranic mythologicals, usually featuring special effects by **Babubhai Mistri**, and the successful Gevacolor film ***Hatimtai***. Married Nadia (1961); sold Basant (1981) and retired.

FILMOGRAPHY: **1931**: *Diler Daku* (St); **1934**: *Veer Bharat*; **1935**: ***Hunterwali***; ***Hind Kesari***; *Sarangadhara*; **1936**: *Jai Bharat*; ***Miss Frontier Mail***; **1937**: *Toofani Tarzan*; **1938**: *Lutaru Lalna*; **1939**: *Punjab Mail*; *Bharat Kesari*; **1940**: ***Diamond Queen***; *Hind Ka Lal*; **1941**: *Bambaiwali*; **1942**: *Jungle Princess*; *Ekta*; **1943**: *Vishwas*; **1945**: *Bachpan*; **1946**: *Amar Raj*; *Flying Prince*; *Sher-e-Baghdad*; **1947**: *Atom Bomb*; **1948**: *Eleven O'Clock*; *Shri Rambhakta Hanuman*; **1949**: *Balam*; *Dhoomketu*; **1950**: *Shri Ganesh Mahima*; **1951**: *Hanuman Pataal Vijay*; **1952**: *Jungle Ka Jawahar*; *Alladdin And the Wonderful Lamp*; **1954**: *Alibaba and the Forty Thieves*; **1956**: ***Hatimtai***; **1958**: *Zimbo*; **1961**: *Zabak*; **1964**: *Char Darvesh*; **1966**: *Alibaba and the Forty Thieves*; **1970**: *Shri Krishna Leela*; *Bhale Goodachari*; **1976**: *Toofan Aur Bijli*; **1978**: *Alladdin and the Wonderful Lamp*.

WADIA, JAMSHED BOMAN HOMI (1901-86)

Hindi director and producer born in Surat, Gujarat. Literary scholar at Bombay University. Worked in a bank while taking a law degree. Major supporter and biographer of Communist (usually referred to as 'radical humanist') reformer M.N. Roy. Founder member of Radical Democratic Party of India (1937). Combined literary and political interests with fascination for US western and stunt films. Wrote and co-produced his first film (*Vasant Leela*, 1928) with **Kohinoor** cinematographer and producer G.S. Devare. Together they ran the

Devare Film Laboratory and the Wadia Film Exchange. Established Young United Players (1931) with his brother **Homi** and made five silent films inspired by the Fairbanks-Niblo *Mark of Zorro* (1920), including one direct adaptation, *Diler Daku*. With support from the Tata industrial family and Manchersha B. Bilimoria, set up **Wadia Movietone** (1933) with his brother Homi. Personally made the Yeshwant Dave and Boman Shroff silents but functioned mainly as studio boss and scenarist. Best-known Wadia Movietone work, the **Fearless Nadia** films, were made by Homi Wadia, who also married the star. Although the Wadia signature is linked to the stunt genre, J.B.H.'s work is marked by his political adherences and the conventions of Parsee theatre (e.g. the Jal Khambatta films, ***Lal-e-Yaman***, *Baag-e-Misar*, *Kala Gulab*). His *Naujawan* (Aspi, 1937) was a rare commercial feature without 'song cushions'. When he insisted on privileging social themes in the production programme, Homi left (1942). Influential documentary and newsreel producer (e.g. his *Short Films of Musical Value*, recording musical performances by the likes of Mallika Pukhraj and the child Kumar Gandharva). President of the **Film Advisory Board** (1941-2). Unsuccessful *Indian Screen Gazette*, modelled on *Pathé Gazette*, with early work by **P.V. Pathy**. Collaborated with ad agency D.J. Keymer on British war-effort films (1940). Apparently made three 30' thrillers for US television in 1949. Also made *All Under the Heaven by Force*, directed by Zul Velani (1964), condemning China's 1962 military operations in India. Established J.B.H. Wadia Publications, issuing, e.g., M.N. Roy's *New Humanism* and wrote *M.N. Roy: The Man* (1983). Wrote his autobiography, *Those Were The Days* (unpublished, 1977), and Urdu poetry. Excerpts of his silent film *Vantolio* survive.

FILMOGRAPHY: 1931: *Diler Daku*; **1932**: *Toofan Mail*; *Sinh Garjana*; **1933**: *Vantolio* (all St); ***Lal-e-Yaman***; *Dilruba Daku* (St); **1934**: *Baag-e-Misar*; *Kala Gulab*; *Vaman Avatar*; **1935**: ***Desh Deepak***; *Noor-e-Yaman*; **1944**: *Krishna Bhakta Bodana*; **1951**: *Madhosh*; **1953**: *Husn Ka Chor*; **1955**: *Veer Rajputani*; **1957**: *Captain Kishore*; **1960**: *Duniya Jhukti Hai*; **1966**: *Tasveer*; **1971**: *Saaz Aur Sanam*.

WADIA MOVIETONE

Studio established in 1933 by **J.B.H. Wadia** and **Homi Wadia** with Manchersha B. Bilimoria (film distributor-exhibitor and agent for the famous Columbia Carbon Arcs) and the Tata family represented by brothers Burjor and Nadirsha. Associated with the Fairbanks-inspired stunt genre in films starring **Fearless Nadia**, Boman Shroff, John Cawas and the villain Sayani. Most were intentionally addressed to the C-grade exhibition sector and tried to recapture J.B.H. Wadia's early cinephiliac fascination with Hollywood serials and westerns. Also known for documentaries and newsreels made during WW2, notably the *Indian Screen Gazette* series, under the **Film Advisory Board**'s overall guidance and continued sporadically until the India-China War of 1962. J.B.H. Wadia was overall studio boss, chief producer and scenarist while Homi Wadia directed films and supervised the editing and sound departments. Shortly before closing, made the **Modhu Bose** dance movie ***Raj Nartaki*** (1941) with a bilingual English version to explore the US market. Wadia Movietone was sold to **V. Shantaram** in 1942, who started **Rajkamal Kalamandir** there, but it continued in the shape of Homi Wadia's Basant Pics, first as a production house (1942), then as a studio (1947-81). In 1990, J.B.H. Wadia's grandson, the actor and playwright Riyad Vinci Wadia, inherited Wadia Movietone which now mainly produces material for television.

WADKAR, HANSA (1923-72)

Marathi and Hindi actress, originally Ratan Salgaonkar. Changed her name in her screen début, aged 11, using the family name of her grandmother and thereby asserted her ancestry in a family of Maharashtrian courtesans. Learnt music and tried to join Shalini Cinetone as a child actress but was rejected by **Tembe**. Introduced to the screen in Lalitkaladarsh's only effort to translate its **Sangeet Natak** to cinema with Mama Warerkar's *Vijayachi Lagne*. She then starred in the Karachi-based Golden Eagle Studio's routine movie *Modern Youth*. Did several B films, e.g. for **Bhagwan**'s Studio (*Bahadur Kisan*, *Criminal*) until she broke through in **Osten**'s ***Durga*** and moved to **Bombay Talkies**. After three years, **Prabhat** brought her back to star against type in **Damle-Fattelal**' ***Sant Sakhu***. Produced and starred in *Dhanyavaad*. Established the demure *ingénue* look that has graced nearly every social in Marathi cinema ever since (see **Jayshree Gadkar**). Went on to pioneer the brashly vulgar Tamasha musical with **Shantaram**'s ***Lokshahir Ramjoshi*** and, towards the end of her career, **Mane**'s ***Sangtye Aika***, both record-breaking hits in Marathi cinema. Subsequently in films by **Paranjpe** (***Pudhcha Paool***), **Dinkar D. Patil** (*Patlacha Por*), **Bhalji Pendharkar** (*Shilanganache Sone*, *Naikinichi Sajja*) and Mane. Had a difficult and tempestuous personal life, including a series of relationships which she wrote about in a remarkably candid autobiography, serialised in the popular journal *Manoos* (1966) and later published as *Sangtye Aika* (1970), which caused a major sensation. A fictionalised version was the source of **Benegal**'s ***Bhumika*** (1976).

FILMOGRAPHY: 1936: *Vijayachi Lagne/Shadi Ka Mamla*; **1937**: *Modern Youth*; **1938**: *Bahadur Kisan*; *Sneh Lagna*; *Zamana*; **1939**: ***Durga***; *Criminal*; ***Navjeevan***; **1940**: ***Azad***; **1941**: ***Sant Sakhu***; **1942**: *Apna Paraya*; *Dillagi*; *Mera Gaon*; **1944**: ***Ramshastri***; *Meena*; **1945**: *Aarti*; *Main Kya Karun*; **1946**: *Behram Khan*; **1947**: ***Lokshahir Ramjoshi/Matwala Shayar Ramjoshi***; *Gaurav*; **1948**: *Dhanyavaad*; *Dhanwale*; *Mere Lal*; **1949**: *Pandharicha Patil*; *Sant Janabai*; *Shilanganache Sone*; **1950**: *Kalyan Khajina*; *Navara Baiko*; ***Pudhcha Paool***; *Sonyachi Lanka*; *Vanshacha Diva*; *Shri Krishna Darshan*; **1951**: *Hi Majhi Lakshmi*; *Maya Machhindra/Gorakhnath*; *Patlacha Por*; *Parijatak/Shri Krishna Satyabhama*; **1952**: *Shri Gurudev Dutt*; **1954**: *Khel Chalala Nashibacha*; *Reshmachya Gaathi*; **1955**: *Mi Tulas Tujhya Angani*; **1956**: *Mulga*; **1957**: *Naikinichi Sajja*; **1958**: *Lokshahir Anantphandi*; *Matevin Bal*; **1959**: ***Sangtye Aika***; **1961**: ***Manini***; *Rangapanchami*; **1963**: *Naar Nirmite Nara*; **1964**: *Kai Ho Chamatkar*; **1966**: *Hi Naar Rupasundari*; **1967**: *Shrimant Mehuna Pahije*; **1968**: *Dharmakanya*.

WALKER, JOHNNY (b. 1925)

Revered Hindi comedian born Badruddin Jamaluddin Kazi; son of a millworker. Took his screen name from the whisky brand. Moved to Bombay (1942) doing odd jobs and was discovered by **Balraj Sahni**, who apparently met him as a bus conductor regaling the passengers with an uncanny ability to hold his audience with improvised speech. Made his mark in ***Baazi*** and ***Jaal*** playing **Dev Anand**'s ally; then best known for **Guru Dutt**'s films, often (in the mid-50s) carrying the second love interest (e.g. ***Aar Paar***, ***Kaagaz Ke Phool***). Developed a characteristic style as the hero's comic sidekick within the classic Indian film comedy tradition, relying on his pencil-thin moustache, facial grimaces and nasal drawl (cf *Sar jo tera chakraye* sung by **Mohammed Rafi** in ***Pyaasa***). He stuck to his style even when this might contradict the character he had to play: e.g. the misogynist playboy in ***Kaagaz Ke Phool*** or the nawab in ***Chaudhuvin Ka Chand***. Although he was unable to retain his popularity into the 80s, he pioneered a tradition of stand-up comedy often practised by successors who followed his idiosyncratic screen name: Tony Brandy, Johnny Whisky or Johnny Lever. Turned to direction with *Pahunche Huye Log*.

FILMOGRAPHY: 1951: *Hulchul*; ***Baazi***; **1952**: ***Aandhiyan***; ***Jaal***; **1953**: *Aag Ka Dariya*; *Armaan*; *Baaz*; *Humsafar*; *Thokar*; **1954**: ***Aar Paar***; *Baraati*; *Lalpari*; ***Munna***; *Shaheed-e-Azam Bhagat Singh*; ***Taxi Driver***; **1955**: *Albeli*; *Bahu*; ***Devdas***; *Jashan*; *Jawab*; *Joru Ka Bhai*; *Marine Drive*; *Mast Kalandar*; *Milap*; *Miss Coca Cola*; ***Mr and Mrs '55***; *Musafirkhana*; ***Railway Platform***; *Shahi Mehmaan*; *Shehzada*; *Society*; **1956**: *Anjaan*; *Awara Shehzadi*; *Chandrakant*; *Choo Mantar*; ***Chori Chori***; ***CID***; *Insaaf*; *Naya Andaz*; *Rajdhani*; *Samundari Daku*; *Shrimati 420*; *Twenty-Sixth January*; **1957**: *Changhez Khan*; *Do Roti*; *Duniya Rang Rangili*; *Ek Saal*; *Johnny Walker*; *Maibaap*; *Mr X*; ***Naya Daur***; ***Pyaasa***; *Qaidi*; **1958**: *Aakhri Dao*; *Aji Bas Shukriya*; *Amar Deep*; *Chandan*; *Detective*; *Ghar Sansar*; *Khota Paisa*; *Light House*; ***Madhumati***; *Mr Qartoon MA*; *Mujrim*; *Naya Paisa*; *Sitaron Se Aage*; *Zindagi Ya Toofan*; **1959**: *Black Cat*; *Bhai Bahen*; *Jawani Ki Hawa*; ***Kaagaz Ke Phool***; *Mr John*; *Pehli Raat*; ***Paigham***; ***Satta Bazaar***; *Zara Bachke*; **1960**: *Basant*; ***Chaudhvin Ka Chand***; *Ek Phool Char Kaante*; *Ghar Ki Laaj*; *Kala Admi*; ***Mughal-e-Azam***; *Rickshawala*; **1961**: *Chhote Nawab*; *Modern Girl*; *Suhaag Sindoor*; **1962**: *Aashiq*; *Baat Ek Raat Ki*; *Girls' Hostel*; *Neeli Aankhen*; *Sachche Moti*; **1963**: *Ghar Basake Dekho*; *Kahin Pyar Na Ho Jaye*; *Kaun Apna Kaun Paraya*; ***Mere Mehboob***; *Mulzim*; *Phool Bane Angarey*; *Pyar Ka Bandhan*; *Ustadonke Ustad*; **1964**: *Door Ki Awaz*; *Shehnai*; **1965**: *Bombay Race Course*; *Zindagi Aur Maut*; **1966**: *Baharen Phir Bhi Aayengi*; ***Dil Diya Dard Liya***; *Dillagi*; *Dulhan Ek Raat Ki*; *Pati Patni*; *Preet Na Jane Reet*; *Suraj*; **1967**: *Bahu Begum*; *Jaal*; *Milan Ki Raat*;

Nawab Siraj-ud-Dowla; *Night in London*; *Noorjehan*; *Palki*; *Raju*; *Wahan Ke Log*; **1968**: *Baazi*; *Dil Aur Mohabbat*; *Duniya*; ***Hasina Maan Jayegi***; *Kahin Din Kahin Raat*; *Mere Huzoor*; *Shikar*; **1969**: *Admi Aur Insaan*; *Nannha Farishta*; *Pyar Ka Sapna*; *Sachaai*; **1970**: ***Anand***; *Gopi*; **1971**: *Hangama*; *Memsaab*; *Sanjog*; **1972**: *Ek Bechara*; *Ek Hasina Do Diwane*; *Raja Jani*; *Yeh Gulistan Hamara*; **1973**: *Dil Ki Raahein*; *Pyar Ka Rishta*; **1974**: *Aarop*; *Badla*; *Dawat*; *Imaan*; *Jurm Aur Sazaa*; *Mera Vachan Geeta Ki Kasam*; **1975**: *Teri Meri Ik Jindri*; *Dhoti Lota Aur Chowpatti*; *Kaagaz Ki Nao*; *Pratigya*; *Sewak*; *Vandana*; *Zakhmi*; *Ganga Ki Kasam*; **1976**: *Bandalbaaz*; *Santan*; *Uranchoo*; **1977**: *Farishta Ya Qatil*; *Khel Khiladi Ka*; **1979**: *Madine Ki Galiyan*; **1980**: *Jayen To Jayen Kahan*; *Shaan*; **1983**: *Bindiya Chamkegi*; **1984**: *Mera Dost Mera Dushman*; *Hum Dono*; **1985**: *Pahunche Huye Log* (also d); **1987**: *Mera Karam Mera Dharam*; **1988**: *The Perfect Murder*.

YAGNIK, INDULAL

Gujarati scenarist and producer. Best known as a Gujarati politician for his long association with Gandhi, his 50s trade union work and his involvement in the regionalist Mahagujarat movements. His brief encounter with film as scenarist and producer stemmed from a desire to give it intellectual legitimacy. As editor of the *Hindustan* newspaper, he made both Indian and foreign film a subject of lively debate, e.g. through contributions from **Chaturbhuj Doshi**, then a journalist. Extended this commitment to a popular column in the *Bombay Chronicle*. Entered film as a scenarist (e.g. for **Sharda** Studio). After an abortive attempt to launch the Classical Pics Corp. with G.S. Devare, turned producer with Young India Pics (**Nagendra Majumdar**'s *Goddess Mahakali*, 1928, which he also wrote). The company used his scripts, which were, from available descriptions, largely romances. He faced bankruptcy following the failure of Majumdar's *Kashmir Nu Gulab* (1931) and was rescued by **Imperial**'s financier, Abu Hasan. His productions introduced film-makers Majumdar and Ramakant-Gharekhan, and featured stars Madhuri and Navinchandra. Other script credits include **Manilal Joshi**'s *Ajabkumari* (1926), **Bhavnani**'s *Daya Ni Devi* (1927) and **B.P. Mishra**'s *Jay Bharati* (1929). Major six-volume autobiography published between 1955-73.

Yatrik *see* **Majumdar, Tarun**

YESUDAS, K. J. (b. 1940)

Best-known playback singer in Malayalam cinema. Born in Cochin. Dominated Malayalam music since the 60s and created a parallel music industry with the Tarangini audiocassette label. Made a big cultural impact on, e.g., the popular 'devotional'. Son of Augustine Joseph, a major stage actor and early Malayalam film star (and among the first Christians to be successful in Malayalam theatre and music), his early career was in professional Gana Mela troupes (groups singing film and film-derived compositions during religious festivals). Claimed to be the disciple of the classical musician Chembai Vaidyanatha Bhagavathar, but probably only accompanied him on a few occasions. Early hits include the **Baburaj**-composed songs for **Vincent**'s ***Bhargavi Nilayam*** (1964). Occasionally imitated the Carnatic maestro Balamurali Krishna, mainly as a formal affectation. Most famous for his light classical devotionals addressed to the icons of Ayyappa at Sabarimalai (the centre of an aggressive lumpenised youth culture) and Guruvayoor. His cassette releases are intended for Hindu and sometimes Christian festivals. Sang in almost every Malayalam film since the early 70s. Also did Hindi songs for **Basu Chatterjee** in the 70s, one of which, *Jab deep jale aana* in *Chit Chor* (1976) was a hit. Among the films he scored are **Sethumadhavan**'s *Azhakulla Saleena* (1973); **Madhu**'s *Theekkanal* (1976); Shrikumaran Thampi's *Malika Paniyunnavar* (1978) and **P.N. Menon**'s *Udhayam Kizhakku Thanne* (1976).

YOGANAND, D. (b. 1922)

Telugu and Tamil director born in Madras. Son of the estate manager of an Andhra nawab; adopted at an early age by D. Subbaiah of Bandar, owner of a watch-repairing and photography shop. Studied radiology briefly while developing his skills as a photographer. Joined films as assistant to **Ramabrahmam**'s editor, Manikyam (*Mayalokam*, 1945). Also assisted famous South Indian technicians Jiten Bannerjee and Rehman. After Ramabrahmam, worked with **L.V. Prasad**, whose notions of the reformist social left its imprint on his films. In his use of genre he is perhaps the most inventive of the post-Prasad film-makers: his début, the sentimental ***Ammalakulu***, is a musical hit attacking feudalist practices; his second film, ***Todu Dongalu***, produced by and starring **NTR**, is an influential realist melodrama which flopped. Telugu and Hindi star **Waheeda Rehman** débuted in his folk musical *Jayasimha*. Best-known 50s film is the successful Tamil folk legend ***Madurai Veeran***, one of **MGR**'s most influential roles.

FILMOGRAPHY: 1953: ***Ammalakulu/Marumagal***; **1954**: ***Todu Dongalu***; **1955**: *Jayasimha/Jaisingh*; *Vijayagauri*; *Kaveri*; **1956**: *Ilavelpu*; *Shri Gauri Mahatyam*; ***Madurai Veeran***; **1958**: *Bhuloka Rambha/Bhuloka Rambhai*; *Anbu Engay*; **1959**: *Kaveriyin Kanavan*; *Pelli Sandadi/Kalyana Penn*; *Vachina Kodulu Nachindi*; **1960**: ***Parthiban Kanavu***; *Engal Selvi*; **1962**: *Rani Samyuktha*; **1963**: *Parisu*; *Pareeksha*; **1964**: *Pasamum Nesamum*; **1967**: *Ummadi Kutumbam*; **1968**: *Tikka Shankaraiah*; *Baghdad Gajadonga*; **1969**: *Mooganomu*; **1970**: *Jai Jawan*; *Kodalu Diddina Kapuram*; **1971**: *Thangaikkaga*; **1972**: *Rani Yar Kulandai?*; **1973**: *Dabbuku Lokam Dasoham*; *Vaade Veedu*; **1974**: *Thayi*; **1975**: *Katha Nayakuni Katha*; *Ee Kalam Dampathulu*; *Vemulavada Bhimakavi*; **1976**: *Grihapravesham*; **1978**: *General Chakravarthi*; *Justice Gopinath*; **1979**: *Naan Vazhavippen*; **1980**: *Yamanukku Yaman*; **1982**: *Oorukku Oru Pillai*; *Vaa Kanna Vaa*; **1983**: *Sumangali*; *Simham Navindi*; **1984**: *Charitra Nayakan*.

Yusufali, Abdulali *see* **Esoofally, Abdulally**

ZILS, PAUL (1915-79)

Director born in Wuppertal, Germany. Influential figure in documentary Indian cinema. Worked at Ufa, Germany (1933-7), where he was a favourite of Goebbels and was often used by Ufa to secure Nazi governmental approval for scripts. Defected in 1937. Travelled to Africa and the USA (1939), where he worked with William Dieterle and Max Reinhard in Hollywood and persuaded Paramount to fund a film he wanted to make in Bali. During shooting he was arrested by the British (1941) and, with other Germans, interned in a prisoner of war camp in Bihar. After the war, because of his prior film experience and also because of some impressive stage spectacles in the POW camp, he was offered the job of heading the external unit of **Information Films Of**

Kishore Sahu (on table), Jagdev, Mahendranath and Dev Anand (partially lit, right) in Paul Zils' *Zalzala* (1952)

India (1945-8). Then started his own Documentary Films of India. Sponsored quarterly journal *Indian Documentary* (1949). Became an Indian national for a few years before reverting to his German nationality. Documentarists **Fali Bilimoria** and **P.V. Pathy** started as his assistant and cameraman respectively. Made three features for Art Films of Asia, starring **Dev Anand**. His second one, *Zalzala*, was adaptated from **Tagore**'s controversial novel *Char Adhyay*. Returned to documentaries, setting up the Documentary Unit: India in collaboration with Fali Bilimoria, for which they made several films sponsored by, e.g., Shell, the UN and the USIS. Best-known for his *Major Industries In India* series for Burmah Shell. **Sukhdev** regarded Zils as his teacher. Returned to Germany in 1959 where he ran the Deutsche Condor (Munich) and the Erlangen Film Institute, occasionally making films in India as well. Worked in Sri Lanka (1968-9) on behalf of the German government and made some films about Buddhism. Except for the 1950-2 titles, all are documentaries.

FILMOGRAPHY (* co-d. F. Bilimoria): **1945**: *Bombay-The Story of the Seven Isles*; **1947**: *India's Struggle for National Shipping*; **1947-8**: *Mother/Child/Community**; **1949**: *Kurvandi Road*; *White Magic**; *The Last Jewel**; *General Motors in India**; *A Tiny Thing Brings Death**; *Two Worlds*; **1950**: ***Hindustan Hamara***; **1952**: *Zalzala*; *Shabash*; **1954**: *A Family In Bangalore*; *Ujala**; **1955**: *Fisherfolk Of Bombay*; **1956**: *The School*; *The Ripening Seed*; **1957**: *New Life of a Displaced Person*; *Maa-The Story of an Unwed Mother*; *Fifty Miles from Poona**; **1958**: *The Vanishing Tribe**; *Oraons of Bihar*; *Martial Dances of Malabar*.

ZUBEIDA (1911-90)

Actress born in Surat as a Muslim princess, daughter of the Nawab of Sachin and **Fatma Begum** (later India's first woman director). Started in silent films at **Kohinoor** aged 12. Early career was dominated by her extraordinarily beautiful sister Sultana, a better-known star in the 20s. Her second sister, Shehzadi, also became a teenage actress. Zubeida's best silent work was for **Manilal Joshi** at the Kohinoor and Laxmi Studios. Played the lead in ***Alam Ara***, India's first sound film. Identified with courtesan roles in big Urdu, stage-derived costume pictures, a tradition extended by **Meena Kumari**. Developed the tragic dimension of her image in several of **Naval Gandhi**'s socials including the prestigious **Tagore** adaptation ***Balidan***. Freelanced at the **Ranjit** and **Sagar** Studios and in her mother's films: ***Bulbul-e-Paristan***, *Heer Ranjha*, *Milan Dinar*. Set up Mahalakshmi Cinetone (1934) with the film-maker **Nanubhai Vakil**. Retired at the height of her stardom in the late 30s, doing only a few films later on.

FILMOGRAPHY: **1922**: ***Veer Abhimanyu***; **1924**: ***Gul-e-Bakavali***; ***Kala Naag***; *Manorama*; ***Prithvi Vallabh***; ***Sati Sardarba***; **1925**: *Kala Chor*; *Devadasi*; *Indrasabha*; *Ra Navghan*; *Rambha Of Rajnagar*; *Desh Na Dushman*; *Yashodevi*; *Khandani Khavis*; *Sati Simantini*; **1926**: ***Neera***; ***Bulbul-e-Paristan***; *Kashmeera*; *Raja Bhoj*; *Indrajal*; *Sati Menadevi*; **1927**: *Laila Majnu*; ***Nanand Bhojai***; ***Balidan***; **1928**: *Chamakti Chanda*; *Samrat Ashok*; *Golden Gang*; *Heer Ranjha*; **1929**: *Kanakatara*; *Mahasundar*; *Milan Dinar*; *Shahi Chor*; *Jai Bharati*; *Rangilo Rajavi*; **1930**: *Devadasi*; *Garva Khandan*; *Joban Ni Jadu*; *Veer Rajput*; **1931**: *Meethi Churi*; *Diwani Duniya*; *Roop Sundari*; *Hoor-e-Misar*; *Karmano Kaher*; *Nadira* (all St); ***Alam Ara***; *Meri Jaan*; *Veer Abhimanyu*; **1932**: *Meerabai*; *Subhadra Haran*; *Zarina*; **1933**: *Harijan* (St); *Bulbul-e-Punjab*; *Pandav Kaurav*; **1934**: ***Gul Sanobar***; *Nanand Bhojai*; *Radha Mohan/Nand Ke Lala*; ***Rashk-e-Laila***; *Maa*; *Seva Sadan*; **1935**: *Birbal Ki Beti*; *Gulshan-e-Alam*; **1936**: *Mr and Mrs Bombay*; **1937**: *Aurat Ki Zindagi*; *Kiski Pyari*; **1946**: *Paraye Bas Mein*; **1948**: *Nek Dil*; **1949**: *Nirdosh Abla*.

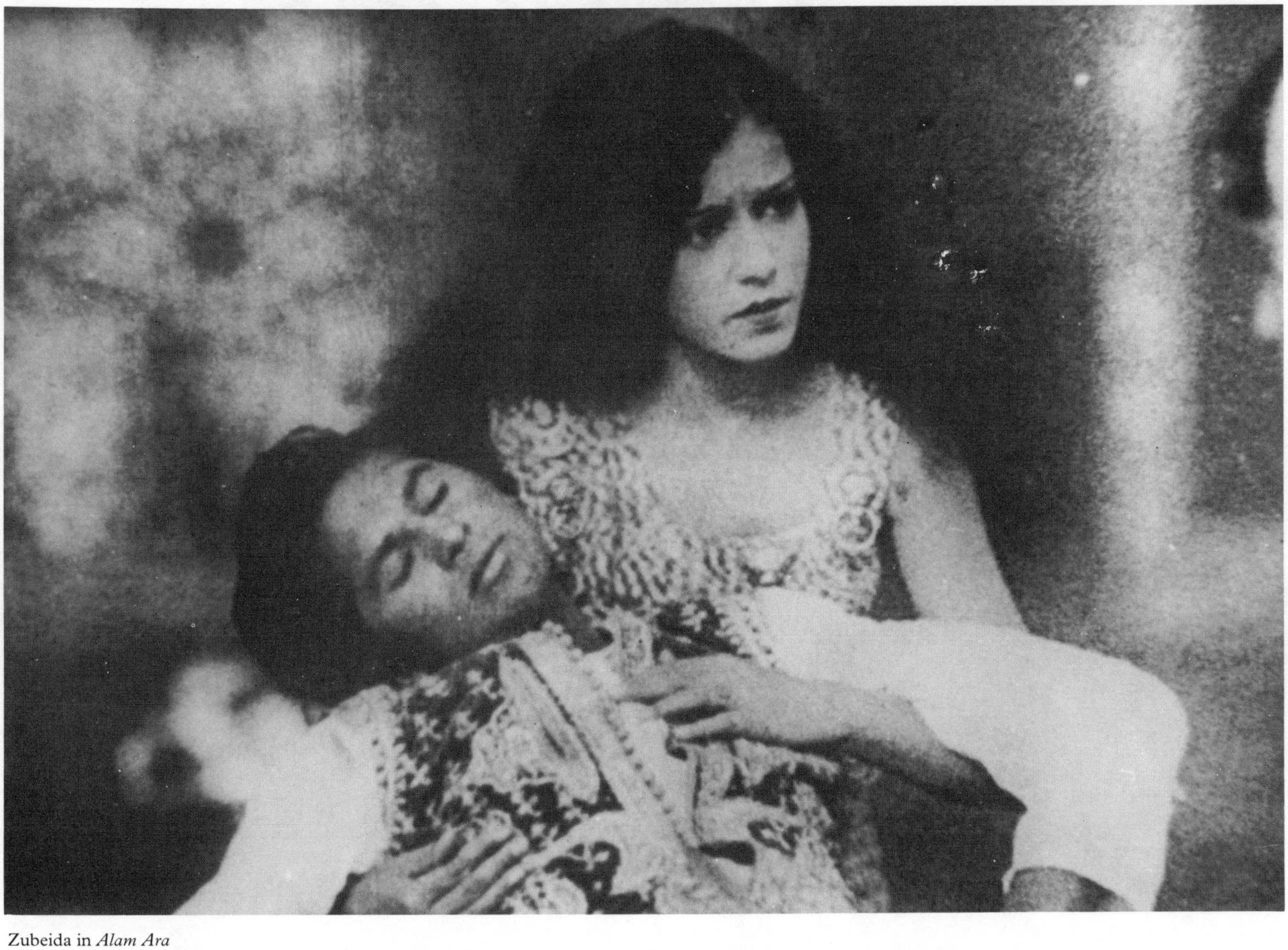

Zubeida in *Alam Ara*

Sathyan and Sheela in *Chemmeen*

PUNDALIK
1912 St c.12' b&w
d P.R. Tipnis, N.G. Chitre *c* Johnson?

Often presented as the first Indian film. Usually credited to **R.G. Torney**, but recent research suggests he was only marginally involved. Made jointly by N.G. Chitre, the manager of the Coronation Cinematograph in Bombay, and P.R. Tipnis, later a major Delhi-based distributor. The film about the Hindu saint is based, according to Harish Booch (1964), on Ramrao Kirtikar's Marathi play as staged by the Shripad Sangeet Mandali of Nasik. Shot on location in Bombay's Grant Road area by a **Bourne & Shepherd** crew and released at the Coronation on 18 May, 1912. For the record, it must be pointed out that film-makers such as **Hiralal Sen** had made similar films of stage plays before *Pundalik*.

RAJA HARISHCHANDRA
aka *King Harishchandra*
1913 St 3700 ft b&w
d/s/p **D.G. Phalke** *pc* **Phalke Films** *c* Trymbak B. Telang.
lp D.D. Dhabke, P.G. Sane, Bhalchandra D. Phalke, G.V. Sane, Dattatreya Kshirsagar, Dattatreya Telang, Ganpat G. Shinde, Vishnu Hari Aundhkar, Anna Salunke, Nath T. Telang.

Commonly performed and often-filmed *Mahabharata* legend. Definitive stage version by Vinayak Prasad 'Talib' for the Baliwala Victoria **Parsee theatre** group (1884). The homage to the upright King Harishchandra (Dhabke) who almost sacrifices his kingdom for his love of truth, opens with a **Ravi Varma**-like tableau showing the king, his wife Taramati (P.G. Sane) and his young son, to whom he is teaching archery. Derived from the **Sangeet Natak**, continuity is defined through juxtaposition of spatial planes (e.g. the space of the family idyll and the space 'beyond', while off-screen space functions like stage wings) which allow the narrative to be condensed into spaces against, and into, which the viewer's gaze traces a logic of movement. The hunt proceeds into and conquers the space beyond. Then the king blunders into a contiguous area controlled by the sage Vishwamitra (G.V. Sane), a mystical space opposed to the king's physical one. To atone for his mistake, the king is banished. In his play, Talib had introduced an ***Indrasabha***-like fairy to seduce the king into renouncing his kingdom. In the film, this figure surfaces in the form of the three furies caught in flames whom Harishchandra tries to rescue. The hunt sequence, as well as the reduction of Nakshatra, Vishwamitra's disciple, into a comic character, are faithful to the play. The king endures much hardship before a *deus ex machina* (here literally a god) emerges at the join of the horizon and the gaze (cf ***Shri Krishna Janma***, 1917) to reasssure everyone that the whole narrative was merely a test of the king's integrity. The cast was drawn from non-professionals and although Phalke wanted to cast women in the female roles (breaking with stage tradition), no women agreed to perform. The film, often celebrated as India's first feature (cf ***Pundalik***, 1912), was released on 3 May 1913 in Bombay and was a commercial and critical success. Phalke remade it at **Hindustan Films** as *Satyavadi Raja Harishchandra* (1917) shortened to 2944 ft. Only 1475 ft of the original film appear to have survived.

LANKA DAHAN
aka *Lanka Aflame*
1917 St 3000 ft b&w
d/p/s **D.G. Phalke** *pc* **Phalke Films** *c* Trymbak B. Telang.
lp Anna Salunke, Shinde, Mandakini Phalke

Phalke Films' last production is a mythological retelling of the familiar *Ramayana* story of Rama's (Salunke) wife Seeta being abducted by Ravana, the demon king of Lanka, and Rama's triumph with the aid of men and monkeys. The available footage of the film, 501 ft, offers sophisticated parallel cutting between three spaces: the tulasi platform where Seeta is held captive in Lanka, the villain, Ravana, coming to molest her and the brave Hanuman (Shinde) atop a tree witnessing the tragic scene below. Instead of editing according to a temporal narrative logic, Phalke uses a spatial logic: Seeta's space is physically and emotionally isolated, conveyed in foreground/background contrasts. Ravana moves towards her in two daring long shots, from right background to left foreground, first across his palace garden and along his pool (locating his characters in the way **stage backdrops** in Marathi theatre functioned), then through two elaborate circular movements as he jettisons his royalty and moves into the no-man's-land around Seeta, with Hanuman performing an athletic dance in rage and grief at the villain's progress. The film proved a success after opening at the Aryan cinema, Pune and at the West End, Bombay.

Shri Krishna Janma
aka *Birth of Shri Krishna*
1917 St 5500 ft b&w
d/s **D.G. Phalke** *pc* **Hindustan Cinema Films**
lp D.D. Dhabke, Purshottam Vaidya, Mandakini Phalke, Bhagirathibai, Neelkanth, P.M. Vaidya

Mandakini, the film-maker's daughter, played the child god Krishna, repeating her role in Phalke's next mythological, ***Kaliya Mardan*** (1919). Beginning with the invocation of 'almighty god', the only available sequence of the film (576 ft), which may in fact be its last episode, opens with a shot of a river from behind the backs of a group of people, echoing the position of the audience vis-a-vis the miraculous appearance of young Krishna rising out of the water astride the demon snake Kaliya. Phalke then cuts 180 degrees across the axis to the audience of the scene, an editing pattern he repeats several times, locking the two spaces into each other at right angles. The viewer enters Yashoda's space as she rocks the sleeping Krishna's crib and imagines the god as Gopala, generating a fantasy space in which the evil Kamsa imagines Krishna threateningly duplicated many times around him. Kamsa then imagines himself dead as his severed head rises up out of the frame and descends again, a matte effect that was one of the film's highlights. The end has people of all castes paying obeisance to the deity and Phalke inserted the title-card: 'May this humble offering be accepted by the Lord'. Adverts included a reference to a 'spectacular' scene of 'the heavenward flight of Maya in the form of lightning'. Released to great acclaim in Bombay.

KALIYA MARDAN
1919 St 6000 ft b&w
d/s **D.G. Phalke** *pc* **Hindustan Cinema Films**
lp Mandakini Phalke, Neelkanth

Introducing Phalke as the 'Pioneering Cine-Artist of the East', the most complete Phalke film extant opens with a series of shots demonstrating the 7-year-old Mandakini Phalke's acting skills through a series of facial expressions. The playmates of Krishna (Mandakini) are insulted by a female villager who splashes water on them. They take revenge by stealing butter from her house. When they are beaten up by the woman, they again take revenge. Krishna receives a gift of fruit and gives it away, 'an act which foreshadows his future benevolent inclination'. The film's most elaborately plotted sequence has Krishna entering the room of a wealthy merchant and his wife at night and tying the man's beard to his wife's hair. These exploits lead to a large crowd complaining of Krishna's antics to his foster parents. The film ends with Krishna vanquishing the demon snake Kaliya in a fierce underwater battle, intercut (cf ***Shri Krishna Janma***, 1917) with the faces of anxious observers. Krishna eventually rises triumphant with the slain demon's tail on his shoulder, garlanded by the now liberated wives of the demon.

SAIRANDHRI
1919 St 4958 ft b&w
d/s **Baburao Painter** *pc* **Maharashtra Film** *c* **S. Fattelal**
lp Balasabeb Yadav, Zunzharrao Pawar, Kamaladevi, Ganpatrao Bakre, Ansuyabai, **Baburao Pendharkar**, Gulabbai, Ravji Bhaskar

Painter's second film, a mythological alluding to contemporary politics, tells the *Mahabharata* story of the villainous Keechak's (Pawar) lusting after Sairandhri (Kamaladevi), the persona adopted by Draupadi in her 13th year of exile. As a maid who is supposed to be Swaraksita, she claims the protection of King Veerat (Bakre). Keechak, with the covert complicity of his sister Sudeshna, attacks the heroine and, after a spectacular chase through King Veerat's court, he is gorily beheaded by Bheema (Yadav). Pendharkar appears as Krishna. The published script (in Bhide and Gajbar, 1978) suggests several grand court scenes and a complicated narrative, more intricate than in **Phalke**'s contemporaneous work and with a more flexible use of space. Remade as a sound film by **Shantaram** (1933).

NALA DAMAYANTI

1920 St 4000 ft b&w
d Eugenio De Liguoro *pc* **Madan Theatres** *c* Jyotish Sarkar
lp **Patience Cooper**, Keki Adajania, Eugenio De Liguoro, D. Sarkari

Big-budget film featuring Madan's star, Patience Cooper as Damayanti and Adajania as Nala in an often filmed episode from the *Mahabharata*, relying on special effects, moving from 'Narada's Ascent of Mount Meru to Swarga, the Heaven of Indra, the Transformation in the Clouds of the Four Gods into impersonations of King Nala, Swan Messengers of Love, the Transformation of Kali, the Demon of Evil, into a Serpent, the Meeting of Kali and Dwapor and the Four Gods amidst the Blue Air', etc., according to a *Times of India* advert. De Liguoro, who also played Pushkar, was known in Italy for his Orientalist spectacles (e.g. *Fascino d'Oro*, 1919).

SHAKUNTALA

1920 St c.6000 ft b&w
d/sc **Suchet Singh** *pc* Oriental Film *st* Kalidasa's *Shakuntala c* Baron Von Rayvon (Roy Vaughan?)
lp Dorothy Kingdom, Goharjaan, Sampson, Mrs Sutria

Suchet Singh's debut, adapting Kalidas' Sanskrit play, features the American import Dorothy Kingdom in the title role, triggering a major **Swadeshi** debate with **S.N. Patankar** announcing a rival production in the *Bombay Chronicle* of 24 January 1920: *Shakuntala, or The Fateful Ring* (1920), adapted 'strictly in accordance with the drama'. **Hindustan Cinema Films** joined in claiming that its *Usha Swapna* was 'produced by Indian Artistes, by Indian Labour and Without Foreign Assistance'. Singh's film was a major success running for 40 consecutive days in Bombay. The cameraman was probably Roy N. Vaughan, an American import.

BHAKTA VIDUR

aka *Dharma Vijay*
1921 St 6835 ft b&w
d **Kanjibhai Rathod** *pc* **Kohinoor Film** *s* **Mohanlal G. Dave** *c* Gajanan S. Devare
lp Dwarkadas Sampat, Sakina, Maneklal Patel, **Homi Master**, Prabhashankar, Gangaram

One of the most famous silent mythologicals proposing a politically subversive allegory, causing a major censorship row. The *Mahabharata* story was advertised as a 'series of events between Pandavas and Kauravas, which led to the decline and downfall of the ancient empire and culminated in terrible war between the two rival factions. A **Swadeshi** film. Glory of the East, portrayed with a skill of acting which defies European art.' (*Bombay Chronicle*, 13 August 1921). Starred the studio's owners, Dwarkadas Sampat as Vidur and Maneklal Patel as Krishna, with Homi Master as Duryodhan. Initially successful in Bombay, it was first banned in Karachi, then in Madras, for being 'a thinly veiled resume of political events in India, Vidur appearing as Mr Gandhi clad in Gandhi-cap and khaddar shirt' (quoted in *ICC Report*, 1928). It was made partially in the wake of the anti-Rowlatt Act (1919) agitations and continued the studio's political documentaries representing Sampat's Gandhian nationalist adherences. Also known for a specially written music score performed live with every show, esp. the stridently nationalistic song in praise of the *charkha* (spinning wheel and Congress Party symbol) *Rudo maro rentiyo, rentiyama nikle taar, taare taare thai Bharatno udhaar*. Re-released as *Dharma Vijay* in 1923. Rathod and Dave courted notoriety again with ***Mahasati Ansuya*** (1921).

BILET PHERAT

aka *The England Returned*
1921 St c.4000 ft b&w
d/co-s N.C. Laharry *pc* Indo-British Film *p/co-s* **Dhirendranath Ganguly** *c* Jyotish Sarkar
lp Dhirendranath Ganguly, Manmatha Pal, Kunjalal Chakra, Sushilabala

Dhirendranath Ganguly made his acting debut in this famous satire contrasting conservative Bengali culture with that of the colonial elite. Advertised as a story about 'a young Indian [who] returns to his native land after a long absence and is so mightily impressed with his foreign training that, at his parental home, he startles everybody with his quixotic notions of love and matrimony' (*Bombay Chronicle*, 20 August 1921). Ganguly's acting incorporated Hollywood slapstick and a number of 19th century performance traditions from Calcutta. A long time in the making, the film was promoted as the first Bengali film, with a live 'all-Bengali' band to accompany the screening.

DHRUVA CHARITRA

aka *Triumph of Devotion*
1921 St c.4000 ft b&w
d Eugenio De Liguoro *pc* **Madan Theatres** *s* Shaida
lp **Patience Cooper**, Master Mohan, Signora Dorros, James Magarth, Master Manilal, Dadabhai Sarkari, **Aga Hashr Kashmiri**, Mrs Manelli, P. Manelli, Master Surajram

Mythological based on the Pauranic legend of the boy Dhruva whose quest for eternal salvation was rewarded when he became the brightest star in the heavens (the pole star is known as the Dhruvatara). As part of Madan's bid for an international breakthrough (cf ***Nala Damayani***, 1920, also by De Liguoro), the cast featured many Europeans with Cooper in the lead as Suniti. The *Times of India* (11 June 1921) noted that it offered 'directions in which a greater appeal may be made to the Westernised mind in trying to picture modern India.' The playwright Aga Hashr Kashmiri, then a Madan employee, played a small role (Dharmadev) and may have written some of the script, uncredited. The Indian version was successful but the film became better known in a shorter version adapted for Europe.

MAHASATI ANSUYA

aka *Birth of Shri Dattatreya*
1921 St 6927 ft b&w
d **Kanjibhai Rathod** *pc* **Kohinoor Film** *s* **Mohanlal G. Dave** *c* **V.B. Joshi**
lp Lina Valentine, Vaidya, Sakina

Successful Kohinoor mythological consolidating the partnership between Rathod and Dave (e.g. ***Bhakta Vidur***, 1921). It retells the *Ramayana* tale of Ansuya, who, with her husband Atri, shelters Rama, Seeta and Lakshmana during their banishment from Ayodhya. It gained notoriety for a nude shot of Sakina.

ANDHARE ALO

aka *The Influence of Love*
1922 St c.5000 ft b&w
d **Sisir Bhaduri, Naresh Mitra** *pc* Taj Mahal Film *st* Saratchandra Chatterjee *c* Nani Sanyal
lp Sisir Bhaduri, Naresh Mitra, Jogesh Choudhury, Durga Rani

Typical Saratchandra love-triangle short story provided the plot for Taj Mahal Film's debut production. An upper-class Bengali hero, the son of a zamindar, Satyendra, experiences the conflict between familial duty and the modern world in terms of his desire for an 11-year-old virgin bride, Radharani, and the nurturing and self-sacrificing courtesan Bijli. This is the first exploration in Bengali cinema of this plot's melodramatic potential (cf the films of Saratchandra's ***Devdas*** in 1928, 1935, 1955). The journal *Bijli* (1923) commended the acting in the emotionally charged scenes. **Painted backdrops** were used and, although Sourindramohan Mukherjee (in *Bangla Bioscope*) felt the film deployed several stereotypical scenes (drunkenness, a courtesan's dance), he recommended adapting more Saratchandra stories.

PATI BHAKTI

aka *Human Emotions*
1922 St 11710 ft b&w
d J.J. Madan *pc* **Madan Theatres** *s* Shaida
lp **Patience Cooper**, Master Mohan

Major Madan hit starring Cooper as Leelavati in a social advocating that women should be devoted to their husbands. A highlight in her career and a significant prototype of the genre (cf ***Gunsundari***, 1927). In Madras, the censor demanded that an 'obscene' dance sequence be removed.

VEER ABHIMANYU

aka *Virat Swaroop*
1922 St c.6500 ft b&w
d **Manilal Joshi** *pc* Star Films *s* **Mohanlal G. Dave** *c* V.B. Joshi
lp Sultana, **Fatma Begum**, Madanrai Vakil

Big-budget mythological by first-time producers **Ardeshir Irani** and Bhogilal

Dave, director Joshi and silent star Sultana (sister of **Zubeida**). Adverts in the *Bombay Chronicle* emphasised the 'expense of more than 100,000 rupees. More than 5000 people have taken part in the production of this film'. The plot is from the *Mahabharata* tale about Abhimanyu who learns of the Chakravyuha or battle formation of the Kauravas while in the womb of his mother, Subhadra (Fatma). The film was acclaimed for its war scenes. Sultana plays Uttara and Vakil is Krishna.

CATECHIST OF KIL-ARNI, THE

1923 St 5 reels b&w
co-d/c **R.S. Prakash** *co-d/co-s/p* Thomas Gavin Duffy *co-s* Bruce Gordon

Catholic propaganda film produced and written by the Irish lay-priest Thomas Gavin Duffy together with Bruce Gordon as a fund raiser for the Paris Foreign Mission Society in Pondicherry. Although there was a village called Kil-Arni nearby, the film was shot in March and April 1923 in the village of Sattiamangalam inhabited by Catholic Untouchables to avoid problems of caste and religious dissent. The plot tells of a reprobate called Ram who is converted to Catholicism by the exemplary conduct of the local priest (Duffy himself) during an epidemic. The main interest of the film resides in its location footage showing the landscapes and farming practices in the Velantangal district. The non-professional cast was recruited locally. The film was processed in Boston where it was premiered on 25 October 1923.

SAVITRI

aka *Savitri Satyavan*
1923 St 1634m b&w
d/sc Giorgio Mannini *p* Cines (Rome), **Madan Theatres** *s* Ferdinando Paolieri, Aldo de Benedetti *c* Gioacchino Gengarelli
lp Rina de Liguoro, Angelo Ferrari, Gianna Terribili-Gonzales

Described as India's first international co-production (cf **Nala Damayanti**, 1920; ***Dhruva Charitra***, 1921), this much-touted Madan film was shot in Rome with an Italian cast in 1923 and released in 1925. Italian sources do not mention the involvement of Madan Theatres. Some sources credit T. Marconi, who later shot ***Indrasabha*** (1932), with the cinematography and the original story is said to be by the indologist A. De Gubernati whose narrative was first translated into Gujarati by Ranina and thence into Hindi. The love-is-stronger-than-death story sees Savitri (de Liguoro), the daughter of King Ashwapati and a goddess, fall for Satyavan (Ferrari) who is destined to die within a year. He is killed by a tree and his soul is gathered by the god Yama (Terribili-Gonzales) but he returns to life and there is a happy ending for the lovers. Contemporary Italian critics described it both as a medieval legend transported to the Orient and a *1001 Nights* story. It was regarded as a colourful spectacle, promoted as Italy's most 'daring' film to date. Its delayed release and the short running time suggest that the film may have been re-edited, losing some nudity and other 'erotic' images to satisfy the censor.

SINHAGAD

1923 St 6880 ft b&w
d **Baburao Painter** *pc* **Maharashtra Film** *s* Hari Narayan Apte's novel *Gad Aala Pan Simha Gela* *c* **S. Fattelal**
lp Balasaheb Yadav, Kamaladevi, Miss Nalini, Baburao Painter, **V. Shantaram**, Zunzharrao Pawar, **Keshavrao Dhaiber**, **Narayanrao D. Sarpotdar**

India's first full-scale historical and the Maharashtra Studio's costliest film to date. Based on a classic by the best-known 19th/early 20th-C. Marathi novelist, it retells a famous episode in the military career of the 17th-C. Maratha emperor Shivaji (Painter) and his lieutanant, the folk hero Tanaji Malusare (Yadav). It features Tanaji's invasion of Fort Sinhagad in the dead of night, using his pet lizard to run up the wall with a rope, and his death in victory. The film was a major influence on subsequent Marathi cinema and on **Prabhat** films when Maharashtra Film's key technicians worked there. It was remade by V. Shantaram (1933).

BISMI SADI

aka *Twentieth Century*
1924 St 9170 ft b&w
d **Homi Master** *pc* **Kohinoor Film** *st* **Mohanlal G. Dave** *c* D.D. Dhabke
lp **Raja Sandow**, Noor Mohammed

Homi Master's directorial debut at Kohinoor is a **social** attacking Bombay's industrial parvenu class, initiating the realist-reformist **melodrama** as a genre. It tells of the street hawker Devidas, who goes to the city to make his fortune but, once successful, becomes an exploitative cotton mill owner and a callous snob knighted by the British. His wife, the kindly Hirabai, is made to suffer and his daughter Rukmini is dishonoured. The happy ending sees his deathbed repentance and Rukmini is saved by the real heir to the business. Location shots filmed on board a steamer and the mise en scene of a factory workers' violent revolt figured prominently in the film's marketing campaign.

GUL-E-BAKAVALI

1924 St 7997 ft b&w
d **Kanjibhai Rathod** *pc* **Kohinoor Film** *s* **Mohanlal G. Dave**
lp **Zubeida**, **Fatma Begum**, Sultana, Khalil, Abdul Ghani, Noor Mohamed, Raja Babu, Miss Moti, Jamna

One of the most successful silent films tells the legend of the fairy Bakavali (Zubeida), her deivi pushp (or divine flower) Gul known for its healing powers, and the Eastern prince Taj-ul-Mulk (Khalil), who wants the flower to cure his blind father. The origins of this popular legend vary. One version claims it was introduced into India by Nihal Chand Lahori's *Mazhab-e-Ishq*, written around the turn of the 19th C. under the influence of his British teacher John Gilchrist at the Fort William College in Calcutta. Another traces it to Abley Sheikh's narration of the story in 1513 couplets from which it was adapted by several Kashmiri writers into Urdu couplets in the Masnavi form. It was a favourite on the Parsee stage, esp. the scenes where Taj-ul-Mulk faces his villainous brothers who steal the flower as Bakavali is turned to stone and installed in a temple, and her human re-birth. It was often filmed, including in several South Indian languages (**Dhirubhai Desai**'s *Paristan*, 1957; a Tamil version starring **M.G. Ramachandran** in 1955; a Telugu one, *Gul-e-Bakavali Katha*, starring **N.T. Rama Rao** in 1962). This version, made in 97 scenes, featured Kohinoor superstars Zubeida and Khalil. It was one of the first films to embrace the folk-fantasy mode as opposed to e.g. Rathod and Dave's mythologicals (***Bhakta Vidur***, ***Mahasati Ansuya***, both 1921).

KALA NAAG

aka *Kalyug Ki Sati* aka *Triumph of Justice*
1924 St 8200 ft b&w
d **Kanjibhai Rathod** *pc* **Kohinoor Film** *s* **Mohanlal G. Dave** *c* Gajanan S. Devare, D.D. Dhabke
lp Sultana, **Homi Master**, Ibrahim, Moti, Savita, Tara, Behram Vasunia, Vaidya, **Zubeida**, **Fatma Begum**, Khalil

There is some debate about whether this film was made by Rathod or by Homi Master, its male star. It claimed realist intent, mainly for its thinly veiled allusions to a major scandal in Bombay known as the Champsi-Haridas murder case. Vihari, the son of a rich mill owner, falls into the clutches of crooks led by Kalidas, aka the Black Cobra, who also has designs on Nirmala, Vihari's wife. The *Bombay Chronicle* (5 January 1924) advertised the film as a 'thrilling plot revealing various styles of treacherous fraud of the modern civilisation and dreadful assassination for the ardent desire of wealth or passions and rape and ravishment by atrocious villains'.

KALYAN KHAJINA

aka *The Treasures of Kalyan*
1924 St 9440 ft b&w
d **Baburao Painter** *pc* **Maharashtra Film** *c* **S. Fattelal**
lp Chimasaheb Bhosle, K.P. Bhave, Sultana, **Master Vithal**, Kamaladevi, Miss Nalini, Bedi, Zunzharrao Pawar, **Baburao Painter**

Quasi-historical adventure movie based on the exploits of the 17th-C. Maratha emperor Shivaji (Bhosle). A large part of the film was shot in a cave where Shivaji meets the Subedar of Kalyan (Bhave). The design of the cave is often hailed as an art-directorial triumph for the studio. The film's dramatic highlight occurs when, inspecting stolen Mughal wealth, Shivaji suddenly confronts not a box-full of coins but a fair maiden (Sultana) emerging from one of the crates full of treasure. It is also stunt superstar Master Vithal's debut, apparently in the role of a dancing-girl.

PAAP NO FEJ

aka *The Debt of Sin*
1924 St 6782 ft b&w
co-d **Ardeshir Irani** *co-d/st* **Naval Gandhi** *pc* Majestic Film *c* Bhogilal K.M. Dave
lp **B.P. Mishra**, Tara, Asooji, Elizer

The best-known Gandhi-Irani co-direction at Majestic is a moralistic social in a contemporary setting, successfully translating

Hollywood conventions (e.g. parallel cutting). The plot concerns a young woman, Sarojini (Tara), who, under the influence of her jailbird cousin Jairam (Mishra) swindles her aged husband and ruins her lover, the next door neighbour Thakurdas (Asooji). In spite of the moralism, the film's interest and energy derive from the depiction of moral turpitude and modernity represented by a race course, the cotton market and bars. Highlights include a car chase and Jairam's narrow escape from the police while Sarojini and Thakurdas end up in jail.

POONA RAIDED

aka *Poona Par Hallo*
1924 St 7453 ft b&w
d/s Mama Warerkar *pc* Deccan Pics *c* Ramrao Anandkar
lp Miss Bhawani, Krishnarao Ketkar, Shankarrao Sahasrabuddhe, Shankarrao Moghe, **Vishnupant Pagnis**, Miss Kaiser, Krishnarao Pethkar, Baburao Sansare, Datta Varane, Haripant Kulkarni, Narayanrao Phaterphekar, Shankarrao Shinde, Pandharinath Kale, Lakshmanrao Rane, Mohammed Arab, Shuplani Mukherjee, Ratansha Vakil, Miss Dulari, **Sundarrao Nadkarni**

This expensive historical, the most ambitious production of the Pune-based Deccan Pics, is a seminal item in Marathi cinema's influential tradition later continued by **Sarpotdar** and inherited by **Bhalji Pendharkar**: the Right-wing valorisation of the 17th-C. Maratha emperor Shivaji. It was also the best-known directorial effort by one of the Marathi theatre's major playwrights, B.V. (Mama) Warerkar, whose play *Satteche Gulam* (1922), transformed the Marathi stage with the first full-blown instance of Ibsenite stage naturalism. This film retells the legendary episode, a favourite of numerous popular historians of Maratha glory, of Mughal emperor Aurangzeb's (Sahasrabuddhe) attack on the fort city of Poona and of how Shivaji (Ketkar) repelled it. Although it shared the scale of, e.g., **Painter**'s ***Sinhagad*** (1923), it was probably made with greater awareness of the contemporary anti-imperialist metaphors of the historical genre and the ideological Hindu and Marathi-chauvinist dimensions of the era. Apart from Sarpotdar, who continued in this vein when he acquired Deccan, the other film-maker to launch his career was Sundarrao Nadkarni, appearing in a minor role.

PRITHVI VALLABH

aka *The Lord of Love and Power*
1924 St 7456 ft b&w
d **Manilal Joshi** *pc* Ashoka Pics *sc* Sirur based on **K.M. Munshi**'s novel *c* V.B. Joshi
lp **P.Y. Altekar**, Wagle Sandow, **Fatma Begum**, **Zubeida**, Sultana, Miss Jaina

Seminal silent historical and the first film adaptation of Gujarati novelist K.M. Munshi. Just before the film was made, the story was serialised in the journal *Vismi Sadi* and its allusions to current events became controversial. Gandhi criticised it for departing from the principles of non-violence and abstinence. The story features King Munja, ruler of Aranti, famed warrior and patron of the arts who Munshi saw as 'the gay, amoral man radiating power and love - extracting joy from every moment - true to himself, under all conditions, in conquest, defeat, in prison, in love, when betrayed and sentenced to death. Critics fell on me like voracious tigers - Munja was so immoral! The truth was that in him the readers saw the man who lived as most people wanted to live but dared not.' (Munshi in a speech, 1947). Munja (Sandow) falls into the hands of his arch enemy Tailap, who received assistance from Bhillam (Altekar), king of Dharavati. Tailap orders that Munja be put to death but is held back by Tailap's powerful sister Minalvati (Fatma Begum), a widow who first wants to break Munja's spirit. Instead, she and Munja fall in love. Learning of Munja's plan to escape with Minalvati, Tailap has Munja trampled to death by his elephants. Manilal Joshi's film was also an ambitious launch for the new Ashoka Pics set up as an independent technicians' co-operative. The big production shot mainly around the Makkarpura palace in Baroda with sets designed by **R.S. Choudhury**, had climactic scenes featuring the elephant stampede and created a sensation. It was also noted for its costume design. Joshi defended the film's technical defects and implausibilities in a note published when it was released, claiming all this would be excused when India one day 'finds its place in the pantheon of world cinema'. It was remade by **Sohrab Modi** as a spectacular in 1943.

SADGUNI SUSHILA

aka *Sushila the Virtuous* aka *Triumph of Truth*
1924 St 7997 ft b&w
d **Kanjibhai Rathod**? *pc* **Kohinoor Film** *s* **Mohanlal G. Dave**

Attributed to Rathod, this is a love story claiming to uphold the tradition of domesticated female virtue and a classic example of a reform novel-derived plot being transmuted into a thriller melodrama using elaborate references to the freedom struggle. Story tells of virtuous Sushila and her debauched husband Pratap, who leads a peaceful life until her former suitor Jaswant arrives on a social call. His appearance prompts Pratap to suspect his wife's marital fidelity and he drives the visitor away. Returning to retrieve his belongings, Jaswant surprises a gang of burglars who shoot him dead. The leader of the gang, the police chief Vinayak, frames Pratap for the murder. Pratap runs away and what appears to be his corpse is found in a well. Vinayak now makes amorous advances to Sushila who is resigned to widowhood (performing symbolically laden acts like weaving on the charkha). After some years, Pratap reappears having discovered the truth about Vinayak's criminal deals (but apparently unrepentant about his own nasty behaviour towards his wife).

SATI PADMINI

aka *Beauty of Rajasthan*, aka *Siege of Chittor*
1924 St 5990 ft b&w
d **Baburao Painter** *pc* **Maharashtra Film** *c* **S. Fattelal**
lp Bedi, Ganpat Bakre, Balasaheb Yadav, Nalini, **V. Shantaram**, Zunzharrao Pawar, Dwarka

Painter moved outside his favourite Maratha history for this story of the legendary Rajput queen Padmini of Chittor. At the turn of the century, Rajput history, often drawn from the *Raso* sagas (corresponding to medieval European lays of prowess and chivalry), together with Maratha history were the most popular sources of screen historicals evoking pre-colonial grandeur. The story is set against the violent siege of Chittor, the Rajput capital, by the sultan of Delhi, Allauddin Khilji (Bedi), which temporarily saw the end of the Chauhan dynasty (14th C.). According to legend, during a state visit to Chittor, Khilji caught sight of a reflection of Queen Padmini and became so infatuated that he attacked the Chittor fortress, defeating the Rajputs. However, Padmini, with her entire entourage, had committed sati (ritual suicide) by the time Khilji arrived. The film capitalised on its screening at the British Empire exhibition at Wembley and received some favourable reviews in the British press, a fact always mentioned in references to the film in autobiographies or film histories.

SATI SARDARBA

1924 St 8747 ft b&w
d/s **Nanubhai Desai** *pc* Saraswati Film *c* Bhogilal K.M. Dave
lp **Zubeida**, Sultana, Mohanlala, **Fatma Begum**

The debut production of Saraswati Film, an offshoot of **Irani**'s Star Studio. Mulraj (Mohanlala), an alcoholic and gambler, wagers his sister Sardarba (Zubeida) to a bunch of crooks and loses her. The rest of the film focuses on Sardarba's tormented life and how she comes through her trials with her virtue intact. Apart from the sisters Zubeida and Sultana and their star mother Fatma Begum, the film features a rare screen appearance of Gujarati stage star Mohanlala (cf ***Narasinh Mehta***, 1932).

BAAP KAMAI

aka *Fortune and Fools*
1925 St 8927 ft b&w
d **Kanjibhai Rathod** *pc* **Krishna Film** *st* Shaida *c* **Chimanlal Luhar**
lp Gulab, **Gohar**, Ermeline, Gangaram, Nandram, Putli

Seth Madhavadas's only son Laxmidas aka Bachuseth (Gangaram) is brought up with affection but also strict discipline. Surviving on a small allowance, he cannot sustain his expensive habits, particularly after he is befriended by the scoundrels Harilal and Chiman who try to exploit his family's wealth. Madhavadas dies leaving his son in the care of his trusted manager. Bachuseth then meets the actress Roshanara, a lady of ill repute who, with Harilal and Chiman, entices him to a gambling den. The villains tell Bachuseth that his wife is having an affair with Kundan, the son of his manager-guardian. Bachuseth dismisses the manager and his son and, gradually, Harilal and Chiman take over the business, including the inherited wealth, leaving Bachuseth a pauper. He is eventually helped by the sacked Kundan. The film is mainly remembered as Gohar's film debut, albeit in a minor role. Based on a novel by the

Gujarati writer Shaida, the film illustrates a genre of popular fiction addressing the urban experience in colonial India, a fertile terrain to dramatise the encounter between traditional cultural values and those of the West.

BAJIRAO MASTANI

1925 St 7679 ft b&w
d/s **Bhalji Pendharkar** *pc* **Sharda Film** *c* Bhogilal K.M. Dave
lp **Master Vithal**, Yakub, Nanasaheb Phatak, Miss Jones

Pendharkar's film debut, foreshadowing his later use of Maratha history, focuses on the Maratha Peshwai (18th C.). It is an uncharacteristic production launching the silent era's most famous manufacturer of stunt movies, Sharda Film, and features the legendary Marathi stage actor, Nanasaheb Phatak.

CINEMA QUEEN

aka *Love's Sacrifice*
1925 St 8550 ft b&w
d **Mohan Bhavnani** *pc* **Kohinoor Film** *st* **Mohanlal G. Dave** *c* V.B. Joshi
lp **Sulochana**, Khalil, Putli

Bhavnani's directorial debut and one of Sulochana's first big films also inaugurated the very popular 'lives of the stars' genre. This film was about a poor painter named Chandrakant (Khalil) who is about to commit suicide when he meets the film star Manjiri (Sulochana). He is creatively rejuvenated by the fantasies she inspires. Manjiri's modelling sessions are used to narrate her biography: her mother was a prostitute with a heart of gold who made sure her daughter was well educated. Chandrakant and Manjiri fall in love, but he is already married and his vampish, ill-tempered wife will not set him free. Exploiting the autobiographical ambiguities generated by a star playing a star, the film shows how Sulochana's image was being moulded for exploitation at Kohinoor and later at the **Imperial** Studio.

FANKDO FITURI

aka *Handsome Blackguard*
1925 St 16400 ft b&w
d **Homi Master** *pc* **Kohinoor Film** *st* Pijam *sc* **Mohanlal G. Dave** *c* D.D. Dhabke, Gajanan S. Devare
lp **Homi Master**, Athavale, Miss Moti, Boman Behram, Fram Sethna, Yakbal, Thelma Wallace, Yvonne Wallace

One of the first elaborate film translations of the **Parsee theatre**, the film is based on a popular novel by Pijam (aka P.J. Marzban), editor of the newspaper *Jam-e-Jamshed* and playwright. Released as a two-part serial, the adverts summarised the story as: 'A charming heiress, a good-looking but villainous doctor, a timid lover, a crafty detective, a singing girl, a Nawab in his dotage and a dancing woman from the gutter. A photodrama that rings with love, hate, villainy, and fidelity'; 'The magnificent Parsee-Hindu-Muslim screen romance, from the extremely popular and sensational novel, [a] fascinating and thrilling story of social life of today, starring the beautiful and emotional artists Miss Thelma Wallace and Miss Yvonne Wallace'. It helped consolidate its maker and lead actor, Homi Master, playing Yakub the detective, as the top-selling film-maker at Kohinoor. Athavale played the eponymous handsome blackguard.

KULIN KANTA

1925 St 9144 ft b&w
d **Homi Master** *pc* **Kohinoor Film** *st* **Mohanlal G. Dave** *c* Gokhale
lp Miss Moti, Jamna, Khalil, Boman Behram, Ganibabu, Yakbal

Advertised as a 'dramatic version of love, jealousy and loyalty along with disastrous results of superstition and hot-headedness and the miseries of a deserted and ill-treated Hindu wife' and a 'story of Hindu superstition and its ruinous results', this film extends Homi Master's tendency (***Bismi Sadi***, 1924) to weave major social scandals into a fast-paced narrative with socially critical pretensions. The plot is derived from the Bawla murder case. The maharaja of Holkar fell in love with a dancing girl named Mumtaz (played by Moti) who spurned his advances because she loved another man. In fact, the maharaja had the man kidnapped in full public view and killed, a scene included in the film, shot on the Chowpatty waterfront in Bombay. The film was presented as critiquing the behaviour of religious leaders while showing communal unity among the lower classes. It equally valorises the love between brother and sister as well as between sisters-in-law. Reviewers often commended Master for his ability to elaborate highly complicated plots.

LANKA NI LAADI

aka *Fairy of Ceylon*
1925 St 9101 ft b&w
d **Homi Master** *pc* **Kohinoor Film** *st* **Mohanlal G. Dave** *c* Gajanan S. Devare
lp Jamna, **Gohar**, Khalil

This fantasy, with overtones of Greek legend, is Gohar's first major hit and grossed more than any other film in 1925. The story is set in Lanka, present-day Sri Lanka and a site for some of the most important action of the *Ramayana* epic. The king is told that he will be killed by his grandson and that his daughter will marry a brave shepherd. When bandits come to steal cows from the royal park, the princess (Gohar) gives chase and is helped by a passing shepherd (Khalil). They fall in love and the shepherd claims her hand in marriage. The king then sends the shepherd on a series of dangerous adventures around the globe, hoping that he will die. However, the shepherd cures the ailing king of neighbouring Ghoga and is declared the heir to the kingdom, an event that enables the union of the couple and the realisation of the two predictions. The highlight is said to be a scene where the wounded shepherd is fed milk by a lioness.

MAHARACHI POR

aka *Dher Ni Chhokri* aka *Two Little Untouchables* aka *The Untouchables*
1925 St 7986 ft b&w
d **Narayanrao D. Sarpotdar** *pc* United Pics Syndicate *c* Pandurang Talegiri
lp **P.Y. Altekar**, Joshi, Miss Jones, Dattoba Rajwade

Influential reformist social about an Untouchable girl who marries a Brahmin. The film draws its influence from a strand of Ibsenite naturalism pioneered on the Marathi stage by playwright Mama Warerkar. Warerkar had, the previous year, made ***Poona Raided*** for Deccan Pics, predecessors of United Pics, with Sarpotdar. This was a brief occasion for the convergence of Left progressives with mainstream Hindu reformism, e.g. in the journalism of N.S. Phadke, associate of Sarpotdar and an influence on the Natyamanwantar group (1933, cf **K. Narayan Kale**). It did not last long, as Sarpotdar's work revealed in its increasing assimilation of Hindu Mahasabha-inspired religious and regional Marathi chauvinism.

MOJILI MUMBAI

aka *The Slaves of Luxury*
1925 St 8220 ft b&w
d/s **Manilal Joshi** *pc* **Kohinoor Film** *c* D.D. Dhabke
lp Yakbal, **Raja Sandow**, Jamna, Ganibabu, Moti, Nur Mohammed, Saraswati

Joshi's best-known film and, with ***Bismi Sadi*** (1924), his most successful attempt to locate the narrative in the present day. Presented as a comment on the lifestyle of Bombay's rich, the film tells of the wealthy Mr Nanavati (Sandow) who is attracted to a dancer, Roshanara (Yakbal) who in turn is represented by a Dalal (agent or, more precisely, pimp) named Chhotalal (Nur Mohammed). Chhotalal plans to rob Nanavati and seizes his chance when the rich man buys a gold necklace as a present for his daughter's birthday. Chhotalal tempts Nanavati to visit Roshanara, who then seduces him and obtains the necklace. When Nanavati realises that he has been duped, he accuses Chhotalal, who has by then switched the necklace for a fake. The film led to a debate in the pages of the journal *Be-Ghadi Mouj* about the meaning of realism in film between Shaida, the editor and himself a scenarist, and Joshi. Joshi denied any critical intent, claiming he merely wished to point to an all-too-common incident in Bombay. The only other interesting thing about the characters is the continual reapparance in Kohinoor's film themes (e.g. ***Baap Kamai***, 1925), of a dancer of ill repute named Roshanara, based, apparently, on a real cabaret dancer of that name.

MUMBAI NI MOHINI

aka *Social Pirates*, aka *Night Side of Bombay*
1925 St 8879 ft b&w
d **Nanubhai Desai** *pc* Saraswati Film *st* Nirbhayshankar Thakkar *c* Bhogilal K.M. Dave
lp **Fatma Begum**, Mohanlala, Dorabji, Mewawala

Millionaire Ratanlal (Mohanlala) is an old man without an heir. He marries the rich, Western-educated Mohini. He has two managers, the sincere and faithful

Dhairyadhar and the Anglicised crook Manhar. Mohini, bored with her marriage, falls in love with Manhar who embezzles Rs 50,000 from Ratanlal's office and frames Dhairyadhar for the crime, who is imprisoned. Mohini's affair with Manhar develops and they decide to eliminate old man Ratanlal but they are caught. In the end the two schemers die. The title, which in translation simply means Mohini of Bombay, is also a pun on the phrase 'the Charms of Bombay'. It preceded by a few months **Kohinoor**'s ***Mojili Mumbai***, the best-known example of a thriller set amongst Bombay's colonial bourgeoisie. Desai's film ran into a legal problem when the noted Gujarati novelist Gopalji Delwadkar claimed that he had written the script, commissioned by Bhogilal Dave's Star Film and that it was based on his novel *Chandrakala* (possibly adapted from Baron Lytton's play *Night And Morning*). Nirbhayshankar Thakkar, officially credited with the story, claimed that he had written it drawing on his own experiences as a poor medical student in Bombay.

SANAMANI SHODHMA

aka *Looking for Love*
1925 St 7468 ft b&w
d R.N. Vaidya *pc* **Saurashtra Film** *s/c* **Chimanlal Luhar**

Love fantasy from the short-lived but culturally influential Saurashtra Studio. Two young men, Naval and Mavji, dream of their ideal love. Naval's fantasy draws upon the *Laila Majnu* story while Mavji's is from the *Arabian Nights*. Trying to realise their dreams, Mavji falls for a woman he sees in a horse-drawn carriage. Naval meets Dolar, the daughter of Seth Kapurchand, who is trying to escape from an oppressive home. Mavji steals jewels which Naval had bought for Dolar, but the lovers overcome adversity and live happily ever after.

SAVKARI PASH

aka *Indian Shylock*
1925 St 5984 ft b&w
d **Baburao Painter** *pc* **Maharashtra Film** *s* **Narayan Hari Apte** *c* **S. Fattelal**
lp **V. Shantaram**, Zunzharrao Pawar, Kamaladevi, **Narayanrao Sarpotdar**

The Marathi cinema's first explicit **social**, written by one of Maharashtra's most popular novelists in this genre. A peasant (Shantaram) loses his land to a greedy money-lender and moves to the city where he becomes a mill worker. Taking its cue from the realist tradition, the film counterposes an idyllic rural life (destroyed by the greedy money-lender who uses forged papers to steal the peasant's land) with the harsh city life. In spite of its high melodrama, the film was hailed as a realist breakthrough. Critics noted the poetic combination of visuals evoking sound and light, singling out the shot of a hut accompanied by a howling dog as one of the most memorable moments of the Indian cinema to date. The ending intercuts the money-lender snoring with his head on his safe while the poor peasant turned proletarian

PREM SANYAS

aka *The Light of Asia* aka *Die Leuchte Asiens*
1925 St 9437 ft b&w
d **Franz Osten** *pc* Great Eastern Film, Emelka Film (Munich), The Indian Players *sc* **Niranjan Pal** *st* Edwin Arnold *c* Josef Wirsching, Willi Kiermeier
lp **Seeta Devi**, **Himansu Rai**, Sarada Ukil, Rani Bala, Prafulla Roy, Dayanananda, **Modhu Bose**

Osten's Indian debut launched the Indo-German unit which grew into **Bombay Talkies**. Pal's adaptation of Arnold's 1861 Orientalist epic opened with documentary shots of tourists in Bombay watching street performers. Then a white-bearded old man sitting under the bodhi tree tells the tourists the story of Gautama (Rai), son of King Suddhodhana (Ukil) and Queen Maya (Bala), who left his consort Gopa (Seeta) and became a wandering teacher credited with founding Buddhism. The religious epic, with its idealised figures, takes up the narrative in flashback and ends with Gopa kneeling before Gautama asking to become his disciple. The film suggests that the real aim of Buddhism is the de-sexualisation of women. Released in India in 1926, it also received a major release in Germany with a score written by I.L. Fischer and Hans-Heinrich Dransmann. The film was hyped, mainly by Osten, as the 'first specifically Indian film' and the production was aided by a wealthy maharaja who contributed the use of his subjects, dressed in valuable old costumes, and 30 richly decorated elephants. One of the film's highlights, besides Seeta Devi's performance, is Wirsching's use of deep focus, as in the scene where Gopa watches a spectacular contest between Gautama and Devadatta (Roy) in the royal court. A key influence on the film's style was probably the costume and set designer, and future director, **Charu Roy**. A 90' version was screened in the US in 1928, shortly after the wedding of a Nancy Miller to a maharajah. Some sources credit Himansu Rai as co-director. The discrepancy in the film's length may be due to different Indian and European versions.

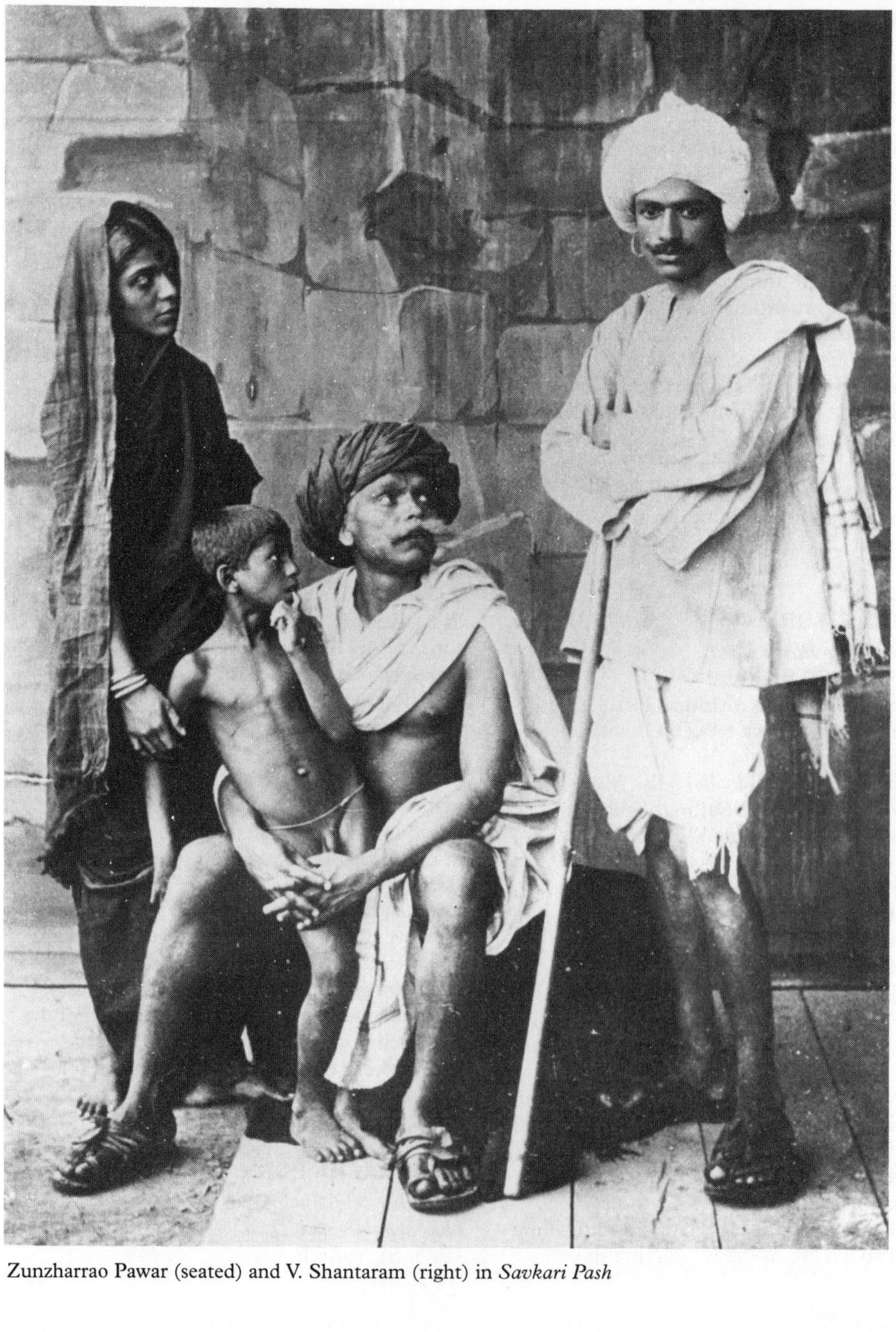

Zunzharrao Pawar (seated) and V. Shantaram (right) in *Savkari Pash*

trudges the streets. It was remade in 1936, hyping the drama with scenes showing the money-lender with a sexy courtesan.

VEER KUNAL

1925 St 7235 ft b&w
d/s **Manilal Joshi** *pc* **Kohinoor Film** *c* D.D. Dhabke
lp **Raja Sandow**, Yakhbal, Miss Moti, Athavale, Bachubabu

This legend drawn from the *Asokavadana* stories is set at the time of the Maurya empire (3rd C. B.C.). Kunal (Sandow), son of Emperor Ashoka (Athavale) and Queen Padmavati, has beautiful eyes but a prediction says he will go blind. The villainous Tishyaraksha (Yakhbal) gains Ashoka's confidence and plots to have Kunal blinded and killed. The official executioners spare Kunal and he becomes a wandering singer accompanied by his favourite wife Kanchanmala (Moti). In Pataliputra, Ashoka hears Kunal's song, realises that Kunal's misfortune may have been a punishment for some past sin of the emperor himself and condemns Tishyaraksha to death, restoring Kunal to the court. The film acquired an avant-garde reputation for breaking with convention using close shots and with Dhabke's camera deploying a sophisticated range of grey tones. It can be seen as a distant ancestor to the psycho-historicals of **Mehboob**: one concrete connecting link was **R.S. Choudhury**, apprenticed to Joshi for this film.

BHAKTA PRAHLAD

1926 St 7447 ft b&w
d/s **Dadasaheb Phalke** *pc* **Hindustan Cinema** *c* Salunke
lp Bhapurao Datar, Bachu, Gangaram, Yamuna Gole

Drawn from the *Vishnu Purana*, this legend tells of Prahlad (Gangaram), the son of the demon tyrant Hiranyakashapu (Bachu). Prahlad disobeys his father by worshipping the latter's hated enemy, Vishnu (Datar). He undergoes tortures, including being burnt in oil, trampled beneath an elephant and poisoning, until, finally, Vishnu appears from a pillar in his Narasimha guise to overwhelm the demon. Available footage: 519 ft.

BULBUL-E-PARISTAN

1926 St 9427 ft b&w
d/s **Fatma Begum** *pc* Fatma Film *c* Pandurang Naik, Rustom Irani
lp **Zubeida**, **Sultana**, Putli, Madame Tosca, Madanrai Vakil, Athavale

Probably the first Indian feature directed by a woman. Available information suggests it was a big-budget fantasy abounding with special effects set in a Parastan or fairyland. **Ardeshir Irani** may have helped with the trick photography.

NEERA

aka *Beautiful Snake of Aravalli*
1926 St 9217 ft b&w
co-d/s **R.S. Choudhury** *co-d* **R.G. Torney** *pc* Lakshmi Film *c* Pandurang Naik
lp **Raja Sandow**, **Zubeida**, Putli, Baba Vyas, Ghory

Choudhury's influential directorial debut breaks new generic ground, depicting tribals and presenting mysticism and sexuality as primal powers. Neera (Zubeida), a temple priest's daughter, lives amongst tribals. A Kapalik (Sandow), i.e. a devotee of Kali said to possess mystical powers, uses them to acquire tribal lands. The conflict is between his powers and the shield of innocence around Neera, leading to the villain's destruction. Conflict over land rights was later used extensively by Choudhury's apprentice, **Mehboob** (e.g. ***Roti***, 1942).

SUVARNA KAMAL

aka *Kalika Murti* aka *Golden Lotus*
1926 St 10176 ft b&w
d/s K.P. Bhave *pc* **Sharda Film** *c* Naval P. Bhatt
lp **Master Vithal**, Marie, Shiraz Ali Hakim, Janibabu, Heera, Miss Rosy

Typical Vithal-Sharda stunt film featuring a masked adventurer in quest of a golden lotus, which involves placating the terrible goddess Mahakali. The film teemed with Bhatt' special effects (e.g. giant genies) and showed the influence of Douglas Fairbanks's work as well as of folk-fantasies (***Gul-e- Bakavali***, 1924; ***Indrasabha***, 1932) while continuing in the vein of the studio's earlier successes, *Ratan Manjari* and *Madan Kala*, both 1926.

TELEPHONE GIRL, THE

1926 St 8427 ft b&w
d **Homi Master** *pc* **Kohinoor Film** *st* **Mohanlal G. Dave** *c* **Narayan G. Devare**
lp **Sulochana**, **Gohar**, Khalil, **Raja Sandow**, Jamna

Sulochana's most famous silent film sees her as a telephone operator, a job she used to do in real life, who becomes the love object of a leading lawyer (Sandow). The problems of inter-community marriage are highlighted, as is the value of patriotism through the character of Peter, the heroine's brother (Khalil). The film also refers to a collectivisation movement among farmers (inspired by events in the USSR). Writer Dave was commended for his ability to entwine disparate narrative strands while introducing contemporary references. For his debut as cameraman, Devare pioneered the use of real locations, shooting in the Grant Road telephone exchange in Bombay.

VANDE MATARAM ASHRAM

1926 St 6590 ft b&w
d/s/co-p **Bhalji Pendharkar** *co-p* **Baburao Pendharkar** *pc* Vande Mataram Film *c* D.D. Dhabke
lp Yamunadevi, **P.Y. Altekar**, Baburao Pendharkar

Independently produced by Bhalji and his brother Baburao Pendharkar in between leaving **Maharashtra Film** and joining **Prabhat**, this was a major silent political film influenced by the Hindu ideals of the nationalist leaders Lala Lajpat Rai and Madan Mohan Malaviya (the founder of Benares Hindu University). It criticises the British education policies and counterposed a defence of 'traditional' Indian teaching systems. The film was repeatedly censored, even banned briefly, and eventually released in a mutilated version.

BALIDAN

aka *Bisarjan* aka *Sacrifice*
1927 St 8282 ft b&w
d **Naval Gandhi** *pc* Orient Pics *st* **Rabindranath Tagore**'s play *sc* Jamshed Ratnagar *c* Naval P. Bhatt
lp **Sulochana**, **Zubeida**, **Master Vithal**, Sultana, Jal Khambatta, Janibabu

The Indian Cinematograph Committee of 1928 used *Balidan* and ***Janjirne Jankare*** (1927) to show how 'serious' Indian cinema could match Western standards. Based on Tagore's play of 1887, the film's advertising emphasised the high literary quality of its source. The plot of this quasi-mythological is set in the fictional land of Tippera and features Queen Gunavati (Sulochana), King Govinda, Aparna the beggar girl (Zubeida) and the priest Raghupati who runs a Kali temple. The story addresses the conflict between reformist enlightenment and obsolete, inhuman ritual, questioning the contemporary validity of traditional rituals. The dramatic pivot is the conflict between the king who has banned animal sacrifice, and the priest who calls for the king's own blood. Emotionally, the film revolves around the childless queen and a beggar girl whose pet goat has been taken for the sacrifice and who loves a servant in the temple. Except for the temple scenes, much of the film was shot on location in Rajasthan.

BHANELI BHAMINI

aka *Educated Wife*
1927 St 9882 ft b&w
d **Homi Master** *pc* **Kohinoor Film** *st* **Mohanlal G. Dave** *c* **Narayan G. Devare**
lp **Gohar**, **Raja Sandow**, Vaidya

Advertised in the *Bombay Chronicle* as 'an excellent warning to the younger generation to beware of venereal disease and take necessary precautions. [I]t not only brings ruin to himself but to the innocent members of his family.' This didactic Gohar-Sandow production set the tone for the message-oriented socials for which the duo became famous. It was also an important predecessor of ***Gunsundari*** (1927).

GAMDANI GORI

aka *Village Girl*
1927 St 10128 ft b&w
d **Mohan Bhavnani** *pc* **Imperial Film** *st* **Nanubhai Desai** *c* Rustom Irani
lp **Sulochana**, Mazhar Khan, W.M. Khan, Hussain, Madanrai Vakil, **Raja Sandow**

This important film in Sulochana's career at the Imperial Studio cast her as Sundari, the innocent village beauty with an ineffectual father, adrift in the big, bad city where she is preyed upon by lustful men seeking to force her into prostitution. The hero, Navichand, is a film actor and the film milieu is represented by a studio boss and a comedian, Gazdar, nicknamed Charlie Chaplin. Other features of the urban landscape, besides 'electric trains, motor cars and buses, the giant wheel, cinemas and theatres', as the publicity pamphlet claims, include a corrupt policeman, a racecourse and the fictional Bachelors' Club whose members see Sundari and promptly postpone their collective pledge never to marry. The film was part of Imperial's calculated and successful effort to manufacture a star image for the actress.

GUNSUNDARI

aka *Why Husbands Go Astray*
1927 St 9452 ft b&w
d **Chandulal Shah** *pc* **Kohinoor Film** *st* Dayaram Shah *c* **Narayan G. Devare**
lp **Gohar**, **Raja Sandow**, Rampiary, Jamuna, Vaidya

Shah's best-known silent film established the core unit of the **Ranjit** Studio and the signature role of its lead star, Gohar. She plays a dutiful wife whose husband refuses to take his share of the domestic responsibilities, claiming that he has enough problems at the office. Frustrated with his housewifely spouse, he takes up with a dancing-girl. The wife is spurred into an active social life, discovering a world beyond the confines of the home. The tale sought to tell modern women that they owed it to their husbands to be more than domestic drudges. Ranjit believed the story to be commercially infallible. it was remade by Shah himself in 1934 and again by **Punatar** in 1948 when the studio was branching out into Gujarati.

JANJIRNE JANKARE

aka *At the Clang of Fetters*
1927 St 13496 ft b&w
d **Harshadrai Mehta** *pc* **Krishna Film** *st* Champsi Udeshi *sc/c* **Chimanlal Luhar**
lp Gulab, Hydershah, P.R. Joshi, Nandram, Gangaram, Sultan Alam

Together with ***Balidan*** (1927), this Rajput romance was often cited by the I.C.C as an example of the Indian cinema's technical achievements matching those of the West. Commander Ambar of Ajaygarh triumphs over neighbouring Ramgarh capturing its king and the beautiful Princess Rama (Gulab). Ambar falls for her but problems arise when the king of Ajaygarh wants to give his own daughter in marriage to the victorious commander. Ambar covertly helps Rama and her father escape but he is killed in the process and dies in Rama's arms. The major portion of the film deals with Ambar's imprisonment at the hands of his own patron, remaining seven days without food. Drawn from Udeshi's story serialised a year earlier in the popular journal *Navchetan*, highlights included spectacular battle scenes.

NANAND BHOJAI

aka *The Victim of Society*
1927 St 9370 ft b&w
d/s **Manilal Joshi** *pc* Excelsior Film *c* D.D. Dhabke
lp Thatte, Rani, S. Nazir, **Zubeida**, Udvadia, Takle, Miss Mani, Nargis, Gangaram

After his successful ***Mojili Mumbai*** (1925), Joshi again used a real-life incident as the basis for a typical melodramatic plot locating reformist concerns in large joint families riven by tensions between in-laws. A greedy brother forces his educated sister to marry a rich old man. She rebels, goes to court and succeeds in preventing the marriage. The film was shot in Surat, where the original incident took place. A reviewer of the period noted that 'this is one of the few films to show Western women as not all bad'.

WILDCAT OF BOMBAY

1927 St 9724 ft b&w
d **Mohan Bhavnani** *pc* **Imperial Film**
lp **Sulochana**, **D. Bilimoria**

One of the best-known hits of Imperial's top-selling duo. Sulochana said in an interview (*Screen*, 1951) that she had eight separate roles in this film: a gardener, a policeman, a Hyderabadi gentleman, a street urchin, a European blonde, an old banana-seller and an expert pickpocket who gives her money to charity. Remade as a sound film, ***Bambai Ki Billi*** (1936), also with Sulochana.

DEVDAS

1928 St c.8000 ft b&w
d Nitish Chandra Mitra *pc* Eastern Films Syndicate *st* Saratchandra Chatterjee *c* **Nitin Bose**
lp **Phani Burma**, **Naresh Mitra**, Mani Ghosh, Tinkari Chakraborty, Kanaknarayan Bhup, Miss Light, Niharbala, Rama Devi

First version of Saratchandra's novel later filmed by **New Theatres** (1935). A review in the Bengali journal *Nachghar* said that despite its 'theatrical ruggedness', the film was well scripted and showed a distinct Bengali touch as against the **Madan** style. Mitra was praised for his attempt to express character through mise en scene.

KELOR KIRTI

1928 St 10665 ft b&w
d Sudhangshu Mustafi *pc* **Aurora Film** *st* Bhupen Bannerjee *c* Debi Ghosh
lp Lalu Bose, Belarani, Niharbala

Calcutta's Aurora Studio embarked on its first feature, *Ratnakar* (1921), when **Madan Theatres** started *Bilwamangal* (1919), the latter sometimes being presented as the first Bengali feature in spite of Madan's *Satyavadi Raja Harishchandra* in 1917. The comedy *Kelor Kirti*, roughly meaning A Scandal, tells of Kalbhairab Bose aka Kelo, part clown part idiot and an incorrigible romantic. He rescues the heroine Manukumari from drowning and falls in love with her. Her father allows the marriage if Kelo first earns Rs 5000, triggering a series of adventures. He wins the money at the races but loses it when he swallows his winning ticket; he tries to have an accident to collect the insurance but is knocked down by a car driven by his future brother-in-law. He eventually gets the insurance and marries Manukumari. The film continues the efforts by locally owned Calcutta studios to create an indigenous cinematic idiom distinct from the idiom of Madan Theatres' ***Bilet Pherat*** (1921) or of Taj Mahal's ***Andhare Alo*** (1922).

LOVES OF A MUGHAL PRINCE, THE

1928 St 9525 ft b&w
co-d Prafulla Roy, **Charu Roy** *pc* Great Eastern Film Corp. *st* Imtiaz Ali Taj's play *Anarkali* *sc* Hakim Ahmed Shuja *c* V.B. Joshi
lp Prafulla Roy, **Seeta Devi**, Maya Devi, Shakuntala, Swarn Singh, Imtiaz Ali Taj, Dewan Sharar

Punjabi capital's first major bid for the national market used the seminal Urdu historical play of 1922, with the author himself playing the 16th-C. Mughal emperor Akbar. It recounts the love story between Prince Salim (Singh), Akbar's son, and the slave girl Anarkali (Seeta). Following on from the **Osten-Rai** Orientalist dramas, and produced by the Indian partners responsible for ***Prem Sanyas*** (1925), it also features Seeta Devi as the heroine and is the directorial debut of *Prem Sanyas*' art director and the lead actor of ***Shiraz*** (1928), Charu Roy. The big-budget picture was beaten to the screen that same year by the rival and more successful **Imperial** version starring **Sulochana** and directed by **R.S. Choudhury** (*Anarkali*, 1928), who remade it in 1935. **Jaswantlal** made it again in 1953 but the most famous version remains **K. Asif**'s ***Mughal-e-Azam*** (1960).

SHIRAZ

aka *Das Grabmal einer groszen Liebe*
1928 St 8402 ft/2561 m b&w
d **Franz Osten** *pc* British Instructional Films/Ufa/Himansu Rai Film *st* **Niranjan Pal**'s play *sc* W.A. Burton *m* Arthur Guttmann *c* Emil Schunemann, H. Harris
lp **Himansu Rai**, **Charu Roy**, **Seeta Devi**, Enakshi Rama Rao, Maya Devi, Profulla Kumar

After ***Prem Sanyas*** and some German films, Osten returned to India for his second collaboration with Rai, a historical romance set in the Mughal Empire, subtitled, like ***Prapancha Pash*** (1929), A Romance of India. Selima (Enakshi) is a princess-foundling raised by a potter and loved by her brother, Shiraz (Rai). She is abducted and sold as a slave to Prince Khurram, later Emperor Shah Jehan (Roy), who also falls for her, to the chagrin of the wily Dalia (Seeta Devi). When Selima is caught with Shiraz, the young man is condemned to be trampled to death by an elephant. A pendant reveals Selima's royal status and she saves her brother, marries the prince and becomes Empress Mumtaz Mahal while Dalia is banned for her machinations against Selima. When Selima dies (1629), the emperor builds her a monument to the design of the now old and blind Shiraz, the Taj Mahal. The film contains a number of passionate kissing scenes. The cinematography received favourable comment, introducing a baroque camera style that became inescapably linked with the genre of Mughal romances (e.g. Charu Roy's ***Loves of a Mughal Prince*** and **Choudhury**'s *Anarkali*, both also 1928). The art direction was by Promode Nath. The German release had a music score by Arthur Guttmann. The US release credited the assistant director V. Peers as co-director of an 80' version in 1929.

VIGATHAKUMARAN

1928 St ? b&w
d/p/sc J.C. Daniel
lp J.C. Daniel

Hailed as the first Malayalam film, released in November 1928 in Trivandrum. Its lack of success ruined the director and no literature about, or footage from, the film appear to have survived.

GOPAL KRISHNA

1929 St 9557 ft b&w
d **V. Shantaram** *pc* **Prabhat Film** *st* Shivram Vashikar *c* **S. Fattelal**
lp Suresh, Kamaladevi, Anant Apte

Shantaram's successful debut as a solo director (*Netaji Palkar*, 1927, had been co-directed with **K. Dhaiber**) signalled the first appearance of the famous Prabhat emblem, the profile of a woman (Kamaladevi) playing the tutari, the Indian equivalent of MGM's Leo The Lion. In his autobiography (1986) Shantaram said that he wove topical allusions into this Pauranic tale about the antics of Krishna as a child. The conflict between Krishna and the evil Kamsa, king of Mathura, was to be seen as representing the conflict between the Indian people and the British rulers in a manner enabling him to avoid censorship. The playful family film's highlight, apparently, is when the loin cloth of a little boy playing on the swing with Krishna came loose and revealed his penis. This, Shantaram says, went unnoticed in the shooting but was applauded for its bold realism and became seen as his unique directorial 'touch'.

HATIMTAI

1929 St 35891 ft b&w
d Prafulla Ghosh *pc* **Krishna Film** *c* Chaturbhai Patel.
lp Rampiary, A.R. Pahelwan, Gulab, Motibai, Hydershah, Haridas, Durga

After **Patankar** Friends' *Ram Vanvas* (1918), this was the second big-budget, four-part serial. The Krishna Studio's production was based on *The Arabian Nights* with sets designed by M.D. Shah. It tells of the traveller Hatim and his encounters with the fairy Gulnar, a popular **Parsee theatre** story.

KONO VAK?

aka *Whose Fault?*
1929 St 12861 ft b&w
d **Kanjibhai Rathod** *pc* **Krishna Film** *st* **K.M. Munshi** *c* Gordhanbhai Patel.
lp Gulab, Bapurao Apte

Based on a K.M. Munshi story, this typical transformation of a reform novel into a social substantially determined Rathod's authorial signature. It tells of Mani (Gulab), a child bride widowed aged eight and treated as a slave by her in-laws until she is cast out for bearing an illegitimate child. Her destitution is alleviated by a young lawyer, Muchkund, who nevertheless is forced to marry his father's choice, Kashi. Mani devotes herself to Muchkund, even sacrificing her own child, and finally marries the lawyer after Kashi's death. Gulab's performance made her a star.

PITRU PREM

aka *Father's Love*
1929 St 9868 ft b&w
d/s Harilal M. Bhatt *pc* Mahavir Photoplays
lp Miss Mani, Gaby Hill, Mr Dave, Mr Yusuf, Y.L. Chichulkar, S.P. Niphadkar, Madanlal

Arguing for communal harmony and filial piety, the film tells of Madhumal (Dave), a rich zamindar, his beloved son Shashibhushan (Yusuf), his loving daughter Annapurna (Mani) and his adopted son Madhav (Chichenkar). When Madhumal picks up a wounded child swathed in bandages, a title says 'nay - Hindus and Mohammedans are but the children of one loving father - God'. In close-up, Madhumal is shown donating equally to the Aligarh Muslim and Benares Hindu universities. In contrast, his dissolute son Shashibhushan falls into the clutches of the villain Gadbaddas and the courtesan Nurjehan (Hill).

PRAPANCHA PASH

aka *A Throw of Dice* aka *Schicksalswurfel*
1929 St 2523m b&w
d **Franz Osten** *pc* British Instructional Film/Himansu Rai Film/Ufa *st* **Niranjan Pal** *sc* W.A. Burton, Max Jungk *m* Willy Schmidt-Gentner *c* Emil Schunemann
lp **Seeta Devi**, **Himansu Rai**, **Charu Roy**, **Modhu Bose**, Sarada Gupta, Lala Bijoykishen, Tinkari Chakraborty

The third Osten-Rai collaboration (***Prem Sanyas***, 1925; ***Shiraz***, 1928, the latter also subtitled 'A Romance of India') no longer used existing legends but proposed a new one: two rival kings addicted to gambling, Ranjit (Roy) and the evil Sohan (Rai), also vie for the same woman, Sunita (Seeta Devi), Kanwa the hermit's (Gupta) daughter. Ranjit loses his kingdom and his love and becomes Sohan's slave through a crooked game of dice. The conflict is eventually resolved when the trickery is exposed and Sohan plunges to his death from a cliff after the people, led by Ranjit, revolt. The happy ending is sealed by a passionate kiss between the lovers. The lavish production with art direction by Promode Nath uses over 10,000 extras, a thousand horses and fifty elephants, benefiting from the largesse of the Royal houses of Jaipur, Udaipur amd Mysore. Unusually, star and producer Rai played the villain.

Seeta Devi and Charu Roy (atop camel) in *Prapancha Pash*

CINEMA GIRL

1930 St 10925 ft b&w
d/s **B.P. Mishra** *pc* **Imperial Film** *c* Rustom Irani.
lp Ermeline, **Prithviraj Kapoor**, Akbar Nawaz, Mazhar Khan, Baburao Sansare

In contrast to ***Cinema Queen***'s (1925) exploitation of voyeurism or ***Daily Mail***'s (1930) kiss-and-tell approach to the cinema, this film presented a fictionalised biography of its maker. One of the major characters is a producer modelled on **Kohinoor**'s proprietor, D.N. Sampat, including a reference to the real-life occasion when the studio, on the verge of bankruptcy, survived only because its employees donated money and gold ornaments to keep it afloat. Another character referred to a financier at the Imperial Studio. The plot also touched on the way a producer can curtail the freedom of a director.

DAILY MAIL

1930 St 11925 ft b&w
d **Narayan G. Devare** *pc* **Kohinoor** United

Artists *st* A.S. Desai
lp Kumudini, Janina, Thomas, Alawali, Bhopatkar

By the mid-20s, satirical prose and journalism had merged to create popular film gossip columns in most Marathi and Gujarati papers. KUA, an independent, employee-run group, produced this controversial film about the daily *Hindustan* thinly disguised as the fictional *Daily Mail*, edited by a character constructed as a composite portrait of *Hindustan*'s owner Lotwala and editor **Indulal Yagnik**. It also lampooned the patron of the **Ranjit** Studio, Jamsaheb of Jamnagar, and his studio boss **Chandulal Shah** in a plot designed as a scabrous expose of the film industry's ethics.

GIRIBALA

1930 St c.8000 ft b&w
d **Modhu Bose** *pc* **Madan Theatres** *st* **Rabindranath Tagore** *c* Jatin Das
lp **Dhiraj Bhattacharya, Naresh Mitra**, Tinkari Chakraborty, Lilabati, Shanti Gupta, Lalita

Renamed after the lead character, this was Madan Theatres' remake of Taj Mahal Film's *Maanbhanjan* (1923). The rich Gopinath ignores his beautiful wife Giribala, preferring the company of the stage actress Labanga. Tired of her only pastime, dressing up in narcissistic solitude, Giribala one night follows her husband to the theatre where a new world opens up for her. When Gopinath runs off with Labanga, Giribala joins the stage in Labanga's place and becomes famous. The hypocrisy of men's moral double standards is revealed when Gopinath recognises his wife on stage when her veil drops. Tagore was apparently closely involved with the making of the film and may have written the intertitles.

UDAYKAL

aka *Thunder of The Hills*
1930 St 10804 ft b&w
d **V. Shantaram** *pc* **Prabhat Film** *s* **Baburao Pendharkar** *c* **S. Fattelal, Keshavrao Dhaiber**
lp V. Shantaram, Baburao Pendharkar, Kamaladevi, Bazarbattoo, Mane, Vaghya the Dog

According to Shantaram (1986) this was the first film which explicitly politicised the figure of the enormously popular 17th-C. Maratha emperor Shivaji (Shantaram), a staple figure of the Marathi historical. **Bhalji Pendharkar**, whose sound films would confirm Shivaji as a contemporary icon, worked as a scenarist at Prabhat at this time but his brother Baburao received the script credit for this effort in addition to a starring role. Shantaram played the lead himself, a pattern he would often repeat. The film was originally titled *Swarajyacha Toran* (*The Garland of Freedom*) but the censors objected to the use of the word 'freedom' and forced many additional changes after the premiere screening. Key scenes included Shivaji's invocation of the goddess Bhawani who blesses his sword, and Shivaji putting up the saffron flag on the Sinhagad fort at the film's climax, another point objected to by the censors. Many of the battle scenes were shot with two cameras.

ALAM ARA

1931 124' b&w Hindi-Urdu
d/co-s **Ardeshir Irani** *pc* **Imperial Movietone** *co-s* Joseph David *c* Adi M. Irani, Wilford Deming *m* Ferozshah M. Mistri, B. Irani
lp **Master Vithal**, **Zubeida**, Jilloo, Sushila, **Prithviraj Kapoor**, Elizer, Wazir Mohammed Khan, Jagdish Sethi, **L.V. Prasad**

India's first sound film, released on 14 March 1931 at the Majestic Theatre, Bombay, narrowly beating ***Shirin Farhad*** (1931) to the screens. It established the use of music, song and dance as the mainstay of Indian cinema. The film is a period fantasy based on Joseph David's popular Parsee theatre play and told of the ageing king of Kumarpur, his two queens, Navbahar and Dilbahar, and their rivalry when a fakir predicts that Navbahar will bear the king's heir. Dilbahar unsuccessfully tries to seduce the army chief Adil (Vithal) and vengefully destroys his family, leaving his daughter Alam Ara (Zubeida) to be raised by nomads. Eventually, Alam Ara's nomad friends invade the palace, expose Dilbahar's schemes, release Adil from the dungeon and she marries the prince of the realm. The film was made on the Tanar single-system camera, recording image and sound simultaneously, which was difficult esp. for the seven songs which were its highlights. Wazir Mohammed Khan's rendering of a wandering minstrel's number, *De de khuda ke naam par pyare*, was particularly popular and pioneered the use of a commentating chorus, a device adopted in several later films. Although **Mehboob** was scheduled to play the lead, Master Vithal from the **Sharda** Studio got the part. When Sharda sued Vithal for breach of contract, he was defended by M.A. Jinnah. **Nanubhai Vakil** remade the film in 1956 and '73. Playwright David was later known for his **Wadia Movietone** scripts, including ***Hunterwali*** (1935).

BHAKTA PRAHLADA

1931 108' b&w Telugu
d **H.M. Reddy** *pc* Bharat Movietone *s/lyr* **Surabhi** Nataka *m* H.R. Padmanabha Sastry
lp **Surabhi Kamalabai**, **L.V. Prasad**, Munipalle Subbaiah, B.V. Subba Rao, Darasami Naidu

The first sound film in Telugu is a classic mythological drawn from the *Vishnu Purana*. Prahlada, the son of the demon Hiranyakashapu (Subbaiah), defies his father and worships Vishnu. He is imprisoned but Vishnu protects him. The film adapts a stage production by one of the Surabhi Theatre troupes, which was taken to Bombay's **Imperial** Studio to shoot the film. The verses and the dialogue were left intact. Its success prompted many more adaptations from plays, e.g. **Badami**'s *Paduka Pattabhisekham* and *Shakuntala* (both 1932).

DEVI DEVAYANI

1931 150' b&w Hindi
d **Chandulal Shah** *pc* **Ranjit Movietone** *s* **Narayan Prasad Betaab** *c* Pandurang Naik *m* Jhande Khan
lp **Gohar**, Miss Kamala, **D. Bilimoria**, M. Bhagwandas, Keki Adajania, S. Baburao, Baba Vyas, Mr Thatte

Shah's first sound hit, a mythological, inaugurated the famous Ranjit Studio productions and the use of Audio-Camex sound equipment. A cosmic battle between gods and demons reaches stalemate when the sage Shukracharya (Adajania) instantly restores every fallen demon to life. The god Indra (Baburao), on advice from Brahaspati (Vyas), sends Kacha (Bhagwandas) to the sage to learn his magic secret. Shukracharya's daughter, Devayani (Gohar) likes Kacha and the latter is accepted as the sage's disciple. The demon Vrisha Parva (Thatte) tries to kill Kacha but the youth is rescued by Devayani until the demons succeed in dissolving Kacha's body in alcohol and make Shukracharya drink the brew. Shukracharya then teaches Kacha the secret chant so that when he dies and Kacha emerges from his stomach, Kacha may bring him back to life again. Kacha's duties now conflict with a love-triangle, as Devayani marries Yayati who loves Sharmistha (Kamala).

DILER JIGAR

aka *Gallant Hearts*
1931 St 9632 ft b&w
d/s G.P. Pawar *pc* Agarwal Film *c/p* Shyam Sundar Agarwal
lp **Lalita Pawar**, Hamir, Ezak Daniel, Gopinath

Along with ***Ghulami Nu Patan*** (1931), also made by the Pune-based Agarwal Film, this is one of the few surviving silent films. It opens with shots of a hand distributing charity from a silver plate to a waiting crowd and tells of the good king of Magadh's fight with his evil ministers. The king is poisoned by his brother, the evil Kalsen and the infant prince Chandrapratab, smuggled out by the loyal sardar Satyapal, grows up in a forest to become the acrobat Hamir (Hamir) in love with his partner, the beautiful Saranga (Pawar, credited as 'Ambu'). Saranga is kidnapped by Kalsen's son Ramanaraj, described as 'the perfect libertine', but Kalsen takes her away from his son and attempts to seduce Saranga with promises of wealth. The fearless Hamir fights dozens of soldiers, in amateurishly staged fights, trying to liberate her. In the end Saranga, rejected by her lover for having been tempted by Kalsen's promises of wealth, dons a mask and turns into a Zorro-type avenger. Hamir is eventually recognised by the royal tattoo on his shoulder and restored to the throne as well as reunited with Saranga. A dramatic moment in the film is Hamir's assumption that Saranga has fallen for Kalsen's wiles. The threatening seduction (rape) attempt is shown through a series of dissolves from the villain's face to that of the heroine. Other dissolves are effectively used to convey fantasies and desires, although the use of fades-to-black are used erratically, even within action scenes. One of the more technically elaborate scenes is Saranga's kidnapping, involving a trick bed descending through a trapdoor.

DRAUPADI

1931 124' b&w Hindi
d/s **B.P. Mishra** *pc* **Imperial Movietone** *c* Adi M. Irani
lp Khalil, Ermeline, Jilloo, Jagdish, Hadi, Elizer, Rustom Irani, **Prithviraj Kapoor**

After its success with ***Alam Ara*** (1931), the studio made this big-budget *Mahabharata* adaptation starting with Duryodhana's (Jagdish) scheme to appropriate the kingdom of Hastinapur by eliminating his Pandava cousins. When the Pandavas return from banishment with Draupadi (Ermeline), won by Arjuna (Kapoor) in a tournament, they establish their capital at Indraprastha. The film shows the Rajasuya Yagna ceremony and culminates in the famous dice game in which Duryodhan, backed by his scheming Uncle Shakuni (Hadi), wins the Pandavas' kingdom and then Draupadi herself, whom Yudhishthira (Elizer) then wagers and loses. Duryodhan commands that Draupadi be stripped naked in open court but Krishna (Khalil) saves her honour with a miracle. Irani plays Bhim and Jilloo is Kunti.

GHULAMI NU PATAN

aka *The Fall of Slavery*
1931 St 10627 ft b&w
d/sc/c/p Shyam Sundar Agarwal *pc* Agarwal Film *st* Baburao Thatte
lp Vatsala, Ezak Daniel

With ***Diler Jigar*** (also 1931), this is the second silent film by the Pune-based Agarwal Film to have survived. More ambitious than the former, it is set in the Marwar region in 1818 and addresses the notorious 'Gola' system of slavery. The fantasy adventure, leavened with realistic scenes showing the slaves' working conditions, tells of Kumar Umedhsingh of Kadeempur (Daniel) who institutes a usurious tax mainly to obtain power over the beautiful peasant girl Kamalbala (Vatsala). However, she is protected by Kartarsingh of Amargarh, whom she once nursed to health and who has vowed to liberate all slaves. Kartarsingh is imprisoned but eventually defeats the villain and rescues the heroine. A (presumably Rajput) emperor arrives, censures the villain and lets the lovers marry. Extensive chase sequences on horseback and complicated plotting show that, by the end of the silent era, the Indian cinema had achieved considerable narrative dexterity.

JAMAIBABU

1931 St 3000' b&w
d/s Kalipada Das *pc* Hira Film *c* D.R. Barodkar
lp Kalipada Das, Pravat Coomar, Sivapada Bhowmick, Radharani, Amulya Bandyopadhyay, Rajen Baruah, Sadhana Devi

The only surviving silent Bengali film was accidentally discovered by **Mrinal Sen**'s film unit while shooting on location in 1980. The comedy has a country bumpkin hero Gobardhan (Das) visiting his parents-in-law in Calcutta. Mistaking a 'No Nuisance' sign for an address, he gets lost trying to find his friend Amal's (Baruah) room. His subsequent adventures take him to famous locations including Howrah Bridge, the Victoria Memorial and the Maidan. These scenes are intercut with fast-paced shots of life in the city and of crowds, evidently gathered to watch the shooting. Gobardhan eventually finds his in-laws, feigns illness to prolong his stay, is beaten up when he tries to sneak into his wife's (Radharani) room and gets mistaken for a thief. The sequence of Gobardhan kissing his wife, somewhat abruptly introduced, probably evokes a tradition of pre-censorship pornographic film using Anglo-Indian actresses. As director and lead actor, Das mostly restricts his gags to stumbling in various ways. The erratic cinematography and editing betrays a general lack of technical control.

KALIDAS

1931 c.10000 ft b&w Tamil
d **H.M. Reddy** *pc* **Imperial Film**, Select Pics *lyr* **Bhaskara Das**
lp **T.P. Rajalakshmi**, Thevaram Rajambal, T. Sushila Devi, J. Sushila, P.G. Venkatesan, M.S. Santhanalakshmi, **L.V. Prasad**

The first Tamil sound feature, made by the director of ***Bhakta Prahlada*** (1931), was released in Madras on 31 October 1931, but shot in Bombay like most Tamil films between 1931 and '34. It tells the familiar tale of Kalidas, the legendary 3rd-C. Sanskrit poet and playwright. A minister at the court of King Vijayavarman of Thejavathi wants Princess Vidhyadhari (Rajalakshmi) to marry his son. She refuses and the minister tricks her into marrying a cowhand. The duped princess invokes the help of Kali, who appears to the couple and endows the cowhand with literary talent, allowing him to become Kalidas (Venkatesan). Although mostly in Tamil, including its 50 or so songs, some characters spoke in Telugu to accommodate actors from **Surabhi Theatres** and in Urdu. Rajalakshmi sang some numbers she had made popular on the stage as well as two nationalist songs unconnected with the plot, linking the film to the Civil Disobedience Movement of the period: one song called for national unity, the other was in praise of the spinning wheel. The film was released with what is probably the first Tamil sound film, a four-reel short called *Korathi Dance and Songs*, starring the gypsy dancer Jhansi Bai.

KHUDA KI SHAAN

aka *Wrath*
1931 St 10540 ft b&w
d/s **R.S. Choudhury** *pc* **Imperial Film** *c* Adi M. Irani
lp **Sulochana**, Raghunath Jagtap, Makanda, Salvi, Elizer, Sushila

Ramaki (Sulochana), a poor scheduled caste girl, has an illegitimate daughter by Manekchand, the son of the wealthy Krishnadas. She seeks refuge with a nautch girl. Krishnadas, who also wants to posses Ramaki, dies trying to kill her. Ramaki then seeks shelter with a young Muslim but they perish in a fire. Her daughter, along with the Muslim's son (Jagtap), is raised by a nomad, Garibdas Sadhu (Makanda), a character made to look like Gandhi. The youngsters are hired as factory hands by Manekchand who unwittingly falls in love with his own daughter and appropriates land belonging to Garibdas. When the latter finally curses the greedy Manekchand, a dam bursts, wiping out Manekchand and his property. Although the film focused on the evils of the caste system, censorship troubles arose from Garibdas' deliberate resemblance to Gandhi.

MARTANDA VARMA

1931 St 11905 ft b&w
d/s P.V. Rao *pc* Shri Rajeshwari Films, Nagercoil, R. Sunderraj *st* C.V. Raman Pillai's novel (1891) *c* P.E. Naik
lp Jaidev, A.V.P. Menon, V. Naik, V.C. Kutty, S.V. Nath, Devaki, Padmini, Sundaram Iyer

The second Malayalam feature, based on the novel that effectively launched the prose tradition in Travancore. It was the first of a series by Raman Pillai (followed by *Dharmaraja*, 1913; *Premamritam*, 1915; *Ramaraja Bahadur*, 1920) dealing with Travancore's royalty in a style that Ayyappa Panicker claims (1987) drew directly on Walter Scott's *Waverly* novels. It features Jaidev as Martanda Varma (1706-58), the legendary founder of the Travancore State (now Kerala), telling the story of the love between Anantha Padmanabham (Menon) and Parukutty (Padmini), the political conspiracy of Padmanabha Thampi (Naik) and the heads of the eight Nair Houses against Martanda Varma. It opens with newsreel coverage of the aarattu procession of the Travancore maharaja Chitta Thirunal, including elephants, cavalry and the Nair Brigade before embarking on the story of the king's ancestor. Scenes from the young Martanda Varma's youth are intercut with well-known episodes from the novel. The Malayalam intertitles, taken from the novel, are also translated into high-flown English. The opening title proclaims: 'Most Puissant Sovereign, born to carve a State Anew, and rid it clean of Marshalled Hate, released by Fractious Chiefs with Heartless Swords to seize thy realm'. The film may have included references to the contemporary Congress-led nationalism in, e.g., titles like 'Enough of this age-long tyranny. Ye! Freedom-loving sons of the soil! Gird up your loins and fight for your birthright. Rise up from your slumber. Awake, arise and stop not, till the goal is reached.' There was a copyright dispute with the publishers of the original novel, so that the film was never released and the producer went bankrupt. This also prevented the novel from being filmed later. The available version, minus one reel, was salvaged by the NFAI.

PREM JOGAN

aka *Drums of Love*
1931 St 13477 ft b&w
d **Nandlal Jaswantlal** *pc* **Ranjit Film** *st* **Mohanlal G. Dave** *c* Pandurang Naik
lp Shantakumari, **D. Bilimoria**, Thatte, Putli, Ishwarlal

Amar (Bilimoria) and Ila's (Shantakumari) love is disrupted by the dashing Samar (Ishwarlal). The rivals get embroiled in the Kashmir war and Samar dies in Amar's arms. Amar returns to find that Ila has become an ascetic but they eventually get married. This is an early Jaswantlal-Naik collaboration which elaborated the use of the close-up, esp. in melodramas. Naik had started with **Phalke**, assisted cameramen Gajanan S. Devare and Dhabke and turned cameraman with ***Neera*** (1926). He later toured Europe with Jaswantlal (1933). They went on to make some classic **Imperial** sound films together.

SHIRIN FARHAD

1931 120'(11000 ft) b&w Hindi
d J.J. Madan *pc* **Madan Theatres** *lyr* **Aga Hashr Kashmiri** *m* Vrijlal Verma
lp Master Nissar, Jehan Ara, Kajjan, Mohammed Hussain, Abdul Rehman Kabuli, Mohan, Miss Sharifa

Narrowly beaten to the screen by ***Alam Ara*** (1931) as India's first sound feature, this is a big-budget musical narrating a legend from the *Shahnama*. The Persian sculptor Farhad falls in love with Queen Shirin. The shah Khusro, who had promised Farhad a reward for having built a canal, agrees to let him marry Shirin provided he first single-handedly demolishes the Besutun mountain. Shirin and Farhad are finally united in death as Farhad's tomb miraculously opens to accept Shirin. The film proved a bigger hit than ***Alam Ara*** and, unlike the Tanar single-system camera used by **Irani**, recorded sound and image separately, a technique widely adopted later because it offered greater aesthetic flexibility.

AYODHYECHA RAJA/AYODHYA KA RAJA

aka *King of Ayodhya*
1932 146'[M]/152'[H] b&w Marathi/Hindi
d/ed **V. Shantaram** *pc* **Prabhat Film** *st/co-dial*[M] N.V. Kulkarni *co-dial*[H] Munshi Ismail Farooque *c* **Keshavrao Dhaiber** *lyr/m* **Govindrao Tembe**
lp **Govindrao Tembe, Durga Khote, Baburao Pendharkar, Master Vinayak**, Nimbalkar, Shankarrao Bhosle, Digambar

Shantaram's and Prabhat's first sound film may also have been the first Marathi talkie, although *Sant Tukaram* by Babajirao Rane was released a few months earlier. A big-budget mythological, it tells a famous *Ramayana* tale. The truth-loving Harishchandra (Tembe), king of Ayodhya, is tested when the sage Vishwamitra challenges him to sacrifice his kingdom and offer alms of a thousand coins earned through his own labour. After many hardships, Harishchandra, Taramati (Khote) and their son Rohileshwara (Digambar) earn the money when the king and queen are sold as slaves in the city of Kashi. When the queen's new owner, Ganganath (Pendharkar), tries to assault her, her son intervenes and is killed. Taramati is accused of the killing and is sentenced to be executed by her husband. The Kashi-Vishveshwara deity intervenes, brings the boy back to life, declares the king

Govindrao Tembe (centre) and Durga Khote (right) in *Ayodhyecha Raja*

to have proved himself and returns him to his throne. Shantaram cast the untrained actress and singer Khote when it was still controversial in Marathi theatre to use actresses. Shot on elaborate plaster sets designed by **Fattelal**, the film had some bravura shots like a burning forest and a tree falling to the ground barely missing the hero. Despite its occasional 'miracle' scenes and its stage-derived frontal compositions, there was an attempt at a realist idiom, esp. in the scenes where the king and queen are shown trying to earn their money. Shantaram's characteristic use of extended pauses and elaborate gesture may here still be due to the technical limitations of the sound equipment (**Damle** was the sound man), although he later elaborated this acting style into an expressionist technique. Tembe sang most of the songs while Khote performed the hit *Bala ka jhop yeyina*.

CHANDIDAS

1932 133'(118') b&w Bengali
d/s **Debaki Bose** *pc* **New Theatres** *c* **Nitin Bose** *m* **Rai Chand Boral**
lp **Durgadas Bannerjee**, **K.C. Dey**, Manoranjan Bhattacharya, **Amar Mullick**, Dhirendra Bandyopadhyay, Chani Dutta, Umasashi, Sunila

Classic New Theatres **saint film** about Chandidas, a legendary 15th-C. Bengali Vaishnavite poet whose biography remains obscure but is credited as an influence on the better documented Chaitanya (1486-1533), a school teacher who promoted the Vaishnavite ideology in Bengal, mostly through hymns about the Radha-Krishna legend. Chandidas may have been one of three possible poets: Badu Chandidas, who wrote the *Shri Krishna Keertan* adapted mainly from the *Geet Govind* (13th C.); Dwija Chandidas or Deena Chandidas. The film mainly adapted Aparesh Chandra Mukherjee's successful stage musical of the same title, performed first at the Star Theatre in Calcutta (1926), and stressed the poet's teachings through the love story between Chandidas (Bannerjee) and a low-caste washerwoman, Rami (Umasashi). The conventional villain of the saint film genre, who represents the established order threatened by the outsider's revolutionary influence on common people, is the rapacious upper-caste merchant Bijoynarayan. When Rami rejects his advances, he persuades the high priest to insist that Chandidas must repent or be punished for associating with a low-caste woman. Chandidas agrees to repent but when he sees the injuries Rami has suffered at the hands of the merchant's goons, he rejects institutionalised religion in favour of the higher Vaishnavite call for a more democratic god and leaves the village with Rami. Stylistically, the film broke new ground for the studio, distancing itself from the theatre by stressing the poet's ever popular lyrics. However, the acting remained stilted and used more straight frontal shots than, e.g., Debaki Bose's later films at New Theatres (***Bidyapati***, 1937). It was the studio's first major hit. There were several more versions of the story, including Hiren Bose's *Rami Dhoban* (1953), told from a woman's point of view. The film is also noted for its breakthroughs in recording sound with Mukul Bose overcoming the problems of an optical track with varying densities by spacing out dialogue and modulating frequencies.

INDRASABHA

1932 211' b&w Hindi
d J.J. Madan *pc* **Madan Theatres** *st* Sayed Aga Hasan Amanat's play (1853) *c* T. Marconi *m* Nagardas Nayak
lp Nissar, Jehan Ara, Kajjan, A.R. Kabuli, Mukhtar Begum

Big-budget adaptation of Sayed Aga Hasan Amanat's *Indrasabha* written in 1853 for the Lucknow court of Nawab Wajid Ali Shah. The often staged play had elaborated the Rahas style, adapted from the Ras-Lila form of Hindi folk theatre and brought specific music and dance conventions into Urdu prose theatre. This new style gradually amalgamated, says Somnath Gupta (1969), 'The Hindi Devmala [Hindi Pantheon] with the Islami Ravaiyat' and crystallised into a plot structure revolving around a benevolent king whose moral fibre is tested by celestial powers as they cause an apsara (a fairy) to appear before him as a fallen woman begging for mercy. The language assimilated the Urdu ghazal, Hindustani, Brajbhasa and dialects usually spoken by women (zanani boli). As performed in the **Parsee theatre**, this performance style also absorbed aspects of European opera, esp. its neo-classical visuals which already contained a measure of baroque Orientalism. The 70 songs, familiar from the stage productions, suggested an Indian equivalent of the *Ziegfield Follies*. Madan also drew on his Italian connections (***Savitri***, 1923) and asked his Italian cinematographer to model the complex choral mise en scene on the venerable Italian epics. The film repeated the popular singing duo of Nissar and Kajjan from ***Shirin Farhad*** (1931). Marconi later shot and probably directed the Tamil feature ***Vimochanam*** (1939).

JALTI NISHANI/AGNIKANKAN

aka *The Branded Oath*
1932 129'[M]/136'[H] b&w Marathi/Hindi
d **V. Shantaram** *pc* **Prabhat Film** *dial/lyr/m* **Govindrao Tembe** *c* **Keshavrao Dhaiber**
lp Shankarrao Bhosle, Kamaladevi, **Master Vinayak**, Budasaheb, Nimbalkar, Leela, **Baburao Pendharkar**

Shantaram followed ***Ayodhyecha Raja*** (1932) with this adventure movie about a king (Bhosle) who is overthrown by the perfidy of his villainous Commander (Pendharkar). The young prince (Vinayak) eventually defeats the villain, reclaims the throne and restores his father's honour. Shot on Shantaram's (and set designer **Fattelal**'s) trademark sets of large palaces and neoclassical decor, the film has more sophisticated lighting than its predecessor but the stodgy, static acting style dominates despite Vinayak's acrobatic swordplay in his first important film role. Shantaram returned to the story for his ambitious ***Amritmanthan*** (1934).

MADHURI

1932 155' b&w Hindi
d **R.S. Choudhury** *pc* **Imperial Film** *c* Adi M. Irani *m* Pransukh M. Nayak
lp **Sulochana**, Ghulam Mohammed, Vinayakrao Patwardhan, Jamshedji, Hadi, Chanda

Adventure spectacular set in the 4th-C. Gupta period during the battles between the kingdoms of Ujjain and Kanauj. Features the heroic Amber (Patwardhan) and the craven Prince Tikka (Mohammed), both from the Malwa, and the scheming commander of Kanauj, Mahasamant (Jamshedji). Highlights includes extensive swordplay by the heroine, Madhuri (Sulochana), who defeats Mahasamant in a duel and later dresses as a male soldier to rescue Amber. Many songs by classical singer Patwardhan.

MAYA MACHHINDRA

aka *Illusion*, aka *Triya Rajya*
1932 154'[M]/158'[H] b&w Marathi/Hindi
d **V. Shantaram** *pc* **Prabhat Film** *st* Mani Shankar Trivedi's play *Siddhasansar dial* N.V. Kulkarni, **Govindrao Tembe**[M], Narbada Prasad 'Aasi'[H] *m* Govindrao Tembe *c* **Keshavrao Dhaiber**
lp Govindrao Tembe, **Durga Khote**, **Master Vinayak**, Leela Chandragiri, Rajarambapu Purohit, Bazarbattoo, Nimbalkar, **Baburao Pendharkar**, Tanibai, Hirabai

Shantaram's 3rd collaboration with actor-musician Tembe was based on an often-filmed Tantric legend about the guru Machhindranath (Tembe) and his disciple Gorakh (Master Vinayak) on the subject of 'maya' (belief in the illusory nature of worldly temptations). The guru appears to his student to have entered the kingdom of man-hating women, married the queen (Khote) and abandoned his commitment to celibacy and pure thoughts. Gorakh sets out to rescue him but the entire experience turns out to be an 'illusion' set up by the master. There are many special effects, including the classic shot of Gorakh's beheading with his head rolling back and rejoining his body. In addition to the conventional use of dissolves and travelling matte effects for 'miracle' scenes, Shantaram attempted optical superimpositions for the first time, with animated sparks of fire coming out of swords, or when enemy troops are encircled by flames and lightning. The film includes a spectacular celebration of Vasantotsav (spring festival).

NARASINH MEHTA

1932 139' b&w Gujarati
d **Nanubhai Vakil** *pc* **Sagar Movietone** *s* **Chaturbhuj Doshi** *c* Faredoon Irani *m* Rane
lp Mohanlala, Marutirao, Master Manhar, Master Bachu, Umakant Desai, Trikam Das, Miss Jamna, Miss Mehtab, Miss Thatun, Miss Devi

The first Gujarati feature is a **saint film** about the life of Narasinh Mehta (1408-75), played by Marutirao. Known for his evocative Prabhatiyan (morning hymns) and especially for his composition *Vaishnava jana to* ('The Vaishnav is he who knows the pain of others') made popular by Gandhi, who also adapted the poet's term Harijan (children of god) for the nation's Untouchables. According to the writer Anandashankar Dhruv, Vakil's film adhered to the Gandhian interpretation of Narasinh Mehta's work, avoiding e.g. miracle scenes. The quasi-realistic sets were designed by Ravishankar Rawal.

NATIR PUJA

1932 117' b&w Bengali
d/s **Rabindranath Tagore** *pc* **New Theatres** *c* **Nitin Bose** *m* Dinendranath Tagore
lp Students of Shantiniketan

Widely advertised as a film directed by Tagore, this was, according to B. Jha (1990), a simple recording of Tagore's 1926 dance drama based on a Buddhist legend, staged on his 70th birthday at the Old Empire, Calcutta. Sound recorded by Mukul Bose.

RADHA RANI

aka *Divine Lady*
1932 176' b&w Hindi
d **Chandulal Shah** *pc* **Ranjit Film** *s* **Narayan Prasad Betaab** *c* Pandurang Naik *m* Jhande Khan
lp **Gohar**, Bhagwandas, Keki Adajania, S. Baburao

Betaab's best-known script tells of Radha (Gohar), a carefree rural belle who is supposed to marry childhood friend Gopal, but instead falls in love with a stranger who turns out to be the missing Prince Vijaysingh. When the king despatches soldiers to recover the prince, Vijaysingh discards the pregnant Radha. She is attacked by the villagers for her immorality and eventually appears before the prince, her fomer lover, in court where she refuses to denounce him. Her child dies, she becomes a prostitute and eventually dies in the arms of the prince.

SATI SAVITRI

1932 153' b&w Gujarati/Hindi
d/st **Chandulal Shah** *pc* **Ranjit Movietone** *sc* **Chaturbhuj Doshi** *c* Pandurang Naik *m* Jhande Khan
lp Bhagwandas, Ghori, Keki Adajania, Alladdin, S. Baburao, **Gohar**, Shanta, Kamal, Tara

Ranjit's debut in Gujarati uses the *Mahabharata* tale of how Savitri (Gohar) saves her husband Satyavan (Bhagwandas) from the clutches of Yama, the god of death. The film opened up a lucrative regional market for the producers, consolidated by the films of, e.g., **Ratibhai Punatar** and **V.M. Vyas**.

SATI SONE

aka *Champraj Hado*, aka *Sone Rani*
1932 134' b&w Hindi
d Madanrai Vakil *pc* **Imperial Film** *s* Joseph David *c* Rustom Irani
lp Jamshedji, Boman Shah, Hadi, Jilloo, Mushtari

Champraj, king of Bundi (Jamshedji), boasts in the court of the maharaja Karansingh of his wife Sone's (Jilloo) purity and fidelity. The villainous Sher Singh (Hadi) claims to prove otherwise and, through trickery, appropriates a dagger and a handkerchief by which Sone had said she would remember her husband in his absence. Champraj, who stakes his life on his wife's fidelity, is about to be beheaded when Sone herself, dressed as a dancing-girl, exposes the truth. Based on a script by David, a Parsee theatre playwright, author of ***Alam Ara*** (1931) and future **Wadia Movietone** stunt movies.

SHYAM SUNDAR

1932 121'[M]/129'[H] b&w Marathi/Hindi
d/s/lyr **Bhalji Pendharkar** *pc* Saraswati Cinetone *c* D.G. Gune *m* Bapurao Ketkar
lp **Shahu Modak**, **Shanta Apte**, Bandopant Sohoni, Bapurao Ketkar, Sandow, Bapurao Apte

Children's mythological drawn from the *Vishnu Purana* telling of the child Krishna (Modak). The film intercuts Krishna's rural escapades with Pendya and other childhood friends with palace intrigues in Mathura, where Kans receives a divine warning that the boy Krishna shall be the cause of his death. Although the film follows the style of the ***Gopal Krishna*** (1929 and '38) versions by **Prabhat**, it was a breakthrough in other ways: it was the first film made in Pune, apparently the first Indian film with a continuous run of more than 25 weeks (at the New West End, Bombay) and the first to introduce the marketing technique of adding a new sequence after the release to attract a repeat audience (the sequence in which Kans is killed). It is also the screen debut of **Prabhat** stars Apte and Modak as child actors. Pendharkar continued the story's motifs in his next film, ***Akashwani*** (1934).

ZALIM JAWANI

aka *The Youth* aka *Chandraprabha*
1932 139' b&w Hindi
d/s **B.P. Mishra** pc **Imperial Cinetone** *c* Adi M. Irani
lp **Master Vithal**, Ermeline, Jamshedji, Rustom Poonawala, Hadi, Saku

Mishra, who died in 1932, followed his ***Draupadi*** (1931) with this historical fantasy establishing the studio's trademark genre. The story is drawn from the Rajput war sagas and features the despotic Jaisingh (Poonawala) who usurps the throne of Achalgarh. The court intrigues involve the good Pratap (Vithal), lover of Princess Chandraprabha (Ermeline), hidden testaments from the dead King Udaybhanu, fortune tellers and a swayamvar (a public contest) to claim the princess as a bride. The film's treatment of sexuality receives an unusual twist when the misogynist Sher Singh (Hadi), a friend of Pratap, is forced to impersonate a woman to protect Chandraprabha from the villain Ranamal (Jamshedji). The main highlights are Master Vithal's swordplay.

KARMA/NAGAN KI RAGINI

aka *Fate* aka *Song of Serpent*
1933 73'(68')[E]/76'[H] b&w Hindi/English
d J.L. Freer-Hunt *pc* Indian & British Film Prods *p* **Himansu Rai** *s* Diwan Sharar *m* Ernest Broadhurst
lp **Devika Rani**, **Himansu Rai**, Abraham Sofaer, Sudharani, Diwan Sharar

Himansu Rai continued addressing the European markets with this effort directed by an ex-Royal Navy captain better known for Navy propaganda and training films. The simple plot has the maharani (Devika Rani) fall in love with the neighbouring prince (Rai) despite her father's disapproval. Shot and synchronised at Stoll Studios in London, it is presented as an Orientalist fantasy with a by Indian standards scandalously prolonged kiss. Devika Rani's melodious English was a major selling point, with songs like *Now The Moon Her Light Has Shed* and an advertising blurb quoting the *London Star*: 'You will never hear a lovelier voice or diction or see a lovelier face'. *Variety* (30 May 1933) described it as 'a sort of modern American romance done against an Indian background.' The film flopped, encouraging Rai to concentrate on **Bombay Talkies**.

LAL-E-YAMAN

aka *Parviz Parizad*
1933 158' b&w Hindi
d/sc **J.B.H. Wadia** *pc* **Wadia Movietone** *st/co-lyr/m* Joseph David *dial/co-lyr* Munshi Ashik *co-dial* Munshi Sefta *m* Master Mohammed *c* Vasant B. Jagtap, **Homi Wadia**
lp Jal Khambatta, Karimja, Padma, Feroze Dastur, Master Mohammed, Sayani, Nazir, B. Khan, Boman Shroff, Mohini, Kamala, Mayuri, Lola

Classic Parsee theatre-derived Oriental fantasy. The heir to the Yemeni throne, Prince Parviz (Karimja), is falsely imprisoned by his stepmother (Mohini) who claims power. Parviz receives a magic dagger from a mystic sufi fakir (Mohammed) to liberate himself and his people. The dagger makes him invisible. He kills the Apeman (Shroff) and the genii (Khan), rescues the captive Princess Parizad (Padma) and, finally, overwhelms the soldiers sent to recapture him. The king (Khambatta) learns the truth and repents. Lalarukh (Kamala), Parviz' wife who dresses in male clothes to rescue her husband, sacrifices her life so that he may marry the princess.

MEERABAI/RAJRANI MEERA

1933 131'[B]/151'[H] b&w Bengali/Hindi
d/s[H] **Debaki Bose** *pc* **New Theatres** *co-s*[B] Hiren Bose, Basanta Chatterjee *c* **Nitin Bose** *m* **Rai Chand Boral**
lp **Pahadi Sanyal**, Molina Devi, **Durgadas Bannerjee**[B]/**Prithviraj Kapoor**[H], **Amar Mullick**[B], Manoranjan Bhattacharya[B], Sailen Pal[B], Chandrabati Devi[B]/**Durga Khote**[H], Nibhanani Devi[B], **K.L. Saigal**[H], Ansari[H]

Big-budget **saint film** on the life of Meera (Chandrabati Devi/Khote), a princess of the Rajput kingdom of Chittor married to the king of Mewad (Bannerjee/Kapoor). She is persecuted by her husband and her brother-in-law when she abandons worldly possessions to become a devotee of Krishna. She undertakes a journey of penance and performs a miracle which the king attributes to the machinations of the evil army chief Abhiram. After being imprisoned, vilified and accused of infidelity, she dies and is united with her god. The film launches Chandrabati Devi (1903-92) as a major Bengali star, while Khote, already established at **Prabhat**, went to Calcutta to do the Hindi version (cf ***Meera***, 1945).

MISS 1933

1933 176' b&w Hindi
d **Chandulal Shah** *pc* **Ranjit Movietone** *c* Pandurang Naik *m* Jhande Khan
lp **Gohar**, Mehtab, E. Bilimoria, Keki Adajania, Dixit, Ghory, Yakub

Gohar in a classic modernisation **melodrama** exploring the consequences of female autonomy. Kusum (Gohar) rejects her avaricious uncle's decision to marry/sell her to a rich man and is adopted by Seth Kisandas (Adajania). She meets his urbanised son Jayant (E. Bilimoria) and his friends Ramesh (Yakub) and Kishori (Mehtab). The love story of Kusum and Jayant explores the complications ensuing from a woman's freedom to choose. The issue is resolved only after Ramesh molests her: she defends herself and is tried for attempted murder.

PRITHVI PUTRA

1933 154' b&w Telugu
d Potina Srinivasa Rao *pc* Saraswati Cinetone
lp **K. Raghuramaiah**, Parepalli Satyanarayana, **Surabhi Kamalabai**

The Pauranic story of Narakasura, the demon who, when slayed by Krishna, asks that the day of his death be celebrated by mankind and that he be allowed to descend to earth every year to witness the festivity. Financed by an AP exhibitor, the film, made at the Saraswati Cinetone, was probably the first locally financed Telugu film.

PURAN BHAKT

1933 159' b&w Hindi
d **Debaki Bose** *pc* **New Theatres** *c* **Nitin Bose** *m* **Rai Chand Boral**
lp Choudhury Mohammed Rafiq, Kumar, Anwari, **K.C. Dey**, Umasashi, Kapoor, Tara, **K.L. Saigal**, Molina Devi, Ansari

The legend of Prince Puran, born under King Silwan of Sialkot's curse which binds his parents never to set eyes on him until he is 16. Accused of leading a debauched life by an evil general and by the king's second wife, Puran is sentenced to death. Rescued by the mystic Gorakhnath, he becomes an ascetic. When the king is overthrown, Puran rises from his meditations to depose the general who has seized power, before returning to his life of renunciation. Saigal only appears during his own song sequences.

SAVITHRI

1933 125' b&w Telugu
d **C. Pullaiah** *pc* **East India Film**
lp Ramatilakam, **Vemuri Gaggaiah**, Nidumukkala Subba Rao, **Surabhi Kamalabai**

Mahabharata legend in which Princess Savitri marries Satyavan despite a curse that foretells his death within a year. She manages to get Yama (Gaggaiah), the god of death, to restore her husband to life. With this film the Calcutta-based studio tried to compete with the entry of Bombay studios into the nascent Telugu cinema, inaugurated by **H.M. Reddy**'s ***Bhakta Prahlada*** (1931) using actors from the **Surabhi theatres** troupe. Pullaiah's version introduces the star Gaggaiah.

SINHAGAD

1933 135' b&w Marathi
d **V. Shantaram** *pc* **Prabhat Film** *st* Hari Narayan Apte's novel *Gad Aala Pan Sinha Gela* *sc/dial/m* **Govindrao Tembe** *c* **Keshavrao Dhaiber**, V. Avadhoot
lp Keshavrao Dhaiber, Shinde, Shankarrao Bhosle, Bazarbattoo, **Baburao Pendharkar**, Budasaheb, **Master Vinayak**, Leela Chandragiri, Prabhavati

Based on a Marathi literary classic, but more immediately on **Baburao Painter**'s 1923 silent version, the film focuses on the 17th-C. Maratha emperor Shivaji's lieutenant (and folk hero) Tanaji Malusare (Bhosle). Here Kamalkumari, about to commit sati (self-immolation), is captured by Udaybhanu (Pendharkar) and taken to his fort at Kondana. Tanaji dies during his successful attack on the fort with only 50 soldiers. This scene, although not a great piece of action choreography, is imaginatively lit with torches in the background, followed by remarkable shots of Shivaji's (Shinde) ascent up the hill on horseback. The music was memorable for the songs in the militant Powada form: *Mard maratha mawalcha* and Tanaji's strident defence of his king as representing 'Hindu' ideals, *Jyachi kirti saarya jagaat*. Dhaiber had acted in B. Painter's version (1923) as well.

YAHUDI KI LADKI

1933 137' b&w Hindi-Urdu
d **Premankur Atorthy** *pc* **New Theatres** *sc* **Aga Hashr Kashmiri** from his play *Misarkumari* *c* **Nitin Bose** *m* **Pankaj Mullick, Rai Chand Boral**
lp **K.L. Saigal, Pahadi Sanyal**, Rattan Bai, Gul Hamid, Nawab, Nemo, Ghulam Mohammed, Radharani, Tara

Costume epic and the most faithful adaptation of Kashmiri's Parsee theatre classic also filmed by **Bimal Roy** (***Yahudi***, 1958). The play was written by Kashmiri in 1915, but the movie's immediate formal ancestor was the Bengali stage version of Kashmiri's play, Baradaprasanna Dasgupta's *Misarkumari* (1919). The familiar story features the rivalry between the Roman priest Brutus and the oppressed Jewish merchant, Prince Ezra. Brutus sentences Ezra's son to death and Ezra in turn kidnaps and raises Brutus' only daughter, Decia. When the daughter, renamed Hannah (Rattan Bai), grows up, the Roman Prince Marcus (Saigal) falls in love with her. To court her, he disguises his Roman identity. When his religion is discovered, he is ejected from Ezra's house. Marcus then agrees to marry Princess Octavia (Tara) as arranged, but Hannah denounces him in open court and he is sentenced to death by his own father, the emperor. When Hannah and Ezra respond to Octavia's pleas and retract their accusations, they in turn are sentenced to death by Brutus. Ezra reveals to Brutus that Hannah, who is about to be killed, is in fact Brutus' own daughter. The costumed spectacular was one of the early New Theatres' most elaborate productions, with 19 songs including Saigal's Ghalib number *Nuktanchi hai gham-e-dil usko sunaye na bane*.

ZEHARI SAAP

1933 156' b&w Hindi
d J.J. Madan *pc* **Madan Theatres** *s/lyr* **Narayan Prasad Betaab** from his play *c* T. Marconi *m* Vrijlal Verma
lp **Patience Cooper**, Kajjan, Sorabji Kerawala, Sheela, Rosy, A.R. Kabuli, Ghulam Hussain

Typical Cooper vehicle about a medieval chieftain's revolt against the good Nawab Bakar Malik. The nawab's outlaw son vows revenge and the adventures end with the royal family reunited. The dramatic pivot is the chieftain's demand to marry the princess whom he had raised as his own daughter. The theme of incestuous aggression, present in many stories (e.g. ***Khuda Ki Shaan***, 1931), is prevalent in Parsee historicals (as it was in the Elizabethan theatre which fed into that form) and culminated in **Mehboob**'s ***Humayun*** (1945). Cooper provided the matrix for roles later associated with **Nargis**, evoking an uneasily innocent sexuality upon which competing males, representing conflicting social-historical forces, make proprietorial claims.

AKASHWANI

1934 151'[M]/149'[H] b&w Marathi/Hindi
d/s/lyr **Bhalji Pendharkar** *pc* **Kolhapur Cinetone** *c* V.B. Joshi *m* Gundopant Walavalkar
lp Leela, Nanasaheb Phatak, **Master Vinayak**, Dr Sathe, **Baburao Pendharkar**, Master Vasant, Shirodkar, Bhadre

Pendharkar's anti-imperialist version of the *Vishnu Purana* legend tells of the villainous Kans (Phatak) plotting to marry Devaki (Leela) to Dikpal (Pendharkar), commander of Magadh's army. The people of Mathura fear that Magadh will destroy their city-state and foil Kans' scheme as Devaki marries the beggar Vasudev (Vinayak). The heavens forecast, accurately, that Devaki's eighth son Krishna (Shirodkar) shall cause Kans' death. This is the debut production of Kolhapur Cinetone, launched as a rival to **Prabhat** and featuring Phatak, Pendharkar and Vinayak in roles evoking their screen images established at Prabhat.

AMRITMANTHAN

aka *The Churning of the Oceans*
1934 155' b&w Marathi/Hindi
d/dial **V. Shantaram** *pc* **Prabhat Film** *s* **Narayan Hari Apte** from his novel *Bhagyashree* *lyr* **Shantaram Athavale** *c* **Keshavrao Dhaiber** *m* **Keshavrao Bhole**
lp **Chandramohan**[H]/**Keshavrao Date**[M], Nalini Tarkhad, Sureshbabu Mane, **Shanta Apte**, Kelkar, Kulkarni, Varde, Budasaheb, Desai

Shantaram's classic opens with a sensational low-angle circular track movement as Chandika cult followers meet in a dungeon of flickering lights and deep shadow. As the more rationalist King Krantivarma (Varde) banned human or animal sacrifices from the increasingly fanatical festivals dedicated to the goddess, the cult's high priest (Chandramohan/Date) orders the hapless Vishwasgupta (Kelkar) to kill the king. He obeys but is then betrayed by the perfidious priest and caught. His son Madhavgupta (Mane) and daughter Sumitra (Apte) together with the princess (Tarkhad) and the people finally overthrow the priest. There are several famous scenes, including the twice-told legend of the churning of the seas, once by the priest to show how evil must be exorcised, and again by a good general to show how demons often appear disguised as gods. Although invoking divine intervention when Madhavgupta is about to be sacrificed, the film's strongly political thrust has the people rise in revolt. Shantaram had just returned from Germany and used several techniques from that expressionist cinema, including the systematic recourse to artificial light, even bleaching the film in places, and, in its most famous shot, the telephoto lens focused on the priest's right eye in his opening declaration. Prabhat's first all-India hit introduced names later associated with several of the studio's productions, with screen debuts from both Date in the Marathi version and Chandramohan in the Hindi. Date perhaps gives his best performance ever, while Apte plays her first adult role. It is composer Bhole's first professional film. **Fattelal** and **Damle** are responsible for the art direction and the sound.

BHAKTA DHRUVA

1934 142' b&w Kannada
d **P.Y. Altekar** *pc* Jayavanti Talkies *s/lyr* from a play by the Ratnavali Natak Co. *m* Harmonium Sheshgiri Rao
lp Master Muthu, T. Dwarkanath, H.S.

Rattan Bai (centre) and K.L. Saigal (foreground, right) in *Yahudi Ki Ladki*

Krishnamurthy Iyengar, G. Nagesh, M.G. Mari Rao, T. Kanakalakshamma

Regarded as the first Kannada feature, though ***Sati Sulochana*** (1934) was released earlier. Pauranic mythological about the child Dhruva (Muthu) who eventually finds solace when he becomes a star in the heavens. The film was made by the Marathi stage and film director Altekar, of the Natyamanwantar group, as a tribute to the Kannada theatre personality A.V. Varadachar who died in 1933. Varadachar's grandson played the lead, surrounded by several actors from his grandfather's Ratnavali company.

CHANDIDAS

1934 128' b&w Hindi
d/c **Nitin Bose** *pc* **New Theatres** *dial/lyr* **Aga Hashr Kashmiri** *m* **Rai Chand Boral**
lp **K.L. Saigal**, Umasashi, **Pahadi Sanyal**, Nawab, M. Ansari, H. Siddiqui, Parvati, Ansaribai

Hindi remake of **Debaki Bose**'s 1932 film by its cameraman. The film stars Saigal as Chandidas and Umasashi as Rami, featuring several of their popular duets (e.g. *Prem nagar mein banaongi ghar main*) and other songs with Sanyal. Released at Chitra and New Cinema, Calcutta, it became the studio's first Hindi success.

GUL SANOBAR

1934 154' b&w Hindi
d/st **Homi Master** *pc* **Imperial Film** *sc* **Mohanlal G. Dave** *c* Rustom Irani *m* Pransukh M. Nayak
lp **Sulochana**, **D. Bilimoria**, **Zubeida**, Jilloo, Chanda, Lakshmi, Ghulam Mohammed, Peerjan, Hadi, Abdul Kader, Syed Ahmed

Adventure drama based on a Persian legend. Mubarak (Kader) kidnaps Sanobar (Mohammed), the son of the king of Yemen (Peerjan) and raises him in the forest. Prompted by Mubarak, Sanobar attacks the king returning from a hunt, but is caught, condemned to be locked in a box and thrown into the sea. A fakir teaches the king the language of the animals, warning him not to pass on the skill to any other humans. Listening to two birds, the king realises that Sanobar is his own son. The queen (Jilloo), learning that the king has special linguistic powers, forces him to teach them to her as well. He does so and becomes paralysed. Only a flower from the mouth of Meherangez, the princess of Sistan (Sulochana) can save him. Umar (Bilimoria), the good prince, attempts the task. Zubeida plays the helpful fairy, Gul.

GUNSUNDARI

1934 185' b&w Hindi
d/s **Chandulal Shah** *pc* **Ranjit Movietone** *c* Pandurang Naik *m* Rewashankar Marwadi, Gangaprasad Pathak
lp E. Bilimoria, **Gohar**, Keki Bawa, Gangaprasad Pathak, Dixit, Ghory, Ram Apte, Shanta, Charubala, Rampiary, Kamala

Shah's first remake of his silent hit ***Gunsundari*** (1927) presents a more traditional, though complicated, version of the original plot. A joint family headed by Seth Shyamaldas (Bawa) includes two sons Chandrakant (Bilimoria) and Vinu (Apte) and daughter Kusum (Shanta). The stories of the father and each of the three children unfold and in each Gunsundari (Gohar), Chandrakant's dutiful wife, appears as the saviour. Shyamaldas (Bawa) is a drunkard, accused of fathering an illegitimate child. Chandrakant becomes a drunk falling into the clutches of both the villain Madanrai (Gangaprasad) and the prostitute Bansari (Rampiary) who try to steal his property. Sister-in-law Sushila (Kamala) is unhappily married to Vasantrai (Ghory) who pawns her necklace. Gunsundari gives her some money and later gets into trouble because she is sworn to secrecy and cannot account for the money. As in the silent version, Gunsundari tries to entice her husband back from Bansari, but eventually finds herself on the streets, destitute. She finally meets Chandrakant, who is also on the streets. Eventually all ends happily when they discover, through coincidence, that the dead Shyamaldas has left all his property to his estranged son.

INDIRA MA

1934 158' b&w Hindi
d **Nandlal Jaswantlal** *pc* **Imperial Films** *s* **Mohanlal G. Dave** *lyr* Dhani Ram 'Prem' *c* Pandurang Naik *m* Pransukh M. Naik
lp **Sulochana**, **D. Bilimoria**, **Raja Sandow**, Jamshedji, Jilloo, Hadi

Imperial's remake of their silent Sulochana hit, *Indira BA* (1929), presents an East-West conflict in the form of a love triangle. Indira (Sulochana), with an MA from Oxford, rejects the 'idiot' Kishore (Sandow) chosen for her by her alcoholic father, the leading lawyer Bansilal (Jamshedji), and falls for the playboy Pyarelal (Bilimoria). However, Pyarelal is a philanderer and the marriage ends in divorce while Kishore remains devoted to his beloved, proving that parents instinctively choose the right man for their daughters. The climactic scene has the father defending the innocent Kishore in court and publicly accusing himself for his daughter's misfortune, blaming alcohol and his decision to have her educated abroad.

LAVAKUSA

1934 c.165' b&w Telugu/Tamil
d **C. Pullaiah** *pc* **East India Film** *s* Ramanamurthy *lyr* Balijepalli Lakshmikanta Kavi *m* Prabhala Satyanarayana
lp Parepalli Subba Rao, **Sriranjini Sr.**, Master Bhimarao, Malleshwara Rao, Parepalli Satyanarayana, Bhushana Sastry

Made apparently on the used sets of **Debaki Bose**'s *Seeta* (1934). It is the *Ramayana* story of Seeta (Sriranjini) who retires to the forest and gives birth to twin boys, Lava (Bhimarao) and Kusa (M. Rao), who later take on the might of Rama (Subba Rao) unaware that he is their father. Probably the first film to receive a wide release in the AP countryside, it was singer Sriranjini's film debut and a major hit running in some theatres for over a year. Pullaiah remade the film (1963) with **N.T. Rama Rao** and **Anjali Devi**.

MAZDOOR

aka *The Mill*
1934 155' b&w Hindi
d/sc **Mohan Bhavnani** *pc* Ajanta Cinetone *s* Munshi Premchand *c* B.C. Mitra *m* B.S. Hoogan
lp Bibbo, S.B. Nayampalli, P. Jairaj, Tarabai, Khalil Aftab, Amina, S.L. Puri

One of the first realistic treatments of industrial working-class conditions and the only engagement with cinema of the best-known 20th-C. Urdu and Hindi novelist, Munshi Premchand. In his biography, *Premchand: A Life* (1982), Amrit Rai noted that Premchand had to accept Bhavnani's offer for financial reasons after the closure of his journal *Jagran*. In Bombay for a year, Premchand wrote: 'What they want are thrilling and sensational films. Without endangering my reputation I shall try and go along with the directors as far as I can, for that I shall be obliged to do. [I]dealism demands a high price and one is occasionally obliged to suppress it.' Premchand later elaborated his position on the film industry in his essay *Cinema Aur Sahitya* (publ. in *Lekhak*, Allahabad, 1935). Shot on location in a Bombay textile mill, the schematic plot opens with the death of a benevolent mill owner whose good daughter Padma (Bibbo) and drunken playboy son Vinodh (Nayampalli) must now run the business jointly. Vinodh's ruthlessly exploitative management prompts Padma and her protege Kailash (Jairaj) to lead a strike against her brother. Vinodh turns violent, goes to prison and the mill closes. With the workers' support and a providential order, Padma restarts the business in a humanitarian way and marries Kailash. The president of the Mill Owners Association was a member of the censor board in Bombay and tried to get the film banned. The Punjab Board cleared the film initially, but following near-riots after it was released in Lahore, banned it. The Delhi ban was followed by a central government decree that the film had an inflammatory influence on workers. The film was a commercial failure, sinking the Ajanta Studio.

PIYA PYARE

aka *My Man*
1934 144' b&w Hindi
d **R.S. Choudhury** *pc* **Imperial Film** *sc* **Ardeshir Irani** *st* **Mohanlal G. Dave** *c* Adi M. Irani *m* Pransukh M. Nayak
lp **Sulochana**, **D. Bilimoria**, Jilloo, Lakshmi, Chanda, Jamshedji, Ghaznavi

Classic R.S. Choudhury adventure fantasy setting the studio's top box office duo in an unnamed Rajput-style court. The king's younger wife Taramati (Jilloo) is condemned to death for infidelity and her son Chandrakumar (Ghaznavi) is brought up by a distant uncle. The elder wife has twins, the lovely Princess Chanda (Sulochana) and the nasty Jaisingh, who turns out not to be their son after all. Rohil (Bilimoria) is the romantic outlaw who is revealed to be the long lost son of the good chief Sajjan Singh (Jamshedji). Rohil helps restore order in the kingdom to Princess Chanda's delight. Elaborately filmed scenes of a tiger hunt, the cheetah who takes away Rohil when still an infant and lavish palace scenes contributed to its success.

RASHK-E-LAILA

aka *Jaaneman*
1934 153' b&w Hindi
d/s **Nanubhai Vakil** *pc* Mahalakshmi Cinetone *dial* G.K. Mehta *c* V.V. Date *m* Master Dinkar
lp **Zubeida**, Bhai Desa, Master Gulab, Hiroji, Pawar, Master Yusuf, Master Joshi

One of the best-known films of Mahalakshmi, a sound film studio set up jointly by star Zubeida and director Vakil. The costumed love fantasy derived from the *Arabian Nights* and tells of Laila (Zubeida), a gypsy dancer who falls in love with the Persian soldier Asghar (Desa). The villain, who lusts after Laila, is Sardar Sagi (Gulab), right-hand man to the grand vizir (Joshi) who has political ambitions of his own.

SAMAJ KI BHOOL

1934 143' b&w Hindi
d **Homi Master** *pc* **Imperial Film** *st/dial* Munshi Zameer *c* Adi M. Irani *m* Pransukh M. Nayak
lp Ghaznavi, Dulari, Jamshedji, Syed Ahmed, Abdul Kader, Inayat, Jilloo, Lalita

Unusually violent film for its time advocating widows' right to remarry. The crooked Daulatram (Jamshedji) sells his daughter Chandramukhi (Dulari) in marriage to Banwarilal. Distraught, her mother commits suicide. Banwarilal is poisoned by his nephew who fears the new wife might produce an heir, and Chandramukhi is forced into prostitution. Her father, now a beggar, chances to see his daughter in this condition and he too commits suicide. The nephew then kills Chandramukhi's brother Dayaram (Kader) in an argument and Chandramukhi is arrested for the murder. The sorry tale ends happily when the good lawyer Raghuvir (Ghaznavi), Chandramukhi's original suitor, rescues her in court. The film ends with debates for and against widow remarriage and with Raghuvir marrying Chandramukhi.

SATI SULOCHANA

1934 c.170' b&w Kannada
d **Y.V. Rao** *pc* South India Movietone *st* a play by Shri Sahitya Samrajya Nataka Mandali *sc* **Bellave Narahari Sastry** *m* **R. Nagendra Rao**
lp R. Nagendra Rao, **M.V. Subbaiah Naidu**, Lakshmibai, Tripuramba, C.T. Sheshachalam, Y.V. Rao

First major Kannada film, released before though made after ***Bhakta Dhruva*** (1934). Based on a play by R. Nagendra Rao and Subbaiah Naidu's theatre group, the first of many the duo translated to the screen, it is a *Ramayana* mythological told from the viewpoint of Sulochana, daughter-in-law of the villain Ravana. Her husband Indrajit, who wounds Lakshman, is eventually killed by Rama, leaving her a widow. According to M.V. Ramakrishnaiah (1992), the film was made in a Kolhapur studio with 2000 extras and spectacular war sequences were shot with two cameras.

SEETA BIBAHA

1934 ?' b&w Oriya
d/p Mohan Sunder Dev Goswami *dial* Advaitacharan Mohanty *m* Haricharan Mohanty
lp Makhanlal Bannerjee, Mohan Sunder Dev Goswami, Krishnachandra Singh, Prabhavati, Buddhimati, Radharani

Oriya cinema's first feature is a *Ramayana* mythological telling of Rama's wedding to Seeta. Made on the initiative of an amateur theatre group in Puri, it was sponsored by **Priyanath Ganguly**'s Kali Film Studio in Calcutta and cost Rs 30,000. Director Goswami apparently ran a Rasadala group (boys specialising in performing the *Krishna Leela*). Although the film did well at the box office, the next Oriya film, *Lalita*, was released only in 1949.

SEETA KALYANAM

1934 c.133' b&w Telugu
d **Ch. Narasimha Rao** *pc* **Vel Pics** *c* **K. Ramnoth** *m* Galipenchala Narasimha Rao
lp Master Kalyani, **Bezawada Rajarathnam**, Madavapeddi Venkatramaiah, T. Venkateshwarulu

The Vel Studio's debut production is a Telugu adaptation of **Prabhat**'s Tamil mythological, *Seeta Kalyanam* (1933). Believed to be the first Telugu film to use outdoor sequences, it is the first independent production of cameraman Ramnoth and art director A.K. Sekhar, later crucial to the **Vauhini** and **Gemini** Studios.

SHAHER KA JADOO

aka *Lure Of the City*
1934 144' b&w Hindi
d/s **Kaliprasad Ghosh** *pc* **Sagar Movietone** *c* Ambalal Patel *m* **K.C. Dey**
lp Sabita Devi, M. Kumar, **Motilal**, K.C. Dey, Kamalabai, **Sitara Devi**

After some silent successes ((*Nishiddha Phal*, 1928; *Kanthahaar*, 1930), this is Kaliprasad Ghosh's sound debut during his brief stint at the Sagar Studio. A seminal Sabita Devi social critiquing decadent urban values, it tells of Sundarlal (Kumar) who leaves his wife Lalita (Kamalabai) and children to make a living in the city where he succumbs to depravity and vice. His son dies and his beautiful daughter Sarju (Sabita Devi) defends her virtue and tries to support her mother in conditions of extreme misery. Dressed as a man and accompanied by the blind Baldev (Dey), she scours the city in search of her father, encountering difficulties, including a drunken millionaire she rescues and with whom she falls in love even though he mistakes her for a boy. Dey, a **New Theatres** singer, moved to Bombay to act in and score this film which saw Motilal's debut. Ghosh later became better known for 40s/50s Bengali films such as *Vidyasagar* (1950) and *Kar Papey* (1952).

SITAMGARH

aka *The Tyrant*
1934 158' b&w Hindi
d/co-s **Jayant Desai** *pc* **Ranjit Movietone** *co-s/dial/lyr* **Narayan Prasad Betaab** *co-s* **Chaturbhuj Doshi** *c* G.G. Gogate *m* Banne Khan, Rewashankar Marwadi
lp E. Bilimoria, Keki Bawa, Ghory, Charlie, Dixit, Ishwarlal, Bhupatrai, Ram Apte, Madhuri, Khatoon

The tyrant Jabbar (Bawa) attacks the village where lives the famously devout Sayyed (Bhupatrai) and kidnaps his son Iqbal (Bilimoria). Iqbal grows up to become the commander of Jabbar's army and is as tyrannical as his mentor, campaigning to force the people to accept Jabbar as the true god. He comes upon a camp of 'true' religious believers led by Sadiq, his daughter Sadika (Madhuri) and a Princess Hamida (Khatoon). The latter falls in love with him, much to the chagrin of Shaddad (Ishwarlal), her suitor. Eventually Iqbal learns of his real ancestry and joins the true believers. He then proceeds to attack those who do not share his religion, nor his belief in Jabbar. When Jabbar realises that his own family now opposes him, he commits suicide. The Ranjit Studio hit evokes the successful ***Amritmanthan*** of the same year.

VEER BABRUWAHAN

1934 144' b&w Hindi
d **Jayant Desai** *pc* **Ranjit Movietone** *st* Dayaram Shah, **Narayan Prasad Betaab** *c* G.G. Gogate *m* Jhande Khan, Rewashankar Marwadi, Gangaprasad Pathak
lp E. Bilimoria, Madhuri, Bhagwandas, Khatoon, Keki Adajania, Ghory, Ishwarlal, Dixit, Tarabai

Bilimoria's best-known mythological. Babruwahan (Bilimoria), son of Arjuna (Adajania) and Chitrangada (Tarabai), fights heroically in the *Mahabharata* war and returns to his mother who despairs at the strife between her son and her husband. He stops a horse that belongs to Arjuna's army, which is a sign of defiance that leads to further bloodshed. Babruwahan defeats and beheads his own father and is about to follow his mother in an act of ritual suicide when Krishna (Bhagwandas) descends to earth and instructs him to go to the land of the serpents and fetch the mythical Sanjivani Mani to bring Arjuna back to life. This pits Babruwahan against Ullupi (Khatoon), daughter of the serpent king and a former wife of Arjuna. After another battle she is forced to surrender the sanjivani mani, but instead she captures the dead Arjuna's head. Krishna has to intervene again to resolve matters. One of the most adventure-laden of the epics, this tale is popular among producers of mythologicals. It was first made by **Phalke** (*Babruwahan*, 1923), then by **Nanabhai Bhatt** in Hindi (1950) and most recently by **Hunsur Krishnamurthy**, starring Kannada superstar **Rajkumar** (*Babruvahana*, 1977).

BARRISTER'S WIFE

aka *Barrister Ki Bibi*
1935 158' b&w Hindi
d **Chandulal Shah** *pc* **Ranjit Movietone** *dial/lyr* **Narayan Prasad Betaab** *c* G.G. Gogate *m* Rewashankar Marwadi, Banne Khan
lp **Gohar**, E. Bilimoria, Keki Bawa, **Raja Sandow**, Ram Apte, Ishwarlal, Bhanumathi,

Charlie, Dixit, Bhupatrai, Khatoon, Kamala, Shanta

Lily (Gohar) and her college lover Vasant (Bilimoria) vow to commit suicide should circumstances prevent their marriage. Lily's father forces her to marry a barrister (Bawa) but she persuades Vasant not to kill himself. When Vasant becomes an invalid, she looks after him, causing her husband to disown and ban her from meeting their daughter. Years later, Lily becomes a servant while her daughter Indu (Gohar again) returns from England having become a lawyer. Lily meets Vasant again, who coincidentally is painting a portrait of her daughter. Their encounter leads to a renewal of their death pact but only Vasant dies while Lily is arrested for his murder. In the long trial scenes, Indu defends Lily, the prosecutor is Indu's boyfriend (Sandow) and the judge is Lily's ex-husband and Indu's father.

Chandrasena

BHIKHARAN

aka *Song of Life*
1935 143' b&w Hindi
d/s **Premankur Atorthy** *pc* **Kolhapur Cinetone** *c* V.B. Joshi *m* H.C. Bali
lp Rattan Bai, **Master Vinayak**, I.A. Hafizji, Pramila, Raja Pandit, Pheroze Bai, Pawar, Gundopant Walavalkar

After quitting **New Theatres** and moving to Western India, the noted Bengali writer-director Atorthy's first Hindi film was this bid by Kolhapur Cinetone to enter the Hindi mainstream. It is a four-handed melodrama: Kedar (Hafizji) asks Madhavi (R. Bai) to leave home so that he may marry the rich Chandra (Pramila). But Chandra is only obeying her parents: in fact she loves the painter Kumar (Vinayak). Madhavi, now a beggar singing for alms, becomes Kumar's model and lover while Chandra tries to get away from Kedar. She enlists Kumar's help, pushing Madhavi out again. The latter becomes a stage actress while the distraught Kumar becomes a mad street singer. Eventually, Madhavi and Kumar get married. The film belongs mainly to Rattan Bai, a New Theatres singing star recruited to the cinema by Atorthy in ***Yahudi Ki Ladki*** (1933).

CHANDRASENA

1935 136' b&w Marathi/Hindi/Tamil
d **V. Shantaram** *pc* **Prabhat Film** *s/dial* Shivram Vashikar *lyr* **K. Narayan Kale** *c* **Keshavrao Dhaiber** *m* **Keshavrao Bhole**
lp Nalini Tarkhad, Rajani, Sureshbabu Mane, Kulkarni, Mane Pahelwan, Kelkar, Manajirao, Budasaheb, Shantabai, Azoorie

After his epochal ***Amritmanthan*** (1934), Shantaram returned to familiar territory with this special-effects-laden episode from the *Ramayana*. Indrajit, son of Ravana, initiates an attack on Rama (Mane) and Lakshmana (Kulkarni) in which they are captured by Mahi (Kelkar). They escape with the assistance of Rama's disciple, the monkey-god Hanuman (Manajirao). The narrative foregrounds Chandrasena (Tarkhad), wife of Mahi, who reveres Rama but disapproves of the bacchanalian orgies and the celebration of liquor that is the norm in his kingdom. She helps resolve the stalemate of the battle when Mahi (who can duplicate himself and his dead soldiers) proves invincible, by revealing the secret formula that will kill her husband. In addition to the usual flying figures and magic arrows mandatory for a *Ramayana* mythological, there is an effective scene of a gigantic Hanuman picking up a miniaturised human figure. A Tamil version was also made alongside the Marathi and Hindi ones.

DESH DASI

1935 167' b&w Hindi
d **Chandulal Shah** *pc* **Ranjit Movietone** *c* G.G. Gogate
lp **Gohar**, E. Bilimoria, **Raja Sandow**, Keki Bawa, Dixit, Ghory, Charlie, Ishwarlal, Khatoon, Shanta, Ram Apte, Baby Bhanumathi

Shah gave this melodramatic Gohar/Bilimoria/Sandow love triangle a nationalistic twist. Leading a life of boredom typical of the colonised leisure class, Vinakumari (Gohar) and her lover Dr Rasik (Bilimoria) suddenly come across a Gandhian ashram run by Dilip Kumar (Sandow) and other social workers. Vinakumari dedicates herself to the cause of the poor while the ashram faces problems: an entertainment carnival set up by urban businessmen leads the villagers into temptation, a famine breaks out and rapacious landlords, including Bakshiji (Bawa), Vinakumari's guardian, demand money. Eventually Dr Rasik too joins the group, providing much-needed medical assistance to the workers in the disease-stricken countryside.

DESH DEEPAK

aka *Josh-e-Watan*
1935 160' b&w Hindi
d/sc **J.B.H. Wadia** *pc* Wadia Bros. *st/lyr/co-dial* Joseph David *co-dial* Munshi Sarfaraz *c* Vasant B. Jagtap *m* Master Mohammed
lp Sharifa, Iqbal, Sardar Mansoor, Sayani, **Fearless Nadia**, Parsee Charlie, Husn Bano, Puri, Master Mohammed, Boman Shroff, John Cawas, Master Jaidev, Bashir Qawal

Unusual Parsee theatre-influenced costume thriller written by noted stage and film writer Joseph David (***Alam Ara***, 1931). Two sisters vie for power in a kingdom. The elder one (Iqbal), though hampered by a perfidious general (Sayani), wins and persecutes the younger one (Sharifa) who has the support of the elder one's husband (Sardar Mansoor). She captures her brother-in-law but he refuses to abandon his patriotic ideals. The nasty general's daughter (Bano), having lost her lover (Puri) in the war, mobilises the army for a pacifist campaign with the support of an adventurous duo (Nadia and Parsee Charlie) who penetrate the enemy fortress disguised as dancers. Director J.B.H. Wadia saw this film as representing anti-war propaganda and included, in his directorial credit, another one for the 'pacifistic incidents in the scenario'.

DEVDAS

1935 141'[H]/139'[B] b&w Hindi/Bengali
d/sc **P.C. Barua** *pc* **New Theatres** *st* Saratchandra Chatterjee's novel (1917) *c* **Bimal Roy**[H]/Yusuf Mulji, Sudhin Majumdar, Dilip Gupta[B] *dial/lyr*[H] **Kidar Sharma** *m* **Rai Chand Boral, Pankaj Mullick**[H]/**Timir Baran**[B]
lp **K.L. Saigal**[H]/P.C. Barua[B], Jamuna, **K.C. Dey**, Kshetrabala, Rajkumari[H], A.H. Shore[H], Nemo[H], Biswanath Bhaduri[H], Ramkumari[H], **Pahadi Sanyal**[H], **Kidar Sharma**[H], Bikram Kapoor[H], **Amar Mullick**[B], Dinesh Das[B], Manoranjan Bhattacharya[B], Nirmal Bannerjee[B], Sailen Pal[B], Ahi Sanyal[B], Chandrabati Devi[B], Lila[B], Kishori[B], Prabhavati[B]

Devdas (Saigal/Barua), son of a zamindar, and Parvati (aka Paro) (Jamuna), his poor neighbour's daughter, are childhood sweethearts. Status and caste differences prevent their marriage and Devdas is sent to Calcutta while Paro is married off to an aged but rich widower. In Calcutta the hero meets the prostitute Chandramukhi (Rajkumari/Chandrabati Devi) but remorse drives him to alcohol and (after a long train journey in which he attempts to run away from himself) he comes to die in front of his true love's house. Saratchandra's classic novel, which touched a sensitive nerve with its implied criticism of the spinelessness of the feudal elite, later became a favourite source for films after Saigal's influential performance. The weak and narcissistic hero, esp. as played by Saigal (confirmed by his major hit song *Dukh ke din ab beetat nahin*), later grew into a *Werther*-type cult figure as the story, first filmed in the silent period by **Naresh Mitra** (1928), was remade in Hindi by Bimal Roy with **Dilip Kumar** (1955) and twice in Telugu (by **Vedantam Raghavaiah** in 1953 with **A. Nageshwara Rao**; and by **Vijayanirmala** in 1974 starring **Krishna**). The film has become a mythological reference point for Hindi melodrama: in Ramesh Saigal's realist ***Phir Subah Hogi*** (1958), **Raj Kapoor** is taunted for 'being a Devdas' and **Guru Dutt** used the story as an undercurrent for both ***Pyaasa*** (1957) and ***Kaagaz Ke Phool*** (1959). Bimal Roy's hyperactive camera and sophisticated lighting techniques (e.g. the use of green filters to create a negative effect of black sky above white bushes and grass) contrasts with the static acting style, generating an uncanny emotional resonance reinforced by the dynamic, even distorted editing. Barua's Hindi version is strictly a remake of the original Bengali in which Barua played the lead. This version was believed lost until a print was recently discovered in Bangladesh. Saigal, who plays Devdas in the Hindi version, had a sensational walk-on part in the Bengali film as one of the visitors to a brothel, singing *Kahare je jodathe chai* and *Golab huey uthuk phutey*. This was his Bengali debut and the producers, unsure of his accent and whether a non-Bengali singing Bengali songs would be acceptable to the audience, got the author Saratchandra's personal approval (his argument in favour was apparently that Bengalis were not the only people who frequented brothels). Saigal later acted in several Bengali films at New Theatres. Most contemporary critics mention the use of parallel cutting, suggesting this technique had a startling impact at the time. The montage of Devdas crying out in delirium, Parvati stumbling and then Devdas falling from his berth in the train, was described as a 'telepathic' sequence, sometimes commended for its essential 'Indianness' in conveying fate's dominion over individual destiny. **Ritwik Ghatak** admired the film greatly and often used it to teach film students about cinematography.

DHARMATMA

1935 144'[M]/152'[H] b&w Marathi/Hindi
d **V. Shantaram** *pc* **Prabhat Film** *s* **K. Narayan Kale** *dial/lyr*[H] Narottam Vyas *c* V. Avadhoot *m* **Master Krishnarao**
lp **Bal Gandharva**, Ratnaprabha, K. Narayan Kale, Master Chhotu, **Chandramohan**[H]/Kelkar[M], Vasanthi

Playing the only male role of his career, the Marathi stage legend Bal Gandharva's film debut in one of Prabhat's elite Shantaram-directed releases made this saint film one of the most eagerly awaited productions of the year. He acted Sant Eknath (1533-99), a major Marathi poet, author of the *Eknathi Bhagavata* and of numerous *abhangas* evoking folk poetry, esp. the *bharuda* form of solo performances. The film focuses on Eknath's humanitarian defence of the 'untouchable' castes. Opposed by the evil Mahant (Kelkar/Chandramohan), Eknath becomes a social outcast when he arranges to have the lower-caste people fed before the Brahmins during a prayer meeting at his house, compounding the offence by going to eat in one of their houses. The drama is heightened by Eknath's son Hari Pandit (Kale) who joins the ranks of the opposition. The happy ending occurs when the film transcends the food motif and Eknath defends himself by reading his poems to the Pradyananda Shastri of Kashi. The ambitious film enjoyed a larger budget than e.g. ***Sant Tukaram*** (1936). Its key author was Kale who intended it as a political film and played down the mandatory 'miracle' scenes while drawing an explicit analogy between Eknath and Gandhi. The film was originally titled *Mahatma* but the title was changed after the censor objected. Shantaram's direction brought it into the Hindi mainstream, making e.g. the Mahant into an ordinary film villain with a nervous tic in one eye, while continuing on another level his expressionist preoccupations with several high-angle close-ups. The only character contrasting Gandharva's bland performance, extended into most of the other 'goodies', is the wisecracking Shrikhandya (Chhotu).

DHOOP CHHAON/BHAGYA CHAKRA

1935 129'[H]/125'[B] b&w Hindi/Bengali
d/sc/c **Nitin Bose** *pc* **New Theatres** *st/lyr* Sudarshan *m* **Rai Chand Boral**
lp Bishwanath Bhaduri, Bikram Kapoor[H]/**Durgadas Bannerjee**[B], **K.C. Dey**, Ajmat Bibi, Nawab, **Kidar Sharma**, **Pahadi Sanyal**, Umasashi, Devbana, Nagendra Bala, Girdharilal Vaid, Indu Mukherjee, Shyam Laha, **Sardar Akhtar**, **Amar Mullick**[B], Boken Chatterjee[B], Ahi Sanyal[B]

Shyamlal (Bhaduri) kidnaps Deepak (P. Sanyal), the son of his elder brother Hiralal (Kapoor/Bannerjee), to get a larger share in Hiralal's will. Deepak is raised by the blind singer and stage performer Surdas (Dey). Deepak grows up and falls in love with Rupkumari (Umasashi). Plagued by the uncertainty of his parentage, they decide to elope and are chased by detectives (Mukherjee and Laha) employed by Hiralal. Following an accident, Deepak loses his memory, only to regain it when he sees Surdas on the stage. The film is dominated by Dey's powerful singing and the Umasashi-Sanyal love interest. It was the first Indian film to introduce systematically the technique of playback singing (Nitin Bose later claimed it to be one of the first films in the world to do so).

DR MADHURIKA

aka *Modern Wife*
1935 171' b&w Hindi
d **Sarvottam Badami** *pc* **Sagar Film** *st* **K.M. Munshi** *dial/lyr* Waqif *c* Faredoon Irani *m* Pransukh M. Nayak, Ashok Ghosh
lp Sabita Devi, **Motilal**, Padma Shaligram, Pesi Patel, Gulzar, Baby Indira, Pande, Bhudo Advani

Dr Madhurika (Sabita) is a 'modern' young woman dedicated to her profession who advocates birth control to limit population growth. She marries Narendra (Motilal) on condition that he foregoes children, and does not interfere with her practice or with her choice of friends. The film then presents her as neglecting her home and provoking her husband's jealousy with her relationship with a smarmy colleague, Dr Gaurish (Patel). When Narendra attends to Dr Gaurish's suffering wife and then to a starving stranger, Indu (Shaligram), Madhurika gets jealous and agrees to become a dutifully domesticated wife. Using one of Munshi's rare original scripts, the film exemplifies the Sagar Studio's commitment to the morality tale disguised as a reformist social.

DO GHADI KI MAUJ

1935 153' b&w Hindi
d/st **Homi Master** *pc* **Imperial Film** *sc* **Mohanlal G. Dave** *dial* Munshi Zameer *c* Adi M. Irani
lp **Sulochana, D. Bilimoria**, Jilloo, Jamshedji, Lalita, Baby Mayuri, Syed Ahmed, Gani, Sohrab, Gulam Rasool

Master's remake of **Kohinoor**'s silent-era hit *Be Ghadi Mouj* (1927) starred Imperial's top star duo. Hero Kishenprasad (Bilimoria) is an upright engineer with a large family, including his wife Lakshmi (Sulochana), mother Valibai (Jilloo), sister Asha (Lalita) and son Bachoo (Mayuri). He gambles away his happiness and is about to be jailed for embezzlement when he is saved by an honest fellow employee, Hamid (Jamshedji), who takes the blame. The villains are his secretary Kassum (Ahmed) and Sukhlal (Gani), a rich man who wants to marry Asha. When his advances are spurned, he alleges that he had an affair with Kishenprasad's wife, Lakshmi.

FASHIONABLE INDIA

1935 169' b&w Hindi
d/s/lyr Mohan Sinha *pc* **Krishna Film** *c* Haribhai K. Patel, Sadashiv J. Vyas *m* Badri Prasad
lp Pushpa, R.D. Shukla, O.K. Dhar (aka Jeevan), Wadilal, B.L. Ganju, Badriprasad, Bhusharan Sharma, Dhanjit Shah

Big-budget drama with 'special photographic tricks, story, dialogues, songs and the entire production idealised' by the director. The idealistic Kusum (Pushpa) believes in the 'fashionable way of modern civilisation' and writes a play extolling the virtues of modernisation. It is produced by her lover and fellow university student, Ramesh (Shukla), bringing him into conflict with the villainous Madhav (Dhar). The other major character is a local Raja (Wadilal) who also loves Kusum and plans to marry her by settling her father's debts. This leads to kidnappings and murders before the happy end. Known mainly as a musical spectacular containing English ditties like *Daisy, Daisy* and *Jolly Good Fellow* and the film that sank the Krishna Film Studio. Well-known Hindi screen villain Jeevan acts under the name O.K. Dhar, retaining the name for the sequel, ***Romantic India*** (1936).

GHAR JAMAI

1935 177'[G]/155'[H] b&w Gujarati/Hindi
d/sc **Homi Master** *pc* Premier Cinetone *st* **Mohanlal G. Dave** *dial*[H] Munshi Sagar Hussain*c* Rustom Irani
lp Heera, Jamuna, Baby Nurjehan, Amoo, Alimiya, Jamshedji, Syed Ahmed, Ghulam Rasool, Chemist

Master's big hit was an unusual slapstick remake of his own 1925 film. Mafatlal (Alimiya) is an unemployed adventurer thrown out of his home and told not to return until he has made some money. He responds to an ad for a 'resident son-in-law for wealthy heiress', tries to earn commission from a lawyer by instigating lawsuits, impersonates a station-master to dodge the fare, gets chased by cops and a fisherwoman, and gets robbed. Eventually, he is chosen by the original advertiser, Heeralaxmi (Heera), a woman with 'advanced views' on everything. Other characters include a phalanx of women standing for election on outlandish platforms. The socially conservative comedy betrayed the anxieties of sexually insecure men when faced with the possibility of the emancipation of women.

HIND KESARI

1935 141' b&w Hindi
d **Homi Wadia** *pc* **Wadia Movietone** *st* H.E. Khatib *sc* **J.B.H. Wadia** *lyr* Joseph David *c* M.A. Rehman *m* Master Mohammed
lp Husn Banu, Sardar Mansoor, Dilawar, Gulshan, Jal Khambatta, Tarapore

The Wadias' remake of their 1932 silent film is a Ruritanian drama mainly featuring the stunts of the horse Punjab-Ka-Beta. Good King Mansingh (Tarapore) is dethroned by evil minister Zalim Singh (Khambatta). Princess Hansa (Husn Banu) transforms lover Prince Randhir (Sardar Mansoor) from an easy-going youth into the masked Hind Kesari, saviour of the poor.

HUNTERWALI

aka *The Lady with the Whip*
1935 164' b&w Hindi
d/sc **Homi Wadia** *pc* **Wadia Movietone** *st* **J.B.H. Wadia** *dial/lyr* Joseph David *c* Balwant Dave *m* Master Mohammed
lp **Fearless Nadia**, Sharifa, Gulshan, Boman Shroff, John Cawas, Master Mohammed, Sayani Atish, Jaidev

The stunt movie that established the Wadias and Fearless Nadia. Preceded by a legend describing its heroine as a 'Brave Indian girl who sacrificed royal luxuries to the cause of her people and her country', the story opens with a prologue showing Krishnavati (Sharifa) and her infant son being thrown out of the house in a thunderstorm by the wicked Prime Minister Ranamal who also killed her brother. 20 years later the now adult son, Jaswant (Schroff), is hit by a royal motor car and given a bag of gold in compensation. His refusal of the gift attracts the admiration of Princess Madhuri (Nadia). When the nasty Ranamal, who wants to marry her, imprisons her father the king (Mohammed), she becomes the masked Hunterwali, 'protector of the poor and punisher of evildoers', and performer of stunts like jumping over a moving cart and fighting 20 soldiers at once. She steals Jaswant's prize horse, Punjab, but returns it later. Jaswant chances upon a nude Hunterwali bathing in the river (a rare sequence for Nadia) and after a long duel captures her and takes her to Ranamal to claim his reward. She escapes, but later they join forces and triumph over the villain. There are several bhajans by Govind Gopal, one of them (*Hunterwali hai bhali duniya ki sudh leth*) in praise of its masked star. Jaidev, later a noted composer, appears here as her sidekick, Chunnoo. J.B.H. Wadia's original scenario was developed by Joseph David, also known for India's sound debut ***Alam Ara*** (1931).

INQUILAB

aka *After the Earthquake*
1935 144' b&w Hindi
d/s **Debaki Bose** *pc* **New Theatres** *lyr* **Kidar Sharma** *c* Krishna Gopal *m* **Rai Chand Boral**
lp **Durga Khote**, **Prithviraj Kapoor**, Syed Mohammed, Nawab, **K.C. Dey**, H. Siddiqui, Mehera, **Kidar Sharma**, Surama, Malina, Nirmal Bannerjee

Prabhat star Durga Khote's foray into Calcutta's New Theatres is a drama set amid an earthquake in Bihar. Miss Renee (Khote) looks after the victims while her lover, the businessman Sardar (Mohammed), wants to make money from the disaster. She comes under the spell of the blind itinerant Musafir (Dey in his usual persona) whose low opinion of the depravity of the wealthy provides the film's moral backbone. She eventually discovers that as a child she had been promised to Musafir but had been rejected by his family for being of a lower caste. In a dramatic finale, fighting the villainous Sardar's henchmen, she dies in the itinerant's arms.

JAWANI KI HAWA

aka *Leichtsinn der Jugend*
1935 148' b&w Hindi
d **Franz Osten** *pc* **Bombay Talkies** *s* **Niranjan Pal** *dial* J.S. Casshyap, S.I. Hassan *co-lyr/m* **Saraswati Devi** *co-lyr* J.S. Casshyap, Najmul Hussain, Bare Agha, Dhansukhlal K. Mehta *c* Josef Wirsching
lp **Devika Rani**, Najmul Hussain, Chandraprabha, Kamta Prasad, J.S. Casshyap, P.F. Pithawala, Talpade, Bhaskar Dev, Mukherjee, Azoori, Sunita Devi, Solanki, Masiha, Khosla

Osten's first Hindi sound film was the debut production of Bombay Talkies. It is a romantic crime thriller. Kamala (Rani) elopes on her wedding day with her childhood friend Ratanlal (Hussain). Her father Maganlal chases the couple and catches them on a train. His furious exchanges with Ratanlal are interrupted by gunfire and in the mysterious gloom of the evening a body is thrown off the train. The suspects are Ratanlal, who cannot furnish an alibi, Kamala, who insists on being the murderess, ex-convict Sukhdev (Dev), who confesses to the murder claiming robbery to be the motive, and the lunatic Tarachand, who also admits his guilt. The film caused a major scandal by employing two sisters from the conservative Parsee community: composer Saraswati Devi and actress Chandraprabha. The Parsee Federal Council tried to ban it and organised demonstrations at the Imperial cinema. Eventually the predominantly Parsee board of Bombay Talkies' trustees mediated with the leaders of the community and got the film released without censorship.

JEEVAN NATAK

aka *Life is a Stage*
1935 139' b&w Hindi
d/s **Debaki Bose** *pc* Jayant Pics *dial/lyr* Narottam Vyas *c* Y.D. Sarpotdar, Haribhai Patel *m* Harishchandra Bali
lp **Durga Khote**, Rampiary, Alaknanda, Shivrani, Lavji Lavangia, Nirmal Bannerjee, Nandkishore Mehra, Trikamlal, Gulam Jilani Sham, Pahelwan

The plot is set in two historical epochs, 1735 and 1935. The spirited Miss Queen (Khote), performing in a period play, recalls a previous incarnation when she was the actual person she is now acting on the stage. She inherited the throne because the state of Ranigarh had no constitutional male heirs and her horoscope was deemed auspicious. Instead of being merely a figurehead, she opposes the corrupt minister Jairaj and army commander Mubarak and, following the advice of the court poet (Pahelwan), she makes sure the royal court is accessible to the suffering people.

JOYMATI

1935 c.14,000 ft b&w Assamese
d/s/m/lyr **Jyotiprasad Agarwala** *pc* Chitralekha Movietone *st* Lakhindranath Bezbaruah's play *Joymati Kunwari c* Bhopal Shankar Mehta
lp Phanu Barua, Asaideo Handige, Mohini Rajkumari, Swargajyoti Datta, **Phani Sarma**, Manabhiram Barua, Sneha Chandra Barua, Naren Bordoloi, Rana Barua, Shamshul Haque, Gajen Barua, Putul Haque, Pratap Barua, Rajkumari Gohain, Lalit Mohan Choudhury, Banamali Das, Prafulla Chandra Barua, Kamale Prasad Agarwala

The Assamese cinema debut feature made in an improvised studio built by Jyotiprasad Agarwala on the Bholaguri tea estate. Set in 17th-C. Assam, it tells of the sacrifice of Joymati, a medieval princess who is tortured and killed by the evil prime minister for refusing to betray her husband. The event is interpreted in contemporary patriotic terms and calls for a greater harmony between the people of the hills and the plains (the former represented by Dalimi, a Naga tribesman who shelters the fugitive Prince Gadapani). Available footage was used in **Bhupen Hazarika**'s commemorative film *Rupkonwar Jyotiprasad Aru Joymati* (1976) devoted to Agarwala.

JUDGEMENT OF ALLAH

aka *Al Hilal*
1935 158' b&w Urdu
d/s **Mehboob** *pc* **Sagar Movietone** *dial/lyr* Munshi Ehsan Lucknowi *c* Faredoon Irani *m* Pransukh M. Nayak
lp Kumar, Indira, Yakub, **Sitara Devi**, Pande, Wallace, Asooji, Razak, Kayamali, Azoorie

Mehboob's directorial debut was one of Sagar's classic period movies, better known until then for its reformist socials. It is set in the Ottoman empire where Caesar's (Pande) Roman armies clash with the Muslim kingdoms. Ziyad (Kumar), the son of the sultan (Asooji), is captured by the Romans. Rahil (Indira), a Roman princess, falls in love with him and asks the Muslim woman Leila (Sitara) to guard him. Leila smuggles a message written in her blood to the sultan. Ziyad eventually escapes with Rahil's help and the film culminates in an elaborate chase sequence. The film probably drew from the influential style of **K.M. Munshi** (cf ***Prithvi Vallabh***, 1924), combining historical fantasies with a reformist sensibility.

KARWAN-E-HAYAT

1935 122' b&w Urdu
d **Premankur Atorthy, Hemchandra Chunder** *pc* **New Theatres** *dial* Hakim Ahmed Shuja *c* Krishna Gopal *m* Mihirkiran Bhattacharya, **Rai Chand Boral**
lp **K.L. Saigal**, Rajkumari, **Pahadi Sanyal**, Shyama Zutshi, Nawab, Hamid, Rana, Rattan Bai

Adventure movie featuring Saigal as the wild Pervez, heir to the throne of Kascand. In protest at the marriage with the princess (Rajkumari) of neighbouring Bijapore arranged by his mother (Zutshi) and the vizir (Hamid), he leaves and joins a band of travelling gypsies where Zarina (Rattan Bai) falls in love with him. The bad Tikkim, who wants to marry the princess himself, has her kidnapped by the gypsies. In the gypsy camp, Pervez sees her as a dancing girl. They fall in love and defeat the villain while Zarina resigns herself to the class difference between her and the prince.

KEEMTI AANSOO

1935 154' b&w Hindi
d **Chandulal Shah** *pc* **Ranjit Movietone** *sc/lyr* **Narayan Prasaad Betaab** *m* Rewashankar Marwadi, Banne Khan
lp **Gohar**, E. Bilimoria, Ishwarlal, Khatoon, Ram Apte, Bhanumathi, Charubala

A tearful melodrama about a progressive writer, Pushpa (Gohar), and her weak husband, Kulin (Bilimoria). She has to fight her domineering mother-in-law and the tyrannies of a conservative household. When falsely accused of theft and infidelity by her wayward sister-in-law Gulab, Pushpa is forced out of the house. In her final state of penury, she recalls the examples of the great female Saint-Poets of Indian history, like Meerabai. Secondary characters are used to caricature Bombay's merchant class, e.g. Mahatma Ramanand Adambar, a fortune-teller who suspects his wife of infidelity, and a gold collector called Prof. Pyarelal.

KHOON KA KHOON

aka *Hamlet*
1935 122' b&w Urdu
d **Sohrab Modi** *pc* Stage Film *s* Mehdi Ahsan from his Urdu adaptation of *Hamlet* *m* Kanhaiya Pawar
lp **Sohrab Modi**, Naseem Banu, Shamshadbai, Ghulam Hussain, Obali Mai, Fazal Karim, Eruch Tarapore, Ghulam Mohiyuddin, Shamshad, Rampiary, Gauhar, B. Pawar

Modi's debut featured him as Hamlet in the film version of his highly popular stage performance surrounded by the same principal cast: Banu as Ophelia, Shamshadbai as Gertrude, etc. The play had been made popular by the Parsee Theatre actor and producer Cowasji Khatau. Modi's film won acclaim mostly for the qualities of the play, esp. the Urdu dialogue. A *Times of India* review (10.1.1936) noted that Modi's performance so dominated the film 'that the other characters do not matter very much' and criticised the 'protracted clowning with which the director has attempted to provide relief from the tragic atmosphere'.

MANMOYEE GIRLS' SCHOOL

1935 152' b&w Bengali
d **Jyotish Bannerjee** *pc* Radha Films Co *st* Rabindranath Maitra's play *c* D.G. Gune *m* Anath Basu, Mrinal Ghosh, Kumar Mitra
lp **Tulsi Chakraborty**, Radharani, **Jahar Ganguly, Kanan Devi**, Jyotsna Gupta, Kumar Mitra

Veteran **Madan Theatres** director Bannerjee's comedy adapting one of the most successful Bengali plays ever, staged originally by Star Theatres (1932). The zamindar Damodar Chakraborty (Chakraborty) starts a school named after his wife and recruits a married couple as teachers. Manas (Ganguly in the role which had made him a stage star) and Niharika (Kanan Devi) pretend to be married in order to get the jobs. Their imposture, together with the fact that he is Hindu while she is Christian, produces complications. Eventually the couple fall in love and get married. The film is remembered mainly as an acting *tour de force* with Kanan Devi matching Tulsi Chakraborty's comic talent. The introduction of various small-town stereotypes gives the film an appealing sense of a village populated by laid-back, slightly crazy but basically benevolent denizens. The film was a hit and was remade several times: in Bengali by **Hemchandra Chunder** (1958), and then, with a partially altered plot, by **L.V. Prasad** in Tamil (***Missiamma***, 1955), Telugu (***Missamma***, 1955) and Hindi (*Miss Mary*, 1957). **Anant Mane** also made a Marathi version, *Jhakli Mooth* (1957).

SHRI KRISHNA LEELALU

1935 199' b&w Telugu
d **Ch. Narasimha Rao** *pc* **Vel Pics** *s* A.T. Raghavachari *m* Galipenchala Narasimha Rao
lp **Vemuri Gaggaiah, Sriranjini Sr.**, Ramatilakam, **Saluri Rajeshwara Rao**, Parepalli Satyanarayana, Parepalli Subba Rao, Master Avadhani, **Lakshmirajyam**

Playful mythological featuring the antics of the child Krishna (Rajeshwara Rao) from his birth to his victory over the evil Kamsa (Gaggaiah). It is the film debut of future composer Rajeshwara Rao and one of Gaggaiah's best-known films.

SILVER KING

1935 161' b&w Hindi
d/s **Chimanlal Luhar** *pc* **Sagar Film** *dial* Waqif *c* Faredoon Irani *m* Pransukh Nayak
lp Sabita Devi, **Motilal**, Asooji, Yakub, Tara, Jamoo Patel

One of the best-known costumed stunt movies made at Sagar, in the **Mehta**-Luhar silent tradition. The king of the idyllic royal state of Jayanagar is kidnapped by his wily commander (Yakub). Ajit, aka the Silver King (Motilal), who leads a band of patriots, frees the king with the aid of the Princess Krishna (Sabita). In the end Ajit is revealed as the crown prince of the kingdom.

THAKICHA LAGNA

1935 52' b&w Marathi
co-d/co-p/sc **Vishram Bedekar** *co-d/co-p* V.N. Bhatt *st* Ram Ganesh Gadkari's play *dial* **P.K. Atre** *c* Nana Ponkshe, Anant Marathe
lp **Damuanna Malvankar**, Balwantrao Pethe, Shankarrao Majumdar, Vithu, Balkoba Gokhale

The noted reformist Marathi playwright Gadkari is known mainly for his classic tragedy on alcoholism, *Ekach Pyala* (1919), and less so for the humourous prose which he often wrote under assumed names. This film version of his play fields a variety of Maharashtrian rural comedy stereotypes: Nana, Balkya and Balakram use a number of ploys to arrange the marriage of Thaki, the virtually unmarriageable daughter of Timbunana. Scripted by Atre and featuring Marathi comedian Malvankar in his first major screen role, the film pioneered a tradition in Marathi comedy later associated with **Vinayak**, Atre, and the Hans/**Navyug** production companies.

USHA

1935 122' b&w Marathi/Hindi
d **Baburao Painter** *pc* Shalini Cinetone *c* K.V. Machve *m* **Govindrao Tembe**
lp Usha Mantri, Govindrao Tembe, Ratnaprabha, K. Vasudeo, D. Dudhale, Sushila Devi, Karnakar, Kale

The film with which Baburao Painter re-established himself after the closure of **Maharashtra Film** is a fiction film deploying aspects of the mythological. The demonic King Banasur (Dudhale), a devout disciple of Shiva, wants to eliminate Vishnu and his followers in the guise of Krishna (Tembe), king of Dwarka and an incarnation of Vishnu. Krishna overcomes Banasur's designs by getting his daughter Usha (Mantri) to fall in love with Aniruddha (Vasudeo). Painter was also responsible for the art direction.

VILASI ISHWAR/NIGAH-E-NAFRAT

aka *Orphans of the Storm*
1935 140'[M]/148'[H] b&w Marathi/Hindi

d **Master Vinayak** *pc* **Kolhapur Cinetone** *st* Mama Warerkar *sc* R.S. Junnarkar *c* V.B. Joshi *m* Gundopant Walavalkar
lp **Master Vinayak, Baburao Pendharkar,** Bal Dhavale, **Shobhana Samarth,** Indira Wadkar, Gundopant Walavalkar, Manohar Mainkar

Master Vinayak's directorial debut was scripted by Warerkar, noted Marathi playwright and film-maker (***Poona Raided***, 1924). It is a melodrama about the rich and callous Vilas (Pendharkar), who abandons girlfriend Shama (Wadkar) when he discovers that she is pregnant. She raises her son Nandu (Mainkar) with the help of her younger brother and the film's hero, Sanjeev (Vinayak). When Vilas re-enters their lives, it is with a new name, Ishwar, and with the intention of seducing the rich Princess Indira (Samarth) who loves Sanjeev. Ishwar has a bad accident and an attack of amnesia that also leads to a confession of his past deeds. The film, which was also actress Shobhana Samarth's debut, includes an English song, *Puff Puff the Engine Said* and is apparently the Marathi cinema's first full-length social (two years before ***Kunku/Duniya Na Mane***, 1937). The Hindi version contained 12 songs.

YASMIN

aka *Bewafa Ashq*
1935 119' b&w Hindi
d H.K. Shivdasani *pc* Eastern Arts *dial/lyr* Gauri Shankarlal Akhtar *c* Gordhanbhai Patel *m* Chandiram
lp Rattan Bai, Amirbai Karnataki, H. Siddiqui, Gope Kamlani, M. Mirza, D. Manek, Hamid, Alexander

Parsee Theatre-derived adventure fantasy about an old man, Gias Baig (Manek) who wants his daughter Zubeida (Karnataki) to marry the rich merchant Shaukat (Mirza) although she loves Rashid (Siddiqui). Zubeida and Rashid plan to elope but are intercepted by Gias Baig who promptly dies of heart failure. Accused by Shaukat of murder, Rashid escapes to a gypsy camp where the beautiful Yasmin (Rattan Bai) entertains him, much to the envy of the gypsy chief Behram (Hamid). When Rashid is arrested, Yasmin's men rescue him and make him the new clan chief. Hamid (Alexander), a nomad who belongs to Yasmin's group, rescues Zubeida from Shaukat's clutches by killing the villain and bringing her to the camp. This creates a love triangle solved only when Yasmin sacrifices her life to save Rashid. Writer-director **Atorthy** was credited with the 'personal supervision' of the film.

ACHHUT KANYA

aka *The Untouchable Girl*
1936 142' b&w Hindi
d **Franz Osten** *pc* **Bombay Talkies** *s* **Niranjan Pal** *dial/lyr* J.S. Casshyap *c* Josef Wirsching *m* **Saraswati Devi**
lp **Devika Rani, Ashok Kumar,** P.F. Pithawala, Kamta Prasad, Kishori Lal, Kusum Kumari, Pramila, Anwar, Ishrat

A circular story, told in flashback, in which eternal repetition is only interrupted by death in the form of a relentlessly linear railway engine. The film opens at a railway crossing where a man is about to kill his wife when the narrative spins into the past via a song. The central story is of the unhappy love affair between Kasturi (Devika Rani), the Harijan (Untouchable) daughter of the railway level-crossing guard Dukhia (Prasad), and Pratap (Kumar), the Brahmin son of the grocer Mohan (Pithawala). At first, rumour and mob violence are deployed to lethal effect in order to maintain a 'traditional', oppressive morality. Later, when the main protagonists are about to conform and marry selected partners, rumour and maliciousness again intervene to trigger renewed violence until the on-rushing train of fate stops the strife. Enhanced by Wirsching's contrasted imagery, the plot suggests that both conformity and nonconformity are equally impossible options, the latter being punished by society, the former unable to suppress what it oppresses. The standard formal conflict between circular/traditional time and linear/modernising time is undercut by the suggestion that social-ethical change is as untenable as social stasis. Even fate, associated with the archetypal symbol of modernity and progress, is denied its ultimate victory: the spirit of the defeated lingers, haunting the crossroads, testifying to the ineradicability of desire. The film's narrative structure and its eruptions into visual stylisation can be seen as a more intelligently complex way of addressing the encounter between Indian and European notions of history than many an attempt to take East-West differences as an explicit theme. With this film, Bombay Talkies also invented its Anglicised fantasy of an Indian village which became a studio stereotype (***Janmabhoomi***, 1936; ***Durga*** and ***Kangan***, both 1939; ***Bandhan***, 1940), resisting the generic shifts in the formula initiated by S. Mukherjee and **Amiya Chakravarty**. Hero Ashok Kumar later said that he felt his acting in this film to be 'babyish'.

AMAR JYOTI

aka *The Immortal Flame*
1936 166' b&w Hindi
d **V. Shantaram** *pc* **Prabhat** Cinetone *sc* **K. Narayan Kale** *dial/lyr* Narottam Vyas *c* V. Avadhoot *m* **Master Krishnarao**
lp **Durga Khote, Shanta Apte,** Vasanthi, Aruna Devi, **Chandramohan,** K. Narayan Kale, B. Nandrekar

Remarkable Prabhat adventure classic featuring Durga Khote's most memorable role as the pirate Queen Saudamini. Faced with extreme patriarchal laws in an ancient seaport kingdom and denied the legal custody of her infant son Sudhir, Saudamini becomes a pirate declaring war on the state and especially on its tyrannical minister of justice, Durjaya (Chandramohan). She attacks a royal ship and captures Durjaya, inadvertently also taking Princess Nandini (Apte). In captivity, Durjaya declares his love for Nandini but she falls for a shepherd boy (Nandrekar) who turns out to be Saudamini's long-lost son Sudhir. Durjaya's men then capture Saudamini and a palace intrigue ensues marked by her emancipatory rhetoric and the universal humanist arguments of her adviser Shekhar (Kale). The swordplay and stunt action distinguish this film from Prabhat's other work although Kale's story bears some resemblance to the plot of e.g. ***Amritmanthan*** (1934), with Chandramohan replaying some of his role in the earlier film.

Durga Khote and Chandramohan in *Amar Jyoti*

ANSUYA

1936 100' b&w Telugu
d **C. Pullaiah** *pc* **East India Film** *s* Balijepalli Lakshmikanta Kavi *m* Prabhala Satyanarayana
lp **C. Krishnaveni**, Prakash Rao, Suryanarayana, Narayanarao, P. Sundaramma, **R. Balasaraswathi**

Ansuya was made and released by Pullaiah as a double bill with *Dhruva* (1936)(65'), two mythologicals made exclusively with children and telling the stories of ***Sati Ansuya*** and ***Bhakta Dhruva***. The films were commended by reviews for their realism in script and casting.

BALAYOGINI

aka *Child Saint*
1936 c.210' b&w Tamil/Telugu
d/p/s **K. Subramanyam** *pc* Madras United Artistes Corp[Ta]/Mahalakshmi Studios[Te] *dial/lyr* **Papanasam Sivan**[Ta], B.T. Raghavacharyar[Te] *c* Kamal Ghosh *m* Moti Babu, Maruthi Seetaramayya
lp **K. Vishwanathan** (aka Vathsal)[Ta], Bharath[Ta], Mani Bhagavathar[Ta], V.R. Chellam[Ta], C.V.V. Panthulu[Ta], K.N. Rajalakshmi[Ta], Baby Saroja, **R. Balasaraswathi**[Ta], Rukmini[Ta], Brahadambal[Ta], Arani Satyanarayana[Te], Vangara[Te], Kamala Kumari[Te], Tilakam[Te], **S. Varalakshmi**[Te]

Although there had been some films with a 'contemporary' setting (*Kausalya*, featuring a pistol-wielding heroine; *Dambachari*, about a playboy, both 1935), this was one of Tamil cinema's first reformist socials (cf ***Iru Sahodarargal***, 1936) with an original script. A Brahmin widow (Chellam) and her daughter (Saroja) are cast out by wealthy relatives. She seeks shelter in the house of a low-caste servant, causing the enraged Brahmins of the village to set the servant's house on fire. The film, made by Brahmins, launched Baby Saroja as a legendary star and infringed many caste taboos, including the casting of an actual Brahmin widow in the lead. A group of Brahmins met in Thanjavur and declared the director an outcast. He replied with *Bhakta Cheta* (1940), glorifying a Harijan saint. In ***Seva Sadan*** (1938) he defended the cause of women's equality and went on to make the classic reformist social ***Thyagabhoomi*** (1939). However, in the context of Periyar E.V. Ramaswamy Naicker's strident anti-Brahminism, Subramanyam's humanist attack on the irrationality of caste prejudices was very moderate. The lead role was played by the director's brother, K. Vishwanathan.

BAMBAI KI BILLI

aka *Wildcat*
1936 170' b&w Hindi
d **Nandlal Jaswantlal** *pc* **Imperial Film** *m* Pransukh M. Nayak
lp **Sulochana, D. Bilimoria**, Jilloo, Lakshmi, Pramilla, Abdul Kader, Ali Dadan, Syed Ahmed

A remake of **Bhavnani**'s silent Sulochana hit crime melodrama, ***Wildcat of Bombay*** (1927), again featuring Sulochana as the mysterious criminal nicknamed the Wildcat who is pitted against police Inspector Suresh (Bilimoria). She masquerades as Usha, a medical student, and in this guise falls in love with Suresh. Eventually the Wildcat, after cleaning up the nefarious activities of Pratap and getting arrested for the murder of his henchman Kapoor (Kader), turns out to be the daughter of Judge Biharilal, kidnapped years ago in an effort to blackmail the judge in a murder case.

BANGALEE

1936 142' b&w Bengali
d **Charu Roy** *pc* Shri Bharatlaxmi Pics *st* Bhupendranath Bannerjee *c* Bibhuti Das *m* Tulsi Lahiri
lp Manoranjan Bhattacharya, Nirmalendu Lahiri, Tulsi Lahiri, **Dhiraj Bhattacharya**, Sarat Chatterjee, Mani Ghosh, Kartick Roy, Bhanu Roy, Manorama, Meera Dutta, Charuvala, Kamala Jharia

One of the first Bengali films to attempt a realist idiom with a story about a lower-middle-class family, praised by **Satyajit Ray** for its ability to 'steer clear from Hollywood'. The family consists of Dinadas the father, a mother and some sons, only one of whom earns money. It opens with a series of dissolves presenting each son: one is smoking a cigar and trains for an acting career reciting Michael Madhusudhan Dutt; the next is an aspirant writer smoking a hukka (a bubble-pipe); the third wants to be a dancer and smokes a bidi (reed). The mother complains that there is no peace in the house; the father returns from the market to find everything in a mess; the earning brother prefers to spend his money buying expensive cosmetics. The story shows a rivalry with the family of Sukhadas, first over who Dinadas's only daughter will marry, and then, more seriously, over the Anglo-Indian prostitute Flora, with whom the sons of both patriarchs fall in love. In an interview reprinted along with excerpts of *Bangalee*'s script in *Chitravas* (1987), Charu Roy claimed that this was the first film using source lighting as a shooting principle, deploying a tonal range as practised by **Osten**'s German crew. Tulsi Lahiri, who acted in and scored this film, was also a prominent Bengali film-maker (*Happy Club*, 1936) and became a key figure in the film industry's assimilation of the **IPTA**-influenced realist idiom (e.g. via his acting in **Sushil Majumdar**'s *Dukhir Iman*, 1954).

CHHAYA

aka *Holy Crime*
1936 150'[M]/152'[H] b&w Marathi/Hindi
d **Master Vinayak** *pc* Huns Pics *st/dial/lyr*[M] **V.S. Khandekar** *sc* R.S. Junnarkar *dial/lyr*[H] Indra *c* Pandurang Naik *m* Annasaheb Mainkar, Dhamman Khan
lp Master Vinayak, **Leela Chitnis**, Indira Wadkar, **Baburao Pendharkar**, Hardikar, Ratnaprabha, Vaishampayan, N.G. Pandit Rao, Anant Marathe

Vinayak's second film, which was also his regular scenarist Khandekar's debut with a celebrated melodrama, launched Huns Pictures. A bank employee who steals money to buy medicine for his dying wife is caught, jailed and dies of shame. His eldest son Prakash (Vinayak) publishes a poem in the very newspaper that publicised his father's crime. The judge (Hardikar) who convicted Prakash's father gives him a poetry prize and the judge's daughter Chhaya (Chitnis) happens to fall in love with him. But when she learns of Prakash's family history, Chhaya allows her father and her suitor, Dr Atul (Pendharkar), to accuse Prakash of molesting her and sends him to prison. Prakash's destitute sister Kala (Ratnaprabha) becomes a prostitute to pay for the younger brother Suman's (Marathe) medical bills levied by the ambitious Dr Atul. Kala bears a child and has to kill it. Prakash escapes from jail and works as a porter in a small town. His anonymous existence ends when his autobiographical novel is published. The police eventually catch up with both Prakash and Kala and the two are sent back to jail.

DECCAN QUEEN

1936 158' b&w Hindi
d **Mehboob** *pc* **Sagar Movietone** *lyr* **Zia Sarhadi** *c* Faredoon Irani *m* Pransukh Nayak, Ashok Ghosh
lp Surendra, Aruna Devi, Ramchandra, Pande, Pesi Patel, M.A. Mani, Kayamali, Bhudo Advani, Mehdi Raza, Gulzar, Kamala

Mehboob's only full-scale stunt movie, made presumably after **Luhar** introduced the genre at Sagar Studio. The crooked trustees of Lala Niranjanmal's estate try to eliminate its two heirs: the daughter (Aruna Devi) is jailed and the son becomes a penniless wanderer. When released, the daughter becomes the mysterious Deccan Queen, nemesis of evildoers. The plot gets complicated when a clerk in an insurance company, Vrinda (Aruna Devi again), turns out to be the wanted woman's double. Vrinda falls in love with Inspector Suresh (Surendra), but then later so does the Deccan Queen. The triangle takes unusual turns when the queen impersonates Vrinda and demands that Suresh marry her at once. Apart from the fast-paced stunt action, Aruna Devi's dual role is the film's major attraction. It is also the debut of Surendra, a well-known Mehboob singing star (e.g. ***Anmol Ghadi***, 1946).

DO DIWANE/BE KHARAB JAN

aka *Gay Birds*
1936 171'[H]/153'[G] b&w Hindi/Gujarati
d **Chimanlal Luhar** *pc* **Sagar Film** *s* **K.M. Munshi** *lyr* Raghunath Brahmbhatt *c* Keki Mistry *m* Pransukh Nayak
lp **Shobhana Samarth, Motilal**, Yakub, Rama Devi, Aruna Devi, Kamalabai, Kayam Ali, Pande, Temuras, Pessi Patel, Raza, Kantilal Nayak, Kamla, Sankatha

The noted Gujarati writer Munshi's acclaimed comedy, adapted from a popular play, contrasts contemporary culture with the values prevailing 50 years earlier. Dr Mohanlal (Motilal) and Miss Rambha (Shobhana) see themselves as revolutionaries handicapped by being born into conservative families. On the other hand, the millionaire Ramdas opposes his culture although experiencing some discomfort with the adoption of Western values. The film was the first featuring the celebrated star pair of Motilal and Shobhana.

DRAUPADI MANASAMRAKSHANAM

1936 159' b&w Telugu
co-d S. Jagannath, Ramanamurthy *pc* Lakshmi Films *m* Papatla Kantaiah
lp **Ballari Raghava**, S. Rangaswamy, Sivarakrishna Rao, H.N. Choudhury, Daita Gopalam, Jandhyala Gaurinatha Sastry, Banda Kakalingeshwara Rao, **Surabhi Kamalabai**, Padmavati Devi, Shrihari, Leela
Lakshmi Films' owner Kavali Gupta signed noted stage actor Raghava to play Duryodhana. At Saraswati Talkies, **H.V. Babu** was making ***Draupadi Vastrapaharanam*** at the same time, although on a smaller budget. Both films told the same *Mahabharata* episode in which Draupadi is publicly humiliated by the Kauravas and rescued by Krishna. In spite of Raghava's star presence, the film was not as successful as its rival.

DRAUPADI VASTRAPAHARANAM

1936 185' b&w Telugu
d/sc **H.V. Babu** *pc* Saraswati Talkies *s* Malladi Achutha Ramana Sastry *m* **B. Narasimha Rao**
lp Yadavalli Suryanarayana, **C.S.R. Anjaneyalu**, Dommeti Suryanarayana, Dommeti Satyanarayana, Nelluri Nagaraja Rao, Arani Satyanarayana, Nagabhushanam, **Vemuri Gaggaiah**, Parabhrama Sastry, **P. Kannamba**, Ramatilakam, Katari Shakuntala, Puvvula Nagarajakumari, Puvvula Nagabhushanam

Made in competition with ***Draupadi Manasamrakshanam*** (1936), this *Mahabharata* mythological is the debut feature of Saraswati Talkies, a partnership between Parepalli Sheshaiah, K. Subba Rao and director **Ramabrahmam**. The film was a hit, noted especially for Anjaneyalu's performance as Krishna, and for a new generation of Telugu stars, including Kannamba and Gaggaiah, who collectively overshadowed **Ballari Raghava**'s star draw in the rival production. Y. Suryanarayana plays Duryodhana and D. Suryanarayana plays Bhima.

GRAMA KANYA

aka *Village Girl*
1936 167' b&w Hindi
d **Sarvottam Badami** *pc* **Sagar Film** *st* Jayant Shyam *dial* Waqif *c* Faredoon Irani *m* Rao
lp Sabita Devi, Aruna, Surendra, Yakub, Jamoo Patel, Kayamali, Gulzar, Sankatha, Baby Indira, Pande

Well-known Sagar social with a coincidence-ridden plot structured around the studio's star Sabita Devi. Hero Kumar (Surendra) studies at university with money borrowed by his poor father from Dinanath (Kayamali) who in return expects Kumar to marry his daughter Bansari (Sabita). Although he makes a city girl, Vilas (Aruna), pregnant, Kumar is forced to wed Bansari, which leaves Vilas at the mercy of the villainous Vinod (Yakub). Then Kumar accidentally kills his father in a car crash and Vilas's father commits suicide after driving his pregnant daughter out of his house. Bansari, the staunchly faithful village girl, then goes to the city to recover her husband. The film claimed to modernise traditional Hindu ideals.

GRIHADAH/MANZIL

1936 144'[B]/151'[H] b&w Bengali/Hindi
d **P.C. Barua** *pc* **New Theatres** *st* Saratchandra Chatterjee *dial/lyr* Arzoo Lucknowi, A.H. Shore[H] *c* **Bimal Roy** *m* **Rai Chand Boral, Pankaj Mullick**
lp P.C. Barua, **Prithviraj Kapoor, K.C. Dey**, Boken Chatto, Jamuna, Molina Devi, Ahi Sanyal

The poor but educated Mahim and his childhood friend, the rich but conservative Suresh, both fall in love with the same woman, the liberated Achala. Mahim marries her and they move to a village but she cannot forget Suresh. Her smouldering unhappiness takes the form of a resentment towards the orphaned Mrinal, raised by Mahim's father, and receives a dramatically visual embodiment when their house burns down. Mahim falls ill, is rescued by Suresh and nursed back to health by Achala. On a train (a metaphor for the irreversibly linear course of life) to a health-resort where Mahim is supposed to convalesce, Suresh on a rainswept night gives in to temptation and elopes with Achala. At the end of the film, there is a dubious reconciliation as Achala is shown following Mahim down a dark road. Much of the film contrasts Mahim's 'good' traditionalism with Saratchandra's barely concealed hostility towards Achala's liberated Brahmo Samaj upbringing, which is eventually punished.

HAMARI BETIYAN

aka *Our Darling Daughters*
1936 154' b&w Hindi
d/s **R.S. Choudhury** *pc* **Imperial Film** *c* Adi M. Irani *m* Annasaheb Mainkar
lp Rose, Kumar, Jilloo, Pramila, Mubarak, Baby Shri, Baba Vyas

An epic drama idealising Indian womanhood. Prince Madan (Kumar) loves university colleague Radha (Rose). The villain Lalsingh (Mubarak) and his sister Vasanthi (Pramila) get him banned from the realm by the king (Vyas), but he marries his beloved anyway. Radha's estranged mother (Jilloo) becomes a priestess distributing free grain. When Radha goes blind, she is abandoned by her husband and unknowingly meets her mother. An earthquake restores Radha's sight and allows her to find a buried treasure. Masquerading as the wealthy Princess Chandni, Radha teaches a lesson to all her tormentors, including the king, the prince and the villain.

IRU SAHODARARGAL

aka *Two Brothers*
1936 144' b&w Tamil
d **Ellis R. Duncan** *p* Ramasamy *pc* Parameshwar Sound, Coimbatore
sc S.D.S. Yogi
lp K.P. Kesavan, K.K. Perumal, T.S. Baliah, S.N. Kannaman, M.M. Radhabai, S.N. Vijayalakshmi, **P.U. Chinappa, M.G. Ramachandran**

Shot in Bombay at **Sagar Movietone** by the American expatriate Duncan, who also edited it, this film was billed as only the 2nd social (cf ***Balayogini***, 1936) in a Tamil industry dominated by mythologicals. The plot addresses the joint family system: two

P.C. Barua (left), Molina Devi (centre) and Jamuna (right) in *Grihadah*

brothers, Sabapathi and Pasupathi, and their wives fight over the family property. The happy resolution requires the introduction of an angel in the shape of a maid. The most interesting aspect of the film is its depiction of the world of commercial drama, the most popular form of urban mass entertainment in 30s Tamil Nadu. Duncan reduced the envisaged 30-5 songs to 13, tightened the editing and integrated the comedy into the narrative rather than leaving it as an autonomous sub-plot. He also endeavoured to get the actors to adopt the rhythms of everyday speech. The producer was a Congress Party sympathiser responsible for the nationalist flavouring of the songs. The film received the blessing of nationalist leaders like S. Sathyamurthy and C. Rajagopalachari. **Bhagwan** made a Hindi version of the film, ***Albela*** (1951).

JAGRAN

aka *The Awakening*
1936 152' b&w Hindi
d/p **Mohan Bhavnani** *s/lyr* Narottam Vyas *m* S.P. Mukherji, Walter Kaufmann
lp Enakshi Rama Rao, Navin Yagnik, S.B. Nayampalli, Prabha, Narottam Vyas, S.L. Puri, N.N. Tuli, A.S. Gyani, Abu Baker, Shiv Rani Ghosh

Bhavnani's sequel to the Premchand-scripted ***Mazdoor*** (1934) is a melodrama about unemployment. Blackmailer Rasik (Nayampalli) is pitted against the good deeds of Prof. Ramanand, who opens an ashram for the unemployed. The struggles of hero Narayan (Yagnik) and heroine Kokila (Rama Rau) and their tales of sacrifice and starvation before they are united in the ashram, make up the bulk of the narrative. Written by Vyas, an admirer of Premchand, the title evokes the journal *Jagran* Premchand edited (1932-4). Produced independently by Bhavnani, the film was made at the **Wadia Movietone** Studio.

JANMABHOOMI

1936 139' b&w Hindi
d **Franz Osten** *pc* **Bombay Talkies** *sc* **Niranjan Pal** *dial/lyr* J.S. Casshyap *c* Joseph Wirsching *m* **Saraswati Devi**
lp **Devika Rani, Ashok Kumar**, Pramila, Khosla, Chandraprabha, N.M. Joshi, Kamta Prasad, H.S. Naik, Jhaverbhai Kaiser, P.F. Pithawala

Following on from ***Jeevan Naiya*** (1936) with the same starring duo, this was a nationalist rural drama by Osten who had just joined the Nazi Party in India. The plot has Ajay (Kumar) and his girlfriend Protima (Devika Rani) working on behalf of Indian villagers, incurring the enmity of the local zamindar (Kaiser) and the villainous Sanatan (Pithawala). Ajay's relentless goodness eventually persuades the zamindar to bequeath his property to the hero, and general well-being reigns as class conflict is transmuted into class collaboration. The film includes the nationalist song *Jai jai janani janmabhoomi* and other choruses with a similar thrust.

JEEVAN NAIYA

1936 140' b&w Hindi
d **Franz Osten** *pc* **Bombay Talkies** *s* **Niranjan Pal** *dial/lyr* J.S. Casshyap *c* Josef Wirsching *m* **Saraswati Devi**
lp **Devika Rani, Ashok Kumar**, Kamta Prasad, Anwari Begum, Kusum Kumari, K.J. Joshi, S.N. Tripathi

Lata (Devika Rani), daughter of a dancing girl, is brought up by social worker Mathuradas (Prasad) and is engaged to marry the rich Ranjit (Ashok Kumar) when the villain Chand (S.N. Tripathi) arrives to blackmail her with her undisclosed ancestry. Lata is forced to disclose the truth to Ranjit and the assembled wedding guests. Ranjit disowns her but they are reunited when Ranjit, blinded by an explosion, is nursed back to health by a devoted woman who turns out to be his wife. This was Ashok Kumar's screen debut.

LAGNA BANDHAN

aka *Achhuta Daman* aka *Forbidden Bride*
1936 157' b&w Hindi
d/s **Kaliprasad Ghosh** *pc* **Sagar Film** *dial* Munshi Ahsan *c* Faredoon Irani *m* Pransukh Nayak
lp Sabita Devi, **Motilal**, Aruna Devi, Leelavati, Azoorie, Gulzar, Sankatha, Ansari, Pesi Patel

A period adventure with Motilal in a famous dual role. Judhajit (Sankatha), the outlawed brother of the king of Udayanagar, wants revenge on the royal family. He had left the palace with one of the king's twin sons who grew up as Indrajit, the twin of the drunken and debauched Prince Shatrujit (both Motilal) due to marry Princess Chanda (Sabita Devi). Indrajit is sent to kidnap her as part of the vendetta but the two fall in love. Shatrujit is too drunk to go through the marriage procedure and the dewan (Ansari) asks Indrajit to impersonate his brother. Indrajit is now torn between his love for Chanda and his promise to the dewan, but the story ends happily.

MANMOHAN

1936 147' b&w Hindi
d **Mehboob** *pc* **Sagar Film** *s/lyr* **Zia Sarhadi** *c* Faredoon Irani *m* Ashok Ghosh
lp Bibbo, Surendra, Yakub, Ashalata, Ramchandra, Bhudo Advani, Pande, Pesi Patel, Kayamali, Mehdi Raza, Zia Sarhadi

The first of Mehboob's socials at Sagar (e.g. ***Jagirdar***, 1937) using Bibbo in an early example of his woman-centred films interrogating aspects of feudal patriarchy. The painter Ashok (Surendra) who loves the orphaned Vimala (Bibbo) is distressed to learn that she is due to marry Jagdish (Yakub). He paints Vimala's portraits with a frenzied obsession and becomes a famous artist. Jagdish tries to get Ashok killed. Paralleling this love story is the decline in Ashok's family fortunes, which eventually leaves him homeless and penniless with only the rich Shanti (Ashalata) who stands by him. Mehboob often liberates his characters from feudal ties by making them orphans (***Deccan Queen***, 1936; ***Ek Hi Raasta***, 1939), later extending this into the format of structuring the guilt of the woman into a love triangle (*Jagirdar*, ***Hum Tum Aur Woh***, 1938), transforming his melodramas into social parables (cf also **R.S. Choudhury**'s ***Hamari Betiyan***, 1936).

MAYA

1936 122'[B]/132'[H] b&w Bengali/Hindi
d/sc **P.C. Barua** *pc* **New Theatres** *st* **Sukumar Dasgupta** *lyr*[H] A.H. Shore *c* **Bimal Roy** *m* **Rai Chand Boral, Pankaj Mullick**
lp **Pahadi Sanyal**, Jamuna, **K.C. Dey**, Azoorie, Boken Chatto[B], Ahi Sanyal[B], Nawab[H], Nemo[H], Vaid[H], Jagdish Sethi[H]

Maya (Jamuna) is the poor cousin of rich socialite Shanta (Azoorie). Shanta is supposed to marry the equally rich Pratap (P. Sanyal), but he falls in love with Maya and fathers her child before going abroad. Shanta causes a separation by intercepting Pratap's letters to Maya. When he returns, a successful lawyer, he is unable to trace her, while her efforts to meet him are foiled. Later, Maya is accused of murder and is prosecuted in court by Pratap, before the dramatic reconciliation in the courtroom.

MISS FRONTIER MAIL

1936 161' b&w Hindi
d **Homi Wadia** *pc* **Wadia Movietone** *s* **J.B.H. Wadia** *c* Vasant Jagtap *m* Master Mohammed
lp **Fearless Nadia**, Gulshan, Sardar Mansoor, Master Mohammed, Sayani, John Cawas, Jal Khambatta, Jaidev, Minoo The Mystic

This follow-up of ***Hunterwali*** (1935) was Nadia's best-known 'train movie'. Savita (Nadia), aka Miss 1936, is an amateur hunter while her brother Jayant (Jaidev, later a noted lyricist) is an amateur film-maker. Their father, Maganlal (Mohammed), arrested for the murder of a station-master, is defended by their uncle Shyamlal (Sayani), who is in fact the mysterious Signal X. Shyamlal causes a major train smash-up (convincingly shot with miniatures) so as to promote his new airline. He then implicates hero Sundar (Mansoor), son of the railway president, in the crime. Savita overcomes the nasty Signal X, whose henchmen are caught on film by Jayant as they sabotage a bridge. Nadia indulges in extensive fist-fights, set to heavy sound effects, and a famous battle alongside Sundar atop a moving train. The film evokes Walter Forde's British hit *The Ghost Train* (1931), combined with Feuillade-type deserted houses and mysterious radio messages.

PRABHU KA PYARA

aka *God's Beloved*
1936 149' b&w Hindi
d **Chandulal Shah** *pc* **Ranjit Movietone** *dial/lyr* **Narayan Prasad Betaab** *c* G.G. Gogate, D.K. Ambre *m* Jhande Khan, Banne Khan
lp **Gohar, Raja Sandow**, E. Bilimoria, Khatoon, Charubala, Kamala, Keki Bawa
A melodrama suggesting that atheism is not a

desirable option. Heroine Kusum (Gohar), the daughter of atheist millionaire Gumanchand (Bawa), is forced on to the streets when her father is jailed for fraud. She eventually meets the rich Rasiklal (E. Bilimoria), joins the stage and encounters her father once more when he tries to save her from a fire. The atheist father invokes the Almighty to save his daughter, but although she is saved she loses her eyesight. Other characters include the God-fearing but crooked tutor Indulal (Sandow) who later turns into a nice man after all, and Padma (Khatoon), who exploits Rasiklal's alcoholism to the benefit of her lover, Pyarelal.

PREMAVIJAYAM

1936 c.133' b&w Telugu
d/s Krithiventi Nageshwara Rao *pc* Indian Art Cinetone *lyr* Vedula Satyanarayana Sastry *m* Munuvanty Venkata Rao
lp P. Krishnamurthy, P.S. Sharma, P. Rama Rao, K. Ranga Rao, M. Ramchandramurthy, Bhanumathi, Nookaraju, Rajyam, B. Rajalakshma Bhagavathar

Based on the director's original stage play and regarded as the first non-mythological Telugu film, the melodrama tells of two lovers who have to overcome parental obstruction to their eventual union. The film is sometimes seen as an early ancestor of the Rohini and **Vauhini** Telugu melodramas.

PUJARIN

1936 137' b&w Hindi
d Prafulla Roy *pc* International Filmcraft, **New Theatres** *st* Saratchandra Chatterjee's novel *Dena Paona* *m* **Timir Baran**
lp **K.L. Saigal**, Chandra, **Pahadi Sanyal**, Rajkumari, Nawab, Babulal, Kailash, Jagdish, **Kidar Sharma**, Shyam Laha, **K.C. Dey**

The Hindi remake of Atorthy's *Dena Paona* (1931), **New Theatres**' first sound film. The wastrel Jibananda (Saigal) marries Alaknanda (Chandra) for her money, but ends up falling in love with her. Wanted by the police, he has to abandon her only to reappear years later a wealthy man. He soon turns into an oppressive landlord and comes into conflict with the pujarin (priestess) of the local temple who leads a popular revolt against him. She turns out to be his wife. Eventually Jibananda has a change of heart and the couple are reunited. Dey plays his usual role of a blind beggar.

RAJPUT RAMANI

1936 138' b&w Hindi
d **Keshavrao Dhaiber** *pc* **Prabhat Film** *st* **Narayan Hari Apte** *dial/lyr* Narottam Vyas *c* V. Avadhoot *m* **Keshavrao Bhole**
lp Nalini Tarkhad, Nanasaheb Phatak, **Shanta Apte**, Kelkar, Sureshbabu Mane, Budasaheb, Master Chhotu

Prabhat's adventure movie, set in a medieval Rajput court, mainly addresses Rajput notions of chivalry. The legendary warrior Mansingh (Phatak) is the nation's strong man but he is cordially hated even by his own people. Claiming to have been offended by Taramati (Tarkhad), he insists to her eminent father that only a marriage (on terms insulting to her) can placate him. He becomes a tyrant imprisoning large numbers of people, and eventually Taramati's father, also in prison, leads a popular revolt, threatening to kill his son-in-law. Only Taramati's decision to protect her husband resolves the conflict. The film has a rare appearance of the Marathi stage legend, Nanasaheb Phatak. Apte played the heroine's sidekick, Kesar, repeating the two stars' earlier screen relationship in ***Amritmanthan*** (1934). This is ex-cameraman Dhaiber's best-known directorial effort.

ROMANTIC INDIA

aka *Romance*
1936 161' b&w Hindi
d Mohan Sinha *pc* Rajputana Films *m* Badriprasad
lp Nurjehan, Radharani, Snehalata, Lily, O.K. Dhar (aka Jeevan), Prem, Shyamsunder, D.P. Bhargava, Badriprasad, Munshi Ratanlal Khanjar, S. Gulab

Exotic adventure drama juxtaposing feudal pleasures with a new world imagery represented by American modernity. Heroine Chandrakala (Nurjehan), daughter of the dewan of a native king, is educated in England and lives in America. She refuses to marry the prince of her ancestral state, an insult that causes her father to be dismissed. She makes amends by disguising herself as a man and becoming the prince's secretary. A noted sequence set in America features an Indian pilot, Premsingh, who loves Chandrakala and offers to fly her entourage back to India in a Zeppelin, but a mid-flight drama forces the passengers to parachute to safety.

SAMPOORNA RAMAYANAM

1936 c.200' b&w Telugu
co-d E. Nagabhushanam, S.B. Narayana *pc* Nidamarthy Bros, Durga Cinetone
lp Pushpavalli, Kadaru Raju

Made locally in AP by a Rajahmundhry-based producer, this mythological features tales from the *Ramayana*. The film later acquired curiosity value for its primitive technique: workers from the Godavari canals were recruited to play Rama's (Kadaru Raju) monkey brigade; a train comes into a shot of Rama, Seeta and Lakshmana during their exile in the forest. Kadaru Raju may be **Kadaru Nagabhushanam** in his days as a major theatre personality.

SAMSARA NAUKA

1936 c.185' b&w Kannada
d/s **H.L.N. Simha** *pc* Devi Films *c* D.T. Telang, D.B. Chauhan *m* M. Madhava Rao
lp **B.R. Panthulu, M.V. Rajamma**, Dikki Madhava Rao, S.K. Padmadevi, M.S. Madhava Rao

Simha's melodrama, adapted from his successful Chandrakala Natak Mandali play (1933), introduces the theatre group's emphasis on reformist realism into Kannada cinema. Hero Sundar (Panthulu) marries Sarala against the wishes of his grandfather and is disowned by his family. His troubles, which include harsh treatment by his in-laws and the loss of his job, climax when he is accused of having murdered Sushila, the woman his grandfather originally wanted him to marry. The actor Panthulu later became the most influential Kannada film director in the reformist tradition.

SANT TUKARAM

1936 131' b&w Marathi
d **V. Damle, S. Fattelal** *pc* **Prabhat Film** *s* Shivram Vashikar *lyr* **Shantaram Athavale** *c* V. Avadhoot *m* **Keshavrao Bhole**
lp **Vishnupant Pagnis**, Gauri, Bhagwat, B. Nandrekar, Shankar Kulkarni, Kusum Bhagwat, Shanta Majumdar, Master Chhotu, Pandit Damle

This classic film chronicles the life of Tukaram (17th C.), one of Maharashtra's most popular saint poets, activating the 20th-C. resonances of his turning away from courtly Sanskrit towards vernacular rhythms of religious poetry which constituted the first major emancipatory movement against brahminical caste domination. The episodic plot pits Tukaram (Pagnis) against the Brahmin Salomalo (Bhagwat), who pretends to be the true author of Tukaram's songs while calling for his ostracisation. In showing Tukaram's growing popularity and his willing acceptance of the suffering heaped on him and his family by his oppressors, the movie binds song, gesture, rhythm and camera together with character and crowd behaviour denoting the spiritual connection between the poet and the people while separating off the members of the brahminical caste. One of the studio's cheaper productions, it adheres to most of the conventions of the genre, including numerous 'miracle' scenes in which the poet's god intervenes to demonstrate the truth of Tukaram's teachings. However, it endows these conventions with an unusual degree of conviction, as in the song *Adhi beej ekale*, written for the scene in which Tukaram celebrates the fertility of nature and composed in the poet's own ovi form of 31/2 beats, paralleling the work rhythm of women churning a grindstone. Scholars mistook it for an original, hitherto unknown Tukaram composition. The film breaks new ground with Gauri's earthy portrayal of Tukaram's wife, Jijai, who energetically squeezes cow-dung cakes for fuel and refuses to ascend to heaven, preferring to stay on earth and look after the children. Other innovations include the extraordinary tracking shot introducing Rameshwar Shastri to the town, showing the people working to the cadence of a song. Gauri, a familiar figure in Prabhat films mainly in walk-on roles, had her first major break in the film and went on to several fine performances in, e.g. ***Manoos/Admi*** (1939) and ***Sant Sakhu*** (1941). **Kumar Shahani** (1981) pointed to erotic elements in the devotional fervour, e.g. in the scenes of the prostitute who is converted by the saint and in Pagnis's own performance. Art historian Geeta Kapur wrote (1987):'[It] belongs [t]o a sub-genre of special significance. The saints' lives are, as legends, quasi-biographical material [e]xpressly adaptable to historical ends' in the light of their manifest commitment to spiritual equality and their validation of demotic speech patterns.

SARALA

1936 157' b&w Hindi
d/sc **Premankur Atorthy** *pc* **Imperial Film** *st* I.A. Hafizji *c* Rustom Irani *m* H.C. Bali
lp Rattan Bai, Kumar, I.A. Hafizji, Jilloo, Pramila, Anant Marathe, Chemist, Asooji, **Ahindra Choudhury**

Melodrama warning women to be dutifully subordinated wives and not to be tempted by modernising trends towards individual emancipation. The orphaned Sarala (Rattan Bai) is estranged from her loving husband Ramdas (Kumar) by the wiles of villain Avilash (Hafizji). She runs away and, following divine intervention in the form of an earthquake, escapes the villain's clutches. Living as a beggar, she finally dies in the arms of her husband begging forgiveness.

SIPAHI KI SAJNI/SIPAHINI SAJNI

aka *Soldier's Sweetheart*
1936 134' b&w Hindi/Gujarati
d/s **Chandulal Shah** *pc* **Ranjit Movietone** *dial/lyr* **Narayan Prasad Betaab** *c* G.G. Gogate *m* Rewashankar Marwadi, Banne Khan
lp **Gohar**, E. Bilimoria, Ram Apte, Keki Bawa, Ishwarlal, Dixit, Charlie, Ghory, Kesari, Bhupatrai

Gohar-centred adventure movie. She is the ruthless Princess Hansa determined to acquire a treasure map from rival King Sujansingh (Bawa). She daringly steals the map but the king's misogynist son, Dilipsingh (Bilimoria), manages to get it back. Together they are caught by the outlaw Vijay (Ishwarlal) who also wants the treasure. The film was replete with sword fights, tribal magic and a horse battle at the end when Sujansingh attacks his former friend Vijay to find his imprisoned son.

SONAR SANSAR/SUNEHRA SANSAR

1936 156'[B]/167'[H] b&w Bengali/Hindi
d/s **Debaki Bose** *pc* **East India Film** *dial* N.K. Mehra[H] *lyr* Vijay Kumar[H] *c* Sailen Bose *m* **K.C. Dey**
lp Menaka Devi, Azoorie, **Ahindra Choudhury**[B], **Dhiraj Bhattacharya**[B], **Chhaya Devi**[B], Bhumen Roy[B], **Jahar Ganguly**[B], Rampiary[H], Kamala Jharia[H], Gul Hamid[H], Mazhar Khan[H], Vijay Kumar[H], Nandkishore[H], Bedi[H], K.N. Singh[H]

A parable about human suffering and capitalist enterprise. The village headman has bandits attack the house of Ramesh to settle a feud. They kidnap the man's wife Roma, and abandon their infant son in the forest. Years later, Roma works as the nurse of a kind millionaire while the boy Raghunath shares a neighbourhood house with other unemployed youths who collectively dream of starting a soap factory. The father is a beggar on the streets. None of them know of each other's existence until circumstances bring the family together and the millionaire eventually funds the soap factory.

ALIBABA

1937 119' b&w Bengali
d **Modhu Bose** *pc* Shri Bharatlaxmi Pics *st* Khirode Prasad Vidyavinode's play *c* Bibhuti Das, Geeta Ghosh *m* Franco Polo, Nagardas Nayak
lp Modhu Bose, **Sadhona Bose**, Suprava Mukherjee, Indira Roy, Bibhuti Ganguly, Preeti Majumdar

Dancer Sadhona Bose made her feature debut in Modhu Bose's acclaimed *Arabian Nights* musical. Vidyavinode's play, first staged in 1897 by the Classic Theatre with Nripen Basu and Kusum Kumari, remained one of the most popular pre-WW1 Bengali plays. It tells of the Baghdadi woodcutter Alibaba (M. Bose) and his magic 'Open Sesame' formula; of the hero's jealous brother Kasim and of the slave girl Marjina (S. Bose). The film adapts the Calcutta Art Players' orientalist stage version, giving it a Hollywood-derived exotic flavour. An improvised 'modern' dance is inserted, Sadhona Bose's trademark due to her theatrical work with composer **Timir Baran**. The slow, mannered acting and the frontally framed tableau shots are enlivened by the dance scenes, esp. the Marjina-Abdallah sequence which long set the standard for film musicals (cf Lila Desai's dance in ***Bidyapati***, 1937). The surviving copy is probably incomplete.

AMBIKAPATHY

1937 c.210' b&w Tamil
d **Ellis R. Duncan** *pc* Salem Shankar Films *sc* **Elangovan** *c* Krishna Gopal *lyr/m* **Papanasam Sivan** *m* **K.C. Dey**
lp **M.K. Thyagaraja Bhagavathar**, Serukalathur Sama, P.B. Rangachari, T.S. Baliah, **N.S. Krishnan**, M.R. Santhanalakshmi, T.A. Mathuram

After *Raja Desingu* (1936), this is the 2nd major South Indian **historical**. It tells of the poet Kambar who wrote the *Ramayanam* in Tamil at Karikala Chola's court and draws on George Cukor's *Romeo and Juliet* (1936), including the balcony scene, for the love story between the poet's son, Ambikapathy (Bhagavathar) and the Princess Amaravathy (Santhanalakshmi). However, class distinctions are maintained as the young lover fails the test of will imposed by the king as a precondition for the marriage. Shot at the **New Theatres** Studio in Calcutta, the background music was by the blind singer-composer K.C. Dey, and the film was a landmark in the careers of Bhagavathar (esp. the song *Bajanai seivay maname*), Santhanalakshmi and Baliah, who played an army commander. Duncan was fond of 'return' scenes: this film opened with the victorious return of Kulothunga Chola to the city of Woriur; in his *Shakuntalai* (1940) there was the Sage Kanwar's return from pilgrimage and in ***Manthiri Kumari*** (1950) he staged the return home of a marriage party. The scenarist Elangovan, making his debut here, initiated the trend of privileging dialogue over songs.

ANATH ASHRAM

1937 136' b&w Hindi
d/s **Hemchandra Chunder** *pc* **New Theatres** *dial/lyr* **Kidar Sharma** *c* Yusuf Mulji *m* **Rai Chand Boral**
lp Umasashi, Najmul Hussain, Jagdish Sethi, **Prithviraj Kapoor**, Nawab, Master Satu, Trilok Kapoor, Nemo, Manorama

New Theatres' reformist melodrama about widow-remarriage. Jai Narain (Sethi), owner of a colliery, forms a happy family with his wife (Manorama), his daughter Saroj (Umasashi), son-in-law Kailash (T. Kapoor), an engineer at the colliery, and their son Nannha (Satu). Kailash dies in a colliery accident caused by Jai Narain. Nannha is sent to an orphanage and Saroj marries Ramesh, who loves her but is unaware of her previous marriage or of being a stepfather, while Saroj misses her dead husband and longs for her absent son. A former suitor, Ranjit (P. Kapoor) appears, knowing her past history. Repeated scenes show Nannha pining for his mother. The problem is finally resolved when Ramesh, who discovers the truth, saves the lonely child's life in a train accident

BIDYAPATI/VIDYAPATI

1937 141'[B]/152[H] b&w Bengali/Hindi
d/co-s/dial[H] **Debaki Bose** *pc* **New Theatres** *co-s* **Kazi Nazrul Islam**[H] *lyr*[H] **Kidar Sharma** *c* Yusuf Mulji *m* **Rai Chand Boral**
lp **Pahadi Sanyal, Chhaya Devi, Kanan Devi, K.C. Dey**, Leela Desai, **Durgadas Bannerjee**[B]/**Prithviraj Kapoor**[H], **Amar Mullick**[B], Debabala[B], Ahi Sanyal[B], Sailen Pal[B], K.N. Singh[H], Nemo[H], Kidar Sharma[H], Rampiary[H], Mohammed Ishaq[H]

New Theatres' classic celebration of Mithila's King Shiva Singha's (Bannerjee/Kapoor) love for his wife while chronicling the influence of the pacifist court poet Bidyapati (Sanyal). Invited to the royal court by the king, Bidyapati arrives with his faithful follower Anuradha (Kanan Devi). Queen Laxmi (Chhaya Devi) falls in love with the poet, much to the distress of the king. The king falls ill and starts neglecting his royal duties until Anuradha persuades him that true love does not need reciprocation. The queen, equally distressed by her divided loyalties, contemplates suicide, encouraged by the prime minister who is worried by the nefarious impact of Bidyapati's poetry on the king. Both the king and queen sacrifice their lives before the statue of the god Vishnu who appears to weep at the tragedy. Kanan Devi's unusually intense performance dominates the film, aided by a fast-moving script that broke with the convention of the static, frontal camera style of Indian film-devotionals. The sustained use of filmic close-ups allows Bidyapati's poetry to take on an autonomous motivational function in the plot, almost as though his art, rather than he himself, is the story's true protagonist.

DHARMAVEER

1937 156' b&w Marathi/Hindi
d **Master Vinayak** *pc* Huns Pics *st/dial*[M]*/lyr*[M] **P.K. Atre** *sc* R.S. Junnarkar *c* Pandurang Naik *m* Annasaheb Mainkar

lp Ratnaprabha, Master Vinayak, **Baburao Pendharkar**, Indira Wadkar, Javdekar, Datar

Atre's comedy launched a long collaboration with Master Vinayak (e.g. ***Brahmachari***, 1938; ***Brandichi Batli/Brandy Ki Botal***, 1939). The hypocritically pious philanthropist Dinanath (Pendharkar) drinks alcohol claiming it to be holy water, womanises and swindles people in private. He is contrasted with common man Jagadish (Vinayak), abused by all for having failed his matriculation exam eight times and who is loved by the poor flower-girl Kasturi (Ratnaprabha). Jagadish eventually becomes the instrument for the public exposure of Dinanath which makes him a popular hero. He remains unaffected by this turn of events and remains Kasturi's faithful admirer.

DIDI/PRESIDENT

aka *Badi Bahen*
1937 140'[B]/153[H] b&w Bengali/Hindi
d/s/c **Nitin Bose** *pc* **New Theatres** *m* **Rai Chand Boral, Pankaj Mullick**
lp **K.L. Saigal**, Leela Desai, Debabala, **Durgadas Bannerjee**[B]/**Prithviraj Kapoor**[H], **Amar Mullick**[B], Bhanu Bannerjee[B], Indu Mukherjee[B], Chandrabati Devi[B]/Kamlesh Kumari[H], Prabha[B], Nawab[H], Jagdish Sethi[H], Bikram Kapoor[H], Shabbir Ali[H]

A famous Saigal musical narrating a strange love story set against 1930s industrialisation and worker-management relations. The 16-year-old Prabhavati (Chandrabati Devi/Kumari) inherits a mill and turns it into an extremely profitable enterprise. Prakash (Saigal) is a worker who designs a more efficient machine for the factory for which he first gets sacked and then is re-employed. He falls in love with Prabhavati's sister Sheila (Desai), who later makes way for Prabhavati who is also in love with Prakash. Her withdrawal distresses Prakash, causing him to bully the workers who then go on strike. Prabhavati realises the problem and presumably commits suicide (she disappears into an office and locks the door) for the good of her sister and of the business. The unmistakable thrust of the story is that the 'personal' (i.e. relations with women) should not be allowed to interfere in male pursuits like business or management, equated with social good. The film has Saigal's classic number *Ek bangla bane nyara*. The plot echoes the **Guru Dutt** script for the unfinished *Baharain Phir Bhi Ayengi*.

GANGAVATARAN

aka *The Descent of Ganga*
1937 142'[M]/134'[H] b&w Marathi/Hindi
d/s/dial/lyr **D.G. Phalke** *co-d* Madhukar Bavdekar *pc* **Kolhapur Cinetone** *c* Vasudev Karnataki *m* Vishwanathbua Jadhav
lp **Chitnis**, Suresh Pardesi, Kusum Deshpande, Bhagwat, Shankarrao Bhosle, Pathan, Ibrahim, Gawli, Dongre, Barchi Bahadur, Mahananda, Leela Mishra, Ansuyabai, **Shanta Hublikar**

Nearly 70 years old and ailing, Phalke came out of retirement in 1934 to make this, his only sound film, at the invitation of Shahu Maharaj of Kolhapur. With a massive budget and two years' shooting, Phalke made the Pauranic tale which, by all accounts, was a grand mythological spectacle full of miracles and fantasy scenes with special effects credited to Phalke's son, Babaraya Phalke. **Narayan Hari Apte**, fresh from his success with ***Amritmanthan*** (1934), was hired for the script but he is not credited on screen. The film failed at the box-office and took the studio down with it.

(From left) Bikram Kapoor, Kamlesh Kumari and K.L. Saigal in *President*

HURRICANE HANSA

1937 151' b&w Hindi
d R.N. Vaidya *pc* **Wadia Movietone** *s* **J.B.H. Wadia** *dial* Dunyan *c* R.A. Rehman *m* Master Mohammed
lp **Fearless Nadia**, Husn Banu, Sardar Mansoor, Sayani Atish, Master Mohammed, Minoo The Mystic, John Cawas, Master Chhotu

Hansa (Nadia), daughter of Veer Singh (Mohammed), escapes an attack on her family by the villain Zalim Singh (Sayani) in which her mother is killed, her father injured and her sister Padma (Husn Banu) abducted. Growing up as a Harijan (an untouchable) she transforms the word to 'Hurricane', dons a mask and overthrows Zalim. She falls in love with Zalim's good son Diler (Mansoor). The horse Punjab-Ka-Beta features in its usual key role, rescuing Hansa when she hangs from a cliff, leaping over a wall of fire and aiding the love angle by nudging Diler into the pond where Hansa is having a bath.

JAGIRDAR

aka *Landlord*
1937 166' b&w Hindi
d **Mehboob Khan** *pc* **Sagar Film** *st* Babubhai A. Mehta *dial/lyr* **Zia Sarhadi** *c* Keki N. Mistry *m* **Anil Biswas**
lp Surendra, **Motilal**, Yakub, Zia Sarhadi, Pesi Patel, Bhudo Advani, Bibbo, Maya, Pande

The follow-up to ***Manmohan*** (1936) again starred Surendra and Bibbo. She is Neela, he plays Jagirdar Surendra. They secretly marry and have a child. When Jagirdar is presumed dead in a shipwreck, the child is considered illegitimate. The poor peasant Shripat (Pande) helps Neela by marrying her and raising her son Ramesh (Motilal). The husband eventually returns and violently quarrels with Shripat about who 'owns' Neela. When the villain Banwarilal kills Shripat, the husband is framed for the killing. The real problem, however, is the son's rejection of his father, solved when together they face the gangsters in Narayanlal's (Yakub) den. The orphan motif, repeated from *Manmohan*, contrasts with the woman's apparent state of 'illegitimacy' and both are used to elaborate a narrative able to question feudal patriarchy (cf also ***Hum Tum Aur Woh***, 1938) in contrast with e.g. **Shantaram**'s ***Kunku*** (1937), ***Manoos*** (1939) or the later ***Dahej*** (1950), all of which strongly affirm feudal patriarchy.

JEEVAN PRABHAT

1937 144' b&w Hindi
d **Franz Osten** *pc* **Bombay Talkies** *s* **Niranjan Pal** *dial/lyr* J.S. Casshyap *c* Josef Wirsching *m* **Saraswati Devi**
lp **Devika Rani**, Mumtaz Ali, **Kishore Sahu**, Renuka Devi, Chandraprabha, Maya Devi, Vimala Devi, Aloka, Tarabai Solanki, Saroj Baokar, Kamta Prasad, P.F. Pithawala, M. Nazir, N.M. Joshi, G.S. Vaishampayan

Osten returns to the familiar terrain of rural caste divisions (***Achhut Kanya***, 1936), adding polygamy to the theme in this story of Uma (Devika Rani), born in an orthodox

Brahmin family. To the despair of her parents she values her friendship with low-caste potters, esp. with Ramu (Sahu). When she marries Nandlal (Ali), a man from her own caste, her potter friends are happy for her - until they learn that Nandlal is taking a second wife, Padma, with Uma's consent. The problem is that Uma is thought to be infertile. Uma returns to her parents' home mainly because Nandlal is paying no attention to his new wife, and when she returns she meets Ramu again. Nandlal overhears a conversation between Ramu and Uma and, when Uma suddenly discovers that she is pregnant after all, he doubts her fidelity. The problem is only solved by Padma's generous withdrawal from the scene.

KANHOPATRA

1937 147' b&w Marathi
d/s/c/lyr **Bhalji Pendharkar** *c* K.V. Machwe, S.P. Shinde *m* Balaji Chougule
lp Leela Chandragiri, Chintamanrao Kolhatkar, Indubala, Sunubai, Gangadharpant Londhe, Jaishankar Danve, **Raja Paranjpe**, Dinkar Kamanna, Vidyadhar Joshi, **Shanta Hublikar**

Pendharkar's social deals with a prostitute who decides to rebel against tradition and the individuals who oppress her. Society, represented by encounters with a variety of males, makes it virtually impossible for her to maintain any dignity. The film was admired for its use of colloquial language.

KISAN KANYA

1937 130' col Hindi
d **Moti B. Gidwani** *pc* **Imperial Film** *s* M. Ziauddin *sc/dial* **Sadat Hasan Manto** *c* Rustom M. Irani *m* Ram Gopal Pandey
lp Padmadevi, Jilloo, Gulam Mohammed, Nissar, Sayed Ahmed, Gani

Rural crime drama featuring an exploitative landlord (Gani) and a good peasant Ramu (Nissar) who is accused of murdering the landlord. Remembered mainly for being one of India's first colour films, using the Cinecolour process imported by Imperial.

KUNKU/DUNIYA NA MANE

aka *The Unexpected*
1937 162'[M]/166'[H] b&w Marathi/Hindi
d **V. Shantaram** *pc* **Prabhat Film** *s* **Narayan Hari Apte** from his Marathi novel *Na Patnari Goshta lyr*[M] **Shantaram Athavale** *dial/lyr*[H] Munshi Aziz *c* V. Avadhoot *m* **Keshavrao Bhole**
lp **Shanta Apte**, **Keshavrao Date**, **Raja Nene**, Vimala Vasishta, Shakuntala Paranjpye, Vasanthi, Gauri, Master Chhotu, Karmarkar

Neera[M]/Nirmala[H] (Apte) is trapped into marrying the old widower Kakasaheb (Date). He is a progressive lawyer with a son and a daughter of Neera's age. She refuses to consummate the union, claiming repeatedly that while suffering can be borne, injustice cannot. After facing many hurdles including an aunt (Vasishta), her mother-in-law, and a lascivious stepson Pandit[M]/Jugal[H]) (Nene), her husband has a change of heart and magnanimously commits suicide, enjoining Neera to marry someone more suitable. The change occurs mainly through his widowed daughter Chitra[M]/Sushila[H] (Paranjpye, a noted social worker off screen) who provides a forcefully feminist moment in a speech to the young bride. Apte sings the combative song *In the world's broad field of battle...Be not like dumb, driven cattle* written by Longfellow. The original novel was a landmark in Maharashtra's social reform movement denouncing arranged and venal marriages that ignore women's rights. Shantaram's version stresses melodramatic overtones while indulging in some bravura visual stylisations, e.g. in the editing (he edited his own films) of the brief marriage sequence or the shattered mirror scene returning multiple laughing faces to the distraught old man gazing into the mirror, the leitmotif of the ticking clock, etc., many of these stylised images referring obliquely to the old man's sexual impotence. Apte's performance in her first leading role displays a modern freshness ahead of its time which established her as India's foremost singing star of the 30s. The veterans **Fattelal** and **Damle** did the art direction and the sound respectively. The Hindi title translates literally as 'The world will not accept...' while the Marathi title refers to the vermilion mark adorning the forehead of a married woman.

MINNALKODI

aka *Bolt of Lightning*
1937 157' b&w Tamil
d **K. Amarnath** *pc* Mohan Pics
lp K.T. Rukmini, B. Srinivasa Rao, Coco, Gogia Pasha
The Tamil debut of Bombay-based producers making cheaper versions of **Wadia Movietone** stunt films such as C. Parekh's *Jungle Ka Jawan* (1938) or Amarnath's *Chashmawali* (1939). Left fatherless and swindled by a nasty uncle, young Mohini (Rukmini) and her servant (Coco, aka Pasubulti Ramulu Naidu, a circus artiste turned comedian) come across the injured dacoit Minnalkodi. When he dies, Mohini takes on his identity and becomes a feared Robin Hood-type figure pursued by Inspector Jayakumar (Srinivasa Rao) who falls in love with her, reforms and marries her. The accent is on Mohini imitating **Fearless Nadia** as a dacoit: fighting, riding horses and, unusually for the genre, motorcycles. Rukmini models herself on the Hindi cinema's Gohar, even draping her sari in the Gujarati style.

MOHINI RUGMANGADA

1937 c.165' b&w Telugu
d **Ch. Narasimha Rao** *pc* National Movietone *s/lyr* **Tapi Dharma Rao** *c* Boman D. Irani *m* **B. Narasimha Rao**
lp **Vemuri Gaggaiah**, T. Suryanarayana, Ramatilakam, Pulipati, Vemuri Parabrahma Sastry, Saraswathi, Pushpa, Hemavathi, Kumpatla Subba Rao, Krithiventi Subba Rao, T. Ramakrishna Sastry, Susarla Ramchandra Rao, **C. Krishnaveni**

Proselytising mythological advocating the ekadashi 'vrat' (a ritual fast on the 11th day of the lunar month). Strongly promoted, it claimed to bring a new variety to Telugu cinema, featuring scenes from heaven (Brahmalok) and hell (Yamalok), 'moulded strictly according to ancient traditions' (ad in the *Andhra Patrika*). T. Ramakrishna Sastry, playing Narada, sings his musical forte, Tarangini, with the numbers *Ehi mudam dehi* and *Veekshe kada devadevam* in the traditional style.

MUKTI

aka *The Liberation of the Soul*
1937 139'[B]/155'[H] b&w Bengali/Hindi
d/sc **P.C. Barua** *pc* **New Theatres** *st/dial* Sajanikanta Das, *dial/co-lyr*[H] A.H. Shore *co-lyr*[H] Arzoo *c* **Bimal Roy** *m* **Pankaj Mullick**
lp P.C. Barua, **Kanan Devi**, Menaka, Nawab[H]/**Amar Mullick**[B], Sailen Choudhury[B], Ahi Sanyal[B], Jagdish Sethi[H], Bikram Kapoor[H], Pankaj Mullick[B]

Barua's classic adultery story tells of an artist, Prasanta (Barua) presented in the stereotypically romantic image: dedicated to his vocation, paying no heed to his scandalous reputation (he paints nude models) and with a cavalier attitude to his conservative father-in-law's demands for good social behaviour. He is married to the rich Chitra (Kanan Devi). The couple are in love but neither partner is prepared to compromise their ideals. The marriage falls apart. Prasanta concedes his wife's demand for a divorce and goes to the jungles of Assam, where for many years his closest associates are a wild elephant and Jharna (Menaka), the wife of an innkeeper named Pahari (Nawab/Mullick). He also makes a sworn enemy of a local trader. Chitra marries the millionaire Bipul and they go on an elephant hunt. They kill Prasanta's pet elephant. Since Chitra believes Prasanta to be dead he avoids meeting her, but he is forced to rescue her from the villainous trader. Prasanta succeeds but dies at Chitra's feet. The film interprets his death as Chitra's final achievement of the freedom she had craved. Barua contrasts the regressive story presented as static and unresolved, both as narrative and as performance, with a hyperactive environment that overwhelms the trivial nature of the lead couple's desires. There are many sequence shots tracking through walls and from interior to exterior, while nature is exemplified by mountains, trees, wind and charging elephants. This was one of the first elaborate filmic uses of **Tagore**'s lyrics, mostly using the poet's original tunes, but one of the film's big hits, *Diner sheshe ghumer sheshe*, was composed originally by Mullick.

PRATIBHA

1937 124' b&w Marathi/Hindi
d **Baburao Painter** *pc* Shalini Cinetone *st/co-dial*[M] **Narayan Hari Apte**, from his novel *Hridayachi Shrimanti co-dial/co-lyr*[H] Anandkumar *m/co-lyr*[M] **Govindrao Tembe** *c* K.V. Machwe
lp **Durga Khote**, **Keshavrao Date**, Miss Heera, Hirabai Badodekar, Nanasaheb Phatak, Master Shyam, Vishnupant Aundhkar, S.D. Danve, V.S. Jog, **Raja Paranjpe**, V.B. Date

The poet Prasad (K. Date) lives far from the city in a forest, enjoying only the company of his wife Pratibha (Khote). The court poet Kaveeshwar (Phatak) of a neighbouring kingdom discovers Prasad's poetry and, more importantly, his beautiful wife, and invites them to his palace, promising fame and glory. Against Pratibha's advice, Prasad succumbs to temptation, only to see his work plagiarised and his wife harassed. One of Painter's biggest films at Shalini (and one of the few to have been preserved) shows his control over big sets, lighting and crowd scenes, cf the princess's birthday scene with Prasad amid the crowd outside while his poetry is being recited inside, and the film's emotional highlight when a distressed Prasad and Pratibha leave the palace in a raging storm. The well-known classical singer Hirabai Badodekar sings three songs.

RAJAMOHAN

1937 c.210' b&w Tamil
d Fram Sethna *pc* National Movietone *s* V.M. Kothainayaki Ammal *c* Boman D. Irani *m* Yanai Vaidhyanatha Iyer, H.H. Sharma
lp K.P. Kesavan, **P.U. Chinappa**, A.K. Rajalakshmi, M.M. Radhabai, Kali N. Rathnam

Stagey musical reform melodrama by a Calcutta-based director, adapting a well-known novel by the female novelist Kothainayaki Ammal. When his poor mother, a vegetable vendor, becomes too frail to work, the hero, Mohan (Kesavan), drops out of school and becomes a proofreader of a popular journal. Mohan falls in love with the proprietor's daughter, Rajam, and ends up as editor. When the proprietor is killed Mohan is accused, but he eventually clears himself. The noted actor-singer of stage mythologicals P.U. Chinappa makes a rare appearance in a contemporary setting as Krishnan, the proprietor's villainous son. The music was mainly Carnatic and, following the stage convention, Kali N. Rathnam provided comedy relief. In keeping with convention, the film opens with a song in praise of the producers and asks Ganesh to make the venture a success.

SAVITRI

1937 136' b&w Hindi
d **Franz Osten** *pc* **Bombay Talkies** *s* **Niranjan Pal** *dial/lyr* J.S. Casshyap *c* Josef Wirsching *m* **Saraswati Devi**
lp **Devika Rani**, **Ashok Kumar**, Chandraprabha, Sunita Devi, Vimala Devi, Maya Devi, Sushila, Aloka, Madhurika Devi, Tarabai Solanki, Kamta Prasad, Mumtaz Ali, P.F. Pithawala, M. Nazir

Unusual mythological from the unit best known for ruralist reform dramas. The love story from the *Mahabharata*, already told as a silent film in the Italian co-production ***Savitri*** (1923), features Devika Rani as the heroine born through divine benediction to Ashwapati, and Ashok Kumar as Satyavan, son of an exiled and blinded hermit. Although Satyavan is scheduled to die soon, Savitri marries him and eventually propitiates Yama, the god of death, to return Satyavan's life and to restore her father-in-law's sight.

TALKIE OF TALKIES

aka *Dasturmoto Talkie*
1937 c.135' b&w Bengali
d/co-s **Sisir Bhaduri** *pc* Kali Films *co-s* Jaladhar Chattopadhyay's play *Reetimata Natak* (1936) *c* Suresh Das
lp Sisir Bhaduri, **Ahindra Choudhury**, **Jahar Ganguly**, Kankabati, Ranibala, Sailen Choudhury, Surabala

A film derived from a play about life imitating art. Prof. Digambar Majumdar's sister Shanta defies her brother's wishes and marries Biren, whom she nursed to health after knocking him down in her car. Shanta and Biren join the stage, to the consternation of her brother, and come to a tragic end when it is revealed that Biren already has a wife and son. Shanta dies trying to save Biren from committing suicide. Bhaduri's film version, which follows the old Taj Mahal film style, ignores all the developments in film technique and provides a straight stage adaptation using painted backdrops.

WAHAN

aka *Beyond the Horizon*
1937 130' b&w Hindi
d/s **K. Narayan Kale** *pc* **Prabhat** Cinetone *dial/lyr* Narottam Vyas *c* V. Avadhoot *m* **Master Krishnarao**
lp **Shanta Apte**, **Leela Chitnis**, Prahlad, Aruna Devi, **Chandramohan**, Ulhas, Master Chhotu, **Vasant Desai**

Kale's debut direction mixes Prabhat's baroque period movie style (cf ***Amritmanthan***, 1934) with the primitivist iconography of Hollywood's biblical epics. The setting vaguely evokes an ancient Aryan society ruled by Kodandavarma (Chandramohan), a dictator committed to the ideals of Aryan justice. A stone statue of Justice collapses, threatening to crush many slaves. The situation is saved by the youthful Jeevan (Prahlad), the king of an aboriginal tribe. Jeevan then falls in love with Princess Jayanti (Chitnis). Although mainly a romance, the film also addresses ideals of justice and morality. Its key characters include the villainous vice boss Madhuvrat (Chhotu) who plots against Kodandavarma and entraps Uttam (Ulhas), the designated heir to the throne, and the dancing girl Lata (Apte) who is forced to seduce Uttam so as to alleviate the slaves' suffering. The film was known even at the time of its release for Kale's innovative screenplay and esp. for the nonsense rhymes of the drinkers at Madhuvrat's bar.

ABHIGYAN/ABHAGIN

1938 143'[B]/151'[H] b&w Bengali/Hindi
d Prafulla Roy *pc* **New Theatres** *st* Upendranath Ganguly *sc* **Phani Majumdar** *dial*[H] A.H. Shore *lyr* Ajoy Bhattacharya[B]/Munshi Arzoo[H] *c* **Bimal Roy** *m* **Rai Chand Boral**
lp Molina Devi, **Prithviraj Kapoor**[H]/**Jiban Ganguly**[B], Vijay Kumar[H]/Sailen Choudhury[B], Nemo[H]/Manoranjan Bhattacharya[B], Bikram Kapoor[H]/Bhanu Bannerjee[B], Devbala, Manorama, Hashmat, Menaka, Rajlakshmi, **Pankaj Mullick**

A tenant attacks the villainous landlord Jawaharlal Choudhury (Nemo/Bhattacharya), injures his son Priyalal (Kumar/Choudhury) and abducts his daughter-in-law Sandhya (Molina Devi). Sandhya escapes unharmed to her relative, the engineer Prakash (B. Kapoor/Bannerjee), but her father-in-law refuses to take her back, believing her to be 'damaged goods'. Sheltered by the kindly Promode (P. Kapoor/Ganguly), her husband eventually accepts her back although she feels torn between affection for her saviour and her marital obligations. Based on a story by Bengali novelist Upendranath Ganguly (1881-1960), who was a follower of the best-known novelist of the reformist Bengali social, Saratchandra Chatterjee, Majumdar's script is the high point of the film, working with a literary authenticity often attempted but not always achieved by New Theatres.

ABHILASHA

aka *Postman*
1938 134' b&w Hindi
co-d/s/lyr **Zia Sarhadi** *co-d* Mahendra Thakore *pc* **Sagar Film** *c* Rajnikant Pandya *m* **Anil Biswas**
lp Kumar, Bibbo, Maya, Yakub, Bhudo Advani, Sankatha

Sarhadi's directorial debut constituted a move towards a didactic cinema, following, e.g., **R.S. Choudhury**'s ***Hamari Betiyan*** (1936), later extended by **Mehboob**. Postman Shishir (Kumar) is obsessed by the desire to own a car. He meets the crook Vinod (Yakub) who promises him a car if he will become his accomplice. The film includes a character named Devdas (Advani) obsessed with violins, who provokes the failure of Vinod's plot to have Shishir framed for the murder of Sushila (Bibbo).

ADHIKAR

1938 133'[B]/132[H] b&w Bengali/Hindi
d/s **P.C. Barua** *pc* **New Theatres** *dial/lyr*[B] Ajoy Bhattacharya *lyr*[H] Munshi Arzoo, Rashid *c* Yusuf Mulji *m* **Timir Baran**
lp P.C. Barua, Jamuna, **Pahadi Sanyal**, **Pankaj Mullick**, Rajalakshmi, Menaka Devi, Sailen Choudhury[B], Indu Mukherjee[B], Molina Devi[B], Chitralekha[B], Ushabati[B], Jagdish Sethi[H], Bikram Kapoor[H]

Melodrama about lineage and property questions. Nikhilesh (Barua) loves heiress Indira (Jamuna). A poor orphan girl, Radha (Menaka Devi), arrives claiming to be Indira's stepsister and therefore part inheritor of the family estate. Indira agrees to share her inheritance but then Radha makes a play for Nikhilesh. Ultimately, Radha turns out to be the real and sole heir. Love proves to be stronger than material possession as Indira and Nikhilesh get married and Radha finds happiness with Ratan, a man she had known and loved during her days of poverty. As each character returns to the class of his/her birth, the message hammered home is a warning to people never to transcend their social status. Barua continues his emphasis on the contrast between poverty and wealth, stylising the opulence of the wealthy interiors. Radha becomes 'unnatural' away from the realism of her slum while Indira's problem, threatened with the potential loss of her property, is seen mainly as one of alienation. The film also continues Barua's fascination with showing the urban-rural (read modern-traditional) split through the contrasting personalities of two women, a device inaugurated in ***Devdas*** (1935) and repeated even in his last major film ***Shesh Uttar/Jawab*** (1942), although *Adhikar* is probably the most confused and cynical of its many versions.

BAGHBAN

1938 159' b&w Hindi
d/sc/dial **A.R. Kardar** *pc* **General Films** *st* Begum Ansari *lyr* Mirza Musharraf *c* Kukde *m* Mushtaq Hussain
lp Bimala Kumari, B. Nandrekar, **Sitara Devi**, Yasmin, Putlibai, Ashraf Khan, Nazir, Lala Yakub, K.N. Singh, R. Wasti, Mirza Musharraf

The naive Saroop (Nandrekar) romantically renounces earthly pleasures under the influence of a sadhu (Ashraf Khan). Arrested at a fairground and jailed, fellow convicts change his view of the world. Working in the prison's garden, he meets the superintendent Sohanlal's (Nazir) daughter Durga (Kumari), who was married as a child to a boy now believed dead. Ranjit (Singh) covets her and on her wedding day to the nasty Ranjit, it is discovered that Saroop was her child-husband. Kardar's fascination with sexually deviant behaviour and the violence just below the surface of reformism (cf ***Pagal***, ***Pooja***, both 1940) is manifest in one of his first Bombay films.

BALAN

1938 180'(16,235 ft) b&w Malayalam
d S. Nottani *prod* **T.R. Sundaram** *pc* **Modern Theatres** *st/co-dial* A. Sundaram *sc/co-dial/lyr* **Muthukulam Raghavan Pillai** *c* Bado Gushwalkar
lp K.N. Laxmikutty, A.K. Kamalam, K.K. Aroor, Aleppey Vincent, A.B. Pious, Master Madan, Gopal, Miss Malathy, C.O.N. Nambiar, M.V. Sanku, Gopinathan Nair, Parukutty

Described as the first Malayalam sound film, made at the Modern Theatres, Salem. The story features the struggles of two orphaned children, Balan and his younger sister, oppressed and exploited by an evil stepmother until they are rescued by a kindly lawyer. The film ends with Balan sacrificing his happiness for that of his sister. Many of the stereotypes, esp. the wicked stepmother taking over the ancestral property of her spineless husband, and the helpless children, dominated the early Malayalam cinema for some time after they were introduced there. Apparently initiated by a Nagercoil resident, A. Sundaram, who got the Modern Theatres to back his project of filming his story *Mrs Nair and Fate*, was later eased out by the studio who recommissioned the script to playwright Pillai. Director Nottani also directed the next attempt in the campaign by Tamil producers to capture a Malayalam market, with ***Gnanambika*** (1940).

BHAKTA JAYADEVA

1938 c.155' b&w Telugu
d Hiren Bose *pc* Andhra Cinetone
lp Rentachintala Satyanarayana, **Surabhi Kamalabai**, Shantakumari, V. Venkateshwarulu

Big-budget but unsuccessful saint film about Jayadeva (12th C.), the author of the *Geet Govind*. The story shows the enmity between Jayadeva and Taranatha, who first burns down Jayadeva's house and then imprisons his wife. Help comes in the form of bandits who rob the villain's house and blind him.

BHUKAILASA

1938 189' b&w Tamil
d/p **Sundarrao Nadkarni** *pc* Sundaram Sound Studios *st Ramayana dial* Ayyulu Somayajulu *lyr* Yanai Vaidyanatha Iyer
lp Hansa Damayanti, T.S. Santhanam, Mahadeva Iyer, Master Mani, Azoorie

The first film version of this celebrated *Ramayana* episode features the evil Ravana (Santhanam) and Mandodhari (Damayanti). Although a hit, it was eclipsed by **Meiyappan**'s multilingual 1940 version of the same story. For the plot, cf ***Bhukailasa***, 1958.

BRAHMACHARI

1938 152'[M]/156'[H] b&w Marathi/Hindi
d **Master Vinayak** *pc* Huns Pics *s/lyr*[M] **P.K. Atre** *dial/lyr*[H] Indra *c* Pandurang Naik *m* Dada Chandekar
lp Master Vinayak, Meenakshi, V.G. Jog, Salvi, **Damuanna Malvankar**, Javdekar

Vinayak's Atre-scripted film initiated his best-known series of political satires (***Brandichi Batli/Brandy Ki Botal***, 1939; ***Sarkari Pahune***, 1942). The title means 'The Celibate' and addresses the Rashtriya Swayamsevak Sangh (RSS), a Hindu organisation emphasising celibacy and discipline, which became the power base of the right-wing Bhartiya Janata Party (BJP). An ordinary young man Audumbar (Vinayak), inspired by a militant lecture on bachelorhood and nationalism by the Deshbhakta Jatashankar (Javdekar), renounces sexual desire, throws away his collection of movie star posters, starts exercising his muscles in the tradition of Hanuman's disciples and joins the Self-Help Institute of the Acharya Chandiram (Malvankar). All his discipline comes to nought in the face of Kishori (Meenakshi). The film was the first to feature actors most associated with Vinayak's brand of satire: V.G. Jog and Damuanna Malvankar (the duo in the film-maker's legendary *Chimanrao* series). Malvankar's tremendously popular role in the film was his first big success. Meenakshi also makes her first appearance in a Vinayak film and here she sings, dressed in a bathing costume in a pool, the sensational seduction number *Yamuna jali khelu khela*.

DESHER MATI/DHARTI MATA

aka *The Motherland*
1938 163'[B]/165'[H] b&w Bengali/Hindi
d/sc/c/co-st/co-dial **Nitin Bose** *co-st/dial*[B] Benoy Chatterjee, **Sailajananda Mukherjee**, Sudhir Sen *lyr*[H] Sudarshan *m* **Pankaj Mullick**
lp **K.L. Saigal**, **K.C. Dey**, Umasashi, Pankaj Mullick, Shyam Laha, **Durgadas Bannerjee**[B], Indu Mukherjee[B], **Amar Mullick**[B], **Kanu Bannerjee**[B], Chandrabati Devi[B], Ahi Sanyal[B], Kamlesh Kumari[H], Nemo[H], Nawab[H], **Prithviraj Kapoor**[H], Jagdish Sethi[H]

Inspired apparently by Dovzhenko's cinema, Nitin Bose's call for a technological revolution in the agrarian sector through collective farming is presented in the guise of a love story. Ashok (Saigal) goes to a village, mobilises the peasants, fights the oppression of the village headman and achieves bumper crops. Childhood friend Ajoy (Sethi) goes to England to study mining technology and is determined to make a success of a mining project in the rural area where Ashok is working. Each has radically different ideas about what is best for an independent nation. Ajoy's sister Protibha (Kumari), who loves Ashok, secretly finances Ajoy's rural modernisation endeavours. Ajoy, unaware of this, falls in love with Gauri (Umasashi), daughter of the social outcast Kunja (Dey). When Ajoy returns from England, he discovers that the best coalfields lie directly beneath Ashok's land. The crisis is manifested in a drought that threatens to destroy Ashok's work and prove Ajoy's contentions right. Ajoy starts buying up the land but the rains arrive just in time to resurrect Ashok's rural-socialist dreams. The music credit is shared by Pankaj Mullick, Umasashi and K.C. Dey, but Saigal dominates the film in spite of singing only two songs, *Kisne yeh sab khel rachaya* and *A main ka karun kith jaoon*.

DOUBLE CROSS

1938 142' b&w Hindi
d/s/p **Mohan Bhavnani** *dial* Rai Mohan *c* F. Berko, Dara R. Mistry *m* Badri Prasad
lp Bimala Kumari, S.B. Nayampally, Fatty Prasad, Amina, David, Kishore, A.S. Gyani, R. Dilawar, Master Hussain, Rai Mohan

Bhavnani moved away from his reformist ambitions (***Mazdoor***, 1934; ***Jagran***, 1936) when he turned independent producer with this film. This modernisation drama tells of Prof. Mukherjee (David), the inventor of a diamond manufacturing process. His uncle, the stockbroker Romesh Chandra (Gyani) who invests in diamond mines, faces bankruptcy because Sardar Mulkraj (Nayampally) plots to ruin the mine owner Rangnath (Mohan) and take power in the feudal state of Panipur. The invention can alter the power struggle if either of the factions gets hold of it. The conflict is eventually solved by a masked stranger who turns out to be a policeman.

DUNIYA KYA HAI

aka *Resurrection*
1938 146' b&w Hindi
d/s G.P. Pawar *pc* Diamond Pics *st* Lev Tolstoy's *Resurrection lyr* Munshi Aziz *c* Kukde, Ahmedullah *m* Annasaheb Mainkar, Kikubhai Yagnik

lp **Lalita Pawar**, Madhav Kale, Bulbule, Ghanshyam, Indira Wadkar, **Fatma Begum**, Mankame, Bipin Mehta

An independent production by Lalita Pawar starring herself as a mistreated orphan called Lalita in this rare example of a melodrama drawn from a non-Indian literary source. Madhav (Kale), the son of the family, impregnates Lalita and promises to marry her on his return from Bombay. Years later, Madhav returns married, and refuses to recognise her. To feed her son, Lalita becomes a prostitute and is accused of a murder that takes place in the brothel. The prosecutor turns out to be Madhav.

DUSHMAN/JIBAN MARAN

aka *The Enemy*
1938 144' b&w Hindi/Bengali
d/sc/c **Nitin Bose** *st/co-dial*[B] **Sailajananda Mukherjee**, Benoy Chatterjee, *co-dial*[H] Sudarshan *lyr* Munshi Arzoo *m* **Pankaj Mullick**
lp **K.L. Saigal**, Leela Desai, Najam, Shiraz Farooque, Nemo, Devbala, Manorama, Elias Chowla, Jagdish Sethi, Dhumi Khan, Boken Chatto, Bhanu Bannerjee, Indu Mukherjee

Made at the invitation of the governmental Tuberculosis Fund in the context of Lady Linlithgow's immunisation programme. Mohan (Saigal), a radio singer, and Kedar (Najam), a doctor, both love Geeta (Desai). Mohan falls ill and makes way for Kedar, who eventually marries Geeta. After wandering in a delirium, Mohan is admitted to a sanatorium where he is cured of TB. He is then employed in the same institution. In a campaign to set up more sanatoria, Mohan agrees to sing on the radio to raise funds while Kedar persuades Geeta to give a dance recital. Geeta hears Mohan's broadcast and rushes to him followed by Kedar. To heighten the emotions for the climax of the story, Geeta has a bad accident and is admitted to the very sanatorium where Mohan works. The Hindi version was a major hit and led to a virtually identical Bengali remake. Seen today, however, it appears hopelessly dated, stringing together shots of carefully lit individual figures but indicating no control over its rambling narration.

GOPAL KRISHNA

1938 132' b&w Marathi/Hindi
d **V. Damle**, **S. Fattelal** *pc* **Prabhat Film** *s/dial* Shivram Vashikar *lyr* **Shantaram Athavale** *c* V. Avadhoot *m* **Master Krishnarao**
lp Ram Marathe, **Shanta Apte**, Parashuram, Shankar, Ganpatrao, Haribhau, Manajirao, Sophia

Damle and Fattelal followed up their hit ***Sant Tukaram*** (1936) with this remake of **Shantaram**'s silent mythological ***Gopal Krishna*** (1929). It tells of the playful child Krishna (Marathe) and his battle against the evil King Kamsa (Ganpatrao) who rules the city of Gokul. The stories, mainly from the popular *Bhagvat* and *Vishnu Purana*, also show Krishna vanquishing Keshi (Haribhau), Kamsa's general who arrives in disguise to capture him. Finally, when Kamsa unleashes rain and flood over the city (in a departure from the original legend where Indra caused the natural disaster), Krishna raises the mountain Govardhan over the people to protect them. From its opening sequences showing the cows and cowherds returning at sunset, the milking of the animals and the churning of the milk, the film develops a strongly materialist flavour, playing down 'miracle' scenes until the climactic storm and the raising of the mountain. The fast-paced dialogue and esp. the antics of Krishna's sidekick Pendya (Parashuram) help to make this a family favourite which made the child actor (and later noted classical musician) Ram Marathe famous.

GRAMOPHONE SINGER

1938 148' b&w Hindi
co-d/s **Ramchandra Thakur** *co-d* V.C. Desai *pc* **Sagar Film** *st* Sudarshan *dial/lyr* **Zia Sarhadi** *c* Keki Mistry *m* **Anil Biswas**
lp Surendra, Bibbo, Prabha, Bhudo Advani, Sankantha, Pande, Jamu Patel, Pesi Patel, Kayamali, Sawant, Kanhaiyalal, Gulzar, Durga, Agashe, Master Devdas, Naval

Thakur's music-dominated debut tells of a love triangle involving the famous gramophone singer Sundardas (Surendra) who is happily married to Mohini (Prabha), and the even more popular singer Tilottama (Bibbo), who falls in love with Sundardas's voice and wants them to sing a duet and have an affair. Ghosh Babu (Advani) is the manager of the record label.

GRIHALAKSHMI

1938 184' b&w Telugu
d **H.M. Reddy** *pc* Rohini Pics *s/lyr* **Samudrala Raghavacharya** *c* **K. Ramnoth** *m* Prabhala Satyanarayana
lp **Chittor V. Nagaiah**, Gauripathy Sastry, Ramanujachari, Govindrajulu Subbarao, **P. Kannamba**, **Kanchanmala**, Sarala, Mohini

Debut production of **Vauhini**'s predecessor, Rohini Pics, launching a local, Madras-based Telugu film industry with the first Telugu reformist social made in the same year as the equally influential ***Raitu Bidda*** (1939). The film tells of a decadent dancer, Madhuri (Kanchanmala), who seduces the upright Dr Krishna Rao (Ramanujachari) into leaving his good wife Radha (Kannamba). The doctor becomes an alcoholic and is framed for the murder of Vishwasa Rao, the trustee of his father's estate. Krishna Rao's brother-in-law Gopinath (Nagaiah) helps the hero and later offers shelter to a destitute Radha. Radha has a scuffle with Madhuri, falls down the stairs and becomes mentally unbalanced, ending up walking the streets of Madras denouncing god, truth and justice. Nagaiah's sensational debut included the two hits *Kallu manandoyi* (*Leave this drinking*) and the upbeat nationalist *Lendu bharata veerulara* (*Arise, soldiers of India*). The film's narrative style became a key model for Vauhini's sprawling melodramas, among the best-known Indian films in the genre. The film was apparently adapted from the popular stage play *Rangoon Rowdy*.

HUM TUM AUR WOH

aka *We Three*
1938 157' b&w Hindi-Urdu
d **Mehboob Khan** *pc* **Sagar** Movietone *s/co-lyr* Wajahat Mirza *co-lyr* **Zia Sarhadi** *c* Faredoon Irani *m* **Anil Biswas**
lp **Motilal**, Maya, Rose, Yakub, Bhudo Advani, Harish, Sankantha, Pande, Sunalini Devi

Mehboob presents the autonomous passion of Leela (Rose) for Moti (Motilal) who is promised to another woman, Bina (Maya). Leela is portrayed as irresponsible and impulsive as she acknowledges her desire for Moti and has a child by him. Bina then releases Moti from his promise. Moti suffers when he is told by Bina's father (Sankantha) that she is dead, while Leela's father (Pande) enjoins his daughter to commit suicide if Moti does not marry her. In spite of the film's endorsement of 'traditional', lethally oppressive patriarchal mores, incarnated by the women's fathers, Mehboob's narrative at least dares to depict a woman who refuses to feel guilty about her desire.

JAILOR

1938 150' b&w Hindi-Urdu
d **Sohrab Modi** *pc* **Minerva Movietone** *st/lyr* Ameer Haider Kamal **[Kamal Amrohi]** *sc* J.K. Nanda *c* Y.D. Sarpotdar *m* Mir Sahib
lp Sohrab Modi, **Leela Chitnis**, Sadiq Ali, Eruch Tarapore, Abu Baker, Sheila, Sharifa, Kumari Kamala, Kusum Deshpande

Modi's first psychodramatic role as a liberal man becoming a tyrannical jailer (remade with **Geeta Bali** in 1958). He loses his wife to a lover who then goes blind. The jailer locks up his wife, Kanwal, in their own home, forbidding any contact with their child, Bali. Later the jailer himself falls in love with a blind woman, Chhaya, only to lose her as well.

JWALA

1938 161'[M]/165'[H] b&w Marathi/Hindi
d **Master Vinayak** *pc* Huns Pics *s/dial/lyr*[M] **V.S. Khandekar** *dial*[H] Indra *c* Pandurang Naik *m* Dhamman Khan, Dada Chandekar
lp **Chandramohan**, Ratnaprabha, Ashalata, **Master Vinayak**, Chandrakant, Rajani, Dhavale, Bulbule

Vinayak changes from his usual melodramas to a period fantasy with this tale of a good general Angar (Chandramohan) who is corrupted by ambition. Echoing *Macbeth*, the loyal Angar is told by the witch Kuntala (Ashalata) that his king (Bulbule) shall die and that he shall be king instead. Angar then kills the king and seizes power. Departing from *Macbeth*, Angar's wife Mangala (Ratnaprabha) and his friend Tarang (Chandrakant) do not approve and they eventually join forces with the people against Angar. The dying Angar is seen crawling towards the throne which lies just beyond his reach. A rare Marathi film by the Hindi actor Chandramohan who seems ill at ease with the language. The big-budget film was a major flop from which Huns Pics never recovered, despite the success of their next production, ***Brahmachari*** (1938).

KAMBAR

1938 177' b&w Tamil
d C.S.U. Sankar *pc* **Vel Pics**, **Madan Theatres**
lp S.V. Subbaiah Bhagavathar, C.S. Swarnambal, Narayan Rao, R.P. Yagneshwaran, Devuluri, Venkataraju

Vel Pics' **Saint Film** on the legend of Kamban, the 9th-C. Tamil poet who left the Chola court to become a wanderer and composed the best-known Tamil adaptation of Valmiki's *Ramayana*. The film's major attraction was the starring actor Bhagavathar's music.

MALAPILLA

aka *The Outcast Girl*
1938 c.175' b&W Telugu
d **Gudavalli Ramabrahmam** *pc* Sarathi Studio *co-s* Gudipati Venkatachalam (aka Chalam) *co-s/co-lyr* **Tapi Dharma Rao** *co-lyr* Basavaraja Apparao *c* Sailen Bose *m* **B. Narasimha Rao**
lp Govindrajulu Subbarao, **Kanchanmala**, Sundaramma, Suribabu, Gali Venkateshwara Rao, Venkatasubbaiah, M.C. Raghavan, Hemalathamma Rao, Gangarathnam, P. Laxmikantamma, Teku Ansuya, Puvvula Ansuya, Bhanumathi

Radical director Ramabrahmam's debut feature tells of a Harijan woman (Kanchanmala) who falls in love with a Brahmin (Gali Venkateshwara Rao) in a direct critique of exploitative Brahmin rituals. The musical hit including songs like *Nallavade golla pillavade* and *Aa mubbu ee mubbu* established the poet Basavaraja Apparao as a film lyricist. Addressing the problem of caste, a major issue in South Indian politics, it was dedicated to the maharajah of Travancore who had passed a law allowing members of all castes to enter temples. On its release, the film caused a sensation, rejecting the stage-derived mythological genre dominating 1930s Telugu cinema.

MAZHA MULGA/MERA LADKA

aka *My Son*
1938 161' b&w Marathi/Hindi
d **K. Narayan Kale** *pc* **Prabhat Film** *s* Y.G. Joshi *lyr* **Shantaram Athavale**[M], Sampatlal Srivastava 'Anuj'[H] *c* V. Avadhoot *m* **Keshavrao Bhole**
lp **Shanta Hublikar**, **Shahu Modak**[M], Ulhas[H], Mama Bhatt, Vasant Thengadi, Vatsalabai Joshi, Balakram, Master Chhotu, Sundarabai

Radical journalist Diwakar (Modak) runs a printing press and edits a newspaper, much to the disapproval of his authoritarian middle-class father who believes that all respectable youths should get a job and settle down. Diwakar's scheming politician friend Vithalrao (Thengadi) incites a strike and acquires the press and the paper with the help of Diwakar's father, causing Diwakar to leave home in disgust. His rich girlfriend Nalini (Hublikar) also enters politics, first on the side of the corrupt Vithalrao, then campaigning for Diwakar who represents the slum-dwellers for the municipal elections. Although Diwakar's father campaigns on behalf of Nalini, she tells people not to vote for her but to elect Diwakar instead. Although Nalini wins, the film presents Diwakar's loss as a moral victory. Director Kale, himself a former radical journalist, made his first contemporary story as a critique of Maharashtrian middle-class materialism. He also published a long essay on the film, 'Mazha Mulgachya Nimittane', (1939). Launching the star combination of Modak and Hublikar, repeated in Shantaram's hit ***Manoos*** (1939), the film essayed a realist idiom new to the Prabhat Studio (esp. in the scenes at the printing press). Hit songs included *Pahu re kiti vaat* (Hublikar) and *Ya sagle jan laukar ya* (Modak).

Mazha Mulga

MOHINI BHASMASURA

1938 183' b&w Telugu
d **C. Pullaiah** *pc* Andhra Talkies *lyr* D. Venkatavadham *c* G.V. Bhadsavale
lp Pushpavalli, Dasari Kotiratnam, A.V. Subba Rao, Nagarajakumari, Tungala Chalapathi Rao

Pullaiah's widely advertised mythological about the demon Bhasmasura who comes to earth armed with a boon from Shiva and causes mayhem until Vishnu, in the guise of Mohini (Pushpavalli), brings about the demon's self-destruction. The film's main attraction was the star Pushpavalli, promoted as a divine beauty come down to earth. The advertising, by the London Film Exchange (which controlled distribution rights), also stressed the location scenes and their 'natural scenic beauty'.

NANDAKUMAR

1938 156' b&w Tamil
d **Narayanrao D. Sarpotdar** *p* **A.V. Meiyappan** *pc* Pragati Pics *c* Pai *m* Ramaswamy
lp V.A. Chelappa, C.V.V. Panthulu, **T.P. Rajalakshmi**, T.R. Mahalingam, Krishnamurthy, G.S. Sandow, T.S. Rajalakshmi

The breakthrough for producer A.V. Meiyappan (see **AVM Film**) is also the Marathi director Sarpotdar's only venture into Tamil. The mythological features the birth, childhood and the early antics of Krishna (Mahalingam), culminating in the death of Kamsa. The mandatory miracle scenes gave ample scope for special effects in a narrative format that had by now congealed into a formula (cf **Damle** and **Fattelal**'s ***Gopal Krishna*** made the same year). The Tamil film historian Randor Guy claimed there was a link with the **Prabhat** production, although the two films have different technical credits. This was the famous Carnatic musician T.R. Mahalingam's film debut, aged 14, his powerful singing voice being among its star attractions. The sound was recorded by Y.S. Kothare and C.E. Biggs.

SARBAJANIN BIBAHOTSAB

1938 c.130' b&w Bengali
d **Satu Sen** *pc* Kali Films *s* Sachindranath Sengupta *c* Suresh Das *m* **Kamal Dasgupta**
lp **Jiban Ganguly**, **Dhiraj Bhattacharya**, **Jahar Ganguly**, Nabadwip Haldar, Haridhan Mukherjee, Santosh Sinha, Ranibala, Sabitri, Usha, Bina

Stage director and technician Satu Sen's best-known film is an elaborately plotted farce written by noted playwright Sengupta (1892-1961), better known for his historicals and reformist melodramas (*Siraj-ud-Dowla*, 1938; *Janana*, 1933). The story features five couples: stage actor Bimal is loved by actress Chameli but prefers Kamala. When Kamala announces her marriage with Pranadhan, Chameli disguises herself and tries to implicate Pranadhan in a scandal. He escapes by disguising himself as an old man, but winds up in the clutches of Banalata. Departing from the conventions of the Bengali comedy of manners, this film about acting vertiginously multiplies the 'disguise' motif and culminates in a quintuple wedding. According to contemporary reviews, excessive plotting detracted from the film's success.

SEVA SADAN

1938 210' b&w Tamil
d **K. Subramanyam** *pc* Chandraprabha Cinetone, Madras United Artists *st* Premchand's novel *Bazaar-e-Husn* (1919) *c* Sailen Bose.
lp M.S. Subbulakshmi, F.G. Natesa Iyer, Mrs Jayalakshmi, Varadachar, Rampiary, Pattu Iyer, Mani Bhagavathar, A.K. Kamalam, Jolly Kittu

Written originally in Urdu, the novel's translation became Premchand's first Hindi work of fiction. The writer was distressed by **Nanubhai Vakil**'s film version (1934) and Subramanyam's Tamil film put it back into its original reformist shape. The novel deals with prostitution and women's emancipation. While retaining its political thrust, Subramanyam made it a musical, casting the debuting Subbulakshmi in the lead as Suman. Both her performance and that of her co-star, Natesa Iyer as Gajadhar Pande, won acclaim. The music was very popular and served partly to blunt the anticipated conservative opposition to the plot's feminist overtones. Subbulakshmi's *Shyamasundara madana mohana* was a major hit and remains popular today. Actress Rampiary was imported from Bombay for the film.

STATE EXPRESS

1938 171' b&w Hindi
d **Vijay Bhatt** *pc* Prakash Pics *dial/lyr* Sampatlal Srivastava 'Anuj' *m* Lallubhai Nayak
lp Jayant, **Sardar Akhtar**, Umakant, Shirin, Zaverbhai, M. Zahur, Lallubhai, Ismail, Jehangir, Chhotejaan, Vithaldas, Athavale

Successful stunt movie featuring a vivacious prince (Jayant), his evil uncle, and a masked girl (Akhtar). Its major attractions, apart from Akhtar who also sings all the songs, is a performing gorilla. Together with e.g. ***Leatherface*** (1939), this is the best known of mythological specialist Bhatt's early stunt work.

STREET SINGER/SAATHI

1938 135'[H]/144'[B] b&w Hindi/Bengali
d/s **Phani Majumdar** *pc* **New Theatres** *dial*[H] A.H. Shore *lyr* Munshi Arzoo Lucknowi[H], Ajoy Bhattacharya[B] *c* Dilip Gupta, Sudhish Ghatak *m* **Rai Chand Boral**
lp **K.L. Saigal**, **Kanan Devi**, Boken Chatto, Rekha, Jagdish[H], Bikram Kapoor[H], Shabbir[H], A.H. Shore[H], Chamanlal[H], Vaid[H], Abdul Rehman[H], Vrij Paul[H], Ramkumari[H], Rani[H], **Amar Mullick**[B], Sailen Choudhury[B], Bhanu Bannerjee[B], Ahi Sanyal[B], Khagen Pathak[B], Sukumar Pal[B], Shyam Laha[B], Benoy Goswami[B], Kamala Jharia[B], Poornima[B]

Majumdar's directorial debut is a classic musical and one of Saigal's most famous films. The story tells of two childhood friends, Bhulwa (Saigal) and Manju (Kanan Devi), who grow up to become street singers in Calcutta. Bhulwa dreams of becoming a stage star but it is Manju who succeeds. At the height of her fame Manju almost forgets Bhulwa until at the end - in an obviously symbolic landscape (literally showing a boat washed ashore in a storm) the two are united. The Hindi version, where this sequence illustrates Saigal's all-time hit *Babul mora*, is the better known.

TALAAQ

aka *Divorce*
1938 127' b&w Hindi
d **Sohrab Modi** *pc* **Minerva Movietone** *co-st* **Gajanan Jagirdar** *dial/lyr/co-st* Anand Kumar *c* S.D. Patil *m* Mir Saheb
lp Naseem Banu, Gajanan Jagirdar, Navin Yagnik, Prem Adib, Khwaja Sabir, Sheela, Vimala Vasishta, Shanta Dutt, Abu Baker, Khan Mastana
An early Modi psychodrama condemning the divorce law as iniquitous to Hinduism. Roopa (Banu), wife of politician Niranjan (Yagnik), leaves her husband to fight for more progressive divorce laws. She is helped for exploitative reasons by Chhabilelal (Jagirdar), the editor of the radical journal *Aandhi*. Roopa gets her divorce but is disillusioned by her legal achievement when Amarnath (Adib), whom she marries, uses the same law against her. Niranjan rescues and falls in love with the married Shanta (Sheela); since he does not approve of the divorce law, they cannot marry. Modi's late 30s films focus on the issue of sexual infidelity (***Jailor***, 1938; ***Bharosa***, 1940), chronicling with almost gleeful misogyny how the guilty women are made to suffer for their temerity.

THREE HUNDRED DAYS AND AFTER

aka *Teen Sau Din Ke Baad*
1938 158' b&w Hindi
d **Sarvottam Badami** *pc* **Sagar Film** *st* Babubhai A. Mehta *dial* Wajahat Mirza, Waqif *lyr* **Zia Sarhadi** *c* Faredoon Irani *m* **Anil Biswas**
lp Sabita Devi, **Motilal**, Bibbo, Yakub, Sankatha, Pesi Patel, Pande, Gulzar, Yusuf, Wasker, Rukmini, Piroj Wadkar

Young, bored millionaire (Motilal) has a bet with his doctor that he will go out into the world without taking any money and survive for 300 days. The story of his adventures was a big hit, including two songs by Motilal himself: *Ghar apna yeh kursi apni* and *Ik tum na hui to kya hua*.

WATAN

1938 168' b&w Hindi
d/s/co-st **Mehboob Khan** *pc* **Sagar Film** *co-st/dial/lyr* Wajahat Mirza *c* Faredoon Irani *m* **Anil Biswas**
lp Kumar, Bibbo, Maya Bannerjee, Yakub, **Sitara Devi**, Kayamali, Sankatha, H. Siddiqui, Pande, Mirza, Ramchandra, Agashe

Ostensibly a Central Asian war fantasy about a conflict between the Cossacks and the Tartars, Mehboob's film proposes a tale advocating national independence. The Cossacks are oppressed by the despotic Russian king (Siddiqui) and his minister Jabir (Kayamali), who has Tartar blood in him. General Murad (Kumar) covertly sides with the opposition, gets arrested for treason and escapes. He meets the wild Gulnar (Sitara Devi) and gets her to spy as a maid of Princess Nigar (Bibbo). Nigar falls for Murad and Gulnar withdraws from the scene for the sake of her nation. Eventually Nigar, at the head of an army of women, helps defeat the villains.

ADHURI KAHANI

aka *The Unfinished Tale*
1939 148' b&w Hindi
d **Chaturbhuj Doshi** *pc* **Ranjit Movietone** *st* Gunwantrai Acharya *sc/dial/lyr* J.S. Casshyap *c* L.N. Verma *m* Gyan Dutt
lp **Durga Khote**, **Prithviraj Kapoor**, Rose, **Keshavrao Date**, Ila Devi, Ishwarlal, Meera, Lala Yakub, Khatoon, Mirza Musharraf, T. Zadi

Based on a story by the noted Gujarati novelist Acharya (author of *Daryalal*, *Allabeli* et al.), this modernisation fable is one of Chaturbhuj Doshi's best early films at Ranjit. The educated and liberal Harbala (Khote) is oppressed by her conservative husband Seth Gopaldas (Date). Determined that her children Somnath (Kapoor) and Neelam (Rose) shall lead freer lives, she is frustrated by Gopaldas's authoritarian traditionalism and commits suicide. Neelam and Somnath, haunted by guilt, join her in death. The film leaves open the possibility that in the future a less oppressive society will be achieved: literally translated, the title means 'The Unfinished Tale'.

BARDIDI/BADI DIDI

1939 128'[B] b&w Bengali/Hindi
d **Amar Mullick** *pc* **New Theatres** *st* Saratchandra Chatterjee *dial/lyr*[H] **Kidar Sharma** *lyr* Ajoy Bhattacharya, **Pashupati Chatterjee**, Jibanmoy Roy[B] *c* **Bimal Roy** *m* **Pankaj Mullick**
lp[B]: Jogesh Choudhury, Nirmal Bannerjee, Sailen Choudhury, Bhanu Bannerjee, Indu Mukherjee, Keshto Das, Ahi Sanyal, Naresh Babu, Benoy Sanyal, Sailen Pal, Dhiren Das, Kali Ghosh, Paresh Chatterjee, Chhabi Roy, Nibhanani Devi, Ranibala, Poornima; [H]: Molina Devi, **Pahadi Sanyal**, Chandrabati Devi, Jagdish Sethi, Zainab, Gulab, Bela, Nawab, Bikram Kapoor, Rajlakshmi, Menaka, Pannalal, Nemo, Chimanlal, Rani, Renuka Devi, **Kidar Sharma**

After ***Devdas*** (1935), this is one of New Theatres' best-known films based on Saratchandra's writing. Suren (P. Sanyal), prevented by his family from pursuing a university career, leaves home and becomes a tutor to Pramila (Zainab). He falls in love with her widowed elder sister Madhavi (Molina Devi) who, although returning his love, has him sacked to save the situation. Years later, Suren becomes a big zamindar and, unknown to him, Madhavi is one of his tenants suffering under the oppression of his staff, a plot device providing ample opportunities for emotional drama about how 'traditional' social conventions lay waste to people's lives. The end, as a terminally ill Suren makes up with Madhavi before dying on her lap, evokes *Devdas*.

BRANDICHI BATLI/BRANDY KI BOTAL

1939 147'[M]/146'[H] b&w Marathi/Hindi
d **Master Vinayak** *pc* Huns Pics *s/lyr*[M] **P.K. Atre** *c* Pandurang Naik *m* Dada Chandekar
lp **Damuanna Malvankar**[M]/Master Vinayak[H], V. Jog, Salvi, Meenakshi, Javdekar

Vinayak and Atre's classic sequel to the hit ***Brahmachari*** (1938) addresses prohibition and Gandhian morality. The naively innocent bachelor Bagaram (Malvankar/Vinayak), a clerk in a municipal office, has to find some brandy to restore the ill son of his boss, who is also the brother of Malati (Meenakshi), whom he secretly loves. Not knowing what brandy is, Bagaram gets embroiled in adventures, including a famous scene in a crowded bar. He eventually procures a bottle but his beloved persists in regarding him merely as 'a brother'. Documentary footage of Vallabhbhai Patel making a speech about abstinence (included with his permission) had to be removed because of censor objections, as was the ambiguous line by Bagaram who, surrounded by young women, implored the god Krishna to 'give me a break too'. The film was widely attacked for its irreverence towards Hindu tradition but went on to become a perennial commercial hit, establishing Atre's scripts as an independent stellar attraction.

DEVATA

1939 148' b&w Marathi
d **Master Vinayak** *pc* Huns Pics *s/co-lyr* **V.S. Khandekar** *co-lyr* B.R. Tambe *c* Pandurang Naik *m* Dada Chandekar
lp **Baburao Pendharkar**, Indira Wadkar, Meenakshi, Salvi, **Damuanna Malvankar**, Miss Sardar, Vibhavati, Baby Vimal, Patankar

One of Marathi actress-singer Wadkar's most famous roles as Sushila, who marries an old widower, Dasopant (Salvi), in order to pay for her younger brother's education. Dasopant already has a son, the social worker and professor Ashok (Pendharkar), who is horrified at his father's decision and begs Sushila to reconsider, but she marries the old man anyway. Sushila later admits to Ashok (now her stepson) that it was a mistake, and when she has to take refuge in his room to escape from her husband she is accused of adultery with Ashok, who then becomes a social outcast to the distress of his girlfriend Pushpa (Meenakshi). Sushila leaves having written letters explaining all to Ashok and Pushpa. Years later she is heard singing on a radio station. The film repeats Khandekar's favourite themes of bravely borne suffering (inevitably that of an older sister on behalf of younger siblings) and the self-revealing act at the end: in ***Chhaya*** (1936) the hero publishes an autobiographical novel thus betraying himself to the police; here Sushila craves anonymity yet she sings an autobiographical song on the radio drawing the family's attention back to her.

DURGA

1939 135' b&w Hindi
d **Franz Osten** *pc* **Bombay Talkies** *s* Sardindu Bannerjee *dial/co-lyr* Narottam Vyas *co-lyr* Narendra Nath Tuli *c* Josef Wirsching *m* **Saraswati Devi**
lp **Devika Rani**, Rama Shukul, **Hansa Wadkar**, Vishnupant Aundhkar, P.F. Pithawala, Saroj Borkar, Enver, Kiran Singh Shashi

Rural melodrama about Durga (Devika Rani), an adolescent child of nature, living with her aged mother Heera. Unable to get the medicine required to prevent her mother's death, one misfortune after another befalls the heroine in spite of the sympathies of the newly arrived village doctor, Jawahar (Shukul). In the absence of **Niranjan Pal**, the studio's main scenarist and author of its best-known rural dramas (***Achhut Kanya***, ***Janmabhoomi***, both 1936), the tale reduces itself to a purely familial narrative. It is nevertheless a key production in Devika Rani's self-projection of urbane charm clothed in primal innocence. Osten followed it with **Leela Chitnis**'s first big film, ***Kangan*** (1939). Wadkar was promoted to lead actress again opposite Shukul in in her next big film, ***Navjeevan*** (1939).

EK HI RAASTA

aka *The Only Way*
1939 149' b&w Hindi
d **Mehboob Khan** pc **Sagar Movietone** *s* Babubhai A. Mehta *dial* Wajahat Mirza *lyr* Indra *c* Faredoon Irani *m* **Anil Biswas**
lp Arun, Sheikh Mukhtar, Anuradha, Jyoti, Harish, Kanhaiyalal, Mohan, A. Banbasi, Jagdish Rai, Devi, Wasker, Gani

Mehboob uses a didactic style to address contemporary topics, a concern extended in e.g. ***Roti*** (1942). The orphan and shipwreck survivor Raja (Arun) works as a coolie forming a trio of friends with Mangoo (Sheikh Mukhtar), a pickpocket, and Vithal (Mohan), a hansom cab driver. Mala (Anuradha) and her father (Gani) come to the city where she is kidnapped by Banke (Kanhaiyalal) and sold to a rich man while her father accuses Mangoo of theft. Mangoo kills the father. Mala escapes and finds shelter with Raja, with whom she falls in love. The problems of the trio increase when they enlist in the army for WW 2. The film opposes religious faith to atheistic fatalism (the latter exemplified by Mangoo whose mother dies in an accident and he becomes a killer) and dares to present a couple openly living together as Mala stubbornly rejects the pressures of her stepmother (Devi) and her villainous cousin Madan (A. Banbasi).

JAWANI KI REET/PARAJAY

1939 144'[H]/136'[B] b&w Hindi/Bengali
d/sc **Hemchandra Chunder** *pc* **New Theatres** *st* Ranajit Sen *dial* Benoy Chatterjee[B], Amjad Hussain, **Kidar Sharma**[H] *lyr* Ajoy Bhattacharya[B], Arzoo Lucknowi[H] *c* Yusuf Mulji *m* **Rai Chand Boral**
lp **Kanan Devi**, Rajalakshmi, Chhabirani, A.H. Shore, Bhanu Bannerjee[B], **Amar Mullick**[B], Sailen Choudhury[B], Indu Mukherjee[B], Jiban Bose[B], Biren Das[B], Sailen Pal[B], **Jiban Ganguly**[B], Najmul Hussain[H], Jagdish Sethi[H], Nemo[H], Bikram Kapoor[H], Bipin Gupta[H], Kalavati[H], Nandkishore[H]

Seminal film on the inheritance theme (cf ***Udayer Pathey***, 1944, and ***Andaz***, 1949). The lawyer Bholanath Roy adopts Anita (Kanan Devi) who grows up into a beautiful and fashionable teenager. She meets Dilip, the lawyer's estranged son, working on a flood-relief programme and they fall in love. Their lineage problems (she does not know hers, he keeps his a guilty secret) are solved when Bholanath dies, leaving his estate to Dilip and thus rehabilitating him as well as their relationship.

JAYAPRADHA

aka *Pururava Chakravarthi*
1939 c.190' b&w Telugu
d **Ch. Narasimha Rao** *pc* Sharada-Rayalseema Films *dial/lyr* Varanasi Seetarama Sastry, Ch. Hanumantha Rao *m* **Saluri Rajeshwara Rao**
lp **C.S.R. Anjaneyalu**, K. Pichhaiah, Narasimha Rao, Lalita, Sampurna, Sheshu, Chitti, Seeta, Yashoda, **T. Suryakumari**, Rajakumari, Anjamma, Ramudu, Saluri Rajeshwara Rao

By way of an ***Ayodhyecha Raja*** (1932) type of story, the film offers an invented legend as a nationalist allegory aligned with the Gandhian opposition (including a scene showing Jayapradha using the spinning-wheel associated with Gandhi's campaign). Rather than resorting to violence to defend his country, the peace-loving Emperor Pururava leaves his palace with his wife Jayapradha and his two sons. The royal couple attempt manual labour, which is abhorrent to the wife, and face the evil machinations of the merchant Navakoti Narayana Shetty. When Shetty captures and tries to molest Jayapradha, his house is accidentally set on fire. Rajeshwara Rao's first full assignment as composer.

JEEVAN SAATHI

aka *Comrades*
1939 157' b&w Hindi
d **Nandlal Jaswantlal** *pc* **Sagar Film** *s* Babubhai Mehta *dial/co-lyr* **Zia Sarhadi** *co-lyr* Kanhaiyalal *c* Faredoon Irani *m* **Anil Biswas**
lp Surendra, Maya Bannerjee, Harish, Jyoti, Jilloo, Sankatha, Kayamali, Bhudo Advani, Jamu Patel A mildly socialist realist (esp. in the music) family drama exemplifying the spirit of camaraderie and sacrifice. Seth Madhavlal's household includes two sons, Jatin (Surendra) and Kiran (Harish), and the adopted orphan Rekha (Maya). When the trio grow up, both Jatin and Kiran love Rekha. To solve the dilemma Jatin becomes a social outlaw. The love duets of Surendra and Maya Bannerjee are emotionally contrasted with Surendra's political addresses, the solo *Hame hua hai desh nikala* and his duet with Jyoti, *Aan base pardes sajanava*, both being songs of exile.

KANGAN

1939 139' b&w Hindi
d **Franz Osten** *pc* **Bombay Talkies** *p* S. Mukherjee *st* Gajendra Kumar Mitra's *Rajanigandha* *sc* Saradindu Bannerjee, S. Mukherjee *dial/co-lyr* Narottam Vyas *co-lyr* Pradeep *c* Josef Wirsching, R.D. Parineeja *m* **Saraswati Devi**, Ramchandra Pal
lp **Leela Chitnis, Ashok Kumar**, V.H. Desai, P.F. Pithawala, Mubarak, Saroj Borkar, Nana Paliskar, Pratima

Leela Chitnis' first big film at Bombay Talkies is a love story between the beautiful village belle Radha (Chitnis) and Kamal (Kumar), the son of the village zamindar who wants to be a great poet. The zamindar sends his son to the city where Kamal becomes a noted novelist and playwright while Radha is persecuted by the zamindar and his henchman Banwari. She feigns suicide but in fact goes to join her beloved in the city (on the same train as the now repentant father). When she eventually reaches Kamal's house, she hears him declaring his love to a woman. Unaware that he is merely reading lines from his latest play, Radha withdraws, but eventually the father brings about the happy end. Unlike the studio's **Niranjan Pal** melodramas written for **Devika Rani**, this production ignored the reformist dimensions of the story and opts for a conventional romance. Chitnis's acting style, continued in ***Bandhan*** (1940) and in ***Jhoola*** (1941), both S. Mukherjee productions, heralded a new era for Bombay Talkies and culminated in **Filmistan**'s seductive performance techniques.

LEATHERFACE

aka *Farzande Watan*
1939 166' b&w Hindi
d **Vijay Bhatt** *pc* Prakash Pics *s* Batuk Bhatt *dial/lyr* Sampatlal Srivastava 'Anuj' *c* G.N. Shirodkar *m* Shankarrao Vyas, Lallubhai Naik *lp* Jairaj, Mehtab, Shirin, Jal Writer, M. Zahoor, Lallubhai Naik, Bholaram, Faizy

The remake of Royal Film's silent *Badmash Ka Beta* (1933) is a typical example of Vijay Bhatt's stunt-film origins. Hero Samar (Jairaj) singlehandedly takes on the might of the oppressive state led by the warlord chief (M. Zahoor). He falls in love with the chief's sister Ila (Mehtab) and fights his revolution from the tavern of Dulari (Shirin) with little more than a band of adventurers, a leather face mask, his faithful dog Tiger, and horse Bahadur.

MALLI PELLI

1939 187' b&w Telugu
d/st **Y.V. Rao** *pc* Jagdish Films *dial/lyr* Balijepalli Lakshmikanta Kavi *m* Ogirala Ramchandra Rao
lp Y.V. Rao, Balijepalli Lakshmikanta Kavi, **Kanchanmala, Bezawada Rajarathnam**, Rangaswamy, K. Satyanarayana, Natesa Iyer, Manikyamma

Reformist melodrama about widow remarriage made to upstage **Vauhini**'s film on the same theme, ***Sumangali*** (1940). Villain Janardhanarao Panthulu has his 6-year-old daughter Lalitha married to an old man who dies shortly after. Lalitha (Kanchanmala) is brought up by her father under the strictures of widowhood. She meets the reformist Sundarrao (Y.V. Rao) who eventually defies tradition and marries her. Probably the first instance in Telugu cinema of the use of playback, according to music historian V.A.K. Ranga Rao, who also notes that it is the composer Ogirala who sings the duet with Kanchanmala, *Na sundara suruchira roopa*, although the record credits the male voice to hero Y.V. Rao.

MANOOS/ADMI

aka *Life is for the Living*
1939 160'[M]/164'[H] b&w Marathi/Hindi
d **V. Shantaram** *pc* **Prabhat Film** *st* A. Bhaskarrao *sc/dial/lyr*[M] Anant Kanekar *dial/lyr* Munshi Aziz[H] *c* V. Avadhoot *m* **Master Krishnarao**
lp **Shahu Modak, Shanta Hublikar**, Sundarabai, Budasaheb, Ram Marathe, Gauri, Manju, Narmada, Ganpatrao, **Raja Paranjpe**, Manajirao

Shantaram's classic adaptation of the Kammerspiel style is a love tragedy featuring a policeman, Ganpat[M]/Moti[H] (Modak) and a prostitute, Maina[M]/Kesar[H] (Hublikar). Ganpat saves Maina from a police raid on a brothel and they fall in love. Her reputation and sense of guilt resist his attempts to rehabilitate her. Ganpat's respectable middle-class mother (Sundarabai) symbolises all that Maina would like to be, but she is arrested for murdering her evil uncle and refuses Ganpat's offer to release her from prison. The film ends on a falsely positive tone with a song set to the rhythm of marching policemen. The film is shot entirely on sets including street corners, alleys, corridors, etc., and consists mainly of night scenes often in heavy shadows. The only location sequence is the film's romantic duet (*Hum premi premnagar mein jaayen*) as the loving couple blunder on to a film set. Shantaram uses the occasion to include a surprising spoof on the **Bombay Talkie** style of cinema: hero and heroine sit by a tree in a posture similar to **Ashok Kumar** and **Devika Rani** in the *Main ban ka panchhi* song of ***Achhut Kanya*** (1936), after which the Anglo-Indian heroine, who speaks and sings with an English accent, throws off her sari to walk away in Western dress. Shantaram deploys the expressionist technique of making physical spaces represent mental states, perhaps because Modak and Hublikar use a fairly restrained gestural repertoire rare in Shantaram's work. The film's classic number *Ab kis liye kal ki baat* (Hublikar's seduction number) is also a kind of spoof set in five different languages (Tamil, Telugu, Bengali, Gujarati and Punjabi in addition to its Marathi/Hindi refrain) alluding to familiar stereotypes from the corresponding film centres. There were suggestions that the plot was borrowed from Robert Sherwood's *Waterloo Bridge* (James Whale, 1931).

MATHRU BHOOMI

aka *Motherland*
1939 c.200' b&w Tamil
d **H.M. Reddy** *pc* **Vel** Pics, Al. Rm. Company, Madras *st* Dwijendralal Roy's play *Chandragupta* (1911) *c* E.R. Cooper *lyr* **Papanasam Sivan** *m* K. Subba Rao
lp T.S. Santhanam, **P.U. Chinappa**, Kali N. Rathnam, C.S.D. Singh, K.K. Permal, T.V. Kumudini, A.K. Rajalakshmi, P. Saradambal, M.S.J. Kamalam, Devulu Venkataraju

Reddy, the director of the first Tamil talkie (***Kalidas***, 1931), adapted Roy's important Bengali play for this nationalist allegory about an Indian king's resistance to Alexander the Great. It was briefly banned by the British. Greek general Seleucus Nicator, here called Minander (C.S.D. Singh), is left in charge by Alexander. He is opposed by Ugrasen (Santhanam), the king of Udaygiri and the founder (321BC) of the Maurya dynasty. Minander's daughter Helen (Rajalakshmi)

Shanta Hublikar in *Manoos*

falls in love with the king and eventually marries him after Minander has been defeated and returns to Greece. The real heroine is Kumudini, making her screen debut as a fiercely nationalist character of the same name who throws out her husband Jayapala (Santhanam again, in a dual role) when she learns that he is a Greek spy. Her brother Prathapan is played by the future star Chinappa. Although the costumes bear scant relation to history, the battle scenes are shot at the actual forts of Gingee and Krishnagiri in Tamil Nadu. Two songs proved particularly popular: *Bharatha desam* ('The Country of Bharat') and *Namadhu Janma bhoomi* ('The Land of our Birth'), the latter becoming a marching song widely used in schools.

NAVJEEVAN

1939 134' b&w Hindi
d **Franz Osten** *pc* **Bombay Talkies** *s* Saradindu Bannerjee *dial/co-lyr* J.S. Casshyap *co-lyr* L. Meghani, Narottam Vyas *c* Josef Wirsching *m* **Saraswati Devi**
lp **Hansa Wadkar**, Rama Shukul, V.H. Desai, Mumtaz Ali, Saroj Borkar, P.F. Pithawala, Rai Mohan, M. Nazir, Pratima, Lalita Devulkar

Osten followed ***Durga*** (1939) with this musical fantasy, giving Wadkar her first lead role in a big studio production. Although Mahendra (Shukul) belongs to a clan of proud warriors, he is a hypochondriac. This poses a problem when he woos Menaka (Wadkar) who is fixated on swashbuckling heroics and appears more impressed with Mahendra's rival Jeevan. The 'hero' overcomes his cowardice by taking a magic pill and dreaming that he is his own ancestor, overthrowing a band of robbers (led by Jeevan) and rescuing the damsel (Menaka). The enacted dream, which occupies most of the film's 2nd half, transforms the hero. Wadkar sings four songs in the film.

NETAJI PALKAR

1939 136' b&w Marathi
d/s/p/lyr **Bhalji Pendharkar** *pc* Arun Pics *c* Saju Naik *m* C. Balaji
lp **Lalita Pawar**, Bakulabai, Bhapurao Datar, **Master Vithal**, I.T. Nimbalkar, G.R. Sandow, Krishnarao Gote, Shahir Nanivadekar, Anandrao, Sheikh

The debut production of Pendharkar's Arun Pics is also the first of his major Maratha historicals focusing on Shivaji (cf ***Thoratanchi Kamala***, 1941; ***Chhatrapati Shivaji***, 1952). The villainous Subedar of Kalyan, in his effort to defeat 17th-C. Maratha emperor Shivaji, abducts a Maratha damsel (Pawar). However, Shivaji and his trusted lieutenant, the equally legendary Netaji Palkar, overcome this threat.

PUKAR

1939 151' b&w Urdu
d **Sohrab Modi** *pc* **Minerva Movietone** *s/lyr* **Kamal Amrohi** *c* Y.D. Sarpotdar *m* Mir Sahib
lp Sohrab Modi, **Chandramohan**, Naseem Banu, Sheela, **Sardar Akhtar**, Sadiq Ali

One of Kamal Amrohi's best-known scripts and the first of the megabudget epics characteristic of Modi and his Minerva Studio (***Sikandar***, 1941; ***Jhansi Ki Rani***, 1953). Set at the court of the harsh Mughal Emperor Jehangir (Chandramohan), the film tells two seperate love stories: the first of Mangal Singh (Ali) and Kanwar (Sheela) amid the violent feud raging between their families, and the second, the famous one of Jehangir and Nurjehan (Banu). Mangal kills the brother and father of his lover. His father, the loyal Rajput chieftain Sangram Singh (Modi), captures his son and Jehangir passes the death sentence. Jehangir's claim that the law knows no class distinction is put to the test when a washerwoman (Akhtar) accuses Queen Nurjehan of having inadvertently killed her husband during a hunt. Jehangir offers his own life but the washerwoman magnanimously forgives him. The queen and the emperor then in turn pardon Mangal Singh, thus proving that class position does count after all (or, since the film was made in 1939, suggesting that the death penalty should never be applied). The film was known mainly for some of the most spectacular scenes of palace grandeur in the Indian cinema.

RAITU BIDDA

1939 c.175' b&w Telugu
d/s **Gudavalli Ramabrahmam** *pc* Sarathi Films *lyr* **Kosaraju, Tapi Dharma Rao, Samudrala Raghavacharya** *m* **B. Narasimha Rao**
lp **Ballari Raghava**, G. Sitapathy, B. Narasimha Rao, Suribabu, Padmavati, **T. Suryakumari**, Nellore Nagaraja Rao, Sundaramma, **S. Varalakshmi**

Ramabrahmam's best-known work is a seminal reformist melodrama critiquing the zamindari system from the viewpoint of the Kisan Sabha agitations in rural AP. Small-time landowner Narsi Reddy borrows money from a shavukar (money-lender) who is also the major zamindar of the village. When Narsi Reddy votes for a peasant candidate rather than for the political party supported by the landlord, his son is attacked and he is publicly humiliated. Divine intervention in the form of a flood comes to the aid of the peasant. The film highlighted the ruling nexus of absentee landlords, the police and revenue authorities, and deployed several militant songs written by Kisan Sabha activist N. Venkatrama Naidu. Although it received a censor certificate, the film's release led to numerous protests by powerful zamindar groups; it was first banned in Nellore, then in Madras. The Bobbili and Venkatagiri royals threatened to sue the producer, who was also a member of the landed elite, while copies of the print were publicly burnt.

RAJAT JAYANTI

1939 140' b&w Bengali
d/s **P.C. Barua** *pc* **New Theatres** *lyr* Ajoy Bhattacharya *c* Sudhin Majumdar *m* **Rai Chand Boral**
lp P.C. Barua, **Pahadi Sanyal**, Bhanu Bannerjee, Sailen Choudhury, Dinesh Ranjan Das, Indu Mukherjee, Shore, Satya Mukherjee, Barin Das, Molina Devi, Menaka Devi

Barua's successful elaboration of a short comedy into a feature about intrigue and internecine warfare within families. The simple-minded Rajat (Barua) loves neighbour Jayanti (Molina Devi). He is advised on how to court her by his streetsmart cousin Bishwanath (Sanyal) and Bishwanath's friend Samir (Bannerjee). Bishwanath and Samir try to get Rajat's miserly guardian Bagalcharan (Choudhury) to loan them money so that Samir can make a 'European-style art film'. The guardian is admitted to the clinic of a doctor Gajanan (Ranjan Das) where he falls into the clutches of two professional crooks Natoraj (Indu Mukherjee) and Supta (Menaka Devi). Supta wants Rajat and they try to kidnap her but they are outsmarted. One of the best-known comedies of pre-war Indian film, this one reveals Barua's flair for comedy, most notably in the way he sends up his own established screen persona, introducing himself via a glamourously back-lit close-up, evoking his romantic ***Devdas*** (1935) and ***Mukti*** (1937) roles, but then revealing his character to be ridiculously inept and nervous in what may well be the star's most accomplished performance, ably supported by Sanyal, Molina Devi, Indu Mukherjee and Sailen Choudhury.

SACH HAI

aka *It's True*
1939 157' b&w Hindi
d/s **R.S. Choudhury** *pc* Saraswati Cinetone *dial* Niranjan Sharma Ajit *c* M.M. Purohit, S.P. Shinde *m* Suresh Babu
lp **Motilal**, Rose, Shakir, Sethi, Ramakrishna Choube, Chandani, Usha

A melodrama set in the holy city of Benares exploring issues of caste status. Chandan (Motilal) is the son of Kashipati, the head of an influential brahminical sect. His hedonistic brother Shripati (Sethi) wants to get his hands on the sect's assets while the evil Guru (Choube) - who publicly opposes Chandan's rebellions against traditional casteism - wants to abduct the poor Mangala (Chandani), daughter of a blind traveller. Chandan's declared love for Roopa (Rose), an Untouchable woman, causes major consternation. Adding to the drama is a scene of the flooding river, perceived as a kind of divine judgement for all the misdeeds in the name of religion.

SANT TULSIDAS

1939 154' b&w Hindi/Marathi
d **Jayant Desai** *pc* **Ranjit Movietone** *s/co-dial*[M] Shivram Vashikar *dial/lyr*[H] Indra, P.L. Santoshi *lyr*[M] S.A. Shukla *c* Krishna Gopal *m* **Vishnupant Pagnis**, Gyan Dutt
lp Vishnupant Pagnis, **Leela Chitnis, Keshavrao Date**, Vasanthi, Ram Marathe, Bandopant Sohoni, Dixit, Kantilal

Ranjit Studio's big-budget miracle-laden saint film on Tulsidas (16th C.) who rewrote Valmiki's *Ramayana* in Hindi. To the despair of his teacher Narahari Guru (Sohoni), who hopes that Tulsidas (Pagnis) will make the classic text accessible to the people, the poet spends time with his beloved wife Ratnavali (Chitnis). The dramatic pivot of the story comes when Tulsidas discovers his life's vocation amid howling wind and a river in spate. He becomes an ascetic and settles down in Benares where his translation threatens the brahminical clergy, until then sole proprietors of the wisdom of the Sanskrit text. Their representative, Batteshwar Shastri (Date), persecutes Tulsidas who is rescued through divine intervention. Ranjit hired both the actor Pagnis and the writer Vashikar of **Prabhat**'s classic ***Sant Tukaram*** (1936). Pagnis also scores the songs.

SAPUREY/SAPERA

aka *The Snake-charmer*
1939 123'[B]/128'[H] b&w Bengali/Hindi
d/sc **Debaki Bose** *pc* **New Theatres** *st/co-lyr*[B] **Kazi Nazrul Islam** *dial*[H] Lalchand Bismil *co-lyr* Ajoy Bhattacharya[B], **Kidar Sharma**[H] *c* Yusuf Mulji *m* **Rai Chand Boral**
lp **Pahadi Sanyal**, **Kanan Devi**, **K.C. Dey**, Menaka Devi, Shyam Laha, Satya Mukherjee, Manoranjan Bhattacharya[B]/Nawab[H], Rathin Bannerjee[B], Ahi Sanyal[B], Prafulla Mukherjee[B], **Prithviraj Kapoor**[H], Bikram Kapoor[H]

Primitivist love story set among the Shaivite clan of snake-charmers. Renowned snake-charmer Jahar (Bhattacharya/Nawab), the survivor of 99 snakebites thanks to rigorous self-discipline including sexual abstinence, rescues a young girl from snakebite and raises her as a boy called Chandan (Kanan Devi). As he starts feeling sexually attracted to 'him', the clan discovers that Jahar is sheltering a young woman and so they seek to depose him as chief. Meanwhile, the young Jhumro (Sanyal) elopes with Chandan and in a fit of fury Jahar sends a deadly snake in pursuit of the couple. The snake bites Jhumro and only Jahar's powers can save the boy, which poses a major dilemma for the patriarch.

SEVA SAMAJ

aka *Service Limited*
1939 145' b&w Hindi
d **Chimanlal Luhar** *pc* **Sagar Film** *co-dial* P. Razdan *co-dial/co-lyr* **Zia Sarhadi** *co-lyr* Indra *c* Keki Mistry *m* **Anupam Ghatak**
lp Maya Bannerjee, Surendranath, Bibbo, Yakub, Bhudo Advani, Sanktha Prasad

Heiress Shobhana Devi (Bannerjee) starts a campaign, with the help of the three trustees of her fortune, to capture the crook Jagmohandas (Yakub). They start a detective agency, Service Ltd, and take clients who have all been victims of Jagmohandas' criminal endeavours. Eventually, when Jagmohandas gets hold of an international trade treaty, Shobhana Devi dons a disguise, infiltrates the gang and captures the villain.

SHRI VENKATESHWARA MAHATYAM

aka *Balaji*
1939 171' b&w Telugu
d **P. Pullaiah** *pc* Famous Films *dial* D. Ramireddy *lyr* Buchanna Sastry, Vishwanathan *c* Machwe *m* Akula Narasimha Rao, B. Kumaraswamy
lp **C.S.R. Anjaneyalu**, Shantakumari, Rajeshwari Devi, Buchanna Sastry, T. Venkateshwarulu, Sanjiva Kumari, Nagmani, Nagamma

Pullaiah's original version of **N.T. Rama Rao**'s legendary 1960 film of the same title is a mythological about the life of the deity at Tirupati, notorious as India's richest temple shrine. Made at the Mahalakshmi Studio, Bombay, the film featured Pullaiah's wife and Telugu star Shantakumari as the consort of the 'Lord of the Seven Hills', Venkateshwara (Anjaneyalu).

SITARA

1939 169' b&w Hindi
d **Ezra Mir** *pc* Everest Pics *dial/lyr* Munshi Dil *c* P.G. Kukde *m* Rafiq Ghaznavi
lp Rattan Bai, Khurshid, Nazir, Mubarak, Jamshedji, Ashok Hussain, K.N. Singh, Sunalini

Romantic drama set in a fantasy version of a gypsy camp telling of an amorous rivalry spanning two generations. Azurie (Rattan Bai) marries Zamorra (Jamshedji) rather than his rival Eureka (Mubarak). Later, Zamorra accuses his wife of adultery with his rival and she dies in the 'dance of death' inflicted on her as punishment. Her infant daughter Sitara (Khurshid), abandoned in the forest, grows up as the adopted daughter of Suresh but is unable to reconcile her gypsy habits with bourgeois society: she paints canvasses with titles like 'Gypsy Blood'. She unknowingly gets embroiled in the ancestral rivalry when Eureka's wild son Tanzi (Nazir) falls in love with her and kidnaps her. The brutal tactic works and she marries him, which also leads her to discover her own ancestry.

THOKAR

aka *The Kick*
1939 161' b&w Hindi
d **A.R. Kardar** *pc* **Ranjit Movietone** *s* M. Sadiq *lyr* P.L. Santoshi *c* Gordhanbhai Patel *m* Gyan Dutt
lp Madhuri, Kumar, Charlie, Yakub, Ishwarlal, Wahidan, Dikshit, Ram Marathe, Suresh, K.N. Singh, Wasti

A cautionary tale about wealth not bringing happiness. The blind Mohan (Kumar) lives in a village with his ward Radha (Madhuri). He wins a fortune with a sweepstake ticket sold to him by the tramp Ramesh (Charlie), who claims his due and begins to take over Mohan's life, making him move to the city and getting him married to Chinta, a prostitute. When Mohan's eyesight is restored, he finds that his wife is having an affair with Ramesh. Mohan takes revenge and eventually lands up in his old village, a poor man, but with Radha still unchanged, waiting for him.

THYAGABHOOMI

aka *The Land of Sacrifice*
1939 194' b&w Tamil
d/p **K. Subramanyam** *pc* Madras United Artists *s* R. Krishnamurthy **[Kalki]** *c* Sailen Bose *m* **Papanasam Sivan**, Mothi Balan
lp S.D. Subbulakshmi, Papanasam Sivan, Baby Saroja, A.K. Kamalam, K.J. Mahadevan

Subramanyam's best-known film and Tamil cinema's biggest 30s hit is a spirited contribution to the Independence movement, deploying Gandhian themes. Sambhu Sastry (Sivan) is portrayed as the Gandhi of Tamil Nadu, sitting on a dais spinning with a charkha. The film includes inserts from documentary footage of Gandhi. The story, first published in the journal *Ananda Vikatan*, tells of Sastry the Brahmin priest and his daughter Savithri (Subbulakshmi). It opens with Harijans waiting in front of a closed temple during a cyclone. Sastry is punished for sheltering them and he goes to Madras where, together with the Harijan Nallan, he embarks on Gandhian social uplift programmes including picketing liquor shops. The main plot focuses on daughter Savithri, married to the evil Sridharan who prefers to live in

Papanasam Sivan (left), Baby Saroja (centre) and S.D. Subbulakshmi in *Thyagabhoomi*

'Western' luxury in Calcutta and mistreats his wife. Sastry, who sells his property to pay for the dowry, finds himself on the streets while his abandoned daughter, who returns to find her ancestral home gone, gives birth to a daughter Charu (Saroja) in a free hospital. Eventually Savithri becomes the wealthy Uma Rani, devoting herself to charity. In her new guise she rejects her husband who sues for the restoration of his 'marital rights'. She loses the case, but her husband sees the light and becomes a nationalist. In the end, Savithri is imprisoned for disregarding the court's verdict, preferring her life as a nationalist agitator. Outside her prison the national flag is raised. Pioneering the integration of melodrama with a symbol-laden political idiom later adopted by the **DMK film**, it has many scenes that resonate with local political meanings: the shot of Harijans standing outside the temple relates to the Temple Entry movement in the state; and footage of the Congress volunteers's march (which briefly caused the film to be banned) is presented as the will of the goddess Ambikai, repeatedly invoked in the film by the religious Sastry. The child Saroja, playing Sastry's granddaughter, had been launched in ***Balayogini*** (1936) and soon achieved legendary status.

VANDE MATARAM

aka *Mangalsutram*
1939 222' b&w Telugu
d/st **B.N. Reddi** from his short story *Mangalsutram* *pc* **Vauhini** Pics *sc/c* **K. Ramnoth** *dial/lyr* **Samudrala Raghavacharya** *m* **Chittor V. Nagaiah**
lp Chittor V. Nagaiah, **Kanchanmala**, Lingamurthy, Kalyani, Sheshamamba, Usha, Rani, **Sriranjini Sr**.

Vauhini's debut production is also that of the pioneering Telugu film-maker Reddi. The elaborate melodrama, based on Reddi's own unpublished short story, presented problems of uneven development in terms of an emotional conflict between an innocent feudal rural female and a worldly-wise capitalist urban male. Hero Raghu (Nagaiah), an unemployed graduate, insists on marrying the village girl Janaki (Kanchanmala) despite the opposition of his scheming mother who wants a dowry. Raghu's unemployment problems continue despite his migration to the city, leaving his wife in the clutches of her mother-in-law. When Raghu wins a lottery for Rs 5 lakhs and returns home, he finds his wife and infant son have left. Although his mother insists he marry again, Raghu goes to the city and dedicates himself to social work, including building factories in order to create employment opportunities. In this he is assisted by his rich female college friend, provoking gossip about their relationship. Raghu's wife, now a poor flower seller, sees her husband with his new friend and believes he has remarried. Eventually the misunderstanding is resolved. A major commercial hit, the film engages the agenda of the reform and nationalist movements: Raghu names a lottery-ticket seller Vande Mataram, meaning 'Hail to the mother' and one of India's national anthems, and tramples underfoot his 'foreign' degree in a scene that caused censorship problems. The film also introduces numerous stereotypes, e.g. the suave urban crook and the stage-struck villager (who marries the hero's sister).

VARAVIKRAYAM

1939 194' b&w Telugu
d **C. Pullaiah** *pc* **East India Film** *st* Kallakuri Narayanrao's play *dial/lyr* Balijepalli Lakshmikanta Kavi *c* Biren De *m* Durga Sen
lp Balijepalli Lakshmikanta Kavi, Daita Gopalam, K. Satyanarayana, M. Ramchandramurthy, T. Chalapathi Rao, A.V. Subba Rao, **Relangi Venkatramaiah**, **Sriranjini Sr**, Dasari Kotirathnam, Pushpavalli, **P. Bhanumathi**, Subhadra

Pullaiah, making Telugu films in Calcutta, abandons his usual mythologicals for this reformist social about the iniquitous dowry system. Although opposed to the dowry system, the retired government official Purshottama Rao borrows money to get his eldest daughter Kalindi (Bhanumathi) married, against her wishes, to the thrice-married Lingaraju. Kalindi commits suicide before the marriage can take place and when Lingaraju refuses to return the dowry, Purshottama's second daughter Kamala (Pushpavalli) agrees to marry him. Eventually she takes her husband and father-in-law to court, winning her point and restoring family honour while avenging her sister's death. Remembered mainly as the 16-year-old Telugu star Bhanumathi's screen debut, although she may have appeared earlier as a child actress.

VIMOCHANAM

1939 160' b&w Tamil
d A.N. Kalyanarayan *pc* Jaya Films, Hindustan Films *c* T. Marconi

Tamil reformist melodrama probably directed as well as shot by the Italian cameraman T. Marconi. The film took up Gandhi's call for temperance, adopted in Tamil Nadu following the Salem Congress. The plot has the male lead, Arumugham, sell his wife's jewellery to buy alcohol until prohibition in the Salem district offers much-needed relief. The hero goes to jail for trying to brew liquor illicitly. On his release, he finds the liquor shop has become a tea-stall and his wife destitute, leading to his reform. The film featured girl students from the Sangeetha Vidyalaya high school.

ABHINETRI/HAAR JEET

1940 131' b&w Bengali/Hindi
d/sc **Amar Mullick** *pc* **New Theatres** *st* Upendranath Ganguly *dial* **Pashupati Chatterjee**[B], Parimal Ghosh, A.H. Shore[H] *lyr* Munshi Arzoo, **Kidar Sharma**[H] *c* **Bimal Roy** *m* **Rai Chand Boral**
lp **Kanan Devi**, **Pahadi Sanyal**, Meera Dutta, **Chhaya Devi**, Sailen Choudhury[B], Bhanu Roy[B], Indu Mukherjee[B], Santosh Sinha[B], Harimohan Bose[B], Biren Pal[B], Boken Chatto[B], Naresh Bose[B], Benoy Goswami[B]; Nawab[H], Nemo[H], Pannalal[H], Madho Shukla[H], Arvind[H]

A vehicle for the vocal talents of Sanyal and Kanan Devi set in the early 20th-C. **Calcutta Theatres** industry. Kamala (Kanan Devi) is the star of the Ruby Theatre owned by her guardian Maheshbabu. Narendra (Sanyal) is the equally popular star in the rival Bina Theatre, which he abandons to join the Ruby repertory when he falls in love with Kamala. In a lyrical sequence in the countryside, they marry in a poor peasant setting. Narendra then shows his true colours and forbids Kamala to continue her acting career. She returns to the stage anyway while Narendra stays among the peasants. He later returns to the Bina Theatre and its success is intercut with the bankrupcy of the Ruby Theatre. Kamala's symbolic punishment for refusing to become a dutiful housewife ministering to her man's needs is worked through the conduit of establishing the moral superiority of a lyrical/utopian peasantry against the corrupt city.

ACHHUT

aka *The Untouchable*
1940 141' b&w Hindi/Gujarati
d/s **Chandulal Shah** *pc* **Ranjit Film** *lyr* P.L. Santoshi *c* Krishna Gopal *m* Gyan Dutt
lp **Gohar**, **Motilal**, Vasanthi, Charlie, Rajkumari, **Sitara Devi**, Mazhar Khan, Dixit, T. Kapur, Lala Yakub, Bhupatrai, Ibrahim

Promoted as a nationalist film addressing Gandhi's anti-untouchability campaign, it was endorsed by Gandhi and Vallabhbhai Patel even before it was made. Denied access to a well reserved for the upper castes, Lakshmi's (Gohar) Harijan father turns Christian while his wife prefers to remain a Hindu. Lakshmi is adopted by a rich businessman, becomes friends with his daughter Savita, completes her education and finds social acceptance in the urban upper class. When both Lakshmi and Savita fall in love with the same man, Savita's father resolves the matter by sending Lakshmi back to her impoverished Harijan family where she meets her childhood friend Ramu (Motilal) and together they lead the Harijans' revolt. Lakshmi is jailed, her best friend falls ill and her boyfriend dies, but eventually the village temple is opened to all castes.

APNI NAGARIYA

aka *Mud*
1940 144' b&w Hindi
d/p Dada Gunjal *pc* Hindustan Cinetone, Gunjal Prod *st* **Sadat Hasan Manto** *dial* S. Khalil *lyr* Safdar 'Aah', Indra *c* S. Hardip *m* Rafiq Ghaznavi
lp **Shobhana Samarth**, Nazir, Jayant, Singh, Madhavi, Shanta Dutt, Majid, Keki Bawa, Bibi, Baby Sushila

Manto's reformist story tells of Sushila (Samarth), the daughter of the authoritarian factory owner Seth Ramdas who is in conflict with militant workers led by Keshav. Sushila is caught up in an angry confrontation and rescued by the worker Prithvi, who is victimised by the management for his action. In love with her, he nurses her during a plague epidemic when her own family deserts her, but she spurns his attentions and later becomes a tool in the exploitative hands of her fiance Shambhu, who declares a factory lock-out. The disillusioned Prithvi becomes a dangerous hoodlum. To solve her own problems, Sushila must first acknowledge the injustice of the class divide.

ARDHANGI/GHAR KI RANI
aka *The Better Half*
1940 152'[M]/161'[H] b&w Marathi/Hindi
d **Master Vinayak** *pc* Huns Pics *s/dial/lyr*[M] **P.K. Atre** *dial/lyr*[H] Indra *c* Pandurang Naik *m* Dada Chandekar
lp Master Vinayak, Meenakshi, **Baburao Pendharkar, Damuanna Malvankar, Leela Chitnis**

Huns Pics' last film transferred the *Mahabharata* Savitri tale about marital devotion to a modern Maharashtrian middle-class setting exploiting anti-Western feelings to advocate a traditionalist misogynist ideology. Satyavan (Vinayak), a university professor, admires the beautiful, English-speaking and cigarette-smoking Arundhati (Chitnis), wife of a colleague. He hires a tutor to train his own wife Savitri (Meenakshi) in Western manners. When Satyavan succeeds in having an affair with Arundhati, she humiliates him by making him do domestic chores and then abandons him for the rich Z. Marutrao (Pendharkar). Satyavan finally comes to his senses and asks the gods to intervene, which reunites him with the faithful Savitri.

AURAT
aka *Woman*
1940 154' b&w Hindi
d **Mehboob Khan** *pc* National Studios *st* Babubhai A. Mehta *dial* Wajahat Mirza *lyr* Safdar 'Aah' *c* Faredoon Irani *m* **Anil Biswas**
lp **Sardar Akhtar**, Surendra, Yakub, Jyoti, Harish, Arun, Vatsala Kumthekar, Brij Rani

The original version of Mehboob's classic ***Mother India*** (1957). The heroine Radha (Akhtar) works her fingers to the bone to pay off the villainous moneylender Sukhilala. She and husband Shamu (Arun) have three sons, and when she gets pregnant yet again Shamu removes himself from the scene and leaves her to battle against starvation and the advances of the villain. The two eldest sons die, leaving Radha with the diligent Ramu (Surendra) and her favourite, temperamental Birju (Yakub) who goes astray and becomes a bandit chieftain, which causes the family to be ostracised by the village. Birju murders Sukhilala and attempts to abduct his childhood sweetheart, Tulsi (Brij Rani). Radha then kills her son. The film lacks the psychoanalytic dimension and the overtones of socialist realism present in its famous remake, but Akhtar's extraordinary performance endows it with an earthiness rooted in North Indian agrarian feudalism that seems to be missing from *Mother India*'s attempt at nationalist allegory.

AZAD
1940 140' b&w Hindi
d **N.R. Acharya** *pc* **Bombay Talkies** *st* Saradindu Bannerjee *dial/lyr* J.S. Casshyap *c* R.D. Pareenja *m* **Saraswati Devi**, Ramchandra Pal
lp **Leela Chitnis, Ashok Kumar, Hansa Wadkar**, Rama Shukul, Mumtaz Ali, Nazir Bedi, Arun, Ramchandra Pal, D.V. Surve

For his directorial debut, scripted by **Osten**'s regular collaborator Casshyap, Acharya orchestrates an allegory of contemporary political attitudes presented in terms of differing approaches to the institutionalisation of sexuality: marriage. There are three college friends: the liberal Vijay, the conservative Loknath and Jagdish, a careerist. Vijay rescues a damsel in distress and marries her. Later, his son Anand repeats his father's history by rescuing Jagdish's daughter from a bandit and marrying her, resolving the differences between the three friends. The film was overshadowed by the spectacular success of Acharya's ***Bandhan*** that same year, but its commentative approach to contemporary politics was further elaborated in his ***Naya Sansar*** (1941).

BANDHAN
1940 154' b&w Hindi
d **N.R. Acharya** *pc* **Bombay Talkies** *p* S. Mukherjee *sc* **Gyan Mukherjee, Amiya Chakravarty** *dial* J.S. Casshyap *lyr* Pradeep *c* R.D. Parineeja *m* **Saraswati Devi**, Ramchandra Pal
lp **Leela Chitnis, Ashok Kumar**, Suresh, P.F. Pithawala, V.H. Desai, Shah Nawaz, Purnima Desai, Jagannath, Arun Kumar

Acharya followed ***Azad*** (1940) with this tale about Beena (Chitnis), the daughter of the zamindar (Pithawala). Beena is to marry Suresh (Shah Nawaz) but loves Nirmal (Ashok Kumar), the head of a village school funded by the zamindar. Suresh and his father Gokul try to blackmail Nirmal and eventually accuse him of murdering Gauri (P. Desai), daughter of schoolteacher Bholanath (V.H. Desai), who is actually killed by Suresh. Producer S. Mukherjee adapted the by-now standard Bombay Talkies type of orientalist fiction about Indian feudalism into simplified, single-location melodramas, a virtually infallible formula both there and at **Filmistan**. This commercial hit is enlivened mainly by the songs performed by the actors themselves, esp. Ashok Kumar's full-throated *Chal chal re naujawan*, Arun Kumar's *Chana jor garam* and several Leela Chitnis numbers (e.g. *Manabhavan, lo sawan aya re, Apne bhaiya ko naach nachaoongi*).

BHAROSA
1940 147' b&w Hindi
d **Sohrab Modi** *pc* **Minerva Movietone** *s/lyr* Lalchand Bismil *c* Y.D. Sarpotdar *m* G.P. Kapoor
lp **Chandramohan, Sardar Akhtar**, Mazhar Khan, Sheela, Maya Devi, Naval, Eruch Tarapore, Gulab, Menaka, Abubakar

Modi's tale of incest starts when Gyan (Khan) goes to Africa and entrusts his wife Shobha (Akhtar) to his bosom pal Rasik (Chandramohan). The two have an affair resulting in the child Indira (Sheela). On his return, Gyan assumes the child to be his and he is delighted when later she falls in love with Rasik's son Madan (Naval), much to Rasik and Shobha's consternation. As in his other social melodramas (e.g. ***Jailor***, 1938 and 1958), Modi deploys a pathological sexuality to present feudal values as laws of nature.

BHUKAILASA
1940 c.185' b&w Telugu
d **Sundarrao Nadkarni** *pc* Saraswati Cine Films *st* **R. Nagendra Rao**'s play *Bhukailasa* *dial* Balijepalli Lakshmikanta Kavi *m* R. Sudarshanam
lp R. Nagendra Rao, **M.V. Subbaiah Naidu**, Lakshmibai, Kamalabai, Master Vishwam

Second and, to some, best-known film version of the *Ramayana* episode staged earlier by R. Nagendra Rao. Sundarrao Nadkarni's adaptation of his earlier Tamil film was one of the hits produced by **A.V. Meiyappan** before setting up the **AVM Film** Studio. The film, which Randor Guy describes as a unique collaboration between a Tamil producer, Marathi director, Telugu scenarist and Kannada actors, was initially a failure when released at Bezwada, but then went on to become one of the biggest commercial successes of the year. AVM remade it as a high-profile trilingual in 1958. For the plot, cf ***Bhukailasa***, 1958.

CHANDIKA
1940 184' b&w Telugu
d **R.S. Prakash** *pc* Bhawani Pics *st* Alexandre Dumas's *Three Musketeers* *c* Kamal Ghosh *m* Kopparapu Subbarao
lp **P. Kannamba, Vemuri Gaggaiah, Ballari Raghava**, Lalitha Devi, Peddapuram Raju, Arani Satyanarayana, Puvvula Ratnamala

The forthright Chandika (Kannamba) plans to kill villainous womaniser Giriraju (Gaggaiah). Although she decides to do so on principle, she attempts the deed only when he tries to molest her. He is rescued by Veeramallu (Raghava) who has him jailed. Unusual melodrama loosely derived from Dumas's novel and set in an undefined feudal era where royalty survives amid democratic state institutions. Although rehearsing the usual pieties about Hindu women, the film is remembered for its unorthodox heroine.

DHARMAPATNI
aka *Pativrata*
1940 170' b&w Telugu/Tamil
d **P. Pullaiah** *pc* Famous Films *st* **V.S. Khandekar**'s story *dial* **Chakrapani** *lyr* Daita Gopalam *c* S.K. Pai *m* Annasaheb Mainkar, **Timir Baran**
lp Shantakumari, **P. Bhanumathi**, Peddappuram Raju, Lakshminarasimha, Hemalatha, Hanumantha Rao, **A. Nageshwara Rao**, Adinarayanaiah, Achari, Himam

Elaborate melodrama with several typical Khandekar characters: the good prostitute, the irredeemably evil man, the vacillating youth. The prostitute Sridevi, charged with looking after the orphaned Radha, arranges for Radha's marriage to Mohan. The evil Ananda Rao, who covets Radha, reveals Sridevi's past to Mohan's father and the wedding is called off. Mohan marries the independent-minded Uma, and when he is framed for murder by Ananda Rao it is Uma who eventually brings the original couple together. Shot in Kolhapur for a Bombay-based film company, the film derives from e.g. Marathi cinema's Huns Pics, adapted into Telugu by scenarist Chakrapani (making his film debut). It is also remembered as Telugu superstar A. Nageshwara Rao's first film, as a teenage actor.

DIAMOND QUEEN

1940 155' b&w Hindi
d **Homi Wadia** *pc* **Wadia Movietone** *s* **J.B.H. Wadia** *dial/lyr* Munshi Sham *c* R.P. Master *m* Madhavlal D. Master
lp **Fearless Nadia**, John Cawas, Radha Rani, Sayani, Nazira, Fatma, Sardar Mansur, Dalpat, Kunjru, Boman Shroff, Minoo the Mystic

Nadia is Madhurika who, flanked by her horse Punjab-ka-Beta, her sidekick the reformed brigand Diler (Cawas), and her magic car Rolls-Royce-ki-Beti, cleans up Diamond Town. Like ***Hunterwali*** (1935), ***Miss Frontier Mail*** (1936) and ***Carnival Queen*** (1955), this is a stunt film featuring all Nadia's Zorro-like swashbuckling skills, including the obligatory fight atop a speeding carriage. Its expressionist beginning, showing distorted facial close-ups, leads on to several theatrical devices, e.g. the extensive use of back-projection when the house burns down, or later when Nadia and Cawas are saved by her horse from a waterfall in spate. Several indigenous symbols, like the glorified Bajrang, the Swastika (a tantric symbol) and physical exercises resembling those of Hanuman devotees are intended to contrast the obvious Western origins of the Wadias' stunt idiom. Nadia performed her own stunts in this film combining elements from westerns, serials and sword-fighting pictures. Her difficulties with Hindi required her dialogues to be kept to a minimum.

GEETA

1940 163'[M]/164'[H] b&w Marathi/Hindi
d/sc **P.Y. Altekar** *pc* CIRCO *st* Minoo Katrak *dial/lyr* Mama Warerkar[M], S.K. Kalla[H] *c* Govardhanbhai Patel *m* Datta Koregaonkar [K. Dutta]
lp **Chandramohan**, **Durga Khote**, Anant Marathe, S. Prahlad, Keki Bawa, Ashalata, Vatsala Kumthekar, Trilok Kapoor

The Marathi stage personality and film-maker Altekar's moral fable about the law. The naive, saintly Durga (Khote) uses the *Bhagavad Gita* as an ethical guidebook while her husband Shankar and later her son Mohan (Chandramohan in both roles) become professional villains. When her second son Kumar (Kapoor), an English-trained lawyer, returns he becomes a public prosecutor. He finds he must prosecute his own brother. Subplots include Sundari (Kumthekar), Mohan's prostitute girlfriend whose pimp Keshavlal (Prahlad) killed Mohan's father and whose sister Lata (Ashalata) is Durga's disciple. The dialogues and songs of the Marathi version were written by major Marathi playwright Warerkar.

GNANAMBIKA

aka *Jnanambika* aka *Raga Leela*
1940 c.190' b&w Malayalam
d S. Nottani *pc* Shyamala Pics *s* C. Madhavan Pillai from his novel *lyr* Puthankavu Mathan Tharakan
lp Sebastian Kunju Kunju Bhagavathar, C.K. Rajam, Aleppey Vincent, M.V. Shankar, K.K. Aroor, C. Madhavan Pillai, Chellappan Pillai, A.B. Pious, P.K. Kamalakshi, T.A. Rose, L. Ponnamma, C.A. Seetalakshmi, K. Ammini, C. Lakshmikutty, C.P. Devaki

Made at the Newtone Studio, Madras, this was after ***Balan*** (1938) the director's 2nd effort to capture the Malayalam market on behalf of his Tamil backers. The plot is similar to its predecessor with an unscrupulous second wife of a mild-mannered husband, who exploits his daughter by his first marriage. The wife and her lover want to appropriate the husband's property. Eventually the wife is brought to justice and Gnanambika, the daughter, marries in traditional style. The film, using extensive outdoor locations from the Trivandrum zoo and museum complex, was succesful. The lyrics by Puthankavu Mathan Tharakan were the first instance of a noted Malayalam poet writing verse for the cinema. ***Prahladan*** (1941) was the third in the venture of Tamil producers entering the Malayalam market.

HINDUSTAN HAMARA

aka *Our India*
1940 136' b&w Hindi
d Ram Daryani *pc* Film Corp of India *lyr* Arzoo *m* Bhishmadev Chatterjee
lp Jamuna, Padmadevi, Nandrekar, Gope, Hari Shivdasani, Badri Prasad, Ram Dulari, Rajendra, Dewaskar

Feudal melodrama: Veena (Jamuna), daughter of an exploitative landlord and wife of the drunkard Chunilal (Shivdasani), defies her family and fights for the exploited peasantry. In the process she falls in love with the poor Madhu (Nandrekar). When her evil husband cannot undermine the peasants' unity he commits suicide. The heroine is disinherited by her father, but remains committed to nationalism. The film prominently deploys Gandhian symbols (e.g. the spinning-wheel), and contrasts an idyllic notion of erstwhile India to the penury of its people today.

HOLI

1940 137' b&w Hindi
d **A.R. Kardar** *pc* **Ranjit Movietone** *s/dial* M. Sadiq *lyr* D.N. Madhok *c* Krishna Gopal *m* **Khemchand Prakash**
lp **Motilal**, Khurshid, Ishwarlal, **Sitara Devi**, **Keshavrao Date**, Dixit, Ghory, Lala Yakub, Tarabai, Manohar Kapoor

A Motilal star vehicle featuring him as a villain turning into a good guy. The evil Chand (Motilal) and his rich father Mangaldas (Date) persecute the nice Sunder (Ishwarlal): he kidnaps Sunder's sister Kokila (Khurshid) and frames him for theft. Sunder is jailed. The abducted Kokila succumbs to the villain's charms and her love reforms him. When released, Sunder, unaware of the fact that his enemy has reformed, seeks revenge on the very day that Chand and Kokila are to marry.

KUMKUM/KUMKUM THE DANCER

1940 150'[B]/142'[H] b&w Bengali/Hindi
d **Modhu Bose** *pc* **Sagar Film** *st* Manmatha Ray *dial*[H] W.Z. Ahmed *lyr*[H] Sudarshan *c* Jaigopal Pillai *m* **Timir Baran**
lp **Sadhona Bose**, **Dhiraj Bhattacharya**, Priti Majumdar, Padmadevi, Moni Chatterjee, Shashadhar Chatterjee, Lalit Roy, Binita Gupta, Labanya Palit, Abani Mitra, Rabi Ray[B], Bhujanga Ray[B], Kira Devi[B], Jasobant Agashi[B], Shanta Majumdar[B], Bechu Singha[B], M. Ishaq[H], Kamta Prasad[H], Bhudo Advani[H], Kayamali[H], Jamu Patel[H], Kamal[H], Agashe[H]

Dance film idealising poverty made mainly to showcase Bose's talents. Labour leader Suryashankar is jailed for trade union activities and, when released, finds that his friend Jagdish has stolen his property and plagiarised his play *Bhookh* (*Hunger*). To take revenge on behalf of the poor, Suryashankar's daughter Kumkum (Bose) marries Jagdish's son Chandan (Bhattacharya). Later she collaborates in staging a play meant to expose Jagdish's evil past. The film's publicity slogan was 'She robbed her husband to feed the poor!'

LAGNA PAHAVE KARUN

1940 150' b&w Marathi
d **Master Vinayak** *pc* **Navyug Chitrapat** *st* C.V. Joshi's short story *sc/dial/co-lyr* **V.S. Khandekar** *co-lyr* B.R. Tambe *c* Pandurang Naik *m* Dada Chandekar
lp **Damuanna Malvankar**, V. Jog, Shakuntala Bhome, Vasant Eric, Vatsala Kumthekar, Damayanti Joshi
Navyug Chitrapat started with Vinayak's first adaptation of C.V. Joshi's popular satires featuring the bumbling duo Chimanrao (Malvankar's best-known film role) and Gundyabhau (Jog). In order to marry off his sister Chimni, Chimanrao must first get married himself but he is tricked by his prospective father-in-law. He then arranges a marriage between Chimni and a post office clerk who soon turns into a routinely selfish male. Shot mainly as a comedy about arranged marriages in early 20th-C. feudal Maharashtra, the film has a loose, episodic narrative with Gundyabhau addressing the viewer directly in the beginning and at the end. Much of it concerns 'traditional' attitudes evoked through e.g. technological novelties like still photography (the girl's photograph to show to her prospective groom is taken in flat tones and a characteristic **Ravi Varma**-like posture), through caricatures of other communities (e.g. the Gujarati businessman from Kathiawar, the Englishman) and sometimes through the music (the sister knows one devotional song to show off her voice to elderly people and one love song if her audience is young).

LAPANDAV

1940 133' b&w Marathi
d **K. Narayan Kale** *pc* **Navyug Chitrapat** *s/lyr* **P.K. Atre** *c* Pandurang Naik *m* Dada Chandekar

lp **Baburao Pendharkar**, **Master Vinayak**, Dada Salvi, Bapurao Pawar, Vanamala, Meenakshi

Comedy representing the best years of the Atre-Vinayak-Pendharkar combination at Navyug and addressing cultural modernisation problems in feudal Maharashtra. The crusty patriarch Raobahadur has two beautiful daughters. Both fall in love with men beneath their father's social standing: one wants to marry an instructor at a driving school, the other falls for a building contractor.

NARSI BHAGAT

1940 179' b&w Hindi
d **Vijay Bhatt** *pc* Prakash Pics *st* **Mohanlal G. Dave** *sc* Vishnupant Aundhkar *lyr* Sampatlal Srivastava 'Anuj', Balam *c* G.N. Shirodkar *m* Shankarrao Vyas
lp **Vishnupant Pagnis**, **Durga Khote**, Pande, V. Adikhar, Vimala Vasishta, Amirbai Karnataki, Ram Marathe, Baby Indira

Vijay Bhatt's **Saint film** was built around Pagnis who had defined the genre through his performance in ***Sant Tukaram*** (1936). Narasinh Mehta (1408-75), a major Gujarati poet (Pagnis), is excluded from the community and, with his wife Manekbai, lives in extreme deprivation in Junagadh and Mangrol. His poems praising Krishna, often in the erotic and devotional Ras Lila form, also address the condition of Untouchables. Much of the film is based on his autobiographical statements which have now become part of popular legend. Key figures including his wife Manekbai (Khote), his evil sister-in-law, and her brother Sarangadhar (Pande), who persecute him. The film also features the Dewan of Warnagar, who chooses Narasinh's son as the groom for his daughter. The plot requires Narasinh to sacrifice his son to save the prince as well as defend himself against accusations of sorcery. Bhatt's largely descriptive camera emphasises physical movement while the elaborate set design contrasts with the sophisticated use of frontal shooting in *Sant Tukaram*. Apart from several Pagnis solos, other songs are by Amirbai Karnataki (esp. *Jhulna jhulave nandalal*) and one is by the young Ram Marathe (*Ghanshyam rang ran javoon*).

NARTAKI

1940 133'[B]/150'[H] b&w Bengali/Hindi
d/s **Debaki Bose** *pc* **New Theatres** *dial*[H] A.H. Shore *lyr* Ajoy Bhattacharya[B], Munshi Arzoo[H] *c* Yusuf Mulji *m* **Pankaj Mullick**
lp Leela Desai, Bhanu Bannerjee[B], Sailen Choudhury[B], **Chhabi Biswas**[B], Utpal Sen[B], Pankaj Mullick[B], Indu Mukherjee[B], Jyoti[B], Naresh Bose[B], Najam[H], Jagdish Sethi[H], R. Wasti[H], R.P. Kapoor[H], Nandkishore[H], Dhruba Kumar[H], Rajani Rani[H], Kalabati[H]

Period movie apparently set in the 16th C. The story pits the famous dancer Roopkumari (Desai), backed by the court, against a temple monastery ruled by the authoritarian ascetic priest Gyanananandji. The temple forbids the entry of women and Roopkumari is determined to avenge such an insult. She seduces the priest's son Satyasunder but she also falls in love with him. The film suggests that love transcends both political and religious authoritarianism. The Bengali version uses extensive songs by the 15th-C. Bengali saint poet Chandidas.

PAGAL

1940 142' b&w Hindi
d/s **A.R. Kardar** *pc* **Ranjit Movietone** *lyr* D.N. Madhok, P.L. Santoshi *c* Krishna Gopal *m* **Khemchand Prakash**
lp Madhuri, **Prithviraj Kapoor**, Charlie, Khatoon, **Sitara Devi**, Lala Yakub

Kardar went against the studio's usual brand of family melodrama with this story about a psychotic doctor in an asylum. Tricked into marrying Chhaya (Khatoon), believing he is to marry her more beautiful sister Parvati (Madhuri), Dr Vasant (Kapoor) becomes a sexually obsessed maniac who injects Parvati with a drug that renders her insane. He then keeps her in his asylum where he continues to brutalise her. Intended as a critique of resurgent neo-traditionalism among the educated younger generation, the grotesque depiction of masculinity associated with modern medicine severely undercuts the implied critique of the methods used to arrange marriages, while women simply remain victims. In fact, the victimisation of women is portrayed with such gusto that the film ends up raising more disturbing questions about the way grotesque masculine sexuality pervades the very fabric of the film. Kardar's ***Pooja*** (also 1940) offers a more considered treatment of the ravages wrought by feudal sexual codes.

POOJA

1940 191' b&w Hindi-Urdu
d **A.R. Kardar** *pc* National Studios *st/dial* M. Sadiq *lyr* Khan Shatir Ghaznavi *c* P.G. Kukde *m* **Anil Biswas**
lp **Sardar Akhtar**, **Sitara Devi**, Zahur Raja, Jyoti, Sankatha, Satish, Sunalini Devi, Bhudo Advani

In contrast to his lurid depiction of women's suffering under feudal patriarchy in ***Pagal*** (1940), Kardar achieves a more complex treatment of sexual oppression in rural North India via Sadiq's script. It was made the same year and by the same studio as **Mehboob**'s ***Aurat***, also starring Akhtar. *Pooja* tells of two lonely sisters, Rama (Akhtar) and Lachhi (Sitara Devi), giving vent to their frustrations by persecuting each other. When Rama's wedding to Darpan (Raja) falls through and she marries another, Darpan rapes Lachhi in revenge, although the rape is presented ambiguously, suggesting she might be complicit in wanting to take something from her sister. Lachhi has a child, Bina (Jyoti), and ends up living with her sister, the now widowed Rama. Bina is led to believe that Rama is her mother. Only later does Bina realise her real mother was her aunt's servant. Kardar's film set the tone for Mehboob's later and better-known depictions of crumbling family relations and thwarted sexualities. It is more ambitious than Mehboob's work of the time, with a fairly sparing use of melodramatic effects. The theme evoked radical Urdu literature's critiques of feudal sexual mores, placed on the official literary agenda after the 1936 **PWA** conference whence writers like **Ismat Chughtai** drew their initial inspiration.

SANT DNYANESHWAR

1940 139' b&w Marathi/Hindi
d **V. Damle**, **S. Fattelal** *pc* **Prabhat Film** *s* Shivram Vashikar *dial*[H] Anand *lyr* **Shantaram Athavale**[M], P.L. Santoshi, Mukhram Sharma 'Ashant'[H] *c* V. Avadhoot *m* **Keshavrao Bhole**
lp **Shahu Modak**, **Datta Dharmadhikari**, Pandit, Malati, Tamhankar, Shanta Majumdar, Sumati Gupte, Bhagwat

An effort to repeat the success of ***Sant Tukaram*** (1936) with a bigger budget and enlarged canvas. Dnyaneshwar (1275-96) was the first of the Marathi saint poets and wrote the *Dnyaneshwari* as a commentary of the *Bhagavad Gita* in the rhythm of the ovi form, using popular language for the first time in Marathi literature, the culmination of the regional literary works that emerged throughout India after the 7th C. More closely associated with the performance of miracles than Tukaram or Eknath, Dnyaneshwar's exploits are narrated in the keertan form of religious storytelling. Crowd scenes, elaborate sets and complicated miracle scenes (shot by Pralhad Dutt and Harbans) signal the film's spectacular ambitions. Like the directors' last saint film, ***Sant Sakhu*** (1941), this effort at times finds an effective *mise en scene* using frontally shot imagery while allowing the action to expand around the fixed point of the god's position which, as the film progresses, Dnyaneshwar (Modak) gradually comes to occupy.

SUMANGALI

1940 194' b&w Telugu
d **B.N. Reddi** *pc* **Vauhini** Pics *st/c* **K. Ramnoth** *dial/lyr* **Samudrala Raghavacharya** *m* **Chittor V. Nagaiah**
lp Chittor V. Nagaiah, Giri, Kumari, Malathi, Lingamurthy, Sheshamamba, Doraiswamy

This typical Vauhini melodrama is made by the unit responsible for Rohini's ***Grihalakshmi*** (1938): writer/cameraman Ramnoth, designer A.K. Sekhar, scenarist Raghavacharya and composer/lead star Nagaiah. Mobilising one of reformism's main motifs, widow remarriage, the film tells of the progressive Sathyam (Giri) who is loved by two women: his rustic cousin Parvati (Malathi) and the educated, fashionable and rich Saraswathi (Kumari). When Saraswathi discovers that she had been married and widowed as a child, preventing her from marrying again, all three protagonists are plunged into emotional turmoil. Eventually Parvati sacrifices her life so that Sathyam and Saraswathi can marry after all. Making plentiful use of symbols (e.g. the crucifix when Saraswathi is the victim of attempted rape), the film apparently drew inspiration from the Telugu reformist writer Kandakuri Veerashaligram Panthulu (1848-1919) (Nagaiah plays a white-haired character called Panthulu).

Despite innovative camerawork and several musical hits by Nagaiah (e.g. *Ada grathuke madhuram*, *Pasupukunkuma*), the film flopped when first released, almost sinking the Vauhini Studio.

THIKADAR

1940 c.145' b&w Bengali
d Prafulla Roy *pc* Shri Bharatlaxmi Pics *s/m* Tulsi Lahiri *c* Bibhuti Das
lp Tulsi Lahiri, **Durgadas Bannerjee**, **Jiban Ganguly**, Satya Mukherjee, Renuka Roy, Chitra Devi, Kamala Jharia, Santosh Sinha, Rabi Ray, Sudhir Mitra, Girin Chakraborty

Melodrama featuring a thikadar (forest contractor), a somewhat remote figure like the landscape in which he operates. The villain is the plantation-owner named Abani Haldar, with a beautiful daughter, Latika. The thikadar saves Haldar in an accident, while later it is revealed that Haldar killed the thikadar's father and left his wife and children for dead. Latika, who loves the thikadar, succeeds in preventing the forester from taking revenge for those crimes. The playwright Tulsi Lahiri, an influential figure who helped introduce realism to the post-WW2 Bengali theatre with plays like *Chhenra Tar*, *Pathik* and *Dukhir Iman* (the latter two were also filmed, in 1939/1953 and 1954 respectively), wrote, scored and acted in this film noted for its extensive location shooting and crowd scenes showing the lives of plantation workers.

VISHWAMOHINI

1940 195' b&w Telugu
d/st **Y.V. Rao** *pc* Jagdish Pics *dial/lyr* Balijepalli Lakshmikanta Kavi *m* Ogirala Ramchandra Rao
lp Y.V. Rao, **Chittor V. Nagaiah**, Lalitha Devi, **Bezawada Rajarathnam**, Rangaswamy, Kakinada Rajarathnam, Doraswamy, Gangarathnam, Sampurna, Suryanarayana

A love triangle satirising the film industry. Purshottam (Y.V. Rao) embezzles money from a firm of brokers owned by Padmanabham in order to get his son Mohan Rao married to Hemalatha, daughter of the millionaire Vishalakshamma (B. Rajarathnam). The now impoverished Padmanabham partially gets his own revenge when his daughter Sushila (Lalitha Devi) becomes the film star Vishwamohini, introduced by the film producer Pashupati, brother of Vishalakshamma. The star Vishwamohini falls in love with Mohan Rao and her father agrees to their marriage provided Mohan can find a job. He pretends to have done so and the two get married. Hemalatha offers Vishwamohini money to go away and free Mohan, which, in an emotional scene, she refuses to do. The hit film continued director/star Y.V. Rao's trailblazing work at Jagdish (his earlier film for them, ***Malli Pelli***, 1939, was also a hit) and includes long comedy sequences such as the satirical depiction of a film director (Nagaiah).

ZINDAGI

1940 120' b&w Hindi
d/c **P.C. Barua** *pc* **New Theatres** *co-dial/co-lyr* **Kidar Sharma** *co-dial* Javed Hussain *co-lyr* Arzoo Lucknowi *m* **Pankaj Mullick**
lp **K.L. Saigal**, **Pahadi Sanyal**, Ashalata, Jamuna, Shyam Laha, Nemo, **Sitara Devi**, Bikram Kapoor, Rajni Rani

Following on from **Mehboob**'s ***Ek Hi Raasta*** (1939), Barua also shows an unmarried couple living together, one of the most sacrosanct taboos of the Indian cinema. In a park, the vagabond gambler Ratan (Saigal) encounters Shrimati (Jamuna) who has escaped from her brutal husband. They team up and collect numerous donations pretending to belong to a charitable religious trust. They buy a flat and live together until Shrimati's father dies and she inherits his wealth. Renouncing her earlier life, she devotes herself to good works and employs Ratan to tutor an adopted orphan, Lakhia, but he discovers that he cannot live without her, while she, feeling she must pay for her guilty life, rejects him. He returns to being a tramp and she gives her fortune to Lakhia and withdraws to a lonely dwelling awaiting death. To ensure a happy ending, the two meet again as though on the threshhold of a new afterlife. The film had several Sharma songs performed by Saigal, including the famous *So jaa rajkumari*.

Thikadar

FILMS *1941 - 1950*

AMRIT

1941 153'[M]/162'[H] b&w Marathi/Hindi
d **Master Vinayak** *pc* **Navyug Chitrapat** *s/lyr*[M] **V.S. Khandekar** *lyr*[H] Indra *c* Pandurang Naik *m* Dada Chandekar
lp Dada Salvi, **Baburao Pendharkar**, **Lalita Pawar**, **Master Vithal**, **Damuanna Malvankar**, Javadekar, Meenakshi, V. Jog, Master Vinayak

A complicated plot about class differences in a coastal Konkan village. It introduces a typical Khandekar character, the idealistic but dogmatic patriarch who becomes a victim of his beliefs. Here it is Bappa (Salvi) who monopolises the village's palm trees from which toddy is made. He believes in fairness, not in mercy. The story of his urban son Vilas (Vithal), his daughter Lata and her friend Sadanand is intercut with that of a drunken shoemaker Krishna (Pendharkar) and his wife Seeta (Pawar). Vilas, who covets the shoemaker's wife, procures a new hut for them. The son then starts having problems with his father and all the parallel storylines converge when Vilas accidentally kills Seeta's daughter. Bappa, using his political influence, gets her innocent husband arrested instead and Seeta, exploiting Vilas's desire for her, retaliates by making him her virtual slave. Bappa eventually faces up to his moral responsibility in a tale that also warns against the demon drink.

ANJAAN

1941 144' b&w Hindi *d/s* **Amiya Chakravarty** *pc* **Bombay Talkies** *dial* J.S. Casshyap, Shahid Latif *lyr* Pradeep, P.L. Santoshi *c* R.D. Mathur *m* Pannalal Ghosh
lp **Devika Rani**, **Ashok Kumar**, V.H. Desai, Girish, Suresh, P.F. Pithawala, Gulab, Fatty Prasad, Yusuf Sulehman, Syed Mukhtar, David

Bombay Talkies' formula melodrama: villain is hero's rival in love, frames hero with crime, hero vindicates himself (cf ***Janmabhoomi***, 1936; ***Bandhan***, 1940). Dowager Ranima runs the feudal household helped by the family doctor, guardian Ajit (Kumar) and villainous manager Ramnath (Pithawala). Indira (Devika Rani), the children's governess, is wooed by both Ramnath and Ajit. Ranima dies, Ramnath accuses Ajit of having killed her but Ajit vindicates himself after a long courtroom battle. Remembered mainly as Bombay Talkies' star director Amiya Chakravarty's directorial debut and for the celebrated classical flautist Pannalal Ghosh's score.

ASHOK KUMAR

1941 211' b&w Tamil
d **Raja Chandrasekhar** *pc* Murugan Talkie Films *s* **Elangovan** *lyr* **Papanasam Sivan** *c* Jiten Bannerjee *m* Alandur V. Sivasubramanyam
lp **M.K. Thyagaraja Bhagavathar**, **Chittor V. Nagaiah**, **P. Kannamba**, T.V. Kumudini, **N.S. Krishnan**, T.A. Mathuram, **M.G. Ramachandran**, Ranjan

Hit Tamil historical retelling of the famous and often filmed (cf ***Veer Kunal***, 1925) legend of the 3rd-C. BC Mauryan King Ashoka (Nagaiah). His second wife Tishyarakshithai (Kannamba) tries to seduce his son Gunalan (Bhagavathar) but he prefers Pramila (Kumudini). The queen then accuses him of having tried to seduce her and Ashoka exiles his son and has him blinded. Later the emperor repents and the Buddha appears to restore the prince's sight. The film takes many liberties with the legend as it appears in the original *Ashokavadana* (cf Romila Thapar's *Asoka and the Decline of the Mauryas*, 1961), while addressing notions of non-violence and vegetarianism. It is remembered mainly as Bhagavathar's film, at the zenith of his career, singing songs that have become part of Tamil Nadu's social history (e.g. *Boomiyil manida genman*, also sung by the Sri Lankan plantation workers in Dieterle's *Elephant Walk*, 1953). Other hits included songs by Nagaiah making his Tamil debut. Besides recycling the tune of **Pankaj Mullick**'s Hindi song *Piya milan* from the film *Kapal Kundala* (1939), a growing practice at the time, the film also shows the influence of Busby Berkeley in the staging of a dance at court. The action sequences feature an early appearance of MGR in a minor role (as Mahendran). It is the debut of stunt actor Ranjan (who became famous with ***Chandralekha***, 1948). The known Tamil comic duo of Krishnan and Mathuram have a subplot of their own.

M.K. Thyagaraja Bhagavathar and P. Kannamba in *Ashok Kumar*

BAHEN

aka *Sister*, aka *My Sister*
1941 156' b&w Hindi
d **Mehboob** *pc* National Studios *st* **Zia Sarhadi**, Babubhai A. Mehta *sc/dial* Wajahat Mirza *lyr* Safdar 'Aah' *c* Faredoon Irani *m* **Anil Biswas**
lp Sheikh Mukhtar, **Nalini Jaywant**, Harish, Kanhaiyalal, Husn Bano, Swaroop Rani, Shehzadi, R. Choube, Baby Meena (aka **Meena Kumari**), Bhudo Advani, Agashe, Miss Iqbal

Classic Mehboob incest film. Elder brother Amar (Mukhtar) saves the life of his infant sister Bina and raises her, becoming very possessive about her. When Bina grows up (Jaywant), the progressive social activist Rajendra (Harish) wants to marry her. Amar then plots to get a thief, Moti (Kanhaiyalal), to marry and immediately abandon her so that she will forever remain dependent on Amar. Eventually she does get married and the brother's grief is alleviated only when his sister delivers a child (in a remarkable sequence featuring the nurses at the hospital). The incest motif was widely used to represent the complexities of an 'Aryan' agrarian-feudal patriarchy (e.g. the **New Theatres**' ***Meri Bahen***, 1944, and, classically, in **Ghatak**'s ***Subarnarekha***, 1962), but Mehboob was distinctive in making it a central focus.

BHAKTIMALA

1941 186' b&w Telugu
d/s Haribhai Desai *pc* Bhaskar Pics *c* M.A. Rehman *m* Kopparapu Subbarao
lp **B.R. Panthulu**, **P. Bhanumathi**, M. Lingamurthy, Coconada Rajarathnam, Shanta, Venkatagiri, Kutumba Sastry, Annapurna, Kondala Rao, G.V. Sitapathy

Story paying tribute to the Varkari tradition of Marathi saint poets. Radha (Bhanumathi), a devadasi (South Indian form of ritualised prostitution, in which the woman is wedded to god), converts herself into a worshipper of the saints. She is persecuted by the pimp Timmaya Sastry (Kondala Rao) and the villainous Brahmin Ramanujachari (Sitapathy). The hero Mohan (Panthulu) joins her struggle for social reform. When Ramanujachari has her framed for Mohan's murder, she is saved through divine intervention. One of the best-known films of Haribhai Desai, a Gujarati graduate of the J.J. School of Art in Bombay (cf **Art Schools**) and of the New York Institute of Cinematography as well as manager of the Suvarna Studio in Poona and the founder of the influential Bangalore-based Surya Film. This studio became a conduit for other Bombay-based directors (e.g. **Sundarrao Nadkarni**) to work in Tamil, Telugu and Kannada cinemas, bringing their influences of Marathi, Hindi and Gujarati cinema to the South.

CHITRALEKHA

1941 156' b&w Hindi
d/sc/lyr **Kidar Sharma** *pc* Film Corp. of India *st* Bhagwati Charan Verma's novel *c* G.K. Mehta *m* Jhande Khan, A.S. Gyani
lp Mehtab, Nandrekar, A.S. Gyani, Rajendar, Monica Desai, Ram Dulari, Leela Mishra, Ganpatrai Premi

Sharma's first major musical hit contains what is probably the first erotic bathing sequence in Indian cinema. Chitralekha (Mehtab), a dancer at the court of Chandragupta (founder of the 3rd-C. BC Mauryan dynasty, cf ***Ashok Kumar***, 1941), seduces Bijagupta (Nandrekar), a libertarian known as the 'ultimate sinner'. Mrityunjay (Premi), a nobleman who wants his daughter Yashodhara (Desai) to marry Bijagupta, gets his guru, the mystic Kumaragiri (Gyani) to undo Chitralekha's seductive charms but she triumphs over him, causing the guru to commit suicide. Chitralekha then leaves the palace and the lonely Bijagupta goes to the holy city of Gaya to purify himself. However, there he meets and falls in love with Yashodhara. When he loses her as well, he concludes that all women are an illusion (Maya) and becomes a saint. The reformed Chitralekha becomes his disciple. Most of the famous songs are by actress/singer Ram Dulari. Sharma remade it in garish colour with **Meena Kumari** (1964).

CHOODAMANI

1941 211' b&w Telugu/Tamil
d **P.K. Raja Sandow** *pc* Janaki Pics *s* Sadasiva Brahmam *c* Mama Shinde
lp Pushpavalli, **C.S.R. Anjaneyalu**, Narayanrao, Sundaramma, Satyavati, Pulipati

Sandow's elaborately scripted melodrama introduced the complicated Tamil entertainment formula into Telugu cinema. Madhusudhan (Anjaneyalu) is an Oxford graduate and a Madras-based businessman. Choodamani (Pushpavalli) is a beautiful rural orphan who turns down villain Raghava Rao's offer of marriage. The villain is joined by Madhuri, a cranky woman seduced and abandoned by the hero, and they make trouble at Madhusudhan and Choodamani's wedding. Madhuri bears the hero's child but strangles the baby and abandons it in a garbage can but she is caught by Raghava Rao who blackmails the hero into bankrupcy and even causes the hero to suspect his own wife of adultery. In a fit of rage he murders his own child but the infant is magically revived by a holy man. The film has a clown, Girisan, who leaves his wife to adopt a Western lifestyle, ending up as a barber.

DAKSHAYAGNAM

1941 184' b&w Telugu
d **Ch. Narayanamurthy** *pc* Shobhanachala Pics *s/lyr* B.T. Narasimhacharyulu *c* Bhavan *m* Motibabu
lp **Vemuri Gaggaiah**, **C. Krishnaveni**, **Bezawada Rajarathnam**, **G. Varalakshmi**, Kamaladevi, Gopika Devi, Samrajyam, Ramakrishna Shetty, Kumpatla, Sadasiva Rao, Ramana Rao, Kanchi Narasimham

Telugu mythological telling the story of the enmity between Shiva and Daksha, the father of Shiva's consort Uma. When Daksha announces a yagna (ritual sacrifice), Shiva is the only god in the pantheon who is not invited, and Uma arrives alone. This crisis threatens to terminate the yagna before it can start, as Uma gives up her life and is resurrected as Parvati.

DEVATHA

aka *Divinity*
1941 186' b&w Telugu
d **B.N. Reddi** *pc* **Vauhini Pics** *s/c* **K. Ramnoth** *dial/lyr* **Samudrala Raghavacharya** *m* **Chittor V. Nagaiah**
lp Chittor V. Nagaiah, Lingamurthy, **Bezawada Rajarathnam**, Ch. Narayana Rao, **T. Suryakumari**, Subba Rao, Master Ashwathama, Kumari

A big success in spite of its controversial subject-matter and its unusually mobile camerawork breaking with the prevailing theatrical conventions adopted in South Indian cinema. The plot tells of the young Venu (Nagaiah) who returns to his family in the village after studying law in England. He has an affair with Lakshmi (Kumari), the maid, and she becomes pregnant. Due to marry the well-off and 'modern' Vimala (Rajarathnam), Venu tries to get rid of Lakshmi by offering her money but she refuses and leaves. As for Vimala, she lets Venu off the hook by eloping with a phony poet, Sukumar (Narayana Rao), so that Venu, who confessed his pre-marital affair to his mother, can try to make amends by marrying the lower-class Lakshmi. Mother and son, accompanied by the daughter Seeta (Suryakumari), set out in search of Lakshmi and locate her in Madras where she became a prostitute and then was jailed for assaulting the madam. All are reconciled. The film questions both the established class divisions and the sexual mores of its depicted social milieu. As with all of Nagaiah's early films, this is a musical hit with perennial songs like *Adigo andiyala ravani*, *Radhe chali* and *Evaru makinka saati* (by Rajarathnam), and *Vendikanchalalo* and *Kroorakarmammulu* (by T. Suryakumari). The melodrama re-established Vauhini after the financial disaster of ***Sumangali*** (1940), although diluting the reformist commitment of earlier films by the Reddi/Ramnoth/Raghavacharya/A.K. Sekhar combination. A review in *Ananda Vikatan*

Chittor V. Nagaiah (right) in *Devatha*

(20.7.1941) welcomed the film, exclaiming: 'Oh gods and goddesses! We wanted to portray you as heroes and heroines in our films. That's what we said when we produced talkies. No god/goddess objected to that. [T]hen we came down to Puranic characters - on to bhaktas, maharajahs, zamindars, millionaires and thence to the common man. But none had thought to make the servant maid the heroine of a film.' Realism in this context meant deploying a new symbolic lexicon (cf the seduction scene juxtaposed with a montage of sexy covers of glossy foreign magazines, erotic sculpture and calendar art).

DOCTOR

1941 144' b&w Hindi
d Subodh Mitra *pc* **New Theatres** *st* **Shailajananda Mukherjee** *dial/co-lyr* A.H. Shore *co-lyr* Munshi Arzoo *c* Yusuf Mulji *m* **Pankaj Mullick**
lp Pankaj Mullick, **Ahindra Choudhury**, Jyoti Prakash, Master Meenu, Nemo, **Amar Mullick**, Buddhadeb, Indu Mukherjee, Miss Panna, Bharati

Amar Nath (P. Mullick), progressive son of an aristocratic family, becomes a doctor to address the cholera epidemic ravaging his ancestral village. He marries village girl Maya (Panna) against the wishes of his father Seeta Nath (Choudhury), causing a break with his family. Maya dies in childbirth and Amar Nath agrees to let Dayal (A. Mullick), his father's secretary, adopt the infant son on condition that the boy's antecedents are kept secret. The boy Somnath (Prakash) becomes a doctor and, fired by the idealist zeal of Amar Nath but unaware that he is his father, decides to start a drugs factory in the village. The son falls in love with Shibani (Bharati) but this pits him against Seeta Nath, unaware he is his grandfather. The Mukherjee story invokes the standard reformist moral conflict between ancestry and vocation often used to subordinate ideals of progress and modernity (e.g. medicine) to 'tradition'.

GUMASTAVIN PENN

aka *Clerk's Daughter*
1941 183' b&w Tamil
d/co-sc **Balkrishna Narayan Rao** *pc* **TKS Brothers**, Murthy Films-Coimbatore *st* TKS Brothers' play *co-sc* V.S. Vyas *dial* T.K. Muthuswamy *c* Rustom Irani *m* Narayanan, Padmanabhan Party
lp **M.V. Rajamma**, P. Subbaiah Pillai, T.S. Rajalakshmi, M.S. Draupadi, T.K.Shanmugham, T. Seetalakshmi

A melodrama based on a famous play by TKS Bros. Poor but upright Brahmin clerk Ramaswamy Iyer (Pillai), employed by a wealthy zamindar, has two unmarried daughters, Sarasa (Draupadi) and Seeta (Rajamma). Seeta loves the rich Ramu, a match approved by Ramu's widowed mother (Seetalakshmi) but opposed by Ramu who arranges for Seeta to marry someone else. She refuses. Because of the ensuing scandal Seeta finds herself obliged to marry an old widower who fortunately dies directly after the wedding. Then the clerk's evil employer Mani goes after her. He sacks her reluctant father, causing him to die of shock. Ramu later repents and tries to help Seeta's family but she commits suicide leaving him the responsibility of taking care of her sister. Ramu then tries to marry off the younger sister Sarasa, later marrying her himself. This was regarded as an early attempt at realism in Tamil cinema.

JHOOLA

1941 177' b&w Hindi
d/co-s **Gyan Mukherjee** *pc* **Bombay Talkies** *p* S. Mukherjee *co-s* P.L. Santoshi *lyr* Pradeep *c* R.D. Parineeja *m* **Saraswati Devi**
lp **Leela Chitnis, Ashok Kumar**, Shah Nawaz, Aruna Devi, V.H. Desai, Mumtaz Ali, Shahzadi, Rajkumari Shukla

The third consecutive S. Mukherjee-produced hit by Bombay Talkies starring Leela Chitnis and Ashok Kumar (***Kangan***, 1939; ***Bandhan***, 1940) was also Gyan Mukherjee's debut. Two half-brothers, Ramesh (Kumar) and Mahesh, love the same woman, Geeta (Chitnis). Mahesh inherits his father's estate (half of which belongs to Ramesh) while Ramesh works as a postman. Complicating the situation is the presence of Kamala whom Mahesh has promised to marry and who could now wreck his matrimonial designs on Geeta.

KHAZANCHI

aka *The Cashier*
1941 171' b&w Hindi
d **Moti B. Gidwani** *pc* Pancholi Art Pics *st* **Dalsukh M. Pancholi** *lyr* Walli *c* Badri Dass *m* **Ghulam Haider**
lp M. Ismail, Ramola, S.D. Narang, Manorama, Durga, Jankidas, Ajmal

Musical megahit from Lahore often cited as the precursor of the commercial Hindi cinema's editing and sound-mixing style and trend-setter of Hindi-Urdu film music. Shadilal (Ismail), the trusted cashier of a bank, has to transport gold jewellery to Bombay. His son Kanwal (Narang) falls in love with the millionaire Durgadas's (Durga) daughter Madhuri (Ramola). Kanwal finds himself pitted against the villainous Ramesh (Ajmal), Durgadas's secretary and the nephew of Madhuri's stepmother as well as being a rival suitor for Madhuri. The marriage is cancelled when news flashes from Bombay that Shadilal has murdered an actress and absconded with the jewellery.

NAYA SANSAR

1941 158' b&w Hindi
d **N.R. Acharya** *pc* **Bombay Talkies** *p* S. Mukherjee *st/co-sc* **K.A. Abbas** *co-sc* **Gyan Mukherjee** *dial* J.S. Casshyap, Shahid Latif *lyr* Pradeep *c* R.D. Parineeja *m* **Saraswati Devi**, Ramchandra Pal
lp Renuka Devi, **Ashok Kumar**, Mubarak, Shah Nawaz, V.H. Desai, Jagannath, David, Suresh, Sushil Kumar, P.F. Pithawala, Azoorie

Although S. Mukherjee's production team (e.g. Gyan Mukherjee, Shahid Latif) were involved, authorship for this film is usually credited to Abbas. It was his first major film work, in which he used his experiences as a journalist to create the character of the reporter Puran (A. Kumar). Premchand (Mubarak), fearless editor of the radical newspaper *Sansar*, loves Asha (Renuka Devi), an orphan raised by his family. She joins the paper and falls for its ace reporter, the cynical Puran, yet she feels bound to accept her benefactor's marriage proposal. When the editor dilutes his radicalism and starts negotiating with the corrupt Dhaniram, Puran leaves and produces a broadsheet called *Naya Sansar* (*New World*). The editor recognises his mistake, gives his blessing to the couple and even re-employs Puran, promising to stick to his radical stance. There are numerous dances composed and performed by Azoorie promoting solidarity and against Untouchability. Abbas later named his film production unit Naya Sansar Films and made all his films under that banner.

PARICHAY/LAGAN

1941 141'[B]/150'[H] b&w Bengali/Hindi
d/sc/c **Nitin Bose** *pc* **New Theatres** *st* Benoy Chatterjee *lyr*[H] Arzoo *m* **Rai Chand Boral**
lp **K.L. Saigal, Kanan Devi**, Naresh Bose, Rathin Bannerjee[B], Mihir Bhattacharya[B], Shyam Laha[B]/Nawab[H], Nandita Devi[B], Harimohan Bose[B], Jagdish[H], Girdharilal Vaid[H], Nemo[H], Rehmat Bibi[H]

Student Kusum Kumari (Kanan Devi) is a hit at a college concert while her tutor, the composer and poet (Saigal), is ignored. After marrying the rich Deendayal (Laha/Nawab), she realises she loves the poet. Her husband tries to please her by publishing the poet's work, making him famous, which leads to further complications. The film made an important contribution to Saigal's image, helping to define the Indian version of the romantic stereotype of the artist, a figure later mobilised by, e.g., **Guru Dutt** in ***Pyaasa*** (1957).

PAYACHI DASI/CHARNON KI DASI

1941 126'[M]/129'[H] b&w Marathi/Hindi
d **Gajanan Jagirdar** *p/s/lyr*[M] **P.K. Atre** *pc* Atre Pics *dial/lyr*[H] Anand Kumar *c* S. Hardip *m* Annasaheb Mainkar
lp **Durga Khote**, Vanamala, Gajanan Jagirdar, Avinash, Kusum Deshpande, Kelkar

Typical Marathi reform social written and produced by Atre. Evil mother-in-law (Khote) cruelly exploits the young bride Vidya (Vanamala). Husband Murari (Avinash) protests only feebly until finally he decides to revolt and stand by his wife. The film ends with Vidya, now in charge of the house, declaring her commitment to the very tradition that victimised her. The widowed and equally vindictive sister-in-law Champa (Deshpande) and the village flirt Nokheram (played by the director) are the other major characters of this commercial hit.

PRAHLADAN

aka *Bhakta Prahlada*
1941 183' b&w Malayalam
d **K. Subramanyam** *pc* Madras United Artists Corp *s* N.P. Chellappan Nair *lyr* Kilimannoor Madhavaryar *c* Kamal Ghosh
lp Gopinath, Thangamani, Kumari Lakshmi, Master Sadasivam, N.P. Chellappan Nair, P.R. Rajagopala Iyer, K.R.N. Swamy, Sharada, Master Gopi, N. Krishna Pillai
Shot at the **Gemini** Studio by the leading

Tamil director of the time, the mythological retells the familiar tale of the demon Hiranyakashapu and his devout son Prahlada who worships the god Vishnu. The film was noted mainly for its spectacular dances, featuring the famed duo of Gopinath (as Hiranyakashapu) and Thangamani (as his wife Kayadhu). The dance of Yama, god of death, was the film's major highlight. Some of the choreography was set to classical Carnatic music. Master Sadasivam provided the mandatory comedy relief.

RAJ NARTAKI/COURT DANCER

1941 144[B]/126'[H]/86'[E] b&w Bengali/Hindi/English
d/sc **Modhu Bose** *pc* **Wadia Movietone** *st* Manmatha Ray *dial*[H] W.Z. Ahmed *lyr* Indra[H] *c* Jatin Das, Probodh Das *m* **Timir Baran**
lp **Sadhona Bose**, Jyoti Prakash[B]/**Prithviraj Kapoor**[H], **Ahindra Choudhury**, **Protima Dasgupta**, Binita Gupta, Priti Majumdar

Best-known film by the Bose husband and wife team. Set in feudal Manipur, presumably to display Bose's abilities in the famous classical dance form of the region. The story pivots around Prince Chandrakriti's (Prakash/Kapoor) responsibilities to his kingdom requiring him to marry the princess of Tripur although he loves the court dancer Madhuchanda (Bose). The mystical head of a temple sect persuades Madhuchanda to give up her hold on the prince. She does so at the cost of her reputation and becomes a public outcast. One of the few Indian films made also in English and released in the USA.

RISHYASHRINGAR

1941 172' b&w Tamil
d **S. Sounderrajan** *pc* Tamil Nadu Talkies *lyr* Papanasam Rajagopal Iyer *c* Jiten Bannerjee *m* Sharma Bros
lp Vasundharadevi, **S. Balachander**, G. Pattu Iyer, K.N. Kamalam, K.N. Rajalakshmi, M.S. Murugesan, Kumari Rukmini, Ramani, Kumar Murali

A rare mythological celebrating the triumph of desire over religious asceticism. The celibate sage Vibhandaka finds an abandoned child and names him Rishyashringar. He teaches the child all the scriptures but keeps him isolated from all human contact. In a nearby kingdom that faces drought following the curse of a sage, the king is told that only Rishyashringar can bring rain. The king sends the seductive Maya to entice him into the kingdom, which she does. Rishya arrives, brings the rain and marries the princess, much to the dismay of Vibhandaka.

SANT SAKHU

1941 128' b&w Marathi/Hindi
d **V. Damle**, **S. Fattelal**, **Raja Nene** *pc* **Prabhat Film** *s* Shivram Vashikar *dial/co-lyr*[H] P.L. Santoshi *co-lyr*[H] Mukhram Sharma *lyr*[M] **Shantaram Athavale** *c* V. Avadhoot, E. Mohammed *m* **Keshavrao Bhole**
lp **Hansa Wadkar**, Gauri, Shankar Kulkarni, Shanta Majumdar, Sumitra

Gauri and Hansa Wadkar in *Sant Sakhu*

The only woman-centred Saint film at Prabhat with Wadkar in the classic role of Sakhu, a Marathi Saint poet whose existence is mainly legendary as opposed to the better-documented male ones. She is depicted as a devoutly religious woman married to a weak husband (Kulkarni) and oppressed by her cruel mother-in-law Mhalsakaku (Gauri) and sister-in-law Durga (Majumdar). Recognition comes at the end of the film through a series of miracles (including the classic scene where she is tied to a pillar, her disembodied death and reincarnation). Unlike the directors' earlier and better-known films in the genre, this was mainly a family melodrama. The celebratory power of the genre only appears sporadically, e.g. the pilgrims walking to Pandharpur. Unusually, the mandatory miracle scenes were integrated into the plot (instead of merely illustrating saintly power), esp. at the end when the 'real' Sakhu confronts her divine stand-in to confuse everyone in the village and to attract charges of being a ghost. The bizarre publicity included stills showing convoys of military vehicles captioned 'What leads an army - Faith'.

SHEJARI/PADOSI

1941 134'[M]/135'[H] b&w Marathi/Hindi
d **V. Shantaram** *pc* **Prabhat Film** *s* **Vishram Bedekar** *dial/lyr*[H] Sudarshan *lyr*[M] **Shantaram Athavale** *c* V. Avadhoot *m* **Master Krishnarao**
lp **Gajanan Jagirdar**, Balakram, Sumitra, Gopal, **Keshavrao Date**[M]/Mazhar Khan[H], Chandrakant[M], Jayashree[M], Gauri[M], Manajirao[M], Master Chhotu[M], Vatsala[M], Anees Khatoon[H], Balwant Singh[H], Muliya[H], Casshyap[H], Radha Krishna[H], Vasant Thengdi[H], Lajwanti[H], Sarala Devi[H]

Melodrama addressing communal harmony. Mirza (Jagirdar) and Patil (Date/Khan) are close friends and the senior guardians of their village. The industrialist Omkar wants to build a bigger dam but is opposed by the duo. He has Patil sacked and his son excommunicated for allegedly burning a house. This causes a rift between the two old friends, who eventually make up as the giant dam bursts and they die in each other's arms. Shantaram continued his relentlessly emotional and symbolic use of nature, as the stormy scene that accompanies Omkar's decision to split the friendship between Mirza and Patil. This use of nature culminates logically in the film's highlight: the dam bursting with a series of impressive nature-on-the-rampage shots. The Marathi version has some classic hits, including *Radhika chatur bole* and the nicely picturised community number *Lakhlakh chanderi tejachi nyari duniya* shot in torchlight with remarkably controlled deep-focus shots.

SIKANDAR

1941 146' b&w Urdu
d **Sohrab Modi** *pc* **Minerva Movietone** *s/lyr* Sudarshan *c* Y.D. Sarpotdar *m* Mir Saheb, Rafiq Ghaznavi
lp Sohrab Modi, **Prithviraj Kapoor**, Vanamala, Meena, Sheela, Sadiq Ali, Zahur Raja, Shakir, K.N. Singh, Jilloo

Modi's military epic is set in 326BC when Alexander the Great aka Sikandar (Kapoor), having conquered Persia and the Kabul valley, descends to the Indian border at Jhelum with his Macedonian army and encounters King Porus (Modi) of the Punjab who stops the advance with his troops. The plot has Sikandar ignoring his teacher Aristotle's (Shakir) advice and he falls for a Persian woman, Rukhsana (Vanamala). Fearing for Sikandar's life, she goes to Porus's court and extracts a promise that he shall not harm Sikandar. In the battle with the Macedonian army, Porus loses his son Amar (Raja) and meets Sikandar face to face. An elaborate verbal duel follows, then the two kings become friends and Sikandar withdraws. The stilted, declamatory dialogue was pure Parsee Theatre as Modi and Kapoor, well-known Shakespearean actors, give free reign to their histrionic proclivities. Highlights including the scenes of battle on horses and elephants. The film was later dubbed in Persian.

SWAMI

1941 152' b&w Hindi
d **A.R. Kardar** *pc* CIRCO *st* Munshi Premchand's *Triya Charitra sc/dial* Imtiaz Ali Taj *lyr* Shahir Ghaznavi, Indra, Tanveer Naqvi *c* Jatin Das *m* Rafiq Ghaznavi
lp **Sitara Devi**, Jairaj, Yakub, Majid, Badriprasad, Ghulam Rasool

Kardar's ultra-conservative ode to patriarchy tells of Binod (Jairaj) and Indira (Sitara Devi) who were married as children and never meet as adults. Indira grows into a 'modern' young woman while Binod, disinherited when his stepfather has a son, works in a distant village. Indira haughtily refuses a relationship with a pauper but she eventually realises her duties to her husband and goes to meet him disguised as Shanta, a beggar woman. Binod then falls in love with her, not realising she is in fact his wife.

TALLIPREMA

1941 211' b&w Telugu
d Jyotish Sinha *pc* Rajarajeshwari Pics *st* Lakshmi Narasimha Rao *dial* K.L. Narasimha Rao *lyr* Daita Gopalam *c* Kamal Ghosh *m* N.V. Venkatraman, N.B. Dinkar Rao
lp **P. Kannamba**, Hemalatha Devi, Sheshamba, **C.S.R. Anjaneyalu**, **Kalyanam Raghuramaiah**

Marital melodrama promoting the image of the ideal woman as a long-suffering and self sacrificing wife. Santha (Kannamba) is the exemplary but still childless wife of Krishna Rao (Anjaneyalu). When all rituals fail, she accepts her evil sister-in-law Durgabai's (Sheshamba) suggestion that her husband take a second bride, Kamala (Hemalatha). Durgabai and Kamala then combine to eject Santha from the house in spite of her sudden pregnancy. She gives birth to a son but gets separated from the child, which is raised by a local zamindar. Kamala turns out to be the real villain and sends an assassin to kill the child. Eventually the husband has a change of heart and rescues the child himself; Kamala obligingly commits suicide, thus restoring the original happy couple.

TENALI RAMAKRISHNA

1941 198' b&w Telugu
d **H.M. Reddy** *pc* Rohini Pics *s/lyr* Sadasiva Brahmam *c* P. Sridhar *m* Gundopant Walavalkar
lp Master Raju, S.P. Lakshmanaswamy, P. Subba Rao, K.V. Subba Rao, **L.V. Prasad**, T. Hanumantha Rao, P. Koteshwara Rao, Baby Rohini, Kumari Sarala, Tilakam, Ansuya, Gangarathnam, Subbulu

Tenali Ramakrishna (aka Tenali Raman, the hero of many popular morality tales) was a jester in the court of Krishnadeva Raya, who ruled over the Vijayanagara empire at its pinnacle (1509-30). The rather wordy film opens with the child Ramakrishna (Master Raju) being admonished for telling unpalatable truths exposing the duplicity of the elders: when the old and twice-married widower Karanam wants to marry 9-year-old Saubhagyam, Ramakrishna masquerades as the child bride and prevents the marriage. His reputation as a principled prankster grows and as an adult (Lakshmanaswamy) he wins a seat in Krishnadeva Raya's court as a poet by dressing up as a folk entertainer. In the court he comes up against the scheming Brahmin Tatacharya, who interprets divine signs to enhance his own wealth. When the king's aged mother dies leaving an uneaten mango, Tatacharya foretells that her soul will never find peace unless all the Brahmins are given mangoes made of gold. Ramakrishna replies that his own mother died with an unfulfilled desire to be branded with a hot iron, and he arranges to have all the Brahmins branded instead. Ramakrishna's ready wit also saves the king from losing his empire. L.V. Prasad played two roles in the film: the minister Timmarasu and the corrupt matchmaker who arranges the marriage of the 9-year-old girl with the aged Brahmin. Tenali Ramakrishna stories were also filmed in Telugu (e.g. **B.S. Ranga**'s Telugu/Tamil/Kannada trilingual, ***Tenali Ramakrishna/Tenali Raman***, 1956).

THORATANCHI KAMALA

1941 138' b&w Marathi
d/s/lyr **Bhalji Pendharkar** *pc* Famous-Arun Pics *c* Saju Naik *m* Kashalkar-Pyarasaheb
lp Sumati Gupte, Chandrakant, Nanasaheb Phatak, Nimbalkar, Jaishankar Danve, Kamalabai, Shanta, Chitnis, Bapurao Pawar

Famous Marathi historical made originally by **Sarpotdar** (1927), probably with a story credit for Pendharkar, and remade by Madhav Shinde based on Pendharkar's script in 1963. A fictional story set in the 17th-C. Maratha empire of Shivaji (Phatak) extolling the greatness of a Maratha past teeming with beautiful maidens and men of valour. Wounded during a tiger hunt, Shivaji's son Sambhaji (Chandrakant) is looked after by Kamala (Gupte), falls in love and eventually abducts her. When Kamala returns home, her father refuses to accept her and kills himself out of shame. Shivaji has a public trial of his own son and puts him in prison. When Kamala is abducted again, by Yeshwantrao, the man she was supposed to marry, Sambhaji escapes from prison to rescue her but she is killed in the ensuing violence. The musical hit established Chandrakant as a major Marathi star. Pendharkar made a companion work: *Mohityanchi Manjula* (1963).

VENUGANAM

1941 167' b&w Tamil
d **Murugadasa** *pc* Jewel Pics-Coimbatore *st* Manjeri S. Ishwaran *sc* **K. Ramnoth** *dial* Ki-Rai *lyr* **Kambadasan** *c* Sudhish C. Ghatak *m* Govindarajulu Naidu
lp N.C. Vasanthakokilam, A. Shakuntala, V.V. Satagopalan, M.V. Mani, T.V. Krishnaswamy, Sandow Chinnappa Devar, K. Sarangapani

Regarded as a light mythological comedy, it is a rare example of a totally invented mythological. Prince Vindhan (M.V. Mani) hates the god Krishna adored by his sister Mithra (Vasanthakokilam). When Vindhan runs over a child in his chariot, he is tried and sent to prison by his own father but he escapes and stages a coup. He becomes a tyrant with the help of the villainous King Duryodhan. Duryodhan wants Mithra to marry his imbecile brother-in-law Parvatheshwara but Krishna steps in, rescues Mithra and arranges to have his friend disguised as the bride. Krishna and his accomplice are arrested but just then Vindhan's father, the old king, reappears after having escaped from prison, and puts matters right. Vasanthakokilam's songs in praise of Krishna were hits.

APNA GHAR/APLE GHAR

1942 167'[H]/156'[M] b&w Hindi/Marathi
d/s **Debaki Bose** *pc* CIRCO *lyr* Narottam Vyas[H], **Shantaram Athavale**, Shivram Vashikar[M] *c* Govardhanbhai Patel *m* Harishchandra Bali
lp **Shanta Apte**, **Chandramohan**, Maya Bannerjee[H], Kusum Deshpande[M], Jagdish Sethi[H], Nayampalli[M], Jeevan[H], Madhukar Gupte[M], Nimbalkar, Vimala Vasishta, Maruti Rao, Vimal Sardesai, **Mahesh Kaul**, P.R. Joshi, Bibi, Mishra[H], Angre[M]

A melodrama examining the family within nationalism. Forest contractor Narendra (Chandramohan) has an arranged marriage with social reformer Meera (Apte) mainly to keep Meera's ailing father happy. Since her work with the tribal peoples and her attempts to unionise them interferes with his business interests, Narendra demands that she devote herself solely to his comforts. An unwanted relative, Mami (Vasishta), encourages the couple's gradual alienation. Meera leaves home vowing never to return and is believed to have drowned in a river, which prompts a change of heart for Narendra, both towards Meera and to the jungle-folk who have in fact rescued her. **New Theatres**' Debaki Bose ventured into classic **Prabhat** territory with his only Marathi film using Prabhat's stars (Apte and Chandramohan) and writers (Vyas, Athavale and Vashikar).

ARMAAN

1942 127' b&w Hindi
d/s/lyr **Kidar Sharma** *pc* **Ranjit Movietone** *c* D.K. Ambre *m* Gyan Dutt *lp* **Motilal**, Shamim, Nagendra, Rajendra Singh, Meera, Rajkumari, Bhagwandas, A. Shah, Bhupatrai, Nazir Bedi

Sharma's first film at Ranjit is a science fiction romance using nature as a metaphor for inner turmoil and as the model for social morality. Set in 1910, its modern hero, Kanwal (Motilal), invents a ray that records pain and pleasure photographically. His experiments render him blind. Country lass Meera (Shamim) tends to him and they fall in love. Later Meera meets a sage (Shah) who has an expensive magic potion that cures blindness. Unable to afford it, Meera kills the sage, grabs the medicine and goes to Kanwal's house while all nature protests her actions. There the evil Diwan (Bhagwandas) and his accomplices steal the medicine, cure Kanwal and take the credit. Kanwal, who can now see but does not recognise Meera, accuses her of murder but eventually realises the truth.

BALANAGAMMA

1942 c.220' b&w Telugu
d **C. Pullaiah** *p* **S.S. Vasan** *pc* **Gemini** *s/lyr* Balijepalli Lakshmikanta Kavi *c* Sailen Bose *m* **Saluri Rajeshwara Rao**, M.D. Parthasarathy
lp **Kånchanmala**, Pushpavalli, G.V. Subba Rao, Banda, Balijepalli Lakshmikanta Kavi, Ballari Lalitha, Kamaladevi, Lanka Sathyam, **Relangi Venkatramaiah**

Gemini's megahit launched a very popular and uniquely Telugu genre of fantasy films derived from folk theatre (e.g. **K.V. Reddy**'s films, esp. ***Patala Bhairavi***, 1951). The film adapts the Telugu folk Burra Katha to a reformist idiom to tell the story of a woman, Balanagamma (Kanchanmala), who is abducted by an evil magician, Mayala Marathi (Subba Rao). She keeps his amorous advances at bay for twelve years, claiming to be engaged in a ritual act of penance, after which her son rescues her. Known for its spectacular costumes and sets, its music, elaborate special effects and Pushpavalli's dance number (in the role of the villain's sidekick). A lawsuit with Vasan following on from the film halted Kanchanmala's career for almost a decade.

BASANT

1942 146' b&w Hindi
d/s/c **Amiya Chakravarty** *pc* **Bombay Talkies** *dial* J.S. Casshyap *lyr* P.L. Santoshi *c* R.D. Mathur *m* Pannalal Ghosh
lp Mumtaz Shanti, Ulhas, Mumtaz Ali, P.F. Pithawala, Suresh, Jagannath, Kamala, Kanu Roy, Pramila

Establishing both Chakravarty as director and Mumtaz Shanti (she went on to star with **Ashok Kumar** in ***Kismet***, 1943), the film tells of Uma (Shanti) and her brother Babul, two downtrodden servants who dream of becoming singing and dancing stars on the stage. They attract the attention of the impresario Janaki Prasad and Uma marries his spoilt and envious younger brother, Nirmal (Ulhas) who sets out to make his own fortune leaving Uma and their baby to starve. When he returns to find his wife is working on the stage, he abducts the baby and disappears again. After a further 10 years of unhappy stage stardom for Uma, the family is reunited and the happy ending sees her return to being a housewife in accordance with her husband's wishes. The film belonged to the studio's more orthodox production wing run by **Devika Rani** who tried to continue the **Osten** tradition. However, the cameraman R.D. Mathur (who later shot **K. Asif**'s historicals) hadn't mastered Wirsching's use of spotlights: shadows and source reflections interfere constantly with the action. Mumtaz Shanti's dancing and Mumtaz Ali's' minimal gestures belongs to a different actorial generation from the 30s Bombay Talkies, as did the songs, esp. the leitmotif *Aya basant ritu*. Although celebrated flautist Pannalal Ghosh is credited as composer, the music was scored uncredited by **Anil Biswas** while Ghosh played in the orchestra recording.

BHAKTA POTANA

1942 186' b&w Telugu
d **K.V. Reddy** *pc* **Vauhini** Pics *dial/lyr* **Samudrala Raghavacharya** *sc/c* **K. Ramnoth** *m* Chittor V. Nagaiah
lp **Chittor V. Nagaiah**, Malati, C. Hemlatha, Vanaja, Samrajyam, Gaurinatha Sastry, Lingamurthy, **B. Jayamma**

Nagaiah's debut in the saint film genre sees him as Bammera Potanamatya, aka Bhakta Potana, a farmer who, allegedly on orders from Rama, adapted the Sanskrit *Bhagvata* into Telugu. The king insists that Potana should dedicate his translations from Sanskrit to him. The king's efforts to appropriate Potana's text are foiled by divine intervention, once when Hanuman protects him and his family from the king's soldiers, and in the film's finale when the soldiers, trying to demolish Potana's home, find the king's palace being magically destroyed instead. The film was a major hit and including songs like *Sarvamangalanama*, *Nannu vidichi kadalakura* and *Pavanaguna nama*, encouraging Nagaiah to direct a sequel, ***Thagayya*** (1946). The former actress **Bezawada Rajarathnam** sang playback for the dancer Samrajyam.

BHARAT MILAP/BHARAT BHET

1942 170' b&w Hindi/Marathi
d **Vijay Bhatt** *pc* Prakash Pics *s* Vishnupant Aundhkar *dial/co-lyr*[H] Anuj Visharad *co-lyr*[H] Indra, Balam *co-lyr*[M] **Shantaram Athavale** *c* P.G. Kukde *m* Shankarrao Vyas *choreo* Lachchu Maharaj
lp **Shahu Modak**, **Shobhana Samarth**, **Durga Khote**, Prem Adib[H], Chandrakant[M], Vimala Vasishta, Umakant[H], Vinay Kale[M], Nimbalkar, P. Ratnamala, Amirbai Karnataki

Bhatt's first of many films based on the *Ramayana* tried to be the biggest and the most faithful adaptation of the epic to date. Credits include dozens of literary sources and the expertise of several historians and curators. This plot tells of Bharat, the third of Dasharath's four sons, and his unstinting devotion to Rama, his eldest brother. Kaikeyi, incited by her maid Manthara, takes advantage of a royal boon to force Dasharath to exile Rama on the eve of his coronation and to have her own son Bharat made king of Ayodhya. Bharat refuses the throne and goes to the forest to recall Rama. When Rama insists on honouring his father's promise, Bharat spends 14 years waiting for the heir to return and assume his rightful place as king. The film omits most of the mandatory miracle sequences and looks more like a period romance with expensive sets and battle scenes, e.g. when Bharat is attacked by Nishadraj's army. Notwithstanding the film's textual claims to authenticity, its general effect is that of contemporary calendar art with its vaguely neo-classical decor.

DAHA WAJTA/DAS BAJE

aka *10 o'clock*
1942 144' b&w Marathi/Hindi
d **Raja Nene** *pc* **Prabhat Film** *co-s* D.D. Casshyap *co-s/dial*[M] G.K. Pawar *dial/lyr*[H] Mukhram Sharma *lyr*[M] **Shantaram Athavale** *c* E. Mohammed *m* **Keshavrao Bhole**
lp Urmila[H]/P. Ratnamala[M], Paresh Bannerjee[H]/Shankar Kulkarni[M], Manajirao, Vasant Thengdi, Baby Shakuntala

Top university student Dilip (Bannerjee/Kulkarni) falls in love with rich classmate Asha (Urmila/Ratnamala) but her father forces her to marry Dr Ramesh (Thengdi). Dilip falls ill and only Dr Ramesh's surgical skills can save him. 10 o'clock is when the lovers first promise to remember each other and the symbol recurs at various points in the melodrama. A commercially successful film and an important rallying point at Prabhat Studio for the Nene/**Dharmadhikari**/**Mane**/Bhole unit which went independent shortly thereafter.

Daha Wajta

GARIB

1942 152' b&w Hindi
d/st **Ramchandra Thakur** *pc* National Studios *p* **Mehboob Khan** *sc* **Zia Sarhadi** *lyr* Safdar 'Aah' *c* Keki Mistry *m* Ashok Ghosh
lp Surendranath, Rose, Veena Kumari, Sankatha, Ansari, Qayamali, Pesi Patel, Keshav, Waskar

Produced by Mehboob and scripted by Sarhadi, this melodrama about poverty is one of the **Sagar** and National Studio films later acknowledged by **Abbas** as a precursor to his own political cinema. The unemployed graduate Sharad (Surendranath) finds work accompanying a blind beggar. He meets the heiress Sudha (Rose) on the street and later finds that the place where the destitutes find shelter belongs to Sudha's industrialist father Biharilal (Sankatha). He uses his friendship with Sudha to get her father to forego the rent and to start a factory that may employ them all. The factory does well, to the chagrin of Sudha's fiance (and the film's villain) Satish (Ansari). Satish, who simultaneously pursues the beautiful Lata (Veena Kumari), has the factory closed and accuses Sharad of having an affair with Lata. The threat of renewed destitution is avoided only when Sudha and Lata meet and the truth comes out.

GARMIL

1942 141' b&w Bengali
d **Niren Lahiri** *pc* Chitrabani *dial* Nripendra Krishna Chatterjee, Jogesh Choudhury *c* **Ajoy Kar** *m* **Kamal Dasgupta**
lp **Chhabi Biswas**, Jogesh Choudhury, Sheila Haldar, Srilekha, **Jahar Ganguly**, Robin Majumdar, Nripati Chatterjee, **Kanu Bannerjee**, **Tulsi Chakraborty**, Santosh Sinha, Prabhadevi, Shyam Laha

Melodrama confronting the traditionalist Hindu Madhab Thakur and his Westernised neighbour Mukherjee. Mukherjee's son Robi and Thakur's daughter Malati run a school of traditional disciplines which they hope to develop into a nationwide institution. Their plans to marry receive a setback when Malati's elder sister is forced to marry a Brahmin, triggering a revolt by the younger generation of both households. Then Malati's marriage to a wealthy zamindar is arranged but eventually a happy ending and the triumph of modernity are achieved.

GHARANA DONGA

aka *Satyame Jayam* aka *Honest Rogue*
1942 ?' b&w Telugu
d **H.M. Reddy** *pc* Rohini Pics *s/lyr* Sadasiva Brahmam
lp **L.V. Prasad**, Tilakam, Gangarathnam

Folk-tale about a thief (L.V. Prasad) who is scapegoated to divert attention from the real enemy, the decadent minister of a kingdom. The king eventually realises the truth when he goes out in disguise and finds himself assisting the thief in robbing the royal safe, an adventure which shows the thief to be a decent fellow. The film apparently claimed to promote Gandhian ideals.

JAWANI KI PUKAR

aka *Call Of Youth*
1942 140' b&w Hindi
d/co-s **D. Bilimoria** *pc* Artists Combine *co-s* Harbanslal *dial/lyr* A.K. Sindi *c* R.M. Rele, V.G. Sawant *m* Vasant Kumar Naidu
lp D. Bilimoria, Harish, W.M. Khan, Afghan Sandow, Benjamin, Samson, Kalyani, Urmila, Alaknanda, Abdul Ghani, S. Gulab

Adventure film directed by silent star D. Bilimoria about two friends, Balu (Bilimoria) and Harish (Harish), and their faithful servant who set out to seek their fortune in Bombay. The film includes episodes in a film studio that were used to comment on the gangsterism present among the extras and their suppliers, using characters with names like Al Capone (Samson). Much of the action takes place on a ship where they try to rescue the heroine Kanwal (Kalyani) from the clutches of villain Jagat (W.M. Khan).

JEEVANA NATAKA

1942 160' b&w Kannada
d Wahab Kashmiri *p* **Gubbi Veeranna** *pc* Gubbi Films *s* **A.N. Krishnarao** from his play *m* Rama Iyer, Harmonium Sheshgiri Rao
lp Gubbi Veeranna, **Kemparaj Urs**, **Shanta Hublikar**, **B. Jayamma**, D. Jaya Rao, Mohan Kumari

Melodrama in which Anand (Veeranna), proprietor of a theatre group, offers shelter to the orphan Padma (Jayamma) who eventually displaces the star of the company Kamala (Hublikar). When she falls in love with Mohan (Urs), who also lives under Anand's patronage, the proprietor throws both of them out. Driven to alcoholism by his infatuation with Kamala, Mohan almost drives his wife Padma to suicide. She is rescued by Anand, who eventually brings everyone together again. One of the few films scripted by noted Kannada author A.N. Krishnarao, it introduced the noted South Indian actor-director Kemparaj Urs to film and imported the former **Prabhat** star Shanta Hublikar for her only Kannada movie.

KANNAGI

1942 c.220' b&w Tamil
d **T.R. Raghunath** *pc* Jupiter Pics *s* **Elangovan**
lp **P. Kannamba**, **P.U. Chinappa**, **N.S. Krishnan**, T.A. Mathuram, D. Balasubramanyam

Classic Kannamba role as Kannagi, a character from the major Tamil epic and morality tale *Chilapathikaram* (1st C. AD), written by Elango Adigal. Hero Kovalan (Chinappa) marries Kannagi (Kannamba), both being subjects of the Chola kingdom. But Kovalan then falls in love with the dancer Madhavi who causes his ruin. He is rescued by his dutiful wife, who offers to sell her golden anklet to help him restart his business. The anklet, which the king of the neighbouring Pandya kingdom suspects to be stolen, leads to the hero being beheaded by royal command. Kannagi avenges herself by proving the king was mistaken, causing him and his queen to die on the spot. Then in the spectacular finale, she sets the entire Pandyan capital town of Madurai on fire with a curse. Eventually Kannagi ascends to heaven. The film followed an earlier film of an important Tamil legend, *Mani Mekalai* (1940), scripted by A.A. Somayajulu, exploiting the revivalist interest in Tamil literature's Sangam period (1-5 C. AD) promoted by major political/literary figures like Ramalingaswamy (1823-74) who prefigure Periyar E.V. Ramaswamy Naicker's Self-Respect Movement in the state. *Kannagi* extended this trend via Elangovan's strident dialogues. Although Kannagi also figured in popular legends in Tamil Nadu and in Sri Lanka and was subjected to various mutations down the centuries in poetry and theatre, as an icon she came to be identified with Kannamba's image after this successful film.

KHANDAAN

1942 171' b&w Hindi
d/co-s Shaukat Hussain Rizvi *pc* **Pancholi** Art Prod *st/dial* Imtiaz Ali Taj *co-sc* Khadeem Mohiyuddin *c* M.N. Malhotra *m* **Ghulam Haider**
lp **Nurjehan**, Ghulam Mohammed, Manorama, Ajmal, Durga Mota, Baby Akhtar

Written by *Anarkali* author Imtiaz Ali Taj and made in Pancholi's Lahore studio, this was mainly a Nurjehan musical about a man seduced by a gold-digging woman, who then kills her and her lover and is jailed. When he is released, he finds employment as a gardener and becomes a father-figure to his employer's son Anwar and to Anwar's fiancee Zeenat (Nurjehan). This allows him to prevent Anwar from perpetuating precisely the same crime for which he had been jailed as history repeats itself because, so the film alleges, men are constantly threatened by women and only paternal wisdom can save them from the untoward desires of women.

KUNWARA BAAP

aka *Bachelor Father*
1942 134' b&w Hindi
d/co-s **Kishore Sahu** *pc* Acharya Art Prod. *st* D.N. Naik *co-sc* Sardindu Bannerjee *dial/co-lyr* Amritlal Nagar *co-lyr* Balam, Satyakam, Sharma *c* Rajanikant Pandya *m* Ramchandra Pal
lp Kishore Sahu, **Protima Dasgupta**, Baby Lal, Anjali Devi, Dhulia, Manohar Ghatwani, Moni Chatterjee, Jamu Patel, Hadi, Amritlal Nagar

One of Kishore Sahu's better-known films. The comedy concerns a bachelor who is about to marry a pretty girl when he discovers an infant child abandoned in his car. A rare screen contribution by the eminent Hindi novelist and playwright Amritlal Nagar (author of novels such as *Boond Aur Samudra*, 1956; *Shatranj Ke Mohre*, 1959, etc.) who wrote the dialogues and the lyrics as well as acting in the film.

MEENAKSHI

1942 155'[B]/146'[H] b&w Bengali/Hindi
d **Modhu Bose** *pc* **New Theatres** *st* Manmatha Ray *dial*[H] Amjad Hussain *lyr*[H] Bhushan *c* **Bimal Roy** *m* **Pankaj Mullick**

lp **Sadhona Bose, Ahindra Choudhury**, Jyoti Prakash(B)/Najmul Hussain[H], **K.C. Dey, Naresh Mitra**, Debabala, Preeti Majumdar, Panna Devi, Rajalakshmi

This Sadhona Bose star vehicle sees her as Meenakshi, who blunders into the flat of rich playboy Amitabh (Prakash/Hussain) while escaping from a venal marriage arranged by her tyrannical uncle. Amitabh protects her and falls in love. Later, when her presence in his flat is used to blackmail him, he suspects that he has been set up and throws Meenakshi out. They meet again when, coincidentally, she finds shelter with Amitabh's mother. But then Meenakshi starts going blind and runs away again. An operation is performed by the very man to whom she was first betrothed and from whom she had run away. He cures her and ensures the happy ending.

MUQABALA

1942 133' b&w Hindi
d/co-s **Nanabhai Bhatt** *co-d* **Babubhai Mistri** *pc* **Wadia Movietone** *co-s* **J.B.H. Wadia** *lyr* A. Karim *c* Anant Kadam *m* Khan Mastana
lp **Fearless Nadia**, Yakub, Agha, Baby Madhuri, Dalpat

Nadia departed from her Zorro-like persona to make her last film for Wadia Movietone (before it it became Basant Pics), a double role of twin sisters: the good Madhuri and the bad Rita. The villain, rebuffed by the infant twins' mother, kidnaps Rita, whom he raises to be a nightclub singer and gangster's moll. Madhuri is brought up by the good Rai Bahadur. Madhuri impersonates her sister, after holding her up with her own gun-shaped cigarette lighter, and unmasks the villain. The climax has Madhuri's planned assassination at the hands of the villain as part of a magic show, raising tension when Madhuri exchanges places with Rita. Nadia's stilted Hindi and orthodox (by the 40s) performance contrasts sharply with the mobile presence of comedian Agha, playing Yakub's sidekick. The film claims to be the first in India to use a split-screen for a double role, and included some bravura special effects by Mistri, e.g. one sister walking across the other even though the camera establishes both to be Nadia. Other highlights including the spectacular nightclub set that can be transformed into a respectable residence within minutes, using complicated pulleys, whenever cops raid the place.

PAHILA PALNA

1942 144' b&w Marathi
d/s **Vishram Bedekar** *pc* New Huns Pics *lyr* **G.D. Madgulkar**, Bobde *c* Pandurang Naik *m* C. Balaji
lp **Shanta Hublikar**, Indu Natu, Balabhai, Kusum Deshpande, **Baburao Pendharkar**, Dinkar Kamanna, G.D. Madgulkar, Vishnupant Aundhkar

A prime example of the growing popularity in the 40s of a formulaic comedy genre satirising Maharashtrian middle-class aspirations towards modernity. Inspired by the **Vinayak-Atre** style of comedy, Bedekar's film tells the story of Dhananjay (Pendharkar), who belongs to a conventional family, and his modern wife Chitra (Hublikar, in a screen image continued from ***Mazha Mulga***, 1938). Chitra's sister Banu (Natu) and her husband are birth-control zealots. When Chitra and Dhananjay settle down in his ancestral home in the village, a series of vignettes on the theme of married life show Chitra's efforts to change things greatly resisted by the family. This reaches crisis point when she presides over a public meeting on birth control. She leaves to become a schoolteacher. Dhananjay joins her and she gets pregnant, in spite of her sister's admonitions. When the child is born, the proud Dhananjay goes to show it to his dying father. In the end, Chitra is shown accepting the traditionalist strictures imposed on her modernity by Dhananjay's parents. The noted scenarist Madgulkar debuted here as a lyricist (e.g. *Lagle mitaya dole*).

PAHILI MANGALAGAUR

1942 122' b&w Marathi
d R.S. Junnarkar *pc* **Navyug Chitrapat** *st/dial* V.V. Bokil *sc* Achyut Govind Ranade *lyr* Baburao Gokhale *c* Pandurang Naik *m* Dada Chandekar
lp Snehprabha Pradhan, Sudha Apte, **Lata Mangeshkar**, Shobha Kumari, **Shahu Modak**, Dada Salvi, Vishnupant Jog, **Damuanna Malvankar**, Gopinath Sawkar

This comedy about arranged marriages started as a **Vinayak** production, completed by Junnarkar when Vinayak left Navyug. When the handsome doctor Sadashiv (Modak) sets up a new clinic in Pune, he finds himself with no patients but is beseiged with marriage offers. Chintu (Jog), son of the crusty patriarch, tricks him into coming home to examine his supposedly ill sister Sarala (Pradhan). One of the major scenes in the film is a cross-talk as Sadashiv asks medical questions while her father examines him as a prospective son-in-law. Sarala and Sadashiv get married, when suddenly Lily, Sadashiv's old girlfriend who is related to the local village gossip, surfaces. As with all of Huns-Navyug films, the snappy dialogue was crucial to the film, which includes kissing scenes. It is also remembered for Lata Mangeshkar's film debut as actress and singer.

PATNI

1942 194' b&w Telugu
d **Gudavalli Ramabrahmam** *pc* Sarathi Films *s/lyr* **Tapi Dharma Rao** *c* Sudhish Ghatak *m* Kopparapu Subba Rao
lp **K.S. Prakash Rao, Surabhi Kamalabai,** Rushyendramani, Haimavathi, Vangara, Kocherlakota Satyanarayana

Ramabrahmam (***Malapilla***, 1938; ***Raitu Bidda***, 1939) departs radically from his earlier style, adapting the Kannagi legend (cf ***Kannagi***, 1942) with Rushyendramani in the title role and future director Prakash Rao as her husband. Given Ramabrahmam's political inclinations, this version may have addressed the colonial present more directly than Jupiter Pics' version.

RAJA RANI

1942 136' b&w Hindi
d Najam Naqvi *pc* Atre Pics *p/s* **P.K. Atre** *dial* Anand Kumar *c* Surendra Pai *m* Khan Mastana
lp Vanamala, Trilok Kapoor, Sunalini Devi, Maya Devi, Baby Vimal, Mazhar Khan, Navin Yagnik

Atre produced and scripted this melodrama about the fragmentation of a joint family. Raja (Kapoor) and Rani (Vanamala) marry and are welcomed with much ceremony by the family. Gradually dissensions caused mainly through envy lead the couple to set up their own separate home. Their ambition to live beyond their means brings creditors and a financial crisis. An early instance of a predominantly Marathi film unit branching into Hindi cinema.

ROTI

1942 153' b&w Hindi
d **Mehboob Khan** *pc* National Studio *st* **R.S. Choudhury** *sc/co-lyr* Wajahat Mirza *lyr* Safdar 'Aah', Munshi Arzoo Lucknowi, Wajahad Lucknowi *c* Faredoon Irani *m* **Anil Biswas**
lp **Chandramohan**, Sheikh Mukhtar, **Sitara Devi**, Akhtari Faizabadi, Ashraf Khan, Kayamali, Jamshedji, Mirza, Waskar, Choubeji, Nawab, Agha

Mehboob's classic, didactic film counterposing capitalism and primitive tribal communism. The film's crooked commentator (A. Khan) persuades the starving hero (Chandramohan), to impersonate Seth Laxmidas, the long-lost heir of a rich family. In the process, the hero reveals himself as a ruthless entrepreneur and acquires the Laxmidas business empire. He and his girlfriend Darling (Faizabadi, a legendary ghazal singer in a rare film appearance) happen to crash their private plane and wind up in a tribal, sexually liberated community which ignores notions of private property and believes in the basic goodness of all humankind. The tribals Balam (Mukhtar) and Kinari (Sitara Devi) look after the injured capitalist and help him get back to the city by lending him a pair of buffaloes, Changu and Mangu, who are friends rather than beasts of burden. When the animals are not returned, the tribals go to the city to retrieve them. They are astounded by the way capitalism functions; they have no concept of money and get arrested for eating food they cannot pay for. Their gradual descent into bonded labour is intercut with the machinations of Laxmidas, who has his future father-in-law murdered. Eventually, with the help of Darling (who falls in love with Balam), the tribal couple manages to leave, even as Laxmidas, facing disaster, escapes from his outraged shareholders in a car full of gold bricks. He encounters the tribals again in the desert where his car has broken down. In an echo of Stroheim's *Greed* (1925), he refuses their offer of water, preferring to die of thirst. The film's dominant character is the fat, cynical commentator (echoeing a Brechtian device) who manipulates the story, laughs every time disaster strikes and ridicules compassion (*Garibon ki daya karke bada ahsaan karte ho*) in a kind of prose chant. Begum Akhtar aka Akhtari Faizabadi gives a fine performance as Darling, the woman who accepts her role as a sex object and the property of the capitalist while hating him inwardly for the murder of her father.

SARKARI PAHUNE

aka *State Guests*
1942 164' b&w Marathi
d **Master Vinayak** *pc* **Navyug Chitrapat** *st* C.V. Joshi's short story *s* **V.S. Khandekar** *lyr* Rajkavi Yeshwant *c* Vasudev Karnataki *m* Datta Davjekar
lp **Damuanna Malvankar**, Vishnupant Jog, Nandu Khote, Saroj Borkar, Vatsala Kumthekar, Shakuntala Bhome

Vinayak claimed this, his best-known of the Gundyabhau-Chimanrao films and the first one without **Atre**, to be his only truly political film. His earlier satires (***Brahmachari***, 1938; ***Brandichi Batli/Brandy Ki Botal***, 1939) primarily reflected Atre's literary and political attitudes. This film spoofs the still-influential feudal nobility in pre-WW2 Maharashtra. Kautai (Bhome), recently married to Chimanrao (Malvankar) (cf ***Lagna Pahave Karun***, 1940), claims to be a distant relative of the king of a small state and takes her husband and his bachelor-cousin Gundyabhau (Jog) for a family visit to the 'palace'. The fancy Ford sent to collect them from the railway station is pulled by two oxen (the origin of the classic joke about the 'Ox-Ford'). They find their lodgings have no electricity and the servants are less than honest. Gundyabhau, the convinced misogynist, experiences a crisis when faced by a seductive dancer (Kumthekar). Like its prequel, *Lagna Pahave Karun*, the film has an episodic narrative, deploys dialogues with a strong period flavour and has extended comic set pieces like the musical contest between Gundyabhau and the dancer.

SATYABHAMA

1942 183' b&w Telugu
d **Y.V. Rao** *pc* Jagdish Films *dial* Sivasankara Sastry, S.G. Acharya *lyr* Daita Gopalam *m* Gotu Narayana Iyer
lp Y.V. Rao, Addanki, Pushpavalli, Sthanam, Purnima, Kasturi

Y.V. Rao also plays the lead, Krishna, in this mythological derived from the *Mahabharata*. Krishna restores the Syamantak gem from the bear-king Jambavanta to Shatrujit, receiving in return the hand of Shatrujit's daughter in marriage. The film is sometimed presented as an early example of the introduction of low Tamil comedy into Telugu cinema.

SHESH UTTAR/JAWAB

1942 144'[B]/157'[H] b&w Bengali/Hindi
d **P.C. Barua** *pc* MP Prod *st* Shashadhar Dutt *lyr* Buddhichandra Agarwal 'Madhur', Bekal[H] *m* **Kamal Dasgupta**
lp **Kanan Devi**, Jamuna, P.C. Barua, **Ahindra Choudhury**, Devbala, **Jahar Ganguly**, **Tulsi Chakraborty**

Barua's last major film continues his concern with the fortunes of an aimless feudal upper class (***Devdas***, 1935; ***Mukti***, 1937). The rich, self-absorbed and, to his family, deranged Manoj (Barua) is sent to his future father-in-law for a rest cure. However, he loses his way and is offered shelter by a railway station-master with whose daughter he falls in love. The poor, earthy and worldly-wise Meena (Kanan Devi) is contrasted with the hero's rich fiancee Reba (Jamuna) and the eventual confrontation between the two women provides the justification for Manoj's decision to marry the former. The film established Murlidhar Chatterjee's new company as one of the foremost producers of socials in Bengali cinema. The Hindi version included classic Kanan Devi numbers such as *Toofan mail* and *Kuch yaad rahe to sun kar jaa*.

STATION MASTER

1942 157' b&w Hindi
d **Chimanlal Luhar** *pc* Prakash Pics *co-s/co-dial/co-lyr* P.L. Santoshi *co-s* Vishnupant Aundhkar *co-dial/co-lyr* Chaturvedi *co-lyr* Indra, V.R. Sharma *c* G.N. Shirodkar *m* **Naushad**
lp Jagdish Sethi, Prem Adib, P. Ratnamala, Jeevan, Umakant, Kaushalya, Shakir, Amirbai Karnataki, **Suraiya**, Gulab, Pratima Devi

Melodrama by a stunt-film director. The story features various characters employed in a small railway station. Arun, a new guard, loves Uma, daughter of the old station-master. Through the machinations of a clerk to the district traffic superintendent, their marriage cannot take place. The clerk wants his own daughter to marry Arun and he persuades the superintendent, a widower, to marry Uma. Uma's tragic life is woven into a railway accident for which the station-master is held responsible until an investigation acquits him. Arun's injury sustained in the event brings all the subterranean intrigues into the open.

VASANTSENA

1942 167'[M]/166'[H] b&w Marathi/Hindi
d **Gajanan Jagirdar** *pc* Atre Pics *p/s/lyr*[M] **P.K.Atre** *lyr* Neelkanth Tiwari, D.N. Madhok, P.L. Santoshi *c* S. Haridas *m* **Master Krishnarao**
lp Vanamala, Chintamanrao Kolhatkar[M]/Gajanan Jagirdar[H], **Shahu Modak**, Baby Devi, Sunalini Devi, Vimala Tripathi, Rajvishwas, Vijaya, Sudhir Gore, Raja Pandit, Gokhale, Balwant Parchure[M], Vinay Kale[M], Dange[M], Eruch Tarapore[H], Navin Yagnik[H], Nazir Bedi[H]

Based on Shudraka's classic 3rd-C. Sanskrit play *Mrichakatika*, the main plot of the Brahmin Charudatta's (Modak) love for the courtesan Vasantsena (Vanamala) is interwoven with a parallel plot concerning the popular revolt in Ujjain against the despotic King Palaka, whose state is effectively run by his tyranical brother-in-law Shakar (Jagirdar/Kolhatkar). The rebels want to replace him with the Gopalaputra Aryaka. The film belongs mainly to Atre and is one of his occasional departures from comedy to update a classic text into a contemporary idiom.

ZAMINDAR

1942 166' b&w Hindi
d **Moti B. Gidwani** *pc* **Pancholi** Art Pics *s* Imtiaz Ali Taj *lyr* Qamar Jalalabadi, Behzad Lucknowi, Nazim Panipatti, D.N. Madhok *c* M.N. Malhotra *m* **Ghulam Haider**
lp **Shanta Apte**, Manorama, Ghulam Mohammed, M. Esmail, S.D. Narang, M. Ajmal, Baby Akhtar, Durga Mota, Khairati, M. Manzoor, G.N. Butt

Pancholi's sequel to their big hit ***Khazanchi*** (1941) is a murder mystery indicting feudal patriarchy. The tyrannical village zamindar Ganesh (Mohammed) sacks his trusty manager Raghubir (Esmail) with whose daughter Rupa (Apte) the zamindar's son Karan (Narang) is in love. Karan is disinherited when he sides with the tenants. Unable to live with the tyranny, the tenants draw lots to kill Ganesh just when he is starting to repent his actions. Ganesh is killed with Karan's gun and the son is arrested. Rupa then finds a clue identifying the real killer but cannot reveal it to the police inspector (Butt). Only Rambha (Akhtar), a blind woman, knows the ancestral truth that will solve the mystery.

BHAGYA LAKSHMI

1943 192' b&w Telugu
d **P. Pullaiah** *pc* Renuka Films *p/s* Chittor V. Nagaiah *dial/lyr* **Samudrala Raghavacharya** *c* M.A. Rehman *m* **B. Narasimha Rao**
lp **Chittor V. Nagaiah**, Doraiswamy, Umamaheshwara Rao, Giri, Raghavan, Gauripathy Sastry, **N.S. Krishnan**, T.A. Mathuram, Malati, **T. Suryakumari**, Kamala Kotnis

Melodrama about unrequited love. The music teacher Srinivasa Rao (Nagaiah) loves Bhagya Lakshmi (Malati) but her parents arrange for her to marry another man, Vishwanatha Rao (Giri). When the lovesick hero spurns the vamp Kamakshi, she starts a rumour suggesting Srinivasa Rao is having a sexual affair with Bhagya Lakshmi, causing the heroine to be thrown out of her home. Eventually the hero patches up the marriage between Bhagya Lakshmi and Vishwanatha Rao. Nagaiah hired Pullaiah to direct his first independent production designed to refurbish the star's heroic screen image after playing second leads and Saint films at **Vauhini**. The film had one classic Nagaiah song hit, *Asha nirasha*. According to V.A.K. Ranga Rao, this was the first time in Telugu cinema that a playback singer, **R. Balasaraswathi**, received an explicit credit for her Kamala Kotnis songs, acknowledging that actors did not always sing their songs.

CHENCHULAKSHMI

1943 ?' b&w Telugu
d **S. Soundararajan** *pc* Tamil Nadu Talkies *s/lyr* **Samudrala Raghavacharya** *c* Jiten Bannerjee *m* **C.R. Subburaman**, R.N. Chinnaiah
lp Kamala Kotnis, **Chittor V. Nagaiah**, Narayana Rao, Rushyendramani, Lanka Sathyam

Mythological continuing the often-filmed *Vishnu Purana* legend of Prahlada and

Hiranyakashapu. After the demon Hiranyakashapu is destroyed, Vishnu's (Narayana Rao) consort Lakshmi (Kotnis) takes the earthly form of a chenchu (tribal) to soothe and entice Vishnu out of his rage. Her success, marriage and eventual recognition as the goddess forms the major part of the film. Mainly known for Subburaman's innovative score. For his debut film, he drew on Latin American music for the credit sequence and to accompany a tribal dance. Nagaiah plays the tribal woman's father. A 1958 remake starring **A. Nageshwara Rao** and **Anjali Devi** was a major hit (made by B.A. Subba Rao).

DUHAI

1943 120' b&w Hindi
d/s **V.M. Vyas** *pc* Sunrise Pics *s* **Mohanlal G. Dave** *dial* **Zia Sarhadi** *lyr* Bharat Vyas *c* Dwarka Divecha *m* Rafiq Ghaznavi, Pannalal Ghosh, Shanti Kumar
lp **Shanta Apte, Nurjehan**, Kumar, Zarina, Mirza Musharraf, Ansari, Butt Kaser, Kesarbai

Vyas's romantic thriller pivots mainly around the unusual co-presence of the singing stars Apte and Nurjehan. Rural beauty Neela (Apte) loves the urbane Rajendra (Kumar) and they decide to get married against the wishes of her father Jugal Babu (Ansari). Jugal, it turns out, knows the family secret: Rajendra's father had years ago tried to seduce Neela's mother and had been killed by Neela's brother Basant (Kaser), who has been in hiding ever since. The plot gets more complicated when the singer and dancer Urvashi (Nurjehan) falls for Rajendra and, one evening in a nightclub, unable to perform in front of him, is replaced on stage by Neela. The dramatic highlight is when Jugal Babu, telling Neela the terrible past history of her brother, gets her to promise never to reveal the truth to her husband.

GARUDA GARVABHANGAM

1943 178' b&w Telugu
d **Ghantasala Balaramaiah** *pc* Pratibha Pics *s/lyr* **Samudrala Raghavacharya** *m* Galipenchala Narasimha Rao
lp **Vemuri Gaggaiah, P. Bhanumathi**, Ramakrishna Sastry, Mandavalli Sandow, **Vedantam Raghavaiah**

Mythological featuring a contest between Garuda (the eagle) and Hanuman (the monkey god), regarded as Vishnu's two most trusted followers. Although Garuda can see the original Vishnu avatar underneath Vishnu's current incarnation as Rama, Hanuman has greater access to Rama, his temporal master. The film, adapted from a stage play, was noted mainly for Bhanumathi's singing, re-released in HMV's series *Alanati Andaalu*.

JOGAJOG/HOSPITAL

1943 120' b&w Bengali/Hindi
d/co-s **Sushil Majumdar** *pc* MP Prod *st* Manmatha Ray *co-sc* **Premendra Mitra** *dial/co-lyr*[H] Bhushan *co-lyr* Buddhichandra Agarwal 'Madhur' *c* Ajit Sen *m* **Kamal Dasgupta**
lp **Kanan Devi, Ahindra Choudhury**, Robin Majumdar, **Tulsi Chakraborty, Jahar Ganguly**[B], Bhanu Bannerjee[B], **Kanu Bannerjee**[B], Jawahar[H], Krishna[H], Promode[H]

Pratima (Kanan Devi), a nurse, is persuaded by the crooked Jayant to pretend to be his wife for a day, in order to convince his father Dr Dindayal of his need for money. Dr Dindayal likes his new daughter-in-law very much and wants her to accompany him to the country where he runs a charitable hospital in the name of his late wife. There Dr Bhatt, Dindayal's rival, finds out by hiring detectives that Pratima and Jayant are not married. He uses the information to try to oust Dindayal from the hospital. The solution eventually links with Pratima's growing sense of responsibility towards Dr Dindayal's medical endeavours.

KISMET

1943 143' b&w Hindi
d/sc **Gyan Mukherjee** *pc* **Bombay Talkies** *p* S. Mukherjee *st/dial* P.L. Santoshi, Shahid Latif *lyr* Pradeep *c* R.D. Pareenja *m* **Anil Biswas**
lp **Ashok Kumar**, Mumtaz Shanti, Shah Nawaz, Moti, P.F. Pithawala, Chandraprabha, V.H. Desai, Kanu Roy, Jagannath Aurora, Prahlad, Harun, Mubarak, David, Kumari Kamala

The supreme hit, the fourth success in a row for producer Mukherjee (***Kangan***, 1939, ***Bandhan***, 1940; ***Jhoola***, 1941), made by the people who were to launch the **Filmistan** Studio. Pickpocket Shekhar (A. Kumar) befriends an old man (Pithawala) who once owned a theatre and is the father of its star singer, Rani (Shanti). In a fit of greed he made his daughter dance to exhaustion, making her a cripple. Now she is employed by, and indebted to, the theatre's new owner, the villain Indrajit. Shekhar steals Indrajit's wife's valuable necklace and Rani rescues him from the cops. Shekhar and Rani fall in love and he wants to raise the money to cure her disability. The crisis is precipitated when Rani unwittingly wears the stolen necklace and is caught by the police. Shekhar owns up, is arrested, escapes from the police and raids Indrajit's house to pay for Rani's operation. Caught again, Shekhar is saved from a long jail sentence by the revelation that he is Indrajit's long-lost son. Shekhar's newly found brother Mohan is permitted to marry Rani's sister Lila (whom he had made pregnant) and the happy ending sees all protagonists united in the family of the patriarch Indrajit. Known for its musical hits, Kumar's ebullient performance and Shanti's voice, the film assimilates the Warner Bros. realist style with 'expressionist' overtones, esp. in some of its classic, often anthologised sequences, e.g. Shekhar's escape from the cops in a puff of cigarette smoke or the final robbery scene. A contemporary review in *Filmindia* (Feb. 1943) condemned the film for imitating John Cromwell's *Algiers* (1938) while glorifying crime, making it a bad influence on the younger generation. It includes the patriotic song *Aaj himalay ki choti se phir humne lalkara hai*. The film, which ran for 3 consecutive years in the same cinema in Calcutta, is an early example of a pre-Partition 'lost and found' movie rehearsing the familiar pre-capitalist fairy-tale motif of members of a family who are separated by fate or villainy and eventually are 'recognised' and reunited.

Mumtaz Shanti (left) in *Kismet*

KRISHNA PREMA

1943 184' b&w Telugu
d **H.V. Babu** *pc* Famous/Star Combines *s/lyr* **Tapi Dharma Rao** *c* P.S. Selvaraj, Jiten Bannerjee *m* Galipenchala Narasimha Rao
lp Shantakumari, **P. Bhanumathi, T. Suryakumari**, Jayagauri, Himavathi, Parvathibai, Gali Venkateshwara Rao, Addanki, Hirannaya, Sangeetha Rao

This major musical hit, made at the **Vel** Pics Studio in their characteristic mythological genre, tells of Radha's (Shantakumari) devotion for Krishna (Venkateshwara Rao), which is supposed to exemplify divine love. Her love is scorned both by Radha's sister Chandravali (Bhanumathi) and by Krishna's wife Satyabhama (Himavathi). Krishna wins over Chandravali by impersonating her husband Chandragopa (Addanki). He then impersonates Radha herself to prove that divine love transcends sexual difference. The film united the three best-known Telugu actress-singers: Shantakumari, Bhanumathi and T. Suryakumari (as the trouble-making Narada). Between them they had several numbers including *Godumu krishna*, *Chiluka palkuladana Repe vastadanta gopaludu* and *Oogave uyyala* that have become cultural legends.

MAHATMA VIDUR

1943 155' b&w Marathi/Hindi
d **P.Y. Altekar** *pc* CIRCO *st* **Mohanlal G. Dave** *dial/lyr* Narottam Vyas, **Mahesh Kaul**[H], Raja Badhe[M] *c* Dwarkadas Divecha, Purshottam Divecha *m* Harishchandra Bali
lp **Vishnupant Pagnis, Durga Khote**, Nayampalli, S. Prahlad, Manohar Ghatwani, Yashodhara Katju[H], Seeta Jhaveri[M], Kalyani, Nayampalli, Baby Madhuri[H], Sudha Amonkar[M]

Pagnis's last film is a miracle-laden Saint film chronicling a familiar episode from the *Mahabharata*. Vidur (Pagnis) takes a vow of non-violence and renounces his royal position, causing displeasure to the Kaurava kings. The art direction is by the prestigious **Baburao Painter** and V.H. Palnitkar.

MAZHE BAL

1943 122' b&w Marathi
d **Master Vinayak** *pc* Prafulla Pics *s/co-lyr* **V.S. Khandekar** *co-lyr* Madhav Julien *c* Madhav Bulbule *m* Datta Davjekar
lp Master Vinayak, Dada Salvi, Sumati Gupte, Meenakshi, **Lata Mangeshkar, Damuanna Malvankar**, Bhapurao Datar, Damuanna Joshi, Saroj Borker, Baby Nalini, Shripad Joshi, Baburao Athane, Ingavle, Renuka

Khandekar's didactic script for Vinayak continues his preoccupation with the character of a moral man whose principles conflict with practical reality. Manohar (Salvi, who plays this character's earlier version: Bappa in Vinayak's ***Amrit***, 1941) is an alcoholic but idealistic public prosecutor and calls for the death sentence for the nationalist anarchist Ravindra (Vinayak). Ravindra's girlfriend Shashi (Meenakshi) is pregnant and gives birth in an orphanage. She then becomes a nurse and has to look after Manohar who falls for her. She agrees to marry him but keeps her child a secret. When a child is found dead in the orphanage, Manohar prosecutes its humanitarian manager for infanticide. Shashi, who appears as a witness, reveals the truth of her life in court, causing a dramatic change in her husband's world-view.

MOHABBAT

1943 122' b&w Hindi
d/sc **Phani Majumdar** *pc* Laxmi Prod. *st* Bipradas Tagore *c* Jatin Das *m* Hariprasanna Das
lp **Shanta Apte, Pahadi Sanyal**, Jagdish Sethi, Sunalini Devi, Yashodhara Katju, **K.C. Dey**, S. Nazir

A musical advocacy of arranged marriages. Heroine Sujata (Apte) loves hero Jiban (Sanyal) and their parents are for their marrying, except that the villain Madanlal (Nazir) discovers some juicy facts about Sujata's father's past and tries blackmail. The problem is what Jiban's mother (Sunalini Devi), who repudiates her eldest son for marrying outside his caste, will say. This is the only joint appearance of the singing stars Apte and Sanyal. Apte's music included a memorable Meera bhajan, *Main Giridhar ke ghar jaoon*.

NADAAN

1943 118' b&w Hindi
d/s/co-lyr **Zia Sarhadi** *pc* A.B. Prod., Jyoti Studio *co-lyr* Tanvir Naqvi *c* R.M. Rele *m* K. Dutta (aka Dutta Koregaonkar)
lp **Nurjehan**, Maya Devi, Jilloo, Alaknanda, Mumtaz, Masood, Aman

A romantic adventure story about Anil (Masood) and Roopa (Nurjehan) who were promised to each other as children but start off their adult acquaintance on the wrong foot when Anil hands Roopa over to the police for resembling a face on a 'wanted' poster. They meet again when both become journalists on the same newspaper owned by Mukesh (Aman), who also fancies Roopa. The film boasts six Nurjehan numbers, including the famous *Ab to nahin duniya mein apna thikana*.

NAJMA

1943 121' b&w Hindi-Urdu
d/p **Mehboob Khan** *pc* Mehboob Prod. *s* Aga Jani Kashmiri *lyr* Anjum Pilibhiti *c* Faredoon Irani *m* Rafiq Ghaznavi
lp **Ashok Kumar**, Veena, **Sitara Devi**, Kumar, Yakub, Majid, Shantarin, Rajkumari Shukla, Murad

Muslim melodrama set in early 20th-C. Lucknow. The young doctor Yusuf (A. Kumar) loves Najma (Veena), daughter of a nawab. As Yusuf's family is not aristocratic, they cannot marry. Their respective marriages within their own class do not solve the problem. Mukarram (Kumar), Najma's husband, meets with an accident and is injured on his way to killing Yusuf, and Yusuf performs a miraculous operation saving Mukarram's life. Thus peace is restored between the two families. This was Mehboob's debut as independent producer under his own banner.

NAUKAR

1943 121' b&w Hindi-Urdu
d/sc Shaukat Hussain Rizvi *pc* Sunrise Pics *st/dial* **Sadat Hasan Manto** *lyr* Akhtar Sherani, Munshi Shamas, Nazim Panipatti *c* S. Shrivastav *m* Rafiq Ghaznavi, Shantikumar
lp **Shobhana Samarth, Chandramohan, Nurjehan**, Balwant Singh, Yakub, Miss Moti, Mirza Musharraf

A realist tragedy based on a story by the Urdu novelist Manto about Fazlu (Chandramohan), the lifelong servant of the Khwaja Islamuddin. Blamed for the death of Islamuddin's infant son Salim in a railway accident, Fazlu is jailed. Escaping from prison, he finds his wife has given birth to a son whom he believes to be Salim's reincarnation. The film chronicles Fazlu in his old age, when his son, also named Salim (Singh), befriends Nargis (Samarth), Mirza (Musharraf) and Sadiq (Yakub). When Fazlu moves to the city, he helplesly watches the destruction of his family by economic circumstances. Nargis dies in his arms, Mirza is arrested, Sadiq commits suicide and Fazlu ends up once again in prison. Much of the film works through symbols like the whistle of the railway engine evoking traumatic memories.

PAISA BOLTO AAHE/NAGAD NARAYAN

1943 122' b&w Marathi/Hindi
d/s **Vishram Bedekar** *pc* Navhans Chitra *dial*[H] Munshi Dil *lyr* **G.D. Madgulkar**[M], S.A. Shukla[M], Bekal[H], Shamim[H] *c* Pandurang Naik *m* Shridhar Parsekar
lp **Baburao Pendharkar**, Kusum Deshpande, Nalini Dhere[M]/Leela Desai[H], Nayampalli, Samant, Sudha Apte[M], Kanekar[M], P.R. Joshi[M], Bapurao Pawar[M], Dhumal[M], Masood[H], Bose[H], Pratima Devi[H], Shakir[H]

Allegory about the South Asian economy during WW2. Bapuji is an agent for the Rangoon Oil Co. Although he has made his money mainly through the black market, his daughter Vidya (Dhere/Desai) believes in his honesty. She meets a young man whom she scorns as he does not seem to be from her own social class, but then he turns out to be Lalnath, a director of Rangoon Oil. When the Japanese attack Pearl Harbor, Bapuji seizes the opportunity to make money but Lalnath orders an investigation into Bapuji's accounts. However, the rest of the company's Rangoon-based directors, chased out of the country by the Japanese, oppose Lalnath's honesty and throw him out. Eventually Vidya falls in love with Lalnath and sees the truth for herself.

PRITHVI VALLABH

1943 121' b&w Hindi
d **Sohrab Modi** *pc* **Minerva Movietone** *st* **K.M. Munshi** *s/lyr* Sudarshan *c* Y.D. Sarpotdar *m* Rafiq Ghaznavi, **Saraswati Devi**
lp **Sohrab Modi, Durga Khote**, Sankatha Prasad, Jehanara Kajjan, Meena, Sadiq Ali, K.N. Singh, Al Nasir, Navin Yagnik

Big-budget costume drama based on K.M. Munshi's 1920 novel of the same name. Prithvi Vallabh is the good Munja, king of

Avantipur (Modi), whom the evil Tailap (Prasad), rival king of Tailangan, had failed to defeat in repeated battles. Tailap finally succeeds through the machinations of his hard-headed sister Mrinalvati (Khote). The film's major highlights are the confrontations between Munja and the haughty Mrinalvati who tries to humiliate him publicly but then falls in love with him. When Munja has a chance to escape from his prison, he holds back so that Mrinalvati may accompany him but she, apprehensive of losing him, betrays Munja, who is then condemned to be trampled to death by an elephant. Unlike Modi's earlier ventures into big-budget territory (***Pukar***, 1939; ***Sikandar***, 1941), this was not a major success.

RAMRAJYA

aka *Lav Kush*
1943 144' b&w Hindi/Marathi
d **Vijay Bhatt** *pc* Prakash Pics *s/dial*[M] Vishnupant Aundhkar *dial*[H] Sampatlal Srivastava 'Anuj' *lyr* Ramesh Gupta[H], Raja Badhe[M] *c* P.G. Kukde *m* Shankarrao Vyas
lp **Shobhana Samarth**, Yeshwant, Madhusudhan, V.D. Pandit, Amirbai Karnataki, Shantakumari, Ranjana, Leela Pawar, Baby Tara, Prem Adib[H]/Chandrakant[M], Umakant[H], G. Badriprasad[H], Pande[H], Bahadur[H], Vinay Kale[M], Bandopant Sohoni[M], Kelkar[M], Kumari Kamala[M]

Bhatt's best-known and most successful *Ramayana* musical. Rama (Adib/Chandrakant) triumphantly returns from exile having conquered Lanka and rescued Seeta (Samarth), but a washerwoman queries whether Seeta remained chaste during her captivity. To allay suspicions, Rama sends Seeta into the forest where, under the care of Valmiki, she gives birth to twin boys. Later, Rama launches the Ashwamedha Yagna ritual: a horse is let loose as an open challenge for anyone to stop it and do battle with the king. The two adolescent boys, thanks to Valmiki's teachings, succeed in the challenge. The big-budget art direction was a classic contribution by neo-classical kitsch artist Kanu Desai. The final battle with fire spewing magical arrows was the film's highlight. The Marathi version contains the hit song *Ladakya ranila lagale dohale*.

SAMADHAN

1943 c.120' b&w Bengali
d/s **Premendra Mitra** *pc* S.D. Prod. *c* **Ajoy Kar** *m* Rabin Chatterjee
lp **Chhabi Biswas**, Rabin Majumdar, **Dhiraj Bhattacharya**, Sandhyarani, Purnima, Krishnadhan Mukherjee, Indu Mukherjee, Shyam Laha, **Chhaya Devi**

Mitra tells a story familiar from late feudal romances and 19th-C. dime novels. A working-class leader confronts a villainous factory owner, falls in love with the boss's daughter unaware of her family origins and, after many adventures and setbacks, it is revealed that the hero is in fact the official heir to the property the villain had usurped. An influential Bengali novelist acknowledging allegiance to socialism, Mitra's studio-bound film concentrates on showing the milieu of the rich while the dialogues make numerous references to the workers and the poor. **Nitin Bose**'s ***Didi/President*** (1937) and **Bimal Roy**'s ***Udayer Pathey/Hamrahi*** (1944) tell similar stories.

SANJOG

1943 122' b&w Hindi
d/p **A.R. Kardar** *pc* Kardar Prod. *s/co-lyr* Waqif *co-lyr* D.N. Madhok *c* Dwarka Divecha *m* **Naushad**
lp Mehtab, Charlie, Wasti, Ulhas, Anwar Hussain, A. Shah

A romantic musical comedy of mistaken identity. Deepak Raj (Charlie) arrives at the magnificent house of the maharaja of Pahadganj (Shah) and is mistaken for Surendra (Hussain), the maharaja's future son-in-law. Deepak's crooked sidekick Jugal Kishore (Wasti) urges Deepak to continue the masquerade and the Princess Bina Kumari (Mehtab) falls in love with him, believing him to be her fiance. The film has many comic references to military-style discipline, including Surendra's father who is obsessed with holding court-martials. The actress-singer **Suraiya** performs several songs in playback, including *Mori gali more raja*, *Oh oh, ai ai* and *Kaun gali ka chhora pukare*. The film anticipated Kardar's **Kishore Kumar** comedies.

SHAHAR THEKE DOORAY

1943 121' b&w Bengali
d/s **Sailajananda Mukherjee** *pc* Eastern Talkies *c* **Ajoy Kar** *m* Subal Dasgupta
lp **Jahar Ganguly**, **Dhiraj Bhattacharya**, Renuka Roy, **Naresh Mitra**, Molina Devi, **Pashupti Chatterjee**, **Kanu Bannerjee**, Phani Roy, Prabhadevi

Hit rural melodrama confirming the novelist Sailajananda Mukherjee as a film-maker. Ratan (zestfully played by Ganguly), the carefree hero of the village youth, is under pressure from his mother to remarry since his current marriage is childless. The mother chooses Jaya, although Jaya loves the doctor temporarily working in the village. The drama's main villain is the evil president of the union board, and its emotional high points include a savage suicide bid by Ratan's wife before events come to a happy ending. The wordy film (characteristic of Mukherjee's cinema) rehearsed the familiar tensions between country/tradition and city/modernity in the form of a morality tale set in an idyllic rural landscape that becomes the value-laden terrain of the conflict. The film was remade by **Tarun Majumdar** in 1981, one of the main inheritors of the rural melodrama genre.

SHAKUNTALA

1943 122' b&w Hindi
d/p **V. Shantaram** *pc* **Rajkamal Kalamandir** *s/co-lyr* Dewan Sharar *st* Kalidasa's play *co-lyr* Ratanpriya *c* V. Avadhoot *m* **Vasant Desai**
lp Jayashree, **Chandramohan**, Nimbalkar, Zohra, Shantarin, Vidya, Kumar Ganesh, Raja Pandit, Vilas, Amina, Nana Paliskar

Having quit the **Prabhat** Studio, Shantaram inaugurated his new company with this costumed adaptation of Kalidasa's 3rd-C. play. The beautiful Shakuntala (Jayashree) gets pregnant following a romance with King Dushyanta (Chandramohan), but she is rejected when she arrives at his royal court. Abandoned, she bears a son, Bharat (Ganesh), in the forest. When a repentant Dushyanta comes to take her back she refuses, using the same language with which she had been evicted, but the two are eventually reconciled. Shantaram writes that the venture was a major gamble, made during WW2 and in a changed film-industry context. Both the future of his new studio as well as his reputation depended on its success, established when the film became a major hit running for 104 consecutive weeks. Shantaram intended the birth of Bharat to symbolise the newly independent India. The film remains one of the best-known adaptations of the literary classic, and has a quaint period flavour as an early instance of the director's highly decorative use of neo-classical design, which later degenerated into garish calendar art. A 76' version was released in the USA, where *Life* magazine saw it as having a 'touch of *William Tell*'.

SHANKAR PARVATI

1943 122' b&w Hindi
d/s **Chaturbhuj Doshi** *pc* **Ranjit Movietone** *dial/lyr* Indra *c* D.K.Ambre *m* Gyan Dutt
lp **Sadhona Bose**, Aroon, Kamala Chatterjee, Brijmala, Bhagwandas, Rajendra, Rewashankar Marwadi, Mahipal

A dance-based mythological featuring Shankar (Aroon), the triad in the Hindu pantheon (sometimes equated with Dionysus), who dances the Tandava, the dance of destruction, when his wife Sati kills herself after she is humiliated by her father. He then retires into meditation from which he has to be awoken to rid the world of the demon Tarakasura. The seductive powers of Sati, reborn as Parvati (Bose), liven up Shankar but she has to pay for this by doing extensive penance, after which she can be accepted again by her husband as a real wife, partly through the divine intervention of Vishnu. The film highlights Bose's dancing talents but its real interest for contemporary viewers is in the tale's overtly Oedipal overtones together with its status as a blatant allegory about female sexuality as both a life-restoring force and a potential threat to be brought under control by and for men (including highlighting the function of religion in this process of repression).

TANSEN

1943 122' b&w Hindi
d/s **Jayant Desai** *co-dial/co-lyr* D.N. Madhok *co-dial* Munshi Dil *co-lyr* Indra *c* Gordhanbhai Patel *m* **Khemchand Prakash**
lp **K.L. Saigal**, Khurshid, Mubarak, Nagendra, Kamaladevi Chatterjee, Bhagwandas

One of Saigal's best-known later films features him as Tansen, a legendary classical musician at the 16th-C. court of Mughal Emperor Akbar who composed some of the best-known ragas, including the *Darbari* and the *Malhar*. Director Desai, who appears after the credits surrounded by camera equipment, presents the story as a love fantasy between Tansen and a shepherdess, Tani (Khurshid), and rehearses several legends about Indian music, including its ability to calm animals, cause trees to flower and cure gravely ill people. Having joined Akbar's (Mubarak) court, which separates him from his lover, Tansen has to sing the raga *Deepak* to cure Akbar's daughter. Since the raga is supposed to have the power to create fire, it almost consumes the singer and he is saved by Tani's singing of the rainmaking raga *Megh Malhar*. Both songs, *Diya jalao* and *Baraso re*, were big hits. One of the film's 13 songs, Madhok's *Ho dukhia jiyara rote naina* was composed, uncredited, by **Bulo C. Rani**. This is Khurshid's best-known performance, holding her own as a singer alongside the legendary Saigal.

TAQDEER

aka *Destiny*
1943 113' b&w Hindi
d/p **Mehboob Khan** *pc* Mehboob Prod. *st* Ghulam Mohammed *sc/dial* Aga Jani Kashmiri *lyr* Mehrul Kadri *c* Faredoon Irani *m* Rafiq Ghaznavi
lp **Motilal, Chandramohan, Nargis,** Charlie, Jilloo, Kayamali, Ansari

In between his more ambitious ***Najma*** (1943) and ***Humayun*** (1945), Mehboob made this lightweight comedy about Justice Gangaprasad (Chandramohan) and theatre-owner Seth Badriprasad (Charlie) who lose their daughter and son respectively in the Kumbh Mela. The children are exchanged and Gangaprasad brings up Babu (Motilal) as a rich playboy while Badriprasad raises Salma (Nargis) as a dancer in his theatre. Later, the two fall in love, which is a problem in view of the class difference between them. This is resolved when their true parentage is discovered. An interesting though unexplored aspect of the story is that Gangaprasad's wife (played by the silent film star Jilloo), brings up Babu believing him to be a girl. The peasant song *Meri mata bharat mata*, with Nargis holding a sickle and a cloth bundle, intercut with shots of waving fields, foreshadows glimpses of her role in ***Mother India*** (1957).

TASVEER

1943 122' b&w Hindi
d/dial Najmul Hussain (aka Najam) Naqvi *pc* Excelsior Film Exchange *sc* **P.K. Atre** *lyr* Munshi Arzoo *m* Ramchandra Pal
lp **Durga Khote, Motilal,** Swarnalata, David, Azoorie, Navin Yagnik

Romantic comedy about a philandering Dr Ambadas (David), his childless wife Vidya Devi (Khote), the beautiful Kishori (Swarnalata) who meets the couple when her dog chases Ambadas into the river, and the photographer Jayant (Motilal) who loves Kishori. After some standard plot cliches (e.g. Jayant overhears Kishori rehearsing a play but mistakes the lines for an actual conversation), Jayant, Ambadas and Vidya Devi all decide to commit suicide but Jayant's sister Tara (Azoorie) sets things right.

WAPAS

1943 122' b&w Hindi
d **Hemchandra Chunder** *pc* **New Theatres** *s* Benoy Chatterjee *dial* Natwar *lyr* Bhushan, Zakir Hussain, Akhtar Chughtai *c* Sudhin Majumdar *m* **Rai Chand Boral**
lp Asit Baran, Bharati Devi, **Dhiraj Bhattacharya,** Latika Bannerjee, Nawab, Maya Bose, Indu Mukherjee, Nawab

A city/country melodrama telling of the village boy Shyam (Baran) who loves the city girl Shobha (Bharati Devi) who arrives in the village with her retired father (Mukherjee). Their wedding plans are resisted by both families, esp. after Shyam's miserly father (Nawab) insults Shobha's father. Her family returns to the city where she is to marry Rajendra (Bhattacharya), the nephew of her father's employer. Shyam follows her to the city and finds work as Rajendra's coach-driver. The happy ending is achieved by Rajendra agreeing that Shyam should replace him as the groom while he then becomes their chauffeur.

Wapas

BURMA RANI

aka *Escape*
1944 115' b&w/col Tamil
d **T.R. Sundaram** *pc* **Modern Theatres** *s* **Elangovan**, D.V. Chari, Ki.Ra.
lp K.L.V. Vasantha, **Honappa Bhagavathar, N.S. Krishnan,** T.A. Mathuram, T.R. Sundaram, T.S. Baliah

Along with **K. Subrahmanyam**'s *Manasamrakshanam* (also 1944), one of the better-known Tamil war-effort films. Three Indian airmen are forced to land in Burma and eventually free the country from Japanese occupation with the help of an Indian resistance movement in the state. The plot revolves around Rani, an Indian girl in Burma who helps the airmen. T.R. Sundaram played the part of a Japanese commander made-up to look like Hitler. The director of War Publicity in Madras, G.T.B. Havey, presided over the film's premiere.

CHAL CHAL RE NAUJAWAN

1944 122' b&w Hindi
d/s **Gyan Mukherjee** *pc* **Filmistan** *dial* **Sadat Hasan Manto** *lyr* Pradeep *c* Hardip *m* **Ghulam Haider**
lp **Ashok Kumar,** Naseem Banu, Jagdish Sethi, V.H. Desai, Motibai, Rafiq Ghaznavi, Navin Yagnik

Filmistan's much-awaited debut film from the makers of the hit film ***Kismet*** (1943). The title of this story of friendship and betrayal over two generations evokes Ashok Kumar's hit song from ***Bandhan*** (1940). The friends Thakur Jaipal Singh (Sethi) and Jamuna Prasad (Ghaznavi) fall out when Jaipal Singh's wife Savitri (Motibai) finds she shares a common musical interest with Jamuna Prasad. Her husband accuses her of infidelity and throws her out. The framing story has Jaipal Singh's horse-riding daughter Sumitra (Banu) meet Jamuna Prasad's son Arjun (A. Kumar). They briefly work together combating an epidemic and Sumitra meets her mother without recognising her. At the end, when the thakur himself arrives, his wife recognises him. Jamuna Prasad sings a song (*Aya toofan*) amid storm and thunder, and when it settles down Savitri is found dead beneath an uprooted tree. The earlier history, starting the flashback, is told with a strident voice-over narrator following the example of *Citizen Kane* (1941), according to *Filmindia*. The film makes some political allusions equating the thakur's authoritarianism with Nazi rule and includes several nationalist numbers, e.g. *Jai bharat desh* and the communal harmony *Bolo har har mahadev allah-o-akbar* (both Ashok Kumar). Although a minor hit, the film is considered a disappointment compared with *Kismet*.

GAALI

1944 122' b&w Hindi
d/s **R.S. Choudhury** *pc* N.R. Desai Prod. *co-lyr* Ram Murti Chaturvedi, Indra, Sugunapiya, D.N. Madhok *m/co-lyr* Hanuman

Prasad *m* Sajjad Hussain *c* B.S. Jagirdar
lp Nirmala, Karan Dewan, Yakub, Kanhaiyalal, Anand Prasad, Manju, Sunalini Devi, Jilloobai, Kamta Prasad, Chandabai, Gulab, Mehdi Raja, Bibubai, Ram Murti, Khanjar, Mohan, Tuklu, Sachin Ghosh

A successful film by **Mehboob**'s scenarist and ex-**Imperial** director R.S. Choudhury. A quasi-expressionist drama about a blind young widow, Mangala (Nirmala), who lives with her father-in-law Jaggu Chakravarty and her young sister-in-law Lali (Manju). Chakravarty wants Lali to marry Tilak (Dewan), the educated modern landlord, but instead Tilak falls for the widow. The crisis is triggered by the local gossip Baldev (Yakub) and leads to Chakavarty's death at the hands of the villagers. When Tilak and Mangala make love in a temple, her eyesight is magically restored and she is astounded that Tilak is not her dead husband. Eventually Tilak marries Lali while Mangala resigns herself to a life of solitude.

JWAR BHATA

1944 120' b&w Hindi
d/s **Amiya Chakravarty** *pc* **Bombay Talkies** *dial* B.C. Verma *lyr* Narendra Sharma *c* R.D. Mathur *m* **Anil Biswas**
lp Mridula, Shamim, Aga Jaan, **Dilip Kumar**, P.F. Pithawala, K.N. Singh, Arun Kumar, Bikram Kapoor, Jagannath Arora, Naseem Lodhi, C.J. Pande, Khalil, Mumtaz Ali

A musical romance remembered mainly for Dilip Kumar's debut. An old patriarch has two unmarried daughters Rama (Shamim) and Renu (Mridula). Narendra (Aga Jaan), the modern son of an urban millionaire, is to marry Rama. Visiting the family in disguise to sneak a look at his future bride, he mistakes Rama for Renu and they fall in love. The mix-up comes to light only after the wedding. Renu blames god and is thrown out of the house for blasphemy. On a train, she joins some travelling performers led by Jagdish (D. Kumar), and to escape getting caught she pretends to live with him. When Renu goes home again, her sister Rama is pregnant and ill and a choice must be made between the foetus and the mother. Renu makes up with god and through divine intervention Rama's and her child's lives are saved. The film's ten songs include several by singer Parul Ghosh.

MAHAMAYA

1944 ?' b&w Tamii
co-d/co-dial **T.R. Raghunath** *co-d/co-dial/st* **Elangovan** *co-d* R.S. Mani *pc* Jupiter Pics *c* Marcus Bartley *m* Venkatramaiyer
lp **P. Kannamba, N.S. Krishnan**, M.S. Saroja, **P.U. Chinappa**, T.R. Mathuram, Meena Lochani, R. Balasubramanyam, M.G. Chakrapani

Period tragedy in Rajput costume featuring Mahamaya, princess of Gandhara (Kannamba) and Vikram (P.U. Chinappa), prince of a neighbouring kingdom, both students of the same teacher. Mahamaya innocently garlands Vikram's sword unaware of the sexual/political significance of the act. Both get married to other partners, but when they meet again Vikram reminds her of the garland, insists that she give herself to him and abducts her. Although she escapes, she is disowned by her husband, whereupon she kills her child and then herself to prove her chastity. The film is dominated by Kannamba and by its large sets. The Krishnan-Mathuram comedy duo provides light relief.

MERI BAHEN

aka *My Sister*
1944 122' b&w Hindi
d **Hemchandra Chunder** *pc* **New Theatres** *s* Benoy Chatterjee *lyr* Bhushan *c* Sudhin Majumdar *m* **Pankaj Mullick**
lp **K.L. Saigal**, Sumitra Devi, Nawab, Akhtar Jehan, Chandrabati Devi, Hiralal, **Tulsi Chakraborty**, Tandon, A.H. Shore, Rajalakshmi

Poor but upright schoolteacher Ramesh (Saigal) adores his adolescent sister Bimala (Akhtar Jehan). He falls in love with Krishna (Sumitra Devi), the village zamindar's daughter, but he declines to marry her when the zamindar insists that they live in the village. Ramesh moves to Calcutta which is under attack by the Japanese (the time is WW2). There he becomes a singer in the Great Metropolitan Theatre company and its female star Miss Rekha (Chandrabati Devi) falls for him. This is one of Saigal's more technically sophisticated movies at New Theatres and includes some quasi-documentary scenes (e.g. about a blood donation programme) showing life under the bombardment, and the shots showing the theatre devastated by an air raid. Ramesh is injured during the attack and is hospitalised. His beloved sister leaves him. The film intercuts his angst-ridden condition while Rekha dies in the same hospital, unbeknown to Ramesh. The film passes an unusually harsh judgement on Rekha, notwithstanding the convention of damning 'liberated' women in the Indian cinema of the time. Like all Saigal films, it relies heavily on his songs, e.g. *Do naina matware, Chupo na, o pyari sajaniya* (when Saigal serenades Krishna's father, thinking him to be Krishna) and *Ai qatib-e-taqdeer mujhe itna bata de*. Composer Mullick later re-recorded these songs in his own voice for an independent album.

PARAKH

1944 122' b&w Hindi
d **Sohrab Modi** *pc* Central Studios *s/co-lyr* Sudarshan *co-lyr* Munshi Arzoo Lucknowi, Ghafil Harnalvi *c* Y.D. Sarpotdar, Keki Mistry *m* Khurshid Anwar, **Saraswati Devi**
lp Mehtab, Kaushalya, Balwant Singh, Shah Nawaz, Yakub, Sadiq Ali, Pratima Devi, Latika

A class division melodrama centred on Mehtab's histrionics. Kiran (Mehtab) is the daughter of a courtesan. Her lowly origins first destroy her marriage and then threaten to jeopardise her son Prakash's (Singh) ambitions. She is blackmailed for keeping her son's parentage a secret from him, forcing her to return to her ancestral profession. The film was a commercial success.

PHOOL

1944 122' b&w Hindi-Urdu
d **K. Asif** *pc* Famous Films *s* **Kamal Amrohi** *c* Kumar Jaywant *m* **Ghulam Haider**
lp Veena, **Sitara Devi, Suraiya, Prithviraj Kapoor, Durga Khote**, Yakub, Wasti, Mazhar Khan

The directorial debut of K. Asif, best known for his ***Mughal-e-Azam*** (1960), is a big-budget Amrohi drama set in a Muslim joint family. Safdar loses his inheritance through his sister-in-law's machinations but he still has to honour his promise to complete the building of a mosque started by his father. His future son-in-law Salim goes to Turkey to fight in the Balkan wars, where a dancer corrupts him, so the responsibility of building the mosque falls on Safdar's orphaned daughter who has to choose between that responsibility and her freedom.

RAMSHASTRI

1944 122'[H]/108'[M] b&w Marathi/Hindi
co-d **Gajanan Jagirdar, Raja Nene** *co-d/sc* **Vishram Bedekar** *pc* **Prabhat** *st* V.S. Sukhtankar *lyr* S.A. Shukla[M], **Shantaram Athavale**[M], Qamar Jalalabadi[H] *c* Pandurang Naik, E. Mohammed *m* **Keshavrao Bhole**, G. Damle
lp Gajanan Jagirdar, Anant Marathe, Baby Shakuntala, Meenakshi, **Lalita Pawar**, Sudha Apte, **Hansa Wadkar**, Bhagwat, Manajirao, Balkoba Gokhale, Madhu Apte, Ganpatrao Tambat[M], **Master Vithal**[M], Master Chhotu[M], Manjrekar[H], Ram Singh[H]

Prabhat's expensively mounted historical set at a contentious period of the Maratha empire is a biographical of Ramshastri Prabhune (1720-89), chief justice at the court of Madhavrao and later of Nana Phadnavis, and a major figure in the development of an indigenous legal code. The period of the Peshwai (i.e. the council of ministers established by Shivaji, which was by the 18th C. the real power behind the ceremonial throne occupied by his descendents) follows the death of the Peshwa (Prime Minister) Madhavrao in 1772 when Raghoba seized power by killing Narayanrao, the official heir and his own nephew. The film adheres to the legendary version of this episode elaborated in K.P. Khadilkar's Marathi play *Bhaubandhaki* (1902), blaming Raghoba's ambitious and calculating wife Anandibai (Pawar) for the murder. The idealised figure of Ramshastri (Jagirdar) is presented as truth incarnate. Struggling for an education, he eventually becomes the popular chief justice at Madhavrao's court and is the only influential figure in the realm willing to stand up to Raghoba and to denounce his usurpation of the throne. After an intricate palace intrigue, he resigns his judicial post. The studio's last big film in its celebrated 30s style, it was to have been directed by **Shantaram** but others were drafted in to save the film when he left the Prabhat Studio. It carries no director credit and the Marathi version has no credits at all.

RATTAN

1944 118' b&w Hindi
d M. Sadiq *pc* Jamuna Prod. *co-st* **R.S. Choudhury** *co-st/dial/lyr* D.N. Madhok *c* Dwarka Divecha *m* **Naushad**

lp Swarnalata, Karan Dewan, Wasti, Manju, Gulab, Rajkumari Shukla, Badriprasad, Azoorie, Chandabai, Amirbano

Extremely successful love story establishing the careers of both its director and its composer. Two country youths Govind (Dewan) and Gauri (Swarnalata) are in love. Gauri is forcibly married to another but their love does not fade. The film was bought by the Kapurchands for distribution and cheaply resold locally because it was deemed uncommercial. Classic musical score includes the Zohrabai number *Akhiyan mila ke jiya bharma ke chale nahin jaana* and established Naushad's reputation among the leading music directors from the 40s onwards.

TEHSILDAR

1944 ?' b&w Telugu
d/st **Y.V. Rao** *pc* Shri Jagadish Films *dial/lyr* Balijepalli Lakshmikanta Kavi *c* Purshottam *m* H.R. Padmanabha Sastry
lp Y.V. Rao, Ch. Narayana Rao, Balijepalli Lakshmikanta Kavi, Rangaswamy, Krishnayya, Natesayya, B.V.K. Acharya, M.S. Rama Rao, **B.R. Panthulu**, Kamala Kotnis, **P. Bhanumathi**, Hemalatha, **Bezawada Rajarathnam**, Krishnakumari, Tripurasundari, Soudamini, Ch. Narayana Rao

Y.V. Rao's best-known film as actor is a satire on the mania for Westernisation among India's lower-level bureaucrats. A minor tehsildar (revenue collector) (Y.V. Rao) marries the naive, rural Kamala (Bhanumathi) and instantly wants her to adopt Western fashions, learn English and walk in high-heeled shoes. This leads to ludicrous situations and at a tea party hosted by the collector she feels publicly humiliated. The tehsildar rejects Kamala in favour of Rajani (Kotnis), a 'modern' lady who first has Kamala evicted from the house and then goes on to ruin the Tehsildar financially, causing him to be arrested for embezzlment. With, e.g. ***Grihapravesham*** (1946), **L.V. Prasad** later continued the satires on blind Westernisation.

UDAYER PATHEY/HAMRAHI

1944 122'[B]/121'[H] b&w Bengali/Hindi
d/c/co-sc **Bimal Roy** *pc* **New Theatres** *st/dial* Jyotirmoy Roy *co-sc* **Nirmal Dey** *lyr* Zakir Hussain[H] *m* **Rai Chand Boral**
lp Radhamohan Bhattacharya, Binata Basu, Rekha Mitra, Devi Mukherjee, **Tulsi Chakraborty**, Debabala, Mira Dutta, Boken Chatterjee, Maya Basu, Rajalakshmi, Parul Kar, Manorama, Bishwanath Bhadury[B], Hiren Basu[B], Tarapada Choudhury[B], Smritirekha Biswas[B], Leena Bose[B], Aditya Ghosh[B], Bhupendra Kapoor[H], Hiralal[H], Dindayal Luthra[H], Ramesh Sinha[H]

Bimal Roy's directorial debut tells of impoverished novelist Anup who works as a speechwriter for the millionaire Rajendranath, but leaves when he finds that his sister Sumitra had been falsely accused of theft in Rajendranath's house. Anup, increasingly committed to the working class, writes a novel but Rajendranath later publishes it under his own name. The novel becomes a major success. Anup's commitment to the workers' union grows and starts threatening Rajendranath's business interests. During a labour rally Rajendranath has his henchmen severely beat Anup, even as his daughter Gopa, who has fallen in love with Anup, sides with the workers. The film was characteristic of a seminal melodramatic mode of addressing indigenous capitalism as a contradiction between inherited and earned wealth.

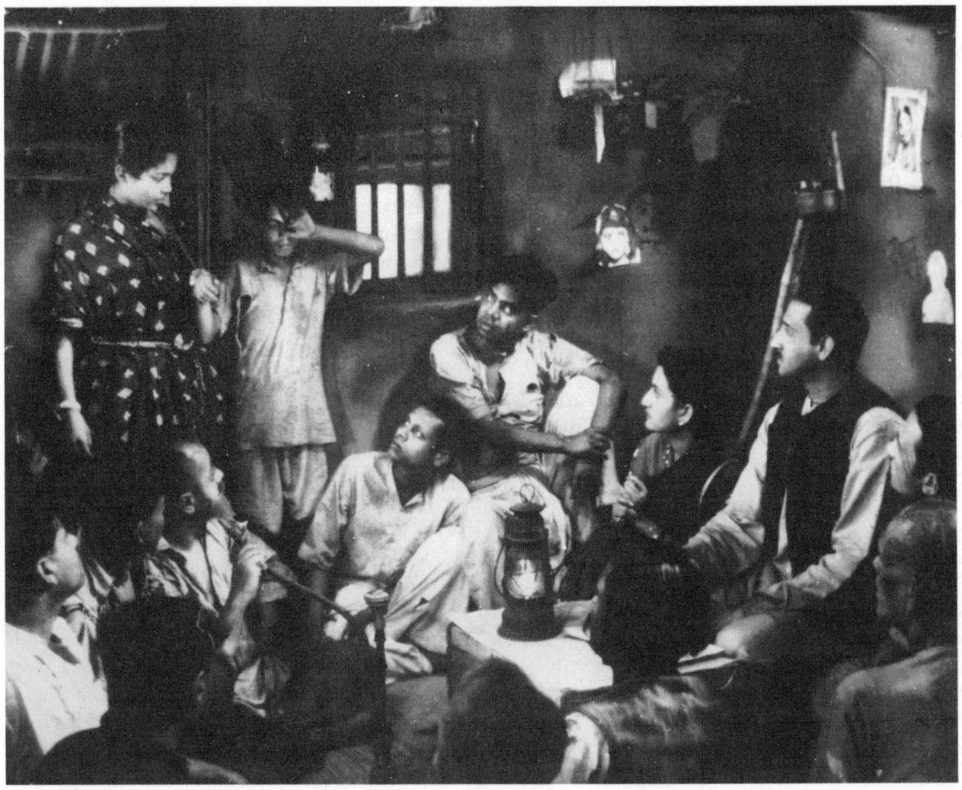

Udayer Pathey

BADI MAA

1945 122' b&w Hindi
d **Master Vinayak** *pc* Prafulla Pics *st* **V.S. Khandekar** *lyr* **Zia Sarhadi**, Anjum Pilibhiti, Raja Badhe, **Dinkar D. Patil** *c* Madhav Bulbule *m* K. Datta
lp **Nurjehan**, Meenakshi, Ishwarlal, Yakub, Alka, **Lata Mangeshkar**, Leela Mishra, **Sitara Devi**, Dada Salvi, **Damuanna Malvankar**, V. Jog, Girish, Datar

Vinayak was forced to make this war-effort movie to keep his company alive during WW2. Durgadas (Salvi) worries about his son Dinesh (Ishwarlal) who is in London during the Blitz. Moneylender Ghanshyam (Girish) agrees to write off a debt provided Durgadas's daughter Usha (Meenakshi) marries his son Rajendra (Yakub), but Rajendra and the dancer Mona (Sitara Devi) are spies for the Japanese. When the Japanese attack the village of Dinapur, Rajendra becomes a patriot and fights for the Allied cause along with Dinesh.

HEMAREDDY MALLAMMA

1945 ?' b&w Kannada
d **S. Soundararajan**, G.R. Rao *p* **Gubbi Veeranna** *pc* Gubbi Films *dial* **Bellave Narahari Sastri** based on his play *m* **Chittor V. Nagaiah**
lp Gubbi Veeranna, **Honappa Bhagavathar**, C.B. Malappa, K.R. Seetarama Sastry, **B. Jayamma**

Veeranna's hit sequel to his ***Jeevana Nataka*** (1942) is based on the Sastri play he had staged with his own theatre group. Told in the **Saint film** idiom, the story shows how the devout Mallamma (Jayamma), burdened by a mentally retarded husband and a tyrannical mother-in-law, eventually transforms everyone around her. Nagaiah made his Kannada debut as composer with several popular songs which, along with the film's elaborate special effects, contributed to its success.

HUMAYUN

1945 118' b&w Hindi-Urdu
d/p **Mehboob Khan** *pc* Mehboob Prod. *st* Waqif *sc* Aga Jani Kashmiri *lyr* Shams Lucknowi, Munshi Arzoo, Anjum Pilibhiti, Buddhichandra Agarwal 'Madhur', Vikaar Ambalvi *c* Faredoon Irani *m* **Ghulam Haider**
lp **Ashok Kumar**, Veena Kumari, **Nargis**, Shah Nawaz, **Chandramohan**, K.N. Singh, Himalaywala, Yusuf Effendi, Abdul Rashid, Abdul Kader, Afghan Sandow, Waskar

Classic spectacular featuring the 16th-C. Mughal emperor Humayun (Kumar). Advocating communal harmony, a policy prompted by contemporary developments, the film stresses the friendship between the victorious Babar (Nawaz) and the defeated Rajputs: he asks the Rajkumari (Veena), daughter of the slain Rajput king, to assume her father's throne and to regard Babar as a father. In the latter part of the story, Humayun sacrifices his kingdom to save the Rajkumari. Hamida Bano (Nargis) is a commoner with whom Humayun falls in love, but who turns down his offer of marriage claiming that women, for all kings, are mere playthings. The major highlights of the film are the elaborate Mughal sets and the spectacular battle scenes with elephants and horses. Cecil B. DeMille described the film, in a letter to the film-maker, as a 'masterpiece of lighting and composition'.

LAKHRANI

1945 122' b&w Hindi
d/s **Vishram Bedekar** *pc* **Prabhat Film** *dial* Sudarshan *lyr* Qamar Jalalabadi *c* Pandurang Naik *m* **Master Krishnarao**
lp **Durga'Khote**, Monica Desai, Azoorie, Sapru, Butt Kaiser, Ganpatrao, Gauri, Karadkar, **Guru Dutt**, Baby Malan, Ramsingh, Urmila

Bichwa (Khote) is the queen of a devout Untouchable community not permitted to enter the temple. Her daughter Lakha, the best dancer in the community, marries the prince of a rival community of atheists and is excommunicated by her own people. The devout group has their devotion tested by economic setbacks and a major conflict erupts between them and the atheists but god materialises on earth, thus solving the problems of belief and its attendant conflicts. Untouchability is abolished and they can all join together to worship in the temple. This transparent piece of religious propaganda saw Guru Dutt's acting debut in the minor role of Lachman, Lakha's brother.

MANE NA MANA

1945 121' b&w Bengali
d/s **Sailajananda Mukherjee** *pc* New Century Prod. *c* Sudhir Basu *m* Sailen Dasgupta
lp **Ahindra Choudhury**, **Jahar Ganguly**, Phani Roy, **Dhiraj Bhattacharya**, **Tulsi Chakraborty**, Santosh Sinha, Renuka Roy, Molina Devi, Sandhyarani, Prabhadevi, Nibhanani Devi

Mukherjee followed his ***Shahar Theke Dooray*** (1943) with this rural joint family melodrama about a woolly-headed but saintly Debnath (a stereotype in Saratchandra's novels) who loves his stepbrother the idle hedonist Bhoothnath, and his stepsister. Debnath's wife would like her sister to marry the step-brother. Debnath finds a job for Bhoothnath with a miserly zamindar but this leads to Bhootnath becoming implicated in a theft and he is jailed. The problems threaten the cohesion of the joint family but the happy end reasserts the permanence of blood ties. A major hit, the film produced fashion spin-offs including *Mane Na Mana* saris. The fashion trend had earlier been introduced into Bengali film mainly around the figure of **Kanan Devi** (e.g. 'Kanbala' earrings), followed by 'Anuradha *bindis*' (forehead dots) after ***Bidyapati*** (1937).

MEERA

1945 136'[T]/120'[H] b&w Tamil/Hindi
d **Ellis R. Duncan** *pc* Chandraprabha Cinetone *sc/dial*[H] Amritlal Nagar *lyr* Narendra Sharma[H], **Kalki**[T] *m* S.V. Venkatraman, Ramnath, Naresh Bhattacharya
lp M.S. Subbulakshmi, T.V. Rajasundaribai, T.S. Santhanam, **Chittor V. Nagaiah**, Radha, Kumari Kamala, **M.G. Ramachandran**

A Saint film about the life of Meera aka Meerabai (1498-1565). Born a Rajasthani princess, she married King Bhoj (Nagaiah), was later persecuted by her brothers-in-law and became an itinerant singer performing mainly in Rajasthani, Brijbhasha and Gujarati (see Kumkum Sangari, 1990). One of India's most famous saint poets, her 1400 or so poems, handed down completely in the oral tradition, often address a demystified ideal of Krishna (played in the film by Kumari Kamala). The film features the famous classical singer M.S. Subbulakshmi known for her Carnatic-style music but also for several other, including North Indian styles. Her rendition of 18 Meera bhajans in Hindi remained for several years the definitive musical version of the lyrics. They have remained an important part of her live concerts ever since. Originally a Tamil hit, the film's very successful Hindi version had the poetess-politician Sarojini Naidu introduce Subbulakshmi to a North Indian audience. The Tamil version has novelist Kalki's best-known work as a lyric writer, esp. *Katrinile varum geetham.*

SAMRAT CHANDRAGUPTA

1945 122' b&w Hindi
d/p **Jayant Desai** *pc* Jayant Desai Prod *st* **Mohanlal G. Dave** *dial* Shahid Latif, Sagar Hussain *lyr* Buddhichandra Agarwal 'Madhur' *c* Dronacharya *m* **C. Ramchandra**
lp Renuka Devi, Ishwarlal, Nayampalli, **Suraiya**, Anil Kumar, Ibrahim, Sulochana Chatterjee, Rewashankar Marwadi, Kantilal, Bhagwandas

Big-budget historical about the founder of the Maurya empire in 321BC The film uses the legend about the Indian emperor who was close to Alexander's Macedonian army but fell out with the Greek and eventually defeated him in battle, establishing his own empire and capital at Pataliputra. The film shows Chandragupta's friendship with the Greek general Seleucus Nicator, whose daughter the Mauryan king is believed to have married. He saves Nicator's life and also his daughter Helen from the evil Antigonus, in return for which he marries Helen. The subsequent political history, e.g. Chandragupta's conquest of the Nandas, is presented as a consequence of the love story. Happiness reigns only after several attempts to overthrow the king are foiled. A key figure is the wily politician Chanakya. The film also had the nationalist number *Mata ki jai, janani ki jai ho.*

SWARGASEEMA

1945 114' b&w Telugu
d/sc **B.N. Reddi** *pc* **Vauhini** *st/dial* **Chakrapani** *lyr* B. Rajanikanta Rao, **Samudrala Raghavacharya** *c* Marcus Bartley *m* **Chittor V. Nagaiah**
lp **P. Bhanumathi**, Chittor V. Nagaiah, **B. Jayamma**, Lingamurthy, K. Shiva Rao, Ch. Narayana Rao

Reddi's best-known film is a remarkable melodrama chronicling the metamorphosis of rural street entertainer Subbi (Bhanumathi) into the urban nymphomaniac Sujata Devi. Murthi (Nagaiah), a married man who loves her, helps her to become a stage star while the heroine breaks up Murthi's marriage to the affectionate Kalyani (B. Jayamma). The film can be read as a comment on the star-manufacturing process in Telugu cinema, with Bhanumathi, supported by Bartley's constantly moving camera, expertly modulating the gradual shifts in gesture, speech accent and make-up as the village beauty is transformed into a 'sexy' star. Allegedly inspired by Shaw's *Pygmalion* and Mamoulian's *Blood and Sand* (1941) starring Rita Hayworth. The film's generic innovativeness is sometimes ascribed to the new unit assembled by the studio after designer A.K. Sekhar and writer/cameraman **K. Ramnoth** left to join **Gemini**. Major new presences include writer Chakrapani (later co-producer with B.N. Reddi at Vauhini), lyricist-composer B. Rajanikanta Rao and singer **Ghantasala**, who makes his singing debut here with the number *Gazulapilla.* According to V.A.K. Ranga Rao, lyricist Rajanikanta Rao introduces Arabic music and Bhanumathi adopts Hayworth's humming from *Blood and Sand* for the classic hit song *Ooh pavurama* as a contrast to the Carnatic number *Manchidinamu nede.*

TADBIR

1945 121' b&w Hindi
d/p **Jayant Desai** *pc* Jayant Desai Prod *st* **Mohanlal G. Dave** *dial* Munshi Sagar Hussain *lyr* Swami Ramanand *c* Dronacharya *m* Lal Mahomed
lp **K.L. Saigal**, **Suraiya**, Mubarak, Jilloo, Rehana, Rewashankar Marwadi, Raja Rani, Shashi Kapoor, Amina, Shalini, Gharpure, Raja Joshi

When Kanhaiyalal (Saigal) is born, an astrologer predicts that upon growing up he shall follow a prostitute, learn to wield a knife and be sentenced to the gallows. The predictions come true but not in the imagined forms: he and his mother find shelter in the house of Saguna (Suraiya), a prostitute who eventually sacrifices her life to save the hero's. The knife-wielding prediction comes true when he becomes a surgeon. Kanhaiyalal and his mother fight poverty and crime, and his evil stepbrother Jwala Prasad. A well-known Saigal and Suraiya musical that claimed to address the phenomenon of destiny.

ANMOL GHADI

aka *Precious Time*
1946 122' b&w Hindi
d/p **Mehboob Khan** *pc* Mehboob Prod *st* Anwar Batalvi *s* Aga Jani Kashmiri *lyr* Tanvir Naqvi *c* Faredoon Irani *m* **Naushad**
lp **Nurjehan**, Surendra, **Suraiya**, Zahur Raja, Leela Mishra, Anwari Begum, Bhudo Advani, Murad, Bibubai, Amir Bano, Noor Mahal, Waskar

A love-triangle romance with reformist overtones set partly in Bombay. Impoverished hero Chander (Surendra) and rich heroine Lata (Nurjehan) are childhood sweethearts separated when Lata's parents move to Bombay. Later, Chander moves there when his rich friend Prakash (Zahur Raja) finds him work in a musical instruments shop. By then, Lata has become a famous poetess going by the name of Renu and is engaged to Prakash. Lata's friend Basanti (Suraiya) falls in love with Chander but he remains true to his childhood girl and walks away into the sunset (with Basanti running after him). Although Mehboob made other triangular romances (***Hum Tum Aur Woh***, 1938; ***Najma***, 1943

Suraiya in *Anmol Ghadi*

etc.), this film started his investigation of patriarchy, shown as masquerading under 'eternal' values (cf ***Anokhi Ada***, 1948; ***Andaz***, 1949). The film deploys a strident rhetoric about class divisions, opposing poverty to eternal human(ist) values such as friendship and love. Languorous gesture and a romantically lit neo-classical decor are used to suggest femininity. Musical hits including Nurjehan's best-known songs, e.g. *Awaaz de kahan hai* (with Surendra) and the solos *Mere bachpan ke saathi*, *Jawan hai mohabbat*.

DHARTI KE LAL

aka *Children of the Earth*
1946 125' b&w Hindi
d/sc/co-p **K.A. Abbas** *co-p* V.P. Sathe *pc* **IPTA** *st* **Bijon Bhattacharya**'s plays *Nabanna* and *Jabanbandi*; **Krishen Chander**'s short story *Annadata* *lyr* Ali Sardar Jafri, Nemichand Jain, Wamiq, Prem Dhawan *c* Jamnadas Kapadia *m* Ravi Shankar
lp **Sombhu Mitra**, **Balraj Sahni**, Usha Dutta, Damayanti Sahni, Anwar Mirza, Tripti Bhaduri, Namid Butt, Pratap Ojha, Rashid Ahmed, Randhir, Zohra Saigal, Mahendranath, Snehaprabha, David, K.N. Singh

Abbas's directorial debut launched a major trend of 'realist' cinema. The film is set during WW2 and the 1943 Bengal famine (a traumatic event often used as source material by left cultural movements) and a growing 'nation-building' ideology. Made during the war, the novice cast and crew were accorded a special licence for a war-effort contribution. The only film actually produced by the IPTA (although it later informally supported several other films), the film is based partly on Sombhu Mitra's landmark production of Bhattacharya's play *Nabanna* for the IPTA. It narrates the story of a family of sharecroppers in Bengal: the patriarch Samaddar, his elder son Niranjan and his wife Binodini, and the younger son Ramu with his wife Radhika. Despite a good harvest and rising grain prices during the war, Samaddar loses his property to a crooked grain-dealing zamindar. Ramu, his wife and their newborn baby go to Calcutta followed soon after by the rest of the family along with thousands of similarly dispossessed peasants. The film intercuts Ramu's frantic search for work with his wife's descent into prostitution. Before dying, the patriarch enjoins his family to return to their native soil where the farmers get together and, in a stridently celebratory socialist-realist ending, opt for Soviet-style collective farming. Ramu is excluded from their world. The film's highly stylised and symbol-laden realism proved extremely influential. It appears to have found a way of narrativising the 1943 famine which set the pattern for many films moving from depictions of deprivation in the country to suffering in the city, e.g. **Nemai Ghosh**'s ***Chinnamul*** (1950) and **Bimal Roy**'s ***Do Bigha Zameen*** (1953). It also initiated a new type of melodrama able to marry actuality to psychoanalytic and political anxieties and desires, as in Abbas's scripts for **Raj Kapoor**.

DR KOTNIS KI AMAR KAHANI

aka *The Journey of Dr Kotnis* aka *Immortal Journey of Dr Kotnis* aka *And One Did Not Come Back*
•1946 127'[H]/100'[E] b&w Hindi
d/p **V. Shantaram** *pc* **Rajkamal Kalamandir** *st/co-s* **K.A. Abbas** from his story *And One Did Not Come Back* *co-s* V.P. Sathe *lyr* Dewan Sharar *c* V. Avadhoot *m* **Vasant Desai**
lp V. Shantaram, Jayashree, Dewan Sharar, **Baburao Pendharkar**, **Master Vinayak**, Ulhas, **Keshavrao Date**, Rajashree, Pratima Devi, Salvi, Jankidass, Hublikar

A chronicle of the real-life story of Dwarkanath Kotnis (V. Shantaram), a member of a medical team sent by India during WW2, an intensely nationalist period, to fight alongside the Chinese during the Japanese invasion. Kotnis goes to China, works almost singlehandedly to provide medical relief to the wounded, meets and marries a Chinese girl, Ching Lan (Jayashree), is captured by the Japanese and eventually dies in battle while developing a cure against an epidemic. Ching Lan and their infant son return to India, symbolising the solidarity of their nationalist struggles. Made along with the **IPTA**-backed ***Dharti Ke Lal*** and ***Neecha Nagar*** (both 1946) under a special WW2 licence as a war-effort film, *Dr Kotnis* is remarkable for its absolute abandonment of any pretence at cinematic realism and its powerful nationalist rhetoric, culminating in the hero's dying speech describing what his wife will see when she goes 'home'. This is intercut with documentary footage of Nehru at a mass meeting. The film succeeded in simultaneously pleasing the Communists, the Congress and the colonial occupation force. Shantaram re-edited a shorter version in English in 1948 in which, according to S. Bannerjee and A. Srivastava (1988), the 'clothing of the Indian characters' was made 'more ethnic to please a Western audience'.

EIGHT DAYS

aka *Aath Din*
1946 141' b&w Hindi
d Dattaram Pai *pc* **Filmistan** *s* **Sadat Hasan Manto** *lyr* Gopal Singh Nepali *c* S. Hardip *m* **S.D. Burman**
lp **Ashok Kumar**, Veera, S.L. Puri, Rama Shukul, Mohsin, Sadat Hasan Manto, Upendranath Ashok, Mehdi Ali Khan, B.M. Dikshit, Ram Nath, Aga Jan, **Master Bhagwan**, Victor Pinto, Leela Mishra, H. Desai

Manto wrote in *Meena Bazar* (1962) that his script was specifically designed as an Ashok Kumar comedy. Effectively directed by the star himself, this early Filmistan production tells of Shamsher Singh (Kumar), a discharged military officer who wants to settle down as a farmer. His marriage is arranged with the educated Neela (Veera) who ditches him at the last minute and goes to the city where she learns that she stands to inherit a fortune if she gets married within 8 days. After rejecting several suitors, she finally falls in love with Shamsher Singh, whom she meets in the city unaware that he is the person to whom she was earlier betrothed. Singh treats her badly and she sues him but in the end the two realise that they love each other. Manto acts in the film as an air force officer.

GRIHAPRAVESHAM

1946 122' b&w Telugu
d **L.V. Prasad** *pc* Sarathi Films *s* **Tripuraneni Gopichand** *c* Jiten Bannerjee *lyr/m* Nalinikanta Rao (aka Balanthrapu Rajanikanta Rao)
lp **P. Bhanumathi**, Hemalatha, **C.S.R. Anjaneyalu**, L.V. Prasad, Rangaswamy, K. Shiva Rao, **Sriranjini Jr**.

The studio associated with **Ramabrahmam**'s work commissioned the new director Prasad to film a reformist story simultaneously critiquing Westernisation and the feudal practice of arranged marriages (representing the views of scenarist Gopichand). Prasad turned it into a satire of the reformist social itself. The film was supposed to contrast the misogynist bachelor Somalingam (Prasad) with the 'modern' Janaki (Bhanumathi) who insists on her equal rights. Instead, it opens with the culturally loaded scene of Janaki playing badminton and her feminism is presented as strident and disruptive. Janaki's stepmother (Hemalatha) tries to force a marriage between her brother the anglophile Ramana Rao (Anjaneyalu) and Janaki, even though Ramana Rao has a girlfriend, Lalita (Sriranjini). Eventually Janaki and Somalingam devise a plot, embroiling them in many hypocrisies, to get Lalita and Ramana Rao married. Middle-class anglophilia is also ridiculed through Anjaneyalu's character, dressed in a three-piece suit and singing a couple of English songs. Bhanumathi's sentimental *Amma nee nayanammulla ashajyothula ninduga velugenamma* was a hit song.

HUM EK HAIN

1946 121' b&w Hindi
d/co-sc/lyr P.L. Santoshi *pc* **Prabhat Film** *st* Saleh Mohammed Qureshi *co-sc* Tony Lazarus *c* Surendra Pai *m* **Husnlal-Bhagatram**
lp **Durga Khote**, Kamala Kotnis, **Dev Anand**, Alka Achrekar, Rehana, Rehman, Ranjit Kumari, Rane, Ram Singh, Gokhale, Ganpatrao, Manajirao Karadkar, Bhagwat, Baby Usha

A national unity parable choreographed by **Guru Dutt** but more significant as Dev Anand's debut. The old landlady of a village supports its people during a famine and raises three orphaned children of differing religions. The children, although encouraged to practice their separate religions, are taught to remain united at all times. The villain Chhote Babu, who wants to marry the girl who is engaged to the eldest of the three boys, sows discord and hatred, causing great enmity between the trio until reason prevails and they reunite.

JEEVAN YATRA

1946 134' b&w Hindi
d **Master Vinayak** *pc* **Rajkamal Kalamandir** *p* **V. Shantaram** *st* N.S. Phadke's novel *sc/lyr* Dewan Sharar *c* Madhav Bulbule *m* **Vasant Desai**
lp Nayantara, Pratima Devi, **Lata Mangeshkar**, Shantarin, Sunalini Devi, Meher Sultana, Sundarabai, Vijaya, Yakub, **Baburao Pendharkar**, Dixit, Chandrakant, **Damuanna Malvankar**

Shantaram, who had given him his first break, also produced Vinayak's last film. It features a large number of characters travelling on a bus to Benares. A storm forces the passengers to take shelter in an abandoned temple where a prostitute tries to seduce Raja (Yakub) and he is left behind. The bus later breaks down and when Raja rejoins the group a local bandit, Vishwas (Pendharkar), attacks it. Eventually the bandit turns out to be Raja's father and the husband of an old woman, Kalindi (Protima Devi), another passenger on the bus. Vinayak's only film in the mainstream Hindi cinema, it included the collective number *Ao azadi ke geet gate chalein* and Lata Mangeshkar's *Chidiya bole choo choo*. Mangeshkar plays a village girl.

NAUKA DUBI/MILAN

1946 147'[B]/144'[H] b&w Bengali/Hindi
d **Nitin Bose** *pc* **Bombay Talkies** *st* **Rabindranath Tagore**'s novel *Nauka Dubi* (1916) *sc* Sadhanikanta Das *lyr* Arzoo, P.L. Santoshi[H] *c* Radhu Karmakar *m* **Anil Biswas**
lp **Dilip Kumar**[H]/**Abhi Bhattacharya**[B], Ranjana[H]/Meera Sarkar[B], Meera Mishra, **Pahadi Sanyal**, Moni Chatterjee, Shyam Laha

The hero Ramesh (Kumar/Bhattacharya) agrees to marry a woman he's never met, unknown to his real lover Hemnalini (Ranjana/Sarkar). The wedding party is hit by a storm when travelling across a river; the hero's father and the bride are drowned while the hero survives. He later meets Kamala (Meera Mishra), whose husband (like Ramesh's wife) had died shortly after their marriage. Their respective bereavements bring the two closer until Kamala's husband is discovered to be still alive. Eventually Ramesh marries Hemnalini. The classic Tagore novel was Nitin Bose's debut at Bombay Talkies, and his most ambitious Hindi film to date. Reviews attacked it for its slow pace, but generally commended its extensive night shooting.

NEECHA NAGAR

1946 122' b&w Hindi
d **Chetan Anand** *pc* India Pics *s* Hyatullah Ansari *st* M. Gorky's *The Lower Depths* *lyr* Vishwamitter Adil, Manmohan Anand *c* Bidyapati Ghosh *m* Ravi Shankar
lp Rafiq Anwar, Uma Anand, Rafi Peer, Kamini Kaushal, Hamid Butt, S.P. Bhatia, **Mohan Segal**, Zohra Segal, Prem Kumar

Chetan Anand's **IPTA**-supported film loosely adapted from Gorky's classic forms a trio with **Abbas**'s ***Dharti Ke Lal*** and **Shantaram**'s ***Dr Kotnis Ki Amar Kahani*** (both 1946). Class division is signified by a rich landowner (Rafi Peer) who lives on a mountain while the poor starve in the 'Neecha Nagar', a village in the valley below. The landowner's sewage flows around the poor people's huts, spreading disease. Eventually the rich man dies in a long-drawn-out heart attack. Anand's debut featured several judgemental high- and low-angled shots, sacrificing realism for quasi-expressionist emotional intensity. This film and *Dharti Ke Lal* mark Ravi Shankar's debut as film composer.

RANAKDEVI

1946 123' b&w Gujarati
d/sc **V.M. Vyas** *pc* Sunrise Pics *st* **Mohanlal G. Dave** *dial* Karsandas Manek *lyr* Manasvai Prantijwalla *c* R.M. Rele *m* Chanalal Thakur
lp Anjana, Motibai, Dulari, **Nirupa Roy**, Lilavati, Lila Jayawant, Mallika, Damayanti, Chandrabala, Amubai, Sumati, Daksha, Kavita, Bhagwandas, Pande, Chanalal Thakur, Natwarlal Chohan, Master Dhulia, Shyam, Gangaram, Gautam

Nirupa Roy's first film. The Solanki King Siddharaj Jaisinh (12th C.) wants to marry Ranak, a daughter of the Parmar king of Sind but raised by a potter. However, she marries King Ra'Khengar of Junagadh, triggering a war as Ranak, confined for 12 years, bears two children while refusing to succumb to Siddharaj. When he kills her husband, she commits sati (ritual suicide on her husband's funeral pyre). Based on historical events, the story had become a folk legend. It was the only Gujarat film made that year, but launched a tradition of film adaptations of quasi-historical legends, many of them dealing with Rajput royalty (cf **Raskapur**'s films ***Mulu Manek***, 1955; ***Kadu Makrani***, 1960).

SHAHJEHAN

1946 121' b&w Hindi-Urdu
d/p **A.R. Kardar** *pc* Kardar Prod. *lyr* **Majrooh Sultanpuri**, Kumar Barabankavi *m* **Naushad**
lp **K.L. Saigal**, Kanwar, Ragini, Nasreen, Jairaj, Himalay, Nazir Bedi, Azoorie, Kesarbai, Anwari, Munir Sultana, Rehman, Peerjaan

Kardar's costume drama set in Mughal Emperor Shah Jehan's court is Saigal's last film and the debut of new-generation set designer M.R. Achrekar (later associated mainly with **Raj Kapoor**) and lyricist Sultanpuri. The melodrama stresses the two motifs usually associated with Shah Jehan: his commitment to justice and the Taj Mahal, which he built as a monument of love for his wife Mumtaz. The poet Sohail (Saigal) writes a love song (*Mere sapnon ki rani*) in praise of the beauteous Ruhi, daughter of Rajput general Jwala Singh. The song becomes so popular that it seriously inconveniences its subject: some lovelorn youths disrupt her wedding procession and five of her brothers are killed. Shah Jehan adopts Ruhi into the royal court and offers her in marriage to the one who can create a work of art that 'replicates heaven on earth'. Sohail wins the contest with the song *Kar lijiye chal kar meri jannat ke nazare* but she is in love with the Persian sculptor Shiraz (Jairaj). The dilemma causes a split between

Shah Jehan and his wife, only resolved when Mumtaz, on her deathbed, asks the emperor to build a monument reflecting their love. Shiraz is to build the monument, but he must first experience a loss analogous to Shah Jehan's loss of Mumtaz. And so, Ruhi's father kills Ruhi: the distraught Shiraz then builds the Taj Mahal. Later, it is revealed that Ruhi is still alive as Sohail sacrificed his life to save her. Although Mughal historicals generally fetishise legends about royal masculinity (***Tansen***, 1943; ***Anarkali***, 1928, 1935, 1953) this one goes further, gendering the segregation between personal and political spaces while contrasting declamatory dialogues and large-scale sets with a staccato, documentary narrative. The film includes Saigal's famous song *Jab dil hi tut gaya*.

SUBHADRA

1946 122' b&w Hindi
d **Master Vinayak** *pc* Prafulla Pics *s* **V.S. Khandekar** *lyr* Indra, Moti B.A. *c* Madhav Bulbule *m* **Vasant Desai**
lp **Shanta Apte**, Ishwarlal, Yakub, Prem Adib, Dada Salvi, V. Jog, **Lata Mangeshkar**

Vinayak's only full-scale mythological tells of the argument between Krishna (Prem Adib) and his stepbrother Balaram (Salvi) as to who their sister Subhadra (Apte) should marry. Eventually Krishna has his way and Arjun (Ishwarlal) marries her. Shanta Apte sings a rare duet with Lata Mangeshkar (*Main khili khili phulwari*) for this film.

THYAGAYYA

1946 186' b&w Telugu
d/s/m **Chittor V. Nagaiah** *pc* Renuka Pics *dial* **Samudrala Raghavacharya** *c* M.A. Rehman
lp Chittor V. Nagaiah, Lingamurthy, **B. Jayamma**, Hemalatha, S.V. Rajyam, Sabita Devi

The actor, singer and composer Nagaiah's directorial debut is a classic Saint film about the Telugu saint poet Thyagaraja (1767-1847), author of c.2400 kritis (verses) and the founder of the Carnatic system of classical music. Thyagaraja (Nagaiah) is shown as a villager composing devotional music to Rama while rejecting the court of Serfoji, maharaj of Tanjore, the dominant cultural centre of the region. Turning down invitations and gifts from the maharaj, Thyagaraja provokes the jealous wrath of his brother Japesam (Lingamurthy). The film's climax comes when Japesam destroys Rama's idols, Thyagaraja resurrects them and eventually sacrifices his life to his god. Nagaiah's performance in the title role dominated the hit film together with the music, including 28 of Thyagaraja's kritis culminating in the number *Nidhi chala sukhama*, sung when he rejects the royal gifts. The director-composer also introduced lyrics from Kannada (the *Purandaradasa devara nama* in the film's opening), Tamil (by **Papanasam Sivan** and sung by D.K. Pattamal) and Hindi (sung by Jayavanti Devi).

ELAAN

1947 133' b&w Urdu
d/p **Mehboob Khan** *pc* Mehboob Prod. *s/lyr* **Zia Sarhadi** *c* Faredoon Irani *m* **Naushad**
lp Surendra, Munawar Sultana, Himalaywala, Rehana, Leela Mishra, Zebunissa, Wazir Mohammed Khan, Reeta, Shahida, Shabnam, Gazi

Story of two half-brothers, the evil Sajjad (Himalaywala) and the good Javed (Surendra). Exploited since his childhood by the richer and crueller branch of the family, represented by Sajjad and his mother (Zebunissa), Javed loses his beloved (Munawar Sultana), bought by Sajjad's family wealth. The fortunes of the two brothers change: Sajjad gambles away his wealth while Javed becomes a noted lawyer. In a fit of desperation, Sajjad wants to kill his son but is himself killed by his mother. His widow turns down Javed's offer of marriage and instead starts a school in her family palace, partly to make amends for the family's vile behaviour. This was Mehboob's most stylised Muslim social with quasi-expressionist acting enhanced by an ornate decor and Irani's heavily shaded camerawork. The final song, *Insaan ki tarkeeb*, carried the film's anti-feudal message, addressed to the camera by a purdah-clad Munawar Sultana.

KANJAN

aka *Miser*
1947 170' b&w Tamil
co-d/s/lyr Kovai Ayyamuthu *co-d* T.R. Gopu *pc* Jupiter Pics *c* P. Ramaswamy *m* S.M. Subbaiah Naidu
lp Kamaladevi, S.V. Subbaiah, M.N. Nambiar, P.V. Narasimhabharati, M.S.S. Paickam, R. Malathi, C.K. Saraswati, K.S. Angamuthu

A Tamil chauvinist/revivalist contribution to social reform and the Independence struggle. The womanising widower Kandasamy (Subbaiah) is the miserly zamindar of Amaravathipudur with his crock of gold buried in the house. He covets the actress Maragatham (Kamaladevi), who is his son Kumarasamy's girlfriend, as a 2nd wife and plans to sell his daughter Amaravarthi to a rich old man. The sale of women, miserliness and black marketeering having been duly criticised, the film has a happy ending. The playwright Ayyamuthu (his *Inbasagaran* had been staged by the famous Nawab Rajamanikkam Co) was a pro-Congress nationalist associated with the controversial chief minister C. Rajagopalachari. He wrote the film's popular Tamil chauvinist hit *Indha ulanginil irukkum* ('Of all the people on this earth, the Tamils are the best'), released as a record and broadcast only by Tiruchi, Madras and Colombo radio stations. All the songs are based on classical Hindustani or Carnatic music. The film's release in the year of India's independence was accompanied by a two-reeler showing Gandhi visiting Palani and the Independence Day celebrations in Coimbatore.

LOKSHAHIR RAMJOSHI/MATWALA SHAYAR RAMJOSHI

1947 123'[M]/132'[H] b&w Marathi/Hindi
d **Baburao Painter, V. Shantaram** *pc* **Rajkamal Kalamandir** *s/co-lyr* **G.D. Madgulkar** *co-lyr* Shahir Ramjoshi *c* G. Balkrishna *m* **Vasant Desai**
lp Jayaram Shiledar, **Hansa Wadkar**, Shakuntala, Parashuram, G.D. Madgulkar, Sudha Apte, Samant, Gundopant Walavalkar, Jayaram Desai, Kanase, Sawalram, Vaidya, Abhyankar

Classic Marathi Tamasha musical telling the life story of Ramjoshi (1758-1812) (Shiledar), a poet, keertan and lavani performer who later became extraordinarily popular notably with the lavani and the militant powada forms. The film narrates the poet's history, his descent into alcoholism and his eventual rise to greatness. The main dramatic pivot is his love for the Tamasha dancer Baya (Wadkar). Several scenes extensively illustrate Shantaram's symbol-laden expressionism, e.g. the scene where he drops the liquor jug to the floor, it hooks on to his clothing and thus does not 'let go of him'. These are combined with the scenes for which the film is famous, e.g. the sawal-jawab (musical question and answer contest) sequence, and numerous other lavani song-picturisations featuring Madgulkar's lyrics in his script debut. Shantaram had originally commissioned his mentor, Painter, to direct the film, but later sacked him and completed it himself. The film went on to become the biggest post-war success in the Marathi cinema, inaugurating the Tamasha genre in Marathi (followed by D.S. Ambapkar's *Jai Malhar* the same year, and **Mane**'s ***Sangtye Aika***, 1959). All three films, and indeed the genre itself, remained indelibly linked to Madgulkar's songwriting. A sequence from the movie is reconstructed in the opening of **Benegal**'s Wadkar biographical ***Bhumika*** (1976).

NAM IRUVAR

aka *We Two*
1947 153' b&w Tamil
d/p **A.V. Meiyappan Chettiar** *pc* **AVM** *s* **P. Neelakantan** from his play *lyr* Subramanya Bharati *c* T. Muthusamy *m* R. Sundarshanam
lp T.R. Mahalingam, **B.R. Panthulu**, T.R. Ramchandran, V.K. Ramaswamy, K. Sarangapani, T.A. Jayalakshmi, K.R. Chellam, Kumari Kamala

Political melodrama establishing the famed AVM Prod. and the debut of Neelakantan, its scenarist and assistant director. The original play had been a stage success produced by S.V. Sahasranamam for the comedian **N.S. Krishnan**'s theatre troupe. The film is replete with nationalist symbols, which proliferated in Tamil films following the installation of a popular government (1945) and the lifting of WW2 censorship. It begins with a Subramanya Bharati anniversary and ends with Gandhi's 77th-birthday celebrations, characters greeting each other with the 'Jai Hind' salute. The story, adapted from the earlier film ***Iru Sahodarargal*** (1936), features a blackmarketeer and his two sons Vijayakumar (Panthulu) and Sukumar (Mahalingam). The latter is a wastrel who loves Kannamma (Jayalakshmi), the daughter of his father's partner. The partner is a rapacious movie producer. The stagey, studio-bound film spoken in chaste (literary) Tamil used Bharati's nationalist songs and love poems. The younger sister of the heroine

(Kumari Kamala) dances on a decorated drum with national flags draped behind her to Bharati's famous *Kottu murase* ('Let the drum sound'), prefiguring the climactic scenes of ***Chandralekha*** (1948).

NEEL KAMAL

1947 116' b&w Hindi
d/s/lyr **Kidar Sharma** *pc* Oriental Pics *c* Gordhanbhai Patel *m* B. Vasudev *lp* **Madhubala, Raj Kapoor**, Begum Para, Rajinder, Shanta Kumar, Nifis Khilili, Nazira, Pesi Patel, Subhashini, Inquilab, Radha, Karan Singh, Baby Indira, Kumar Sahu, Dilip Kumar

Seminal melodrama, although a commercial flop, introducing Raj Kapoor and Madhubala. The love triangle and drama about atheism is set in an undefined Rajput court. The king and queen are killed when the king's evil brother-in-law seizes power. Both their daughters escape. The younger princess, Kamala (Madhubala), is rescued and adopted by a clan of Untouchables. She meets and nurses to health a young atheist sculptor, Madhusudhan (Kapoor), who falls in love with both Kamala and her sister (Begum Para), forcing Kamala to commit suicide. In Sharma's classic romantic idiom, a lotus flower grows where she died.

PALNATI YUDDHAM

1947 168' b&w Telugu
d **Gudavalli Ramabrahmam, L.V. Prasad** *pc* Sharada Prod *s/lyr* **Samudrala *R*aghavacharya** *c* Jiten Bannerjee *m* Galipenchala Narasimha Rao
lp G.V. Subba Rao, **P. Kannamba,** Shrivatsava Venkateshwara Rao, Lingamurthy, G.V. Sitapati, D.S. Sadasivarao, **A. Nageshwara Rao**, Vangara, **S. Varalakshmi**, Chandra, Narimani, Rajabala, Annapurna, Gangarathnam, P. Vishweshwaramma

Ramabrahmam died before he could complete his dream project, a historical foreshadowing India's independence, and L.V. Prasad finished it. The film tells of warfare and rivalries within the kingdom of Palnadu, causing the kingdom to split and numerous bloody caste and religious conflicts. The minister Brahmanayudu (G.V. Subba Rao), a wily political visionary, opens the doors of the Chenna Keshava temple to people of all castes, leading to a revolt from the military instigated by the royal matriarch Nagamma. The kingdom splits and early contests for dominance give way to full-scale battle among the second generation of the warring clans. The opening title directly alludes to Partition, referring to the fate of a nation 'whose soil has been converted into a rudrabhoomi [a cremation ground] by the vengeful attitudes of warring brothers'.

RAMER SUMATI/CHHOTA BHAI

1947 131'[B]/144'[H] b&w Bengali/Hindi
d **Kartick Chattopadhyay** *pc* **New Theatres** *st* Saratchandra Chatterjee *sc* Sudhiranjan Mukherjee *dial*[H] Mohanlal Bajpai *lyr*[H] Romesh Panday *c* Sudhin Majumdar *m* **Pankaj Mullick**
lp Molina Devi, Master Shakoor[H]/Master Swagat[B], Rajalakshmi, Paul Mohinder[H], Sisir Batabyal[B], Asit Sen, Khurshid, Phani Roy[B], Chhabi Roy

Kartick Chattopadhyay's debut adapts a Saratchandra story about a typically affectionate sister-in-law. Narayani (Molina Devi) raises her husband's young stepbrother Ramlal (Shakoor/Swagat), and is the only person who can control him when he becomes a notorious prankster. Problems develop between Ramlal and Narayani's visiting mother, and Ramlal attempts to run away, before he is reconciled with Narayani.

RATNAMALA

1947 165' b&w Telugu
d **P.S. Ramakrishna Rao** *pc* Bharani Pics *s/co-lyr* **Samudrala Ragavacharya** *co-lyr* Rajanikanta Rao *c* Jiten Bannerjee, P.S. Selvaraj *m* **C.R. Subburaman**
lp **P. Bhanumathi**, G.V. Subba Rao, **C.S.R. Anjaneyalu**, **A. Nageshwara Rao,** Hemalatha, Arani Satyanarayana, Suryanarayana, Seetaram, Ramanatha Sastry, Venkumamba, Koteshwara Rao, Narayana, Baby Sumitra

The first film from Bhanumathi's independent production concern, set up with her husband, director Ramakrishna. Cast in a folk-tale idiom, the story tells of Ratnamala (Bhanumathi) who is tricked into marrying the infant Prince Chandrakantha. She raises her 'husband' in a forest but when he is 7 years old he is kidnapped by bandits for a ritual sacrifice. Ratnamala follows him and the robber chieftain tries to molest her. The couple are eventually rescued by the king, Ratnamala's father. When he refuses to believe that the boy is indeed her husband, the gods Shiva and Parvathi descend to earth to sort out the confusion. The film is famous composer C.R. Subburaman's first independent assignment and includes several hit songs: *Anandadayini* and, when Ratnamala goes in search of her husband, *Niluva needa leka*. The film also featured compositions by **Saluri Rajeshwara Rao, Ghantasala** and Rajanikanta Rao, all uncredited.

SAMAJ KO BADAL DALO

1947 133' b&w Hindi
d **Vijay Bhatt** *pc* Prakash Pics *s* Girish *lyr* Roopdas, Indra, Qamar Jalalabadi *c* Yusuf Mulji *m* **Khemchand Prakash**
lp Aroon, Mridula, Yakub, Shantarin, Umakant, Lila Pawar, Ramesh Sinha, Bikram Kapoor, Prem Dhawan, Shabnam

Bhatt's unusually strident marital melodrama made with the informal help of the **IPTA** (choreographers Santi Bardhan, Sachin Shankar, Narendra Sharma et al.), mounting an IPTA-style attack on social conventions in the context of the Independence movement's promises of liberation. Heroine Manorama (Mridula), daughter of a clerk, cannot marry hero Kishore (Aroon) because her father can't afford the dowry. Manorama marries the evil widower Jayant (Yakub) who tortures her. Kishore marries the rich Champa (Lila Pawar), but then magnanimously allows her to remarry the man she really loves, Naresh. Kishore's goodness eventually clashes with Jayant's villainy and in a frenzied sequence he kills both Jayant and Manorama. He is pronounced insane and arrested.

SHEHNAI

1947 133' b&w Hindi
d/s/lyr P.L. Santoshi *pc* **Filmistan** *c* K.H. Kapadia *m* **C. Ramchandra**
lp Rehana, Indumati, Naseer Khan, Dulari, Mumtaz Ali, Niranjan Sharma, Leela Mishra, Kumkum, Rekha, S.L. Puri, **Kishore Kumar**, Shobha Thakur, Radha Kishen, Srinath, V.H. Desai

Hit musical by the famous duo of lyricist Santoshi and composer Ramchandra. Marital drama featuring the four daughters of a comedian (V.H. Desai), their rival, the arrogant daughter of the zamindar (Indumati), and the various men in their lives: the zamindar's secretary (Radha Kishen), the police inspector (Kishore Kumar) etc. The film had Ramchandra's all-time hit *Aana meri jaan Sunday ke Sunday* (sung by Meena Kapur and Shamshad Begum with the composer) and several other songs, including the bhajan *Jai Krishna hare Krishna* (sung by Veenapani Mukherjee) and the railway number *Jawani ki rail chale jai re* (sung by **Geeta Dutt, Lata Mangeshkar** and the composer).

YOGI VEMANA

1947 174' b&w Telugu
d **K.V. Reddy** *pc* **Vauhini** *s/lyr* **Samudrala Raghavacharya** *c* Marcus Bartley *m* **Chittor V. Nagaiah**, Ogirala Ramchandra Rao
lp Chittor V. Nagaiah, **M.V. Rajamma**, Parvathibai, M. Lingamurthy, Kantamani, Baby Krishnaveni, Rami Reddy, Seeta, K. Doraiswamy

Nagaiah's third Saint film made by the same unit that produced his first one, the hit ***Bhakta Potana*** (1942). Vemana, a 17th-C. poet born in the Reddy community, attacked social inequality although adhering to the conventional Hindu views on women. The film attempts to inject realism into the Telugu version of the genre, showing, e.g., the relationship between Vemana (Nagaiah) and a courtesan, Mohanangi (Rajamma). Vemana, the younger brother of a local chieftain, steals his sister-in-law's diamond necklace for Mohanangi. He next steals the money meant for the king's tribute, causing his brother to be imprisoned. He and his friend Abhiram (Lingamurthy) successfully manufacture gold by using alchemy. His moment of revelation comes when he brings this gold home to find his niece Jyoti (Baby Krishnaveni), his only real friend, dead. The film dissolves her face on to a skeleton, adding shots of people in their daily work routine, set to the song *Idena inthena* ('Is this all that life is?'). Vemana then becomes a mendicant, advocating an ideology earlier demonstrated when he takes the silk cloak covering an idol in a temple and drapes it over an old woman shivering in the cold. The film is often compared with **Shantaram**'s **Prabhat** biographical of Eknath, ***Dharmatma*** (1935).

Raj Kapoor and Premnath in *Aag*

AAG

aka *Fire*
1948 138' b&w Hindi
d/p **Raj Kapoor** *pc* R.K. Films *s* **Inder Raj Anand** *lyr* Behzad Lucknowi, Saraswati Kumar Deepak, **Majrooh Sultanpuri** *c* V.N. Reddy *m* Ram Ganguly
lp Raj Kapoor, **Nargis**, Premnath, Kamini Kaushal, Nigar Sultana, Kamal Kapoor, B.M. Vyas, Vishwa Mekra, **Shashi Kapoor**, Indumati

Raj Kapoor said he would never forget this film, his directorial debut, 'because it was the story of youth consumed by the desire for a brighter and more intense life. And all those who flitted like shadows through my own life, giving something, taking something, were in that film.' The hero is Kewal (Kapoor), a country boy disfigured by a self-inflicted scar on his face who dreams of running a theatre. He is cast out by his father and eventually builds his own theatre where Nimmi (Nargis) becomes a star. Shashi Kapoor plays the part of Raj Kapoor as a young boy. Announcing the baroque imagery of ***Barsaat*** (1949) and ***Awara*** (1951), Kapoor fills his film with shadows evoking the influence of the **Osten**/Wirsching brand of chiaroscuro.

AJIT

aka *Rangeen Zamana*
1948 133' col Hindi
d/p **Mohan Bhavnani** *pc* Bhavnani Prod. *st* Snilloc's novel *Asir of Asirgarh lyr* Phani *m* Govind Ram
lp Monica Desai, Premnath, Yashodhara Katju, Gope, Nayampalli, Badri Prasad, Ram Kamlani

Bhavnani's last feature is described in a *Times of India* review (18.12.1949) as a 'Rajput story fraught with great drama and tender romance'. It is India's first colour film using Kodachrome 16mm blown up to 35mm in the USA.

ANJANGARH

1948 126'[B]/139'[H] b&w Bengali/Hindi
d/s **Bimal Roy** *pc* **New Theatres** *st* Subodh Ghosh's *Fossil dial*[H] Mohanlal Bajpai *lyr*[H] Bhushan, Ramesh Panday *c* Kamal Bose *m* **Rai Chand Boral**
lp Sunanda Bannerjee, **Tulsi Chakraborty**, Parul Kar, Manorama Jr., Chhabi Roy, Bipin Gupta, Asit Sen, Purnendu Mukherjee, **Jahar Roy**, Sunil Dasgupta, Prafulla Mukherjee, Ramakrishna Chatterjee, Devi Mukherjee[B], Amita Basu[B], Phalguni Roy[B], Shankar Sen[B], Raja Ganguly[B], Kalipada Sarkar[B], Bhanu Bannerjee[B], Manoranjan Bhattacharya[B], Rama Nehru[H], Hirabai[H], Hiralal[H], Ajay Kumar[H], Raimohan[H], Bhupendra Kapoor[H]

Roy's New Theatres sequel to his remarkable debut ***Udayer Pathay/Hamrahi*** (1944), this is a political allegory about collusion in colonial times between the aristocracy and a rising indigenous bourgeoisie. The despotic ruler of the small Anjangarh kingdom comes into conflict with a mining syndicate which pays its workers a decent wage and allows the unionisation of the workforce. This bodes ill for the ruler. Eventually the syndicate joins with the despot in naming an innocent reformist collective set up for the welfare of the workers as the real culprit behind the popular unrest. Subodh Ghosh's powerful story *Fossil* is a savagely ironic account of a fictional kingdom allegorically representing the socio-economic rise of the native colonial state. The big-budget film includes the key characters of the novel (e.g. the bourgeois liberal Mukherjee who dreams of a future land when the bones of the dead workers will, with the quartz and granite, yield mineral deposits a million years from now; the peasant leader Dulal Mahato), while placing in greater prominence the love story between the peasant leader Shubha and Mukherjee. It also has a 'Vivek', a singing minstrel used as a narrative chorus, a device borrowed from the traditional Jatra form.

ANOKHI ADA

1948 141' b&w Hindi-Urdu
d/p **Mehboob Khan** *pc* Mehboob Prod. *st* **Zia Sarhadi** *sc* Aga Jani Kashmiri *lyr* Shakeel Badaiyuni, Anjum Pilibhiti *c* Faredoon Irani *m* **Naushad**
lp Naseem Banu, Surendra, Prem Adib, Zeb Kureshi, Cuckoo, Nawab, Pratima Devi, Murad, Bhudo Advani

An updating of the ***Anmol Ghadi*** (1946) love triangle, this time featuring mainly the heroine's amnesia. The rivals for her love are an adventurer (Adib) who calls himself Laatsaheb (i.e. Lord Sahib) and a professor (Surendra). Each is associated with her life on either side of her memory divide, giving each a particular stake in whether she be allowed to recall her past or not. Remarkably shot in heavy chiaroscuro, esp. in the backdrops at the professor's house where the heroine battles with her amnesia.

BHULI NAAI

1948 157' b&w Bengali
d **Hemen Gupta** *pc* National Progressive Pics *st* Manoj Bose *c* **Ajoy Kar** *m* **Hemanta Mukherjee**
lp Radhamohan Bhattacharya, Pradeep Kumar, Nibedita Das, **Tulsi Chakraborty**, Sudipta Roy

Ex-terrorist Gupta's first film in his best-known style (cf ***'42***, 1949) celebrates the patriotic terrorist movements in pre-Independence Bengal. Markedly different from the film biographies of political personalities, Gupta's angry tone conveys opposition to the nationalist leadership coming into power at the time. Faithfully following Manoj Bose's original story, it opens with the 1905 Swadeshi upsurge: the burning of imported garments, the anti-Partition rallies etc. Mahananda, Ajit and Anandakishore are in a procession which is attacked by the police. Their leader Masterda (borrowed from the chronologically later Surya Sen) absconds with Anupama when Mahananda betrays the group of insurgents. The young Anandakishore is killed and Ajit is arrested. He escapes from jail, kills the informer and is sentenced to death, reaffirming his faith in nationalism shortly before he is hanged. The episode, evoking the real-life incident of a terrorist vendetta against Naren Gosain, is followed by documentary shots of Gandhi and Subhash Chandra Bose (apparently added following censor strictures) that remain somewhat out of place in the main drama.

BIPLABI

aka *The Revolutionary*
1948 c.140' b&w Assamese
d/c **Asit Sen** *pc* Shri Krishna Films *co-lyr/m* Siba Bhattacharya *co-lyr* Malin Bora, Bhupen Bhattacharya
lp Anupama Bhattacharya, Chandra Phukan, Rani Nath, Jagat Bezbaruah

In his debut film, the noted Bengali and Hindi director Asit Sen tells of a young radical who sacrifices his life for the nation. Several Assamese films, often featuring former **IPTA** members, broached the theme of radical martyrdom and nationalism, but this is technically very accomplished and remained for some years a standard work in the genre.

CHANDRALEKHA

1948 207' b&w Tamil/Hindi
d/p **S.S. Vasan** *pc* **Gemini** *s* Gemini Story Dept. *dial* K.J. Mahadevan, Kothamangalam Subbu, Sangu, Kittu, Naina[T], Indra, Aga Jani Kashmiri[H]
lyr **Papanasam Sivan**, Kothamangalam Subbu[T], Indra, Bharat Vyas[H] *c* Kamal Ghosh *m* **Saluri Rajeshwara Rao**, Balkrishna Kalla
lp T.R. Rajkumari, M.K. Radha, Ranjan, Sundaribai, L. Narayan Rao, P. Subbaiah Pillai, V. Janaki, **N.S. Krishnan**[T], T.A. Mathuram[T], T.E. Krishnamachariar[T], N. Seetaraman[T], Pottai Krishnamurthy[T], Yashodhara Katju[H], H.K. Chopra[H]

One of India's most famous films, started in 1943 and costing a massive Rs 3m this was the first major effort of a Tamil studio to attempt an all-India distribution. The film's nationwide success encouraged many others, e.g. **AVM** and **Prasad**, to follow suit. It is a period adventure film sometimes compared with *The Prisoner of Zenda* (1922, 1937). The basic plot is one of sibling rivalry between two princes, the good Veer Singh (Radha) and the bad Shashank (Ranjan). The object of desire and bone of contention between them is state power equated with the possession of the village maiden Chandralekha (Rajkumari). In the process, the hero and the heroine become circus artistes. The villain grabs the girl and enforces a wedding. She agrees provided there be an elaborate drum dance: the enormous drums, in the Indian cinema's most anthologised sequence, contain the hero's soldiers who burst out of the drums after the dance overwhelming the baddies followed by the longest sword duel in Indian cinema. Although the genre itself was not new to the Tamil cinema, its aggressive redefinition of entertainment mobilised Hollywood-style orientalism for an indigenist mass culture and became a landmark in the codification of an Indian mass entertainment ideology after Independence. Many of the spectacular dance sequences can be seen as continuations of the choreography in Uday Shankar's ***Kalpana*** (1948), shot earlier that year at Gemini by many of the same technicians. The choreography was arranged by Jaya Shankar, Mrs Rainbird, Natanam Nataraj and Niranjala Devi. T.G. Raghavacharya started directing the film and probably shot most of it. Vasan took over direction later. According to Randor Guy, the initial plot stems from G.M.W. Reynolds's novel *Robert Macaire, or The French Bandit in England* (1848). V.A.K. Ranga Rao notes that the film's music shows influences from Carnatic, Hindustani, Bharatnatyam, Latin American and Portuguese folk music as well as a Strauss waltz. The chorus by the circus members apparently adapts the *Donkey Serenade* from R.Z. Leonard's film *The Firefly* (1937).

DROHI

1948 179' b&w Telugu
d **L.V. Prasad** *pc* Swatantra Pics *s/lyr* **Tapi Dharma Rao** *c* Sridhar *m* **Pendyala Nageshwara Rao**
lp **G. Varalakshmi**, **Lakshmirajyam**, **K.S. Prakash Rao**, **L.V. Prasad**, Rallabandi, Prabhakar Rao, K. Sivarao, Venkumamba, Surabhi Balasaraswathi

Melodrama deploying the later **New Theatres** idiom of addressing the rise of a corrupt class of usurers in plots revolving around disease. The villain in the village is the wealthy and corrupt Gangadhara Rao (Rallabandi). His Westernised daughter Saroja (Varalakshmi) loves the crook Raja (Prabhakar). Driving her car, Saroja knocks down an old man who later dies of his injuries. The old man's granddaughter Seeta (Lakshmirajyam) is adopted by Prakash (K.S. Prakash Rao), a local doctor, who marries Saroja. When Saroja finds out Seeta's relationship with the accident victim, she has her thrown out on charges of theft. At this point an epidemic spreads through the village and the doctor has to work for long hours with the people. He also starts representing their interests to the political authorities. This threatens the villains Gangadhara Rao and Raja, who set fire to the village. The angry villagers are restrained by Seeta, but in the ensuing confrontation Seeta dies, accidentally killed by Gangadhara Rao. Saroja now turns over a new leaf and has her father and her ex-lover arrested, and she offers charity in the name of the dead Seeta. This is the first production of actor (and later director) K.S. Prakash Rao, and the debut of composer Pendyala. The other major director in the Prasad tradition, **T. Prakash Rao**, joined films here as assistant to Prasad, directing the scenes in which Prasad acted.

GHAR KI IZZAT

1948 136' b&w Hindi
d Ram Daryani *pc* Murli Movietone *st* K.S. Daryani *dial/lyr* I.C. Kapoor *c* Kumar Jaywant *m* Pundit Gobindram
lp Mumtaz Shanti, **Dilip Kumar**, Manorama, Jeevan, Dixit, Suleman, Gulab, Gope

Daryani's domestic drama features two couples, each cutting across the urban-rural divide. Radhika, daughter of Seth Chunilal, and her husband Chaman leave her father's house to start an insurance business in the countryside. They meet Roopa (Shanti), poor but happy and living with her two brothers. Chanda (Kumar), Radhika's brother, falls in love with Roopa; they get married and move to the city where Roopa lives an unhappy life, taunted by her parents-in-law about her former poverty. The weak Chanda, concerned about his wife's unhappiness, leaves home and becomes a drunk and a gambler until, on a full-moon night, all differences are resolved.

GOPINATH

1948 155' b&w Hindi
d/s **Mahesh Kaul** *pc* Shanti Lokchitra *lyr* poems by the saint-poets Surdas and Meerabai, Ram Murthy *c* Chandu *m* Ninu Majumdar
lp **Raj Kapoor**, Tripti Mitra, Latika, Nand Kishore, Sachin Ghosh, Randhir, Anwaribai, Feroze, Mahesh Kaul, Baby Zubeida, Niranjan Tiwari

Tragic tale of Gopi (Mitra), a village woman virtually abandoned by her brother in the home of Mohan (Kapoor) and his ageing mother. The lower-caste Gopi secretly loves Mohan but he pines for the movie star Neela Devi. Eventually the frustrated Gopi goes mad just when Mohan, fed up with his star's whims, returns to Gopi. The film belongs to the Bengali tradition of literary melodramas, an association enhanced by Tripti Mitra's remarkable performance. In shifting the tragedy from a ***Devdas***-type male anxiety to the woman's condition, the film chronicles the behavioural and moral restrictions besetting a woman caught in a 'traditional' environment. Mitra's performative idiom rises above the story's vindication of tradition as superior to the liberated but hollow freedoms of the film star.

KALPANA

aka *Imagination*
1948 164' b&w Hindi
d/s/choreo Uday Shankar *pc* Stage & Screen Presentations *dial* Amritlal Nagar *lyr* Sumitranandan Pant *c* **K. Ramnoth** *m* Vishnudas Shirali
lp Uday Shankar, Amala Shankar, Lakshmi Kanta, G.V. Subba Rao, Birendra Bannerjee, Swaraj Mitter Gupta, Anil Kumar Chopra, **Padmini**

A dance spectacular, four years in the making, orchestrated by India's most famous modern dancer (and brother of Ravi Shankar). The narrative of the surreal fantasy is embedded within a framing story of a writer telling a story to a film producer, who eventually declines to make the movie. The writer tells of Udayan (Shankar) and Kamini (Kanta) and the young man's dream of establishing an art centre, Kalakendra (a fictional equivalent of Shankar's India Cultural Centre at Almora) in the Himalayas. Shot in the **Gemini** Studios in Madras, this ode to creative imagination mobilises the vocabulary of traditional dancing, which doubles as a metaphor for the dreams invested in the newly independent India. The choreography was specifically designed for the camera, with semi-expressionist angles and chiaroscuro effects, and became a model for later dance spectaculars like ***Chandralekha*** (also made at Gemini and shot by Ramnoth, 1948) and the dream sequence in **Raj Kapoor**'s ***Awara*** (1951). For many years, the unusual film was seen as exemplifying a successful fusion of Indian modernism and the cinema. Shankar, who had danced with Pavlova, was lauded by James Joyce in a letter to his daughter: 'He moves on the stage like a semi-divine being. Believe me, there are still some beautiful things left in this poor old world.' A 122' version was shown in the US although one reviewer noted that the Indian government seemed reluctant to let it be seen abroad.

SIRAJ

1948 ?' b&w Assamese
d Bishnu Rabha, **Phani Sarma** *st* Lakhidhar Sarma *lyr* Siba Bhattacharya, **Bhupen Hazarika** *c* Sudesh Ghatak *m* Bishnu Rabha
lp Phani Sarma, Bishnu Rabha, Chandradhar Goswami, Bhupen Hazarika, Anupama Bhattacharya, Nirupama, Ambika Patwari, Bhabha Hazarika

National integration movie made by former associates of the Assamese **IPTA**, calling for communal harmony through its central character Siraj (Sarma), a kind-hearted Muslim who raises an orphaned Hindu child. Composer and actor Bhupen Hazarika, making his debut here, remade the film in 1988, but four decades later the plot, lacking its initial conviction and performative authenticity, seemed maudlin.

SUHAAG RAAT

1948 143' b&w Hindi
d/sc/lyr **Kidar Sharma** *pc* Oriental Pics *st* F.A. Mirza, V. Sharma *c* D.C. Mehta, D.K. Ambre, Machwe *m* Snehal
lp Begum Para, Bharat Bhushan, **Geeta Bali**, Pesi Patel, S. Nazir, Rajinder, Nazira, Shanta Kumar, D. Kumar

Geeta Bali's debut is a classic love triangle. The child Bali is placed under the guardianship of the evil and greedy stepbrother Rahu: he pushes Bali over a cliff in order to get the entire family inheritance. Bali (Bhushan) survives, protected by an old murderer, Jaggu, whose beautiful daughter Kammo (Geeta Bali) falls in love with him although he prefers Paro (Begum Para), daughter of a zamindar with whom he has found employment. The villainous stepbrother re-enters the scene and lays claim to Paro; the lovely Kammo sacrifices her own life to get the lovers, Bali and Paro, together. All the well-known Sharma trademarks are present, including the use of nature as an emotional equivalent for the characters' state of mind, e.g. the scene where Kammo rows the boat through the dark night to enable the lovers to elope. The film has several Geeta Dutt numbers, including *Rum jhum matwale badal chha gaye* and *Balo more payal*.

VADILONA VANKE

1948 132' b&w Gujarati
d **Ramchandra Thakur** *pc* Saras Pics *s/lyr* Prabhulal Dwivedi *c* Gordhanbhai Patel *m* Mohan Jr
lp Motibai, Vasant Nayak, Pratima Devi, Latabai, Ramesh Vyas, Anant Vin, Amrit, Anjana, Neelam, Chunilal Nayak, Master Pransukh, Baby Saroj, Vijaya, Keshav Purohit, Jayshankar, Chhagan Romeo

Melodrama about social modernisation featuring the retired diwan of Kathiawar and his two daughters who have both separated from their husbands. The elder sister, illiterate and a traditionalist, is married to the sophisticated political prisoner Pushkar. The younger sister is married to the aimlessly 'modern' Kirtikumar. The drama of conflicting rights and ambitions is played out by an unusually large number of characters including Pushkar's widowed mother, her younger son, other members of the joint family, a criminal, and the accountants employed by Kirtikumar and the diwan. The film ends with Pushkar's death, leading to the cessation of hostilities. The film is based on a successful play by the Desh Nataka Samaj.

ANDAZ

aka *A Matter of Style* aka *Beau Monde*
1949 148'(142') b&w Hindi
d/p **Mehboob Khan** *pc* Mehboob Prod. *st* Shams Lucknowi *sc* S. Ali Raza *lyr* **Majrooh Sultanpuri** *c* Faredoon Irani *m* **Naushad**
lp **Dilip Kumar, Nargis, Raj Kapoor**, Cuckoo, V.H. Desai, Sapru, Murad, Anwaribai, Amir Banu, Jamshedji

Melodrama using the pivotal figure of a woman to dramatise the contradictory proposition that the new, independent India should value capitalist modernisation while retaining feudal family and moral values. Neeta (Nargis), a modern young woman who dresses in Western style, inherits the business empire of Sir Badriprasad (Sapru). She entrusts its management to her dashing young friend Dilip (Kumar), who misreads her easygoing friendship and assumes that she reciprocates his love. When the man she is engaged to, the spoilt playboy Rajan (Kapoor), returns, she marries him. Dilip's managerial efficiency disintegrates under the pressure of his frustrated desire while the infantile Rajan begins to suspect his wife's fidelity. Eventually the tensions erupt into a violent clash between the two men as Rajan threatens to beat Dilip to death with a tennis racket. When Dilip recovers and advances on Neeta, she shoots him and is jailed for murder. The ensuing trial underlines the moral of the story: all the mayhem is Neeta's fault for not having listened to her father when he warned her to avoid 'modern' ways. A major musical hit with Naushad classics like *Hum aaj kahin dil kho baithe*, *Tu kahe agar*, *Jhoom jhoom ke nacho aaj* (all sung by Mukesh).

APOORVA SAHODARARGAL/APOORVA SAHODHARALU/NISHAN

aka *Strange Brothers*
1949 151' b&w Tamil/Telugu/Hindi
d T.G. Raghavacharya[Ta], **C. Pullaiah**[Te], **S.S. Vasan**[H] *pc* **Gemini** *st* Alexandre Dumas's *The Corsican Brothers* *dial* Gemini Story Dept.[Ta], *co-dial/lyr* Indra[H] *co-dial* J.S. Casshyap *lyr* Kothamangalam Subbu[Ta] *c* Kamal Ghosh[H], P. Ellappa *m* **Saluri Rajeshwara Rao**, M.D. Parthasarathy, Balkrishna Kalla, R. Vaidyanath
lp **P. Bhanumathi**, M.K. Radha[Ta], **R. Nagendra Rao**, G. Pattu Iyer, L. Narayanarao, B.S. Saroja, D. Balasubramanyam, Ranjan[H], J.S. Casshyap[H], Maya Bannerjee[H], Balkrishna Kalla[H], Suryaprabha[H]

Vasan's sequel to the smash hit ***Chandralekha*** (1948) adapted the Douglas Fairbanks Jr version of the Dumas novel, directed by Edward Small (1942). Made as a trilingual, its nearly identical Tamil (*Apoorva Sahodarargal*) and Telugu (*Apoorva Sahodharalu*) versions were nevertheless credited to different directors, while M.K. Radha, who plays the double role of the separated twins in Tamil is replaced by his *Chandralekha* co-star Ranjan for the Hindi film. The villain Zoravar Singh (Nagendra Rao) defeats the rival kingdom of Bhawanigarh and the good doctor Shankar (Casshyap) manages to rescue the twins Vijay and Vikram (Radha/Ranjan), heirs to the throne. Vijay is raised in the city and Vikram in the forest. They grow up to take revenge on Zoravar. Both brothers love the same girl, Ranjana (Bhanumathi), causing a rivalry that generates further intrigues: Zoravar kidnaps the girl as bait to get the two heroes to reveal themselves. The Hindi version was less successful than the Tamil one, which broke several records.

BARSAAT

aka *Rain*
1949 171'(163') b&w Hindi
d/p **Raj Kapoor** *pc* R.K. Films *s* **Ramanand Sagar** *lyr* Hasrat Jaipuri, **Shailendra**, Ramesh Shastri, Jalal Mahilabadi *c* Jal Mistry *m* **Shankar-Jaikishen**
lp Raj Kapoor, **Nargis**, Premnath, K.N. Singh, Cuckoo, Nimmi, V.M. Vyas, Ratan Gaurang, Vishwa Mehra, Dolly Baldev, Pushpa Bimla, Prakash Arora, Susheela Devi, B.N. Khera, Master Sandow

Kapoor's sombre musical classic contrasts different notions of love. The rich and 'sensitive' Pran (Kapoor) passionately loves the poor country girl Reshma (Nargis). Defying her father's objections, who repudiates her, she runs to Pran but apparently drowns on the way. Pran and his philandering friend Gopal (Premnath), who callously jilted the village girl Neela (Nimmi), are driving through the country and happen upon Reshma's wedding to the obsessive fisherman (Singh) who saved her and believes he owns her. Pran crashes his car, stops the wedding and gets Reshma while the repentant Gopal finds that Neela has killed herself. Kapoor's 2nd independent production starring himself and Nargis was the R.K. Studio's first major hit. Its unusually innovative chiaroscuro cinematography (e.g. for **Lata Mangeshkar** and Mukesh's song *Chhod gaye balam*) created deep rather than laterally elaborated spaces and relied heavily on metaphor, as in the shot where the angled rope cut off by Reshma's father aligns with the angle of the violin bow with which Pran nightly serenades Reshma (playing the

Nargis in *Barsaat*

Anniversary Song from *The Jolson Story*, 1946). The dominant metaphor for the flow of desire, evoked by the title, is that of water, cf the love sequence after the song *Mujhe kisise pyar ho gaya* (Lata Mangeshkar) with the waterfall, or the last shot when the smoke from Neela's funeral pyre merges with the rain clouds. The film is remembered above all for Shankar-Jaikishen's music, with numerous all-time hits, including the opening number *Hawa mein udta jaye mera lal dupatta* and *Jiya bekarar hai, Barsaat mein humse mile, Meri aankhon mein bas gaya koi re, Ab mera kaun sahara* (all sung by Lata Mangeshkar). The specially charged Kapoor-Nargis love duets (cf the *Pyar hua ikraar hua* song in ***Shri 420***, 1955) were often singled out as exemplifying the acme of the Indian cinema's romances.

EK THI LADKI

1949 164' b&w Hindi
d **Roop K. Shorey** *pc* Shorey Films *lyr* Aziz Kashmiri *m* Vinod
lp Meena Shorey, **Motilal**, Kuldeep, I.S. Johar, Majnu, Shakuntala, Batra, Shamlal, Gogia Pasha, Agha Miraz

This suspense drama was Shorey's first major Hindi success after his migration from Lahore. Poor and orphaned Meena (Shorey) accidentally witnesses the murder of a businessman in his office. Fleeing the scene, she is caught by the cops but rescued by the two killers who smart-talk their way out of the crisis. The trio check into a fancy hotel where Meena is required to play a princess. Spotting a policeman, she escapes once again and blunders into the office of hero Ranjit (Motilal), who employs her as his stenographer and then falls in love with her, to the annoyance of his boss's daughter Vimala (Kaur). **Geeta Dutt** (then Geeta Roy) sang one of her early numbers *Chandani raat hai*, but the major hit of the movie is **Lata Mangeshkar**'s *La-ra-lappa lai rakhada*: throughout the rest of her career Meena Shorey was known as the La-ra-lappa-girl.

'42

aka *Byalis*
1949 156' b&w Bengali
d/s **Hemen Gupta** *pc* Film Trust of India *lyr* Tarit Kumar Ghosh *c* G.K. Mehta *m* **Hemanta Mukherjee**
lp Bikash Roy, Manju Dey, **Sombhu Mitra**, Suruchi Sengupta, Pradeep Kumar

Gupta's best-known political film addresses the violent agitations against the colonial police in the Midnapore district of Bengal in late 1942. Set against the violent Quit India agitations of the 40s in Midnapore, much of the drama stems from the ambivalence of the local leadership towards Gandhian non-violence. An aged woman activist (a reference to Matangini Hazra of Midnapore) explains that Gandhi advocated non-violence but asked every woman to carry a knife as well, just in case. Ajoy, his wife Bina and aged grandmother are fired with the 'Karenge ya marenge' (Do or die) zeal. Violence erupts when the village blacksmith's daughter is killed. The blacksmith is tortured and killed by the evil army officer Major Trivedi (Bikash Roy, providing one of Bengali cinema's most enduring images of untrammelled villainy). Bina, who becomes a courier for the terrorists, is gang-raped by the army and goes insane, whereupon the entire village rises in anger. The grandmother is shot while leading an unarmed procession. Ajoy is shot too. Finally, in a sequence evoking Eisenstein's *Bronenosets Potemkin* (1925) the army refuses further orders to fire and eventually tramples over the major to join the marchers in raising the Indian tricolour. The tensely constructed and well-acted film, despite occasional hiccups in the dialogue (e.g. the major's line in English, 'You will be killed, killed to death'), encountered censorship problems for its potential to 'excite passion and encourage disorder'. Banned in Bengal, MP, Assam, Bihar and Madras (although cleared in Bombay), it was eventually released, with changes, in 1951.

Gunsundari Katha

GIRLS' SCHOOL

1949 154' b&w Hindi
d/sc **Amiya Chakravarty** *pc* Lokmanya Prod *dial* J.S. Casshyap *lyr* Pradeep *c* V. Babasaheb *m* **C. Ramchandra, Anil Biswas**
lp **Geeta Bali**, Sohan, Shashikala, Sajjan, Mangala, Ramsingh, Vimala Vasishta, Krishna, Harun, Jagannath, Arjun, Gangu, Kesarbai

Rural drama about Meena (Bali) who leaves home rather than submit to an arranged marriage and starts a girls' school in a village, although opposed by the local zamindar. The zamindar's brother-in-law Bipin (Sajjan), who lusts after Meena, is the villain. The hero (Sohan) appears in answer to an advertisement for a schoolteacher and is appointed only because Meena mistakes his name - Shanti Kumar Majumdar - for that of a woman. The zamindar's widowed sister Sumitradevi, a supporter of the school, objects because he is not married. Meena and Shanti Kumar fall in love but he realises the damage he may cause to her school and leaves. Bipin then spreads rumours about Shanti Kumar's morals, which cause a further difficulty that has to be resolved before both the future of the school and of the loving couple may be assured. **Guru Dutt** assisted Chakravarty on this film shot at **Bombay Talkies**.

Gunsundari Katha
1949 172' b&w Telugu
d/co-sc **K.V. Reddy** *pc* **Vauhini** *co-sc* **K. Kameshwara Rao** *st* Shakespeare's *King Lear* *dial/lyr* **Pingali Nagendra Rao** *c* Marcus Bartley *m* Ogirala Ramchandra Rao
lp Govindrajulu Subbarao, Shantakumari, K. Sivarao, Malathi, **Relangi Venkatramaiah, Sriranjini Jr.**, T.G. Kamala, Hemalatha, Jr. **Lakshmirajyam**, Seeta, Balijepalli Lakshmikanta Kavi

Freewheeling adaptation of *Lear* by fantasist K.V. Reddy. The royal patriarch (Subbarao) is offended by his youngest daughter Gunsundari (Sriranjini) when she pledges unconditional loyalty to her future husband. He has her married to a deaf and dumb cripple (Sivarao) who is in fact a perfectly healthy youth living under a curse. The king is stricken with a mysterious illness and his three sons-in-law set out to discover the Mahendramani jewel which will cure him. When the youngest son-in-law finds it, the other two steal it and magically change the third into a bear. Gunsundari eventually succeeds in lifting the curse upon her husband. The music of the big-budget Vauhini film is particularly successful, with V.A.K. Ranga Rao claiming Ogirala's composition *Eevanilo* to be the most unusual song in the history of Telugu cinema. The scenarist K. Kameshwara Rao later remade it in Tamil (*Gunsundari*, 1955) starring **Gemini Ganesh** and **Savithri**.

KANEEZ

1949 140' b&w Hindi-Urdu
d Krishna Kumar *pc* Caravan Pics *s/co-lyr* Hasrat Lucknowi *co-dial/co-lyr* Shahir Ghaznavi *co-lyr* Sarshar Saloni, Harishchandra Akhtar *c* S. Srivastava *m* **Ghulam Haider**, Hansraj Behl, **O.P. Nayyar**
lp Munawar Sultana, Shyam, Urmila, Kuldeep Kaur, Khwaja Sabin, Tiwari, Nazir Kashmiri, Jilloo, Cuckoo, Sinha

This Muslim social became one of 40s star Munawar Sultana's best-known films. She plays Sabira, the daughter of the millionaire Seth Akbar (Sinha) who is swindled and put into an asylum by his villainous manager Hamid (Sabin). Sabira marries Hamid's son Akhtar (Shyam), but it is an unhappy marriage ruined by a sexy urban socialite, Darling (Kaur). Sabira is forced to become a servant in her own home but eventually recovers her rightful place as the household's mistress. Numerous songs by Shamshad Begum and Zeenat Begum also includes early songs by **Geeta Dutt**.

KAVI

1949 151' b&w Bengali
d/sc **Debaki Bose** *pc* Chitramaya *st/dial/lyr* Tarashankar Bannerjee from his novel (1942) *c* Dhiren Dey *m* Anil Bagchi
lp Nilima Das, Anubha Gupta, Robin Majumdar, **Tulsi Chakraborty**, Nitish Mukherjee, Reba Devi

Noted novelist Tarashankar Bannerjee's book addressed the desire for immortality through art. In his own screen adaptation, the railway porter Nitai (Robin Majumdar) develops a reputation as a poet through participating in the choral kabigan (musical debate between poets who improvise in a question-answer contest). The married Thakurjhee (Anubha Gupta) falls in love with him. To avert a scandal he leaves his village and travels with a nomadic Jhumur troupe of dancers and musicians. The prostitute Basan (Nilima Das), whose advances the hero initially rejects, eventually comes to embody the unity of art and desire as theorised in the Vaishnavite system of belief. Her death forces him to return home, where he finds Thakurjhee also dead. The performances of the two women, the mute suffering of the mundane Thakurjhee, counterposed by Basan's delicate frame crippled by a terminal illness, and seen as the two sensuous opposites evoked by the hero's poetry, allow for some graceful moments in the film. Bose's ecstatic soft close-ups, his signature, are available in profusion. He remade the film in Hindi (1954) with **Geeta Bali**, **Nalini Jaywant** and Bharat Bhushan.

KEELUGURAM/MAYA KUDHIRAI

aka *The Magic Horse*
1949 220' b&w Telugu/Tamil
d Rajah of Mirzapur *pc* Shobhanachala Pics *sc* **Ch. Narayanamurthy** *dial/lyr* **Tapi Dharma Rao** *c* D.L. Narayana *m* **Ghantasala Venkateshwara Rao**
lp **Anjali Devi**, **A. Nageshwara Rao**, T. Kanakam, Suryashree, Lakshmirajyam Jr., **Surabhi Kamalabai**, Gangarathnam, M. Subbulu, A.V. Subba Rao, **Relangi Venkatramaiah**, V. Koteshwara Rao

Folk-tale in which the king, out on a hunt, falls in love with a beautiful woman (Anjali Devi) who turns out to be a rakshasi (demoness). The king insists on marrying her, inviting retribution from his son (Nageshwara Rao) by his first queen. The demoness, who is able to devour elephants and horses, sends the hero, her stepson, on a dangerous journey to fetch a rare herb, hoping he will die in the process. He survives with the aid of a magic flying horse and eventually defeats his stepmother in a savage battle. This is one of noted singer Ghantasala's first films as composer. The Rajah of Mirzapur, proprietor of the Shobhanachala Studio, took directorial credit.

LAILA MAJNU

1949 171' b&w Telugu/Tamil
d/sc **P.S. Ramakrishna Rao** *pc* Bharani Pics *dial/lyr* **Samudrala Raghavacharya** *c* **B.S. Ranga** *m* **C.R. Subburaman**
lp **P. Bhanumathi**, **A. Nageshwara Rao**, **C.S.R. Anjaneyalu**, K. Sivarao, **Mukkamala Krishnamurthy**, Arani Satyanarayana, Lalitha, **Padmini**, **Sriranjini Jr**.

The first Telugu version of the classic Sufi legend filmed extensively in Hindi. The rich Laila (Bhanumathi) loves the poor Qais (A. Nageshwara Rao) who is accused of insanity by her family. She is sent to Iraq but, in a reversal of the usually tragic ending, meets and unites with her lover in the desert. Remembered mainly for the two stars' performances and for Bhanumathi's songs *Ninu basipovudana* and *Preme neramauna*, both of which she later claimed to have composed herself. The film is also Malayalam star Padmini's Telugu debut with her sister Lalitha.

MAHAL

1949 162' b&w Hindi-Urdu
d/s **Kamal Amrohi** *pc* **Bombay Talkies** *lyr* Nakshab *c* Josef Wirsching *m* **Khemchand Prakash**
lp **Ashok Kumar**, **Madhubala**, Kumar, Vijayalakshmi, Kanu Roy

Amrohi's debut is now considered a Hindi classic. It is a complicated ghost story psychodrama choreographed by Lachhu Maharaj and featuring hero Shankar (A. Kumar), who moves into an abandoned mansion that has a tragic history. He notices his resemblance to a portrait of the mansion's former owner and sees the ghost of the man's mistress Kamini (Madhubala) who tells him he must either die if they are to be united or that he must marry her reincarnation, the gardener's daughter, Asha. His friend Shrinath (Kumar) tries to break the obsession by arranging Shankar's marriage to Ranjana (Vijayalakshmi). However, Shankar's obsession continues to the distress of his new bride who is expected, among other things, to live in a snake- and bat-infested hut. Ranjana commits suicide, accusing Shankar of the deed, but the truth comes out in the courtroom drama when the gardener's daughter admits to having masqueraded as the ghost. Shankar is nevertheless condemned to death for Ranjana's murder but in a strange reversal of fortunes, transfers his obsession to Asha: instead of being fascinated by a dead woman, he is now the near-ghost fascinated by the living Asha. The deep-focus photography is perhaps German cameraman Wirsching's best work in his career at Bombay Talkies. It is complemented by a remarkably advanced soundtrack. The film includes the song hit, *Ayega aanewala* (sung by **Lata Mangeshkar** and regarded as a turning-point in her career), used as a leitmotif for the ghost.

MANA DESAM

1949 172' b&w Telugu
d **L.V. Prasad** *pc* M.R.A. Prod. *dial/lyr* **Samudrala Raghavacharya** *c* M.A. Rehman *m* **Ghantasala Venkateshwara Rao**
lp **Chittor V. Nagaiah**, Narayana Rao, **N.T. Rama Rao**, **Relangi Venkatramaiah**, Vangara, Ramanatha Sastry, **C. Krishnaveni**, Kanchana, **R. Balasaraswathi**, Hemalatha, Lakshmikantam, **S.V. Ranga Rao**

Produced by the actress Krishnaveni, this is a political melodrama about India's freedom struggle. Shobha (Krishnaveni), a critic of the Congress Party, argues with Madhu (Narayana Rao), a supporter, and they fall in love. Both get caught up in repressive police violence and are arrested. When independence is achieved, Madhu develops amnesia as a result of torture by the police, but his memory returns and eventually he marries Shobha. The film included several symbolic scenes including a prostitute and a bottle of liquor in front of a Gandhi portrait while a Nagaiah song bemoans the speed at which India forgot Gandhi's teachings. Remembered mainly as Telugu megastar N.T. Rama Rao's debut as a police inspector, and as singer Ghantasala's first composing assignment. The film relies heavily on Burrakatha and Oggukatha folk forms, introduced here via songwriter Raghavacharya and widely used in the propagandist theatre of the Praja Natya Mandali (see **IPTA**).

MANGALFERA

1949 139' b&w Gujarati
d **Ratibhai Punatar** *pc* Ajit Pics *st* Vaju Kotak *sc* **Ramchandra Thakur** *c* H.S. Kwatra *lyr/m* **Avinash Vyas**
lp **Nirupa Roy**, Dulari, Sarita Devi, Shanti Madhok, Manhar Desai, Babu Raje, Chhagan Romeo, Bhagwandas, Ibrahim, Maruti, Kamlakant, Barkat Virani, Haridas, Popat

Ajit's remake of the **Ranjit** Studio's *Shadi* (1941). The physically handicapped Mangal (Desai) is seduced away from his loving wife Shobha (Roy) by Mena (Madhok). Shobha tries to commit suicide. When the well-meaning Chandrika (Dulari) tries to seduce the hero again, Mangal begins to believe that he was trapped into marrying a disabled woman and he returns to Shobha. The film was considered a reform social rather than a melodrama and was seen as a worthy successor of Punatar's previous Gujarati hit, *Gunsundari* (1948), confirming him as the leading Gujarati director.

MEETH BHAKAR

1949 125' b&w Marathi
d/s/lyr **Bhalji Pendharkar** *pc* Prabhakar Pics *c* Ganpat Shinde *m* Kashalkar
lp P. Ratnamala, Jayaram Shiledar, **Baburao Pendharkar**, Chintamanrao Kolhatkar, Jayaram Desai, R.V. Rane, Chittaranjan Kolhatkar, Omkar Devaskar, Usha Kiron

Pendharkar's ruralist melodrama and murder mystery. Amrit, the son of proud patriarch Tatyaba, who lives with three sons and a daughter-in-law, is accused of a murder in a gambling den. In return for hushing up the matter, the evil owner of the den enslaves the entire family, forcing them to do menial labour. The happiness of the past is contrasted with the family's downfall, for which fate is blamed, until salvation arrives when the murder victim turns out to be still alive. Pendharkar's lyrics intensified the film's sentimentality, e.g. *Bhar divasa amhi ek swapna pahila.*

NAGAKANNIKA

1949 172' b&w Kannada
d G. Vishwanathan *p* D. Shankar Singh, **B. Vittalacharya** *pc* Mahatma Pics *dial/lyr* **Hunsur Krishnamurthy** *c* G. Dorai *m* Palavangudi Shyama Iyer
lp M. Jayashree, Ballari Ratnamala, B. Raghavendra Rao, U. Mahabala Rao, S.M. Veerabhadrappa, G.R. Sandow, Pratima Devi, Eswarappa

D. Shankar Singh's Mahatma Pics' best-known film is a 'folklore' movie modelled on the Telugu fantasy genre (cf ***Patala Bhairavi***, 1951). An evil magician indulging in human sacrifices changes his protesting daughter into a parrot. He then changes a yogi's daughter into a snake and wants to sacrifice the king of Mahendrapuri but the hero manages to save the king. Co-producer B. Vittalacharya continued the genre in his Kannada and Telugu films.

NALLATHAMBI

1949 199' b&w Tamil
d **Krishnan-Panju** *pc* Eneskay Pics, Uma Films *s* **C.N. Annadurai** *lyr* **Udumalai Narayana Kavi**
lp **N.S. Krishnan**, T.A. Mathuram, S.V. Sahasranamam, **P. Bhanumathi**, Alwar Kuppuswamy

Together with ***Velaikkari*** (1949), this key DMK film initiates Annadurai's film career. The zamindar of Swapnapuri bequeaths his property to his daughter Pushpa (Bhanumathi) and his sister's son, the idealist rebel Nallathambi (Krishnan). The villain Bhoopati, who planned to marry Pushpa to acquire her land, sows discord between Pushpa and Nallathambi while the latter propagates Annadurai's political programme (e.g. advocating prohibition) and defends the people who are oppressed by the zamindari system. While promoting Krishnan as a star, the film's highlight is a fantasy insert in which Bhanumathi becomes Cleopatra.

NAVAJEEVAN/NAVAJEEVANAM

1949 172' b&w Telugu/Tamil
d **Kadaru Nagabhushanam** *pc* Shri Rajarajeshwari Prod. *s/co-lyr* Nagamani *co-lyr* **Kambadasan** *dial*[Ta] Udayakumar *c* P. Ellappa *m* S.V. Venkatraman
lp **Chittor V. Nagaiah**, Mahadevan, **P. Kannamba**, Annapurna, Sriram, **S. Varalakshmi**, Kamala, T.A. Jayalakshmi, Vanaja

Nationalist film contemporaneous with the DMK political film idiom and deploying many Gandhian symbols. It contrasts the benevolent Gandhian playwright Mahadevan (Nagaiah) with his arrogant younger brother Prabhakar (Sriram). When Prabhakar marries the rich Kamala (Kamala) and is entrusted with the estate of his industrialist father-in-law, he becomes an oppressive employer and rejects his brother when Mahadevan argues on the workers' behalf. Kamala surrounds herself with upper-class social engagements, throwing her husband together with his old flame Vanaja. Eventually Kamala and Prabhakar have a change of heart and restore the joint family's feudal collective identity.

PARIBARTAN

1949 c.130' b&w Bengali
d/sc **Satyen Bose** *pc* National Progressive Pics *st/dial* Manoranjan Ghosh *lyr* Bimal Ghosh *c* **Ajoy Kar** *m* **Salil Choudhury**
lp Ajit Bose, Shyamal Bose, Dilip Chatterjee, Sova Sen, Satyabrata, Sandhyarani, Satyen Bose

Satyen Bose and (probably) composer Salil Choudhury's debut is a didactic reformist children's film elaborating two enduring themes of Bengali boyhood novels: life at a boarding school and the semi-tragic experience of growing up. Prankster Ajoy is sent away from his widowed mother to school where he learns to respect people from a different class and becomes bosom pals with the handicapped Shakti. The boys' triumphant encounter with the corrupt school superintendent involves the good teacher Sisirbabu (played by director Bose), a nationalist who is popular with all the students except Ajoy. Their feud is eventually called off when Shakti dies in an accident, leaving Ajoy bereft twice over when Sisirbabu also has to leave the school. The producers were known for their nationalist dramas, including **Hemen Gupta**'s ***Bhuli Naai*** (1948).

RAKSHAREKHA

1949 168' b&w Telugu
d/p/sc **R. Padmanabhan** *pc* R. Padmanabhan Prod. *s/lyr* Balijepalli Lakshmikanta Kavi *c* T. Marconi *m* Ogirala Ramchandra Rao
lp **P. Bhanumathi**, **Anjali Devi**, Lakshmirajyam Jr., T. Kankam, Vijayalakshmi, R. Subbamma, Lakshmidevi, Gangarathnam, **A. Nageshwara Rao**, Balijepalli Lakshmikanta Kavi, K. Sivarao, Ramnatha Sastry, D. Satyanarayana, Vangara

Costumed fantasy, and a rare joint appearance of Telugu cinema's two best-known female stars, Bhanumathi and Anjali Devi. Kalavathi (Bhanumathi), talented and versatile daughter of the king of Simhala, refuses to marry, as does Sudhakar (A. Nageshwara Rao), prince of the neighbouring kingdom of Avanti. While he is asleep, fairies come and transport him in his bed to Kalavathi's chamber and they fall in love. The celestial damsel Chitra (Anjali Devi), envious of Kalavathi, whisks Sudhakar up to heaven, allowing him to return to earth once a week but threatening that his head will explode into a 1000 pieces if he reveals her existence. When Kalavathi gets pregnant, her husband's disappearances lead to rumours accusing her of infidelity and she is forced to leave the palace. Kidnapped by tribals, she escapes dressed as a man. Another princess, Chandrika, believing Kalavathi to be a man, falls in love with her and marries her. In the end, Chitra throws Sudhakar out of heaven and he lands on earth, petrified into a stone statue. A holy man makes him human again and changes Chitra into a witch. Patterned on an earlier hit, **Pullaiah**'s *Gollabhama* (1947), the film became a pioneering example of a genre Telugu film critics call 'folklore films'.

RIMJHIM

1949 144' b&w Hindi
d Ramesh Gupta, Sushil Sahu *pc* Hindustan Chitra *s* **Kishore Sahu** *lyr* Bharat Vyas, Moti, K. Tripathi *c* P. Isaac *m* **Khemchand Prakash**
lp Kishore Sahu, Ramola, Mubarak, Mohna, Jankidass, Jugnu, Mumtaz Ali

Musical comedy romance about Rammo (Ramola) who, scheduled to marry a fat man she hates, runs away on her wedding day dressed as a man. She meets Kamal who falls in love with her. Later they get married, but the niece of their common employer then declares her love for Kamal, creating a triangle. The film includes several classic Shamshad Begum songs.

SHABNAM

1949 154' b&w Hindi
d/sc B. Mitra *pc* **Filmistan** *st* Helen Devi *dial/lyr* Qamar Jalalabadi *c* Marshall Braganza *m* **S.D. Burman**
lp **Dilip Kumar**, Kamini Kaushal, Jeevan, Paro, Mubarak, Rajendar Singh, Harun, Shyama, Cuckoo

Filmistan's musical hit also established the reputation of composer S.D. Burman. Heroine Shanti (Kaushal), her aged father and a young man, Manoj (Kumar), are refugees from the 1942 bombing of Rangoon on their way to Bengal. Shanti initially dresses as a man to avoid being molested. When Manoj discovers that she is a woman they fall in love, although he is ensnared by the charms of a gypsy girl (Paro). Shanti accepts shelter from a rich zamindar (Jeevan) who falls in love with her. She next encounters Manoj when the zamindar hosts a gypsy dance: he is part of the troupe but misunderstands her presence in the palace as a betrayal. The film includes the classic Shamshad Begum *Yeh duniya roop ki chor, bachale mere babu.*

VELAIKKARI

1949 186' b&w Tamil
d **A.S.A. Sami** *p* S.K. Moiyuddin, K. Somasundaram *pc* Jupiter Pics *sc* **C.N. Annadurai** from his play *lyr* **Udumalai Narayana Kavi** *c* M. Masthan *m* **C.R. Subburaman**, S.M. Subbaiah Naidu
lp K.R. Ramaswamy, M.N. Nambiar, T.S. Baliah, V.N. Janaki, **M.V. Rajamma**, Lalitha, **Padmini**

Taking off from the play by the future chief minister of Tamil Nadu, the film's release coincided with the founding of the party he led, the DMK, and set out its programme in dramatic form. Inspired both by the actual Bhowal Sanyasi case and by Dumas's *Count of Monte Cristo*, the plot tells of Anandan (Ramaswamy) who returns from a tea plantation in Sri Lanka to find his father hanging from a tree, hounded to suicide by a rapacious landlord. He takes revenge with a DMK character called Mani (Baliah). A subplot has the landlord's son fall in love with a maid, providing the title as well as opportunities to castigate elitism. The film expounds the DMK's anti-caste and anti-clerical populist ideology with long monologues, flowery language and by showing, e.g., a criminal, Harihara Das (Nambiar) masquerading as a pious leader of an ashram. Sivathamby (1981) commented: 'The rhetoric of Anandan at the temple (of Mariamman) and in the court of law exposed the manner in which the landowners manipulated the entire system to keep themselves in power and authority. The arguments were so radical and heretical that they posed a threat to the very foundations of Tamil rural society.' However, the producers, religious people who only made the film because the play had been a hit, attenuated the atheist thrust and ended the film with a title card affirming 'only one god and only one community'. For his first feature, playwright/scenarist Sami relies heavily on theatrical conventions such as speech to camera, mid-shots and studio settings. The Travancore sisters, Lalitha and Padmini, perform a dance number. Janaki, **MGR**'s wife, who plays the landlord's daughter, briefly became chief minister of Tamil Nadu in 1987 and led one of the two AIADMK factions after her husband died.

AFSAR

1950 121' b&w Hindi
d/s **Chetan Anand** *pc* Navketan *st* N. Gogol's *The Inspector General* *lyr* Vishwamitter Adil, Narendra Sharma *c* V. Ratra *m* **S.D. Burman**
lp **Dev Anand**, **Suraiya**, Ruma Devi, Kanhaiyalal, Rashid, **Mohan Segal**, Krishna Dhawan, Anand Pal, Zohra Segal, Manmohan Krishna

Chetan Anand's 2nd film (after ***Neecha Nagar***, 1946), launching Navketan, continues his engagement with classic Soviet literature, although a *Filmindia* review suggested the film was based on the Henry Koster-Danny Kaye version (1949) of Gogol's play. The journalist Kapur (Dev Anand) comes to a village run by corrupt politicians led by the village tehsildar (Kanhaiyalal). They mistake him for a government inspector and treat him like a VIP. The expose of rural politics is intercut with a love story between Kapur and the tehsildar's sister Bimala (Suraiya). The film substantially determined the style, and the key unit, characteristic of Navketan's 50s productions.

BABUL

1950 142' b&w Hindi
d/p S.U. Sunny *pc* Sunny Art Prod *s* Azm Bazidpuri *lyr* Shakeel Badaiyuni *c* Fali Mistry *m/p* **Naushad**
lp **Nargis**, **Dilip Kumar**, Munawar Sultana, Amar, A. Shah, Jankidass, H. Pahadi, Vinod Ismail, Jugnu, Chandabala, Seema, Meher, Rajbala, Khursheed

Major commercial hit recounting a love triangle in a feudal household between the handsome new postman Ashok (Kumar), Bela (Nargis), the old postman's vivacious daughter and Usha (Sultana), the haughty daughter of the zamindar. Ashok teaches Usha music until Bela warns her to keep away from her man. Usha withdraws and promises to marry a man of her father's choice. One of the most formally elaborate romance dramas of 50s Hindi film, *Babul*'s tragic end forms part of the unusual plot departure of the hero falling in love with a woman who is not the heroine and who, indeed, remains out of sympathy with the audience for the better part of the film. When it turns out that both women have been betrayed by the hero and by their fathers, the film shifts into a completely subjective style, locating the man and two women in three distinct spaces, even separated in one shot by a gigantic wall. In the end, Usha's wedding procession escalates into a whole sequence of tragedies: Bela, in a deranged fit, falls from a tree and is fatally injured, though she insists that Ashok marry her, which he does, minutes before she dies. Her death is shown by a medieval horseman descending from the skies to receive her, as the smoke from her cremation merges with the clouds.

Munawar Sultana in *Babul*

BANWRE NAIN

1950 138' b&w Hindi
d/sc/co-lyr **Kidar Sharma** *pc* Ambitious Pics *st* Akhtar Mirza *c* Pandurang K. Shinde *m* Roshan *co-lyr* Sharada [Himmat Roy], Vrajendranath Gaur
lp **Raj Kapoor**, **Geeta Bali**, Vijayalakshmi, Pesi Patel, Nazira, Cuckoo, Sharada, Banke, Siraj, Prakash, Darpan, Kanta

Extraordinary melodrama distinguished by Geeta Bali's innovative acting. Disinherited Chand (Kapoor) falls in love with village girl Tara (Bali). He leaves for the city promising to return and marry her. Her sister Gangu dies as does her blind mother. She goes to the city to join Chand but Rajani, the woman who was supposed to marry Chand, manages to discredit her and she is mercilessly ejected. Chand marries Rajani while Tara is relegated to join the brass band at the wedding. Rajani dies a horrible death shortly afterwards, confessing to her deceitful action. Chand then goes in search of Tara but he is too late: she is dead. The elaborate plot is perfunctorily wrapped up in the last 15' but the film remains notable for its remarkable camerawork, e.g. in the song *Sun bairi balam*, Sharma and Shinde extend the use of filters pioneered in **Barua**'s ***Devdas*** (1935) to create black skies over a white earth. There is an unrestrained use of the pathetic fallacy with repeated rain and fire motifs, esp. in the song *Teri duniya mein dil lagta nahin*, allowing Sharma to merge a romanticised socialist realism with a mawkish presentation of patriarchy at times slipping into cosmic fantasy (e.g. the dead Tara comes alive to help Chand to enter her world). All the registers are ably sustained in Bali's skilful performance. Sharma later claimed to have written all the lyrics himself.

CHINNAMUL

aka *The Uprooted*
1950 117' b&w Bengali
d/c **Nemai Ghosh** *pc* Desha Pics *s/lyr* Swarnakamal Bhattacharya *m* Kalabaran Das
lp Prematosh Roy, Gangapada Basu, Sova Sen, Shanta Devi, Shanti Mitra, Sushil Sen, Jalad Chatterjee, **Bijon Bhattacharya**, **Ritwik Ghatak**

This seminal film in the evolution of Bengali cinematic realism tells of a large group of farmers from East Bengal who, on Partition, have to migrate to Calcutta. Made with **IPTA** support, the film used several people from refugee camps to represent their fictional equivalents. Its two legendary highlights are the scene of the old woman clinging to the doorpost of her ancestral house, refusing to leave, and the arrival of the peasants at Sealdah station amid thousands of real refugees living on the pavement. Other remarkable scenes include the long train journey, cut to the rocking movement of the passengers as they try to sleep or stand in the crowd. Despite its strong documentary overtones with people enacting their actual experiences (including the old woman), it is the folk-derived IPTA acting style that sets the tone, punctuated by tight close-ups, usually of the hero (Roy), the only politically aware member of the group, who looks for his community on Calcutta's streets. The film came to exemplify realism as consisting, in Ghosh's words, six different principles: no professional actors, no make-up (except whiskers), no out-takes, no songs, concealed camera on all occasions, and dialogue with a strongly regional dialect. Early commentators (including **Mrinal Sen**, writing in *Parichay*) criticised the film for its narrative and stylistic incoherence, although it is much closer to the spirit of IPTA's famed stage production of *Nabanna* than IPTA's own film version of that play, ***Dharti Ke Lal*** (1946). The film was made under trying conditions, including police harassment (e.g. the script was seized following a court order). Post-production censorship imposed some compromises and the film was released only following the intervention of **New Theatres**' B.N. Sircar. It was a commercial failure but recovered its costs when the USSR bought it on Pudovkin's recommendation (cf his long essay in *Pravda*, 6.12.1951), where it was dubbed and retitled *Obejdolni*. This was Ghatak's first extended encounter with cinema, functioning as actor and assistant director. According to Ghosh, **Satyajit Ray**, then an art director with an advertising agency, informally contributed to the initial screenplay.

DAHEJ

1950 149' b&w Hindi
d **V. Shantaram** *pc* **Rajkamal Kalamandir** *s/lyr* Shams Lucknowi *c* V. Avadhoot *m* **Vasant Desai**
lp Jayashree, **Prithviraj Kapoor**, Karan Dewan, **Lalita Pawar**, Ulhas, **Keshavrao Date**

Melodrama about the oppressive consequences of the dowry custom. Chanda (Jayashree), the daughter of the thakur (Kapoor), is to marry Suraj (Dewan) but his greedy mother (Pawar) demands more money than the thakur can afford. Chanda is tormented and eventually expelled from the house while Suraj is forced into a second and more lucrative alliance. Her eventual reconciliation with her husband is premised on her complete abandonment of all progressive ideals and resignation to the role of servile housewife.

DASTAAN

1950 122' b&w Hindi
d **A.R. Kardar** *pc* Musical Pics *s* Prem Bannerjee, Jagdish Kanwal *lyr* Shakeel Badaiyuni *c* Dwarka Divecha *m* **Naushad**
lp **Raj Kapoor**, **Suraiya**, Suresh, Al Nasir, Prem Bannerjee, Pratima Devi, Murad, Lakshman, Surinder, Shakila, Baby Anwari, Veena, Sapru

Melodrama told in flasback about the sexually repressed Rani (Veena) whose life is caught between two historical moments and ends up causing grief to all who knew her. The orphaned Indira (Suraiya) is adopted by the wealthy colonial (Sapru) and becomes a companion to his sons Raj (Kapoor) and Kundan (Nasir) but she is hated by Rani, the household's eldest daughter. Both Raj and Kundan fall in love with Indira, but Rani gets her married to the foreign-returned Ramesh (Suresh) and later causes a rift between the two brothers, resulting in Raj suffering a major accident and indirectly leading to Indira's death. The film starts with Rani's own death, after 25 years of isolation. Her character is placed historically between colonial domination (represented by the father) and independent capitalism's rule with its continuation of traditional patriarchy. She is represented as surrounded by infantile men and logically negative about marriage. Suraiya sang all the nine songs in the film, including the very popular duet *Tara ri yara ri* (with **Mohammed Rafi**).

EZHAI PADUM PADU/BEEDALA PATLU

aka *The Plight of the Poor* aka *Les Miserables*
1950 197'[Ta]/194'[Te] b&w Tamil/Telugu
d **K. Ramnoth** *pc* Pakshiraja Studios *sc* Suddhananda Bharathi, Jawar Seetaraman *st* Victor Hugo's *Les Miserables dial*[Ta] **Elangovan** *lyr* V.A. Gopalakrishnan[Ta], **Arudra**[Te] *c* N. Prakash *m* S.M. Subbaiah Naidu
lp **Chittor V. Nagaiah**, Serukalathur Sama, Jawar Seetaraman, T.S. Baliah, T.S. Dorairaj, Lalitha, **Padmini**, N. Rajam, V. Gopi

Extraordinary melodrama held together by Nagaiah's best-known film performance. This version of Sadanand Bharathi's Tamil translation of Hugo's novel (remade, unacknowledged, as ***Gnana Oli***, 1972), opens with the petty thief Konda (Nagaiah) in jail. He escapes and is rearrested by Inspector Javert (Seetaraman). Konda's wife Rajam, rendered homeless by floods, becomes pregnant when she is raped by the manager of a circus. When released, Konda is reformed by the kind action of a Christian priest, Sadhu Uthaman, becomes a successful glass manufacturer and, after changing his name, is elected the town's mayor. Konda's past catches up with him when Inspector Javert is posted to the town and intends exposing him. During an Independence struggle incident, Konda rescues Javert and the inspector commits suicide, caught in the dilemma of having to work for an imperialist police force but being indebted to a former criminal. The film is dominated by Nagaiah, inviting comparisons with Paul Muni, and by the stage actor and co-scenarist Seetaraman, who became known as Javert (aka Jawar) Seetaraman for the rest of his career. Much of it is shot with heavy expressionist lighting, esp. the jail sequences as the inspector's presence is announced by the sound of stomping boots. The visual effect was extended by Elangovan's dialogue.

GADANO BEL

1950 123' b&w Gujarati
d **Ratibhai Punatar** *pc* Ajit Pics *st* Prabhulal Dwivedi's play *sc* **Ramchandra Thakur** *c* M.G. Jadhav *lyr/m* **Avinash Vyas**
lp **Nirupa Roy**, Dulari, Charubala, Lila Kurle, Hirabai, Maya Devi, Manhar Desai, Babu Raje, Chhagan Romeo, Ramlal, Banke Bihari, Champak Lala, Bhogilal, Ramesh, Girish, Nityananda Ghosh

Realist Gujarati reform social adapting a noted play first staged by the nationalist Desh Natak Samaj. When the head of a family, who is also the main breadwinner, dies of overwork, the joint family disintegrates as the in-laws leave with whatever they can appropriate. Eventually, after the house has been auctioned, the three family members left behind are supposedto put their faith in god.

HAR HAR MAHADEV

1950 137' b&w Hindi
d/p **Jayant Desai** *st* Bachubhai Shukla *dial* Anuj *lyr* Ramesh Sastry, Saraswati Kumar Deepak *c* Saju Naik *m* **Avinash Vyas**
lp **Nirupa Roy**, Trilok Kapoor, Shanta Kumar, Jeevan, Kanta Kumari, Mishra, Meenakshi, Niranjan Sharma

Major mythological hit and Nirupa Roy's best-known film in the genre. King of demons Tarakasur invades the land of the gods to avenge the insult meted out to his mother by Indra. His victory leads to a declaration that he is now king of the cosmos, an imbalance that may only be righted by Shiva (Kapoor). Kama, god of love, is sent to awaken Shiva from his eternal meditation, but gets burnt to ashes. Shiva can only be propitiated by Uma (Roy), daughter of the Himalayas, through an act of penance that leads to Shiva accepting her as his consort.

JOGAN

1950 116' b&w Hindi
d/co-lyr **Kidar Sharma** *pc* **Ranjit** *co-lyr* Indra, Butaram Sharma, Himmatrai Sharma *c* D.C. Mehta *m* **Bulo C. Rani**
lp **Nargis**, **Dilip Kumar**, Pratima Devi, Pesi Patel, Purnima, Baby Tabassum, Anwari, Ramesh Thakur, Durpan, **Rajendra Kumar**

The title refers to religious female mendicants, whose best-known example continues to be the 16th-C. saint poet Meerabai. One of Sharma's most emotionally charged melodramas, it features Surabhi (Nargis), a mendicant whose song by Meerabai *Ghunghat ke pat khole re* (sung by **Geeta Dutt**) attracts Vijay (D. Kumar). Despite her protestations, he keeps following her and she eventually tells him how she escaped her debt-ridden father and alcoholic brother who wanted her to marry an old man; she ran away to die and renounced her earlier life. When she leaves, she tells Vijay not to follow her beyond a particular tree. Later, another jogan arrives, meets Vijay by the tree and gives him a book, saying that Surabhi had entrusted her, before she died, with the task of giving it to a man who would be waiting by a tree. The film has several other Meera bhajans sung by Geeta Dutt which became some of her early hit songs. Bulo C. Rani's most famous film score.

Nargis and Dilip Kumar in *Jogan*

Sabhyata etc. A student at the Hindu College, he wrote his first poems in English (e.g. the narrative poem *Captive Ladie*, 1849). He later wrote the epic *Meghnadbad Kavya*, the Homeric epic *Tilottama Sambhab Kavya* (1860), the Radha and Krishna love story in rhymed verse *Brajangana* (1861) and *Birangana* (1862) in blank verse. Two stage biographicals precede the film: one by Netal Bhattacharya (1943) with the great **Sisir Bhaduri** playing the poet, the other by Mahendra Gupta (1942) featuring Ahindra Choudhury in the lead. Probably following Banaphool's popular play, the film depicts the poet as a romantic rebel and chronicles the high points of his adventure-laden career: his baptism, his romance and marriage to the Frenchwoman Emilia Henrietta, and his tragic death in poverty and oblivion. Most notable for Utpal Dutt's remarkable screen debut as the poet, including several recitations of poetry. Dutt, often credited with having renovated acting in Bengali theatre and film, went on to identify himself with Michael Madhusudhan (cf his play *Danrao Pathikbar*, 1980, harking back to the film's iconography). The popular genre of screen biographicals was continued by Bose in *Bireshwar Vivekananda* (1964), Bijoy Basu's *Raja Rammohun* (1965) and Piyush Bose's *Subhashchandra* (1966).

MANTHIRI KUMARI

aka *The Minister's Daughter*
1950 173' b&w Tamil
d **Ellis R. Duncan**, **T.R. Sundaram** *pc* **Modern Theatres** *st Kundalakesi dial* **M. Karunanidhi** *lyr* **A. Marudakasi**, K.M. Sharif *c* K.G. Vijayan *m* G. Ramanathan *lp* **M.G. Ramachandran**, S.A. Natarajan, M.N. Nambiar, A. Karunanidhi, Madhuri Devi, G. Shakuntala, T.P. Muthulakshmi, Lalitha, **Padmini**, Ragini

One of the most popular Tamil films of the decade, continuing the post-***Velaikkari*** (1949) engagement of top DMK personnel with cinema, scenarist Karunanidhi and star MGR. Shot near Salem in the hill resort of Yercaud, the film is based on an 8th-C. Tamil literary epic, a Buddhist text that, according to Mu. Varadarajan (1988), was a Buddhist propaganda work reflecting the rivalry between Buddhists and Jains in the 1st millenium AD. The original story, of which only 28 verses still exist, tells of a woman from the vaisya caste, a Jain by birth, who kills her husband when he tries to murder her, and is eventually converted to Buddhism. The film is a costumed adventure fantasy attacking royal priests, in line with DMK policy. Parthiban (Natarajan), the son of an imbecilic king's royal priest (Nambiar), commits banditry wearing a Batman-type mask to discredit Veeramohan (MGR), a loyal general and lover of Princess Jeeva (Shakuntala). The minister's daughter is Amudavalli (Madhuri) who tries to reform the treacherous son and ends up killing him in self-defence. The nasty priest then kills her at the durbar. The songs proved enduring, esp. *Vaarai...vaarai* sung by Trichy Loganathan for Parthiban as he leads Amudavalli to a hilltop to kill her. It is also a landmark in playback singer T.M. Soundarrajan's long career. Master Subbaiah, the teenage prodigy who died young, sings a song and appears briefly as a cowherd. The film also introduces one of the most famous Tamil screen villains, Nambiar. Madhuri Devi provides the best performance as a sword-wielding, independently minded heroine, rare in films of the period.

MASHAAL/SAMAR

1950 136' b&w Hindi/Bengali
d **Nitin Bose** *pc* **Bombay Talkies** *st* Bankimchandra Chatterjee *sc* Sajanikanta Das *dial*[H] Sudarshan *lyr*[H] Pradeep *c* Radhu Karmakar *m* **S.D. Burman**, Manna Dey *lp* **Ashok Kumar**, Sumitra Devi, Ruma Ganguly, Kanu Roy, Moni Chatterjee, **Krishnakant**

Based on Bankimchandra's novel *Rajani* (1877), this romance addresses property rights. Samar (Kumar) and Tarangini (Sumitra Devi) are childhood lovers. Samar feels betrayed when she obeys her father's decision and marries a wealthy zamindar. When Samar becomes a successful lawyer, he tries to take revenge on Tarangini and marries a blind flower-girl who, he discovers, owns the property on which the zamindar has built his fortune. The plot is complicated by the fact that the blind girl loves Jatin, the zamindar's son.

MICHAEL MADHUSUDHAN

1950 c.145' b&w Bengali
d/s **Modhu Bose** *pc* I.N.A. Pics *lyr* Pranab Roy *c* G.K. Mehta *m* Chitta Roy *lp* **Utpal Dutt**, Molina Devi, **Ahindra Choudhury**, Debjani, Miss Grace

Biopic of Michael Madhusudhan Dutt (1824-73), a major and colourful Bengali poet. Regarded as the founder of the modern Bengali theatre with his plays *Sarmistha* (1858), staged by the Belgatchia Theatre, followed by *Krishna Kumari*, *Ekey Ki Bole*

NALLATHANKA

aka *The Good Sister*
1950 c.165' b&w Malayalam
d P.V. Krishna Iyer *p* K.V. Koshy, **Kunchako** *pc* K&K Prod. *s* **Muthukulam Raghavan Pillai** *c* A. Shanmugham, P.K. Madhavan Nair *m* **V. Dakshinamurthy**, Rama Rao *lp* Augustine Joseph, Vaikkom Moni, Miss Kumari, Omana, Muthukulam Raghavan Pillai, S.P. Pillai, Matheppan, Joseph Mulawana, Jagadamma, Thankamma, Joy Poonnuran, Balakrishna Pillai, Pallam Joseph, Baby Girija

Melodrama adapting the legend of Nallathanka (aka Nallathangal in Tamil), a pivotal reference in ***Parasakthi*** (1952). The king's sister marries the king of another land and bears him seven children. When drought strikes, she has to appeal to her brother and face the humiliation of an envious sister-in-law. The high point in this melodrama comes when the sister tries to kill herself and all her children by throwing them into a well. The film was a major K&K hit, encouraging Malayalam distributors to give more time to films from their own state.

PARAMANANDAYYA SHISHYULU KATHA

1950 c.200' b&w Telugu
d K. Sivarao *pc* Allied Prod. *s/lyr* **Tapi Dharma Rao** *c* B. Subba Rao *m* Ogirala Ramchandra Rao, S. Dakshinamurthy *lp* **C.S.R. Anjaneyalu**, **A. Nageshwara Rao**, **Lakshmirajyam**, K. Sivarao, **Relangi Venkatramaiah**, Nalla Ramamurthy, Kankanam, D. Hemalatha, Girija

Comedy portraying two bumbling disciples of the eccentric philosopher Paramanandayya (Anjaneyalu). Into this standard folk narrative, scenarist Tapi Dharma Rao weaves a Shakespearean court intrigue while conveying his political concerns in lines like 'It is better to starve than to rob others' and in satirical attacks on political opportunism. Nageshwara Rao and Lakshmirajyam played the romantic leads.

PATTHE BAPURAO

1950 143' b&w Marathi
d/p **Raja Nene** *pc* Raja Nene Prod. *s/lyr* D.K. Kane *c* Dolly Daruwala *m* Vasant Pawar
lp Ranjana, Raja Nene, Shashikala, Jawdekar, Manjrekar, Chandu Gokhale, Govindaswamy Aphale, Vatsalabai, Indirabai

Former **Prabhat** Studio director/actor Nene's best-known film is a biopic of Patthe Bapurao (Nene), Maharashtra's famous composer and author of the folk-classical lavani musical form. He is shown as an upper-caste schoolteacher, absorbed in a musical genre practised by lower-caste people. He partners the dancer Pavala (Ranjana) and together, after many hardships, they popularise the dance-music form throughout the region. Beginning with the typical Tamasha invocation to Ganesh (*Shubhamangali charana gana nachala*), the musical has several hit numbers from the lavani tradition as well as Kane's originals.

PUDHCHA PAOOL

1950 135' b&w Marathi
d **Raja Paranjpe** *pc* Manik Studio *st* Venkatesh Madgulkar *s/lyr* **G.D. Madgulkar** *c* I. Mohammed *m* **Sudhir Phadke**
lp **Hansa Wadkar**, P.L. Deshpande, G.D. Madgulkar, Kusum Deshpande, Vivek, Mohammed Hussain, D.S. Ambapkar, Bal Chitale, Raja Paranjpe, Shakuntala Jadhav, Suman, Ravindra, Baby Neela

Raja Paranjpe's directorial breakthrough features the famous Marathi humourist, playwright and stage star P.L. Deshpande. Krishna (Deshpande) goes to the city looking for work and promptly falls for the folk Tamasha dancer Mogri (Wadkar). She is presented as a gold-digger, as the hero eventually realises after he is beaten up. Paranjpe, writer Madgulkar and composer Phadke became an established team.

RAM RAM PAHUNA

1950 122' b&w Marathi
d/s **Dinkar D. Patil** *pc* Uday Kala Chitra *lyr* P. Sawalram, Shanta Shelke *c* Shankar Savekar *m* **Lata Mangeshkar**
lp **Damuanna Malvankar**, Chandrakant, Baburao Athane, Ratnamala, Kusum Deshpande, Madhu Bhonsle, Shakuntala Bhome, Susheela Devi, Kusum Sukhtankar

The first solo film by Maharashtra's best-known exponent of the 'gramin chitrapat' genre set in a Maharashtrian village frontier area evoking the Western genre. This melodrama, more intimate than some of Patil's later work, features good elder brother Shripati who sends younger brother Jaisingh to his uncle to study English. The wily uncle encourages Jaisingh's affair with his daughter, and she becomes pregnant. Shripati arranges for the two to marry, but the uncle causes a rift between the brothers, causing Shripati and his wife to be evicted from their own home. Jaisingh falls prey to several vices while his uncle takes over the family property, but eventually he makes up with his brother. Lata Mangeshkar, making her debut as composer, scored some melodious tunes, esp. *Bara gava majhya sathi jhurati*.

SAMADHI

1950 165' b&w Hindi
d/s Ramesh Saigal *pc* **Filmistan** *lyr* Rajinder Krishen *c* K.H. Kapadia *m* **C. Ramchandra**
lp **Ashok Kumar**, **Nalini Jaywant**, Shyam, Kuldip Kaur, Mubarak

Patriotic drama addressing Subhash Chandra Bose and the Indian National Army. Following Bose's call on Indian youth to join in the anti-imperialist front, Shekhar (Kumar) abandons his wealth to join the INA. In Singapore his elder brother Suresh (Shyam), who is a captain in the British army, has to collaborate with a British spy ring headed by Boss (Mubarak) and the dancer Dolly (Kaur). Shekhar falls in love with Lily (Jaywant), Dolly's sister. Boss uses this to infiltrate the INA's intelligence. In the war, the two brothers face each other and Shekhar is left for dead. He nevertheless makes it back alive and rounds up the British spies. Shekhar eventually dies in an operation to blow up a bridge on the India-Burma border. The film, which *Filmindia* (May, 1950) described as politically obsolete since India had already achieved independence, included the C. Ramchandra hit *Gore gore o banke chhore* (sung by **Lata Mangeshkar** and Amirbai Karnataki) praising Bose, *Subhash Chandra ke naam se Hindustan ka naam*, as well as the the socialist-realist marching song *Kadam kadam badhaye ja* (both sung by the composer).

SAMSARAM

1950 219' b&w Telugu
d **L.V. Prasad** *pc* Sadhana Pics *st/dial/co-lyr* Sadasiva Brahmam *co-lyr* K.G. Sharma *c* M.A. Rehman, B. Subba Rao *m* S. Dakshinamurthy
lp **N.T. Rama Rao**, **A. Nageshwara Rao**, **Relangi Venkatramaiah**, Nalla Ramamurthy, Doraswamy, **Lakshmirajyam**, Surabhi Balasaraswathi, Suryakantam, Bezawada Kantamma, Pushpalatha, **Savitri**

A major melodrama hit about the fragmentation of a joint family made in the same year as Prasad's seminal ***Shavukaru***. After their joint appearance in *Palletoori Pilla*, also 1950, Telugu cinema's two best-known stars, N.T. Rama Rao and A. Nageshwara Rao, again teamed up for this story about a middle-class government clerk Raghu (NTR), living happily with his wife Manjula (Lakshmirajyam), until his scheming mother Venkamma, his sister Kamakshi (Balasaraswathi) and her cowardly husband (Venkatramaiah) move into his house. Venkamma appropriates all of Raghu's earnings and Kamakshi plots to have Manjula blamed for all that goes wrong in the household. Raghu, unable to pay his pregnant wife's medical fees, loses his job and abandons his family. His brother Venu (Nageshwara Rao), a flirt who lives off his girlfriend Kamala (Pushpalata) and her rich father, eventually traces Raghu and finds him a job as a porter in a mill. Venu also manages to reunite the family. The film borrows the popular Tamil cinema convention of introducing a comic duo (here Venkatramaiah and Suryakantam) into the melodrama. Critic K.N.T. Sastry argued that Prasad's tendency to replace characters with stereotypes in stereotypical situations begins here.

SANGRAM

1950 139' b&w Hindi
d/s **Gyan Mukherjee** *pc* **Bombay Talkies**, Sargam Pics Unit *dial/co-lyr* Vrajendra Gaur *co-lyr* P.L. Santoshi, Raja Mehndi *c* Josef Wirsching *m* **C. Ramchandra**
lp **Ashok Kumar**, **Nalini Jaywant**, Nawab, Tiwari, Sajjan, Ramsingh, Kumud, Bina Paul, Indumati, Baby Tabassum, Shashi Raj

A cop father against criminal son crime drama made in the Indian variant of the film noir style launched by Mukherjee's megahit ***Kismet*** (1943). Kunwar takes to gambling and gets involved in bad company in spite of his father being a policeman. Although Kunwar is reformed by his gentle betrothed, his past catches up with him in the form of his former crooked sidekick. In the end, Kunwar escapes from jail to avenge the betrayal of a man who was supposedly on the right side of the law, and his father faces him with a gun, torn between his responsibilities as a parent and as a cop.

SHAVUKARU

1950 177' b&w Telugu
d **L.V. Prasad** *pc* **Vijaya** *s* **Chakrapani** *lyr* **Samudrala Raghavacharya** *c* Marcus Bartley *m* **Ghantasala Venkateshwara Rao**
lp **Sowcar Janaki**, **N.T. Rama Rao**, Govindrajulu Subba Rao, **S.V. Ranga Rao**, Shri Vatsa, Shantakumari, T. Kanakam, Seeta, Baby Bhanu, Sivaram, Vangara, Joga Rao, **Relangi Venkatramaiah**

Successful ruralist melodrama evoking the **Bombay Talkies** dramas of **Ashok Kumar** and **Leela Chitnis**. Satyam (NTR), the son of the moneylender Chengaiah (Subba Rao), is supposed to marry the daughter, Subbulu (Janaki), of his neighbour, the farmer and village elder Ramaiah (Shri Vatsa). Problems arise and villainies are perpetrated until both men's sons find themselves together in jail. Chengaiah then has a change of heart, the main villain, his helper Ranganna (Ranga Rao), is caught and the village is united again. The film, later remade as ***Enga Veetu Penn*** (1965), begins with a folk Harikatha performance, making a lyrical comment on the theme of miserliness as a social evil. NTR's debut as leading man is often seen as launching a second generation of Telugu melodrama in which, e.g., Ghantasala's 'rooted' music (the song *Palukaradate chiluka*) and Chakrapani's script marked a 'realist' departure from the pre-WW2 reform sagas. More importantly, this is the debut production of Vijaya Studios, demarcating itself from the earlier Vauhini style. Chakrapani's script was later serialised in the journal *Vijayachitra* owned by the studio. Actress 'Sowcar' Janaki makes her film debut here. She appended the film's title to her name from then on.

SHEESH MAHAL

1950 144' b&w Hindi
d **Sohrab Modi** *pc* **Minerva Movietone** *st* Hakim Ahmed Shuja *co-sc* Munshi Abdul Baqui *co-sc/co-lyr* Shams Lucknowi *co-lyr* Hakim Panipati *c* M. Malhotra *m* **Vasant Desai**
lp Sohrab Modi, Naseem Banu, Pushpa Hans, Nigar Sultana, Mubarak, Pran

Modi's big-budget commentary on decaying feudal aristocracy. Old patriarch Jaspal Singh (Modi) lives in the Sheesh Mahal (Palace of Mirrors) and believes only in aristocatic lineage, scorning capitalist enterprise. His contempt for money makes him an easy victim for a moneylender and he eventually has to sell his palace to a labourer turned millionaire, Durgaprasad (Mubarak) while himself turning into a worker to survive. The film contrasts Jaspal Singh's feudal ambitions for his daughters, against what he sees as treacherous bourgeois values, but which are also the only values that come to his aid in the form of Durgaprasad.

SWAPNA SUNDARI

1950 173' b&w Telugu/Tamil
d/s **Ghantasala Balaramaiah** *pc* Pratibha Pics *dial/lyr*[Te] **Samudrala Raghavacharya** *dial*[Ta] Sakshi *lyr*[Ta] Ramaiah Doss *c* P. Sridhar *m* **C.R. Subburaman**
lp **G. Varalakshmi**, **Anjali Devi**, **A. Nageshwara Rao**, K. Sivarao, **K. Mukkamala**, Surabhi Balasaraswathi

'Folklore' fantasy in which a heavenly damsel (Anjali Devi) falls in love with an earthly prince (Nageshwara Rao) and keeps entering his dreams. He stays awake one night in order to capture her, but she is entrapped by a magician (Mukkamala). The hero goes in search of her and rescues her after another woman (from earth, Varalakshmi) sacrifices her life. Both Anjali Devi and Varalakshmi, in the prime of their careers, give highly entertaining performances, which, with the dance compositions of **Vedantam Raghavaiah** and **R. Balasaraswathi**'s songs (as playback for Anjali Devi), comprise this hit's major attractions. Varalakshmi's *Nee sani neevene* number was, in the words of V.A.K. Ranga Rao, a 'sexy delight'.

TATHAPI

1950 122' b&w Bengali
d Manoj Bhattacharya *pc* Chhabi-o-Bani *st* Swarnakamal Bhattacharya *sc* **Bimal Roy** *lyr* **Rabindranath Tagore**, Atul Sen, Shyamal Gupta *c* Jayantilal Jani *m* Rabin Roy
lp Pronoti Ghosh, Sunil Dasgupta, Sova Sen, **Bijon Bhattacharya**, Manoranjan Bhattacharya, Prabhadevi, Sudipta Roy, **Ritwik Ghatak**

A film remembered mainly for introducing several key Bengal **IPTA** figures to the cinema, including Ghatak. Although scripted by Bimal Roy from a story by noted leftist writer Swarnakamal Bhattacharya, the film stands at a tangent from the radical realist initiative launched by Roy's ***Udayer Pathey*** (1944) and which culminated in **Nemai Ghosh**'s ***Chinnamul*** (1950). The plot has a mute heroine (a novelty at the time) named Kalyani (Ghosh, in her debut). Hero Pranabesh (Dasgupta) is tricked into marrying her and insists on continuing to meet his lover Sujata. A rather ugly encounter leads to Kalyani being injured and returning to her village. The hero, having a change of heart, saves Kalyani from committing suicide and brings her back home. Contemporary reviews in *Chitrabani* and *Rupamancha* commend the film's sensitive portrayal of psychological changes and its refreshingly untheatrical observation of life.

Tathapi

AFSANA

1951 168' b&w Hindi
d **B.R. Chopra** *pc* Shri Gopal Pics *s* I.S. Johar *lyr* Asad Bhopali, Chander *c* Rajendra Malone *m* **Husnlal-Bhagatram**
lp **Ashok Kumar**, Veena Kumari, Kuldip Kaur, Pran, Jeevan, Cuckoo, Baby Tabassum, Ratan Kumar, Madan Jamoora, Chaman Puri, Narmada Shankar, Wajid Khan, Uma Dutt, Prem Kohli

Chopra's debut is a story about identical twin brothers, Ratan and Chaman (A. Kumar), separated in childhood. Ratan, raised in an orphanage, grows up to become a noted magistrate. Chaman inherits the family wealth and becomes an arrogant playboy. The two meet as adults when Chaman is on the run, falsely accused of murder. Chaman gets away by impersonating Ratan and when he dies in a car crash everybody believes it is Ratan who is dead. Ratan, whose wife (Kaur) has an affair with his friend Mohan (Pran), wakes up from a drugged sleep to find himself regarded as Chaman. Eventually his memory returns through the help of childhood sweetheart Meera (Veena) and happiness follows upon his fickle wife's suicide and her lover's financial ruin. Continuing Ashok Kumar's association with the **Filmistan** crime movie, newcomer Chopra's direction was extensively commended.

AGNI PAREEKSHA

1951 181' b&w Telugu
d P. Manikyam *pc* Sarathi Films *s* **Tapi Dharma Rao** *lyr* K.G. Sharma *c* B. Subba Rao *m* Galipenchala Narasimha Rao
lp **Kalyanam Raghuramaiah**, **C.S.R. Anjaneyalu**, K. Sivarao, **Lakshmirajyam**, Malathi, Lakshmikantam, **Relangi Venkatramaiah**, Kanakam, Gangarathnam, Suryakantam

Melodrama suggesting a slight modernisation of the devoted wife stereotype in order to refurbish feudal patriarchal values. Heroine Sushila (Lakshmirajyam) loses her husband Kumaravarma (Anjaneyalu) to the charms of the prostitute Kalavati (Lakshmikantam) and fails in her attempt to commit suicide. Sushila then sets out to seduce her husband back. In doing so, it is she rather than he who faces accusations of sexual infidelity and has to undergo a trial by fire to prove her chastity. **Agradoot** made a version of the story in 1954.

ALBELA

1951 158' b&w Hindi
d/p/s **Master Bhagwan** *pc* Bhagwan Art Prod. *dial* Ehsan Rizvi *lyr* Rajendra Krishen *c* Shankar A. Palav *m* **C. Ramchandra**
lp **Geeta Bali**, Master Bhagwan, Badri Prasad, Pratima Devi, Bimala, Nihal, Dulari, Sunder, Usha Shukla

A musical hit and Bhagwan's most successful film as producer and director. A dispatch clerk (Bhagwan) dreams of becoming a stage star. His success as singer and dancer is aided by the reigning star Asha (Bali) with whom he falls in love. The love story is intercut with tragedy in his home, the death of his mother (Pratima Devi), estrangement from his father (Badri Prasad) and the villainy of his brother-in-law (Nihal). The film's highlights are the dances and C. Ramchandra's hit songs *Shola jo bhadke* (set to flickering light and Hawaiian dance choreography), *Bholi surat* and *Shyam dhale*, all sung by the composer with **Lata Mangeshkar**. Bhagwan apparently sold the film's rights cheaply after its initial run and its successful 90s re-release did nothing to benefit its impecunious maker.

AMAR BHOOPALI

aka *Kavi Honaji Bala*
1951 136' b&w Marathi
d/p **V. Shantaram** *pc* **Rajkamal Kalamandir** *st/dial* C.Y. Marathe *sc* **Vishram Bedekar** *lyr* Honaji Bala, Shahir Amar Sheikh *c* G. Balkrishna *m* **Vasant Desai**
lp Panditrao Nagarkar, Sandhya, **Lalita Pawar**, Bhalchandra Pendharkar, Vishwas, Gulab, Jayarampant, Nimbalkar, Ameena, Bandopant Sohoni

Shantaram's hit musical biopic of Honaji Bala (played by Marathi stage star Nagarkar), a legendary Marathi poet from the Gawali caste in the last years of the Pune Peshwai. Known mainly for having popularised the musical dance form of the lavani in Maharashtra and esp. for his classic composition *Ghanashyam sundara shirdhara*, addressing a new dawn in the morning raga *Bhoop*. The piece later acquired revolutionary associations alluded to in the film's anti-British discourse. Set in the Pune-based Maratha empire just before it succumbed to the British, the story shows the poet's involvement with lavani music, which the film associates with prostitutes, winning recognition when the peshwa's wife at the Pune court gives him an award for his Bhoop composition. His love life with Tamasha dancer (Sandhya in her debut) is intercut with the Maratha wars against the British, his music spurring on the soldiers. Shantaram contrasts Honaji's erotic and militant poetry with the prevailing 'decadent' brahminical effusions. Replete with Shantaram-type calendar art compositions (when pigeons descend around Sandhya's body in the forest) the film ends like a mythological, showing the infant Krishna and Yashoda, when his *Ghanashyam* composition is immortalised. Additional songs were written by the radical poet and performer Amar Sheikh, associated with the militant powada form and with the **IPTA**'s left wing in Maharashra.

ANDOLAN

aka *Our Struggle*
1951 146' b&w Hindi
d **Phani Majumdar** *pc* Motwane *co-st/sc* **Krishan Chander** *co-st* Sudhir Sen *lyr* Indivar, Niaz Haidar *c* Roque M. Layton *m* Pannalal Ghosh
lp Shivraj, **Kishore Kumar**, Manju, Pushpa, Sushama, Parashuram, Tiwari Jr., Shekhar, Bhojwani, Sharad, Malhotra, **Krishnakant**, **Rabindranath Tagore**

A stridently nationalistic story of India's freedom struggle, presented through the experiences of a Bengali family from 1885, when the Indian National Congress was established, to 1947. Important events incorporated into the plot were Gandhi's satyagraha (1920), the Simon Commission (1928), Vallabhbhai Patel's Bardoli satyagraha (1928) and the 1942 Quit India agitations. Krishan Chander's script, Sachin Shankar's choreography and the acting styles owed much to the **IPTA** theatre of the 40s. The film, made at **Bombay Talkies**, was produced by the distributors of the Chicago Radio PA systems label. Kishore Kumar plays the militant hero of this quasi-documentary. Motwane included old documentary footage purchased from **Kohinoor** and **Krishna** Film, such as Rabindranath Tagore singing his *Jana Gana Mana* composition, one of India's national anthems.

AWARA

aka *The Tramp* aka *The Vagabond*
1951 193'(170')(82') b&w Hindi
d/p **Raj Kapoor** *pc* R.K. Films *co-st/sc/dial* **K.A. Abbas** *co-st* V.P. Sathe *lyr* Hasrat Jaipuri, **Shailendra** *c* Radhu Karmakar *m* **Shankar-Jaikishen**
lp Raj Kapoor, **Nargis**, **Prithviraj Kapoor**, **Leela Chitnis**, K.N. Singh, **Shashi Kapoor**, Cuckoo, Leela Mishra, Baby Zubeida, Honey O'Brien

Having built his own studio at Chembur in Bombay with the profits of ***Barsaat*** (1949), Kapoor launched his most famous film, collaborating with the unit most closely associated with his work: scenarists Abbas and Sathe, song-writers Shailendra and Hasrat, art director Achrekar, cameraman Karmakar and composers Shankar-Jaikishen. Set in Bombay, the plot concerns Raju (Kapoor), the estranged son of Judge Raghunath (P. Kapoor), who finds a surrogate father in the criminal Jagga (Singh), the dacoit who caused Raju's mother (Chitnis) to be thrown out of her home. Raju eventually kills Jagga and tries to kill Raghunath, before he redeems himself in the eyes of the judge and wins the love of his childhood sweetheart, Rita (Nargis), who is now the lawyer defending him in court. The very intensity of the oedipal melodrama, enacted by the Kapoor family itself, spills over into a kind of hallucinatory pictorialism (the dream sequence, the prison sequence at the end, the design of the judge's mansion) and underpinned some of the most remembered songs of the 50s (*Awaara hoon*, *Ghar aya mera pardesi* and *Dum bharke udhar mooh phere, o chanda*). The spectacular 9' dream sequence which took three months to shoot was apparently added on at the end, to hike up its market value. This was also Kapoor's first fairy-tale treatment of class division in India, whose nexus of authority (power, patriarchy and law) explicitly excludes the hero. Its main tenet, presented through Raghunath, is the feudal notion of status: 'the son of a thief will always be a thief', a view that villain Jagga sets out to disprove by making Raju a thief. Raju's patricide (he kills Jagga and is arrested for

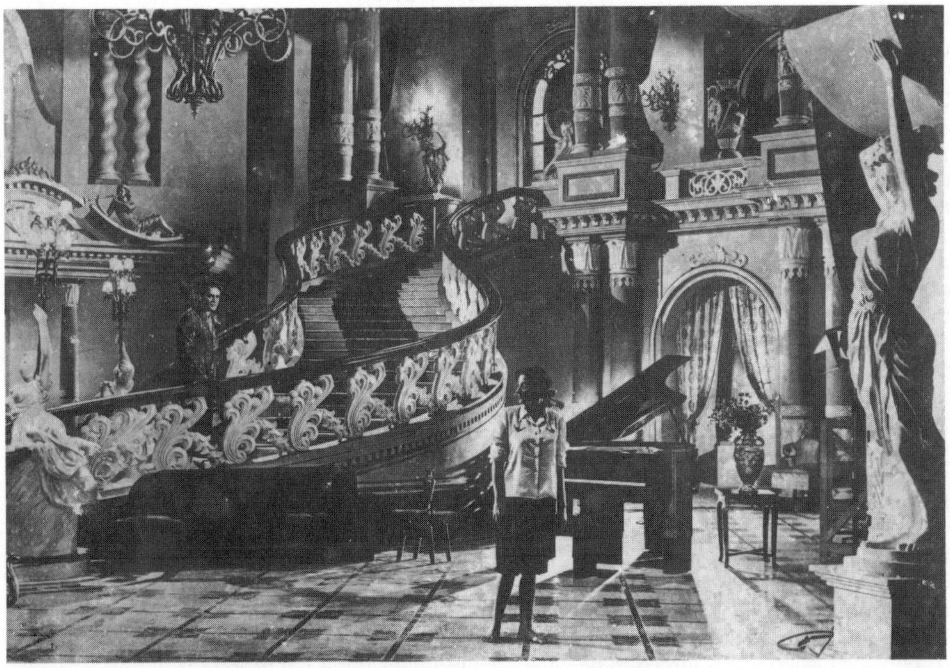

Prithviraj Kapoor and Nargis in *Awara*

attempting to murder Raghunath) tries to break out of the contradiction set against an alternative, post-colonial, reinvention of an infantile Utopia in which everyone can fully 'belong', a condition symbolised by Nargis who is both the hero's conscience and reward. Kapoor's later treatments of the same contradictions increasingly took on the 'frog prince' fairy-tale structure (***Shri 420***, 1955; ***Mera Naam Joker***, 1970), mapped on to the middle/working-class divide. The film launched Kapoor and Nargis as major stars in parts of the USSR, the Arab world and Africa, while the US briefly released an 82' version. Nargis' appearance in a bathing costume is widely but wrongly believed to be the first erotic swimsuit scene. That cliche had earlier been deployed by **Master Vinayak** in ***Brahmachari*** (1938).

BAAZI

aka *A Game of Chance*
1951 143' b&w Hindi
d/co-st **Guru Dutt** *pc* Navketan *co-st/sc/dial* **Balraj Sahni** *lyr* **Sahir Ludhianvi** *c* V. Ratra *m* **S.D. Burman**
lp **Dev Anand, Geeta Bali**, Kalpana Kartik, Roopa Varma, K.N. Singh, K. Dhawan, Srinath, Rashid Ahmed, Abu Baker, Nirmal Kumar, Habib

Guru Dutt's directorial debut was a follow-up of ***Afsar*** (1950), the film with which the brothers Anand launched Navketan and which signalled a transition in Dev Anand's screen persona. Madan (Anand) is a small-time gambler forced into joining the owner of the Star Hotel, a mysterious and shadowy criminal (Singh), to pay for his sister's medical expenses. Other characters are Rajani (Kartik), a doctor, her fiance, the cop Ramesh (Dhawan), and later Leena (Bali), a cabaret dancer who is killed and for whose murder Madan is framed. The elusive villain eventually turns out to be Rajani's father. Madan, condemned to death, is saved by Ramesh who lays a trap to catch the villain. Dutt demonstrates a confident assimilation of the Warner Bros. film noir style, esp. in the lighting, the camera placements and the editing. Even though it was his directorial debut, the film already shows a remarkable talent for song picturisation, something Dutt became famous for. One of the film-makers who apparently fascinated him at this time was John Huston, an inspiration he also used in his second film, ***Jaal*** (1952). Includes **Geeta Dutt**'s famous song *Tadbir se bigdi huyi*.

BABLA

1951 ?' b&w Bengali/Hindi
d **Agradoot** *pc* MP Prod. *st* Souren Mukherjee *lyr*[H] **Sahir Ludhianvi** *c* Bibhuti Laha, Sushanta Maitra *m* Robin Chatterjee
lp Naren Bhattacharya, Sova Sen, **Jahar Ganguly**, Paresh Bannerjee, **Pahadi Sanyal**

Typical instance of the commercially successful realist Bengali melodrama of this period, as a pop variation of what the later **New Theatres** directors were doing after the war. A compositor in a printing press (Bannerjee) brings his wife (Sen) and son Babla (Bhattacharya) to Calcutta. He has an accident and his overworked wife succumbs to tuberculosis. Babla leaves school to work as a newspaper hawker. When he finds a purse full of money, he dutifully returns it to its owner and refuses to be helped. Returing home, he finds his mother dead. Widely advertised in the Hindi market, the film was accurately described in *Filmfare* (16.10.1953) as failing 'from sheer excess'. The film's Malayalam remake, ***Newspaper Boy*** (1955), was much more of a critical success.

BADAL

1951 146' b&w Hindi
d **Amiya Chakravarty** *pc* Varma Films *sc* Rajendra Shankar *dial* Hari Pratap, C.L. Kavish *lyr* **Shailendra**, Hasrat Jaipuri *c* V. Babasaheb *m* **Shankar-Jaikishen**
lp Premnath, **Madhubala**, Purnima, Hiralal, Randhir, S. Nazir, Agha

Commercially successful adventure movie adapting the Robin Hood legend in the character of Badal (Premnath). The hero loses his faith in God and king when Jaisingh, right-hand man of the jagirdar, takes away his property. He forms a band of outlaws, falls in love with the daughter of the jagirdar, Ratna (Madhubala), who is unaware of his identity but who later joins his side. Eventually the conflict between Badal and Jaisingh is resolved when the king ventures out in disguise and sees for himself the tyranny of his ministers.

BAHAR

1951 170' b&w Hindi
d **M.V. Raman** *pc* **AVM** *s* Ramesh Chandra Gupta *dial/lyr* Rajendra Krishen *c* M.V. Muthuswamy *m* **S.D. Burman**
lp **Vyjayanthimala, Padmini**, Karan Dewan, Pran, Om Prakash, Sundar, Shyamlal, Leela Misra, Indira Acharya, Baby Tabassum

Heroine Lata (Vyjayanthimala) is a modern girl, pursued by villain Shekhar (Pran) but in love with novelist Ashok (Dewan) who turns out to be her neighbour called Kumar. Shekhar fathers a child to the country girl Malati (Padmini) who, unable to trace the perfidious Shekhar, abandons the child in Kumar's house. Seeing Kumar playing parent to a mysterious child, Lata misunderstands the situation until the truth is revealed in the end. Pran, playing his usual villain role, undergoes an uncharacteristic change of heart to allow a happy ending for all. Intended mainly to showcase Vyjayanthimala in her Hindi debut, the film features her numerous dances as well as **Kishore Kumar**'s hit song *Kusoor aap ka*. This major hit, adapting Raman's earlier hit *Vazhkai/Jeevitham* (1949), was the Madras-based AVM Studio's big foray into Hindi cinema.

BARJATRI

1951 ?' b&w Bengali
d **Satyen Bose** *pc* National Progressive Pics *st* Bibhutibhushan Mukherjee *co-lyr* Bimal Chandra Ghosh *co-lyr/m* **Salil Choudhury** *c* Bimal Mukherjee
lp **Kali Bannerjee, Anup Kumar**, Arun Choudhury, Satya Bannerjee, Haradhan Bannerjee, Bhabhen Pal

Successful comedy featuring the stammerer Ganesha (K. Bannerjee) and three efforts to find him a bride. In the first, Ganesha goes with his friends to a village to attend a wedding, but they are mistaken for thieves when trying to peek into the bridal chamber. They create another scandal when they arrive at the bride's house 'for negotiations', impersonating their guardians. Ganesha later becomes tutor to the cousin of the girl he loves, but this fails as well, and he gets punished by his despotic uncle.

DEEDAR

1951 130' b&w Hindi
d **Nitin Bose** *pc* Filmkar *s* Azmi Bazidpuri *lyr* Shakeel Badaiyuni *c* Dilip Gupta *m* **Naushad**.
lp **Dilip Kumar**, **Nargis**, **Ashok Kumar**, Nimmi, Baby Tabassum, Murad, Jal Merchant, Parikshit, Baby Anwari, Niharika Devi, Umasashi, Surender, Agha Mehraj, Yakub

Adapting much of the **Saigal** type of melodrama (***Street Singer***, 1938), the tale opens with adolescents Shamu (D. Kumar) and childhood sweetheart Mala (Nargis). Mala's rich father disapproves and when the children have an accident while horse-riding (a portent of the tragedy to come), he has Shamu and his mother evicted. The trauma kills the mother and turns Shamu blind. He is rescued and brought up by Champa (Nimmi) and her canny guardian, Choudhury. Champa loves Shamu but he cannot forget Mala. Dr Kishore (A. Kumar), an eye surgeon moved by the music Shamu sings on the streets, restores the hero's eyesight. Shamu then sees that Mala, to whom he has dedicated his life, is married to his benefactor, Dr Kishore, and he puts his eyes out again. Dilip Kumar's best-known tragic performance clearly evokes the Oedipus legend with blindness signifying an escape from the unbearable present and mourning for a lost innocence. The film, however, splits its lead protagonists, e.g. through turn-wipes repeatedly juxtaposing Dilip against Ashok Kumar and Nargis against Nimmi, a technique that evokes the Bengali literary melodrama (as does the cliche of the eye operation). In spite of the many unimaginative and maudlin sequences, some attempts at realism resemble aspects of **Satyajit Ray**'s approach, e.g. the long track along the kitchen floor in Champa's hovel or the changing light patterns on the ceiling behind Shamu when he sings *Naseeb dar pe tere azmaane aya hoon*. **Bimal Roy** edited the film.

HUMLOG

1951 144' b&w Hindi
d/s **Zia Sarhadi** *pc* **Ranjit** *lyr* Vishwamitter Adil, Uddhav Kumar *m* Roshan
lp **Nutan**, Shyama, **Balraj Sahni**, **Durga Khote**, Anwar Hussain, Sajjan, Kanhaiyalal, Manmohan Krishna, Durrani, Rashid Khan, Master Rattan, Cuckoo

Sarhadi's realist film forms a trilogy with ***Footpath*** (1953) and ***Awaaz*** (1956). It tells of the bank clerk Lala Haricharan Das, who supports a wife and three children on a meagre salary. His son Raj (Sahni) grows up disaffected; daughter Paro gets tuberculosis leading to big medical bills, and youngest son Chhotu drops out of school with no money to pay for his education. Raj steals money belonging to his father's employer and causes the father's imprisonment. Raj now has to look after the family, suffers from overwork and heart disease and ignores his girlfriend Shefali. Paro, kept apart from her boyfriend Anand by her disease, writes the play *Humlog* (*We, The People*). Later, Raj's friend Kundan (Hussain) is killed and Raj is arrested for the murder and dies of a heart attack in court. Paro and Anand, at the end, stage Paro's play as a self-reflexive comment on the film itself.

JEEVITHA NAUKA/JEEVAN NAUKA

aka *Pichaikari*, aka *Life is a Boat*
1951 170' b&w Malayalam/Tamil/Hindi
d K. Vembu *p* K.V. Koshy, **Kunchako** *pc* K&K Prod. *s* **Muthukulam Raghavan Pillai** *lyr* Abhayadev *c* Balasubramanyam, P.B. Mani *m* **V. Dakshinamurthy**
lp **Thikkurisi Sukumaran Nair**, Sebastian Kunju Kunju Bhagavathar, P. Adimoolam, Muthukulam Raghavan Pillai, B.S. Saroja, Pankajavalli, S.P. Pillai, Mathappan, Nanukuttan, Jagadamma, Janamma

Soman (Nair) is married to Laxmi (Saroja), a poor village performer. His brother, employed by the local capitalist, and wicked sister-in-law resent this and break up the joint family. Soman goes to the city while Laxmi, with her infant son, faces local harassment. She follows her husband to the city, but when she sees him in the company of rich women, she misunderstands and keeps away. Soman then searches for his wife and son and the nuclear family is reconstituted, although the sister-in-law is punished when she is forced to become a beggar. The second big production of the famed duo Koshy and **Kunchako** (after ***Nallathanka***, 1950) and the first Malayalam megahit, the film combined the talents of Sebastian Bhagavathar who, with Augustine Joseph, was one of the last great actor-singers from the stage, alongside future stars Nair, Pankajavalli and composer Dakshinamurthy. Both the title and the character of Saroja evoke **Osten**'s ***Jeevan Naiya*** (1936), but the major dramatic influence was probably **Vauhini** Studio's 1940s cinema, which Koshy in his autobiography maintained as his ideal. Tamil and Hindi versions were also made, probably dubbed.

MALLEESHWARI

1951 194' b&w Telugu
d **B.N. Reddi** *pc* **Vauhini** *s/lyr* **Devulapalli Krishna Sastry** *c* Adi M. Irani, B.N. Konda Reddy *m* **Saluri Rajeshwara Rao**, Addepalli Rama Rao
lp **P. Bhanumathi**, **N.T. Rama Rao**, Kumari, T.G. Kamaladevi, Shri Vatsa, Rushyendramani, Baby Mallika, Doraiswamy, Master Venkatramana

Reddi's big-budget fantasy set in the reign of Krishnadeva Raya, king of the Vijayanagara Empire with its capital at Hampi. The beautiful Malleeshwari (Bhanumathi) loves the sculptor Nagaraja (NTR) but class differences keep them apart. The king (Shri Vatsa) secretly observes her dancing in the rain for her lover. When Nagaraja leaves to seek his fortune so that he may claim Malleeshwari's hand, the king summons her to become a court entertainer. The lovers meet again when the hero is hired to build a dancing hall for the queen (Kamaladevi) but they infringe the queen's rule forbidding companions to fall in love and they are sentenced to death. At the last minute, the king forgives them. Apparently one of Reddi's favourite films, it benefits from A.K. Sekhar's sets. The songs by Bhanumathi and **Ghantasala** (singing the playback for NTR) were hits.

MANGALA

1951 182' b&w Telugu
d Chandru *p* **S.S. Vasan** *pc* **Gemini** *st* Gemini Story Dept. *dial/lyr* **Tapi Dharma Rao** *m* M.D. Parthasarathy
lp **P. Bhanumathi**, Ranjan, Suryaprabha, T.R. Ramchandran, Narayanrao, Doraiswamy, Kolatthu Mani, **Surabhi Kamalabai**, Vijayarao

A remake of Gemini's hit *Mangamma Sapatham* (1943), to follow their successful trilingual ***Apoorva Sahodarargal/Nishan*** (1949) starring Bhanumathi and Ranjan. Vasan again claimed directorial credit for the Hindi version. Mangala (Bhanumathi), the daughter of a rich farmer, chases her pet pigeon into a strange land whose prince (Ranjan) instantly falls in love with her. When she resists his advances, he threatens to marry and imprison her for the rest of her life. She responds by threatening that, should they marry, their son would grow up to whip his father. Dressed as a Carmen Miranda gypsy dancer she seduces him, gets pregnant and bears a son who eventually fulfils her prophecy.

MARMAYOGI/EK THA RAJA

aka *The Mysterious Sage*
1951 175' b&w Tamil
d **K. Ramnoth** *pc* Jupiter Pics *sc* **A.S.A. Sami** *st* Robin Hood legend, Marie Corelli's *Vendetta* (1886) *lyr* **Udumalai Narayana Kavi**, **Kannadasan**, K.D. Santhanam *c* M. Masthan *m* **C.R. Subburaman**, S.M. Subbaiah Naidu
lp **M.G. Ramachandran**, Serukalathur Sama, Jawar Seetaraman, S.A. Natarajan, M.N. Nambiar, Madhuri Devi, **Anjali Devi**

A royal fairy tale set in an unspecified place and time (although there is medieval jousting tournament) granting set and costume designers full freedom. A courtesan (Anjali Devi) tries to kill the king and assumes power, but he survives and returns disguised as a ghostly sage while his son Karikalan (MGR) becomes a Robin Hood figure in the forest. After many adventures the king exposes the courtesan, who dies of shock, and the prince becomes a benign ruler after marrying the general's daughter (Madhuri). Sami tailored the script, Flynn/Fairbanks references and all, for his friend MGR, giving him a character named after a legendary Chola king, fitting in with the current wave of Tamil revivalism. The credit sequence freely uses *Ivan the Terrible* imagery. The narration is whimsically misogynist but seems to delight in the unfettered cinematic play with popular imagery and stories. Uncharacteristically for the genre, the film received an Adults Only censor certificate.

NAVALOKAM

aka *New World*
1951 169' b&w Malayalam
d V. Krishnan *pc* Kottayam Popular Prod. *s* **Poonkunnam Varkey** *lyr* **P. Bhaskaran** *c* P.K. Madhavan Nair *m* **V. Dakshinamurthy**

lp Kumari, Sethulakshmi, Lalitha, **Thikkurisi Sukumaran Nair**, Sebastian Kunju Kunju Bhagavathar, Venniyoor Madhavan Nair, **Muthukulam Raghavan Pillai**

A ruthless estate owner, Kuruppu (Nair), sparks off a revolt among his labourers over his callous seduction and discarding of Devaki (Kumari). The woman, who has an independent reputation for her social work, allows her husband to be arrested on charges of assault, but eventually comes to his rescue, and also reconciles differences between the employer and his workers. The film combined the stage and film talents introduced by Koshy-**Kunchako** productions into Malayalam (cf ***Jeevitha Nauka*** the same year) with major figures from the radical literary movements in Kerala, writer Varkey and lyricist Bhaskaran. Despite its stagey effects, including crammed studio interiors, emphasis on dialogue and on entries and exits, the film is seen as the first in Malayalam to shift away from mythologicals and into politically informed realism. Its extension of traditional melodramatic forms, adapted from Tamil and Telugu cinema, to address e.g. industrialisation and class conflict, was to prove an important generic precedent for **Kariat**'s films.

NIRDOSHI/NIRAPARADHI

1951 186'[Te]/182'[Ta] b&w Telugu/Tamil
d **H.M. Reddy** *pc* Rohini Pics *co-st/co-lyr/dial*[Ta] K.G. Sharma *co-st/co-lyr*[Te] **Sri Sri, Acharya Athreya**, Sadasiva Brahmam *dial/co-lyr*[Te] M.S. Subramanyam *c* P.L. Rai *m* **Ghantasala Venkateshwara Rao**, H.R. Padmanabha Sastry
lp **Anjali Devi, K. Mukkamala, G. Varalakshmi**, Lakshmikantam, Doraiswamy, Chandrasekhar, **Madhu**, Pandit Rao, K. Prabhakar Rao

Inaugurating a fresher idiom for 50s Telugu melodrama, this is a love quartet: the rich lawyer Vijay (Mukkamala) marries village girl Nirmala (Anjali Devi), but Tara (Varalakshmi), who wanted to marry Vijay, tries to disrupt the marriage, and Chandrayya, who loved Nirmala, also features in the intrigue. Telugu megastar Anjali Devi's first major lead role and pioneering Telugu director Reddy's last film.

PATALA BHAIRAVI/PATAAL BHAIRAVI

aka *The Goddess from Below the Earth*
1951 195'[Te]/192'[Ta] b&w Telugu/Tamil/Hindi
d **K.V. Reddy** *pc* **Vijaya** *s/lyr*[Te] **Pingali Nagendra Rao** *lyr*[Ta] **Thanjai Ramaiyadas** *lyr*[H] Indra *c* Marcus Bartley *m* **Ghantasala Venkateshwara Rao**
lp **N.T. Rama Rao**, Malati, **S.V. Ranga Rao, C.S.R. Anjaneyalu**, Balakrishna, Padmanabhan, Lakshmikantam, Hemalatha Amma Rao, **Relangi Venkatramaiah**, T.G. Kamaladevi, **Surabhi Kamalabai, Savitri**

Breaking all box-office records in AP, Vijaya quickly made a Tamil version and Gemini Studios followed with a Hindi version, all starring Rama Rao who soon after started his own production house. The poor gardener's son Thota Ramudu (NTR) has to become rich to gain the hand of the Princess Indumati (Malati). The villain is a sorcerer (Ranga Rao) who wants to make the hero, as a fine example of manhood, into a human sacrifice to the underworld Goddess Patala Bhairavi. He entraps the hero with a magic bowl able to generate gold and Thota has to overcome numerous trials (e.g. fighting a crocodile which turns out to be a godly being living under a curse) before he tricks the sorcerer and is able to decapitate him. He thus satisfies Patala Bhairavi's lust for a human sacrifice and receives all the riches he craves from her as a reward. To lengthen the film, the sorcerer is revived and again pursues the hero and is again defeated. The kitschy imagery and studio sets provide an appropriate style for this emphatically Orientalist fairy tale. Ghantasala's music is a key contribution to the film's success. The Hindi version, dubbed from Telugu, included a specially shot colour sequence with a dance by Lakshmikantam. The Telugu film consolidated a local version of the 'folklore' film, a swashbuckling Orientalist fantasy evoking both Alexandre Dumas and Hollywood's Douglas Fairbanks films. Created by the Tamil cinema (cf ***Apoorva Sahodarargal***, 1949; later associated mainly with **MGR**), the genre was successfully transferred into Telugu where established directors like **B.N. Reddi** (formerly associated with reform themes) had to acknowledge its commercial infallibility (***Raja Mukutam***, 1959). The real success of the genre is due to its colourful invention of local pseudo-legends often adapting idioms from the folk theatre, e.g. Burrakatha. Earlier Telugu films in this idiom included ***Balanagamma*** (1942), ***Ratnamala*** (1947) and ***Raksharekha*** (1949).

NTR (centre) in *Patala Bhairavi*

RATNADEEP/RATNADEEPAM

1951 ?' b&w Hindi/Bengali/Tamil
d **Debaki Bose** *pc* Chitramaya *st* Prabhat Kumar Mukherjee's novel *dial* Narottam Vyas, Shekhar Roy[H] *lyr* Mahendra Pran, Buddhichandra Agarwal 'Madhur'[H] *c* Deojibhai *m* Robin Chatterjee
lp A. Gupta, Manju Dey, Molina Devi, **Chhaya Devi, Pahadi Sanyal, Tulsi Chakraborty, Kamal Mitra**, Rajkumar Soni, Sudhir Chakravarty, Gokul Mukherjee, Gaurishankar, **Abhi Bhattacharya**

Bengali-Hindi costume movie (the Tamil version was probably dubbed). The kingdom of Basuligram is in mourning on the 14th anniversary of the disappearance of Prince Bhuvan (after 14 years, a missing person may be pronounced dead). That night, at a nearby railway station, a dismissed station-master Gopal finds the corpse of a Sanyasi (ascetic) bearing a remarkable resemblance to himself. When he realises that this is the missing prince, he impersonates him. Amid joy and celebration in the palace, he meets the young queen whose innocence makes him realise the folly of his deception. The businessman Ghulam, who wanted to marry the queen himself, intends exposing the impostor. The Hindi version had several **Geeta Dutt**, Jutika Roy and Talat Mahmood numbers.

AAN

aka *Savage Princess*
1952 161' col Hindi
d/p **Mehboob Khan** *pc* Mehboob Prod. *sc* **R.S. Choudhury** *dial* S. Ali Raza *lyr* Shakeel Badaiyuni *c* Faredoon Irani *m* **Naushad**
lp **Dilip Kumar**, Nimmi, Premnath, Nadira, Sheela Nayak, Mukri, Murad, Nilambi, Cuckoo, Maya, Abdul, Aga Mehraj, Amir Bano

Mehboob's shift from b&w to colour led to a sweeping narrative style, with a brown and green countryside, neo-classical decor, expansive gestures and valiant horsemen thundering under fiery golden-orange skies, announcing his ***Mother India*** (1957) socialist realism. Hero Jai Tilak (Kumar) belongs to a Rajput clan loyal to the benevolent maharaja (Murad). The villain is the Cadillac-driving Prince Shamsher Singh (Premnath) who tries to usurp power by killing his father, the ruler. Much to the distress of Mangala (Nimmi), who loves him, Jai resolves to tame the proud rajkumari (Nadira) as he tamed her wild stallion in a contest. Shamsher kidnaps Mangala and tries to rape her, causing her to fall to her death. Jai retaliates by capturing the rajkumari, forcing her to take Mangala's place. Eventually it turns out that the maharaja is still alive and Mangala appears in the rajkumari's dream, making the princess realise she loves Jai. Jai and the loyalist forces defeat Shamsher and reassume power. One of Mehboob's first films to receive wide distribution in the West, where it was compared, incongruously, to both LeRoy's *Quo Vadis* (1951) and Powell's *The Red Shoes* (1948), while Dilip Kumar was seen as close to Tarzan. The desert, a set created by art director Achrekar, in which the rajkumari is gunning for Jai quotes the climactic scenes of King Vidor's *Duel in the Sun* (1946). Full of elaborately stylised action (esp. Nimmi's performance), the most spectacular action takes place in a *Ben Hur*-type arena, including the sword-fight between Jai and Shamsher in front of the funeral pyre intended to burn the rajkumari at the stake. Shot in 16mm Gevacolour and blown up in Technicolor, the film's epic style merges remarkably well with Technicolor's tendency to create colour patches, a problem that e.g. **Nitin Bose** failed to solve in his ***Ganga Jumna*** (1961), making ***Aan*** one of India's first successful experiments with colour cinematography. Released in a 105' dubbed French version as *Mangala Fille des Indes* in 1954.

AANDHIYAN

1952 136' b&w Hindi
d/co-st/sc/dial **Chetan Anand** *pc* **Navketan Films** *co-st* Hameed Butt *lyr* Narendra Sharma *c* Jal Mistry *m* Ali Akbar Khan
lp **Dev Anand**, Nimmi, Kalpana Kartik, **Durga Khote**, K.N. Singh, Leela Mishra, Pratima Devi, M.A. Latif, **Johnny Walker**

Chetan Anand's 2nd film at Navketan, made between the more famous ***Afsar*** (1950) and ***Taxi Driver*** (1954), argues for a humane form of capitalism. The honest lawyer Ram Mohan (Anand) wants to marry Janaki (Kartik), daughter of the businessman Din Dayal. The villain is a rival businessman, Kuber Das (Singh), who blackmails Din Dayal into letting him marry Janaki. The entire community comes to the aid of the honest capitalist but to no avail and it remains up to the star, Anand, to ensure the happy ending.

ANANDMATH

1952 176' b&w Hindi
d/sc **Hemen Gupta** *pc* **Filmistan** *st* Bankimchandra Chatterjee's novel (1884) *dial* Krishna Prabhakara *lyr* **Shailendra**, Hasrat Jaipuri *c* Dronacharya *m* **Hemanta Mukherjee**
lp **Prithviraj Kapoor**, **Geeta Bali**, Ranjana, Pradeep, Ajit, Bharat Bhushan

Militant Bengali film-maker Gupta made his Hindi debut at Filmistan with this stridently nationalist biographical of the 18th C. sage Satyanand who led the sanyasi uprising against the British and the subject of Bankimchandra's best-known novel. Alongside Satyanand's heroism, the film, choreographed by Sachin Shankar, develops a murkier tale around the sexual troubles of Satyanand's two lieutenants, Jeevanand and Bhavanand. Jeevanand renounces his wife Shanti when he joins the Math (clan), but finds himself so frustrated that he has to recover her, while Bhavanand covets Kalyani, the refugee queen of Padachinha. Both men die in the uprising, their deaths being presented as a kind of retribution for their sexual weakness.

ANDAMAN KAITHI

aka *The Prisoner of the Andamans*
1952 190' b&w Tamil
d V. Krishnan *pc* Radhakrishna Films *s* Ku. Sa. Krishnamurthy from his play
lp K. Sarangapani, T.S. Baliah, **M.G. Ramachandran**, **Thikkurisi Sukumaran Nair**, P.K. Saraswathi, Santhanalakshmi, M.S. Draupadi

A story about Independence and Partition (shown via newsreel footage) adapted from Krishnamurthy's reformist play as staged by the popular 40s company, **TKS Brothers**. The young trade union activist Nataraj (an early MGR role) tells, in flashback, his cellmate how his villainous uncle, Ponnambalam, a collaborator with the British, swindled Nataraj's mother, killed his father and married his sister, Leela. The family having escaped by train from Karachi to Madras, the villain has Nataraj imprisoned but the hero manages to kill him, earning a further prison term. Set at the time when the labour movement was gaining ground (scenes of food shortage, unemployment, strike calls), the play's reformism was skewed towards a nationalist politics and sexual conservativism: the hero marries a rape victim but the child conveniently dies; his sister Leela is a widow but also a virgin, a difficult condition achieved by feigning madness during marriage. The song *Anju ruba notai* (*A Five Rupee Note*) was a hit and the poet Subramanya Bharati's *Kani nilam vendum* (*I Want a Piece of Land*) also featured. A long dance sequence interrupts the narrative momentum. Some accounts suggest **K. Subrahmanyam** supervised the making of the film.

BAIJU BAWRA

1952 168' b&w Hindi
d **Vijay Bhatt** *pc* Prakash Pics *st* **Ramchandra Thakur** *sc* **R.S. Choudhury** *dial* **Zia Sarhadi** *lyr* Shakeel Badaiyuni *c* V.N. Reddy *m* **Naushad**
lp Bharat Bhushan, **Meena Kumari**, Surendra, Kuldip Kaur, Bipin Gupta, Manmohan Krishna, B.M. Vyas, Mishra, Radhakrishan, Kesari, Ratan Kumar, Bhagwanji, Baby Tabassum, Raimohan, Nadir

Bhatt took considerable liberties with the history of India's classical music for this megahit focusing on an encounter between Tansen (Surendra), court musician in Akbar's (Gupta) Mughal court, and the itinerant Baiju (Bhushan). When Tansen's guards kill Baiju's father (Bhagwanji), he avenges himself by defeating Tansen in a musical contest. Naushad used leading classical singers D.V. Paluskar and Amir Khan as playback voices for the highlight of the movie, the contest itself. This was Meena Kumari's first important role, playing Baiju's self-sacrificing sweetheart, Gauri. Remembered mostly for its music.

BASU PARIVAR

1952 ?' b&w Bengali
d **Nirmal Dey** *pc* MP Prod.
lp **Uttam Kumar**, **Pahadi Sanyal**, Nepal Nag, Bani Ganguly, **Bhanu Bannerjee**, **Sabitri Chatterjee**, **Supriya Choudhury**, **Jahar Roy**

Dey's first film with Bengali superstar Uttam Kumar adapts the Bengali cinema's 1940s realist tendency (e.g. ***Chinnamul***, 1950) to the commercial entertainer's requirements. It tells of a family's economic difficulties during WW2. The father (Sanyal) is an excitable figure mourning the passing of pre-war plenitude; there is a kindly mother (Ganguly) and two sons, Sukhen (Kumar) exercising a restraining influence on his impulsive younger brother Satyen (Nag). The crisis comes when Satyen is arrested for theft. Believing Sukhen did it, Satyen takes the blame. The family suffers severe disruption until the real thief is caught in an implausible ending.

CHHATRAPATI SHIVAJI

1952 156'[M]/170'[H] b&w Marathi/Hindi
d/s/co-lyr **Bhalji Pendharkar** *pc* Prabhakar Chitra *co-lyr* P. Sawalram, **Shailendra** *c* G. Shinde *m* **C. Ramchandra**
lp Chandrakant, **P.Y. Altekar**[M], **Prithviraj Kapoor**[H], **Gajanan Jagirdar**, Leela Chandragiri, **Lalita Pawar**, Ranjana, Ratnamala, Vanamala, **Baburao Pendharkar**, **Master Vithal**, Krishnarao Chonkar, Jaishankar Danve, Sureshnath, Vasantrao Pahelwan, **Lata Mangeshkar**

Pendharkar's biopic of his idol, 17th-C. Maratha emperor Shivaji (Chandrakant), presented as the founder of India's first Hindu kingdom. The film chronicles Shivaji's birth at Shivneri, the evolution of his *Dev-Desh-Dharam* (God, Country and Religion) ethic, his unification of the Maratha people and his celebrated encounters with the Adil Shahi king of Bijapur and with Shahista Khan, the uncle of Mughal King Aurangzeb (Jagirdar). Shivaji's capture by the Mughals and his escape from Agra are also shown. The film establishes the definitive version of the popular iconography clustering around Shivaji's heroic persona (cf the Marathi historical novels of Ranjit Desai or Vasant Kanetkar's stage historicals). Marathi stage actor and film-maker Altekar played Raja Jaisingh, with Kapoor taking the role in Hindi.

CHIMNI PAKHARE/NANNHE MUNNE

1952 c.130' b&w Marathi/Hindi
d **Datta Dharmadhikari** *pc* Alhaad Chitra *s/co-lyr* **G.D. Madgulkar** *co-lyr* Phani *c* Bal Bapat *m* Vasant Pawar, Ramchandra Wadhavkar
lp Baby Shakuntala, **Raja Nene**, Sulochana, Indira Chitnis, Indu Kulkarni, Rambhau Gramopadhye, Dada Mirasi, Raja Gosavi

Typical Dharmadhikari melodrama about a 12 year-old girl who raises her three younger brothers when their father runs away after committing a crime and their mother dies of shock. Several songs intensify the sentimental approach, e.g. *Aai meli baap gela aata sambhali vithala* (*Mother is dead, father is gone, now we're in God's hands*). The film suggests that its melodramatic idiom is really a version of the saint film in a contemporary setting (cf the formal similarities with ***Sant Dnyaneshwar***, 1940).

DAAG

1952 149' b&w Hindi
d/co-s **Amiya Chakravarty** *pc* Mars & Movies *co-s* Rajendra Shankar *dial* **Rajinder Singh Bedi** *lyr* **Shailendra**, Hasrat Jaipuri *c* V. Babasaheb *m* **Shankar-Jaikishen**
lp **Dilip Kumar**, Nimmi, Usha Kiron, **Lalita Pawar**, Kanhaiyalal, Jawahar Kaul, Leela Mishra, Chandrasekhar, **Krishnakant**

In Chakravarty's melodrama about class division and the evils of alcohol, Shankar (Kumar), a nice village youth who makes clay statues, is parted from his sweetheart Parvati (Nimmi) when her family inherits a fortune. In addition, he is an alcoholic who devotes all his wealth, property and even the money for his ailing mother's medicines on drink. The maudlin plot comes alive only through Nimmi's uncanny knack for larger-than-life gestures. The film's remembered song is Talat Mahmood's *Ai mere dil kahin aur chal.*

DAASI

1952 181' b&w Telugu/Tamil
d C.V. Ranganatha Das *pc* Rajyam Pics *c* M. Rehman *m* S. Dakshinamurthy, **C.R. Subburaman**
lp **N.T. Rama Rao**, **Lakshmirajyam**, **S.V. Ranga Rao**, **Relangi Venkatramaiah**, K. Sivarao, Shri Vatsa, Doraswamy, Shantakumari, Kanakam, Vasanthi

Telugu melodrama unusually derived from the Bengali literary idiom. A childless zamindar (Ranga Rao) wants to marry again but his wife (Shantakumari) then feigns pregnancy and adopts her maid's (Lakshmirajyam) child. The film deals with the problems of the maid, and then those of the child (Vasanthi) who discovers her real mother.

JAAL

aka *The Net*
1952 165' b&w Hindi
d/s **Guru Dutt** *pc* Filmarts *dial* M.A. Lateef *lyr* **Sahir Ludhianvi** *c* V.K. Murthy *m* **S.D. Burman**
lp **Dev Anand**, **Geeta Bali**, Ram Singh, Purnima, K.N. Singh, Krishna Kumari, **Johnny Walker**, Rashid Khan, **Raj Khosla**, Raj Matwala

Dutt's classic follow-up to ***Baazi*** (1951) with the same stars. Set in a small Indian enclave still under foreign control (presumably Portuguese Goa), Tony (Anand) is an unscrupulous gold smuggler who seduces the local belle Maria (Bali) and makes her his accomplice. Lisa (Purnima), who was Tony's companion until the police got on her track, tries to warn him. In the end, when Tony is hunted down by the police, Maria stops the shootout and persuades him to go to jail, promising to wait for him. Maria's blind brother Carlo (K.N. Singh) and her fiance Simon (R. Singh) are the other important characters in the story. The film's most remarkable scenes, apart from its wonderfully suspenseful opening on the waterfront, include a very stylish seduction scene as Tony lures Maria to the beach with his song *Yeh raat yeh chandni phir kahan* (sung by Hemanta Mukherjee), and she ends up caught, literally, in his net. The rural Goan fishing community is transformed into a kind of frontier town to provide the setting for the morality tale of sex and religion, summarised in a strangely comic scene with masked dancers at a village fete. Dutt uses the sound of waves as a leitmotif and his renowned crane shots (cf ***Pyaasa***, 1957; ***Kaagaz Ke Phool***, 1959) are already in evidence.

LAKHACHI GOSHTA

1952 133' b&w Marathi
d **Raja Paranjpe** *pc* Gajaraj Chitra *co-s/lyr* **G.D. Madgulkar** *co-s* G.R. Kamat *c* Bal Bapat *m* **Sudhir Phadke**
lp Chitra, Rekha, Raja Gosavi, Indira Chitnis, Ravindra, Sharad Talwalkar, G.D. Madgulkar, Raja Paranjpe, Madan Mohan

A poet loves a kindly radio singer while his painter friend loves the daughter of a millionaire. The millionaire agrees to his daughter's marriage provided the painter can demonstrate his ability to live in luxury by spending Rs 1 lakh (Rs 100,000) within a month. However, the money he spends keeps making profits. The comedy depends mainly on Madgulkar's incisive dialogue and a cast including several well-known Marathi comedians such as Gosavi and Talwalkar. Gosavi, a former bank clerk, made his debut here and went on to become a major Marathi stage and screen comedian, associated with deadpan dialogue.

MAHAPRASTHANER PATHEY/YATRIK

1952 137' b&w Bengali/Hindi
d **Kartick Chattopadhyay** *pc* **New Theatres** *st* Prabodh Kumar Sanyal's novel *dial* Mohanlal Bajpai[H] *c* Amulya Mukherjee *m* **Pankaj Mullick**
lp **Basanta Choudhury**, **Arundhati Devi**, Maya Mukherjee, **Tulsi Chakraborty**[B], **Abhi Bhattacharya**[H], **Kamal Mitra**

Film based on Prabodh Kumar Sanyal's travelogue about his visit, presented as a search for Truth, to the Himalayas and the religious shrines at Kedarnath and Badrinath. Choudhury plays the author in both versions. Arundhati Devi in her film debut plays Rani, the widow on a pilgrimage, while Bhattacharya plays the Brahmachari in the Hindi version. A strongly mystical aura pervades the film, notably in the nature shots.

MR SAMPAT

1952 165' b&w Hindi
d **S.S. Vasan** *pc* **Gemini** *st* R.K. Narayan's novel (1949) *lyr* Indra, Kashyap *m* E. Shankar Sastry, Balkrishna Kalla
lp **Motilal**, **Padmini**, Kanhaiyalal, Swaraj, Vanaja, Agha

The famous R.K. Narayan literary character of the gentleman crook became a classic Motilal role. The suave and fast-talking Mr Sampat hits Bombay as the manager of Seth Makhanlal Jhaverimull Gheewala's (Kanhaiyalal) municipal election campaign. He opens a bank with assistance from a former prince and the Kalamandir Theatre company to impress the woman he wants to win, Malini Devi (Padmini).

NAGARIK

aka *The Citizen*
1952 127' b&w Bengali
d/s **Ritwik Ghatak** *pc* Film Guild *c* Ramananda Sengupta *m* Hariprasanna Das
lp Satindra Bhattacharya, Prabhadevi, Sova Sen, Ketaki Devi, Geeta Shome, Ajit Bannerjee, **Kali Bannerjee**, Keshto Mukherjee, Gangapada Basu, Shriman Pintoo, Parijat Bose, Mumtaz Ahmed Khan, **Anil Chatterjee**

Ghatak's directorial debut was part of a co-operative effort. The film is an ensemble piece featuring a family of migrants to Calcutta, victims of the Partition of Bengal. Ramu (S. Bhattacharya) the eldest son, hopes to get a job to support the family but spends his time gazing wistfully at a flowering tree and dreaming of settling with his girlfriend Uma (K. Devi) in a house resembling one he saw in a calendar painting. His aged father (K. Bannerjee) is disillusioned while his mother (Prabhadevi) passionately regrets the loss of their old mansion; his sister Seeta (Sen) internalises the family's suffering and tries to escape the situation via the lodger, Sagar (A. Bannerjee), they have taken in and who becomes the figure through whom the family articulates its future. Eventually they move into a proletarian slum and abandon their individual aspirations as they become progressively politicised. The film came in the wake of the **IPTA**-derived political cinema in Bengal (e.g. ***Chinnamul***, 1950) and remains Ghatak's most direct call to political action, including his only explicit propaganda scene: the insertion of the Internationale on the sound-track as the family leaves the house while another group 'just like them' comes in presumably to live through similar experiences. Ackowledging for the first time in Indian cinema the melodramatic origins of an apparently realist plot, Ghatak uses wide-angle lenses to make the histories and the social relations crystallised in the urban environment resonate with the fate of the characters, starting with the presentation of the city itself, Calcutta, through a series of pan-dissolves at the film's opening. The development of the relationship between the central characters of the melodramatic plot and the city is gradually inflected by the encounter with peripheral characters: Jatin Babu (K. Mukherjee) who lives under the staircase and whose wife dies; Shefali (G. Shome), Uma's sister, who becomes a prostitute; Sagar, who changes from a rent-payer to an escape route for Seeta. These inflections begin to clarify the relations between broader social processes and the lives of individual characters, opening up the melodrama towards a directly political consciousness of the need for radical change. The film was never released and believed lost, but a restored print, unfortunately showing the extensive decay of the recovered positive, was eventually released in 1977.

PALLETOORU

1952 171' b&w Telugu
d **T. Prakash Rao** *pc* Peoples' Art Prod. *s/co-lyr* S. Vasireddy *co-lyr* **Sri Sri**, V. Shri Krishna *c* Abhayakar *m* **Ghantasala Venkateshwara Rao**
lp **N.T. Rama Rao, Savitri, S.V. Ranga Rao**, T.G. Kamaladevi, Nagabhushanam, Suryakantam

Prakash Rao's debut is a commercial hit introducing a new phase of the Telugu ruralist melodrama. Contrasting scientific enlightenment with backward superstition, the film also pits the progressive hero Chandram (NTR) against the villainous moneylender Ganapati (Ranga Rao). A second plot strand features Kondaiah (Nagabhushanam) who wants to marry heroine Suguna (Savitri). The moneylender tries to close down Chandram's Vishal Andhra (Greater Andhra) library in order to construct a temple in its place. When the village is hit by famine, he starts hoarding food. The hero opposes him, for which he is arrested and tried in court. The long court scene confronts the peasantry that supports Chandram with the rich landlords who persecute him. The film used verite footage of the Sankranti festival shot in the Krishna district and included progressive poet Sri Sri's noted lyric *Polalananni halaladunni*. Other ruralist films followed in its wake: e.g. ***Pedaraitu*** (1952).

PARASAKTHI

aka *The Goddess*
1952 188' b&w Tamil
d **Krishnan-Panju** *p* M.S. Perumal *pc* National Pics *sc/co-lyr* **M. Karunanidhi** *co-lyr* Subramanyam Bharati, **Bharatidasan** *c* Maruthi Rao *m* R. Sudharshanam
lp **Sivaji Ganesan**, S.S. Rajendran, S.V. Sahasranamam, **Sriranjini Jr**, **Pandharibai**, Kannamma

Ganesan's debut in a classic **DMK Film** scripted in line with party policies by the future chief minister of Tamil Nadu. Three brothers, based in Rangoon, go home to Madurai when their youngest sister is to be married. WW2 is declared and the brothers are separated, the eldest, Chandrasekharan (Sahasranamam) becoming a judge, the second, Gnanasekharan (Rajendran), a representative of the beggars' community. Gunasekharan (Ganesan) arrives home to find their father dead and his newly married sister Kalyani (Sriranjini) widowed and homeless. Concealing his identity, he looks after her like a guardian. In the film's dramatic as well as political highlight, he wounds a villainous Brahmin priest who tries to rape Kalyani in the deity Parasakthi's temple. Significantly, for the DMK's anti-religious stance, the hero first pretends to be the temple deity and then reveals it to be just a piece of stone. Gunasekharan's girlfriend Vimala

Sivaji Ganesan in *Parasakthi*

(Pandharibai) represents, with her politically activist brother, the voice of the DMK, esp. that of its chief, **Annadurai**. When she isn't lecturing Gunasekharan on Annadurai's works, she goes boating in the river, thus finding herself well placed to rescue Kalyani's child thrown into the river by its mother (recalling the legend of Nallathangal who threw her seven children into a well). Kalyani, accused of infanticide, comes to trial, in a classic DMK formula, before her eldest brother, the judge. When she tells her story, the brother recognises her and has a heart attack. Gunasekharan, accused of the priest's murder, gets his turn in court to make a speech. This is probably one of the most elaborately plotted melodramas in the Indian cinema and glorifies the Dravidian heritage, contrasted with the 'pitiable' state of contemporary Tamil Nadu. The film advocates (e.g. when Gunasekharan is robbed by a vamp with elitist views on the cinema played by Kannamma) traditional kinship relations while castigating caste discrimination, the Brahmin class, superstition and WW2 black marketeering. The soundtrack, released on record and cassette, was, like the book, extremely popular, as was the music. Almost banned, heavily censored for the temple scene, it was a spectacular commercial hit. Ganesan became the dominant icon of the DMK, replacing Ramaswamy who had achieved that status through Annadurai's film ***Velaikkari*** (1949). The film, its numerous political references, and the circumstances of its making and showing, have been researched by M.S.S. Pandian: 'Parasakthi: Life and Times of a DMK Film' (1991).

PEDARAITU

1952 172' b&w Telugu
d **Kadaru Nagabhushanam** *pc* Rajarajeshwari Films *s/co-lyr* Kopparapu Subbarao *co-lyr* Sambasiva Rao, Babji *c* P. Ellappa *m* H.R. Padmanabha Sastry
lp **P. Kannamba, Anjali Devi**, M. Shri Ramamurthy, **Relangi Venkatramaiah**, Doraswamy, Lingamurthy, D. Sadasivarao, Tulasi, Muthulakshmi

Rural drama in the tradition of ***Palletooru*** (1952). The evil son of the zamindar loves the same girl as the hero (Ramamurthy) and has the hero expelled from the village. The hero manages to return and all zamindar land is eventually redistributed to the poor peasants. There is a parallel comedy story including a prostitute, a manager, the manager's assistant and the assistant's lover.

PEDGAONCHE SHAHANE

1952 131' b&w Marathi
d/p **Raja Paranjpe** *pc* Makarand Films, Raja Paranjpe Prod *s/co-lyr* **G.D. Madgulkar** *dial* G.R. Kamat *co-lyr* Mukhram Sharma *c* Bal Bapat *m* Datta Davjekar
lp Raja Paranjpe, G.D. Madgulkar, Chittaranjan Kolhatkar, Dhumal, Master Dwarkanath, Vasant Shinde, Nalini Nagpurkar, Nayana, Prasad Sawkar, Sadashiv Thakar, Ganpatrao Kelkar, Daldaseth

In his best-known film as director and as actor, Paranjpe plays the bearded Kaka Shahane, a once-famous surgeon who went insane when he performed an unsuccessful operation on his girlfriend. Escaping from the mental asylum, he finds shelter with a family, pretending to be their long-lost uncle back from Zanzibar. The family, corrupted by 'modernity' (mother is a singer, daughter a dancer, one son obsessed by racing) tries to get the presumably rich uncle's money. The madman eventually reforms the family and denounces rationalist notions of sanity.

PELLI CHESI CHOODU/KALYANAM PANNI PAAR

1952 191'[Te]/193'[Ta] b&w Telugu/Tamil
d **L.V. Prasad** *pc* **Vijaya** *s* **Chakrapani** *lyr* **Pingali Nagendra Rao**[Te], Sadasiva Brahmam[Ta] *c* Marcus Bartley *m* **Ghantasala Venkateshwara Rao**
lp **N.T. Rama Rao**[Te], **Gemini Ganesh**[Ta], **G. Varalakshmi**, **Savitri**, **S.V. Ranga Rao**, Suryakantam, Joga Rao, Meenakshi, Doraiswamy, Pushpalata, **Relangi Venkatramaiah**

Major L.V. Prasad hit relying on his best-known comedy formula: complicated middle-class marital relations. Rathamma, mother of hero Raju (NTR/Ganesh), worries about finding a suitable groom for her daughter Ammadu (Varalakshmi). Raju agrees with Viyanna (Ranga Rao) that he will marry Viyanna's daughter Savitri (Savitri) if Viyanna first arranges Ammadu's marriage. Ammadu's wedding with Ramana (Joga Rao) is arranged but broken off at the instigation of Govindaiah who wants Raju to marry his daughter Chitti (Pushpalata). Pretending to go to Madras for a job, Ramana takes Ammadu along and they live together in a village, causing much gossip. When Ramana's father arrives, Raju disguises himself as a doctor and Ammadu as a nurse, while Ramana pretends to be mentally ill. When Ammadu gives birth to a son, more gossip causes the family to be rejected by the village. In the end Govindaiah finds another match for his daughter, allowing Ammadu and Ramana to legitimize their relationship. The film's major hit song is *Povamma balikavamma sanghaniki dayaledamma*. **Hunsur Krishnamurthy** remade the film in Kannada, *Madhuve Madi Nodu* (1965).

PREMA/KATHAL

1952 171'[Te]/169'[Ta] b&w Telugu/Tamil
d **P.S. Ramakrishna Rao** *pc* Bharani Pics *st* **P. Bhanumathi** *dial/lyr* K.G. Sharma *c* Kamal Ghosh *m* **C.R. Subburaman**
lp P. Bhanumathi, **A. Nageshwara Rao**, **K. Mukkamala**, **Sriranjini Jr.**, **Relangi Venkatramaiah**, **Surabhi Kamalabai**, K. Sivarao, Doraiswamy, **C.S.R. Anjaneyalu**

Rich boy-poor girl romance following on from the successful Nageshwara Rao-Bhanumathi hit ***Laila Majnu*** (1949) made by the same production team. The naive village girl Moti (Bhanumathi) meets the rich city youth Raja (Nageshwara Rao) in a rural resort. Moti's father insists that she marry the villain Parashuram (Mukkamala), but she escapes and goes to Raja. When she sees Raja walking with another woman, Lata (Sriranjini), she becomes a beggar, eventually finding a job with a theatre group. The reconciliation takes place when Raja and Lata happen to see the play, and Moti, recognising Raja, swoons on stage. Remembered mainly for Subburaman's music (e.g. the song *Agavoyi maa raja*, sung by Bhanumathi).

RAHI/TWO LEAVES AND A BUD

1952 139' b&w Hindi/English
d/dial/co-sc **K.A. Abbas** *pc* Naya Sansar *st* Mulk Raj Anand's novel *Two Leaves and a Bud* (1937) *co-sc* Mohan Abdullah, V.P. Sathe *lyr* Prem Dhawan *c* Ramchandra *m* **Anil Biswas**
lp **Dev Anand**, **Balraj Sahni**, **Nalini Jaywant**, David, Manmohan Krishna, Achala Sachdev, S. Michael, Rashid Khan, Habib Tanvir, Shaukat Hashmi

A rather confused attempt to equate a nationalist politics (well after Independence) with class politics. Set in pre-Independence Assam, it tells of oppressed, mostly women, tea plantation workers. The villainous English manager (Michael) employs the hero, a former army officer (Anand), to run the plantation with brutal discipline. He is eventually humanised by one of the workers, Ganga (Jaywant), and when the workers rise in revolt the hero joins them. However, Ganga has to pay for the film's simplifications with her life. It was made simultaneously in English and a dubbed Russian version called *Ganga* was released in the USSR.

SANKRANTI

1952 198' b&w Telugu
d **C. Pullaiah** *pc* **East India Film** *s/lyr* Balijepalli Lakshmikanta Kavi *c* N.C. Balakrishnan, Prabhakar, G. Chandran *m* Ashwathama
lp Shantakumari, **Sriranjini Jr**, **Savitri**, K. Sivarao, Ashalata, Vishwam, Ramana Rao, Chandrasekhar, **Rajanala Nageshwara Rao**

Uncharacteristic middle-class melodrama by mythological director Pullaiah, showing the ascendancy of melodrama in 50s Telugu cinema. Matriarch Annapurnamma's (Shantakumari) joint family crumbles when her two sons do not stop their respective wives from quarrelling: one son is henpecked, the other 'too busy' to bother with matters domestic. The preachy film bemoans the loss of 'traditional' male authority required to control women in the family.

SHIN SHINAKI BOOBLA BOO

1952 ?' b&w Hindi
d/p/dial/lyr P.L. Santoshi *pc* Santoshi Prod. *st* **Ramanand Sagar** *sc* Deben Mukherjee *c* L.N. Verma, P.C. Sinha *m* **C. Ramchandra**
lp **Sadhona Bose**, Rehana, Ranjan, Veera, Baby Tabassum, Radhakrishnan, Mumtaz Ali, Tiwari, Samson, Indu Paul, Shama Gulnar

Santoshi based this orientalist fantasy on the modern dance ballets Sadhona Bose had been associated with on stage, using the experiments with jazz and Latin American rhythms of Santoshi's regular composer, Ramchandra. Shin Shinaki (Bose) dreams of killing the man, Taishi, who killed her parents. When the villain dies, she transfers her vengeful energies on to the man's son. The story involves a fortune-teller, Chiang, who only surfaces publicly one day per year. The other key figure is her lover, the bandit Boobla (Ranjan), who eventually falls in with her plans. Classic songs include Sumayati's *Han dai taka lai han dai kali aie* in a kind of question-answer mode using a fast-paced chorus, Shin's number *Aare baba* and her duet with Boobla, *Kuch chahelen ho, kuch charchein ho.* This film was the unlikely first victim of the central government's authority to overrule the censor board, an action enabled by the Indian Cinematograph Act passed that year. Given a Universal certificate by the censors, the Ministry of Information and Broadcasting banned the film because of its 'low moral tone' and because it 'throws the glamour of romance and heroism over criminal characters, treats sacred subjects irreverantly and is, in consequence, opposed to the interests of public decency and morality'. The ban was later revoked but ruined the film's commercial chances.

AAH

1953 150' b&w Hindi
d Raja Nawathe *pc* R.K. Studio *s* **Inder Raj Anand** *lyr* Hasrat Jaipuri, **Shailendra** *c* Jaywant Pathare *m* **Shankar-Jaikishen**
lp **Nargis**, **Raj Kapoor**, Vijayalakshmi, Pran, Ramesh Sinha, Bhupendra Kapoor, Leela Mishra, Sohanlal, Mukesh

Raj (Kapoor), a poet at heart, is the chief engineer in charge of building the Saraswati dam. Raj's father wants him to marry the glamorous Chandra (Vijayalakshmi), but he loves Chandra's sister Neelu (Nargis) who shares his poetic inclinations. Raj discovers that he has tuberculosis. He then pretends never to have loved Neelu and persuades a doctor friend to marry her. Raj also pretends to love Chandra and so to prove to Neelu that he is an untrustworthy man. All his lies create far greater emotional problems than the disease itself but Raj and Neelu do eventually unite. Although one of Kapoor's less memorable films, it remains important as one of the first movies to deploy the very popular melodramatic device of the hero suffering nobly from a terminal disease. Masochistically wallowing in his suffering while arrogantly spreading misery all around, the infantile yet paternalistic hero, presented as a 'realist', denies the heroine, presented as an incurable romantic, the chance to make up her own mind by telling her lies. This device allows for a great variety of twists in the plot and countless displays of emotion. Here, an extra opposition is woven into the plot: the city/country dichotomy, with good tribals and workers being faced with urban profiteers. The ending sees good (country and love) triumph over evil (money and disease). In ***Bobby*** (1973), a tribute Kapoor paid to his own early work, some shots of *Aah* are reprised. He also incorporates a reference to the popular ***Devdas*** (1935) by having the dying hero make his way to his beloved's village in a cart, as Devdas did.

AMMALAKULU/MARUMAGAL

1953 187'[Te]/177'[Ta] b&w Telugu/Tamil
d **D. Yoganand** *pc* Krishna Pics *s* Sadasiva Brahmam *lyr* Samudrala Jr *c* Boman D. Irani *m* **C.R. Subburaman**, Vishwanathan-Ramamurthy
lp Lalitha, **Padmini, N.T. Rama Rao, Relangi Venkatramaiah, B.R. Panthulu,** Sivaramakrishnaiah, Rushyendramani, **Surabhi Kamalabai**

Yoganand's successful debut. The educated Usha (Lalitha), a 50s Telugu stereotype, marries the hero (NTR) despite the protests of her family. She then takes on, and vanquishes, the oppressive feudalist practices of her husband's family. The film concentrates on its female lead, featuring the Ammalakulu (neighbourhood women) indulging in dances, bicycle picnics and pranks before getting down to the story.

AMMALDAR

1953 118' b&w Marathi
d **K. Narayan Kale**, Madhukar Kulkarni *pc* Mangal Pics *st* N. Gogol's *The Government Inspector co-sc/lyr* **G.D. Madgulkar** *co-sc/m* P.L. Deshpande *c* Bal Bapat
lp P.L. Deshpande, G.D. Madgulkar, K. Narayan Kale, Sheila Naik, Leela Ogale, Vinay Kale

With ***Gulacha Ganapati*** and *Devbappa* (both 1953), this is one of the popular Marathi satirist, playwright and stage actor P.L. Deshpande's best-known films. His adaptation of Gogol's play is better anchored in the Indian situation than ***Afsar*** (1950). Various local stereotypes are incisively cast in this tale of Sarjerao (Deshpande), mistaken for a goverment official in a corrupt post-Independence village.

ANARKALI

1953 175' b&w Hindi
d **Nandlal Jaswantlal** *pc* **Filmistan** *st* **Nasir Hussain** *sc* Ramesh Saigal *lyr* **Shailendra**, Hasrat Jaipuri, Rajendra Krishen, Ali Sardar Jafri *c* Marshall Braganza *m* **C. Ramchandra**
lp Bina Rai, Pradeep Kumar, Mubarak, S.L. Puri, **Sulochana**, Kuldeep Kaur

Frequently filmed Mughal romance in which Prince Salim (P. Kumar) falls in love with the common Anarkali (Rai). In Imtiaz Ali Taj's play of 1922 she was a slave girl (cf ***Loves of a Mughal Prince***, 1928); in ***Mughal-e-Azam***, 1960, she is a court attendant. Director Jaswantlal alludes to his precursors by casting **Sulochana**, who played Anarkali in **R.S. Choudhury**'s famous 1928 version, as the hero's mother. The Filmistan production does not acknowledge the play and claims to be a direct, unmediated treatment of the Mughal legend with story and script credited to the emerging directors Hussain (***Tumsa Nahin Dekha***, 1957) and R. Saigal (***Railway Platform***, 1955). Constructed as a fantasy flashback, Jaswantlal opens the film with a big close-up of Rai's lips before going on to the customary establishing shots that set the scene. Sustaining his emphatic use of close-ups throughout, the film intercuts emotional episodes with elaborate war scenes used like fillers in between dramatic sequences. On occasion, the visual flair detected by reviewers of Jaswantlal's work for the **Imperial Studio** emerges in this Filmistan product: the slow crane movement when Akbar (Mubarak) is told of his son's secession threat and the abrupt dimming of the lights when he is confronted by his brother-in-law, the Rajput Raja Man Singh (Puri). The music, which by convention dominates this genre, includes hits like **Mangeshkar**'s *Yeh zindagi usi ki hai.*

AVVAIYYAR

aka *Avaiyar*
1953 173' b&w Tamil
d/s Kothamangalam Subbu *pc* **Gemini** *lyr* Avaiyyar, **Papanasam Sivan** *c* Thambu *m* M.D. Parthasarathy
lp K.B. Sundarambal, Kushala Kumari, G. Pattu Iyer, M.K. Radha, **Gemini Ganesh**

A hagiography of the legendary Tamil saint poetess of the Sangam period (100BC-250AD). Of her 59 surviving lyrics, 33 are in the Puram mode, addressing worldly matters, wars and politics, and 26 in the Akam mode, addressing the 'inner world', often of female desire. Kumari plays her as a young girl, Sundarambal as an adult, while Iyer takes the part of Tirunvalluvar. Starting with the story of her birth to a low-caste woman and being found, like Moses (the film often evokes *The Ten Commandments*, 1923), in a basket adrift in a river, the film chronicles her devotion to her god, Vigneshwara and her wide-ranging travels. She sings her message to all while effectively filmed miracles confirm her sainthood, first revealed when she resists an imposed marriage. There are spectactular scenes, including an army of several hundred stampeding elephants storming a fortress and Avvaiyyar alone facing a massed enemy when a chasm opens creating a barrier they cannot cross. With this 'purposeful' picture, the studio's boss **Vasan** and his close collaborator, the poet Subbu, tried to extend Gemini's reputation for spectacles after ***Chandralekha*** (1948). It is the culmination

Pradeep Kumar and Bina Rai in *Anarkali*

of the 40s Tamil films portraying major folk legend figures (cf ***Kannagi***, 1942) in the context of Tamil Nadu's political/cultural revivalism: a prologue dedicates the film to 'Mother Tamil', while the heroine symbolises Tamil virtues. Remembered mainly for Sundarambal's classic musical performance. The actress and singer, later a Gandhian, made her debut playing a sensational male role in *Nandanar* (1935). *Avvaiyyar* remains her best-known screen performance, putting her among **Vishnupant Pagnis** (Marathi) and **Chittor V. Nagaiah** (Telugu) as actors indelibly linked with the saint film genre.

BHAGYAVAAN

1953 ?' b&w Hindi
d **Datta Dharmadhikari** *pc* Rup Kamal Chitra *st* Dada Mirasi *sc* Mukhram Sharma *lyr* Neelkanth Tiwari, Saraswati Kumar Deepak *c* E. Mahmood *m* **Avinash Vyas**
lp Master Alhaad, **Raja Nene**, Radhakrishen, **Nirupa Roy**, Balraj, Rattan Kumar, Yashodhara Katju, Shakuntala, Baby Mala

The first Hindi film and an uninhibited weepie by the master of the Marathi melodrama, Dharmadhikari. The orphan Chanda (Alhaad) has to survive on the charity of an uncle and an aunt. He has an elder brother Suraj (Nene) who does not like the attention his wife bestows on the boy. After innumerable hardships, Chanda runs on to the railway track to commit suicide but he suddenly notices the oncoming train is hurtling towards a major accident. He manages to stop the train and saves the lives of his tormentors who, coincidentally, happen to be on the train. The excessively melodramatic style, though common in Marathi, was new to the Hindi cinema. It was later practised by **Shantaram** and by the ex-**Prabhat** film-makers involved in this production: Dharmadhikari, Nene and **Anant Mane**, the latter the assistant director on this movie.

CHANDIRANI

1953 165'[Ta]/164'[Te] b&w Tamil/Telugu/Hindi
d/s/co-m **P. Bhanumathi** *pc* Bharani Pics *dial*[Ta] Uday Kumar *dial/lyr*[Te] **Samudrala Raghavacharya** *c* P.S. Selvaraj *co-m* **C.R. Subburaman**, Vishwanathan
lp P. Bhanumathi, **N.T. Rama Rao, Relangi Venkatramaiah, S.V. Ranga Rao**, Amarnath, Vidyavati, **R. Nagendra Rao, C.S.R. Anjaneyalu**

Adventure movie on the pattern of ***Apoorva Sahodarargal*** (1949) replacing the male twins with female twins (Bhanumathi in a double role), daughters of an imprisoned king. One grows up in the forest, learning fencing and unarmed combat (including vanquishing a lion), while the other leads a sheltered life in the palace. Both love the same hero (NTR). The forest girl gets the hero after she defeats the king's evil commander-in-chief. Bhanumathi's debut as director was made as a trilingual but was not a success in Hindi. The duet *O taraka* was, however, a hit in all three languages.

CHANDRAHARAM

1953 174'[Te]/175'[Ta] b&w Telugu/Tamil
d **K. Kameshwara Rao** *pc* **Vijaya** *st* **Chakrapani** *dial/lyr* **Pingali Nagendra Rao** *c* Marcus Bartley *m* **Ghantasala Venkateshwara Rao**
lp **N.T. Rama Rao, Savitri, Sriranjini Jr., S.V. Ranga Rao, Relangi Venkatramaiah**, Joga Rao

Kameshwara Rao's debut is an elaborate costume drama merging Gemini's adventure film genre (***Chandralekha***, 1948) with Vijaya's own type of folk fantasy (cf ***Patala Bhairavi***, 1951). Villain Dhoomketu wants to become the crown prince of Chandanadesam, but his ambition is thwarted by the birth of Chandan (NTR). However, Chandan's life depends on his wearing a magic necklace. He dreams of his unknown beloved, Gauri (Sriranjini), and paints her portrait to show his teacher Mali (Ranga Rao), who then finds the woman. Unfortunately, the search brings the celestial nymph Chanchala (Savitri) into the story. Chanchala promises to lift Chandan's curse of death if he marries her; when he refuses, she removes the necklace and Chandan dies. Dhoomketu's ambitions are thus revived but then Chanchala returns Chandan to life for a brief period. Eventually another goddess, taking pity on the hero, unites Chandan and Gauri. There are many opulent court scenes, dance sequences featuring Apsaras in heaven, scenes of gods and goddesses who lift the hero's curse, and comedy interludes featuring the luckless Dhoomketu and his politician teacher Nikshepараyudu.

DAERA

1953 139' b&w Hindi
d/s **Kamal Amrohi** *pc* Kamal Pics *lyr* **Majrooh Sultanpuri**, Kaif Bhopali *c* M.W. Mukadam *m* Jamal Sen
lp **Meena Kumari**, Nasir Khan, Kumar, Roopmala, Nana Palsikar, Pratima Devi, Kammo, Jankidas

Amrohi's least-known but most elegiac film. Sheetal (Kumari) is married to an old, ailing man repeatedly mistaken for her father. She has an affair with Sharan Kumar (Nasir Khan) and eventually commits suicide. From the outset, when the mismatched couple arrives at the dark, windswept scene where they will face their destiny, the symbol-laden film deploys a baroque style of lighting with sparse dialogue and obsessive characters in the grip of their desires. As in Amrohi's ***Mahal*** (1949), the soundtrack is exceptional, from the opening Mukhtar Begum bhajan introducing Sharan to Sheetal, to the hush marking Sharan's fall from the balcony as the camera cranes over the crowded chaos below into Meena Kumari on a distant terrace.

DEVADASU

1953 191' b&w Telugu/Tamil
d **Vendantam Ragavaiah** *pc* Vinoda Pics *st* Saratchandra Chatterjee *sc/lyr*[Te] **Samudrala Raghavacharya** *lyr*[Ta]) **Udumalai Narayana Kavi** *c* **B.S. Ranga** *m* **C.R. Subburaman**
lp **A. Nageshwara Rao, Savitri**, Lalitha, **C.S.R. Anjaneyalu**, Doraswamy, **Rajanala Nageshwara Rao**

After P.V. Rao's 1937 film, this is the 2nd Tamil and the first Telugu version of Saratchandra's oft-filmed novel about unrequited love. Nageshwara Rao is the weak hero Devadas and Savitri is his tragic beloved Paro while Lalitha takes the role of the golden-hearted prostitute Chandramuki. The hit film was shot mostly at the Narasu Studios in Madras and became one of the best-known films by the mainstream Telugu studio that originated as Jaya Films, sponsored by the Raja of Mirzapuram apparently to counter the radical anti-feudal melodramas of, e.g., **Ramabrahmam**. The 11 songs (in both languages) of Subburaman's last film are regarded as among his best and most popular works, while Narayana Kavi's lyrics enhanced the popularity of the Tamil songs, one of them later providing the title for a **Kamalahasan** film, *Vazhve Mayam* (1982), an update of the **Devdas** plot.

DO BIGHA ZAMEEN

aka *Two Acres Of Land*
1953 142'(134') b&w Hindi
d/p **Bimal Roy** *pc* Bimal Roy Prod. *st/m* **Salil Choudhury** *sc* **Hrishikesh Mukherjee** *dial* Paul Mahendra *lyr* **Shailendra** *c* Kamal Bose
lp **Balraj Sahni, Nirupa Roy**, Rattan Kumar, Murad, Jagdeep, Nana Palsikar, Nasir Hussain, Mishra, Dilip Jr., Nandkishore, Rajlakshmi, Tiwari, Noor, Kusum, Hiralal, Sapru, **Meena Kumari**, Mehmood

Realist drama about a small landowner, Shambhu (Sahni) which opens with a song celebrating the rains that put an end to two seasons of drought, *Hariyala sawan dhol bajata aaya*. Shambhu and his son Kanhaiya (R. Kumar) have to go and work in Calcutta to repay their debt to the merciless local zamindar (Sapru) in order to retain their ancestral two acres of land. The sentimentally portrayed peasants bid farewell to the departing Shambhu and his son with the song *Bhai re, ganga aur jamuna ki dharti kahe pukar ke*. In Calcutta, Shambhu becomes a rickshaw-puller, facing numerous hardships that lead to his near-fatal accident, the death of his wife (N. Roy) who joins him in the city and, inevitably, the loss of his land to speculators who build a factory on it. Although promoted as the epitome of Indian neo-realism, the film is even more melodramatic than, e.g., De Sica's work (sometimes claimed to have influenced Roy's work). The script and the humanist acting styles, including a hard but kind landlady in the Calcutta slum and the happy-go-lucky shoeshine boy (Jagdeep) who takes Kanhaiya under his wing while humming **Raj Kapoor**'s *Awara hoon* number, all find their ancestry in **Nitin Bose**'s ruralist socials at **New Theatres** (cf ***Desher Mati***, 1938) enhanced by **IPTA** overtones in Choudhury's music. The film's neo-realist reputation is almost solely based on Balraj Sahni's extraordinary performance in his best-known film role. Also remarkable is Hrishikesh Mukherjee's editing, virtually eliminating dissolves in favour of, e.g., the unusually hard cut from the falling wheel in the film's famous rickshaw race sequence to Kanhaiya coming to the bedside of his injured father. Mukherjee claims that such a cut from day to night was unprecedented in Indian cinema.

EN VEEDU/NAA ILLU

1953 191'[Ta]/214'[Te] b&w Tamil/Telugu
d/sc/co-m **Chittor V. Nagaiah** *pc* Our India Films *co-dial/co-lyr* **Devulapalli Krishna Sastry** *co-dial* Y. Lakshminarayana *co-lyr* **Samudrala Raghavacharya**, G.S. Casshyap, Mohan *c* M.A. Rehman *co-m* A. Rama Rao
lp Chittor V. Nagaiah, Mudigonda Lingamurthy, Ramasarma, Gopalakrishnan, A.V. Subba Rao, K. Doraswamy, T.R. Rajkumari, Girija, Vidyavati, Chhaya Devi, Master Krishna, Lakshmi

Nagaiah's Tamil directing debut follows his celebrated performance in the epic melodrama ***Ezhai Padum Padu*** (1950), repeating the theme of the honest hero trapped in circumstances beyond his comprehension. The story is adapted from Samuel Butler's autobiographical novel *The Way of All Flesh* (1903) and Louis King's film version (1940). Bank clerk Shivram (Nagaiah giving a ponderously melodramatic performance) and his wife hope to see their two children grow up into classical Carnatic musicians. Trapped in a theft by the banker's corrupt brother-in-law, Shivram is believed to have been killed and his family lives in extreme poverty for decades until Shivram turns up again, arrested for theft while watching his daughter's birthday celebrations from the street. Eventually Shivram manages to unmask the real villains, Dhanraj and the dancer Leela (Vidyavati). Remembered for its extensive use of music, including a classical concert, the playback singing of M.L. Vasanthakumari and the extensive reference to radio via the public-interest broadcasts sponsored by the charitable Balananda Sangham. The Sangham also supports Shivram's starving family, an initiative apparently adopted from this film by All-India Radio. Extending Nagaiah's recourse to cross-cultural musical references, the film's highlights are the two Hindi songs *Pushpon ki rani* and *Main hasti gaati aayi* (both sung by Meena Kapur) which accompany the Bombay-based courtesan Leela's dances. Nagaiah's own hit song is *Adigadigo gaganaseema* sung along with the children.

FOOTPATH

1953 148' b&w Hindi
d/s **Zia Sarhadi** *pc* **Ranjit** *lyr* **Majrooh Sultanpuri**, Ali Sardar Jafri *c* M. Rajaram *m* **Khayyam**
lp **Dilip Kumar**, **Meena Kumari**, Achala Sachdev, Anwar, Kuldip Akhtar, Ramesh Thakur, Janakidas, P. Kailash, Kamalesh Thakkar, Master Romi, Sumati, Maruti, Romesh Thapar

Along with ***Awaaz*** (1956), this is Sarhady's best-known film as director. Set during WW2, it features the honest but poor writer Noshu (D. Kumar) who falls among black marketeers hoarding medicines in a famine-stricken area. Now that money comes easily, Noshu abandons his brother, his lover Mala (Meena Kumari) and his erstwhile principles. In the end, he comes to his senses and abandons his dream of becoming a millionaire. This morality tale extends the genre practised by Sarhady's colleague **Mehboob** in, e.g., ***Roti*** (1942). The film was an influential contribution to Dilip Kumar's reputation for naturalism.

GULACHA GANAPATI

1953 118' b&w Marathi
d/s/m P.L. Deshpande *pc* Swati Chitra *lyr* **G.D. Madgulkar** *c* A.D. Dev
lp P.L. Deshpande, Vinay Kale, Lele Mama, Vasant Shinde, Chitra

Virtual solo effort by best-selling Marathi playwright and humourist P.L. Deshpande. The naive villager Naru (Deshpande) is exploited by all except Leela, whose love allows him to grow up. As in all Deshpande's work, dialogue dominates. Madgulkar's lyric for classical singer Bhimsen Joshi, *Indrayani kathi devachi alandi*, proved very popular and later became a regular piece in the musician's repertoire.

GUMASTA

1953 187'[Te]/184'[Ta] b&w Tamil/Telugu
d/c R.M. Krishnaswamy *pc* Aruna Pics *s/lyr* **Acharya Athreya** from his play *NGO* *m* C.N. Pandurangam, **Chittor V. Nagaiah**, G. Ramanathan
lp Chittor V. Nagaiah, Ramasarma, Sivaram, **Pandharibai**, **B. Jayamma**

Influential realist effort in Telugu and Tamil cinemas based on a major Telugu play (1949) which introduced, along with Vasireddy's *Mundadugu*, a new generation in Telugu theatre. Nagaiah plays a clerk in a government office who looks after a sick father (Ramasarma), an unmarried sister and an unemployed brother (Sivaram) who sells tooth powder on the street. The clerk accepts a bribe, is found out and arrested. The father dies and the younger brother delivers the play's morality lecture on honesty. Athreya added scenes for the film such as the sister's marriage to a man who promptly dies after the wedding.

GUNASAGARI/SATHYA SHODHANAI

1953 199'[K]/159'[Ta] b&w Kannada/Tamil
d **H.L.N. Simha** *pc* Gubbi-Karnataka Films *m* R. Sudarshanam
lp **Honappa Bhagavathar**, **Pandharibai**, **Gubbi Veeranna**, **B. Jayamma**

Melodrama about a traditional heroine who marries the husband (Bhagavathar) selected by her parents. When the husband is away, the heroine has to escape from her vicious in-laws and give birth to her child in the forest. The husband returns, clears up misunderstandings and reintegrates the heroine into the family. The debut production of Veeranna's Gubbi-Karnataka Films, started in collaboration with **AVM** Film.

JHANSI KI RANI

aka *The Tiger and the Flame*
1953 148' col Hindi
d **Sohrab Modi** *pc* **Minerva Movietone** *st* S.R. Dubey *sc* Geza Herczeg, Sudarshan, Adi F. Keeka *dial* Munshi Abdul Baqui, Shams Lucknowi *lyr* **Radheshyam Kathavachak** *c* Ernest Haller *m* **Vasant Desai**
lp Mehtab, Sohrab Modi, Mubarak, Ulhas, Ramsingh, Sapru, Anil Kishore, Baby Shikha

One of the best-known Indian historicals, it is a spectacular account of Rani Laxmibai's (Mehtab) life, the 19th C. queen of Jhansi known as Manu to her friends and who led her armies into battle against the British East India Company during the 1857 rising (known in Britain as 'the Mutiny'). The film chronicles Lord Dalhousie's annexation policies which had forced a treaty upon the aged and childless King Gangadhar Rao (Mubarak). The high priest (Modi), who controls the throne and who had opposed the signing of the treaty, searches for someone capable of leading a revolt and finds the defiant Manu. He persuades the king to marry her, making her the rightful successor to the king instead of the scheming Sadashiv Rao (Ramsingh) who is on the side of the British. Much of the film, shot by Hollywood import Haller, consists of battle scenes, courtesy of the Ministry of Defence and horses, elephants and subjects of the maharajahs of Bikaner and Jaipur.

KANNA TALLI/PETRATHAI

1953 193'[Te]/194'[Ta] b&w Telugu/Tamil
d **K.S. Prakash Rao** *pc* Prakash Prod. *dial*[Te] **Sri Sri**, **Arudra**, Sankara, Vasireddy *dial*[Ta] M.S. Subramanyam *lyr* **Tapi Dharma Rao**, **Acharya Athreya** *c* Jagirdar *m* **Pendyala Nageshwara Rao**
lp **G. Varalakshmi**, **A. Nageshwara Rao**, **Rajanala Nageshwara Rao**, M.N. Nambiar, Vasantha, Mikkilineni, K. Sivarao

Melodrama about a middle-class mother (Varalakshmi) who raises her two children when her husband, unable to repay mounting debts, abandons his family. While the daughter (Vasantha) becomes a good soul, like her mother, the son (Nambiar) goes astray and eventually commits murder. Mother takes the blame for the crime and goes to jail, thus reforming her errant son. At this time in Telugu cinema, 'the struggling mother' is a nationalist as well as a melodramatic stereotype (cf **L.V. Prasad**'s ***Pempudu Koduku***, also 1953).

NATUN YAHUDI

1953 ?' b&w Bengali
d/s/co-lyr Salil Sen from his play *pc* Eastern Artists *co-lyr* Krittivas Ojha, Suresh Choudhury, Dwija Kanai *c* Ramanand Sengupta *m* Chitta Roy
lp **Kanu Bannerjee**, **Bhanu Bannerjee**, Bani Ganguly, **Sabitri Chatterjee**, Nepal Roy

Sen adapted his own play, first staged by the Uttar Sarathi group (1948) to raise funds for refugees from East Bengal (cf **Bhanu Bannerjee**), and part of a genre of 40s 'realist' theatre addressing the 1942-3 Bengal famine and Partition (cf plays like Digin Bandyopadhyay's *Bastubhita*, Tulsi Lahiri's *Banglar Meye*). School-teacher Manmohan Pandit arrives in Calcutta as a refugee from what had become East Pakistan. His eldest son was killed in the freedom struggle and the family is determined to live up to the dead son's idealism: second son Mohan refuses a job out of solidarity for striking workers and becomes a coolie while the father finds employment as a cook. The other son, Duikhya, is rejected by the family when he turns to crime, but he is the only one with money when the father falls ill. Eventually the criminal son and the father die, shortly before the latter's delayed pension arrives from Pakistan. Although a straight adaptation of the play, the film followed ***Chinnamul***'s (1950) example and used Bangladeshi dialect.

PAKKINTI AMMAYI

1953 164' b&w Telugu
d **C. Pullaiah** *pc* **East India Films** *st* Arun Choudhury's *Pasher Bari dial/lyr:* Muddukrishna *c* Biren De *m* Ashwathama
lp **Anjali Devi**, V. Kamaladevi, Mohanakrishna, **C. Krishnaveni**, Shakuntala, Gangarathnam, **Relangi Venkatramaiah**, **C.S. Rao**, V.V. Tatachari, R.K. Rao, A.M. Raja, Addala Narayana Rao

Early Telugu version of a comic Bengali short story first filmed by Sudhir Mukherjee (1952) in Bengali though best known in its Hindi version, ***Padosan*** (1968). Anjali Devi plays the sexy neighbour of Venkatramaiah. The music helped assure its success with a rare on-screen performance by the singer A.M. Raja. It was also remade in 1981 with singer **S.P. Balasubramanyam** and composer Chakravarty playing the two rivals for the heroine's affections.

PARINEETA

1953 151' b&w Hindi
d/sc **Bimal Roy** *pc* Ashok Kumar Prod. *st* Saratchandra Chatterjee *dial* Vrajendra Gaur *lyr* Bharat Vyas *c* Kamal Bose *m* Arun Kumar Mukherjee
lp **Ashok Kumar**, **Meena Kumari**, Asit Baran, Nasir Hussain, Badri Prasad, Pratima Devi, Manorama, S. Bannerjee, Tiwari, Baby Sheela, Manju, Naina, Bhupen Kapoor, Bikram Kapoor, Sailen Bose, Colin Pal

In Calcutta, at the turn of the century, Shekhar (A. Kumar), the son of rich businessman Nabin Rai (Prasad), loves and secretly marries his poor neighbour Lalita (Kumari), the niece of Gurcharan Babu (Hussain). Despite the long friendship between the two families, things deteriorate fast when Nabin Rai insists on Gurcharan Babu repaying an old loan. Gurcharan Babu wants to raise the money by marrying off Lalita. Shekhar misunderstands Lalita's silence as meaning she acquiesces in this scheme. However, she turns down an old benefactor of the family, Girin Babu (Baran). She admits to being already married and, even though she refuses to reveal her husband's name, vows to remain faithful to him all her life. Shekhar recognises her sacrifice just in time to cancel a wedding he had arranged out of resentment and he publicly acknowledges his relationship with Lalita. The film rehearses some of the period effects through costume, architecture and lighting of turn-of-the-century Calcutta, later associated with **Ray**'s ***Charulata*** (1964).

PATHIK

1953 ?' b&w Bengali
d **Debaki Bose** *pc* Chitramaya *s* Tulsi Lahiri from his play *c* Bibhuti Chakraborty *m* Dakshina Mohan Thakur
lp **Sombhu Mitra**, Tripti Mitra, Monica Ganguly, Manoranjan Bhattacharya, Tulsi Lahiri, Gangapada Basu, Kali Sarkar, Sabitabrata Datta

Lahiri's seminal Bengali play, with which Sombhu Mitra launched his Bohurupee theatre group, was first staged when the CPI's 'left-wing deviation' was causing many key **IPTA** figures, including Mitra and **Bijon Bhattacharya**, to leave the organisation. The play continued the IPTA's experiments with realism and was set in a colliery's teashop over two days. The events are mainly seen through the eyes of a failed and disillusioned writer, Ashim Roy (Mitra), who ends up fighting for an injured worker's compensation rights and eventually becomes a heroic figure for the miners. The film version deploys a voice-over quoting from Ashim's diary and features characters speaking in several languages and accents. It deviates from the play in adding an encounter between Ashim and a criminal, Atmaram, and it has an upbeat ending with the workers pushing the wounded Ashim in a broken-down motor car towards the hospital. Bose's tightly edited film orchestrates indoor space via intricate tracking shots and an extensive use of different focal depths, although the studio scenes are not always well integrated into the many outdoor scenes.

Meena Kumari (above) in *Parineeta*

PEMPUDU KODUKU

1953 163' b&w Telugu
d/p **L.V. Prasad** *pc* Prasad Art Pics *st* Varadarajan *dial/co-lyr* Sadasiva Brahmam *co-lyr* **Sri Sri**, Anisetty *c* Adi M. Irani *m* **Saluri Rajeshwara Rao**
lp L.V. Prasad, Pushpavalli, **Sivaji Ganesan**, **S.V. Ranga Rao**, Kumari, Ramamurthy, **Savitri**

The debut of Prasad Art Pics, later run by **T. Prakash Rao** and **Pratyagatma**, is a melodrama about a woman and her two sons. To make ends meet, Mangamma (Pushpavalli) has her younger son Mohan (Ganesan) adopted, raising her first son Muthu while working as a domestic servant. She witnesses a murder in the house, is arrested for the crime and jailed. When released, she finds the decent Muthu has become the enemy of the bad Mohan. **Filmistan**'s ***Munimji*** (1955) rehearsed similar motifs.

POONGOTHAI/PARDESI

1953 171'[Ta]/190'[Te] b&w Tamil/Telugu
d **L.V. Prasad** *pc* Anjali Pixtures *dial/lyr* Sadasiva Brahmam[Ta], Malladi Krishna Sharma[Te] *c* Kamal Ghosh *m* **Adi Narayana Rao**
lp **Anjali Devi**, **Sivaji Ganesan**, **S.V. Ranga Rao**, **A. Nageshwara Rao**, **Pandharibai**, K.A. Thangavelu[Ta], **Relangi Venkatramaiah**[Te], Mohan

The Anjali Pixtures debut is an incest melodrama. Chandram (Nageshwara Rao) becomes a pauper on the death of his father. To support the widow and son of a childhood friend, he finds a job and meets the beautiful flower-girl Lakshmi (Anjali Devi) at a hill resort. Defying her conservative father, they marry. When Chandram has to leave for the city in a hurry, Lakshmi believes that he has deserted her. She is persecuted by a suitor who burns down her house, and when Chandram returns he believes his wife is dead. Years later Lakshmi's daughter and Chandram's adopted son fall in love. In addition, rumour has it that Chandram's adopted son is in fact his illegitimate child by the widow he supported, making the incest motif yet more explicit.

PUTTILLU

1953 176' b&w Telugu
d/st Rajarao *pc* Raja Prod. *dial* Sankara, Vasireddy *c* V.N. Reddy, Ajit Kumar *m* Mohandas, T. Chalapathi Rao

lp **Jamuna**, Rajarao, Perumallu, Mikkilineni, Ramana Reddy, Chadalavada, Suryasri

The noted playwright Vasireddy, the composer Chalapathi Rao, future Telugu star Jamuna and the director all emerged from the **IPTA**'s Andhra Unit, the Praja Natya Mandali. A father insists on having his daughter educated but forbids her to continue studying when she reaches marriageable age. She later leaves her unsuitable husband and the plot also addresses the woman's problematic relationship with her mother-in-law. The makers of this unsuccessful film were sometimes criticised for having sold out to commercialism, although other histories, notably those of the impact of the IPTA on Telugu cinema, continue to ascribe to it a historically significant role.

SHAREY CHUATTAR

1953 ?' b&w Bengali
d/sc **Nirmal Dey** *pc* MP Prod *st/dial* **Bijon Bhattacharya** *lyr* Sailen Roy *m* Kalipada Sen
lp **Uttam Kumar, Suchitra Sen, Tulsi Chakraborty**, Molina Devi, **Bhanu Bannerjee, Jahar Roy**, Nabadwip Haldar

A big hit, this effervescent comedy launches Bengali cinema's most successful star duo ever, Uttam Kumar and Suchitra Sen. Rajanibabu (Chakraborty) runs the Annapurna Boarding House. Into this raucous all-male world of mainly unemployed tenants arrives the beautiful Romola (Sen) with her parents. The hero Rampriti (Kumar) in the end triumphs over his main rival (Bannerjee) and gets the girl. Dey's breakthrough film after ***Basu Parivar*** (1952) expertly orchestrates a large number of characters while sustaining a fast pace.

SHYAMCHI AAI

1953 152' b&w Marathi
d/p/sc/co-lyr **P.K. Atre** *pc* Atre Pics *st* Sane Guruji's novel *co-lyr* Vasant Bapat, Rajkavi Yashwant *c* R.M. Rele *m* **Vasant Desai**
lp Vanamala, Madhav Vaze, Umesh, **Baburao Pendharkar**, Sumati Gupte, Saraswati Bodas, Vasant Bapat, Prabodhankar Thakre, Damuanna Joshi, Nagesh Joshi, Bapurao Mane, Pandurang Joshi, Vimal Ghaisas

Major Marathi melodrama based on one of the most influential 20th C. Marathi novels (1935), a fictionalised account of the childhood years of Sane Guruji (1899-1950). A nationalist influenced by Vinoba Bhave and esp. Gandhi, he was imprisoned repeatedly for his work among the peasantry and participation in the Quit India agitations. His book *Shyamchi Aai*, written in jail, has 45 episodes in which Shyam, a youth living in poverty in Konkan, recalls the teachings of his mother. The film incorporates the heavy nationalist symbolism associated with the mother (Vanamala), a devoutly religious person with an earthy philosophy, as well as the sentimental depiction of her relationship with her son (Vaze). Despite its emphasis on a ruralist realism, the characters remain exemplary and (surprisingly for Atre) humourless stereotypes. The film, like the book, relies on flashbacks as Sane Guruji (D. Joshi) tells the stories in homage to a person to whom he owes everything. Episodes showing the young Shyam's maturation culminate in the mother's death. The hit film has remained a generic landmark in Marathi melodrama, esp. for Vanamala's maternal prototype. The book has been analysed by Shanta Gokhale (1990).

THIRAMALA

aka *Waves*
1953 172' b&w Malayalam
co-d/p P.R.S. Pillai *co-d/m* Vimal Kumar *pc* Kalasagar Films *s* T.N. Gopinathan Nair *lyr* **P. Bhaskaran** *c* V. Ramamurthy
lp Kumari Thangam, Miss Chandni, Kumari Kalyani, M.L. Rajam, P.D. Janaki, Kumari Prabha, T.N. Gopinathan Nair, P. Bhaskaran, Baby Vatsala, **Sathyan**, Thomas Birly, T.S. Muthaiah, **Sasikumar**, Govinda Pillai, **Adoor Bhasi**

Melodrama about separated lovers: Laxmi, the village landlord's daughter, and Venu, the son of the ferryman. Laxmi is married off to a city wastrel and Venu, who followed her to the city and became a waiter at the hotel where Laxmi stays, witnesses her marriage breaking up. The penniless Laxmi also loses her daughter. Laxmi and Venu each having returned to their village, they meet again in a storm as Venu comes to her rescue with his boat to take her to the opposite shore. However, the boat capsizes and, as the storm subsides, the film shows Venu's corpse being washed up on the shore. The Merryland Studio production is choreographed by Chandrasekhar to art direction by M.V. Kochhappu.

AAR PAAR

aka *From One Side to the Other*
1954 146' b&w Hindi
d/p **Guru Dutt** *pc* Guru Dutt Prod. *sc* Nabendu Ghosh *dial* Abrar Alvi *lyr* **Majrooh Sultanpuri** *c* V.K. Murthy *m* **O.P. Nayyar**
lp Guru Dutt, Shyama, Shakila, **Johnny Walker**, Jagdish Sethi, Noor, Beer Sakhuja, Rashid Khan, Jagdeep

With this innovative and, for the period, daring film Guru Dutt enters the happiest phase of his career. He plays Kalu, a taxi driver and mechanic who has served a jail sentence for rash driving and is in love with Nicky (Shyama), the daughter of his boss at the garage. Several subplots are woven into their romance: a gang of safe busters led by Captain, kidnappers employed by Nicky's father and lovable ruffians like Elaichi Sandow (Jagdeep). Considered until recently a relatively minor Guru Dutt film, its bravura song picturisations such as the 'tragic' version of the song *Ja ja ja ja bewafa* (inverting the earlier number *Sun sun sun sun zaalima*), where the camera pans over a series of black pillars hiding heroine Shyama from the viewer, announce ***Pyaasa*** (1957) and the melodramas that followed. Dutt experiments with novel ways of cutting songs into the story, e.g. omitting introductory music. The opening song sequence introduces the Western musical ploy of interposing incidental characters into the narrative choreography as the street urchins energetically dance in the streets of Bombay. As in all Dutt's films, the **Geeta Dutt** songs are perennial hits, including *Babuji dheere chalna*, *Yeh lo main haari piya*, *Mohabbat kar lo, ji bhar lo* (the last a duet with **Mohammed Rafi**). The film exudes a lighthearted cheekiness which, coupled with the elaboration of new generic conventions, divided the contemporary audience, offending the stuffier traditionalists and delighting the others.

AMAR

1954 149' b&w Hindi
d/p **Mehboob Khan** *pc* Mehboob Prod. *st/co-sc* S. Ali Raza *co-st* Mehrish, S.K. Kalla, B.S. Ramaiah *co-sc* Agha Jani Kashmiri *lyr* Shakeel Badaiyuni *c* Faredoon Irani *m* **Naushad**
lp **Madhubala, Dilip Kumar**, Nimmi, Jayant, Ulhas, Mukri, Amar, Husnbano, Murad, Shakeel Nomani

Apparently Mehboob's favourite film in which the cowardly hero Amar (D. Kumar), a lawyer, seduces a milkmaid, Sonia (Nimmi), while engaged to Anju (Madhubala). The hero watches silently as Sonia suffers the consequences of their passionate moment while the villain, Sankat (Jayant), offers her help and comfort. Sankat causes havoc in the village before getting killed in a fight with Amar. Sonia is arrested and defended in court by Amar who eventually marries her. The film continues Mehboob's fascination with a kind of cultural primitivism (cf ***Roti***, 1942) shown here in the harvest number and in the temple sequences with both Anju and Sonia. The melodramatic subject combined with some unusually surreal imagery made the film an oddity in the genre. It was not a commercial success, possibly because the audience refused to accept Dilip Kumar in a negative role.

ANTA MANAVALLE

1954 185' b&w Telugu
d **Tapi Chanakya** *pc* Sarathi Pics *s* Kondepudi Lakshminarayana *lyr* **Tapi Dharma Rao**, Kopparapu Subbarao, Konakalla Venkatrathnam *m* **Master Venu**
lp **C.S.R. Anjaneyalu, S.V. Ranga Rao**, Narasimharao, Ramanareddy, Krishnakumari, **Jamuna**, Hemalatha, Rajasulochana, Suryakantam, Perumallu

'Realist' corruption melodrama about a politician and village headman, Jagannatham (Ranga Rao), the man behind a gang of extortionists including Chidambaram (Anjaneyalu), Vaikuntam and Purniah. Chidambaram dupes the widowed Rathamma, forcing her family into destitution while he builds his bungalow. The fearless editor of the local newspaper (Perumallu) and his daughter (Krishnakumari), who loves the widowed Rathamma's son Sathyam, try to expose the corruption. A review in *Andhra Patrika* compared the film to *Ladri di biciclette* (1948). Chanakya's debut, evoking the earlier radical-reformist cinema of Sarathi Pics, and Master Venu's debut as an independent composer relies heavily on folk-derived music.

BAADBAAN

1954 ?' b&w Hindi
d/st **Phani Majumdar** *pc* **Bombay Talkies** Workers Industrial Coop. Society *sc/dial* Nabendu Ghosh, **Shakti Samanta** *lyr*

Indivar, Uddhav Kumar *c* Roque M. Layton *m* **Timir Baran**, S.K. Pal
lp **Ashok Kumar**, **Dev Anand**, Usha Kiron, **Meena Kumari**, Jairaj, Sheikh Mukhtar, Bipin Gupta, **Leela Chitnis**, Gope, Shivraj, **Krishnakant**, Mehmood

Billed as a 'Workers' Own Enterprise', the film was produced as a last-ditch attempt by its employees to keep Bombay Talkies alive. Lalan, the village headman, leaves to warn fishermen about an impending storm but he disappears followed by his wife Leela. Their child, adopted by the judge Mr Choudhury, grows up to become Naren (Anand). Educated abroad, he is to wed Bina, the daughter of a family friend. Shankar, Naren's friend and Bina's music teacher, also in love with Bina, keeps his feelings to himself. The marriage is called off when Mr Choudhury admits that Naren is not his son. The setting then shifts to the village where Naren decides to dedicate his life to the people, starting, e.g., an ice factory and a workers' co-operative society. He falls in love with the village girl Mohna. Naren and Bina get married anyway, but she is unhappy about his rural activism.

BANGARU PAPA

1954 183' b&w Telugu
d/co-sc **B.N. Reddi** *pc* **Vauhini** *st/co-sc* Palagummi Padmaraju from George Eliot's *Silas Marner* *lyr* **Devulapalli Krishna Sastry** *c* B.N. Konda Reddy *m* A. Rama Rao
lp **S.V. Ranga Rao**, **K. Jaggaiah**, **Jamuna**, Krishnakumari, Ramasarma, Vidyavati, Ramana Reddy, Jayalakshmi, Hemalatha

The rich Manohar (Jaggaiah) marries the poor Shanta (Jamuna), neglecting to inform his conservative and tyrannical father. The father forces him to marry a girl of his choice, even as Shanta dies in a storm leaving an infant daughter behind. The daughter is rescued by the criminal Kotaiah (Ranga Rao) who, while raising her, becomes a reformed character. Manohar suffers, unable to declare the woman to be his daughter. The melodrama is remembered for Ranga Rao's performance. A commercial flop though a success among the urban upper class.

BEDARA KANNAPPA

1954 155' b&w Kannada
d **H.L.N. Simha** *pc* Gubbi Karnataka Films *s* **G.V. Iyer** from his play *m* R. Sudarshanam
lp **Rajkumar**, G.V. Iyer, **Pandharibai**, Narasimhraju

The screen debut of Kannada superstar Rajkumar in this quasi-mythological melodrama, derived from the Telugu 'folklore' genre (cf ***Patala Bhairavi***, 1951), effectively establishes this specifically Kannada genre in which human beings often turn out to be gods and earthly existence comes to function mainly as a metaphor for exclusion rather than as an engagement with reality. The genre, inevitably featuring Rajkumar as the questing hero while the earthier sidekicks Narasimhraju and Balkrishna provide the comic interludes, is continued in, e.g., **Hunsur Krishnamurthy**'s *Shri Kannika Parameshwari Kathe* (1966). Here, Dinna (Rajkumar) and Neela (Pandharibai) are gods banished to earth where they are born to a tribe of hunters. They grow up and become involved with a corrupt temple priest who accuses Dinna of theft. Dinna weathers all the tests, including torture, the gods impose on him. Based on his original play for the Gubbi company, this is G.V. Iyer's film debut.

BIRAJ BAHU

1954 145' b&w Hindi
d **Bimal Roy** *pc* Hiren Choudhury Prod. *st* Saratchandra Chatterjee *sc* Nabendu Ghosh *dial* **Nasir Hussain** *lyr* Prem Dhawan *c* Dilip Gupta *m* **Salil Choudhury**
lp Kamini Kaushal, **Abhi Bhattacharya**, Shakuntala, Pran, Randhir, Bikram Kapoor, Manorama, Kammo, Baby Chand, Iftikhar, Moni Chatterjee, Ravikant

Hindi remake of **Amar Mullick**'s Bengali film for **New Theatres**' *Biraj Bou* (1946). Based on a story by Bengali novelist Saratchandra, the film's narrative pivot is the beautiful Biraj who is committed to the happiness of her husband Nilambar. Left in poverty by the callousness of Nilambar's brother Pitambar and to meet the cost of his sister Punnu's marriage, Biraj slaves away earning money making and selling dolls until an amorous young zamindar starts paying attention to her. Then, her commitment to her family yields to cynicism about the attitudes of all men towards women, including those of her husband. Edited by **Hrishikesh Mukherjee** and with **Asit Sen** as assistant director, this film continued ***Parineeta***'s (1953) effort to transplant themes from Bengali reform literature into the Hindi cinema, influencing the later films of Mukherjee and Sen.

BOOT POLISH

1954 149'(99') b&w Hindi
d Prakash Arora *pc* R.K. Films *p* **Raj Kapoor** *s* Bhanu Pratap *lyr* **Shailendra**, Hasrat Jaipuri, Saraswati Kumar Deepak *c* Tara Dutt *m* **Shankar-Jaikishen**
lp Baby Naaz, Rattan Kumar, David, Chand Burque, Veera, Bhupendra Kapoor, Bhudo Advani, Shailendra, Prabhu Arora, Raj Kapoor

Following his collaboration with **Abbas** on ***Awara*** (1951), Kapoor presided over and allegedly directed most of this social melodrama credited to his assistant. It is a story about two orphan children, Bhola (R. Kumar) and Belu (Naaz), who are forced to become beggars in Bombay by their wicked aunt Kamala Chachi. They are shown the straight and narrow path by the one-legged bootlegger, Uncle John (David), who

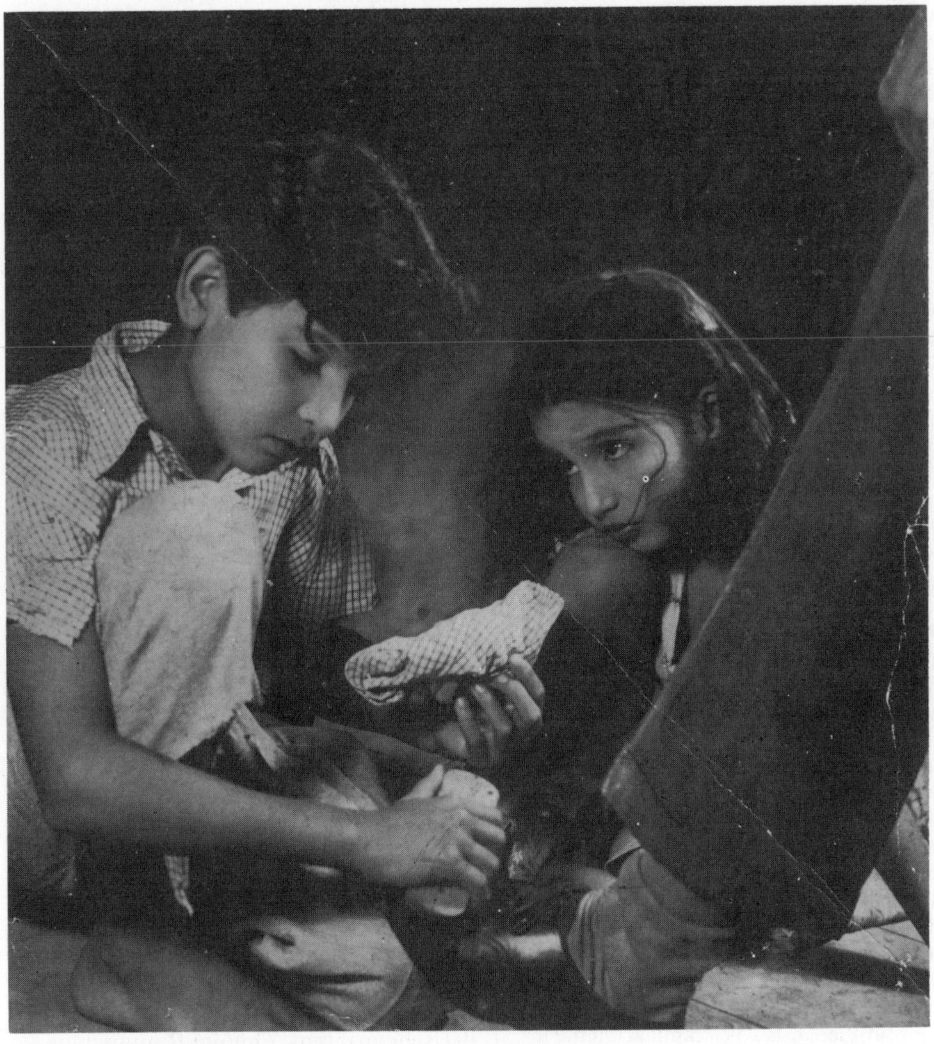

Rattan Kumar and Baby Naaz in *Boot Polish*

encourages them to take up the honest trade of polishing shoes. The film established a realist precedent for, e.g., *Salaam Bombay* (1988), which replaced its sentimental optimism with an unrelenting miserabilism. Kapoor's film can be seen as an allegorical representation of the newly independent 'infant' Indian nation. As the upbeat marching song *Nannhe munne bachche* suggests, children can control their own destiny. Kapoor makes a guest appearance asleep on a train seat, being mistaken by Bhola as 'Raj Kapoor the film star' and silenced by the girl who sensibly remarks: 'Everybody pretends to be Raj Kapoor.' A shortened version was released in the USA in 1958.

CHAKRAPANI

1954 171' b&w Telugu
d **P.S. Ramakrishna Rao** *p/m* **P. Bhanumathi** *pc* Bharani Pics *s/lyr* Ravoori *c* P.S. Selvaraj
lp P. Bhanumathi, T.G. Kamaladevi, Leelakumari, Chhaya Devi, Suryakantam, **A. Nageshwara Rao**, **C.S.R. Anjaneyalu**, Vangara, Sivaramakrishnaiah, Ramana Reddy, Amarnath

When **Vijaya** Studio refused to cast her in their hit comedy ***Missamma*** (1955), Bhanumathi apparently produced this film as a rejoinder. For a star best known for musical melodramas, this is an unusual comedy about an ageing miser named after the scenarist and proprietor of the Vijaya Studio, **Chakrapani** (Anjaneyalu), who promises his wealth to whichever of his two granddaughters (Bhanumathi, Kamaladevi) first bears him a great-grandson. The first is disqualified when she has a daughter while the second attempts to pass off someone else's child as her own, which leads to the arrest of her husband. Eventually a previously unknown grandson appears on the scene, inherits and distributes the property to all. Bhanumathi's first independent work as a composer had six songs, including the hit *Ananda dayini*.

CHAMPADANGAR BOU

1954 ?' b&w Bengali
d/p/c **Nirmal Dey** *pc* Nirmal Dey Prod. *s/lyr* Tarashankar Bannerjee *m* Manabendra Mukhopadhyay
lp Anubha Gupta, **Uttam Kumar**, **Sabitri Chatterjee**, **Kanu Bannerjee**, Premangshu Bose, **Tulsi Chakraborty**, Kobita Sarkar

Hit joint family melodrama in a sentimentalised rural setting, scripted by a noted Bengali novelist. The crusty head of the family, Setap Moral, is contrasted with his irresponsible younger brother Mahatap (Kumar). Their conflicts are usually resolved by the elder brother's efficient and matronly wife Kadambini (Gupta), who is so fond of Mahatap that it causes a scandal. When the showdown between the brothers comes, Setap blames his wife for everything and wants to kill her. However, he relents when he realises Kadambini's commitment is really to the maintenance of the family's unity. A later Hindi version, *Aanchal* (1980), with **Rajesh Khanna** and **Amol Palekar**, emphasised the plot's association with the *Ramayana* legend. The elder sister-in-law's sexual attraction for a younger brother-in-law is a familiar theme in Bengali literature and film (cf **Ray**'s ***Charulata***, 1964).

CHANDNI CHOWK

1954 ?' b&w Hindi
d **B.R. Chopra** *pc* Hira Films *st* D.P. Berry *sc* I.S. Johar *dial* Kamil Rashid *lyr* Saif, **Majrooh Sultanpuri**, Raja Mehdi, **Shailendra** *c* Keki Mistry *m* Roshan
lp **Meena Kumari**, Shekhar, Kumar, Jeevan, Achala Sachdev, Smriti Biswas, Yashodhara Katju, Agha

Chopra's first hit is a costumed musical melodrama addressing Muslim feudal orthodoxy. The nawab Safdar Jung (Kumar), anxious about preserving his aristocratic lineage, turns down a proposal by the scheming Ibrahim Beg (Jeevan) that the nawab's daughter Zarina (Kumari) marry Yusuf (Agha), the rich son of a former vegetable vendor. Beg then tricks the nawab into letting Zarina marry Akbar (Shekhar), a gardener's son. Later, when Safdar Jung realises he was tricked, Akbar is forced to leave home and goes to Cairo where he meets a dancer, Noorie (Biswas), who later dies. The film is best remembered for Meena Kumari's performance, esp. the scene where she writes to her missing husband singing *Aa jaye jane wale* (sung by **Lata Mangeshkar**).

DHULI

1954 163' b&w Bengali
d Pinaki Mukherjee *pc* Aaj Prod. *dial* Narayan Gangopadhyay *m* Rajen Sarkar
lp Robin Majumdar, **Pahadi Sanyal**, Nitish Mukherjee, **Suchitra Sen**, **Mala Sinha**, **Anil Chatterjee**, **Chhabi Biswas**, **Jahar Roy**

Parashar's (Majumdar) grandfather Kunja is the celebrated village performer on the dhol (folk instrument), but his grandson chooses the more respected life of a singer and moves to Calcutta to pursue his profession, where he falls in love with Minati, his music teacher's daughter. Minati defeats the rich Ratri in a musical contest and the latter avenges herself by hiring Parashar as her teacher, thus introducing him into the decadent world of the urban rich. Eventually, a chastened Parashar returns to the village, realising he should never have departed from his ancestral vocation of playing the dhol. As ***Pather Panchali*** (1955) was still in production at the time, this is the film which established the Bengali village as a dominant icon in post-Independence romanticism. Placed outside the histories of famine and Partition, the village becomes a poignantly nostalgic repository of the values threatened by modernity. In the process, the country/city divide gets mapped on to the conflicts of tradition versus modernity, innocence versus evil, good art versus bad and, finally, the good woman versus the bad. Importantly, in this form, virtue triumphs only in defeat and in death.

MALAIKALLAN

1954 186' b&w Tamil
d S.M. Sreeramulu Naidu *pc* Pakshiraja Studio *st/co-lyr* Namakkal Kavingar *dial* **M. Karunanidhi** *co-lyr* **Bharatidasan**, S.P. Balasubramanyam, **Thanjai Ramaiyadas**, Makkalanban *m* S.M. Subbaiah Naidu
lp **M.G. Ramachandran**, **P. Bhanumathi**, M.G. Chakrapani, P.S. Gnanam, Dorairaj, Surabhi Balasaraswathi, Ezhumalai, Balasubramanyam, Sandhya, Sagadevan, Santha

Classic MGR movie about an outlaw who robs the rich to feed the poor while maintaining a double identity as a Muslim merchant. He falls in love with Poonkothai (Bhanumathi) who is later used by the police to entrap the hero. Eventually, the police officer turns out to be the bandit's brother. According to M.S.S. Pandian (1992), in this film MGR established his political persona as a 'superman' imposing his own version of justice. The Karunanidhi script, replete with the customary DMK propaganda, inaugurated the crucial device of hinging its political message in a song: Pandian translates its lines as follows: 'How long will they fool us/in this land of ours?/We'll open schools in every street/and see that none is unlettered/We'll teach many vocations/and banish starvation/Because they don't even get a glimpse/of the hoarded money/Why do they keep yelling/"There is no god"?/Because He has not shown Himself/for far too long'. Written by Bharatidasan and sung by T.M. Soundarrajan, the song was very popular. *Malaikallan* was remade in Hindi by the same studio as ***Azad*** (1955) starring **Dilip Kumar**.

MANOHARA/MANOHAR

1954 199'[Ta]/184'[Te] b&w Tamil/Telugu/Hindi
d/s **L.V. Prasad** *pc* Manohar Pics *st* **P. Sambandam Mudaliar** *dial/lyr*[Ta] **M. Karunanidhi** *dial/co-lyr*[Te] **Acharya Athreya** *co-lyr*[Te] Balijepalli Lakshmikanta Kavi, **Sri Sri** *lyr*[H] Vishwamitter Adil *c* P. Ramasami *m* S.V. Venkatraman
lp **P. Kannamba**, T.R. Rajakumari, **Pandharibai**, Girija, **Sivaji Ganesan**, S.A. Natarajan, S.S. Rajendran, K.A. Thangavelu, Sadasivarao

Costume fantasy allegedly set in the 11th C. at the time of the Chola dynasty. The king (Sadasivarao), seduced by Vasantasena (T.R. Rajakumari), abandons his wife (Kannamba) and his son Manohara (Ganesan). Vasantasena wants Manohara arrested and her own son made heir. She has the king and queen imprisoned while she attempts to seize power. Manohara escapes from prison and leads a popular revolt against Vasantasena and her general Ugrasen. The hit film, scripted by Karunanidhi and featuring a major star cast, helped mould Ganesan's early career.

MAYURPANKH

1954 ?' col Hindi
d/s/p **Kishore Sahu** *pc* Sahu Films *lyr* Hasrat Jaipuri *c* Andre Thomas *m* **Shankar-Jaikishen**
lp Kishore Sahu, Sumitra Devi, Odette Ferguson, Jankidass, Reginald Jackson, Seema, Asha Mathur, Helen, Ramesh Gupta, Cuckoo, Moni Chatterjee

A love story addressing racial division and contrasting European and Indian values. Joan Davis (Ferguson) and William Griffith

(Jackson), who loves Joan, arrive in India as tourists. One night, stranded in a dense forest, they meet Ranjit (Sahu), an aristocrat from Jaipur. Ranjit and Joan fall in love to the silent distress of Ranjit's wife Shanti (Sumitra Devi) as well as that of Griffith but, predictably, ethnic loyalties prevail in the end.

MIRZA GHALIB

1954 145' b&w Urdu
d **Sohrab Modi** *pc* **Minerva Movietone** *st* **Sadat Hasan Manto** *sc* J.K. Nanda *dial* **Rajinder Singh Bedi** *lyr* Shakeel Badaiyuni *c* V. Avadhoot *m* Ghulam Mohammed
lp **Suraiya**, Bharat Bhushan, Ulhas, Nigar Sultana, **Durga Khote**, Mukri, Murad, Baij Sharma

Costume period movie about the life of the best-known poet in the Urdu language, Mirza Asadullah Khan Ghalib (1797-1869) who was also for a while the court poet appointed by the last Mughal King Bahadur Shah Zafar. The film, chronicling Ghalib's (Bhushan) rejection and final acceptance by the royal court is mainly a love story between the poet and a courtesan he calls Chaudhvin (Suraiya). The ever-popular Ghalib poetry is sung here by Suraiya, Talat Mahmood and **Mohammed Rafi**.

MUNNA

1954 139' b&w Hindi
d/s/lp **K.A. Abbas** *pc* Naya Sansar *c* Ramchandra *m* **Anil Biswas**
lp Romi, Sulochana Chatterjee, Shammi, Tripti Mitra, Achala Sachdev, David, Manju, Naaz, Jairaj, Om Prakash, Manmohan Krishna, **Johnny Walker**, Rashid Khan, Nana Palsikar, Jagdeep, Madan Puri, Bhudo Advani

After Wadia Movietone's *Naujawan* (1937), this was the 2nd songless film in the Hindi cinema. The absence of songs has remained one of its main claims to realism. It is a sequel of sorts to Abbas's debut film ***Dharti Ke Lal*** (1946), evoked in the opening sequence. Tripti Mitra is the widowed mother of Munna (Romi), a six-year-old boy. Unable to feed her child in the city, the mother eventually commits suicide, leaving Munna in an orphanage. The child escapes and encounters several characters whom he reforms with his innocence: the pickpocket Bhikudada (David), the crooked Seth Laxmidas, a clerk, a magician, a boy who makes a living pasting posters while nursing an ambition to become the prime minister of India, and a couple who want to adopt him. The film intercuts Munna's adventures with the travails of his mother, the two often narrowly missing each other in various city locations before she kills herself. Later **Chetan Anand** reworked the plot with an even younger child in ***Aakhri Khat*** (1966).

Manju in *Munna*

NAGIN

1954 139' col Hindi
d **Nandlal Jaswantlal** *pc* **Filmistan** *st* **Bijon Bhattacharya** *sc* Hamid Butt *dial/lyr* Rajinder Krishen *c* Fali Mistry *m* **Hemanta Mukherjee**
lp **Vyjayanthimala**, Pradeep Kumar, Mubarak, Jeevan, S.L. Puri, I.S. Johar, Ram Avtar, Krishnakumari, Kamal, Sulochana

A primitivist love fantasy and a big hit for Vyjayanthimala. She and Pradeep Kumar play professional snake catchers for different tribal groups. When they fall in love (encouraged by the hero's villainous rival, played by Jeevan) their respective clans go to war. A snake sent to kill the hero bites the heroine instead, but he then rescues her by sucking the poison out of her body. This skeletal plot holds together the dances choreographed by Sachin Shankar, Yogendra Desai and Hiralal and executed by the sinuous Vyjayanthimala. Major hit songs include *Man dole mera tan dole* sung by **Lata Mangeskhar** and introducing Hemanta Mukherjee as a front-line Hindi composer as well as **Kalyanji**'s clavioline which simulates the snake-charmer's flute. The number was adapted from Bijon Bhattacharya's play *Jiyankanya* which is also a distant source for the plot.

NATASHEKHARA

1954 185' b&w Kannada
d C.V. Raju *pc* Jairaj Films *m* **P. Kalingrao**
lp **Kalyana Kumar**, Sandhya, Vidya, H.R. Sastry, Jayashree, Comedian Guggu

Melodrama about Raja (Kumar) who wants to act in plays and films while his conservative father wants him to study. Raja runs away from home and eventually makes it as a star when he saves the actress Nalini. A big hit and the debut of Kannada star Kalyana Kumar who, like the character he plays, apparently also ran away from home to pursue an acting career.

NAUKRI

1954 ?' b&w Hindi
d/p **Bimal Roy** *pc* Bimal Roy Prod. *st* Subodh Basu *sc* Nabendu Ghosh *dial* Paul Mahendra *lyr* **Shailendra** *c* Kamal Bose *m* **Salil Choudhury**
lp **Kishore Kumar**, Sheila Ramani, Kanhaiyalal, Noor, Achala Sachdev, **Tulsi Chakraborty**, Jagdeep, Bikram Kapoor, **Krishnakant**

This Kishore Kumar musical features him as Ratan, an incurable optimist who believes that on his graduation he will get a good job and achieve a rosy future for his poverty-stricken family. The film chronicles his gradual disillusionment turning to cynicism and eventually his coming to political awareness. It had one musical hit, *Chhotasa ghar hoga* (sung by K. Kumar with Usha Mangeshkar).

NEELAKUYIL

aka *The Blue Koel*
1954 182' b&w Malayalam
co-d/lyr **P. Bhaskaran** *co-d* **Ramu Kariat** *p* K.M. Raja, T.K. Pareekutty *pc* Chandrathara Pics *s* Uroob (aka P.C. Kuttikrishnan) *c* **A. Vincent** *m* K. Raghavan
lp Kumari, Prema, Kodangallur Ammini Amma, **Sathyan**, P. Bhaskaran, Master Vipin, Manavalan Joseph, Balakrishna Menon, Kochappan, Balaraman, J.A.R. Anand, Johnson, V. Abdulla, V. Kamalakshi, Thangamani

The Harijan girl Neeli (Kumari) is found dead with her illegitimate child which is adopted by the postman, a high-caste Hindu (Bhaskaran) to the consternation of the village. The child's real father, a high-caste teacher (Sathyan) with a barren wife, eventually acknowledges paternity, thus breaking the caste barrier. Kariat's direction debut is often presented as the first major breakthrough in the Malayalam cinema. The reformist literature of novelist Uroob was extended into a performance idiom, using new-generation actors like Sathyan alongside Vincent's crisp camerawork to manufacture for the first time a culturally valid and economically succesful indigenous melodrama in Kerala. The film was a musical success, representing the best work of singer **Kozhikode Abdul Qadir**. The trend of realist melodrama inaugurated by this film was to continue for over 20 years, in Kariat's own work and, e.g., in Vincent's **M.T. Vasudevan Nair** films.

NIRUPEDALU

1954 163' b&w Telugu
d **T. Prakash Rao** *pc* Gokul Pics *st* **K. Pratyagatma** *dial/lyr* Anisetty *c* **B.S. Ranga** *m* **T.V. Raju**
lp **A. Nageshwara Rao**, **Jamuna**, Ramana Reddy, Chandalavada, Surabhi Balasaraswathi, Sudhakar, **Rajanala Nageshwara Rao**

This reworking of the ***Ezhai Padum Padu*** (1950) story also had censorship trouble. Apparently the censors, apprehensive of leftist propaganda in a post-Telangana milieu, objected to, among other things, a 'Keep Left' traffic sign.

OON PAOOS

1954 127' b&w Marathi
d **Raja Paranjpe** *pc* Navachitra *s/lyr* **G.D. Madgulkar** *c* Bal Bapat *m* **Sudhir Phadke**
lp Raja Paranjpe, Sumati Gupte, Ranjana, Shanta Modak, Vasant Thengdi, Rajan, Baby Kala, Jayanti, Sanjeev, **Gajanan Jagirdar**, Dhumal, Vasudev Palande, Prabhakar Salvi, Anand Hardikar

Whimsical comedy about Bapu Master (Paranjpe), an old schoolteacher, and his wife Kashibai (Gupte). After the graduation of their two sons and the marriage of their daughter, the much-loved teacher and his wife retire. However, fate intervenes: their house is auctioned and the couple are forced to seek shelter with their children, which forces the aged couple to separate. Eventually a grateful student rather than one of their children helps out and offers them shelter together. With ***Pedgaonche Shahane*** (1952) this is Paranjpe's best-known performance as actor-director and is sometimes seen as a predecessor to **Panthulu**'s ***School Master*** (1958).

PEDDA MANUSHULU

1954 191' b&w Telugu
d **K.V. Reddy** *pc* **Vauhini** *st* Ibsen's *Pillars of Society* *sc* **D.V. Narasaraju** *lyr* **Kosaraju**, Veetukari, N. Raghavaiah *c* B.N. Konda Reddy *m* Ogirala Ramchandra Rao, Addepalli Ramarao
lp Gowrinatha Sastry, Lingamurthy, **Relangi Venkatramaiah**, **Sriranjini Jr.**, Vangara, Sheshamamba, Swarajyalakshmi, Ramchandra Kashyap

With this Ibsen adaptation by the Telugu playwright Narasaraju in his screen debut, the fantasist K.V. Reddy (***Patala Bhairavi***, 1951; ***Maya Bazaar***, 1957) shifted to the realist melodrama which dominated Telugu cinema in the 50s. The central characters are chairman Dharma Rao (Sastry) and a widow who has an affair with a chauffeur (the film's most popular scenes). Other characters include Tikka Shankaraiah (Venkatramaiah) and a newspaper editor (Lingamurthy). The film reintroduced some popular Telugu folk songs, e.g. *Nandamaya guruda nandamaya*.

PEHLI TAREEKH

1954 ?' b&w Hindi
d **Raja Nene** *pc* Kamal Chitra *st/co-sc* Dada Mirasi *co-sc/dial/lyr* Qamar Jalalabadi *co-sc* Madhusudan Kalelkar, G.R. Kamat *c* Bal Bapat, M.N. Kulkarni *m* **Sudhir Phadke**
lp **Nirupa Roy**, Raja Nene, Agha, Yashodhara Katju, Sudha, Ramesh Kapoor, Vasantrao Pahelwan, Javdekar

A realist inversion of Capra's *It's A Wonderful Life* (1947), this is an unusual story about the poor Shamlal (Nene) who, faced with starvation, commits suicide. His soul is not admitted into heaven and he is condemned to return to earth as a disembodied spirit. He has to watch his family face starvation and imprisonment and, in the film's climax, is unable to prevent his wife and daughter from committing suicide as well. The film helped establish Nirupa Roy's realist image. It was made by an ex-**Prabhat** director and actor (***Daha Wajta/Das Baje***, 1942) and contains **Kishore Kumar**'s classic number *Din ho suhana aaj paheli tareekh hai*. It was remade in Kannada and Tamil (***Modalatedi/Mudhal Thedi***, 1955) by **P. Neelakantan**.

SNEHASEEMA

aka *Love's Limits*
1954 165' b&w Malayalam
d S.S Rajan *pc* Associated Prod. *s* **Poonkunnam Varkey** *c* H.S. Venu *lyr* Abhayadev *m* **V. Dakshinamurthy**, A. Ramarao
lp **Padmini**, **Sathyan**, **Kottarakkara Sridharan Nair**, **P.J. Cherian**, G.K. Pillai, Ramankutty, **Muthukulam Raghavan Pillai**, S.P. Pillai

Johnny (Sathyan), raised by a priest, marries Omana (Padmini) against her father's wishes. To escape unpleasantness, he quits his teaching job and joins the army and is reported killed at the front. Omana is forced by her father to marry Baby (Nair), a doctor. When Johnny returns and finds her remarried he commits suicide, and she follows suit. Writer Varkey, noted in his writings for his attacks on the Church and the orthodoxy it represents in Kerala, loosely adapted Tennyson's *Enoch Arden* for this love tragedy set amid the Christian community in Kerala. Made at the **Vauhini** Studios and at Star Combines, the film developed a reputation and enduring appeal mainly for its claim to secular credentials.

TAXI DRIVER

1954 138'(133') b&w Hindi
d/sc **Chetan Anand** *pc* **Navketan** *co-st* Uma Anand *co-st/dial* **Vijay Anand** *lyr* **Sahir Ludhianvi** *c* V. Ratra *m* **S.D. Burman**
lp **Dev Anand**, Kalpana Kartik, Sheila Ramani, **Johnny Walker**, Ratan Gaurang, Rashid Khan, M.A. Lateef, Bhagwan Sinha, Krishen Dhawan, Parveen Paul, Hamid Sayani, Vernon Corke

Dev Anand's best-known 'proletarian' performance as a taxi driver in a story inspired by *film noir*. Mangal, alias Hero (Anand), rescues Mala (Kartik) from some hoodlums. This act of chivalry leads to a series of encounters with a violent criminal gang who, later in the film, steal Mangal's cab to commit a bank robbery. Mala, who has ambitions of becoming a singer in the movies, finds shelter in Mangal's room, which also forces her, in the most dramatic part of the film involving a mysterious sister-in-law who appears and equally suddenly exits from the story, to cut her hair and to masquerade as a man. Mangal teaches her the foul-mouthed habits of the city's proletariat, their swaggering gait and their way of lighting a cigarette. Much of the film's action takes place in a nightclub where an Anglo-Indian cabaret dancer, Sylvie (Ramani), works and who is in love with Mangal. The film climaxes with a shoot-out in the club between the gang, aided by a bunch of film-industry types, and Mangal's friends. The film's explicit invocation of Hollywood is particularly well realised in the character of the flaxen-haired Anglo-Indian drummer in Sylvia's band, Tony (Corke). He also washes cabs, helps to save Mangal's life and, in a remarkable shot, lies resplendent on the roof of Mangal's taxi in the background during a drunken chat between Mangal and his comic sidekick (Walker). Most of the songs were Ramani's cabaret numbers with a few additions: the upbeat 'socialist-realist' taxi drivers' number *Chahe koi khush ho chahe galiyan hazaar de* sung by **Kishore Kumar** and the tragic *Jaye to jaye kahan* sung by Talat Mahmood.

TODU DONGALU

1954 142' b&w Telugu
d **Yoganand** *p* **N.T. Rama Rao** *pc* National Art Theatres *s/lyr* Samudrala Ramanujam *c* M.A. Rehman *m* **T.V. Raju**
lp N.T. Rama Rao, **Gummadi Venkateshwara Rao**, T.G. Kamaladevi, Hemalatha, Gudipati Venkatachalam (aka Chalam), Rita, A. Pundarikakshayya, Sivaramakrishnayya

Realist drama which helped define the image of Telugu megastar and politician NTR. He plays Paramesam, the corrupt manager of the Annapurna Rice Mills, in league with the owner Lokanatham (Gummadi). As a result of the brutal working conditions, the starving and unpaid worker Ramudu dies. The nasty duo get rid of Ramudu's body and claim he committed suicide. However, Paramesam feels guilty and, when another worker helps him when he is ill, joins the workers demanding that the factory pay compensation to Ramudu's family. Eventually Paramesam becomes the owner of the mill and the workers share in its prosperity. NTR's first production flopped but is sometimes presented as a predecessor of the realist 70s New Indian Cinema in Telugu.

VIDUTHALAI

1954 170' b&w Tamil
d **K. Ramnoth** *pc* New Era Prod *dial/co-lyr* Velavan *co-lyr* Kothamangalam Subbu, Arumagam *m* Lakshman Raghunath
lp **Chittor V. Nagaiah**, Manohar, Peer Mohammed, Ganapati Bhatt, Krishnakumari, Vimala

Nagaiah's last major film repeats his role in ***Ezhai Padum Padu*** (1950) for the same director. He plays a crooked lawyer, Periaswamy, who tries to get his brother Chellaiah (Manohar) off a murder charge by framing the poor Murugan (Mohammed), the driver of a horse carriage. Chellaiah, overcome with guilt, donates money he wins in a lottery to Murugan and confesses to his crime in a letter before committing suicide. Periaswamy tries to suppress the letter but he ends up in jail. In this melodrama Nagaiah tried to redefine his screen image but his career went into a long decline. The film included musical hits such as Nagaiah's *Iraivane*.

VIPRANARAYANA

1954 183' b&w Telugu
d **P.S. Ramakrishna Rao** *pc* Bharani Pics *s/lyr* **Samudrala Raghavacharya** *c* M.A. Rehman *m* **Saluri Rajeshwara Rao**
lp **P. Bhanumathi**, **A. Nageshwara Rao**, **Relangi Venkatramaiah**, Allu Ramalingaiah, Vimala, Rushyendramani, Sandhya, K.V. Subba Rao

Bhanumathi's only major Telugu hit of the period continues the Bharani Studios' love stories with her and Nageshwara Rao. A Brahmin maker of flower garlands (Nageshwara Rao) devotes his life to the god Ranganatha but he is seduced by a woman (Bhanumathi) determined to make him break his vow. The musical hit sees the Vijaya composer Rajeshwara Rao making his debut at Bharani replacing their usual composer **Subburaman**. One of the hits, *Ooh tapovana*, recalls the classic *Ooh pavuram* number from ***Swargaseema*** (1945) and was apparently composed, uncredited, by Rajanikanta Rao. A.M. Raja's playback singing for the hero contributes to the film's success, notably his duets with Bhanumathi including the adaptation of 12th C. poet Jayadeva's composition *Savirahe tava deena*.

WARIS

1954 ?' b&w Hindi
d/c **Nitin Bose** *pc* **Minerva Movietone** *st* Hakim Ahmed Shuja *sc* Arjun Dev Rashk *lyr* Qamar Jalalabadi, **Majrooh Sultanpuri** *m* **Anil Biswas**
lp **Suraiya**, Nadira, Talat Mahmood, Jagdish Sethi, Yakub, Sadat Ali, Achala Sachdev

An inheritance melodrama about Kunwar (Mahmood), the son of zamindar Rana Himmat Singh (Sethi). Kunwar marries Shobha (Suraiya) and is disinherited, forcing him to join the army during WW2. When he is reported lost and presumed dead, a repentant Rana invites Shobha to stay with him. However, it is Kanta (Nadira), a young woman betrayed by Rana's villainous secretary Kailash (Yakub), who arrives at the house and is mistaken for Shobha. Masquerading as Shobha, who lives nearby in absolute poverty, Kanta moves in, causing a moral dilemma and generating suspense since she could be caught out any moment. Starring singing stars Talat Mahmood and Suraiya, the film includes several solos by each of them as well as some duets: *Rahi matwale*, *Ghar tera apna ghar laage*.

ALIBABAVUM NARPATHU THIRUDARGALUM

aka *Alibaba and the Forty Thieves*
1955 155' col Tamil
d **T.R. Sundaram** *pc* **Modern Theatres** *dial* Murasoli Maran *lyr* **A. Marudakasi** *m* S. Dakshimanurthy
lp **M.G. Ramachandran**, **P. Bhanumathi**, K. Sarangapani, P.S. Veerappa, K.A. Thangavelu, M.G. Chakrapani, M.N. Rajam, P. Sushila, **Waheeda Rehman**, Vidyavati

The 2nd major adaptation of the popular orientalist fantasy (the 1941 version starred **N.S. Krishnan**) and one of Modern Theatres' best-known films, featuring MGR and his elder brother M.G. Chakrapani. When the soldier Sher Khan abducts the dancer Marjina (Bhanumathi) to Amir Kasim's palace, Alibaba (MGR) rescues her. The woodcutter Alibaba, who is Amir Kasim's brother, has been disinherited but is quickly reinstated after discovering the magical cave full of jewels. When Amir Kasim goes after the jewels, he is apprehended and killed by Abu Hussain (Veerappa), chief of the thieves. Alibaba and Marjina eventually get the thieves and the gold. The first South Indian full-colour feature is remembered mainly for MGR's swashbuckling stunts (it is one of the star's most characteristic 50s genre films), the elaborate group dances and Bhanumathi's very popular song-and-dance routines (e.g. *Unnai vidamatten*). Although the tale and costumes are pseudo-Arabic, Alibaba's wife incongruously refers to Yama, the Hindu god of death. Irises and wipes in the film add to its sense of anachronism. This is probably the Hindi star Waheeda Rehman's screen debut as a dancer.

ARDHANGI/PENNIN PERUMAI

1955 186' b&w Telugu/Tamil
d **P. Pullaiah** *pc* Ragini Films *s* Manilal Gangopadhyay's Bengali novel *Swayamsiddha* *s/lyr/c* **Acharya Athreya** *m* **B. Narasimha Rao**
lp **A. Nageshwara Rao**[Te]/**Gemini Ganesh**[Ta], **K. Jaggaiah**[Te], **Sivaji Ganesan**[Ta], **Savitri**, Surabhi Balasaraswathi, Shantakumari, **S.V. Ranga Rao, Gummadi Venkateshwara Rao, Chittor V. Nagaiah**

A hit Telugu and Tamil ruralist melodrama (the Tamil is technically a remake). The heroine (Savitri, in the film that established her reputation as an actress) is forced to marry a mentally retarded man (Nageshwara Rao/Ganesh) whom she eventually nurses back to health while teaching a lesson to her scheming mother-in-law (Shantakumari) and brother-in-law (Jaggaiah/Ganesan).

AZAD

1955 163' b&w Hindi
d S.M. Sreeramulu Naidu *pc* Pakshiraja Studios *st* Namakkal *dial/lyr* Rajendra Krishen *c* Sailen Bose *m* **C. Ramchandra**
lp **Dilip Kumar**, **Meena Kumari**, Shammi, Achala Sachdev, Pran, Om Prakash, Raj Mehra, Badri Prasad, Randhir, S. Nazir, Murad

Hindi remake of Pakshiraja Studio's major **M.G. Ramachandran** hit, ***Malaikallan*** (1954). D. Kumar takes on the twin roles of Khan Saheb who is an urbane businessman by day but becomes the urban vigilante Azad by night. (It is instructive to note that at this time not even US comics had the temerity to cast businessmen as vigilante superheroes). Heroine Shobha (Kumari) is kidnapped by villains Sunder (Pran), Jagirdar (Murad) and Chunder (Nazir). Azad rescues her and she falls in love with him. Various efforts by the baddies to kidnap her again are foiled by Azad, as are other crimes, while Khan Saheb gives the cops (Prakash and Mehra) the runaround before explaining everything to them. Rather than serving MGR's particular political agenda, the Hindi version portrays capitalist entrepreneurs as the guardians of society. Remembered mainly for Dilip Kumar's change of image and for Ramchandra's songs (including *Kitna haseen hai mausam*, sung by the composer with **Lata Mangeshkar**, *Radha na bole re* and *Aplam chaplam*). The film also relies on the staccato editing prevalent in 50s Madras cinema.

BANDISH

1955 129' b&w Hindi
d **Satyen Bose** *pc* Basu Chitra Mandir *s* Jyotirmoy Roy's novel *Chheley Kar?* *lyr* Jan Nissar Akhtar *c* Madan Sinha *m* **Hemanta Mukherjee**
lp **Ashok Kumar**, **Meena Kumari**, Daisy Irani, Roop Kumar, **Bhanu Bannerjee**, Bipin Gupta, Pratima Devi, Nasir Hussain,

Sajjan, Shammi, Indira Bansal, Mehmood, Narmada Shankar

S. Bose's directorial debut in Hindi is a sentimental comedy about an orphan called Tomato (Irani). Looking for a more congenial guardian in a park, Tomato selects Kamal (A. Kumar) and turns him into her father. Kamal is a blackmail victim and is burdened by many other problems but he and his girlfriend Usha (Kumari) find themselves having to look after the child. In the end, the child helps resolve all the problems. The precocious performance by Daisy Irani, Hindi cinema's best-known child actress, was the film's main highlight.

CARNIVAL QUEEN

1955 ?' b&w Hindi
d Noshir Engineer *pc* Jewel Pics *s* Adi Marzban *dial/lyr* Pritam Dehlvi *c* Aga Hasham, Jehangir Mistry *m* Shafi M. Nagri
lp **Fearless Nadia**, John Cawas, Shanti Madhok, Habib, Sheikh, Prakash, M.S. Khan, Shafi, Aftab, Pritam Dehlvi, Aga Mehraj

This late Nadia-Cawas stunt movie sees her as Asha, a champion with the six-shooter displaying her marksmanship in her father's Great Jewel Carnival. To boost income and to pay off the Carnival's debt to the villain Prasad, she hires the motor-bike stunt rider Ashok (Cawas). Prasad tries sabotaging the bike and various other villainies but Asha eventually catches him after a long chase sequence. Scripted by noted Parsee Theatre director Adi Marzban.

DEVDAS

1955 159' b&w Hindi
d/p **Bimal Roy** *pc* Bimal Roy Prod. *st* Saratchandra Chatterjee's novel *sc* Nabendu Ghosh *dial* **Rajinder Singh Bedi** *lyr* **Sahir Ludhianvi** *c* Kamal Bose *m* **S.D. Burman**
lp **Dilip Kumar**, **Suchitra Sen**, **Vyjayanthimala**, **Motilal**, Kanhaiyalal, Nasir Hussain

This remake of **Barua**'s ***Devdas*** which Roy had shot in 1935 is dedicated to Barua and to **K.L. Saigal**. Roy's version is presented as a formal/technical modernisation of the famous legend, allowing for an extensive use of deep focus and the naturalist underacting of both Dilip Kumar and Motilal, the latter in the role of the corrupting sidekick, Chunni Babu. Paro is played by the Bengali star S. Sen, and Vyjayanthimala is the prostitute Chandramukhi, each bringing with them the connotations accumulated in their respective generic star images. The new approach provides a more resonant historical background to a story usually focused almost exclusively on Devdas's psychological obsessions. In the famous train sequences when Devdas runs away from himself, eventually to die at Paro's doorstep, Roy's version conveys the sense of a savagely tragic journey through an Indian nation determined to rule out the possibility of the hero finding happiness.

DONGA RAMUDU

1955 197' b&w Telugu
d/co-st **K.V. Reddy** *p* A. Nageshwara Rao *pc* Annapurna Pics *co-st* D. Madhusudhana Rao *co-st/dial* **D.V. Narasaraju** *lyr* **Samudrala Raghavacharya** *c* Adi M. Irani *m* **Pendyala Nageshwara Rao**
lp **A. Nageshwara Rao**, **Savitri**, **Jamuna**, **Rajanala Nageshwara Rao**, **S.V. Ranga Rao**, Surabhi Balasaraswathi, **Relangi Venkatramaiah**, **K. Jaggaiah**, Vangara, Suryakantam

The debut production of Nageshwara Rao's company is a melodrama about a good-hearted thief who steals to support his sister. Jailed, and often accused of crimes he did not commit, he is blamed for a murder but eventually succeeds in unmasking the real criminal. One of composer Pendyala's better-known films.

GARAM COAT

1955 80' b&w Hindi
d Amar Kumar *p/s* **Rajinder Singh Bedi** *pc* Cine Co-op *st* N. Gogol's *The Overcoat* *lyr* **Majrooh Sultanpuri** *c* Vaikunth Kunkalekar *m* Amarnath
lp **Balraj Sahni**, **Nirupa Roy**, Vijayalakshmi, Jayant, Rashid Khan, Baij Sharma, Baby Chand

Seminal realist melodrama written, produced and effectively directed by Rajinder Singh Bedi. The postal clerk Giridhari (Sahni) does not have a proper winter coat and cannot afford the tweed jacket displayed in the window of tailor Mirzauddin's shop. During the day, he loses a Rs 100 note, recovers it from an erring customer and loses it again. Desperate and paranoid, he starts imagining that his wife (Roy), who tries to earn extra money doing odd jobs, has become a prostitute. He is about to throw himself under a train when he finds the money in the lining of his old coat. The film relocates Gogol's story in a post-Partition North India in economic crisis, human goodness crumbling in the face of a growing cynicism about state institutions. Depending mainly on Sahni's performance, the film has a notable soundtrack (e.g. the sound of trains merged into the voice of a woman singing). Jayant played the major role of the hero's Pathan friend.

HOUSE NUMBER 44

aka *Ghar Number 44*
1955 ?' b&w Hindi
d M.K. Burman *pc* **Navketan** *s* Vishwamitter Adil *lyr* **Sahir Ludhianvi** *c* V. Ratra *m* **S.D. Burman**
lp **Dev Anand**, Kalpana Kartik, K.N. Singh, Rashid Khan, Anand Pal, Bhagwan Sinha, Kumkum, Sheila Vaz, Zamboora

Continuing in the vein of his ***Taxi Driver*** (1954) image, Anand plays the part of Ashok, a pavement-dweller and pickpocket who falls in with a gang whose hideout is house no. 44. The gang's pretty stooge Nimmo (Kartik) becomes his beloved and, to escape their life of crime, Ashok turns informer. Chased by the gang boss's henchmen and a mysterious figure called Captain, Ashok has to face a kangaroo court at the house but he eventually fights his way to freedom.

INSANIYAT

1955 185' b&w Hindi
d **S.S. Vasan** *pc* **Gemini** *s* Gemini Studio story dept *dial* **Ramanand Sagar**, T. Mukherjee *lyr* Rajendra Krishen *c* P. Ellappa *m* **C. Ramchandra**
lp **Dilip Kumar**, **Dev Anand**, Bina Rai, Vijayalakshmi, Jayant, Jairaj, **Shobhana Samarth**, Badri Prasad, Kumar, Agha, Mohana

A rural adventure drama with Western overtones and the only time the two leading stars of the 50s, D. Kumar and D. Anand, appeared together. Mangal (D. Kumar) is the hero opposing the bandit chief Zangoora (Jayant) and his right-hand man Bhanu (Anand). When Bhanu raids a village, Mangal persuades Bhanu to renounce banditry and Bhanu becomes a leader of the villagers. Zangoora captures Bhanu and, in trying to rescue him and his child, Mangal is killed.

MISSAMMA/MISSIAMMA

1955 181'[Te]/179'[Ta] b&w Telugu/Tamil
d **L.V. Prasad** *pc* **Vijaya** *s* **Chakrapani** *lyr* **Pingali Nagendra Rao**[Te], **Thanjai Ramaiyadas**[Ta] *c* Marcus Bartley *m* **Saluri Rajeshwara Rao**
lp **Savitri**, **Jamuna**, Rushyendramani, **S.V. Ranga Rao**, Doraswamy, **N.T. Rama Rao**[Te], **A. Nageshwara Rao**[Te], **Relangi Venkatramaiah**[Te], Balkrishna[Te], Ramana Reddy[Te], **Gemini Ganesh**[Ta], K.A. Thangavelu[Ta], K. Sarangapani[Ta], Nambiar[Ta], A. Karunanidhi[Ta], Ezhumalai[Ta]

Hit comedy about a village zamindar (Ranga Rao) who advertises for a married couple to run a school set up in memory of his long-lost daughter. The unemployed Rao (NTR/Ganesh) and Mary (Savitri) pretend to be married to get the job. Annoyed by Rao's interest in the zamindar's other daughter (Jamuna), Mary starts teaching music to an amateur detective and the zamindar's future son-in-law (Nageshwara Rao/Thangavelu). Mary feigns pregnancy while the zamindar tries to convert her to Hinduism. Eventually Mary turns out to be the zamindar's lost daughter and she marries Rao. The film adapts Jyotish Bannerjee's classic Bengali comedy ***Manmoyee Girls' School*** (1935). Prasad remade his own version at the AVM Studio in Hindi as *Miss Mary* (1957) starring **Meena Kumari**. **Anant Mane** also did a Marathi version of the story, *Jhakli Mooth* (1957).

MR AND MRS'55

1955 157' b&w Hindi
d/p **Guru Dutt** *pc* Guru Dutt Films *dial* Abrar Alvi *lyr* **Majrooh Sultanpuri** *c* V.K. Murthy *m* **O.P. Nayyar**
lp Guru Dutt, **Madhubala**, **Lalita Pawar**, **Johnny Walker**, Kumkum, Cuckoo, Agha, Yasmin, Uma Devi, Radhika, Anwari, Harun, Moni Chatterjee, Roop Lakshmi, Bir Sakhuja, Al Nasir

Guru Dutt's 5th film as director is a classic social comedy relying on a familiar plot: the heroine must fulfil the terms of her father's will to inherit his wealth. Dutt uses this plot to satirise the reformism of India's urban upper class. Anita (Madhubala) must marry quickly to inherit her father's estate. Her aunt, the authoritarian champion of women's rights, Seeta Devi (Pawar), plots to find a needy bachelor who will marry Anita for money and divorce her immediately afterwards. A poor but lovable scrounger and cartoonist, Preetam Kumar (Dutt), agrees to the plan but he and Anita then fall in love. Pressured by Seeta Devi, Preetam eventually goes through with the divorce and even furnishes faked photographs compromising himself. When Anita discovers the truth, she and Preetam decide to stay together. Dutt's inventiveness is given free rein, esp. in the song picturisations. As the British critic Geoff Brown pointed out: 'Dutt realises the cinematic advantages of India's playback system. The camera never stands still. The first, in which Preetam tells his friend about meeting the heroine, starts in a bar, proceeds to a bus stop and continues on the bus, from which the couple are eventually thrown off. Another song - an argumentative duet between hero and heroine - is imaginatively performed among women drying and shaking out saris. But the most exhilarating number is the heroine's swimming pool song, performed with a smiling chorus line of girls twirling umbrellas, parading around the pool in deliriously tilted shots.' The film included hits such as *Udhar tum haseen ho*, *Jaane kahan mera jigar gaya ji* (both sung by **Geeta Dutt** and **Mohammed Rafi**) and *Thandi hawa kali ghata* (sung by Geeta Dutt).

MODALATEDI/MUDHAL THEDI

aka *The First Day of the Month*
1955 165'[K]/145'[Ta] b&w Kannada/Tamil
d/s **P. Neelakantan** *pc* Padmini Pics *st* **Raja Nene**'s ***Pehli Tareekh*** (1954) *c* V. Ramamurthy *m* T.G. Lingappa
lp **Sivaji Ganesan**[Ta], **B.R. Panthulu**[K], **M.V. Rajamma**[K], M. Madhava Rao[K], Revathi[K], H.R. Sastry[K], Master Hiranayya[K], **N.S. Krishnan**[Ta], R. Balasubramanyam[Ta], **Anjali Devi**[Ta], T.A. Mathuram[Ta]

Kannada hit and debut production of Panthulu's Padmini Pics. A stoic reply to Capra's sentimental optimism, showing that a petty-bourgeois life is far from wonderful. Shivram (Panthulu)/Sivagnanan (Ganesan) is a lowly teller in a bank that goes bust and, unable to find work, he commits suicide so that his wife and children may get the insurance money. In heaven, at the court of Yama, the lord of death, he is punished for his irresponsibility: he is sent back as a disembodied spirit to witness what happens to the family. His son is imprisoned for stealing food, his daughter is molested and his wife, having murdered the molester, drowns herself in a well. Sivagnanam then wakes up screaming, realises it was all a dream and vows to face life's difficulties with courage. The film's style is conventional with elementary studio sets and painted backdrops, often using irises for shot transitions. The novel introduction of mythological elements into the realist tale is handled with much more aplomb in the South Indian version than in the original Hindi (***Pehli Tareekh***, 1954) which was mostly a **Nirupa Roy** melodrama. Here Brahma, lord of creation, becomes the mouthpiece to state the conditions of an unjust world. In the Tamil version the legendary comedy duo Krishnan (playing a carefree government clerk) and Mathuram assume the *kattiyakaran* role of traditional drama, providing comedy relief while offering social comment. Carnatic musician Dandapani Desingar sang two songs in the Tamil. Ganesan, the lead in the Tamil version appears in a minor role in the Kannada version.

MULU MANEK

1955 137' b&w Gujarati
d/sc **Manhar Raskapur** *pc* Vikram Chitra *st/dial* Gunwantrai Acharya from his play *Allabeli* *lyr* Karsandas Manek *c* Manek Mehta *m* Indukumar
lp **Shanta Apte**, Arvind Pandya, Champsibhai Nagda, Shalini, Champak Lala, Ulhas

This film of Acharya's anti-imperialist play, first staged by the **IPTA**, opens Raskapur's series of tales about valorous Rajput clans resisting the British conquest (cf ***Kadu Makrani***, 1960). Set in Okha, Kathiawar, a region taken by the British and controlled by the Gaekwad royalty, in the period preceding and during the 1857 mutiny. In his fight against the British and the Gaekwad family, the courageous Mulu Manek becomes a bandit. The antagonism is exacerbated when the hero's childhood friend Devba joins the enemy after being rejected by Mulu's sister. This is Marathi and Hindi singing star Apte's only Gujarati film. It was remade by Manibhai Vyas in 1977.

MUNIMJI

1955 163' b&w Hindi
d/co-sc **Subodh Mukherjee** *pc* **Filmistan** *st* Ranjan *co-sc/co-dial* **Nasir Hussain** *co-dial* Qamar Jalalabadi *lyr* **Shailendra, Sahir Ludhianvi** *c* Marshall Braganza *m* **S.D. Burman**
lp **Dev Anand, Nalini Jaywant, Nirupa Roy**, Pran, Amita, S.L. Puri, Prabhu Dayal, Kanu Roy, Samar Chatterjee

Whereas most Western melodramas would represent good and evil as conflicting forces within one character, this movie distributes the moral conflict across two half-brothers, Ratan (Pran) and Amar (Anand). The film then goes on to multiply this splitting device to the point of vertigo, making it a text eminently suitable for psychoanalytic interpretation. The process starts with Ram fathering a second son with his second wife. He then repudiates his first wife Malati (N. Roy), but she switches the two infants so that her son Ratan grows up as the heir while Malati and the second son, Amar, become servants in Ram's household. When the two boys grow up, each begins to lead a double life: Amar is a clerk who wears a disguise to hide his good looks, revealing them only when courting the haughty Roopa (Jaywant); Ratan, who is betrothed to Roopa, is also the notorious bandit and blackmailer Kala Ghoda whose schemes are often foiled by Amar. In the end, when Ratan tries to blackmail his own family, Malati denounces him as her real son. The film included the hit *Jeevan ke safar mein rahi* sung by **Kishore Kumar**.

NEWSPAPER BOY

1955 120' b&w Malayalam
d/sc P. Ramadas *p* N. Subramanyam *pc* Adarsha Kala Mandir *dial* Nagavalli R.S. Kurup *lyr* K.L. Pukundam *c* P.K. Madhavan Nair *m* A. Vijayan, A. Ramachandran *lyr* K.L. Poonkunnam *m* A. Vijayan, A. Ramchandran
lp Master Moni, Narendran, Venkateshwaran, Mohan, Baby Usha, Nagavalli R.S. Kurup, Veeran

A highly acclaimed neo-realist experiment telling of Appu (Moni), the son of an industrial worker and a maid. When the father has an accident, is sacked and later dies of

(From left) Dev Anand, Ameeta and Nalini Jaywant in *Munimji*

tuberculosis, Appu has to leave school and become the breadwinner, looking after his two even younger siblings when his mother dies as well. He works as a domestic servant in a rich household and eventually becomes a newspaper vendor. The film adapted the commercially successful 'realist' Bengali-Hindi tearjerker ***Babla*** (1951), esp. in modelling Master Moni's tragic and incorruptible determination to succeed and vindicate his family's good name in the style of Naren Bhattacharya. The director and production unit had no previous film-making experience.

PATHER PANCHALI

aka *Song of the Little Road* aka *Song of the Road*
1955 122'(115') b&w Bengali
d/sc **Satyajit Ray** *pc* West Bengal Govt *st* Bibhutibhushan Bannerjee's novel (1929) *c* Subrata Mitra *m* Ravi Shankar
lp **Kanu Bannerjee**, Karuna Bannerjee, Chunibala Devi, Uma Dasgupta, Subir Bannerjee, **Tulsi Chakraborty**, Runki Bannerjee, Aparna Devi, Binoy Mukherjee, Haren Bannerjee, Harimohan Nag, Nibhanani Devi, Ksirodh Roy, Ruma Ganguly

Ray's classic, internationally successful debut initiated the Apu trilogy (***Aparajito***, 1956; ***Apur Sansar***, 1959) featuring young Apu (S. Bannerjee) and his impoverished family in the Bengali village of Nischintpur in the early 20th C. The Brahmin priest Harihar Rai (Kanu Bannerjee) goes to the city in search of employment, leaving behind his two children Apu and Durga (Uma Dasgupta), his wife (Karuna Bannerjee) and an ancient aunt, Indira Thakurain (Chunibala Devi). At the end of the film, Durga dies and the family leaves the village, moving to Benares. Ray used this meagre plot to elaborate a strikingly innovative narrative, evoking the classic symbols of a newly independent nation, the aftermath of the war and the shift towards Nehruite industrialism. The major scenes in the film, including the children's romp in the fields where they first encounter a telegraph pole and a train belching clouds of smoke, and the death of the old aunt followed by that of Durga after her rain dance, were spectacularly filmed by the debuting Mitra. The final scene of the family leaving in a cart shows the three faces of father, mother and son, virtually summing up the film's achievement: the father's contorted self-pity evokes a long tradition of the pitiable protagonist in Bengali melodrama, while the mother's expression signals 'fortitude', hiding a tragedy too grim for words. Apu, in sharp contrast, cut off at the neck by the frameline in the lower left-hand corner, stares without expression into the distance, suggesting curiosity as well as apprehension at what the future may bring. Ray claimed the influence of Italian neo-realism in what was, despite the presence of several well-known names from Bengali theatre and film, a revolutionary use of performance, and in his shooting style. Within India, the film signals one of the artistic pinnacles of a specifically modernist art enterprise inaugurated by post-war Nehruite nationalism. In the context of later historical developments and the work of the Subaltern Studies group, the film's deployment of a secular, Enlightenment liberalism institutionalised by Nehru combined with a fantasy of pre-industrial village innocence inaugurated a trend in Indian cinema which has been increasingly critiqued. A 115' version was prepared for circulation outside Bengal.

PIOLI PHUKAN

1955 ?' b&w Assamese
d/s **Phani Sarma** *pc* Rupjyoti Prod., Tezpur *c* Subodh Bannerjee *lyr/m* **Bhupen Hazarika**
lp Phani Sarma, Chandradhar Goswami, Hiren Choudhury, Eva Achaw, Jnanada Kakoti, Rebecca Achaw, Bina Das

Nationalist Assamese film providing a fictional account of a legendary Assamese anti-imperialist figure. Pioli Phukan (Sarma), a somewhat wayward 'prince', is transformed into a radical nationalist eventually hanged by the British. The noose turns into a halo as he accepts his fate.

RAILWAY PLATFORM

1955 162' b&w Hindi
d/s Ramesh Saigal *pc* Saigal Prod. *lyr* **Sahir Ludhianvi** *c* Dronacharya *m* **Madan Mohan**
lp **Nalini Jaywant**, **Sunil Dutt**, Sheila Ramani, **Johnny Walker**, Manmohan Krishna, Leela Mishra, Nisha, Nana Palsikar, Jagdeep

Melodramatic parable in a social-realist idiom. A flood forces a train to stop for 24 hours at a remote railway station in the Andher Nagari (land of darkness) kingdom ruled by an authoritarian king whose daughter Princess Indira (Ramani) is among the passengers. Other passengers include the unemployed Ramu (Dutt), his sister and aged mother; Kavi, a long-haired and cynical poet; a laundryman and his formidable wife; and an avaricious Marwari businessman, Nasibchand. When the food runs out, Nasibchand buys the local grocery shop and starts a black market. A Westernised clique, keeping their distance from the others, starts dancing and drinking while a Brahmin priest charges money to perform mandatory religious rituals. Indira falls in love with Ramu and wants to marry him right away, although the grocer's poor daughter Naina (Jaywant) also loves him. The marriage is interrupted by the arrival of Indira's royal father. Eventually Ramu and Naina get married. The film included the hit *Basti basti parbat parbat* (sung by **Mohammed Rafi**) and several catchy numbers by **Lata Mangeshkar** and **Asha Bhosle**.

Chunibala Devi (left) and Uma Dasgupta in *Pather Panchali*

ROJULU MARAYI/KALAM MARIPOCHU

1955 190'[Te]/211'[Ta] b&w Telugu/Tamil
d/co-st **Tapi Chanakya** *pc* Sarathi Pics *co-st* K.L. Narayana, C.V.R. Prasad *dial/co-lyr*[Te] **Tapi Dharma Rao** *co-lyr*[Te] **Kosaraju** *dial/lyr*[Ta] M. Rajamanikam *c* Kamal Ghosh *m* **Master Venu**
lp **A. Nageshwara Rao**[Te], **Gemini Ganesh**[Ta], **Sowcar Janaki**, Perumalu, Hemalatha, **Relangi Venkatramaiah**, **C.S.R. Anjaneyalu**[Te], T.S. Baliah[Ta], **Waheeda Rehman**

Major Telugu/Tamil hit musical and reformist rural melodrama often cited as the film which redefined the formula for commercial success in 50s Telugu cinema. The peasant hero Venu (Nageshwara Rao/Ganesh) takes on the oppressive might of the zamindar (Anjaneyalu/Baliah) and succeeds, helped by a sympathetic police force, in redistributing the land to the peasants. The hero also marries a low-caste woman (Janaki) rejected by his parents. The film was apparently inspired by the Avadi Congress (1955) where Nehru called for a 'socialist pattern of society in which the principle means of production are under social ownership', a view replicated in the film's dialogues and lyrics. The song *Eruvaka sagaloi*, picturised on Waheeda

Rehman who thus became a star, was a megahit in Telugu and is regarded as signalling the advent of a new generation. According to V.A.K. Ranga Rao, the song's tune had been used by **C.R. Subburaman** in *Shri Lakshmamma Katha* (1950), where the folk-singers Seeta and Ansuya claimed authorship, although it was probably adapted from a 20s HMV recording by their teacher Valluri Jagannatha Rao. When the **M.G. Ramachandran** hit ***Madurai Veeran*** (1956) used a similar tune, the producer was sued for plagiarism. The tune was later used for other South Indian lyrics and by **S.D. Burman** in ***Bambai Ka Babu*** (1960) for **Asha Bhosle**'s rendition of *Dekhne mein bhola hai, dil ka salona*.

SANTHANAM

1955 182' b&w Telugu
d C.V. Ranganatha Das *pc* Sadhana Pics *co-s/lyr* Anisetty, Raviraja Pinisetty *m* S. Dakshinamurthy
lp **A. Nageshwara Rao**, **S.V. Ranga Rao**, Amarnath, Gudipati Venkatachalam (aka Chalam), Ramana Reddy, **Savitri**, **Relangi Venkatramaiah**, **Sriranjini Jr**.

Melodrama about a sister and two brothers who believe themselves to be orphans. They grow up doing odd jobs and the elder brother becomes the manager of a touring theatre group, the younger a wrestler and the sister a maid in a rich household. They eventually trace their father and the family is reunited. **Lata Mangeshkar** sang her first Telugu film song, *Nidura pora thammuda*. **L.V. Prasad** is credited with 'direction supervision'.

SHRI 420

aka *Mr 420*
1955 177' b&w Hindi
d/p **Raj Kapoor** *pc* R.K. Films *st/co-sc* **K.A. Abbas** *co-sc* V.P. Sathe *lyr* **Shailendra**, Hasrat Jaipuri *c* Radhu Karmakar *m* **Shankar-Jaikishen**
lp Raj Kapoor, **Nargis**, Nadira, Nemo, **Lalita Pawar**, M. Kumar, Hari Shivdasani, Nana Palsikar, Bhudo Advani, Iftikhar, Sheila Vaz, Ramesh Sinha, Rashid Khan, Pesi Patel

Having played a tramp in ***Awara*** (1951), Kapoor elaborates his vagabond image further with this sentimental story about Raju (Kapoor), a country boy carrying the archetypal bundle on the end of a stick over his shoulder, who tries to make his fortune in Bombay. The city is presented in terms of Abbas's familiar stereotypical contrast between the corruption of the urban rich and the warm-hearted poor (e.g. Pawar as the fruit-seller). Raju falls in love with Vidya (Nargis), a poor schoolteacher who has a paralysed father. Maya (Nadira) is the *femme fatale* who embroils Raju in a decadent life. Raju is seen gambling, playing the trumpet in a club, surrounded by dancing-girls (the number *Mudmud ke na dekh*), and he becomes a conman in the employ of Maya's friend Seth Dharmanand, a ruthless capitalist. When he is used to swindle the homeless, Raju rebels and a lively chase involving a bag of money provides the bridge to the happy ending. Opening with the Chaplin number *Mera Joota hai japani* (sung by Mukesh), the film includes some of the star's most famous star songs: the carnivalesque *Dil ka haal sune dilwala* (sung by Manna Dey) and the best-known Kapoor-Nargis duet, performed in the rain as they fall in love, *Pyar hua ikraar hua* (sung by Manna Dey and **Lata Mangeshkar**).

UDAN KHATOLA

1955 151' b&w Hindi
d S.U. Sunny *pc* Sunny Art Prod. *s* Azmi Bazidpuri *lyr* Shakeel Badaiyuni *c* Jal Mistry *m/p* **Naushad**
lp **Dilip Kumar**, Nimmi, Jeevan, **T. Suryakumari**, Agha, Nawab, Roopmala, Tuntun

Musical hit adapting Capra's *Lost Horizon* (1937). An aeroplane crashes in the lost island of Shanga. Only Kashi (D. Kumar) is saved by Soni (Nimmi), the daughter of the peshwa, i.e. the minister. The two fall in love causing problems for her fiance Shangu (Jeevan). Kashi needs the queen's (Suryakumari) permission to settle in the village but complications arise when the queen falls in love with him too. The queen manipulates a situation in which Soni is sacrificed (set to the song hit *O door ke musafir*), which is followed by the death of the hero as well. Produced by Naushad for the director's company, it includes some of the composer's famous songs: *Mera salaam le ja* and the two numbers sung by **Lata Mangeshkar**, *Hamare dil se na jana* and *Duba tara ummeedonse chhut gaya*. Dubbed in Tamil and released successfully as *Vanaratham* (1956) with new lyrics by **Kambadasan**.

AMARA DEEPAM

aka *The Eternal Lamp*
1956 162' b&w Tamil
d **T. Prakash Rao** *pc* Venus Pics *s* **C.V. Sridhar** *lyr* K.P. Kamakshi, **A. Marudakasi**, K.S. Gopalakrishnan *c* **A. Vincent** *m* T. Chalapathi Rao
lp **Sivaji Ganesan**, M.N. Nambiar, K.A. Thangavelu, **Savitri**, **Padmini**, **Chittor V. Nagaiah**

While rescuing Aruna (Savitri) from kidnappers, Ashok (Ganesan) is hit by a car and loses his memory. Having joined a group of nomads, the gypsy singer Rupa (Padmini) falls for him and her love eventually helps cure his amnesia. He returns to Aruna and Rupa, who turns out to be Aruna's sister, kidnapped as a child, is shot trying to save him from the villains. Scenarist Sridhar later wrote and directed several triangular love stories. The Carnatic music maestro G.N. Balasubramanyam and G. Ramanathan each contributed one composition. One of the songs refers to the landowner-peasant conflict at Thanjavur and the hero, employed for a while in a factory there, is allowed to express some dissatisfaction with the capitalist ethos. The director remade this Tamil hit into Hindi, *Amar Deep* (1958) with **Dev Anand** and **Vyjayanthimala**, produced by the Tamil version's star Ganesan.

APARAJITO

aka *The Unvanquished*
1956 127'(113') b&w Bengali
d/sc **Satyajit Ray** *pc* Epic Films *st* Bibhutibhushan Bannerjee's novels *Pather Panchali* and *Aparajito* *c* Subrata Mitra *m* Ravi Shankar
lp **Kanu Bannerjee**, Karuna Bannerjee, Pinaki Sen Gupta, Smaran Ghoshal, Santi Gupta, Ramani Sengupta, Ranibala, Sudipta Roy, Ajay Mitra, Charuprakash Ghosh, Subodh Ganguly, Mani Srimani, Hemanta Chatterjee, **Kali Bannerjee**, Kalicharan Roy, Kamala Adhikari, Lalchand Bannerjee, K.S. Pandey, Meenakshi Devi, Anil Mukherjee, Harendrakumar Chakravarty, Bhaganu Palwan

Following on from ***Pather Panchali*** (1955), Apu (Pinaki Sen Gupta/Smaran Ghoshal) comes of age. His father, the Brahmin Harihar Rai (Kanu Bannerjee), dies in the family's new home near Benares and his mother, Sarbajaya (Karuna Bannerjee), is forced to accept the charity of a rich uncle (R. Sengupta) in another village in order to educate her son. Apu's insistence on going to school rather than taking up his family's priestly vocation sows the seeds of further tragedy. His departure for a Calcutta college is followed, inevitably, by the death of his mother. The film is more extensively plotted than its predecessor and more melodramatic, e.g. making Apu's refusal to stay with his mother a personal rather than a historical conflict. His life in Calcutta, studying by day and working in a printing press by night, is juxtaposed with his mother's wasting illness. Ray also uses with greater freedom a directly romantic brand of symbolism, such as the mother festooning the house with lights for the Diwali festival shortly before her husband dies, the latter being accompanied by a shot of rising pigeons at dawn. Ray noted that several problems prevented a full realisation of the script, including a defective Arriflex, the need to rush through the editing and difficulties with composer Ravi Shankar which created 'blank moments, [s]lowing down the film'. However, his contemporary **Ghatak** admired precisely this musical sparseness: 'Sarbajaya and Apu are returning to the village from Benares; the train leaves the village behind; soon through the windows one can see the landscape of Bengal. [J]ust then on the soundtrack you hear that [*Pather Panchali*] theme tune. Just once for the whole length of the film, but once is enough. A [c]orrelative between the past and present floods your mind with memories of Nischintpur and Durga and the white cotton fields' ('Sound In Film', in Ghatak, 1987). With the help of Ray's regular art director Bansi Chandragupta, Mitra pioneered the use of bounce lighting to suggest the ambience of Benares houses on studio sets. The film flopped but was re-evaluated after its critical success in Europe.

AWAAZ

1956 146' b&w Hindi
d/s/co-lyr **Zia Sarhadi** *pc* Mehboob Prod. *lyr* **Shailendra**, Vishwamitter Adil, Prem Dhawan *m* **Salil Choudhury**
lp **Nalini Jaywant**, Usha Kiron, Zul Velani, **Rajendra Kumar**, Nasir Hussain, Anwar Hussain, Sapru
Sarhadi's best-known melodrama drew on Pudovkin and Donskoi-style Soviet realism to tell of an oppressive industrialist (Sapru), his trusted foreman, Bhatnagar (N. Hussain) and

the lives of Bhatnagar's family. The foreman obsessed with his daughter Bela's (Kiron) marriage, pretends to have a large sum set aside to secure her future. When the father of her fiance, Ashok (R. Kumar), claims a large dowry, Bhatnagar is distraught. He loses his job and dies of the shock. His son Kishen (Velani), who resented that money had allegedly been saved for his sister, now discovers that there is no money and, in a drunken moment, accuses his own wife Jamuna (Jaywant) of having stolen the cash. Desperate to raise the dowry, Jamuna does odd jobs and falls into the clutches of the old industrialist who had sacked her father. The man promises to give her the money in exchange for sex. She takes the money and then commits suicide. The film contains many references to Soviet film styles, including the heavy-handed use of low and high angles, e.g. the shots of the overcoat-wearing Banke (A. Hussain), a figure representing the organised proletariat (esp. in the militant workers' song *Araram tararam duniya ke kaise kaise gam*) and the family's self-appointed protector. The only print currently available has been reconstructed from fragments of original prints.

AYODHYAPATI

1956 ?' b&w Hindi
d **S. Fattelal** *pc* Pushpa Pics *s* Pushpa Pics Story Dept *lyr* Saraswati Kumar Deepak *c* P. Isaac *m* Ravi
lp Raaj Kumar, Anant Kumar, Balraj Mehta, Ratnamala, Kanchanmala, Rajan Haksar, Gadadhar Sharma, Dar Kashmiri, Amrit Rana, Heera, Nalini, Bhalerao, Dabboo, Roshan Kumari, Kiran, Asha

Fattelal made this mythological after he left the **Prabhat** Studio. The film shows the decay of a genre in which Fattelal used to excel. The story, featuring early episodes from the *Ramayana*, tells how Kaikeyi saves the life of King Dasharatha in a celestial battle between gods and demons and wins two boons. The rest of the story narrates the early life and adventures of Rama.

CHINTAMANI

1956 158' b&w Telugu
d **P.S. Ramakrishna Rao** *pc* Bharani Pics *s/lyr* Ravoor Venkata Satyanarayana Rao *c* Sridhar *m* **P. Bhanumathi**, Addepalli Rama Rao
lp P. Bhanumathi, **N.T. Rama Rao**, **Jamuna**, **S.V. Ranga Rao**, **Relangi Venkatramaiah**, **Kalyanam Raghuramaiah**, Rushyendramani, Lakshmikantam

Bharani Studios' remake of **Y.V. Rao**'s Tamil mythological, ***Chintamani*** (1937). Chintamani (Bhanumathi), forced into prostitution by her mother, falls in love with the merchant Bilwamangal (NTR). The latter reciprocates her feelings, which leads to much tragedy, revealed in mystical imagery: his wife's corpse and a python help Bilwamangal cross a river to be with his beloved. Chintamani is disillusioned, prompting the gods Krishna and Rukmini to descend to earth to show her the right path. The legend was filmed repeatedly, some versions presenting it as a biography of the saint poet Surdas (**Homi Master**'s silent *Bilwamangal*, 1929; Madan Theatres' *Bilwamangal*, 1932). Most Hindi and Bengali versions tell the story from the male perspective, following Girish Ghosh's famous play *Bilwamangal* (1886), but the South Indian films narrate Chintamani's tale. Although at times accused of plagiarising **C. Ramchandra**'s Hindi compositions from ***Azad*** (1955), Bhanumathi's score is successful (e.g. *Ravoyi ravoyi*, *Punnami chakorinoyi*). Kannada actress **B. Saroja Devi** repeated the title role the following year.

CHORI CHORI

1956 158' b&w Hindi
d Anant Thakur *pc* **AVM** *s* Aga Jani Kashmiri *lyr* Hasrat Jaipuri, **Shailendra** *c* V.N. Reddy *m* **Shankar-Jaikishen**
lp **Nargis**, **Raj Kapoor**, Gope, **Master Bhagwan**, **Johnny Walker**, David, Mukri, Raj Mehra, Pran, Indira Bansal, Amir Banoo, Rajasulochana, Kumari Kamala, Sayee, Subbulakshmi

A lively comedy derived from Capra's *It Happened One Night* (1934). A millionaire's daughter affectionately nicknamed Baby (Nargis) wants to marry a man her father knows to be a gold-digger. Annoyed by her father, she runs away and meets the impoverished journalist Suman (Kapoor). Together they journey through South India and they fall in love. This is the last of the romantic duos between Nargis and Kapoor. Nargis only appeared once more in his films: ***Jagte Raho*** (1956) as a final tribute to her collaboration with RK Films.

CID

1956 146' b&w Hindi
d **Raj Khosla** *pc* **Guru Dutt** Films *s* **Inder Raj Anand** *lyr* **Majrooh Sultanpuri** *c* V.K. Murthy *m* **O.P. Nayyar**
lp **Dev Anand**, Shakila, **Waheeda Rehman**, **Johnny Walker**, Kumkum, K.N. Singh, Bir Sakhuja, Jagdish, Prabhuji, Uma Devi, Rajesh Sharma, Paul Sharma

Khosla's first successful film, made in the crime movie tradition of **Navketan** inflected by Guru Dutt's influence. Police Inspector Shekhar (Anand) investigates the death of a newspaper editor when he meets Rekha (Shakila), the daughter of the commissioner (K.N. Singh). Shekhar keeps running into a mysterious woman (Rehman) who, in a cloak-and-dagger encounter, tries to bribe him to release a crook. He meets her again at Rekha's birthday party. The crook she wants released is mysteriously killed in jail and Shekhar is blamed for police torture. He goes into hiding, pursued by the murderer he was investigating as well as by the police. He eventually solves the case in hospital. The film is dominated by Rehman's luminous presence in her first Hindi role, the camera enhancing her mystery with soft-focus over-the-shoulder shots. Her sensuality is particularly well rendered in the scenes where she tries to seduce the crime boss (with the song *Kahin pe nigahen*) in order to facilitate the hero's escape.

ERA BATOR SUR

1956 ?' b&w Assamese
d/s/lyr/m **Bhupen Hazarika**
lp **Phani Sarma**, Bishnu Rabha, Bijoy Shankar, Tasadduf Yusuf, Anil Das, Preetidhara, **Chhaya Devi**, Eva Achaw, Rebecca Achaw, **Balraj Sahni**

Hazarika's debut as director tells of a researcher into folk art and music who meets a young flautist in an Assamese tea garden. They fall in love with the same woman, but the researcher withdraws, saying that he is expendable whereas the 'young man's flute must not be silenced'. Most of the film features the cultural traditions of the labourers in Assam's famous tea gardens and their celebrated folk music.

HATIMTAI

1956 ?' col Hindi
d **Homi Wadia** *pc* Basant Pics *s* **J.B.H. Wadia**, Hakim Lala *lyr* Raja Mehdi, Akhtar Roomani, B.D. Mishra, Chand Pandit *c* Anant Wadadekar *m* S.N. Tripathi
lp Jairaj, Shakila, B.M. Vyas, Naina, Meenakshi, Krishna Kumari, Sheikh, S.N. Tripathi

An *Arabian Nights* tale first filmed by Prafulla Ghosh as a silent 4-part serial in 1929. It tells, in Gevacolor, the story of Hatim who travels in the poverty-stricken Muflisganj, giving clothes and alms to the needy. He meets the Munir Shami, the impoverished prince of Kharzaman. The prince tells Hatim his story: the prince was to marry the daughter of Shah Saudagar Barzukh, but when the shah had cast his 'evil eye' on the fairy Gulnar the fairy turned to stone, promising that the shah's own daughter will also turn to stone on the day of her marriage unless someone solves the Seven Riddles that will free both Gulnar and the princess. Hatim, after many adventures in enchanted woods meeting fairies and giants, solves riddles like 'What I experience once I want to experience again' or 'Do good deeds and throw them in the water'.

JAGTE RAHO/EK DIN RAATRE

aka *Stay Awake* aka *Under Cover of Night* aka *A Night in the City*
1956 149'[H]/153'[B] b&w Hindi/Bengali
d/s **Sombhu Mitra**, Amit Moitra *p* **Raj Kapoor** *pc* R.K. Films *dial* **K.A. Abbas**[H] *lyr* **Shailendra**, Prem Dhawan[H] *c* Radhu Karmakar *m* **Salil Choudhury**
lp Raj Kapoor, Pradeep Kumar, Sumitra Devi, Smriti Biswas, **Pahadi Sanyal**, Nemo, Iftikhar, Sulochana Chatterjee, Daisy Irani, Nana Palsikar, **Motilal**, Moni Chatterjee, Bikram Kapoor, Bhupendra Kapoor, Bhudo Advani, **Krishnakant**, Pran, Ratan Gaurang, Rashid Khan, **Chhabi Biswas**[B], **Nargis**

Two major figures from the Bengali **IPTA**, actor-director Sombhu Mitra and composer Salil Choudhury, collaborated with Raj Kapoor on this expressionist effort that became successful only after a 115' version of the film received the main prize at the Karlovy Vary festival in 1957. Kapoor plays a 'thirsty peasant' wandering through Calcutta looking for a drink of water. He breaks into an apartment block but is discovered and has to dodge the residents, an ingenious narrative device to move the hero from one flat and one milieu to another, allowing for a comic yet critical survey of middle-class Bengali life.

Raj Kapoor in *Jagte Raho*

The film ends with the hero's searing denunciation of a class that places no value on honesty and a fantasy sequence in which Nargis finally offers him water to the tune of a song heralding the dawn, *Jago ujiyara chhaye*. The British critic Geoff Brown noted: 'Kapoor's character is cut from Chaplin's cloth. He starts out sharing food with a dog, squatting on the pavement, and spends most of the film acting in pantomime, darting in and out of rooms, hiding in a drum, shinnying down a drainpipe, periodically pursued by a lively crowd of residents wielding anything from sticks to stringless tennis racquets. The result is one of Kapoor's most diverting films.'

KABULIWALA

1956 116' b&w Bengali
d/sc **Tapan Sinha** *pc* Charuchitra *st* **Rabindranath Tagore** *c* Subodh Ray *m* Ravi Shankar
lp **Chhabi Biswas**, Tinku Thakur, Radhamohan Bhattacharya, Manju Dey

Sinha's version of the Tagore short story (pub. 1918) about an Afghan tribesman, Rehmat (Biswas), who sells spices in Calcutta and befriends a little girl (Thakur in an uninhibited performance) who reminds him of the daughter he left behind. Having killed a man who tried to cheat him, the Kabuliwala is jailed for many years and on his release he finds that the little girl has grown up, prompting the realisation that his own daughter has probably forgotten him. The story was remade in Hindi by **Hemen Gupta** (1961) starring **Balraj Sahni** in a **Bimal Roy** production.

MADURAI VEERAN

aka *The Soldier of Madurai*
1956 165' b&w Tamil
d **Yoganand** *pc* Krishna Pics *s/co-lyr* **Kannadasan** *co-lyr* **Udumalai Narayana Kavi, Thanjai Ramaiyadas** *c* M.A. Rehman *m* S. Dakshinamurthy
lp **M.G. Ramachandran, N.S. Krishnan, P. Bhanumathi, Padmini**, E.V. Saroja, T.A. Mathuram

A megahit version of the legend of Madurai Veeran (played by actor-politician MGR), a popular Tamil Nadu village deity and the subject of numerous ballads and plays, previously filmed in 1938. Set in the 16th C. royal court of the Poligars, the legend offers a variant of the Oedipus myth. Veeran (MGR) is the king's son, abandoned in a forest because of a bad omen, but protected by a snake and an elephant. He is found and raised by a cobbler. He rescues and falls in love with Princess Bommi (Bhanumathi) who is also his father's mistress. When she is about to be forced into a marriage, Veeran kidnaps her. However, Veeran also falls in love with the courtesan Velaiammal (Padmini). He is sentenced to death and killed just before the king realises that the outlaw was his own son. Veeran and his lover ascend to heaven and attain godhood. Scripted by the noted DMK rationalist poet Kannadasan, the film is an early example of the political appropriation of Tamil folk ballads praising heroes like Chinnadan, Chinnathambi, Jambulingam, etc. Most of these heroes, according to Vanamamalai (1981, quoted in Pandian, 1992) are 'low-caste men who protect crops, protect the cattle, protect the rights of lower-caste women, challenge sexual norms, challenge the privilege of the higher-caste groups and demand equal rights for the lower-caste men with talent and skill'. The script sanitises its anti-caste thrust by showing that the apparently lower-caste hero is in fact a prince by birth, allowing MGR to be an underdog, a tragic lover, a nobleman and a god all at once. Neither the costumes nor the props (including a guillotine) bear much relation to the historical period. The film is also remembered for its cinematic obituary to the noted politician and comedian N.S. Krishnan who died during shooting: his death is commemorated with a song in front of his statue.

MALELA JIV

1956 141' b&w Gujarati
d/sc **Manhar Raskapur** *pc* Sadhana Chitra *st/dial/co-lyr* Pannalal Patel *c* Bipin Gajjar, Manek Mehta *co-lyr/m* **Avinash Vyas**
lp Dina Gandhi, Mahesh, Champsibhai Nagda, Vishnukumar Vyas, Babu Raje, Pratap Ojha, Chandrika Thakore, Champak Lala, Tarla Mehta, Leela Jariwala, Vijay Bhatt, Kamlesh Thakar, Manjula, Shobha Joshi, Narmadashankar, Naran Rajgor, **Chandrakant Sangani**, Baby Purnima

Love story scripted by the prominent Gujarati novelist Patel. The hero Kanji, separated from his lower-caste girlfriend Jivi, tries to persuade her into a pro-forma wedding which, he hopes, will allow the couple to continue their relationship. Things take a tragic turn as Kanji is forced to leave the village and Jivi commits suicide. The earthy realism of Patel's descriptions and language is substantially retained.

NEW DELHI

1956 176' b&w Hindi
d **Mohan Segal** *pc* Deluxe Films *s* **Inder Raj Anand**, Radhakishen *lyr* **Shailendra**, Hasrat Jaipuri *c* K.H. Kapadia *m* **Shankar-Jaikishen**
lp **Vyjayanthimala, Kishore Kumar**, Jabeen, Radhakishen, Nasir Hussain, Dhoomal

Segal's remarkable satire, continuing his work with Kishore Kumar, advocates national unity. The North Indian Daulatram Khanna

(N. Hussain) opposes the marriage of his son Anand (K. Kumar) with Janaki (Vyjayanthimala), the daughter of the South Indian Mr Subramanyam. He throws out the Bengali painter Ashok who loves Khanna's other daughter, Nikki (Jabeen). The musical highlight of the deliberate cultural pot-pourri is Kishore Kumar dressed as Fred Astaire with a cane and a top hat singing *Nakhrewali* to an indigenous dance number by Vyjayanthimala. The film included several topical references to contemporary politics.

RANGOON RADHA

1956 192' b&w Tamil
d A. Kasilingam *pc* Mekala Prod *st* **C.N. Annadurai** *dial* **M. Karunanidhi** *m* T.R. Papa
lp **Sivaji Ganesan**, S.S. Rajendran, **P. Bhanumathi**, M.N. Rajam, Rajasulochana

Complicated adventure and murder mystery attacking feudal superstition. A flashback reveals the evil designs of Dharmalinga Mudaliar (Ganesan): though married to Rangam (Bhanumathi), he now wants to marry her sister Thangam (Rajam) as well in order to get their ancestral property. Mudaliar's wife, locked in a room and declared insane, gives birth to a son before she escapes in disguise. She witnesses her husband murdering a tantric conman who promised to reinvigorate Mudaliar's sex drive. In Rangoon, she lives with Naidu and gives birth to a daughter named Radha (Rajasulochana). When the film moves to the present, Nagasundaram (Rajendran), the man who falls in love with the grown-up Radha, is revealed to be the son of Mudaliar, so that Radha is his stepsister. Eventually the two unmask the villain and avenge their mother. Apparently inspired by *Gaslight* (1940), the film offers a rare example of Tamil star Ganesan as a villain.

RARICHAN ENNA PAURAN

aka *Citizen Rarichan*
1956 166' b&w Malayalam
d/lyr **P. Bhaskaran** *p* T.K. Pareekutty *pc* Chandrathara Prod., **Vauhini** *s* Uroob *c* B.J. Reddy *m* K. Raghavan
lp Vilasini, Prema, Miss K.P. Raman Nair, Master Latif, K.P. Ummar, J.A.R. Anand, P. Kunjava, **Ramu Kariat**, Kochappan, Kalamandalam Kalyanikutty Amma, Padmanabhan, Manavalan Joseph

Rarichan (Latif) is an orphan employed by a kindly widow and her daughter in their teashop. When he saves the day by producing the daughter's dowry enabling her to get married, it turns out he stole it and is arrested. Lyricist Bhaskaran's first solo as director in many ways continues the ***Newspaper Boy*** (1955) type of realism, but in more melodramatic form using more songs (including some lilting Mappila folk music from North Malabar). The other film that probably inaugurated this trend of 'heartwarming' realist films featuring children performing adult tasks was ***Boot Polish*** (1954).

SAGARIKA

1956 152' b&w Bengali
d Agragami *pc* S.C. Prod. *s/co-lyr* Nitai Bhattacharya *co-lyr* Pranab Roy, Gouriprasanna Majumdar *c* Bijoy Ghosh *m* Robin Chatterjee
lp **Suchitra Sen, Uttam Kumar**, Jamuna Singha, Namita Sinha, Tapati Ghosh, **Kamal Mitra, Jahar Ganguly, Pahadi Sanyal, Anup Kumar**

Classic Sen/Kumar melodrama evoking, e.g., **Nitin Bose**'s love tragedies with **Dilip Kumar**. Impoverished and orphaned medical student Arun (U. Kumar) falls in love with colleague Sagarika (Sen). Following an act of perfidy by Arun's cousin Sipra, who is also in love with him, Arun loses a scholarship to go to England and has to borrow money on condition that he marry Basanti on his return. The suffering Sagarika has to look after the illiterate Basanti, which means writing Basanti's love-letters to Arun. Arun goes blind after an accident, and on his return Sagarika nurses him back to health, pretending to be Basanti. In the end, the lead couple unite. As in the **Kapoor/Nargis** love stories of the same period, this film is famous for the ecstatic, soft-focus close-ups of the lead pair and esp. of Suchitra Sen, which became classic icons in Bengali popular culture, transcending the characters and suggesting a fantasy of romance in which love can, by its own internal strength, develop an independent destiny. The style, with its poetic, soft-toned b&w images and lyrical scene transitions, evolved further with, e.g., **Ajoy Kar** (cf ***Saptapadi***, 1961), Salil Dutta and **Asit Sen** generating the finest examples of popular film's absorption of the Bengali romantic literary tradition. These films, and others such as ***Saat Pake Bandha*** (1963), are further enhanced by their contrast to the resurgence of traditional values in 80s Bengali cinema, partly through assimilating the 'social' contemporary Jatra, and partly as a means of keeping a distance from the influence of Hindi film.

TAKSAAL

aka *The Mint*
1956 ?' b&w Hindi
d/p/s **Hemen Gupta** *pc* Hemen Gupta Prod. *lyr* Prem Dhawan *c* V.N. Reddy *m* Roshan
lp **Balraj Sahni, Nirupa Roy**, Smriti Biswas, Radhakrishen, Master Jayant

A 'realist' melodrama, independently produced by Gupta in Bombay, bemoaning the power of money. The lawyer Jatin Mukherjee (Sahni) is beset by disasters because of his lack of money: his son dies, his unmarried sister is raped by her employer and commits suicide. These events lead him to believe that only wealth can secure happiness and he proceeds to acquire it through crime.

Tenali Ramakrishna/Tenali Raman
1956 204'[Te]/195'[Ta] b&w Telugu/Tamil/Kannada
d/c **B.S. Ranga** *pc* Vikram Pics *s/lyr* **Samudrala Raghavacharya** *dial* **Kannadasan, Murugadasa** *m* Vishwanathan-Ramamurthy
lp **P. Bhanumathi, Jamuna, N.T. Rama Rao, A. Nageshwara Rao**[Te], **Chittor V. Nagaiah**[Te], Surabhi Balasaraswathi[Te], **Sivaji Ganesan**[Ta], T.S. Dorairaj[Ta], **Rajkumar**[K], **Balkrishna**[K], Sandhya, **K. Mukkamala**

Megabudget trilingual featuring the legendary folk hero and jester in the government of Krishnadeva Raya, king of the Vijayanagara Empire 1509-30. The Bahamani Kingdom, in a protracted war with Vijayanagara, sends the dancer and courtesan Krishnasani (Bhanumathi) to seduce the king (NTR) and to spy on him. The king falls in love with her and only an elaborate ruse by Tenali Ramakrishna (Nageshwara Rao/Ganesan/Rajkumar) and Chief Minister Timmarasu (Nagaiah/Dorairaj/Balkrishna), another legendary figure (and the subject of an independent film biography by **K. Kameshwara Rao** in 1962), in which they disguise themselves as a holy man and his disciple, enables the king to realise the truth. Bhanumathi's musical presence was again the film's star attraction. The story had been filmed by **H.M. Reddy** in 1941.

ADARSHA HINDU HOTEL

1957 141' b&w Bengali
d Ardhendu Sen *pc* Sreelekha Pics *st* Bibhutibhushan Bannerjee's novel (1940) *sc* Jyotirmoy Roy *lyr* Manabendra Mukherjee *m* Ali Akbar Khan
lp **Chhabi Biswas, Dhiraj Bhattacharya, Jahar Ganguly, Tulsi Chakraborty, Jahar Roy, Anup Kumar**, Sandhyarani, **Sabitri Chatterjee**, Sikha Bag, Sova Sen

Based on a novel by Bibhutibhushan Bannerjee, the author of *Pather Panchali* (1929), *Hotel* had already been successfully adapted to the stage for the Rangmahal theatre in Calcutta (1953). The plot revolves around two rival hotels at the Ranaghat railway station. The establishment run by Bechu Chakraborty (Ganguly) is winning because of its excellent cook, Hajari Thakur (Bhattacharya). The maidservant Padma (Sandhyarani), envious of the cook's reputation, steals some utensils from the kitchen and frames the cook, who is arrested. On his release, he starts the Adarsha Hindu Hotel. It becomes popular and he wins the contract to start a restaurant at the railway station itself. In the end, he has the satisfaction of employing his former boss as well as the troublesome Padma, which he does without losing his humility.

AJANTRIK

aka *Pathetic Fallacy* aka *The Unmechanical*
1957 120'(102') b&w Bengali
d/sc **Ritwik Ghatak** *pc* L.B. Films *st* Subodh Ghosh *c* **Dinen Gupta** *m* Ali Akbar Khan
lp **Kali Bannerjee**, Kajal Gupta, Shriman Deepak, Gyanesh Mukherjee, Keshto Mukherjee, Gangapada Basu, Satindra Bannerjee, **Tulsi Chakraborty**, Jhurni, **Anil Chatterjee**, Seeta Mukherjee

Ghatak's 2nd major film explores the romantic trope of the pathetic fallacy (making nature into a metaphor for human emotions), a figure often used in Indian literature and cinema (cf the films of **Shantaram** or **Kidar Sharma**). However,

Ghatak modifies the trope, endowing it with complex historical resonances as tribal culture (here the Oraon culture) and a motor car are put on the side of nature while the 'human emotion' side of the trope is represented by greed in the form of rampant capitalism and industrialisation in the shape of bulldozers and the mining town of Ranchi. The plot revolves around Bimal (K. Bannerjee) and his battered taxi, an old Chevrolet he calls Jagaddal. Because he takes his car to be a living being, many believe Bimal to be mad. In a long sequence, Bimal plies his trade, his world intersecting at various points with that of the Oraon tribals. Industrialisation proceeds relentlessly, sowing discord among the tribals, and Jagaddal breaks down irretrievably. It has to be dismantled and sold for scrap. In the end, a child finds the car horn on the street and plays with it, making it emit the call of the 'Oraon' horn. Many parallel storylines are interwoven into the basic plot, along with extensive sequences and repeated images of both tribal cultures and landscapes. These strands come together in a scene where Bimal first shares in an Oraon feast and then literally burdens his car with objects of nature after which the car breaks down. The other side of the complex trope is represented by imagery evoking the speed of technologically driven change (electric telegraph wires, a train, the village madman's metal basin which is replaced by a gleaming new one at the end). Ghatak commented in 1958: 'The idea of the machine has always had an association of monstrosity for us. It devours all that is good, all that is contemplative and spiritual. It is something that is alien. [T]his apathy may be due to the fact that all change and the very introduction of the machine age was the handiwork of foreign overlords. It may have more comprehensive causes, encompassing all the pangs of Western civilisation. But the end-product of all these causes seems to be an ideological streak which is doing immense harm in all practical spheres of life' ('Some Thoughts on Ajantrik', in Ghatak, 1987). The film itself suggests a more complex position on the question of industrialisation: not that machines are monstrous (Jagaddal is Bimal's love object) but that the forces driving the speed of change disregard and thus destroy the slower, more human tempo at which people adopt and incorporate change into their networks of social relations.

AASHA

1957 171' b&w/col Hindi
d **M.V. Raman** *pc* Raman Studios *s* Jawar Seetaraman *dial/lyr* Rajinder Krishen *c* S. Hardip, Fali Mistry *m* **C. Ramchandra**
lp **Vyjayanthimala, Kishore Kumar**, Pran, Raj Mehra, Minoo Mumtaz, Randhir, Naina, Shivraj, Patanjal, **Lalita Pawar**, Om Prakash

Partly made in colour, this love story and crime drama is a comedy variation of the *Hamlet* theme. The story revolves around an old landowner, Hasmukhlal (Prakash), his son Kishore (K. Kumar) who is accused of murder, and the villain Raj (Pran) who is Kishore's cousin. The love object is Nirmala (Vyjayanthimala), the niece of a millionaire coveted by Raj. Kishore, masquerading as an Arab, launches a theatre company and resolves the conflicts by performing a play in front of the 'real-life' characters to whom the fiction is addressed. Director Raman, star Vyjayanthimala and writer Jawar Seetaraman enlivened a standard **AVM** plot, with Ramchandra's fast-paced music and Kishore Kumar's mainly slapstick acting and relying on his pioneering singing style culminating in the foot-stomping and ever popular number *Ina Mina Dika* (sung in two versions, one by Kishore Kumar and the female version by **Asha Bhosle**).

AMBIKAPATHY

1957 187' b&w Tamil
d **P. Neelakantan** *pc* A.L.S. Prod. *s* **A.P. Nagarajan** *m* G. Ramanathan
lp **P. Bhanumathi, Sivaji Ganesan**, M.K. Radha, M.N. Nambiar, Rajasulochana, **N.S. Krishnan**, T.A. Mathuram, **Chittor V. Nagaiah**

Legendary tale about the 11th C. court poet Kambar, a plot used earlier by **Duncan** (1937). The love story between the lower-caste poet Ambikapathy (Ganesan) and Princess Amaravati (Bhanumathi) is mapped on to a disagreement between Kambar, who is translating the *Ramayana* into Tamil, and his 'modern' disciple, Ambikapathy, who critiques the translation for its acceptance of caste divisions. The spectacular end has the king challenging Ambikapathy to improvise 100 songs in praise of chaste love. The poet miscalculates and his 100th song is a passionate love song addressed to the princess, for which he is sentenced to death.

BANDI

1957 ?' b&w Hindi
d **Satyen Bose** *pc* Shri Pics *dial* Mahendra Pran *lyr* Rajinder Krishen *c* Madan Sinha *m* **Hemanta Mukherjee**
lp **Ashok Kumar**, Bina Rai, **Kishore Kumar**, Anup Kumar, Nanda, Shyama, Kanhaiyalal, Kammo, Mishra, Banerjee, **Krishnakant**

Satyen Bose's melodrama, based on **Sailajananda Mukherjee**'s Bengali film *Bondi* (1942), features the Kumar brothers (Ashok, Kishore and Anup). Madhav (Kishore Kumar) is the innocent and illiterate brother of the educated and married Shankar (Ashok Kumar) who works for an eccentric zamindar, becoming the object of the affections of the zamindar's daughter Mala (Rai). The villain of the piece, Choubeji (Mishra), causes Shankar to be jailed for 15 years. Shankar's wife (Shyama) dies and his younger brother Madhav, now the guardian of Shankar's daughter (Nanda), arranges her marriage to a boy who happens to be the villain's son. When Shankar is released, he marries Mala and sets out to avenge himself on Choubeji, causing violent conflicts in which he nearly kills his own brother. There are several Kishore Kumar solos in this film remembered as one of the comic star's few 'serious' roles. Director Bose immediately went on to cast the three Kumar brothers in the farce ***Chalti Ka Naam Gaadi*** (1958).

BHAGYA REKHA

1957 176' b&w Telugu
d **B.N. Reddi** *pc* Ponnaluri Bros *s* Palagummi Padmaraju *lyr* **Devulapalli Krishna Sastry, Kosaraju**, Adisesha Reddy *c* B.N. Konda Reddy *m* **Pendyala Nageshwara Rao**
lp **N.T. Rama Rao, Jamuna**, D. Hemalatha, Govindrajulu Subbarao, **Sowcar Janaki, Relangi Venkatramaiah**, Lakshmikantam, E.V. Saroja

Reddi's hit film (one of the few films he did not produce himself) tells of the orphan Lakshmi (Jamuna) who is raised by her kindly uncle Nayarana Rao and her evil aunt Jagadamba. Narayana Rao and Jagadamba already have two children: the boy Kotaiah who runs away to join the army and the spoilt daughter Kalyani who wants to marry the manager of a cinema theatre. When Kalyani's fiance falls in love with Lakshmi, Lakshmi leaves and finds a second home when she restores a lost child to its mother. While Lakshmi works as a tutor to a rich girl whose brother Ravi (NTR) falls in love with her, aunt Jagadamba starts spreading malicious rumours, preventing the lovers from marrying and driving Lakshmi away again. Ravi falls ill with frustration but eventually things are set right when the son Kotaiah returns home and discovers the injustice his mother inflicted on the heroine.

CHINTAMANI

1957 187' col Kannada
d/s M.N. Basavarajaiah *pc* Lokeshwari Pics *ph* Kotnis
lp **B. Saroja Devi**, Ashwath, Narasimhraju, Lakshmidevi, **Balkrishna**, M.S.S. Pandit, Master Hirannayya, Sampath, Rajakumari

Kannada remake of the **Bhanumathi** hit (1956), emphasising the melodramatic rather than the mythological aspects of the legend. The prostitute Chintamani (Saroja Devi) entices the saintly Bilwamangal (Ashwath) away from his wife. He is, however, returned to his true purpose in life following a series of calamities including his father's death and wife's suicide. He blinds himself in remorse before reuniting with his lover. The film was also an early experiment in colour in Kannada.

DEKH KABIRA ROYA

1957 141' b&w Hindi
d **Amiya Chakravarty** *pc* Shrirangam *st* Manoranjan Ghosh *sc* Chandrakant *lyr* Rajendra Krishen *c* Ajit Kumar *m* R.L. Suri
lp Anita Guha, Ameeta, Anup Kumar, Daljit, Jawahar Kaul, Shobha Khote, Sundar

A romance masquerading as a debate on art. A painter, a writer and a singer meet three women, each of whom loves one of the art forms they practise. Unfortunately, they are mismatched. The ensuing misunderstandings are resolved only after their respective soul mates have been discovered and their marriages arranged. This is one the the last independent films by A. Chakravarty, formerly of **Bombay Talkies** and the man who discovered **Dilip Kumar** in his first film, ***Jwar Bhata*** (1944).

DILER DAKU

1957 ?' b&w Hindi
d Noshir Engineer *pc* Basant Pics *s* Boman Shroff *co-dial/lyr* Chand Pandit *co-dial* Pritam Dehlvi *c* Anant Wadadekar *m* Shafi M. Nagri
lp **Fearless Nadia**, John Cawas, Samar Roy, Chanda, Boy Prithvi, Julian Gaikwad, Hira Sawant, Sheikh, Kallu Ustad, Rajni, Sardar Mansoor, Boy Sikandar, S. Advani, Vijaya Choudhury, Baby Mangala, Abdulla, Yadav

Remake of the Wadia Bros' 1931 debut feature which launched the stunt genre most closely associated with **Wadia Movietone** and its fearless female star. When the king is overthrown by his commander-in-chief and his minister, Princess Farida (Nadia) is rescued and raised by the old Chacha. Farida becomes an expert swordfighter and horsewoman. With the help of Kamran (Cawas), the minister's good son, she retakes the palace and punishes the villains in hand-to-hand combat.

DO AANKHEN BARAH HAATH

aka *Two Eyes Twelve Hands*
1957 155'(124') b&w Hindi
d **V. Shantaram** *pc* **Rajkamal Kalamandir** *s* **G.D. Madgulkar** *lyr* Bharat Vyas *c* G. Balakrishna *m* **Vasant Desai**
lp V. Shantaram, Sandhya, Uhlas, B.M. Vyas, **Baburao Pendharkar**, Paul Sharma, S.K. Singh, Gajendra, G. Invagle, **Keshavrao Date**, Chandorkar, Thyagaraj, S. Bhosle, Asha Devi, Samar, Suneel

Stylised parable about human virtue. An idealistic cop, Adinath (Shantaram), believing people to be fundamentally good, takes six simple-minded murderers to a desolate area and sets up a farming commune. In spite of the threats of violence, they produce a decent farm and come into conflict with the 'virtuous' citizens in a nearby village who see their economic interests threatened and reveal themselves to be the real nasties. Shantaram's characteristic neo-expressionist imagery is much in evidence, e.g. juxtaposing eyes and palm prints with prison bars, patches of light on parts of the hero's mouth and eyes. In one of the more successful sequences, armed men are depicted in looming shadows against the threatened hero shown in extreme long shot. Sandhya plays Champa, an itinerant seller of children's toys who befriends all the prisoners and the only female in this oppressively male world. About her, Godard reported in a telegram from the Berlin Film Festival (1958): 'Sandhya charming in story Indian jailer.' A 124' version was shown at the San Francisco Festival that same year.

KATHPUTLI

1957 160'(152') b&w Hindi
co-d/s **Amiya Chakravarty** *co-d* **Nitin Bose** *pc* Shrirangam *dial* Chandrakant *lyr* **Shailendra**, Hasrat Jaipuri *c* V. Babasaheb *m* **Shankar-Jaikishen**
lp **Vyjayanthimala**, Kumari Kamala, **Balraj Sahni**, Jawahar Kaul, Agha, Sheila Kashmiri, Poonam

Chakravarty's last film was completed after his death by Bose. It is a melodrama about Pushpa (Vyjayanthimala) who loves and marries a small-time puppeteer (Kaul). She becomes a famous dancer in the theatre of the benevolent Loknath (Sahni) and gets embroiled in the man's tragic life, estranging her from her husband. A Vyjayanthimala vehicle, the film consists of expensively staged dance sequences loosely strung together, including the hit number *Bagad bam baaje damaroo.*

LAL BATTI

1957 ?' b&w Hindi
co-d/s **Balraj Sahni** *co-d* Krishen Chopra *pc* Cine Co-op *p* **Rajinder Singh Bedi** *lyr* **Majrooh Sultanpuri** *c* K. Vaikunth *m* **Salil Choudhury**
lp Balraj Sahni, **Mala Sinha**, Jawahar Kaul, Shashikala, Kamal, Rashid Khan, **Sulochana**

Sahni's only film as director is a suspense movie. It is set in a train and on a lonely railway platform where passengers are forced to spend a night at the time of India's Independence.

MAYA BAZAAR

1957 192' b&w Telugu/Tamil
d **K.V. Reddy** *pc* **Vijaya** *s* **Chakrapani** *lyr* **Pingali Nagendra Rao** *c* Marcus Bartley *m* **Ghantasala Venkateshwara Rao**
lp **N.T. Rama Rao**, **S.V. Ranga Rao**, **A. Nageshwara Rao**, **Relangi Venkatramaiah**, **Gummadi Venkateshwara Rao**, **K. Mukkamala**, **C.S.R. Anjaneyalu**, **Rajanala Nageshwara Rao**, Vangara, Balakrishna, **Savitri**, Rushyendramani, Suryakantam, Chhaya Devi, Sandhya

Major Vijaya mythological following on from Reddy's hit fantasy, ***Patala Bhairavi*** (1951). Taken from the *Mahabharata*, it tells the legend of Abhimanyu's marriage to Sasirekha (Savitri), assisted by Bhima's son Ghatotkacha (Ranga Rao) and opposed by the wily Shakuni (Anjaneyalu) who wants Sasirekha to marry one of the Kauravas. The film featured NTR in his first role as the Hindu god Krishna and includes an early version of one of Indian cinema's favourite special effects: magic arrows spewing fire and water. One of the musical highlights is the wedding feast number *Vivaha bhojanam.* The Tamil version was credited to Chakrapani's direction, which had a slightly different cast, and some compositions by **Saluri Rajeshwara Rao**.

MINNAMINUNG

aka *The Fire Fly*
1957 ?' b&w Malayalam
d/co-p/co-sc **Ramu Kariat** *co-p* Sreenivasan *pc* Chitra Keralam *co-sc* Rafi *dial* K.S.K. Thalikulam *lyr* **P. Bhaskaran** *c* B.J. Reddy *m* **Baburaj**
lp Damayanthi, Seeta, Padmam, Menon, Santha Devi, Mary Eddy, Maggie, Vasudev, Vipin, Lateef, Vakkachhan, Balakrishna Menon, Premji

Mysore's Premier Studio's melodrama about a young woman, Ammini, orphaned because of a greedy doctor's negligence. She becomes a maid and surrogate mother in the new doctor's household but the man's wife feels threatened and has Ammini sacked. However, misunderstandings are cleared up, and in the end Ammini is happily absorbed into the doctor's family and the villagers bid a tearful farewell to the group when the doctor is transferred. The virtually unknown cast is handled competently by the young Kariat who was to develop into one of Kerala's main film-makers. The film was not successful.

MOTHER INDIA

aka *Bharat Mata*
1957 168'(152')(120') col Hindi
d/s/p **Mehboob Khan** *pc* Mehboob Prod *dial* Wajahat Mirza, S. Ali Raza *lyr* Shakeel Badaiyuni *c* Faredoon Irani *m* **Naushad**
lp **Nargis**, **Sunil Dutt**, Raaj Kumar, **Rajendra Kumar**, Kanhaiyalal, Jilloo, Kumkum, Master Sajid, **Sitara Devi**

This film has acquired the status of an Indian *Gone with the Wind* (1939), massively successful and seen as a national epic, although formally the film's rhythms and lyrical ruralism seem closer to Dovzhenko's later work finished by Yulia Solntseva. Radha (Nargis), now an old woman, remembers her past: her happy married life with three sons in a village. The family have to work extremely hard to pay off the avaricious landlord, Sukhilala (Kanhaiyalal) and her husband (Raaj Kumar), having lost both arms in an accident, leaves her. Alone, she has to raise the children while fending off the financial as well as sexual pressures from Sukhilala. One son dies in a flood and in later years her son Birju (Dutt, Nargis's later husband) becomes a rebel committed to direct, violent action, while the other one, Ramu (Rajendra Kumar), remains a dutiful son. In the end, the long-suffering Mother India can only put an end to her rebellious son's activities by killing him, as his blood fertilises the soil. The film is a remake in colour and with drastically different imagery of Mehboob's own ***Aurat*** (1940), notably in the heavy use of psychoanalytic and other kinds of symbolism (the peasants forming a chorus outlining a map of India). Its spectacular commercial success was ironically noted in **Vijay Anand**'s ***Kala Bazaar*** (1960) when **Dev Anand** is shown selling tickets on the black market for *Mother India*'s premiere. *Mother India*'s plot and characters became the models for many subsequent films, including ***Ganga Jumna*** (1961) and ***Deewar*** (1975).

MUSAFIR

aka *Traveller*
1957 151' b&w Hindi
d/s/co-sc **Hrishikesh Mukherjee** *pc* Film Group *co-sc* **Ritwik Ghatak** *dial* **Rajinder Singh Bedi** *lyr* **Shailendra** *c* Kamal Bose *m* **Salil Choudhury**
lp **Suchitra Sen**, Shekhar, Bipin Gupta, **Durga Khote**, **Kishore Kumar**, **Nirupa Roy**, Nasir Hussain, Keshto Mukherjee, Hira Sawant, Daisy Irani, **Dilip Kumar**, Usha Kiron, Paul Mahendra, Mohan Choti, David, Rajlakshmi, Baby Naaz, Rashid Khan

The experienced editor Mukherjee's directorial debut constituted an important attempt to carve out a viable independent production sector in the Hindi cinema at the time. The film was made by a loose collective of mainly Bengali film people, including Ghatak and composer Choudhury who shared a background in radical theatre and were in Bombay mainly through **Bimal Roy**'s patronage. Many of them worked together again on ***Madhumati*** (1958). Set in an old suburban house, presumably in Calcutta, the film narrates three tenuously related Chekhovian stories about three sets of the house's occupants. The first has the Bengali star S. Sen as an orphaned young woman, Shakuntala, who desperately wants her husband Ajay (Shekhar) to make up with his estranged parents so that she may belong to a family once more. The second story has a wayward young man, Bhanu (K. Kumar), desperate to find a job to support his aged father (Hussain) and his widowed sister-in-law (N. Roy). The third and longest story focuses on the shadowy figure of a neighbourhood 'madman' (D. Kumar) who crops up in the previous stories as well. He was in love with Uma (Kiron) who lived in the house but disappeared just before their wedding day. In the end, the madman's death and the miraculous recovery of Uma's paralysed son coincide. The stories invoke a cyclical sequence of marriage, birth, death and rebirth, enhanced by Choudhury's score and some remarkable camerawork.

NAU DO GYARAH

1957 170' b&w Hindi
d/s **Vijay Anand** *p* **Dev Anand** *pc* **Navketan** *lyr* **Majrooh Sultanpuri** *c* V. Ratra *m* **S.D. Burman**
lp Dev Anand, Kalpana Kartik, Shashikala, Jeevan, Krishna Dhawan, Madan Puri, Rashid Khan, **Lalita Pawar**, Helen, M.A. Lateef

Raksha (Kartik) runs away from an arranged marriage to Surjit and meets Madan (Anand) on the road. Madan is on his way to collect an inheritance but he finds that his foster-aunt and cousin Kuldeep (Jeevan) have stolen it. In order to locate the original will, Madan and Raksha disguise themselves and pretend to be married. Madan is later arrested, charged with abducting Raksha but she continues the search for the will and to learn the truth about the death of Madan's uncle. Songs included *Hum hain rahi pyar ke* (sung by **Kishore Kumar**) and *Ankhon mein kya ji* (sung by **Asha Bhosle** and Kishore Kumar). Like ***Chori Chori*** (1956), this film seems to have borrowed plot elements from Capra's *It Happened One Night* (1934).

NAYA DAUR

1957 173' b&w Hindi
d/p **B.R. Chopra** *pc* B.R. Films *s* Akhtar Mirza *dial* Kamil Rashid *lyr* **Sahir Ludhianvi** *c* M.N. Malhotra *m* **O.P. Nayyar**
lp **Dilip Kumar**, **Vyjayanthimala**, Ajit, Chand Usmani, Jeevan, Manmohan Krishna, Nasir Hussain, **Leela Chitnis**, Pratima Devi, **Johnny Walker**, Daisy Irani, Radhakrishen, Kumkum, Minoo Mumtaz

A melodrama about the perils of progress: villain Kundan (Jeevan) introduces an electric saw and cars into an isolated, sylvan village while economic, caste and religious divisions between the rurals are woven into the main story of the rivalry between Shankar (D. Kumar) and Krishna (Ajit) over the heroine Rajani (Vyjayanthimala). The dramatic high point sees everyone joining forces to build a road to prove (via a race between a bus and a horsedrawn carriage) that traditional technology is just as good as the new machinery. Ironically, the nationalist modernisation argument is advanced by the villain while the benevolent father-figure Seth Maganlal (Hussain) hopes that a humanist attitude will abolish all class divisions. The hero Shankar argues for collectivisation as the proletarian way of managing new technology. Classic Nayyar numbers included *Reshmi salwar kurta jaali ka* (sung by **Asha Bhosle** and Shamshad Begum), *Saathi haath badhana* (sung by **Mohammed Rafi** and Asha Bhosle) and the Rafi solo *Main bambai ka babu*.

Ajit and Dilip Kumar in *Naya Daur*

PADATHA PAINGILI

aka *The Parrot That Never Sings*
1957 182' b&w Malayalam
d/p **P. Subramanyam** *pc* Neela Prod. *s* **Mutatthu Varkey** *lyr* Thirunayanar Kurichi, Madhavan Nair *c* N.S. Mani *m* Brother Lakshmanan
lp **Prem Nazir**, Kumari, **Kottarakkara Sridharan Nair**, S.P. Pillai, Vanakutty, Pankajavalli, K.V. Shanti, Muthaiah, Shanta, Aranmulla Ponnamma, Adoor Pankajam, Bahadur

Marriage melodrama around dowry problems. Thankachan (Nazir) wants to marry the poor Chinnamma (Kumari) but his rich father wants a big dowry for the eligible young man. Thankachan's marriage is arranged with Lucy, daughter of a millionaire, on the same day on which Chinnamma is scheduled to marry a poor worker from a beedi factory. Lucy, however, resolves the matter by becoming a nun, leaving the lovers free to marry. One of the first major films featuring the scripts of Mutatthu Varkey, in the paingili brand of popular fiction in Malayalam that later also influenced star Prem Nazir's screen persona.

PARASH PATHAR

aka *The Philosopher's Stone*
1957 111' b&w Bengali
d/sc **Satyajit Ray** *p* Promod Lahiri *pc* L.B. Films *st* Rajasekhar Bose [aka Parashuram] *c* Subrata Mitra *m* Ravi Shankar
lp **Tulsi Chakraborty**, Ranibala Devi, **Kali Bannerjee**, Gangapada Basu, Haridhan, **Jahar Roy**, Bireshwar Sen, Mani Srimani, **Chhabi Biswas**, **Jahar Ganguly**, **Pahadi Sanyal**, **Kamal Mitra**, Tulsi Lahiri, **Amar Mullick**, Nitish Mukherjee, Subodh Ganguly

Ray's first comedy is a low-budget quickie because of the delay on his more ambitious ***Jalsaghar*** (1958). Bank clerk Paresh Dutta (Chakraborty) finds a magic stone that can turn things into gold and becomes a rich man. When Dutta drunkenly reveals his secret at a cocktail party, his downfall follows as he is arrested for gold smuggling. Eventually the stone is swallowed and digested by his lovelorn secretary Priyatosh Henry Biswas (Bannerjee), turning all Dutta's gold back into iron to the delight of his wife. Relying at times on silent film comedy techniques (stop motion, speeded-up movement), the film adapts the short story of Rajasekhar Bose, a famous Bengali humorist, evoking, (mainly via Chakraborty's spectacular performance) a tradition of popular satire featuring the colonial bhadralok (upper middle class): e.g. when the clerk imagines his own heavily garlanded statue amid those of British politicians in Calcutta. Ray later also adapted Parashuram's *Birinchi Baba* in ***Mahapurush*** (1964).

PARDESI

aka *Khozheniye Za Tri Morya* aka *The Foreigner*
1957 110'(76') col Hindi/Russian
co-d/co-sc **K.A. Abbas** *co-d* Vassily M. Pronin *pc* **Naya Sansar**, Mosfilm *co-sc* Maria Smirnova *lyr* Prem Dhawan, Ali Sardar Jafri *c* E. Andrikaniz, V. Nikolaev, Ramchandra Singh *m* **Anil Biswas**
lp **Nargis**, Oleg Strizhenov, **Balraj Sahni**, **Prithviraj Kapoor**, Jairaj, David, Achala Sachdev, Manmohan Krishna, **Padmini**, V. Obuchova, V. Beliachov, S. Kayukov, N. Zhivago

A Nehruite Indo-Soviet co-production made in the wake of the Kruschov 'thaw' about the first Russian to set up a trading mission in India in the 15th C. The Muscovite Afanasi (Oleg) travels to India down the Volga, across Iran's deserts and the Arabian sea. In India he meets the fair maiden Champa (Nargis) through whom he discovers Indian civilisation. The film was shot on numerous tourist locations in India. The Russian version ran for 76' only. Pronin is known mainly for making an early Tadzhik feature in 1947 (*Son Of Tadzhikistan*) and the first Kirghiz feature, *Saltanat* (1955).

PAYING GUEST

1957 157' b&w Hindi
d/s **Subodh Mukherjee** *pc* **Filmistan** *dial* **Nasir Hussain** *lyr* **Majrooh Sultanpuri** *c* Dronacharya *m* **S.D. Burman**
lp **Dev Anand, Nutan, Gajanan Jagirdar**, Sajjan, Shobha Khote, Gyani, Dulari, Rajendra, Chamanpuri, Sailen Bose, Yakub

A mixture of romance and crime with Nutan giving an uninhibited performance in one of her best roles outside **Bimal Roy**'s socials. Hero Ramesh (Anand) masquerades as an old man to be near his beloved Shanti (Nutan). The crime plot in the latter half of the film concerns the faithless Chanchal (Khote) who is disinherited by her husband Dayal and teams up with Shanti's brother-in-law, the villainous Prakash. Shanti is later accused of having murdered Prakash but her innocence is finally established. Dev Anand's antics include an elaborately staged fight between his two guises: as the old man Mirza and as the frisky Ramesh. **Kishore Kumar** sings some of his best-known Dev Anand playback numbers including *Mana janab ne pukara nahin*, *Chhod do aanchal zamana kya kahega* (with **Asha Bhosle**) and *O nigahen mastana*. *Chand phir nikla* was sung by **Lata Mangeshkar**.

PYAASA

aka *Eternal Thirst* aka *The Thirsty One*
1957 153'(139') b&w Hindi
d/p **Guru Dutt** *pc* Guru Dutt Films *dial* Abrar Alvi *lyr* **Sahir Ludhianvi** *c* V.K. Murthy *m* **S.D. Burman**
lp Guru Dutt, **Waheeda Rehman, Mala Sinha, Johnny Walker**, Rehman, Kumkum, Shyam, Leela Mishra, Rajendar, Mayadass, Mehmood, Radhe Shyam, Ashita, Moni Chatterjee

Dutt's classic melodrama was the first in a series addressing the state of the nation and the displaced romantic artist (cf ***Kaagaz Ke Phool***, 1959). Vijay (Dutt) is an unsuccessful poet whose work is sold by his brothers as waste paper. Unable to bear the reigning philistinism, he elects to live on the streets where a young prostitute, Gulab (W. Rehman), falls in love with him and his poetry while Vijay's former girlfriend Meena (Sinha) marries an arrogant publisher, Mr Ghosh (Rehman), for comfort and security. When a dead beggar to whom Vijay gave his coat is mistaken for Vijay, Gulab has his poetry published in a book which becomes a best seller. Everyone who previously rejected Vijay now gathers to pay tribute to the dead poet. Vijay disrupts the celebration with a passionate song denouncing hypocrisy and calling for the violent destruction of a corrupt world (*Jala do ise phook dalo yeh duniya*). According to Dutt the inspiration for this film came from a lyric referring to Homer: 'Seven cities claimed Homer dead/ While the living Homer begged his bread' (cf his essay 'Classics And Cash', in Rangoonwala, 1973). The comic relief scenes with Johnny Walker as Abdul Sattar, an eccentric masseur, do not always fit smoothly into the rest of the film, but Dutt's exploration of the tragic idiom is unprecedented in Hindi cinema and can be compared to some of **Ritwik Ghatak**'s work in the powerful use of a musical chorus and the presentation of characters as archetypes (Vijay repeatedly evokes Christ imagery, e.g. in the song *Jaane woh kaise* and his appearance at the memorial celebration). The film, shot mostly on sets, makes no specific reference to its location but audiences would be able to note the significance of Vijay as an Urdu poet belonging to a Bengali family or the figure of Mr Ghosh evoking a Calcutta or Delhi businessman. Several sequences testify to an astonishing cinematic mastery: the crane movements during Gulab's tender and hesitant move towards a Vijay absorbed in his own thoughts (set to the song *Aaj sajan mohe ang lagalo*) or when Vijay staggers through the red-light district protesting (in the song *Jinhe naaz hai hind par woh kahan hain*) against the existence of such exploitation in a newly independent India.

SUVARNA SUNDARI/MANALANE MANGAYIN BHAGYAM

1957 209'[Te]/211'[Ta] b&w Telugu/Hindi/Tamil
d/sc **Vedantam Raghavaiah** *pc* Anjali Pixtures *st/dial/lyr*[Te] **Samudrala Raghavacharya** *lyr*[H] Bharat Vyas *c* M.A. Rehman *m* **Adi Narayana Rao**
lp **A. Nageshwara Rao, Anjali Devi, Relangi Venkatramaiah**[Te], Mahankali Venkayya[Te], Rajasulochana[Te], **C.S.R. Anjaneyalu**[Te], **Gummadi Venkateshwara Rao**[Te], Ramana Reddy[Te], Balakrishna[Te], Pekati[Te], Shyama[H], Kumkum[H], Daisy Irani[H], Mohana[H], Suryakala[H], Agha[H], Mukri[H], Dhumal[H], Randhir[H], Bipin Gupta[H], Niranjan Sharma[H], **Gemini Ganesh**[Ta], **M.V. Rajamma**[Ta], **B. Saroja Devi**[Ta]

Anjali Devi repeated her role from Balaramaiah's ***Swapna Sundari*** (1950) in this megabudget trilingual fantasy produced by her studio. A celestial fairy descends to earth and is captivated by the charms of a young man. The god Indra puts a curse on the fairy and converts her earthling lover into a stone statue. This is one of the major 50s productions in the uniquely Telugu fantasy-legend genre (cf **K.V. Reddy**'s work or **Bhanumathi**'s hit ***Raksharekha***, 1949). However, when Anjali Pix repeated the formula again with Raghavaiah's *Swarnamanjari/Mangayir Ullam Mangada Selvam* (1962), starring **NTR**, it flopped.

TUMSA NAHIN DEKHA

1957 156' b&w/col Hindi
d/s **Nasir Hussain** *pc* **Filmistan** *lyr* **Majrooh Sultanpuri** *c* Marshall Braganza *m* **O.P. Nayyar**
lp **Shammi Kapoor**, Ameeta, Pran, B.M. Vyas, Raj Mehra, Sheela Vaz, S.K. Singh, Kanu Roy, Ram Avtar, Anjali Devi, Rajendra, Shetty, S.L. Puri

Hussain's directorial debut, a musical partly shot in colour, transformed Shammi Kapoor into a loose-limbed, hip-swinging hero (esp. in the song *Chupne wale samne aa*). The sympathetic criminal Gopal kills his nasty partner and has to go on the run, abandoning his wife and baby son. Twenty years later, safely hidden as a reclusive landlord in Assam, Gopal betrays his whereabouts to his wife via a job advertisement. His grown-up son Shankar (Kapoor), who hates his father for having abandoned his family, applies for the job carrying a letter of introduction from his mother. However, the villainous Sohan (Pran) who covets Gopal's property intercepts and copies the letter so that two young men recommended by his wife turn up on Gopal's doorstep. The old man doesn't know which is his son and which the impostor. Sohan's intrigues are intercut with numerous musical interludes as Shankar woos Meena (Ameeta), Gopal's adopted daughter. The final conflict between the good guys and the bad guys includes several hill tribesmen led by fight-director Shetty. The title number, *Yun to humne lakh haseen dekhe hain, tumsa nahin dekha*, was one of **Mohammed Rafi**'s biggest hits ever. Hussain remade the story as ***Dil Deke Dekho*** (1959).

APPU CHESI PAPPU KOODU/KADAM VANGI KALYANAM

1958 180'[Te]/185'[Ta] b&w/col Telugu/Tamil
d/co-s **L.V. Prasad** *pc* **Vijaya** *co-s* **Chakrapani** *co-s/dial* Sadasiva Brahmam *lyr* **Pingali Nagendra Rao** *c* Marcus Bartley *m* **Saluri Rajeshwara Rao**
lp **S.V. Ranga Rao, Savitri, Jamuna**, E.V. Saroja, **N.T. Rama Rao**[Te], **K. Jaggaiah**[Te], **Relangi Venkatramaiah**[Te], **C.S.R. Anjaneyalu**[Te], Ramana Reddy[Te], K. Sivarao[Te], Girija Suryakantam[Te], **Gemini Ganesh**[Ta], T.R. Ramchandran[Ta], K.A. Thangavelu[Ta], T.S. Baliah[Ta], Meenakshi[Ta], **Rajanala Nageshwara Rao**[Te]

Prasad's comedy for Vijaya continues the genre of ***Pelli Chesi Choodu*** (1952) and ***Missamma*** (1955). Rao Bahadur Ramadas (Anjaneyalu/Baliah) tries to get Diwan Bahadur Mukunda Rao's property by marrying his son to Mukunda Rao's daughter Leela (Jamuna). The latter is also courted by

Raja (NTR/Ganesh), formerly jailed for his Independence movement activities. Raja masquerades as a zamindar, on the instigation of Ramadas' corrupt secretary Bhajagovindam (Venkatramaiah/Thangavelu), while Leela pretends to be a dumb servant in her own home. A further twist in the plot is provided by the reappearance of Leela's childhood husband Raghu who does not recognise his wife. Known for well-scripted comedy scenes between Anjaneyalu and Venkatramaiah, and for Saroja's dance filmed in Gevacolor.

AVAN AMARAN

aka *He Is Immortal*
1958 199' b&w Tamil
d/m **S. Balachander** *pc* People's Films *s* S. Nagarajan *c* **Nemai Ghosh**
lp K.R. Ramasamy, T.S. Baliah, S.V. Subbaiah, Rajasulochana, **P. Kannamba**

Written by a CP ideologue, the plot concerns Arul, the bright son of a mill worker, who marries the mill owner's daughter Lily, becomes a barrister and ends up leading an amalgamation of mill workers' unions in a strike against the introduction of new machinery. He dies while preventing the mill owner from dynamiting a bridge filled with protesting workers. The Veena master Balachander, fresh from his successful *Andha Naal* (1954), achieves some excellent sequences (the workers passing over the Hamilton Bridge near Fort St George in Madras) shot by the Bengali director turned Tamil cameraman Ghosh. The censors cut 1034ft out of the film, including a series of lines spoken by the hero in a court scene and references to class struggle and economic inequality. People's Films with its Mosfilm-type logo is an early effort to define a Tamil Communist cinema, briefly sustained by Ghosh.

BHAKTA PRAHLADA

1958 179' b&w Kannada
d H.S. Krishnaswamy, **M.V. Subbaiah Naidu** *pc* Shri Sahitya Samrajya Nataka Mandali *s* M.S. Bangaramma *lyr* G. Mahalinga Bhagavathar *c* K. Balu *m* L. Mallesh Rao
lp M.V. Subbaiah Naidu, Lakshmibai, **Udaya Kumar**, **Leelavathi**, Narasimhraju, G. Mahalinga Bhagavathar, P.R. Venugopal, Master Loknath

Subbaiah Naidu and **R. Nagendra Rao**'s theatre company staged many mythologicals which had a major influence on South Indian cinema, including *Bhakta Prahlada* and *Bhukailasa*. K. Shankar and **AVM** made the best-known film adaptation of ***Bhukailasa*** (1958), while S. Naidu and Nagendra Rao themselves made the screen adaptation of *Bhakta Prahlada*, their best-known filmed mythological. It tells the *Ramayana*'s Vishnu Purana legend of the demon Hiranyakashapu, his son Prahlada, a devotee of Vishnu, and Vishnu's eventual triumph over the demon in his man-lion avatar.

BHUKAILASA

1958 174'[Te]/169'[K] b&w Telugu/Tamil/Kannada
d K. Shankar *pc* **AVM** *dial/lyr* **Samudrala Raghavacharya**[Te], K.R. Seetarama Sastry[K] *c* Madhav Bulbule *m* R. Sudarshanam, R. Govardhanam
lp **Jamuna**, **B. Saroja Devi**, **S.V. Ranga Rao**, **N.T. Rama Rao**[Te], **A. Nageshwara Rao**[Te], **Vijayanirmala**[Te], **Rajkumar**[K], **Kalyana Kumar**[K], Aswath[K]

Third and biggest film (cf versions of 1938 and 1940) based on the *Ramayana* story originally staged by **R. Nagendra Rao** and **Subbaiah Naidu**. Intended as a major remake of **A.V. Meiyappan**'s 1940 Telugu hit. Ravana, king of Lanka, propitiates the god Shiva and, when he wins a boon, claims in return the latter's phallic powers and his consort Parvati. Narada tells Ravana that the Parvati who has been sent is merely the shadow of the goddess. Ravana marries Mandodhiri believing her to be Parvati, but he is condemned by his mother Kaikasi. As for the *atma-linga*, the symbol of Shiva's magical powers, it is donated on condition that it never be set down on earth. Ravana cannot fulfil the condition and has to accept defeat.

CHALTI KA NAAM GAADI

1958 173' b&w Hindi
d **Satyen Bose** *pc* K.H. Pics *dial* Ramesh Pant, Gobind Moonis *lyr* **Majrooh Sultanpuri** *c* Aloke Dasgupta *m* **S.D. Burman**
lp **Kishore Kumar**, **Ashok Kumar**, Anup Kumar, **Madhubala**, Sajjan, K.N. Singh, Veena, Sahira, Helen, Cuckoo, Mohan Choti, S.N. Bannerjee

Following on from ***Bandi*** (1957), Bose made this crazy comedy with the brothers Kumar which became their best-known ensemble production. The eldest brother (Ashok Kumar) is a misogynist; the second one, Jaggu (Anup Kumar) is the bumbler and the youngest, Mannu (Kishore Kumar), is the romantic. Together they run a garage. Mannu meets Renu (Madhubala) when she arrives in the dead of night to get her car repaired and they fall in love. With the help of the other brothers, they have fight off a gang led by Raja Hardayal Singh (K.N. Singh) and his son Kumar Pradeep (Sajjan) before they can live happily ever after. The film resorts to silent Hollywood comedy techniques like speeded up action and back projection (e.g. the race won by the trio in their ancient 1928 Chevrolet which gives the film its title), and freely digresses into scenes only tenuously related to the narrative (the great-lovers-in-history number, *Paanch rupaiya bara anna*). It features several of Kishore Kumar's jazzy numbers, such as *Babu samjho ishare, horn pukare, Hum the woh thi woh thi hum the*. Very soon after it starts, the film signals its disregard for chronological consistency.

CHENCHULAKSHMI

1958 162'[Te]/190'[Ta] b&w Telugu/Tamil
d B.A. Subba Rao *pc* B.A.S. Prod *s* Sadasiva Brahmam *lyr* **Arudra** *c* C. Nageshwara Rao *m* **Saluri Rajeshwara Rao**
lp **A. Nageshwara Rao**, **Anjali Devi**, **Relangi Venkatramaiah**, **S.V. Ranga Rao**, Master Balaji

Musical mythological, remade from **S. Soundararajan**'s hit of 1943, featuring Vishnu (Nageshwara Rao) in his two best-known incarnations: the boar (Varaha) and the man-lion (Narasimha). Not invited to the celestial marriage of Vishnu and Lakshmi (Anjali Devi), Durvasa banishes Lakshmi's parents to earth as common people. There, Lakshmi is reborn as a tribal. The film intercuts her story on earth with the heavenly tale of Hiranyakashapu (Ranga Rao) who cannot be killed by man or beast. The demon's son Prahlada (Balaji), devoted to Vishnu, survives several murder attempts by his own father until finally Vishnu kills Hiranyakashapu using his Narasimha avatar. The heaven-earth split allows the film to deploy two narrative styles: the mythological one and a folk idiom (cf Anjali Devi as a restrained goddess and a coquettish earthling). Her performance and Rajeshwara Rao's music helped the film's commercial success.

ETTUKU PAI ETTU

1958 ?' b&w Telugu
d **Tapi Chanakya** *pc* Sarathi Pics *s/co-lyr* **Tapi Dharma Rao**, Kondepudi, Chiranjeevi *co-lyr* **Kosaraju** *m* **Master Venu**
lp T.S. Baliah, Janaki, **C.S.R. Anjaneyalu**, **Gummadi Venkateshwara Rao**, **Relangi Venkatramaiah**, **Lakshmirajyam**, V. Narasimha Rao, **Chittor V. Nagaiah**, Chhaya Devi, Hemalatha

Considered an avant-garde film at the time for casting unknown actors in a realist story of two warring elders, Kailasam (Anjaneyalu) and Govindaiah (Gummadi), who are eventually brought together by their sons. The film made Baliah a star.

HOWRAH BRIDGE

1958 153' b&w Hindi
d/p **Shakti Samanta** *pc* Shakti Films *s* Ranjan Bose *dial* Vrajendra Gaur *lyr* Qamar Jalalabadi, Hasrat Jaipuri *c* Chandu *m* **O.P. Nayyar**
lp **Ashok Kumar**, **Madhubala**, Dhumal, K.N. Singh, Om Prakash, Helen, Kammo, Madan Puri, Sundar, **Krishnakant**, Kundan, Bhagwan Sinha, Sailen Bose

This crime movie was one of the first to assimilate the Hong Kong cinema's influence, a trend continued by Samanta's ***China Town*** (1962). Rakesh (Kumar), the son of a Rangoon merchant, comes to Calcutta in search of his brother's killer. With the help of Joe, a restaurant manager, and Edna (Madhubala), a cabaret dancer, he routs the villains Pyarelal (K.N. Singh) and Chiang (Puri). The film ends with a chase sequence over the famous Howrah Bridge in Calcutta and includes **Geeta Dutt**'s famous cabaret number *Mera naam Chin Chin Choo ... Hello mister, how do you do?* performed in the film by Helen.

JAILOR

1958 ?' b&w Hindi
d **Sohrab Modi** *pc* **Minerva Movietone** *st/dial* **Kamal Amrohi** *sc* J.K. Nanda *lyr* Rajinder Krishen *c* Y.D. Sarpotdar *m* **Madan Mohan**

lp Sohrab Modi, Kamini Kaushal, **Geeta Bali**, **Abhi Bhattacharya**, Nana Palsikar, Daisy Irani, Eruch Tarapore, Pratima Devi

Modi's remake of his own 1938 film starring himself as the humanitarian prison warden Dilip whose wife Kanwal (Kaushal) elopes with Dr Ramesh (Bhattacharya), triggering Dilip's transformation into a viciously oppressive maniac (whose image recalls the Hollywood versions of Mr Hyde). Geeta Bali plays the virtuous Chhaya, Dilip's own temptation.

JALSAGHAR

aka *The Music Room*
1958 100' b&w Bengali
d/p/sc **Satyajit Ray** *pc* Satyajit Ray Prod. *st* Tarashankar Bannerjee *c* Subrata Mitra *m* Ustad Vilayat Khan
lp **Chhabi Biswas**, Padmadevi, Pinaki Sengupta, Gangapada Basu, Tulsi Lahiri, Kali Sarkar, Waheed Khan, Roshan Kumari, Bismillah Khan

Ray's critique of decadent colonial feudalism, shot on the property of a zamindar at Nimtita near the river Padma on the (current) border between India and Bangladesh (by coincidence the very family on which novelist Bannerjee had based his fiction). The ageing Bishwambar Roy (Biswas) pawns the family jewels to keep up with the opulence of his ancestors and with his rich upstart neighbour Mahim Ganguly (Basu). Roy's reputation is based on the spectacular concerts of classical music and dance he once hosted, featuring Lucknow's great Kathak dancers and *thumri* singers, one of which is shown in flashback. Another concert, amid ominous thunder and lightning, is followed by news of the death of his wife and son. He withdraws into complete seclusion, only to resurface when his neighbour invites him yet again, and hosts his final show explicitly to upstage Ganguly's. Eventually he rides off on his horse, a shadow of his former grandeur, and dies by the hull of an upturned boat. Ray's nostalgic portrayal of the end of an era that saw feudal oppression but also sustained India's classical arts is often compared to **Guru Dutt**'s film on the same theme, ***Sahib Bibi Aur Ghulam*** (1962), both portraying the feudal elite in sensual terms, reclining amid silk cushions, smoking hookahs and drinking, and because both directors rely on straightforwardly melodramatic idioms. *Jalsaghar* is heavy on symbols: shots of rain announcing death, an insect trapped in a glass, a decaying palace, the neighbour's trucks kicking up dust and obscuring Roy's view of his elephant grazing in the distance, the upturned boat at the end of the patriarch's life. Unlike the rest of the film, which was shot on location, the key locale of the music room was created on sets by Bansi Chandragupta. Ray included a concert by Begum Akhtar, India's greatest 20th C. *ghazal* singer. Other featured artists were *shehnai* maestro Bismillah Khan, singer Waheed Khan and dancer Roshan Kumari. The film boasts Chhabi Biswas's best-known screen performance.

KALA PANI

1958 164' b&w Hindi
d **Raj Khosla** *pc* **Navketan** *st* Anand Pal *sc* G.R. Kamat *dial* Bhappi Sonie *lyr* **Majrooh Sultanpuri** *c* V. Ratra *m* **S.D. Burman**
lp **Dev Anand**, **Madhubala**, **Nalini Jaywant**, **Kishore Sahu**, Nasir Hussain, Sapru, Krishna Dhawan, M.A. Lateef, Rashid Khan, Bir Sakhuja, Mukri, Agha

A crime movie about institutionalised corruption. Hero Karan (Anand) discovers that his father, believed dead, is in fact in jail for a murder he did not commit. Karan sets out to prove his father's innocence with the help of a fearless journalist, Asha (Madhubala). The villain is the corrupt public prosecutor (Sahu). The key witness is a dancer, Kishori, played by Nalini Jaywant who elevates the film beyond its plot. Her own desire, rendered in the hit **Asha Bhosle** number *Nazar laagi raja tore bangle pe*, makes for an ambiguous love triangle that also provides other reasons to that of the hero's vendetta for seeking out the truth. The other song hit *Hum bekhudi me tumko pukare* (sung by **Mohammed Rafi**), in which Kishori unleashes her charms on the drunken hero, was described by **Mahesh Bhatt** (1993) as 'a typical example of a Raj Khosla song and his unique attitude towards sex on the Indian screen'.

LAJWANTI

1958 120' b&w Hindi
d Narendra Suri *pc* Delux Films *s* Sachin Bhan *lyr* **Majrooh Sultanpuri** *c* M. Malhotra *m* **S.D. Burman**
lp **Nargis**, Baby Naaz, **Balraj Sahni**, Prabhu Dayal, Radhakrishnan

Suri's family movie echoes ***Andaz*** (1949): a husband (Sahni) believes his wife (Nargis) to be having an affair with an artist friend and throws her out. In fact, she was having her portrait painted. When a decade later the two get together again, she has to win over her grown-up daughter (Baby Naaz) which she does only when she's on the verge of suicide. Sahni's naturalism as usual considerably tones down the emotional pitch.

MADHUMATI

1958 179'(165') b&w Hindi
d/p **Bimal Roy** *pc* Bimal Roy Prod. *s* **Ritwik Ghatak** *dial* **Rajinder Singh Bedi** *lyr* **Shailendra** *c* Dilip Gupta *m* **Salil Choudhury**
lp **Dilip Kumar**, **Vyjayanthimala**, **Johnny Walker**, Pran, Jayant, Tiwari, Misra, Baij Sharma, Bhudo Advani, Jagdish, Sagar, Ranjeet Sud, Sheojibhai, Tarun Bose

A reincarnation story with the lead actors in multiple roles. Devendra (D. Kumar) shelters from a storm in a deserted house and believes he hears a woman crying. Exploring the house, he finds a painting of its former owner Raja Ugranarayan. Devendra feels he must have painted the portrait in a previous life when he was called Anand. This cues a flashback to Anand's life when he worked as a foreman on a plantation and loved a woman from the village, Madhumati (Vyjayanthimala), who died escaping from the libidinous Raja Ugranarayan (Pran). Then a trap is set for the Raja by means of another woman, Madhavi (Vyjayanthimala again), who looks like the dead Madhumati and could be her reincarnation. The happy ending arrives when the original Madhumati returns from the dead to take her revenge. The film deploys an eerily romantic atmosphere, enhanced by Choudhury's background score and **Hrishikesh Mukherjee**'s editing. Its songs have remained enduringly popular. The film includes the famous *Aja re pardesi* sung by **Lata Mangeshkar**. It was Bimal Roy's biggest commercial success, scripted by Ghatak. Many of the people involved in this film had worked together on Hrishikesh Mukherjee's ***Musafir*** (1957), also based on a Ghatak story. The imagery at times evokes Ghatak's ***Ajantrik*** (1957), linking the beautiful Madhumati with nature and tribal cultures beyond the grasp of capitalist appropriation.

MAYA BAZAAR

1958 ?' b&w Hindi
d/sc **Babubhai Mistri** *pc* **Wadia Movietone** *st* Vishwanath Pande *dial* C.K. Mast *lyr* Gopal Singhnepali, Saraswati Kumar Deepak, Indivar *c* N. Satyanarayan *m* Chitragupta
lp Anita Guha, Mahipal, Vasant Pahelwan, Raaj Kumar, Ulhas, B.M. Vyas, Ramsingh, Indira

Director Mistri created the special effects for his best-known mythological narrating episodes from the *Mahabharata*: e.g. the Rajasuya Yagna, Krishna's killing of Shishupal, the game of dice, and Abhimanyu and Ghatotkach's rescue of Balaram's daughter Surekha from the Kauravas. Mistri remade it in colour in 1984.

NADODI MANNAN

1958 220' b&w/col Tamil
d/p **M.G. Ramachandran** *pc* Emgeeyar Pics *st* R.M. Veerappan, V. Lakshmanan, S.K.D. Sami *co-dial/lyr* **Kannadasan** *co-dial* Ravindran *c* G.K. Ramu *m* S.M. Subbaiah Naidu, N. Balakrishnan
lp M.G. Ramachandran, **P. Bhanumathi**, P.S. Veerappa, M.N. Rajam, M.N. Nambiar, Chandrababu, T.K. Balachandran, **B. Saroja Devi**, T.P. Muthulakshmi

MGR's period adventure fantasy, with 19 songs, and important **DMK** propaganda film repeating his successful screen pairing with Bhanumathi (***Alibabavum Narpatha Thirudargalum***, 1955 and ***Madurai Veeran***, 1956) in a style derived from **Gemini**'s post-***Chandralekha*** (1948) films. The good king Marthandan (MGR) is dethroned by the Rajguru and replaced by a double, the commoner Veerangam (MGR again). Nakedly propagandist (e.g. colour sequences showing the red and black DMK flag and its rising sun party symbol), the film presents the good guys as waiting to overthrow the Rajguru's corrupt rule, a thinly disguised reference to the Congress Party. Its commercial success was followed by a public reception for MGR by the DMK Party, taking him in procession in a 'chariot drawn by four horses, thronged by the people. The chariot had a background of a rising sun on a lotus. At the beginning of the procession there were party volunteers carrying festoons. Elephants garlanded MGR twice' (M.S.S. Pandian, 1992). Apparently **Karunanidhi** read out a poem he wrote about the film at the festivities.

NEEL AKASHER NEECHEY

aka *Under the Blue Sky*
1958 133' b&w Bengali
d/sc **Mrinal Sen** *p/m* **Hemanta Mukherjee** *pc* Hemanta Bela Prod *st* Mahadevi Verma *lyr* Gauriprasanna Chattopadhyay *c* Sailaja Chatterjee
lp **Kali Bannerjee**, Manju Dey, Bikash Roy

Sen's first commercial success, after his financially disastrous debut *Raat Bhore* (1956). Produced by the composer Hemanta Mukherjee, the film is set in the 30s and tells of an honest Chinese hawker, Wang Lu (Bannerjee), who sells silk in Calcutta's streets while refusing to get involved in the opium trade run by his fellow countrymen. A flashback reveals his past history in China's Shantung province: a cruel landlord blackmailed Wang Lu's sister into prostitution, resulting in her suicide. The sequence, including documentary footage shot by Sen in China, is recalled when Wang Lu feels a brotherly affection for Basanti (Dey), the wife of a Calcutta lawyer (Roy). Basanti is committed to Swadeshi and has political disagreements with her husband, who blames Wang Lu for this. Basanti is arrested and imprisoned, causing Wang Lu to become more involved with her political group. When she is released, in 1931, the Japanese invasion of Manchuria makes Wang Lu go back and join the resistance. The story attempts to link India's independence struggle with China's fight against Japan. Sen said that the 30s, which formed much of the CPI's theory on imperialism, was 'enormously exciting ... [w]ith an element of nostalgia' and he returned to the period several times (cf ***Matir Manisha***, 1966). However, the film's non-chauvinist end is as significant as its internationalism in the anti-Chinese hysteria preceding the India-China War of 1962. The sentimental film is remembered mainly for one of composer-singer Mukherjee's most famous songs, *O nadire ekti katha sudhai*, and for Kali Bannerjee's remarkable performance. Shot mainly on sets, the dialogue evokes political and class stereotypes while inscribing several political references, e.g. Basanti's use of homespun Khadi cloth when Wang Lu offers her a piece of silk.

PHIR SUBAH HOGI

1958 168'(154') b&w Hindi
d/co-sc Ramesh Saigal *pc* Parijat Pics *st* Dostoevsky's *Crime and Punishment* *co-sc* Mubarak *dial* D.N. Madhok *lyr* **Sahir Ludhianvi** *c* Krishan Saigal *m* **Khayyam**
lp **Raj Kapoor**, **Mala Sinha**, Rehman, **Leela Chitnis**, Mubarak, Nana Palsikar, Jagdish Sethi, Kamal Kapoor, Mishra

Dostoevsky's story provides only the bare outlines of this emotional plea for social justice in 'Nehruite' India by an influential film-maker of the genre (cf ***Railway Platform***, 1955). Ramu (Kapoor) is a poor law student in love with the even poorer Sohni (Sinha). Sohni's father (Palsikar) is an alcoholic tailor in debt to the villainous Harbanslal who demands to marry Sohni. Ramu must pay off the villain if he is to win Sohni. He is caught robbing the safe of a vicious old moneylender and kills the man in self-defence. When the wrong man is arrested for the crime, a police detective puts pressure on Ramu to confess and save the innocent man from the gallows. Ramu eventually confesses and makes a moving plea on behalf of the dispossessed's right to defend themselves against the real villains in society. The film includes the poet Sahir Ludhianvi's famous critique of Nehru's non-aligned liberalism: *Chin-o-Arab hamara*, with an opening stanza declaring 'China and Arabia are ours/India is ours/We have no roof over our heads/The whole world is ours' (China and Arabia being references to Chou En-Lai and Nasser). This song is picturised at night in Bombay's easily recognisable square opposite the Victoria Terminus where even today, as Kapoor does in the film, one may sleep on the pavement without police interference. Other classic numbers include *Aasman pe hai khuda aur zameen pe hum* ('The Lord is in the heavens and we on earth/And these days He doesn't look our way very often') sung by Kapoor to a cabaret dancer and intercut with the death of Sohni's father. The best-known number is the title refrain heralding a new dawn, *Woh subah kabhi to aayegi*.

POST BOX 999

1958 ?' b&w Hindi
d **Ravindra Dave** *pc* Nagina Films *s/lyr* P.L. Santoshi *c* M.W. Mukadam *m* **Kalyanji**
lp **Sunil Dutt**, Shakila, Purnima, **Leela Chitnis**, Manorama, **Krishnakant**, Gulab, Sadhana, Anwari, Amarnath

Apparently inspired by Hathaway's *Call Northside 777* (1947), this is the best-known and the most successful of Dave's crime thrillers. Journalist Vikas (Dutt) is hired by an old woman (Chitnis) to prove the innocence of her wrongly convicted son Mohan. The investigation of the villainous hotel owner Banarasilal involves Vikas and his girlfriend Nilima (Shakila) posing as magicians while the intrepid mother helps out by going to work in the villain's bird-shop. Mohan's innocence can only be proved via the testimony of Bindiya, supposedly long since dead but believed to be still alive by the investigators.

PUBERUN

1958 139' b&w Assamese
d/sc Prabhat Mukherjee *pc* Kathakali Cine *st* Khagen Roy *c* Ajoy Mitra *m* Faizuddin Ahmed
lp Jnanada Kakoti, Beena Devi, Margaret, Rebecca Achaw, Gautam Borbora, Radha Gobinda Barua, Tasadduf Yusuf, Khagen Roy

Assamese melodrama about motherhood set in the hill-station of Shillong. The mother (Kakoti) extends her love for her child to that of the children of a Christian orphanage. Kakoti's performance was critically acclaimed.

RAI DAICH

1958 112' b&w Sindhi
d J.B. Lulla *pc* Atu Lalwani, D.D. Kripalani *s* Ram Panjwani *lyr* Parsram Zia *c* Chandu *m* **Bulo C. Rani**
lp Shanti Ramchandani, Veena Makhijani, Atu Lalwani, Pratap Maniar, Chandu Shivdasani, Kanmohan, Sajju Kripalani, Minoo Kripalani, Tuntun, Bhudo Advani

(From left) Raj Kapoor, Mubarak and Rehman in *Phir Subah Hogi*

Sindhi folk-tale adapting the Moses and Krishna legends to Rai Daich (Lalwani), the king of Junagadh, who, it is predicted, will be killed by his sister's son. The sister hands her newborn son to her maid who floats him in a box down the river where he is rescued and raised by a shepherd. He grows up to become Bijal (Maniar) whose girlfriend Kamodini (Ramchandani), at the rival King Anerai of Gujarat's request, agrees on Bijal's behalf to behead Rai Dach. Bijal sings before Rai Daich, wins a boon, and asks for his head, triggering a war. Bijal's song suddenly has Anerai's castle bursting into flames. The war is constructed on the editing table with stock shots. This unusual Sindhi film is known mainly for Rani's music.

RAJ TILAK

1958 171' b&w Hindi
d **S.S. Vasan** *pc* **Gemini** *co-st* Kothamangalam Subbu *co-st/dial* **Ramanand Sagar** *co-st/sc* K.J. Mahadevan *lyr* P.L. Santoshi *c* P. Ellappa *m* **C. Ramchandra**
lp **Gemini Ganesh**, **Vyjayanthimala**, Pran, **Padmini**, **Gajanan Jagirdar**, Bipin Gupta

Gemini's fairy-tale adventure continued in the vein of ***Chandralekha*** (1948) and ***Apoorva Sahodarargal*** (1949), involving the same writer (K. Subbu) and art director (A.K. Sekhar). Chander (Ganesh), rescued when still a child from a drifting raft, falls foul of a villainous senapati (chieftain) (Pran). Exiled to a desolate island, he learns that he is the son of the good Sardar Mangal Sen (Jagirdar). He jumps into the sea whence he is rescued by a foreign ship which takes him to its home port. There Chander falls in love with the local princess, Mandakini (Vyjayanthimala). Returning to his homeland, Chander finds that his father has been imprisoned by the villain. To set things right he has to overcome the might of the state.

RANDIDANGAZHI

aka *Two Measures of Paddy*
1958 174' b&w Malayalam
d/p **P. Subramanyam** *pc* Neela Prod *s* Thakazhy Shivashankar Pillai based on his novel *lyr* Thirunayanar Kurichi, Madhavan Nair *c* N.S. Mani *m* Brother Laxmanan
lp Kumari, **P.J. Anthony**, T.S. Muthiah, **Thikkurisi Sukumaran Nair**, **Kottarakkara Sridharan Nair**, S.P. Pillai, Bahadur, Adoor Pankajam, J.A.R. Anand

Seminal political movie by a director better known for mythologicals. Set among the conditions of bonded labour in the Kuttanad province, it tells the story of the peasant Koran, who fights the oppression of the landlord Yusuf along with his wife Chirutha and friend Chatthan. He eventually organises the first peasant union in his area, leading the labourers to freedom. The film was dominated by its script, written by the major novelist Pillai, and prefigures the later achievement of **Kariat**'s ***Chemmeen*** (1965). The genre was akin to many of the stage productions of the radical KPAC (cf **IPTA**), as was some of the music.

RANGA POLICE

1958 ?' b&w Assamese
d **Nip Barua** *pc* Milita Silpi Cine *s* Ramesh Sarin *c* Nalin Duara *m* Nizamuddin Hazarika
lp Jnananda Kakoti, Nip Barua, Munin Burman, **Abdul Majid**, Syed Abdul Malik, Bhola Kakoti, Beena Das

Best-known Assamese director Nip Barua's first major film, made for an amateur theatre group turned film company. Melodrama about an honest policeman who has to weigh his principles against the difficulties faced by his impoverished family. One of the first Assamese films to receive critical attention outside the region. The composer, noted for scoring several numbers in the popular Jyoti Sangeet idiom, is a former colleague of **Jyotiprasad Agarwala**.

SCHOOL MASTER/BADI PANTHULU

1958 185' b&w/col Kannada/Hindi/Telugu
d **B.R. Panthulu** *pc* Padmini Pics *dial* Kanagal Prabhakara Sastry *c* W.R. Subba Rao *m* T.G. Lingappa
lp B.R. Panthulu, **M.V. Rajamma**, Dikki Madhava Rao, **Udaya Kumar**, **Sowcar Janaki**, **B. Saroja Devi**, **Sivaji Ganesan**, **Balkrishna**, Narasimhraju, **Gemini Ganesh**

Panthulu's best-known Kannada film is a reform drama featuring an old but committed schoolteacher (Panthulu) who transforms the students of his native village though his own sons abandon him. He builds a new school, but succumbs to the villainy of the leader of the village panchayat (council) until the entire village comes to his support. Ganesan played a guest role as a police officer. Apparently inspired by the **Raja Paranjpe** melodrama ***Oon Paoos*** (1954), Panthulu dubbed the film in Hindi (1958) and remade it in Tamil (1973), while his disciple **Puttanna Kanagal** made it in Malayalam (1964).

SONE KI CHIDIYA

1958 171' b&w Hindi
d Shaheed Latif *pc* Filmindia Corp. *s/p* **Ismat Chughtai** *lyr* **Sahir Ludhianvi**, **Majrooh Sultanpuri**, **Kaifi Azmi** *c* Nariman A. Irani *m* **O.P. Nayyar**
lp **Nutan**, **Balraj Sahni**, Talat Mahmood, Altaf, Amar, Bikram Kapoor, Pratima Devi, Chandabai, Sarita Devi, Baij Sharma, Hammad Jafri, Zebunissa, Dhumal

The orphaned Lakshmi (Nutan), unwanted by either of her two aunts, suddenly becomes a film star. Her relatives now vie with each other to exploit her new-found earning capacity. Lakshmi falls in love with Amar, a gossip journalist (Mahmood), who ditches her when he realises that Lakshmi's wealth is controlled by her greedy family. On the point of committing suicide, Lakshmi hears the hope-filled song *Raat bhar ka yeh mehmaan andhera* [*Darkness is only a guest for the night*] (written by Ludhianvi and sung by **Mohammed Rafi**) and meets the radical poet Shrikant (Sahni) whom she has idolised for years. After a long digression stigmatising the way the film industry exploits its workforce, Shrikant falls in love with Lakshmi, but when Lakshmi's brothers offer him money to abandon her, he accepts the money and donates it to the Junior Artists' Fund. Lakshmi, believing herself betrayed yet again, realises the truth only at the end of the film when she rejoins Shrikant to the refrain of the 'new dawn' song. Writer and producer Chughtai contrasts the popular cinema's romanticised narratives (cf the soft-focus film-within-the-film song between Amar and Lakshmi) with the hard-edged reality of industrial exploitation underpinning them: the *Saiyan jab se ladi tori akhiyan* song is rapidly followed by the documentary-type Junior Artists' episode. Sahni's imposing presence enhances the film's realist aspirations, e.g. when he reads his poem to a bored producer or when he discovers the reality beneath the industry's glamour.

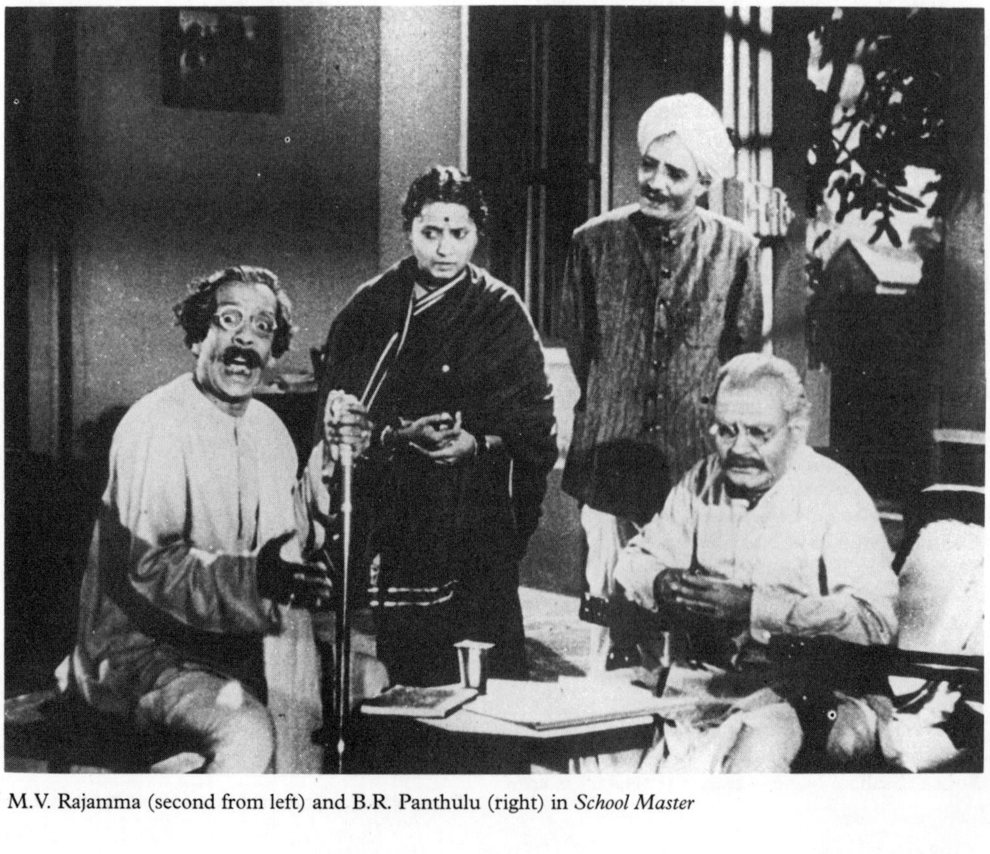

M.V. Rajamma (second from left) and B.R. Panthulu (right) in *School Master*

YAHUDI

1958 161' b&w Hindi
d **Bimal Roy** *pc* Bombay Films *st* **Aga Hashr Kashmiri**'s play *Yahudi Ki Ladki* (1915) *sc* Nabendu Ghosh *dial* Wajahat Mirza *lyr* **Shailendra**, Hasrat Jaipuri *c* Dilip Gupta *m* **Shankar-Jaikishen**
lp **Sohrab Modi**, **Dilip Kumar**, **Meena Kumari**, Nigar Sultana, Nasir Hussain, Anwar Hussain, Minoo Mumtaz, Helen, Cuckoo, Kumari Kamala

Based on Kashmiri's famous and often-filmed play, this version is partially authenticated by former Parsee Theatre actor Modi's presence. The melodrama in fancy dress is set in ancient Rome. The infant son of Ezra the Jew (Modi) is fed to the lions by Brutus (N. Hussain). Ezra's devoted slave Elias then kidnaps Brutus's daughter Lydia, whom Ezra renames Hannah (Kumari) and raises as his own child. The Roman Prince Marcus (D. Kumar) falls in love with Hannah by pretending to be a commoner, but he refuses to convert to Judaism in order to marry her. When, by royal decree, Marcus is to marry Octavia, Hannah and Ezra publicly complain of Marcus's infidelity. Realising that the penalty for infidelity is death, Hannah withdraws her complaint, which in turn entails a death sentence for herself and her father. They are saved only by Ezra's last-minute revelation of Hannah's true ancestry and Marcus blinds himself in atonement for his misbehaviour. The film has many popular songs, including the well-picturised *Yeh mera diwanapan hai* (sung by Mukesh).

ABBA! A HUDGI

1959 190' b&w Kannada
d/s/lyr **H.L.N. Simha** *pc* Shri Jamuna Pics *c* B. Dorairaj *m* **P. Kalingrao**
lp Raja Shankar, Mynavathi, **Rajkumar**, **Leelavathi**, Narasimhraju, **B.R. Panthulu**, **M.V. Rajamma**, **Pandharibai**, H.L.N. Simha, Dikki Madhava Rao

Taming of the Shrew-type drama. The feminist Sarasa, president of the Anti-Marriage League, is tamed by her lover Sarvottam with the assistance of an urban theatre group performing *Samsara Nauka*, one of 20th C. Kannada theatre's most successful plays. The play, which deals with the reforming of a crusty lawyer, is adapted to stage a 'real life' fiction in which Sarvottam is accused of having murdered the theatre group's proprietor. Fear of her lover going to the gallows transforms the woman, as predicted. For the film Simha revived the original stage performance of *Samsara Nauka* by the Chandrakala group, including Panthulu, Rajamma and Simha himself.

ANARI

1959 166' b&w Hindi
d **Hrishikesh Mukherjee** *pc* L.B. Films *s* **Inder Raj Anand** *lyr* **Shailendra**, Hasrat Jaipuri *c* Jaywant Pathare *m* **Shankar-Jaikishen**
lp **Raj Kapoor**, **Nutan**, **Lalita Pawar**, **Motilal**, Shubha Khote, Nana Palsikar, Ashim Kumar, Paul Mahendra, Brahm Bhardwaj, **Sulochana**, Helen

The naive painter Raj (Kapoor) lodges with the devout, rather maternal Mrs D'Sa (Pawar). Raj falls in love with Aarti (Nutan), the niece of the wealthy pharmaceutics manufacturer Ramnath (Motilal) who is Raj's employer. To sidestep class differences, Aarti pretends to be her own maid. This stratagem leads to problems aggravated when Mrs D'Sa dies after taking medicines made by Ramnath's company. Raj is accused of having poisoned her. Eventually Ramnath acknowledges responsibility for the crime. Although directed and edited by Mukherjee, the film's cynical view of capital accumulation betrays Kapoor's authorial signature (cf ***Shri 420***, 1955). The presence of Shailendra, Hasrat and Shankar-Jaikishen, close collaborators of the RK banner, as well as the expected Mukesh solo showing a philosophising tramp (*Kissi ki muskurahaton pe ho nisar*) underline Kapoor's direct influence on the film.

APUR SANSAR

aka *The World of Apu*
1959 117'(106') b&w Bengali
d/p/sc **Satyajit Ray** *pc* Satyajit Ray Prod. *st* Bibhutibhushan Bannerjee's novel *Aparajito* *c* Subrata Mitra *m* Ravi Shankar
lp **Soumitra Chatterjee**, **Sharmila Tagore**, Alok Chakraborty, Swapan Mukherjee, Dhiresh Majumdar, Shefalika Devi, Dhiren Ghoshal

Rather belatedly, Ray decided to add a third film to his ***Pather Panchali*** (1955) and the initially unsuccessful ***Aparajito*** (1956). A grown-up Apu (Chatterjee's debut), now living poorly in Calcutta and dreaming of becoming a great novelist, is persuaded to marry a young village woman, Aparna (the 14-year-old Tagore), to protect her honour when her scheduled marriage is abruptly cancelled. The two live together in Calcutta and fall in love, but when Aparna goes to her maternal home for her first pregnancy, she dies although her son lives. Apu rejects the child and tries to overcome his desperation by working in a remote colliery. He eventually accepts his son. The scenes of the young married couple living in poverty are Ray's first major location shots in contemporary Calcutta, soon to become a leitmotif in his work. Here he also elaborated his way of weaving a complex and suggestive usage of (urban) geography into the cinematic narrative, as in the classic sequences where Apu brings his bride to their new home, a squalid room above a railway line, or the couple's visit to a movie followed by the cab-ride home. Of the remarkable scene in which Apu reclaims his young son Kajal (Alok Chakraborty), standing in front of the river, Geeta Kapur (1993) notes: 'He stands at the crossroads extra tall with his child on his shoulder. [B]ut there is in the very courage of this verticality a disjuncture between the future and the past, and a regret at the alienated space of the present'. It also recalls the young Apu at the beginning of the trilogy.

CHAR DIL CHAR RAAHEIN

1959 160' b&w Hindi
d/st/co-sc/dial **K.A. Abbas** *pc* Naya Sansar *co-sc* **Inder Raj Anand**, V.P. Sathe *lyr* **Sahir Ludhianvi** *c* Ramchandra *m* **Anil Biswas**
lp **Raj Kapoor**, **Meena Kumari**, Ajit, Nimmi, **Shammi Kapoor**, Kumkum, Jairaj, David, Anwar Hussain, Badri Prasad, Shakuntala, Rashid Khan, Nana Palsikar, Baby Naaz, Achala Sachdev

Abbas's only venture into the star-studded Hindi film mainstream. It tells a parable about love and community using three stories, each featuring a hero, his lover and a villain. The Ahir youth Govinda (Kapoor) is prevented from marrying his childhood sweetheart Chavli (Kumari) because she is an Untouchable. Chavli is driven out of the village but Govinda goes and waits for her at a crossroads. Dilawar (Ajit), a Pathan chauffeur, rescues the dancing-girl Pyari (Nimmi) from the clutches of his employer, a villainous nawab, but Pyari refuses to escape without her mother. Pyari then settles down at the same crossroads and starts a small shop, waiting for Dilawar to relent and to accept both of them. The hotel employee Johnny Braganza (S. Kapoor) falls in love with Stella D'Souza (Kumkum) who is coveted by his boss Ferreira (David). Ferreira frames Johnny and has him jailed. Johnny later joins the group at the crossroads and starts a garage. The trade union leader Nirmal Kumar (Jairaj) eventually enlists the trio at the crossroads to help build a road. Blasting through a hill, Govinda finds Chavli again and the whole community walks down 'their' road singing the socialist song *Sathi re kadam kadam se dil se dil mila rahe*. Later, in an interview with Vasudev and Lenglet (1983), Abbas blamed the film's failure on the stars' lack of screen glamour: 'Meena Kumari was blackened, Raj Kapoor was put in a dhoti, Shammi Kapoor was made into a waiter, Nimmi was made into a prostitute'. He never worked with major stars again.

CHHOTI BAHEN

1959 155' b&w Hindi
d **L.V. Prasad** *pc* Prasad Prod. *s* **Inder Raj Anand** *lyr* **Shailendra**, Hasrat Jaipuri *c* Dwarka Divecha *m* **Shankar-Jaikishen**
lp **Balraj Sahni**, Shyama, Nanda, Rehman, Mehmood, Shubha Khote, Sudesh Kumar, Veena, Badri Prasad, Dhumal, Radhakrishen, H. Shivdasani, Tridip Kumar

Prasad's early Hindi hit is a family melodrama featuring Rajendra (Sahni) who must support his younger brother Shekhar (Rehman) and sister Meena (Nanda). Shekhar prefers flirting with Shobha (Shyama) to his studies and Meena goes blind. Shekhar then marries Shobha who starts oppressing her blind sister-in-law, eventually causing her to end up on the streets. Rajendra loses his job and ends up destitute, allowing the film to reiterate its humanist message. It was probably adapted from **Ch. Narayanamurthy**'s earlier *Naa Chellelu* (1953).

DEEP JWELEY JAI

1959 132' b&w Bengali
d/sc **Asit Sen** *pc* Badal Pics *st/dial* Ashutosh Mukherjee *c* Anil Gupta, Jyoti Laha *m* **Hemanta Mukherjee**
lp **Suchitra Sen**, **Basanta Choudhury**, **Pahadi Sanyal**, **Tulsi Chakraborty**, **Anil Chatterjee**, Namita Sinha, Kajari Guha,

Chandrabati Devi, Dilip Choudhury, Shyam Laha

Original version of Sen's **Rajesh Khanna** psychodrama ***Khamoshi*** (1969) and one of Suchitra Sen's best-known performances. She plays Radha, the hospital nurse employed by a progressive psychiatrist. She is expected to develop a personal relationship with the male patients as part of their therapy. The doctor diagnoses Tapash's (B. Choudhury) problem as an unresolved Oedipal dilemma - the inevitable consequence, he says, for men who are denied a nurturing woman. He orders the nurse to play that role, even though on an earlier, similar occasion she fell in love with the patient. Radha bears up to Tapash's violence, wears red-bordered silk saris to impersonate his mother, sings his poetic compositions and, in the process, falls in love yet again. In the end, having brought about Tapash's mental cure, Radha has a nervous breakdown. Suchitra Sen's hauntingly beautiful, often partly lit close-ups set the tone for the film's visual style. Hemanta Mukherjee's music, e.g. *Ei raat tomar amar*, used a whistling chorus as a sort of leitmotif and contributed greatly to the movie's success.

DHOOL KA PHOOL

aka *Blossom of Dust*
1959 153' b&w Hindi
d **Yash Chopra** *pc* B.R. Films *s* Mukhram Sharma *lyr* **Sahir Ludhianvi** *c* Dharam Chopra *m* N. Dutta
lp **Mala Sinha, Rajendra Kumar**, **Ashok Kumar**, Nanda, Susheel Kumar, Manmohan Krishna, **Leela Chitnis**, Daisy Irani, Amirbano, Mohan Choti

Yash Chopra's debut was an epic melodrama about illegitimacy. University colleagues Mahesh Kapoor (R. Kumar) and Meena (Sinha) have an affair which leaves her pregnant. **Mahesh Bhatt** (1993) described the love-making scene as typical of the representation of sex in Indian cinema of the period: 'The real thing is made possible by a studio downpour and the library shots of lightning and thunder.' Under pressure from his autocratic father, Mahesh agrees to marry a rich heiress (Nanda). Meena, helped by her former maid (Chitnis), gives birth to a son and, fearing the stigma of being a single mother, abandons the baby in a forest. The child is found and raised by an old Muslim, Abdul Rasheed (M. Krishna). The grown-up boy (S. Kumar) is ostracised because of his illegitimate birth and falls in with bad company. At the end of the film, the boy's tangled history is revealed when, accused of theft, he has to appear in a court presided over by his father while the defending lawyer (A. Kumar) is his mother's husband. Meena herself acts as a witness. There is a plea for communal harmony when the old Muslim tells the boy not to adhere to any particular religion (*Tu Hindu banega na musalman banega*, sung by **Mohammed Rafi**, i.e. 'You will not grow up to be/a Muslim or a Hindu/You are the son of a man/and a human being you shall be.') The elaborate crane movements (esp. in the scene of Mahesh's wedding procession) and the combination of high-angle 'nature' shots with tightly edited scenes were characteristic of 50s B.R. Films (cf ***Kanoon***, 1960). Well-known songs, including the duet *Tere pyar ka aasra chahata hoon* (by Mahendra Kapoor and **Lata Mangeshkar**) and *Jhukti ghata gaati hawa* (sung by **Asha Bhosle**).

DIL DEKE DEKHO

1959 187' b&w Hindi
d/s **Nasir Hussain** *pc* Filmalaya *lyr* **Majrooh Sultanpuri** *c* Dilip Gupta *m* Usha Khanna
lp **Shammi Kapoor**, Asha Parekh, Sulochana, Raj Mehra, Randhir, Wasti, Rajendranath, Mumtaz Ali, Indira, Tahir Khan, B.K. Mukherjee, Kewal Kapoor, Surendra, Siddhu, Malika

Hussain's reworking of ***Tumsa Nahin Dekha*** (1957) repeats the former film's plot, except that the long-lost father is replaced by a mother. Heiress Jamuna (Sulochana) is deserted by her husband Rana, who takes their son Roop with him. She adopts Kailash (Rajendranath) and Neeta (Parekh) and wants the two to get married. However, Neeta falls in love with a rock singer who turns out to be the grown-up Roop (Kapoor). The villain Harichand persuades Jamuna that her son is in fact his accomplice Sohan, and that Sohan should marry Neeta. The confusion is resolved by way of a shootout during the marriage ceremony. Shammi Kapoor repeats his trademark scene, impersonating a Muslim gentleman (cf the *Dekho kasam se* number in *Tumsa Nahin Dekha*), Professor Saamri, who sings *Do ekam do* while dispensing advice to other characters. The story merely provides a framework for a series of rock numbers including the title song *Dil deke dekho, dil dene walon* and *Pyar ho to keh do Yes* (sung by **Mohammed Rafi**).

GOONJ UTHI SHEHNAI

1959 174' b&w Hindi
d **Vijay Bhatt** *pc* Prakash Pics *s* **G.D. Madgulkar** *dial* Shiv Kumar, Qamar Jalalabadi *lyr* Bharat Vyas *c* Bipin Gajjar *m* **Vasant Desai**
lp **Rajendra Kumar**, Ameeta, Ulhas, I.S. Johar, Manmohan Krishna, Leela Mishra, Prem Dhawan, Pratap Bhansali, Rammurthy, Anita Guha

A successful romance featuring a classical shehnai musician. Kishen (R. Kumar) is a musical prodigy in love with Gopi (Ameeta). Their union is opposed by Gopi's widowed mother Jamuna (Mishra) and by Kishen's adopted music teacher Raghunath (Ulhas) whose daughter Ramkali (Guha) secretly loves the musician. Later, when Kishen is a famous radio musician, his benefactor Shekhar (Bhansali) marries Gopi. In several scenes, the love-stricken Kishen vows never again to play the instrument with which he had wooed Gopi and he drowns his sorrows in alcohol. The film's main asset is the extensive use of the shehnai instrument, performed in playback by 20th C. India's best-known shehnai maestro, Bismillah Khan. In order to try to match the music's classical authenticity, an attempt was made to present the story as a medieval Sanskrit love legend.

GUEST HOUSE

1959 ?' b&w Hindi
d **Ravindra Dave** *pc* Golden Movies *s* K.A. Narayan *dial* Adil Rashid, Rafat Badayuni *lyr* Prem Dhawan *c* Raj Kumar Bhakri *m* Chitragupta
lp Ajit, Shakila, Maruti, **Lalita Pawar**, Vimla Kumari, Tiwari, Pran

A moral fable presented as a crime melodrama. Amar (Ajit) and his cousin Manohar (Pran) are a pair of shifty childhood friends. However, Manohar's father believes his son to be a fine person led astray by Amar. When Amar's dying mother makes her son promise never to tell lies, Manohar, caught by the police, is jailed because Amar refuses to lie to save his friend.

Ameeta and Rajendra Kumar in *Goonj Uthi Shehnai*

Amar is disinherited by his equally shifty guardian and goes to Bombay where he is taken in by Neela (Shakila) and dreams of becoming a saintly figure with his new-found idealism. When Manohar is released, he seeks revenge on his cousin and erstwhile friend. In the process he has to disown his doting father, now a beggar on the streets.

KAAGAZ KE PHOOL

aka *Paper Flowers*
1959 153' b&w/scope Hindi
d/p **Guru Dutt** *pc* Guru Dutt Films *s* Abrar Alvi *lyr* **Kaifi Azmi** *c* V.K. Murthy *m* **S.D. Burman**
lp Guru Dutt, **Waheeda Rehman**, Baby Naaz, **Johnny Walker**, **Mahesh Kaul**, Veena, Minoo Mumtaz, Pratima Devi, Niloufer, Sulochana, Sheila Vaz, Bikram Kapoor

The commercial failure of this film on its initial release prompted Guru Dutt, by some accounts, to stop taking directorial credit for his films. The baroque, quasi-autobiographical fantasy has over time become his best-known film next to ***Pyaasa*** (1957) and could be regarded as India's equivalent of *Citizen Kane* (1941). It tells, in flashback, the story of Suresh Sinha (Dutt), a famous film director. His marriage to Bina (Veena), the daughter of a wealthy parvenue (Mahesh Kaul), is wrecked because film directing is a job lacking in social status. Sinha is denied access to his beloved daughter Pammi (Baby Naaz) who is sent to a private boarding school. On a rainy night Sinha meets Shanti (Rehman) who turns out to be ideally suited to act the part of Paro in Sinha's film *Devdas*. Shanti becomes a star and gossip columns link her with Sinha. The distraught Pammi pleads with Shanti to quit films, which she does, and her withdrawal leads to a rapid decline in Sinha's fortunes. Soon he is a forgotten and destitute man. Eventually, after some painful adventures (reminiscent of Emil Jannings's fate in Sternberg's *The Last Command*, 1928) Sinha is found dead in the director's chair in an empty studio. With a more complex narrative structure than *Pyaasa*, this film can be seen as a meditation on the control of space, itself an eminently cinematic concern and brilliantly rendered by Murthy's astonishing CinemaScope camerawork. The film dramatises the conflict between open and constricted spaces, between spaces controlled by the director and spaces constraining him, spaces he can enter and those from which he is excluded. Eventually these tensions are resolved in the enclosed and womblike but huge and free-seeming space of a deserted film studio. The tragic refrain *Waqt hai meherbaan* of the song *Dekhi zamaane ki yaari*, written by Azmi, repeated throughout the film, endows the narrative with an epic dimension enhanced by Burman's music. The original CinemaScope negative has been damaged and few scope prints survive (two are at European tv stations).

KALYANA PARISU

aka *The Wedding Gift*
1959 194' b&w Tamil
d/s **C.V. Sridhar** *pc* Venus Pics *lyr* **Pattukotai Kalyanasundaram** *c* **A. Vincent** *m* A.M. Raja
lp **Gemini Ganesh**, **A. Nageshwara Rao**, K.A. Thangavelu, **B. Saroja Devi**, Vijayakumari, M. Saroja, S.D. Subbulakshmi

The playwright Sridhar's directorial debut is a melodrama featuring the student Bhaskar (Ganesh) who has a secret liaison with Vasanthi (Saroja Devi), a fellow student in whose house he rents a room. However, he marries her sister Geetha (Vijayakumari), the breadwinner of the family. Vasanthi stays with the couple until Geetha asks her sister to leave. When Geetha dies and leaves Bhaskar a single father, he tries to secure Vasanthi again but finds her already married, so he hands her his child as a 'wedding gift' and disappears into the mist. The film presents the ruthlessly egotistical, wifebeating Bhaskar as a victimised, tragic hero in a story advocating the observance of social convention, with popular songs performed by playback singer and music director A.M. Raja, then at the peak of his career. Its autonomous comic sub-plot also proved very popular and is still sold on audio cassettes. Sridhar went on to make a series of 'eternal triangle' pictures in a similar vein.

MAHISHASURA MARDINI/DURGA MATA

1959 167' b&w Kannada/Hindi
d/c **B.S. Ranga** *pc* Vikram Prod. *s/lyr* Chi. Sadashivaiah *m* **G.K. Venkatesh**
lp **Rajkumar**, **Udaya Kumar**, **Sowcar Janaki**, Sandhya, Narasimhraju, **Chittor V. Nagaiah**, Ashwath, Rajanala, Suryakala

Devi Purana variation of the circumstances that led to the goddess Durga slaying the demon Mahishasura. In the film, told in flashback, he is not a demon but one who was ancestrally wronged when the god Indra slew Karambha, king of Mahishamandala. Karambha's brother Rambha (Udaya Kumar), in retaliation, reaches the Nagaloka and steals the Sanathanakalpa fruit, bringing down a curse on his son: the boy shall never see either of his parents alive. The prophecy comes true as Rambha is killed and his wife Mahishi (Suryakala) commits sati (ritual self-immolation) just after her son Mahishasura is born. Mahishi was in fact a buffalo turned into a beautiful woman by Indra. The orphaned Mahishasura (Rajkumar) is raised by Shukracharya, who tells him the family story in the film's opening. Vowing to take revenge against the invincible Indra, Mahishasura through prayer achieves indestructibility. The celestial impasse is resolved when the goddess Parvati-Durga, gifted with the accumulated power of all the gods, defeats Mahishasura in a nine-day battle.

PAIGHAM

1959 188' b&w Hindi
d **S.S. Vasan** *pc* **Gemini** *s* Kothamangalam Subbu *dial* **Ramanand Sagar**, T. Mukherjee *lyr* Pradeep *c* P. Ellappa *m* **C. Ramchandra**
lp **Dilip Kumar**, **Vyjayanthimala**, Raaj Kumar, **Pandharibai**, **Motilal**, **B. Saroja Devi**, **Johnny Walker**, Minoo Mumtaz

After ***Mr Sampat*** (1952) and ***Insaniyat*** (1955), this multi-star melodrama consolidated S.S. Vasan's efforts to break into the Hindi cinema. Poor heroine Manju (Vyjayanthimala) befriends Malati (Saroja Devi), the daughter of rich millowner Seth Sewakram (Motilal). The engineer Ratanlal (D. Kumar), together with his brother Ramlal (Raaj Kumar), works at Sewakram's mill where he meets Manju again and falls in love with her. The complicated story that ensues involves Ratanlal setting up a union while his brother Ramlal tries to break it under pressure from the boss. The major twist in the plot is that Manju is revealed to be the rich millowner's daughter, whereupon she tries to burn down the mill. Ratanlal, who tries to stop her, is arrested and jailed for arson before the story is eventually resolved.

PRESIDENT PANCHATCHARAM

1959 162' b&w Tamil
d **A. Bhimsingh** *pc* Savithri Pics *st* N. Gogol's *The Government Inspector* *sc* B.S. Ramaiah *c* M. Karnan *m* G. Ramanathan
lp S.S. Rajendran, S.V. Sahasranamam, T.R. Ramchandran, V.R. Rajagopal, **B. Saroja Devi**, S.N. Lakshmi, T.V. Karunanidhi, N. Chandini, D.V. Narayanaswamy

The District Board president (Sahasranamam) meets the unemployed youth Sigamani (Rajendran), who wants a job and says he is in love with the president's daughter (Saroja Devi). However, the president mistakes him for a government representative investigating corruption charges.

RAJA MUKUTAM

1959 179'[Te]/184'[Ta] b&w Telugu/Tamil
d/co-sc **B.N. Reddi** *pc* **Vauhini** *st/dial* **D.V. Narasaraju** *co-sc* Padmaraju, B.S. Ramaiah *lyr* **Devulapalli Krishna Sastry**, **Kosaraju**, Nagaraju *c* B.N. Konda Reddy *m* **Master Venu**
lp **N.T. Rama Rao**, **Gummadi Venkateshwara Rao**, Rajanala, Rajasulochana, **P. Kannamba**

An unacknowledged adaptation of Ramana's 'folkloric' adventure *Pudumaipithan* (1957) by a director known for reformist films. The king is assassinated in the absence of his son Prince Pratap (NTR). When Pratap returns in disguise, he falls in love with the village belle Prameela (Rajasulochana). He becomes a public enemy when he sentences the men who appear to be guilty of the killing, one of whom is Prameela's brother, but the real villain is Prachanda, the prince's uncle. Disguised as an avenging revolutionary known as the Black Snake, Pratap dethrones the villain. The Telugu version of the bilingual (Reddi's only two-language film) was a success, but the director later disowned it for pandering to commercialism.

SANGTYE AIKA

1959 157' b&w Marathi
d **Anant Mane** *pc* Chetana Chitra *st* G.G. Parkhi *s* Venkatesh Madgulkar *lyr* **G.D. Madgulkar** *c* I. Mohammed *m* Vasant Pawar
lp Sulochana, **Hansa Wadkar**, **Jayashree Gadkar**, Ratnamala, Neelam, Pushpa Rane, Chandrakant, **Suryakant**, Dada Salvi, Vasantrao Pahelwan, Vasant Shinde, Kisanrao Agihotri

Mane's major hit is a Wadkar classic, later providing the title for her controversial autobiography (1970). Marathi cinema's best-known Tamasha musical (with Shantaram's ***Lokshahir Ramjoshi***, 1947) is an epic saga narrating a conflict over two generations between the evil Mahadev Patil of Rajuri (Dada Salvi) and folk Tamasha dancer Chima (Wadkar). The good Sakharam and his wife move into the village where he defeats Patil in a bullock-cart race (one of the film's most spectacular sequences). Patil has Sakharam killed and his home burnt down. When Sakharam's wife dies in childbirth, the dancer Chima, who bears Patil's child, switches the two infants. In the second half, the young dancer (Gadkar), now apprenticed to Chima, faces the amorous attentions of Patil's son. The remarkable finale has Chima reveal the truth on stage through song: the young dancer is in fact Patil's own daughter. Sakharam's naivety (cf the song *Jhali bhali pahaat*) is contrasted with the cynical *realpolitik* of the villain, while Wadkar's extraordinary performance holds the story together as well as commenting on the village's history. In a performance recalling Brecht's dramaturgy, she integrates the Tamasha and the Lavni idioms into the melodramatic plot, combining Madgulkar's stereotypes of authenticity with the mythic aspects of the ruralist 'gramin chitrapat' genre. Wadkar's successor in the Tamasha and saint film idioms, Gadkar, here has one of her first major roles.

SATTA BAZAAR

1959 ?' b&w Hindi
d **Ravindra Dave** *pc* Nagina Films *st* **Mohanlal G. Dave** *sc* **K.A. Abbas** *lyr* **Shailendra**, Hasrat Jaipuri, Gulshan Bawra, Indivar *c* W.V. Mukadam *m* **Kalyanji-Anandji**
lp **Meena Kumari**, **Balraj Sahni**, **Johnny Walker**, Suresh, Tiwari, **Krishnakant**, Asit Sen, Savita Choudhury, Vijaya Choudhury

A devout housewife (Kumari) supports her stepdaughter's decision to marry a man not of her own caste, but her husband Ramesh (Sahni) gets mixed up with a bunch of crooks and causes the family much distress.

SIVAGANGAI SEEMAI

aka *The Land of Sivagangai*
1959 173' b&w Tamil
d K. Shankar *p/sc/lyr* **Kannadasan** *pc* Kannadasan Prod. *c* Thambu *m* Vishwanathan-Ramamurthy
lp S.S. Rajendran, T.K. Bhagavathi, M.K. Musthafa, P.S. Veerappa, Kumari Kamala, M.N. Rajam, **S. Varalakshmi**, Wahab Kashmiri

The lyricist and Dravidian ideologue Kannadasan uses a fictionalised account of the British East India Company's subjugation of the Sivagangai kingdom as a vehicle for **DMK** propaganda. Set in 1798, Omaithurai, the brother of Kattabomman who rose against the British, seeks the protection of the Marudu brothers who rule Sivagangai. Col. Welsh (Kashmiri) uses this incident to storm their fort and execute the rulers. In parallel, the film chronicles the tragic love story between Muthazhagu (Rajendran) and Chittu (Kamala). Chittu and another female character die of unspecified causes after their husbands get killed. A young bride whose husband is murdered by robbers commits sati, something the film appears to approve of as the Marudu brothers declare she should be worshipped as a deity. Theatricality, verbosity, angled shots for emotional emphasis and insistent background music weigh the film down, although folk-songs provide a lighter touch.

SUJATA

1959 161'(147') b&w Hindi
d/p **Bimal Roy** *pc* Bimal Roy Prod. *st* Subodh Ghosh *sc* Nabendu Ghosh *dial* Paul Mahendra *lyr* **Majrooh Sultanpuri** *c* Kamal Bose *m* **S.D. Burman**
lp **Nutan**, **Sunil Dutt**, Shashikala, Tarun Bose, Sulochana, **Lalita Pawar**

Roy's classic reformist melodrama about a Harijan (Untouchable) girl whose kinfolk die in a plague epidemic and is raised by an upper-class and caste family. Upendranath Choudhury (Bose) and his wife Charu (Sulochana) have a daughter, Rama (Shashikala), and they adopt Sujata (Nutan), the Harijan orphan. Later, Sujata discovers the truth of her ancestry and must bear the demeaning treatment meted out by Charu and the family friend Giribala (Pawar), whose son Adhir (Dutt) is supposed to marry Rama but falls in love with Sujata. When Sujata donates blood to save Charu's life, even Charu has to abandon her caste prejudice. Nutan gives one of her best performances, surpassed only by her solo tour de force in Roy's ***Bandini*** (1963). Unfortunately, the weak Adhir has to bear the burden of being the only representative of the progressive forces ranged against oppressive tradition. Presumably for its humanist message, the film includes a rather arbitrarily inserted but elaborate stage performance of **Tagore**'s dance drama *Chandalika*. Several classic numbers include **Asha Bhosle**'s *Kali ghata chhaye*, composer S.D. Burman's own *Suno mere bandhu re* and Talat Mahmood's *Jalte hain jiske liye*.

VEERAPANDIYA KATTABOMMAN/AMAR SHAHEED

1959 201' col Tamil/Hindi
d/p **B.R. Panthulu** *pc* Padmini Pics *s* Shakti Krishnaswamy *c* W.R. Subba Rao *lyr* K.M. Balasubramanyam *m* G. Ramanathan
lp **Sivaji Ganesan**, **Gemini Ganesh**, **Padmini**, **S. Varalakshmi**, Ragini, V.K. Ramaswamy

The epic historical and best-known of Ganesan's collaborations with Panthulu. Kattaboman was the ruler of a small kingdom in Tamil Nadu in the 18th C. who heroically fought against the British invaders and is still revered for his rebellion. The plot has the British lure a rival, Ettayappan (Ramaswamy), into betraying the valiant Kattaboman (Ganesan) who is wounded, captured, humiliatingly brought to trial and hanged. The idealised portrait of Kattaboman is interwoven, in Ganesan's first colour picture, with lavish court scenes, temple worship and the taming of bulls. A love interest has been added as well. The film consciously invoked Cecil B. DeMille's spectacles with Panthulu adopting DeMille's tactic of personally introducing the film, on camera.

ANGULIMAL

1960 153' col Hindi
d **Vijay Bhatt** *pc* P.V. Films, Thai Information Service *dial* Sudarshan *lyr* Bharat Vyas *c* V. Avadhoot *m* **Anil Biswas**
lp Nimmi, Bharat Bhushan, Anita Guha, Ulhas, Chandrasekhar, Achala Sachdev, Manmohan Krishna, Prem Adib, Kaisari, Helen

Financed by the Thai Government this film was to celebrate the 2500th anniversary of the Buddha (6th century BC). The tyrannical Angulimal (Bhushan), a bandit wearing a garland of severed human fingers and who engages in bloody mystical rituals to achieve divine power, eventually succumbs to the Buddha's teachings. Nimmi played Angulimal's lover and **Hemen Gupta** was originally announced as the director.

ANURADHA

aka *Love of Anuradha*
1960 141'(120') b&w Hindi
p/d **Hrishikesh Mukherjee** *pc* L.B. Films *st/co-sc* Sachin Bhowmik *co-sc* D.N Mukherjee, Samir Choudhury *dial* **Rajinder Singh Bedi** *lyr* **Shailendra** *c* Jaywant Pathare *m* Ravi Shankar
lp **Balraj Sahni**, **Abhi Bhattacharya**, Leela Naidu, Baby Ranu, Nasir Hussain, Hari Shivdasani, Mukri, Rashid Khan, Asit Sen, Ashim Kumar, Madhav Chitnis, Bhudo Advani

A sentimental variation on *Madame Bovary*: Anuradha Roy (Naidu), a lively and successful singer, marries a dull but idealistic country doctor (Sahni) and soon gets bored. Her former lover, who has an accident while passing through her village, ignites memories of her past and persuades her to return to her former profession. However, a timely visit by a famous and worldly-wise doctor, who recognises her sacrifice as more praiseworthy than the genius of her husband, reconciles her to her new life. Some poetic shots in the film play on life's ironies: while Anuradha looks at palm trees in the moonlight, the doctor gazes at wriggling worms through his microscope. Imaginative cutting (the director is also an expert editor) creates effective narrative ellipses, as when the newly married bride eagerly awaits her husband and he bursts in, years later, tired and irritable. Mukherjee's traditionally conservative fable about marriage is well served by Sahni's underacting, the subtle play of shadows suggesting the flavour of Anuradha'a nostalgia for her former success, and Ravi Shankar's music, including popular songs like *Kaise din beete* and *Hai re woh din kyon na aaye* (sung by **Lata Mangeshkar**).

APNA HAATH JAGANNATH

1960 173' b&w Hindi
d **Mohan Segal** *pc* Deluxe Films *s* **G.D. Madgulkar** *dial* **Rajinder Singh Bedi** *lyr* **Kaifi Azmi** *c* C.S. Puttu *m* **S.D. Burman**
lp **Kishore Kumar**, Sayeeda Khan, **Leela Chitnis**, Nasir Hussain, Jagdev, Nandkishore, Shivraj, Sabita Chatterjee

Following on from his successful ***New Delhi*** (1956), Segal here uses the comedy star Kishore Kumar to address middle-class attitudes to manual labour. Madan (Kumar), the son of an impoverished aristocrat, Dhaniram, is forced to take a labouring job to the disappointment of his father and the disapproval of his future in-laws. However, he makes a success of his printing press and eventually employs his own father in the expanding business. The film has several Kishore Kumar numbers including the bouncy *Permit permit...ke liye mar mit*.

BAISHEY SHRAVAN

aka *The Wedding Day*
1960 110'(98') b&w Bengali
d/s **Mrinal Sen** *pc* Kallol Films *c* Sailaja Chatterjee *m* **Hemanta Mukherjee**
lp Gyanesh Mukherjee, **Madhabi Mukherjee**, Hemangini Devi, Umanath Bhattacharya, Sumita Dasgupta

Set in a Bengal village just before and during the catastrophic famine of 1943 when some 5 million people died of starvation. A middle-aged hawker (G. Mukherjee) marries a beautiful 16-year-old girl (M. Mukherjee) who initially brightens his life. Then the man's mother (H. Devi) dies, WW2 presses upon them and the famine hits Bengal as the couple's marriage and the entire fabric of life disintegrates. In the end, the wife hangs herself. It is a deliberately cruel film about cruel living conditions, with the stark realism heightened through several melodramatic techniques. The mother dies when the roof falls on her head in a violent storm; the marriage breaks up when Priyanath greedily eats up the little rice he can find in the midst of the famine, without leaving any for his wife. The real innovation is that the third party destroying the marriage is not a person but the impact upon the couple of, in Sen's words, 'the men who, as they served colonial bosses in their war efforts, cared only for profiteering and black marketing'.

BAMBAI KA BABU

1960 154' b&w Hindi
d/co-p **Raj Khosla** *co-p/c* Jal Mistry *pc* Naya Films *s* G.R. Kamath *dial* **Rajinder Singh Bedi** *lyr* **Majrooh Sultanpuri** *m* **S.D. Burman**
lp **Dev Anand**, **Suchitra Sen**, Manohar Deepak, Rashid Khan, Jagdish Raj, Lalita Kumari, Prem Khanna, Sailen Bose, Anwaribai, Nasir Hussain

The nice Inspector Malik (Deepak) reforms the criminal Babu (Anand) who is then pursued by the gang boss Bali (Raj) who suspects Babu has become an informer. In a fight, Bali is killed and Babu has to go on the run. A blackmailer, Bhagatji (Khan), forces Babu to impersonate the long-lost son of a rich household in order to steal their jewellery. In the process, Babu falls in love with Maya (Sen), the daughter of the family. After the film's noirish beginning, as in many Dev Anand starrers, it turns into a romance, initially with incestual overtones since Maya believes Babu to be her brother. Eventually, when Babu discovers that the lost son was Bali, whom he has killed, he accepts his responsibilities to the family and that Maya will marry someone else.

CHAUDHVIN KA CHAND

1960 169' b&w/col Hindi-Urdu
d M. Sadiq *p* **Guru Dutt** *pc* Guru Dutt Films *s* Saghir Usmani *lyr* Shakeel Badaiyuni *c* Nariman Irani *m* Ravi
lp **Waheeda Rehman**, Guru Dutt, Rehman, Minoo Mumtaz, **Johnny Walker**, Mumtaz Begum, Praveen Paul, Naazi, Nurjehan, Razia, Zebunissa

Dutt apparently commissioned Sadiq to make this Muslim social to help the maker of ***Rattan*** (1944) out of his impecunious condition. The love triangle pivots around the Islamic practice of purdah, which forbids women to show their face to men outside their immediate family. A nawab (Rehman) catches a brief glimpse of Jamila's (W. Rehman) face and falls in love with her. At his sister's party, he manages to get hold of a torn fragment from Jamila's veil and gives it to a maidservant to trace the identity of its owner. Jamila happens to exchange her veil with that of her friend Bano and so the nawab identifies the wrong woman. This mistake becomes a tragic irony when the nawab, having refused to marry a woman chosen by his ailing mother, persuades his close friend Aslam (Dutt) to marry the maternal choice instead: that woman turns out to be Jamila. When some time later Aslam realises that his friend the nawab is in love with his wife Jamila, he pretends to tire of her, hoping that she will demand a divorce and so will be free to marry the nawab. The nawab soon learns of Aslam's attempted sacrifice and in the tradition of male friendships on the screen, the nawab chooses to die for his friend and commits suicide. In later release prints, two song sequences, one being the famous **Rafi** solo *Chaudhvin ka chand ho, ya aftaab ho*, were rendered in colour although designed for b&w.

Guru Dutt and Minoo Mumtaz in *Chaudhvin Ka Chand*

CHHALIA

1960 112' b&w Hindi
d **Manmohan Desai** *pc* Subhash Pics *s* **Inder Raj Anand** *lyr* Qamar Jalalabadi *c* N. Satyen *m* **Kalyanji-Anandji**
lp **Raj Kapoor**, **Nutan**, Rehman, **Shobhana Samarth**, Pran, Moppet Raja, Ramlal, Gul, Shyamlal

Desai's directorial debut is an unlikely drama about India's Partition. Shanti (Nutan) is married to Kewal (Rehman) in Lahore on the eve of Independence. When the nation is divided, Shanti's family and her husband migrate to Delhi, leaving her behind. She finds shelter for five years with the Afghan bandit Abdul Rehman (Pran) who has a sister of Shanti's age across the border. Shanti bears a son, Anwar (Moppet Raja), and when she travels to Delhi with her child her husband disowns her, as does her father. She finds shelter with another generous criminal, Chhalia (Kapoor), who falls in love with her. Abdul Rehman comes to Delhi to pursue an old feud with Chhalia and threatens to kidnap Shanti. After an extended fight sequence, the two bandits call a truce. On the train back to Pakistan, Rehman is reunited with his sister. Chhalia arranges a reconciliation between Shanti and Kewal, renouncing his own chance at happiness. The film alludes to aspects of realism derived from radical literature as well as from Kapoor's presence (cf ***Phir Subah Hogi***, 1958), but Desai seems impatient with the finer points of plot structure, a tendency that would later lead to his virtual abandonment of temporally coherent plots in the **Bachchan** films of the 70s and 80s. The film had several hit songs including the communal-harmony number *Chhalia mera naam*, sung by Mukesh.

DEVI

aka *The Goddess*
1960 93' b&w Bengali
d/p/sc **Satyajit Ray** *pc* Satyajit Ray Prod. *st* Prabhat Kumar Mukherjee *c* Subrata Mitra *m* Ali Akbar Khan
lp **Chhabi Biswas**, **Soumitra Chatterjee**, **Sharmila Tagore**, Purnendu Mukherjee, Karuna Bannerjee, Arpan Choudhury, **Anil Chatterjee**, Kali Sarkar, Mohammed Israel, Khagesh Chakraborty

Following ***Jalsaghar*** (1958), Ray made a series of period movies featuring strong, well-rounded characters no longer limited to the requirements of melodramatic plot functions. These characters, Bishwambar Roy, Dayamoyee and later ***Charulata*** (1964) were adapted equally from Bengali literary stereotypes and from English literature's notion of psychological realism. Made in the same year as *Devi*, Ghatak's classic ***Meghe Dhaka Tara*** uses the popular Bengali legend associating young married women with Durga, the mythical provider, to reveal how history and culture create the oppressive social spaces determining women's lives. Instead, Ray presented a psychological portrait of a young woman and her zamindar father-in-law set in the mid-19th C. The beautiful Dayamoyee (Tagore) is deemed by her recently widowed father-in-law Kalikinker Roy (Biswas) to be the goddess Kali incarnate, disregarding the rationalist arguments put forth by her husband Umaprasad (S. Chatterjee), a university student. The old man transforms her into an icon for prayer in the village, and she soon develops a reputation for miracle cures. Seduced by her role as divinity, she is reluctant to return with her husband to the city. When the death of her son destroys her illusions, Dayamoyee goes mad and disappears bejewelled into the mist. Much of the film dealt with the barely-concealed sexual relationship between Dayamoyee and the father-in-law as she massages his feet while he reclines with a hookah, or even more explicitly in a prayer sequence that juxtaposes her sitting before the Kali icon with shots of the father-in-law descending for prayer. Ray preferred a cultural and psychological reading, enjoining his Western critics to acquaint themselves thoroughly with, e.g., the cult of the Mother Goddess, the 19th C. Renaissance in Bengal and the position of the Hindu bride. The film is also remembered for Mitra's remarkable camerawork, contrasting the purely psychological exposition with two breathtaking crane shots that show the immersion of the goddess during the Puja festival and capture the manic hold exerted by the Durga/Kali legend in Bengal.

GANGA

aka *The River*
1960 151' b&w Bengali
d/sc **Rajen Tarafdar** *pc* Cine Art Prod. *st* Samaresh Bose *c* **Dinen Gupta** *m* **Salil Choudhury**
lp Niranjan Ray, Gyanesh Mukherjee, Sandhya Roy, Ruma Guha-Thakurta, Seeta Devi, Mani Srimani, Namita Sinha

Following in the wake of **Satyajit Ray**'s idyllic rural realism, Tarafdar's best-known film is an epic drama about a young fisherman of the Sundarbans, Bilash (Ray), who has to overcome fear and superstition to make his way down the river to the sea. Old Panchu (Mukherjee) witnessed, shown in flashback, the horrifying disappearance into the sea of his elder brother and former leader of the fishermen. His impulsive nephew Bilash has an affair with a married woman, rejects the love of Gamli Panchi (Roy) and finally wants to marry Himi (Guha-Thakurta), daughter of the unscrupulous moneylender Damini. When Bilash decides to 'go south' to the sea too, evoking an ominous pattern all too familiar to his uncle Panchu, Himi refuses to follow him. The story meanders through several detours chronicling in detail the fisherfolk's dangerous lives and their struggles with storms, floods, hunger and indebtedness. Its primitivist iconography extends to the depiction of women as both home-makers and destroyers, and to aligning the men's thirst for life with nature rites. **Chidananda Das Gupta** critiqued the film for its lyricism, which for him detracted from the story's epic potential and pushed it towards melodrama. The film established Tarafdar as a major film-maker, but he still had problems finding work in the industry.

HOSPITAL

1960 164' b&w Bengali
d **Sushil Majumdar** *pc* Shri N.C.A. Pics *m* Amal Mukherjee
lp **Ashok Kumar**, **Suchitra Sen**, **Pahadi Sanyal**, **Chhabi Biswas**, Sushil Majumdar, **Bhanu Bannerjee**

A medical story complicated by caste differences. Saibal (A. Kumar) and Sarbari (Sen) are surgeons in a hospital. Their marriage is prevented by her lower-caste status. When she discovers that she is pregnant, Sarbari goes to work in a small town where she gives birth to a son. She then discovers that she suffers from cancer. Saibal comes to perform the operation that saves her. Not to be confused with the bilingual ***Jogajog/Hospital***(B/H) (1943) by the same film-maker.

JAALI NOTE

1960 155' b&w Hindi
d **Shakti Samanta** *pc* S.P. Pics *lyr* Raja Mahendra, Anjaan *m* **O.P. Nayyar**
lp **Dev Anand**, **Madhubala**, Om Prakash, Helen, Madan Puri, Bipin Gupta, Kundan

A crime thriller featuring Inspector Dinesh (Anand) who tracks down a gang of counterfeiters with the assistance of a fearless journalist, Renu (Madhubala). He puts on a variety of disguises and masquerades as a prince who runs a counterfeiting business. In the end the main villain (Gupta) turns out to be the hero's long-lost father. One of Samanta's lesser-known detective movies.

JAGACHYA PATHIVAR

1960 147' b&w Marathi
d/st **Raja Paranjpe** *pc* Shripad Chitra *sc/lyr* **G.D. Madgulkar** *c* Bal Bapat *m* **Sudhir Phadke**
lp Raja Paranjpe, Seema, G.D. Madgulkar, Dhumal, Mai Bhide, Vinay Kale, Raja Gosavi, Ramesh Dev, Sharad Talwalkar, Rajdutt

Melodrama evoking Chaplin's *City Lights* (1931). Poor hero, in search of employment, meets blind heroine who sings and dances in the street for a living. He looks after her until her millionaire father rediscovers her. There are some classic hit songs by Phadke, e.g. *Jag he bandishala* and *Nahi kharchali kavadi damadi*.

JIS DESH MEIN GANGA BEHTI HAI

1960 167' b&w Hindi
d Radhu Karmakar *p* **Raj Kapoor** *pc* R.K. Films *s* Arjun Dev Rashk *lyr* **Shailendra**, Hasrat Jaipuri *c* Tara Dutt *m* **Shankar-Jaikishen**
lp **Raj Kapoor**, **Padmini**, Pran, Tiwari, Nayampalli, Chanchal, Raj Mehra, **Lalita Pawar**, Sulochana Chatterjee, Nana Palsikar, Vishwa Mehra, Amar

A pacifist film directed by Kapoor's cameraman since ***Awara*** (1951). Set among the bandits of central India and by the banks of the Ganges, the story tells of Raju (Kapoor), a wandering innocent who believes in the purity of the Ganga and abhors violence (a trait influenced by the philosophies of Acharya Vinoba Bhave and Gandhi). He rescues a man who turns out to be a bandit chieftain and then reforms the gang after complicated negotiations with the police. In the process, he has to overcome the gang's lieutenant, Raka (Pran), and falls in love with the chief's daughter (Padmini). The film emphasised scenic shots, beginning with several slow pans over the Ganges and ending with a spectacular sequence in a valley when the outlaws finally lay down their arms and surrender to the law. Its most typical movement is a slow crane movement upwards, leaving the audience to 'judge' the characters and their contradictory ideologies. Kapoor, distinctly older than in his 50s classics, moves with the stilted gestures of a marionette in his characteristic role of the innocent country lad who ends up reforming the world.

KADU MAKRANI

1960 148' b&w Gujarati
d/sc **Manhar Raskapur** *pc* Sadhana Chitra *st* Gunwantrai Acharya *co-lyr/m* **Avinash Vyas** *co-lyr* Apa Hamir *c* Bipin Gajjar
lp Arvind, Shalini, Champsibhai Nagda, Mahesh Desai, Babu Raje, Bhudo Advani, Champak Lala, Radha, **Sulochana**, Ulhas, Jaya Bhatt, Honey Chhaya, Vishnu Vyas, Padmakumar Joshi, Ajit Soni, Mukand Desai, Devika Roy, Bhimjibhai, **Upendra Trivedi**, Gunvant Kayastha, Bagla, Manjula Moti

Raskapur's best-known film is an anti-imperialist fantasy historical, his favourite genre (cf his ***Mulu Manek***, 1955). Unlike most Indian royals, the Makranis of Junagadh defy the British who retaliate by invading Inaj, a Makrani settlement. Four members of the royal clan become bandits. The main one, Kadar Baksh aka Kadu Makrani, causes major problems for the British who order the local police chief, one of Kadar's boyhood friends, to capture him. After a furious battle Kadu is captured in Karachi and hanged. The film was remade by Manu Desai in 1973.

KALA BAZAAR

1960 163' b&w Hindi
d/s **Vijay Anand** *pc* **Navketan** Films *lyr* **Shailendra** *c* V. Ratra *m* **S.D. Burman**
lp **Dev Anand, Waheeda Rehman**, Nanda, **Leela Chitnis**, Vijay Anand, **Kishore Sahu**

Hero Raghuvir (D. Anand) becomes Bombay's top black marketeer in film tickets and falls in love with Alka (Rehman) who shuns 'black' money. The hero reforms and starts a 'white market' [Safed Bazaar] with his now legitimate gang of touts. Vijay Anand's characteristic use of realism as a counterweight to the release of fantasy is exemplified in the visual and sound montage that opens the film and in the remarkably picturised *Suraj ke jaisi golayi, chanda se thandak bhi payi* set in top-angle camera among sleeping pavement-dwellers. Dev Anand may have had this strategy in mind when he declared that films should be 'brought as close as possible to the reading of a newspaper'. The film includes several classic songs, e.g. *Na main dhan chahun* (sung by **Geeta Dutt** and Sudha Malhotra) and *Khoya khoya chand* (sung by **Mohammed Rafi**).

KANOON

1960 150' b&w Hindi
d/p **B.R. Chopra** *pc* B.R. Films *s* C.J. Pavri *dial* **Akhtar-ul-Iman** *c* M.N. Malhotra *m* **Salil Choudhury**
lp **Ashok Kumar, Rajendra Kumar**, Nanda, Nana Palsikar, Mehmood, Om Prakash

Chopra's courtroom drama and suspense movie tells of the progressive Judge Badriprasad (A. Kumar) whose daughter Meena (Nanda) is married to the equally progressive Public Prosecutor Kailash Khanna (R. Kumar). Kailash witnesses his father-in-law commit a murder. His dilemma grows when a petty thief is arrested and tried in Badriprasad's court. Eventually, when Badriprasad is forced to step down and submit to a new investigation, the killer is found to be an identical look-alike of the judge. The unlikely ending is shored up by a strong plea against capital punishment. The long court sequences are alleviated by extensive film noir passages (cf the crane movements along walls and corridors), and the film's association with Hollywood models is enhanced by the absence of songs.

KSHUDISTA PASHAN

aka *Hungry Stones*
1960 117' b&w Bengali
d/sc **Tapan Sinha** *pc* Eastern Circuit *p* Hemen Ganguly *st/lyr* **Rabindranath Tagore** *m* Ali Akbar Khan *c* Bimal Mukherjee
lp **Soumitra Chatterjee, Arundhati Devi**, Radhamohan Bhattacharya, **Chhabi Biswas**, Padmadevi, Dilip Roy, Bina Chand, Rasaraj Chakraborty

Sinha continues his adaptations of Tagore (***Kabuliwala***, 1956) with this ghost story shot in Bhopal, Bikaner and in the hills of MP although the story is set in the village of Barich in Hyderabad. A young tax collector (S. Chatterjee) decides to live in a deserted 250-year-old palace on the banks of the Susta river. The palace is said to be haunted and the villagers warn the prosaic taxman not to spend a single night there. Gradually, he falls under the spell of the place. Its hallucinatory world takes him over, in the form of a beautiful female apparition (A. Devi). His obssession gets to the point where his everyday life appears unreal as he vividly relives episodes from the fantasised history. In the fantasy, he is the trader Imtiaz Ali who gave the slave girl to the emperor but then fell in love with her. The palace used to be Emperor Mahmud Shah II's pleasure den and its stones seem to have absorbed the untold anguish suffered by the aristocratic potentate's female victims, a suffering so intense that it overwhelms those who dwell there. The film and its lyrical imagery can be read as metaphors for the remnants of feudal oppression still active in contemporary society. Alternatively, the feudal palace can be seen as triggering the eroticised fantasies of power of modern middle-class men.

MEGHE DHAKA TARA

aka *The Cloud-capped Star* aka *Hidden Star*
1960 134' b&w Bengali
d/sc **Ritwik Ghatak** *pc* Chitrakalpa *st* Shaktipada Rajguru *c* **Dinen Gupta** *m* Jyotirindra Moitra
lp **Supriya Choudhury, Anil Chatterjee, Bijon Bhattacharya**, Geeta De, Niranjan Ray, Geeta Ghatak, Dwiju Bhawal, Gyanesh Mukherjee, Ronen Ray Choudhury

One of Ghatak's most powerful and innovative melodramas revolving around the self-sacrificing Neeta (S. Choudhury), a figure analogous to the women in Mizoguchi's work. A family of refugees from the Partition of Bengal live in a shanty town near Calcutta, surviving on the earnings of the eldest daughter Neeta. Her elder brother Shankar (A. Chatterjee) hopes to become a classical singer, and Neeta postpones her marriage to the scientist Sanat (N. Ray) to support the family and to pay for Shankar's studies. Eventually, with the tacit encouragement of Neeta's mother (De), Sanat marries her younger sister Geeta (G. Ghatak). The family is beset by misfortunes as the father (B. Bhattacharya) and the younger brother Montu (Bhawal) both suffer accidents, forcing Neeta to remain the sole breadwinner in spite of her worsening tuberculosis. Finally Shankar, having achieved his ambition, takes her to a mountain resort for treatment. There, terminally ill and having sacrificed her best years, she finally cries out into the silence of the mountains her will to live. The story is familiar in Bengali melodrama (cf **Arundhati Devi**'s ***Chhuti***, 1967), a link stressed by the casting of Bengali star Supriya Choudhury. However, into this plot Ghatak weaves a parallel narrative evoking the celebrated Bengali legends of Durga who is believed to descend from her mountain retreat every autumn to visit her parents and that of Menaka. This double focus, condensed in the figure of Neeta, is rendered yet more complex on the level of the film language itself through elaborate, at times non-diegetic sound effects working alongside or as commentaries on the image (e.g. the refrain *Ai go Uma kole loi*. i.e. *Come to my arms, Uma, my child*, used through the latter part of the film, esp. on the face of the rain-drenched Neeta shortly before her departure to the sanatorium). This approach allows the film to transcend its story by

Supriya Choudhury in *Meghe Dhaka Tara*

opening it out towards the realm of myth and to the conventions of cinematic realism (evoked, e.g., in the Calcutta sequences). The characters, their actions and the way both are represented acquire an epic dimension: characters, without losing their singularity, are presented as figures caught in the web of historical (and therefore changeable) forces while the limits of mythic and of 'traditional' melodramatic narrative idioms are exceeded by a new, specifically cinematic mode of discourse. For instance, Neeta cuts across both the mythic and the melodramatic stereotypes of 'the nurturing mother', an association elaborated further musically by the Baul folk number, the Khayal compositions and a spectacularly filmed **Tagore** song; the oppression/seduction/nurture triangle which structures the Durga legend as derived from Tantric abstractions, is projected on to the mother, Geeta and Neeta, inscribing these abstractions back into history and thus making them available for critical reconsideration. **Kumar Shahani** addressed the film's achievements in his major essay 'Violence and Responsibility' (cf Shahani, 1986).

MEHNDI RANG LAGYO

1960 151' b&w Gujarati
d **Manhar Raskapur** *pc* Varsha Chitra *s* **Chaturbhuj Doshi** *c* Bipin Gajjar *lyr/m* **Avinash Vyas**
lp **Rajendra Kumar**, Usha Kiron, Chandravadan Bhatt, Satish Vyas, Keshav, Toral Divetia, Krina Lal, **Chandrakant Sangani**, Honey Chhaya, Jayesh Desai, B.M. Vyas, Bhimjibhai, Narayan Ragjor, Jaya Bhatt, Niharika Divetia, **Upendra Trivedi**, Madan Saigal, Mamta Bhatt, Nitin Shah

The beautiful and innocent exemple of Gujarati womanhood Alka (Kiran) loves and marries Anil (Kumar). However, Anil becomes an alcoholic and ends up in jail. Alka finds a job in a college in Calcutta and raises her two children. Anil, released from prison, happens to become a gardener at the college and is thus able to rescue Alka from rapists. This hit musical, made with government assistance in the newly formed state of Gujarat, continues Raskapur's attempts to fantasise an identity for his native state (cf ***Mulu Manek***, 1955; ***Kadu Makrani***, 1960). The film dwells on several historical sites in Ahmedabad and on the Sabarmati jail where nationalist leaders were imprisoned during the freedom struggle.

MUGHAL-E-AZAM

1960 173' b&w/col Urdu
d/co-sc **K. Asif** *pc* Sterling Investment Corp. *co-sc/co-dial* Aman *co-dial* **Kamal Amrohi**, Ehsan Rizvi, Wajahat Mirza *lyr* Shakeel Badaiyuni *c* R.D. Mathur *m* **Naushad**
lp **Prithviraj Kapoor, Dilip Kumar, Madhubala, Durga Khote**, Nigar Sultana, Ajit, Kumar, Murad, Jilloo, Vijayalakshmi, S. Nazir, Surendra, Gopi Krishna, Jalal Agha, Baby Tabassum, **Johnny Walker**

K. Asif's classic megabudget spectacular and best-known historical romance was nine years in the making. Opening with the voice-over words 'I am Hindustan' spoken over a map of India, the film retells in flashback the popular story (cf ***Loves of a Mughal Prince***, 1928; ***Anarkali***, 1953) of the Mughal Emperor Akbar (P. Kapoor) and his Rajput wife Joda Bai (Khote) who finally manage to have a son, Prince Salim (D. Kumar). Salim grows up into a weak and pleasure-loving youth. Having proved himself in battle, Salim receives a sculpture of a beautiful female slave. He falls in love with the 'live' statue, Anarkali (Madhubala), and wants to marry her. Akbar pressurises Anarkali to give up Salim, humiliating and imprisoning her, but to no avail: in the film's best-known Sheesh Mahal (Palace of Mirrors) sequence, shot in colour, she defies Akbar through song: *Pyar kiya to darna kya* ('What is there to fear? All I have done is to love', sung by **Lata Mangeshkar**). Salim remains devoted to her and disobeys his father to the point of rebelling against the emperor and challenging him to battle. Akbar defeats Salim and condemns him to death. Anarkali is allowed to sacrifice her life to save Salim. However, contrary to the legend which has Anarkali walled in alive, Akbar spares her unbeknown to Salim. The film is remembered mainly for Amrohi's dialogues, esp. the confrontations between Kapoor and Kumar. Naushad's music includes the songs by noted classical singer Bade Ghulam Ali Khan (*Shubh din aaye* and *Prem jogan ban ke chali*) and Mathur's expansive camerawork interrupt the statically and frontally shot dialogues. **Mahesh Bhatt** (1993) drew attention to the memorable love scene 'shot in extreme close-ups of just faces in which Dilip Kumar tickles the impassioned face of Madhubala with a white feather. This was perhaps the most sensitively portrayed erotic scene on the Indian screen.'

Prithviraj Kapoor in *Mughal-e-Azam*

PADHAI THERIYUDU PAAR

1960 168' b&w Tamil
d/c **Nemai Ghosh**, V. Ramamurthy *pc* Kumari Films *lyr* K.C.S. Arunachalam, Jayakantan *m* **M.B. Srinivasan**
lp K. Vijayan, S.V. Sahasranamam, V. Gopalakrishnan, S.V. Subbaiah, T.K. Balachandran, R. Muthuraman

Set up by Nemai Ghosh, Srinivasan and others as a co-operative venture, with contributions from over 50 shareholders and collectively scripted in line with CPI ideology, most of the film addressed the trade union movement as seen through the eyes of a worker on the Southern Railway (Vijayan). The novelist Jayakantan contributed the hit song *Thennan keethu oonjalile* set to unusual music by Srinivasan using a xylophone. Randor Guy writes that internal dissensions spoiled the film's release and caused it to flop.

PARTHIBAN KANAVU

aka *Parthiban's Dream*
1960 219' b&w Tamil
d **D. Yoganand** *pc* Jubilee Films *st* novel by R. Krishnamurthy [aka **Kalki**] *s* **Kannadasan** *c* P.S. Selvaraj *m* Veda
lp **S.V. Ranga Rao, Gemini Ganesh**, P.S. Veerappa, S.V. Subbaiah, T.S. Baliah, **Vyjayanthimala**, Malathi, Kamala Kumari, Ragini, **B. Saroja Devi**

Verbose Tamil historical with a relentless music track, adapting one of Kalki's Walter Scott-like historicals. King Parthiban (Ashokan), 8th C. Chola king, dies in battle against the Pallavas and his son Vikraman (Ganesh) tries to realise his father's dream of an autonomous and unified Tamil kingdom. He achieves this with the help of a wise Pallava king, Narasimhavarman I (Ranga Rao), whose daughter Kundhavi (Vyjayanthimala) he marries. Together they defeat the Chalukyan King Pulakesin II and overcome the latter's nasty priests. An abridged version of another Kalki novel, *Sivakamiyin Sabatham* [*The Vow of Sivakami*], has been incorporated, clumsily, as a dance drama. The film, like many other South Indian historicals, overlaps with the stage, here including painted backdrops and simulated shrines (except one shot of the Pallava monument of Mahabalipuram).

RANADHEERA KANTEERAVA

1960 191' b&w Kannada
d N.C. Rajan *pc* Kannada Chalana Chitra Sangha *s/lyr* **G.V. Iyer** *c* B. Dorairaj *m* **G.K. Venkatesh**
lp **Rajkumar**, Sandhya, **Leelavathi**, Narasimhraju, Ashwath, G.V. Iyer, Veerabhadrappa, Eshwara Rao, Rama Devi, Ramchandra Sastry, Krishna Sastry, M.S. Subbanna, Soorat Ashwath, **Balkrishna**

This epochal Rajkumar historical is the prototype for many of the star's costume epics, often written by G.V. Iyer (cf Rajan's *Immadi Pulakesi*, 1967). The film evokes the Mysore royalty's intrigues to address Kannada national chauvinism. Rajkumar plays Kanteerava, supported as an alternative ruler by the villain Dalavayi Vikrama Raya, but Kanteerava defeats the villains using his legendary physical prowess in the service of the official monarch. Made as a co-operative venture by actors Balkrishna and Narasimhraju, the directors Iyer and T.V. Singh Thakore, et al. Although this co-operative made only one film, it featured in several 60s Rajkumar films, effectively constituting the Kannada film industry. Some of G.V. Iyer's filmographies credit him with directing this film.

SHRI VENKATESHWARA MAHATYAM

aka *Balaji*
1960 204' b&w Telugu
d **P. Pullaiah** *pc* Padmasri Pics *s/co-lyr* **Acharya Athreya** *co-lyr* Malladi Ramakrishna Sastry, **Arudra**, Narasa Reddy *c* P.L. Rai *m* **Pendyala Nageshwara Rao**
lp **N.T. Rama Rao, Savitri, S. Varalakshmi, Gummadi Venkateshwara Rao**, Ramana Reddy, Surabhi Balasaraswathi, P. Samibaba, Rushyendramani, **Chittor V. Nagaiah, Sowcar Janaki, Rajanala Nageshwara Rao, Ghantasala Venkateshwara Rao, Relangi Venkatramaiah**

Pullaiah's remake of his 1939 biographical of the Tirupati temple deity is a milestone in NTR's acting career. Made as a mythological telling the legend of Balaji, an incarnation of Vishnu, the film included very popular special effects sequences like Rama Rao physically emanating from the idol and walking towards the viewer. The marketing suggested that viewing the film was a substitute for visiting India's richest shrine, and papier mache replicas of the icon were placed outside movie theatres soliciting donations in the name of the god (apparently the temple authorities later sued the film's producers). According to Rama Rao's hagiographer S. Venkatnarayan (1983), the star's politicisation stems from this period when thousands of pilgrims from the Tirupati temple visited his Madras house. NTR later produced and directed another Venkateshwara version, *Shri Tirupati Venkateshwara Kalyanam* (1979), featuring himself and

ARAPPAVAN

aka *Half a Sovereign*
1961 158' b&w Malayalam
d K. Shankar *pc* Seva Films *p* K. Kumar *s/lyr* Kothamangalam Sadanandan *c* Thambu *m* **G.K. Venkatesh**
lp **Sathyan**, Prem Nawaz, Kalakkal Kumaran, S.P. Pillai, T.S. Muthaiah, G.K. Pillai, Sreenarayana Pillai, Kothamangalam Sadanandan, Pattom Sadan, Sulochana, Ambika

Set in the working-class milieu of toddy tappers and coir workers in Kerala. Paramu, the son of a toddy tapper, marries Kallu, a woodcutter's daughter. As Kallu did not bring the promised dowry of half a sovereign, Paramu's domineering mother harasses the new bride until she returns to her own parents and the lovers are reduced to meeting on the sly until the dowry issue has been settled. Kallu becomes pregnant and a local toddy-shop owner tries to rape her, resulting in rumours in the village that her child is illegitimate. When Kallu's brother returns having earned the money for her dowry, he rejects his sister and Kallu commits suicide. The grim melodrama, realistically filmed, was not successful on its initial release.

BABASA RI LAADI

1961 ?' b&w/col Rajasthani
d B.K. Adarsh *pc* Adarshlok *st/co-dial/lyr* Indra *co-dial* Naval Mathur *c* D.R. Dadhicha *m* Shivram
lp P. Kailash, Hiralal, Rajkumar, Mohan Modi, Rajdeep, Kiran Lal, Saraswati Devi, Sarita Devi, Champak Lala, Dhannalal, Helen, Nana Palsikar

The second Rajasthani film (after G.P. Kapoor's *Nazrana*, 1942) and its first hit. Feudal melodrama about the virtuous landlord Dharamdas, representing an idealised Marwari business community, who adopts a deceased employee's daughter, Saraswati. She and Dharamdas's son Ramesh fall in love, but her villainous uncle, who wants Ramesh to marry his flippant daughter Vaijayanti, uses his familial authority to arrange Saraswati's marriage with the handicapped son of a greedy shah. The tragic consequences of feudal patriarchal powers are eventually overcome and the lead couple unite in the end.

BHABHI KI CHUDIYAN

1961 168' b&w Hindi
d Sadashiv J. Row Kavi *pc* Sadashiv Chitra *st* Y.G. Joshi *sc* Srinivas Joshi *lyr* Narendra Sharma *c* Arvind Laad *m* **Sudhir Phadke**
lp **Meena Kumari**, **Balraj Sahni**, Seema, Ratnamala, Master Aziz, Sailesh Kumar, Sulochana, **Durga Khote**, Om Prakash

A sentimental melodrama which helped establish Kumari's image as 'the queen of tragedy'. Shyam's (Sahni) wife Geeta (Kumari) is like a foster-mother to her young brother-in-law, Mohan (S. Kumar). Mohan's filial devotion becomes an erotic obsession, to the distress of his new bride. The virtuous Geeta tirelessly serves and mothers the men in the family until she dies of exhaustion. The relations between a wife and her younger brother-in-law, echoing Seeta and Lakshman from the *Ramayana*, were often used in films to titillate the audience's expectation of images of sexual impropriety.

BHAKTA KUCHELA

1961 165' b&w Malayalam
d/p **P. Subramanyam** *pc* Neela Prod *s* Nagavalli R.S. Kurup *lyr* Thirunayanar Kurichi *c* N.S. Mani *m* Brother Lakshmanan
lp **Thikkurisi Sukumaran Nair**, **Kottarakkara Sridharan Nair**, S.P. Pillai, T.K. Balachandran, Kumari, Ambika, Shanti, Shashi, Kushalakumari, Jose Prakash, Hari, C.S. Kantha Rao, Adoor Pankajam, Vinodhini, Vilasini, Satheesh

The first big mythological by a director who, having put the radicalism of ***Randidangazhi*** (1958) behind him, would be increasingly associated with the devotional genre through the 60s (including Biblical themes, e.g. *Snapaka Yohannan*, 1963). Krishna's childhood friend and devotee, the Brahmin Kuchela, grows up to father 27 children even as he pines to meet his idol. His worship of Krishna causes enmity with King Shishupala. With his several offspring on the verge of starvation, he goes on a pilgrimage to Dwarka, where he meets his friend and master. To his astonishment Krishna sends him away empty-handed, but Kuchela returns home to find that his modest hut has miraculously been turned into a palace. The film did much to establish a bigger-budgeted version of the B-movie mythologicals routinely churned out by studios in Alleppey and Trivandrum.

GANGA JUMNA

1961 178' col Hindi-Bhojpuri
d **Nitin Bose** *pc* Citizens Films *s/p* **Dilip Kumar** *dial* Wajahat Mirza *lyr* Shakeel Badaiyuni *c* V. Babasaheb *m* **Naushad**
lp Dilip Kumar, **Vyjayanthimala**, Nasir Khan, Azra, Kanhaiyalal, Anwar Hussain, Nasir Hussain, S. Nazir, **Leela Chitnis**, Praveen Paul, Helen, Husn Bano, Ranjit Sud, Khwaja Sabir, Amar, Bihari, Harun, Narbada Shankar, Fazlu, Ram Kumar, Akashdeep, Baby Aruna, Baby Naaz

Dilip Kumar produced, wrote and starred in this story, shot in garish Technicolor, of two brothers on opposite sides of the law, Ganga (D. Kumar) and Jumna (played by D. Kumar's real-life brother, N. Khan). Having been framed by a zamindar (A. Hussain) for a crime he did not commit, Ganga becomes a criminal living in the mountains with his girlfriend Dhanno (Vyjayanthimala). His brother, educated on Ganga's money in the city, becomes a policeman. When years later Ganga is to become a father, he decides to return to the village to ask people's forgiveness, but he has to face his righteous brother Jumna who shoots him dead. Dhanno also dies in the gun battle. This dacoit drama, resembling a cross between 30s Hollywood gangster films and westerns, pioneered a widely copied action film formula (cf ***Deewar***, 1975). The most significant difference from the Hollywood stories is that the two main protagonists are brothers instead of 'kids from the same block' or 'erstwhile bosom buddies'. Dilip Kumar uses Bhojpuri instead of Hindi to liberate himself from his usual, more restrained persona while at the same time equating naturalism with a distinct class attitude against which, in this film, he rebels. This strategy was later followed by, e.g., **Bachchan** (*Ganga Ki Saugandh*, *Don*, both 1978). The songs *Nain lad gayi re* (sung by **Mohammed Rafi**), *Do hanson ka joda*, *Dhoondo dhoondo re saajana* and *Na maanon re* (sung by **Lata Mangeshkar**), were major hits though little can be said for their picturisation.

HIRO SALAAT

1961 129' b&w Gujarati
d **Ramchandra Thakur** *pc* Vishva Rang Chitra *c* Bipin Gajjar *lyr/m* **Avinash Vyas**
lp Vijay Datt, Nalini Chonkar, Champsibhai Nagda, Madhumati, Babu Raje, Tuntun, Ishwarlal

Famed sculptor Hiro Salaat is commissioned by King Siddharaj to build the fort at Darbhavati (now called Dabhoi). When he does so, the king, anxious that he should never surpass this spectacular achievement, buries the sculptor alive in one of its walls. The film, claiming to address the troubled relations between artist and patron, is remembered for artist and designer Kanu Desai's realistic sets, e.g. the replication of the fort in the Mohan Studio.

HUM DONO

aka *We Two*
1961 164'(95') b&w Hindi
d Amarjeet *pc* **Navketan** Films *p* **Dev Anand** *st* Nirmal Sircar *sc* **Vijay Anand** *lyr* **Sahir Ludhianvi** *c* V. Ratra *m* Jaidev
lp Dev Anand, Nanda, Sadhana, **Lalita Pawar**, **Gajanan Jagirdar**, Prabhu Dayal, Jagdish Raj, Rashid Khan, **Leela Chitnis**

Dev Anand plays two identical-looking soldiers, the comrades in arms Capt. Anand and Major Verma, in this (for Navketan) unusually excessive melodrama and major hit. Anand is in love with Mita (Sadhana) while Verma is married to Ruma (Nanda). When Verma is presumed dead, Anand has to take care of Ruma, endangering his relationship with Mita, esp. since Ruma mistakes Anand for her real husband. When Verma turns up again, severely crippled, he believes Anand has taken his place in his home. The resolution comes when all four characters meet in a temple. Some of the film's most successful songs including **Asha Bhosle** and **Mohammed Rafi**'s duet *Abhi na jao chhod kar* and **Lata Mangeshkar**'s bhajan *Allah tero naam*.

JAB PYAR KISISE HOTA HAI

1961 ?' b&w Hindi
d/p/s **Nasir Hussain** *pc* Nasir Hussain Films *lyr* Hasrat Jaipuri, **Shailendra** *c* Dilip Gupta *m* **Shankar-Jaikishen**
lp **Dev Anand**, Asha Parekh, Sulochana, Mubarak, Raj Mehra, Wasti, Rajendernath, Tahir Hussain, Dulari, Bhishan Khanna, Ramavtar

Musical cross-class romance featuring Sunder (Anand) and Nisha (Parekh) whose childhood betrothal is broken off by the boy when the girl's father becomes a millionaire. Sunder then woos Nisha, pretending to be the rich Popatlal, and she falls in love with him. Her father exposes Sunder and the two families are reconciled only through the intervention of a kindly aunt. Known mainly for its hit songs *Yeh aankhen oof yumma* and *Jiya ho jiya*, both sung by **Mohammed Rafi**, the former being a duet with **Lata Mangeshkar**.

JAGADEKA VEERUNI KATHA/JAGATHALA PRATHAPAN

1961 187' b&w Telugu/Tamil
d/sc **K.V. Reddy** *pc* **Vijaya** *dial/lyr* **Pingali Nagendra Rao** *c* Marcus Bartley *m* **Pendyala Nageshwara Rao**
lp **N.T. Rama Rao**, **Relangi Venkatramaiah**, Rajanala, **C.S.R. Anjaneyalu**, **K. Mukkamala**, Lanka Sathyam, **B. Saroja Devi**, Vijayalakshmi, Jayanthi, **P. Kannamba**, Rushyendramani, Girija

This characteristic Reddy fantasy is based on an earlier Tamil film, *Jagathala Prathapan* (1944) starring **P.U. Chinappa**. A king tests his two sons by asking what they desire most. Jagajittu says that he would wish to use the moonlit night to slay his enemies in their sleep. Jagadeka replies that he wishes to be with four heavenly angels. The latter, banished from home, has to make his wish come true by freeing a distressed angel cursed by Indrakumari before he can be readmitted.

JHUMROO

1961 171' b&w Hindi
d Shanker Mukerji *pc* K.S. Films *st/m* **Kishore Kumar** *sc* Vrajendra Gaur *dial* Madhusudan Kalelkar *lyr* **Majrooh Sultanpuri** *c* K.H. Kapadia
lp Kishore Kumar, **Madhubala**, Jayant, **Lalita Pawar**, Anoop Kumar, Chanchal, M. Kumar, Sajjan

One of Kishore Kumar's best-known comedies, containing the song exemplifying his yodelling style, *Main hun jhum-jhum-jhum-jhum jhumroo*. The zany stylistic *melange* tells the love story of the tribal Jhumroo (K. Kumar) who falls in love with the evil landowner's daughter (Madhubala). In the end, Madhubala is shown to be the daughter of Kamli (Pawar) and Jhumroo, the son of the upper-class landowner's friend. In the process, the film proposes the craziest notions of tribal identity in Indian cinema: one song is a variant of *Tequila*, another introduces rock into a Cossack dance, and the Kathmandu/Timbuctoo number sees the hero adopting a Fu Manchu look to rescue the heroine. The film has some of Kishore Kumar's most famous songs, e.g. the *Jhumroo* number, *Thandi hawa yeh chandni suhani* and *Koi humdum na raha*.

JUNGLEE

1961 150' col Hindi
d/p/s **Subodh Mukherjee** *pc* Subodh Mukherjee Prod. *dial* Agha Jani Kashmiri *lyr* **Shailendra**, Hasrat Jaipuri *c* N.V. Srinivas *m* **Shankar-Jaikishen**
lp **Shammi Kapoor**, Saira Banu, Shashikala, Anup Kumar, Azra, **Lalita Pawar**, Helen

Shammi Kapoor's best-known film featuring him in his Yahoo persona in songs like *Chahe koi mujhe junglee kahe* and *Aai aai ya suku suku*. The rich bachelor Shekhar (S. Kapoor) returns from abroad and refuses to laugh until he meets Kashmiri belle Rajkumari (Banu) who eventually changes his view of the world. The film can be seen as heralding the colour films that came to be the mainstay of the popular cinema (cf **Manmohan Desai**'s work) after the 50s **Filmistan** genre products. Previously, colour had been reserved for big spectacles only. After *Junglee*, intimate family romances also had to be in colour. The movie is still regarded as a cult item because of Shammi Kapoor's youthful and rebellious performance.

KABULIWALA

1961 95' b&w Hindi
d **Hemen Gupta** *pc* **Bimal Roy** Prod *sc* **Vishram Bedekar** *st* **Rabindranath Tagore** *dial* S. Khalil *lyr* **Gulzar**, Prem Dhawan *c* Kamal Bose *m* **Salil Choudhury**
lp **Balraj Sahni**, Usha Kiron, Sajjan, Asit Sen, Paul Mahendra, Sonnu

Tagore's story (pub. 1918) of the Pathan tribesman Rehman (Sahni) who journeys from Kabul to Calcutta seemed tailor-made for a naturalist acting challenge. It tells the tale of a seller of spices called Kabuliwala (the man from Kabul) in Calcutta who befriends a little girl because she reminds him of his own daughter. After years in jail for murder, Rehman finds the girl has grown up and realises that his own daughter may have forgotten him as well. Gupta's film, like **Tapan Sinha**'s Bengali version (1956), depends mainly on star performances. Here, Sahni's colourful mannerisms contrast with the static camera, tableau-like shots and extensive dissolves intended to evoke geographic expanse and memory time. The music by Salil Choudhury includes numbers like **Hemanta Mukherjee**'s *Ganga aaye kahan se* and one of Manna Dey's best-known songs *Ai mere pyare watan*. The fake Persian music with its copious mandolin effects is rather intrusive.

KANDAM BACHA COAT

aka *The Patched-up Coat*
1961 156' col Malayalam
d/p **T.R. Sundaram** *pc* **Modern Theatres** *st* T. Mohammed Yusuf's novel *sc* K.T. Mohammed *lyr* **P. Bhaskaran** *c* T.M. Sundarababu *m* **Baburaj**
lp T.S. Muthaiah, **Thikkurisi Sukumaran Nair**, Prem Nawaz, Ambika, Pankajavalli, Aranmulla Ponnamma, S.P. Pillai, P.K. Bahadur, Kothamangalam Sadanandan, Nellikode Bhaskaran, Kottayam Chellappan, Muttatha Soman, Chandni, Aisha, Omana

The kind-hearted Muslim cobbler Mohammed Kaka saved his life's earnings in the pockets of his ancient coat to fulfil his dream of going to Mecca. He offers shelter to Kunjubibi when her scheduled marriage to Ummar breaks down following a dowry

Balraj Sahni (right) in *Kabuliwala*

dispute. Arranging the marriage of the lovers, he offers his life's savings as a dowry, an act that causes the evil parents of the couple to have a change of heart. Made at the Modern Theatres, Salem, the film was known mainly as the first colour feature in Malayalam.

KAPPALOTIYA THAMIZHAN

aka *The Tamil who Launched a Ship*
1961 197' b&w Tamil
d **B.R. Panthulu** *pc* Padmini Pics *lyr* Bharathi
lp **Sivaji Ganesan**, S.V. Subbaiah, **Gemini Ganesh**, T.S. Shanmugam, **Savitri**, Rukmini, Bharathi, Subramaniya Siva, **S.V. Ranga Rao**

A disappointingly filmed episode of the life of Va. Vu. Chidambaram Pillai (Ganesan), a nationalist businessman who launched the Swadeshi Steam Navigation Company to break the British monopoly in shipping at the turn of the century, which earned him the honorific title Kappalotiya Thamizhan or 'The Tamil who launched a ship'. An important film in Ganesan's post-**DMK** project of wrapping himself in nationalist colours and one of Tamil cinema's rare excursions into recent history. Set in Tirunelveli district, it features cultural celebrities like Subramaniya Siva and the poet Bharati (whose poems were set to music and became popular songs). According to some sources, nationalist politicians Tilak, Salem Vijayaraghavachariar and Pondithurai Thevar made cameo appearances in the original release prints. Little effort is made to recreate the look and ambience of the period. The mandatory duets and romance are updated via references to historical events like the killing of the British collector Ashe, the burning of imported cloth, the Tuticorin riots and the Harvey Mills strike. The launching of the first Tamil ship is the climax. In line with the film's political ambitions, the dialogue attempts to move away from the high-flown rhetoric of, e.g., **Elangovan**'s 40s style by having some characters speak Tirunelveli dialect, but most still declaim their lines in written, theatrical Tamil.

KITTUR CHANAMMA/RANI CHANAMMA

1961 187' b&w Kannada/Tamil
d **B.R. Panthulu** *pc* Padmini Pics *c* W.R. Subba Rao, M. Karnan *m* T.G. Lingappa
lp **Rajkumar**, **B. Saroja Devi**, **M.V. Rajamma**, **Leelavathi**, **Balkrishna**, Narasimhraju, Chindodi Leela

Panthulu's big-budget historical about the legendary Queen Chanamma of Kittur (Saroja Devi in her best-known role) who led her people into battle against the British and eventually sacrificed her life. It features much palace intrigue as some Kittur royals invite the British to represent them; others, led by Chanamma, refuse to pay the British taxes. In the end the Kittur state is abolished.

KOMAL GANDHAR

aka *E-Flat*
1961 134' b&w Bengali
d/s **Ritwik Ghatak** *pc* Chitrakalpa *c* Dilip Ranjan Mukhopadhyay *m* Jyotirindra Moitra
lp **Supriya Choudhury**, Abanish Bannerjee, **Anil Chatterjee**, Geeta De, Satindra Bhattacharya, Chitra Mondol, **Bijon Bhattacharya**, Mani Srimani, Satyabrata Chattopadhyay, Gyanesh Mukherjee

Ghatak's innovatively filmed critique of both the **IPTA** style of radical theatre and of Partition caused a major political controversy in Bengal, apparently prompting the director to look for work outside the state. Set in the contentious 50s, the film's plot is structured around the rivalry of two radical theatre groups. One is led by Bhrigu (A. Bannerjee), the other by Shanta (G. De), while Shanta's niece Ansuya (S. Choudhury) participates in Bhrigu's work to the disapproval of her own group. When the two groups join together for a production, Shanta deliberately sabotages it. Bhrigu and Ansuya discover they are both refugees separated from their country (Bangladesh) by a river and they fall in love. Eventually Ansuya, scheduled to marry Samar and move to France, decides to stay with Bhrigu. As in Ghatak's earlier ***Meghe Dhaka Tara*** (1960), the story is interrupted by sound effects including ancient marriage songs, sounds of gunshots and sirens. Music and sound effects mark particularly emotive political moments, as in one of the film's classic shots: a tracking movement along a disused railway ending abruptly at the national border with a fishermen's chant rising to a powerful crescendo. Appropriately for a film dealing with both political and geographical division, the most intense interactions of sound and image occur in spaces which simultaneously divide and connect, as in the aforementioned tracking shot or in the 360-degree camera pans showing a theatre group singing in boats on the river Padma which marks the border between India and Bangladesh. Spatial divisions are further elaborated as a critique of the theatre groups with their cramped and fragmented proscenium spaces and cavernous rehearsal rooms and the claustrophobic, expressionistically lit urban scenes. The overall effect, as noted by **Kumar Shahani**, is the creation of a space-in-formation, a dynamic though static-looking space animated by history.

MANINI

1961 127' b&w Marathi
d **Anant Mane** *pc* Kala Chitra *st* Mahadevshastri Joshi *sc* Venkatesh Madgulkar *lyr* **G.D. Madgulkar**, Bahinabai Choudhury *c* V. Bargir *m* Vasant Pawar
lp **Jayashree Gadkar**, Chandrakant Gokhale, **Hansa Wadkar**, Dada Salvi, Indira Chitnis, Vasant Shinde, Ratnamala, Ramesh Dev, Sharad Talwalkar

Mane's urban melodrama with stagey realist overtones, although formally very different from the Tamasha hit ***Sangtye Aika*** (1959) made by the same crew, almost matched its success. Heroine Malati (Gadkar) marries poor hero Madhav and is disowned by her wealthy aristocratic family. Her father Annasaheb tries to force her to abandon her husband. When she refuses, reprisals ensue: she and her husband are accused of theft and publicly humiliated at her younger sister's wedding. Malati eventually breaks away from her oppressive feudal family (until then portrayed as the guardians of traditional virtue in Marathi film). The film includes hit numbers like *Are sansar sansar* (saying you must first burn your fingers on the stove before you get bread to eat). Gadkar's performance as a demure, exemplary daughter-in-law helps the film to relocate a neo-traditional value system into the emerging urban middle class. **A. Vincent** remade the film in Malayalam as ***Abhijathyam*** (1971), and **Krishnakant** in Gujarati (*Maa Dikri*, 1977).

MUDIYANAYA PUTHRAN

aka *The Prodigal Son*
1961 148' b&w Malayalam
d **Ramu Kariat** *p* T.K. Pareekutty *pc* Chandrathara Prod. *s* **Thoppil Bhasi** *lyr* **P. Bhaskaran** *c* **A. Vincent**, P. Sundaram *m* **Baburaj**
lp **Sathyan**, Ambika, Kumari, **P.J. Anthony**, Kambisseri, Kottayam Chellappan, P.A. Thomas, **Adoor Bhasi**

A story mapping good/bad brother relations on to employer/worker relations. The delinquent Rajan (Sathyan) loses his girl Radha (Ambika) to his more serious brother Gopal Pillai and is eventually ordered out of the parental home by his mother. When Rajan is ambushed and beaten, a Harijan girl he once molested, Chellamma (Kumari), nurses him back to health. Workers, led by Vasu, who also assisted Rajan, are persecuted and attacked by the 'good' brother who nurses old jealousies and believes his wife still to be in love with Rajan. Vasu organises a strike and Rajan is blamed by his brother for knifing one of his thugs. Overcome by the affection the people seem to have for him, Rajan becomes 'good' and turns himself in to the police. Kariat's first major film adapted a Thoppil Bhasi play to inaugurate a uniquely Malayali brand of political melodrama, in which existential aimlessness is extended into a pervasive sense of guilt as feudal institutions crumble and political activism becomes a form of atonement for bad faith. The film was actively supported by the Kerala CPI, with many of its members acting in and otherwise helping with the production. **Gopalakrishnan**'s melodrama ***Mukha Mukham*** (1984) is a retrospective comment on this tradition of melodrama as much as it is on the radical political history it chronicles. Sathyan's remarkable performance as the delinquent younger brother was later the definitive element in Kariat's directorial signature (cf ***Chemmeen***, 1965).

PASAMALAR

1961 197' b&w Tamil
d **A. Bhimsingh** *pc* Rajamani Pics *st* **K.P. Kottarakkara** *sc* G. Balasubramanyam *dial* Arur Das *c* G. Vittal Rao *lyr* **Kannadasan** *m* Vishwanathan-Ramamurthy
lp **Sivaji Ganesan**, **Gemini Ganesh**, **Savitri**, K.A. Thangavelu, M.N. Rajan, Rajasulochana, M.N. Nambiar

Barely camouflaged incest story about the orphaned Rajasekharan (Ganesan) who is devoted to his sister Radha (Savitri). However, she marries Anand (Ganesh), a worker and colleague of Rajasekharan. The lonely brother is struck with blindness and spends the rest of the film trying to unite with his beloved sister, eventually dying in her arms. One of the earliest and best known of Malayalam scenarist/producer K.P. Kottarakkara's Tamil films.

PAVAMANIPPU

aka *Forgiveness of Sins*
1961 196' b&w Tamil
d **A. Bhimsingh** *pc* Buddha Pics *dial* M.S. Solaimani *c* G. Vittal Rao *lyr* **Kannadasan** *m* Vishwanathan-Ramamurthy
lp **Sivaji Ganesan**, M.R. Radha, **Chittor V. Nagaiah**, T.S. Baliah, Kothamangalam Subbu, **Savitri**, **M.V. Rajamma**, Devika, **Gemini Ganesh**

Melodrama with religious stereotypes and symbols about a Hindu diamond merchant, a Muslim village doctor and a Christian do-gooder, combining Tamil Nadu's three main religions in an effort to promote communal harmony. Extra twists are provided by a love story between a Muslim boy and Christian girl alongside an all-Hindu love story. In the end it turns out that all the protagonists descended from the greedy Hindu merchant and from his equally high-caste Hindu chauffeur's family, providing ample material for tearful recognition scenes but also suggesting that the Muslim and Christian communities are cases of mistaken identities. The confused attempt to advocate religious equality is given poignant expression by Rahim (Ganesan), the main protagonist in a Kannadasan song wondering why religion was invented at all. Kannadasan belonged to the **DMK**'s Rationalist Group and included ironic lines which redeem the preachy didacticism of the script. The star studded cast ensured the film's success and Bhimsingh went on to establish himself as the main purveyor of moralising all-star movies in the 60s.

PRAPANCHA

aka *Family Life*
1961 138'(97') b&w Marathi
d Madhukar Pathak *pc* Indian National Pics *s/lyr* **G.D. Madgulkar** *c* K.B. Kamat, Ghanekar *m* **Sudhir Phadke**
lp Sulochana, Amar Sheikh, Kusum Deshpande, Jayant Dharmadhikari, Seema, Shrikant Moghe, Shankar Ghanekar

A miserabilist story about a poor Marathi village potter who tries to feed his wife (Sulochana) and six children in the hope that things will improve when younger brother Shankar completes his education. But they don't and, to foil Shankar's plans to start a porcelain factory, the local moneylender starts legal proceedings to claim the family house. The potter dies, causing the younger brother's marriage to his beloved Champa (Seema) to be cancelled. Eventually the potter's widow migrates with her children to the big city, so as not to be a burden. Shot mostly on location, it was screened in the USSR and in the West in two versions, one subtitled, the other with a voice over.

PUNASHCHA

aka *Over Again*
1961 120' b&w Bengali
d/p/sc **Mrinal Sen** *st* Ashish Burman *c* Sailaja Chatterjee *m* **Hemanta Mukherjee**
lp **Soumitra Chatterjee**, Kanika Majumdar, **Pahadi Sanyal**, **Kali Bannerjee**, Shefali Bannerjee, N. Vishwanathan

After the harrowing exploration of a marriage broken by social-historical pressures on rural life in ***Baishey Shravan*** (1960), Sen returned to the same issue in an urban context. The problems arise as the established patriarchal relations in a family are disrupted when the wife has to leave the domestic space to join the workforce. The resulting impact of a changing economic system on both male and female subjective attitudes and anxieties forms the substance of the plot. Sen contents himself with simply though critically setting out the problems without offering a solution. In this respect, his film allows for a level of ambiguity usually denied (in favour of an unambiguous validation of 'traditional values') in most Indian films with similar themes.

RABINDRANATH TAGORE

1961 54' b&w English/Bengali
d/co-p/s **Satyajit Ray** *co-p* **Films Division**, Anil Choudhury *c* Soumendu Roy *m* Jyotirindra Moitra
lp Raya Chatterjee, Shovanial Gangopadhyay, Smaran Ghoshal, Purnendu Mukherjee, Kallol Bose, Subir Bose, Phani Nan, Norman Ellis

Ray's semi-documentary on his mentor commissioned for the centenary of **Tagore**'s birth. The extraordinarily diverse literary and visual output of Tagore, the Shantiniketan experiment and the Tagore family's contributions to India's freedom struggle are condensed into one hour, relying on a voice-over commentary that eschews historical analysis in favour of a fairly reverential approach. Ray includes some re-enactements of episodes in Tagore's life together with images of paintings, photographs, documents, etc. Criticism of the film tends to focus on the perfunctory treatment of Tagore's poetry, mentioning neither the Vaishnavite Bhakti tradition nor the Baul-inspired style that informed his literature.

SAPTAPADI

1961 163' b&w Bengali
d/sc/c **Ajoy Kar** *pc* Alochhaya Prod. *st* Tarashankar Bannerjee *m* **Hemanta Mukherjee**
lp **Uttam Kumar**, **Suchitra Sen**, **Chhabi Biswas**, **Tulsi Chakraborty**, Tarun Kumar, Preeti Majumdar, **Chhaya Devi**, Padmadevi, Seeta Mukherjee, Swagata Chakraborty, Sabita Roy Choudhury

Set in WW2, the Jesuit Rev. Krishnaswamy (U. Kumar) runs a military hospital in Bankura. A wounded woman soldier, Rina Braun (Sen), arrives and he recognises his former lover, triggering a long flashback showing them as fellow medical students. She is an exotic Eurasian and the hero wins her while playing Othello to her Desdemona in a college performance. His orthodox father forbids their marriage. The hero converts to Christianity and exiles himself. Rina discovers that she is the illegitimate daughter of a Hindu maid and becomes an alcoholic, eventually joining the army. Back in the present, Rina tries to kill herself when she regains consciousness but the lovers are united in the midst of the war (Tarashankar's original story ended tragically). This Kumar/Sen hit (cf ***Sagarika***, 1956), including their characteristic low-angle, soft-focus close-ups and stylised movements, yielded one of the most popular song picturisations of the decade, the classic motor bike scene number *Ei path jadi na shesh hoi*.

TEEN KANYA

aka *Three Daughters*, aka *Two Daughters*
1961
56'(*Postmaster*)/61'(*Monihara*)/56'(*Samapti*) b&w Bengali
d/p/sc/m **Satyajit Ray** *pc* Satyajit Ray Prod. *st* **Rabindranath Tagore** *c* Soumendu Roy
lp (*Postmaster*) **Anil Chatterjee**, Chandana Bannerjee, Nripati Chatterjee, Khagen Pathak, Gopal Roy; (*Monihara*) **Kali Bannerjee**, Kanika Majumdar, Kumar Roy, Govinda Chakravarty; (*Samapti*) **Soumitra Chatterjee**, Aparna Das Gupta (aka **Aparna Sen**), Seeta Mukherjee, Gita Dey, Santosh Dutta, Mihir Chakravarty, Devi Neogi

Three short films adapted from three Tagore stories compiled for the writer's centenary. Western versions usually omit *Monihara*. In *Postmaster*, the most sentimental of the stories, Nandalal the postman (A. Chatterjee) is assigned the 10-year-old orphan Ratan (Bannerjee) as his assistant. Ill treated by his predecessor, she develops an attachment to Nandalal as he teaches her to read and write. Their acquaintance is abruptly ended when the postman falls ill and is transferred. Their wordless parting, as his rupee tip is rejected, was widely commended. *Monihara* is narratively the most complicated and the closest Ray has come to horror film. A schoolteacher (Chakravarty) tells of Manimalika (Majumdar), the jewellery-crazy wife of a zamindar (Bannerjee). When her husband has financial difficulties, Manimalika offers to sell her jewellery and then disappears with the shady Madhusudhan (Roy). When the zamindar returns to a deserted house and opens the new box of jewels he brought for his wife, manic laughter resounds and Manimalika's ghost appears to snatch the jewels. Returning to the storyteller, we discover that the hooded figure to whom the tale is addressed is the husband, who questions its accuracy and then vanishes. In *Samapti*, university graduate Amulya (Chatterjee) prefers to marry the extrovert Mrinmoyee (Das Gupta) rather than the woman chosen by his family. The wedding is both preceded and followed by a series of comic situations, first as Mrinmoyee disrupts the formal meeting with Amulya and his official bride-to-be and makes off with his shoes, and then on their wedding night when she escapes down a tree to sleep on her favourite perch by the river. Eventually the couple is reconciled as she promises to abandon her childish ways. Ray composed his own music score, combining Tagore and folk compositions with a much greater emphasis on 'musicalised' sound effects than in his earlier work.

TERO NADIR PAREY

aka *Beyond Thirteen Rivers*
1961 82' b&w Bengali
d/sc/c Barin Saha *pc* Ramdhanu Pics *st* Nirmal Ghosh *m* Gyan Prakash Ghosh
lp Gyanesh Mukherjee, Priyam Hazaraka, Narayan Chandra Mondal, Nanda Adhikari

A quiet and intimate Bengali story set in a travelling circus prey to the pressures of commercialism. A clown (Mukherjee) resists the privileging of crowd-pleasing dancing-girls in the circus programme and resents the arrival of a new dancer (Hazarika). When he suffers a drunken accident the dancer nurses him, but he remains unable to reconcile himself to the change and becomes virtually insane. This is the only feature by Barin Saha (1925-93), a former **IPTA** activist who studied film-making in France and Italy. The film was not released until 1969 and its commercial failure forced its director to abandon film-making in favour of rural activism. It was shot entirely on location at the Tero Nadi aka the Haldi river in Midnapore, and included scenes of remarkable energy, including the arrival of the dancing-girl in the bazaar (a long subjective shot), the sweeping pans over the river and night shots at the end, evoking **Ghatak**'s work.

THAYILLA PILLAI

1961 173' b&w Tamil
d **L.V. Prasad** *pc* Prasad Movies *s* **M. Karunanidhi** *lyr* **Kannadasan**, Kothamangalam Subbu, **A. Marudakasi** *m* K.V. Mahadevan
lp T.S. Baliah, G. Muthukrishnan, **Kalyana Kumar**, S. Ramarao, Manohar, **M.V. Rajamma**, Vijayalakshmi, Madhuri, Sandhya, T.P. Muthulakshmi, Nagesh, C.V.V. Panthulu, Seetalakshmi

The conservative Brahmin Patanjali Sastry severs relations with his modern brother-in-law Dr Bharati. When Sastry's wife, who had had two miscarriages, finds herself pregnant, she goes to her brother to get medical aid and incurs the displeasure of her husband. The wife gives birth to a son but simultaneously adopts the son of a lower-caste woman who died in childbirth, creating some confusion for Sastry as to which baby is his son. Eventually the couple raise the adopted child while their own son becomes a rickshaw-puller. The two boys grow up and become friends. Following scenarist Karunanidhi's anti-caste politics, the family is reunited in the end.

UNNIYARCHA

1961 138' b&w Malayalam
d/p **Kunchako** *pc* Udaya Studios *s* Sarangapani *lyr* **P. Bhaskaran** *c* T.N. Krishnan Kutty Nair *m* K. Raghavan
lp Ragini, **Prem Nazir**, **Thikkurisi Sukumaran Nair**, **Sathyan**, Kottayam Chellappan, Sunny, S.P. Pillai, Bahadur, Reetha, Kanchana

One of the most succesful of Kunchako's early 60s films at Udaya Studio, the film features Ragini, one of the dancing Travancore sisters, as Unniyarcha, a warrior princess and part of North Kerala folklore. Born into the aristocracy, she is married to the kind-hearted Kunjiraman (Nazir) to whom she bears two sons. When her fearless brother is killed by the evil Chandu (Chellappan), she trains her sons in the martial arts so they can carry out her revenge mission. Shot in the Kerala backwaters, the film led to a major trend of adapting legends of folk heroes from the ballads of the Malabar region.

ABHIJAAN

aka *The Expedition*
1962 150' b&w Bengali
d/sc/m **Satyajit Ray** *pc* Abhijatrik *st* Tarashankar Bannerjee's novel *c* Soumendu Roy
lp **Soumitra Chatterjee**, **Waheeda Rehman**, Ruma Guha-Thakurta, Gyanesh Mukherjee, Charuprakash Ghosh, **Robi Ghosh**, Arun Roy, Sekhar Chatterjee, Ajit Bannerjee, Reba Devi, Abani Mukherjee

Taking over from some friends who lost confidence after one day's shooting, Ray made his first straight melodrama, set in Northern Bihar. Hero Narsingh (So. Chatterjee), a taxi driver who loses his licence, gets involved in drug smuggling and with two women, the missionary teacher Mary Nilima (Guha-Thakurta) and the prostitute Gulabi (Rehman's only appearance in a Ray movie). Conflicts of class with feudal Rajput honour inform the story about the villain Sukhanram (C. Ghosh) who is redeemed by the good Joseph (G. Mukherjee), Mary's brother. The urbane and upper-class Soumitra Chatterjee is cast against type as the rough, bearded Rajasthani driver.

ARADHANA

1962 167' b&w Telugu
d V. Madhusudhana Rao *pc* Jagapathi Prod. *co-dial/co-lyr* Chiranjeevi *co-dial* **Athreya** *co-lyr* **Sri Sri**, **Arudra**, **Kosaraju** *c* C. Nageshwara Rao *m* **Saluri Rajeshwara Rao**
lp **A. Nageshwara Rao**, **Savitri**, Girija, **Relangi Venkatramaiah**, Ramana Reddy, **K. Jaggaiah**, **Gummadi Venkateshwara Rao**

Popular 60s love story and lukewarm remake of the **Uttam Kumar** and **Suchitra Sen** Bengali classic ***Sagarika*** (1956). Gopi (Nageshwara Rao) meets Anuradha (Savitri) while at medical college. Gopi agrees to marry a woman of his parents' choice (Girija) because the dowry will allow him to study medicine in the USA. While he is away, Anuradha moves in with Gopi's family and impersonates his fiance whenever he telephones and also writes the fiance's love-letters to Gopi. This, and the fact that his fiance wanted to marry another man anyway, leads to the happy ending.

BEES SAAL BAAD

1962 158' b&w Hindi
d Biren Nag *pc* Geetanjali Pics *p/m* Hemant Kumar [**Hemanta Mukherjee**] *s* Dhruva Chatterjee *dial* Devkishen *lyr* Shakeel Badaiyuni *c* Marshall Braganza
lp **Waheeda Rehman**, Biswajeet, Manmohan Krishna, Sajjan, Asit Sen, Madan Puri, Devkishen, Lata Sinha

Suspense movie allegedly derived from *The Hound of the Baskervilles*. Kumar (Biswajeet) is the last in a long line of Chandangarh zamindars. He returns to his lonely ancestral manor where his father had been mysteriously killed after he was lured into the fields by the sound of anklets and a woman crying. Rumours abound of the ghost of a woman raped and killed by Kumar's ancestor. Kumar falls for the local belle Radha (Rehman) and meets a gallery of dubious characters: an ex-con servant, a bearded doctor and a man on crutches who turns out to be a disguised policeman. The first half of the film builds up the suspense, mostly using the soundtrack according to generic conventions. The plot then becomes a whodunit until the murderer is revealed: Radha's guardian (M. Krishna),

Aradhana

the father of the woman killed 20 years ago. Waheeda's seduction number, associating her with the ghost, is the classic *Kahin deep jale kahin dil* (sung by **Lata Mangeshkar**).

BHOODANA

1962 161' b&w Kannada
co-d/s **G.V. Iyer** *co-d* P.S. Gopalakrishna *pc* Ananthalakshmi Pics *c* B. Dorairaj *m* **G.K. Venkatesh**
lp **Rajkumar**, **Kalyana Kumar**, **Udaya Kumar**, Ashwath, **Leelavathi**, **Balkrishna**, Narasimraju, H.R. Sastry, Adavani Lakshmi, Mahalinga Bhagavathar

Iyer's debut is a political melodrama made in the context of the Bhoodana (land-gift) movement started by the Gandhian Vinoba Bhave, calling on all large land owners to donate 1/6th of their land for redistribution to the landless. Exploitative landlord Lakshmipati controls the bonded labourer Dasanna and his two sons Rama and Lakshmana. When he donates his sixth, the land is allotted to this trio who exploit it successfully. The landlord later reappropriates the land, causing Dasanna to go insane. One of the first Kannada political films, it is the only film to feature all three Kannada top male stars: Rajkumar, Kalyana Kumar and Udaya Kumar.

CHINA TOWN

1962 151' b&w Hindi
d/p **Shakti Samanta** *pc* Shakti Films *s* Ranjan Bose *dial* Vrajendra Gaur *lyr* **Majrooh Sultanpuri** *c* Dwarka Divecha *m* Ravi
lp **Shammi Kapoor**, Shakila, Helen, Madan Puri, S.N. Bannerjee, Mridula, Jeevankala, Gautam Mukherjee, Kanu Roy

Crime movie with 'Far Eastern' atmosphere following on from Samanta's ***Howrah Bridge*** (1958) and *Singapore* (1960). It is set in a township outside Calcutta inhabited by Chinese refugees from WW2, with smoke-filled bars, cabarets, criminals stalking the streets and skulking in alleys and gangland businessmen sporting fat cigars. Kapoor plays a double role of twins separated at birth who meet again as Shekhar, a cabaret entertainer in love with the aristocratic millionairess Rita, and Mike, the gangster. The police use the resemblance to get Shekhar to impersonate Mike in order to track down the gang boss. Only the shoemaker Ching Lee is wise to the substitution. Kapoor's imitation of Presley is most visible in the hit number *Bar bar dekho*, sung by **Mohammed Rafi**.

DHEUER PARE DHEU

aka *Waves after Waves*
1962 100'? b&w Bengali
co-d/co-p/co-sc/c B.K. Sanyal *co-d/co-sc* Smritish Guha-Thakurta *co-p* M. Dutta Gupta *pc* Renaissance Films *st* S. Dey *m* Ravi Shankar
lp Shankar, Shampa, Badal

Most of the cast and crew headed by the former photographer Sanyal were new to cinema when they made this low-budget film in the wake of **S. Ray**'s pioneering work in Bengal (Ravi Shankar had also scored Ray's *Apu Trilogy*). Set in a small fishing village, it tells of the fisherman Natal (Shankar) and his friend Loton (Badal). Natal marries their childhood companion, Padma (Shampa), but is later feared drowned in a fishing accident. Padma then marries Loton. When Natal returns, observing their happiness through the window of their home, he goes away again and drowns himself. The film's narrative pace is virtually static but the acting, the music and the extremely aestheticised imagery keep the viewer interested.

GANGA MAIYA TOHE PIYARI CHADHAIBO

1962 ?' b&w Bhojpuri
d Kundan Kumar *pc* Nirmal Pics *s* **Nasir Hussain** *lyr* **Shailendra** *c* R.K. Pandit *m* Chitragupta
lp Kumkum, Ashim Kumar, Nasir Hussain, Tiwari, Mishra, Helen, Leela Mishra, Bhagwan Sinha, Tuntun, Kumari Padma

The first feature of the now thriving Bhojpuri cinema, the rhythmic and flowery Central Indian dialect of Hindi approximating Brijbhasha, the language associated with North Indian classical music. In this melodrama Sumitra (Kumkum) is married, according to the film's publicity, 'in the style to which all young women aspire', only to find herself widowed soon after. A variety of villains include her father, the drunken Lakhan Singh, her father-in-law and other members of the village who see her as a harbinger of bad luck, but she eventually overcomes these obstacles and causes the village to revise its orthodox assumptions.

GUNDAMMA KATHA

aka *Manidan Maravalli* aka *Manithan Maravillai*
1962 166' b&w Telugu/Tamil
d **K. Kameshwara Rao** *pc* **Vijaya** *st* **Chakrapani** *s* **D.V. Narasaraju** *lyr* **Pingali Nagenda Rao** *c* Marcus Bartley *m* **Ghantasala Venkateshwara Rao**
lp **N.T. Rama Rao**[Te]/**Gemini Ganesh**[Ta], **A. Nageshwara Rao**, **S.V. Ranga Rao**, **Savitri**, Vijayalakshmi, **Jamuna**, **Relangi Venkatramaiah**

The old woman Gundamma has a son, an exploited stepdaughter and a spoilt daughter for whom she hopes to get a 'resident' son-in-law who can also look after the rest of the family. She gets two: the brothers Anji and Raja, who teach the old woman a lesson. Producer Chakrapani credited himself with the direction of the film's Tamil version *Manithan Maravillai* but it was a failure, unlike the major success of the original Telugu. Regarded as the last film of Vijaya's 'golden age'.

GYARAH HAZAAR LADKIYAN

1962 152' b&w Hindi
d/st/co-sc **K.A. Abbas** *pc* Film Friends *p/co-sc* Ali Sardar Jafri *lyr* **Majrooh Sultanpuri** *c* Ramchandra *m* N. Dutta
lp **Mala Sinha**, Bharat Bhushan, Helen, Jugnu, Baby Farida, Baby Vidyarani, Baby Vijay, Soni Sultana, Nirmala Mansukhani, Minal, Noor, Nadira, David, Madhavi, Imtiaz

The noted Urdu poet Ali Sardar Jafri co-wrote and produced Abbas's film set among journalists. Puran (Bhushan) rebels against his millionaire father and joins a progressive journal. Reporting on working women, he falls in love with Asha (Sinha), a clerk in a food-rationing office. When his father forces Puran to leave his job, he starts his own paper. With the end of rationing after the war, Asha loses her job and her younger sister Uma becomes a cabaret dancer. In self-defence, Uma kills the lecherous nightclub boss and Asha takes the blame. Puran defends Asha in court where his speeches extol working women.

HALF TICKET

1962 168' b&w Hindi
d Kalidas *pc* Cine Technicians Prod. *st* Surid Kar *sc* Ramesh Pant *lyr* **Shailendra** *c* Apurba Bhattacharjee *m* **Salil Choudhury**
lp **Kishore Kumar**, Pran, **Madhubala**, Manorama, Om Prakash, Helen, Shammi, Tuntun, Moni Chatterjee, Sailen Bose, Dilip Mukherjee, Anil Ganguly, B.R. Kapoor, Mauji, Zeb Rehman

Slapstick crime thriller parodying the genre with Indian cinema's weirdest and most sustained chase sequence. Raja Babu (Pran) stuffs stolen diamonds into the hip pocket of Vijay (Kumar), standing in front of him in a railway ticket queue. Vijay, a rich man's socialist son with a bizarre way of organising protests, is running away from home dressed in shorts and a schoolboy cap to obtain the half-price ticket available to schoolchildren. Throughout the rest of the film, Raja Babu chases Vijay and keeps making ineffectual grabs at the hero's hip pocket as they go through Bombay, visit a Cossack stage dance with Helen, a nautanki performance and eventually wind up in a crane, a hot-air balloon and an aeroplane that lands them atop a palm tree. The crazy plot recalls the Tashlin/Lewis films and the Marx Brothers as well as the boisterous traditions of Indian urbanised folk theatre.

HANSULI BANKER UPAKATHA

aka *Folk Tales of River Bend*
1962 122' b&w Bengali
d/sc **Tapan Sinha** *p* S.L. Jalan *st* Tarashankar Bannerjee *c* Bimal Mukherjee *m* **Hemanta Mukherjee**
lp **Kali Bannerjee**, Dilip Roy, Ranjana Bannerjee, Ansuya Gupta, Lily Chakraborty, **Robi Ghosh**

Following in the wake of **S. Ray**'s films set in Bengali villages (cf ***Dheuer Pare Dheu***, 1962), Sinha situates his film in 1941 in a village by the Kopai river. The isolated, bamboo-surrounded village is dominated by a greedy zamindar and an ineffectual chief, Banwari (K. Bannerjee). Young Karali (Roy) leads the drive for change, abandoning the fields for the railroad yard, which eventually succeeds when Banwari is killed and WW2 makes its impact on the village. Sinha uses pathetic fallacy imagery (a monsoon) to signal the advent of a new era and deploys a flowery style for scenes depicting the past while the present is filmed in an earthier, more humorous manner. The music track is enhanced by folk melodies.

HARIYALI AUR RAASTA

1962 168' b&w Hindi
d **Vijay Bhatt** *pc* Prakash Pics *s* Dhruva Chatterjee *dial* Qamar Jalalabadi *lyr* Hasrat Jaipuri, **Shailendra** *c* Bipin Gajjar *m* **Shankar-Jaikishen**
lp **Mala Sinha**, **Manoj Kumar**, Shashikala, Krishnakumari, Manmohan Krishna, Surendranath, Aroon, Chopra, Samar Roy, Om Prakash

A hit musical melodrama set in Darjeeling's tea plantations and one of Sinha's best-known films. Shankar (M. Kumar) falls in love with Shobhana (Sinha), the daughter of the plantation supervisor Shivnath (Krishna). However, Shankar is due to marry the vampish Rita (Shashikala). To make life simpler at the plantation, Shobhana uses a train accident to disappear and to start a new life as Kamala, a hospital nurse. Shankar marries the spendthrift Rita and when their son Ramesh falls ill the boy is nursed back to health by 'Kamala'. Then Shankar himself falls ill and Shobhana's second rescue act brings the couple together again. Hits include *Ibtyade-ishq hum sari raat jaage* and the title number *Yeh hariyali aur yeh raasta*, both sung by **Lata Mangeshkar** (the former being a duet with Mukesh).

KANCHANJUNGHA

1962 102' col Bengali
d/s/m **Satyajit Ray** *pc* N.C.A. Prod. *c* Subrata Mitra
lp **Chhabi Biswas**, **Anil Chatterjee**, Karuna Bannerjee, Anubha Gupta, Subrata Sen, Sibani Singh, Alaknanda Roy, Arun Mukherjee, N. Vishwanathan, **Pahadi Sanyal**, Nilima Chatterjee, Vidya Sinha

Ray's first colour film and his first original script is a naturalist drama set in 'real time' (shot at a ratio of 1:21/4) over an afternoon in the tourist hill-station of Darjeeling (cf a similar plot structure in Ray's next original script, ***Nayak***, 1966). Indranath Roy Choudhury (Biswas), whom Ray described as a 'domineering British title-holding father', heads a large upper-class family on the last day of their holiday in Darjeeling surrounded by snowcapped mountains and swirling mists. His long-suffering wife Labanya (Bannerjee) is relegated to a secondary role while he encourages a possible marriage between their youngest daughter Monisha (Roy) with the pompous, foreign-returned Engineer Pranab Bannerjee (Vishwanathan). The elder daughter Anima (Gupta) confronts her alcoholic husband Shankar (Sen), openly acknowledging her affair with another man. The philandering son Anil (A. Chatterjee) loses one girlfriend and acquires another. Brother-in-law Jagdish (Sanyal) is only interested in bird-watching. The lower-class Sibsankar Roy, Anil's former tutor, tries to inveigle a job for his nephew Ashok (Mukherjee) from the patriarch, but when a job is offered the nephew turns it down, striking up a close friendship with Monisha instead, the latter having rejected her father's choice for a husband. The most significant aspect of the film is not the much-touted non-judgemental humanism nor the 'rounded' characters in this ensemble piece, but the mobilisation of a suspense formula (patterned on the country house murder mystery) in which something 'dramatic' always seems about to happen but never does. In the end, the only 'crime' committed in this indirect tribute to Hitchcock's *Rope* (1948) is the wealthy patriarch's insistence on exerting a 'traditional' authority in a new, independent and industrial era. The film is remarkable for its use of pastel colours (unfortunately, the original negative has been damaged and existing prints do not always reproduce Ray's and Mitra's intended colour schemes) and the sound effect at the end when the humming of a Nepali boy suddely expands to echo through the valleys dominated by the Kanchanjungha peak.

KING KONG

1962 ?' b&w Hindi
d **Babubhai Mistri** *pc* Santosh Prod. *s* V. Pande, Madhur, Masterji *dial* M.R. Nawab *lyr* **Majrooh Sultanpuri** *c* Keki Mistry *m* Chitragupta
lp **Dara Singh**, Kumkum, Chandrasekhar, Pravin Choudhury, Sheila Kashmiri, Kamal Mehra, Leela Mishra, Paul Sharma, Uma Dutt

Dara Singh's best-known 60s stunt movie. King Kong is the title that King Hingoo bestows upon the strongest man in his kingdom. The reigning King Kong discovers a mysterious man (Singh) in a forest who appears to be stronger than he and who eventually defeats him. It emerges that the new King Kong is the son of the strong man deposed by Hingoo. The new prince is imprisoned but breaks out and defeats the entire palace.

KULAGOTHRALU

1962 166' b&w Telugu
d **K. Pratyagatma** *pc* Prasad Arts Pics *dial* **Acharya Athreya** *lyr* **Kosaraju**, **Sri Sri**, C. Narayana Reddy, Dasarathi *c* **A. Vincent** *m* **Saluri Rajeshwara Rao**
lp **A. Nageshwara Rao**, Krishnakumari, **Relangi Venkatramaiah**, Suryakantam, **Gummadi Venkateshwara Rao**, Nirmala, Mikkilineni, **G. Varalakshmi**, Ramana Reddy, Sandhya, Girija, Padmanabham

Pratyagatma's 2nd film is a musical melodrama and tells of hero Ravi who decides to marry a lower-caste woman and has to leave home to do so. The film included several comedy interludes featuring Venkatramaiah and established Krishnakumari as a major Telugu star while confirming the director's signature in the **Prasad** tradition of musical family melodramas.

MAHAMANTRI TIMMARASU

1962 177' b&w Telugu
d **K. Kameshwara Rao** *pc* Gowthami Prod. *m* **Pendyala Nageshwara Rao**
lp **N.T. Rama Rao**, **Gummadi Venkateshwara Rao**, Lingamurthy, Vijayalakshmi, **S. Varalakshmi**, A.V. Subba Rao, Devika, **Relangi Venkatramaiah**, **Shobhan Babu**, Rakashri, **K. Mukkamala**

One of the many costumed spectacles featuring the Vijayanagara Emperor Krishnadeva Raya and his court (cf the popular ***Tenali Ramakrishna*** films of 1941 and 1956). The king (NTR) marries two women, Chinna Devi (Vijayalakshmi) and Tirumaladevi (Varalakshmi). The only way he can end his war with Veerabhadra Gajapathi is to claim Annapurna (Devika) in marriage as well. The war drama and court intrigue includes a murder for which Timmarasu (Gummadi) is falsely accused. The musical consolidated Kameshwara Rao's reputation for making box-office hits in the genre.

SAHIB BIBI AUR GHULAM

aka *Master, Mistress, Servant* aka *King, Queen, Knave* aka *King, Queen and Slave*
1962 152'(120') b&w Hindi-Urdu
d/sc Abrar Alvi *p* **Guru Dutt** *pc* Guru Dutt Films *st* Bimal Mitra's novel *Saheb Bibi Golam* (1952) *lyr* Shakeel Badaiyuni *c* V.K. Murthy *m* Hemant Kumar [**Hemanta Mukherjee**]
lp **Meena Kumari**, Guru Dutt, **Waheeda Rehman**, Rehman, Nasir Hussain, Sapru, Sajjan, S.N. Bannerjee, Dhumal, Krishan Dhawan, Jawahar Kaul, Harindranath Chattopadhyay, Minoo Mumtaz, Pratima Devi, Ranjit Kumari, Bikram Kapoor

After the failure at the box office of ***Kaagaz Ke Phool*** (1959), Guru Dutt had let M. Sadiq direct his ***Chaudhvin Ka Chand*** (1960) before making this elegiac movie which he credited to his long-term collaborator and scenarist, Alvi. Taken from a classic Bengali novel, the story is set in the 19th C. zamindari milieu of the Choudhury household. It is seen through the eyes of the lower-class but educated Bhoothnath (Dutt) who arrives in colonial Calcutta looking for work (while British troops loot the shops). Through his city relative Bhoothnath finds accomodation in the Choudhury haveli (ancestral mansion) while working at the Mohini Sindoor factory, which allows the narrative to move from the aristocratically indolent world of the zamindars to the more prosaic one of the Brahmo Samaj. The plot has the hero being fascinated by the lady of the house Chhoti Bahu (M. Kumari), whose husband (Rehman) prefers the company of dancing-girls and all-night drinking bouts. The film gradually gives way to a darker mood as the family loses its fortune and descends to ruin while Chhoti Bahu becomes an alcoholic. At times compared to **Satyajit Ray**'s ***Jalsaghar*** (1958) as a commentary on Bengal's decaying feudalism, Dutt's film is a romantic and somewhat nostalgic tale about a bygone era, presenting the past and the future through the contradictory attitudes of two female figures. Meena Kumari's skilful performance, redolent with sensuality (e.g. the scene where she entices her husband to stay by her side through the song *Na jao saiyan*, sung by **Geeta Dutt**), is counterpointed by Waheeda Rehman's robust and girlish presence (esp. in the *Bhanwra bada nadaan* number sung by **Asha Bhosle**). The film itself is told entirely in flashback and the long shadows of history invade the images in sequences such as the *Saakiya aaj mujhe neend* number (sung by Asha Bhosle) where all the dancers are seen in shadow while the singing courtesan (Minoo Mumtaz) is bathed in light.

SAUTELA BHAI

1962 ?' b&w Hindi
d/co-sc **Mahesh Kaul** *pc* Alok Bharati *st* Saratchandra Chatterjee's novel *Boikunther Will* *co-sc/dial* Deo Kishen *lyr* **Shailendra** *c* R.L. Nagar *m* **Anil Biswas**
lp **Guru Dutt**, Pronoti Bhattacharya, Bipin Gupta, Raaj Kumar, Ranibala, Asit Sen, Bela Bose, Radheshyam, Samar Chatterjee, Ratna Kanhaiyalal, Lakshman Singh

Melodrama about an extended family in Bengal. Baikunth Majumdar (Gupta), who has a son by a previous marriage, remarries. His new wife Bhawani raises her stepson Gokul along with her own son Vinod. When they grow up Vinod (Raaj Kumar) goes to the city to study while Gokul (Dutt) manages the family shop. Vinod turns bad in the city and his parents decide to leave the family property to Gokul. Vinod returns and contests the will. The battle between the stepbrothers over 'mother' and the will is resolved by Gokul's other-worldly innocence which succeeds in uniting the family.

SHRI KRISHNARJUNA YUDDHAM

1962 174' b&w Telugu/Tamil
d/st **K.V. Reddy** *pc* Jayanti Pics *dial/lyr* **Pingali Nagendra Rao** *m* **Pendyala Nageshwara Rao**
lp **N.T. Rama Rao, A. Nageshwara Rao, B. Saroja Devi, S. Varalakshmi, Sriranjini** Jr., Chhaya Devi, Rushyendramani, Balasaraswathi, **Gummadi Venkateshwara Rao**, Kantarao, Allu Ramalingaiah

Big-budget hit Telugu mythological derived from the *Mahabharata*. Krishna (NTR) has to confront his disciple Arjuna (Nageshwara Rao) in order to sustain the war. NTR, who made a career playing Krishna roles, here shifts the icon away from the romantic into the warlike, apparently a first in Telugu film. The music of Pendyala and lyricist Pingali was as usual successful, particularly the comedy hit *Anchelanchelu* sung by B. Gopalam and Swarnalatha.

SIRI SAMPADALU

1962 167' b&w Telugu
d **P. Pullaiah** *pc* Padmasri Pics *s* Pinisetty *lyr* **Athreya, Kosaraju, Sri Sri** *m* **Master Venu**
lp **N.T. Rama Rao, A. Nageshwara Rao, Chittor V. Nagaiah, Gummadi Venkateshwara Rao**, Gudipati Venkatachalam (aka Chalam), Ramana Reddy, **Savitri**, Shantakumari, Suryakantam, Girija, Vasanthi, Surabhi Balasaraswathi, **Relangi Venkatramaiah**

Family melodrama about the decline of a feudal patriarch and the rise of a new generation with different values. The head of the family, Nayudu (Nagaiah), severs relations with his sister's family since he holds his brother-in-law responsible for his father's death. He also refuses to let his son Prasad (Nageshwara Rao) marry Padma (Savitri). The family becomes impoverished and Prasad has to restore both his father's honour and the family fortunes. He also marries Padma. Released at the same time as ***Kulagothralu*** (1962), also a family melodrama interspersed with comedy routines, Pullaiah's film flopped despite his reputation in Telugu cinema.

SUBARNAREKHA

1962 143' b&w Bengali
d/sc **Ritwik Ghatak** *pc* J.J. Films *st* Radheshyam Jhunjhunwala *c* Dilip Ranjan Mukhopadhyay *m* Bahadur Khan
lp **Abhi Bhattacharya, Bijon Bhattacharya, Madhabi Mukherjee**, Geeta De, Sriman Tarun, Satindra Bhattacharya, Abanish Bannerjee, **Jahar Roy**

One of Ghatak's most impressive and complex films, released in 1965, tells of Ishwar Chakraborty (A. Bhattacharya) and his young sister Seeta who start out in a refugee camp after Partition. After a brief scene ironically evoking the vagaries of nationalism, the two rescue the boy Abhiram (Tarun) when his mother Kausalya (De) is abducted. A businessman appoints Ishwar to run a foundry and he takes the two children to the new abode. Abhiram is sent to school and returns years later (S. Bhattacharya) intent on becoming a writer and marrying Seeta (M. Mukherjee). As Abhiram is an Untouchable, Ishwar finds his job prospects threatened and he asks the boy to leave, arranging for Seeta to marry someone else. She elopes with Abhiram and they, with their baby son, live in a shack in Calcutta until Abhiram dies in an accident and Seeta is forced to turn to prostitution. The lonely old Ishwar contemplates suicide and with his old friend Harprasad (B. Bhattacharya) he goes on a drinking binge in Calcutta, culminating in a visit to a brothel. He is ushered into his own sister's room. Ishwar is devastated and Seeta kills herself, watched by her son. At the end of the film, an aged Ishwar is leading Seeta's child to the promised 'new house' by the river which forms the visual leitmotiv throughout the film. Ghatak endowed virtually every sequence with a wealth of historical overtones through an iconography of violation, destruction, industrialism and the disasters of famine and Partition. Most of the dialogue and the visuals are a patchwork of literary and cinematic quotations enhanced by Ghatak's characteristic redemptive use of music. This strategy ensconces the characters and their behaviour deep into the fabric of history itself, constantly referring their actions to forces playing on a broader canvas than the space-time occupied by an individual. A famous example is the sequence set on an abandoned airstrip with the wreck of a WW2 aeroplane where the children playfully reconstruct its violence until they come up against the frightening image of the goddess Kali (who turns out to be a rather pathetic travelling performer). Later, in dappled light, the older Seeta sings a dawn raga on the airstrip. In a classic dissolve, the old Ishwar throws a newspaper showing Yuri Gagarin's space exploration into the foundry where it bursts into flames which then dissolve into the rainwater outside Seeta's hovel. Harprasad, who had earlier rescued Ishwar from committing suicide by quoting from **Tagore**'s *Shishu Tirtha*, later in the night club parodies an episode from the Upanishads using an East Bengal dialect. Other quotes from this extraordinary sequence including Eliot's *The Waste Land* (1922) and, through the music, Fellini's *La Dolce Vita* (1960). **Kumar Shahani** pointed out that when brother and sister confront each other in the brothel, Ghatak's sudden and brutal recourse to the highly conventionalised codes of melodrama abruptly stresses the usually hidden theme of incestuous aggression in the commercial Indian cinema while also commenting on the brutalisation of India's revered classical heritage (cf Shahani, 1986).

Madhabi Mukherjee and Satindra Bhattacharya in *Subarnarekha*

BABA RAMDEV

aka *Baba Ramdev Peer*, aka *Ramdev*
1963 ?' b&w Rajasthani
d Manibhai Vyas *pc* Ranglok *s* Naval Mathur *c* Narottam *m* Shivram

lp Mahipal, Anita Guha, Lalita Desai, Ratna, B.M. Vyas, Mohan Modi, Deepak, Madhumati, Dalda, Sarita

Rajasthani Saint film and mythological made by a Gujarati director known for mythologicals like *Satyavan Savitri* (1949) and *Bhakta Tulsidas* (1951). Featuring two of the most prominent Hindi stars associated with the genre, Mahipal and Guha, the film tells of Ramdev, a 13th C. Vaishnavite saint poet, unusually presented as a reincarnation of Vishnu (most Saint films usually emphasise the earthly origins of their subjects). Disgusted with his god when famine besets his kingdom, the king of Pokharan tries to commit suicide by jumping into the sea but he is placated by Vishnu who is reborn as the king's son. A variety of genres are telescoped into this miracle-laden film as Ramdev rescues his future wife, the Princess Netal, from bandits, and then saves his sister from her mother-in-law's tyranny. He also defeats the orthodox Yogiraj Kumbheshwar while espousing the cause of the lowest Untouchable castes.

BANDINI

1963 157'(120') b&w Hindi
d/p **Bimal Roy** *pc* Bimal Roy Prod. *st* Jarasandha [Charuchandra Chakraborty] *sc* M. Ghosh *lyr* **Shailendra** *c* Kamal Bose *m* **S.D. Burman**
lp **Nutan**, **Ashok Kumar**, **Dharmendra**, **Raja Paranjpe**, Tarun Bose, Asit Sen, Chandrima Bhaduri, Moni Chatterjee, Leela, Bela Bose, Iftikhar, Hiralal

Nutan's best-known film is set in the women's ward of a pre-independence prison. The story is based on a book by Jarasandha, a former Alipore central jail superintendent who wrote fictional versions of his experiences (*Louha-Kapat*, 1953; *Tamasha*, 1958; *Nyaydanda*, 1961). The gentle inmate Kalyani (Nutan), imprisoned for murder, appears determined to serve her full sentence, resisting the kind overtures of the prison doctor (Dharmendra). Her past is told in flashback. In a 30s Bengal riddled with revolutionary terrorists, she had become involved with the anarchist Bikash Ghosh (A. Kumar), and tries to save his life by claiming to be his wife. Her father (Paranjpe) insists that for her honour's sake she must really marry the man. Bikash disappears and Kalyani later learns that he has married another woman. To avoid her father's dishonour she leaves the village and becomes a servant in a nursing home where she encounters a particularly obnoxious patient who is revealed to be Bikash's wife. Regarding her as the cause of all her and her father's suffering, Kalyani poisons the woman and assumes her guilt. The sentimental story, which suggests a straight link between terrorism and patricide, is redeemed by the most accomplished cinematography Bimal Roy ever achieved and by Nutan's performance, perhaps the only consistent expression in Indian film of female guilt.

BLUFF MASTER

1963 ?' b&w Hindi
d/sc **Manmohan Desai** *pc* Subhash Pics *st* Madhusudan Kalelkar *dial/lyr* Rajendra Krishen *c* N. Satyen *m* **Kalyanji-Anandji**
lp **Shammi Kapoor**, Saira Banu, Pran, **Lalita Pawar**, Mohan Choti, Tuntun, Rashid Khan, Niranjan Sharma, Santosh Kumar, Ramlal, Shyamlal, Jugal Kishore, Charlie Walker

Desai inaugurates his characteristic 'performance masquerade' style with this virtual Shammi Kapoor solo act. Ashok (Kapoor) is a chronic liar who lives by his wits. As a gossip columnist he takes and publishes a photograph of a woman slapping a man in the street. The woman, Seema (Banu), is the boss's daughter. After many adventures, including an impromptu stage performance when he masquerades as his own father and violent encounters with Seema's villainous suitor Kumar (Pran), Ashok wins the woman. The film consistently emphasises a lumpenised street counter-culture culminating in the boisterous and popular number *Govinda ala re ala* performed by Kapoor on the city streets with numerous drunken youths.

Raja Paranjpe and Nutan in *Bandini*

GUMRAH

1963 155' b&w Hindi
d/p **B.R. Chopra** *pc* B.R. Films *dial* **Akhtar-ul-Iman** *lyr* Sahir Ludhianvi *m* Ravi
lp **Ashok Kumar**, **Mala Sinha**, **Sunil Dutt**, Shashikala, **Nirupa Roy**, Nana Palsikar, Vandana

Chopra's melodrama about marital infidelity sees Meena (Sinha), who loves Rajinder (Dutt), forced to marry her widowed brother-in-law Ashok (A. Kumar). Most of the story is occupied by a blackmailer (Shashikala) who, it transpires at the end of the film, was prompted by Ashok. The film features some famous Mahendra Kapoor songs (*In havaon mein, in fizaon mein*; *Yeh hawa, yeh fiza*; *Chalo ek baar phir se ajnabi ban jayen hum dono*).

IRUVAR ULLAM

1963 165' b&w Tamil
d/p **L.V. Prasad** *pc* Prasad Movies *s* **M. Karunanidhi** *lyr* **Kannadasan** *m* K.V. Mahadevan
lp **Sivaji Ganesan**, **B. Saroja Devi**, M.R. Radha, **S.V. Ranga Rao**, T.R. Ramchandran, T.P. Muthulakshmi, Sandhya, **Padmini**, Priyadarshini, **Lakshmirajyam**, A. Karunanidhi

Medical student Selvam (Ganesan) falls for the wiles of Vasanthi who only appears to covet his ancestral wealth. Later Selvam meets the schoolteacher Shanta (Saroja Devi) who is forced by her parents to marry him. However, she refuses to live with her husband because of his earlier affair. When Selvam is accused of murdering his former girlfriend, the crisis reconciles the couple. Prasad produced the Hindi version made by **T. Prakash Rao** as *Sasural* (1961) starring **Rajendra Kumar**.

ITO SITO BOHUTO

1963 113' b&w Assamese
d/s/m **Brojen Barua** *pc* J.P. Cine Art *lyr* Navakanta Barua, Keshab Mahanta *c* Shankar Bannerjee
lp **Phani Sarma**, Brojen Barua, Sarat Das, Muazzin Ali, Girin Barua, Probin Bora, Beena Das, Manideepa

Barua's remarkable debut is Assam's first comedy feature. It tells of an eccentric retired army major (Sarma) who clings to his authority and continues to expect military discipline. The fast-paced film is remembered mainly for Sarma's best-known, albeit uncharacteristic, film role.

MAHANAGAR

aka *The Big City*
1963 131' b&w Bengali
d/sc/m **Satyajit Ray** *p* R.D. Bansal pc R.D.B.

& Co. *st* Narendranath Mitra's *Abataranika c* Subrata Mitra
lp **Anil Chatterjee**, **Madhabi Mukherjee**, Jaya Bhaduri, Haren Chatterjee, Shefalika Devi, Prasenjit Sarkar, Haradhan Bannerjee, Vicky Redwood

Ray's first major incursion into the Calcutta environment after the brief sequence in ***Apur Sansar*** (1959). The film chronicles the shift from feudal social arrangements to Independent capitalism and urban mass culture. Middle-class clerk Subrata Majumdar (A. Chatterjee) persuades his wife Arati (Mukherjee) to take a job as a saleswoman. The large joint family is horrified at the thought of a working woman in their midst. For Arati, going door-to-door selling knitting machines opens up a new world which includes an Anglo-Indian friend, Edith (Redwood), and her employer Mukherjee. Earning money changes Arati's status in the family, causing further problems, especially when her husband loses his job. When Edith is unjustly sacked for racial reasons, Arati resigns in protest and throws the family into crisis. The film ends with an almost socialist-realist idiom as the camera cranes up to show the couple striding with determination into the teeming proletariat on the street. Different characters stand in for the conflicting ideologies: the father-in-law (Bannerjee) expects feudal loyalty from his former students; the entrepreneur Mukherjee espouses ruthless business ethics and the salesgirl Edith exemplifies the orthodox bias against working women as 'Westernised' and with loose morals. Ray often adapts a shooting style to suit the different locales represented by these individuals, using, e.g., expressionist low and wide-angle shots in Mukherjee's office and in the conversation between the two women in the ladies' rest room, whereas 'period' realism prevails for life in the family house. In between the sets designed by Bansi Chandragupta are the location shots, beginning with shots of tramlines and ending with the sweeping upward crane. Madhabi Mukherjee's performance dominates the film, as it would again in ***Charulata*** (1964).

MERE MEHBOOB

1963 164' col Urdu
d/co-sc **H.S. Rawail** *pc* Rahul Theatres *st/dial/co-sc* Vinod Kumar *lyr* Shakeel Badaiyuni *c* G. Singh *m* **Naushad**
lp **Ashok Kumar**, **Rajendra Kumar**, Sadhana, Nimmi, **Johnny Walker**, Pran, Sunder, Ameeta

A romance presumably set in early 20th C. Lucknow. Anwar (R. Kumar) glimpses the veiled Husna (Sadhana) and composes a love song for her while he sings at a college concert. Their subsequent meetings are bedevilled by class differences and family intrigues. The Eastmancolor musical, shot entirely in studios, effectively uses artifice to convey nostalgia for the elaborate courtly manners of a bygone (colonial) era. Naushad's music enhanced this approach with, e.g., the famous title number *Mere mehboob tujhe meri mohabat ki kasam* (sung in two versions by **Mohammed Rafi** and **Lata Mangeshkar**).

MOODUPADAM

1963 161' b&w Malayalam
d **Ramu Kariat** *p* T.K. Pareekutty *pc* Chandrathara Prod. *st* S.K. Pottakkad *dial* K. Padmanabhan Nair, K.T. Mohammed *lyr* **P. Bhaskaran**, Yusuf Ali Kacheri *c* **A. Vincent** *m* **Baburaj**
lp **Sathyan**, Nellikode Bhaskaran, Sheela, Premji, K. Balakrishnan Menon, **Madhu**, **Adoor Bhasi**, Poppu, Venu, Kothamangalam Ali, Kunjam, Ambika, Santha Devi

Kariat's film made at the Vijaya-Vauhini Studio dramatises Hindu-Christian and Hindu-Muslim relations: sexual relations between the former seem possible but sadly not between the latter. The four children of two working-class neighbours, one Hindu family and one Muslim family, grow up together. The Hindu boy Appu and the Muslim girl Ameena are in love but social taboos keep them apart. Having enabled his sister to marry a Christian man, Appu goes to Bombay where he becomes a respected playwright. Ameena's brother Ali is killed by communalist fanatics in Bombay but Appu withholds the news from the Muslim family, sending them money and gifts in Ali's name. Appu eventually arranges his beloved Ameena's marriage to a Muslim soldier.

MOOGAMANUSHULU

1963 164' b&w Telugu
d/sc **Adurthi Subba Rao** *pc* Babu Movies *co-st/co-dial/co-lyr* **Acharya Athreya** *co-st/co-dial* Mullapudi Venkatramana *co-lyr* Dasarathi, **Kosaraju** *c* P.L. Roy *m* K.V. Mahadevan
lp **A. Nageshwara Rao**, **Savitri**, **Jamuna**, Suryakantam, **Gummadi Venkateshwara Rao**, Padmanabham, Allu Ramalingaiah, Annapoorna

Hit Telugu musical about rebirth. Boatman Gopi (Nageshwara Rao) ferries Radha (Savitri) every day across the Godavari river and falls in love with her although he is due to marry Gowri (Jamuna), a woman from his own class. Radha marries a rich man (Padmanabham) and later reappears as a widow. Her relationship with Gopi, which causes a scandal, is presented as a continuation of their relationship in a previous life, shown in flashbacks. The film established the reputation of its composer, Mahadevan, and his long-term collaboration with Athreya and Subba Rao, the latter remaking the film as *Milan* (1967) with **Sunil Dutt** and **Nutan**.

NINAMANNINNYA KALAPADAKAL

aka *Bloodstained Footsteps*
1963 165' b&w Malayalam
d N.N. Pishareddy *pc* Navarathna Prod. *s* Parappuram *lyr* **P. Bhaskaran** *c* U. Rajagopal *m* **Baburaj**
lp **Prem Nazir**, **P.J. Anthony**, Ambika, **Madhu**, Sheela, Kambisseri, S.P. Pillai, Bahadur, **Adoor Bhasi**, Adoor Bhawani, Shantakumari, Kottayam Shantha, Mavelikkara L. Ponnamma, Susheela

A relentless melodrama about neighbours and childhood sweethearts tragically separated when their fathers die. He joins the army and she has to rely on another man's financial help. Wounded at the front and comforted by a friendly nurse, he returns to find his girl married to the drunken village butcher. He returns to the war, sees his best friend die and marries the man's sister but has to go back to the front before consummation can take place. The film adapted a story by Parappuram, who specialised in military stories (cf ***Anveshichu Kandatiyilla***, 1967) and was the first effort at making a war movie in the language, although much of the action was shot on sets.

NIRJAN SAIKATE

1963 130' b&w Bengali
d/s **Tapan Sinha** *pc* New Theatres (Exhibitors) *st* Samaresh Bose *c* Bimal Mukherjee *m* Kalipada Sen
lp **Anil Chatterjee**, **Sharmila Tagore**, Ruma Guha-Thakurta, **Chhaya Devi**, Renuka Roy, Bharati Devi, **Pahadi Sanyal**, **Jahar Ganguly**, **Robi Ghosh**, **Amar Mullick**, Upamanyu Chatterjee

A leisurely tale using a narrative format reminiscent of Ophuls's *Le Plaisir* (1952) with the coachload of women transposed to a railway carriage. A young writer meets four widows and a jilted young woman on the train to Puri. The rest of the film consists of their interactions, the revelation of their backgrounds and the touristic scenery (including the temple of Konarak).

PARASMANI

1963 ?' b&w/col Hindi
d **Babubhai Mistri** *pc* Movieland *s* Vishwanath Pande, Madhur *dial* C.K. Mast *lyr* Asad Bhopali, Farooq Kaiser, Indivar *c* Peter Pereira *m* **Laxmikant-Pyarelal**
lp Geetanjali, Mahipal, Manhar Desai, Nalini Chonkar, Maruti, Nazi, Uma Dutt, Jugal Kishore, Aruna Irani, Ajit Soni, Shekhar Purohit, Jeevankala, Helen

A special-effects fantasy about the son of a princely state's army Chief. Jettisoned from a ship by his father during a storm, the son grows into the fearless Paras who falls in love with the princess of the realm. The king is told by a fortune-teller that his son-in-law will cause his death unless the mythical Parasmani diamond, owned by the witch queen of Mayanagari, is acquired. After many adventures, Paras obtains the jewel. The film, although in the tradition of cheap Hindi *Arabian Nights* fantasies, seems to take its cue from Tamil costume dramas. The inexpensive effects include a fight between Paras and his father on what looks like a cross between a magic carpet and a spaceship. Remembered mainly as the debut of the celebrated composers **Laxmikant-Pyarelal**, with hits such as *Ooi ma yeh kya ho gaya* and *Hansta hua nurani chehra*, filmed in colour.

PUNARJANMA

1963 164' b&w Telugu
d/sc **K. Pratyagatma** *pc* Prasad Art Pics *st* Gulshan Nanda *sc* **Acharya Athreya** *lyr* **Sri Sri**, Dasarathi, C. Narayana Reddy, **Kosaraju** *c* P.S. Selvaraj *m* T. Chalapathi Rao
lp **A. Nageshwara Rao**, Krishnakumari, **Gummadi Venkateshwara Rao**, Ramana

Reddy, Padmanabham, Prabhakara Reddy, Vasanthi, Suryakantham, Sandhya, Chandalavada

Melodrama about Gopi, an artist (Nageshwara Rao) who goes crazy when an electrical short circuit destroys his sculpture. The doctor has the dancer and singer Vasanthi (Krishnakumari) move in to restore the sculptor to sanity. The two plan to marry, but his return to health also causes an attack of amnesia. The hero can only recognise his lover when a second accident reminds him of his first illness.

RAKTHA TILAKAM

1963 166' b&w Tamil
d Dada Mirasi *pc* National Movies *s/lyr* **Kannadasan** *c* Jagirdar *m* K.V. Mahadevan *lp* **Sivaji Ganesan**, G.K. Nagesh, M.N. Kannappa, K. Shanmughasundaram, **Savitri**, C.R. Parthiban, Pushpalata, Veerasamy, Manorama, S.R. Janaki, Saradambal

Ganesan's nationalist war movie against the background of the 1962 India-China conflict. The hero Kumar (Ganesan) and heroine Kamala (Savitri) are colleagues at university. She begins to appreciate him when he rescues a play she directs by understudying her brother in the role of Othello. Kamala then joins her father in Beijing while Kumar joins the Indian Army. In Beijing Kamala marries a Chinese Army doctor and accompanies him to the 1962 war as a nurse by day and an Indian spy by night. Kumar captures her and she is to be shot at dawn when her espionage activities come to light. She is killed by her Chinese husband. Kumar dies in battle holding on to the Indian flag. The film is an important turning-point in Ganesan's and scenarist Kannadasan's efforts to repudiate their DMK associations by valorising Congress nationalism.

RUSTOM SOHRAB

1963 ?' b&w Hindi-Urdu
d **Vishram Bedekar** *pc* Ramsay Prod *s* Kumar **Ramsay** *co-dial* Iqbal Nadeem, Masood Mashedi, Jagdish Gautam, Sardar Illham *co-dial/lyr* Qamar Jalalabadi *co-lyr* Jan Nissar Akhtar *c* Nariman Irani *m* Sayed Hussain
lp **Prithviraj Kapoor**, **Suraiya**, Premnath, Mumtaz, Sajjan, Shah Agha, Marilyn

Kumar Ramsay, a member of the family best known for their horror films, scripted this version of the classic Persian legend drawn from the 10th C. *Shahnama* which was a staple item in the Parsee theatre. Rustom (Kapoor in a role reminiscent of his performance in ***Mughal-e-Azam***, 1960) is the king of Persia whose wife Tehmina (Suraiya) bears him a son while he is away fighting wars. The son Sohrab (Premnath) grows into a powerful warrior and ends up challenging his father. Unaware of each other's identity, they confront each other on the battlefield where, in true feudal tradition, Rustom triumphs over his son.

SAAT PAKE BANDHA

1963 133' b&w Bengali
d/s **Ajoy Kar** *pc* R.D. Bansal *c* Bishu Chakraborty *m* **Hemanta Mukherjee** *lp* **Suchitra Sen**, **Soumitra Chatterjee**, **Pahadi Sanyal**, **Chhaya Devi**, Molina Devi, Tarun Kumar, Prasanta Kumar

Suchitra Sen gives a major performance in this marital melodrama. The independent Archana (Sen) tries to overcome her domineering and snobbish mother by marrying Sukhendu (Chatterjee), a serious university lecturer, but mother continues to interfere, reminding her son-in-law of his poverty. Suffering from divided loyalties, Archana's problems are aggravated when her husband insists that she sever all ties with her parents. She separates from her husband and decides to complete her studies while living independently. When she finally accepts her wifely duties and returns home it is too late, as Sukhendu has resigned his job and gone abroad. Sen's finely honed performance often undercuts the ideology her character is supposed to exemplify, evoking the possibility of a more egalitarian representation of women in Bengali cinema. Despite the conservatism of the story, issues of marital compatibility are extensively discussed without invoking conventional patriarchal moralism.

SHAHER AUR SAPNA

aka *Shehar Aur Sapna* aka *The City and the Dream*
1963 140'(120') b&w Hindi
d/s **K.A. Abbas** *pc* **Naya Sansar** *lyr* Ali Sardar Jafri *c* Ramchandra *m* J.P. Kaushik *lp* Dilip Raj, Surekha Parkar, Nana Palsikar, Manmohan Krishna, David, Anwar Hussain, Rashid Khan, Asit Sen

Abbas's romantic view of Bombay's pavement-dwellers tells of a man (Roy) who arrives from a poor Punjabi village to find a job. Amazed at the city's opulence he soon realises the main problem is to find shelter. He finally settles down with his wife (Surekha) in an unused water pipe where she gives birth to their child. The activities of slum landlords and thieves open the way for property developers and bulldozers and the pavement-dwellers again have to find shelter elsewhere, but this time they act together. For the next decade, this film's sentimentalised way of showing urban class divisions became the standard, popular idiom for these motifs, extending into Abbas's own documentaries (cf ***Char Shaher Ek Kahani***, 1968) and into, e.g., **Sukhdev**'s influential 'progressive' featurettes (***And Miles To Go ...***, 1965).

TERE GHAR KE SAAMNE

1963 149' b&w Hindi
d/s **Vijay Anand** *pc* Navketan *lyr* Hasrat Jaipuri *c* V. Ratra *m* **S.D. Burman**
lp **Dev Anand**, **Nutan**, Harindranath Chattopadhyay, Om Prakash, Praveen Choudhury, Zareen, Rashid Khan, Rajendranath

After ***Paying Guest*** (1957), this is the best-known Dev Anand-Nutan vehicle. Two

Dilip Raj in *Shaher Aur Sapna*

feuding millionaires, Seth Karamchand (Chattopadhyay) and Lala Jagannath (Prakash), want to build their houses in front of each other. Jagannath's son, the architect Rakesh Kumar (D. Anand), is commissioned to construct both houses. In addition, he falls in love with Karamchand's daughter Sulekha (Nutan). A frothy musical comedy with some classic hits such as *Dil ka bhanwar kare pukar* (sung by **Mohammed Rafi**), *Yeh tanhaai hai re hai* (sung by **Lata Mangeshkar**) and bravura song picturisations including the *Dil ka bhanwara* number on the steps of the Qutub Minar in Delhi, and the title song, performed by Rafi and **Mangeshkar**, in which an imagined Nutan appears in miniature in Anand's whisky glass as they sing the duet.

VEERA KESARI/BANDHIPOTU

1963 177' col Kannada/Tamil
d **B. Vittalacharya** *pc* Rajalakshmi Prod. *dial* Sorat Ashwath *lyr* K.R. Seetarama Sastry *c* Ravikant Nagaich *m* **Ghantasala Venkateshwara Rao**
lp **Rajkumar**[K], **Leelavathi**[K], **Udaya Kumar**[K], **R. Nagendra Rao**[K], **N.T. Rama Rao**[Te], Krishnakumari[Te]

Vittalacharya's big-budget return to Kannada cinema is a Rajkumar costumed adventure movie with a complicated plot, characteristic of all the star's films. King Satyasena of Gandhara is overthrown by his evil stepbrother Shurasena (Kumar). The masked hero Veera Nayaka, who leads the oppressed people, attacks the palace of Princess Mandara Male (Leelavathi), but she is rescued by the masked man's brother Narasimha Nayaka (Rajkumar/NTR). Veera Nayaka is killed together with his benevolent father Dharma Nayaka (Nagendra Rao) by Shurasena. This episode introduces a second masked man, revealed to be Narasimha Nayaka's brother. The princess tries to apprehend him but is herself caught. She is then told the truth about the palace intrigues. Narasimha Nayaka is captured, escapes, and eventually overthrows the evil empire of Shurasena. Vittalacharya simultaneously made a Telugu version, *Bandhipotu*, starring **NTR** and Krishnakumari.

AROHI

aka *Aarohi*, aka *Ascent*
1964 124' b&w Bengali
d/sc **Tapan Sinha** *p* Asim Pal *st* Banaphool *c* Bimal Mukherjee *m* **Hemanta Mukherjee**
lp **Kali Bannerjee**, Dilip Roy, Sipra Mitra, Bikash Roy, Tapan Bhattacharya, Shyam Laha, **Chhaya Devi**

The romanticised story of a peasant (Bannerjee) who lives in a small village. He learns to read and is befriended by a doctor (D. Roy) who helps him improve his status in the community. The film concentrates on atmospherics and the character of the somewhat irascible peasant anxious that others should accept the knowledge he gained from his readings.

AMADA BATA

aka *The Untrodden Road*
1964 144' b&w Oriya
d/sc Amar Ganguly *p* Babulal Doshi *st* Basanti Kumar Pattanayak's novel *dial* Gopal Chatray *c* Deojibhai *m* Balakrishna Das
lp Geeta, **Jharana Das**, Lakhmi, Menaka, Kiran, Krishnapriya, Umakant, Akhyay, Sharat, Brindavan

The debut of pioneering Oriya producer Doshi tells of the rebellious Maya (Das) who disapproves of her sister-in-law's meek assent to the role of obedient housewife. However, the latter's attitude is merely a ploy to get her husband to split from his family. When Maya gets married, the curtailment of her freedom causes her intense suffering. The moral of the story is that by meekly submitting to her husband, a woman can achieve greater happiness. This reactionary critique of women's desire for emancipation, adapted from a book by one of Orissa's first female novelists, is best remembered for Das's performance.

AMARASHILPI JAKANACHARI/AMARASHILPI JAKANNA

1964 161' col Kannada/Telugu
d/c **B.S. Ranga** *pc* Vikram Prod. *s/co-lyr*[Te] **Samudrala Raghavacharya** *co-lyr*[Te] Dasarathi, **Kosaraju**, C. Narayana Reddy *dia/lyr*[K] Chi. Sadashivaiah *m* **Saluri Rajeshwara Rao**
lp **Kalyana Kumar**[K]/**A. Nageshwara Rao**[Te], **B. Saroja Devi**, **Udaya Kumar**, **Chittor V. Nagaiah**, Narasimhraju, Rama Devi, Girija, Pushpavalli, H.P. Saroja, **Relangi Venkatramaiah**[Te]

The first Kannada colour movie is a costume spectacule about the sculptor Jakanachari (K. Kumar/Nageshwara Rao) who is apparently responsible for the impressive 12th C. temple sculptures of Belur and Halebid during the reign of the Hoysala King Vishnuvardhana, now a major Karnataka tourist attraction. The sculptor is shown to be inspired by his love for Manjari (Saroja Devi), who is seperated from him by a political conspiracy. Later, Jakanachari has a contest with a young sculptor unaware that the youth is his own son. Kalyana Kumar's best-known screen role.

BHARGAVI NILAYAM

1964 175' b&w Malayalam
d **A. Vincent** *prod* T.K Pareekutty *pc* Chandrathara Prod. *s* Vaikom Mohammed Basheer *lyr* **P. Bhaskaran** *c* P. Bhaskar Rao *m* **Baburaj**
lp **Prem Nazir**, **Madhu**, **Vijayanirmala**, **P.J. Anthony**, Pappu, Kothamangalam Ali, Baby Shanta, Malashanta, Parvati, **Adoor Bhasi**

Mystery story, and rare script by noted Malayalam novelist Basheer (whose diaries were later filmed by **Adoor Gopalakrishnan**, as ***Mathilukal***, 1989). Set in a desolate mansion, it has a novelist (Madhu) who comes to stay and encounters the beautiful ghost Bhargavi (Vijayanirmala). He starts writing her story, a tragic tale about her love for a poet (Nazir) and her evil cousin (Anthony) who ruined the affair. As the novelist reads out the story to the ghost, the cousin turns up and tries to kill the novelist. They fall into a well but the ghost helps the hero out, leaving the villain to drown. Vincent's directorial debut, and the first ghost story in Malayalam, the film was noted for its elegiac camerawork adapting a highly symbolic script. It was also the first big role of future Telugu star and director Vijayanirmala.

CHARULATA

aka *The Lonely Wife*
1964 117' b&w Bengali
d/sc/m **Satyajit Ray** *p* R.D. Bansal *pc* R.D.B. *st* **Rabindranath Tagore**'s *Nastaneer* (1901) *c* Subrata Mitra
lp **Soumitra Chatterjee**, **Madhabi Mukherjee**, Sailen Mukherjee, Shyamal Ghosal, Gitali Roy, Bholanath Koyal, Suku Mukherjee, Dilip Bose, Subrata Sen Sharma, Joydeb, Bankim Ghosh

Ray considered this film, structured like a musical rondo, to be his best work. Set in 1879 during the social reform movement in Calcutta, it tells of Charulata (M. Mukherjee), the bored and neglected upper-class wife of the reformer Bhupati Dutta (S. Mukherjee) who pursues a political career while editing a progressive English weekly newspaper, *The Sentinel*. He invites her older brother Umapada (Ghosal) and his wife Manda to move in to provide company for Charulata. Bhupati's cousin, the literary-minded Amal (Chatterjee) also moves in. Charulata and Amal become increasingly intimate, but their acquaintance is abruptly terminated when Umapada embezzles money and disappears. Amal too leaves, guilty about Bhupati's increasing dependence on him, given his relationship with Charulata. The married couple try to reunite at the end, after she overcomes her loss and he overcomes his feeling of betrayal. The ending, which departs from Tagore's, freezes their gesture as they reach out to one another. From the opening, as Charulata observes a series of Bengali stereotypes with her opera-glasses through the shutters of her windows, the film boasts some of Ray's most cinematic sequences: the card game with an incantatory voice-over keeping score; Amal serenading Charulata with the famous Tagore song *Ami chini-go-chini*, and Charulata daydreaming in the garden. Except for the garden sequence, the film refers to the outside world only via the dialogue, with references to the novelist Bankimchandra, to Gladstone, Disraeli and the dominant political issues of the 1880s which preoccupy Bhupati. The freeze-frames at the end, showing the couple uniting again, were inspired by the ending of Truffaut's *Les Quatre Cents Coups* (1959). The French New Wave apparently also influenced the extensive use of the tracking camera, sometimes across rooms (ironically Ray was to attack **Mrinal Sen** the following year, and New Indian Cinema directors in 1972, for being influenced by French cinema). *Charulata* also has the finest film work of several Ray regulars, including designer Bansi Chandragupta, cameraman Mitra and actors S. Chatterjee and Madhabi Mukherjee.

CHITRALEKHA

1964 ?' col Hindi
d **Kidar Sharma** *pc* Pushpa Pics *s* Rajinder Kumar Sharma *lyr* **Sahir Ludhianvi** *c* D.C. Mehta, A. Lateef *m* Roshan

lp **Ashok Kumar, Meena Kumari**, Pradeep Kumar, Mehmood, Minoo Mumtaz, Zeb Rehman, Bela Bose, Achala Sachdev, Naseem, Neeta, Rehana, Shobhana

Sharma's opulent costume drama set in the Gupta period (4th C.) is a remake of his 1941 film. With Kumari in the title role of the court dancer, her romance with Samant Beejagupta leads to questions of infidelity, the futility of love and corrupt ascetics. The film contributed to Meena Kumari's image as the archetypal courtesan in costume spectaculars (cf ***Pakeezah***, 1971), although its garish colours and costume design betray the degeneration of Sharma's work since his b&w romances.

DOOR GAGAN KI CHHAON MEIN

1964 153' b&w Hindi
d/p/s/co-lyr/m **Kishore Kumar** *pc* Kishore Films *co-lyr* **Shailendra** *dial* Ramesh Pant *c* Aloke Dasgupta
lp Kishore Kumar, **Supriya Choudhury**, Amit Ganguly, Raj Mehra, Sajjan, Shashikala, Nana Palsikar, Iftikhar, Leela Mishra, Harilal

The demobbed soldier Shankar (Kumar) returns to find his family perished in a fire and his infant son Ramu (Ganguly) struck dumb by the catastrophe. When he is attacked by the villainous Thakur's men, Shankar is rescued by Meera (Choudhury) and they fall in love, provoking further trouble from the Thakur whose son Jagga wants to marry Meera. For his directorial debut, the comedian Kishore Kumar cast himself in a tragic role (his own productions were never comedies). The film is remembered mainly for its classic song *A chalke tujhe main le ke chalun* written by the star for himself.

DOSTI

aka *Friendship*
1964 163' b&w Hindi
d **Satyen Bose** *pc* Rajshri Prod. *sc* Govind Moonis *st* Ban Bhatt *lyr* **Majrooh Sultanpuri** *c* Marshall Braganza *m* **Laxmikant-Pyarelal**
lp Sushil Kumar, Sudhir Kumar, Nana Palsikar, **Leela Chitnis, Abhi Bhattacharya**, Baby Farida, Leela Mishra, Sanjay, Uma, Aziz

A crippled boy (Sushil Kumar) and a blind boy (Sudhir Kumar) become close friends in Calcutta and help each other to survive. They befriend a sick rich child (Farida). Famous for its numerous hit songs by **Mohammed Rafi** including *Jaane vaalon zara mud ke dekho mujhe* and *Chahoonga main tujhe*.

HAQEEQAT

1964 184' b&w Hindi
d/s **Chetan Anand** *pc* Himalaya Films *lyr* **Kaifi Azmi** *c* Sadanand Sengupta *m* **Madan Mohan**
lp **Balraj Sahni, Dharmendra**, Priya Rajvansh, **Vijay Anand**, Jayant, Indrani Mukherjee, Sanjay Khan, Chand Usmani, Achala Sachdev, Gulab, **Sulochana**, Sudhir Jagdev, Levy Aaron, Nasreen

A propaganda film dedicated to Nehru and trading on the resurgence of nationalist sentiment in the wake of the India-China war of 1962 which provides the film's setting. The war had led to a sobering awareness of India's military capability and contributed to major schisms about Nehruite notions of non-alignment while accelerating the split in the CPI between Moscow- and Beijing-aligned groups. Made by former Marxists Anand, Sahni et al., the film's main plot concerns a small platoon of Indian soldiers presumed dead but rescued by Kashmiri gypsies and by Capt. Bahadur Singh (Dharmendra) and his tribal girlfriend (Rajvansh) who die holding the Chinese at bay while their comrades retreat to safety. Rhetorical highlights including the platoon commander (Sahni) excoriating Mao's *Little Red Book* which a soldier spears with a bayonet; the commanding officer (Jayant) denouncing the Chinese to documentary footage of Chou En-Lai landing in Delhi and being given a guard of honour; Kaifi Azmi's song *Kar chale hum fida jaan-o-tan saathiyon* (sung by **Mohammed Rafi**) cut to more documentary shots of Nehru addressing the troops and of the Republic Day parade. Shot on location on the Ladakh border, the film had one other song hit, the soldiers' qawali *Ho ke majboor mujhe usne bulaya hoga* (sung by Mohammed Rafi, Bhupendra, Talat Mahmood, Manna Dey and a chorus).

Priya Rajvansh (left) in *Haqeeqat*

KARNAN/KARNA/DAANVEER KARNA

1964 177'[Ta]/187'[Te] b&w Tamil/Telugu/Hindi
d/p **B.R. Panthulu** *pc* Padmini Pics *sc* A.S. Nagarajan *dial* Shakti Krishnaswamy *lyr* **Kannadasan** *c* V. Ramamurthy *m* Vishwanathan-Ramamurthy
lp **Sivaji Ganesan, N.T. Rama Rao, Savitri**, Devika, **M.V. Rajamma**, Sandhya, Jawar Seetaraman, Ashokan

The big-budget follow-up to Panthulu's multilingual Ganesan hit ***Veerapandiya Kattaboman*** (1959) tells the tragic *Mahabharata* tale of Karnan (Ganesan), Kunti's eldest son, known for his charitable nature and archery expertise. Although a brother of the Pandavas, he remains faithful to Duryodhana who raised him and fights his kinfolk until Krishna overcomes him. Shot with three camera units at Jaipur, the massive action scenes such as the Kurukshetra battle required the participation of the 61st Cavalry, 80 elephants and 400 horses. Tamil and Telugu stars Ganesan and NTR had worked together in K. Somu's hit mythological *Sampoorna Ramayanam* (1958).

KASHMIR KI KALI

1964 168' col Hindi
d/p **Shakti Samanta** *pc* Shakti Films *s* Ranjan Bose *dial* Ramesh Pant *lyr* S.H. Bihari *c* V.N. Reddy *m* **O.P. Nayyar**
lp **Shammi Kapoor, Sharmila Tagore**, Pran, Anup Kumar, Nasir Hussain, Sundar, Madan Puri, Padmadevi, Mridula, Tuntun, Bir Sakhuja, Robert, Padma Chavan, Sujata, Neeta, Samar Chatterjee, Aruna, Hamida

Taking its title from the hit song *Kashmir ki kali hoon main* sung by **Lata Mangeshkar** in Kapoor's successful ***Junglee*** (1961), this is an exotic comedy romance in colour deploying Shammi Kapoor's established persona as the rich youth who spurns his family's wealth and after some adventures falls in love with a woman not of his social class who cares little for his wealth. Rajib (Kapoor), constantly criticised by his mother for crazy decisions (e.g. announcing an award of Rs 500,000 to the family's mill employees), leaves when there is talk of arranging a marriage for him and goes to Kashmir where he falls in love with a flower-girl (Tagore). Rajib lives in his family's bungalow, sneakily rented out by the caretaker, and is regarded as weak in the head. Kapoor had put on some weight and his physical gyrations are less elegant than they were in his b&w **Nasir Hussain** films, but the influence of rock music, the exotic locales and the emphasis on upper-class youth culture continues from his previous films. The film includes several **Mohammed Rafi** hits in the Kapoor style (*Kisi na kisise*, *Yeh chand sa roshan chehra*).

KOHRAA

1964 153' b&w Hindi
d/sc Biren Nag *pc* Geetanjali Pics *st* R. Sawant *dial/lyr* **Kaifi Azmi** *c* Marshall Braganza *p/m* Hemant Kumar [**Hemanta Mukherjee**]
lp **Waheeda Rehman**, Biswajit, Manmohan Krishna, **Abhi Bhattacharya**, Badri Prasad, Madan Puri, Tarun Bose, Chand Usmani, Asit Sen, Samar Roy, Dev Kishen

The former art director Nag (e.g. for Navketan films) tells a ghost story about Rajashree (Rehman), a new bride who arrives at an ancestral mansion to find that it is pervaded by the spirit of her husband Amit's first wife, Poonam. Known for its classic songs such as **Lata Mangeshkar**'s *Jhoom jhoom dhalti raat*.

MAHAPURUSH

aka *The Holy Man*
1964 65' b&w Bengali
d/sc/m **Satyajit Ray** *p* R.D. Bansal *pc* R.D.B. *st* Rajasekhar Bose's [aka Parashuram] *Birinchi Baba* *c* Soumendu Roy
lp Charuprakash Ghosh, **Robi Ghosh**, Prasad Mukherjee, Gitali Roy, Satindra Bhattacharya, Soumyen Bose, Santosh Dutta, Renuka Roy

First of two short films often shown as *Kapurush-o-Mahapurush*. Returning to the farces of Parashuram (cf ***Parash Pathar***, 1957) and to the comedy team of ***Abhijaan*** (1962), Charuprakash and Robi Ghosh. The widower Gurupada Mitter (Mukherjee) becomes the disciple of the yogic godman Birinchi Baba (C. Ghosh), followed by his daughter Buchki (G. Roy) who breaks her engagement with Satya (Bhattacharya). Satya and members of an informal club unmask the godman as a fraud. This broadly played, verbose comedy is full of puns, often in English, as the godman claims to have been present in ancient Babylon, argued with Plato and taught Einstein the relativity theory, claiming that the crucifixion of Christ was crucifact because he saw it with his own eyes. The film evokes the popular 50s/60s Calcutta fashion of groups meeting in coffee-houses to swap stories and argue about politics.

MURALI KRISHNA

1964 169' b&w Telugu
d **P. Pullaiah** *pc* Padmasri Prod. *st* P. Radha *s/co-lyr* **Acharya Athreya** *co-lyr* Dasarathi, C. Narayana Reddy *c* Madhav Bulbule *m* **Master Venu**
lp **A. Nageshwara Rao**, **Jamuna**, **S.V. Ranga Rao**, **Gummadi Venkateshwara Rao**, Haranath, Geetanjali, **Sharada**, Suryakantam, Vijayalakshmi

A comedy of mistaken (gender) identity in which the bluff, retired military man (Ranga Rao) raises his daughter Murali (Jamuna) as though she were a son. She loves and is to marry Krishna (Nageshwara Rao) when a painter, Lakshmikantam (Haranath), appears. Murali had written letters of appreciation believing him to be a woman. When Lakshmikantam wants to marry Murali, she persuades her friend Srilatha (Sharada) to pretend to be Murali, a subterfuge that works until the painter turns out to be a friend of Murali's fiance.

NANDI

1964 162' b&w Kannada
d **N. Lakshminarayan** *pc* Shri Bharati Chitra *c* R.N.K. Prasad *m* **Vijayabhaskar**
lp **Rajkumar**, Harini, **Kalpana**, **Balkrishna**

Melodrama about deaf-mute people. Murthy's (Rajkumar) wife dies in childbirth, and when his daughter becomes deaf and mute, Murthy marries a deaf-mute, learns to lip-read and starts a school for the handicapped. When his daughter dies, his wife joins him in running the school. Eventually, the wife delivers a normal baby. The debut of Kannada cinema's first self-proclaimed successor to **Satyajit Ray**, the hit film established Kalpana as a Kannada star.

PATHLAAG

1964 123' b&w Marathi
d **Raja Paranjpe** *pc* Shripad Chitra *st* Jayant Devkule's novel *Asha Parat Yete* *sc/dial/lyr* **G.D. Madgulkar** *c* Datta Gorle *m* Datta Davjekar
lp Bhavana, Kashinath Ghanekar, Ishwar Agarwal, Vasant Thengadi, Ganpat Patil, **Raja Nene**

Hit suspense thriller introducing the future Marathi stage and film stars Bhavana and Ghanekar. When the noted lawyer Balasaheb Panse (Ghanekar) goes abroad, he receives a telegram informing him of the sudden death of his wife Asha (Bhavana). After she has been cremated and he is still in mourning, a woman arrested as a member of a criminal gang by the police claims to be Asha, whom she resembles absolutely (Bhavana again). She keeps telling Panse intimate details about their lives, expresses surprise that anyone could have thought her dead and implores him to have her released, causing a major emotional dilemma for the hero. Eventually, in an unconvincing end that deflates the suspense, the second woman is revealed as indeed his wife, while the woman who died was her hitherto unmentioned twin sister. An early success by composer Davjekar, the film also included the hit song *Ya dolyachi don pakhare*. The film was remade as *Mera Saaya* (1966) by **Raj Khosla**.

POOJAPALAM

1964 156' b&w Telugu
d **B.N. Reddi** *pc* Shri Sambhu Films *st* Munipalle Raju's novel *Pujari* *sc/dial* **D.V. Narasaraju** *lyr* **Devulapalli Krishna Sastry**, C. Narayana Reddy, **Kosaraju** *c* U. Rajagopal *m* **Saluri Rajeshwara Rao**
lp **A. Nageshwara Rao**, **Gummadi Venkateshwara Rao**, **Relangi Venkatramaiah**, Ramana Reddy, **Savitri**, **Jamuna**, Vijayalakshmi, Rajashree, **K. Jaggaiah**

Love story about the shy and sensitive Madhu (Nageshwara Rao), a lover of music, who meets and has affairs with three women, each making a radically different kind of sexual proposition. The first, Vasanthi (Jamuna), represents romantic love leading to several musical compositions in her praise; the second, Seeta (Savitri), is the devoted partner who restores his emotional health when Vasanthi leaves, and the third, Neelanagini (Vijayalakshmi), is the seductive courtesan from a family of entertainers. Eventually Madhu selects Seeta. The performances of the leading duo were praised in the popular press, esp. Nageshwara Rao's as the lovesick poet, continuing his ***Devadasu*** (1953) image. The music includes work of the celebrated violinist Paravur Gopalakrishnan.

RAJKUMAR

1964 178' col Hindi
d K. Shankar *pc* Saravana Films *st* **Manmohan Desai** *sc* **Ramanand Sagar** *lyr* **Shailendra**, Hasrat Jaipuri *c* G. Singh *m* **Shankar-Jaikishen**
lp **Shammi Kapoor**, Sadhana, **Prithviraj Kapoor**, Om Prakash, Pran, Master Babloo, Ravi Shivdasani, Achala Sachdev, Rajindernath, Manorama

Made in Madras and written by the star combination of Manmohan Desai and Ramanand Sagar, this is one of India's few successful parodies. It satirises the historical/costumed adventure fantasy, practised in Madras by, e.g., the influential fictions generated at **Modern Theatres**. The king (P. Kapoor) awaits the return of the prince (S. Kapoor) in a direct quote from his role at the beginning of the classic ***Mughal-e-Azam*** (1960), but on his arrival from Paris in a two-seater plane the son greets the welcoming committee sent by his father with 'bonsoir'. A major palace intrigue involves the king's second wife (Manorama) and her brother (Pran) who plot to overthrow him. The prince tries to foil the villains by pretending to be eccentric. He also falls in love with a tribal princess (Sadhana) with a predilection for singing complicated love songs while standing, e.g., at the edge of a giant waterfall. Hit numbers include *Aaja aai bahar dil hai bekaraar* (sung by **Lata Mangeshkar**) and the title refrain *Aage peeche zara hoshiyar yahan ke hum hain Rajkumar* (sung by **Mohammed Rafi**).

SANGAM

aka *The Confluence*
1964 238' col Hindi
d/p **Raj Kapoor** *pc* R.K. Films *s* **Inder Raj Anand** *lyr* **Shailendra**, Hasrat Jaipuri *c* Radhu Karmakar *m* **Shankar-Jaikishen**
lp Raj Kapoor, **Vyjayanthimala**, **Rajendra Kumar**, **Lalita Pawar**, Achala Sachdev, Iftikhar, Nana Palsikar, Raj Mehra

Kapoor's first colour film is presented as a glossy love triangle but can equally well be seen, along with many Indian triangle dramas, as a romance between two men interrupted by a woman. Sunder (Kapoor) is from a lower class than his childhood friends Gopal (Kumar) and Radha (Vyjayanthimala). Although both men, bosom pals, are in love with Radha, Sunder ignores the fact that he and Gopal share the same object of desire. When Sunder finally wins and marries Radha by joining the air force and becoming a national hero, Gopal puts male bonding and his passion for his friend above his attachment to Radha and withdraws. However, Sunder is obsessed by thoughts of Radha's possible infidelity. In the end, Gopal reassures Sunder of Radha's fidelity and then commits suicide.

The film includes a plea by Radha for fairer treatment of women but the logic of the story demonstrates that the most valuable relationship a man can have is with another man. **Mahesh Bhatt** (1993) commented that the hit song *Bol radha bol, sangam ho ga ke nahin*, sung by Mukesh, 'triggers off memories of a beautiful woman in a picturesque setting dressed in a swimsuit (while) Raj Kapoor, clad in shorts, hangs from a tree with a bagpipe under one arm and begs his beloved Radha for an orgasmic release'. Another hit was *Ye mera prem patra*, sung by **Rafi**. One of the early films to use locations in Europe as exotic backdrops as Sunder and Radha honeymoon in snowy Switzerland and 'decadent' Paris, where, to the song *Main kya karoon ram mujhe buddha mil gaya*, Radha behaves like a prostitute to taunt her husband's virility.

SERVER SUNDARAM

1964 165' b&w Tamil/Telugu
d **Krishnan-Panju** *pc* Guhan Films *sc* **K. Balachander** from his play *c* S. Maruthi Rao *lyr* **Kannadasan** *m* Vishwanathan-Ramamurthy
lp Nagesh, Muthuraman, Major Sundarrajan, K.R. Vijaya, S.N. Lakshmi

One of the future director Balachander's plays with an urban middle-class setting is used in this rags-to-riches story set in the film industry. Sundaram (Nagesh, introducing the anti-hero to Tamil film with this semi-autobiographical fiction) is an inept waiter in a coffee-shop who falls for rich girl Radha (Vijaya). Through his friend Raghavan (Muthuraman) he gets a break in movies and becomes a star, only to see his beloved become his friend's fiancee. Nagesh, at the peak of his career as the 'server', evokes Chaplin via **Raj Kapoor** and accentuates the sentimentality in the Tamil cinema's standard mother-son scenes. Balachander provides witty, fast-paced dialogues and the comedy sequences are integrated into the main narrative, giving the film a modern feeling, confirmed by the scenes showing film production and song recording. Also released in a (probably dubbed) Telugu version.

VIVAHABANDHAM

1964 166' b&w Telugu
d **P.S. Ramakrishna Rao** *pc* Bharani Pics *st* Ravoori *sc* Atluri Picheshwara Rao *lyr* C. Narayana Reddy *c* Annayya *m* **M.B. Srinivasan**
lp **N.T. Rama Rao, P. Bhanumathi, Chittor V. Nagaiah**, Suryakantam, Hemalatha, Padmanabham, Prabhakara Reddi, Vasanthi, Balaiah

Telugu remake of **Ajoy Kar**'s **Suchitra Sen** hit ***Saat Pake Bandha*** (1963), substantially diluting both the performance and plot of the original. Idealists Bharati (Bhanumathi) and Chandrasekhar (NTR) get married against the wishes of Bharati's mother who wants a richer son-in-law. Chandrasekhar refuses to meet Bharati's parents and later Bharati falls out of favour with Chandrasekhar's stepmother. The couple decide to divorce before things work out in the end. The film reunited the successful team of Bhanumathi and NTR at the Bharani Studio. Bhanumathi's only duet with P.B. Srinivas, *Neetilona*, was appreciated.

WOH KAUN THI

aka *Who Was She?*
1964 140' b&w Hindi
d **Raj Khosla** *p* N.N. Sippy *pc* Prithvi Pics *s* Dhruva Chatterjee *dial* Ehsan Rizvi *lyr* Mehdi Ali Khan *c* K.H. Kapadia *m* **Madan Mohan**
lp Sadhana, **Manoj Kumar**, Praveen Choudhury, K.N. Singh, Raj Mehra, Dhumal, Mohan Choti, Ratnamala, Helen, Prem Chopra

A rare big-budget excursion into the thriller genre, the plot concerns a young doctor, Anand (Kumar), obsessed by a woman (Sadhana) who appears to him with different names and in different guises, making him doubt his senses. Like *Vertigo* (1958), the story evokes the supernatural and madness but eventually the hero unravels the plot. The villain of the piece is Anand's friend Dr Ramesh (Chopra) who concocts the plot to drive Anand insane in order to get hold of an inheritance. The enigmatic, sexually repressed figure played by Sadhana ranges from a ghostlike apparition to Anand's future wife (with a seduction scene where she momentarily turns 'human' to the song *Lag jaa gale*). In spite of the often woefully inadequate soundtrack and the fact that the suspense hinges mainly on the repeated use of the song *Naina barse rimjhim* (sung by **Lata Mangeshkar**), it remains one of director Khosla's favourites. The film was remade in Tamil as *Yar Nee* by Sathyam (1966).

YAADEIN

aka *Only the Lonely*
1964 113' b&w Hindi
d **Sunil Dutt** *pc* Ajanta Arts *st* **Nargis** Dutt *sc* Omkar Sahib *dial* **Akhtar-ul-Iman** *lyr* **Anand Bakshi** *c* Ramchandra *m* **Vasant Desai**
lp Sunil Dutt, Nargis

Sunil Dutt's directorial debut was a bizarre 'One actor movie monument' according to the opening credit. Anil (Dutt), a successful businessman, returns to his palatial home to find his wife Priya and their two sons are out. This sets off an extraordinary two-hour soliloquy, shot entirely in the flat, describing the days when he first met his wife, how they got married, when they had their two children, the children's first birthdays, their misunderstandings, his meeting of a new girlfriend, Salma, the nights when they fought, when they made love, and so on. We gather that his wife had many reasons for leaving and he takes this opportunity to accuse her in order to justify himself before committing suicide, hanging himself with her wedding sari. A depressingly uninhibited demonstration of male infantilism and neurosis, the film adopts a naturalist acting idiom played against props such as Mario Miranda cartoon characters animated in the background or balloons representing people whenever the presence of other characters is required. The film's most interesting moment comes when Dutt is attacked by a bunch of toys berating him for his lack of concern for his family. The only living presence other than Dutt occurs at the end when Nargis, playing Priya, is shown in silhouette.

Manoj Kumar and Sadhana in *Woh Kaun Thi*

AASMAAN MAHAL

1965 172' b&w Hindi
d **K.A. Abbas** *pc* Naya Sansar *s* **Inder Raj Anand** *c* Ramchandra *m* J.P. Kaushik
lp **Prithviraj Kapoor**, Dilip Raj, Surekha Parkar, Nana Palsikar, Mridula, David, Anwar Hussain, Madhukar, Irshad Panjatan, Rashid Khan

Shot on location in a dilapidated mansion, Abbas's film suggests that the old feudal order must be allowed to fade away with dignity while its descendants must take their cue from 'the people' rather than from entrepreneurs. An old nawab, Aasmaan (Kapoor), refuses the wealth offered by capitalists who want to turn his palace into a hotel. His dissolute playboy son Salim (Roy) is ultimately reformed by a virtuous young woman, Salma (Parkar).

AKASH KUSUM

aka *Up in the Clouds*
1965 115'(110') b&w Bengali
d/co-sc **Mrinal Sen** *pc* Purbachal Film *st/co-sc* Ashish Burman *c* Sailaja Chatterjee *m* Sudhin Dasgupta
lp **Aparna Sen**, **Soumitra Chatterjee**, Subhendu Chatterjee, Haradhan Bannerjee, Sova Sen, Sati Devi, Prafullabala Devi, Gyanesh Mukherjee

After seeing Truffaut's *Les Quatre Cents Coups* (1959) and *Jules et Jim* (1961) early in 1965, Sen felt inspired to make this bitter-sweet romance set in Calcutta. The lower-middle-class Ajay (Soumitra Chatterjee) finds himself having to pretend to be a successful businessman in order to win the hand of Monica (Sen), the daughter of an affluent family. In the end he is exposed as a con man, his own business dealings go wrong and the romance comes to grief, destroyed by the social and psychological effects of class difference. Sen later said that he wanted a film that would 'physically look youthful', scripting in his street scenes, ragged camera and emphasis on unrehearsed sound effects. It sparked a major debate in the press between Burman, Sen, **Satyajit Ray** and others about notions of topicality, with Ray arguing that despite the 'modish narrative devices and [s]ome lively details of city life', and despite the film-makers' belief 'that they have made an angry film about struggling youth assailing the bastion of class', the hero's behaviour in fact 'dates back to antiquity' (cf Sen, 1977). Ray later continued his tirade against what he thought was the French cinema-inspired 'new wave' of the 70s (cf **New Indian Cinema**).

AND MILES TO GO...

1965 14' b&w English
d/p **S. Sukhdev** *c* K. Vaikunth, K. Ghanekar *m* **Vasant Desai**

Sukhdev's first major propaganda film 'dedicated to all the forces of rationalist thought that are opposed to the path of violence'. After a parallel montage of stereotypical rich/poor oppositions, the camera cuts to the face of the film-maker looking angry. After some shots of street violence in negative images, a voice declaims 'The people speak with the voice of history'. After some fast cuts of a police blockade and sounds of gunfire comes the film's message calling for rational thought: the real enemy is greed and corruption, not the State.

BANGARU PANJARAM

1965 168' b&w Telugu
d **B.N. Reddi** *pc* **Vauhini** *s* Palagummi Padmaraju *lyr* **Devulapalli Krishna Sastry**, **Sri Sri** *c* B.N. Konda Reddy, C.A.S. Mani, Madhav Bulbule *m* **Saluri Rajeshwara Rao**, B. Gopalam
lp **Shobhan Babu**, **Vanisree**, Geetanjali, **Sriranjini Jr**, Ravi Kondala Rao, Pushpavalli

Marital melodrama. Hero Venu (S. Babu) marries the poor Neela (Vanisree) despite his crooked employer Rangaiah who tries to prevent the marriage. Venu's uncle Ramakoti and Ramakoti's daughter Padma, who loves Venu, plant the maid Mangamma in Venu's house. Mangamma spreads rumours that lead to marital discord and Neela is forced to leave home. She is in a train accident and her husband believes her to be dead although she finds shelter in the house of a doctor. When Venu falls ill he is taken to that very doctor and husband and wife are reconciled. Reddi's and the old Vauhini production unit's last film was not a commercial success though it included some popular music such as **S. Janaki**'s *Pagalai the doravera*.

CHEMMEEN

aka *Wrath of the Sea*, aka *The Shrimp*
1965 140'(120') col Malayalam
d **Ramu Kariat** *p* Babu Ismail *pc* Kanmani Films *s* Thakazhy Shivashankar Pillai from his novel *dial* **S.L. Puram Sadanandan** *lyr* **Vyalar Rama Varma** *c* Marcus Bartley, U. Rajagopal *m* **Salil Choudhury**
lp **Sathyan**, Sheela, **Madhu**, **Kottarakkara Sridharan Nair**, S.P. Pillai, Adoor Bhawani, Adoor Pankajam, Lata, Kottayam Chellappan, Rajakumari, J.A.R. Anand, Paravoor Bharathan, Kothamangalam Ali, Philomina

Melodrama that put Malayalam cinema on the map. Chambankunju (Nair) manages to prosper as a fisherman thanks to his daughter Karuthamma (Sheela) and to the man she loves, the Muslim trader Pareekutty (Madhu). In order to obey tradition, she cannot marry the trader and so she becomes the wife of the remote stranger Palani (Sathyan). Although Palani accepts that she never slept with the trader, the village does not believe it and Palani is censured. One day Karuthamma meets her old boyfriend again and they make love, even as Palani, out battling a shark on the high seas, dies in a whirlpool that is attributed to Kadalamma, the goddess of the sea, exacting vengeance for an infringment of prevailing chastity codes. The film ends with the dead shark lying on the beach. Known mainly for the remarkable performances of its entire lead cast (notably Sathyan), the film was made as a sprawling epic matching the scale of one of Malayalam literature's most famous novels. The editing, done by **Hrishikesh Mukherjee** virtually as a salvation job for a production that had apparently got out of hand, is extremely tight, but the film still retains the frontier realism of a fishing community battling the forces of nature, myth and uncontrolled emotion as dictated by the script. Novelist Pillai's highly mystical end in the book, as Palani battles the shark while his wife betrays him, nevertheless remains too complex for predominantly realist melodrama. Composer Salil Choudhury's Malayalam debut was remarkably successful, and both songs and background score are integral to the scale of the drama.

CID

1965 172' b&w Telugu
d **Tapi Chanakya** *pc* **Vijaya** *sc* **Chakrapani** *dial* **D.V. Narasaraju** *lyr* **Pingali Nagendra Rao** *c* Madhav Bulbule *m* **Ghantasala Venkateshwara Rao**
lp **N.T. Rama Rao**, **Jamuna**, **Gummadi Venkateshwara Rao**, **Pandharibai**, Ramana Reddy, Meena Kumari, Mikkilineni

The gamber Chalapathi (Gummadi) is presumed dead by the police when they find a corpse wearing his clothes on a railway track. His wife and son are supported by Ramadasu (Mikkilineni) and the son grows up to become a policeman (NTR). Chalapathi, who is not dead, has become the leader of a gang of thieves and becomes the prey of his own son. The film was considered a major let-down from Telugu cinema's most high-profile banner.

DAHAM

aka *Thirst*
1965 130' b&w Malayalam
d/sc **K.S. Sethumadhavan** *p* M.P. Anand, P. Rangaraj *pc* Thirumugham Pics *dial* **Muthukulam Raghavan Pillai**, B.K. Pottakkad *lyr* **Vyalar Rama Varma** *c* P. Ramaswamy *m* **P. Devarajan**
lp **Sathyan**, Sheela, K.P. Ummar, Bahadur, Sreenarayana Pillai, B.K. Pottakkad, Vijayan, Murali, M.M. Babu, Kunjan, Pratap Chandran, Kaviyoor Ponnamma, Indira, Parvathy

This melodrama, made in 21 days at the Venus Studio, tells of the redemption of Jayarajan, who killed his young wife and her lover in a fit of jealousy and is sent to jail. Transferred to a hospital for an operation, the convict's humanity is rekindled by a kind widow and her son who turn out to be the family of the man Jayarajan killed. However, the hero dies and the script does not allow a new nuclear family to be formed at the end of the film.

ENGA VEETU PENN

1965 177' col Tamil
d B. Nagi Reddy *pc* **Vijaya** *sc* **Chakrapani** *dial* S. Ayyapillai *lyr* **Kannadasan**, Alangudi Somu *c* Marcus Bartley *m* K.V. Mahadevan
lp M.R. Radha, S.V. Subbaiah, A.V.M. Rajan, Jaishankar, K.A. Thangavelu, Nagesh, **Chittor V. Nagaiah**, O.A.K. Thevar, Nirmala (aka **Vijayanirmala**), Vasantha, Manorama, Madhavi

Tamil remake of the Vijaya unit's own Telugu film ***Shavukaru*** (1950), modernising the tale of two warring groups in an Andhra village, with, e.g., more urban references. M.R.

Radha played G. Subbarao's role of the moneylender. Remembered mainly for the star entry of Nirmala, who changed her name to Vijayanirmala with this film in tribute to the studio.

GUIDE

1965 183'(120') col Hindi
d/sc **Vijay Anand** *pc* **Navketan** *st* R.K. Narayan's novel (1958) *lyr* **Shailendra** *c* Fali Mistry *m* **S.D. Burman**
lp **Dev Anand, Waheeda Rehman, Leela Chitnis, Kishore Sahu,** Anwar Hussain, Ulhas, **Gajanan Jagirdar**, Rashid Khan

Adapted from a classic novel written in English, the plot is structured around two processes of transformation. Rosie (Rehman) who belongs to a family of courtesans, is seduced away from her tyrannical archaeologist husband Marco (Sahu) by the brash tourist guide Raju (Anand). Raju helps her to realise her dream of becoming a successful dancer, realising his own ambition to become wealthy at the same time. Their life together is ended when he is jailed for forging Rosie's signature on a cheque. Released from jail, he becomes a drifter and is mistaken for a holy man. Raju uses his newfound respectability to provide a school, a hospital and other facilities for the villagers. Forced to demonstrate his messianic status when there is a drought, he manages to fast for 12 days and the rain comes, confirming his holy status in the eyes of the villagers (and of the audience) as he dies of starvation. The film can be seen as a regressive comment on 'national culture', e.g. the shift from colonial tourism to capitalist enterprise to religious faith, from mass cultural commodification and spectacle to pre-colonial naivety and ritual. There is also a discourse about stardom: starting out as a man of the people, the hero transgresses conventional moral codes and fulfils his dream of wealth, then finds this unsatisfying and, having been freed from material possessions (and women), he ends up fulfilling others' wishes and finds apotheosis as a god in death. The film's quasi-expressionist, garish use of colour and of calender art sets provides its own comment on notions of national popular culture, highlighted in the sequence when Raju changes from a fast-talking tourist guide to a saintly figure through dissolves awash with blue and yellow light spots and in the rhythmic cutting of the song *He ram hamare ramachandra*. Disowned by the novelist Narayan, the film has been attacked mainly for its thematic deviations, esp. the transformation of Rosie: in the novel she is a *devadasi* (temple dancers and prostitutes liberated by a reformist political movement leading to the Devadasi Bill in 1927 in Madras), a condition defended by orthodox historians for having preserved the South Indian classical Bharat Natyam dance tradition. Gayatri Chakravorty Spivak's essay 'Once Again a Leap into the Postcolonial Banal' (1990) addresses the irony of a novel, written originally in English and critical of that orthodoxy, itself being assimilated by the orthodox literary establishment in order to attack the film. She suggests a different version of colonial historical continuity than the one dominated by ideas of (literary, historical) authenticity. The film was a musical success with major hits such as *Gaata rahe mera dil* and *Aaj phir jeene ki tamanana hai*. A substantially altered 120' English version (*co-sc* Pearl S. Buck *p/d/co-sc* Tad Danielewski) was released in the USA in 1965. It introduced new characters and much enlarged the role of, e.g., a bitchy US television reporter played by Sheila Burghart. It also added new scenes (including a sequence in the US Embassy in Delhi). Although the Indian version has Pathe colour, the US version has US-processed Eastmancolor.

KAPURUSH

aka *The Coward*
1965 74' b&w Bengali
d/sc/m **Satyajit Ray** *p* R.D. Bansal *pc* R.D.B. *st* **Premendra Mitra**'s *Janaiko Kapuruser Kahini* *c* Soumendu Roy
lp **Soumitra Chatterjee, Madhabi Mukherjee,** Haradhan Bannerjee, Premendra Mitra

Ray's morality play, usually shown with ***Mahapurush*** (1964), continues his ensemble play format. Both films were dubbed in Hindi and commercially released. Movie writer Amitabha Roy (Chatterjee) finds shelter with a tea magnate (Bannerjee) in Darjeeling when his car breaks down. He finds that the magnate is married to his former lover Karuna (Mukherjee). The film intercuts the banal conversation of the long evening and a picnic the next day with flashbacks showing how Roy had once betrayed Karuna. He offers, in a hurriedly written note, to marry her if she wishes to leave her husband. She turns him down, arriving at their rendezvous simply to recover a bottle of sleeping pills. Critic **Chidananda Das Gupta** saw the film as a sequel to ***Charulata*** (1964), replaying the man's inability to defy social norms.

KAVYA MELA

1965 138' b&w Malayalam
d M. Krishnan Nair *p* T.E. Vasudevan *pc* Jayamaruthi Prod. *st* A.K.V. *sc* **S.L. Puram Sadanandan** *lyr* **Vyalar Rama Varma** *c* C.J. Mohan *m* **V. Dakshinamurthy**
lp **Prem Nazir**, Sheela, **Adoor Bhasi, Muthukulam Raghavan Pillai**, Nellikode Bhaskaran, S.P. Pillai, Murali, Ramesh, Nilambur Aisha

Tear-jerking Malayalam adaptation of **Guru Dutt**'s ***Pyaasa*** (1957) and one of Prem Nazir's classic tragic lover performances. He plays Jayadevan, a blind poet, who is starved of the love of his family by a cruel sister-in-law. He strikes up a relationship with Shridevi (Sheela) whose doctor father restores his eyesight but forbids a marriage. His best friend steals Jayadevan's poetry and publishes it in his own name, thus becoming rich and famous while the original author suffers in a cruel world. In the end, when Jayadevan is recognised as the writer and offered a major award, he rejects the honour.

KELA ISHARA JATA JATA

1965 157' b&w Marathi
d **Anant Mane** *pc* Chetana Chitra *s* Shankar Patil *lyr* Jagdish Khebudkar *c* Vasant Shinde *m* Ram Kadam
lp Leela Gandhi, Arun Sarnaik, Usha Chavan, Barchi Bahadur, Ganpat Patil, Aminabai, Kamal Begadkar, Kamal Dunbale, Maya Jadhav, Kausalya Jadhav, Rajan Salvi

Marathi Tamasha musical by its best-known exponent, Mane (***Sangtye Aika***, 1959). It is a story about two dancing-girls, the sisters Bakul and Shevanti, who are given a break by drummer Ganpat (Sarnaik). Both sisters fall in love with their benefactor, which causes a split in the theatre group. Shevanti joins the rival Tamasha faction led by Sonbai, sharpening the already fierce competition between the two groups. Much of the film consists of Tamasha numbers, culminating in the long Sawal-Jawab (question and answer) contest where Bakul defeats Sonbai and then her own sister to claim her man.

MALAJANHA

aka *The Dead Moon*
1965 164' b&w Oriya
d/sc **Nitai Palit** *pc* Raja Saheb of Ali *st* Upendra Kishore Dash's novel *dial* Govind Senapati, Bhim Singh *lyr* Kabisurya Baladev Rath *c* **Dinen Gupta** *m* Akshay Mohanty
lp **Jharana Das,** Manimala, Geeta, Akshay Kumar, Sarat Poojary, Pira, Bhima, Purna Singh

Epic melodrama often presented as Oriya cinema's coming of age. The sensitive Sati (Das) is forced to marry an old man but refuses to consummate the marriage. She is thrown out of the house when she takes shelter with Nath (Kumar) after a storm. Her parents die in a cholera epidemic and Nath takes her to the city where they live together, fighting unemployment and poverty. On their return to the village they are shunned and, unable to bear further humiliations, Sati drowns herself (in an understated dawn sequence simply showing her footsteps leading to the river). A long, slow-moving film renowned for Bengali cinematographer (later director) Gupta's sensitive camerawork, for the famous Kabisurya Baladev Rath's pastoral lyrics and for being probably the first Oriya film to pay attention to its soundtrack (notwithstanding the overuse of flute and sitar). However, the main plaudits go to Jharana Das's remarkable performance which showed the oppression of women in traditional Oriya society without glorifying suffering womanhood.

MURAPPENNU

aka *Bride by Right* aka *The Betrothed One*
1965 176' b&w Malayalam
d **A. Vincent** *p* K. Parameshwaran Nair *pc* Roopavani *s* **M.T. Vasudevan Nair** *lyr* **P. Bhaskaran** *c* A. Venkat *m* B.A. Chidambaranath
lp **Prem Nazir, Madhu, P.J. Anthony,** K.P. Ummar, S.P. Pillai, **Adoor Bhasi,** Jyothilakshmi, **Sharada,** Nellikode Bhaskaran, Shanta Devi, Bharati Menon, Kaliamma

A relentless joint family melodrama about the social impotence of righteous people. Balan (Nazir) is mercilessly exploited and defrauded by his uncle (Anthony), his cousin and his own brother, even as he dutifully looks after his mother and teenage sister. He sacrifices his own love for Bhagi (Sharada), the daughter of his uncle, so that a complicated (but not unusual) arrangement with the evil uncle can result in Bhagi marrying the hero's younger brother, in return for a marriage between his sister and the uncle's son. However, the uncle's son betrays Balan's sister at the last minute. Balan, forced to borrow money for a dowry, is too late to prevent his sister from committing suicide. The end leaves him an utterly defeated man. This was one of novelist Vasudevan Nair's first major scripts, adapting to the cinema his well-known literary format of the hero caught in a vicious but declining feudal system. It was also the debut of his long-term association with director Vincent, creating a distinct brand of melodrama as social critique in Malayalam.

ODEYIL NINNU

aka *From The Gutter*
1965 175' b&w Malayalam
d **K.S. Sethumadhavan** *p/c* P. Ramaswami *pc* Swami Thirumugham Pics *s* P. Kesavadev *lyr* **Vyalar Rama Varma** *m* **P. Devarajan**
lp **Sathyan**, K.R. Vijaya, **Prem Nazir**, **Adoor Bhasi**, S.P. Pillai, **Thikkurisi Sukumaran Nair**, Kaviyoor Ponnamma, Adoor Pankajam, Kottayam Chellappan, Baby Padmini

The rickshaw man Pappu (Sathyan) adopts the baby girl Lakshmi (Baby Padmini/Vijaya) having rescued her, as the title suggests, from the 'gutter'. Having dropped out of school and earlier worked as a railway porter, he now works hard to provide Lakshmi with an education and with all her needs. She marries a rich man, Gopi (Nazir), which does not, contrary to expectations, signify the end of her foster-father's struggles, for now she is ashamed of her humble origins. In the end, after Pappu has declined her offer to live in her new home, her husband censures her, and she is punished by fate for her ingratitude when Pappu falls terminally ill. The 'punishment' is further heightened by forcing on the woman the guilt of a barely-concealed incest relationship since she insists on seeing Pappu as a parental figure. Sethumadhavan's first critically acclaimed film featured a rare contribution by noted Malayalam novelist Kesavadev, integrated into **Bimal Roy**-type realist melodrama. The film was remade in Tamil as *Babu* (1971).

OONCHE LOG

1965 144' b&w Hindi
d/sc **Phani Majumdar** *pc* Chitrakala (Madras) *st* **K. Balachander**'s play *Major Chandrakant* *dial* Arjun Dev Rashk *lyr* **Majrooh Sultanpuri** *c* Kamal Ghosh *m* Chitragupta
lp **Ashok Kumar**, Raaj Kumar, Feroz Khan, Kanhaiyalal, Tarun Bose, K.R. Vijaya

Melodrama about an upright father, the blind Major Chandrakant (A. Kumar), with a good son, the policeman Srikanth (R. Kumar), and the other son the dissolute playboy Rajnikant (Khan). Rajnikant impregnates and then abandons a woman who commits suicide as a result. The woman's brother Mohan (Bose) kills Rajnikant and wants to hide from the pursuing policeman, Srikanth. He is sheltered by the sympathetic major. The melodramatic pivot contrasts the father's revulsion for his son's murderer with his even greater revulsion at his son's callous philandering. Srikanth has to arrest his own father for having sheltered a killer. One of the more successful adaptations of a play to the screen, the film is shot like a thriller, using emphatic 'suspense' music to bridge the extended 'realistic' longueurs. Made at the Vijaya-Vauhini Studios in Madras, it adapted K. Balachander's best-known play, filmed by Balachander himself (*Major Chandrakant*) the following year.

PANDAVA VANAVASAM

1965 188' b&w Telugu/Tamil
d **K. Kameshwara Rao** *pc* Madhavi Prod *s/co-lyr* **Samudrala Raghavacharya** *co-lyr* **Arudra**, **Kosaraju** *c* C. Nageshwara Rao *m* **Ghantasala Venkateshwara Rao**
lp **N.T. Rama Rao**, **Savitri**, **S.V. Ranga Rao**, **Gummadi Venkateshwara Rao**, Kanta Rao, T.S. Baliah, Haranath, Satyanarayana, Rajanala, Lingamurthy, Mikkilineni, Prabhakara Reddy, **K. Mukkamala**, Ramana Reddy, Padmanabham, Vijayalakshmi, Sandhya, Baby Sasirekha, Rajasulochana, **Chittor V. Nagaiah**, Ajit Singh, **Vanisree**

Kameshwara Rao's *Mahabharata*-based hit mythological has NTR playing Bhima, Ranga Rao as Duryodhan and Savitri in one of her better-known mythological performances as Draupadi. Ghantasala's music also became a hit. A version of the film, dubbed in Hindi and starring **Hema Malini**, was released in 1973, presumably with extra footage cut into the film.

ROSY

1965 140' b&w Malayalam
d/st **P.N. Menon** *p* Mani *pc* Vrindavan Pics *sc* **P.J. Anthony** *lyr* **P. Bhaskaran** *c* E.N. Balakrishnan *m* Job
lp P.J. Anthony, Kaviyoor Ponnamma, **Prem Nazir**, Nirmala, **Thikkurisi Sukumaran Nair**, T.S. Muthaiah, D.K. Chellappan, Johnson, C.P. Anthony, M.M. Narayanan Nair, Sushil Kumar, E. Madhavan, Susheela

The former art director Menon's directorial debut stars the scenarist of this crime melodrama. Having unintentionally murdered a man to save his sister's honour, Thumman flees and finds shelter in a fisherman's hut where he falls in love with his benefactor's daughter Rosy. In spite of the obstacles, the lovers decide to marry. When a police inspector appears in the village, Thumman and the pregnant Rosy escape to the mountains and are sheltered by a Muslim friend. Eventually, Rosy dies giving birth and Thumman, having buried his family, calmly allows himself to be arrested.

SADHI MANSE

1965 134' b&w Marathi
d/s **Bhalji Pendharkar** *pc* Gayatri Chitra *lyr* Yogesh, Jagdish Khebudkar *c* Arvid Laad *m* Anandadhan [pseud. of **Lata Mangeshkar**]
lp **Jayashree Gadkar**, Chandrakant, **Master Vithal**, Sulochana, Barchhi Bahadur, Rajshekhar, Chandrakant Gokhale

Pendharkar inflects his regional chauvinist approach, dominant in his historicals, to contrast an idyllic rural Maharashtra with urban corruption. The happy Shankar (Chandrakant) and his wife Parvati (Gadkar) find their lives disrupted when they accept the offer of a truck driver to find them better prospects in the city. Shankar goes to jail when the driver involves him in a crime. Parvati is imprisoned when she kills the villain, just as Shankar is released. The film's effort at realism was restricted to, e.g., having the characters, incarnated by mainstream Marathi stars, act without make-up.

SATYA HARISHCHANDRA

1965 221' b&w Kannada/Telugu
d/s/lyr[K] **Hunsur Krishnamurthy** *d*[Te] **K.V. Reddy** *pc* **Vijaya** *dial/lyr*[Te] **Pingali Nagendra Rao** *c* Madhav Bulbule *m* **Pendyala Nageshwara Rao**
lp **Rajkumar**[K], **Udaya Kumar**[K], Aswath[K], Narasimhraju[K], M.P. Shankar[K], **Balkrishna**[K], Baby Padmini[K], Dwarkeesh[K], **N.T. Rama Rao**[Te], **K. Mukkamala**[Te], **Chittor V. Nagaiah**[Te], Rajashree[Te], **S. Varalakshmi**, Vijayalakshmi, **Vanisree**, **Pandharibai**, **Relangi Venkatramaiah**

Famous *Ramayana* legend of the truth-seeking king of Ayodhya, his banishment and suffering as he is tested by Vishwamitra, culminating in his dilemma of having either to kill his own wife who is accused of murder or to forsake his principles. The elaborate costume drama featured the two top stars of Kannada and Telugu cinemas, Rajkumar and NTR, playing the king. The successful Kannada version credited to **Hunsur Krishnamurthy** was a hit, but the Telugu one by **K.V. Reddy** failed.

SHEVATCHA MALUSARA

1965 144' b&w Marathi
d/p Vasant Joglekar *st* Sumati Joglekar *sc* **Datta Keshav** *dial* Madhusudan Kalelkar *lyr* Jagdish Khebudkar *c* Bal Joglekar *m* Datta Davjekar
lp Ramesh Dev, Uma, Shrikant Moghe, Chandrakant Gokhale, Chitrarekha, Sunanda, Master Sachin, **Ashok Kumar**

An unusual Marathi war movie which mobilises and updates a historical/regional chauvinism associated with 17th-C. Maratha emperor Shivaji. Major Subhanrao Malusare, a direct descendant of Shivaji's legendary lieutenant Tanaji Malusare, continues a proud family tradition by winning the Victoria Cross as an Allied officer fighting against Italian fascists in WW2. When he dies, his wife Savitri (Uma) vows that their son will never join the army. However, during the India-China conflict (1962), when her son's friend is killed, she enjoins her son to fight for the nation even though the boy's death would mean the end of the ancient clan. The film updated the rousing sentimentalism associated with Shivaji historicals into the present via songs such as *He bharatiyano aika balidan katha veeranchi*.

THENE MANUSHULU

1965 174' col Telugu
d **Adurthi Subba Rao** *pc* Babu Movies *co-st* Mullapudi Venkatraman, K.R.K. Mohan *co-st/co-dial* **K. Vishwanath**, *co-dial/co-lyr* **Acharya Athreya** *co-lyr* Dasarathi *c* P.S. Selvaraj *m* K.V. Mahadevan
lp Rammohan, **Krishna**, Chalapathi Rao, Sandhyarani, Sukanya, K.V. Ramamurthy, G.S.R. Murthy, Koneshwara Rao

Subba Rao's 'experimental' film announces his co-productions with **Nageshwara Rao** (*Sudigundalu*, 1967; ***Maro Prapancham***, 1970). Narasaraju (Murthy) steals money from his friend Srinivasarao (K. Rao) to pay for his daughter's wedding, leaving Srinivasarao unable to finance his own daughter Bhanumathi's (Sukanya) marriage and compelling him to abandon his family and run away. To earn a living, Bhanumathi goes to the city where she meets Basavaraju (Krishna), the man she was to have married, and the two fall in love. Of the several new actors making their debuts, only Krishna became a major star.

WAQT

1965 206' col Hindi
d **Yash Chopra** *pc* B.R. Films *st* F.A. Mirza *sc* B.R. Films Story Dept. *dial* **Akhtar-ul-Iman** *lyr* **Sahir Ludhianvi** *c* Dharam Chopra *m* Ravi
lp **Sunil Dutt**, Raaj Kumar, Sadhana, **Sharmila Tagore**, **Shashi Kapoor**, **Balraj Sahni**, Shashikala, **Motilal**, Rehman, Achala Sachdev, Madan Puri, Jeevan

A contribution to the 'lost and found' genre (cf ***Kismet***, 1943; ***Awara***, 1951) later associated with **Manmohan Desai**'s films. The old and prosperous merchant Lala Kedarnath (Sahni) sees his family split and his house wrecked by an earthquake. Trying to trace one of his sons, he learns that the boy was ill treated by an evil orphanage warden (Jeevan) and he kills the warden, earning himself a 20-year stretch in jail. The son is raised by the crook Chinoy (Rehman) and becomes the suave thief Raja (Kumar). Kedarnath's other sons are the fun-loving Ravi (Dutt) who becomes a lawyer and the hard-working but poor Vijay (Kapoor) who looks after their ailing mother. Vijay is hired as a chauffeur by his girlfriend Renu (Tagore) while Ravi and Raja love the same woman, Meena (Sadhana). After advocating a fatalist approach to the passage of time, the film turns into a suspense and courtroom drama when Chinoy frames Raja for murder. Raja is defended in court by Ravi. Eventually the family is reunited. The film was a major hit, exemplifying a kitschy colour aesthetic (denoting wealth) that was to become popular in Hindi films: a series of living-rooms in pink and blue, with fountains and circular beds in bedrooms, motor boats and fancy cars in which the rich race each other to get the girl in between attending huge parties. Hit songs included *Ai meri zohrajabeen* (sung by Manna Dey), *Din hai bahar ke* (sung by **Asha Bhosle** and Mahendra Kapoor) and *Aage bhi jane na tu* (sung by Asha Bhosle).

AAKHRI KHAT

1966 153' b&w Hindi
d/s **Chetan Anand** *pc* Himalaya Films *lyr* **Kaifi Azmi** *c* Jal Mistry *m* **Khayyam**
lp **Rajesh Khanna**, Indrani Mukherjee, Naqi Jehan, Bunty, Nana Palsikar, Manavendra Chitnis

A social-realist melodrama about a man (Khanna in his debut) who secretly marries a gypsy girl from the hills (Mukherjee). They have a son (Bunty) but misunderstandings arise and the wife ends up living on the streets of Bombay with the child. She dies, leaving the boy wandering the city's streets, having his own little adventures while his distraught father searches for him. With its extensive actuality footage of Bombay's slums, suburban trains and working-class life, the film evokes, e.g., **K.A. Abbas**'s urban melodramas (***Munna***, 1954; ***Shaher Aur Sapna***, 1963). The film deploys a simple set of oppositions to signal good and bad: jazzy music and discotheques signify the callous and modern rich while the poor display their human warmth through acts of kindness to the child. Although the soundtrack adheres to the 'realist' principle of using the pilot dialogue track for all speech except that of the hero and heroine, it occasionally inserts suspense music to plug the narrative gaps in the plot.

ANUPAMA

1966 148' b&w Hindi
d/st **Hrishikesh Mukherjee** *pc* L.B. Films *p* L.B. Lachman *sc* Bimal Dutt, D.N. Mukherjee *dial* **Rajinder Singh Bedi** *lyr* **Kaifi Azmi** *c* Jaywant Pathare *m* Hemant Kumar [**Hemanta Mukherjee**]
lp **Dharmendra**, **Sharmila Tagore**, Shashikala, Deven Verma, **Durga Khote**, David, Surekha Pandit, Dulari, Naina, Brahm Bhardwaj, Amar, Tarun Bose

Although dedicated to **Bimal Roy**, known for his reformist socials, this is a psychodrama. Throughout her life Uma (Tagore), the daughter of Mohan Sharma (Bose), is blamed for her mother dying while giving birth to her. The guilt-laden Uma is contrasted with the flippant, upper-class Anita (Shashikala). Other characters include Arun (Verma), Anita's boyfriend who returns from abroad, and his idealist friend Ashok (Dharmendra), a writer who loves Uma and eventually rescues her after writing a novel based on his imagination of her life. Classic songs composed and performed by Hemanta Mukherjee include the well-picturised *Ya dil ki suno*, and **Lata Mangeshkar**'s *Dheere dheere machal*.

CHITTHI

1966 177' b&w Tamil
d/s K.S. Gopalakrishnan *pc* Chitra Prod. *lyr* **Udumalai Narayana Kavi**, **Kannadasan** *c* R. Sampath
lp **Padmini**, M.R. Radha, Muthuraman, **Vijayanirmala**, Nagesh, Vijayashree, V.R. Rajagopal, S.D. Subbulakshmi

In her comeback film, Padmini plays the suffering Meenakshi, the eldest daughter in a large family. To look after her dumb sister and her medical-student brother Balu (Muthuraman), she spurns a rich lover since his property is under litigation, preferring the financial security promised by an ageing widower (Radha). The man's son disapproves and becomes a cab driver, while the widower's daughter (Vijayanirmala) falls in love with Balu. B.A. Subba Rao's *Pinni* (1967) is the Telugu version.

DIL DIYA DARD LIYA

1966 169' col Hindi
d **A.R. Kardar** *pc* Kay Prod. *st* Kay Prod. Story Dept. *dial* Kaushal Bharti *lyr* Shakeel Badaiyuni *c* Dwarka Divecha *m* **Naushad**
lp **Dilip Kumar**, **Waheeda Rehman**, Pran, **Johnny Walker**, Rehman, Shyama, Sajjan, Rani, S. Nazir, Sapru, Amar, Dulari

Allegedly borrowing the characters of *Wuthering Heights*, the film tells of the tyrannical Ramesh (Pran), son of the thakur, who falls into bad company while Shankar (Kumar), a farm-hand employed by Ramesh, is unaware that he is the real heir to the kingdom. Shankar loves Ramesh's sister Roopa (W. Rehman) and vows to earn enough money to win her hand. However, Ramesh's men beat him up and leave him for dead. Having survived, Shankar later returns a rich but bitter man and he uses a dancing-girl (Shyama) to make Roopa jealous, before things sort themselves out. According to the actress Shyama's reminiscences (in *Movie*, Bombay, Sept. 1991), Kardar's comeback film was directed by Dilip Kumar, uncredited, following a major falling out between the director and the star.

GABAN

1966 169' b&w Hindi
co-sc/co-d Krishan Chopra *co-d* **Hrishikesh Mukherjee** *pc* B.I. Prod. *st* Munshi Premchand's novel (1930) *co-sc* Bhanu Pratap *dial* Baij Sharma, **Akhtar-ul-Iman** *lyr* Hasrat Jaipuri, **Shailendra** *c* K. Vaikunth *m* **Shankar-Jaikishen**
lp **Sunil Dutt**, Sadhana, Zeb Rehman, Kanhaiyalal, Agha, Anwar Hussain, Meenu Mumtaz, Badri Prasad, P. Kailash, Kamal Kapoor, Mishra, Pratima Devi, Leela Mishra, Brahm Bhardwaj, B.B. Bhalla, Surekha Pandit

Set in Allahabad, 1928, in the anti-British terrorist actions that peaked between the Simon Commission and the Gandhi-Irwin Pact (1929), Premchand's story tells of Ramnath (Dutt), son of a small-time clerk in the Allahabad court, who borrows large amounts of money in order to satisfy his wife's desire for jewellery. This forces him to embezzle money at the court, and gets the police after him. On the run, and unaware that his wife has repaid the embezzled money, he is blackmailed by a repressive police force into presenting a false eyewitness account that would convict non-violent nationalists for terrorist acts. One of Dutt's better-known screen performances holds together a film that was patched together by Mukherjee following the death of the original director, Chopra.

GALLAN HOYIAN BEETIYAN

1966 117' b&w Dogri
d/sc Kumar Kuldip *pc* Tawi Films *st* Narendra Khajuria's play *Pyasi Dharti* *dial* Ramnath

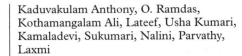

Shastri *lyr* Yash Sharma, Kehari Singh 'Madhukar'
lp Ram Kumar Abrol, Jitender Sharma, Kaberi, Veena Kotwal

The only film made to date in the language of the Dogra community, which comprises c.25% of the Kashmiri people. Made mainly on the initiative of several well-known Dogri writers, the melodrama revolves around the problems of intermarriage between two villages and of water scarcity in the Kandli area of Duggar. A canal is dug between two villages when the marriages of a village chieftain's brother and sister are arranged with their counterparts from the other community. The sister Shano's marriage takes place, but when her brother dies, negotiations over the water-sharing agreement break down. Trying to resolve the resulting drought Shano is killed and, in the dramatic finale, her dead body reaches her marital home at the same time as the water from the reopened canal. The film is best-known for evoking Khajuria's realist idiom.

KAA

1966 165' b&w Oriya
d/sc Siddharth *p* **Parbati Ghosh** *st* Kanhucharan Mohanty *c* Deojibhai, Bijoy De *m* Shrikumar
lp Guruprasad, Chandana Geeta, Manimala, Sarat Pujari, Byomkesh, Sudhangsu

Oriya melodrama based on Mohanty's popular fiction. According to some sources, the film was pseudonymously directed by **Ramchandra Thakur**. Nandika, childless after eight years of marriage, persuades her husband Sunanda to remarry. Both Nandika and the second wife Lalita are unhappy though superficially affectionate. After Lalita and Sunanda move to the city, Nandika finds herself pregnant and follows them. The tensions are resolved when Nandika dies in childbirth. This is the first production of Parbati Ghosh, actress and director (*Chamana Atha Guntha*, 1986) and known for producing, with husband Gauraprasad Ghosh, quality Oriya cinema (cf **Nitai Palit**'s *Bhai Bhai*, 1956; Sharada Prasanna Nayak's *Lakhmi*, 1962).

KALAPI

1966 137' b&w Gujarati
d **Manhar Raskapur** *pc* Pragya Pictures *st* Prabodh Joshi *co-lyr* Kalapi *c* Shankar Bakel *co-lyr/m* **Avinash Vyas**
lp Sanjeev Kumar, Padma Rani, Aruna Irani, Vishnukumar Vyas, P. Kharsani, Pratap Ojha, Nandini Desai, Narayan Rajgor, Dineshkumar, D.S. Mehta, Ashok Thakkar, Premshankar Bhatt, Ajit Soni, Nutan, Manoj Purohit, Jayant Vyas, Miss Jayashree, Madhumati

Film based in the life of Kalapi (1874-1900), a Gujarati romantic poet who died aged 26 leaving one anthology, *Kalapino Kelkrav*, consisting mainly of love poems, apparently addressed to his wife's maid. Some evoke the legend of Bilwamangal, while others adapt Wordsworth, Shelley and Keats into a local idiom. Prince Sursinhji Takthasinghji Gohil (Hindi star Sanjeev Kumar), the ruler of Lathi, marries two princesses on the same day. However, Rama, the princess he loves, is more interested in power than in him. The prince rejects the throne, becomes a poet and falls in love with Rama's maid Shobhana (Irani).

KAYAMKULAM KOCHHUNNI

aka *The Dear One of Kayamkulam*
1966 131' b&w Malayalam
d/p P.A. Thomas *dial* Jagathi N.K. Achari *lyr* **P. Bhaskaran**, Abhayadev *c* P.B. Mony *m* B.A. Chidambaranath
lp **Sathyan, Thikkurisi Sukumaran Nair**, K.P. Ummar, **Adoor Bhasi**, Manavalan Joseph, **Muthukulam Raghavan Pillai**, Kaduvakulam Anthony, O. Ramdas, Kothamangalam Ali, Lateef, Usha Kumari, Kamaladevi, Sukumari, Nalini, Parvathy, Laxmi

A story featuring Central Travancore's Robin Hood-type folk hero, Kochhunni (Sathyan), an expert in Kerala's martial arts who became a notorious dacoit, allegedly with a golden heart. Betrayed by his lover, the palace maid Janaki, he escapes, settles the score with Janaki and her accomplice and then gives himself up to the law.

KUMARI PENN

aka *Kanne Pilla*
1966 154' b&w Tamil
d Ramanna *pc* E.V.R. Pics *lyr* **Kannadasan** *c* G. Dora *m* M.S. Vishwanathan
lp **Jayalalitha**, Ravichandran, Madhavi, **S.V. Ranga Rao**

Early Jayalalitha hit featuring her in body-hugging tights and sexy numbers like the train song *Varushattai paru arubatthi aaru*. She plays Shyamala, whose rich but ailing grandfather (Ranga Rao) insists she marry before he dies. She passes off an illiterate shepherd (Ravichandran) as her chosen groom to keep the old man happy, but eventually marries the man.

KUNJALI MARAKKAR

1966 147' b&w Malayalam
d S.S. Rajan *pc* Chandrathara Prod. *s* K. Padmanabhan Nair *lyr* **P. Bhaskaran** *c* C.A.S. Mani *m* B.A. Chidambaranath
lp **Kottarakkara Sridharan Nair, Prem Nazir, Adoor Bhasi**, S.P. Pillai, Kottayam Chelappan, **P.J. Anthony**, G.K. Pillai, Sathyapal, Premji, Nellikode Bhaskaran, Jyothilakshmi, Sukumari, Nalini

Major Malayalam historical telling the story of the legendary 16th C. naval captain Kunjali Marakkar (Nair). Following Vasco da Gama's landing in Calicut (1498) the Portuguese dominated the Malabar trade for the next century, opposed only by the Zamorin of Calicut (Premji). In the film, the zamorin's evil nephew (Anthony) sides with the Portuguese. Marakkar defeats the imperialist enemy in several sea battles, but the perfidy of the nephew and a scheming Namboodiri priest causes the zamorin's downfall. Marakkar is arrested and killed. The film belonged to Nair in his best-known role, supported by Nazir playing the double role of the Portuguese Antonio and Narayana Nair.

MATIR MANISHA

aka *Two Brothers*
1966 113' b&w Oriya
d/sc **Mrinal Sen** *p* Babulal Doshi *pc* Chhayaloke Prod. *st* Kalindi Charan Panigrahi's novel (1930) *dial* Gopal Chatray *c* Sailaja Chatterjee *m* Srikanth
lp Sarat Pujari, **Prashanta Nanda**, Ram Mania, Sujata, Dukhiram, Bhim Singh, Kartick Ghosh, Bhanumathi, Snehalata, Meera

Sen's only feature in Oriya, based on a major Oriya novel, tries to elaborate a new way of

Kaa

representing rural India. The director wrote his script and dialogues in Bengali, first translating them into Oriya, then adapting and modifying the text during the shooting on advice from the actors and the local villagers. Set in a small Orissa village in the late 30s as WW2 breaks out and the Indian economy is neglected in favour of the war effort, the film contrasts different attitudes, exemplified by two brothers, Baraju (Pujari) and Chakkadi (Nanda), to tradition and modernity, an important debate within nationalist politics at the time. Sen's film was criticised for its symbolic imagery and for bringing a 'Communist' angle to the Gandhian fable (referred to via the elder brother's character), but it remains a pioneering attempt to inscribe a rural world into history, divesting it of both nostalgia and idealisation. Produced by Oriya's main producer Doshi, Pujari and Nanda later became the top male stars in the language.

MOTOR SUNDARAM PILLAI

1966 160' b&w Tamil
d Balu *pc* **Gemini** *s* Vembattur Kittu *lyr* Kothamangalam Subbu *c* P. Ellappa *m* M.S. Vishwanathan
lp **Sivaji Ganesan**, **Sowcar Janaki**, Manimala, Kanchana, Asha, **Jayalalitha**, **Pandharibai**, **Chittor V. Nagaiah**

Motor magnate Sundaram Pillai (Ganesan) disappears on weekdays to his workplace, leaving his wife (Sowcar Janaki) behind, until it is revealed that he has a second wife (Manimala) at another residence. The Gemini Studio production was a remake of **Kishore Sahu**'s *Grihasthi* (1963).

NAYAK

aka *The Hero*
1966 120' b&w Bengali
d/s/m **Satyajit Ray** *p* R.D. Bansal *pc* R.D.B. *c* Subrata Mitra
lp **Uttam Kumar**, **Sharmila Tagore**, Bireshwar Sen, Soumyen Bose, Nirmal Ghosh, Premangshu Bose, Sumita Sanyal, Ranjit Sen, Bharati Devi, Lali Choudhury, Kamu Mukherjee, Sushmita Mukherjee, Subrata Sen Sharma, Jamuna Sinha, Hiralal, Jogesh Chatterjee, Satya Bannerjee, Gopal Dey

Ray's first original script since ***Kanchanjungha*** (1962) seems inspired by Bergman's *Smullstronstallet* (1957) and uses an ensemble piece with the structure of a suspense plot: a group of characters interact during a 24-hour train journey between Calcutta and Delhi. The film is dominated by its insecure male lead, movie megastar Arindam Mukherjee (played by Bengali megastar Uttam Kumar). In nightmares he drowns in a sea of banknotes amid jangling telephones operated by skeletons. On the train, he tells his story to Aditi (Tagore), the sexy but severe (her intelligence is signalled conventionally by her glasses, her beauty equally conventionally by having her remove her glasses) editor of a women's magazine. In the end, she destroys her notes because journalists should respect the privacy even of film stars. As in *Kanchanjungha*, the bizarre protagonist, the dream sequences and the flashbacks constantly suggest an impending dramatic event: e.g. the tensely edited sequence in which he gets drunk, contemplates suicide, gets the attendant to call Aditi, starts confessing to her about his affair with a married woman, etc. The presence of a small set of bit players, including an advertising man, a religious guru who wants to advertise his business, an old writer who sees the hero as exemplifying contemporary decadence and a businessman with his family, are typical of the whodunit ploy of creating a small but varied set of potential murder suspects. Here, unlike *Kanchanjungha* or the film that would use the format with greater skill, ***Aranyer Din Ratri*** (1969), the 'clues' to the unfolding drama point not to a crime but to a notion of cultural identity hidden in verbal, gestural and dress nuances (e.g. when Aditi gets off the train, Arindam puts on his dark sunglasses again). Ray made his first real thriller the following year, ***Chidiakhana*** (1967).

RANGULA RATNAM

1966 181' b&w Telugu
d **B.N. Reddi** ***pc*** **Vauhini** *st* Palagummi Padmaraju *dial* **D.V. Narasaraju** *lyr* Dasarathi, C. Narayana Reddy, **Kosaraju** *c* U. Rajagopal *m* **Saluri Rajeshwara Rao**, B. Gopalam
lp **Anjali Devi**, Pushpavalli, **Rekha**, Chandramohan, Rammohan, **Vanisree**, **Vijayanirmala**, Sukanya, Ramana Reddy, Kakarala, Radhakumari

Hit family melodrama about a formerly rich but now impoverished rural family that migrates to the city. The father dies, leaving behind his widow (Anjali Devi), two sons and a daughter. The elder son Suryam (Rammohan) marries the daughter of a corrupt politician. Younger son Vasu (Chandramohan) starts working at a young age to help his mother but retains his idealism and he eventually comes to represent the oppressed classes. The two brothers clash, first ideologically and then physically, during an election in which they fight on opposite sides. The mother tries to intervene and is injured, leading to a family reconciliation. Reddi cast several newcomers, some of whom (Kakarala, Chandramohan, Vanisree) later became stars. Hindi star Rekha debuted in this film as child actress Baby Bhanurekha, acting alongside her mother Pushpavalli.

TEESRI KASAM

aka *The Third Vow*
1966 159' b&w Hindi
d **Basu Bhattacharya** *p/co-lyr* **Shailendra** *pc* Image Makers *st/dial* Phanishwar Nath Renu's *Mare Gaye Gulfam sc* Nabendu Ghosh *co-lyr* Hasrat Jaipuri *c* Subrata Mitra *m* **Shankar-Jaikishen**
lp **Raj Kapoor**, **Waheeda Rehman**, Dulari, Iftikhar, Asit Sen, C.S. Dubey, Krishen Dhawan, Vishwa Mehra, Samar Chatterjee, Nabendu Ghosh, Keshto Mukherjee

Wonderfully photographed by Mitra, who shot **S. Ray**'s early films, this musical melodrama sees Kapoor return to his role as a country bumpkin called Hiraman, a bullock-cart driver. Transporting a Nautanki dancer, Hirabai (Rehman) to join a performing troupe, he wins her affection with his old songs and by treating the 'dancing-girl' as a respectable woman. Hiraman eventually finds out that a dancing-girl in a troupe is in no position to refuse sex with local potentates. However, his innocence has persuaded her to fight off unwanted advances and to leave the Nautanki theatre. She bids farewell to Hiraman at the railway station and invites him to come and see her in a different show. The film ends with Hiraman taking his third vow, telling his bullocks that he will never carry a Nautanki dancer again. The sentimental story touches on the gross sexual oppression of women but in the end places its sympathies with the disillusioned Hiraman rather than with the woman. The film is notable mostly for its seamless, lyrical imagery and for Kapoor's best performance of his archetypal persona.

TEESRI MANZIL

1966 172' col Hindi
d **Vijay Anand** *pc* United Producers, Nasir Hussain Films *s/p* **Nasir Hussain** *lyr* **Majrooh Sultanpuri** *c* N.V. Srinivas *m* **R.D. Burman**
lp **Shammi Kapoor**, Asha Parekh, Premnath, Helen, K.N Singh, Raj Mehra, Prem Chopra, Laxmi Chhaya, Neeta, Sabina, Salim, Rashid Khan

Musical love story repeating the star pairing of the hit ***Dil Deke Dekho*** (1959) as well as its locales, the hill-station and the hotel dance-floor. Sunita (Parekh) goes to Mussoorie with her college hockey team. She is also determined to avenge the death of her sister Rupa, who had apparently committed suicide when she was rejected by her lover Rocky (Kapoor), a drummer in the hotel's jazz band. Rocky meets her and, wise to her intentions, disguises his identity. The two fall in love. The story picks up again when a policeman reveals that Rupa was murdered. The dancer Ruby (Helen), who is in love with Rocky, and Rupa's jealous fiance are prime suspects. In the end, a subplot is quickly developed and the murderer caught. The film included classic **Mohammed Rafi** and **Asha Bhosle** duets such as *O hasina zulfonwali*, *Aaja aaja*, *O mere sona re sona re* and the quixotic Rafi solo, *Diwana mujhsa nahin*, energetically picturised on the ageing but lively lead duo.

AADA PADUCHU

1967 162' b&w Telugu
d K. Hemambharadhara Rao *pc* Subhashini Art Pics *sc* **L.V. Prasad** *dial* **K. Pratyagatma** *lyr* Dasarathi, **Kosaraju**, **Sri Sri**, C. Narayana Reddy, **Arudra** *c* M.G. Singh, M.C. Sekhar *m* T. Chalapathi Rao
lp **N.T. Rama Rao**, **Relangi Venkatramaiah**, Padmanabham, **Shobhan Babu**, Chandrakala, **Vanisree**, Geetanjali

Melodrama written by noted Telugu directors Prasad and Pratyagatma. Satyam (NTR) looks after his sister Sharada (Chandrakala) and younger brother Shekhar (Shobhan Babu). The sister has an accident and goes blind just before her marriage. The younger brother gets married and takes to drinking and gambling. Satyam finally succeeds in bringing the family together and restores his sister's sight. The film adapted two earlier versions of the same plot, **C. Narayanamurthy**'s *Naa Chellelu* (1953) and Prasad's own ***Chhoti Bahen*** (1959).

AGNIPUTHRI

1967 144' b&w Malayalam
d M. Krishnan Nair *p* Prem Nawaz *pc* Prem and Balaji Movies *s* **S.L. Puram Sadanandan** *lyr* **Vyalar Rama Varma** *c* N.S. Mani *m* **Baburaj**
lp **Prem Nazir**, T.S. Muthaiah, T.K. Balachandran, S.P. Pillai, **Adoor Bhasi**, Bahadur, Sheela, Vasantha, Aranmulla Ponnamma, Baby Usha, T.R. Omana, Meena

Melodrama taking Malayalam cinema's fascination with incest to its limit. The respectable college teacher Rajan (Nazir) marries Sindhu (Sheela), the orphaned inmate of a home for destitutes. The feudal conservative hypocrisies of the hero's family are graphically criticised: Rajan's cousin Chandran admits he once had sex with Sindhu, and Rajan's snooty brother, the doctor Jayadev, fathered Sindhu's daughter Bindu. Sindhu further confesses on her wedding night that she suffers from venereal disease, and eventually dies. The gruesome film is adapted from a popular play by Nazir's brother Prem Nawaz. The theatrical gestures and painted backdrops were maintained in the film version. The film was remade in Hindi as *Darpan* (1970) starring **Sunil Dutt** and **Waheeda Rehman**.

ANTONY FIRINGEE

1967 157' b&w Bengali
d Sunil Bannerjee *p* B.N. Roy *lyr* Pranab Roy *c* Bijoy Ghosh *m* Anil Bagchi
lp **Uttam Kumar**, Tanuja, Lolita Chatterjee, Asit Baran, **Chhaya Devi**, Haridhan, Ruma Guha-Thakurta, **Jahar Roy**, Ashim Kumar

Reformist musical recounting the legend of a Portuguese-Indian who in the early 19th C. became a famous Bengali poet-musician (in the Kabigan genre). Antony Firingee [Antony the Foreigner] (U. Kumar) falls in love with the famous courtesan Shakila (Tanuja). At first she rejects him, but later reveals her tragic story: she is a widow who escaped when she was forced to commit sati (ritual immolation) and was later raped. She then agrees to marry Antony and they try to overcome social ostracisation when, under her tutelage, he defeats a series of famous poets in the tradition of the Kabir Larai (contest between poets emphasising improvisation). However, he returns home to find his wife killed by a mob and resigns himself to being a social outcast, 'the fate of all poets and foreigners'. Bagchi's music was the film's most successful feature.

ANVESHICHU KANDATIYILLA

aka *Sought But Didn't Find*
1967 150' b&w Malayalam
d/lyr **P. Bhaskaran** *p* K. Ravindranathan Nair *pc* Kollam General Pics *s* Parappuram *c* E.N. Balakrishnan *m* **Baburaj**
lp **Sathyan**, **Madhu**, **Thikkurisi Sukumaran Nair**, **P.J. Anthony**, T.S. Muthaiah, **Adoor Bhasi**, Bahadur, G.K. Pillai, Latif, K.R. Vijaya, **Vijayanirmala**, Kaviyoor Ponnamma, Mavelikara Ponnamma, Meena, Sukumari, **Sharada**, Baby Sheela, Baby Kausalia, Nellikode Bhaskaran

Emotional drama about a woman's unsuccessful search for happiness, made as a reply to the biblical homily, 'seek and ye shall find'. Susamma (Vijaya), born eight months after her parents' marriage, is for this reason rejected by her father and ridiculed by her village community. She eventually becomes a nurse during WW2 and falls for a dashing captain who turns out to be a philanderer. He is killed and she returns home where she has a relationship with Anthony, who turns out to be a married man. Disillusioned, she finds peace in the very hospital where she used to be a nurse. Bhaskaran's biggest film to date, with a major star cast, adapting one of Parappuram's war stories (cf ***Ninamanninnya Kalapadakal***, 1963). Bahadur and Bhasi have independent comedy routines.

ARUNDHATI

1967 145' b&w Oriya
d/sc Prafulla Sengupta *p* Dhiren Patnaik *st* Gurukrishna Goswami *dial* Anand Shankar Das *c* Bishu Chakraborty *m* Shantanu Mahapatra
lp Minati Mishra, Sarat Poojari

Ambitious but unsuccessful big-budget Oriya musical extravaganza. Arundhati (Mishra), studying dance at her father's performing arts establishment, loves Manoj (Poojari), a singer whom her father hopes will become his successor. The industrialist Biswajit claims Arundhati is his wife Madhu, believed to have died in a train accident. He presents various kinds of proof and accuses the bewildered Arundhati of infidelity. Eventually a twin sister, lost when still a child, turns out to have been the cause of the confusion. The skeletal plot was mainly an excuse for several classical dance numbers by Mishra, choreographed by the legendary Odissi dancer Guru Kelucharan Mahapatra.

ASHWAMEDHAM

aka *The Liberation Ritual*
1967 135' b&w Malayalam
d/c **A. Vincent** *p* Hari Pothan *pc* Supriya Pics *s* **Thoppil Bhasi** *lyr* **Vyalar Rama Varma** *m* **P. Devarajan**
lp **Sathyan**, **Prem Nazir**, **Madhu**, Sheela, Indira Thambi, Sukumari, **P.J. Anthony**, **Adoor Bhasi**, G.K. Pillai, T.R. Omana, Bahadur, Kambisseri Karunakaran

Vincent's reform drama adapted a noted Bhasi play about attitudes to disease. Sarojan's (Sheela) marriage to lover Mohan (Nazir) is called off when she contracts leprosy. She is cured in six months, but neither her lover nor her own family accept her back. Eventually she returns to the sanatorium that cured her, and finds happiness helping others afflicted by the disease. Sathyan plays the good doctor Thomas.

AVAL

aka *She*
1967 142' b&w Malayalam
d Aziz *p* Mohammed Sarkar *pc* Beena Films *s* **Thoppil Bhasi** *lyr* **Vyalar Rama Varma** *c* Ravi Varma *m* **P. Devarajan**
lp Usha Nandini, **Madhu**, K.P. Ummar, **Adoor Bhasi**, Bahadur, Kothamangalam Ali, Ramchand, Maya, Meena, Shanta, Baby Waheeda, Kaduvakkulam Anthony, Krishnan Kutty, Shanta Devi

Bizarre Bhasi melodrama about sexual impotence, divorce and a social system that is shown as riddled with incestuous relationships. Sridevi (Usha Nandini) becomes a schoolteacher in a remote village in the mountains, where a widower falls in love with her. This leads to a long story in flashback, where she tells him about how she was betrayed by her lover (Madhu). It appears that her brother had rejected his sister, and in retaliation he does the same to her. She marries a second man even through she is pregnant by her first lover. Her new husband turns out to be sexually impotent. When she delivers her child, she is told that it is dead, but the child survives and is adopted by its biological father. In the end she has to choose between her duties to her new husband and her maternal desire to raise her own child. The problem is solved by the generosity of her husband who accepts her with her baby. This film was the debut of former **FTII** student Aziz, at this time a member of an informal collective.

BAMBAI RAAT KI BAHON MEIN

1967 136' b&w Hindi
d/s/p **K.A. Abbas** *pc* Naya Sansar *lyr* Hasan Kamal *c* Ramchandra *m* J.P. Kaushik
lp Surekha, Vimal Ahuja, Jalal Agha, Madhavi, David, Persis Khambatta, Irshad Panjatan

Characteristic of many CPI ideologues' work in the 60s (cf **Sukhdev**), this is a demagogic melodrama bewailing the city's effect on 'traditional' values. The city is represented by nightclubs, swindlers and drunken women. The hero is Amar Kumar (Ahuja), a crusading journalist under pressure to accept a bribe to kill his story about corruption in high places. Returning from Delhi, he meets a bootlegger named Johnny (Agha) on the plane. An old passenger, Sevakram (Panjatan), dies and leaves a wad of money he stole from a bank. Amar, debating the future with his estranged wife Asha, winds up in Bombay at a nightclub. At Toto's house, Amar meets the cabaret singer Lily (Khambatta) and the drunk Rosy (Madhavi). Although Rosy loves Johnny, he loves Lily. Eventually it transpires that Johnny strangled the old man and as the police chase him through Bombay, his car runs over Rosy and he is caught.

BELLIMODA

1967 163' b&w Kannada
d/s **S.R. Puttana Kanagal** *pc* Srinivasa Arts *st* Triveni *c* R.N.K. Prasad *m* **Vijayabhaskar**
lp **Kalpana**, **Kalyana Kumar**, **Pandharibai**, Ashwath, **Balkrishna**

Kanagal's Kannada debut is a classic melodrama inaugurating his characteristic type of expressionist psychodrama. The story is set in a hilly orchard belonging to Indira's (Kalpana) father Sadashiva (Ashwath). She loves Mohan (Kumar), who goes abroad to study sponsored by Indira's father. Although the two are supposed to marry, a problem arises when Indira's mother Lalitha (Pandharibai) dies giving birth to a son, the official heir to Sadashiva's property. Believing himself too indebted to her father and socially beneath her, Mohan refuses to marry Indira. In the film's extraordinary end, Indira hacks a tree to pieces and rises 'to catch a rainbow'. Although mobilising the Kannada version of Mills & Boon romances, Kanagal's work evokes the psychotic undertone of these lower middle-class fictions, e.g. Indira nurses her infant brother as she would her own child, intensifying Mohan's envy. The lush orchard is disturbingly filmed with a hand-held camera and the film's imagery repeatedly refers to calendar art: the stars, the moon, curved wash-stands and a fan-shaped bed, painted backdrops, etc. The film established Kalpana as Kannada cinema's reigning star, and composer Vijayabhaskar. Kanagal remade the film in Malayalam as *Swapnabhoomi* (1967) with **Prem Nazir** and Sheela.

BHAMA VIJAYAM/BHALE KODALU

1967 179' b&w Tamil/Telugu
d **K. Balachander** *pc* Manohar Pics *lyr* **Kannadasan** *c* P.N. Sundaram, K.S. Prakash *m* M.S. Vishwanathan, **T.V. Raju**
lp Rajshree, Nagesh, Muthuraman, Sundarrajan, T.S. Baliah, Jayanthi, Kanchana, **Sowcar Janaki**, **K. Mukkamala**, **N.T. Rama Rao**

Balachander's satire is reminiscent of his stage work. A movie star Bhama (Rajshree) moves into the neighbourhood where a joint family of three husbands (Nagesh, Muthuraman, Sundarrajan) and their wives (Jayanthi, Kanchana, Janaki) live. Her presence sends the wives into a spending spree as they buy television sets, radios and fancy goods in order to keep up with their glamorous neighbour, while accusing their husbands of being more than friendly with the star. Balachander made a simultaneous Telugu version, *Bhale Kodalu*, with **S.V. Ranga Rao**.

CHHUTI

1967 119' b&w Bengali
d/sc/m **Arundhati Devi** *pc* Purnima Pics *st* Bimal Kar *c* Bimal Mukherjee
lp Nandini Maliya, Mrinal Mukherjee, Ajitesh Bannerjee, Romi Choudhury, Debabrati Sen, Dipali Chakraborty, Tinku

Actress Arundhati Devi's directorial debut is a lyrical melodrama. When Bhramar's (Maliya) father (Bannerjee) remarries, she does not get on with her stern stepmother (Sen). She falls ill but hides her illness, which develops into tuberculosis. Into this family arrives Amal (Mukherjee) and the two fall in love. In the end Bhramar is taken to hospital and Amal, aware she is terminally ill, promises to wait for her. An elegiac film in the tradition of **Tapan Sinha**'s **Tagore**an film-novelettes with a startling thematic resemblance to aspects of **Ghatak**'s ***Meghe Dhaka Tara*** (1960), revealing that film's origins in popular Bengali romantic fiction. Unlike Ghatak, however, Arundhati Devi offers a nostalgic, sylvan landscape to contrast with the painful experience of the contemporary.

Chhuti

CHIDIAKHANA

aka *Chiriakhana* aka *The Zoo*
1967 125' b&w Bengali
d/sc/m **Satyajit Ray** *p* Harendranath Bhattacharya *pc* Star Prod. *st* Saradindu Bannerjee's novel *Chidiakhana c* Soumendu Roy
lp **Uttam Kumar**, Sailen Mukherjee, **Sushil Majumdar**, Kanika Majumdar, Subhendu Chatterjee, Shyamal Ghosal, Prasad Mukherjee, Subira Roy, Nripati Chatterjee, Subrata Chatterjee, Gitali Roy, Kalipada Chakravarty, Chinmoy Roy, Ramen Mullick, Brajadas, Nilatpal Dey

This relatively unknown Ray film, made to help out some friends, is his first real detective thriller (cf ***Sonar Kella***, 1974; ***Joi Baba Felunath***, 1978) although he had deployed the generic narrative structure often before (cf **Kanchanjunga**, 1962). The detective Byomkesh Bakshi (Kumar) is hired by a retired judge to trace a former screen actress who lives in a colony for social outcasts (run by the judge to atone for sentencing several convicts to death). Bakshi ends up investigating the mysterious death of his own client. He unmasks the culprit when he notices that, in a series of tape-recorded interviews with the inhabitants, a woman betrays her identity by her accent. The woman turns out to be the former film actress, whose career was ruined by her lover when he changed her looks with plastic surgery.

CHITRAMELA

Aka *Image Festival*
1967 172' b&w Malayalam
d T.S. Muthaiah *pc* Shri Movies *s Nagarathinte Mukhangal*: M.K. Mani, **S.L. Puram Sadanandan**; *Penninte Prapancham*: T. Vasudevan, Bharathan Kutty; *Apaswarangal*: Shrikumaran Thampi *c* N.S. Mani *m* **P. Devarajan**
lp Nagarathinte Mukhangal: Sheela, K.P. Ummar, Kottayam Chelappan, Baby Rajani, Baby Usha; *Penninte Prapancham*: S.P. Pillai, **Adoor Bhasi**, Bahadur, Manavalan Joseph, Shri Nagendra Pillai, Meena, Khadija, C.R. Lakshmi; *Apaswarangal*: **Prem Nazir**, **Sharada**, **Thikkurisi Sukumaran Nair**, Sukumari, G.K. Pillai, Nellikode Bhaskaran, T.R. Omana, Wahab Kashmiri

Malayalam cinema's first portmanteau film, consisting of three short films, is also Tamil/Malayalam actor Muthaiah's debut as director. *Nagarathinte Mukhangal* [*Faces of the City*] (38') shows the tragic fate of children left at home by pleasure-loving parents who frequent nightclubs. *Penninte Prapancham* [*A Woman's World*] (39') is a Laurel and Hardy-inspired comedy speculating on life 50 years in the future when sex-change operations become commonplace. The longest story, *Apaswarangal* [*Discordant Notes*] (95'), is a tragic love story between a street singer and a blind woman. To achieve success, the street singer has to accept the patronage of a famous dancer, which estranges him from his girl. In the end she dies in his arms.

INDIA 67

aka *An Indian Day*, aka *India Today*
1967 57' col wordless
d **S. Sukhdev** pc **Films Division**

Sukhdev's best-known documentary was a more muted work than his more demagogic ***And Miles To Go*** ... (1965). A wordless montage strings together shots from various parts of the country, moving from the village to the city. Sequences include well-known political figures, e.g. Bal Thackeray, now head of the notorious right-wing Shiv Sena, making a streetside speech. Some shots were admired by **S. Ray**: the drop of sweat on the nose of a perspiring Rajasthani musician, followed by an ant on the desert sand, or the dog urinating on a bicycle. The film consciously recalls Rossellini's *India 57* (1958). The film was recut into shorter versions with alternative titles.

IRUTINTE ATMAVU

aka *The Soul of Darkness*
1967 147' b&w Malayalam
d/lyr **P. Bhaskaran** *p* P.I. Muhammad Kasim *pc* Sony Pics *s* **M.T. Vasudevan Nair** *c* E.N. Balakrishnan *m* **Baburaj**
lp **Prem Nazir, Thikkurisi Sukumaran Nair, P.J. Anthony**, T.S. Muthaiah, Balaji, **Sharada**, Ushakumari, M.S. Namboodiri, Shankaradi, **Adoor Bhasi**, Shanta Devi, Philomina, **Padmini**, Selina, Rukmini, Shobha

One of scenarist Vasudevan Nair's best-known scripts, critiquing the feudal values of a declining Nair community in Kerala. The key figure prising out the biases and attitudes of the family headed by the karanavar (Thikkurisi Sukumaran Nair) is the partiarch's mentally retarded nephew Velayudhan (Nazir). To the family his condition symbolises the curse that has led to its decline. He has a good relationship with Ammukutty (Sharada), his cousin and traditionally his future bride. When she is molested by a foreign-returned relative, he protests his innocence but is chained and locked up in a cage. She is married off to an old widower, but when she too rejects his pleas to reconsider her decision, Velayudhan finally acknowledges defeat and agrees to be defined as mad. The film was also cut out as an actorial challenge for megastar Nazir, playing his role with aplomb in scenes such as the one where he swings in ecstacy from one areca tree to another, and generally exploits the tearjerking sympathy generated by his character.

JEWEL THIEF

1967 186' col Hindi
d/sc **Vijay Anand** *pc* **Navketan Films** *st* K.A. Narayan *lyr* **Majrooh Sultanpuri, Shailendra** *c* V. Ratra *m* **S.D. Burman**
lp **Dev Anand, Ashok Kumar, Vyjayanthimala**, Tanuja, Helen, Fariyal, Anju Mahendru, Nasir Hussain, Sapru, Pratima Devi

Hero Vinay (Anand), son of the police commissioner (Hussain), finds himself repeatedly mistaken for notorious jewel thief Amar. He is accused by Shalini (Vyjayanthimala) of being the man who had promised to marry her, and the accusation is substantiated by her brother (Ashok Kumar). Vinay masquerades as Amar to try to crack the gang, even as it appears that Amar too masquerades as Vinay, leaving the audience guessing for most of the film on the identity of the hero. Eventually Amar turns out to be a piece of fiction, created by the real thief, Shalini's brother, who turns out not to be her brother at all. This cult movie, using concealed bars, moving walls and hidden safes, snowlifts and aeroplanes, determined the look and the fashions of much of late 60s Hindi cinema. Vijay Anand's direction, demonstrating a greater control over colour than, e.g., ***Guide*** (1965), goes well with the taut editing despite a meandering plot. Song hits include *Yeh dil na hota bechara* (sung by **Kishore Kumar**), *Rulake gaya sapna mera* and *Hoton pe aisi baat main dabake chali aayi* (both by **Lata Mangeshkar**).

KANDAN KARUNAI

1967 149' b&w Tamil
d/s **A.P. Nagarajan** *p* M.M.A. Chinnappa Devar *pc* ALS Prod. *lyr* K.B. Sundarambal, Sirkhazi Govindaraja *c* K.S. Prasad
lp **Sivaji Ganesan, Savitri, Gemini Ganesh**, K.R. Vijaya, **Jayalalitha**, Ashokan, Balaji, V. Gopalakrishna, Nagesh, K.B. Sundarambal, Shakuntala, Manorama

Major Nagarajan mythological with Ganesan unusually starring as a minor local deity, Muruga, introduced into Tamil cinema, according to Sivathamby (1981), by the producer. Muruga is born to earth specifically to eliminate the evil Soorasura, and the film includes spectacular footage of the war between the two kings Athaigaman and Malayaman, halted by Avvaiyyar's pacificist speech. The dialogue was noted for its lofty classical Tamil idiom.

KAVALAM CHUNDAN

aka *The Racing Boat* aka *Fisherman Chundan*
1967 136' b&w Malayalam
d/st **Sasikumar** *p* V.P.M. Manikkam *pc* Bhagawathi Pics *sc* **Thoppil Bhasi** *lyr* **Vyalar Rama Varma** *c* U. Rajagopal, Benjamin *m* **P. Devarajan**
lp **Sathyan, Sharada**, Aranmulla Ponnamma, **P.J. Anthony**, Pankajavally, S.P. Pillai, **Adoor Bhasi**, Manavalan Joseph, Joseph Chacko, Adoor Pankajam, Adoor Bhawani, Radha, Kadhija

Family melodrama set in one of the most spectacular festivals in Kerala, the traditional boat race during the festival of Onam (and a major tourist attraction). Kavalam Chundan is the name of a famous racing boat, the symbol of the village's pride, strength and unity. Saraswathi Kunjamma (Ponnamma), a widow, owns the boat. Her son Chandran (Sathyan) loves his cousin, the woman traditionally destined to be his bride, Sharada (Sharada), but when his sister comes home pregnant the family is torn apart by disputes over succession and property rights, including the right to the racing boat. The drama involves the entire village, leading to gory scenes when Sharada's jealous father gains the traditional secret of how the boat is made, after which the master carpenter kills his own son-in-law for having divulged the knowhow. In the end, Chandran's rights are restored and he wins the race thereby also signalling the victory of traditional values, after which he dedicates the boat to the entire village.

KOTTAYAM KOLA CASE

1967 143' b&w Malayalam
d **K.S. Sethumadhavan** *pc* Jayamaruthi Prod. *st* Chembil John *dial* **S.L. Puram Sadanandan** *lyr* **Vyalar Rama Varma** *c* C. Namashivaya *m* B.A. Chidambaranath
lp **Prem Nazir**, Sheela, **Kottarakkara Sridharan Nair, Adoor Bhasi**, T.K. Balachandran, G.K. Pillai, Kamaladevi, Sukumari, Shankaradi, Shanta Devi, Indira Priyadarshini

Sethumadhavan changed his style to make this joint family melodrama that turns into murder mystery. The two brothers Shekhar and K.G. Nair part ways when the latter refuses a loan. Shekhar, who leaves his wife to live with his mistress, is mysteriously murdered. Police investigations disrupt the marriage ceremony of Shekhar's son Prabhakaran. When Nair's son Rajan is the next to get killed, the police accuse Prabhakaran. He, however, evades arrest and eventually catches the real criminal, Nair himself.

MADHUCHANDRA

1967 148' b&w Marathi
d **Rajdutt** *pc* Madhuvasant Chitra *s* Madhusudan Kalelkar *lyr* **G.D. Madgulkar** *c* Datta Gorle *m* N. Datta
lp Kashinath Ghanekar, Uma, Shrikant Moghe, Raja Pandit, Barchi Bahadar, Nana Palsikar, Master Sachin, **Raja Paranjpe**

Poor hero Dinu Khare (Ghanekar) elopes with rich girlfriend Malu (Uma), using a false railway pass. Malu's rich father searches for the missing couple but they are caught by the railway authorities and have to spend their wedding night in jail. Rajdutt's debut is a whimsical comedy. The highlight is the hero and heroine, interned in two seperate cells in the prison, singing a love duet to each other, the hit number *Madhu ithe ani chandra tithe*. The film made Ghanekar, a noted stage actor, a major Marathi film star.

PRANAMITHRULU

1967 177' b&w Telugu
d **P. Pullaiah** *pc* Padmasri Pics *s* Mullapudi Venkatramana *lyr* **Athreya**, Dasarathi, C. Narayana Reddy *c* P.S. Selvaraj *m* K.V. Mahadevan
lp **A. Nageshwara Rao, K. Jaggaiah, Savitri**, Shantakumari, Kanchana, Girija, Geetanjali, **Relangi Venkatramaiah, Gummadi Venkateshwara Rao**

Melodrama about two friends, Babu (Jaggaiah), a third-generation owner of a business, and his best friend, his employee and childhood friend Chinna (Nageshwara Rao). When Babu wills all his property to his friend, the diwan (Venkateshwara Rao), who runs the company's affairs, leaves and Babu's mother Jagadamba (Shantakumari) tries to break up the friendship. This happens anyway when the diwan incites a workers' strike and Chinna becomes a labour leader opposed to Babu. Chinna is eventually shot dead by a killer hired by the diwan. First of the several versions of Peter Glenville's *Becket* (1964) adapted to contemporary conditions, and the original version of Mukherjee's ***Namak Haram*** (1973) with **Bachchan** and **Rajesh Khanna** in Jaggaiah's and Nageshwara Rao's roles.

RAM AUR SHYAM

1967 171' col Hindi
d **Tapi Chanakya** *pc* **Vijaya** International *st* **D.V. Narasaraju** *lyr* Shakeel Badaiyuni *c* Marcus Bartley *m* **Naushad**

lp **Dilip Kumar**, **Waheeda Rehman**, Mumtaz, Pran, **Nirupa Roy**, Kanhaiyalal, Nasir Hussain, Zebunissa

A successful Hindi remake of Chanakya's equally successful Telugu *Ramudu Bheemudu* (1964, with **NTR**) and Tamil *Enga Veetu Pillai* (1965, with **MGR**). In a double role Dilip Kumar plays twins separated at birth who grow up to become the timid Ram, who is terrified of villain Gajendra (Pran), and the boisterous Shyam. They are mistaken for each other, even by their respective girlfriends Anjana (Rehman) and Shanta (Mumtaz).

SAAKSHI

1967 142' b&w Telugu
d/sc **Bapu** *pc* Nandana Films *st/dial* Mullapudi Venkatramana *lyr* **Arudra**, Dasarathi *c* P.S. Selvaraj *m* K.V. Mahadevan
lp **Krishna**, **Vijayanirmala**, Jagga Rao, Ramana Panthulu, Rajababu, Sivarakrishna, Chalapathi Rao, Saakshi Rangarao

Bapu's debut is regarded as an 'experimental' movie (it flopped) about rural politics. The villain Fakir (Jagga Rao), a truck driver paid by a local politician, kills two men. A boatman (Krishna) witnesses the murders and the entire village, hoping to get Fakir imprisoned, supports the witness when the case comes to court. However Fakir claims self-defence and he gets a light jail sentence. When Fakir comes out, he publicly announces his intention to kill the boatman. When he does so, nobody in the village dares to help the victim. The film introduced the then unknown lead pair of Krishna and Vijayanirmala acting without make-up in outdoor sequences, a standard aspect of New Indian Cinema realism.

SHRI KRISHNAVATARAM

1967 211' b&w Telugu/Tamil
d **K. Kameshwara Rao** *p* N.T. Rama Rao *pc* Tarakarama Pics *s/co-lyr* **Samudrala Raghavacharya** *co-lyr* C. Narayana Reddy *c* Annaiah *m* **T.V. Raju**
lp **N.T. Rama Rao**, **Shobhan Babu**, Satyanarayana, Rajanala, **Chittor V. Nagaiah**, Lingamurthy, **K. Mukkamala**, Dhoolipala, Devika, Kanchana, Sukanya, Rushyendramani, Krishnakumari, Vijayalakshmi, Geetanjali, Sandhya Rani, **S. Varalakshmi**, Chhaya Devi

This big-budget mythological is one of the best known of NTR's screen versions of the Krishna myth and recounts several of the *Mahabharata*'s well-known episodes, including Krishna's childhood in Dwarka, the slaying of Shishupala, the visit of Kuchela, the killing of Kansa, etc. Raju's score, adapting the *Tirupati Venkatakavulu*, was widely admired.

TAQDEER

aka *Destiny*
1967 108' b&w Hindi
d/sc A. Salaam *pc* Rajshri *lyr* **Anand Bakshi** *c* Nariman Irani *m* **Laxmikant-Pyarelal**
lp Bharat Bhushan, Shalini, Kamal Kapoor, Farida Jalal

All this film shares with **Mehboob Khan**'s ***Taqdeer*** (1943) is its title. The plot concerns a music teacher who leaves wife and children to try to earn money abroad. When his wife hears that her husband's ship has been wrecked, she tries to make ends meet by marrying a rich, villainous mine owner. Later, the husband, who suffers from amnesia, returns and the nasty industrialist tries to kill him. In the end, the villain gets killed and the musician's family is reunited. The film's main interest resides in its nostalgic music track.

THANGAI

1967 168' b&w Tamil
d/sc A.C. Trilogchander *pc* Sujata Cine Arts *dial* Aroor Das *lyr* **Kannadasan** *c* Muthuswamy *m* M.S. Vishwanathan
lp **Sivaji Ganesan**, Balaji, K.R. Vijaya, Nagesh, Kanchana, Sundarrajan, Baby Kausalya, Ramadas

Madan (Ganesan), sent to jail in his teens for a crime he did not commit, is released and becomes a gambler to support his sister. He falls in love with the rich Leela (Vijaya) who is, however, supposed to marry Sridhar (Balaji), the cop who wants to bust the gambling racket. Fellow gambler Lalitha (Kanchana) also loves Madan. When an argument at the gambling tables leads to a fight, a gang leader shoots at Madan but kills Lalitha instead.

THANGA THAMBI

1967 139' b&w Tamil
d Francis Ramanath *pc* Unmayal Prod. *st/dial* **M. Karunanidhi**
lp Sundarrajan, Ravichandran, **Vanisree**, Bharati, Nagesh, Manorama, O.A.K. Devar

Karunanidhi's domestic melodrama about two loving brothers torn apart by their respective wives. Elder brother Varadan (Sundarrajan) marries Sundari (Vanisree). He wants younger brother Venu (Ravichandran) to marry a rich woman, but Sundari wants a poor and obedient sister-in-law. Although Sundari initially refuses pregnancy for fear of ruining her looks, she eventually bears a child at the same time as the meek sister-in-law Parvathi (Bharati). Parvathi raises both children, causing an estrangement between the brothers.

THAIKKU THALAIMAGAN

1967 159' b&w Tamil
d/dial M.A. Thirumugham *pc* Devar Films *sc* M.M.A. Chinnappa Devar *lyr* **Kannadasan** *c* N.S. Varma *m* K.V. Mahadevan
lp **M.G. Ramachandran**, **Jayalalitha**, **Sowcar Janaki**, Manorama, **S.V. Ranga Rao**, Nagesh, Manohar, M.M.A. Chinnappa Devar, S.N. Lakshmi

A good and bad brother morality play. Younger brother Maradhur (MGR) marries the rich Malathi (Jayalalitha) but refuses to move into his father-in-law's (Ranga Rao) house. Elder brother Somu uses this impasse to persuade Maradhur's father-in-law to finance a new garage and to have the entire family move in, forcing Maradhur to follow suit, but the plan is foiled when Somu falls in love with a dancing-girl, driving his family into poverty. Both Somu and the brothers' beloved mother (Lakshmi) die. MGR's melodrama, enlivened by several fight sequences, deploys his usual persona of the working-class hero who marries a rich heiress and wins his battles by virtue of his sterling lower-class morality.

UPKAAR

aka *Good Deed*
1967 172' col Hindi
d/s **Manoj Kumar** *pc* Vishal Pics *lyr* Prem Dhawan, Indivar, Gulshan Bawra Qamar Jalalabadi *c* V.N. Reddy *m* **Kalyanji-Anandji**
lp Asha Parekh, Manoj Kumar, Pran, Kamini Kaushal, Prem Chopra, Kanhaiyalal, Madan Puri, Manmohan Krishna, David

Stridently nationalistic melodrama with which Manoj Kumar launched a series casting himself as good hero Bharat, contrasting his son-of-the-soil simplicity with Westernised decadence (cf *Purab Aur Paschim*, 1970). He tends to the family fields to pay for bad younger brother Puran's (Chopra) education, but Puran spends it all in a dissolute life in the city. When the villain (Puri), who had killed their father, encourages enmity between the brothers, Bharat surrenders all his property and joins the Indian Army. The villain follows him into the war and tries to kill him, but he is rescued by the crippled soldier Malang Baba (Pran, attampting a change of screen image). Meanwhile Puran, who heads a nationwide network of smugglers and black marketeers, recants and helps the government to crack the gang. Bharat is saved in a medical operation performed by his girlfriend (Asha Parekh). Much of the strident rhetoric along with the peasant-and-soldier iconography (illustrating the *Jai jawan jai kisan* slogan) is in the context of India's war with Pakistan the previous year. The film's nationalism is encapsulated in its theme song *Mere desh ki dharti* (sung by Mahendra Kapoor), and the other hit is **Lata Mangeshkar**'s *Har khushi ho wahan*.

ADHYAPIKA

1968 139' b&w Malayalam
d/p **P. Subramanyam** *pc* Neela Prod. *s* **Kanam E.J.** *lyr* Balamurali *c* E.N.C. Nair *m* **V. Dakshinamurthy**
lp **Padmini**, **Madhu**, Ambika, S.P. Pillai, Bahadur, Shanti, Aranmulla Ponnamma, Leela, Meena, Shobha, **Thikkurisi Sukumaran Nair**, **Kottarakkara Sridharan Nair**, Piravam Many, Ramakrishna, T.K. Balachandran

Unremittingly tragic melodrama, drawing on the paingili type of popular sentimental fiction, about a middle-class schoolteacher, Saramma (Padmini). She supports her father and two siblings, but receives nothing but ingratitude. The only man in her life marries her sister, her brother refuses all responsibilities to the family when he completes his education, and her father prevents her marriage for fear of losing his only source of income. Eventually she dies of tuberculosis, sad and lonely, apparently loved

Padmini (right) in *Adhyapika*

only by her dog (the pet featured prominently in the poster campaign for the film). The film is designed to show off Padmini's melodramatic talents and remains one of her best-known Malayalam weepies.

APANJAN

1968 123' b&w Bengali
d/sc/m **Tapan Sinha** *pc* K.L. Kapoor Prod. *st* Indramitra *lyr* **Rabindranath Tagore**, Atulprasad Sen *c* Bimal Mukherjee
lp **Chhaya Devi**, Swarup Dutta, Samit Bhanja, Partha Mukherjee, Kalyan Chatterjee, **Robi Ghosh**, **Bhanu Bannerjee**, Dilip Roy, Premangshu Bose

Tapan Sinha's violent and cynical melodrama in response to the **Naxalite** student movement in Bengal (cf **Satyajit Ray**'s ***Pratidwandi***, 1970 and ***Seemabaddha***, 1971; **Mrinal Sen**'s Calcutta trilogy). An old woman, Anandamoyee (Chhaya Devi), 'adopts' a group of lumpenised political activists, sensing the emotional vulnerability beneath their violent reduction of democracy to a series of gang wars. Two gangs clash when their respective political leaders (representing also the ongoing conflict between 'local' people and post-Partition migrants from East Bengal) fight an election. Anandamoyee eventually dies trying to save one of the students from a bullet. The hit film is remembered for its tightly edited portrayal of the farcical election campaign and for its climactic confrontation. The film was remade by **Gulzar** (***Mere Apne***, 1971) with **Meena Kumari** emulating Chhaya Devi's performance.

ASHIRWAD

aka *The Blessing* aka *Aashirwaad*
1968 146'- col Hindi
d/s **Hrishikesh Mukherjee** *p* N.C. Sippy *dial/co-lyr* **Gulzar** *co-lyr* Harindranath *c* T.B. Seetaram *m* **Vasant Desai**
lp **Ashok Kumar**, Sanjeev Kumar, Sumita Sanyal, Veena, Sajjan, **Abhi Bhattacharya**

A flamboyant melodrama about a poet, Shivnath (A. Kumar) who studies folk-songs but is married to a woman who owns much land and ruthlessly extorts taxes from the local Untouchables. She even threatens to burn down their village unless they pay. At this point, the mild husband rebels and kills one of his wife's allies, which earns him a spell in jail. When he is released, he is a broken old man. He attends his daughter's wedding and offers his blessings without telling her that he is her father.

ASURAVITHU

1968 158' b&w Malayalam
d **A. Vincent** *pc* Manoj Pics *s* **M.T. Vasudevan Nair** *lyr* **P. Bhaskaran** *c* A. Venkat *m* K. Raghavan
lp **Prem Nazir**, **Adoor Bhasi**, **P.J. Anthony**, Shankaradi, N. Govindankutty, Nilambur Balan, **Sharada**, Kaviyoor Ponnamma, Shanta Devi

Political melodrama sometimes considered to make a Vasudevan Nair trilogy with Vincent's ***Murappennu*** (1965) and Bhaskaran's ***Irutinte Atmavu*** (1967) about life in feudal Kerala. This one is set in the communally charged situation of violence between Hindu and Muslim communities. The rich Shankaran Nair tries to bribe his brother-in-law, the good hero Govindankutty (Nazir), to marry his daughter Meenakshi. The reason for the haste is that Meenakshi is pregnant by Govindankutty's wayward nephew Kochuppan. Govindankutty, however, refuses, and is thrown out by the family. He moves in with his Muslim friend Kunjarikkar (Anthony), a daring thing to do given the prevailing political atmosphere. He eventually converts to Islam, renaming himself Abdullah.

BANGARU PICHIKA

1968 145' b&w Telugu
d **Bapu** *pc* Shri Ganesh Pics *s* Mullapudi Venkatramana *lyr* **Arudra** *c* Kannappa *m* K.V. Mahadevan
lp Shantakumari, **Vijayanirmala**, Padmanjali, Chandramohan, Ramana Panthulu, Rajababu, Chalapathi Rao, Sakshi Rangarao

The rich mother (Shantakumari) of hero (Chandramohan) wants him to marry but his worldly-wise father advises him to escape from his mother's clutches and to seek his own fortune. He runs away, pursued by several people seeking to collect the reward offered by his mother for locating him. A criminal gang uses one of its female members (Vijayanirmala) to lure the hero into its control. Eventually she falls in love with her target and proves to be his only true friend. The fast-paced movie is noted for its racy script, although Vijayanirmala claimed it as an art-house movie since she wore the same costume throughout.

CHAR SHAHER EK KAHANI

aka *A Tale of Four Cities*
1968 16' b&w English/Hindi
d/sc/p **K.A. Abbas** *pc* Naya Sansar

Abbas's best-known political documentary and a notorious censorship case. Fast-paced editing intercuts touristic images of India's 'achievements' in industry and agriculture with verite long shots of Bombay's red-light area. Rhetorical devices include a shot of the first indigenously launched rocket, from the Thumba base, which freezes a missile in mid-air and turns the image into its negative to a distorted soundtrack. Shot in Bombay, Calcutta, Delhi and Madras, the film also has a dramatised sequence enacted by a real-life prostitute. Abbas was a member of the G.D. Khosla Committee on Film Censorship (New Delhi: 1969) and writes that he made the film during the committee's investigations especially to put its proclaimed political liberalism to the test. The Censor Board objected mainly to the prostitution scenes, alleging them to be pornographic. Abbas fought the case up to the Supreme Court, rejecting even the compromise of an Adult certificate, and when he won his case he shifted his legal argument to claim all forms of censorship as *ultra vires*, leading to Chief Justice Hidaytullah's landmark judgment on safeguards in the censorship process, including the setting up of an appellate tribunal. When Abbas later released the short, along with his ***Saat Hindustani*** (1969), he shot the mandatory censor certificate at the beginning of the copy with a zoom lens and used suspense music.

EZHU RATHRIKAL

aka *Seven Nights*
1968 140' b&w Malayalam
d **Ramu Kariat** *p* Babu Ismail *pc* Kammani Films *s* Kaladi Gopi from his play *lyr* **Vyalar Rama Varma** *c* Kamal Bose *m* **Salil Choudhury**
lp Aalammood, Chachhappan, Nellikode Bhaskaran, Govindan Kutty, Shihaab, J.C. Kuttikkad, Kamalamma, Kamaladevi, Latha, Radhamony, K.R. Rajam, Kothamangalam Ali, Kuttan Pillai, Raghava Menon, Aravindan, Kaduvakkulam Anthony

Kariat's film follows Kaladi Gopi's play in weaving together a number of melodramatic plots, realist acting conventions and the theatrical device of enclosing disparate characters into a socially ambiguous space. A number of vagabonds and social outcasts shelter every night in a dilapidated house, the dim, municipal light setting the atmosphere for their interactions. Characters include the hypocritical Pashanam Varky who exploits religious bigotry; Maria the street vendor; the ex-con Ikka, an old Muslim who murdered his unfaithful wife and is now searching for his daughter; a blind and victimised young woman; Abu, who went to jail to protect his girlfriend's father but lost his girl in the process, and the hunchback Paramu, who acts as a metaphor for a crippled but still decent moral universe. In the end, the blind girl turns out to be Ikka's long-lost daughter, tying up some of the diverse narrative strands designed to give a picture of contemporary social problems.

GOOPY GYNE BAGHA BYNE

aka *The Adventures of Goopy and Bagha*
1968 132'(118') b&w Bengali
d/sc/m **Satyajit Ray** *p* Nepal Dutta, Ashim Dutta *pc* Purnila Pics *st* Upendra Kishore Roy-Choudhury *c* Soumendu Roy
lp Tapan Chatterjee, **Robi Ghosh**, Santosh Dutta, **Jahar Roy**, Santi Chatterjee, Harindranath Chattopadhyay, Chinmoy Roy, Durgadas Bannerjee, Govinda Chakravarty, Prasad Mukherjee, Haradhan Mukherjee, Abani Chatterjee, Khagen Pathak, Binoy Bose, Prasad Mukherjee

Ray's children's fantasy is his first commercial success and became a cult movie in Bengal. It is a fairy-tale about ghosts and kings written originally by his grandfather and published in 1914. The impoverished amateur musicians Goopy (T. Chatterjee) and Bagha (R. Ghosh), banished for their inept playing, receive a magic pair of slippers from an animated ghost-king which allow them to travel anywhere they like. They can also conjure up food. They become master performers, arriving in the kingdom of Shundi whose king (Dutta) makes them his court musicians. The twin brother of this king (Dutta again), who rules neighbouring Halla, is held prisoner by his despotic and warlike prime minister (J. Roy). The musical duo are captured by the prime minister but they escape and, with a series of magical effects, overthrow the villain and live 'happily ever after' having married two princesses. The film mobilises a melange of sources from Lewis Carroll to the bawdy Bengali jatra, held together by the sheer cinephilia which animates the performances, the sets and the soundtrack. The high point is the spectacular ghost dance followed by the rhyming dialogue of the ghost-king amid flashing lights. The dance, nearly 7' long and set to percussion music, calls on mime, shadow puppetry and **Pat painting** traditions and is shot with shimmering effects and negative images to tell of the four classes of colonial society: well-fed Brahmins, kings, peasantry and the colonial bureaucracy. Ray felt the film was probably unique, although it coincides with French, British and Italian comic-strip-inspired films of the mid-60s. Ray made a sequel, ***Hirak Rajar Deshe*** (1980), and his son Sandeep continued with *Goopy Bagha Phere Elo* (1991). Salman Rushdie, in a tribute to the enduring appeal of this loveable duo, introduced them briefly in his children's novel *Haroun and the Sea of Stories* (1990).

HANNELE CHIGURIDAGA

1968 161' b&w Kannada
d M.R. Vittal *pc* Srikanth & Srikanth Enterprises *st* Triveni's novel *dial/lyr* R.N. Jayagopal *c* Srikanth Kumar *m* M. Ranga Rao
lp **R. Nagendra Rao**, **Rajkumar**, **Kalpana**, Arun Kumar, B.V. Radha

An orthodox patriarch (Nagendra Rao) is upset when one of his five sons wants to marry a theatre actress. The old man's friend, a widower, wants to marry the patriarch's widowed daughter, which would infringe the old man's traditional values. However, he transforms himself and agrees to both marriages. One of veteran Kannada thespian Nagendra Rao's best-known roles.

HASINA MAAN JAYEGI

1968 165' col Hindi
d/co-lyr **Prakash Mehra** *pc* Mangatram Films *s* S.M. Abbas *co-lyr* Qamar Jalalabadi, Akhtar Roomani, Kafeel Azar *c* N. Satyen *m* **Kalyanji-Anandji**
lp **Shashi Kapoor**, Babita, **Johnny Walker**, Ameeta, Yunus Pervez, Manmohan Krishna, Niranjan Sharma, Hari Shivdasani, Sapru, Brahm Bhardwaj

Two identical look-alikes Kamal and Ramesh (Kapoor in both roles) love Archana (Babita). She loves Kamal, but often mistakes the one for the other. The evil Ramesh tries to take advantage of this resemblance to have Kamal kidnapped on the day of their marriage, but becomes the victim of his own ploy when his henchmen make the same error as everyone else. The plot expands to take in the India-China War (1962), as Kamal enlists and Ramesh once again tries to kill him. When only one of the two emerges from a muddy pond, the audience is inducted into the confusion as Archana, who initially accepts the man as her husband, starts getting suspicious and eventually has him arrested for impersonation. It is only when Ramesh reappears that the man she has been living with is revealed to be indeed her husband. Mehra (cf ***Zanjeer***, 1973, ***Muqaddar Ka Sikandar***, 1978) in his debut reveals only one element of his trademark plotting in this convoluted film, that of Kamal's illegitimacy and unknown parentage.

KANAVAN

1968 152' b&w Tamil
d **P. Neelakantan** *pc* Vali Films *st* **M.G. Ramachandran** *dial* Sornam *lyr* Alangudi Somu, **Vali**
lp M.G. Ramachandran, **Jayalalitha**, Vijayakumari, Vasantha, Kannan, Ashokan, Manohar, Cho, Manorama, Rama Rao

The self-willed Rani (Jayalalitha) does not want to marry, but according to her father's will she cannot inherit her property until she does. She marries Valaiyan (MGR), a prisoner on death row, but Valaiyan is acquitted of the murder charge when a documentary showing a Prosperity Brigade rally proves his alibi.

LEELUDI DHARTI

1968 138' col Gujarati
d Vallabh Choksi *pc* K.V. Films *st* Chunilal Madia *sc* Manu Desai *dial* Jitubhai P. Mehta *lyr* **Avinash Vyas** *c* A.G. Dhanik *m* Purushottam Upadhyay, Gaurang Vyas
lp Daisy Irani, Mahesh Desai, Kala Shah, Champsibhai Nagda, Upendra Kumar, Kishore Bhatt, Mahendra Zaveri, Shashikant Bhat, Veena Prabhu, Vanlata Mehta, Shirin, Sudha Zaveri, Arvind Kamdar, Suvarna Kapadia

The first Gujarati colour feature mixes fertility rituals with rural melodrama in an adaptation of Chunilal Madia's short story. One of the three sons of farmer Hada Patel falls in love with the accursed Santu Rangili, accused of having caused a drought. The accusation is confirmed when her child is stillborn. She and her marriage are rehabilitated when an other woman abandons her own child in favour of Santu. Eventually, when another of the farmer's sons returns, having become a holy man, the family settles down 'to make the earth greener'.

MAHATMA - LIFE OF GANDHI 1869-1948

1968 330' b&w English
d/s Vithalbhai Jhaveri *pc* Gandhi National Memorial Fund *m* Vishnudas Shirali

Landmark compilation documentary on Gandhi, made with the assistance of D.G. Tendulkar, the author of the 8 vol. biography *Mahatma*, which is the source of the film's narrative. Edited down from over 50 hours of footage assembled by Gandhi's son Devdas, the film chronicles political events with little analysis, e.g. the famous salt agitation, the Swadeshi movement, village reconstruction programmes, Gandhi's march through the communal riots in Noakhali, his fast which almost singlehandedly forced an end to the Partition riots, etc. These events are intercut with footage revealing Gandhi's unfamiliarity with world literature, his controversially conservative positions on birth control and his statement that under socialism all property would belong to God. Although there is very little material of Gandhi actually speaking, the film has been used as a standard reference for Gandhian iconography (cf Attenborough's biographical). Tendulkar, known mainly for his biography, studied film in Germany and Moscow and may briefly have been a student of Eisenstein. Director Jhaveri is a former jeweller and freedom fighter.

PADOSAN

1968 157' col Hindi
d Jyoti Swaroop *pc* Mehmood Prod. *st* Arun Choudhury's *Pasher Bari sc/dial/lyr* Rajinder Krishen *c* K.H. Kapadia *m* **R.D. Burman**
lp **Sunil Dutt**, Saira Banu, **Kishore Kumar**, Mehmood, Om Prakash, Mukri, Agha, Keshto Mukherjee

Slapstick musical comedy in which the innocent Bhola (Dutt) gives up his commitment to celibacy when he falls for sexy neighbour Bindu (Saira Banu). His rivals in love are his own uncle (Prakash) and Bindu's traditionalist Carnatic music teacher

(Mehmood). He, however, wins his girl with the assistance of the crooked guru (K. Kumar), when he serenades her using the guru for a musical playback. The high point of the film is a zany take-off on the *jugalbandi* (musical contest) between the guru and the Carnatic musician (*Ek chatur naar karke singaar*, sung by Manna Dey and Kumar). The original Bengali story had previously been filmed by Sudhir Mukherjee (*Pasher Bari*, 1952) and by **C. Pullaiah** (***Pakkinti Ammayi***, 1953).

PUDHIYA BHOOMI

1968 144' b&w Tamil
d **Tapi Chanakya** *pc* Jayaar Movies *sc* V.C. Guhanathan *lyr* **Kannadasan**, Poovai Chenkuttiyuvan *m* M.S. Vishwanathan
lp **M.G. Ramachandran**, **Jayalalitha**, M.N. Nambiar, Ashokan, Muthaiah, Sheila, Trichy Sundarrajan

Bandits kidnap Dr Katheeravan (MGR) to treat their ailing leader in his secret lair and send him back, attaching a bomb to his car. Katheeravan survives the blast and is nursed to health by a girl in a remote village, Kannamma (Jayalalitha). He sets up a hospital in the village, causing problems for the bandit chief Kankeyan (Nambiar), who informs Katheeravan's urban fiancee (Sheila) of her lover's village affair. Eventually, Kannamma turns out to be the bandit's daughter. Although not a mainstream DMK film, it included the mandatory political symbology: the hero's name Katheeravan (the sun) refers to the DMK party symbol; the hero reveals his social consciousness as much through his medical commitment to the villagers as through rejecting his city-bred fiancee to marry a rural woman.

SANGHARSH

1968 ?' col Hindi
d/co-sc **H.S. Rawail** *pc* Rahul Theatres *st* Mahashweta Devi's story *co-sc* Anjana Rawail *dial* **Gulzar**, Abrar Alvi *lyr* Shakeel Badaiyuni *c* R.D. Mathur *m* **Naushad**
lp **Dilip Kumar**, **Vyjayanthimala**, **Balraj Sahni**, Sanjeev Kumar, Jayant, **Durga Khote**, Sulochana, Sundar, Iftikhar, Sapru, Mumtaz Begum, Padma, Urmila, Mehmood Jr., Master Arun, Kamaldeep, Jagdish Raj, Master Levy, Ram Mohan

Big melodrama set in the 19th C. Thuggee, a cult of bandits in Central India. Bhawani Prasad (Jayant), a legendary bandit whose own relatives have threatened to destroy him, adopts his grandson Kundan against the wishes of his wife (Khote) in order to initiate him into the ancestral profession. The boy, however, grows up (D. Kumar) into a pacificist. When his cousins (Sahni, Sanjeev Kumar) try to kill him, he is saved by a mysterious dancer (Vyjayanthimala). The original story was by noted Marxist novelist Mahashweta Devi.

SARASWATICHANDRA

1968 156' b&w Hindi
d **Govind Saraiya** *pc* Sarvodaya Pics *st* Govardhanram Tripathi's novel *sc* Vrajendra Gaur *dial* Ali Raza *lyr* Indivar *c* Nariman Irani *m* **Kalyanji-Anandji**
lp **Nutan**, Manish, Vijaya Choudhury, Sulochana, Sulochana Chatterjee, Ramesh Dev, Seema, B.M. Vyas, Surendra, Babu Raje, Jeevan Kala, Madhumati

Set in the 19th C. and adapting the most important reform novel in Gujarati (1887-1901). The rich Saraswatichandra (Manish) is to marry Kumud (Nutan), daughter of a neighbouring dewan. Initially committed to nationalism and reluctant to marry, he changes his mind when he falls in love with his fiancee. However, a jealous sister-in-law forces him to leave his ancestral residence, and Kumud is forced into marrying a drunk and a debauchee (Dev). She tries to commit suicide but is rescued by the nuns in a reformist charitable mission. Here she once again meets her former betrothed. Following the death of her degenerate husband, she is free to remarry, and is indeed encouraged by her family to do so, but instead she dedicates her life to charitable work. The 19th C. novelist Tripathi had been personally opposed to widow remarriage, contradicting his otherwise progressive reformism (cf Sudhir Chandra, 1992). Extraordinarily, a century later, the film endorses this attitude with a variety of melodramatic effects, making a contemporary love story with silhouetted split-lighting and a sentimental soundtrack even though the story is periodised by a commentary and 'period' decor. One of Nutan's typical performances of reformist romance fiction, the film is known for some major song hits including *Phool tumhe bheja hai khat mein*, *Chandan sa badan* and *Main to bhool chali babul ka des*.

THILLANA MOHANAMBAL

aka *Dancer Mohanambal*
1968 175' col Tamil
d **A.P. Nagarajan** *pc* Shri Vijayalakshmi Pics *s* Kothamangalam Subbu *c* K.S. Prasad *lyr* **Kannadasan** *m* K.V. Mahadevan
lp **Sivaji Ganesan**, T.S. Baliah, **Padmini**, Manorama, A.V.M. Rajan, M.N. Nambiar

Set in the Kaveri delta in TN, the nursery of many dance and music traditions, the plot features a musical contest and love story between dancer Mohanambal (Padmini) and the nadaswaram (clarinet-like instrument) player Sikkal Shanmughasundaram (Ganesan). The love story, overcoming many hurdles presented mainly by the dancer's mother and her rich suitor Nagalingam, reaches a happy ending and the couple bids farewell to the audience from the wedding dais when 'tradition', so crucial to Nagarajan's revivalism, has been valorised. Although the film claimed to represent 'classical' art, using noted nadaswaram players Sethuraman and Ponnuswamy dubbing the hero's performances,

Nutan and Manish in *Saraswatichandra*

and Padmini in probably her most elaborate Bharat Natyam film performance, its aesthetics are borrowed mainly from the commercial theatre with a mise en scene using mostly frontal shots, even lining up the characters to deliver their lines facing the camera. Nagarajan, a former **TKS Brothers** employee, pays tribute to Sankaradas Swamigal (a major theatrical figure from whom the TKS group traced its ancestry) by naming a drama company after him and providing cameo roles for many old stage actors (Baliah, K. Sarangapani, **Chittor V. Nagaiah**, M.N. Nambiar, S.V. Sahasranamam, E.R. Sahadevan, P.T. Sambandham, K.A. Thangavelu and A. Karunanidhi). References to the courtesan tradition, horse-drawn carriages and palaces suggest a 19th C. setting, but contemporary images of Madurai and Thanjavur railway junctions belie this. Similarly, actual locations are mixed in with a fictional town, Madanpur, ruled by an achkan-clad king with a Western wife, turning the entire film into a fantasy scene.

THIRICHADI

1968 145' b&w Malayalam
d/p **Kunchako** *pc* Excel Prod. *st* **Kanam E.J.** *sc* **S.L. Puram Sadanandan** *lyr* **Vyalar Rama Varma** *c* Dattu *m* Sudarshanam
lp **Prem Nazir**, Govindankutty, **Kottarakkara Sridharan Nair**, **Adoor Bhasi**, S.P. Pillai, Bahadur, Manavalan Joseph, Kaduvakkulam, Sheela, Pankajavalli, Adoor Pankajam, Kanchana, Devaki

The vagabond and petty thief Kuttappan (Nazir) goes to the city to discover and settle scores with his unknown father. The father had abandoned his pregnant wife and moved in with another woman. Kuttappan finds the father, and also a look-alike stepbrother, the policeman Venu (Nazir again). His way of taking revenge is to impersonate the cop and commit crimes. He also kidnaps Venu's fiancee. Major Nazir double role, and typical 60s Kanam script for the Excel Studio.

THULABHARAM

1968 152' b&w Malayalam
d **A. Vincent** *p* Hari Pothain *pc* Supriya Pics *s* **Thoppil Bhasi** *lyr* **Vyalar Rama Varma** *c* Bhaskar Rao *m* **P. Devarajan**
lp **Prem Nazir, Madhu, Thikkurisi Sukumaran Nair, Adoor Bhasi**, Nellikode Bhaskaran, Paravoor Bharathan, Thoppil Bhasi, Sheela, **Sharada**, Adoor Bhawani

Vincent's political melodrama, based on Bhasi's play staged by the KPAC, tells of two friends, Vijaya (Sharada) and Vatsala (Sheela), who part ways when Vatsala's father, a lawyer, causes Vijaya's father, a businessman, to lose a case which leads to the man's death. Vijaya is forced to marry the trade unionist Ramu (Nazir) who leads a strike but dies when the strike turns violent. The suffering Vijaya kills her three starving children and is arrested before she can commit suicide. She is sent to the gallows by her former friend Vatsala, now a noted lawyer. The film is the best known of the Vincent/Bhasi collaborations (cf ***Ashwamedham***, 1967). It was remade with great success by Madhusudhana Rao in Telugu (*Manushulu Marali*, 1969) and in Hindi (***Samaj Ko Badal Dalo***, 1970). All three films featured Sharada, and collectively they represent her best-known screen image.

VARAKATNAM

1968 176' b&w Telugu
d/s **N.T. Rama Rao** *pc* Ramakrishna/NAT Combines *dial* Maddipatla Suri, Samudrala Ramanujacharya *lyr* **Kosaraju**, C. Narayana Reddy *c* Ravikant Nagaich *m* **T.V. Raju**
lp N.T. Rama Rao, Krishnakumari, Nagabhushanam, Hemalatha, **Savitri**, Satyanarayana, Chandrakala, Suryakantam, **Relangi Venkatramaiah**, Padmanabham, Ravikondala Rao

Anti-dowry melodrama in which Meesala Venkaiah (Nagabhushanam), who wants his son Devasimha (NTR) to marry in a manner befitting the father's social status, demands a dowry of Rs 50,000. The marriage is stopped just before the ceremony is completed. Eventually the groom marries the bride, after overcoming the oppressive attitudes of his family. The film includes a parallel narrative of another groom who, in a situation similar to the hero's, marries the bride anyway, which leads to the woman being exploited by her husband's family in various ways.

ADIMAGAL

aka *Slaves*
1969 145' b&w Malayalam
d **K.S. Sethumadhavan** *p* M.O. Joseph *pc* Manjilas Cine Ents *s* **Thoppil Bhasi** from M.K. Menon's novel *lyr* **Vyalar Rama Varma** *c* Mehli Irani *m* **P. Devarajan**
lp **Sathyan, Prem Nazir**, Sheela, **Sharada**, Adoor Bhawani, **Adoor Bhasi**, Shankaradi, Bahadur, Jaycee, N. Govindankutty, Bharathan, Ammini, Kuttan Pillai, **Padmini**, Kumudam

Ponnamma (Sharada), the beautiful servant of the devout Saraswathi Amma, is seduced and made pregnant by Saraswathi's brother Anandan, an office worker. Ponnamma is thrown out of Saraswathi's house, but finds shelter with a progressive-minded neighbour, Appukuttan (Sathyan), who brings the absconded Anandan back and forces him to offer to marry Ponnamma. She refuses and prefers to marry the deaf-mute odd job man Raghavan (Nazir) who has loved her all along. Saraswathi finally realises that her religious gullibility caused much suffering, and she discards her saffron robes in favour of a new life (to be reached by train) with the tolerant Appukuttan. The film is adapted from a novel by Pammen aka M.K. Menon.

APARICHITA

1969 ?' b&w Bengali
d/sc Salil Dutta *pc* R.D. Prod. *st* Samaresh Bose *lyr* Pranab Roy *c* Bijoy Ghosh *m* Robin Chatterjee
lp **Uttam Kumar, Soumitra Chatterjee, Aparna Sen**, Sandhya Roy, Bikash Roy, **Utpal Dutt**, Haradhan Bannerjee, Dilip Roy

Bizarre and spectacular psychodrama based on Samaresh Bose's novel with overtones of Dostoevsky's *The Idiot*. Sunita (Sen), forced into prostitution by her 'respectable' politician-employer Priyanath, is abducted by the gangster Ranjan (Kumar) from a nightclub. She travels with Ranjan as though in a dream, and when she is rescued meets a similarly disoriented and unbelievably naive Sujit (Chatterjee) who has just recovered from a mental breakdown. When Sunita's marriage is arranged, mainly to avoid scandal, she tries to elope with Sujit but Ranjan prevents it. Eventually, Ranjan, unable to subdue her, kills Sunita and lands in jail, while Sujit has a second breakdown. The film is known mainly for Chatterjee's remarkable performance.

ARADHANA

1969 169' col Hindi
d/p **Shakti Samanta** *pc* Shakti Films *s* Sachin Bhowmick *dial* Ramesh Pant *lyr* **Anand Bakshi** *c* Ashoke Dasgupta *m* **S.D. Burman**
lp **Rajesh Khanna, Sharmila Tagore**, Sujit Kumar, **Pahadi Sanyal**, Anita Dutt, **Abhi Bhattacharya**, Madan Puri, Asit Sen, **Subhash Ghai**, Farida Jalal

The musical romance about non-family-sanctioned sex that established Khanna as a major star backed by the singing voice of **Kishore Kumar** and Burman's music. The film helped set the pattern for 70s entertainment cinema. Arun (Khanna), an Air Force officer, secretly marries Vandana (Tagore) who bears him a son. Arun dies in an air crash. Vandana is rejected by Arun's family as his legal wife. To safeguard her son's honour, she decides to let him be adopted by a childless couple while making sure she is responsible for raising the child by becoming his nanny. She devotes the rest of her life to raising her son to become an air force pilot like his father. Khanna plays both father and son. Remembered mainly for its music with, e.g., *Mere sapnon ki rani* and *Kora Kaagaz*. The film's best-known song, *Roop tera mastana* (sung by Kishore Kumar), was picturised in a single 4' take deploying the conventional cloudburst as a metaphor for sex as the drenched heroine, clad only in a blanket, succumbs to the hero's advances after a sexual encounter in the next room has been shown in silhouette. This sequence was for years presented to students of Indian film schools as the definitive example of mise en scene.

ARANYER DIN RATRI

aka *Days and Nights in the Forest*
1969 115' b&w Bengali
d/sc/m **Satyajit Ray** *p* Nepal Dutta, Ashim Dutta *pc* Priya Films *st* Sunil Ganguly's novel *c* Soumendu Roy, Purnendu Bose
lp **Soumitra Chatterjee**, Subhendu Chatterjee, Samit Bhanja, **Robi Ghosh**, **Pahadi Sanyal**, **Sharmila Tagore**, Kaberi Bose, Simi Garewal, **Aparna Sen**

Four young male Bengali urban stereotypes leave Calcutta for a holiday in the forest of Palamau, Bihar: the suave executive and former political activist Ashim (Soumitra Chatterjee), the middle-class Sanjoy (Subhendu Chatterjee), the sportsman Hari (Bhanja) and the insecure comedian Sekhar (Ghosh). They bribe a caretaker and hire a government bungalow in the forest where they meet the sophisticated Aparna (Tagore) and her widowed sister-in-law, Jaya (Bose). Completing the ensemble is the sexy Santhal tribal Duli (Garewal). The film moves in a series of episodes as Ashim falls for Aparna and then has some embarassing encounters which shake his patriarchal attitudes. The climactic sequence takes place at a village fair as the group splits up into couples: Hari seduces the tribal woman, Sanjoy is unable to accept Jaya's overtures, Aparna's tragic autobiography causes Ashim to replay some of the anxieties of his predecessors in previous Chatterjee roles in Ray's films (cf ***Charulata***, 1964; ***Kapurush***, 1965). The many references to Bengali literature, colonial history and recent political events provide the viewer with an array of clues to some pervasive but unspoken off-screen enigma which has taken the place of the 'crime' which usually powers this type of plot. This use of a suggested trauma, indirectly shaping the lives of the characters as they try not to deal with it, was taken up by other Bengali New Indian Cinema directors (cf **B. Dasgupta**'s work) to deal with middle-class ambivalence and guilt in the face of the political events of the 70s (cf **Naxalite**). It also informed Ray's own Calcutta trilogy, begun shortly after this film.

BANDHAN

1969 159' col Hindi
d/s **Narendra Bedi** *pc* Sippy Films *dial* **Rajinder Singh Bedi** *lyr* Anjaan, Indivar *c* K. Vaikunth *m* **Kalyanji-Anandji**
lp **Rajesh Khanna**, Mumtaz, Anju Mahendroo, Jeevan, Kanhaiyalal, Achala Sachdev, Aruna Irani, Sundar, Ratnamala, Sapru, Kamal Kapoor, Meena, Birbal, Rajindernath, Keshav Rana, Roopesh Kumar, Narbada Shankar, Baldev Mehta

Ruralist melodrama featuring Khanna as Dharma who grows up haunted by a thieving, alcoholic, wife-beating father, Jeevanlal (Jeevan), who even steals his own daughter's jewels on her wedding day. Dharma manages a meagre living tilling his land until his father assigns it to the wicked moneylender Malik Ram (Kanhaiyalal), whose daughter Gauri (Mumtaz) is Dharma's beloved. Malik Ram takes over Dharma's field, and when his father is killed Dharma is arrested for the murder until the truth emerges. The film continued the ***Do Raaste*** (1969) star combination of Khanna and Mumtaz, with several musical hits including *Bina badara ke bijuriya kaise chamke* (sung by Mukesh).

BHUVAN SHOME

1969 111'(96') b&w Hindi
d/p/sc **Mrinal Sen** *pc* Mrinal Sen Prod. *st* Banaphool *dial* Satyendra Sharat, Badrinath *c* K.K. Mahajan *m* Vijay Raghava Rao
lp Suhasini Mulay, **Utpal Dutt**, Sadhu Meher, Shekhar Chatterjee, Rochak Pandit, Punya Das; voice over by **Amitabh Bachchan**

Sen's breakthrough film, a low-budget, **FFC**-sponsored hit, is sometimes seen as the origin of New Indian Cinema. The story, set in the late 40s just after Independence, was sarcastically summarised by **Satyajit Ray** as 'Big Bad Bureaucrat Reformed by Rustic Belle'. It is a satirical comedy about the upright Bengali railway officer Bhuvan Shome (Dutt). He sacks a corrupt ticket collector (Meher) before going off on a duck-shooting expedition in Gujarat. There, in the dunes of Saurashtra, he meets the village belle Gauri (Mulay) who turns out to be the wife of the man he sacked. He has a long, and unstated, sexual/cultural encounter with her, enjoying the attention she lavishes upon him even as he remains anxious about his sudden loss of authority. He returns determined to enjoy life to the full. Sen described his first Hindi feature as Tati-inspired nonsense and suggested that the ending, with the 'humanised' bureaucrat boisterously disrupting the office routine, is difficult to grasp 'unless you grant Mr Shome a certain touch of insanity. As you examine the sequence, you will see that the same can be said about the editing pattern, all erratic and illogical.' Mulay went on to become a noted maker of radical documentaries while occasionally acting in independent films.

BUDDHIMANTHUDU

1969 187' b&w Telugu
d **Bapu** *pc* Chitrakalpana Films *s* Mullapudi Venkatramana *lyr* **Arudra, Kosaraju**, Dasarathi, C. Narayana Reddy *c* Venkatarathnam *m* K.V. Mahadevan
lp **A. Nageshwara Rao**, Nagabhushanam, Krishnamraju, Sakshi Rangarao, **Vijayanirmala**, Sandhyarani, Suryakantam, Shantakumari, **Shobhan Babu, Gummadi Venkateshwara Rao**

Bapu's rationalist critique of religion. Madhavacharya (Nageshwara Rao), a temple priest, goes into mystic trances when he encounters the god Krishna. Consequently, he is both believed to have magic powers and ridiculed for his mystic mumbo-jumbo. His brother (Nageshwara Rao again, in a double role), a rationalist, argues that it is not temples but schools that will lead to progress. There is also a love story subplot between the rationalist brother and the virtuous village belle (Vijayanirmala).

DO RAASTE

1969 165' col Hindi
d/p **Raj Khosla** *pc* Raj Khosla Films *st* Chandrakant Kakodkar's novel *Nilambiri sc* G. R. Kamath *lyr* **Anand Bakshi** *m* **Laxmikant-Pyarelal**
lp **Rajesh Khanna**, Mumtaz, **Balraj Sahni**, Prem Chopra, Bindu, Kamini Kaushal, Veena, Mohan Choti, Asit Sen, Randhir, Birbal, Leela Mishra, Shivraj, Shah Agha, Uma Dutt, Ravikant, Anand Tiwari, Kumud Bole, Jayant, **Krishnakant**

Along with ***Aradhana*** (1969), this film, released within weeks of the former title, established Khanna as a major star. Navendu's (Sahni) stepmother (Veena) treats him like her own son. When his father dies, Navendu has the responsibility of looking after his stepmother and stepbrothers (Khanna and Chopra) which leads to conflict when one of them (Chopra) decides to marry a shrewish 'modern' girl (Bindu). Most of the film is a Khanna-Mumtaz romance culminating in the famous *Bindiya chamkegi* song sung by **Lata Mangeshkar**.

ITTEFAQ

1969 104' col Hindi
d **Yash Chopra** *pc* B.R. Films *st* B.R. Films Story Dept *dial* **Akhtar-Ul-Iman** *c* Kay Gee *m* **Salil Choudhury**
lp **Rajesh Khanna**, Nanda, Sujit Kumar, Bindu, **Gajanan Jagirdar**, Madan Puri, Iftikhar, Shammi, Jagdish Raj, Alka

Low-budget, songless suspense drama in which the hero Dilip Roy (Khanna), accused of having murdered his wife and pronounced mentally insane, escapes from an asylum and finds refuge in the house of a young but married woman. He sees the corpse of her husband in the bathroom, but it disappears. Shot mainly on sets, the taut editing keeps the whodunit plot enigmatic until the ending resolves the suspense. It is one of Khanna's pre-***Aradhana*** (1969) hits. Apparently, he appeared unshaven in Raj Khosla's ***Do Raaste*** (1969) because he had to be unshaven for *Ittefaq* and was shooting the two films simultaneously.

JANMABHOOMI

aka *Motherland*
1969 130' b&w Malayalam
d/s John Shankaramangalam *pc* Rooparekha *lyr* **P. Bhaskaran** *c* Ashok Kumar *m* B.A. Chidambaranath
lp **Kottarakkara Sridharan Nair**, S.P. Pillai, **Madhu**, Manavalan Joseph, Janardhanan, T.R. Ramchand, Ushakumari, Shobha, T.R. Omana, Snehalatha, L.V. Sharada Rao, Baby Saroja

A melodrama about acculturation as a poor family of Christian Syrians from Central Travancore resettle on a jungle farm in the wilds of Wynad in North Malabar. After succumbing to social pressures (incarnated by the local zamindar) and to natural ones (some of the family's children are drowned in a local river, others are trampled by a rogue elephant), the family's heroic son, Johnny, finally overcomes the rogue elephant and returns in triumph to the village where henceforth he will assume his rightful position in the community.

KANKU

1969 148'(99') b&w Gujarati
d/p/sc **Kantilal Rathod** *pc* Akar Films *st* Pannalal Patel *c* Kumar Jaywant *m* Dilip Dholakia
lp Pallavi Mehta, Kishore Jariwala, Kishore Bhatt, Arvind Joshi

Reformist Gujarati tale introducing New Indian Cinema to the language. Kanku (Mehta) is a village maiden widowed while she is still pregnant. The rather static and verbose film tells of her relationship with a local grocer, Malakchand (Bhatt). Refusing to remarry, she devotes her life to her son and arranges his marriage with the grocer's help. Afterwards, she and the grocer make love, which would normally have led to their ostracism, but Kanku struggles to retain her honour.

KAVAL DAIVAM

aka *The Guardian Deity*
1969 145' b&w Tamil
d K. Vijayan *pc* Ambal Prod. *sc* Jayakanthan's *Kai Vilangu* [*Handcuffs*] *c* R. Vijayan *m* S. Devarajan
lp S.V. Subbaiah, **Sivaji Ganesan**, Nagesh, Sivakumar, M.N. Nambiar, Lakshmi, **Sowcar Janaki**

One of the better-known filmic translations of Jayakantan's fiction, the noted Tamil novelist and former CPI member who later joined the Congress and who also had a brief film career as scenarist and producer. Mainly an ode to the humanity of a childless jail warden Raghavan (Subbaiah) who treats the prisoners as his children, equating him with Ayyanar, the guardian deity of Tamil villages. The main plot features the farmer Manikam (Sivakumar), a peasant who wounds his brutal rival and becomes a prisoner. There is a second plot, added especially for the film, with a toddy-tapper (Ganesan) who killed the two men who raped his daughter. He is caught and hanged. The film's highlight was the inclusion of several of Tamil Nadu's best-known folk forms, the therukoothu (including its famous exponent Purisai Natesathambiran performing *The Destruction of Hiranyan*), the karagam dance and the villupattu. The film has only two songs and emphasises village life and rural forms of worship, unusual in Tamil cinema.

KHAMOSHI

1969 127' b&w Hindi
d **Asit Sen** *pc* Geetanjali Pics *st* Ashutosh Mukherjee *dial/lyr* **Gulzar** *c* Kamal Bose *m* **Hemanta Mukherjee**
lp **Rajesh Khanna, Waheeda Rehman, Dharmendra**, Nasir Hussain, **Lalita Pawar**, Snehalata, Iftikhar

The first of Sen's tragic melodramas with Hindi star Khanna (followed by *Safar*, 1970). The nurse Radha (Rehman) has to pretend to fall in love with her male patients, as part of the therapy in a mental asylum. The first time she does this, she actually falls in love, and is devastated when her cured patient (Dharmendra) merely thanks her and leaves to marry his fiancee. When it threatens to happen once again, with a few variations, with her second patient (Khanna), the nurse goes insane. Hindi remake of Sen's classic ***Deep Jweley Jai*** (1959), rescued like its predecessor mainly by soft-focus b&w photography and classic songs like composer Mukherjee's *Tum pukar lo, tumhara intezar hai* and *Woh shyam kuch ajeeb thi* (sung by **Kishore Kumar**).

MATTUKKARA VELAN

1969 173' col Tamil
d **P. Neelakantan** *pc* Jayanthi Films *s* A.L. Narayanan *c* Ramamurthy
lp **M.G. Ramachandran, Jayalalitha**, Lakshmi, **S. Varalakshmi**

Classic MGR double role where he plays the title role of the cowherd Velan and the urbane lawyer Raghu. Their lovers (Jayalalitha and Lakshmi respectively) mistake the men for each other, providing the cowherd with an opportunity to help locate a murderer in a case that has baffled the lawyer, and also to claim the rich heiress whose father had earlier thrown him out of his house. The MGR political formula, which M.S.S. Pandian (1992) describes as 'the hero's use of literacy as a weapon of struggle against oppression [c]ontrasted with its use as a weapon of oppression in the hands of the elite' (cf *Padakottai*, 1964; *Enga Veetu Pillai*, 1965) is most typically demonstrated in this film. It was remade as cinematographer turned director Ravikant Nagaich's *Jigri Dost* (1969) starring **Jeetendra**.

MEGH-O-ROURDA

aka *Sun and Showers*
1969 116' b&w Bengali
d/sc/m **Arundhati Devi** *p* Ajitesh Bandyopadhyay *pc* K.L. Kapur Prod. *st* **Rabindranath Tagore** *c* Bimal Mukherjee
lp Nripati Chatterjee, Hashu Bannerjee, Prahlad Brahmachari, Prasad Mukherjee, Swaroop Datta, Gautam Ghosh, Sushil Chakravarty, Bankim Ghosh, Monojit Lahiri, Bhabharup Bhattacharya, Balai Sen, Satu Majumdar, Samar Nag

Following **Tapan Sinha**'s example, in whose Tagore adaptation ***Kshudista Pashan*** (1960) she acted, Arundhati Devi aka Mukherjee embarked on her directing career with a Tagore-style story, ***Chhuti*** (1967). *Megh-o-Roudra* is her 2nd feature and tells of a strong young woman in British-ruled 19th C. Bengal. Struggling to affirm her human dignity in her village, she learns to read and write under the tutorship of a stubborn and impetuous law student who constantly challenges the British colonists and is eventually jailed. By the time he is released, the woman has become a prosperous widow. When they meet, she bows courteously to pay homage to the bedraggled man who helped her achieve self-confidence.

NADHI

1969 133' col Malayalam
d **A Vincent** *pc* Supriya Prod. *st* **P.J. Anthony** *sc* **Thoppil Bhasi** *lyr* **Vyalar Rama Varma** *c* P.N. Sundaram, A. Venkat *m* **P. Devarajan**
lp **Prem Nazir, Madhu, Thikkurisi Sukumaran Nair, P.J. Anthony, Adoor Bhasi**, Shankaradi, Nellikode Bhaskaran, **Sharada**, Ambika, Kaviyoor Ponnamma, Adoor Bhawani

Vincent's colour debut also represented a more dramatic style of plotting than his **Thoppil Bhasi** and **Vasudevan Nair** b&w scripts. The families of Varkey and Thomman rekindle their ancient feud when they happen to hire adjacent boathouses on the Alwaye lake. However, Varkey's daughter Stella (Sharada) falls in love with Thomman's son Johnny (Nazir). The dramatic highlight, when the infant daughter of Stella's sister falls and is drowned, also leads to the reconciliation. Several songs were major hits.

NAM NAADU

1969 186' col Tamil
d Jambulingam *pc* Vijaya International *st* M. Venkatramana *dial* Swarnam *lyr* **Vali** *c* B.N. Konda Reddy *m* M.S. Vishwanathan
lp **M.G. Ramachandran, Jayalalitha, S.V. Ranga Rao**, K.A. Thangavelu, S.A. Ashokan, Nagesh, Bhagavati, S.V. Ramadas, Manohar, **Thanjai Ramaiyadas, Pandharibai**, Baby Padmini

MGR, who would soon be expelled from the DMK, here turned the DMK propaganda discourse against the Party. The philanthropists and pillars of society, a doctor, a builder and a merchant, led by the rich Dharmalingam, are in fact villains dealing in

Megh-o-Roudra

crime and the black market. They are exposed when the nationalist Dorai (MGR) masquerades as a foreign-returned millionaire dealing in contraband. He gets the villains to confess to their deeds before a hidden camera. The film was remade in Hindi with **Rajesh Khanna** as *Apna Desh* (1972).

NANAK NAAM JAHAZ HAI

1969 140' col Punjabi
d/s Ram Maheshwari *p* Pannalal Maheshwari *c* D.K. Prabhakar *m* S. Mahindra
lp **Prithviraj Kapoor**, Vimi, Nishi, Som Dutt, Suresh, Veena, I.S. Johar

Epic fable with a major cultural impact on Punjabi Sikhs at home and abroad. It is also the last of the great **Saint films**, although not a biographical of Guru Nanak but a devotional movie addressing his teachings. Made for the 500th anniversary of the saint's birth and apparently inspired by legends around the Golden Temple in Amritsar, the film tells of Gurmukh Singh (Kapoor) and his equally devout son Gurmeet (Dutt). Gurmukh treats his partner Prem Singh as a younger brother until a business dispute ends their relationship. Prem Singh's wife Ratan Kaur (Nishi), influenced by the villain Shukha, wants the son Gurmeet to marry her niece Channi (Vimi); however, in an argument she accidentally blinds him. The blind Gurmeet, a repentant Ratan Kaur and Gurmeet's fiancee Channi (dressed as a man) set out on a pilgrimage of atonement to all the Sikh shrines. The troubled relationship and unconsummated marriage between Gurmeet and Channi is eventually resolved at the Golden Temple where, in answer to Channi's prayers, a miracle causes Gurmeet's eyesight to return while destroying that of the original villain Shukha. The classic musical, extensively quoting from the basic Sikh text, the *Granth Sahib*, is the first big hit in post-Independence Punjabi cinema, badly hit by Partition and the loss of its Lahore base as well as by the Pakistan government's decision (1953) to ban the import of Indian films. Much of its devotional fervour comes from the region's troubled political history (references include a documentary opening showing the festival celebrating Nanak's anniversary in the presence of Abdul Gaffar Khan and the Dalai Lama).

NATUN PATA

aka *The New Leaf*
1969 121' b&w Bengali
d/c **Dinen Gupta** *pc* Gora Pics *st* Prativa Bose *sc* Ajitesh Bannerjee *m* Bahadur Khan
lp Arati Ganguly, Kajal Gupta, Ajitesh Bannerjee, Samit Bhanja, Indranath Chatterjee, **Sombhu Mitra**, Sipra Mitra, Geeta Dey, **Jahar Roy**, Chinmoy Roy, Sikha Roy Choudhury

Lyrical ruralist melodrama building on, e.g., **Satyajit Ray**'s *Samapti* episode of ***Teen Kanya*** (1961) to tell the story of a mischievous 14-year-old young girl, Savitri, and how she is 'tamed' into marriage and conventional behaviour. Forced by her guardian-aunt to marry the son of the stationmaster, she runs away from her marital home but finds herself unwelcome everywhere. Her husband eventually rescues her just before she tries to commit suicide on a railway line (the railway track is used as a recurring symbol through the film). Disturbingly, the film presents this socially sanctioned form of child abuse as a painful but ultimately positive experience as the girl 'grows up' to be a woman who accepts her domestic and marital duties. Noted cinematographer Gupta's debut as director.

NINDU HRIDAYALU

1969 188' b&w Telugu
d/co-lyr **K. Vishwanath** *pc* S.V.S. Films *st* Nagercoil Padmanabham *sc/co-lyr* Samudrala Jr *dial* **Devulapalli Krishna Sastry** *co-lyr* C. Narayana Reddy *c* S.S. Lall *m* **T.V. Raju**
lp **N.T. Rama Rao**, **Shobhan Babu**, Gudipati Venkatachalam (aka Chalam), Satyanarayana, **Vanisree**, Geetanjali, **Relangi Venkatramaiah**, Chhaya Devi, **G. Varalakshmi**

Gopi, when a child, witnesses his father's murder at the hands of Veeraju and vows to take revenge. However, when he grows up, circumstances make it necessary for him to extend his protection to Veeraju's wife and son, and he also falls in love with Veeraju's daughter Sharada. The hit film is Vishwanath's breakthrough work.

OLAVUM THEERAVUM

aka *Waves and Shore*
1969 120' b&w Malayalam
d **P.N. Menon** *p* **P.A. Backer** *pc* Asha Films, Charuchitra *s* **M.T. Vasudevan Nair** *lyr* **P. Bhaskaran** *c* Ravi Varma *m* **Baburaj**
lp **Madhu**, Jose Prakash, Nellikode Bhaskaran, Usha Nandini, Paravoor Bharathan, Kunjava, Philomina, Mala, Nilambur Aisha, Nilambur Balan

Independently produced by future director Backer, Menon's debut is often considered the first film to have introduced an art-house New Indian Cinema aesthetic to Kerala. Noted mainly for Nair's classic script and unusual dialogue style evoking local accents, as well as for its extensive use of outdoor locations. The Muslim trader Bapputti (Madhu) loves Nabisa (Usha Nandini), and tries to earn money that would enable them to live in comfort after marriage. However, when the rich stranger Kunjali arrives, Nabisa's money grabbing mother forces her to marry him. The film ends with Nabisa's dramatic suicide when Bapputti, rejected by her family, leaves only to find her swollen corpse washed ashore. The 'tragic' realism in this art-house movie and commercial hit was later to prove definitive to a whole generation of Malayalam directors including Backer himself, **K.G. George** (cf ***Kolangal***, 1980), scenarist Vasudevan Nair's own directions or the work of, e.g., **Padmarajan**.

SAAT HINDUSTANI

1969 144' b&w Hindi
d/p/s **K.A. Abbas** *pc* Naya Sansar *st* Madhukar *lyr* **Kaifi Azmi** *c* Ramchandra *m* J.P. Kaushik
lp Shahnaz, **Madhu**, **Utpal Dutt**, Madhukar, Anwar Ali, **Amitabh Bachchan**, Jalal Agha, Surekha, Sukhdeo, Prakash Thapa, Irshad Panjatan, Dina Pathak, Surekha, A.K. Hangal, Anjali

Remembered as one of Bachchan's first feature films, this is a non-violent variation of the *Dirty Dozen* (1967) with moralistic comments about contemporary India. Six men from different parts of the country join Maria (Shahnaz), a native of Portuguese-occupied Goa, to raise nationalist sentiment in that state by hoisting Indian flags on Portuguese forts and buildings. In the process they find unity and abandon their religious and regional differences. The film begins with a dying Maria who summons her former comrades and ends with the comrades assembling before her and reiterating their faith in nationalism. The film was released together with the controversial short ***Char Shaher Ek Kahani*** (1968). Apart from Bachchan, it was also the first Hindi film by Malayalam star Madhu, who played the Bengali commando.

SARA AKASH

aka *The Big Sky* aka *The Whole Sky*
1969 99'(96') b&w Hindi
d/sc **Basu Chatterjee** *pc* Cine Eye Films *st* Ravindra Yadav *c* K.K. Mahajan *m* **Salil Choudhury**
lp Rakesh Pandey, Madhu Chakravarty, Tarala Mehta, Dina Pathak, A.K. Hangal, **Mani Kaul**, Jalal Agha, Nandita Thakur

A realist critique of arranged marriages and patriarchy set in North India. The film chronicles the relationship of Samar (Pandey), whose parents (Pathak and Hangal) coveted the dowry his marriage would bring, and his wife Prabha (Chakravarty). Samar shuns his wife because he is afraid her presence might hinder his educational ambitions. She thus has to accept being confined largely to the joint family's kitchen or to return to her parental home for long visits. She commits the *faux pas* of washing the vessels with the clay symbolising a deity designed for use only during the religious ceremony of her sister-in-law's (Thakur) newborn child. Together with **Sen**'s ***Bhuvan Shome*** and Kaul's ***Uski Roti***, made in the same year, this film set the pattern for what the media described as New Indian Cinema. All three films were shot by cinematographer K.K. Mahajan who had just graduated from the **FTII** and who received his first national award for *Sara Akash*.

SATYAKAM

1969 160' col Hindi
d **Hrishikesh Mukherjee** *pc* Panchi Art *sc* Bimal Datta *st* Narayan Sanyal's novel *dial* **Rajinder Singh Bedi** *lyr* **Kaifi Azmi** *c* Jaywant Pathare *m* **Laxmikant-Pyarelal**
lp **Ashok Kumar**, **Dharmendra**, **Sharmila Tagore**, **Robi Ghosh**, David, Sanjeev Kumar, Tarun Bose, Sapru, Rajan Haksar, Baby Sarika, Manmohan, Uma Dutt, Dina Pathak, Paul Mahendra, Kanu Roy, O.P. Kohli, Anand Mama, Abhimanyu Sharma

Nationalist melodrama using the metaphor of illegitimacy. When Satyapriya is born his mother dies (cf Mukherjee's ***Anupama***, 1966). His father turns into a sanyasi (ascetic) and he is raised with strong nationalist feelings by his grandfather, a Sanskrit scholar. He grows up (Dharmendra) to become an engineer at the time of India's independence. Employed by a princely state, he discovers that few of his nationalist-utopian dreams have been realised. The critique of the state of the nation is illustrated by the unfortunate Ranjana (Tagore) who has been raped by the prince and is pregnant. Satyapriya marries her and she gives birth to the child. The rest of the film concerns the aged grandfather's refusal to accept a child born of sin and refers to a mythological tale from the *Upanishads*: Gautam accepted Jabala's son, Satyakam, under similar circumstances.

TEEN BHUBHANER PAREY

1969 151' b&w Bengali
d/sc Ajitesh Bannerjee *pc* Satirtha Prod. *st* Samaresh Bose *co-lyr* Pulak Bannerjee *co-lyr/m* Sudhin Dasgupta *c* Ramanand Sengupta
lp **Soumitra Chatterjee**, Tanuja, **Kamal Mitra**, Tarun Kumar, Sulata Choudhury, Subrata Chatterjee, Padmadevi, Aparna Devi, **Robi Ghosh**, Sumita Sanyal

Factory clerk Subir, aka Montu (Soumitra Chatterjee) falls in love with schoolteacher Sarasi (Tanuja), transgressing the class barrier between them. She marries him, partly intending to 'improve' him through education. Her disapproval of his working-class friends causes problems for the marriage, but the real crisis occurs when the tables are turned. Once educated, Subir becomes a bespectacled and grey-haired professor, and also an opportunist who plans to take up a lucrative post in a new city. Event ıally his arguments for conformism, merging with the greyness of his urban environment, become increasingly unreal (underlined by make-up and acting style). Soumitra Chatterjee's classic performance is supported by Sengupta's intricate camerawork as Subir moves through different spaces on his socially upward journey. Samaresh Bose's scathingly critical novel is softened into a typically reformist presentation of education as the solution to all social ills.

USKI ROTI

aka *A Day's Bread* aka *Our Daily Bread*
1969 110'(95') b&w Hindi
d/sc **Mani Kaul** *p* Rochak Pandit *st* Mohan Rakesh's short story *c* K.K. Mahajan
lp Gurdeep Singh, Garima, Richa Vyas, Lakhanapal, Savita Bajaj

Kaul's debut is an adaptation of a short story by the noted Hindi author Mohan Rakesh and is perhaps the first consistently formal experiment in Indian cinema. The burly bus driver Sucha Singh (G. Singh) travels through the dusty, flat Punjabi countryside. His wife Balo (Garima) spends long hours waiting for him at the bus-stop with his food packet. One day her younger sister is sexually molested, causing Balo to arrive late at the bus-stop. Sucha Singh is upset by her late arrival, rejects her food and drives away. She remains standing at the roadside until nightfall. The original story uses many stereotypes for both its characters and situations. The film, however, integrates the characters into the landscape, evoking an internalised yet distanced kind of realism reminiscent of Robert Bresson, cf the shots from within the bus showing the road and the countryside going by while a little sticker on its window intrudes in the corner of the frame. Kaul wanted to discover 'what was truly cinematic in the filming of a play' (1974) and he used a minimum of gestures to enact the rigidly notated script. The two registers of Balo's physical and mental environment are represented by two camera lenses: the 28mm wide-angle deep-focus lens and the 135mm telephoto lens leaving only a minute section of the frame in focus. This schema was gradually reversed through the film, making it Indian cinema's most controlled achievement in image composition. Its use of spatial volume refers to the large canvases of the modernist painter Amrita Sher-Gil while the soundtrack isolates individual sounds to match the equally fragmented visual details. The film, financed by the **FFC**, was violently attacked in the popular press for dispensing with familiar cinematic norms and equally strongly defended by India's aesthetically sensitive intelligentsia.

UYYALE

aka *The Swing*
1969 163' b&w Kannada
d **N. Lakshminarayan** *pc* Bharat Ents *c* N.G. Rao *m* **Vijayabhaskar**
lp **Rajkumar**, Aswath, **Kalpana**, **Balkrishna**, Rama Devi

Marital melodrama about a professor (Aswath) who, engaged in his researches, neglects his domestic life. His indifference alienates his wife (Kalpana), especially when their daughter dies. The wife becomes attracted to the professor's friend Krishna (Rajkumar) who eventually goes away to preserve the marriage of his friend.

VAA RAJA VAA

1969 152' b&w Tamil
d/s **A.P. Nagarajan** *pc* C.N.V. Prod. *c* W.R. Subba Rao *m* Kannakkudi Vaidyanathan
lp Master Prabhakar, Baby Shanti, V.S. Raghavan, Rukmini

The hero (Prabhakar) is a tourist guide at the Mahabalipuram shrine. His friend and mentor is a sculptor who keeps a pillar in his yard on which there are sayings affirming the truths of past wisdom. The hero tries to see if these bits of wisdom are valid in today's world and finds that they are. Neo-traditionalism Nagarajan style.

ADINA MEGHA

1970 154' b&w Oriya
d/sc Amit Moitra *p* Babulal Doshi *st* Kuntala Kumari Acharya *dial* Gopal Chatray *c* Sailaja Chatterjee *m* Balakrishna Das
lp **Prashanta Nanda, Jharana Das**, Sandhya, Geeta, Bhanumathi, Niranjan, Dukhiram, Sagar, Janaki

Hit Oriya musical melodrama by Bengali director Moitra. University student Suresh (Nanda) loves Champak (Jharana Das), though his brother and sister-in-law would like him to marry Alka. Suresh ends up marrying a third woman, Bina, as an act of chivalry when she is abandoned by her fiance. Champak is heartbroken while Alka marries, becomes a widow almost immediately and ends up educating tribal children. Eventually, she is the one who brings Suresh and Bina together. One of the best-known films by the famous Oriya star duo Nanda and Das, and also known for hit numbers like *Ae bhara janha raati* and *Boulo ki kahibi*.

ANAND

1970 122' col Hindi
d/st/co-sc **Hrishikesh Mukherjee** *pc* Rupam Chitra *co-sc/dial/co-lyr* **Gulzar** *co-sc* D.N. Mukherjee *co-lyr* Yogesh *c* Jaywant Pathare *m* **Salil Choudhury**
lp **Rajesh Khanna**, **Amitabh Bachchan**, Sumita Sanyal, Ramesh Dev, Seema, **Johnny Walker**, **Dara Singh**

The Khanna hit which launched the 70s melodrama formula of endowing the central character with a terminal disease. In this way, a typical emotional highlight of the melodramatic genre, the death of the hero could be spun out across the entire length of the film. Anand (Khanna) zestfully fights intestinal cancer, determined to extract as much pleasure from his remaining lifespan as possible despite the physical pain. The moral of the story is emphasised via the recording of the hero's voice, replayed minutes after his actual death, enjoining the audience to value a large-hearted life over a merely long one. The film retained a commercial repeat value as one of Bachchan's early starring roles. He plays the brooding Dr Bhaskar who tends to Anand in his last days and then writes a book on him which wins a literary prize. The award ceremony provides the framing narrative of Anand's story told in flashback. Choudhury's music also contributed to the film's success, e.g. *Kahin door* sung by Mukesh. Mukherjee cast the popular Bengali actress Sanyal (***Ashirwad***, 1968; *Chena Achena* and *Chiradiner*, both 1969; and esp. ***Guddi***, 1971) in her first major Hindi role. He remade the film, with less success, as *Mili* (1975), featuring a terminally ill heroine, Jaya Bhaduri, opposite a cynical and alcoholic Bachchan.

APARAJEYA

1970 108' b&w Assamese
d Chaturanga *pc* Madhab Films *lyr* Keshab Mahanta, Phani Talukdar *c* D.K. Prabhakar *m* **Salil Choudhury**
lp Rakhi, Prasanta Hazarika, Parag Chaliha, Punya Das, Prasannalal Chowdhe, Rajen Das

Assamese communal harmony movie set among the region's marginalised fishermen's community, consisting mainly of Bengali immigrants. The film is remembered mainly as an unusual collective experiment, directed by **Atul Bordoloi**, poet-playwright Phani Talukdar, Gauri Burman and Munin Bhuyan, and for its unusual 'frontier' cultural promitivism.

ARANAZHIKANERAM

aka *Just Half An Hour*
1970 168' b&w Malayalam
d **K.S. Sethumadhavan** *p* M.O. Joseph *pc* Manjilas *s* Parappuram, from his novel *lyr* **Vyalar Rama Varma** *c* Mehli Irani *m* **P. Devarajan**

lp **Kottarakkara Sridharan Nair**, **Sathyan**, **Prem Nazir**, **Adoor Bhasi**, Ragini, K.P. Ummar, Sheela, Ambika, Meena, Bahadur, Shankaradi, Bharathan, **Muthukulam Raghavan Pillai**, Govindan Kutty, Jose Prakash, Santosh Kumar, P.R. Menon

Sethumadhavan's bizarre portrayals of deviant sex, seen from the 'tragic' viewpoint of decaying but good tradition, became increasingly the standard for his 'middle-of-the-road' Malayalam cinema (cf ***Odeyil Ninnu***, 1965; ***Adimagal***, 1969; *Chattakkari*, 1974). The story features the reminiscences of the good octogenarian Kunjochanam (Nair), whose history is narrated as well as that of his five offspring. Shortly after succumbing to a paralytic stroke, he discovers his 'bad' daughter-in-law carrying on with an evil opium dealer. The old man believes death to be 'half an hour away', but this does not stop the villain from poisoning him as well. Eventually the daughter-in-law, like her predecessor in *Odeyil Ninnu*, commits suicide. The film was noted mainly for Kottarakkara's florid performance accompanied by some unusual make-up.

DASTAK

1970 140' b&w Hindi
d/s **Rajinder Singh Bedi** *pc* Dachi Films *lyr* **Majrooh Sultanpuri** *c* Kamal Bose *m* **Madan Mohan**
lp Sanjeev Kumar, Rehana Sultan, Anju Mahendroo, Shakila Bano Bhopali, Anwar Hussain, Manmohan Krishna, Niranjan Sharma, Kamal Kapoor, Yash Kumar, Jagdev

Author Bedi uses his own outstanding script for his directorial debut financed by the **FFC** as part of early New Indian Cinema. Hamid (S. Kumar), a clerk in Bombay, and his bride Salma (Sultan) live next to the red-light district in a small apartment formerly inhabited by the famous prostitute Shamshad (Bhopali). Clients still turn up, to the annoyance of the young couple who strive to achieve respectability. In contrast to the abstract commands of 'respectable' morality, the grossly materialist economics of prostitution offering more concrete and immediate benefits acquire liberating overtones for the couple. When Hamid refuses a bribe and finds himself unable to buy his own house or to raise money for his sister-in-law's marriage, he displaces his anger and frustration into sexual exploitation. He rapes his wife and fantasises her as a whore in order to be able to respond to her sexually. For Salma, it is the association between prostitution and classical music which provides the link to her family inheritance. Eventually the two realise that there is no escape from prostitution (in reality or as a metaphor) in the urban world. Commercially, the theme had obvious voyeuristic attractions exploited fully in its publicity: the notorious scene where Salma lies on the floor, naked, features prominently in the advertising campaign. Unfortunately, the script, published as a book (1971) with considerable literary merit, was greatly marred by the screen adaptation. Songs include *Bahian na dharo* and *Hum hain mataye-kuch-o-bazaar ki tarah*, both sung by **Lata Mangeshkar**.

Sanjeev Kumar and Rehana Sultan in *Dastak*

ENGAL THANGAM

aka *Our Darling*
1970 174' col Tamil
d **Krishnan-Panju** *pc* Mekala Pics *c* S. Maruthi Rao *m* M.S. Vishwanathan
lp **M.G. Ramachandran**, **Jayalalitha**, Cho Ramaswamy, A.V.M. Rajan, Manorama, S.R. Janaki

MGR film made at the height of his popularity, typical of his own propaganda idiom as he broke from the **DMK** (1972). A concerned and law-abiding truck driver Thangam (MGR) tracks down Murthy (Rajan), the rapist of his blind sister Sumathi. Out of loyalty to the man's mother, he forces Murthy to reform and to marry Sumathi (the blind girl's feelings about having to marry the man who brutally raped her are glossed over). Thangam himself first rescues Kala (Jayalalitha), daughter of a policeman, from a gang of robbers and marries her, having brought the culprits to justice. MGR was the Deputy Chairman of Small Savings in Tamil Nadu's State Assembly at the time, reflected in the film's opening sequence where he is called Vathiar ('teacher', a term used by his fans) at the opening of a Savings Bank. The film includes footage of a speech by **C.N. Annadurai** while MGR literally wraps himself in the colours of the DMK: claiming to be the true inheritor of Annadurai's mantle, MGR often uses the red and black DMK colours in his wardrobe. He also depicts himself as the protector of the poor while preaching against alcohol and smoking. In a highlight of the film he rises from a coffin to sing 'I died and came back alive, I laughed at Yama', the god of death, referring to his 'rebirth' when he survived a gunshot wound inflicted by fellow actor M.R. Radha in 1967. The incident was earlier referred to, to enhance his heroic image, in *Vivasayee* (1967).

EZHUTHATHA KATHA

aka *Unwritten Story*
1970 153' b&w Malayalam
d A.B. Raj *p* T.E. Vasudevan *pc* Jaimaruthy Pics *st* E.P. Kurien *sc* V. Devan *dial* Jagathy N.K. Achary *lyr* Harippad Sreekumar Thampy *c* Ashok Kumar *m* **V. Dakshinamurthy**
lp **Prem Nazir**, Sheela, Ummar, T.R. Omana, **Adoor Bhasi**, **Thikkurisi Sukumaran Nair**, G.K. Pillai, Shankaradi, Bharathan, Nellikode Bhaskaran, Chandrakala, **Muthukulam Raghavan Pillai**, T.K. Balachander, A. Abbas

A story simultaneously exposing venality in the press and corruption among stage stars and politicians. A former prostitute and stage star, Kamalamma, lives on her memories and the income of her daughter Meena, a successful singer. When Prathapan, the editor of a local newspaper, wants to publish Kamalamma's memoirs, her former clients panic and seek to prevent publication by various means including bribery and violence. Prathapan eventually discovers that his own uncle, a respected political leader, is in fact Meena's father. A CID agent masquerading as a journalist uncovers an old plot to accuse Kamalamma of a murder committed by politicians and overwhelmed by the pressures, Kamalamma collapses. Meena is taken into Prathapan's family. Although Kamalamma is presented as a former stage star, her story also evokes the shady past of some film stars.

GEJJE POOJE

aka *The Mock Marriage*
1970 154' b&w Kannada
d/sc **S.R. Puttana Kanagal** *pc* Chitra Jyothi *st* M.K. Indira's novel *c* S.V. Srikanth *m* **Vijayabhaskar**
lp **Kalpana**, Gangadhar, **Leelavathi**, **Arathi**, **Pandharibai**

Kanagal's best-known film outside Karnataka. Aparna (Leelavathi), an orphan raised by a brothel madam, has an affair and bears a daughter whom the madam hopes to make into a prostitute. To prevent this outcome,

Aparna brings up her daughter Chandra (Kalpana) in a different city among respectable neighbours Lalita (Arathi) and her brother Somu, who falls in love with Chandra. When Chandra's father resurfaces, her inability to explain the presence of a stranger becomes the cause of her broken engagement and her return to prostitution. Continuing Kanagal's fascination with tragic heroines, incarnated until ***Sharapanjara*** (1971) by Kalpana and then by Arathi, who makes her debut here, the film has two distinct camera styles which also influence the performances: the style used to portray the 'normal' world of middle-class orthodoxy is rendered increasingly brittle in both image and sound by a second aesthetic in which the worlds of Aparna and Chandra are shown through tight close-ups, expressions of terror and low-angle shots of exploitative men. The musical leitmotiv, associated with the violin that Aparna plays when she remembers her father, extends into expressionist sound effects. In Kanagal's later work (***Ranganayaki***, 1981; *Manasa Sarovara*, 1982) he used colour not only to make films about corruption but a cinema that is in itself corrupted. The film's Telugu remake is *Kalyana Mandapam* (1971).

INTERVIEW

1970 101'(78')(85') b&w Bengali
d/sc **Mrinal Sen** *pc* D.S. Pics *st* Ashish Burman *c* K.K. Mahajan *m* Vijay Raghava Rao
lp Ranjit Mullick, Karuna Bannerjee, Shekhar Chatterjee, Mamata Bannerjee, Bulbul Mukherjee, Umanath Bhattacharya, Amal Chakravarty, Tapan Dasgupta, Bimal Bannerjee, Satyen Ghosh

The first of Sen's Calcutta trilogy (***Calcutta '71***, 1972; ***Padatik***, 1973) marking the director's turn to a more explicitly political address. While the overt symbols of colonial rule are being dismantled, the internalised residues of colonialism still blight the country, as Ranjit (Mullick) finds out when he cannot get a middle-class job because he cannot get hold of his only suit. The narrative structure is humorous and episodic as the mishaps and frustrations accummulate within one dawn-to-dusk period until the protagonist rebels and destroys a genteel, Western-looking mannequin in a shop window, the symbol of aspirations out of touch with actuality. Inspired by Brecht's approach to the theatre, Sen includes newsreels and an argument between the protagonist and a voice representing the audience, inviting the viewer to adopt the stance of a critical interlocutor. Not to be confused with **Sasikumar**'s Malayalam titillation melodrama *Interview* (1973).

JOHNNY MERA NAAM

1970 159' col Hindi
d/sc **Vijay Anand** *pc* Trimurti Films *st* K.A. Narayan *lyr* Rajinder Krishen, Indivar *c* Fali Mistry *m* **Kalyanji-Anandji**
lp **Dev Anand**, **Hema Malini**, Premnath, Jeevan, I.S. Johar, Pran, Sajjan, Padma, Randhawa, Iftikhar, Sulochana

The policeman father of Mohan and Sohan is killed by villain Ranjit Singh (Premnath) who later abducts Mohan. Mohan grows up to become Moti (Pran), the lieutenant in Ranjit Singh's gang, while brother Sohan (Anand) becomes a cop who tries to infiltrate the gang calling himself Johnny. He succeeds with the help of Rekha (Hema Malini), whose father is held hostage by the villain. Eventually the brothers reunite and destroy the gang. Vijay Anand, noted for earlier crime dramas (***Jewel Thief***, 1967), adopts the dominant Hindi film style (rapid editing and a noisy soundtrack) and several quotes caricaturising the box-office 'formula', e.g. a quadruple role for the comedian Johar. The script contains attacks on classical music (the gang exploits the foreign 'craze' for Indian music by exporting drugs hidden in musical instruments) and religion (the burglary of a temple with Pran dressed as a holy man and Malini as a jogan). Although the film has several **Kishore Kumar** hit songs such as *Pal bhar ke liye koi hame pyar kar le*, Vijay Anand's famed song-picturising skills are evident only in the opening number, *Vaada to nibhaya*, sung by Kishore Kumar and **Asha Bhosle**.

KAVIYATH THALAIVI

1970 166' b&w Tamil
d/s **K. Balachander** *p* **Sowcar Janaki** *pc* Selvi Films *lyr* **Kannadasan** *c* N. Balakrishnan *m* M.S. Vishwanathan
lp **Sowcar Janaki**, **Gemini Ganesh**

The heroine Devi (Janaki, who also produced the film) loves the lawyer Suresh (Ganesh) but circumstances force her to marry the gambler and alcoholic Paranthaman. Trying to escape from her evil husband, Devi becomes a dancer in Hyderabad where she gives birth to a daughter. When her husband tries to kidnap the child, she has Suresh adopt her. Later, when her husband's blackmail threatens her daughter's marriage, Devi kills him. Remake of **Asit Sen**'s Hindi film *Mamata* (1966).

MARO PRAPANCHAM

1970 155' b&w Telugu
d **Adurthi Subba Rao** *pc* Chakravarthi Chitra *st* B.S. Thapa *sc* **K. Vishwanath** *dial* Modukuri Johnson *lyr* **Sri Sri** *c* K.S. Ramakrishna Rao *m* K.V. Mahadevan
lp **Savitri**, **A. Nageshwara Rao**, **K. Jaggaiah**, **Gummadi Venkateshwara Rao**, Padmanabham, **Jamuna**

Second and last of the 'experimental' co-productions featuring Subba Rao, star Nageshwara Rao and scenarist K. Vishwanath (cf *Sudigundalu*, 1967). The earlier film had attacked the flaws in the legal system, and had won the state award of best film. Here, a revolutionary group calls for an end to all poverty and the social systems that curtain freedom of thought. The film used Sri Sri's lyrics to push through their radical message. The commercial failure of this film ended both the experiment and Chakravarthi Chitra.

MERA NAAM JOKER

aka *I Am a Clown*
1970 240' col Hindi
d/p **Raj Kapoor** *pc* R.K. Films *s* **K.A. Abbas** *lyr* **Shailendra**, Hasrat Jaipuri, Neeraj, Prem Dhawan, Shailey Shailendra *c* Radhu Karmakar *m* **Shankar-Jaikishen**
lp Raj Kapoor, **Manoj Kumar**, Rishi Kapoor, **Dharmendra**, **Dara Singh**, **Rajendra Kumar**, **Padmini**, Ksiena Rabiankina, Simi Garewal, Achala Sachdev, Om Prakash, members of the Soviet State Circus and of the Gemini Circus

A mammoth film apparently inspired by Chaplin's *Limelight* (1951), featuring Raj Kapoor as Raju the circus clown in a sprawling tale often seen as the star's autobiographical fantasy. Initially conceived as three separate films, the 3-part story abounds with allusions to Kapoor's own life and work. It starts with the young Raju (Rishi Kapoor), the son of a trapeze artist, falling in love with his schoolteacher Mary (Simi), and dreaming of becoming a famous clown. In Part 2, Raju joins a Russian circus where he falls in love with Marina (Rabiankina). The climax of this part comes when Raju's mother (Sachdev), seeing him on a trapeze and remembering his father's fatal fall, collapses, forcing the anguished Raju to finish the routine with a smile. Using the Soviet State Circus and portraying Marina as devoted to the title number of ***Awara*** (1951) since childhood, Kapoor intended to signal his gratitude to the USSR for the popularity he had enjoyed there since the 50s. In Part 3, Raju befriends the young Mina (Padmini) who, disguised as a boy, pastes cinema posters while dreaming of becoming a film star. The film's conclusion shows the three women in his life witnessing, as special guests, Raju's grand circus finale. Kapoor constantly deploys emphatically symbolic images, like a clown doll abandoned in the hut where Raju and Mina used to meet, a cracked mirror showing a laughing face, etc. If Kapoor's 50s films projected the attainment of political freedom as a loss of innocence and a yearning for a new world, this film projects an uninhibited infantile narcissism combined with a mother fixation which not only determines his acrobatic demands for affection but also programmes the proliferation of female figures whose approval the leading character craves. Its commercial failure is often cited as the reason for Kapoor's lapse into a cynical use of sexploitation in his post-70s films, as if the rejection of the film had been translated into a vengeful recourse to demeaning images of women thrown at an unworthy public.

MUKTI

1970 145' b&w Kannada
d **N. Lakshminarayan** *pc* Navodaya Chitra *st* V.M. Inamdar's novel *Shapa* *c* Meenakshi Sundaram *m* **Vijayabhaskar**
lp **Kalpana**, Rajasekhar, **Udaya Kumar**, **B. Jayamma**

Prostitution melodrama involving the hero Madhava (Rajasekhar) and the heroine Sarojini (Kalpana), who want to marry. He discovers that his recently deceased father had an affair with Sarojini's mother (Jayamma), a former prostitute. When Sarojini's mother falls ill, it is discovered she has a venereal disease, which she passed on to her daughter. Madhav thus finds himself in love with his diseased stepsister.

NINGALENNE COMMUNISTAKI

aka *You Made Me a Communist*
1970 155' b&w Malayalam
d/s **Thoppil Bhasi** *p* **Kunchako** *pc* Udaya Studios (Alleppy) *lyr* **Vyalar Rama Varma** *m* **P. Devarajan**
lp **Sathyan**, **Prem Nazir**, Sheela, Ummar, Jayabharati, Kottyam Chellappan, S.P. Pillai, Thoppil Krishna Pillai, Lalitha, Adoor Pankajam, P. Rajamma, Vijayakumari, Alumoodan, Kundara Bhasi

Bhasi's version of his own landmark socialist realist play (1952) popularising official CPI ideology in Kerala. Gopalan, after obtaining a college degree, devotes himself to trade union work to the distress of his father, the tradition-bound Paramu Pillai whose family fortune has been eroded. Gopalan and his working-class friend Mathew oppose the evil landlord Kesavan Nair's schemes to obtain ever more land through fraud and intimidation. They are beaten up by the landlord's hired thugs and hospitalised. In the end, Paramu Pillai, radicalised by the need to defend himself against the landlord, emerges from his house brandishing a red flag and joining the collective struggle against exploitation. A subplot has Gopalan in love with Kesavan Nair's daughter although the one who truly loves him is Mala, the daughter of a poor, aged tenant farmer also about to be evicted by the villain. The film, produced by the owner of Udaya Studios, was not as successful as the play. Bhasi went on in the same agit-prop vein, backed by the CPI, with, e.g., ***Enippadikal*** (1973).

PENN DAIVAM

1970 164' b&w Tamil
d M.A. Thirumugham *pc* Dandayuthapani Films *st* A. Abdul Muthalif *dial* Arur Doss *lyr* Alangudi Somu, **Kannadasan** *c* P. Bhaskar Rao *m* V. Kumar
lp Lakshmi, Jaishankar, **Padmini**, Sundarrajan, S.P. Muthuraman, Nagesh, Thenjai Srinivasan, Udayachandrika

Elaborate Padmini melodrama marking her change to mother roles. Ponnamma (Padmini) is the suffering wife of a criminal (Sundarrajan) who leaves her and forces their son (Muthuraman) into a life of violent crime. Their daughter (Lakshmi), placed in a home for destitutes, is adopted and raised by a rich man in whose house Ponnamma becomes a servant. Later, the criminal father tries to kidnap his daughter and is confronted by his wife. The criminal son dies. The film's love interest is integrated into the crime melodrama when the daughter falls in love with a police inspector (Jaishankar).

PRATIDWANDI

aka *The Adversary*, aka *Siddhartha and the City*
1970 110' b&w Bengali
d/sc/m **Satyajit Ray** *p* Nepal Dutta, Ashim Dutta *pc* Priya Films *st* Sunil Ganguly's novel *c* Soumendu Roy, Purnendu Bose
lp **Dhritiman Chatterjee**, Indira Devi, Debraj Roy, Krishna Bose, Kalyan Choudhury, Jayshree Roy, Shefali, Shoven Lahiri, Pishu Majumdar, Dhara Roy, Mamata Chatterjee

The first of Ray's Calcutta trilogy, coinciding with **Mrinal Sen**'s, addresses his native Calcutta's turbulent politics. The student movement aligned with the **Naxalite** rebellion is invoked through the younger brother (Debraj Roy) of the film's protagonist Siddhartha (D. Chatterjee) and informs the plot repeatedly, e.g. with the **Films Division** newsreel about Indira Gandhi's budget speech and, most importantly, by Siddhartha's search for self-realisation and a job in Calcutta, an enterprise presented as inherently tragic. Siddhartha fails to get a job by answering that the greatest achievement of mankind in the 60s is the courage of the Vietnamese people rather than the NASA moon landing. In such an atmosphere, defined by the endless waiting for job interviews in stiflingly oppressive and humiliating conditions, he is eventually driven to leave Calcutta and his lover Keya (J. Roy). Ray introduces for him unprecedented narrative devices such as the voice-over of an unseen political activist (Ray's own voice) who offers advice to Siddhartha, two film clips (the newsreel and a boring European art-house movie shown by the local film society) and the encounter with a prostitute which is shown in negative. Ray also includes, in the background as the lovers part, footage of a big political rally on Calcutta's Maidan. Unlike Sen, however, whose use of similar devices was accompanied by a more sophisticated understanding of Brecht, Ray's protagonist leaves only after performing a cathartic act of rebellion: he upsets an office in which yet another set of job interviews are being conducted. The film intercuts these episodes with a relatively more familiar pattern of flashbacks, e.g. Siddhartha's fantasies about his childhood before being disturbed by American hippies, or the flashback which interrupts the argument he has with his sister (K. Bose) about her opportunistic affair with her employer. The 2nd title in the trilogy is ***Seemabaddha*** (1971).

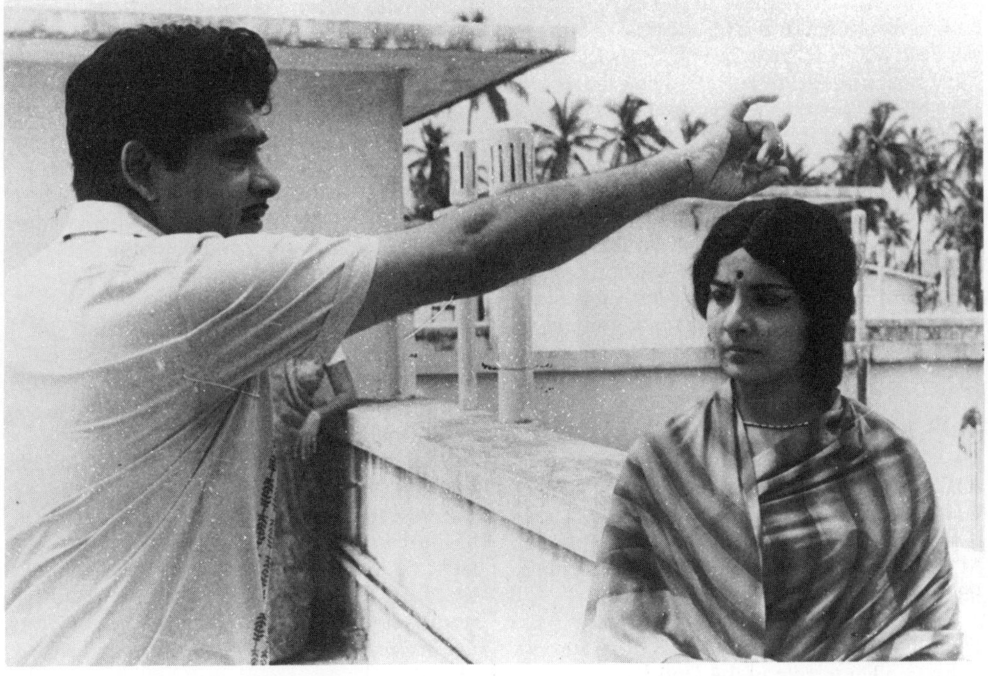

Madhu and Lily Chakraborty in *Priya*

PREM PUJARI

1970 192' col Hindi
d/s **Dev Anand** *pc* Navketan *lyr* Neeraj *c* Fali Mistry *m* **S.D. Burman**
lp Dev Anand, **Waheeda Rehman**, Zaheeda, Prem Chopra, Nasir Hussain, Siddhu, Madan Puri, Achala Sachdev, Sajjan, Ulhas, Master Sachin

The first film Dev Anand officially signed as director is a nationalist and militarist pot-pourri of war and international espionage, partly shot in Spain, France and Britain. Ram (Anand), a soldier descending from a long line of famous army men, is a pacificist. Court-martialed for disobeying orders he is jailed but escapes. On the run, he encounters Rita (Zaheeda) whose single-seater plane has crashed and who embroils him in a spy ring he is determined to expose. This involves impersonating a Tibetan and a Portuguese and travelling to many international tourist spots before he destroys the spy ring which was leaking information about India's military deals. However, he is too late to prevent Pakistan from attacking India in 1965 and, abandoning his pacifism, he rushes back to fight the enemy and to win back his girl (Rehman). The film is mainly notable for its aggressive exoticisation of the West (bullfights in Spain; cabarets, restaurants and boulevards in Paris; the Embankment and Scotland Yard in London).

PRIYA

1970 152' b&w Malayalam
d **Madhu** *p* N.P. Ali, N.P. Abu *pc* Jammu Pics *s* C. Radhakrishnan *lyr* Yusuf Ali Kacheri *c* U. Rajagopal, Benjamin, Ramchandra, L.C. Kapoor *m* **Baburaj**
lp Madhu, Jayabharati, **Adoor Bhasi**, Bahadur, Lily Chakraborty, Shankaradi, Veeran, Sukumari, Kadeeja, Meena

Malayalam star Madhu's directorial art-house debut, edited by **Hrishikesh Mukherjee** in his first association with Malayalam cinema. Gopan (Madhu) becomes a sexual debauchee when he gets a job in a Bombay advertising agency. He married his cousin Devi against the objections of her father. Migrating to

Bombay, he gets his typist Thulasi pregnant, forcing her into prostitution. Later, he visits a brothel and meets Thulasi again, who has renamed herself Priya, but he does not recognise her. She entices him into her room and kills him, tearing him to pieces with her poisoned nails. She is jailed and Gopan's disillusioned wife accepts the care of her husband's illegitimate child. The story is told in flashback as Gopan's friend (Bhasi) tries to trace Gopan in Bombay. Madhu attempted a change of image in this negative role, also casting Bengali star Lily Chakraborty in her only Malayalam film. The film was critically acclaimed in Kerala for its realism and for confirming the conventional image of Bombay as sin city, where most of the film is shot on location, with numerous dingy night scenes.

SACHCHA JHUTHA

1970 143' col Hindi
d **Manmohan Desai** *pc* V.R. Films *s* J.M. Desai *dial* Prayag Raj *lyr* Indivar, Gulshan Bawra, Qamar Jalalabadi *c* Peter Pereira *m* **Kalyanji-Anandji**
lp **Rajesh Khanna**, Mumtaz, Naaz, Vinod Khanna, Faryal, Prayag Raj, Kamal Kapoor, Jagdish Raj

Desai's Khanna hit was, together with, e.g., ***Hum Dono*** (1961) and many others, an example of the popular 'double role' Hindi films. Good guy and village simpleton Bhola (R. Khanna) looks like the gangster Ranjit (also R. Khanna). Ranjit uses the resemblance to deceive the police until Bhola finally gets wise and impersonates Ranjit, leading to the gangster's downfall. The film includes a highly sentimental subplot about Bhola's reciprocated love for his disabled sister (Naaz) with the **Kishore Kumar** number *Meri pyari bahenia*.

SAMAJ KO BADAL DALO

1970 162' col Hindi
d V. Madhusudhana Rao *pc* **Gemini Studio** *st* **Thoppil Bhasi** *dial* Mukhram Sharma *lyr* **Sahir Ludhianvi** *c* Thyagaraj Pendharkar *m* Ravi
lp **Sharada**, Kanchan, Aruna Irani, Parikshit Sahni, Shammi, Jayashree T., Praveen Paul, Pran, Mehmood

An unusual political film made by the mainstream Gemini Studio, the Telugu commercial director Rao, the Malayalam communist Bhasi and the Telugu/Malayalam star Sharada. Chhaya (Sharada), whose father once owned a textile mill but was swindled by his partner, now finds happiness as the wife of a mill worker. The couple have to contend with trade union blacklegs and the villainous owners who persecute Chhaya's husband. Songs include *Dharti mata ka maan hamara pyara lal nishan*, stridently praising the red flag, and the miserabilist beggar song *Amma ek roti de* which later became popular among real beggars in Bombay. The film is not a remake of **Vijay Bhatt**'s ***Samaj Ko Badal Dalo*** (1947) but of **Vincent**'s ***Thulabharam*** (1968), and was adapted by Madhusudhana Rao in Telugu (*Manushulu Marali*, 1969) before he made it in Hindi.

SAMSKARA

aka *Funeral Rites*
1970 113' b&w Kannada
d/p **Pattabhi Rama Reddy** *pc* Ramamanohara Chitra *st* U.R. Ananthamurthy's novel (1966) *sc* **Girish Karnad** *c* Tom Cowan *m* Rajeev Taranath
lp Girish Karnad, Snehalata Reddy, **P. Lankesh**, B.R. Jayaram, Dasharathi Dixit, Lakshmi Krishnamurthy

The Telugu director and poet Reddy's landmark adaptation of an early story written by his family's friend, the noted Karnataka novelist Ananthamurthy whose work is an important source for many young Kannada film-makers, launching a cinematic version of the literary **Navya Movement**. Shot on location in the mountains of Mysore by a visiting Australian cameraman, this morality tale set among orthodox Madhava Brahmins tells of a rebellious but charismatic Brahmin who rejects his caste's religion. Plague erupts in a village claiming as its first victim Naranappa (Lankesh), a Brahmin notorious for eating meat, drinking and for his low-caste mistress Chandri (Snehalata Reddy). None of the Brahmins are willing to cremate him until Chandri appeals to the scholar Praneshacharya (Karnad), who cannot find a solution to the problem in the scriptures. Praneshacharya seduces Chandri and his subsequent guilt induces him to assume responsibility when the entire village becomes plague infested. He is lectured on the reality principle by a talkative commoner (Jayaram) and eventually returns to cremate Naranappa himself, rejecting brahminical bigotry. The film's backbone is the playwright Karnad's script (here making his film debut) which adopted the novel's very localised idiom. A censor ban was averted through the personal intervention of the Information and Broadcasting Minister I.K. Gujral. Ananthamurthy approved of the film but noted that in his story, the corpse is soon buried secretly by Naranappa's Muslim friend, so that the scholar's dilemma is purely a matter of brahminical beliefs: by burning the corpse, it becomes an ancestor to be worshipped. The novelist commented that when the scholar 'realises all he has in common with his rival after making love to the dead man's mistress, he becomes the other man himself, thus embodying the presence of the other within himself. The scriptwriter and the director felt that the body should be kept for the protagonist to return to after his wanderings, cremating it himself as an act of expiation.' The film in effect dismisses religious subtleties in favour of simple humanitarian values. Following a year after Sen's ***Bhuvan Shome*** (1969), this film helped New Indian Cinema gain a foothold in the South.

SHRI KRISHNADEVARAYA

1970 216' col Kannada
d **B.R. Panthulu** *pc* Padmini Pics *s* **A.N. Krishnarao** *m* T.G. Lingappa
lp **Rajkumar, B.R. Panthulu**, Narasimhraju, **M.V. Rajamma, R. Nagendra Rao**, Bharati, Jayanti

Panthulu's last big Kannada historical returns to his familiar terrain of the 16th C. Vijayanagara Empire with its best-known king, Krishnadeva Raya (Rajkumar), his canny minister Thimmarasu (Panthulu) and the wise buffoon Tenali Ramakrishna, all famous figures in the Kannada historical genre.

THURAKATHA VATHIL

aka *The Unopened Door*
1970 143' b&w Malayalam
d/lyr **P. Bhaskaran** *p* A. Raghunath *pc* Sanjay Prod. *s* K.T. Mohammed *c* N. Rajagopal, Benjamin *m* K. Raghunath
lp **Prem Nazir, Madhu**, Bahadur, Ragini, Jayabharati, Philomina, K.T. Mohammed, Raghava Menon, Nellikode Bhaskaran, Ramankutty, B.K. Pottekkad, C.A. Balan

One of K.T. Mohammed's best-known scripts, this sentimental movie was part of a growing trend in 70s Malayalam cinema, showing the infantile hero sacrificing his happiness to fulfil his obligations towards his sister, which involves asking his best friend to live the life he had planned for himself. The simple-minded Bappu (Nazir) leaves for the city to earn money that would allow him to fulfil his two ambitions: to get his sister happily married, and to himself marry Sulekha (Ragini). In the city he meets and befriends Vasu (Madhu). When Bappu is injured and about to die, he asks Vasu to complete the course he had embarked upon. Vasu goes to Bappu's village, arranges the sister's marriage, and, in a poignant moment at the end of the film, seeks out Bappu's girlfriend, who immediately realises what happened and its implications for her future.

VAZHVE MAYAM

aka *World of Illusion*
1970 153' b&w Malayalam
d **K.S. Sethumadhavan** *p* M.O. Joseph *pc* Manjilas Cine Ents *s* **Thoppil Bhasi** from P. Ayyaneth's novel *lyr* **Vyalar Rama Varma** *c* Mehli Irani *m* **P. Devarajan**
lp **Sathyan**, Sheela, Ummar, Kadeeja, Bahadur, K.P.A.C. Lalitha, **Adoor Bhasi**, Shankaradi, N. Govindankutty, C.A. Balan, Ammini, Kuttan Pillai, **Muthukulam Raghavan Pillai**, Paravoor Bharathan, Philomina

The team responsible for ***Adimagal*** (1969) followed on with this unusual love story featuring three neighbouring couples working in the electricity supply industry: Sudhi who is madly in love with his wife Sharada, Sudhi's younger colleague and friend Sasidharan and his wife Kamalakshmi, and Kuttappan, the department's lineman, and his wife Gauri. The insecure and jealous Sudhi suspects his wife of being unfaithful with Sasidharan and he spies on her, causing an indignant Sharada, pregnant with their daughter, to pack her bags and return to her family, where her father makes matters worse and the loving couple end up agreeing to a divorce. Sudhi eventually finds out that it was Sasidharan's wife who was having an affair, but by that time Sharada has remarried and Sudhi goes mad. Years later, the couple meet again at their daughter's wedding. After blessing his daughter, Sudhi returns home and dies. Sharada goes to pay her last respects to her former husband and dies as well.

Sivaji Ganesan and Padmini in *Vietnam Veedu*

VIETNAM VEEDU
aka *Vietnam House*
1970 164' b&w Tamil
d P. Madhavan *p* Sivaji Ganesan *pc* Sivaji Prod. *s* Sundaram, from his play *c* P.N. Sundaram *lyr* **Kannadasan** *m* K.V. Mahadevan
lp **Sivaji Ganesan**, Nagesh, Srikanth, K.A. Thangavelu, **Padmini**, Ramaprabha, V.S. Raghavan, **P. Bhanumathi**

Traditionalist melodrama focusing on the traumas of retirement and generational change (a suitable transition towards 'mature' roles for the ageing producer and star Ganesan). The dignified old company executive known as Prestige Padmanabha Iyer (Ganesan) is forced to retire and experiences hostility and indifference in his new life at the head of a family including his wife, two sons and a daughter. He devoted the best years of his life to pay for the children's upbringing, only to end up in a lonely and complicated retirement. The film's high points are the subtly erotic relationship between the ageing couple and some big dance numbers intended to show the generation gap as college girls prance around in miniskirts. Originally a play staged by Ganesan's troupe, the film opens with the patriarch introducing all the characters. The action is set inside the old man's ancestral house, named Vietnam Veedu (Vietnam House) because of the constant fighting and arguing in the family.

Kaviyoor Ponnamma and Master Babloo in *Abhijathyam*

ABHIJATHYAM

aka *False Pride*
1971 164' b&w Malayalam
d **A. Vincent** *p* R.S. Prabhu *pc* Shri Rajesh Films *s* **Thoppil Bhasi** *lyr* **P. Bhaskaran** *c* Surya Prakash *m* A.T. Ummar
lp **Thikkurisi Sukumaran Nair**, Kaviyoor Ponnamma, Veeran, **Sharada**, **Madhu**, Raghavan

An adaptation of Anant Mane's ***Manini*** (1961). Malathi (Sharada) is the daughter of a wealthy family. She forces her father Shankara Menon (Nair) to let her marry a poor music teacher, Madhavan (Madhu), claiming to be pregnant by him. The father rejects the couple, who manage to make a meagre living in the husband's village. The mother dies of grief and her spirit visits the daughter, soon followed by a repenting father. P.K. Nair suggests that the end sequence echoes Mizoguchi's *Ugetsu Monogatari* (1953).

ANDAZ

1971 166' col Hindi
d **Ramesh Sippy** *pc* Sippy Films *s* Sachin Bhowmick *dial* **Gulzar** *lyr* Hasrat Jaipuri *c* K. Vaikunth *m* **Shankar-Jaikishen**
lp **Shammi Kapoor**, **Hema Malini**, Achla Sachdev, Aruna Irani, Simi Garewal, **Rajesh Khanna**, Roopesh Kumar, Randhawa, Sonia Sahni

Ramesh Sippy's haltingly meandering debut film bears no resemblance to the classic ***Andaz*** (1949). A spendthrift widower (Kapoor) falls in love with a woman (Malini) who, in a long flashback, secretly married her lover (Khanna) but soon became a widow. His villainous, womanising younger brother (Kumar) makes life difficult for all concerned. When the villain rapes a hill woman (Irani) and she commits suicide, his nastiness is at last exposed and the two brothers' doting mother (Sachdev) sees the light. Rajesh Khanna, then at the peak of his popularity, is billed as a guest star and sings the hit motorbike number *Zindagi ek safar hai suhana* (sung by his regular playback **Kishore Kumar**). The vaguely Westernising dimension, necessary to justify a widow falling in love, is provided by the rather ludicrous presence of several Caucasians and by the priest who gives the widow permission to remarry.

ANUBHAV

1971 139' b&w Hindi
d/s **Basu Bhattacharya** *pc* Arohi Film Makers *co-dial* Sagar Sarhadi *co-dial/co-lyr* Kapil Kumar *co-lyr* **Gulzar** *c* Nandu Bhattacharya *m* Kanu Roy
lp Sanjeev Kumar, Tanuja, Dinesh Thakur, A.K. Hangal

Bhattacharya's best-known film after ***Teesri Kasam*** (1966) began a series of melodramas about the problems of married couples (cf *Avishkar*, 1973). The newspaper editor Amar (Kumar) grows distant from his wife Meeta (Tanuja) because his new assistant is her former lover Shashi (Thakur). Amar cannot accept that his wife is no longer enamoured of Shashi. The film is part of the early **FFC**-sponsored 'art-house' cinema. It is shot on location in one of Bombay's best-known and most expensive high-rise apartment blocks. The soundtrack rather crudely takes its cue from Godard, interrupted by radio advertising jingles, combined with the leitmotiv of a ticking clock in addition to two popular **Geeta Dutt** songs, *Mera dil jo mera hota* and *Koi chupke se aake sapne sulake*.

ANUBHAVANGAL PALICHAKAL

aka *Shattered Experience*
1971 133' b&w Malayalam
d **K.S. Sethumadhavan** *p* M.O. Joseph *pc* Manjilas *st* Thakazhy Shivashankar Pillai's novel *sc* **Thoppil Bhasi** *lyr* **Vyalar Rama Varma** *c* Mehli Irani *m* **P. Devarajan**
lp **Sathyan**, **Prem Nazir**, Sheela, **Adoor Bhasi**, Sankaradi

Following on from Sethumadhavan's typical formula (cf ***Odeyil Ninnu***, 1965; ***Aranazhikaneram***, 1970, *Chattakkari*, 1974) of viewing sexually deviant behaviour as being the consequence of the 'tragic' decay in feudal values, he tells a story here of a conscientious worker (Sathyan) who suspects his wife's (Sheela) fidelity when she wants to go out to work. This becomes the reason for him getting involved in a murder, which forces him to abscond and thus to abandon his family. The wife survives with the help of a friend (Nazir). When the husband reappears, he now discovers his wife apparently living with his friend. Trapped between the decay of the feudal values he upholds and an equally oppressive legal system, he surrenders to the police. Based on a Thakazhy story, the film adheres to some of the detailed realism of the original, but the performances of the male leads remain extreme. Sathyan, in his last film, replays to some extent the tragic condition of being married to an unfaithful wife in ***Chemmeen*** (1965), also a Thakazhy story. This was also the last film by the Manjilas production group, responsible for memorable Malayalam films in the 60s (cf *Aranazhikaneram*).

ARANYA

1971 107' b&w Assamese
d/s Samarendra Narayan Deb *pc* United Club, Mangaldoi *lyr* Keshab Mahanta *c* Ramanand Sengupta *m* Sudhin Dasgupta
lp Biju Phukan, Bidya Rao, Tasadduf Yusuf, Kashmiri, Beena Barwati, Bijoy Shankar, Punya Das, Deuti Barua, Bishnu Khargaria

Conservationist drama protesting the poaching of the one-horned Assamese rhinoceros. Set in the famed Assamese Kaziranga sanctuary, the film indicts the local elite and exposes the cruelties of the poachers.

ASHAD KA EK DIN

aka *A Monsoon Day*
1971 114' b&w Hindi
d/sc **Mani Kaul** *pc* **FFC** *st* Mohan Rakesh's play (1958) *c* K.K. Mahajan
lp Arun Khopkar, Rekha Sabnis, Om Shivpuri, Pinchoo Kapoor, Anuradha Kapur

Kaul's 2nd film continued his exploration of cinematic form via this adaptation of Rakesh's play featuring the legendary Sanskrit playwright Kalidasa (*Abhignan Shakuntala*, *Kumarasambhava*, *Meghdoot*), a figure tentatively identified as a court poet in the reign of Chandragupta II (3rd C. AD). The play presents the ethical dilemmas of an artist by requiring Kalidasa to choose between his lover Mallika and his duties at the court of Ujjain. The film is set in a small hut on a hillside and concentrates on three characters: Kalidasa (Khopkar), Mallika (Sabnis) and their friend Vilom (Shivpuri). The characters' lines, mostly monologues, were pre-recorded and played back during shooting, freeing the actors from any vestiges of theatrical conventions. The sparse realism of ***Uski Roti*** (1969) is replaced by Mahajan's sensuously shot landscapes and languid camera movements, minutely registering light changes within the frame, at times by slowly shutting the aperture.

DO BOOND PANI

1971 141' col Hindi
d/s/p **K.A. Abbas** *pc* Naya Sansar *lyr* **Kaifi Azmi**, Balkeshav Bairagi *m* Jaidev
lp Simi Garewal, Jalal Agha, Prakash Thapa, Madhu Chanda, Sajjan, KiranKumar, Rashid Khan, Pinchoo Kapoor, Amrit Oberoi

The Rajasthan Ganga Sagar Canal Project, intended to transform the state's vast barren desert, was one of the Nehru government's show pieces. Shot on the canal building site, this distant echo of King Vidor's *Our Daily Bread*(1934) endorses Indira Gandhi's slogans while deploying the developmentalrhetoric and Nehruite iconography of dams, bridges and industrialisation.Ganga Singh (Agha) lives in a drought-stricken village in Rajasthan and leaves his wife Gauri (Simi), sister Sonki (Chanda) and father Hari Singh(Sajjan) to dedicate himself to the canal project. He learns of the projectvia a government propaganda newsreel in a touring cinema. The story intercuts Ganga Singh's struggle for progress at work with the direpre-industrial conditions at home: his father dies, his sister is raped by the bandit Mangal Singh (Thapa) and Gauri waits for her husband to return.Ganga Singh sacrifices his life to avert a disaster at the site but eventually industrial progress triumphs and the life-giving water arrives.

DUSHMAN

1971 177' col Hindi
d Dulal Guha *pc* Suchitra *s* Virender Sinha *lyr* **Anand Bakshi** *c* M. Rajaram *m* **Laxmikant-Pyarelal**
lp **Meena Kumari**, **Rajesh Khanna**, Mumtaz, Nana Palsikar, Kanhaiyalal, K.N. Singh, Anwar Hussain, Sajjan, **Abhi Bhattacharya**, Rehman, Bindu

Khanna plays a truck driver who in a drunken accident kills a man. Sentenced to work in his victim's village and to look after the family that lost its sole breadwinner, he enters a hostile environment. The hero eventually makes himself loved by tackling the real villains (a gang of hoarders and criminals), gets the heroine (Mumtaz) and wins the affection of his implacable foe, the widow (Kumari) of the man he killed. With classic Khanna-**Kishore Kumar** numbers such as *Tumhari zulf hai ya sadak ka mod hai ye*, the film was also a musical success. The film was remade in Tamil as *Neethi* (1972) starring **Sivaji Ganesan** in Rajesh Khanna's role.

EK ADHURI KAHANI

aka *An Unfinished Story*
1971 115'(110') b&w Hindi
d/sc **Mrinal Sen** *p* Arun Kaul/**FFC** *st* Subodh Ghosh *c* K.K. Mahajan *m* Vijay Raghava Rao
lp **Utpal Dutt**, Shekhar Chatterjee, Arati Bhattacharya, Vivek Chatterjee

The novelist Ghosh (filmed earlier by **Bimal Roy** in ***Anjangarh***, 1948 and ***Sujata***, 1959) provided the story for Sen's exploration of the ravages wrought by capitalism in a rural economy. Set in 1929 in a Bihar sugar mill, a middle-class outsider becomes the factory's cashier. When the Depression hits, the apparently benevolent factory owners reveal their true colours as the workers and the peasants desperately try to defend their livelihood by any means at their disposal, including violence. The outcome of the struggle and the ending of the film are left open, suggesting that they have to be provided by real rather than represented struggles. However, the mood of the 'unfinished story' is far from triumphant and stresses the soul-destroying aspects of having to battle against overwhelming odds.

GUDDI

aka *Darling Child*
1971 121' col Hindi
d/co-sc **Hrishikesh Mukherjee** *pc* Rupam Chitra *st/lyr/co-sc* **Gulzar** *co-sc* D.N. Mukherjee *c* Jaywant Pathare *m* **Vasant Desai**
lp Jaya Bhaduri, **Dharmendra**, Sumita Sanyal, Vijay Sharma, **Utpal Dutt**, Samit, A.K. Hangal, Keshto Mukherjee

Teenaged and miniskirted Kusum aka Guddi (Bhaduri) has such a crush on Hindi film star Dharmendra that her family arranges for her to meet the star. A rare Hindi film about film-making, *Guddi* appears to want to deconstruct the myth of the star and to show not only how films are made but the poverty, the exploitation and the transitory nature of stardom. What it does do, however, is produce a small parade of stars playing 'themselves'. The film's tentative critique of stardom involves drawing a comparison between contemporary screen idols and gods: Kusum adores Dharmendra like the legendary saint poet Meerabai was unconditionally devoted to Krishna. The film made Bhaduri into a major 70s star as the bouncy teenager with an ear-splitting laugh, repeated, e.g., in *Jawani Diwani* (1972).

HARE RAMA HARE KRISHNA

1971 149' col Hindi
d/s **Dev Anand** *pc* Navketan *lyr* **Anand Bakshi** *c* Fali Mistry *m* **R.D. Burman**
lp Dev Anand, Mumtaz, **Zeenat Aman**, Prem Chopra, **Kishore Sahu**, Achala Sachdev, Iftikhar

Set among Hare Krishna cultists, presented as dope-smoking hippies fronting for drug smugglers, Anand's call for a return to nationalist Indian values was dominated by Zeenat Aman in her first starring role. She is the hero's sister, parted from him by an unhappy family life and now in the clutches of long-haired freaks in Nepal. His attempt to rescue her involves encounters with pop ideologies of liberation, crooks and rapists before the final reconciliation. Mumtaz, a sexy local belle, provides the hero's love interest but she is overshadowed by Aman. The smash hit *Dum Maro Dum*, sung by **Asha Bhosle** and blues singer Usha Iyer, remains the film's main claim to fame.

JESAL TORAL

1971 137' col Gujarati
d **Ravindra Dave** *p* Kanti R. Dave, T.J. Patel *pc* Kirti Films *st* Himmat Dave *sc* Jitubhai Mehta *dial* Ramesh Mehta *c* Pratap Dave *lyr/m* **Avinash Vyas**
lp Anupama, **Upendra Trivedi**, Arvind Trivedi, Ramesh Mehta, Jayant Bhatt, Mulraj Rajda, Mukund Pandya, Laxmi Patel, Sarala Dand, Induben Rajda, Lily Patel, Vandana, Suryakant, Umakant, Veljibhai Gajjar, Jayashree T.

A big Gujarati hit in Eastmancolor renovating the tradition of the adventure folk-tale. It adapts a famous Kutchhi legend (first filmed, with great success, by **Chaturbhuji Doshi** in 1948) featuring the dreaded bandit Jesal (U. Trivedi) and the devout god-woman Toral (Anupama) who reforms him. Director Dave's Gujarati debut sees the star Upendra Trivedi in one of his best-known performances.

MERE APNE

1971 134' col Hindi
d/sc/lyr **Gulzar** *pc* Uttam Chitra *st* Indra Mitra *c* K. Vaikunth *m* **Salil Choudhury**
lp **Meena Kumari**, Vinod Khanna, Shatrughan Sinha, Paintal, Asrani, Danny Denzongpa, Yogesh Chhabda, Dinesh Thakur, Mehmood, Yogita Bali, Deven Verma, Leela Mishra

Story of an old widow (Kumari) who becomes a silent witness to two violent eras in India's history: the Partition riots and the criminal politics amid gang warfare in the 60s. Persuaded by an acquaintance to move from her tranquil village home to the city to look after their child, the old woman finds herself lost on the streets until she is offered shelter by Shyam (Khanna), a notorious gangster fighting with the leader of a rival gang (Sinha). The widow's tales, and her maternal concern for Shyam's criminal friends, make her an oasis of peace amid the prevailing violence. In the end she becomes the unintended victim of their violence, restoring peace in her death. The story is intercut with flashbacks of the widow's oppressive marriage to a Nautanki performer (Verma) during the Partition riots which led to the death of her husband. Gulzar's directorial debut adapted Sinha's controversial ***Apanjan*** (1968), relocating the plot from its original **Naxalite** Bengal into a North Indian milieu. The film is held together mainly by Meena Kumari in what was, together with ***Pakeezah*** (1971), one of her last major screen performances.

MOHAMMED-BIN-TUGHLAQ

1971 136' b&w Tamil
d/s Cho Ramaswamy *pc* Prestige Prod. *lyr* **Vali** *m* M.S. Vishwanathan
lp Cho Ramaswamy, Sukumari, Ambi

Best-known satirical film, adapted from his own play, by Ramaswamy, now better known as a civil liberties activist and editor of the anti-DMK journal *Tughlaq*. The graves of two historical figures are unearthed by the commoner Rangachari (Ambi): Ibn Batuta, a mid-14th C. African Arab who travelled through India and wrote a travelogue, and Mohammed-bin-Tughlaq, a 14th C. king of the Tughlaq dynasty who sought to shift his capital from Delhi to Daulatabad trying to consolidate an all-India empire. To Rangachari's amazement, the two men are still alive. He brings them to Madras where Tughlaq wins the mid-term elections, eventually becoming Prime Minister. Seduced by power, he breaks his promise to Ibn Batuta and refuses to reveal his true identity. When Ibn Batuta threatens to expose both Tughlaq and himself as cheats impersonating politicians, Tughlaq has Ibn Batuta murdered. As a critique of the **DMK** (and of its leading politicians), the party tried to get the film banned by the Information & Broadcasting ministry. It was remade the following year by B.V. Prasad in Telugu.

ORU PENNINTE KATHA

aka *Story of a Woman*
1971 147' b&w Malayalam
d **K.S. Sethumadhavan** *p* K.S.R. Murthy *pc* Chitranjali Films *st* Moses *sc/dial* **S.L. Puram Sadanandan** *lyr* **Vyalar Rama Varma** *c* Mehli Irani *m* **P. Devarajan**
lp **Sathyan**, Sheela, Ummar, Jayabharati, **Adoor Bhasi**, Govindan Kutty Jr, Bharathan, Kaviyoor Ponnamma, T.R. Omana

Sethumadhavan's formula of the decay of feudalism with a sex motive here yields his most bizarre female lead yet, Gayatri Devi (Sheela), who carries out a remorseless vendetta against a feckless former lover, Madhavan Thambi (Sathyan), as she returns to her native village of Moonnar. She buys Madhavan's estate and his bungalow and harasses him in various ways until Madhavan's wife asks for mercy. Then, in flashback, Gayatri reveals the story of her past relationship with Madhavan.

PAKEEZAH

aka *Pure Heart*
1971 175'(125') col/scope Urdu
d/s/p/co-lyr **Kamal Amrohi** *pc* Mahal Pics *lyr* Kaif Bhopali, **Majrooh Sultanpuri**, **Kaifi Azmi** *c* Josef Wirsching *m* Ghulam Mohammed, **Naushad**
lp **Ashok Kumar**, **Meena Kumari**, Raaj Kumar, Pratima Devi, Altaf, Parveen Paul, Lotan, Chandabai, Meenakshi, Chandramohan, Zebunissa, Nadira, Veena

As shown by the presence of 40s **Bombay Talkies** cameramen Wirsching and R.D. Mathur as well as the composers Ghulam Mohammed and Naushad, Kumari's best-known film had been planned by her and her husband Amrohi as their most cherished project since 1958, when Amrohi intended to star in it himself. The film started production in 1964. When the star and her director-husband separated, the filming was postponed indefinitely. After some years, during which Kumari suffered from alcoholism, she agreed to complete the film. The plot is a classic courtesan tale set in Muslim Lucknow at the turn of the century. The dancer and courtesan Nargis (Kumari) dreams of escaping her dishonourable life but she is rejected by the family of her husband Shahabuddin (A. Kumar) and dies, in a graveyard, giving birth to a daughter, Sahibjaan. The daughter grows up to become a dancer and a courtesan as well (Kumari again). Sahibjaan's guardian, Nawabjaan (Veena), prevents Sahibjaan's father from seeing her or knowing who she is. Later, Sahibjaan falls in love with a mysterious, noble stranger who turns out to be her father's nephew, Salim (R. Kumar). Salim's father forbids his ward to marry a courtesan. The film's climax occurs when Sahibjaan dances at Salim's arranged wedding where her own father also discovers her identity and claims her as his child. Finally her desires are fulfilled and she marries Salim, leaving her past behind. The film's main merit, however, resides in its delirious romanticism enhanced by saturated colour cinematography. Includes the all-time **Lata Mangeshkar** hit songs *Chalte chalte* and *Inhe logone ne*.

RESHMA AUR SHERA

1971 158'(85') col/scope Hindi
d/p **Sunil Dutt** *pc* Ajanta Arts *st/co-sc* Ali Raza *co-sc* Ajanta Arts Story Dept *lyr* Balkavi Bairagi, Neeraj, Udhav *c* Ramchandra *m* Jaidev
lp Sunil Dutt, **Waheeda Rehman**, Raakhee, Jayant, Sulochana, K.N. Singh, Amrish Puri, **Amitabh Bachchan**, Vinod Khanna, Padma Khanna

Sunil Dutt's best-known film as director, shot in the desert at Jaisalmer, retells the Rajasthani legend about the love of Reshma (Rehman) and Shera (Dutt) amid violent feudal conflict between their clans. Also remembered as an early Bachchan appearance in the role of Chotu, Shera's sharpshooting 'kid brother' who, ordered by their vengeful father, shoots Reshma's father and her recently married brother. Unable to bear the grief of the widowed bride, Shera kills his own father believing he actually pulled the trigger. Trying to save Shera from grief and destructive madness, Reshma marries Chotu. In the end, Shera tries to redeem his patricidal act and commits suicide. Reshma also dies, rolling down a sand-dune towards his dead body. A sandstorm comes to cover their bodies, united in death. The film's sweeping desert shots dwarf the actors among the enormous dunes. Thematically, the film was unusual in its refusal to sanction the traditional, macho values of bloody revenge: Reshma refuses revenge and, prompted by the goddess Durga, finds a way out of the dilemma while remaining true to her lover. The man, however, chooses to avenge the bride turned widow and rejects love in favour of keeping his word.

SEEMABADDHA

aka *Company Limited*
1971 110' b&w Bengali
d/sc/m **Satyajit Ray** *p* Jung Bahadur Rana *pc* Chitranjali *st* Shankar's novel *c* Soumendu Roy
lp Barun Chanda, **Sharmila Tagore**, Paromita Choudhury, Harindranath Chattopadhyay, Haradhan Bannerjee, Indira Roy, Promod

Ray's follow-up to ***Pratidwandi*** (1970) sees contemporary Calcutta through the eyes of a dull sales manager in a fan factory. Shyamalendu Chatterjee (Chanda), whose life story is briefly narrated in a voice-over in the beginning, leads a well-off life among Calcutta's newly rich, apparently untouched by the political turmoil around him. He gets involved in a deal with his corrupt personnel manager, to the disappointment of his sexy sister-in-law (Tagore), but the company rewards him with a promotion. The film's moral points about the corrosive effects of a social system based on greed are made mainly through a series of markedly symbolic shots, such as the zoom into the telephone wire through which the corrupt deal is being hatched and, at the end, the high-angle shot from above the ceiling fan. The final film in Ray's Calcutta trilogy would be ***Jana Aranya*** (1975).

SHANTATA! COURT CHALU AAHE

aka *Silence! The Court is in Session*
1971 138'(118') b&w Marathi
d/co-p Satyadev Dubey *pc* Satyadev-Govind Prod. *s* **Vijay Tendulkar** from his Marathi play based on Friedrich Durrenmatt's *Die Panne* (1956) aka *A Dangerous Game c/co-p* **Govind Nihalani** *m* Jeetendra Abhishekhi
lp Sulabha Deshpande, Arvind Deshpande, Eknath Hattangadi, Saroj Telang, **Amol Palekar**, Narayan Pai, Arvind Karkhanis, Arun Kakde, Vinod Doshi, Amrish Puri, Savant

Marathi cinema's first explicitly avant-garde film. It is based on one of Tendulkar's best-known plays first staged by the well-known experimental theatre collective Rangayan. Stranded in a village, the members of a low-brow theatre group decide to pass the time by mounting a mock trial. One member of the group, Leela Benare (S. Deshpande), is expected to defend herself against a series of charges. These so disconcert the woman that the game gradually turns more serious, revealing the false veneer and the propensity to violence of the middle-class performers. The film features several of the Rangayan cast, including Sulabha Deshpande in the central role. Noted avant-garde stage director Dubey shot it using extensive jump-cuts, repeatedly fragmenting the action and the sound into a series of isolated units. Although the film depicts some of the fictional accusations, it follows the play's strategy of not revealing to the audience whether the charges are in fact true or false. It was the debut of several noted film personalities, including Tendulkar himself, **Amol Palekar**, Amrish Puri and director/cinematographer Govind Nihalani who co-produced the film in addition to shooting it. The film was apparently admired by **Ritwik Ghatak**.

SHARAPANJARA

1971 180' col Kannada
d **S.R. Puttana Kanagal** *pc* Vardini Arts *st* Triveni's novel *sc* Kanagal Prabhakara Sastry *c* D.V. Rajaram *m* **Vijayabhaskar**
lp **Kalpana**, Gangadhar, Chindodi Leela, Narasimhraju, Aswath, Shivaram, M.N. Lakshmidevi, **Leelavathi**

The culmination of Kalpana's long association with Kanagal (cf ***Bellimoda***, 1967; ***Gejje Pooje***, 1970). The happily married Kaveri (Kalpana) becomes pregnant and suffers an attack of hysteria in which she recalls having gone to Nanjangud on a picnic with an unnamed man. She returns to the picnic spot and frantically searches for something she believes she 'lost' there. Her husband (Gangadhar) has her interned in an asylum and starts an affair with an office colleague (Leela). Released from the asylum, Kaveri finds that everyone keeps reminding her of her 'insanity', including the new cook (Shivaram), the neighbours, her father (Aswath) and her mother-in-law. She eventually has to return to the hospital for the rest of her life. Kalpana's spectacular performance and the film's blatant but unacknowledged psychoanalytic dimension holds the story together. The conflict between virtue and unconscious desire is given a mythological dimension in the song *Hadi nalaku varusha* comparing Kaveri to Seeta returning from exile in the *Ramayana*. Kanagal's neo-expressionist idiom is most in evidence in the scenes of Kaveri's hysteric episode, the mysterious boyfriend's presence being confined to the soundtrack only.

SINDOORACHEPPU

aka *Sindoor Box*
1971 150' b&w Malayalam
d **Madhu** *p/s/lyr* Yusuf Ali Kacheri *c* Benjamin, Master Aloysius, Vasant B.N. *m* **P. Devarajan**
lp Madhu, Shankaradi, Jayabharati, Bahadur, Philomina, Radhamani, Shobha

Directed by Malayalam star Madhu, the film was dominated by its producer and writer, the poet Kacheri. It used the rich Kerala landscape and folklore as a backdrop for his love songs in a story humanising elephants and poking fun at soothsayers and simple village folk. The star of the sometimes violent film is the elephant Gopi who behaves a little like a golem, rebelling against being maltreated and blindly enacting a code of social justice. A soothsayer claims that the beloved elephant will kill three people and the mahout's daughter, Ammalu, fills her sindoor box with ants which she then puts into Gopi's trunk to kill him. Years later, the village has been modernised but the prediction has not been forgotten. When the mahout Shankaran Nair drunkenly annoys Gopi, the elephant kills a man and is to be destroyed. A wandering mahout, Keshavan, saves Gopi's life and becomes Ammalu's lover. When Keshavan is about to marry Ammalu, Gopi goes mad with anger and Ammalu again puts ants in his trunk. Gopi kills her and Keshavan leaves the village as the police come to shoot the elephant. Kacheri went on to make another animistic film, ***Maram*** (1972).

SONGADYA

1971 142' b&w Marathi
d Govind Kulkarni *p/co-lyr* **Dada Kondke** *pc* Sadiccha Chitra *s/co-lyr* Vasant Sabnis *co-lyr* Jagdish Khebudkar *c* Arvind Laad *m* Ram Kadam
lp Usha Chavan, **Dada Kondke**, Ratnamala, Nilu Phule, Ganpat Patil, Gulab Mokashi, Sampat Nikam

Marathi comedian Kondke's first independent production inaugurates his particular style: a vaguely Tamasha-derived ribald comedy featuring an innocent bumbling hero, a sexy heroine and dialogues replete with sexual puns and innuendo. The script is by Sabnis, whose Tamasha-derived stage hit *Vichcha Majhi Puri Kara* (1965) saw Kondke's breakthrough performance. The innocent Namya (Kondke), the son of the tough Shitabai, is taken by his friends to see a Tamasha performance. He gets so excited by the *Mahabharata* scene of Draupadi's vastraharan (in which the enemy Kauravas try forcibly to disrobe her) that he jumps on stage disrupting the performance. He goes to the next village to see the performance again, where (as the actor who is to play the monkey-god Hanuman gets drunk) he is invited to understudy the part. Namya's distraught mother kicks him out of the house, but the dancer Kalavati (Chavan, Kondke's usual female lead) offers him shelter. The clutch of hit songs includes the duet *Malyachya malya madhi kon ga ubhi*.

TERE MERE SAPNE

1971 175' col Hindi
d/sc/p **Vijay Anand** *pc* Navketan, Vijay Anand Prod. *st* Kaushal Bharti's story based on A.J. Cronin's *The Citadel* *lyr* Neeraj *c* V. Ratra *m* **S.D Burman**
lp **Dev Anand**, Mumtaz, **Mahesh Kaul**, Vijay Anand, Agha, **Hema Malini**, Tabassum, Premnath

Dev Anand is the young, idealistic doctor who moves to the village with his wife, a rural schoolteacher (Mumtaz). When his pregnant wife meets with an accident caused by a rich car driver who then bribes the authorities, the hero loses faith in his idealism and returns to the city. There he becomes rich and falls in love with the film star Malatimala (Hema Malini). He is reconciled with his wife when their long-awaited son is born. Shot mainly in studios (except for the picturisation of the hit song *Maine kasam li*), the film resembles a tv drama. Notable mainly for Burman's music.

VAMSHA VRIKSHA

1971 166' b&w Kannada
co-d **B.V. Karanth** *co-d/dial* **Girish Karnad** *p* **G.V. Iyer** *st* S.L. Byrappa's novel *c* U.M.N. Sharief *m* Bhaskar Chandavarkar
lp Venkata Rao Talegiri, L.V. Sharada Rao, B.V. Karanth, Girish Karnad, Chandrasekhar, Uma Sivakumar, G.V. Iyer

The debut feature of directors Karnad and Karanth, in the wake of ***Samskara*** (1970), interrogates the legitimacy of tradition: a proud Brahmin scholar (Talegiri) looks after his widowed daughter-in-law (Sharada) and grandson until she falls in love with her English lecturer (Karnad) and remarries. She loses custody of her son, and her guilt feelings are aggravated by her son (Chandrasekhar) who becomes her student but refuses to acknowledge her as his mother. Eventually the old partiarch discovers that he himself was illegitimate and he foregoes his wealth to prove to the heroine, on her deathbed, that she was right to insist on inventing her own notion of tradition.

UMMACHU

1971 162' b&w Malayalam
d/lyr **P. Bhaskaran** *pc* Rajshri Prod. *s* Uroob *m* Raghunath
lp Sheela, **Madhu**, Nellikode Bhaskaran, Shankaradi, Bahadur, Vidhubala

Convoluted drama adapting a famous Uroob novel. The Muslim girl Ummachu (Sheela in a major role) has two suitors, Mayan (Madhu) and Beeran (Bhaskaran). She marries the rich Beeran, who ill-treats her. In retaliation Mayan kills Beeran and marries Ummachu, even as an innocent man is arrested for the crime. Many years later the truth comes out, after which Mayan commits suicide and his son by Ummachu marries the daughter of the man accused of Mayan's crime.

VIDYARTHIKALE ITHILE ITHILE

aka *This Way Students* aka *Students Today*
1971 174' b&w Malayalam
d **John Abraham** *p* Minnal *pc* Mehboob Prod. *s* M. Azad *lyr* **Vyalar Rama Varma** *c* Ramchandra *m* **M.B. Srinivasan**
lp **Adoor Bhasi**, Manorama, **S.V. Ranga Rao**, Jayabharati, S.P. Pillai, M.R.R. Vasu, T.K. Balachandran, Paravoor Bharathan, Kuthiravattom Pappu, Philomina, Santha Devi

Abraham's first feature is a politically pessimistic but ethically optimistic story advocating practical forms of solidarity with victimised or threatened colleagues. While playing football, some schoolboys break the statue of the school's founder and the culprit, Raju, must pay for the damage or face expulsion. The boys get together and earn the money polishing boots, selling lottery tickets and so on. The school's principal (Ranga Rao) is so impressed that he gets the management to repair the statue and spends the money paid by the boys on a school trip for them. Shortly afterwards, during another game of football, the ball hits and breaks the statue again. Apparently inspired by Louis Daquin's *Nous les gosses* (1941).

ANTA MANA MANCHIKE

aka *All for the Best*
1972 176' b&w Telugu
d/s/co-m **P. Bhanumathi** *pc* Bharani Pics *dial* **D.V. Narasaraju** *lyr* Dasarathi, **Arudra**, **Devulapalli Krishna Sastry** *c* Laxman Gore *co-m* Sathyam
lp P. Bhanumathi, **Krishna**, Nagabhushanam, Krishnamraju, **Chittor V. Nagaiah**, T. Padmini, Suryakantam, Rushyendramani, Chhaya Devi, Sandhya Rani, **K. Mukkamala**

Bhanumathi's return to direction (cf ***Chandirani***, 1953) is a melodrama with nine songs. A young widow, Savitri, raises her sister, Seeta. When Seeta grows up she gets a job with the villain Phanibhushana Rao, not knowing that he was the cause of her parents' poverty and death. She also falls in love with the man's son. The villain tries to trap Savitri into prostitution and has her imprisoned when she attacks his associate. Eventually Savitri is freed and Seeta marries her beloved.

BANGARADA MANUSHYA

1972 180' col Kannada
d/sc Siddalingaiah *pc* Rajkamal Arts *st* T.K. Ramarao's novel *dial/co-lyr* **Hunsur Krishnamurthy** *co-lyr* R. Jayagopal, Vijayanarasimha *c* D.V. Rajaram *m* **G.K. Venkatesh**
lp **Rajkumar**, Bharati, **Balkrishna**, **Arathi**, M.P. Shankar, B.V. Radha, Srinath, Dwarkeesh, Vajramuni, Lokanath, Lakshmidevi

Ruralist frontier melodrama in which hero Rajiv (Rajkumar) abandons his urban career to help his widowed sister and her impoverished family reestablish themselves. Overcoming the ingratitude of his elder brother (Lokanath) and the self-serving opposition of several villagers, he builds a garish home symbolising his family's success. However, his wife (Bharati), wearing her red wedding sari, is chased by a bull, falls into a well and drowns. His two nephews, Sethuram and Chakrapani (introduced as a comedy duo), accuse him of bigamy with the woman (Arathi) who later is revealed to be the illegitimate daughter of his late brother-in-law whom Rajiv secretly protected. In the end, Rajiv leaves and renounces all his worldly possessions. The film recalls the upwardly-mobile and gaudy neo-traditionalism associated with Rajkumar as well as **Rajesh Khanna** (cf ***Bandhan***, 1969, and ***Dushman***, 1971). From the opening, as Rajkumar steps out of the train dressed in red and black singing the homecoming song *Nagunaguta nali nali* to the bizarre sequence showing his decision to abandon his family (camera tilting down to his uneaten meal), the film constructs a fantasy village as the authentic underpinning of urban values, echoing the formally more sophisticated ruralist realism of the contemporary New Indian Cinema. Rajkumar's biggest 70s hit and one of the top grossers of Kannada cinema.

BILET PHERAT

1972 145' b&w Bengali
d/p/s/m **Chidananda Das Gupta** *pc* C. Das Gupta Prod. *lyr* Jaidev *c* Dhrubajyoti Basu, Kamal Nayak
lp Nirmal Kumar, **Anil Chatterjee**, **Soumitra Chatterjee**, **Aparna Sen**, Dulal Ghosh, Shyamal Ghosh, Sohag Sen, Anuradha Lahiri, Neeta Ghosh, Ashok Mitra, Krishna Kundu, Sonali Sen, Neela Khan

Noted critic Das Gupta's critically acclaimed solo feature reworks the theme of one of the first Bengali films, **Dhiren Ganguly**'s ***Bilet Pherat*** (1921) satirising colonial India's 'foreign-returned' youth. The film tells three separate short stories, all written by the director and featuring young men who prove unsuccessful in getting their idealism to work in present-day India. The best known of the three, *Rakta*, was later re-issued as a separate film. In it, a young man (S. Chatterjee) who returns to Calcutta from Oxford University is forced by the conservatism of his family to quit his job as lecturer and then his job as executive in a British firm. He rebels and starts his own business, converting animal blood into fertiliser, but loses that as well when it is taken over by multinational interests. The film combined fiction with documentary sequences, which continued Das Gupta's fascination with Calcutta first in evidence in his b&w documentary *Portrait of a City* (1961) using the remarkable camerawork of Barin Saha.

CALCUTTA '71

1972 132' b&w/col Bengali
d/sc/co-st **Mrinal Sen** *pc* DS Pics *p* D.S. Sultania *co-st* Manik Badyopadhyay, Prabodh Sanyal, Samaresh Bose, Ajitesh Bannerjee *c* K.K. Mahajan *m* Ananda Shankar
lp Ranjit Mullick, **Utpal Dutt**, Geeta Sen, **Madhabi Mukherjee**, Sadhana Roy Choudhury, Satya Bannerjee, Snigdha Majumdar, Ajitesh Bannerjee, Debraj Ray, **Robi Ghosh**, Raju, Suhasini Mulay, Binota Ray

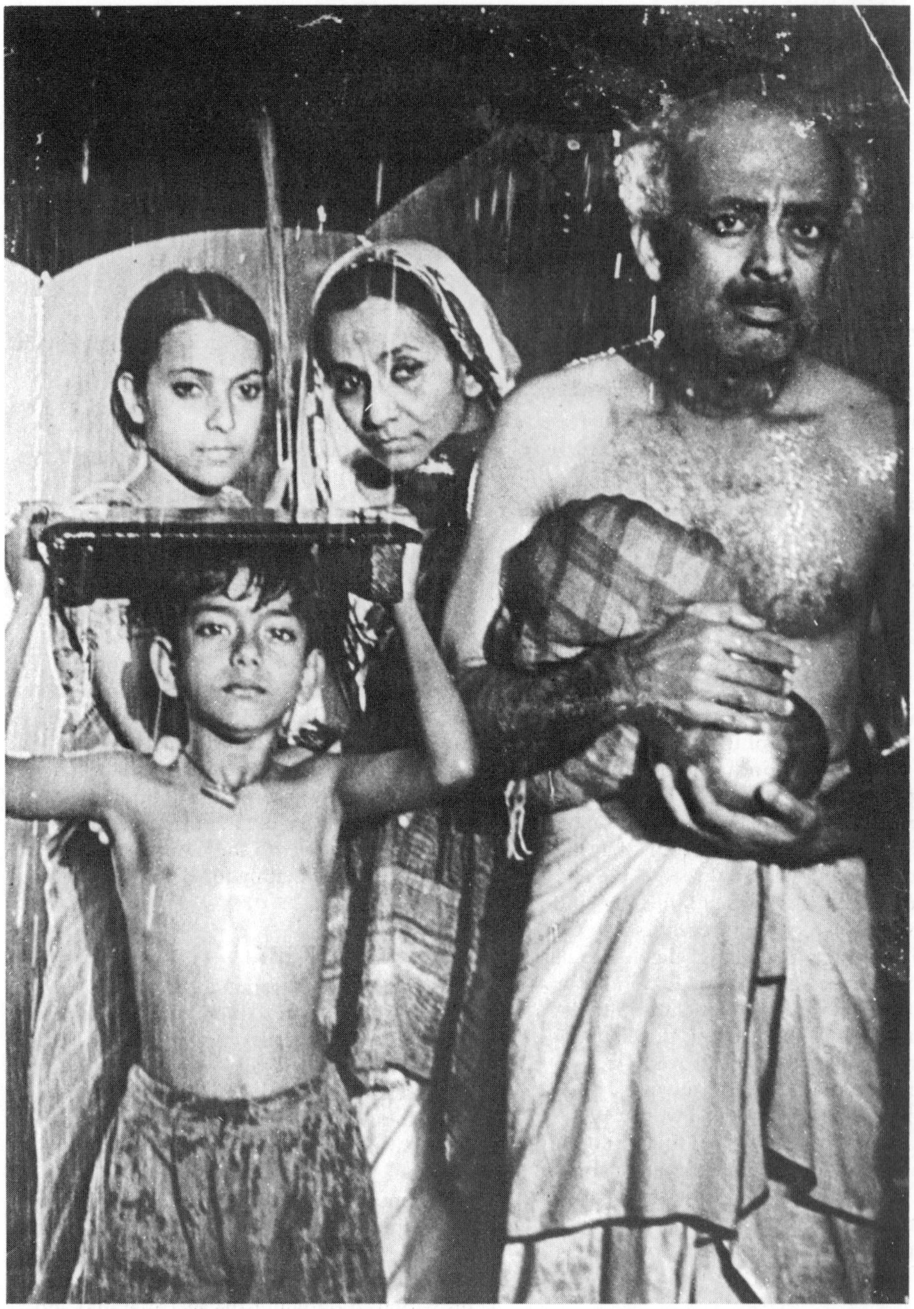

Snigdha Majumdar (left, rear), Sadhana Roy Choudhury (centre) and Satya Bannerjee (right) in *Calcutta '71*

Sen set out the aims of his 2nd film in the Calcutta trilogy (***Interview***, 1970; ***Padatik***, 1973): 'As long as you present poverty as something dignified, the establishment will not be disturbed. We wanted to define history and put poverty in its right perspective.' Extending his anti-naturalist approach in order to explore more freely and with greater complexity the way history shapes the texture of people's lives, the film recounts three famous Bengali stories by three Bengali authors together with two contemporary episodes, each presenting an aspect of poverty and exploitation: an angry young man on trial in 1971, a rainstorm in a slum in 1933, a lower-middle-class family during the 1943 famine, teenage smugglers in 1953 and, back again in 1971, a middle-class group in a posh hotel. The events are linked by an imaginary figure who, by 1971, has gained an insight into the dynamics of history and urges action for change. Often described as 'propagandistic', the film is more didactic in the Brechtian sense, encouraging audiences to learn from the representations rather than telling people what to think. The film became a major cultural rallying point for student radicals, its screenings at the Metro Theatre in Chowringhee, Calcutta, being placed constantly under police surveillance.

CHEMPARATHI

1972 142' b&w Malayalam
d **P.N. Menon** *p* S.K. Nair *pc* New India Films *s* Malayattoor Ramakrishnan *lyr* **Vyalar Rama Varma** *c* Ashok Kumar *m* **P. Devarajan**
lp **Madhu**, Raghavan, Sudhir, Balan K. Nair, Bharathan, **Adoor Bhasi**, Bahadur, **Kottarakkara Sridharan Nair**, Shobhana, Adoor Bhawani, Rani Chandra, Radhamani

Menon followed up his critically acclaimed realist drama ***Olavum Theeravum*** (1969) with this love tragedy and murder mystery. The beautiful teenager Shantha (Shobhana), daughter of a gatekeeper, loves the student Dinesh who lives in the main lodge along with Prof. Balachandran. However, the rich villain Rajappan rapes and then kills Shantha. Dinesh, who witnesses the murder and is haunted by Shantha's ghost, kills the villain in turn. Shot largely in close-up and mid-shot, the film includes several suspense-inducing sequences like Shantha's corpse floating in a well, or Dinesh being haunted by what he saw, to shift an otherwise conventional Malayalam storyline into a new genre.

DHAKAM

aka *Thirst*
1972 144' b&w Tamil
d/s Babu Nathencode *pc* Kavya Chitra *sc* K.K. Raman *st/c* T. Vaiyadurai *lyr* Bharati, Poovai Senguttovan *m* **M.B. Srinivasan**
lp C. Muthuraman, Nandita Bose, Sundarrajan, **Pandharibai**, Rajakokila, Renuka Parvathi, Jayaseelam

The blind Sekhar (Muthuraman) lives with other orphans in a Gandhian ashram, where he forms a special bond with little Sharada (Bose). They eventually get married and she tries to make a living as a saleswoman in Madras, but city life is too much for them and they return to the ashram. Sharada dies, having donated her eyes to a blind person. Nathencode and Vaiyadurai devised this film while on the staff at the Madras Film Institute and shot it in Gandhigram against the beautiful Sirumalai hills. Composer Srinivasan's speciality of the group song is evident in the hits *Vanam namadhu thanthai* and *Bharata samudayam*.

GNANA OLI

aka *The Light of Wisdom*
1972 158' b&w Tamil
d P. Madhavan *pc* Jayaar Movies *s* Vietnam Veedu Sundaram *lyr* **Kannadasan** *c* P.N. Sundaram *m* M.S. Vishwanathan
lp **Sivaji Ganesan**, **Sharada**, Major Sundarrajan, M.R.R. Vasu, Srikanth, Jaya Kausalya, V.K. Ramaswamy, Seetalakshmi, **Vijayanirmala**, Manorama, Gokulnath

The golden-hearted ex-criminal Anthony (Ganesan) works with the Rev. Adaikalam (Gokulnath) who has raised him. When his daughter Mary (Sharada) is impregnated and abandoned by her lover Bhaskar (Srikanth), Anthony kills Bhaskar and gets a life sentence. He escapes, with the priest's assistance, and becomes the millionaire philanthropist Arun, wearing a black eyepatch and white gloves as a disguise. Inspector Lawrence, who has pursued his former schoolfriend Anthony for years, eventually arrests his prey at the wedding of Anthony's granddaughter (Jaya Kausalya) with the cop's son. Loosely based on Victor Hugo's *Les Miserables* (cf ***Ezhai Padum Padu***, 1950), the film was shot around the Church of the Immaculate Lady at Poondi near Thanjavur and was released on the centenary of St Thomas's arrival in India, an important Christian festival in India. Anthony's song, *En devene Ennai parungal*, was the hit of the year.

GRAHAN

1972 121' b&w Hindi
d/p/c Arvind Kumar Sinha *st* Bimal Kumar *m* **Vasant Desai**
lp **Nutan**, **Subhash Ghai**, Suhasini Mulay, **Basanta Choudhury**

Art-house melodrama with a complicated plot. The notoriously principled scientist marries a young woman. His assistant falls in love with his superior's wife. The assistant's wife causes further problems when she reveals a past affair that the scientist once had with her sister. Financed by the **FFC**, the film was for a while exhibited as an instance of the 'parallel' or 'new-wave' cinema of the 70s (cf **New Indian Cinema**).

Inner Eye, The

1972 20' col English/Bengali
d/sc/m **Satyajit Ray** *c* Soumendu Roy

After an unfortunate experience with the documentary *Sikkim* (1971), produced by the Chogyal of Sikkim (whose widow, Hope Cooke, may possess a copy) but banned by the Indian Government, Ray made this documentary on the noted Bengali painter and muralist Binode Behari Mukherjee. Extensive footage of the artist as a (blind) old man is intercut with shots of paintings and stock footage of Shantiniketan where he worked. The best moments in the film are the shooting of Mukherjee's best-known work, the *Medieval Hindi Saints* mural on the walls of the Hindi Bhavan, Shantiniketan.

KOSHISH

1972 125' col Hindi *d/st/co-sc/lyr* **Gulzar** *co-sc* Mohini N. Sippy *c* K. Vaikunth *m* **Madan Mohan**
lp Sanjeev Kumar, Jaya Bhaduri, Om Shivpuri, Dina Pathak, Asrani, Nitin Sethi, Seema, Urmila Bhatt, Atam Prakash

Melodrama about a deaf and dumb couple who, with the aid of a blind man, overcome the odds of living in a hostile and uncaring society. Haricharan (Kumar) and Aarti (Bhaduri) are plagued by Aarti's evil brother (Asrani) as they struggle to bring up their son notwithstanding their disabilities. When their son refuses to marry a disabled girl, Haricharan forces a happy ending. Probably Gulzar's most heavy-handed drama, further weighed down by an emphatic score.

MARAM

aka *Tree*
1972 131' b&w Malayalam
d/p/co-lyr Yusuf Ali Kacheri *pc* Anjana *s* N.P. Mohammed *co-lyr* Sateeshan *c* U. Rajagopal *m* **P. Devarajan**
lp **Prem Nazir**, K.P. Ummar, Jayabharati, Nellikode Bhaskaran, K.P.A.C. Lalitha, T.S. Muthaiah, **Adoor Bhasi**, Bahadur, Philomina

Melodrama in which a young Muslim woman, Ameena (Jayabharati), believes her husband Ibrahim (Nazir) to have been killed at the front. She consents to marry a coarse but rich mill owner. When her first husband returns, she has a problem, resolved when she rejoins her true love. The film was a musical hit with songs by **Yesudas**, **P. Susheela** et al., one of which, *Pathinalam ravudichathu*, was a hit.

MAYA DARPAN

aka *Mirror of Illusion*
1972 107' col Hindi
d/p/sc **Kumar Shahani** *pc* **FFC** *st* Nirmal Varma *c* K.K. Mahajan *m* Bhaskar Chandavarkar
lp Aditi, Anil Pandya, Kanta Vyas, Iqbalnath Kaul

Shahani's extraordinary but controversial debut feature marks both the culmination and the end of the brief **NFDC**-sponsored renewal of Indian cinema. With great formal rigour and beauty, the film extends Ghatak's ***Meghe Dhaka Tara*** (1960; quoted on two occasions on the soundtrack), making female sexuality and the very textures of living the focus of a conflict between oppressive feudal norms and a changing industrialised landscape. Taran (Aditi), the younger unmarried daughter of the zamindar (Kaul) in a Rajasthani mansion, violates the social codes dictating class and gender segregation by her sexual encounter with an engineer (Pandya). Shahani, who later evolved a theory of epic cinema, develops a uniquely cinematic orchestration of time and space through, e.g., the rigid cyclical rhythms of lyric poetry: cf the tracking shots through the ancient house while Vani Jayaram sings the lullaby *Lal bichhona* or the repeated reading of her brother's letter about fertile Assam as she walks through the arid industrial landscape around her home. In the end, the circular form is broken as the Chhou dancers, dressed in black and red, are shot with gigantic tilt-down camera movements and the film closes with a linear flight-line (fantasy escape) towards a green shore, but filmed through the constricting portholes of a boat. Taran moves through a landscape that mirrors her state of mind: a barren desert that was once owned by a warrior caste now reduced to effete rituals of self-purification, and handed over without protest to a new era of technological colonisers. The effects of capitalist modernisation are presented as both ruthless and incomprehensible, reducing an articulate cultural landscape into a mere natural resource. Taran's fantasies of Assam are contrasted with the engineer's radical notion of change as he quotes Engels's famous line 'freedom is the recognition of necessity'. Images and soundtrack are at times punctuated by violent eruptions of anger at the suffocation of desire: e.g. gunfire, war (in an explosion of yellow), the hushed reference to working-class agitations. Taran's own rebellion is prefigured by a breathtaking shot of herself annointed with the ultramarine blue of Kali against an urban skyline. Her recognition of 'necessity' is followed by her absorption into the Chhou performance as the dancers invoke fertility on the desert sand. The film also constitutes the only successful colour experiment of New Indian Cinema.

NAGARA HAAVU

1972 184' col Kannada
d/sc **S.R. Puttana Kanagal** *pc* Shri Eswari Prod. *st* T.R. Subbarao *co-dial/co-lyr* Chi. Udayashankar *co-dial* Vijayanarasimha *co-lyr*

R.N. Jayagopal *c* R. Chittibabu *m* **Vijayabhaskar**
lp **Vishnuvardhan**, **Arathi**, Shobha, K.S. Aswath, Shivaram, Ambareesh, M.P. Shankar, **Leelavathi**, Loknath, H.R. Sastry, B. Raghavendra Rao

Kanagal's colour debut continues his neo-expressionist psychodramas. Ramachari (Vishnuvardhan), Kanagal's first male protagonist, is a 'cobra', i.e. a hunched, unpredictable, phallocentric creature, disinterested in his studies and dreaded by his teachers and neighbours. He falls in love with Alamelu (Arathi), but the relationship is discouraged by his teacher, the only man able to influence him. The cobra then falls in love with Margaret (Shobha). Alamelu marries another man and Ramachari discovers, in the lobby of a hotel with a gaudy fountain, that she has become a prostitute. Eventually, Ramachari pushes his teacher off a cliff and commits suicide along with his Christian girlfriend. Characteristically, Kanagal uses the skeletal plot to elaborate a long drama, set in the mountainous wilds of the Chitradurga region. Its major constituent is the stylised, reptilian performance of Vishnuvardhan, making his film debut. It extends into several fantasy sequences of women running in slow motion in a rocky landscape, the rebellious *Nanna rosha* number set to a marching beat, and the climactic hotel sequence as Alamelu bursts into song to explain her condition. Subbarao, aka Ta.Ra.Su., wrote the original story but later disowned the film, causing furious supporters of Kanagal to attack him for not having understood his own story. It was remade by Kanagal in Hindi as *Zehreela Insaan* (1974), starring Rishi Kapoor.

NINE MONTHS TO FREEDOM: THE STORY OF BANGLADESH

1972 72' col English
d **S. Sukhdev** *pc* **Films Division** *collaboration by* Sohrab Boga, **Tapan Bose**, Jagmohan, Gopal Maharesh, Bina Puri, Abdullah Khan, B.I. Maisuriya, Subrata Bannerjee, **Harisadhan Dasgupta**, Pratap Sharma, N.V.K. Murthy, Pyare Shivpuri

Sukhdev's biggest documentary is a partisan chronicle of the history of Pakistan to the point where Bangladesh, led by Sheikh Mujibur Rehman, demanded its freedom. Then it narrates the events after 25 March 1971, when Yahya Khan sent in the raping and rampaging Pakistani army, the heroic struggle of Bangladesh's Mukti Bahini and finally the Indian Army's defeat of Pakistan and the liberation of Bangladesh. The highlights of the film are its refutation of a clip from Pakistan tv with a strong voice-over, and the interview with an enraged Andre Malraux saying he wants to pick up a rifle and join the war against Yahya Khan's army. Large parts of the story are told using a montage of stills, including newspaper headlines. In addition to footage from BBC tv and Pakistan tv, the film uses sequences of the massacre in Bangladesh (including the opening shot of a dog ripping apart a human corpse).

PADI PISHIR BARMI BAKSHA

aka *Aunt Padi's Burmese Box*
1972 118' b&w/col Bengali
d/sc/m **Arundhati Devi** *pc* Anindiya Chitra *st* Leela Majumdar *lyr* **Kazi Nazrul Islam** *c* Bimal Mukherjee
lp **Chhaya Devi**, Tapan Bhattacharya, Chinmoy Roy, Ajitesh Bannerjee, **Robi Ghosh**, **Jahar Roy**, Haridhan Mukherjee, Ketaki Dutta, Nirmal Kumar, Padmadevi, Rudraprasad Sengupta

Enjoyable though uneven adaptation of Leela Majumdar's classic children's novel. Young hero Khokha, on the way to his uncle's house, is told the tale of his famed Aunt Padipishi. A formidable widow, she once tamed a bandit uncle of hers who passed himself off as a saint, extracting a precious Burmese box in return for her silence. Back in the present, a private detective follows the young hero as the entire family searches for the missing treasure. Eventually the box is found in the attic, where it had been hidden by Padipishi's no-good son Gaja. The film's flashbacks, showing the exploits of the aunt, are in colour. The zany shooting and acting styles mix naturalism with a stylised, operatic direct address.

PANDANTI KAPURAM

1972 178' col Telugu
d/sc P. Laxmi Deepak *pc* Jayaprada Pics *st* Prabhakara Reddy *dial* Madipatla Suri *lyr* Dasarathi, C. Narayana Reddy, **Kosaraju**, Gopi, Appulacharya *c* V.S.R. Swamy *m* S.P. Kodandapani
lp **Krishna**, **Vijayanirmala**, **S.V. Ranga Rao**, Devika, **Gummadi Venkateshwara Rao**, **Jamuna**, Prabhakara Reddy, **B. Saroja Devi**, Rajbabu, Sandhyarani, Ram Mohan, **Pandharibai**, Mikkilineni, Sujatha, Allu Ramalingaiah, Radhakumari

Traditionalist joint family tale by a star better known for his indigenous adaptations of James Bond thrillers. Four brothers, who love each other dearly, get married and find their wives less than inclined to share their notions of family collectivity.

PARICHAY

1972 145' col Hindi
d/co-sc/dial/lyr **Gulzar** *pc* Tirupati Pics *st* R.K Mitra *co-sc* D.N. Mukherjee *c* K. Vaikunth *m* **R.D. Burman**
lp **Jeetendra**, Jaya Bhaduri, Pran, Sanjeev Kumar, Vinod Khanna, A.K. Hangal, Veena, Leela Mishra, Keshto Mukherjee, Asrani, Master Ravi, Master Kishore, Baby Pinky, Master Raju

Sound of Music (1965) adaptation turning the tutor into a man (Jeetendra) who arrives at Rai Saheb's (Pran) regimental household to 'civilise' the orphaned grandchildren: a brat pack and their elder sister Rama (Bhaduri). The children's father was the talented singer Nilesh (Kumar) who had been told to leave the house when he married against his father's wishes, and the brood hold their rich grandfather responsible for their father's penury and death from tuberculosis. The tutor eventually befriends the children and changes their attitude towards their grandfather. Rama falls in love with him and Rai Saheb blesses their wedding. The Hindi version of the *Do re mi* number was *Sa-re ke sa-re ga-ma*, sung by **Asha Bhosle** and **Kishore Kumar**.

PINJRA

1972 175'[Mar]/186'[H] col Marathi/Hindi
d/p **V. Shantaram** *pc* V. Shantaram Prod. *s* **Anant Mane** *dial* Shankar Patil *lyr* Jagdish Khebudkar *c* Shivaji Sawant *m* Ram Kadam
lp Sandhya, Shriram Lagoo, Nilu Phule, Vatsala Deshmukh, Govind Kulkarni, Manikraj, Krishnakant Dalvi, Sarla Yevlekar

Shantaram's remake of Sternberg's *Der blaue Engel* (1930) is a belated homage to his German neo-expressionist influences. He set the story in the popular (esp. in scenarist Mane's own films) Marathi genre of the Tamasha musical. The upright teacher (Shriram Lagoo), vehemently opposed to what he considers degenerate entertainment, is seduced by a Tamasha actress (Sandhya). The two fall in love, forcing the teacher to change his identity. In his new guise he ends up being accused, and sentenced to death, for having murdered the teacher, i.e. himself. Known mainly for its numerous hit songs, the film uninhibitedly rehearses the emphatic symbologies of Shantaram's early days. Ironically, the film also chronicles Shantaram's own dissolution as a film-maker closely linked to the formal misery of contemporary Marathi cinema, performing lok-natya music to garish colour and Sandhya's actorial contortions. This is the film debut of Dr Lagoo, who was making a big impact at the time on the Marathi stage with his highly charged naturalist style.

SHAYAR-E-KASHMIR MAHJOOR

1972 153' col Hindi
d/p/sc Prabhat Mukherjee *pc* Tas Films, Govt. of Jammu and Kashmir *dial* **Balraj Sahni**, Pran Kaul *lyr* Prem Dhawan, **Kaifi Azmi** *c* Ajoy *m* Prem Dhawan
lp Balraj Sahni, Parikshit (aka Ajay) Sahni, Miss Kaul, Kalpana Sahni, Pran Kishore Kaul, Badgami, Raja Hamid, Kishori Kaul, Rajni Gupta, Geetanjali Desai, Sajda Zameer Ahmed, Gulam Mohammed Pandit

Although regarded as a Kashmiri production, this Hindi film is a biographical of Ghulam Ahmed Mahjoor (1885-1952), the Kashmiri poet often presented as the greatest writer in the language after Habba Khatoon's 16th-C. romantic lyrics, which strongly marked the writer's early work. In the 40s, influenced by the radical literary movements of the **PWA**, he wrote poems addressing contemporary Kashmir and his death triggered state-wide mourning rituals. In 1953 he was declared the official national poet of Kashmir. The film presents Mahjoor's (Sahni) chequered early life until he switches from writing in Persian and Urdu to Kashmiri, after which his image becomes fused with the official iconography of the Jammu and Kashmir government. However, under Sahni's influence, the film also offers a nationalist critique of the regime of Sheikh Abdullah, jailed by the Delhi government in 1953 shortly after Kashmir officially joined the Republic.

SWAYAMVARAM

aka *One's own Choice* aka *Betrothal by Choice*
1972 131' b&w Malayalam
d/co-sc/st **Adoor Gopalakrishnan** *p* Kulathoor Bhaskaran Nair *pc* Chitralekha Film Co-op *co-sc* **K.P. Kumaran** *c* Ravi Varma *m* **M.B. Srinivasan**
lp **Sharada, Madhu, Thikkurisi Sukumaran Nair**, Adoor Bhawani, Lalitha, **Gopi**, P.K. Venukuttan Nair, Janardhan Nair, B.K. Nair, Vaikom Chandrasekharan Nair, G. Shankara Pillai

In Gopalakrishnan's debut feature, Viswam (Madhu) and Seeta (Sharada) come to the city as eloped lovers, but although the social pressures to conform may be less stifling, the economic pressures make their survival increasingly precarious. They move from their expensive hotel to a cheaper one, and eventually to a slum, with a smuggler, a rice seller and a prostitute for neighbours. Viswam, who is also a writer, has his novel turned down, and then loses his job as a lecturer. Eventually he dies in poverty, leaving Seeta a destitute widow with a small baby. In the end, as she puts the child to sleep, she hears a knock at the door and looks up into camera. This shot is held for a while, raising the question of the viewers' implication in the conditions portrayed in the film. A bitter drama redeemed by the passion the lovers bear for each other, represented by the child which deserves a better deal out of life than the parents received. The immiseration of the couple is not presented as a punishment for infringing some repressive moral code, which is a refreshing change in this type of melodrama in Kerala; instead, Gopalakrishnan raises the issue of collective responsibility in an impressively cinematic manner.

TATA MANUVUDU

1972 177' b&w Telugu
d/s **Dasari Narayana Rao** *pc* Pratap Art Prod. *lyr* C. Narayana Reddy, **Kosaraju**, Shankara *c* Kannappa *m* Ramesh Naidu
lp **S.V. Ranga Rao, Gummadi Venkateshwara Rao**, Rajababu, Satyanarayana, **Anjali Devi, Vijayanirmala**, Rajasulochana, Renuka, Allu Ramalingaiah, Manjula

Dasari Narayana Rao's debut is a melodrama featuring three generations of a rural family. A villager educates his son who then moves to the city, forgetting all about his responsibilities to his parents until his own son resumes a relationship with the grandfather.

TRISANDHYA

1972 133' b&w/col Hindi
d/p Raj Marbros *st* Uroob *c* Sudarshan Nag *m* Bahadur Khan
lp **Waheeda Rehman**, Bhaskar, Lata Menon, P.K. Abraham

Art-house movie adapting an Uroob novel and set in Kerala. Bhaskar (Bhaskar) falls in love with Indu (Rehman), but she marries his elder brother and business partner. The elder brother dies and Bhaskar has a paralytic attack. He is attended to by his former lover, who has now become a professional nurse. The only significant feature of an otherwise unremarkable film was that **John Abraham** was employed, early in his career, to assist Marbros.

ZER TO PIDHAN JANI JANI

1972 127' b&w Gujarati
d/sc **Upendra Trivedi** *pc* Rangbhoomi Prod. *st* Manubhai Pancholi 'Darshak' *lyr/m* **Avinash Vyas** *c* Pratap Dave
lp Anupama, Upendra Trivedi, Arvind Trivedi, Vishnukumar Vyas, Narhari Jani

Trivedi, the main star of Gujarati cinema, directed this version of Pancholi's novel after first adapting it to the stage. A man retires to rural life and becomes a benevolent agriculturist. His daughter and her childhood boyfriend, a city-bred son of a barrister, fall into a complex family drama against the backdrop of India's freedom struggle.

ABACHURINA POST OFFICE

1973 114' b&w Kannada
d/sc **N. Lakshminarayan** *pc* Chitra Shilpi *st* Purnachandra Tejasvi *dial* Navarathna Ram *c* N.G. Rao *m* **Vijayabhaskar**
lp B.N. Narayanan, Girija Lokesh, Jayaram, Shanta, Katte Ramchandra, Ramesh Bhatt

Bobanna works on a coffee plantation and doubles up as the village postman. He becomes involved with the lives of the illiterate villagers who ask him to write or read out their letters. Although he scrupulously respects people's privacy, his evil mother-in-law leaks the contents of an anonymous letter and causes a scandal. The village turns against Bobanna, who has to leave.

ANKUR

aka *The Seedling*
1973 136' col Hindi
d/s **Shyam Benegal** *p* Lalit M. Bijlani *pc* Blaze Film *dial* Satyadev Dubey *c* **Govind Nihalani** *m* **Vanraj Bhatia**
lp **Anant Nag, Shabana Azmi**, Sadhu Meher, Priya Tendulkar, Mirza Qadir Ali Baig, Agha Mohammed Hussain, Hemant Jeshwantrao, Shesham Raju, Aslam Akhtar, Syed Yakub, Jagat Jeevan

Benegal's successful feature debut is set in feudal AP and consolidated the New Indian Cinema movement. The politically inflected melodrama tells of a newly married urban youth, Surya (Nag, in his Hindi film debut), who is sent alone to his rural home to look after his ancestral property. Finding himself in the role of the traditional landlord, he has an affair with Lakshmi (Azmi, in her extremely powerful film debut), the young wife of a deaf-mute labourer (Meher), and she becomes pregnant. Her husband, believing the child to be his, goes to tell the landlord the good news but Surya, consumed by his guilt and afraid of being exposed, beats the man almost to death. Lakshmi then turns on her former lover with a passionate speech calling for a revolutionary overthrow of feudal rule. In the last shot, a young boy throws a stone at Surya's house and then the screen turns red. Azmi and Nag launched a new style of naturalist acting deploying regionalised Hindi accents (here Hindi inflected by a Hyderabadi accent) that came to be associated with Benegal's subsequent work. It also helped define a 'middle-of-the-road' cinema which adapted psychological realism and regionalism (emphasised in the fluid camera style) to the conventions of the mainstream Hindi movie. Having cherished the project to make this film for a long time, Benegal eventually found a producer, a distributor of advertising films for whom he had previously made commercials. The producer also backed Benegal's next films.

ASHANI SANKET

aka *Distant Thunder*
1973 101' col Bengali
d/sc/m **Satyajit Ray** *p* Sarbani Bhattacharya *pc* Balaka Movies *st* Bibhutibhushan Bannerjee's novel *c* Soumendu Roy
lp **Soumitra Chatterjee**, Babita, Ramesh

Shabana Azmi (left, in crowd) in *Ankur*

Mukherjee, Chitra Bannerjee, Govinda Chakravarty, Sandhya Roy, Noni Ganguly, Seli Pal, Suchita Roy, Anil Ganguly, Debatosh Ghosh

Ray returns to the village setting of his early films, but in lush colour, with this Bibhutibhushan novel set in 1942 in the run-up to the catastrophic 1943 Bengal famine (evoked in many films, cf **Mrinal Sen**'s ***Calcutta '71***, 1972). A Brahmin, Gangacharan (Chatterjee), and his beautiful wife Ananga (Bangladesh actress Babita) find their village, despite a successful harvest, overrun by famine. The rice shop of Gangacharan's former benefactor, Biswas (Mukherjee), is attacked by starving villagers, while strangers who have profited from WW2 try to subjugate the local women. Chutki (Sandhya Roy), who had earlier protected Ananga from a sexual assault, has to resort to prostitution in return for rice. The famine forces Gangacharan to abandon his priestly identity and his bourgeois aspirations and the film ends with his family, including his pregnant wife, sharing what little food they have with a large family of refugees. Footage of starving people in silhouette, with a caption reminding viewers that over five million died in the famine, closes the film. In sharp contrast to Ray's 50s ruralism based on Bibhutibhushan stories, this film is closer to **Benegal**'s ***Ankur*** (also 1973) in its use of realist plotting and performance within a melodramatic structure. Several critics had problems with the use of colour, e.g. the lush green environments and blazing sunsets. Although sometimes defended as an appropriate device to emphasise the artificial nature of the man-made tragedy, it could also be due to laboratory processing in India which tends towards highly saturated effects in line with the demands of the commercial mainstream and advertising film.

BOBBY

1973 168' col Hindi
pc R.K. Films *d/p* **Raj Kapoor** *st/co-sc* **K.A. Abbas** *co-sc* V.P. Sathe *dial* Jainendra Jain *lyr* **Anand Bakshi**, Vithalbhai Patel, Inderjit Singh Tulsi *c* Radhu Karmakar *m* **Laxmikant-Pyarelal**
lp Rishi Kapoor, Dimple Kapadia, Pran, Premnath, Sonia Sahni, **Durga Khote**, Shashi Kiran, Pinchoo Kapoor, Jagdish Raj, Prem Chopra, Aruna Irani, Farida Jalal

Very successful kitschy teenage love story deploying the urban 'pop' iconography of mid-60s middle-class teenage fashions and Annette Funicello beach movies (including the display of a variety of bathing suits). The 18-year-old Raj Nath (Rishi Kapoor), son of a wealthy businessman (Pran) and a rough but prosperous Goan fisherman's (Premnath) 16-year-old daughter, Bobby Braganza (Kapadia), have a romance despite their respective fathers feuding over class status. The numerous love songs include the famous *Hum tum ek kamre mein band ho* (sung by Shailendra Singh and **Lata Mangeshkar**). Although the original script required a tragic ending confirming its Romeo and Juliet model, the distributors insisted on a happy one. Their wishes were met by a manifestly fake conclusion in which celebrated screen villain Chopra appears as himself, and kidnaps the heroine so that the hero may rescue her and unite the two families through his heroism. Raj Kapoor includes many references to his own famous love scenes with **Nargis**, casting his son Rishi (fresh from his appearance in ***Mera Naam Joker***, 1970) in the lead opposite the debuting Dimple. Apparently Dimple was chosen because of her resemblance to Nargis. The couple's first meeting in the film recreates Kapoor's often-recounted first meeting with Nargis: Dimple comes through the kitchen door with dough on her hands which she absentmindedly rubs into her hair. Hit songs by the new singer Shailendra Singh include *Main shayar to nahin* and his duets with **Lata Mangeshkar**, *Mujhe kuch kehna hai* and *Jhoot bole kauva kaate*. Rishi Kapoor and Dimple, who had been absent from the screen for a while, starred together again in **Ramesh Sippy**'s *Sagar* (1985).

BON PALASHIR PADABALI

1973 224' b&w Bengali
d/sc **Uttam Kumar** *pc* Silpi Sangsad *st* Ramapada Choudhury *dial* Jayadeb Basu *lyr* Gouriprasanna Majumdar, Ruby Bagchi *c* Madhu Bhattacharya, Kanai Dey *m* **Nachiketa Ghosh**, Satinath Mukherjee, Dwijen Mukherjee, Adhir Bagchi, Shyamal Mitra
lp Uttam Kumar, **Supriya Choudhury**, Basabi Nandi, Bikash Roy, Molina Devi, **Anil Chatterjee**, **Jahar Roy**, Nirmal Kumar, Kalipada Chakravarty, **Madhabi Chakraborty**

The Bengali matinee idol Uttam Kumar's massive melodrama about passion, violence and politics in the small village of Bon Palashi. The film is narrated through two sets of characters whose stories are intercut and eventually merged. The first is the family of Girijaprasad, a retired and now impoverished school principal. His inability to invest in the progress of the village has the natives looking for a new leader in his former schoolmate, the businessman Abani. A long flashback, featuring the tragic history of Abani's old aunt, serves to frame Girijaprasad's present crisis: his scheming brother offers the fiance of Girijaprasad's daughter Bimala a larger dowry to marry his own daughter instead. The second protagonist is the peasant Udas, who loves the good Padma but is forced to marry the neurotic Laxmi in order to be allowed to learn to drive a bus. Laxmi kills Padma's father and then commits suicide. Udas tries to get Padma to elope with him but he ends up trying to rape her and, eventually, he kills Padma. Plans to develop the village loom large in the melodrama but the film impresses mainly through its scale (the title means *The Songs of Bon Palashi*) and its recourse to several acting idioms, including folk theatre.

DAAG

aka *The Stain* aka *Stigma*
1973 146' col Hindi
d/p/co-sc **Yash Chopra** *pc* Yash Raj Films *st/co-sc* Gulshan Nanda *dial* **Akhtar-ul-Iman** *lyr* **Sahir Ludhianvi** *c* Kay Gee *m* **Laxmikant Pyarelal**
lp **Sharmila Tagore**, **Rajesh Khanna**, Raakhee, Baby Pinky, Raju, Manmohan Krishna, Madan Puri, Iftikhar, Karan Dewan, Prem Chopra, Padma Khanna, Achala Sachdev, Surendranath

A convoluted melodrama about Sunil (Khanna) who is charged with murder. He kills his boss's villainous son (Chopra) in self-defence when the latter attacks his wife Sonia (Tagore). On his way to jail the hero has an accident and is believed dead while Sonia bears his child. Later, after she loses her job as a schoolteacher, Sonia and her child are given refuge by Chandni (Raakhee). Chandni is married to Sonia's husband, Sunil, who did not die and now lives under an assumed name. Sunil is elected mayor but a policeman discovers his real identity and a trial ensues. Sunil and Sonia are eventually united again.

DHUND

aka *Fog*
1973 130' col Hindi
d/p **B.R. Chopra** *pc* B.R. Films *sc* B.R. Films Story Dept *dial* **Akhtar-ul-Iman** *lyr* **Sahir Ludhianvi** *c* Dharam Chopra *m* Ravi, Gyan Varma
lp Sanjay Khan, **Zeenat Aman**, Danny Denzongpa, Urmila Bhatt, Madan Puri, Jagdish Raj, Nana Palsikar, Padma Khanna, **Ashok Kumar**, Navin Nischol

A love-triangle suspense film. The heroine (Aman) is married to a vicious, crippled tyrant (Denzongpa) who is killed in the beginning of the film (shot from the killer's subjective point of view). The heroine and her secret lover (Khan) are the prime suspects. Their story is shown in flashbacks alternating with the progress of the police investigation. In the end, another man (Nischol) confesses to the crime: the old tyrant had raped the man's wife and she became a nun.

DUVIDHA

aka *In Two Minds* aka *Two Roads*
1973 83' col Hindi
d/p/sc **Mani Kaul** *pc* Mani Kaul Prod. *st* Vijaydan Detha's short story *c* Navroze Contractor *m* Ramzan, Hammu, Saki Khan, Latif
lp Ravi Menon, Raisa Padamsee, Hardan, Shambhudan, the villagers of Barunda

Kaul's third film, financed by the **FFC** and an independent multi-arts co-op led by the noted painter Akbar Padamsee. Derived from a Rajasthani folk-tale, it tells of a merchant's son (Menon) who returns home with his new bride (Padamsee), only to be sent away again on family business. A ghost witnesses the bride's arrival and falls in love with her. He takes on the absent husband's form and lives with her. She has his child, which poses a problem when the real husband returns home. A shepherd traps the ghost in a bag. The film focuses on the wife's life and dispenses with almost any dialogue, developing the characters through parallel, historically uneven and even contradictory narratives. The classical styles of the Kangra and Basohli miniature paintings inform the colour schemes, the framing and the editing, as well as the somewhat melancholic atmosphere of the film. This is contrasted by the full-blooded folk-music score. Kaul skilfully orchestrates the way classical and folk forms (apparently) contradict each other in the way they present each other's fantasy worlds, an opposition with many ramifications in the realm of everyday behaviour. It is one of Kaul's best-known films and was widely shown in Europe. It was also sharply attacked by **Satyajit Ray** who preferred what he took to be the 'realism' of **Benegal** and **M.S. Sathyu**'s work.

ENIPPADIKAL

aka *Staircases*
1973 164' b&w Malayalam
d/sc **Thoppil Bhasi** *p* Kambiseri Karunakaran *pc* K.P.A.C. *st* Thakazhy Shivashankar Pillai *lyr* **Vyalar Rama Varma**, Iraiyamman Thampi *c* P. Ramaswami *m* **P. Devarajan**
lp **Madhu**, **Sharada**, Jayabharati, Sankaradi, Kaviyoor Ponnama, K.P.A.C. Lalitha, **Adoor Bhasi**, **Kottarakkara Sridharan Nair**

Classic Thoppil Bhasi socialist realism backed by the official CPI, continuing his agit-prop stage and screen work starting from ***Ningalenne Communistaki*** (*You Made Me A Communist*, 1970). The film adapts a Thakazhy story set in the oppressive pre-Independence bureaucracy of the diwan C.P. Ramaswamy Aiyer. Erstwhile farmer Kesava Pillai (Madhu) gets a clerical job in the government secretariat advocating and administering the savage repression of the popular CPI uprising. Although married in his village to Karthiyani, in the city he has an affair with Thankamma (Sharada), the daughter of an influential bureaucrat. Thankamma eventually discovers his selfish hypocrisy and becomes a sanyasini. The strength of the people's movement forces his voluntary retirement when his family, personal and professional relationships are all in ruins.

GARAM HAWA

aka *Hot Winds*
1973 146' col Urdu
d/co-p **M.S. Sathyu** *co-p* Abu Siwani *co-p/c* Ishan Arya *pc* Unit 3 MM. *st* **Ismat Chughtai**'s short story *co-sc/dial/lyr* **Kaifi Azmi** *co-sc* Shama Zaidi *m* Bahadur Khan
lp **Balraj Sahni**, Dinanath Zutshi, Badar Begum, Geeta Siddharth, Shaukat Kaifi, Abu Siwani, Farouque Shaikh, Jamal Hashmi, Yunus Parvaiz, Jalal Agha, Kalpana Sahni, Shanta Agarwal, A.K. Hangal

The **FFC**-sponsored film debut of the **IPTA** stage director Sathyu is one of the last titles by the generation of 50s Marxist cultural activists (Sahni, Azmi and **Chughtai**) and chronicles the plight of the minority Muslims in North India. Set in Agra after the first major Partition exodus, the film tells of an elderly Muslim shoe manufacturer, Salim Mirza (Sahni) and his family who must decide whether to continue the ancestral business or to migrate to the newly formed state of Pakistan. Salim's brother Halim (Zutshi) migrates but Halim's son Kazim (Hashmi) returns illegally across a sealed border to marry Salim Mirza's daughter, Amina (Siddharth). He is arrested and sent back. The family loses its ancestral property which under new laws is allocated to a Sindhi businessman; refugees from Pakistan start competing with Salim's business while moneylenders refuse to invest in someone who might emigrate; Amina commits suicide after yet another lover leaves her to go to Pakistan. These adversities persuade the old patriarch to leave as well, leading to a poignant scene where his ancient mother (Badar Begum) hides herself to try to stay in her 'home'. On the way to the station, the family comes across a communist rally proclaiming the unity of all the dispossessed, regardless of religion or caste. Salim's son Sikandar (Shaikh) abandons his emigration plan and joins the rally, determined to stay in India. The film, with its lovingly re-created portrait of Agra's Muslim milieu, is dominated by Sahni's remarkable performance in his last major role.

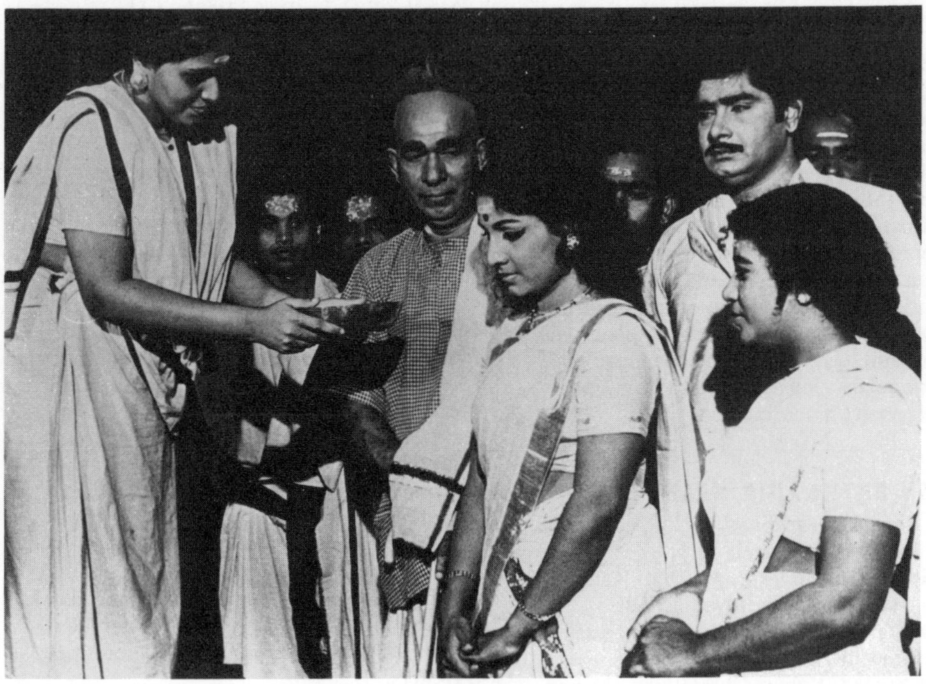
Kottarakkara Sridharan Nair ((2nd from left, foreground), Jayabharati (centre) and Madhu (2nd from right) in *Enippadikal*

KAADU

1973 141' b&w Kannada
d/sc **Girish Karnad** *p* G.N. Lakshmipathi, K.N. Narayan *pc* L.N. Combines *st/dial* Shrikrishna Alanahalli *c* **Govind Nihalani** *m* **B.V. Karanth**
lp Amrish Puri, Nandini, Lokesh, G.K. Govinda Rao, G.S. Nataraj, B. Sudha Belwadi, Kalpana Sirur, Uma Shivakumar, **T.S. Nagabharana**, Sunderrajan

Girish Karnad's first solo direction is a violent rural drama about rivalry between two villages as seen through the eyes of a young boy, Kitti (Nataraj). The boy, who is temporarily staying with his uncle Chandre Gowda (Puri) and aunt Kamali (Nandini), notices his uncle's secret visits to his mistress in the next village. This affair escalates into a larger confrontation between Chandre Gowda and his rival Shivaganga (Lokesh), which eventually leads to violence, the death of Aunt Kamali and the arrival of the police. The boy cannot distinguish the specifically man-made violence that surrounds him from the more primeval threats presented by the dense forest which, according to legend, contains a killer bird that calls out its victims by name. In a fantasy ending, the boy imagines the bird calling him and he follows the call, ignoring the frantic voices of his parents who want to take him home. Shot by Nihalani and starring Amrish Puri, both key figures in **Shyam Benegal**'s cinema, the film anticipates many conventions later associated with Benegal-style ruralism. Karanth did the art direction as well as the music while T.S. Nagabharana designed the costumes.

MANZILEIN AUR BHI HAIN

aka *Jail is still Ahead*
1973 112' col Hindi
d/st **Mahesh Bhatt** *p* Johnny Bakshi, R.H. Jain *pc* Cine Guild *sc* Rakesh Sharma *dial* Satyadev Dubey *c* Pravin Bhatt *m* Bhupinder Soni *lyr* Yogesh
lp Prema Narayan, Kabir Bedi, Gulshan Arora, Purnima, Sudhir, Shah Aga, Mukesh Bhatt, Soni, Ranvir Raj, Viju Khote, Kirti Kumar, Uma Dutt

Bhatt described his first feature as revolving around 'an unusual sexual relationship between a prostitute (Narayan) and two criminals on the run. The film was a box-office disaster.' The fast paced thriller proclaims its violation of morality codes, as noted theatre personality Dubey's aggressive dialogues sometimes evoke the **Abbas** or **Sukhdev**-type rhetoric attacking corruption. It was banned for 14 months by the censors for mocking the 'sacred institution of marriage'.

NAMAK HARAM

aka *Traitor* aka *The Ungrateful*
1973 146' col Hindi
d/st **Hrishikesh Mukherjee** *p* Raja Ram, Satish Wagle, Jayendra Pandya *pc* RSJ Prod. *co-sc/dial* **Gulzar** *co-sc* D.N. Mukherjee *lyr*

Anand Bakshi *c* Jaywant Pathare *m* **R.D. Burman**
lp **Rajesh Khanna, Amitabh Bachchan, Rekha**, Simi Garewal, Asrani, A.K. Hangal, Jayashree T, Om Shivpuri, **Durga Khote**, Raza Murad

Mukherjee repeats his successful pairing of Khanna and Bachchan in ***Anand*** (1970) with this buddy melodrama in an industrial working-class setting. When his father (Asrani) falls ill, the rich playboy Vikram (Bachchan) has to manage the Bombay factory. He insults a union leader and triggers a strike which he can end only by publicly apologising. Vikram asks his friend Somu (Khanna) to help avenge this humiliation and Somu joins the workforce. Somu becomes involved with a female union activist and changes his views about the conflict and sides with the workers. Vikram's father exposes him as a management stooge and Somu is killed. Vikram takes the blame, is jailed and, when released, decides to champion workers' rights to honour Somu's memory. Based loosely on Peter Glenville's *Becket* (1964) with a contemporary plot, it attempted a hard-edged realism in its dialogue, with several references to debates and political action from the Left in the late 60s.

NIRMALAYAM

aka *The Offering* aka *The Blessed Offering*
1973 134' b&w Malayalam
d/p/s **M.T. Vasudevan Nair** *pc* Novel Films *lyr* Edassery *c* K. Ramachandra Babu *m* K. Raghavan
lp **P.J. Anthony**, Kaviyoor Ponnamma, Ravi Menon, Sukumaran, Sumitra, Shankaradi, Devidasan, K.R. Sumithra, Shanta Devi, S.P. Pillai, **Kottarakkara Sridharan Nair**

The directorial debut of noted novelist and screenwriter Vasudevan Nair is an art-house movie about Kerala at the crossroads of modernisation. The ancient temple is neglected and in ruins, tended only by the old oracle, Velichapad (Anthony) and the man who picked flowers for its garden, Variyar (Kottarakkara). When the priest leaves to start a teashop, one of the trustees sends his cook's son (Sukumaran) as the new priest, but the young man is not really interested in the job and forms a relationship with the oracle's teenage daughter, Ammini. The oracle's son is caught trying to sell the sacred sword and has to leave the village. When smallpox breaks out, the villagers return to the temple and prepare a big festival to appease the goddess, to Velichapad's delight. But on the festive day, he discovers that his daughter has been seduced by the young priest and that his wife (Ponnamma) sells herself to a moneylender to feed the family. The film ends on an expressionist scene of the oracle performing the final ceremony of the temple, as he dances before the goddess, spitting at her for letting him down and striking his forehead with the sacred sword until he draws blood. He finally collapses, dead. Stage and film actor Anthony creates with great conviction a larger-than-life character made anachronistic by a changing world.

PADATIK

aka *The Guerrilla Fighter* aka *The Rank And File*
1973 98'(93') b&w Bengali
d/p/s/co-st **Mrinal Sen** *co-st* Ashish Burman *c* K.K. Mahajan *m* Ananda Shankar *lp* Simi Garewal, **Dhritiman Chatterjee, Bijon Bhattacharya**, Jochan Dastidar, Dhruba Mitra, Ashima Singh, Kamal Kidwai, Farida Kidwai, Tapan Das

Completing his Calcutta trilogy (***Interview***, 1970; ***Calcutta '71***, 1972) with a story more conventionally coherent than its predecessors, Sen presents the lessons adumbrated in the two previous instalments in a reflection on practical politics and party organisation after the Moscow-Beijing split of the early 60s and the **Naxalite** rising. An urban political activist (Chatterjee) escapes from police custody and is sheltered by an upper-class woman (Simi) who also defies the constraints of 'traditional' oppression: she left her husband and lives alone in a comfortable flat. The two are visited by a prudish and dogmatic party official (Mitra). The activist, though loyal to the movement for political liberation, uses his enforced isolation to reassess the political situation in Bengal. Eventually the activist leaves the flat to visit his ailing mother and learns that his father (Bhattacharya) refuses to be coerced into signing a no-strike agreement at his factory. Sen's lucid if at times naive assessment of party politics and leadership questions caused considerable controversy at the time, partly because, via the figure of the activist's father, Sen suggests that the Naxalite rising against the Indian State was an extension of the Independence struggle.

SHARADA

1973 166' b&w Telugu
d **K. Vishwanath** *pc* Annapurna Cine Ents *dial* Bollimunta *lyr* C. Narayana Reddy, Dasarathi, Veeturi, **Arudra** *c* G.K. Ramu, V.K. Gopal *m* K. Chakravarty
lp **Shobhan Babu, Sharada**, Jayanthi, Satyanarayana, Raj Babu, Allu Ramalingaiah, Ravu Gopala Rao, Saradhi, Baby Dolly, Shanta Devi

Vishwanath's psychodrama in the Annapurna tradition (cf **Adurthi Subba Rao**'s work). A woman (Sharada) goes insane after her husband's (Shobhan Babu) death on their wedding night. A doctor who resembles the husband (Shobhan Babu again) pretends to be the husband as part of the therapy. The treatment eventually fails when she realises the truth and, upholding what the film presents as the glorious Indian tradition of female virtue, dies in a boat on a river at the very place where the husband died. The music enhanced the film's popularity and launched Vishwanath towards an art-house cinema.

TITASH EKTI NADIR NAAM

aka *A River Named Titash*
1973 159' b&w Bengali
d/sc **Ritwik Ghatak** *pc* Purba Pran Katha Chitra (Bangladesh) *st* Advaita Malla Burman's novel *c* Baby Islam *m* Bahadur Khan, Ahid-ul-Haq
lp Rosy Samad, Kabari Choudhury, Roshan Jamil, Rani Sircar, Sufia Rustam, Banani Choudhury, Prabir Mitra, Chand

Ghatak's film, considered by some to be his masterpiece, is a Bangladesh production made shortly after its independence. The tale is set among Malo fishermen living by the Titash river. Kishore's (Mitra) bride is abducted by river bandits. She escapes and is rescued by the fisherfolk, with whom she lives and raises her child. Kishore becomes a madman and is offered shelter by his wife but they recognise each other only before they die. The child is raised by Basanti (Samad) while the river starts silting up and urban traders drive out the fisherfolk. **Kumar Shahani** devoted an essay to the film, 'The Passion of a Resurrected Spring' (1985), suggesting that the tightly cut beginning of the abduction sequence has the closed structure of a myth which the film gradually opens out into history, especially through the archetypally constructed male and female spaces. Kishore represents an unprecedented amalgamation of Christ and Shiva, usually regarded as contradictory figures, while the thrice-born female figure, associated with the motif of the nurturing river, constitutes a movement of both historical displacement and deliverance. For Shahani the only precedent for such a construction is classical Indian sculpture's use of volume: the film works entirely through planar rather than perspectival depth while condensing opposites such as 'natural' and highly evolved cultural forms into the same image. The film, which works according to an iconographic rather than a narrative logic, places those hybrid images at the end of a civilisation (the drying up of the river), anticipating a future overshadowed by industrial encroachments on nature. The film exists in two versions, the second being c.30' shorter and apparently cut by Ghatak himself.

27 DOWN

aka *Sattawis Down* aka *The Train to Benares* aka *27 Down Bombay-Varanasi Express*
1973 123'(115') b&w Hindi
d/p/sc Avtar Krishna Kaul *pc* Avtar Kaul Prod. *st/dial* Ramesh Bakshi *lyr* Nand Kishore Mittal *c* Apurba Kishore Bir *m* Bhuban Hari
lp M.K. Raina, Raakhee, Rekha Sabnis, Om Shivpuri, Madhvi, Manjula, Nilesh Velani

The promising young Kaul's only feature, financed by the **NFDC** and finished shortly before he died trying to save someone from drowning. An engine driver (Shivpuri), incapacitated after an accident, forces his son Sanjay (Raina) to join the railways and to stifle his artistic ambitions beneath a conductor's uniform. Sanjay befriends the commuting typist Shalini (Raakhee) but his father pressures Sanjay to marry a village belle (Sabnis) who resembles the buffaloes she brings as her dowry. Sanjay escapes in yet another train journey (the Bombay-Benares train that provides the film's title as well as the framing scene for the flashback narrative). When Sanjay meets Shalini again, he finds they have nothing in common any more. The train motif dominates the film's highly contrasted imagery and generated one classic high-angle shot of an empty platform filled within seconds by thousands of commuting travellers.

ULAGAM SUDURUM VALIBAN

1973 184' col Tamil
d/p **M.G. Ramachandran** *pc* Emgeeyar Pics *st* R.M. Veerappan, S.K.T. Samy, Vidwan V.E. Lakshmanan *sc* Emgeeyar Pics Story Dept *dial* K. Sornam *lyr* **Kannadasan**, **Vali**, Pulamai Pithan *c* V. Ramamurthy *m* M.S. Vishwanathan
lp M.G. Ramachandran, M.N. Nambiar, S.A. Ashokan, R.S. Manohar, Nagesh, Thenjai Srinivasan, V. Gopalakrishnan, San Chai, Selvi, Chandrakala, Manjula, Lata, Meta Rungrat

MGR's last major self-produced film is a James Bond-style drama shot in Hong Kong, Singapore, Kuala Lumpur and Thailand. The scientist Murasan (MGR) invents a way of harnessing the energy of lightning. The crooked Prof. Bhairavan offers him a a fortune but Murasan donates the secret to a Buddhist monk in Japan. Murasan is believed to be murdered, after which his brother, a Central Bureau of Investigation official, unmasks the international gang of villains.

YAADON KI BARAAT

aka *Procession of Memories*
1973 164' col Hindi
d/p/dial **Nasir Hussain** *pc* Nasir Hussain Films *s* **Salim-Javed** *lyr* **Majrooh Sultanpuri** *c* Munir Khan *m* **R.D. Burman**
lp **Dharmendra**, **Zeenat Aman**, Vijay Arora, Tariq, Ajit, Anamika, Imtiaz, Ravinder Kapoor, Nasir Khan, Shyam Kumar, Neetu Singh, Jalal Agha, Shetty, Satyendra

Vendetta movie and teenage love story inaugurating the influence of Western rock music in Hindi cinema associated with the Americanised persona of Zeenat Aman. While escaping from the murderers of their parents, three brothers get separated. The eldest, Shankar (Dharmendra), a professional thief for whom the traumatic murder remains associated with the motif of a train, pursues the killer (Ajit). The second brother (Arora) has a love affair with a rich woman (Aman), while the youngest (Tariq) becomes a rock star. The 'lost and found' fairy-tale formula, often deployed in Indian cinema (cf the films of **Desai**) is adapted here to allow for various encounters between the brothers before they all recognise each other when the rock star sings the film's title refrain, a song they learned from their mother as children. An interestingly fetishistic aspect is that the villain is recognised by his shoes. Although the film recalls Hussain's own earlier musicals with **Shammi Kapoor** and **Dev Anand**, its main 'merit' is Aman's guitar-strumming introduction of the disco era. Hits include Burman's *Chura liya hai tumne jo dil ko*, sung by **Asha Bhosle** and **Mohammed Rafi**.

ZANJEER

aka *The Chain*
1973 145' col Hindi-Urdu
d/p/co-lyr **Prakash Mehra** *pc* Prakash Mehra Prod. *s* **Salim-Javed** *co-lyr* Gulshan Bawra *c* N. Satyen *m* **Kalyanji-Anandji**
lp **Amitabh Bachchan**, Jaya Bhaduri, Ajit, Bindu, Pran, Om Prakash, Iftikhar, Ram Mohan, Yunus Pervez, Purnima, Gulshan Bawra, Keshto Mukherjee

First of many films to cast Bachchan as an angry young man, although this still seems a transitional movie: the hero evolves from a cop into a vigilante, the latter being closer to the star's subsequent persona. As a child, Vijay witnesses the murder of his parents by a faceless killer wearing a chain around his wrist. Haunted by the image of the chain, the adult Vijay (Bachchan) becomes a cop determined to clean up Bombay. He befriends the Pathan gambler Sher Khan (Pran) who becomes his ally. Although romantically involved with Mala (Bhaduri), Vijay singlemindedly roots out evildoers and finally identifies his parents' killer: Teja (Ajit). Taking the law into his own hands, he avenges the murders. The film, which introduced the Salim-Javed style, the real authors behind the Bachchan persona, was a great success and set the trend for later revenge and vigilante movies to which the director, the scenarists and the stars of this film would continue to contribute throughout the 70s. Mehra continued the theme in ***Muqaddar Ka Sikandar*** (1978).

ALLURI SEETARAMARAJU

1974 187' col/scope Telugu
d V. Ramachandra Rao *p* Krishna *pc* Padmalaya Pics *dial* Maharathi *lyr* C. Narayana Reddy, **Arudra**, **Kosaraju**, **Sri Sri** *c* V.S.R. Swamy *m* **Adi Narayana Rao**
lp **Krishna**, **Gummadi Venkateshwara Rao**, Kantha Rao, Chandramohan, **K. Jaggaiah**, M. Prabhakara Reddy, Jagga Rao, **Vijayanirmala**, Jayanthi, Manjula, Allu Ramalingaiah, Mikkilineni, Ravu Gopala Rao, **Pandharibai**

Telugu star Krishna produces this big-budget film which introduces CinemaScope to Telugu cinema. He stars as the famous revolutionary Alluri Seetaramaraju, an anti-imperialist tribal leader who founded the early peasant movements in the state before he was sentenced to death by the British. Remembered for the lyrics by radical poet Sri Sri, the film's success spawned a wave of biopics of historical as well as mythological figures, usually presented as major challenges to the star actors.

AMANUSH

1974 165'[B]/153'[H] col Bengali/Hindi
d/p/co-sc **Shakti Samanta** *pc* Shakti Films *st/co-sc* Shaktipada Rajguru *dial* Prabhat Roy[B], Kamleshwar[H] *lyr* Gouriprasanna Majumdar[B], Indivar[H] *c* Aloke Dasgupta *m* Shyamal Mitra
lp **Uttam Kumar**, **Sharmila Tagore**, **Utpal Dutt**, **Abhi Bhattacharya**, **Anil Chatterjee**, Prema Narayan, Manmohan, Asit Sen

Samanta's hit with an all-Bengali star cast reconnects with the Bengali-Hindi bilinguals and signifies to some extent the powerful Bombay production sector's cultural takeover of the Bengali cinema. In the village of Dhaniakhali, the new police chief Bhuvan Sen finds corruption and decay personnified by the dissolute Madhusudhan Roy Choudhury (Kumar), the zamindar's son. However, the cause of the rot is not the persistence feudalism in the village but the presence of the sophisticated and mild-mannered Mahim Babu, cast as the villain who turns the head of Madhusudhan's girlfriend Lekha (Tagore). The policeman eventually restores the old feudal power relations, rehabilitates the hero and restores Lekha to him. This reactionary parable was celebrated for the performance of Bengali megastar Uttam Kumar. The Hindi version has the hit song *Dil aisa kisine mera toda*, sung by **Kishore Kumar**.

AVALUM PENN THAANE

aka *She Too Is A Woman*
1974 164' b&w Tamil
d/s **Durai** *pc* Shri Panduranga Prod. *c* V. Manohar *lyr* **Vali** *m* M.S. Vishwanathan
lp C. Muthuraman, M.R.R. Vasu, Thenjai Srinivasan, S.A. Ashokan, S.V. Sahasranamam, Sunithra, Manorama, M.N. Rajam, **Pandharibai**, Kutti Padmini, V.K. Ramaswamy, S.V. Ramdas, Adithan, Dasarathan, Ambathur Mani

Durai's first film tells of Seeta, a prostitute, and her attempt to quit the trade. Muthu, a young businessman from a mofussil town finds her in a Madras brothel and proposes marriage but her pimp ruins her chances and she commits suicide. Only two songs and a comic subplot help maintain the narrative momentum of the melodrama. In contrast to Tamil cinema's archetypes, the film offers some well-drawn characters with distinct caste identities, speaking with pronounced regional accents: the Chettiar money lender and his young wife interested in pornography, Kanagu the vegetable vendor and Sambandham the bicycle mechanic.

BEHIND THE BREADLINE

1974 29' col English
d/p **S. Sukhdev** *s* Tanvier Farouqe, **Tapan Bose** *c* Govind Maharesh *m* **Vanraj Bhatia**

Propaganda film with emphatic graphics (e.g. a large question mark cut out of newspaper) for Indira Gandhi's 'Garibi Hatao' (Away with Poverty) agricultural policies. Opening with shots of demonstrators led by the Mumbai Mazdoor Sabha being confronted by police, the film cuts to paddy-fields and suggests that the main political and economic problem facing the country is the presence of Sukhdev's favourite enemy: black marketeers and hoarders. Shots of peasants at work are juxtaposed with food-laden plates at tourist resorts, and the mechanical sieving of wheat in Punjab is accompanied by bhangra folk-dance music. The film ends with a governmental raid on black marketeers staged for the film.

BHOOMIKOSAM

1974 176' col Telugu
d/co-s K.B. Tilak *pc* Anupama Films *co-s/dial/co-lyr* Shankara *co-s/co-lyr* **Sri Sri** *co-lyr* **Arudra**, Rimjhim, Srikanth *c* Ramakrishna *m* **Pendyala Nageshwara Rao**
lp Gudipati Venkatachalam (aka Chalam), **K. Jaggaiah**, **Gummadi Venkateshwara Rao**, Thyagaraj, **Ashok Kumar**, Ramana Reddy, Prabhakar Reddy, Prabha, **Jamuna**, Vijaya

The film propagates a CPI(ML) (cf **Naxalite**) ideology and is dedicated to the director's brother, Narasimha Rao, a member of the party. Set in rural post-Independence AP, it presents the struggle of the peasantry against the rich zamindar, continued at the end by the son of a martyred peasant. Shot on location in Telangana, it included several of Sri Sri's radical lyrics, e.g. the title song *Bhoomikosam buktikosam saage raitula poratam* and *Evaro vastharani edo chestarani eduruchoosi mosapokuma*.

BRISTI

1974 122' b&w Assamese
d/s Deuti Barua *pc* Jayashree Prod. *lyr* **Bhupen Hazarika** *m* Jayanta Hazarika
lp Biju Phukan, Bishnu Khargaria, Ila Kakati, Deuti Barua, Rudra Goswami

Unusual film by noted playwright Deuti Barua. The middle-class hero's diffidence for the girl he loves is contrasted with the lofty idealism of a friend, and the more humane promise of marriage another friend makes to a lonely, elderly woman. The film, accused of upholding the very middle-class conservatism it seeks to critique, was acclaimed for its unusual scripting style.

CHORUS

1974 124' b&w Bengali
d/p/co-sc **Mrinal Sen** *co-sc/lyr* Mohit Chatterjee *c* K.K. Mahajan *m* Ananda Shankar
lp **Utpal Dutt**, Subhendu Chatterjee, Asit Bannerjee, Haradan Bannerjee, Shekhar Chatterjee, Satya Bannerjee, Snighda Majumdar, **Robi Ghosh**, Rasuraj Chakraborty, Geeta Sen, Dilip Roy, Moon Moon Sen, Nirmal Ghosh

Starting out as a fantasy mythological with the gods, entrenched in their fortress, deciding to create 100 jobs, the film becomes an exemplary fairy tale when 30,000 applicants start queuing up for work. The fairy tale then becomes a didactic tragedy with realist sequences (media men interviewing individuals in the crowd of applicants) when the people realise the job scheme is grossly inadequate and popular discontent grows into a desire to storm the citadel. Freely mixing different styles and modes of storytelling including direct address to the camera, with the chorus both as narrator and as political agitator, Sen continues exploring the possibilities of a cinematic narrative that would be both enlightening and emotionally involving without descending into authoritarian sloganising. Having gone as far in this direction as he could, Sen deploys the lessons of his experiments with complex and stylistically diverse cinematic idioms in his next feature, ***Mrigaya*** (1976).

JADU BANSHA

1974 167' b&w/col Bengali
d/sc/co-st/co-dial/m Partha Prathim Choudhury *pc* Montage Films *co-st/co-dial* Bimal Kar *lyr* Atulprasad Sen, **Rabindranath Tagore** *c* Krishna Chakraborty, Kanai Das
lp **Sharmila Tagore**, **Uttam Kumar**, **Aparna Sen**, **Dhritiman Chatterjee**, Santosh Dutta, Siddhartha Dutta, Dulal Ghosh, Mihir Pal, **Robi Ghosh**

Modernist critique of decadent rationalism by the former critic and film society organiser Choudhury. A group of young people live in an unnamed, culturally insecure town where they interact with a series of characters, e.g. an old shopkeeper whom they torture and humiliate but who remains their staunchest ally until his death. The self-indulgent style is occasionally interrupted by lively scenes such as the encounter with a deaf politician, the ransacking of a shop and the number picturised on an Atulprasad Sen lyric, *Ar kata kal thakbo basey*.

JUKTI TAKKO AAR GAPPO

aka *Reason, Debate and a Story* aka *Argument and a Story*
1974 119' b&w Bengali
d/p/s/m **Ritwik Ghatak** *pc* Rit Chitra *c* Baby Islam
lp Ritwik Ghatak, Tripti Mitra, Shaonli Mitra, **Bijon Bhattacharya**, Saugata Burman, Gyanesh Mukherjee, **Utpal Dutt**, Ananya Ray, Shyamal Ghosal

Ghatak's last film featured himself as the drunken and spent intellectual Neelkantha who goes on a picaresque journey through Bengal to reconcile himself with his wife. He is accompanied by Nachiketa (Burman) and Bangabala (S. Mitra), a young refugee from Bangladesh. On the way they are joined by a Sanskrit teacher, Jagannath (Bhattacharya). The episodic narrative also includes encounters with Shatrujit (Dutt) who was once a noted writer but who now writes pornography; a ranting trade union leader and Panchanan Ustad (Mukherjee) who makes masks for Chhou dancers (a sequence is devoted to showing the famous dance). Jagannath is shot by a landlord when the group stumbles upon a land-grab action. The film ends with Neelkantha meeting a group of **Naxalite** students wanted by the police: he argues politics with them and is shot in a police ambush the next morning. Filmed while Ghatak was ill and suffering from alcoholism shortly before his death, *Jukti* is an inventive and lucid though pessimistic testament film, acted with elegance and irony by the director. With an astonishing sense of freedom Ghatak weaves together different styles and images ranging from gross calendar art (the courtship of his wife) to an almost abstract dance of death; from the elaborate Chhou performance where the goddess Durga slays the demon to lyrical depictions of nature; from inserted bits of leader footage to a Baul song. The encounters with the pornographer and the Naxalites add up to a devastating critique of contemporary politics. In the end, Ghatak offers a disabused but stubborn politics of the everyday: Neelkantha dies with a quote from a Manik Bandyopadhyay story about a weaver who wove an empty loom because 'one must do something'. Geeta Kapur's essay 'Articulating the Self into History' (1989) is the most extended study on the film.

RAJANIGANDHA

aka *Tube Rose*
1974 110' col Hindi
d/sc/dial **Basu Chatterjee** *pc* Devki Chitra *st* Manu Bhandari's short story *Yeh Sach Hai lyr* Yogesh *c* K.K. Mahajan *m* **Salil Choudhury**
lp Vidya Sinha, **Amol Palekar**, Dinesh Thakur, Rajita Thakur, Master Chikkoo, Rajprakash, Gopal Dutia, Naresh Suri

The novelist Manu Bhandari (*Mahabhoj*, *Aapka Banti*) was also associated with the 50s literary Nai Kahani movement in Hindi. Her story chronicles the life of a working woman, Deepa (Sinha) torn between two lovers: her intended husband, the gregarious bank clerk Sanjay (Palekar) and Navin (Thakur) whom she meets in Bombay when applying for a teaching job. Palekar's debut performance in Hindi established his best-known screen image as a bumbling common-man hero. The

Utpal Dutt in *Chorus*

film's claim to represent realistically the middle class through Sanjay's persona is belied by an extensive use of glamourous soft-focus imagery. It was Basu Chatterjee's breakthrough into mainstream Hindi cinema, encouraging the notion that low-budget art-house films can be commercially successful.

SHRI RAMANJANEYA YUDDHAM

1974 166' col Telugu
d **Bapu** *pc* Shri Lakshminarayana Films *s* Gabbita Venkatarao *lyr* **Arudra**, C. Narayana Reddy, Dasarathi, **Kosaraju** *c* K.S. Prasad *m* K.V. Mahadevan
lp **N.T. Rama Rao**, Arja Janardana Rao, Kantarao, Dhulipada, **B. Saroja Devi**, Jayanthi, Rajshri, Hemalatha, Jaikumari, **K. Mukkamala**, Kashinath Tata, Sridhar, Nagaraju, Ramesh, P.J. Sharma, Ch. Krishnamurthy, Ashok Kumar

Costumed mythological featuring a contest between Shiva and Parvati to ascertain whether Shakti (physical prowess) is stronger than Bhakti (devotion). The issue will be decided through a test of Hanuman's devotion to Rama. The film, which includes the *Paduka Pattabhishekham* and the *Yayati* episodes from the *Ramayana*, offers an important example of NTR's god-on-earth political image, here playing Rama.

SONAR KELLA

aka *The Golden Fortress*
1974 120' col Bengali
d/s/m **Satyajit Ray** *pc* West Bengal Govt. *c* Soumendu Roy
lp **Soumitra Chatterjee**, Santosh Dutta, Siddhartha Chatterjee, Kushal Chakraborty, Sailen Mukherjee, Ajoy Bannerjee, Kamu Mukherjee, Santanu Bagchi, Harindranath Chattopadhyay, Sunil Sarkar, Suili Mukherjee, Haradhan Bannerjee, Rekha Chatterjee, Ashok Mukherjee, Bimal Chatterjee

The first film featuring the detective Feluda from the Sherlock Holmes pastiches which Ray had published and illustrated since 1965 in his magazine *Sandesh*. The 6-year-old Mukul (Chakraborty) is obsessed with memories of a previous life in a golden fortress with pigeons, peacocks and camels. Parapsychologist Dr Hazra (Sailen Mukherjee) guesses that the location of Mukul's past life is in Rajasthan and takes the child there to find it. Two crooks, Burman (Ajoy Bannerjee) and Bose (Kamu Mukherjee), read about the expedition in a local paper and, sensing there is a fortune to be made, try to kidnap Mukul. This brings the famed detective Feluda (Soumitra Chatterjee) and his sidekick Topse (Siddhartha Chatterjee) into the case. In an extended chase through Rajasthan, the detective is joined by the thriller writer Jatayu (S. Dutta) as the action, energetically orchestrated via parallel cutting, moves from cars to camels and a train. The film is dominated by the remarkable performance of Kushal Chakraborty as the boy, as well as Santanu Bagchi's extraordinary cameo as the boy who gets kidnapped by mistake and then explains what happened to the detective. Ray made another Feluda story, ***Joi Baba Felunath*** (1978).

UTTARAYANAM

aka *Throne of Capricorn*
1974 117' b&w Malayalam
d/co-sc **Govindan Aravindan** *p* Karunakaran *pc* Ganesh Movie Makers *st/co-sc* Thikkodiyan *c* Ravi Varma *m* Raghavan, **M.B. Srinivasan**
lp Mohandas, Kunju, Balan K. Nair, **Adoor Bhasi**, Sukumaran, Mallika, Radhamani, Shanta Devi

Aravindan's debut extended a 60s Calicut modernism into cinema, drawing on the work of the writer Pattathiruvila Karunakaran, who produced the film, and the satirical playwright Thikkodiyan, who co-scripted it. The plot is about a disabused young man, Ravi, who has a series of ironic encounters while looking for a job. One of his mentors, Kumaran Master, and his now critically ill friend Setu had participated in the 1942 Quit India agitations with Ravi's father (shown in flashback). The lawyer Gopalan Muthalaly, also a participant in those events, has become a rich contractor and an example of the corrupt post-Independence bourgeoisie. Ravi abandons the city and, in a mystical ending, is initiated into 'eternal truths' by a godman meditating on a mountain. The figures of the father and the ailing friend form a composite portrait of Sanjayan, a political activist, spiritualist and satirist, and major influence on the Calicut artists who participated in the film. Aravindan's approach to his lead characters and his framing evoke the cartoon characters Ramu and Guruji from his *Small Man and Big World* series.

AANDHI

1975 133' col Hindi
d/sc/lyr **Gulzar** *pc* Filmyug, Om Prakash *st* Kamleshwar's novel *c* K. Vaikunth *m* **R.D. Burman**
lp **Suchitra Sen**, Sanjeev Kumar, Om Shivpuri, Manmohan, A.K Hangal, Om Prakash, Rehman

A combination of marital romance and political intrigue. A woman politician, Aarti Devi (Sen), fights an election against the powerful Chandersen. Her headquarters are in a hotel owned and managed by her estranged husband J.K. (Kumar). Their memories of life together are intercut with the election campaign, the opposition turning her nightly meetings with her ex-husband into a scandal. She eventually wins the election following an impassioned speech from Chandersen's platform in which she proclaims the man to be her husband and insists on her right to marital privacy. The Bengali musical superstar Suchitra Sen's last Hindi film role is controversial because of her character's obvious references, during the Emergency, to Indira Gandhi (e.g. the streak of white hair; the reference to an ambitious father who caused her marriage to break up), producing some mild censorship problems. There were some popular **Kishore Kumar** and **Lata Mangeshkar** duets such as *Is mod se jaate hain*, *Tere bina zindagi* and *Tum aa gaye ho noor aa gaya hai.*

APOORVA RAGANGAL

1975 144' b&w Tamil
d/sc **K. Balachander** *pc* Kalakendra Films *lyr* **Kannadasan** *c* B.S. Lokanathan *m* M.S. Vishwanathan
lp **Kamalahasan**, Sundarrajan, Nagesh, **Rajnikant**, Shrividya, Jayasudha, Kanaga Durka, Kannadasan

Melodrama in which the lovers end up exchanging parents. The rebellious Prasanna leaves his home after quarrelling with his father and finds shelter with the singer Bhairavi whose illegitimate daughter also leaves home and finds shelter at Prasanna's father's house. The problem becomes acute when the young couple want to marry. Rajnikant's debut film also re-launched Kamalahasan. Lyric writer Kannadasan plays himself.

CHARANDAS CHOR

aka *Charandas the Thief*
1975 156' b&w Hindi
d **Shyam Benegal** *pc* **CFS** *s* Shama Zaidi, Habib Tanvir *lyr/m* Nandkishore Mittal, Gangaram, Swarnakumar *c* **Govind Nihalani**
lp Lalu Ram, Madanlal, Bhakla Ram, Ramnath, Thakur Ram, Malabai, Fidabai, Ram Ratan, Hira Ram, Habib Tanvir, **Smita Patil**, Anjali Paingankar, Sadhu Meher

Benegal's adaptation of the classic Chattisgarhi dialect folk play by the noted stage director Habib Tanvir. Remembered mainly for celebrated folk theatre actors Fidabai and Madanlal and as Smita Patil's film debut (in the role of a princess). The crazy comedy is about petty thieves in a village who keep eluding the bumbling police until the central character, Charandas (Lalu Ram), is executed for being honest rather than for being a criminal.

CHHOTISI BAAT

aka *A Little Affair*
1975 123' col Hindi
d/s **Basu Chatterjee** *pc* B.R. Films *lyr* Yogesh *c* K.K. Mahajan *m* **Salil Choudhury**
lp **Amol Palekar**, Vidya Sinha, **Ashok Kumar**, Asrani, Nandita Thakur, Rajen Haksar, Rajindernath, Komilla Wirk

Chatterjee's sequel to ***Rajanigandha*** (1974) continues his middle-class love stories. This is a comic tale about a lovesick clerk, Arun Pradeep (Palekar), who is too shy to declare his love to Prabha (Sinha). He is coached in assertiveness by a bluff ex-officer (Kumar) and then succeeds, besting his cocky rival and winning the woman. The film intercuts this story with Arun's fantasies and boasts one hit song, *Jaaneman jaaneman tere do nayan*, sung by Yesudas and **Asha Bhosle**.

CHOMANA DUDI

aka *Choma's Drum*
1975 140'(120') b&w Kannada
d/m **B.V. Karanth** *pc* Praja Films *s* K. Shivrama Karanth from his novel (1933) *c* S. Ramchandra
lp M.V. Vasudeva Rao, Jayaran, Honnaiah, Padma Kumtha, Sunderrajan, Nagaraja, Nagendra, Shankar Bhat, Lakshmibai, Sarojini, Venkatesh, Mahalakshmi, Govind Bhatt

A relentlessly miserabilist but well-scored and

acted story set among the *mari holeya*, a caste of Untouchables in Southern Karnataka who are forbidden from owning or tilling their own land. This rigid law prevents old Choma (Vasudeva Rao) repaying a long-standing debt to the landlord despite owning two buffaloes he found in the forest. The film chronicles the disintegration of Choma's family: two of his three sons die (one drowns because Brahmins refuse to touch him), the third seeks to escape his social status by converting to Christianity. The daughter is seduced by the landlord's secretary and then submits to the landlord himself hoping to settle the debt. Choma's only way of transcending his grim situation is by playing his little drum nightly, sometimes accompanied by his daughter. When Choma discovers his daughter's relationship with the landlord, he goes to the forest, releases his precious buffaloes, breaks his plough and dies a lonely old man madly playing his drum. Brilliantly carried by the performance of Vasudeva Rao, the film is one of the most successful examples of a ruralist New Indian Cinema, elevating the post-**Satyajit Ray** invocation of primitivist authenticity into something like a productive principle.

DEEWAR

aka *The Wall* aka *I'll Die for Mama*
1975 174' col Hindi
d **Yash Chopra** *p* Gulshan Rai *pc* Trimurti Films *s* **Salim-Javed** *lyr* **Sahir Ludhianvi** *c* Kay Gee *m* **R.D. Burman**
lp **Amitabh Bachchan**, **Shashi Kapoor**, **Nirupa Roy**, Neetu Singh, Parveen Babi, Manmohan Krishna, Madan Puri, Iftikhar, Sudhir, Rajpal, Jagdish Raj, Kuljit Singh, Rajkishore, A.K. Hangal

Boasting one of the best-known Salim-Javed scripts, Bachchan's hit crime film, told in flashback, relies on the familiar plot of two brothers, one of which is an exemplary cop, Ravi (Kapoor), the other a criminal, Vijay (Bachchan). The bridge between them is the mother they both adore, Sumitra (Roy) but whom Vijay cannot later visit for fear of being arrested. Vijay is the focus of the narrative as he works hard at menial jobs and suffers many humiliations to pay for his younger brother's education. Embittered by the prevailing social iniquities, Vijay is recruited by a dockyard gang of smugglers and rises to become their leader. Ravi has to arrest him. Vijay decides to marry his pregnant lover, the dancer Anita (Babi), and go straight but she is murdered, causing him to become a ruthless vigilante while his mother gives Ravi permission to hunt down his wayward brother. Eventually a dying Vijay, shot by his brother, keeps his tryst at a temple with his mother. A phenomenal hit, the film repeats the 'traditional' proposition that kinship laws must prevail over legality at a very sensitive political and cultural moment: the year the Emergency was declared. Salim-Javed apparently modelled Bachchan's character on the notorious smuggler Haji Mastan Mirza (a media celebrity as public enemy number one jailed during the Emergency and making a dramatic self-criticism afterwards). Although his fight scenes seem calibrated on those in Hong Kong action films, Bachchan's sultry performance in the discursive scenes humanises the gangster, thus also humanising the contemporary nationalist law and order rhetoric used to legitimise dictatorial oppression. The mother-as-nation cliche, an extension of the nation-as-family cliche, both often deployed in Hindi films (cf **Mehboob**'s emblematic ***Mother India***, 1957), was mobilised here for a more ambiguous purpose: although the audience's sympathies are directed towards the working-class rebel, the mother-nation reluctantly sanctions the legalised persecution of her well-meaning but misguided son, an action with obvious parallels in the political situation of the time.

GANGA CHILONER PANKHI

1975 105' b&w Assamese
d/co-sc/m **Padum Barua** *pc* Rupjyoti Films *st* Laxmi Nandan Bora *co-sc* Mohammed Sadulla *lyr* Shankardev *c* Indukalpa Hazarika
lp Beena Baruwati, Basanta Saikia, Basanta Duara, Mohini Rajkumari, Aideo Handique, Bipul Barua, Beena Das Manna, Bhola Kakoti

Landmark Assamese political melodrama set shortly after Independence. A petty trader refuses to let his sister marry the man she loves because he has supported a rival candidate in a local election. Instead, he forces her to marry another man, who dies tragically when he learns of his wife's past. The bulk of the film addresses the young widow's difficult life as she defies her family only to be rejected by the man she loves. A decade in the making, this remains the director's only film to date.

HAMSA GEETHE

aka *The Swan Song*
1975 150' col Kannada
d/sc **G.V. Iyer** *pc* Ananthalakshmi Films *st* T.R. Subbarao *lyr* Muthuswamy Dikshitar, Shama Sastry, Sadasiva Brahmendra, Uthukadu Venkatasubbaiah Iyer, Jayadeva *c* **Nemai Ghosh** *m* **B.V. Karanth**, Balamurali Krishna
lp **Anant Nag**, Rekha Rao, Narayana Rao, Mysore Mutt, G.S. Rama Rao, B.V. Karanth, Chandrasekhar, Balasubramanyam, Girimaji, **Prema Karanth**, Jayalakshmi Eswaran, Meenakshi, Saroja, Ramkumar

Veteran director Iyer's first art-house film is a musical version of the legendary tale of the 19th C. Carnatic singer Bhairavi Venkata Subbaiah (Nag, in his first major screen role), who received the patronage of Chitradurga royalty and at one time defied Tipu Sultan. The singer apparently cut out his tongue to prove that 'music is nobody's slave'. The film presents the singer according to the conventional Romantic model of the artist: a musician who rebels against his teacher, wanders aimlessly and asks a beggar to become his new guru, attains glory, falls in love and 'sells' two of his compositions to survive. With less than 15' of dialogue, the film's sequence shots emphasise the barren, rocky outback of Chitradurga as an analogy for the musician's quest for aesthetic rigour. One of Iyer's first attempts to fulfil the old Mysore royalty's search for a brahminical classicism to legitimate their British-backed rule. In this respect, Iyer's film is at the opposite pole, in contemporary Karnataka politics, of anti-brahminical films such as ***Samskara*** (1970). Iyer's revivalist project, which led him later to make Saint films, is repeated by **K. Vishwanath**'s Telugu films after ***Shankarabharanam*** (1979).

JAI SANTOSHI MAA

aka *In Praise of Mother Santoshi*
1975 145' col Hindi
d Vijay Sharma *pc* Bhagyalakshmi Chitra Mandir *s* R. Priyadarshini *lyr* Pradeep *c* Sudhendu Roy *m* C. Arjun
lp Anita Guha, Ashish Kumar, Kanan Kaushal, Trilok Kapoor, Mahipal, Manhar Desai, B.M. Vyas, Bharat Bhushan, Anant

Rekha Rao in *Hamsa Geethe*

Marathe, Rajan Haksar, Dilip Dutt, Johnny Whisky, Shri Bhagwan, Leela Mishra, Asha Poddar, Lata Arora, Neelam, Surendra Mishra

Starting life as a routine B picture, the film made history by becoming one of the biggest hits of the year (with ***Sholay*** and ***Deewar***), and made a little-known mother goddess into one of the most popular icons esp. among the urban working-class women who started observing the goddess's ritual fast on 12 consecutive Fridays and made offerings of chick-peas. The foremost earthly disciple of the deity Santoshi (Guha) is Satyavati (Kaushal). When Satyavati marries the itinerant Birju, the wives of the celestial trio Brahma, Vishnu and Shiva feel envious and create a series of problems intended to test Satyavati's devotion. After Santoshi has made the heavens literally rock with her rage, Satyavati emerges from her trials with her faith untarnished and so allows Santoshi to be accepted into the cosmic pantheon. The movie was lucidly analysed by the anthropologist Veena Das in her essay 'The Mythological Film and its Framework of Meaning' (1980). I. Masud noted some revealing differences between this mythological and its classic predecessors, showing this film to be far closer to 'daily preoccupations' than its generic models (e.g. gods also engage in frenetic quarrels).

JANA ARANYA

aka *The Middleman*
1975 131' b&w Bengali
d/sc/m **Satyajit Ray** *p* Subir Guha *pc* Indus Films *st* Shankar's novel *c* Soumendu Roy
lp Pradip Mukherjee, Satya Bannerjee, Dipankar Dey, Lily Chakraborty, **Aparna Sen**, Gautam Chakraborty, Sudeshna Das, **Utpal Dutt**, **Robi Ghosh**, Bimal Chatterjee, Arati Bhattacharya, Padmadevi, Soven Lahiri, Santosh Dutta, Bimal Deb, Ajeya Mukherjee, Kalyan Sen, Alokendu Dey

The final film in Ray's Calcutta trilogy (cf ***Pratidwandi***, 1970; ***Seemabaddha***, 1971) is also his most disaffected melodrama. Further elaborating the theme of corruption which runs through the entire trilogy and would return later in, e.g., ***Shakha Proshakha*** (1990), the film features the young Somnath Bannerjee (P. Mukherjee) who, unfairly assessed in his graduate examination, cannot get a job. He goes into partnership with Bishuda (Dutt) and becomes a corporate 'middleman' or dalal (also the term for a pimp) buying and selling. Since the purchasing officer of a mill, Goenka (Lahiri), requires a call-girl as a bribe, Somnath and his new mentor, Mitter (Ghosh), explore Calcutta's underworld. Several comic failures later, he finally meets the prostitute Juthika (Das), the sister of a former colleague Sukumar, (G. Chakraborty), although she is too ashamed to admit to this. With this grimly comical tale Ray abandoned the gentle humanism with which he chronicled the follies of his well-meaning but sometimes ill-equipped liberal intelligentsia. Even the mild sympathy he felt for the radical movements reflected in *Pratidwandi* now disappear before a hero willing to be led unquestioningly through life by mentors like Bishuda or Mitter. The 'upright' father-figure (Satya Bannerjee) now belongs to a different world from this new generation. For the next decade, Ray concentrated on children's stories and period melodramas, turning away from the contemporary.

JULIE

1975 145' col Hindi
d **K.S. Sethumadhavan** *pc* **Vijaya** *st* Pamman's novel *Chattakari dial* **Inder Raj Anand** *lyr* **Anand Bakshi**, Harindranath Chattopadhyay *m* Rajesh Roshan
lp Laxmi, Om Prakash, **Utpal Dutt**, Vikram, Jalal Agha, **Sulochana**, **Sridevi**

Sethumadhavan and Tamil star Laxmi's best-known Hindi film is a remake of the director's Malayalam hit *Chattakkari* (1974). The Anglo-Indian Julie (Laxmi) abandons her boyfriend to have an affair with Shashi (Vikram) and becomes pregnant, providing an excuse for several shots detailing the star's body. She tries to contain the scandal by sending her son to a far-away place. The film claimed to address the attitudes of India's Anglo-Indians but its major attraction, apart from the voyeurism, is Harindranath Chattopadhyay's English song, *My heart is beating*, sung by Preeti Sagar.

KABANI NADI CHUVANNAPPOL

aka *When the Kabani River Turned Red*
1975 87' b&w Malayalam
d/s **P.A. Backer** *pc* Saga Movie Makers *m* **P. Devarajan**
lp T.V. Chandran, Raveendran, J. Siddiqui, Salam, Pailunni, Bharati, Dawn

Backer's debut telling the love story between a young woman and a radical political activist. The relationship 'humanises' an idealist who is declared to be a criminal. The featurette ends with police killing the hero, a tragedy the woman learns about through the newspapers. Several young Malayalam directors were strongly influenced by the film, notably T.V. Chandran (***Alicinte Anveshanam***, 1989), who plays the lead, and Raveendran, who worked on it.

KATHA SANGAMA

1975 144' b&w Kannada
d/sc **S.R. Puttana Kanagal** *pc* Vardhini Art Pics *st* Giraddi Govindaraj, Veena Yelburgi, Eshwar Chandra *dial* Yoganarasimha *lyr* Vijayanarasimha *c* B.N. Haridas *m* **Vijayabhaskar**
lp G.K. Govinda Rao, **B. Saroja Devi**, **Arathi**, Loknath, Manjula Rao, **Kalyana Kumar**, **Leelavathi**, Gangadhar, **Rajnikant**

Portmanteau film based on three short stories. *Hangu* is about a poor university professor presented with a bribe just when his son is ill and requires expensive medical treatment. The second episode, *Atithi*, tells of an old spinster who once refused to marry the man who loved her and now sees him marrying her student. The third, *Munithayi*, has a wealthy man marrying a blind girl (Arathi) out of pity, but in his absence she is raped by an adolescent youth and later blackmailed. The husband eventually ' forgives' her for having been raped.

MAMATA

1975 124' b&w Oriya
d/sc Byomkesh Tripathi *pc* Peekay Prod. *st* **Prashanta Nanda** *co-lyr* Madhusudhana Rao, Sibabrata Das, Gopal Krishna Das *co-lyr/m* Prafulla Kar *c* Deojibhai
lp Prashanta Nanda, Suresh, Asima, Dhira Biswal, Dinabandhu, Bhanumathi, Radha Panda

Melodrama celebrating the love between a woman and her brother-in-law. Mohan goes to the city and marries Chitra. They become parent figures for Mohan's younger brother, the rustic Ramu. When Mohan dies, gossip about an affair between Chitra and Ramu forces her to leave but she returns to take care of Ramu. This Oriya hit, largely for Prafulla Kar's music, is regarded as having revived the region's film industry.

MAUSAM

1975 156' col Hindi
d/co-sc/lyr/ **Gulzar** *pc* Sunandini Pics, P. Mallikarjuna Rao *st* Kamleshwar *co-sc* Bhushan Banmali *c* K. Vaikunth *m* **Madan Mohan**
lp **Sharmila Tagore**, Sanjeev Kumar, Om Shivpuri, Agha, Satyen Kappu, Dina Pathak, Lily Chakraborty

The successful doctor Amarnath Gill (Kumar) returns to a hill resort where 20 years ago he had an affair with the local beauty Chanda (Tagore). He learns that she had gone crazy waiting for him, married unhappily and died shortly after giving birth to a daughter. He now encounters the fiery prostitute Kajli (Tagore again) who turns out to be the daughter. Without revealing his identity, he tries to make her a socially respectable woman in several comic and, to him, embarrassing situations recalling Shaw's *Pygmalion*. Kajli, who hates the man who jilted her mother and caused her death, eventually relents and leaves with the hero. Tagore's lively performance is the highlight of the film.

MUTHYALA MUGGU

1975 165' col Telugu
d/sc **Bapu** *pc* Shri Rama Chitra *st/dial* Mullapudi Venkatramana *lyr* **Arudra**, C. Narayana Reddy *c* Ishan Arya *m* K.V. Mahadevan
lp Sridhar, Sangeetha, T.L. Kantha Rao, Ravu Gopala Rao, **K. Mukkamala**, Suresh, Allu Ramalingaiah, Vara Prasad, Suryakantam, Purnima, Jaya Malini, Kalpana, Baby Radha, Master Murali, Arja Janardana Rao

Although the author of mythologicals (cf ***Shri Ramanjaneya Yuddham***, 1974; ***Seeta Kalyanam***, 1976), Bapu is better known for his updating of the genre as a critique of modernity (cf ***Hum Paanch***, 1980). This is a contemporary version of the Rama legend. Sridhar (Sridhar), the son of Raja Ramadas, marries Laxmi (Sangeetha) who is earlier seen with a pet monkey (evoking the monkey god Hanuman). The villain (Mukkamala) and his daughter (Malini) seek out a modern Ravana (Gopala Rao), who hides a person in the wife's bedroom so that her husband will suspect an affair. Eventually the couple's twins bring their parents together and wreak revenge on the

Ravana figure. Gopala Rao's stylised performance together with the twins' 'cute' pranks assured the film's entertainment value.

NISHANT

aka *Night's End*
1975 144' col Hindi
d **Shyam Benegal** *p* Freni M. Variava, Mohan J. Bijlani *pc* Blaze Film Ents *s* **Vijay Tendulkar** *dial* Satyadev Dubey *lyr* Mohammed Quli Qutb Shah *c* **Govind Nihalani** *m* **Vanraj Bhatia**
lp **Girish Karnad, Shabana Azmi, Anant Nag**, Amrish Puri, **Smita Patil**, Satyadev Dubey, Kulbhushan Kharbanda, Mohan Agashe, **Naseeruddin Shah**, Savita Bajaj, Sadhu Meher

Based on Tendulkar's original play, apparently inspired by an actual event and written for **Utpal Dutt**, the film extends the ***Ankur*** (1973) theme of rural oppression in AP. A poor schoolmaster (Karnad) and his young wife (Azmi) come to a village dominated by a villainous family of zamindars, consisting of four brothers who abduct and rape his wife. The distraught schoolteacher, helped by an old priest (Dubey), finally succeeds in mobilising the villagers and they slaughter their oppressors. Although not as big a success as *Ankur*, the film enabled many of the actors to trade on their naturalist authenticity to become mainstream Hindi stars including the debuting Naseeruddin Shah and Amrish Puri, who plays the eldest and nastiest brother and is now the highest-priced screen villain in Hindi cinema.

PALANKA

1975 128' b&w/col Bengali
d/dial **Rajen Tarafdar** *pc* Film Arts, Anis Film Corp [Bangladesh] *st* Narendranath Mitra *c* Sailaja Chattopadhyay *m* Sudhin Dasgupta
lp **Utpal Dutt**, Sandhya Roy, Anwar Hussain

This Indo-Bangladesh co-production sees the return to prominence of Tarafdar (***Ganga***, 1960). In East Bengal during Partition, the Hindu patriarch Rajmohan (Dutt), aka White Boss because of his fair complexion, stays behind when his family emigrates to Calcutta. His only companion, the poor Maqbool (Hussain), ridicules him for staying in what is now Pakistan. Rajmohan's daughter-in-law, facing poverty in Calcutta, asks him to sell a giant four-poster bed that had once been her dowry, and to send her the money. The opulent bed, renowned throughout the village for its size and elaborate craftsmanship, is bought by Maqbool (who dreams of making love to his wife on it). This sparks a major controversy among the Muslim gentry in the village as Maqbool is accused of trying to transcend his class position. The quarrel is eventually resolved and Rajmohan imagines Maqbool's two children sleeping on the bed in the manner of the infant Krishna. The film moves into colour as the scene shifts to the present, as the sons of Maqbool and Rajmohan continue their fathers' relationship. With fluent dialogue and memorable acting, esp. by Dutt and Hussain, the recourse to the bed as a metaphor within a realist idiom allows the film to address the fantasy dimensions inherent in questions of class and religion.

Utpal Dutt (right) in *Palanka*

PANDU HAVALDAR

1975 143' b&w Marathi
d/co-lyr **Dada Kondke** *pc* Sadiccha Chitra *s/co-lyr* Rajesh Majumdar *co-lyr* Jagdish Khebudkar *c* Arvind Laad *m* Ram-Lakshman
lp Dada Kondke, Usha Chavan, Ashok Saraf, Lata Arun, Ratnamala, Gulab Mokashi, Mohan Kothivan

Kondke's ribald crazy comedy hit, a change from his usual rural Tamasha-derived formula, continues the director-star's fondness for sexual puns, as in the song *Aho havaldar majhya kulupachi chavi haravli* ('I lost the key to my lock'). Pandu Havaldar (Kondke) is a corrupt cop, a comical figure whose costume undermines any effort to appear authoritative, and an ally of Paru Kelewali, a fruitseller with links to a smuggling ring. The gang is smashed and the cop humanised through the unashamedly sentimental use of a deaf-and-dumb woman he rescues.

SAAMNA

aka *Samna* aka *Confrontation*
1975 151' b&w Marathi
d/co-lyr **Jabbar Patel** *pc* Giriraj Pics *s* **Vijay Tendulkar** *lyr* Aarti Prabhu [aka C.T. Khanolkar], Jagdish Khebudkar *c* Suryakant Lavande *m* Bhaskar Chandavarkar
lp Shriram Lagoo, Nilu Phule, Vilas Rakate, Mohan Agashe, Lalan Sarang, Usha Naik, Sanjeevani Bidkar, **Smita Patil**, Asha Patil, Rajani Chavan

Tendulkar's first independent Marathi script and Jabbar Patel's debut is set in Maharashtra's notorious sugar co-operatives, the power base of the state's Congress Party. In his best-known screen role the noted Marathi stage and film actor Phule plays Hindurao Dhonde Patil with the familiar body language of the arrogantly corrupt politician secure in his power. He covers up an incident involving the military officer Maruti Kamble (Agashe) until a mystic hobo, a former schoolteacher, amateur magician and drunkard (Lagoo) challenges the politician's might. The film's high points are the actorial duel between the two biggest names of the Marathi theatre, Lagoo and Phule, and characters which a literary critic would describe as rounded. The film continues directly from Tendulkar's 70s theatre (cf *Sakharam Binder*, 1971) but glorifies cinema's ability to show actual locations. Lagoo sang the hit song *Kuni tari ashi phataphat.*

SANSAR SIMANTEY

1975 126' b&w Bengali
d/co-lyr **Tarun Majumdar** *pc* Samakalin Pics *st* **Premendra Mitra** *s* **Rajen Tarafdar** *co-lyr* Pulak Bannerjee, Hridayesh Pandeya, Himansu Sekhar Sen *c* K.A. Reza *m* **Hemanta Mukherjee**
lp Sandhya Roy, **Soumitra Chatterjee**, Shekhar Chatterjee, **Robi Ghosh**, Sulata Choudhury, Samita Biswas, **Utpal Dutt, Kali Bannerjee**

Endearingly realist love story between a prostitute and a thief. Rajani, a streetwalker, shelters the thief Aghor but he steals her money. She has him beaten up by a mob and then nurses him back to health. Aghor gives her a stolen necklace and is then chased by his own gang for failing to share the booty. Eventually Rajani agrees to marry Aghor and he promises to buy her from her pimp, but he gets caught by the police. Major scenes include Aghor taking Rajani on a tour of Calcutta, the hand-held shot showing the police searching the corpse of Rajani's friend Manada, and cameraman Reza's controlled bounce-lighting technique. The love story does not, except at the end, interfere with the film's intention of showing life in the red-light area through a series of characters like the madam, the doctor, the vendors, the hoodlums, the landlord's agent who comes for his weekly rent, and the 'respectable' neighbours.

SHOLAY

aka *Flames of the Sun* aka *Embers*
1975 199' col Hindi
d **Ramesh Sippy** *p* G.P. Sippy *pc* Sippy Films *s* **Salim-Javed** *lyr* **Anand Bakshi** *c* Dwarka Divecha *m* **R.D. Burman**
lp **Dharmendra**, Sanjeev Kumar, **Amitabh Bachchan, Hema Malini**, Jaya Bhaduri, Amjad Khan, Iftikhar, A.K. Hangal, Leela Mishra, Macmohan, Sachin, Asrani, Helen, Keshto Mukherjee

Massively popular adventure film shot in 70mm. India's best-known 'curry' western patterned on Italian westerns with admixtures of romance, comedy, feudal costume drama and musicals. In addition, it is peppered with elements from, e.g., Burt Kennedy, Sam Peckinpah, Chaplin and *Butch Cassidy and the Sundance Kid* (1969). The revenge plot has two adventurous crooks, Veeru (Dharmendra) and Jaidev (Bachchan) who are hired by ex-cop Thakur Baldev Singh (Kumar) to hunt down the dreaded dacoit Gabbar Singh (Amjad Khan) who massacred Thakur's family. The film tells its story in two long flashbacks, the first showing the meeting between Thakur and the crooks followed by a long sequence of bandits attacking a train; the second shows Thakur arresting Gabbar Singh, who retaliates by wiping out Thakur's entire family, except for his younger daughter-in-law Radha (Jaya Bhaduri). This episode introduces the third and final encounter when Thakur, whose two arms have been cut off, kicks the bandit into submission. In keeping with his romantic screen image, Jaidev/Bachchan is also killed (which also allowed the film to adhere to the Hindi cinema's norm that the widowed Radha may not remarry). A technically accomplished film, it uses its spectacular cinematography panning and craning over rocky heights and barren quarries, often under menacing clouds, mainly to build up its major legend, the evil Gabbar Singh. Amjad Khan's best-known screen role includes dialogues that became famous throughout the country (an edited soundtrack of the film was released as an LP). The kaleidoscopic approach to the plot structure allowed the film-maker to anthologise the highlights of various genre narratives (e.g. *How the West Was Won*, 1962) and to combine them into a single film, a privilege usually reserved for crazy comedies but here held together by its intensely emotional current, sustained not only by the high-energy shooting styles but also by the music and savoury dialogues. The end result resembles a skilfully designed shopping mall with the viewer being propelled past successive window displays, each exhibiting an eye-catching presentation of some aspect of the popular cinema's history. W. Dissanayake and Malti Sahai (1992) published a book-length commentary on the film.

SWAPNADANAM

aka *Journey through a Dream* aka *Somnambulism*
1975 121' b&w Malayalam
d/co-sc **K.G. George** *pc* K.R. Films *st* E. Mohammed *co-sc* Pamman *m* Bhaskar Chandavarkar
lp Mohandas, M.G. Soman, P.K. Abraham, Isaac Thomas, Venukuttan Nair, Rani Chandra, T.R. Omana, Prema, Mallika, Sonia

George's commercially successful art-house debut is a marital psychodrama without the usual songs and dances. Hero Gopi (Mohandas, a medical practitioner as well as an actor) is unhappily married to Sumitra (Rani Chandra), his cousin and traditional bride. The problem is complicated by his indebtedness to her father who sponsored his education. The film works through extensive use of flashbacks (George's favourite storytelling device) as the hero is treated by a psychiatrist, haunted by memories of the woman he loved at university. He ends up in a mental asylum.

TANARIRI

1975 120' col Gujarati
d/sc **Chandrakant Sangani** *pc* Geeta Chitra *st/dial* Harin Mehta *lyr* Kanti Ashok *c* Vishnukumar Joshi *m* Mahesh-Naresh
lp **Sohrab Modi**, Kanan Kaushal, Bindu, Nareshkumar, Urmila Bhatt, Vishnukumar Vyas, Naran Rajgor, Leela Jarivala

A version of the often-filmed legend associated with the 16th musician Tansen (cf ***Tansen***, 1943) at Mughal Emperor Akbar's (Modi) court and one of the founding figures of North Indian classical music. After singing the raga *Deepak* (associated with light), Tansen himself burns from within and can be saved only by an equally competent singer performing the *Malhar* (a raga associated with the monsoon). The two women, Tana and Riri, daughters of the head of the Nagar community and victims of Akbar's imperialism, can do so but they turn down the invitation from Akbar. This leads to royal retribution and eventually forces the two women to commit suicide.

WAVES OF REVOLUTION

aka *Kranti Ki Tarangein*
1975 30' b&w English
d/co-c **Anand Patwardhan** *co-p* Pradeep Krishen, Ved Prakash

Patwardhan's first full documentary, made on Super-8, inaugurated the independent documentary movement in India. It chronicles the Navnirman students' movement in Gujarat (1974) which eventually led to the mass movement of Jayaprakash Narayan in Bihar, culminating in the Emergency being declared (26 June 1975). The film interprets the JP agitation as a latter-day and more radicalised version of Gandhi's call for non-violent land reform, this time directed against Indira Gandhi's rule. It includes several speeches by Narayan himself, and one direct interview, and shows the rallies he led in Patna (1974) and New Delhi (1975). Completed before the declaration of the Emergency, it has an epilogue on the early days of the state crackdown in the months of June and July. Extensively screened by underground groups during the Emergency, the film inaugurates several of the director's typical documentary strategies, including the use of his own voice and his interviews while holding the camera. Along with its sequel, ***Prisoners of Conscience*** (1978), the film represents definitive coverage of the political conflicts, as well as the rhetoric, characterising those turbulent years.

ANNAKKILI

aka *Annam the Parrot*
1976 133' b&w Tamil
d Devaraj-Mohan *pc* SPT Films *st* Selvaraj *sc/lyr* Panchu Arunachalam *c* A. Somasundaram *m* **Ilaiyaraja**
lp Sivakumar, S.V. Subbaiah, Srikanth, Thenjai Srinivasan, Sujatha, Jayalakshmi, Murthy, Senthamarai, M.N. Rajam

Eternal-triangle story set and shot on location in the picturesque village of Thengumarada in a valley near Sathyamangalam. The young village midwife Annam (Sujatha) falls for the new schoolteacher, but he marries her friend Sumathi (Jayalakshmi), the rich landlord's daughter. The owner of the local cinema is the villain: he abducts the teacher's son to blackmail Annam into marrying him. She sets fire to his cinema and rescues the infant but dies in the process. Silent Tamil film shows often had live attractions on the programme and this aspect was later incorporated into the films, e.g. as a special dance drama. Here, two long extracts from other films were worked into the plot by having the heroine go to her local cinema and watch **Padmini** dancing as Andal, the mythical devotee offering flowers to her god, and **Kannamba** playing the title part in ***Kannagi*** (1942) where she burns the city of Madurai after proving the innocence of her husband. Both sequences dovetail with elements of the main plot. The film also launched Ilaiyaraja's phenomenal career as a music director with the songs *Annakkili unnai thedudhu* and *Machanai partheengala*, two extremely popular and long-lasting hits in TN.

BHUMIKA

aka *The Role*
1976 142' col Hindi
d/co-sc **Shyam Benegal** *p* Lalit M. Bijlani, Freni M. Variava *pc* Blaze Film Ents *st* **Hansa Wadkar**'s *Sangtye Aika* (1970) *co-sc* **Girish Karnad** *dial* Satyadev Dubey *lyr* **Majrooh Sultanpuri**, Vasant Dev *c* **Govind Nihalani** *m* **Vanraj Bhatia**
lp **Smita Patil, Anant Nag**, Amrish Puri, **Naseeruddin Shah**, Sulabha Deshpande, Kulbhushan Kharbanda, Baby Rukhsana, **Amol Palekar, B.V. Karanth**

Benegal abandons his rural settings for this cinephile fantasy based on the autobiography of the Marathi/Hindi actress Hansa Wadkar. Uma (Patil, in the role of Wadkar) is taught music by her grandmother. She tries to become a film actress as a child and eventually becomes a star in adulthood, a trajectory inflected by the four men she meets at various points in her life: husband Keshav (Palekar), narcissistic male co-star Rajan (Nag), effete film-maker Sunil Verma (Shah) with whom she makes an unsuccessful suicide pact, and the landowner Kale (Puri) whose second wife she becomes. Many aspects of the story allow the question of women's oppression to be raised although, tragically, Uma seems to end up identifying herself with the romantic cliche of the self-sacrificing heroine, defeated by the patriarchal mores that have weighed on her since early childhood (shown in sepia flashbacks). The film opens with scenes alluding to the making of Wadkar's best-known title, ***Lokshahir Ramjoshi*** (1947). The music test which **Govindrao Tembe** and **Baburao Painter** gave the young Wadkar at Shalini Cinetone is reconstructed, a rather poignant moment since Wadkar hates the very music which elevates her to stardom. However, film history is treated with poetic licence as the story roams through some pre-WW2 genres: **Bombay Talkies** is evoked through Sunila Pradhan who is made up to look like **Devika Rani**; a quote from ***Kismet*** (1943) and allusions to **Wadia**'s masked stunt films seem arbitrarily inserted. The soundtrack uses radio broadcasts about Pearl Harbor and other events to provide historical markers.

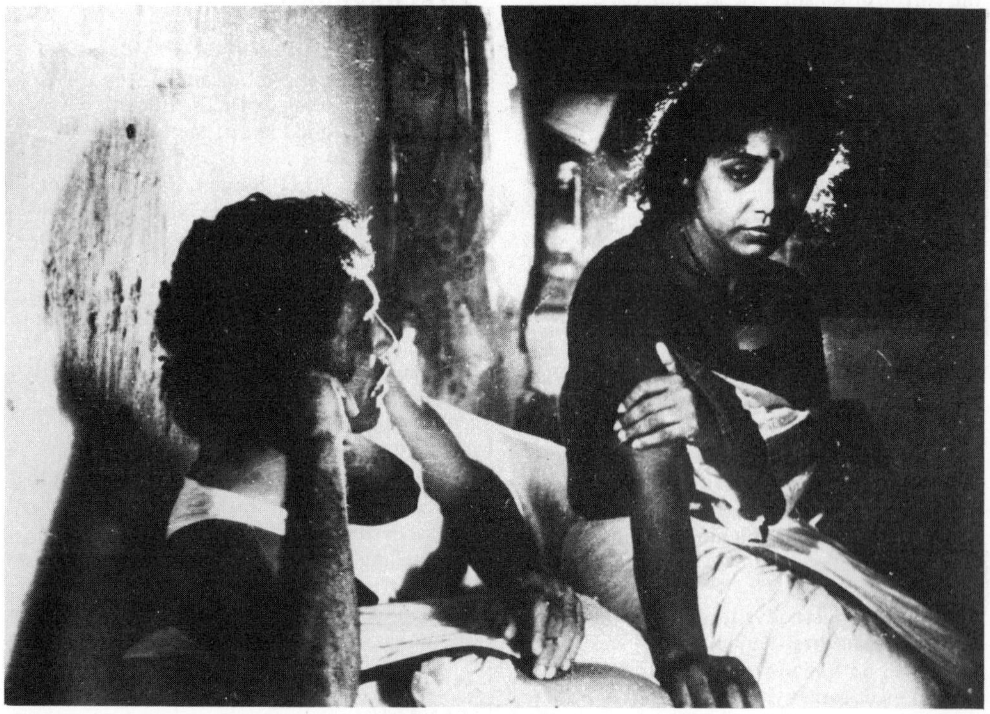

Chuvanna Vithukal

CHHATRABHANG

aka *The Divine Plan*
1976 80' col Hindi
d/co-p/s Nina Shivdasani *co-p* Asha Sheth, Vashketu Foundation *c* Apurba Kishore Bir *m* Edgar Varese
lp Amrish Puri

An allusive documentary shot in 1975 with a commentary written by Vinay Shukla and narrated by Puri, India's notorious screen villain. The film uses an aestheticised, painterly shooting style to meditate on the iniquities of the caste system esp. in rural areas. The focus of the story is the fictional reconstruction of a real-life episode in which Harijans confront Brahmin elites and eventually the police, when their well dries up. It ends with some documentary interviews with real people involved in the original struggle. Born in Bombay (1946), Shivdasani was trained as a painter and a photographer in New York and Los Angeles. She is probably the first Indian woman director of experimental films. After four short films, this is her first feature-length work.

CHUVANNA VITHUKAL

aka *Red Seedling*
1976 96' b&w Malayalam
d/s **P.A. Backer** *p* Salam Karasheri *pc* Navadhara Movie Makers *c* Vipin Das *m* **P. Devarajan**
lp Shantakumari, Rehman, Zeenat, Nilambur Aisha, V.V. Anthony, Siddiqui, Nilambur Balan, Sethu

Melodrama about two sisters. Bharati (Shantakumari) works as a prostitute for Madam Rudrama and tries to secure a better life for her younger sister Lekha, but the prostitute is caught in a police raid and jailed while Lekha disappears with a dubious young man. After she is released, Bharati plies her trade on the streets. A truck driver, Keshavan, is kind to her and a new life seems possible when a haggard Lekha suddenly arrives on Bharati's doorstep, holding a baby and explaining that her lover has left her. The older sister sees their chance of a better life vanish as new burdens are placed on them.

GALPA HELEBI SATA

1976 148' col Oriya
d Nagen Ray *pc* Swati Films *st/dial* Basanta Mahapatra *sc/c* P.D. Shenoy *lyr* Gurukrishna Goswami *c* Surendra Sahu *m* Bhubhan, Hari
lp Banaja, Sudharani, Harish, Suresh, Soudamini, Tanuja

Wealthy hero meets local belle while touring the famous temples of Konarak, Orissa. He marries her and then goes home, promising to return. When he fails to do so, the woman traces him to his home. After first rejecting her he eventually accepts her as his wife. Oriya cinema's first colour film is better known for its music, composed by Hari, i.e. the noted flautist Hariprasad Chaurasia, and Bhubhan. Hit song hits include *E banara chai* and *E mora dost*, sung by **Kishore Kumar**'s son Amit Kumar, and *Sathi re jaa kahi*, sung by Suman Kalyanpur.

GHASHIRAM KOTWAL

1976 108'(98') col Marathi
pc Yukt Film Co-op *d* K. Hariharan, **Mani Kaul**, Kamal Swaroop, **Saeed Mirza** *s/lyr* **Vijay Tendulkar** from his play *c* Binod Pradhan, Rajesh Joshi, Manmohan Singh, Virendra Saini *m* Bhaskar Chandavarkar
lp Mohan Agashe, Rajani Chavan, **Om Puri**, Vandana Pandit, Shriram Ranade, Ravindra Sathe

This remarkable avant-garde experiment in collective film-making is based on one of the most celebrated plays in contemporary Indian theatre, staged in 1972 by the Theatre Academy, Pune (members of which participate in the film's cast). The play used Marathi folk forms like the Gondhal and the Keertan in an elaborately choreographed musical featuring the legendary Nanasaheb Phadnavis, the prime minister of Peshwa Madhavrao II and the real power behind Maharashtra's Peshwa throne (1773-97). The original play, a transparent allegory referring to Indira Gandhi's reign, was adapted in order to comment on Maratha and Indian history, starting from the enthronement of the child Peshwa Madhavrao II, until the final decline of the empire and the arrival of the British (cf ***Ramshastri***, 1944). It presents the decadent Nanasaheb (Agashe) and his lieutenant Ghashiram (Puri), a Brahmin from Kanauj, whom he uses to mount a reign of terror in the capital city of Pune. The main plot concerns Nana's spy network, the rout of the British at Wadgaon (1779), Ghashiram's rise and his fall when Nana sacrifices him, and the popular revolt against Nana's henchman leaving the prime minister (and true culprit) unscathed. The film's main significance resides in the way it adapts theatre to investigate cinema itself, a point underlined by the chorus at the beginning of the movie and, at the end, the quote from Glauber Rocha's *Antonio das Mortes* (1969) as the sutradhara (chorus) suddenly enters into the present when a truck leaves the quarry. The collective of former **FTII** students made one more film, Saeed Mirza's debut ***Arvind Desai Ki Ajeeb Dastaan*** (1978) before folding. *Ghashiram Kotwal* itself was subject to a court order from the bank which loaned the production finance, delaying its general screening after the premiere in Madras in January 1977.

HUNGRY AUTUMN

1976 75' b&w English
d/c **Gautam Ghosh** *pc* Cine 74

Ghosh's first major film is a documentary about the 1974 Bengal famine, analysing how famines come about and chronicling their impact in the cities and the villages of India. Made on a Paillard Bolex by a group calling itself the 'Joris Ivens collective', it was one of the first Indian documentaries to face censorship under the Emergency. Much of the footage reflects Ghosh's preoccupation, later developed in his features, with people surviving on the margins of society.

KABHI KABHIE

1976 177' col Hindi-Urdu
d/co-sc **Yash Chopra** *pc* Yash-Raj Films *st* Pamela Chopra *co-sc/dial* Sagar Sarhadi *lyr* **Sahir Ludhianvi** *c* Kay Gee, Romesh Bhalla *m* **Khayyam**
lp **Amitabh Bachchan**, **Shashi Kapoor**, **Waheeda Rehman**, Raakhee, Neetu Singh, Rishi Kapoor, Naseem, Simi Garewal, Parikshit Sahni

The poet Amit (Bachchan) loves Pooja (Raakhee) but she, under pressure from her parents, marries another (S. Kapoor). The resulting tensions between the two families are resolved only in the next generation: Pooja's son (Rishi Kapoor) will choose the partner he prefers. According to the film, the object of his desire also chooses him. Remembered for Mukesh's rendering of the title song *Kabhi kabhie mere dil main khayal ata hai.*

MANIMUZHAKKUM

aka *Tolling of the Bell*
1976 112' b&w Malayalam
d/sc **P.A. Backer** *pc* Anaswara Chitra *st* Sara Thomas *m* **P. Devarajan**
lp Hari, Cyril, Veeran, Prabhakaran, Urmila, Charulata, Vani

Backer's 2nd film is a melodrama about an infantile youth, Jose Paul, whose love life is blighted by his early years in a Christian orphanage. Born a Hindu, he is imbued with Christian beliefs by a kindly priest, Father Francis. Later he is adopted by a rich Hindu uncle, who renames him and urges him to change his religion. Jose Paul's problems with his own sense of identity are dramatised in terms of his relations with women: rejected by a rich woman for his complicated past, he is refused next by a Hindu woman for having been a Christian and again by the daughter of his Christian employer in Madras for having been a Hindu.

MANMATHA LEELAI

1976 161' col Tamil
d/sc **K. Balachander** *pc* Kalakendra Movies *lyr* **Kannadasan** *c* B.S. Lokanathan *m* M.S. Vishwanathan
lp **Kamalahasan**, Y.G.P. Mahendran, Y.G. Parthasarathy, M.R.R. Ravi, Harihara Subramanyam, Halam, Y. Vijaya, Jayapradha, Hema Choudhury

Balachander's melodrama about a rich company director who has everything but a child. He compulsively has affairs until he comes to terms with his infertility just in time to save his marriage.

MANTHAN

aka *The Churning*
1976 134' col Hindi
d/co-st **Shyam Benegal** *pc* Sahyadri Films *co-st* V. Kurien *sc* **Vijay Tendulkar** *dial* **Kaifi Azmi** *lyr* Niti Sagar *c* **Govind Nihalani** *m* **Vanraj Bhatia**
lp **Girish Karnad**, **Smita Patil**, **Naseeruddin Shah**, Sadhu Meher, **Anant Nag**, Amrish Puri, Kulbhushan Kharbanda, Mohan Agashe, Savita Bajaj, Abha Dhulia, Anjali Paingankar

Although the film suggests in its opening title, '500,000 farmers of Gujarat present ...', that it was publicly financed, it was in fact made through the National Dairy Development Board (NDDB), an enormously controversial organisation headed by Dr V. Kurien, who shares a script credit. Established in 1965 to regularise milk co-operatives and to enhance their productivity with new technology, the NDDB was accused of aggravating India's foreign debt and of diverting resources destined to help the rural poor into servicing the urban upper-class market. Made during this controversy to enhance the NDDB's image, *Manthan* tells a version of the organisation's early years when corrupt local politicians, middlemen and an uneducated community's prejudices had to be overcome to create local co-operatives. Karnad plays what is presumably a fictional version of Dr Kurien himself while Kharbanda is the villainous Sarpanch (village head). Shah and Patil represent the voices of progress among the peasantry. The Andhra Hindi spoken in ***Ankur*** (1973) and ***Nishant*** (1975) is here replaced by Gujarati Hindi.

MRIGAYA

aka *The Royal Hunt*
1976 119' col Hindi
d/co-sc **Mrinal Sen** *p* Rajeshwara Rao *pc* Udaya Bhaskar *co-sc* Mohit Chattopadhyay *st* Bhagavati Charan Panigrahi *c* K.K. Mahajan *m* **Salil Choudhury**
lp **Mithun Chakraborty**, Robert Wright, Mamata Shankar, Gyanesh Mukherjee, Sajal Roy Choudhury, Samit Bhanja, Ann Wright, Sadhu Meher

After a series of stylistically complex, politically oriented experiments with modes of cinematic storytelling, Sen achieved this controlled yet seductive allegorical tale shot in vibrant colours. Set in the 30s in Orissa with echoes of the Santhal revolt, a tribal hunter, Ghinua (Chakraborty) feels a kinship with a middle-aged British colonial administrator (Wright) who is equally passionate about hunting and perhaps also attracted to the vigorous young man. Protected by colonial notions of law and order, the moneylender Bhuban Sardar (Meher) pursues a tribal rebel (Bhanja) and legally murders him, taking his head to the Administrator for his reward. When Ghinua's wife (Shankar) is seized by the greedy moneylender in lieu of payment, the young man hunts down the villain and proudly takes the villain's head as a hunting trophy to the British officer, claiming he has rid the jungle of its most savage beast. The young hero in his turn becomes the prey of colonial justice. Made during the Emergency, the film's ramifications go beyond the depiction of a clash of cultures, advocating resistance against the imposition of an administrative tyranny that ends up recompensing the perpetrators of injustice. First major role by Mithun Chakraborty, later a Hindi cinema star associated with disco musicals.

PALLAVI

1976 128' b&w Kannada
d/s **P. Lankesh** *pc* Indira Lankesh Prod. *c* S. Ramchandra *m* Rajeev Taranath
lp Vimala Naidu, T.S. Seetaram, P. Lankesh, Pandu, Shashidhar, Shankara Swamy, Parvathavani

For his film debut, the noted Kannada novelist Lankesh tells of Shanta (Naidu), a bouncy university teenager who wants to grow her hair as long as that of **Vyjayanthimala** and is as idealistic as her boyfriend Chandru. The two apply for the same job, which Shanta gets. She eventually marries her boss, Jagannathan (Lankesh), but continues working. Her old boyfriend suddenly resurfaces, a fugitive from justice, and accuses her of having sold out in return for security. The film tells her life story in flashback, returning to the present to show the boyfriend being caught by the cops.

RUSHYA SHRINGA

1976 112' col Kannada
d/sc V.R.K. Prasad *pc* Young Cinema *st/lyr* **Chandrasekhar Kambhar** from his play *dial* **G.V. Iyer** *c* S. Ramchandra *m* **B.V. Karanth**
lp Rathna, **Suresh Heblikar**, Sundarshree, Kavitha, Shanta, Swarnamma

Melodrama derived from a folk-tale. In a rainless village, a demon possesses the headman and the local deity prophesies that only Balappa can solve the problem. On his arrival, Balappa embarrasingly fails until he meets his father's ghost. When he takes on the headman, the man's wife appears as a goddess, gives him a necklace and tells him that if he sleeps with a virgin wearing the necklace, the rain will come. Eventually Balappa does indeed bring rain and rids the village of its demon.

SEETA KALYANAM

aka *Seeta's Wedding*
1976 134' col Telugu
d **Bapu** *p* P. Ananda Rao *pc* Ananda Lakshmi Art Pics *s* Mullapudi Venkatramana *c* K.S. Prasad *lyr* **Arudra**, C. Narayana Reddy *c* K.S. Prakash, Ravikant Nagaich *m* K.V. Mahadevan
lp Ravi Kumar, Jayapradha, Sathyanarayana, **Gummadi Venkateshwara Rao**, **Jamuna**, **K. Mukkamala**, Mikkilineni, Kanta Rao, Thyagaraj, Hemalatha, P.R. Varalakshmi, Mamata

Bapu's lavish and successful colour mythological with special effects supervised by the cinematographer and director Ravikant Nagaich and art direction by K. Nageshwara Rao, is one of the best-known 70s Telugu films in the genre. The story is the *Ramayana* tale leading up to the wedding between Rama (Kumar, who also plays the part of Vishnu) and the Princess Seeta (Jayapradha, who also plays Lakshmi). The villainous interloper is King Ravana (Sathyanarayana).

SHESHA SHRABANA

1976 129' col Oriya
d/sc **Prashanta Nanda** *pc* Shri Jagannath Films *st* Basant Mahapatra's play *co-lyr* Sibabrata Das *co-lyr/m* Prafulla Kar *c* Rajan Kinagi
lp Prashanta Nanda, Mahashweta, Mohammed Mohsin, Hemant Das, Banaja Mohanty

Oriya star Nanda's successful directorial debut and the second Orissa colour film. The Brahmin woman Manika (Mahashweta in her screen debut) is rescued in a flood by the fisherman Sania (Nanda). When he takes her home, their class differences cause problems in the village. When the brutish village head tries to rape Manika, she jumps into the river and Sania goes insane.

SILA NERANGALIL SILA MANITHARGAL

aka *Some People Sometimes*
1976 130' b&w Tamil
d/sc **A. Bhimsingh** *pc* A.B.S. Prod. *st/dial/lyr* Jayakantan's novel and the story *Agnipravesam* *c* D.S. Pandian *m* M.S. Vishwanathan
lp Laxmi, Srikanth, Y.G. Parthasarathy, Nagesh, Neelakantan, Rajasulochana, Sukumari, Sundaribai, Jai Geetha

Noted Tamil writer Jayakantan (cf ***Kaval Daivam***, 1969) wrote this novel as a justification for his ending of the controversial story *Agnipravesham* (*Ordeal by Fire*). The film incorporates both works. Ganga (Laxmi) is raped and the stigma condemns her to remain unmarried, living with her widowed mother (Sundaribai) where her uncle sexually harasses her. Years later she tracks down the rapist: Prabhu (Srikanth), a chain-smoking, wealthy, lower-caste businessman, married and father of a teenage daughter. Ganga insists on him being 'her man' although the relationship remains platonic. She refuses his suggestion that she marry an old middle-class widower. The film reproduces the novel's long conversations but somewhat dilutes their impact: nadaswaram music, traditionally played during marriages, is played over the rape in the car, and at the end Ganga, dressed in white like a widow, is compared in a voice-over to the pure and serene Ganges. The acting by Laxmi and Sundaribai convey the force and the underlying bitterness of the story. The film was hailed for bringing Tamil film up to the level of quality literature and for showing a married man in a relationship with an unmarried woman. That he is also a rapist seems not to have been so important to the critics.

SIRI SIRI MUVVA

1976 144' col Telugu
d/s **K. Vishwanath** *pc* Geetha Krishna Combines *co-dial* Jandhyala *co-dial/lyr* Veeturi Sundara Ramamurthy *c* V.S.R. Swamy *m* K.V. Mahadevan
lp Chandramohan, Jayapradha, Devadas, Sakshi Rangarao, Ramaprabha, Kavitha, Satyanarayana, Allu Ramalingaiah

The first of Vishwanath's several 'classical' musicals (cf ***Shankarabharanam***, 1979) is a love story between Hema (Jayapradha), a pretty deaf-mute dancer, and Samba (Chandramohan), a talented drummer. Their love has to overcome the prejudices suffered by the disabled woman, esp. from her stepmother. The film has 10 songs and was a hit mainly for Mahadevan's music. Remade by the director in Hindi as *Sargam* (1979) starring Rishi Kapoor and Jayapradha.

SONBAINI CHUNDADI

1976 152' col/scope Gujarati
d/sc Girish Manukant *pc* R.J. Films *st* Kantilal Jagjivan Mehta's play *lyr/m* **Avinash Vyas** *c* Rajen Kapadia
lp Dilip Patel, Ranjitraj, Sohil Virani, Narayan Rajgor, Premshankar Bhatt, Jay Patel, Ashvin Patel, Girija Mitra, Anjana, Vrinda Trivedi, Parul Parekh, Priti Parekh

Adapted from Mehta's stage version of a gruesome Gujarati folk legend addressing early capitalism and the fragmentation of the feudal joint family. Four of the little Son's seven brothers leave home in search of employment, leaving Son's cruel sister-in-law Bhadra free to inflict her tyranny upon the remaining members of the family. One of her brothers-in-law, Shambhu, is killed but his ghost reappears to try to protect the defenceless Son. Bhadra and her new lover try to kill her but in the process her own son loses his life. Eventually Bhadra too dies and the seven brothers reunite. A musical melodrama with 10 songs, and Gujarati cinema's first CinemaScope film.

THUNDER OF FREEDOM

1976 31' col English
d/c **S. Sukhdev** *pc* Films Division, Film-20 Series *made with* Gopal Maharesh, Govind Maharesh, B.L. Maisuriya, M. Michael, Salim Sheikh

Sukhdev's Emergency propaganda documentary is the best known of the Film-20 series illustrating the benefits of Indira Gandhi's Twenty-point Economic Programme. Shot mainly in and around New Delhi, the film presents the pre-Emergency period as riddled with riots and disruptions, in which 'almost anyone' could bring all legal processes to a standstill. It interviews a factory owner who praises the absence of labour agitation and two noted journalists, Dileep Padgaonkar and Abu Abraham, both of whom express some doubt about the loss of fundamental human rights while agreeing that the breakdown of the State infrastructure prior to the Emergency was not a situation to which the country would wish to return.

AGRAHARATHIL KAZHUTHAI

aka *Agraharathil Oru Kazhuthai* aka *Donkey in a Brahmin Village*
1977 96' b&w Tamil
d/co-p/co-sc **John Abraham** *co-p* Charly John *pc* Nirmiti Films *co-sc* Venkat Swaminathan *dial* Sampath *c* Ramchandra *m* **M.B. Srinivasan**
lp M.B. Srinivasan, Swathi, Savitri, Raman Veerarghavan, Krishnaraj, S. Gopali, Rajan, Shri Lalitha, Lalithambal, Narasimhan, Thilairajan

Abraham's 2nd feature, his only one in Tamil, is an acid satire told in an innovative, surreal narrative style making excellent use of repetitions for comic effect, on brahminical bigotry and superstition. It was shot around Kunrathur near Chingelpet and at the Loyola College in Madras. A donkey strays into the brahminical enclave in a village and is adopted as a pet by Prof. Narayanaswami (Srinivasan). Ridiculed by his caste fellows, he asks the mute village girl Uma to look after it. When the girl's stillborn baby is deposited outside the temple, the donkey is blamed and killed. Guilt then induces the priests to start seeing miracles. The dead donkey becomes an object of veneration and is ritually burned. In a symbolic sequence recalling Bunuel, the fire spreads and engulfs the entire village. Only the girl and the professor survive. Although Brahmin bigots tried to have the film banned, it is more a morality fable about innocence (Abraham claimed Bresson's *Au Hasard Balthazar*, 1966, as an inspiration) and guilt, recalling parts of ***Ajantrik*** (1957) by Abraham's FTII teacher **Ghatak**. Although the film received a national award, the Tamil press remained cool. Even in late 1989, **Doordarshan** thought it prudent to cancel a scheduled tv screening.

AMAR AKBAR ANTHONY

1977 186' col Hindi
d **Manmohan Desai** *pc* MKD Films *st* Mrs J.M. Desai *sc* Prayag Raj *dial* Kadar Khan *lyr* **Anand Bakshi** *c* Peter Pereira *m* **Laxmikant-Pyarelal**
lp **Vinod Khanna**, Rishi Kapoor, **Amitabh Bachchan**, Neetu Singh, **Shabana Azmi**, Parveen Babi, **Nirupa Roy**, Jeevan, Pran, Helen, Nadira, Pratima Devi, Madhumati

Desai's breakthrough film started his long collaboration with Bachchan and established his characteristic style: a series of episodic 'highlights' (as the director describes them) edited into an extravagant fantasy spectacle. Hunted by Robert (Jeevan), the ex-convict Kishenlal (Pran) is forced to abandon his wife Bharati (Roy) and his three sons who get separated by a combination of fate and villainy. The sons grow up to become Amar (Khanna), raised by a Hindu cop; Akbar (Kapoor), looked after by a Muslim tailor; and Anthony (Bachchan), sheltered by a Catholic priest. The convoluted story has Kishenlal become a crime boss while gangsters led by Robert and his sidekick Zebisco interfere in the story on various occasions to trigger more action. A close friendship develops between the three brothers and their separated parents before the family is reunited. Starting with a pre-credit sequence where, in high-angle shots, all three heroes are seen simultaneously donating blood for their injured mother, each of them unaware of their relationship with the other, the plot merely provides a formal skeleton for the narrative spectacle. The substance of the movie is not in its ostensible plea for religious tolerance but in the Bachchan-dominated star turns, esp. the famous *My name is Anthony Gonsalves* song (by **Kishore Kumar** and Bachchan) that has Bachchan step out of an Easter egg, and his drunken dialogue with a mirror reflection. The film, which on one occasion involves divine intervention (when their mother Bharati's eyesight is restored), ends with all three brothers in various disguises (cop Amar as a one-man band,

Akbar as a tailor and Anthony as a priest) pursuing the same villains. Bachchan speaks in a dialect coloquially described as Bombay Hindi, a vernacular and body language usually associated with the city's lumpenised underclass. The masquerade presented by the film helped create an autonomous cult image for the star which, because not anchored in a coherent narrative, could be deployed henceforth as a brand image in disparate contexts. The action sequences are shot rather perfunctorily.

AVARGAL

aka *Characters*
1977 167' b&w Tamil
d/s **K. Balachander** *pc* Kalakendra Movies *lyr* **Kannadasan** *c* B.S. Lokanathan *m* M.S. Vishwanathan
lp **Kamalahasan**, **Rajnikant**, Ravikumar, Sujatha, **Leelavathi**, Kumari Padmini

Lovers Anu and Bharani separate and Anu is forced to marry Ramnath, the sadistic boss of her dying father. After she has a child she gets a divorce and finds a job in Madras. Her old lover Bharani is now her neighbour and their affair is resumed. When her former husband reappears to destroy again her aspirations for a new life, her repentant mother-in-law is the only person who stands by her.

BABA TARAKNATH

1977 159' b&w Bengali
d Sunil Bannerjee, Baren Chatterjee *pc* Sulochana Art Int. *co-s/lyr* Gouriprasanna Majumdar *co-s/dial* Bibhuti Mukherjee *co-s* Shantiranjan Ghosh Dastidar *c* Anil Gupta, Jyoti Laha *m* Neeta Sen
lp Sandhya Roy, Biswajeet, Sulochana Chatterjee, Gurudas Bannerjee, Sukhen Das, **Anup Kumar**

Bengali hit mythological comparable with the more famous Hindi ***Jai Santoshi Maa*** (1975). The film addresses the shrine of Taraknath (a version of Shiva) at Tarakeshwar, represented by a phallic stone over which pilgrims pour holy water. The extremely simplistically presented conflict between religion and science has an urban scientist (Biswajeet) marry a devout rural belle (Sandhya Roy) against his will. An astrologer foretells much misfortune, which comes true when the scientist, fed up with superstition, returns to his experiments with snake poison and is bitten by one of his snakes. The wife saves her husband by undertaking a long and hazardous pilgrimage to Tarakeshwar, where the deity sends a snake that sucks the poison out of her husband's body. The film adhered to the tenets of the communal mythological, e.g. linking religious faith and female chastity, and evoked the popular legend of Behula and Lakhinder from the *Manasa Mangal*, a legend promptly filmed within a month of *Baba Taraknath*'s success (*Behula Lakhinder*, 1977). Frenzied crowds attending screenings left their footwear outside and many poured the ritual water over a make-believe shrine in the theatre lobby. The film sparked a new wave of pilgrimages to the shrine, esp. by women.

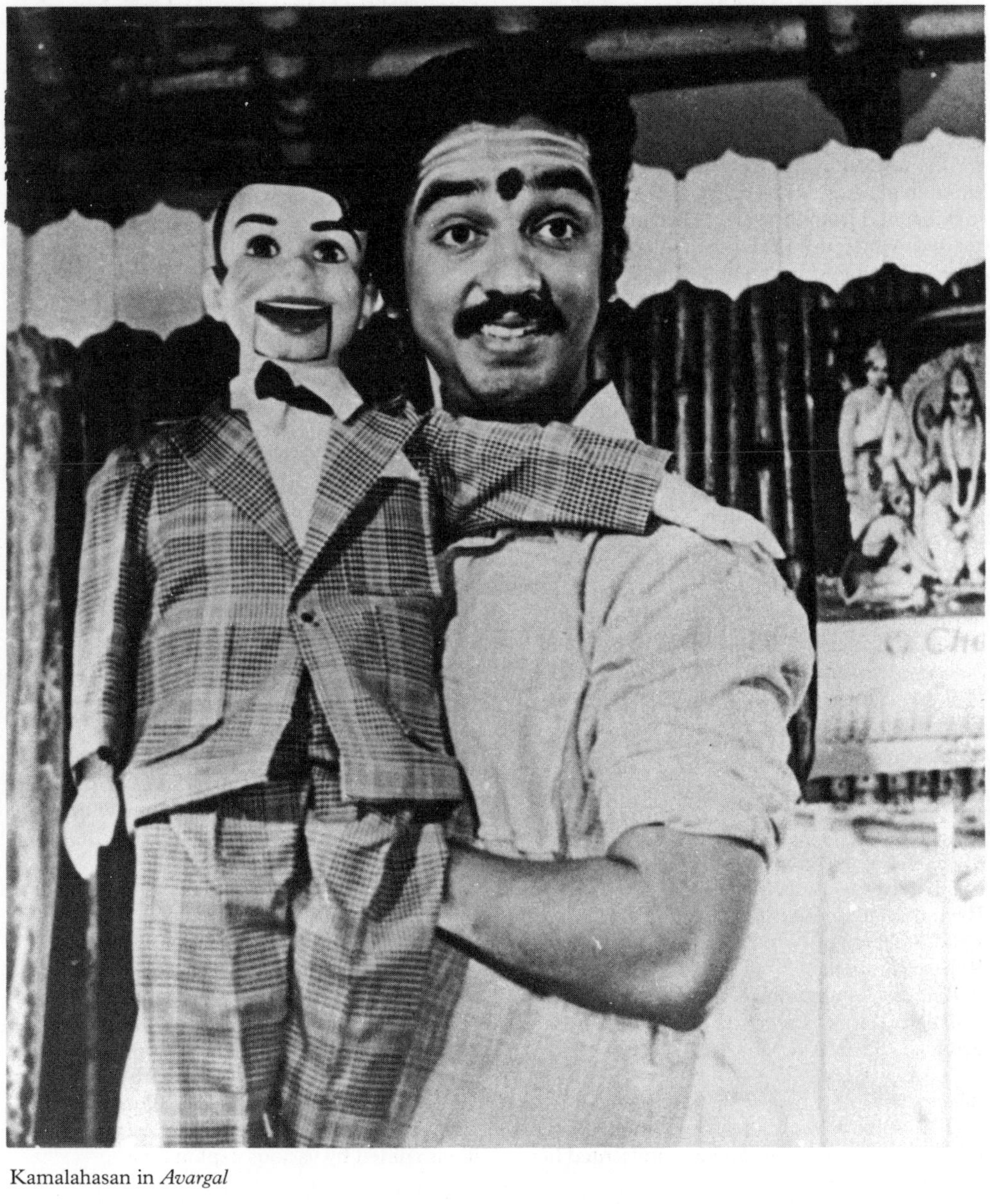

Kamalahasan in *Avargal*

CHAANI

1977 134'[M]/136'[H] col Marathi/Hindi
d/sc/p **V. Shantaram** *pc* V. Shantaram Prod. *st* C.T. Khanolkar *dial* Vrajendra Gaur *lyr* Bharat Vyas *c* Shivaji Sawant *m* Hridaynath Mangeshkar
lp Ranjana, Sushant Ray, Yeshwant Dutt, Premkumar, Gauri Kamat, Durga Senjit, Arvind Deshpande

Shantaram intended the film to be part of New Indian Cinema's vanguard, adapting a difficult work from the innovative contemporary Marathi writer C.T. Khanolkar. The story, written in 1970 and set on the Konkan coast, features a woman born of an 'incident' between an Englishman and a local fisherwoman, now only discussed as a hushed rumour except by a boatman who loudly curses the girl whenever he ferries his boat across the river. Shantaram's garish colour photography and emphatic dialogue make the story into a bizarre calendar-art curiosity with a plump, blue-eyed, blonde fisherwoman (Ranjana), a caricature of the original literary character.

CHAKRADHARI

aka *Panduranga Mahima*
1977 153' col Telugu
d V. Madhusudhana Rao *pc* Lakshmi Film Combines *dial/co-lyr* **Acharya Athreya** *co-lyr* C. Narayana Reddy, *c* P.S. Selvaraj *m* **G.K. Venkatesh**
lp **A. Nageshwara Rao**, Satyanarayana, Allu Ramalingaiah, **Vanisree**, Jayapradha, Ramaprabha, **Vijayanirmala**, Jayamalini

Saint film featuring the Marathi poet Gora Kumbhar (Nageshwara Rao), whose devotion to his god causes much hardship to his wife Lakshmi (Vanisree). It also leads to the death of their son, whom his god, descending to earth, brings back to life. The film included cabaret items by Jayamalini and Jayapradha, indicating changes in the genre from its pre-Independence heyday.

CHILAKAMMA CHEPPINDI

1977 155' b&w Telugu
d Eranki Sharma *pc* Gopikrishna Int. *sc* **K. Balachander** *dial* Ganesh Patro *lyr* **Athreya**, Veeturi Sundara Ramamurthy *c* B.S. Lokanathan *m* M.S. Vishwanathan
lp Narayana Rao, **Rajnikant**, Lakshmi Kant, P.L. Narayana, Sripriya, Sangeetha, Seetalatha, Lakshmi, Hemsunder

Melodrama about a village girl in the city. The heroine Malli (Sripriya) prompted by a fortune-teller, sets out to seek her fortune in the city. She is seduced by Madhu (Narayana Rao), who quickly abandons her when she becomes pregnant. Madhu's man-hating sister Bharati (Sangeetha) initially helps her, but then abandons her when she falls in love with a neighbour. Eventually a chastened Malli finds happiness with Kasi (Rajanikant), a rural simpleton who loves her. Eranki Sharma's debut was praised for its b&w photography and rustic songs.

DAANA VEERA SHURA KARNA

1977 233' col Telugu
d/s **N.T. Rama Rao** *pc* Ramakrishna Cine Studios *dial/co-lyr* Kondaveeti Venkata Kavi *co-lyr* C. Narayana Reddy, Dasarathi, *Thirupati Venkatakavulu* *c* Kannappa *m* **Pendyala Nageshwara Rao**
lp N.T. Rama Rao, M. Satyanarayana, Rajanala, **S. Varalakshmi**, **B. Saroja Devi**, **Sharada**, Prabha, Mikkilineni, Dhulipala Sivarama Sastry, Kanchana, Deepa, Prabhakara Reddy, Balakrishna, **K. Mukkamala**

NTR's best-known film as director is a mammoth mythological about the life of Karna, a character from the *Mahabharata* born to Kunti, brought up among the Kauravas and eventually killed in the great battle by Arjuna when his chariot wheel gets stuck in the ground. NTR plays three roles in this special-effects-laden movie: Krishna, Duryodhana and Karna. It was later resurrected as part of the propaganda for NTR's Telugu Desam Party. After the film's success, he directed himself in several multiple-role mythologicals, e.g. ***Shri Rama Pattabhishekham*** (1978); he plays five roles in *Shrimad Virat Veerabrahmendra Swamy Charitra* (1984).

DHARAM VEER

1977 165' col Hindi
d **Manmohan Desai** *pc* S.S. Movietone *st* J.M. Desai, Pushpa Sharma *sc* Prayag Raj, K.B. Pathak *dial* Kadar Khan *lyr* **Anand Bakshi**, Vithalbhai Patel *c* N.V. Srinivas *m* **Laxmikant-Pyarelal**
lp **Dharmendra**, **Jeetendra**, **Zeenat Aman**, Neetu Singh, Pran, Indrani Mukherjee, Jeevan, Ranjeet, Sujit Kumar, Dev Kumar, Chand Usmani, Pradeep Kumar

A **Manmohan Desai**-style fairy-tale adventure story freely mixing elements from different film genres and historical periods. A lone hunter (Pran) secretly marries the maharani (Mukherjee) of a princely state. In a scene crying out for a psychoanalytic reading, a wild tigress manifests herself during their wedding night. The bride believes her husband to have died as a result and marries a more powerful man, a prince (P. Kumar). Before the maharani gives birth to twin boys, her husband is killed; his dying wish is that the boys' parentage be kept secret. The twins are separated: Dharam (Dharmendra) is raised by a woodcutter while Veer (Jeetendra) becomes the heir-apparent to the throne. Unaware of their relationship, the two become buddies and go through a series of adventures. Dharam woos the haughty princess (Aman) of a neighbouring kingdom and Veer falls for a gypsy girl (Singh). The maharani's evil brother (Jeevan) provides complications to the plot and the key action scene, presided over by the haughty princess, is a jousting tournament won by Dharam. When the victorious knight is captured, Veer, disguised as a gypsy, rescues him. The end of the film includes a spectacular battle between two pirate ships. The film also features a trained hawk, which was responsible for saving Dharam as a child and which intervenes several times on behalf of the good guys.

GHATTASHRADDHA

aka *The Ritual*
1977 144' b&w Kannada
d/sc **Girish Kasaravalli** *pc* Suvarnagiri Films *st* U.R. Ananthamurthy *dial* K.V. Subbanna *c* S. Ramchandra *m* **B.V. Karanth**
lp Ajit Kumar, Meena Kuttappa, Ramaswamy Iyengar, Shanta, Jagannath, Suresh, Jagadish, Narayana Bhatt, M.D. Subba Rao, Gopala Krishna, S.M. Shetty, Ramakrishna

Set in the 20s in a rural orthodox Brahmin Karnataka village, Kasaravalli's first feature tells the story of a child widow through the eyes of a young boy. The widowed Yamuna (Kuttappa) lives with her father Udupa (Iyengar), who runs a traditional scripture school for young Brahmins. The student Nani (Kumar), bullied by his colleagues, is protected by Yamuna. When she becomes pregnant after an affair with a teacher, Nani becomes a horrified witness to her attempts to induce an abortion and then to commit suicide. The climactic moments of the film show her achieve the abortion, helped by an Untouchable, to the sound and images of drunken tribals, the terror of Nani, the guilty schoolteacher leaving the village in the night, and the villagers looking for Yamuna and Nani. Udupa then imposes the ghatashraddha ritual on his daughter: breaking a pot (a metaphor for the womb) as an expulsion and humiliation ritual that leaves her isolated, clad in a white sari, banned from the village. Having thus made amends, the old Udupa ogles a 16-year-old girl hoping to start a new family. Although Kasaravalli acknowledges the influence of the **Navya** literary movement and ***Samskara*** (1970), this is a major cinematic achievement: the dark woods (where Yamuna expresses her sexual desires and tries to kill herself by sticking her hand into a snake's nest) and the harrowing, torch-lit night pierced by cries of pain during the abortion while the villagers obsessively bang their drums, contain more human kindness and honesty than the glaring sunlight exposing the rejected Yamuna in her white sari, a desolate figure with shaven head sitting under a tree while her only friend, a small child, is dragged away from her. Kasaravalli's film was anticipated in his student diploma featurette *Avasesh* (1975) where the little Brahmin boy first appears.

KANCHANA SEETA

aka *Golden Seeta*
1977 90' col Malayalam
d/sc **Govindan Aravindan** *p* K. Ravindranathan Nair *pc* General Pics *st/dial* C.N. Sreekantan Nair *c* **Shaji N. Karun** *m* Rajeev Taranath
lp Ramdas, Venkateshwaralu, Chinna Pullaiah, Keshav Panicker, Krishnan, Pottiah, Rangiah, Shobha Kiran, Annapurna

Aravindan's most enigmatic film to date is his version of the *Ramayana* episode about Rama (Ramdas) and his bride Seeta, represented here only as aspects of nature such as the rustling of the wind in the trees or as rain bringing harmony where discord threatens. Derived from Sreekantan Nair's play and Valmiki's epic, the film alludes to the golden image of Seeta which Rama sets by his side for the Ashwamedha Yagya, the ritual sacrifice of a horse to Agni, the god of fire. The poet Valmiki (Panicker) is cast as a witness to the mythical events which move him to compose the story of Rama as an epic. The film's epilogue shows Rama's last journey as he walks into the River Saraya and becomes one with Seeta, i.e. nature. Aravindan's nature mysticism finds expression in Shaji's pellucid images prefiguring some of the associations of nature in his later ***Estheppan*** (1979) and ***Chidambaram*** (1985)). The director's most daring gesture is his attempt to renovate the mythological as a genre, partly by his interpretation of Seeta's presence but also by casting Rama Chenchus, tribals from AP where the film was shot, as the mythological figures.

KISSA KURSI KA

1977 142' col Hindi
d Amrit Nahata *pc* Dhwani Prakash *st/lyr* Rakesh *sc* Shivendra Sinha *m* Raghunath Seth
lp **Utpal Dutt**, **Shabana Azmi**, Chaman Bagga, Raj Babbar, Surekha Sikri, Deena Nath, Rajeshwar Nath, Master Champalal

Gross political satire renowned mainly as a censorship scandal during the Emergency. The original version of the film attacking Indira Gandhi's rule was apparently destroyed by Sanjay Gandhi's men. Its fate was later linked to the Turkman Gate carnage in Delhi as examples of the authoritarianism of the regime. Nahata remade the film after the Emergency was lifted. The film has its villainous politician (Dutt) mouthing flowery rhetoric, usually addressing a character who stands for 'the people', Janata (Azmi). After several allusions to the Emergency, the politician rapes Janata. Nahata, who introduced the remake, later joined the Congress Party and disowned the film.

KODIYETTAM

aka *The Ascent*
1977 137'(118') b&w Malayalam
d/s **Adoor Gopalakrishnan** *p* Kulathoor Bhaskaran Nair *pc* Chitralekha Film Co-op *c* Ravi Varma
lp **Gopi**, Lalitha, Aziz, **Thikkurisi Sukumaran Nair**, Adoor Bhawani, Kaviyoor Ponnamma, Vilasini, Susheela, Radhamani

Gopalakrishnan's 2nd and to many his best feature, made five years after ***Swayamvaram***, tells of the growth to adulthood of a wide-eyed village simpleton, Sankarankutty (an admirable performance by Gopi). Affectionately treated as a fool, the man begins to come to terms with real human relationships through an encounter with a truck driver prone to most human weaknesses. Sankarankutty begins to accept that a wife (Lalitha), or indeed any woman, should not be regarded solely as a provider of food and comforts. The most tragic figure in the story is the lonely widow Kamalamma (Ponnamma) who mothers the central character but whose life is ruined by various exploitative relationships, and she ends up by committing suicide. The film has an innovative soundtrack, esp. with Kathakali drums, and unfolds at the slow, rhythmical pace of a village festival which provides the opening imagery of the tale. The main character's maturation can be seen as a parallel to social and historical changes in Kerala: the erosion of a matriarchal system and the rise of a competitive world conventionally coded as masculine, the impact of technology and so on. Blending realism and lyricism, the film achieved both artistic and commercial success.

KONDURA/ANUGRAHAM

aka *The Boon* aka *Sage from the Sea* aka *Manas Ka Maharshi*
1977 137'[H]/136'[T] col Hindi/Telugu
d/co-sc **Shyam Benegal** *pc* Raviraj Int. *st* C.T. Khanolkar's novel *Kondura* (1966) *co-sc* **Arudra**, **Girish Karnad** Satyadev Dubey *lyr* Vasant Dev[H], Arudra[T] *c* **Govind Nihalani** *m* **Vanraj Bhatia**
lp **Anant Nag**, **Vanisree**, **Smita Patil**, Venu, Shekhar Chatterjee, Amrish Puri[H], Satyadev Dubey, Ravu Gopala Rao[T], A.R. Krishna[T]

Benegal's only film in the language of the Northern AP region in which his early political dramas (***Ankur***, 1973; ***Nishant***, 1975) are located. Continuing his interest in the politics of rural exploitation, this is a morality tale linking religious illusions with personal frustrations. Adapting a mystical Marathi novel, it tells of the Brahmin Parashuram (Nag) who meets the sage Konduraswamy (Puri) and receives a boon: in exchange for a vow of celibacy he receives a root able to terminate pregnancies. Parashuram's wife (Vanisree) reluctantly goes along with her husband's new convictions and soon he becomes known as a holy man. In his dreams, the 'holy man' covets the daughter-in-law of a rich scoundrel and, mistakenly assuming that the scoundrel impregnated her, Parashuram administers the abortive root to the woman with disastrous results. Disillusioned, Parashuram realises his asceticism was an act of naivety and he proceeds to rape his own wife who then commits suicide. The Telugu version ended with a voice-over instructing the audience to consider the implications of the story. The original novel, set in the culturally primitive Konkan, uses its central mythic narrative to create different states of perception so that the viewer is constantly asked to interrogate the protagonist's experiences, leaving open the question of whether the frustrated and exploited Parashuram Tatya ever really saw what he says he saw. The film sidesteps this level of complexity and settles for a more standard political critique of feudalism.

KULAVADHU

1977 148' col Gujarati
d **Krishnakant** *pc* Chitrakala Mandir *s* Gulshan Nanda *dial* Harin Mehta *lyr* Barkat Virani, Kanti Ashok, Manubhai Gadhvi *c* Aloke Dasgupta *m* **Kalyanji-Anandji**
lp Asha Parekh, Navin Nischol, Rita Bhaduri, Kiran Kumar, Champsibhai Nagda, Dulari, Aga, Saroj Oza, Dinu Trivedi

Pioneering melodrama in a cinema dominated by quasi-historicals and folk legends. The rich but unfortunate Chandan (Parekh) suffers for previous sexual misdemeanours when she marries Anil (Nischol). A flashback introduces the cruel Pankaj who has an affair with both Chandan and her sister-in-law Bindu. When Bindu becomes pregnant, Chandan offers to sacrifice herself. Eventually she kills Pankaj and goes to jail. Her magnanimous husband forgives her. The film belonged to Hindi star Asha Parekh in one of her infrequent appearances in her native Gujarati language.

MUKTI CHAI

1977 55' b&w Bengali
d/p **Utpalendu Chakraborty** *c* Sanjay Brahma, Shekhar Tarafdar

Chakraborty's debut was a strident denunciation of the Indian State from a CPI(ML) position. It argued that the laws of the colonial regime, against which India's nationalists fought their freedom struggle, were then duplicated by the Indian State, culminating in the Emergency and its MISA (Maintenance of Internal Security Act) ordinance. Along with **Patwardhan**'s and **Gautam Ghosh**'s early films, this is one of the major documentaries to emerge from the Emergency experience.

NAGARHOLE

1977 170' col Kannada
d/sc **S.V. Rajendra Singh** *pc* Mahatma Prod. *st/dial* H.V. Subba Rao *lyr* Udayashankar *m* Satyam
lp **Vishnuvardhan**, Bharati, Shivaram, Ambarish, B.V. Radha, Uma Sivakumar, Sundarkrishna Urs

Enormously popular children's film by a director best known for violent cop movies. Madhu (Bharati) takes four children, including her son, to visit the Nagarhole wildlife sanctuary. Her son is killed by a tiger, but her husband, believed dead but in fact captured by tribals, resurfaces and saves the other children.

OKA OORIE KATHA

aka *The Outsiders*, aka *Story of a Village*
1977 116' col Telugu
d/co-sc **Mrinal Sen** *p* A. Parandhama Reddy *pc* Chandrodaya Art *co-sc* Mohit Chattopadhyay *st* Munshi Premchand's *Kafan* (The Shroud) *dial* Veerendranath *lyr* **Devulapalli Krishna Sastry** *c* K.K. Mahajan *m* Vijay Raghava Rao
lp M.V. Vasudeva Rao, G. Narayana Rao, Mamata Shankar, Pradeep Kumar, A.R. Krishna, Krishnamurthy, Kondala Rao, Rama Devi, Siddapa Naidu, Lakshmi Devdas, D. Ramgopal, C. Ramesh, Vijayalakshmi

After the masterful ***Mrigaya*** (1976), Sen's first Telugu film continues exploring the contradictions of resistance. Set in UP by Premchand but shifted to Telangana for the film, the story tells of old Venkaiah (Vasudeva Rao), an obstinate eccentric fighting social oppression through determined indolence, and his son Kistaia (Narayana Rao) who follows in his father's footsteps. However, their individual resistance depends on the backbreaking work of the son's wife Nilamma (Shankar) who desperately tries to achieve a more civilised lifestyle. The sterility of the two men's rebellion is cruelly demonstrated when they refuse to help the pregnant Nilamma when her labour goes wrong and she is left to die in agony. Convinced they are right in rejecting society but unable to comprehend the import of their own actions, the two men sink into demented fantasies. The film replaces the end of the original story, where they spend their money drinking in a bar, with a more rhetorical style featuring the father-in-law's soliloquy, the

Mamata Shankar in *Oka Oorie Katha*

image of the dead woman, and a song about how only fools toil in the fields while the rich reap the harvest. Premchand's cruellest story was adapted by the playwright Chattopadhyay and the dialogue was translated into a widely understood, non-dialect Telugu. Sen acknowledged the help of a local political activist, Krishnamurthy, in adapting the film to its regional setting. The film is dominated by the savage performance of Vasudeva Rao, chosen by Sen after seeing him in **Karanth**'s ***Chomana Dudi*** (1975), 'for his coiled energy, sarcasm and fury'. The work prompted several New Indian Cinema directors from other languages to work in Telugu since that region's displaced peasantry and absentee landlordism adhered to the stereotypes of 70s ruralist political films about feudal oppression: cf Benegal's ***Kondura*** (also 1977), Raveendran's *Harijan* (1979) and Gautam Ghosh's ***Maabhoomi*** (1979), continuing the local trend of e.g. ***Bhoomikosam*** (1974) and ***Tharam Marindi*** (1977).

PATHINARU VAYATHINILE

aka *16 Vayathiniley* aka *Sweet 16*
1977 139' col Tamil
d/s **Bharathirajaa** *pc* Shri Amman Creations *dial* P. Kalaimani *lyr* **Kannadasan**, Alangudi Somu, Gangai Amaran *c* Niwas *m* **Ilaiyaraja**
lp **Kamalahasan, Rajnikant**, Shabir Ahmed, Raghunath, Kavandamani, Isaac Senapathi, S.V. Subbaiah, Balagiri, **Sridevi**, Kanthimathi, Gemini Rajeshwari

Sometimes considered the second film (after ***Annakkili***, 1976) to take the Tamil cinema out of the studio, Bharathirajaa's debut is a love story in which a young maiden (Sridevi) has fantasies about marrying a fashionable urban youth. Her dreams come true when the shy villager (Kamalahasan) she marries is transformed when he rescues her from the local bully (Rajnikant). Unfortunately he kills the bully and has to go to jail but she will wait for him. The musical established Sridevi as a major Tamil star.

RAM RAM GANGARAM

1977 160' col Marathi
d/p/co-lyr **Dada Kondke** *pc* Dada Kondke Prod. *s/co-lyr* Rajesh Majumdar *c* Arvind Laad *m* Ram-Lakshman
lp Dada Kondke, Ashok Saraf, Usha Chavan, Dhumal, Anjana, Ratnamala, **Master Bhagwan**

Gangaram (Kondke) becomes a millionaire after the death of a rich uncle and leaves his village to go to Bombay where he has to face his uncle's corrupt manager and his gullible, illiterate mother. Disillusioned, he gives up his wealth and returns to the village and to his lover Gangi (Chavan). Kondke's film had a censorship problem apparently because the original version (entitled *Gangaram Vis Kalmi*) referred to Indira Gandhi's Twenty-point Economic Programme during the Emergency, and the film itself was intended as a political satire. A partially re-edited version was released under this new title. Kondke's style, however, remains intact, including the song *Gangu tarunya tuzha befaam jasa ishkacha atom bomb*.

SANDHYA RAAG

aka *The Evening Song*
1977 159' b&w Assamese
d/p/s/co-m **Bhabendranath Saikia** *c* Indukalpa Hazarika *co-m* Ramen Choudhury, Indreshwar Sharma, Prabhat Sharma
lp Runu Devi, Arun Sharma, Maya Barua, Ishan Barua, Aarti Barua, Kashmri Saikia, Purnima Pathak, Ananda Mohan Bhagwati

Saikia's debut reveals a remarkable sense for realist, ethnographic detail in this unusually complex treatment of the cultural tensions between an impoverished village and a modern city. The two daughters of the widowed Putali go to the city as domestic servants in two upper-class households. The elder sister, Charu, is treated like a member of the family and gets used to the urban lifestyle. The younger sister, Taru, has to ward off the amorous advances of her employer's son. When the sisters are of marriagable age, they return to their village but are unable to adjust to the poor and restricted life in the village. Charu agrees to marry her former employer's chauffeur even though he is sexually impotent. Her mother and sister join her in the city.

SEETA GEETA DATITHE

1977 140' b&w Telugu
d/sc **C.V. Sridhar** *pc* C.P.R. Prod. *st* Balamurugan *dial* Ganesh Patro *lyr* **Acharya Athreya, Arudra**, Veeturi Sundara Ramamurthy *c* Balakrishnan *m* K.V. Mahadevan
lp Sridhar, Chakrapani, Gavaraju, Kavitha, Bhawani, Nirmala, Y. Vijaya, Potti Prasad, Ravi Kondala Rao, Jayamalini, Jyothilakshmi

Marital infidelity drama regarded as an art-house film. Ravi is more interested in literary debate with his friends than in his wife Seeta. Their friends Deepa and Venu also have marital difficulties. Venu draws near to Seeta and both husbands suspect each other of sleeping with the other's wife.

SHATRANJ KE KHILADI

aka *The Chess Players*
1977 129'(124') col Urdu
d/sc/m **Satyajit Ray** *p* Suresh Jindal *pc* Devki Chitra *st* Premchand *c* Soumendu Roy
lp Sanjeev Kumar, **Saeed Jaffrey**, Amjad Khan, Richard Attenborough, **Shabana Azmi**, Farida Jalal, Veena, David Abraham, Victor Bannerjee, Farouque Sheikh, Tom Alter, Lila Mishra, Barry John, Samarth Narain, Bhudo Advani

Ray's so-called Hindi debut (in fact, it is in Urdu with some English dialogues) is set in 1856 at the court of Wajid Ali Shah in Lucknow, the capital of Oudh. It features two parallel narratives: the first, based on Premchand's short story, shows the interminable games of chess played by two hookah-smoking zamindars, Mir Roshan Ali (Jaffrey) and Mirza Sajjad Ali (S. Kumar); the other dramatises the conflict between Wajid Ali Shah (A. Khan) and General Charles Outram (Attenborough) who represents Lord Dalhousie's treacherously implemented annexation policies. Wajid Ali, shown as a politically weak and effete figure who stimulated the revival of the Kathak classical dance and the musical Raas-leela (cf ***Indrasabha***, 1932), in the end surrenders to the British without a fight. The colourful period drama about colonialism and indigenous culture begins with an animated cartoon (with **Amitabh Bachchan**'s voice) about the British annexation policy, and ends with the apolitical duo playing chess in the wilderness - since they can get no peace at home - fighting with each other while the British army marches into their capital. Although he cast major Hindi stars, Ray's film was refused a normal commercial release by local distributors because of the director's Calcutta art-house reputation.

SWAMI

1977 129' col Hindi
d/sc **Basu Chatterjee** *p* Jaya Chakraborty *pc* Jaya Sarathy Combine *st* Saratchandra Chatterjee's novel (1918) *dial* Manu Bhandari *lyr* Amit Khanna *c* K.K. Mahajan *m* Rajesh Roshan
lp **Girish Karnad**, **Shabana Azmi**, Vikram, Dhiraj Kumar, Shashikala, **Utpal Dutt**

Chatterjee extends his usual middle-class romances into a more jaundiced view of marriage based on a novel by the Bengali fountainhead of reformist writing, Saratchandra. Saudamini (Azmi) is a pampered girl until she is forced to marry the widower Ghanshyam (Karnad) and move into his large household. Saudamini cannot cope with her husband's overbearing and greedy stepmother and pines after the man she really loved and had to abandon, Narendra (Vikram). Although she resents the husband imposed on her by custom, she gradually discovers that Ghanshyam is a tolerant, wise and progressive man. In the end, she prefers to stay with Ghanshyam rather than to leave with her former suitor, and so the wisdom of 'traditional' conventions is affirmed.

THARAM MARINDI

1977 143' b&w Telugu
d/sc **Singeetham Srinivasa Rao** *pc* Vishwabharati Movies *st* Madireddy Sulochana *dial* **C.S. Rao** *lyr* **Sri Sri**, Kopalle Sivaram *c* **Balu Mahendra** *m* **G.K. Venkatesh**
lp Sridhar, G.S.R. Murthy, Dasarathi, Prasadrao, G. Satyanarayana, M. Panchanadam, Lakshmikant, Pradeep, Pallavi, Shobha, Rajakumari, Sithalatha, Satyavati, Sudha, Lakshmamma

Realist melodrama. An old man has his daughter Chenna (Shobha) married to an aged drunkard because of a promised dowry. The old man's progressive son opposes this 'trade' and further defies his father by marrying Parvati. The son has to set up house in the Harijan section of the village and is forced to become involved in corrupt village politics. Along with T. Madhava Rao's *Chillara Devullu* (1975) and B.S. Narayana's *Voorummadi Brathukulu* (1976), which also address rural Telangana politics, this film constitutes a current of realist New Telugu cinema.

AGNI

aka *Fire* aka *Anger which Burns*
1978 117' b&w Malayalam
d/s C. Radhakrishnan *p* P.M.K. Babu, Hassan *pc* Sheeba Arts *lyr* Shakuntala *c* U. Rajagopal *m* A.T. Ummar
lp **Madhu**, Vidhubala, Balan K. Nair, Bahadur, Vilasini, Abubakar, Manavalan Joseph, Shanta Devi, Master Suku

The novelist Radhakrishnan (cf ***Ottayadi Paathakal***, 1990) used one of his own novels for his directorial debut telling of a headstrong butcher, Moosa (Nair, in one of his most impressive roles), whose daughter Amina (Vidhubala) elopes with Suleman (Madhu), a man accused of parricide. The butcher furiously pursues the lovers but he eventually realises his now-pregnant daughter's strength of feeling and blesses the couple.

AKBAR SALEEM ANARKALI

1978 139' col Telugu
d/s **N.T. Rama Rao** *pc* Tarakarama Films *dial/lyr* C. Narayana Reddy *m* **C. Ramchandra**
lp N.T. Rama Rao, **Gummadi Venkateshwara Rao, Jamuna**, Deepa, Madhavi, Sridhar, Chalapathi Rao

In a rare departure from the mythologicals he directed at Tarakarama, NTR's big-budget Mughal historical retells the often-filmed love story between Prince Salim and the slave girl Anarkali. This version ends with both Salim and Anarkali being saved when the court singer Tansen persuades Akbar (NTR) to forgive the lovers. The film marks the belated entry into Telugu by the Hindi/Marathi composer C. Ramchandra with hit songs like *Reyi agiponi* and *Vela eringa doravunte*, echoes his own memorable score for **Filmistan**'s ***Anarkali*** (1953) over two decades previously. The film recalls Muddu Krishna's stage version of the story which was also NTR's first theatrical success in the early 40s.

ARVIND DESAI KI AJEEB DASTAAN

aka *The Strange Fate of Arvind Desai*
1978 118' col Hindi
d/co-s **Saeed Akhtar Mirza** *pc* Yukt Film Coop *co-s/co-dial* Cyrus Mistry *co-dial* **Vijay Tendulkar** *c* Virendra Saini *m* Bhaskar Chandavarkar
lp Dilip Dhawan, Anjali Painganakar, Shriram Lagoo, **Om Puri**, Sulabha Deshpande, Rohini Hattangadi

Mirza's first and most experimental feature tries to elaborate its own political film language. The somewhat wimpish young Arvind Desai (Dhawan), the son of a businessman (Lagoo), occasionally dates the company's secretary (Paingankar) and discusses politics and art with a Marxist colleague (Puri). However, the film constantly juxtaposes Desai's views with other information: e.g. his views on his sister's marriage are contrasted with his acquiescence in an arranged marriage; when luxurious carpets are hung in the family's shop, the film shows the weavers who made the carpets. Critic Bikram Singh suggested influences of Antonioni, Ben Barka's politics and, for the epilogue (summing up and placing the central character), *La hora de los hornos* (1967). This was the second and last film by the Yukt Co-op, a group started by **FTII** film-makers and technicians (***Ghashiram Kotwal***, 1976).

ASHWATHAMA

aka *Wandering Soul*
1978 121' b&w Malayalam
d **K.R. Mohanan** *p* P.T.K. Mohammed *pc* Mohan Mohammed Films *sc* P. Raman Nair *st/dial* Madampu Kunjukuttan from his own novel *c* Madhu Ambat *m* A. Anantha Padmanabhan
lp Madampu Kunjukuttan, Vidhubala, Vatsala, Ravi Menon, Savitri, Kuthulli, Ravi Menon, M.S. Valliattan

A contemporary fable about a man who is cursed to live on earth for 3000 years like Ashwathama in the *Mahabharata*. He lives as a teacher, Kunjuni (played by the author of the original novel, Kunjukuttan) and finds himself so frustrated by the prevailing customs and orthodoxies in his milieu that he becomes an alcoholic and begins to lead a dissolute life. Trying to reform and to become like 'other people', the respected scholar marries but his virtuous wife turns out to be an epileptic and the man returns to his wayward behaviour, which means mostly drinking himself into a stupor. In addition, the woman he originally loved finds herself with a broken marriage and discovers she has cancer. Ambat uses diffused lighting in keeping with the mood of the characters who feel torn in a changing world.

AVAL APPADITHAN

aka *She Is Like That*
1978 114' b&w Tamil
d/st/co-sc C. Rudraiah *p* Ragamanjari *pc* Kumar Arts *dial* Vannanilavan, Somasundareshwar *lyr* **Kannadasan**, Gangai Amaran *c* Nallasamy, Gyanasekharan *m* **Ilaiyaraja**
lp **Kamalahasan, Rajnikant**, Sripriya, Sivachandran, Indrani, S.R. Rajkumari, Nalini

A cautionary tale about an independently minded woman, Manju (Sripriya), who works in advertising for a male chauvinist boss (Rajnikant). Weary of men, she keeps her distance from her sensitive boyfriend Arun (Kamalahasan), who makes vox-pop documentaries. Arun eventually accepts an arranged marriage and Manju declares her love for him when it is too late. The film leaves her a lonely figure on Madras's Marina beach. The collaboration between modernist writer Vannanilavan and Rudraiah, a graduate from the Madras Film Institute, is an early engagement with the 'independent woman' motif in South India. The music is fairly unobtrusive and the fluid narrative style mixes flashbacks with vox-pop (students and women workers interviewed about the status of women) and glossy pictorialism.

CHITHEGU CHINTHE

aka *The Restless Corpse*
1978 129' col Kannada
d **M.S Sathyu** *p* G.N. Lakshmipathy *pc* Savan Movies *s* N. Rama Swamy, Javed Siddiqui *c* Ashok Gunjal *m* B.G. Ramanath, Prabhakar Badri, **G.K. Venkatesh**
lp C.R. Simha, Sivaram, MacMohan, Manjula, Paula Lindsay, Ram Prakash, Padma Shri, Uma Sivakumar

A crazy comedy using the conventions of mainstream Hindi cinema and set on a mythical island, Gajadweepa. The plot features crooked politicians and revolves around a gangster, Thimmaya alias T.K., ensconced in a home for the blind to cover up his criminal activities, and a popular film star Gajasimha (Simha). The star keeps escaping the traps set for him and becomes a successful politician. Good guys Avinash, a karate expert, and Mary (Lindsay), a foreign secret agent, take on the villains. Director Sathyu, better known for his poignant Partition drama ***Garam Hawa*** (1973), uses an idiom associated mainly with his stage career at **IPTA**.

DOORATWA

aka *Distance*
1978 96' b&w Bengali
d/lp/sc **Buddadhev Dasgupta** *st* Sirsendu Mukherjee *c* Ranajit Roy *m* Ain Rasheed Khan, Mahmud Mirza
lp Mamata Shankar, Pradip Mukherjee, **Bijon Bhattacharya**, Niranjan Roy, Snigdha Bannerjee, Provosh Sarkar

Dasgupta's feature debut is a story about a young man's growth into maturity. A Calcutta college teacher and former revolutionary of the late 60s generation, Mondar (P. Mukherjee), marries a young woman, Anjali (Shankar). When the former rebel learns that Anjali is a single mother, he leaves her. He also refuses shelter to a **Naxalite** on the run. The lonely teacher forms a relationship with a working-class woman and her insane mother, but class differences prevent this from going any further. In the end, he finds that the woman he rejected is mature enough to accept him as a friend and their relationship shows renewed promise as he tries to shed his prejudices. The film continued the Bengali cinema's fascination with the Naxalite uprising of the late 60s and 70s, often using symbolic imagery as in the opening shot of a newly paved VIP road and the commentary linking the annihilation of 'troublemakers' with the 'beautification' of the city. The film recalled aspects of Ray's 70s Calcutta films in its extensive use of silence and its consistently lyrical emphasis on the protagonist's subjectivity.

GAMAN

aka *Going*
1978 119' col Hindi
d/p/s **Muzaffar Ali** *pc* Integrated Film *dial* Hriday Lani *lyr* Makhdoom Mohiyuddin, Shahryar *c* Nadeem Khan *m* Jaidev
lp Farouque Shaikh, **Smita Patil**, Geeta Siddharth, Jalal Agha, Devi Mishra, Nana Patekar, Arun Bhuthnath, Amir Bano, Hameed, Sulabha Deshpande, Arvind Deshpande, Nitin Sethi

The uneducated and landless Ghulam Hussain (Shaikh) leaves his wife Khairun

(Patil) in his native village in UP to go to Bombay in search of work. He becomes a cab driver and the film intercuts his struggles in the city with those of his wife while she awaits his infrequent letters and remittances. The film's best moments are in the sequences with the close-knit group of cabbies who operate a kind of subterranean jungle-telegraph. Muzaffar Ali's **FFC**-sponsored debut features a typical and characteristically sensitive Smita Patil performance as a rural belle.

GANADEVATA

aka *The People*
1978 172' col Bengali
d/co-sc/co-lyr **Tarun Majumdar** *pc* West Bengal Govt *st/co-lyr* Tarashankar Bannerjee from his novel (1942) *co-sc* **Rajen Tarafdar** *co-lyr* Pulak Bandyopadhyay, Mukul Dutta, Gangacharan Sarkar *c* Shakti Bannerjee *m* **Hemanta Mukherjee**
lp **Soumitra Chatterjee**, Sandhya Roy, **Madhabi Mukherjee**, Samit Bhanja, Ajitesh Bannerjee, Anup Kumar Das, Debraj Roy, **Robi Ghosh**, Purnima Devi, Sumitra Mukherjee

This adaptation of Bannerjee's main novel is Majumdar's most ambitious film. Set in pre-WW2 rural Bengal, it chronicles the revolution incited by two villagers, a blacksmith and a tanner, who refuse to work on the traditionally established rates of barter. A rapacious village landlord, a radicalised schoolteacher, a revolutionary sought by the British and a group of corrupt policemen lead a large ensemble of characters in a film whose political message is made to order for its sponsors.

GORANTHA DEEPAM

1978 154' col Telugu
d **Bapu** *pc* Chitrakalpana Films *st* Nerella Ramalakshmi *sc* Mullapudi Venkatramana *lyr* C. Narayana Reddy, **Arudra**, Dasarathi *c* Ishan Arya *m* K.V. Mahadevan
lp Sridhar, Mohan Babu, Ravu Gopala Rao, T.L. Kantha Rao, Allu Ramalingaiah, **Vanisree**, Suryakantam, **G. Varalakshmi**

Telugu melodrama about feudal marital life. The young bride Padmavati (Vanisree, in one of her best-known performances) is sent to her new home with injunctions to regard her husband as father, god, teacher and so on and always to 'earn' her keep. What she finds is an exploitative mother-in-law, an uncaring husband and a family friend who tries to rape her. However, her exemplary virtuousness eventually transforms everyone.

GRAHANA

aka *The Eclipse*
1978 121' b&w Kannada
d/co-s **T.S. Nagabharana** *p* D. Sivaram, D. Venkatesh, D. Rame Gowde *pc* Harsha Pics *co-s* T.S. Ranga *st* Kodalli Shivaram *c* S. Ramchandra *m* **Vijayabhaskar**
lp Anand Paricharan, Govind Rao, Venkatramane Gowde, S.N. Rotti, B.S. Achar, Katte Ramchandra, Shobha Jyoti, Malati Rao

Nagabharana's first feature is a critique of the caste system and of 'traditional' mores (cf ***Samskara***, 1970). The story is based on the Hebbaramma Festival celebrated in some Karnataka districts where Nagabharana shot the film on location (after bribing the local high priest to obtain permission). The plot concerns an annual village ritual in which a small number of Untouchables are selected to be Brahmins, for two weeks only, provided they mortify themselves throughout this period, often in extremely cruel fashion, as a kind of purification ceremony performed by ritual scapegoats. One of the scapegoats dies as a result and his body cannot be buried by members of either caste. The village headman's son, Puttuswamy, calls in the police who remove the corpse. Puttuswamy then lives with the Harijans for a while. Since this infringes the rules of the ritual and of caste behaviour, the headman commits suicide. In spite of these traumas, the next year's ritual goes ahead with the full participation of all villagers. However, the rebellious Puttuswamy joins the selected Harijans in the temple and tries to prevent the ritual. The Harijans throw him out to the angry Brahmin crowd and he is beaten to death. **Girish Kasaravalli**, who assisted on this film while still an **FTII** student, apparently directed most of it.

JAGAN MOHINI

1978 163' col Telugu
d/s **B. Vittalacharya** *pc* Vittal Prod. *dial* G. Krishnamurthy, Karpoorapu Anjaneyalu *lyr* C. Narayana Reddy, Datlam Ramarao *c* H.S. Venu *m* Vijaya Krishnamurthy
lp Narasimhraju, Prabha, Jaya Malini, Vijayalakshmi, Saradhi, Dhulipala, **Savitri**, A. Satyanarayana, Bhoosarapu, Jayavani, Attili Lakshmi, Varanasi, **K. Mukkamala**, Balkrishna

In a year marked by spectacular flops (e.g. V.B. Rajendra Prasad's gangster movie *Ramakrishnulu* with megastars **NTR** and **A. Nageshwara Rao**), the surprise Telugu hit was this mid-budget ghost film. A woman betrayed by a king reappears in his next life as a ghost (the cabaret dancer Jaya Malini) intent on possessing him. On the advice of a priest, the king marries a pious woman who matches her devotional prowess against the ghost's seductions and wins.

JOI BABA FELUNATH

aka *The Elephant God*
1978 112' col Bengali
d/s/m **Satyajit Ray** *p* R.D. Bansal *pc* R.D.B. *c* Soumendu Roy
lp **Soumitra Chatterjee**, Santosh Dutta, Siddhartha Chatterjee, **Utpal Dutt**, Jit Bose, Haradhan Bannerjee, Bimal Chatterjee, Biplab Chatterjee, Satya Bannerjee, Moloy Roy, Santosh Sinha, Manu Mukherjee, Indubhushan Gujral, Kamu Mukherjee

Following on from ***Sonar Kella*** (1974), here the trio of detective Feluda (Soumitra Chatterjee), his sidekick Topse (Siddhartha Chatterjee) and thriller writer Jatayu (Dutta) become involved in a grimmer story set in the Bengali quarter of the holy city of Benares. Feluda, on holiday, is hired to track down a stolen gold statuette of Ganesh, the elephant god, harbinger of good fortune and worshipped by the mercantile middle class. Feluda finally gets the villains: the evil Maganlal Meghraj (Dutt), a Marwari businessman and smuggler, and his partner in crime, the yogic godman Machli Baba (Manu Mukherjee). With less action than *Sonar Kella*

Ganadevata

and more direct confrontation between the good and evil, the film's main departure from Ray's earlier children's movies is the portrait of the villain who Ray described as 'polished and ruthless, [c]ertainly the most ferocious character that I have created'.

JUNOON

aka *The Obsession* aka *Possessed* aka *A Flight of Pigeons*
1978 141' col Hindi
d/sc **Shyam Benegal** *p* **Shashi Kapoor** *pc* Film Valas *st* Ruskin Bond's short story *A Flight of Pigeons* *dial* Satyadev Dubey, **Ismat Chughtai** *lyr* Yogesh Praveen, Jigar Muradabadi, Amir Khusro, Sant Kabir *c* **Govind Nihalani** *m* **Vanraj Bhatia**, Kaushik
lp Shashi Kapoor, **Shabana Azmi**, Jennifer Kendal, **Naseeruddin Shah**, Kulbhushan Kharbanda, Jalal Agha, Benjamin Gilani, Tom Alter, Pearl Padamsee, Nafisa Ali, Ismat Chughtai, Geoffrey Kendal, Deepti Naval

Shashi Kapoor's debut as producer is set at the time of the 1857 'Mutiny' and weaves a passionate love story into the historical fresco. Javed Khan (Shashi Kapoor) is a Pathan whose wife (Azmi) has not yet borne a child. Javed falls madly in love with a half-caste Anglo-Indian girl, Ruth Labadoor (Nafisa Ali), who lives with her mother (Jennifer Kendal). After Javed's brother-in-law (Shah) and a band of mutineers attack and massacre the English garrison, Javed takes the women under his protection. Marriage with Ruth is impossible because Javed's family objects to the 'English' woman becoming Javed's second wife. The irony is that the Labadoor family represents the Raj to the Indians even though they are equally suspect in the British milieu. In the end, Javed is killed and Ruth returns to Britain where she dies an old maid. The film touches on the complex relationships between people from three different religions (Muslim, Hindu and Christian) and from different classes as well as ethnic groups. The story opens strongly with an entranced fakir overwhelming his audience with his vision of love and war, but this is quickly overcome with acting styles that are either 'passionate' and loud (Shah, Kapoor) or standing still with backlit profiles (Ali, but also the older women). Although the film claimed to offer the first authentic depiction of the 'Mutiny' (e.g. every formal, well-drilled attack ends in bloody chaos), it sidesteps any engagement with the issues underpinning what is often described as the first Indian war of independence and opts for a colonial-sexual fantasy instead.

KAADU KUDURE

aka *The Wild Horse*
1978 117' col Kannada
d/st/co-lyr **Chandrasekhar Kambhar** *pc* Wheel Prod. *sc* Shama Zaidi *co-lyr* M.N. Bangalore *c* Sundarnath Suvarna *m* Bhaskar Chandavarkar
lp Manu, Benglori, Mariappa, Krishnappa, Narayana, Ramchandra, Silpa, Swarnamma, Sundarashri, Maithili, Malati Rao, Shashikala

Folklorist Kambhar's remarkable debut feature, adapting Lorca's *House of Bernarda Alba* into a surrealist fable. The film tells, through extensive use of verse, the story of Huligonda (Manu), a handsome youth who falls in love with the youngest daughter of a village chief. To marry her he first has to break in the chief's wild horse. Having done that, the chief tricks him into marrying, not the girl he loves, but her ugly elder sister. He is virtually trapped in the household, representing different kinds of freedom for each of the three sisters and their formidable mother. When the youngest sister is to be married off to a loutish youth, she decides to elope with Huligonda. They sit astride the wild horse, which refuses to move, and are shot dead by the mother.

KALLOL

aka *Kollol* aka *The Wave*
1978 94' b&w Assamese
d/s **Atul Bordoloi** *pc* Gati Chitra *lyr/m* Rudra Barua *c* Nalin Duara
lp Chandra N. Barua, Lachit Phukan, Bishnu Khargharia, Bina Saikia, Muhidhar Gohain, Ranen Saha, Bharat Rajkhowa, Pratima Mahanta, Moihuddin Ahmed

Revolutionary, symbol-laden film about class conflict in a feudal fishing community. When the fishermen fail to capture a giant shark, the local landlord Anangaprasad Choudhury (Barua), who claims most of the fishermen's catch for himself, is enraged, esp. when a defiant youth, Mani (Phukan), sets out to catch the fish by himself. Eventually the youth leads a rebellion against the landlord. The wordy film was playwright Bordoloi's first independent movie.

MANNU

aka *The Soil*
1978 134' col Malayalam
d **K.G. George** *pc* Susmitha, Thiruvalluvar *s/lyr* Dr Pavithran *c* Ramchandra *m* A.T. Ummar
lp Soman, **Sharada**, P.K. Abraham, **Adoor Bhasi**, Kuthiravattom Pappu, Nellikode Bhaskaran, Nilambur Balan, Sukumaran, Mallika, Shanta Devi

George returned to the idiom of his teacher, **Kariat**, in this strident feudal melodrama of greed and superstition. The poor Damu (Soman) gets into a legal fight, supported by a CPI activist, with the rapacious landlord Krishnan Nair over tenancy rights. The matter takes a religious turn when the landlord announces his decision to build a temple on Damu's land. Damu kills the landlord and goes into hiding. The film shifts the moral dilemma to the son of the landlord, a patriotic army officer who has to decide whether to continue the ancestral dispute: the officer makes peace with Damu and his wife (Sharada).

MARO CHARITHRA

1978 169' b&w Telugu
d/s **K. Balachander** *pc* Andal Prod. *dial* Ganesh Patro *lyr* **Acharya Athreya** *c* B.S. Lokanathan *m* M.S. Vishwanathan
lp **Kamalahasan**, Saritha, Jaya Vijaya, Shyamala, Madhavi, Saroja, Ramanamurthy, P.L. Narayana, Adams, Chaitanya, Bhaskara Raju, Janardana Murthy

Tamil director Balachander's Telugu film is a love story between a Tamil man (Kamalahasan) and a Telugu woman (Saritha). Their families interfere and ask them to remain separate for a whole year. Balachander remade the film for **L.V. Prasad** in Hindi, *Ek Duuje Ke Liye* (1981), again starring Kamalahasan.

MULLUM MALARUM

aka *A Thorn and a Flower*
1978 143' col Tamil
d/s **J. Mahendran** *pc* Ananthi Films *st* Uma Chandran *lyr* **Kannadasan**, Panju Arunachalam, Gangai Amaran *m* **Ilaiyaraja**
lp **Rajnikant**, Sarath Babu, Jaya Lakshmi, Shobha

Echoing ***Pasamalar*** (1961), the successful playwright and director Mahendran's debut feature provides a low-key version of the orphaned brother and sister theme. The short-tempered Kali (Rajnikant) is a worker at a power station and possessively protects his sister Valli. In a clash with the new engineer, Kumaran, he is fired, gets drunk and loses his hand trying to save some tribals from a tiger. Encouraged by Kali's wife Manga, Kumaran forms a relationship with Kali's sister and Kali eventually matures enough to realise he cannot monopolise her for ever.

MUQADDAR KA SIKANDAR

1978 189' col Hindi
d/p/co-lyr **Prakash Mehra** *pc* Prakash Mehra Prod. *st* Lakshmikant Sharma *sc* Vijay Kaul *dial* Kadar Khan *co-lyr* Anjaan *c* N. Satyen *m* **Kalyanji-Anandji**
lp **Amitabh Bachchan**, Raakhee, Vinod Khanna, **Rekha**, Amjad Khan, Shriram Lagoo, R.P. Sethi, Madhu Malini, **Nirupa Roy**, Kadar Khan

Bachchan reprises his typical persona of the doomed loner with a mother fixation living and fighting in an urban jungle. A homeless urchin, he receives his name, Sikandar, from his foster-mother (N. Roy). He is raised to be a servant of Kaamna (Raakhee), with whom he falls in love, but her father Ramanath (Lagoo) accuses him of theft and he is cast out. Sikandar befriends a lawyer, Vikas (Khanna), which presents him with a second parental figure and a new responsibility: to ensure Vikas's happiness. Vikas falls in love with Kaamna, pre-empting Sikandar's own declaration of love when he goes to find her. Forewarned by the suicide of the only other woman in his life, the prostitute Zohra (Rekha), Sikandar arranges Vikas's marriage to Kaamna before he dies at the hands of the villain Bilawal (Amjad Khan), a former lover of Zohra. In spite of the film's aesthetic shortcomings, with rapid and jumpy editing usually to cover up limitations in the shooting, the story's rootedness in Bombay and Bachchan's extraordinary performance confirmed him as the icon of Bombay's industrialised lumpen proletariat.

ONDANONDU KALADALLI

aka *Once Upon A Time*
1978 154' col Kannada
d/co-s **Girish Karnad** *p* G.N. Lakshmipathy, K.N. Narayan *pc* L.N. Combines *co-s* Krishna

Basrur *dial* G.B. Joshi *lyr* **Chandrasekhar Kambhar** *c* A.K. Bir *m* Bhaskar Chandavarkar
lp **Shankar Nag**, Sundarkrishna Urs, Akshata Rao, Sushilendra Joshi, Ajit Saldanha, Rekha Sabnis, Anil Thakkar, Vasantrao Nakkod, V. Ramamurthy, Sundarrajan

A tribute to Kurosawa's samurai stories, resurrecting a South Indian martial arts technique which survives mainly in the Kerala-based form of the Kalaripayattu. The film is set in 13th C. Karnataka during the Hoysala dynasty (AD1073-1327), when small princelings fought each other for domination, often hiring martial arts experts. The plot focuses on the war between two rival brothers, Kapardi (Thakkar) and Maranayaka (Nakkod), who had already disposed of their elder sibling. The terrain is the margin between the Deccan plains and the Malnad jungles. Nag's Kannada debut appearance sees him in the Mifune-inspired role of the cynical and individualistic mercenary Gandugali whose main antagonist is the equally proficient but more tradition-bound Permadi (Urs), the general of the opposing force. When the rival brothers betray their own soldiers, Ganduguli and Permadi join forces to fight the pretenders to the throne. Gandugali dies in the epic battle but Permadi succeeds in saving the real heir to the throne, Jayakeshi (Joshi), and peace is restored to the kingdom. The exuberant action consists mainly of swordplay, martial arts training and duels. The art directors **Jayoo** and **Nachiket Patwardhan**, architects who turned film-makers in their own right, researched the period details for this ballad-like tale. Karnad claims the film sets out to transcend the narrowly anti-brahminical agenda of most Kannada New Cinema's independents at the time.

ONDU OORINA KATHE

1978 127' b&w Kannada
d/s/lyr Baraguru Ramchandrappa *c* Sundarnath Suvarna *m* **B.V. Karanth**
lp Pramila, Vimalakshi, Uma, M.V. Vasudeva Rao, M.S. Umesh, Lohiteshwara, Prasanna, Mailari Rao

Noted Kannada writer Ramchandrappa's directorial debut is a ruralist drama about caste exploitation, showing that economic exploitation goes beyond orthodox caste divides: when in power, rich Harijans (Untouchables) exploit people as ruthlessly as their erstwhile Brahmin masters did. Sometimes construed as a reply to the relentless anti-brahminism of the **Navya** writers and film-makers.

ORU NADIGAI NADAGAM PARKIRAL

aka *An Actress Views Her Life*
1978 131' b&w Tamil
d **A. Bhimsingh** *pc* Girnar Films *s/lyr* D. Jayakantan *c* B. Kaman *m* M.S. Vishwanathan
lp Laxmi, Srikanth, Y.G. Parthasarathy, Nagesh, Mahendran, Thenjai Srinivasan, Rajani, Kanthimati

The director's last, posthumously released film is a social comedy about women's independence. The 33-year-old Kalyani (Laxmi) marries the widowed Ranga (Srikanth), a drama critic. She refuses to be a subservient housewife, pursuing her stage career instead. The husband cannot cope but in the comic highlight of the movie, they visit a lawyer whose questioning makes them realise they belong together after all. When Kalyani has a paralytic stroke, they finally unite. Together with Bhimsingh's ***Sila Nerangalil Sila Manithargal*** (1976), this is one of Tamil star Laxmi's best-known performances.

ORU VEEDU ORU ULAGAM

1978 130' b&w Tamil
d/sc **Durai** *pc* Movie Int. *dial* 'Vietnam Veedu' Sundaram *st* Lalitha *lyr* **Vali**, Alangudi Somu, Pulamai Pithan *m* M.S. Vishwanathan
lp Srikanth, Major Sundararajan, Delhi Ganesh, Surilirajan, Shobha, **Pandharibai**, Manorama

Melodrama about the travails of a daughter, Gowri, of a piously Brahmin household. She has to overcome considerable parental resistance to be allowed access to higher education. She falls in love with A.R.K., a lecturer, then she marries the man's son, Murali. When her husband is accidentally drowned, her parents insist on her leading the austere and repressed life of a widow. Thankfully, A.R.K. intervenes and manages to get his daughter-in-law remarried.

PARASHURAM

aka *The Man With The Axe*
1978 100' col Bengali
d/co-sc **Mrinal Sen** *pc* West Bengal Govt Dept of Information *co-sc* Mohit Chatterjee *st* Sudhendu Mukherjee's sociological report *c* Ranjit Roy *m* **B.V. Karanth**
lp Arun Mukherjee, Sreela Majumdar, Biswas Chakraborty, Jayanta Bhattacharya, Sajal Roy Choudhury, Nilanta Sengupta, Nirmal Ghosh

Named after the mythical hero Parashuram who avenged his father's death by raising his axe 21 times, killing the king's men with every blow, an axe-wielding dispossessed peasant (Mukherjee) arrives in the city and finds shelter in a hovel in an abandoned cemetery together with a beggar (J. Bhattacharya). Parashuram is haunted by his encounter with a tiger and is prone to fantasies of heroic actions although he lives in fear of authority and petty criminals. Into the world of the destitute a young woman appears, Alhadi (Majumdar), deserted by her husband. She and Parashuram live side by side for a while but then she leaves, presumably because she feels strong enough to look for a better life. The lonely Parashuram sinks into his fantasies and ends up madly wielding his axe against the darkness overwhelming him. The film developed partly from an earlier play, *Jagannath*, adapting Lu Xun's *Ah Q*, staged in Bengal with the film's lead Mukherjee.

PRISONERS OF CONSCIENCE

1978 45' b&w English/Hindi
d/p/co-c **Anand Patwardhan** *m* Shamla and Friends, Calcutta Peoples' Choir *co-c* Pramod Mathur, Balan S., **Govind Nihalani** et al.

Patwardhan's first documentary to be widely screened in India contains clandestinely filmed footage and features the arrest and detention of political prisoners during the Emergency. It emphasises the widespread practice of arrest and torture both before and after Indira Gandhi's dictatorial crackdown. The film has interviews with several activists, including Jasbir Singh, member of the youth wing of the Socialist Party; D.P. Tripathi, member of the Students Federation of India; Mary Tyler, an Englishwoman who spent five years in prison and wrote the book *My Years in an Indian Prison*; Dev Nathan and Vasanthi Raman, intellectuals and supporters of the CPI(ML); and several others, alongside a humane commentary in the director's voice.

RATHI NIRVEDHAM

aka *Adolescent Desire*
1978 124' col Malayalam
d **Bharathan** *p* **Prathap Pothan** *pc* Supriya Creations *s* **Padmarajan** *lyr* Kavalam Narayana Panicker *c* Ramchandra *m* **P. Devarajan**
lp Soman, Krishnakumar, **Adoor Bhasi**, Bahadur, Kaviyoor Ponnamma, Manohar, Baby Sumathi, V.J. Jose, Jayabharati, Meena, T.R. Omanna

The painter and sculptor's 3rd feature tells of Pappu, an adolescent boy, and his sexual awakening, with a scenic tea plantation estate as backdrop, as he falls in love with the slightly older girl next door, Rathi. The consummation of the relationship is treated in high Gothic style with thunder and lightning accompanying the midnight union in a deserted cobra shrine, culminating in the woman being bitten by a snake and dying. Next morning, presumably feeling like a real man at last, he sets out for college and a new life. The most disturbing aspect of the film is not that sexuality is seen as some cataclysmic event but that the death of a woman is presented both as the price paid for sex by women and as a price worth paying by a boy to achieve manhood.

SARVASAKSHI

aka *The Omniscient*
1978 135' b&w Marathi
d/p/st/co-sc Ramdas Phutane *pc* Giriraj Pics *co-sc* Meena Chandavarkar *lyr* Viroba, Aarti Prabhu, Indira Sant, Shanta Shelke *c* Sharad Navle *m* Bhaskar Chandavarkar
lp **Smita Patil**, Jairam Hardikar, Anjali Paingankar, Vijay Joshi, Datta Bhatt, Vilas Rakte, Nilu Phule, Ram Nagarkar, Leela Gandhi, Kamini Bhatia, **Shankar Nag**, Dilip Kulkarni, Ashok Joshi, Rajan Kalekar, Suresh More

Phutane, a former journalist, art teacher, poet and actor, had produced **Patel**'s ***Saamna*** (1975), inaugurating New Indian Cinema productions in Marathi. This is his debut feature and, like **Palekar**'s ***Aakriet*** (1981), it deals with mystical rituals calling for human sacrifice in the context of the notorious Manwat murders in Maharashtra. The idealistic schoolteacher Ravi (Hardikar) and his wife Rekha (Paingankar) move to a village and come up against local superstition. When Rekha becomes pregnant, she has a premonition of death. A bhagat (witch-doctor) confirms the premonition and suggests a human sacrifice to stave off death. Rekha dies in childbirth. Ravi's problems are further heightened when he is arrested for the murder of one of the bhagat's ritual victims. In jail, he has a premonition of another sacrifice and is able to tip off the police who arrest the bhagat.

SATI ANSUYA

1978 132' col Oriya
d/sc A. Sanjiva Rao *pc* Madhav Pics *dial/co-lyr* Saubhagya Chandra Das *co-lyr* Loknath Patnaik *co-lyr/m* Prafulla Kar *c* Babu Rao
lp Chakrapani, Narendra Mishra, Roja Ramani, Mahashweta, Rita

Hit mythological made by a Telugu company and director showing Sati Ansuya narrating her story to Seeta during Rama's banishment. Her chastity is questioned by the gods, but her devotion to her husband gives her the power to transform the Hindu trinity of Brahma, Vishnu and Mahesh into children and to stop the sun from rising for seven days. The film is adapted from two successful Oriya plays, *Lakhyahira* and *Na Pahu Rati Na Maru Pati*. Its success persuaded more Telugu and other South Indian producers to explore the Oriya market.

SATYAM SHIVAM SUNDARAM

aka *Love Sublime* aka *Love Truth Beauty*
1978 172' col Hindi
d/p **Raj Kapoor** *pc* R.K. Films *s* Jainendra Jain *lyr* Narendra Sharma, Vithalbhai Patel, **Anand Bakshi** *c* Radhu Karmakar *m* **Laxmikant-Pyarelal**
lp **Zeenat Aman**, **Shashi Kapoor**, Kanhaiyalal, A.K. Hangal, David, Hari Shivdasani, **Leela Chitnis**, Sheetal, Baby Padmini Kolhapure

Kapoor's most sexploitative movie features Roopa (Aman) as the emphatically sexual woman unfortunately burdened with guilt (her mother died giving birth to her) and with half her face scarred by fire. However, she has an angelic voice which bewitches the engineer Rajiv (Kapoor) who marries her. Refusing to believe that this scarred woman is the figure of his dreams, he rejects the pregnant Roopa who curses her husband. The curse materialises in the form of a dam bursting, causing floods. Eventually, Rajiv accepts the 'real' Roopa and his conflict between sacred (ideal) and profane (earthy and imperfect) love is resolved. Aman, a former pin-up girl and advertising model, is presented as a sex object embodying the 'modernity' contemporary India has to come to terms with (resulting in censorship problems). In the process, the representation of what has been lost, 'tradition', also becomes corrupted, as can be seen from the glitzy temple architecture in the opening bhajan (devotional story) featuring Roopa as a child (Padmini Kolhapure) and in which ejaculatory symbols are inflated to gigantic dimensions. The film also showed a husband kissing his wife, several times.

SHRI RAMA PATTABHISHEKHAM

1978 196' col Telugu
d/s **N.T. Rama Rao** *pc* Ramakrishna Cine Studios *dial* **Samudrala Raghavacharya** *lyr* **Devulapalli Krishna Sastry**, C. Narayana Reddy *c* M.A. Rehman *m* **Pendyala Nageshwara Rao**
lp N.T. Rama Rao, Ramakrishna, Satyanarayana, Prabhakara Reddy, **Jamuna**, Sangeetha, Kanchana, Pushpalata, Saikumari, Suryakantam, Sridhar, Arja Janardana Rao, Thyagaraju, Mamata, Halam

Ramayana mythological featuring the life of Rama (NTR): his childhood, his banishment to the forests for 14 years, his war with the villainous Ravana (NTR again), his return to Ayodhya and Seeta's trial by fire to prove her chastity.

THAMPU

aka *The Circus Tent*
1978 129' b&w Malayalam
d/s **Govindan Aravindan** *p* K. Ravindranathan Nair *pc* General Pics *lyr* Kavalam Narayana Panicker *c* **Shaji N. Karun** *m* M.G. Radhakrishnan
lp **Gopi**, Venu, Shriraman, Jalaja, members of the Great Chitra Circus

Aravindan's finest b&w film chronicles three days with a circus in a small town in Kerala. A series of high-angle shots, as the circus drives into its new location, introduce us to the village. Several sequences use a remarkable quasi-documentary effect combined with minutely choreographed action, e.g. the sunset as the manager (Gopi) directs the raising of the big top. The episodic film tells of a soldier who befriends the circus strong man in a toddy bar and shows how the bizarre characters from the circus including the dwarf merge with the local populace. Much of the imagery is genuinely poetic, accompanied by some remarkable b&w work by Shaji, sustained by a narrative that consistently replaces conventional storytelling with a sense of the cultural geography of the village. The film's documentary style, including direct address to camera, is in sharp contrast with Aravindan's previous feature, ***Kanchana Seeta*** (1977), also shot by Shaji, although the same reverence for nature animates both works.

TRISHUL

1978 167' col Hindi
d **Yash Chopra** *pc* Trimurti Films *s* **Salim-Javed** *lyr* **Sahir Ludhianvi** *m* **Khayyam**
lp **Amitabh Bachchan**, Sanjeev Kumar, Raakhee, **Shashi Kapoor**, Prem Chopra, **Hema Malini**, Sachin, Poonam, Manmohan Krishna, **Waheeda Rehman**

In this story, Bachchan plays a character, Vijay, obsessed with his mother whom he believes to have been abandoned by his father Raj, alias R.K. Gupta (S. Kumar). Vijay plans an Oedipal revenge by trying to ruin his father, a prominent businessman. Chopra's apparent sequel to ***Deewar*** (1975), with the same star and scenarists, deploys Bachchan's familiar persona in a big-budget spectacular culminating in a massive fight sequence set in what looks like a giant aircraft hangar.

YARO ORAL

aka *Someone Unknown*
1978 111' b&w Malayalam
d/s **V.K. Pavithran** *pc* Saga Movies *c* Madhu Ambat *m* **Govindan Aravindan**
lp Ravi, Protima, A.C.K. Raja Varma, Pavithran, Javed Siddiqui, Sathyabhama, Ramani, Baby Preetha

Melodrama about death. The gynaecologist Malathi is childless. To remedy her condition she divorces her husband and marries his friend. At the end of the film she gives birth to a child just before she commits suicide. Her former husband tries to find salvation in religion, while the second husband dies shortly after his wife. The cynical film has an art-house reputation in Kerala, known for Aravindan's score and being Pavithran's debut. Some of the film takes its cue from ***Thampu*** (1978) for its quasi-documentary b&w chronicling of village life, which it deflects in the direction of a perennialist fatalism.

AUR KAUN

1979 136' col Hindi
d Tulsi and Shyam **Ramsay** *p* F.U. Ramsay *pc* Ramsay Pics *st* Kumar Ramsay *dial* Kafil Azar *lyr* Amit Khanna *c* Gangu and Keshu Ramsay *m* **Bhappi Lahiri**
lp Sachin, Rajni Sharma, Padmini Kapila, Roopesh Kumar, Sudhir, Vimal Sahu, Kanchan Mathu, Om Shivpuri, Madan Puri, Nasir Hussain

A necrophilia film by India's foremost horror film-makers. Teenager Raj (Sachin) is left alone in his father's grand, isolated villa. He loves the innocent Kamal but is seduced by Mona, who dies before she was able to reach sexual satisfaction. Her corpse continues to mesmerise Raj, as it appears to demand the sexual fulfilment he was unable to provide. The rest of the film consists of Raj trying to rid himself of the sexually demanding female: first he tries to 'cool' her by putting her in the refrigerator, then he buries her and finally he disposes of the body in a lake.

CHERIYACHENTE KROORA KRITHYANGAL

aka *The Wicked Deeds of Cheriyachan*, aka *The Evil Deeds of Cherian*
1979 107' b&w Malayalam
d/s **John Abraham** *pc* Janasakthi Films *c* Madhu Ambat
lp **Adoor Bhasi**, Kaviyoor Ponnamma, Purnima, Jayaram, Abraham Joseph

Released briefly in 1981, Abraham's 3rd feature is set in the Kuttanad rice-fields of Kerala, the director's home province. Cheriyachan (Bhasi) is a typical landlord who feels threatened by industrialisation and by left activists. When he witnesses the police massacring poor peasants, he takes upon himself the guilt of his class, as well as the guilt of the voyeur. He is last seen up a coconut tree trying to keep away from the police. It is Abraham's achievement that this figure, steeped in the local mix of feudal and Christian traditions, becomes understandable as a frightened victim of history whereas most films would cast him as a one-dimensional villain or a grotesquely comic character. The film is Abraham's most controlled, opening with a series of sweeping shots on the famed backwaters of the region as it establishes both the strongly realist and quasi-mythic flavour necessary to allow for the transference of economic oppression into the condition of Cheriyachan's guilt. It also leads the film into a far more contentious aspect of Kerala's political cinema and literature, addressing the common phenomenon of presenting the responsibility of intervention in highly romanticised and even directly sexualised terms, or in other ways implicating individual responsibility towards history in the voyeuristic, infantile guilt of the passive observer.

EK DIN PRATIDIN

aka *And Quiet Flows the Dawn* aka *And Quiet Rolls the Day*
1979 95' col Bengali
d/p/sc **Mrinal Sen** *pc* Mrinal Sen Prod. *st* Amalendu Chakravarty's *Abiroto Chene Mukh* *c* K.K. Mahajan *m* **B.V. Karanth**
lp Satya Bannerjee, Geeta Sen, Mamata Shankar, Sreela Majumdar, Umanath Bhattacharya, Arun Mukherjee, Tapan Das, Nalini Bannerjee, Kaushik Sen, Tupur Ghosh, Gautam Chakraborty, Biplab Chatterjee

Sen uses a thriller format for this tale set among Calcutta's petty bourgeoisie. A young woman, Chinu (Shankar), is the sole breadwinner supporting a family of seven headed by a retired clerk (S. Bannerjee) and his wife (G. Sen). One night, she does not return home from the office and, as the hours pass, the family grows increasingly distraught as each member, including the independent-seeming university student Minu (Majumdar), begins to realise how dependent they are on Chinu's labour. Filmed by Sen with a mastery of mise en scene in cramped surroundings, the story graphically illustrates how profound insecurities underpin a precarious, egotistical moral code that refuses to acknowledge the real place of women in the social network. When Chinu returns by taxi in the morning, nobody dares question her since this would involve each family member having to betray the selfishness of their concern. With amazing resilience, the facade is restored. There are some echoes of Sen's previous stylistic devices (e.g. direct address to camera by the characters when they visit a hospital to check on missing persons), but the film leaves an indelible impression of the cavernous courtyard surrounded by claustrophobic apartments and, beyond the gate, a teeming and indifferent metropolis making its presence felt mainly on the soundtrack. Sen claimed that the film started his interest in the 'inward' investigation into middle-class life, away from the explicitly political language of his earlier 70s films.

ESTHEPPAN

aka *Stephen*
1979 94' col Malayalam
d/co-st/co-sc/co-m **Govindan Aravindan** *p* K. Ravindranathan Nair *pc* General Pics *co-st* Kavalam Narayana Panicker *co-sc/lyr* Isaac Thomas Kotukapally *c* **Shaji N. Karun** *co-m* Janardhan
lp Rajan Kakkanadan, Krishnapuram Leela, Sudharma, Shobha, Catherine, Balakrishnan Nair, Ganeshan, Gopalakrishnan, M.R. Krishan, Francis David

Estheppan (Kakkanadan) is a strange and mysterious figure, allegedly immortal, in a Christian fishing village in Kerala. Although a more earthly version of ***Kummatty*** (1979: the subject of his previous film), all manner of virtues and magical powers are ascribed to the Christ-like worker of miracles (including printing his own money and drinking whisky without getting drunk). The director says it was made as a rejoinder to the criticism levelled against him and his scenarist Panicker for the emphasis on folk ritual in their theatre. An extra dimension is given to the central character, adapted from stories about religious mystics of all stripes, by casting Kakkanadan, a Malayalam tantric-modernist painter, in the role. The final sequence of the miracle play alludes to the *Chavittu Natakam*, a form derived from Portuguese passion-plays on the west coast. However, contrary to the director's stated intention sympathetically to explore religious mysticism, the film can be seen as celebrating confusion, jumbling together religious iconography, pop music, tourism and garish calendar-art colours and artistic creativity. This cultural levelling out is further heightened by more than one 'version' of Estheppan's activities, each bidding for plausibility but also undercutting whatever conviction the plot might have. The fragmented narrative helps to convey a critique of the conventions of psychological realism prevalent in 'quality' cinema by refusing to present an individual as a complex but ultimately coherent and knowable character. However, by also refusing to show the individual as a historically formed figure, an option chosen, e.g., by **Ghatak**, **Shahani** and **Abraham**, Aravindan ends up relativising his characters completely, dissolving them either into creatures of gossip, as in the movie, or into the timeless and eternally unknowable flow of nature.

JHOR

aka *The Storm*
1979 100' col Bengali
d/s **Utpal Dutt** *pc* West Bengal Govt *c* **Dinen Gupta** *m* Prasanta Bhattacharya
lp Ujjal Sengupta, Indrani Mukherjee, Sagarika Adhikari, Kaushik Bannerjee, **Robi Ghosh**

The noted leftist theatre director and film star's tale about the introduction of Western-style rationalism in Bengal in 1829 and its conflicts with religious and traditional reaction. The focus of the plot is the Hindu College run by a Portuguese Indian, Henry Derozio, and his students who save a woman from the sati ritual. The students lose their battle against obscurantist authorities and Derozio is sacked, but the initial impetus for change has been given. The film is edited by **Hrishikesh Mukherjee**.

KALA PATTHAR

1979 176' col Hindi
d/p **Yash Chopra** *pc* Yashraj Films *s* **Salim-Javed** *lyr* **Sahir Ludhianvi** *c* Kay Gee *m* Rajesh Roshan, **Salil Choudhury**
lp **Shashi Kapoor**, Raakhee Gulzar, **Amitabh Bachchan**, Shatrughan Sinha, Neetu Singh, Parveen Babi, Prem Chopra, Parikshit Sahni, Romesh Sharma, Poonam Dhillon, Manmohan Krishna, Iftikhar, Madan Puri

A coal-mining tale about three main characters who try to avert a mining disaster in a colliery owned by Seth Dhanraj (Chopra). Vijay (Bachchan) is a court-martialled merchant navy officer who abandoned his ship during a storm and is riddled with guilt. He works as a miner to forget his past. Mangal (S. Sinha) is a dacoit hiding from the police among the miners. Ravi Malhotra (S. Kapoor) is an engineer working for Seth Dhanraj. He discovers his greedy employer's scheme that will endanger the lives of hundreds of miners in a coal-rich shaft. The men meet women who transform their lives. Vijay falls in love with Sudha (Raakhee), a doctor. Mangal flirts with a bangle seller (Singh) and then rescues her from rapists. Ravi meets his old flame Anita (Parveen Babi) who is now a journalist and has come to do a story about the mines. The wall of the mine shaft collapses and there is a deluge, leading to a long disaster-movie sequence as Mangal atones by sacrificing his life for his fellow miners. Vijay and Ravi survive after rescuing many workers. The film refers to several mining disasters in Dhanbad and Chasnala where organised criminal gangs, often masquerading as trade unions, had become major political issues in the pre-Emergency period. Despite these references, most of the script is largely subordinated to the necessity of providing each of the several stars with equal footage and a hand in the action.

KASHINO DIKRO

1979 146' col Gujarati
d Kanti Madia *pc* Cine India Int. *st* Vinodini Neelkanth *sc* Prabodh Joshi *lyr* Balmukund Dave, Ravji Patel, Madhav Ramanuj, Anil Joshi *c* Barun Mukherjee *m* Kshemu Divetia
lp Rajiv, Ragini, Rita Bhaduri, Giresh Desai, P. Kharsani, Tarla Joshi, Lila Jariwala, Vatsala Deshmukh, Mahavir Shah, Arvind Vaidya, Saroj Nayak, Jagdish Shah, Pushpa Shah, Javed Khan, Shrikant Soni, Dilip Patel, Kanti Madia

Debut and sole feature by theatre director and actor Madia, revitalising a Gujarati cinema inaugurated by **Rathod**'s **FFC**-supported ***Kanku*** (1969). The sentimental melodrama adapted from a noted writer's story by Gujarat's two leading stage personalities, Madia and Joshi, tells of Kashi (Ragini) who raises her husband's (Desai) adolescent younger brother (Rajiv). The young man dies on his wedding night of snakebite. His widowed bride Rama (Bhaduri) is later raped by Kashi's husband and becomes pregnant. Kashi saves the family's and Rama's 'honour' by pretending to be pregnant herself and adopting the child as her own. Kashi dies in the end as an icon of saintly motherhood. The rather slow moving narrative promotes a conservative notion of Gujarat's brahminical joint family culture.

KUMMATTY

aka *The Bogeyman*
1979 90' col Malayalam
d/co-sc/co-m **Govindan Aravindan** *p* K. Ravindranathan Nair *pc* General Pics *st/co-s/lyr/co-m* Kavalam Narayana Panicker *c* **Shaji N. Karun** *co-m* M.G. Radhakrishnan
lp Ramunni, Master Ashokan, Vilasini Reema, Kothara Gopalakrishnan, Sivasankaran Divakaran, Vakkil, Mothassi, Shankar

Made shortly after the quasi-documentary ***Thampu*** (1978), this film adapts an age-old Central Kerala folk-tale featuring a partly mythic and partly real magician called Kummatty (played by the famous musician and dancer Ramunni in his screen debut) who comes to entertain a group of village children with dancing, singing and magic tricks. In a game, he changes them into animals. One boy, changed into a dog, is chased away and misses the moment when the magician breaks the spell restoring the children to their human form. The dog-boy has to wait a year until Kummatty returns to the village. Aravindan claimed the film to be his favourite and referred to the international legend of the bogeyman which parents use to frighten their children, except that, in Kerala, the bogeyman is often shown as a compassionate person.

MAABHOOMI

aka *Our Land* aka *The Motherland*
1979 152' b&w Telugu
d/co-sc/co-m **Gautam Ghosh** *co-p* G. Ravindranath *co-p/co-sc* **B. Narasinga Rao** *pc* Chaitanya Chitra *co-sc* Partha Bannerjee, Pran Rao *st* **Krishan Chander**'s novel *Jab Khet Jaage* (1948) *c* Kamal Naik *co-m* Vinjanuri Seeta
lp Kakarala, Saichand, Rami Reddy, Bhopal Reddy, Yadagini, Pokala, Rajeshwari, Hansa, Prasad Rao, Pradeep Kumar, Lakshmana Rao

Set during one of India's main peasant risings, the Telangana insurrection between 1945 and 1951 in the pre-Independence state of Hyderabad, the Bengali director's first feature tells the story of Chander's best-known novel from the peasant's point of view. A young peasant, Ramiah, rebels against the corrupt rule of the nizam, and when his girlfriend has to submit to the potentate's sexual coercion, Ramiah leaves. He befriends a Marxist activist (the rising was CPI-inspired) and participates in the Independence struggle. When the peasants take over the village after Independence, their anger boils over and they perpetrate a massacre. In 1948 the Indian army marched into Hyderabad and suppressed the rising. Many of the ousted landlords returned to power by becoming Congress officials, so that the peasants had to face the same struggle all over again. The film is made in a documentary style inspired by Latin American political cinema but also uses Indian folk idioms such as the Burrakatha style (cf the political education sequence with the union leader Maqbool). The film's view of the rising is mostly an uncritical one, esp. in comparison with recent analyses by historians sympathetic to political groups currently working in Telangana.

NAXALITES, THE

1979 141' col Hindi
d/s/co-dial **K.A. Abbas** *pc* Naya Sansar *co-dial* **Inder Raj Anand** *lyr* Ali Sardar Jafri *c* Ramchandra *m* Prem Dhawan
lp **Mithun Chakraborty**, **Smita Patil**, Nana Palsikar, Imtiaz Khan, Priyadarshini, Jalal Agha, Tinnu Anand, Dilip Raj, Pinchoo Kapoor

Abbas's political drama about the Naxalbari peasant uprising (see **Naxalite**) and student movement borrows from several real-life characters including Ajitha (Patil), an activist from Kerala, Charu Majumdar (Palsikar) et al. The complexities of the historical issues are reduced to an interplay of simplistic attitudes while the sensationalist aspects are intensified (e.g. police torture shown in silhouette). In typical Abbas-style social realism, efforts to convey an insight into the historical events have been replaced by efforts to manipulate the viewers' emotions, as in the sequence where Majumdar's speech reverberates through the countryside while the police gather for the final assault, or in the finale, played with great skill by Smita Patil, where she walks to the gallows to the farewells of her fellow inmates. The reasons why young people became part of the Naxalite movements are presented in titillating images of rape, torture and corruption, with the sexual threats to women providing the main motive for male rebelliousness. Partly because of Abbas's prior political history and the CPI's rejection of the movement, the film faced some censorship problems. Abbas claimed that unsympathetic political groups waged a vendetta against the film.

NEEM ANNAPURNA

aka *Bitter Morsel*
1979 95' b&w Bengali
d/p/sc **Buddhadev Dasgupta** *st* Kamal Kumar Majumdar *c* Kamal Nayak
lp Manidipa Ray, Sunil Mukherjee, Jayita Sarkar, Manojit Lahiri

A married man loses his job in a small town so he takes his family to the city in search of work. To make ends meet, they rent out part of their hovel to an old beggar. When the father fails to find work and his eldest daughter is tempted by prostitution, the mother steals a sack of rice from the beggar who has a heart attack and dies. She disposes of the body and serves up a delicious meal. Guilt prevents her from eating and she goes out to vomit as the film ends. Dasgupta's 2nd feature evokes a 1950s **Ray** style in using slow action, making the plot secondary to extensive and extended mid-shots and realist detailing. The director claimed the influence of Godard in some sequences.

PASI

aka *Hunger*
1979 138' col Tamil
d/st/s **Durai** *pc* Sunitha Cine Arts *c* V. Ranga *m* Shankar-Ganesh
lp Shobha, Delhi Ganesh, Vijayan, Tambaram Lalitha, Praveena, Elangovan, Rajendran, Surulirajan, Narayanan, Sathya, S.N. Parvathy, Jayabharati

Durai's best-known film is a low-life drama set among Madras's shanty dwellers, people who in most films are cast as comic relief for

Smita Patil (centre) in *The Naxalites*

their 'Madras Tamil' dialect or as villains. The teenage ragpicker Kuppamma (Shobha) and her father Muniyandi (Ganesh), a cycle-rickshawalla with many mouths to feed, are the main characters. She gets pregnant by a lorry driver who turns out to be married, and dies in childbirth. Other vignettes include the owner of a cycle shop (Narayanan) who plays records to attract the attention of Kuppamma whenever she passes by, a narrative device that compensates for the absence of songs in the film. Spoken in genuine Madras Tamil and shot on location, at times with concealed cameras, the film has an authentic city flavour. Shobha, who committed suicide the following year, received a national award for her intense performance.

PERUVAZHIYAMPALAM

aka *A Dead End* aka *Wayside Inn*
1979 118' b&w Malayalam
d/s **P. Padmarajan** *p* Prem Prakash *pc* Bhadra Movie Makers *lyr* Kavalam Narayana Panicker *c* A. Kannan Narayanan *m* M.G. Radhakrishnan
lp Ashok, **Gopi**, Aziz, Jose Prakash, Lalitha, Geeta, Adoor Bhawani

Set in a village, Raman (Ashok) is a rather simple boy living with his sister. The villainous bully, rapist and ex-con Prabhakaran Pillai (Aziz), a married man with children, covets the sister and persecutes Raman who, alone, stands up to the bully and kills him in a knife fight. He has to hide from the police and from the villagers, with the help of a teashop owner (Gopi) and a prostitute, Devayani (Lalitha), who thus express their hatred for the bully they did not dare confront themselves. It emerges that the villain enjoyed a grudging respect for his 'macho' qualities: by killing him, Raman has become the one who is both respected and feared. In the end, Raman is struck with remorse when faced by the children of the man he killed. The novelist Padmarajan's feature has a taut script in which women are expected to pay the price for demonstrations as well as critical examinations of manliness.

PRATYUSHA

aka *Before Dawn* aka *Dawn*
1979 90' b&w Telugu
d/co-s Jatla Venkataswamy Naidu [V.N. Jatla] *p* B. Nagabhushanam, S. Nagaiah, B. Sailu *pc* Swairi Films *co-s* K. Shiva Reddy *c* R.S. Agarwal
lp Kadambini, Gangaram, Godavari, Tulasi

Jatla's first feature is a critique of the 'Jogu' custom practised in some villages where a possessed devadasi (temple prostitute and dancer) selects, in the name of religion, another woman who shall succeed her as a prostitute. The film, performed by non-professionals and shot in documentary style on location in Binola in Nizamabad, focuses on a mother who refuses to hand over her chosen daughter and, because she cannot afford to pay the fine for this infringement against 'religious' duty, kills the child.

PUTHIYA VARPUGAL

aka *The New Moulds*
1979 143' col Tamil
d **Bharathirajaa** *pc* Manoj Creations *s* **K. Bhagyaraj** *lyr* **Kannadasan** *c* P.S. Srinivas *m* **Ilaiyaraja**
lp **K. Bhagyaraj**, Kavundamani, G. Srinivasan, Chandrasekhar, Rati Agnihotri, Usha Rani

A newly arrived village teacher becomes the rival of the local elder and feudal bully for the beautiful Jyothi, the daughter of a temple musician. The elder frames the teacher for murder and gets his factotum, Amavasai, to marry Jyothi so as to have access to her. She, however, knifes him and is caught in the act by both the teacher and Amavasai, who has an instant change of heart: he disposes of the corpse in a village ritual bonfire, lit by the dead man's son, and releases Jyothi to escape with her true love. The film is typical of Bharathirajaa's work, featuring his trade-mark scene of a group dance of white-clad women and following his set narrative structure: a new arrival in a rural location, love at first sight, rivalry with the socially powerful villain and resolution against the background of a village ritual. The locations around Mysore provide a convincing setting.

SANGHAGANAM

aka *Chorus*
1979 83' b&w Malayalam
d **P.A. Backer** *p* Salam Karasseri *pc* Navadhara Movie Makers *s* M. Sukumaran *c* Vipin Das *m* **P. Devarajan**
lp Srinivasan, **Ramu Kariat**, P.R. Nambiar, Madhu Master, Rani Tankam

A symbolic story continuing Backer's effort to provide a geneology of political activists (cf ***Kabani Nadi Chuvannappol***, 1975; ***Chuvanna Vithukal***, 1976). This story is structured as a quest for a reliable leader called Goutama. The educated but cynical hero meets different men bearing that name but all reject him until he meets a CP union activist being tortured in a police cell. Only after he sees the activist killed in a lathi charge does the hero realise that he must take responsibility for his own actions and rebel against injustice rather than put his faith in a charismatic figure.

SHANKARABHARANAM

aka *The Jewel of Shiva*
1979 143' col Telugu
d/s **K. Vishwanath** *p* Edida Nageshwara Rao *pc* Poornodaya Art Creations *dial* Jandhyala *lyr* Veeturi Sundara Ramamurthy *c* **Balu Mahendra** *m* K.V. Mahadevan
lp J.V. Somayajulu, Manju Bhargavi, Allu Ramalingaiah, Pushpakumari, Tulasi Ram, Chandramohan, Rangarao, Baby Varalakshmi, Rajyalakshmi, Jhansi

Vishwanath's musical hit is often presented as the film that transformed the Telugu film industry in the 80s. It borrows extensively from classical Carnatic music to tell the story of a relationship between a Carnatic guru and a prostitute. The prostitute Ratnaprabha (Bhargavi) runs away from home and is reluctantly accepted as a student, which brings the guru Shankara Sastry (Somayajulu) into social disrepute. When Ratnaprabha is forced to return to her ancestral vocation, she murders her customer but nevertheless finds herself pregnant. She gives birth to a son (Tulasi), who now studies under the guru although they are ostracised. Eventually Ratnaprabha becomes rich and she builds an auditorium in the name of her guru. During the opening performance, he has a heart attack and the son replaces the guru on stage, extending the tradition. It is the first Telugu film to attempt a redefinition of mass culture, using calendar-art aesthetics in several garish dance sequences by Manju Bhargavi - many of them in front of temples - and classical music (the guru out-shouts the rock music created by his detractors). Successful mainly for its anti-Tamil and anti-North view of an indigenist Telugu classicism (cf **G.V. Iyer**'s work in Kannada at the same time), spawning a whole genre: cf **Bapu**'s ***Thyagayya*** (1981), **Dasari Narayana Rao**'s ***Megha Sandesam*** (1982), **Singeetham Srinivasa Rao**'s *Sangeetha Samrat* (1984), **Vamsy**'s ***Sitara*** (1984) and Vishwanath's own sequels ***Sagara Sangamam*** (1983) and *Swati Muthyam* (1985). Somayajulu later played many similar roles, his presence being enough to invoke the *Shankarabharanam* legacy. Vishwanath remade his Telugu film in Hindi as *Sur Sangam* (1985) with **Girish Karnad** and Jayapradha.

SINHASAN

aka *The Throne*
1979 170' b&w Marathi
d/co-p **Jabbar Patel** *co-p* D.V. Rao *pc* Sujata Chitra *st* Arun Sadhu's novels *Mumbai Dinank* and *Simhasan* *sc* **Vijay Tendulkar** *lyr* Suresh Bhatt *c* Suryakant Lavande *m* Hridayanath Mangeshkar
lp Arun Sarnaik, Nilu Phule, Shriram Lagoo, Datta Bhatt, Madhukar Toradmal, Satish Dubhashi, Shrikant Moghe, Madhav Watve, Mohan Agashe, Jairam Hardikar, Nana Patekar

A film that sets out to elaborate a new genre derived from the language of political journalism. Based on two novels by the noted political correspondent Arun Sadhu, and scripted by a former journalist, Tendulkar, the plot addresses Maharashtra's political corruption linked with Bombay's entrepreneurial sector. The main protagonist is a newspaper correspondent, Digu Tipnis (Phule), who uncovers a network of telephone tapping and espionage, relations between trade union leaders and politicians, etc. Many of the characters were thinly-veiled references to real-life figures: Chief Minister Jivajirao (Sarnaik) refers to Maharashtra's former Chief Minister Vasantrao Naik, while the trade union leader Da Costa (Dubhashi) refers to George Fernandes. In the end, the journalist appears to go crazy. The cast includes many of the Marathi theatre and cinema's most famous names.

SPARSH

aka *The Touch*
1979 145' col Hindi
d/s **Sai Paranjpye** *p* **Basu Bhattacharya** *pc* Arohi Film Makers *lyr* Indu Jain *c* Virendra Saini *m* Kanu Roy
lp **Naseeruddin Shah**, **Shabana Azmi**, **Om**

Puri, Sudha Chopra, Pran Talwar, Arun Joglekar, Mohan Gokhale, Lakshman Tandon, I.V. Sambhani, Arun Sachdev, Tapan Kumar Nandi, Baladutt Sharma, Amjad Ali Khan

Paranjpye's first full-scale art-house feature tells a love story set among the blind. The blind Anirudh Parmar (Shah) runs a school for blind children and is particularly touchy about the notion that the children might be perceived as less than self-sufficient. Kavita (Azmi), who takes up charitable causes after the death of her husband, becomes involved with the school and falls in love with Anirudh. They are to marry, but Anirudh cannot get rid of the suspicion that she is doing it out of pity. This humanist though sentimental story was commended by reviewers for the performances of the children and the several comic moments that enlivened the script.

22 JUNE 1897

1979 121' col Marathi
d/p/co-s **Nachiket Patwardhan** *co-d* **Jayoo Patwardhan** *pc* Sanket *co-s* **Shankar Nag** *dial* **Vijay Tendulkar** *c* Navroze Contractor *m* Anand Modak
lp Prabhakar Patankar, Ravindra Mankani, Udayan Dixit, Rod Gilbert, John Irving, Sadashiv Amarapurkar

The co-directors, who are also architects and art directors (***Ondanondu Kaladalli***, 1978) retell the famous Pune legend of the Chaphekar brothers, the militant Hindu chauvinist followers of Bal Gangadhar Tilak whose violent anti-British activities led to their martyrdom. Mr Rand imposed martial law in Pune because of an outbreak of the plague in January 1897, and the eldest brother, Damodar, kills Rand on 22 June. In retaliation, Inspector Brewin starts a massive manhunt using former colleagues of the three brothers as informers. Damodar is hanged, despite Tilak's personal appeal to the British. When the youngest brother, Vasudev, kills the informers who helped Brewin, he and the remaining brother, Balkrishna, are also sentenced to hang. The directors rely heavily on a version of method acting which was then seeping into the Marathi avant-garde theatre, emphasising minimal movement, deep voices and meaningful looks. The cast includes members of Pune's Theatre Academy, including its most promising performer, Mankani. Contractor's sophisticated lighting combined with the directors' architectural sensibilities provide the film with a sense of place. However, a disturbing question hangs over the film: to celebrate, in 1979, anti-colonial activities is uncontroversial whereas the glorification of fanatical Hindu chauvinists at that time is troubling.

VETAGADU

1979 161' col Telugu
d **K. Raghavendra Rao** *pc* Roja Movies *s* Jandhyala *lyr* Veeturi Sundara Ramamurthy *c* K.S. Prakash *m* Chakravarty
lp **N.T. Rama Rao, Sridevi**, Satyanarayana, Ravu Gopala Rao, Pushpalatha, Allu Ramalingaiah, **Pandharibai**, Nagesh, Mamatha, Shrilakshmi

With this film, together with ***Yugandhar*** (1979), NTR tried to change his image and to assimilate conventions of Hindi cinema. He plays a police officer who hunts down a gang of smugglers in a forest. The combination of NTR and the future Hindi star Sridevi caused a sensation.

YUGANDHAR

1979 169' col Telugu
d K.S.R. Doss *pc* Gajalakshmi Arts *st* **Salim-Javed** *dial* **D.V. Narasaraju** *lyr* C. Narayana Reddy, **Acharya Athreya**, Veeturi Sundara Ramamurthy *c* U.C. Shekhar *m* **Ilaiyaraja**
lp **N.T. Rama Rao, K. Jaggaiah**, Prabhakara Reddy, Kantarao, Thyagaraj, Jayasudha, Jayamalini, Sheela, Satyanarayana

Early example of the impact of the **Prakash Mehra** and **Salim-Javed** styles on Telugu cinema, an idiom assimilated by NTR in his later work (cf ***Vetagadu***, 1979). A kind smuggler unfortunately kills Ramesh, whose sister Jaya vows revenge, but then falls in love with the hero. This genre confirmed several female stars (e.g. **Sridevi** and Jayapradha) who went on to perform the same roles in Hindi, and provided welcome platforms for 50s stars like **Anjali Devi** or **G. Varalakshmi** to play tearful mother roles. The genre also includes cabaret scenes with Jayamalini and Silk Smitha.

AAKROSH

aka *Cry of the Wounded*
1980 145' col Hindi
d/c **Govind Nihalani** *p* Devi Dutt, Narayan Kenny *pc* Krsna Movies *s* **Vijay Tendulkar** *dial* Satyadev Dubey *lyr* Vasant Dave, Suryabhanu Gupta *m* Ajit Varman
lp **Naseeruddin Shah**, Amrish Puri, **Om Puri**, Arvind Deshpande, **Smita Patil**, Mohan Agashe, Achyut Potdar, Nana Palsikar, Bhagyashree Kotnis, Mahesh Elkunchwar, Vihang Nayak

Cinematographer Nihalani's directorial debut with a classic Tendulkar script based on an actual incident in Bhiwandi, a small town outside Bombay. The central character is a young lawyer, Bhaskar Kulkarni (Shah) appointed to defend a tribal, Lahanya Bhiku (Om Puri, who emerged as a star in this film), who is accused of murdering his wife Nagi (Patil) but refuses to speak a word. Kulkarni investigates and finds that the man's wife had been raped and killed by a group of politicians and businessmen during their revels. He also finds that the police and his own boss (A. Puri) are implicated in the cover-up and the framing of Lahanya. When Lahanya is allowed to attend the funeral of his father, he takes the opportunity to kill his young sister to protect her from the fate that befell his wife. In the end, Lahanya gives vent to his suffering and to his helpless anger with a cry of anguish. The part of a left activist who assists Kulkarni's investigations is played by the playwright Elkunchwar whose play ***Party*** Nihalani adapted to the screen (1984). Nihalani's film extended Tendulkar's interest in an expressionist fictional reconstruction of real-life political incidents (cf **Benegal**'s ***Nishant***, 1975) and greatly influenced the way cinema in the 80s approached political issues, using tight close-ups, fast-paced editing and dramatic lighting. Nihalani's 3rd film, ***Ardh Satya*** (1983) went on to focus on police brutality.

AJALI NABOU

1980 153' col Assamese
d **Nip Barua** *lyr* Keshab Mahanta *c* Nalin Duara *m* **Ramen Barua**
lp Biju Phukan, Nipon Goswami, Ila Kakoti, Prasanta Hazarika, Purabi Sarma, Purnima Pathak, Bidya Rao, Pranjal Saikia, Biswajit Chakraborty

The first mainstream Assamese Eastmancolor film with a star cast is a melodramatic middle-class musical fantasy. It made Nip Barua the top commercial attraction in Assamese cinema.

AKALER SANDHANEY

aka *In Search of Famine*
1980 124' col Bengali
d/sc **Mrinal Sen** *p* Dhiresh Kumar Chakraborty *pc* D.K. Films *st* Amalendu Chakravarty *c* K.K. Mahajan *m* **Salil Choudhury**
lp **Dhritiman Chatterjee, Smita Patil**, Sreela Majumdar, Geeta Sen, Dipankar Dey, **Rajen Tarafdar**, Radhamohan Bhattacharya, Devika Mukherjee, Sajal Roy Choudhury, Jochan Dastidar, Siddhartha Dutta, Reba Roy Choudhury, Umanath Battacharya, Nirmal Ghosh

In 1980 a film crew from Calcutta headed by a director (D. Chatterjee) arrives in a small Bengali village to make a 'social conscience' film set in the 1943 famine (setting of his earlier ***Baishey Shravan***, 1960). They stay in a dilapidated mansion inhabited by a woman and her incapacitated old husband. The crew, including star Patil (playing herself), begins to make contact with villagers such as the admiring Haren (Tarafdar), the last surviving weaver, and the local teacher (R. Bhattacharya). The villagers observe the preparations with undisguised curiosity but gradually the voyeuristic implications of a big film crew coming to address 'local history' in a village become unbearable to all concerned. Conflicts erupt and the film has to be abandoned. The double time levels involved in the 1943-1980 structure of the tale, with ample parallels between the two periods emerging as the film progresses (e.g. a villager accuses the crew of starting a new famine as they buy up food for the film unit's lavish meals; or the village notables used to be or are descended from famine profiteers), is further complicated by a village woman, Durga (S. Majumdar) whose intimations of the future disorient the city-dwellers even further. Bansi Chandragupta's art direction is particularly notable for the way he orchestrates the encroachment of set-like qualities into the village location, giving the cultural and temporal disjunctions in the narrative a palpably physical dimension. Sen commented that the film made 'a confession of our incapacities. We speak of the crisis in the arts when we hesitate to confront reality or fail to catch its true bearings.'

ALBERT PINTO KO GUSSA KYON AATA HAI

aka *What Makes Albert Pinto Angry*
1980 113' col Hindi
d/p/co-s **Saeed Akhtar Mirza** *pc* Saeed Mirza Prod. *co-s* **Kundan Shah** *lyr* Hriday Lani, Madhosh Bilgrami *c* Virendra Saini *m* Manas Mukherjee, Bhaskar Chandavarkar
lp **Naseeruddin Shah, Shabana Azmi, Smita Patil,** Dilip Dhawan, Sulabha Deshpande, Arvind Deshpande

Mirza later acknowledged that the film, which addresses India's minorities, is set in a catholic Bombay milieu because at the time he lacked the courage to deal with the Muslim issues (this he did later in his ***Salim Langde Pe Mat Ro***, 1989). Albert Pinto (Shah) is a garage mechanic from Goa who dreams of owning the expensive cars he drives for clients. His girlfriend Stella (Azmi) upsets him with her casual and pragmatic attitude to his colleagues as well as to their employer's sexual interest in her. Albert's father (Deshpande) joins a textile workers' strike and stimulates his son's political awareness. Mirza wanted the film to be acceptable to the mainstream Hindi cinema and to that end included some songs, e.g. the scene of the garage workers praising an expensive car, *Paanch lakh ki gaadi hai* ('The car costs 500,000 rupees'), shot in a single take. Several characteristic Mirza sequences are introduced into the film, such as the hero examining himself in a mirror, or the workers being searched as they leave the factory (shot with a concealed camera).

BANCHARAMER BAGAN

aka *The Garden of Bancharam*
1980 133' col Bengali
d/sc/lyr/m **Tapan Sinha** *p* Dhiresh Kumar Chakraborty *st* Manoj Mitra's play *c* Bimal Mukherjee
lp Manoj Mitra, Nirmal Kumar, Dipankar Dey, **Robi Ghosh**, Bishwa Guha-Thakurta, Debika Mukherjee, Donald F. Sihan, **Bhanu Bannerjee, Madhabi Chakraborty**

Sinha's excursion into the fairy-tale genre tells of an old peasant, Bancharam, who defeats the tyrannical landlord Chhakari. Inheriting a dry patch of land, Bancharam converts it into a fabulous garden. The British magistrate supports him when Chhakari attempts to acquire the garden, after which he dies. Chhakari's son Nakari tries a new strategem: he promises Bancharam Rs 100 every month provided Bancharam bequeaths his garden to the landowner by a specific date. Bancharam agrees but amazingly becomes healthier with every passing day, repeatedly promising to die but failing to do so. Come the appointed day, Nakari arrives with the funeral band and finds Bancharam glowing with health. Nakari collapses on the prepared funeral bed and dies instead. The film used several theatrical techniques, including direct address and rhyming dialogue, and has fine performances by Mitra, the author of the popular play, and Dipankar Dey.

BARA/SOOKHA

aka *The Famine* aka *Drought* aka *Dushkal*
1980 135'[K]/119'[H] col Kannada/Hindi
d/p **M.S. Sathyu** *st* U.R. Ananthamurthy's story *sc* Shama Zaidi, Javed Siddiqui *c* Ashok Gunjal *m* Kuldeep Singh
lp **Anant Nag**, Lavlin Madhu, Nitin Sethi, Veeraj Byakod, Uma Shivshankar

The noted **Navya** Movement writer Ananthamurthy (cf ***Samskara***, 1970) provided the story for this tale about political chicanery set in the Bidar district of Karnataka, a famine-ridden area. The film weaves together the farmers' daily reality with scenes of the political rivalry between two ministers, represented at local level by the clash between Gangadhar, president of the grain merchants' association, and Bhimoji, a small-time politician. When Satish Chandra (Nag), a deputy commissioner, resorts to a crazy water diviner to relieve the situation, a crisis erupts and a major riot ensues, leading to a ministerial resignation. The rival minister, by being the first to order much-needed grain to be rushed to the famine-stricken area, thereby consolidates his political hold.

BHAVNI BHAVAI/ANDHER NAGARI

aka *A Folk Tale* aka *The Bhavai of Life*
1980 140'[G]/125'[H] col Gujarati/Hindi
d/s **Ketan Mehta** *pc* Sanchar Film *st* Folk-tale *Achhut No Bhavai Vesh* *c* Pammy *m* Gaurang Vyas
lp **Naseeruddin Shah, Smita Patil,** Mohan Gokhale, **Om Puri**, Dina Pathak, Suhasini Mulay, Benjamin Gilani, Nimesh Desai, Gopi Desai

Mehta's debut is a remarkably successful transposition of the folk performance idiom to the screen. It is dedicated to Brecht, Goscinny and to the inventor of the Bhavai, Asait Thakore, who was a Gujarati Brahmin cast out from his community. He proceeded to live among the lower castes and his descendents, the targalas, are the traditional Gujarati performers of the plays he wrote and dedicated to Amba, a mother goddess. The Bhavai evolved into one of India's most

Bancharamer Bagan

energetic folk music and dance dramas. It has an episodic structure consisting of Veshas (playlets set in medieval Gujarat stressing masquerades and offering much scope for improvisation) and mobilises a wealth of religious, political and mythological references, usually held together by a male Rangla and female Rangli chorus. The film deploys a 'chinese box' structure. In the framing narrative, a group of persecuted Harijans (Untouchables) are migrating to the city and pause for the night. To the accompaniment of Malo's (Puri) music, a story is told of the time when Harijans had to have broomsticks tied to their backs in order to erase their footsteps while walking. The tale is of a king (Shah) with two wives. When the elder queen delivers a male heir, the younger one (Mulay) conspires to have the child killed. But the child survives and, raised by Malo, grows up into the handsome Jivo (Gokhale). The climax of the film combines Jivo's sexual awakening in response to the wild tribal woman Ujaan (Patil) with the digging of a well by the Untouchables to propitiate the gods, so that the king may have another heir. However, in a traditional happy ending, the well yields water, Jivo is saved and the people freed. This ending of Malo's story is disputed by his audience, who suggest an alternative: Jivo is beheaded and Malo jumps into the dry well cursing the king with his dying breath; his sacrifice results in a flood that washes away the evil rulers (this ending is intercut with documentary footage of India's freedom struggle). The film's own end shifts back into realism showing the Harijans approaching the city. The film succeeds mainly through the extraordinary performances of, e.g., Shah, Gilani (the commander) and Mulay, enhanced by comic-strip-style camera angles and exotic locations. Its several contemporary references include violent caste riots in Ahmedabad and the severe drought in Northern Gujarat.

CHAKRA

aka *Vicious Circle*
1980 135' col Hindi
d/sc **Rabindra Dharmaraj** *p* Manmohan Shetty, Pradeep Uppoor *pc* Neo Films *st* Jaywant Dalvi's Marathi novel (1963) *lyr* Madhosh Bilgrami *c* Barun Mukherjee *m* Hridayanath Mangeshkar
lp **Smita Patil, Naseeruddin Shah**, Kulbhushan Kharbanda, Ranjit Choudhury, Anjali Paingankar, Savita Bajaj, Uttam Sirur, Rohini Hattangadi

Predating *Salaam Bombay* (1988) by several years, Dharmaraj's only feature (he died in 1981) provides a less idealised look at Bombay's slum-dwellers. Amma (Patil) and her son Benwa (Choudhury) move to Bombay's slums when her husband killed a moneylender who tried to rape her. The husband was then shot trying to steal some tin to build a hut. In Bombay, she lives with the vain pimp and petty crook Lukka (Shah), Benwa's idol. Lukka is banned from Bombay by the police and Benwa marries the young Chenna (Paingankar). Amma acquires another lover, a truck driver (Kharbanda), and becomes pregnant. Lukka reappears, ravaged by syphilis and drugs; he kills a chemist to feed his habit and hides in Amma's hut. The cops find him and arrest both him and Benwa, beating them up in the process. Amma has a miscarriage in the scuffle. In the end, bulldozers arrive to flatten the entire slum area. Patil gives her best 'realistic' performance and some shots of her moving unrecognised among Bombay's slum-dwellers were taken with a hidden camera (***Do Bigha Zameen***, 1953, had made the same claims).

CHANN PARDESI

1980 147' col Punjabi
d Chitrarath Singh *co-p* Swarn Seedha, J.S. Cheema *co-p/s* Baldev Gill *c* Manmohan Singh *m* Surinder Kohli
lp Raj Babbar, Rama Vij, Kulbhushan Kharbanda, **Om Puri**, Amrish Puri

One of the few Punjabi hits is an epic melodrama spanning two generations of feudal warfare. The peasant Nekh (Kharbanda) loves Kammo (Vij), but she is seduced by the landlord Joginder Singh (A. Puri). Kammo gives birth to Singh's baby after she is married to Nekh, leading to Nekh's lifelong vendetta against Singh. Nekh becomes a bandit and on several occasions tries to attack Singh's house, which leads to his arrest and life imprisonment. Years later, Kammo's son (Babbar) falls in love with Singh's daughter, Channi, unaware that she is his half-sister. Eventually, after Nekh's release and complications involving Singh's blackmailing secretary (O. Puri) and Channi's wedding, the outlaw is reconciled with his wife. All leading players were imported from the Hindi cinema, inaugurating a new trend of commercially successful Bombay-based Punjabi movies as an offshoot of the Hindi industry.

DADAR KIRTI

1980 154' col Bengali
d/sc **Tarun Majumdar** *p* Ram Gupta *st* Saradindu Bandyopadhyay *lyr* **Rabindranath Tagore**, Pulak Bandyopadhyay, Hridesh Pandey *c* Shakti Bannerjee *m* **Hemanta Mukherjee**
lp Tapas Paul, Mahua Roy Choudhury, Ayan Bannerjee, Debashree Roy, **Kali Bannerjee**, Satya Bannerjee, **Anup Kumar**, Ruma Guha-Thakurta, Shefali Bannerjee, Sulata Choudhury

Hit melodrama about a simple-minded youth's growth into adulthood. Kedar (Paul) is sent to study with his smarter cousin Santu in the hope of improving his university results. Kedar falls in love with next-door neighbour Saraswati, but also comes under the nefarious influence of the local bully Bhombhal, who also estranges Kedar from Saraswati. The problems are resolved only at the end. Paul, whose debut this was, went on to become a major Bengali star in the 80s playing the naive, sacrificing hero almost to the point of masochism (cf ***Guru Dakshina***, 1987). His 'loveable' image is often pointedly in contrast to the 80s Hindi cinema's emphasis on machismo.

DOORATHU IDHI MUZHAKKAM

aka *Faraway Thunder*
1980 125' col Tamil
d/p K. Vijayan *pc* Jai Sudha Films *s* Somasoodan *c* N. Balakrishnan *m* **Salil Choudhury**
lp Poornima, Vijayakant, Peelisivam, A.K. Veeraswamy, Jagadeesan

A village melodrama about a fisherman, Ponnan (Vijayakant), believed lost at sea whose girlfriend Chelli (Poornima) marries a relative, Mari (Peelisivam), and has a child. Assuming she had been unfaithful, Mari and a nasty magician plan to sacrifice the child ritually to obtain wealth. Ponnan resurfaces and saves the child but both the men in Chelli's life die, leaving her to sail off into the sunset with her baby.

GEHRAYEE

1980 131' col Hindi
d/st/co-sc Aruna-Vikas *pc* N.B. Kamat, Avikam *co-sc* **Vijay Tendulkar** *dial* Hafeez *lyr* **Gulzar** *c* Barun Mukherjee *m* **Laxmikant-Pyarelal**
lp Shriram Lagoo, **Anant Nag**, Padmini Kolhapure, Indrani Mukherjee, Amrish Puri, Rita Bhaduri, Sudhir Dalvi, Suhas Bhalekar, Shobha Joshi, Satyendra, Satya Kumar Patil, Shetty

Uma (Kolhapure), the daughter of a businessman (Lagoo), spews abuse and reveals uncomfortable secrets from her father's past. The father arranges psychiatric treatment for her, including electric shocks, to the disapproval of the mother (Mukherjee) and son Nandu (Nag) who prefer the more traditional interpretation that Uma is possessed by a rogue demon. To perform the exorcism, they employ a potentially dangerous Tantric (Puri) who practises black magic on virgins. The daughter's exorcism is then followed by the son's effort to track down the demon whom he finds living in the body of a woman. He strangles her as the film ends, literally, with a question mark. Although *The Exorcist* (1973) was an unofficially acknowledged influence, the film is more a mystificatory engagement with religious ritual than with the conventions of the horror film.

GREESHAMAM

aka *Summer*
1980 122' col Malayalam
d/s V.R. Gopinath *p* Sumathy Ayyapan *pc* Mayflower Movie Makers *c* Madhu Ambat *m* **M.B. Srinivasan**
lp Rajendran, **Gopi**, Ravi Menon, Jalaja, Rekha Rao, Pratima, Ramu

K.G. George-type drama about Hari (Rajendran), a psychology student with remarkably little psychological sensitivity who is obsessed by a 16-year-old girl, Rathi (Jalaja). When he discovers that she is not the daughter but the mistress of his university professor, the student is so traumatised and preoccupied with himself that he is unable to develop any real relationship with other women like the prostitute Anitha (Pratima) or his former colleague Malini (Rekha Rao). The story, told in flashbacks, ends with a dreamlike reconciliation between Hari and Rathi, suggesting that Hari remains stuck in his adolescent fantasies.

HIRAK RAJAR DESHE

aka *The Kingdom of Diamonds*
1980 118' col Bengali
d/s/m **Satyajit Ray** *pc* West Bengal Govt *c* Soumendu Roy
lp **Soumitra Chatterjee**, **Utpal Dutt**, Tapan Chatterjee, **Robi Ghosh**, Santosh Dutta, Promod Ganguly, Alpana Gupta, Robin Majumdar, Sunil Sarkar, Nani Ganguly, Ajoy Bannerjee, Kartick Chattopadhyay, Haridhan Mukherjee

Continuing the adventures of ***Goopy Gyne Bagha Byne*** (1968), Ray's musical is at times a hard-hitting satire. The lead duo Goopy (T. Chatterjee) and Bagha (R. Ghosh) face up to the despotic king of Hirak (Dutt) who tries to brainwash his subjects with the help of a scientist (Dutta) and shuts down the only school in the kingdom, forcing the idealist schoolteacher Udayan (S. Chatterjee) to become a terrorist in hiding. Goopy and Bagha eventually plunder the diamond treasury, bribe the soldiers, rescue Udayan and defeat the king. The Emergency (1975-7) and Sanjay Gandhi's fascist programmes are directly referenced in, e.g., the scene where poor people are to be evicted so that tourists may not see them, while the king's attempt to brainwash all his subjects by means of rhymed couplets inculcating good behaviour evokes the many official slogans launched at the time enjoining people to mind their own business, to 'be Indian buy Indian' and to follow the then prime minister's Twenty-point Programme.

HUM PAANCH

1980 163' col Hindi
d **Bapu** *pc* S.K. Film Ents *st* **S.R. Puttanna Kanagal** *sc* **M.V. Raman** *dial* Rahi Masoom Raza *lyr* **Anand Bakshi** *c* Sharad Kadwe *m* **Laxmikant-Pyarelal**, **S.P. Balasubramanyam**
lp Sanjeev Kumar, **Shabana Azmi**, **Mithun Chakraborty**, **Naseeruddin Shah**, Deepti Naval, Raj Babbar, Gulshan Grover, Amrish Puri, Kanhaiyalal

Bapu's first Hindi film remade **Puttanna Kanagal**'s *Paduvarahalli Pandavaru* (1978), derived from a popular *Mahabharata* legend set in feudal UP. The villainous zamindar Veer Pratap Singh (Puri) is Duryodhan, his sidekick Lala (Kanhaiyalal) is Shakuni and their opponents are the drunken holy man Krishna (Kumar), Bhima (Chakraborty), Arjun (Babbar), etc. The good and the bad perform with straightfaced conviction (which prevents the film from becoming a comedy) a story reduced to a series of action thrills. In many respects this feudal drama ironically echoed **Benegal**'s ***Nishant*** (1975), a resemblance reinforced by the presence of Puri, Azmi and Shah.

INSAAF KA TARAZU

aka *The Scales of Justice*
1980 146'(112') col Hindi
d/p **B.R. Chopra** *pc* B.R. Films *s* Sharad Kumar *lyr* **Sahir Ludhianvi** *c* Dharam Chopra *m* Ravindra Jain
lp **Zeenat Aman**, Padmini Kolhapure, **Dharmendra**, Raj Babbar, Deepak Parashar, Shriram Lagoo, Iftikhar, Simi Garewal, Jagdish Raj, Om Shivpuri

This notorious rape movie followed in the wake of growing feminist activism in India in the 70s after the Mathura and Maya Tyagi rape cases, the amendment to the Rape Law and the impact of, e.g., the Forum Against Rape which offered legal assistance to rape victims. The film has been analysed by Susie Tharu in her essay 'On Subverting a Rhetoric: Media Versions of Rape' (in *Olympus*, 9 August 1981). The pre-credit sequence shows a rape in shadow play. The story then shows the advertising model Bharati (Aman) being raped by the millionaire Ramesh (Babbar). When he is arrested, Bharati is unable to get a conviction in court. Bharati and her sister Nita (Kolhapure) move to another city where Nita, answering a job advertisement, is also raped by Ramesh. Bharati shoots Ramesh dead and once again faces the legal process, presided over by the same judge and prosecuted by the lawyer who had earlier defended Ramesh. The argument gets bogged down in legal technicalities until it is emotionally resolved with a passionate outburst from Nita. The three rape sequences shown in the film, staged with voyeuristic relish, no doubt contributed to its commercial success. **Bapu** remade the film in Telugu as *Edi Nyayam Edi Dharmam* (1982).

KALYUG

aka *The Machine Age*
1980 152' col Hindi
d/co-s **Shyam Benegal** *p* **Shashi Kapoor** *pc* Film Valas *co-s* **Girish Karnad** *c* **Govind Nihalani** *m* **Vanraj Bhatia**
lp Shashi Kapoor, **Rekha**, **Anant Nag**, Raj Babbar, Kulbhushan Kharbanda, Victor Bannerjee, Vinod Doshi, **Vijaya Mehta**, Supriya Pathak, Sushma Seth

Following on from the work of **Ghatak** and **Shahani**, Benegal essayed an 'epic' movie by transferring famous episodes from the *Mahabharata* to contemporary industrial society in order to explore, in his words, 'human values as they exist today in the modern world'. The result is a crime movie about a feud between two industrial families, the Puranchands and the Khubchands, which escalates into violence and murder by contract. Karan Singh (Kapoor) is killed while changing a car tyre, referring to Karna, the tragic son of Kunti and the Sun god in the original epic, who was killed when his chariot wheel got stuck; other mythological characters become income tax inspectors raiding the Rekha's character's house, rummaging in her cupboard and fingering her underwear.

KARZ

1980 159' col Hindi
d **Subhash Ghai** *pc* Mukta Films *st* Mukta Films Story Dept. *sc* Sachin Bhowmick *dial* Rahi Masoom Raza *lyr* **Anand Bakshi** *c* Kamalakar Rao *m* **Laxmikant-Pyarelal**
lp Rishi Kapoor, Tina Munim, Simi Garewal, Raj Kiran, Premnath, Pran, **Durga Khote**, Pinchoo Kapoor, Abha Dhulia, Iftikhar, Aruna Irani

Rebirth story with echoes of **Bimal Roy**'s ***Madhumati*** (1958). The day after his wedding, Ravi Varma (Kiran) is killed by his calculating wife Kamini (Garewal) on instructions from Sir Judas. Years later a rock singer, Monty (Rishi Kapoor), who is in love with Tina (Munim), is haunted by images of a woman killing a man. Eventually realising himself to be Varma's reincarnation, he takes belated revenge on Kamini, now the queen of Ooty. The film had the electronic rock-music-inspired hit *Om Shanti Om*, performed on a stage resembling a giant gramophone record.

KOLANGAL

aka *Caricatures*
1980 133' col Malayalam
d/s **K.G. George** *p* K.T. Varghese, D. Philip *pc* Falcon Movies *st* **P.J. Anthony** *c* Ramchandra *m* **M.B. Srinivasan**
lp Menaka, Rajam K. Nair, Gladys, D. Philip, Venu Nagavalli, Nedumudi Venu

A story set in a Kerala village where rumour and gossip spread like wildfire. Kunjamma (Menaka), the only daughter of an overbearing mother (Nair) with a biscuit stall in the market, sells milk to the villagers. When she befriends a passing cosmetics salesman, gossip ruins her reputation and her mother threatens suicide if Kunjamma does not agree to marry the only man still willing to accept her as a wife: an old but well-off lecherous drunk (Philip). Set in the Kerala matriarchy, the film presents its several village characters as not always good but essentially benign, contrasting this edenic world with the corruption introduced by the urban salesman (shown wearing garish clothes and dark glasses). The contrast is, however, undone by the mode of filming itself, with continuously saturated colour and emphatic performance modes.

LORRY

1980 114' col/scope Malayalam
d **B.G. Bharathan** *p* Rajamma Hari *pc* Supriya Films *s* **Padmarajan** *c* Ashok Kumar *m* M.S. Vishwanathan
lp Balan K. Nair, Nitya, Achan Kunju, **Prathap Pothan**

Continuing the collaboration between director Bharathan and writer Padmarajan, the film features the villainous Velan who kidnaps and forcibly blinds village children to turn them into fellow circus performers. He falls in love with one of his victims, the beautiful Rani, as does his hard drinking lorry-driver friend Ouseph. Eventually Ouseph and Velan kill each other allowing Rani to escape with the man she really loves, a lorry cleaner.

MINCHINA OTA

1980 135' col Kannada
d **Shankar Nag** *pc* Sanket Prod. *s* **Girish Karnad** *c* B.C. Gowri Shankar *m* Prabhakar Badri
lp **Anant Nag**, Shankar Nag, Ramesh Bhat, Priya Tendulkar, Loknath, Somu, Mandip Roy

Story of three petty thieves, Katte (S. Nag), Tony (A. Nag) and Tatha (Loknath), attempt a daring jailbreak because Tony wants to be with his pregnant wife (Tendulkar) when she has her baby. Shankar Nag's directing debut, apparently based on a real-life incident.

OPPOL

aka *Elder Sister*
1980 143' col Malayalam
d **K. S. Sethumadhavan** *pc* Rosamma George *s* **M.T. Vasudevan Nair** *c* Madhu Ambat *m* **M.B. Srinivasan**
lp Menaka, Master Arvind, Balan K. Nair, Sankaradi, Master Sivaprasad

Sethumadhavan's best-known film outside Kerala. The 6-year-old Appu (Arvind) is the illegitimate son of Malu (Menaka) and knows her as his elder sister. He becomes intensely jealous when Malu marries the hard-drinking ex-military man Govindan (Nair). Appu attacks him during the honeymoon. When Malu scolds him, the boy applies emotional blackmail by running away. Much of the film deals with the bizarre love triangle, which ends only when the little Oedipus triumphs by driving away the husband so that he can keep the mother all to himself. The film, and Vasudevan Nair's script, which apparently legitimises a woman's love for her illegitimate son, broke new ground with the characterisation (and performance) of the little boy who dominates the film.

PIKOO

aka *Pikoo's Day*
1980 26' col Bengali
d/s/m **Satyajit Ray** *pc* Henri Fraise *c* Soumendu Roy
lp Arjun Guha-Thakurta, **Aparna Sen**, Soven Lahiri, Promod Ganguly, Victor Bannerjee

Short film made as a companion piece for ***Sadgati*** (1981). It is a sad fairy-tale about an upper-class Bengali family seen through the eyes of the little boy Pikoo (Guha-Thakurta). One afternoon, Pikoo's father discovers that his wife (A. Sen) is having an affair. The mother makes love to her boyfriend (V. Bannerjee) while the grandfather (Ganguly) dies of a heart attack in another room and Pikoo sketches flowers in the garden with his new crayons.

SATAH SE UTHATA ADMI

aka *Arising from the Surface*
1980 114' col Hindi
d/p/sc **Mani Kaul** *pc* Infrakino Film, Madhya Pradesh Kala Parishad *st* texts by Gajanan Madhav Muktibodh *c* Virendra Saini *m* Fariduddin Dagar *lp* **Gopi**, M.K. Raina, Vibhuti Jha, Kulbhushan Billori, Satyen Kumar

Kaul's film addresses the writings of Gajanan Madhav Muktibodh (1917-69), one of the main representatives of the Nai Kavita (New Poetry) movement in Hindi (*Tar Saptak*, 1943; *Chanda Ka Mooh Tedha Hai*, 1954). Muktibodh also wrote several short stories, one of which (1971) provides the film with its title, and critical essays. The film integrates episodes from Muktibodh's writings with material from other sources, including a reinvented neo-realism derived from Muktibodh's literary settings. The narrative is constructed around three characters. Ramesh (Gopi) is the one who speaks and enacts Muktibodh's writings, functioning as the first-person voice of the text; his two friends, Madhav (Jha) and Keshav (Raina), are Ramesh's antagonists and interlocutors esp. in the debates about modernity. Kaul gradually minimises the fictional settings until, in the remarkably shot sequences of the factory, the audience is directly confronted with the written text itself. Kaul had begun his studies of Dhrupad music, the classical North Indian music known mainly for its extreme austerity, and derived a number of cinematic styles from this musical idiom which have influenced all his films since: e.g. the continuously mobile camera, the use of changing light patterns and the importance of improvisation.

YAGAM

1980 111' b&w Malayalam
d/c Sivan *p* B. Chandramani Bai *pc* Saritha Films *st* N. Mohan *sc* K.S. Namboodiri *m* M.G. Radhakrishnan
lp Babu Nathencode, Premji, Jalaja, Kalpana, Sreelatha

The sentimental melodrama, allegedly critiquing the extreme-left CPI(ML), has the middle-class namboodiri hero Unni join a political group committed to violent struggle. He abandons his studies, slavishly obeys the group's leaders and kills a fellow activist as well as a religiously inclined local landlord. Moving to Madurai, he falls in love with Kannamma, the daughter of a factory worker. In the end, following Party instructions, he blows up a train but discovers too late that one of the victims is Kannamma's father.

Master Arvind (left) in *Oppol*

Amol Palekar in *Aakriet*

AAKRIET

aka *The Misbegotten*
1981 135' col Marathi
d **Amol Palekar** *pc* Dnya Films *s* **Vijay Tendulkar** *c* S.D. Deodhar *m* Bhaskar Chandavarkar, Ashok Patki
lp Amol Palekar, Chitra Palekar, Rekha Sabnis, Dilip Kulkarni

Film star and stage director Palekar's directorial debut is based on a series of brutal ritual murders among tribals in Manwat, Maharashtra. The central characters are the corrupt Mukutrao Shinde (A. Palekar), an influential trader, fence and smuggler, and his mistress Ruhi (C. Palekar). The middle-aged Ruhi, desperate to consolidate her hold on her husband, wants to become pregnant and initiates the ritual murders of five young virgins to facilitate the desired event. The greedy Mukutrao's hope to become rich on completion of the ritual stifles his fear of being caught. The fast-moving, confidently edited story quickly abandons its initial realism in favour of the suspense.

ADHARSHILA

aka *The Foundation Stone*
1981 154' col Hindi
d/p/s Ashok Ahuja *pc* Ashok Films *c* Sharad Navla *m* Ranjit Kapoor, Uttam Singh
lp **Naseeruddin Shah**, Anita Kanwar, Devki Nandan Pandey, Anil Kapoor, Madhu Malati

An example of a genre rarely practised in Indian feature films: autobiography. Ahuja features the existential dilemmas of an **FTII** graduate who wants to express himself through art movies. Ajay (Shah) takes his new bride Asha (Kanwar) on a tour of the Film Institute, narrating its history (it was the former **Prabhat** Studio). The two set up home and do reasonably well except that Ajay is haunted by disturbing desires to make films.

ANTHA

1981 143' col Kannada
d **S.V. Rajendra Singh** *pc* Parimala Art Prod *c* K.S. Prakash *m* **G.K. Venkatesh**
lp Ambarish, Lakshmi, Prabhakar, Jayamala, Vajramuni, Sudhir, Shakti Prasad, Musari Krishnamurthy, Seetaram

Violent Kannada cop-on-rampage film (cf ***Zanjeer***, 1973; ***Ardh Satya***, 1983), dubbed into Telugu, Malayalam and Tamil and remade in Hindi as *Meri Awaaz Suno* (1981). The film became a notorious censorship case. A police officer (Ambarish) tracks down a gang of smugglers, leading to some gruesome encounters (the cop's pregnant wife is tortured, his nails are torn out, etc). He discovers that his own superiors are involved in the gang, massacres the villains and drives their corpses into the courtroom. The promotion for the original Kannada version enjoined viewers to 'see it before it is banned' and created a series of controversies which finally led to a parliamentary debate on the Hindi version (starring **Jeetendra** and **Hema Malini**). There were claims of it being a political movie for exposing the connections between criminals, the police and politicians, but the censor cuts apparently had nothing to do with the movie's alleged politics, bearing mainly on nude scenes, a fire and a gory abortion.

APARNA

1981 97' b&w Malayalam
d/co-p/s Padmakumar *co-p* Vijayan *pc* Sahya Film Makers *c* Bipin Mohan *m* Ananda Padmanabhan
lp **Prathap Pothan**, Sudharshana, Kanakalatha, Master Tony, Balakrishna Pillai

The tale of a young woman, Aparna (Sudharshana), who invests all her hopes and dreams in the illusion of loving Ramesh (Pothan) while her real life becomes progressively more unbearable. She clings to memories and attaches herself to a little boy, Ramu (Tony), who bears the nickname she gave to her lost love. When she sets out to find Ramesh again, she reaches a banyan tree where Ramesh was said to have taken refuge one day and she realises that everything, happiness and misery, even death itself, have been manifestations of 'maya', illusion. The ambiguous ending suggests that Aparna too may have disintegrated into an illusion. The film evokes the myth of Aparna's love for Shiva, which was transformed into an intense and concentrated tapasya (a form of ritual penance).

CHAALCHITRA

aka *The Kaleidoscope*
1981 92' col Bengali
d/s **Mrinal Sen** *p* Dhiresh Kumar Chakraborty *pc* D.K. Films Enterprise *c* K.K. Mahajan *m* Aloke Dey
lp Anjan Dutt, Geeta Sen, **Utpal Dutt**, Debapratim Dasgupta

The lower-middle-class Calcutta milieu critically examined in ***Ek Din Pratidin*** (1979) here becomes the setting for an affectionate comedy with a sting in the tail. A talented young writer, Dipu (A. Dutt), is asked by a newspaper editor (U. Dutt) to write in two days a short story about everyday life. Dipu starts enthusiastically but each situation he addresses appears to have ramifications too wide to deal with in a short impressionistic sketch. He wants to write about families living in overcrowded apartment blocks using coal stoves for cooking because they cannot afford gas. This means the small rooms are constantly filled with smoke. At one point, Dipu's little brother innocently asks: 'How many coal stoves are there in the city?' Dipu, despairing of his ability to deal with the subject in the format commissioned by the newspaper, has an angry wish fulfilment dream which he writes up and presents to the editor who prints the story suitably toned down. Sen returns to the same problem in his next film, ***Kharij*** (1982).

CHASHME BUDDOOR

aka *Touch Wood* aka *Shield against the Evil Eye*
1981 145' col Hindi
d **Sai Paranjpye** *p* Gul Anand *pc* PLA Prod. *c* Virendra Saini *m* Raj Kamal
lp Farouque Shaikh, Deepti Naval, **Saeed Jaffrey**, Rakesh Bedi, Leela Mishra, Ravi Baswani

A light romantic comedy about three students who share a flat in Delhi. Jomo (Bedi) and Omi (Baswani) are forever chasing women in the city but it is the shy Siddharth (Shaikh) who finds a woman he can love. The film also pokes fun at the way mainstream Hindi cinema portrays love relationships. **Amitabh Bachchan** puts in a guest appearance here, as he seems to do in all Gul Anand productions (*Jalwa*, 1986; *Hero Hiralal*, 1988).

DAKHAL

aka *The Occupation*
1981 72' col Bengali
d/co-sc/m/c **Gautam Ghosh** *pc* West Bengal Govt *st* Sunil Jana *co-sc* Partha Bannerjee
lp Mamata Shankar, Robin Sengupta, Sunil Mukherjee, Sajal Roy Choudhury, Bimal Deb

Ghosh's first Bengali featurette tells of Andi (Shankar), a member of a nomadic tribe of scavengers, and her struggle against a local landlord. Andi is married to the peasant Joga from a different tribe. When Joga dies, the landlord, who wants Andi's land, incites Andi's nomadic tribe to declare her marriage illegal so that the landlord may appropriate her land. Eventually, the tribe sees through the manipulation and apologises to Andi, offering her the tribe's protection. However, she refuses to rejoin the nomads and decides to fight for her land. Set among Bengal's most marginalised people, the film presents a poeticised (cf the soft-focus twilight shots in the beginning) image, with allegorical rather than miserabilist overtones, of a struggle for bare survival (cf ***Paar***, 1984) in an elemental, raw nature shorn of cultural associations.

ELIPPATHAYAM

aka *The Rat Trap*
1981 126' col Malayalam
d/s **Adoor Gopalakrishnan** *p* K. Ravindranathan Nair *pc* General Pics *c* Ravi Varma *m* **M.B. Srinivasan**
lp Karamana Janardanan Nair, **Sharada**, Jalaja, Rajam K. Nair, Prakash, Soman, John Samuel, Balan K. Nair, Joycee, Thampi

Unni (Karamana) is a middle-aged relic, the head of a parasitic family of the Nair community of ex-rent collectors in a decaying feudal society. His eldest sister Janamma (R.K. Nair) fights for her own family's share of the feudal spoils; the obedient younger sister Rajamma (Sharada) is condemned to be both the slave and the surrogate mother of the indolent Unni until she collapses under the strain. The youngest sister Sridevi (Jalaja) is a student, defiantly pragmatic in her rejection of the old system. Confronted with any difficult situation, Unni withdraws like a rat into a dark hole and eventually sinks into paranoia. The film uses an obsessive, numbing rhythm and an intricate tapestry of close-ups, long shots and isolated sounds to convey the last gasp of a dying order as Unni runs through his house like a rat in a trap. As with ***Mukha Mukham*** (1984), his next film, the performance is pitched between naturalism and metaphor, e.g. when Unni tries to make an inquisitive cow go away or shows a pathological fear of getting mud on his clothes. The director acknowledged autobiographical elements in the film, likening Unni's house to his own ancestral home, but he added that the film is in fact about Kerala's emergence into modernity.

ILAKKANGAL

aka *The Emotional Upsurge*
1981 114' col Malayalam
d/co-dial Mohan *p* David Kachapally, Innocent *pc* Sathru Films *s* M. Raghavan *co-dial* John Paul *lyr* Kavalam Narayana Panicker *c* U. Rajagopal *m* **M.B. Srinivasan**
lp Nedumudi Venu, Shankaradi, Innocent, Kaviyoor Ponnamma, **Adoor Bhasi**, Sudha

Unni, a young man working in the city, returns to his village for a holiday and has to cope with the adolescent yearnings of a 15-year-old girl, Amminikutty, who had built many of her fantasies around him and his presumed big city lifestyle. Unaware of the depth of her feelings, he returns to the city casually giving her a tip for having washed his clothes. One of art director Mohan's better-known films.

IMAGI NINGTHEM

aka *My Son, My Precious*
1981 110' b&w Manipuri
d **Aribam Syam Sharma** *pc* X-Cine Prod. *s* M.K. Binodini Debi *c* K. Ibohal Sharma *m* Khundrakpam Joykumar
lp Leikhendro, Rashid, Ingdam Mangi

The breakthrough film of Manipur's best-known director, made in collaboration with the writer and art patron maharajkumari M.K. Binodini Debi (they collaborated again on ***Ishanou***, 1990). The sensitive schoolteacher Dhani helps Thoithoi, the illegitimate son of Dinachandra, to be adopted by Dinachandra's legitimate wife Ekashini. The legal aspects of the child's adoption are intercut with the child's growth, presented with mythological overtones (e.g. Thoithoi plays the infant Krishna in the folk *Raas-Leela*).

NASEEB

Destiny
1981 197' col Hindi
d/p **Manmohan Desai** *pc* MKD Films, Aasia Films *st* Prayag Raj *sc* K.K. Shukla, Kadar Khan *lyr* **Anand Bakshi** *c* Jal Mistry *m* **Laxmikant-Pyarelal**
lp **Amitabh Bachchan**, **Hema Malini**, Shatrughan Sinha, Rishi Kapoor, Reena Roy, Kim, Pran, Amrish Puri, Kader Khan, Amjad Khan, Shakti Kapoor, Prem Chopra, **Lalita Pawar**, Jagdish Raj, **Raj Kapoor**, **Shammi Kapoor**, **Dharmendra**, **Rajesh Khanna**, **Mala Sinha**, **Waheeda Rehman**, **Sharmila Tagore**, Shubha Khote, Om Shivpuri

Desai's most extravagantly plotted film to date. Namdev (Pran), a waiter, a band musician (Jagdish Raj), Damodar (A. Khan) the photographer and Raghubir (K. Khan) the hack driver jointly win a lottery ticket. After being framed for the murder of the musician, Namdev is presumably killed by Damodar and Raghubir who use the money to set up a criminal empire. The story then switches to the second generation: John Jani Janardan (Bachchan) and Sunny (Rishi Kapoor), are the sons of Namdev; John's buddy is Damodar's son Vikram (S. Sinha); the dead band musician had two daughters: the singer Asha (Malini) and schoolgirl Kim (Kim). Namdev was not killed after all and later resurfaces as the henchman of the ultimate crime boss, Don (Puri). Unlike Desai's other Bachchan films (cf ***Amar Akbar Anthony***, 1977), the convoluted plot and the multitude of characters overwhelms the superstar along with everyone else in the film. The film's shots gradually become shorter and by the second half of the story, two seconds seems an average shot-length. The dialogue accompanying the surfeit of physical action merely conveys information as quickly as possible. Desai's virtual abandonment of narrative structure is complemented by innumerable references to his own as well as to other films and tv commercials. Bachchan sings at a celebration of Desai's earlier ***Dharam Veer*** (1977); Charles Bronson's *Hard Times* aka *The Streetfighter* (1975) is replicated in Bachchan's second profession as a boxer; *The Towering Inferno* (1974) is evoked as a revolving restaurant goes up in flames; in the last song the heroes are dressed as a matador (Bachchan), a cossack (Sinha) and as Chaplin (Rishi Kapoor).

ORIDATHORU PHAYALWAN

aka *There Lived a Wrestler*
1981 128' col Malayalam
d/s **P. Padmarajan** *pc* Thundathil Films *c* Vipin Das *m* Johnson
lp Rashid, Jayanthi, K.G. Devakiamma, Venu

Lightweight folk parable, apparently derived from the director's childhood memories, about success and failure in the life of a wrestler (Rashid). Partronised by the village tailor, he becomes a local hero when he overcomes all opponents and claims the prettiest woman (Jayanthi) as his wife. One of the cinematic highlights is the hero's primitive courtship dance in the traditional wrestling style, flexing his muscles as he throws his new bride in the air. However, his muscular prowess is offset by sexual inadequacy, and he has to leave the village. A novelist and frequent collaborator of **B.G. Bharathan**, Padmarajan presents the wrestler as a catalyst for change: the sleepy tailor transforms into a shrewd businessman and an old woman learns to guard her hens which kept disappearing whenever the wrestler grew hungry.

PEHLA ADHYAY

aka *Pahala Adhyay*
1981 130' col Hindi
d/co-sc **Vishnu Mathur** *pc* Dhwanyalok Films *st/co-sc* C.S. Lakshmi aka Ambai, from her Tamil short story, *Milechan* *c* Navroze Contractor
lp Dinesh Shakul, Jyoti Ranadive, Madan Jain, Rashmi Sethi, Madan Bawaria, Debu Parekh, P.C. Sethi, Kamala Sethi, Anant Bhave, Madhav Sathe

Mathur's debut is an avant-garde feature about Ravi (Dinesh Shakul), a young man from a small village who goes to Bombay University and finds himself unable to relate to life in the city. Unable to connect with the city, Ravi tries to establish contact with a fellow student but his sense of being 'out of place' remains until his pent-up anxieties and fears explode into a violent physical outburst and breakdown. The film ends on a cautious note of optimism as Ravi seems to recover. Mathur tries to make the lived and obscurely threatening sensations of displacement into the very substance of the film. He avoids the way questions of belonging are usually formulated in communitarian terms (religion, class, national or regional identity, etc.). The film was not released. Mathur's next major film, made years later, was ***The Flying Bird*** (1989).

POKKUVEYIL

aka *Twilight*
1981 106' col Malayalam
d/co-s **Govindan Aravindan** *p* K. Ravindranathan Nair *pc* General Pics *co-s* Dr Ramesh *c* **Shaji N. Karun** *m* Rajeev Taranath
lp Balachandran Chullikad, Satish, Ansar, Kalpana, Vijayalakshmi, V.P. Nair

A poignant story of urban life showing a young artist living with his father, a radical friend and a music-loving young woman. The father dies, the radical has to flee and the woman is taken by her family to another city. The boy's world collapses: he becomes prey to hallucinations and ends up in an asylum where he is visited by his mother. The film, mostly told in flashback, betrays the nature-mystic Aravindan's distrust of urban living.

RAJA PARVAI

1981 144' col Tamil
d **Singeetham Srinivasa Rao** *pc* Haazan Bros. *s* Hazan K, Santhanabharaty *lyr* **Kannadasan**, **Vairamuthu**, Gangai Amaran *c* Barun Mukherjee *m* **Ilaiyaraja**
lp **L.V. Prasad**, **Kamalahasan**, Madhavi, Nirmala, KPAC Lalitha, Y.G. Mahendran, Delhi Ganesh

A major Kamalahasan melodrama in which he plays a blind musician oppressed since infancy by his evil stepmother. Nancy (Madhavi) falls in love with him, but her father David forces her to marry someone else. The happy ending sees the lovers elope on a scooter with the aid of Nancy's grandfather (Prasad). Kamalahasan apparently persuaded the producer, director and ex-actor Prasad to come out of retirement for this role. Both the direction and Kamalahasan's performance are unabashedly melodramatic, milking the hero's disability for all its worth, and Srinivasa Rao's notorious zooms and cutaways underlined by rapid and awkward editing are fully in evidence. Unusually, the credits list everyone in a single rolling title sequence without assigning individual credits.

RANGANAYAKI

1981 196' col/scope Kannada
d **S.R. Puttana Kanagal** *pc* Ashok Arts *c* Maruthi Rao *m* M. Ranga Rao
lp **Arathi**, Ashok, Ambarish, Rajanand, Ramakrishna, Musari Krishnamurthy

Kanagal's epic features Arathi's most famous performance: she plays a stage actress in the folk theatre who marries a rich man (Ramakrishna) and ostensibly adapts to the required upper-class lifestyle. Her intense desire to perform on the stage is rekindled when her old theatre group arrives in her city. She agrees to replace one of the actresses in an emergency. The sexual release she experiences in acting emerges forcefully during a street procession when she appears to be ' possessed', to the intense embarrassment of her husband. Her obsession with acting leads to a divorce and her husband gets custody of their son. Having become a film star, she has an affair (coyly presented in the film) with a sexy young man (Ashok) who turns out to be her son. In a drawn out climax, the son tries to reconcile his parents but arrives too late to prevent his mother's suicide. Kanagal extensively used hand-held camerawork and a distorting wide-angle lens which, in a CinemaScope frame, creates a disturbingly unsettling space, aggravated by the primary colour schemes. The film's publicity claimed it showed the backstage world of the old **Company Natak**.

SADGATI

aka *Deliverance*
1981 52' col Hindi
d/sc/co-dial/m **Satyajit Ray** *pc* **Doordarshan** *st* Munshi Premchand *co-dial* Amrit Rai *c* Soumendu Roy
lp **Om Puri**, Mohan Agashe, **Smita Patil**, Richa Mishra, Geeta Siddharth, Bhaiyalal Hedao

Short film, derived from a Premchand short story, made as a companion piece to ***Pikoo*** (1980) for **Doordarshan**. The indolent Brahmin Ghashiram (Agashe) gets the low-caste bonded labourer Dukhi (Puri) to perform several onerous tasks while denying him food. While chopping a giant log with a blunt axe, as instructed, Dukhi dies of exhaustion, leaving a grieving widow (Patil) and child in the village. Ghashiram, in a muddy and rain-soaked landscape, is last seen dragging the corpse away. In casting actors associated with the Bombay-based New Indian Cinema (Puri, Agashe, Patil) for this rural drama, Ray made a belated contribution to the 70s rural-exploitation melodrama, a genre eventually adopted by Doordarshan.

SEETHAKOKA CHILAKA

1981 140' col Telugu
d/st **Bharathirajaa** *pc* Poornodaya Movie Creations *dial* Jandhyala *lyr* Veeturi Sundara Ramamurthy *c* Kannan *m* **Ilaiyaraja**
lp Murali Karthik, Aruna, **K. Jaggaiah**, Sarat Babu, Janaki Jr, Smita

Musical fantasy addressing communal harmony. Raghu (Karthik), the son of a Brahmin widow, falls in love with the Christian woman Karuna (Aruna). Karuna's brother (Sarat Babu), who does not like Raghu, warns him to keep away from his sister and to leave the village. Later the priest of the local church intervenes and both Raghu and Karuna abandon their respective religions to be able to live together.

SILSILA

1981 182' col Hindi
d/co-sc **Yash Chopra** *pc* Yash Raj Films *st* Preeti Bedi *co-sc* Sagar Sarhadi *lyr* **Javed Akhtar**, Rajendra Krishan, Hassan Kamal, Nida Fazli, Harivanshrai Bachchan *c* Kay Gee *m* Shiv-Hari
lp **Amitabh Bachchan**, **Shashi Kapoor**, Jaya Bhaduri, **Rekha**, Sanjeev Kumar

Shobha (Bhaduri) is in love with the air force officer Shekhar (Kapoor). Shekhar's younger brother Amit (Bachchan) writes poetry and plays and woos Chandni (Rekha). Shekhar dies in the war, leaving Shobha pregnant. Amit sacrifices his love for Chandni to marry Shobha and save her reputation. Chandni marries a doctor (Kumar) in the town where Amit and Shobha live. The ex-lovers meet in an accident in which Shobha loses her baby. Amit and Chandni have an affair while their marital partners suffer in silence. The lovers elope after a highly stylised confrontation between the two women (the two rivals standing back to back). The film features Bachchan's alleged offscreen lover Rekha and his wife Bhaduri (who came out of retirement to play the part). Several scenes appear designed to fuel or to exploit the gossip journalism which underpins and surrounds film careers. In the end, the sanctity of marriage triumphs and the original married couples are restored. Bachchan sang his own songs and declaimed numerous poetic couplets addressed to Chandni, fully exploiting a key aspect of his star persona: his deep baritone voice. Songs picturised in Dutch tulip fields help promote Rekha's image as a glamorous but unattainable object of desire.

SUPATTAR BINANI

1981 153' col Rajasthani
d/sc Satyen *pc* Amrit Kalash Prod. *st/dial/lyr/m* Mahendra Pujari *c* Balbir
lp Shirish Kumar, Neelu, Kshitij, Vijaya, Atmaram, Manjula, Padma Khanna

After a long commercially fallow period, Satyen's hit re-established the Rajasthani cinema. The modern Ramakant (Kumar) is forced by his rich orthodox father to marry the illiterate Munga (Neelu). Ramakant's greedy uncle and aunt urge him to abandon his wife and to marry the modern Kavita who stands to inherit a fortune. Ramakant almost kills his exemplary, long-suffering wife before orthodoxy triumphs. Neelu went on to become Rajasthan's top star with neo-traditionalist melodramas like *Chokho Lage Sasariyo* (1983), ***Nanand Bhojai*** (1985), *Bhikaoo Tordo* (1987) and *Lichhmi Ayi Angane* (1992).

THANNEER THANNEER

aka *Water Water*
1981 143' col Tamil
d/sc **K. Balachander** *pc* Kalakendra Movies *st* **Komal Swaminathan**'s play *lyr* **Vairamuthu** *c* B.S. Lokanathan *m* M.S. Vishwanathan
lp Saritha, V.K. Veeraswami, Shanmugham, M.R. Radha Devi

Shot on location and set in Athipattu, a drought-stricken hamlet in Southern TN, Balachander's political film tells of the villagers' desperate attempts to obtain water in the face of corrupt politicians and their servants, including the police. The villagers protect a communist fugitive from justice and later give him money to buy a bullock with which to bring water from a spring 20 miles away. The man persuades them to dig a canal, an initiative obstructed by government officials. The villagers then decide to boycott elections (a tactic tried in Thanjavur a year after the film's release), but in the end the police act against them for defying orders and corruption triumphs. The film's effort at a stark realism, esp. in the use of Southern Tamil dialect, goes alongside an agit-prop stage style borrowed from Swaminathan's original play, e.g. when villagers hand a

Saritha in *Thanneer Thanneer*

petition to a minister, he gives it to his assistant, who hands it to a district collector, who passes it to his orderly, who puts it in his pocket. The Tamil Nadu Information Minister, R.M. Veerappan, calling for a ban on the film, said that 'the law enforcement ministry had never used arms against people who made efforts to get their water supply'.

36 CHOWRINGHEE LANE

1981 122'(113') col English
d/s **Aparna Sen** *p* **Shashi Kapoor** *pc* Film Valas *c* Ashok Mehta *m* **Vanraj Bhatia**
lp Jennifer Kendal, **Dhritiman Chatterjee**, Debashree Roy, Geoffrey Kendal, Soni Razdan, Dina Ardeshir, Fae Soares, Reny Roy, Sylvia Philips

Aparna Sen's directorial debut, made in English, relies heavily on Bansi Chandragupta's art direction for her film on loneliness and old age. An Anglo-Indian schoolteacher, Violet Stoneham (Kendal) lives a solitary life teaching Shakespeare, her major obsession, to schoolgirls. She invites Samaresh (Chatterjee) to write his novel in her house but instead he uses the place to make love to his girlfriend Nandita (D. Roy). The couple constitute Violet's principal interaction with the outside world. The lovers get married and no longer need the flat. The teacher reconciles herself to further loneliness on Christmas Day while the soundtrack plays *Silent night, holy night*. Presented as a European-style character study (reminiscent of Rene Allio's *La Vieille dame indigne*, 1965, and of the Merchant-Ivory films with which producer Kapoor was also associated), the film has often elicited charges of colonial nostalgia. The Indian version includes scenes removed from the British release version, e.g. a sequence with Violet's cat atop the lavatory cistern.

THYAGAYYA

1981 143' col Telugu
d **Bapu** *pc* Navata Cine Arts *sc* Mullapudi Venkatramana *c* Baba Azmi *m* K.V. Mahadevan
lp J.V. Somayajulu, Ravu Gopala Rao, Rallapalli, M.B.K.V. Prasada Rao, K.R. Vijaya, Rohini

Bapu's remake of **Chittor V. Nagaiah**'s classic **Saint film** (1946) adapted his mythological style to the notion of classicism proposed by **Vishwanath**'s ***Shankarabharanam*** (1979). The latter film's star, Somayajulu, here plays the Telugu saint Thyagaraja (1767-1847) who defies Serfoji, the king of Tanjore. When the hero's sister-in-law Ganga steals his precious deity and throws it in the Kaveri river, the saint goes on a pilgrimage in search of his god. Several divine interventions later (filmed in Bapu's typical frontal-address mythological style) and following the death of his wife Kamala, the saint eventually transforms into a sanyasi, a renouncer. Unlike the pre-Independence versions of the genre, this film exemplifies the essential requirement of a neo-traditional 'authenticity' in terms of contemporary caste for the cinema Vishwanath and others pioneered. Here **S.P. Balasubramanyam**, who sang the kritis of Thyagaraja, was criticised by Carnatic vocalists for not being classical enough: this attack, unlike those pointing to the performance or soundtrack as the far more obvious instances of pandering to popular taste in the name of 'high' art, appeared to be seen as far more damaging to the film.

UMBARTHA/SUBAH

aka *Threshold* aka *Dawn*
1981 151'[M]/135'[H] col Marathi/Hindi
d/co-p **Jabbar Patel** *co-p* D.V. Rao *pc* Sujatha Chitra *st* Shanta Nisal's novel *Beghar* *sc* **Vijay Tendulkar** *lyr* Vasant Bapat, Suresh Bhatt *c* Rajan Kinagi *m* Hridayanath Mangeshkar
lp **Smita Patil, Girish Karnad**, Shrikant Moghe, Ashalata, Daya Dongre, Kusum Kulkarni, Manorama Wagle, Jayamala Kale, Ravi Patwardhan, Shriram Ranade, Satish Alekar, Purnima Ganu

Smita Patil's best-known screen role features her as Sulabha, the wife of the progressive lawyer Subhash (Karnad). Upset by her husband's willingness to blacken the name of a rape victim in order to benefit his client, accused of committing the rape, Sulabha decides to take charge of a Mahilashram (women's home). There she has to contend with the gross corruption and greed which further exploits and victimises the women in her care. The governors of the institution eventually make life so difficult for Sulabha that she has to resign. When she returns home, her husband informs her that he has taken a mistress and intends to keep her. Sulabha leaves her home determined to make a life for herself. Based on an autobiographical work by Shanta Nisal, the film was given a feminist value by Smita Patil's performance and by her use of the film in campaigns for women's rights. The feminist historian Susie Tharu expressed reservations about the film's presentation of the lead character: 'The filmic focus, emphasised by several close-ups of Sulabha sitting, toying with her glasses, looking up, walking, sitting again [e]stablishes her as the central character as well as the problem (the disruption, the enigma) the film will explore and resolve. In *Umbartha* it is clear that to search herself is, for a woman, a tragic enterprise. An enterprise in which she is doomed to fail, but can fail bravely and heroically. Such a perspective [i]nevitably poses the problem in such a way that the solutions come from the individual, more specifically from the individual's personality or character. We sense a vague structural similarity [b]etween Sulabha's own predicament and that of the destitute or abandoned women in the Home. But the parallel is never clear because while one motif is explored psychologically the other is given a rather crude sociological interpretation' (1986).

UMRAO JAAN

1981 145' col Urdu
d/co-sc **Muzaffar Ali** *pc* Integrated Films *st* Meer Hadi Hassan Rusva's novel *Umrao Jaan Ada* (1899) *sc* Shama Zaidi, Javed Siddiqui *lyr* Shahryar *c* Pravin Bhatt *m* **Khayyam**
lp **Rekha**, Farouque Shaikh, **Naseeruddin Shah**, Raj Babbar, Prema Narayan, Shaukat Kaifi, Dina Pathak, Leela Mishra, **Gajanan Jagirdar**

Based on the first major Urdu novel and possibly (there is controversy about this) the autobiography of a legendary mid-19th C. tawaif (a courtesan who was also an accomplished and respected musician and dancer) from Lucknow. Abducted as a child and sold in Lucknow, Umrao Jaan (Rekha) is trained in music and dance. She grows up to become immensely popular with the elite of the city, falls in love with an aristocrat nawab (Shaikh), then finds companionship with her childhood friend Gauhar Mirza (Shah), finally escaping her claustrophobic life with the bandit Faiz Ali (Babbar). Aijaz Ahmad (1992) notes about the novel that: 'The scandal of Rusva's text is its proposition that since such a woman depends upon no one man, and because many depend on her, she is the only relatively free woman in our society. Rusva was a very traditional man, and he was simply tired of certain kinds of moral posturing'. Ahmad sees the continuation of this motif of the free woman in the work of the **PWA** in the 30s. Muzaffar Ali recreated the image of the Urdu costume spectacular around the star Rekha while Bansi Chandragupta's sets and Khayyam's music endow the film with a sense of opulence enhancing the star's performance (as well as overshadowing her limitations as a dancer). Includes many popular ghazals sung by **Asha Bhosle**, e.g. *Dil cheez kya hai* and *In ankhon ki masti*.

VALARTHU MRUGANGAL

aka *Performing Beasts*
1981 148'(125') col Malayalam
d **T. Hariharan** *pc* Priyadarshini Movies *s* **M.T. Vasudevan Nair** *c* Mehli Irani *m* **M.B. Srinivasan**
lp Balan K. Nair, Sukumaran, Madhavi, Nagesh

A bleak melodrama involving murder among circus performers. The members of a financially ailing circus troupe join a bigger circus, and find the employees exploited. Trapeze performer Janu falls for a stuntman who is also the employees' representative in their fight for better work conditions. The stuntman is killed in a simulated accident, and his girlfriend tries to commit suicide. The plot was originally written as a short story by scenarist Vasudevan Nair. Director Hariharan was one of the most prolific in the 70s Malayalam cinema, with over 60 features since his debut, *Ladies' Hostel* (1973).

AAROHAN

aka *The Ascending Scale* aka *The Ascent*
1982 147' col Hindi
d **Shyam Benegal** *pc* West Bengal Govt *sc* Shama Zaidi *dial/lyr* Niaz Haidar *c* **Govind Nihalani** *m* Purnadas Baul
lp **Om Puri**, Sreela Majumdar, Victor Bannerjee, **Rajen Tarafdar**, Geeta Sen, Pankaj Kapoor, Khoka Mukherjee

The small farmer Hari Mondal (Puri) supports an extended family working on his little plot of land. When he tries to obtain a loan from his absentee landlord living in Calcutta, Mondal finds himself ensnared in a lengthy legal battle, lasting from 1967 to 1977, to preserve his political rights as a sharecropper. In the process, his family is destroyed. One of the better known of several films produced by the communist government of West Bengal to portray through fiction their political programmes: in this case, Operation Barga, a successful campaign of land for landless tillers. Benegal starts the film with Om Puri introducing himself, the cameraman, scenarist and other crew members who are to enact the performance to follow. The rest of the film, however, once it starts, attempts no further alienation devices except perhaps a spectacular and stagey scene of lightning and floods.

APAROOPA/APEKSHA

1982 124' col Assamese/Hindi
d/p/st/co-sc **Jahnu Barua** *co-sc* J.S. Rao *dial* Jogen Chetia *c* Binod Pradhan *m* **Bhupen Hazarika**
lp Suhasini Mulay, Biju Phukan, **Girish Karnad**

Barua's technically accomplished debut feature is a stylish low-key melodrama set in the colonial upper-class society of Assam's tea gardens. Aparoopa (Mulay) foregoes her education to marry the rich Mr Barua to whom her father owes money. Her boredom and anxiety become unbearable on the arrival of an old college friend and military officer who offers her an escape route.

ARTH

1982 143' col Hindi
d/st/dial/co-sc **Mahesh Bhatt** *pc* Anu Arts *co-sc* Sujit Sen *lyr* **Kaifi Azmi** *c* Pravin Bhatt *m* Chitra Singh, Jagjit Singh
lp **Shabana Azmi**, **Smita Patil**, Kulbhushan Kharbanda, Raj Kiran, Rohini Hattangadi, Siddharth Kak, Geeta Siddharth

Inder Malhotra (Kharbanda), a fashionable film-maker, is married to Pooja (Azmi) when he starts an affair with film star Kavita (Patil). Pooja leaves him and experiences the social insecurities of a single working woman. Her dilemmas are highlighted by the parallel story of her cleaning lady (Hattangadi) who, abandoned by her husband, kills him and is arrested. Kavita, who suffers from guilt and eventually succumbs to schizophrenia, leaves Inder. Bhatt's breakthrough film benefited both from gossip suggesting, with Bhatt's assistance, that it was autobiographical, and of a much-publicised rivalry between actresses Patil and Azmi. Bhatt continued producing sensationalised versions of wicked upper-class Bombay life, peppered with inane talk about art cinema (as in this film's party sequence), paralleling, e.g., gossip columnist Shobha De's novels set in the film and advertising industries.

CHOKH

aka *The Eyes*
1982 98' col Bengali
d/s/m **Utpalendu Chakraborty** *pc* West Bengal Govt *c* Shakti Bannerjee
lp **Om Puri**, Shyamanand Jalan, **Anil Chatterjee**, Sreela Majumdar, Asit Mukherjee, Dipak Sarkar, **Madhabi Chakraborty**

When in 1975, during the Emergency, a union leader, Jadunath, is falsely accused of murder and hanged, he bequeaths his eyes to a blind worker. The surgeon Dr Mukherjee, who has to perform the operation, is put under severe pressure by the factory owner Diethyl who instigated the judicial killing of Jadunath and who now wants an eye donor for his own son. When Diethyl learns who the eyes belonged to, he orders them to be destroyed in the hope that the revolutionary fire that burned in them may be extinguished forever. The surgeon resists the order but eventually has to comply while outside the hospital, Jadunath's widow and demonstrating workers advance on the police cordon surrounding the surgery. The demagogic film by-passes the cinematic potential of the motif of 'vision' in favour of low-angle shots with wide-angle lenses together with a high-volume expressionist soundtrack.

DHRUPAD

1982 72' col Hindi
d/p **Mani Kaul** *pc* Infrakino Film *c* Virendra Saini
lp Zia Mohiuddin Dagar, Zia Fariduddin Dagar

Kaul's documentary on Dhrupad, the famous North Indian form of classical music. Its foremost living practitioners are members of the Dagar family. The film features the director's own music teachers, Zia Mohiuddin Dagar on the rudra veena and his younger brother Fariduddin Dagar as vocalist. The music itself, unlike its successor form, the khayal, is austere and rigidly defined with, e.g., precise rules for its elaboration from the formalist alaap (which includes no words and no external rhythmic accompaniment) to the faster and more celebratory drut. Its central tenet is that of freedom achieved within a rigid rule-bound structure through a continuous musical scale and the use of notes mainly as approximations rather than as absolutes (as in Western traditions). The film attempts to explore the musical form through the cinematic orchestration of space and light. It includes sequences suggesting Dhrupad's tribal musical origins and some remarkable scenes in Jaipur's Jantar Mantar observatory. The bravura ending has a long shot descending from the sky into the urban metropolis, weaving through concrete rooftops as the camera pulls slowly out of focus. The critic Shanta Gokhale commented: 'Classical Indian music is to Mani Kaul the purest artistic search. The alaap or slow unfolding of a raga (melody) to get its innermost swaroop (form), is its finest expression. Just as a good musician has mastered the musical method of construction which saves his delineation of a raga from becoming formless, so a good film-maker has a firm control over cinematic methods of construction and can therefore allow himself to improvise.'

EE NADU

1982 181' col/scope Malayalam
d **I.V. Sasi** *pc* Geo Movie Prod. *p* N.G. John *s* T. Damodaran *lyr* Yusuf Ali Kacheri *c* S.S. Chandramohan, C.E. Babu *m* Shyam
lp **Mammootty**, Balan K. Nair, T.G. Ravi, Ratheesh, Anjali, Surekha, Vanitha, Krishnachandran

Sasi's opus about Kerala politics. Karunakaran (Ravi), the corrupt Congress politician, and Venu (Ratheesh), a member of the Legislative Assembly, run a major nexus of crime with the assistance of the police and state bureaucracy. Karunakaran's son, a student gangster, tries to rape the girlfriend of his colleague Shashi in the college, leading to her suicide. In order to defeat their Left opponents, the corrupt politicians engineer the mass distribution of adulterated liquor, causing large-scale deaths. Eventually Salim (Mammootty), a Dubai-returned youth impoverished by prevalent conditions, leads a revolution, along with Krishna Pillai (Balan K. Nair), the good trade unionist/politician and a reference to the Kerala CPI leader P. Krishna Pillai. The people are successful, however, only because Karunakaran's wife Sridevi offers evidence of her husband's murderous activities. From the titles, which are intercut with a CPI(M) march, to the final confrontation as Venu is forced by the people to withdraw his bid for the chief minister's post, the film unabashedly locates the villains as representing the corrupt Congress governments that have ruled the state. The good, on the other hand, become politicised in support of the Left for a variety of reasons that include religious, caste and economic oppression. Much of the plot makes direct reference to contemporary events, including the notorious 'blade' finance companies and the liquor deaths, that have been (with the corruption) key issues in Kerala politics. The film packs in a massive number of characters in a variety of situations including political meetings, backdoor bargaining, press conferences and the inevitable drinking sessions, which it usually wraps up with a few fast-paced talking heads shots, with the demagoguery underlined by a relentless music track.

EZHAVATHU MANITHAN

aka *The Seventh Man*
1982 125' col Tamil
d/sc K. Hariharan *p/st* Palai N. Shanmugham *pc* Lata Creations *dial* Somasundareswar, Arunmozhi *lyr* Subramanya Bharati *c* Dharma *m* Vaithilaxman
lp Raghuvaran, Ratna, Satyajit, Deepak, Anita Mathews, Satyendra, Ranga

First feature of Hariharan, a former member of the YUKT Film Coop (***Ghashiram Kotwal***, 1976), who went on to become an eminent Tamil film critic. The film tells of labour/management conflicts in a Tirunelveli district village, the home of the legendary late 19th C. Tamil poet Bharati (cf **DMK Film**) whose poems are featured in the movie, contrasting his utopian vision with contemporary conditions. The central figure is an engineer, Anand (Raghuvaran), who becomes the main activist for social justice in a cement factory with connections to a callous moneylender and his cronies. In line with traditional Tamil plot structures, the villain Seth and the hero are after the same woman, Gouri. The villains even plan to set the factory on fire hoping to blame the workers and to claim the insurance, but the plan misfires. The film was apparently inspired by Martin Ritt's *Norma Rae* (1979).

GRIHAJUDDHA

aka *Crossroads*, aka *The Crossroad*
1982 98' col Bengali
d/sc/m **Buddhadev Dasgupta** *pc* West Bengal Govt *st* Dibyendu Palit *c* Sambit Bose
lp Anjan Dutt, Mamata Shankar, Gautam Ghosh, Prabir Guha, Manoj Mitra, Monidipa Roy, Sunil Mukherjee

Costa-Gavras-type political thriller continuing Dasgupta's efforts to address the nexus between private lives and politics, evolving a kind of morality fable about sexual and comradely relationships (e.g. ***Dooratwa***, 1978). The corrupt owner of a steel factory has his labour officer killed and then hires thugs to murder Prabir, a left-wing trade union worker. Prabir's impoverished sister Nirupama (Shankar) loves her brother's friend and comrade Bijon. The journalist Sandipan's investigation is blocked by the paper's owners and eventually he too is killed. Bijon, now a successful salesman in distant Nasik, finds the gulf between himself and the politically committed Nirupama too wide to allow their marriage.

KATHA

aka *The Tale* aka *The Fable*
1982 141' col Hindi
d/s **Sai Paranjpye** *pc* Devki Chitra *lyr* Indu Jain *c* Virendra Saini *m* Rajkamal
lp **Naseeruddin Shah**, Farouque Shaikh, Deepti Naval, Mallika Sarabhai, Leela Mishra, Nitin Sethi, Arun Joglekar, Winnie Paranjpye-Joglekar

Satire adapted from the director's own play *Sakkhe Shejari*, and inspired by the tale of the hare and the tortoise. Set in a lower-middle-class tenement in Bombay, it features the slow-but-sure upwardly mobile clerk Rajaram (Shah), who loves his neighbour Sandhya (Deepti Naval). The energetic Basu (Shaikh) arrives and dazzles everyone with his go-getting charm. He rapidly acquires three girlfriends: Sandhya, Anuradha (Sarabhai), Rajaram's boss's 2nd wife, and Jojo, the boss's daughter. When things get too hot, Basu departs for new pastures and life settles down again in the tenement. The fairly successful musical included signs on the screen officially censoring some of the lewd jokes presumably being told.

KHARIJ

aka *The Case is Closed*
1982 95' col Bengali
d/sc **Mrinal Sen** *pc* Neelkanth Films *st* Ramapada Choudhury *c* K.K. Mahajan *m* **B.V. Karanth**
lp Anjan Dutt, Mamata Shankar, Indranil Moitra, Debrapatim Dasgupta, Sreela Majumdar, Nilotpal Dey, Bimal Chatterjee, Chakruprakash Ghosh

Whereas ***Chaalchitra*** (1981) addresses the middle-class living conditions in Calcutta as a comedy, here Sen returns to the same theme in a darker mood. A young servant boy is locked in the kitchen in an apartment block and dies. The social networks prevailing in the neighbourhood are thrown into relief during the police investigation. Selfishness and guilt create a nightmarish atmosphere heightened by the arrival of the boy's father from a small village. In the end, the post-mortem reveals the boy died of carbon monoxide poisoning caused by a coal stove in the cramped room. In an ending reminiscent of ***Ek Din Pratidin*** (1979), as soon as the protagonists feel let off the hook, all the problems are promptly swept back under the carpet. In this second Calcutta trilogy, Sen deploys a critical yet compassionate look at his own social milieu and described the films as a form of autocritique. The flamboyant narrative style of the earlier Calcutta trilogy (starting with ***Interview***, 1970) has been replaced by a more reflective but equally intense approach relying on framing and camera movement to emphasise the interactions between people's mentality and their living conditions. The relations between people and the spaces they inhabit (a series of Chinese boxes) becomes the driving force of a narrative proceeding with a sense of coiled energy constantly threatening to tear the fabric of daily life.

MARMARAM

aka *Rumbling*
1982 113' col Malayalam
d **Bharathan** *pc* P.N. Films *sc* John Paul *st* Vijayan Karot *c* Ramchandra *m* M.S. Vishwanathan
lp Nedumudi Venu, **Gopi**, Jalaja, Jose, Saira Banu

A sensitive and progressive headmaster, Narayana Iyer (Venu), falls in love with the school's music teacher, the lower-caste Nirmala (Jalaja), whose husband is a political activist (Gopi) on the run and whose child is looked after by her parents in her home village. Narayana overcomes his own prejudices and endures his orthodox mother's disapproval. When Nirmala's husband is shot by the police, Narayana consoles Nirmala and their love for each other triumphs over all social and emotional obstacles. The young but prolific director described the film as, 'The melodious murmur of two people who love each other with all their hearts'.

MASOOM

aka *Innocent*
1982 143' col Hindi
d **Shekhar Kapur** *pc* Krsna Movies Ents *s/lyr* **Gulzar** *c* Pravin Bhatt *m* **R.D. Burman**
lp **Shabana Azmi, Naseeruddin Shah, Saeed Jaffrey**, Tanuja, Supriya Pathak, Jugal Hansraj, Urmila, Aradhana, P. Jairaj, Rajan, Satish Kaushik, Pran Talwar, Anila Singh

Marital melodrama featuring Shah as D.K. Malhotra, living happily with his wife Indu (Azmi) and their two daughters, Rinky and Minnie, when a boarding school asks him to come and fetch his son. Replying that he has no son, he later realises that the boy Rahul (Hansraj) is the fruit of a brief affair he had with the terminally ill Bhavna (Pathak). Unbeknown to D.K., Bhavna had raised the child. Now she is dead and D.K. and his wife are forced to adopt the boy, shattering the couple's peaceful life. Indu finally accepts the boy and D.K. at last has a male child in his family. Kapur's glossy directing debut benefits by the children's uninhibited performances which endeared the film to a predominantly urban middle-class audience. Although the film addresses the question of illegitimacy in a humane manner, it also sidesteps the knottier aspects of the problem by making the illegitimate child a boy and by requiring the wife to accept the fruit of her husband's infidelity rather than the other way around.

MEGHA SANDESAM

aka *The Cloud Messenger*
1982 151' col Telugu
d/s/co-lyr **Dasari Narayana Rao** *pc* Dasari Padma, Taraka Prabhu Films *co-lyr* **Devulapalli Krishna Sastry**, Veeturi Sundara Ramamurthy, Palagummi Padmaraju *c* P.S. Selvaraj *m* Ramesh Naidu
lp **A. Nageshwara Rao**, Jayapradha, Jayasudha, **K. Jaggaiah**, Subhashini

Dasari's art-house melodrama shows the influence of ***Shankarabharanam*** (1979) on Telugu film. It invents a legend recalling Sternberg's *Der blaue engel* (1930): an upright and much-loved poet, Ravindrababu (Nageshwara Rao) falls in love with the courtesan Padma (Jayapradha). He composes several poems praising her, proving to his wife that he needs Padma to survive as an artist. Sacrificing herself to his talent, the wife urges her husband to move in with his lover. However, when the poet's daughter marries, Padma persuades him to go back to his wife. Overcome with remorse, Ravindrababu dies. Padma dies at the same time to confirm their profound unity. It remains Dasari's best-known film outside AP. Apparently a homage to the Telugu lyricist Devulapalli Krishna Sastri who died shortly before the film was made and whose songs (e.g. *Akulo akunai, Sigalo avi virulo, Mundu telisena*) were reset to music by Ramesh Naidu and became very popular.

MOONDRAM PIRAI

1982 143' col Tamil
d/s/c **Balu Mahendra** *pc* Satyajyothi Films *lyr* **Vairamuthu** *m* **Ilaiyaraja**
lp **Kamalahasan, Sridevi**, Silk Smitha

Mahendra's best-known film is a morality tale about a schoolteacher (Kamalahasan) who rescues a mentally deranged woman (Sridevi) from a brothel and looks after her in his hillside home. While the crazed woman becomes devoted to him, he struggles to keep his sexual desire in check. The libidinal tensions culminate in an orgiastic dream sequence attributed to the headmaster's sexually frustrated wife (Silk Smitha) who desires the hero: she erupts into a sinuous, hip-swinging dance around a tree (and the teacher) on a bare hill. According to film-maker and critic K. Hariharan, the plot's main problem, left in suspension, is not that the hero rescues the heroine from a brothel, but that he visits the brothel in the first place, which puts a different light on the ending when the prostitute recovers and departs, leaving the hero on the verge of insanity. Mahendra remade the film with its original cast in Hindi as *Sadma* (1983).

Gopi (standing, left) and Madhavi (centre) in *Ormakkayi*

ORMAKKAYI

aka *In Your Memory*
1982 113' col Malayalam
d/co-s **Bharathan** *p* David Kachapally, Innocent *pc* Pankaj Movie Makers *co-s* John Paul *lyr* Madhu Alleppey *c* Vasant Kumar *m* Johnson
lp **Adoor Bhasi**, Madhavi, **Gopi**, Nedumudi Venu, Krishnachandran, Ramu, Innocent, Lalitha

The story, told in flashback during a scooter ride through the city on a bleak and rainy day, of Susanna's (Madhavi) tragic life. Recently released from prison, she looks for her little daughter in the city's orphanage. Her story involves the death of her pleasure-loving Anglo-Indian father, her marriage to the kindly deaf-and-dumb painter Nandagopal and the unwelcome advances of the pop singer Peter Lal. In a scuffle, both Peter and Nandagopal are killed, causing Susanna to be put in jail and her daughter in an orphanage.

PHANIYAMMA

1982 118' col Kannada
d/p/sc **Prema Karanth** *pc* Babukodi Movies *st* M.K. Indira *c* Madhu Ambat *m* **B.V. Karanth**
lp L.V. Sharada Rao, Baby Pratima, Pratibha Kasaravalli, Archana Rao, Dasharathi Dixit, H.N. Chandru, Vishwanath Rao, Kesargodu Chinna, Shri Pramila, **Anant Nag**

Stage personality Prema Karanth's directorial debut, adapting a major novel by Kannada author M.K. Indira (1976). The novel's protagonist, a mid-19th C. widow, resurrects a stereotype from reformist fiction, drawing 'its emotional capital from powerful and deeply embedded cultural formations and is emblematic of the way Swadeshi formulations of gender, nation and indeed feminism have reappeared and are renotated in the literature of the late 70s and 80s' (Susie Tharu/K. Lalitha, 1993). Based on the actual life story of Phaniyamma who from 1870 to her death in 1952 lived in the village of Hebbalige in Malnad, Karnataka. The woman's story was told to M.K. Indira's mother when Phaniyamma came to help her give birth to a child. Born into an upper-caste and respected family, Phani (Sharada Rao) is married aged 9 to a young relative who dies shortly afterwards. Having suffered the cruel conventions imposed upon widows throughout her childhood, Phani eventually grows into a strong, quiet and wise woman to whom many people come for help and advice. Flouting caste rules, she helps an Untouchable woman give birth to a child and stands by a young woman who, when widowed at the age of 16, rebels against the harsh norms imposed by an orthodox society. Mostly told in flashback, the film conveys the spirit of the original work through Sharada Rao's dignified performance, suggesting not a radical critique of orthodox society but a purification of tradition adapted to modern conditions (evoked in the film through tight close-ups, e.g. in the opening childbirth sequence, and fast-paced editing).

SEETA RAATI

aka *Winter Night*
1982 105' b&w Oriya
d/co-s **Manmohan Mahapatra** *pc* Varatee Pics *co-s* Bibhuti Patnaik *c* Ranajit Ray *m* Shantanu Mahapatra
lp Arun Nanda, Mahashweta Roy, Hemanta Das, Sadhu Meher, Subrat Mahapatra, Samuel Sahu, Pinku

Melancholy film-novelette set in rural Orissa. The rich Pranab (Nanda) loves the poor Aruna (Roy) but class differences keep them apart. Their story is woven into the cultural divide between the city and the village and into rural politics. Eventually the woman realises that the class gap cannot be overcome and she resigns herself to her fate. Mahapatra's feature debut inaugurated the New Indian Cinema type of ruralist realism in Oriya.

SHELTER

1982 42' b&w English
d/s/c Uma Segal *pc* **FTII**

The only film, made while still a student, by the promising cinematographer and director Uma Segal, who died in 1991. The film deals with slum demolition in Bombay, a major political issue in the early 80s (and also the subject of **Patwardhan**'s ***Hamara Shaher***, 1985). It intercuts interviews with various concerned individuals, and ends with documentary shots of an actual demolition.

VEENA POOVU

aka *Fallen Flower*
1982 133' col Malayalam
d/sc Ambili *p* Surya Prakash *pc* Mithra Film Makers *st* Ravishankar *c* Bipin Mohan *m* Vidyadharan
lp Nedumudi Venu, Shankar Mohan, Babu, Uma, Namboodiri, Seeta, Sukumari

Ambili was a leading art director when he turned director with this film about a young musician who falls in love with Sumangala, the daughter of an impoverished Brahmin in a village of the Namboodiri community. Obeying her father, the young woman marries a mentally retarded member of her own community. The drama is further heightened by first equating Sumangala with the mystificatory folk rituals the musician sets out to discover, and then by the book of poems in which he expresses her condition. The lovers remain separated, with dire consequences, especially for the woman.

YAVANIKA
aka *The Curtain Falls*
1982 147' col Malayalam
d/st/co-sc **K.G. George** *p* Henry *pc* Carolina Films *co-s* **S.L. Puram Sadanandan** *c* Ramchandra *m* **M.B. Srinivasan**
lp **Gopi**, Jalaja, **Mammootty**, Venu Nagavalli, Nedumudi Venu, Tilakan, Jagathi, Shrikumar, Ashok

A story, told like a thriller, about touring players and the sense of claustrophobia that encompasses their violent lives. The plot is structured around the search for the unpopular tabla player of the Bhavana Touring Theatre in Kerala. He turns up as a murder victim. The subsequent police investigation reveals the complicated sexual rivalries and internal dissensions within the group, yielding several possible suspects. George said that in using the thriller form, situated in a theatrical context, he wanted to contextualise and thereby overcome the conventionally 'stagey' format of Malayalam film.

ABHILASHA
1983 159' col Oriya
d/p/co-st/sc Sadhu Meher *pc* Shanti Films *co-st* Ramesh Mohanty *dial* Purna Mohanty *lyr/m* Saroj Patnaik *c* Suresh Patel
lp Uttam Mohanty, Aparajita, Sujata, Jaya, Byomkesh Tripathi, Niranjan, Satapathy, Sadhu Meher

Medical students Chinmay (Mohanty) and Anuradha (Aparajita) get married but disagree on their professional priorities: Chinmay starts a clinic in the village while his wife stays in the city. The hero faces opposition from the local medicine man (Meher) and from Gajanan, the villainous son of the zamindar, who eventually has Chinmay killed. Anuradha continues the hero's good work. The debut feature of Meher, better known as the Hindi actor who played Shabana Azmi's handicapped husband in ***Ankur*** (1973) and in several **Benegal** films. Meher continued his mentor's style of dialogue, of a naturalist performance idiom and his use of rural locations.

ADAMINTE VARIYELLU
aka *Adam's Rib*
1983 142' col Malayalam
d/st/co-sc **K.G. George** *pc* St Vincent Movies *co-sc* Kallikkadu Ramachandran *lyr* **O.N.V. Kurup** *c* Ramchandra *m* **M.B. Srinivasan**
lp **Suhasini**, Shrividya, Soorya, Rajan K. Nair, **Gopi**, Venu Nagavalli, **Mammootty**, Thilakan

An emphatic film graphically depicting the relentless oppression of women in urban milieus which are presumed to be more liberal than the Draconian conditions prevailing in rural India. The plot tells of three women. Vasanthi has to mother three generations of her family in addition to her daytime job; she eventually escapes into madness and experiences the asylum as a kind of liberation. Alice is married to a ruthless businessman (Gopi) and seeks solace in affairs. When she is refused a divorce, she prefers suicide. Both the middle-class women push their rebellion to self-destruction. The third, however, overcomes her condition: Ammini is a brutally exploited maid in Alice's home. She ends up in a home for women where, in a powerfully utopian ending, she helps her fellow women break out of the suffocating institution and rush right past the camera crew waiting in front of the gates, to freedom.

ADI SHANKARACHARYA
aka *The Philosopher*
1983 156' col Sanskrit
d/s **G.V. Iyer** *pc* **NFDC** *dial* Benanjaya Govindacharya *lyr* Balamurali Krishna *c* Madhu Ambat *m* **B.V. Karanth**
lp Sarvadaman D. Bannerjee, M.V. Narayana Rao, Manjunath Bhatt, Leelamma Narayana Rao, L.V. Sharada Rao, Bharat Bhushan, **T.S. Nagabharana**, Srinivasa Prabhu, Gopal, V.R.K. Prasad, Gopalakrishna, Gayathri Balu, Balasubramanyam, Balu Bhargava

The first film made in Sanskrit. Set in 8th C. Kerala, it tells of Shankara aka Adi Shankaracharya, the best-known Advaita Vedanta (Monism) philosopher to whom over 300 Sanskrit texts are attributed and the subject of numerous biographies. He established a series of religious sites at Badrinath (in the Himalayas), Puri (in Orissa), Dwarka (on the west coast) and Sringeri in South India. The film begins with Shankara as a boy in a village inducted into brahminical rituals. When his father dies, the boy turns to philosophy to try to understand the great mysteries of life and death. He lives as a mendicant and studies Vedic texts. Later, he shies away from marriage and promises his mother that he will remain a devoted son while living as a wandering scholar. The teacher Govinda entrusts Shankara (Bannerjee) with the composition of new Vedic commentaries. Having glimpsed the inner truth of the texts, Shankara becomes an ascetic and travels to the peaks of the Himalayas. Everywhere he goes he is received as a man of infinite wisdom. He eventually founds his own monastery having transcended all earthly illusions, including the rituals of the Brahmin community, and, at the age of 32, he rises from his sickbed and wanders away towards the mountains so that his soul may become one with the Brahma. Continuing his effort after ***Hamsa Geethe*** (1975) towards a brahminical revivalism, Iyer claimed to have made the film in Sanskrit to do justice to the abstractions of Shankara's philosophical thought. The film does away with the miracle scenes typical of the genre and deploys several symbolic figures (e.g. death and wisdom are both personified). The extensive musical track consists of Vedic chants. Iyer went on to make two more **Saint films** featuring two of Shankara's main disciples, *Madhavacharya* (Kannada, 1986) and *Shri Ramanujacharya* (Tamil, 1989). The film did not get a commercial release in India but apparently did very well in foreign markets.

AKKARE
aka *The Other Shore*
1983 118' col Malayalam
d/p/s K.N. Sasidharan *pc* Sooryarekha Film *c* N. Diwakar Menon *m* **M.B. Srinivasan**
lp **Gopi**, Madhavi, **Mammootty**, Nedumudi Venu, Rani Padmini, Baby Vandana, **Mohanlal**, Master Prasad Babu

FTII graduate Sasidharan's debut satirising the phenomenon of Malayalis emigrating to the Gulf States and the rise of a culturally degenerate neo-rich class. Honest clerk Gopinath (Gopi) tries to learn typing and tailoring in an effort to emulate the success of men like Johnny (Venu) and Ismail (Mammootty). His ambitious wife (Madhavi) lusts for the consumer objects with which her neighbourhood is awash, but this gets the clerk into a series of difficulties. He has an encounter with a prostitute that leads to a scandal, is cheated by a labour agent and ends up as a porter carrying the luggage of Keralites returning from the Gulf. The film was important to future megastar Mammootty, establishing a generic context for many of his thrillers (cf ***Ee Nadu***, 1982, where he plays a Dubai-returned Muslim youth).

AMERICA AMERICA
1983 148' col/scope Malayalam
d **I.V. Sasi** *pc* Vijayatara Movies *st* Radhika Vijayan *sc* T. Damodaran *lyr* Bichu Thirumala *c* C.E. Babu *m* Shyam
lp **Mammootty**, Lakshmi, Seema, Ratheesh, Prathap, Balan K. Nair, K.P. Ummar

Complicated melodrama, adventure movie and whodunit set mainly in Florida. This definitive Malayalam hit established the combination of star Mammootty and director Sasi. He plays Ramesh, an undercover investigator checking the murder of Albert, the captain of a ship and husband of heroine Radha. He also investigates the loss of the ship *Kaikeyi*. The film's main highlight includes strippers in Miami, and shootouts on American streets, before the final confrontation with an international gang and the triumphant return of the good guys. The film's three songs included the *Never on Sunday* tune from Jules Dassin's *Pote Tin Kyriaki* (1960).

ARDH SATYA
aka The *Half-truth*
1983 130' col Hindi
d/c **Govind Nihalani** *p* Manmohan Shetty, Pradeep Uppoor *pc* Neo Films Associates *st* S.D. Panwalkar's short story *sc/dial* **Vijay Tendulkar**, Vasant Dev *m* Ajit Varman
lp **Om Puri**, **Smita Patil**, Amrish Puri, **Naseeruddin Shah**, Sadashiv Amrapurkar, Achyut Potdar, Shafi Inamdar

Nihalani followed his ***Aakrosh*** (1980) with this variation on Siegel's *Dirty Harry* (1971). The son of a brutally violent cop (A. Puri), Anant Welankar (O. Puri) is a sub-inspector in the Bombay police. Wanting to arrest the big gangster and powerful politician Rama Shetty (Amrapurkar), Welankar is constantly frustrated and vents his anger on less prominent targets, to the distress of his humane girlfriend Jyotsna (Patil). Although the example of the ex-cop Lobo (Shah), now an alcoholic wretch, is pointed out to him, Welankar cannot control his temper and he eventually kills a petty thief. Forced to ask Shetty for protection, he kills him instead and surrenders to the police. The fast-paced film, with almost continuous action interspersed with tightly framed close-ups of the lead character, was very successful and spawned numerous cop-on-rampage movies sharing none of this one's serious intent. Its best-known remake is K. Vijayan's *Kaval* (Tamil, 1985).

BANKER MARGAYYA

aka *Margayya, the Banker*
1983 145' col Kannada
d/co-p/sc **T.S. Nagabharana** *co-p* B.S. Somasundar *pc* Komal Prod. *st* R.K. Narayan's novel *The Financial Expert* (1952) *lyr* Vijaya Narasimha *c* S. Ramchandra *m* **Vijayabhaskar**
lp Lokesh, Jayanthi, Master Manjunath, Sundarraj, Sundarkrishna Urs, Vijayaranjini, Surekha, Ponni, Musari Krishnamurthy

An ironic morality tale about an entrepreneur whose endeavours are constantly ruined by his son. Margayya (Lokesh) starts out as a moneylender sitting under a banyan tree opposite a co-operative bank, filling in forms, and offering advice to the villagers of Narayan's fictional village of Malgudi, usually on how to circumvent the bank's bureaucratic process of offering loans. His career as a banker is ruined when his son Balu (Sundarraj) throws away all the account books. Then Margayya publishes a sex manual with its author, a Dr Pal (Urs). The venture is very profitable and Margayya becomes wealthier than all the banks in the area. But Balu is the victim of the salacious book and starts visiting prostitutes. Dr Pal manoeuvres to keep all the profits for himself and Margayya has to start all over again under his banyan tree, with the threatening but beloved presence of his son by his side. Narayan, who had earlier disowned the Navketan production of his story ***Guide*** (1965), claimed this film to be the only 'authentic' screen version of his fiction.

CHENGATHEM

1983 160' col Malayalam
d Bhadran *pc* Divya *lyr* Puthyakam Murali *c* Vipin Das *m* Ravi
lp **Mammootty**, Murali, Satyakala, Captain Raju

Early Mammootty crime movie. Telephone operator Anne marries rich criminal Tony (Mammootty), discovering his occupation only after their marriage. His illegal dealings are however presented as a consequence of his childhood experiences, when his mother was killed by villains and he was imprisoned. When Anne is raped by another man, Daniel, Tony kills Daniel and becomes a fugitive from justice, this time chased by sadistic cops not very different from the villains of his childhood. He is eventually caught. Although similar in many ways to **Bachchan**-type themes, e.g. with **Prakash Mehra**, what is often noted with Mammootty is the extent to which corruption, crime and violence are treated as a fact of life and with remarkably little moral posturing. The violence of law enforcement agencies is, likewise, treated on a par with that of organised crime, distinguished only by the assumed goodness of the hero and those in his protection.

COOLIE

1983 177' col/scope Hindi
co-d **Manmohan Desai** *co-d/co-st* Prayag Raj *pc* M.K.D. Films Combine *co-st* Pushpa Raj Sharma *sc* K.K. Shukla *dial* Kadar Khan *lyr* **Anand Bakshi** *c* Peter Pereira *m* **Laxmikant-Pyarelal**
lp **Amitabh Bachchan, Waheeda Rehman**, Rishi Kapoor, Rati Agnihotri, Shoma Anand, Suresh Oberoi, Kadar Khan, Om Shivpuri, Satyen Kappoo, Nilu Phule, Goga, Puneet Issar

Remembered mainly as the film in which Bachchan suffered a near-fatal accident. The frame recording the incident is frozen as the legend of his injury flashes on to the screen. It is also Manmohan Desai's most aggressively communal film. Iqbal (Bachchan) is orphaned when the villain Zafar (Khan) kills his father and rapes his mother Salma (Rehman). Zafar also bursts a dam killing hundreds of people. Iqbal grows up to become a leader of the coolies (porters) at a railway station. Other characters are the drunken journalist Sunny (Kapoor), a foster-child of the villain who befriends Iqbal, and the rich heroine Julie (Agnihotri) whose father was also killed by the villain. The end of the film, shot at the Haji Ali mosque in Bombay, makes an appeal to the lumpenised Muslim underclass when an injured Iqbal invokes the power of Allah to deal the death blow to the villain. Iqbal also enjoys an electoral triumph over Zafar, foreshadowing Bachchan's election as an MP in 1984. Not to be confused with the Malayalam film *Coolie* (also 1983) directed by Ashok Kumar.

ENTE MAMATTUKUTTIYAMA

aka *For my Mamattukuttiama*
1983 116' col Malayalam
d/s **Fazil** *p* Appachan *pc* Navodaya *lyr* Bichu Thirumala *c* Ashok Kumar *m* Jerry Amaldev
lp Baby Shalini, **Gopi**, Sangeetha Naik, **Mohanlal**, Purnima Jayaram, Tilakan, Baby Manju

A regressive melodrama deploying all the myths about motherhood to make a plea on behalf of children born out of wedlock. Sethu (Naik) and Vinod (Gopi), distraught by the death of their own child, focus all their emotions on their adopted child, little Mamattukuttiyama, Tintu for short (Shalini). However, Tintu's real father Alex (Mohanlal) reclaims the child, explaining that his wife Mercy (Jayaram) had been forced to give away the illegitimate child and had gone insane as a result. Only reunification with her daughter will cure her. Overcoming her feelings, Sethu in the end personally hands over the child to its biological mother. Fazil remade the film in Tamil as *En Bommu Kutti Ammavukku* (1988). It was also an instance of the negative roles Mohanlal played in his early career.

GODAM

aka *Warehouse*
1983 140' col Hindi
d/s/co-dial/m Dilip Chitre *pc* **NFDC** *st* Bhau Padhye *co-dial* Vasant Deo *lyr* Sharatchandra Arolkar, Sushama Shreshtha *c* **Govind Nihalani**
lp Satyadev Dubey, K.K. Raina, Trupti, Vijaya Chitre

A tragic story about a woman's relentless suffering in an isolated village. Yesu (Trupti) is a child bride married to the retarded son of a lecherous old man who threatens to rape her. She kills the old man and hides in a disused warehouse where she is protected but sexually exploited by the caretaker Edekar (Raina) and his helper Dharma (Dubey). One morning, Edekar opens the warehouse to find Yesu has hanged herself. Almost the entire film is set in the abandoned warehouse, atop an isolated and

Jayanthi (centre) and Lokesh (right) in *Banker Margayya*

rocky hill, intended to provide a hallucinatory, mystical experience. The hyperactive camera, with montage cut-outs of Queen Victoria and the monkey god Hanuman, and soundtrack, where Sharatchandra Arolkar's music jostles with John Coltrane, presents an excess that contrasts with the spartan setting. Noted Marathi poet Chitre's only feature.

HERO

1983 173' col Hindi
d **Subhash Ghai** *pc* Mukta Arts *st* Mukta Ghai *sc* Ram Kelkar *lyr* **Anand Bakshi** *m* **Laxmikant-Pyarelal**
lp Jackie Shroff, Meenakshi Sheshadri, Sanjeev Kumar, **Shammi Kapoor**, Amrish Puri, Bindu, Shakti Kapoor

The orphan Jackie (Shroff) is raised by notorious criminal Pasha (Puri). When Pasha is arrested, he asks Jackie to silence the main prosecution witness, a retired police officer, Mathur (Shammi Kapoor). Jackie kidnaps Radha (Sheshadri), Mathur's daughter, who then falls in love with him and asks him to give himself up. The obstacles are Mathur, who hates Jackie, and Jackie's rival (Shakti Kapoor). Jackie has to save both Mathur and Radha from Pasha in the violent climax before he can be forgiven. Ghai's independent hit marketed its unknown lead, Jackie Shroff, via a major advertising campaign using a series of teaser ads. The film includes several of Ghai's trade-mark song picturisations in mountainous locales (e.g. *Ding-a-dong baby sing-a-song*).

HOLI

aka *Festival of Fire*
1983 116'(120') col Hindi
d/co-sc/co-lyr **Ketan Mehta** *pc* Film Unit, Neo Film Associates *st/co-sc/co-dial* Mahesh Elkunchwar based on his play *co-dial/co-lyr* Hriday Lani *c* Jehangir Choudhury *m* Rajat Dholakia
lp Sanjeev Gandhi, Manoj Pandya, Rahul Ranade, Ashutosh Gowarikar, Amole Gupte, **Om Puri**, **Naseeruddin Shah**, Deepti Naval, Shriram Lagoo, Aamir Khan, Mohan Gokhale

Mehta's first Hindi film addresses the increasing lumpenisation of university students featuring scenes of victimisation reminiscent of Volker Schloendorff's *Der junge Toerless* (1966). Forced to attend a lecture on India's cultural heritage while on holiday, the boys rebel. The violence gradually escalates into a major battle with the authorities as the colourful and anarchistic pre-Vedic spring festival, Holi, turns into a menacing festival of fire with burning school furniture. The college principal induces a boy to denounce the leaders of the rebellion. The informer is publicly humiliated and is forced to commit suicide. Mehta decided to shoot almost all the scenes in sequence shots, often using a crab-dolly or a steadycam, and using synch sound rather than playback or post-synched sound (in spite of the complicated songs and the musical accompaniment). The film's enthusiastic and hallucinatory participation in student violence (of which it is supposedly critical) allows it to move away from its original political thrust, conveying existential despair instead. The film enjoyed a cult audience in New Delhi for a short period.

INIYENKILUM

1983 201' col Malayalam
d **I.V. Sasi** *pc* Geo Movie Prod. *st* Rose *dial* T. Damodaran *lyr* Yusuf Ali Kacheri *c* Jayanan Vincent *m* Shyam
lp **Mammootty**, **Mohanlal**, Lalu Alex, Ratheesh, Ravindran, T.G. Ravi, Seema, Rani Padmini, Sunitha Sharma, Balan K. Nair

Extraordinary and long-drawn out melodrama contrasting conditions in Kerala with those in Japan. A group of performers from Kerala are invited to Japan, but they are left stranded when their criminal host disappears. With the assistance of Nambiar, a benevolent Tokyo-based Malayali, they learn about the Japanese economy, initiating - on their return - a series of reformist movements that end up with the revolutionary overthrow of corrupt leadership. The film continued Sasi's tendency (***America America***, also 1983) to set his plots in exotic foreign locales, and also his 'hard-hitting' and often satirical collaborations with Marxist writer Damodaran (cf ***Angadikkapurathu***, 1985; ***Vartha*** 1986).

JAANE BHI DO YAARON

aka *Who Pays the Piper*
1983 143'(130') col Hindi
d/s **Kundan Shah** *pc* **NFDC** *co-s* Sudhir Mishra *dial* Ranjit Kapoor, Satish Kaushik *c* Binod Pradhan *m* **Vanraj Bhatia**
lp **Naseeruddin Shah**, Ravi Baswani, Bhakti Bharve, **Om Puri**, Satish Shah, Pankaj Kapoor, Satish Kaushik, Neena Gupta, Deepak Qazir, Rajesh Puri, Zafar Sanjari, Vidhu Vinod Chopra

Extraordinary slapstick comedy, a genre almost unknown in Indian cinema since **Kishore Kumar**'s early films. Two bumbling photographers, Vinod Chopra (N. Shah) and Sudhir Mishra (Baswani), are employed by Shobha (Bharve), the editor of a scandal sheet, *Khabardar*. They have to spy on millionaire property developer Tarneja (Kapoor) and police commissioner D'Mello (S. Shah). The photographers uncover dirty business between Tarneja and his equally unsavoury rival Ahuja (O. Puri). The commissioner is killed by one of the builders who, as a result, wins the contract to build a flyover that collapses shortly afterwards. The photographers get hold of D'Mello's corpse in order to prove that he was murdered, but they lose it, which gives rise to an extended sequence where everyone chases everyone else. In the end, the photographers are framed for the collapse of the fly-over. The film, set in the same early 80s of, e.g., **Anand Patwardhan**'s documentary ***Hamara Shaher*** (1985), refers directly to specific corrupt Bombay politicians of the period. The collapse of the flyover, shown in a video clip in the film, is in fact footage of the actual Byculla Bridge in Bombay which collapsed shortly before the film was made. Commissioner D'Mello refers to the then police chief Julio Ribeiro (who appears in the Advertising Club meeting in Patwardhan's documentary), Tarneja and Ahuja are a composite picture of Bombay's biggest builder Raheja, while the Shobha who runs a scandal sheet is an allusion to Shobha Kilachand, aka Shobha De, former editor of a film gossip and city magazine. In addition, the film repeatedly refers to, e.g., Antonioni's *Blow Up* (1966) and to New Indian Cinema, including some of Shah's former **FTII** colleagues: film-makers Vinod Chopra (on whose *Sazaaye Maut*, 1981, Shah had been a production manager) and Sudhir Mishra, who lend their names to the photographer duo. The *Albert Pinto* code-word of the two amateur sleuths refers to **Saeed Mirza**'s film (1980). Large posters of **Kumar Shahani**'s ***Maya Darpan*** (1972) and **Mani Kaul**'s ***Uski Roti*** (1969) can be seen pasted on the walls during the chase. The film was a mild commercial success and influenced mainly a brand of tv comedy (cf Shah's tv series *Yeh Jo Hai Zindagi*, 1985, and one he made together with Mirza, *Nukkad*, 1987).

KATTATHE KILIKOODU

aka *Bird's Nest in the Wind*
1983 136' col Malayalam
d **Bharathan** *pc* Grihalakshmi Prod. *sc* T. Damodaran *st* Nedumudi Venu *lyr* Kavalam Narayana Panicker *c* Vasant Kumar *m* Johnson
lp **Gopi**, **Mohanlal**, Shrividya, Revathi, Lalitha, Santhakumari, Master Prashab, Baby Poonambili, Baby Anju, Baby Preetha, Krishna Swamy

Melodrama about the fears of young women's sexuality (a recurrent Bharathan theme, cf ***Rathi Nirvedham***, 1978; ***Ormakkayi***, 1982). A callous and immature teenage girl, Asha, who sets out to turn a middle-aged professor's (Gopi) head and nearly destroys his entire family. In the end, the girl marries the boy she wanted from the beginning, Unni (Mohanlal), the college's athletics coach.

KHANDHAR

aka *The Ruins*
1983 108' col Hindi
d/sc **Mrinal Sen** *p* Jagadish and Pushpa Chokhani *pc* Shri Bharatlaxmi Pics *st* **Premendra Mitra**'s *Telenapota Abishkar* (*The Discovery Of The Village Telenapota*) *c* K.K. Mahajan *m* Bhaskar Chandavarkar
lp **Shabana Azmi**, **Naseeruddin Shah**, Geeta Sen, Pankaj Kapoor, Annu Kapoor, Sreela Majumdar, **Rajen Tarafdar**

Three friends from the city visit some ruins where an aged mother (Sen) and her daughter Jamini (Azmi) live. The mother awaits the arrival of a distant cousin to marry Jamini but the man is already married and living in Calcutta. The photographer Subhash (Shah) takes pity on the family and pretends to be the awaited suitor. The mother dies contented but when the threesome leave again, Jamini stays behind facing a life of loneliness in the ruins. The second Sen film to receive a Hindi release, its passive storyline and heavy emphasis on meaningful looks was a major departure from his political cinema of the 70s. Sen commented that 'The film is partly memory and partly fantasy punctuated by bits of instant happenings', and created an

Shabana Azmi and Naseeruddin Shah in *Khandhar*

expressionist set of broken walls and ruins to replicate the woman's state of mind. Claiming the influence of Robert Bresson, he also said that with this film he finally put the **IPTA** influence behind him, something he had aimed to do since the communist government returned to power in Bengal in 1977 which made the IPTA aesthetic into official policy.

KOODEVIDE?

aka *Where is the Nest?* aka *In Whose Nest?*
1983 150'(103') col Malayalam
d/s **P. Padmarajan** *pc* Prakash Movietone *st* Vasanthy *lyr* **O.N.V. Kurup** *c* **Shaji N. Karun** *m* Johnson
lp **Mammootty, Suhasini**, Rahman, Jose Prakash, Prem Prakash, Sukumari, Rajani Menon

A story of ambition and resigned frustration set in Kerala's old Syrian Christian community, a milieu unfamiliar to the noted Malayalam novelist, scenarist and director Padmarajan. Alice (Suhasini), who lives with her brother (P. Prakash), is a teacher at the reputable Ootacamund convent school. An MP, Xavier Puthooran (J. Prakash), sacrifices his wife and son for his career. The MP's neglected and unruly son Ravi (Rahman in his debut role), is foisted upon the school and Alice manages to turn him into a prize student. Her boyfriend Capt. Thomas (Mammootty) feels intensely jealous of the attention Alice bestows upon Ravi. He kills the boy apparently by accident, but later surrenders to the police, leaving Alice frustrated in all aspects of her life.

LEKHAYUDE MARANAM ORU FLASHBACK

aka *Lekha's Death a Flashback*
1983 172' col/scope Malayalam
d/s **K.G. George** *p* David Kachapally, Innocent *pc* Sathru Int. *dial* **S.L. Puram Sadanandan** *lyr* **O.N.V. Kurup** *c* **Shaji N. Karun** *m* **M.B. Srinivasan**
lp Nalini, **Gopi, Mammootty**, Subha, Jayashri, Jayachitra, **Sharada**, Nedumudi Venu, John Varghese, Adoor Bhawani, Thilakan, Venu Nagavalli, Innocent, Meena

Controversial film embroiled in lawsuits because of its alleged exploitation of the well-publicised suicide of the Tamil actress Shobha. When a poor Kerala family moves to Madras, their young daughter Santhamma becomes the teenage film star Lekha (Nalini). However, the young girl hangs herself. The film recounts the events leading up to her decision, including a stint as a prostitute and the merciless exploitation she suffers from her alcoholic father (Varghese) and her pushy mother (Subha) as well as from her professional colleagues, esp. from her lover, the unhappily married Suresh (Gopi), a director of art-house films. The film depended heavily on the real-life events and characters to whom it alluded, while continuing the director's fascination with the thriller format (***Yavanika***, 1982).

MALAMUKALILE DAIVAM

aka *The God Atop the Hill*
1983 111' col Malayalam
d **P.N. Menon** *pc* Suryamudra Films *s/lyr* Kalpatta Balakrishnan *c* Deviprasad *m* Johnson
lp Sudharani, Master Suresh, Kunjandi, Balasingh, Lakshmi Geetha, Subramanyam, Unni Mary, Sathyendra, Ranjith, Gabriel, Rani Abraham

Symbolic tale set in a tribal village at the foot of the Banasuran Mountains in Kerala. Religious superstition and ignorance maintain stasis in the village. A relentlessly intelligent boy escapes its oppressive confines and later returns, determined to bring enlightenment to the village. The event is represented in terms of a torchlight procession up the forbidding, god-guarded mountains shielding the villagers from the 'outside'.

MANDI

aka *The Marketplace*
1983 167' col Hindi
d/co-sc **Shyam Benegal** *p* Freni M. Variava, Lalit M. Bijlani *pc* Blaze Film Ents *co-sc* Satyadev Dubey, Shama Zaidi *lyr* Mir Taqi Mir, Bahadur Shah Zafar, Insha, Makhdoom Mohiuddin, Talwar Danda, Ila Arun *c* Ashok Mehta *m* **Vanraj Bhatia**
lp **Shabana Azmi, Smita Patil, Naseeruddin Shah**, Amrish Puri, Kulbhushan Kharbanda, **Saeed Jaffrey, Om Puri**, Sreela Majumdar, Harish Patel, Neena Gupta, Soni Razdan, Ila Arun, Geeta Siddharth, Aditya Bhattacharya

Apparently inspired by *The Best Little Whorehouse in Texas* (Colin Higgins, 1982), Benegal's rare venture into comedy touches on religion and politics via the motif of prostitution. Brothel madam Rukmini (Azmi) tries to make her 'girls' conform to the time-honoured traditions of a kotha (a brothel where music and dance flourish). The women's mischievousness forces the establishment to find another home. Problems arise when Sushil, the son of Major Agarwal (Jaffrey), a local notable, falls in love with the prostitute Zeenat (Patil), Agarwal's illegitimate daughter. Instead, Sushil is supposed to marry the neurotic daughter of Mr Gupta (Kharbanda), a property developer who makes the brothel shift locations yet again in order to separate Sushil from Zeenat.

MAYA MIRIGA

aka *Maya Mriga* aka *The Mirage*
1983 115' col Oriya
d/sc/co-st **Nirad N. Mohapatra** *pc* Lotus Prod. *co-st/dial* Bhiputi Patnaik *c* Rajagopal Mishra *m* Bhaskar Chandavarkar
lp Bansidhar Satpathy, Manimala, Binod Mishra, Manaswini, Sampad Mohapatra, Sujata, Vivekananda Satpathy, Kishore Debi, Managaraj, Shriranjan Mohanty, Kunumuni, Tikina

FTII-graduate Mohapatra's low-key first feature, shot on 16mm with non-professional actors in Puri, a small coastal town in Orissa. The plot concerns the break-up of a middle-class extended family. The former freedom fighter Raj Kishore (Satpathy), now an elderly school headmaster, lives with his four sons and only daughter. The eldest son Tuku (Mishra) and his wife Prabha (Manaswini) are expected to help pay for the education of the younger siblings while the second son Tutu (Mohapatra) marries a well-off woman (Sujata) who insists on a separate household. In the end, Tuku refuses to keep shouldering the burdens of the extended family and the unit disintegrates. The director, a noted teacher and writer of film theory, acknowledges the influence of Yasujiro Ozu's editing style.

MHARI PYARI CHANANA

1983 130' col Rajasthani
d/sc Jatin Kumar *pc* Jayashree Ents *st* Bharat Vyas's play *Ramu Chanana dial/co-lyr* Suraj Dadhich *c* H. Lakshminarayan *m* Narayan Dutt
lp Satyajit Puri, Pooja Saxena, Ramesh Tiwari, Bina Shyam, Ajay Sinha, Suraj Dadhich, Ritu Khanna, S.D. Chavan, Hakim Keranvi, Master Anil

Successful Rajasthani melodrama adapted from Vyas's stage hit. Poor Ramu (Puri) and rich Chanana (Saxena) are childhood lovers but class differences keep them apart as her desires conflict with the need to maintain her father's social standing. The film evokes the Laila-Majnu and Shirin-Farhad legends with overtones of ***Devdas*** thrown in for good measure.

NAYANMONI

1983 140' col Assamese
d **Suprabha Debi** *pc* Rajendra Chalachitra *sc* Guna Sindhu Hazarika *c* Indukalpa Hazarika *m* Jitu-Tapan
lp Nipon Goswami, Bidya Nair, Vandana Sharma, Girija Das, Ishan Barua, Gauri Barua

Debut feature by Assam's first woman director. Moina marries the rich Arup although his parents disapprove. She insists on a separate establishment away from her husband's joint family, which creates difficulties when her husband dies. Her lone struggle to bring up her children eventually wins her the affection of her estranged in-laws.

ORU INDHIYA KANAVU

aka *An Indian Dream*
1983 141' col Tamil
d/s **Komal Swaminathan** *p* T.P. Varadarajan, Vijayalakshmi Desikan *pc* Shri Muthiallammal Creations *lyr* **Vali**, **Vairamuthu** *c* M. Kesavan *m* M.S. Vishwanathan
lp **Suhasini**, Rajeev, R.K. Raman, Samikkannu, Lalitha

The celebrated playwright and scenarist of ***Thanneer Thanneer*** (filmed in 1981) turned director with *Yuddha Kandam* (1983) and this emphatic reformist melodrama is his 3rd effort. It tells of a woman intellectual, Anamika (Suhasini), who, when exposed to tribal authenticity, becomes an activist on behalf of the tribals in the Javadhi Hills. Overcoming the extremes of political persecution with the help of an honest and therefore victimised policeman, Muthuvel (Rajeev), she exposes the rapist of a tribal woman (Lalitha): the son of a powerful politician who stops at nothing to cover up his son's crime.

RACHANA

aka *Writing* aka *Rachna*
1983 149' b&w Malayalam
d Mohan *p* Sivan Kunnamppilly *pc* Thushara Films *sc/dial* John Paul *st* Eastman Anthony *lyr* Mullahakshmi *c* Vasant Kumar *m* **M.B. Srinivasan**
lp Nedumudi Venu, Shrividya, **Gopi**, **Mammootty**, Poornima Jayaram, Vijay Menon, Jagathy Shrikumar, Ramu, Isaac Thomas

The story, told in flashback, of a writer, Shriprasad (Gopi), who uses his wife Sharada (Shrividya) to get to know a simple-minded man, Unni (Venu), so that he may use him as source material for his next novel. The duped simpleton finds out the truth and commits suicide, leaving the wife insane with guilt and the writer a broken man even though the author of a highly acclaimed novel. The director is a well-known playwright and stage director as well as a prolific film-maker.

RANGULA KALA

aka *Colourful Dreams*
1983 136' col Telugu
d/st/co-sc/co-m **B. Narasinga Rao** *pc* Suchitra Int. *co-sc/co-lyr* Devi Priya *co-sc* Uppala Narasimham *co-sc/dial* S.M. Pran Rao *co-lyr* Gaddar, Angaiah *c* Venugopal K. Thakker *co-m* Janardan
lp B. Narasinga Rao, G. Narayana Rao, T. Saichand, Kakarala, Chandra, Venkata Reddy, Roopa, Shakuntala, Shesham Raju, Sangeetha Behal, Rajyalakshmi, Usha Sheikh, Haritha, Amar Mohan

Narasinga Rao's debut is an existential melodrama with the director playing a romantic painter, Ravi, whose friends include a trade union leader (Kakarala), an auto-rickshaw driver, a Marxist journalist (Narayana Rao) and a glib, successful painter (Saichand) whose success contrasts with Ravi's inability to sell his own work. His neighbour Kankamma, who rejects an evil landlord's advances, is evicted from her house; the trade unionist is killed in police custody; and Ravi starts exhibiting his work on the streets to indicate his growing politicisation to the satisfaction of his Marxist friend. The film is geared to the CPI(ML)-led political movements in Northern AP and included the compositions and songs of the region's best-known radical poet and performer, Gaddar.

SAGARA SANGAMAM

aka *The Confluence*
1983 160' col Telugu
d/st **K. Vishwanath** *p* Edida Nageshwara Rao *pc* Poornodaya Movie Creations *dia* Jandhyala *lyr* Veeturi Sundara Ramamurthy *c* P.S. Nivas *m* **Ilaiyaraja**
lp **Kamalahasan**, Jayapradha, Sarathbabu, S.P. Sailaja, Sakshi Rangarao, Venkayala, Janaki, Arunkumar, Bhoomeswararao, Potti Prasad, Manju Bhargavi, Mohan Sharma

Vishwanath's sequel to ***Shankarabharanam*** (1979) concentrated on classical dance. The drunken dance critic Balakrishna Bhagavatar (Kamalahasan) writes a review denouncing a mediocre but much-touted dancer (Sailaja). It turns out, in a flashback, that the dancer is the daughter of the reviewer's old flame Madhavi (Jayapradha). Madhavi persuades Balakrishna to teach her daughter. He eventually dies of a broken heart but his pupil achieves mastery in classical dance so that the classical art (cf *Shankarabharanam*) will live on. The film is dominated by Kamalahasan, who demonstrated a remarkable, unexpected skill to dance the Bharat Natyam, although the rest of the film's classicism is pure kitsch.

SAGARAM SHANTHAM

1983 126' col Malayalam
d P.G. Vishwambaran *pc* Premadevas Films *st* Sara Thomas *sc* John Paul *lyr* **O.N.V. Kurup** *c* Ramchandra *m* **M.B. Srinivasan**
lp **Mammootty**, Nedumudi Venu, Sreenath, Ramu, Shanti Krishna, Sukumari, Manochitra

Early Mammootty melodrama establishing some of the key tenets of his later screen persona: his commitment to helpless women, as well as his penchant for taking on the role of an avenging angel. He is the motor mechanic Anandan, who is rejected by his childhood friend Sridevi because of class differences. However, she marries a villain and gets thrown out on the streets, pregnant and penniless. Anandan takes revenge on her husband and ends up in jail, while she promises to wait for his release to marry him.

SANAKEITHEL

aka *Golden Market*
1983 131' col Manipuri
d M.A. Singh *pc* Th. Dorendra Singh *st/m* N. Pahari *c* Sooresh Patel
lp A. Memi, Master Tony, Somorendra, Manao, Upen, Ingochouba, Anwar Ali, Shahnawaz Khan, Holkhomang, Ibechaobi, Bijoy, Meena, Meim Chaoba, Maharaj Okendrajit, G. Ibeyaima Devi

Melodrama featuring criminal violence in Imphal, the (for most Indians) exotic capital of Manipur. It addresses issues like unemployment, drugs and the nexus between an oppressive state power and an entrenched feudal elite through the story of a widow, Nungshi (Memi), and her son Ibungobi (Master Tony). When the independent-minded Nungshi is gang-raped and becomes a crazed beggar, her son joins a group of criminals operating in Imphal's 'Golden Market'. Ibungobi eventually realises that the beggar is his mother, but is too late to help her even though one of his criminal friends is a local politician. Shot under very difficult conditions, the film is a courageous effort to go beyond the exotic and miserabilist stories featured in many art-house films originating in India's smaller film industries.

SMRITICHITRE

aka *Memory Episodes*
1983 135' col Marathi
d **Vijaya Mehta** *pc* **Doordarshan** *st* Laxmibai Tilak's autobiography *sc* Mangesh Kulkarni *lyr* Laxmibai Tilak *c* R.C. Mapakshi *m* Mohan
lp Vijaya Mehta, Suhas Joshi, Pallavi Patil, Ravindra Mankani, Shirish Joshi, Mangesh Kulkarni, Vishwas Mehendale, Rekha Kamat, Sudhir Joshi

Vijaya Mehta's debut is a tv film based on the legendary Marathi autobiography of Laxmibai Tilak (1868-1936), a major social reform text evoking the life of her husband, the philosopher Narayan V. Tilak (Mankani and, as an older man, Sudhir Joshi). The film covers 20 years of her life (1890-1900), from her marriage to her conversion to her husband's religion, Christianity. It also tells of her childhood, the loss of her two children, her self-education and her husband's conversion in Ahmednagar while she spent another five years in the same town rigidly adhering to her Hindu beliefs. The predominantly theatrical actors contribute to a theatrical film. The main character is played by three different actors: for the childhood scenes, Patil takes the role; as a young woman she is played by Suhas Joshi and as an old woman by Mehta herself.

ACCIDENT

1984 121' col Kannada
d **Shankar Nag** *pc* Sanket Prod. *s* Vasant Mokashi *dial* G.S. Sadashiv *c* Shankar Deodhar *m* **Ilaiyaraja**
lp **Anant Nag**, Shankar Nag, Ashok Mandanna, Srinivas Prabhu, Ramesh Bhatt, Arundhati Rao

Fast-paced crime movie with two rich young men getting involved in a major accident that could threaten the election prospects of the corrupt politician Dharmadhikari. A police inspector is forced to withdraw from the case but a courageous journalist eventually reveals the political connections. Like Shankar Nag's previous film, ***Minchina Ota*** (1980), it is apparently based on a true-life incident.

ACHAMILLAI ACHAMILLAI

aka *Fearless*
1984 161' col Tamil
d/s **K. Balachander** *pc* Kavithalaya Prod. *lyr* **Vairamuthu**, Erode Tamizhanban *c* B.S. Lokanathan *m* V.S. Narasimhan
lp Saritha, Rajesh, Delhi Ganesh, Pavithra, Ahalya, Prabhakar, Vairam Krishnamurthy, Veeraiah, Jayagopi, Charley T.

After the critical success of ***Thanneer Thanneer*** (1981), Balachander pushes his jaundiced view of (Tamil but also general Indian) politics further with this grotesque drama symbolising the conditions of life in independent India. The central character is Thenmozhi (Saritha), a textile worker, who loves and marries Ulaganathan, a pragmatic politician whose daily compromises eventually lead to provoking communal riots and callous corruption. A strong and lively woman, Thenmozhi ends up killing her corrupt husband. The film repeatedly evokes, in its political references, the old tradition of political propaganda in Tamil film, with numerous symbols and clear distinctions between good and evil: most notably in the climactic sequence when the wife, stepping on to a dais to garland her husband, has a knife hidden in the garland with which she publicly stabs him. Sridhar Rajan described the film's opening as 'a stunning surrealist streetside strewn with corpses [a]nd, later, we see the evocative visuals of men with loudspeakers growing out of their throats, each vying democratically to down the other vocally in the battle of the ballot'. The grotesque side of the story is evident in, e.g., Thenmozhi's deformed brother born on Independence Day and named Swatantram (i.e. Independence) and in her blind father, a former freedom fighter who is corrupted by Ulaganathan's promise to pay for an operation to restore his sight.

ADMI AUR AURAT

aka *Man and Woman*
1984 56' col Hindi
d/sc **Tapan Sinha** *pc* **Doordarshan** *st* Prafulla Roy *c* Kamal Nayak *m* Ashish Khan
lp **Amol Palekar**, Mahua Roy Choudhury, Kalyan Chatterjee, Nirmal Ghosh, Parimal Sengupta, Sudhir K. Singh, Dipak Sanyal, Samir Mukherjee

A simple tv drama about a young, pregnant Muslim woman who walks 20 miles through the Vakilgunga hills to a hospital to deliver her baby. A kind Hindu poacher helps her to overcome geographical obstacles and inclement weather. In the end, when the child is born, the hunter learns that the woman is a Muslim, but he nevertheless takes the news of her son's birth back to the woman's husband.

ALKOOTTATHIL THANIYE

aka *Alone in the Crowd*
1984 139' col Malayalam
d **I.V. Sasi** *pc* Century *s* **M.T. Vasudevan Nair** *lyr* Kavalam Narayana Panicker *c* Jayanan Vincent *m* Shyam
lp Balan K. Nair, **Mammootty**, Seema, Subha, Sumitra, Unni Mary, **Mohanlal**, Pappu, Lalu Alex, **Adoor Bhasi**, Prashob

A film from a prolific sexploitation director advocating adherence to old-style family values and unconditional submission to patriarchy. A dying father's three children rush to his bedside but, as the old man clings on to life, his two daughters return to their busy urban lives and his son's wife leaves for fear of missing out on her Harvard fellowship. The son, Rajan (Mammootty), stays and the old man's niece Ammukkutty (Seema), a schoolteacher who helped Rajan in his education but was not allowed to marry him, is summoned to come and look after the men. With exemplary devotion Ammukkutty tends to their needs while reconciling all members of the family with each other. The happy ending demonstrates the transcendent value of filial piety.

ANDHI GALI

aka *Blind Alley* aka *Dead End*
1984 152' col Hindi
d/sc/m **Buddhadev Dasgupta** *pc* K.B.S. Films *st* Dibyendu Palit's novel *Ghar Bari*
dial/lyr **Gulzar** *c* Kamal Nayak
lp Kulbhushan Kharbanda, Deepti Naval, M.K. Raina, **Anil Chatterjee**, Mahesh Bhatt, Satya Bannerjee, Shyamanand Jalan, Anuradha Tandon

The final part of the director's trilogy dealing with contemporary middle-class Bengali politics (***Dooratwa***, 1978; ***Grihajuddha***, 1982) is his first film in Hindi. Set in Calcutta in the early 70s, the central figure is a left activist and schoolteacher, Hemanta. Narrowly escaping being murdered by the police, Hemanta finds his political organisation in disarray and flees to Bombay where he leads a quiet life though his nerves are still shattered by his Calcutta experiences. Through a friend, Rakesh, Hemanta meets Jaya and they marry. To help raise money to buy a flat, Jaya reluctantly becomes a model for advertisement photographs. Obsessed with the desire to secure a middle-class lifestyle, Hemanta forces Jaya to take on demeaning photographic assignments and, to impose his will on her, he rapes her. Jaya commits suicide and Hemanta finds himself facing the police again.

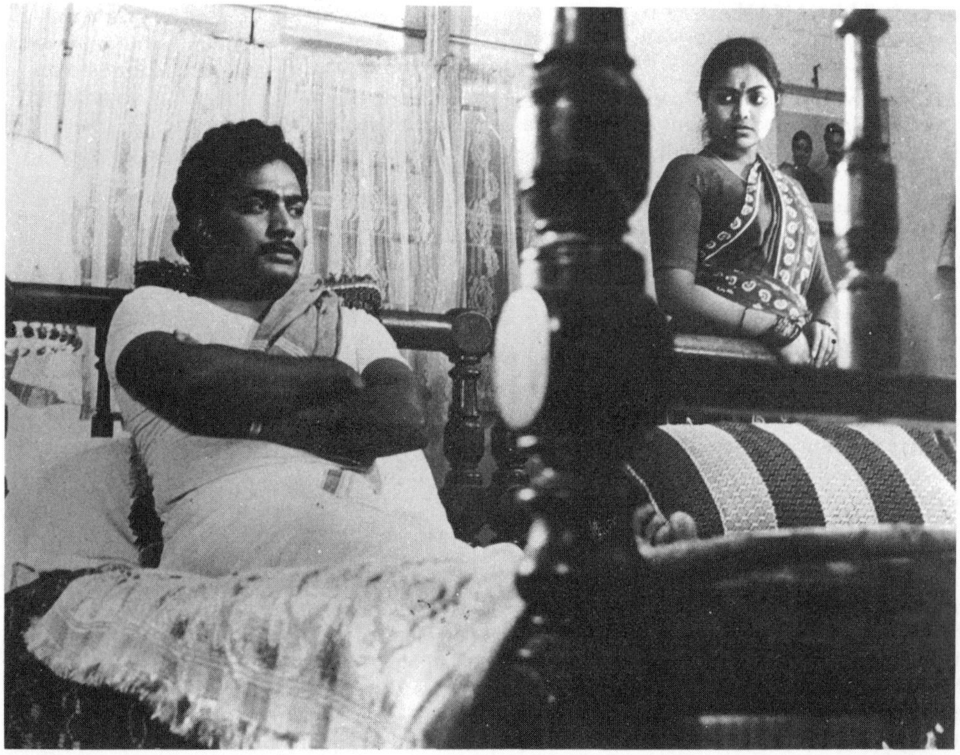

Saritha (right) in *Achamillai Achamillai*

ANKAHEE

aka *The Unspoken*
1984 135' col Hindi
d/p **Amol Palekar** *pc* Suchimisha *sc* Jayant Dharmadhikari, Basu Bhagat, S.G. Akolkar *st* C.T. Khanolkar's play *Kalaya Tasmeya Namaha dial* Kamalesh Pande *c* Debu Deodhar *m* Jaidev
lp Amol Palekar, Deepti Naval, Shriram Lagoo, **Anil Chatterjee**, Dina Pathak, Devika Mukherjee, Vinod Chopra, Seema, Vinod Mehra

Palekar follows his Marathi film ***Aakriet*** (1981) with this Hindi melodrama about fatalism, adapted from a noted experimental play. Nandu's (Palekar) father (Lagoo) is an astrologer who stoically lives with the knowledge that his predictions mostly come true. Nandu resents his father's fatalistic attitude and rebels when his father predicts that Nandu's first wife will die in childbirth, which puts a damper on Nandu's marriage plans with Sushma, a rational woman prepared to take the risk. Instead, Nandu marries the retarded but curable Indu (Naval), hoping to circumvent his father's prediction. Indu is taken to hospital to give birth and she survives, but Sushma commits suicide to assert her right to determine her own destiny.

APRIL 18

aka *April Pathinettu*
1984 153' col Malayalam
d/s **Balachandra Menon** *pc* Sathosh Films *lyr* Bichu Thirumala *c* Bipin Mohan *m* A.T. Ummar
lp Balachandra Menon, Venu Nagavalli, **Adoor Bhasi**, **Gopi**, Shobhana, Jose Prakash, Raju, Santosh, Shankaradi, Srinath, Unnimary, Adoor Bhawani, Sukumari, Shrilatha

A melodrama about a conscientious policeman, played by the director, whose visits to a convict's wife (Unnimary) are misunderstood by his wife (Shobhana) who leaves home in protest. His father-in-law (Bhasi), who never liked his daughter's choice for a husband, pushes for divorce. However, the unpleasant nature of the legal proceedings plus the nostalgic memories of their first meeting reconcile the couple.

CHIRAI

aka *Sirai*
1984 143' col Tamil
d/sc R.C. Sakthi *pc* Ananthi Films *st* Anuradha Ramanan *lyr* Pulamai Pithan, Muthulingam *c* Vishwam Nataraj *m* M.S. Vishwanathan
lp Rajesh, Prasanna, Pandian, Lakshmi, Elavarasi, S.S. Chandran

The drunken landlord Anthony (Rajesh) rapes Bhagirathi (Lakshmi), wife of the village Brahmin priest. When her husband rejects her, encouraged by a kindly policeman she moves in with her rapist and eventually develops an attachment to him. When he dies she prefers to be known as the man's widow and refuses to rejoin her husband. A parallel story has a farm-worker courting a local politician's daughter, providing an opportunity to show the corrupt relationships between politicians and police. The story's impact is diluted by gross comedy, cabarets, and a fight sequence inserted for box-office reasons. Lakshmi gives an accomplished repeat performance of a rape victim (cf ***Sila Nerangalil Sila Manithargal***, 1976). The film upset Brahmin organisations, which campaigned against it.

DAMUL

aka *Bonded until Death*
1984 141'(125') col Hindi
d/p/sc **Prakash Jha** *pc* Prakash Jha Prod *dial/st* Shaiwal based on his story *Kaabutra c* Rajan Kothari *m* Raghunath Seth
lp Manohar Singh, Sreela Majumdar, Annu Kapoor, Deepti Naval, Pyare Mohan Sadhay, Braj Kishore, Gopal Sharan, Om Prakash

Melodrama set in Bihar addressing poverty, rural exploitation and the politics of Untouchability. Madho (Manohar Singh), the village head, uses the conventional system of bonded labour (i.e. labourers have to sign a paper assuming the debts of their ancestors) to subjugate the Harijan labourer Sanjeevan (Kapoor). Madho also runs an extortion racket based on stealing cattle and then requiring the owners to buy them back. Sanjeevan's story is intercut with Madho's multifarious misdeeds and the equally nefarious doings of Madho's rival, the politician Bachcha Singh. Madho's younger brother heads the gang of thugs who enforce the headman's will, including rigging the elections, raping and killing the widow Mahatmeen when she threatens to expose him in court, framing Sanjeevan for the crime, etc. In the end, Sanjeevan's wife Rajuli kills Madho. Jha's 2nd film uses a continuously circling camera, converting the melodrama into a frontier tale of crime, sex and revenge, with colourful clothes and exotic accents.

DHARE AALUA

aka *Ray of Light*
1984 162' b&w Oriya
d/sc Saghir Ahmed *pc* Garuda Cinemagraphics *st* Manorama Das *dial* Sanjide Tayab *lyr* Suryamani Tripathi *c* Bidushree Bindhani *m* Harihar Panda
lp Prithviraj Mishra, Soumitra, Hemanth, Purna Bindhani, Dipen Ghosh, Soumendu Tripathi, Amrita Ahmed, Shivani Mahapatra

A courageous low-budget feature by Saghir Ahmed who teaches script writing at the **FTII**. The film addresses questions of rural oppression in ways markedly different from its usual treatment in Oriya cinema (cf **Manmohan Mahapatra**). A joint family is partially fragmented when the patriarch's only son (Mishra), a political activist, has to spend much of his time avoiding the police. The family informally adopts two children and is then blamed when one of them commits suicide while escaping from Panchanan (Ghosh), the children's oppressive legal guardian. The children's mostly absent journalist father (Mahapatra) causes the activist to be arrested, but eventually all the players of the drama come together. The director's daughter Amrita Ahmed played one of the two children.

GHARE BAIRE

aka *Home and The World*
1984 140' col Bengali
d/sc/m **Satyajit Ray** *pc* **NFDC** *st* **Rabindranath Tagore**'s novel *c* Soumendu Roy
lp **Soumitra Chatterjee**, Victor Bannerjee, Swatilekha Chatterjee, Gopa Aich, Jennifer Kendal, Manoj Mitra, Indrapramit Roy, Bimal Chatterjee

Twenty years after ***Charulata*** (1964) Ray returned to Tagore, in colour, adapting a controversial novel that had increased in stature over the years. Set during the terrorist movements following the first communal partition of Bengal (1905), the book tells a triple story, interweaving the diaries of the nationalist zamindar Nikhil (V. Bannerjee) with the stories of the man's wife Bimala (Sw. Chatterjee) and of their guest, the fiery activist Sandeep (So. Chatterjee). Sandeep and Bimala become involved with one another, which for her leads to a sense of liberation. In the end, Nikhil is able to accept his wife's new-found sense of individuality while Sandeep is shown to be an opportunist. Ray played down the novel's political overtones in favour of a straight love triangle enacted in a meticulously researched period setting. The film, written by Tagore in 1948 and which Ray had intended as his debut work, recalls *Charulata* in many ways. By the time Ray rewrote and shot the film in 1984, it had become somewhat anachronistic. Ray's son, Sandeep, completed the post-production after Ray suffered his first heart attack.

KAANAMARAYATHU

aka *The Invisible One*
1984 137' col Malayalam
d **I.V. Sasi** *pc* Vici Films *s* **P. Padmarajan** *lyr* Bichu Thirumala *c* Jayanan Vincent *m* Shyam
lp **Mammootty**, Lalu Alex, Rehman, Bahadur, Shobhana, Sabitha, Seema, Kaviyoor Ponnamma, Sukumari, Noorjehan, Unnimary

Best known for starting the sexploitation genre in Malayalam cinema, Sasi adapts a script of the novelist and director Padmarajan (***Koodevide?***, 1983), a story of an aging, brutally practical businessman who reluctantly pays for the education of an orphaned girl originally sponsored by his father. The schoolgirl falls madly in love with the middle-aged businessman who, when the girl is about to be sent to a nunnery, allows himself to accept her love.

KONY

1984 131' col Bengali
d/sc/co-dial Saroj De *pc* West Bengal Govt *co-dial* Jayanta Bhattacharya *st* Moti Nandy *lyr* **Rabindranath Tagore** *c* Kamal Nayak *m* Chinmoy Chatterjee
lp **Soumitra Chatterjee**, Sreeparna Bannerjee, Moushumi Roy, Sarmishta Mukherjee, Subrata Sen, Swaroop Dutta

A sporting melodrama about a wayward but determined swimming coach, Kshitish Sinha (Chatterjee), and his star disciple, the female street urchin Kony (Bannerjee). Under her coach's tutelage, Kony overcomes all adversities, including hostile sports administrators, and wins her race. Adapted from a story by the noted sports journalist and novelist Moti Nandy (cf the novel *Striker*, filmed in 1978). Both the realism and the political references mandatory in Bengali cinema (club rivalry, Sinha becoming a speechwriter for a politically ambitious industrialist) are present, and Kony's general defiance of both gender and class oppression keeps the sentimentalism within bounds. Director Saroj De was associated with the famous Agragami collective.

LAKSHMANA REKHA

1984 113' col Malayalam
d **I.V. Sasi** *pc* Murali Movies *s* P.V. Kuriakose *lyr* Bichu Thirumala *c* Jayanan Vincent *m* A.T. Ummar
lp **Mammootty**, **Mohanlal**, K.P. Ummar, P.K. Abraham, **Adoor Bhasi**, Seema, Kalaranjini, Kaviyoor Ponnamma

Bizarre Sasi melodrama exploiting the Kerala convention of marriage between cousins. Two brothers, Sukumaran and Sudhakaran both love their cousin Radha. She marries one of them, but her husband has an accident on their wedding night and is paralysed for life. A psychiatrist recommends that the wife has sex with her brother-in-law to solve her emotional problems. The paralysed husband, unable to handle this new development, is then killed by his father in order to end his misery. The father is arrested.

MANIK RAITONG

aka *Manik the Miserable*
1984 149' col Khasi
d/sc **Ardhendu Bhattacharya** *p/st* Rishan Rapseng *pc* Neo Cine Prod. *dial* Humphrey Blaah *lyr* Skendrowel Syiemlih *c* Bijoy Anand Sabharwal *m* Kazu Matsui
lp William Rynjhah, Sheba Diengdoh, Gilbert Synnah, Veronica Nongbet, Benjamin Khongnor, Diamond Matthew

Documentarist Bhattacharya's feature debut is the first film in the North-Eastern language of Khasi. It is a folk-tale about a poor man, Manik, and his beloved Lieng who is forced to marry the tribal chief Syiem. She refuses to live with her husband and at one time has a sexual encounter with Manik which leaves her pregnant. She raises the child, but her lover is condemned to death. She jumps into Manik's funeral pyre and dies with him. Reputed to be one of Meghalaya's most ancient legends, relating to the origins of the region when seven of the sixteen families with privileged access to heaven decide to live on earth. In spite of some awkward acting, the film evokes the sad fatalism of marginalised people's folk idiom in India.

MATI MANAS

aka *Mind of Clay* aka *Terracotta*
1984 92' col Hindi
d/p/co-s **Mani Kaul** *pc* Infrakino Film Prod. *co-sc* Kamal Swaroop *c* Venu *m* T.R. Mahalingam
lp Anita Kanwar, Robin Das, Ashok Sharma

Episodic film about the ancient Indian tradition of terracotta sculpture and pottery and the several legends associated with this tradition. The artefacts involved include some of the oldest items of Indian civilisation (from the Indus Valley, 2500BC) and have been, together with the legends associated with terracotta techniques, central to historical research into, e.g., the origins of patriarchy, the shift from pastoral to agrarian systems, etc. The film enacts a series of such legends. The first is of the Sariya Mata or cat mother whose kittens remained safe in the interior of the baked pot, a legend associated with Harappan archaeological sites which had human skeletons buried in womb-like pots. The second legend revolves around the Kala-Gora (Black-White) icon produced in the village of Molella, Rajasthan, and features the witch Gangli who transforms Gora into a bull by day, making him work in her oil-press, until finally Kala beheads Gangli. The film connects this tale with the Mesopotamian legend of Gilgamesh and Enkidu. The third, and best-known, legend features Parashuram who beheads his own mother Renuka with his axe. Interwoven with these tales are stories narrated by the potters themselves and fictional sequences featuring three contemporary historians who recall the legends while looking at the terracotta artefacts, often through the eyepiece of a camera or from behind glass panes in a museum. Shot throughout Central, South and Eastern India, the film deliberately suppresses its variety of locations to achieve the idea of an integrated civilisation endowed with a sense of immortality through cultural (pro)creativity. At the same time, the techno-cultural process of film-making is presented as an extension of similar craft traditions.

MOHAN JOSHI HAAZIR HO!

aka *A Summons for Mohan Joshi*
1984 123'(130') col Hindi
d/p/co-st/co-sc/co-dial **Saeed Akhtar Mirza** *pc* Saeed Akhtar Mirza Prod *co-st/co-sc* Yusuf Mehta *co-dial* Ranjit Kapoor *co-st/co-sc* Sudhir Mishra *lyr* Madhosh Bilgrami *c* Virendra Saini *m* **Vanraj Bhatia**
lp **Naseeruddin Shah**, Deepti Naval, Bhisham Sahni, Dina Pathak, Rohini Hattangadi, Amjad Khan, Mohan Gokhale, Satish Shah, Pankaj Kapoor, Arvind Deshpande

Mirza's parody on housing legislation tells of Mohan Joshi (Sahni, the well-known novelist and brother of **Balraj Sahni** in his screen debut), a retired clerk who lives with his wife (Pathak) in an old Bombay tenement. Joshi sues his landlord, the evil property developer Kundan Kapadia (Khan), which starts a complicated and expensive legal procedure conducted by the slick lawyer Malkani (N. Shah). Eventually Joshi realises that one cannot win against entrenched economic powers. In the end, when the judge comes to see the condition of the building for himself, Kapadia's men quickly cover its rickety walls with a coat of paint and Joshi, unable to control his anger, goes berserk and demolishes the place, making it collapse on to his own head. Mirza's allegorical approach, using a crudely Brechtian idea of surface realism, allows him to cast the noted screen villain Amjad Khan (cf ***Sholay***, 1975) as the property developer with lather dripping from his chin or eating a leg of mutton.

MUKHA MUKHAM

aka *Face to Face*
1984 106' col Malayalam
d/s **Adoor Gopalakrishnan** *p* K. Ravindranathan Nair *pc* General Pics *c* Ravi Varma *m* **M.B. Srinivasan**
lp P. Ganga, Balan K. Nair, Kaviyoor Ponnamma, Krishna Kumar, Karamana Janardanan Nair, Thilakan, Vishwanathan, Ashokan, Lalitha, Vembayam, Krishnakutty Nair, John Samuel, Shanmugham Pillai, Thambi

Gopalakrishnan's melodrama that opened up a new direction in the genre in Malayalam film while looking at the unpalatable aspects of radical populism in Kerala. The first part is set in the 1945-55 period just prior to the short-lived 1957 CPI electoral victory in the

Bhisham Sahni and Dina Pathak in *Mohan Joshi Hazir Ho!*

State. The 2nd part is ten years later, after 1964, when the CPI split in two, later fragmenting even further. The central character is Sridharan (Ganga), a trade union leader who plays a key role in winning a strike against mechanisation. He is mercilessly beaten by thugs and has to go underground. This episode is told from the point of view of an idealist radical, Sudhakaran (Vishwanathan as a boy, Ashokan as a man). Years later, the old radicals have made their compromises and Sridharan has become a legendary emblem of integrity on whom the defeated survivors have projected their erstwhile radicalism. When he returns, there follows bitter disappointment at the discovery of the legendary hero's human weaknesses. His name is invoked by all factions as a rallying cry, making his presence all the more embarrassing. One day, he is found killed. With the man safely out of the way, his image can once again be mobilised, untarnished by the complexities of real life. Violently attacked by the CPI(M) establishment in Kerala, the film works on several layers: in critiquing the state's left establishment it also critically evokes a tradition of political melodrama in Kerala (cf **Thoppil Bhasi**'s scripts). It suggests that its protagonist in all his roles - fiery leader, spent force, political legend - is inescapably reduced into stereotypical functioning, in the popular melodramatic sense, of one kind or another. The film thereby shifts the entire critique into one where the mass culture generated by incomplete capitalist growth merges with the rhetoric of left activism, the whole masking what the director suggests to be the major problem: the absence of a valid indigenous culture able to define the terms of its engagement with capitalist systems.

MY DEAR KUTTICHATHAN/CHHOTA CHETAN

1984 96' col Malayalam/Hindi
d Jijo *pc* Navodaya *sc* Raghunath Paleri *st* Navodaya's script team *lyr* Bichu Thirumala *c* Ashok Kumar *m* **Ilaiyaraja**
lp **Kottarakkara Sridharan Nair**, Alumoodan, Dalip Tahil, Arvind, Mukesh, Suresh, Sonia

Made by the veteran director Appachan's son, this box-office hit is a fantasy film designed to show off its special effects in India's first 3-D movie. Kuttichathan is a mischievous genie living in an abandoned house. He is accidentally summoned by a group of children and appears in the guise of a boy who carries out all their wishes. This allows the director to stage scenes of children walking on the ceiling, speeded-up rickshaw rides and various other spectacular episodes. Sentiment is catered for by having the genie cure one child's father of alcoholism. The geni eventually changes into a fox-bat and flies off. A dubbed Hindi version, *Chhota Chetan*, was also successful.

NEERAB JHADA

aka *The Silent Storm*
1984 119' b&w Oriya
d/sc **Manmohan Mahapatra** *pc* Chayadhwani Prod. *st* Nandlal Mahapatra *c* Raj Sekhar, B. Bindhani *m* Shantanu Mahapatra
lp Hemanta Das, Niranjan Patnaik, B. Tripathi, R. Das, Jaya Swami, Manimala

Mahapatra's melancholic rural realism, deployed on an expanded canvas, tells of three peasants confronting a dastardly landlord. One of the friends goes crazy trying to find buried treasure in order to recover his land; another goes to the city where he finds even worse forms of exploitation; the third has a more complicated problem: his daughter falls in love with an employee of the landlord. He too loses his land and has to migrate, but in the process delivers the film's 'voice of hope', suggesting that if sufficient numbers of people feel the way he does, the future might still be bright.

NOKKETHA DHOORATHU KANNUM NATTU

aka *Looking at Infinity*
1984 130' col Malayalam *d/s* **Fazil** *pc* Bodhi Chitra *lyr* Bichu Thirumala *c* Ashok Kumar *m* Jerry Amaldev
lp **Padmini**, Nadia Moidu, Sukumari, **Mohanlal**, Nedumudi Venu, Thilakan, K.P. Ummar, Fazil, Raju

Contemporary melodrama about a young girl incongruously called Girly (Moidu) who brightens the life of her embittered grandmother, Kunjoojamma Thomas (Padmini). As the girl requires a critical operation, the grandmother finds that once more the story of her life repeats itself: the people she loves are invariably taken away from her. Actress Padmini, who had been living in the USA for many years, made her comeback with this film.

NOORAVATHUNAAL

1984 133' col Tamil
d/s Manivannan *pc* Thirupathiswamy Pics *lyr* **Vairamuthu**, Mutthulingam, Pulamai Pithan *m* **Ilaiyaraja**
lp Mohan, Vijayakanth, Thenjai Srinivasan, Sathyaraj, Nalini, Ponni, Y. Vijaya

An efficient crime thriller notable as the film which the unemployed psychotic murderer Jayaprakash cited as the inspiration for his slaughter of a large family in Madras. The claim hit the headlines and ensured the film's box-office success. The plot concerns a wayward son, Kumar, of an equally wayward father. Kumar steals museum pieces with the help of a security officer. He kills a young woman and marries the victim's sister, Devi, who finds out about her husband's criminal activities and, with the help of her brother-in-law, exposes Kumar to the police.

PAAR

aka *The Crossing*
1984 141'(120') col Hindi
d/co-sc/c/m **Gautam Ghosh** *pc* Orchid Films *co-sc* Partha Bannerjee *st* Samaresh Bose's short story *Paarhi dial* S.P. Singh.
lp **Naseeruddin Shah**, **Shabana Azmi**, **Utpal Dutt**, **Om Puri**, Mohan Agashe, **Anil Chatterjee**, Ruma Guha-Thakurta, Sunil Mukherjee, Kamu Mukherjee

One of the photo-journalist and documentarist Ghosh's best-known films, it features a familiar New Indian Cinema cast: Shah, Puri and Azmi. A fable of exploitation in rural Bihar, in which the landlord's men wreck a village and kill the benevolent schoolmaster who was its progressive force. The labourer Naurangia (Shah) breaks with a tradition of passive resistance and retaliates by killing the landlord's brother. Naurangia and his wife Rama (Azmi) become fugitives from justice. After many efforts to find sustenance elsewhere, the two decide to return home. To earn the fare, they agree to drive a herd of pigs through a river, causing the pregnant Rama to believe she has lost her baby. At the end of the film Naurangia puts his ear to her belly and listens to the heartbeats of the unborn child. The original short story dealt mainly with the river crossing and the film was criticised for not adequately integrating this episode with the others. With this film Ghosh joined the trend of 70s ruralist realism, although the river-crossing episode achieves a wider metaphoric resonance.

PANCHAVADIPPALAM

1984 140' col Malayalam
d/s **K.G. George** *pc* Jansuk Gandhimati Films *st/lyr* Chuvalloor Krishnankutty *dial* Yesudasan *c* **Shaji N. Karun** *m* **M.B. Srinivasan**
lp **Gopi**, Nedumudi Venu, Thilakan, K.P. Ummar, Jagathy Shrikumar, Venu Nagavalli, Alumoodan, Srinivasan, V.D. Rajappan, Innocent, Chandran Nair, Sukumari, Subha, Shrividya, Kalpana

A satirical comedy about political corruption and vanity. A henpecked politician wants his name attached to a new bridge, even if that means destroying another, perfectly serviceable bridge. The new bridge collapses during its official opening and kills a bystander.

PARTY

1984 118'(155') col Hindi
d/c **Govind Nihalani** *pc* **NFDC** *s* Mahesh Elkunchwar from his Marathi play
lp Rohini Hattangadi, Manohar Singh, **Vijaya Mehta**, Deepa Sahi, K.K. Raina, Soni Razdan, Shafi Inamdar, **Om Puri**, Amrish Puri, Akash Khurana, **Naseeruddin Shah**, Gulan Kripalani, Pearl Padamse

An exemplary tale set in a middle-class artistic milieu inaugurating Nihalani's long-term project of filmed theatre. Mrs Rane (Mehta) hosts a party for the recipient of a literary prize (Singh). The gathered 'intelligentsia' are revealed to be shallow hypocrites compared with the absent poet Amrit (Shah), who abandoned his literary career to become an activist among the tribals. The original Marathi play was criticised for its superficial depiction of the Bombay intelligentsia and the film does not really improve matters. Nihalani commented about the differences between the play and the film: 'There is a major difference in the thrust. The play is concerned with the question of art versus life. The film goes a bit further and tries to see whether a person can have two contrary sets of morality: one as an artist and the other as a human being.'

SAARANSH

aka *The Gist*
1984 137' col Hindi
d/st/co-sc/co-dial **Mahesh Bhatt** *pc* Rajshree Prod. *co-sc* Sujit Sen *co-dial* Amit Khanna *lyr* Vasant Deo *c* Adeep Tandon *m* Ajit Varman
lp Rohini Hattangadi, Anupam Kher, Soni Razdan, Madan Jain, Suhas Bhalekar, Nilu Phule

Bhatt follows his successful ***Arth*** (1982) with this expressionistic psychodrama about old age, fading idealism and political corruption. Old Pradhan (Kher, in his debut performance), a retired headmaster, and his wife Parvati (Hattangadi) learn that their son, studying in New York, has been mugged and killed. Pradhan goes through the trauma of bureaucratic corruption to receive his cremated son's ashes at the airport. Their tenant Sujata (Razdan), a young actress, is in love with Vilas (Jain), whose father is the corrupt politician Chitre (Phule). When Sujata finds herself pregnant, Pradhan and Parvati believe that it is their son reborn and protect Sujata from Chitre's threats. The problem of bureaucratic ineptitude is solved when Pradhan goes to meet a minister who turns out to be his former student and still retains his old teacher's sense of integrity. In the end, the old couple are reconciled to the loss of their son. The film has an oppressive soundtrack, with heavy music and effects underlining the states of loneliness, fear and frustration.

SITARA

aka *A Star*
1984 144' col Telugu
d/sc **Vamsy** *pc* Poornodaya Movie Creations *dial* Sainath *lyr* Veeturi Sundara Ramamurthy *c* M.V. Raghu *m* **Ilaiyaraja**
lp Sudhakar, Suman, Sarath Babu, Sriram, Prabhakar Reddy, Bhanupriya, Chamundeshwari, Saroja, J.V. Somayajulu, Sakshi Ranga Rao

Sexual fantasy in the **Vishwanath** style made by the producers of ***Sagara Sangamam*** (1983). The photographer Devadas (Sudhakar) offers shelter to a mysterious woman he names Sitara (Bhanupriya). She later becomes a film star and he her manager. Her secretiveness about her past is broken when she shows she is terrified by caged birds and cannot bear to work in an abandoned palace. It turns out that she used to live in that palace, a virtual prisoner of her impoverished but proud zamindar brother (Sarath Babu), until she was rescued by a group of travelling performers. At the end of the film, the cynical manager writes an unauthorised biography of Sitara and she once again has to abandon her home and seek her future elsewhere.

SWATI

aka *The Pearl*
1984 144' col Telugu
d/s Kranthi Kumar *pc* Shri Kranthi Chitra *dial* Ganesh Patro *lyr* Veeturi Sundara Ramamurthy *c* Hari Anumolu *m* Chakravarty
lp **Suhasini, K. Jaggaiah**, Bhanuchander, P.L. Narayana, Sarat Babu, Rajendra Prasad, Subhalekha Sudhakar, **Sharada**, Samyuktha, Ramaprabha, Anuradha

Kranthi Kumar's directorial debut is an episodic melodrama about an aggressive young woman, Swati (Suhasini), who looks after her divorced mother (Sharada) while defending herself against predatory males in the street. Having arranged her mother's second marriage with an old widower (Jaggaiah), Swati has problems with her new stepsister. When one of Swati's friends is raped, local gossip blames the victim's husband for failing to prevent the attack and the couple commit suicide. In the end, Swati's father turns up wanting to meet his former wife once more before his death. He is allowed only to see her from a distance, while she is not told that he is still alive. One of Tamil star Suhasini's best-known Telugu films. The director remade the film in Hindi in 1986 with **Shashi Kapoor, Sharmila Tagore** and **Madhuri Dixit**, with a score by **Laxmikant-Pyarelal**.

TARANG

aka *Wages and Profit* aka *The Wave*
1984 171' col Hindi
d/co-sc **Kumar Shahani** *pc* **NFDC** *co-sc* Roshan Shahani *dial* Vinay Shukla *lyr* Raghuvir Sahay, **Gulzar** *c* K.K. Mahajan *m* **Vanraj Bhatia**
lp **Smita Patil, Amol Palekar**, Shriram Lagoo, **Girish Karnad, Om Puri**, Jalal Agha, Rohini Hattangadi, Kawal Gandhiok, M.K. Raina, Sulabha Deshpande, Arvind Deshpande, Jayanti Patel

Made 12 years after ***Maya Darpan*** (1972), Shahani's biggest film to date is an elaborately plotted melodrama precisely realising his theory of epic cinema. An industrial family headed by the patriarch Sethji (Lagoo) is split when his son-in-law Rahul (Palekar) falls out with the industrialist's nephew Dinesh (Karnad). Sethji, who became rich as a war profiteer, regards 'wealth creation' as a goal in itself and ruthlessly administers his personal fiefdom accordingly. Rahul, regarded by the family as a mere caretaker until Sethji's grandson is ready to take over, is a more modern 'nationalist' capitalist committed to developing indigenous technology and minimum welfare arrangements for his workers. Dinesh, on the other hand, acts (illegally) on behalf of transnational interests which stand to profit by destabilising India's sovereignity. These conflicts are mirrored in ironically identical ways within the working class: the corrupt Patel (Patel) is a trade union leader presumably aligned to the Congress Party who sells out to the management; the worker Namdev (Puri) finds his more radical union leader Kalyan (A. Deshpande) equally inclined to opportunism while another worker, Abdul (Raina), believes the established forms of political struggle to be inadequate and joins a more extreme left group which is also betrayed by his erstwhile leader. The only figure transcending these mirrored divisions is the remarkable Janaki (Patil). Widowed when her activist husband is killed, her commitment to the nurturing of a progressive force is repeatedly exploited by different factions and conflicting ideologies: reduced to prostitution, she is manipulated by Rahul's sexually frigid wife Hansa (Gandhiok) into becoming her husband's mistress. The money she thus obtains from Rahul is used to support the working-class movement. Forced by Rahul to become his accomplice in a plot to kill his father-in-law, she is made the scapegoat when the family conflict escalates into virtual gang war. At the end, the film shifts into a mythic discourse and Janaki becomes the elusive voice of history. Accusing Rahul of trying to manipulate what he never understood, she claims the forces of change to be 'faster than the fleeting wind'. This sequence replays lines from the Urvashi-Pururavas legend from the

Smita Patil and M.K. Raina in *Tarang*

Rig Veda as analysed by the historian D.D. Kosambi in his book *Myth And Reality* (1962/1983). The film adheres to Kosambi's view that in India, the epic has often been the most precise language available for history itself, and much of the plotting is informed by the structure of the *Mahabharata*. In a narrower sense, however, the film is also a definitive comment on India's nationalist enterprise, and on the tradition of cinematic melodrama that saw itself, and its formal assimilations, as the cultural vanguard of a modernising nation-state.

TASVEER APNI APNI

Their Own Faces
1984 66' col Hindi
d/p/s **Mrinal Sen** *pc* **Doordarshan** *c* Sambit Bose
lp M.K. Raina, K.K. Raina, Shyamand Jalan

A minor work made for tv about an employee (K.K. Raina) who desperately tries to persuade the office manager (M.K. Raina) not to sack him. The story is interrupted by dialogues between the narrator (Jalan) and the character suggesting that we are all playthings in games beyond our control.

THIRAKKIL ALPA SAMAYAM

1984 134' col Malayalam
d P.G. Vishwambaran *pc* Vijaya and Vijaya *st* **Kanam E.J.** *sc* Pappanamcode *dial* Sharief *lyr* Chunakkara *c* C.E. Babu *m* Shyam
lp **Madhu**, Thilakan, **Mammootty**, Shankar, T.G. Ravi, Seema, Menaka, Shubha, Meena

Communal melodrama about a conflict of generation and class that also involves three religions. The Hindu Shankaran Nair falls out with his friend, the Muslim Khadir Haji, when the latter arranges a marriage between Nair's daughter Sarala and her poor Christian lover Anthony (Mammootty). The ensuing battle, which splits the village, escalates when Haji pulls his daughter out of school and virtually forces her into an arranged marriage; the daughter eventually marries a man of her choice with the help of Sarala and Anthony. Playing a major role as a social force is Anthony's working-class trade union of rickshaw-drivers, which helps re-establish amity.

UTSAV

aka *The Festival*
1984 145' col Hindi
d/co-sc **Girish Karnad** *p* **Shashi Kapoor** *co-p* Dharampriya Das *pc* Film Valas *st* Sudraka's play *Mrichchakatikam* aka *The Little Cart* and Bhasa's play *Charudatta co-sc* Krishna Basrur *dial* Sharad Joshi *lyr* Vasant Dev *c* Ashok Mehta *m* **Laxmikant-Pyarelal**
lp Shashi Kapoor, **Rekha**, Anuradha, **Shankar Nag**, Shekhar Suman, Amjad Khan, Kunal Kapoor, Annu Kapoor, Neena Gupta, Kulbhushan Kharbanda, Anupam Kher

An exuberant but unsuccessful picaresque film set in the 4th C., when Sudraka is supposed to have written one of the most famous plays in Indian history, a love story between the Brahmin merchant Charudatta (Suman) and the beautful courtesan Vasantsena (Rekha). Karnad also introduced Vatsyayana (Amjad Khan) as a voyeuristic lecher peeking into various brothel chambers to write his famous *Kama Sutra*. Vasantsena, a beautiful prostitute of Ujjain, runs away from the villain Samasthanaka (S. Kapoor), the libidinous brother-in-law of the king, and hides in the house of Charudatta, a music-lover, with whom she falls in love. She loses her golden necklace in Charudatta's house and when it is stolen, Charudatta's affair with the prostitute is exposed. Samasthanaka, who believes he killed Vasantsena when he tried to rape her, accuses Charudatta of the deed. When Charudatta is sentenced to hang for Vasantsena's murder, she turns up, alive and well, to try to save her lover's life. Just then, a horseman arrives to declare that a new king has been crowned and has pardoned all prisoners. Charudatta is reunited with his wife while the populace turns on the villainous Samasthanaka. He drags himself to Vasantsena's house who, this time, accepts him. Karnad uses the conventions of the Hindi movie to explore the rasas of Shringar (the erotic) and Hasya (the comic), on which India's classical aesthetic theory of performance is based, and intended the film as a celebration of life and love. The location scenes, filmed in Karnataka and Bharatpur because of the traditional architectural styles available there, were completed by studio scenes shot in Bombay. Apparently a more explicitly erotic version of the film was created for the Western market. This expensive film was producer Shashi Kapoor's last effort at an art-house production.

AGNISNAN

aka *Ordeal*
1985 186' col Assamese
d/p/s **Bhabendranath Saikia** *c* Kamal Nayak *lyr/m* Tarun Goswami
lp Malaya Goswami, Biju Phukan, Arun Nath, Kashmiri Barua, Sanjib Hazarika, Ananda Mohan Bhagawati, Arun Guha-Thakurta, Nilu Chakraborty, Indra Bania, Ashok Deka

The Assamese physicist and writer Saikia used one of his own novels, set in 30s feudal-colonial Assam, for this extended film about a woman's emancipation. The well-off and British-supported rice mill owner Mohikanta is married to the quiet Menoka and has four children by her. When Mohikanta takes a second wife, Kiran, and makes her pregnant, the angry Menoka starts a secret affair with the village thief, Madan, and becomes pregnant. Unaware of his double standards, Mohikanta feels betrayed and demands an explanation for Menoka's refusal to have sexual relations with him ever since Kiran moved into their home. Menoka simply points out that since Mohikanta had expected her to put up with his infidelities, so he must accept hers. The final confrontation between husband and wife, set in the rice mill, provides an unusual ending to this tale about patriarchal hypocrisy as the initially submissive Menoka self-confidently affirms her right to fully equal status with her husband.

AKALATHE AMBILI

1985 157' col Malayalam
d Jesey *pc* Centaur Art Prod. *s* S.N. Swamy *lyr* M.D.R. *c* Vipin Das *m* Shyam
lp **Mammootty**, Mukesh, Manian Pillai Raju, Supriya Pathak, Rohini, Mala Aravindan, Santosh, Thilakam

Standard Mammootty adventure movie. He plays Ajayan, a successful businessman with a rags-to-riches background, in love with his secretary Ambili. His rival in love, Ashok, is kidnapped by their mutual enemies, but Ajayan rescues Ashok and eventually (in characteristic Mammootty style) sacrifices his own happiness for that of his friends.

Angadikkapurathu
1985 155' col Malayalam
d **I.V. Sasi** *pc* Jeyemje Arts *s* T. Damodaran *lyr* Bichu Thirumala *m* Sathyam
lp **Mammootty, Mohanlal**, Rehman, Mahalakshmi, Lily

Early instance of the fast-paced satires of director Sasi and writer Damodaran, also featuring the combined presence of Malayalam megastars Mammootty and Mohanlal. Babu (Mohanlal), a poor orphan, wins a rigged lottery ticket by accident, and encounters a new world of crime, double-dealing and dishonesty. He eventually realises that he has no use for the money, and prefers to get rid of it and return to his earlier lifestyle. Mammootty plays a political activist in a film liberally peopled with gangsters, crooked lawyers with dubious morals, drug addicts and (Sasi's regular feature) cabaret dancers.

ANKUSH

1985 149' col Hindi
d/sc/co-dial **N. Chandra** *pc* Shilpa Movies *st* Debu Sen *co-dial* Sayyad Sultan *lyr* Abhilash *c* H. Laxminarayan *m* Kuldeep Singh
lp Madan Jain, Nana Patekar, Arjun Chakraborty, Suhas Palshikar, Nisha Singh, Ashalata, Dinkar Kaushik, Mahavir Shah, Rabia Amin, Ravi Patwardhan, Master Bobby, Raja Bundela, Sayyed

Chandra's debut film propagates the cause of the fanatic Hindu party, the Shiv Sena, a link emphasised by the Hindi film debut of Nana Patekar. A gang of four educated but unemployed men are a law unto themselves. Reformed by a female guardian angel (Singh), the four briefly attempt an entrepreneurial life until the woman is raped by the very gang leader (and his masters) against whom the youths are fighting. Revenge is swift, as is their repentance, creating a cyclical story of violence and regret. The film unashamedly rehearses Bombay's Shiv Sena ideologies: unemployment is the devil's workshop, industry is controlled by 'rootless outsiders' (North Indians, mainly) who persecute and exploit 'the natives'. The relentless violence culminates in the four thugs, presented as 'heroes', being martyred as they are hanged in a manner reminiscent of India's nationalist freedom fighters.

CHIDAMBARAM

1985 102' col Malayalam
d/sc **Govindan Aravindan** *pc* Suryakanthi Film Makers *st* C.V. Shriraman *c* **Shaji N. Karun** *m* **P. Devarajan**
lp **Gopi, Smita Patil**, Srinivas, Mohan Das, Murali, Chandran Nair

Unfolding in exquisitely photographed poetic rhythms and coloured landscapes, this is the simple but cynical tale of Muniyandi (Srinivas), a labourer on the Indo-Swiss Mooraru farm in Kerala. He brings a wife, Shivagami (Patil), from the temple town of Chidambaram. She befriends Shankaran (Gopi), the estate manager and amateur photographer with a shady past. Their friendship transgresses the hypocritical but deeply felt behavioural codes the local men inherited from previous social formations: i.e. that women are to be denied what men are allowed to enjoy. The tragedy that ensues (Muniyandi's suicide, Shankaran's descent into alcoholism and Shivagami's withering into a worn-out old woman) condenses the tensions between socio-economic change (as tractors and machinery invade the landscape) and people's refusal to confront the corresponding need to change their mentality. The tension is, however, most graphically felt in the way Shivagami's life-force is extended into the naturescape, which is shot around her with garish colour (e.g. purple flower-beds) suggesting that the very nature of Kerala's beauty and fertility, as she represents it, has been irredeemably corrupted from within. The film then shifts to the equally oppressive cloisters of the Chidambaram temple, as Shankaran and Shivagami meet once more: he is there to purify himself through religious ritual while she is now employed to look after the footwear of devotees and tourists. The nihilist film ends with a rising crane shot as the camera can only avert its gaze and escape, tilting up along a temple wall towards an open sky.

DEBSHISHU

aka *The Child God*
1985 100' col Hindi
d/s/m **Utpalendu Chakraborty** *pc* **NFDC** *c* Soumendu Roy
lp **Smita Patil**, Sadhu Meher, Rohini Hattangadi, **Om Puri**, Shyamanand Jalan, Sushant Sanyal

Intended as an indictment of religious intolerance, the film is set on the frontier between West Bengal and Bihar. In a fairground, a child with three heads is exhibited as a miracle-performing child god. A poor peasant, Raghubir (Meher), and his wife Seeta (Patil) hope that the child will alleviate their suffering. However, Raghubir then discovers that the misshapen child was borne by his own wife who sold the infant for 30 rupees. Raghubir indignantly demands to be given half of that sum and, when he cannot get it, he beats Seeta in the hope that she will give birth to another misshapen child.

GHULAMI

1985 199' col/scope Hindi
d/s **J.P. Dutta** *pc* Habib and Faruq Nadiadwala *dial* O.P. Dutta *lyr* **Gulzar** *c* Ishwar Bidri *m* **Laxmikant-Pyarelal**
lp **Dharmendra**, Reena Roy, **Smita Patil**, Om Shivpuri, Mazhar Khan, Bharat Kapoor, Anita Raj, Kulbhushan Kharbanda, Raza Murad, **Mithun Chakraborty**, **Naseeruddin Shah**

Violent ruralist melodrama about Rajput oppression in the desert of Rajasthan. The hero Ranjit Singh (Dharmendra), son of a Jat farmer, leads a popular rebellion against the corrupt zamindar (Shivpuri) and his three nephews. The hero is aided by a policeman (Kharbanda) whose son had been killed by the nephews, and an army officer from a Jat regiment (Chakraborty) who decides to use his military skills to defend his community from the rapacious Thakurs. On the side of the zamindar is his son-in-law, the police officer Sultan Singh (Shah). However, the cop's wife Sumitra (Patil) is sympathetic to Ranjit Singh's cause. The Jats' objective is to capture and burn the account ledgers of the moneylending thakur community to free themselves from bonded labour. They eventually succeed though the hero dies, leaving his wife Moran (Reena Roy) and infant son to continue the struggle. Rajasthan's arid desert landscape, its vultures and shots of the famous folk fair at Pushkar (a major tourist attraction) give the film both an exotic and a primitivist atmosphere. However, it went beyond poetic metaphor in several inflammatory scenes addressing the region's charged communal situation. The scene where the hero's mother rushes into the villain's house to save her son without taking off her slippers, and is then humiliated by being forced to put the slippers on her head and walk out, led to riots in several small cities in Rajasthan.

HAMARA SHAHER

aka *Bombay Our City*
1985 82' col Hindi/Tamil/English/Marathi
d/p/s/co-c **Anand Patwardhan** *co-c* Vijay Khambati, Pervez Mehrwanji, Venugopal Thakker *Hindi voice-over* Deepa Arora, Rita Bhatia, Supriya Pathak, **Om Puri**, **Naseeruddin Shah**, Rahul Varma

Patwardhan's most acclaimed documentary, made on 16mm, tells of Bombay's millions of pavement-dwellers. Throughout the early 80s there were several brutal efforts to evict families who lived in illegal tenements and on pavements although they provided the city with the casual (esp. construction) labour crucial to its economy. The film looks at the culture of Bombay's elite, often contrasting what they say with the physical conditions in which they say it: the former municipal commissioner bemoans the lack of space in the city while his pet dog trots around his spacious garden; the Police Commissioner Julio Ribeiro, in a speech at the Advertising Club, talks about the poor as 'low-quality, low-intelligence' people. The pavement-dwellers work in the construction industry in the city's expensive Nariman Point area on land reclaimed from the sea, while massing clouds on the horizon evoke the possibility of an unbalanced environment which may cause tidal waves to wash away their seaside huts. The film achieves epic dimensions in three remarkable sequences. Street urchins sell the Indian flag on a rainy Independence Day, keeping their precious commodities dry while the huge Gothic facade of the Victoria Terminus presides over a police march-past; in the thick of the monsoon, a child in one of the homeless families dies; a woman pavement-dweller's angry outburst at the film-makers, all highlight the issues involved in the making of this type of documentary.

IRAKAL

aka *Victims*
1985 142' col Malayalam
d/s **K.G. George** *p* M. Sukumaran *c* Venu *m* **M.B. Srinivasan**
lp Ganesan, Sukumari, Shrividya, Thilaka, Chandran Nair, **Gopi**, Ashokan, Nedumudi Venu, Venu Nagavalli

A ruthless rubber baron, Mathukutty (Thilakan), disregards the prevailing moral standards and spawns criminal sons as well as

Hamara Shaher

a sexually wayward daughter, Annie (Shrividya). His son, called Baby (Ganesan), is a psychotic strangler using a nylon wire and is eventually brutally shot dead by his repentant father. In Kerala, excessively flexible morality is called 'rubber morality'.

KILIPPATTU

aka *Song of the Parrot*
1985 121' col Malayalam
d/sc Raghavan *pc* Revathy Chitra *st/dial/lyr* K.M. Raghavan Nambiar *c* Vipin Das *m* **M.B. Srinivasan**
lp Nedumudi Venu, Sukumaran, K.P. Ummar, Sabitha Anand, Balan K. Nair, **Adoor Bhasi**, Chandran Nair, Philomina, Manavalan Joseph

The prolific actor Raghavan's directorial debut is set at festival time in a North Kerala village. The corpse of a young woman, presumed to be the temple-keeper's daughter, is found in a well. A trade union activist is arrested and dies in police custody, after which the temple-keeper's daughter turns up alive to everyone's embarrassment. However, she is later killed and her body found in the well during the next festival. In an ending reminiscent of ***Nirmalayam*** (1973), the distraught temple-keeper frenziedly strikes himself with a sacred sword during the performance of his ritual duties.

KLANTA APARANHA

aka *Tired Afternoon*
1985 93' col Oriya
d/sc **Manmohan Mahapatra** *pc* Dynamic Studios *st* Nandlal Mahapatra *c* Ranajit Ray *m* Shantanu Mahapatra
lp Sachidananda Rath, Kanak Panigrahi, Madhukar, Kishori Devi, Master Sushil

Two parallel tragic love stories continue Mahapatra's bleak portrayal of rural Orissa. Two local schoolteachers, Niru and Sandhya, see their respective marriage proposals break down. Niru is the daughter of the poor landowner Adikanta, who mortgages his land to raise the dowry for his daughter's marriage to an urban youth; however, the dowry offered is not enough. Sandhya loves Ashok who moves to the city, but she cannot move with him since her family depends on her income for its survival. The best moments are with Niru's ancient grandmother (Kishori Devi), esp. in the film's most spontaneous sequence when she is presented with a pair of spectacles.

MARD

1985 177' col Hindi
d **Manmohan Desai** *pc* MKD Films, Aasia Films *st* Prayag Raj *sc* K.K. Shukla *dial* **Inder Raj Anand** *lyr* Rajinder Krishan *c* Peter Pereira *m* Annu Malik
lp **Amitabh Bachchan**, Amrita Singh, **Nirupa Roy**, **Dara Singh**, Prem Chopra

The son, Raju Tangewala (Bachchan), of a dispossessed rajah is given the name 'Mard', i.e. Man, and has it tattooed on his chest as a sign of virility. Mard rebels against the British who are presented as robbers and property developers, the favourite Hindi film villains of this period. In keeping with a characteristic Desai plot device, Raju is raised by foster-parents who, just before dying, inform their adopted son of his 'real' ancestry. The leather-clad daughter (Amrita Singh) of a doctor in the service of the British first whips the hero and then falls in love with him. The British villains are called Dyer and Simon, names still associated with the general responsible for the Jallianwala Bagh massacre (referred to in the film) and the leader of the Simon Commission. Desai juxtaposes these references with the more arbitrary introduction of Roman gladiators and Mexican bandits. Made immediately after ***Coolie*** (1983), marked by Bachchan's near fatal accident, *Mard* went to unusual lengths to demonstrate the invincibility of the hero, invoking colonialism and feudal oppression to affirm that he whom the gods protect cannot be destroyed.

MAYURI

1985 142' col Telugu
d/co-sc **Singeetham Srinivasa Rao** *pc* Usha Kiron Movies *st* Usha Kiron Movies Unit *co-sc/dial* Ganesh Patro *lyr* Veeturi Sundara Ramamurthy *c* A. Hari *m* **S.P. Balasubramanyam**
lp Sudha Chandran, Subhakar, P.L. Narayana, Y. Vijaya, Nirmala

Melodrama about a classical dancer who, after an accident, has a leg amputated. With an artificial leg known as the Jaipur foot, she returns to dancing and regains her earlier reputation. The film was promoted as a fictionalised version of the real-life story of its lead actress, Sudha Chandran. Other characters include a henpecked father, a cruel stepmother and a boyfriend who is the cause of the accident and promptly abandons Mayuri when she becomes a cripple, adding to her determination to regain her lost self-respect.

MEENAMASATHILE SOORYAN

aka *Midsummer Sun*
1985 117' col Malayalam
d/s **Lenin Rajendran** *p* C.G. Bhaskaran *pc* Sauhudra Chitra *c* **Shaji N. Karun** *m* **M.B. Srinivasan**
lp **Gopi**, Venu Nagavalli, Vijay Menon, Murali, Ravi, Shobhana

Told in flashback, this is the story of how four fine young men achieved communist political consciousness in a peasant rising against a villainous landlord in 1943 in Kerala. The men, played by Menon, Murali, Nagavalli and Ravi, receive the revolutionary word from the schoolteacher (Gopi) and spread the message among the ignorant villagers. They end up as revered heroes condemned to be hanged by the British for treason. When asked for their last wish, they all ask to see their beloved teacher once more. Director Rajendran later contested two general elections backed by the Kerala CPI(M), from whose viewpoint he tells this tale.

MIRCH MASALA

aka *Spices*
1985 128' col Hindi
d **Ketan Mehta** *pc* **NFDC** *st* Chunilal Madia *sc* Hriday Lani, Tripurari Sharma *lyr* Babubhai Ranpura *c* Jehangir Choudhury *m* Rajat Dholakia
lp **Naseeruddin Shah**, **Smita Patil**, **Om Puri**, Suresh Oberoi, Deepti Naval, Benjamin Gilani, Raj Babbar, Mohan Gokhale, Supriya Pathak, Dina Pathak, Ratna Pathak, Ram Gopal

Following its commercial release in New York this became Mehta's best-known film outside India. Intended as an allegory of colonial oppression but presented as a sex-and-violence drama, the film is set in pre-Independence Saurashtra. The despotic tax collector Subedar (Shah), dressed in a way that evokes British 19th C. catchpenny prints and Daumier's cartoons, imposes his rule on a village. All the villagers try to satisfy his every whim, except for the protesting schoolteacher (Gilani). The drama starts when the beautiful Sonbai (Patil) is to be surrendered to the lecherous Subedar. She takes refuge in the courtyard of a spice factory run entirely by women and is protected by an aged watchman (Om Puri) who closes the gates to Subedar's men. Although made in Hindi, the film draws on Gujarati verbal and performative idioms. Mehta explicitly deployed stock literary melodrama characters, but these cliches from contemporary popular culture lack the historical resonance achieved by the more complex figures Mehta used in his extraordinary ***Bhavni Bhavai*** (1980).

MUHURTAM AT 11.30

1985 138' col Malayalam
d Joshi *pc* Saj Prod. *s* Kalloor Dennis *lyr* Poovachal Kader *c* N.A. Tara *m* Shyam
lp **Mammootty**, Ratheesh, Prathap Chandran, Saritha, Baby Shalini, Surekha, Lalitha, Lalu Alex, Kunjan, V.D. Rajappan, Jagathy Shrikumar

Melodrama by one of Malayalam cinema's foremost practitioners in the art. Love triangle featuring the good doctor Haridas (Mammootty), his new receptionist and ex-wife Indu and his rival (and Indu's cousin) Jayan. The doctor believes that the child born to Indu is not his. Jayan dies of a heart attack, shortly after a major operation, followed by Indu: the doctor realises his suspicions were groundless, but is too late to prevent the tragedy.

MUTHAL MARIYATHAI

aka *A Matter of Honour* aka *Prime Honour*
1985 161' col Tamil
d/p/sc **P. Bharathirajaa** *pc* Manoj Creations *st/dial* R. Selvaraj *lyr* **Vairamuthu** *c* B. Kannan *m* **Ilaiyaraja**
lp **Sivaji Ganesan**, Radha, Vadivukkarasi, Ranjini, Janakaraj, Deepan, Veeraswamy, Aruna

A relentless melodrama told in flashback as the saintly landlord Malaichami (Ganesan) lies dying. Beset by a shrewish wife, Ponnatha, who cannot cook and who was pregnant by another man when she married the hero, Malaichmi fell in love with a fisherman's young daughter, Kuyil, and eventually accepts her love, clinging to life

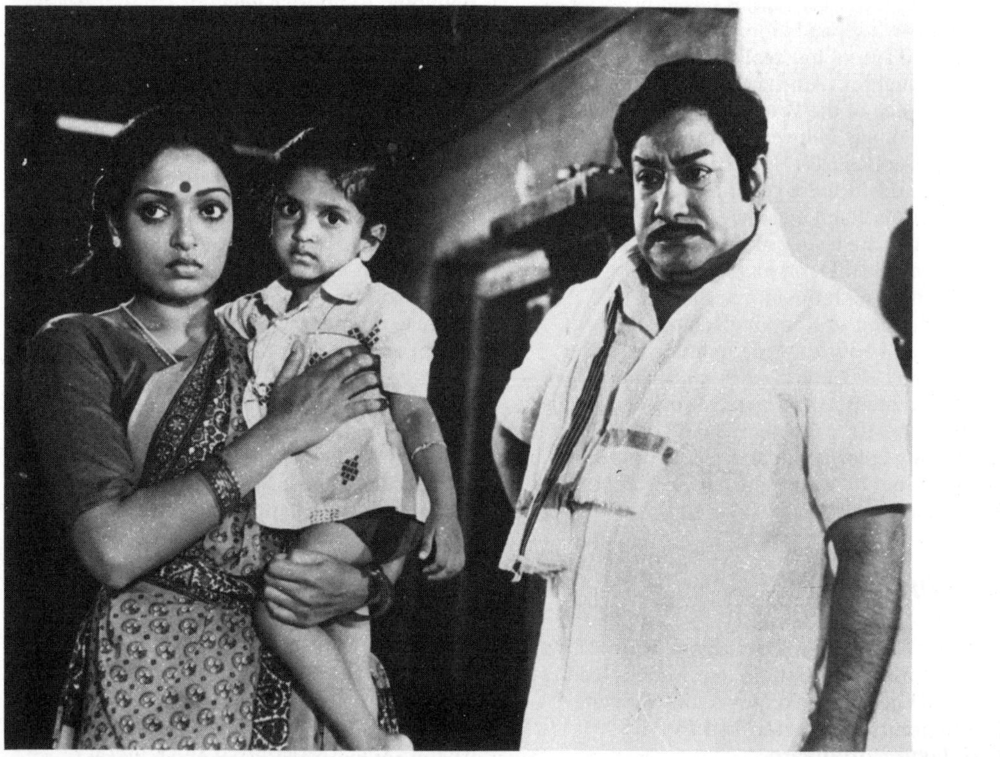

Sivaji Ganesan (right) in *Muthal Mariyathai*

until she returns, under police escort, to hold his hand as he dies. A second tragic love story involves Malaichami's evil son-in-law who is a rapist and a murderer. Ganesan deploys the florid acting style and declamatory agility for which he is revered.

NANAND BHOJAI

1985 161' col Rajasthani
d/sc Prabhakar Mandloi *pc* Kamal Kala Mandir *st* Ansuya Vyas *dial* Madhukar Mandloi, Kundan Kishore *lyr* B.L. Vyas *c* Arvind Dave *m* Jugalkishore-Tilakraj
lp Neelu, Dheraj Kumar, Gouri, Sunil Pandey, Adi Irani, Satyen Kappoo, Shubha Khote, Ramesh Dev, Bharat Bhushan, Aruna Irani

Neo-traditionalist melodrama pivoting on the relationship between sisters-in-law, but also including brotherly and parental relations. Poonam (Neelu), with the financial help of her Muslim friend Rasool, marries Vijay (Dheraj) despite the evil machinations of her rejected suitor Rocky. When Vijay goes to look for work in the city, Vijay's sister, manipulated by the villainous Rocky, persecutes the heroine. The familiar theme (esp. in Gujarati cinema: cf **Punatar**'s bilingual of the same title, 1948) confirmed Rajasthani star Neelu's image of 'goodness' in family melodramas (cf ***Supattar Binani***, 1981, and ***Bai Chali Sasariye***, 1988). Made with mainly Bombay film actors and modelled on Hindi cinema except for some narrative emphases such as the approach to the dowry problem: in Hindi films, dowries are increasingly seen as anti-modern and assigned to oppressive feudalism, whereas it is a more urgent issue in Rajasthan.

NEW DELHI TIMES

1985 123' col Hindi
d/co-st Ramesh Sharma *pc* P.K. Communications *co-st* K. Bikram Singh *co-st/sc* **Gulzar** *c* Subrata Mitra *m* Louis Banks
lp **Shashi Kapoor**, **Sharmila Tagore**, **Om Puri**, Kulbhushan Kharbanda, A.K. Hangal, Manohar Singh, M.K. Raina, Farokh Mehta

A political thriller examining the links between crime and politics in a north Indian state. The editor of the English-language *New Delhi Times*, Vikas Pande (Kapoor) has to confront the politician Ajay Singh (Puri) who is associated with a powerful lobby of illicit liquor manufacturers. The trail of murders, sequestrations in insane asylums, beatings and the instigation of communal riots by political henchmen eventually leads to the corrupt chief minister, D.N. Trivedi. Made in the style of Costa-Gavras's films and of Pakula's *All the President's Men* (1976), the film is inspired by the case of the *Indian Express* whose editor Arun Shourie exposed the criminal links of Maharashtra's chief minister, A.R. Antulay. The owner of the *Indian Express*, R.N. Goenka, is the figure evoked in the film by Vikas's boss, the publisher Jagannath Poddar (M. Singh). The film faced official censorship when **Doordarshan** initially refused to broadcast it.

PAROMA/PARAMA

1985 134'[B]/138'[H] col Bengali/Hindi
d/s **Aparna Sen** *pc* Usha Ents *lyr* **Gulzar** *c* Ashok Mehta *m* Bhaskar Chandavarkar
lp Raakhee, Sandhya Rani Chatterjee, Aparna Sen, Mukul Sharma, Dipankar De, **Anil Chatterjee**, Bharati Devi, Chitti Ghosal, Manas Mukherjee Jr, Arjun Guha-Thakurta

Sen followed up her directorial debut, ***36 Chowringhee Lane*** (1981) with this story about a 40-year-old married woman, Parama (Raakhee) who falls in love with Rahul (Sharma), an expatriate photo-journalist working for glossy magazines who photographs her making her look glamorous. Their affair, and the invasion of the glamour machine into her life, becomes a problem when some of the photographs, earlier admired by the family, are published in a journal. Parama is rejected by her husband and has a mental breakdown. In the end, a doctor suggests prescribing psychiatric treatment and when Parama adamantly refuses any sense of guilt, her young daughter comes and gives her mother moral support. The film is notable mainly for its emancipatory thrust, undermined by a class-inflected sense of nostalgia for 'belonging', rather than for its cinematic qualities which are akin to the kitschy style of glossy consumer magazines. The Bengali version, shown in Calcutta amid much controversy, was successful; the Hindi version was never properly released.

SAMANDARAM

aka *Parallel*
1985 117' col Malayalam
d/sc John C. Shankaramangalam *pc* Sudarshan *st* Ms M. Shankaramangalam *c* Prabhat Parida, Santosh Sivan *m* Jerry Amaldev
lp Soorya, Babu Namboodiri, Sai Das, Balan K. Nair, T.R.K. Menon, Mathews, Leela Panicker

A film by the dean of the **FTII** warning against student romances. The university student Susan notices disturbing signs of cowardice in her boyfriend Jose but marries him anyway. He turns into a brutal business executive and a wife-beater. The husband's deterioration is further emphasised in contrast with communist radical Mohan, Susan's former hero. After suffering her husband's brutalities as long as she can bear, she finally plucks up the courage to leave him on Christmas Eve.

SINDHU BHAIRAVI

1985 159' col Tamil
d/s **K. Balachander** *p* Rajam Balachander, V. Natarajan *pc* Kavithalaya Prod. *lyr* **Vairamuthu** *c* Raghunatha Reddy *m* **Ilaiyaraja**
lp Sivakumar, Delhi Ganesh, Janakaraj, T.S. Raghavendran, **Prathap Pothan**, **Suhasini**, Sulakshana, Manimala

Musical melodrama in the genre of **Dasari Narayana Rao**'s ***Megha Sandesam*** (1982) and **K. Vishwanath**'s revivalist stories advocating 'traditional' notions of 'classical' artistry. The classical singer J.K. Balaganapathi (Sivakumar) falls in love with Sindhu, a folk-music teacher. His barren wife Bhairavi attempts suicide and he renounces his affair, only to seek refuge in drink, which entails degrading scenes such as a forced strip tease and the singing of pop songs in exchange for alcohol. Bhairavi then sacrifices herself for the sake of her husband's music and asks Sindhu to help save the artist. Nevertheless, the film follows the convention of passing off male infantilism as evidence of a commitment to 'traditional values'. Women sacrificing themselves for the sake of an immature man's singing ability can be seen, against the grain of the film, as raising critical questions about arrogantly patriarchal fantasies, mainly through the performances of the two main female protagonists, esp. Suhasini.

THINKALAZHCHA NALLA DIVASAM

aka *Monday the Good Day*
1985 126' col Malayalam
d/s **P. Padmarajan** *pc* Sunitha prod. *c* Vasant Kumar *m* Shyam
lp Kaviyoor Ponnamma, **Mammootty**, Karamana Janardanan Nair, Sasangan, Shrividya, Unnimary, Ashokan, Kukku Parameswaran, Madhavikutty

A family gathers in its spacious ancestral home to celebrate their lonely mother's (Ponnamma) 60th birthday. Jealousies and rivalries erupt focusing on who will inherit the house. The old mother is placed in an institution for geriatrics and dies, leaving the next generation guilt-ridden, but her grandchildren nevertheless appreciate living in the big house.

TRIKAAL

aka *Past, Present and Future*
1985 137' col Hindi
d/sc **Shyam Benegal** *p* Lalit M. Bijlani, Freni M. Variava *pc* Blaze Film Ents *dial* Shama Zaidi *lyr* Ila Arun *c* Ashok Mehta *m* **Vanraj Bhatia**
lp Leela Naidu, **Naseeruddin Shah**, Neena Gupta, Anita Kanwar, Dalip Tahil, Soni Razdan, Sushama Prakash, K.K. Raina, Keith Stevenson, Kulbhushan Kharbanda, Maqsoom Alie, Sabira Merchant

Ruiz Pereira (Shah) returns to his native Goa and visits the old mansion where he spent his youth. The film nostalgically evokes in flashback the hybrid Portuguese-Indian colonial world in terms of adolescent passions and complicated wedding arrangements. Intended as a Bergman-like saga of a family, using extensive quotations from his film-making style including candle-lit sequences as the entire family sits down to a festive dinner. Goa's best-known pop singer Remo Fernandes wrote the number *Panch vorsam* in Konkani for this film, but it was actually used in an adapted Hindi version.

YATHRA

1985 124' col Malayalam
d/sc/c **Balu Mahendra** *pc* Prakkat Films *st/dial* John Paul *lyr* **O.N.V. Kurup** *m* **Ilaiyaraja**
lp **Mammootty**, Shobhana, **Adoor Bhasi**, Thilakan, Kunjan

Tragic love story between a forest officer (Mammootty) and village belle Tulsi (Shobhana). Arrested for the murder of his best friend, a crime he did not commit, the forest officer goes to jail while freeing his fiancee from any commitment to their planned marriage. However, when he is finally released she is waiting for him. Apparently inspired partly by Alan Parker's *Midnight Express* (1978), Yoji Yamada's *Shiawase No Kiiroi Hankuchi* [*Yellow Handkerchief of Happiness*] (1978) and *The Sound of Music* (1965) the love story reinforces much of the fatalism often associated with Mammootty's screen persona.

AMMA ARIYAN

aka *Report to Mother*
1986 115' b&w Malayalam
d/s **John Abraham** *pc* Odessa Movies *c* Venu *m* Sunitha
lp Joy Mathew, Maji Venkitesh, Nilambur Balan, Harinarayanan, Kunhulakshmi Amma, Itingal Narayani, Nazim, Ramachandran Mokeri, Kallai Balan, Thomas, Venu C. Menon

Abraham's last and most complex film is told in the form of an open letter from a son, Purushan (Mathew), to his mother (Kunhulakshmi) while interweaving fact and fiction with fragments of memory. Purushan sets out for Delhi with his friend Paru (Venkitesh), who is researching a thesis on Durga, the mother goddess, a figure traditionally though ambiguously representing the cohesive forces of nature. Along the way they find a hanged man who seems hauntingly familiar, a suicide. Reconstructing the identity of the corpse takes Purushan, and a growing body of young men who all have a stake in the youth's history, from the northern highlands of Kerala to Southern Cochin and ends with a re-evaluation of a generation's radical past. Along the way, Abraham filmed an actual quarry workers' strike, echoing Kerala's troubled 70s, and manages to endow both the journey and the central character with broader historical resonances in a manner reminiscent of the director's master, **Ritwik Ghatak**'s ***Jukti Takko Aar Gappo*** (1974): a style full of irony and with a free-wheelingly innovative approach to sound and to narrative structures. The first production of the Odessa group, it was made entirely through raising funds from public contributions. Abraham's death, shortly after the film was made, elevated it to cult status while also merging together the fate of the director with that of the main protagonist, both strongly inflected with Christian themes of innocence and martyrdom.

ANJUMAN

1986 140' col Hindi
d/s **Muzaffar Ali** *p* Shobha M. Doctor *c* Ishan Arya *m* **Khayyam**
lp **Shabana Azmi**, Farouque Shaikh, Rohini Hattangadi, Shaukat Kaifi, Mushtaq Khan

Social melodrama about the plight of chikan-embroiderers in decaying Lucknow, the setting of Ali's ***Umrao Jaan*** (1981). The sensitive Anjuman (Azmi) does chikan work to augment her extended family's income. She is courted by a phoney poet, Banke Nawab (Khan), who has control over the chikan workers, but she falls in love with her wealthy but weak neighbour Sajjid (Shaikh). Encouraged by her doctor friend Suchitra Sharma (Hattangadi), Anjuman demands fair treatment for the chikan workers but the pressure on her to marry the exploitative Banke grows. She finally says 'No' during the wedding ceremony and has to face the wrath of Banke who incites a riot among the Muslims in the town. Anjuman then becomes a feminist labour activist and earns the admiration of her beloved Sajjid.

AVANAZHI

1986 156' col/scope Malayalam
d **I.V. Sasi** *pc* Saj Prod. *s* T. Damodaran *c* V. Jayaram *m* Shyam
lp **Mammootty**, Geetha, Nalini, Seema, Captain Raju, Paravoor Bharathan, **Thikkurisi Sukumaran Nair**, Janardhanan, Jagannath Varma, Sukumaran, Sattar

Sasi's demented melodrama repeating his theme of corruption in Kerala politics (cf ***Ee Nadu***, 1982; ***Vartha***, 1986), and seminal text determining Mammootty's screen persona. He plays the police inspector Balaram, who is personally honest but not opposed in principle to corruption. Framed for the murder of the student Unni, who died in police custody, Balaram loses his girlfriend Usha (Nalini) and faces the enduring hostility of Unni's sister Radha (Seema). The film's key villain is the businessman and politician Vincent, whose partner, the corrupt lawyer Jayachandran, happens to be Usha's new husband. Completing the key ensemble is the prostitute Seeta (Geetha), who was forced by the bad guys into prostitution and now lives with Balaram. In a relentless series of brutal encounters, personal vendettas merge with political rivalries. In the end, the true killer of the student turns out to be the politically influential murderer Sathyaraj (Captain Raju). Balaram hunts him down, and in the process becomes responsible for the killing of the pregnant Seeta. The most notable aspect of the film is its view of corruption as something that has seeped into every aspect of Kerala society, to a point where even the film is unable to restrict its subject-matter. The hero is presented throughout as essentially unpleasant, who warns Usha not to take up a job as university lecturer, and later refuses to acknowledge having fathered Seeta's child. The film's plot in both instances vindicates the hero's stand (e.g. when Usha is attacked by a student) without making any effort to render it in any way morally palatable. Sasi's usual alternative is an enormous excess of plot, as the complicated roles of different characters merge and interconnect to the point of vertigo. Like his other films, here too there are no neat endings, as the hero's arrest (repeating an enhanced version of Don Siegel's *Dirty Harry*, 1971) leaves the futures of most of the characters largely unresolved.

EK PAL

aka *A Moment*
1986 135' col Hindi
d/co-p/co-sc **Kalpana Lajmi** *pc* **Atma Ram** Films *co-p/m* **Bhupen Hazarika** *st* Maitreyi Devi *co-sc/dial/lyr* **Gulzar** *c* K.K. Mahajan
lp **Shabana Azmi**, **Naseeruddin Shah**, Farouque Shaikh, Shriram Lagoo, Dina Pathak, Sreela Majumdar

Kalpana Lajmi's directorial debut tells a story of extramarital sex in the tea gardens of Assam. Priyam (Azmi), married to the staid but loving Ved (Shah), has an affair with her former boyfriend Jeet (Shaikh) while her husband is away. She becomes pregnant. Having already had one miscarriage, she is determined to keep the baby despite her boyfriend's protests. On his return, Ved eventually accepts both his unfaithful wife and her baby. Lajmi explained that she set the story in Assam to link the heroine's innocence and later loneliness with the environment, but the easier if less sympathetic explanation is reviewer Aloknanda Datta's (in *Splice*, July 1986) suggestion that the gardens merely provide an exotic backdrop. Famous Assamese singer-composer Hazarika contributes some fine compositions, overcoming the mandatory emphasis on regional folk-music in films set in exotic locales.

GANDHINAGAR 2ND STREET

1986 137' col Malayalam
d/s Sathyan Andhikkad *pc* Casino Prod. *lyr* Bichu Thirumala *c* Bipin Mohan *m* Shyam
lp **Mohanlal**, Srinivasan, Seema, **Mammootty**, Karthika, Tilakan

Mohanlal comedy and one of Andhikkad's biggest hits. The simpleton Sethu (Mohanlal) finds employment as a security guard, hired by a street neighbourhood. The first part of the film is a straightforward sit-com as his friend Madhavan (Srinivasan) masquerades as a thief to raise Sethu's stock with his employers; the plan misfires and Madhavan gets a sound thrashing. Things take a more serious turn as Sethu's former girlfriend Maya (Karthika) moves into one of the houses on the street with her police chief father (Tilakan). The lovers had parted when Sethu tried to seduce Maya, following misguided advice that the best way to get her father to agree to their marriage was to get her pregnant first. Sethu makes an enemy of the entire neighbourhood when he uses violence to rescue Maya from the unwanted attentions of one of the street denizens. He is protected by the schoolteacher Nirmala (Seema), leading to allegations of an illicit sexual relationship between them. However, her husband (Mammootty) arrives from the Gulf, and sorts everything out. The plot somewhat gratuitously reveals Maya at the end to be a widow, whose husband died a week after their wedding. It does so mainly to allow the film to end on a tragic note, as Sethu too leaves for the Gulf unable to make concrete promises to his reconciled girl. The film is dominated by Mohanlal's energetic performance and the comic dialogue (interspersing Hindi with Malayalam).

GENESIS

1986 109' col Hindi
d/co-p/sc **Mrinal Sen** *pc* Scarabee Films (Paris), Mrinal Sen Prod. (Calcutta), Les Films de la Dreve (Brussels), Cactus Films (Zurich) *co-pc* Film Four (London), SSR (Berne) *co-p* Marie Pascale Osterrieth, Palaniappan Ramasamy, Eliane Stutterheim, Jean-Jacques Andrien *co-sc* Mohit Chattopadhay *st* Samaresh Bose *dial* Surendra P. Singh, Umashankar Pathik *c* Carlo Varini *m* Ravi Shankar
lp **Shabana Azmi**, **Naseeruddin Shah**, **Om Puri**, M.K. Raina

Whereas Sen's best work derived much strength from being rooted in a specific time and place, giving historical resonances to the particular shapes of the conflicts he depicted, this international co-production mostly financed by European television channels is set in a purely symbolic and timeless space: some ruins in the middle of a desert. A farmer (Shah) and a weaver (Puri) exchange their products for goods provided by a regularly passing trader (Raina). A woman (Azmi) arrives, focusing the two men's desires but also urging them to obtain more recompense from the trader. After a visit to a village fair (exuberantly shot with telling details reminiscent of Sen's earlier work) the two men become more acquisitive and jealousies break out over the now pregnant woman who simply ups and leaves. As the two men fight each other, the trader's men attack and enslave the workers again. The film closes with shots of bulldozers and modern machinery clearing the ground. Sen's timeless parable about the genesis of capitalism, although acted with conviction by the cast, suffers from its abstraction, transforming the characters into stereotypes and reducing the complexities of history to simplified generalities. G. Chakravorty Spivak (1993) provides a postcolonial reading of the film.

KARMA

1986 193' col/scope Hindi
d **Subhash Ghai** *pc* Mukta Arts *lyr* **Anand Bakshi** *m* **Laxmikant-Pyarelal**
lp **Dilip Kumar**, **Nutan**, **Dara Singh**, Anupam Kher, Jackie Shroff, **Naseeruddin Shah**, Anil Kapoor, Tom Alter, Poonam Dhillon, **Sridevi**, Shakti Kapoor

Dirty Dozen (1967) -style film invoking 'terrorists' backed by 'neighbouring' states. Rana Vishnu Pratap Singh (Kumar) is a benevolent warden of a jail who feels that people become criminals either because they are forced into crime by a corrupt society (in which case they should get a second chance) or through greed (which is unpardonable). His main hatred is reserved for Dr Dang (Kher), head of the Black Star Organisation, a group of international terrorists. The obstreperous Dang arranges to bomb the jail, killing inmates, and during his escape bid Dang massacres Rana's family, except for his wife Seeta (Nutan), who goes dumb with shock, and his youngest son. Rana is put in charge of a special anti-terrorist squad comprising murderers condemned to death: Baiju Thakur (Shroff), Khairu (Shah) and Johnny (A. Kapoor). Rana trains them at a border post in the farmhouse of the former criminal Dharma (Dara Singh). The relationship between the condemned men and their leader forms the bulk of the film, interspersed with love affairs, until the quartet eventually overwhelms the villain's heavily guarded military retreat.

LOVE AND GOD

1986 141' col Urdu
d **K. Asif** *p* K.C. Bokadia, Akhtar Asif *s* Wajahat Mirza *lyr* Kumar Barabankvi, Asad Bhopali *c* R.D. Mathur *m* **Naushad**
lp Nimmi, Sanjeev Kumar, Simi Garewal, Jayant, Agha, Nasir Hussain, Pran

This often-filmed Arab love legend of Laila and her lover, released in 1986, could have been Asif's most formally ambitious film had it been completed during his lifetime. As with his ***Mughal-e-Azam*** (1960) and in keeping with his grandiose film style, it was in the making for over a decade. When **Guru Dutt**, who played the lead, died in 1964, the film had to be reshot with Sanjeev Kumar in the lead. When the director died as well, the film was abandoned, then revived by his widow, Akhtar Asif, and finally released in incomplete form. The composer Naushad contributes songs such as *Hame kuch raahein khuda de de*, *Yeh nadanon ki duniya hai yeh diwanon ki mehfil hai*. Cameraman R.D. Mathur, formerly of **Bombay Talkies**, developed his baroque style almost exclusively for Asif's period epics: his camera moves over elaborate desert vistas and complicated sets, including a bravura tracking crane shot lasting almost ten minutes when Qais is rejected by Laila and leaves, the whole town turning out to witness his departure.

MALAYA MARUTHA

aka *A Morning Melody*
1986 180' col/scope Kannada
d Ravi (aka K.S.L. Swami) *p* C.V.L. Sastry *pc* Sastry Movies *c* B. Purshottam *m* **Vijayabhaskar**
lp **Vishnuvardhan**, Madhavi, Saritha, Shivram, Dinesh, R.K. Suryanarayana, M.S. Umesh, Saikumar

Classical Carnatic revivalist musical in the ***Shankarabharanam*** (1979) formula. When the great musician Vidwan Shrikantaiah dies in a road accident, his artistic soul is transferred into his disciple Vishwanath (Vishnuvardhan), who founds a music school. This commitment interferes with his more worldly attractions for Sharada, his mentor's daughter, and for Girija, a dancer whose father exploits Vishwanath's abilities. One interesting twist is that, since the hero inherited the teacher's soul, his relationship to Sharada might be incestuous. The singers include **S.P. Balasubramanyam**, **Yesudas** and Vani Jayaram.

MASSEY SAHIB

1986 124' col Hindi
d/sc/co-dial **Pradeep Krishen** *p* Ravi Malik *pc* **NFDC** *co-dial* Raghuvir Yadav *c* R.K. Bose *m* **Vanraj Bhatia**
lp Raghuvir Yadav, Barry John, Arundhati Roy, Jacqueline Garewal, Sudhir Kulkarni, Virendra Saxena, Madan Lal, Francis King, Lalloo Ram, Hemant Mishra, Vasant Joglekar, James Ure, David Maurice

Satirical comment on colonial India set in 1929 and featuring a government clerk named Francis Massey (Yadav). Because of his constant interactions with the British, Massey fancies himself to be just like an Englishman. However, he has to deploy extreme financial ingenuity to keep the wolf from the door. When Massey's boss Charles Adam (Barry John) lacks the funds to complete his dream project of building a road through the forest, Massey manages to get the scheme finished through financial skullduggery, rpersuasion and threats. To his surprise, an unofficial road tax he levies is considered to be corruption by the very boss who had condoned Massey's earlier shenanigans. Frustrated and humiliated, Massey attacks and kills his old friend Banaji when the latter refuses to help.

Massey is arrested for murder and Adam advises him to plead guilty to accidental manslaughter, but Massey refuses, assuming that his colonial associations will get him off the hook. Krishen's feature debut reveals many technical inadequacies, but Yadav's fine performance inaugurated a screen image he has maintained ever since.

MOUNA RAGAM

aka *Silent Raga*
1986 145' col Tamil
d/s **Mani Rathnam** *pc* Sujatha Prod. *c* P.C. Sriram *m* **Ilaiyaraja**
lp Mohan, Revathi, Karthik

Rathnam's art-house melodrama just prior to his big-budget breakthrough hit ***Nayakan*** (1987). Divya (Revathi) is unable to resign herself to a forced marriage with Chandra Kumar (Mohan). She dreams, in flashback, of her carefree days with her first boyfriend, Manmohan (Karthik), who died. She seeks a divorce, but as the law requires the couple to stay together for a year, they decide to live separately in the same house. After she has nursed her husband back to health following a murderous attack by an employee, the couple decide to stay together. Much of the film is taken up with the boyfriend and the repressive politics he tries to overcome. The film's main merit is Sriram's use of chiaroscuro effects. Not to be confused with Ambili's Malayalam *Mouna Ragam* (1983).

OOMAI VIZHIGAL

aka *The Dumb Eyes*
1986 176' col Tamil
d R. Aravindraj *pc* Thirai Chirpi *st/dial/lyr* Aabavanan *c* A. Rameshkumar *m* Manoj Gyan
lp Vijayakanth, Jaishankar, Karthik, Chandrasekhar, Arunpandian, Kokila, Saritha, Ilavarasi

An exploitative expose film by a group of film students using hand-held camera, emphatic lighting and location sound techniques. A man with good political and criminal connections kills women who come and picnic near his mansion. After much bloodletting, the villains are eliminated by an honest cop and a fearless newspaper editor as the cop pumps his bullets, in slow motion, into the slasher's body. The gory film is leavened with song and dance numbers and references to violent incidents of Tamil Nadu political life: e.g. the storming of the newspaper office followed by the editor's performance of a song often used at political and trade union demonstrations.

ORIDATHU

aka *Somewhere* aka *And There Was a Village*
1986 112' col Malayalam
d/s **Govindan Aravindan** *pc* Suryakanti Film Makers *c* **Shaji N. Karun**
lp Nedumudi Venu, Srinivasan, Thilakan, Vineet Krishnakutty Nair, Surendra Babu, Kunhandi, Chandran Nair, Soorya, Sitara

Set in the 50s in a remote part of Travancore Cochin, the story tells of a village, rather like the one in Aravindan's ***Thampu*** (1978), threatened by electrification. Although the absurdities and the small-minded hypocrisies of village life are depicted with humour, the film produces a strange impression since the conclusion it reaches, that life is better without electricity, also condemns the very existence of cinema as a legitimate means of expression. The key to the film can be found in Aravindan's statement that in the small village where he was born there was no electricity until he was ten years old, and that he felt nostalgic for those pre-pubertal times marked by the memory of people moving about with torches.

PANCHAGNI

aka *Five Fires*
1986 141' col Malayalam
d **T. Hariharan** *p* G.P. Vijay Kumar, M.G. Gopinath *pc* Seven Arts Films *s* **M.T. Vasudevan Nair** *c* **Shaji N. Karun** *m* Ravi
lp Geeta, **Mohanlal**, Nadia Moidu, Thilakan

As in the romantic socialist realism of ***Meenamasathile Sooryan*** (1985), this film extols the virtues of radical political activists but, contrary to **Rajendran**'s film, Hariharan exploits the unpleasant aspects of revolutionary violence. The central figure is Indira (Geeta), imprisoned for murder and on hunger strike. Allowed to visit her dying mother, a former activist in the Independence struggle, on a two-week pass, she encounters unmitigated hostility from some members of her family although her old mother welcomes her warmly. Persecuted by the villagers as well as by the police, Indira eventually turns to a journalist, Rashid (Mohanlal), to unburden herself, recounting the circumstances of her crime. In the politically turbulent 60s in Kerala, she had been a welfare officer who had led a group people which hacked to death a particularly vicious landowner. Later, when she is released, she shoots the husband of her best friend for participating in a brutal gang rape of a servant girl. Then she calmly awaits being imprisoned again. The film was a commercial hit.

PANDAVAPURAM

1986 93' col Malayalam
d/p/co-sc G.S. Panicker *pc* Neo Films *st/co-sc* Sethu *c* Divakara Menon *m* Mohan
lp Jamila, Appu, James, Master Deepak

Based on Sethu's magic-realist novel adapted by the author to the screen, the film refuses to make clear distinctions between quasi-realist, fantastic and symbolic registers of fiction. It tells of a woman teacher in her 30s, Devi (Jamila), whose young son keeps asking questions about his absent father. Devi often loses herself in fantasies which appear to come true. She spends much time on the station platform of the small village, awaiting the arrival of a man from Pandavapuram (it is left unclear whether such a place exists). Someone turns up called Jaran (Appu), meaning 'lover'. Jaran claims to know her and to want to renew their friendship. As the villagers, and especially Devi's friend Unni (James), put pressure on Jaran to leave, Devi locks him in her house. One night, dressed in red, she frenziedly rapes him claiming to be the avenging goddess Durga. The morning after, Jaran vanishes and everybody claims no such man ever arrived in the village. Devi then recommences her ritual of waiting on the station platform.

PAPORI

1986 144' col Assamese
d/sc **Jahnu Barua** *pc* Patkai Films *st* Heu-En Barua *c* Binod Pradhan *m* Satya Barua, P.P. Vaidyanathan
lp Biju Phukan, Gopi Desai, Sushil Goswami, Dulal Roy, Runjun, Amulya Kakoti

Grim melodrama set in the context of the All-Assam Students' Union agitations during the 1983 elections, a familiar setting for mainstream Assamese cinema of the period (cf Hem Bora's *Sankalpa*, 1986). Papori's (Desai) husband Binod (Goswami) is falsely arrested for murder. Her daughter is in hospital, where she eventually dies. Papori's only support, a police inspector (Phukan), finds the true murderer but cannot arrest him because the killer enjoys political protection. Papori is raped by a smuggler, her husband is convicted of murder and only an arbitrarily added epilogue, claiming that the husband is eventually freed and the good inspector promoted, brings a glimmer of relief. In his later ***Halodiya Choraye Baodhan Khaye*** (1987), Barua again weaves contemporary political events into a melodramatic plot.

PHERA

aka *The Return*
1986 94' col Bengali
d/sc/p **Buddhadev Dasgupta** *st* Narendranath Mitra *c* Dhrubajyoti Basu *m* Jyotish Dasgupta
lp Subrata Nandy, Alaknanda Dutt, Alaknanda Dasgupta, Aniket Sengupta, Sunil Mukherjee, Debika Mukherjee, Biplab Chatterjee, Kamu Mukherjee, Pradeep Sen

The story of Sasanka (Nandy), a lonely, misanthropic playwright who finds his talent for writing, producing and starring in Bengali jatra theatre waning. His wife Jamuna (D. Mukherjee) leaves the crotchety artist and only his servant Rashu (S. Mukherjee) keeps him company. Into his dessicated environment comes his widowed sister-in-law Saraju (A. Dutt) and her small son Kanu (A. Sengupta). Sexual desire and the friendship of the child restore Sasanka's creative powers.

RAO SAHEB

1986 123' col Hindi
d/s **Vijaya Mehta** *p* Pahlaj Bajaj *st* Jaywant Dalvi *c* Adeep Tandon *m* Bhaskar Chandavarkar
lp Anupam Kher, Vijaya Mehta, Nilu Phule, Tanvi, Mangesh Kulkarni

Based on the popular play *Barrister* (1977) by Dalvi, Mehta's film is set in the 20s in a small Maharashtrian town. Rao Saheb (Kher), an English-educated but orthodox barrister, lives with his elder brother and his widowed but vivacious aunt Mausi (Mehta) in an old mansion. Mausi befriends the equally lively young bride living next door, Radhika (Tanvi), who also becomes a widow. Radhika rebels against her bigoted father's attempt to make her conform to the orthodox Brahmin rituals imposed on widows and she becomes a close friend of Rao Saheb. However, he cannot break free from Brahmin custom and marry her. Instead, unable to act according to his convictions, he goes insane while Radhika resigns herself to the cruel existence of a Brahmin widow. The (like all Mehta's cinema) stagey film evokes the plight of progressive liberals who support reform movements regarding widow remarriage but are themselves unable to overcome the social and moral pressures exerted by orthodox traditions.

SAMSARAM ATHU MINSARAM

aka *Married Life is like Electricity*
1986 145' col Tamil
d/s Visu *pc* AVM Prod. *lyr* **Vairamuthu** *c* N. Balakrishnan *m* Shankar-Ganesh
lp Visu, Raghuvaran, Chandrasekhar, Manorama, Laxmi, Ilavarasi, Madhuri, Kamala Kamesh

Visu's caste-conscious urban middle-class family dramas overtly advocate the subordination of women, often justifying the beating of women in stories mixing sentiment and comedy. Here he plays Ammaiyappa Mudaliar, a salaried employee with a wife, a daughter and three sons, making for four couples in a single household. The daughter, who aspires to a measure of freedom in her marriage, is contrasted with an obediently traditional daughter-in-law; both are beaten for talking back and forced to endure life with their husbands. The story approves of Christian-Hindu marriage, clearly features caste identities (e.g. the trouble-shooter figure of the servant, played brilliantly by Manorama) and refuses to hide reactionary family ideologies under a progressive cloak.

SULTANAT

1986 153' col/scope Hindi
d/s **Mukul S. Anand** *pc* Kapleshwar Films, Arjun Hingorani *dial* Kadar Khan *lyr* Anjaan, Hasan Kamal *c* Pravin Bhatt *m* **Kalyanji-Anandji**
lp **Dharmendra**, Sunny Deol, Amrish Puri, **Sridevi**, Shakti Kapoor, Tom Alter, Karan Kapoor, Dalip Tahil, Juhi Chawla, Padma Khanna

Spectacular *Arabian Nights* revenge fantasy set in a vaguely identifiable Middle East and deploying the exoticism associated with Spielberg's adventure films. The shah's General Khalid (Dharmendra) thwarts the coup for the throne attempted by Razaulli (Puri). Razaulli kidnaps Khalid and his pregnant wife on their way to the hospital. Khalid's wife dies in childbirth and Razaulli proclaims Khalid's son as his own, swapping the infant for his stillborn daughter. Khalid remarries and has another son, Samir (Karan Kapoor), whom he sends abroad vowing never to set eyes on him until Khalid has avenged the death of his first wife. Razaulli's secretly adopted son Sultan (Deol) grows up and falls in love with the shah's daughter, Princess Yasmin (Sridevi). In a complicated denouement, Khalid kills Razaulli and recalls Samir; Shakkir, an ambitious vassal, kills the shah and intercepts the returning Samir and emprisons him. Khalid is taken prisoner by Sultan and they engage in a bloody duel till Razaulli's wife tells them that Khalid is Sultan's real father. Khalid, Sultan and Samir then kill Shakkir. Only then can Khalid die in peace surrounded by his sons. Anand does not shrink from spectacular anachronisms which have become his trademark (cf his ***Khuda Gawah***, 1992), as he mixes contemporary scenes into this commercially unsuccessful period movie tale.

SUSMAN

aka *The Essence*
1986 140' col Hindi
d/p **Shyam Benegal** *pc* Association of Co-operatives and Apex Society of Handloom, Sahyadri Films *sc* Shama Zaidi *c* Ashok Mehta *m* Sharang Dev, **Vanraj Bhatia**
lp **Om Puri**, **Shabana Azmi**, Neena Gupta, Kulbhushan Kharbanda, K.K. Raina, Annu Kapoor, Harish Patel, Mohan Agashe, Ila Arun

A tribute to the 'Ikat' handloom weavers of Pochampally in AP. The film tells of Ramulu (Puri), a master of silk weaving, his family and their tribulations with the co-operative they work in. The drama is sparked off by internal rivalries and the arrival of a government official, a woman (Gupta) looking for items to send to an exhibition in Paris. Complications are provided by Ramulu, who secretly uses some of his allotted silk to make a wedding sari for his daughter, leading to his temporary disgrace. The contrast between artisanal craftsmanship and mass-production techniques is illustrated by the life of Ramulu's son-in-law, who moves away from the family and finds work in a textile factory. The moral of the story is underlined in an interview between a French journalist and Ramulu, the latter trying to explain that a craftsman pours the essence of his soul into his craft. Unlike, e.g., **Mani Kaul** (cf ***Mati Manas***, 1984) whose 80s work is also animated by similar concerns for dying craft traditions, Benegal's cinema makes no effort to mediate, demystify or even understand the nature of that 'essence'. Produced, like his earlier ***Manthan*** (1976), by a marketing co-operative, the film also capitalised on a specifically 80s orientalism brought about by the several Festivals of India and trade fairs of traditional craft in Europe and the USSR.

TABARANA KATHE

aka *Tabara's Tale*
1986 179' col Kannada
d/sc **Girish Kasaravalli** *pc* Apoorva Chitra *dial* Poornachandra Tejaswi from his short story *c* Madhu Ambat *m* L. Vaidyanathan
lp Charuhasan, Nalina Murthy, Krishnamurthy, Jayaram, Master Santosh

Kasaravalli's multiple-point-of-view melodrama tells the story of Tabara (Charuhasan), a low-ranking worker in a municipal office who espouses colonial views despite his obvious pride in his job in a post-Independence government. Tabara gets into financial trouble when his honesty causes enmity among the coffee planters, and his pension is held up because he has not remitted some taxes that he was supposed to have collected. His wife falls ill and his 'case' becomes a mere file number in a bureaucratic office. The film is narrated from different points of view: the colonial point of view, the bureaucratic one, the view of those who believe Tabara to be mentally deranged and, mainly, the view of the orphan Babu through whose eyes the steel and concrete urban future is presented. Although primarily told in a realist idiom, at times (e.g. the shots of Bangalore and in the municipal office) the camerawork anticipates the surrealism of the sequel, ***Mane/Ek Ghar*** (1990).

THALAVATTAM

1986 147' col Malayalam
d/s Priyadarshan *pc* Seven Arts Prod. *lyr* Poovachal Kader, Pantalam Sudhakaran *c* S. Kumar *m* Raghukumar, Rajamani, Johnson
lp **Mohanlal**, Karthika, Nedumudi Venu, M.G. Soman

Priyadarshan's highly adapted version of **Asit Sen**'s ***Deep Jweley Jai*** (1959) and ***Khamoshi*** (1969). Mentally deranged hero Vinu (Mohanlal) is admitted to an asylum, where he is befriended by one of the doctors (Venu) who happens to be a childhood buddy. Heroine Savithri (Karthika), also employed in the hospital, falls for the hero in the process of curing him. However, Savithri's tyrannical father (Soman), who owns the asylum, cruelly performs a lobotomy operation on the hero because he fears for his daughter's future. Like all Priyadarshan films, this one too works extensively with flashbacks, using the various drastic shock treatments meted out to the hero as an excuse for some psychedelic musical effects.

UPPU

aka *Salt*
1986 115' col Malayalam
d **Pavithran** *pc* Eranadan Films *s/p* K.M.A. Rahim *c* Madhu Ambat *m* Saratchandra Maratte
lp Mohammad, Vijayan Kottarathil, C.V. Shriraman, Madhavan, Jayalalitha, Sadiq Renu Nair, Bharati, Valsala Menon, Mullenezhi

The wealthy Meleri Moosa (Kottarathil) ruins himself with obsessive litigation. With his daughter Amina (Jayalalitha) and her husband Abu (Mohammad), Meleri crosses the Bharathapuzha river to settle in a new area. There, the wealthy Moidutty Mudalali (Madhavan), with the benediction of the local kazi (religious leader, played by Shriraman), sends his own wife away, lays claim to Amina and marries her, ignoring Abu's protests. Twenty years later, Amina lives alone in a tomb-like mansion while her father happily indulges in civil litigation cases. In addition, her son leads a dissolute life and her daughter elopes with the chauffeur. Scenarist Rahim claimed the film to be a critique of the controversial Muslim personal law in India.

VARTHA

1986 163' col/scope Malayalam
d **I.V. Sasi** *pc* Grihalakshmi Prod. *s* T. Damodaran *lyr* Bichu Thirumala *c* Jayanan Vincent *m* A.T. Ummar, Johnson
lp **Mammootty**, **Mohanlal**, Seema, Rehman, Nalini

The fearless newspaper editor Madhavan Kutty (Mammootty) takes on Kerala's corrupt political establishment in order to vindicate his sweetheart Radha (Seema), the district collector accused of illegal practices. The villain is the owner of the Manikyam financial group, who appears to control the state's entire bureaucratic and political apparatus. Personal rivalries weave into political conflict as Manikyam implicates Radha's kid brother Unni in a smuggling operation. Eventually, when all legal means fail, the editor, the kid brother and Vasu (Mohanlal), a reformed gangster formerly in Manikyam's employ, establish a secret hideout where they assemble the documents that would appear to indict virtually everybody in power of criminal conspiracies. The film's dramatic and wholly unexpected end has all the good guys gunned down by corrupt cops, making the fight for justice a virtually hopeless cause.

ANANTARAM

aka *Monologue*
1987 125' col Malayalam
d/s **Adoor Gopalakrishnan** *p* K. Ravindranathan Nair *pc* General Pics *c* Ravi Varma *m* **M.B. Srinivasan**
lp Ashokan, **Mammootty**, Shobana, Balan K. Nair, Bahadur, Vempayan, Sooraj, Sudheesh, Kaviyoor Ponnamma, Chandran Nair

Gopalakrishnan's experiment with subjective storytelling. The film centres on a young man (Ashokan) who narrates two stories about himself in the first person. He was abandoned by his mother, raised by a doctor, and proved himself a consistent misfit. Much of his fantasy, into which the 'reality' of his second story merges, revolves around the figure of his foster-brother's wife. The film marks a major shift from the director's previous ***Mukha Mukham*** (1984) which, despite its critical depiction of politics, retained Gopalakrishnan's commitment to developing a tradition of Kerala melodrama. *Anantaram* is much more cynical, descending into a subjectivity bordering on the paranoid. Gopalakrishnan says that the film attempts to 'relate an experience', nothing more, of a 'state of intense despair and angst'.

ANTARJALI JATRA/MAHAYATRA

aka *The Voyage Beyond*
1987 140'[B]/123'[H] col Bengali/Hindi
d/sc/c/m **Gautam Ghosh** *p* Ravi Malik, Debashish Majumdar *pc* **NFDC** *st* Kamal Kumar Majumdar's novel *Antarjali Jatra* (1960)
lp Shatrughan Sinha, Promode Ganguly, **Robi Ghosh**, Mohan Agashe, Shampa Ghosh, **Basanta Choudhury**, Sajal Roy Choudhury, Kalyan Chatterjee

In 1829, in the context of various reform movements associated with Raja Rammohan Roy, sati (the widow immolating herself on her husband's funeral pyre) was outlawed by the British. The film, based on the noted Bengali writer Kamal Kumar Majumdar's best-known fiction, is set after that date and addresses the cruelty of a patriarchal practice which continues even today. The Brahmin Seetaram (Ganguly) is dying and an astrologer (Robi Ghosh) assures the dying man and his relatives of finding happiness after death on condition that his wife commits sati on his death. The villagers defy the law and persuade an impoverished Brahmin (Choudhury) to marry his daughter Yashobati (Shampa Ghosh) to the dying man so that she may commit Sati. The only dissident is Baiju (Sinha), a drunken Untouchable who tends to the cremation grounds. Baiju persuades Yashobati to flee. In the end, on a moonlit night, Baiju tries to kill old Seetaram. The superstitious Yashobati tries to prevent the deed and the two struggle on the muddy banks of the Ganges. The struggle changes into lovemaking but the river in spate eventually carries away both Seetaram and Yashobati. The film's end sums up a major controversy surrounding Ghosh's filming of a difficult text. Yashobati's death, which in effect constitutes the act of sati, is shown as a combination of accident and desire, further contrasting her 'holy' condition with Baiju's traditionless bestialism. Much of this is revealed in the original novel through broken syntax, interior monologue and a dense, graphic style of disjointed phrases, from which Ghosh assembled something like a coherent story. Gayatri Chakravorty Spivak (1992) contrasts the book with the film, suggesting that Majumdar's novel 'takes as understood a fully formed ideological subject (and thus) a question that can only be asked by us, as Hindus, of ourselves. This text is exactly not for the outsider who wants to enter with nothing but general knowledge, to have her ignorance sanctioned'. The film, on the other hand, 'shatters this project by staging the burning ghat as a realistic referent carrying a realistic amount of local colour, a stage for a broadly conceived psychodrama played out by easily grasped stock characters.' She accuses the film of being 'an abdication of the responsibility of the national artist, trafficking in national identity (in the name of woman) for international consumption'. Ghosh used another, and equally difficult, literary text for his next film ***Padma Nadir Majhi*** (1992), this time by Manik Bandyopadhyay.

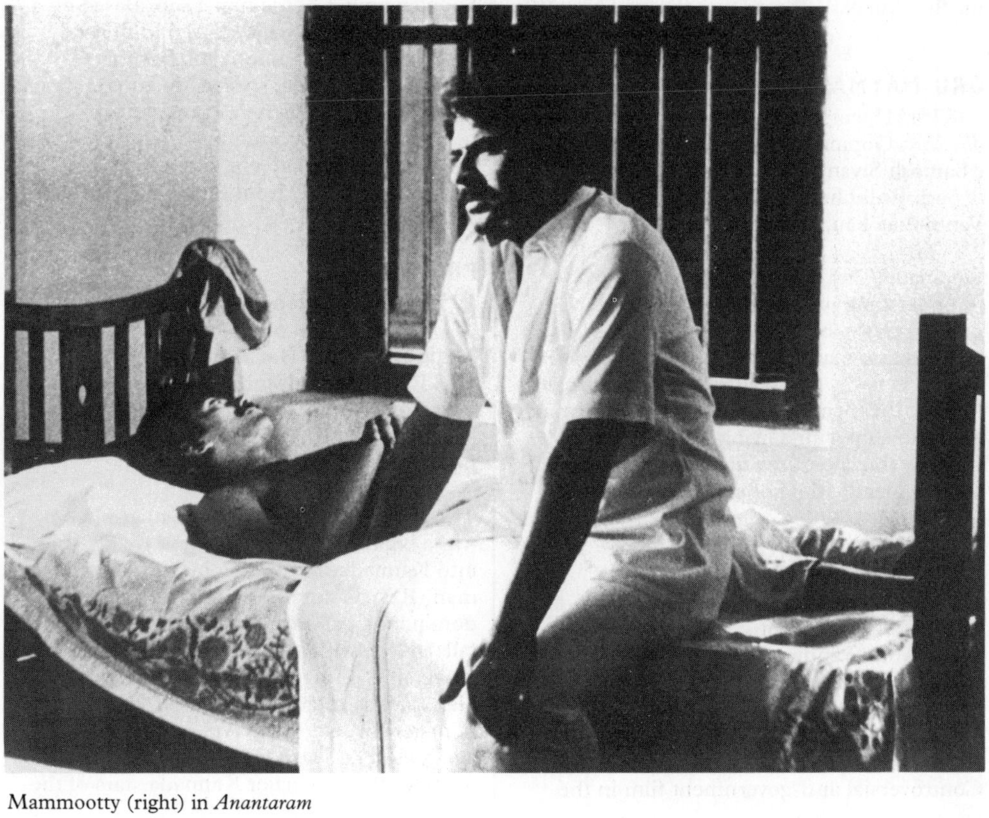

Mammootty (right) in *Anantaram*

CHINNA THAMBI PERIYA THAMBI

1987 145' col Tamil
d/s Manivannan *pc* Chamba Creations *lyr* **Vali** *c* Sabhapathy *m* Gangai Amaran
lp Satyaraj, Prabhu, Nadia, Sudha Chandran

Melodrama about good and evil in a country/city conflict. The twin brothers (Prabhu and Satyaraj) live in a village. They are deliberately insulted by their haughty urban cousin (Nadia) who is to marry the villain, a rich, America-returned millionaire. When Nadia's parents die, creditors take all her wealth and her fiance now refuses to marry her. She is forced to find a job in the factory of the villain who tries to make her his mistress. Both twins love their cousin (by Indian convention, one of them should have married her) and try to court her. When one of the twins is charged with theft by the villain, the other kills him and goes to jail, from where he emerges white-haired to see the other twin married to the cousin. The film reiterates, in the words of a *Deep Focus* review, the conventional commitment to relationships of a 'familiar and communal nature as against secular relationships between individuals'.

GURU DAKSHINA

1987 ?' col Bengali
d/sc Anjan Choudhury *p/st* Bhabesh Kundu *c* Girish Padidhar *m* **Bhappi Lahiri**
lp Tapas Paul, Ranjit Mullick, Shatabdi Roy, **Kali Bannerjee**, Shaktimala Barua, Soumitra Bannerjee, Bhabesh Kundu, Ishani Bannerjee

Major hit by the most successful Bengali director of the 80s. The poor Jayanta (Paul) loves Rupa, the rich daughter of the local zamindar, but is also indebted to his music teacher. When Jayanta upstages Rupa in a music contest, the zamindar uses his financial hold over the music teacher to extract a promise that Jayanta will never sing again. Eventually, when Jayanta shows he wants to keep his promise come what may, the zamindar relents and allows his daughter to marry Jayanta. The film borrows from a bawdy latter-day version of the folk jatra with its often lewd speech (an idiom associated particularly with this director), cueing the editing to the dialogue. Lahiri departed from his usual electronic rock score and composed several hits in a 'classical' style.

HALODIYA CHORAYE BAODHAN KHAYE

aka *The Catastrophe*
1987 120' col Assamese
d/sc **Jahnu Barua** *pc* Patkai Films *st* Hemen Borgohain *c* Anup Jotwani *m* Satya Barua
lp Indra Bania, Purnima Pathak Saikia, Badal Das, Hemen Choudhury, Pabitra Kumar Dekha

A happy, innocent farmer (Bania) is conned out of his landholding by an evil landlord. Forced to sell his cattle and to make innumerable trips to sort out bureaucratic problems, the farmer eventually meets that ultimate rarity, a 'good' bureaucrat who helps him get his land back. This story is set amid the din and cacophony of Assamese politics, leading at one point to the protagonist literally going berserk. Barua's best-known film, renowned for Bania's performance.

MR INDIA

1987 179' col/scope Hindi
d **Shekhar Kapur** *pc* Narsimha Ents *st/dial/lyr* **Javed Akhtar** *c* Baba Azmi *m* **Laxmikant-Pyarelal** *lp* Anil Kapoor, **Sridevi**, Amrish Puri, Sarat Saxena, Bob Christo, **Ashok Kumar**, Satish Kaushik

Shekhar Kapur's biggest movie tells an 'invisible man' story. One of Indian film's most exotic villains yet, the blond dictator Mogambo (Puri, resembling Marty Feldman in Nazi uniform) is defeated by a common-man hero (Kapoor) who can render himself invisible. The film moves through a series of sketches: break-dancing kids, heroine Sridevi playing a journalist while performing her famous *Hawa Hawaii* routine (quoted in *Salaam Bombay*, 1988) and her popular Chaplin imitation. Referring to what is regarded as Sridevi's sexiest film scene (the solo number *Karte hain hum pyar Mr India se*), Ravi Vasudevan writes (1992): 'Perhaps it is no coincidence that in the most sexual of her performances [s]he is sensualised by the lovemaking of an invisible man. It could be argued that this empty space invites the insertion of the male spectator [b]ut it is somehow still consistent with the narcissistic, auto-erotic regime of sexuality implied in the persona of this female star.'

NAYAKAN

aka *Hero*
1987 155' col Tamil
d/s **Mani Rathnam** *pc* Mukta Films *dial* Balakumaran *lyr* Pulamai Pithan *c* P.C. Sriram *m* **Ilaiyaraja**
lp **Kamalahasan**, Saranya, Vasudeva Rao, Janakaraj, Delhi Ganesh, Karthik, Nizhalgal Ravi, Tinnu Anand

Rathnam's controversial breakthrough film is a version of *The Godfather* (1972), based on the life of the Bombay gangster Varadarajan Mudaliar, played by Kamalahasan (at times explicitly imitating Brando). Seeing his **Naxalite** father brutally murdered by the police in Madras, the son runs away to Bombay and becomes Velu Naicker, the ruthless Godfather with a Robin Hood streak in the Dharavi slums, assisted by Ganesh in the Robert Duval role. Velu becomes Bombay's minority Tamil population's 'Nayakan' (hero/star/leader) and saviour. His daughter Charu (Saranya) walks out and marries the assistant chief of police. Velu is eventually shot by a mentally retarded youth (Anand) he had taken into his care. Although Kamalahasan's performance was widely lauded, critics like K. Hariharan noted that the degree to which the star monopolises the film made 'other characters seem either underdeveloped or perfunctory'. The cinematography takes its cue from Storaro while Thotha Tharani's art direction follows the conventions of Hollywood gangster films and concentrates on cars and decors. However, the film is more than a Hollywood pastiche: it draws on 30 years of Tamil Nadu's star/politician images (including the spotless, all-white uniform of the Tamil politician, chewing betel-leaf) and directly plays to Tamil people's anti-Hindi feelings when Velu, beaten up, gives the hugely popular reply in Tamil to a Hindi-speaking Bombay cop: 'If I ever hit you, you will die.' The latter half of the film virtually abandons Bombay as a location in favour of studio interiors and goes to Madras for the climax.

ORU MAYMASAPPULARAYIL

1987 151' col Malayalam
d/sc V.R. Gopinath *p* Alex Kapadvil *st* Renjith *c* Santosh Sivan *m* Ravindran
lp Sari, **Balachandra Menon**, Nedumudi Venu, Ashokan, Murali

Gopinath's 2nd film tells of two men who try to understand why a woman threw herself under a train: the cricket star she loved believes that marrying her was a bad career move. As in his first feature, ***Greeshamam*** (1980), the men are still incapable of forming a relationship with a living woman but this time, by the end of the film, they have gained some understanding of a dead one.

ORE ORU GRAMATHILE

aka *Once Upon a Time in a Village*
1987 137' col Tamil
d/s K. Jyothi Pandian *pc* Aries Pics *c* V. Ranga *m* **Ilaiyaraja**
lp Laxmi, Poornam Vishwanathan, Delhi Ganesh, Arundhati

Controversial anti-government film in the tradition of the **DMK** propaganda melodrama, evoked, e.g., in the opening cyclone scenes recalling ***Thyagabhoomi*** (1939). Produced in association with the publishers of Madras's mainstream daily *The Hindu*, the film attacks the government's positive discrimination policy in favour of 'scheduled' castes, better known as the Mandal Commission Recommendations which helped bring down the Janata Dal government (1990). The impoverished upper-caste Brahmin woman Karupayi (Laxmi) masquerades as a low-caste Harijan in order to receive a good education and a good job. She is blackmailed by a tramp-like figure and eventually arrested and brought to court. As in the DMK genre, the trial becomes the place to expound the pros and cons of the policy and for the heroine to make her fervent plea that it is unfair to ask talented upper-caste people to suffer so that low-caste people may get decent jobs. In addition, the script places feminist ideas in its heroine's speech to bolster its elitist message. The film uses several folk-music tunes as part of the rural drama and has a convincing performance by Laxmi. It was briefly banned but the Supreme Court eventually cleared it for public screening.

PESTONJEE

1987 110' col Hindi
d/co-sc **Vijaya Mehta** *pc* **NFDC** *st/co-sc* B.K. Karanjia *c* A.K. Bir *m* **Vanraj Bhatia**
lp Anupam Kher, **Naseeruddin Shah**, **Shabana Azmi**, Kiran Thakur Singh Kher

Melodrama about two old Parsee friends, the extrovert Pesi (A. Kher) and the shy Piroj (Shah), both in love with Jeroo (Azmi). Pesi marries Jeroo and also draws close to the widowed lawyer Soona (K. Kher). Piroj is transferred away from Bombay for five years and returns to find Jeroo had a miscarriage and that Pesi now prefers Soona's company. When Pesi dies, his funeral is paid for by Soona who has borne him a son. Based on a short story by Karanjia written in the early 50s, the film is set among the Bombay Parsees. The acting, speech, decor and much of the storyline adheres to popular perceptions of a community often caricatured as idiosyncratic. The film often slips into flashbacks, usually from Piroj's point of view.

PREMALOKA

1987 154' col/scope Kannada
d V. Ravichandran *pc* Sri Eswari Prod. *c* R. Madhusudhan *m* **Hamsalekha**
lp V. Ravichandran, Juhi Chawla, **Vishnuvardhan**, Ambarish, Prabhakar, Srinath, Lokesh, K. Vijaya, Urvashi, Jayachitra, **Leelavathi**

The actor Ravichandran's directorial debut was a big hit bringing disco and rock music into Kannada film. A rich but timid young man (Ravichandran), oppressed by dominating parents, is transformed when he falls in love with an independent-minded university colleague (Chawla). Composer Hamsalekha established himself with a series of major hit songs, e.g. *Nimbeyanta hudugi bantu nodu nee nodu*. The supporting cast includes the two major Kannada stars of the time, Vishnuvardhan and Ambarish (who rarely perform in the same film). The film introduced Juhi Chawla, who became the emblem of the teen love-and-rock formula with the Aamir Khan hit ***Qayamat Se Qayamat Tak*** (1988).

PURUSHARTHAM

aka *Purge*
1987 111' col Malayalam
d/sc **K.R. Mohanan** *p* P.T.K. Mohammed *st* C.V. Sriraman's *Irikkapindam* *c* Madhu Ambat *m* **M.B. Srinivasan**
lp Sujata Mehta, **Adoor Bhasi**, Madampu Kunjukuttan, Jebin George, Dr Rama, Rana Muttalali, Bhargaviyamma, Baby Nandita

After his directorial debut with ***Ashwathama*** (1978), Mohanan had to wait almost a decade for his 2nd feature to be finished. It tells of an urban widow, Bhadra Vasudev (Mehta), who, with her son, returns to her dead husband's village to perform the ritual that will free her from the turbulent corpse that seems to persecute her and whose death she may have caused. The story unfolds from her son Vineet's point-of-view as he becomes progressively estranged from his mother, ending up throwing sacrificial rice balls at her and her new friend Ninan. The title refers to the four purusharthas, the goals of mankind according to Hindu ethical philosophy.

PUSHPAK/PUSHPAKA VIMANA

aka *The Love Chariot*
1987 130' col Wordless (Kannada)
d/s **Singeetham Srinivasa Rao** *p* Srinagar Nagaraj *pc* Mandakini Chitra *c* B.C. Gowri Shankar *m* L. Vaidyanathan
lp **Kamalahasan**, Amala, Tinnu Anand, Samir Khakhar, K.S. Ramesh

Apparently taking its cue from Mel Brooks's *Silent Movie* (1976), this wordless comedy helped change Kamalahasan's screen image. An unemployed youth (Kamalahasan) sees a drunken man (Khakhar) with a fancy hotel's room key dangling from his pocket. The youth kidnaps the drunk and ties him up in his own tenement room, making elaborate arrangements to allow his prisoner to perform his daily toilet (he cuts a hole in the prisoner's chair and gift-wraps the excrement). The youth then checks into the hotel where he immediately becomes the target of a hoodlum (Anand) who tries to murder him with knife-shaped ice cubes (when the ice melts, the murder weapon would vanish).

RUTHUBHEDAM

aka *Hrithubhedam* aka *Change of Seasons*
1987 126' col Malayalam
d **Prathap Pothan** *p* Verghese Abraham *s* **M.T. Vasudevan Nair** *c* Ashok Kumar *lyr* Thakazhy Shankaranarayanan *m* Shyam
lp **Balachandra Menon**, Nedumudi Venu, Murali, Sankaradi, Vieneth, Geetha, Monisha, Manimala

Echoing aspects of **Gopalakrishnan**'s ***Elippathayam*** (1981), Vasudevan Nair's script tells of the decline of a family of former Nair rent collectors as various members give way to greed and other weaknesses. The dramatic trigger is provided by a government compensation payment for confiscated forest lands, and the rapacious members of the family go to extraordinary lengths to appropriate as much compensation money as they can get by means both fair and foul. The story is told mainly through the eyes of a poor village lad, Keshu, returning from the city. The well-known director, B. Menon, can here be seen as an actor.

SACRIFICE OF BABULAL BHUIYA, THE

aka *Babulal Bhuiya Ki Qurbani*
1987 63' col Oriya
d Manjira Dutta *pc* Media Workshop *c* Ranjan Palit

A poetic documentary about the tribals around Bihar's Mailgora collieries who survive by recycling the pits' coal slurry. In February 1981, Babulal Bhuiya, one of the workers, was shot dead by the Industrial Security Force. The film goes into the circumstances of his death via covering Communist Party rallies in the area. Much of the story is intercut with painterly shots on the body of an anonymous male worker in the quarry.

Swathi Thirunal
1987 133' col/scope Malayalam
d/co-s **Lenin Rajendran** *p* G.P. Vijay Kumar *pc* Seven Arts Films *co-s* Varaham Balakrishnan *c* Madhu Ambat *m* **M.B. Srinivasan**
lp **Anant Nag**, Shrividya, Ambika, Ranjini, Nedumudi Venu

Biographical fantasy about Swathi Thirunal, best-known of the 19th C. Travancore kings. The British treaty (1795) established Travancore as an independent state figureheaded by its royalty. As with, e.g., the Mysore state and other capitals of former rulers reduced to ceremonial function, this period saw a major revival of classical music and performing arts. However, Swathi Thirunal's reign has received special attention, as a relatively uncomplicated era preceding Travancore's decline into the 20th C. rule of the despotic Diwan C.P. Ramaswamy Aiyer against whom the 1940s communist uprising was directed. The big-budget CinemaScope film, by a director noted for his CPI(M) sympathies, is an unrepentantly revivalist effort to appropriate a 'golden age' in Travancore history. Its resemblance to G.V. Iyer's ***Hamsa Geethe*** (1975) in this regard is further heightened by the presence of leading man Nag, whose naturalist underplaying of the king contrasts with the elaborate period decor. After establishing the king's credentials as lover and patron of art and music, and as staunch anti-imperialist, the film devolves into a love story with the Tanjore dancer Sugandhavalli (Shrividya). The escalating political crisis is represented by the arrival of a new general, and ends with the king's death.

TAMAS

aka *Darkness*
1987 297' col Hindi
d/sc/co-c **Govind Nihalani** *pc* Blaze Ents *st* Bhishm Sahni's novel *co-c* V. K. Murthy *m* **Vanraj Bhatia**
lp **Om Puri**, Deepa Sahi, Dina Pathak, Bhishm Sahni, Amrish Puri, Uttara Baokar, Surekha Sikri, **Saeed Jaffrey**, Ila Arun, K.K. Raina

Nihalani's controversial five-hour tv series deals with the Partition of India and led to major communal confrontations when the Hindu BJP organisations threatened to set tv stations afire and caused rioting in Hyderabad and Bombay. Based on one of Hindi author Bhishm Sahni's best-known recent novels, the epic tale is seen mainly through the eyes of a

Tamas

tanner named Nathu (Om Puri) and his pregnant wife Karmo (Sahi). An effort to cause a communal conflict (one of the commonest strategies is to place a dead pig in a mosque) escalates into the pre-1947 conflagration throughout Punjab. The film effectively lumps together the activities of all the various political groups involved, including the British colonial powers and Hindu as well as Muslim communal fronts, which it contrasts with individual expressions of human concern that serve sometimes to dilute a notoriously complex historical episode into no more than a conflict between common good and politically motivated bad.

THORANAM

1987 103' col Malayalam
d/s Joseph Madapally *p* V. Rajan *c* Ravi Varma *m* **P. Devarajan**
lp Nedumudi Venu, Soman, Janardanan, Jamuna, Kunjandi

Directorial debut of a journalist and novelist with a film about a crippled soldier who settles in a village in Kerala. He adopts a little Muslim boy and befriends a woman (Jamuna) relentlessly pursued by misfortune. The old soldier's benevolence is misconstrued by the villagers but the woman repays his kindness and a kind of family situation is maintained.

VEDHAM PUDITHU

aka *New Vedas*
1987 144' col Tamil
d/sc **P. Bharathirajaa** *pc* Janani Art Creations *st/dial/c* B. Kannan from his play *Jatikal Illayadi Papa* *lyr* **Vairamuthu** *m* Devendran
lp Satyaraj, Sarita, Raja, Nizhalgal Ravi, Charuhasan, Amala, Master Dasarathi

Melodrama supposedly critiquing Tamil Brahminism and a major censorship case when the Madras Tamil Brahmins' Association's call to have it banned was apparently supported by the then-President of India, R. Venkatraman. Balu Thevar (Satyaraj), a non-Brahmin atheist and the village chief, has a feud with the Brahmin Neelkanth Sastry (Charuhasan) who teaches the Vedas to Thevar's son Sankara Pandi, the latter also being in love with Sastry's daughter. Pandi gets killed, as does Sastry, allowing another character to emerge: a widowed forest ranger who confronts the girl's Brahmin suitor as well as the film's villain. The ranger eventually wins the girl. Bharathirajaa's practice of setting a love story in the context of village ritual yields an unusually violent story with several killings in a film purporting to advocate humanist values against religious bigotry.

VEEDU

aka *The House* aka *Home and the World*
1987 110' col Tamil
d/sc/c **Balu Mahendra** *p* Kala Das *pc* Shri Kala Int. *st* Ahila Balu Mahendra *m* **Ilaiyaraja**
lp Archana, Bhanuchander, M.A. Chokkalinga Bhagavathar, Sathiya, Indu

Released in the International Year of Shelter, the film tells of Sudha (Archana), a government clerk in Madras, who lives with her sister and grandfather Murugesan (Bhagavathar), a retired music teacher. They look for a new home and are advised to build one instead. Helped by her friend Gopi (Bhanuchander), she encounters harassment, corruption and obstruction wherever she turns until, in the end, the Water Authority appropriates her new house and she is last seen in a freeze-frame seeking redress through the courts. The director claimed it to be a true story, inspired by the experiences of his mother. As his own cinematographer, Mahendra uses hand-held techniques and atmospheric source lighting to great effect. There are no song and dance sequences but the movie lovingly shows the old man singing beloved Tamil songs. The music is taken largely from Ilaiyaraja's album *How to Name It*. Archana's and especially Bhagavathar's performances stand out, while the overly emphatic figure of building worker Mangatha strikes a false note.

AGNI NAKSHATRAM

1988 146' col Tamil
d/s **Mani Rathnam** *pc* Sujatha Prod. *lyr* **Vali** *c* P.C. Sriram *m* **Ilaiyaraja**
lp Karthik, Prabhu, Amala, Nirosha, G. Umapathi, Janakaraj, V.K. Ramaswamy

Rathnam's hit follow-up to ***Nayakan*** (1987) is a music video-type fantasy with rapid cutting, hazy images and flared lights. It also boasts one of the most sexually explicit song picturisations to date: the camera slithers along, peeking at a woman autoerotically engaged in an indoor swimming pool. The plot involves two stepbrothers, one a cop (Prabhu) and the other a streetwise hood (Karthik), the two mothers, and the shared father who runs separate family establishments for them. After the unsatisfactory conflict between the brothers, one realises, in the critic K. Hariharan's words, 'that the real hero of the film is actually behind the camera [p]ulling out every gimmick available in the ad-man's repertoire'.

APARAN

1988 115' col Malayalam
d/s **P. Padmarajan** *pc* Supriya International *c* Venu *m* Johnson
lp Poornima Jayaram, Shobhana, Parvathy, Jalaja, **Madhu**, Soman

A story of mistaken identity: an innocuous good guy is mistaken for a gangster boss who may well have been his twin brother. Most Western versions of this plot, e.g. featuring Jerry Lewis or Fernandel, explore the situation's comic potential. However, Padmarajan sees the plot as a psychological drama.

AYARTHI THOLLAYIRATHI IRUPATHONNU

aka *1921*
1988 197' col/scope Malayalam
d **I.V. Sasi** *p* Mohammed Mannil *pc* Mannil Films *s* T. Damodaran *c* V. Jayaram *m* Shyam
lp **Mammootty, Madhu**, K.P. Ummar, Suresh Gopi, Bahadur, Parvathy, Jagannath Varma, Janardhanan, T.G. Ravi, Seema, Balan K. Nair, Tom Alter, Rohini, Bhaskaran, Urvashi

Designed as an action melodrama blockbuster to follow the successful ***Ee Nadu*** (1982). The film addresses the 1921 Moplah rebellion when poor peasants, mostly Muslim, rose against the landowning aristocrats, mostly Hindu, while the British operated their characteristic divide-and-rule policy after the defeat of Tipu Sultan. The historical and political contexts of the rising are treated in terms of a catalogue of cartoon-like cliches and stirring nationalist speeches. The meat of the movie is in the rapes, battles and other nastiness perpetrated upon the innocent. The film-makers explicitly stated their wish not to support nor to contradict any possible interpretation of the historical events to which they allude.

BAI CHALI SASARIYE

1988 151' col Rajasthani
d/sc/co-dial Mohansingh Rathod *pc* Sundar Films *st* Keshav Rathod *co-dial* Mahendra Singh Jodha *co-dial/co-lyr* Kundan Kishore *co-lyr* Diwakar *c* Chandu Desai *m* O.P. Vyas
lp Alankar, Neelu, Gnan Shivpuri, Priyanka, Ramesh Tiwari, Bhairavi Shah, Devyani Thakkar, Prahlad Pawar, **Lalita Pawar**, Jagdeep

Rajasthani star Neelu reprises her familiar role as a virtuous victim in a neo-traditionalist melodrama. Lakshmi's (Neelu) mother dies giving birth to her; when her millionaire father remarries, she is raised like an outsider in her own family. Her only support (in an unusual twist) is her stepbrother, who assumes the familial responsibility in arranging her marriage. However, her misfortunes continue as her in-laws heap more suffering on her and eventually cause her death. The film purported to be against feudalism and superstition.

BANNADA VESHA

1988 110' col Kannada
d/s **Girish Kasaravalli** *pc* **Doordarshan** (Bangalore) *c* G.S. Bhaskar *m* **B.V. Karanth**
lp Sridhar, Smitha Kasaravalli, A.B. Jayaram, Narayana Bhatt, Shantamma, Loknath, Shankar

Folk-theatre-derived melodrama set in the famed Karnataka tradition of the Yakshagana, a variant of the Kathakali style involving complicated make-up and rigorous dance codes, patronised mainly by temples which invite groups to perform for worship and to raise revenue. The central character, Shambhu (Shankar), a member of such a group, is a traumatised and guilt-ridden figure usually relegated to minor roles but with the driving ambition of playing the male lead by displacing the arrogant Sheshappa. When he is allowed to play the demonic Jhunjhutti, he pretends to be possessed by the demon and uses his new-found reputation to start an alternate theatre group sponsored by the financially ailing Kapileshwara temple. His performative limitations, and the secondary problems caused by his having to live a fake identity, intensify his emotional crises and the film ends on a tragic note after he is revealed to be a fraud. Kasaravalli's stylised idiom, the film's most attractive aspect, is restricted to the performances while routine realism prevails in the rest of the story.

CHITHRAM

1988 171' col Malayalam
d/s Priyadarshan *pc* Shirdi Sai Creations *p* P.K.R. Pillai *lyr* Shibu Chakravarty *c* S. Kumar *m* Kannoor Rajan, Johnson
lp **Mohanlal**, Nedumudi Venu, Ranjini, Raju, Srinivasan

Along with *Kilukkam*, the same year, Mohanlal established his collaborations with director Priyadarshan as among the most infallible in the commercial Malayalam cinema. When Kalyani's (Ranjini) rich father returns from abroad on a brief holiday to settle the inheritance of his property, Kalyani's uncle (Venu) hires a thief and con man, Vishnu (Mohanlal), to masquerade as her husband. The reason for this impersonation is to keep the father's property from falling into the hands of a bunch of baddies (Srinivasan, Raju) who run the estate. Most of the film exploits the several comic possibilities of a spirited woman and a crazy hero being forced to pretend to be married. The story takes a tragic turn when Mohanlal is revealed as a murderer facing a death sentence, and he tells his tale in flashback. He had killed his deaf-mute girlfriend Revathi, when he mistook her **Naxalite** brother as being her lover. His child by Revathi was put into an orphanage when he was arrested. At the end, Vishnu and Kalyani, having fallen in love, are parted by the law, as he goes off to his death sentence while she is saddled with the responsibility of raising his orphaned child. The film adheres to the sometimes inexplicable tendency, for viewers unfamiliar with its generic codes, of 80s Kerala melodrama to end in tragedy.

DAASI

aka *Bonded Woman*
1988 94' col Telugu
d/s/m **B. Narasinga Rao** *pc* Little India *c* A.K. Bir
lp Archana, Roopa, Bhopal Reddy, Sidappa Naidu, Shilpa

Political melodrama set in the 20s addressing the practice of purchasing slave girls, often given as dowry in a marriage, by zamindar families under the rule of the Nizam of Hyderabad. Kamakshi (Archana), a daasi bonded to Jayasimha Rao, becomes pregnant by her owner. At the command of the zamindar's self-indulgent and childless wife, Kamakshi is forced to have an abortion. The film uses a neo-expressionist style, e.g. the dark servants' quarters, the drumbeats announcing the pregnancy of the landlord's sister counterpointed with the daasi's screams as the midwife terminates her pregnancy, etc.

EK DIN ACHANAK

aka *Suddenly One Day*
1988 105' col Hindi
d/sc **Mrinal Sen** *pc* **NFDC**, **Doordarshan** *st* Ramapada Choudhury *c* K.K. Mahajan *m* Jyotishka Dasgupta
lp Shriram Lagoo, Uttara Baokar, **Shabana Azmi**, **Aparna Sen**, Roopa Ganguly, Arjun Chakraborty, **Anil Chatterjee**, Manohar Singh, Lily Chakraborty, Anjan Dutt

Closely echoing the plot of ***Kharij*** (1982), Sen tells of a retired professor (Lagoo) who suddenly disappears. His wife, children and friends start to worry when he does not return and wait months for him. Their memories, as each tries to reconstruct their view of the man, provide the film with a patchwork of fragments building into a composite but never quite coherent picture of the professor. Some critics saw it as Sen's most autobiographical film.

IDU NAMMA ALU

1988 165' col Tamil
d Balakumaran *pc* Bhagavathi Creations
st/sc/m **K. Bhagyaraj** *lyr* **Vali**
lp K. Bhagyaraj, Shobhana

Although credited to the novelist Balakumaran, this caste comedy belongs to the established director and actor Bhagyaraj, here playing an unemployed son of a village barber who, assisted by a con man, enters an orthodox Brahmin household and marries the daughter (Shobhana). His lower-caste status is not discovered until after the wedding. The broad comedy is often irreverent towards established caste traditions.

IN WHICH ANNIE GIVES IT THOSE ONES

1988 112' col English
d **Pradeep Krishen** *pc* Grapevine Media *s* Arundhati Roy *c* Rajesh Joshi
lp Arjun Raina, Arundhati Roy, Rituraj, Roshan Seth, Isaac Thomas, Divya Seth, Idres Malik, Moses Uboh, Himani Shivpuri

TV film comedy about college life in Delhi. Set in an architecture college, the hero, Anand Grover aka Annie keeps failing his exams because he made fun of his college head. Nevertheless he retains his idealist vision of planting fruit trees to prevent people defecating near railway lines. Other characters are Annie's Ugandan room-mate and the outrageously dressed Radha. In the end, Annie manages to pass his exams thanks to a trick played by the students. The film suggests the hero goes on to become the head of the department.

KADAL THEERATHU

aka *On the Seashore*
1988 83' col Malayalam
d/p/sc T. Rajeevnath *pc* Rasika Films *st* O.V. Vijayan *c* Santosh Sivan *m* **Govindan Aravindan**, Kavalam Narayana Panicker
lp Amir Abbas, Leelamma Verghese

With stylised images and the familiar flashback structure, Rajeevnath uses the writer and cartoonist Vijayan's story to show the journey and the memories of a father, Vellayiappan, on his way to the coast to visit his imprisoned son Kandunni, condemned to death for killing a gangsterish landlord. The story echoes aspects of **Shaji N. Karun**'s ***Piravi*** (1988).

KHAYAL GATHA

aka *Khayal Saga*
1988 103' col Hindi
d/s **Kumar Shahani** *pc* Madhya Pradesh Film Dev. Corp., Bombay Cinematograph *dial* Ashmaki Acharya, Kamal Swaroop *c* K.K. Mahajan *m supervision* Roshan Shahani
lp Mita Vasisht, Birju Maharaj, Alaknanda Samarth, Rajat Kapoor, Navjot Hansra, Mangal Dhillon

Rather than imbuing stories about contemporary conditions with epic dimensions (cf ***Maya Darpan***, 1972; ***Tarang***, 1984), Shahani here addresses the epic forms directly in a film about the Khayal, a form of classical music established in the 18th C., based on the earlier Dhrupad which it then adapted, mobilising elements of other classical and folk literatures and music. For Shahani, the crucial relevance of this music to the cinema resides in its theory of the shruti, the subdivisions between given notes in a raga which eventually yield a continuous scale and prove that 'you can only name approximations, never absolutes' (1986). By

Meeta Vasisht and Pushpamala in *Khayal Gatha*

emphasising sequence rather than discrete notes or the rhythmic cycle, musical elaboration could be based on improvisation so that, like jazz or other musical forms emerging from oppression, it was able to resist all efforts at encoding while remaining free to assimilate the widest range of musical elements from as far as Central Asia, Turkey and Persia. The film merges the history of the Khayal form with several legends associated with it: e.g. the legends of Rani Rupmati (Vasisht) and Baaz Bahadur (Dhillon), Heer-Ranjha, Nala-Damayanti and others (some invented for the film). These legends are then worked into some of the key figurations determining the Khayal narrative, such as the *nayika* and the object of the address, and the *sakhi*. A music student (Kapoor) moves through these epochs and legends. The result is a visually stunning narration condensing legend, history and poetry, emphasising hybridity in all cultural practices. The key musical contributions are by some of the foremost musicians from the Gwalior *gharana*, the oldest of the several that exist, including Krishnarao Shankar Pandit, Sharatchandra Arolkar, Jal Balaporia and Neela Bhagwat. Shahani also uses the dance of Birju Maharaj, India's top Kathak dancer.

KOLAHAL

aka *The Turmoil*
1988 118' col Assamese
d/p/s **Bhabendranath Saikia** *c* Kamal Nayak *m* Mukul Barua
lp Runu Devi Thakur, Arun Nath, Bibhu Ranjan Choudhury

Realist melodrama based on an original radio play by the director. The child Moti keeps himself and his mother from starvation by stealing rice from trucks. His mother Kiran tries to work in a warehouse with a little support from her neighbours. Moti is killed when a truck capsizes and the driver tries to bribe Kiran's mother with a sack of rice marked by the blood of her son. When later she discovers that her long-absent husband is living with another woman in the city, she succumbs to the advances of Badal, the truck-cleaner.

MARATTAM

aka *Masquerade* aka *Faces and Masks*
1988 90' col Malayalam
d **Govindan Aravindan** *pc* **Doordarshan** *s/lyr* Kavalam Narayana Panicker based on his own play *c* **Shaji N. Karun**
lp Sadanandan Krishnamurthy, Kalamdalam, Keshavan, Urmila Gupta

Panicker's one-act play deals with the relation of identification between an actor and his or her role. Aravindan put the stress on the relations between the viewer and the actor/role dualities. The action takes place on the eve of the last act of the Kathakali piece *Keechakavadham* (*The Killing of Keechaka*). The events surrounding the performance uncannily echo events in the play. One character even claims to have killed the lead actor of the play because he detested the character the man portrayed. However, the three different accounts that are presented of the same plot are never resolved or reconciled with each other. Each version is accompanied by a different style of folk-music: the tune and rhythm of southern Kerala's thampuran pattu, the pulluvan pattu and the ayappan pattu. The performers were drawn from the theatre and from Kathakali. In southern India, with its plethora of politicians using their film images to acquire inordinate wealth and power, Aravindan's tv film bears on an eminently sensitive political as well as aesthetic issue.

OM DAR-B-DAR

1988 101' col Hindi
d/p/s/lyr Kamal Swaroop *pc* **NFDC** *c* Ashwani Kaul, Milind Ranade *m* Rajat Dholakia
lp Anita Kanwar, Gopi Desai, Lalit Tiwari, Aditya Lakhia, Bhairav Chandra Sharma, Lakshminarayan Shastri, Ramesh Mathur, Manish Gupta, Peter Morris

One of the most unusual independent films of the 80s, Kamal Swaroop's debut briefly suggested the possibility of an avant-garde. Set in a mythical small town in Rajasthan, akin to the Jhumri Talaiya whence stem the largest number of requests for film music singles addressed All India Radio's commercial channel, the film tells of a boy, Om, growing into adolescence. The son of a fortune teller and the younger brother of Gayatri, Om's major problem is that, riddled with guilt about his voyeurism, he believes hilmself to be responsible for everything that happens around him. Gayatri is courted by Jagdish as she dreams of a future that would allow her to ride a bicycle or to sit in the men's section of a movie theatre. Many of Om's fantasies about sexuality and death are graphically realised in remarkable song sequences: a science teacher dissecting a frog expands into the Felliniesque *Rana Tigrina* number, or the moonwalk on a terrace on the night that Neil Armstrong landed on the moon. This double-edged satire acquires a further dimension with the entry of Phoolmati (Kanwar), whose sexuality sends out beguiling and horrifying messages evoking, for Jagdish, the world of cheap Hindi novelettes. Then war is declared as the Diwali firecrackers become real explosions, the father's diamonds hoarded for black-market purposes are lost on the sethji's property where they are swallowed by frogs. In the end, Om atones by enacting the traditional legend of Brahma's descent to earth, the origin of the Pushkar fair which today is a major tourist attraction in Rajasthan. Om learns the art of breathing underwater and turns into a tourist exhibit. The jerky, fast-moving and witty film proceeds by way of symbolic imagery including tadpoles, skeletons and fantasies derived from Hindi movies, advertising, television and the popular Hindi novel. The music and soundtracks are remarkably inventive (e.g. the transformation of *Come September* into the number *A-a-a mohabbat humsafar ho jaye*).

ORU CBI DIARY KURUPPU

1988 137' col Malayalam
d K. Madhu *pc* Sunitha Prod. *p* M. Mani *s* S.N. Swamy *c* Vipin Das *m* Shyam
lp **Mammootty**, Urvashi, Suresh Gopi, Janardhanan, Sukumaran

Among the best known (with ***Avanazhi***, 1986) of Mammootty's cop movies. Omana, the daughter-in-law of prominent businessman Ouseph, dies under mysterious conditions. The officer investigating the crime is transferred when he rejects the official conclusion of suicide. Omana's father and sister (Urvashi) petition the Supreme Court, which orders the CBI (Central Bureau of Investigation) to re-examine the case. CBI officer Sethuraman (Mammootty), with crack lieutenants Vikram and Harry, unearths the truth. Much of the film deals with the illegal financial activities of Ouseph and his gang, their extensive political contacts and their control over the local police (who consistently oppose the CBI officers). The end, however, develops from a relatively less explored aspect of the script: Omana's sexual oppression in an all-male household. The criminal is revealed as one of Ouseph's henchmen, and the pretence of suicide is meant to cover up a rape.

PIRAVI

aka *Birth*
1988 110' col Malayalam
d/co-sc **Shaji N. Karun** *pc* Filmfolk *co-sc/st* S. Jayachandran Nair *co-sc* Raghu *c* Sunny Joseph *m* Mohan Sitara, **Govindan Aravindan**
lp Premji, Archana, Lakshmiamma, C.V. Sriraman, Mullenezhi, Chandran Nair

A visually engrossing yet austere directorial debut by Kerala's leading cinematographer. The plot is taken from actuality and concerns a frail but dogged old man, Chakyar (Premji), who obsessively searches for his vanished son, Raghu, venturing even into bewildering Trivandrum to seek an audience with the Home Minister. The man's daughter learns that her brother probably died in police custody after being tortured, but she cannot bear to tell her father who continues to hope and to search. However, the old man's grip on reality is slipping fast and he begins dreaming that his son is with him. The story is based on the disappearance of Rajan, a Naxalite sympathiser, during the Emergency. Rajan's father later sued the Congress-I Government. The film's force comes from its skilful orchestration of time and space into fascinating rhythmical patterns interacting with land- and cityscapes, drawing the viewer into the father's obsessive search in everyday, indifferent surroundings. It is also highly mystical, and deflects a major real-life incident with direct political repercussions into a brand of orientalist fatalism.

QAYAMAT SE QAYAMAT TAK

1988 162' col/scope Urdu
d Mansoor Khan *p/s* **Nasir Hussain** *lyr* **Majrooh Sultanpuri** *c* Kiran Deohans *m* Anand-Milind
lp Aamir Khan, Juhi Chawla, Ravinder Kapoor, Goga Kapoor, Dalip Tahil, Aloknath, Asha Sharma, Reema Lagoo, Beena, Ajit Vachhani, Raj Zutshi

The biggest box-office hit of 1988 relaunched its producer/writer (and some sources claim also director), and gave new life to glossy teen romances shot in advertising styles (cf ***Maine Pyar Kiya***, 1989). It also established the 90s star Aamir Khan. The film combines a Romeo and Juliet theme with the standard Nasir Hussain pop musical. Raj (Khan) and Rashmi (Chawla) fall in love, defying a major ancestral conflict between their families. They elope and create a kind of utopia in an abandoned temple on an isolated mountain, living on love, fresh air and burnt food. Having to buy provisions in a nearby town (the 'real' world), they are betrayed and die. The film presents the act of falling in love as an illusory individuation, but perhaps the only form of culturally acceptable rebellion available. Its strongly neo-traditional thrust is underlined by Khan's nostalgic evocation of classic Nasir Hussain heroes (e.g. **Shammi Kapoor**, **Dev Anand**), in the teenage hero's dilemma: whether to follow the idolised father, incarnated in the film's hit song *Papa kehte hain*, or to follow a different heroic vocation and fall in love. The film rapidly became a cult, fondly referred to by teenagers as 'QSQT'. Khan starred again in the follow-up, ***Dil*** (1990).

RAAKH

1988 153' col Hindi
d/st/co-sc Aditya Bhattacharya *pc* Emotion Pics, Second Image Ents *co-sc/dial* Nuzhat Khan *c* Santosh Sivan *m* Ranjit Barot
lp Aamir Khan, Pankaj Kapoor, Supriya Pathak, Naina Balsavar, Homi Wadia, Chandu Parkhi

Aamir Khan's first starring role prior to his breakthrough with ***Qayamat Se Qayamat Tak*** later in the year. The story, told in flashback, focuses on a young man whose interior monologue accompanies the film. The hero (Khan) helplessly watches his girlfriend (Pathak) being gang-raped. To refurbish his male pride (the woman's suffering is trivialised in the film), he spends the rest of the film, aided by a good cop (Kapoor), avenging the slighting of his manhood by the gangster and his henchmen responsible for the rape. The revenge story is presented as a fatalist meditation on 'meaning of life'. Using close-ups, flashing lights and throbbing music (composed by the rock drummer Ranjit Barot) under the dialogue, the film tries to induce the viewer to wallow in the choreography of violence.

RIHAEE

1988 158' col Hindi
d/s **Aruna Raje** *pc* Gaahimedia *dial* Suraj Sanim *lyr* Babu Rangpura, Suraj *c* S.R.K. Moorthy *m* Sharang Dev
lp **Hema Malini**, **Naseeruddin Shah**, Vinod Khanna, Kulbhushan Kharbanda, Ila Arun

First solo feature by Aruna Raje whose previous films were co-directed with Vikas Desai and signed jointly as Aruna-Vikas. It is set in a Rajasthan village where the men migrate to Bombay to seek work (and visit prostitutes) while their wives at home become victims of rapacious outsiders like Mansukh (Shah). Mansukh seduces the virtuous Taku (Malini) who becomes pregnant. When her husband (Khanna) returns, she informs him of her decision to defy the village elders' diktat and to have her child. The husband supports her against a group of villagers determined forcibly to terminate her pregnancy. Addressing the still unexplored theme of female sexuality, the film allows itself to be derailed into a conventional morality tale.

TEZAAB

1988 173' col/scope Hindi
d/s/p **N. Chandra** *pc* Aarti Ents Bombay, N. Chandra Prod. *lyr* **Javed Akhtar** *c* Baba Azmi *m* **Laxmikant-Pyarelal**
lp Anil Kapoor, Chunky Pandey, **Madhuri Dixit**, Anupam Kher, Kiran Kumar, Suresh Oberoi, Mandakini, Annu Kapoor

Chandra, the maker of the Shiv Sena propaganda film ***Ankush*** (1985), had his first hit with this Bombay low-life crime movie. Munna (Anil Kapoor) is in love with the dancer Mohini (Dixit). Mohini's father (Kher) is an alcoholic gambler who lives off his daughter's earnings. To prevent the lovers marrying, he helps Lotiya Khan (Kumar), a criminal hostile to Munna. Lotiya Khan's brother tries to rape Munna's sister and Munna kills him, earning himself a year in jail. On his release, Munna is persecuted by Lotiya Khan, Mohini's father and the police. Forced by his bail conditions to remain outside Bombay's city limits, Munna becomes a noted criminal. Mohini's father and Lotiya Khan quarrel and Mohini is kidnapped by Khan. Munna rescues her and defeats the villains. Most of the film is told in flashback, narrating the romance between Munna and Mohini and the violence it engenders (the film is subtitled 'A violent love story'). The main title, meaning 'Acid', refers to the way Mohini's father disfigures his wife and causes her to commit suicide, threatening to assault his daughter in the same way. Chandra places much of the action in recognisable parts of the city. However, the film's spectacular opening sequence at a rock concert, featuring the hit song *Ek do teen* showing Mohini's kidnap by a bunch of motor-cyclists weaving through the crowded streets, is shot in a studio and presents a fantasy version of New York's Times Square. The fanatic communalism evident in Chandra's *Ankush* is echoed here: the hero, identified as a Maharashtrian, disposes of several 'outside' thugs suggesting that 'local' Maharashtrian criminals are revered by the people who dislike outsiders interfering with their home-grown racketeers.

YATEEM

1988 173' col Hindi
d/s **J.P. Dutta** *pc* Bikramjeet Films, **Dharmendra** *dial* O.P. Dutta *lyr* Hasan Kamal *m* **Laxmikant-Pyarelal**
lp Sunny Deol, Farha, Kulbhushan Kharbanda, Amrish Puri, Sujata Mehta, Danny Denzongpa, Dina Pathak

Dutta returned to his favourite Rajasthan desert locale with camerawork placing people in huge spaces for this revivalist tale of a policeman, Shivkumar Yadav (Kharbanda). Responsible for the death of Krishna's bandit parents, he adopts the boy (Deol) who goes to a police academy and returns home a commissioned officer to find his foster-father remarried. Yadav's new wife Chanchal (Sujata Mehta) mistreats her stepdaughter Gauri (Farha), Krishna's lover, while lusting for Krishna and having an affair with a junior officer, Girivar Mathur (Denzongpa). Rejected by Krishna, Chanchal accuses him of attempted rape and has him jailed. Krishna escapes and lives as a fugitive with Gauri until he is captured by a bandit. Escaping again, Gauri gives birth to a child which forces Krishna to surrender to his foster father. Earlier, Chanchal had been shot by Girivar, who blamed Yadav for the killing and is later killed himself by Krishna. Yadav dies protecting Krishna who then kills the bandits.

ALICINTE ANVESHANAM

aka *Alice's Search*, aka *The Search of Alice*
1989 132' col Malayalam
d/s T.V. Chandran *pc* Neo Vision, **NFDC** *c* Sunny Joseph *m* Ouseppachan
lp Jalaja, Ravindranath, Nedumudi Venu, C.V. Sriraman, Nilambur Balan, P.T.K. Mohammed

Set in a northern Kerala Catholic milieu, the film tells of a college lecturer's wife, Alice (Jalaja), who searches for her vanished husband and slowly discovers disturbing aspects of the man's life including his descent from his earlier radicalism into 'bourgeois' degeneracy. In the end, she abandons the search and decides to take responsibility for her own life. Third and best-known film by former actor (***Kabani Nadi Chuvannappol***, 1975) and assistant to **Abraham** and **Backer**.

BAGH BAHADUR

aka *The Tiger Dancer*
1989 91' col Hindi
d/p/sc **Buddhadev Dasgupta** *pc* **Doordarshan** *st* Prafulla Roy *c* Venu *m* Shantanu Mahapatra
lp Pavan Malhotra, Archana, Vasudev Rao, Biplab Chatterjee, Rajeshwari Roy Choudhury, Masood Akhtar

Inspired by the atmosphere of folk-tales, the film tells of Ghunuram (Malhotra), a quarry worker who returns to his native village of Nonpura to participate in its annual festival as the celebrated Tiger Dancer and to marry Radha (Archana), the daughter of the drummer Sibal (Rao). However, Ghunuram's dance is eclipsed by a real-life leopard show staged by a circus. In addition, Archana falls in love with a circus performer. In desperation and encouraged by Sibal's drumming, Ghunuram enters the leopard's cage and challenges it to a duel, which he loses.

BANANI

aka *The Forest*
1989 108' col Assamese
d **Jahnu Barua** *pc* Purbanchal Film Co-op *s* Sushil Goswami *c* Anoop Jotwani *m* Satya Barua, Prasanta Bordoloi
lp Mridula Barua, Sushil Goswami, Bishnu Kharghoria, Golap Dutta, Lakshmi Sinha, Munim Sharma, Jyoti Bhattacharya, Shasanka Debo Phukan

With this ecological drama, Assam's leading director Jahnu Barua continues exploring the conflict between corrupt state politics and a determined individual (cf ***Halodiya Choraye***

Baodhan Khaye, 1987). The forest ranger (Goswami) confronts illegal timber merchants and contractors on behalf of impoverished tribals. The honest ranger's activities get him into trouble and he is constantly transferred from one post to another, to the annoyance of his wife who wants him to settle down and look after their ailing child. Eventually she supports her husband's fight and the tribals realise they need weapons to defend themselves against rapacious outsiders. The film's simple plot is interrupted by long didactic speeches.

BATWARA

1989 201' col/scope Hindi
d/s **J.P. Dutta** *pc* 786 Aftab Pics *dial* O.P. Dutta *lyr* Hasan Kamal *c* Ishwar Bidri *m* **Laxmikant-Pyarelal**
lp **Dharmendra**, Vinod Khanna, Kulbhushan Kharbanda, Vijayendra Ghatge, Nina Gupta, Dimple Kapadia, **Shammi Kapoor**, Asha Parekh, Poonam Dhillon, Mohsin Khan, Amrish Puri, Amrita Singh

Amitabh Bachchan's celebrated baritone introduces in voice-over the film's political context: new laws limiting land ownership introduced after Independence threaten the zamindar class. One of them, Bade Thakur (Kapoor), has a son, Vikram Singh aka Vicky (Khanna) who is friendly with Sumer Singh (Dharmendra), a member of the hated Jat community. Vicky's younger brother, the arrogant Devan (Ghatge), is killed by irate villagers and Vicky in turn murders several villagers, including the brother of Sumer's girlfriend (Dimple). The friends turn into mortal enemies as Sumer becomes the farmers' leader. Both Sumer and Vicky are sought by the police, especially by Rajendra Pratap Singh (Khan), a principled officer despite being the youngest son of Bade Thakur. Rajendra Pratap's disdain for caste differences irks his junior officer Hanumant Singh (Puri), who plans to kill him. The film continues J.P. Dutta's concern with Rajastan's communal and caste wars, the feudal lifestyle of the zamindars, their scant respect for human life and the image of a powerful, charismatic leader who unites the people against the oppressive thakurs. The visuals are replete with horses racing across the desert, camels, palaces, elaborate costumes, sand-dunes, ravines and the mandatory vultures.

CHANDNI

1989 186' col Hindi
d **Yash Chopra** *pc* Yash Raj Films *st* Kamna Chandra *sc* Unmesh Kalba, Arun Kashyap *lyr* **Anand Bakshi** *c* Manmohan Singh *m* Shiv-Hari
lp Vinod Khanna, Rishi Kapoor, **Sridevi**, **Waheeda Rehman**, Anupam Kher, Mita Vasisht

Yash Chopra returns to his familiar brand of romances (cf ***Silsila***, 1981) in exotic locations with this tale of Chandni (Sridevi). She is seen - and for a large part of the film, also imagined - only through the eyes of her lover Rohit (Kapoor), who decorates the walls of his room with the countless snapshots he takes of her. Later, while showering his beloved with flowers from a helicopter, he falls and is partially paralysed, prompting him to break off the relationship. However, his sexually charged fantasies of Chandni eventually rekindle his desire to live. After an expensive operation in a hospital abroad, he is cured and re-enters Chandni's life just when she is about to marry her boss, Lalit (Khanna). The film and its marketing campaign revolve entirely around Sridevi, confirming her as India's top female star. Arguably, the whole film can be seen as an extended advertisement promoting Sridevi as the Indian film consumers' ideal fantasy of womanhood. including the popular song by **Lata Mangeshkar**, *Mere haathon main nau nau churiyan*.

CHHANDANEER

aka *The Nest of Rhythm*
1989 130' col Bengali
d/s/m **Utpalendu Chakraborty** *pc* Abhishek Prod. *c* Girish Padhiar
lp Anjana Bannerjee, Dipak Sarkar, **Madhabi Chakraborty**, Satya Bannerjee, **Anup Kumar**, Sreela Majumdar, Gyanesh Mukherjee, Ratna Ghoshal, Kanika Majumdar

A classical dance film focusing on the performance skills of Anjana Bannerjee who plays the central character, Seema, an internationally acclaimed Bharat Natyam dancer with a comfortable middle-class background. Rejecting the man her parents chose as her husband, she marries a wonderful but blind musician, Anyan, and they stage shows together. However, to earn more money, Anyan compromises his talent and works for pop singers and commercial film producers, causing Seema to walk out on him so as to remain devoted to the purity of her classical dance tradition.

FLYING BIRD, THE

1989 90' col English
d/co-s **Vishnu Mathur** *p/co-s* C.S. Lakshmi *c* K.K. Mahajan
lp Savithri Rajan

A beautifully crafted and meditative documentary portrait shot on 16mm of the 80-year-old Madras-based Savithri Rajan, a virtuoso veena player who never performed in public. She was the disciple of the legendary musicians Tiger Varadachari and Veenai Dhanammal. The film is built around her music and family memories with K.K. Mahajan's sensuous camera gliding through the spaces of her life or simply recording the aged but lively Rajan's voice and music. Savithri Rajan's extraordinary presence is the film's focus, but Mathur manages to convey the complex interrelations between personal, familial, artistic and social rhythms of change, achieving the rare feat of doing justice to the accomplishments of the individual artist while at the same time suggesting how social elements constrained as well as nourished her life and her art. An exemplary documentary about an admirable woman.

GANASHATRU

aka *An Enemy of the People*
1989 99' col Bengali
d/sc/m **Satyajit Ray** *pc* **NFDC** *st* Henrik Ibsen's play *c* Barun Raha
lp **Soumitra Chatterjee**, Ruma Guha-Thakurta, Mamata Shankar, **Dhritiman Chatterjee**, Dipankar Dey, Subhendu Chatterjee, Manoj Mitra, Vishwa Guha-Thakurta, Rajaram Yagnik, Satya Bannerjee, Gobinda Mukherjee

Having suffered a heart attack, Ray returned to cinema, extensively assisted by his son Sandeep, with a short documentary on his father, *Sukumar Ray* (1987), and with this first of three features set in contemporary Bengal, addressing, like his earlier trilogy, the theme of corruption. For his first contemporary story since ***Jana Aranya*** (1975), Ray transposes the Ibsen play into the story of Dr Ashok Gupta (Soumitra Chatterjee) who protests when the holy water in a temple turns out to be contaminated by bad plumbing and produces a jaundice epidemic. The doctor meets with powerful opposition from the temple trustees and the villagers. The plot device of making the holy water in a temple the cause of disease evoked the rise of the Hindu religious right wing in Indian politics. The film is shot predominantly in close-ups and mid-shots and seems to bear the stamp of Ray's continuing ill health.

GEETANJALI

1989 142' col Telugu
d/s **Mani Rathnam** *pc* Bhagyalakshmi Ents *lyr* Veeturi Sundara Ramamurthy *c* P.C. Sriram *m* **Ilaiyaraja**
lp Nagarjuna, Girija, Vijayakumar, Vijayachander, Sumithra, Velu, Disco Shanthi, Chandramohan, **Sowcar Janaki**, Smita

Rathnam's first Telugu film was the biggest hit of the year in Telugu as well as in Tamil (in a dubbed version, *Idhayathe Thirudathe*). It tells an unusual love story about a young collegiate gangster (Nagarjuna) who meets the wild Geetanjali (Girija). Both are terminally ill, he with leukaemia and she with heart disease. These afflictions appear to liberate the duo from social constraints. Most of the film is shot in exotic, fog-bound locations and includes several rock numbers (e.g. *Om Namaha* which uses an amplified heartbeat as background rhythm). The critic Tejaswini Niranjana (1991) points out that the heroine is the 'new woman, the strong heroine, the inheritor of a refracted modernity in a context where feminity is once again being redefined [placing on her] the burden of saviour and teacher [w]ho has to be the one to provide support, when the hero in a similar situation [sings] sad songs. However, [s]he is allowed to take the initiative in the relationship because in spite of her shoulder-length hair she is 'Indian' and a signifier of the good modernity.'

HATHYAR

1989 186' col/scope Hindi
d/st **J.P. Dutta** *p* H.A. Nadiadwala *dial* O.P. Dutta *lyr* Hasan Kamal *c* Ishwar Bidri *m* **Laxmikant-Pyarelal**

lp **Dharmendra**, Rishi Kapoor, Sanjay Dutt, Amrita Singh, Sangeeta Bijlani, Kulbhushan Kharbanda, Paresh Rawal

One of Sanjay Dutt's early hits in his current loner mould. In distant Rajasthan, Avinash (Dutt) and Suman (Singh) are married as children. As they grow up, feudal clan rivalry between their families causes Avinash to leave his wife and to move to Bombay with his pacifist parents (Kharbanda and Rawal) where he becomes involved in gang violence. The fearsome Khushal Khan (Dharmendra), protector of Avinash's family, has a weakness: his good younger brother Samiulla Khan (Kapoor) will not talk to him. Eventually, a third storyline emerges as the 'real' villain comes on the scene: a Tamil gangster (Rawal) who caused Khushal Khan to become a criminal. All the characters struggle to achieve a degree of control over their circumstances while the director undercuts their efforts by resorting to 'mythic', overpowering Bombay locations (**N. Chandra** and **Mukul S. Anand** territory) which nevertheless give the impression of being sets because of the patchy lighting, the overbearing soundtrack or the relentless shot-reverse-shot editing pattern.

KAAL ABHIRATI

aka *Time Addiction*
1989 172' col Bengali
d/co-p Amitabh Chakraborty *co-p* Mandira Mitra *pc* Ayonija Films *dial* Moinak Biswas *c* Shashikant Anantachari *m* Prasun Mitra
lp Somo Dev Basu, Badal Sircar, Jogesh Datta, Rajavati Sircar, Rita Chakraborty, Sunil Mukherjee

Experimental feature debut by a young **FTII** graduate. The opening shot sets the tone, holding for nearly 10' a static frame with an outstretched palm and occasional passers-by seen through a door in the distance. The film has four main characters, an artist-hero, his girlfriend, a garrulous and cynical avuncular figure (played by Badal Sircar), and a sound technician who records their conversation (and sometimes represents the film-maker). The occasional stretches of dialogue between the man and woman in a partially constructed building and in the zoo, or the rowdy drunken conversation in a bar, serves to heighten the surreal effects arrived at with immense Kali figures on Calcutta's streets, clouds of smoke and ghostly figures wandering through cavernous 19th C. mansions. At the end of the film, in a dawn shot, the hero sets his works of art afire, and joins the other characters in a Dionysian dance. The highly theatrical film depends mainly on a rigorous symmetry of volumes and long duration shots that are either static or move in a slow track. Remarkably, the main set, the city of Calcutta, is physically drained of all human presence other than the actual actors. The presence of Badal Sircar, one of Bengal's best-known playwrights (*Evam Indrajeet*) and proponent of a Grotowskian 'Third Theatre' concept, serves partially to contextualise the theatrical origins of the language.

MAI

1989 ?' col Bhojpuri
d/co-sc Rajkumar Sharma *pc* Shiv Ganga Prod. *st* Ashok Sinha *co-sc* Narayan Bhandari *dial* Shiv Munjal *lyr* Shaktikishore Dubey *c* Surjeet Cheema *m* Ram Babu
lp Padma Khanna, Sheila David, Pankaj Sharma, Vijay Khare, Hari Shukla, Brijkishore, Narayan Bhandari, Shraddha Sinha

Bhojpuri hit melodrama invoking a Gorky-type mother figure in the village of Karitpur in Central India. She and her family, notably her younger brother-in-law Kundan and her sister-in-law Radha, come up against the evil violence of the young local zamindar who tries to appropriate the village land. One-time Hindi actress Padma Khanna, now a major Bhojpuri star, plays the lead.

MAINE PYAR KIYA

aka *I Have Fallen in Love* aka *When Love Calls*
1989 192' col/scope Hindi
d/sc Sooraj Barjatya *pc* Rajshri Prod. *st* S.M. Ahale *lyr* Asad Bhopali, Dev Kohli *c* Arvind Laad *m* Ram-Lakshman
lp Salman Khan, Bhagyashree, Alok Nath, Rajiv Verma, Rima Lagoo, Ajit Vachani, Harish Patel, Deep Dhillon, Huma Khan, Pervin Dastur, Mohnish Behl, Laxmikant Berde

A typical, very successful rich-boy/poor-girl romance launching the career of 90s star Salman Khan as a teenage hero. The hero, Prem (Khan), falls in love with Suman (Bhagyashree). Obstacles are provided by Krishen (Vachani), Prem's businessman father who is also Suman's guardian. Suman is the daughter of a village motor-mechanic (Nath), which evokes suggestions of class as well as city/country divisions in the love story which initiated the now-popular convention of the slow fade-out on the embrace of the couple's fathers. The film's novelty is due mainly to its adoption of advertising imagery: rich, saturated colour effects constantly emphasising surface, trendy costumes (the cooks wear red-check coats), green fields full of footballs, mountainsides of red apples, neon signs, ice falling into glasses of Coke, a heroine with fluffy toys and a leather-jacketed hero who loves motor-bikes, posters of American pop icons (including a poster of Salman Khan himself). The soundtrack, which uses an 'I love you' refrain throughout the film, includes the hit song *Kabutar ja ja* with a carrier pigeon hitching a ride in a car to convey a love letter. The film's songs broke all sales records. It was dubbed into several languages, eg. *Inapravugal* (Malayalam, 1991).

MARHI DA DEEVA/DEEP

aka *The Lamp of the Tomb*
1989 115' col Punjabi/Hindi
d/sc Surinder Singh *pc* **NFDC**, **Doordarshan** *st* Gurdial Singh *c* Anil Sehgal *m* Mohinderjit Singh
lp Raj Babbar, Deepti Naval, Kanwaljit, Parikshit Sahni, Asha Sharma, Pankaj Kapoor

The first Punjabi art-house film is a melodrama about feudalism based on a popular novel, also adapted to the stage, by Gurdial Singh. The story chronicles the shift from feudal sharecropping to capitalist farming over two generations of the region's rural elite. Hero Jagsir, the son of the sharecropper Thola, is treated as a brother by landlord Dharam Singh. The landlord's son, however, does not continue this family tradition. As Jagsir's mother belongs to a nomad caste (preventing the son, by custom, from ever marrying), the hero's love for the bride of the impotent barber Nika is fraught with problems. Symbolically, the building of Jagsir's father's tomb (also a means of marking out the land that rightfully belongs to the family) and then of his own tomb precedes Jagsir's physical deterioration and death. Insightful links between masculinity and land ownership provide a good example of how melodrama can address difficult political realities.

Deepti Naval and Raj Babbar in *Marhi Da Deeva*

MATHILUKAL

aka *The Walls*
1989 119' col Malayalam
d/p/sc **Adoor Gopalakrishnan** *pc* **Doordarshan** *st* Vaikom Mohammed Basheer *c* Ravi Varma *m* **Vijayabhaskar**
lp **Mammootty**, Thilakan, Murali, Ravi Vallathol, Karamana Janardanan Nair, Srinath, Babu Namboodiri, Jagannath Varma, Vempayan, Aziz, P.C. Soman

Based on the prison diaries of the well-known Kerala writer Basheer, this is a love story, set in the 40s, between the imprisoned Basheer and a woman from the neighbouring prison compound. They are separated by a high wall so that they never see each other and have to devise ingenious ways of communicating. Produced for tv, the story is played out in confined spaces with a sense of claustrophobia and suppressed violence which enhances the emotional impact of the moving love story.

NAZAR

aka *The Gaze*
1989 124' col Hindi
d/p **Mani Kaul** *pc* Infrakino *st* Dostoevsky's *The Meek Creature* *sc* Sharmistha Mohanty *c* Piyush Shah *m* D. Wood, Vikram Joglekar
lp **Shekhar Kapur**, Shambhavi, Surekha Sikri

Kaul's first fiction film since ***Duvidha*** in 1973 is based on both Dostoevsky's story and Bresson's version of it, *Une Femme douce* (1969). Set in Bombay but effacing its geographic location, the film starts, like Bresson's film, with the suicide of a young bride (Shambhavi, the director's daughter). Then we learn of her marriage to a middle-aged antique dealer (Kapur) and her growing estrangement. The only other major character in the film is the heroine's impoverished relative (Sikri), initially a go-between before the couple's marriage, and later a crucial third figure from whose perspective the disintegrating marriage can be viewed. The major part of the film chronicles the young wife's alienation, as she first resists and then succumbs to the order of things in a world in which her place is determined regardless of her efforts to intervene. This aspect of the narrative is elaborated in terms of a remarkable orchestration of cinematic space, including the construction of 'virtual', unsuspected spaces within the frame. This device makes the narrative space itself dramatic, as claustrophobic situations are juxtaposed with 'a reality' within which spaces can suddenly acquire extra dimensions. The fragmented dialogue, often functioning as an interiorised soliloquy, is counterpointed by the extraordinary use of the camera's focalisations which at times take the place of editing. Kaul continued his exploration of Dostoevsky with a vastly enlarged canvas in ***Idiot*** (1991).

ORU VADAKKAN VEERAGATHA

aka *A Northern Ballad*
1989 168' col Malayalam
d **T. Hariharan** *pc* Grihalakshmi Prod. *s* **M.T. Vasudevan Nair** *c* Ramchandra *m* Ravi
lp **Mammootty**, Suresh Gopi, Balan K. Nair, Madhavi, Captain Raju

A martial arts drama reminiscent of Hong Kong's Kung Fu tales. This one is set in a 16th C. northern Kerala village. Two young men from a clan of Kalaripayattu fighters challenge the recluse Chandu to a fight, to avenge an ancient feud. The film presents the legend associated with the dispute as well as the facts, weaving in elements of caste and kinship rivalry.

PARINDA

1989 154' col/scope Hindi
d/p/st Vidhu Vinod Chopra *pc* Vidhu Vinod Chopra Films *sc* Shivkumar *dial* Imtiaz Hussain *lyr* Khursheed Hallauri *c* Binod Pradhan *m* **R.D. Burman**
lp Anil Kapoor, Jackie Shroff, **Madhuri Dixit**, Nana Patekar, Anupam Kher, Kader Khan, Suresh Oberoi, Tom Alter

Chopra's biggest mainstream movie, known mainly for his thrillers (*Sazaaye Maut*, 1981; *Khamosh*, 1985) and the famous Pepsi commercial announcing the multinational's entry into India. A spectacular, lyrical opening introduces the viewer to Bombay in this postmodern variation of the Hindi crime movie. With low-angle tracking shots and swiftly changing volumes in the image, the film tells of a mentally unbalanced villain, Anna (Patekar) and his henchman Kishen (Shroff) who supports his innocent brother Karan (Kapoor). Karan is used as a bait to trap the cop (Kher) and is eventually killed on his wedding night. Elder brother Kishen, until then divided between his responsibilities to his brother and to Anna, finally turns against his employer and sets him on fire. The film flopped but was critically acclaimed for its soundtrack, its use of CinemaScope and for Patekar's streetwise performance.

PERCY

1989 128' col Gujarati
d Pervez Mehrwanji *pc* **NFDC** *st/co-sc* Cyrus Mistry *co-sc* Jill Misquitta *c* Navroze Contractor *m* **Vanraj Bhatia**
lp Ruby Patel, Hosi Vasunia, Kurush Deboo, Sharad Smart, Zenobia Shroff, Roshan Tirandaz

The only feature by Pervez Mehrwanji, a noted documentary and tv director who died shortly afterwards, is a melodrama set among Bombay's minority Parsee community. Percy (Deboo) is an awkward youth dominated by his mother (Patel) and emasculated by the memory of a gross, pleasure-loving father (Vasunia). Employed by a small pharmaceutical business, he is tormented by a lumpenised Maharashtrian (through whom the film refers to Maharashtra's Hindu Shiv Sena Party). When the hero causes the other man to be sacked, he is beaten up on the street. He finds some solace for his loneliness by joining a motley bunch of Western classical music enthusiasts. The film intercuts his actual experiences with his dreams and fantasies, the last one (in which he resurrects a dead school friend, Dara) urging him to jettison his pervasive sense of guilt. The two realities are separated and merged mainly via Contractor's masterful camerawork. The film has several well-known actors from Bombay's Parsee theatre and deploys the characteristic self-mocking idiom of Parsee popular plays.

RAM LAKHAN

1989 186' col Hindi
d/st **Subhash Ghai** *p* Ashok Ghai *pc* Suneha Arts *sc* Ram Kelkar *lyr* **Anand Bakshi** *c* Ashok Mehta *m* **Laxmikant-Pyarelal**
lp Raakhee, Jackie Shroff, Anil Kapoor, Amrish Puri, Gulshan Grover, **Madhuri Dixit**, Dimple Kapadia, Paresh Rawal, Annu Kapoor, Anupam Kher, **Saeed Jaffrey**, Satish Kaushik, Raza Murad, Sonika Gill, Dalip Tahil

A family feud mixed with large-scale villainy. Thakur Pratap Singh is killed by his own cousin and his family loses its ancestral home. His wife Sharda (Raakhee) swears that she will immerse his ashes in the Ganges only when her sons Ram (Shroff) and Lakhan (Anil Kapoor) have avenged their father. Ram becomes an honest cop, Lakhan a corrupt one who wants to get rich quick. Both have totally different notions of revenge. Lakhan eventually repents when his mother almost destroys his house accusing him of betraying his primary duty, to avenge his father. The story refers to the *Ramayana* via the names of the brothers (Ram and Lakshman) and labelling the villains 'a set of Ravanas'. Sharda, dressed in black whenever she confronts the villains, refers to the myth of the female black cobra who avenges the death of her mate. The film was a big success.

SALIM LANGDE PE MAT RO

aka *Don't Cry for Salim the Lame*
1989 111' col Hindi
d/s **Saeed Akhtar Mirza** *pc* **NFDC** *c* Virendra Saini *m* Sharang Dev
lp Pawan Malhotra, Makarand Deshpande, Ashutosh Gowarikar, Vikram Gokhale, Surekha Sikri

Mirza's investigation ('My own self, split 500 times') of what it means to be a Muslim in a working-class Bombay neighbourhood controlled by criminals. Set in Bombay's Do Tanki area, the film features Salim, a petty thief, in a world peopled by policemen, smugglers and an assortment of crooks. Salim's father still suffers the after-effects of Bombay's famous textile strike (1982) and his mother earns some money as an outworker sewing, but Salim has to support both of them as well as his sister Anees. He reforms after meeting Aslam, Anees's poor but educated suitor, but is eventually killed in a fatalistic ending. Despite the film's technical excellence, the presentation of a doomed hero via a quasi-documentry, street-level realism makes the film a voyeuristic experience allowing viewers to feel sorry for the unfortunates in their city.

SANDHYA RAGAM

aka *The Evening Raga*
1989 100' col Tamil
d/p/s/c **Balu Mahendra** *pc* **Doordarshan** *m* L. Vaidyanathan
lp Archana, Chokkalinga Bhagavathar, Santhanam Rajalakshmi

Emotional yet humorous tale of an old man (Bhagavathar) who leaves his village after his wife's death and goes to live with his nephew in Madras. To spare his nephew the extra cost, he then moves into a home for the aged before being reunited with his nephew's family. As old age is akin to early childhood, the old man forms a special relationship with the child of the house and causes major problems of adjustment for the adults. A member of the well-known Boy's Company theatre group, the 83-year-old Bhagavathar came out of retirement to play the lead in only his second film appearance (cf ***Veedu***, 1987).

SATI

1989 140' col Bengali
d/co-s **Aparna Sen** *pc* **NFDC** *co-s* Arun Bannerjee *c* Ashok Mehta *m* **Chidananda Das Gupta**
lp **Shabana Azmi**, **Kali Bannerjee**, Pradeep Mukherjee, Arindam Ganguly, Ketaki Dutta, Shakuntala Barua, Arun Bannerjee, Ajit Bannerjee, Bimal Dev, Manu Mukherjee, Dipankar Raha, Ratna Ghoshal

Primitivist melodrama set prior to 1829 when sati (a woman's religiously enforced immolation on her husband's funeral pyre) was made illegal by the British. Uma (Azmi), a mute and orphaned young Brahmin woman, is saddled with an ominous horoscope and is given in marriage to a tree. Seduced by a local schoolteacher, Uma becomes pregnant and is ostracised by the villagers. One night, while sheltering from a storm under her tree, lightning strikes them and she is found in the morning, blood on her forehead like bridal vermillion. The tree, the only sign of real virility in a society of cowardly superstition, protected its bride.

SIDDHESHWARI

1989 123' col/b&w Hindi
d/p/s **Mani Kaul** *pc* Infrakino Film Prod., **Films Division** *c* Piyush Shah
lp Mita Vasisht, Ranjana Shrivastava, Shravani Mukherjee, Mohor Biswas, Narayan Mishra, Anoop Mishra, Raman Shankar Pandy, Malviya, Manmohan Chibber

Kaul continues his interest in a cinema in between fiction and documentary with this magnificently shot feature about Siddheshwari Devi (1903-77) of the Benares gharana. She was the most extraordinary 20th C. singer in the classical thumri tradition which, according to legend, goes back to a eunuch at Indra's court, cursed for failing to return a lady's love. As a young woman, Siddhi silently absorbed the music listening to the artful performances of Siyaji Maharaj. Thrown out of her aunt's house for daring to ask questions, she painfully tries to survive in the streets of Benares, the city of rituals, suffering and death but also of passion, transformation and the sublime. Eventually, accepted as a disciple by Maharaj, she started performing at 16 years of age and became a uniquely popular singer condensing a lifetime of horror and joy in the grain of her voice, singing thumri music in addition to its variants in the Kajri, Chaiti and Jhoola folk idioms. The narrative is structured like a thumri piece: it presents key motifs (of Siddhi's life as well as of myths and locations) and elaborates on and around them with different songs, moods, camera movements, etc., until the whole becomes a moving tapestry celebrating the transfiguration of life into music. Shot in colour and monochrome, the film proceeds by means of metaphors, evoked rather than named: an ultramarine boat floats on the Ganges, a dropped metal utensil produces musical overtones, etc. The intoxicants mandatory to the euphoria of a (sexual) meeting are contrasted with the labour that went into practising the difficult art of music. There is something of Lewis Carroll's cat about the movie: as it evokes Siddhi's life, her physical presence becomes more and more elusive, even escaping the actress (Vasisht) who tries to embody her existence. Towards the end, archive footage of Siddheshwari's sole tv appearance offers a glimpse of the singer, an image which seems to recede into the technology of the recording until only the eerily intense voice remains.

Mita Vasisht in *Siddheshwari*

THAZHVARAM

aka *The Valley*
1989 130' col/scope Malayalam
d/m **Bharathan** *pc* Anugraha Cine Arts *s* **M.T. Vasudevan Nair** *c* Venu
lp **Mohanlal**, Sumalatha, Anju, Sankaradi

A tale of revenge involving four characters in a small rural community. The remote stranger Balan (Mohanlal) arrives in a deserted valley to take revenge on the wily Rajan, who is employed on a farm run by Nanu and his daughter Koochutti. When Balan's effort to kill Rajan is thwarted and Balan is injured, he is nursed by Koochutti. Rajan, who had earlier robbed Balan and murdered his wife, now makes off with Koochutti's ornaments as well, adding to the satisfaction when the hero gets the villain in the end. The CinemaScope production excels in spacious long-shots, coupled with minimal dialogue, building Mohanlal into a brooding Leone-Eastwood 'man with no name'-type stranger.

UCHI VEYIL

aka *High Noon*
1989 100' col Tamil
d/s Jayabharati *pc* Jwala *c* Ramesh Vyas *m* L. Vaidyanathan
lp Kuppuswamy, Uma, Delhi Ganesh, Vijay, Shrividya, Usha, Preeta, Baby Rukmini, Rajamani, Saranath

A gentle village family drama shot in real time (emphasised by a ticking clock). An old grandfather and former Gandhian freedom-fighter, Doraiswamy (Kuppuswamy), lives with his impecunious married son and granddaughter Mallika. To make a little money they take a lodger, a young executive, Shankar (Vijay). The old man falls ill but nevertheless sets out for the city with Mallika and Shankar to be honoured for his services to the Independence struggle. He then disappears. An understated story performed by non-star actors, using Madras street noises and the ticking clock instead of songs. It is the best-known film by the noted writer (cf his *Oomai Janangal*, 1984) about bonded labourers in the British Raj.

UNDA MITTERANDI YAAD PYARI

aka *In Memory of Friends*
1989 60' col Punjabi/Hindi/English
d/p/c **Anand Patwardhan** *m* Navnirman, Jaimal Singh Padda

Patwardhan's extraordinary 16mm documentary on terrorist activity in Punjab inaugurated a series of films (the second is ***Ram Ke Naam***, 1992) addressing the growing communalism of Indian politics. The film follows a group of Hindi and Sikh socialists campaigning against both a repressive state government (which not long ago encouraged communalism as a divide-and-rule tactic) and communalist fanatics. The focus of their campaign is the legacy of Bhagat Singh, a young socialist hanged by the British (1931) and now claimed both by the state as a patriot and by the separatists as a Sikh militant. The film-maker includes his own interpretation of Bhagat Singh, emphasising his rationalist atheism. As in his earlier work, the director isolates the false rhetoric of professional politicians, contrasting it with images and sounds of ordinary people in their daily lives (e.g. the sound of the woman making chapatis). He also debunks the pompousness of offical politics together with its representations: when a central government minister lands in a helicopter, the event is first shown on a **Doordarshan** tv clip, including its declamatory voice track; then the film cuts to Patwardhan's own footage of the event, presenting a less glorious arrival. The film ends with noted communist leader Jaimal Singh Padda, who communicated his universalist message through speech and song in the film shortly before he was shot dead. The film is an extraordinary document with unforgettable images showing murderous stupidity blazing in the eyes of the fundamentalists as well as the astonishing courage of those trying to build a socialist politics in that situation.

AGNEEPATH

1990 174' col Hindi
d **Mukul S. Anand** *p* Yash Johar *pc* Dharma Prod. *s* Santosh Saroj *lyr* **Anand Bakshi** *c* Pravin Bhatt *m* **Laxmikant-Pyarelal**
lp **Amitabh Bachchan, Mithun Chakraborty**, Danny Denzongpa, Neelam, Madhavi, Rohini Hattangadi, Tinnu Anand, Archana Puran Singh, Alok Nath

The hero Vijay Chauhan aka 'Bhai' (Bachchan) witnesses his schoolmaster father (Nath) being falsely implicated in a scandal with a prostitute and lynched by the villagers. Bhai grows up to become a gangster and encounters the main villain Kancha Cheena (Denzongpa) in a luxurious place in Mauritius. He joins the villain's gang only to have him arrested by the police. When Cheena is released (by arranging to have a key eyewitness killed), the hero murders Cheena after negotiating the 'path of fire' referred to in the film's title. The most violent of Bachchan's recent films, it was also the most sustained effort to rehabilitate the politically discredited star. The title and opening sequences borrow from a poem by Bachchan's father Harivanshrai Bachchan, and show today's New Man walking through the fires of hell to redeem a brutalised world and make it into a new utopia. The mother obsession of Bachchan's previous films is still in evidence. In spite of Mukul Anand's usual fast-moving camera and distorted perspectives, the film occasionally lapses into earlier cinematic idioms (e.g. the foot-stomping song picturisation of Archana Puran Singh's *Alibaba* song). Anand's familiar anachronisms suggest that very different historical epochs are 'actually' very similar: an exotic James Bond-type tourist resort and the blood and stench of Bombay's gang wars. Although still playing the vigilante hero, Bachchan initially abandoned his well-known baritone voice to suggest an older man speaking in a heavy 'Bombay Hindi' accent, but he later had to re-dub the voice when the experiment proved unpopular. The film was not a major hit.

ANJALI

1990 123' col/scope Tamil/Hindi
d/s **Mani Rathnam** *pc* G.V. Films *lyr* **Vali** *c* Madhu Ambat *m* **Ilaiyaraja**
lp Raghuvaran, Revathi, Baby Shyamali, Prabhu, Master Tarun, Baby Anthony

Anjali (Shyamali) is a mentally handicapped girl who, after her father sends her away for a few years, is brought home to live with her parents and two healthy siblings. The movie chronicles the love given and received by the little girl until she dies just after calling out the name of her mother for the very first time. The family is helped by a mysterious stranger (Prabhu) who appoints himself their guardian angel. The high points of the film are the numerous songs, mainly featuring the neighbourhood children, elaborately choreographed and including some fantasy numbers. The film shows the extent to which Rathnam absorbed the influence of music videos.

APARAHNAM

aka *The Late Afternoon*
1990 116' col Malayalam
d/s M.P. Sukumaran Nair *pc* Rachana Films *c* Ashwini Kaul *m* Jerry Amaldev
lp Baby Anthony, Jalaja, Kaviyoor Ponnamma, Babu Namboodiri

An elegy for a defeated middle-class radical and veteran of the **Naxalite** rising. Released from prison, Nandakumar remains a suspect and is unable to settle into a job. He refuses advice to emigrate to the Gulf and suffers harassment both from the police and from his erstwhile comrades. During the Emergency in the mid-70s, he is imprisoned again. In the end, all he has left are his increasingly fanciful memories of his days as a young radical. Much of the film's storytelling, performance and lighting evokes the elegaic naturalism of the director's mentor, **Adoor Gopalakrishnan**.

DIL

1990 172' col/scope Hindi
d Indra Kumar *pc* Vinod Doshi, Maruti Int. *s* Rajiv Kaul, Praful Parekh *dial* Kamlesh Pandey *lyr* Sameer *c* Baba Azmi *m* Anand-Milind
lp Aamir Khan, **Madhuri Dixit, Saeed Jaffrey**, Anupam Kher, Deven Verma

The top Hindi hit of 1990 reprises the classic dilemmas of Aamir Khan's earlier ***Qayamat Se Qayamat Tak*** (1988): a love story leading to the estrangement between the families of a loving couple, thus gradually replacing the problems of individual romance with those of interfamilial relationships. Hero Raja (Khan) has a miserly father Hazari Prasad (Kher) who plans to increase his wealth by persuading the millionaire Mehra (Jaffrey) to allow his daughter Madhu (Dixit) to marry Raja. Madhu and Raja are in love anyway and indulge in high-school squabbles, a popular plot motif since *Grease* (1978). The marriage plans come unstuck when Mehra discovers that Hazari Prasad is not the industrialist he claims to be, but the young lovers defy their respective families and marry anyway. Raja becomes a labourer and has a major accident, allowing the two rich fathers to make their peace with each other. The ending replays the end of **Guru Dutt**'s ***Mr And Mrs '55*** (1955) at the airport. One of the many disco numbers, *Ladki hai ya chhadi hai*, is a version of Elvis Presley's *Blue Suede Shoes*, while another adapted **Ilaiyaraja**'s *O Priya Priya* number from ***Geetanjali*** (1989). Like ***Maine Pyar Kiya*** (1989), the film deploys an advertising film style, esp. for the soundtrack and the editing, several sequences winding up with a direct address to the audience. Following the success of his next film, *Beta*

(1992), Indra Kumar became the top-grossing director of 90s Hindi cinema.

DISHA

aka *The Uprooted Ones*
1990 135' col Hindi
d/p/s **Sai Paranjpye** *pc* Sai Paranjpye Films *c* Madhu Ambat, G.S. Bhaskar *m* Anand Modak
lp **Shabana Azmi**, Nana Patekar, Raghuvir Yadav, **Om Puri**, Nilu Phule, Rajshree Sawant

Paranjpye's sentimental tale of migrant workers in Bombay, caught between urban displacement and a changing rural reality. Farm labourers Vasant (Patekar) and Soma (Yadav) move to Bombay following drought in their village. Soma becomes a millhand. Vasant, who has come mainly to pay off his marriage debts, returns to find his wife having an affair with her employer, the owner of a bidi (reed) factory. Soma also plans to go home, because his brother (Puri) has finally dug a well which yields water. The film uses extensive tracking shots presenting panoramic views of the Dadar region in central Bombay with its textile mills and apparently Asia's most populated square mile. Location shots taken in the textile mills provide a quasi-documentary background for the fiction.

DRISHTI

aka *Vision*
1990 171' col Hindi
d/co-s/c **Govind Nihalani** *pc* Udbhav *co-s* Shashi Deshpande *m* Kishori Amonkar
lp **Shekhar Kapur**, Dimple Kapadia, Mita Vasisht, Vijay Kashyap, Irfan

Marital melodrama informally adapting Ingmar Bergman's *Scener ur ett Aktenskap* (*Scenes from a Marriage*, 1974). Sandhya (Dimple), employed by a children's publisher, and her husband Nikhil (Shekhar Kapur), a research scientist, celebrate their 8th wedding anniversary. Sandhya feels attracted to the singer Rahul. Nikhil has an affair with Vrinda (Mita Vasisht) and, amid some unexpressed doubt about whose child the pregnant Sandhya is bearing, the couple agree to a divorce. A year later, when Nikhil's affair with Vrinda is over, the couple meet again and Sandhya convinces Nikhil that her aborted child was his. This is the first of several theatre-derived dialogue movies Nihalani made after ***Party*** (1984). Nihalani says the film is constructed in eleven movements, each signalled by a song by its composer, the noted Jaipur gharana Khayal singer Kishori Amonkar.

FIGURES OF THOUGHT

1990 33' col English
d/p/s Arun Khopkar *c* Piyush Shah *m* Rajat Dholakia

Remarkable documentary about the paintings of Bhupen Khakhar, Nalini Malani and Vivan Sundaram. The three artists had participated in the landmark show *Place for People* (1981, cf Chronicle) which helped transform the notion of contemporary art in India. The film takes off from a mural they jointly made on commission from a Bombay industrialist and represents the paintings of the three artists, innovatively using reframing and lighting effects while interweaving shots of the artists's working environment. Khopkar is well known as a teacher of film theory and an authority on Eisenstein, whose essay 'A Figure of Speech or a Figure of Thought?' provided the film's title.

GHAYAL

1990 163' col Hindi
d/s Raj Kumar Santoshi *p* **Dharmendra** *pc* Vijayta Films *dial* Dilip Shukla *lyr* Anjaan, Indivar *c* Rajen Kothari *m* **Bhappi Lahiri**
lp Sunny Deol, Meenakshi Sheshadri, Amrish Puri, Raj Babbar, Moushumi Chatterjee, Kulbhushan Kharbanda, **Om Puri**, Shabbir Khan, Sudesh Berry, Mitwa

Produced by Dharmendra, Deol's father, and designed to create a definitive screen image for Deol as the urban Rambo-type vigilante (like Stallone, Deol has in every film, at least once and sometimes on several occasions, a scene where he is chained, insulted and physically tortured as the camera lingers over his sweating and bulging muscles). Here Deol plays Ajay, whose elder brother Ashok (Babbar) becomes involved with drug-dealing villains led by the politician Balwant Rai (A. Puri). When the politician collaborates with legal top brass to convict Ajay for murdering his own brother, Ajay becomes a one-man army against the state. He kidnaps the police commissioner (Kharbanda), informs Balwant Rai that the day of judgement is at hand and finally gets his man in a huge Coney Island-style amusement park. The film established Raj Kumar Santoshi, the son of P.L. Santoshi, song-writer and director of **C. Ramchandra** musicals, as a director in his own right.

ISHANOU

aka *The Chosen One*
1990 94' col Manipuri
d/p/m **Aribam Syam Sharma** *pc* Aribam Syam Sharma Prod. *s* M.K. Binodini Debi *c* Girish Padhiar
lp Kiranmala, Tomba, Manbi, D. Hiren, Baby Molly, Baby Premita

Manipuri family melodrama combining upward mobility with the strange ritualism of the matriarchal Meitei cult. This cult, according to the film, claims its female adherents through a series of mystical signals which the chosen woman cannot ignore. A small and happy family lives in the Manipur Valley under the care and protection of an old woman. Suddenly the young wife Tampha (Kiranmala) becomes possessed by the divinity Maibi and leaves her home to be initiated by the guru of the Maibi sect. Much of the film's second half features the exotic dance rituals, ending with a brief encounter between Tampha, her now estranged husband and grown-up child.

KASBA

1990 121' col Hindi
d/co-sc **Kumar Shahani** *pc* **NFDC, Doordarshan** *st* Anton Chekov's *In The Ravine* *co-sc* Farida Mehta *c* K.K. Mahajan *m* **Vanraj Bhatia**
lp Shatrughan Sinha, Mita Vasisht, Manohar Singh, Alaknanda Samarth, Navjot Hansra, Raghuvir Yadav

Shahani's remarkable melodrama, based on Chekov's little-known short story, tells of Maniram (Singh), an old-style entrepreneur in a small township in the mountains of Kangra, who made his fortune adulterating food. His business is run by the canny Tejo (Vasisht), the wife of his mentally retarded younger son (Yadav) and the Shakespearean fool in the story. His elder son Dhani (Sinha) is doing well in a government-related business in Delhi which turns out to be the printing of counterfeit currency. Dhani is brought back and married, in local style, to Tara (Hansra); however, he gets drunk on his wedding night, scatters some counterfeit notes and leaves for the city, his marriage still unconsummated. Tara is impregnated by a local fixer (Raina) and

Alaknanda Samarth and Shatrughan Sinha in *Kasba*

gives birth to a son who stands to inherit the family property. News of Dhani's arrest and the police crackdown on Maniram's corrupt enterprise is accompanied by Tejo's ruthless take-over of local power. She kills Tara's child, builds an electric substation on her father-in-law's land and seduces the vacuous son of a local industrialist into becoming her partner. Her machinations are intercut with the aimless travels of a benumbed Tara holding her dead child, finding solace among the wandering minstrels and the hill tribes. Much of the film deploys a savage irony, as, e.g., Shatrughan Sinha, a major Hindi star effectively playing 'himself', is presented as a small-town braggart trying to imitate his own swaggering style, or the poignant budha bhangda (dance for elderly Sikhs) playing over a drunken Maniram among the flashing lights of his son's ostentatious marriage. The melodrama verges repeatedly on the satirical, chronicling a decaying nationalism and the end of modernist dreams of self-reliance, epitomised by Maniram's manic second wife (Samarth) spouting religious mumbo-jumbo, which in no way detracts from these ideologies' political power. The only characters who find their way out of the cultural quagmire are the 'moonstruck' younger son and the fixer, in the song at the end when he clutches a tree in the nude. The film's main generic achievement is to recall to the melodrama its original function, of integrating marginalised peoples and their languages into a mainstream culture. It also provides the film's most crucial ironic edge in its implicit suggestion that in order to do so melodrama has to first invent a mainstream.

KUTTY JAPANIN KUZHANDAIGAL

aka *Children of Mini-Japan*
1990 63' col Tamil
d/s Chalam Bennurkar *pc* Janamadhyam *c* R.V. Ramani

Documentary about the Sivakasi region known for its artisanal industries and for providing the national supply of matchboxes, fireworks and gaudy calendars. Known locally as 'Mini-Japan', Sivakasi is also one of the worst exploiters of child labour anywhere in India: 70% of its workforce are pre-puberty girls. The film juxtaposes these unsavoury labour conditions with Sivakasi's association with 'popular art'.

LEKIN ...

aka *But ...*
1990 171' col Hindi
d/s/lyr **Gulzar** *pc* Dinanath Kala Mandir, **Lata Mangeshkar** *c* Manmohan Singh *m* Hridaynath Mangeshkar
lp Vinod Khanna, Dimple Kapadia, Amjad Khan, Alok Nath, Manohar Singh, Beena, **Hema Malini**

Story of an unhappy ghost, Rewa (Kapadia), who haunts the palace of Raja Param Singh of Jasod which is now government property. Samir (Khanna), the curator of a government museum, is sent to salvage the valuables in the sealed palace where he encounters the ghost. Rewa's ability to recreate the past brings alive her tragic story, making Samir determined to liberate her even at the risk of own life. Parapsychology is touted as proof of the reality of the encounter and his 'Why me?' is answered by a possible encounter in their previous lives. Rewa is finally liberated when, with his help, she completes the journey through a desert that claimed her life on earth. The film adds to the horror iconography (ruins, dungeons, suggestive music and fluttering pigeons) several sequences involving the tribal Banjaras, a community presented as practising witchcraft.

MANE/EK GHAR

1990 137' col Kannada/Hindi
d/sc **Girish Kasaravalli** *pc* Apoorva Chitra *c* S. Ramchandra *m* L. Vaidyanathan
lp **Naseeruddin Shah**, Deepti Naval, Rohini Hattangadi, Mico Chandru, B.S. Achar

Rajanna (Shah) and Geeta (Naval) move into their newly rented house, a badly built room in a compound also housing a noisy motor-mechanic's shop, allowing no sleep. The couple seek the help of Geeta's aunt (Hattangadi), who knows a senior police officer. When the mechanic's shop is closed down, it is replaced by the policeman's nephew's equally noisy video games parlour. Rajanna works in a factory building large earth-moving vehicles: in the end, when the couple decide to move into a slum, these vehicles are seen in a slum-clearance drive led by the police. The film lavishly deploys surreally symbolic images: a giant four-poster bed in a small room, colour continuities between tractors, large metal drums in the street and the haldi (saffron) which the couple put on the walls to keep pests away, the yawning vehicles in the garage and the destructive imagery of the video games. Kasaravalli's first explicitly urban film.

MATTI MANUSHULU

1990 87' col Telugu
d/s/m **B. Narasinga Rao** *pc* Little India *c* A.K. Bir
lp Archana, Moin Ali Beg

The story of a peasant couple who migrate to the city following drought in their Telangana village and become construction workers. The husband becomes an alcoholic and abandons his wife who is harassed sexually and financially until she dies a pauper, leaving her orphaned child behind.

MUTHINA HARA

1990 161' col Kannada
d **S.V. Rajendra Singh** *pc* Rohini Pics *c* D.V. Rajaram *m* **Hamsalekha**
lp **Vishnuvardhan, Suhasini**, K.S. Aswath, Ramkumar

Rajendra Singh's big-budget war film has the brave hero (Vishnuvardhan) fight a series of wars, starting with WW2 in Burma, then with China and Pakistan after Independence, before losing his life protecting his fellow soldiers. His wife (Suhasini), enlisted as a nurse, eventually makes a fervently pacificist plea.

OTTAYADI PAATHAKAL

aka *The Narrow Footpaths*
1990 96' col Malayalam
d/s C. Radhakrishnan *p* Vincent Chittilappilly *pc* St Vincent Movies *c* Sunny Joseph *m* Mohan Sithara
lp **Madhu**, Sreenath, Revathi, Kaviyoor Ponnamma, Isac Thomas, Somasundaran, Chandran Nair, Paul Neelankavil, Rahim

A heavy-handed, **NFDC**-financed melodrama shot in Trichur and featuring a group of characters: an old judge, Bhaskara Menon (Madhu), his daughter Sati and his mentally retarded son, and the nephew, Anup Kumar, who covets the daughter. However, Sati refuses to marry Anup and devotes herself to mothering her father and brother. The dramatic event is the death of the son, Suku, a mercy-killing by electrocution by his father, the judge. The latter goes crazy (indicated by, e.g., the fact that he makes an abstract painting) and, apparently sleepwalking, jumps to his death. Sati and Anup get together after all. The film mainly showcased an ageing Madhu playing the tearful judge. The director, educated as a scientist, is best known as a novelist.

SHAKHA PROSHAKHA

aka *Branches of the Tree*
1990 130' col Bengali
d/s/m **Satyajit Ray** *p* Daniel Toscan du Plantier, Gerard Depardieu *pc* Erato Films, DD Prod., Soprofilms *c* Barun Raha
lp Ajit Bannerjee, Haradhan Bannerjee, **Soumitra Chatterjee**, Dipankar De, Ranjit Mullick, Lily Chakraborty, Mamata Shankar

Following the unsatisfactory ***Ganashatru*** (1989) and his critique of contemporary corruption, Ray's first international co-production looks more like a tv movie and continues the realist Ibsenite idiom with this story about a Bengali joint family. The honest old patriarch Ananda Majumdar (A. Bannerjee), who rose from government clerk to real-estate developer building a small township, has a heart attack on his 70th birthday, causing the large family to gather: his four sons, their wives and children. The eldest son, Probodh (H. Bannerjee), is a corrupt businessman, to the great disappointment of the old man who finds he is closest to his mentally retarded second son, the music-loving Prashanto (S. Chatterjee).

THODASA RUMANI HO JAYE

aka *Let there be a Wee Bit of Romance* aka *Let's Get Romantic*
1990 160' col Hindi
d/p **Amol Palekar** *pc* **Doordarshan** *sc* Chitra Palekar *c* Debu Deodhar *lyr* Kamlesh Pande *m* Bhaskar Chandavarkar
lp Anita Kanwar, Vikram Gokhale, Nana Patekar, Dilip Kulkarni, Arun Joglekar, Deepa Lagoo, Aparajita Krishna, Riju Bajaj, Shashank Shanker, Vijay Shirke, Hemant Desai

Palekar's mass-entertainment musical featuring Binny (Kanwar), an unmarried woman whose condition is reflected by the barren and rainless town in which she lives with her family. A stranger comes, bringing rain and romance into her life. The film uses music extensively, often weaving spoken words into songs.

VASTHUHARA

aka *The Dispossessed*
1990 103' col Malayalam
d/sc **Govindan Aravindan** *pc* Paragon Movie Makers *st* C.V. Shriraman *c* Sunny Joseph *m* **Salil Choudhury**
lp **Mohanlal**, Neelanjana Mitra, Neena Gupta, **Padmini**

Aravindan's last film is based on a story by the author of ***Chidambaram*** (1985). Making a virtually unprecedented, and deeply moving, departure from a cinematic tradition that has always emphasised regional identity, the film is set in Calcutta. The story tells of Venu (Mohanlal), a Malayali officer in the rehabilitation ministry of the Andaman Islands, who selects candidates for a refugee aid programme enabling them to settle in the islands with state assistance. He meets an old Bengali widow (Mitra) who is not eligible for the programme, but he discovers that she is the abandoned wife of his uncle from Kerala. Re-establishing family links, he also befriends her hostile daughter (Gupta) and her son, a political refugee. Their brief acquaintance ends at a shipyard where he hoards his emigrant refugees on deck and leaves for the islands once more. From its remarkable opening sequence, as the camera tracks through abandoned refugee shelters built during the 1943 famine and Partition, with a voice-over in Malayalam recapitulating that tragic history and the Kerala peoples' commitment to the plight of the Bengalis, Aravindan makes clear his intention to transcend a localised and increasingly cynical view (cf ***Chidambaram*** and ***Oridathu***, 1986) and to move towards something like a national perspective on the contemporary. In the process he also abandons much of his early pictorialism in favour of, e.g., the remarkable shots of Mohanlal walking through the crowded Calcutta streets, or standing on the terrace of his cheap hotel, and especially in the last sequence aboard an ancient and grossly overcrowded ship overrun with impoverished refugees, as Venu tries to bring some order into the chaos. Several well-entrenched naturalist conventions, however, prevent a further formal elaboration of the style, such as the dialogue problems (Mohanlal speaks in Malayalam and English, Neelanjana Mitra in Bengali, highly accented Malayalam and English, and Neena Gupta only in English), but the acting is uniformly in tune with Joseph's deliberately rough-edged camera.

Shobhana in *Vasthuhara*

VEMBANAD

aka *A Lake in Central Kerala*
1990 91' col Malayalam
d/s Sivaprasad *pc* Anna Cine Creations *c* Ashwini Kaul *m* Louis Banks
lp Aziz, Ranjini, Jayabharati, Babu Namboodiri

An obsessive tale of incest, either consummated or desired, on an island community of fisherfolk. A fisherman rescues a teenage girl from drowning, and is obsessed by her. He rapes her, and in the end, repeating the opening sequences, watches her drown. The narrative strategy is both engrossingly ambiguous and alienating as sequences with images of uncertain status (fantasy, desire, dream, reality) coalesce to form an undifferentiated discourse of a father's desire for his teenage daughter together with his denial of that desire.

WOSOBIPO

aka *The Cuckoo's Call*
1990 138' col Karbi
d/s Gautam Bora *pc* Wojaru Cine Trust Karbi Anglong *c* Vivek Bannerjee *m* Sher Choudhury
lp Elsie Hanse, Bubul Terang, Raman Rongpi, Langbiram Engti

The first film in Karbi, a north-eastern dialect, traces the gradual politicisation of a native schoolteacher, Sarthe Ronghang, who moves beyond a romantic and nostalgic sense of his land into an awareness of the region's real contemporary problems. The director is a graduate of the Konrad Wolf Institute (Potsdam), a documentarist and former assistant to **Bhabendranath Saikia** (***Agnisnan***, 1985).

AGANTUK

aka *The Stranger*
1991 120' col Bengali
d/s/m **Satyajit Ray** *pc* **NFDC** *c* Barun Raha *lp* Dipankar De, Mamata Shankar, Bikram Bhattacharya, **Utpal Dutt, Dhritiman Chatterjee, Robi Ghosh**, Subrata Chatterjee, Promod Ganguly, Ajit Bannerjee

Ray's last film continues his critique of decaying values in the Bengali middle class (cf ***Ganashatru***, 1989; ***Shakha Proshakha***, 1990). Into the lives of Sudhindra Bose (De) and his wife Anila (Shankar) arrives Anila's uncle whom she last met 35 years ago. This stranger, Manomohan Mitra (Dutt), lived abroad and worked with tribal communities in various parts of the world. When Sudhindra's lawyer, who does not care about tribals, accuses Mitra of coveting Anila's inheritance, Mitra leaves, having donated his share of the family property to his niece.

BHAVANTARANA

1991 63' col Oriya
d/s **Kumar Shahani** *pc* Bombay Cinematograph *c* Alok Upadhyay

A spectacular part-fictional documentary on India's famous Odissi dance, seen via its foremost living exponent, Guru Kelucharan Mahapatra. The film shows how living traditions and modes of social initiation can turn into classical forms. Described by the director as a film 'about hunger', it returns the dance to both the labour that it celebrates and the improvisations that continue to defy codification and control. Many of the dances, including the spectacular *Navarasa* sequence at the end, were choreographed specially for the cinema.

HUM

1991 184' col/scope Hindi
d **Mukul S. Anand** *pc* Romesh Films *s* Ravi Kapoor, Mohan Kaul *dial* Kader Khan *lyr* **Anand Bakshi** *c* W.B. Rao *m* **Laxmikant-Pyarelal**
lp **Amitabh Bachchan**, Kimi Katkar, **Rajnikant**, Anupam Kher, Danny Denzongpa, Kader Khan, Govinda, Deepa Sahi, Shilpa Shirodkar, Romesh Sharma, Annu Kapoor

Beginning with silhouetted scenes (cf Sam Fuller's *Underworld USA*, 1960) in the Bombay dockyards recalling ***Deewar*** (1975) and ending with the star's bloodshot eyes advancing towards the quivering villain, Mukul Anand's hit provides a lexicon of Bachchanalia. Tiger (Bachchan), a petty collector of protection money, changes sides when his friend Gonsalves (Sharma) leads the exploited dockers against Mr Big, Bakhtawar (Denzongpa). The perfidious Inspector Giridhar (Kher) and his sidekick (Kapoor) manipulate the bloody confrontations so that Bakhtawar is jailed for Gonsalves' murder, his family is exterminated and Tiger, together with his two brothers (Rajnikant and Govinda) and their families, is banished from the city. Years later, after idyllic family scenes and a complicated plot involving high-level scams in the Indian Army, the Bachchan clan has to go into action against a bunch of terrorists in pseudo-hippy costumes and equipped with an assortment of armaments. The high point of the film, refurbishing an ageing Bachchan image, is the big musical number *Jumma chumma* (taken from Mori Kante's *Akwaba Beach* album) with Kimi Katkar performing in a bar filled with sweaty, beer-swilling and foot-stomping dockers whose collective ejaculation takes the form of spraying the star with whatever liquid is available. The scene is repeated, as the gang-rape connotations are replaced by those of movie-star mania, when Katkar becomes a star and both she and Bachchan are mobbed by crazed fans. The film received an unprecedented saturation release in over 400 cinemas.

IDIOT

1991 180' col Hindi
d **Mani Kaul** *pc* **Doordarshan** *st* Fyodor Dostoevsky's novel *sc* Anup Singh *dial* Hemendra Bhatia, Rajeev Kumar *c* Piyush Shah *m* D. Wood, Vikram Joglekar
lp Ayub Khan Din, Shah Rukh Khan, Mita Vasisht, Navjot Hansra, Vasudeo Bhatt, Deepak Mahan, Babulal Bora, Meenakshi Goswami, Zul Velani, Amritlal Thulal

With this *tour de force* of control over a bewilderingly complex narrative and a massive cast of characters (more than 50 key roles) constantly shifting about in both geographic and cinematic spaces, Mani Kaul continues exploring Dostoevsky's fiction (cf ***Nazar***, 1989), faithfully following the novel's original plot transposed into a scathing depiction of a feudal elite, largely bypassed by history, located in Bombay and Goa. The story begins with the return of Myshkin (Ayub Khan), having spent many years in London undergoing treatment for epilepsy. He encounters the beautiful Nastasia (Vasisht), a *femme fatale* pursued by the rich Pawan Raghujan (Shah Rukh Khan) and the ambitious Ganesh (Mahan). The wealthy milieu seems to live in a vacuum, alongside a formerly productive generation, such as the businessman Mehta (Velani) and his proud daughter Amba (Hansra) or the retired, drunken colonel (Bora) who is accompanied by characters like Killer and the cynical and suicidal Shapit (Thulal) on the beaches of Goa. At Nastasia's party both Ganesh and Myshkin propose to her, but she leaves with Raghujan who throws a bundle of banknotes at her which she proceeds to burn. After the central sequence in Goa, the colonel leaves home and dies, and Myshkin becomes engaged to Amba. However, he suffers an epileptic fit and the next day Nastasia breaks the engagement, claiming Myshkin for herself. Just before their wedding she again runs away to Raghujan who eventually kills her, after which he spends the night with Myshkin awaiting the police. In the end Myshkin is revealed to have gone mad. Kaul coolly orchestrates with great virtuosity the continuously mobile, elusive points of 'stress' (in Kaul's phrase) as they shift from geographic location to cinematic space and back again, from the editing and gestural rhythms to the discontinuous soundtrack, achieving a multi-layered cinematic texture that at times threatens to stretch beyond the boundaries of the frame. The innovative approach to plot and narration keeps the film on a precarious edge between formal control and random collisions of speech and identity. Much of the film's successful use of characters as 'independent vertices' (as the director describes them) follows the extraordinary performance of British Asian actor Ayub Khan who uses his difficulties with Hindi to considerable advantage as the nervous and culturally dislocated epileptic. The director commented: 'Whereas for years I dwealt on rarefied wholes where the line of the narrative often vanished into thin air, with *Idiot* I have plunged into an extreme saturation of events. [P]ersonally, I find myself on the brink, exposed to a series of possible disintegrations. Ideas, then, cancel each other out and the form germinates. Content belongs to the future, and that's how it creeps into the present'. The film was made as a four part tv series running 223' and edited down to feature length.

(From left) Ayub Khan Din, Navjot Hansra, Mita Vasisht in *Idiot*

KSHANA KSHANAM

1991 158' col/scope Telugu
d/s Ramgopal Varma *pc* NRP Films *p* N. Ravindranath *dial* Gopalram *c* S. Gopal Reddy *m* M.M. Keeravani
lp Venkatesh, **Sridevi,** Paresh Rawal, Rami Reddy

When the sexy working woman Sridevi happens upon a clue to some hidden loot, she is targeted by a gang led by the villain (Rawal). Teaming up with a petty crook (Venkatesh), the pair are chased through the film by both the criminals and the police. This megabudget chase film opens with a suspenseful bank raid, moves to surreal forest scenes as the couple rough it beside a camp fire, and climaxes as the hero fights the gangsters atop a moving train. Director Varma shows himself able to assimilate recent Hollywood styles influenced by tv advertising and music clips (cf John Badham's *Bird on a Wire*, 1990). Most of the songs are inserted with no connection whatever to the plot, unusual even in a tradition noted for the autonomy of its song picturisations. Film critic Rajeev Velicheti (1992) used the film to identify a recent trend of consumerist cinema in AP calibrated on the linguistic-regional attitudes of a Hyderabad-based middle-class. The film was dubbed in Hindi as *Hairaan*.

MAHAPRITHIBI

aka *World Within, World Without*
1991 105' col Bengali
d/sc **Mrinal Sen** *pc* G.G. Films *st* Anjan Dutta *c* Shashi Anand *m* **B.V. Karanth,** Chandan Roy Choudhury
lp Victor Bannerjee, **Soumitra Chatterjee,** Anjan Dutta, **Aparna Sen,** Gita Sen, Anasuya Majumdar

With this film Sen returned to his most congenial setting, Calcutta, and to one of his favourite plot formulas: the sudden disappearance of a family member causes the others to reflect on themselves and their lives. Here Sen considers the lives of a Bengali middle-class family against the background of 'the new world order' with the defeat of the USSR in the cold war and the unification of Germany. When the elderly mother of a Calcutta family hangs herself, her husband, her youngest son, her mentally unbalanced daughter and her widowed daughter-in-law are distraught but do not have the courage to read the old woman's diary. When the eldest son returns from Germany, his anxious questioning brings to light the disorientation experienced by the family and the way world history penetrates into the fabric of individual lives. In the end the daughter, with silent anger and resentment, burns the mother's diary, unread.

NARASIMHA

1991 214' col Hindi
d/p/s **N. Chandra** *pc* N. Chandra Prod. *lyr* **Javed Akhtar** *c* Binod Pradhan *m* **Laxmikant-Pyarelal**
lp Sunny Deol, Dimple Kapadia, **Om Puri,** Urmila, Ravi Behl, Babban Yadav, Satish Shah, Guddi Maruti, Sharat Saxena, Usha Nadkarni, Shafi Inamdar, Om Shivpuri, Nivedita Joshi, Brij Gopal, Shail Chaturvedi

Baapji (Om Puri) is the self-styled king of a township. His loyal lieutenant Narasimha (Sunny Deol) commits the crimes for him. Baapji kills the only honest policeman who attempts to arrest him, and the cop's son, who is in love with Baapji's daughter, is severely beaten. Baapji's daughter drives off a mountainside and declares that she will do worse if her father does her boyfriend any more harm. When Baapji asks Narasimha to expel the policeman's family from the town, Narasimha recalls his own homeless past, reforms and turns against his mentor. The film updates *Vishnu Purana*'s legend: Narasimha, half man and half lion, bursts out of a pillar to destroy the evil Hiranyakashapu. Sunny Deol, acting in the Rambo-style, performs the mythological act shortly after he has been chained and whipped, and then goes on almost single-handedly to destroy Baapji's mansion, allowing the young lovers to be united. The villain is killed through divine intervention as he is impaled by the falling hand of a giant clock. Chandra's visceral camerawork matches the performance of the muscular Deol and together they amount to a savage argument in defence of a revivalist mass culture.

PRAHAAR

1991 166' col/scope Hindi
d/co-s Nana Patekar *pc* Divya Films Combine *co-s* Sujit Sen *dial* Hriday Lani *lyr* Mangesh Kulkarni *c* Debu Deodhar *m* **Laxmikant-Pyarelal**
lp Nana Patekar, Dimple Kapadia, **Madhuri Dixit,** Habib Tanvir

Patekar's weirdly fascist fantasy of a military Pied Piper followed by naked boys about to be transformed into a glorious army of bullies which will sort out the mess created by 'emasculated' people in the real world. The first half of the film lovingly portrays a dictatorial Major Chouhan (Patekar himself) subjecting the youthful male bodies to some gruelling tests. We learn that the major's Messianism is rooted in a tragic childhood: his mother was sold as a prostitute and he spends the rest of his life compensating for the helplessness he felt then. When one of the major's wards is killed by gangsters extracting protection money from his father, the local baker, Patekar confronts the thugs, but the ordinary folk in the area do not understand the need for drastic action and the hero is forced to massacre the villains in the dead of night, watched only by the widow of one of their former victims. The climax is, in the light of subsequent events in Bombay, a chillingly deliberate orgy of violence. The ensuing court case sentences Patekar to a lunatic asylum, where he fantasises about his naked, pubescent army.

SAUDAGAR

1991 213' col/scope Hindi
d/st **Subhash Ghai** *pc* Mukta Arts *sc* Sachin Bhowmick *dial* Kamlesh Pandey *lyr* **Anand Bakshi** *c* Ashok Mehta *m* **Laxmikant-Pyarelal**
lp **Dilip Kumar,** Raaj Kumar, Vivek Mushran, Manisha Koirala, Anupam Kher, Gulshan Grover, Dina Pathak, Jackie Shroff, Deepti Naval, Dalip Tahil, Mukesh Khanna, Anand Balraj, Amrish Puri

Billed as a clash of titans between the 60s stars Raaj and Dilip Kumar, the conflict between two ageing patriarchs is told as a parable by Mandhari (Kher). The two are bosom buddies in their youth and Bir Singh aka Biru (Dilip Kumar) is supposed to marry Thakur Rajeshwar Singh's (Raaj Kumar) sister. However, he has to abandon her because honour requires him to save a woman who has been rejected on the eve of her wedding. The thakur's sister commits suicide and the buddies become bitter enemies, pursuing their feud over two decades while their respective families proliferate on either side of the Beas river. Each maintains a private army to counter the other's threat. The real villain, Rajeshwar Singh's brother-in-law Chuniya (Puri), has Biru's eldest son Vishal (Shroff) killed when he tries to make peace. Vishal's son Vasu (Mushran), sent to an ashram to prepare for joining his grandfather's army, now falls in love with the enemy's granddaughter Radha (Koirala) and the two eventually bring the warring clans together. The partiarchs die in each other's arms. Dialogue reigns supreme in the film but the love interest between Vasu and Radha (played by newcomers) culminates in the hit song *Ilu ilu*.

SOMETHING LIKE A WAR

1991 63' col English
d Deepa Dhanraj *pc* D&N Prod., Equal Media *c* Navroze Contractor

Noted feminist documentary addressing the Indian government's controversial family planning programme. After the infamous Sanjay Gandhi-led forced sterilisation programmes during the Emergency (1975-6), the programme ran into trouble again promoting injectable contraception, hormonal implants and abortifacient pills, often on the recommendation of international population control agencies dominated by multinational corporate interests. The film concentrates on the experience of the women subjected to the programme, contrasting this with the official discourse and the well-known government-sponsored advertising jingles ('small family happy family'). The women speak with, for Indian film, unprecedented candour. The rapid tv-style editing sometimes undoes the fine camerawork but the film manages to convey that the invocation of Western-style notions of individual freedom in the very different context of Indian women's lived conditions can be oppressive, esp. when women are socially denied the right to control their fertility and do not have access to appropriate post-operative health care systems.

CHELUVI

aka *The Flowering Tree*
1992 102' col Hindi
d/s/co-dial **Girish Karnad** *pc* Sadir Media, **Doordarshan** *p* B.V. Ramachandra *co-dial* Padmavati Rao *lyr* Vasant Dev *c* Rajiv Menon *m* Bhaskar Chandavarkar
lp Sonali Kulkarni, Gargi Yakkundi, Prashant Rao, Geetanjali Kirloskar, B. Jayashree, Sushma, Poornima Chikkerur, Girish Karnad, Padmavati Rao, Appayya, Sivdasan, Suresh Kulkarni, Vijaya Yakkundi

Karnad retells a Karnataka folk-tale, dubbed in Hindi, usually told by women while feeding children or putting them to bed, a time when other women would also be present. A young woman, Cheluvi (Kulkarni), living in abject poverty with her mother and sister, can turn herself into a tree yielding an endless supply of blossoms as long as they are picked very carefully. The son, Kumar (Prashant Rao), of the village headman (Karnad), seduced by the scent of the flowers, marries Cheluvi and they enjoy her flowering in strict privacy. During Kumar's absence, the headman's young daughter Shyama (G. Yakkundi) forces Cheluvi to disclose her secret. Unable to comprehend the delicacy and beauty of the event, the children destroy the tree, leaving Cheluvi's body as a mutilated tree-stump. In the end, Kumar disconsolately leaves carting off the Cheluvi-stump. The folklorist A.K. Ramanujan pointed out that in Sanskrit and in Kannada the same word is used for 'flowering' and 'menstruation'. Art direction is provided by **Jayoo** and **Nachiket Patwardhan**.

HUN HUNSHI HUNSHILAL

aka *Love in the Time of Malaria*
1992 140'(133') col Gujarati
d Sanjiv Shah *pc* Karanar Prod. *s/lyr* Paresh Naik *c* Navroze Contractor *m* Rajat Dholakia
lp Dilip Joshi, Renuka Shahane, Manoj Joshi, Mohan Gokhale, Arvind Vaidya

Gujarati musical allegory about politics. The middle-class scientist Hunshilal (Joshi), mainly through the actions of his scientist-girlfriend Parveen (Shahane), is pitted against a despotic politician, King Bhadrabhoop II of Khojpuri (Gokhale) whose subjects are bitten by a mysterious breed of mosquitoes and become restless. Hunshilal is employed by the Queen's Laboratory to eradicate the mosquitoes but he defects, with Parveen, to the side of the bugs. He is caught and brainwashed but Parveen escapes the kingdom and sets out for the land of the mosquitoes beyond the Black Hills. The rulers are portrayed as indolent oppressors who spend their time playing with toy guns and toy trains. The film's somewhat forced effort to assimilate a postmodern aesthetic is mainly evidenced in an unprecedentedly large number of songs cut into an already overcrowded soundtrack.

KAMALABAI

1992 46' col Marathi/Hindi
d/p Reena Mohan *c* Ranjan Palit, K.U. Mohanan

Remarkable documentary about the Marathi theatre and screen actress Kamalabai Gokhale who also played the lead in **Phalke**'s *Mohini Bhasmasur* (1914). Based on interviews with the octogenarian in her Pune flat and with several clips from Phalke films, Mohan captures some revealing moments with complex cinematic reverberations: e.g. Kamalabai informally re-enacts roles she played in the 20s and, at the end of the film, she suddenly realises that the camera has been filming her all that time. Made over a three-year period, the film chronicles changing seasons and times of day with a finely tuned soundtrack and innovative camerawork.

KHUDA GAWAH

1992 193' col/scope Hindi
d **Mukul S. Anand** *pc* Glamour Films *s/co-dial* Santosh Saroj *co-dial* Rajkumar Bedi *lyr* **Anand Bakshi** *c* W.B. Rao *m* **Laxmikant-Pyarelal**
lp **Amitabh Bachchan, Sridevi**, Danny Denzongpa, Nagarjuna, Vikram Gokhale, Shilpa Shirodkar, Kiran Kumar

Bachchan and the successful team that had made ***Hum*** (1991) went on to make this film which starts in an unspecified period in tribal Afghanistan. The hero Badshah Khan (Bachchan) goes to India to avenge the killing of heroine Benazir's (Sridevi) father. He does so, but in the process becomes involved in an honour pact with a Rajput police officer (Gokhale), which eventually forces Badshah to take responsibility for the cop's death when the latter is murdered by a drug-smuggling bandit (Kumar). Later, when an old Badshah is released from jail, his daughter, whom he has never seen, has grown into a second Benazir (Sridevi again), forcing Badshah to come to terms with his past. He overwhelms the narcotics bandit with the help of two young police officers (Nagarjuna and Shirodkar) who are more or less his wards by virtue of the old honour pact. Badshah's action also reconciles him with his by-now nearly demented wife Benazir. The complicated plot is told via an extravagant camera style including numerous shots, often from a helicopter, of deserts and mountain vistas. The film is dedicated to **Manmohan Desai**.

PADMA NADIR MAJHI

aka *Boatman of the River Padma*
1992 126' col Bengali
d/c/s/co-m **Gautam Ghosh** *pc* West Bengal Film Development Corp. *st* Manik Bandyopadhyay's novel *co-m* Alauddin Ali
lp Asaad, Champa, Rupa Ganguly, **Utpal Dutt, Robi Ghosh**, Abdul Khaer, Hasan Imam, Sunil Mukherjee

Set in pre-Partition Bengal in 1947, Ghosh used Bandyopadhyay's classic novel to tell the story of a man's struggle against the oppressive forces of nature, society and of his own desires. The spectacularly beautiful banks of the Padma, functioning as the metaphor for 'the river of life', form the backdrop. The main character in the fishing village is the boatman Kuber (Asaad), and the episodic film chronicles his tension-ridden encounters with the wealthy Muslim trader Hussain (Dutt), who wants to transform an island in the Padma delta into a haven free from communal strife. The women in the film are mainly metaphors for the eternally mysterious forces of nature.

PHOOL AUR KAANTE

1992 173' col/scope Hindi
d Kuku Kohli *p* Dinesh Patel *pc* Sonu Films *s* Iqbal Durrani *lyr* Sameer, Rani Malik *c* Thomas A. Xavier *m* Nadeem-Shravan
lp Amrish Puri, Ajay Devgun, Jagdeep, Madhu Raghunath, Arif Khan, Aruna Irani, Satyen Kappu, Raza Murad

The hit film that introduced Devgun as a new star for the 90s. The plot is a drama about machismo in which the orphaned Ajay (Devgun) battles the drug-peddling son of his college trustee. When violence breaks out, he is mysteriously saved by a mafia don (Puri) who, it turns out, is his unacknowledged father. Ajay marries and has a son who is kidnapped, first by the gangster-father and then again by the don's enemies. Ajay is reconciled with his father and together they eventually confront the real villains of the story. Much of the film's violence is choreographed more effectively than is usual in Hindi films (cf the locker-room fight in the men's hostel and the hero's *Mad Max*-type motor-cycle stunts). The virtual absence of a romantic sub-plot is typical of the aggressive crime thriller, using extensive political references, that came to dominate 90s Hindi cinema (cf ***Prahaar***, 1991). The several musical hits confirmed the music directors Nadeem-Shravan as major film composers of the early 90s.

RAM KE NAAM

aka *In the Name of God*
1992 90' col Hindi
d/p/c **Anand Patwardhan**

The 2nd part of Patwardan's investigation of communalism in contemporary India (***Unda Mitterandi Yaad Pyari***, 1989). The film, shot on 16mm, addresses the rise of a fanatic Hindu right wing and its exploitation of the Ayodhya temple in its bid for power. The *Ramayana* suggests Ayodhya was the God Ram's birthplace. In 1528, one of the Mughal Emperor Babar's noblemen built the Babri Masjid mosque there. In the late 19th C., both Hindus and Muslims began claiming the site as a place of worship. Since 1984, the Vishwa Hindu Parishad, a militant Hindu organisation allied with the BJP, rekindled and converted the old dispute into a nationwide political programme, affirming that the very spot where the mosque was built marks Ram's birthplace. They called for the mosque to be demolished and for a Hindu temple to be erected instead. In 1990, the BJP's leader, L.K. Advani, went on a 'Rath Yatra', a chariot procession from Somnath to Ayodhya, inciting violent communal riots en route. Advani's arrest led to the downfall of V.P. Singh's minority Janata Dal government and, later that year, to the violent Kar Seva (reconstruction) programme that saw, amid several killings, VHP men take over the mosque. Since then the Hindu fanatics have used the issue as a bargaining ploy against the ruling Congress regime. Patwardhan follows some of the infamous Rath Yatra and documents the Kar Seva itself, exposing the link between the local police and the militant mobs. Interviewing his subjects while operating the camera, Patwardhan has most of his speakers address the camera directly, revealing, often indirectly, their actual motivations. Patwardhan also includes the confession of the man who was employed to aggravate communal strife by placing idols in the temple and the remarkable statements of the priest in charge of the temple (and who was later assassinated for his anti-communalist position).

ROJA

1992 137'(114') col/scope Tamil
d/s **Mani Rathnam** *pc* Kavithalaya Prod. *c* Santosh Sivan *m* A.R. Rehman
lp Aravind Swamy, Madhubala, Pankaj Kapur, Janakaraj, Nazar

Unusually, Mani Rathnam's Tamil hit also became a success in its Hindi dubbed version. A politically controversial film set mainly in Kashmir, it recalls the real-life incident of a Kashmiri terrorist kidnapping of an Indian Oil official in 1993. In a spectacular opening the Indian army captures the dreaded Kashmiri terrorist Wasim Khan. In return, militants abduct the film's hero, the Tamilian cryptologist Rishi Kumar (Swamy). Roja (Madhubala) is Rishi Kumar's Tamil-speaking wife, left alone and unable to communicate in a land where nobody speaks her language. Eventually, just as she manages to convince a minister to agree to an exchange of prisoners, Rishi Kumar is released while the terrorist leader Liaqat (Kapur) is 'humanised' in an unconvincing ending. The lead couple's marriage in the sylvan surroundings of the cryptologist's native Tamilian village, evokes the rhetoric of Tamil nationalism, a contentious issue in the context of Rajiv Gandhi's assassination by Sri Lankan Tamils and the DMK's avowed past seperatism. Rathnam then displaces this nationalism by inflating it to the dimensions of Indian and, more specifically, uncritically Hindu chauvinism contrasted with the presentation of the Kashmiris as religion obsessed, bellicose and profoundly 'unreasonable'. In one famous scene, the tied-up hero, offended by the Kashmiris' burning of the Indian flag, crashes through a window and tries to extinguish the flames with his body to the tune of a Subramanyam Bharati lyric. In Hyderabad, the film's Telugu version sparked an outbreak of anti-Muslim slogans. Billed as a 'patriotic love story', India's election commissioner T.N. Seshan took the most unusual step of officially endorsing the film. The music was also a hit, esp. the rap number *Rukmini* sung in Hindi version by Baba Sehgal. Tejaswini Niranjana analysed the film's political address in her essay *Integrating Whose Nation?* (1994).

SURAJ KA SATWAN GHODA

aka *The Seventh Horse of the Sun*
1992 130' col Hindi
d **Shyam Benegal** *pc* **NFDC** *s* Shama Zaidi from Dharamvir Bharati's novel *c* Piyush Shah *m* **Vanraj Bhatia**
lp Amrish Puri, Neena Gupta, K.K. Raina, Pallavi Joshi, Raghuvir Yadav

In Allahabad in UP, every evening, the bachelor Manek Mulla (Puri) tells stories to a group of friends gathering at his house. Over two evenings, he tells three stories: apparently about his own boyhood, adolescence and adulthood. Each centres on a relationship with a woman and they rehearse the notions of romance, love and separation. After the stories, the friends discuss them. This bitter-sweet comedy, shot by one of India's most outstanding cinematographers, about a man's smug but immature attitudes towards women also raises questions about the distinctions between memory, reality and fantasy.

THEVAR MAGAN

1992 168' col/scope Tamil
d **B.G. Bharathan** *pc* Kaajkamal Films *p/s* **Kamalahasan** *lyr* **Vali** *c* P.C. Sriram *m* **Ilaiyaraja**
lp Kamalahasan, **Sivaji Ganesan**, Gauthami, Revathi, Nazar, K. Radhakrishnan, S.N. Lakshmi, Prasanthi

The Tamil megastar Kamalahasan produced and wrote this *Godfather*-type hit described by the star as 'a Sicilian drama', set in the feudal Madurai district controlled by big landlords who employ their own gangs and often indulge in expensive feuds with their neighbours. The star explained that this environment was part of his childhood experience. He plays Shaktivelu, the modern son of Peria-thevar (Ganesan), who returns to his ancestral home to introduce his girlfriend (Gauthami) to his family. He becomes involved in the bloody feuds between different members of the clan led by Maya-thevar (Nazar), and when his father dies he assumes the godfather's mantle. The rival family is eventually annihilated in a gory ending. Kamalahasan's performance, especially in the second half, pays tribute to the patriarchal figure of Ganesan, the focus of a neo-traditionalist discourse woven into a film primarily devoted to the star's own image.

BIBLIOGRAPHY

GENERAL BOOKS & ESSAYS

Acharya, R. N., *Television in India: A Sociological Study of Policies and Perspectives*, Delhi: Manas Publishers, 1987.

Agarwal, Binod C., *Satellite Instructional Television Experiment: Television Comes to Villages*, Bangalore: ISRO, 1978.

Agarwal, Binod C., *Television Studies in India: The State of the Art*, unpublished paper, 1985.

Agarwal, Binod C., Joshi, S. R. and Sinha, Arabind (eds), *Communication Research for Development: The ISRO Experience*, Delhi-Ahmedabad: Concept Publishing-DECU, ISRO, 1986.

Agyaat, Dr, *Bharatiya Rangabhoomika Vivechanatmak Itihas*, Kanpur: Pustak Sansthan, 1978 (Hindi).

Ahmad, Aijaz, *In Theory: Classes Nations Literatures*, London: Verso, 1992.

Ali, Imran, *The Punjab under Imperialism, 1885-1947*, New Delhi: Oxford University Press, 1989.

Amin, Shahid, 'Gandhi as Mahatma: Gorakhpur District, Eastern U. P.,1921-2' in R. Guha (ed.), *Subaltern Studies*, vol. 3, 1984.

Anon., *Rabindranath Tagore 1861-1941*, Paris: Bibliotheque Nationale de Paris, 1961.

Apte, M. L. (ed.), *Mass Culture, Language and Arts in India*, Bombay: Popular Prakashan, 1978.

Archer, Mildred, *Indian Popular Paintings in the India Office Library*, London: HMSO, 1977.

Archer, W. G., *Bazaar Paintings of Calcutta*, London: Victoria and Albert Museum, 1953.

Archer, W. G., *Kalighat Drawings*, Bombay: Marg Publications, 1962.

Balagopal, K., *Probings in the Political Economy of Agrarian Classes and Conflicts* (compiled by G. Haragopal), Hyderabad: Perspectives, 1988.

Bannerjee, Sumanta, *In the Wake of Naxalbari*, Calcutta: Subarnarekha, 1980.

Bannerjee, Sumanta, *The Parlour and the Streets: Elite and Popular Culture in Nineteenth-Century Calcutta*, Calcutta: Seagull Books, 1989.

Baruah, U. L., *This is All-India Radio*, New Delhi: Publications Division, Ministry of Information and Broadcasting, 1983.

Bhabha, Homi K., 'The Other Question ...: The Stereotype and Colonial Discourse', *Screen*, vol. 24, no. 6, London, November-December 1983.

Bhabha, Homi K. (ed.), *Nation and Narration*, London: Routledge, 1990.

Bhabha, Homi K., *The Location of Culture*, London: Routledge, 1994.

Bharucha, Rustom, *Rehearsals of Revolution: The Political Theatre of Bengal*, Honolulu: University of Hawaii Press, 1983.

Bhatkhande, V. N., *Hindustani Sangeet Paddhati*, Hathras: Sangeet Karyalaya, 1921 (Hindi).

Bhattacharya, Malini (ed.), *Manik Bandyopadhyay: Selected Stories*, Calcutta: Thema, 1988.

Bhattacharya, Rinki (ed.), *Uncertain Liaisons: Sex, Strife and Togetherness in Urban India*, New Delhi: Penguin Books India, 1993.

Bhattacharya, Sachidananda, *A Dictionary of Indian History*, Calcutta: University of Calcutta, 1967.

Bhattacharje, S. P. (ed.), *Encyclopaedia of Indian Events and Dates*, New Delhi: Sterling Publishers, 1986.

Blackburn, Robin (ed.), *Explosion in a Subcontinent*, Harmondsworth: Penguin, 1975.

Chandra, Sudhir, *The Oppressive Present: Literature and Social Consciousness in Colonial India*, New Delhi: Oxford University Press, 1992.

Chatterjee, Partha, *Bengal 1920-1947: The Land Question*, Calcutta: Centre for Studies in Social Sciences/K.P. Bagchi, 1984.

Chatterjee, Partha, *Nationalist Thought and the Colonial World: A Derivative Discourse*, New Delhi: Oxford University Press, 1986.

Chatterjee, Partha and Pandey, Gyanendra, *Selected Subaltern Studies*, vol. 7, New Delhi: Oxford University Press, 1992.

Chatterjee, Ratnabali, *From the Karkhana to the Studio: Changing Social Roles of Patron and Artist in Bengal*, New Delhi: Books and Books, 1990.

Chaudhury, M. M., 'India: From SITE to INSAT', *Media in Education and Development*, vol. 19 no. 3, 1986.

Chinappa, B. N., 'B. Puttaswamaiah Navaras Natakagalu', in Sriranga (ed.), *Kannada Rangabhoomiya Nadedubanda Daari*, Bangalore: Kannada Sahitya Parishat, 1983 (Kannada).

Chopra, P. N. and Chopra, Pratibha, *Encyclopaedia of India*, vols 1-2, Delhi: Agam Prakashan, 1988.

Choudhury, Asim, *Private Economic Power in India*, New Delhi: People's Publishing House, 1975.

Coomaraswamy, Ananda K., *Art and Swadeshi*, Madras: Ganesh Press, 1911.

Coomaraswamy, Ananda K., 'Young India', *The Dance of Shiva: Fourteen Indian Essays* [1918], New Delhi: Munshiram Manoharlal, 1977.

Datta, Amaresh (ed.), *Encyclopaedia of Indian Literature*, vol. 1 (1987), vol. 2 (1988), vol. 3 (1989), New Delhi: Sahitya Akademi.

Deodhar, B. R., 'Interview', *Pravinya*, Bombay: 1933.

Deodhar, B. R., *Gayanacharya Pandit Vishnu Digambar*, Bombay: Akhil Bharatiya Gandharva Mahavidyalaya Mandal, 1971 (Marathi).

Desai, A. R., *Social Background of Indian Nationalism*, Bombay: Popular Prakashan, 1948.

Dhanagare, D. N., 'Social Origins of the Peasant Insurrection in Telangana, 1946-51', in A. R. Desai (ed.), *Peasant Struggles in India*, New Delhi: Oxford University Press, 1979.

Dhawan, B. D., *Economics of Television in India*, New Delhi: S. Chand, 1974.

Dhillon-Kashyap, Perminder, 'Locating the Asian Experience', *Screen*, vol. 29, no. 4, London, Autumn 1988.

Engineer, Asghar Ali (ed.), *The Shah Bano Controversy*, Hyderabad: Orient Longman, 1987.

Frankel, Francine, *India's Political Economy 1947-1977: The Gradual Revolution*, Princeton: Princeton University Press, 1978.

Gandhi, M. K., 'Cent Per Cent Swadeshi', in D. G. Tendulkar (ed.), *Mahatma, Life of Mohandas Karamchand Gandhi*, vol. 3, New Delhi: Publications Division, Govt of India, 1961.

Gandhi, M. K., *The Gospel of Swadeshi*, (compiled by A. T. Hingorani), Bombay: Bhartiya Vidya Bhavan, 1967.

Gokhale, Shanta, 'Mother in Sane Guruji's *Shyamchi Ai*', *Economic and Political Weekly*, Bombay, 20 October 1990.

Guha, Amalendu, 'Parsee Seths as Entrepreneurs, 1750-1850', *Economic and Political Weekly*, vol. 5, no. 35, Bombay, 29 August 1970.

Guha, Amalendu, 'The Comprador Role of Parsee Seths', *Economic and Political Weekly*, vol. 5, no. 48, Bombay, 28 November 1970.

Guha, Amalendu, *Planter-Raj to Swaraj: Freedom Struggle and Electoral Politics in Assam 1826-1947*, New Delhi: People's Publishing House, 1977.

Guha, Ranajit, *Elementary Aspects of Peasant Insurgency in Colonial India*, New Delhi: Oxford University Press, 1983.

Guha, Ranajit (ed.), *Subaltern Studies:* vol. 1 (1982), vol. 2 (1983), vol. 3 (1984), vol. 4 (1985), vol. 5 (1987), vol. 6 (1989), New Delhi: Oxford University Press.

Guha, Ranajit and Spivak, Gayatri Chakravorty (eds), *Selected Subaltern Studies*, Foreword by Edward Said, New York: Oxford University Press, 1988.

Guha-Thakurta, Tapati, *The Making of a New 'Indian' Art: Artists, Aesthetics and Nationalism in Bengal, c.1850-1920*, Cambridge: Cambridge University Press, 1992.

Gupta, Parthasarathy, *Music and Political Consciousness (Regional, Pan-Indian and Communal): A Critical Study of Dwijendralal Roy and Nazrul Islam*, New Delhi: Nehru Memorial Museum and Library, 2nd series, no. 15, 1988.

Gupta, Somnath, *Parsee Theatre: Udbhav Aur Vikas*, Allahabad: Lokbharati Prakashan, 1969 (Hindi).

Gutman, Judith Mara, *Through Indian Eyes: Nineteenth and Early Twentieth Century Still Photography in India;* New York: Oxford University Press/International Centre of Photography, 1982.

Hari Singh, Master, *Punjab Peasant in Freedom Struggle*, New Delhi: People's Publishing House, 1984.

Havell, E. B., 'Indian Administration And Swadeshi', *Essays on Indian Art, Industry and Education*, Madras: G. A. Natesan and Co., 1901.

Irschick, Eugene F., *Tamil Revivalism in the 1930s*, Madras: Cre-A, 1986.

Jain, Jyotindra and Chandra, Lokesh (eds), *Dimensions of Indian Art: Pupul Jaykar Seventy*, New Delhi: Agam Kala Prakashan, 1986.

Joshi, G. B. and Kurthakoti, K. D., *Nadedu Banda Dari*, 3 vols, Dharwar: Manohar Granthalaya, 1959 (Kannada).

Joshi, G. N., *Down Memory Lane*, Bombay: Orient Longman, 1984.

Kagal, Ayesha et al., *Nukkad: Hope for the Indian Serial?*, Bombay: Centre For Education and Documentation, 1987.

Kapur, Geeta, *Contemporary Indian Artists*, New Delhi: Vikas, 1978.

Kapur, Geeta, *K. G. Subramanyam*, New Delhi: Lalit Kala Akademi, 1987.

Kapur, Geeta, 'Ravi Varma: Representational Dilemmas of a Nineteenth

Century Indian Painter', *Journal of Arts and Ideas*, New Delhi, nos. 17-18, June 1989.

Kapur, Geeta, 'Contemporary Cultural Practice: Some Polemical Categories', *Social Scientist*, vol. 18, no. 3, New Delhi, March 1990.

Kapur, Geeta, 'The Place of the Modern in Contemporary Cultural Practice', *Economic and Political Weekly*, vol. 26, no. 49, Bombay, 7 December 1991.

Kapur, Geeta, 'When Was Modernism in Indian-Third World Art?', *The South Atlantic Quarterly*, vol. 92, no. 3, Durham, NC: Duke University Press, Summer 1993.

Kashyap, Subhash C., *Political Events Annual 1987*, New Delhi: Lok Sabha Secretariat, 1989.

Kashyap, Sunbhash C., *Political Events Annual 1988*, Delhi: National Publishing House, 1990. Kaul, Vimala, *India Since Independence: Chronology of Events*, vol. 1 (1947-1966), vol. 2 (1967-1977), vol. 3 (1978), vol. 4 (1979), vol. 5 (1980), vol. 6 (1981), vol. 7 (1982), vol. 8 (1983), vol. 9 (1984), Delhi: Sagar Publications, 1977-88.

Keer, Dhananjay, *Rajarshi Shahu Chhatrapati*, Bombay: Popular Prakashan, 1979 (Marathi).

Khosla, G. D., *Pornography and Censorship in India*, New Delhi: Indian Book Co., 1976.

Kosambi, D. D., *An Introduction to the Study of Indian History*, Bombay: Popular Prakashan, 1956 and 1980.

Kosambi, D. D., 'Social and Economic Aspects of the *Bhagavad Gita*', *Myth and Reality*, Bombay: Popular Prakashan, 1962 and 1983.

Kosambi, D. D., *On History and Society: Problems of Interpretation*, (compiled by A. J. Syed), Bombay: Department of History, University of Bombay, 1985.

Krishnan, Prabha and Dighe, Anita, *Affirmation and Denial: Construction of Femininity on Indian Television*, New Delhi: Sage, 1990.

Kumar, Dharma and Desai, Meghnad (eds), *The Cambridge Economic History of India*, vol. 2: c.1757-c.1970, Cambridge: Cambridge University Press, 1982.

Kumar, Kewal J., *Mass Communications in India*, Bombay: Jaico, 1981.

Kumar, Ravinder, 'The Two "Revolutions" in the Panjab', *Essays in the Social History of Modern India*, Calcutta: Oxford University Press, 1983.

Lakshmi, C. S., *The Face Behind the Mask: Women in Tamil Literature*, New Delhi: Vikas, 1984.

Lal, Dr Lakshminarayan, *Parsee Hindi Rangmanch*, New Delhi: Rajpal and Sons, 1973 (Hindi).

Luthra, H. R., *Indian Broadcasting*, New Delhi: Ministry of Information and Broadcasting, 1986.

Mahilabadi, Josh, *Yaadon Ki Baraat*, Delhi: Rajpal and Sons, s.d..

Marulasiddappa, K. M., *Adhunika Kannada Nataka*, Bangalore: Printers Prakashana, 1983 (Kannada).

Masani, M., *Broadcasting and the People*, New Delhi: National Book Trust, 1975.

Mehra, Parshottam, *A Dictionary of Modern Indian History: 1707-1947*, Delhi: Oxford Unversity Press, 1985.

Menon, N., 'Traditional Culture, New Mediums, Interaction and Diffusion', in J. R. Roach (ed.), *India 2000: The Next 15 Years*, Riverdale: Riverdale, 1986.

Mirchandani, G. C., *India Backgrounders: Television in India*, New Delhi: Vikrant Press, 1976.

Mitra, Ananda, *Television and Popular Culture in India: A Study of the Mahabharat*, New Delhi: Sage, 1993.

Mugali, R. S., *History of Kannada Literature*, New Delhi: Sahitya Akademi, 1975.

Mukherjee, Meenakshi, *Realism and Reality: The Novel and Society in India*, New Delhi: Oxford University Press, 1985.

Mukherjee, Sushil Kumar, *The Story of the Calcutta Theatres: 1753-1980*, Calcutta: K. P. Bagchi and Co., 1980.

Nagar, Amritlal, *Tukde Tukde Dastaan*, Delhi: Rajpal and Sons, 1986 (Hindi). 'Nairang', Abdul Qadus, *Agha Hashr Aur Natak*, Lucknow: Uttar Pradesh Sangeet Natak Akademi, 1978 (Hindi).

NAMEDIA, *A Vision for Indian Television: Report of a Feedback Project, Indian Television Today and Tomorrow*, New Delhi: NAMEDIA, 1986.

Namboodiripad, E. M. S., *Marxisavum Malayala Sahityavum*, Trivandrum: Chintha, 1974 (Malayalam).

Nandakumar, R., 'Ravi Varma and His Relevance: An Art-Historical Revaluation', *Samskara Keralam*, Delhi: Dept of Cultural Publications, Govt of Kerala, July-September 1989 (Trivandrum).

Narayana, Birendra, *Hindi Drama and Stage*, New Delhi: Bansal and Co., 1981.

Narayanan, Andal, *The Impact of TV on Viewers: A Case Study of Bombay TV Viewers*, Bombay: Somaiya, 1987.

Nayak, H. M., *Kannada Vishwakosha*, Mysore: Institute of Kannada Studies, University of Mysore, 1975 (Kannada).

Niranjana, Tejaswini, Sudhir, P. and Dhareshwar, Vivek (eds), *Interrogating Modernity: Culture and Colonialism in India*, Calcutta: Seagull Books, 1993.

Nossiter, T. J., *Communism in Kerala: A Study in Political Adaptation*, New Delhi: Oxford University Press, 1982.

Pandey, Gyanendra, *The Construction of Communalism in Colonial North India*, New Delhi: Oxford University Press, 1990.

Pandey, Gyanendra, 'In Defence of the Fragment: Writing about Hindi-Muslim Riots in India Today', *Economic and Political Weekly*, Bombay, vol. 26 nos. 11-12 (Annual), 1991.

Panicker, Ayyappa, *A Short History of Malayalam Literature*, Trivandrum: Dept of Public Relations, 1987.

Panikkar, K. N., *Against Lord and State: Religion and Peasant Uprisings in Malabar, 1836-1921*, Delhi: Oxford University Press, 1989.

Paul, Ashit, (ed.), *Woodcut Prints of Nineteenth-Century Calcutta*, Calcutta: Seagull Books, 1983.

Political Events Annual 1989, New Delhi: Lok Sabha Secretariat, Research and Information Division, Larrdi Service, 1990.

Pradhan, Sudhi (ed.), *Marxist Cultural Movement in India: Chronicles and Documents*, vol. 1 (1936-1947), Calcutta: Santi Pradhan/National Book Agency, 1979; vol. 2 (1947-1958), Calcutta: Navana, 1982; vol. 3 (1943-1964), Calcutta: Santi Pradhan-Pustak Bipani, 1985.

Raha, Kiranmoy, *Bengali Theatre*, Calcutta: National Book Trust, 1978.

Rai, Amrit, *Premchand: A Life*, New Delhi: People's Publishing House, 1982.

Ramakrishna, V., *Social Reform in Andhra (1848-1919)*, New Delhi: Vikas, 1983.

Ramakrishna Rao, A. (ed.), *Telugu Novel*, vol. 1, Secunderabad: Yuva Bharati, 1975.

Ramamurti, P., *The Freedom Struggle and the Dravidian Movement*, Madras: Orient Longman, 1987.

Ranade, Ashok D., *Stage Music of Maharashtra*, New Delhi: Sangeet Natak Akademi, 1986.

Raychoudhury, Tapan and Habib, Irfan (eds), *The Cambridge Economic History of India*, vol. 1: c.1200-c.1750, Cambridge: Cambridge University Press, 1982.

Ross-Barnett, Margaret, *The Politics of Cultural Nationalism in South India*, Princeton: Princeton University Press, 1976.

Ryerson, Charles, *Regionalism and Religion: The Tamil Renaissance and Popular Hinduism*, Madras: The Christian Literature Society, 1988.

Sangari, Kumkum, *Mirabai and the Spiritual Economy of Bhakti*, Occasional Papers on History and Society, 2nd Series, no. 28, New Delhi: Nehru Memorial Museum and Library, June 1990.

Sarkar, Sumit, *Modern India: 1885-1947*, New Delhi: Macmillan, 1983.

Sarkar, Sumit, *'Popular' Movements and Middle-Class Leadership in Late Colonial India: Perspectives and Problems of a History from Below*, Calcutta: Centre for Studies in Social Sciences-K. P. Bagchi, 1983.

Sarkar, Tanika, *Bengal 1928-1934: The Politics of Protest*, New Delhi: Oxford University Press, 1987.

Seetharamaiah, H. V., *Karnatakada Ranga Kalavidaru*, Bangalore: Kala Sahitya Prakashana, 1983 (Kannada).

Sen, Samar et al. (eds), *Naxalbari and After: A Frontier Anthology*, 2 vols, Calcutta: Kathashilpa, 1978.

Sharma, Dr Devendra, *Hindi Rangmanch Ke Vikas Mein Bambai Ka Yog*, Bombay: Bambai Hindi Vidyapeeth, 1987 (Hindi).

Sheikh, Gulam Mohammed, 'Mobile Vision', *Journal of Arts and Ideas*, no. 5, New Delhi, October-December 1983.

Sheikh, Gulam Mohammed, 'Viewer's View: Looking at Pictures', *Journal of Arts and Ideas*, no. 3, New Delhi, April-June 1983.

Sheikh, Gulam Mohammed et al. (eds), *Paroksha: Coomaraswamy Centenary Seminar Papers*, New Delhi: Lalit Kala Akademi, 1984.

Thapar, Romila, *Asoka and the Decline of the Mauryas*, New Delhi: Oxford University Press, 1961.

Thapar, Romila, *A History of India*, vol. 1, Harmondsworth: Penguin Books, 1966.

Thapar, Romila, *From Lineage to State*, Delhi: Oxford University Press, 1984.

Tharu, Susie and Lalitha, K., *Women Writing in India*, vol. 1 (1991); vol. 2 (1993), New York: The Feminist Press.

Thomas, G., *History of Photography in India 1840-1980*, Andhra Pradesh State Akademi of Photography, 1981.

Vanaik, Achin, *The Painful Transition: Bourgeois Democracy in India*, London: Verso, 1990.

Varadarajan, Mu., *A History of Tamil Literature*, New Delhi: Sahitya Akademi, 1988.

Vishwanathan, Gauri, *Masks of Conquest: Literary Study and British Rule in India*, London: Faber and Faber, 1989

Wilkins, W. J., *Hindu Mythology* [1882], Calcutta: Rupa and Co., 1975.

REPORTS

1922: Evans, W., *Survey of the Cinema Industry*, Letter 1237 Law (G), 12-5-1922 (M/S), London: India Office Library.

1928: *Report of the Indian Cinematograph Committee 1927-28*, 5 vols [T. Rangachariar Chairman] Calcutta: Govt Of India Central Publications Branch, 1928.

1951: *Report of the Film Enquiry Committee* [S. K. Patil Chairman], New Delhi: Govt of India Press, 1951.

1961: UNESCO, *The Present-Day Situation and Future Prospects of the Feature Film in India*, Paris: UNESCO, 1961.

1966: *Report on Documentary Films and Newsreels*, New Delhi: Ministry of Information and Broadcasting, 1966.

1966: *Report on Employment Conditions in the Film Industry*, [P. G. Kher Chairman], Bombay: Govt of Maharashtra, 1966.

1968: *Film Enquiry Committee Report 1962-63*, Calcutta: Govt of West Bengal, 1968.

1969: *Report of the Enquiry Committee on Film Censorship* [G. D. Khosla Chairman], New Delhi: Govt of India, 1969.

1969: *Audience Reaction to Films Screened in Villages. A Report on a Study of the Impact of Documentary Films in Tamil, Hindi and Bengali*, New Delhi: Indian Institute of Mass Communications, 1969.

1974: *Estimates Committee 58th Report (1973-74) of the Ministry of Information and Broadcasting*, New Delhi: Lok Sabha Secretariat, 1974.

1975: *Estimates Committee 80th Report (1975-76) of the Ministry of Information and Broadcasting*, New Delhi: Lok Sabha Secretariat, 1975.

1976: *79th Report, Committee on Public Undertakings (1975-76): Film Finance Corporation*, New Delhi: Lok Sabha Secretariat, 1976.

1976: *Report of the Minimum Wage (Revision) Committee for Employment in the Cinema Exhibition Industry*, Bombay: Govt of Maharashtra, 1976.

1980: *Report of the Working Group on National Film Policy* [K. S. Karanth Chairman], New Delhi: Govt of India, Ministry of Information and Broadcasting, 1980.

1984: *Report of the Working Group on Software for Doordarshan* [P. C. Joshi Chairman], 'Summary', *Mainstream*, 14, 21 and 28 April, 5 May 1984; 'Recommendations', *A Vision for Indian Television*, New Delhi: NAMEDIA, 1986.

BOOKS/SCREENPLAYS

Abbas, Khwaja Ahmad, *I Am Not An Island: An Experiment in Autobiography*, New Delhi: Vikas Publishing, 1977.

Abbas, Khwaja Ahmed, *Mad, Mad World of Indian Films*, New Delhi: Hind Pocket Books, 1977.

Abbas, Khwaja Ahmed, *How Films are Made*, New Delhi: National Book Trust, 1977.

Abbas, Khwaja Ahmed, *Mera Naam Joker*, New Delhi: Hind Pocket Books, s.d.

Abraham, John, *John Parayumu*, Vadakara: Odessa Pravartagar, 1987 (Malayalam).

Adarsh, B. K. (ed.), *Film Industry of India*, Bombay: Trade Guide Publications, 1963.

Agarwal, Pralhad, *Adhi Hakikat Adha Phasana*, New Delhi: Radhakrishna Prakashan, 1984 (Hindi).

Agnihotri, Ram Avtar, *Social and Political Study of Modern Hindi Cinema: Past, Present and Future Perspectives*, New Delhi: Commonwealth Publishers, 1990.

Agnihotri, Ram Avtar, *Artists and their Films of Modern Hindi Cinema: Cultural and Socio-Political Impact on Society, 1931-1991*, 3 vols, New Delhi: Commonwealth Publishers, 1992.

Akhtar, Javed and Khan, Salim, *Amar Akbar Anthony*, Ahmedabad: Guide Pocket Books, 1977.

Alekar, Vasant, *Chanderi Baat-Cheet*, Bombay: Rohan Prakashan, 1986 (Marathi).

Amur, G. S., *A. N. Krishnarao*, Makers of Indian Literature Series, New Delhi: Sahitya Akademi, 1983.

Anandan, 'Filmnews' (ed.), *Thiraikkalai Thoguppu*, Madras: Sivagami Publications, 1978 (Tamil).

Anandur, Satyamurthy, *Singeetham Srinivasa Rao*, Bangalore: Karnataka Chalanachitra Patrakartara Parishat, 1988 (Kannada).

Ananthamurthy, Sindhuvalli, *Gubbi Company*, Mysore: Suruchi Prakashana, 1979 (Kannada).

Anon., *Indian Talkie 1931-56, Silver Jubilee Souvenir*, Bombay, 1956.

Anon., *Indian Talkie 1936-56*, Bombay: Film Federation of India, 1956.

Anon., *Faces in the Dark: Advertising and Sales Promotion Survey on Cinema Audiences*, Bombay: Advertising and Sales Promotion, 1963.

Anon., *Sahityakara Directory*, Trichur: Kerala Sahitya Akademi, 1976.

Anon., *25 Years 1938-1963 of Service to the Motion Picture Industry of India: Silver Jubilee Souvenir*, Bombay: Indian Motion Picture Producers Association, 1963.

Anon., *Documentary in National Development*, New Delhi: Indian Institute of Mass Communication, 1967.

Anon., *Malayala Cinema Directory*, Kottayam: Commercial Art Centre, 1970 (Malayalam).

Anon., *Symposium on Cinema in Develping Countries*, New Delhi: Ministry of Information and Broadcasting, 1979.

Anon., *Infrastructure, Production Values and Marketing of the Other Cinema*, Madras: Hindustan Photo Films, 1979.

Anon., *Bombay Cinemas (Regulation) Act, 1953*, Bombay: Maharashtra State Govt Printing, Stationery and Publications, 1982.

Anon., *Regional Cinema*, Hyderabad: Secunderabad Film Society, 1983.

Anon., *Cinemasia '85 - I Film*, XXI Mostra Internazionale del Nuovo Cinema, Pesaro, 1985.

Anon., *FTII Films 1964-1987*, Pune: FTII, 1987.

Anon., *The Film in India and South-East Asia: A Documentation*, Mannheim: Internationale Filmwoche, 1979.

Anvalikar, Sudhakar, *Bhulaye Na Bane*, Bombay: Aarti Prakashan, 1984 (Hindi).

Apte, Shanta, *Jau Mi Cinemaat?*, Bombay: B. Govind, 1940 (Marathi).

Aravindan, G., *Cheriya Manushyarum Valiya Lokavum*, Trivandrum: Bees Books, 1978 (Malayalam).

Athavale, Shantaram, *'Prabhat' Kaal*, Pune: Venus Prakashan, 1965 (Marathi).

Atorthy, Premankur, *Mahasthavir Jatak*, Calcutta: Indian Associated Publishing, 1922 (Bengali).

Atorthy, Premankur, *Nirvak Juger Chayaloker Katha, Basumati Journal, 1952-53*, Calcutta: Bishwabani Prakashani, 1990 (Bengali).

Atre, P. K., *Karheche Pani*, Bombay: Parchure Prakashan, 1965-7 (Marathi).

Bafna, C. L., *Law Relating to Cinemas in India*, Jaipur: Bafna Law Publishers, 1978.

Baji, A. R. (ed.), *Indian Talkie, 50 Years - 1931-81*, Madras: South Indian Chamber of Commerce, 1981.

Balakrishnan, P. E., *Makkal Kavignar Pattukottai Kalyanasundaram Padalgal*, Madras: New Century Book House, 1965 (Tamil).

Bandyopadhyay, Bidhubhushan, *Chhayachhabir Marmakatha*, Calcutta: The Book Stall, 1934 (Bengali).

Bandyopadhyay, Janaki Kumar, *Satyajit, Fellini, Godard*, Calcutta: India International, 1975 (Bengali).

Bandyopadhyay, Ranjan, *Bishoy Satyajit*, Calcutta: Navana, 1988 (Bengali).

Bandyopadhay, Samik (ed.), *Govind Nihalani*, Jamshedpur: Celluloid Chapter, 1992.

Bannerjee, Haimanti, *Ritwik Kumar Ghatak: A Monograph*, Pune: NFAI, 1985.

Bannerjee, Shampa and Srivastava, Anil (eds), *One Hundred Indian Feature Films: An Annotated Filmography*, New York and London: Garland Publishing, 1988.

Bannerjee, Shampa (ed.), *New Indian Cinema*, New Delhi: Directorate of Film Festivals, 1982.

Bannerjee, Shampa (ed.), *Ritwik Ghatak*, New Delhi: Directorate of Film Festivals, 1982.

Bannerjee, Shampa (ed.), *Profiles: Five Film-makers from India*, New Delhi: Directorate of Film Festivals, 1985.

Baokar, Purshottam, *Brahmachari*, Bombay: Aradhana Prakashan, 1972 (Marathi).

Baokar, Ratnakar and Vashikar, Purshottam, *Tyacha Velu Gela Gaganavari*,

Bombay: Aradhana Prakashan, 1970 (Marathi).

Bapu and Ramana, *Bapu Ramaneeyam*, Vijaywada: Navodaya Publishers, 1990 (Telugu).

Barjatya, Tarachand, *A Handbook Detailing some of the Problems of the Indian Film Industry*, Bombay: Rajshri Pictures, 1975.

Barnouw, Eric and Krishnaswamy, S., *Indian Film*, New York: Columbia University Press, 1963; rev. edn. Oxford University Press, 1980.

Baskaran, S. Theodore, *The Message Bearers: Nationalist Politics and the Entertainment Media in South India 1880-1945*, Madras: Cre-A Publishers, 1981.

Bawa, Mohan, *Actors and Acting: 14 Candid Interviews*, Bombay: India Book House, 1978.

Bedekar, Vishram, *Ek Jhaad Ani Don Pakshi*, Bombay: Popular Prakashan, 1985 (Marathi).

Bedi, Rajinder Singh, 'A Note on the Creative Process and the Art of ShortStory', *Selected Short Stories*, New Delhi: Sahitya Akademi, 1989.

Bedi, Rajinder Singh, *Dastak* (Screenplay), Delhi: Hind Pocket Books, 1971 (Hindi).

Berger, J., Gregor, E. and Schoenberner, G. (eds), *Panorama des neuen indischen Films*, Berlin: Internationales Forum des jungen Films/ Freunde der Deutschen Kinemathek, 1979.

Bhagat, Bhai, *Namankit Nat Nati*, Bombay: Jhavbachi Wadi, 1954 (Marathi).

Bhagat, Bhai, *Digdarshak Raj Kapoor*, Bombay: Shalaka Prakashan, 1992 (Marathi).

Bhalekar, Vasant, *Sulochana*, Bombay: G. P. Parchure Prakashan, 1969 (Marathi).

Bhalekar, Vasant, *Chanderi Baatcheet*, Bombay: Rohan Prakashan, 1986 (Marathi).

Bhardwaj, Vinod, *Naya Cinema*, New Delhi: Veni Prakashan, 1985 (Hindi).

Bharucha, B. D. (ed.), *Indian Cinematograph Yearbook 1938*, Bombay: Motion Picture Society of India, 1938.

Bhattacharya, Basu, *Avishkar* (Screenplay), New Delhi: Hind Pocket Books, 1975 (Hindi).

Bhattacharya, Dhiraj, *Jakhan Nayak Chhilam*, Calcutta: Indian Associated Publishing, 1956 (Bengali).

Bhattacharya, Dilip Kumar, *Jibanshilpi Satyajit Ray*, Calcutta: Haraf Prakashan, 1969 (Bengali).

Bhattacharya, Rinki, *Bimal Roy*, Bhopal: Madhya Pradesh Film Development Corp., 1989 (Hindi).

Bhide, G. R. and Gajbar, Baba, *Kalamaharshi Baburao Painter*, Kolhapur: Meenal Prakashan, 1978 (Marathi).

Bhole, Keshavrao, *Mazhe Sangeet: Rachana Ani Digdarshan*, Bombay: Mauz Prakashan, 1964 (Marathi); Ashish Rajadhyaksha (tr.), 'Keshavrao Bhole: Excerpts from his *Mazhe Sangeet*', *Sangeet Natak*, no. 100, New Delhi, April-June 1991.

Binford, Mira Reym (ed.), *Media Policy as a Catalyst to Creativity: The Role of Government in the Development of India's New Cinema*, Madison: University of Wisconsin-Madison, unpublished.

Booch, Harish S., *Green Leaves*, Bombay: Harish S. Booch Memorial Committee, 1964.

Bora, Prafulla, *Cinema in Assam*, Gauhati: Performing Arts Centre, 1978.

Bose, Modhu, *Amar Jeeban*, Calcutta: Vak-Sahitya, 1967 (Bengali).

Bose, Sadhona, *Silpir Atmakatha*, Calcutta: Granthaprakash, 1963 (Bengali).

Burra, Rani (ed.), *Looking Back 1896-1960*, New Delhi: Directorate of Film Festivals, 1981.

Burra, Rani (ed.), *Indian Cinema: 1980-1985*, New Delhi: Directorate of Film Festivals, 1985.

Burra, Rani (ed.), *Ashok Kumar: Green to Evergreen*, New Delhi: Directorate of Film Festivals, s.d. [1990].

Chaddha, Manmohan, *Hindi Cinema Ka Itihas*, New Delhi: Sachin Prakashan, 1990 (Hindi).

Chajlani, Abhay (ed.), *Lata Mangeshkar*, Indore: Nai Duniya, 1983 (Hindi).

Chakravarty, Rudraprasad, *Solar Kella Sandhaney*, Calcutta: New Book Stall, 1977 (Bengali).

Chakravarty, Sumita S., *National Identity in Indian Popular Cinema 1947-1987*, Austin: University of Texas Press, 1993.

Chatterjee, Bishwanath (ed.), *Hindi Film Geet Kosh 1971-1980*, Kanpur: Satinder Kaur, 1991.

Chatterjee, Gaur and Bandyopadhyay, Sunil, *Chitrabani Chitrabashiki*,

Calcutta: Chitrabani Prakashan, 1951 (Bengali).

Chattopadhyay, Amitabh, *Chalachitra Samaj-o-Satyajit Ray*, Asansol: Film Technique Centre, 1980 (Bengali).

Chattopadhyay, Dilip, *Satyajit*, Calcutta: Banishilpa, 1986 (Bengali).

Chaturvedi, Brijbhushan (ed.), *Suchitra Film Directory 1991-92*, Indore: Suchitra Prakashan, 1992 (Hindi).

Chellangatti, Gopalakrishnan, *Cinemayude Charitram*, Shertellai: Prathap Publications, 1972 (Malayalam).

Chinappa, B. N., *Natakaratna Gubbi Veeranna*, Bangalore: Bangalore University, 1982 (Kannada).

Chiranjeevi, *Kannada Chalanachitra Patrikodyama: Nadedu Banda Dari*, Bangalore: Karnataka Chalanachitra Patrakartara Parishat, 1988 (Kannada).

Chitnis, Leela, *Chanderi Duniyet*, Pune: Srividya Prakashan, 1981 (Marathi).

Choudhury, Ahindra, *Nijere Haraye Khunji*, vol 1, Calcutta: Indian Associated Publishers, 1962 (Bengali).

Choudhury, Ishwar Prasad, *Jyotiprasad Agarwala*, New Delhi: Builders of Modern Indian Series, Publications Division, Ministry of Information and Broadcasting, 1986.

Chouhan, Mahavir Singh (ed.), *Chulbuli Rekha*, Delhi: Punjabi Pustak Bhandar, 1978 (Hindi).

Chouhan, Mahavir Singh, *Great Showman - Raj Kapoor*, New Delhi: Star Pocket Books, 1982.

Chughtai, Ismat, *The Quilt and Other Stories*, New Delhi: Kali For Women, 1990. da Cunha, Uma (ed.), *Film India: The New Generation 1960-1980*, New Delhi: Directorate of Film Festivals, 1981.

Daithota, Eswar, *D. V. Rajaram*, Bangalore: Karnataka Chalanachitra Pratakartara Parishat, 1988 (Kannada).

Das, Nandini (ed.), *An Anthology of Articles on Indian Cinema*, New Delhi: Directorate of Film Festivals, 1985.

Das, Shyamal Kanti (ed.), *Lekhak Satyajit Ray*, Calcutta, Shibarani Prakashani, 1986 (Bengali).

Dasgupta, Buddhadev, *Swapna Samay Cinema*, Calutta: Banishilpa, 1991 (Bengali).

Das Gupta, Chidananda, Majumdar, Kamal and Ray, Satyajit et al. (eds), *Chalachitra: Pratham Paryay*, Calcutta: Signet Press, 1950 (Bengali).

Das Gupta, Chidananda, *The Cinema of Satyajit Ray*, New Delhi: Vikas Publishing, 1980.

Das Gupta, Chidananda, *Talking about Films*, New Delhi: Orient Longman, 1981.

Das Gupta, Chidananda (ed.), *Satyajit Ray*, New Delhi: Directorate of Film Festivals, 1981.

Das Gupta, Chidananda and Kobe, Werner, *Kino in Indien*, Freiburg in Breisgau: Verlag Wolf Mersch, 1986.

Das Gupta, Chidananda, *The Painted Face: Studies in India's Popular Cinema*, New Delhi: Roli Books, 1991.

Dasgupta, Manasi, *Chhabir Naam Satyajit*, Calcutta: Ananda, 1984 (Bengali).

Datta, Dilip Kumar, *Bhupen Hazarika Geet Aru Jiban Rath*, Calcutta: Sribhumi, 1982 (Assamese).

David, C. R. W., *Cinema as a Means of Communication in Tamil Nadu*, Madras: Christian Literature Society, 1983.

Desai, Vasant Shantaram, *Bal Gandharva: Vyakti Ani Kala*, Pune: Venus Prakashan, 1959 (Marathi).

Deshpande, Rekha, *Smita Patil*, Pune: Srividya Prakashan, 1987 (Marathi).

Devi, Kanan, *Sabare Ami Nomi* (compiled by Sandhya Sen), Calcutta: M. C. Sirkar and Sons, 1973 (Bengali).

Dharap, B. V., *Indian Films 1972*, Bombay: B. V. Dharap Motion Picture Enterprises, s.d.; *Indian Films 1973*, ibid., 1974; *Indian Films 1974*, ibid., 1975; *Indian Films 1975*, ibid., 1976; *Indian Films 1976*, ibid., 1977; *Indian Films 1977* and *1978*, ibid., 1979; *Indian Films 1983*, Pune: NFAI, 1985; *Indian Films 1984*, ibid., 1985; *Indian Films 1985* (roneo) Pune: NFAI.

Dickey, Sara, *Cinema and the Urban Poor in South India*, Cambridge: Cambridge University Press, 1993.

Dissanayake, Wimal (ed.), *Cinema and Cultural Identity: Reflections on Films from Japan, India and China*, Lanham: University Press of America, 1988.

Dissanayake, Wimal and Sahai, Malti, *Raj Kapoor's Films: Harmony of Discourses*, New Delhi: Vikas, 1988.

Dissanayake, Wimal and Sahai, Malti, *Sholay: A Cultural Reading*, Honolulu: Wiley East-West, 1992.

Dissanayake, Wimal (ed.), *Melodrama and Asian Cinema*, Cambridge: Cambridge University Press, 1993.

Doddanegowda, Joladarashi, *Natyakala Prapoorna T. Raghavaru*, Mysore: Mysore Rajya Sangeet Natak Akademi, 1972 (Kannada).

Doraiswamy, V. (ed.), *Asian Film Directory and Who's Who*, Bombay: Mrs Jaya Doraiswamy, 1956.

Doshi, Sunil and da Cunha, Uma (eds), *Film Catalogue: National Centre of Films for Children and Young People*, Bombay: N'CYP, 1993.

Dutt, Utpal, *Towards a Revolutionary Theatre*, Calcutta: M. C. Sarkar and Sons, 1982.

Ekbote, Vidya, *Economics of the Indian Film Industry with Special Reference to the Marathi Film Industry (1974-85)*, Pune: University of Pune, unpublished, 1986.

Fazalbhoy, Y. A., *The Indian Film: A Review*, Bombay: Bombay Radio Press, 1939.

Fazalbhoy, Y. A., *Indian Film*, Bombay: Motion Picture Society of India, 1950.

Ferrario, Davide (ed.), *Mrinal Sen e il cinema indiano*, Bergamo Film Meeting, 1983.

Gadkar, Jayashree, *Ashi Mi Jayashree*, Bombay: Rohan Prakashan, 1986 (Marathi).

Gala, Manilal and Gangar, Amrit, *Gujarati Chalachitron: 1982 Na Aare*, Bombay: Screen Unit, 1982 (Gujarati).

Ganguly, Dhiren, *Biye*, Calcutta: Sisir Publishing House, 1922 (Bengali).

Garga, B. D., *The Present-Day Situation and Future Prospects of the Feature Film in India*, Paris: UNESCO, 1961.

Garga, B. D., *Sound Track in the Indian Film*, Paris: UNESCO, 1966.

Gaur, Madan, *Other Side of the Coin: An Intimate Study of the Indian Film Industry*, Bombay: Trimurti Prakashan, 1973.

Ghatak, Ritwik, *Chalachitra Manash Ebam Aro Kichhu*, Calcutta: Sanadan Samabaya Prakashani, 1975 (Bengali).

Ghatak, Ritwik, 'Jukti Takko Aar Gappo (Screenplay)', in Sen, Anil (ed.), *Chitrabikshan*, Annual Number, Calcutta, 1975.

Ghatak, Ritwik, *Cinema And I*, Calcutta: Ritwik Memorial Trust/Rupa, 1987.

Ghosh, Debiprasad (ed.), *Bangla Bhashay Chalachitra Charcha 1923-33*, Calcutta: Cine Club, 1990 (Bengali).

Ghosh, Gaurangaprasad, *Sonar Daag*, Calcutta: Johumaya Prakashan, 1982(Bengali).

Ghosh, Kartick Kumar, *Oriya Chalachitrara Itihas*, Cuttack: Govind Charan Patra, Orissa Bookstore, 1984 (Oriya).

Ghosh, Sital Chandra and Roy, Arun Kumar (eds), *Twelve Indian Directors*, Calcutta: People's Book Publishing, 1981.

Gopal, S. R., *Madras Talkie Register 1939*, Madras: S.R. Gopal, 1939.

Gopalakrishnan, Adoor, *Cinemayude Lokam*, Trivandrum: Trivandrum State Institute of Languages, 1983 (Malayalam).

Gopalakrishnan, Adoor, *Face To Face - Mukhamukham*, transl. Shampa Bannerjee, Calcutta: Seagull Books, 1985.

Gopalakrishnan, Adoor, *The Rat Trap - Elippathayam*, transl. Shampa Bannerjee, Calcutta: Seagull Books, 1985.

Gopalan, Lalitha, *Wogs, Natives, Heroes: Postcolonial Inquiry into Sexuality and Nationalism*, Unpublished, University of Rochester, 1992.

Govindacharya, Bananje, *G. V. Iyer*, Bangalore: Karnataka Chalanachitra Patrakartara Parishat, 1988 (Kannada).

Grover, Ashok (ed.), *Filmon ke Rashtriya Geet*, Meerut: Ratan Pocket Books, 1985 (Hindi).

Gulavani, V. N. (ed.), *Films Division Catalogue of Films: 1949-1972*, Bombay: Films Division, 1974.

Gupta, Dhruba, Das Sharma, Biren and Bandyopadhyay, Samik (eds), *Indian Cinema: Contemporary Perceptions from the Thirties*, Jamshedpur: Celluloid Chapter, 1993.

Guy, Randor, *B. N. Reddi: A Monograph*, Pune: NFAI, 1985.

Guy, Randor (ed.), *History of Tamil Cinema*, Madras: International Film Festival of India, 1991.

Haldar, Gopal, *Kazi Nazrul Islam*, New Delhi: Sahitya Akademi, Makers of Indian Literature series, 1973.

Haldar, Sukumar and Ghosh, Netai (eds), *Sabakchitra*, Calcutta: Basumati Sahitya Mandir, 1935 (Bengali).

Hardgrave Jr, Robert L., *When Stars Displace the Gods: The Folk Culture of Cinema in Tamil Nadu*, Austin: University of Texas, 1975.

Hatkanagalekar, M. D., *V. S. Khandekar*, New Delhi: Sahitya Akademi, 1986.

Hauff, R., *Ten Days in Calcutta: A Portrait of Mrinal Sen* (Screenplay), Calcutta: Seagull Books, 1987.

Hazarika, Bhupen, *Jilikabo Luyitare Paar*, Calcutta: Hemango Biswas, 1955 (Assamese).

Hazarika, Bhupen, *Sangram Legne Aaji*, Guwahati: Gatiprakash, 1962 (Assamese).

Hazarika, Bhupen, *Sundarar Na-digantar*, Calcutta: Bichitranarayan Datta Barua, 1967 (Assamese).

Hazarika, Bhupen, *Bhupen Mamar Geete Mate: A-Aa-Ka-Kha*, Calcutta: Bhawani Publishing, 1976 (Assamese).

Hazarika, Bhupen, *Sundarar Sarubar Aliyedi*, Dibrugarh: Banimandir, 1980 (Assamese).

Hazarika, Bhupen, *Samayer Pakhi Ghonrat Uthi*, Dibrugarh: Banimandir, 1981 (Assamese).

Hublikar, Shanta, *Kashyala Udyachi Baat*, Pune: Srividya Prakashan, 1990 (Marathi).

Indian Cinema 1965, New Delhi: Govt of India Publications, s.d. *Indian Cinema 77/78*, Rani Burra (ed.), New Delhi: Directorate of Film Festivals, 1978. *Indian Cinema 78/79*, Uma da Cunha (ed.), New Delhi: Directorate of Film Festivals, s.d.

Indian Cinema 79/80, Uma da Cunha (ed.), New Delhi: Directorate of Film Festivals, s.d.

Indian Cinema 80/81, Uma da Cunha (ed.), New Delhi: Directorate of Film Festivals, s.d.

Indian Cinema 81/82, Kironmoy Raha (ed.), New Delhi: Directorate of Film Festivals, s.d.

Indian Cinema 82/83, Aruna Vasudev (ed.), New Delhi: Directorate of Film Festivals, s.d.

Indian Cinema 83/84, Uma da Cunha (ed.), New Delhi: Directorate of Film Festivals, s.d.

Indian Cinema 1984, Shampa Bannerjee (ed.), New Delhi: Directorate of Film Festivals, 1985.

Indian Cinema 1985, P. K. Nair, (ed.) New Delhi: Directorate of Film Festivals, 1986.

Indian Cinema 1986, Rani Burra (ed.), New Delhi; Directorate of Film Festivals, s.d.

Indian Cinema 1987, Ashish Rajadhyaksha (ed.), New Delhi: Directorate of Film Festivals, 1988.

Indian Cinema 1988, Jag Mohan (ed.), New Delhi: Directorate of Film Festivals, 1989.

Indian Cinema 1989, Shampa Bannerjee (ed.), New Delhi: Directorate of Film Festivals, 1990.

Indian Cinema 1990, K. N. T. Sastry (ed.), New Delhi: Directorate of Film Festivals, 1991.

Indian Cinema 1991, Shampa Bannerjee (ed.), New Delhi: Directorate of Film Festivals, 1992.

Indira, M. K., *Kannada Chitrashilpi Puttana Kanagal*, Bangalore: Hemantha Sahitya, 1986 (Kannada).

Ivory, James (ed.), *Autobiography of a Princess: Also Being the Adventures of an American Film Director in the Land of the Maharajas*, New York: Harper and Row, 1975.

Iyer, G. V., *Mooru Chitra Mooru Daari*, Bangalore: Navkarnataka, 1984 (Kannada).

Jag Mohan (ed.), *Two Decades of the Films Division*, Bombay: Ministry of Information and Broadcasting, Films Division, 1969.

Jag Mohan (ed.), *Dr P.V. Pathy: Documentary Film-maker*, Pune: NFAI, 1972.

Jag Mohan, *S. Sukhdev Film-maker. A Documentary Montage*, Pune: Ministry of Information and Broadcasting, Films Division, NFAI, 1984.

Jag Mohan, *Documentary Films and India's Awakening*, New Delhi: Publications Division, Ministry of Information and Broadcasting, 1990.

Jagirdar, Gajanan, *Sandhyakal*, Pune: Raj Hans Prakashan, 1971 (Marathi).

Jagirdar, Gajanan, *Abhinay Kasa Karava*, Pune: India Book Company, 1983 (Marathi).

Jagirdar, Gajanan, *Paool Khuna*, Bombay: Majestic Prakashan, 1986 (Marathi).

Jain, Rikhab Das, *The Economic Aspects of the Film Industry in India*, Delhi: Atma Ram and Sons, 1960.

Jayasimha, S., *Vijayabhaskar*, Bangalore: Karnataka Chalanachitra Patrakartara Parishat, 1988 (Kannada).

Jha, Bagishwar (ed.), *Indian Motion Picture Almanac*, Calcutta: Shot, 1986.

Jha, Bagishwar, *Nitin Bose: Flowering of a Humanist Film-maker*, Calcutta: Asian Art Foundation, 1986.

Jha, Bagishwar (ed.), *B. N. Sircar*, Calcutta: NFAI and Seagull Books, 1990.

Jhony, O. K. (ed.), *Aravindante Kala*, Kozhikode: Bodhi, 1991 (Malayalam).

Jog, N. G. (ed.), *Screen Yearbook and Who's Who*, Bombay: Express Newspapers, 1956.

Jog, V. V., *Natashreshta Keshavrao Date*, Bombay: Parchure Prakashan, 1976 (Marathi).

Joshi, Badriprasad (ed.), *Hindi Cinema Ka Sunehra Safar*, Bombay: Cinevani Prakashan, 1988 (Hindi).

Joshi, P. C. (ed.), *Balraj Sahni: An Intimate Portrait*, New Delhi: Vikas Publications, 1974.

Kabir, Nasreen, *Les Stars du cinema indien*, Paris: Centre Pompidou/ Centre National de la Cinematographie, 1985.

Kakatkar, Balakrishna, *Shankar Nag*, Bangalore: Karnataka Chalanachitra Patrakartara Parishat, 1988 (Kannada).

Kale, K. Narayan, *Natyavimarsh*, Bombay: Popular Book Depot, 1961 (Marathi).

Kale, K. Narayan et al. (eds), *Marathi Rangabhoomi Marathi Natak*, Bombay: Mumbai Marathi Sahitya Sangh, 1971 (Marathi).

Kale, K. Narayan, *Bhoomika Shilpa/Abhinay Sadhana*, Bombay: Maharashtra Rajya Sahitya Sanskriti Mandal, 1976 (Marathi).

Kale, K. Narayan, *Pratima, Roop Ani Rang*, Pune: Nutan Prakashan, 1976 (Marathi).

Kambhar, Chandrasekhar (ed.), *Kannada Folklore Dictionary*, Bangalore: Kannada Sahitya Parishat, 1984.

Karanjia, B. K., *A Many Splendoured Cinema*, Bombay: New Thacker's Fine Art Press, s.d.

Kasaravalli, Girish (ed.), *Cinema Kale-Nele*, Bangalore: Navkarnataka, 1983 (Kannada).

Kathavachak, Radheshyam, *Mera Natak Kaal*, Bareilly: Shri Radheshyam Pustakalaya, 1957 (Hindi).

Kelkar, M. W., *Master Vinayak*, New Delhi: Wiley Eastern, 1991.

Kesavalu, V. (ed.), *Impact of MGR Films*, Madras: Movie Appreciation Society, 1989 (Tamil/English).

Khanna, Satendra, *Indian Cinema and Indian Life*, Los Angeles: University of California Press, 1980.

Khedekar, Padma and Durgaram, *Padadyamagil Bal Gandharva*, Pune: Venus Book Stall, 1968 (Marathi).

Kher, Sanjeevani, *Mayadarpan*, Pune: Srividya Prakashan, 1989 (Marathi).

Khopkar, Arun, *Guru Dutt: Teen Anki Shokantika*, Bombay: Granthali, 1985 (Marathi).

Khote, Durga, *Mee Durga Khote*, Bombay: Majestic Book Stall, 1982 (Marathi).

Kinikar, Shashikant (ed.), *Dastan-e-Naushad*, Pune: Chandrakala Prakashan, 1991 (Marathi).

Kiron, Usha, *Ushakkal*, Pune: Srividya Prakashan, 1989 (Marathi).

Koch, Gerhard, *Franz Osten's Indian Silent Films*, New Delhi: Max Mueller Bhavan, 1983.

Kondala Rao, Ravi, *Shavukaru-Chakrapani*, Vijaywada: Navodaya, ?.

Koshy, K. V., *Ente Cinemasmaranakal*, Kottayam: NBS, 1968 (Malayalam).

Kozhikodan, *Chalachitra Sallappam*, Kottayam: D. C. Books, 1982 (Malayalam).

Krishnakumari, K. V., *Manishi Lo Manishi Dr Akkineni*, Hyderabad: Man, 1992 (Telugu).

Krishnarao, A. N., *Pragitisila Sahitya*, Dharwad: Karnataka Sahitya Mandir, 1944 (Kannada).

Krupanidhi, Uma and Srivastava, Anil (eds), *Montage* Special Issue Satyajit Ray, Bombay, July 1966.

Kulkarni, Shyama Sundar, *Hunsur Krishnamurthy*, Bangalore: Karnataka Chalanachitra Patrakartara Parishat, 1988 (Kannada).

Kulkarni, Shyama Sundar, *Dr Rajkumar*, Bangalore: Karnataka ChalanachitraPatrakartara Parishat, 1988 (Kannada).

Kumar, Prashant (ed.), *Gulzar: Ek Shaksiyat*, Allahabad: Tagore Prakashan, 1973 (Hindi).

Kumar, Uttam, *Amar Ami*, Calcutta: Mitra and Ghosh, 1979 (Bengali).

Lahiri, Sandeep and Rahman, Hafizur (eds), *Satyajit, Ritwik, Mrinal*, Calcutta, Cut-Zoom-Pan, 1982 (Bengali).

Maheshwari, Omkarprasad, *Hindi Chitrapat Ka Geeti Sahitya*, Agra: Vinod Pustak Mandir, 1978.

Mahmud, Hameedduddin, *The Kaleidoscope of Indian Cinema*, New Delhi: Affiliated East-West Press, 1974.

Malhotra, Ramesh (ed.), *Film India Directory 1990*, Bombay: Division of Bombay Trade Information, 1990.

Mammootty, *Chamayangalillathe*, Kottayam: Labour India Publications, ? (Malayalam).

Mane, Anant, *'Anant' Athvani*, Chandrakant Mane (ed.), Pune: Indrayani Sahitya, 1987 (Marathi).

Manimekalai Editorial Board, Monographs on: *T. Rajendar* (1990), *Rajnikant* (1987), *K. Balachander* (1987), *P. Bharathirajaa* (1989), *K. Bhagyaraj* (1983), *Kamalahasan* (1985), *Jayalalitha* (1990), Madras: Manimekalai Prasuram (Tamil).

Manto, Sadat Hasan, *Kingdom's End and Other Stories*, London: Verso, 1987.

Manto, Sadat Hasan, *Meena Bazar* [1962], New Delhi: Rajkamal Publications, 1984 (Hindi).

Mathew, Manarcadu, *Chalachitraswaroopam*, Kottayam: M. Mathew, 1984 (Malayalam).

Marudakasi, A., *Tirai Kavithalam Kavignar A. Marudakasi Padalgal*, Madras: Bhawani Publishers, 1988 (Tamil).

Mehta, Ketan, *Bhavni Bhavai* (Screenplay), Calcutta, Seagull Books, 1986.

Mehta, Ushakant, *Gujarati Chalachitra Parampara: Saat Dashak*, Krishnanagar-New Delhi: Rajesh Prakashan, 1991 (Hindi).

Mehta, Vinod, *Meena Kumari*, Bombay: Jaico, 1972.

Meiyappan, A. V., *Enadhu Vazhkai Anubhavangal*, Madras: Vanadhi Padhipagam, 1974 (Tamil).

Menon, I. K., and Chandavarkar, S. G., *Handbook of the Indian Film Industry*, Bombay: Motion Picture Society of India, 1949.

Menon, I. K. and Chandavarkar, S. G., *Indian Motion Picture Almanac and Who's Who*, Bombay: Film Federation of India, 1953.

Menon, Raghava R., *K. L. Saigal: The Pilgrim of the Swara*, New Delhi: Clarion Books, 1978; new edn.: Hind Pocket Books, 1989.

Merchant, Ismail, *Hullabaloo in Old Jeypore: The Making of Shakespeare Wallah*, London: Viking, 1988.

Mhambre, Gangadhar, *Mounankit Chitrapat Maharshi Phalke Hyanche Charitra*, Bombay: Popular Prakashan, 1976 (Marathi).

Micciollo, Henri, *Guru Dutt*, Paris: Anthologie du cinema, vol. 9, 1978.

Micciollo, Henri, *Satyajit Ray: Pather Panchali*, Paris: L'Avant-scene du cinema no. 214, 1980.

Micciollo, Henri, *Satyajit Ray*, Paris: L'Age d'Homme, 1981.

Mitra, Kamal, *Flashback*, Calcutta: Mandal & Sons, 1989 (Bengali).

Mitra, Premendra, *Snake and Other Stories*, Calcutta: Seagull Books, 1990.

Moholkar, Madhav, *Geetayatri*, Bombay: Mauj Prakashan, 1977 (Marathi).

Mudaliar, Gangadhar, *Jayanthi*, Bangalore: Karnataka Chalanachitra Patrakartara Parishat, 1988 (Kannada).

Mudaliar, P. Sambandam, *Handbook for Tamil Talkies*, Madras: Peerless Press, 1937.

Mudaliar, P. Sambandam, *Talkie Experience in Tamil*, Madras: Peerless Press, 1937 (Tamil).

Mujawar, Isak, *Maharashtra: Birthplace of Indian Film Industry*, Bombay: Govt of Maharashtra, 1965.

Mujawar, Isak, *Dev Anand*, Bombay: Priya Prakashan, 1977.

Mujawar, Isak, *Albela Master Bhagwan*, Bombay: Shalaka Prakashan, 1991 (Marathi).

Mukherjee, Hemanta (with Shankarlal Bhattacharya), *Amar Ganer Swaralipi*, Calcutta, 1988 (Bengali).

Mukherjee, Hrishikesh, *Anand: Hindi Film Script*, New Delhi: Hind Pocket Books, 1971.

Mukherjee, Hrishikesh, *Ashirwad: Film Script*, New Delhi: Hind Pocket Books, 1972.

Mukherjee, Nishit, *Bangla Sahitya-o-Bangla Chalachitra*, Calcutta: Ananda Dhara, 1986 (Bengali).

Mukherjee, Nishit, *Bangla Chalachitrakaar*, Calcutta: Standard, 1987 (Bengali).

Mukherjee, Nishit, *Pramathesh Barua-o-Bangla Chalachitra*, Calcutta: Ananya Prakashan, 1987 (Bengali).

Mukherjee, Probhat, *Hiralal Sen: India's First Film-Maker*, Calcutta: Cine Central, 1966.

Mukherjee, Sailajananda, *Je Katha Bola Hoy Ni*, (compiled by Nakul Chatterjee), Calcutta: Prakash Bhavan, 1968 (Bengali).

Mukhopadhyay, Dilip, *Satyajit*, Calcutta: Banisilpa, 1986.

Mukhopadhyay, Kalish, *Bangla Chalachitra Shilper Itihas 1897-1947*, Calcutta: Rupamancha, 1962 (Bengali).

Mukhopadhyay, Subhash (ed.), *Chalachitra: Barshiki*, Calcutta: Signet Press, 1959 (Bengali).

Muller, Marco (ed.), *Le Avventurose storie del cinema indiano: 1. Scritture e contesti*, Venice: Marsilio, 1985.

Mullick, Pankaj, *Amar Jug Amar Gaan*, Calcutta: Firma KLM, 1980 (Bengali).

Nadkarni, Mohan, *Bal Gandharva: The Nonpareil Thespian*, New Delhi: National Book Trust, 1988.

Nagaiah, Chittor, V., *Swiya Charitra*, Madras: Inturi Venkateshwara Rao, 1983 (Telugu).

Nair, P. K. (ed.), *Fifty Years of Malayalam Cinema*, Trivandrum: Filmotsav 1988 and Kerala State Film Development Corp., 1988.

Namra, Vidyavati, *Hindi Rangmanch Aur Pandit Narayan Prasad 'Betaab'*, Varanasi: Vishwavidyalaya Prakashan, 1972 (Hindi).

Nanda, Ritu, *Raj Kapoor: His Life and His Films*, Bombay: R. K. Films, 1991.

Nandi, Alok B. (ed.), *Satyajit Ray 70 ans. Photographs by Nemai Ghosh*, Brussels: Ed. Eiffel, 1991.

Narayanan, Aranthai, *Tamil Cinemavin Kathai*, Madras: New Century Book House, 1981 (Tamil).

Narayanan, Aranthai, *Nagarikakomal N. S. Krishnan*, Madras: New Century Book House, 1992 (Tamil).

Narwekar, Sanjit (ed.) *Films Division and the Indian Documentary*, Bombay: Publications Division, 1992.

Narwekar, Sanjit (ed.), *Directory of Indian Film-Makers and Films*, London: Flicks Books, 1994.

Natarajan Pillai, T. B., *Cinemavin Thennattu Varalaru*, Thanjavur: ?, 1958 (Tamil).

Nazir, Prem, *Enne Thediyetha Kathapatrangal*, Trivandrum: Prabhath Book House, ? (Malayalam).

Nerurkar, Vishwas (ed.), *Lata Mangeshkar Gandhar Swarayatra*, Kalwa: Smt.

Nerurkar, 1989 (Hindi).

Nyce, Ben, *Satyajit Ray: A Study of his Films*, New York: Praeger, 1988.

Ojha, Rajendra (ed.), *75 Glorious Years of Indian Cinema: Complete Filmography of all Films (Silent and Hindi) Produced between 1913-1988*, Bombay: Screen World, 1988.

Oomen, M. A. and Joseph, K. V., *Economics of Film Industry in India*,

Gurgaon: Academic Press, 1981.

Oomen, M. A. and Joseph, K. V., *Economics of Indian Cinema*, New Delhi: IBH, 1991.

Padgaonkar, Dilip, *L'Esthetique traditionelle indienne appliquee au cinema*,

Paris: University of Paris, unpublished, 1968.

Padgaonkar, Dilip et al. (eds), *Flashback: Cinema in 'The Times of India'*, Bombay: Times of India, 1990.

Paidapaala, *Telugu Cinemapaata*, Madras: Sneha Prachuranalu, 1992 (Telugu).

Pandian, M. S. S., *The Image Trap: M. G. Ramachandran in Film and Politics*, New Delhi: Sage, 1992.

Pandit, Girija, *Rajesh Khanna: Ek Abhineta*, New Delhi: Star, 1973 (Hindi).

Pandit, Prakash (ed.), *Sahir Ludhianvi Aur Unki Shayari*, New Delhi: Rajpal and Sons, 1976 (Hindi).

Pandit, Prakash (ed.), *Shakeel Badaiyuni Aur Unki Shayari*, New Delhi: Rajpal and Sons, s.d. (Hindi).

Paradhaman, *Kalaivanar Vazhvile*, Madras: Paradhaman Publications, 1985 (Tamil).

Parrain, Philippe, *Regards sur le cinema indien*, Paris: Le Cerf, 1969.

Passek, Jean-Loup (ed.), *Le Cinema indien*, Paris: L'Equerre-Centre Georges Pompidou, 1983.

Patel, Baburao (ed.), *Stars of the Indian Screen*, Bombay: Parker and Sons, 1953.

Patil, Dinkar D., *Master Vinayak: Digdarshakancha Digdarshak*, Bombay: Sindhu Prakashan, 1971 (Marathi).

Patil, Dinkar D., *Patlacha Por*, Pune: Prestige Prakashan, 1986 (Marathi).

Patil, Dinkar D., *Ruperi Padada: Tantra Ani Mantra*, Bombay: Majestic

Prakashan, 1988 (Marathi).

Paul, A. (ed.), *Kerala Film Guide*, Calicut: Chitravedi, 1966 (Malayalam).

Paul, Chandra R., *Film and Society: A Study Carried out and Written about Cinema for UNESCO with Reference to the Film Language as Inheritor of Oral and Visual Traditions in India*, New Delhi: UNESCO, s.d.

Pendharkar, Baburao, *Chitra Ani Charitra*, Pune: Vishakha Prakashan, 1961/1983 (Marathi).

Pendharkar, Bhalji, *Sadha Manoos*, Bombay: Mauj Prakashan, 1993 (Marathi).

Perala, Vasanthakumara, *R. Madhusudhan*, Bangalore: Karnataka Chalanachitra

Patrakartara Parishat, 1988 (Kannada).

Pfleiderer, Beatrix and Lutze, Lothar, *The Hindi Film: Agent and Re-Agent of Cultural Change*, New Delhi: Manohar, 1985.

Phadke, Sudhir (ed.), *Chitrasharada*, Bombay: Maharashtra Chitrapat Mahamandal, 1982 (Marathi).

Poddar, N. L. (ed.), *All-India Film Guide*, Calcutta: Kalakunj, 1968.

Pradhan, Snehaprabha, *Snehankita*, Bombay: Popular Prakashan, 1973 (Marathi).

Prasad, Chalasani (ed.), *Sri Sri Upanyasulu*, Hyderabad: Virasam, 1990 (Telugu).

Pym, John, *The Wandering Company. Twenty-One Years of Merchant Ivory Films*, London: British Film Institute, 1983.

Radha Bai, C. A., *An Economic Survey of the Cinematographic Industry in Madras Presidency*, Madras: Madras University, unpublished, 1940.

Radhakrishnan, M. G. (ed.), *Malayalam Cinema: 50 Years*, Bombay: Sahrudaya Film Society, 1989.

Raghava, Ballari, *The South Indian Stage and Other Lectures*, (compiled by V. Srinivasa Sarma and K. Dasapathi Rao), Hyderabad, 1976.

Raghuvanshi, Harish, *Mukesh Film Geet Kosh*, Surat: Audio Vision, 1985 (Hindi).

Raha, Kiranmoy, *Bengali Cinema*, Calcutta: Nandan, 1991.

Rai, Hemendra Kumar, (compiled by Debiprasad Ghosh), *Jatrapathe Chalachitra*, Calcutta: Agami, 1990 (Bengali).

Rajadhyaksha, Ashish, *Ritwik Ghatak: A Return to the Epic*, Bombay: Screen Unit, 1982.

Rajadhyaksha, Ashish and Gangar, Amrit (eds), *Ghatak: Arguments/Stories*, Bombay: Sceen Unit-Research Centre for Cinema Studies, 1987.

Rajadhyaksha, Ashish (ed.), *The Sad and the Glad of Kishore Kumar*, Bombay:

Research Centre for Cinema Studies, 1988.

Rajadhyaksha, Ashish, 'Debating the Third Cinema', in Jim Pines and Paul Willemen (eds), *Questions of Third Cinema*, London: British Film Institute 1989, pp. 170-8.

Rajamohan, O. P., *Adhunika Cinema Moolayavum*, Tellicherry: 1985 (Malayalam).

Ramachandran, T. M, (ed.), *Indian Talkie 1931-81: Fifty Years of Indian Talkies, A Commemorative Volume*, Bombay: Indian Academy of Motion Picture Arts and Sciences, 1981.

Ramachandran, T. M. (ed.), *70 Years of Indian Cinema, 1913-1983*, Bombay: Cinema India-International, 1985.

Ramakrishnaiah, M. V., *Rajendra Singh Babu*, Bangalore: Karnataka Chalanachitra Patrakartara Parishat, 1988 (Kannada).

Ramakrishnaiah, M. V., *R. Nagendra Rao*, Bangalore: Karnataka Chalanachitra Patrakartara Parishat, 1988 (Kannada).

Ramakrishnaiah, M. V. and Narahari Rao, H. H., *A Glimpse of Kannada Cinema*, Bangalore: Suchitra Film Society, 1992.

Ramankutty, K. V., *Malayalam Cinema*, Trivandrum: Govt of Kerala Public Relations Dept, 1988.

Ramankutty, K. V., *Adhunika Malayala Cinema*, Trivandrum: Kerala State Institute of Languages, 1989 (Malayalam).

Rama Rao, Veeranki, *Madras Film Diary*, Madras: 1953/1957.

Ramchandra, C., *Majhya Jeevanacha Sargam*, Pune: Inamdar Bandhu Prakashan, 1977 (Marathi).

Ranga Rao, V. A. K. (ed.), *Bhuvanavijayamu: A Compilation of Ghantasala Venkateshwara Rao's Lyrics*, Madras: Ooha Enterprises, 1972 (Telugu).

Rangaswami, S. (ed.), *Who is Who in Indian Filmland*, Madras: Happy India Office, 1933.

Rangoonwalla, Firoze, *Indian Films Index (1912-1967)*, Bombay: J. Udeshi, 1968.

Rangoonwalla, Firoze, *Indian Filmography: Silent and Hindi Films (1897-1969)*, Bombay: Rangoonwalla-J. Udeshi, 1970.

Rangoonwala, Firoze, *Guru Dutt: 1925-1965*, Pune: NFAI, 1973.

Rangoonwalla, Firoze, *Seventy-Five Years of Indian Cinema*, New Delhi: Indian Book Company, 1975.

Rangoonwalla, Firoze (ed.), *Phalke Centenary Souvenir*, Bombay: Phalke Centenary Celebrations Committee, 1978.

Rangoonwalla, Firoze, *Pictorial History of Indian Cinema*, London: Hamlyn,1979.

Rangoonwalla, Firoze, *Satyajit Ray's Art*, Delhi: Clarion Books, 1980.

Rangoonwalla, Firoze, *Indian Cinema*, New Delhi: Clarion Books, 1983.

Rao, R. Nagendra, *Idu Nanna Kathe: Autobiography* (as told to C. Sitharam), Bangalore: H. V. S. Kala Sahitya Prakashana, 1974 (Kannada).

Ray, Mriganka Sekhar (ed.), *Chalachitra Samiksha*, Calcutta: Federation of Film Societies of India Eastern Zone, 1983 (Bengali).

Ray, R. M. (ed.), *Sangeet Natak Akademi Film Seminar Report: 1955*, New Delhi, Sangeet Natak Akademi, 1956.

Ray, Satyajit, *Autres nouvelles du Bengale*, Paris: Presses de la Renaissance, 1989.

Ray, Satyajit, *Bisoy Chalachchitra* [On Cinema], Calcutta: Ananda, 1976 (Bengali).

Ray, Satyajit, *Bravo! Professor Shonku*, transl. Kathleen M. O'Connell, Calcutta: Rupa, 1986.

Ray, Satyajit et al. (eds), *Chalachitra*, vol. 1, Calcutta: Signet, 1950.

Ray, Satyajit, *Ekei Bole Shooting* [We Call It Shooting], Calcutta: Newscript, 1979 (Bengali).

Ray, Satyajit, *Jakhan Choto Chhilam* [When I Was Small], Calcutta: Ananda, 1982 (Bengali).

Ray, Satyajit, *Kanchanjungha* (Screenplay), Calcutta: Mitra and Ghosh, 1972 (Bengali).

Ray, Satyajit, *La Nuit de l'indigo et autres nouvelles*, Paris: Presses de la Renaissance, 1987.

Ray, Satyajit, *Les Pieces d'or de Jahangir*, Paris: Presses de la Renaissance, 1990.

Ray, Satyajit, *Nayak* (Screenplay), Calcutta: Bengal Publications, 1973.

Ray, Satyajit, *Nonsense Rhymes: Translations of Sukumar Ray's Poetry*, Calcutta: Writers Workshop, 1970.

Ray, Satyajit, *Our Films, Their Films*, Calcutta: Orient Longman, 1976.

Ray, Satyajit, *Pather Panchali* (Satish Bahadur, ed.), Pune: NFAI, 1981.

Ray, Satyajit, *Pather Panchali*, transl. Lila Ray, Calcutta: Cine Central, 1984.

Ray, Satyajit, *Phatikchand*, transl. Lila Ray, Delhi: Orient Paperbacks, 1983.

Ray, Satyajit, *Sera Satyajit*, Calcutta: Ananda, 1991 (Bengali).

Ray, Satyajit, *Sera Sandesh*, Calcutta: Ananda, 1981 (Bengali).

Ray, Satyajit, *Stories*, London: Secker and Warburg, 1987/ *The Unicorn Expedition and Other Fantastic Tales of India*, New York: E.P. Dutton, 1987.

Ray, Satyajit and Basu, Partha (eds), *Sukumar Sahitya Samagra*, 3 vols, Calcutta: Ananda, 1973 (Bengali).

Ray, Satyajit, *The Adventures of Feluda*, New Delhi: Penguin-India, 1985.

Ray, Satyajit, *The Apu Trilogy*, transl. Shampa Bannerjee, Calcutta: Seagull Books, 1985.

Ray, Satyajit, *The Chess Players and Other Screenplays* (Andrew Robinson ed.), London: Faber and Faber, 1989.

Razdan, C. K. (ed.), *Bare Breasts and Bare Bottoms: Anatomy of Film Censorship in India*, Bombay: Jaico Publishing, 1975.

Redi, Ricardo (ed.), *Le Avventurose storie del cinema indiano: 2. Estetiche e industria*, Venice: Marsilio, 1985.

Reddy, Pattabhi Rama, *Pattabhi Panchangam*, Mysore: Telugu Association, 1974 (Telugu).

Reddy, Pattabhi Rama, *Kaita Na Daita*, Nellore: Nellore Progressive Union,1978 (Telugu).

Rehmatullah, Dr, *Parsee Rangmanch Aur Aga Hashr Kashmiri*, Kanpur: Vidyavihar, 1985 (Hindi).

Reuben, Bunny, *Raj Kapoor: The Fabulous Showman, An Intimate Biography*, Bombay: NFDC, 1988.

Roberge, Gaston, *Chitra Bani: A Book on Film Appreciation*, Calcutta: Chitra Bani Publications, 1974.

Roberge, Gaston, *Another Cinema for Another Society*, Calcutta: Seagull Books, 1985.

Roberge, Gaston, *Films for an Ecology of Mind*, Calcutta: Firma KLM, 1978.

Roberge, Gaston, *Mediation: The Action of the Media in our Society*, New Delhi: Manohar Book Service, 1978.

Robinson, Andrew, *Satyajit Ray: The Inner Eye*, London: Andre Deutsch, 1989.

Roy, Arunkumar and Ghosh, Sital, *Satyajit Ray Binna Chokha*, Calcutta: Bharti Book Stall, 1980 (Bengali).

Roy, Arunkumar and Ghosh, Sital, *Twelve Indian Directors*, Calcutta: People's Book Publishing, 1981.

Roy, Arunkumar, *Rabindranath-o-Chalachitra*, Calcutta: Chitralekha, 1986 (Bengali).

Roy, Arunkumar, *Buddhadev Dasgupta*, Calcutta: Cine Society, 1987.

Roy, Biren, *Chalachitra*, Calcutta: Sujit Kumar Dasgupta, 1934 (Bengali).

Roy, Rajat (ed.), *Ritwik-o-Taar Chhabi*, vol. 1, Calcutta: Sampratik, 1979;vol. 2, Calcutta: Annapurna Pustak Mandir, 1983 (Bengali).

Roy, Rajat (ed.), *Filmography of Sixty Eminent Indian Movie-Makers*, Mosaboni: Cinema Society, 1983.

Sahni, Balraj, *Rusi Safarnama*, New Delhi: Rajpal and Sons, 1971 (Hindi).

Sahni, Balraj, *Yaadein*, New Delhi: Major Paper Books, 1972 (Hindi).

Sahni, Balraj, *Meri Film Atamakatha*, New Delhi: Star Pocket Books, 1971 (Hindi); English transl.: *Balraj Sahni By Balraj Sahni*, New Delhi: Hind Pocket Books, 1979.

Samanta, Shakti, *Anuraag Film Script*, New Delhi: Star, 1973.

Saraswathy, M., *Malayalam Cinema-Aranoottandu*, Madras: Perspective, 1987 (Malayalam).

Sarkar, Bidyut, *The World of Satyajit Ray*, New Delhi: UBSPD, 1992.

Sarkar, Kobita, *Indian Cinema Today*, New Delhi: Sterling, 1975.

Sarkar, Kobita, *You Can't Please Everyone: Film Censorship - The Inside Story*, Bombay: IBH Publishing, 1982.

Sastry, K. N. T. (ed.), *Telugu Cinema*, Hyderabad: Cinema Group, 1986.

Sastry, K. N. T., *L. V. Prasad: A Monograph*, Delhi: NFAI/Wiley Eastern, 1993.

Sathe, Vasant (ed.), *Chitrasampada*, Bombay: Jagatik Marathi Parishad, 1989 (Marathi).

Sathe, V. P., *Raj Kapoor Ani Tyache Chitrapat*, Bombay: Granthali, 1978 (Marathi).

Sen, Mrinal, *The Cheat*, Calcutta: Pustakalaya, 1946 (Bengali).

Sen, Mrinal, *Charlie Chaplin*, Calcutta: Shatabdi, 1951 (Bengali).

Sen, Mrinal, *Ami Ebam Chalachitra*, Calcutta: Granthajagat, 1956 (Bengali).

Sen, Mrinal, *Views on Cinema*, Calcutta: Ishan, 1977.

Sen, Mrinal, *Chalachitra Bhut Bartaman Bhabhishya*, Calcutta: Granthaprakash, 1977 (Bengali).

Sen, Mrinal, *In Search of Famine/Akaler Sandhaney* (Screenplay), Calcutta: Seagull Books, 1983.

Sen, Mrinal, *The Ruins/Khandhar* (Screenplay), Calcutta: Seagull Books, 1984.

Sen, Mrinal, *Cinema Adhunikata*, Calcutta: Pratikshan, 1992

Sen, Satu, *Atmasriti-o-Anyanya Prasanga*, Calcutta: Asha Prakashan, 1976 (Bengali).

Sengupta, Bandhan, *Ritwik Chalachitra Katha*, Calcutta: Nabajatak Prakashan, 1982 (Bengali).

Sengupta, Bandhan (ed.), *Indubala*, Calcutta: Moushumi Prakashan, 1983 (Bengali).

Sethna, Phiroze, *Indian Film Industry Today and Tomorrow*, Bombay: Motion Picture Society of India, 1936.

Seton, Mary, *Portrait of a Director: Satyajit Ray*, London: Dennis Dobson, 1971.

Shah, Panna, *The Indian Film*, Bombay: Motion Picture Society of India, 1950; Westport, Conn.: Greenwood Press, 1981.

Shahane, Narmada (transl.), *Studies in Film History: Research Papers on D. G. Phalke*, Pune: FTII, 1970.

Shahane, N. and Bahadur, Satish (eds), *Phalke Centenary Volume*, Pune: FTII, 1971.

Shantaram, V., *Shantarama : The Autobiography of V. Shantaram* (as told to Madhura Jasraj), Bombay: Rajkamal Kalamandir, 1986 (Marathi/Hindi).

Sharda, Ratan (ed.), *Collections (1991-92)*, New Delhi: Update Video, 1991.

Shastri, Devdutt (ed.), *Prithviraj Kapoor Abhinandan Granth*, Allahabad: Vishal Manch, 1963 (Hindi).

Sheth, Ajit (ed.), *Guzar Gaya Woh Zamana*, Bombay: Pankaj Mullick Foundation, 1981 (Gujarati).

Shinde, M. K., *Shinde's Dictionary of Cine Arts and Crafts*, Bombay: Popular Prakashan, 1962.

Singh, Har Mandir (ed.), *Hindi Film Geet Kosh 1931-40; 1941-50; 1951-60; 1961-70*, 4 vols, Kanpur: Satinder Kaur, 1988, 1984, 1980, 1986 respectively (Hindi).

Singh, R. P., *Talat Geet Kosh*, Kanpur, 1992.

Sivathamby, Karthigesu, *The Tamil Film as a Medium of Political Communication*, Madras: New Century Book House, 1981.

Som, Ashim (ed.), *Chalachitra Katha*, Calcutta: Ruprekha, 1969 (Bengali).

Spivak, Gayatri Chakravorty, *Outside in the Teaching Machine*, New York and London: Routledge, 1993.

Srinivas Rao, Srirangam, *Mahaprasthanam*, Hyderabad: Vishal-Andhra, 1950 (Telugu).

Srivastava, Bachchan, *Bhartiya Filmon Ki Kahani*, New Delhi: Rajpal and Sons, 1962 (Hindi).

Srivastava, Rajiv, *Mukesh: Surile Safar Ki Kahani*, Sultanpur: Mamata Rajiv, 1993 (Hindi).

Subba Rao, V. N., Ramakrishnaiah, M. V. and Dr Vijaya (eds), *Kannada Cinema*, Bangalore: Karnataka Chamber of Commerce, 1992.

Sundaresan, V., *Cinema Innale Innu*, Trivandrum: Geethanjali, 1986 (Malayalam).

Suresha, B., *P. Bhaktavatsalam*, Bangalore: Karnataka Chalanachitra Patrakartara Parishat, 1989 (Kannada).

Sureshchandra, Lingenahalli, *Rajan-Nagendra*, Bangalore: Karnataka Chalanachitra Patrakartara Parishat, 1988 (Kannada).

Suryakant, *Dhakti Pati*, Pune: Purandara Prakashan, 1986 (Marathi).

Swaminathan, Venkat, *Agraharathil Kazhuthai* (Screenplay), Trivandrum: Sruti, 1979 (Malayalam).

Tamhane, Lalitha, *Smita Smit Ani Mi*, Pune: Sankalp Prakashan, 1989 (Marathi).

Tembe, Govindrao, *Mazha Sangeet Vyasanga* (compiled by Vamanrao

Deshpande), Bombay: Maharashtra Rajya Sahitya Sanskriti Mandal, 1984 (Marathi).
Tendulkar, Vijay, *The Churning/Manthan* (Screenplay), Calcutta: Seagull Books, 1984.
Tendulkar, Vijay, *The Threshold/Umbartha* (Screenplay), Calcutta: Seagull Books, 1985.
Tesson, Charles, *Satyajit Ray*, Paris: Cahiers du cinema, 1992.
Thiranavukarasu, Ka., *Dravidar Iyakkamum Thiraipada Ulagamum*, Madras: Manivasahar Publications, 1990 (Tamil).
Thomas, M. F. (ed.), *Adoorinte Lokam*, Calicut: Mulberry Books, 1976 (Malayalam).
Toeplitz, Jerzy, *Indian Films and Western Audiences*, Paris: UNESCO, 1964.
Ullaha, Dr Rahmat, *Parsi Rangmanch Aur Aga Hashr Kashmiri*, Kanpur: Vidyavihar, 1985.
Urs, Kemparaj, *Alvat Varshalu* (date unknown, private publication) and *Naanu*, 1979. (Kannada).
Valicha, Kishore, *The Moving Image: A Study of Indian Cinema*, Hyderabad: Orient Longman, 1988.
Vallachira, Aravindan, *Athmanintayude Pookkal*, Kozhikode: Kerala, Poorna Pubs, 1991 (Malayalam).
Vasudev, Aruna, *Liberty and Licence in the Indian Cinema*, New Delhi: Vikas, 1978.
Vasudev, Aruna, *The Role of the Cinema in Promoting Popular Participation in Cultural Life in India*, Paris: UNESCO, 1981.
Vasudev, Aruna, *The Film Industry's Use of the Traditional and Contemporary Performing Arts*, Paris: UNESCO, 1982.
Vasudev, Aruna and Lenglet, Philippe (eds), *Indian Cinema Superbazaar*, New Delhi: Vikas, 1983.
Vasudev, Aruna and Lenglet, Philippe (eds), *Les cinemas indiens*, Paris: Le Cerf-CinemAction, 1984.
Vasudev, Aruna, *The New Indian Cinema*, Delhi: Macmillan India, 1986.
Vasudevan, Ravi, *Errant Males and the Divided Woman: Melodrama and Sexual Difference in the Hindi Social Film of the 1950s*, 2 vols, unpublished, University of East Anglia, Norwich, 1991.
Vasudevan Nair, M. T., *Catching an Elephant and Other Stories*, transl. V. Abdulla, Calcutta: Rupa and Co., 1991.
Veeranna, Gubbi, *Kaleye Kayaka*, Mysore: Suruchi Prakashana, 1967.
Velavam, Sanghai (ed.), *Udumalai Narayana Kavi*, Madras: Dravidar Kazhagam, 1986 (Tamil).
Venkateshwara Rao, Inturi, *Nagaiah Smaraka Sanchika*, Madras: 1977.
Venkatnarayan, S., *NTR: A Biography*, New Delhi: Vikas, 1983.
Venkatramana, Mullapudi, *Andala Ramudu*, Vijaywada: Sakshi Books/Navodaya, 1973 (Telugu).
Verma, Madanlal, *Nirupa Roy Ki Abhinay Kala*, Agra: Vidyarthi Prakashan, 1954 (Hindi).
Vijaya et al. (eds), *Kannada Vakchitra Suvarna Mahotsava: 1934-1984 Smarana Sanchike*, Bangalore: Karnataka Chalanachitra Vanijya Mandal, 1984 (Kannada).
Vijayalakshmi, S., *The Impact of Film*, Madras: Centre for Social Research, 1974.
Vijaykrishnan, *Karuppum Veluppum Varnangalum*, Trivandrum: Soorya, 1986 (Malayalam).
Vijaykrishnan, *Malayala Cinemayude Katha*, Trivandrum: Kerala State Film Development Corp., 1987 (Malayalam).
Vindhan, *M. K. T. Bhagavathar Kadhai*, Madras: Madras Poothaga Poonga, 1983 (Tamil).
Wadia, J. B. H., *Looking Back on my 'Romance' with Films*, Bombay: Jayant Art Printers, 1955.
Wadia, J. B. H., *Those Were the Days: Being a Romanticised Account of my Early Years and Career as a Silent Film-maker between 1928 and 1933*, unpublished MS, Pune: NFAI, 1977.
Wadia, J. B. H., *M. N. Roy - The Man: An Incomplete Royana*, Bombay: Popular Prakashan, 1983.
Wadkar, Hansa, *Sangtye Aika: Autobiography* (as told to Arun Sadhu), Pune: Rajhans Prakashan, 1970 (Marathi).
Watve, Bapu, *V. Damle and S. Fattelal*, Pune: NFAI, 1985.
Willemen, Paul and Gandhy, Behroze (eds), *Indian Cinema*, London: British Film Institute, 1980.
Willemen, Paul and Pines, Jim (eds), *Questions of Third Cinema*, London: British Film Institute, 1989.
Yadav, Yogesh S., *Hindi Film Singers 1931-1981*, Baroda: Y. S. Yadav, 1987 (Hindi).
Yagnik, Indulal, *Atmakatha*, vols 1-3, Nenpur: Vatrak Khedut Vidyalaya, 1955; vols 4 and 5, Ahmedabad: Gurjar Granth Rathna Karyalaya, 1969-71; vol. 6, Ahmedabad: Mahagujarat Seva Trust, 1973 (Gujarati).

ESSAYS/JOURNALS/CATALOGUES

Abbas, Khwaja Ahmed, 'Supreme Court Judgment on *A Tale of Four Cities*', *Screen*, Bombay, 4, 11 and 18 December, 1970.
Ahmed, Akbar S., 'Bombay Films: The Cinema as Metaphor for Indian Society and Politics', *Modern Asian Studies*, vol. 26, no. 2, May 1992.
Ali, Abdul (ed.) *Mehboob Revisited*, Bombay: Cine Society, 1977.
Ali, Abdul (ed.) *New Theatres*, Bombay: Cine Society, 1979.
Ali, Abdul (ed.), *Prakash Pictures*, Bombay: Cine Society, 1984.
Ali, Abdul (ed.), *J. B. H. Wadia*, Bombay: Cine Society, 1987.
Ali, Abdul (ed.), *A. R. Kardar*, Bombay: Cine Society, 1990.
Ali, Abdul (ed.), *Phani Majumdar*, Bombay: Cine Society, 1992.
Ali, Abdul (ed.), *Fearless Nadia*, Bombay: Cine Society, 1993.
Arora, Poonam, 'The Woman Caught between *The Home and The World*: The Erotics of Regionalism and Nationalism in Satyajit Ray's Film', unpublished paper, 1992.
Atre, P. K., 'Mi Patakatha Lekhak Kasa Jhalo', *Huns Film Number*, Bombay, August 1949 (Marathi).
Bal Gandharva, 'Autobiographical Statement', in J. S. Tilak (ed.), *Kesari*, Diwali Special, Pune: October 1962.
Barua, P. C., 'Barua Memorial Issue', *Shot*, Calcutta, B. Jha (ed.), December 1951-January 1952.
Benimadhab (ed.), *Shilpir Preithibi: Dr Bhupen Hazarika Bishesh Sankhya*, special issue on Bhupen Hazarika, Guwahati, October 1981 (Assamese).
Bhaduri, Sisir, 'Sisir Bhaduri on Independence: Independence and our Stage', in Sudhi Pradhan (ed.), *Marxist Cultural Movement: Chronicles and Documents*, vol. 2, Calcutta: Navana, 1982.
Bhatt, Mahesh, 'Sex in Indian Cinema: Only Bad People Do It', in Rinki Bhattacharya (ed.), *Uncertain Liaisons: Sex, Strife and Togetherness in Urban India*, New Delhi: Penguin Books India, 1993.
Bhatt, Vijay, 'Nirmatani Najare Rooperi Srishti: Autobiography', *Janmabhoomi*, Bombay, 7 January 1968 (Gujarati).
Bhavnani, Mohan, 'Enlightening the Nation with the Documentary', *Filmfare*, Bombay, 21 March 1952.
Bhide, G. R., 'Bhalji Pendharkar', *Sahyadri*, Pune, May 1949 (Marathi).
Bhowmik, Someswar, 'The State of the Indian Film Industry', *Splice*, no. 2, Calcutta, July 1986.
Binford, Mira Reym, 'The Two Cinemas of India', in John H. D. Downing (ed.), *Film and Politics in the Third World*, New York: Automedia Inc., 1987.
Binford, Mira Reym, 'Innovation and Initation in the Indian Cinema', in Wimal Dissanayake (ed.), *Cinema and Cultural Identity - Reflections on Films from Japan, India and China*, Lanham: University Press of America, 1988, pp. 77-92.
Binford, Mira Reym (ed.), 'Indian Popular Cinema', *Quarterly Review of Film and Video*, vol. 11, no. 3, Los Angeles, 1989.
Breur, W. et al., *A Retrospective of Films by Paul Zils*, New Delhi: Max Muller Bhavan, 1981.
Chajlani, Abhay (ed.), *Sargam Ka Safar*, Indore: *Nai Duniya* Film Special, June 1989 (Hindi).
Chajlani, Abhay (ed.), *Parde Ki Pariyan: 1913-1990*, Indore: *Nai Duniya* Film Special 1990 (Hindi).
Chajlani, Abhay (ed.), *Nayak Mahanayak*, Indore: *Nai Duniya*, 1992 (Hindi).
Chakravarty, Sumita S., 'National Identity and the Realist Aesthetic: Indian Cinema of the Fifties', *Quarterly Review of Film and Video*, vol.11, no. 3, Los Angeles, 1989.
Chandavarkar, Bhaskar, 'The Tradition of Music in Indian Cinema', *Cinema in India*, vol. 1, no. 2 (April 1987) to vol. 3, no. 3 (July-September 1989), Bombay.
Chatterjee, Partha, 'Ray's Home, Ray's World: Calcutta', *Cinemaya*, no. 20, New Delhi, Summer 1993.
Chatterjee, Pashupati, 'Banglar Chalachitra Shilpa', in Ashim Som (ed.), *Chalachitra Katha*, Calcutta: Ruprekha, 1969 (Bengali).
Chopra, B. R., 'NFDC: The Dividing Line', *Screen*, Bombay, 3 May, 1985.
Choudhury, Salil, 'Modern Bengali Music in Crisis', in S. Pradhan (ed.), *Marxist Cultural Movement in India*, vol. 3, Calcutta: Santi Pradhan-Pustak Bipani, 1985.

Das, Veena 'The Mythological Film and its Framework of Meaning: an Analysis of *Jai Santoshi Maa*', *India International Centre Quarterly*, vol. 8, no. 1, New Delhi, March 1980.

Dasgupta, Buddhadev, 'Poetry in Cinema', *Cinema in India*, Bombay, January-April 1988.

Dasgupta, Buddhadev, 'The Poetry and Politics of Cinema', Interview with Samik Bandyopadhyay, *Splice*, Calcutta, January-March 1986.

Das Gupta, Chidananda, 'The Cultural Basis of Indian Cinema' (1968), *Talking about Films*, New Delhi: Orient Longman, 1981.

Das Gupta, Chidananda, 'The Painted Face of Politics: The Actor Politicians of South India', in Wimal Dissanayake (ed.), *Cinema and Cultural Identity: Reflections on Films from Japan, India and China*, Lanham:

University Press of America, 1988, pp. 127-48.

Datt, Gopal (ed.), *Close-Up: The Indian Film Scene*, special issue, vol. 3, nos. 5-6, Bombay: Film Forum, 1970.

Desai, Chimanlal B., *Presidential Address, Second All-India Motion Picture Convention*, Madras, 1936.

Desai, Vasant, 'Bas Jhali Sangeetachi Gulamgiri', *Huns Film Special*, Bombay, 8 May 1950 (Marathi).

Dhondy, Farrukh, 'Keeping Faith: Indian Film and its World', *Daedalus*, Fall 1985.

Dutt Utpal, 'An Armoured Car on the Road to Proletarian Revolution', Interview with Mihir and Malini Bhattacharya, *Journal of Arts and Ideas*, no. 8, New Delhi, July-September 1984.

Gandhy, Behroze and Thomas, Rosie, 'Three Indian Film Stars', in Christine

Gledhill (ed.), *Stardom: Industry of Desire*, London: Routledge, 1991.

Ganguly, Dhirendranath, 'Evidence', *Indian Cinematograph Committee 1927-28*, vol. 2, Calcutta: Central Publications Branch, Govt of India, 1928.

Ghatak, Ritwik, 'An Interview with Ritwik Ghatak', Ravi Ojha and Judhajit Sarkar, *Film Miscellany*, Pune: FTII, 1976.

Ghosh, Bishnupriya, 'Satyajit Ray's *Devi*: Constructing a Third-World Feminist Critique', *Screen*, vol. 33, no. 2, London, Summer 1992.

Ghosh, Gautam, 'Cinema of the Dispossessed', Interview with Khalid Mohammed, *Cinema in India*, Bombay, April-June 1988.

Ghosh, Gautam, 'Closing in on the Elemental', Interview with Samik Bandyopadhyay, *Splice*, no. 4, Calcutta: Seagull Books, 1988.

Ghosh, Kaliprasad, 'Jiban Sriti', *Rupamancha*, Calcutta: Poush-Magh, 1956.

Ghosh, Nemai, 'In Memory of Nemai Ghosh', *Chitravas* special issue, Calcutta: North Calcutta Film Society, Nemai Ghosh Festival Special, 1990.

Gopalan, Lalitha, 'Gangsterism and Regionalism: *Nayakan*, Masculinity in India Cinema', unpublished paper, 1992.

Gopal Singh, Madan, 'Ray and the Realist Conscience', *Cinemaya*, no. 20, New Delhi, Summer 1993.

Gupta, Udayan, 'New Visions in Indian Cinema', in John H. D. Downing (ed.), *Film and Politics in the Third World*, New York: Automedia Inc., 1987.

Guy, Randor, 'Once upon a City', weekly column in *Aside*, Madras, 1988-9.

Hameeduddin Mahmood, 'Sulochana', *Filmfare*, Bombay, 15-28 October 1976.

Hansen, Kathryn, 'Hindi New Cinema: Basu Chatterjee's *Sara Akash*', *South Asia*, new series, vol. 4, no. 1, 1981.

Hansen, Kathryn, '*Tisri Kasam*: The Story and the Film', *Journal of South Asian Literature*, vol. 23, no. 1, 1981.

Hardgrave Jr, Robert L., 'The Celluloid God: M. G. R. and the Tamil Film', *South Asian Review*, vol. 4, July 1971.

Hardgrave Jr, Robert L. and Neidhart, Anthony C., 'Film and Political Consciousness in Tamil Nadu', *Economic and Political Weekly*, Bombay, 1 January 1975.

Hirlekar, K. S., *The Place of Film in National Planning*, Bombay: Visual Education Society, 1938.

Jaffrey, Saeed, 'Memories of Ray', *Sight and Sound*, vol. 2, no. 4, London, August 1992.

Jag Mohan (ed.), *The Sukhdev Retrospective: An Introduction to the Man and his Documentary Films*, Bombay: Ministry of Information and Broadcasting, Films Division, 1990.

Jha, Prakash, 'Going Back to Grassroots', Interview with Deepa Gahlot, *Cinema in India*, Bombay, April 1987.

Joshi, Manilal, 'Directing Yane Film Directorni Jokhamdari', *Mouj Majah*, Bombay, 21 April 1926 (Gujarati).

Joshi, Manilal, *Mouj Majah* special issue, Bombay, 10 April 1934 (Gujarati).

Kak, Siddharth (ed.), *Cinema Vision* (4 issues), Bombay, 1980.

Kale, K. Narayan, 'Rangabhoomi 1940-1970: Simhavalokan Ani Samalochan', in Kale et al. (eds), *Marathi Rangabhoomi Marathi Natak*, Bombay: Mumbai Marathi Sahitya Sangh, 1971 (Marathi).

Kale, K. Narayan, 'Mazha Mulgachya Nimittane', *Sahyadri*, Pune, February 1939.

Kale, K. Narayan, 'Majhya Parichayache Shriyut Keshavrao Date', *Sahyadri*, Bombay, November 1950 (Marathi).

Kale, Pramod, 'Ideas, Ideals and the Market: A Study of Marathi Films', *Economic and Political Weekly*, Bombay, 1 September 1979.

Kapoor, Raj, 'Efflorescence of Little Man Image in *Joker*', *Screen*, Bombay, 18 December 1970.

Kapur, Geeta, 'Mythic Material in Indian Cinema', *Journal of Arts and Ideas*, nos. 14-15, New Delhi, July-December 1987.

Kapur, Geeta, 'Articulating the Self into History', in Jim Pines and Paul Willemen (eds), *Questions of Third Cinema*, London: BFI, 1989, pp. 179-94.

Kapur, Geeta, 'Cultural Creativity in the First Decade: The Example of Satyajit Ray', *Journal of Arts and Ideas*, nos. 23-24, New Delhi, January 1993.

Karanjia, B. K., 'The State's Responsibility to Cinema', *Cinema in India*, Bombay, July-September 1987.

Kararkasis, Pantelis, Ntritzou, Katerian and Sava, Vasso, 'Das Andere Kino in Indien', *Filmfaust*, nos. 28-29, Frankfurt am Main, 1982.

Kaul, Mani, 'Communication', *Seminar*, New Delhi, 1974.

Kaul, Mani, 'Exploration in New Film Techniques', *Indian Film Culture*, no. 8, Bombay, Federation of Film Societies of India, Autumn 1974.

Kaul, Mani, 'Seen from Nowhere', in Kapila Vatsyayan (ed.), *Concepts ofSpace: Ancient and Modern*, New Delhi: Indira Gandhi National Centre For Art/Abhinav Publications, 1991.

Khan, Pervaiz, 'Ritwik Ghatak and Some Directions for the Future', *Sight and Sound*, vol. 1, no. 5, London, September 1991.

Koch, Gerhard, 'Franz Osten's Role in the German Cinema', *German Studies in India*, vol. 8, nos. 2-3, Trivandrum: University of Kerala, 1984.

Koch, Gerhard, 'Franz Osten: Regisseur', *Cinegraph: Lexikon zum deutschsprachigen Film*, Munich: Hans-Michael Bock, 1985.

Krishen, Pradeep (ed.), 'Indian Popular Cinema: Myth, Meaning and Metaphor', special issue of *India International Centre Quarterly*, vol. 8, no. 1, New Delhi, March 1980.

Krishen, Pradeep, 'Knocking at the Doors of Public Culture: India's Parallel Cinema', *Public Culture*, vol. 4, no. 1, Philadelphia, Fall 1991.

Lakshmi, C. S., 'Seduction, Speeches and Lullaby: Gender and Cultural Identity in a Tamil Film', unpublished paper, 1992.

Lakshminarayan, N., 'Kannada Cinema towards World Show Window', *Kannada Films Supplement*, Bangalore: Directorate of Information and Publicity, 1977.

Lankesh, P. (ed.), *Lankesh Patrike*, Bangalore: Deepavali Film Special Issues, 1986, 1987, 1988.

Majumdar, Swapan, (ed.), *Satyajit Ray Retrospective Souvenir*, vol. 1, Calcutta, 1975, vol. 2, 1979.

Mir, Ezra, 'What is a Good Documentary Film?', in T. M. Ramachandran (ed.), *Fifty Years of Indian Talkies (1931-1981)*, Bombay: Indian Academy of

Motion Picture Arts and Sciences, 1981.

Mishra, Vijay, 'Towards a Theoretical Critique of Bombay Cinema', *Screen*, vol. 26, nos. 3-4, London, May-August 1985.

Mishra, Vijay, Jeffrey, Peter and Shoesmith, Brian, 'The Actor as Parallel Text in Bombay Cinema', *Quarterly Review of Film and Video*, vol. 11, no. 3, Los Angeles, 1989.

Mitra, Ananda, 'Interconnection and Cross-Overs Between Film and Television in India', unpublished paper, 1988.

Mordekar, Raghavendra, 'Bhalji Pendharkaranche Marathi Bolpat', *Yeshwant*, Bombay, June 1941 (Marathi).

Mordekar, Raghavendra, 'Shriyut Khandekaranche Marathi Bolpat', *Yeshwant*, Bombay, August 1941 (Marathi).

Muller, Marco (ed.), *Ritwik Ghatak: The Burning Tiger*, Rotterdam Film Festival/NFM/IAF, 1990.

Munshi, Leelavati, 'Women and Film Industry', in Shyam Kumari Nehru (ed.), *Our Cause: A Symposium by Indian Women*, pp. 158-164, Allahabad: Kitabistan, 1938.

Nandy, Ashish, 'How "Indian" is Ray?', *Cinemaya*, no. 20, New Delhi, Summer 1993.

Niranjana, Tejaswini, 'Cinema, Femininity and the Economy of Consumption', *Economic and Political Weekly*, vol. 24, no. 43, Bombay, 26 October 1991.

Niranjana, Tejaswini, 'Integrating Whose Nation: Tourists and Terrorists in *Roja*', *Economic and Political Weekly*, vol. 24, no. 3, Bombay, 15 January 1994.

Noorani, A. G., 'Censoring *Behind The Barricade*', *Economic and Political Weekly*, vol. 27, no. 36, Bombay, 4 September 1993.

Padukone, Vasanthi, 'My Son Gurudutt', *Imprint*, Bombay: Business Press, April 1979.

Painter, Baburao, 'Rangabhoomi Ani Vastralankaar', *Pravinya Film Special*, Bombay, October-November 1933 (Marathi).

Painter, Baburao, 'Interview', *Screen*, Bombay, 23 May, 1952.

Pal, Niranjan, 'Such Is Life', excerpted in *Screen*, Bombay, 28 September 1984 and in *Filmfare*, Bombay, 16-31 December 1983.

Pandian, M. S. S., '*Parasakthi*: Life and Times of a DMK Film', *Economic and Political Weekly*, vol. 26 nos 11-12, Bombay, March 1991.

Paranjpe, Raja, 'Majhya Shabdaat Mi', *Rudravani*, Pune, 25 June 1975 (Marathi).

Patil, Dinkar D., 'Marathi Kautumbik Chitrache Pravartak: Datta Dharmadhikari', *Rasrang*, Nasik, 15 January 1983 (Marathi).

Pendakur, Majunath, 'New Cultural Technologies and the Fading Glitter of Indian Cinema', *Quarterly Review of Film and Video*, vol. 11, no. 3, Los Angeles, 1989.

Pendakur, Manjunath, 'India', in John A. Lent, *The Asian Film Industry*, Bromley: Christopher Helm, 1990, pp. 229-252.

Pendharkar, Bhalji, *Rasarang* special issue, Nasik, 15 August 1981 (Marathi).

Phalke, Dadasaheb, 'Interview', *Kesari*, Pune, 19 August 1913.

Phalke, Dadasaheb, 'Evidence', *Indian Cinematographic Committee 1927-28*, vol. 3, Calcutta: Central Publications Branch, 1928.

Phalke, Dadasaheb, 'Bharatiya Chitrapat', *Navyug*, Bombay, November-December 1917, February/September 1918 (Marathi); transl. in Firoze Rangoonwalla (ed.), *Phalke Centenary Souvenir*, Bombay: Phalke Centenary Celebrations Committee, 1978.

Phalke, Dadasaheb, 'Swadeshi Moving Pictures', transl. N. S. Shahane, *Continuum*, vol. 2, no. 1, Perth, 1988-9, pp. 51-73.

Premchand, Munshi, 'Cinema Aur Sahitya', *Lekhak*, Allahabad, 1935.

Rajadhyaksha, Ashish, 'Neo-Traditionalism', *Framework*, nos. 32-33, London, 1986.

Rajadhyaksha, Ashish, 'The Phalke Era: Conflict of Traditional Form and Modern Technology', *Journal of Arts and Ideas*, nos. 14-15, New Delhi, July-December 1987.

Rajadhyaksha, Ashish, 'Beyond Orientalism', *Sight and Sound*, vol. 2, no. 4, London, August 1992.

Rajadhyaksha, Ashish, 'Satyajit Ray, Ray's Films and Ray-movie', *Journal of Arts and Ideas*, nos. 23-24, New Delhi, 1993.

Rajadhyaksha, Ashish, 'Fundamental Films', *Sight and Sound*, vol. 3, no. 10, London, October 1993.

Rajadhyaksha, Ashish, 'The Epic Melodrama: Themes of Nationality in Indian Cinema', *Journal of Arts and Ideas*, nos. 25-26, New Delhi, 1993.

Ranade, Ashok, 'Popular Culture and Music', *International Pop Culture: India*, special issue, vol. 2, no. 1.

Ranade, Ashok (ed.), *Sangeet Natak*, special issue *Hindi Film Music*, no. 100, New Delhi: Sangeet Natak Akademi, April-June 1991.

Ranga Rao, V. A. K., 'Cultural Dissemination through Cinema', in *Indian Cinema 1990*, K. N. T. Sastry (ed.), New Delhi: Directorate of Film Festivals, 1991, pp. 1-13.

Roy, Charu, 'Interview', *Chitravas*, Calcutta: North Calcutta Film Society, vol. 21, nos. 3-4, July-December 1987.

Sandow, Raja, 'The Memoirs of Raja Sandow', *The Movie Mirror*, vol. 2, nos. 7/8, Madras, 1928.

Sen, Anil (ed.), *Chitrabikshan*, Annual Number, Calcutta, 1975.

Sen, Anil (ed.), *Chitrabikshan*, special issue on Ghatak, Calcutta: January-April 1976.

Sen, Mrinal, 'Towards Another Moment of Truth', *Cinema in India*, Bombay, October-December, 1987.

Shahani, Kumar, 'The Saint Poets of Prabhat' (1981), in T. M. Ramachandran (ed.), *70 Years of Indian Cinema, 1913-1983*, Bombay: Cinema India-International, 1985.

Shahani, Kumar, 'Dossier', *Framework*, nos. 30-31, London, 1986.

Shahani, Kumar, 'In the Forest of the Night', *Times Of India*, Bombay, 5 July 1987.

Shahani, Kumar, 'The Passion of a Resurrected Spring' (1985), in Rajadhyaksha, Ashish and Gangar, Amrit (eds), *Ghatak: Arguments/Stories*, Bombay: Sceen Unit-Research Centre for Cinema Studies, 1987.

Shahani, Kumar, 'Film As A Contemporary Art', *Social Scientist*, vol. 18, no. 3, New Delhi, March 1990.

Shahani, Kumar, 'Interrogating Internationalism', *Journal of Arts and Ideas*, no. 19, New Delhi, May 1990.

Sharma, Kidar, 'Cupid Directs the Film', *Filmfare*, Bombay, 8 August 1952.

Sheth, Ajit, 'Tagore And Cinema', *National Centre for the Performing Arts Quarterly Journal*, vol. 10, no. 3, Bombay, September 1981.

Singh, Anup, 'Mani Kaul, *The Idiot*: Senses/Spaces', *Pix*, no. 1, London, Winter 1993-94.

Singh, Anup, 'Time as the Play of Subjectivity: A Note on Mani Kaul's *Siddheshwari*, *Deep Focus*, vol. 3, no. 2, Bangalore, 1990.

Singh, Bikram, 'More about the Indian New Wave', *Filmfare*, Bombay, 14 January 1971.

Sinha, Tapan, 'The Director of Today', *Screen*, Bombay, 24 September 1971.

Sinha, Tapan, 'Popular Cinema With A Conscience', *Splice*, no. 2, Calcutta, 1986.

Skillman, Teri, 'Songs in Hindi Films: Nature and Function', in Wimal Dissanayake (ed.), *Cinema and Cultural Identity: Reflections on Films from Japan, India and China*, Lanham: University Press of America, 1988, pp. 149-58.

Slingo, Carol J., 'The Malayalam Commercial Cinema and the Films of Mammootty', *Asian Cinema*, vol. 5, no. 1, Hamden, Conn.: Asian Cinema Studies Society, Quinnipiac College, 1990.

Spivak, Gayatri Chakravorty, 'Once again a Leap into the Postcolonial Banal', in Peter Collier and Helga Geyer-Ryan (eds), *Literary Theory Today*, Cambridge: Polity Press, 1990.

Spivak, Gayatri Chakravorty, 'Acting Bits, Identity Talk', *Critical Inquiry*, no. 18, Summer 1992, pp. 770-803.

Spivak, Gayatri Chakravorty, 'Marginality in the Teaching Machine' and '*Sammy and Rosie Get Laid*', in *Outside in the Teaching Machine*, New York and London: Routledge, 1993.

Srivatsan, R., 'Looking at Film Hoardings: Labour, Gender, Subjectivity and Everyday Life in India', *Public Culture*, vol. 4, no. 1, Philadelphia, Fall 1991.

Sundar, Shiv, 'Nirbak Chalachitra Pariyalochana', *Bharati*, vol. 1, Calcutta 1923 (Bengali).

Talwalkar, Govind (ed.), 'Bal Gandharva Janma Shatabdi Visheshank', *Maharashtra Times Special*, Bombay, 1987 (Marathi).

Tarafdar, Rajen, 'Rajen Tarafdar Issue', *Chitravas*, vol. 24, nos. 2-4, Calcutta, North Calcutta Film Society, April-December 1989.

Tembe, Govindrao, 'Chalachitrapat: Chitrapatache Kathanak', in N. S. Phadke (ed.), *Ratnakar*, Pt. 1, pp. 654-9 (1930); Pt. 2, pp. 918-24 (1930); Pt. 3, pp. 305-14 (1931), Pune (Marathi).

Tharu, Susie, 'Third World Women's Cinema: Notes on Narrative, Reflections on Opacity', *Economic and Political Weekly*, Bombay, 17 May 1986.

Thomas, Rosie, 'Indian Cinema: Pleasures and Popularity', *Screen*, London, vol. 26, nos. 3-4, 1985.

Thomas, Rosie, 'India: Mythologies and Modern India', in William Luhr (ed.), *World Cinema Since 1945*, pp. 301-29, New York: Ungar, 1987.

Thomas, Rosie, 'Sanctity and Scandal: The Mythologisation of *Mother India*', *Quarterly Review of Film and Video*, vol. 11, no. 3, Los Angeles, 1989.

Toeplitz, Jerzy, 'National Characteristics of the Indian Cinema', *Close-up*, vol. 3, nos. 5-6, Bombay, 1970.

Vasudev, Aruna, 'The Woman: Myth and Reality in the Indian Cinema', in Wimal Dissanayake (ed.), *Cinema and Cultural Identity: Reflections on Films from Japan, India and China*, Lanham: University Press of America, 1988, pp. 107-26.

Vasudevan, Ravi, 'The Melodramatic Mode and the Commercial Hindi Cinema: Notes on Film History, Narrative and Performance in the 1950s', *Screen*, London, vol. 30, no. 3, 1989.

Vasudevan, Ravi, 'Glancing Off Reality', *Cinemaya*, New Delhi, Summer, 1992.

Vasudevan, Ravi, 'Shifting Codes, Dissolving Identities: The Hindi Social Film of the 1950s as Popular Culture', *Journal of Arts and Ideas*, nos. 23-24, New Delhi, 1993.

Velicheti, Rajeev, 'Women, Violence and Telangana: Changing Constructions in Telugu Cinema', Hyderabad: Anveshi/Subaltern Studies Conference, unpublished paper, 1993.

INDEX

A

Abhayam Thedi (**I.V. Sasi**, Mal, 1986)
Abhi (Apurba Mitra, B, 1980)
Abhi Abhi (S.P. Rajaram, H, 1992)
Abhigyan/Abhagin (Prafulla Roy, B/H, 1938)
Abhijaan (*aka* The Expedition: **Satyajit Ray**, B, 1962)
Abhijaan (Sujit Singh, A, 1973)
Abhijathyam (*aka* False Pride: **A. Vincent**, Mal, 1971)
Abhijatya (**Sukumar Dasgupta**, B, 1949)
Abhijeet (K.V. Raju, K, 1993)
Abhijog (**Sushil Majumdar**, B, 1947)
Abhilasha (Mahendra Thakore/**Zia Sarhadi**, H, 1938)
Abhilasha (Amit Bose, H, 1968)
Abhilasha (A. Kodandarami Reddy, Tel, 1983)
Abhilasha (Sadhu Meher, O, 1983)
Abhimaan (Binoy Bannerjee, B, 1949)
Abhimaan (**Mahesh Kaul**, H, 1957)
Abhimaan (**Hrishikesh Mukherjee**, H, 1973)
Abhimaan (Sadhu Meher, O, 1977)
Abhimaan (Sujit Guha, B, 1986)
Abhimana (P.N. Srinivas, K, 1989)
Abhimanam (**C.S. Rao**, Tel, 1960)
Abhimanam (**Sasikumar**, Mal, 1975)
Abhimanavanthulu (K.S. Rami Reddy, Tel, 1973)
Abhimanavathi (P. Dhoondy, Tel, 1975)
Abhimanyu (A. Kasilingam, Tam, 1948)
Abhimanyu (**Mahesh Bhatt**, H, 1980)
Abhimanyu (**Tapan Sinha**, B, 1983)
Abhimanyu (**Priyadarshan**, Mal, 1987)
Abhimanyu (Tony Juneja, H, 1989)
Abhimanyu (Raviraj, K, 1990)
Abhimanyudu (**Dasari Narayana Rao**, Tel, 1984)
Abhinandana (Ashok Kumar, Tel, 1988)
Abhinandanam (**I.V. Sasi**, Mal, 1976)
Abhinav (*aka* Nishir Dak: **Debaki Bose**, B, 1940)
Abhinaya (**Modhu Bose**, B, 1938)
Abhinayam (Baby, Mal, 1981)
Abhinay Nay (**Sailajananda Mukherjee**, B, 1945)
Abhinay Nay (Archan Chakraborty, B, 1983)
Abhinetri/Haar Jeet (**Amar Mullick**, B/H, 1940)
Abhinetri (Amar Ganguly, O, 1965)
Abhinetri (**Subodh Mukherjee**, H, 1970)
Abhinetri (TV: Sandip Ray, H, 1985)
Abhinivesam (**I.V. Sasi**, Mal, 1977)
Abhisar (Hemanta Gupta, B, 1943)
Abhisar (Sanat Dutta, B, 1989)
Abhisarika (**Dhiren Ganguly**, B, 1938)
Abhisarika (Kamal Majumdar, B, 1962)
Abhishap (Benoy Bannerjee, B, 1959)
Abhishap (Biresh Chatterjee, B, 1986)
Abhishapta (Digambar Chatterjee, B, 1951)
Abhishapta Chambal (Manju Dey, B, 1967)
Abhishek (Prafulla Roy, St, 1931)
Abhishek (Chitra Pali, B, 1957)
Abhishek (Subhash Mukhopadhyay, B, 1984)
Abhi To Jee Lein (Roshan Taneja, H, 1977)
Abhiyatri (**Hemen Gupta**, B, 1947)
Abhoya-o-Srikanta (Haridas Bhattacharya, B, 1965)
Abhoyer Biye (**Sukumar Dasgupta**, B, 1957)
Abichar (Bishwajeet Chatterjee, B, 1981)
Abidah (Nazir, H, 1947)
Abil Gulal (Rajani Nandlal, G, 1984)
Abir (Kamal Majumdar, B, 1987)
Abirey Rangano (Amal Dutta, B, 1972)
Abirvab (Amitava Dasgupta, B, 1977)
Abkari (**I.V. Sasi**, Mal, 1988)
Ab Kya Hua (Sawan Kumar, H, 1977)
Ab Meri Bari (Bhagwant S. Thakur, H, 1989)
Abode of Kings: Rajasthan (**Shyam Benegal**, E, 1990)
Abodh (Hiren Nag, H, 1984)
Abola Rani (*aka* The Queen that Would Not Speak: **Manilal Joshi**, St, 1926)
Abol Haiyan (Egbert Christie, G, 1984)
Aboli (**Anant Mane**, Mar, 1953)
Abu Hasan *see* Baghdad Ki Raatein
Abu Hossain (Ratan Chatterjee, B, 1952)
Abu Kaliya (C.K. Kader, H, 1990)
Abul Hasan (Prafulla Ghosh, H, 1931)
Acceptance, The *see* **Grahan**
Accident (Ravi Kapoor, H, 1965)
Accident (**Shankar Nag**, K, 1984)
Ace of Diamonds *see* Chokadika Ekka
Ace of Spades *see* Hukum Ka Ekka *or* Kalina Ekka
Ace of Swords *see* Talwar Ka Pati
Achamillai Achamillai (**K. Balachander**, Tam, 1984)
Achan (M.S. Mani, Mal, 1952)
Achanak (**S.S. Gulzar**, H, 1973)
Achani (**A. Vincent**, Mal, 1973)
Achani (Karaikudi Narayanan, Tam, 1978)
Achannum Bappayum (**K.S. Sethumadhavan**, Mal, 1972)
Achannum Maganam (Vimal Kumar, Mal, 1957)
Achante Bharya (**Thikkurisi Sukumaran Nair**, Mal, 1971)
Acharam Ammini Osaram Omana (**Adoor Bhasi**, Mal, 1977)
Acharya Nandalal (**Harisadhan Dasgupta**, E, 1984)
Acharya Prafulla Chandra Ray (**Harisadhan Dasgupta**, E, 1961)
Achena Atithi (Sukhen Das/Gnanesh Mukherjee, B, 1973)
Achena Mukh (Ajit Lahiri, B, 1984)
Achha Bura (Mohammed Hussain, H, 1972)
Achha Bura (**Hrishikesh Mukherjee**, H, 1983)
Achhaji (S.H. Tharani, H, 1950)
Achhut (**Chandulal Shah**, H/G, 1940)
Achhuta Daman *see* **Lagna Bandhan**
Achhut Kanya (**Franz Osten**, H, 1936)
Achhyo Jayo Giglo *see* Bhikaoo Tordo
Achin Priya (**Dhiren Ganguly**, B, 1938)
A Chitrashalabham Paranotte (A. Balthazar, Mal, 1970)
Achuvettante Veedu (**Balachandra Menon**, Mal, 1987)
Action for Calcutta (**Santi P. Choudhury**, E/B/H, 1971)
Actor (Ramji Acharya, H, 1951)
Actor Prepares, An (**Saeed Mirza**, E, 1976)
Actress (*aka* Bambai Ki Mohini: **Balwant Bhatt**, H, 1934)
Actress (Najam Naqvi, H, 1948)
Actress Kyon Bani (G.R. Sethi, H, 1939)
Actress Views Her Life, An *see* **Oru Nadigai Nadagam Parkiral**
Ada (Devendra Goel, H, 1951)
Adab Arz (*aka* Thank You: Virendra Desai, H, 1943)
Ada Bomma (B. Satyanaidu, Tel, 1988)
Adadani Adrushtam (G.V.R. Sheshgiri Rao, Tel, 1975)
Adadani Saval (K.S.R. Doss, Tel, 1983)
Adadarite Alusa (M. Mallikarjuna Rao, Tel, 1978)
Adade Adharam (Visu, Tel, 1988)
Adadi Gadapa Datithe (B.S. Narayana, Tel, 1980)
Adalat (Vasant Joglekar, H, 1948)
Adalat (Kalidas, H, 1958)
Adalat (Dilip Deka, A, 1976)
Adalat (**Narendra Bedi**, H, 1976)
Adalat-o-Ekti Meye (**Tapan Sinha**, B, 1981)
Adalu Badalu (C.V. Rajendran, K, 1979)
Adambaralu Anubandhalu (**C.S. Rao**, Tel, 1974)
Adaminte Variyellu (**K.G. George**, Mal, 1983)
Adam Ka Janam (B. Raj, H, 1989)
Adamkhor (Aakkoo, H, 1955)
Adamkhor (Joginder, H, 1985)
Adam's Rib *see* **Adaminte Variyellu**
Adapillale Thandri (K. Vasu, Tel, 1974)
Adapillale Mayam (Vejalla Satyanarayana, Tel, 1985)
Adarkalam (D. Rajendra Babu, Mal, 1985)
Adarsh (T. Chamanlal, H, 1983)
Adarsha Hindu Hotel (Ardhendu Sen, B, 1957)
Adarsha Kutumbam (**K. Pratyagatma**, Tel, 1969)
Adarsham (**H.V. Babu**, Tel, 1952)
Adarsham (Joshi, Mal, 1982)
Adarsham (Mouli, Tel, 1992)
Adarsha Ramani (*aka* An Ideal Woman: Bannerjee?, Mahavir Photoplays, St,1930)
Adarshasati *see* Nagula Chaviti
Adarshavanthudu (Kodi Ramakrishna, Tel, 1989)
Adarsha Veerangana *see* Roop Sundari
Adarsh Mahila (?, Ideal Films, Calcutta, H, 1937)
Adavalle Aligithe (Vejalla Satyanarayana, Tel, 1983)
Adavallu Apanindalu (B.S. Narayana, Tel, 1976)
Adavallu Meeku Joharlu (**Dasari Narayana Rao**, Tel, 1981)
Adavi Donga (**K. Raghavendra Rao**, Tel, 1985)
Adavilo Abhimanyudu (Anil, Tel, 1989)
Adavi Manushulu (G.K. Murthy, Tel, 1978)
Adavi Raja (K. Muralimohana Rao, Tel, 1986)
Adavi Ramudu (**K. Raghavendra Rao**, Tel, 1977)
Adavi Simhalu (**K. Raghavendra Rao**, Tel, 1983)
Adavi Veerulu (**P. Subramanyam**, Tel, 1971)
Adavukal-18 (Vijayanand, Mal, 1978)
Addadari (**Hunsur Krishnamurthy**, K, 1968)
Addala Meda (**Dasari Narayana Rao**, Tel, 1981)
Addeham Enna Eddaham (Viji Thampi, Mal, 1993)
Ade Hridaya Ade Mamathe (M.N. Prasad, K, 1969)
Ade Kannu (Chi. Dattaraj, K, 1985)
Adhaar (Pannalal Ghosh, H, 1945)
Adhaar (**Raja Paranjpe**, Mar, 1969)
Adha Din Adhi Raat (Dhoondy, H, 1977)
Adharam (George Kithoo, Mal, 1992)
Adharm (Aziz Sajawal, H, 1992)
Adharmoddhar *see* Bhakta Lakshmidas
Adharshila (Ashok Ahuja, H, 1981)
Adhayalam (K. Madhu, Mal, 1991)
Adhi Kalas Mag Paya (**Raja Paranjpe**, Mar, 1961)
Adhikar (**P.C. Barua**, B/H, 1938)
Adhikar (**Mohan Segal**, H, 1954)
Adhikar (**Dinkar D. Patil**/Arun Karnataki, Mar, 1971)
Adhikar (S.M. Sagar, H, 1971)
Adhikar (Vijay Sadanah, H, 1986)
Adhikar (TV: **Jahnu Barua**, H, 1988)
Adhikaram (Chandrakumar, Mal, 1980)
Adhikari (P. Vasu, Tam, 1991)
Adhiko Alladiko (Kodi Ramakrishna, Tel, 1984)
Adhipathi (**Sibi Malayil**, Mal, 1990)
Adhipathyam (Shrikumaran Thampi, Mal, 1983)
Adhi Raat (S.K. Ojha, H, 1950)
Adhi Raat (**Chandrakant**, H, 1957)
Adhi Raat Ke Baad (**Nanabhai Bhatt**, H, 1965)
Adhivaram Amavasya (Babu, Tel, 1993)
Adhi Velli (Ramanarayanan, Tam, 1990)
Adhiyayam Odhu Mudhal (Sathyan Andhikkad, Mal, 1985)
Adholokam (Chellappan, Mal, 1988)
Adhu Anthakalam (Valampuri John, Tam, 1988)
Adhura Armaan *see* Kul Kasumbo Ne Kanya
Adhuri Kahani (**Chaturbhuj Doshi**, H, 1939)
Adhyapika (**P. Subramanyam**, Mal, 1968)
Adhyathe Anuragam (V.S. Nair, Mal, 1983)
Adhyathe Katha (**K.S. Sethumadhavan**, Mal, 1972)
Adikkurippu (**Madhu**, Mal, 1989)
Adimachangala (A.B. Raj, Mal, 1981)
Adimagal (**K.S. Sethumadhavan**, Mal, 1969)
Adimagal Udumagal (**I.V. Sasi**, Mal, 1987)
Adimai Penn (K. Shankar, Tam, 1969)
Adimakachavadam (**T. Hariharan**, Mal, 1978)
Adi Manav/Adi Manavulu (G.K. Murthi, H/Tel, 1976)
Adi Manavulu *see* Adi Manav
Adi Mimansa (A.K. Bir, H, 1991)
Adina Megha (Amit Moitra, O, 1970)
Adinathan Kanavu (**T.R. Sundaram**, Tam, 1948)
Adipan (K. Madhu, Mal, 1989)
Adipapam (**K.P. Kumaran**, Mal, 1979)
Adipapam (?, Mal, 1988)
Adi Parasakthi (**K.S. Gopalakrishnan**, Tam, 1971)
Adiperaku (K. Shankar, Tam, 1962)
Adisaya Manithan (Prabhakar, Tam, 1990)
Adisaya Piravi (S.P. Muthuraman, Tam, 1990)
Adisaya Piravigal (R. Thyagarajan, Tam, 1982)
Adisaya Ragam (Mohanraj-Suresh, Tam, 1979)
Adisaya Thirudan *see* Bandaramudu
Adi *see* Aadi
Adi Shankaracharya (**G.V. Iyer**, Sanskrit, 1983)
Adithyan (Baskarraj, Tam, 1992)
Aditya 369 (**Singeetham Srinivasa Rao**, Tel, 1991)
A Divasam (M. Mani, Mal, 1982)
Adivasiyon Ka Jeevan Srot (**Ritwik Ghatak**, H, 1955)
Adiverukkal (?, Mal, 1986)
Adiyozhukkukal (**I.V. Sasi**, Mal, 1984)
Adiyug (Prasad, H, 1978)
Adl-e-Jehangir (*aka* Justice of Jehangir: A.P. Kapur, St, 1930)
Adl-e-Jehangir (*aka* Nyayi: K. Sardar, H, 1934)
Adl-e-Jehangir (**G.P. Sippy**, H, 1955)
Admi *see* **Manoos**
Admi (Navneet Rai, H, 1957)
Admi (**A. Bhimsingh**, H, 1968)
Admi (Arshad Khan, H, 1993)
Admi Aur Aurat (**Tapan Sinha**, H, 1984)
Admi Aur Insaan (**Yash Chopra**, H, 1969)
Admi Khilona Hai (J. Om Prakash, H, 1993)
Admi Sadak Ka (Devendra Goel, H, 1977)
Adolescent Desire *see* **Rathi Nirvedham**
Adooray Chheley (*aka* Pampered Youth: **J.J. Madan**, St, 1925)
Ados Pados (TV: **Sai Paranjpye**, H, 1985)
Adrishtakaran (Venunath, Tam, 1978)
Adrishya Manush (Amar Dutta, B, 1953)
Adrushta Deepudu (**S. Soundararajan**, Tel, 1950)
Adrushta Jathakudu (K. Hemambharadhara Rao, Tel, 1971)
Adrushtavanthalu (V. Madhusudhana Rao, Tel, 1969)
Adrushtavanthudu (G.C. Sekhar, Tel, 1980)
Adrushtavanthuralu (Chakraborty, Tel, 1977)
Adugal Nanaigindrana (P. Madhavan, Tam, 1981)
Adugu Jadalu (**Tapi Chanakya**, Tel, 1966)
Adukkan Entheluppam (?, Classic Arts, Mal, 1986)
Adukku Malli (**K.S. Gopalakrishnan**, Tam, 1979)
Adu Pembey (Amirtham, Tam, 1979)
Aduthaduthu (Sathyan Andhikkad, Mal, 1984)
Aduthathu Albert (G.N. Rangarajan, Tam, 1985)
Adutha Varisu (S.P. Muthuraman, Tam, 1983)
Adutha Veedu (Ramanarayanan, Tam, 1986)
Adutha Veetu Penn (**Vedantam Raghavaiah**, Tam, 1960)
Advaitham (**Priyadarshan**, Mal, 1991)
Advantha Daivam (**P. Neelakantan**, Tam, 1960)
Adventure of Robin Hood and Bandits (B.J. Patel, H, 1965)
Adventures of a Sugar Doll (**Kantilal Rathod**/K. Gopal Krishnan E, 1965)
Adventures of Goopy and Bagha, The *see* **Goopy Gyne Bagha Byne**
Adventures of Tarzan *see* Tarzan
Adversary, The *see* **Pratidwandi**
Adwitiya (**Nabyendu Chatterjee**, B, 1968)
Adya Kiranangal (**P. Bhaskaran**, Mal, 1964)
Adyapadam (**Adoor Bhasi**, Mal, 1977)
Adyashakti Mahamaya (Purnendu Roy Choudhury, B, 1968)
Ae Chhilo Mone (Subir Sarkar, B, 1983)
Ae Jahar Sey Jahar Noy (Kanak Mukherjee, B, 1959)
Ae Juger Meye (Kamal Chatterjee, B, 1952)
Ae Korechho Bhalo (Ajit Bannerjee, B, 1970)
Ae Prithibi Pantha Niwas (Aravind Mukherjee, B, 1977)
Ae Satyi (Suresh Haldar, B, 1954)
Ae To Jiban (Dhiresh Ghosh, B, 1946)
Ae To Sansar (Kanak Mukherjee, B, 1980)
Afghan Abla (*aka* Throne of Delhi: **N.G. Devare**, St, 1931)
Afghan Abla (*aka* Fugaane Abla: **J.P. Advani**, H, 1934)
Aflatoon (Pesi Karani, H, 1937)
Aflatoon (Jaswant Jhaveri, H, 1950)
Aflatoon (Basu/Douglas?, H, 1967)
Aflatoon Abla (*aka* Bondage: G.S. Devare, St, 1931)

Aflatoon Aurat (*aka* Amazon, Veerangana: Kikubhai Desai, H, 1940)
Africa (K. Kant, H, 1954)
Africadalli Sheela (Dwarkeesh, K, 1986)
Africa Mein Hind *see* India in Africa
Afsana (*aka* Madhur Milan: **Zia Sarhadi**, H, 1938)
Afsana (**B.R. Chopra**, H, 1951)
Afsana (Brij Sadanah, H, 1966)
Afsana Do Dilon Ka (**K.S. Sethumadhavan**, H, 1982)
Afsana Pyar Ka (Shahjehan, H, 1991)
Afsar (**Chetan Anand**, H, 1950)
After Ten Years (**Santi P. Choudhury**, E, 1973)
After the Death *see* Maraner Pare
After the Earthquake *see* **Inquilab**
After the Eclipse (**S. Sukhdev**, E, 1964)
After the Silence (**S. Sukhdev**, E, 1977)
Afzal (*aka* Hoor-e-Haram: **M. Bhavnani**, H, 1933)
Agam (Rajeevnath, Mal, 1992)
Agaman (**Muzaffar Ali**, H, 1983)
Agaman (**Tarun Majumdar**, B, 1988)
Agamanam (Jesey, Mal, 1980)
Agami Kal (Tapan Saha, B, 1983)
Agantuk (**Satyajit Ray**, B, 1991)
Agantuka (**Suresh Heblikar**, K, 1985)
Agar (*aka* If: Esmayeel Shroff, H, 1977)
Agar Tum Na Hote (Lekh Tandon, H, 1983)
Agathiar (**A.P. Nagarajan**, Tam, 1972)
Agaya Gangai (?, Tam, 1982)
Agayathamaraigal (A.Alagappan, Tam, 1985)
Agent Gopi (K.S.R. Doss, Tel, 1978)
Agent 1-2-3 *see* Putani Agents 1-2-3
Agent 777 (Satish Khurana, H, 1988)
Agent Vinod (Deepak Bahry, H, 1977)
Age of the Earth, The (**Pradeep Krishen**, E, 1979)
Aggibarata (**B. Vittalacharya**, Tel, 1966)
Aggidora (**B. Vittalacharya**, Tel, 1967)
Aggimada Guggilam (G. Vishwanathan, Tel, 1968)
Aggipidugu (**B. Vittalacharya**, Tel, 1964)
Aggiraju (B. Bhaskara Rao, Tel, 1985)
Aggiramudu (S.M. Sreeramulu Naidu, Tel, 1954)
Aggiramudu (S.S. Ravichandra, Tel, 1990)
Aggirava (**K. Bapaiah**, Tel, 1981)
Aggiveerudu (**B. Vittalacharya**, Tel, 1969)
Aghaat *see* Aaghat
Aghaton Ajo Ghatey (Amal Mitra, B, 1989)
Aghnayam (P.G. Vishwambaran, Mal, 1993)
Agla Mausam (?, H, 1989)
Agnathavasam (A.B. Raj, Mal, 1973)
Agneepath (**Mukul S. Anand**, H, 1990)
Agni (C. Radhakrishnan, Mal, 1978)
Agni (J. Om Prakash, H, 1988)
Agni (**K. Raghavendra Rao**, Tel, 1989)
Agni Banya (Jayadrath, B, 1964)
Agni Bhramar (Ajit Ganguly, B, 1973)
Agnichirakulla Thambi (P.K. Krishnan, Mal, 1988)
Agnidah (Arun Kumar, H, 1985)
Agni Gundam (Kranthi Kumar, Tel, 1984)
Agni Jwala (B. Subba Rao, Tel, 1983)
Agnikaal (Abbas-Mastan, H, 1990)
Agnikankan *see* **Jalti Nishani**
Agnikanya (Gopal Kundu, B, 1990)
Agni Keratalu (**T. Rama Rao**, Tel, 1988)
Agni Kshetram (P.T. Rajan, Mal, 1980)
Agnimrigam (M. Krishnan Nair, Mal, 1971)
Agnimuhurtam (?, Navayuga Prod, Mal, 1987)
Agni Nakshatram (**A. Vincent**, Mal, 1977)
Agni Nakshatram (**Mani Rathnam**, Tam, 1988)
Agni Nakshatram (Sarath, Tel, 1989)
Agni Nilavu (N. Shankaran Nair, Mal, 1991)
Agni Panjara (Srinivasa, K, 1992)
Agni Pareeksha (P. Manikyam, Tel, 1951)
Agni Pareeksha (**Agradoot**, B, 1954)
Agni Pareeksha (M. Krishnan Nair, Mal, 1968)
Agni Pareeksha (K. Varaprasadarao, Tel, 1970)
Agni Pareeksha (Balai Sen, O, 1980)
Agni Pareeksha (Kamal Majumdar, H, 1981)
Agni Pareekshe (Srinivasa, K, 1986)
Agni Parva (Sundaranath Suvarna, K, 1987)
Agni Parvai (P. Madhavan, Tam, 1992)
Agni Parvatham (Chandrakumar, Mal, 1979)
Agni Parvatham (**K. Raghavendra Rao**, Tel, 1985)
Agnipath *see* **Agneepath**
Agni Poolu (**K. Bapaiah**, Tel, 1981)
Agni Pravesham (Karaikudi Narayanan, Tam, 1978)
Agni Pravesham (K. Madhu, Mal, 1989)
Agni Pravesham (Yandamuri, Tel, 1989)
Agni Pushpam (Eranki Sharma, Tel, 1987)
Agni Pushpan (Jesey, Mal, 1976)
Agniputhri (M. Krishnan Nair, Mal, 1967)
Agni Putrudu (**K. Raghavendra Rao**, Tel, 1987)
Agni Rekha (**Mahesh Kaul**, H, 1973)
Agni Samadhi (K.S.R. Doss, Tel, 1983)
Agnisambhaba (**Sushil Majumdar**, B, 1959)
Agni Sanket (Sanjib Chattopadhyay, B, 1988)
Agni Sanskar (**Agradoot**, B, 1961)
Agnisaram (A.B. Raj, Mal, 1981)
Agni Satchi (**K. Balachander**, Tam, 1982)
Agni Shuddhi (Sachin Adhikari, B, 1984)
Agnisikha (**Rajen Tarafdar**, B, 1962)
Agnisnan (**Bhabendranath Saikia**, A, 1985)
Agniswar (Aravind Mukherjee, B, 1975)
Agni Teertham (?, B. Jayahandran, Tam, 1990)
Agni Trishna (Prabhat Roy, B, 1989)
Agnivyuham (P. Chandrakumar, Mal, 1979)
Agniyudham (?, Mal, 1981)
Agni Yuger Kahini (Bhupen Roy, B, 1969)
Agnyathavasa (Janakiram, K, 1984)
Agradani (Palash Bannerjee, B, 1982)
Agraham (Rajasenan, Mal, 1984)
Agraham (M. Rosi Raju, Tel, 1985)
Agraham (Kodi Ramakrishna, Tel, 1991)
Agraharathil Kazhuthai (**John Abraham**, Tam, 1977)
Agra Road (**Ravindra Dave**, H, 1957)
Agreement (Anil Ganguly, H, 1980)
Agreement (Manivannan, Tel, 1992)
Agun (**Asit Sen**, B, 1962)
Agun (Victor Bannerjee, B, 1988)
Aguner Phulki (Kushali Goshti, B, 1976)
Ahalya (K. Rangarao, Tel, 1934)
Ahalya (**Jyotish Bannerjee**, B, 1936)
Ahalya (Thomo, Mal, 1978)
Ahana Pellanta (Jandhyala, Tel, 1987)
Ahankaram (D. Sasi, Mal, 1983)
Ahankari (**Dasari Narayana Rao**, Tel, 1992)
Ahankar Vijay *see* Samudra Manthan
Aher (Namdev Vhatkar, Mar, 1957)
Ahilyoddhar *see* Patit Pawan
Ahilyoddhar (G.V. Sane, St, 1919)
Ahi-Mahi Vadh *see* Hanuman Pataal Parakram
Ahimsa (Rajaram, H, 1947)
Ahimsa (Chand, H, 1979)
Ahimsa (**I.V. Sasi**, Mal, 1981)
Ahimsa Path (**Keshavrao Dhaiber**, H, 1949)
Ahimsa Yuddham (*aka* Gandhiji: **T.R. Sundaram**, Tam, 1948)
Ahiravan Mahiravan Vadh (G.V. Sane, St, 1922)
Ahista Ahista (Esmayeel Shroff, H, 1981)
Ahmedabad Congress (**Dadasaheb Phalke**?, St, 1922)
Ahsaas (S.K. Puri, H, 1979)
Ahuti (**Dhiren Ganguly**, B, 1941)
Ahuti (*aka* Anokhi Qurbani: Kulbhushan, H, 1950)
Ahuti (Ashok Bhushan, H, 1978)
Ahuti (**T.S. Nagabharana**, K, 1984)
Ahuti (Probir Mitra, B, 1984)
Ahuti (M.S. Reddy, Tel, 1987)
Ahwan (Aravind Mukherjee, B, 1961)
AIDS (?, Aji Films, Mal, 1987)
Aidu Beralu (S.R. Rajan, K, 1971)
Aijani Sarudhan (Kudala Kumar Bhattacharya, A, 1983)
Aika *see* Suniye
Ai Meri Bekhudi (Chanchal Kumar, H, 1993)
Aindhu Laksham (G. Ramakrishnan, Tam, 1969)
Air Hostess (Chandrakumar, Mal, 1980)
Airmail (A. Rashid, H, 1946)
Airmail (B.J. Patel, H, 1960)
Aisa Bhi Hota Hai (Kamran, H, 1971)
Aisa Kyon (A.K. Chatterjee, H, 1947)
Aisa Pyar Kahan (Vijay Sadanah, H, 1986)
Aitbaar (**Mukul S. Anand**, H, 1985)
Aitya Bilavar Nagoba (Murlidhar Kapdi, Mar, 1979)
Aiye (Yakub, H, 1947)
Ajabkumari (**Manilal Joshi**, St, 1926)
Ajab Teri Sarkar *see* Jagriti
Ajab Tujhe Sarkar (**Raja Thakur**, Mar, 1971)
Ajagajanthara (Kashinath, K, 1991)
Ajali Nabou (**Nip Barua**, A, 1980)
Ajamil (**Kanjibhai Rathod**, St, 1922)
Ajamil (A.R. Kabuli, H, 1934)
Ajamil (Jamnadas Kapadia, G/H, 1948)
Ajana Kahini (Sunil Baran, B, 1960)
Ajana Shapath (Salil Sen, B, 1967)
Ajanma Brahmachari (B. Padmanabham, Tel, 1972)
Ajanta (?, Super Films, Mal, 1987)
Ajanta and Ellora (**Saeed Mirza**, E, 1992)
Ajantay (Aravind Mukherjee, B, 1984)
Ajantrik (**Ritwik Ghatak**, B, 1957)
Ajasra Dhanyabad (Aravind Mukherjee, B, 1976)
Ajatashatru (**Vijayanirmala**, Tel, 1989)
Ajayanum Vijayanum (**Sasikumar**, Mal, 1976)
Aj Di Heer *see* Aaj Di Heer
Ajeeb Ittefaq (Jyoti Swaroop, H, 1989)
Ajeeb Ladki (Mohammed Ehsan, H, 1952)
Ajeya (Siddalingaiah, K, 1985)
Ajeyudu (G. Rama Mohana Rao, Tel, 1987)
Aji Bas Shukriya (Mohammed Hussain, H, 1958)
Ajit (**M. Bhavnani**, H, 1948)
Ajit (V. Somasekhar, K, 1982)
Ajit Yoddho (*aka* The Protector: ?, Kohinoor/Meghji Jeevanji, St, 1934)
Ajker Nayak (**Dinen Gupta**, B, 1972)
Ajnabi (Hari Khanna, H, 1966)
Ajnabi (**Shakti Samanta**, H, 1974)
Ajnatha Theerangal (M. Krishnan Nair, Mal, 1979)
Ajooba (**Shashi Kapoor**, H, 1991)
Ajooba Kudrat Ka (Tulsi/Shyam **Ramsay**, H, 1991)
Ajvadi Raat Amasni (Chandravan Seth, G, 1981)
Akacheede Kunjuvava (Sajan, Mal, 1985)
Akaij Neeku Joharlu (N. Ramachandra Rao, Tel, 1984)
Akalangalil (**Sasikumar**, Mal, 1986)
Akalangalil Abhayam (Jesey, Mal, 1980)
Akalathe Ambili (Jesey, Mal, 1985)
Akale Akasam (**I.V. Sasi**, Mal, 1977)
Akaler Sandhaney (**Mrinal Sen**, B, 1980)
Akali Rajyam (**K. Balachander**, Tel, 1981)
Akalmand (**Roop K. Shorey**, H, 1966)
Akalmand (Raj Bharath, H, 1984)
Akalmand Bewaqoof (*aka* Foolish Wisdom: Dada Sarkari, **Madan Theatres**, St,1929)
Akal Vilakku (R. Selvaraj, Tam, 1979)
Akan (Gouri Burman, A, 1980)
Akanksha (?, Vijay Kapoor, H, 1988)
Akarshan (Tanvir Ahmed, H, 1988)
Akasar Akhi (Pankaj Pani, O, 1989)
Akash (Manmohan Sabir, H, 1953)
Akashakottayile Sultan (Jayaraj, Mal, 1991)
Akasharaju (Jyotish Sinha, Tel, 1951)
Akasharamana (G. Vishwanathan, Tel, 1965)
Akash Chhoan (**Rajen Tarafdar**, B, 1967)
Akashdeep (**Phani Majumdar**, H, 1965)
Akashganga (**Bhalji Pendharkar**, Mar, 1959)
Akash Ganga (?, H, 1989)
Akash Kusum (**Mrinal Sen**, B, 1965)
Akash Pari (Mohan Sinha, H, 1958)
Akash-Patal (Prabhat Mukherjee, B, 1960)
Akash Pradeep (Kanak Mukherjee, B, 1963)
Akashwani (**Bhalji Pendharkar**, Mar/H, 1934)
Akasmika (**T.S. Nagabharana**, K, 1993)
Akayla *see* Akela
Akbar Saleem Anarkali (**N.T. Rama Rao**, Tel, 1978)
Akela (*aka* Alone: Pesi Karani, H, 1941)
Akela (Jay Bee, H, 1963)
Akela (*aka* Akayla: **Ramesh Sippy**, H, 1991)
Akeli Mat Jaiyo (**Nandlal Jaswantlal**, H, 1963)
Akhanda Brahmacharigalu (Vishukumar, K, 1980)
Akhand Chudlo (B.J. Patel, Gl, 1982)
Akhand Saubhagya (**Chaturbhuj Doshi**, G, 1950)
Akhand Saubhagyavati (**Manhar Raskapur**, G, 1963)
Akhand Saubhagyavati (Rakesh Nahata, H, 1981)
Akhani Poratam (**K. Raghavendra Rao**, Tel, 1988)
Akhantudu (V. Ramachandra Rao, Tel, 1970)
Akher Jamla (**Datta Dharmahikari**, Mar, 1952)
Akhiyon Ke Jharokhon Se (Hiren Nag, H, 1978)
Akka (Madurai Thirumanam, Tam, 1976)
Akkachellelu (A. Sanjivi, Tel, 1970)
Akkaldama (**Madhu**, Mal, 1975)
Akkal Na Bardan (**Homi Master**, G, 1936)
Akka Mogadu Chelleli Kapuram (K. Subba Rao, Tel, 1983)
Akka Peddadanam Chelleli Kapuram (**Dasari Narayana Rao**, Tel, 1993)
Akkarai Pachai (N. Venkatesh, Tam, 1974)
Akkarai Seemaiyile (Radhabharati, Tam, 1993)
Akkarapacha (M.M. Nesan, Mal, 1972)
Akkare (K.N. Sasidharan, Mal, 1983)
Akkare Ninnoru Maran (Girish, Mal, 1985)
Akka Tammudu (**Krishnan-Panju**, Tel, 1972)
Akka Thangai (M.A. Thirumugham, Tam, 1969)
Akraman (J. Om Prakash, H, 1975)
Akramana (**Girish Kasaravalli**, K, 1980)
Akramanam (Shrikumaran Thampi, Mal, 1981)
Akrava Avatar (**Keshavrao Dhaiber**, Mar, 1939)
Akrosha (Tiptur Raghu, K, 1983)
Akrosham (A.B. Raj, Mal, 1982)
Akshadhoodu (**Sibi Malayil**, Mal, 1993)
Aksharangal (**I.V. Sasi**, Mal, 1984)
Aksharathettu (**I.V. Sasi**, Mal, 1989)
Akshaya Pathram (**Sasikumar**, Mal, 1977)
Akshintalu (Mouli, Tel, 1987)
Akshi Tritiya (Babulal Doshi, O, 1981)
Alaap (**Hrishikesh Mukherjee**, H, 1977)
Alabhama (**Vamsy**, Tel, 1986)
Alag Alag (**Shakti Samanta**, H, 1985)
Alaigal (**C.V. Sridhar**, Tam, 1973)
Alaigal Oyvathillai (**Bharathirajaa**, Tam, 1981)
Alai Osai (Sirimughai Ravi, Tam, 1985)
Alai Payum Nenjangal (H. Ramesh, Tam, 1983)
Alajadi (Tammareddy Bharadajwa, Tel, 1990)
Alakadalinakkare (Joshi, Mal, 1984)
Alakal (M.D. Mathews, Mal, 1974)
Alakh Kishori (*aka* Sisters: **Dhirubhai Desai**, St, 1931)
Alakhna Otle (Dinesh Rawal, G, 1980)
Alakh Niranjan *see* Gorakhnath
Alakh Niranjan (*aka* Raja Gopichand: Dada Gunjal, H, 1950)
Alakh Niranjan (**Babubhai Mistri**, H, 1975)
Alakh Niranjan (Dilip Bhatt, G, 1981)
Alaknanda (Ratan Chatterjee, B, 1947)
Alam Ara (**Ardeshir Irani**, H/Urdu, 1931)
Alam Ara (**Nanubhai Vakil**, H, 1956)
Alam Ara (**Nanubhai Vakil**, H, 1973)
Alam Ara Ki Beti (**Nanubhai Vakil**, H, 1960)
Alangari (Gopu, Tam, 1979)
Alapiranthavan (**Nanabhai Bhatt**, Tam, 1963)
Alapiranthavan (K. Vijayan, Tam, 1987)
Alasyam (?, Sai Devi Films, Mal, 1991)
Alavattam (Raju Ambaran, Mal, 1993)
Alaya Deepam (**C.V. Sridhar**, Tam/Tel, 1984)
Alayam (Thirumalai-Mahalingam, Tam, 1967)
Alayam (D. Madhusudhana, Tel, 1980)
Alayamani (K. Shankar, Tam, 1962)
Alayashikharam (Kodi Ramakrishna, Tel, 1983)
Alay Toofan Daryala (Jaywant Pathare, Mar, 1973)
Albela (**Master Bhagwan**, H, 1951)
Albela (A. Shamsheer, H, 1971)
Albela Mastana (B.J. Patel, H, 1967)
Albeli (R.C. Talwar, H, 1945)
Albeli (Devendra Goel, H, 1955)
Albeli (Karunesh Thakur, H, 1974)
Albeli Mumbai (*aka* Bombay the Mysterious: **Nanubhai Vakil**, St, 1931)
Albeli Naar (S.J. Talukdar, G, 1981)
Albelo Sawar (*aka* Beloved Rogue: **Nagendra**

Majumdar, St, 1930)
Albert Pinto Ko Gussa Kyon Aata Hai (**Saeed Mirza**, H, 1980)
Alemane (Mohan Kumar, K, 1981)
Alexander (K. Ranga Rao, Tel, 1992)
Aleya (Nabendusundar, B, 1943)
Aleyar Alo (Mangal Chakraborty, B, 1970)
Al Hilal *see* **Judgement of Allah**
Al Hilal (Ram Kumar, H, 1958)
Ali Angavar (**Dada Kondke**, Mar, 1982)
Alibaba (**Modhu Bose**, B, 1937)
Alibaba (**Mehboob**, H/P bil, 1940)
Alibaba (**Nanubhai Vakil**, H, 1946)
Alibaba (Mohammed Hussain, H, 1976)
Alibaba and Forty-one Thieves (*aka* Alibabavum 41 Kalamarnum: **Sasikumar**, Mal, 1975)
Alibaba and the Forty Thieves *see* **Alibabavum Narpathu Thirudargalum**
Alibaba and the Forty Thieves (**Hiralal Sen**, St, 1903)
Alibaba and the Forty Thieves (**B.P. Mishra**, St, 1927)
Alibaba and the Forty Thieves (*aka* Alibaba Aur Chalis Chor, **J.J. Madan**, H, 1932)
Alibaba and the Forty Thieves (*aka* Alibaba Aur Chalis Chor, **Homi Wadia**, H, 1954)
Alibaba and the Forty Thieves (**Homi Wadia**, H, 1966)
Alibaba Aur Chalis Chor *see* Alibaba and the Forty Thieves
Alibaba Aur Chalis Chor (Umesh Mehra/L. Faiziev, H, 1980)
Alibaba 40 Dongalu (**B. Vittalacharya**, Tel, 1970)
Alibaba Marjina (Kedar Kapoor, H, 1977)
Alibabavum 40 Thirudargalum (K.S. Mani, Tam, 1941)
Alibabavum 41 Kalamarnum *see* Alibaba and Forty One Thieves
Alibabavum Narpathu Thirudargalum (**T.R. Sundaram**, Tam, 1955)
Ali Badusha (?, Universal Talkies, Tam, 1936)
Alibha Daga (Ramaraman Padhi, O, 1980)
Alice's Search *see* **Alicinte Anveshanam**
Alicinte Anveshanam (T.V. Chandran, Mal, 1989)
Alif Laila (*aka* Arabian Nights: Shanti J. Dave/**Balwant Bhatt**, H, 1933)
Alif Laila (**K. Amarnath**, H, 1953)
Alik Babu (*aka* Master Liar: **Dhiren Ganguly**, St, 1930)
Ali Lahar Kela Kahar (Arun Karnataki, Mar, 1984)
Alila Kuruvigal (**S.L. Puram Sadanandan**, Mal, 1988)
Alimaya (Kishore Sarja, K, 1993)
Alingan (*aka* The Embrace: C.L. Dheer, H, 1974)
Alingan (Tapan Saha, B, 1990)
Alinganam (**I.V. Sasi**, Mal, 1976)
Alippazhangal (?, Geodaya Prod, Mal, 1987)
Aliya Bhogasi (**Datta Dharmadhikari**, Mar, 1957)
Aliya Geleya (**B.R. Panthulu**, K, 1971)
Alkoottathil Thaniye (**I.V. Sasi**, Mal, 1984)
All About Teeth (**Govind Saraiya**, E, 1957)
Alladdin (**Nanubhai Vakil**, H, 1945)
Alladdin and the Magic Lamp *see* Hoor-e-Arab
Alladdin and the Wonderful Lamp *see* Allavudeenum Albutha Velakkum *or* Tarzan Aur Jadui Chirag
Alladdin and the Wonderful Lamp (**B.P. Mishra**, St, 1927)
Alladdin and the Wonderful Lamp (Jal Ariah, St, 1931)
Alladdin and the Wonderful Lamp (*aka* Jadu Ka Chirag, Tilasmi Chirag, Alladdin Aur Jadui Chirag: **J.J. Madan**?, Madan Theatres, H, 1933)
Alladdin and the Wonderful Lamp (**Nanubhai Vakil**, H, 1938)
Alladdin and the Wonderful Lamp (*aka* Alladdin Aur Jadui Chirag, **Homi Wadia**, H, 1952)
Alladdin and the Wonderful Lamp (**Homi Wadia**, H, 1978)
Alladdin Aur Jadui Chirag *see* Alladdin and the Wonderful Lamp
Alladdin Ka Beta *see* Son of Alladdin
Alladdin Ka Chirag *see* Allavudeenum Arputha Vilakkum
Alladdin Ki Beti (**Nanubhai Vakil**, H, 1949)
Alladdin Laila (A.M. Khan, H, 1941)
Alladdin Laila (Lekhraj Bhakri, H, 1957)
Alladdin-o-Ashcharya Pradeep (Bijon Sen, B, 1952)
Alladdin-II (*aka* Aaj Ka Alladdin: **Nagendra Majumdar**, H, 1935)
Allah Ka Pyara (*aka* The Guarding Angel: K.P. Bhave, St, 1927)
Allah Nine Nine Ishwara (Vasanthakumar Goni, K, 1983)
Allah-o-Akbar (Moidu Padiath, Mal, 1976)
Allah Rakha (Ketan Desai, H, 1986)
Allari Ammayilu (Tamavanan, Tel, 1972)
Allari Bhava (P. Sambasiva Rao, Tel, 1980)
Allari Bullodu (G.C. Shekhar, Tel, 1978)
Allari Krishnayya (N. Ramesh, Tel, 1987)
Allari Mogadu (**K. Raghavendra Rao**, Tel, 1992)
Allari Pandavulu (M. Baliah, Tel, 1987)
Allari Pilla (Kodi Ramakrishna, Tel, 1992)
Allari Pillalu (**C.S. Rao**, Tel, 1978)
Allari Priyudu (**K. Raghavendra Rao**, Tel, 1993)
Allauddin Adbhuta Deepam *see* Allavudeenum Arputha Vilakkum
Allavudeenum Albutha Velakkum/Allavudeenum Arputha Vilakkum/Alladdin and the Wonderful Lamp (**I.V. Sasi**, Mal/Tam/H, 1979)
Allavudeenum Arputha Vilakkum *see* Allavudeenum Albutha Velakkum
Allavudeenum Arputha Vilakkum/Allauddin Adbhuta Deepam/Alladdin Ka Chirag (**T.R. Raghunath**, Tam/Tel/H, 1957)
All for a Son *see* Takraar
All for Love *see* Maanbhanjan *or* Diwano
All for Money *see* Paisa Na Gulam
All for the Best *see* **Anta Mana Manchike**
All for the Crown *see* Khooni Taj
All God's Children (**Vishram Bedekar**, E, 1964)
Alli (S.S.R., Tam, 1964)
Alli Arjuna (?, Saraswathi Cinetone, Tam, 1935)
Alli Darbar (K.M. Balakrishnan, Tam, 1978)
All in the Family (**Ketan Mehta**, E, 1992)
Alli Petra Pillai (K.Somu, Tam, 1959)
Alli Ramachari Illi Brahmachari (B. Ramamurthy, K, 1992)
Alli Vijaam (**Harshadrai Mehta**, Tam, 1942)
All Quiet on the Maratha Front *see* Amar Shaheed
All Rounder (Mohan Kumar, H, 1984)
All-Star Tragedy (Ashu Bannerjee, B, 1944)
Alludochadu (**K. Pratyagatma**, Tel, 1976)
Alludu Diddina Kapuram (**Ghantamneni Krishna**, Tel, 1991)
Alludugaru (**K. Raghavendra Rao**, Tel, 1990)
Alludu Kosam (M.S. Kotareddy, Tel, 1987)
Alludu Menalludu (**P. Pullaiah**, Tel, 1970)
Alludu Pattina Bharatham (**K. Vishwanath**, Tel, 1980)
Allulostunnaru (**K. Vishwanath**, Tel, 1984)
All Under the Heaven by Force (Zul Velani, E, 1964)
Alluri Seetaramaraju (V. Ramachandra Rao, Tel, 1974)
Almaram (**A. Vincent**, Mal, 1969)
Almarottam (Venu, Mal, 1978)
Alo Amar Alo (Pinaki Mukherjee, B, 1972)
Alo Andhare (Dhruba Chatterjee, B, 1973)
Alochhaya/Aandhi (*aka* The Tempest; The Storm: Dinesh Ranjan Das, B/H, 1940)
Alochinchandi (Narayana Murthy, Tel, 1988)
Alo Hasi Gaan (Amar Ghosh, B, 1973)
Alolam (M. Mohan, Mal, 1982)
Alone *see* Akela
Alone in the Crowd *see* **Alkoottathil Thaniye**
Along the Brahmaputra (**Kalpana Lajmi**, E, 1981)
Along the Jumna (**P.V. Pathy**, E, 1946)
Alo-o-Chhaya (**Gurudas Bagchi**, B, 1973)
Alor Pipasa (**Tarun Majumdar**, B, 1965)
Alor Thikana (Bijoy Basu, B, 1974)
Alorungi Arangorungi (Chellappan, Mal, 1986)
Aloye Phera (Ajit Ganguly, B, 1983)
Alphonsa (O. Jose Thottan, Mal, 1952)
Althara (**P. Subramanyam**, Mal, 1964)
Alukkoru Asai (S.P. Muthuraman, Tam, 1977)
Alukkoru Veedu (M. Krishnan, Tam, 1960)
Aluku (K.S.L. Swamy, K, 1978)
Always Tell Your Wife *see* Miya Bibi
Amada Bata (Amar Ganguly, O, 1964)
Aman (Mohan Kumar, H, 1967)
Amanat (Lalit Chandra Mehta, H, 1943)
Amanat (Aravind Sen, H, 1955)
Amanat (**A. Bhimsingh**, H, 1975)
Amanat (Santanu Bhowmick, B, 1989)
Aman Ke Farishte (?, H, 1992)
Amanush (**Shakti Samanta**, B/H, 1974)
Amanusha (Nanjunde Gowda, K, 1989)
Amar (**Mehboob**, H, 1954)
Amara Bharathi (B. Krishan, K, 1971)
Amara Deepam (**T. Prakash Rao**, Tam, 1956)
Amara Deepam (**K. Raghavendra Rao**, Tel, 1977)
Amarajeevi (J.K. Murthy, K, 1965)
Amarajeevi (Jandhyala, Tel, 1983)
Amarakavi (F. Nagoor, Tam, 1952)
Amarakaviyam (Amirtham, Tam, 1981)
Amar Akbar Anthony (**Manmohan Desai**, H, 1977)
Amaram (**B.G. Bharathan**, Mal, 1991)
Amara Madhura Prema (Ramdas Naidu, K, 1982)
Anaran (K. Rajeshwar, Tam, 1991)
Amara Prema (Saiprakash, K, 1992)
Amara Prema (**T. Rama Rao**, Tel, 1978)
Amara Sandesham (**Adurthi Subba Rao**, Tel, 1954)
Amar Asha (*aka* Immortal Hope: **Harshadrai Mehta**, St, 1926)
Amar Asha (*aka* Eternal Hope: Sailen Ghosh, H, 1942)
Amar Asha (**V.M. Vyas**, H, 1947)
Amarashilpi Jakanachari/Amarashilpi Jakanna (**B.S. Ranga**, K/Tel, 1964)
Amaravathi (Selva, Tam, 1993)
Amar Bandhan (Tapan Saha, B, 1986)
Amar Bhoopali (**V. Shantaram**, Mar, 1951)
Amar Bou (Khagen Roy, B, 1956)
Amar Deep (**T. Prakash Rao**, H, 1958)
Amar Deep (K. Vijayan/R. Krishnamurthy, H, 1979)
Amar Desh (Anath Mukherjee, B, 1947)
Amar Devidas (Dinesh Rawal, G, 1981)
Amar Geeti (Hiren Bose, B, 1940)
Amar Geeti (**Tarun Majumdar**, B, 1983)
Amar Ghar (**Nip Barua**, A, 1959)
Amari Gaan Jhua (Vinay Bannerjee, O, 1953)
Amar Jyoti (**V. Shantaram**, H, 1936)
Amar Jyoti (Raman Desai, H, 1965)
Amar Jyoti (Gurdeep Singh, H, 1984)
Amar Kahani (Baij Sharma, H, 1949)
Amar Keertan (K.C. Pandit, H, 1954)
Amar Kirti (*aka* Immortal Glory: Prafulla Ghosh, St, 1930)
Amar Lenin (**Ritwik Ghatak**, B, 1970)
Amarnath (K. Manimurugan, K, 1978)
Amar Prem *see* Himalaya Ki Beti
Amar Prem (*aka* Diler Dilbar: Natwar Shyam, H, 1936)
Amar Prem (*aka* Radha Krishna: N.M. Kelkar, H, 1948)
Amar Prem (Mahendra Gupta, B, 1954)
Amar Prem (Ramanna, H, 1960)
Amar Prem (**Shakti Samanta**, H, 1971)
Amar Prem (Gopal Ghosh/Palash Bannerjee, O, 1976)
Amar Prithibi (Bimal Bhowmick, B, 1985)
Amar Pyar (?, J.R. Prod, Calcutta, H, 1958)
Amar Rahe Taro Chandlo (Rakesh Nahata, G, 1981)
Amar Rahe Yeh Pyar (Prabhu, H, 1961)
Amar Raj (**Homi Wadia**, H, 1946)
Amar Rakhdi (Keshav Rathod, G, 1981)
Amar Saigal (*aka* The Immortal Singer: **Nitin Bose**, H, 1955)
Amar Shaheed *see* Marathyatil Duhi
Amar Shaheed *see* Veerapandiya Kattaboman
Amar Shaheed (*aka* Shamsher-e-Jung, All Quiet on the Maratha Front: Balasaheb Yadav, H, 1936)
Amar Shakti (Harmesh Malhotra, H, 1978)
Amarsham (**I.V. Sasi**, Mal, 1978)
Amar Shapath (Prabhat Roy, B, 1989)
Amar Shilpi (Chitrashilpi, H, 1977)
Amarsinh Daggar (*aka* Marwad's Moti: **B.P. Mishra**, St, 1925)
Amarsinh Rathod (Jaswant Jhaveri, H, 1957)
Amarsinh Rathod (**Babubhai Mistri**, G, 1979)
Amar Suhagin (**Babubhai Mistri**, Bh, 1978)
Amar Tumi (Bimal Roy, B, 1989)
Amar Yoddho (**Dhirubhai Desai**?, St, 1931)
Amavas Ki Raat (Mohan Bhakri, H, 1990)
Amayaka Chakravarthi (Janardhan, Tel, 1983)
Amayukudu (A. Narayana Rao, Tel, 1968)
Amayukudu Kadu Aggi Bharothalu (R. Thyagarajan, Tel, 1984)
Amayukudu Kadhu Asadhyudu (**Vijayanirmala**, Tel, 1983)
Amayakuralu (B.A. Subba Rao, Tel, 1971)
Amazon *see* Aflatoon Aurat
Amazon, The *see* Dilruba Daku
Amba (Mohan Kumar, H, 1990)
Amba Ambika Ambalika (**P. Subramanyam**, Mal, 1976)
Ambadi Thannilorunni (?, Shiny Films, Mal, 1986)
Ambalakkara Panchayath (Kabir Rowther, Mal, 1988)
Ambalapravu (**P. Bhaskaran**, Mal, 1970)
Ambala Vilakku (Shrikumaran Thampi, Mal, 1980)
Ambar *see* Amber
Ambarish (Dada Gunjal, H, 1934)
Ambeda Gnane (Anthony Eastman, Mal, 1985)
Ambe Maa Jagadambe Maa (**Sukhdev Ahluwalia**, H, 1980)
Amber (*aka* Ambar: **Jayant Desai**, H, 1952)
Ambigai Neril Vandhal (Manivannan, Tam, 1984)
Ambikapathy (**Ellis Duncan**, Tam, 1937)
Ambikapathy (**P. Neelakantan**, Tam, 1957)
Ambili Ammavan (?, Yuvaraja Films, Mal, 1986)
Ambri (Bill Sikand, P, 1983)
Ame Evaru (B.S. Narayana, Tel, 1966)
Ame Katha (**K. Raghavendra Rao**, Tel, 1977)
Ame Neelgagan Na Pankheru (Ramesh Gupta, G, 1979)
Ame Pardeshi Pan (Mahesh Desai, G, 1977)
America Abbayi (**Singeetham Srinivasa Rao**, Tel, 1987)
America Alludu (K. Vasu, Tel, 1985)
America America (**I.V. Sasi**, Mal, 1983)
America Ammayi (**Singeetham Srinivasa Rao**, Tel, 1976)
Amhi Doghe Rajarani (Kamalakar Torne, Mar, 1986)
Amhi Jato Amuchya Gava (Kamalakar Torne, Mar, 1968)
Ami-Baro-Habo (**Sailajananda Mukherjee**, B, 1957)
Amina (?, Kali Films, H, 1934)
Amina Tailors Sajan, Mal, 1991)
Amir (Chandu, H, 1954)
Amir Admi Gareeb Admi (Amjad Khan, H, 1985)
Ami Ratan (Ajit Bannerjee, B, 1977)
Amir Garib (Mohan Kumar, H, 1974)
Amiri (**P.C. Barua**, H, 1945)
Amiri Garibi (Harmesh Malhotra, H, 1990)
Amir Khan (Shinde, St, 1931)
Amir of Kabul's Procession (?, Elphinstone Bioscope, St, 1907)
Amirzadi (A.R. Kabuli, H, 1934)
Ami Sey-o-Sekha (Mangal Chakraborty, B, 1975)
Ami Sirajer Begum (Sushil Mukherjee, B, 1973)
Amma (**Niranjan Pal**, Tel, 1939)
Amma (K. Vembu, Mal, 1952)
Amma (**B.R. Panthulu**, K, 1968)
Amma (M.S.N. Murthy/Pamarthy, Tel, 1975)
Amma (M. Krishnan Nair, Mal, 1976)
Amma (Rajasekhar, Tam, 1982)
Amma (*aka* Mother: Jiten, H, 1986)
Amma (Suresh Krishna, Tel, 1991)
Amma Ariyan (**John Abraham**, Mal, 1986)
Amma Engay (G. Vishwanathan, Tam, 1964)
Amma Enna Stree (**K.S. Sethumadhavan**, Mal, 1970)

Amma Evarikaina Amma (R. Thyagarajan, Tel, 1979)
Amma Irukka (Major Sundarrajan, Tam, 1983)
Ammaiyappan (**A. Bhimsingh**, Tam, 1954)
Amma Kadupo Chellaga (Bolena Subba Rao, Tel, 1991)
Amma Koduku (?, Nalini Cine Chitra, Tel, 1993)
Ammakorumma (Shrikumaran Thampi, Mal, 1981)
Amma Kosam (B.V. Prasad, Tel, 1970)
Ammalakulu/Marumagal (**Yoganand**, Tel/Tam, 1953)
Ammaldar (**K. Narayan Kale**/Madhukar Kulkarni, Mar, 1953)
Amma Manasu (**K. Vishwanath**, Tel, 1974)
Amma Mata (V. Ramachandra Rao, Tel, 1972)
Amma Nana (T. Lenin Babu, Tel, 1975)
Amman Arul (Pattu, Tam, 1973)
Amman Koil Kizhakkale (R. Sundarrajan, Tam, 1986)
Amman Koyil Thiruvizha (?, Shri Bhairav Combines, Tam, 1990)
Amma Pillai (R.C. Sakthi, Tam, 1990)
Amma Ponnu (Arun, Tam, 1993)
Ammavandachu (P. Vasu, Tam, 1992)
Ammavanu Pattiya Amali (Augustine Prakash, Mal, 1989)
Ammavum Neeye Appavum Neeye (S.P. Muthuraman, Tam, 1985)
Ammayana Sathyam (**Balachandra Menon**, Mal, 1993)
Ammayi Amma (M. Masthan, Mal, 1977)
Ammayila Sabatham (G.V.R. Sheshgiri Rao, Tel, 1975)
Ammayilu Jagratha (P. Sambhasiva Rao, Tel, 1975)
Ammayi Manasu (C. Krishna Rao, Tel, 1985)
Ammayi Mogadu Mamaku Yamadu (Amrutam, Tel, 1980)
Ammayi Pelli (**P. Bhanumathi**, Tel, 1974)
Ammayum Malakum (Stanley Jose, Mal, 1980)
Amme Anupame (**K.S. Sethumadhavan**, Mal, 1977)
Amme Bhagavathi (?, Devi Prod, Mal, 1987)
Amme Narayana (Suresh, Mal, 1984)
Ammeye Kannan (**P. Bhaskaran**, Mal, 1963)
Ammini Ammavan (**T. Hariharan**, Mal, 1976)
Ammu (N.N. Pishareddy, Mal, 1965)
Ammuvinte Attinkutty (**Ramu Kariat**, Mal, 1978)
Amor Kantak (Sukhen Das, B, 1986)
Amor Prem (Sujit Guha, B, 1989)
Amor Sangi (Sujit Guha, B, 1987)
Ampal Poovu (Harikumar, Mal, 1981)
Amrapali (**Nandlal Jaswantlal**, H, 1945)
Amrapali (Shri Tarashankar, B, 1959)
Amrapali (Lekh Tandon, H/E, 1966)
Amrit (**Master Vinayak**, Mar/H, 1941)
Amrit (Mohan Kumar, H, 1986)
Amrita (Dilip Mukherjee, H, 1976)
Amrita Kumbher Sandhaney (Dilip Roy, B, 1982)
Amritam Gamaya (**T. Hariharan**, Mal, 1987)
Amriter Swad (Parimal Bhattacharya, B, 1975)
Amritha Chumbanam (Venu, Mal, 1979)
Amritha Geetham (Baby, Mal, 1982)
Amritha Vahini (**Sasikumar**, Mal, 1976)
Amrit Ki Zaher (*aka* Madira Mohini, Wine and Woman: **Nagendra Majumdar**, St, 1928)
Amritmanthan (**V. Shantaram**, Mar/H, 1934)
Amritmanthan (S.N. Tripathi, H, 1961)
Amru Hindustan (*aka* Our Hindustan, Our India: C.H. Shah?, Elphin Cinema, St, 1928)
Amrutha Bindu (**Vamsy**, K, 1989)
Amrutha Galige (**Puttanna Kanagal**, K, 1984)
Amrutha Kalasham (Giduturi Satyam, Tel, 1981)
Amrutha Sindhu (S.R. Bhatt, K, 1993)
Amudha (K. Venkatraman, Tam, 1975)
Amudha Ganam (K. Rangaraj, Tam, 1985)
Amudhavalli (A.K. Sekhar, Tam, 1959)
Ana (P. Chandrakumar, Mal, 1983)
Anaaj (?, Cine Art Pics., H, 1952)
Anadha Silpangal (M.K. Ramu, Mal, 1971)
Anadhai Anandan (**Krishnan-Panju**, Tam, 1970)
Anadhai Penn (*aka* Orphan's Daughter: **Raja Sandow**, St, 1929)
Anadhai Penn (*aka* Orphan Girl: **R.S. Prakash**, Tam, 1938)
Anadhika Adathi (Anilkumar, Tel, 1986)
Anaganaga Oka Thandri (**C.S. Rao**, Tel, 1974)
Anakh Jattan Di (Ravinder Ravi, P, 1990)
Anakkalari (A.B. Raj, Mal, 1978)
Anakkorumma (M. Mani, Mal, 1985)
Anal Katru (**Komal Swaminathan**, Tam, 1983)
Anaam (Ramesh Modi, H, 1992)
Anami (Abani Mitra, B, 1952)
Anamika (**Hemen Gupta**, H, 1967: Incomplete)
Anamika (*aka* Girl Without a Name: Raghunath Jhalani, H, 1973)
Anand (**Hrishikesh Mukherjee**, H, 1970)
Anand (C.V. Rajendran, Tam, 1987)
Ananda (**Singeetham Srinivasa Rao**, K, 1986)
Ananda Aradhanai (Dinesh Babu, Tam, 1987)
Ananda Ashramam (C.V. Raman, Tam, 1939)
Ananda Bashpa (**R. Nagendra Rao**, K, 1963)
Ananda Bhairavi (Mohan Gandhiram, Tam, 1978)
Ananda Bhairavi (Jandhalya, Tel/K, 1983)
Anandada Aramane (V. Somasekhar, K, 1982)
Ananda Jyoti (V.N. Reddy/**A.S.A. Sami**, Tam, 1963)
Ananda Jyoti (?, Shiva Chithralaya, K, 1993)
Anandakanda (A.C. Narasimhamurthy/T. Dwarkanath, K, 1968)
Ananda Kannir (K. Vijayan, Tam, 1986)
Anandakummi (Balakrishnan, Tam, 1983)
Ananda Math (Satish Dasgupta, B, 1951)
Ananda Mela (Mangal Chakraborty, B, 1976)
Anandam Paramanandam (**I.V. Sasi**, Mal, 1977)
Ananda Nilayam (B.S. Narayana, Tel, 1971)
Ananda Sagara (V.T. Thyagarajan, K, 1983)
Anand Ashram (**Shakti Samanta**, H/B, 1977)
Ananda Tandavam (A. Raghurami Reddy, Tel, 1987)
Anand Aur Anand (**Dev Anand**, H, 1984)
Anand Bhavan (S.M. Yusuf, H, 1953)
Anandhan (S.D.S. Yogi, Tam, 1942)
Anandha Ragam (Bharani, Tam, 1982)
Anandi (**P. Neelakantan**, Tam, 1965)
Anandi Anand (**Rajdutt**, Mar, 1987)
Anandi Dhara (*aka* The Unending Flow: **G. Aravindan**, E, 1988)
Anand Mangal (Honey Chhaya, G, 1979)
Anandmath (**Hemen Gupta**, H, 1952)
Anangsena (**Moti Gidwani**, H, 1931)
Anantana Avanthara (Kashinath, K 1989)
Ananta Prema (T. Janardhan, K, 1990)
Anantara (Tararakere?, K, 1989)
Anantaram (**Adoor Gopalakrishnan**, Mal, 1987)
Ananthasayanam (**K. Subramanyam**, Tam, 1942)
Ananthasayanam (K. Sukumaran, Mal, 1972)
Anant Vrat (G.V. Sane, St, 1925)
Anantyatra (**Jayoo/Nachiket Patwardhan**, H, 1985)
Ananya (Sabhyasachi, B, 1949)
Anappachan (**A. Vincent**, Mal, 1978)
Anar (?, K.K. Films, H, 1989)
Anarbala (*aka* Fairy of Anardesh: **B.P. Mishra**, St, 1929)
Anarbala (A.M. Khan, H, 1940)
Anarbala (Raja Yagnik, H, 1961)
Anari (**Hrishikesh Mukherjee**, H, 1959)
Anari (**Asit Sen**, H, 1975)
Anari (K. Muralimohana Rao, H, 1993)
Anarkali (*aka* Monument of Tears: **R.S. Choudhury**, St, 1928)
Anarkali (**R.S. Choudhury**, H, 1935)
Anarkali (**Nandlal Jaswantlal**, H, 1953)
Anarkali (**Vedantam Raghavaiah**, Tam/Tel, 1955)
Anarkali (**Kunchako**, Mal, 1966)
Anashchadanam (M. Krishnan Nair, Mal, 1969)
Anaswara Ganangal (?, Excel Combines, Mal, 1986)
Anaswaram (Joemon, Mal, 1991)
Anatha (J.D. Thottan, Mal, 1970)
Anath Abala (*aka* Charkha, Spinning Wheel, Unprotected Woman: **Kanjibhai Rathod**, St, 1925)
Anath Ashram (**Hemchandra Chunder**, H, 1937)
Anathavagalu (V. Prabhakar, Tel, 1982)
Anaval Modhiram (G.S. Vijayan, Mal, 1991)
Anavaranam (**A. Vincent**, Mal, 1976)
Anaya Vilakku (**Krishnan-Panju**, Tam, 1975)
Anayum Ambariyum (Mani, Mal, 1978)
Anbai Thedi (V. Sinivasan, Tam, 1974)
Anbalipu (A.C. Trilogchander, Tam, 1969)
Anban (**Niren Lahiri**, H, 1944)
Anbe Aruyere (A.C. Trilogchander, Tam, 1975)
Anbe Daivam *see* Premada Putri
Anbe Odi Vaa (R. Ranjith Kumar, Tam, 1984)
Anbe Sangeetha (Karaikudi Narayanan, Tam, 1979)
Anbe Vaa (A.C. Trilogchander, Tam, 1966)
Anbin Alaigal (M. Mastan, Tam, 1978)
Anbin Mukavari (Manivannan, Tam, 1985)
Anbu (M. Natesan, Tam, 1953)
Anbu Engay (**Yoganand**, Tam, 1958)
Anbu Kattalai (Kannan, Tam, 1989)
Anbukkarangal (K. Shankar, Tam, 1965)
Anbukkor Anni (**T.R. Raghunath**, Tam, 1960)
Anbukku Naan Adimai (M.A. Thirumugham, Tam, 1980)
Anbukku Oru Annan (N.S. Manian, Tam, 1971)
Anbulla Appa (A.C. Trilogchander, Tam, 1987)
Anbulla Athan (Kanmani Subbu, Tam, 1981)
Anbulla Malare (B.R. Ravi Shankar, Tam, 1984)
Anbulla Rajanikant (K. Nataraj, Tam, 1984)
Anbu Magan (**T. Prakash Rao**, Tam, 1961)
Anbu Roja (Devaraj-Mohan, Tam, 1974)
Anbu Sahodarargal (Lakshmi Deepak, Tam, 1973)
Anbu Thangai (S.P. Muthuraman, Tam, 1974)
Anbu Vazhi (M. Natesan, Tam, 1968)
Anchara Ki Laaj (?, Bh, 1989)
Andagadu (?, Tel, 1982)
Andala Ramudu (**Bapu**, Tel, 1973)
Andal Thirukalyanam (**R.S. Prakash**, Tam, 1937)
Andamaina Anubhavam (**K. Balachander**, Tel, 1979)
Andaman Ammayi (V. Madhusudhana Rao, Tel, 1979)
Andaman Kaithi (V. Krishnan, Tam, 1952)
Andaman Kathali (Muktha V. Srinivasan, Tam, 1977)
Andame Anandam (**Singeetham Srinivasa Rao**, Tel, 1977)
Andam Kosam Pandem (A. Sheshgiri Rao, Tel, 1971)
Andar Bahar (Raj N. Sippy, H, 1984)
Andarikante Ghanudu (**C.V. Sridhar**, Tel, 1987)
Andarikante Monagadu (T. Krishna, Tel, 1985)
Andariki Monagadu (M. Mallikarjuna Rao, Tel, 1971)
Andaru Bagundali (**P. Pullaiah**, Tel, 1975)
Andaru Dongale (V.B. Rajendra Prasad, Tel, 1974)
And at Last *see* Abasheshe
Andavan Kathali (K. Shankar, Tam, 1964)
Andavan Sothu (M. Karnan, Tam, 1985)
Andaz (**Mehboob**, H, 1949)
Andaz (**Ramesh Sippy**, H, 1971)
And Bones Do Blossom *see* Asthikal Pookkunnu
Andha Atit (Hiren Nag, B, 1972)
Andha Diganta (**Manmohan Mahapatra**, O, 1989)
Andha Inteqam (Swaroop Kumar, H, 1993)
Andha Kanoon (**T. Rama Rao**, H, 1983)
Andhakar *see* Mano Na Mano
Andhala Magto Ek Dola (**Raja Paranjpe**, Mar, 1956)
Andhala Marto Dola (Dinesh, Mar, 1973)
Andhali Phoolwali *see* Asha
Andha Naal (**S. Balachander**, Tam, 1954)
Andha Oru Nimidam (Major Sundarrajan, Tam, 1985)
Andha Ratrikku Satchi Illai (R. Sundarrajan, Tam, 1982)
Andhare Alo (**Sisir Bhaduri/Naresh Mitra**, St, 1922)
Andhare Alo (Haridas Bhattacharya, B, 1957)
Andhar Periye (**Tapan Sinha**, B, 1973)
Andhar Surya (Sudhir Mukherjee, B, 1969)
Andharu Manchivare (S.S. Balan, Tel, 1975)
Andha Ezhu Natkal (**K. Bhagyaraj**, Tam, 1981)
Andha Sila Natkal (Venkat, Tam, 1983)
Andhasthu (R. Thyagarajan, Tam, 1985)
Andha Uravukku Satchi (R. Pattabhiraman, Tam, 1984)
Andha Yudh (Dayal Nihalani, H, 1988)
Andhera (Aspi, H, 1943)
Andhera (Tulsi/Shyam **Ramsay**, H, 1975)
Andhergardi (Ashok Tyagi, H, 1989)
Andheri Duniya (**Vishram Bedekar**, H, 1936)
Andheri Raat Mein Diya Tere Haath Mein (**Dada Kondke**, H, 1986)
Andher Nagari *see* **Bhavni Bhavai**
Andher Nagari Choupat Raja (Shamim Bhagat, H, 1955)
Andhi Duniya (?, Zenith Pics., H, 1943)
Andhi Gali (**Buddhadev Dasgupta**, H, 1984)
Andhi Jawani *see* **Gumrah**
Andhi Mayakkam (Bhanudasan, Tam, 1981)
Andhi Varum Neram (?, G.S. Prod, Tam, 1990)
Andhiveyilille Ponnu (Radhakrishnan, Mal, 1982)
Andhon Ka Sahara (Vasantrao Tungare, H, 1948)
Andhon Ki Duniya (**Keshavrao Date**, H, 1947)
Andhra Kesari (Thirumalai-Vijaychandar, Tel, 1983)
And Man Created (**Adoor Gopalakrishnan**, E, 1968)
And Miles to Go... (**S. Sukhdev**, E, 1965)
Andolan (**Phani Majumdar**, H, 1951)
Andolan (Lekh Tandon, H, 1975)
And One Did Not Come Back *see* **Dr Kotnis Ki Amar Kahani**
And Quiet Flows the Dawn/And Quiet Rolls the Day *see* **Ek Din Pratidin**
Andru Kanda Mukham (?, New India Prod, Tam, 1968)
Andru Moodal Indru Vari (?, Tam, 1981)
Andru Moodal Innu Varai (Kayyen, Mal, 1992)
Andru Sindhia Ratham (R. Sundaram, Tam, 1976)
And There Was a Village *see* **Oridathu**
A Neram Alpa Dooram (Thampi Kannamthanam, Mal, 1985)
Angachamayam (Rajaji-Babu, Mal, 1982)
Angadi (**I.V. Sasi**, Mal, 1980)
Angadi Bomma (V. Madhusudhana Rao, Tel, 1978)
Angadikkapurathu (**I.V. Sasi**, Mal, 1985)
Angai (Keshav Toro, Mar, 1968)
Angaiyalli Apsara (C.R. Simha, K, 1993)
Angalai Nambathe (Alex Pandian, Tam, 1987)
Angam (Joshi, Mal, 1983)
Angar (Ashok Roy, H, 1980)
Angar (Govind Kulkarni, Mar, 1988)
Angar (Srinivas Chakraborty, B, 1989)
Angar (K. Shashilal Nair, H, 1992)
Angarey (K.B. Lall, H, 1954)
Angarey (**Govind Saraiya**, H, 1975)
Angarey (Rajesh Seth, H, 1986)
Angathattu (**T.R. Raghunath**, Mal, 1973)
Angathavasam (A.B. Raj, Mal, 1972)
Anger Which Burns *see* **Agni**
Angi Trishna (Prabhat Roy, B, 1989)
Angikar (Sushil Ghosh, B, 1966)
Angikar (Probin Bora, A, 1985)
Angikaram (**I.V. Sasi**, Mal, 1977)
Angoor (**S.S. Gulzar**, H, 1981)
Angoorbala (Nadeem Siddiqui, H, 1947)
Angoori (**Mahesh Kaul**, H, 1943)
Angootha Chhaap (**Sai Paranjpye**, H, 1988)
Angoothi (B. Mitra, H, 1943)
Angrejjan (Subhash Bhakri, P, 1982)
Ang Se Ang Lagale (Shiv Kumar, H, 1974)
Angulimal (**Vijay Bhatt**, H, 1960)
Anhonee (*aka* The Impossible: **K.A. Abbas**, H, 1952)
Anhonee (Ravi Tandon, H, 1973)
Anibarya (Ratan Chatterjee, B, 1952)
Anicha Malar (Vijayakumar, Tam, 1981)
Animal Reproduction and Artificial Insemination in Bovines (**Shyam Benegal**, E, 1983)
A Nimisham (**I.V. Sasi**, Mal, 1977)

Anindita (**Hemanta Mukherjee**, B, 1972)
Anirban (Soumyen Mukherjee, B, 1948)
Anirban (**Bhabendranath Saikia**, A, 1981)
Anirikshita (B. Nagesh Babu, K, 1970)
Anita (**Raj Khosla**, H, 1967)
Anivar (K. Vijayan, Tel, 1981)
Aniyara (**B.G. Bharathan**, Mal, 1977)
Aniyatha Valakkal (**Balachandra Menon**, Mal, 1980)
Anjaam (*aka* Ishwari Nyay: **Kanjibhai Rathod**, H, 1940)
Anjaam (Shanti Kumar, H, 1952)
Anjaam (Shiv Kumar, H, 1968)
Anjaam (Kishore Khanna, H, 1978)
Anjaam (**T. Hariharan**, H, 1986)
Anjaam Khuda Jaane (Tahir Akhtoon, H, 1989)
Anjaan (**Amiya Chakravarty**, H, 1941)
Anjaan (M. Sadiq, H, 1956)
Anjaana (Sam Poppet, H, 1948)
Anjaana (Mohan Kumar, H, 1969)
Anjaan Hai Koi (**Babubhai Mistri**, H, 1969)
Anjaan Raahein (Mohan, H, 1974)
Anjada Gandu (Renuka Sharma, K, 1988)
Anjal Petty 520 (T.N. Balu, Tam, 1969)
Anjali (**Chetan Anand**, H, 1957)
Anjali (**I.V. Sasi**, Mal, 1977)
Anjali (Anjan Choudhury, B, 1988)
Anjali (**Mani Rathnam**, Tam/H, 1990)
Anjane Mehmaan (Gyanesh Mukherjee, H, 1975)
Anjane Mein (Samir Ganguly, H, 1978)
Anjangarh (**Bimal Roy**, B/H, 1948)
Anjatha Nenjangal (R. Thyagarajan, Tam, 1981)
Anju Sundarigal (M. Krishnan Nair, Mal, 1968)
Anjuman (Akhtar Hussain, H, 1948)
Anjuman (**Muzaffar Ali**, H, 1986)
Ankahee (*aka* The Unspoken: **Amol Palekar**, H, 1984)
Ankhen *see* Aankhen
Ankhijal (Kalipada Das, St, 1932)
Ankiliyude Tharattu (Cochin Haniffa, Mal, 1987)
Ankitam (P. Eswara Rao, Tel, 1990)
Ankur (**Shyam Benegal**, H, 1973)
Ankuram (?, Mal, 1982)
Ankuram (Uma Maheshwara Rao, Tel, 1992)
Ankur Maina Aur Kabutar (Madan Bawaria, H, 1989)
Ankush (**Tapan Sinha**, B, 1954)
Ankush (**N. Chandra**, H, 1985)
Ankusham (Kodi Ramakrishna, Tel, 1989)
Anmol (Ketan Desai, H, 1993)
Anmol Ghadi (**Mehboob**, H, 1946)
Anmol Moti (Shanti Kumar, H, 1949)
Anmol Moti (Nirmal Srivastava, H, 1965)
Anmol Moti (S.D. Narang, H, 1969)
Anmol Rattan (M. Sadiq, H, 1950)
Anmol Sahara (Amar Dutt, H, 1952)
Anmol Sitara (Geethapriya, H, 1982)
Anmol Tasveer (**Satyen Bose**, H, 1978)
Anna (**K.S. Sethumadhavan**, Mal, 1964)
Anna Attige (M.R. Vittal, K, 1974)
Anna Chellalu (**B. Vittalacharya**, Tel, 1960)
Anna Chellalu (Raviraja Pinisetty, Tel, 1988)
Annadadidi (?, Neo Films, H, 1987)
Anna Dammula Anubandham (S.D. Lall, Tel, 1975)
Anna Dammula Katha (D.S. Prakash Rao, Tel, 1975)
Anna Dammula Saval (K.S.R. Doss, Tel, 1978)
Anna Damulu (V. Ramachandra Rao, Tel, 1969)
Annadata (Ismail Memon, H, 1952)
Annadata (**Vedantam Raghavaiah**, Tel, 1954)
Annadata (**Asit Sen**, H, 1972)
Annai/Penchina Prema (**Krishnan-Panju**, Tam/Tel, 1962)
Annai Abhirami (G.N. Velumani, Tam, 1972)
Annai Bhoomi (R. Thyagarajan, Tam, 1985)
Annai En Daivam (R. Krishnamurthy, Tam, 1986)
Annai Illam (P. Madhavan, Tam, 1963)
Annai Oru Alayam (R. Thyagarajan, Tam, 1979)
Annai Vayal (Ponnvannan, Tam, 1992)
Annai Velanganni (K. Thankappan, Tam, 1971)
Annaiyah (D. Rajendra Babu, K, 1993)
Annaiyin Aanai (**Ch. Narayanamurthy**, Tam, 1958)
Annaiyin Madiyil (S. Rajguru, Tam, 1992)
Annaiyum Pithavum (**Krishnan-Panju**, Tam, 1969)
Annakkili (Devaraj-Mohan, Tam, 1976)
Annakkili Sonna Kathai (S. Devaraj, Tam, 1989)
Annakutti Kodambakkam Vilikkunnu (Jagathy Shrikumar, Mal, 1989)
Anna Lakshmi (S. Srinivasan, Tam, 1978)
Annamalai (Suresh Krishna, Tam, 1992)
Annamitta Kai (M. Krishnan, Tam, 1972)
Annam the Parrot *see* **Annakkili**
Annanagar Muthal Theru (M.N. Balu Anand, Tam, 1988)
Annan Ennada Thambi Ennada (Vijaykrishna Raj, Tam, 1992)
Annan Kattiya Vazhi (K.S. Madhangan, Tam, 1991)
Annan Oru Koyil (K. Vijayan, Tam, 1977)
Annanukkey Jey (Gangai Amaran, Tam, 1989)
Annaparavai (R. Pattabhiraman, Tam, 1980)
Anna Poornammagari Alludu (M. Rosi Raju, Tel, 1988)
Annapoorni (**Krishnan-Panju**, Tam, 1978)
Annapurna (?, Bengal Movie Pictures, St, 1933)
Annapurna (V. Madhusudhana Rao, Tel/Tam, 1960)
Annapurna (Aruru Pattabhi, K, 1964)
Annapurna (Sadashiv J. Row Kavi, Mar, 1968)
Annapurnar Mandir (Tinkari Chakraborty, B, 1936)
Annapurnar Mandir (**Naresh Mitra**, B, 1954)
Anna Thamudu (**C.S. Rao**, Tel, 1958)
Anna Thamudu (**Ghantamneni Krishna**, Tel, 1991)
Anna Thamma (Ravi, K, 1968)
Anna Thangi (K.R. Seetarama Sastry, K, 1958)
Annavin Asai (Dada Mirasi, Tam, 1966)
Anney Anney (Mouli, Tam, 1983)
Anni (Kartick Raghunathan, Tam, 1985)
Anni *see* Deeksha *or* Kusirthikuttan
Annoru Ravil (M.R. Joseph, Mal, 1985)
Anokha (Jugal Kishore, H, 1975)
Anokha Aspatal (Mukesh Sharma, H, 1989)
Anokha Bandhan (**Mehul Kumar**, H, 1982)
Anokha Daan (**Asit Sen**, H, 1972)
Anokha Darr (Tulsi/Shyam **Ramsay**, H, 1989)
Anokha Insaan (M.F. Kashyap, H, 1986)
Anokha Jungle (*aka* Zanzibar: Sultan, H, 1956)
Anokha Milan (Jagannath Chatterjee, H, 1972)
Anokha Mod (Kamal Chandiok, H, 1985)
Anokha Prem (F.R. Irani, H, 1934)
Anokha Pyar (M.I. Dharamsey, H, 1948)
Anokha Rishta (**I.V. Sasi**, H, 1986)
Anokha Shivbhakt (**Bapu**, H, 1978)
Anokhi Ada (**Mehboob**, H, 1948)
Anokhi Ada (Kundan Kumar, H, 1973)
Anokhi Mohabbat (Ramnik Desai, H, 1934)
Anokhi Pehchan (**Satyen Bose**, H, 1972)
Anokhi Qurbani *see* Ahuti
Anokhi Raat (**Asit Sen**, H, 1968)
Anokhi Seva (Safdar Mirza, H, 1949)
Anolkhi (Kamalakar Torne, Mar, 1973)
Anpadh (Mohan Kumar, H, 1962)
Anpadh (S.M. Sagar, H, 1978)
Anpillai Singham *see* Aan Pillai Singam
Anru Peitha Malayil (Ashok Kumar, Tam, 1989)
Ansuya (**Ahindra Choudhury**, Tel, 1935)
Ansuya (**C. Pullaiah**, Tel, 1936)
Ansuyammagari Alludu (A. Kodandarami Reddy, Tel, 1986)
Anta Mana Manchike (**P. Bhanumathi**, Tel, 1972)
Anta Manavalle (**Tapi Chanakya**, Tel, 1954)
Antaral (**Agradoot**, B, 1965)
Antarala (**Suresh Heblikar**, K, 1983)
Antaraley (Shantanu Mitra, B, 1985)
Antaranga (**Dinen Gupta**, B, 1988)
Antardhan (**Tapan Sinha**, B, 1991)
Antardhanam (**I.V. Sasi**, Mal, 1977)
Antareen (**Mrinal Sen**, B, 1993)
Antaricha Diva (Madhav Shinde, Mar, 1960)
Antariksha (**Rajen Tarafdar**, B, 1957)
Antarjali Jatra/Mahayatra (**Gautam Ghosh**, B/H, 1987)
Antarnaad (**Shyam Benegal**, H, 1992)
Antarpat (Shantaram Savant, Mar, 1987)
Antastulu (V. Madhusudhana Rao, Tel, 1965)
Ante Kavali (**K.S. Prakash Rao**, Tel, 1955)
Antha (**S.V. Rajendra Singh**, K, 1981)
Antham/Drohi (Ramgopal Varma, Tel/H, 1992)
Antham Choosina Adadi (J. Williams, Tel, 1983)
Antham Kadidi Arambham (**Vijayanirmala**, Tel, 1981)
Anthappuram (Chandrakumar, Mal, 1980)
Antharala *see* Antarala
Antharangam (Muktha V. Srinivasan, Tam, 1975)
Antharangam Oomaiyanthu (G. Premkumar, Tam, 1980)
Anthaveyilile Ponnu (?, Mal, 1982)
Anthi Chuvappu (Kuriyan Varnasala, Mal, 1984)
Anthuleni Katha (**K. Balachander**, Tel, 1976)
Antima Ghatta (Janakiram, K, 1987)
Antima Theerpu (A.T. Raghu, K, 1987)
Antima Theerpu (Joshi, Tel, 1988)
Anti-Memoirs (**Manmohan Mahapatra**, E, 1975)
Antim Ichha (F. Makrani, G, 1984)
Antim Nyay (Sukhwant Dhadda, H, 1993)
Antinta Gandu Naanalla (Srinivasa, K, 1989)
Antony Firingee (Sunil Bannerjee, B, 1967)
Antony Mor Naam (**Nip Barua**, A, 1986)
Anu (**P.N. Menon**, Tam, 1982)
Anubandha (V.L. Acharya, K, 1978)
Anubandhalu (**P.S. Ramakrishna Rao**, Tel, 1963)
Anubandham (A. Kodandarami Reddy, Tel, 1984)
Anubandham (**I.V. Sasi**, Mal, 1985)
Anubavai Raja Anubavai (**K. Balachander**, Tam, 1967)
Anubhav (**Basu Bhattacharya**, H, 1971)
Anubhava/Anubhav (Kashinath, K/H, 1984)
Anubhavam (**I.V. Sasi**, Mal, 1976)
Anubhavam Pudhumai (C.V. Rajendran, Tam, 1967)
Anubhavangal Palichakal (**K.S. Sethumadhavan**, Mal, 1971)
Anubhavangale Nandi (**I.V. Sasi**, Mal, 1979)
Anubhootikalude Nimisham (P. Chandrakumar, Mal, 1978)

Vijayalakshmi and Sajjan in *Toofan* (1954)

Anugraha (**H.L.N. Simha**, K, 1971)
Anugraham *see* **Kondura**
Anugraham (Malattoor Ravi Varma, Mal, 1977)
A Nuhen Kahani *see* E Nuhen Kahani
Anujathi (M. Krishnan Nair, Mal, 1955)
Anukunnadhi Sadhishta (P. Chandrasekhara Reddy, Tel, 1978)
Anumodhanam (**I.V. Sasi**, Mal, 1978)
Anupallavi (Baby, Mal, 1979)
Anupama (**Agradoot**, B, 1955)
Anupama (Hrishikesh Mukherjee, H, 1966)
Anupama (Renuka Sharma, K, 1981)
Anuraag (Madhusudhan, H, 1950)
Anuraag (Jatin Das, B, 1951)
Anuraag (**Shakti Samanta**, H, 1972)
Anuraag (**Nitai Palit**, O, 1980)
Anuraag (Jahar Biswas, B, 1990)
Anuradha (Mohan Sinha, H, 1940)
Anuradha (Pranab Roy, B, 1949)
Anuradha (Hrishikesh Mukherjee, H, 1960)
Anuradha (Aruru Pattabhi, K, 1967)
Anuradha (P. Chandrasekhara Reddy, Tel, 1971)
Anuradha (Shashidhar, O, 1980)
Anuradha (Yatrik, B, 1986)
Anuragabandham (Srinivas Chakraborty, Tel, 1985)
Anuraga Devatha (**T. Rama Rao**, Tel, 1982)
Anuraga Kodathi (**T. Hariharan**, Mal, 1982)
Anuragalu (K.S. Rami Reddy, Tel, 1975)
Anurager Choa (Jahar Biswas, B, 1986)
Anuragha Aralitu (M.S. Rajashekhar, K, 1986)
Anuragha Bandhana (Geethapriya, K, 1978)
Anuraghada Alegalu (S. Narayan, K, 1993)
Anuragham (G. Ramineedu, Tel, 1963)
Anuragi (**I.V. Sasi**, Mal, 1988)
Anurakthe (Maruti Shivram, K, 1980)
Anurodh (**Shakti Samanta**, H, 1977)
Anurodh (Jayanta Bhattacharya, B, 1987)
Anurupa (**P. Lankesh**, K, 1977)
Anusandhan *see* Barsaat Ki Ek Raat
Anustup Chhanda (Piyush Bose, B, 1964)
Anutaap (**Atul Bordoloi**, A, 1973)
Anutaap (Jalal Adeni, O, 1977)
Anveshan (Shankar Bhattacharya, B, 1984)
Anveshan (TV: **Basu Bhattacharya**, H, 1985)
Anveshana (**Vamsy**, Tel, 1985)
Anveshanam (**Sasikumar**, Mal, 1972)
Anveshane (**T.S. Nagabharana**, K, 1980)
Anveshichu Kandatiyilla (P. Bhaskaran, Mal, 1967)
Anya (**Girish Kasaravalli**, K, 1975)
Anya Mati Anya Rang (Ramprasad Chakraborty, B, 1971)
Anyarude Bhoomi (Nilambur Balan, Mal, 1979)
Anyay (*aka* Injustice: J.S. Casshyap, H, 1949)
Anyay (Satish Ranadive, Mar, 1987)
Anyay Abichar *see* Aar Paar
Anyaya Sahibi Nahin (Ashok Sharma, O, 1988)
A Okati Adakku (E.V.V. Satyanarayana, Tel, 1992)
Apabaad (Jatin Das, B, 1950)
Apahrita (*aka* The Kidnapped Girl: **Kaliprasad Ghosh**, St, 1929)
Apala (Ishwarlal, H, 1949)
Apaman (Chandan Mukherjee, B, 1988)
Apan Ghare (Pinaki Mukherjee, B, 1987)
Apanindalu Adavallakena (Vejalla Satyanarayana, Tel, 1984)
Apanjan (Tapan Sinha, B, 1968)
Aparadh (**Phani Majumdar**, B, 1942)
Aparadh (Anup Sarkar, B, 1960)
Aparadh (**Rajdutt**, Mar, 1969)
Aparadh (Feroz Khan, H, 1972)
Aparadha (**I.V. Sasi**, Mal, 1992)
Aparadhi (**Debaki Bose**, St, 1931)
Aparadhi (Dada Gunjal, H, 1935)
Aparadhi (?, Movie Technicians, H, 1942)
Aparadhi (Yeshwant Pethkar, H, 1949)
Aparadhi (**Sushil Majumdar**, B, 1955)
Aparadhi (Jugal Kishore, H, 1974)
Aparadhi (P.N. Sundaram, Mal, 1976)
Aparadhi (V.R. Swamy, K, 1976)
Aparadhi (P. Sambhasiva Rao, Tel, 1984)
Aparadhi (Nandan Dasgupta, B, 1988)
Aparadhi (K. Ravi Shankar, H, 1992)
Aparadhi Abla (F.R. Irani, H, 1935)
Aparadhi Kaun (**Asit Sen**, H, 1957)
Aparadhi Kaun (Mohan Bhakri, H, 1982)
Aparadhini (**P. Bhaskaran**, Mal, 1968)
Aparadhini (Vinod Sharma, H, 1990)
Aparahnam (M.P. Sukumaran Nair, Mal, 1990)
Aparajeya [Chaturanga(**Atul Bordoloi**), A, 1970]
Aparajitha (**Sasikumar**, Mal, 1977)
Aparajithe (Veerabhadraiah, K, 1970)
Aparajito (Partha Sarathy, B, 1951)
Aparajito (Satyajit Ray, B, 1956)
Aparajito (Amitabha Dasgupta/Ramesh Joshi, B, 1975)
Aparan (P. Padmarajan, Mal, 1988)
Aparanher Alo (**Agradoot**, B, 1989)
Aparanji *see* Daasi
Aparanji (Ravindranath, K, 1984)
Aparichita (Salil Dutta, B, 1969)
Aparichita (Kashinath, K, 1978)
Aparichita (Sadhu Meher, O, 1980)
Aparichita (TV: **Utpalendu Chakraborty**, B, 1986)
Aparna (Padmakumar, Mal, 1981)
Aparoopa/Apeksha (Jahnu Barua, A/H, 1982)
Aparoopa (Bidesh Sarkar, B, 1983)
Aparoopada Atithagalu (Kashinath, K, 1976)
Aparoopada Kathe (Vemagal Jagannatha, K, 1986)
Apath Bandhava (A.T. Raghu, K, 1987)
Apath Bandhavulu (Y. Eshwara Reddy, Tel, 1983)
Apath Bandhavulu (*aka* The Saviour: **K. Vishwanath**, Tam, 1992)
Apatkaal (V Subba Rao, H, 1993)
Apavadu (**Gudavalli Ramabrahmam**, Tel, 1941)
Apeksha *see* **Aparoopa**
Aplam Chaplam (**Roop K. Shorey**, H, 1961)
Aplech Daat Aplech Oth (**Rajdutt**, Mar, 1982)
Aple Ghar *see* **Apna Ghar**
Apli Manse (V.K. Naik Mar, 1979)
Apmaan (Ami Asthana, H, 1982)
Apmaan Ki Aag (S.J. Talukdar, H, 1990)
Apna Bana Lo (J. Om Prakash, H, 1982)
Apna Banake Dekho (Jagdish Nirula, H, 1962)
Apna Bhi Koi Hota (Girish Ranjan, H, 1984)
Apna Desh/Nam Naadu (**V. Shantaram**, H/Tel, 1949)
Apna Desh (Jambulingam, H, 1972)
Apna Desh Paraye Log (Pradeep Hooda, H, 1989)
Apna Farz (K.S.R. Doss, H, 1973)
Apna Ghar/Aple Ghar (Debaki Bose, H/Mar, 1942)
Apna Ghar (Ram Pava, H, 1960)
Apna Ghar (Kalpataru, H, 1989)
Apna Ghar Apni Kahani (*aka* Pyaas: **Phani Majumdar**, H, 1968)
Apna Haath Jagannath (Mohan Segal, H, 1960)
Apna Jahan (?, Preeti Films, H, 1987)
Apna Khoon *see* **Taqdeer**
Apna Khoon (B. Subhash, H, 1978)
Apna Khoon Apna Dushman (Kamran, H, 1969)
Apnapan (J. Om Prakash, H, 1977)
Apna Paraya (**Ramchandra Thakur**, H, 1942)
Apne Apne (Ramesh Behl, H, 1987)
Apne Begane (Madhu Tejpal, H, 1989)
Apne Dushman (Kailash Bhandari, H, 1975)
Apne Huye Paraye (Ajit Chakraborty, H, 1964)
Apne Paraye (**Basu Chatterjee**, H, 1980)
Apne Rang Hazaar (Ravi Tandon, H, 1975)
Apni Chhaya (P.L. Santoshi, H, 1950)
Apni Izzat (**Nanabhai Bhatt**, H, 1952)
Apni Nagariya (Dada Gunjal, H, 1940)
Apon Amar Apon (**Tarun Majumdar**, B, 1990)
Apoorva Chintamani *see* 1000 Thalaivangi Apoorva Chintamani
Apoorva Kanasu (P. Balachandra, K, 1976)
Apoorvam Silar (Kala Adoor, Mal, 1991)
Apoorva Nagam (Chozharajan, Tam, 1991)
Apoorva Piravigal (G. Vishwanathan, Tam, 1967)
Apoorva Ragangal (K. Balachander, Tam, 1975)
Apoorva Sahodaralu (C. Pullaiah, Tel, 1950)
Apoorva Sahodaralu (**K. Raghavendra Rao**, Tel, 1986)
Apoorva Sahodarargal/Nishan (T.G. Raghavacharya/**S.S. Vasan**, Tam/H, 1949)
Apoorva Sahodarargal/Appu Raja (**Singeetham Srinivasa Rao**, Tam/H, 1989)
Apoorva Sahodarigal (R. Thyagarajan, Tam, 1983)
Apoorva Sangama (Y.R. Swamy, K, 1984)
Apostle of Truth, The *see* Harishchandra
Appa Amma (Malliyam Rajagopal, Tam, 1974)
Appagintalu (V. Madhusudhana Rao, Tel, 1962)
Appa Tata (Malliyam Rajagopal, Tam, 1972)
Appiko (**Prema Karanth**, K, 1988)
Appooppan (**P. Bhaskaran**, Mal, 1976)
Appothe Sonnene Kettiya (V.T. Arasu, Tam, 1976)
Appothi Adigal (**R. Padmanabhan**/Fram Sethna, Tam, 1941)
Appu Chesi Pappu Koodu/Kadam Vangi Kalyanam (L.V. Prasad, Tel/Tam, 1958)
Appula Apparao (E.V.V. Satyanarayana, Tel, 1991)
Appunni (Sathyan Andhikkad, Mal, 1984)
Appu Raja *see* Apoorva Sahodarargal
Aprakavil Appu (?, Tam, 1986)
April 18 (Balachandra Menon, Mal, 1984)
April Fool (**Subodh Mukherjee**, H, 1964)
April 1 Vidudala (**Vamsy**, Tel, 1991)
April Pathinettu *see* **April 18**
Apsara (**V.M. Vyas**, H, 1961)
Apsara Urvashi (?, British India Film, St, 1931)
Apta Mithrulu (**Kadaru Nagabhushanam**, Tel, 1963)
Apur Sansar (Satyajit Ray, B, 1959)
Apyo Jadro (Himmat Dave, G, 1979)
Arabian Knight, The *see* Sher-e-Arab
Arabian Nights *see* Alif Laila
Arabian Nights, The (?, **Madan Theatres**, St, 1927)
Arabian Nights (**Niren Lahiri**, H, 1946)
Arabian Nights (*aka* Panic in Baghdad, Baghdad Ki Raatein: **Nanabhai Bhatt**, H, 1967)
Arabic Hansa (?, Basant Pics, Arabic, 1943)
Arabikadal (**Sasikumar**, Mal, 1983)
Arab Ka Chand (Naseem Siddiqui, H, 1946)
Arab Ka Lal (A. Shamsheer, H, 1964)
Arab Ka Saudagar (S.D. Narang, H, 1956)
Arab Ka Sitara (**Nanubhai Vakil**, H, 1946)
Arab Ka Sitara (P.K. Rehman, H, 1961)
Arada Gaya (V. Somasekhar, K, 1980)
Aradhana (V. Madhusudhana Rao, Tel, 1962)
Aradhana (Shakti Samanta, H, 1969)
Aradhana (B.V. Prasad, Tel, 1976)
Aradhana (**Madhu**, Mal, 1977)
Aradhana (**Bharathirajaa**, Tel, 1987)
Aradhanai (Prasad, Tam, 1981)
Aradhane (Deepak Balraj, K, 1984)
Aradhika (B.K. Pottekkad, Mal, 1973)
Aradi Manninte Janmi (**P. Bhaskaran**, Mal, 1972)
Araichi Mani (*aka* Manu Neethi Cholan: **Raja Sandow**, Tam, 1942)
Arakallan Mukkal Kallan (**P. Bhaskaran**, Mal, 1974)
Arakillam (N. Shankaran Nair, Mal, 1967)
Arakshaniya (**Pashupati Chatterjee**, B, 1948)
Aralida Hoovugalu (Chi Dattaraj, K, 1991)
Aram (D.D. Kashyap, H, 1951)
Aram + Aram = Kinnaram (**Priyadarshan**, Mal, 1985)
Arambh (Gyan Kumar, H, 1976)
Arambham (Joshi, Mal, 1982)
Aram Haram Aahe (Kamalakar Torne, Mar, 1976)
Aranazhikaneram (K.S. Sethumadhavan, Mal, 1970)
Arangetram (**K. Balachander**, Tam, 1973)
Arangetra Velai (**Fazil**, Tam, 1990)
Arangu (Chandrasekharan, Mal, 1991)
Arangum Aniyarayum (Chandrakumar, Mal, 1980)
Arani Mantulu (K. Vasu, Tel, 1980)
Aranjanam (?, Mal, 1982)
Aranmanai Kili (Rajkiran, Tam, 1993)
Arante Mulla Kochu Mulla (**Balachandra Menon**, Mal, 1984)
Aranya (Samarendra Narayan Deb, A, 1971)
Aranya Amar (**Tarun Majumdar**, B, 1985)
Aranyadalli Abhimanyu (Bhargava, K, 1991)
Aranyak (Ajit Lahiri, B, 1973)
Aranyakam (**T. Hariharan**, Mal, 1988)
Aranyakanda (Kranthi Kumar, Tel, 1987)
Aranyakandam (**Sasikumar**, Mal, 1975)
Aranyam (P. Gopikumar, Mal, 1981)
Aranyer Din Ratri (Satyajit Ray, B, 1969)
Arappatta Kettiya Gramathil (**P. Padmarajan**, Mal, 1985)
Arappavan (K. Shankar, Mal, 1961)
Arasa Kattali (**Chakrapani**, Tam, 1967)
Arasilankumari (**A.S.A. Sami**, Tam, 1961)
Arathi (?, Mal, 1981)
Arathi Edungadi (?, Murali Cine Arts, Tam, 1990)
A Rathri (Joshi, Mal, 1983)
Arati (J.H. Sattar, O, 1981)
Arati (Ashim Das, A, 1985)
Arattu (**I.V. Sasi**, Mal, 1979)
Aravalli (S.V. Krishna Rao, Tam, 1957)
Aravalli Sooravalli (C.V. Raman, Tam, 1946)
Aravam (**B.G. Bharathan**, Mal, 1978)
Archana (**K.S. Sethumadhavan**, Mal, 1966)
Archana (Piyush Ganguly, B, 1972)
Archana (Satpal, H, 1973)
Archana (Manimurugan, K, 1982)
Archana Aradhana (Sajan, Mal, 1985)
Archana IAS (A. Jagannathan, Tam, 1991)
Archanai Pookkal (Gokulakrishna, Tam, 1982)
Archana Teacher (**P.N. Menon**, Mal, 1981)
Archer, The *see* Tirandaz
Ardhanari (**T.R. Raghunath**, Tam, 1945)
Ardhangi/Ghar Ki Rani (Master Vinayak, Mar/H, 1940)
Ardhangi/Pennin Perumai (P. Pullaiah, Tel/Tam, 1955)
Ardhangi (A. Mohan Gandhi, Tel, 1977)
Ardhangi (**Rajdutt**, Mar, 1985)
Ardhangini (Bikash Roy, B, 1955)
Ardhangini (Ajit Chakraborty, H, 1959)
Ardha Rathri (P. Sambhasiva Rao, Tel, 1969)
Ardha Rathri (Ashakhan, Mal, 1986)
Ardha Rathri Swatanthiram (R. Narayanamurthy, Tel, 1986)
Ardh Satya (Govind Nihalani, H, 1983)
Are Sansar Sansar (**Rajdutt**, Mar, 1981)
Areyappedatha Rahasyam (Venu, Mal, 1981)
Arghya (**Debaki Bose**, B, 1961)
Argument and a Story *see* **Jukti Takko Aar Gappo**
Arikkari Ammu (Shrikumaran Thampi, Mal, 1981)
Arishina Kumkuma (Ravi, K, 1970)
Arising from the Surface *see* **Satah Se Uthata Admi**
Arivali (A.T. Krishnaswamy, Tam, 1963)
Arivu (Katte Ramachandra, K, 1979)
Ariyatha Veethigal (**K.S. Sethumadhavan**, Mal, 1984)
Ariyum Perumal *see* Thamizhariyum Perumal
Arjun (Inder Sen, B, 1975)
Arjun (**Rahul Rawail**, H, 1985)
Arjun (A.T. Raghu, K, 1988)
Arjun Dennis (?, Mal, 1988)
Arjun Pandit (**Hrishikesh Mukherjee**, H, 1976)
Armaan (Kidar Sharma, H, 1942)
Armaan (Fali Mistry, H, 1953)
Armaan (*aka* The Desires: Anand Sagar, H, 1981)
Arodum Parayaruthu (A.J. Rogers, Mal, 1985)
Aro Ekjan (Srijan, B, 1980)
Arogyaniketan (Bijoy Bose, B, 1969)
Arohanam (A.I. Rishi, Mal, 1980)
Arohi (*aka* Ascent: **Tapan Sinha**, B, 1964)
Aromalunni (**Kunchako**, Mal, 1972)
Aroodam (**I.V. Sasi**, Mal, 1983)
Arorumariyathe (**K.S. Sethumadhavan**, Mal, 1984)
Around the World (*aka* Duniya Ki Sair: Pachhi, H, 1967)
Arpan (J. Om Prakash, H, 1983)
Arpan (Srinivas Chakraborty, B, 1987)

Arpita (Aravind Mukherjee, B, 1983)
Arrival (**Mani Kaul**, E, 1979)
Arrow of Destiny *see* Taqdeer Ka Teer
Artanad (Chanda Mukherjee, B, 1986)
Arth (**Mahesh Bhatt**, H, 1982)
Artham (Johnson, Mal, 1989)
Arthamulla Asaigal (Babu Maharaja, Tam, 1985)
Arthanadam (M.V. Raghu, Tel, 1989)
Arthangal Ayiram (Rajkannan, Tam, 1981)
Arulirundhu Arupadhu Varai (S.P. Muthuraman, Tam, 1979)
Arul Theram Ayappan (Dasarathan, Tam, 1987)
Arumai Makal Abirami (V. Krishnan, Tam, 1959)
Arumbugal (Jupiter Chinnadurai, Tam, 1979)
Aruna Raga (K. Vijayaram, K, 1986)
Arunagiri Nathar (Raja Yagnik, Tam, 1937)
Arunagiri Nathar (Ramanna, Tam, 1964)
Arun Barun-o-Kiranmala (Barun Kabasi, B, 1979)
Arundhati (**Raja Chandrasekhar**, Tam, 1943)
Arundhati (Prafulla Sengupta, O, 1967)
Arundivide Chodikkan (Manoj Babu, Mal, 1986)
Arunodaya (*aka* Rising Sun: **B.P. Mishra**, St, 1930)
Arunodaya/Arunodhayam (C. Srinivasan, K/Tam, 1968)
Arup Katha *see* Bedeni
Aruthu (Ravi, Mal, 1976)
Arutperunjyothi (T.S. Balachandran/A.T. Krishnaswamy, Tam, 1971)
Aruvadainal (G.M. Kumar, Tam, 1986)
Aruvathu Naal Aruvathu Nimidham (?, Kalaichirpi Films, Tam, 1990)
Arvind Desai Ki Ajeeb Dastaan (**Saeed Mirza**, H, 1978)
Arya Kanya (Gokhale, St, 1930)
Arya Mahila (*aka* The Ideal Wife: **N.D. Sarpotdar**, St, 1928)
Aryamala (S.M. Sreeramulu Naidu, Tam, 1941)
Aryan (**Priyadarshan**, Mal, 1988)
Aryankavu Kallasangham (R. Velappan, Mal, 1969)
Arzoo (R.M. Vaidya/M. Issa, H, 1942)
Arzoo (Shaheed Latif, H, 1950)
Arzoo (*aka* Love in Kashmir: **Ramanand Sagar**, H, 1965)
Asa (Augustin Prakash, Mal, 1982)
Asabarna (Pinaki Mukherjee, B, 1956)
Asadharan (Piyush Bose, B, 1976)
Asadhya Aliya (Bhargava, K, 1979)
Asadhyudu (V. Ramachandra Rao, Tel, 1968)
Asadhyudu (M.S. Kota Reddy, Tel, 1985)
Asahya Sooran (G. Vishwanathan, Tam, 1965)
Asai (**R. Padmanabhan**, Tam, 1937)
Asai (M. Natesan, Tam, 1956)
Asai Alaigal (**A.S.A. Sami**, Tam, 1963)
Asai Anna Arumai Thambi (G.R. Ram, Tam, 1955)
Asai Arubathu Naal (**Durai**, Tam, 1976)
Asai Kiliye Kobanna (T.K. Prasad, Tam, 1991)
Asaikku Vayasilai (Gopu, Tam, 1979)
Asai Machan (Karaikudi Narayanan, Tam, 1985)
Asai Magan (G.R. Rao, Tam, 1953)
Asai Manaivi (K. Sornam, Tam, 1977)
Asai Mukham (**P. Pullaiah**, Tam, 1965)
Asamapta (Ratan Chatterjee, B, 1956)
Asambhav (Jagdish Bannerjee, H, 1985)
Asamshakalode (Vijayan/Karot, Mal, 1983)
Asati (Salil Dutta, B, 1974)
Asattu Veeran Manaivi (?, Yessel Films, Tam, 1938)
Asayam (A. Mohan Gandhi, Tel, 1993)
Ascending Scale, The *see* **Aarohan**
Ascent *see* **Arohi** *or* **Aarohan** *or* **Kodiyettam**
Aseer-e-Hawas (Pandit Shiv Kumar, H, 1936)
Aseer-e-Hirs (*aka* Nemesis of Lust: ?, Surya Film, St, 1931)
Asel Mazha Hari (**Datta Keshav**, Mar, 1971)
Ash, The *see* Charam
Asha *see* **Aasha**
Asha (*aka* Andhali Phoolwali: **R.S. Choudhury**, St, 1926)
Asha (Parry David/Ranjit Sen, H, 1938)
Asha (Meghani, H, 1948)
Asha (Haridas Bhattacharya, B, 1956)
Asha (J. Om Prakash, H, 1980)
Asha (A.T. Raghu, K, 1983)
Asha (V.T. Thyagarajan, Tam, 1985)
Asha (Sajal Deb/Hiralal Das, B, 1989)
Asha Asavya Suna (Harisut, Mar, 1981)
Ashabari (Apurba Mitra, B, 1949)
Asha Chakram (R. Seetaramaswamy, Mal, 1973)
Ashadabhooti (Fram Sethna, Tam, 1941)
Ashadabhooti (D. Shankar Singh, K, 1955)
Asha Deepam (G.R. Rao, Mal, 1953)
Ashadhi Beej (Dinesh Rawal, G, 1979)
Ashad Ka Ek Din (**Mani Kaul**, H, 1971)
Ashajeevulu (**B.S. Ranga**, Tel, 1962)
Asha Jyoti (**T. Prakash Rao**, Tel, 1981)
Asha Jyoti (**Dasari Narayana Rao**, H, 1984)
Asha Kirana (B.N. Haridas, K, 1984)
Ashani Sanket (**Satyajit Ray**, B, 1973)
Ashanka (Hari Atma, H, 1983)
Ashant (Keshu **Ramsay**, H, 1993)
Ashanta Ghoorni (Pinaki Mukherjee, B, 1964)
Ashanta Graha (Sarat Pujari, O, 1982)
Ashanti (Umesh Mehra, H, 1982)
Ashanti Shantidas (TV: **Atma Ram**, H, 1977)
Asha-o-Bhalobasha (Sujit Guha, B, 1989)
Ashapura Matani Chundadi (Radhakant, G, 1978)
Ashar Akash (Gadadhar Putti, O, 1983)
Ashar Alo (S. Bannerjee, B, 1973)
Ashasundari/Ramasundari (**Hunsur Krishnamurthy**, K/Tel, 1960)
Ashay Bandhinu Ghar (Kanak Mukherjee, B, 1961)
Ashiana (**Sukumar Dasgupta**, H, 1936)
Ashiana (B. Trilochan, H, 1952)
Ashiana (*aka* Ek Mausam Chhota Sa: Syed Hasan, H, 1974)
Ashiana (**Mahesh Bhatt**, H, 1986)
Ashich Ek Ratra Hoti (**Anant Mane**, Mar, 1971)
Ashi Hi Banavabanvi (Sachin, Mar, 1987)
Ashi Hi Sataryachi Tarha (Murlidhar Kapdi, Mar, 1974)
Ashi Rangali Ratra (Govind Kulkarni, Mar, 1970)
Ashirvadam (R. Devarajan, Tam, 1972)
Ashirvadam (**I.V. Sasi**, Mal, 1976)
Ashirwad (**Ramchandra Thakur**, H, 1943)
Ashirwad (**Hrishikesh Mukherjee**, H, 1968)
Ashirwad (Biresh Mukherjee, B, 1986)
Ashirwada (Kunigal Nagabhushan, K, 1975)
Ashite Ashio Na (Jayadrath, B, 1967)
Ashlilatar Daye (Umanath Bhattacharya, B, 1982)
Ashok (Ajay Bhattacharya, B, 1942)
Ashoka (*aka* Samrat Ashoka: ?, **Madan Theatres**, St, 1922)
Ashoka Chakravarthi (S.S. Ravichandra, Tel, 1989)
Ashokante Ashwathikutti (Vijayan Karot, Mal, 1989)
Ashokavanam (M. Krishnan Nair, Mal, 1978)
Ashok Kumar (**Raja Chandrasekhar**, Tam, 1941)
Ashramam (K.K. Chandran, Mal, 1978)
Ashray (Dulal Roy, A, 1979)
Ashray (Biplab Roy Choudhury, H, 1984)
Ashrayam (K. Ramachandran, Mal, 1983)
Ashru Diye Lekha (Amal Dutta, B, 1966)
Ashtabandham (?, Arifa Combines, Mal, 1986)
Ashtalakshmi Vaibhavamu (**K. Kameshwara Rao**, Tel, 1986)
Ashtalli (**S.P. Bakshi**, P, 1954)
Ashtamangalyam (P. Gopikumar, Mal, 1977)
Ashtami Rohini (A.B. Raj, Mal, 1975)
Ashtamudikayal (K.P. Pillai, Mal, 1978)
Ashtapadi (Ambili, Mal, 1983)
Ashta Vinayak (**Rajdutt**, Mar, 1979)
Ashtram (V.V.L.V. Prasad, Tel, 1991)
Ashwamedha (C.R. Simha, K, 1990)
Ashwamedham (**A. Vincent**, Mal, 1967)
Ashwamedham (**K. Raghavendra Rao**, Tel, 1992)
Ashwamedher Ghora (Shankar Bhattacharya, B, 1980)
Ashwaratham (**I.V. Sasi**, Mal, 1980)
Ashwathama (**Dadasaheb Phalke**, St, 1923)
Ashwathama (**K.R. Mohanan**, Mal, 1978)
Ashwathama (B. Gopal, Tel, 1988)
Ashwini (Mouli, Tel, 1991)
Asiai Sitara (*aka* Star of Asia: ?, Surya Film, St, 1932)
Asiai Sitara (Haribhai Desai, H, 1937)
Asia '72 (**Santi P. Choudhury**, E, 1974)
Asla Navara Nako Ga Bai (**Anant Mane**, Mar, 1977)
Aslilatar Daye (Umanath Bhattacharya, B, 1983)
Asli Naqli (**Hrishikesh Mukherjee**, H, 1962)
Asli Naqli (Sudarshan Nag, H, 1986)
Asliyat (Raghunath Singh, H, 1974)
Asmat *see* Ismat
Asmat Ka Moti (*aka* Chirag-e-Arab: Fram Sethna, H, 1935)
Asmat Ki Devi *see* Nirdosh Abla
Asomoy (Inder Sen, B, 1976)
Assembly Rowdy (B. Gopal, Tel, 1991)
Astaraga (Sarat Pujari, O, 1982)
Asthamayam (P. Chandrakumar, Mal, 1978)
Asthamikkatha Pakalukal (Sharief, Mal, 1981)
Asthikal Pookkunnu (*aka* And Bones Do Blossom: P. Shrikumar, Mal, 1988)
Asthi Kosam (G.K. Suryam, Tel, 1975)
Asthikoru Anum Asaikkoru Pennum (K. Somu, Tam, 1962)
Asthivaram (T. Thirunnavukkarasu, Tam, 1982)
Asthram (**P.N. Menon**, Mal, 1983)
Astiparulu (V. Madhusudhana Rao, Tel, 1966)
Astulu Antastulu (V. Ramachandra Rao, Tel, 1969)
Astulu Antastulu (B. Bhaskara Rao, Tel, 1988)
Asuchi Mo Kalia Sune (Raju Mishra, O, 1989)
Asuran (Hassan, Mal, 1983)
Asuravithu (**A. Vincent**, Mal, 1968)
Asuri Lalsa (*aka* Passion: **Nanubhai Desai**, St, 1927)
Aswathi (Jesey, Mal, 1974)
Aswamedham *see* **Ashwamedham**
As You Please *see* Aap Ki Marzi
Atabommalu (G. Vishwanathan, Tel, 1966)
Atal Jaler Ahwan (**Ajoy Kar**, B, 1962)
Atanikante Ghanudu (G.C. Shekhar, Tel, 1978)
Atanka (**Tapan Sinha**, B, 1986)
Atanka (Saiprakash, K, 1992)
Atash Behram (**H.S. Bhatavdekar**, St, 1901)
Atashi Toofan (*aka* Storm of Death: ?, Pioneer Films, H, 1933)
Atha Naan Pasaitten (?, Anitha Pics, Tam, 1990)
Athai Magal (I.N. Murthy, Tam, 1969)
Athaimadi Methaiyadi (**K.S. Gopalakrishnan**, Tam, 1989)
Athaivida Rahasyam (K. Shankar, Tam, 1978)
Atham Chithira Chothi (?, Salimbabu-Clarion, Mal, 1986)
Atha Sommu Alludu Dhanam (Y. Nageshwara Rao, Tel, 1992)
Atha Un Kovilile (Kasturiraja, Tam, 1991)
Athaya Mamiya (Gopu, Tam, 1974)
Athimadhura Anuraga (P.H. Vishwanath, K, 1992)
Athinti Kapuram *see* Attinti Kapuram
Athinumappuram (Chellappan, Mal, 1987)
Athiranthudu (A. Chandra, Tel, 1991)
Athiratha Maharatha (Perala, K, 1987)
Athirathan (Pradeep Kumar, Mal, 1991)
Athirathnam (**I.V. Sasi**, Mal, 1984)
Athirishtam (*aka* Luck: S.D.S. Yogi, Tam, 1939)
Athirishtam Azhaikkirathu (A. Jagannathan, Tam, 1976)
Athirthigal (J.D. Thottan, Mal, 1988)
Athirupa Amaravathi (C.V. Raman, Tam, 1935)
Athisaya Penn (**M.V. Raman**, Tam, 1959)
Athisaya *see* Adisaya
Athmiyudu (**T. Rama Rao**, Tel, 1977)
Athora Atha (Managadu Ramachandran, Tam, 1984)
Athuleni Vintha Katha (Mohandas, Tel, 1979)
Athyey Kangal (Thirulok Atishbaaz, Tam, 1967)
Ati Shahana Tyacha (**Datta Keshav**, Mar, 1966)
Atishbaaz (Mukhtar Ahmed, H, 1990)
Atithi (**Tapan Sinha**, B, 1965)
Atithi (**K.P. Kumaran**, Mal, 1974)
Atithi (Aravind Sen, H, 1978)
Atma (**Prathap Pothan**, Tam, 1993)
Atma Bal (*aka* Sundar Kamdar: ?, Majestic Film, St, 1924)
Atmabalam (V. Madhusudhana Rao, Tel, 1964)
Atmabalam (T. Prasad, Tel, 1985)
Atma Bandhana (Srikant Nahata, K, 1992)
Atma Bandhavulu (**Dasari Narayana Rao**, Tel, 1987)
Atma Bandhuvu (**P.S. Ramakrishna Rao**, Tel, 1962)
Atmadaan (?, P.S. Films Intl, H, 1989)
Atmadarshan (Surendra Ranjan Sarkar, B, 1955)
Atmagauravam (**K. Vishwanath**, Tel, 1965)
Atmakatha (V. Madhusudhana Rao, Tel, 1988)
Atmaram (Sohanlal Kanwar, H, 1979)
Atmarpanam (G.R. Rao, Mal, 1956)
Atmasakhi/Priyasakhi (G.R. Rao, Mal/Tam, 1952)
Atmashanti (Joseph Taliath, Mal, 1952)
Atmashakti (Raja, K, 1978)
Atma Tarang (**Sohrab Modi**, H, 1937)
Atma Vishwas (Manohar Shetty, H, 1985)
Atmaya (**Nabyendu Chatterjee**, B, 1990)
Atmiyulu (V. Madhusudhana Rao, Tel, 1969)
Atom Bomb (**Homi Wadia**, H, 1947)
Atom Bomb (Taru Mukherjee, B, 1954)
Atom Bomb (**P. Subramanyam**, Mal, 1964)
Attagadu (**T. Rama Rao**, Tel, 1980)
Attagaru Kottakodalu (A. Sanjivi, Tel, 1968)
Attagaru Swagatham (Kodi Ramakrishna, Tel, 1986)
Attagaru Zindabad (Kodi Ramakrishna, Tel, 1987)
Attahasam (K.S. Gopalakrishnan, Mal, 1984)
Attakatha (Williams, Mal, 1987)
Attaki Yamudu Ammayiki Mugudu (A. Kodandarami Reddy, Tel, 1989)
Attakkalasam (**Sasikumar**, Mal, 1983)
Attalu Kodallu (P. Chandrasekhara Reddy, Tel, 1971)
Attamari (**Sasikumar**, Mal, 1981)
Atta Mechina Alludu (Kodi Ramakrishna, Tel, 1989)
Attannikkare (S.L. Puram Sadanandan, Mal, 1989)
Atta Okinti Kodale (K.B. Tilak, Tel, 1958)
Attaracha Phaya (Gangadhar Rawal, Mar, 1984)
Attatar Din Pare (Ajit Lahiri, B, 1971)
Attavarillu (**K. Pratyagatma**, Tel, 1976)
Attege Takka Sose (Y.R. Swamy, K, 1979)
Attegondukala Sosegondukala (Y.R. Swamy, K, 1968)
Attention (M. Navewala, H, 1947)
Atthanu Diddina Kodalu (B.S. Narayana, Tel, 1972)
At the Altar of Love *see* Shirin Farhad
At the Clang of Fetters *see* **Janjirne Jankare**
At the Service of Small Industries (**Vishram Bedekar**, E, 1968)
Attinti Kapuram (Acharya M. Mastan, Tel, 1952)
Attintlo Adde Mogadu (Relangi Narasimha Rao, Tel, 1992)
Attraction, The *see* Kashish
Attuvanchi Ulanjappol (Bhadran, Mal, 1984)
Atukkara Alamelu (R. Thyagarajan, Tam, 1977)
Atyachar (Bhaskar Chandavarkar, Mar, 1982)
Atyachar (C.P. Sharma, H, 1978)
August 15 Rathri (P.N. Ramachandra Rao, Tel, 1988)
August 1 (**Sibi Malayil**, Mal, 1988)
Aukshavanta Ho Bala (Madhukar Kulkarni, Mar, 1953)
Aulad *see* Dil Hi To Hai
Aulad (**Mohan Segal**, H, 1954)
Aulad (Kundan Kumar, H, 1968)
Aulad (Vijay Sadanah, H, 1987)
Aulad Ke Dushman (Rajkumar Kohli, H, 1993)
Aulad Ki Khatir (Kanwar Jagdish, H, 1989)
Aulia-e-Islam (A. Shamsheer, H, 1979)
Aunda Lagin Karaychay (Krishna Patil, Mar, 1974)
Aundhi Khopdi *see* Lal Buzakkad
Aunt Padi's Burmese Box *see* **Padi Pishir Barmi Baksha**
Auntie Na Vajavili Ghanti (Dinesh Sakhare, Mar, 1989)
Aurat (**Mehboob**, H, 1940)

Aurat (B. Verma, H, 1953)
Aurat (**S.S. Vasan**/S.S. Balan, H, 1967)
Aurat (**B.R. Ishara**, H, 1986)
Aurat Aur Patthar (Anil Kumar, H, 1989)
Aurat Ka Dil *see* Pati Seva
Aurat Ka Dil (*aka* Patitoddhar: H.E. Sonie, H, 1933)
Aurat Ka Inteqam (*aka* Rape: **B.R. Ishara**, H, 1984)
Aurat Ka Inteqam (Ashok Malhotra/Anil Singh, H, 1990)
Aurat Ka Pyar (**A.R. Kardar**, H, 1933)
Aurat Ki Zindagi (*aka* Life of a Lady: F.R. Irani, H, 1937)
Aurat Pair Ki Jooti Nahin Hai (Prithviraj Chatterjee, H, 1985)
Aurat Teri Yahi Kahani (**Chaturbhuj Doshi**, H, 1954)
Aurat Teri Yahi Kahani (Mohanji Prasad, H, 1988)
Aur Kaun (Tulsi/Shyam **Ramsay**, H, 1979)
Aut Ghatkecha Raja *see* Awara Shehzada
Automobile Industry in India, The (**Harisadhan Dasgupta**, E, 1969)
Auto Raja (Vijay, K, 1980)
Avadellam Pennale (?, Sunrise Films, Tam, 1990)
Avaghachi Sansar (**Anant Mane**, Mar, 1960)
Avaiyyar *see* **Avvaiyyar**
Avakasham (A.B. Raj, Mal, 1978)
Avakashi (Anthony Mithradas, Mal, 1954)
Aval (Aziz, Mal, 1967)
Aval (A.C. Trilogchander, Tam, 1972)
Aval (J.V. Rukmangadhan, Tam, 1991)
Avala Antaranga (R.N. Jayagopal, K, 1984)
Avala Hejje (Bhargava, K, 1981)
Avalai Cholli Kutramillai (?, Velan Creations, Tam, 1986)
Avalakku Maranamilla (Malathoor Ravi Varma, Mal, 1978)
Avalalppam Vaikippoi (John Shankaramangalam, Mal, 1971)
Avala Neralu (A.T. Raghu, K, 1983)
Aval Appadithan (C. Rudraiah, Tam, 1978)
Avale Nanna Hendthi (Umesh Prabhakar, K, 1988)
Aval Etriya Deepam (?, Tam, 1982)
Avali Javali (A.V. Sheshgiri Rao, K, 1981)
Aval Kanda Lokam (M. Krishnan Nair, Mal, 1978)
Aval Kathirunnu Avanum (?, Ganesh Prod, Mal, 1986)
Aval Mela Chirithal (M.N. Jaisundar, Tam, 1988)
Aval Niraparadhi (Masthan, Mal, 1979)
Aval Oru Athisayam (B.V. Srinivasan, Tam, 1977)
Aval Oru Devalayam (A.B. Raj, Mal, 1977)
Aval Oru Kaviyam (**Durai**, Tam, 1981)
Aval Oru Nadodi (Gopikumar, Mal, 1979)
Aval Oru Pachchai Kuzhandhai (S.C. Sekhar, Tam, 1978)
Aval Oru Thodarkathai/Aval Oru Thodarkatha/Aaina (**K. Balachander**, Tam/Mal/H, 1974)
Aval Oru Vasantham (?, Sharmila Creations, Tam, 1991)
Aval Sumangalithan (Visu, Tam, 1985)
Aval Thantha Uravu (**Durai**, Tam, 1978)
Avalude Pathikaran (Venu, Mal, 1979)
Avalude Ravukal (*aka* Her Nights: **I.V. Sasi**, Mal, 1978)
Avalukendru Ore Manam (**C.V. Sridhar**, Tam, 1971)
Avalukku Ayiram Kangal (Ramanna, Tam, 1975)
Avalukku Nihar Avale (Madurai Thirumanam, Tam, 1974)
Avalum Penn Thaane (**Durai**, Tam, 1974)
Avalum Thayanal (Mohammed Ali, Tam, 1981)
Aval Vishwasthayayirunnu (Jesey, Mal, 1978)
Aval Yar (K.J. Mahadevan, Tam, 1959)
Avan (Sozharajan, Tam, 1985)
Avana Evan (**S. Balachander**, Tam, 1962)
Avan Amaran (**S. Balachander**, Tam, 1958)
Avan Aval Adhu (Muktha V. Srinivasan, Tam, 1980)
Avanazhi (**I.V. Sasi**, Mal, 1986)
Avane Nanna Ganda (S. Umesh/K. Prabhakar, K, 1989)
Avanga Namma Uru Ponnunga (?, Santhana Cine Arts, Tam, 1990)
Avano Atho Avalo (Baby, Mal, 1979)
Avan Oru Ahankari (Rajasekharan, Mal, 1980)
Avan Oru Charitram (**K.S. Prakash Rao**, Tam, 1976)
Avan Pithana (**P. Neelakantan**, Tam, 1966)
Avanthan Manithan (A.C. Trilogchander, Tam, 1975)
Avanukku Nigar Avane (M. Karnan, Tam, 1982)
Avan Varunnu (M.R.S. Mani, Mal, 1954)
Avarampu (**B.G. Bharathan**, Mal, 1992)
Avare En Daivam (?, Meenakshi-Sundareshwara Films, Tam, 1969)
Avar Enakke Sontham (Pattu, Tam, 1977)
Avargal (**K. Balachander**, Tam, 1977)
Avar Jeevikkunu (P.G. Vishwambaran, Mal, 1978)
Avarunarunnu (N. Shankaran Nair, Mal, 1956)
Avasara Kalyanam (V.T. Thyagarajan, Tam, 1972)
Avasarakkari (Mathangan, Tam, 1981)
Avasara Police 100 (**K. Bhagyaraj**, Tam, 1990)
Avasesh (**Girish Kasaravalli**, K, 1975)
Avasthe (Krishna Masadi, K, 1987)
Avatar (**Premankur Atorthy**, B, 1941)
Avatar (Saikat Bhattacharya, B, 1977)
Avatar (Mohan Kumar, H, 1983)
Avatara Purusha (Raj Kishore, K, 1989)
Avatharam (P. Chandrakumar, Mal, 1981)
Avayer Biye (**Sushil Majumdar**, B, 1942)
Avedana (**I.V. Sasi**, Tel, 1989)
Ave Kallu (A.C. Trilogchander, Tel, 1967)
Avemin Pudhumai Penn (**Bharathirajaa**, Tel, 1983)
Avenging Angel *see* Golibar
Avenging Blood *see* Khoon Ka Badla
Avenging Tears *see* Ver Na Aansoo
Avesha (Perala, K, 1990)
Avesham (Vijayanand, Mal/Tel, 1979)
Avhaan (Sushila Kamat, Mar, 1982)
Avidathepole Ivideyum (**K.S. Sethumadhavan**, Mal, 1985)
Avinash (Umesh Mehra, H, 1986)
Avirice (Harilal Bhatt, St, 1930)
Avishkar (**Basu Bhattacharya**, H, 1973)
Avishkar (Salil Dutta, B, 1990)
Avvaiyyar (Kothamangalam Subbu, Tam, 1953)
Awaam (**B.R. Chopra**, H, 1987)
Awaara *see* **Awara**
Awaargi (**Mahesh Bhatt**, H, 1990)
Awaaz (Rafiq Rizvi, H, 1942)
Awaaz (**Zia Sarhadi**, H, 1956)
Awaaz (**Shakti Samanta**, H, 1984)
Awaaz De Kahan Hai (Sibte Hasan Rizvi, H, 1990)
Awakening, The *see* **Jagran**
Awakening Song, The *see* Unarthupattu
Awara (**Raj Kapoor**, H, 1951)
Awara Abdulla (Tara Harish, H, 1963)
Awara Baap (Sohanlal Kanwar, H, 1985)
Awara Badal (Kedar Kapoor, H, 1964)
Awaragardi (Swaroop Kumar, H, 1990)
Awara Ladki (?, Skyland Prod, H, 1967)
Awara Ladki (B.J. Patel, H, 1975)
Awara Raqasa *see* Bhatakta Joban
Awara Shehzada/Aut Ghatkecha Raja (*aka* Vagabond Prince: **Master Vithal**, H/Mar, 1933)
Awara Shehzadi (Pyarelal, H, 1956)
Awara Zindagi (?, ADM Films, H, 1989)
Awwal Number (**Dev Anand**, H, 1990)
Ayaash (**Shakti Samanta**, H, 1982)
Ayalakkari (**I.V. Sasi**, Mal, 1976)
Ayalathe Athdegam (Rajasenan, Mal, 1992)
Ayalathe Sundari (**T. Hariharan**, Mal, 1974)
Ayalvasi Oru Dharithavasi (**Priyadarshan**, Mal, 1986)
Ayanam (Harikumar, Mal, 1985)
Ayananta (Sondhani, B, 1964)
Ayarthi Thollayirathi Irupathonnu (**I.V. Sasi**, Mal, 1988)
Ayega Aanewala (Kewal Mishra, H, 1967)
Ayesha (**Kunchako**, Mal, 1964)
Ayinavalu (K. Eshwara Rao, Tel, 1975)
Ayiram Abhilashangal (Soman Ambat, Mal, 1984)
Ayiram Janmangal (P.N. Sundaram, Mal, 1976)
Ayiram Janmangal (**Durai**, Tam, 1978)
Ayiram Kaigal (A.V. Babu, Tam, 1983)
Ayiram Kalathu Payir (T.S. Dorairaj, Tam, 1963)
Ayiram Kannudayal (K. Shankar, Tam, 1986)
Ayiram Muthangal (Devarajan, Tam, 1982)
Ayiram Nilave Vaa (A.S. Prakasham, Tam, 1983)
Ayiram Pookal Malarattum (E. Ramadoss, Tam, 1986)
Ayiram Poyi (V. Srinivasan, Tam, 1969)
Ayiram Roopai (**K.S. Gopalakrishnan**, Tam, 1964)
Ayiram Vasal Ithayam (A. Jagannathan, Tam, 1980)
Ayirappara (Venu Nagavalli, Mal, 1992)
Ayirathil Oruthi (Avinashi Mani, Tam, 1975)
Ayirathil Oruvan (**B.R. Panthulu**, Tam, 1965)
Ayisu Nooru (Ponmanirajan, Tam, 1987)
Ayitham (Venu Nagavalli, Mal, 1988)
Ayodhya (P.N. Sundaram, Mal, 1975)
Ayodhya Ka Raja *see* Ayodhyecha Raja
Ayodhyapati (**S. Fattelal**, H, 1956)
Ayodhyecha Raja/Ayodhya Ka Raja (**V. Shantaram**, Mar/H, 1932)
Ayodhyechi Rani (K.P. Bhave, Mar, 1940)
Ayudham (P. Chandrakumar, Mal, 1982)
Ayul Kaidhi (K. Subhash, Tam, 1991)
Ayushkalam (Kamal, Mal, 1992)
Ayyalo Brahmaiah (Aakella, Tel, 1992)
Ayyappa Swami Mahatyam (K. Vasu, Tel, 1989)
Azad (**N.R. Acharya**, H, 1940)
Azad (S.M. Sreeramulu Naidu, H, 1955)
Azad (Pramod Chakraborty, H, 1978)
Azad Abla (*aka* Daring Damsel: Saqi, St, 1933)
Azad Abla (A.P. Kapur, H, 1935)
Azad Desh Ke Gulam (S.A. Chandrasekharan, H, 1990)
Azad Hindustan (**Nanubhai Vakil**, H, 1948)
Azadi (*aka* Ghunghat Ke Pat Khol: R. Sharma, H, 1935)
Azadi-e-Watan (*aka* Desh Sevak: **D. Bilimoria**, H, 1940)
Azadi Ke Baad (D.K. Chatterjee, H, 1951)
Azadi Ke Deewane *see* Sher Dil Aurat
Azadi Ki Or (P.S. Prakash, H, 1985)
Azadi Ki Raah Par (*aka* Swatantrata Ke Path Par: Lalit Mehta, H, 1948)
Azadi Nu Jung (*aka* Bugles of War: **Nanubhai Vakil**, St, 1931)
Azad Jeevan (Harish, H, 1947)
Azad Mohabbat *see* Free Love
Azad Veer (*aka* Revenge: Rasik Bhatt, H, 1936)
Azhagan (**K. Balachander**, Tam, 1991)
Azhagarmalai Kalvan (**Kemparaj Urs**?, Tam, 1959)
Azhage Unnai Aradikiran (**C.V. Sridhar**, Tam, 1979)
Azhagi (**Sundarrao Nadkarni**, Tam, 1953)
Azhagiya Kanney (**J. Mahendran**, Tam, 1982)
Azhagu (K. Vijayan, Tam, 1984)
Azhagu Nila (S. Raghavan, Tam, 1962)
Azhaithal Varuven (P.R. Somu, Tam, 1980)
Azhakulla Saleena (**K.S. Sethumadhavan**, Mal, 1973)
Azhi (Pappan Kunchako, Mal, 1985)
Azhimukham (P. Vijayan, Mal, 1972)
Azhiyada Kolangal (**Balu Mahendra**, Tam, 1979)
Azhiyatha Bandhangal (**Sasikumar**, Mal, 1985)
Azmaish (S.H. Tharani, H, 1952)

B

Baadbaan (**Phani Majumdar**, H, 1954)
Baag-e-Misar (*aka* Shaan-e-Islam: **J.B.H. Wadia**, H, 1934)
Baaje Ghunghroo (Shivraj Srivastava, H, 1962)
Baaje Shehnai Hamaar Angna (Javed Rehman, Bh, 1980)
Baalu Belagithu (Siddalingaiah, K, 1970)
Baap Bahu Aur Beta *see* Hamara Adhikar
Baap Bete (**Raja Paranjpe**, H, 1959)
Baap Beti (**Bimal Roy**, H, 1954)
Baap Dikro (Subhash Shah, G, 1983)
Baap Ka Bol (*aka* Faithful Heart: ?, Bhartiya Films, H, 1933)
Baap Kamai (**Kanjibhai Rathod**, St, 1925)
Baap Mazha Brahmachari (**Dinkar D. Patil**, Mar, 1962)
Baap Numbri Beta Dus Numbri (Aziz Sajawal, H, 1990)
Baap Re Baap (**A.R. Kardar**, H, 1955)
Baarish (Shankar Mukherjee, H, 1957)
Baarish (Narendra Grewal, H, 1993)
Baat Ban Jaye (Bharat Rangachary, H, 1986)
Baat Ek Raat Ki (Shankar Mukherjee, H, 1962)
Baat Hai Pyar Ki (?, Godsons, H, 1987)
Baaton Baaton Mein (**Basu Chatterjee**, H, 1979)
Baaz (**Guru Dutt**, H, 1953)
Baaz (B. Subhash, H, 1992)
Baaz Bahadur *see* Rani Rupmati
Baaz Bahadur (*aka* Hawk: **Sundarrao Nadkarni**, St, 1931)
Baaz Bahadur (*aka* Hawk, Haribhai Desai, H, 1936)
Baaz Bahadur (Kuldeep Sharma, H, 1959)
Baazi (**Guru Dutt**, H, 1951)
Baazi (Moni Bhattacharya, H, 1968)
Baazi (Raj N. Sippy, H, 1984)
Baba (**Harisadhan Dasgupta**, E, 1965)
Babai Abbai (Jandhyala, Tel, 1985)
Babai Hotel (Jandhyala, Tel, 1992)
Babanchi Bayko (*aka* Papa's Wife: **N.D. Sarpotdar**, St, 1926)
Babar (**Hemen Gupta**, H, 1960)
Baba Ramdev (S.P. Kalla/Manibhai Vyas, R, 1963)
Baba Ramdev Peer *see* **Baba Ramdev**
Baba Ramdev Peer (Sushil Vyas, G, 1976)
Babasa Ri Laadi (B.K. Adarsh, R, 1961)
Baba Taraknath (Sunil Bannerjee/Baren Chatterjee, B, 1977)
Baba Taraknath (A.K. Chatterjee, H, 1980)
Babla (**Agradoot**, B/H, 1951)
Babruvahana (**R.S. Prakash**, Tel, 1942)
Babruvahana (**Samudrala Raghavacharya**, Tel, 1964)
Babruvahana (**Hunsur Krishnamurthy**, K, 1977)
Babruwahan (**Dadasaheb Phalke**, St, 1923)
Babu (A.C. Trilogchander, Tam, 1971)
Babu (**K. Raghavendra Rao**, Tel, 1975)
Babu (A.C. Trilogchander, H, 1983)
Babua Hamaar (Adarsh Jain, Bh, 1986)
Babuji (**Master Bhagwan**, H, 1950)
Babul (S.U. Sunny, H, 1950)
Babul (Govind Moonis, H, 1986)
Babul (**Phani Majumdar**, H, 1989)
Babula (Sadhu Meher, O, 1985)
Babul Da Vedha (Satish Bhakri, P, 1985)
Babul Ki Galiyan (Satyadev Narang, H, 1972)
Babulugadi Debba (K. Vasu, Tel, 1984)
Babu Mon (**T. Hariharan**, Mal, 1975)
Babu Moshai (Salil Dutta, B, 1977)
Baby (R.S. Junnarkar, Mar, 1954)
Baby Bride *see* Balika Badhu
Bachche Teen Aur Daku Chhe *see* Tran Treniya Chha Chhabila Baharvatiya
Bachchon Ka Khel (**Raja Nene**, H, 1946)
Bachelor Father *see* **Kunwara Baap**
Bachelor Husband *see* Kunwara Pati
Bachha-i-Sakka (*aka* Josh-e-Jawani, Romance of a Youth, Bhisti: **Moti Gidwani**, St, 1930)
Bachchon Se Baatein (**Kidar Sharma**, H, 1957)
Bachke Rehna (**Master Bhagwan**, H, 1949)
Bachpan (**Homi Wadia**, H, 1945)
Bachpan (Nazar, H, 1963)
Bachpan (**K.P. Atma**, H, 1970)
Bada Admi (Kaushal Raj, H, 1961)
Bada Bhai (**K. Amarnath**, H, 1957)
Bada Bhauja (Rajnikant, O, 1988)
Bada Kabutar (Deven Verma, H, 1973)
Badal (Zahur Raja, H, 1942)
Badal (**Amiya Chakravarty**, H, 1951)
Badal (Aspi, H, 1966)
Badal (Anand Sagar, H, 1985)
Badal Aur Bijli (Morris?, H, 1956)
Badalte Rishte (Raghunath Jhalani, H, 1978)
Badalti Duniya (Mohan Sinha, H, 1943)

Badan Barpukhan (Kamal Choudhury, A, 1947)
Bad Aur Badnaam (Feroz Chinoy, H, 1984)
Badavara Bandhu (Vijay, K, 1976)
Baddi Bangaramma (Kommineni, K, 1984)
Bade Bhaiya (Aspi, H, 1951)
Bade Dil Wala (Bhappi Sonie, H, 1983)
Bade Ghar Ki Bahu (Kundan Kumar, H, 1960)
Bade Ghar Ki Beti (Kalpataru, H, 1989)
Bade Ghulam Ali Khan Saheb (**Harisadhan Dasgupta**, E, 1964)
Bade Log *see* Panihari
Bade Nawab Saheb (Vedi, H, 1944)
Bade Saheb (G.P. Pawar, H, 1951)
Bade Sarkar (**Kishore Sahu**, H, 1957)
Badhe Chalo (*aka* Forward March: Mohan Sinha, H, 1937)
Badhti Ka Naam Daadhi (**Kishore Kumar**, H, 1974)
Badhu Nirupama (Jugal Debata, O, 1987)
Badi (G. Ram Suresh, Tel, 1988)
Badi Baat (Mazhar Khan, H, 1944)
Badi Bahen *see* **Didi**
Badi Bahen (D.D. Kashyap, H, 1949)
Badi Bahen (Kalpataru, H, 1993)
Badi Bahu (S. Bhagat, H, 1951)
Badi Basavaiah (B. Subba Rao, Tel, 1980)
Badi Didi *see* **Bardidi**
Badi Didi (Narendra Suri, H, 1969)
Badi Maa (**Master Vinayak**, H, 1945)
Badi Maa (Ram Gabale, H, 1974)
Badi Panthulu *see* **School Master**
Badi Panthulu (P. Chandrasekhara Reddy, Tel, 1972)
Bad-kaar (Shivkumar, H, 1987)
Badla *see* Manchali
Badla (**Master Bhagwan**, H, 1943)
Badla (Vijay, H, 1974)
Badla (*aka* Sood: **Datta Keshav**, Mar, 1977)
Badla Aur Balidan (Kewal Sharma, H, 1980)
Badle Ki Aag (Rajkumar Kohli, H, 1982)
Badmash (*aka* Rascal: **R.S. Choudhury**, St, 1931)
Badmash (A. Karim, H, 1944)
Badmash (B.J. Patel, H, 1969)
Badmash Ka Beta (*aka* Leatherface: Shanti Dave, St, 1933)
Badmashon Ka Badmash (Satish Bhakri, H, 1979)
Badnaam (D.D. Kashyap, H, 1952)
Badnaam (Dilip Bose, H, 1975)
Badnaam (?, Giridhar Art, H, 1989)
Badnaam (Shibu Laha, B, 1990)
Badnaam Basti (Prem Kapoor, H, 1971)
Badnaam Farishte (Qamar Naqvi, H, 1971)
Badnami (Majnu, H, 1946)
Badnaseeb (Shiv Kumar, H, 1985)
Badrinatha Darshanam (**K. Kameshwara Rao**, Tel, 1985)
Badrinath Dham (Ashish Kumar, H, 1980)
Badrinath Yatra (**Dhirubhai Desai**, H, 1967)
Badshah (**Amiya Chakravarty**, H, 1954)
Badshah (**Agradoot**, B, 1963)
Badshah (**Chandrakant**, H, 1964)
Badshah Salamat (Prem Sinha, H, 1956)
Badtameez (*aka* Budtameez: **Manmohan Desai**, H, 1966)
Baduku Bangaravayithu (A.V. Sheshgiri Rao, K, 1976)
Badukuva Daari (**K.S. Prakash Rao**, K, 1966)
Baeelweda (**K. Narayan Kale**, Mar, 1943)
Baeelweda (**Prabhakar Nayak**, Mar, 1979)
Bagalar Bangadarshan (**Ritwik Ghatak**, B, 1964: Incomplete)
Bagdipar Diye (Mihir Chatterjee, B, 1984)
Bagga Daku (Satish Bhakri, P, 1983)
Bagha Jatin (Hiranmoy Sen, B, 1958)
Bagha Jatin (**Harisadhan Dasgupta**, E, 1977)
Baghavat (?, Rajma Pics, H, 1951)
Baghavat (**B. Vittalacharya**, H, 1971)
Baghavat (*aka* The Rebellion: **Ramanand Sagar**, H, 1982)
Bagh Bahadur (**Buddhadev Dasgupta**, H, 1989)
Baghban (**A.R. Kardar**, H, 1938)
Bagh Bandi Khela (Piyush Bose, B, 1975)
Baghdad *see* Baghdad Thirudan
Baghdad (**Nanabhai Bhatt**, H, 1952)
Baghdad (Shyam Chakraborty, B, 1952)
Baghdad Gajadonga (**Yoganand**, Tel, 1968)
Baghdad Ka Badmash (*aka* Fighting Vagabond: **Nanubhai Vakil**, St, 1932)
Baghdad Ka Chor *see* Thief of Baghdad
Baghdad Ka Chor (Sulemani Setranji: D.N. Madhok, H, 1934)
Baghdad Ka Chor (**Nanubhai Vakil**, H, 1946)
Baghdad Ka Chor (Shriram, H, 1955)
Baghdad Ka Jadu (*aka* Magic of Baghdad: John Cawas, H, 1956)
Baghdad Ki Raatein *see* Arabian Nights
Baghdad Ki Raatein (*aka* Abu Hasan: **Nanabhai Bhatt**, H, 1962)
Baghdad Nu Baharvatiyo (*aka* Bandit of Baghdad: **N.G. Devare**, St, 1929)
Baghdad Nu Bulbul (*aka* Siren of Baghdad: **Nanubhai Vakil**, St, 1931)
Baghdad Perazhagi (Ramanna, Tam, 1973)
Baghdad Thirudan/Baghdad (**T.R. Sundaram**, Tam, 1960)
Baghi (*aka* Bandkhor, Sarfarosh: **Dhirubhai Desai**, H, 1939)
Baghi (Anant Thakur, H, 1953)
Baghi (Ram Dayal, H, 1964)
Baghi (Deepak Shivdasani, H, 1990)
Baghi Hasina (Ram, H, 1965)
Baghi Lutera (A.C. Trilogchander, H, 1975)
Baghi Sultania (R. Thakur, H, 1993)
Baghini (Bijoy Bose, B, 1968)
Baghi Sardar (Majnu, H, 1956)
Baghi Shahzada (Maruti, H, 1964)
Baghi Sipahi (**A.R. Kardar**, H, 1936)
Baghi Sipahi (Bhagwan Das Varma, H, 1958)
Bagula Baguli (**Prashanta Nanda**, O, 1986)
Bagula Bhagat (Harmesh Malhotra, H, 1979)
Bahadur (**Master Bhagwan**, H, 1944)
Bahadur (**Ratibhai Punatar**, H, 1953)
Bahadur Baharvatiyo (*aka* Terror of the Hills, **Dhirubhai Desai**, St, 1929)
Bahadur Beti (*aka* She: A.P. Kapur, St, 1931)
Bahadur Beti (*aka* Bahadur Ladki, Dashing Girl: A.R. Kabuli, H, 1935)
Bahadur Daku (Jugal Kishore, H, 1966)
Bahadur Gandu (A.V. Sheshgiri Rao, K, 1976)
Bahadur Hennu (A.V. Sheshgiri Rao, K, 1992)
Bahadur Jeevan (Harish, H, 1948)
Bahadur Kisan (Chandrarao Kadam/**Master Bhagwan**, H, 1938)
Bahadur Ladki *see* Bahadur Beti
Bahadur Ladkiyan (K.S.R. Doss, H, 1973)
Bahadur Lutera (**K.C. Dey**, H, 1960)
Bahadur Naresh (K.L. Khan, H, 1948)
Bahadur Pratap (**Master Bhagwan**, H, 1947)
Bahadur Ramesh (*aka* Brave Heart, Volunteer: **K. Amarnath**, H, 1939)
Bahadur Shah Zafar (TV: **B.R. Chopra**, H, 1986)
Bahagar Duparia (Jones Mahalia, A, 1985)
Bahaklela Brahmachari (**R.G. Torney**, Mar, 1941)
Bahaklela Brahmachari (C. Raghuvir, Mar, 1971)
Bahana (A.M. Khan, H, 1942)
Bahana (Kumar, H, 1960)
Bahar *see* Jeevan
Bahar (**M.V. Raman**, H, 1951)
Bahar (?, Vishwakarma, H, 1988)
Bahar Aane Tak (Tariq Shah, H, 1990)
Baharen Phir Bhi Aayengi (Shaheed Latif, H, 1966)
Bahar-e-Sulemani (**J.P. Advani**, H, 1935)
Baharon Ke Sapne (**Nasir Hussain**, H, 1967)
Baharon Ki Manzil (Y.H. Rizvi, H, 1968)
Baharon Ki Manzil (Madhava Rao, H, 1991)
Baharon Phool Barsao (Umesh Mathur, H, 1972)
Baharvatiyo (**V.M. Vyas**, G, 1947)
Baharvatiyo Behram (*aka* Behram the Bandit: Saqi, St, 1930)
Baharvatiyo Ni Beti (*aka* Daughter of an Outlaw: **N.G. Devare**, St, 1930)
Bahen (*aka* Sister, my Sister: **Mehboob**, H, 1941)
Bahen Ka Prem (*aka* Benoor Aankhen: J.K. Nanda, H, 1935)
Baheri Zindagi (*aka* Jazz of Life: ?, Rohini Film, St, 1931)
Bahina Tohare Khatir (Hasmukh Rajput, Bh, 1986)
Bahirji Naik (**Bhalji Pendharkar**, Mar, 1943)
Bahroopia (Rajesh Nanda, H, 1971)
Bahu (**Shakti Samanta**, H, 1955)
Bahu Begum (M. Sadiq, H, 1967)
Bahu Beti (C.L. Dheer, H, 1952)
Bahu Beti (**T. Prakash Rao**, H, 1965)
Bahu Betiyan (?, N.R. Desai Prod, H, 1946)
Bahubrihi (Jaladhar Chatterjee, B, 1949)
Bahudoorapu Batasari (**Dasari Narayana Rao**, Tel, 1983)
Bahu Heba Emti (Bijoy Bhaskar, O, 1988)
Bahu Ho To Aisi (Kantilal Dave, H, 1982)
Bahu Ki Awaaz (Shashilal Nair, H, 1985)
Bahurani (R.S. Junnarkar/Mubarak, H, 1940)
Bahurani (S.M. Yusuf, H, 1950)
Bahurani (**T. Prakash Rao**, H, 1963)
Bahurani (S.S. Rawal, Haryanvi, 1983)
Bahurani (Manik Chatterjee, H, 1989)
Bahuriya (Tejesh Akhouri, Bh, 1987)
Bahuroopi Bazaar (*aka* Vanity Fair: **Nagendra Majumdar**, St, 1932)
Bahurupi (Ramnik Vaidya, G, 1969)
Bahurupi (Satish Ranadive, Mar, 1984)
Bahut Din Huye (**S.S. Vasan**, H, 1954)
Bai Chali Sasariye (Mohansingh Rathod, R, 1988)
Baidurya Rahasya (**Tapan Sinha**, B, 1985)
Baiju Bawra (**Vijay Bhatt**, H, 1952)
Baiko Asavi Ashi (Murlidhar Kapdi, Mar, 1983)
Baiko Maheri Jaate (**Raja Paranjpe**, Mar, 1963)
Baiko Pahije (Raja Joshi, Mar, 1950)
Baikocha Bhau (Madhav Bhoit, Mar, 1962)
Baikunther Will (Manu Sen, B, 1950)
Baikunther Will (Sushil Mukherjee, B, 1985)
Baimanaik (Shyam Chakraborty, B, 1953)
Bai Mi Bholi (Krishna Patil, Mar, 1967)
Bai Mothi Bhagyachi (**Datta Keshav**, Mar, 1968)
Baine Kela Sarpanch Khula (Krishna Patil, Mar, 1981)
Bairaag (**Asit Sen**, H, 1976)
Bairi Sawan (Raj Jalandhi, Bh, 1984)
Baisaheb (Datta Mane/Dattaram Tawde, Mar, 1983)
Baisakhi (*aka* Vaisakhi: Rajendra Sharma, P, 1951)
Baisakhi Megh (**Utpal Dutt**, B, 1981)
Baisa Ra Jatan Karo (R.K. Joshi, R, 1989)
Baishey Shravan (**Mrinal Sen**, B, 1960)
Baji Prabhu Deshpande (*aka* Valley of the Immortals: **Baburao Painter**, St, 1929)
Baji Prabhu Deshpande (Balasaheb Yadav, Mar, 1939)
Bajirao Mastani (**Bhalji Pendharkar**, St, 1925)
Bajiravacha Beta (**Raja Thakur**, Mar, 1971)
Bajrang Bali (Manibhai Vyas, H, 1956)
Bajrang Bali (**Chandrakant**, H, 1976)
Bakavali (*aka* Taj-ul-Mulk (Mohanlal Shah, St, 1930)
Ba Ki Yaad Mein (**Ketan Mehta**, H, 1985)
Baksha Badal (Nityananda Dutta, B, 1965)
Baksheesh (Brijmohan/A. Jadhav, H, 1950)
Baksiddha (Bireshwar Bose, B, 1957)
Bakul *see* Bokul
Bakulbasar (TV: **Dinen Gupta**, B, 1990)
Bala (Satyajit Ray, E, 1976)
Bala Bandhana (Pekati Shivram, K, 1971)
Bala Bharatam (**K. Kameshwara Rao**, Tel, 1972)
Bala Gau Kashi Angaai (Kamalakar Torne, Mar, 1977)
Bala Gopaludu (Kodi Ramakrishna, Tel, 1989)
Balaji *see* **Shri Venkateshwara Mahatyam**
Balaji Nimbalkar (**Dadasaheb Phalke**, St, 1926)
Bala Joban (Baburaj Patel, H, 1934)
Bala Jo Jo Re (**Datta Dharmadhikari**, Mar, 1950)
Bala Ki Raat (*aka* One Fatal Night, Khaufnak Raat: **Modhu Bose**, H, 1936)
Balak (Adarsh, H, 1969)
Balak Aur Jaanwar (**Nanabhai Bhatt**, H, 1975)
Balak Dhruv (Himmat Dave, H, 1974)
Balak Gadadhar (Hiranmoy Sen, B, 1969)
Balak Saratchandra (Jayanta Saha, B, 1976)
Balam (**Homi Wadia**, H, 1949)
Balamani (P.V. Rao, Tam, 1937)
Balamithrula Katha (K. Varaprasad Rao, Tel, 1972)
Balam Pardesia (**Nasir Hussain**, Bh, 1979)
Balamurali Maa (M. Ramakrishna, Tel, 1988)
Balan (S. Nottani, Mal, 1938)
Balanagamma (**C. Pullaiah**, Tel, 1942)
Balanagamma (**Vedantam Raghavaiah**, Tel/Tam, 1959)
Balanagamma (P.R. Kaundinya, K, 1966)
Balanagamma (K. Shankar, Tam/Mal, 1981)
Balanandam (**K.S. Prakash Rao**, Tel, 1954)
Balapanjara (M.R. Vittal, K, 1970)
Balapareekshanam (Anthikad Mani, Mal, 1978)
Balarajana Kathe (Venunath, K, 1965)
Balaraju (**G. Balaramaiah**, Tel, 1948)
Balaraju Katha (**Bapu**, Tel, 1970)
Balaram Krishnudu (Raviraja Pinisetty, Tel, 1992)
Balarampurer Pala (Samiran Dutta, B, 1983)
Balaram Shri Krishna (**Chandrakant**, H, 1968)
Balasanyasamma Katha (P. Subbarao, Tel, 1956)
Bala Sanyasi *see* Mani Mekalai
Bala Yesu (V. Rajan, Tel, 1984)
Balay Gras (Pinaki Mukherjee, B, 1954)
Balayogini (**K. Subramanyam**, Tam/Tel, 1936)
Balayogi Upamanyu (Harsukh Bhatt, H, 1958)
Balbiro Bhabhi (Virendra, P, 1981)
Bal Gopal (*aka* Keshi Vadha: ?, British India Film, St, 190)
Bal Hatya (*aka* Khoon-e-Nahak: Ram Daryani, H, 1935)
Bali (**V.K. Pavithran**, Mal, 1991)
Balidan (**Naval Gandhi**, St, 1927)
Balidan (*aka* Price of a Woman, Woman's Faithfulness: Prafulla Roy, H, 1935)
Balidan/Do Kaliyan (**Raja Paranjpe**, Mar/H, 1948)
Balidan (?, Navbharat Chitra, H, 1962)
Balidan (Ravi Tandon, H, 1971)
Balidan (**Prashanta Nanda**, O, 1978)
Balidan (S.A. Chandrasekharan, H, 1985)
Balidanam (S.A. Chandrasekharan, Tel, 1982)
Balika Badhu (*aka* Baby Bride: P.T. Shaida, St, 1920)
Balika Badhu (**Tarun Majumdar**, H, 1976)
Balika Bodhu (**Tarun Majumdar**, B, 1967)
Balina Guri (**K.S. Prakash Rao**, K, 1979)
Balipeetam (**Dasari Narayana Rao**, Tel, 1975)
Balipeetampi Bharatanari (T. Krishna, Tel, 1989)
Bali Raja *see* Vaman Avatar
Baliya Baapji *see* Baliya Dev
Baliya Dev (*aka* Baliya Baapji: Nitin Shah, G, 1989)
Baliyagna (V.K. Pattani, St, 1924)
Balkrishna Leela (Sushil Vyas, G, 1976)
Ballathapahayan (Shri Muthaiah, Mal, 1969)
Balloon (?, Mal, 1982)
Balma (Harbans, H, 1948)
Balma (Lawrence D'Souza, H, 1993)
Balma Bada Nadaan (Baldev R. Jhingan, R, 1964)
Balma Nadaan (Akbar Alam, Bh, 1982)
Bal Mazha Navasacha (Madhav Shinde, Mar, 1955)
Balo (Kuldeep, P, 1951)
Balondu Bhavageethe (Geethapriya, K, 1988)
Balondu Uyyale (Amirtham, K, 1985)
Bal Ramayan *see* Ramayan
Bal Shivaji (Prabhakar Pendharkar, Mar, 1981)
Bal Shringee (?, Eastern Film, Baroda, St, 1924)
Balu Aparupa Nam Jodi (Janakiram, K, 1978)
Balu Bangara (Geethapriya, K, 1981)
Balu Belagithu (Siddalingaiah, K, 1970)
Baluchari (Ajit Ganguly, B, 1968)
Balu Jenu (Balan/Kunigal Nagabhushan, K, 1976)
Baluve Ninagagi (L. Satya, K, 1974)
Balwan (Deepak Anand, H, 1992)
Balyakalasakhi (**P. Bhaskaran**, Mal, 1967)
Balya Pratignya (Nagarajan, Mal, 1972)
Balya Sakhi (Anthony Mithradas, Mal, 1954)
Balya Vivaham ('1000 Faces' Ramkumar, Tam, 1940)

Balyogi Upamanyu (Harsukh Bhatt, H, 1958)
Bama (Aakkoo, H, 1952)
Bambai Ka Babu (**Raj Khosla**, H, 1960)
Bambai Ka Chor (S.D. Narang, H, 1962)
Bambai Ka Maharaja (Shibu Mitra, H, 1980)
Bambai Ki Billi (**Nandlal Jaswantlal**, H, 1936)
Bambai Ki Billi (*aka* Wildcat: Zahur Ahmed, H, 1960)
Bambai Ki Mohini *see* Actress
Bambai Ki Sair *see* Holiday in Bombay
Bambai Ki Sethani (Rasik Bhatt, H, 1935)
Bambai Raat Ki Baahon Mein (**K.A. Abbas**, H, 1967)
Bambaiwali (**Homi Wadia**, H, 1941)
Bammamata Bangaru Pata (Rajasekhar, Tel, 1989)
Bamuner Meye (Sabhyasachi, B, 1949)
Banabasar (Sushil Mukherjee, B, 1979)
Banahansa (**Abdul Majid**, A, 1977)
Bana Hansi (**Kartick Chattopadhyay**, B, 1953)
Banajyotsna (Dinen Gupta. B, 1969)
Banani (**Jahnu Barua**, A, 1989)
Ba Nanna Preethisu (?, K, 1992)
Banaphul (Ghanshyam Mahapatra, O, 1985)
Banarasi (Arup Guha-Thakurta, B, 1962)
Banarasi Babu (Shankar Mukherjee, H, 1973)
Banarasi Thug (M. Srinivasan/M.C. Rangaswamy, H, 1936)
Banarasi Thug (Lekhraj Bhakri, H, 1962)
Banaria Phool (**Atul Bordoloi**, A, 1973)
Banashankari (K.S.L. Swamy, K, 1977)
Banawat (?, Bihari F., Calcutta, H, 1950)
Bancharamer Bagan (**Tapan Sinha**, B, 1980)
Banchita (**Jyotish Bannerjee**, B, 1948)
Bandada Hoovu (K.V. Jayaram, K, 1982)
Bandagi (K. Shankar, H, 1972)
Bandalbaaz (**Shammi Kapoor**, H, 1976)
Banda Nana Ganda (Rajkishore, K, 1992)
Banda Nawaz *see* Sultan-e-Deccan
Banda Nawaz (Saini?, Galaxy Films, H, 1988)
Bandaramudu/Adisaya Thirudan (**P. Pullaiah**, Tel/Tam, 1959)
Bandar Mera Saathi (**Gajanan Jagirdar**, H, 1966)
Band Darwaza *see* Bandh Darwaza
Bande Mataram *see* Vande Mataram
Bandham (Vijayanand, Mal, 1983)
Bandham (K. Vijayan, Tam, 1985)
Bandham (Rajachandra, Tel, 1986)
Bandha Mukti (K.V. Raju, K, 1987)
Bandhan (**N.R. Acharya**, H, 1940)
Bandhan (**Hemchandra Chunder**, H, 1956)
Bandhan (Ardhendu Mukherjee, B, 1962)
Bandhan (**Narendra Bedi**, H, 1969)
Bandhan (**Nitai Palit**, O, 1969)
Bandhan (Manu Sen, B, 1980)
Bandhan (**Anant Mane**, Mar, 1991)
Bandhana (**S.V. Rajendra Singh**, K, 1984)
Bandhanam (**M.T. Vasudevan Nair**, Mal, 1978)
Bandhan Anjana (Prabhat Roy, H, 1985)
Bandhani (**Ketan Mehta**, H, 1987)
Bandhan Kachche Dhaagon Ka (Anil Sharma, H, 1983)
Bandhan Pheron Ka (Ashok Neemaria, H, 1985)
Bandhan Vachna Ro (Nizam Sayyad Peer, R, 1991)
Bandha Pasam (**A. Bhimsingh**, Tam, 1962)
Bandhavya (Ratnakar-Madhu, K, 1971)
Bandhavyulu (S.V. Ranga Rao, Tel, 1968)
Bandh Darwaza (Tulsi/Shyam **Ramsay**, H, 1990)
Bandhe Haath (O.P. Goyal, H, 1973)
Bandh Honth (Raj Marbros, H, 1984)
Bandhi (Kodi Ramakrishna, Tel, 1985)
Bandhipotu *see* **Veera Kesari**
Bandhipotu Bhayankara (**Tapi Chanakya**, Tel, 1972)
Bandhipotu Bhimanna (M. Mallikarjuna Rao, Tel, 1969)
Bandhipotu Dongalu (**K.S. Prakash Rao**, Tel, 1968)
Bandhipotu Mutha (M. Karnan, Tel, 1978)
Bandhipotu Rudramma (K.S. Rami Reddy, Tel, 1983)
Bandhobi (Shankar Bhattacharya, B, 1989)
Bandhu (Chitta Bose, B, 1958)
Bandhukkal Chatrukkal (Shrikumaran Thampi, Mal, 1993)
Bandhulu Anubandhulu (**C.S. Rao**, Tel, 1974)
Bandhulu Anubandhulu (Bhargava, Tel, 1983)
Bandhuluvosthannuru Jagratha (Sarat, Tel, 1989)
Bandhu Mohanty (**Nitai Palit**, O, 1977)
Bandhur Path (Chitta Bose, B, 1949)
Bandi (**Satyen Bose**, H, 1957)
Bandi (Alo Sircar, B/H, 1978)
Bandi Balaka (Inder Sen, B, 1981)
Bandi Bidhata (Prabhat Mukherjee, B, 1975)
Bandini (**Bimal Roy**, H, 1963)
Bandini (Sujit Guha, B, 1989)
Bandini Kamala (Bimal Bhowmick, B, 1982)
Bandish (**Satyen Bose**, H, 1955)
Bandish (Charandas Shokh, H, 1969)
Bandish (**K. Bapaiah**, H, 1980)
Bandit of Baghdad *see* Baghdad Nu Baharvatiyo
Bandit of the Air (*aka* Hawai Daku: A.R. Choudhury, H, 1936)
Bandivaan Mi Hya Sansari (Arun Karnataki, Mar, 1988)
Band Kamre Mein *see* Bedroom Story
Bandkhor *see* Baghi
Band Master (**Ravindra Dave**, H, 1963)
Band Master (K.S. Ravikumar, Tam, 1993)
Bandodu Gundamma (**Dasari Narayana Rao**, Tel, 1980)
Bandook Dahej Ke Seene Par (Ram Gopal, H, 1989)
Bandookbaaz *see* Gunfight
Bandookbaj (Gautam Gupta, B, 1987)
Bandookwali (**K. Amarnath**, H, 1944)
Bangabala (Dwarka Khosla?, Graphic Arts, St, 1929)
Bangalee (**Charu Roy**, B, 1936)
Bangalore Bhootha (A.B. Jagan Mohan Rao, K, 1975)
Bangalore Mail (L.S. Narayana, K, 1968)
Bangarada Gudi (K.S.R. Doss, K, 1976)
Bangarada Hoovu (Arasukumar, K, 1967)
Bangarada Jinke (**T.S. Nagabharana**, K, 1980)
Bangarada Kalla (D. Shankar Singh, K, 1973)
Bangarada Mane (Basavaraj Kestur, K, 1981)
Bangarada Manushya (Siddalingaiah, K, 1972)
Bangarada Panjara (V. Somasekhar, K, 1973)
Bangarakka (**Dasari Narayana Rao**, Tel, 1977)
Bangari (**G.V. Iyer**, K, 1963)
Bangar Patler (Richard Castellino, Tulu, 1993)
Bangaru Babu (V.B. Rajendra Prasad, Tel, 1972)
Bangaru Bhava (K. Subba Rao, Tel, 1980)
Bangaru Bhoomi *see* Ponnavayal
Bangaru Bhoomi (P. Chandrasekhara Reddy, Tel, 1982)
Bangaru Bommalu (V.B. Rajendra Prasad, Tel, 1977)
Bangaru Bullodu (Raviraja Pinisetty, Tel, 1993)
Bangaru Chellalu (B. Subba Rao, Tel, 1979)
Bangaru Chilaka (Anil Kumar, Tel, 1985)
Bangaru Gajulu (**C.S. Rao**, Tel, 1968)
Bangaru Gudi (K.S.R. Doss, Tel, 1979)
Bangaru Kalalu (**Adurthi Subba Rao**, Tel, 1974)
Bangaru Kanuka (V. Madhusudhana Rao, Tel, 1982)
Bangaru Kapuram (P. Chandrasekhara Reddy, Tel, 1984)
Bangaru Koduku (K.S.R. Doss, Tel, 1982)
Bangaru Kutumbam (K.S.R. Doss, Tel, 1971)
Bangaru Lakshmi (R. Thyagarajan, Tel, 1980)
Bangaru Mama (Muthyala Subbaiah, Tel, 1992)
Bangaru Manishi (**A. Bhimsingh**, Tel, 1976)
Bangaru Manushulu (K.S. Rami Reddy, Tel, 1973)
Bangaru Panjaram (**B.N. Reddi**, Tel, 1965)
Bangaru Papa (**B.N. Reddi**, Tel, 1954)
Bangaru Pichika (**Bapu**, Tel, 1968)
Bangaru Sankellu (G. Ramineedu, Tel, 1968)
Bangaru Talli (**Tapi Chanakya**, Tel, 1971)
Bangaru Timmaraju (G. Vishwanathan, Tel, 1964)
Banglar Kabigan (**Santi P. Choudhury**, B, 1978)
Banglar Mandirey Terracotta (**Santi P. Choudhury**, B, 1961)
Banglar Meye (**Naresh Mitra**, B, 1941)
Banglar Nari (**Sailajananda Mukherjee**, B, 1954)
Banhi Sikha (Piyush Bose, B, 1976)
Banjaran (Harmesh Malhotra, H, 1991)
Banjare (Hiren Bose, H, 1948)
Banjarin (Jaswant Jhaveri, H, 1960)
Banjui (**Abdul Majid**, A, 1978)
Bankalekha (Chitta Bose, B, 1948)
Bankelal (*aka* Nagar Vadhu Jo Bani Kulavadhu, Rasiya: Ratan Kumar, H, 1972)
Banker Margayya (**T.S. Nagabharana**, K, 1983)
Banke Savaria (*aka* Prince Charming: **Jayant Desai**, St, 1931)
Banke Savaria (*aka* Vagabond Lover: **Nanubhai Vakil**, H, 1938)
Banke Savaria (Dhanpat Rai, H, 1962)
Banke Sipahi (*aka* Desh Sevak, Patriot: R.N. Vaidya, H, 1937)
Ban Ki Chidiya (*aka* Nightingale: **Jayant Desai**, H, 1938)
Bank Manager (Rakhan, H, 1959)
Bank Robbery (Maruti, H, 1969)
Banmalir Prem (Amar Dutta, B, 1941)
Banmanush (Kamran, H, 1979)
Bannada Gejje (**S.V. Rajendra Singh**, K, 1990)
Bannada Vesha (**Girish Kasaravalli**, K, 1988)
Banni Ondasala Nodi (S. Umesh, K, 1991)
Banno (S.S. Rawal, H, 1987)
Bano (C.M. Amla, H, 1949)
Banphool (**Niren Lahiri**, H, 1945)
Banphool (**Vijay Bhatt**, H, 1971)
Banprastha (**Sukumar Dasgupta**, B, 1950)
Bansari (**Jayant Desai**, H, 1943)
Bansari (Ashim Bannerjee, B, 1980)
Bansaria (Ram Narayan Dave, H, 1949)
Bansaria Baaje Ganga Teer (Rakesh Pandey, Bh, 1984)
Bansari Bala (*aka* Fairy of the Flute: A.P. Kapur, St, 1927)
Bansari Bala (A.M. Khan, H, 1936)
Bansari Bala (**Nanubhai Vakil**, H, 1957)
Banser Kella (Sudhir Mukherjee, B, 1953)
Banshayya *see* Bhishma Pitamah
Bansi Birju (Prakash Varma, H, 1972)
Banthrotu Bharya (**Dasari Narayana Rao**, Tel, 1974)
Banto (Baldev R. Jhingan, P, 1962)
Banwasi (Kumar Chandrasekhar, H, 1948)
Banwra (G. Rakesh, H, 1950)
Banwre Nain (**Kidar Sharma**, H, 1950)
Banwri (A.C. Trilogchander, H, 1982)
Banyabapu (Govind Kulkarni, Mar, 1977)
Banyan Deer (**Govind Saraiya**, E, 1959)
Bapu Ne Kaha Tha *see* Kashmir Hamara Hai
Bapu Ne Kaha Tha (**Vijay Bhatt**, H, 1962)
Bara/Sookha (**M.S. Sathyu**, K/H, 1980)
Baraat (Dada Gunjal, H, 1942)
Baraat (**K. Amarnath**, H, 1960)
Baraati (J.K. Nanda, H, 1954)
Barababu (Jyotish Mukherjee, B, 1937)
Bara Bou (Suhrid Ghosh, B, 1950)
Baradari (**K. Amarnath**, H, 1955)
Barah Baje *see* Twelve o'clock
Barah Ghante (N.C. Chakraborty, H, 1975)
Bara Maa (**Niren Lahiri**, B, 1957)
Bara Varshe Saha Mahine Teen Divas (Vasant Painter, Mar, 1967)
Baravase (H.S.J. Mekmoon, K, 1982)
Barbela (Kalpataru, B, 1954)
Bar Bodhu (Bijoy Chatterjee, B, 1977)
Bardidi/Badi Didi (**Amar Mullick**, B/H, 1939)
Bardidi (**Ajoy Kar**, B, 1957)
Bare Nanna Muddina Rani (Siddalingaiah, K, 1990)
Bargad Dada (?, Word & Vision, H, 1987)
Bari Palyam Bullodu (Bheeram Mastan Rao, Tel, 1979)
Bari Theke Paliye (*aka* The Runaway: **Ritwik Ghatak**, B, 1959)
Barjatri (**Satyen Bose**, B, 1951)
Bar Ke Pobar (*aka* A Wager in Love: **H.M. Reddy**, St, 1931)
Barkha (**Krishnan-Panju**, H, 1959)
Barkha Bahar (Amar Kumar, H, 1973)
Barna Bibarna (Bipal Roy Choudhury, B, 1975)
Barnachora (Aravind Mukherjee, B, 1963)
Barnali (**Ajoy Kar**, B, 1963)
Baro Bhai (Sushil Mukherjee, B, 1980)
Barood (Aspi, H, 1960)
Barood (Pramod Chakraborty, H, 1976)
Barrister (Harish, H, 1947)
Barrister Ki Bibi *see* **Barrister's Wife**
Barrister Parvatisham (**H.M. Reddy**, Tel, 1940)
Barrister's Wife (**Chandulal Shah**, H, 1935)
Barsaat (**Raj Kapoor**, H, 1949)
Barsaat Ki Ek Raat (G. Singh, H, 1948)
Barsaat Ki Ek Raat/Anusandhan (**Shakti Samanta**, H/B, 1981)
Barsaat Ki Raat (P.L. Santoshi, H, 1960)
Baruar Sansar (**Nip Barua**, A, 1970)
Basabdatta (Satish Dasgupta, B, 1935)
Basant (**Amiya Chakravarty**, H, 1942)
Basant (Bibhuti Mitra, H, 1960)
Basanta Bahar (Bikash Roy, B, 1957)
Basanta Bilap (**Dinen Gupta**, B, 1972)
Basanta Prabha *see* Vasant Prabha
Basanta Rasa (Gurudas/Bansidhar Phanda, O, 1984)
Basant Bahar (Raja Nawathe, H, 1956)
Basanti Apa (S.K. Kalim, O, 1987)
Basanti Purnima (**Sushil Majumdar**, B, 1937)
Basanti Tangewali (Kanti Shah, H, 1992)
Basant Panchami (**Jayant Desai**, H, 1956)
Basera (Inayat, H, 1950)
Basera (Ramesh Talwar, H, 1981)
Bases of Progress (**P.V. Pathy**, E, 1958)
Basre Ki Hoor (Majnu, H, 1956)
Bastab (Phani Ganguly, B, 1953)
Basti Aur Bazaar (Rajdeep, H, 1973)
Basti Bulbul (G.V.R. Sheshgiri Rao, Tel, 1971)
Basti Kiladilu (G.V.R. Sheshgiri Rao, Tel, 1970)
Bastra Haran (**Sisir Mishra**, O, 1991)
Basu Parivar (**Nirmal Dey**, B, 1952)
Bata Abata (Brindaban Jena, O, 1980)
Batasari/Kanal Neer (**P.S. Ramakrishna Rao**, Tel/Tam, 1961)
Batasi (Agantuk, B, 1980)
Batasi Jhada (Ramesh Mohanty, O, 1981)
Bate Boo (Harish Kataria, Haryanvi, 1985)
Bathilukku Bathil (Jambulingam, Tam, 1972)
Bathing Ghat: Howrah (?, Elphinstone Bioscope, St, 1906)
Batighara (Abhiyatrik, O, 1976)
Battalion of the Blunder *see* Rao Saheb
Battle *see* Maidan-e-Jung
Batwara (Karunesh Thakur, H, 1961)
Batwara (Virendra, P, 1983)
Batwara (**J.P. Dutta**, H, 1989)
Bava Bava Panneru (Jandhyala, Tel, 1991)
Bava Diddina Kapuram (G. Ramakrishna, Tel, 1972)
Bava Maradallu (Padmanaba Rao, Tel, 1961)
Bava Maradallu (A. Kodandarami Reddy, Tel, 1984)
Bava Maradhula Saval (C.V. Ganesh, Tel, 1988)
Bawarchi (**Hrishikesh Mukherjee**, H, 1972)
Bayalu Dari (Dorairaj-Bhagavan, K, 1976)
Bayan (?, R.K. Enterprises, H, 1979)
Bayano Navare Sambhala (**Datta Keshav**, Mar, 1974)
Bayasade Banda Bhagya (R. Ramamurthy, K, 1977)
Bazaar (**K. Amarnath**, H, 1949)
Bazaar (Sagar Sarhadi, H, 1982)
Bazaar Band Karo (**B.R. Ishara**, H, 1974)
Bazaar-e-Husn *see* Seva Sadan
Bazaar Rowdy (A. Kodandarami Reddy, Tel, 1988)
Bazarbattu *see* Rani Saheba
Bazigar (Manibhai Vyas, H, 1938)
Bazigar (**Nanabhai Bhatt**, H, 1959)
Bazigar (Karunesh Thakur, H, 1972)
Bazigar (Abbas-Mastan, H, 1993)
Bazooband (*aka* Bracelet: **Ramanand Sagar**, H, 1954)
Beaabroo (Shivkumar, H, 1983)
Beau Monde *see* **Andaz**
Beautiful Snake of Aravalli, The *see* **Neera**

Beauty Caravan *see* Karwan-e-Husn
Beauty from Hell, The *see* Pataal Padmini
Beauty of Rajasthan *see* **Sati Padmini**
Bebas (Bhagwan Hajele, H, 1950)
Bebbuli (V. Madhusudhana Rao, Tel, 1980)
Bebbuli Veta (M. Rosi Raju, Tel, 1985)
Bechain (Kawal Sharma, H, 1993)
Becoming *see* Sahaja
Bedaag (R. Bhattacharya, H, 1965)
Beda Pyar (Harish, H, 1944)
Bedara Kannappa (**H.L.N. Simha**, K, 1954)
Bedard (B.N. Chouhan, H, 1949)
Bedard Zamana Kya Jaane (**Babubhai Mistri**, H, 1959)
Bedardi (**Kidar Sharma**, H, 1951)
Bedardi (Krishnakant Pandya, H, 1993)
Bedaru Bombe (Bhargava, K, 1984)
Bedeni (*aka* Arup Katha; **Ritwik Ghatak/Nirmal Dey** et al, B, 1952: Incomplete)
Be Dhari Talwar (*aka* Do Dhari Talwar, Challenge: **B.P. Mishra**, St, 1929)
Bedi (V. Somasekhar, K, 1987)
Bedi Bandhavalu (C. Srinivasan, K, 1968)
Be Din Ni Badshahi (*aka* A Crown for Two Days: **Harshadrai Mehta**, St, 1926)
Bedroom Story (*aka* Band Kamre Mein: D. Raman, H, 1988)
Beedala Asti (D.L. Ramachandar, Tel, 1955)
Beedala Patlu *see* **Ezhai Padum Padu**
Beedala Patlu (**B. Vittalacharya**, Tel, 1972)
Beedhi Basavanna (**B.R. Panthulu**, K, 1967)
Beedi Kunjamma (Rajasekharan, Mal, 1982)
Beena (Karaikudi Narayanan, Mal, 1978)
Been Ka Jadu (N. Rajesh, H, 1963)
Beera Shera (Pradeep A. Nayyar, Haryanvi, 1973)
Beesida Bale (B.A. Arasukumar/Sastan Philip Louis, K, 1973)
Bees Saal Baad (Biren Nag, H, 1962)
Bees Saal Baad (Raj Kumar Kohli, H, 1988)
Bees Saal Pehle (Probir Roy, H, 1972)
Beeswa Oonth (TV: **Atma Ram**, H, 1990)
Beete Din (**Ezra Mir**, H, 1947)
Before Dawn *see* **Pratyusha**
Before my Eyes (**Mani Kaul**, Wordless, 1988)
Before Taking Leave *see* Vidaparayum Munpe
Begaar (**Sai Paranjpye**, H, 1975)
Begana (Sadashiv Rao Kavi, H, 1963)
Begana (Ambarish Sangal, H, 1986)
Beggar Girl *see* Bhikharan *or* Rehana
Beggar Girl of Agra (?, Bengal United Film, St, 1932)
Beggar Meets Beggar *see* Rajdoot
Be Ghadi Mouj (*aka* Pleasure Mad: **N.G. Devare**, St, 1927)
Begum (**Sushil Majumdar**, H, 1945)
Beguman Ashiq (*aka* The Gallant: ?, Chandrakala Film, St, 1930)
Begunah (**Gajanan Jagirdar**, H, 1937)
Begunah (B.R. Mudnaney, H, 1949)
Begunah (Narendra Suri, H, 1957)
Begunah (Shivkumar, H, 1970)
Begunah Qaidi (V.K. Sobti, H, 1982)
Behind the Breadline (**S. Sukhdev**, E, 1974)
Behind the Veil *see* Burkhawali
Behke Kadam (Dharmesh Dutt, H, 1971)
Behram Daku (Aakkoo, H, 1959)
Behram Khan (**Gajanan Jagirdar**, H, 1946)
Behram Khan (?, Standard Pics, Persian, 1947)
Behram the Bandit *see* Baharvatiyo Behram
Behula (C. Legrand, St, 1921)
Behula Lakhinder (Amal Dutta, B, 1977)
Beimaan (Sohanlal Kanwar, H, 1972)
Beinsaafi (?, H, 1981)
Bejoy Ragar (Tulsi Lahiri, B, 1936)
Bekaraar (V.B. Rajendra Prasad, H, 1983)
Bekar Nashan (**Jyotish Bannerjee**, B, 1938)
Bekhabar (**Nanabhai Bhatt**, H, 1965)
Bekhabar (Kedar Kapoor, H, 1983)
Be Kharab Jan *see* **Do Diwane**
Bekhudi (**Rahul Rawail**, H, 1992)
Bekkina Kannu (S.N. Singh, K, 1983)
Bela (**Chaturbhuj Doshi**, H, 1947)
Belagaam (Naval Kishore, H, 1987)
Belaku (**N. Lakshminarayan**, K, 1987)
Belbhandar (Achyut Ranade, Mar, 1952)
Belgian Emperor's Visit to India (**Nitin Bose**, St, 1921)
Belle, La *see* Qatil Kathiyani
Belle of Baluchistan *see* Mohtaj Mashuq
Belle of Bombay *see* Dilruba
Belliappa Bangarappa (Poornapragna, K, 1992)
Bellimoda (**Puttanna Kanagal**, K, 1967)
Bellimodalu (K.V. Raju, Mal, 1992)
Beloved *see* Sajni
Beloved Blade *see* Pyari Katar
Beloved Rogue *see* Albelo Sawar
Belt Mathai (T.S. Mohan, Mal, 1983)
Beluvalada Madilalli (Geethapriya, K, 1975)
Bemisal (**Hrishikesh Mukherjee**, H, 1982)
Benaam (**Narendra Bedi**, H, 1974)
Benaam Badshah (K. Ravishankar, H, 1991)
Benaam Rishte (Shyam Gupta, H, 1992)
Benarasi's Secret (**Santi P. Choudhury**, E, 1968)
Benazir (S. Khalil, H, 1964)
Benevolent Bravery *see* Shoorana Sangram
Bengal Famine (**Bimal Roy**, E, 1943)
Bengali Fisherman, The (**Hiralal Sen**, St, 1904)
Bengali Bomb, The *see* Vasant Bengali
Bengal 1983 (**P.C. Barua**, B/H, 1932)
Bengal Partition Film, The (**Hiralal Sen**, St, 1905)
Benki Alli Aralida Hoovu (**K. Balachander**, K, 1983)
Benki Birugali (Tiptur Raghu, K, 1984)
Benki Chendu (Manimurughan, K, 1982)
Benkiya Bale (Dorairaj-Bhagavan, K, 1983)
Benoor Aankhen *see* Bahen Ka Prem
Benz Vasu (Hassan, Mal, 1980)
Bepanah (Jagdish Sadanah, H, 1985)
Beqasoor (**K. Amarnath**, H, 1950)
Beqasoor (Kamran, H, 1969)
Berahem (Raghunath Jhalani, H, 1980)
Beretha Jeeva (K.R. Seetarama Sastry, K, 1965)
Berozgar (*aka* Jai Leela: Rajhans, H, 1936)
Besahara (**B.R. Ishara**, H, 1987)
Beshaque (Kashinath, H, 1980)
Besharam (Deven Verma, H, 1978)
Besuge (Geethapriya, K, 1976)
Beta (Indra Kumar, H, 1992)
Betaab (Harbans, H, 1952)
Betaab (**Rahul Rawail**, H, 1983)
Betaaj Badshah *see* Raj Mukut
Bete (V. Somasekhar, K, 1986)
Bethaala Gudda (B.A. Arasukumar, K, 1971)
Beti (**Jayant Desai**, H, 1941)
Beti (Suraj Prakash, H, 1957)
Beti (Harmesh Malhotra, H, 1969)
Beti Bete (**L.V. Prasad**, H, 1964)
Beti Rajasthan Ri (Naval Mathur, R, 1989)
Beti Tumhare Jaisi (Mahendra Nath, H, 1969)
Beti Udhar Ke (?, Bh, 1990)
Betrayer, The *see* Dagabaaz Dushman
Betrothal By Choice *see* **Swayamvaram**
Betrothed One, The *see* **Murappennu**
Bettada Bhairava (M.N. Srinivas, K, 1973)
Bettada Hoovu (**N. Lakshminarayan**, K, 1985)
Bettada Huli (A.V. Sheshgiri Rao, K, 1965)
Bettada Kalla (S.M. Sreeramulu Naidu, K, 1957)
Bettada Thayi (Perala, K, 1986)
Bettale Seve (K.V. Jayaram, K, 1982)
Better Half, The *see* Ardhangi
Bevu Bella (Jambulingam, K, 1963)
Bewafa (M.L. Anand, H, 1952)
Bewafa Ashq *see* **Yasmin**
Bewafa Ashq (*aka* Discarded Love: Dr Alvaro, St, 1931)
Bewafai (R. Thyagarajan, H, 1985)
Bewafa Qatil (*aka* Tiger: Dada Gunjal, St, 1932)
Bewafa Se Wafaa (Sawan Kumar, H, 1992)
Bewaqoof (I.S. Johar, H, 1960)
Beyond the Horizon *see* **Wahan**
Beyond the River Padma *see* Durbargati Padma
Beyond Thirteen Rivers *see* **Tero Nadir Parey**
Bezubaan (Ram Kamlani, H, 1962)
Bezubaan (**Bapu**, H, 1981)
Bezwada Bebbuli (**Vijayanirmala**, Tel, 1983)
Bhabhi (**Franz Osten**, H, 1938)
Bhabhi (**Krishnan-Panju**, H, 1957)
Bhabhi (D. Himmat, G, 1976)
Bhabhi (Kishore Vyas, H, 1991)
Bhabhi-Kaal (**Niren Lahiri**, B, 1945)
Bhabhi Ki Chudiyan (Sadashiv J. Row Kavi, H, 1961)
Bhabhina Het (**V.M. Vyas**, G, 1948)
Bhabhina Het (Vijay B. Chauhan, G, 1986)
Bhabho (?, Monar Films, P, 1990)
Bhadada Hoo (K.V. Jayaram, K, 1982)
Bhadar Tara Vehta Pani (**Ravindra Dave**, G, 1975)
Bhadil Solval Bhadrakali (S. Jagadeeshan, Tam, 1986)
Bhadra Bhamini (*aka* Test of Chastity: **Nanubhai Desai**, St, 1925)
Bhadrachitta (Kalil, Mal, 1988)
Bhadra Deepam (M. Krishnan Nair, Mal, 1973)
Bhadrakali (A.C. Trilogchander, Tam/Tel, 1976)
Bhadram Koduko (K. Kutumba Rao, Tel, 1991)
Bhadraveshi Goonda (*aka* Gentleman Loafer: ?, Royal Art Studio, St, 1926)
Bhaduri Mashai (Prafulla Roy, B, 1956)
Bhadwa Mata (Mukundi Trivedi, Malvi, 1982)
Bhagambhag (**Master Bhagwan**, H, 1956)
Bhagapirivinai (**A. Bhimsingh**, Tam, 1959)
Bhagasthulu (**A. Bhimsingh**, Tel, 1975)
Bhagat Dhanna Jat (**Dara Singh/Chandrakant**, P, 1974)
Bhagat Surdas *see* Bilwamangal
Bhagavad Geeta (**G.V. Iyer**, Sanskrit, 1992)
Bhagavathipuram Railway Gate (R. Selvaraj, Tam, 1983)
Bhagini Nivedita (Bijoy Basu, B, 1962)
Bhagirathi (T.V. Singh Thakore, K, 1969)
Bhagirathi Ganga (*aka* Gangavataran: ?, **Madan** Theatres, St, 1922)
Bhag Ke Lekha (Navin Joshi, Bh, 1990)
Bhago Bhoot Aaya (Krishna Naidu, H, 1985)
Bhagta Bhoot (*aka* Galloping Ghost: Ramanlal Desai, H, 1943)
Bhagwa Jhenda (K.P. Bhave, St, 1926)
Bhagwa Jhenda (**N.D. Sarpotdar**, Mar, 1939)
Bhagwan (?, Trident Arts Intl., Mal, 1986)
Bhagwan (Satya Reddy, Tel, 1989)
Bhagwan Aur Shaitan (Manmohan Sabir, H, 1959)
Bhagwan Balaji *see* **Shri Venkateshwara Mahatyam**
Bhagwan Dada (J. Om Prakash, H, 1986)
Bhagwan Parashuram (**Babubhai Mistri**, H, 1970)
Bhagwan Samaye Sansar Mein (*aka* Kan Kan Mein Bhagwan: Satish Kumar, H, 1976)
Bhagwan Shri Krishna (Raja Yagnik, H, 1950)
Bhagwan Shri Krishna (Ramkumar Bohra, G, 1984)
Bhagwan Shri Krishna Chaitanya/Chaitanya Mahaprabhu (**Debaki Bose**, B/H, 1954)
Bhagwan Shri Saibaba (Sai Om Prakash, K, 1993)
Bhagwan Shri Shri Ramakrishna (Prafulla Chakraborty, B, 1955)
Bhagwata Bhakta Damaji (**Baburao Painter**, St, 1922)
Bhagwat Mahima (Vithaldas Panchotia, H, 1955)
Bhagya Chakra *see* **Dhoop Chhaon**
Bhagya Chakra (*aka* Wheel of Fate: ?, Surya Films, H, 1933)
Bhagya Chakra (**Y.V. Rao**, K, 1956)
Bhagya Chakra (Ajit Kar, B, 1980)
Bhagyachakram (**K.V. Reddy**, Tel, 1968)
Bhagyada Bagilu (Ravi, K, 1968)
Bhagyada Belaku (K. Kutumba Rao, K, 1981)
Bhagyada Lakshmi Baramma (**Singeetham Srinivasa Rao**, K, 1985)
Bhagya Devatha/Bhagya Devathai (**Tapi Chanakya**, Tel/Tam, 1959)
Bhagya Devathe (Ratnakar-Madhu, K, 1968)
Bhagya Jatakam (**P. Bhaskaran**, Mal, 1962)
Bhagya Jyothi (K.S.L. Swamy, K, 1975)
Bhagya Lakshmi (*aka* Wife's Destiny: **Kaliprasad Ghosh**, St, 1932)
Bhagya Lakshmi (**P. Pullaiah**, Tel, 1943)
Bhagya Lakshmi (**Sarvottam Badami**, H, 1944)
Bhagya Lakshmi (K.V. Srinivasan, Tam, 1961)
Bhagya Lakshmi (**Anant Mane**, Mar, 1962)
Bhagya Lakshmi (**Ravindra Dave**, G, 1978)
Bhagya Lakshmi (Kommineni, Tel, 1984)
Bhagya Leela (**K. Amarnath**, Tam, 1938)
Bhagyalipi (Niranjan Dey, B, 1978)
Bhagyamudra (M.A.V. Rajendran, Mal, 1967)
Bhagya Rekha (**Shantaram Athavale**, Mar, 1948)
Bhagya Rekha (**B.N. Reddi**, Tel, 1957)
Bhagya Tara (Dwarkanath, Tam, 1938)
Bhagyavaan (**Datta Dharmadhikari**, H, 1953)
Bhagyavaan (S. Subhash, H, 1993)
Bhagyavaan Bharwad (*aka* Son of a Shepherd: Hiralal Doctor, St, 1930)
Bhagyavantha (**B.S. Ranga**, K, 1981)
Bhagyavantharu (H.R. Bhargava, K, 1977)
Bhagyavanthudu (**C.S. Rao**, Tel, 1971)
Bhagyavati (**L.V. Prasad**, Tam, 1957)
Bhagyavati Mi Hya Sansari (R. Tipnis, Mar, 1971)
Bhagyodaya (*aka* Destiny at Play: R.N. Vaidya, St, 1930)
Bhagyodaya (P.V. Babu, K, 1956)
Bhai (K.D. Mehra, H, 1944)
Bhai Aakhir Bhai Hota Hai (R.C. Nanda, H, 1983)
Bhai Bahen (**V.M. Vyas**, G, 1948)
Bhai Bahen (Ram Daryani, H, 1950)
Bhai Bahen (**G.P. Sippy**, H, 1959)
Bhai Bahen (**A. Bhimsingh**, H, 1969)
Bhai Bahen Chalya Mosal (Madhavi Pandya, G, 1980)
Bhaibandhi (**Ravindra Dave**, G, 1976)
Bhai Bhai *see* Sona Chandi
Bhai Bhai (**M.V. Raman**, H, 1956)
Bhai Bhai (**Nitai Palit**, O, 1956)
Bhai Bhai (Raja Nawathe, H, 1970)
Bhai Bhai (Biju Phukan, A, 1988)
Bhai Bhauja (Sarathi, O, 1967)
Bhai Bone (Indumadhab Bhattacharya, B, 1948)
Bhaichara (*aka* Brotherhood, Fraternity: G.K. Mehta, H, 1943)
Bhaidooj (Narottam Vyas, H, 1947)
Bhai Ho To Aisa (**Manmohan Desai**, H, 1972)
Bhaijan (S. Khalil, H, 1945)
Bhai Ka Dushman Bhai (Sudesh Issar, H, 1987)
Bhai Ka Pyar *see* Phir Bhi Apna Hai
Bhai Ki Kasam (*aka* His Father's Honour: Ramakant-Gharekhan/Vaidya, St, 1928)
Bhairab Mantra (Mani Ghosh, B, 1951)
Bhairavi (**Dinkar D. Patil**, Mar, 1960)
Bhairavi (M. Bhaskar, Tam, 1978)
Bhairavi (Ramanarayanan, K, 1991)
Bhairu Pahelwan Ki Jai (Kamalakar Torney, Mar, 1978)
Bhai Saheb (**Ravindra Dave**, H, 1954)
Bhaiti (Kamal Choudhury, A, 1972)
Bhaiya (**Phani Majumdar**, Magadhi, 1961)
Bhaiya Bhouji Ke Dulaar (A.B. Tiwari, Bh, 1991)
Bhaiya Dooj (Qamar Narvi, Bh, 1984)
Bhaiyaji (Om Prakash, P, 1950)
Bhaiya Nangal (N.S. Thapa, E, 1958)
Bhakta Ambarish (**Kanjibhai Rathod**, St, 1922)
Bhakta Ambarish (B. Subba Rao, Tel, 1959)
Bhakta Arunagiri (*aka* Saint Arunagiri: S.D.S. Yogi, Tam, 1937)
Bhakta Bilwamangal (Shantikumar, H, 1948)
Bhakta Bilwamangal (Pinaki Mukherjee, B, 1954)
Bhakta Bodana *see* Jai Ranchhod
Bhakta Bodana (*aka* Shri Ranchhodrai: **S.N. Patankar**, St, 1922)
Bhakta Cheta (*aka* Cheta Chamar: Shrikrishna, H, 1936)
Bhakta Cheta (**K. Subramanyam**, Tam, 1940)
Bhakta Cheta (M.B. Ganesh, K, 1961)
Bhakta Damaji (**Dadasaheb Phalke**, St, 1928)
Bhakta Damaji (K.B. Athavale, Mar, 1937)
Bhakta Damaji (**Bhalji Pendharkar**, Mar, 1942)
Bhakta Dhruva (**P.Y. Altekar**, K, 1934)
Bhakta Dhruva (Shantikumar, H, 1947)
Bhakta Dhruva (Dada Gunjal, H, 1957)
Bhakta Dhruva Markandeya (**P. Bhanumathi**, Tel/Tam, 1982)

Bhakta Dhruvakumar (**Dhirubhai Desai**, H, 1964)
Bhakta Dnyanadeva (**Hunsur Krishnamurthy**, K, 1982)
Bhakta Gauri (S. Nottani, Tam, 1941)
Bhakta Gopal Bhaiya (Shantikumar, H, 1948)
Bhakta Gora Kumbhar (?, Gopalakrishna Pics, Tam, 1940)
Bhakta Gora Kumbhar (Dinesh Rawal, G/H, 1978)
Bhakta Gora Kumbhara (Boman D. Irani/**P. Pullaiah**, K, 1949)
Bhakta Hanuman (C.V. Raman, Tam, 1944)
Bhakta Hanuman (Ganga, Mal, 1980)
Bhakta Jana (**P. Pullaiah**, Tam, 1948)
Bhakta Jayadeva (?, Ramban Films, Tam, 1937)
Bhakta Jayadeva (Hiren Bose, Tel, 1938)
Bhakta Jayadeva (P. Ramarao, Tel, 1961)
Bhakta Kabir (Rameshwar Sharma, H, 1942)
Bhakta Kabir (**Ch. Narayanamurthy**, Tel, 1944)
Bhakta Kalathi (**R. Padmanabhan**, Tam, 1945)
Bhakta Kanakadasa (Y.R. Swamy, K, 1960)
Bhakta Kannappa (**Bapu**, Tel, 1976)
Bhakta Ke Bhagwan (*aka* Raja Shriyal, Raja Mordhwaj: Dada Gunjal, H, 1934)
Bhakta Ke Bhagwan (**V.M. Vyas**, H, 1947)
Bhakta Kuchela (**K. Subramanyam**, Tam, 1936)
Bhakta Kuchela (**P. Subramanyam**, Mal, 1961)
Bhakta Kumaran (*aka* Raja Yogi: K. Rangarao, Tam, 1939)
Bhakta Kumbhara (**Hunsur Krishnamurthy**, K, 1974)
Bhakta Lakshmidas (*aka* Adharmoddhar: Khodidas Chunilal Panchal, St, 1933)
Bhakta Mallikarjuna (C.V. Raju, K, 1955)
Bhakta Markandeya (*aka* Chiranjeev: G.B. Bhonsle, Mar, 1944)
Bhakta Markandeya (**B.S. Ranga**, K/Tam/Tel, 1956)
Bhakta Meera (**Y.V. Rao**, Tam, 1938)
Bhakta Muldas (S.J. Rajdev, G, 1982)
Bhakta Namdev (Dhrupad Roy, Tam, 1938)
Bhakta Nandan (*aka* Nandanar; **R.S. Prakash**, St, 1923);
Bhakta Nandanar (**S. Soundararajan**, Tam, 1942)
Bhakta Naradar *see* Naradar
Bhakta Narasinh Mehta (Vijay B. Chauhan, G, 1984)
Bhakta Narsaiyon (Jamnadas Kapadia, G, 1952)
Bhakta Pipaji (Dinesh Rawal, G, 1980)
Bhakta Potana (**K.V. Reddy**, Tel, 1942)
Bhakta Potana (G. Ramineedu, Tel, 1966)
Bhakta Prahlad (**S.N. Patankar**, St, 1917)
Bhakta Prahlad (**Baburao Painter**, St, 1926)
Bhakta Prahlad (**Dadasaheb Phalke**, St, 1926)
Bhakta Prahlad (*aka* Narasinh Avatar: **Kanjibhai Rathod**, H, 1932)
Bhakta Prahlad (K.P. Bhave/**R.G. Torney**, H/Mar, 1933)
Bhakta Prahlad (**Dhirubhai Desai**, H/G, 1946)
Bhakta Prahlad (**Nip Barua**, A, 1958)
Bhakta Prahlad (Raja Yagnik, H, 1959)
Bhakta Prahlad (Kamal Sharma, H, 1965)
Bhakta Prahlad (Ramkumar Bohra, G, 1980)
Bhakta Prahlada *see* **Prahladan**
Bhakta Prahlada (**H.M. Reddy**, Tel, 1931)
Bhakta Prahlada (**Ch. Narayanamurthy**, Tel, 1942)
Bhakta Prahlada (**K. Subramanyam**, K, 1942)
Bhakta Prahlada (H.S. Krishnaswamy/M.V. Subbaiah Naidu, K, 1958)
Bhakta Prahlada (**Ch. Narayanamurthy**, Tel/Tam/H, 1967)
Bhakta Prahlada (Vijay, K, 1983)
Bhakta Pundalik (**Dhirubhai Desai**, G/H, 1949)
Bhakta Pundalik (**Datta Dharmadhikari**, Mar, 1975)
Bhakta Puran (**Chaturbhuj Doshi**, G, 1949)
Bhakta Puran (*aka* Parasmani: **Dhirubhai Desai**, H, 1952)
Bhakta Purandaradasa (Baburao Chavan, Tam/K, 1937)
Bhakta Raaj (**Jayant Desai**, H, 1943)
Bhakta Raaj (**V.M. Vyas**, H, 1960)
Bhakta Raghunath (Devnarayan Gupta, B, 1951)

Chitra in *Sakhi Hatim* (1955)

Bhakta Raghunath (**Samudrala Raghavacharya**, Tel, 1960)
Bhakta Raidas (**Keshavrao Dhaiber**, H, 1943)
Bhakta Ramadas (**Kemparaj Urs**, K, 1948)
Bhakta Ramadasa (**Murugadasa**, Tam, 1935)
Bhakta Salabega (Radha Panda, O, 1983)
Bhakta Shabari (**Ch. Narayanamurthy**, Tel/Tam/K, 1960)
Bhakta Shiromani *see* Rajrishi Ambarish
Bhakta Shri Ranima Rudima (Shantilal Soni, G, 1980)
Bhakta Siriyala (**P.S. Ramakrishna Rao**, Tel, 1948)
Bhakta Siriyala (**Hunsur Krishnamurthy**, K, 1980)
Bhakta Sudama (**Dadasaheb Phalke**, St, 1927)
Bhakta Sudhanva (?, Star Film, St, 1923)
Bhakta Surdas *see* Bilwamangal
Bhakta Surdas (**Chaturbhuj Doshi**, H, 1942)
Bhakta Surdas (Shanti Dave, G, 1947)
Bhakta Tukaram (V. Madhusudhana Rao, Tel, 1973)
Bhakta Tulsidas (**Raja Chandrasekhar**, Tam, 1937)
Bhakta Tulsidas (**B.S. Ranga**, Tam, 1940)
Bhakta Tulsidas (Lanka Sathyam, Tel, 1946)
Bhakta Tulsidas (**B.S. Ranga**, Tam, 1947)
Bhakta Tulsidas (Manibhai Vyas, G, 1951)
Bhaktavatsala (*aka* Bhakta Vatsalam, Durvas Garvabhangam: **Raja Sandow**, St, 1931)
Bhakta Vidur (**Kanjibhai Rathod**, St, 1921)
Bhakta Vijaya (*aka* Sati Vijaya: ?, Shri Ramesh Film, St, 1933)
Bhakta Vijaya (Aruru Pattabhi, K, 1956)
Bhakti (**Murugadasa**, Tam, 1940)
Bhakticha Mala/Mali (**Keshavrao Date**, Mar/H, 1944)
Bhakti Mahima (K. Shankar, H, 1960)
Bhaktimala (Haribhai Desai, Tel, 1941)
Bhakti Mein Shakti/Dhyanoo Bhagat (**Dara Singh**, H/P, 1978)
Bhakti Prabhav *see* Gorakhnath
Bhala Admi (**Master Bhagwan**, H, 1958)
Bhalai (Nazir, H, 1943)
Bhala Manus (Vishwamitter Adil, H, 1979)

Bhale Abbayilu (Pekati Shivram, Tel, 1969)
Bhale Adrushtavo Adrushta (Ravi, K, 1971)
Bhale Alludu (P. Chandrasekhara Reddy, Tel, 1977)
Bhale Ammayilu/Iru Sahodarargal (**Vedantam Raghavaiah**, Tel/Tam, 1957)
Bhale Basava (**B.S. Ranga**, K, 1969)
Bhale Bhaskar (R. Ramamurthy, K, 1971)
Bhale Bhatta (Kanagal Prabhakara Sastry, K, 1974)
Bhale Bhava (Rajanikanth, Tel, 1957)
Bhale Chatura (?, Pragathi Enterprises, K, 1990)
Bhale Dampathulu (Kodi Ramakrishna, Tel, 1989)
Bhale Donga (A. Kodandarami Reddy, Tel, 1989)
Bhale Dongalu (K.S.R. Doss, Tel, 1976)
Bhale Ethu Chivaraku Chittu (**Vedantam Raghavaiah**, Tel, 1970)
Bhale Goodachari (**Homi Wadia**, Tel, 1970)
Bhale Huchcha (Y.R. Swamy, K, 1972)
Bhale Huduga (T.R. Ramanna, K, 1978)
Bhale Jodi (Y.R. Swamy, K, 1970)
Bhale Kaidheelu (B.L.V. Prasad, Tel, 1992)
Bhale Kapuram (N. Gopalakrishna, Tel, 1982)
Bhale Keshava (Vijaya Shetty, K, 1992)
Bhale Kiladi (S. Nagaraja Singh, K, 1970)
Bhale Kodalu *see* **Bhama Vijayam**
Bhale Krishnudu (**K. Raghavendra Rao**, Tel, 1980)
Bhale Mastaru (S.D. Lall, Tel, 1969)
Bhale Mithrulu (A. Mohan Gandhi, Tel, 1986)
Bhale Mogudu (Relangi Narasimha Rao, Tel, 1987)
Bhale Monagadu (**B. Vittalacharya**, Tel, 1968)
Bhale Mosagadu (P. Sambasivarao, Tel, 1972)
Bhale Pandian (**B.R. Panthulu**, Tam, 1962)
Bhale Papa (**K.S. Prakash Rao**, Tel, 1971)
Bhale Pelli (S. Jagannath, Tel, 1941)
Bhale Raja (Y.R. Swamy, K, 1969)
Bhale Ramudu/Prema Pasham (**Vedantam Raghavaiah**, Tel/Tam, 1956)
Bhale Ramudu (K.S.R. Doss, Tel, 1984)
Bhale Rangudu (**T. Rama Rao**, Tel, 1969)
Bhale Rani (Vijaya Satyam, K, 1971)

Bhale Tammudu (B.A. Subba Rao, Tel, 1969)
Bhale Tammudu (Parchuri bros., Tel, 1985)
Bhalobasha (Tulsi Lahiri, B, 1941)
Bhalobasha (**Debaki Bose**, B, 1955)
Bhalobasha Bhalobasha (**Tarun Majumdar**, B, 1985)
Bhalu (**Rajdutt**, Mar, 1980)
Bhalyachi Duniya (Govind Ghanekar, Mar, 1955)
Bhama Kalapam (Relangi Narasimha Rao, Tel, 1988)
Bhama Parinayam (**Y.V. Rao**, Tam, 1936)
Bhama Rukmini (**K. Bhagyaraj**, Tam, 1980)
Bhama Vijayam (M.L. Tandon, Tam, 1934)
Bhama Vijayam (**C. Pullaiah**, Tel, 1967)
Bhama Vijayam/Bhale Kodalu (**K. Balachander**, Tam/Tel, 1967)
Bhamta (**Dinkar D. Patil**, Mar, 1982)
Bhamto Bhoot (*aka* Wandering Phantom: **M. Bhavnani**, St, 1926)
Bhaneli Bhamini (**Homi Master**, St, 1927)
Bhaneli Vahu (**Homi Master**, G, 1948)
Bhangagara (**Sushil Majumdar**, B, 1954)
Bhangan (Mohan Biswas, B, 1973)
Bhangela Shikkano Bhed (*aka* The Broken Coin: Saqi, St, 1931)
Bhangra (Jugal Kishore, P, 1959)
Bhannat Bhanu (Sushama Shiromani, Mar, 1982)
Bhanu Goenda Jahar Assistant (Purnendu Roy Choudhury, B, 1971)
Bhanumathigaru Mogudu (A. Kodandarami Reddy, Tel, 1987)
Bhanu Pelo Lottery (M.G.S. Pictures Unit, B, 1958)
Bhanwar (Madhu Patel, H, 1947)
Bhanwar (Bhappi Sonie, H, 1976)
Bhanwara (*aka* Harjaai: **Kidar Sharma**, H, 1944)
Bhanwar Chameli (Gulu Sachdev, Haryanvi, 1985)
Bharari the Bandit (Dada Gunjal, St, 1931)
Bharatamlo Arjundu (**T. Prakash Rao/K. Raghavendra Rao**, Tel, 1987)
Bharatamlo Balachandurudu (Kodi Ramakrishna, Tel, 1988)
Bharatamlo Oka Ammayi (**Dasari Narayana Rao**, Tel, 1975)
Bharatamlo Sankharavam (B. Bhaskara Rao, Tel, 1984)
Bharatanari (Muthyala Subbaiah, Tel, 1989)
Bharata Natyam (**Ramu Kariat**, Mal, 1956)
Bharat Bandh (Kodi Ramakrishna, Tel, 1991)
Bharat Bhet *see* **Bharat Milap**
Bharat Darshan (**K.A. Abbas**, H, 1972)
Bharat Ek Khoj (*aka* Discovery of India; TV; **Shyam Benegal**, H, 1988-89)
Bharater Pher (*aka* Wheel of Fortune: ?, Star of India Film, St, 1930)
Bharater Sadhik (Suhrid Ghosh, B, 1965)
Bharathada Rathna (T.V. Singh Thakore, K, 1973)
Bharatham (*aka* Symphony: **Sibi Malayil**, Mal, 1991)
Bharathan (S.D. Saba, Tam, 1992)
Bharatha Vilas (A.C. Trilogchander, Tam, 1973)
Bharati *see* Twenty Sixth January
Bharati (R.M. Veerabhadraiah, K, 1949)
Bharati (Veeturi, Tel, 1975)
Bharati Bala *see* Dukhtar-e-Hind
Bharati Balak (Aga Hashr Kashmiri, H, 1931)
Bharat Ka Bhavishya *see* Krishna Shishtai
Bharat Ka Jeevan (*aka* Life of India: M.D. Shah, H, 1937)
Bharat Ka Lal (*aka* Hot Blood: S.M. Yusuf, H, 1936)
Bharat Kesari (**Homi Wadia**, Tam, 1939)
Bharat Ke Shaheed (**Vishram Bedekar**, H, 1972)
Bharat Ki Beti (**Premankur Atorthy**, H, 1935)
Bharat Ki Devi *see* Snehlata
Bharat Ki Santaan (Bhagwat S. Anand, H, 1980)
Bharat Ki Sati (?, **Madan** Theatres, H, 1937)
Bharat Mata *see* **Mother India**
Bharat Milap/Bharat Bhet (**Vijay Bhatt**, H/Mar, 1942)
Bharat Milap (**Babubhai Mistri**, H, 1965)
Bharatni Vani (**V.M. Vyas**, G, 1958)

Bharat Ramani (**Jyotish Bannerjee**, St, 1930)
Bharat Veer (*aka* Knight Errant: **Harshadrai Mehta**, St, 1932)
Bhargava (P.S. Ramaraju, Tel, 1991)
Bhargava Ramudu (A. Kodandarami Reddy, Tel, 1987)
Bhargavi Nilayam (**A. Vincent**, Mal, 1964)
Bhari Bharjari Bete (**S.V. Rajendra Singh**, K, 1981)
Bharjaee (K. Chandra, P, 1964)
Bharjari Gandu (Renuka Sharma, K, 1992)
Bharmayalo Bharthar (*aka* Foolish Husbands: **N.G. Devare**, St, 1928)
Bharosa (**Sohrab Modi**, H, 1940)
Bharosa (Ravi, H, 1963)
Bharthavu (M. Krishnan Nair, Mal, 1964)
Bhartrahari (A.P. Kapur, H, 1932)
Bhartrahari (**Chaturbhuj Doshi**, H, 1944)
Bhartrahari (*aka* Raja Bhartrahari: **K. Subramanyam**, Tam, 1944)
Bharya (**Kunchako**, Mal, 1962)
Bharya (**K.S. Prakash Rao**, Tel, 1968)
Bharya Bartulu (**K. Pratyagatma**, Tel, 1961)
Bharya Bartulu (K. Murali Mohana Rao, Tel, 1988)
Bharya Bharthala Bandham (V.B. Rajendra Prasad, Tel, 1985)
Bharya Bharthala Saval (P. Chandrasekhara Reddy, Tel, 1983)
Bharya Biddalu (**T. Rama Rao**, Tel, 1971)
Bharya Illatha Rathri (Babu Nathencode, Mal, 1975)
Bharyamani (Vijaya Bapineedu, Tel, 1984)
Bharyamar Sukshikuka (**K.S. Sethumadhavan**, Mal, 1968)
Bharya Oru Devatha (N. Shankaran Nair, Mal, 1984)
Bharya Oru Manthri (Raju Mahendra, Mal, 1986)
Bharya Vijayam (A.B. Raj, Mal, 1977)
Bharyaye Avasyamundu (M. Krishnan Nair, Mal, 1979)
Bharyayum Kamukiyum (**Sasikumar**, Mal, 1978)
Bhasmasur (Tarapada Saha, St, 1930)
Bhasmasur Mohini (**Kanjibhai Rathod**, H, 1932)
Bhasmasur Mohini (**Sundarrao Nadkarni**, Tam, 1937)
Bhasmasur Vadh (*aka* Prithvi Putra: G.S. Devare, St, 1926)
Bhasmasur Vadha *see* Jai Shri Shankar
Bhatak Bhawani (**Dinkar D. Patil**, Mar, 1987)
Bhatakta Joban (*aka* Wandering Dancer, Awara Raqasa: **A.R. Kardar**, St, 1931)
Bhatakti Jawani (Inderjit Doshi, H, 1988)
Bhatakti Maina (Sadiq Nizami, H, 1947)
Bhathiji Maharaj (*aka* Varachhada Dada: Shantilal Soni, G, 1980)
Bhatke Rahee (Nasir Imam, H, 1984)
Bhatti Vikramarka (Jampana, Tel, 1960)
Bhaubeej (Rajan Kumar, Mar, 1955)
Bhauji Maay (**Mehul Kumar**, Maithili, 1985)
Bhava Bhava Maruthi (Sarat, Tel, 1993)
Bhavai of Life, The *see* **Bhavni Bhavai**
Bhavani (T.P. Ramanna, Tam, 1967)
Bhavantarana (**Kumar Shahani**, O, 1991)
Bhav Bhavna Bheru (Ramkumar Bohra, G, 1981)
Bhavna (Karunesh Thakur, H, 1972)
Bhavna (Pravin Bhatt, H, 1984)
Bhavni Bhavai/Andher Nagari (**Ketan Mehta**, G, 1980)
Bhav Tethe Dev (Prabhakar Pendharkar, Mar, 1961)
Bhavya Bharata (Shivram Gangatgar, K, 1993)
Bhawani Junction (Dinesh, H, 1985)
Bhawani No Bhog (*aka* Temple of Tortures: **Dhirubhai Desai**, St, 1930)
Bhawani Talwar (*aka* Sword of Victory: **N.D. Sarpotdar**, St, 1932)
Bhayam Bhayam (N. Ramchandra Rao, Tel, 1986)
Bhayanak (S.Y. Sayed, H, 1979)
Bhayankara Bhasmasura (**C.S. Rao**, K, 1983)
Bhayankar Bakasarudu (P.S. Prakash, Tel, 1985)
Bhayyaji (Lekhraj Bhakri, P, 1950)
Bhed (?, Amba Cinetone, H, 1950)
Bhedbhav (Navin Kumar, H, 1985)
Bhedi Bungla (*aka* House of Mystery: **Master Bhagwan**, H, 1949)
Bhedi Burkha (*aka* Hooded Terror: A.H. Issa, H, 1938)
Bhedi Daku (M. Isamuddin, H, 1950)
Bhedi Dushman (Ramjibhai Arya, H, 1946)
Bhedi Khanjar (*aka* Three Daggers: Dada Gunjal, St, 1932)
Bhedi Khavis *see* Uthavgar
Bhedi Khazana (S. Usman, H, 1946)
Bhedi Kumar (Chunilal Parekh, H, 1939)
Bhedi Lutera (B. Azimabadi, H, 1955)
Bhedi Rajkumar (*aka* Mysterious Prince: **Harshadrai Mehta**, St, 1932)
Bhedi Rajkumar/Thaksen Rajputra (*aka* Rajputra Thagsen, Mysterious Prince: **R.G. Torney**, H/Mar, 1934)
Bhedi Sawar (*aka* Masked Cavalier: A.P. Kapur, St, 1929)
Bhedi Trishul (*aka* Hidden Treasure: **Nanubhai Desai**, St, 1927)
Bhedi Trishul (A.M. Khan, H, 1938)
Bhediya Ka Bhoot (?, CFS, H, 1980)
Bhediyon Ka Samooh (M.K. Shankar, H, 1991)
Bheegi Palkein (**Sisir Mishra**, H, 1982)
Bheegi Raat (Kalidas, H, 1965)
Bheema (Dinesh Saxena, H, 1984)
Bheeman (?, Mal, 1982)
Bhikaoo Tordo (*aka* Achhyo Jayo Giglo: Pradeep Saxena, R, 1987)
Bhikaran (?, Mal, 1988)
Bhikara Nimishankal (M. Krishnan Nair, Mal, 1970)
Bhikari (*aka* Satyanarayan: Kumar Sahu/R. Vishnuram, H, 1949)
Bhikari Ramudu (Padmaraju, Tel, 1961)
Bhikharan (*aka* Beggar Girl: **Chandulal Shah**, St, 1929)
Bhikharan (**Premankur Atorthy**, H, 1935)
Bhimanjaneya Yuddham (S.D. Lall, Tel, 1966)
Bhim Bhawani (TV: **Basu Chatterjee**, H, 1986)
Bhim Garjana (*aka* Dr Babasaheb Ambedkar 1: ?, Vikrant Chitra, H, 1989)
Bhim Sanjeevan (*aka* How Bhim Was Brought Back to Life: G.V. Sane, St, 1926)
Bhimsen *see* Veer Bhimsen
Bhimsen the Mighty (**N.D. Sarpotdar**, St, 1930)
Bhingri (**Datta Keshav**, Mar, 1977)
Bhintila Kan Astaat (Kamalakar Torne, Mar, 1962)
Bhishma (**Jyotish Bannerjee**?, **Madan** Theatres, St, 1922)
Bhishma (*aka* Sher Ki Garaj: ?, Frontier Films, H, 1937)
Bhishma (**Jyotish Bannerjee**, B, 1942)
Bhishma (**Ch. Narayanamurthy**, Tel, 1944)
Bhishma (B.A. Subba Rao, Tel/Tam, 1962)
Bhishmakar *see* **Meeth Bhakar**
Bhishma Pitamah (*aka* Banshayya: ?, Star Film, St, 1922)
Bhishma Pratigna (**P.Y. Altekar**, Tam, 1936)
Bhishma Pratigya *see* Matsyagandha
Bhishma Pratigya (**R.S. Prakash**, St, 1921)
Bhishma Pratigya (Vasant Painter, H, 1950)
Bhisti *see* Bachha-i-Sakka
Bhoga Bhagyalu (P. Chandrasekhara Reddy, Tel, 1981)
Bhogimanthulu (**Vijayanirmala**, Tel, 1981)
Bhoja Kalidasa (**H.V. Babu**, Tel, 1940)
Bhojan (L.S. Ramachandran, Tam, 1948)
Bhola Bhala (Satpal, H, 1978)
Bhola Master (**Niren Lahiri**, B, 1956)
Bhola Moira (Piyush Ganguly, B, 1977)
Bhola Raja *see* Rickshawala
Bhola Shankar (**Vishram Bedekar**, H, 1951)
Bhola Shankarudu (**Dasari Narayana Rao**, Tel, 1980)
Bhola Shikar (*aka* Brand of Fate: Ramakant-Gharekhan, St, 1930)
Bhola Shikar (*aka* Easy Victim: **Jayant Desai**, H, 1933)
Bhola Shikar (Aakkoo, H, 1958)
Bhole Bhale (*aka* Poor Sweethearts: **Zia Sarhadi**, H, 1939)
Bhole Bhale (**Master Bhagwan**, H, 1949)
Bhole Piya (Jaswant Jhaveri, H, 1949)
Bholi (Ram Daryani, H, 1949)
Bholi Bhabdi (**Rajdutt**, Mar, 1973)
Bholi Bhikharan (*aka* Garib Ki Ladki: Babubhai Jani, H, 1936)
Bholi Lutaran (A.M. Khan, H, 1940)
Bhombhol Sardar (Nripen Ganguly, B, 1983)
Bhomli (Mohansingh Rathod, R, 1991)
Bhoodana (**G.V. Iyer**/P.S. Gopalakrishna, K, 1962)
Bhoodi Muchida Kenda (G. Shivamurthy, K, 1982)
Bhookamp (Gautam Adhikari, H, 1993)
Bhookh (Safdar Aah, H, 1947)
Bhookh (Dinesh-Ramanesh, H, 1978)
Bhookha (Sabhyasachi Mahapatra, O, 1989)
Bhool (V. Avadhoot, H, 1948)
Bhool (Tej Saran, H, 1984)
Bhoola Bhatka (Ashwini Kumar, H, 1975)
Bhool Bhulaiyan (*aka* Comedy of Errors: **Jayant Desai**, H, 1933)
Bhool Bhulaiyan (Taimur Behramshah, H, 1949)
Bhoole Bhatke (Brij Mohan, H, 1952)
Bhool Ka Bhog (*aka* Irony of Fate: T.G. Lalwani, H, 1935)
Bhool Ka Shikar (Maheshchandra, H, 1950)
Bhool Na Jana (*aka* Forget Me Not: A.E. Charlie, H, 1947)
Bhool No Bhog (*aka* The Victim: **Harshadrai Metha**, St, 1926)
Bhoolokadalli Yamaraja (Siddalingaiah, K, 1979)
Bhoolokamlo Rambha Urvashi Menaka (B. Bhaskara Rao, Tel, 1989)
Bhoolokamlo Yamalokam (G. Vishwanathan, Tel, 1966)
Bhoomidevi Pushpiniyayi (**T. Hariharan**, Mal, 1974)
Bhoomige Banda Bhagavanta (Ravi, K, 1981)
Bhoomigeetham (Kamal, Mal, 1993)
Bhoomikosam (K.B. Tilak, Tel, 1974)
Bhoomi Thayane (Raj Kishore, K, 1988)
Bhoomiyile Malakha (P.A. Thomas, Mal, 1965)
Bhoomiyile Rajakkanmar (?, Jubilee Prod, Mal, 1987)
Bhoopathiranga (Geethapriya, K, 1970)
Bhooporatam (R. Narayanamurthy, Tel, 1989)
Bhoot Bangla (Mehmood, H, 1965)
Bhoot Mera Sathi (Shahid Lal, H, 1974)
Bhootnath (**Nanabhai Bhatt**, H, 1963)
Bhoot Rajya (*aka* Devil Land: ?, Usha Pics., St, 1931)
Bhopal: Beyond Genocide (**Tapan Bose**, E, 1986)
Bhor Hoye Elo (**Satyen Bose**, B, 1953)
Bhouji (Kundan Kumar, Bh, 1965)
Bhoy (Gouranga Prasad Basu, B, 1960)
Bhranti (**Jyotish Bannerjee**, St, 1928)
Bhranti (Prafulla Chakraborty, B, 1959)
Bhranti Bilas (Manu Sen, B, 1963)
Bhrashtachar (**Ramesh Sippy**, H, 1989)
Bhrashtachar Murdabad (**Manhar Raskapur**, G, 1977)
Bhrashthu (Tripprayar Sukumaran, Mal, 1978)
Bhuchaal (Rakesh Kashyap, H, 1993)
Bhugolam Thiriyunnu (Shrikumaran Thampi, Mal, 1974)
Bhujang (Murlidhar Kapdi, Mar, 1982)
Bhujangayana Dashavtara (Lokesh, K, 1991)
Bhukailasa (**Sundarrao Nadkarni**, Tam, 1938)
Bhukailasa (**Sundarrao Nadkarni**, Tel, 1940)
Bhukailasa (K. Shankar, Tel/Tam/K, 1958)
Bhukambam (Joshi, Mal, 1983)
Bhula Na Dena (Harsh Kohli, H, 1980)
Bhulekha (Chander, P, 1983)
Bhuler Baluchare (Jaladhar Chatterjee, B, 1949)
Bhuler Sheshe (**Amar Mullick**, B, 1952)
Bhuli Huena (Ashok Swain, O, 1987)
Bhuli Naai (**Hemen Gupta**, B, 1948)
Bhuloka Rambha (**Balkrishna Narayan Rao**, Tam, 1940)
Bhuloka Rambha/Bhuloka Rambhai (**Yoganand**, Tel/Tam, 1958)
Bhuloka Rambhai *see* Bhuloka Rambha
Bhumika (**Shyam Benegal**, H, 1976)
Bhutacha Bhau (Sachin, Mar, 1989)
Bhutia Mahal (*aka* Haunted House: **Jayant Desai**, H, 1932)
Bhuvana Oru Kelvi Kuri (S.P. Muthuraman, Tam, 1977)
Bhuvana Sundari Katha (**C. Pullaiah**, Tel, 1967)
Bhuvan Shome (**Mrinal Sen**, H, 1969)
Bibaha Bibhrat (**Jyotish Bannerjee**, St, 1931)
Bibaha Bibhrat (Ashim Bannerjee, B, 1969)
Bibhas (Binu Bardan, B, 1964)
Bibhranta (Chitta Mukherjee, B, 1959)
Bibhrat (Phani Talukdar, A, 1972)
Bichar/Paraya Dhan (**Nitin Bose**, B/H, 1943)
Bichar (Ajit Ganguly, B, 1980)
Bicharak (*aka* The Judge: **Sisir Bhaduri**, St, 1929)
Bicharak (Devnarayan Gupta, B, 1948)
Bicharak (Prabhat Mukherjee, B, 1959)
Bichhade Balam (Manibhai Vyas, H, 1948)
Bidaai (**L.V. Prasad**, H, 1974)
Biday (Ajit Ganguly, B, 1989)
Bideshini (**Premendra Mitra**, B, 1944)
Bidesia (S.N. Tripathi, Bh, 1963)
Bid for the Throne *see* Namak Haram Kon
Bidhilipi (Manu Sen, B, 1955)
Bidhira Bidhan (Mohammed Mohsin, O, 1989)
Bidrohi (**Dhiren Ganguly**, B/H, 1935)
Bidrohi (Anjan Choudhury, B, 1987)
Bidugade (Y.R. Swamy, K, 1973)
Bidugadeya Bedi (Dorairaj-Bhagavan, K, 1985)
Bidushi Bharya (**Naresh Mitra**, B, 1949)
Bidyapati/Vidyapati (**Debaki Bose**, B/H, 1937)
Bidyasundar (*aka* The Lover's Trance: Surendra Narayan Roy, St, 1922)
Bidyasundar (**Priyanath Ganguly**, B, 1935)
Big City, The *see* **Mahanagar**
Bigde Dil (A.M. Khan, H, 1949)
Bighalita Karuna Janhabi Jamuna (Hiren Nag, B, 1972)
Bigraha (*aka* The God and the Image: **Charu Roy**, St, 1930)
Big Sky, The *see* **Sara Akash**
Bihari (K.D. Katkar/A.R. Zamindar, H, 1948)
Bihari Babu (Dilip Bose, Bh, 1985)
Bihar Ke Darshaniya Sthan (**Ritwik Ghatak**, H, 1955)
Bijli (*aka* Miss Lightning: Gharekhan, St, 1931)
Bijli (**Balwant Bhatt**, H, 1939)
Bijli (Sushil Sahu, H, 1950)
Bijli (Ram Kumar, H, 1972)
Bijli (Anant Marathe, Mar, 1986)
Bijli Aur Badal (Mohan T. Gehani, H, 1991)
Bijli Aur Toofan (Praveen Bhatt, H, 1988)
Bijli Chamke Jamna Paar (Jaswant Jhaveri, H, 1962)
Bijoya (Dinesh Ranjan Das, B, 1935)
Bijoy Basant *see* Bimata
Bijoyini (Tulsi Lahiri, B, 1941)
Bijoyini (Palash Bannerjee, B, 1982)
Biju in Hyderabad (**Santi P. Choudhury**, E, 1971)
Bikalpa (TV: **Utpalendu Chakraborty**, B, 1988)
Bikele Bhorer Phool (Piyush Bose, B, 1974)
Bikhare Moti (*aka* Crash: Jayant Dalal, H, 1935)
Bikhare Moti (S.M. Yusuf, H, 1951)
Bikhare Moti (**Tapi Chanakya**, H, 1971)
Bilambita Lay (Agragami, B, 1970)
Bile Naren (Rabi Basu, B, 1988)
Bilet Pherat (N.C. Laharry, St, 1921)
Bilet Pherat (**Chidananda Das Gupta**, B, 1972)
Biley Naren (Robi Bose, B, 1974)
Bilhana (*aka* Kaviyin Kathal: T.V. Srinivasan/**Balkrishna Narayan Rao**, Tam, 1948)
Biligiriya Bandalalli (Siddalingaiah, K, 1980)
Bili Hendthi (**Puttanna Kanagal**, K, 1975)
Billa (R. Krishnamurthy, Tam, 1980)
Billa Ranga (K.S.R. Doss, Tel, 1982)
Billi (*aka* The Cat: **Jayant Desai**, H, 1938)
Billi (Nari Ghadiali, H, 1949)
Billo (Shankar Mehta, P, 1961)
Billoo Badshah (**Sisir Mishra**, H, 1989)
Bilwamangal (*aka* Bhagat Surdas; Rustomji Dotiwala, St, 1919)
Bilwamangal (*aka* Bhakta Surdas: **Homi Master**, St, 1929)
Bilwamangal (*aka* Bhakta Surdas: Fram Madan, H, 1932)

Bilwamangal (Tinkari Chakraborty, B, 1933)
Bilwamangal (D.N. Madhok, H, 1954)
Bilwamangal (Gobinda Ray, B, 1976)
Bimata (*aka* Bijoy Basant, Stepmother: **Dhiren Ganguly**, St, 1922)
Binani (Subhash Shah, R, 1992)
Binani Bot Denane Chali (Sudarshan Lal, R, 1990)
Bin Badal Barsaat (Jyoti Swaroop, H, 1963)
Bindiya (**Chimanlal Luhar**, H, 1946)
Bindiya (Shamim Bhagat, H, 1955)
Bindiya (**Krishnan-Panju**, H, 1960)
Bindiya Aur Bandook (Shibu Mitra, H, 1973)
Bindiya Chamkegi (Tarun Dutt, H, 1983)
Bindu (Mookkanur Sebastian, Mal, 1984)
Bindur Chheley (Chitta Bose, B, 1952)
Bindur Chheley (**Gurudas Bagchi**, B, 1973)
Binimoy (Dilip Nag, B, 1963)
Bin Kamacha Navara (Murlidhar Kapdi, Mar, 1984)
Bin Maa Ke Bachche (**Satyen Bose**, H, 1979)
Bin Phere Hum Tere (Rajat Rakshit, H, 1979)
Binsati Janani (Khagen Roy, B, 1964)
Bipasha (**Agradoot**, B, 1962)
Biplabi (**Asit Sen**, A, 1948)
Biplabi Kshudiram (Hiranmoy Sen, B, 1951)
Biradari (Ram Kamlani, H, 1966)
Biraha (Tinkari Chakraborty, B, 1935)
Biraj Bahu (**Bimal Roy**, H, 1954)
Biraj Bou (**Amar Mullick**, B, 1946)
Biraj Bou (Manu Sen, B, 1972)
Birbal Ki Beti (**Nanubhai Vakil**, H, 1935)
Birbal my Brother (**Raja Thakur**, E, 1972)
Birbal Paristan *see* Jalti Nishani
Bird of Prey *see* Pyari Mamta
Bird of Time, The (**Gautam Ghosh**, E, 1991)
Bird's Nest in the Wind *see* **Kattathe Kilikoodu**
Biresh Lahiri (Bechu Sinha, B, 1950)
Bireshwar Vivekananda (**Modhu Bose**, B, 1964)
Birha Ki Raat (**Gajanan Jagirdar**, H, 1950)
Birha Ki Raat (Lalji Yadav, Bh, 1988)
Bir Hambir (Shyam Dass, B, 1955)
Birhan (Kailash Bhandari, H, 1948)
Birinchi Baba (Manu Sen, B, 1944)
Birju Ustad (Manu Desai, H, 1964)
Birth *see* **Piravi**
Birthday (**Phani Majumdar**, H, 1965)
Birth of a Pea Plant (**Dadasaheb Phalke**, St, 1913)
Birth of Hanuman, The *see* Sati Anjani
Birth of Kalika *see* Shatamukh Ravan Vadh
Birth of Shivaji *see* Shivaji Nu Janma
Birth of Shivaji (?, Gajanan Film, St, 1930)
Birth of Shri Dattatreya *see* **Mahasati Ansuya**
Birth of Shri Krishna *see* **Shri Krishna Janma**
Birth of the Himalayas, The (Pradeep Krishen, E, 1978)
Birthright *see* Janma Haq
Bisarjan *see* **Balidan**
Bisarjan (Bireshwar Bose, B, 1974)
Bisathi Babu (Aruru Pattabhi, Tulu, 1972)
Bisesh Erati (Upen Kakoti, A, 1979)
Bishabriksha (**Jyotish Bannerjee**?, Madan Theatres, St, 1922)
Bishabriksha (*aka* The Poison Tree: **Jyotish Bannerjee**, St, 1928)
Bishabriksha (**Phani Burma**, B, 1936)
Bishabriksha (Shantipriya Mukherjee, B, 1953)
Bishabriksha (**Ajoy Kar**, B, 1984)
Bish Bichar Agey (Gunamaya Bannerjee, B, 1948)
Bisher Dhoan (Atanu Bannerjee, B, 1949)
Bishkanya (Shri Jayadhrata, B, 1961)
Bishnupriya (**Hemchandra Chunder**, B, 1949)
Bishyut Barer Barbela (Debi Ghosh, St, 1930)
Bisilu Beladingalu (Kodi? Ramakrishna, K, 1989)
Bismil Ki Arzoo (B.S. Hijle, H, 1937)
Bismillah Ki Barkat (K. Sharief, H, 1983)
Bismi Sadi (**Homi Master**, St, 1924)
Bistar (R. Thakur, H, 1986)
Biswi Sadi *see* **Sone Ki Chidiya**
Biswi Sadi (**M. Bhavnani**, H, 1945)
Bitiya Bhail Sayan (?, Bh, 1982)
Bitiya Chalal Sasural (Dilip Bhatt, Bh, 1986)
Bitter Autumn with a Scent of Mango, the *see* Horky Podzim S Vuni Manga
Bitter Morsel *see* **Neem Annapurna**
Biwi (Kishore Sharma, H, 1950)
Biwi Aur Makaan (**Hrishikesh Mukherjee**, H, 1966)
Biwi Ho To Aisi (J.K. Bihari, H, 1988)
Biwi Kiraye Ki (Ajit Kumar, H, 1975)
Biwi-o-Biwi (**Rahul Rawail**, H, 1981)
Biyer Bazaar (*aka* Marriage Market: Chittaranjan Goswami, St, 1922)
Biyer Khata (Niranjan Dey, B, 1960)
Black and White (S.M. Raza, H, 1946)
Black Archer (?, **Madan Theatres**, St, 1930)
Black Arrow (Mehmood, H, 1965)
Black Bandit *see* Chalak Chor
Black Belt (Mani, Mal, 1978)
Black Box (*aka* Harfan Maula: R.N. Vaidya, H, 1936)
Black Cat (N.A. Ansari, H, 1959)
Black Cobra (K.S.R. Doss, H?, 1981)
Black Eagle *see* Gayab-e-Garud
Black Ghost *see* Kalo Bhoot
Blackguard, The *see* Mumbaino Mawali
Black Heart *see* Kala Jigar
Blackmail (*aka* Kala Dhandha: **Vijay Anand**, H, 1973)
Blackmail (Crossbelt Mani, Mal, 1985)
Blackmailer (**G.P. Sippy**, H, 1957)
Black Market (S.H. Tharani, H, 1947)
Black Market (S.N. Singh, K, 1967)
Black Money (Achyut Lahakar, A, 1974)
Black Mountain *see* Chernaya Gora
Blackout (Nari Ghadiali, H, 1942)
Black Rider *see* Kala Sawar
Black Rider (*aka* Safed Ghoda Kala Sawar: Mehmood, H, 1960)
Black Rose *see* Kala Gulab
Black Shadow (Madan Mohan Mehra, H, 1961)
Black Shirt (Framji Havewala, H, 1946)
Black Terror (?, Mohan Pics, H, 1949)
Black Thief *see* Chin Ka Sahukar *or* Kala Chor
Black Tiger *see* Kala Wagh *or* Kalo Wagh
Black Tiger (Aakkoo, H, 1960)
Black Tiger (**Dasari Narayana Rao**, Tel, 1989)
Blessed Offering, The *see* **Nirmalayam**
Blessing, The *see* **Ashirwad**
Blind Alley *see* **Andhi Gali**
Blind Girl, The *see* Rajani Chandra
Blind God, The *see* Panchasar
Blind Lane (**Sailajananda Mukherjee**, B, 1953)
Bliss (**N. Lakshminarayan**, Wordless, 1961)
Blood Feud *see* Josh-e-Inteqam
Blood Feud (?, University Art Federation, St, 1931)
Blood for Blood *see* Raktacha Sood
Bloodstained Footsteps *see* **Ninamanninnya Kalapadakal**
Blossom of Dust *see* **Dhool Ka Phool**
Blue Koel, The *see* **Neelakuyil**
Bluff Master (**Manmohan Desai**, H, 1963)
Boatman of the River Padma *see* **Padma Nadir Majhi**
Bobanum Molyum (**Sasikumar**, Mal, 1971)
Boba Sanai (Ajit Ganguly, B, 1988)
Bobbili Brahmana (**K. Raghavendra Rao**, Tel, 1984)
Bobbili Puli (**Dasari Narayana Rao**, Tel, 1982)
Bobbili Raja (B. Gopal, Tel, 1990)
Bobbili Rowdy (Kishore, Tel, 1993)
Bobbili Yuddham (C. Seetaram, Tel, 1964)
Bobby (**Raj Kapoor**, H, 1973)
Bodhan (Amal Dutta, B, 1982)
Bodhodaya (**Niranjan Pal**, B, 1951)
Bodhu (Bhupen Roy, B, 1962)
Bodhu Baran (Dilip Nag, B, 1967)
Bodku Mathu (*aka* Indulal Advocate: **Kanjibhai Rathod**, St, 1928)
Boeing Boeing (**Priyadarshan**, Mal, 1985)
Bogeyman, The *see* **Kummatty**
Bogi Manthulu (Seenu, Tel, 1981)
Bohurupee (Mithu Chattopadhyay, B, 1972)
Bokul/Bakul (Bholanath Mitra, B/H, 1954)
Bola Dajiba (Krishna Patil, Mar, 1987)
Bolavita Dhani (**Raja Thakur**, Mar, 1953)
Bolki Bahuli (Raja Bargir/Daftardar, Mar, 1961)
Bolki Tapeli (*aka* Talking Pot: **Dadasaheb Phalke**, St, 1929)
Bolo He Chakradhari (**Chandrakant**, H, 1977)
Bol Radha Bol (David Dhawan, H, 1992)
Bolt of Lightning *see* **Minnalkodi**
Bolti Bulbul (*aka* Shahi Fakir: **Dhirubhai Desai**, H, 1942)
Bolti Bulbul (*aka* Wooing Nightingale: **Kanjibhai Rathod**, St, 1926)
Bolto Kagal *see* Pak Daman
Bolto Lekh *see* Sati Menadevi
Bombata Rendthi (?, R.S. Prod., K, 1992)
Bombat Huduga (K.V. Raju, K, 1993)
Bombay *see* Bambai
Bombay (C.R. Bajaj, H, 1949)
Bombay By Nite (A. Shamsheer, H, 1976)
Bombay Calling (Raja Yagnik, H, 1942)
Bombay Central (R.K. Balam, H, 1960)
Bombay 405 Miles (Brij Sadanah, H, 1980)
Bombay Ka Chor (S.D. Narang, H, 1962)
Bombay Mail (*aka* Burkhawala: R.P. Bhatt, H, 1935)
Bombay Mail (B. Sampathkumar, Tam, 1939)
Bombay Mail (T.P. Sundaram, Tam, 1980)
Bombay Our City *see* **Hamara Shaher**
Bombay Race Course (Kedar Kapoor, H, 1965)
Bombay Talkie (James Ivory, E, 1970)
Bombay-The Story of the Seven Isles (**Paul Zils**, E, 1945)
Bombay the Mysterious *see* Albeli Mumbai
Bombay to Goa (S. Ramanathan, H, 1972)
Bombay War (Dnyandev Aroskar, H, 1990)
Bomb, The *see* Vasant Bengali
Bomb Blast (Deepak Balraj Vij, H, 1993)
Bombshell (*aka* Khabardar: Ishwarlal/Dinkar Rao, H, 1935)
Bomma Borusa (**K. Balachander**, Tel, 1971)
Bomma Borusa Jeevam (Kommineni, Tel, 1979)
Bommai (**S. Balachander**, Tam, 1964)
Bommai Kalyanam *see* Bommalapelli
Bommala Koluvu (Kommineni, Tel, 1980)
Bommalapelli/Bommai Kalyanam (R.M. Krishnaswamy, Tel/Tam, 1958)
Bommalattam (V. Srinivasan, Tam, 1968)
Bommalu Cheppina Katha (G. Vishwanathan, Tel, 1969)
Bommarillu (Rajachandra, Tel, 1978)
Bondage *see* Aflatoon Abla
Bondam Pelli (**H.M. Reddy**, Tel, 1940)
Bonded Until Death *see* **Damul**
Bonded Woman *see* **Daasi**
Bondi (**Sailajananda Mukherjee**, B, 1942)
Bondita (Hemanta Gupta, B, 1945)
Bondman *see* Ghulami Zanjeer
Bond 303 (Ravi Tandon, H, 1986)
Bonga (**Kundan Shah**, H, 1976)
Bono Basar (Sushil Mukherjee, B, 1978)
Bon Palashir Padabali (**Uttam Kumar**, B, 1973)
Boodha Bubukh (?, **Madan Theatres**, St, 1922)
Books That Talk (**Sai Paranjpye**, E, 1981)
Boom Boom Madu (Adaikalavan, Tam, 1982)
Boon, The *see* **Kondura**
Boond Jo Ban Gaye Moti (**V. Shantaram**, H, 1967)
Boothayyana Maga Ayyu (Siddalingaiah, K, 1974)
Boot Polish (Prakash Arora, H, 1954)
Bordoisila (Dara Ahmed, A, 1989)
Boregowda Bangaloruge Banda (B.A. Arasukumar, K, 1970)
Born Hero *see* Kuldeepak
Bot Lavin Tithe Gudgudlya (**Dada Kondke**, Mar, 1978)
Bottu Kattuka (Durga Nageshwara Rao, Tel, 1979)
Boudi (Dilip Bose, B, 1968)
Boudir Bone (Khagen Roy, B, 1953)
Bouma (Sujit Guha, B, 1986)
Bou Thakuranir Haat (**Naresh Mitra**, B, 1953)
Bowari (Siva Prasad Thakur, A, 1982)
Boxer (Radhakant, H, 1965)
Boxer (Raj N. Sippy, H, 1983)
Boy and the Parrot, The *see* Raju Aur Gangaram
Boy Friend (Naresh Saigal, H, 1961)
Boy Friend (Venu, Mal, 1975)
Boy Friend (Ramesh U. Lakhiani, H, 1993)
Bracelet *see* Bazooband
Brahma (B. Gopal, Tel, 1992)
Brahmachari (**Master Vinayak**, Mar/H, 1938)
Brahmachari (Bhappi Sonie, H, 1968)
Brahmachari (**T. Rama Rao**, Tel, 1968)
Brahmachari (**Sasikumar**, Mal, 1972)
Brahmachari (Muktha V. Srinivasan, Tam, 1991)
Brahmacharigal (Sornamurthy, Tam, 1983)
Brahma Ghotala (**P.K. Atre**, Mar, 1949)
Brahma Mudi (**Dasari Narayana Rao**, Tel, 1985)
Brahma Nayudu (**Dasari Narayana Rao**, Tel, 1987)
Brahman Kanya *see* Khandani
Brahman Kanya (**Niranjan Pal**, B, 1941)
Brahma Puthrudu (**Dasari Narayana Rao**, Tel, 1988)
Brahma Ratham (**Ch. Narayanamurthy**, Tel, 1947)
Brahma Ratham (**Ch. Narayanamurthy**, Tel, 1949)
Brahmarishi Vishwamitra (N. Jagannath, Tam, 1947)
Brahmarishi Vishwamitra (**N.T. Rama Rao**, Tel, 1991)
Brahma Rudralu (Murali Mohana Rao, Tel, 1986)
Brahmastham (G. Rammohan Rao, Tel, 1986)
Brahmastra (Perala, K, 1986)
Brahma Vishnu Mahesh (**Babubhai Mistri**, H, 1971)
Brahma Vishnu Maheshwara (Rajachandra, K, 1988)
Brajabuli (Piyush Bose, B, 1977)
Branches of the Tree *see* **Shakha Proshakha**
Branded Oath, The *see* **Jalti Nishani**
Brandichi Batli/Brandy Ki Botal (**Master Vinayak**, Mar/H, 1939)
Brand of Fate *see* Bhola Shikar
Bratacharini (Kamal Ganguly, B, 1955)
Brathuke Oka Panduga (P. Chandrasekhara Reddy, Tel, 1975)
Bratuku Theruvu (**P.S. Ramakrishna Rao**, Tel, 1953)
Brave Do Not Die, The (**Harisadhan Dasgupta**, E, 1978)
Brave Heart *see* Bahadur Ramesh
Brave Hearts *see* Sarfarosh
Brave Lion *see* Sinh Ki Pyaas
Brave Warrior *see* Shooro Sainik
Bride By Right *see* **Murappennu**
Bridegrooms Wanted *see* Shadi Ki Raat
Bride of God *see* Devadasi
Bridge *see* Pul
Bridging of Ocean *see* Setu Bandhan
Briefless Barrister (**Homi Master**, St, 1926)
Brij Bhoomi (Shiv Kumar, Brij Bhasha, 1982)
Brij Sundari (?, Nirakar Films, H, 1989)
Brindaban Leela (Panchajanya, B, 1958)
Brindavana (S.P. Rajagopal, K, 1969)
Brindavanamu (**Singeetham Srinivasa Rao**, Tel, 1992)
Bristi (Deuti Barua, A, 1974)
Brojendra Gee Luhungha (S.N. Chand 'Sajatia', Manipuri, 1972)
Broken Coin, The *see* Bhangela Shikkano Bhed
Broken Hearts *see* Nirdosh Abla or Zakhmi Jigar
Broken Journey, The *see* Uttoran
Broken Promise (?, Chitrakala Movietone, Sinhalese, 1947)
Broker Bhishmachari (B.C. Srinivas, K, 1969)
Brotherhood *see* Bhaichara
Brother to Brother *see* Tarunina Tarang
Brown Landscape, The (**G. Aravindan**, Mal, 1985)
Buchi Babu (**Dasari Narayana Rao**, Tel, 1980)
Buddhadev (*aka* Lord Buddha: **Dadasaheb Phalke**, St, 1923)
Buddha Mil Gaya (**Hrishikesh Mukherjee**, H, 1971)
Buddhibal *see* Vikram Charitra
Buddhimanthudu (**Bapu**, Tel, 1969)
Buddhu Aur DCM (**Kantilal Rathod**, H, 1959)

Budhiman Balwan Ivan (K.S. Mani, Tam, 1940)
Budtameez *see* Badtameez
Bugles of War *see* Azadi Nu Jung
Buker Bojha (*aka* The Burden: **Nitin Bose**, St, 1930)
Bulandi (Esmayeel Shroff, H, 1980)
Bulbul (A. Rasheed, H, 1951)
Bulbul-e-Baghdad (*aka* Fairy of Baghdad: **Nanubhai Vakil**, H, 1932)
Bulbul-e-Baghdad (**K. Amarnath**, H, 1941)
Bulbul-e-Iran (Faredoon R. Irani, H, 1936)
Bulbul-e-Iran (?, Mohan Pics, H, 1947)
Bulbul-e-Paristan (**Fatma Begum**, St, 1926)
Bulbul-e-Paristan (**Dhirubhai Desai**, H, 1934)
Bulbul-e-Punjab (*aka* Fairy of Punjab, Sassi Punnu, Punjab Ki Padmini: **Nanubhai Vakil**, H, 1933)
Bulbul-e-Shiraz (?, Bharat Pics., St, 1931)
Bulldog (Dwarka Khosla, H, 1937)
Bullemma Bullodu (Naganjaneyalu, Tel, 1971)
Bullemma Sabatham (Vijay, Tel, 1975)
Bullet (**Vijay Anand**, H, 1976)
Bullet (Crossbelt Mani, Mal, 1984)
Bullet (**Bapu**, Tel, 1985)
Bullet Bullodu (T.N. Balu, Tel, 1972)
Buniyaad (Dileep Kumar, H, 1950)
Buniyaad (Virendra Sinha, H, 1972)
Buniyaad (TV: **Ramesh Sippy**, H, 1987-88)
Burden, The *see* Buker Bojha
Buripalem Bullodu (Bheeram Mastan Rao, Tel, 1979)
Burkhawala *see* Bombay Mail
Burkhawali (*aka* Veiled Enemy, Behind the Veil: **Kanjibhai Rathod**, St, 1926)
Burkhewala (*aka* White Devil: Shantilal Dave, St, 1932)
Burma Rani (**T.R. Sundaram**, Tam, 1944)
Burma Road (Tara Harish, H, 1962)
Burmar Pathey (Hiranmoy Sen, B, 1947)
Burning Train, The (Ravi Chopra, H, 1980)
Bus Conductor (Dwarka Khosla, H, 1959)
Business As Usual (**Anand Patwardhan**, E, 1972)
Business Is People (**Kantilal Rathod**, E, 1975)
But... *see* **Lekin...**
But Tarash (?, Butkada Prod, H, 1947)
Butterflies (Rajeev Anjal, Mal, 1993)
Butterfly *see* Parwana
Buzdil (Shaheed Latif, H, 1951)
Byabadhan (**Phani Burma**, B, 1940)
Byabadhan (Dilip Mukherjee, B, 1990)
Byalis *see* **'42**
Byapika Biday (Archan Chakraborty, B, 1980)
Byathar Dan (Hemanta Gupta, B, 1936)
Byomkesh Bakshi (TV: **Basu Chatterjee**, H, 1993)
By Sheer Valour *see* Shiraz-ud-Dowla
By Word of Mouth (Pradeep Krishen, E, 1981)

C

Cabaret Dancer (?, Sasthakrupa Prod, Mal, 1986)
Calcutta (**Santi P. Choudhury**, E, 1966)
Calcutta After Midnight (*aka* Madhyaraat Ka Kalkatta: A.R. Kabuli, H, 1937)
Calcutta After Midnight (*aka* Night in Calcutta *aka* Kalkatta Ki Raat: Amrit Mahendra, H, 1970)
Calcutta my Eldorado (**Mrinal Sen**, E, 1990)
Calcutta '71 (**Mrinal Sen**, B, 1972)
Call Girl (Vijay Kapoor, H, 1974)
Call of Satan *see* Mumbai Ni Sethani
Call of the Jungle *see* Jungle Ki Pukar
Call of the Motherland *see* Swarg Se Sundar Desh Hamara
Call of the Soul *see* Hridaya Manthan
Call of Youth *see* **Jawani Ki Pukar**
Cancer Aur Guptrog (?, Sastha Prod, H, 1982)
Cancerum Laingika Rogangalum (P.R.S. Pillai, Mal, 1981)
Can't Help It *see* Naseeb
Captain *see* Sipahsalaar
Captain (S. Narayan, K, 1993)
Captain Azad (Ram Rasila, H, 1964)
Captain Barry (Surjit Gill, H, 1984)
Captain India (C. Kant, H, 1960)
Captain Kirti Kumar (**Chimanlal Luhar**, H, 1937)
Captain Kishore (**J.B.H. Wadia**, H, 1957)
Captain Kishori (**K. Amarnath**, H, 1940)
Captain Krishna (K.S.R. Doss, Tel, 1979)
Captain Lakshmi (**Sai Paranjpye**, E, 1977)
Captain Magal (**Bharathirajaa**, Tam, 1992)
Captain Nagarjuna (V.B. Rajendra Prasad, Tel, 1986)
Captain Prabhakaran (R.K. Selvamani, Tam, 1991)
Captain Ranjan (T.P. Sundaram, Tam, 1969)
Captain Sheroo (Dharam Kumar, H, 1963)
Caravan (Aspi, H, 1944)
Caravan (Rafiq Rizvi, H, 1964)
Caravan (**Nasir Hussain**, H, 1971)
Carey Shaheber Munshi (Bikash Roy, B, 1961)
Caricatures *see* **Kolangal**
Carnival, The (**B. Narasinga Rao**, E, 1984)
Carnival (P.G. Vishwambaran, Mal, 1989)
Carnival Queen (Noshir Engineer, H, 1955)
Car Thief (Sameer Malkan, H, 1990)
Cartoon (**Dhiren Ganguly**, B, 1949)
Case is Closed, The *see* **Kharij**
Cashier, The *see* **Khazanchi**
Castles in the Air *see* Sheikhchilli
Castor (**S. Sukhdev**, E, 1962)
Cat, The *see* Billi
Catastrophe, The *see* **Halodiya Choraye Baodhan Khaye**
Catechist of Kil-Arni, The (**R.S. Prakash**/Thomas Gavin Duffy, St, 1923)
Cavalier of Love *see* Chit Chor
CBI Vijay (Umashankar, K, 1991)
Celestial Lotus *see* Pandav Patrani
Central Rowdy (B. Ramamurthy, K, 1991)
Ceramics (**Buddhadev Dasgupta**, E, 1986)
Certain Childhood, A (**Kumar Shahani**, Wordless, 1969)
Chaalbaaz (**Nanabhai Bhatt**, H, 1958)
Chaalbaaz (Kamran, H, 1969)
Chaalbaaz (Hari Mehta, H, 1980)
Chaalbaaz (Pankaj Parashar, H, 1989)
Chaalbaaz Leader (Ajit Singh, H, 1970)
Chaalchitra (**Mrinal Sen**, B, 1981)
Chaal Majhya Payaat (Bal Saraf, Mar, 1960)
Chaani (**V. Shantaram**, Mar/H, 1977)
Chabukne Chamkare (*aka* Flogged into Love: Baburao, St, 1930)
Chabuk Sawar (*aka* The Whipman: Chunilal Parekh, St, 1930)
Chabuk Sawar (M. Udwadia, H, 1937)
Chabuk Sawar (K. Narayan Rao, H, 1947)
Chabukwali *see* **Hunterwali**
Chabukwali (A.M. Khan, H, 1938)
Chacha Bhatija (**Manmohan Desai**, H, 1977)
Cha Cha Cha (Chandrasekhar, H, 1964)
Chacha Choudhury (**Raja Paranjpe**, H, 1953)
Chacha Zindabad (Om Prakash, H, 1959)
Chadastrapu Mogudu (Sarat, Tel, 1986)
Chadhi Jawani Budhe Nu (A. Salaam, P, 1976)
Chaduranga (N.C. Rajan, K, 1969)
Chaduranga (V. Somasekhar, K, 1985)
Chadurangam (J.D. Thottan, Mal, 1958)
Chadurangam (S.V. Ranga Rao, Tel, 1967)
Chadurangam (**Durai**, Tam, 1978)
Chadurangam (B. Bhaskara Rao, Tel, 1984)
Chadurida Chitragalu (N.T. Jayarama Reddy, 1981)
Chaduvukonna Ammayilu (**Adurthi Subba Rao**, Tel, 1963)
Chaduvukonna Bharya (**H.M. Reddy**, Tel, 1940)
Chaduvukonna Bharya (**Kadaru Nagabhushanam**, Tel, 1965)
Chaduvu Samskaram (Rajshri, Tel, 1974)
Chahat (Homi Bhattacharya, H, 1971)
Chahoonga Main Tujhe (Kamal, H, 1993)
Chain Jaipal (Ramanarayanan, Tam, 1985)
Chain, The *see* **Zanjeer**
Chain Reaction (**Govind Saraiya**, E, 1971)
Chains of Bondage (**Gautam Ghosh**, E, 1976)
Chairman Chalamayya (G. Ramineedu, Tel, 1974)
Chaitali (**Hrishikesh Mukherjee**, H, 1975)
Chaitanya (**Prathap Pothan**, Tel, 1991)
Chaitanya Mahaprabhu *see* Bhagwan Shri Krishna Chaitanya
Chaitanya Ratham (Dhavala Sathyam, Tel, 1987)
Chaka Akhi Sabu Dekhuchi (Raju Mishra, O, 1989)
Chakara (P.G. Vishwambaran, Mal, 1980)
Chakkarauma (Sajen, Mal, 1984)
Chakkar Pe Chakkar (Ashok Roy, H, 1977)
Chakma (?, N.N. Shukla/R.N. Tiwari, H, 1987)
Chakori (Ram Nayaran Dube, H, 1949)
Chakra (**Rabindra Dharmaraj**, H, 1980)
Chakradhari (K.S. Gopalakrishnan, Tam, 1948)
Chakradhari (Raman B. Desai, H, 1954)
Chakradhari (V. Madhusudhana Rao, Tel, 1977)
Chakram (A. Kasilingam, Tam, 1968)
Chakrapani (**P.S. Ramakrishna Rao**, Tel, 1954)
Chakra Teertha (Pekati Shivram, K, 1967)
Chakravakam (**Thoppil Bhasi**, Mal, 1974)
Chakravakam (V. Madhusudhana Rao, Tel, 1974)
Chakravalam Chuvannappol (**Sasikumar**, Mal, 1983)
Chakravarthi (**Krishnan-Panju**, Tam, 1977)
Chakravarthi (Raviraja Pinisetty, Tel, 1987)
Chakravarthi (D. Rajendra Babu, K, 1990)
Chakravarthini (Charles Ayampally, Mal, 1977)
Chakravarthi Thirumagal (**P. Neelakantan**, Tam, 1957)
Chakravyuha (**Basu Chatterjee**, H, 1978)
Chakravyuha (V. Somasekhar, K, 1983)
Chakravyuham (**Balu Mahendra**, Tel, 1992)
Chakrayudham (K. Raghunath, Mal, 1978)
Chalachal (**Asit Sen**, B, 1956)
Chalagara (C.N. Krishna, K, 1981)
Chalak (T.N. Sharma/R.K. Bannerjee, H, 1973)
Chalak Chor (*aka* Black Bandit: **Raja Sandow**, H, 1936)
Chalaki Chellamma (Janakiram, Tel, 1982)
Chalaki Mogadu Chadasthapu Pellamu (Relangi Narasimha Rao, Tel, 1989)
Chalaki Rani Kiladi Raja (Vijay, Tel, 1971)
Chala Murari Hero Banne (Asrani, H, 1977)
Chalanam (N.R. Pillai, Mal, 1975)
Chalar Pathe (Batakrishna Dalal, B, 1948)
Chala Utha Lagna Kara (**Prabhakar Nayak**, Mar, 1965)
Chal Chal Gurram (K. Saradadevi, Tel, 1988)
Chal Chal Re Naujawan (**Gyan Mukherjee**, H, 1944)
Chale Hain Sasural (Dharam Kumar, H, 1966)
Chali Cheemalu (Devadas Kanakala, Tel, 1978)
Chalis Baba Ek Chor (P.L. Santoshi, H, 1954)
Chalis Chor (Shashikumar, H, 1976)
Chalis Din (*aka* Forty Days: Dwarka Khosla, H, 1959)
Chalis Karod (*aka* Forty Crores: **Nanabhai Bhatt**, H, 1945)
Chalitil Shejari (D.K. Kale, Mar, 1950)
Challani Needa (**T. Rama Rao**, Tel, 1968)
Challani Ramayya Chakkani Seetamma (Kodi Ramakrishna, Tel, 1986)
Challani Talli (K.S. Rami Reddy, Tel, 1975)
Challenge *see* Be Dhari Talwar *or* Chalta Purza *or* Lalkaar
Challenge (**Balwant Bhatt**, H, 1937)
Challenge (B.J. Patel, H, 1964)
Challenge (A. Kodandarami Reddy, Tel, 1984)
Challenge Gopalakrishna (Saiprakash, K, 1990)
Challenge Ramudu (T.L.V. Prasad, Tel, 1980)
Chal Mohanaranga (**C. Pullaiah**, Tel, 1938)
Chal Mohanaranga (B. Bhaskara Rao, Tel, 1978)
Chal Re Lakshya Mumbaila (Satish Ranadive, Mar, 1987)
Chalta Purza (*aka* The Zombie, Passing Show: **Balwant Bhatt**, St, 1932)
Chalta Purza (*aka* The Invincible: R.N. Vaidya, H, 1934)
Chalta Purza (*aka* Challenge: Ravi Kapoor, H, 1958)
Chalta Purza (Bhappi Sonie, H, 1977)
Chalta Putla (**N.D. Sarpotdar**, H, 1935)
Chalte Chalte (*aka* On the Way: S.K. Malik, H, 1947)
Chalte Chalte (Sundar Dar, H, 1976)
Chalti Duniya *see* Chalu Zamana
Chalti Duniya (Dada Gunjal/B. Murzban, H, 1940)
Chalti Ka Naam Gaadi (**Satyen Bose**, H, 1958)
Chalti Ka Naam Zindagi (**Kishore Kumar**, H, 1981)
Chalu Mera Naam (Krishna Naidu, H, 1977)
Chalu Zamana (*aka* Chalti Duniya: ?, **Krishna Film**, St, 1925)
Chamak Chandni (Manibhai Vyas, H, 1957)
Chamakti Bijli (**Homi Master**, H, 1946)
Chamakti Chanda (M. Udvadia, St, 1928)
Chamakti Shamsheer *see* Flashing Sword
Chaman (**Roop K. Shorey**, P, 1948)
Chamana Atha Guntha (**Parbati Ghosh**, O, 1986)
Chamaram (**B.G. Bharathan**, Mal, 1979)
Chamatkar (Rajiv Mehra, H, 1992)
Chamatkar (**Suresh Heblikar**, K, 1992)
Chamayam (**B.G. Bharathan**, Mal, 1993)
Chambal Ka Badshah (S. Dinesh, H, 1986)
Chambal Ke Daku (S. Azhar, H, 1982)
Chambal Ki Kasam (Ram Maheshwari, H, 1979)
Chambal Ki Rani (Radhakant, H, 1979)
Chambalkulam Thachan (Kamal, Mal, 1992)
Chambe Di Kali (R.C. Talwar/**Phani Majumdar**?, P, 1941)
Chambe Di Kali (B.S. Glaad, P, 1965)
Chambu Gabale (Shivdas Ghodke, Mar, 1989)
Cham Chama Cham (P.L. Santoshi, H, 1952)
Chameli Ki Shaadi (**Basu Chatterjee**, H, 1986)
Chameli Memsaab (**Abdul Majid**, A, 1975)
Chameli Memsaab (Ajit Lahiri, H, 1979)
Chameli Memsahib (Inder Sen, B, 1978)
Chamki (J.K. Nanda, H, 1952)
Chammak Challo (Subhash Bhakri, P, 1982)
Champa (Barkat Mehra, H, 1945)
Champa Chameli (Bhagwat Thakur, Bh, 1987)
Champadangar Bou (**Nirmal Dey**, B, 1954)
Champakali (**Nandlal Jaswantlal**, H, 1957)
Champalakadu (Rajasekharan, Mal, 1982)
Champion (M. Karnan, Tel, 1984)
Champion (Y. Nageshwara Rao, Tel, 1992)
Champraj Hado *see* **Sati Sone**
Champraj Hado (**Nanubhai Desai**, St, 1923)
Chamundeshwari (Dhrupad Roy, Tam, 1937)
Chamundeshwari Mahime (Addala Narayana Rao, K, 1974)
Chamundi (Manoj Kumar, Tam, 1992)
Chanakya (**Sisir Bhaduri**, B, 1939)
Chanakya (Saila Barua, A, 1959)
Chanakya (A. Somasekhar, K, 1984)
Chanakya Chandragupta (**N.T. Rama Rao**, Tel, 1977)
Chanakyam/Chanakyan (Rajeev Kumar, Tel/Mal, 1989)
Chanakya Sapatham (**K. Raghavendra Rao**, Tel, 1986)
Chanchala (S. Babu, Mal, 1974)
Chanchala (Mysore Girish, K, 1981)
Chanchala Kumari (D. Shankar Singh, K, 1953)
Chanchal Ka Sapna (Sachidanand Sen Majumdar, H, 1966)
Chand (D.D. Kashyap, H, 1944)
Chand (Lekhraj Bhakri, H, 1959)
Chanda Aur Bijli (**Atma Ram**, H, 1969)
Chanda Ki Chandni (Dwarka Khosla, H, 1948)
Chandal Chaukadi *see* Char Chakram
Chandal Chaukadi (*aka* Gangster: R.N. Vaidya, St, 1933)
Chandal Chaukadi (**Prabhakar Nayak**, Mar, 1978)
Chandamama (Relangi Narasimha Rao, Tel, 1982)
Chandamama Raave (Mouli, Tel, 1987)
Chanda Marutha (**Pattabhi Rama Reddy**, K, 1977)
Chandan (**Dhirubhai Desai**, H, 1941)
Chandan (**M.V. Raman**, H, 1958)
Chandan (Kewal Mishra, H, 1971)
Chandana (B. Giri Babu, Tel, 1974)
Chandanachi Choli Ang Ang Jaali (Ravindra, Mar, 1975)

Chandanachola (Jesey, Mal, 1975)
Chandanada Gombe (Dorairaj-Bhagavan, K, 1979)
Chandana Katru (Manivannan, Tam, 1990)
Chandan Chawali (Joshi-More, G, 1981)
Chandane Shimpit Ja (Kamalakar Torne, Mar, 1982)
Chandan Ka Palna (Ismail Memon, H, 1967)
Chandan Malayagiri (**Naval Gandhi**, St, 1924)
Chandan Malayagiri (Dinesh Rawal, G, 1978)
Chandar Kalanka/Rani (**P.C. Barua**, B/H, 1943)
Chanda Sasanudu (**N.T. Rama Rao**, Tel, 1983)
Chanda Tare Chandane (Mohan Kaviya, R, 1989)
Chand Aur Suraj (Dulal Guha, H, 1965)
Chandavalliya Tota (T.V. Singh Thakore, K, 1964)
Chandbibi (*aka* Queen of Ahmednagar: **N.D. Sarpotdar**, St, 1931)
Chand Chakori (**Kidar Sharma**, H, 1945)
Chander Kachhakachhi (Yatrik, B, 1976)
Chandi Chamundi (K.S. Rami Reddy, Tel, 1983)
Chandi Chamundi (V. Somasekhar, K, 1983)
Chandidas (*aka* Shri Krishna's Devotee: **Jyotish Bannerjee**, St, 1927)
Chandidas (**Debaki Bose**, B, 1932)
Chandidas (**Nitin Bose**, H, 1934)
Chandika (**R.S. Prakash**, Tel, 1940)
Chandi Ki Deewar (Dilip Kumar Bose, H, 1964)
Chandi Priya (V. Madhusudhana Rao, Tel, 1980)
Chandi Puja (Raman B. Desai, H, 1957)
Chandirani (**P. Bhanumathi**, Tam/Tel/H, 1953)
Chandirani (P. Chandrasekhara Reddy, Tel, 1983)
Chandi Sona (Sanjay Khan, H, 1977)
Chand Ka Tukda *see* Pardesi Saiyan
Chand Ki Duniya (Mohan Sinha, H, 1959)
Chand Mere Aaja (Ram Daryani, H, 1960)
Chandni (**Jayant Desai**, H, 1942)
Chandni (**Yash Chopra**, H, 1989)
Chandni Chowk (**B.R. Chopra**, H, 1954)
Chandni Raat (M. Ehsan, H, 1949)
Chandoba Chandoba Bhaglas Ka? (Madhukar Pathak, Mar, 1978)
Chando Ugyo Chowkma (Bhupen Desai, G, 1981)
Chand Par Chadhai *see* Trip to the Moon
Chandra *see* Modern Girl
Chandrabimbam (N. Shankaran Nair, Mal, 1980)
Chandragupta (?, Star Film, St, 1923)
Chandragupta (**A.R. Kardar**, H, 1934)
Chandragupta Chanakya (C.K. Sachi, Tam, 1940)
Chandraharam (**K. Kameshwara Rao**, Tel/Tam, 1953)
Chandrahari (K.S. Mani, Tam, 1941)
Chandrahasa (**Kanjibhai Rathod**, St, 1921)
Chandrahasa (**Kanjibhai Rathod**, St, 1928)
Chandrahasa (**Dadasaheb Phalke**, St, 1929)
Chandrahasa (**Sarvottam Badami**, H, 1933)
Chandrahasa (Prafulla Ghosh, Tam, 1936)
Chandrahasa (M.L. Rangaiah, Tel, 1941)
Chandrahasa (S. Patil, K, 1947)
Chandrahasa (Dada Gunjal, H, 1947)
Chandrahasa (**B.S. Ranga**, Tel/K, 1965)
Chandrahasam (Baby, Mal, 1980)
Chandra Hota Sakshila (**Rajdutt**, Mar, 1978)
Chandrakant (*aka* Filial Duty: **Harshadrai Mehta**, St, 1925)
Chandrakant (**G.P. Sippy**, H, 1956)
Chandrakantha (**Raja Sandow**, Tam, 1936)
Chandrakantham (Shrikumaran Thampi, Mal, 1974)
Chandra Kiran (S.S. Rawal, Haryanvi, 1985)
Chandrakumara (N.S. Varma, K, 1963)
Chandralekha (**S.S. Vasan**, Tam/H, 1948)
Chandramani (*aka* Necklace: Mohanlal Shah, St, 1931)
Chandramohana (**Raja Chandrasekhar**, Tam, 1936)
Chandramukhi (**Chandulal Shah**, St, 1929)
Chandramukhi (**Ramchandra Thakur**, H, 1960)
Chandramukhi (Debaloy Dey, H, 1993)
Chandrarao More (Arolkar, Mar, 1938)
Chandranath (**Naresh Mitra**, St, 1924)
Chandranath (**Kartick Chattopadhyay**, B, 1957)
Chandraprabha *see* **Zalim Jawani**
Chandrarao More (**N.D. Sarpotdar**, St, 1925)
Chandrasekhar (**Debaki Bose**, B/H, 1947)
Chandrasekhar Azad (Jagdish Gautam, H, 1963)
Chandrasena (**V. Shantaram**/K. Dhaibar, St, 1931)
Chandrasena (**V. Shantaram**, Mar/H/Tam, 1935)
Chandrasena (**Babubhai Mistri**, H, 1959)
Chandravali (*aka* The Crown of Virtue: **Fatma Begum**, St, 1928)
Chandravanka (Jiten Bannerjee, Tel, 1951)
Chandrawal (Jayant Prabhakar, Haryanvi, 1984)
Chandrika (V.S. Raghavan, Tam/Mal, 1950)
Chandrodyam (K. Shankar, Tam, 1966)
Chand Saudagar (Prafulla Roy, B, 1934)
Chand Sitare (I.C. Kapoor, H, 1948)
Chand Tara (Mahesh Chandra, H, 1945)
Chandu (Majnu, H, 1958)
Chandu Jamadar (**Mehul Kumar**, G, 1977)
Change Mande Tere Bande (Subhash Bhakri, P, 1976)
Change of Seasons *see* **Ruthubhedam**
Changhez Khan (*aka* Chenghiz Khan: Kedar Kapoor, H, 1957)
Changu Mangu (Bipin Warty, Mar, 1988)
Chan Mahi (Anwar Kamal, P, 1962)
Chan Mera Mahi (Subhash Bhakri, P, 1987)
Channachara (Anjan Mukherjee, B, 1988)
Chann Pardesi (Chitrarath Singh, P, 1980)
Chantabbayi (Jandhyala, Tel, 1986)
Chanwa Ke Take Chakor (**Nasir Hussain**, Bh, 1981)
Chaos *see* Jallad
Chaowa-Pawa (Yatrik, B, 1959)
Chappa (**P.A. Backer**, Mal, 1982)
Chappala Channigaraya (Bhargava, K, 1990)
Char Aankhen (**Sushil Majumdar**, H, 1944)
Charachar (**Buddhadev Dasgupta**, B, 1993)
Characters *see* **Avargal**
Charam (*aka* The Ash: **P.A. Backer**, Mal, 1981)
Charanadasi *see* Mathurkula Manikyam
Charandas (B.S. Thapa, H, 1977)
Charandas Chor (**Shyam Benegal**, H, 1975)
Charan Data (**T. Hariharan**, Mal, 1989)
Charan Kabi Mukundadas (Nirmal Choudhury, B, 1968)
Charas (**Ramanand Sagar**, H, 1976)
Char Bhondu *see* Char Chakram
Char Chakram (*aka* Chandal Chaukadi, Char Bhondu, Four Rascals: **Jayant Desai**, H, 1932)
Char Chakram (Sultan, H, 1965)
Char Chand (A. Karim, H, 1953)
Char Darvesh/Shri Gouranga (*aka* Merchant of Arabia: Prafulla Ghosh, H/B, 1933)
Char Darvesh (**Homi Wadia**, H, 1964)
Char Dil Char Raahein (**K.A. Abbas**, H, 1959)
Char Din (M. Sadiq, H, 1949)
Char Divas Sasuche Char Divas Suneche (Kamalakar Torne, Mar, 1962)
Char Diwari (Krishan Chopra, H, 1961)
Char Dost (**Nitin Bose**, H, 1956)
Charitable Outlaw *see* Dharmi Daku
Charithram (G.S. Vijayan, Mal, 1989)
Charitra (**B.R. Ishara**, H, 1973)
Charitraheen (**Dhiren Ganguly**, St, 1931)
Charitraheen (**Shakti Samanta**, H, 1974)
Charitra Heenulu (**K. Bapaiah**, Tel, 1977)
Charitra Nayakan (**Yoganand**, Tam, 1984)
Charkha *see* Anath Abala
Char Maharathi (S. Waris Ali, H, 1985)
Char Minar (**Ravindra Dave**, H, 1956)
Charmurti (Umanath Bannerjee, B, 1978)
Charnon Ki Dasi *see* **Payachi Dasi**
Charnon Ki Dasi (Ramesh Vyas, H, 1959)
Charnon Ki Saugandh (**K. Bapaiah**, H, 1988)
Charotarni Champa (S.J. Talukdar, G, 1982)
Char Paise (N.K. Ziri, H, 1955)
Char Shaher Ek Kahani (**K.A. Abbas**, H, 1968)
Charulata (**Satyajit Ray**, B, 1964)
Chasher Meye (*aka* Farmer's Daughter: Prafulla Roy, St, 1931)
Chashmawali (**K. Amarnath**, H, 1939)
Chashme Buddoor (**Sai Paranjpye**, H, 1981)
Chaska (Mohan Kaul, P, 1981)
Chastity Versus Unchastity *see* Keshavkant BA
Chatak Chandani (Prakash Bhende, Mar, 1982)
Chathriyan (Subhash, Tam, 1990)
Chatpatee (V. Ravindra, H, 1982)
Chatra Bakavali (**S.N. Patankar**, St, 1926)
Chatra Bakavali (**J.J. Madan**, H, 1932)
Chatra Bakavali (?, Kapoor Films, Punjab, H, 1941)
Chatra Bakavali (?, Goodwin Pics, Tam, 1947)
Chatta (**B.G. Bharathan**, Mal, 1981)
Chattagram Astraghar Lunthan (Nirmal Choudhury, B, 1949)
Chattakkari (**K.S. Sethumadhavan**, Mal, 1974)
Chattam (K. Vijayan, Tam, 1983)
Chattambi Kalyani (**Sasikumar**, Mal, 1975)
Chattambi Kavala (N. Shankaran Nair, Mal, 1969)
Chattambi Krishnan (?, Mal, 1981)
Chattam En Kaiyil (T.N. Balu, Tam, 1978)
Chattamtho Chadarangam (K. Muralimohana Rao, Tel, 1988)
Chattamtho Poratam (**K. Bapaiah**, Tel, 1985)
Chattaniki Kallulevu (S.A. Chandrasekharan, Tel, 1981)
Chattaniki Veyi Kallu (**Vijayanirmala**, Tel, 1983)
Chattan Singh (Kedar Kapoor, H, 1974)
Chattathurukku Oru Saval (M. Karnan, Tam, 1983)
Chatujye-Banrujye (Bangsi Ash, B, 1955)
Chatur Balak (*aka* Wise Child: **Shantaram Athavale**, H, 1963)
Chatur Kanya (Ramakant-Gharekhan, St, 1928)
Chatur Sundari (*aka* Wily Heroine: **N.D. Sarpotdar**, St, 1930)
Chaturthicha Chandra (*aka* Moon Cursed By Ganapati: **Dadasaheb Phalke**, St, 1925)
Chaturvedam (**Sasikumar**, Mal, 1977)
Chaubis Ghante (*aka* 24 Ghante: Dwarka Khosla, H, 1958)
Chaudhary *see* Choudhury
Chaudhvin Ka Chand (M. Sadiq, H, 1960)
Chaudi Chandlo (Jamnadas Kapadia, G, 1950)
Chauhani Talwar (*aka* Fighting Cavalier: Baburao, St, 1930)
Chavhata (Arun Karnataki, Mar, 1984)
Chavi (Kartick Raghunathan, Tam, 1985)
Chavukkadi Chandrakantha (A.L. Narayanan, Tam, 1960)
Cheat, The (*aka* Farebi: Suresh Issar, H, 1974)
Cheats, The (**Govind Saraiya**, E, 1971)
Chechi (T. Janakiram, Mal, 1950)
Checkpost (J.D. Thottan/Devi Thottan, Mal, 1973)
Check to the King *see* Shahala Shah
Cheekh (Mohan Bhakri, H, 1985)
Cheenavala (**Kunchako**, Mal, 1975)
Chehra (R. Sharma, H, 1946)
Chehre Pe Chehra (Raj Tilak, H, 1980)
Chekkaran Oru Chilla (**Sibi Malayil**, Mal, 1986)
Chekuthante Kotta (M.M. Nesan, Mal, 1967)
Cheleta (Santosh Ghosal, B, 1986)
Chelisada Sagara (Vijay, K, 1983)
Chelisuva Modagalu (**Singeetham Srinivasa Rao**, K, 1982)
Chellakkili (K.M. Balakrishnan, Tam, 1978)
Chella Kutty (K. Nataraj, Tam, 1987)
Chella Penn (K. Krishnamurthy, Tam, 1969)
Chellapillai (**M.V. Raman**, Tam, 1955)
Chelleli Kapuram (**K. Vishwanath**, Tel, 1971)
Chellida Rakta (B. Subba Rao, K, 1982)
Chellikosam (M. Mallikarjuna Rao, Tel, 1968)
Cheluvi (**Girish Karnad**, H, 1992)
Chembaruthi (R.K. Selvamani, Tam, 1992)
Chemmeen (**Ramu Kariat**, Mal, 1965)
Chemparathi (**P.N. Menon**, Mal, 1972)
Chena Achena (Hiren Nag, B, 1969)
Chena Achena (Pinaki Choudhury, B, 1983)
Chenchulakshmi (**S. Soundararajan**, Tel, 1943)
Chenchulakshmi (B.A. Subba Rao, Tel/Tam, 1958)
Chenda (**A. Vincent**, Mal, 1973)
Chengalva Poodanda (Janardan Maharishi, Tel, 1991)
Chengathem (Bhadran, Mal, 1983)
Chenghiz Khan *see* Changhez Khan
Chennai Valarthiya Kutty (**Kunchako**, Mal, 1976)
Chennapatnam Chennollu (S.P. Reddy, Tel, 1989)
Chenra Tamsukh (Purnendu Pattrea, B, 1974)
Cheppadivida (G.S. VBijayan, Mal, 1993)
Cheppindi Cheshta (M.S. Gopinath, Tel, 1978)
Cheppu (**Priyadarshan**, Mal, 1987)
Cheppu Kilukina Sangadhi (Kaladharan, Mal, 1991)
Cheran Pandian (K.S. Ravikumar, Tam, 1991)
Cheriyachente Kroora Krithyangal (**John Abraham**, Mal, 1979)
Chernaya Gora (*aka* Black Mountain: Alexander Zguridi/**M.S. Sathyu**, Russian/E, 1971)
Cherupukura Chedevu (B. Bhaskara Rao, Tel, 1955)
Chesina Basalu (K.S.R. Doss, Tel, 1980)
Chess Players, The *see* **Shatranj Ke Khiladi**
Cheta Chamar *see* Bhakta Cheta
Chetak (**Kidar Sharma**, H, 1960)
Chetak and Rana Pratap (Sultan, H, 1958)
Cheti Ka Poster (?, Prakash Prod, H, 1987)
Chetna (**B.R. Ishara**, H, 1970)
Chetna Dorahe Par (K. Sharief, H, 1980)
Chettathi (**Puttanna Kanagal**, Mal, 1965)
Chettukinda Pleader (**Vamsy**, Tel, 1989)
Chevalier Mikhail (P.K. Baburaj, Mal, 1992)
Chevilo Puvvu (E.V.V. Satyanarayana, Tel, 1989)
Chevrolet 1936 (*aka* Toofani: G.P. Pawar, H, 1937)
Cheyithi Jai Kottu (Kommineni, Tel, 1979)
Chhabi (**Niren Lahiri**, B, 1959)
Chhabila (?, Avinash Bhatnagar, H, 1955)
Chhabili (Shobhna Samarth, H, 1960)
Chhadiyan Di Doli (Lal S. Kelsay, P, 1963)
Chhadmabeshi (Ajay Bhattacharya, B, 1944)
Chhadmabeshi (**Agradoot**, B, 1971)
Chhai (Shankar Mehta, P, 1950)
Chhaila Babu (K. Parvez, H, 1967)
Chhaila Babu (Joy Mukherjee, H, 1977)
Chhail Gabhru (Arvind Kumar, Haryanvi, 1985)
Chhail Gailyan Jaangi (Aravind Kumar, Haryanvi, 1984)
Chhakke Panje (V.K. Naik, Mar, 1987)
Chhalia (**Manmohan Desai**, H, 1960)
Chhalia (Mukul Dutt, H, 1973)
Chhamia (**Protima Dasgupta**, H, 1945)
Chhandaneer (**Utpalendu Chakraborty**, B, 1989)
Chhandapatan (**Gurudas Bagchi**, B, 1972)
Chhanda Preetichi (Madhav Bhoit, Mar, 1968)
Chhaon (?, P, 1967)
Chhappan Churi (*aka* Dagger Devil: Ramakant Rangnath, H, 1934)
Chhat Maiya Ki Mahima (Tapeshwar Prasad, H, 1979)
Chhatra Bakavali *see* Chatra Bakavali
Chhatrabhang (Nina Shivdasani, H, 1976)
Chhatrapati Sambhaji (**N.D. Sarpotdar**, St, 1925)
Chhatrapati Sambhaji (**P.Y. Altekar**, Mar, 1934)
Chhatrapati Shivaji (**Bhalji Pendharkar**, Mar/H, 1952)
Chhatrapati Shivaji (Ram Gabale, H, 1961)
Chhattis Ghante (*aka* 36 Ghante: Raj Tilak, H, 1974)
Chhattis Nakhrewali (Kamalakar Torne, Mar, 1980)
Chhau Dances of Mayurbhanj (**Nirad Mahapatra**, E, 1986)
Chhaya (**Master Vinayak**, M/H, 1936)
Chhaya (**Hrishikesh Mukherjee**, H, 1961)
Chhaya (Hanuman Prasad, Tel, 1979)
Chhaya (Sanjeevi, K, 1981)
Chhayam (**P.N. Menon**, Mal, 1972)
Chhaya Path (Gunamoy Bannerjee, B, 1957)
Chhaya Sangini (Bidyapati Ghosh, B, 1956)
Chhaya Surya (Partha Prathim Choudhury, B, 1963)
Chhayatir (Sushil Biswas, B, 1972)
Chhed Chhaad (*aka* Sweet Lie: **K. Amarnath**, H, 1943)

Chheen Le Azadi (Aspi, H, 1947)
Chhelbatao *see* Mohana Rani
Chhel Chhabili Sonal (S.J. Talukdar, G, 1981)
Chhel Chhabilo Gujarati (S.J. Talukdar, G, 1983)
Chheley Kaar (Chitta Bose, B, 1954)
Chhogala Chhaganlalno Varghodo (G.K. Mehta, G, 1965)
Chhoo Mantar (M. Sadiq, H, 1956)
Chhora Chhori (**Kidar Sharma**, H, 1955)
Chhora Jat Ka (Arvind Swami, Haryanvi, 1985)
Chhori Gaon Ki (Rajkumar Trivedi, H, 1981)
Chhota Admi (**Krishnakant**, H, 1986)
Chhota Baap (Shantilal Soni, H, 1977)
Chhota Bhai *see* Ramer Sumati
Chhota Bhai (**K.P. Atma**, H, 1966)
Chhota Chetan *see* **My Dear Kuttichathan**
Chhota Chor (*aka* Petit Brigand: ?, **Sharda Film**, St, 1932)
Chhota Jawan (Ram Gabale, Mar, 1963)
Chhote Babu (Harsukh Bhatt, H, 1957)
Chhote Bade (TV: **Sai Paranjpye**, H, 1985)
Chhote Nawab (S.A. Akbar, H, 1961)
Chhote Sarkar (*aka* Warisdaar: **Homi Master**, H, 1938)
Chhote Sarkar (K. Shankar, H, 1974)
Chhoti Bahen *see* Majboori
Chhoti Bahen (**L.V. Prasad**, H, 1959)
Chhoti Bahen (Girish Manukant, H, 1977)
Chhoti Bahu *see* Sanskar
Chhoti Bahu (K.B. Tilak, H, 1971)
Chhoti Bhabhi (Shanti Kumar, H, 1950)
Chhoti Chhoti Baatein (Motilal, H, 1965)
Chhoti Duniya (?, Kiran Film Exchange, H, 1953)
Chhoti Maa (*aka* Nurse: **Chaturbhuj Doshi**, H, 1943)
Chhoti Maa (**Hemchandra Chunder**, H, 1952)
Chhotisi Baat (**Basu Chatterjee**, H, 1975)
Chhotisi Duniya (B.S. Rajhans, H, 1939)
Chhotisi Mulaqat (Alo Sircar, H, 1967)
Chhoto Bakulpurer Jatri (Purnendu Pattrea, B, 1987)
Chhoto Bou (Satish Dasgupta, B, 1955)
Chhoto Bou (Anjan Dey, B, 1988)
Chhoto Jignasa (?, Trio Films, B, 1968)
Chhoto Maa (Shakti Chatterjee, B, 1982)
Chhoto Nayak (Shakti Bannerjee, B, 1975)
Chhupa Chhupi (Arun Jaitly, H, 1981)
Chhupa Rustom (*aka* Mysterious Shadow: R.N. Vaidya, H, 1936)
Chhupa Rustom (Aakkoo, H, 1965)
Chhupa Rustom (**Vijay Anand**, H, 1973)
Chhupi Chhupi Ashey (**Premendra Mitra**, B, 1960)
Chhuti (**Arundhati Devi**, B, 1967)
Chhutir Din (?, Aurora Film, B, 1951)
Chhutir Ghanta (Barun Kabasi, B, 1974)
Chhutir Phande (Salil Sen, B, 1974)
Chhutki Bahu (?, Bh, 1989)
Chidambaram (**G. Aravindan**, Mal, 1985)
Chidambara Rahasyam (Visu, Tam, 1985)
Chidiakhana (**Satyajit Ray**, B, 1967)
Chief Guest (A.B. Raj, Mal, 1974)
Chikamma (R. Sampath, K, 1969)
Chikati Velugulu (**K.S. Prakash Rao**, Tel, 1975)
Chikitsa Sankat (Binoy Seyene, B, 1953)
Chikkadu Dorakudu (**B. Vittalacharya**, Tel, 1967)
Chikkadu Dorakudu (Relangi Narasimha Rao, Tel, 1988)
Chikka Yajamanaru (Ravichandran, K, 1992)
Chik Mik Bijuli (**Bhupen Hazarika**, A, 1969)
Chilaka-Gorinka (**K. Pratyagatma**, Tel, 1966)
Chilaka Joshyam (M. Parthasarathy, Tel, 1983)
Chilakamma Cheppindi (Eranki Sharma, Tel, 1977)
Chilampoli (G.K. Ramu, Mal, 1963)
Chilampu (**B.G. Bharathan**, Mal, 1986)
Chilanthivala (?, Mal, 1982)
Child God, The *see* **Debshishu**
Child of the Streets, A (**Shyam Benegal**, E, 1967)
Children of Desired Sex (TV: **Mira Nair**, E, 1987)
Children of Mini-Japan *see* **Kutty Japanin Kuzhandaigal**
Children of the Earth *see* **Dharti Ke Lal**
Children of the Storm *see* Toofan
Child Saint *see* **Balayogini**
Child Widow (Baheram, St, 1925)
Chilika Teere (Biplab Roy Choudhury, O, 1978)
Chilipi Dampathulu (Relangi Narasimha Rao, Tel, 1988)
Chilipi Krishnudu (B. Subba Rao, Tel, 1978)
Chilipi Yavanam (Ramnarayan, Tel, 1985)
Chillara Devullu (T. Madhava Rao, Tel, 1975)
Chillarakottu Chittamma (**Dasari Narayana Rao**, Tel, 1977)
Chillara Mogudu Allari Koduku (Relangi Narasimha Rao, Tel, 1992)
Chillu (**Lenin Rajendran**, Mal, 1982)
Chillukottaram (K.G. Rajasekharan, Mal, 1984)
Chilman (Changhezi, H, 1949)
Chimanrao Gundyabhau (Vinay Dhumale, Mar, 1979)
Chimni Ka Dhuan (*aka* Prayashchit: Prabhat Mukherjee, H, 1973)
Chimni Pakhare/Nannhe Munne (**Datta Dharmadhikari**, Mar/H, 1952)
Chimnyanchi Shala (**Anant Mane**, Mar, 1962)
Chimukla Pahuna (Shubha Khote Balsavar, Mar, 1967)
Chimukla Sansar (Vasan Joglekar, Mar, 1943)
Chinababu (A. Mohan Gandhi, Tel, 1988)
Chinan Chiru Kiley (K. Chandra Bose, Tam, 1980)
China Siragugal (Ramanarayanan, Tam, 1982)
China Town (**Shakti Samanta**, H, 1962)
Chiner Putul (Partha Sarathy, B, 1951)
Chingari (**Sarvottam Badami**, H, 1940)
Chingari (*aka* Paraya Ghar: S. Srivastava, H, 1955)
Chinha Achinha (Kumar Anand, O, 1979)
Chini Jadugar (Rasheed Pervez, H, 1947)
Chini Jadugar (Noshir Engineer, H, 1959)
Chin Ka Sahukar (*aka* Black Thief: Chunilal Parekh, H, 1935)
Chinna Chinna Asaigal (Muktha S. Sunder, Tam, 1989)
Chinna Chinna Veedu Katti (Yuvaraja, Tam, 1980)
Chinnachiru Ulagam (**K.S. Gopalakrishnan**, Tam, 1966)
Chinna Chittu (Manivarma, Tam, 1992)
Chinnada Gombe/Muradhan Muthu (**B.R. Panthulu**, K/Tam, 1964)
Chinnadanta Maga (K.S.R. Doss, K, 1983)
Chinnadurai (T.R. Mahalingam, Tam, 1952)
Chinna Gounder (R.V. Udayakumar, Tam, 1991)
Chinna Jamin (Rajkapoor, Tam, 1993)
Chinna Kannamma (R. Raghu, Tam, 1992)
Chinnakodalu (**G. Balaramaiah**, Tel, 1952)
Chinna Kuyil Padhutthu (P. Madhavan, Tam, 1987)
Chinna Mappillai (Santhana Bharati, Tam, 1992)
Chinna Marumagal (Prasanna Kumar, Tam, 1992)
Chinnamma Katha (S.V.S. Ramarao, Tel, 1952)
Chinnamul (**Nemai Ghosh**, B, 1950)
Chinnamul Periamul (Rajmohan, Tam, 1981)
Chinnanati Kalalu (T. Lenin Babu, Tel, 1974)
Chinnanati Snehitulu (**K. Vishwanath**, Tel, 1971)
Chinna Ninna Muddaduve (A.M. Samiulla, K, 1977)
Chinna Paravaikale (P.K.S. Maniraj, Tam, 1993)
Chinna Pasanga Nanga (Rajkapoor, Tam, 1992)
Chinnapatra (Yatrik, B, 1972)
Chinnappadas (C.V. Rajendran, Tam, 1989)
Chinna Poovai Killathe (Senthilnathan, Tam, 1992)
Chinna Poove Mella Pesu (Robert-Rajasekharan, Tam, 1987)
Chinnari Chittibabu (K. Subba Rao/Gopalakrishnan, Tel, 1981)
Chinnari Mudhulapapa (Vasireddy, Tel, 1991)
Chinnari Mutha (TV: **T.S. Nagabharana**, K, 1993)
Chinnari Papalu (**K. Savitri**, Tel, 1968)
Chinnari Puttana (**B.R. Panthulu**, K, 1968)
Chinnari Sneham (Mutyala Subbaiah, Tel, 1989)
Chinna Thambi (P. Vasu, Tam, 1991)
Chinna Thambi Periya Thambi (Manivannan, Tam, 1987)
Chinnathayi (S. Ganeshraj, Tam, 1992)
Chinnavan (Gangai Amaran, Tam, 1992)
Chinna Veedu (**K. Bhagyaraj**, Tam, 1985)
Chinni Krishnudu (Jandhyala, Tel, 1988)
Chinnodu Peddodu (Relangi Narasimha Rao, Tel, 1988)
Chino Haar (Hari Bhanja, B, 1936)
Chintamani (**Dhiren Ganguly**, St, 1922)
Chintamani (**Kanjibhai Rathod**, H, 1931)
Chintamani (?, **Madan** Theatres, H, 1933)
Chintamani (K. Sadasiva Rao, Tel, 1933)
Chintamani (**Y.V. Rao**, Tam, 1937)
Chintamani (**P.S. Ramakrishna Rao**, Tel, 1956)
Chintamani (M.N. Basavarajaiah, K, 1957)
Chintamani (Kotnis, K, 1957)
Chintamani Surdas (Ram Pahwa, H, 1987)
Chiradiner (**Agradoot**, B, 1969)
Chirag (Ram Daryani, H, 1943)
Chirag (**Raj Khosla**, H, 1969)
Chirag-e-Arab *see* Asmat Ka Moti
Chirag-e-Chin (C.M. Trivedi/G.P. Pawar, H, 1955)
Chirag-e-Husn (*aka* Lamp of Beauty: G.K. Mehta, H, 1935)
Chirag-e-Kohistan (*aka* Lamp of the Hut: A.P. Kapur, St, 1929)
Chirag Kahan Roshni Kahan (Devendra Goel, H, 1959)
Chirai (R.C. Sakthi, Tam, 1984)
Chirai Kadhavukal (T.R, Selvam, Tam, 1991)
Chirakumar Sabha (**Premankur Atorthy**, B, 1932)
Chirakumar Sabha (**Debaki Bose**, B, 1956)
Chirakumari (?, **Madan** Theatres, H, 1932)
Chirakumari (Amar Choudhury, B, 1932)
Chiranjeev *see* Bhakta Markandeya
Chiranjeevi (K.P. Bhave, K, 1936)
Chiranjeevi (**K. Savitri**, Tel, 1969)
Chiranjeevi (**A. Bhimsingh**, K, 1976)
Chiranjeevi (K. Shankar, Tam, 1984)
Chiranjeevi (C.V. Rajendran, Tel, 1985)
Chiranjeevi Rambabu (**T. Prakash Rao**, Tel, 1977)
Chiranjeevi Sudhakara (**Singeetham Srinivasa Rao**, K, 1988)
Chiranjeevulu (**Vedantam Raghavaiah**, Tel, 1956)
Chirantan (**Gurudas Bagchi**, B, 1979)
Chirantani (Bidhayak Bhattacharya, B, 1953)
Chiriakhana *see* **Chidiakhana**
Chirikuduka (A.B. Raj, Mal, 1976)
Chiriyo Chiri (**Balachandra Menon**, Mal, 1982)
Chirutha (Tanvir Ahmed, H, 1980)
Chitadano Chor (S.J. Rajdev, G, 1980)
Chit Chor (*aka* Cavalier of Love: Fram Sethna, St, 1930)
Chit Chor (**Basu Chatterjee**, H, 1976)
Chithegu Chinthe (**M.S. Sathyu**, K, 1978)
Chithirame Chithirame (**K. Bhagyaraj**, Tam, 1985)
Chithrai Pookkal (Kanmani Subbu, Tam, 1991)
Chithram (**Priyadarshan**, Mal, 1988)
Chitra (Wahab Kashmiri, Tam, 1945)
Chitra Bandhayya (M.S. Rajasekhar, K, 1993)
Chitrada Premanjali (?, M.C. Prod, K, 1992)
Chitrakathi (**Mani Kaul**, H, 1976)
Chitralekha (**Kidar Sharma**, H, 1941)
Chitralekha (**Kidar Sharma**, H, 1964)
Chitralekha (V. Somasekhar, K, 1992)
Chitram Bhalare Vichitram (V. Ramachandra Rao, Tel, 1991)
Chitramela (T.S. Muthaiah, Mal, 1967)
Chitranaliyam (D. Ramireddy, Tel, 1938)
Chitrangada (**Hemchandra Chunder**/Souren Sen, B/H, 1954)
Chitrangi (R.S. Mani, Tam, 1964)
Chitra Pournami (P. Madhavan, Tam, 1976)
Chitrasenotakhyam *see* Galava Rishi
Chitra Sevanam (N.C. Chakraborty, Tam, 1979)
Chitta Banhiman (Dhiren Seal, B, 1952)
Chittemma Chilakamma (P. Brahmananda Rao, Tel, 1975)
Chitthi (*aka* Letter: **Niranjan Pal**, B, 1941)
Chitthi (**K.S. Gopalakrishnan**, Tam, 1966)
Chitthi (**Nabyendu Chatterjee**, B, 1972)
Chitti Chellalu (M. Krishnan, Tel, 1970)
Chitti Talli (G.K. Murthy, Tel, 1972)
Chitti Tamudu (K.B. Tilak, Tel, 1962)
Chittor Ni Veerangana (*aka* Valiant Angel: **Dhirubhai Desai**, St, 1930)
Chittor Rani Padmini (**Ch. Narayanamurthy**, Tam, 1963)
Chittor Vijay (Mohan Sinha, H, 1947)
Chittu Kuruvi (Devaraj-Mohan, Tam, 1978)
Chivalry *see* Daan-e-Dushman
Chiviraku Migiledi (G. Ramineedu, Tel, 1960)
Chocolate (Steven, H, 1950)
Choice is Yours, The (**Kantilal Rathod**, E, 1982)
Choice of a Bride *see* Kishori
Chokadika Ekka (*aka* Ace of Diamonds: Chunilal Parekh, St, 1933)
Choka Melar (C.V. Raman, Tam, 1942)
Chokh (**Utpalendu Chakraborty**, B, 1982)
Chokher Aloye (Sachin Adhikari, B, 1989)
Chokher Bali (**Satu Sen**, B, 1938)
Chokho Lage Sasariyo (Siyyad Peer, R, 1983)
Chola Heritage, The (**Adoor Gopalakrishnan**, E, 1980)
Choli Daman (TV: **M.S. Sathyu**, H, 1988)
Chollu Kanna Chollu (T.M. Thirumalaisamy Nadar, Tam, 1977)
Chomana Dudi (**B.V. Karanth**, K, 1975)
Choodamani (**Raja Sandow**, Tel/Tam, 1941)
Choodata Pookal (M.S. Baby, Mal, 1985)
Choondakari (P. Vijayan, Mal, 1976)
Choopulu Kalisina Subavela (Jandhyala, Tel, 1988)
Choothatham (K. Sukumaran Nair, Mal, 1981)
Chopper (**Nabyendu Chatterjee**, B, 1985)
Chor (A.P. Kapur, H, 1950)
Chorabali (Tulsi Lahiri, B, 1947)
Chora Chuvanna Chora (Gopalakrishnan, Mal, 1980)
Chorachya Manaat Chandana (Kamalakar Torne, Mar, 1984)
Chorakku Chora (Crossbelt Mani, Mal, 1985)
Choran Noon Mor (?, P, 1980)
Chor Aur Chand (Pawan Kaul, H, 1993)
Choravar Mor (Yeshwant Pethkar, Mar, 1958)
Choravar Mor (Murlidhar Kapdi, Mar, 1980)
Chor Bazaar (P.N. Arora, H, 1954)
Chor Chor (Prem Prakash, H, 1974)
Chor Chor Chhupja *see* Kalla Kalla Bachitko
Chor Darwaza (Pradeep Nayyar, H, 1965)
Chore (**Kartick Chattopadhyay**, B, 1956)
Chorekanta (**Charu Roy**, St, 1931)
Chor Ho To Aisa (Ravi Tandon, H, 1978)
Choricha Mamla (Babasaheb S. Fattelal, Mar, 1976)
Chori Chori (Anant Thakur, H, 1956)
Chori Chori (Kewal P. Kashyap, H, 1973)
Chori Mera Kaam (Brij Sadanah, H, 1975)
Chorina Fera Char (Mulraj Rajda, G, 1979)
Chor Ka Bhai Chor (K.S.R. Doss, H, 1978)
Chor Ke Ghar Chor (Vijay Sadanah, H, 1978)
Chor Ke Wafadaar (*aka* In Shackles: Haribhai Desai, St, 1932)
Chor Machaye Shor (Ashok Roy, H, 1974)
Chor Mandli (C.L. Rawal, H, 1982)
Chorni (Jyoti Swaroop, H, 1981)
Choron Ka Chor (Mohammed Hussain, H, 1970)
Choron Ki Baraat (Pradeep Nayyar, H, 1960)
Choron Ki Baraat (Harmesh Malhotra, H, 1980)
Choron Ki Rani Haseenon Ka Raja (V. Menon, H, 1990)
Chor Pe Mor (Kapil Kapoor, H, 1990)
Chor Police (Amjad Khan, H, 1983)
Chor Sipahi (Prayag Raaj, H, 1977)
Choru (Ramanarayanan, Tam, 1986)
Chorus *see* **Sanghaganam**
Chorus (**Mrinal Sen**, B, 1974)
Chosen One, The *see* **Ishanou**
Chottanikara Amma (Mani, Mal, 1976)
Choubeji *see* Hip Hip Hurray
Choudhury (Niranjan, H/P, 1941)

Choudhury Harphul Singh (Sushil Kumar Vyas, Haryanvi, 1974)
Choudhury Karnail Singh (Krishan Kumar, P, 1962)
Chow Chow (**T.R. Sundaram**?, **Modern Theatres**, Tam, 1944)
Chowkada Deepa (**G.V. Iyer**, K, 1969)
Chowkidar (Shyam Ralhan, H, 1974)
Chowki No. 11 (V.K. Sobti, H, 1978)
Chowringhee (S. Fazli/Nabendusundar, H/B, 1942)
Chowringhee (Pinaki Mukherjee, B, 1968)
Christian Kumari *see* The Mission Girl
Christmas Rathri (**P. Subramanyam**, Mal, 1961)
Chuda Tujha Savitricha (Govind Kulkarni, Mar, 1971)
Chudi Chandlo (Bharat Patel, G, 1979)
Chudiyan (K.J. Parmar/L.J. Bhatt, H, 1942)
Chudiyan (**Sai Paranjpye**, H, 1993)
Chukki Chandramma (Najunde Gowda, K, 1993)
Chukku (**K.S. Sethumadhavan**, Mal, 1973)
Chula (**Sasikumar**, Mal, 1979)
Chul Ani Mul (**Vishram Bedekar**, Mar, 1947)
Chumadu Thangi (**P. Bhaskaran**, Mal, 1975)
Chunadi (Ramesh Modi, R, 1992)
Chunaria (**Ravindra Dave**, H, 1948)
Chunauti (Satpal, H, 1979)
Chundadi Chokha (**Ratibhai Punatar**, G, 1961)
Chundadini Laaj (Mahendra Shah, G, 1985)
Chundadino Rang (*aka* Lakhanshini Katar: Jasubhai Trivedi, G, 1976)
Chundadi Odhi Tara Namni (**Ravindra Dave**, G, 1978)
Chunnu Munnu (R.D. Rajput, H, 1949)
Chup (*aka* Hush: Hiren K. Bose, St, 1931)
Chupke Chupke (Vaij Sharma/K.C. Verma, H, 1948)
Chupke Chupke (**Hrishikesh Mukherjee**, H, 1975)
Churi Chikanna (R. Ramamurthy, K, 1969)
Churning, The *see* **Manthan**
Churning of the Ocean, The *see* Samudra Manthan
Churning of the Sea *see* Samudra Manthan
Chutki Bhar Senur (**Nasir Hussain**, Bh, 1983)
Chuttalabbai (Kodi Ramakrishna, Tel, 1988)
Chuttalunnaru Jagratha (B.V. Prasad, Tel, 1980)
Chuttarikalu (Pekati Shivram, Tel, 1968)
Chuvanna Chirakukal (Shankaran Nair, Mal, 1979)
Chuvanna Sandhyakal (**K.S. Sethumadhavan**, Mal, 1975)
Chuvanna Vithukal (**P.A. Backer**, Mal, 1976)
Chuvappu Thalam (Babu Radhakrishnan, Mal, 1991)
Chuzhali (Madhu Mohan, Mal, 1991)
Chuzhi (Triprayar Sukumaran, Mal, 1973)
CID (M. Krishnan Nair, Mal, 1955)
CID (**Raj Khosla**, H, 1956)
CID (**Tapi Chanakya**, Tel, 1965)
CID (Ajay Goel, H, 1990)
CID Agent *see* Puraskaar
CID Agent 302 (S. Azeem, H, 1968)
CID Girl (**Ravindra Dave**, H, 1959)
CID in Jungle (G.P. Kamath, Mal, 1971)
CID Inspector *see* Private Detective
CID Nazir (Venu, Mal, 1971)
CID 909 (Mohammed Hussain, H, 1967)
CID 116 *see* Goodachari 116
CID Rajanna (R. Ramamurthy, K, 1970)
CID Raju (K.S.R. Doss, Tel, 1971)
CID 72 (Ravi, K, 1973)
CID Shankar (R. Sundaram, Tam, 1970)
CID Shankar (P. Nanjundappa, K, 1989)
Cinema Cinema (Krishna Shah, H, 1978)
Cinema Cinema (Gajendar, Tam, 1986)
Cinema Girl (**B.P. Mishra**, St, 1930)
Cinema Ki Rani *see* Cinema Queen
Cinema Paithiyam (V. Srinivasan, Tam, 1975)
Cinema Queen (**M. Bhavnani**, St, 1925)
Cinema Queen (*aka* Cinema Ki Rani: Rajendra Raj Gaur, H, 1934)
Cinema Shrushti (*aka* Filmland: Hiralal G. Doctor, St, 1931)
Circus Girl (Ramanlal Desai, H, 1943)
Circus King (?, Bharat Prod, Tel, 1944)
Circus King (B.R. Mudnaney, H, 1946)
Circus Ki Sundari (*aka* Circus Queen: **Balwant Bhatt**, H, 1941)
Circus Queen *see* Circus Ki Sundari
Circus Queen (Noshir Engineer, H, 1959)
Circus Ramudu (**Dasari Narayana Rao**, Tel, 1980)
Circus Sundari (C.M. Trivedi/**Chandrakant**, Tam, 1958)
Circus Tent, The *see* **Thampu**
Circuswale (**Balwant Bhatt**, H, 1950)
Citizen, The *see* **Nagarik**
Citizen Rarichan *see* **Rarichan Enna Pauran**
Citizens and Citizens (**Shantaram Athavale**, E, 1962)
City, The (**B. Narasinga Rao**, E, 1985)
City and the Dream, The *see* **Shaher Aur Sapna**
City in History, A (**Santi P. Choudhury**, E, 1966)
City of Silence *see* Khooni Jadugar
Civilisation *see* Dagabaaz Duniya
Civil Marriage (**Ramchandra Thakur**, H, 1940)
CK Sen's Jaba Kusum Oil (**Hiralal Sen**, St, 1905)
Clerk (**Manoj Kumar**, H, 1989)
Clerk's Daughter *see* **Gumastavin Penn**
College Bullodu (Sarat, Tel, 1992)
College Girl (Sudhir Mukherjee, St, 1933)
College Girl (*aka* College Kanya: **Jayant Desai**, H, 1935)
College Girl (**T. Prakash Rao**, H, 1960)
College Girl (**T. Hariharan**, Mal, 1974)
College Girl (Shantilal Soni, H, 1978)
College Girl (Surendra Gupta, H, 1990)
College Hero (Chandrahasa Alva, K, 1990)
College Kanya *see* College Girl
College Kumari (G.G. Mama Shinde, Tam, 1942)
Collegeranga (**Puttanna Kanagal**, K, 1976)
Collegian (Dada Gunjal, St, 1929)
Collegian (**Balwant Bhatt**, H, 1944)
Colonel and Collector (M.M. Nesan, Mal, 1976)
Colonial Exposition: Paris (**P.V. Pathy**, E, 1934)
Colourful Dreams *see* **Rangula Kala**
Colourful Pattern of Life, A *see* Rangoli
Combat, The *see* Solanki Shamsher
Comedy of Errors *see* Bhool Bhulaiyan *or* Hanste Rehna
Comet, The *see* Dhoomketu
Commander (Kedar Kapoor, H, 1959)
Commander (Rakesh Kumar, H, 1981)
Commando (B. Subhash, H, 1988)
Commercial Pilot Officer (?, Deepak-Jyoti, H, 1963)
Common Accidents (**Phani Majumdar**, E, 1990)
Communication Security (**Vishnu Mathur**, E, 1977)
Companion *see* Savangadi
Company Limited *see* **Seemabaddha**
Comparative Religions (**Fali Bilimoria**, E, 1962)
Compromise *see* Haq Insaaf
Comrades *see* Jeevan Saathi
Confluence, The *see* **Sagara Sangamam** *or* **Sangam**
Confrontation *see* **Saamna**
Confrontation (**Nirad Mahapatra**, E, 1971)
Congratulations Miss Anita Menon (Tulsidas, Mal, 1992)
Congress Session in Bombay (**Baburao Painter**, St, 1919)
Congress Session 1947 (**Fali Bilimoria**, E, 1947)
Congress Session 1948 (**Fali Bilimoria**, E, 1948)
Conqueror, The *see* Veer Na Ver
Constable Koothuru (**Tapi Chanakya**, Tel, 1962)
Contemporary Indian Sculpture (**Buddhadev Dasgupta**, E, 1987)
Continent of Love (**Buddhadev Dasgupta**, E, 1969)
Contours of a Linear Rhythm (**G. Aravindan**, E, 1987)
Coolie (Ashok Kumar, Mal, 1983)
Coolie (**Manmohan Desai**, H, 1983)
Coolie (Chakraborty, Tel, 1988)
Coolie No 1 (**K. Raghavendra Rao**, Tel, 1991)
Coolies at Bombay Central (**Ketan Mehta**, E, 1975)
Co-operation is Success (**S. Sukhdev**, E, 1973)
Coral Queen *see* Pavalakkodi
Coronation Ceremony and Durbar (**Hiralal Sen**, St, 1903)
Coronation of Maharaja Holkar at Indore (?, Gaumont, St, 1912)
Corpses (*aka* Murde: **Saeed Mirza**, H, 1976)
Costly Couplet *see* Sati Menadevi
Country Calls *see* Watan Ki Pukar
Country Girl (*aka* Dehati Ladki: **Dhiren Ganguly**, H, 1936)
Country Teacher, The *see* Nai Taleem
Court Dancer *see* **Raj Nartaki**
Courtesans of Bombay, The (Ismail Merchant, E, 1982)
Coward, The *see* **Kapurush**
Cowboy Kulla (Vijay Reddy, K, 1973)
Cowboy No. 1 (K.S.R. Doss, Tel, 1986)
Crack, The *see* Daraar
Crash *see* Bikhare Moti
Cricketer (Bish Mehey, H, 1983)
Crime and Punishment *see* Paper Parinam
Criminal (*aka* Gunehgaar: **Master Bhagwan**, H, 1939)
Criminals, The (*aka* Hum Sub Chor Hain: Maruti, H, 1973)
Criminals (S. Babu, Mal, 1975)
Crisis on the Campus (**Rabindra Dharmaraj**, E, 1971)
Cross Belt (Mani, Mal, 1970)

Ameeta (above) in *Raj Singhasan* (1958)

Close to Nature (**Shyam Benegal**, E, 1967)
Cloud Capped Star, The *see* **Meghe Dh*aka* Tara**
Cloud Messenger, The *see* **Megha Sandesam**
Cloven Horizon (**Kantilal Rathod**, E, 1965)
Clue, The *see* Suraag
Cobbler, The (**Roop K. Shorey**?, H, 1942)
Cobra (Batra Mohinder, H, 1980)
Cobra Girl (*aka* Naag Rani: **Nanabhai Bhatt**, H, 1963)
Cochin Express (M. Krishnan Nair, Mal, 1967)
Cocoanut Fair (?, St, 1897)
Coffee House (Hari Valia, H, 1957)
Coir Worker (**Fali Bilimoria**, E, 1961)
Collectorgari Abbayi (B. Gopal, Tel, 1987)
Collector Janaki (S.S. Balan, Tel, 1972)
Collector Malathi (M. Krishnan Nair, Mal, 1967)
Collector Vijaya (**Vijayanirmala**, Tel, 1987)

Crossing, The *see* **Paar**
Crossroad, The *see* **Grihajuddha**
Crown for Two Days, A *see* Be Din Ni Badshahi
Crown of Virtue, The *see* Chandravali
Cruelties of Society *see* Rank Ramani
Cry for Life *see* Mujhe Jeene Do
Cry of the Wounded *see* **Aakrosh**
Cuckoo's Call, The *see* **Wosobipo**
Culprit *see* Gunehgaar
Cultured Criminal *see* Sudheral Shaitan
Current (K. Hariharan, H, 1991)
Curse, The *see* Garibni Hai
Curse of Durvas *see* Durvas Shaap
Curses of Cupid *see* Inteqam
Curtain Falls, The *see* **Yavanika**
Customs Diary (T.S. Suresh Babu, Mal, 1993)
Cyclewali (A.M. Khan, H, 1958)
Cyclone Girl *see* Toofani Taruni
Cynic Ke Shaitan (*aka* Devil's Disciple: ?, Sun Art Film, St, 1931)

D

Daabi (**Dhiren Ganguly**, B, 1943)
Daabi (Kanak Mukherjee, B, 1973)
Daag (**Amiya Chakravarty**, H, 1952)
Daag (**Yash Chopra**, H, 1973)
Daaj (Dharam Kumar, P, 1976)
Daaka (**Nanabhai Bhatt**, H, 1959)
Daak Babu (Lekhraj Bhakri, H, 1954)
Daal Mein Kala (**Satyen Bose**, H, 1964)
Daana Shura Karna (Dwarkanath, Tam, 1940)
Daana Veera Shura Karna (**N.T. Rama Rao**, Tel, 1977)
Daan-e-Dushman (*aka* Chivalry: Ramakant-Gharekhan, St, 1931)
Daan Veer Karna *see* **Karnan**
Daari Thappinte Manishi (B. Narasimha Rao, Tel, 1981)
Daasi (*aka* Aparanji: **Balkrishna Narayan Rao**, Tam, 1944)
Daasi (Hiren Bose, H, 1944)
Daasi (C.V. Ranganatha Das, Tel/Tam, 1952)
Daasi (**Raj Khosla**, H, 1981)
Daasi (**B. Narasinga Rao**, Tel, 1988)
Daasi Penn (**Ellis Duncan**, Tam, 1943)
Daasi Putra (Devnarayan Gupta, B, 1949)
Daasi Ya Maa (Shaukat Hussain Rizvi, H, 1946)
Daata (Sultan Ahmed, H, 1989)
Dabar Chal (Kumar Choudhury, B, 1987)
Dabbu Bhale Jabbu (K.S. Rajendra, Tel, 1992)
Dabbu Evariki Chedhu (Relangi Narasimha Rao, Tel, 1986)
Dabbuku Lokam Dasoham (**Yoganand**, Tel, 1973)
Dabbur Kelenkari (Debi Ghosh, St, 1921)
Dabcherry Milk Project (TV: **Sai Paranjpye**, E, 1976)
Dabukku Thha Dongala Muttha (**P. Subramanyam**, Tel, 1971)
Dacait (**Rahul Rawail**, H, 1987)
Dacoit *see* Lutaru
Dacoit's Damsel *see* Lutaru Lalna
Dada (Harish, H, 1949)
Dada (Kedar Kapoor, H, 1966)
Dada (Jugal Kishore, H, 1978)
Dada (P. Vasu, K, 1988)
Dada Dadi Ki Kahaniyan (TV: Moti Sagar, H, 1986-87)
Dadagiri (Deepak Shivdasani, H, 1987)
Dada Ho Dikri (Honey Chhaya, G, 1977)
Dada Khetrapal (Ramkumar Bohra, G, 1978)
Dada Moni (Sujit Guha, B, 1984)
Dadar Kirti (**Tarun Majumdar**, B, 1980)
Dada Thakur (Sudhir Mukherjee, B, 1962)
Daddy (TV: **Mahesh Bhatt**, H, 1989)
Daddy (Sangeeth Sivan, Mal, 1992)
Dadi Maa (**L.V. Prasad**, H, 1966)
Dadosa Ri Ladli (Mohansingh Rathod, R, 1990)
Dadu (Ajit Ganguly, B, 1969)
Dadu Nati-o-Hati (**Nip Barua**, B, 1985)
Daera (**Kamal Amrohi**, H, 1953)
Dafaa 302 (*aka* IPC Section 302: K. Shrivastava, H, 1975)
Daga (Vasant Painter, Mar, 1977)
Dagabaaz (Shiv Kumar, H, 1970)
Dagabaaz Ashiq (Pesi Karani, H, 1932)
Dagabaaz Balma (Aarti Bhattacharya, Bh, 1988)
Dagabaaz Bhai (*aka* Tainted Heart: Asooji, St, 1932)
Dagabaaz Doctor *see* Dagabaaz Dost
Dagabaaz Dost (S.M. Ibrahim, H, 1947)
Dagabaaz Duniya (*aka* Way of the World: Harihar Diwana, St, 1926)
Dagabaaz Duniya (*aka* Civilisation: ?, Ganesh Movies, H, 1936)
Dagabaaz Dushman (*aka* The Betrayer: Kantilal Patel, St, 1931)
Dagakhor Dilbar (*aka* King's Paramour: ?, British-India Film, St, 1929)
Dagger Devil *see* Chhappan Churi
Dagudu Moothulu (**Adurthi Subba Rao**, Tel, 1964)
Dagudu Moothulu (Ravindra Babu, Tel, 1986)
Daha (D.V.K. Murthy, K, 1979)
Daham (**K.S. Sethumadhavan**, Mal, 1965)
Daha Wajta/Das Baje (**Raja Nene**, Mar/H, 1942)
Dahej (**V. Shantaram**, H, 1950)
Dahlia (**Modhu Bose**, St, 1930)
Dahshat (Tulsi/Shyam **Ramsay**, H, 1981)
Daily Mail (**N.G. Devare**, St, 1930)
Daily Passenger (Sadhan Sarkar, B, 1958)
Dainee (Manoj Bhattacharya, B, 1961)
Daisy (**Prathap Pothan**, Mal, 1988)
Daivabalam (Vasantkumar Reddy, Tel/Tam, 1959)
Daivacha Khel (C. Mohan, Mar, 1964)
Daivache Bhaksha *see* Shaitan Ki Shikar
Daiva Janile Kuni (Krishna Patil, Mar, 1967)
Daiva Kuzhandigal (S.P. Muthuraman, Tam, 1973)
Daivaleele (Krishnakumar, K, 1962)
Daivam (M.M.A. Chinappa Devar, Tam, 1972)
Daivamagan (A.C. Trilogchander, Tam, 1969)
Daivamasam (K. Vijayam, Tam, 1973)
Daivame Thunai (**Ch. Narayanamurthy**, Tam, 1959)
Daivam Pesuma (?, Bhanu Chitra Jagath, Tam, 1971)
Daiva Neethi (M.L. Tandon, Tam, 1947)
Daiva Penn (?, Savitri Pics., Tam, 1970)
Daiva Piravi (**Krishnan-Panju**, Tam, 1960)
Daiva Piravi (R. Krishnamurthy, Tam, 1985)
Daiva Sankalpa (M.B. Ganesh, K, 1956)
Daiva Sankalpam (P.R. Somu, Tam, 1972)
Daiva Seyal (M.G. Balu, Tam, 1967)
Daiva Shakti (Renuka Sharma, K, 1987)
Daivat (Govind Kulkarni, Mar, 1982)
Daivatare (M.S. Rajashekhar, K, 1985)
Daivathai (P. Madhavan, Tam, 1964)
Daivathe Orthu (R. Gopi, Mal, 1985)
Daivathin Daivam (**K.S. Gopalakrishnan**, Tam, 1962)
Daivathinte Vikrithikal (**Lenin Rajendran**, Mal, 1992)
Daiva Thirumagal (M.M.A. Chinappa Devar, Tam, 1964)
Daiva Thirumanangal (K. Shankar/**K. Kameshwara Rao**/**P. Neelakantan**, Tam, 1981)
Daiva Vakku (M.S. Madhu, Tam, 1992)
Daiveega Ragangal (A. Veerappan, Tam, 1980)
Daiveega Uravu (Sathyam, Tam, 1968)
Daivi Khadga (*aka* Divine Sabre: Zunjharrao Pawar, St, 1930)
Daivi Khajina (*aka* Divine Treasure: G.P. Pawar, St, 1933)
Daiviyin Thirumanam (P. Madhavan, Tam, 1977)
Daiviyin Thiruvilaiyadal (**K.S. Gopalakrishnan**, Tam, 1982)
Dakather Hatey Bulu (**Santi P. Choudhury**, B, 1963)
Dak Bangla (M. Sadiq, H, 1947)
Dak Bangla (Govind Ranjan, H, 1974)
Dak Bangla (Keshu **Ramsay**, H, 1987)
Dak Diye Jai (Ranjit Mull Kankaria, B, 1978)
Dak Ghar (Zul Velani, H, 1965)
Dakhal (**Gautam Ghosh**, B, 1981)
Dak Harkara (Agragami, B, 1958)
Dakhine Bagh (Bibhuti Das, B, 1949)
Dakinir Char (**Premendra Mitra**, B, 1955)
Daksha Yagna (G.V. Sane, St, 1927)
Daksha Yagna (*aka* Sati, Sati Parvati: **Jyotish Bannerjee**, B/H, 1934)
Daksha Yagna (Bhabani Basu Mullick, B, 1980)
Dakshayagnam (**Raja Chandrasekhar**, Tam, 1938)
Dakshayagnam (**Ch. Narayanamurthy**, Tel, 1941)
Dakshayagnam (**Kadaru Nagabhushanam**, Tel/Tam, 1962)
Dakshina Haryana (**Santi P. Choudhury**, H, 1972)
Daktar *see* Doctor
Daktar Babu (Bishu Dasgupta, B, 1958)
Daktar Bou (Jagadish Mandal, B, 1986)
Daku (Aspi, H, 1955)
Daku (**Basu Bhattacharya**, H, 1975)
Daku (V.V.S. Reddy, Tel, 1984)
Daku Aur Bhagwan (**Dhirubhai Desai**, H, 1975)
Daku Aur Jawan (Sunil Dutt, H, 1978)
Daku Aur Mahatma (Ravi Nagaich, H, 1977)
Daku Bijli (Ritu Raj, H, 1986)
Daku Hasina (Ashok Roy, H, 1987)
Daku Ka Ladka (**Charu Roy**, H, 1935)
Daku Ke Dilbar (*aka* Laughing Cavalier: **Harshadrai Mehta**, St, 1930)
Daku Ki Ladki (**Moti Gidwani**, H, 1933)
Daku Ki Ladki (Harish, H, 1954)
Daku Mangal Singh (Chand, H, 1966)
Daku Mansingh (**Babubhai Mistri**, H, 1971)
Daku Mansoor (*aka* Karishma-e-Kudrat: **Nitin Bose**, Urdu, 1934)
Daku Mansoor (Kuldeep Sharma, H, 1961)
Daku Raja (B.K. Adarsh, H, 1987)
Dakurani (K.S. Rami Reddy, Tel, 1986)
Dakurani Ganga (**Krishnakant**, G/Bh, 1976)
Daku Shamsher Singh (Pushp Raj, P, 1975)
Dalaal (Partho Ghosh, H, 1993)
Dalapathi (**Mani Rathnam**, Tam, 1991)
Dalimbi (G.G. Bhosle, Mar, 1982)
Dalit Kusum (Shame of the Nation: Michael Ormalev/M.L. Tandon, H, 1936)
Daliyappukal (Pratap Singh, Mal, 1980)
Dallali (D. Shankar Singh, K, 1952)
Damaad (Brij Rani, H, 1951)
Damaad (Rajat Rakshit, H, 1978)
Daman (*aka* Lok Laaj: **Nanabhai Bhatt**, H, 1951)
Daman Aur Aag (Vinod Kumar, H, 1973)
Dambachari (M.L. Tandon, Tam, 1935)
Damini (Rajkumar Santoshi, H, 1993)
Dam Kari Kaam (**Prabhakar Nayak**, Mar, 1971)
Damnit Katha Addam Thirigindi (Relangi Narasimha Rao, Tel, 1987)
Dampathiam Oru Sangeetham (Venkat, Tam, 1982)
Dampathiyaru (H.P. Jayaprakash, K, 1983)
Dampati (**Niren Lahiri**, B, 1943)
Dampati (Anil Ghosh, B, 1976)
Dampati (S.N. Rao, H, 1980)
Dampatyam (E. Apparao, Tel, 1957)
Dampatyam (A. Kodandarami Reddy, Tel, 1985)
Dampatyam (K. Vijayan, Tam, 1987)
Damsel of Patan *see* Patan Ni Paniari
Damul (**Prakash Jha**, H, 1984)
Dana Pani (**V.M. Vyas**, H, 1953)
Dana Pani (Deven Verma, H, 1989)
Danavudu (Kodi Ramakrishna, Tel, 1984)
Dance Dance (B. Subhash, H, 1987)
Dance of Life *see* Hridaya Veena
Dance of Shiva, The (**Chidananda Das Gupta**, E, 1968)
Dancer (Kishore Vyas, H, 1991)
Dancer Mohanambal *see* **Thillana Mohanambal**
Dancer of the Temple *see* Pujarini
Dances from Alibaba (**Hiralal Sen**, St, 1903)
Dancing Girl *see* Gutter Nu Gulab *or* Naachwali
Dancing of Indian Nautch Girls (?, Elphinstone Bioscope, St, 1906)
Dancing Scenes from the Flower of Persia (**Hiralal Sen**, St, 1898)
Danda Balunga (Mohammed Mohsin, O, 1984)
Dandanai (Ramanarayanan, Tam, 1985)
Dandayatra (**K. Bapaiah**, Tel, 1984)
Daner Maryada (**Sushil Majumdar**, B, 1956)
Danga Fasaad (Sunil Agnihotri, H, 1990)
Dangal (Rati Kumar, Bh, 1977)
Danger at Your Doorstep (**Adoor Gopalakrishnan**, E, 1968)
Danger Biscuit (A.B. Raj, Mal, 1969)
Dangerous Woman *see* Khatarnak Aurat
Danger Signal (**K. Amarnath**, Tam/H, 1937)
Dangeyedda Makkalu (Vadiraj, K, 1979)
Dani Samrat *see* Vaman Avatar
Danka (**J.P. Advani**, H, 1954)
Danka (Baldev R. Jhingan, H, 1969)
Dao Pe Dao (?, Gayatri Cine Enterprises, H, 1980)
Dara (Harish, H, 1953)
Daraar (*aka* The Crack: Ved Rahi, H, 1972)
Dara Singh (*aka* The Iron Man: Kedar Kapoor, H, 1964)
Dara the Ape Man *see* Khooni Khazana
Darban (S.M. Yusuf, H, 1946)
Darbar (**Nanubhai Vakil**, H, 1955)
Dard (**A.R. Kardar**, H, 1947)
Dard (Ambarish Sangal, H, 1981)
Darde Budedi (?, Tulu, 1971)
Dard-e-Dil (*aka* Romance: **M. Bhavnani**/Moti Jhangiani, H, 1934)
Dard-e-Dil (**Nitin Bose**, H, 1953)
Dard-e-Dil (Suraj Prakash, H, 1983)
Dard-e-Jigar (*aka* Songs of Sorrow: **Harshadrai Mehta**, St, 1931)
Dard-e-Ulfat (*aka* The Pangs of Love: **Dhirubhai Desai**, H, 1935)
Dardi (*aka* Faithful Heart: **Niranjan Pal**, St, 1932)
Dard Ka Rishta (**Sunil Dutt**, H, 1982)
Daredevil *see* Jung Bahadur *or* Himmat-e-Mard
Darinda (Kaushal Bharti, H, 1977)
Daring Damsel *see* Azad Abla
Daring Detective (Mohammed Hussain, H, 1948)
Daring Rathod *see* Veer Rathod
Dari Tappida Maga (Pekati Shivram, K, 1975)
Dariya Dil (K. Ravishankar, H, 1987)
Dariyai Devangana (*aka* Sea Goddess: **Dhirubhai Desai**, St, 1931)
Darja Donga *see* Dharja Donga
Darkness *see* **Tamas**
Darkness to Light (?, Bapsy Sabavala, St, 1931)
Dark Street (Naresh Saigal, H, 1961)
Darling Child *see* **Guddi**
Darling Darling (Gogi Anand, H, 1977)
Darling Darling Darling (**K. Bhagyaraj**, Tam, 1982)
Darmam Thalai Kakum (M.A. Thirumugham, Tam, 1963)
Darodekhor (Kamalakar Torne, Mar, 1980)
Darogaji (Akhtar Hussain, H, 1949)
Darpachurna (Ashok Chatterjee, B, 1951)
Darpachurna (Dilip Roy, B, 1980)
Darpan (A.H. Essa, H, 1941)
Darpan (**Adurthi Subba Rao**, H, 1970)
Darpan (TV: **Basu Chatterjee**, H, 1985)
Darpok Ki Dosti (**Prakash Jha**, H, 1977)
Darr (**Yash Chopra**, H, 1993)
Darshan (**Chimanlal Luhar**, H, 1941)
Darshana (Uma Maheshwara Rao, Tel, 1989)
Darshanam (**P.N. Menon**, Mal, 1973)
Darwaza (Shaheed Latif, H, 1954)
Darwaza (Tulsi/Shyam **Ramsay**, H, 1978)
Daryai Lutera (A.R. Zamindar, H, 1952)
Dasara (B.Y. Ramadas, K, 1949)
Dasara Bullodu (V.B. Rajendra Prasad, Tel, 1971)
Dasarathan (Manivasagam, Tam, 1993)
Dasarathanukku Onbathu Pengal (M.S. Basu, Tam, 1984)
Dasa Thirigindi (K. Subba Rao, Tel, 1979)
Dasavataramulu (K.P. Bhave/**C. Pullaiah**, Tel, 1937)
Das Baje *see* **Daha Wajta**
Dasharatham (**Sibi Malayil**, Mal, 1989)
Dasharathi Ram (Sane Mama, St, 1929)
Dashavtar (**R.S. Prakash**, St, 1927)
Dashavtar (**Jayant Desai**, H, 1951)
Dashavtara (P.G. Mohan, K, 1960)

Dashavatharam (Sheshayya?, Jayabheri Films, Tam, 1934)
Dashavatharam (**K.S. Gopalakrishnan**, Tam, 1976)
Dashing Devil *see* Sher Dil
Dashing Girl *see* Bahadur Beti
Dashing Hero *see* Jawan Mard
Dashing Youth *see* Das Lakhno Dallo *or* Sher-e-Jawan
Dashyumohan (Ardhendu Mukherjee, B, 1955)
Dasi *see* Daasi
Das Lakh (D.C. Goyal, H, 1966)
Das Numbri (Madan Mohla, H, 1976)
Dassehra (**Chaturbhuj Doshi**, H, 1956)
Dastaan (**A.R. Kardar**, H, 1950)
Dastaan (**B.R. Chopra**, H, 1972)
Dastaan-e-Laila Majnu (R.L. Desai, H, 1974)
Dastak (**Rajinder Singh Bedi**, H, 1970)
Dastoor (Anil Matto, H, 1991)
Dasturmoto Talkie *see* Talkie of Talkies
Dasyu Ratnakara (Prabhat Mukherjee, O, 1962)
Data Karna (**Phani Burma**, B, 1957)
Datta (Soumyen Mukherjee, B, 1951)
Datta (**Ajoy Kar**, B, 1976)
Datta Janma (*aka* Sati Ansuya: G.V. Sane, St, 1924)
Dattak (Kamal Ganguly, B, 1955)
Dattaputhrudu (T.L. Babu, Tel, 1972)
Dattuputhran (**Kunchako**, Mal, 1970)
Daughter-in-Law *see* Kulavadhu
Daughter of an Outlaw *see* Baharvatiyo Ni Beti
Daughter of God *see* Dev Kanya
Daughter of Himalaya *see* Himalaya Ki Beti
Daughter of Hunterwali *see* Hunterwali Ki Beti
Daughter of India *see* Dukhtar-e-Hind
Daughter of Shripur *see* Krishna Kumari
Daughter of Sinbad *see* Sinbad Ki Beti
Daughter of the Jungle (*aka* Vanasundari: Ramanlal Desai, H, 1942)
Daughter of the Maharattas, The (**N.D. Sarpotdar**, St, 1928)
Daughter of the Sea *see* Sagar Kanya
Daughters of India (**V.M. Vyas**, H, 1939)
Daughters of India *see* Princess Rajba
Daughters of Today (G.K. Mehta, St, 1928)
Daulat (S.M. Yusuf, H, 1937)
Daulat (**Sohrab Modi**, H, 1949)
Daulat (**Mohan Segal**, H, 1981)
Daulat Ka Nasha (*aka* Money: Pesi Karani, H, 1931)
Daulat Ke Liye (A. Rashid, H, 1947)
Daulat Ki Jung (S.A. Kader, H, 1992)
Dauntless *see* Randhir
Dauthiyam (Anil, Mal, 1989)
Davedar (?, H, 1982)
David, David, Mr David (Viji Thampi, Mal, 1988)
David Uncle (Guna, Tam, 1992)
Dav Pech *see* Ganimi Kava
Dav Pech (*aka* The Web: **Moti Gidwani**, St, 1930)
Dav Pech (Kawal Sharma, H, 1989)
Dawat (*aka* Invitation: M. Nazir, H, 1943)
Dawat (**B.R. Ishara**, H, 1974)
Dawn of Life *see* Jeevan Prabhat
Dawn *see* **Pratyusha** *or* **Umbartha** *or* Savera
Dayalan (Anthony Mithradas, Tam, 1941)
Dayamayudu (Vijaya Chander, Tel, 1987)
Daya Ni Devi (*aka* The Nurse: **M. Bhavnani**, St, 1927)
Dayar-e-Habib (Hira Singh, H, 1956)
Dayar-e-Madina (A. Shamsheer, H, 1975)
Dayavan (Feroz Khan, H, 1988)
Days and Nights in the Forest *see* **Aranyer Din Ratri**
Day's Bread, A *see* **Uski Roti**
Dayyala Meda (Ramnarayan, Tel, 1985)
Dead End *see* **Andhi Gali** *or* **Peruvazhiyampalam**
Dead Moon, The *see* **Malajanha**
Death of Narayanrao Peshwa, The (**S.N. Patankar**, St, 1915)
Debabrata Biswas (**Utpalendu Chakraborty**, B, 1983)
Debarshi Narader Sansar (Panchaboot, B, 1960)
Debibaran (Srikanta Guha-Thakurta, B, 1988)
Debi Choudhrani (**Priyanath Ganguly**, St, 1931)
Debi Choudhrani (Satish Dasgupta, B, 1949)
Debi Choudhrani (**Dinen Gupta**, B, 1974)
Debigarjan (Piyush Kanti Ganguly, B, 1984)
Debjani (**Phani Burma**, B, 1939)
Debshishu (**Utpalendu Chakraborty**, H, 1985)
Debt of Sin, The *see* **Paap No Fej**
Debts of Honour *see* Inteqam
Deccan Queen (**Mehboob**, H, 1936)
Deccan Queen (Aakkoo, H, 1962)
December Evening, The (P.K. Shivkumar, H, 1973)
December Pookkal (R. Bhoopati, Tam, 1986)
December 31st (Mano Bala, K, 1988)
Decision Divine *see* Kudrat Ka Faisla
De Danadan (Mahesh Kothare, Mar, 1987)
Deedar (**Nitin Bose**, H, 1951)
Deedar (Jugal Kishore, H, 1970)
Deedar (Pramod Chakravarty, H, 1992)
Deedar-e-Yaar (**H.S. Rawail**, H, 1982)
Deed Shahane (Raja Bargir, Mar, 1979)
Deeksha/Anni (**K.S. Prakash Rao**, Tel/Tam, 1951)
Deeksha (**K. Pratyagatma**, Tel, 1974)
Deeksha (Arun Kaul, H, 1991)
Deen Aur Imaan (*aka* Koran Aur Imaan: A. Shamsheer, H, 1979)
Deen-o-Duniya (H.R. Sethi, H, 1936)
Deep *see* **Marhi Da Deeva**
Deepa (S.V. Rajendran, K, 1977)
Deepak (Dwarka Khosla, H, 1940)
Deepak (Chandrasekhar, H, 1951)
Deepak (Harsukh Bhatt, H, 1963)
Deepak Mahal (**Nanubhai Vakil**, H, 1940)
Deepam (K. Vijayan, Tam, 1977)
Deepam (Chandrakumar, Mal, 1980)
Deeparadhana (**Dasari Narayana Rao**, Tel, 1980)
Deeparadhana (Vijayanand, Mal, 1983)
Deepar Prem (**Arundhati Devi**, B, 1983)
Deepavali (Rajanikant, Tel, 1960)
Deep Jalta Rahe (**Datta Dharmadhikari**, H, 1959)
Deep Jweley Jai (**Asit Sen**, B, 1959)
Deepjyoti (Pradyut Basu, A, 1985)
Deep Nebhey Noy (Kanak Mukherjee, B, 1964)
Deergha Sumangali (A.C. Trilogchander, Tam, 1974)
Deergha Sumangali (K. Hemambharadhara Rao, Tel, 1974)
Deer on the Lake, The (**Aribam Syam Sharma**, E, 1989)
Dee Vale Ee Dikra (Kishore Vyas, G, 1982)
Deewana *see* Diwana
Deewane (Chander Sharma, H, 1991)
Deewangee (Samir Ganguly, H, 1976)
Deewar (S. Khalil, H, 1955)
Deewar (**Yash Chopra**, H, 1975)
Defeat *see* Main Hari
Dehati (*aka* Villager: Narayanbhai Patel, H, 1947)
Dehati Ladki *see* Country Girl
Dehleez (Ravi Chopra, H, 1986)
Deity in Distress *see* Niradhar Nira
Deiva *see* Daiva
Dekha Jayega (**J.P. Advani**, H, 1939)
Dekha Jayega (O.P. Khanna, H, 1960)
Dekha Pyar Tumhara (K. Parvez, H, 1963)
Dekha Pyar Tumhara (Virendra Sharma, H, 1985)
Dekhi Teri Bambai (Kailash Bhandari, H, 1961)
Dekh Kabira Roya (**Amiya Chakravarty**, H, 1957)
Dekh Khabar Rakh Nazar (Kumar Anand, O, 1983)
Dekhoji (Walli, H, 1947)
Delhi Durbar (?, American Biograph, St, 1903)
Delhi Durbar (**Chandrakant**, H, 1956)
Delhi Durbar and Coronation (?, Gaumont, St, 1911)
Delhi Durbar and Coronation (?, Imperial Bioscope, St, 1912)
Delhi Durbar of Lord Curzon (**H.S. Bhatavdekar**, St, 1903)
Delhi Express (Madanrai Vakil, H, 1935)
Delhi Express (**Balwant Bhatt**, H, 1949)
Delhi Junction (Mohammed A. Hussain, H, 1960)
Delhi Ka Dada (R.S. Tara, H, 1962)
Delhi Ka Thug (*aka* White Devil: **Dhirubhai Desai**, H, 1935)
Delhi Ka Thug (S.D. Narang, H, 1958)
Delhi Ki Kahani (Rajendra Sharma, H, 1960)
Delhi Mappillai (Devan, Tam, 1968)
Delhi No Thug (*aka* Thief of Delhi: **Homi Master**, St, 1926)
Delhi to Madras (I.N. Murthy, Tam, 1972)
Deliverance *see* **Sadgati**
Demon Land *see* Vethala Ulagam
Dena Paona (**Premankur Atorthy**, B, 1931)
Dena Paona (Sukhen Das, B, 1988)
Deoghar (**Raja Paranjpe**, Mar, 1956)
Deoghar (Govind Kulkarni, Mar, 1981)
Dera Ashiqan Da (Pavan Dev, P, 1979)
Derani Jethani (Mohansingh Rathod, R, 1985)
Derby Ka Shikar (N. Bulchandani, H, 1936)
Derso Khokhar Kando (Kamal Ganguly, B, 1959)
Desadanakkili Karayilla (**P. Padmarajan**, Mal, 1986)
Desamante Manasuloi (**C.S. Rao**, Tel, 1970)
Desamlo Dongaru Paddaru (T. Krishna, Tel, 1985)
Descent of Ganga, The *see* **Gangavataran**
Desert Damsel *see* Mojili Mashuq
Deserted Son of Kunti *see* Karna
Desert of a Thousand Lines (**Mani Kaul**, H, 1981)
Desert Queen *see* Registan Ki Rani
Deshabhaktan (S.M. Sreeramulu Naidu, Mal, 1952)
Desha Drohigal *see* Deshadrohulu
Deshadrohulu/Desha Drohigal (B. Subbarao, Tel/Tam, 1964)
Desha Munnetram (Mahendra Thakur/A.N. Kalyanasundaram, Tam, 1938)
Deshawato (*aka* The Exiled Prince, The Exiled Prince of Ujjain: ?, Indian Pics., St, 1925)
Deshbandhu (G.R. Sethi, St, 1931)
Deshbandhu Chittaranjan (Ardhendu Mukherjee, B, 1970)
Desh Bhakt (*aka* Patriot: A.H. Issa, H, 1940)
Deshbhakti (?, Prakash Pics, Tam, 1940)
Desh Dasi (**Chandulal Shah**, H, 1935)
Desh Deepak (*aka* Patriot: **Nanubhai Vakil**, St, 1930)
Desh Deepak (**J.B.H. Wadia**, H, 1935)
Desh Drohi (**Prakash Mehra**, H, 1980)
Desher Daabi (Samar Ghosh, B, 1947)
Desher Mati/Dharti Mata (**Nitin Bose**, B/H, 1938)
Desh Ke Dushman (Swaroop Kumar, H, 1989)
Desh Na Dushman (*aka* The Divine Punishment: **Manilal Joshi**, St, 1925)
Deshoddharakulu (**C.S. Rao**, Tel, 1973)
Deshoddharakulu (A. Kodandarami Reddy, Tel, 1986)
Desh Premi (**Manmohan Desai**, H, 1982)
Desh Seva (**Nanubhai Vakil**, H, 1948)
Desh Sevak *see* Azadi-e-Watan *or* Banke Sipahi
Desh Shatru (Vijayendar Mittal, H, 1983)
Deshwasi (Rajeev Goswami, H, 1989)
Desire *see* Meri Khwaish
Desires, The *see* Armaan
Des Pardes (**Dev Anand**, H, 1978)
Destiny *see* Honhar *or* **Naseeb** *or* **Taqdeer** *or* Karmadevi *or* Swaham
Destiny at Play *see* Bhagyodaya
Destiny Defied *see* Lekh Par Mekh
De Taali (**Datta Keshav**, Mar, 1989)
Detective *see* Jasoos
Detective (**Shakti Samanta**, H, 1958)
Detective Kumar (Dada Athavale, St, 1927)
Detective Narada (M.V. Raghu, Tel, 1992)
Detective 909 Keralathil (Venu, Mal, 1970)
Determination *see* Sankalp
Deva (Vijay, K, 1989)
Devacha Kaul (Raja Joshi, Mar, 1952)
Devadasi (*aka* Bride of God: **Manilal Joshi**, St, 1925)
Devadasi (*aka* Bride of God: **Naval Gandhi**, St, 1930)
Devadasi (Prafulla Ghosh, B, 1935)
Devadasi (**Phani Majumdar**, H, 1945)
Devadasi (T.V. Sundaram, Tam, 1948)
Devadasi (C.V. Raju, K, 1978)
Devadasu (**Vedantam Raghavaiah**, Tel/Tam, 1953)
Devadasu (**Vijayanirmala**, Tel, 1974)
Devadasu Malli Puttadu (**Dasari Narayana Rao**, Tel, 1978)
Devagharcha Lena (D.M. Ambapkar, Mar, 1957)
Devajani (Byomkesh Tripathi, O, 1981)
Devakannika (G.R. Rao, K, 1954)
Devakanya (**R. Padmanabhan**, Tam, 1943)
Devakanya (K. Hemambharadhara Rao, Tel, 1968)
Devaki (**N.D. Sarpotdar**, Mar/H, 1934)
Devaki (R.S. Mani, Tam, 1951)
Devaki Nandan Gopala (**Rajdutt**, Mar, 1977)
Deval Devayat (Ramkumar Bohra, G, 1985)
Devalaya (A.R. Sabhapati Devar, K, 1984)
Devalayam (S. Ramanathan/N.S. Muthukumar, Mal, 1964)
Devalayam (**Ghantamneni Krishna**, Tel, 1985)
Deva Manava (Jambu, K, 1966)
Devamanohari (A.T. Krishnaswamy, Tam, 1949)
Devanthakudu (**C. Pullaiah**, Tel, 1960)
Devanthakudu (S.A. Chandrasekharan, Tel, 1984)
Deva Pudhe Manoos (Baburao Rokade, Mar, 1980)
Devar (**Jyotish Bannerjee**, B, 1943)
Devar (S.M. Yusuf, H, 1946)
Devar (**Mohan Segal**, H, 1966)
Devara Aata (V. Somasekhar, K, 1981)
Devara Duddu (K.S.L. Swamy, K, 1976)
Devara Gedda Manava *see* Devuni Gelichina Manavudu
Devara Gudi (R. Ramamurthy, K, 1974)
Devara Kannu (Y.R. Swamy, K, 1975)
Devara Makkalu (Y.R. Swamy, K, 1970)
Devara Tirpu (B.S. Badrinath, K, 1983)
Devar Bhabhi (Kedar Kapoor, H, 1958)
Devare Dikku (Basavaraj Kestur, K, 1977)
Devarelliddane (V. Somasekhar, K, 1985)
Devaru Kotta Thangi (Ravi, K, 1973)
Devaru Kotta Vara (R. Ramamurthy, K, 1975)
Devar Veetu Ponnu (Ramanarayanan, Tam, 1992)
Devashapath Khara Sangen (Bhaskar Jadhav, Mar, 1985)
Devasundari (N. Nambiar, Mal, 1957)
Devasundari (C.V. Raju, K, 1962)
Devasundari (**H.V. Babu**, Tel, 1963)
Devasuram (**I.V. Sasi**, Mal, 1993)
Devata (**Master Vinayak**, Mar, 1939)
Devata (Pattanna, H, 1956)
Devata (S. Ramanathan, H, 1978)
Devata (Kamalakar Torne, Mar, 1983)
Devatar Deep (Prabhat Mukherjee, B, 1965)
Devatha (**B.N. Reddi**, Tel, 1941)
Devatha (K. Padmanabhan Nair/W.R. Subbarao, Mal, 1965)
Devatha (K. Hemambharadhara Rao, Tel, 1965)
Devatha (**K. Raghavendra Rao**, Tel, 1982)
Devathai (**P.N. Menon**, Tam, 1979)
Devathalara Deevinchandi (Kommineni, Tel, 1977)
Devatha Manushya (**Singeetham Srinivasa Rao**, K, 1988)
Devatra (Haridas Bhattacharya, B, 1955)
Deva Tujhi Sonyachi Jejuri (Raja Bargir, Mar, 1967)
Devayani (Pandurang Talegiri, Mar, 1940)
Devbala (Bapurao Apte, H, 1938)
Devbappa (Ram Gabale, Mar, 1953)
Devdas (Nitish Chandra Mitra, St, 1928)
Devdas (**P.C. Barua**, B/H, 1935)
Devdas (P.V. Rao, Tam, 1936)
Devdas (**Bimal Roy**, H, 1955)
Devdas (Dilip Roy, B, 1979)
Devdas (Ownbelt Mani, Mal, 1989)
Devdoot (Atanu Bannerjee, B, 1948)
Development in Irrigation (**Gautam Ghosh**, E, 1981)
Devi (**Satyajit Ray**, B, 1960)

Devi (?, Thirumalai Films, Tam, 1968)
Devi (V. Madhusudhana Rao, H, 1970)
Devi (**K.S. Sethumadhavan**, Mal, 1972)
Devi (Sambhu Gupta/Dara Ahmed, A, 1984)
Devi Ahalyabai (**B.P. Mishra**, St, 1925)
Devi Devayani (**Chandulal Shah**, H, 1931)
Devi Dharisanam (K. Shankar, Tam/Tel, 1981)
Devifullara (Tinkari Chakraborty, B, 1938)
Devi Hothal *see* Hothal Padmini
Devika (Anil Ghosh, B, 1985)
Devi Kanyakumari (**P. Subramanyam**, Mal, 1974)
Devi Lalithamba (G.N. Velumani, Tel, 1973)
Devil and the Damsel *see* Peyum Pennum
Devil Land *see* Bhoot Rajya
Devil May Care *see* Khaufnak Khiladi
Devil of the Cave *see* Math No Sadhu
Devil's Dagger *see* Khooni Khanjar
Devil's Dice *see* Shaitan Ka Pash
Devil's Disciple *see* Cynic Ke Shaitan
Devimalini (**Niren Lahiri**, B, 1955)
Devi Navagraha Nayaki (**K. Kameshwara Rao**, Tel, 1986)
Devi Shri Karumariamman (Vietnam Veedu Sundaram, Tam, 1974)
Devi Sridevi (Gangai Amaran, Tam, 1983)
Devi Sridevi (Rajachandra, Tel, 1983)
Devi Tirtha Kamrup Kamakshya (Manu Sen, B, 1967)
Devi Todi (**Kanjibhai Rathod**, St, 1922)
Devi Ya Danvi *see* Pyar Ki Maar
Dev Jaga Aahe (**Dinkar D. Patil**, Mar, 1957)
Devkanya (*aka* Daughter of God: **Kanjibhai Rathod**, St, 1928)
Devkanya (**Dhirubhai Desai**, H, 1946)
Devkanya (Srinath Tripathi, H, 1963)
Dev Manoos (**Rajdutt**, Mar, 1970)
Devotee *see* Prem Diwani
Devotion's Reward *see* Shri Markandeya Avatar
Dev Pavla (Ram Gabale, Mar, 1950)
Devudamma (K.V. Nandan Rao, Tel, 1972)
Devude Digivaste (**Dasari Narayana Rao**, Tel, 1975)
Devude Gelichadu (**Vijayanirmala**, Tel, 1976)
Devudichina Bharta (P. Padmaraju, Tel, 1969)
Devudichina Koduku (K.S.R. Doss, Tel, 1980)
Devudu Chesina Bommali (Hanuman Prasad, Tel, 1976)
Devudu Chesina Manushulu (V. Ramchandra Rao, Tel, 1973)
Devudu Chesina Pelli (**T. Rama Rao**, Tel, 1974)
Devudulanti Manishi (**C.S. Rao**, Tel, 1975)
Devudu Mamayya (K. Vasu, Tel, 1981)
Devudunadu Jagratha (K.S.R. Doss, Tel, 1977)
Devuni Gelichina Manavudu/Devara Gedda Manava (**Hunsur Krishnamurthy**, Tel/K, 1967)
Devuni Roopalu (Rammohan Rao, Tel, 1983)
Devyani (Vasant Painter, H, 1952)
Deya Neya (Sunil Bannerjee, B, 1963)
DG Movie Pioneer (**Kalpana Lajmi**, E, 1978)
Dhaar (Amar Bhattacharya, H, 1992)
Dha Cha Maa (*aka* The Murder of Narayanrao Peshwa: **N.D. Sarpotdar**, St, 1926)
Dhadha (L.N. Ramachandra Reddy, Tel, 1987)
Dhadkan (Zahur Raja, H, 1946)
Dhadkan (Devendra Goel, H, 1972)
Dhagala Lagali Kala (Kamalakar Torne, Mar, 1985)
Dhairyalakshmi (Gopu, Tam/K, 1979)
Dhairyavanthudu (Laxmi Deepak, Tel, 1986)
Dhakam (Babu Nathencode, Tam, 1972)
Dhake Ki Malmal (J.K. Nanda, H, 1956)
Dhakti Bahin (**Rajdutt**, Mar, 1970)
Dhakti Jau (**Anant Mane**, Mar, 1958)
Dhakti Mehuni (**Datta Dharmadhikari**, Mar, 1978)
Dhakti Soon (N.S. Vaidya, Mar, 1986)
Dhamaka (Jagdish, H, 1980)
Dhamal Bablya Ganpyachi (**Datta Keshav**, Mar, 1990)
Dhamki (**Ravindra Dave**, H, 1945)
Dhamki (K. Parvez, H, 1973)
Dhana Amaravathi (B.S. Ramesh, Tam, 1947)
Dhanalakshmi (K.S.S. Narayan, K, 1977)
Dhanam (**Sibi Malayil**, Mal, 1991)
Dhanama? Daivama? (**C.S. Rao**, Tel, 1973)
Dhananjay (**Raja Thakur**, Mar, 1966)
Dhanapishachi (S.N. Singh, K, 1967)
Dhanavanthulu Gunavanthulu (K. Varaprasada Rao, Tel, 1974)
Dhan Daulat (Harish Shah, H, 1980)
Dhandha Gopuram (P. Chandrakumar, Mal, 1981)
Dhandhal Bhatjiche Gangasnaan (**Dadasaheb Phalke**, St, 1917)
Dhandhora (Charlie, H, 1941)
Dhania Munia (A.A. Darpan, Bh, 1991)
Dhani-Lugai (Adarsh, R, 1964)
Dhanna Bhagat (**Kidar Sharma**, H, 1945)
Dhanraj Tamang (Piyush Bose, B, 1978)
Dhanurbhanga *see* Janaki Swayamvar
Dhanwale (Ramanlal Desai, H, 1948)
Dhanwan (*aka* Mazdoor Ki Beti: **Premankur Atorthy**, H, 1937)
Dhanwan (**V.M. Vyas**, H, 1946)
Dhanwan (Surendra Mohan, H, 1981)
Dhanwan (**K. Vishwanath**, H, 1993)
Dhanya (**Fazil**, Mal, 1981)
Dhanya Te Santaji Dhanaji (**Dinkar D. Patil**, Mar, 1968)
Dhanyavaad (**Gajanan Jagirdar**, H, 1948)
Dhanyi Meye (Aravind Mukherjee, B, 1971)
Dhara (V.N. Gajarajan, K, 1983)
Dharam *see* Dharma
Dharam Adhikari (**K. Raghavendra Rao**, H, 1986)
Dharam Aur Kanoon (Joshi, H, 1984)
Dharam Bhai (Shantilal Soni, R, 1987)
Dharamjeet (**Sukhdev Ahluwalia**, P, 1975)
Dharam Ka Insaaf (Sunil Nayyar, H, 1993)
Dharam Kanta (Sultan Ahmed, H, 1982)
Dharam Karam (*aka* Duty and Deed: Randhir Kapoor, H, 1975)
Dharam Ki Devi (*aka* Suhaag Ki Raat: Hiren Bose, H, 1935)
Dharam-Sankat (N.D. Kothari, H, 1991)
Dharam Shatru (Harmesh Malhotra, H, 1985)
Dharam Veer (**Manmohan Desai**, H, 1977)
Dharam Yuddh (TV: **Rahul Rawail**, H, 1988)
Dharamyudh (Sudarshan Nag, H, 1988)
Dharanimandala Madhyadolage (**Puttanna Kanagal**, K, 1983)
Dharavi (Sudhir Mishra, H, 1991)
Dhare Aalua (Saghir Ahmed, O, 1984)
Dharisanam (V.T. Arasu, Tam, 1970)
Dharitri (**Nitai Palit**, O, 1972)
Dharja Donga (Manivannan, Tel, 1985)
Dharma *see* Dharam
Dharma (Ramnik Desai, H, 1945)
Dharma (Chand, H, 1973)
Dharma (K.S.R. Doss, Tel, 1990)
Dharma Bandhan (*aka* Duty: **J.P. Advani**, H, 1940)
Dharma Chakram (Laxmi Deepak, Tel, 1980)
Dharma Dari Tappitu (Bhandaru Giribabu, K, 1982)
Dharmadatha (A. Sanjeevi, Tel, 1970)
Dharma Devadai (S.P. Muthuraman, Tam, 1986)
Dharma Devan (A.L.N. Mohan, Tam, 1989)
Dharmadevata (**P. Pullaiah**, Tel/Tam, 1952)
Dharmadurai (Rajasekharan, Tam, 1990)
Dharmakai (Bhaben Das, A, 1977)
Dharmakanya (Madhav Shinde, Mar, 1968)
Dharmakartha (K.V.R., Tam, 1984)
Dharmakshetre Kurukshetre (**Kunchako**, Mal, 1975)
Dharmam (R. Thyagarajan, Tam, 1986)
Dharmam Dari Thappita (Srinivasa Reddy, Tel, 1980)
Dharmam Engay (A.C. Trilogchander, Tam, 1972)
Dharmam Thalai Kakum (M.A. Thirumugham, Tam, 1963)
Dharmam Vellum (K. Rangaraj, Tam, 1989)
Dharmane Jayam (**Kadaru Nagabhushanam**, Tel, 1960)
Dharmangada (**H.V. Babu**, Tel, 1949)
Dharmapatni (**Jyotish Bannerjee**, St, 1926)
Dharmapatni (**A. Narayanan**, St, 1929)
Dharmapatni (C.K. Rajagopal, Tam, 1935)
Dharmapatni (**P. Pullaiah**, Tel/Tam, 1940)
Dharmapatni (**Ramchandra Thakur**, H, 1953)
Dharmapatni (Govind Ghanekar, Mar, 1968)
Dharmapatni (B.A. Subba Rao, Tel, 1969)
Dharmapatni (Aruru Pattabhi, K, 1972)
Dharmapatni (Ameerjan, Tam, 1986)
Dharmapatni (T. Prasad, Tel, 1987)
Dharmapatni (M.S. Rajashekhar, K, 1988)
Dharma Peetam Daddarillindi (**Dasari Narayana Rao**, Tel, 1986)
Dharma Poratam (B. Subba Rao, Tel, 1983)
Dharmapuri Rahasyam (*aka* The Traitor: G.R. Sethi, Tam, 1938)
Dharmaputra (**Yash Chopra**, H, 1961)
Dharma Raja (M.A. Thirumugham, Tam, 1980)
Dharmaseelan (Cheyyar V. Ravi, Tam, 1993)
Dharmasere (**Puttanna Kanagal**, K, 1979)
Dharmasethram (A. Kodandarami Reddy, Tel, 1992)
Dharma Teja (Perala, Tel, 1988)
Dharmathin Thalaivan (S.P. Muthuraman, Tam, 1988)
Dharmathmudu (B. Bhaskara Rao, Tel, 1983)
Dharmatma (**V. Shantaram**, Mar/H, 1935)
Dharmatma (Feroz Khan, H, 1975)
Dharmatma (?, Shrisarvashakti Prod, Tel, 1988)
Dharmatma (A. Jagannathan, K, 1988)
Dharma Vadi (K.B. Tilak, Tel, 1982)
Dharmaveer (**Master Vinayak**, Mar/H, 1937)
Dharmaveeran (B. Sampathkumar, Tam, 1941)
Dharma Vijay *see* Bhakta Vidur
Dharma Vijaya (N. Jagannath, K, 1959)
Dharma Yuddha (A.T. Raghu, K, 1983)
Dharma Yuddham (**A. Vincent**, Mal, 1973)
Dharma Yuddham (R.C. Sakthi, Tam, 1979)
Dharmi Balak *see* Garib Ki Duniya
Dharmi Daku (*aka* Charitable Outlaw: Jeetendra Mehta, St, 1931)
Dharmo (**Krishnakant**, G, 1982)
Dharti (Manibhai Vyas, H, 1946)
Dharti (**C.V. Sridhar**, H, 1970)
Dharti Akash (?, Shivani Films, H, 1987)
Dhartichi Lekre (Neelkanth Magdoom, Mar, 1970)
Dharti Kaamp (*aka* Thunder: **Harshadrai Mehta**, St, 1931)
Dharti Kaamp (Saqi, H, 1934)
Dharti Kahe Pukar Ke (Dulal Guha, H, 1969)
Dharti Ke Lal (**K.A. Abbas**, H, 1946)
Dharti Ki Awaaz (K.D. Singh, Bh/H, 1987)
Dharti Ki God Mein (Kewal Mishra, H, 1971)
Dharti Ki Pukaar (**K.A. Abbas**, H, 1967)
Dharti Maiya (Qamar Naqvi, Bh, 1981)
Dharti Mata *see* **Desher Mati**
Dharti Mata (**Nanabhai Bhatt**, G, 1976)
Dhartina Ami (Jashubhai Trivedi, G, 1984)
Dhartina Chhoru (Babubhai Thakar, G, 1970)
Dhartiputra (Iqbal Durrani, H, 1993)
Dharti Saddi Ma (**Surinder Singh**, P, 1976)
Dharti Veeran Di (Baldev R, Jhingan, P, 1965)
Dhatri Debata (**Kaliprasad Ghosh**, B, 1948)
Dhat Tere Ki (Meraj, H, 1983)
Dhauligiri Shantistupa (**Nirad Mahapatra**, O, 1975)
Dhavani Kanavugal *see* Thavani Kanavukal
Dheem Tharikita Thom (**Priyadarshan**, Mal, 1986)
Dheera (Joshi, Mal, 1982)
Dheeran (?, Mal, 1987)
Dhee Rani (Balbir Begumpari, P, 1988)
Dheere Sameere Yamuna Theere (**Madhu**, Mal, 1976)
Dher Chalaki Jin Kara (**Datta Keshav**, Bh, 1971)
Dher Ni Chhokri *see* **Maharachi Por**
Dheuer Pare Dheu (Bhupendra Kumar Sanyal/Smritish Guha-Thakurta, B, 1962)
Dhiraj (**Chaturbhuj Doshi**, H, 1942)
Dhobi Doctor (**Phani Majumdar**, H, 1954)
Dhokhebaaz (R. Shivraj, H, 1946)
Dhokhebaaz (Chand, H, 1984)
Dholak (**Roop K. Shorey**, H, 1951)
Dhola Maru (**N.R. Acharya**, H, 1956)
Dhola Maru (**Mehul Kumar**, G, 1983)
Dhola Marwan (Manibhai Vyas, R, 1964)
Dholer Raja Khirode Natta (**Buddhadev Dasgupta**, B, 1973)
Dholi (**Mehul Kumar**, G, 1982)
Dhol Jani (Rajesh Nanda, P, 1962)
Dhondi Dhondi Pani De (Arun Karnataki, Mar, 1986)
Dhongee (Ashok Roy, H, 1976)
Dhool Ka Phool (**Yash Chopra**, H, 1959)
Dhool Parakudhu (K. Hariharan, Tam, 1993)
Dhoomam (Chandrasekharan Thampi, Mal, 1984)
Dhoom Dhaam (Rajaram, H, 1949)
Dhoomketu *see* Impostor *or* Dhumketu
Dhoomketu (*aka* The Comet: **Sundarrao Nadkarni**, St, 1930)
Dhoomketu (*aka* The Comet: **Homi Wadia**, H, 1949)
Dhoomketu (Gouranga Prasad Basu, B, 1958)
Dhoomketu (Gopal Krishnan, H, 1985)
Dhoop Chhaon/Bhagya Chakra (**Nitin Bose**, H/B, 1935)
Dhoop Chhaon (S.M. Raza, H, 1954)
Dhoop Chhaon (Prahlad Sharma, H, 1977)
Dhoop Chhaya (Chitta Bose, B, 1962)
Dhoorau Kondalu (Prasad Nallam Reddy, Tel, 1987)
Dhoti Lota Aur Chowpatti (Mohan Choti, H, 1975)
Dhrupad (**Mani Kaul**, H, 1982)
Dhruva (**Jyotish Bannerjee**, H, 1933)
Dhruva (Satyen Dey, B, 1934)
Dhruva (**R. Padmanabhan**, Tam, 1935)
Dhruva (**C. Pullaiah**, Tel, 1936)
Dhruva (D.K. Kale, Mar, 1938)
Dhruva (Chandrasekhar Bose, B, 1953)
Dhruva Charitra (Eugenio De Liguoro, St, 1921)
Dhruva Charitra (**Jyotish Bannerjee**, H, 1933)
Dhruva Kumar *see* **Bhakta Dhruva**
Dhruva Kumar (K.P. Bhave, Mar/H, 1938)
Dhruvam (Joshi, Mal, 1992)
Dhruvanakshatram (Y. Nageshwara Rao, Tel, 1989)
Dhruvanakshatram (Raja, Tam, 1993)
Dhruva Narayan (?, British India Film, St, 1930)
Dhruva Sangamam (**Sasikumar**, Mal, 1981)
Dhruva Tare (M.S. Rajashekhar, K, 1985)
Dhuaan (R.L. Malhotra, H, 1953)
Dhuaan (Dulal Guha, H, 1981)
Dhuen Ki Lakeer (**Kishore Sahu**, H, 1974)
Dhular Dharani (Ardhendu Sen, B, 1956)
Dhuli (Pinaki Mukherjee, B, 1954)
Dhumdhadaka (Mahesh Kothare, Mar, 1985)
Dhumketu (R.N. Jayagopal, K, 1968)
Dhumrapan Leela (**Dadasaheb Phalke**, St, 1916)
Dhumuha (**Phani Sarma**, A, 1957)
Dhun (Kumar, H, 1953)
Dhund (**B.R. Chopra**, H, 1973)
Dhuwandhaar (Sukumar Chatterjee, H, 1935)
Dhwani (A.T. Abu, Mal, 1988)
Dhyanoo Bhagat *see* Bhakti Mein Shakti
Dial 100 (S. Ramanathan, H, 1982)
Dial 2244 (R.M. Krishnaswamy, Mal, 1968)
Diamond King (?, Chitrabharati, H, 1961)
Diamond Necklace *see* Kanthahaar
Diamond Queen (**Homi Wadia**, H, 1940)
Diary of a Racehorse (**Jahnu Barua**, E, 1974)
Diba Ratrir Kabya (Bimal Bhowmick/Narayan Chakraborty, B, 1970)
Didh Shahane (Raja Bargir, Mar, 1979)
Didi/President (**Nitin Bose**, B/H, 1937)
Didi (Mukund Masurekar, H, 1948)
Didi (**K. Narayan Kale**, H, 1959)
Didi (Swadesh Sarkar, B, 1984)
Digambara Swamiyar (**T.R. Sundaram**, Tam, 1950)
Digbhranta (**Sushil Majumdar**, B, 1950)
Digvijay (Asooji, St, 1931)
Digvijaya (Somu, K, 1987)
Digvijayam (M. Krishnan Nair, Mal, 1980)
Dikadari (Tulsi Lahiri, B, 1935)

Dikkatra Parvathi (**Singeetham Srinivasa Rao**, Tam, 1973)
Dikri Chali Sasariye (Dilip Bhatt, G, 1985)
Dikri Ne Gaay Dore Tyan Jaay (Shantilal Soni, G, 1979)
Diksha *see* Deeksha
Dikshul (**Premankur Atorthy**, B, 1943)
Dil (S.F. Hasnain, H, 1946)
Dil (Indra Kumar, H, 1990)
Dil Aakhir Dil Hai (Esmayeel Shroff, H, 1982)
Dil Apna Aur Preet Parayi (**Kishore Sahu**, H, 1960)
Dil Apna Aur Preet Parayi (K. Vinod, H, 1993)
Dilara (**J.P. Advani**, H, 1934)
Dil Aram (**Nanubhai Desai**, St, 1926)
Dil Ashna Hai (**Hema Malini**, H, 1991)
Dil Aur Deewar (**K. Bapaiah**, H, 1978)
Dil Aur Mohabbat (Anand Dutta, H, 1968)
Dil Aur Patthar (Kanak Mishra, H, 1977)
Dilawar (**R.G. Torney**, St, 1931)
Dilawar (**M. Bhavnani**, H, 1936)
Dilawar (Harish Khatri, H, 1966)
Dilawar (Ramesh Bedi, H, 1984)
Dilbar (Rajaram, H, 1951)
Dil Bhi Tera Hum Bhi Tere (A. Hingo, H, 1960)
Dildaar (*aka* Gypsy Girl: Ramakant-Gharekhan, St, 1933)
Dildaar *see* Gypsy Girl
Dildaar (R. Shivraj, H, 1947)
Dildaar (**K. Bapaiah**, H, 1977)
Dil Dariya (Tarapada Saha, St, 1930)
Dil Daulat Duniya (P.N. Arora, H, 1972)
Dil Deke Dekho (**Nasir Hussain**, H, 1959)
Dil Diwana (**Narendra Bedi**, H, 1974)
Dil Diya Dard Liya (**A.R. Kardar**, H, 1966)
Dil-e-Dilar (*aka* Stunt King: Haribhai Desai, St, 1932)
Dil Ek Mandir (**C.V. Sridhar**, H, 1963)
Dil-e-Nadaan (**A.R. Kardar**, H, 1953)
Dil-e-Nadaan (**C.V. Sridhar**, H, 1981)
Diler (K.S.R. Doss, H, 1979)
Diler Daku (*aka* Thunderbolt: **J.B.H. Wadia/Homi Wadia**, St, 1931)
Diler Daku (Noshir Engineer, H, 1957)
Diler Dilbar *see* Amar Prem
Diler Hasina (?, Bhagwati Productions, H, 1960)
Diler Jigar (G.P. Pawar, St, 1931)
Dilfarosh (Udwadia, St, 1927)
Dilfarosh (*aka* Three Warriors: D.N. Madhok, H, 1937)
Dil Hai Betaab (K.C. Bokadia, H, 1993)
Dil Hai Ke Maanta Nahin (**Mahesh Bhatt**, H, 1991)
Dil Hi Dil Mein (Desh Gautam, H, 1981)
Dil Hi To Hai (*aka* Aulad: **Kidar Sharma**, H, 1939)
Dil Hi To Hai (P.L. Santoshi/C.L. Rawal, H, 1963)
Dil Hi To Hai (Asrani, H, 1993)
Diljala (**Bapu**, H, 1987)
Diljani (*aka* Mastana, Kunwari: **Charu Roy**, H, 1935)
Dil Ka Daku (D.N. Madhok, H, 1936)
Dil Ka Heera (Dulal Guha, H, 1979)
Dil Ka Kya Kasoor (Lawrence D'Souza, H, 1992)
Dil Ka Raja (P. Madhavan, H, 1972)
Dil Ka Saathi Dil (N. Shankaran Nair, H, 1982)
Dil Ki Awaaz (**Krishan Chander**, H, 1948)
Dil Ki Baat (*aka* Romance: **P.K. Atre**, H, 1944)
Dil Ki Baazi (Anil Ganguly, H, 1993)
Dil Ki Basti (Waheed Qureshi, H, 1949)
Dil Ki Duniya (Mazhar Khan, H, 1949)
Dil Ki Pyaas (**J.J. Madan**/Sohrab Kerawala, H, 1935)
Dil Ki Raahein (**B.R. Ishara**, H, 1973)
Dil Ki Rani (Mohan Sinha, H, 1947)
Dil Lagake Dekho (**K. Raghavendra Rao**, H, 1988)
Dillagi (**Balwant Bhatt**, H, 1942)
Dillagi (**A.R. Kardar**, H, 1949)
Dillagi (S. Bannerjee, H, 1966)
Dillagi (**Basu Chatterjee**, H, 1978)
Dilli *see* Delhi
Dilli Babu (Chitralaya Gopu, Tam, 1989)
Dilli Theke Kolkata (Sushil Ghosh, B, 1961)
Dil Ne Phir Yaad Kiya (C.L. Rawal, H, 1966)
Dil Ne Pukara (Mohan, H, 1967)
Dilruba *see* Neelam
Dilruba (*aka* Belle of Bombay: **Harshadrai Mehta**, St, 1929)
Dilruba (Dwarka Khosla, H, 1950)
Dilruba (Mohammed A. Hussain, H, 1967)
Dilruba Daku (*aka* The Amazon: **J.B.H. Wadia**, St, 1933)
Dilruba Tangewali (S.R. Pratap, H, 1987)
Dil Se Mile Dil (Bhishm Kohli, H, 1978)
Dil Tera Aashiq (Lawrence D'Souza, H, 1993)
Dil Tera Diwana (**B.R. Panthulu**, H, 1962)
Dil Tujhko Diya (Rakesh Kumar, H, 1985)
Dilwala (K. Murli Mohana Rao, H, 1986)
Dilwale (Ramanlal Desai, H, 1948)
Dilwale Dulhania Le Jayenge (Rajinder Singh Atish, H, 1980)
Dilwale Kabhi Na Hare (V. Menon, H, 1992)
Dimple (Vijay Singh, H, 1977)
Dinabandhu (M.L. Bandal, Tel, 1942)
Din Amader (**Agradoot**, B, 1977)
Dinanter Alo (Mangal Chakraborty, B, 1965)
Dinarathrangal (Joshi, Mal, 1988)
Din Dahade (Yash Chouhan, H, 1990)
Diner Par Din (Jyotirmoy Roy, B, 1949)
Din Jay (Manu Sen, B, 1983)
Din Raat (**Roop K. Shorey**, H, 1945)
Dipshikha (Amal Nag, B, 1988)
Director (S. Shafaqat, H, 1947)
Discarded Love *see* Bewafa Ashq
Discipline on the Road (**Vishnu Mathur**, E, 1975)
Disco Dancer (B. Subhash, H, 1982)
Disco Disco (**I.V. Sasi**, Tel, 1984)
Disco King (T. Prasad, Tel, 1984)
Discovery of India *see* Bharat Ek Khoj
Disha (**Sai Paranjpye**, H, 1990)
Dispossessed, The *see* **Vasthuhara**
Distance, The *see* **Dooratwa** *or* Faasla
Distances *see* Dooriyan
Distant Thunder *see* **Ashani Sanket**
Dista Tasa Nasta (**Dinkar D. Patil**, Mar, 1956)
Dista Tasa Nasta (Shakir Sheikh/Ramesh Jain, Mar, 1988)
Ditiya Path (**Niranjan Pal**, B, 1940)
Di Vaale Ee Dikra (Kishore Vyas, G, 1982)
Divadandi (**Balwant Bhatt**, G, 1950)
Divine Dowry *see* Mrignayani
Divine Lady *see* **Radha Rani** *or* Meri Mashuq
Divine Lovers *see* Mahiari
Divine Lute *see* Madhu Bansari
Divine Plan, The *see* **Chhatrabhang**
Divine Punishment, The *see* Desh Na Dushman
Divine Sabre *see* Daivi Khadga
Divine Sacrifice *see* Keemti Qurbani
Divine Treasure *see* Daivi Khajina
Divinity *see* **Devatha**
Divorce *see* **Talaaq**
Divorce (N.D. Kothari, H, 1982)
Divya Darshanam (**Sasikumar**, Mal, 1973)
Divyashakti (Sameer Malkan, H, 1993)
Diwali (**Jayant Desai**, H, 1940)
Diwali Ki Raat (Deepak Asha, H, 1956)
Diwana (**A.R. Kardar**, H, 1952)
Diwana (**Mahesh Kaul**, H, 1967)
Diwana (Raj Kanwar, H, 1992)
Diwana Mujhsa Nahin (Y. Nageshwara Rao, H, 1990)
Diwana Tere Naam Ka (Gautam Bhatia, H, 1987)
Diwan Bahadur (**T.R. Sundaram**, Tam, 1943)
Diwan Bhamasha (*aka* Lion of Mewar: **M. Bhavnani**, St, 1926)
Diwani (*aka* Tapasi: D.N. Madhok, H, 1934)
Diwani (Y.D. Sarpotdar, H, 1947)
Diwani Dilbar (*aka* My Darling: **Chandulal Shah**?, St, 1930)
Diwani Duniya *see* Rang Bhoomi
Diwani Duniya (*aka* Underworld: **Naval Gandhi**, St, 1931)
Diwanji (G.K. Desai, H, 1950)
Diwano (*aka* All for Love: **Nagendra Majumdar**, St, 1931)
Diyar Bhojai (Sushil Vyas, G, 1984)
Diyarvatu (Mulraj Rajda, G, 1980)
Dnyanba Tukaram (V. Avadhoot, Mar, 1958)
Do Aankhen (Ajay Biswas, H, 1974)
Do Aankhen Barah Haath (**V. Shantaram**, H, 1957)
Do Admi (Dwarka Khosla, H, 1960)
Do Anjaane (Dulal Guha, H, 1976)
Do Auratein (*aka* Two Women: **Moti Gidwani**, H, 1937)
Do Aur Do Paanch (Rakesh Kumar, H, 1980)
Do Baatein (**H.S. Rawail**, H, 1949)
Do Bachche Dus Haath (K. Parvez, H, 1972)
Do Badan (**Raj Khosla**, H, 1966)
Do Badmash (*aka* Two Impostors: **Jayant Desai**, H, 1932)
Do Bahadur (Baburao, H, 1953)
Do Behnen (*aka* Phool Aur Kaanta: Kedar Kapoor, H, 1959)
Do Bhai (Munshi Dil, H, 1947)
Do Bhai (**Vishram Bedekar**, H, 1961)
Do Bhai (Brij Sadanah, H, 1969)
Do Bigha Zameen (**Bimal Roy**, H, 1953)
Do Boond Pani (**K.A. Abbas**, H, 1971)
Do Chattane (G.H. Sareen, H, 1974)
Do Chehre (Kewal Mishra, H, 1977)
Do Chor (Padmanabh, H, 1972)
Doctor (**Phani Majumdar**, B, 1940)
Doctor (Subodh Mitra, H, 1941)
Doctor (M.S. Mani, Mal, 1963)
Doctoramma (Sournam, Tam, 1974)
Dr Ambedkar (Bharath, Tel, 1992)
Dr Anand (V. Madhusudhana Rao, Tel, 1966)
Dr Babasaheb Ambedkar *see* Bhim Garjana
Dr Babasaheb Ambedkar (**Jabbar Patel**, E, 1991)
Dr Babu (T. Lenin Babu, Tel, 1973)
Dr Bangaru (?, Saraswathi Films, Tam, 1940)
Dr Bezbarua (**Brojen Barua**, A, 1969)
Dr Bhawani (B. Gopal, Tel, 1989)
Dr Chakravarthi (**Adurthi Subba Rao**, Tel, 1964)
Doctor Cineactor (**Vijayanirmala**, Tel, 1982)
Doctorgari Abbayi (P.N. Ramachandra Rao, Tel, 1988)
Dr Iqbal (**K.A. Abbas**, H, 1978)
Dr Kotnis Ki Amar Kahani (**V. Shantaram**, H, 1946)
Doctor Krishna (Phani Ramchandra, K, 1989)
Dr Kumar (Kishore Sharma, H, 1944)
Dr Madhurika (**Sarvottam Badami**, H, 1935)
Doctor Pagal (**Suchet Singh**, St, 1920)
Doctor Rekha (Khalil Dhantejvi, G, 1977)
Dr Savithri (R.M. Krishnaswamy, Tam, 1955)
Dr Shaitan (Shriram, H, 1960)
Doctor Siva (A.C. Trilogchander, Tam, 1975)
Dr Vidya (Rajendra Bhatia, H, 1962)
Dr X (B. Gupta, H, 1970)
Dr Z (Jal, H, 1959)
Doddamane Estate (C. Chandrasekhar, K, 1980)
Do Dhari Talwar *see* Be Dhari Talwar
Dodh Dahyo (Subhash Shah, G, 1983)
Do Dil (Jagdish Sethi, H, 1947)
Do Dil (**Hrishikesh Mukherjee**, H, 1965)
Do Dil Diwane (C.V. Rajendran, H, 1981)
Do Dilon Ki Dastaan (Pradeep Kumar, H, 1966)
Do Dilon Ki Dastaan (A.C. Trilogchander, H, 1984)
Do Dilwale (*aka* Ek Dil Do Diwane: Mehmood, H, 1977)
Do Dishayen (Dulal Guha, H, 1982)
Do Diwane/Be Kharab Jan (**Chimanlal Luhar**, H/G, 1936)
Do Dooni Char (Debu Sen, H, 1968)
Do Dost *see* Prem Ki Jyot
Do Dost (K. Anand, H, 1960)
Do Dulhe (K.J. Mahadevan, H, 1955)
Do Dushman (Mohammed Hussain, H, 1967)
Do Gaz Zameen Ke Neeche (Tulsi/Shyam **Ramsay**, H, 1972)
Do Ghadi Ki Mauj (**Homi Master**, H, 1935)
Do Gulab (**Durai**, H, 1983)
Do Gunde (**V.M. Vyas**, H, 1959)
Do Haath Sau Bandooken (Saraswati Kumar, H, 1974)
Do Hanson Ka Joda (Anup Malik, H, 1992)
Do Hawaldar (Kedar Kapoor, H, 1979)
Do Jasoos (Naresh Kumar/Karaikudi Narayanan, H, 1975)
Do Jhooth (Jitu Thakur, H, 1975)
Do Juari (Jambu, H, 1974)
Do Kaliyan *see* Balidan
Do Kaliyan (**Krishnan-Panju**, H, 1968)
Do Khiladi (Jugal Kishore, H, 1976)
Dokhtare Lor Ya Irane Diruz Va Emruz *see* Dukhtar-e-Lur
Do Lachhiyan (Jugal Kishore, P, 1960)
Do Ladke Dono Kadke (**Basu Chatterjee**, H, 1978)
Do Ladkiyan (**K.P. Atma**, H, 1976)
Dolgobinder Karcha (Sarathi, B, 1966)
Doli (S.K. Ojha, H, 1947)
Doli (**Adurthi Subba Rao**, H, 1969)
Dolls of Clay *see* Mitti Ka Putla
Dolna (Partha Prathim Choudhury, B, 1965)
Dolonchapa (Sujit Guha, B, 1987)
Dolti Naiya (Dhrupad Rai, H, 1934)
Dolti Naiya (Mirza Musharraf, H, 1950)
Do Madari (Mohan Bhakri, P, 1983)
Do Mastane (Harish, H, 1958)
Do Matwale (Kamran, H, 1966)
Do Matwale (Ajay Kashyap, H, 1991)
Dombara Krishna (H.M.K. Murthy, K, 1979)
Do Musafir (Devendra Goel, H, 1978)
Don (Chandra Barot, H, 1978)
Do Naina (M. Bhatia, H, 1947)
Don Baika Phajiti Aika (**Anant Mane**, Mar, 1982)
Donga (A. Kodandarami Reddy, Tel, 1985)
Dongagaru Swagatham (G. Rammohan Rao, Tel, 1987)
Donga Kapuram (Kodi Ramakrishna, Tel, 1988)
Donga Kollu (Vijaya Bapineedu, Tel, 1988)
Dongala Dopidi (M. Mallikarjuna Rao, Tel, 1978)
Dongalaku Donga (K.S.R. Doss, Tel, 1977)
Dongalaku Saval (K.S.R. Doss, Tel, 1979)
Dongala Veta (K.S.R. Doss, Tel, 1978)
Dongalo Dora (Chengaiah, Tel, 1957)
Dongalo Dora (Vijaya Bapineedu, Tel, 1985)
Dongalu Baboi Dongalu (K.S.R. Doss, Tel, 1984)
Dongalunnaru Jagratha/Thirudargal Jagrathi (**Bhimavarapu Narasimha Rao**, Tel/Tam, 1958)
Dongalunnaru Jagratha (Sathya Reddy, Tel, 1992)
Donga Mogudu (A. Kodandarami Reddy, Tel, 1987)
Donga Pelli (Raviraja Pinisetty, Tel, 1988)
Donga Police (K.S. Prakash, Tel, 1992)
Donga Ramudu (**K.V. Reddy**, Tel, 1955)
Donga Ramudu (**K. Raghavendra Rao**, Tel, 1988)
Dongarchi Maina (**Anant Mane**, Mar, 1969)
Don Ghadicha Dav (**Anant Mane**, Mar, 1958)
Dongoduchhadu (Kodi Ramakrishna, Tel, 1987)
Donhi Gharcha Pahuna (**Gajanan Jagirdar**, Mar, 1971)
Donkey in a Brahmin Village *see* **Agraharathil Kazhuthai**
Don't Cry for Salim the Lame *see* **Salim Langde Pe Mat Ro**
Don't Pinch the Heart *see* Nenjathai Killathey
Do Number Ke Ameer (P.D. Shenoy, H, 1974)
Doodh Bhaat (Ram Gabale, Mar, 1952)
Doodh Ka Karz (Ashok Gaikwad, H, 1990)
Dooja Vivah (Atul Bhogal, P, 1984)
Dooj Ka Chand (**Nitin Bose**, H, 1964)
Doomed Soul *see* Kangal Qaidi
Doom of the Yadavas *see* Yadav Vinas
Doongar Ro Bhed (**Kantilal Rathod**, R, 1985)
Doorada Betta (Siddalingaiah, K, 1973)
Dooram Adhigamillai (Robert Rajasekharan, Tam, 1983)
Dooram Arike (Sharif, Mal, 1980)
Doorathu Idhi Muzhakkam (K. Vijayan, Tam, 1980)
Dooratwa (**Buddhadev Dasgupta**, B, 1978)
Door Chalein (**Phani Majumdar**, H, 1946)
Door Desh (Ambarish Sangal, H, 1986)
Door Die (*aka* Zindagi Ya Maut: Harbans, H, 1944)

Door Door Paas Paas (Darshan Laad, H, 1985)
Doore Doore Koodu Kottam (**Sibi Malayil**, Mal, 1986)
Door Gagan Ki Chhaon Mein (**Kishore Kumar**, H, 1964)
Doorie (?, Shahbaaz Films, H, 1989)
Dooriyan (*aka* Distances: Bhimsain, H, 1979)
Door Ka Rahi (**Kishore Kumar**, H, 1971)
Door Ki Awaz (Devendra Goel, H, 1964)
Door Nahin Manzil (Hari Valia, H, 1973)
Door Wadiyon Mein Kahin (**Kishore Kumar**, H, 1982)
Doosra Admi (Ramesh Talwar, H, 1977)
Doosri Dulhan (Lekh Tandon, H, 1983)
Doosri Seeta (Gogi Anand, H, 1974)
Doosri Shadi (Ram Daryani, H, 1947)
Do Pal (Ravi Rai, H, 1991)
Do Phool (**A.R. Kardar**, H, 1958)
Do Phool (S. Ramanathan, H, 1973)
Dopidi Dongalu (S.A. Chandrasekharan, Tel, 1984)
Do Posti (Chaman Nillay, P, 1981)
Do Premi (**Raj Khosla**, H, 1980)
Do Qaidi (Ajay Kashyap, H, 1989)
Dora (**Prashanta Nanda**, O, 1984)
Do Raaste (**Raj Khosla**, H, 1969)
Dora Babu (**T. Rama Rao**, Tel, 1974)
Dora Bidda (Sath Dhavala, Ananthalakshmi Films, Tel, 1986)
Doragaru Intilo Dongalu (Kodi Ramakrishna, Tel, 1988)
Do Raha (Bal Chhabda, H, 1952)
Do Raha (Firoz Chinoy, H, 1971)
Dorakani Donga (K.S.R. Doss, Tel, 1988)
Doralu Dongalu (K.S.R. Doss, Tel, 1976)
Dorangia Daku (*aka* Gangsters: **H.S. Rawail**, H, 1940)
Dorangi Duniya (*aka* Robes and the Rags: **S.N. Patankar**, St, 1926)
Dorangi Duniya (*aka* Merry-go-round: Pesi Karani, H, 1933)
Dorikite Dongalu (V. Subramanyam, Tel, 1965)
Dorikite Dongalu (K. Muralimohana Rao, Tel, 1989)
Do Roti (Ismail Memon, H, 1957)
Do Saudagar (M.M. Billoo, H, 1950)
Do Shatru (Kewal Mishra, H, 1976)
Do Sher (**Sukhdev Ahluwalia**, P, 1974)
Doshi (?, Dhoopchaya Films, H, 1950)
Do Shikari (Kuljit Pal, H, 1978)
Doshi Nirdoshi (Y. Nageshwara Rao, Tel, 1990)
Do Sholay (**Sukhdev Ahluwalia**, H, 1977)
Do Sitare (D.D. Kashyap, H, 1951)
Dost (Shaukat Hussain Rizvi, H, 1944)
Dost (Rajendra Sharma, H, 1954)
Dost (Dulal Guha, H, 1974)
Dost (K. Murali Mohana Rao, H, 1989)
Dostana (**Raj Khosla**, H, 1980)
Dost Asava Tar Asa (Devendra Goel, Mar, 1978)
Dost Aur Dushman (Kewal Mishra, H, 1971)
Dost Garibon Ka (C.P. Dixit, H, 1989)
Dosti (**Master Bhagwan**, H, 1946)
Dosti (**Satyen Bose**, H, 1964)
Dosti Dushmani (**T. Rama Rao**, H, 1986)
Dosti Ki Saugandh (Mohanji Prasad, H, 1993)
Dost Magarmach *see* Mudhalai
Dost Mazha Mast (Gajanan Sarpotdar, Mar, 1989)
Do Tana (Amulya Bannerjee, B, 1945)
Do Thug (B.J. Patel, H, 1970)
Do Thug (S.D. Narang, H, 1975)
Double Cross (**M. Bhavnani**, H, 1938)
Double Cross (Gogi Anand, H, 1972)
Double Face (M. Udwadia, H, 1946)
Doubt *see* Shaque
Dour (Shankar Bhattacharya, B, 1979)
Do Ustad (Tara Harish, H, 1959)
Do Ustad (S.D. Narang, H, 1982)
Do Waqt Ki Roti (?, Satyendra Films, H, 1988)
Do Yaar (Kewal Mishra, H, 1972)
Do You Know? (**Ezra Mir**, E, 1958)
Dozakh (Suhas Khandke, H, 1987)
Draupadi (**B.P. Mishra**, H, 1931)
Draupadi (Baburao Patel, H, 1944)
Draupadi Bhagya (**R.S. Prakash**, St, 1924)
Draupadi Manasamrakshanam (S. Jagannath/Ramanamurthy, Tel, 1936)
Draupadi Swayamvar (Vishnupant Divekar, St, 1922)
Draupadi Vastraharan (**Dadasaheb Phalke**, St, 1927)
Draupadi Vastraharan (W. Garcher, H, 1952)
Draupadi Vastrapaharanam (**R. Nataraja Mudaliar**, St, 1917)
Draupadi Vastrapaharanam (**A. Narayanan/R.S. Prakash**?, Tam, 1934)
Draupadi Vastrapaharanam (P.V. Rao, Tam, 1934)
Draupadi Vastrapaharanam (**H.V. Babu**, Tel, 1936)
Draupadi Veni Bandhan (*aka* Veni Bandhan, Gada Yuddha, Fall of the Kauravas: Vishnupant Divekar, St, 1922)
Dravidan (Billa Krishnamurthy, Tam, 1989)
DR Bendre (**Girish Karnad**, E, 1973)
Dream Damsel *see* Swapna Sundari
Dream Girl (Pramod Chakraborty, H, 1977)
Dreamland *see* Khwab Ki Duniya *or* Swarga Vihar
Dream of Life *see* Sansar Swapna
Dreams of Mouji Ram, The (**Govind Saraiya**, E, 1967)
Driksakshi (P.G. Vasudevan, Mal, 1973)
Drikung: A Faith in Exile (**Ramesh Sharma**, E, 1981)
Drishti (Chitta Bose, B, 1955)
Drishti (**Atul Bordoloi**, A, 1990)
Drishti (**Govind Nihalani**, H, 1990)
Drishtidaan (**Nitin Bose**, B, 1948)
Drishtidaan (Bijoy Chatterjee, H, 1988)
Drishti Jagachi Aahe Nirali (Baburao Athane, Mar, 1962)
Driver Babu (B. Subba Rao, Tel, 1986)
Driver Hanumanthu (Ravi, K, 1980)
Driver Madyapichirunnu (Subhash, Mal, 1979)
Driver Ramudu (**K. Raghavendra Rao**, Tel, 1979)
Drohi *see* Antham
Drohi (**L.V. Prasad**, Tel, 1948)
Drohi (**K. Bapaiah**, Tel, 1970)
Drohi (?, Mal, 1982)
Drought *see* **Bara**
Drought in Maharashtra (**Vishnu Mathur**, E, 1973)
Drums of Love *see* **Prem Jogan**
Drums of War, The *see* Ranabheri
Dub De Mon Kali Bole (Samir Ghosh, B, 1979)
Dudde Doddappa (**B.R. Panthulu**, K, 1966)
Du Dhara (Anami, B, 1950)
Dudubasavanna (B.V. Prasad, Tel, 1978)
Duhai (**V.M. Vyas**, H, 1943)
Dui Adhyay (Gautam Mukherjee, B, 1986)
Dui Bandhu (Amar Dutta, B, 1947)
Dui Bari (Ashim Pal, B, 1963)
Dui Bechara (Dilip Bose, B, 1960)
Dui Beyai (**Premendra Mitra**, B, 1953)
Dui Bhai (Sudhir Mukherjee, B, 1961)
Dui Bone (Chandrasekhar Bose, B, 1955)
Dui Bone (Sachin Adhikari, B, 1975)
Dui Nari (Jiban Ganguly, B, 1963)
Dui Parba (Binu Bardhan, B, 1964)
Dui Prithibi (Piyush Bose, B, 1980)
Dui Purush (Subodh Mitra, B, 1945)
Dui Purush (Sushil Mukherjee, B, 1978)
Du-Janay (**Nirmal Dey**, B, 1955)
Du-Janay (Ardhendu Chatterjee, B, 1983)
Duja Vyah (Avtar Bhogal, P, 1984)
Dukh Bhanjan Tera Naam (B.S. Thapa, P, 1972)
Dukhda Khame Ee Dikri (**Ravindra Dave**, G, 1981)
Dukh Dard (Syed Hasan, H, 1988)
Dukhe Jader Jiban Gara (Himadri Choudhury, B, 1946)
Dukhiari (*aka* Street Girl: **V.M. Vyas**, St, 1930)
Dukhiari (Manibhai Vyas, H, 1937)
Dukhiari (D.K. Ratan, H, 1948)
Dukhir Iman (**Sushil Majumdar**, B, 1954)
Dukhiyon Ki Aah *see* Aah-e-Mazluman
Dukh Sukh (Ram Daryani, H, 1942)
Dukh Sukh (Majeed Maqbool, H, 1974)
Dukhtar-e-Hind (*aka* Daughter of India, Bharati Bala; A.P. Kapur, H, 1934)
Dukhtar-e-Lur (*aka* Dokhtare Lor Ya Irane Diruz Va Emruz: **Ardeshir Irani**, Farsi, 1933)
Dulari (**Manilal Joshi**, St, 1926)
Dulari (**A.R. Kardar**, H, 1949)
Dulari Bibi (**Debaki Bose**, Urdu, 1933)
Dulha (Manibhai Vyas, H, 1946)
Dulha Bikta Hai (Anwar Pasha, H, 1981)
Dulha Dulhan (**Ravindra Dave**, H, 1964)
Dulha Ganga Paar Ke (Rajkumar Sharma, Bh, 1986)
Dulhan (**Premankur Atorthy**, H, 1938)
Dulhan (Dada Gunjal, H, 1943)
Dulhan (**V.M. Vyas**, H, 1958)
Dulhan (C.V. Rajendran, H, 1974)
Dulhan Ek Raat Ki (D.D. Kashyap, H, 1966)
Dulhan Wahi Jo Piya Man Bhaye (Lekh Tandon, H, 1977)
Dulhin (Ashokchand Jain, Bh, 1986)
Dulla Bhatti (**Roop K. Shorey**, P, 1940)
Dulla Bhatti (Baldev R. Jhingan, P, 1966)
Duniya (S.F. Hasnain, H, 1949)
Duniya (**T. Prakash Rao**, H, 1968)
Duniya (Ramesh Talwar, H, 1984)
Duniya Chalti Hai (S.S. Gaikwad, H, 1976)
Duniyadari (K.P. Shahani/Krishen Advani, H, 1948)
Duniyadari (Ram Kelkar, H, 1977)
Duniya Diwani (K.L. Kahan, H, 1943)
Duniya Ek Sarai (**Kidar Sharma**, H, 1946)
Duniya Ek Tamasha (Dwarka Khosla, H, 1942)
Duniya Gol Hai (Om Prakash, H, 1955)
Duniya Hai Dilwalon Ki (Jain, H, 1966)
Duniya Jhukti Hai (**J.B.H. Wadia**, H, 1960)
Duniya Ka Mela (Kundan Kumar, H, 1974)
Duniya Kari Salaam (**Anant Mane**, Mar, 1979)
Duniya Ki Sair *see* Around the World
Duniya Kya Hai (G.P. Pawar, H, 1938)
Duniya Kya Jaane (**C.V. Sridhar**, H, 1971)
Duniya Meri Jeb Mein (Tinnu Anand, H, 1979)
Duniya Nachegi (K. Parvez, H, 1967)
Duniya Na Mane *see* **Kunku**
Duniya Na Mane (V. Avadhoot, H, 1959)
Duniya Pagal Hai (?, Indigo Movies, H, 1987)
Duniya Rang Rangili (M. Sadiq, H, 1957)
Duniya Tumhari Hai (G.P. Pawar, H, 1942)
Dupatta (Mohinder Wahi, P, 1970)
Duranir Rong (Johns Moholia, A, 1979)
Duranta Charai (Jagannath Chatterjee, B, 1969)
Duranta Jay (Ardhendu Mukherjee, B, 1972)
Durbargati Padma (*aka* Beyond the River Padma: **Ritwik Ghatak**, B, 1971)
Durga (**Franz Osten**, H, 1939)
Durga (**Kunchako**, Mal, 1974)
Durga (Shibu Mitra, H, 1984)
Durga (**Basu Chatterjee**, H, 1989)
Durga (Ramanarayanan, Tam, 1990)
Durga Devi (Ra. Shankaran, Tam, 1977)
Durga Devi (N. Harishchandra Rao, Tel, 1983)
Durga Durgati Nashini (Parimal Bhattacharya, B, 1981)
Durga Maa (K.S. Rami Reddy, H, 1986)
Durga Mata *see* **Mahishasura Mardini**
Durga Puja (**Dhirubhai Desai**, H, 1954)
Durga Puja (Adarsh, H, 1962)
Durgashtami (Geethapriya, K, 1991)
Durgesh Nandini (**Priyanath Ganguly**, St, 1927)
Durgesh Nandini (**Amar Mullick**, B, 1951)
Durgesh Nandini (B. Mitra, H, 1956)
During and After Air Raid (**Mani Kaul**, E, 1970)
Durlav Janma (Prafulla Chakraborty, B, 1955)
Durvas Garvabhangam *see* Bhakta Vatsalam
Durvas Shaap (*aka* Curse of Durvas: **S.N. Patankar**, St, 1923)
Dushkal *see* **Bara**
Dushman *see* Katto Dushman
Dushman/Jiban Maran (**Nitin Bose**, H/B, 1938)
Dushman (Raj Rishi, H, 1957)
Dushman (Dulal Guha, H, 1971)
Dushman (**Shakti Samanta**, H, 1990)
Dushman Devata (Anil Ganguly, H, 1991)
Dushman-e-Iman (**Homi Master**, St, 1931)
Dushmani (S. Upendra, H, 1950)
Dushmani (Dinesh Saxena, H, 1982)
Dushmani Di Aag (Virendra, P, 1990)
Dushman Ki Raat (*aka* Night of Terror: Balasaheb Yadav, St, 1931)
Dushman Ni Dikri *see* Kashmeera
Dushman Zamana (Jagdish Sharma, H, 1992)
Dust the Killer (**Govind Saraiya**, E, 1962)
Dustu Mishti (Rajkumar Roy Choudhury, B, 1981)
Dustu Prajapati (Shyam Chakraborty, B, 1967)
Duti Mon (Piyush Basu, B, 1970)
Duti Pata (Bimal Roy, B, 1983)
Duty *see* Dharma Bandhan
Duty (Ravi Nagaich, H, 1986)
Duty and Deed *see* Dharam Karam
Duvidha (**Mani Kaul**, H, 1973)
Dwairath (Bijon Sen, B, 1950)
Dwanda (**Hemen Gupta**, B, 1943)
Dwanda Yuddham (C.V. Hariharan, Mal, 1981)
Dwarkadheesh (Natwar Shyam, H, 1956)
Dweep (**Ramu Kariat**, Mal, 1976)
Dwibachan (TV: **Utpalendu Chakraborty**, B, 1989)
Dwipantar (**Dhiren Ganguly**, B, 1936)
Dwiper Nam Tiya Rang (**Gurudas Bagchi**, B, 1963)
Dynamite *see* Fauladi Jigar
Dynamite (*aka* Kiske Sajan: **Chimanlal Luhar**, H, 1938)

E

Eagle (Ambili, Mal, 1991)
Earth and Water (**P.V. Pathy**, E, 1956)
Easy Victim *see* Bhola Shikar
Ebbani Karagitu (K.V. Jayaram, K, 1983)
Echil Iravugal (A.S. Prakasham, Tam, 1982)
Eclipse, The *see* **Grahana**
Ecology of the Western Ghats (**Suresh Heblikar**, E, 1984)
Edadugula Anubandham (Laxmi Deepak, Tel, 1979)
Edadugula Bandham (**Dasari Narayana Rao**, Tel, 1985)
Edakallu Guddada Mele (**Puttanna Kanagal**, K, 1973)
Edantastulameda (**Dasari Narayana Rao**, Tel, 1980)
Edavazhiyile Pucha Mindappucha (**T. Hariharan**, Mal, 1979)
Edavellakku Sesham (Joshi, Mal, 1984)
Eden Thottam (Chandrakumar, Mal, 1980)
Edeyuru Siddhalingeshwara/Siddhalingeshwara Mahima (**Hunsur Krishnamurthy**, K/Tel, 1981)
Edhirkatru (Amirjan, Tam, 1990)
Edi Nijam (**S. Balachander**, Tel, 1956)
Edi Nyayam Edi Dharmam (**Bapu**, Tel, 1982)
Edi Papam Edi Punyam (K. Vasu, Tel, 1979)
Edo Saritha (**K. Balachander**, Tel, 1979)
Educated Actress (?, Imperial Film, H, 1938)
Educated Wife *see* **Bhaneli Bhamini** *or* Grihalakshmi
Educated Wife (?, **Madan** Theatres, H, 1932)
Edu Kondalaswamy (**K. Kameshwara Rao**, Tel, 1991)
Eduppar Kayi Pillai (K. Vijayan, Tam, 1975)
Edureetha (B.S. Narayana, Tel, 1963)
Edureetha (V. Madhusudhana Rao, Tel, 1977)
Edurinti Mogudu Pakkinti Pellam (Relangi Narasimha Rao, Tel, 1991)
Eduruleni Manishi (**K. Bapaiah**, Tel, 1975)
Eduruleni Monagalu (K. Vasu, Tel, 1984)
Edurumaneli Ganda Pakkadmaneli Hendthi (Relangi Narasimha Rao, K, 1992)
Edward's Anti-malarial Specific (**Hiralal Sen**, St, 1905)
Ee Bandha Anubandha (Janakiram, K, 1987)
Ee Chaduvulu Makodu (Vejalla Satyanarayana, Tel, 1984)
Ee Charika (?, Shri Sathya Srinivasa Movies, Tel, 1986)
Ee Charithra Ee Sivato (Vejalla Satyanarayana, Tel, 1982)
Ee Desamlukaroju (Vejalla Satyanarayana, Tel, 1983)

Eedu Jodu (K.B. Tilak, Tel, 1963)
Ee Ganam Marakkumo (N. Shankaran Nair, Mal, 1978)
Ee Jeeva Ninagagi (V. Somashekhar, K, 1986)
Ee Kaikalil (?, Prekshaka, Mal, 1986)
Ee Kalam Dampathulu (**Yoganand**, Tel, 1975)
Ee Kalam Katha (Raja Sridhar, Tel, 1984)
Ee Kalapu Pillalu (Laxmi Deepak, Tel, 1975)
Ee Kanni Koodi (**K.G. George**, Mal, 1990)
Ee Lokam Ivide Kure Manushyar (P.G. Vishwambaran, Mal, 1985)
Ee Manohara Theeram (**I.V. Sasi**, Mal, 1978)
Ee Nadu (**I.V. Sasi**, Mal, 1982)
Ee Nadu (P. Sambhasiva Rao, Tel, 1982)
Eenati Bandham Yenatido (K.S.R. Doss, Tel, 1977)
Een Meen Sadeteen (Balkrishna, Mar, 1954)
Ee Nootandile Maharogam (?, Sastha Prod, Mal, 1987)
Eent Ka Jawab Patthar (Pachhi, H, 1982)
Eenum (**B.G. Bharathan**, Mal, 1983)
Ee Pillaku Pellavuthunda (Vejalla Satyanarayana, Tel, 1983)
Ee Poratam Marpu Kosam (L. Radhakrishna, Tel, 1985)
Eeramana Rojave (Kaayar, Tam, 1991)
Eeran Sandhya (Jesey, Mal, 1985)
Ee Samajam Maakodu (G. Rajkumar, Tel, 1985)
Ee Saritha Inkenallu (Rajachandra, Tel, 1984)
Ee Shabdam Ennathe Shabdam (P.G. Vishwambaran, Mal, 1985)
Eeshwar (**K. Vishwanath**, H, 1989)
Eetapuli (Mani, Mal, 1983)
Ee Thalamura Inganna (Roche Alex, Mal, 1985)
Ee Thalanil Ithirineram (P.G. Vishwambaran, Mal, 1985)
Ee Tharam Illalu (**Bharathirajaa**, Tel, 1985)
Ee Tharam Manishi (V. Madhusudhana Rao, Tel, 1977)
Ee Theerpu Illaladi (T. Prasad, Tel, 1984)
Eetti (Rajasekhar, Tam, 1985)
Eettillam (**Fazil**, Mal, 1983)
Ee Vazhimathram (Ravi Guptan, Mal, 1983)
Ee Yugam (Suresh, Mal, 1983)
E-Flat *see* **Komal Gandhar**
Ehsan (R. Sharma, H, 1954)
Ehsan (Shiv Kumar, H, 1970)
Ei Aama Sansar (**Sisir Mishra**, O, 1986)
Eid Mubarak *see* Id Mubarak
Eight Days (Dattaram Pai, H, 1946)
Eighteen Fifty-Seven (Mohan Sinha, H, 1946)
Eighth Incarnation *see* Krishna Sambhav
Ei Ta Duniya (Mohammed Mohsin, O, 1987)
Ek Aadmi *see* Mr X
Ek Aasman Kai Dishayen (?, Chandrakant Sharda, H, 1987)
Ek Abla (*aka* Sainted Devil: **B.P. Mishra**, St, 1928)
Ekada (**P.C. Barua**, St, 1932)
Ekadashi *see* Mohini
Ekadashi (Dada Gunjal, H, 1955)
Ekadashi Mahima *see* Indrasan
Ek Adhuri Kahani (**Mrinal Sen**, H, 1971)
Ekaj Chumban (*aka* Fatal Kiss: Athavale, St, 1928)
Ek Akar (**S.S. Gulzar**, E, 1985)
Ekaki (Panna Hussain, B, 1990)
Ekakini (G.S. Paniker, Mal, 1975)
Ekalaivan (Shaji Kailash, Mal, 1993)
Ekalavya (**Jyotish Bannerjee**, B, 1938)
Ekalavya (**K. Kameshwara Rao**, Tel, 1982)
Ekambavanan (**Balkrishna Narayan Rao**, Tam, 1947)
Ekanaina Marandi (Gangadhar, Tel, 1983)
Ekanto Apon (Biresh Mukherjee, B, 1987)
Ek Armaan Mera (Dada Gunjal, H, 1959)
Ekati (**Raja Thakur**, Mar, 1968)
Ek Aurat (S.D. Narang, H, 1948)
Ek Aur Ek Gyarah (Ashok Roy, H, 1981)
Ek Aur Itihas (**Prakash Jha**, H, 1987)
Ek Aur Khoon (Ramesh Bedi, H, 1985)
Ek Aur Sangram (R.P. Swamy, H, 1982)
Ek Aur Sikandar (Bhaskar Shetty, H, 1985)
Ekaveera (**C.S. Rao**, Tel, 1969)
Ek Baap Chhe Bete (Mehmood, H, 1978)
Ek Baar Chale Aao (Jagdish Sadanah, H, 1983)
Ek Baar Kaho (Lekh Tandon, H, 1980)
Ek Baar Muskurado (Ram Mukherjee, H, 1972)
Ek Baar Phir (*aka* Once Again: **Vinod Pande**, H, 1979)
Ek Bechara (S.M. Abbas, H, 1972)
Ek Bindu Sukh (Ajit Lahiri, B, 1977)
Ek Chadar Maili Si (Sukhwant Dhadda, H, 1986)
Ek Chitthi Pyar Bhari (Vijay Sadanah, H, 1984)
Ek Daku Shaher Mein (Kalidas, H, 1985)
Ek Dao Bhutacha (Ravi Namade, Mar, 1982)
Ek Desh Mor Desh (?, A, 1986)
Ek Dhaga Sukhacha (**Datta Dharmadhikari**, Mar, 1961)
Ek Dil Do Diwane *see* Do Dilwale
Ek Dil Sau Afsane (R.C. Talwar, H, 1963)
Ek Din Achanak (**Mrinal Sen**, H, 1988)
Ek Din Adhi Raat (Kawal Sharma, H, 1971)
Ek Din Bahu Ka (Desh Gautam, H, 1983)
Ek Din Ka Badshah (*aka* King for a Day: Rajhans, H, 1933)
Ek Din Ka Badshah (Jugal Kishore, H, 1964)
Ek Din Ka Sultan (**Sohrab Modi**, H, 1945)
Ek Din Pratidin (**Mrinal Sen**, B, 1979)
Ek Din Raatre *see* **Jagte Raho**
Ek Din Surya (Nitish Mukherjee, B, 1973)
Ek Doctor Ki Maut (**Tapan Sinha**, H, 1990)
Ek Don Teen (Ashok Tate, Mar, 1964)
Ek Do Teen (**Roop K. Shorey**, H, 1953)
Ek Duuje Ke Liye (**K. Balachander**, H, 1981)
Ek Gao Bara Bhangadi (**Anant Mane**, Mar, 1968)
Ek Gaon Ki Kahani (Dulal Guha, H, 1957)
Ek Gaon Ki Kahani (S.S. Balan, H, 1975)
Ek Ghar *see* **Mane**
Ek Ghat Ki Kahani (**Gautam Ghosh**, H, 1987)
Ek Gunah Aur Sahi (Yogi Kathuria, H, 1980)
Ekhane Amar Swarga (Jahar Biswas, B, 1990)
Ekhane Pinjar (Yatrik, B, 1971)
Ekhani (**Tapan Sinha**, B, 1971)
Ek Hans Ka Joda (Avtar Bhogal, H, 1975)
Ek Hasina Do Diwane (S.M. Abbas, H, 1972)
Ek Hi Bhool (**Vijay Bhatt**, H, 1940)
Ek Hi Bhool (**T. Rama Rao**, H, 1981)
Ek Hi Maqsad (Praveen Bhatt, H, 1988)
Ek Hi Raasta (**Mehboob**, H, 1939)
Ek Hi Raasta (**B.R. Chopra**, H, 1956)
Ek Hi Raasta (**Mohan Segal**, H, 1977)
Ek Hi Raasta (Deepak Bahry, H, 1993)
Ek Hota Raja (Baburao Gokhale, Mar, 1952)
Ek Hota Vidushak (**Jabbar Patel**, Mar, 1992)
Eki Ange Eto Rup (**Harisadhan Dasgupta**, B, 1965)
Eki Gramer Chhele (**Sailajananda Mukherjee**, B, 1950)
Ek Jaan Hain Hum (Rajiv Mehra, H, 1983)
Ek Je Chhilo Bagh (Umaprasad Moitra, B, 1973)
Ek Je Chhilo Desh (**Tapan Sinha**, B, 1976)
Ek Jhalak (Kalidas, H, 1957)
Ek Kadam (Ramnik Desai, H, 1947)
Ek Kahani (TV: **Jahnu Barua**, H, 1986)
Ek Kali Muskayi (Vasant Joglekar, H, 1968)
Ek Ke Baad Ek (Raj Rishi, H, 1960)
Ek Khiladi Bawan Patte (Ravi Khanna, H, 1972)
Ek Kunwari Ek Kunwara (**Prakash Mehra**, H, 1973)
Ek Ladka Ek Ladki (Vijay Sadanah, H, 1992)
Ek Ladki Saat Ladke (**Roop K. Shorey**, H, 1961)
Ek Mahal Ho Sapnon Ka (Devendra Goel, H, 1975)
Ek Main Aur Ek Tu (Ravi Tandon, H, 1986)
Ek Masoom (Akhtar Khalid, H, 1969)
Ek Mati Anek Nati (Krishna Patil, Mar, 1968)
Ek Mausam Chhota Sa *see* Ashiana
Ek Musafir Ek Hasina (**Raj Khosla**, H, 1962)
Ek Mutthi Aasmaan (Virendra Sinha, H, 1973)
Ek Nai Paheli (**K. Balachander**, H, 1984)
Ek Nannhi Munni Ladki Thi (**Vishram Bedekar**, H, 1970)
Ek Nao Do Kinare (**B.R. Ishara**, H, 1973)
Ek Nari Do Roop (Madhusudhan, H, 1973)
Ek Nari Ek Brahmachari (**K.P. Atma**, H, 1971)
Eknath (**Harshadrai Mehta**, Tam, 1938)
Ek Naya Itihaas (B.S. Narayan, H, 1983)
Ek Naya Rishta (**Vinod Pande**, H, 1988)
Ek Nazar (O.P. Dutta, H, 1951)
Ek Nazar (**B.R. Ishara**, H, 1972)
Ek Number Ka Chor (Tajdar Amrohi, H, 1988)
E Kon? (*aka* Who?: Jhaveri, St, 1927)
Ek Paheli (Naresh Kumar, H, 1971)
Ek Pal (**Kalpana Lajmi**, H, 1986)
Ek Phool Char Kaante (Bhappi Sonie, H, 1960)
Ek Phool Do Mali (Devendra Goel, H, 1969)
Ek Raat (W.Z. Ahmed, H, 1942)
Ek Raaz (**Shakti Samanta**, H, 1963)
Ek Roz (Dawood Chand, H, 1947)
Ek Ruka Hua Faisla (**Basu Chatterjee**, H, 1985)
Ek Saal (Devendra Goel, H, 1957)
Ek Saal Pahele (Dharam Kumar, H, 1965)
Ek Saas Zindagi (**Basu Bhattacharya**, H, 1991)
Ek Sapera Ek Lutera (Naresh Kumar, H, 1965)
Ek Se Badhkar Ek (Brij Sadanah, H, 1976)
Ek Se Bhale Do (**S.V. Rajendra Singh**, H, 1985)
Ek Shola (Chander Saigal, H, 1958)
Eksho Noi Dhara (Apurba Mitra, B, 1950)
Ek Shriman Ek Shrimati (Bhappi Sonie, H, 1969)
Ekta (**Homi Wadia**, Sindhi, 1942)
Ekta (**Kidar Sharma**, H, 1959)
Ekta Jeev Sadashiv (Govind Kulkarni, Mar, 1972)
Ektara (Hiren Bose, B, 1957)
Ek Teri Nishani (B.K. Sagar, H, 1947)
Ek Tha Alibaba (Harbans, H, 1963)
Ek Tha Chhotu Ek Tha Motu (**M.S. Sathyu**, Wordless, 1967)
Ek Tha Ladka (Roop Sanware, H, 1951)
Ek Tha Raja *see* **Marmayogi**
Ek Thi Ladki (**Roop K. Shorey**, H, 1949)
Ek Thi Rita/A Girl Named Rita (**Roop K. Shorey**, H/E, 1971)
Ektikatha (Tulsi Lahiri, B, 1936)
Ekti Raat (Chitta Bose, B, 1956)
Ek Tukro Agun (Binu Bardhan, B, 1963)
Ek Tuku Basa (**Tarun Majumdar**, B, 1965)
Ek Tuku Chhoya Lage (Kamal Majumdar, B, 1965)
Elaan (**Mehboob**, Urdu, 1947)
Elaan (K. Ramanlal, H, 1971)
Elaan-e-Jung (*aka* Ultimatum: **J.P. Advani**, H, 1936)
Elaan-e-Jung (Anil Sharma, H, 1989)
Elakkangal *see* Ilakkangal
Elamai Vunjaladugiradhu (**C.V. Sridhar**, Tam, 1978)
Elam Singam (**S.V. Rajendra Singh**, Tam, 1985)
Elaneer (Sitara, Mal, 1981)
Elan Kanru (Ameerjan, Tam, 1985)
Elaya Rani Rajalakshmi (Madurai Thirumaran, Tam, 1978)
Elder Sister *see* **Oppol**
Electricity in the Service of Man (**Govind Saraiya**, E, 1956)
Electric Moon (TV: **Pradeep Krishen**, E, 1991)
Electrocine (**Santi P. Choudhury**, E, 1966)
Elephant Boy *see* Mahout
Elephant God, The *see* **Joi Baba Felunath**
Elephant Queen (*aka* Hathi Ki Rani: Rajendra, H, 1961)
Elevation of the Downtrodden, The *see* Nandanar
Eleven O'clock (*aka* Gyarah Baje: **Homi Wadia**, H, 1948)
Elippathayam (**Adoor Gopalakrishnan**, Mal, 1981)
Ella Hanakkagi (B.C. Lal, K, 1977)
Ellai Kodu (S. Raghavan, Tam, 1972)
Ellai Kodu (K. Jothipandian, Tam, 1987)
Ellaisamy (K. Rangaraj, Tam, 1992)
Ellam Avale (Amirtham, Tam, 1977)
Ellame En Thangachi (Bala Ganesh, Tam, 1989)
Ellam En Kairasi (M.A. Thirumugham, Tam, 1980)
Ellam Inbamayam (Jiten Bannerjee/**R. Padmanabhan**, Tam, 1955)
Ellam Inbamayam (C.N. Rangarajan, Tam, 1981)
Ellam Ninakku Vendi (**Sasikumar**, Mal, 1981)
Ellam Unnakkaga (Saravanabava/Unity Pics, Tam, 1961)
Ellellu Nane (M.S. Gopinath, K, 1969)
Ellindalo Bandavaru (**P. Lankesh**, K, 1980)
Ellora Caves (**Dadasaheb Phalke**, St, 1925)
Ellorum Innattu Mannar (**T. Prakash Rao**, Tam, 1960)
Ellorum Nallavare (S.S. Balan, Tam, 1975)
Ellorum Vazhavendum (B.V. Acharya, Tam, 1962)
Elusive Dream, An (Gopal Singh, H, 1976)
Emarantha Sonagiri (?, Madurai Meenakshi Films, Tam, 1937)
Emayam (Muktha V. Srinivasan, Tam, 1979)
Embers *see* **Sholay**
Embrace, The *see* Alingan
Emmadi Pulakesi *see* Immadi Pulakesi
Emme Thammanna (**B.R. Panthulu**, K, 1966)
Emotional Upsurge *see* Ilakkangal
Emperor Ashok *see* Samrat Ashok
En (Ramanna, Tam, 1970)
Enaitha Kodugal (Balaji, Tam, 1985)
Enakkaga Kathiru (Nivas, Tam, 1981)
Enakkoru Magan Perappan (M. Krishnan, Tam, 1975)
Enakkul Oruvan (S.P. Muthuraman, Tam, 1984)
Enakku Nane Needipathi (S.A. Chandrasekharan, Tam, 1986)
Enakku Oru Neethi (?, Tam, 1990)
En Annan (**P. Neelakantan**, Tam, 1970)
En Arugil Nee Irundhal (Sundar Vijayan, Tam, 1991)
En Arumai Manaivi (Jayakumar, Tam, 1989)
En Asai Unnoduthan (K. Narayanan, Tam, 1983)
Enbaralli Preeti Erali (P.N. Srinivas, K, 1979)
En Bommu Kutti Ammavukku (**Fazil**, Tam, 1988)
Enchanted Pills, The *see* Vichitra Gutika
Enchanting Illusion, The *see* Maya Memsaab
Enchantress, The *see* Zalim Jadugarin
Ende Nandini Kutty (Valsan, Mal, 1984)
Ende Ponnu Thamburan (A.D. Abu, Mal, 1992)
Endina Bharata (T. Krishna, K, 1984)
Endina Ramayana (Rajachandra, K, 1984)
Endrum Anbudan (Bhagyanathan, Tam, 1992)
Endu Ninnavane (**Kalyana Kumar**, K, 1966)
Enemy, The *see* **Dushman** *or* Katto Dushman
Enemy of the People, An *see* **Ganashatru**
Enemy's Daughter, The *see* Kashmeera
Energy (**Suresh Heblikar**, E, 1984)
Enga Chinna Rasa (**K. Bhagyaraj**, Tam, 1987)
Engalamum Mudiyum (**T. Prakash Rao**, Tam, 1983)
Engal Annan Varattum (R. Krishnamurthy, Tam, 1989)
Engalayum Vazha Vidungal (P.S. Prakash, Tam, 1985)
Engal Kudumbam Parisu (**B.R. Panthulu**, Tam, 1958)
Engal Kula Daivam (P.R. Somu, Tam, 1974)
Engal Kula Daivi (**Adurthi Subba Rao**, Tam, 1959)
Engal Sami Ayappan (?, Deepa Hari Films, Tam, 1990)
Engal Selvi (**Yoganand**, Tam, 1960)
Engal Thaikulame Varuga (?, Tam, 1986)
Engal Thangam (**Krishnan-Panju**, Tam, 1970)
Engal Thanga Raja (V.B. Rajendra Prasad, Tam, 1973)
Engal Thanga Raja (V.B. Rajendra Prasad, Tam, 1980)
Engal Thayi (Malliyam Rajagopal, Tam, 1973)
Engalukam Kalamvaryam (**A. Vincent**, Tam, 1967)
Engalukkum Kathal Varum (R. Vittal, Tam, 1975)
Enga Mama (A.C. Trilogchander, Tam, 1970)
Engamma Maharani (M.A. Kaja, Tam, 1981)
Engamma Sabatham (S.P. Muthuraman, Tam, 1974)
Enga Muthalaly (Liaqat Ali Khan, Tam, 1993)
Engane Nee Marakkum (M. Mani, Mal, 1983)
Enganeundasane (Balu Kiriyath, Mal, 1984)
Enga Oor Rasathi (N.S. Rajendran, Tam, 1980)
Enga Ooru Attukkaran (Sripriya, Tam, 1990)
Enga Ooru Kannagi (**K. Balachander**, Tam, 1981)
Enga Ooru Kavalkaran (T.P. Gajendran, Tam, 1988)
Enga Ooru Mappillai (T.P. Gajendran, Tam, 1989)

Enga Ooru Pattukaran (Gangai Amaran, Tam, 1987)
Enga Ooru Raja (P. Madhavan, Tam, 1968)
Enga Ooru Sipoy (Manimurugan, Tam, 1991)
Enga Papa (**B.R. Panthulu**, Tam, 1966)
Enga Pattan Sothu (M. Karnan, Tam, 1975)
Enga Thambi (S.D. Saba, Tam, 1993)
Engatta Modathe (**R. Soundarrajan**, Tam, 1990)
Enga Vathiar (**Durai**, Tam, 1980)
Enga Veetu Daivam (T.R. Ramesh, Tam, 1989)
Enga Veetu Mahalakshmi *see* Maa Inti Mahalakshmi
Enga Veetu Penn (B. Nagi Reddy, Tam, 1965)
Enga Veetu Pillai (**Tapi Chanakya**, Tam, 1965)
Enga Veetu Ramayanam (?, Tam, 1987)
Enga Veetu Velan (**T. Rajendar**, Tam, 1992)
Enge Kadavul (V.S. Rao, Tam, 1965)
Engeyo Ketta Kural (S.P. Muthuraman, Tam, 1982)

Shakila in *Madam XYZ* (1959)

Engineers (India) Limited (**Harisadhan Dasgupta**, E, 1973)
Engirundalum Vazhga (Parambai R. Selvaraj, Tam, 1985)
Engiruthu Vandhal (A.C. Trilogchander, Tam, 1970)
England Returned, The *see* **Bilet Pherat**
Enikku Gnan Swantham (P. Chandrakumar, Mal, 1979)
Enikkum Oru Divasam (Shrikumaran Thampi, Mal, 1982)
Enikku Visakkunu (**P. Bhaskaran**, Mal, 1983)
Enipadigal (P. Madhavan, Tam, 1979)
Enippadikal (**Thoppil Bhasi**, Mal, 1973)
En Jeevan Paduthu (R. Soundarrajan, Tam, 1988)
En Kadamai (M. Natesan, Tam, 1964)
En Kadhali (Dwarkanath, Tam, 1938)
En Kanavar (*aka* My Husband: **S. Balachander**, Tam, 1948)
En Kanavar (Ashwini Kumar, Tam, 1989)
En Kathal Kanmani (?, Progressive Cine Arts, Tam, 1990)
En Kelvikku Enna Bathil (P. Madhavan, Tam, 1978)
Enki Nayudu Bava (B. Subba Rao, Tel, 1978)
En Magal (K.V.R. Acharya/M.K.R. Nambiar, Tam, 1954)
En Magan (R.S. Mani, Tam, 1945)
En Magan (C.V. Rajendran, Tam, 1974)
En Manaivi (*aka* My Wife: **A.V. Meiyappan/Sundarrao Nadkarni**, Tam, 1942)
Ennadi Meenakshi (Karaikudi Narayanan, Tam, 1979)
Ennai Paar (G.R. Nathan, Tam, 1961)
Ennaipar En Azhagai Paar (N.S. Manian, Tam, 1983)
Ennai Petha Rasa (Siraj, Tam, 1989)
Ennai Pol Oruvan (T.R. Ramanna, Tam, 1976)
Ennai Veetu Pogathe (T.K. Bose, Tam, 1988)
Enna Mudalali Sowkiyama (Malliyam Rajagopal, Tam, 1972)
Ennathan Mudivu (?, Ravi Prod, Tam, 1965)
Enna Thavam Saithen (**Krishnan-Panju**, Tam, 1976)
Enne Snehikku Enne Mathram (P.G. Vishwambaran, Mal, 1981)
Ennodishtam Koodama (Kamal, Mal, 1992)
Ennum Kannettante (**Fazil**, Mal, 1986)
Ennum Nammagal (Sathyan Andhikkad, Mal, 1991)
En Oyir Tholan *see* En Uyir Thozhan
En Purushanthan Enakkum Mattumthan (Manobala, Tam, 1989)
En Rasavin Manisile (Kasturiraja, Tam, 1991)
En Rathithin Rathame (K. Vijayan, Tam, 1989)
En Sabatham (S.A. Chandrasekharan, Tam, 1986)
En Selvame (S.P. Muthuraman, Tam, 1985)
Enta Ghattu Prayamo (P. Sambhasiva Rao, Tel, 1982)
Ente Ammu Ninte Thulasi Avarude Chakki (**Balachandra Menon**, Mal, 1985)
Ente Bhava Mariyanu (Relangi Narasimha Rao, Tel, 1992)
Entede Bhanta (D. Rajendra Babu, K, 1992)
Ente Entethu Mathram (?, Beegees Films, Mal, 1986)
Ente Gramam (T.K. Vasudevan/Moolanagaram Vijayan, Mal, 1983)
Ente Kalithozhen (M. Mani, Mal, 1984)
Ente Kannakuyil (**Sasikumar**, Mal, 1985)
Ente Katha (P.K. Joseph, Mal, 1983)
Ente Mamattukuttiamma (**Fazil**, Mal, 1983)
Ente Mohanangal Poovaninju (?, Mal, 1982)
Ente Neela Akasham (**Thoppil Bhasi**, Mal, 1978)
Entertainers of Rajasthan (**Santi P. Choudhury**, E, 1968)
Ente Shabdam (?, Mal, 1986)
Ente Shatrukkal (?, Mal, 1982)
Ente Sneham Ninakku Mathram (S.L. Puram Sadanandan, Mal, 1979)
Ente Suryaputhrikku (**Fazil**, Mal, 1991)
Ente Upasana (**B.G. Bharathan**, Mal, 1984)
En Thambi (A.C. Trilogchander, Tam, 1968)
En Thamil En Makkal (Santhana Bharati, Tam, 1988)
En Thangachi Padichaval (P. Vasu, Tam, 1988)
En Thangai (**Ch. Narayanamurthy**/M.K.R. Nambiar, Tam, 1952)
En Thangai (A. Jagannathan, Tam, 1989)
En Thangai Kalyani (**T. Rajendar**, Tam, 1988)
Enthino Pookunna Pookal (Gopinath Babu, Mal, 1982)
Enticement *see* Maya Na Rang
Entravathu Oru Naal (Balu, Tam, 1986)
Entu Nathante Nimmi (?, Vijaya Movies Prod, Mal, 1986)
E Nuhen Kahani (*aka* A Nuhen Kahani: K.H.D. Rao, O, 1977)
En Uyir Kannamma (Sivachandran, Tam, 1988)
En Uyir Thozhan (**Bharathirajaa**, Tam, 1990)
En Vazhi Thani Vazhi (V. Azhagappan, Tam, 1988)
En Veedu/Naa Illu (**Chittor V. Nagaiah**, Tam/Tel, 1953)
En Veedu En Kanavar (?, Tam, 1990)
Environment, An (**Santi P. Choudhury**, E, 1973)
Enzhai Vazhavan (**Kadaru Nagabhushanam**, Tam, 1952)
Epar Opar (**Sukumar Dasgupta**, B, 1941)
Epar Opar (Ashutosh Bannerjee, B, 1973)
Epilepsy (**Shyam Benegal**, E, 1975)
Episode from the Ramayana, An (?, Cinema De Luxe, St, 1912)
Epistle (Shankar V. Giri, E, 1961)
Era Bator Sur (**Bhupen Hazarika**, A, 1956)
Eradu Kanasu (Dorairaj-Bhagavan, K, 1974)
Eradu Mane Meena (V. Balakrishna, K, 1990)
Eradu Mukha (M.R. Vittal, K, 1969)
Eradu Nakshatragalu (**Singeetham Srinivasa Rao**, K, 1983)
Eradu Rekhegalu (**K. Balachander**, K, 1984)
Era-Ek-Jug (Archan Chakraborty, B, 1976)
Era Kara (Bireshwar Bose, B, 1964)
Era Matti (Dhavala Satyam, Tel, 1985)
Erandu Manam (K. Nataraj, Tam, 1985)
Eratha Tilagam (?, Tam, 1963)
Erattai Manithan (K. Shankar, Tam, 1982)
Era Vizhi Kaviyangal (B.R. Ravishankar, Tam, 1982)
Erikkarai Poongatre (?, Leo Pics, Tam, 1990)
Erimalai (Gopikrishna, Tam, 1985)
Ernakulam Junction (Vijayanarayanan, Mal, 1971)
Errakota Veerudu (M.S. Parthasarathy, Tel, 1973)
Erramandaram (Muthyala Subbaiah, Tel, 1991)
Erulu Hagalu (Rajmohan, K, 1980)
Erumanam Kalanthal Thirumanam (Jampana/G. Vishwanathan, Tam, 1960)
Erumpazhikal (A.B. Raj, Mal, 1979)
Escape *see* **Burma Rani**
Essence, The *see* **Susman**
Estheppan (**G. Aravindan**, Mal, 1979)
Eswari (Ramanarayanan, Tam, 1991)
Etawah Story, The (**P.V. Pathy**, E, 1956)
Eternal Hope *see* Amar Asha
Eternal Lamp, The *see* **Amara Deepam**
Eternal Music *see* Mahageet
Eternal Thirst *see* **Pyaasa**
Etha Ennumuthal (Raji, Mal, 1984)
Ethanai Konam Ethanai Parvai (B. Lenin, Tam, 1983)
Etharkum Thuninthavan (M. Karnan, Tam, 1976)
Ethayum Thangam Idayam (**P. Neelakantan**, Tam, 1962)
Ethiraligal (Joshi, Mal, 1982)
Ethirikal Jakkirathi (R. Sundaram, Tam, 1967)
Ethirkalam (M.S. Solaimalai, Tam, 1970)
Ethir Neechal (**K. Balachander**, Tam, 1968)
Ethiroli (**K. Balachander**, Tam, 1970)
Ethirparadathu (**Ch. Narayanamurthy**, Tam, 1954)
Ethirparatha Mutham *see* Ponmudi
Ethirpukkal (Oonni Aranmulla, Mal, 1984)
Ethir Veetu Jannal (Kalainathan, Tam, 1980)
Etho Enthan Daivam (A.C. Trilogchander, Tam, 1972)
Etho Mogam (T.K. Manian, Tam, 1984)
Etho Oru Swapnam (Shrikumaran Thampi, Mal, 1978)
Ettikku Potti (Govindarajan, Tam, 1987)
Ettuku Pai Ettu (**Tapi Chanakya**, Tel, 1958)
Etu Ediretu (Manimurugan, K, 1981)
Etwa (Jyotirmoy Roy, H, 1988)
Evadabba Somu (K.S.R. Doss, Tel, 1979)
Eval Oru Seethai (A. Jagannathan, Tam, 1978)
Evandi Avide Ochindi (E.V.V. Satyanarayana, Tel, 1993)
Evandi Shrimathigaru (Relangi Narasimha Rao, Tel, 1982)
Evar (**I.V. Sasi**, Mal, 1980)
Evariki Vare Yamuna Theere (**Dasari Narayana Rao**, Tel, 1974)
Evaru Devudu (**A. Bhimsingh**, Tel, 1977)
Evaru Monagaru (R. Sundaram, Tel, 1968)
Evedayo Oru Sathru (**T. Hariharan**, Mal, 1983)
Evening in Paris, An (*aka* Paris Ki Ek Shyam: **Shakti Samanta**, H, 1967)
Evening Raga, The *see* **Sandhya Ragam**
Evening Song, The *see* **Sandhya Raag**
Ever Ready (*aka* Garma Garam: Nari Ghadiali, H, 1946)
Evide Ee Theerath (P.G. Vishwambaran, Mal, 1985)
Evil Deeds of Cherian, The *see* **Cheriyachente Kroora Krithyangal**
Evolution and Races of Man, The (**S. Sukhdev**, E, 1961)
Excuse Me, Sir (**Dhiren Ganguly**, B, 1934)
Ex-husband *see* Soneri Jaal
Exiled Prince, The *see* Deshawato
Exiled Prince of Ujjain, The *see* Deshawato
Exile of Shri Rama *see* Ram Vanvas
Expedition, The *see* **Abhijaan**
Experience India (**Ketan Mehta**, E, 1977)
Expression, An (**Prakash Jha**, E, 1988)
Extra Girl (B.A. Joshi, H, 1947)
Eye for an Eye *see* Meethi Churi
Eyes, The *see* **Chokh**
Ezhaikkum Kalam Varum (S. Rajendra Babu, Tam, 1975)
Ezhai Jaathi (Liaqat Ali Khan, Tam, 1993)
Ezhai Padum Padu/Beedala Patlu (**K. Ramnoth**, Tam/Tel, 1950)
Ezhai Pangalan (K. Shankar, Tam, 1963)
Ezham Kadalinakkare (**I.V. Sasi**, Mal, 1979)
Ezham Rathri (Krishnakumar, Mal, 1982)
Ezhamuthal Onpathuvare (**Sasikumar**, Mal, 1985)
Ezhanda Kadal (K.S. Mani, Tam, 1941)
Ezhara Ponnara (Tulasidas, Mal, 1992)
Ezhavathu Manithan (K. Hariharan, Tam, 1982)
Ezhayin Asthi (P.L. Ramchandra, Tam, 1955)
Ezhunallathu (Harikumar, Mal, 1991)
Ezhu Rathrikal (**Ramu Kariat**, Mal, 1968)
Ezhuthantha Sattangal (K. Shankar, Tam, 1984)
Ezhuthapurangal (**Sibi Malayil, Mal, 1987**)
Ezhuthatha Katha (A.B. Raj, Mal, 1970)

F

Faasla (*aka* Faslah, The Distance: **K.A. Abbas**, H, 1974)

Faasle (**Yash Chopra**, H, 1985)
Fable, The *see* **Katha**
Face to Face *see* **Mukha Mukham**
Faces (**K.G. George**, E, 1971)
Faces after the Storm (**Prakash Jha**, E, 1982)
Faces and Masks *see* **Marattam**
Fair Folk, Folk Fair (**Ketan Mehta**, E, 1983)
Fair Warrior, A *see* Shoor Killedarin
Fairy of Anardesh *see* Anarbala
Fairy of Baghdad *see* Bulbul-e-Baghdad
Fairy of Ceylon *see* **Lanka Ni Laadi**
Fairy of Delhi *see* Rangmahal Ni Ramani
Fairy of Punjab *see* Bulbul-e-Punjab
Fairy of Sinhaldwip *see* Sinhaldwip Ni Sundari
Fairy of the Flute *see* Bansari Bala
Faisla (Apurva Mitra, H, 1947)
Faisla (Jugal Kishore, H, 1965)
Faisla (?, K. Zaidi, H, 1988)
Faithful Heart *see* Baap Ka Bol *or* Dardi
Fakhr-e-Islam (*aka* Pride of Islam: **Nanubhai Vakil**/Safdar Mirza, H, 1937)
Fakira (Kumar Chandrasekhar, Mar, 1963)
Fakira (C.P. Dixit, H, 1976)
Fakir Badshah (Subhash, H, 1987)
Fakiron Ki Basti (?, Ajit Singh Pics, H, 1962)
Falak (Shashilal Nair, H, 1988)
Falak Numa (*aka* Triumph of Love, Saundarya Jwala: M.K. Smart, St, 1929)
Falgu (Satish Dasgupta, B, 1956)
Fallen Flower *see* **Veena Poovu**
Fall of Pavagarh *see* Goddess Mahakali
Fall of Pride *see* Garva Khandan
Fall of Slavery *see* **Gulami Nu Patan**
Fall of the Kauravas *see* Draupadi Veni Bandhan
Fall of the Mauryas *see* Maurya Patan
Fall of Vijayanagar *see* Mast Fakir
False Pride *see* **Abhijathyam**
Family Feuds (?, Madan Theatres, St, 1931)
Family in Bangalore, A (**Paul Zils**, E, 1954)
Family Life *see* **Prapancha**
Famine, The *see* **Bara**
Fankdo Fituri (**Homi Master**, St, 1925)
Fankdo Fituri (**Homi Master**, G/H, 1939)
Fansi (**Utpalendu Chakraborty**, B, 1989)
Faraar (**Phani Majumdar**, H, 1955)
Faraar (Pinaki Mukherjee, H, 1965)
Faraar (Shankar Mukherjee, H, 1975)
Faraib (Shaheed Latif/**Ismat Chughtai**, H, 1953)
Faraib (Rajat Rakshit, H, 1983)
Farari (*aka* Outlaw: Y.D. Sarpotdar?, St, 1931)
Farari (**Anant Mane**, Mar, 1976)
Farari (?, Flower Films, H, 1988)
Faraway Thunder *see* **Doorathu Idhi Muzhakkam**
Farebi *see* The Cheat
Farebi Duniya (*aka* Mysterious Man: **J.P. Advani**, H, 1935)
Farebi Jaal (*aka* Trapped: **M. Bhavnani**, H, 1931)
Farebi Shahzada (*aka* Shepherd: **A.R. Kardar**, St, 1930)
Farishta (**Ravindra Dave**, H, 1958)
Farishta (Kedar Kapoor, H, 1968)
Farishta (Sunil Sikand, H, 1983)
Farishta Ya Qatil (S.M. Abbas, H, 1977)
Farishte (Anil Sharma, H, 1991)
Fariyad (**Jayant Desai**, H, 1942)
Fariyad (**Kidar Sharma**, H, 1964)
Fariyad (Bijoy Bose, B, 1971)
Fariyadi (Habib Sarhadi, H, 1953)
Farmaish (B.K. Sagar, H, 1953)
Farmer's Daughter *see* Chasher Meye
Farz (Niranjan, H, 1947)
Farz (Ravi Nagaich, H, 1967)
Farzande Hind (*aka* Phantom of the Hills: **Ezra Mir**, H, 1934)
Farzande Watan *see* **Leatherface**
Farz Aur Kanoon (**K. Raghavendra Rao**, H, 1982)
Farz Aur Mohabbat *see* Nausherwan-e-Adil
Farz-e-Ada (*aka* Loyalty: A.M. Khan, H, 1936)
Farz-e-Islam (?, Ganesh Prasad Movies, H, 1980)
Farz Ki Jung (R.P. Swamy, H, 1988)
Farz Ki Keemat (Sudhir Wali, H, 1983)
Fashion (S.F. Hasnain, H, 1943)
Fashion (Lekhraj Bhakri, H, 1957)
Fashionable India (Mohan Sinha, H, 1935)
Fashionable Wife (**Dhirubhai Desai**, H, 1938)
Fashionable Wife (Adarsh, H, 1959)
Faslah *see* Faasla
Fatal Anklet *see* Kovalan
Fatal Arrow *see* Khooni Teer
Fatal Garland *see* Haiyan No Haar
Fatal Kiss *see* Ekaj Chumban
Fatal Marriage *see* Kal Parinaya
Fate *see* **Karma**
Fateful Ring, The *see* Shakuntala
Fateh (Talat Jani, H, 1991)
Fateh Imaan *see* Insaan Ya Shaitan
Father (Dilip Mukherjee, B, 1981)
Father India *see* Hamarun Hindustan
Father o'Mine *see* Pita Ke Parmeshwar
Father's Love *see* **Pitru Prem**
Fattak (Kamal Ganguly, B, 1955)
Fauji (Joginder, H, 1976)
Fauji Chacha (Dharam Kumar, P, 1980)
Faulad (Mohammed Hussain, H, 1963)
Fauladi Firman (*aka* Fiats of Steel: Baburao, St, 1931)
Fauladi Jigar (*aka* Dynamite: Behram Vasunia, St, 1932)
Fauladi Mukka (R.N. Vaidya, H, 1936)
Fauladi Mukka (S. Azeem, H, 1965)
Fauladi Pahelwan (*aka* Iron Man: **Jayant Desai**, St, 1931)
F Cycle, The (**Jahnu Barua**, E, 1974)
Fear (**Ritwik Ghatak**, H, 1965)
Fearless *see* **Achamillai Achamillai**
Fearless Phantom (?, Shri Vijay Film, St, 1926)
Fearless-The Hunterwali Story (Riyad Vinci Wadia, E, 1993)
Female Feet *see* Rajwadana Ranga
Ferry *see* Kashti
Festival *see* **Mela** *or* **Utsav**
Festival of Fire *see* **Holi**
Festival of India (**Shyam Benegal**, E/French, 1985)
Fever Mixture (Tulsi Lahiri, B, 1940)
Few More Questions, A (**S. Sukhdev**, E, 1974)
Fiats of Steel *see* Fauladi Firman
Fida-e-Tauheen (?, Shankar Movietone, H, 1934)
Fida-e-Watan (*aka* Tasveer-e-Wafaa: G.R. Sethi, H, 1936)
Fidelity *see* Wafadari
Field Marshal *see* Mard-e-Maidan
15th August (Vicky Ranawat, H, 1993)
Fifty-Fifty (R.L. Malhotra, H, 1956)
Fifty-Fifty (Shomu Mukherjee, H, 1981)
Fifty Miles from Poona (**Fali Bilimoria**/**Paul Zils**, E, 1957)
Fighter Sheila (Vijay, H, 1972)
Fighting Blade *see* Khooni Khanjar
Fighting Blood *see* Josh-e-Jawani *or* Lal Panjo
Fighting Cavalier *see* Rangila Nawab *or* Chauhani Talwar
Fighting Hero (Keshav K. Talpade, H, 1946)
Fighting Queen (Nari Ghadiali, H, 1956)
Fighting Vagabond *see* Baghdad Ka Badmash
Fight Unto Death *see* Khandana Khel
Figures of Thought (Doc: Arun Khopkar, E, 1990)
Filial Duty *see* Chandrakant
Film Gaze (**Vishnu Mathur**, Wordless, 1970)
Film Hi Film (Hiren Nag, H, 1983)
Filmland *see* Cinema Shrushti
Firaun *see* Shah-e-Misar
Firdaus (V. Joglekar/H. Ahluwalia, H, 1953)
Fire *see* **Aag** *or* **Agni**
Fire (**Phani Majumdar**, E, 1990)
Fire in the Belly (**Kumar Shahani**, E, 1973)
Firey Chalo (Atanu Kumar, B, 1966)
Firingoti (**Jahnu Barua**, A, 1991)
Firman (**Nanubhai Vakil**, H, 1942)
First Bell (P.G. Vishwambaran, Mal, 1992)
First Day of the Month, The *see* **Modalatedi**
First Love (Ved-Madan, H, 1961)
First Love Letter (Shiva, H, 1991)
First Step, The *see* Pehla Kadam
Fisherfolk of Bombay (**Paul Zils**, E, 1955)
Fishergirl, The *see* Jaler Meye
Fisherman's Boy, The (**Hiralal Sen**, St, 1904)
Fishermen of Sundarban (**Buddhadev Dasgupta**, E, 1970)
Fitness for Fun Fitness for Everyone (**Amol Palekar**, E, 1989)
Five Divine Wands *see* Panchdanda
Five Fires *see* **Panchagni**
Five Rifles (I.S. Johar, H, 1974)
Fix it Right (**Shantaram Athavale**, E, 1960)
Flag of Honour *see* Nishan Danka
Flame of Love *see* Shama Parwana
Flame of Love (*aka* When Love Blazes: ?, **Madan Theatres**, St, 1926)
Flames of Flesh *see* Kamaner Aagun
Flames of the Sun *see* **Sholay**
Flaming Soul *see* Jalta Jigar
Flaming Youth *see* Jawani Diwani
Flashing Sword (*aka* Chamakti Shamsheer: **J.P. Advani**, H, 1934)
Flat No. 9 (Ramesh Sharma, H, 1961)
Flight of Pigeons, A *see* **Junoon**
Flight to Assam (Kawal Sharma, H, 1961)
Flirting Wife *see* Vilasi Kanta
Flogged into Love *see* Chabukne Chamkare
Flower Bird *see* Pardesi Pankhi
Flower Garden (**Shyam Benegal**, E, 1969)
Flowering Tree, The *see* **Cheluvi**
Flower of Heaven, The *see* Parijatak
Flower of Rajasthan *see* Krishna Kumari
Flowers and Thorns *see* Phool Aur Kaante
Flying Bird, The (**Vishnu Mathur**, E, 1989)
Flying Express (**Nanubhai Vakil**, H, 1949)
Flying Goods Wagon (**Fali Bilimoria**, E, 1949)
Flying Horse *see* Panch Kalyani
Flying Horse (*aka* Udta Ghoda: Trimoorti, H, 1963)
Flying Man (*aka* Hawai Insaan: **Nanubhai Vakil**, H, 1947)
Flying Man (*aka* Hawai Insaan: Pradeep Nayyar, H, 1965)
Flying Prince *see* Hawai Swar
Flying Prince (**Homi Wadia**, H, 1946)
Flying Rani (Aspi, H, 1939)
Flying Rani (**Nanubhai Vakil**, H, 1959)
Flying Surface (Dhanpat Rai, H, 1965)
Fog *see* **Dhund**
Folk Fair at Tarnetar (**Ketan Mehta**, E, 1982)
Folk Dances of India (**M. Bhavnani**, E, 1953)
Folk Instruments of Rajasthan (**Santi P. Choudhury**, E, 1965)
Folk Tale, A *see* **Bhavni Bhavai**
Follies of the Rich *see* Reshmi Sari
Food Front, The (**S. Sukhdev**, E, 1975)
Foolish Husbands *see* Bharmayalo Bharthar
Foolish Wisdom *see* Akalmand Bewaqoof
Football (Radhakrishnan, Mal, 1982)
Football Champion (V. Devan, Mal, 1973)
Footpath (**Zia Sarhadi**, H, 1953)
Footpathni Rani (S.J. Talukdar, G, 1982)
For a Happier Tomorrow (**S. Sukhdev**, E, 1975)
Forbidden Bride *see* **Lagna Bandhan**
Forbidden Fruit *see* Nishiddha Phal
Forbidden Love *see* Hoor-e-Baghdad
For Country's Sake *see* Gunial Gulab
Foreigner, The *see* **Pardesi**
Forest, The *see* **Banani**
Forget Me Not *see* Bhool Na Jana
Forgiveness of Sins *see* **Pavamanippu**
For Whom the Sun Shines (**Bhupen Hazarika**, E, 1974)
For Ladies Only (*aka* Titali: Bedi, H, 1951)
For Mother's Sake *see* Matri Prem
Forms and Design (**Mani Kaul**, E, 1968)
For My Mamattukuttiamma *see* **Ente Mamattukuttiamma**
Forsaken Love *see* Prem Nirasha
Forsaken Wife *see* Tajayali Taruni
Forts of Maharashtra *see* Sea Forts
Fortune and Fools *see* **Baap Kamai**
Fortune Hunters *see* Manik Jorh
Forty Crores *see* Chalis Karod
Forty Days *see* Chalis Din
47 Natkal/47 Rojulu (*aka* 47 Days: **K. Balachander**, Tam/Tel, 1981)
'42 (*aka* Byalis: **Hemen Gupta**, B, 1949)
Forward March *see* Badhe Chalo
Foundations of Progress (**Shyam Benegal**, E, 1972)
Foundation Stone, The *see* **Adharshila**
Four Devils *see* Prabhu Na Chor
Four Faces (**Govind Saraiya**, E, 1980)
Four Families (**Fali Bilimoria**, E, 1960)
Four Plus Four (?, Mal, 1987)
Four Rascals *see* Char Chakram
420 (M. Sathyakumar, Tel, 1991)
Fraternity *see* Bhaichara
Freedom Freedom (**Kantilal Rathod**, E, 1971)
Freedom from Fear (**Sai Paranjpye**, E, 1978)
Freedom on Wheels (**Govind Saraiya**, E, 1957)
Free Love (*aka* Azad Mohabbat: Batra Kaushalraj, H, 1974)
Free Souls *see* Sher Dil Aurat
Friend in Need, A *see* Geeta Rahasya
Friend or Fiend *see* Sanmitra Ki Shaitan
Friendship *see* **Dosti**
Friends Together (**Prakash Jha**, H, 1978)
From Behind the Barricade (**Tapan Bose**, E, 1993)
From One Side to the Other *see* **Aar Paar**
From the Gutter *see* **Odeyil Ninnu**
Frontiers of Freedom (**S. Sukhdev**, E, 1964)
Fugaane Abla *see* Afghan Abla
Fuji Lama (S.H. Tharani, H, 1954)
Fun with Matchsticks *see* Aagkadyancha Mauja
Funeral Rites *see* **Samskara**
Funtoosh (**Chetan Anand**, H, 1956)

G

Gaai Aur Gori (M.A. Thirumugham, H, 1973)
Gaal Gulabi Nain Sharabi (Devi Sharma, H, 1974)
Gaali (**R.S. Choudhury**, H, 1944)
Gaath Padli Th*aka* Th*aka* (**Raja Paranjpe**, Mar, 1956)
Gaavgund (Vasant Kulkarni, Mar, 1951)
Gaban (Krishan Chopra/**Hrishikesh Mukherjee**, H, 1966)
Gabbar Singh (M. Karnan, H, 1976)
Gabhroo (?, New Naubahar, H, 1951)
Gabhroo Desh Punjab De (D. Sohna, P, 1966)
Gabhroo Punjab Da (Jagjeet, P, 1986)
Gadano Bel (**Ratibhai Punatar**, G, 1950)
Gadasari Attaha Sosagari Kodalu (K. Subba Rao, Tel, 1981)
Gada Yuddha *see* Draupadi Veni Bandhan
Gadbad Ghotala (Raja Bargir, Mar, 1986)
Gadbidi Ganda (V.S. Reddy, K, 1993)
Gaddar (Harmesh Malhotra, H, 1973)
Gad Jejuri Jejuri (Ram Kadam, Mar, 1985)
Gaduggayi (Sarath, Tel, 1989)
Gadusu Ammayi (**K. Pratyagatma**, Tel, 1977)
Gadusu Pillodu (**K. Bapaiah**, Tel, 1977)
Gadusu Pindam (Karaikudi Narayanan, Tel, 1984)
Gafil Musafir (**J.P. Advani**, H, 1934)
Gagana (Dorairaj-Bhagavan, K, 1989)
Gaibi Gola (?, **Madan** Theatres, H, 1935)
Gaibi Insaan (**Dadasaheb Gokhale**, H, 1935)
Gaibi Sawar (*aka* Masked Rider: Vithaldas Panchotia, St, 1930)
Gaibi Sitara (Wilford Deming, H, 1935)
Gaibi Talwar (A.M. Khan, H, 1948)
Gair Kanooni (Prayag Raj, H, 1989)
Gajab Bhaile Ram (K.P. Shukla, Bh, 1984)
Gajabhau (**Master Vinayak**, Mar/H, 1944)
Gajab Tamasha (Ranjeet, H, 1992)
Gajadonga (**K. Raghavendra Rao**, Tel, 1980)
Gaja Gauri (**Baburao Painter**, St, 1926)
Gaja Gauri (**Raja Thakur**, H, 1958)
Gajandravache Bhagya (**Dadasaheb Phalke**, St, 1922)
Gajara Maru (**Nanabhai Bhatt**, G, 1981)
Gajarni Pipudi (Sushil Vyas, G, 1979)
Gajendra (V. Somasekhar, K, 1984)
Gajendra Moksham (**R.S. Prakash**, St, 1923)

Gajendra Moksham (**R.S. Prakash**, St, 1930)
Gajre (R.D. Mathur, H, 1948)
Gaju Bommalu (Ravindranath, Tel, 1983)
Gajula Kishtayya (**Adurthi Subba Rao**, Tel, 1975)
Galate Samsara (C.V. Rajendran, K, 1977)
Galat Faimi (*aka* Miss 1949: ?, Pancholi, H, 1949)
Galatta Kalyanam (C.V. Rajendran, Tam, 1968)
Galava Rishi (*aka* Chitrasenotakhyam: T.C. Vadivelu Naicker/**Sarvottam Badami**, Tam, 1932)
Galigopura/Gali Medalu (**B.R. Panthulu**, K/Tel, 1962)
Galimathu (Dorairaj-Bhagavan, K, 1981)
Gali Medalu *see* Galigopura
Gali Patalu (**T. Prakash Rao**, Tel, 1974)
Gali Theke Rajpath (Prafulla Chakraborty, B, 1959)
Galivana (Adiraju Ananda Mohan, Tel, 1979)
Galiyon Ka Badshah (Sher Jung Singh, H, 1989)
Gallan Hoyian Beetiyan (Kumar Kuldip, Dogri, 1966)
Gallant, The *see* Beguman Ashiq
Gallant Girl *see* Shoorveer Sharada
Gallant Hearts *see* **Diler Jigar**
Galli Te Dilli (**Anant Mane**, Mar, 1982)
Galloping Ghost *see* Bhagta Bhoot
Galpa Helebi Sata (Nagen Ray, O, 1976)
Galpa Holeo Satti (**Tapan Sinha**, B, 1966)
Galyachi Shapath (R.V. Rane, Mar, 1949)
Gaman (*aka* Going: **Muzaffar Ali**, H, 1978)
Gamble of Life *see* Zindagi Nu Jugar
Gambler *see* Juari *or* Jugal Jugari
Gambler (Dwarka Khosla, H, 1960)
Gambler (Amarjeet, H, 1971)
Gamdani Gori (**M. Bhavnani**, St, 1927)
Gamdani Gori (**Mehul Kumar**, G, 1981)
Game (Anil Matoo, H, 1993)
Game of Chance, A *see* **Baazi**
Gammathu Goodacharulu (**Singeetham Srinivasa Rao**, Tel, 1978)
Gammat Jammat (Sachin, Mar, 1987)
Ganadevata (**Tarun Majumdar**, B, 1978)
Ganam (Shrikumaran Thampi, Mal, 1982)
Ganam Courtar Avargale (Manivannan, Tam, 1988)
Ganamela (Ambili, Mal, 1991)
Ganana Ghunghroo Haravala (Datta Mane, Mar, 1970)
Ganapati Bappa Morya (Ajit Jhala, G, 1986)
Ganapati Festival, The (?, Cinema De Luxe, St, 1912)
Ganashatru (**Satyajit Ray**, B, 1989)
Ganda Bherunda (**S.V. Rajendra Singh**, K, 1984)
Ganda Hendthi (**K.S. Prakash Rao**, K, 1977)
Gandandre Gandu (V. Somasekhar, K, 1989)
Gandanige Thakka Hendthi (Bhargava, K, 1991)
Gandaragandudu (K.S.R. Doss, Tel, 1969)
Gandhadagudi (Vijay, K, 1973)
Gandhara Golam (**Singeetham Srinivasa Rao**, Tel, 1980)
Gandhari (Sunil, Mal, 1993)
Gandhariyin Pulambal (*aka* Lament of Gandhari: **R.S. Prakash**, St, 1930)
Gandharva (Rajasekhar?, Husain Pics., K, 1992)
Gandharvagiri (N.S. Dhananjaya, K, 1983)
Gandharva Kanya (*aka* The Reunion: ?, **Krishna Film**, St, 1927)
Gandharva Kanya (**B. Vittalacharya**, Tel, 1979)
Gandharva Kanye (D. Shankar Singh, K, 1955)
Gandharvakshetram (**A. Vincent**, Mal, 1972)
Gandharvam (Balakrishnan Pottekkad, Mal, 1977)
Gandharvam (Sangeeth Sivan, Mal, 1993)
Gandhi (Richard Attenborough, E/H, 1982)
Gandhiji *see* Ahimsa Yuddham *or* Mahatma Gandhi
Gandhinagar Rendava Veedhi (**P.S. Ramakrishna Rao**, Tel, 1987)
Gandhinagar 2nd Street (Sathyan Andhikkad, Mal, 1986)
Gandhinagara (K.S.L. Swamy, K, 1968)
Gandhi Puttina Desam (Laxmi Deepak, Tel, 1973)
Gandikota Rahasyam (**B. Vittalacharya**, Tel, 1969)
Gandipeta Rahasyam (Prabhakara Reddy, Tel, 1989)
Gandondu Hennaru (**B.R. Panthulu**, K, 1969)
Gandugalli Rama (Bhargava, K, 1983)
Ganesh (A.K. Films Unit, A, 1973)
Ganesha Mahime (Manimurughan, K, 1981)
Ganeshana Madhuve (Phani Ramchandra, K, 1990)
Ganesha Subramanya (Phani Ramchandra, K, 1992)
Ganesh Avatar (G.V. Sane, St, 1922)
Ganesh Janma (Jal Ariah, St, 1930)
Ganesh Utsav (**Dadasaheb Phalke**?, St, 1925)
Gang Leader (Vijaya Bapineedu, Tel, 1991)
Ganga (**Rajen Tarafdar**, B, 1960)
Ganga (Kundan Kumar, Bh, 1965)
Ganga (M. Karnan, Tam, 1972)
Ganga (Jagdev Bhambhri, H, 1974)
Ganga (Balaji, K, 1984)
Ganga Abad Rakhi Sajanwa Ke (Rajeev Ranjan, Bh, 1987)
Ganga Aur Gauri (Jagdish Singh, Bh, 1988)
Ganga Aur Geeta (?, Vikrant International, H, 1979)
Ganga Aur Sarju (Akbar Alam, Bh, 1981)
Ganga Aur Suraj (A. Salaam, H, 1980)
Ganga Bani Shola (Kanti Shah, H, 1992)
Ganga Bhawani (**T. Prakash Rao**, Tel, 1978)
Ganga Bridge, The (**Fali Bilimoria**, E, 1982)
Ganga Chiloner Pankhi (**Padum Barua**, A, 1975)
Ganga Dham (B.S. Thapa, H, 1980)
Ganga Gauri (**B.R. Panthulu**, Tam, 1973)
Ganga Gauri Samvadam (V.N. Reddy, Tel, 1958)
Ganga Ghat (Rajpati, Bh, 1981)
Ganga Hamaar Mai (Dilip Bose, Bh, 1986)
Ganga Jaisan Bhouji Hamaar (Dilip Bose, Bh, 1986)
Ganga Jamuna Ki Lalkaar (Kanti Shah, H, 1991)
Ganga Jamuna Saraswathi (Uma Maheshwara Rao Tel, 1977)
Ganga Jamuna Saraswati (**Manmohan Desai**, H, 1988)
Ganga Jumna (**Nitin Bose**, H, 1961)
Ganga Jwala (Ashwini Kumar, Bh, 1987)
Ganga Ka Vachan (Gulshan Ashta, H, 1992)
Ganga Ke Teere Teere (Rajpati, Bh, 1986)
Ganga Ki Beti (K.D. Singh, Bh, 1986)
Ganga Ki Kasam (**B.S. Ranga**, H, 1975)
Ganga Ki Lehren (**Kidar Sharma**, H, 1957)
Ganga Ki Lehren (Devi Sharma, H, 1964)
Ganga Kinare (Kailash Advani, H, 1985)
Ganga Kinare Mora Gaon (Dilip Bose, Bh, 1983)
Ganga Ki Saugandh (Sultan Ahmed, H, 1978)
Ganga Maang Rahi Balidan (Radhakant, H, 1981)
Ganga Maiya (**Chandrakant**, H, 1955)
Ganga Maiya Bharde Acharwa Hamaar (Dilip Bose, Bh, 1982)
Ganga Maiya Bharde Godiya Hamaar (Jagdish Singh, Bh, 1991)
Ganga Maiya Kardo Milanwa Hamaar (Prem Singh, Bh, 1988)
Ganga Maiya Tohar Kiraya (Naresh Kumar, Bh, 1985)
Ganga Maiya Tohe Piyari Chadhaibo (Kundan Kumar, Bh, 1962)
Ganga Manga (**Tapi Chanakya**/V. Ramchandra Rao, Tel, 1973)
Ganga Meri Maa (Shyam Ralhan, H, 1982)
Gangapurni Ganga (S.J. Talukdar, G, 1980)
Ganga Sagar (Ashish Kumar, H, 1978)
Gangasangamam (Poonkunnam Varkey, Mal, 1971)
Ganga Sati (Dinesh Rawal, G, 1979)
Ganga Se Nata Ba Hamaar (Dilip Bose, Bh, 1991)
Ganga Tera Pani Amrit (Virendra Sinha, H, 1971)
Ganga Tere Desh Mein (Vijay Reddy, H, 1988)
Ganga Teri Shakti Apaar (**Muzaffar Ali**, H, 1985)
Ganga the Redeemer *see* Pitroddhar
Ganga Tulsi (Ram Singh, Bh, 1986)
Gan Gaulan (**Anant Mane**, Mar, 1969)
Gangavataran *see* Bhagirathi Ganga
Gangavataran (**Dadasaheb Phalke**/Madhukar Bavdekar, Mar/H, 1937)
Gangavatarana (**Babubhai Mistri**, Tel, 1984)
Gangavathar (C.K. Sachi, Tam, 1942)
Ganga Yamuna Kaveri (K. Sornam, Tam, 1978)
Gange Gauri (**B.R. Panthulu**, K, 1967)
Ganges at Your Doorstep *see* Gher Betha Ganga
Ganget Ghoda Nhala (**Raja Paranjpe**, Mar, 1955)
Gangor (Kamal Dadhich, R, 1964)
Gangor (Harish Tak, R, 1982)
Gangster *see* Chandal Chaukadi
Gangsters *see* Dorangia Daku
Gangu (Pramod Chakraborty, H, 1962)
Gangvaa (Rajshekhar, H, 1984)
Gang War (Kodi Ramakrishna, Tel, 1992)
Ganimi Kava (*aka* Dav Pech, Guerilla Tactics: **N.D. Sarpotdar**, St, 1928)
Ganimi Kava (**Bhalji Pendharkar**, Mar, 1981)
Ganwaar *see* Middle Fail
Ganwaar (Naresh Kumar, H, 1970)
Ganyer Meye (Gunamaya Bannerjee, B, 1951)
Gaon (Dwarka Khosla, H, 1947)
Gaon Hamara Shaher Tumhara (Naresh Kumar, H, 1972)
Gaon Ki Gori *see* Village Girl
Gaon Ki Kahani (**Harisadhan Dasgupta**, E, 1953)
Gao Tasa Changla Pan Veshila Tangla (**Anant Mane**, Mar, 1985)
Garabini (**Niren Lahiri**, B, 1950)
Garambicha Bapu (Baba Mazgavkar, Mar, 1980)
Garam Coat (Amar Kumar, H, 1955)
Garam Hawa (**M.S. Sathyu**, H, 1973)
Garam Khoon (A. Salaam, H, 1980)
Garam Masala (Aspi, H, 1972)
Garam Masala (Gopal Nandori, Tel, 1985)
Garbh Gyan (?, Ayyappan Prod, H, 1981)
Garden of Bancharam, The *see* **Bancharamer Bagan**
Garden Party of Sir Shapurji Broacha (Excelsior Cinematograph, St, 1912)
Gardish (**Priyadarshan**, H, 1993)
Garh Nasimpur (Ajit Lahiri, B, 1968)
Garib (**Ramchandra Thakur**, H, 1942)
Gariba Gharchi Lek (Kamalakar Torne, Mar, 1962)
Garibanche Rajya (Master Chhotu/S.V. Tunge, Mar, 1948)
Gariber Meye (Ardhendu Mukherjee, B, 1960)
Garibi (**Ramchandra Thakur**, H, 1949)
Garibi Hatao *see* Prarthana
Garibi Hatao (R.K. Midha, H, 1973)
Garib Ka Lal (*aka* Prince of Paupers: **V.M. Vyas**, H, 1939)
Garib Ka Pyara *see* Kala Wagh
Garib Ki Duniya (*aka* Dharmi Balak: Sorabji Kerawala, H, 1934)
Garib Ki Ladki *see* Bholi Bhikaran
Garib Ki Ladki (Jyotish Mukherjee, H, 1941)
Garib Ki Tope *see* Khudai Khidmadgar
Garibni Hai (*aka* The Curse: Asooji, St, 1930)
Garibon Ka Daata (Ramesh Ahuja, H, 1989)
Garib Parwar (**M. Bhavnani**, H, 1936)
Garijinchina Ganga (Kommineni, Tel, 1989)
Garjana (Anil Kumar, Tel, 1985)
Garjanai/Garjanam/Garjane (C.V. Rajendran, Tam/Mal/K, 1981)
Garma Garam *see* Ever Ready
Garma Garam (P.L. Santoshi, H, 1957)
Garm Hawa *see* **Garam Hawa**
Garmil (**Niren Lahiri**, B, 1942)
Garuda Dhwaja (Raj Bharath, K, 1991)
Garuda Garvabhangam (*aka* Pride of Satyabhama: **A. Narayanan**, St, 1929)
Garuda Garvabhangam (**R. Padmanabhan**/Fram Sethna, Tam, 1936)
Garuda Garvabhangam (**G. Balaramaiah**, Tel, 1943)
Garuda Rekhe/Garuda Rekha (P.S. Prakash, K/Mal, 1982)
Garuda Sowkiyama (**K.S. Prakash Rao**, Tam, 1982)
Garudi Ke Govind *see* Jadunath
Garva Khandan (*aka* Fall of Pride: M. Udvadia, St, 1930)
Garvi Naar Gujaratni (**Mehul Kumar**, G, 1981)
Garvo Garasiyo (**Chandrakant Sangani**, G, 1979)
Gaslight Mangamma (N.S. Maniam, Tam, 1977)
Gateway of India (Om Prakash, H, 1957)
Gaud Bangal (*aka* Magicians of Bengal, Kamroo Deshni Kamini: K.P. Bhave, St, 1925)
Gauhar (F.H. Hasan, H, 1953)
Gauna (**Amiya Chakravarty**, H, 1950)
Gauna (Tejesh, Bh, 1992)
Gauracha Navara (Usha Chavan, Mar, 1988)
Gaurav (K.J. Parmar, H, 1947)
Gauravam (Vietnam Veedu Sundaram, Tam/Tel, 1973)
Gauravamma (Ramanarayanan, Tel, 1992)
Gauravar (Joshi, Mal, 1992)
Gauri (**Kidar Sharma**, H, 1943)
Gauri (S.K. Ananthachari, K, 1963)
Gauri (**A. Bhimsingh**, H, 1968)
Gauri (P. Chandrasekhara Reddy, Tel, 1974)
Gauri (Dhira Biswal, O, 1979)
Gauri (A.C. Trilogchander, Tam, 1983)
Gauri Ganda (**Sundarrao Nadkarni**, K, 1968)
Gauri Ganesha (Phani Ramchandra, K, 1991)
Gauri Kalyana (Dwarkeesh, K, 1991)
Gauri Kalyanam (K. Shankar, Tam, 1966)
Gauri Kalyanam (Visu, Tam, 1983)
Gauri Manohari (T.S. Krishnakumar, Tam, 1992)
Gauri Puja (Vinod Desai, H, 1956)
Gauri Shankar (Ananda Mohan Roy, St, 1932)
Gauri Shankar (**Raja Nene**, H, 1958)
Gautama the Buddha (**Bimal Roy**/Rajbans Khanna, H, 1967)
Gautam Govinda (**Subhash Ghai**, Hind, 1979)
Gauthami (Kranthi Kumar, Tel, 1987)
Gavachi Izzat (Madhukar Bavdekar, Mar, 1962)
Gavran Gangu (Prakash Kashikar, Mar, 1989)
Gawah (A. Salaam, H, 1979)
Gawahi (Anant Balani, H, 1989)
Gawaiya (H.P. Sharma, H, 1954)
Gayab-e-Garud (*aka* Black Eagle: Harilal M. Bhatt, St, 1931)
Gayak (Shantanu Bhowmick, B, 1987)
Gayali Gangamma (Bheeram Mastan Rao, Tel, 1980)
Gayatri (**P.N. Menon**, Mal, 1973)
Gayatri (R. Pattabhiraman, Tam, 1977)
Gayatridevi Ente Amma (Sathyan Andhikkad, Mal, 1986)
Gayatri Madhuve (B. Mallesh, K, 1983)
Gayatri Mahatmya (*aka* Venukumar: ?, Star Films, St, 1923)
Gayatri Mahima (Harsukh Bhatt, H, 1977)
Gay Bandit *see* Laheri Lutera *or* Laheri Lutaru
Gay Birds *see* **Do Diwane**
Gay Cavalier, The *see* Rangila Rajput
Gay Prince *see* Rangila Raja
Gazab (?, Chitra Leela, H, 1951)
Gaze, The *see* **Nazar**
Gazi Diler (G.K. Mehta/K. Shah, H, 1936)
Gazi Salauddin (I.A. Hafizji, H, 1939)
Gedda Maga (S.A. Chandrasekharan, K, 1983)
Geddavalu Nane (Aruru Pattabhi, K, 1977)
Geet (S.U. Sunny, H, 1944)
Geet (*aka* The Song: **Ramanand Sagar**, H, 1970)
Geet (Partho Ghosh, H, 1992)
Geeta (Tinkari Chakraborty, St, 1931)
Geeta (**P.Y. Altekar**, Mar/H, 1940)
Geeta Ki Saugandh (Reetu Raj, H, 1988)
Geeta Mera Naam (Sadhna Nayyar, H, 1974)
Geetanjali (T. Hanumantha Rao, Tel, 1948)
Geetanjali (K. Rangaraj, Tam, 1985)
Geetanjali (**Mani Rathnam**, Tel, 1989)
Geetanjali (**Chandrakant Sangani**, G, 1993)
Geetanjali (**Shakti Samanta**, H, 1993)
Geeta Rahasya (*aka* A Friend in Need: K.P. Bhave, St, 1928)
Geet Baharan De (Henry Julius, P, 1964)
Geet Gata Chal (Hiren Nag, H, 1975)
Geet Gaya Pattharone (*aka* A Poem in Stone: **V.**

Shantaram, H, 1964)
Geet Govind (**Ramchandra Thakur**, H, 1947)
Geetha (G.K. Murthy, Tel/Tam, 1973)
Geetha (**Shankar Nag**, K, 1981)
Geetha Gandhi (**K. Subramanyam**, Tam, 1949)
Geetham (?, Centaur Art Prod, Mal, 1986)
Geetha Oru Shenbagapoo (S.A. Kannan, Tam, 1980)
Geetha Sangeetha (M.S. Kotareddy, Tel, 1977)
Geetha Saram *see* Navayuvan
Geet Milan Ke Gaate Rahenge (Qamar Hajipuri, H, 1992)
Gehra Daag (O.P. Ralhan, H, 1963)
Gehra Raaz (?, Saleem Productions, H, 1971)
Gehrayee (?, Shri Ram Krishna Films, Calcutta, H, 1954)
Gehrayee (**Aruna Raje**/Vikas Desai, H, 1980)
Gehra Zakhm (Deepak Bahry, H, 1981)
Gehri Chaal (**C.V. Sridhar**, H, 1973)
Gejje Naada (Vijay Nanjundappa, K, 1993)
Gejje Pooje (**Puttanna Kanagal**, K, 1970)
Geluvu Nannade (S. Chandrasekhar, K, 1983)
Gem City of India *see* Mysore Gem City of India
General Chakravarthi (**D. Yoganand**, Tam, 1978)
General Motors in India (**Paul Zils/Fali Bilimoria**, E, 1949)
Genesis (**Mrinal Sen**, H, 1986)
Genova (F. Nagoor, Mal/Tam, 1953)
Gentleman (Shivkumar/Vinod K. Verman?, H, 1989)
Gentleman (Shankar, Tam, 1993)
Gentleman Daku (Ram Daryani, H, 1937)
Gentleman Daku (A. Shamsheer, H, 1960)
Gentleman Loafer *see* Bhadraveshi Goonda
Ghabrahat (?, Kapoor Movies, H, 1989)
Ghalib (**M.S. Sathyu**, H, 1969)
Ghamand (Deepak Asha, H, 1955)
Ghamandi (Ramesh Bedi, H, 1980)
Ghanchakkar *see* Sheikh Chilli
Ghar (*aka* Home: **V.M. Vyas**, H, 1945)
Ghar (Manik Chatterjee, H, 1978)
Ghar Aakhir Ghar Hai (Pawan Kumar, H, 1988)
Ghara Bahuda (Sona Mukherjee, O, 1972)
Gharana (S. Bhatia, H, 1949)
Gharana (**S.S. Vasan**, H, 1961)
Gharana (K. Ravishankar, H, 1989)
Gharana Donga (**H.M. Reddy**, Tel, 1942)
Gharana Donga (**K. Raghavendra Rao**, Tel, 1980)
Gharana Gaja Dongalu (Vijay Reddy, Tel, 1985)
Gharana Gangulu (K. Subba Rao, Tel, 1981)
Gharana Mogudu (?, Devi Film, Tel, 1992)
Gharana Rowdy (Rajasekhar Reddy, Tel, 1984)
Ghara Sansara (Gopal Ghosh/Byomkesh Tripathi, O, 1973)
Ghar Aya Mera Pardesi (Ravindra Peepat, H, 1993)
Gharbar *see* The Householder
Gharbar (?, Hind Pics, H, 1948)
Gharbar (**Dinkar D. Patil**, H, 1953)
Ghar Basake Dekho (**Kishore Sahu**, H, 1963)
Gharcha Bhedi (Kantilal Dave, Mar, 1984)
Gharcha Jhala Thoda (**Raja Thakur**, Mar, 1957)
Gharchi Rani (**Rajdutt**, Mar, 1968)
Ghardhani (Ram Gabale, Mar, 1952)
Ghar Divdi (Manukant Patel, G, 1961)
Ghar Dwar (?, J.K. Films Raipur, Chattisgarhi, 1971)
Ghar Dwar (Kalpataru, H, 1985)
Ghare Baire (**Satyajit Ray**, B, 1984)
Ghar Ek Mandir (**K. Bapaiah**, H, 1984)
Ghar Ek Mandir (TV: **Chandrakant Sangani**, H, 1988)
Gharer Baire Ghar (Salil Dutta, B, 1980)
Gharer Math (Aaj Productions, B, 1957)
Ghar Gangechya Kathi (Madhav Bhoit, Mar, 1975)
Ghar Ghar Ki Baat (**Ravindra Dave**, H, 1959)
Ghar Ghar Ki Kahani (Balu Damania, H, 1947)
Ghar Ghar Ki Kahani (**T. Prakash Rao**, H, 1970)
Ghar Ghar Ki Kahani (Kalpataru, H, 1988)
Ghar Ghar Mein Diwali (**Gajanan Jagirdar**, H, 1955)
Ghar Gharni Vaat (Arun Bhatt, G, 1983)
Ghar Grihasthi (Dada Gunjal, H, 1958)
Ghar Ho To Aisa (Kalpataru, H, 1990)
Ghar Jamai (*aka* Henpecked Husband: **Homi Master**, St, 1925)
Ghar Jamai (**Homi Master**, G/H, 1935)
Ghar Jamai (Arun Bhatt, H, 1992)
Gharjavai (Kumarsen Samarth, Mar, 1941)
Gharjavai (Arun Karnataki, Mar, 1981)
Ghar Ka Chirag (Jagdev Bhambhri, H, 1967)
Ghar Ka Chirag (Sikandar Bharti, H, 1989)
Ghar Ka Sukh (Kalpataru, H, 1987)
Ghar Ki Bahu (**N.G. Devare**/G.K. Devare, H, 1947)
Ghar Ki Izzat (Ram Daryani, H, 1948)
Ghar Ki Laaj (**V.M. Vyas**, H, 1941)
Ghar Ki Laaj (**V.M. Vyas**, H, 1960)
Ghar Ki Laaj (**B.R. Ishara**, H, 1979)
Ghar Ki Lakshmi (*aka* The Wife: **Kanjibhai Rathod**, H, 1931)
Ghar Ki Numaish (Vithaldas Panchotia, H, 1949)
Ghar Ki Rani *see* Ardhangi
Ghar Ki Shobha (**Harshadrai Mehta**/Ramesh Saigal, H, 1944)
Gharkul (**Raja Thakur**, Mar, 1970)
Ghar Mein Raj Lugayan Ko (Sandeep Vaishnav, R, 1989)
Ghar Mein Ram Gali Mein Shyam (Subhash Sonik, H, 1987)
Gharni Shobha (Ratilal Thakar, G, 1963)
Ghar Number 44 *see* **House Number 44**
Gharoa (Mani Ghosh, B, 1947)
Gharonda *see* Nai Zindagi
Gharonda (*aka* The Nest: Bhimsain, H, 1977)
Ghar Parivar (Mohanji Prasad, H, 1990)
Ghar Sansar (**V.M. Vyas**, H, 1942)
Ghar Sansar (**V.M. Vyas**, H, 1958)
Ghar Sansar (**Krishnakant**, G, 1978)
Ghar Sansar (Siva Prasad Thakur, A, 1983)
Ghar Sansar (**K. Bapaiah**, H, 1986)
Gharwali (**Homi Master**/Nautam Trivedi, G, 1948)
Gharwali Baharwali (S.P. Rajaram, H, 1989)
Ghashiram Kotwal (**Mani Kaul**, K. Hariharan et al, Mar, 1976)
Ghatana (Mahesh Shaundilya, H, 1974)
Ghatana (Dharani, Tel, 1990)
Ghatkali (Bimal Roy, B, 1979)
Ghattashraddha (**Girish Kasaravalli**, K, 1977)
Ghayal (**Ramchandra Thakur**, H, 1951)
Ghayal (Raj Kumar Santoshi, H, 1990)
Ghazab (C.P. Dixit, H, 1982)
Ghazal (Zahur Raja, H, 1945)
Ghazal (Ved-Madan, H, 1964)
Ghazal (Rehman-Naushad, H, 1985)
Ghazal (Kamal, Mal, 1993)
Gher Betha Ganga (*aka* Ganges at Your Doorstep: **Shyam Benegal**, G, 1962)
Gher Gher Matina Chula (Dayabhai Bhagat, G, 1977)
Gholat Ghol (Vinay Laad, Mar, 1988)
Ghoom (Agrani, B, 1957)
Ghoom Bhangar Gaan (**Utpal Dutt**, B, 1965)
Ghor Pratigna (*aka* Sarojini: ?, **Kohinoor Film**, St, 1928)
Ghoshayatra (G.V. Sane, St, 1928)
Ghulami (*aka* Rape of Burma: M. Wadhwani, H, 1945)
Ghulami (**J.P. Dutta**, H, 1985)
Ghulami Ki Zanjeeren (C.P. Sharma, H, 1947)
Ghulami Nu Patan (*aka* Fall of Slavery: Shyam Sundar Agarwal, St, 1931)
Ghulami Zanjeer (*aka* Bondman: Prafulla Ghosh, St, 1931)
Ghumiye Ache Gram (**Sailajananda Mukherjee**, B, 1948)
Ghunghat (Shantikumar, H, 1946)
Ghunghat (*aka* The Veil: **Ramanand Sagar**, H, 1960)
Ghunghat (Jasubhai Trivedi, G, 1974)
Ghunghat (Satyapal Bagga, H, 1988)
Ghunghat Aur Ghunghroo *see* Paise Ki Gudiya
Ghunghat Ke Pat Khol *see* Azadi
Ghunghatwali (*aka* Painted Angel: **Nandlal Jaswantlal**, St, 1931)
Ghunghatwali (**Kanjibhai Rathod**, H, 1938)
Ghunghroo (Hiren Bose, H, 1952)
Ghunghroo (Ram Sethi, H, 1983)
Ghunghroo Ki Awaaz (Tulsi/Shyam **Ramsay**, H, 1981)
Giddh (T.S. Ranga, H, 1984)
Giddha (B.S. Shaad, P, 1978)
Gift of Sight (**Shantaram Athavale**, E, 1961)
Gijagana Goodu (T.S. Ranga, K, 1977)
Gili Bette (Vemala Jgannatha Rao, K, 1992)
Gili Gili Ge (Ishwar Chakraborty, B, 1989)
Ginny Aur Johnny (Mehmood, H, 1976)
Gipsy Meye (Binoy Bannerjee, B, 1950)
Giraftaar (Prayag Raaj, H, 1985)
Gir Game Sanctuary (**K.A. Abbas**, E, 1961)
Giribala (**Modhu Bose**, St, 1930)
Giribala (**Modhu Bose**, H, 1947)
Giri Bale (B. Mallesh, K, 1985)
Giridhar Gopal Ki Meera (Prafulla Roy, H, 1949)
Girija Kalyanam (K.S.R. Doss, Tel, 1981)
Girikanye (Dorairaj-Bhagavan, K, 1977)
Girl Friend (**Satyen Bose**, H, 1960)
Girl Mad *see* Pagal Premi
Girl Named Rita, A *see* Ek Thi Rita
Girls' Hostel (**Ravindra Dave**, H, 1962)
Girls' School (**Amiya Chakravarty**, H, 1949)
Girl Without a Name *see* Anamika
Girnar No Sinh (*aka* The Lion of Girnar: R.N. Vaidya, St, 1933)
Girno Gamar (*aka* Hill Man: ?, Arvind Pics., St, 1932)
Gist, The *see* **Saaransh**
Glass (Pradeep Krishen, E, 1979)
Glass Factory at Talegaon (**Dadasaheb Phalke**, St, 1915)
Glass Pane, The (**Kumar Shahani**, H, 1966)
Glimpse of Light of a Flying Fireball *see* **Oru Minnaminuginte Nurungu Vettam**
Glimpses of India (**Harisadhan Dasgupta**, E, 1965)
Glimpses of Kerala (**P.N. Menon**, E, 1983)
Glittering Sword *see* Tati Talwar
Glory of India *see* Noor-e-Watan
Glory of Virtue *see* Sheel Prabhav
Glowing Embers (Parts 1/2: **Girish Kasaravalli**, E, 1986)
Gnana Kuzhandhai (**K. Kameshwara Rao**, Tam, 1979)
Gnanambika (S. Nottani, Mal, 1940)
Gnanangal Jayikum Gnanangal Bharikum (V. Somasekhar, Mal, 1985)
Gnanangal Jeikattum *see* Nyayangal Jeyikattum
Gnana Oli (P. Madhavan, Tam, 1972)
Gnana Paravai (Vietnam Veedu Sundaram, Tam, 1991)
Gnanasoundari (**A. Narayanan**, Tam, 1935)
Gnanasoundari (F. Nagoor/Joseph Taliath, Tam, 1948)
Gnanasoundari (**Murugadasa**, Tam, 1948)
Gnana Sundari (**A. Narayanan**, St, 1929)
Gnana Sundari (**K.S. Sethumadhavan**, Mal, 1961)
Gnan Ekananu (P. Chandrakumar, Mal, 1982)
Gnan Gandharvan (**P. Padmarajan**, Mal, 1991)
Gnan Gnanalla (?, Mal, 1981)
Gnan Gnan Mathram (**I.V. Sasi**, Mal, 1978)
Gnan Kathorthirikkum (?, Mal, 1986)
Gnan Ninne Premikkunu (K.S. Gopalakrishnan, Mal, 1975)
Gnan Oru Parayatte (K.A. Venugopalan, Mal, 1982)
Gnan Piranna Natil (P. Chandrakumar, Mal, 1985)
Gnaval Pazhangal (Aziz, Mal, 1976)
Goadalli CID 999 (Dorairaj-Bhagavan, K, 1968)
Goat Sacrifice at Kalighat (?, Elphinstone Bioscope, St, 1906)
Godam (Dilip Chitre, H, 1983)
Godan (Trilok Jetly, H, 1963)
Godana (Vinay Shukla, Bh, 1987)
God and the Image, The *see* Bigraha
God atop the Hill, The *see* **Malamukalile Daivam**
Goddess, The *see* **Devi** *or* **Parasakthi**
Goddess from Below the Earth, The *see* **Patala Bhairavi**
Goddess Mahakali (*aka* Fall of Pavagarh: **Nagendra Majumdar**, St, 1928)
Goddess of Love (**Fatma Begum**?, St, 1927)
Goddess of Luck *see* Naseeb Ni Devi
Goddess of War *see* Ranchandi
Godhuli *see* Tabbaliyu Neenade Magane
Godhuli (**Kartick Chattopadhyay**, B, 1955)
Godhuli Belaye (Chitta Bose, B, 1964)
God of War *see* Ranadevata
God's Beloved *see* **Prabhu Ka Pyara**
God's Own Man *see* Ram Bharose
Gogaji Peer (Anand Kumar Dasani, R, 1969)
Gogola (Balwant Dave, H, 1966)
Goharjaan (Hiralal Doctor, St, 1931)
Going *see* **Gaman**
Gokul (Vasant Painter, H, 1946)
Gokul (**Arundhati Devi**, H, 1985)
Gokula Dasi (**K. Subramanyam**, Tam, 1948)
Gokulam (Vikraman, Tam, 1993)
Gokulcha Raja (Bal Gajbar, Mar, 1950)
Gokul Ka Chor (Vasant Painter, H, 1959)
Gokul Ka Raja (Bal Gajbar, H, 1954)
Gola Barood (David Dhawan, H, 1989)
Golamgiri (**Prashanta Nanda**, O, 1987)
Golanagamma (P.V. Raju, Tel, 1981)
Golap Bou (Shakti Bannerjee, B, 1977)
Golconda Ka Qaidi *see* Prisoner of Golconda
Gold *see* Sona
Golden City *see* Sone Ka Shaher
Golden Dagger *see* Khooni Katar
Golden Fortress, The *see* **Sonar Kella**
Golden Gang *see* Sunehri Toli
Golden Gang (*aka* Soneri Toli: K.P. Bhave, St, 1928)
Golden Grain of Bharatkhand, The (**P.V. Pathy**, E, 1942)
Golden Hair *see* Sunehra Baal
Golden Lotus *see* **Suvarna Kamal**
Golden Market *see* **Sanakeithel**
Golden Pathway (?, Royal Art Studio, St, 1930)
Golden River, The (**P.V. Pathy**, E, 1954)
Golden Seeta *see* **Kanchana Seeta**
Gold Medal, The (Ravi Nagaich, H, 1979)
Golibar (*aka* Avenging Angel: **B.P. Mishra**, St, 1931)
Golibar (*aka* Gorakhdhandha: **Nanubhai Vakil**, H, 1940)
Golibar (Sivamani, K, 1993)
Golkonda Abbulu (**Dasari Narayana Rao**, Tel, 1982)
Gollabhama (**C. Pullaiah**, Tel, 1947)
Golmaal (**Hrishikesh Mukherjee**, H, 1979)
Golmaal Bhaga 2 (Saiprakash, K, 1991)
Golmaal Govindan (**T. Rama Rao**, Tel, 1992)
Golmaal Radhakrishna (Saiprakash, K, 1990)
Gol Nishan (*aka* Mark of Zero: M. Udwadia, H, 1936)
Gomata (*aka* Sacred Cow: ?, **Madan Theatres**, St, 1924)
Gomatha En Kulamatha (M. Krishnan, Tam, 1973)
Gomathiyin Kathali (**P. Neelakantan**, Tam, 1955)
Gomti Ke Kinare (Sawan Kumar, H, 1972)
Gomtini Sakhe (Dinesh Rawal, G, 1978)
Gondhalat Gondhal (V.K. Naik, Mar, 1981)
Gonjamil (Sudhirbandhu Bannerjee, B, 1944)
Goodachari 116/CID 116 (M. Mallikarjuna Rao, Tel/Tam, 1966)
Goodachari 117 (Kodi Ramakrishna, Tel, 1989)
Goodachari No. 1 (Kodi Ramakrishna, Tel, 1983)
Goodbye Kingship *see* Virni Vibhuti
Goodbye Marriage *see* Nakoga Bai Lagna
Good Deed *see* **Upkaar**
Good Sister, The *see* **Nallathanka**
Goodu Putani (Laxmi Deepak, Tel, 1972)
Goonda (Mohammed Hussain, H, 1969)
Goonda (A. Kodandarami Reddy, Tel, 1984)
Goonda Rajya (Vijay, K, 1992)
Goonda Rajyam (Kodi Ramakrishna, Tel, 1989)
Goonj (**Phani Majumdar**, H, 1952)
Goonj (S.U. Syed, H, 1974)
Goonj (Jalal Agha, H, 1989)

Goonj Uthi Shehnai (**Vijay Bhatt**, H, 1959)
Goopy Bagha Phere Elo (Sandeep Ray, B, 1991)
Goopy Gyne Bagha Byne (**Satyajit Ray**, B, 1968)
Gopal Bhanar (Bikramjit, B, 1953)
Gopal Bhanar (Amal Sur, B, 1980)
Gopal Krishna (**V. Shantaram**, St, 1929)
Gopal Krishna (G. Bhosle, Tam, 1935)
Gopal Krishna (**V. Damle/S. Fattelal**, Mar/H, 1938)
Gopal Krishna (D. Raman, H, 1965)
Gopal Krishna (Vijay Sharma, H, 1979)
Gopala Krishnudu (A. Kodandarami Reddy, Tel, 1982)
Gopaler Kirti Borer Chaal (Niron Moya Sen, B, 1984)
Gopalraogari Abbayi (Manivannan, Tel, 1989)
Gopalraogari Ammayi (K. Vasu, Tel, 1980)
Gopaludu Bhoopaludu (G. Vishwanathan, Tel, 1967)
Gopi (**A. Bhimsingh**, H, 1970)
Gopichand (Ishwarlal, H, 1958)
Gopichand Bhartrahari (Manibhai Vyas, R, 1965)
Gopichand Jasoos (Naresh Kumar, H, 1981)
Gopi Krishna (Ravichandran, K, 1992)
Gopinath (**Mahesh Kaul**, H, 1948)
Goppari Pondam (Ravitheja Katragadda, Tel, 1991)
Goppavari Gothralu (A. Apparao, Tel, 1967)
Gopurangal Saivathillai (Manivannan, Tam, 1982)
Gopura Vasalile (**Priyadarshan**, Tam, 1991)
Gora (**Naresh Mitra**, B, 1938)
Gora (Desh Gautam, H, 1987)
Gora Aur Kala (Naresh Kumar, H, 1972)
Gorakh Aya (**Chaturbhuj Doshi**, H, 1938)
Gorakh Dhandha (Jasubhai Trivedi/Vaju Kotak, G, 1949)
Gorakh Dhandha (Ramesh Bedi, P, 1979)
Gorakhdhandha *see* Golibar
Gorakhnath *see* **Maya Machhindra**
Gorakhnath (*aka* Bhakti Prabhav: Chauhan, St, 1931)
Gorakhnath/Alakh Niranjan (**Bhalji Pendharkar**, Mar/H, 1940)
Gorakhnath Baba Tohe Khichdi Chadhaibe (Surendra Choudhury, Bh, 1986)
Gora Kumbhar (G.V. Sane, St, 1923)
Gora Kumbhar (Pandit Anandkumar, Mar, 1942)
Gora Kumbhar (Raman B. Desai, G, 1950)
Goral Garasni (Dilip Bhatt, G, 1981)
Gorantha Deepam (**Bapu**, Tel, 1978)
Gori (Sudhakar Sharma, H, 1992)
Gori Bala (*aka* Hell's Paradise: **P.Y. Altekar**, 1929)
Gori Diyan Jhanjharan (Subhash Bhakri, P, 1980)
Gorilla (Aakkoo, H, 1953)
Gorintaku (**Dasari Narayana Rao**, Tel, 1979)
Goshayatra (G.S. Vijayan, Mal, 1993)
Goshta Dhamal Namyachi (Girish Ghanekar, Mar, 1982)
Goswami Tulsidas (**Kanjibhai Rathod**, St, 1923)
Goswami Tulsidas (B.K. Adarsh, Avadhi, 1964)
Govardhan Dhari (G.V. Sane, St, 1921)
Government Mappillai (Manivannan, Tam, 1992)
Govinda Ala Re Ala (Govind Kulkarni, Mar, 1981)
Govindadas (Prafulla Chakraborty, B, 1956)
Govula Gopanna (**C.S. Rao**, Tel, 1968)
Gowandhi (G.R. Sethi, P, 1942)
Graduate (*aka* Parivartan: Harilal Doctor/Raja Yagnik, H, 1936)
Grahan (Arvind Kumar Sinha, H, 1972)
Grahan (**Atul Bordoloi**, A, 1990)
Grahana (**T.S. Nagabharana**, K, 1978)
Graher Pher (**Charu Roy**, B, 1936)
Gramadevathulu (**C.S. Rao**, Tel, 1968)
Grama Kanya (**Sarvottam Badami**, H, 1936)
Gramathu Adhiyayam (C. Rudraiah, Tam, 1980)
Gramathu Kilikal (Sanjeevi Ganesh, Tam, 1983)
Gramathu Kuyil (?, Tam, 1987)
Gramophone Singer (V.C. Desai/**Ramchandra Thakur**, H, 1938)
Grand Delhi Coronation Durbar (**Hiralal Sen**, St, 1912)
Grand Hotel *see* Hotel
Grand Masonic Procession (?, Elphinstone Bioscope, St, 1906)
Grandma, The *see* Nani Maa
Grand Pareshnath Procession (?, Elphinstone Bioscope, St, 1906)
Great Bengal Partition Movement (Jyotish Sarkar, St, 1905)
Great Cricket Match (Pathe Freres, St, 1912)
Great Day, A (**Adoor Gopalakrishnan**, H, 1965)
Great Delhi Durbar and Presentation of Colours (Excelsior Cinematograph,
St, 1911)
Great Devotee, The *see* King Shriyal
Great Devotee of Shri Krishna *see* Narasinh Mehta
Greatest Sacrifice, The *see* Samrat Shiladitya
Great Gambler, The (**Shakti Samanta**, H, 1979)
Great Problem, A (**Govind Saraiya**, E, 1960)
Great Show of India, The *see* Circus Sundari
Green Horizon (**Santi P. Choudhury**, E, 1972)
Greeshamam (V.R. Gopinath, Mal, 1980)
Greeshma Jwalakal (?, Mal, 1981)
Grihadah/Manzil (**P.C. Barua**, B/H, 1936)
Grihadah (Subodh Mitra, B, 1967)
Grihadevata (Madhav Shinde, Mar, 1957)
Grihajuddha (*aka* The Crossroad: **Buddhadev Dasgupta**, B, 1982)
Grihalakshmi (*aka* Sansar: **Chandulal Shah**, St, 1928)
Grihalakshmi (*aka* Educated Wife: **Sarvottam Badami**, H, 1934)
Grihalakshmi (**H.M. Reddy**, Tel, 1938)
Grihalakshmi (Gunamaya Bannerjee, B, 1945)
Grihalakshmi (Sewak, H, 1949)
Grihalakshmi (**H.V. Babu**, Tam, 1955)
Grihalakshmi (Raman B. Desai, H, 1959)
Grihalakshmi (**P. Bhanumathi/P.S. Ramakrishna Rao**, Tel, 1967)
Grihalakshmi (Vijaya Satyam, K, 1969)
Grihalakshmi (?, Mal, 1981)
Grihalakshmi (B. Bhaskara Rao, Tel, 1984)
Grihalakshmi (**C.S. Rao**, O, 1985)
Grihalakshmi (B. Subba Rao, K, 1992)
Grihapravesh (**Ajoy Kar**, B, 1954)
Grihapravesh (*aka* The Housewarming: **Basu Bhattacharya**, H, 1979)
Grihapravesham (**L.V. Prasad**, Tel, 1946)
Grihapravesham (**D. Yoganand**, Tam, 1976)
Grihapravesham (B. Bhaskara Rao, Tel, 1982)
Grihapravesham (Mohandas, Mal, 1992)
Griha Sandhaney (Chitta Bose, B, 1966)
Grihasthi (S.M. Yusuf, H, 1948)
Grihasthi (**Kishore Sahu**, H, 1963)
Grihasthi (**Prashanta Nanda**, H, 1984)
Growing Wings (**Govind Saraiya**, E, 1956)
Growth for a Golden Future (**Shyam Benegal**, E, 1982)
Gruhini (Vijaya Satyam, K, 1974)
Guardian Deity, The *see* **Kaval Daivam**
Guarding Angel, The *see* Allah Ka Pyara
Guddi (Jugal Kishore, P, 1961)
Guddi (**Hrishikesh Mukherjee**, H, 1971)
Guddo (Naval Kishore, P, 1985)
Guddu (Prem Lalwani, H, 1993)
Gudigantalu (V. Madhusudhana Rao, Tel, 1964)
Gudigantalu Mrogayi (Dhavala Satyam, Tel, 1984)
Gudippu Manasu (**K. Balachander**, Tel, 1979)
Gudiya (R. Pandya/A. Ranade, H, 1947)
Gudugu Sidilu (Shankar Narayana, K, 1988)
Guerilla (K.S. Gopalakrishnan, Mal, 1986)
Guerilla Fighter, The *see* **Padatik**
Guerilla Tactics *see* Ganimi Kava
Guest, The *see* Mehmaan
Guest House (Tulsi/Shyam **Ramsay**, H, 1980)
Guest House (**Ravindra Dave**, H, 1959)
Guha (M.R. Jose, Mal, 1981)
Guide (**Vijay Anand**, H, 1965)
Gujaratan (F.R. Irani, G, 1965)
Gulab Ka Phool (**Kidar Sharma**, H, 1958)
Gulacha Ganapati (P.L. Deshpande, Mar, 1953)
Gulam (*aka* Slave: **Moti Gidwani**, St, 1931)
Gulam Begum Badshah (Jugal Kishore, H, 1956)
Gulam Begum Badshah (Jambu, H, 1973)
Gulam Daku (**Moti Gidwani**, H, 1936)
Gulami *see* Ghulami
Gul Badan (**Harshadrai Mehta**, St, 1928)
Gul Badan (**Kanjibhai Rathod**, H, 1937)
Gul Bahar (**Nanubhai Vakil**, H, 1954)
Gul Bakavali (Rustom Modi, H, 1947)
Gul Baloch (?, Zaman Prod, P, 1944)
Gulchhadi (Sushama Shiromani, Mar, 1984)
Gul-e-Arab (?, Venus Film, St, 1930)
Gul-e-Bakavali *see* Paristan
Gul-e-Bakavali (**Kanjibhai Rathod**, St, 1924)
Gul-e-Bakavali (A.R. Kapoor, H, 1932)
Gul-e-Bakavali (**S. Soundararajan**, Tam, 1935)
Gul-e-Bakavali (K. Sadasiva Rao, Tel, 1938)
Gul-e-Bakavali (B.R. Mehra, P, 1939)
Gul-e-Bakavali (Ramanna, Tam/H, 1955)
Gul-e-Bakavali (Jugal Kishore, H, 1963)
Gul-e-Bakavali Katha (**K. Kameshwara Rao**, Tel, 1962)
Gulenar (D.A. Dandekar, St, 1930)
Gulenar (Harbans, H, 1950)
Gullopelli (**K.S. Prakash Rao**, Tel, 1961)
Gulmohar (**Kartick Chattopadhyay**, B, 1965)
Gulru Zarina (**J.J. Madan**, H, 1932)
Gul Sanobar (**Homi Master**, St, 1928)
Gul Sanobar (**Homi Master**, H, 1934)
Gul Sanobar (Aspi, H, 1953)
Gulshan *see* Jannat
Gulshan-e-Alam (**Nanubhai Vakil**, H, 1935)
Gulshan-e-Arab (K.P. Bhave, St, 1929)
Gulshan-e-Havas *see* Shikari
Gulzar (*aka* The Horrors of Slavery: **Nanubhai Desai**, St, 1927)
Gumasta (S.M. Yusuf, H, 1951)
Gumasta (R.M. Krishnaswamy, Tam/Tel, 1953)
Gumastavin Magal (**A.P. Nagarajan**, Tam, 1974)
Gumastavin Penn (**Balkrishna Narayan Rao**, Tam, 1941)
Gumnaam (Raja Nawathe, H, 1965)
Gumnaam Hai Koi (Yash Kapoor, H, 1983)
Gumrah (?, Ajit Pics, H, 1948)
Gumrah (**B.R. Chopra**, H, 1963)
Gumrah (Prem Manik, H, 1976)
Gumrah (**Mahesh Bhatt**, H, 1993)
Gumsum (Dayanand, H, 1982)
Guna (Santhana Bharati, Tam, 1991)
Gunah (**Kidar Sharma**, H, 1953)
Gunah (**Mahesh Bhatt**, H, 1993)
Gunah Aur Kanoon (**B.R. Ishara**, H, 1970)
Gunahon Ka Devta (Devi Sharma, H, 1967)
Gunahon Ka Devta (Kawal Sharma, H, 1990)
Gunahon Ka Faisla (Shibu Mitra/Pahlaj Nihalani, H, 1988)
Gunahon Ke Raaste (Radhakant, H, 1970)
Gunahon Ke Shatranj (**Chandrakant Sangani**, H, 1988)
Gunanodi Hennu Kodu (A.V. Sheshgiri Rao, K, 1982)
Gunasagari/Sathya Shodhanai (**H.L.N. Simha**, K/Tam, 1953)
Gunavanthudu (**Adurthi Subba Rao**, Tel, 1975)
Gunavathi (**B.S. Ranga**, Tam, 1960)
Gundammagari Krishnudu (Relangi Narasimha Rao, Tel, 1987)
Gundamma Katha/Manidan Maravalli (**K. Kameshwara Rao**, Tel, 1962)
Gundana Madhuve (G.K. Mudduraj, K, 1993)
Gundelu Thesina Monagadu (Chakraborty, Tel, 1974)
Gunehgaar *see* Criminal
Gunehgaar (*aka* Culprit: Shanti J. Dave/**Balwant Bhatt**, St, 1933)
Gunehgaar (*aka* Kalankini, the Sinner: H.R. Soni/Baba Kesar Singh, H, 1936)
Gunehgaar (S. Khalil, H, 1953)
Gunehgaar (R. Thaker, H, 1967)
Gunehgaar (**Rahul Rawail**, H, 1980)
Gunehgaar Kaun (Ashok Gaikwad, H, 1991)
Gunfight (*aka* Bandookbaaz: ?, Firdaus Films, H, 1960)
Gunfighter Johnny (K.S.R. Doss, H, 1972)
Gunial Gujaratan (**V.M. Vyas**, G, 1949)
Gunial Gulab (*aka* Patighatini Sati, For Country's Sake: Harihar Diwana, St,
1926)
Gunjan (V. Desai, H, 1948)
Gunsundari (*aka* Why Husbands Go Astray: **Chandulal Shah**, St, 1927)
Gunsundari (**Chandulal Shah**, H, 1934)
Gunsundari (**Ratibhai Punatar**, G/H, 1948)
Gunsundari (**K. Kameshwara Rao**, Tam, 1955)
Gunsundari Katha (**K.V. Reddy**, Tel, 1949)
Gunsundari No Ghar Sansar (**Govind Saraiya**, G, 1972)
Gupchup Gupchup (V.K. Naik, Mar, 1983)
Guppedu Manasu *see* Gudippu Manasu
Gupta Ratna (*aka* Hidden Treasure: B.S. Rajhans, St, 1931)
Gupt Gyan (B.K. Adarsh, H, 1973)
Gupt Shastra (Shriram Bohra, H, 1975)
Gurbani Jatt Di (?, Super Arts, P, 1990)
Guri (Vasu, K, 1986)
Gurjar Veer (**Dhirubhai Desai**, St, 1932)
Gurjoki Maar (*aka* Sword of Allah: ?, Surya Prakash Film, St, 1931)
Guru (**I.V. Sasi**, Tam/Tel, 1980)
Guru (Shrikant Nahata, K, 1989)
Guru (Umesh Mehra, H, 1989)
Guru Aur Chela (Chand, H, 1973)
Guru Bhakti (Rajendra Kumar, H, 1960)
Guru Bhakti (K.N. Chandrasekhar Sharma, K, 1984)
Guru Brahma (B. Gopal, Tel, 1986)
Guru Chengannur (**Adoor Gopalakrishnan**, E, 1974)
Guruchi Vidya Gurula? (Krishna Patil, Mar, 1958)
Guru Dakshina (?, Rajasthan Studios, H, 1950)
Guru Dakshina (Baby, Mal, 1983)
Guru Dakshina (Anjan Choudhury B, 1987)
Guru Dakshina (Dayal Nihalani, H, 1988)
Gurudakshinai (**A.P. Nagarajan**, Tam, 1969)
Gurudev (Vinod Mehra, H, 1993)
Guru Dronacharya (**Dadasaheb Phalke**, St, 1923)
Guru Ghantal (*aka* Shareef Badmash: Kikubhai Desai, H, 1937)
Guru Ghantal (S.M. Yusuf, H, 1956)
Guru Ho Jaa Shuru (Shiv Kumar, H, 1979)
Guru Jagadguru (A.T. Raghu, K, 1985)
Guruji Oru Vakku (Rajan Shankaradi, Mal, 1985)
Gurukilli (**Raja Paranjpe**, Mar, 1966)
Guru Machhindranath (*aka* Streeyaraj: **S.N. Patankar**, St, 1923)
Guru Manio Granth (S.R. Kapoor, P, 1977)
Guru Sarvabhowma Shri Raghavendra Karune (**Hunsur Krishnamurthy**, K, 1980)
Guru Shishyan (S.P. Muthuraman, Tam, 1988)
Guru Shishyaru (Bhargava, K, 1981)
Guru Shishyulu (**K. Bapaiah**, Tel, 1981)
Guru Shishyulu (S.P. Muthuraman, Tel, 1990)
Guru Suleman Chela Pahelwan (Radhakant, H, 1980)
Guru, The (James Ivory, E, 1969)
Guruvayoor Kesavan (**B.G. Bharathan**, Mal, 1977)
Guruvayoor Mahatmiyam (**P. Bhaskaran**, Mal, 1984)
Guruvuniminchina Shishyudu (**B. Vittalacharya**, Tel, 1963)
Gustakhi Maaf (*aka* Kshama Yachana: Rajkumar Bedi, H, 1969)
Gutiloni Ramachiluka (G. Rammohan Rao, Tel, 1980)
Gutter Nu Gulab (*aka* Dancing Girl: **B.P. Mishra**, St, 1927)
Guzara (S.M. Yusuf, H, 1954)
Gwalan (*aka* Milk Maid: **Nagendra Majumdar**, St, 1931)
Gwalan (Baburao Patel, H, 1946)
Gyanbachi Mekh (Vasant Painter, Mar, 1979)
Gyaniji (Chaman Nillay, H, 1977)
Gyarah Baje *see* Eleven o'clock
Gyarah Hazaar Ladkiyan (**K.A. Abbas**, H, 1962)
Gypsy *see* Pardesia
Gypsy Girl *see* Dildaar
Gypsy Girl (*aka* Dildaar, Sher Dil: Aakkoo, H, 1961)
Gypsy Love *see* Aatishe Ishq

H

Haadsa (Akbar Khan, H, 1983)
Haan (Lolit Chakraborty, B, 1954)
Haan Nu Haan Pyara (Avtar Bhogal, P, 1983)
Haar Jeet *see* **Abhinetri**
Haar Jeet (Tulsi Lahiri, B, 1939)
Haar Jeet (Juggi Rampal, H, 1954)
Haar Jeet (Manu Sen, B, 1957)
Haar Jeet (C.P. Dixit, H, 1972)
Haar Jeet (Avtar Bhogal, H, 1990)
Haar Mana Haar (Salil Sen, B, 1972)
Haat Baraley Bandhu (**Sukumar Dasgupta**, B, 1960)
Haath Ki Safai (**Prakash Mehra**, H, 1974)
Haath Lavin Tithe Sona (Datta Mane, Mar, 1973)
Haathon Ki Lakeeren (**Chetan Anand**, H, 1985)
Haavu Eni Aata (V.R.K. Prasad, K, 1985)
Habari (Sher Jung Singh, H, 1978)
Haddina Kannu (A.V. Sheshgiri Rao, K, 1980)
Hafta Bandh (Deepak Balraj Vij, H, 1991)
Ha Ha Hee Hee Hoo Hoo (P.L. Santoshi, H, 1955)
Hai Hai Nayaka (Jandhyala, Tel, 1989)
Hai Jani *see* Jamuna Paar
Hai Mera Dil (Ved-Madan, H, 1968)
Hai Meri Jaan (Roopesh Kumar, H, 1991)
Hai Padosan (Deep Rahi, H, 1984)
Haisiyat (**Dasari Narayana Rao**, H, 1984)
Haiwan (Ram Rano, H, 1977)
Haiwan (?, Popular Pictures, H, 1940)
Haiyana Daan (Vinod Parmar, G, 1985)
Haiyan No Haar (*aka* Fatal Garland: **B.P. Mishra**, St, 1928)
Ha Khel Savalyancha (Vasant Joglekar, Mar, 1976)
Hakim Babu (Pranab Das, O, 1985)
Halaal Ki Kamai (Swaroop Kumar, H, 1988)
Halaat (Raman Kumar, H, 1986)
Halaat (Naresh Nagpal, H, 1990)
Halahal (Shankar Kinagi, Mar, 1988)
Halaku (D.D. Kashyap, H, 1956)
Halaman Jethvo *see* Sati Sone
Halaman Jethvo (*aka* Sati Sone: Dinesh Rawal, G, 1977)
Hal Aur Bandook (Anup Malik, H, 1989)
Halbangala (**Dhiren Ganguly**, B, 1938)
Haldia Dock Complex (**Harisadhan Dasgupta**, E, 1978)
Haldi Kunku (**Anant Mane**, Mar, 1979)
Half Ticket (Kalidas, H, 1962)
Half-truth, The *see* **Ardh Satya**
Haliya Surasuraru (?, K, 1990)
Halkatha (**Dhiren Ganguly**, B, 1934)
Halla Gulla (**Master Bhagwan**, H, 1954)
Halla Gulla (Bhaskar Jadhav, Mar, 1988)
Halli Haidha (Amirtham, K, 1978)
Halli Krishna Delhi Radha (P.V. Raju, K, 1992)
Halli Mestru (Mohan Manju, K, 1992)
Halli Rambhe Belli Bombe (M.S. Rajasekhar, K, 1991)
Halodiya Choraye Baodhan Khaye (**Jahnu Barua**, A, 1987)
Halu Jenu (**Singeetham Srinivasa Rao**, K, 1982)
Hamaan (Sorabji Kerawala, H, 1934)
Hamaar Betwa (Kishore Kumar Singh, Bh, 1990)
Hamaar Bhauji (Kalpataru, Bh, 1983)
Hamaar Dulha (?, Bh, 1989)
Hamaar Sansar (Naseem, Bh, 1965)
Hamara Adhikar (*aka* Baap Bahu Aur Beta: Devi Sharma, H, 1970)
Hamara Desh (A.M. Khan, H, 1940)
Hamara Ghar (**Nanabhai Bhatt**, H, 1950)
Hamara Ghar (**K.A. Abbas**, H, 1964)
Hamara Haj (Ahmed Essa, H, 1957)
Hamara Khandaan (Anwar Pasha, H, 1988)
Hamara Sansar (Shanti Kumar, H, 1945)
Hamara Sansar (**T. Prakash Rao**, H, 1978)
Hamara Shaher (**Anand Patwardhan**, H/E, 1985)
Hamara Watan (**Jayant Desai**, H, 1956)
Hamare Gham Se Mat Khelo (Kunwar Shankar Tomar/Pal Premi, H, 1967)
Hamare Tumhare (Umesh Mehra, H, 1979)
Hamari Baat (M.I. Dharamsey, H, 1943)
Hamari Bahu Alka (**Basu Chatterjee**, H, 1981)
Hamari Beti (**Shobhana Samarth**, H, 1950)
Hamari Betiyan (**R.S. Choudhury**, H, 1936)
Hamari Dulhania (Shri Gopal, Bh, 1987)
Hamari Duniya (Sushil Sahu, H, 1952)
Hamari Jung (Rajesh Bhaduri, H, 1987)
Hamari Kismat (Nari Ghadiali, H, 1949)
Hamari Manzil (O.P. Dutta, H, 1949)
Hamari Shaan (**Balwant Bhatt**, H, 1951)
Hamari Shadi (**Basu Chatterjee**, H, 1990)
Hamari Yaad Ayegi (*aka* Jawan Mohabbat: **Kidar Sharma**, H, 1961)
Hamarun Hindustan (*aka* Father India: **R.S. Choudhury**, St, 1930)
Ha Mazha Marg Ekala (**Raja Paranjpe**, Mar, 1963)
Hameer Hath (Jaswant Jhaveri, H, 1964)
Hame Khelne Do (Rajendra Sharma, H, 1962)
Hamidabai Ki Kothi (TV: **Vijaya Mehta**, H, 1987)
Hamla (**N. Chandra**, H, 1991)
Hamlet *see* Khoon-e-Nahak *or* **Khoon Ka Khoon**
Hamlet (**Kishore Sahu**, H, 1954)
Hamraaz (**B.R. Chopra**, H, 1967)
Hamrahi *see* **Udayer Pathey**
Hamrahi (**T. Prakash Rao**, H, 1963)
Hamrahi (Sawan Kumar Tak, H, 1974)
Hamsa Geetham (**I.V. Sasi**, Mal, 1981)
Hamsa Geethe/Aakhri Geet (**G.V. Iyer**, K/H, 1975)
Hana Balavo Jana Balavo (Vijay, K, 1981)
Hanabari (**Premendra Mitra**, B, 1952)
Hand Held (Anil Tejani, H, 1975)
Handicrafts of Assam (**Santi P. Choudhury**, E, 1964)
Handicrafts of Rajasthan (**Santi P. Choudhury**, E, 1967)
Handsome Blackguard *see* **Fankdo Fituri**
Handsome Prisoners *see* Shamsherbaaz
Hands Up *see* Toofani Tamacha
Hangama (Ram Kamlani, H, 1952)
Hangama (S.M. Abbas, H, 1971)
Hangama Bombay Ishtyle (Siraj-Ayesha Sayani, H, 1978)
Hannele Chiguridaga (M.R. Vittal, K, 1968)
Hansamithun (Partha Prathim Choudhury, B, 1968)
Hansaraj (Ajit Ganguly, B, 1975)
Hanso Hanso Ai Duniyawalon (Dwarka Khosla, H, 1942)
Hanste Aansoo (K.B. Lall, H, 1950)
Hanste Khelte (Dayanand, H, 1984)
Hanste Rehna (Mohammed Hussain, H, 1950)
Hanste Zakhm (**Chetan Anand**, H, 1973)
Hansuli Banker Upakatha (**Tapan Sinha**, B, 1962)
Hantakulostannuru Jagratha (S.D. Lall, Tel, 1966)
Hanthakana Sanchu (B. Krishnan, K, 1980)
Hanthakulu Devanthakulu (K.S.R. Doss, Tel, 1972)
Hanuman Chalisa (?, Basant Pics, H, 1969)
Hanuman Janma *see* Sati Anjani
Hanuman Janma (**Dadasaheb Phalke**, St, 1927)
Hanuman Janma (*aka* Sati Anjani: **Raja Nene**, H, 1954)
Hanuman Pataal Parakram (*aka* Ahi-Mahi Vadh: ?, Kalika Film, St, 1931)
Hanuman Pataal Vijay (**Homi Wadia**, H, 1951)
Hanuman Pathal Vijayan (**Babubhai Mistri**, Tam, 1960)
Hanuman Vijay (?, British India Film, St, 1930)
Hanuman Vijay (*aka* Jai Shri Ram: **Babubhai Mistri**, H, 1974)
Happy Club (Tulsi Lahiri, B, 1936)
Happy Warrior *see* Sher Ka Bachcha
Haq (*aka* Haque: Harish Bhosle, H, 1991)
Haqdaar (Rafiq Rizvi, H, 1946)
Haqdaar (P.S. Wagle, H, 1964)
Haqdaar (S.K. Luthra, H, 1981)
Haqeeqat (**Chetan Anand**, H, 1964)
Haqeeqat (**T. Rama Rao**, H, 1985)
Haq Insaaf (*aka* Compromise: Kohinoor U.A., St, 1931)
Haque (Harish Bhosle, H, 1991)
Haradhaner Meye (Bijoy Chatterjee, B, 1983)
Hara Gauri (**Dhiren Ganguly**, St, 1922)
Harake (K. Nagesh, K, 1977)
Harakeya Kuri (K.S.L. Swamy, K, 1992)
Haranath Pandit (Panchanan Chakraborty, B, 1953)
Haranidhi (Tinkari Chakraborty, B, 1937)
Harano Prapti Niruddesh (Swadesh Sarkar, B, 1975)
Harano Prem (Ashim Bannerjee, B, 1966)
Harano Sur (**Ajoy Kar**, B, 1957)
Harathi (Laxmi Deepak, Tel, 1974)
Haraye Khunji (Subhash Chakraborty, B, 1973)
Hare Kaanch Ki Chudiyan (**Kishore Sahu**, H, 1967)
Hare Krishna Hello Radha (**C.V. Sridhar**, Tel, 1980)
Hare Rama Hare Krishna (**Dev Anand**, H, 1971)
Harfan Maula *see* Black Box
Harfan Maula (S.M. Sagar, H, 1976)
Har Har Gange *see* Sati Narmada
Har Har Gange (**Babubhai Mistri**, H, 1968)
Har Har Gange (**Babubhai Mistri**, H, 1979)
Har Har Mahadev (**Jayant Desai**, H, 1950)
Har Har Mahadev (**Chandrakant**, H, 1974)
Har Har Mahadev (Girish Manukant, G, 1983)
Hari Bhakta (T.V. Singh Thakore, K, 1956)
Hari Bhakti (*aka* Shri Gouranga Leela: Prafulla Ghosh, H, 1934)
Hari Darshan (Raman B. Desai, H, 1953)
Hari Darshan (**Chandrakant**, H, 1972)
Haridas (**Sundarrao Nadkarni**, Tam, 1944)
Haridhayame Sakshi (Shariff, Mal, 1977)
Harihara Maya (**T.R. Sundaram**, Tam, 1940)
Harihara Puthran (M.N. Balu, Mal, 1992)
Harihar Bhakti (C. Raghuvir, H, 1956)
Harijan (*aka* The Untouchable: ?, British-India Film, St, 1933)
Harijan (Raveendran, Tel, 1979)
Harijana Penn (*aka* Harijan Girl: C.V. Raman, Tam, 1937)
Harijana Simham (*aka* Lion of Harijans: Battling Mani, Tam, 1938)
Harijan Girl *see* Harijana Penn
Harilakshmi (Ardhendu Chatterjee, B, 1953)
Hari Maya (**Y.V. Rao**, St, 1932)
Harishchandra *see* Raja Harishchandra
Harishchandra (*aka* The Apostle of Truth: **Kanjibhai Rathod**, H, 1931)
Harishchandra (**Raja Chandrasekhar**/**Sarvottam Badami**, Tam, 1932)
Harishchandra (Rajopadhyay/**P. Pullaiah**, Tel, 1935)
Harishchandra (Prafulla Ghosh, B/Tam, 1935)
Harishchandra (**Kadaru Nagabhushanam**, Tam, 1943)
Harishchandra (Anthony Mithradas, Mal, 1955)
Harishchandra (Jampana, Tel, 1956)
Harishchandra (**Phani Burma**, B, 1957)
Harishchandra (**Dhirubhai Desai**, H, 1958)
Harishchandra (**K.S. Prakash Rao**, Tam, 1968)
Harishchandra Shaibya (Ardhendu Chatterjee, B, 1984)
Harishchandra Taramati (Adarsh, H, 1963)
Harishchandra Taramati (Adarsh, H, 1970)
Harishchandra Taramati (**Babubhai Mistri**, G, 1974)
Haritalika (G.V. Sane, St, 1922)
Hariya (Rajendra Sharma, H, 1958)
Hariyali Aur Raasta (**Vijay Bhatt**, H, 1962)
Harjaai *see* Bhanwara
Harjaai (Ramesh Behl, H, 1981)
Harmonium (**Tapan Sinha**, B, 1975)
Harsha Bhashpam (P. Gopi Kumar, Mal, 1977)
Harsiddh Mata (Subhash Shah, G, 1982)
Harya Narya Zindabad (Govind Kulkarni, Mar, 1972)
Haseenon Ka Devta (Ravi Nagaich, H, 1971)
Haseen Qatil *see* Nagan
Hashi Sudhu Hashi Noy (Santosh Guha Roy, B, 1963)
Hasida Hebbuli (S. Chandrasekhar, K, 1983)
Hasina (**J.P. Advani**, H, 1955)
Hasina Maan Jayegi (**Prakash Mehra**, H, 1968)
Hasiru Kaibisi Karedavo (**Chandrasekhar Kambhar**, K, 1990)
Hasiru Thorana (T.V. Singh Thakore, K, 1970)
Hasrat (Shaila Mukherjee, H, 1946)
Hastamelap (Jasubhai Trivedi, G, 1969)
Hasti (Ashok Gaikwad, H, 1993)
Hasyabhishekham (K. Hemambharadhara Rao, Tel, 1985)
Hasyarathna Ramakrishna (**B.S. Ranga**, K, 1982)
Hatamari Hennu Kiladi Gandu (?, Sri Nimishamba Prod., K, 1992)
Hatekhari (**Niranjan Pal**, B, 1939)
Hatey Bazarey (**Tapan Sinha**, B, 1967)
Hatey Roilo Tin (Sarit Bannerjee, B, 1977)
Hathat Dekha (Nityananda Dutta, B, 1967)
Hathi Ke Daant (**B.R. Ishara**, H, 1973)
Hathi Ki Rani *see* Elephant Queen
Hathili Dulhan (*aka* Taming of the Shrew: **J.J. Madan**, H, 1932)
Hathi Mere Saathi (Sandow M.M.A. Chinappa Devar, H, 1971)
Hathkadi (Sudarshan Bhatia, H, 1958)
Hathkadi (Surendra Mohan, H, 1981)
Hathyar (**J.P. Dutta**, H, 1989)
Hatimtai *see* Saat Sawaal
Hatimtai (Prafulla Ghosh, St, 1929)
Hatimtai (G.R. Sethi, H, 1933)
Hatimtai (G.R. Sethi, H, 1947)
Hatimtai (**Homi Wadia**, H, 1956)
Hatimtai (**Babubhai Mistri**, H, 1990)
Hatimtai Ka Beta *see* Noor-e-Yaman
Hatimtai Ki Beti (**Nanubhai Vakil**, H, 1940)
Hatimtai Ki Beti (*aka* Son of Hatimtai: **Nanubhai Vakil**, H, 1945)
Hatimtai Ki Beti (**Nanubhai Vakil**, H, 1955)
Hatya (Kirti Kumar, H, 1988)
Hatyakanda (Mohammed Ghousi, K, 1991)
Hatyara (Surendra Mohan, H, 1977)
Hatyare (Sunil Kumar, H, 1989)
Hatyarin (Vinod Talwar, H, 1991)
Haunted House *see* Bhutia Mahal
Hausla (Satyabham Sinha, H, 1984)
Havada Hoovu (N.T. Jayarama Reddy, K, 1983)
Haveli (Sudarshan Babbar, H, 1970)
Haveli (Keshu **Ramsay**, H, 1985)
Haveli Bulund Thi (TV: **Vijaya Mehta**, H, 1987)
Havina Hedde (V. Somasekhar, K, 1981)
Havina Hejje (K. Manimurugan, K, 1978)
Hawai Daku *see* Bandit of the Air
Hawai Insaan *see* Flying Man
Hawai Khatola (A.M. Khan/Sultan Alam, H, 1946)
Hawai Swar (*aka* Flying Prince: **M. Bhavnani**, St, 1929)
Hawalaat (Surendra Mohan, H, 1987)
Hawa Mahal (B.J. Patel, H, 1962)
Hawas (Sawan Kumar, H, 1974)
Hawk *see* Baaz Bahadur
Hazaar Haath (Rajdeep, H, 1978)
Hazaar Pariyan (**Balwant Bhatt**, H, 1957)
Hazaar Raatein (**Jayant Desai**, H, 1953)
Headmaster (Agragami, B, 1959)
Health in the Village (**K.G. George**, E, 1971)
Heart of a King *see* Raj Hriday
Heart Thief *see* Prem Masaa
Heat and Dust (James Ivory, E, 1983)
Hech Mazha Maher (**Rajdutt**, Mar, 1984)
He Daan Kunkvache (Vasant Painter, Mar, 1983)
Heer (Hameed Butt, H, 1956)
Heer (J.C. Anand, H, 1957)
Heera (Ishwarlal, H, 1947)
Heera (Sultan Ahmed, H, 1973)
Heera Aur Patthar (**Vijay Bhatt**, H, 1977)
Heera Ka Haar *see* Mangalsutra
Heeralal Pannalal (Ashok Roy, H, 1978)
Heera Moti (Krishan Chopra, H, 1959)
Heera Moti (Chand, H, 1979)
Heera Panna (**Dev Anand**, H, 1973)
Heera Sundari (A.P. Kapur, St, 1928)
Heere Ki Titali (**S.P. Choudhury**, H, 1970)
Heerer Prajapati (**Santi P. Choudhury**, B, 1968)

Heeron Ka Chor (S.K. Kapoor, H, 1982)
Heer Ranjha (**Fatma Begum**, St, 1928)
Heer Ranjha (*aka* Hoor-e-Arab: **R.S. Choudhury**/Pesi Karani, St, 1929)
Heer Ranjha (**J.P. Advani**, H, 1931)
Heer Ranjha (*aka* Hoor-e-Punjab: **A.R. Kardar**, H/P, 1932)
Heer Ranjha (Walli, H, 1948)
Heer Ranjha (**Chetan Anand**, H, 1970)
Heer Ranjha (Harmesh Malhotra, H, 1992)
Heer Syal (Krishnadev Mehra, P, 1938)
Heer Syal (**S.P. Bakshi**, P, 1960)
He Is Immortal *see* **Avan Amaran**
Hello Darling (A.B. Raj, Mal, 1975)
Hello Darling (Mouli, Tel, 1992)
Hello Madras Girl (J. Williams, Mal, 1983)
Hello Mister Zamindar (?, Sudarshanam Pics, Tam, 1965)
Hello my Dear-Wrong Number (**Priyadarshan**, Mal, 1986)
Hello Partner (K. Krishnamurthy, Tam, 1972)
Hello Yaar Pesarathu (A. Ramarajan, Tam, 1985)
Hell's Paradise *see* Gori Bala
He Maha Manab (Gunamoy Bannerjee, B, 1956)
Hema Hemeelu (**Vijayanirmala**, Tel, 1979)
Hemantha Rathri (P. Balthazar, Mal, 1978)
Hemareddy Malamma (**S. Soundararajan**/G.R. Rao, K, 1945)
Hemareddy Malamma (N.C. Rajan/T.V. Singh Thakore, K, 1973)
Hemavathi (Siddalingaiah, K, 1977)
Hemavin Kathalargal (T.V. Chandran, Tam, 1984)
Hendthi Beku Hendthi (Anil Anand, K, 1985)
Hendthige Helabedi (Dinesh Babu, K, 1989)
Hendthi Helikare Kelbeku (Relagi Narasimha Rao, K, 1992)
Henna (Randhir Kapoor, H, 1991)
Henne Ninagenu Bandhana (Ravindranath, K, 1986)
Hennina Balu Kanneru (**Y.V. Rao**, K, 1963)
Hennina Koogu (Dorairaj-Bhagavan, K, 1986)
Hennina Saubhagya (T.V. Panchakshari, K, 1984)
Hennina Sedu (A.M. Samiulla, K, 1981)
Hennu Huli (Rajasekhar, K, 1982)
Hennu Onnu Mannu (Basavaraja Kestur/M.V. Varadaraj, K, 1971)
Hennu Samsarada Kannu (A.V. Sheshgiri Rao, K, 1975)
Henpecked Husband *see* Ghar Jamai
Hera Pheri (**Prakash Mehra**, H, 1976)
Hercules (Shriram, H, 1964)
Her Fer (Amal Bose/Shanti Bhattacharya/Sudhansu Mukherjee, B, 1949)
Her Highness *see* Rani Saheba
Her Highness (**Balwant Bhatt**, H, 1946)
Her Last Desire *see* Uski Tamanna
Her Nights *see* Avalude Ravukal
Hero *see* **Nayakan** *or* **Nayak**
Hero (**Shyam Benegal**, H, 1975)
Hero (**Subhash Ghai**, H, 1983)
Hero (Vijaya Bapineedu, Tel, 1984)
Hero Hiralal (**Ketan Mehta**, H, 1988)
Hero No 1 (*aka* Sardar-e-Awwal: **Balwant Bhatt**, H, 1939)
Hero No 1 (?, Jawahar Films, H, 1959)
Hero of the Wilds *see* Jungle Ka Jawan
Hero Worship *see* Veer Pujan
He's in the Navy Now (**P.V. Pathy**, E, 1940)
Hicha Kay Chukla (Hemant Kadam, Mar, 1986)
Hich Khari Daulat (Babasaheb S. Fattelal, Mar, 1980)
Hidden Star *see* **Meghe Dhaka Tara**
Hidden Treasure *see* Bhedi Trishul *or* Gupta Ratna
Hide and Seek *see* Aankh Micholi
Hides and Strings (**John Abraham**, E, 1969)
Hidimb Bakasur Vadha (**Dadasaheb Phalke**, St, 1925)
Hifazat *see* In Custody
Hifazat (K.S.R. Doss, H, 1973)
Hifazat (Prayag Raj, H, 1987)
High Heel (Dilip Bose, B, 1963)
High Noon *see* **Uchi Veyil**
Hilal-e-Id *see* Hoor-e-Samundar
Hill Man *see* Girno Gamar
Hill Station (**Shakti Samanta**, H, 1957)
Hi Majhi Lakshmi (**P.K. Atre**, Mar, 1951)
Himalayan Tapestry, The (**M. Bhavnani**, E, 1957)
Himalay Ki Beti (*aka* Amar Prem, Daughter of Himalaya: **M. Bhavnani**, H, 1938)
Himalay Ki God Mein (**Vijay Bhatt**, H, 1965)
Himalay Se Ooncha (B.S. Thapa, H, 1975)
Himam (Joshi, Mal, 1983)
Himavahini (P.G. Vishwambaran, Mal, 1983)
Himmat (**Roop K. Shorey**, H, 1941)
Himmat (Ravi Nagaich, H, 1970)
Himmat Aur Mehnat (**K. Bapaiah**, H, 1987)
Himmat-e-Mard (*aka* Daredevil: Prafulla Ghosh, St, 1930)
Himmat-e-Mard (*aka* Lord of the Jungle: G.P. Pawar, H, 1935)
Himmatwala (**K. Raghavendra Rao**, H, 1983)
Himmatwali (Ratilal, H, 1947)
Himmatwali (G. Suryam, H, 1974)
Hi Naar Rupasundari (**Prabhakar Nayak**, Mar, 1966)
Hind Ka Lal (**Homi Wadia**/Ramji Acharya, H, 1940)
Hind Kesari (**Homi Master**, St, 1932)
Hind Kesari (**Homi Wadia**, H, 1935)
Hind Ke Tare (*aka* Stars of the East: Aseer, H, 1931)
Hind Mahila (*aka* Women's Challenge: **Premankur Atorthy**, H, 1936)
Hind Mail (**Nanubhai Vakil**, H, 1948)
Hindu Bathing Festival at Allahabad (**Hiralal Sen**, St, 1913)
Hindustan (?, Madan Theatres, H, 1972)
Hindustan Hamara (Ram Daryani, H, 1940)
Hindustan Hamara/Our India (**Paul Zils**, H, 1950)
Hindustan Hamara (**K.A. Abbas**, H, 1983)
Hindustan Ki Kasam (**Chetan Anand**, H, 1973)
Hip Hip Hurray (*aka* Choubeji: Aravind Sen, H, 1948)
Hip Hip Hurray (**Prakash Jha**, H, 1984)
Hira Aur Patthar *see* Heera Aur Patthar
Hirak Jayanti (Anjan Choudhury, B, 1990)
Hirak Rajar Deshe (**Satyajit Ray**, B, 1980)
Hiral Hamir (B.J. Patel, G, 1979)
Hira Moti Manika (J. Adeni, O, 1981)
Hiranne Kanthe (**Mehul Kumar**, G, 1984)
Hirasat (Surendra Mohan, H, 1987)
Hirer Angti (Rituparno Ghosh, B, 1992)
Hirer Shikal (Murari Chakraborty, B, 1988)
Hirey Manik (Salil Dutta, B, 1978)
Hirji Kamdar (**Homi Master**, St, 1925)
Hiro Ghoghe Jai Avyo (Arun Bhatt, G, 1981)
Hiro Salaat (**Ramchandra Thakur**, G, 1961)
Hirva Chuda (Kamalakar Torne, Mar, 1966)
Hisab Khoon Ka (Surendra Mohan, H, 1989)
Hisab Nikas (**Prashanta Nanda**, O, 1982)
His Father's Honour *see* Bhai Ki Kasam
His Highness *see* Ran Haq
His Highness (**Balwant Bhatt**, H, 1937)
His Highness (Anand Joshi, H, 1964)
His Highness Abdullah (**Sibi Malayil**, Mal, 1990)
His Love Affair (Raphael Algoet, St, 1931)
His Old Debt *see* Mard Ki Zabaan
Historical Sketch of Indian Women (**Mani Kaul**, E, 1975)
History of Indian Jute (**Buddhadev Dasgupta**, E, 1990)
Hitler Umanath (P. Madhavan, Tam, 1982)
Hi Vaat Pandharichi *see* Johar Maibaap
Holavu Gelavu (Bhargava, K, 1977)
Holi (**A.R. Kardar**, H, 1940)
Holi (**Ketan Mehta**, H, 1983)
Holi Aayee Re (Harsukh Bhatt, H, 1970)
Holiday in Bombay (*aka* Bambai Ki Sair: **Sarvottam Badami**, H, 1941)
Holiday in Bombay (P.L. Santoshi, H, 1963)
Holy Crime *see* **Chhaya**
Holy India *see* Teerthayatra
Holy Man, The *see* **Mahapurush**
Homage of Love *see* Premanjali
Homage to Lal Bahadur Shastri (**S. Sukhdev**, E, 1967)
Homage to the Teacher (**Mani Kaul**, E, 1967)
Hombisilu (Geethapriya, K, 1978)
Home *see* Ghar
Home and the World *see* **Veedu** *or* **Ghare Baire**
Homecoming, The (**Shantaram Athavale**, E, 1962)
Home Front (**P.V. Pathy**, E, 1943)
Honee Anhonee (TV: **Rahul Rawail**, H, 1988)
Honest Rogue *see* **Gharana Donga**
Honey (Sheetal, H, 1982)
Honeymoon *see* Sunehri Raatein
Honeymoon (Hiren Nag, H, 1973)
Honeymoon (A.B. Raj, Mal, 1974)
Honeymoon (Surendra Mohan, H, 1992)
Hong Kong (Pachhi, H, 1962)
Honhar (*aka* Destiny: **Gajanan Jagirdar**, H, 1936)
Hoo Bisilu (T.V. Singh Thakore, K, 1971)
Hooded Terror *see* Bhedi Burkha
Hoor-al-Bahar *see* Jal Kumari
Hoor-e-Arab *see* Heer Ranjha
Hoor-e-Arab (*aka* Alladdin and the Magic Lamp: ?, **Madan** Theatres, St, 1928)
Hoor-e-Arab (P.N. Arora, H, 1955)
Hoor-e-Baghdad (*aka* Forbidden Love: **B.P. Mishra**, St, 1928)
Hoor-e-Baghdad (R.N. Vaidya, H, 1934)
Hoor-e-Baghdad (A.M. Khan, H, 1946)
Hoor-e-Haram *see* Afzal
Hoor-e-Hind (**Harshadrai Mehta**, St, 1932)
Hoor-e-Jungle (*aka* Jungle Girl: Jaswamt Jhaveri, H, 1946)
Hoor-e-Misar (*aka* Land of Pyramids: Prafulla Ghosh, St, 1931)
Hoor-e-Misar (**Homi Master**, H, 1932)
Hoor-e-Murakak (?, B.I. Quality Films, H, 1934)
Hoor-e-Punjab *see* Heer Ranjha
Hoor-e-Roshan (*aka* Roshan Ara: **Nanubhai Vakil**, St, 1931)
Hoor-e-Samundar (*aka* Hilal-e-Id: **Dhirubhai Desai**, H, 1936)
Hoovu Mullu (A.V. Sheshgiri Rao, K, 1968)
Horky Podzim S Vuni Manga (*aka* The Bitter Autumn with a Scent of Mango:
Jiri Sequens/**Basu Bhattacharya**, Czech, 1983)
Horrors of Slavery, The *see* Gulzar
Hosa Baalu (N.T. Nagendrappa, K, 1985)
Hosa Belaku (Dorairaj-Bhagavan, K, 1982)
Hosa Itihasa (D. Rajendra Babu, K, 1984)
Hosa Jeevana (Bhargava, K, 1990)
Hosa Kalla Hale Kulla (Dwarkeesh, K, 1992)
Hosa Love Story (?, V.S.R. Prod., K, 1993)
Hosa Neeru (K.V. Jayaram, K, 1985)
Hosa Raga (K.V. Jayaram, K, 1992)
Hosa Teerpu (**Shankar Nag**, K, 1983)
Hoshiyar (**K. Raghavendra Rao**, H, 1985)
Hosilu Mettida Hennu (V.T. Thyagarajan, K, 1975)
Hospital *see* **Jogajog**
Hospital (**Sushil Majumdar**, B, 1960)
Hot Blood *see* Bharat Ka Lal
Hotel (*aka* Grand Hotel: Manmohan Sabir, H, 1956)
Hotel (Tulsi/Shyam **Ramsay**, H, 1981)
Hotel Highrange (**P. Subramanyam**, Mal, 1968)
Hotel Snow Fox (Yatrik, B, 1976)
Hotel Sorgam (G. Ramakrishna, Tam, 1974)
Hothal Padmini (**Harshadrai Mehta**, St, 1925)
Hothal Padmini (**Kanjibhai Rathod**, H, 1934)
Hothal Padmini (*aka* Devi Hothal: Maheshchandra Chunawala, G, 1947)
Hothal Padmini (**Ravindra Dave**, G, 1974)
Hot Winds *see* **Garam Hawa**
House, The *see* **Veedu**
Householder, The (*aka* Gharbar: James Ivory, E/H, 1963)
House Number 44 (M.K. Burman, H, 1955)
House Number 13 (Baby, H, 1991)
House of Mystery *see* Bhedi Bungla
House that Ananda Built, The (**Fali Bilimoria**, E, 1967)
Housewarming, The *see* Grihapravesh
How Bhim Was Brought Back to Life *see* Bhim Sanjeevan
How Films Are Made (**Dadasaheb Phalke**, St, 1917)
Howrah Bridge (**Shakti Samanta**, H, 1958)
Howrah Express (Kawal Sharma, H, 1961)
How to Vote (**Shantaram Athavale**, E, 1961)
Hoysala (C.V. Shivashankar, K, 1975)
Hoysala and Chalukyan Architecture of Karnataka (**T.S. Nagabharana**, E, 1984)
Hrad (Ardhendu Sen, B, 1955)
Hridaya Bandhana (?, Shakti Creations, K, 1993)
Hridaya Deepa (C.S. Subbarayan, K, 1980)
Hridaya Geethe (Bhargava, K, 1989)
Hridaya Hadithu (M.S. Rajasekhar, K, 1991)
Hridaya Jwala (*aka* A Woman's Vengeance: Vaidya, St, 1930)
Hridaya Manthan (*aka* Call of the Soul: **Jaddanbai**, H, 1936)
Hridayame Sakshi (**I.V. Sasi**, Mal, 1977)
Hridayam Oru Kshetram (**P. Subramanyam**, Mal, 1976)
Hridayam Padunnu (G. Premkumar, Mal, 1980)
Hridayar Proyojan (Gouri Burman, A, 1972)
Hridayasangama (Rashi Sahodararu, K, 1972)
Hridayathil Nee Mathram (Govindan, Mal, 1979)
Hridayathinte Nirangal (**P. Subramanyam**, Mal, 1979)
Hridaya Triputi *see* Manorama
Hridaya Veena (*aka* Dance of Life: **Harshadrai Mehta**, St, 1931)
Hrithubedham *see* **Ruthubhedam**
Hua Savera (Kulbhushan Agarwal, H, 1948)
Hudugathada Hudugi (Amrutham, K, 1976)
Hukum Ka Ekka (Shanti J. Dave, H, 1939)
Hukum Ka Ekka (*aka* Ace of Spades: Ravindra Vyas, H, 1964)
Hukumat (Raja Yagnik, H, 1954)
Hukumat (Anil Sharma, H, 1987)
Hulare (O.P. Dutta, P, 1957)
Hulchul (S.K. Ojha, H, 1951)
Hulchul (O.P. Ralhan, H, 1971)
Huli Bantu Huli (C. Chandrasekhar, K, 1978)
Huli Hebbuli (Vijay, K, 1987)
Huli Hejje (Ravi, K, 1984)
Huliyada Kala (**B.S. Ranga**, K, 1984)
Huliya Halina Mevu (Vijay, K, 1979)
Hullabaloo over Georgie and Bonnie's Pictures (James Ivory, E, 1978)
Hulusthul (Aravind Mukherjee, B, 1985)
Hum (**Mukul S. Anand**, H, 1991)
Human Emotions *see* **Pati Bhakti**
Humayun (**Mehboob**, H, 1945)
Hum Bachche Hindustan Ke (Dhanpat Mehta, H, 1984)
Hum Bhi Insaan Hain (**Phani Majumdar**, H, 1948)
Hum Bhi Insaan Hain (Ranjan Majumdar, H, 1959)
Hum Bhi Insaan Hain (Manivannan, H, 1989)
Hum Bhi Kuch Kam Nahin (Ramanlal Desai, H, 1958)
Hum Bhi Kuch Kam Nahin (M.S. Gopinath, H, 1979)
Humdard (S. Bhagat, H, 1953)
Hum Diwane (**Master Bhagwan**, H, 1965)
Hum Do Daku (**Kishore Kumar**, H, 1967)
Hum Do Hamare Do (**B.R. Ishara**, H, 1984)
Hum Dono (Amarjeet, H, 1961)
Hum Dono (B.S. Glaad, H, 1984)
Humdum (Krishna Malik, H, 1984)
Hum Ek Hain (P.L. Santoshi, H, 1946)
Hum Ek Hain (Daljeet, H, 1969)
Hum Farishte Nahin (Jatin Kumar, H, 1988)
Hum Hain Kamaal Ke (Vijay Reddy, H, 1993)
Hum Hain Lajawaab (**Mohan Segal**, H, 1984)
Hum Hain Rahi Pyar Ke (**Mahesh Bhatt**, H, 1993)
Hum Hindustani (Ram Mukherjee, H, 1960)
Hum Hindustani (TV: **Hrishikesh Mukherjee**, H, 1986)
Hum Intezar Karenge (Prabhat Roy, H, 1989)
Humjoli (Ismail Memon/Lukman, H, 1946)
Humjoli (Ramanna, H, 1970)
Hum Jungli Hain (**P. Subramanyam**, H, 1973)
Humkadam (Anil Ganguly, H, 1980)
Hum Kahan Ja Rahe Hain (**Nitin Bose**, H, 1966)
Hum Kisise Kum Nahin (**Nasir Hussain**, H, 1977)
Humlaa *see* Hamla

Humlog (**Zia Sarhadi**, H, 1951)
Humlog (TV: Kumar Vasudev, H, 1984-85)
Hum Matwale Naujawan (L.R. Asthana, H, 1961)
Hum Nahin Sudhrenge (Asrani, H, 1980)
Hum Naujawan (**Dev Anand**, H, 1985)
Hum Paanch (**Bapu**, H, 1980)
Hum Panchhi Ek Dal Ke (P.L. Santoshi, H, 1957)
Hum Rahe Na Hum (Ketan Anand, H, 1984)
Humrahi *see* Hamrahi
Humsafar (A.N. Bannerjee, H, 1953)
Humsaya (Joy Mukherjee, H, 1968)
Humse Badhkar Kaun (Deepak Bahry, H, 1981)
Humse Hai Zamana (Deepak Bahry, H, 1983)
Humse Na Jeeta Koi (Shibu Mitra, H, 1983)
Humse Na Takrana (Deepak Bahry, H, 1990)
Humshakal (Jambu, H, 1974)
Humshakal (Kalpataru, H, 1992)
Hum Sub Chor Hain *see* The Criminals
Hum Sub Chor Hain (I.S. Johar, H, 1956)
Hum Sub Qatil Hain *see* The Killers
Hum Sub Ustad Hain (Maruti, H, 1965)
Hum Tere Aashiq Hain (Prem Sagar, H, 1979)
Hum To Chale Pardes (Ravindra Peepat, H, 1988)
Hum Tum Aur Woh (**Mehboob**, H-Urdu, 1938)
Hum Tum Aur Woh (Shiv Kumar, H, 1971)
Hun Hunshi Hunshilal (Sanjiv Shah, G, 1992)
Hunger *see* **Pasi**
Hungry Autumn (**Gautam Ghosh**, E, 1976)
Hungry Stones *see* **Kshudista Pashan**
Hunimeya Rathriyalli (Rajasekhar, K, 1980)
Hunterwali (**Homi Wadia**, H, 1935)
Hunterwali (*aka* Chabukwali: B.J. Patel, H, 1959)
Hunterwali (Mohan Choti, H, 1977)
Hunterwali Ki Beti (*aka* Daughter of Hunterwali: Batuk Bhatt, H/Arabic, 1943)
Hurricane Express (M.H. Doctor, H, 1961)
Hurricane Hansa (R.N. Vaidya, H, 1937)
Hurricane Special (Chunilal Parekh, H, 1939)
Husain (**Santi P. Choudhury**, E, 1980)
Husband and Wife *see* Pati Patni
Hush *see* Chup
Husn Ara (Mohanlal Shah, St, 1930)
Husn Aur Ishq (Naresh Kumar, H, 1966)
Husn Bano (Aakkoo, H, 1956)
Husn De Hulare (?, Filmmakers Int., P, 1987)
Husn Ka Chor (**J.B.H. Wadia**, H, 1953)
Husn Ka Daku (*aka* Mysterious Eagle: **A.R. Kardar**, St, 1929)
Husn Ka Gulam (*aka* Passion: ?, Paramount, H, 1933)
Husn Ka Gulam (Kedar Kapoor, H, 1966)
Husn Pari (*aka* Queen of Fairies: A.P. Kapur/M.D. Shah?, **Sharda Film**, St, 1931)
Hyalach Mhantat Prem (Madhav Velkar, Mar, 1964)
Hyderabad Ki Nazneen (S.M. Yusuf, H, 1952)
Hyoch Navara Pahije (**Dada Kondke**, Mar, 1980)

I

I Am a Clown *see* **Mera Naam Joker**
Ibbani Karagitu (K.V. Jayaram, K, 1983)
Ibrat (M. Inamuddin, H, 1954)
Ice Cream (?, Simna Movies, Mal, 1986)
Ichhamoti (Amar Bhattacharya, B, 1983)
Ichhapuran (*aka* Wish Fulfilment: **Mrinal Sen**, B, 1969)
Ida Lokam (**K.S. Prakash Rao**, Tel, 1973)
Idanazhiyil Oru Kalocha (Bhadran, Mal, 1987)
Ida Nilangal (**I.V. Sasi**, Mal, 1985)
Ida Prapancham (M. Subbaiah, Tel, 1987)
Idavela (Mohan, Mal, 1982)
Idaya Deepam (B. Nithyanandan, Tam, 1989)
Idaya Geetham (Joseph Taliath, Tam, 1950)
Idayakkani (A. Jagadeeshan, Tam, 1975)
Idaya Koyil (**Mani Rathnam**, Tel, 1985)
Idayam (Kadir, Tam, 1991)
Idaya Malar (**Gemini Ganesh**/Thamaraimanalan, Tam, 1976)
Idayam Parkirathu (A. Jagannathan, Tam, 1974)
Idaya Thamarai (K. Rajeshwar, Tam, 1990)
Idayathil Nee (V. Srinivasan, Tam, 1963)
Idaya Vasal (Chandranath, Tam, 1991)
Idaya Veenai (**Krishnan-Panju**, Tam, 1972)
Idd *see* Id
Iddaru Ammayilu (**Puttanna Kanagal**, Tel, 1970)
Iddaru Dongalu (**K. Raghavendra Rao**, Tel, 1984)
Iddaru Iddare (V. Madhusudhana Rao, Tel, 1976)
Iddaru Iddare (Vijaya Bapineedu, Tel, 1990)
Iddaru Kiladilu (Relangi Narasimha Rao, Tel, 1983)
Iddaru Kodakulu (Kotta Subba Rao, Tel, 1982)
Iddaru Mithralu (**Adurthi Subba Rao**, Tel, 1961)
Iddaru Monagallu (**B. Vittalacharya**, Tel, 1967)
Iddaru Monagallu (M.R. Vijaychandra, Tel, 1985)
Iddaru Pellala Muddula Police (Relangi Narasimha Rao, Tel, 1991)
Iddaru Pellalu (Nagoor, Tel, 1954)
Iddaru Pellam Mudhula Mogudu (Relangi Narasimha Rao, Tel, 1991)
Ideal Wife, The *see* Arya Mahila
Ideal Woman, An *see* Adarsha Ramani
Ideal Womanhood *see* Roop Sundari
Idekaddi Nyayam (**Dasari Narayana Rao**, Tel, 1977)
Ide Mahasudina (B.C. Srinivas, K, 1965)
Idem Pellam Baboyi (K. Ravi Teja, Tel, 1990)
Ide Naa Ghattam (K.S.R. Doss, Tel, 1985)
Ide Naa Nyayam (M. Nandakumar, Tel, 1986)
Ide Naa Samadhanam (Rajachandra, Tel, 1986)
Ide Police Belt (Muthuraj, K, 1991)
Idhayathe Thirudathe *see* **Geetanjali**
Idhu *see* Idu
Idhu Enga Bhoomi (M. Karnan, Tam, 1984)
Idhu Engal Needhi (S.A. Chandrasekharan, Tam, 1988)
Idhu Engal Rajyam (M.S. Madhu, Tam, 1985)
Idhu Enga Nadu (Ramanarayanan, Tam, 1983)
Idhu Oru Thodarkathai (Anumohan, Tam, 1987)
Idhuthanda Sattam (Senthilnathan, Tam, 1992)
Idhu Ungal Kudumbam (S. Umesh, Tam, 1989)
Idhya Kamalam (?, Prasad Prod, Tam, 1965)
Idi Kadhu Mugimpu (Vejalla Satyanarayana, Tel, 1983)
Idi Kathakadu (**K. Balachander**, Tel, 1979)
Idimuzhakam (Shrikumaran Thampi, Mal, 1980)
Idiot (**Mani Kaul**, H, 1991)
Idiot Son (?, Deccan Cinetone, Tam, 1943)
Idi Pellantara (Vijaya Bapineedu, Tel, 1982)
Idiyum Minnalum (P.G. Vishwambaran, Mal, 1982)
Id Ka Chand (A.P. Kapur, H, 1933)
Id Ka Chand (**Nanubhai Vakil**, H, 1964)
Id Ka Salaam (K. Mallik, H, 1976)
Id Mubarak (ak Eid Mubrak: **K.A. Abbas**, H, 1960)
Id Mubrak (Ramesh Malhotra, H, 1988)
Ido Prema Charitra (Ameer John, Tel, 1985)
Idu Namma Alu (Balakumaran, Tam, 1988)
Idu Namma Bhoomi (P. Vasu, Tam, 1992)
Idu Namma Desha (A.R Sabhapati, K, 1974)
Idu Saadhya (Dinesh Babu, K, 1989)
Idu Sathiyam (K. Shankar, Tam, 1963)
If *see* Agar
I Have Fallen in Love *see* **Maine Pyar Kiya**
Ijaazat (**S.S. Gulzar**, H, 1987)
Ikanaina Marandi (D. Gangadhar, Tel, 1983)
Ik Musafir (**R.L. Shorey/Roop K. Shorey**, P, 1940)
Ilaka (Aziz Sejawal, H, 1989)
Ilakkangal (*aka* Elakkangal, Emotional Upsurge: Mohan, Mal, 1981)
Ilamai (Ramanarayanan, Tam, 1985)
Ilamai Kalangal (Harivannan, Tam, 1983)
Ilamaikolam (N. Venkatesh, Tam, 1980)
Ilanjippookkal (?, Pushpa & Pushpa Prod, Mal, 1986)
Ilanjodigal (Ramanarayanan, Tam, 1982)
Ilankeswaran (T.R. Ramanna, Tam, 1987)
Ilavarasan (Senthilnathan, Tam, 1991)
Ilavelpu (**Yoganand**, Tel, 1956)
Ilaya Piravigal (A. Hridayaraj, Tam, 1983)
Ilaya Thalaimurai (**Krishnan-Panju**, Tam, 1976)
Illala Sandadi (Relangi Narasimha Rao, Tel, 1982)
Illale Devatha (T. Prasad, Tel, 1985)
Illaliko Pariksha (T. Prasad, Tel, 1985)
Illali Korikalu (G. Rammohan Rao, Tel, 1982)
Illali Muchatlu (M.S. Kota Reddy, Tel, 1979)
Illali Pratigna (Tatineni Prasad, Tel, 1986)
Illali Sapadham (Gangai Amaran, Tel, 1985)
Illalu (**Gudavalli Ramabrahmam**, Tel, 1940)
Illalu (Sanjeevi, Tel, 1965)
Illalu (**T. Rama Rao**, Tel, 1981)
Illalu Priyuralu (A. Kodandarami Reddy, Tel, 1984)
Illalu Vardhilu (Rajachandra, Tel, 1985)
Illam (**I.V. Sasi**, Tam, 1988)
Illara Jyothi (G.R. Rao, Tam, 1954)
Illara Jyoti *see* Jyoti
Illarame Nallaram (**P. Pullaiah**, Tam, 1958)
Illarikam (**T. Prakash Rao**, Tel, 1959)
I'll Die for Mama *see* **Deewar**
Illu Illalu (P. Chandrasekhara Reddy, Tel, 1972)
Illu Illalu Priyuralu (Visu, Tel, 1988)
Illu Pelli (Mutyala Subbaiah, Tel, 1993)
Illusion *see* **Maya Machhindra**
Illu Vakili (P.D. Prasad, Tel, 1976)
I Love India (Pavithran, Tam, 1993)
I Love You (B.L. Nandan Rao/Vayunanda Rao, Tel/K/Mal, 1979)
I Love You (Varaprasad, H, 1992)
Ilzaam (R.C. Talwar, H, 1954)
Ilzaam (Kamran, H, 1970)
Ilzaam (Shibu Mitra, H, 1986)
Imaan (**Atma Ram**, H, 1974)
Imaan Dharam (Desh Mukherjee, H, 1977)
Imaan Farosh (B.S. Rajhans, H, 1937)
Imaandar (G.R. Sethi, H, 1939)
Imaandar (Sushil Malik, H, 1986)
Image Festival *see* **Chitramela**
Imagination *see* **Kalpana**
Imagi Ningthem (**Aribam Syam Sharma**, Manipuri, 1981)

Sivaji Ganesan in *Amar Prem* (1960)

Imaigal (R. Kishnamurthy, Tam, 1983)
Iman Kalyan (Shantimoy Bannerjee, B, 1982)
Imitator *see* Krishna Kausalya
Immadi Pulakesi (N.C. Rajan, K, 1967)
Immortal Flame, The *see* **Amar Jyoti**
Immortal Glory *see* Amar Kirti
Immortal Hope *see* Amar Asha
Immortal Journey of Dr Kotnis, The *see* **Dr Kotnis Ki Amar Kahani**
Immortal Singer, The *see* Amar Saigal
Immortal Stupa (**Bimal Roy**, E, 1961)
Imperial Mail (Safdar Mirza, H, 1939)
Impossible *see* Na Honewali Baat *or* Naamumkin *or* Anhonee
Impostor (*aka* Dhoomketu: **Satu Sen**, B, 1936)
Imtehan (Mohan Sinha, H, 1949)
Imtehan (Madan Sinha, H, 1974)
Ina (**I.V. Sasi**, Mal, 1982)
Inaam (Harish, H, 1946)
Inaam (M.I. Dharamsey, H, 1955)
Inaam Dus Hazaar (Jyotin Goel, H, 1987)
Inainda Kaikal (N.K. Vishwanathan, Tam, 1990)
Inaindha Duruvangal (Delhi Gopalakrishnan, Tam, 1980)
Inakkilli (Joshi, Mal, 1984)
Ina Mina Dika (Raju Parsekar, Mar, 1989)
Inapravugal (**Kunchako**, Mal, 1965)
Inaye Thedi (Anthony Eastman, Mal, 1981)
Inbavalli (S. Nottani, Tam, 1949)
Incarnation *see* Punarjanma
In Custody (*aka* Hifazat, Muhafiz: Ismail Merchant, H-Urdu, 1993)
India: An Unusual Environment for Meetings (**Muzaffar Ali**, E, 1985)
India Cabaret (**Mira Nair**, E, 1985)
India in Africa (*aka* Song of the Wilds, Africa Mein Hind, Jungle Geet:
Hiren Bose, H, 1939)
India in Glory *see* Shaan-e-Hindustan
Indian Airlines ... Pride of India (**Rabindra Dharmaraj**, E, 1976)
Indian Charlie (?, G.N. Butt, St, 1933)
Indian Day, An *see* **India 67**
Indian Dream, An *see* **Oru Indhiya Kanavu**
Indian Engineering (**Santi P. Choudhury**, E, 1972)
Indian Iron and Steel *see* The Story of Steel
Indian Journey, An (**Santi P. Choudhury**, E, 1971)
Indian Life and Scenes (**Hiralal Sen**, St, 1903)
Indian National Congress at Gauhati (**A. Narayanan**, St, 1927)
Indian Science Marches Ahead (**Buddhadev Dasgupta**, E, 1984)
Indian Screen Gazette (**P.V. Pathy**, E, 1938)
Indian Shylock *see* **Savkari Pash**
Indian Story, An (**Tapan Bose**, E, 1981)
Indian Theatre (**Jabbar Patel**, Mar, 1988)
Indian Youth: An Exploration (**Shyam Benegal**, E, 1968)
India on the Move (**Buddhadev Dasgupta**, E, 1985)
India 67 (**S. Sukhdev**, Wordless, 1967)
India's Struggle for National Shipping (**Paul Zils**, E, 1947)
India Today *see* Aaj Ka Hindustan *or* **India 67**
Indigenous Games of Manipur (**Aribam Syam Sharma**, E, 1991)
Indina Bharatha (P. Krishna, K, 1984)
Indira (**Jyotish Bannerjee**, St, 1929)
Indira (Tarit Bose, B, 1937)
Indira (**Ardhendu Bhattacharya**, B, 1950)
Indira (**Dinen Gupta**, B, 1983)
Indira (Nripen Mohla, H, 1991)
Indira BA (**R.S. Choudhury**, St, 1929)
Indira Gandhi (**Ritwik Ghatak**, B, 1972)
Indira MA (**Nandlal Jaswantlal**, H, 1934)
Indra Bhavanam (**Ghantamneni Krishna**, Tel, 1991)
Indradhanu (Deepak Bose, B, 1960)
Indradhanush (Rajasekharan, Mal, 1979)
Indra Dhanushu (**K. Bapaiah**, Tel, 1977)
Indra Dhanushu (K. Ranga Rao, Tel, 1988)
Indra En Selvam (**R. Padmanabhan**, Tam, 1962)
Indrajal (*aka* Missing Bracelet: **B.P. Mishra**, St, 1926)
Indrajal (Amar Dutta, B, 1950)
Indrajalam (?, Chalana Chitra, Mal, 1990)
Indrajit (**Dhiren Ganguly**, St, 1922)
Indrajit (K.V. Raju, K, 1989)
Indrajit (K.V. Raju, H, 1991)
Indra Kumari (?, Star Film, St, 1923)
Indra Leela (Rajendra Sharma, H, 1956)
Indramalati (**Jyotiprasad Agarwala**, A, 1939)
Indranath (Prabhat Mitra, B, 1950)
Indranath Srikanta-o-Annadadidi (Haridas Bhattacharya, B, 1959)
Indrani (**Niren Lahiri**, B, 1958)
Indrasabha (*aka* Sabz Pari: **Manilal Joshi**, St, 1925)
Indrasabha (**J.J. Madan**, H, 1932)
Indrasabha (**A. Narayanan/R.S. Prakash**?, Tam, 1936)
Indrasabha (**Nanubhai Vakil**, H, 1956)
Indrasan (*aka* Ekadashi Mahima: **Raja Nene**, H, 1952)
Indra the Victorious *see* Vratrasur Vadha
Indrudu Chandrudu (Suresh Krishna, Tel, 1989)
Indru Nee Nalai Naan (Major Sundarrajan, Tam, 1983)
Indru Pol Endrum Vazhga (K. Shankar, Tam, 1977)
Indru Poyi Nalai Vaa (**K. Bhagyaraj**, Tam, 1981)
Indulal Advocate *see* Bodku Mathu
Indulekha (Kalanilayam Krishnan Nair, Mal, 1967)
Industrial India *see* Nirala Hindustan
Influence of Love, The *see* **Andhare Alo**
Ingeet (Taru Mukherjee, B, 1961)
Ingeyum Manithargal (A.L. Narayanan, Tam, 1975)
Ingeyum Oru Gangai (Manivannan, Tam, 1984)
Ini Aval Urangatte (**K.G. George**, Mal, 1978)
Inikilabinde Puthri (Jayadevan, Mal, 1988)
Inikkum Ilamai (M.A. Kaja, Tam, 1979)
Inimai Idho Idho (R. Ramalingam, Tam, 1983)
In India Today (Abdul Sattar, H, 1991)
Ini Oru Janmam Tharu (K. Vijayan, Mal, 1972)
Ini Oru Sudhanthiram (Manivannan, Tam, 1987)
Iniyaraja (V. Ganeshpandian, Tam, 1993)
Ini Yathra (Shrini, Mal, 1979)
Iniya Uravu Poothathu (**C.V. Sridhar**, Tam, 1987)
Iniyavaley Vaa (N.C. Chakraborty, Tam, 1982)
Iniyenkilum (**I.V. Sasi**, Mal, 1983)
Iniyethra Sandhyakal (Sukumaran Nair, Mal, 1979)
Iniyum Kanam (Charles, Mal, 1979)
Iniyum Katha Thudarum (Joshi, Mal, 1985)
Iniyum Kurukshetram (**Sasikumar**, Mal, 1986)
Iniyum Marichittillatha Nammal (Ravindran, Mal, 1980)
Iniyum Puzha Ozhukum (**I.V. Sasi**, Mal, 1978)
Injakadan Mathayi and Sons (Kallur Dennis, Mal, 1993)
Injustice *see* Anyay
Inkaar (Sudhir Sen, H, 1943)
Inkaar (Raj N. Sippy, H, 1977)
In Memory of Friends *see* **Unda Mitterandi Yaad Pyari**
Innale (*aka* Season: **P. Padmarajan**, Mal, 1989)
Innale Innu (**I.V. Sasi**, Mal, 1977)
Innalenkil Nale (**I.V. Sasi**, Mal, 1982)
Innaleyude Baaki (**P.A. Backer**, Mal, 1987)
Inner Eye, The (**Satyajit Ray**, E, 1972)
Innethe Programme (P.G. Vishwambaran, Mal, 1991)
Innisai Mazhai (Shobha, Tam, 1992)
Innocent *see* **Masoom**
Innocent Dancer *or* Innocent Raqasa *see* Pak Daman Raqasa
In Panchgani (**Vishnu Mathur**, E, 1970)
In Praise of Mother Santoshi *see* **Jai Santoshi Maa**
Inquilab *see* Sarai Ke Bahar
Inquilab (**Debaki Bose**, H, 1935)
Inquilab (Kedar Kapoor, H, 1956)
Inquilab (**T. Rama Rao**, H, 1984)
Inquilab Ke Baad (**Utpal Dutt**, H, 1984)
Inquilab Zindabad (**K.S. Sethumadhavan**, Mal, 1971)
Insaaf (**J.P. Advani**, H, 1937)
Insaaf (*aka* Justice, Nyay: **Phani Majumdar**, H, 1946)
Insaaf (Kedar Kapoor, H, 1956)
Insaaf (Radhakant, H, 1966)
Insaaf (**Adurthi Subba Rao**, H, 1973)
Insaaf (**Mukul S. Anand**, H, 1987)
Insaaf Kahan Hai (**Hemen Gupta**, H, 1959)
Insaaf Ka Khoon (?, N.C. Films, H, 1988)
Insaaf Ka Mandir (**B.R. Ishara**, H, 1969)
Insaaf Ka Tarazu (**B.R. Chopra**, H, 1980)
Insaaf Kaun Karega (Sudarshan Nag, H, 1987)
Insaaf Ki Awaaz (D. Rama Naidu, H, 1986)
Insaaf Ki Devi (S.A. Chandrasekharan, H, 1992)
Insaaf Ki Jung (M.G. Hashmat, H, 1987)
Insaaf Ki Manzil (Brij Bhushan, H, 1988)
Insaaf Ki Pukar (**T. Rama Rao**, H, 1987)
Insaaf Ki Tope (Vithaldas Panchotia, H, 1934)
Insaaf Main Karoonga (Shibu Mitra, H, 1985)
Insaan (Babubhai Jani, H, 1944)
Insaan (Jagdish Sethi, H, 1952)
Insaan (**Narendra Bedi**, H, 1982)
Insaan Aur Shaitan (Aspi Irani, H, 1970)
Insaan Bana Shaitan (Mohan Bhakri, H, 1992)
Insaan Jaag Utha (**Shakti Samanta**, H, 1959)
Insaan Ya Shaitan (*aka* Fateh Imaan: **Moti Gidwani**, H, 1933)
Insaniyat (**S.S. Vasan**, H, 1955)
Insaniyat (Prayag Raj, H, 1974)
Insaniyat Ka Devata (K.C. Bokadia, H, 1993)
Insaniyat Ke Dushman (Rajkumar Kohli, H, 1986)
In Search of Famine *see* **Akaler Sandhaney**
In Search of Happiness *see* Sukhacha Shodh
In Self Defence (**P.V. Pathy**, E, 1941)
In Shackles *see* Chor Ke Wafadaar
Inspector (R.S. Mani, Tam, 1953)
Inspector (**Shakti Samanta**, H, 1956)
Inspector (M. Krishnan Nair, Mal, 1968)
Inspector (Chand, H, 1970)
Inspector Ashwini (Mouli, Tel, 1993)
Inspector Balram (**I.V. Sasi**, Mal, 1991)
Inspector Dhanush/Police Mattu Dada (Tulsi/Shyam **Ramsay**, H/K, 1991)
Inspector Eagle (Vishwamitter Adil, H, 1978)
Inspector Jhansi (Balaji, Tel, 1993)
Inspector Krantikumar (A.T. Raghu, K, 1987)
Inspector Lakshmi (Ramnarayanam, Tel, 1985)
Inspector Manaivi (S. Rajendra Babu, Tam, 1976)
Inspector Pratap (M. Subbaiah, Tel, 1988)
Inspector Rudra (**Ghantamneni Krishna**, Tel, 1990)
Inteha (Shibu Mitra, H, 1984)
Inteha Pyar Ka (J.K. Bihari, H, 1992)
Inteqam (*aka* Revenge: K.P. Bhave, St, 1930)
Inteqam (*aka* Debts of Honour: Haribhai Desai, St, 1931)
Inteqam (*aka* Curses of Cupid, Mohabbat Ki Maar: J.K. Nanda, H, 1933)
Inteqam (Naushir Engineer, H, 1947)
Inteqam (R.K. Nayyar, H, 1969)
Inteqam (Raj Kumar Kohli, H, 1988)
Inteqam Ki Aag (Shivkumar, H, 1986)
International Crook (*aka* Kala Bazaar: Pachhi, H, 1974)
Interview (**Mrinal Sen**, B, 1970)
Interview (**Sasikumar**, Mal, 1973)
Interview with Jawaharlal Nehru (**Fali Bilimoria**, E, 1958)
Intezaar *see* Sneh Bandhan
Intezaar (Mohan Sinha Kavia, H, 1973)
Intezaar (TV: **Saeed Mirza** et al, H, 1988)
Intezaar Ke Baad (G.P. Pawar, H, 1947)
In the Name of God *see* **Ram Ke Naam**
Inti Donga (Kodi Ramakrishna, Tel, 1987)
Inti Dongalu (K. Hemambharadhara Rao, Tel, 1973)
Inti Gauravam (**Bapu**, Tel, 1970)
Intiguttu (**Vedantam Raghavaiah**, Tel, 1958)
Intiguttu (**K. Bapaiah**, Tel, 1984)
Intiki Deepam Illale (Ramanna, Tel, 1961)
Inti Kodalu (Laxmi Deepak, Tel, 1974)
Intiko Rudramma (S.A. Chandrasekharan, Tel, 1985)
Intilo Pilli Veedhilo Puli (P.S. Ramchandra Rao, Tel, 1991)
Intilo Ramayya Vidhilo Krishnayya (Kodi Ramakrishna, Tel, 1981)
Intinti Bhagavatham (**Dasari Narayana Rao**, Tel, 1988)
Intinti Katha (K. Satyam, Tel, 1974)
Intinti Ramayanam (P. Sambasiva Rao, Tel, 1979)
Into the Antiquity (K.R. Mohanan, E, 1972)
In Two Minds *see* **Duvidha**
Invention *see* Shareef Badmash
Invincible, The *see* Chalta Purza
Invisible One, The *see* **Kaanamarayathu**
Invitation *see* Dawat
In Which Annie Gives it Those Ones (TV: Pradeep Krishen, E, 1988)
In Whose Nest? *see* **Koodevide?**
In Your Memory *see* **Ormakkayi**
IPC Section 302 *see* Dafaa 302
Ippadiyum Oru Penn (**P. Bhanumathi**, Tam, 1975)
Iqraar (*aka* Tyaag: Manibhai Vyas, H, 1942)
Iqraar (Kailash Advani, H, 1979)
Iraada (S. Shamsuddin, H, 1944)
Iraada (Rajdeep, H, 1971)
Iraada (Indrajit Singh, H, 1990)
Iraivan Irukkindran (H.S. Venu, Tam, 1973)
Iraivan Kodutha Varam (**A. Bhimsingh**, Tam, 1978)
Irakal (**K.G. George**, Mal, 1985)
Irandil Onru (V. Azhagappan, Tam, 1988)
Iran Ka Shah *see* Shah-e-Iran
Iran Ki Ek Raat (**P.C. Barua**, H, 1949)
Iraq Ka Chor *see* Thief of Iraq
Iraq Ka Chor (*aka* Thief of Iraq: K.P. Bhave, St, 1931)
Irasaal Karti (Pitambar Kale, Mar, 1987)
Ira Thedunna Manushyan (?, Madeena Prod, Mal, 1981)
Irattaival Kuruvi (**Balu Mahendra**, Tam, 1987)
Irattimadhuram (Shrikumaran Thampi, Mal, 1982)
Iravum Pagalum (Joseph Taliath, Tam, 1965)
Iravu Pannirandu Mani (S. Rajendran, Tam, 1978)
Iravu Pookkal (Sridhar Rajan, Tam, 1986)
Iravu Suryan (Senthilnathan, Tam, 1991)
Irayilukku Neramachu (Bharathi Mohan, Tam, 1988)
Iron and Steel (**Fali Bilimoria**, E, 1956)
Iron Man *see* Fauladi Pahelwan *or* Dara Singh
Irony of Fate *see* Bhool Ka Bhog
Irsha (Suryakant, Mar, 1978)
Irshad Panjatan (**M.S. Sathyu**, E, 1969)
Irugu Porugu (I.S. Murthy, Tel, 1963)
Iru Kodukal (**K. Balachander**, Tam, 1969)
Irulum Valiyum (**Puttana Kanagal**, Tam, 1971)
Iru Malargal (A.C. Trilogchander, Tam, 1967)
Irumbu Pookkal (G.M. Kumar, Tam, 1991)
Iru Methaigal (Muktha V. Srinivasan, Tam, 1984)
Irumpazhigal (?, Shri Sai Prod, Mal, 1979)
Irumputhirai (**S.S. Vasan**, Tam, 1960)
Irupatham Noottandu (?, Mal, 1987)
Iru Sahodarargal *see* Bhale Ammayilu
Iru Sahodarargal (**Ellis Duncan**, Tam, 1936)
Iru Thuruvam (?, Tam, 1971)
Irutinte Atmavu (**P. Bhaskaran**, Mal, 1967)
Iru Vallavarkal (K.V. Srinivasan, Tam, 1966)
Iruvar Ullam (**L.V. Prasad**, Tam, 1963)
Isabella (Mohan, Mal, 1988)
Isai Padum Thendrai (Devaraj-Mohan, Tam, 1986)
Isa Masih *see* Jesus
Is Anybody Listening (**Saeed Mirza**, E, 1987)
Ishanou (**Aribam Syam Sharma**, Manipuri, 1990)
Ishara (J.K. Nanda, H, 1943)
Ishara (**K. Amarnath**, H, 1964)
Ishq Aur Inteqam (Sunil Kumar, H, 1993)
Ishq-e-Punjab (*aka* Mirza Sahiban: ?, Hindmata Cinetone, P, 1935)
Ishq Ishq Ishq (**Dev Anand**, H, 1974)
Ishq Ke Parwane *see* Madan Manjiri
Ishq Nimana (Vinod Talwar, P, 1984)

Ishq No Anjam (*aka* Kingdom of Love: Baburao/**Sundarrao Nadkarni**, St, 1931)
Ishq Par Zor Nahin (Ramesh Saigal, H, 1970)
Ishrat Ki Maut (*aka* 100 Lashes: M. Murtaza, H, 1935)
Ishtamanu Pakshe (**Balachandra Menon**, Mal, 1980)
Ishtapraneshwari (Sajan, Mal, 1979)
Ishwar *see* Eeshwar
Ishwar Allah Tera Naam (Vasant Kumar Soni, H, 1982)
Ishwar Bhakti (*aka* Shani Mahatmya: Dada Gunjal, H, 1951)
Ishwari Nyay *see* Anjaam
Isi Ka Naam Duniya Hai (**Shakti Samanta**, H, 1962)
Isi Ka Naam Zindagi (Kalidas, H, 1992)
Ismat (*aka* Asmat: S. Fazli, H, 1944)
Is Paar Ya Us Paar (Govind Singh, H, 1990)
ITA Story, The (**Harisadhan Dasgupta**, E, 1981)
ITC Tube: The Lifetimer (**Santi P. Choudhury**, E, 1972)
Itha Ivide Vare (**I.V. Sasi**, Mal, 1977)
Ithanende Vazhi (M. Krishnan Nair, Mal, 1978)
Itha Oru Dhikkari (?, Mal, 1981)
Itha Oru Manushyan (**I.V. Sasi**, Mal, 1978)
Itha Oru Pennkutty (?, Mal, 1988)
Itha Oru Theeram (P.G. Vishwambaran, Mal, 1979)
It Happened on a Saturday (**Govind Saraiya**, E, 1964)
Itha Samayamani (?, Royal Films, Mal, 1987)
Ithayam Pesugirathu (S.A. Chandrasekharan, Tam, 1982)
Ithayithal Oru Edam (Prasad, Tam, 1980)
Ithe Naa Saval (Puratchidasan, Tel, 1984)
Ithente Neethi (?, Mal, 1987)
Ithikkara Pakki (**Sasikumar**, Mal, 1980)
Ithile Iniyum Varum (P.G. Vishwambaran, Mal, 1986)
Ithile Vannavar (Chandrakumar, Mal, 1980)
Ithiri Neram Othiri Karyam (**Balachandra Menon**, Mal, 1982)
Ithiri Poove Chuvannapoove (**B.G. Bharathan**, Mal, 1984)
Itho Varugiren (K.C. Krishnamurthy, Tam, 1982)
Ithra Martham (P. Chandrakumar, Mal, 1986)
Ithrayum Kalam (?, Shabana & Diana Prod, Mal, 1987)
Ithu Eppadi Irukku (R. Pattabhiraman, Tam, 1978)
Ithu Gnangalude Katha (P.G. Vishwambaran, Mal, 1982)
Ithu Ivarkalin Kathai (T.P. Arunachalam, Tam, 1975)
Ithu Manushiano? (Thomas Burlie, Mal, 1973)
Ithum Oru Jeevitham (Veliyan Chandran, Mal, 1982)
Ithu Nalla Thamasa (Kailashnath, Mal, 1985)
Ithu Nijama (Krishna Gopal, Tam, 1948)
Ithu Oru Thodakkam Mathram (Baby, Mal, 1986)
Ithuthan Arambam (Rajbarath, Tam, 1988)
Itihaas (Krishna Dehlvi, H, 1987)
Itihasam (Joshi, Mal, 1981)
Itni Jaldi Kya Hai (**P. Bhanumathi**, H, 1986)
Itni Si Baat (Madhu M, H, 1981)
Ito Sito Bohuto (**Brojen Barua**, A, 1963)
It's True *see* **Sach Hai**
Ittefaq (**Yash Chopra**, H, 1969)
Ival Ee Vazhi Ithu Vare (Rajasekharan, Mal, 1980)
Ivalentha Hendthi (?, Rohan Film, K, 1990)
Ival Oru Pournami (T.P.K., Tam, 1987)
Ivan Avanethan (T.G. Raj, Tam, 1960)
Ivanente Priyaputhran (**T. Hariharan**, Mal, 1977)
Ivan Oru Simham (Suresh, Mal, 1982)
Ivare Sookshikukka (?, Mal, 1987)
Ivargal Ilandiarygal (S. Jagadeeshan, Tam, 1987)
Ivargal Varunkala Thoongal (Venkat, Tam, 1987)
Ivargal Vithyasamanavargal (Mouli, Tam, 1980)
Ivide Ellavarkkum Sukham (Jesey, Mal, 1987)
Ivide Ingane (Joshi, Mal, 1984)
Ivide Kattinnu Sugandham (Vishwabharan, Mal, 1979)
Ivide Thodangannu (**Sasikumar**, Mal, 1984)
Iyambathilum Asaivarum (P. Kalaimani, Tam, 1991)
Iyarkayin Athisayangal (R. Mahesh, Tam, 1984)
Iye Marathyachi Nagari/Ladki Sahyadri Ki (**V. Shantaram**, M/H, 1965)
Izhaar (Yashpal, H, 1989)
Izzat (**Franz Osten**, H, 1937)
Izzat (Taimur Behramshah, H, 1952)
Izzat (**T. Prakash Rao**, H, 1968)
Izzat (Ashok Gaikwad, H, 1991)
Izzat Aabroo (Chhotu Arya, H, 1989)
Izzatdar (**K. Bapaiah**, H, 1990)
Izzat Ki Roti (K. Kappu, H, 1993)

J

Jaa Devi Sarva Bhuteshu/Nyaya Chakra (**Prashanta Nanda**, O/B, 1989)
Jaago (Chandrakant Bhanta, H, 1985)
Jaag Punjabi Shera (Anil Gandotra, P, 1987)
Jaag Utha Insaan (**K. Vishwanath**, H, 1984)
Jaal (**Guru Dutt**, H, 1952)
Jaal (Moni Bhattacharya, H, 1967)
Jaal (Umesh Mehra, H, 1986)
Jaali Note (**Shakti Samanta**, H, 1960)
Jaalsaaz (Aravind Sen, H, 1959)
Jaalsaaz (Mohammed Hussain, H, 1969)
Jaal Sanyasi (Salil Sen, B, 1977)
Jaanam (Vikram Bhatt, H, 1993)
Jaanbaaz (Feroz Khan, H, 1986)
Jaanbaaz Mallika (*aka* Queen of Hearts: N.G. Bulchandani, H, 1936)
Jaandaar (S.K. Luthra, H, 1979)
Jaane Anjane (**Shakti Samanta**, H, 1971)
Jaan-e-Alam (TV: **Muzaffar Ali**, Urdu, 1986)
Jaan-e-Alam Anjuman Ara (**Nanubhai Desai**, St, 1927)
Jaan-e-Alam Anjuman Ara (*aka* Prem Purnima: M.R. Kapoor, H, 1935)
Jaan-e-Bahar (Prakash Kapoor, H, 1979)
Jaane Bhi Do Yaaron (**Kundan Shah**, H, 1983)
Jaan-e-Jaan (Ramesh Behl, H, 1983)
Jaaneman *see* **Rashk-e-Laila**
Jaaneman (**Chetan Anand**, H, 1976)
Jaan-e-Wafaa (Rukun, H, 1989)
Jaan Hatheli Pe (Raghunath Jhalani, H, 1987)
Jaan Hazir Hai (Manhar Nath Rangroo, H, 1975)
Jaani Dost (**K. Raghavendra Rao**, H, 1983)
Jaani Dushman (?, Shivraj Prod, H, 1957)
Jaani Dushman (Rajkumar Kohli, H, 1979)
Jaan Ki Baazi (Ajay Kashyap, H, 1985)
Jaan Ki Kasam (Sushil Malik, H, 1991)
Jaan Lada Denge (Dilip Gulati, H, 1990)
Jaanoo (Jainendra Jain, H, 1985)
Jaan Pehchan (Fali Mistry, H, 1950)
Jaan Pe Khel Kar (S.A. Khan, H, 1993)
Jaan Se Pyara (Anand, H, 1992)
Jaan Tere Naam (Deepak Balraj Vij, H, 1992)
Jaanwar (Bhappi Sonie, H, 1965)
Jaanwar (Ali Raza, H, 1982)
Jaanwar Aur Insaan (**Tapi Chanakya**, H, 1972)
Jaban (Palash Bannerjee, B, 1972)
Jab Andhera Hota Hai (Deepak Bahry, H, 1974)
Jabanbandi (Amar Dutta, B, 1952)
Jabanbandi (Pranab Bannerjee, B, 1983)
Jab Jab Phool Khile (Suraj Prakash, H, 1965)
Jab Pyar Kisise Hota Hai (**Nasir Hussain**, H, 1961)
Jabse Tumhe Dekha Hai (Kedar Kapoor, H, 1963)
Jab Yaad Kisiki Aati Hai (Naresh Saigal, H, 1967)
Jackie (**Bapu**, Tel, 1985)
Jackpot (Joe Simon, Mal, 1993)
Jadagantalu (K.S. Rami Reddy, Tel, 1984)
Jadhikoru Needhi (S. Shankaran, Tam, 1981)
Jadi Jantem (Yatrik, B, 1974)
Jadiketha Moodi (Umesh-Prabhakar, Tam, 1988)
Jadu (**A.R. Kardar**, H, 1951)
Jadu (B. Gupta, H, 1966)
Jadu Bansha (Partha Prathim Choudhury, B, 1974)
Jadubhatta (**Niren Lahiri**, B, 1954)
Jadu-e-Mohabbat (*aka* Magic of Love: **Harshadrai Mehta**, St, 1931)
Jadugar *see* Maya Jaal
Jadugar (A.P. Kapur, H, 1946)
Jadugar (Mohammed Hussain, H, 1954)
Jadugar (**Prakash Mehra**, H, 1989)
Jadugar Daku (**Chandrakant**, H, 1962)
Jadugarin (Niranjan Arya, Mar, 1937)
Jadui Angoothi (*aka* Magic Ring: A.M. Khan, H, 1948)
Jadui Angoothi (*aka* Magic Ring: A.M. Khan, H, 1964)
Jadui Bandhan (**Nanubhai Vakil**, H, 1941)
Jadui Bansari (**Nanubhai Vakil**, H, 1948)
Jadui Chitra (Jaswant Jhaveri, H, 1948)
Jadui Danda (*aka* Magic Wand: Dwarka Khosla, H, 1935)
Jadui Jhoola (A.M. Khan, H, 1943)
Jadui Jung (*aka* Khooni Katar, Phantom Foe, Naagdand: R.N. Vaidya, St, 1934)
Jadui Kangan (**Nanubhai Vakil**, H, 1940)
Jadui Kismat (A.M. Khan, H, 1944)
Jadui Putli (Ramanlal Desai, H, 1946)
Jadui Ratan (Natwar Shyam, H, 1947)
Jadui Sandook *see* Magic Box
Jadui Shatranji *see* Magic Carpet
Jadui Shehnai (Nasim Sadiq?, H, 1948)
Jadui Sindoor (Nasim Sadiq?, H, 1949)
Jadui Topi *see* Magic Cap
Jadu Ka Chirag *see* Alladdin and the Wonderful Lamp
Jadu Ka Shankh (**Sai Paranjpye**, H, 1973)
Jadu Mahal (Aakkoo, H, 1962)
Jadu Nagari (*aka* Magic City: Bapurao Apte, H, 1940)
Jadu Nagari (Radhakant, H, 1961)
Jadu Nagari (K. Shankar, H, 1986)
Jadunath (*aka* Juggler, Garudi Ke Govind: **S.N. Patankar**, St, 1922)
Jadu Tona (Ravi Nagaich, H, 1977)
Jaga Balia (**Prashanat Nanda**, O, 1984)
Jaga Bhadyane Dene Aahe (Achyut Ranade, Mar, 1949)
Jagachya Pathivar (**Raja Paranjpe**, Mar, 1960)
Jagadeka Veera (?, K, 1991)
Jagadeka Veerudu Attilokasundari (**K. Raghavendra Rao**, Tel, 1990)
Jagadeka Veeruni Katha/Jagathala Prathapan (**K.V. Reddy**, Tel/Tam, 1961)
Jagadguru Adi Shankaran (**P. Bhaskaran**, Mal, 1977)
Jagadguru Shankaracharya (**S. Fattelal**, H, 1955)
Jagadguru Shrimad Shankaracharya (*aka* The World Teacher: **P.Y. Altekar**, St, 1928)
Jaga Hatare Pagha (Mohammed Mohsin, O, 1985)
Jagajyothi Basaveshwara (T.V. Singh Thakore, K, 1959)
Jagal Bhag Hamaar (S.N. Tripathi, Bh, 1980)
Jaga Mechida Huduga (Bhargava, K, 1992)
Jaga Mechida Maga (**Hunsur Krishnamurthy**, K, 1972)
Jagame Maya (I.N. Murthy, Tel, 1973)
Jagamondi (V. Madhusudhana Rao, Tel, 1981)
Jagan (**Dasari Narayana Rao**, Tel, 1984)
Jaganmatha (Dhana Koteshwara Rao, Tel, 1987)
Jagan Mohini (D. Shankar Singh, K, 1951)
Jagan Mohini (**B. Vittalacharya**, Tel, 1978)
Jagannathan and Sons (Anil Kumar, Tel, 1992)
Jagannatha Rathachakralu (**Dasari Narayana Rao**, Tel, 1982)
Jagannathakam (Shobhandirao, Tel, 1960)
Jagannathakam (A. Mohan Gandhi, Tel, 1991)
Jagannath Pandit *see* Lavangi
Jagapishi (Janaki Bhattacharya, B, 1938)
Jagaran (Bibhuti Chakraborty, B, 1947)
Jagathala Prathapan *see* **Jagadeka Veeruni Katha**
Jagathala Prathapan (S.M. Sreeramulu Naidu, Tam, 1944)
Jagathala Prathapan (Shankar-Ganesh, Tam, 1990)
Jagath Jentreelu (Laxmi Deepak, Tel, 1971)
Jagath Jettelu (K.V. Nandanrao, Tel, 1970)
Jagath Kiladilu (I.N. Murthy, Tel, 1969)
Jagat Janani Jagadamba *see* Maa Durga
Jagat Kesari (**Homi Master**, H, 1937)
Jagat Mohini (**Homi Master**, St, 1933)
Jagat Mohini (?, **Madan Theatres**, H, 1936)
Jagat Mohini (Chunilal Parekh, H, 1940)
Jagavegali Goshta (Madhukar Kulkarni, Mar, 1956)
Jagavegali Prem Kahani (**Anant Mane**, Mar, 1984)
Jag Biti (M. Sadiq, H, 1946)
Jag Chanan Hoya (Subhash Bhakri, P, 1986)
Jagdev Parmar *see* Sati Veermati
Jagga (Jugal Kishore, P, 1964)
Jagga Daku (B.S. Rajhans, P, 1940)
Jagga Daku (**Chandrakant**, H, 1959)
Jaggu (Jagdish Sethi, H, 1952)
Jaggu (Samir Ganguly, H, 1975)
Jaggu (P. Chandrasekhara Reddy, Tel, 1982)
Jaggu (B. Vijay Gujjar, K, 1983)
Jagir (Jag Mohan Mattu, H, 1959)
Jagir/Teen Murti (Pramod Chakraborty, H/B, 1984)
Jagirdar (**Mehboob**, H, 1937)
Jagmagti Jawani (*aka* Sparkling Youth: **Nagendra Majumdar**, St, 1930)
Jago Hua Savera (Shaukat Jamali, H, 1986)
Jagran (**M. Bhavnani**, H, 1936)
Jagran (?, B, 1947)
Jagrata Bharat (Pushpitanath Chatterjee, B, 1950)
Jagratha (K. Madhu, Mal, 1989)
Jagrihi (Hiten Majumdar, B, 1954)
Jagriti (Manohar Ghatwai, H, 1949)
Jagriti (**Satyen Bose**, H, 1954)
Jagriti (*aka* Ajab Teri Sarkar: Rajendra Bhatia, H, 1977)
Jagriti (Suresh Krishna, H, 1992)
Jagruthi (**C.V. Sridhar**, K, 1975)
Jagte Raho/Ek Din Raatre (**Sombhu Mitra**/Amit Moitra, H, 1956)
Jagwal (Tulsi Dhimire, Garhwali, 1983)
Jagwala Mela (Kamal Sahni, P, 1988)
Jagya Tyanthi Savar (**Ravindra Dave**, G, 1981)
Jahaku Rakhibe Anant (Ashim Kumar, O, 1988)
Jahan Ara (F.R. Irani, H, 1935)
Jahan Ara (Vinod Kumar, H, 1964)
Jahan Bahe Ganga Ki Dhar (Shyam Kaushal, Bh, 1983)
Jahan Pyar Mile (Lekh Tandon, H, 1969)
Jahan Sati Wahan Bhagwan (Satish Kumar, H, 1965)
Jahazi Lutera (Akkoo, H, 1957)
Ja Hoy Na (Promod Dasgupta, B, 1949)
Jai *see* Jay
Jai Ambe (Shanti Kumar, H, 1957)
Jai Ambe Maa (*aka* Sati Ahilya: Jal, H, 1977)
Jai Baba Amarnath (**B.R. Ishara**, H, 1983)
Jai Baba Baidyanath (Prahlad Sharma, H, 1979)
Jai Baba Balak Nath (Satish Bhakri, P, 1981)
Jai Bahucharma (Ramkumar Bohra, G, 1980)
Jai Bajrang *see* Vanarsena
Jai Bajrang Bali *see* Bajrang Bali
Jai Bethala (B.V. Srinivas, Tel, 1985)
Jai Bhadrakali (W.D. Garcher, G, 1962)
Jai Bhadrakali (Sushil Vyas, G, 1979)
Jai Bharat (**Homi Wadia**, H, 1936)
Jai Bharati (*aka* Young India: **B.P. Mishra**, St, 1929)
Jai Bhawani (K.P. Bhave, St, 1934)
Jai Bhawani (Jaishankar Danve, Mar, 1947)
Jai Bhawani (**Vedantam Raghavaiah**, Tam, 1959)
Jai Bhawani (**Dhirubhai Desai**, H, 1961)
Jai Bhawani (B.J. Patel, G/Bh, 1982)
Jai Bhim (**Anant Mane**, H, 1949)
Jai Chandi Chamunda (Bhupen Desai, G, 1985)
Jai Chittor (Jaswant Jhaveri, H, 1961)
Jai Dwarkadheesh (Sushil Kumar Gupta, H, 1977)
Jai Ganesh (R.N. Mandloi, H, 1977)
Jai Gantalu (**Singeetham Srinivasa Rao**, Tel, 1981)
Jai Hanuman (**Ramchandra Thakur**, H, 1948)
Jai Hanuman (Manu Desai, H, 1973)
Jai Hanuman (Ramkumar Bohra, G, 1984)
Jai Hari Vithal *see* Sant Tukaram
Jai Hind *see* Netaji Subhash

Jai Hind (*aka* Sipahi: Ramnik Vaidya, H, 1948)
Jai Ho Mohabbat Ki (Vithaldas Panchotia, H, 1962)
Jai Jagannath (?, Utkal Chalachitra Prathisthan, H, 1963)
Jai Jawan (**Yoganand**, Tel, 1970)
Jai Jawan Jai Makan (**Vishram Bedekar**, H, 1971)
Jai Jwala (*aka* Pooja Aur Payal: Manohar Deepak, H, 1972)
Jai Karnimata (S.P. Kalla, R, 1991)
Jai Karoli Maa (Raam Pahwa, H, 1988)
Jai Khodiyar Ma (Ramkumar Bohra, G, 1976)
Jail (**Kunchako**, Mal, 1966)
Jailbirds *see* Jail Ke Parinde
Jai Leela *see* Berozgar
Jail Ke Parinde (*aka* Jailbirds: Munshi Abbas, St, 1931)
Jailor (**Sohrab Modi**, H-Urdu, 1938)
Jailor (**Sohrab Modi**, H, 1958)
Jailor Jagannath (A.T. Raghu, K, 1993)
Jailpully (**P. Subramanyam**, Mal, 1957)
Jailupakshi (Kodi Ramakrishna, Tel, 1986)
Jail Yatra (*aka* Pilgrimage to Prison: **Gajanan Jagirdar**, H, 1947)
Jail Yatra (Bhappi Sonie, H, 1981)
Jai Mahadev (**Ramchandra Thakur**, H, 1955)
Jai Mahakali (*aka* Vikram Betaal: **Dhirubhai Desai**, H, 1951)
Jai Mahakali (**Babubhai Mistri**, G/H, 1978)
Jai Mahalakshmi (**Nanubhai Vakil**, H, 1951)
Jai Mahalakshmi Maa (Vijay Sharma, H, 1976)
Jai Malhar (D.S. Ambapkar, Mar, 1947)
Jai Mata Chintpurni (Satish Bhakri, P, 1983)
Jai Mata Di (Daljit, P, 1977)
Jai Mata Sheran Wali (**Sukhdev Ahluwalia**, P, 1978)
Jaimini (*aka* Learning Versus Passion: **S.N. Patankar**, St, 1918)
Jain Teertha Kshetra Darshan (Anant Hiregowder, H, 1975)
Jai Phoola (Siddharth, O, 1984)
Jai Radhe Krishna (Yeshwant Pethkar, H, 1974)
Jai Ranchhod (**Homi Master**/Nautam Trivedi, G, 1948)
Jai Ranchhod (*aka* Bhakta Bodana: **Manhar Raskapur**, G, 1975)
Jai Randalma (**Ravindra Dave**, G, 1977)
Jai Renukadevi Yellamma (Keshav Toro, Mar, 1985)
Jai Santoshi Maa (Vijay Sharma, H, 1975)
Jaise Ko Taisa (Murugan-Kumaran, H, 1973)
Jai Shankar (Ishwarlal, H, 1951)
Jai Shri Ram *see* Hanuman Vijay
Jai Shri Shankar (*aka* Bhasmasur Vadha: ?, British India Film, St, 1930)
Jaisi Karni Waisi Bharni (Vimal Kumar, H, 1989)
Jaisingh *see* Jayasimha
Jai Somnath (**Harshadrai Mehta**, St, 1929)
Jai Swadesh (Aspi, H, 1940)
Jaithra Yathra (?, Shri Lakshmi Creations, Mal, 1987)
Jait Re Jait (**Jabbar Patel**, Mar, 1977)
Jai Tulaja Bhawani (Govind Kulkarni, Mar, 1981)
Jaitya Yatra (V. Narayana Rao, Tel, 1991)
Jai Vijay (**N.D. Sarpotdar**, St, 1930)
Jai Vijay (**L.V. Prasad**, H, 1977)
Jai Vithal (*aka* Sant Tukaram: ?, Hind Vijay Film, St, 1931)
Jajabara (Trimurti, O, 1975)
Jajsaheber Nathni (**Kaliprasad Ghosh**, B, 1943)
Jakher Dhan (Hari Bhanja, B, 1939)
Jakhmi Vaghin (Vasant Painter, Mar, 1984)
Jakkamma (M. Karnan, Tam, 1972)
Jako Rakhe Saiyan (Hardev Raj Rishi, P, 1986)
Jala (Shrivatsa Ranganath/J.V.S. Narayana, K, 1981)
Jaladurga/Karkottai (**Kemparaj Urs**, K/Tam, 1953)
Jalaja (G.K. Sheshgiri, Tam, 1938)
Jalakam (*aka* Window: Harikumar, Mal, 1986)
Jalakanyaka (M.S. Mani, Mal, 1971)
Jalamsang Jadeja (Narendra Trivedi, G, 1976)
Jalan (**Master Bhagwan**, H, 1948)
Jalan (H.A. Rahi, H, 1978)
Jalandhar Vrinda (G.V. Sane, St, 1920)
Jalatarangam (P. Chandrakumar, Mal, 1977)
Jal Bin Machhli Nritya Bin Bijli (**V. Shantaram**, H, 1971)
Jaldeep (*aka* Light House: **Kidar Sharma**, H, 1956)
Jaler Meye (*aka* The Fishergirl: **Jyotish Bannerjee**, St, 1925)
Jaliat (Shri Vaskar, B, 1953)
Jalim Jawani *see* **Zalim Jawani**
Jal-Jangal (**Kartick Chattopadhyay**, B, 1959)
Jal Kumari (*aka* Hoor-al-Bahar: **Harshadrai Mehta**, St, 1925)
Jallad (*aka* Chaos: **Harshadrai Mehta**, St, 1933)
Jallad (J.B., H, 1956)
Jallianwala Bagh (Balraj Tah, H, 1987)
Jallianwala Bagh Ki Jyot (**R.S. Choudhury**, H, 1953)
Jalli Kattu (Manivannan, Tam, 1987)
Jal Mahal (Raghunath Jhalani, H, 1980)
Jalpari *see* Tarzan Aur Jalpari
Jalpari (Mohan Sinha, H, 1952)
Jalsa (Kamalakar, H, 1948)
Jalsa Bullodu (S.P. Muthuraman, Tel, 1985)
Jalsaghar (**Satyajit Ray**, B, 1958)
Jalsarayudu (**Tapi Chanakya**, Tel, 1960)
Jalsarayudu (S.P. Muthuraman, Tel, 1984)
Jalta Jigar (*aka* Flaming Soul: G.P. Pawar, St, 1933)
Jal Tarang (Rajendra Sharma, H, 1949)
Jalte Badan (*aka* Sizzling Bodies: **Ramanand Sagar**, H, 1973)
Jalte Deep (Deepak Asha, H, 1950)
Jalti Nishani/Agnikankan (**V. Shantaram**, H/Mar, 1932)
Jalti Nishani (*aka* Birbal Paristan: Harish, H, 1957)
Jalwa (**Roop K. Shorey**, H, 1955)
Jalwa (Pankaj Parashar, H, 1986)
Jamadagni (**Bharathirajaa**, Tel, 1988)
Jamaibabu (Kalipada Das, St, 1931)
Jamairaj (Vijaydev, G, 1965)
Jamai Raja (A. Kodandarami Reddy, H, 1990)
Jamai Sasthi (Amar Choudhury, B, 1931)
Jama Masjid Street Journal (**Mira Nair**, E, 1979)
Jambalakadi Pampa (E.V.V. Sathyanarayana, Tel, 1992)
Jambam (Jhaveri/V. Kumaraswamy, Tam, 1947)
Jambu (M. Karnan, Tam, 1980)
Jambulingam (?, Premier Cinetone, Tam, 1945)
Jambulingam (**Sasikumar**, Mal, 1982)
Jambu Savari (Lalith Ravi, K, 1993)
James Bond 999 (P. Chandrasekhara Reddy, Tel, 1984)
James Bond 777 (K.S.R. Doss, Tel, 1971)
Jamuna Bani Jagadamba (S.J. Talukdar, G, 1982)
Jamuna Kinare (Laxminarayan Garg, Brajbhasha, 1984)
Jamuna Paar (*aka* Hai Jani: A.R. Zamindar, H, 1946)
Jamuna Puliney/Radha Krishna (**Priyanath Ganguly**/Tulsi Lahiri?, B/H, 1933)
Jana (**Priyanath Ganguly**, St, 1927)
Jana Aranya (**Satyajit Ray**, B, 1975)
Janakeeya Kodathi (Hasan, Mal, 1985)
Janaki (Datta Mane, Mar, 1969)
Janaki (Vasant Joglekar, Mar, 1979)
Janaki Ramudu (**K. Raghavendra Rao**, Tel, 1988)
Janaki Sabatham (Avinashi Mani, Tam, 1975)
Janaki Swayamvar (*aka* Dhanurbhanga: **Dadasaheb Phalke**, St, 1926)
Janaki Thediya Raman (K. Shanmugham, Tam, 1983)
Janak Nandini (**Phani Burma**, B, 1939)
Janak Videhi *see* Videhi Janak
Janam (**Mahesh Bhatt**, H, 1985)
Janam Janam (Vijay Sadanah, H, 1988)
Janam Janam Ka Naata *see* Sati Vaishalini
Janam Janam Ke Phere (*aka* Sati Annapurna: Manu Desai, H, 1957)
Janam Janam Ke Saathi (Nand Kishore, H, 1965)
Janam Janamna Saathi (Manibhai Vyas, G, 1962)
Janam Janamna Saathi/Phir Janam Lenge Hum (**Mehul Kumar**, G, 1977)
Janam Manam (D. Mohan Doss, Tel, 1984)
Janamtep (Firoze A. Sarkar, G, 1973)
Jana Nayaka (Bhargava, K, 1988)
Janangalude Shraddhakku (?, Mal, 1987)
Janani (Dhiresh Ghosh, B, 1943)
Janani (Ajit Ganguly, B, 1971)
Janani (Mohammed Mohsin, O, 1984)
Janani (Netaji, Tam, 1985)
Janani (**Utpalendu Chakraborty**, B, 1989)
Janani Janma Bhoomi (**K. Vishwanath**, Tel, 1984)
Janara Jana (G.K. Murthy, K, 1967)
Janasanstha (**Santi P. Choudhury**, B, 1972)
Janata (Ram Prakash, H, 1947)
Janata Havaldar (Mehmood, H, 1979)
Janatar Adalat (Madhukar, B, 1972)
Janeta (F.R. Irani, G, 1947)
Janetana Sogand (Kishore Vyas, G, 1987)
Jangi Jawan (Dawood, H, 1943)
Janhavi (Sona Pathare/Kamat, Mar, 1959)
Jani *see* Johnny
Janjirne Jankare (**Harshadrai Mehta**, St, 1927)
Jankar (?, B, 1989)
Janmabhoomi (**Franz Osten**, H, 1936)
Janmabhoomi (John Shankaramangalam, Mal, 1969)
Janmabhoomi (G. Vishwanathan, Tel, 1970)
Janmabhoomi (Piyush Kanti Ganguly, B, 1973)
Janmachi Gaath (Madhukar Bavdekar, Mar, 1949)
Janmadata (K.H.D. Rao, O, 1978)
Janma Haq (*aka* Birthright: **P.Y. Altekar**, St, 1931)
Janma Ha Tuzhsathi (V.S. Rao, Mar, 1972)
Janma Janmada Anubandha (**Shankar Nag**, K, 1980)
Janma Janmala Bandham (P. Chandrasekhara Reddy, Tel, 1977)
Janmandaram (Thampi Kannathanam, Mal, 1988)
Janmantar (Ashim Bannerjee, B, 1959)
Janma Patri (K.P. Shahani, H, 1949)
Janma Rahasya/Janma Rahasyam (S.P.N. Krishna, K/Mal, 1972)
Janma Rahasyam *see* Janma Rahasya
Janmashatru (?, Mal, 1988)
Janmashthami (**Nanabhai Bhatt**, H, 1950)
Janmatithi (Dilip Mukherjee, B, 1957)
Janmejaya's Serpent Sacrifice *see* Raja Parikshit
Jannat (*aka* Gulshan: Murtaza Changhezi, H, 1949)
Jannat (Mohan Sinha, H, 1957)
Jan Nissar (**Kanjibhai Rathod**, H, 1934)
Jantar Mantar (Radhakant, H, 1964)
Jantarwalo Jeevan (Raman B. Desai, G, 1978)
January 1 (Manivannan, Tam/Tel, 1984)
January Oru Orma (Joshi, Mal, 1987)
Japanil Kalyanaraman (S.P. Muthuraman, Tam, 1985)
Jara Japoon (**Raja Paranjpe**, Mar, 1950)
Jarasandha (**Ch. Narasimha Rao**, Tel, 1938)
Jarasandha Vadha (**Dadasaheb Phalke**, St, 1923)
Jaribidda Jana (Y.R. Swamy, K, 1980)
Jarigina Katha (K. Baburao, Tel, 1969)
Jar Je Priyo (Salil Dutta, B, 1987)
Jar Jetha Ghar (**Chhabi Biswas**, B, 1949)
Jaruguthunna Katha (G. Sheshgiri Rao, Tel, 1976)
Jasal (**Harshadrai Mehta**/Bapurao Apte?, St, 1933)
Jashaas Tase (Ram Gabale, Mar, 1951)
Jashan (S. Shamsuddin, H, 1955)
Jasoos (*aka* Detective: T.V. Trivedi, H, 1947)
Jasoos (R.D. Rajput, H, 1955)
Jasoos 007 *see* SOS Jasoos 007
Jatagadu (B. Subba Rao, Tel, 1981)
Jatakam *see* Jataka Phala
Jataka Phala/Jatakapalam/Jatakam (**R. Nagendra Rao**, K/Tam/Tel, 1953)
Jatakarathna Gunda Joisa/Jatakarathnam (B. Padmanabhan, K, 1971)
Jata Mat Tata Path (**Gurudas Bagchi**, B, 1979)
Jatara (Satyam, Tel, 1980)
Jatayu (Uttarsuri, B, 1976)
Jat-e-Sharif *see* Zaat-e-Sharif
Jathakam (Suresh Unnithan, Mal, 1989)
Jathi Malli (**K. Balachander**, Tam, 1992)
Jatt Da Gandasa (Mohan Bhakri, P, 1991)
Jatti (J.D. Talwar, P, 1961)
Jatti (Mohan Bhakri, P, 1980)
Jatt Jeona Mor (Ravinder Ravi, P, 1992)
Jatt Punjab Da (Yograj Singh, P, 1992)
Jatt Punjabi (Satish Bhakri, P, 1979)
Jatt Surmey (Veerendra, P, 1988)
Jatt Te Zameen (Veerendra, P, 1989)
Javai Mazha Bhala (Neelkanth Magdum, Mar, 1962)
Javai Vikat Ghene Aahe (**Raja Thakur**, Mar, 1973)
Javal Ye Laju Nako (Arun Karnataki, Mar, 1976)
Javayachi Jaat (Kamalakar Torne, Mar, 1979)
Jawab *see* **Shesh Uttar**
Jawab (Ismail Memon, H, 1955)
Jawab (Ramanna, H, 1970)
Jawab (Ravi Tandon, H, 1985)
Jawab (Jyoti Prakash Roy, B, 1987)
Jawab Ayega (**Ismat Chughtai**, H, 1968)
Jawabdaar (**Krishnakant**, G, 1982)
Jawabdari (Virendra Patel, G, 1950)
Jawab Hum Denge (Vijay Reddy, H, 1987)
Jawahar (?, Kuldeep Prod, H, 1960)
Jawahar (Kumar Kiran, H, 1989)
Jawahir-e-Hind (*aka* Modern Hero: **Dhirubhai Desai**, St, 1931)
Jawahir-e-Hind (Chunilal Parekh, H, 1937)
Jawani (Wajahat Mirza, H, 1942)
Jawani (Ramesh Behl, H, 1984)
Jawani Diwani (*aka* Flaming Youth: **Nandlal Jaswantlal**, St, 1929)
Jawani Diwani (*aka* Flaming Youth: Shanti J. Dave, H, 1934)
Jawani Diwani (**Narendra Bedi**, H, 1972)
Jawani Ka Nasha (Manzoor Ahmed/Nazim Azmabadi, H, 1935)
Jawani Ka Rang *see* Stree
Jawani Ke Gunah (?, Victory Movies, H, 1988)
Jawani Ki Aag (**H.S. Rawail**, H, 1951)
Jawani Ki Bhool (Dorai, H, 1981)
Jawani Ki Hawa (**Franz Osten**, H, 1935)
Jawani Ki Hawa (M. Sadiq, H, 1959)
Jawani Ki Kahani (K.R. Ragan, H, 1986)
Jawani Ki Lehren (Sanil Khosla, H, 1988)
Jawani Ki Pukar (**D. Bilimoria**, H, 1942)
Jawani Ki Reet/Parajay (**Hemchandra Chunder**, H/B, 1939)
Jawani Zindabad (Arun Bhatt, H, 1990)
Jawan Mard *see* Navbharat
Jawan Mard (*aka* Dashing Hero: **Jayant Desai**, St, 1930)
Jawan Mard (Ishwarlal, H, 1966)
Jawan Mohabbat *see* Hamari Yaad Ayegi
Jawan Mohabbat (Bhappi Sonie, H, 1971)
Jawbreakers *see* Taj Ke Talwar
Jaya (Chitta Bose, B, 1965)
Jaya Bharati (Raja Yagnik, Tam, 1939)
Jayabheri (**P. Pullaiah**, Tel, 1959)
Jayadeb (Shiba Bhattacharya, O, 1963)
Jayadeb (Shyamal Mukherjee, O, 1987)
Jayadratha Vadh (G.V. Sane, St, 1924)
Jaya Gopi (**B.S. Ranga**, Tam, 1955)
Jayakkodi (**K. Amarnath**, Tam, 1939)
Jaya Maa Mangala (Akshay Mohanty, O, 1980)
Jayam Manade (**T. Prakash Rao**, Tel, 1956)
Jayam Manade (**K. Bapaiah**, Tel, 1986)
Jayammu Nischayammura (Jandhyala, Tel, 1989)
Jaya Nee Jayichuthey (A. Jagannathan, Tam, 1979)
Jayant (**Nagendra Majumdar**, St, 1929)
Jaya Parvati Vrat (**Nanabhai Bhatt**, G, 1982)
Jayapradha (**Ch. Narasimha Rao**, Tel, 1939)
Jayashree (Balchandra Shukla/Harsukh Bhatt, H, 1956)
Jayashree Yamuna Maharani (Vishnukumar Vyas, G, 1977)
Jayasimha/Jaisingh (**Yoganand**, Tel/H, 1955)
Jayasimha (P. Vasu, K, 1987)
Jayasudha (K.V. Nandana Rao, Tel, 1982)
Jayaveeran/Jayavijaya (**B. Vittalacharya**, Tam/Tel, 1959)
Jayavijaya *see* Jayaveeran
Jaya Vijaya (A.V. Sheshgiri Rao, K, 1973)

Jayen To Jayen Kahan (Anil Kumar, H, 1980)
Jayikkanai Janichavan (**Sasikumar**, Mal, 1978)
Jayjatra/Vijay Yatra (**Niren Lahiri**, B/H, 1948)
Jay Jayanti (S. Mullick, B, 1971)
Jay Parajay (Chandan Mukherjee, B, 1983)
Jazbaat (Suraj Prakash, H, 1980)
Jazeerey (**Govind Nihalani**, H, 1989)
Jazz of Life *see* Baheri Zindagi
Jazz of Life (**H.M. Reddy**, St, 1932)
Jeb Katra (*aka* Pickpocket: Nari Ghadiali, H, 1946)
Jebu Donga (V. Madhusudhana Rao, Tel, 1975)
Jebu Donga (A. Kodandarami Reddy, Tel, 1987)
Jedara Bale (Dorairaj-Bhagavan, K, 1968)
Jeejaji (Baldev R. Jhingan, P, 1961)
Jeeja Sali (Mohan Bhakri, P, 1985)
Jeena Hai Pyar Mein (Krishna Naidu, H, 1983)
Jeena Isi Ka Naam Hai (P.D. Shenoy, H, 1982)
Jeena Marna Tere Sangh (Vijay Reddy, H, 1992)
Jeena Seekho (Heera Singh, H, 1946)
Jeena Teri Gali Mein (?, Super Cassettes, H, 1991)
Jeena Yahan (**Basu Chatterjee**, H, 1979)
Jeene Do (Adi F. Keeka/K.A. Majid, H, 1948)
Jeene Do (Rajesh Sethi, H, 1990)
Jeene Ki Arzoo (Rajashekhar, H, 1981)
Jeene Ki Raah (**L.V. Prasad**, H, 1969)
Jeene Ki Sazaa (Nazir Herekar, H, 1991)
Jeene Nahin Doonga (Rajkumar Kohli, H, 1984)
Jeet (Mohan Sinha, H, 1949)
Jeet (**Adurthi Subba Rao**, H, 1972)
Jeete Hain Shaan Se (Kawal Sharma, H, 1988)
Jeete Raho (C.S. Krishna Kumar, H, 1949)
Jeet Hamari (R. Thyagarajan, H, 1983)
Jeet Kiski (Vasant Joglekar, H, 1952)
Jeeto (Ramesh Bedi, P, 1972)
Jeeva (Raj N. Sippy, H, 1986)
Jeeva (**Prathap Pothan**, Tam, 1988)
Jeevajyoti (K.M. Multani, Tam, 1947)
Jeevan (*aka* Bahar: M. Sadiq, H, 1944)
Jeevana Chakra (H.R. Bhargava, K, 1985)
Jeevana Chitra (Dorairaj-Bhagavan, K, 1992)
Jeevanadhi (A.K. Subramanyam, Tam, 1970)
Jeevanadhi (Sanjai-Bhaskar, Tam, 1986)
Jeevana Ganga (Mouli, Tel, 1988)
Jeevana Jokaali (Geethapriya, K, 1972)
Jeevana Jyothi (P. Vasu, K, 1987)
Jeevana Jyoti (D. Ch. Kameshwara Rao, Tel, 1940)
Jeevana Jyoti (**K. Vishwanath**, Tel, 1975)
Jeevana Jyoti (Relangi Narasimha Rao, Tel, 1988)
Jeevanamsam (Malliyam Rajagopal, Tam, 1968)
Jeevana Mukti (Lanka Sathyam, Tel, 1942)
Jeevana Nataka (Wahab Kashmiri, K, 1942)
Jeevana Poratam (Rajachandra, Tel, 1986)
Jeevana Rangam (V.V. Prasad, Tel, 1986)
Jeevana Sathi (Prabhat Mukherjee, O, 1964)
Jeevana Taranga (Bangararaju, K, 1963)
Jeevana Tarangulu (**T. Rama Rao**, Tel, 1973)
Jeevana Theeralu (G.C. Shekhar, Tel, 1977)
Jeevana Vauhini (Rajashri, Tel, 1984)
Jeevan *see* Jiban
Jeevan Chhaya *see* Kul Kalank
Jeevan Daata (Swaroop Kumar, H, 1991)
Jeevan Dhara (**T. Rama Rao**, H, 1982)
Jeevan Ek Paheli (P. Razdan?, Central India Theatres: H, 1938)
Jeevan Ek Sangharsh (**Rahul Rawail**, H, 1990)
Jeevan Jyoti (M.R. Kapoor, H, 1937)
Jeevan Jyoti (Vijay Mohan Gupta, H, 1949)
Jeevan Jyoti (**Mahesh Kaul**, H, 1953)
Jeevan Jyoti (Murugan-Kumaran, H, 1976)
Jeevan Ki Nadiyan *see* Rivers of Life
Jeevan Ki Shatranj (S.A. Chandrasekharan, H, 1993)
Jeevan Lata (**Sarvottam Badami**, H, 1936)
Jeevan Mrityu (**Satyen Bose**, H, 1970)
Jeevanmukt (Sudhendu Roy, H, 1977)
Jeevan Naiya (**Franz Osten**, H, 1936)
Jeevan Natak (**Debaki Bose**, H, 1935)
Jeevan Nauka *see* **Jeevitha Nauka**
Jeevan Palto (Hiralal Doctor/Amritlal Thakar, G, 1948)
Jeevan Prabhat (*aka* Dawn of Life: Santosh K. Hazra, St, 1931)
Jeevan Prabhat (**Franz Osten**, H, 1937)
Jeevan Rekha (**Nanabhai Bhatt**, H, 1974)
Jeevan Saathi (**Nandlal Jaswantlal**, H, 1939)
Jeevan Saathi (*aka* Prem Ki Kahani: M.D. Baig, H, 1949)
Jeevan Saathi (R.S. Tara, H, 1957)
Jeevan Saathi (?, Tilak Movies, H, 1988)
Jeevan Sangeet (?, Cultural Film Society, H, 1973)
Jeevan Sangharshana (S. Venugopal, K, 1993)
Jeevan Sangram (*aka* Struggle: **Ezra Mir**, H, 1936)
Jeevan Sangram (Rajbans Khanna, H, 1974)
Jeevan Suravi (Naresh Kumar, A, 1984)
Jeevan Swapna (*aka* Journey's End: **Jaddanbai**, H, 1937)
Jeevan Swapna (*aka* Main Awara: A. Karim/Sultan Mirza, H, 1946)
Jeevan Tara (Joseph Taliath, H, 1951)
Jeevante Jeevan (J. Williams, Mal, 1985)
Jeevan Yatra (**Master Vinayak**, H, 1946)
Jeevikan Anuvadhikuka (P.A. Thomas, Mal, 1967)
Jeevikkan Marnupoya Shree (**K.S. Sethumadhavan**, Mal, 1974)
Jeevikkan Patikkanam (?, Mal, 1981)
Jeevit Amche Ashe (**Y.V. Rao**, Konkani, 1950)
Jeevitha Bandham (M.S. Gopinath, Tel, 1968)
Jeevitha Chakram (**C.S. Rao**, Tel, 1971)
Jeevithalu (V.S. Murthy, Tel, 1968)
Jeevitham *see* Vazhkai
Jeevitham (**K.S. Prakash Rao**, Tel, 1973)
Jeevitham (K. Vijayan, Mal, 1984)
Jeevithame Oka Cinema (Phani Ramchandra, Tel, 1992)
Jeevithame Oka Natakam (**Dasari Narayana Rao**, Tel, 1977)
Jeevithamlo Vasantham (U.S.V. Pani, Tel, 1977)
Jeevitham Oru Ganam (Shrikumaran Thampi, Mal, 1979)
Jeevitham Oru Ragam (U.V. Raveendranath, Mal, 1989)
Jeevitha Nauka/Jeevan Nauka (K. Vembu, Mal/Tam/H, 1951)
Jeevitha Nauka (**K. Vishwanath**, Tel, 1977)
Jeevitha Rangamu (P.D. Prasad, Tel, 1974)
Jeevitha Ratham (V. Madhusudhana Rao, Tel, 1981)
Jeevithasayam (**K. Kameshwara Rao**, Tel, 1974)
Jeevitha Yatra (**Sasikumar**, Mal, 1965)
Je Jekhane Danriye (Agragami/Saroj De, B, 1974)
Jekara Charanva Mein Lagle Paranva (B.K. Adarsh, Bh, 1964)
Jennikara (Raghuram, K, 1992)
Jenugudu (Y.R. Swamy, K, 1963)
Jesal Toral (**Chaturbhuj Doshi**, G, 1948)
Jesal Toral (**Ravindra Dave**, G, 1971)
Jesus/Isa Masih (P.A. Thomas, Mal/H, 1973)
Jevichhun Tevi (G.K. Mehta, G. 1963)
Jewelled Arrow *see* Poonam No Chand
Jewel of Manipur (**Prema Karanth**, E, 1985/1986)
Jewel of Mewar *see* Panna Ratna
Jewel of Rajputana *see* Mewad Nu Moti
Jewel of Shiva *see* **Shankarabharanam**
Jewel Thief (**Vijay Anand**, H, 1967)
Jhakli Mooth (**Anant Mane**, Mar, 1957)
Jhakmari (Kalipada Das, B, 1953)
Jhakol (Shreeram Lagoo, Mar, 1980)
Jhala Gela Visroon Ja (Yeshwant Pethkar, Mar, 1957)
Jhalak (Raja Yagnik, H, 1947)
Jhala Mahar Pandharinath (Kamalakar Torne, Mar, 1970)
Jhamela (**Master Bhagwan**, H, 1953)
Jhanak Jhanak Payal Baaje (**V. Shantaram**, H, 1955)
Jhanda Ooncha Rahe Hamara (?, Movie Mandir, H, 1964)
Jhanjavaat (Dada Paranjpe, Mar, 1954)
Jhanjhar (**Kidar Sharma**, H, 1953)
Jhanjhar (**V. Shantaram**, H, 1986)
Jhankar (S. Khalil, H, 1942)
Jhansi Ki Rani (**Sohrab Modi**, H, 1953)
Jhansi Rani (M. Karnan, Tam, 1985)
Jhansi Rani (Satyanand, Tel, 1988)
Jharer Parey (Apurba Mitra, B, 1947)
Jharer Parey (Debnarayan Gupta, B, 1955)
Jharkhand (**Tapan Bose**, E, 1993)
Jharna (**Protima Dasgupta**, H, 1948)
Jheel Ke Us Paar (Bhappi Sonie, H, 1973)
Jhep (**Rajdutt**, Mar, 1971)
Jhiati Seeta Pari (Bidhubhushan Nand, O, 1983)
Jhilimili (K.H.D. Rao, O, 1978)
Jhinder Bandi (**Tapan Sinha**, B, 1961)
Jhinjhinyar Jer (**Phani Burma**, B, 1936)
Jhoola (**Gyan Mukherjee**, H, 1941)
Jhoola (K. Shankar, H, 1962)
Jhoom Utha Akash (Y.N. Kapoor, H, 1973)
Jhootha Kahin Ka (Ravi Tandon, H, 1979)
Jhootha Sach (Esmayeel Shroff, H, 1984)
Jhoothi (**Hrishikesh Mukherjee**, H, 1986)
Jhoothi Kasmein (**H.S. Rawail**, H, 1948)
Jhoothi Shaan (Ranjan Bose, H, 1992)
Jhoothi Sharm (*aka* Naked Truth: **M. Bhavnani**, H, 1940)
Jhoothi Sharm (?, H, 1989)
Jhor (Anjan Das, B, 1978)
Jhor (**Utpal Dutt**, B, 1979)
Jhuk Gaya Aasmaan (Lekh Tandon, H, 1968)
Jhumke (J.K. Nanda, H, 1946)
Jhumroo (Shankar Mukherjee, H, 1961)
Jhunz *see* Zunz
Jiban (Palash Bannerjee, B, 1972)
Jiban (Ardhendu Chatterjee, B, 1986)
Jiban Je Rakam (Swadesh Sarkar, B, 1979)
Jiban Jignasa (Piyush Basu, B, 1971)
Jiban Kahini (**Rajen Tarafdar**, B, 1964)
Jiban Maran *see* **Dushman**
Jiban Maran (Sukhen Das, B, 1983)
Jiban Marer Prante (Sadhan Choudhury, B, 1976)
Jiban Mrityu (Hiren Nag, B, 1967)
Jiban Niye (Ramaprasad Choudhury, B, 1974)
Jiban Rahasya (Salil Roy, B, 1973)
Jiban Saikat (Amar Dutta, B, 1950)
Jiban Saikate (Swadesh Sarkar, B, 1972)
Jiban Sangeet (Aravind Mukherjee, B, 1968)
Jiban Sangini (Gunamaya Bannerjee, B, 1942)
Jiban Sangram (Prabhat Chakraborty, B, 1972)
Jiban Sangram (Jiban Mahanta, O, 1984)
Jiban Sathi (Adhir Bhattacharya, B, 1985)
Jiban Trishna (**Asit Sen**, B, 1957)
Ji Chahta Hai (Bibhuti Mitra, H, 1964)
Jidda (**Datta Keshav**, Mar, 1980)
Jiddu (D. Rajendra Babu, K, 1984)
Jigar (**Master Bhagwan**, H, 1949)
Jigar (Faroque Siddiqui, H, 1992)
Jigar Ane Ami (**Chandrakant Sangani**, G, 1970)
Jigarme Gha (*aka* Rajput Ramani, Wronged Wife: Pesi Karani, St, 1930)
Jigarwala (Swaroop Kumar, H, 1991)
Jighansa (**Ajoy Kar**, B, 1951)
Jigra Jatt Da (Satish Bhakri, P, 1992)
Jigri Dost (Ravi Nagaich, H, 1969)
Jigri Yaar (K. Pappu, P, 1984)
Jigu Jigu Rail (Manivannan, Tam, 1986)
Ji Haan (*aka* Yes Please, Ticket Master: R.Vaidya/**Babubhai Mistri**, H, 1945)
Jimmy (Melattur Ravi Varma, Mal, 1979)
Jimmygallu (Ravi, K, 1982)
Jindri Yar Di (Dharam Kumar, P, 1978)
Jingo (Brij Mohan, H, 1952)
Jini Ram Tini Krishna Ek Dehe Ram Krishna (Niranjan Dey, B, 1983)
Jis Desh Mein Ganga Behti Hai (Radhu Karmakar, H, 1960)
Jise Tu Kabool Karle (Chetana?, H, 1980)
Jism Ka Rishta (?, Anu Arts, H, 1988)
Jisne Tera Naam Liya *see* Tere Dwar Khada Bhagwan
Jithro Bhabho (Lalit Gajra, G, 1983)
Jivacha Sakha (**Raja Paranjpe**, Mar, 1948)
Jivachi Mumbai (Achyut Ranade, Mar, 1952)
Jivakke Jiva (K.S.R. Doss, K, 1981)
Jivhala (Ram Gabale, Mar, 1968)
Jivi Rabaran (Shridhar Prasad, G, 1980)
Jivno Jugari (Dinesh Rawal, G, 1963)
Jiyo Aur Jeene Do (B. Mastan, H, 1969)
Jiyo Aur Jeene Do (Shyam Ralhan, H, 1982)
Jiyo Raja (Nari Ghadiali, H, 1949)
Jiyo To Aise Jiyo (Kanak Mishra, H, 1981)
Jnanambika *see* **Gnanambika**
Joban Nu Jadu (*aka* Love Angel: **Jayant Desai**, St, 1930)
Job Charnaker Bibi (Jayanta Bhattacharya, B, 1978)
Jockey (B. Subba Rao, K, 1989)
Jode Rejo Raaj (Subhash J. Shah, G, 1989)
Jodi Chenthachu (Lakshmi, Tam, 1992)
Jodidar (**Balwant Bhatt**, H, 1950)
Jodi Jeeva (Geethapriya, K, 1982)
Jodipura (V.K. Ramaswamy, Tam, 1983)
Jogajog/Hospital (**Sushil Majumdar**, B/H, 1943)
Jogajog (**Nitin Bose**, B, 1958)
Jogan (**Kidar Sharma**, H, 1950)
Jog Biyog (Pinaki Mukherjee, B, 1953)
Jog Biyog (Bibhan Barua, A, 1971)
Jog Biyog (Pinaki Mukherjee, B, 1984)
Jogi (Huda Bihari, H, 1982)
Jogidas Khuman (**Manhar Raskapur**, G, 1948)
Jogidas Khuman (**Manhar Raskapur**, G, 1962)
Jogidas Khuman (**Manhar Raskapur**, G, 1975)
Jog Sanjog (**Krishnakant**, G, 1980)
Jog Sanjog (*aka* Bai Ra Bhag: R.K. Joshi, R, 1988)
Johar-e-Shamsheer *see* Raj Nandini
Johar-e-Shamsheer (**J.P. Advani**, H, 1934)
Johari (Niranjan, H, 1951)
Johar in Bombay (Shantilal soni, H, 1967)
Johar In Kashmir (I.S. Johar, H, 1966)
Johar Maibaap (*aka* Sant Chokhamela, Hi Vaat Pandharichi: Ram Gabale, Mar, 1950)
Johar Mehmood in Goa (I.S. Johar, H, 1965)
Johar Mehmood in Hong Kong (S.A. Akbar, H, 1971)
John Jaffer Janardhan (**I.V. Sasi**, Mal, 1982)
John Jani Janardan (**T. Rama Rao**, H, 1984)
Johnny (*aka* Jani: **J. Mahendran**, Tam, 1980)
Johnny I Love You (Rakesh Kumar, H, 1982)
Johnny Mera Naam (**Vijay Anand**, H, 1970)
Johnny Walker (Ved-Madan, H, 1957)
Johnny Walker (Jayaraj, Mal, 1992)
Jo Hua So Bhool Jao (Yeshwant Pethkar, H, 1960)
Joi (**Gurudas Bagchi**, B, 1976)
Joi Baba Felunath (**Satyajit Ray**, B, 1978)
Joi Bangla (Umaprasad Moitra, B, 1971)
Joi Bangla Desh (*aka* Aage Badho: I.S. Johar, H, 1971)
Joi Maa Mangalchandi (Prabhat Chakraborty, B, 1980)
Joi Ma Tara (Ajit Ganguly, B, 1978)
Jo Jeeta Wohi Sikandar (Mansoor Hussain, H, 1992)
Joker (**Balwant Bhatt**, H, 1949)
Joker (**Vamsy**, Tel, 1993)
Joker Mama Super Alludu (K. Vasu, Tel, 1992)
Jonakir Alo (**Asit Sen**, B, 1958)
Joradighir Choudhury Paribar (Ajit Lahiri, B, 1966)
Jore Barat (**Jyotish Bannerjee**, B, 1931)
Jorjar Mulak Tar (Raju Mishra, O, 1987)
Jor Jatt Da (Sukhjinder Shera, P, 1991)
Joru Ka Bhai (**Chetan Anand**, H, 1955)
Joru Ka Gulam (**A. Bhimsingh**, H, 1972)
Josh (A. Karim, H, 1950)
Josh (Raj N. Sippy, H, 1981)
Josh-e-Inteqam (*aka* Blood Feud: Prafulla Roy, H, 1935)
Josh-e-Islam (Dawood, H, 1939)
Josh-e-Jawani *see* Bachha-i-Sakka
Josh-e-Jawani (*aka* Fighting Blood: Dwarka Khosla, H, 1935)
Josh-e-Mohabbat (?, **New Theatres**, H, 1932)
Josh-e-Watan *see* **Desh Deepak**
Joshila (**Yash Chopra**, H, 1973)
Joshilay (**Shekhar Kapur**, H, 1985)
Josh Jawani Da (Surinder Kapoor, P, 1981)
Jotugriha (**Tapan Sinha**, B, 1964)
Journey of Dr Kotnis, The *see* **Dr Kotnis Ki Amar Kahani**
Journey's End *see* Jeevan Swapna

Journey through a Dream *see* **Swapnadanam**
Joutuk (Jiban Ganguly, B, 1958)
Joyar Bhanta (**Dhiraj Bhattacharya**, B, 1936)
Joydev (**Jyotish Bannerjee**, St, 1926)
Joydev (**Jyotish Bannerjee**, B, 1933)
Joydev (**Phani Burma**, B, 1954)
Joymakali Boarding (Sadhan Sarkar, B, 1955)
Joymati (**Jyotiprasad Agarwala**, A, 1935)
JP (**Atma Ram**, H, 1988)
Juari (*aka* Gambler, Jugari: G.K. Mehta, H, 1939)
Juari (Suraj Prakash, H, 1968)
Judaai (**T. Rama Rao**, H, 1980)
Judagadu (V. Madhusudhana Rao, Tel, 1979)
Judge, The *see* Bicharak
Judgement (A. Mohan Gandhi, Tel, 1990)
Judgement of **Allah** (*aka* Al Hilal: **Mehboob**, Urdu, 1935)
Judge Saheb (Piyush Deb Nath, B, 1989)
Judigigari Kodalu (V. Madhusudhana Rao, Tel, 1977)
Jue Ka Nateeja *see* Shadi Se Pehle
Jugadevata (Bidhayak Bhattacharya, B, 1950)
Jugalangriya (**Jyotish Bannerjee**, St, 1930)
Jugalbandi (Datta Gorle, Mar, 1984)
Jugal Jodi (Arun Bhatt, G, 1982)
Jugal Jugari (*aka* Gambler: Fram Sethna, St, 1930)
Jugari Dharma (*aka* Royal Gambler: **P.Y. Altekar**, St, 1927)
Juggler *see* Jadunath
Jug Jug Jiyo More Lal (?, Bh, 1991)
Jugni (Rajinder Sharma, P, 1953)
Jugnu (Shaukat Hussain Rizvi, H, 1947)
Jugnu (Pramod Chakraborty, H, 1973)
Juhu (TV: **K.A. Abbas**, H, 1973)
Jukti Takko Aar Gappo (**Ritwik Ghatak**, B, 1974)
Julia Dalia (*aka* The Mughal Prince: ?, United Pics Syndicate, St, 1929)
Julie (**K.S. Sethumadhavan**, H, 1975)
Jumbish (Salauddin Pervez, H, 1986)
Juna Te Sona (Yeshwant Pethkar, Mar, 1967)
Jung Aur Aman (**Nanabhai Bhatt**, H, 1968)
Jungbaaz (**Mehul Kumar**, H, 1989)
Jung Bahadur (*aka* Daredevil: **M. Bhavnani**, H, 1935)
Jung Bahadur (G.P. Pawar, H, 1958)
Jung-e-Azadi *see* Veer Pujan
Jung-e-Azadi (Chandrarao Kadam, H, 1940)
Jung-e-Daulat (*aka* Lust for Gold: A.P. Kapur, St, 1931)
Jung-e-Jawani *see* Modern Youth
Jung-e-Jawani (*aka* Love of Youth: Maneklal Thakkar, St, 1932)
Jung-e-Ulfat *see* Maya Jaal
Jungle, The (*aka* Kaadu: William Berke/**Ellis R. Duncan**, E/Tam, 1952)
Jungle Beauty (Dilip Gulati, H, 1991)
Jungle Boy (S. Pal, H, 1963)
Jungle Boy (?, Karthikeya Films, Mal, 1987)
Junglee (**Subodh Mukherjee**, H, 1961)
Jungle Geet *see* India in Africa
Jungle Girl *see* Hoor-e-Jungle
Jungle Goddess (Nari Ghadiali, H, 1948)
Jungle Ka Beta (Sunil Kumar, H, 1992)
Jungle Ka Jadu (Nari Ghadiali, H, 1955)
Jungle Ka Jawahar (**Homi Wadia**, H, 1952)
Jungle Ka Jawan (*aka* Hero of the Wilds: Chunilal Parekh, St, 1931)
Jungle Ka Jawan (Chunilal Parekh, H, 1938)
Jungle Ka Sher (Harbans, H, 1946)
Jungle Ki Beti (R. Thakur, H, 1987)
Jungle Ki Duniya (B.N. Chouhan, H, 1959)
Jungle Ki Hoor (S.M. Sheikh, H, 1967)
Jungle Ki Ladki (*aka* Maid of the Forest: Omkar Lalit, H, 1941)
Jungle King (Nari Ghadiali, H, 1939)
Jungle King (Masood, H, 1959)
Jungle Ki Pukar (*aka* Call of the Jungle: Ramji Arya, H, 1946)
Jungle Ki Rani *see* Jungle Queen
Jungle Love (V. Menon, H, 1990)
Jungle Man (Harbans, H, 1950)
Jungle Mein Mangal (Baburao Badodekar, H, 1947)
Jungle Mein Mangal (Rajendra Bhatia, H, 1972)
Jungle Ni Jadibuti (*aka* Love Rewarded: **Manilal Joshi**, St, 1926)
Jungle Princess (**Homi Wadia**, H, 1942)
Jungle Princess (A.R. Zamindar, H, 1958)
Jungle Queen (*aka* Jungle Ki Rani: **Nandlal Jaswantlal**, H, 1936)
Jungle Queen (Nari Ghadiali, H, 1956)
Jungle Queen (K. Chandra, H, 1991)
Jungli Raja (Vishwanath, H, 1963)
Junoon (**Shyam Benegal**, H, 1978)
Junoon (**Mahesh Bhatt**, H, 1992)
Jurm (**Mahesh Bhatt**, H, 1990)
Jurmana (*aka* Penalty: M.S. Asif, H, 1947)
Jurmana (**Hrishikesh Mukherjee**, H, 1979)
Jurm Aur Sazaa (N.A. Ansari, H, 1974)
Jurrat (David Dhawan, H, 1989)
Just Half-an-hour *see* **Aranazhikaneram**
Justice *see* Insaaf *or* Prem Samadhi
Justice (Vedi, St, 1925)
Justice Chakravarthy (**Dasari Narayana Rao**, Tel, 1984)
Justice Choudhury (**K. Raghavendra Rao**, Tel/H, 1982)
Justice Gopinath (**D. Yoganand**, Tam, 1978)
Justice of Jehangir *see* Adl-e-Jehangir
Justice of Vikram *see* Manthan
Justice Raja (R. Krishnamurthy, Mal, 1983)
Justice Rudramma Devi (K. Ranga Rao, Tel, 1990)
Justice Vishwanathan (G.R. Nathan, Tam, 1971)
Juwanina Zer (Raju Bhatt/Kiran Bhrambhatt, G, 1985)
Jwain Pua (**Dinen Gupta**, O, 1982)
Jwala (**Master Vinayak**, Mar/H, 1938)
Jwala (M. Krishnan Nair, Mal, 1969)
Jwala (**M.V. Raman**, H, 1970)
Jwala (Ravi Raja Pinisetty, Tel, 1985)
Jwala (Sudesh Issar, H, 1986)
Jwala (G.K. Mudduraj, K, 1993)
Jwala Dahej Ki (Chaman Nillay, H, 1983)
Jwala Daku (R.P. Swamy, H, 1981)
Jwaladeepa Rahasyam (**B. Vittalacharya**, Tel, 1965)
Jwala Mohini (S.N. Singh, K, 1973)
Jwalamukhi (D.N. Madhok, H, 1936)
Jwalamukhi (**Prakash Mehra**, H, 1980)
Jwalamukhi (**Singeetham Srinivasa Rao**, K, 1985)
Jwar Bhata (**Amiya Chakravarty**, H, 1944)
Jwar Bhata (**Adurthi Subba Rao**, H, 1973)
Jyothi (Manivannan, Tam, 1983)
Jyothi Malar (Ramnarayanan, Tam, 1986)
Jyothi Ramalingaswamy *see* Ramalinga Swamigal
Jyoti/Illara Jyoti (Sridhar-Tilak, Tel/Tam, 1954)
Jyoti (**Ramchandra Thakur**, H, 1969)
Jyoti (Dulal Guha, H, 1969)
Jyoti (**K. Raghavendra Rao**, Tel, 1976)
Jyoti (Pramod Chakraborty, H, 1981)
Jyoti (Manohar Reddy, K, 1982)
Jyotibacha Navas (Kamalakar Torne, Mar, 1975)
Jyoti Bane Jwala (**Dasari Narayana Rao**, H, 1980)
Jyoti Lakshmi (K.S. Rami Reddy, Tel, 1973)
Jyoti Malar *see* Thasippen
Jyotishi (Chitta Bose, B, 1955)
Jyot Jale (**Satyen Bose**, H, 1968)
Jyotsna Ratri (Mrinal Bhattacharya, B, 1983)

K

Kaa (Siddharth, O, 1966)
Kaadu *see* The Jungle
Kaadu (**Girish Karnad**, K, 1973)
Kaadu (**P. Subramanyam**, Mal, 1973)
Kaadu (**Durai**, Tam, 1980)
Kaadu Kudure (**Chandrasekhar Kambhar**, K, 1978)
Kaagaz Ke Phool (**Guru Dutt**, H, 1959)
Kaagaz Ki Nao (**B.R. Ishara**, H, 1975)
Kaal Abhirati (Amitabh Chakraborty, B, 1989)
Kaala Patthar *see* **Kala Patthar**
Kaalchakra (Dilip Shankar, H, 1987)
Kaalia *see* Kaliya
Kaalsrote (**Sushil Majumdar**, B, 1964)
Kaamchor (**K. Vishwanath**, H, 1982)
Kaamshastra (Prem Kapoor, H, 1975)
Kaamyaab (**K. Raghavendra Rao**, H, 1984)
Kaamyabi (Pervez Malik, H, 1987)
Kaanamarayathu (**I.V. Sasi**, Mal, 1984)
Kaanch Aur Heera (Charandas Shokh, H, 1972)
Kaanch Ki Deewar (M.N. Yasin, H, 1986)
Kaanch Ki Gudiya (**H.S. Rawail**, H, 1961)
Kaangoo (G. Karimbhai, H, 1946)
Kaanike (Satyam, K, 1969)
Kaani Nilam (*aka* A Piece of Land: S. Arunmozhi, Tam, 1987)
Kaaran (**B.R. Ishara**, H, 1980)
Kaash (**Mahesh Bhatt**, H, 1987)
Kabani Nadi Chuvannappol (**P.A. Backer**, Mal, 1975)
Kabaristan (Mohan Bhakri, H, 1988)
Kabeela *see* Rain Basera
Kabeela (Bolu Khosla, H, 1976)
Kabhi Ajnabi The (Vijay Singh, H, 1985)
Kabhi Andhera Kabhi Ujala (C.P. Dixit, H, 1958)
Kabhi Dhoop Kabhi Chhaon (**Chandrakant**, H, 1971)
Kabhi Door Kabhi Paas (TV: **Mrinal Sen**, H, 1987)
Kabhi Haan Kabhi Naa (**Kundan Shah**, H, 1993)
Kabhi Kabhie (**Yash Chopra**, H, 1976)
Kab Hoihain Gavanava Hamaar (P.L. Santoshi, Bh, 1964)
Kabi (Sunit Bannerjee, B, 1973)
Kabir (?, Oriental Film, Tel, 1936)
Kabir Kamal (**S.N. Patankar**, St, 1919)
Kabir Kamal (G.V. Sane, St, 1930)
Kabi Samrat Upendra Bhanja (*aka* Upendra Bhanja: N. Gopal, O, 1978)
Kabita (Bharat Shumsher Jung Bahadur Rana, B, 1977)
Kab Kyon Aur Kahan (Arjun Hingorani, H, 1970)
Kaboye Alludu (Relangi Narasimha Rao, Tel, 1987)
Kab Tak Chup Rahungi (**T. Prakash Rao**, H, 1988)
Kabuli Khan (**K. Amarnath**, H, 1963)
Kabuliwala (**Tapan Sinha**, B, 1956)
Kabuliwala (**Hemen Gupta**, H, 1961)
Kabzaa (**Mahesh Bhatt**, H, 1988)
Kacha Devayani (**S.N. Patankar**, St, 1919)
Kacha Devayani (*aka* Vidya Haran: **S.N. Patankar**, St, 1926)
Kacha Devayani (**Dadasaheb Phalke**, St, 1929)
Kacha Devayani (D.Ch. Kameshwara Rao, Tel, 1938)
Kacha Devayani (**K. Subramanyam**/C.S.V. Iyer, Tam, 1941)
Kacha Devayani (**K. Subramanyam**, K, 1956)
Kachaghara (Byomkesh Tripathi, O, 1981)
Kachcha Chor (Jambu, H, 1977)
Kachche Dhaage (**Raj Khosla**, H, 1973)
Kachche Heere (**Narendra Bedi**, H, 1981)
Kachhi Dhoop (TV: **Amol Palekar**, H, 1987)
Kachhi Kali (K.R. Rangan, H, 1987)
Kachi Matina Kodiyan (Kantilal Dave, G, 1984)
Kachi Samsad (Jyotish Mukherjee, B, 1936)
Kadaikan Parvai (Rajsridhar, Tam, 1986)
Kadai Karantha Oduthi (Mandhurai Babuji, Tam, 1979)
Kadaklakshmi (Murlidhar Kapdi, Mar, 1980)
Kadakti Bijli (*aka* Thunderbolt: G.R. Sethi, H, 1936)
Kadal (**P. Subramanyam**, Mal, 1968)
Kadaladu Vadaladu (**B. Vittalacharya**, Tel, 1969)
Kadalamma (**Kunchako**, Mal, 1963)
Kadalikka Neramillai (**C.V. Sridhar**, Tam, 1964)
Kadalithu Paar (?, Tam, 1982)
Kadali Vachina Kanakadurga (K.S. Rami Reddy, Tel, 1982)
Kadalkattu (P.G. Vishwambaran, Mal, 1980)
Kadal Meengal (G.N. Rangarajan, Tam, 1981)
Kadalora Kattu (?, Sharon Pics., Mal, 1991)
Kadalora Kavathaikal (**Bharathirajaa**, Tam, 1986)
Kadalpalam (**K.S. Sethumadhavan**, Mal, 1969)
Kadalpura (Babu Ganesh, Tam, 1993)
Kadal Theerathu (T. Rajeevnath, Mal, 1988)
Kadamai (Ramanarayanan, Tam, 1984)
Kadamai Kanniyam Kattupadu (Santhana Bharati, Tam, 1987)
Kadamai Nenjam (**Durai**, Tam, 1979)
Kadamattathachan (Father George/K.R. Nambiar, Mal, 1966)
Kadamattathachan (Suresh, Mal, 1984)
Kadamba (**P.N. Menon**, Mal, 1982)
Kadambam (L.S. Ramchandran/K.S. Mani, Tam, 1941)
Kadambari (**Nandlal Jaswantlal**, H, 1944)
Kadambari (H.K. Verma, H, 1975)
Kadambari (Kodulu Ramakrishna, K, 1993)
Kadam Vangi Kalyanam *see* **Appu Chesi Pappu Koodu**
Kadana (K.V. Raju, K, 1991)
Kadapa Redamma (Bharatwaja, Tel, 1990)
Kadarkarai Dhagam (Elango, Tam, 1988)
Kadathanattu Maakkam (Appachan, Mal, 1978)
Kadathu (P.G. Vishwambaran, Mal, 1981)
Kadatthukaran (M. Krishnan Nair, Mal, 1965)
Kadavu (**M.T. Vasudevan Nair**, Mal, 1991)
Kadavul Amaitha Medai (S.P. Muthuraman, Tam, 1979)
Kadavulai Nambungal (Dasarathan, Tam, 1984)
Kadavulin Theerpu (C. Shanmugham, Tam, 1981)
Kadavul Mama (K. Singhamuthu, Tam, 1974)
Kadavulukku Oru Kaditham (Kalanithi, Tam, 1982)
Kadavunin Kuzhandai (Dada Mirasi, Tam, 1960)
Kade Dhoop Kade Chhaon (Kunwar Shorey, P, 1967)
Kadedullu Ekaram Nela (Jampana, Tel, 1960)
Kadgichhu (S.N. Singh, K, 1976)
Kadhal *see* Kathal
Kadhalithal Pothumma (K.V. Srinivas, Tam, 1967)
Kadhija (M. Krishnan Nair, Mal, 1967)
Kadhi Karishi Lagna Mazhe (Yeshwant Pethkar, Mar, 1965)
Kadima Kallaru (Vijay, K, 1982)
Kadina Benki (**Suresh Heblikar**, K, 1988)
Kadina Rahasya (Geethapriya, K, 1969)
Kadina Raja (A.T. Raghu, K, 1985)
Kadinjul Kalyanam (Rajasenan, Mal, 1991)
Kadinte Makkal (P.S. Prakash, Mal, 1985)
Kadivalam (Balamurali/Ram Shankar, Tam, 1984)
Kadu Makrani (**Manhar Raskapur**, G, 1960)
Kadu Makrani (Manu Desai, G, 1973)
Kaduvaye Pidicha Kiduva (A.B. Raj, Mal, 1977)
Kaduvulai Kandan (**A.S.A. Sami**, Tam, 1963)
Kafan (Dhirendra Bohra, H, 1990)
Kafila (Aravind Sen, H, 1952)
Kafila (Sudhanshu Hakku, H, 1989)
Kafir-e-Ishq *see* Zan Mureed
Kagida Odam (Ramnarayanan, Tam, 1986)
Kahalam (Joshi, Mal, 1981)
Kahan Gaye (?, Maheshwari Pics, H, 1946)
Kahan Hai Kanoon (Deepak Balraj Vij, H, 1989)
Kahan Hai Manzil Teri (S.M. Yusuf, H, 1939)
Kahani Hum Sub Ki (Rajkumar Kohli, H, 1973)
Kahani Kismat Ki (Arjun Hingorani, H, 1973)
Kahani Phoolwati Ki (Ashok Roy, H, 1984)
Kahan Kahan Se Guzar Gaye (**M.S. Sathyu**, H, 1986)
Kahan Tak Aasmaan Hai (Mehmood Kureshi, H, 1984)
Kahi Khara Nahi (Manohar Rele, Mar, 1956)
Kahin Aar Kahin Paar (Maruti, H, 1971)
Kahin Aur Chal (**Vijay Anand**, H, 1968)
Kahin Debe Sandes (?, Chitra Sansar, Chhatisgarhi, 1965)
Kahin Din Kahin Raat (Darshan, H, 1968)
Kahin Pyar Na Ho Jaye (K. Parvez, H, 1963)
Kahyagaro Kanth (**Manhar Raskapur**, G, 1950)
Kaidhi (**S. Balachander**, Tam, 1951)
Kaidhi Kanniyiram (**A.S.A. Sami**, Tam, 1960)
Kaifi Azmi (Raman Kumar, E, 1979)
Kai Ga Sakhu (Shankarrao Chavan, Mar, 1982)
Kai Ho Chamatkar (**Anant Mane**, Mar, 1964)
Kaikeyi (**I.V. Sasi**, Mal, 1983)

Kaikoduppal Karpagambal (S. Jagadeeshan, Tam, 1988)
Kaikodutha Daivam (**K.S. Gopalakrishnan**, Tam, 1964)
Kailash (*aka* Land of Martyrs: G.P. Pawar, St, 1932)
Kailash Kumari (**Nanubhai Desai**, St, 1927)
Kailashpati (**Dhirubhai Desai**, H, 1962)
Kainattu (V.C. Guhanathan, Tam, 1988)
Kai Raja Kai (Parchuri Bros., Tel, 1984)
Kairasi (K. Shankar, Tam, 1960)
Kairasikaran (S.S.K. Shankar, Tam, 1984)
Kaisan Banaula Sansar (?, Bh, 1989)
Kaise Kahun (**Moti Gidwani**, H, 1945)
Kaise Kahun (**Atma Ram**, H, 1964)
Kaise Kaise Log (D.S. Azad, H, 1983)
Kaise Kaise Rishte (Akash Mehra, H, 1993)
Kaithapoova (Raghunathan, Mal, 1977)
Kaithiyin Kathali (A.K. Velan, Tam, 1963)
Kaithiyin Theerpu (Vijayabharati, Tam, 1986)
Kaivara Mahatme (T.V. Singh Thakore, K, 1961)
Kaivari (Kamalakar Torne, Mar, 1981)
Kai Varisai (Prem Kumar, Tam, 1983)
Kaiveesu Amma Kaiveesu (Vinodh, Tam, 1989)
Kaiyethum Doorathu (?, Rajasarasa Prod, Mal, 1987)
Kajal (M. Sadiq, H, 1948)
Kajal (Sunil Bannerjee, B, 1962)
Kajal (Ram Maheshwari, H, 1965)
Kajal Lata (Bikash Roy, B, 1975)
Kajari (**Niren Lahiri**, B, 1953)
Kajari (Kirankant, Bh, 1989)
Kajla Didi (Kaushik, B, 1983)
Kaka Mala Vachva (**Raja Paranjpe**, Mar, 1967)
Kakana Kote (C.R. Simha, K, 1976)
Kakasahebanchya Dolyat Jhanjhanit Anjan (*aka* Kakasaheb Outwitted: **Dadasaheb Phalke**, St, 1925)
Kakathampurati (**P. Bhaskaran**, Mal, 1970)
Kakka (P.N. Sundaram, Mal, 1982)
Kakkaji Kahin (TV: **Basu Chatterjee**, H, 1988)
Kakkatholayiram (V.R. Golakrishnan, Mal, 1991)
Kakki Chattai (Rajasekhar, Tam, 1985)
Kakkum Karangal (A.C. Trilogchander, Tam, 1965)
Kakothikavile Appuppan Thadigal (Kamal, Mal, 1988)
Kaksha (V.C. Guhanathan, Tel, 1980)
Kala Admi (Ved-Madan, H, 1960)
Kala Admi (Ramesh Lakhanpal, H, 1978)
Kal Aaj Aur Kal (Randhir Kapoor, H, 1971)
Kalabaaz (Ashok Roy, H, 1977)
Kalabaaz Ashaq (*aka* Wooing Tactics: V.K. Pattani, St, 1926)
Kala Bazaar *see* International Crook
Kala Bazaar (**Vijay Anand**, H, 1960)
Kala Bazaar (Rakesh Roshan, H, 1989)
Kalabhimani (B. Srinivas, K, 1989)
Kala Bhoot (A.M. Khan, H, 1937)
Kalachakra (D. Rajendra Babu, K, 1991)
Kalachakram (K. Narayanan, Mal, 1973)
Kala Chashma (K. Vinod, H, 1962)
Kala Chor (*aka* The Black Thief: **Manilal Joshi**, St, 1925)
Kala Chor (Ravi Kapoor, H, 1956)
Kala Coat (Mehmood Khan, H, 1993)
Kala Dhandha *see* Blackmail
Kala Dhandha Goray Log (Sanjay Khan, H, 1986)
Kaladi Osai (M. Madhu, Tam, 1984)
Kala Ghoda (A. Shamsheer, H, 1963)
Kalagi Tura (S. Chavan, Mar, 1955)
Kala Gulab (*aka* Black Rose: **J.B.H. Wadia**, H, 1934)
Kalai Arasi (A. Kasilingam, Tam, 1963)
Kalai Kovil (**C.V. Sridhar**, Tam, 1964)
Kalaingan (G.B. Vijay, Tam, 1993)
Kalaivanan (**P. Pullaiah**, Tam, 1959)
Kala Jadu (Mehmood, H, 1963)
Kala Jigar (*aka* Black Heart: A.M. Khan, H, 1939)
Kalakaar (Karim, H, 1942)
Kalakaar (**Anant Mane**, H, 1954)
Kalakaar (P. Sambasiva Rao, H, 1983)
Kalalu Kane Kallu (Balu, Tel, 1984)
Kalam (Hemachander, Tam, 1983)
Kalamadi Kalam (Gopu, Tam, 1976)
Kalamati (**Tapan Sinha**, B, 1958)
Kalam Bathil Sollum (Amirtham, Tam, 1980)
Kalamegham (**Ellis Duncan**, Tam, 1940)
Kalamellam Un Mediyil (Rajasekhar, Tam, 1986)
Kalam Kathu Ninilla (A.B. Raj, Mal, 1979)
Kalam Mari Katha Mari (?, Jai Jaya Combines, Mal, 1987)
Kalam Marindi (**K. Vishwanath**, Tel, 1972)
Kalam Maripochu *see* **Rojulu Marayi**
Kalam Marudhu (?, Tam, 1987)
Kalam Marunnu (R. Velappan, Mal, 1955)
Kalamorukkam (V.S. Indira, Mal, 1991)
Kalam Orunal Marum (N.A. Panneerselvam, Tam, 1981)
Kalam Vellum (M. Karnan, Tam, 1970)
Kala Naag (**Kanjibhai Rathod**, St, 1924)
Kala Naag (Adi Irani/B. Murzban, H, 1934)
Kalangalil Aval Vasantham (S.P. Muthuraman, Tam, 1976)
Kalanjukuttiya Thangam (**Puttanna Kanagal**, Mal, 1964)
Kalanka (Shanti Ghosh Dastidar, B, 1990)
Kalanka Bhanjan (Amar Choudhury, B, 1933)
Kalanka Shobha (**Datta Dharmadhikari**, Mar, 1961)
Kalankari Vilakkam (K. Shankar, Tam, 1965)
Kalankini *see* Gunehgaar
Kalankini (**Jyotish Bannerjee**, B, 1945)
Kalankini (**Dinen Gupta**, B, 1981)
Kalankini Kankabati (**Uttam Kumar**, B, 1981)
Kalankini Nayika (Shuven Sarkar, B, 1988)
Kalanki Raat (Chitratanu Unit, B, 1966)
Kalankita Nayak (Salil Dutta, B, 1970)
Kalank Shobha *see* Vikram Shashikala
Kalanthakulu (**K. Vishwanath**, Tel, 1978)
Kala Pahad (*aka* Masked Terror: **Nanubhai Desai**, St, 1927)
Kala Pahad (*aka* Masked Terror: Bapurao Apte, H, 1933)
Kala Pani (**Raj Khosla**, H, 1958)
Kala Pani (Shibu Mitra, H, 1980)
Kalapani No Kaidi *see* Return of Kala Naag
Kala Parvat (**M.S. Sathyu**, H, 1970)
Kala Patthar (**Yash Chopra**, H, 1979)
Kalapi (**Manhar Raskapur**, G, 1966)
Kala Ranjani (P. Shekhar, Tel, 1984)
Kalarathri (?, Mal, 1987)
Kalarathrilo Kanna Pilla (?, N.V. Chandrasekhar, Tel, 1992)
Kalaridhudu (K. Subba Rao, Tel, 1985)
Kala Samundar (R.P. Ashq, H, 1962)
Kalasapurada Hudugaru (Gurudas A.L. Acharya, K, 1982)
Kala Sawar (*aka* Black Rider: W. Garcher, H, 1935)
Kalasina Manushulu (**K. Kameshwara Rao**, Tel, 1968)
Kalasivunte Kaladu Sukham (**Tapi Chanakya**, Tel, 1959)
Kalasochina Kalam (Ranga Rao/Mangalapalli, Tel, 1973)
Kala Sona (Ravi Nagaich, H, 1975)
Kalasopana (Ashwin Sebastian, Mal, 1981)
Kala Suraj (Desh Gautam, H, 1985)
Kalathai Venravan (Mohan Gandhiram, Tam, 1989)
Kalathinde Shabdam (Asha Khan, Mal, 1987)
Kalathur Kannamma (**A. Bhimsingh**, Tam, 1960)
Kalavanta Vikne Aahe (Jayant Dharmadhikari, Mar, 1971)
Kalavanteen (**Anant Mane**, Mar, 1978)
Kalavari Kodulu (K. Hemambharadhara Rao, Tel, 1964)
Kalavari Kutumbam (G.V. Prabhakar, Tel, 1972)
Kalavari Samsaram (K.S. Rami Reddy, Tel, 1982)
Kalavathi (L.S. Ramachandran, Tam, 1951)
Kalavati (T.V. Singh Thakore, K, 1964)
Kalavidha (Sohanlal, K, 1949)
Kala Wagh (*aka* Black Tiger, Kalo Wagh: **Harshadrai Mehta**, St, 1931)
Kala Wagh (*aka* Black Tiger, Garib Ka Pyara: **Nagendra Majumdar**, H, 1934)
Ka Lawei Ha Ki Ktijong Ngi (**Dhritiman Chatterjee**, Khasi, 1983)
Kala Yamudu (N. Harishchandra Rao, Tel, 1983)
Kalayum Neeye Malayum Neeye (R. Sundarrajan, Tam, 1988)
Kale Badal (Anant Thakur, H, 1951)
Kaleidoscope, The *see* **Chaalchitra**
Kaleyum Kaminiyum (**P. Subramanyam**, Mal, 1963)
Kal Hamara Hai (S.K. Prabhakar, H, 1959)
Kal Hamara Hai (Girish Ranjan, H, 1989)
Kali (**I.V. Sasi**, Tam, 1980)
Kali Baiko (**Dinkar D. Patil**, Mar, 1970)
Kali Basti (Sudesh Issar, H, 1985)
Kalicha Narad (*aka* Ram Maruti Yuddha, aka Quarrel Game of Narad: Shinde, St, 1923)
Kalicharan (**Subhash Ghai**, H, 1976)
Kalicharan (Raja, Tam, 1988)
Kalidas (*aka* Life Story of Kalidas: **S.N. Patankar**, St, 1922)
Kalidas (**H.M. Reddy**, Tam, 1931)
Kali Ganga (Raj Sippy, H, 1989)
Kali Ghata (**Kishore Sahu**, H, 1951)
Kali Ghata (Ved Rahi, H, 1979)
Kalika (**Balachandra Menon**, Mal, 1980)
Kalikalam (A. Mohan Gandhi, Tel, 1991)
Kalikalam (Panju Arunachalam, Tam, 1992)
Kalikala Minor (**T.R. Sundaram**, Tam, 1944)
Kalika Murti *see* **Suvarna Kamal**
Kalika No Kop (*aka* Royal Savage: **Sundarrao Nadkarni**, St, 1930)
Kalika's Vengeance *see* Madan Kokila
Kalikecha Janma *see* Shatamukh Ravan Vadh
Kalimilemulu (G. Ramineedu, Tel, 1962)
Kali Mohini (**Muzaffar Ali**, H, 1986)
Kalina Ekka (*aka* Ace of Spades: **Nagendra Majumdar**, St, 1930)
Kali Nagin (?, Indian Pics., St, 1925)
Kalindi (**Naresh Mitra**, B, 1955)
Kalinga (V. Somasekhar, K, 1980)
Kalinga Mardanam (**R. Nataraja Mudaliar**, St, 1920)
Kalinga Sarpa (D. Rajendra Babu, K, 1984)
Kalippava (A.B. Raj, Mal, 1972)
Kali Raat (Shriram Bohra, H, 1977)
Kalisochina Adrushtam (**K. Vishwanath**, Tel, 1968)
Kalitharu Henne (N.C. Rajan, K, 1963)
Kalithozhen (M. Krishnan Nair, Mal, 1966)
Kalithozhi (D.M. Pottekkad, Mal, 1971)
Kali Topi Lal Rumal (Tara Harish, H, 1959)
Kali Waghan (*aka* Wild Tigress: R.N. Vaidya, St, 1933)
Kali Waghan (*aka* Wild Tigress: ?, Kumar Movietone, H, 1935)
Kaliya (Tinnu Anand, H, 1981)
Kaliyalla Kalyanam (A.B. Raj, Mal, 1968)
Kaliya Mardan (**Dadasaheb Phalke**, St, 1919)
Kaliya Mardan/Muraliwala (**Bhalji Pendharkar**, H/Mar, 1935)
Kaliyamardhanam (J. Williams, Mal, 1982)
Kaliyan (**Kidar Sharma**, H, 1944)
Kaliyankattu Nili (M. Krishnan Nair, Mal, 1979)
Kaliyil Alpan Karyam (Sathyan Andhikkad, Mal, 1984)
Kaliyodam (**P. Subramanyam**, Mal, 1965)
Kaliyuga (Rajachandra, K, 1984)
Kaliyuga Abhimanyudu (S.S.Ravichandra, Tel, 1990)
Kaliyuga Daivam (M. Rosi Raju, Tel, 1983)
Kaliyuga Kannan (**Krishnan-Panju**, Tam, 1974)
Kaliyuga Karnudu (**Ghantamneni Krishna**, Tel, 1988)
Kaliyuga Krishnudu (T. Krishna, Tel, 1986)
Kaliyugam (V.S. Dhrupad, Tam, 1952)
Kaliyugam (**K.S. Sethumadhavan**, Mal, 1973)
Kaliyugam (K. Subhash, Tam, 1988)
Kaliyugam (Relangi Mallick, Tel, 1992)
Kaliyuga Mahabharatam (Hanuman Prasad, Tel, 1979)
Kaliyuga Ramudu (**K. Bapaiah**, Tel, 1982)
Kaliyuga Ravana Surudu (**Bapu**, Tel, 1980)
Kaliyuga Seethe (?, Sree Durga Art, K, 1992)
Kaliyuga Stree (P. Sambhasiva Rao, Tel, 1978)
Kaliyugni Seeta (Sunil Prasad, G, 1989)
Kalka (Loksen Lalwani, H, 1983)
Kalkatta Ki Raat see Calcutta After Midnight
Kal Ki Awaaz (Ravi Chopra/**B.R. Chopra**, H, 1992)
Kal Ki Baat (*aka* A Tale of Yesterday: **R.S. Choudhury**, H, 1937)
Kal Ki Baat (**K.A. Abbas**, H, 1973)
Kalkut (*aka* Kismet Ki Bhool: D.K. Kale, H, 1935)
Kalkut (Batra Mohinder, B, 1981)
Kal Kya Hoga (Ramesh Dheeraj, H, 1958)
Kalla Kalla Bachitko/Chor Chor Chhupja (**B.V. Karanth**, K/H, 1975)
Kalla Kulla (K.S.R. Doss, K, 1975)
Kalla Malla (Saiprakash, K, 1991)
Kallan Kappalil Thanne (Prashanth, Mal, 1992)
Kallan Pavithran (**P. Padmarajan**, Mal, 1981)
Kallanum Polisum (**I.V. Sasi**, Mal, 1992)
Kallara Kala (M.P. Shankar, K, 1970)
Kalli Chelamma (**P. Bhaskaran**, Mal, 1969)
Kalli Koyil Vapali (R. Sundaram, Tam, 1979)
Kallimullu (Mohammed Ghazali, Mal, 1985)
Kallinte Katha (*aka* A Tale of Toddy: **V.K. Pavithran**, Mal, 1990)
Kallipennu (P.A. Thomas, Mal, 1966)
Kallol (**Atul Bordoloi**, A, 1978)
Kalloori Kanavugal (P.J. Mohan, Tam, 1985)
Kallu (M.V. Raghu, Tel, 1988)
Kallu Karthiyani (P.K. Joseph, Mal, 1979)
Kallukkul Eram (**Bharathirajaa**, Tam, 1980)
Kallum Kaniyakum (K. Shankar, Tam, 1968)
Kalluri Kanavugal (Anumohan, Tam, 1988)
Kallu Sakkare (**Kalyana Kumar**, K, 1967)
Kalluveene Nudiyitu (Tiptur Raghu, K, 1983)
Kalo Bhoot (*aka* Black Ghost: Shanti Dave, St, 1932)
Kalo Bou (Silpi Sangha, B, 1955)
Kalo Chhaya (**Premendra Mitra**, B, 1948)
Kalo Chokher Tara (Palash Bannerjee, B, 1980)
Kalo Ghora (**Jyotish Bannerjee**, B, 1948)
Kalo Sawar (*aka* Black Rider: **Harshadrai Mehta**, St, 1932)
Kalo Wagh *see* Kala Wagh
Kalpadukal (K.S. Anthony, Mal, 1962)
Kalpana (P. Sandeyal, B, 1939)
Kalpana (Uday Shankar, H, 1948)
Kalpana (Rakhan, H, 1960)
Kalpana (**K.S. Sethumadhavan**, Mal, 1970)
Kalpana (**K. Raghavendra Rao**, Tel, 1977)
Kalpana House (P. Chandrakumar, Mal, 1989)
Kal Parinaya (*aka* Fatal Marriage: **Priyanath Ganguly**, St, 1930)
Kal Parinaya (**Priyanath Ganguly**, B, 1936)
Kalpa Vruksha (K.R. Seetaramá Sastry, K, 1969)
Kalpa Vruksha (**Sasikumar**, Mal, 1978)
Kal Ratrinu Khuni Khanjar (*aka* Vile Woman: **Kanjibhai Rathod**, St, 1928)
Kalsap (Khagen Roy, B, 1951)
Kaltay Pan Valat Nahi (Dattaram Tawade, Mar, 1987)
Kalthoon (Major Sundarrajan, Tam, 1981)
Kal Tumi Aleya (Sachin Mukherjee, B, 1965)
Kal Udaas Na Hogi (*aka* No Sad Tomorrow: **S. Sukhdev**, E/H, 1965)
Kal Vadiyum Pookal (V. Karthikeyan, Tam, 1983)
Kalvanin Kadhali (V.S. Raghavan, Tam, 1955)
Kalyana Agathigal (**K. Balachander**, Tam, 1985)New ALL-IN-1 mail for LAURENCE MCAREE from NORMA LEIGHTON
Kalyana Chakravarthi (M.S. Kotireddy, Tel, 1980)
Kalyana Jyothi (R. Ganesh, Tel, 1980)
Kalyana Kacheri (Manivannan, Tam, 1987)
Kalyana Kalam (Robert-Rajasekhar, Tam, 1982)
Kalyana Kanavugal (K. Sivarajan, Tam, 1984)
Kalyanamam Kalyanam (K. Krishnamurthy, Tam, 1974)
Kalyanamanavare Sowkyama (Janakiram, Tam, 1983)
Kalyana Mandapam (?, Dhanalakshmi Theatres, Tam, 1965)
Kalyana Mandapam (V. Madhusudhana Rao, Tel, 1971)
Kalyana Mantapa (?, K, 1991)

Sivaji Ganesan and S.S. Rajendran in *Alayamani* (1962)

Kalyanam Oru Kalkattu (S. Jayachander, Tam, 1985)
Kalyanam Panni Paar *see* Pelli Chesi Choodu
Kalyanam Panniyum Brahmachari (**P. Neelakantan**, Tam, 1954)
Kalyanam Saidhukko (R. Chandar, Tam, 1955)
Kalyana Pandhal (P. Balakrishnan, Mal, 1975)
Kalyana Paravaigal (?, Tam, 1988)
Kalyana Parisu (**C.V. Sridhar**, Tam, 1959)
Kalyana Penn *see* Pelli Sandadi
Kalyanaphoto (J.D. Thottan, Mal, 1965)
Kalyanaraman (G.N. Rangarajan, Tam, 1979)
Kalyana Rasi (?, Shankaralaya Pics, Tam, 1990)
Kalyana Rathriyil (M. Krishnan Nair, Mal, 1966)
Kalyana Rekha (M.S. Rajasekhar, K, 1993)
Kalyana Saugandhikam (Vijayan, Mal, 1974)
Kalyana Tambulam (**Bapu**, Tel, 1986)
Kalyana Tilakam (B. Bhaskara Rao, Tel, 1985)
Kalyana Urvalam (**K.S. Sethumadhavan**, Tam, 1970)
Kalyana Veena (Giridhar, Tel, 1983)
Kalyani (**Premankur Atorthy**, H, 1940)
Kalyani (Acharya M. Mastan, Tam, 1952)
Kalyani (**Niren Lahiri**, B, 1954)
Kalyani (Geethapriya, K, 1971)
Kalyani (**Dasari Narayana Rao**, Tel, 1979)
Kalyani (Samiran Dutta, B/O, 1983)
Kalyanikku Kalyanam (**A.S.A. Sami**, Tam, 1959)
Kalyanin Kanavan (S.M. Sreeramulu Naidu, Tam, 1963)
Kalyan Khajina (**Baburao Painter**, St, 1924)
Kalyan Khajina (Balasaheb Pathak, Mar, 1950)
Kalyug (Nazir, H, 1942)
Kalyug (**Shyam Benegal**, H, 1980)
Kalyug Aur Ramayan (**Babubhai Mistri**, H, 1987)
Kalyug Ki Sati *see* **Kala Naag**
Kamadhenu (**Nandlal Jaswantlal**, Tam, 1941)
Kamadhenu (**Sasikumar**, Mal, 1976)
Kamagni (Ashok Kumar, H, 1987)
Kamal (Surya Kumar, H, 1949)
Kamala *see* Kamla
Kamala (Chimanlal Trivedi, H, 1946)
Kamala (C.V. Rajendran, K, 1979)
Kamalabai (Reena Mohan, Mar, 1992)
Kamala CID *see* Shaitan Ka Pash
Kamala Ki Maut (**Basu Chatterjee**, H, 1989)
Kamala Kumari (*aka* Sabur Shah: **B.P. Mishra**, St, 1928)
Kamalamma Kamatam (**K. Pratyagatma**, Tel, 1979)
Kamalathalam (**Sibi Malayil**, Mal, 1992)
Kamale Kamini (*aka* Maid of the Lotus: **Sisir Bhaduri**, St, 1922)
Kamale Kamini (**Phani Burma**/Nirmal Goswami, B, 1940)
Kamale Shamsheer (Ramakant-Gharekhan, St, 1930)
Kamal Ke Phool (D.D. Kashyap, H, 1950)
Kamallata (**Kanjibhai Rathod**, St, 1925)
Kamallata (**Harisadhan Dasgupta**, B, 1969)
Kamam Krodham Moham (**Madhu**, Mal, 1975)
Kamana (Nabendusundar, B, 1949)
Kamana (K. Chatterjee, H, 1972)
Kamana Billu (Chi. Dattaraj, K, 1983)
Kamaner Aagun (*aka* Flames of Flesh: Dinesh Ranjan Das, St, 1930)
Kaman Pandigai (H.S. Venu, Tam, 1983)
Kama Purta Mama (**Dinkar D. Patil**, Mar, 1965)
Kamar-al-Zaman *see* Noor Mahal *or* Princess Budur
Kamar-al-Zaman (Shah G. Agha, St, 1931)
Kama Sasthiram (Balamurugan, Tam, 1979)
Kamatchiyin Karunai (K. Narayanaswamy, Tam, 1978)
Kamavalli (*aka* Nandini: Manikan, Tam, 1948)
Kambar (C.S.U. Shankar, Tam, 1938)
Kambojuraju Katha (**K. Kameshwara Rao**, Tel, 1967)
Kamini (Subair, Mal, 1973)
Kamla (*aka* Kamala: Jagmohan Mundhra, H, 1984)
Kamli (**S.P. Bakshi**, P, 1946)
Kampana (V. Rajan, K, 1982)
Kamra Number Nau *see* Room Number Nine
Kamroo Desh Ki Kamini (A.R. Kabuli, H, 1935)
Kamroo Deshni Kamini *see* Gaud Bangal
Kamsena Lilavati (?, Excelsior Film, St, 1928)
Kamsin (Usman Khan, H, 1992)
Kamumara Prayam (Gopalakrishnan, Mal, 1979)
Kanakachilanka (M. Krishnan Nair, Mal, 1966)
Kanakadurga Puja (**B. Vittalacharya**, Tel, 1960)
Kanakalata (Ghanshyam Mahapatra, O, 1974)
Kanakambara (Shridhar Kshirsagar, K, 1976)
Kanakambarangal (K. Raghavan, Mal, 1988)
Kanakangi (?, State Prod, Tam, 1949)
Kanaka Purandaradasa (**Girish Karnad**, E, 1988)
Kanakatara (**Fatma Begum**?, St, 1929)
Kanakatara (**H.V. Babu**, Tel, 1937)
Kanakatara (Rajanikanth, Tel, 1956)
Kanak Kanta (*aka* Navalakh Haar: A.P. Kapur, H, 1928)
Kanak Kesari (*aka* The Lionhearted: **Dhirubhai Desai**, St, 1931)
Kanalattam (C. Radhakrishnan, Mal, 1979)
Kanal Katru (Sathyan Andhikkad, Mal, 1991)
Kanalkkattakal (A.B. Raj, Mal, 1978)
Kanal Neer *see* Batasari
Kanamachi (Tas Unit/Bhaben Das, B, 1961)
Kanasu Nanasu (Amrutham, K, 1976)
Kanathaya Pennkutty (K.N. Sasidharan, Mal, 1985)
Kanavan (**P. Neelakantan**, Tam, 1968)
Kanavane Kan Kanda Daivam (**T.R. Raghunath**, Tam, 1955)
Kanavan Manaivi (**A. Bhimsingh**, Tam, 1976)
Kanavu (P.V. Krishnan, Tam, 1954)
Kanavugal Karpanaigal (A.L.S. Kannappan, Tam, 1982)
Kanavu Palithamma (S. Ramanathan, Tam, 1965)
Kancha-Mithey (Jyotirmoy Roy, B, 1957)
Kanchan (Manibhai Vyas, H, 1941)
Kanchan (Baij Sharma, H, 1955)
Kanchana (S.M. Sreeramulu Naidu, Tam/Mal, 1952)
Kanchana Ganga (V. Madhusudhana Rao, Tel, 1984)
Kanchana Seeta (**Dasari Narayana Rao**, Tel, 1988)
Kanchana Seeta (**G. Aravindan**, Mal, 1977)
Kanchan Ane Ganga (**Mehul Kumar**, G, 1978)
Kanchan Aur Ganga (**Mehul Kumar**, H, 1981)
Kanchanganga (Madhav Shinde, Mar, 1954)
Kanchanjungha (**Satyajit Ray**, B, 1962)
Kanchan Kanya (Sukhendu Chakraborty, B, 1963)
Kanchanmulya (Nirmal Mitra, B, 1961)
Kanchan Ranga (Amar Ganguly, B, 1964)
Kancher Swarga (Yatrik, B, 1962)
Kanchghar (Piyush Ray/Bijoy Choudhury, A, 1975)
Kanchika Cheerani Katha (**P. Subramanyam**, Tel, 1979)
Kanchi Thalaivan (A. Kasilingam, Tam, 1963)
Kanch Kata Hirey (**Ajoy Kar**, B, 1966)
Kanchu Kagada (A. Kodandarami Reddy, Tel, 1984)
Kanchu Kavacham (Rajashekhar Reddy, Tel, 1985)
Kanchukota/Pallava Sevangal (**C.S. Rao**, Tel/Tam, 1967)
Kanchukuravu (Vinayan, Mal, 1992)
Kandam Bacha Coat (**T.R. Sundaram**, Mal, 1961)
Kandan Karunai (**A.P. Nagarajan**, Tam, 1967)
Kandatham Kettatham (**Balachandra Menon**, Mal, 1988)
Kandavarundo (M. Mallikarjuna Rao, Mal, 1972)
Kandhar Alangaram (K. Sundaram, Tam, 1979)
Kandu Kandarinju (Sajan, Mal, 1985)
Kaneez (Krishna Kumar, H, 1949)
Kaneril Ezhuthanthe (Gangaikondan, Tam, 1981)
Kangal (**Krishnan-Panju**, Tam, 1953)
Kangal Qaidi (*aka* Doomed Soul: ?, Majestic Film, St, 1925)
Kangan (**Franz Osten**, H, 1939)
Kangan (**Nanabhai Bhatt**, H, 1959)
Kangan (K.B. Tilak, H, 1971)
Kangsa (Emkeji Unit, B, 1958)
Kanhaiya (Om Prakash, H, 1959)
Kanhaiya (Khalid Samy, H, 1981)
Kanhopatra (**Bhalji Pendharkar**, Mar, 1937)
Kanikalum Neram (Rajasenan, Mal, 1987)
Kanimuthu Papa (S.P. Muthuraman, Tam, 1972)
Kanjan (Kovai Ayyamuthu/T.R. Gopu, Tam, 1947)
Kankabatir Ghat (Chitta Bose, B, 1955)
Kankal (**Naresh Mitra**, B, 1950)
Kankana (V.R.K. Prasad, K, 1975)
Kankanam (S.K. Vasagan, Tam, 1947)
Kan Kanda Daivam (**K.S. Gopalakrishnan**, Tam, 1967)
Kankan De Ohle (Om Bedi, P, 1971)
Kan Kan Mein Bhagwan *see* Bhagwan Samaye Sansar Mein
Kan Kan Mein Bhagwan (**Babubhai Mistri**, H, 1963)
Kankantala Light Railway (**Premendra Mitra**, B, 1950)
Kankatchi (**A.P. Nagarajan**, Tam, 1971)
Kanku (**Kantilal Rathod**, G, 1969)
Kanku Ane Kanya (Jashwant Jhaveri, G, 1962)
Kankuni Kimat (Kartik Mehta, G, 1983)
Kanmalar (Pattu, Tam, 1970)
Kanmanikal (**Sasikumar**, Mal, 1966)
Kanmani Poonga (Visu, Tam, 1982)
Kanmani Raja (Devraj-Mohan, Tam, 1974)
Kanmaniye Pesu (Rakasekhar, Tam, 1986)
Kanna (Agragami, B, 1962)
Kannada Kayi (K. Seetaram, K, 1973)
Kannadi (M.A. Kaja, Tam, 1981)
Kannadi Maligal (N.N.C. Swamy/Mahesh, Tam, 1962)
Kannagi (**T.R. Raghunath**, Tam, 1942)
Kannaiah Chittaiah (Relangi Narasimha Rao, Tel, 1993)
Kannai Thorakanum Sami (R. Govindaraj, Tam, 1986)
Kanna Koduku (Krishnarao, Tel, 1961)
Kanna Koduku (V. Madhusudhana Rao, Tel, 1973)
Kannamma (M. Lakshmanan, Tam, 1972)
Kannamma En Kadhali (Kothamangalam Subbu, Tam, 1945)
Kanna Moochi (R. Pattabhiraman, Tam, 1978)
Kanna Nalama (**K. Balachander**, Tam, 1972)
Kannan En Kathalan (**P. Neelakantan**, Tam, 1968)
Kannan Oru Kayi Kuzhanthai (N. Venkatesh, Tam, 1978)

Kannan Varuvan (I.N. Murthy, Tam, 1970)
Kannappa Nayanar (?, Kalidas Films, Tam, 1938)
Kannappanunni (**Kunchako**, Mal, 1977)
Kannaram Pothi Pothi (Hasan, Mal, 1985)
Kanna Talli/Petrathai (**K.S. Prakash Rao**, Tel/Tam, 1953)
Kanna Talli (T. Madhavarao, Tel, 1972)
Kannatha Veshankal (M. Krishnan Nair, Mal, 1967)
Kannavari Illu (**K. Pratyagatma**, Tel, 1978)
Kannavari Kalalu (S.S. Balan, Tel, 1973)
Kanneer Pookal (Rajeshwar, Tam, 1981)
Kanneeru (B.M. Shankar, K, 1970)
Kanne Kaniamuthe (?, Shri Amaravati Cine Creations, Tam, 1979)
Kanne Kanni Amudhe (Sakthi-Kannan, Tam, 1986)
Kanne Manushulu (**Adurthi Subba Rao**, Tel, 1966)
Kanne Papa (P. Madhavan, Tam, 1969)
Kanne Radha (Ramanarayanan, Tam, 1982)
Kanneshwara Rama (**M.S. Sathyu**, K/H, 1977)
Kanne Vayasu (O.S.R. Anjaneyalu, Tel, 1973)
Kannika (S.M. Sreeramulu Naidu, Tam, 1947)
Kannil Theriyum Kathaigal (Devaraj-Mohan, Tam, 1980)
Kanni Mahamayi (M. Duraithangam, Tam, 1981)
Kannin Manigal (T. Janakiram, Tam, 1956)
Kanni Paruvathinile (B.V. Balaguru, Tam, 1979)
Kanni Penn (A. Kasilingam, Tam, 1969)
Kanni Pilla (?, Tam, 1966)
Kanniraindha Kanavan (**T. Prakash Rao**, Tam, 1959)
Kanni Rasi (R. Pandiarajan, Tam, 1985)
Kannithai (M.A. Thirumugham, Tam, 1965)
Kanni Theevu (Ramanna, Tam, 1981)
Kanniyin Kathali (**K. Ramnoth**, Tam, 1949)
Kanniyin Sabatham (**T.R. Raghunath**, Tam, 1958)
Kannodu Kann (**Ghantamneni Krishna**, Tam, 1982)
Kannu Muchale (M.R. Vittal, K, 1969)
Kannukal (Gopikumar, Mal, 1979)
Kannukku Mai Ezhuthu (**J. Mahendran**, Tam, 1986)
Kannulapanduga (Anisetty, Tel, 1969)
Kannum Karalum (**K.S. Sethumadhavan**, Mal, 1962)
Kannur Deluxe (A.B. Raj, Mal, 1969)
Kannu Terasida Hennu (Manimurughan, K, 1982)
Kanoon (**A.R. Kardar**, H, 1943)
Kanoon (**B.R. Chopra**, H, 1960)
Kanoon Apna Apna (B. Gopal, H, 1989)
Kanoon Aur Mujrim (Shyam Jethani/Jeevan Kumar, H, 1981)
Kanoonige Saval (C.S. Manju, K, 1984)
Kanoon Kanoon Hai (Arvind Kumar, H, 1987)
Kanoon Ka Shikar (Shankar Kinnagi, H, 1978)
Kanoon Ki Awaaz (R. Kumar, H, 1990)
Kanoon Ki Zanjeer (P. Lakshman, H, 1990)
Kanoon Kya Karega (**Mukul S. Anand**, H, 1984)
Kanoon Meri Mutthi Mein (K. Prasad, H, 1984)
Kan Simittun Nerum (Kalaivanan Ksan, Tam, 1988)
Kan Sivanthal Man Sivakkum (Sridhar Rajan, Tam, 1983)
Kans Vadh (G.V. Sane, St, 1920)
Kantakma Gulab *see* Padmalata
Kanta Taar (Bireshwar Mukherjee, B, 1964)
Kanthahaar *see* Khooni Kaun
Kanthahaar (*aka* Diamond Necklace: **Kaliprasad Ghosh**, St, 1930)
Kanthahaar (**Jyotish Bannerjee**, B, 1935)
Kanthavalayam (**I.V. Sasi**, Mal, 1980)
Kantheredu Nodu (T.V. Singh Thakore, K, 1961)
Kan Thiranathathu (K.V. Srinivasan, Tam, 1959)
Kanwarlal (S.S. Ravichandra, H, 1988)
Kanyadaan (Arun Mohanty, O, 1988)
Kanyadaan (**V.M. Vyas**, H, 1940)
Kanyadaan (**Ratibhai Punatar**, G, 1951)
Kanyadaan (Madhav Shinde, Mar, 1960)
Kanyadaan (**Mohan Segal**, H, 1968)
Kanyadaan (**Phani Majumdar**, Maithili, 1965)
Kanyadana/Kanyadanam (**B. Vittalacharya**, K/Tel, 1954)
Kanyadanam (**T. Hariharan**, Mal, 1976)
Kanya Dweep (Ramanna, H, 1982)
Kanyaka (**Sasikumar**, Mal, 1978)
Kanyakumari (**K.S. Sethumadhavan**, Mal, 1974)
Kanya Kumari (**Dasari Narayana Rao**, Tel, 1977)
Kanyakumariyil Oru Kavitha (Vinayan, Mal, 1993)
Kanya Ratna (J.D. Thottan, K, 1963)
Kanyashulkam (**P. Pullaiah**, Tel, 1955)
Kanya Viday (Subhash Shah, G, 1986)
Kanya Vikraya (*aka* Sharada: V.S. Nirantar, St, 1924)
Kanya Vikraya (*aka* Lobhi Pita, Lobhi Baap: Mohammed Hussain, H, 1934)
Kanya Vikraya Ni Kahani (*aka* Navi Sethani: **Homi Master**, St, 1924)
Kapalika (Mani, Mal, 1973)
Kapal Kundala (**Priyanath Ganguly**, St, 1929)
Kapal Kundala (**Premankur Atorthy**, B, 1933)
Kapal Kundala (**Phani Majumdar**, H, 1939)
Kapal Kundala (Ardhendu Mukherjee, B, 1952)
Kapal Kundala (Pinaki Mukherjee, B, 1981)
Kappalotiya Thamizhan (**B.R. Panthulu**, Tam, 1961)
Kappu Bilapu (**Puttanna Kanagal**, K, 1969)
Kappu Kola (K. Nagesh, K, 1980)
Kapurush (**Satyajit Ray**, B, 1965)
Karadi (T.K. Mohan, Tam, 1980)
Karagatta Karan (Gangai Amaran, Tam, 1989)
Karaikkal Ammaiyar (C.V. Raman, Tam, 1943)
Karaikkal Ammaiyar (**A.P. Nagarajan**, Tam, 1973)
Karaiyellam Shenbagappu (G.N. Rangarajan, Tam, 1981)
Karakanakadal (**K.S. Sethumadhavan**, Mal, 1971)
Karama Bai (U.K.G. Purohit 'Tendu', R, 1988)
Karamdata (Shashilal Nair, H, 1986)
Karam Kasauti (?, U.P. Chalachitra Nigam, H, 1989)
Karamyoddha (Dayal Nihalani, H, 1992)
Karan Ghelo (**S.N. Patankar**, St, 1924)
Karan Ghelo (Narayan Patel, G, 1948)
Karasthan (Keshav Talpade, Mar, 1947)
Karate (Deb Mukherjee, H, 1983)
Karate Girls (?, Mal, 1988)
Karate Kamala (K.S. Giri, Tam, 1978)
Karavali (Vishnukumar, K, 1976)
Karava Tasa Bharava (Raja Bargir, Mar, 1975)
Karayai Thodatha Alaigal (P. Madhavan, Tam, 1985)
Kar Bhala (**Master Bhagwan**, H, 1956)
Kare Shaheber Munshi (Bikash Roy, B, 1961)
Kari Diye Kinlam (Biresh Chatterjee, B, 1989)
Karigar (Vasant Joglekar, H, 1958)
Karimbana (**I.V. Sasi**, Mal, 1980)
Karimbin Poovinakkare (**I.V. Sasi**, Mal, 1985)
Karimbu (**Ramu Kariat**/K. Vijayan, Mal, 1979)
Karimedi Karivayan (Ramanarayanan, Tam, 1986)
Karimpoocha (?, Mal, 1981)
Karinaga (Basavaraj Kestur, K, 1981)
Karinagam (K.S. Gopalakrishnan, Mal, 1986)
Karinizhakal (J.D. Thottan, Mal, 1971)
Kari-o-Komal (Moni Ghosh/Amal Dutta, B, 1957)
Kari Puranda Jeevithangal (**Sasikumar**, Mal, 1980)
Karishma (**I.V. Sasi**, H, 1984)
Karishma-e-Kudrat *see* Daku Mansoor
Karishma Kali Ka (Ashok Punjabi, H, 1990)
Karishma Kudrat Ka (Sunil Hingorani, H, 1985)
Kariyam Nisaram (**Balachandra Menon**, Mal, 1983)
Kariyavar (**Chaturbhuj Doshi**, G, 1948)
Kariyavar (Kantilal Dave, G, 1977)
Kariyila Kattu Pole (**P. Padmarajan**, Mal, 1986)
Karkottai *see* Jaladurga
Karm (**B.R. Chopra**, H, 1977)
Karma/Nagan Ki Ragini (J.L. Freer Hunt, E/H, 1933)
Karma (**Subhash Ghai**, H, 1986)
Karmadevi (*aka* The Destiny: **Kanjibhai Rathod**, St, 1923)
Karmakhali (**Dhiren Ganguly**, B, 1940)
Karmano Kaher (*aka* Toll of Destiny: Pesi Karani, St, 1931)
Karmaphal (Kalipada Das, B, 1949)
Karmaveer (*aka* True Warrior: ?, Kohinoor U.A., St, 1931)
Karmaveer (*aka* Mard Bano: Vithaldas Panchotia, H, 1938)
Karmayili Kali (*aka* Tainted Virtue: **R.S. Choudhury**, St, 1927)
Karmayogi (Ram Maheshwari, H, 1978)
Karmika Kallanalla (K.S.R. Doss, K, 1982)
Karm Yudh (Swaroop Kumar, H, 1985)
Karna *see* **Karnan**
Karna (*aka* Deserted Son of Kunti: **S.N. Patankar**, St, 1922)
Karna (Bhargava, K, 1986)
Karnama (Ranjit, H, 1990)
Karnan/Karna/Daanveer Karna (**B.R. Panthulu**, Tam/Tel/H, 1964)
Karnaparvam (Babu Nathancode, Mal, 1977)
Karnarjun (**Jyotish Bannerjee**/Satish Dasgupta, B, 1941)
Karna the True Battler *see* Maharathi Karna
Karodpati (*aka* Millionaire: **Hemchandra Chunder**, H, 1936)
Karodpati (**Mohan Segal**, H, 1961)
Karo Kankuna (**Govind Saraiya**, G, 1980)
Karotti Kannan (R. Pattu, Tam, 1975)
Karpagam (**K.S. Gopalakrishnan**, Tam, 1963)
Karpagam Vandhachu (Billa Krishnamurthy, Tam, 1993)
Kar Papey (**Kaliprasad Ghosh**, B, 1952)
Karpura Arathi (V. Ramchandra Rao, Tel, 1969)
Karpura Deepam (A. Jagannathan, Tam, 1985)
Karpura Deepam (Rajachandra, Tel, 1986)
Karpurakarasi (**A.S.A. Sami**, Tam, 1957)
Karpuram (C.N. Shanmugham, Tam, 1967)
Karpura Mullai (**Fazil**, Tam, 1991)
Kartavya (**Mohan Segal**, H, 1979)
Kartavya (K.S.R. Doss, K, 1985)
Kartavyada Kare (Sunand, K, 1973)
Kartavyam (Joshi, Mal, 1982)
Kartavyam (Madhu Babu, Tel, 1983)
Kartavyam (A. Mohan Gandhi, Tel, 1990)
Karthavarayan Katha (Ramanna, Tel, 1958)
Karthika (M. Krishnan Nair, Mal, 1968)
Karthika Deepam (Laxmi Deepak, Tel, 1979)
Karthikai Deepam (A. Kasilingam, Tam, 1965)
Karthika Pournami (A. Kodandarami Reddy, Tel, 1987)
Kartiki (Datta Mane, Mar, 1974)
Kartiki Purnima Utsav (**Dadasaheb Phalke**, St, 1916)
Kartoot (?, Tabassum Art, H, 1988)
Karudiddina Kapuram (Mouli, Tel, 1986)
Karulina Kare (**Puttanna Kanagal**, K, 1970)
Karuna (Thankappan, Mal, 1966)
Karunai Ullam (**A. Bhimsingh**, Tam, 1978)
Karunai Vel (Vijai, Tam, 1980)
Karuna Kumari (**Harshadrai Mehta**, St, 1928)
Karunamayi (Ardhendu Chatterjee, B, 1978)
Karunamayi (Bhargava, K, 1987)
Karunamayudu (**A. Bhimsingh**, Tel, 1978)
Karune Illada Kannu (Ravi, K, 1983)
Karuneye Kutumbada Kannu (T.V. Singh Thakore, K, 1962)
Karuninchina Kanakdurga (**B. Vittalacharya**, K, 1992)
Karunkuyil Kunrathu Kolai *see* Maragatham
Karunthel Kanniyiram (R. Sundaram, Tam, 1972)
Karuppu Panam (G.R. Nathan, Tam, 1964)
Karuppu Sattaikaran (M. Karnan, Tam, 1985)
Karuppu Vellai (Manobala, Tam, 1993)
Karutha Kayi (M. Krishnan Nair, Mal, 1964)
Karutha Pournami (Narayanan Kutti Vallam, Mal, 1968)
Karutharathrigal (Mahesh/N. Shivankutty Nair, Mal, 1967)
Karwa Chouth (Ramlal Hans, H, 1980)
Karwan-e-Hayat (**Premankur Atorthy/Hemchandra Chunder**, U, 1935)
Karwan-e-Husn (*aka* Beauty Caravan: Choudhury M. Raji, H, 1935)
Karwat (Prakash, H, 1949)
Karz (**Subhash Ghai**, H, 1980)
Kasak (**K. Bapaiah**, H, 1992)
Kasa Kai Patil Bara Hai Ka? (Datta Mane, Mar, 1972)
Kasam (*aka* Oath: M.D. Baig, H, 1947)
Kasam (Ramesh Bedi, H, 1976)
Kasam (Umesh Mehra, H, 1988)
Kasam Dhandhe Ki (Gautam Bhatia, H, 1990)
Kasam Gangajal Ki (Dilip Bose, Bh, 1990)
Kasam Kali Ki (Qamar Narvi, H, 1991)
Kasam Khoon Ki (Ashok Roy, H, 1977)
Kasam Paida Karne Wale Ki (B. Subhash, H, 1984)
Kasam Suhaag Ki (**Mohan Segal**, H, 1989)
Kasam Teri Kasam (Raman Kumar, H, 1993)
Kasam Vardi Ki (Shibu Mitra, H, 1989)
Kasappum Inippum (C.R. Devaraj, Tam, 1983)
Kasarkode Kadarbai (Tulsidas, Mal, 1992)
Kasauti (*aka* Supreme Test: Haribhai Desai?, St, 1931)
Kasauti (**Ramchandra Thakur**, H, 1941)
Kasauti (Aravind Sen, H, 1974)
Kasavuthattam (**Kunchako**, Mal, 1967)
Kasba (**Kumar Shahani**, H, 1990)
Kasethan Kadavulada (Chitralaya Gopu, Tam, 1972)
Kashala Udyachi Baat (Datta Keshav, Mar, 1983)
Kashasathi Premasathi (Pitambar Kale, Mar, 1987)
Kashinath (Gunamoy Bannerjee, B, 1937)
Kashinath (**Nitin Bose**, B/H, 1943)
Kashino Dikro (Kanti Madia, G, 1979)
Kashish (*aka* The Attraction: Amin Choudhury, H, 1980)
Kashi Yatra (S.P. Muthuraman, Tam, 1973)
Kashi Yatra (V. Madhusudhana Rao, Tel, 1983)
Kashmakash (Feroz Chinoy, H, 1973)
Kashmeera (*aka* Dushman Ni Dikri, Enemy's Daughter: **Manilal Joshi**, St, 1926)
Kashmeera (**Nandlal Jaswantlal**, H, 1934)
Kashmeera (**Sukhdev Ahluwalia**, P/H, 1983)
Kashmir (Rajendra Jolly, H, 1951)
Kashmir Bullodu (**Krishnan-Panju**, Tel, 1975)
Kashmir Hamara Hai (*aka* Bapu Ne Kaha Tha: K.K. Varma, H, 1950)
Kashmiri Sundari (?, **Madan** Theatres, St, 1925)
Kashmir Kathali (Mathioli Shanmugham, Tam, 1983)
Kashmir Ki Kali (Jagannath Dhar, H, 1946)
Kashmir Ki Kali (**Shakti Samanta**, H, 1964)
Kashmir Nu Gulab (*aka* Rose of Kashmir: **Nagendra Majumdar**, St, 1931)
Kashti (*aka* Ferry: **Hemen Gupta**, H, 1954)
Kashti (*aka* Kishti: K. Devendra Rao, H, 1984)
Kashtipathar (Aravind Mukherjee, B, 1964)
Kasidre Kailasa (Janakiram, K, 1971)
Kasme Vade (Ramesh Behl, H, 1978)
Kasturi (Vrajendra Gaud, H, 1954)
Kasturi (Bimal Dutt, H, 1978)
Kasturi (?, O, 1987)
Kasturi Manjal (J.B. Rajaravi, Tam, 1992)
Kasturi Nivasa (Dorairaj-Bhagavan, K, 1971)
Kasturi Tilakam (Malliam Ragagopal, Tam, 1970)
Kasturi Vijaya (Srikanth, K, 1975)
Kasturi Vijayam (P. Madhavan, Tam, 1975)
Kasulaperu (**C. Pullaiah**, Tel, 1938)
Kasumbino Rang (G.K. Mehta, G, 1965)
Kasu Thanga Kasu (Mohammed Raj, Tam, 1992)
Ka Swariti *see* Pratidhwani
Kata Ajanare (**Ritwik Ghatak**, B, 1959: Incomplete)
Ka-Taba-Kanta (Bidhayak Bhattacharya, B, 1952)
Katakam (T.G. Raghavacharya, Tam, 1947)
Katakatala Rudraiah (**Dasari Narayana Rao**, Tel, 1978)
Kataryu Gap (Dinshaw P. Jhaveri, St, 1926)
Katha (**Sai Paranjpye**, H, 1982)
Kathai Kathayam Karanaman (Y.G. Mahendran, Tam, 1987)
Katha Ithuvare (Joshi, Mal, 1985)
Kathak (**S. Sukhdev**, E, 1970)
Katha Kao (**Sailajananda Mukherjee**, B, 1955)

Kathakku Pinnil (**K.G. George**, Mal, 1987)
Kathal *see* **Prema**
Kathal Ennum Nadhiyinile (M. Sukumaran, Tam, 1989)
Kathalikka Vanga (I.N. Murthy, Tam, 1972)
Kathal Jyothi (Thirumalai-Mahalingam, Tam, 1970)
Kathal Kathal Kathal (M.A. Kaja, Tam, 1980)
Kathal Kiligal (A.C. Trilogchander, Tam, 1980)
Kathal Oviyam (**Bharathirajaa**, Tam, 1982)
Kathal Oyvathillai (Manivannan, Tam, 1989)
Kathal Paduthum Padu (Joseph Taliath, Tam, 1966)
Kathal Paravai (A.V. Sheshgiri Rao, Tam, 1967)
Kathal Parisu (A. Jagannathan, Tam, 1987)
Kathal Vaghanam (M.A. Thirumugham, Tam, 1968)
Katha Madhopur Ki (**Prakash Jha**, H, 1989)
Katha Nayaka (Vasu, K, 1986)
Katha Nayakan (Muktha V. Srinivasan, Tam, 1988)
Kathanayaki (**K. Ramnoth**, Tam, 1955)
Katha Nayakudu (K. Hemambharadhara Rao, Tel, 1969)
Katha Nayakudu (K. Muralimohana Rao, Tel, 1984)
Katha Nayakudu Katha (**B.R. Panthulu**, Tel, 1965)
Katha Nayakuni Katha (**Yoganand**, Tel, 1975)
Katha Nayakuralu (G. Suryam, Tel, 1971)
Katha Nayika Molla (Padmanabham, Tel, 1970)
Katha Parayum Kayal (?, Mal, 1986)
Kathari Veera (Y.R. Swamy, K, 1966)
Katha Sagar (TV: **Shyam Benegal**, H, 1986)
Katha Sangama (**Puttanna Kanagal**, K, 1975)
Kathavai Thatteya Mohini Paye (M.A. Rajaraman, Tam, 1975)
Kathavarayan (T.R. Ramanna, Tam, 1958)
Kathayariyathe (Mohan, Mal, 1981)
Kathin Maya (**Sushil Majumdar**, B, 1961)
Kathirmandapam (K.P. Pillai, Mal, 1979)
Kathiruna Divasam (P.K. Joseph, Mal, 1983)
Kathiruna Nikkah (M. Krishnan Nair, Mal, 1965)
Kathirunda Kankal (**T. Prakash Rao**, Tam, 1962)
Kathodu Kathoram (**B.G. Bharathan**, Mal, 1985)
Kathoduthan Naan Pesuvan (M.A. Kaja, Tam, 1982)
Kathputli (**Amiya Chakravarty**/**Nitin Bose**, H, 1957)
Kathputli (Brij Sadanah, H, 1971)
Kathrina Nimisham (Baby, Mal, 1978)
Kathula Kondaiah (N.B. Chakraborty, Tel, 1985)
Kathula Poo (G.K., Tam, 1984)
Kathula Rathaiah (K.S.R. Doss, Tel, 1972)
Kati Patang (**Shakti Samanta**, H, 1970)
Kato Bhalobasha (**Dinen Gupta**, B, 1991)
Kato Door (Chitta Bose, B, 1945)
Katorabhar Khoon (*aka* The Stinger Stung: **S.N. Patankar**, St, 1920)
Katrinile Varum Geetham (S.P. Muthuraman, Tam, 1978)
Katrukku Enna Veli (K.N. Subbu, Tam, 1982)
Kattaboman (Manivasagam, Tam, 1993)
Kattalai (Liaqat Ali Khan, Tam, 1993)
Kattaruvi (**Sasikumar**, Mal, 1983)
Kattathe Kilikoodu (**B.G. Bharathan**, Mal, 1983)
Katthi (V.P. Muhammed, Mal, 1983)
Katthiruna Nikah (M. Krishnan Nair, Mal, 1965)
Kattiki Kankanam (K.S.R. Doss, Tel, 1971)
Kattile Pattu (**K.P. Kumaran**, Mal, 1982)
Kattilla Thottilla (Malliyam Rajagopal, Tam, 1973)
Katto Dushman (*aka* Dushman, The Enemy: Mohanlal Shah, St, 1931)
Kattukallan (P. Chandrakumar, Mal, 1981)
Kattukurangu (**P. Bhaskaran**, Mal, 1968)
Kattu Maina (M. Krishnan Nair, Mal/Tam, 1963)
Kattumallika/Kattu Malligai (**P. Subramanyam**, Mal/Tam, 1966)
Kattupookal (Thankappan, Mal, 1965)
Kattu Rani (?, Dhandhayuthapani Films, Tam, 1965)
Kattu Rani (A.T. Raghu, Mal, 1985)
Kattu Roja (**Adurthi Subba Rao**, Tam, 1963)
Katturumpinium Kathukudu (Girish, Mal, 1986)
Kattuthulasi (M. Krishnan Nair, Mal, 1965)
Kattu Vithachavan (Suvi, Mal, 1973)
Kauke Bolo Na (Vishwanath Mukherjee, B, 1983)
Kaul De Re Khanderaya (Krishna Patil, Mar, 1972)
Kaun Apna Kaun Paraya (Niranjan, H, 1963)
Kaun Dilan Diyan Jaane (S.P. Puri, P, 1985)
Kaun Hai Woh (Qamar Narvi, H, 1983)
Kaun Hamara (**Chaturbhuj Doshi**, H, 1947)
Kaun Ho Tum (Amrit Kapahi, H, 1970)
Kaun Jeeta Kaun Hara (Rakesh Kumar, H, 1987)
Kaun? Kaise? (Anil Ganguly, H, 1983)
Kaun Kare Qurbani (Arjun Hingorani, H, 1991)
Kaun Kisika (**Chimanlal Luhar**, H, 1939)
Kaun Kitne Paani Mein (Shibu Mitra, H, 1987)
Kaun Pardesi (J.V. Trivedi, H, 1947)
Kaun Sachcha Kaun Jhootha (Jankiram, H, 1972)
Kaurav Pandav (S. Dossani, H, 1970)
Kausalam (T.S. Mohan, Mal, 1993)
Kausalya (C.S.V. Iyer, Tam, 1935)
Kausalya Parinayam (**K. Subramanyam**/C.S.V. Iyer, Tam, 1937)
Kavacham (K. Madhu, Mal, 1992)
Kaval (K. Vijayan, Tam, 1985)
Kavalai Illatha Manithan (K. Shankar, Tam, 1960)
Kavalam Chundan (**Sasikumar**, Mal, 1967)
Kavalan Anan Kovalan (Visu, Tam, 1987)
Kaval Daivam (K. Vijayan, Tam, 1969)
Kavaleradu Kulavondu (T.V. Singh Thakore, K, 1965)
Kaval Geetham (S.P. Muthuraman, Tam, 1992)
Kaval Kadhigal (Ramanarayanan, Tam, 1984)
Kavalkaran (**P. Neelakantan**, Tam, 1967)
Kaval Madam (Chandrakumar, Mal, 1980)
Kaval Nilayam (Senthilnathan, Tam, 1991)
Kaval Poonaigal (Kalaipuli Shekharan, Tam, 1989)
Kavalukku Kannillai (Ashwin Kumar, Tam, 1992)
Kavalukku Kettikaran (Santhanabharati, Tam, 1990)
Kavariman (S.P. Muthuraman, Tam, 1979)
Kaveri (**Yoganand**, Tam, 1955)
Kaveri (H.N. Reddy, K, 1975)
Kaveri (Rajeevnath, Mal, 1986)
Kaveriyin Kanavan (**Yoganand**/A.K.Velan, Tam, 1959)
Kavi (**Debaki Bose**, B, 1949)
Kavi (**Debaki Bose**, H, 1954)
Kavi Chandrabati (Hiren Nag, B, 1952)
Kavi Honaji Bala *see* **Amar Bhoopali**
Kavi Joydev (Hiren Bose, B, 1941)
Kavi Kalidas (S.N. Tripathi, H, 1959)
Kavikuyil (Devaraj-Mohan, Tam, 1977)
Kavilamma (N. Shankaran Nair, Mal, 1977)
Kaviraja Kalamegham (G.R. Nathan, Tam, 1978)
Kavirathna Kalidas (?, Ganesh Pics, Tam, 1937)
Kavirathna Kalidas (Renuka Sharma, K, 1983)
Kavi Sammelan (**Kidar Sharma**, H, 1972)
Kavita (K.J. Parmar/Maheshchandra Chunawala, H, 1944)
Kavitha (**T.R. Raghunath**, Tam, 1962)
Kavitha (**Vijayanirmala**, Mal, 1973)
Kavitha (**Vijayanirmala**, Tel, 1975)
Kavithai Pada Neramillai (Yugisethu, Tam, 1987)
Kavithai Padum Alaigal (?, K.B. Arts, Tam, 1990)
Kaviyath Thalaivan (**K.S. Gopalakrishnan**, Tam, 1992)
Kaviyath Thalaivi (**K. Balachander**, Tam, 1970)
Kaviyin Kathal *see* Bilhana
Kavya Mela (M. Krishnan Nair, Mal, 1965)
Kaya Hiner Kahini (**Ajoy Kar**, B, 1973)
Kayalkarayil (N. Prakash, Mal, 1968)
Kayalum Kayarum (K.S. Gopalakrishnan, Mal, 1979)
Kayam (P.K. Joseph, Mal, 1982)
Kayamkulam Kochunni (P.A. Thomas, Mal, 1966)
Kayamkulam Kochunniyude Maghan (**Sasikumar**, Mal, 1976)
Kayam Thalayum Purathidaruthu (P. Shrikumar, Mal, 1985)
Kaya Palat (**Satyen Bose**, H, 1983)
Kayar (TV: **M.S. Sathyu**, H, 1991)
Kayda Kanoon (Pradeep Maini, H, 1993)
Kayi Kodukkum Kayi (**J. Mahendran**, Tam, 1984)
Kayi Niraya Kasu (A.B. Raj, Tam, 1974)
Kayi Pidithaval (**A. Bhimsingh**, Tam, 1978)
Kayyale Ammayi Kalavari Abbayi (Venkata Ganesh, Tel, 1982)
Kayyum Thalayum Purathidaruthu (Shrikumar, Mal, 1985)
Kazhachakkapuram (V.R. Gopalakrishnan, Mal, 1991)
Kazhaki (Prakash Arora, H, 1966)
Kazhak Ki Ladki (Sultan Mirza/S. Varman, H, 1937)
Kazhugu (S.P. Muthuraman, Tam, 1981)
Kazhugu Mallaikallan (Rajasekhar, Tam, 1988)
Kazhukan (A.B. Raj, Mal, 1979)
Kazhumaram (A.B. Raj, Mal, 1982)
KD No 1 (**K. Raghavendra Rao**, Tel, 1978)
KD No 1 (?, Ravi-Chitra Films, K, 1986)
Kecha Sone (**Phani Sarma**, A, 1959)
Kedar Gouri (**Nitai Palit**, O, 1954)
Kedar Raja (Bolai Sen, B, 1967)
Kee Banu Duniya Da (Jagjeet, P, 1986)
Keechaka Vadh (G.V. Sane, St, 1926)
Keechaka Vadha *see* Sairandhri
Keechaka Vadha (*aka* Sairandhri: **Baburao Painter**, St, 1928)
Keechaka Vadha (Yeshwant Pethkar, Mar/H, 1959)
Keechaka Vadham *see* Sairandhri
Keechaka Vadham (**R. Nataraja Mudaliar**, St, 1916)
Keechuralu (Geetakrishna, Tel, 1991)
Keelu Bommalu (**C.S. Rao**, Tel, 1965)
Keeluguram/Maya Kudhirai (Raja of Mirzapur, Tel/Tam, 1949)
Keemat (Nazir Ajmeri, H, 1946)
Keemat (Hira Singh, H, 1956)
Keemat (Ravi Nagaich, H, 1973)
Keemti Aansoo (**Chandulal Shah**, H, 1935)
Keemti Aansoo (*aka* Precious Tears: **Harshadrai Mehta**, St, 1927)
Keemti Qurbani (*aka* Divine Sacrifice: **Balkrishna Narayan Rao**, H, 1935)
Kehte Hain Mujhko Raja (Biswajeet, H, 1975)
Keibul Lamjao National Park (**Aribam Syam Sharma**, E, 1988)
Kela Ishara Jata Jata (**Anant Mane**, Mar, 1965)
Kelkatha Shabdam (**Balachandra Menon**, Mal, 1982)
Kelor Kirti (Sudhangshu Mustafi, St, 1928)
Kelviyum Nane Bathilum Nane (N. Murugesh Tam, 1982)
Kempu Gulabi (Vijay, K, 1990)
Kempu Hori (B.M. Madhavaiah, K, 1982)
Kempu Soorya (A.T. Raghu, K, 1990)
Kenaram Becharam (Aravind Mukherjee, B, 1985)
Keni (?, Mal, 1982)
Kerala Lesari (M.R. Vittal, Mal, 1951)
Keralida Hennu (A.V. Sheshgiri Rao, K, 1983)
Keralida Simha (Chi. Dattaraj, K, 1981)
Keranir Jiban (?, Shri Bharatlakshmi Pics, B, 1934)
Keranir Jiban (Dilip Mukherjee, B, 1953)
Keranir Mas Kabar (**Jyotish Bannerjee**, St, 1931)
Ke Sapne Ka Jikar (Sansarsingh Pavar, Haryanvi, 1984)
Kesarbhina (Dineshkumar Padia, G, 1978)
Kesar Chandan (Arvind Bhatt, G, 1986)
Kesarina Kamala (R.N. Jayagopal, K, 1973)
Kesar Kathiyani (Ramkumar Bohra, G, 1980)
Keshavkant BA (*aka* Chastity Versus Unchastity: **Harshadrai Mehta**, St, 1927)
Keshi Vadha *see* Bal Gopal
Kesudano Rang (Vibhakar Mehta, G, 1987)
Ketakichya Banaat (**Raja Nene**/**Anant Mane**, Mar, 1950)
Kettikkaran (Venu, Tam, 1971)
Ketti Malam (Visu, Tam, 1985)
Ketugadu (**Dasari Narayana Rao**, Tel, 1980)
Ketumi (Shyam Chakraborty, B, 1964)
Khaak Ka Putla (G.R. Sethi, H, 1934)
Khabardar *see* Bombshell
Khabardar (*aka* Terror: Dada Gunjal, St, 1931)
Khabardar (S.J. Talukdar, G, 1982)
Khada Na Khel (**Manilal Joshi**/**Nagendra Majumdar**, St, 1927)
Khadga Veera (T. Vishwanathan, Tel, 1970)
Khaidi (A. Kodandarami Reddy, Tel, 1983)
Khaidi (K.S.R. Doss, K, 1984)
Khaidi (A. Jagannathan, Tel, 1987)
Khaidi Baba (T. Krishna, Tel, 1973)
Khaidi Kalidas (**P. Subramanyam**, Tel, 1977)
Khaidi Kannayya (**B. Vittalacharya**, Tel, 1962)
Klaidi No. 407 (Y. Krishnamraju, K, 1993)
Khaidi No. 786 (Vijaya Bapineedu, Tel, 1988)
Khaidi No. 77 (V. Hanuman Prasad, Tel, 1978)
Khaidi Rani (K.S.R. Doss, Tel, 1986)
Khaidi Rudraiah (A. Kodandarami Reddy, Tel, 1986)
Khakaan (Aspi, H, 1965)
Khalifa (**Prakash Mehra**, H, 1976)
Khalnayak (**Subhash Ghai**, H, 1993)
Khalnayika (*aka* Khalnaaika: Sawan Kumar, H, 1993)
Khalsa Mera Roop He *see* Sachcha Mera Roop Hai
Khamma Mara Lal (Bhupen Desai, G, 1983)
Khamma Mara Veera (Shantilal Soni, G, 1976)
Khamosh (Vidhu Vinod Chopra, H, 1985)
Khamoshi (R.C. Talwar, H, 1952)
Khamoshi (**Asit Sen**, H, 1969)
Khamosh Nigahen (**Moti Gidwani**, H, 1946)
Khamosh Sipahi (Ram Kamlani/D.N. Madhok, H, 1950)
Khana (**Jyotish Bannerjee**, B, 1938)
Khana (Baidyanath Bannerjee, B, 1962)
Khana Baraha (Bijoy Basu, B, 1981)
Khan Bahadur (**Sohrab Modi**, H, 1937)
Khandaan (Shaukat Hussain Rizvi, H, 1942)
Khandaan (M.L. Anand, H, 1955)
Khandaan (**A. Bhimsingh**, H, 1965)
Khandaan (Anil Ganguly, H, 1979)
Khandaan (TV: Shridhar Kshirsagar, H, 1985)
Khandalyacha Ghat (**Dadasaheb Phalke**, St, 1925)
Khandana Khel *see* Rangila Nawab
Khandana Khel (*aka* Fight Unto Death: **Nagendra Majumdar**/Maneklal Joshi, St, 1930)
Khandani (*aka* Brahman Kanya: Dada Gunjal, H, 1947)
Khandani Khavis (*aka* The Noble Scamp: **Manilal Joshi**, St, 1925)
Khandavideko Mamsavideko (**P. Lankesh**, K, 1979)
Khandhar (**Mrinal Sen**, H, 1983)
Khandobachi Aan ((**Prabhakar Nayak**, Mar, 1968)
Khan Dost (Dulal Guha, H, 1976)
Khanjar (**Atma Ram**, H, 1979)
Khanjarwali (A.M. Khan, H, 1943)
Khapro Jhaveri (Dineshwar Vyas, G, 1977)
Khara Kadhi Bolu Naye (Ravi Namade, Mar, 1987)
Khara Kharino Khel (Ramkumar Bohra, G, 1983)
Khara Khota (**B.R. Ishara**, H, 1981)
Khara Varasdar (Bipin Warty, Mar, 1986)
Kharidar (Kartik Mehta, H, 1988)
Kharij (**Mrinal Sen**, B, 1982)
Khasdakhal (Romesh Chandra Datta, B, 1935)
Khatarnak (Bharat Rangachary, H, 1988)
Khatarnak Aurat (*aka* Dangerous Woman: ?, **Madan** Theatres, H, 1938)
Khatron Ke Khiladi (**T. Rama Rao**, H, 1988)
Khatta Meetha (**Basu Chatterjee**, H, 1977)
Khat Thang Lamjel (?, Asha Tongbra, Manipuri, 1979)
Khatyal Sasu Nathal Soon (N.S. Vaidya, Mar, 1987)
Khaufnak Aankhen (M. Nawaz, H, 1947)
Khaufnak Jungle (?, H, 1955)
Khaufnak Khiladi (*aka* Devil May Care: Sanat Kumar Vin, St, 1933)
Khaufnak Raat *see* Bala Ki Raat
Khayal Gatha (**Kumar Shahani**, H, 1988)

Khazana (*aka* The Treasure: S.N. Bhende, St, 1934)
Khazana (M. Sadiq, H, 1951)
Khazana (Harmesh Malhotra, H, 1984)
Khazanchi (Moti Gidwani, H, 1941)
Khazanchi (P.N. Arora, H, 1958)
Khazanchi Ka Beta (Nari Ghadiali, H, 1943)
Khedan De Din Char (Manohar Deepak/Jugal Kishore, P, 1962)
Khedda (**M. Bhavnani**, St, 1929)
Khed Pritan De (Joginder Samra, P, 1967)
Khel (S.M. Nawab, H, 1950)
Khel (Rakesh Roshan, H, 1992)
Khela Bhangar Khela (Ratan Chatterjee, B, 1957)
Khelaghar (Soumyen Mukherjee, B, 1951)
Khelaghar (**Ajoy Kar**, B, 1959)
Khelar Putul (**Tarun Majumdar**, B, 1981)
Khel Chalala Nashibacha (Shrikant Sutar, Mar, 1954)
Khel Khel Mein (Ravi Tandon, H, 1975)
Khel Khiladi Ka (Arjun Hingorani, H, 1977)
Khel Kismat Ka (S.K. Luthra, H, 1977)
Khel Muqaddar Ka (Veerinder, H, 1980)
Khemro Lodan *see* Prem Samadhi
Khemro Lodan (Bakul, G, 1976)
Kheya (Rupak, B, 1967)
Khichadi (V.K. Naik, Mar, 1985)
Khidki (P.L. Santoshi, H, 1948)
Khilaaf (Rajeev Nagpal, H, 1990)
Khiladi (A.H. Essa, H, 1945)
Khiladi (Hansraj Behl, H, 1950)
Khiladi (B.J. Patel, H, 1961)
Khiladi (**Homi Wadia**, H, 1968)
Khiladi (Abbas-Mastan, H, 1992)
Khilona (*aka* The Toy: **Sarvottam Badami**, H, 1942)
Khilona (Chander Vora, H, 1970)
Khilonewala (**S. Sukhdev**, H, 1971)
Khilte Suman *see* Sajre Phool
Khizan (**Muzaffar Ali**, H, 1991)
Khod Modali (**Dadasaheb Phalke**, St, 1925)
Khoj (**Balwant Bhatt**, H, 1953)
Khoj (Jugal Kishore, H, 1971)
Khoj (Pulak Gogoi, A, 1975)
Khoj (Keshu **Ramsay**, H, 1989)
Khokha Babu (Chittaranjan Goswami, St, 1923)
Khokha Babur Pratyabartan (**Agradoot**, B, 1960)
Kholano Khundnar (Harsukh Bhatt, G, 1976)
Khol De Meri Zabaan (**Dada Kondke**, H, 1989)
Khonjel (M. Nilamani Singh, Manipuri, 1981)
Khoon Aur Pani (Chand, H, 1981)
Khoon Aur Sazaa (Hariprasad Reddy, H, 1984)
Khoon Baha Ganga Mein (Praveen Bhatt, H, 1988)
Khoon Bhari Maang (Rakesh Roshan, H, 1988)
Khoon-e-Jigar (*aka* Within the Law: Ramakant-Gharekhan, St, 1931)
Khoon-e-Nahak *see* Bal Hatya
Khoon-e-Nahak (*aka* Hamlet: Dada Athavale?, Excelsior Film, St, 1928)
Khooni (K.L. Kahan, H, 1946)
Khooni (Manivannan, Tel, 1985)
Khooni Darinda (?, Dhirubhai Dakshini, H, 1987)
Khooni Jadugar (*aka* City of Silence, Shaher-e-Khamosha: **Roop K. Shorey**, H,
1939)
Khooni Katar *see* Jadui Jung
Khooni Katar (*aka* Golden Dagger: **A.R. Kardar**, St, 1931)
Khooni Kaun (*aka* Kanthahaar: G.R. Sethi, H, 1936)
Khooni Kaun (Chakraborty, H, 1974)
Khooni Khanjar (*aka* Fighting Blade: **V. Shantaram**/K. Dhaibar, St, 1930)
Khooni Khanjar (*aka* Devil's Dagger: K.B. Desai/R.N. Vaidya, H, 1935)
Khooni Khazana (*aka* Dara the Ape Man: A. Shamsheer, H, 1974)
Khooni Kon? (*aka* Not Guilty: Saqi, St, 1929)
Khooni Lash (?, Amrit Pics, H, 1943)
Khooni Mahal (Mohan Bhakri, H, 1987)
Khooni Murda (Mohan Bhakri, H, 1989)
Khooni Panja (Vinod Talwar, H, 1991)
Khooni Raat (J.D. Lawrence, H, 1991)

Khooni Saya (A. Zahur, H, 1970)
Khooni Taj (*aka* All for the Crown, Raktacha Rajmukut: Pandurang Talegiri,
St, 1930)
Khooni Teer (*aka* Fatal Arrow: A.P. Kapur, St, 1930)
Khoon Ka Badla (*aka* Avenging Blood: ?, Shri Ramesh Film, St, 1933)
Khoon Ka Badla Khoon (K. Parvez, H, 1978)
Khoon Ka Karz (**Mukul S. Anand**, H, 1991)
Khoon Ka Khoon (Sohrab Modi, U, 1935)
Khoon Ka Khoon (Kamran, H, 1966)
Khoon Ka Rishta (Samir Ganguly, H, 1981)
Khoon Ka Sindoor (Ambarish Sangal, H, 1993)
Khoon Kharaba (Deepak Bahry, H, 1980)
Khoon Khoon (Mohammed Hussain, H, 1973)
Khoon Ki Keemat (Shibu Mitra, H, 1974)
Khoon Ki Pukar (Ramesh Ahuja, H, 1978)
Khoon Ki Pyaasi (K. Chandra, H, 1990)
Khoon Ki Takkar (Harish Chawla, H, 1981)
Khoon Pasina (Rakesh Kumar, H, 1977)
Khordani Khandani (Honey Chhaya, G, 1980)
Khota Paisa (M. Sadiq, H, 1958)
Khote Sikkay (**Narendra Bedi**, H, 1974)
Khubsoorat (S.F. Hasnain, H, 1952)
Khubsoorat (**Hrishikesh Mukherjee**, H, 1980)
Khubsoorat Bala (*aka* Society Butterfly: **Kanjibhai Rathod**, St, 1926)
Khubsoorat Bala (*aka* Ramani Ki Rakshasi, Sherni Ki Garaj: D.N. Madhok/M.R.
Kapoor/B.D. Kamer, H, 1933)
Khubsoorat Dhokha (Ram Prakash, H, 1959)
Khubsoorat Duniya (Mohan Sinha, H, 1947)
Khubsoorat Khawasan (*aka* Sweetheart: **Nagendra Majumdar**, St, 1932)
Khubsoorat Taapoo *see* Sitamgarh
Khudadad (?, New Pioneer Pics, H, 1935)
Khuda Dost (G.R. Sethi, H, 1932)
Khuda Gawah (Mukul S. Anand, H, 1992)
Khuda Hafiz (**Kidar Sharma**, H, 1983)
Khudai Khidmadgar (*aka* Garib Ki Tope: Vithaldas Panchotia, H, 1937)
Khuda Ka Banda (**Chaturbhuj Doshi**, H, 1957)
Khuda Ka Insaaf *see* Kudrat Ka Faisla
Khuda Kasam (Lekh Tandon, H, 1981)
Khuda Ki Shaan (R.S. Choudhury, St, 1931)
Khuda Parasta (Shinde, St, 1930)
Khuddar (Ravi Tandon, H, 1982)
Khudgarz (Rakesh Roshan, H, 1987)
Khudha (Panchamrita, B, 1960)
Khufia Mahal (Aakkoo, H, 1964)
Khukhari (L. Bhattarai, H, 1976)
Khule Aam (Arun Dutt, H, 1992)
Khuli Khidki (P. Chandrakumar, H, 1989)
Khul Jaa Sim Sim (**Nanubhai Vakil**, H, 1956)
Khunje Berai (Salil Dutta, B, 1971)
Khushboo (Rana Indu Shamsher, H, 1954)
Khushboo (**S.S. Gulzar**, H, 1975)
Khush Naseeb (Vithaldas Panchotia, H, 1946)
Khush Naseeb (?, Our Films, H, 1964)
Khush Naseeb (Vijay Deep, H, 1982)
Khush Raho (Harbans, H, 1949)
Khwab (**Shakti Samanta**, H, 1980)
Khwab-e-Hasti (*aka* Magic Flute: **M. Bhavnani**, St, 1929)
Khwab-e-Hasti (*aka* Magic Flute: **Homi Master**, H, 1934)
Khwab Ki Duniya (*aka* Dreamland: **Vijay Bhatt**, H, 1937)
Khwaish *see* Meri Khwaish
Khwaja Ki Duniya (Akbar Balam, H, 1954)
Khyapa Thakur (Ananta Chattopadhyay, B, 1987)
Khyber (Kedar Kapoor, H, 1954)
Khyber Falcon (**Modhu Bose**, St, 1932)
Khyber Pass (Gul Hamid, H, 1936)
Kichhukshan (Aurobindo Mukherjee, B, 1959)
Kichu Smriti Kichu Anubhooti (**Manmohan Mahapatra**, O, 1988)
Kick, The *see* **Thokar**
Kicks of Kismet *see* Naseeb Ni Lili
Kidappadam (M.R.S. Mani, Mal, 1954)
Kidnap (Abir Basu, B, 1988)
Kidnapped Bride *see* Kunwari Kanya
Kidnapped Girl, The *see* Apahrita

Kie Kahara (**Nitai Palit**, O, 1968)
Kiklee (Bekal Amritsari, P, 1964)
Kiladaivam (**Krishnan-Panju**, Tam, 1956)
Kiladi Aliya (Vijay, K, 1985)
Kiladi Bullodu (Nandamuri Ramesh, Tel, 1972)
Kiladi Jodi (**S.V. Rajendra Singh**, K, 1978)
Kiladi Kanmani (Vasanth, Tam, 1990)
Kiladi Kittu (K.S.R. Doss, K, 1978)
Kiladi Krishnudu (**Vijayanirmala**, Tel, 1980)
Kiladi Ranga (**G.V. Iyer**, K, 1966)
Kiladi Singanna (I.N. Murthy, Tel, 1971)
Kilikonchal (V. Ashok Kumar, Mal, 1984)
Kilinjalgal (**Durai**, Tam, 1981)
Kilipetchu Ketkava (**Fazil**, Tam, 1993)
Kilippattu (A. Raghavan, Mal, 1985)
Killer (**Fazil**, Tel, 1992)
Killers, The (*aka* Hum Sub Qatil Hain: Maruti, H, 1969)
Kilukilukkam (**Balachandra Menon**, Mal, 1982)
Kilukkam (**Priyadarshan**, Mal, 1988)
Kilungatha Changalakal (C.N. Venkatasami, Mal, 1981)
Kimiagar (**Nagendra Majumdar**, H, 1936)
Kimti Qurbani *see* Keemti Qurbani
Kinara (Ambalal Dave, H, 1949)
Kinara (**S.S. Gulzar**, H, 1977)
Kinare Kinare (**Chetan Anand**, H, 1963)
Kindara Jogi (Ravichandran/Renuka Sharma, K, 1989)
Kindred of the Dust *see* Soneri Khanjar
King Bhartrahari (**S.N. Patankar**, St, 1922)
King Bhoj (**Y.V. Rao**, St, 1930)
King Coal (**Pradeep Krishen**, E, 1977)
Kingdom of Diamonds, The *see* **Hirak Rajar Deshe**
Kingdom of Love *see* Ishq No Anjam
King for a Day *see* Ek Din Ka Badshah
King Gopichand (Vishnupant Divekar, St, 1921)
King Harishchandra *see* **Raja Harishchandra**
Kinginikombu (Jayan Adiyat, Mal, 1983)
King Kong (Babubhai Mistri, H, 1962)
King of ayodhya *see* **Ayodhyecha Raja**
King of Carnival (T. Prasad, H, 1963)
King of Forest *see* Shah-e-Jungle
King of Hearts *see* Shah-e-Jigar
King of the Jungle *see* Vanraj
King, Queen and Slave/Knave *see* **Sahib Bibi Aur Ghulam**
King Shriyal (*aka* The Terrific Ordeal: **S.N. Patankar**, St, 1918)
King Shriyal (*aka* The Great Devotee: ?, Asian Film, St, 1929)
King's Justice *see* Rajdanda
King's Paramour *see* Dagakhor Dilbar
King's Visit to Bombay (Barker Motion Photography/Excelsior Cinematograph,
St, 1911)
King Uncle (Rakesh Roshan, H, 1993)
King Vallalah *see* Vallai Maharaja
Kinkini (A.N. Thampi, Mal, 1992)
Kinnaram (Satyan Andkikkad, Mal, 1983)
Kinu Goyalar Gali (O.C. Ganguly, B, 1964)
Kirai Alludu (M. Balaiah, Tel, 1984)
Kirai Dada (A. Kodandarami Reddy, Tel, 1987)
Kirai Kotigadu (A. Kodandarami Reddy, Tel, 1983)
Kirai Mogadu (Rajasekhar, Tel, 1986)
Kirai Rowdylu (A. Kodandarami Reddy, Tel, 1981)
Kiran (**Gajanan Jagirdar**, H, 1944)
Kirat Arjun (**Manilal Joshi**, St, 1923)
Kirat Arjun (?, Venus Pics, Tam, 1939)
Kirataka (V. Somashekhar, K, 1988)
Kirathakudu (A. Kodandarami Reddy, Tel, 1985)
Kiratham (K.S. Gopalakrishnan, Mal, 1985)
Kirayedaar (**Basu Chatterjee**, H, 1986)
Kireedam (**Sibi Malayil**, Mal, 1989)
Kirti (Dada Gunjal, H, 1942)
Kirti Garh (Soumyen Mukherjee, B, 1956)
Kirti Kantha Kankanam (U. Vishweshwara Rao, Tel, 1983)
Kisan Aur Bhagwan (**Chandrakant**, H, 1974)
Kisan Kanya (Moti Gidwani, H, 1937)
Kishen Kanhaiya (Rakesh Roshan, H, 1990)

Kishori (*aka* Choice of a Bride: Haribhai Desai, St, 1929)
Kishti *see* Kashti
Kisi Ek Phool Ka Naam Lo (TV: **Ketan Mehta**, H, 1985)
Kisi Ki Yaad (**Chaturbhuj Doshi**, H, 1950)
Kisise Na Kehna (Krishna Gopal/**Keshavrao Date**, H, 1942)
Kisise Na Kehna (**Hrishikesh Mukherjee**, H, 1983)
Kiske Sajan *see* Dynamite
Kiski Biwi (M.A. Mirza, H, 1942)
Kiski Jeet (Safdar Mirza, H, 1948)
Kiski Pyari (*aka* Whose Darling: Akhtar Nawaz, H, 1937)
Kis Liye (?, Imperial Films, H, 1938)
Kismat Palat Ke Dekh (*aka* Zara Palat Ke Dekh: C.S. Dubey, H, 1961)
Kismatwala (**Nanubhai Vakil**, H, 1944)
Kismatwala (S.D. Narang, H, 1986)
Kismatwali (Behram Mukadam, H, 1947)
Kisme Kitna Hai Dum (Mahendra Sandhu, H, 1992)
Kismet (Baburao Patel, H, 1932)
Kismet (Gyan Mukherjee, H, 1943)
Kismet (**Nanabhai Bhatt**, H, 1956)
Kismet (**Manmohan Desai**, H, 1968)
Kismet (Bhishm Kohli, H, 1980)
Kismet Ka Dhani (Ramanlal Desai, H, 1946)
Kismet Ka Khel (**Kishore Sahu**, H, 1956)
Kismet Ka Shikar (*aka* Victims of Fate: ?, **Madan Theatres**, St, 1924)
Kismet Ka Shikar (?, Pioneer Films, H, 1934)
Kismet Ka Sitara (**Nanubhai Vakil**, H, 1947)
Kismet Ki Bhool *see* Kalkut
Kismet Ki Kasauti (Pesi Karani, H, 1934)
Kissa Kursi Ka (Amrit Nahata, H, 1977)
Kiss Bai Kiss (Murlidhar Kapdi, Mar, 1988)
Kitaab (**S.S. Gulzar**, H, 1977)
Kite, The *see* Patang
Kite Fight (*aka* Woh Kata: Mohan Kaul, H, 1965)
Kiti Hasaal (Vasant Joglekar, Mar, 1942)
Kitna Badal Gaya Insaan (I.S. Johar, H, 1957)
Kitne Paas Kitne Door (D.S. Sultania, H, 1976)
Kittu Puttu (C.V. Rajendran, K, 1977)
Kittur Chanamma/Rani Chanamma (B.R. Panthulu, K/Tam, 1961)
Kitturina Huli (Saiprakash, K, 1991)
Kiye Jite Kiye Hare (**Nitai Palit**, O, 1981)
Kizhakkan Pathrose (T.G. Suresh Babu, Mal, 1992)
Kizhakke Pokum Rayil (**Bharathirajaa**, Tam, 1978)
Kizhakku Aprikavil Sheela (Dwarkeesh, Tam, 1987)
Kizhakku Karai (P. Vasu, Tam, 1991)
Kizhakkum Merkum Sandhikindrana (R. Pattabhiraman, Tam, 1979)
Kizhakkunarum Pakshi (Venu Nagavalli, Mal, 1991)
Kizhakku Seemayile (**Bharathirajaa**, Tam, 1993)
Kizhakku Vasal (B.V. Udayakumar, Tam, 1990)
Kizhakku Veethi (M.R. Bhoopathi, Tam, 1992)
Kizhakku Velutthachu (Dalapathi, Tam, 1992)
Kizhattu Mappillai (**T.R. Raghunath**, Tam, 1936)
Kizhvanam Sivakkam (Muktha V. Srinivasan, Tam, 1981)
Klanta Aparanha (Manmohan Mahapatra, O, 1985)
Knife, The *see* Qatil Katari
Knight Errant *see* Bharat Veer
Known Yet Not Known (**Basu Bhattacharya**, E, 1977)
Kobbari Bondam (Raviteja Katragada, Tel, 1991)
Kochaniyathi (**P. Subramanyam**, Mal, 1971)
Kochu Kochu Thettukal (Mohan, Mal, 1980)
Kochumon (K. Padmanabhan Nair, Mal, 1965)
Kochu Thampuratti (Alex, Mal, 1979)
Kochuthemmadi (**A. Vincent**, Mal, 1985)
Kodai Idi Kumaran (G. Suryam, Tam, 1968)
Kodai Malai (Muktha Sundar, Tam, 1986)
Kodalu Diddina Kapuram (**Yoganand**, Tel, 1970)
Kodalu Kavali (Giridhar, Tel, 1983)
Kodalu Pilla (M. Mallikarjuna Rao, Tel, 1972)

Kodalu Vastunaru Jagratha (K. Subba Rao, Tel, 1980)
Kodama Simham (K. Muralimohana Rao, Tel, 1990)
Kodandhari Ram (*aka* Seeta Swayamvar: ?, United Pics Syndicate, St, 1929)
Kodarikam (K. Ramachandra Rao/K. Vembu, Tel, 1953)
Kodathi (Joshi, Mal, 1984)
Kodeduddulu Ekaramnela (Jampana, Tel, 1960)
Kode Naagu (**K.S. Prakash Rao**, Tel, 1974)
Kode Shah (**S.P. Bakshi**, P, 1953)
Kodetharachu (A. Kodandarami Reddy, Tel, 1984)
Kodhaiyin Kadal (?, Shakti Films, Tam, 1941)
Kodimalar (**C.V. Sridhar**, Tam, 1966)
Kodiparakkuthu (**Bharathirajaa**, Tam, 1988)
Kodiyettam (**Adoor Gopalakrishnan**, Mal, 1977)
Kodugal Illatha Kolam (L. Balu, Tam, 1983)
Koduku Diddina Kapuram (**Ghantamneni Krishna**, Tel, 1989)
Koduku Kodalu (**P. Pullaiah**, Tel, 1972)
Kodumudikal (.**Sasikumar**, Mal, 1981)
Kodungalluramma (**Kunchako**, Mal, 1968)
Kodungattu (Joshi, Mal, 1983)
Koduthu Vaithaval (**P. Neelakantan**, Tam, 1963)
Koel (**Roop K. Shorey**, P, 1943)
Kohinoor (S.U. Sunny, H, 1960)
Kohraa (Biren Nag, H, 1964)
Kohraa (Kuku Kohli, H, 1991)
Kohraa (Partho Ghosh, H, 1993)
Koi Hai (Lalit Ahluwalia, H, 1985)
Koi Jeeta Koi Haara (Samir Ganguly, H, 1976)
Koil *see* Koyil
Koilamma Koosindi (Y.R. Babu, Tel, 1977)
Koil Manai Osai (Gangai Amaran, Tam, 1988)
Koi Na Jaane Re (Prasun Bannerjee, H, 1986)
Koino Ladakvayo (**Ravindra Dave**, G, 1980)
Koinu Mindhal Koina Hathe (Mulraj Rajda, G, 1979)
Koka Deuta Nati Aru Hati (**Nip Barua**, A, 1983)
Kokhono Megh (**Agradoot**, B, 1968)
Kokila (**Sarvottam Badami**, H, 1937)
Kokila (**Balu Mahendra**, K, 1977)
Kokila (Geetakrishna, Tel, 1989)
Kokilam (P.N. Sundaram, Mal, 1981)
Kokilamma (**K. Balachander**, Tel, 1983)
Kokilavani (S.A. Natarajan, K/Tam, 1956)
Kokkarako (Gangai Amaran, Tam, 1983)
Kolahal (**Bhabendranath Saikia**, A, 1988)
Kola Komban (**Sasikumar**, Mal, 1983)
Kolangal (**K.G. George**, Mal, 1980)
Kollaikaran Magal (A.V. Sehshgiri Rao, Tam, 1968)
Kolleti Kapuram (K.B. Tilak, Tel, 1976)
Kollol *see* **Kallol**
Kollura Shri Mookambika (Renuka Sharma, K, 1993)
Kollur Kala (saiprakash, K, 1991)
Kolusu (K.S. Madhangan, Tam, 1985)
Komal Gandhar (**Ritwik Ghatak**, B, 1961)
Komalner Ni Kusum (*aka* Rose of Komalner: **Dhirubhai Desai**, St, 1930)
Komaram (J.C. George, Mal, 1982)
Komberi Mookan (A. Jagannathan, Tam, 1984)
Komilla (?, St, 1929)
Konarak: The Sun Temple (**Harisadhan Dasgupta**, E, 1949)
Konarak: The Sun Temple (**Manmohan Mahapatra**, E, 1983)
Konaseema Kurrodu (Raviraja Pinisetty, Tel, 1986)
Kondagali (**Ramu Kariat**, Tel, 1978)
Kondapalli Raja (Raviraja Pinisetty, Tel, 1993)
Kondaveeti Donga (A. Kodandarami Reddy, Tel, 1989)
Kondaveeti Nagulu (Rajasekharan, Tel, 1984)
Kondaveeti Raja (**K. Raghavendra Rao**, Tel, 1986)
Kondaveeti Rowdy (Satya Reddy, Tel, 1990)
Kondaveeti Simham (**K. Raghavendra Rao**, Tel, 1981)
Kondi Kshetrayya (?, Tel, 1985)
Kondi Mogutte Penkipellam (K. Subba Rao, Tel, 1980)
Kondura/Anugraham (**Shyam Benegal**, H/Tel, 1977)
Kongu Chatu Krishnudu (K.S. Rama Rao, Tel, 1992)
Kongumudi (Vijaya Bapineedu, Tel, 1985)
Konjum Kili (T.P. Gajendran, Tam, 1993)
Konjum Kumari (G. Vishwanathan, Tam, 1963)
Konjum Salangai (**M.V. Raman**, Tam, 1962)
Kon Kunacha (Yeshwant Pethkar, Mar, 1953)
Konku Nattu Thangam (M.A. Thirumugham, Tam, 1961)
Kono-Ek-Din (Ashim Bannerjee, B, 1960)
Kono Vak? (**Kanjibhai Rathod**, St, 1929)
Konte Kapuram (Relangi Narasimha Rao, Tel, 1986)
Konte Kodalu (Kommineni, Tel, 1983)
Kontemogudu Penki Pellam (Relangi Narasimha Rao, Tel, 1980)
Kony (Saroj De, B, 1984)
Koodanayum Kattu (?, Prakkat Films, Mal, 1986)
Koodapirappu (J.D. Thottan, Mal, 1956)
Koodevide? (**P. Padmarajan**, Mal, 1983)
Koodi Balona (M.R. Vittal, K, 1975)
Koodi Yedamma Ayithe (T.L.V. Prasad, Tel, 1979)
Koodum Thedi (Paul Babu, Mal, 1985)
Koodu Thedunna Parava (P.K. Joseph, Mal, 1984)
Koogu (K.V. Raju, K, 1985)
Koothuru Kapuram (Shobhandirao, Tel, 1959)
Koothuru Kodalu (Laxmi Deepak, Tel, 1971)
Koottinilangili (Sajan, Mal, 1984)
Koottu Puzhakkal (R.C. Sakthi, Tam, 1987)
Kootukar (**Sasikumar**, Mal, 1966)
Kootu Kudumbam (**K.S. Sethumadhavan**, Mal, 1969)
Kora Aanchal (Somesh Joshi/V. Bhatre, H, 1973)
Kora Badan (B.S. Ghad, H, 1974)
Korada Rani (K.S. Rami Reddy, Tel, 1972)
Kora Kagaz (Anil Ganguly, H, 1974)
Koran Aur Imaan *see* Deen Aur Imaan
Korikile Gurralaite (**Dasari Narayana Rao**, Tel, 1979)
Koritharicha Naal (**Sasikumar**, Mal, 1982)
Koro Kosii (**Aribam Syam Sharma**, Manipuri, 1988)
Koroti (Ajoy Bannerjee, B, 1988)
Kortachi Pairi (**Dinkar D. Patil**, Mar, 1970)
Korukunna Mogadu (K. Subba Rao, Tel, 1982)
Koshish (Rafiq Rizvi, H, 1943)
Koshish (**S.S. Gulzar**, H, 1972)
Kotala Rayudu (Vasu, Tel, 1979)
Kotalo Paga (**B. Vittalacharya**, Tel, 1975)
Koteshwaran (**Sundarrao Nadkarni**, Tam, 1955)
Koteshwaran Magal (A.K. Reddy, Tam, 1981)
Koteshwarudu (Kommineni, Tel, 1983)
Kote Udugore (Baraguru Ramchandrappa, K, 1989)
Kotha Alludu (P. Sambhasiva Rao, Tel, 1979)
Kotha Dampathulu (K. Vasu, Tel, 1984)
Kotha Jeevithulu (**Bharathirajaa**, Tel, 1980)
Kotha Kapuram (P. Chandrasekhara Reddy, Tel, 1975)
Kotha Kodalu (K. Hemambharadhara Rao, Tel, 1979)
Kotha Neeru (**K.S. Prakash Rao**, Tel, 1982)
Kothapeda Rowdy (P. Sambhasiva Rao, Tel, 1980)
Kotha Pelli Koothuru (K.S. Rami Reddy, Tel, 1985)
Kotigadu (N. Ramchandra Rao, Tel, 1986)
Kotikokkadu (Kommineni, Tel, 1983)
Kottaivasal (Selva Vinayakam, Tam, 1992)
Kottaram Vilakkanundu (K. Suku, Mal, 1975)
Kottayam Kola Case (**K.S. Sethumadhavan**, Mal, 1967)
Kottum Kuravayum (?, Surabhi Films, Mal, 1987)
Kotwal Saab (**Hrishikesh Mukherjee**, H, 1977)
Kovai Thambiyin Uyire Unakkaga (K. Rangaraj, Tam, 1986)
Kovalan (**R.S. Prakash**, St, 1928)
Kovalan (*aka* Fatal Anklet: **R.S. Prakash/A. Narayanan**, St, 1929)
Kovalan (**Raja Sandow**, Tam, 1933)
Kovalan (?, Royal Talkie Distributors, Tam, 1934)
Kowmara Swapnangal (K.S. Gopalakrishnan, Mal, 1991)
Koyil Kalai (Gangai Amaran, Tam, 1992)
Koyil Pura (K. Vijayan, Tam, 1981)
Koyil Yanai (Kandasami Singaram, Tam, 1986)
Koyna Nagar (**John Abraham**, E, 1967)
Kozhi Kuvutthu (Gangai Amaran, Tam, 1982)
Krama (Asar Abid, K, 1991)
Kranthiyogi Basavanna (Ravi, K, 1983)
Kranti (M. Bhimeshwara Rao, Tel, 1981)
Kranti (**Manoj Kumar**, H, 1981)
Kranti Ki Tarangein *see* Waves of Revolution
Krantiveera (R. Ramamurthy, K, 1972)
Krantiveera Sangolli Rayanna (Ananth Hiregowda, K, 1967)
Krantiveer Vasudev Balwant (**Vishram Bedekar**, Mar, 1950)
Kripa Santoshi Maani (Thakur C.K. `Mast', G, 1977)
Krishan (Ardhendu Mukherjee, B, 1950)
Krishan Avatar (Ashok Gaikwad, H, 1993)
Krishna (TV: **Ramanand Sagar**, H, 1989)
Krishna Arjuna (**A. Narayanan/R.S. Prakash**?, Tam, 1935)
Krishna Arjuna Yuddha (?, Star Films, St., 1923)
Krishnabarna Tirandaz (B.S. Rajhans, St, 1930)
Krishna Bhakta Bodana (**J.B.H. Wadia**, H, 1944)
Krishna Bhakti (R.S. Mani, Tam, 1948)
Krishnagaradi (Vijaya Bapineedu, Tel, 1985)
Krishnagari Abbayi (V. Madhusudhana Rao, Tel, 1989)
Krishna Guruvaroorappa (Suresh, Mal, 1984)
Krishna Janma *see* Nand Kishore
Krishna Jarasandha *see* Jarasandha
Krishna Kanhaiya (**Sundarrao Nadkarni**, H, 1952)
Krishna Kanhaiya (Hridayesh Pandeya, Bh, 1984)
Krishnakanter Will (**Priyanath Ganguly**, St, 1926)
Krishnakanter Will (**Jyotish Bannerjee**, B, 1932)
Krishnakanter Will (Khagen Roy, B, 1952)
Krishna Kausalya (*aka* Imitator: ?, Mahavir Photoplays, St, 1929)
Krishna Kaveri (Bidhayak Bhattacharya, B, 1949)
Krishna Krishna (**Chandrakant**, H, 1986)
Krishna Kuchela (**Ch. Narayanamurthy**, Tel, 1961)
Krishna Kuchela (**Kunchako**, Mal, 1961)
Krishna Kumar *see* Pradyumna
Krishna Kumar (*aka* Sacho Haqdaar: **Harshadrai Mehta**, St, 1925)
Krishnakumar (S.D.S. Yogi, Tam, 1941)
Krishna Kumari (*aka* Daughter of Shripur: ?, Kohinoor Film, St, 1924)
Krishna Kumari (*aka* Flower of Rajasthan: Maneklal Joshi, St, 1930)
Krishna Leela (?, Angel Film, Tam, 1934)
Krishna Leela (*aka* Radha Krishna Prem: **Debaki Bose**, H, 1946)
Krishna Leela (Raviraja Pinisetty, Tel, 1987)
Krishna Leelalu (Jampana, Tel, 1959)
Krishnaleele (C.V. Raju, K, 1947)
Krishna Maya *see* Madari Mohan
Krishna Maya (**Kanjibhai Rathod**, St, 1921)
Krishna Murari (?, Sudarshan Talkie Phone, Tam, 1934)
Krishna Naradi (K.P. Bhave, St, 1927)
Krishna Naradi (**R.S. Prakash**, Tam, 1936)
Krishna Nee Begane Baaro (Bhargava, K, 1986)
Krishnankutty (T.V. Chandran, Mal, 1980)
Krishnan Thoothu (C.V. Raman, Tam, 1940)
Krishnan Vandhan (K. Vijayan, Tam, 1987)
Krishna Paramatma (**Vijayanirmala**, Tel, 1986)
Krishna Parunthu (Ramadas, Mal, 1979)
Krishnapidaran (C.V. Raman, Tam, 1941)
Krishna Prema (**H.V. Babu**, Tel, 1943)
Krishna Prema (**Adurthi Subba Rao**, Tel, 1961)
Krishnarajunulu (**Dasari Narayana Rao**, Tel, 1982)
Krishnarjun Yuddha (**Vishram Bedekar**/Chintamanrao Kolhatkar/V.N. Bhatt,
Mar/H, 1934)
Krishna Rukmini (H.R. Bhargava, K, 1988)
Krishna Sakha (**Ahindra Choudhury**, St, 1926)
Krishna Sambhav (*aka* Eighth Incarnation: **N.D. Sarpotdar**, St, 1927)
Krishna Satyabhama (*aka* Samantak Mani: **S.N. Patankar**, St, 1923)
Krishna Shishtai (*aka* Bharat Ka Bhavishya: Mama Mane, H, 1935)
Krishna Sudama (**Jayant Desai**, H, 1933)
Krishna Sudama (**Phani Burma**, B, 1936)
Krishna Sudama (**K. Subramanyam**, K, 1943)
Krishna Sudama (**Nitai Palit**, O, 1976)
Krishna Sudama (R. Bajaj, H, 1947)
Krishna Sudama (Raman B. Desai, G, 1947)
Krishna Sudama (Shanti Kumar, H, 1957)
Krishna Sudama (Ardhendu Chatterjee, B, 1979)
Krishna Sudama (Kedarnath Agarwal, H, 1979)
Krishnattam (**Adoor Gopalakrishnan**, E, 1982)
Krishna Tula (Vishnupant Divekar, St, 1922)
Krishna Tulabharam (**A. Narayanan**, Tam, 1937)
Krishna Under Charge of Theft *see* Simantak Mani
Krishnavatar (Maneklal Patel/K. Pritamlal, H, 1932)
Krishnavatar (S. Dossani, H, 1964)
Krishnavataram (**Bapu**, Tel, 1982)
Krishnaveni (V. Madhusudhana Rao, Tel, 1974)
Krishna Vijayam (**Sundarrao Nadkarni**, Tam, 1949)
Kritiman (Akhil Niyogi, B, 1936)
Krodh (Shashilal Nair, H, 1990)
Krodham (A. Jagannathan, Tam, 1982)
Krodhi (**Subhash Ghai**, H, 1981)
Krusinka (*aka* The Terror: ?, Kumar Film, St, 1930)
Kshama Yachana *see* Gustakhi Maaf
Kshamichu Ennoru Vakku (?, Jaybee Combines, Mal, 1986)
Kshan Aala Bhagyacha (**Datta Dharmadhikari**, Mar, 1962)
Kshanakathu (**Sibi Malayil**, Mal, 1990)
Kshana Kshanam (Ramgopal Varma, Tel, 1991)
Kshaniker Atithi (**Tapan Sinha**, B, 1959)
Kshatriya (**J.P. Dutta**, H, 1992)
Kshatriyan (Subhash, Tam, 1990)
Ksheera Sagara (**Singeetham Srinivasa Rao**, K, 1992)
Kshitij (Prem Kapoor, H, 1974)
Kshudista Pashan (**Tapan Sinha**, B, 1960)
Kuasha (**Premendra Mitra**, b, 1949)
Kuber (M.G. Rangnekar, Mar, 1947)
Kuberache Dhan (Balkrishna, Mar, 1953)
Kubera Kuchela (?, Jupiter Pics, Tam, 1943)
Kubera Theevu (G. Vishwanathan, Tam, 1963)
Kubi Mattu Iyala (Sadanand Suvarna, K, 1992)
Kuchela (K. Sadasiva Rao, Tel, 1935)
Kuch Naya (Ninu Majumdar, H, 1948)
Kudi Balidare Swargasukha (Siddalingaiah, K, 1981)
Kudiruntha Koil (K. Shankar, Tam, 1968)
Kudisai (Jayabharati, Tam, 1979)
Kudivazhanthal Kodi Nanmai (D.S. Rajagopal, Tam, 1959)
Kudrat (**Chetan Anand**, H, 1981)
Kudrat Ka Faisla (*aka* Khuda Ka Insaaf, Decision Divine: Sultan Alam, H,
1936)
Kudrat Ka Kanoon (S.A. Chandrasekharan, H, 1987)
Kudre Motte (**G.V. Iyer**, K, 1977)
Kudre Mukha (Y.R. Swamy, K, 1977)
Kudumba Enna Swargam (N. Shankaran Nair, Mal, 1984)
Kudumbam (?, Tel, 1954)
Kudumbam (M. Krishnan Nair, Mal, 1967)
Kudumbam (S.A. Chandrasekharan, Tam, 1984)
Kudumbam Namakku Sreekovil (**T. Hariharan**, Mal, 1978)
Kudumbam Oru Kadambam (Visu, Tam, 1981)
Kudumbam Oru Koyil (K. Vijayan, Tam, 1987)
Kudumba Puranam (Sathyan Andhikkad, Ma, 1988)
Kudumba Thalaivan (M.A. Thirumugham, Tam, 1962)
Kudumba Vilakku (F. Nagoor, Tam, 1956)
Kudumbini (P.A. Thomas, Mal, 1964)

Kue Yaar Mein (**Muzaffar Ali**, H, 1984)
Kuhak (**Agradoot**, B, 1960)
Kuhasa (Amarendra Sinha, H, 1980)
Kuheli (Abhimanyu, B, 1971)
Kuhelika (Ramesh Bose, B, 1950)
Kuhu-o-Keka (**Charu Roy**, B, 1936)
Kuhuri (**Manmohan Mahapatra**, O, 1986)
Kuk Doo Doo (Parvati Menon, H, 1985)
Kukkakatuku Cheppu Debba (Eranki Sharma, Tel, 1979)
Kulachandrama (K.H.D. Rao, O, 1978)
Kuladaivam (Kabir Das, Tel, 1960)
Kuladaivat (**Dinkar D. Patil**, Mar, 1955)
Kulagaurava/Kulagauravam (Pekati Shivram, K/Tel, 1971)
Kula Gauravam (Pekati Shivram, Tam, 1974)
Kulagothralu (**K. Pratyagatma**, Tel, 1962)
Kulakkozhudu (Ramanna, Tam, 1981)
Kulala Kurukshetram (Sarath, Tel, 1987)
Kulamagal Radhai (**A.P. Nagarajan**, Tam, 1963)
Kulama Kunama (**K.S. Gopalakrishnan**, Tam, 1971)
Kulambadigal (Crossbelt Mani, Mal, 1986)
Kulapathi (Nahas, Mal, 1993)
Kulaputra (T.R. Ramanna, K, 1981)
Kulaswamini Ambabai (**Anant Mane**, Mar, 1984)
Kulavadhu (*aka* Daughter-in-Law: **Sarvottam Badami**, H, 1937)
Kulavadhu (T.V. Singh Thakore, K, 1963)
Kulavadhu (**Krishnakant**, G, 1977)
Kulavilakku (**K.S. Gopalakrishnan**, Tam, 1969)
Kuldeep (N. Vaswani, H, 1946)
Kuldeepak (*aka* Born Hero: **Kanjibhai Rathod**, St, 1927)
Kuldeepak (A.M. Khan, H, 1937)
Kuldeepak (Ramanlal Desai, G, 1978)
Kulhara (Manu Sen, B, 1951)
Kulikkaran (Rajasekhar, Tam, 1987)
Kulin Kanta (**Homi Master**, St, 1925)
Kul Kalank (*aka* Jeevan Chhaya: **Nanubhai Vakil**, H, 1945)
Kul Kasumbo Ne Kanya (*aka* Adhura Armaan: Hiren Goswami, G, 1988)
Kulla Agent 000 (Ravi, K, 1972)
Kulla Kulli (Bhargava, K, 1980)
Kulli Yaar Di (Ved Mehra, P, 1970)
Kumaon Hills (**M. Bhavnani**, E, 1952)
Kumaraguru (?, Chitrakala Movietone, Tam, 1946)
Kumara Kulathunga (I. Raja Rao, Tam, 1939)
Kumara Raja (G.K. Ramu, Tam, 1961)
Kumara Raja (P. Sambhasiva Rao, Tel, 1978)
Kumara Sambhavam (**P. Subramanyam**, Mal, 1969)
Kumara Vijayam (A. Jagannathan, Tam, 1976)
Kumari (**R. Padmanabhan**, Tam, 1952)
Kumari Kottam (?, Kayceey Films, Tam, 1971)
Kumari Millche Shuddhikaran (**Dadasaheb Phalke**, St, 1928)
Kumari Mon (Chitra Rath, B, 1962)
Kumari Penn (Ramanna, Tam, 1966)
Kumari Pennin Ullathiley (Ra. Shankaran, Tam, 1980)
Kumbakkarai Thangaiah (Gangai Amaran, Tam, 1991)
Kumkum/Kumkum the Dancer (**Modhu Bose**, B/H, 1940)
Kumkumabhagya (Subba Rao, K, 1993)
Kumkumabharina (**Vedantam Raghavaiah**, Tel, 1968)
Kumkuma Chimizh (R. Sundarrajan, Tam, 1985)
Kumkuma Kodu (V. Azhagappan, Tam, 1988)
Kumkumam (**Krishnan-Panju**, Tam, 1963)
Kumkumam Kadhai Solgiradhu (K. Shankar, Tam, 1978)
Kumkuma Pottu (Ranjith Kumar, Tam, 1986)
Kumkuma Rakshe (S.K. Ananthachari, K, 1977)
Kumkumarekha (**Tapi Chanakya**, Tel, 1960)
Kumkuma Thanda Saubhagya (A.V. Sheshgiri Rao, K, 1985)
Kumkuma Tilakam (B. Bhaskara Rao, Tel, 1983)
Kumku Pagala (Manu Desai, G, 1972)
Kummatty (**G. Aravindan**, Mal, 1979)
Kumsin Hasina (S.A. Rajan, H, 1992)
Kumudam (**Adurthi Subba Rao**, Tam, 1961)
Kumud Kumari (**Nanubhai Vakil**/Vaidya, St, 1929)
Kundalakesi (Boman Irani, Tam, 1946)
Kundan (**Sohrab Modi**, H, 1955)
Kundan (Prayag Raaj, H, 1972)
Kundan (K.C. Bokadia, H, 1993)
Kundukkili (T.R. Ramanna, Tam, 1954)
Kunikitta Kozhi (Viji Thampi, Mal, 1992)
Kunjali Marakkar (S.S. Rajan, Mal, 1966)
Kunjatta Kiligal (**Sasikumar**, Mal, 1986)
Kunjikaikkal (?, Mal, 1972)
Kunj Kishori (?, Gujarat Film, St, 1928)
Kunj Vihari (**Homi Master**, St, 1925)
Kunku/Duniya Na Mane (**V. Shantaram**, Mar/H, 1937)
Kunku Mazha Bhagyacha! (**Dinkar D. Patil**, Mar, 1972)
Kunkvacha Dhani (**Datta Dharmadhikari**, Mar, 1951)
Kunkvacha Karanda (Datta Mane, Mar, 1971)
Kunkvacha Tila (**Dinkar D. Patil**, Mar, 1981)
Kunwara Baap (**Kishore Sahu**, H, 1942)
Kunwara Baap (Mehmood, H, 1974)
Kunwara Badan (Vimal Tewari, H, 1973)
Kunwara Jeeja (Subhash Bhakri, P, 1985)
Kunwara Mama (**Sukhdev Ahluwalia**, P, 1979)
Kunwara Pati (*aka* Bachelor Husband: C.M. Trivedi, H, 1950)
Kunwarbainu Mameru (**V.M. Vyas**, G, 1947)
Kunwarbainu Mameru (**Ravindra Dave**, G, 1974)
Kunwari *see* Diljani
Kunwari (S.N. Tripathi, H, 1966)
Kunwari Bahu (Kumar Vasudev, H, 1984)
Kunwari Kanya (*aka* Kidnapped Bride: V.K. Pattani, St, 1931)
Kunwari Patni *see* Meri Bhool
Kunwari Satino Kesariyo Kanth (Anant Brahmbhatt, G, 1979)
Kunwari Yaa Vidhwa (Pandit Sudarshan/Prafulla Roy, H, 1935)
Kuppathu Ponnu (Feroz Sharief, Tam, 1982)
Kuppathu Raja (Ramanna, Tam, 1979)
Kuppivala (S.S. Rajan, Mal, 1965)
Kura Cheshtalu (Rajachandra, Tel, 1984)
Kurathi Magan (**K.S. Gopalakrishnan**, Tam, 1972)
Kurinchi Malar (Chavi?, Tam, 1980)
Kurisuyuddham (Baby, Mal, 1984)
Kurmai (J.K. Nanda, P, 1941)
Kurmai (?, Dhere Shah Films, P, 1987)
Kurubara Lakka (**Hunsur Krishnamurthy**?, K, 1981)
Kurukkan Rajavayi (?, Rohini Films, Mal, 1987)
Kurukkante Kalyanam (Sathyan Andhikkad, Mal, 1982)
Kurukshetra (Balasaheb Yadav, Mar, 1933)
Kurukshetra (R. Sharma, H, 1945)
Kurukshetra (**Babubhai Mistri**, G, 1983)
Kurukshetra (Bhargava, K, 1987)
Kurukshetra (Shriram Panda, O, 1988)
Kurukshetram (**P. Bhaskaran**, Mal, 1970)
Kurukshetramlo Seeta (B.V. Prasad, Tel, 1983)
Kurukshetramu (**K. Kameshwara Rao**, Tel, 1977)
Kurumbukaran (Amirjan, Tam, 1991)
Kuruthikalam (A.K. Sahadevan, Mal, 1969)
Kuruvi Koodu (P. Madhavan, Tam, 1980)
Kurvandi Road (**Paul Zils**, E, 1949)
Kurvanji (A. Kasilingam, Tam, 1960)
Kusirthikuttan/Anni (M. Krishnan Nair, Mal/Tam, 1966)
Kusum Kumari (?, Little Film, St, 1928)
Kusum Kumari (?, **Madan Theatres**, St, 1929)
Kusum Lata (*aka* Lily of the Valley: **Dhirubhai Desai**, St, 1929)
Kutra (K.S.R. Doss, Tel, 1986)
Kutravali (Raja, Tam, 1989)
Kutravaligal (Ramanarayanan, Tam, 1985)
Kuttapathram (R. Chandru, Mal, 1991)
Kuttavali (**K.S. Sethumadhavan**, Mal, 1970)
Kuttavum Sitshayum (M. Mastan, Mal, 1976)
Kutte Ki Kahani (Harsukh Bhatt, H, 1964)
Kuttichathan (Mani, Mal, 1975)
Kuttikkuppayam (M. Krishnan Nair, Mal, 1964)
Kuttiyedathi (**P.N. Menon**, Mal, 1971)
Kutty (T.P. Kailasam, Tam, 1937)
Kutty Japanin Kuzhandaigal (Chalam Bennurkar, Tam, 1990)
Kutumba Bandham (M. Jayadev, Tel, 1985)
Kutumba Gauravam (**B.S. Ranga**, Tel/Tam, 1957)
Kutumba Gauravam (Rajachandra, Tel, 1984)
Kutumbam (Jampana, Tam, 1954)
Kuva Kuva Vathukal (Manivannan, Tam, 1984)
Kuyile Kuyile (Shrini, Tam, 1984)
Kuyiline Thedi (M. Mani, Mal, 1983)
Kuzhandaigal Kanda Kudiyarasu *see* Makkala Rajya
Kuzhandaikaka (P. Madhavan, Tam, 1968)
Kuzhandai Ullam (**K. Savitri**, Tam, 1969)
Kuzhandai Yesu (V. Rajan, Tam, 1983)
Kuzhandayai Thedi (R. Pattabhiraman, Tam, 1979)
Kuzhanthiyum Daivamum (**Krishnan-Panju**/Jawar Seetarama, Tam, 1965)
Kya Baat (?, Surya Film, St, 1932)
Kyabla (Amar Dutta, B, 1941)
Kya Yeh Bambai Hai (*aka* Yeh Bambai Hai: **Nanubhai Vakil**, H, 1959)
Kyon Ji (Nari Ghadiali, H, 1952)(B)

L

Laadla (Surya Kumar, H, 1954)
Laadla (**Krishnan-Panju**, H, 1966)
Laadli (**J.P. Advani**, H, 1949)
Laadli (Uttam Tulsi, P, 1978)
Laagi Nahin Chhute Ram (Kundan Kumar, Bh, 1963)
Laaj (Shehzade Ayaz/Munawar H. Kasim, H, 1946)
Laajo (Jugal Kishore, P, 1963)
Laajo (Veerendra, P, 1983)
Laaj Rakho Rani Sakhi (Kantilal Dave, R, 1973)
Laath Marin Tithe Pani (**Prabhakar Nayak**, Mar, 1981)
Laatsaab (Sunil Agnihotri, H, 1992)
Laat Saheb (K.P. Bhave, H, 1946)
Laat Saheb (Hari Valia, H, 1967)
Labbaik (Ahmed Kabir, H, 1980)
Labela (**Master Bhagwan**, H, 1966)
Lachak (M.I. Dharamsey, H, 1951)
Lachhi (Rajendra Sharma, P, 1949)
Lachhi (Satish Bhakri, P, 1977)
Lachit Barphukan (Sarbeshwar Chakraborty, A, 1960)
Ladaai (Deepak Shivdasani, H, 1989)
Ladaai Ke Baad (R.S. Junnarkar, H, 1943)
Ladaaku (Dinesh-Ramanesh, H, 1981)
Laddo Basanti (Jayant Prabhakar, Haryanvi, 1985)
Ladies' Hostel (**T. Hariharan**, Mal, 1973)
Ladies Only (**Sarvottam Badami**, H, 1939)
Ladies' Seat (Arun Choudhury, B, 1954)
Ladies Special (Jandhyala, Tel, 1991)
Ladies' Tailor (Khalid Akhtar, H, 1981)
Ladies' Tailor (**Vamsy**, Tel, 1986)
Ladka Ladki (Som Haksar, H, 1966)
Ladke Baap Se Badhke (Subhash Mukherjee, H, 1979)
Ladki *see* Penn
Ladki Bholi Bhali (Ashok Rai, H, 1976)
Ladki Jawan Ho Gayi (Anand Dasani, H, 1977)
Ladki Pasand Hai (C.L. Rawal, H, 1971)
Ladki Sahyadri Ki *see* Iye Marathyachi Nagari
Lado Rani (Niranjan, P, 1963)
Ladusingh Taxiwala (TV: **Atma Ram**, H, 1976)
Lady Cavalier, The *see* Ratna Lutari
Lady Doctor (Walli, H, 1944)
Lady Doctor (K. Sukumar, Mal, 1967)
Lady from Lanka *see* Ratnavali
Lady James Bond (P. Chandrasekhara Reddy, Tel, 1986)
Lady Killer (B.J. Patel, H, 1968)
Lady of the Lake *see* Sarovar Ki Sundari
Lady of the Lake (A.M. Khan, H, 1960)
Lady of the Landing (**Shaji Karun**, E, 1974)
Lady Robin Hood (R.N. Vaidya, H, 1946)
Lady Robin Hood (B.J. Patel, H, 1959)
Lady Teacher (**Dhiren Ganguly**, St, 1922)
Lady with the Whip, The *see* Hunterwali
Lafanga Langoor (**M. Bhavnani**, St, 1931)
Lafange (Harmesh Malhotra, H, 1975)
Lagaam (Desh Gautam, H, 1976)
Lagal Chunari Mein Daag (?, Bh, 1988)
Lagan *see* **Parichay**
Lagan (O.P. Dutta, H, 1955)
Lagan (Ramanna, H, 1971)
Lagan Na Umedvar (**Homi Master**, G, 1948)
Lagebandhe (Govind Kulkarni, Mar, 1979)
Lagna Adhi Ghataspot (Manohar Rele, Mar, 1958)
Lagna Bandhan (**Kaliprasad Ghosh**, H, 1936)
Lagna Bandhan (Shamim Bhagat, G, 1951)
Lagnala Jato Mi (Datta Kulkarni, Mar, 1960)
Lagna Mandap (**N.R. Acharya**, G, 1950)
Lagna Pahave Karun (**Master Vinayak**, Mar, 1940)
Lagna Patrike (K.S.L. Swamy, K, 1967)
Lahari (?, Mal, 1982)
Laher (?, Parvati Films, H, 1933)
Laherein *see* Lehren
Laheri Badmash (Nari Ghadiali, H, 1944)
Laheri Cameraman (Nari Ghadiali, H, 1944)
Laheri Jawan (*aka* Laughing Cavalier: Shanti J. Dave, H, 1935)
Laheri Jeevan (S.M. Yusuf, H, 1941)
Laheri Lala (**Jayant Desai**, H, 1936)
Laheri Lutaru (*aka* Gay Bandit: R.N. Vaidya, St, 1932)
Laheri Lutera (*aka* Gay Bandit: **Nagendra Majumdar**, H, 1937)
Lahini Sagar (Arun Bhatt, G, 1980)
Lahore (M.L. Anand, H, 1949)
Lahu Ke Do Rang (**Mahesh Bhatt**, H, 1979)
Lahu Ki Awaaz (Akash Jain, H, 1989)
Lahu Pukarega (S.N. Tripathi, H, 1968)
Lahu Pukarega (**Akhtar-ul-Iman**, H, 1980)
Lai Haraoba (**Aribam Syam Sharma**, E, 1992)
Laila (Naseem Siddiqui, H, 1954)
Laila (Sawan Kumar, H, 1984)
Laila (**T. Rama Rao**, Tel, 1989)
Laila Majnu (**J.J. Madan**, St, 1922)
Laila Majnu (**Manilal Joshi**, St, 1927)
Laila Majnu (**Kanjibhai Rathod**, H, 1931)
Laila Majnu (**J.J. Madan**, H, 1931)
Laila Majnu (?, East India Film, Persian, 1936)
Laila Majnu (Dharamveer Singh, P, 1940)
Laila Majnu (?, Sarhad Pics, Pushtu, 1941)
Laila Majnu (Nayyar/Nazir, H, 1945)
Laila Majnu (**P.S. Ramakrishna Rao**, Tel/Tam, 1949)
Laila Majnu (F. Nagoor, Tam, 1950)
Laila Majnu (**K. Amarnath**, H, 1953)
Laila Majnu (**P. Bhaskaran**, Mal, 1962)
Laila Majnu (**H.S. Rawail**, H, 1976)
Laila Majnu (Sachin Adhikari, B, 1976)
Laila Majnu Ki Nai Nautanki (**Muzaffar Ali**, H, 1982)
Laiye Tod Nibhaye (Satish Chhabra, P, 1966)
Lajawaab (**J.P. Advani**, H, 1950)
Lajjavathi (Premkumar, Mal, 1979)
Lajjo (Virinder, P, 1983)
Lajwanti (*aka* Radio Singer: **Premankur Atorthy**?, H, 1942)
Lajwanti (Narendra Suri, H, 1958)Lakeeren (Harbans, H, 1954)
Lake in Central Kerala, A *see* **Vembanad**
Lakhachi Goshta (**Raja Paranjpe**, Mar, 1952)
Lakha Loyan (Dinesh Rawal, G, 1975)
Lakhan (Dinesh-Ramanesh, H, 1979)
Lakhanshini Katar *see* Chundadino Rang
Lakhat Ashi Dekhani (Kamalakar Torne, Mar, 1971)
Lakheni Laaj (Shiraz Burmawala, G, 1977)
Lakhimi (Bhaben Das, A, 1957)
Lakhmi (Sharada Prasanna Nayak, O, 1962)
Lakhon Ki Baat (**Basu Chatterjee**, H, 1984)
Lakhon Mein Ek (Taimur Behramshah, H, 1947)
Lakhon Mein Ek (Hira Singh, H, 1955)
Lakhon Mein Ek (S.S. Balan, H, 1971)
Lakho Phulani (?, Royal Art/Lokmanya Film?, St, 1928)

Lakho Phulani (Narendra Dave, G, 1976)
Lakho Vanjaro (**Homi Master**, St, 1926)
Lakho Vanjaro (Anand Joshi, G, 1963)
Lakhpati (?, National Pics, H, 1941)
Lakhpati (Ravindra Jaykar, H, 1948)
Lakhrani (Vishram Bedekar, H, 1945)
Lakh Taka (**Niren Lahiri**, B, 1953)
Lakshadhikari (V. Madhusudhana Rao, Tel, 1963)
Laksha-Hira (Chittaranjan Mitra, B, 1956)
Lakshaprabhu (**P. Bhaskaran**, Mal, 1968)
Lakshmamma (**T. Gopichand**, Tel/Tam, 1950)
Lakshmana Rekha (N. Gopalakrishna, Tel, 1975)
Lakshmana Rekha (I.V. Sasi, Mal, 1984)
Lakshman Joshi (**Jabbar Patel**, Mar, 1989)
Lakshman Rekha (Sunil Sikand, H, 1991)
Lakshman Resha (Manohar Desai, Mar, 1970)
Lakshmi (Mohan Sinha, H, 1940)
Lakshmi (**Kadaru Nagabhushanam**, Tel/Tam, 1953)
Lakshmi (G.P. Pawar, H, 1957)
Lakshmi (**Sasikumar**, Mal, 1977)
Lakshmi (**Anant Mane**, Mar, 1978)
Lakshmi (T.K. Mohan, Tam, 1979)
Lakshmi (B.V. Prasad, Tel, 1981)
Lakshmi (B.S. Thapa, H, 1982)
Lakshmi Aala Ghara (Madhav Shinde, Mar, 1965)
Lakshmicha Galicha (**Dadasaheb Phalke**, St, 1916)
Lakshmiche Khel (**Vishram Bedekar**, Mar, 1938)
Lakshmichi Paoole (G.G. Bhosle, Mar, 1982)
Lakshmi Kalyanam (G.R. Nathan, Tam, 1968)
Lakshmi Kataksha (B. Subba Rao, K, 1985)
Lakshmi Kataksham (**B. Vittalacharya**, Tel, 1970)
Lakshmi Narayan (**Nanabhai Bhatt**, H, 1951)
Lakshmi Narayan (Nirmal Choudhury, B, 1961)
Lakshmi Nirdoshi (**C.V. Sridhar**, Tel, 1975)
Lakshmi Nivasa (K.S.R. Doss, K, 1977)
Lakshminivasam (V. Madhusudhana Rao, Tel, 1968)
Lakshmi Pooja (**Jayant Desai**, H, 1957)
Lakshmi Pooja (Kommineni, Tel/H, 1979)
Lakshmi Pooja (**B. Vittalacharya**, Tel, 1982)
Lakshmi Saraswathi (Ravi, K, 1970)
Lakshmi Vandhachu (Rajasekhar, Tam, 1986)
Lakshmi Vijayam (Boman Irani, Tam, 1947)
Lakshmi Vijayam (**K.P. Kumaran**/Devadas, Mal, 1976)
Lakshyam (Jipsen, Mal, 1972)
Lalach (**Master Bhagwan**, H, 1948)
Lalach (R.D. Rajput, H, 1960)
Lalach (**Shankar Nag**, H, 1983)
Lalaji (L. Mehta/C. Gandhi, H, 1942)
Lal Americayil (Sathyan Andhikkad, Mal, 1989)
Lalan Fakir (Shakti Chattopadhyay, B, 1987)
Lalan Vanjari (Maneklal Patel, St, 1925)
Lala Rukh (Akhtar Siraj, H, 1958)
Lalat (**Raja Nene**, H, 1947)
Lal Bangla (Jugal Kishore, H, 1966)
Lal Batti (*aka* Red Light: Nari Ghadiali, H, 1947)
Lal Batti (Balraj Sahni/Krishan Chopra, H, 1957)
Lal Buzakkad (*aka* Aundhi Khopdi: Kanti Patel, H, 1938)
Lal Chitta (*aka* Red Panther: **Dhirubhai Desai**, H, 1935)
Lal Chitthi (*aka* Red Letter: Niranjan Bhardwaj, H, 1935)
Lal Chooda (Subhash Bhakri, P, 1984)
Lal Chunaria (Sudarshan Lal, H, 1983)
Lal Dupatta (K.B. Lall, H, 1948)
Lal-e-Yaman (J.B.H. Wadia, H, 1933)
Lal-e-Yaman (**Nanubhai Vakil**, H, 1956)
Lal Golap (Jahar Biswas, B, 1984)
Lal Haveli (K.B. Lall, H, 1944)
Lalita (Kalyan Gupta, O, 1949)
Lalitha (Valampuri Somanathan, Tam, 1976)
Lalitha (Valampuri Somanathan, Tel, 1983)
Lalithangi (?, Royal Talkie Distributors, Tam, 1935)
Lalkaar (**Jayant Desai**, H, 1944)
Lalkaar (**Nanubhai Vakil**, H, 1956)
Lalkaar (*aka* Challenge: **Ramanand Sagar**, H, 1972)
Lal Kothi (Kanak Mukherjee, B/H, 1977)
Lal Kunwar (**Ravindra Dave**, H, 1952)
Lallooram (Shiv Kumar, H, 1984)
Lal Mahal (Sumit Guha, B, 1986)
Lal Nishan (Prakash, H, 1959)
Lal-o-Gauhar *see* Payame Ulfat
Lal Pan Bibi (**Prashanta Nanda**, O, 1988)
Lal Panja (K.B. Desai, H, 1936)
Lal Panjo (*aka* Fighting Blood: **Dhirubhai Desai**, St, 1931)
Lalpari (Kedar Kapoor, H, 1954)
Lalpari (Hanif Chhipa, H, 1991)
Lal Patthar (**Sushil Majumdar**, B, 1964)
Lal Patthar (**Sushil Majumdar**, H, 1971)
Lal Qila (**Nanabhai Bhatt**, H, 1960)
Lal Salaam (Narayanamurthy, Tel, 1992)
Lal Swar (*aka* Red Rider: **Jayant Desai**, St, 1932)
Lalten (Harish, H, 1956)
Lalu Bhulu (**Agradoot**, B, 1959)
Lalu Ustad (A. Shamsheer, H, 1956)
Lalwadi Phoolwadi (Radhakant, G, 1979)
Lambadolla Ramadasu (K. Babu Rao, Tel, 1978)
Lambardarni (Veerendra, P, 1980)
Lambe Haath (Krishna Mukllik, H, 1960)
Lamboo in Hong Kong (Harsukh Bhatt, H, 1966)
Lambu Dada (Sharad Choudhury, H, 1992)
Lament of Gandhari *see* Gandhariyin Pulambal
Lamhe (**Yash Chopra**, H, 1991)
Lamja Parashuram (**Aribam Syam Sharma**, Manipuri, 1974)
Lamp in the Niche (Part 1/2: **Girish Karnad**, E, 1989)
Lamp of Beauty *see* Chirag-e-Husn
Lamp of the Hut *see* Chirag-e-Kohistan
Lamp of the Tomb, The *see* **Marhi Da Deeva**
Lancha Lancha Lancha (Ravindranath, K, 1985)
Lanchavatharam (**Dasari Narayana Rao**, Tel, 1985)
Landing of Sir M.M. Bhownuggree (**H.S. Bhatavdekar**, St, 1901)
Landlord *see* **Jagirdar**
Land of Bengal (**Fali Bilimoria**, E, 1957)
Land of Lust, The *see* Lanka
Land of Martyrs *see* Kailash
Land of Pyramids *see* Hoor-e-Misar
Land of Sacrifice, The *see* Thyagabhoomi
Land of Sand Dunes, The (**Gautam Ghosh**, E, 1986)
Land of Sivagangai, The *see* **Sivagangai Seemai**
Langlen Thadoi (**M.A. Singh**, Manipuri, 1984)
Lanka (*aka* The Land of Lust: **Baburao Painter**, St, 1930)
Lanka Aflame *see* **Lanka Dahan**
Lanka Dahan (Dadasaheb Phalke, St, 1917)
Lanka Dahan (**Kanjibhai Rathod**, H, 1933)
Lanka Dahan (**Raja Nene**, H, 1952)
Lanka Dahana (*aka* Ram Doota: **R.S. Prakash**, St, 1930)
Lanka Dahanam (*aka* Maruthi Vijayam: **R.S. Prakash**, Tam, 1935)
Lanka Dahanam (K. Sadasiva Rao, Tel, 1936)
Lanka Dahanam (**Sasikumar**, Mal, 1971)
Lanka Lakshmi (**Homi Master**, St, 1929)
Lanka Ni Laadi (Homi Master, St, 1925)
Lankani Ladi Ghoghano Var (Girish Manukant, G, 1979)
Lanke Bindelu (**Vijayanirmala**, Tel, 1983)
Lankeshwarudu (**Dasari Narayana Rao**, Tel, 1989)
Lapandav (K. Narayan Kale, Mar, 1940)
Laparwah (*aka* The Undaunted: Haribhai Desai, St, 1933)
Laparwah (Ravi Nagaich, H, 1981)
Laralappa (?, Sams Prod, P, 1953)
Lashkar (Jagdish Kadar, H, 1989)
Last Jewel, The (**Paul Zils/Fali Bilimoria**, E, 1949)
Last Kiss (A.P. Gupta, St, 1931)
Last Message, The *see* Aakhri Paigam
Last Mistake *see* Aakhri Galti
Last Raja (**Fali Bilimoria**, E, 1972)
Last Tiger (Premsingh Verma, H, 1983)
Late Afternoon, The *see* **Aparahnam**
Lathi (**Hrishikesh Mukherjee**, H, 1988)
Lathi (Gunasekhar, Tel, 1992)
Lati Ghati (**Bhupen Hazarika**, A, 1966)
Lattu (Ajit Ganguly, B, 1978)
Laughing Cavalier *see* Daku Ke Dilbar *or* Laheri Jawan
Laurels of Loyalty *see* Vijay Danka
Lava (**T. Hariharan**, Mal, 1980)
Lava (Ravindra Peepat, H, 1985)
Lavakusa (**R. Nataraja Mudaliar**, St, 1919)
Lavakusa (**S. Soundararajan**, Tam, 1934)
Lavakusa (C. Pullaiah, Tel/Tam, 1934)
Lavakusa (**C. Pullaiah/C.S. Rao**, Tel/Tam, 1963)
Lavangi (**Y.V. Rao**, Tam, 1946)
Lavangi (*aka* Jagannath Pandit: **Y.V. Rao**, H, 1950)
Lavanya (G.R. Lakshmanan, Tam, 1951)
Lavanya Preeti (A.K. Bir, H, 1993)
Lava Phutiya (Shankar Mehta, P, 1967)
Lav Kush *see* **Ramrajya**
Lav Kush (**Nanabhai Bhatt**, H, 1951)
Lav Kush (Ashoke Chatterjee, B, 1966)
Lav Kush (S.N. Tripathi, H, 1967)
Lav Kush (**K.A. Abbas**, H, 1971)
Lav Kush (Narendra Mistry, G, 1978)
Lawaris (**Prakash Mehra**, H, 1981)
Law of Love *see* Prem Pash
Lawyara Magalu (**G.V. Iyer**, K, 1963)
Lawyer Bharti Devi (K. Rama Mohan Rao, Tel, 1987)
Lawyer Suhasini (**Vamsy**, Tam, 1987)
Lawyer Vishwanath (S.D. Lall, Tel, 1978)
Layam (Ben Marcus, Mal, 1982)
Layanam (Tulasidas, Mal, 1989)
Laylo Nihar (Remino J. Asher, H, 1936)
Leader (Ram Mukherjee, H, 1964)
Leader Vishwanath (Manimurughan, K, 1981)
Learning Versus Passion *see* Jaimini
Leatherface *see* Badmash Ka Beta
Leatherface (Vijay Bhatt, H, 1939)
Leela (Dattaram Pai, H, 1947)
Leela (**Govind Saraiya**, E, 1969)
Leela Kanka (Satish Dasgupta, B, 1958)
Leelavathi Sulochana (P.V. Rao, Tam, 1935)
Leeludi Dharti (Vallabh Choksi, G, 1968)
Leena Meena Reena (A. Shanmugham, Tam, 1983)
Lehren (*aka* Laherein: **H.S. Rawail**, H, 1953)
Leila the Star of Mingrelia (**R.S. Prakash**, St, 1931)
Lek Chalali Sasarala (H.N. Vaidya, Mar, 1984)
Lekh (G. Rakesh, H, 1949)
Lekha's Death a Flashback *see* **Lekhayude Maranam Oru Flashback**
Lekhayude Maranam Oru Flashback (K.G. George, Mal, 1983)
Lekhne Mathe Mekh (Shantilal Soni, G, 1982)
Lekh Par Mekh (*aka* Destiny Defied: **Homi Master**, St, 1928)
Lekin... (S.S. Gulzar, H, 1990)
Les Miserables *see* **Ezhai Padum Padu**
Lest We Forget (**M. Bhavnani**, E, 1951)
Letamanushulu (**Krishnan-Panju**, Tel, 1966)
Letter *see* Chitthi
Let There Be a Wee Bit of Romance *see* **Thodasa Rumani Ho Jaye**
Libaas (**S.S. Gulzar**, H, 1988)
Liberation of the Soul, The *see* **Mukti**
Liberation Ritual, The *see* **Ashwamedham**
Lichhmi Ayi Angane (Mohansingh Rathod, R, 1992)
Lieutenant (Nari Ghadiali, H, 1944)
Life *see* Vazhkai
Life After Death (?, Oriental Players, St, 1931)
Life And... (K.R. Mohanan, E, 1972)
Life and Message of Swami Vivekananda (**Bimal Roy**, E, 1964)
Life Divine *see* Punar Janma
Life is a Boat *see* **Jeevitha Nauka**
Life is a Comedy *see* Laheri Jeevan
Life is a Comedy: S.M. Yusuf, H, 1941)
Life is a Stage *see* **Jeevan Natak**
Life is for the Living *see* Manoos
Lifeline (TV: **Vijaya Mehta**, H, 1990)
Life of a Lady *see* Aurat Ki Zindagi
Life of India *see* Bharat Ka Jeevan
Life of Lord Buddha (?, **Madan Theatres**, St, 1923)
Life of the Enlightened One (?, **Madan Theatres**, St, 1926)
Life Story of Kalidas *see* Kalidas
Light House *see* Jaldeep
Light House (**G.P. Sippy**, H, 1958)
Light House (A.B. Raj, Mal, 1976)
Light of Asia, The *see* **Prem Sanyas**
Light of Love *see* Noor-e-Ishq
Light of the Deccan *see* Noor-e-Deccan
Light of the World *see* Noorjehan
Light of Wisdom, The *see* **Gnana Oli**
Lillipookkal (T.S. Mohan, Mal, 1979)
Lilo Chaman (Rajeev Bhushan, Haryanvi, 1984)
Lily (F. Nagoor, Mal, 1958)
Lily in the Mud *see* Padmalata
Lily of the Valley *see* Kusum Lata
Line Bus (**K.S. Sethumadhavan**, Mal, 1971)
Lioness *see* Shuri Sinha
Lionhearted, The *see* Kanak Kesari
Lion Jagapathy Rao (Saiprakash, K, 1991)
Lion Man *see* Sinh Garjana
Lion of Baghdad *see* Sher-e-Baghdad
Lion of Girnar, The *see* Girnar No Sinh
Lion of Harijans *see* Harijana Simham
Lion of Maharashtra *see* Nara Kesari
Lion of Mewar *see* Diwan Bhamasha
Lion of Punjab *see* Punjab Kesari
Lion of Sagar *see* Sagar Ka Sher
Lion's Claw *see* Sinh No Panja
Lion's Cub *see* Sinh Santaan
Little Affair, A *see* **Chhotisi Baat**
Little Tea Shop, The (TV: **Sai Paranjpye**, E, 1972)
Living Corpse, A *see* Zinda Lash
Living Soil, The (**Atma Ram**, E, 1960)
Liza (Baby, Mal, 1978)
Loafer (**A. Bhimsingh**, H, 1973)
Lobhi Baap *see* Kanya Vikraya
Lobhi Pita *see* Kanya Vikraya
Locket (Ramesh Ahuja, H, 1985)
Log Kya Kahenge (**B.R. Ishara**, H, 1982)
Loguttu Perumallukeruka (K.S.R. Doss, Tel, 1966)
Loha (Raj N. Sippy, H, 1986)
Loha Singh (Kundan Kumar, Bh, 1966)
Lohe Ke Haath (S.S. Arora, H, 1990)
Lohi Bhini Chundadi (Subhash Shah, G, 1986)
Lohika Lilam (*aka* Soul of Slave: **Manilal Joshi**, St, 1927)
Lohini Vasulat *see* Raktacha Sood
Lohinu Tilak (Iqbal Sheikh, G, 1983)
Lohit Kinare (TV: **Kalpana Lajmi**, H, 1988)
Local Scenes Bombay (P.A. Stewart, St, 1899)
Lokaneethi (R. Velappan, Mal, 1953)
Lokayat (K. Hariharan, H, 1976)
Lokeshilpay Terracottay Ramayan (**Santi P. Choudhury**, B, 1961)
Lok Laaj *see* Daman
Lokmanya Bal Gangadhar Tilak (**Vishram Bedekar**, H, 1951)
Lok Parlok (**T. Rama Rao**, H, 1979)
Lokshahir Anantphandi (D.K. Kane, Mar, 1958)
Lokshahir Ramjoshi/Matwala Shayar Ramjoshi (Baburao Painter/V. Shantaram,
Mar/H, 1947)
Lolita (**Brojen Barua**, A, 1972)
Lolita (Tapan Choudhury, B, 1984)
London Express (B.J. Patel, H, 1968)
Lonely Wife, The *see* **Charulata**
Long Da Lishkara (Harpal Tiwana, P, 1983)
Look at Us Now (**Fali Bilimoria**, E, 1974)
Looking at Infinity *see* **Nokketha Dhoorathu Kannum Nattu**
Looking Back (**Prakash Jha**, E, 1987)
Looking for Love *see* **Sanamani Shodhma**
Lookochuri (Kamal Majumdar, B, 1958)
Look to the Sky (**P.V. Pathy**/Clement Baptista/Vishnu M. Vijayakar, E, 1957)

Loose Loose Araperi Loose (Pressi Malloor, Mal, 1988)
Lootmaar (**Dev Anand**, H, 1980)
Lora Nee Evide (**T.R. Raghunath**, Mal, 1971)
Lord Buddha *see* Buddhadev
Lord of Love and Power, The *see* **Prithvi Vallabh**
Lord of the Jungle *see* Himmat-e-Mard
Lore of Faith *see* Shiv Ratri
Lorie (Vijay Talwar, H, 1984)
Lorry (**B.G. Bharathan**, Mal, 1980)
Lorry Driver (S. Bhavanarayana, Tam, 1966)
Lorry Driver (Perala, K, 1987)
Lorry Driver (B. Gopal, Tel, 1990)
Lorry Driver Rajakannu (A.C. Trilogchander, Tam, 1981)
Lost, The *see* Gumrah
Lost in Midstream *see* Manjdhar
Lost Ring, The *see* Shakuntala
Lottery (G. Singh, H, 1949)
Lottery Ticket (A.B. Raj, Mal, 1970)
Lottery Ticket (C.V. Rajendran, Tam, 1982)
Lotus of Kashmir *see* Pamposh
Louha-Kapat (**Tapan Sinha**, B, 1957)
Love, The *see* Pak Daman
Love (Suresh Krishna, H, 1991)
Loveable Enemy, A *see* Pyara Dushman
Love and God (**K. Asif**, U, 1986)
Love and Murder (**Raja Paranjpe**, H, 1966)
Love and Romance *see* Mohabbat Ke Musibat
Love and War *see* Mohabbat Aur Jung
Love Angel *see* Joban Nu Jadu
Love Birds *see* Premi Pankhida
Love Chariot, The *see* **Pushpak**
Love 86 (Esmayeel Shroff, H, 1986)
Love Flame *see* Sneh Jyoti
Love Immortal *see* Rani Rupmati
Love in Andhra (Ravi, Tel, 1969)
Love in Bangalore (Sampath Kumar, K, 1966)
Love in Bombay (Shomu Mukherjee, H, 1975)
Love in Canada (S. Ramanathan, H, 1979)
Love in Goa (Harsh Kohli, H, 1983)
Love in Kashmir *see* Arzoo
Love in Kerala (**Sasikumar**, Mal, 1968)
Love in Simla (R.K. Nayyar, H, 1960)
Love in Singapore (Baby, Tel, 1980)
Love in Singapore (Chandrakumar, Mal, 1980)
Love in the Time of Malaria *see* **Hun Hunshi Hunshilal**
Love in Tokyo (Pramod Chakraborty, H, 1966)
Love is Blind *see* Raja Ne Gami Te Rani
Love is Life *see* Mohabbat Zindagi Hai
Love Letter (P. Balakrishnan, Mal, 1975)
Love Letter (Sekhar?, K, 1990)
Love Life *see* Prem Jeevan
Love Love Love (**K. Balachander**, Tel, 1984)
Love Love Love (B. Subhash, H, 1989)
Lovely (Shankaran Nair, Mal, 1979)
Love Marriage *see* Sneh Lagna
Love Marriage (**Subodh Mukherjee**, H, 1959)
Love Marriage (**T. Hariharan**, Mal, 1975)
Love Marriage (T. Lenin Babu, Tel, 1978)
Love Marriage (**Mehul Kumar**, H, 1984)
Love Master (P.D. Prasad, Tel, 1986)
Love of Anuradha *see* **Anuradha**
Love of a Slave *see* Zameen Ka Chand
Love of Youth *see* Jung-e-Jawani
Love Path *see* Preet Ki Reet
Lover Boy (Shomu Mukherjee, H, 1985)
Love Rewarded *see* Jungle Ni Jadibuti
Lovers *see* Pardesi Saiyan *or* Prem Ni Pratima
Lovers (**Bharathirajaa**, H, 1983)
Lover's Trance, The *see* Bidyasundar
Love's Limits *see* **Snehaseema**
Loves of a Mughal Prince, The (Prafulla Roy/**Charu Roy**, St, 1928)
Loves of Prince Mohammed *see* Ulfat-e-Mohammed
Lovesongs (**Pradeep Krishen**, E, 1978)
Love's Sacrifice *see* **Cinema Queen**
Love Story (**Rajendra Kumar**/**Rahul Rawail**, H, 1981)
Love Story (Sajan, Mal, 1986)
Love Sublime/Love Truth Beauty *see* **Satyam Shivam Sundaram**

Nadira in *Madam Zorro* (1962)

Love Training (B. Ramamurthy, K, 1992)
Love Triumphant *see* Mohabbat Nu Phool
Loyalty *see* Farz-e-Ada
Lubna (Kabir Rauthar, H, 1981)
Luck *see* Athirishtam
Lucky Friends *see* Taqdeerwale
Lucky Number (Manmohan Sabir/Mohan Rathod, H, 1961)
Lure of Gold *see* Sharafi Loot
Lure of the City *see* **Shaher Ka Jadoo**
Lure of the Lust *see* Moh-jaal
Lust for Gold *see* Jung-e-Daulat
Lutaru (*aka* Dacoit: K.G. Gokhale/A.S. Desai, St, 1931)
Lutaru Lalna (*aka* Dacoit's Damsel: **Homi Master**, St, 1929)
Lutaru Lalna (**Homi Wadia**, H, 1938)
Lutera (*aka* Outlaw: Vishnu Kumar Joshi, H, 1947)
Lutera (**Ravindra Dave**, H, 1955)
Lutera (Harbans, H, 1965)
Lutera Aur Jadugar (D. Raman, H, 1968)
Lutere (Dharmesh Darshan, H, 1993)

M

Maa (Prafulla Ghosh, B/H, 1934)
Maa (**Bimal Roy**, H, 1952)
Maa (Prabhat Mukherjee, B, 1956)
Maa (**Nitai Palit**, O, 1959)
Maa (Chitta Bose, B, 1961)
Maa (M.A. Thirumugham, H, 1976)
Maa (**Utpal Dutt**, B, 1983)
Maa (Ajay Kashyap, H, 1991)
Maa (**Prashanta Nanda**, O, 1992)
Maa Amba Gabbarvali (Babubhai Thakkar, G, 1976)
Maa Annapurna (Hari Bhanja, B, 1954)
Maa Aur Mamta (**Asit Sen**, H, 1970)
Maa Avret Jivrat (**Ravindra Dave**, G, 1977)
Maa Baap (**V.M. Vyas**, H, 1944)
Maa Baap (**V.M. Vyas**, H, 1960)
Maa Baap (Kishore Vyas, H/G, 1977)
Maa Baap (Arun Bhatt, H, 1978)
Maa Baap Ki Laaj (**Nanabhai Bhatt**, H, 1946)
Maa Babu (**T. Prakash Rao**, Tel, 1960)
Maa Bahen Aur Biwi (Harbans Kumar, H, 1973)
Maa Beta (Lekhraj Bhakri, H, 1962)
Maa Beti (Kalpataru, H, 1987)
Maabhoomi (**Gautam Ghosh**, Tel, 1979)
Maa Bipat Tarini Chandi (Amar Bhattacharya, B, 1981)
Maa Boot Bhawani (Vinod Parmar, G, 1987)
Maa Chinnamasta (Sailen Nath, B, 1978)
Maa Daivam (S.S. Balan, Tel, 1976)
Maa Da Laadla (Subhash Bhakri, P, 1973)
Maa Dashama (Ajitsingh Jhala, G, 1987)
Maa Dikri (**Krishnakant**, G, 1978)
Maa Durga (*aka* Jagat Janani Jagadamba: **Jyotish Bannerjee**?, St, 1921)
Maa Ek Mandir (Sukhen Das, B, 1988)
Maaf Kijiyega (Nari Ghadiali, H, 1946)
Maa Gopi (**B.S. Ranga**, Tel, 1954)
Maahi Mera Chann Varga (**Sukhdev Ahluwalia**, P, 1987)
Maa Iddari Katha (Nandamuri Ramesh, Tel, 1977)
Maa Ilavelpu (G.V.R. Sheshgiri Rao, Tel, 1971)
Maa Inti Devatha (B. Padmanabham, Tel, 1980)
Maa Inti Devudu (V. Prasad, Tel, 1975)
Maa Inti Jyothi (**A. Bhimsingh**, Tel, 1972)
Maa Inti Katha (Muthyala Subbaiah, Tel, 1990)
Maa Intiki Randi (Kodi Ramakrishna, Tel, 1983)
Maa Inti Kodalu (Srikanth, Tel, 1972)
Maa Inti Lakshmi (?, Tel, 1979)
Maa Inti Mahalakshmi/Enga Veetu Mahalakshmi (G. Ramineedu, Tel/Tam, 1959)
Maa Inti Maharaju (Vijaya Bapineedu, Tel, 1988)
Maa Inti Premayanam (Aluri Ravi, Tel, 1983)
Maa Inti Velugu (Vijay, Tel, 1972)
Maa Intiyina Katha (K.V. Panindha, Tel, 1983)
Maa Ka Aanchal (Jagdev Bhambhri, H, 1970)
Maa Kali Pavavali (S.J. Rajdev, G, 1982)
Maa Kalyaneshwari (Shri Krishna, B, 1982)
Maa Ka Pyar (Ram Daryani, H, 1949)
Maa Kasam (Shibu Mitra, H, 1985)
Maa Kasam Badla Loonga (Sudesh Issar, H, 1990)
Maa Ke Aansoo (**Dhirubhai Desai**, H, 1959)
Maa Khodal Taro Khamkaro (Dinesh Rawal, G, 1989)
Maa Ki Mamta (*aka* Mother Love: **J.J. Madan**, H, 1936)
Maa Ki Pukar (**S. Sukhdev**, H, 1975)
Maa Ki Saugandh (**Mukul S. Anand**, H, 1986)
Maa Koini Marsho Nahin (S.J. Rajdev, G, 1983)
Maaku Swatantriyam Kavali (P.S. Prakash, Tel, 1985)
Maa Manchi Akkaiah (V. Ramchandra Rao, Tel, 1970)
Maa Mane Sambhre Chhe (Dinesh Acharya, G, 1984)
Maa Meldi (Vinod Parmar, G, 1985)
Maa Mhane Kyun Parnai (Surendra Bohra, R, 1989)
Maan (Safdar Aah, H, 1954)
Maana Aansoo (S.J. Rajdev, G, 1984)
Maan Abhiman (Sukhen Das, B, 1978)
Maan Abhiman (Hiren Nag, H, 1980)
Maa Nanna Nirdoshi (K.V. Nandanarao, Tel, 1970)
Maan Apmaan (N.V. Deshpande, H, 1979)
Maanbhanjan (*aka* All for Love: **Naresh Mitra**, St, 1923)
Maang (Saghir Usmani, H, 1950)
Maan Gaye Ustad (Shibu Mitra, H, 1981)
Maang Bharo Sajana (**T. Rama Rao**, H, 1980)
Maan Jaiye (**B.R. Ishara**, H, 1972)
Maan Maryada (R.P. Swamy, H, 1985)
Maanu Mangalsutra (S.J. Rajdev, G, 1985)
Maanwan Thandian Chhanwan (**Sukhdev Ahluwalia**, P, 1984)
Maa-o-Chhele (Gunamaya Bannerjee, B, 1954)
Maa-o-Mamata (**Prashanta Nanda**, O, 1980)

Maa-o-Mati (Ardhendu Sen, B, 1972)
Maa-o-Meye (Sunil Bannerjee, B, 1969)
Maa Ooru (**B. Narasinga Rao**, Tel, 1987)
Maa Pallelo Gopaludu (Kodi Ramakrishna, Tel, 1985)
Maa Rakho Laaj Mhari (Nizam Sayyad Peer, R, 1991)
Maarpu (U. Vishweshwara Rao, Tel, 1977)
Maa Shitala (Debnarayan Gupta, B, 1958)
Maa Telugu Talli (Parachuri Bros, Tel, 1988)
Maa Te Maa (Kishore Vyas, G, 1979)
Maa: The Story of an Unwed Mother (**Paul Zils**, E, 1957)
Maa Umiya Annapurna (Vallabh Choksi, G, 1978)
Maa Vadina (**K. Pratyagatma**, Tel, 1967)
Maa Vaibhav Lakshmi (Subhash J. Shah, G, 1989)
Maavari Gola (Vidyasagar Reddy, Tel, 1985)
Maavari Manchithanam (B.A. Subba Rao, Tel, 1979)
Maavari Pelli (Ramanarayanan, Tel, 1993)
Maaveeran (?, Padmalaya Pics, Tam, 1986)
Maaveeran Jayaseelan (Padmaraj, Tam, 1969)
Maa Vina Suno Sansar (**Mehul Kumar**, G, 1982)
Maavoori Ammayi (**A. Bhimsingh**, Tel, 1961)
Maavoori Ganga (K.S.R. Doss, Tel, 1975)
Maavoori Maagadu (**K. Bapaiah**, Tel, 1987)
Maavoori Monagallu (Vijay, Tel, 1972)
Maavullo Manashivudu (Rajachandra, Tel, 1979)
Machakaran (Rajbharath, Tam, 1986)
Machanai Parthingala (V.C. Guhanathan, Tam, 1978)
Macharekhai (**P. Pullaiah**, Tam, 1950)
Machavatar (?, Peninsular Film Service, St, 1927)
Machhu Tara Vehta Pani (Vibhakar Mehta, G, 1984)
Machine Age, The *see* **Kalyug**
Madadgaar (Raja Ram, H, 1947)
Madadgaar (Ramnesh Puri, H, 1987)
Madakkayatra (George Vettom, Mal, 1985)
Madalasa (G.V. Sane, St, 1927)
Madalasa (**Ch. Narayanamurthy**, Tel, 1948)
Madalasa (J. Williams, Mal, 1978)
Madam Fashion (**Jaddanbai**, H, 1936)
Madam X (Deepak Shivdasani, H, 1993)
Madam XYZ (**Nanabhai Bhatt**, H, 1959)
Madam Zapata (Ram Rasila, H, 1962)
Madam Zorro (Aakkoo, H, 1962)
Madana Gopaludu (P.S. Krishnamohana Reddy, Tel, 1987)
Madanakamarajan (**Balkrishna Narayan Rao**, Tam, 1941)
Madana Kamaraju Katha (**B. Vittalacharya**, Tel, 1962)
Madanamala (K. Vembu, Tam, 1947)
Madana Malligai (K. Vijayan, Tam, 1976)
Madana Manjiri (**B. Vittalacharya**, Tel, 1980)
Madana Mohini (M.L. Pathi, Tam, 1953)
Madan Kala (Harihar Diwana, St, 1926)
Madan Kokila (*aka* Kalika's Vengeance: V.H. Palnitkar, St, 1930)
Madan Manjari (*aka* Wise Fool: Pesi Karani, St, 1928)
Madan Manjiri (*aka* Ishq Ke Parwane: Chhotubhai Desai, H, 1935)
Madan Manjiri (Jasubhai Trivedi, H, 1961)
Madan Mohan (Amal Kumar Basu, B, 1956)
Madan Mohana *see* Roop Basant
Madanolsavam (N. Shankaran Nair, Mal, 1977)
Madappura (S.A. Subramanyam, Tam, 1962)
Madari (Rajinder Sharma, P, 1950)
Madari (**Babubhai Mistri**, H, 1959)
Madari Mohan (*aka* Krishna Maya: Baburao Pokal/R. Varde, H, 1940)
Mada Sambrani (**A. Narayanan**, Tam, 1938)
Madatharuvi (P.A. Thomas, Mal, 1967)
Madathipatti Magal (?, Tam, 1962)
Madcap *see* Premi Pagal
Madhabi Kankan (*aka* Slave Girl of Agra: **Jyotish Bannerjee**, St, 1932)
Madhabir Biya (**Santi P. Choudhury**, B, 1964)
Madhabir Jonye (**Nitin Bose**, B, 1957)
Madhavacharya (**G.V. Iyer**, K, 1986)
Madhavi (Krishna Rao, Tam, 1959)
Madhavi (**Tapi Chanakya**, H, 1969)
Madhavikutty (**Thoppil Bhasi**, Mal, 1973)
Madhav Kam Kundala (**Chandulal Shah**, St, 1926)
Madhav Malati *see* Malati Madhav
Madh Bhare Nain (**Hemchandra Chunder**, H, 1955)
Madhbhar Mohini (*aka* Magic Flame: **Nanubhai Vakil**, St, 1930)
Madhosh (**J.B.H. Wadia**, H, 1951)
Madhosh (Desh Gautam, H, 1974)
Madh Raat Ka Mehmaan (*aka* Midnight Man: Kikubhai Desai, H, 1938)
Madhsurya (**Ketan Mehta**, H, 1975)
Madhu (**Gyan Mukherjee**/S. Bannerjee, H, 1959)
Madhubala (Prahlad Dutt, H, 1950)
Madhuban (**Ajoy Kar**, B, 1984)
Madhu Bansari (*aka* Divine Lute: Sh, ?, **Krishna Film**, St, 1926)
Madhu Bansari (A.P. Kapur, St, 1929)
Madhu Bansari (**Nanubhai Vakil**, H, 1939)
Madhuchandra (**Rajdutt**, Mar, 1967)
Madhuchandra (Ramesh-Shivram, K, 1979)
Madhuchandrachi Ratra (Ramesh Salgaonkar, Mar, 1989)
Madhuganjer Sumati (Agantuk, B, 1988)
Madhu Maasa (V. Narayanaswamy, K, 1989)
Madhumalar (Bharati Vasu, Tam, 1981)
Madhu Malathi (S.K.Ananthachari, K, 1966)
Madhu Malati (**Niren Lahiri**, B, 1957)
Madhu Malati (**Basu Bhattacharya**, H, 1978)
Madhumati (**Bimal Roy**, H, 1958)
Madhumati (Agathiyan, Tam, 1993)
Madhumoy (Partha Prathim Choudhury, B, 1986)
Madhura Bandhavya (Anootan, K, 1986)
Madhura Geetham (V.C. Guhanathan, Tam, 1977)
Madhura Milana (S.K. Ananthachari, K, 1969)
Madhuram Thirumadhuram (E.N. Balakrishnan, Mal, 1976)
Madhura Nagarilo (Kodi Ramakrishna, Tel, 1991)
Madhura Pathinezhu (**T. Hariharan**, Mal, 1975)
Madhura Sangama (T.P. Venugopal, K, 1978)
Madhura Swapnam (M. Krishnan Nair, Mal, 1976)
Madhura Swapnam (**K. Raghavendra Rao**, Tel, 1982)
Madhurati (Shyam Das, B, 1952)
Madhureno (Shanti Bannerjee, B, 1961)
Madhuri (**R.S. Choudhury**, St, 1928)
Madhuri (**R.S. Choudhury**, H, 1932)
Madhurikuna Rathri (P.G. Vishwambaran, Mal, 1978)
Madhur Milan *see* Afsana
Madhur Milan (K.G. Punwani, H, 1955)
Madhur Murali (?, **Madan** Theatres, H, 1933)
Madhusudhan (**Balwant Bhatt**, H, 1941)
Madhuve! Madhuve!! Madhuve!!! (Geethapriya, K, 1969)
Madhuve Madi Nodu (**Hunsur Krishnamurthy**, K, 1965)
Madhuve Madu Tamashe Nodu (Satyam, K, 1984)
Madhuvidhu (N. Shankaran Nair, Mal, 1970)
Madhu Vidhurathri (A.K. Swamy, Mal, 1985)
Madhu Vidhu Theerum Munpe (K. Ramachandran, Mal, 1984)
Madhyaraat Ka Kalkatta *see* Calcutta After Midnight
Madhya Rater Tara (Pinaki Mukherjee, B, 1961)
Madidunno Maraya (D. Shankar Singh, K, 1954)
Madi Madidavaru (K.M. Shankarappa, K, 1974)
Madi Mane Kahevade (Ram Rasila, G, 1968)
Madina Jaya (Shantilal Soni, G, 1976)
Madine Ki Galiyan (Meraj Ansari, H, 1979)
Madira Mohini *see* Amrit Ki Zaher
Madi Tara Aghor Nagara Vage (Vibhakar Mehta, G, 1987)
Madi Veetu Ezhai (Amirtham, Tam, 1981)
Madi Veetu Mappillai (S.K. Ananthachari, Tam, 1967)
Mad Man *see* Paithiakaran
Madmust (Jagdish Pant, H, 1953)
Madras Express (?, Madras Pics, Tam, 1939)
Madrasille Mohan (**Sasikumar**, Mal, 1982)
Madras Mail (**K. Amarnath**, Tam, 1936)
Madras to Pondicherry (Thirumalai-Mahalingam, Tam, 1966)
Madras Vathiyar (Vijayabhaskar, Tam, 1984)
Maduraikara Thambi (V.C. Guhanathan, Tam, 1988)
Madurai Manuvan (**B. Vittalacharya**, Tam, 1966)
Madurai Meenakshi (Amirthan, Tam, 1993)
Madurai Sooran (M.R. Vijayachander, Tam, 1984)
Madurai Veeran (**T.P. Rajalakshmi**, Tam, 1938)
Madurai Veeran (**D. Yoganand**, Tam, 1956)
Madurai Veeran Engasami (?, K.B. Films, Tam, 1990)
Maduraiyai Meeta Sundara Pandian (**M.G. Ramachandran**, Tam, 1977)
Mafia (Shaji Kailas, Mal, 1993)
Magaadu (S.D. Lall, Tel, 1976)
Magadhraj (**R.S. Choudhury**, H, 1946)
Magale Un Samathu (D.S. Rajagopal, Tam, 1964)
Magalukkaga (M. Krishnan, Tam, 1974)
Maga Mommaga (Y.R. Swamy, K, 1974)
Magane Kel (V. Srinivasan, Tam, 1965)
Magane Magane (K.N. Lakshmanan, Tam, 1982)
Magane Nee Vazhga (M. Krishnan, Tam, 1969)
Magarantham (**K.S. Gopalakrishnan**, Tam, 1981)
Magathalanattu Mary (S.S. Rajan, Tam, 1957)
Magavari Mayalu (Shobhandirao, Tel, 1960)
Magha Chithram (Suresh Unnithara, Mal, 1991)
Magic Box (*aka* Jadui Sandook: B.J. Patel, H, 1963)
Magic Cap (*aka* Jadui Topi: J. Arastani, H, 1946)
Magic Carpet (*aka* Jadui Shatranji: **Babubhai Mistri**, H, 1964)
Magic City *see* Jadu Nagari *or* Mayavi Nagari
Magic Flame *see* Madhbhar Mohini
Magic Flute *see* Khwab-e-Hasti
Magic Hands, The (**Santi P. Choudhury**, E, 1978)
Magic Horse, The *see* **Keeluguram**
Magic Horse (Kanu Shukla/Raja Yagnik, H, 1935)
Magicians of Bengal *see* Gaud Bangal
Magic of Baghdad *see* Baghdad Ka Jadu
Magic of Love *see* Jadu-e-Mohabbat
Magic of South India (?, Madras United Artists, E, 1943)
Magic Ring *see* Jadui Angoothi
Magic Valley *see* Maya Mahal
Magic Wand *see* Jadui Danda
Magiya Kanasu (K.S.L. Swamy, K, 1977)
Magroor (R.D. Mathur, H, 1950)
Magroor (Brij Sadanah, H, 1979)
Magudam (**Prathap Pothan**, Tam, 1992)
Magudi (Chakki, Tam, 1984)
Mahaan (S. Ramanathan, H, 1983)
Maha Badmash (R.J. Thakkar, H, 1977)
Mahabali (*aka* Vaman Avatar: G.K. Bhaskar, Tam, 1948)
Mahabali (**Sasikumar**, Mal, 1983)
Mahabali Hanuman (**Babubhai Mistri**, H, 1980)
Mahabaludu (Ravi Nagaich, Tel, 1969)
Mahabharat *see* Pandav Kaurav
Mahabharat (**Jyotish Bannerjee**?, St, 1920)
Mahabharat (**Babubhai Mistri**, H, 1965)
Mahabharat (TV: Ravi Chopra/**B.R. Chopra**, H, 1988-90)
Mahabharatam (**S. Soundararajan**, Tam, 1936)
Maha Biplabi Aurobindo (Dipak Gupta, B, 1971)
Maha Chor (**Narendra Bedi**, H, 1976)
Mahadan (Chandrasekhar Bose, B, 1949)
Mahadeshwala Poojaphala (Sangram Singh, K, 1974)
Mahadev (Raj Sippy, H, 1989)
Mahadevacha Nandi (Dinesh Sakhare, Mar, 1978)
Mahadevi (**Sundarrao Nadkarni**, Tam, 1957)
Mahadheerudu (Vijaya Bapineedu, Tel, 1986)
Mahadimane (C.V. Shivashankar, K, 1971)
Mahageet (*aka* Eternal Music: Hiren Bose, H, 1937)
Mahaguru (S.S. Ravichandra, H, 1985)
Mahajan (**Baburao Painter**, Mar, 1953)
Mahakaal (Tulsi/Shyam **Ramsay**, H, 1993)
Mahakal (Dhiresh Ghosh, B, 1948)
Mahakavi Girishchandra (**Modhu Bose**, B, 1956)
Mahakavi Kalidas (**Niren Lahiri**, B/H, 1942)
Mahakavi Kalidas (Sudhir Sen, H, 1944)
Mahakavi Kalidas (R.R. Chandran, Tam, 1966)
Mahakavi Kalidasa (K.R. Seetarama Sastry, K, 1955)
Mahakavi Kalidasa (**K. Kameshwara Rao**, Tel/Tam, 1960)
Mahakavi Kirtibas (Ashoke Chatterjee, B, 1970)
Mahakavi Kshetrayya (**Adurthi Subba Rao/C.S. Rao**, Tel, 1976)
Maha Kumbh (**S. Sukhdev**, H, 1978)
Mahal (**Kamal Amrohi**, H, 1949)
Mahal (Shankar Mukherjee, H, 1969)
Mahal (Keshu **Ramsay**, H, 1989)
Mahalagna (Kanak Mukherjee, B, 1965)
Mahalakhmi Pooja (Vishwanath Naik, O, 1959)
Mahalakshmi (A. Narayanan, Tam, 1960)
Mahalakshmi (R. Pattabhiraman, Tam, 1979)
Mahalakshmi (Rajachandra, Tel, 1980)
Mahalakshmi Races (Excelsior Cinematograph, St, 1912)
Maha Maharaju (Vijaya Bapineedu, Tel, 1983)
Mahamanishi (M. Balaiah, Tel, 1985)
Mahamantri Timmarasu (**K. Kameshwara Rao**, Tel, 1962)
Mahamaya (Dada Gunjal, H, 1936)
Mahamaya (**T.R. Raghunath**, **Elangovan**, R.S. Mani, Tam, 1944)
Mahamayi (**Babubhai Mistri**, Tam, 1991)
Mahamilan (**Dinen Gupta**, B, 1987)
Mahanagar (**Satyajit Ray**, B, 1963)
Mahanagaramlo Mayagadu (Vijaya Bapineedu, Tel, 1984)
Mahananda (**Dadasaheb Phalke**, St, 1923)
Mahananda (D. Ch. Kameshwara Rao, Tel, 1939)
Mahananda (T. Janakiram, K, 1947)
Mahananda (Mohan Kavia, H, 1984)
Mahananda (K.G. Koregaonkar, Mar, 1984)
Mahanisha (**Naresh Mitra**, B, 1936)
Mahanisha (**Sukumar Dasgupta**, B, 1956)
Mahanubhavudu (K. Hemambharadhara Rao, Tel, 1976)
Mahapavan Teerth Yatra (Vijay Sharma, H, 1975)
Mahapith Tarapith (**Gurudas Bagchi**, B, 1989)
Maha Pooja (Shanti Kumar, H, 1954)
Maha Prachandaru (Joe Simon, K, 1981)
Mahaprasthanam (K. Hemambharadhara Rao, Tel, 1982)
Mahaprasthaner Pathey/Yatrik (**Kartick Chattopadhyay**, B/H, 1952)
Mahaprithibi (**Mrinal Sen**, B, 1991)
Mahapurush (**Satyajit Ray**, B, 1964)
Mahapurusha (Joe Simon, K, 1985)
Maha Purushudu (Laxmi Deepak, Tel, 1981)
Maharachi Por (**N.D. Sarpotdar**, St, 1925)
Maharaja (Naresh Saigal, H, 1970)
Maharajashri Mayagadu (Vijaya Bapineedu, Tel, 1988)
Maharaja Vikram (Shrinath Tripathi, H, 1965)
Maharaj Nandakumar (Barin Das, B, 1953)
Maharaju (Vijaya Bapineedu, Tel, 1985)
Maharana Pratap (**Jayant Desai**, H, 1946)
Maharani (Baburao Patel, H, 1934)
Maharani (A. Karim, H, 1957)
Maharani Jhansi (Jagdish Gautam, H, 1952)
Maharani Meenal Devi (Chimanlal Trivedi, H, 1946)
Maharani Padmini (Jaswant Jhaveri, H, 1964)
Maharani Yesubai (**Bhalji Pendharkar**, Mar, 1954)
Mahara Pihar Sasra (Sudarshan Jal, Haryanvi, 1985)
Maharasan (G.N. Rangarajan, Tam, 1993)
Maharashtra (**Jabbar Patel**, Mar, 1986)
Maharasi Vazhga (Balamurugan, Tam, 1976)
Maharathi Karna (*aka* Karna the True Battler: **V. Damle/S. Fattelal**, St, 1928)
Maharathi Karna (**Bhalji Pendharkar**, H, 1944)
Maharshi (**Vamsy**, Tel, 1988)
Maharudra *see* Maha Shaktiman
Mahasagar Nu Moti (*aka* The Pearl: Mohanlal Shah, St, 1931)

Mahasampad (Surendraranjan Sarkar, B, 1950)
Mahasangram (**Mukul S. Anand**, H, 1988)
Maha Sangramam (A. Kodandarami Reddy, Tel, 1985)
Mahasati Ansuya (**Kanjibhai Rathod**, St, 1921)
Mahasati Ansuya (**Kanjibhai Rathod**, St, 1927)
Mahasati Ansuya (*aka* Sati Ansuya: **V.M. Vyas**, H, 1943)
Mahasati Ansuya (Ramnik Desai, G, 1948)
Mahasati Ansuya (**B.S. Ranga**, K, 1965)
Mahasati Ansuya (**Dhirubhai Desai**, H, 1965)
Mahasati Arundhati (Aruru Pattabhi, K, 1968)
Mahasati Behula (Shanti Kumar, H, 1964)
Mahasati Madalasa *see* Maya Nagari
Mahasati Mena Sundari (Vijay Sharma, H, 1979)
Mahasati Sabitri (Sona Mukherjee, O, 1983)
Mahasati Savitri (Ramnik Vaidya, H, 1955)
Mahasati Savitri (**Chandrakant**, H, 1973)
Mahasati Savitri (Girish Manukant, G, 1982)
Mahasati Tulasi (Radhakant, H, 1985)
Mahasati Tulasi Vrinda (Ishwarlal, H, 1947)
Mahashakti (Kommineni, Tel/H, 1980)
Maha Shaktiman/Maharudra (V.S.R. Swamy, H/B, 1985)
Mahashakti Mariamman (**K.S. Gopalakrishnan**, Tam, 1986)
Mahashilpi (H.B. Jwalanaiah, K, 1966)
Mahashivratra (V.S. Nirantar, St, 1925)
Maha Shivratri (Shantilal Soni, H, 1972)
Mahashweta (Pinaki Mukherjee, B, 1967)
Mahashweta Kadambari (*aka* Shap Sambhram: **S.N. Patankar**, St, 1922)
Mahasundar (?, Precious Pics, St, 1929)
Maha Tapasvi (C.V. Shivshankar, K, 1977)
Mahateerth (**Kidar Sharma**, H, 1961)
Maha Thyaga (Maruti Shivram, K, 1974)
Mahatirtha Kalighat (Bhupen Roy, B, 1964)
Mahatma (**Datta Dharmadhikari**, H/Mar/E, 1953)
Mahatma Gandhi (*aka* Gandhiji: **P.V. Pathy**, H, 1948)
Mahatma Gandhi Vazhkai/Mahatma Gandhi Jeevitham (A.K. Chettiar/**P.V. Pathy**, Tam/Tel, 1940)
Mahatma Kabir (**R. Nagendra Rao**, K, 1947)
Mahatma Kabir (**Gajanan Jagirdar**, H, 1954)
Mahatma Kabir (P. Srinivas, K, 1962)
Mahatma Kabirdas (**R.S. Prakash**, St, 1925)
Mahatma Kabirdas (**A. Narayanan**, Tam, 1936)
Mahatma-Life of Gandhi 1869-1948 (Vithalbhai Jhaveri, E, 1968)
Mahatma Muldas (Chandrahas Thakore, G, 1949)
Mahatma Phule (**P.K. Atre**, Mar, 1954)
Mahatma Udhangar (G. Pattu Iyer, Tam, 1947)
Mahatma Vidur (**P.Y. Altekar**, Mar/H, 1943)
Mahatmudu (M.S. Gopinath, Tel, 1976)
Mahaveera (Naresh Saigal, H, 1988)
Mahaveera Bheeman (S.A. Subburaman, Tam, 1961)
Mahayagnam (Vijayan, Tel, 1991)
Mahayanam (Joshi, Mal, 1989)
Mahayatra *see* **Antarjali Jatra**
Maha Yuddha (M.D. Kaushik, K, 1989)
Mahendra Varma (?, Sri Soundarya Films, K, 1993)
Maherchi Manse (Kamalakar Torne, Mar, 1984)
Maheshwara (Dinesh Babu, K, 1990)
Maheshwari (**T.R. Raghunath**, Tam, 1955)
Mahiari (*aka* Divine Lovers: **Homi Master**, St, 1932)
Mahigir Ki Ladki *see* Matsyagandha
Mahila Mahal (Binu Bardhan, B, 1954)
Mahima Sati Savitricha (Shashikant Nalavade, Mar, 1986)
Mahi Munda (Jarnail Singh, P, 1979)
Mahiravana (**Ch. Narayanamurthy**, Tel, 1940)
Mahiravana (G. Nataraj, K, 1957)
Mahiravana (B.A. Subba Rao, Tel, 1964)
Mahisagarne Aare (Girish Manukant, G, 1989)
Mahishasura Mardini/Durga Mata (**B.S. Ranga**, K/H, 1959)
Mahishasura Mardini (?, K, 1973)
Mahishasur Badh (Hari Bhanja, B, 1952)
Mahiyarni Chundadi (Vibhakar Mehta, G, 1983)
Mahizhampoo (V.T.Arasu, Tam, 1969)
Mahjoor *see* Shayar-e-Kashmir Mahjoor
Mahout (*aka* Elephant Boy: M.A. Thirumugham, H, 1961)
Mahua (Hiren Bose, B, 1934)
Mahua (Bibhuti Mitra, H, 1969)
Mahut Bandhu Re (**Bhupen Hazarika**, B, 1959)
Mai (Rajkumar Sharma, Bh, 1989)
Mai Baap (M. Sadiq, H, 1957)
Maibaap (Sachin, Mar, 1982)
Maidan-e-Jung (*aka* Battle: Appu Mehta, St, 1931)
Maid of the Forest *see* Jungle Ki Ladki
Maid of the Lotus *see* Kamale Kamini
Maid of the Mountains *see* Pahadi Kanya
Mai Ka Anchara (?, Bh, 1986)
Mai Ka Lal (Rajpati, Bh, 1979)
Maikhana (**Kidar Sharma**, H, 1967)
Main Abla Nahin Hoon (**Shantaram Athavale**, H, 1949)
Mainajan (Deb Kumar Barua, A, 1980)
Mainakam (K.G. Rajasekharan, Mal, 1984)
Mainatharuvi Kola Case (**Kunchako**, Mal, 1967)
Main Aur Mera Bhai (Dharam Kumar, H, 1961)
Main Aur Mera Hathi (R. Thyagaraj, H, 1981)
Main Aur Tum (Harihar, H, 1987)
Main Awara *see* Jeevan Swapna
Main Awara Hoon (Ashim Samanta, H, 1983)
Main Azaad Hoon (Tinnu Anand, H, 1989)
Main Balwan (**Mukul S. Anand**, H, 1986)
Main Bhi Ladki Hoon (A.C. Trilogchander, H, 1964)
Main Bhi Maa Hoon (?, Indian National Pics, H, 1965)
Main Chor Hoon (V. Madhusudhana Rao, H, 1976)
Main Chup Nahin Rahungi (I.M. Kunnu, H, 1985)
Main Chup Rahungi (**A. Bhimsingh**, H, 1962)
Maine Jeena Seekh Liya (Satish Nigam, H, 1959)
Maine Jeena Seekh Liya (Bhishm Kohli, H, 1982)
Maine Pyar Kiya (Sooraj Barjatya, H, 1989)
Main Hari (*aka* Defeat: **Gajanan Jagirdar**, H, 1940)
Main Hoon Alladdin (Mohammed Hussain, H, 1965)
Main Hoon Geeta (Yash Chouhan, H, 1992)
Main Hoon Jadugar (Jugal Kishore, H, 1965)
Main Hoon Sherni (Suresh Bohra, H, 1992)
Main Inteqam Loonga (**T. Rama Rao**, H, 1982)
Main Jatti Punjab Di (Baldev R. Jhingan, P, 1964)
Main Khilona Nahin (Qamar Narvi, H, 1985)
Main Kya Karun (Ninu Majumdar, H, 1945)
Main Nashe Mein Hoon (Naresh Saigal, H, 1959)
Main Papi Tum Bakshanhar (Subhash Bhakri, P, 1976)
Main Qatil Hoon (?, R.S. Movies, H, 1985)
Main Shaadi Karne Chala (**Roop K. Shorey**, H, 1962)
Main Suhagan Hoon (Kundan Kumar, H, 1964)
Main Sundar Hoon (**Krishnan-Panju**, H, 1971)
Main Tera Dushman (Vijay Reddy, H, 1989)
Main Tera Hoon (R.S. Junnarkar, H, 1947)
Main Tere Liye (**Vijay Anand**, H, 1988)
Main Tulsi Tere Aangan Ki (**Raj Khosla**, H, 1978)
Main Woh Hoon (A. Shamsheer, H, 1966)
Main Zinda Hoon (Sudhir Mishra, H, 1988)
Maisaheb (K.P Bhave, Mar, 1953)
Maithili Ennai Kathali (**T. Rajendar**, Tam, 1986)
Maitreyi Vijayam *see* Mayil Ravana
Maitri (M.R.K. Murthy, K, 1978)
Majaal (**K. Bapaiah**, H, 1987)
Majboor (Nazir Ajmeri, H, 1948)
Majboor (Narendra Suri, H, 1964)
Majboor (Ravi Tandon, H, 1974)
Majboor (**T. Rama Rao**, H, 1989)
Majboori (*aka* Chhoti Bahen: Ram Daryani, H, 1954)
Majboor Ladki (Ram Pahwa, H, 1991)
Majhi Aai (**Dinkar D. Patil**, Mar, 1961)
Majhi Ladki (**R.G. Torney**, Mar, 1939)
Majhi Zameen (**Bhalji Pendharkar**, Mar, 1953)
Majhli Didi *see* Manjhli Didi
Majib Pahacha (**Manmohan Mahapatra**, O, 1987)
Majiyara Haiya (Mahesh Desai, G, 1969)
Majjach Majja (Satish Ranadive, Mar, 1988)
Majnu (**Dasari Narayana Rao**, Tel, 1987)
Majnu 1935 (**Roop K. Shorey**, H, 1935)
Major Chandrakant (**K. Balachander**, Tam, 1966)
Major Chandrakant (**K. Raghavendra Rao**, Tel, 1993)
Makale Maapu Tharu (**Sasikumar**, Mal, 1984)
Makam Piranna Manka (N.R. Pillai, Mal, 1977)
Makan Ente Makan (**Sasikumar**, Mal, 1985)
Makara Vilakku (P.K. Joseph, Mal, 1980)
Makarshar Jaal (Pashupati Kundu, B, 1953)
Mak Aru Morom (**Nip Barua**, A, 1957)
Makheechoos (**Ramchandra Thakur**, H, 1956)
Makkal (**K.S. Sethumadhavan**, Mal, 1975)
Makkala Bhagya (K.S.L. Swamy, K, 1976)
Makkalai Petra Maharasi (K. Somu, Tam, 1957)
Makkal Anaiyittal (Ramanarayanan, Tam, 1988)
Makkala Rajya/Pillalu Techina Chalana Rajyam/Kuzhandaigal Kanda Kudiyarasu (**B.R. Panthulu**, K/Tel/Tam, 1960)
Makkala Sainya (Lakshmi, K, 1980)
Makkale Devaru (R.N. Jayagopal, K, 1983)
Makkale Manege Manikya (A.V. Sheshgiri Rao, K, 1969)
Makkal En Pakkam (Kartick Raghunathan, Tam, 1987)
Makkaliralavva Mane Thumba (**T.S. Nagabharana**, K, 1984)
Makkal Kural (U. Rajendran, Tam, 1978)
Makkal Mahatmiyan (Paulson, Mal, 1992)
Makkane Ninakku Vendi (E.N. Balakrishnan, Mal, 1971)
Makkar (Krishna Sethi, H, 1986)
Makutamleni Maharaju (**K. Bapaiah**, Tel, 1987)
Mala (**Balwant Bhatt**, H, 1941)
Mala (?, Bharat Art Prod, H, 1951)
Malabar Story (**Harisadhan Dasgupta**, E, 1965)
Mala Dev Bhetla (**Datta Keshav**, Mar, 1973)
Mala Gheoon Chala (**Dada Kondke**, Mar, 1988)
Malaicharal (Rajan, Tam, 1991)
Malaicharalil Oru Poonguyil (Thangavayal Murthy, Tam, 1985)
Malai Itta Mangai (G.R. Nathan, Tam, 1958)
Malaikallan (S.M. Sreeramulu Naidu, Tam, 1954)
Malaikalvan (A.S. Jakal, Tam, 1951)
Malaimangai (?, Bhaskar Pics, Tam, 1947)
Malai Nattu Mangai (**P. Subramanyam**, Tam, 1973)
Malai Sooda Va (C.V. Rajendran, Tam, 1975)
Malaiyur Mambattiyan (Rajasekhar, Tam, 1983)
Malajanha (**Nitai Palit**, O, 1965)
Malamaal (Kawal Sharma, H, 1988)
Malamukalile Daivam (**P.N. Menon**, Mal, 1983)
Malan (**V.M. Vyas**, H, 1942)
Malancha (Prafulla Roy, B, 1953)
Malancha (Purnendu Pattrea, B, 1982)
Mala Oru Mangala Vilakku (S. Mukherjee, Tam, 1959)
Malapilla (**Gudavalli Ramabrahmam**, Tel, 1938)
Malare Kurinje Malare (A. Parthiban, Tam, 1993)
Malargale Malarungal (Babu, Tam, 1980)
Malargalile Aval Malligai (R. Anand, Tam, 1983)
Malargal Naniginrana (S. Chidambaram, Tam, 1985)
Malargindra Paruvathile (L. Vaidyanath, Tam, 1980)
Malarum Kiliyum (K. Madhu, Mal, 1986)
Malarum Ninaivugal (**Krishnan-Panju**, Tam, 1985)
Malashree Mamashree (Saiprakash, K, 1992)
Mala the Mighty (*aka* Sher-e-Jungle: John Cawas, H, 1948)
Malathi (**K.S. Gopalakrishnan**, Tam, 1970)
Malathi Madhava (**B.R. Panthulu**, K, 1971)
Malathi Madhavam (**C. Pullaiah**, Tel, 1940)
Malati Madhav (**Kanjibhai Rathod**, St, 1922)
Malati Madhav (**Dadasaheb Phalke**, St, 1929)
Malati Madhav (A.P. Kapur, H, 1933)
Malati Madhav (M. Neelkanth, H, 1951)
Mala Tumchi Mhana (P. Bhalchandra, Mar, 1970)
Malavarcha Phool (Ramesh Salgaonkar, Mar, 1982)
Malavikagnimitra (**Dadasaheb Phalke**, St, 1929)
Malavpati Munj (*aka* Prithvi Vallabh: **Ravindra Dave**, G, 1976)
Malayadaan (**Ajoy Kar**, B, 1971)
Malaya Marutha (Ravi, K, 1986)
Maldar (Amit Maitra, H, 1951)
Male Bantu Male (P.S. Prakash, K, 1984)
Malela Jiv (**Manhar Raskapur**, G, 1956)
Maleya Makkalu (K. Shivrama Karanth, K, 1978)
Malgudi Days (TV: **Shankar Nag**, H, 1987)
Malhar (Harish, H, 1951)
Malhari Martand (Shinde, St, 1928)
Malhari Martand (**Dinkar D. Patil**, Mar, 1965)
Mali *see* Bhakticha Mala
Mali Chooda Va *see* Malai Sooda Va
Malik (S.M. Yusuf, H, 1958)
Malik (**A. Bhimsingh**, H, 1972)
Malika Paniyunnavar (Shrikumaran Thampi, Mal, 1978)
Mali Methan (Subhash Shah, G, 1984)
Malkin (O.P. Dutta, H, 1953)
Mallamma Katha (A. Sanjeevi, Tel, 1973)
Mallammana Pavada (**Puttanna Kanagal**, K, 1969)
Mallanum Mathevanum (**Kunchako**, Mal, 1976)
Mallaraj (*aka* Tiger of Rajputana: R.N. Vaidya, St, 1932)
Malleeshwari (**B.N. Reddi**, Tel, 1951)
Mallela Manushulu (K.V. Nandanarao, Tel, 1975)
Mallepandari (Jandhyala, Tel, 1982)
Mallepoovu (V. Madhusudhana Rao, Tel, 1978)
Malligai Mohini (**Durai**, Tam, 1979)
Malligai Poo (N.S. Maniam, Tam, 1973)
Mallige Hoove (Rajkishore, K, 1992)
Mallige Sampige (R.N. Jayagoal, K, 1979)
Mallika (A.R. Qureshi, H, 1947)
Mallika (Majnu, H, 1956)
Mallika (Joseph Taliath, Tam, 1957)
Mallika-e-Alam Nurjehan (Dada Gunjal, H, 1954)
Mallika Salome (Mohammed Hussain, H, 1953)
Malli Madhuve (G.R. Nathan, K, 1963)
Malli Pelli (**Y.V. Rao**, Tel, 1939)
Malli Pelli (**C.S. Rao**, Tel, 1970)
Malliyam Mangalam (?, Tamil Nadu Talkies, Tam, 1961)
Mall Road (Viren Dableish, H, 1962)
Mallu Vetti Minor (?, Everest Films, Tam, 1990)
Mal Masala (Satish Ranadive, Mar, 1989)
Malo Naagde (**Ravindra Dave**, G, 1985)
Malootty (**B.G. Bharathan**, Mal, 1992)
Malsaram (K. Narayanan, Mal, 1975)
Mama Alludu (**Dasari Narayana Rao**, Tel, 1990)
Mama Allula Saval (K.S.R. Doss, Tel, 1980)
Mama Bhanja (Naresh Kumar, H, 1977)
Mamagaru (Mutyala Subbaiah, Tel, 1991)
Mamaji (Narottam Vyas, H, 1942)
Mamaji (Roshan Bhardwaj, P, 1964)
Mamakaram (**Adurthi Subba Rao**, Tel, 1963)
Mama Kodalu (**Dasari Narayana Rao**, Tel, 1993)
Mama Kodalu Saval (B. Bhaskara Rao, Tel, 1986)
Mamaku Tagga Alludu (**Vedantam Raghavaiah**, Tel, 1960)
Mamaku Tagga Kodalu (**C.S. Rao**, Tel, 1969)
Mamalakalkkappuruthu (?, Mal, 1988)
Mamala Poricha (Ramesh Salgaonkar, Mar, 1988)
Mamankam (Appachan, Mal, 1979)
Maman Machan (Ramanarayanan, Tam, 1984)
Maman Magal (R.S. Mani, Tam, 1955)
Mamata (*aka* Mother: **Franz Osten**, H, 1936)
Mamata (I.A. Hafizji, H, 1942)
Mamata (Dada Gunjal, H, 1952)
Mamata (Prabhat Mukherjee, B, 1957)
Mamata (**Phani Majumdar**, H, 1965)
Mamata (**Asit Sen**, H, 1966)
Mamata (Nalin Duara, A, 1973)

Mamata (Byomkesh Tripathi, O, 1975)
Mamata (Tapan Bhattacharya, B, 1983)
Mamata Ki Chhaon Mein (**Kishore Kumar**/Amit Kumar, H, 1989)
Mamatala Kovela (Mutyala Subbaiah, Tel, 1989)
Mamata Mage Mula (Amiya, O, 1985)
Mamata Ra Dori (Mohammed Mohsin, O, 1989)
Mamatha (P. Chandrasekhara Reddy, Tel, 1973)
Mambazhathu Vandu (R.C. Sakthi, Tam, 1979)
Mame Bhache (Datta Mane, Mar, 1979)
Mamiyar (K. Vembu, Tam, 1953)
Mamiyara Marumagala (A.K. Subramanyam, Tam, 1982)
Mamiyargal Jagrithi (Ramanarayanan, Tam, 1986)
Mamiyar Meetriya Marumagal (**Krishnan-Panju**, Tam, 1959)
Mamiyarum Oru Veetu Marumagale (?, Anupama Films, Tam, 1961)
Mamiyar Veedu (N. Krishnamurthy, Tam, 1977)
Mamiyar Veedu (S. Ganeshraj, Tam, 1992)
Mamiyar Vijayam (Madurai Thirumaran, Tam, 1975)
Mamla Garbar Hai (Hari Dutt, P, 1983)
Mamlar Phal (**Pashupati Chatterjee**, B, 1956)
Mammathe (Y.R. Swamy, K, 1968)
Mammatheya Bandhana (B.S. Narayana, K, 1966)
Mana Akasha (**Nitai Palit**, O, 1974)
Manab Aru Danab (Indukalpa Hazarika, A, 1971)
Manacha Kunku (Govind Kulkarni, Mar, 1981)
Manacha Mujra (Raja Bargir, Mar, 1969)
Manacha Pan (A.R. Sheikh, Mar, 1949)
Manade Gundalu (**K. Bapaiah**, Tel, 1979)
Manadesam (**L.V. Prasad**, Tel, 1949)
Manadhil Urudhi Vendhum (**K. Balachander**, Tam, 1987)
Managara Kaval (M. Thyagarajan, Tam, 1991)
Manager (I.P. Tiwari, H, 1947)
Manaivi (G.K. Ramu, Tam, 1969)
Manaivi Illatha Neram (A. Jagannathan, Tam, 1983)
Manaivi Oru Manikam (Cholarajan, Tam, 1990)
Manaivi Oru Manthiri (Ramanarayanan, Tam, 1988)
Manaivi Ready (A. Pandiyarajan, Tam, 1987)
Manaivi Solle Mandiram (Ramanarayanan, Tam, 1983)
Manaivi Uruvahiral (N.S. Ravishankar, Tam, 1983)
Manaiviye Manithanin Manikkam (K. Vembu, Tam, 1959)
Manakanakku (R.C. Sakthi, Tam, 1986)
Manakkale Thatta (Babu Korulla, Mal, 1985)
Manalane Mangayin Bhagyam *see* **Suvarna Sundari**
Manal Kayiru (Visu, Tam, 1982)
Manamadurai Malli (Madurai Thirumaran, Tam, 1982)
Manamagal/Pelli Koothuru (N.S. Krishnan, Tam/Tel, 1951)
Manamagale Vaa (Panju Arunachalam, Tam, 1988)
Manamagal Thevai *see* Varudukavali
Manamalai (**Ch. Narayanamurthy**, Tam, 1958)
Mana Maligai (T.V. Swamy, Tam, 1942)
Manamara Vazhthungal (G. Subramaniya Reddiar, Tam, 1976)
Mana Mechhida Madadi (K.R. Seetarama Sastry, K, 1963)
Mana Mechhida Sose (B. Ramamurthy, K, 1992)
Manam Oru Kurangu (A.T. Krishnaswamy, Tam, 1967)
Manampola Mangalyam (**P. Pullaiah**, Tam, 1953)
Manamulla Maratharam (W.R. Subba Rao/S. Ramanathan, Tam, 1958)
Man and his Destiny *see* Raja Bhoj
Man and Monkey (**H.S. Bhatavdekar**, St, 1899)
Man and Woman *see* **Admi Aur Aurat**
Mananthal Mahadevan (Ramanarayanan, Tam, 1989)
Manappandanal (V.N. Reddy, Tam, 1961)
Man Aru Maram (Bibhan Barua, A, 1980)
Manasada Hoovu (**Puttanna Kanagal**, K, 1985)
Manasadevi (?, Madras Films, Tam, 1940)
Manasakshi (G. Vishwanath, Mal, 1954)
Manasakshi (S.K. Ananthachari, K, 1968)
Manasakshi (T.N. Balu, Tam, 1969)
Manasakshi (P. Sambhasiva Rao, Tel, 1976)
Manasamaina Varu (?, Ragamayi Arts, Mal, 1987)
Manasamrakshanam (**K. Subramanyam**, Tam, 1944)
Mana Samsaram (**C.S. Rao**, Tel, 1968)
Manasa Paris Mendhre Bari (**Prabhakar Nayak**, Mar, 1977)
Manasara Vazhthungalen (Parthibaraman, Tam, 1991)
Manasariyathe (Soman Ambattu, Mal, 1984)
Manasa Sarovara (**Puttanna Kanagal**, K, 1982)
Manasa Vacha Karmana (**I.V. Sasi**, Mal, 1979)
Manasa Veena (Babu Nathancode, Mal, 1976)
Manasa Veena (**Relangi Narasimha Rao**, Tel, 1984)
Manase Mandiram (**C.V. Sridhar**, Tel, 1966)
Manase Ninakku Mangalam (A.B. Raj, Mal, 1984)
Manashanti (M.S. Nayak, K, 1969)
Manashi (Balai Sen, A, 1981)
Manasi (Malay Mitra, O, 1981)
Manasi (Anjan Mukherjee, B, 1990)
Manasiddare Marga (M.R. Vittal, K, 1967)
Manasinante Mangalya (Giri Babu, K, 1977)
Manasinte Teertha Yatra (Thamban, Mal, 1981)
Manasi Oru Mahasamudram (P.K. Joseph, Mal, 1983)
Manasi Oru Manimuthu (?, Mal, 1985)
Manas Ka Maharshi *see* **Kondura**
Manas Kanya (Phani Talukdar, A, 1985)
Manas Oru Mayil (P. Chandrakumar, Mal, 1977)
Manasu (Hamid Kakassery, Mal, 1973)
Manasukketha Maharaja (Deendayal, Tam, 1989)
Manasukku Etra Mappillai (?, Amudasurabhi Pics, Tam, 1990)
Manasukkul Mathapu (Robert-Rajasekharan, Tam, 1988)
Manasu Mamatha (Mouli, Tel, 1990)
Manasu Mangalyam (**K. Pratyagatma**, Tel, 1970)
Manaswini (**P. Bhaskaran**, Mal, 1968)
Manava Danava (Janakiram, K, 1985)
Manavadharmam (**Sasikumar**, Mal, 1979)
Manavadi Kosam (**P. Bhanumathi**, Tel, 1976)
Manavadusthunnadu (Kodi Ramakrishna, Tel, 1987)
Manavallakurchi: My Village (**K.G. George**, E, 1973)
Manavan (M.A. Thirumugham, Tam, 1970)
Manavano Aliyano (K.N. Chandrasekhar Sharma, K, 1985)
Manavaralli Pelli (P.N. Ramchandra Rao, Tel, 1992)
Manavata (**Tapi Chanakya**, H, 1972)
Manavati (**Y.V. Rao**, Tel, 1952)
Manavatti (**K.S. Sethumadhavan**, Mal, 1964)
Manav Hatya (?, Goldie Films, H, 1987)
Manavidu Osthannadu (Kodi Ramakrishna, Tel, 1987)
Manavoori Katha (K. Hemambharadhara Rao, Tel, 1976)
Manavoori Pandavalu (**Bapu**, Tel, 1978)
Manavude Mahaniyudu (Kodi Ramakrishna, Tel, 1980)
Manavudu Danavudu (P. Chandrasekhara Reddy, Tel, 1972)
Manavudu Danavudu (Ramanababu, Tel, 1986)
Manavu Manasu (P. Chinappa Reddy, Tel, 1973)
Manchala (**Jayant Desai**, H, 1953)
Manchala Muhame Varuha (V.C. Guhanathan, Tam, 1975)
Manchali (R.C. Talwar, H, 1943)
Manchali (*aka* Badla: ?, Filmsaz, H, 1962)
Manchali (Raja Nawathe, H, 1973)
Manchi Babai (T. Krishna, Tel, 1978)
Manchi Chedu (Ramanna, Tel, 1963)
Manchi Donga (**K. Raghavendra Rao**, Tel, 1987)
Manchiki Maro Peru (**C.S. Rao**, Tel, 1976)
Manchiki Maro Peru (T. Prasad, Tel, 1983)
Manchi Kutumbam (V. Madhusudhana Rao, Tel, 1968)
Manchi Kutumbam (G. Ram Mohan Rao, Tel, 1989)
Manchi Manasu (**K. Pratyagatma**, Tel, 1978)
Manchi Manishi (**K. Pratyagatma**, Tel, 1964)
Manchi Manishi (N. Ravindra Reddy, Tel, 1984)
Manchi Manushuku Manchi Roju (**C.S. Rao**, Tel, 1958)
Manchi Manushulu/Penn Manam (**Adurthi Subba Rao**, Tel/Tam, 1962)
Manchi Manushulu (V.B. Rajendra Prasad, Tel, 1974)
Manchi Mithrulu (**T. Rama Rao**, Tel, 1969)
Manchini Penchali (T. Maharathi, Tel, 1977)
Manchi Roju (M.S. Sriram, Tel, 1977)
Manchi Roju (Mouli, Tel, 1991)
Manchi Rojulu Vastai (G. Vishwanathan, Tel, 1963)
Manchi Rojulu Vastai (V. Madhusudhana Rao, Tel, 1972)
Manchi Vadu (V. Madhusudhana Rao, Tel, 1973)
Manchivallaku Manchivadu (K.S.R. Doss, Tel, 1972)
Manchivaru Maavaru (**I.V. Sasi**, Tel, 1989)
Manchu Pallaki (**Vamsy**, Tel, 1982)
Mandala Dheesudu (Prabhakara Reddy, Tel, 1987)
Mandanda (Ratan Chatterjee, B, 1950)
Mandanda (Pinaki Choudhury, B, 1990)
Mandanmar Londonil (Satyan Andhikkad, Mal, 1983)
Mandaravathi (T. Marconi/**H.V. Babu**, Tam, 1941)
Mandayarkal Sandhippu (**A. Narayanan**, Tam, 1936)
Mandhira Punnagai (V. Tamizhalagan, Tam, 1986)
Mandi (**Shyam Benegal**, H, 1983)
Mandir (**A.R. Kardar**, H, 1937)
Mandir (**Phani Burma**, B, 1947)
Mandir (**Master Vinayak/Dinkar D. Patil**, H, 1948)
Mandir (Chandrasekhar Bose, B, 1952)
Mandir (Bakul Majumdar, B, 1987)
Mandira (Sujit Guha, B, 1990)
Mandir Masjid (Mohammed Hussain, H, 1977)
Mane/Ek Ghar (**Girish Kasaravalli**, K/H, 1990)
Mane Aliya (S.K. Ananthachari, K, 1964)
Mane Belagida Sose (Srikanth, K, 1973)
Mane Belaku (Y.R. Swamy, K, 1975)
Mane Devaru (Ravichandran, K, 1993)
Manegebanda Mahalakshmi (B.V. Acharya/Govindaiah, K, 1959)
Manegebanda Mahalakshmi (Geethapriya, K, 1983)
Mane Katti Nodu (Shri Sadguru, K, 1966)
Manekthamb (Ramkumar Bohra, G, 1978)
Maneli Ramanna Beedhili Kamanna (Amrutham, K, 1983)
Mane Mane Kathe (Rajachandra, K, 1981)
Mane Na Mana (**Sailajananda Mukherjee**, B, 1945)
Mane Thumbida Hennu (**B. Vittalacharya**, K, 1958)
Maneyalli Ili Beediyalli Huli (Saiprakash, K, 1991)
Maneye Manthralaya (Bhargava, K, 1986)
Mangai Oru Gangai (Hariharan, Tam, 1987)
Mangaiyar Ullam Mangada Selvam *see* Swarnamanjari
Mangala (**S.S. Vasan**, H, 1950)
Mangala (Chandru, Tel, 1951)
Mangala (M.N. Prasad, K, 1979)
Mangala Gauri (**T.R. Sundaram**, K, 1953)
Mangala Gauri (G. Giridhara Rao, Tel, 1980)
Mangala Lakshmi (Thiruchengodu Lakshmi, Tam, 1981)
Mangalam Nerunne (Mohan, Mal, 1984)
Mangala Muhurta (M.R. Vittal, K, 1964)
Mangala Nayakan (K. Raghunath, Tam, 1992)
Mangala Nayaki (**Krishnan-Panju**, Tam, 1980)
Mangala Toranalu (**Singeetham Srinivasa Rao**, Tel, 1979)
Mangala Vadyam (K. Shankar, Tam, 1979)
Mangal Dada (Ramesh Gupta, H, 1986)
Mangaldip (Haranath Chakraborty, B, 1989)
Mangalfera (**Ratibhai Punatar**, G, 1949)
Mangalfera (Iqbal Sheikh, G, 1985)
Mangal Nila (Ranjith, Tam, 1982)
Mangal Pandey (Harmesh Malhotra, H, 1982)
Mangalsutra (*aka* Heera Ka Haar: Dada Gunjal, H, 1947)
Mangalsutra (Shabab, G, 1951)
Mangalsutra (**Chandramohan**, K, 1959)
Mangalsutra (Ashok Tate, Mar, 1968)
Mangalsutra (B. Vijay, H, 1981)
Mangalsutra (Rajesh Kumar, K, 1981)
Mangalsutram *see* **Vande Mataram**
Mangalsutram (D.S. Kotnis, Tel, 1946)
Mangalsutram (A.K. Velan, Tel, 1966)
Mangalya (B. subba Rao, K, 1991)
Mangalya Balam/Manjal Magimai (**Adurthi Subba Rao**, Tel/Tam, 1959)
Mangalya Balam (B. Subba Rao, Tel, 1985)
Mangalya Bandham (K. Subba Rao, Tel, 1985)
Mangalya Bandhana (Bhagwan, K, 1993)
Mangalya Bhagya (Vijaya Satyam, K, 1976)
Mangalya Bhagyam (**T.R. Raghunath**, Tam, 1958)
Mangalya Bhagyam (**Padmanabham**, Tel, 1974)
Mangalyam (K. Somu, Tam, 1954)
Mangalyam (B.S. Narayana, Tel, 1960)
Mangalyam Thandunane (Ravidasan, Tam, 1991)
Mangalyaniki Maro Peru (**K. Vishwanath**, Tel, 1976)
Mangalya Yoga (P.K. Lal, K, 1958)
Mangammagari Manavudu (Kodi Ramakrishna, Tel, 1984)
Mangamma Sapatham (T.G. Raghavacharya, Tam, 1943)
Mangamma Sapatham (**B. Vittalacharya**, Tel, 1965)
Mangamma Sapatham (K. Vijayan, Tam, 1985)
Mangayar Karasi (Jiten Bannerjee, Tam, 1949)
Mangayar Thilakam (**L.V. Prasad**, Tam, 1955)
Mangayir Ullam Mangada Selvam *see* Swarnamanjari
Mangetar (Rupa Sain, H, 1972)
Mangti (**Roop K. Shorey**, P, 1942)
Mangu (N.A. Ansari, H, 1954)
Mangu Dada (Maruti, H, 1970)
Mangudi Minor (V.C. Guhanathan, Tam, 1978)
Mani-Aar-Manik (**Sailajananda Mukherjee**, B, 1954)
Manidan Maravalli *see* **Gundamma Katha**
Manihar (Salil Sen, B, 1966)
Manik (Bijoli Baran Sen, B, 1961)
Manikajodi (Prabhat Mukherjee, O, 1964)
Mani Kanchan (Tulsi Lahiri, B, 1934)
Manikavasagar (**T.R. Sundaram**, Tam, 1939)
Manikchand (Ajit Ganguly, B, 1981)
Manikjore (Kalipada Das, B, 1952)
Manik Jorh (*aka* Fortune Hunters: **Jyotish Bannerjee**, St, 1930)
Manikka Thothil (P. Madhavan, Tam, 1974)
Mani Koyakuruppu (Devadas, Mal, 1979)
Manik Raitong (**Ardhendu Bhattacharya**, Khasi, 1984)
Manik the Miserable *see* **Manik Raitong**
Manikuyil (Rajavarman, Tam, 1993)
Manikya Kottaram (U. Rajagopal, Mal, 1966)
Manima (**Nip Barua**, B, 1978)
Mani Makudam (S.S.R., Tam, 1966)
Manimala (Gautam Chakraborty, B, 1989)
Mani Mekalai (*aka* Bala Sanyasi: **K. Subrahmanyam**/Boman Irani, Tam, 1940)
Mani Mekalai (V.S. Raghavan, Tam, 1959)
Manimuzhakkum (**P.A. Backer**, Mal, 1976)
Manini (**Anant Mane**, Mar, 1961)
Manini (**K.S. Sethumadhavan**, K, 1979)
Mani Osai (P. Madhavan, Tam, 1963)
Manippayal (A. Jagannathan, Tam, 1973)
Maniram Dewan (Sarbeshwar Chakraborty, A, 1963)
Manishada (**Kunchako**, Mal, 1975)
Manishichina Maguva (**A. Bhimsingh**, Tel, 1969)
Manishiki Maroperu *see* Manchiki Maro Peru
Manishiku Charithra (T. Prasad, Tel, 1982)
Manishilo Manishi (**P. Subramanyam**, Tel, 1977)
Manishi Mrugham (?, Tel, 1976)
Manishi Rodduna Paddadu (C.V. Ramanji, Tel, 1976)

Manithali (M. Krishnan Nair, Mal, 1984)
Manithan (**K. Ramnoth**, Tam, 1953)
Manithan (S.P. Muthuraman, Tam, 1987)
Manithanin Maru Pakkam (K. Rangaraj, Tam, 1986)
Manithan Maravillai *see* **Gundamma Katha**
Manithan Marivittan (Manivannan, Tam, 1989)
Manithanum Daivamagalam (P. Madhavan, Tam, 1975)
Manithanum Mrigamum (K. Vembu/S.D. Sundaram, Tam, 1953)
Manitharil Ithanai Nirangala (R.C. Sakthi, Tam, 1978)
Manithiral Manikam (C.V. Rajendran, Tam, 1973)
Manivathoorile Ayiram Sivarathrikal (**Fazil**, Mal, 1987)
Maniyan Pillai Athava Maniyan Pillai (**Balachandra Menon**, Mal, 1981)
Maniyara (M. Krishnan Nair, Mal, 1983)
Maniyaro (**Krishnakant**, G, 1980)
Manjal Kumkumam (Pattu, Tam, 1973)
Manjal Magimai *see* Mangalya Balam
Manja Mandarangal (?, Mal, 1987)
Manjari (**Moti Gidwani**, H, 1934)
Manjari (**Y.V. Rao**, Tel, 1953)
Manjari Opera (**Agradoot**, B, 1970)
Manjdhar (*aka* Lost in Midstream: **Sohrab Modi**, H, 1947)
Man Jeete Jag Jeet (B.S. Thapa, P, 1973)
Manjhli Didi (*aka* Majhli Didi: **Hrishikesh Mukherjee**, H, 1967)
Manjil Virinja Pookkal (**Fazil**, Mal, 1980)
Manju (*aka* Sharadasandhya: **M.T. Vasudevan Nair**, Mal, 1982)
Manju Moodal Manju (**Balu Mahendra**, Mal, 1980)
Man Ka Aangan (**I.V. Sasi**, H, 1979)
Man Ka Meet (**Ratibhai Punatar**, H, 1950)
Man Ka Meet (**Adurthi Subba Rao**, H, 1968)
Mankhano Melo (Vibhakar Mehta, G, 1985)
Man Ki Aankhen (Raghunath Jhalani, H, 1970)
Man Ki Jeet (*aka* Tan Ki Haar: W.Z. Ahmed, H, 1944)
Manku Dinne (K.S.L. Swamy, K, 1968)
Mankuthimma (Bhargava, K, 1980)
Manla Tar Dev (Datta Chavan, Mar, 1970)
Manmadha Leela Kamaraju Gula (Relangi Narasimha Rao, Tel, 1987)
Manmadha Ragangal (K. Shankar, Tam, 1980)
Manmadha Samrajyam (Tamma Reddy, Tel, 1988)
Manmadha Sarangal (Baby, Mal, 1991)
Manmadha Vijayam (G. Pattu Iyer, Tam, 1939)
Manmad Passenger (**Kumar Shahani**, H, 1967)
Man Mandir (**Tapi Chanakya**, H, 1971)
Manmani (**Sarvottam Badami**, H, 1947)
Manmatha Leelai (**K. Balachander**, Tam, 1976)
Manmatha Rajakkal (Ramanarayanan, Tam, 1984)
Manmauji (**Krishnan-Panju**, H, 1962)
Manmohan (**Mehboob**, H, 1936)
Manmoyee Girls' School (**Jyotish Bannerjee**, B, 1935)
Manmoyee Girls' School (**Hemchandra Chunder**, B, 1958)
Mannan (P. Vasu, Tam, 1991)
Mannarai Katha Maaveeran (G. Vishwanathan, Tam, 1968)
Mannathai Mannan (M. Natesh, Tam, 1960)
Mannavan Vandanadi (P. Madhavan, Tam, 1975)
Mannemlo Monagadu (Kodi Ramakrishna, Tel, 1986)
Mannina Doni (M.S. Rajasekhar, K, 1992)
Manninamaga (Geethapriya, K, 1968)
Mannina Magalu (**B.S. Ranga**, K, 1973)
Manninte Maril (**P.A. Backer**, Mal, 1979)
Mannippu (M. Krishnan, Tam, 1969)
Manno Manigar (Jasubhai Trivedi, G, 1977)
Mann Soru (Kandaswamy Singaram, Tam, 1984)
Mannu (**K.G. George**, Mal, 1978)
Mannukketha Ponnu (A. Ramarajan, Tam, 1985)
Mannukkul Vairam (**Manoj Kumar**, Tam, 1986)
Mann Vasanai (**Bharathirajaa**, Tam, 1983)
Man of Valour, A (**Govind Saraiya**, E, 1963)
Manohar *see* **Manohara**
Manohara (**P. Sambandam Mudaliar**, Tam, 1936)
Manohara/Manohar (**L.V. Prasad**, Tam/Tel/H, 1954)
Manokamna (Kedar Kapoor, H, 1979)
Manomati (Rohini Barua, A, 1941)
Mano Na Mano (*aka* Andhakar: ?, Bhuvi Entertainers, H, 1955)
Manonmani (**T.R. Sundaram**, Tam, 1942)
Manoos/Admi (**V. Shantaram**, Mar/H, 1939)
Manorama (*aka* Hridaya Triputi: **Homi Master**, St, 1924)
Manorama (**Jayant Desai**, H, 1944)
Manorama (Kamal Ghosh, Tel, 1959)
Manoranjan (**Shammi Kapoor**, H, 1974)
Manoratham (P. Gopikumar, Mal, 1978)
Manoshakti (S. Krishnamraju, Tel, 1986)
Manovijaya (**S.N. Patankar**, St, 1926)
Man Pasand (**Basu Chatterjee**, H, 1980)
Manpeda (Aziz, Mal, 1971)
Manraksha (Satish Dasgupta, B, 1956)
Mansai Na Diva (**Govind Saraiya**, G, 1984)
Mansala Pankh Astaat (Madhav Shinde, Mar, 1961)
Mansarovar (Mahesh Chandra, H, 1946)
Man Tera Tan Mera (**B.R. Ishara**, H, 1971)
Manthan (*aka* Justice of Vikram: Ramji Arya, H, 1941)
Manthan (**Shyam Benegal**, H, 1976)
Man the Creator (**S. Sukhdev**, E, 1962)
Manthiri Kumaran (**B. Vittalacharya**, Tam, 1963)
Manthiri Kumari (**Ellis Duncan/T.R. Sundaram**, Tam, 1950)
Manthoppu Kiliyey (M.A. Kaja, Tam, 1979)
Manthrakodi (M. Krishnan Nair, Mal, 1972)
Manthravadi (**P. Subramanyam**, Mal, 1956)
Mantradandam (K. Ramachandra Rao, Tel, 1951)
Mantradandam (Kommineni, Tel, 1985)
Mantralaya Mahatme (T.V. Singh Thakore, K, 1966)
Mantralaya Shri Raghavendra Vaibhavam (M.R. Nag, Tel, 1982)
Mantramugdha (**Bimal Roy**, B, 1949)
Mantramugdha (Aravind Mukherjee, B, 1977)
Mantra Shakti (**Satu Sen**, B, 1935)
Mantra Shakti (Chitta Bose, B, 1954)
Mantra Shakti (**Hunsur Krishnamurthy**, K, 1975)
Mantrigari Viyankudu (**Bapu**, Tel, 1983)
Mantrikudu Shivabhaktudu (P.S. Prakash, Tel, 1984)
Mantrumurthi (M. Apparao, Tel, 1972)
Mantryanchi Soon (**Dinkar D. Patil**, Mar, 1980)
Manu Neethi Cholan *see* Araichi Mani
Manuni Masi (Chandravadan Bhatt, G, 1952)
Manushiyan (Raveendran, Mal, 1979)
Manushulanta Okkate (**Dasari Narayana Rao**, Tel, 1976)
Manushulo Devadu (B.V. Prasad, Tel, 1974)
Manushulu Chesina Dongalu (M. Mallikarjuna Rao, Tel, 1977)
Manushulu Mamathalu (**K. Pratyagatma**, Tel, 1965)
Manushulu Marali (V. Madhusudhana Rao, Tel, 1969)
Manushulu Matti Bommalu (B. Bhaskara Rao, Tel, 1974)
Manushya Bandhangal (Mani, Mal, 1972)
Manushyamrigam (Baby, Mal, 1980)
Manushya Puthran (Rishi/Baby, Mal, 1973)
Manuski (Shankar Kinargi, Mar, 1983)
Manu the Great (Manu Narang, H, 1987)
Manu Uncle (Dennis Joseph, Mal, 1988)
Man with the Axe, The *see* **Parashuram**
Manyalle Ramanna Bheedili Kamanna (Amrutham, K, 1983)
Manya Mahajanangale (A.T. Abu, Mal, 1985)
Manyashri Vishwamithran (**Madhu**, Mal, 1974)
Manzil *see* **Grihadah**
Manzil (Mandi Burman, H, 1960)
Manzilein Aur Bhi Hain (**Mahesh Bhatt**, H, 1973)
Manzil (**Basu Chatterjee**, H, 1979)
Manzil Manzil (**Nasir Hussain**, H, 1984)
Manzoor (Subodh Mitra, H, 1949)
Maphicha Sakshidar (**Rajdutt**, Hemhira Chitra, Mar, 1986)
Mappillai (**T.R. Raghunath**, Tam, 1952)
Mappillai (Rajasekhar, Tam, 1989)
Mappillai Azhaippu (**T.R. Raghunath**, Tam, 1972)
Mappillai Singam (Cumbum Durai, Tam, 1985)
Mappillai Sir (D.S. Balakan, Tam, 1988)
Mappillai Vanthachu (Sasi Mohan, Tam, 1992)
Mappusakshi (**P.N. Menon**, Mal, 1971)
Maqsad (**K. Bapaiah**, H, 1984)
Maradalu Pelli (**K. Mukkamala**, Tel, 1951)
Maradno Mandvo (**Mehul Kumar**, G, 1983)
Maragatham (*aka* Karunkuyil Kunrathu Kolai: S.M. Sreeramulu Naidu, Tam, 1959)
Maragatha Veenai (Gokulakrishna, Tam, 1986)
Maraka Mudiyuma (Murasoli Maran, Tam, 1966)
Marakkailo Rikalum (**Fazil**, Mal, 1983)
Marakka Matten (A. Ramarajan, Tam, 1986)
Marali Goodige (K.R. Shantharam, K, 1984)
Maralu Sarapani (K.V. Jayaram, K, 1979)
Maram (Yusuf Ali Kacheri, Mal, 1972)
Maram (Bibhan Barua, A, 1978)
Maram Trishna (**Abdul Majid**, A, 1968)
Marana Homam (A. Kodandarami Reddy, Tel, 1987)
Marana Mridanga (B. Ramamurthy, K, 1992)
Marana Mridangam (A. Kodandarami Reddy, Tel, 1988)
Marana Samsaram (S.S. Ravichandra, Tel, 1987)
Maraner Pare (*aka* After the Death: A.K. Roy, St, 1931)
Maraner Pare (Satish Dasgupta, B, 1954)
Marapurani Manishi (**T. Rama Rao**, Tel, 1973)
Marapurani Talli (D.S. Prakash Rao, Tel, 1972)
Maratha Tituka Melavava (**Bhalji Pendharkar**, Mar, 1964)
Maratha War Cry *see* Namak Haram
Marathyachi Mulgi (Pandurang Talegiri, Mar, 1938)
Marathyatil Duhi/Amar Shaheed (Balasaheb Yadav, Mar/H, 1932)
Maratodu Na Mogudu (A. Kodandarami Reddy, Tel, 1992)
Marattam (**G. Aravindan**, Mal, 1988)
Maravan (Manoj Kumar, Tam, 1993)
Maravil Thiruvu Sukshikuha (**Sasikumar**, Mal, 1972)
Marchandi Mana Chattalu (Vejalla Satyanarayana, Tel, 1984)
Mard (**Manmohan Desai**, H, 1985)
Mardangi (S.R. Pratap, H, 1988)
Mardani (Govind Kulkarni, Mar, 1983)
Mard Bano *see* Karmaveer
Mard-e-Maidan (*aka* Field Marshal: Anant Desai, H, 1935)
Mard-e-Punjab (Rajhans, H, 1940)
Mar Dhaad (Yash Chauhan, H, 1988)
Mard Ka Bachcha (*aka* Valiant: Prafulla Ghosh, St, 1930)
Mard Ka Bachcha (*aka* Valiant: M. Udwadia, H, 1936)
Mard Ki Zabaan (*aka* His Old Debt: N.G. Kamatmukar, St, 1929)
Mard Ki Zabaan (**K. Bapaiah**, H, 1987)
Mard Maratha (Keshavrao Talpade, Mar, 1951)
Mardna Gha (*aka* Master Stroke: **Kanjibhai Rathod**, St, 1927)
Mardon Wali Baat (Brij Sadanah, H, 1988)
Mareez-e-Ishq *see* Prem Pujari
Mare Javun Pele Paar (**Chandrakant Sangani**, G, 1968)
Marelayagada Kathe (V. Somasekhar, K, 1982)
Mareyada Deepavali (R. Sampath, K, 1972)
Mareyada Haadu (A.N. Jayagopal, K, 1981)
Mareyada Manikya (Vijay, K, 1985)
Mareyade Mahalu (A.V. Sheshgiri Rao, K, 1984)
Margadarshi (M.R. Vittal, K, 1969)
Margayya the Banker *see* **Banker Margayya**
Marhi Da Deeva/Deep (**Surinder Singh**, P/H, 1989)
Mariakutty (**P. Subramanyam**, Mal, 1958)
Mariamman (L.S. Ramachandran, Tam, 1948)
Mariamman Thiruvizha (Venkatesh, Tam, 1978)
Maria my Darling (**Durai**, Tam/K, 1980)
Mari Bena (Shantilal Soni, G, 1980)
Marichika (Amulya Manna, A, 1972)
Marichika (?, Neeraj Prod, H, 1988)
Marich Sangbad (Arun Mukherjee, B, 1983)
Mari Dhaniyani (*aka* My Wife: **Homi Master**, St, 1925)
Mari Hel Utaro Raj (**Manhar Raskapur**, G, 1977)
Marikkozhunthu (Pudhiyavan, Tam, 1991)
Marikkunnilla Gnan (P.K. Radhakrishnan, Mal, 1988)
Mari Laaj Rakhje Veera (Shantilal Soni, G, 1987)
Marina Manishi (**C.S. Rao**, Tel, 1970)
Mari Nanandino Vir (M.N. Siddiqui, G, 1979)
Marine Drive (**G.P. Sippy**, H, 1955)
Marjina Abdallah (**Dinen Gupta**, B, 1972)
Markandeya (*aka* Shiv Leela: **R. Nataraja Mudaliar**, St, 1923)
Markandeya (**Baburao Painter**, St, 1923)
Markandeya (**Murugadasa/K. Ramnoth**, Tam, 1935)
Markandeya (**Ch. Narayanamurthy**, Tel, 1938)
Marketplace, The *see* **Mandi**
Mark of Zero *see* Gol Nishan
Marmabani (**Sushil Majumdar**, B, 1958)
Marmagal (Kartick Raghunathan, Tam, 1988)
Marmaram (**B.G. Bharathan**, Mal, 1982)
Marmaveeran (**T.R. Raghunath**, Tam, 1956)
Marmayogi/Ek Tha Raja (**K. Ramnoth**, Tam/H, 1951)
Marmayogi (B.A. Subba Rao, Tel, 1964)
Mar Mitenge (Kawal Sharma, H, 1988)
Maro Charithra (**K. Balachander**, Tel, 1978)
Maro Maya Bazaar (**C.S. Rao**, Tel, 1983)
Maro Monagadu (G.C. Shekhar, Tel, 1985)
Maro Prapancham (**Adurthi Subba Rao**, Tel, 1970)
Maro Rasiyo Sajan (Vijay B. Chauhan, G, 1986)
Maro Seeta Katha (N. Gopalakrishnan, Tel, 1979)
Marriage and After (**Shantaram Athavale**, E, 1962)
Marriage Bureau (Subroto Bannerjee, H, 1983)
Marriage Market *see* Biyer Bazaar
Marriage Market (Bachubabu, St, 1926)
Marriage Tonic, The (**Dhiren Ganguly**, St, 1923)
Married Life is like Electricity *see* **Samsaram Athu Minsaram**
Martanda Varma (P.V. Rao, St, 1931)
Marte Dam Tak (**Mehul Kumar**, H, 1987)
Martial Dances of Malabar (**Paul Zils**, E, 1958)
Martyr *see* Qurbani
Martyrs of Love *see* Sneh Samadhi
Marudu Nattu Veeran (**T.R. Raghunath**, Tam, 1961)
Marudu Pandi (**Manoj Kumar**, Tam, 1990)
Maruepiravi (Ramanna, Tam, 1973)
Marumagal *see* **Ammalakulu**
Marumagal (S.K. Chari, Mal, 1952)
Marumagal (Kartick Raghunathan, Tam, 1986)
Marumagaley Varuga (**L.V. Prasad**/Kalindhi, Tam, 1982)
Marumalarchi (Lanka Sathyam/**K.S. Prakash Rao**, Tam, 1956)
Marunattil Oru Malayali (A.B. Raj, Mal, 1971)
Marupadiyam (**Balu Mahendra**, Tam, 1993)
Marupakkam (**K.S. Sethumadhavan**, Tam, 1990)
Marupatta Konangal (Erode N. Murugesh, Tam, 1983)
Maruppacha (S. Babu, Mal, 1982)
Marupurani Katha (V. Ramchandrao Rao, Tel, 1967)
Maruthanattu Ilavarasi (A. Kasilingam, Tam, 1950)
Maruthani (A. Ramarajan, Tam, 1985)
Maruthi (K.V. Thyagarajan, Tam, 1986)
Maruthi Vijayam *see* Lanka Dahanam
Marutirtha Hinglaj (Bikash Roy, B, 1959)
Marutrisha (Suresh Roy, B, 1964)
Marvel Man (B.J. Patel, H, 1964)
Marwad's Moti *see* Amarsinh Daggar

Marwarni Malan (Shridatt Vyas, G, 1988)
Maryada (Digambar Chatterjee, B, 1950)
Maryada (Aravind Sen, H, 1971)
Maryada (Chiranjit, B, 1989)
Maryade Mahalu (A.V. Sheshgiri Rao, K, 1984)
Masala (Srinivas Krishna, E, 1991)
Masappadi Mathupilla (A.N. Thampi, Mal, 1973)
Mashaal/Samar (**Nitin Bose**, H/B, 1950)
Mashaal (**Yash Chopra**, H, 1984)
Mashuq (Humayun Mirza/Sharukh Mirza/Mahrukh Mirza, H, 1992)
Mashuqa (Shanti Kumar, H, 1953)
Mashuqa (Arati Bhattacharya, H, 1987)
Masked Cavalier *see* Bhedi Sawar
Masked Rider *see* Gaibi Sawar
Masked Terror *see* Kala Pahad
Masoom (S.F. Hasnain, H, 1941)
Masoom (**Satyen Bose**, H, 1960)
Masoom (**Shekhar Kapur**/Sibte Hasan Rizvi, H, 1982)
Masquerade *see* **Marattam**
Massey Sahib (Pradeep Kishen, H, 1985)
Mastan (Ashim Samanta, B, 1989)
Mastana *see* Diljani
Mastana (**H.S. Rawail**, H, 1954)
Mastana (**Adurthi Subba Rao**, H, 1970)
Mastana Mashuq (A.M. Khan, H, 1936)
Mastana Mehboob (*aka* Wild Rose: Prafulla Ghosh, St, 1931)
Mastan Dada (**Satyen Bose**, H, 1977)
Mastani (**Dhirubhai Desai**, H, 1955)
Master Carpenter, The *see* Perumthachan
Masterji (Krishna Gopal, H, 1943)
Masterji (**Durga Khote**/Neelkanth Magdum, H, 1964)
Masterji (**K. Raghavendra Rao**, H, 1985)
Master Kiladi (M.M. Rao, Tel, 1971)
Master Liar *see* Alik Babu
Master Madras (V. Ramachandra, Tam, 1968)
Master Man *see* Ustad
Master, Mistress, Servant *see* **Sahib Bibi Aur Ghulam**
Masterpiece, The *see* Shahkar
Master Stroke *see* Mardna Gha
Master Villain *see* Uthavgar
Mast Fakir (*aka* Fall of Vijayanagar: **Homi Master**, St, 1930)
Mast Fakir (D.N. Madhok, H, 1934)
Mastikhor Mashuq (*aka* Sweet Angel: G.P. Pawar, St, 1932)
Mast Kalandar (Kedar Kapoor, H, 1955)
Mast Kalandar (**Rahul Rawail**, H, 1991)
Mastuto Bhai (**Dhiren Ganguly**, B, 1933)
Mata (*aka* Mother: Dada Gunjal, H, 1942)
Mata Agameshwari (Arun Choudhury, B, 1983)
Mata Da Darbar (Kunwar Jagdish, P, 1982)
Mata Gomata (Ramanarayanan, Tam, 1992)
Mata Mahakali (**Dhirubhai Desai**, H, 1968)
Matamgi Manipur (Deb Kumar Bose, Manipuri, 1972)
Mata Vaishno Devi (Satish Kumar, H, 1971)
Matevin Bal (Madhav Velankar, Mar, 1958)
Mathangal 7 (Yugi Sethu, Tam, 1993)
Mathavi Vandal (Nathigam Ramaswamy, Tam, 1980)
Mathe Hadithu Kogile (Bhargava, K, 1990)
Matheye Maha Mandira (B.C. Srinivas, K, 1968)
Mathilukal (**Adoor Gopalakrishnan**, Mal, 1989)
Mathiyum Mamathaiyum (G.M. Basheer, Tam, 1954)
Math No Sadhu (*aka* Devil of the Cave: **Kanjibhai Rathod**, St, 1930)
Mathondu Charithre (B. Mallesh, K, 1986)
Mathru Bhoomi (**H.M. Reddy**, Tam, 1939)
Mathru Bhoomi (M.S. Gopinath, K, 1969)
Mathrudevata (**K. Savitri**, Tel, 1969)
Mathru Devo Bhava (N.S. Dhananjaya, K, 1988)
Mathru Devo Bhava (K. Ajayakumar, Tel, 1993)
Mathru Dharma *see* Tamil Thayi
Mathru Murthi (Manapuram Appa Rao, Tel, 1972)
Mathulai Muthukal (K.M. Balakrishnan, Tam, 1982)
Mathur (Sudhirbandhu Bannerjee, B, 1957)
Mathura Vijay (A. Sanjivi, O, 1979)
Mathurkula Manikyam/Charanadasi (**T. Prakash Rao**, Tam/Tel 1956)
Mati Manas (**Mani Kaul**, H, 1984)
Mati Mange Khoon (**Raj Khosla**, H, 1984)
Mati-o-Manush (Sudhirbandhu Bannerjee, B, 1948)
Matir Ghar (Hari Bhanja, B, 1944)
Mati Ri Aan (?, Kangaroo Pics, Bikaner: R, 1990)
Matir Manisha (*aka* Two Brothers: **Mrinal Sen**, O, 1966)
Matir Swarga (Anil Choudhury, A, 1963)
Matir Swarga (Bijoy Bose, B, 1982)
Matlabi (**Master Bhagwan**, H, 1948)
Matlabi (?, Prerana Movies, H, 1989)
Matlabi Duniya (*aka* Neglected Wife: **Jayant Desai**, H, 1936)
Matlabi Duniya (Radhakant M. Thakur, H, 1961)
Matran Thottathu Malligai (Vijayasarathi, Tam, 1984)
Matravai Neril (Mouli, Tam, 1980)
Matribhakta Ramprasad (Manu Sen, B, 1980)
Matrihara (Gunamaya Bannerjee, B, 1946)
Matri Prem (*aka* For Mother's Sake: **M. Bhavnani**, St, 1925)
Matri Sneh (*aka* A Mother's Devotion: **Jyotish Bannerjee**?, St, 1922)
Matru Bhakti *see* Aankh Ka Tara
Matrubhoomi (*aka* My Hero: **Nagendra Majumdar**, St, 1932)
Matrubhoomi (Ishwarlal, H, 1949)
Matsyagandha (*aka* Bhishma Pratigya, Mahigir Ki Ladki: Dakubhai Mehta, H, 1934)
Matsya Varah Avatar (?, Star Films, St, 1923)
Matter of Honour, A *see* **Muthal Mariyathai**
Matter of Style, A *see* **Andaz**
Matte Vasantha (Ravi, K, 1983)
Mattilo Manikyam (B.V. Prasad, Tel, 1971)
Matti Manushulu (**B. Narasinga Rao**, Tel, 1990)
Mattoli (**A. Bhimsingh**, Mal, 1978)
Mattoral (**K.G. George**, Mal, 1988)
Mattoru Karnan (**Sasikumar**, Mal, 1978)
Mattoru Pranaye Katha (?, Mal, 1988)
Mattoru Seeta (**P. Bhaskaran**, Mal, 1975)
Mattukkara Mannaru (?, Tam, 1986)
Mattukkara Velan (**P. Neelakantan**, Tam, 1969)
Mattuvin Chattangale (Rajsharan, Mal, 1982)
Matu Tappada Maga (Pekati Shivram, K, 1978)
Matwala (M.A. Thirumugham, H, 1958)
Matwala Shayar Ramjoshi *see* **Lokshahir Ramjoshi**
Matwale (**Master Bhagwan**, H, 1947)
Matwali Jogan (**K. Amarnath**, H, 1936)
Matwali Meera (*aka* Meerabai: Prafulla Roy/K. Sharma, P, 1940)
Mauj (Batuk Bhatt/**Babubhai Mistri**, H, 1943)
Maujan Dubai Diyan (Subhash Bhakri, P, 1985)
Mauji Jeevan (Poonawala, H, 1944)
Mauj Majah (**Nanubhai Vakil**?, H, 1944)
Maula Jatt (Mohan Bhakri, P, 1988)
Maurya Patan (*aka* Fall of the Mauryas: **R.S. Choudhury**, St 1929)
Mausam (**S.S. Gulzar**, H, 1975)
Mausi (Prabhat Kumar, H, 1958)
Maut Ka Toofan (*aka* Storm of Death: Henry Dargowitz, H, 1935)
Maut Ki Sazaa (Devendra Khandelwal, H, 1989)
Mavalli Circle (T.N. Narasimhachari, K, 1986)
Mavana Magalu (S.K. Ananthachari, K, 1965)
Mavanige Thakka Aliya (V. Govinda Rao, K, 1992)
Mavano Aliyano (K.N. Chandrasekhar Sharma, K, 1985)
Mava Sose Saval (Amrutham, K, 1982)
Mavtar (Himmat Dave, G, 1981)
Mavva Gopaludu (Kodi Ramakrishna, Tel, 1987)
Mawaali (**K. Bapaiah**, H, 1983)
Maya (**P.C. Barua**, B/H, 1936)
Maya (D.D. Kashyap, H, 1961)
Maya (Nirmal Sarvajna, B, 1969)
Maya (**Ramu Kariat**, Mal, 1972)
Maya *see* Maya Memsaab
Maya Bazaar (**Baburao Painter**, St, 1925)
Maya Bazaar (*aka* Surekha Haran: **Nanubhai Vakil**, H, 1932)
Maya Bazaar (*aka* Vatsala Kalyanam: **R. Padmanabhan**, Tam, 1935)
Maya Bazaar (*aka* Sasirekha Parinayam: P.V. Dasu, Tel, 1936)
Maya Bazaar (G.P. Pawar, Mar, 1939)
Maya Bazaar (*aka* Vatsala Haran: **Datta Dharmadhikari**, H/Mar, 1949)
Maya Bazaar (**K.V. Reddy**, Tel/Tam, 1957)
Maya Bazaar (**Babubhai Mistri**, H, 1958)
Maya Bazaar (?, Sadashiv Chitra, H, 1971)
Maya Bazaar (**Babubhai Mistri**, G/H, 1984)
Mayabee (*aka* Mystery Man: Becharam Ghosh, St, 1930)
Mayabha Mahtari (Mansingh, Bh, 1984)
Mayabini Lane (Kanak Mukherjee, B, 1966)
Mayadari Alludu (K.S.R. Doss, Tel, 1981)
Mayadari Krishnudu (R. Thyagarajan, Tel, 1980)
Mayadari Malligadu (**Adurthi Subba Rao**, Tel, 1973)
Mayadari Maridi (Leela Varaprasad, Tel, 1985)
Mayadari Mogudu (**K. Bhagyaraj**, Tel, 1984)
Mayadari Mosagadu (Y. Nageshwara Rao, Tel, 1993)
Maya Darpan (**Kumar Shahani**, H, 1972)
Mayadore (?, Ramakrishna Films, Calcutta, H, 1949)
Mayagadu (B.L.V. Prasad, Tel, 1983)
Maya Jaal (*aka* Satan Weeps, Jung-e-Ulfat: Shanti L. Dave, H, 1933)
Maya Jaal (*aka* Jadugar: **Babubhai Mistri**, H, 1962)
Mayajal (Amar Dutta, B, 1949)
Maya Jyothi (**R. Padmanabhan**, Tam, 1941)
Maya Kajal (Tulsi Lahiri, B, 1937)
Maya Kanan (**P.C. Barua** et al., B, 1953)
Mayakkari *see* Mayalamari
Mayakkum Mohini (?, A.K. Films, Tam, 1971)
Maya Kudhirai *see* **Keeluguram**
Mayalaadi (P. Chandrasekhara Reddy, Tel, 1985)
Mayalamari/Mayakkari (P. Sridhar, Tel/Tam, 1951)
Mayalokam (**Gudavalli Ramabrahmam**, Tel, 1945)
Maya Machhindra (**V. Shantaram**, Mar/H, 1932)
Maya Machhindra (**Raja Chandrasekhar**, Tam, 1939)
Maya Machhindra (**C. Pullaiah**, Tel, 1945)
Maya Machhindra/Gorakhnath (Aspi, H/Mar, 1951)
Maya Machhindra (**Babubhai Mistri**, H, 1960)
Maya Machhindra (*aka* Illusion: S.N. Tripathi, H, 1975)
Maya Machhindra (**Babubhai Mistri**, Tel, 1975)
Maya Madhusudan (Sheshaiah?, **General Pics**.; St, 1931)
Maya Mahal (*aka* Magic Valley: **Nanubhai Desai**, St, 1928)
Maya Mahal (K. Talpade, H, 1949)
Maya Mahal (**Chandrakant**, H, 1963)
Mayamalai *see* Tilottama
Maya Manithan (T.P. Sundaram, Tam, 1958)
Maya Manushya (K.V.S. Kutumba Rao, K, 1976)
Maya Mayavan (B. Sampathkumar, Tam, 1938)
Maya Mayuram (**Sibi Malayil**, Mal, 1993)
Maya Memsaab (*aka* The Enchanting Illusion: **Ketan Mehta**, H, 1992)
Maya Miriga (**Nirad Mahapatra**, O, 1983)
Maya Mohini (?, Gujarat Film, St, 1928)
Maya Mohini (Kommineni, Tel, 1985)
Maya Mothiram (B.V. Srinivas, Tam, 1967)
Maya Mriga *see* **Maya Miriga**
Maya Mriga (Kali Chakraborty, B, 1941)
Maya Mriga (Chitta Bose, B, 1960)
Maya Nagari (*aka* Mahasati Madalasa: **Dhirubhai Desai**, H, 1944)
Maya Nagari (A.M. Khan, H, 1957)
Maya Na Rang (*aka* Enticement: **Dhirubhai Desai/Sundarrao Nadkarni**, St, 1928)
Mayandi (R. Pattabhiraman, Tam, 1979)
Mayangurikal Oru Madhu (S.P. Muthuraman, Tam, 1975)
Mayani Mamata (**K. Kameshwara Rao**, Tel, 1970)
Mayapilla (**R.S. Prakash**, Tel, 1951)
Maya Rambha/Maya Rambai (**T.R. Sundaram**, Tel/Tam, 1950)
Mayar Sansar (Kanak Mukherjee, B, 1962)
Maya Sundari (**A.S.A. Sami**, H, 1967)
Mayavathi (**T.R. Sundaram**, Tam, 1949)
Mayavi (G.K. Ramu, Mal, 1965)
Mayavi (Rajakumar, Tel, 1976)
Mayavi Jaal (TV: **Chandrakant Sangani**, H, 1992)
Mayavi Nagari (*aka* Magic City: **Dhirubhai Desai**, St, 1929)
May Bahini (**Dinkar D. Patil**, Mar, 1952)
Mayecha Pazhar (Madhav Shinde, Mar, 1952)
Mayer Ashirbad (Parimal Ghosh, B, 1982)
Mayer Dak (Sukumar Mukherjee, B, 1948)
Mayer Pran (**P.C. Barua**, B, 1941)
Mayeya Musuku (B.Y. Ramadas, K, 1980)
Mayil (**Durai**, Tam, 1981)
Mayiladum Kunnu (S. Babu, Mal, 1972)
Mayilanji (M. Krishnan Nair, Mal, 1982)
Mayil Ravana (*aka* Maitreyi Vijayam: **R. Nataraja Mudaliar**, St, 1918)
May I Think Sir? (**Prakash Jha**, E, 1983)
May Maooli (Yeshwant Pethkar, Mar, 1971)
Mayor Meenakshi (Madurai Thirumaran, Tam, 1976)
Mayor Muthanna (Siddalingaiah, K, 1969)
Mayor Nair (**Puttanna Kanagal**, Mal, 1966)
Mayura (Vijay, K, 1975)
Mayurdhwaja (V.T. Choudhury, Tam, 1938)
Mayuri (Biren Bhattacharya, H, 1978)
Mayuri (Birendra, H, 1985)
Mayuri (**Singeetham Srinivasa Rao**, Tel, 1985)
Mayurpankh (**Kishore Sahu**, H, 1954)
Mazaaq (Zahur Raja, H, 1943)
Mazaaq (A. Kumar, H, 1975)
Mazdoor (**M. Bhavnani**, H, 1934)
Mazdoor (**Nitin Bose**, H, 1945)
Mazdoor (Ravi Chopra, H, 1983)
Mazdoor Ki Beti *see* Dhanwan
Mazdoor Zindabad (Naresh Kumar, H, 1976)
Maze Le Lo (Kumar Vasudev, H, 1975)
Mazha Hoshil Ka? (**Anant Mane**, Mar, 1963)
Mazhai Megam (A.S. Prakasham, Tam, 1976)
Mazhakkala Megham (Rajendran, Mal, 1985)
Mazhakkaru (**P.N. Menon**, Mal, 1974)
Mazhalai Pattalam (Lakshmi, Tam, 1980)
Mazha Mulga/Mera Ladka (**K. Narayan Kale**, Mar/H, 1938)
Mazha Mulga (Yeshwant Pethkar, Mar, 1976)
Mazha Pati Karodpati (Sachin, Mar, 1988)
Mazha Peyyunnu Maddalam Kottunnu (**Priyadarshan**, Mal, 1986)
Mazha Ram (Dada Gunjal, Mar, 1949)
Mazhavil Kavadi (Sathyan Andhikkad, Mal, 1989)
Mazhe Bal (**Master Vinayak**, Mar, 1943)
Mazhe Ghar Majhi Manse (**Raja Thakur**, Mar, 1956)
Mazhe Ghar Mazha Sansar (**Rajdutt**, Mar, 1986)
Mazhu (?, Manjulay Films, Mal, 1982)
Mazloom (C.P. Dixit, H, 1986)
Mechanic Alludu (B. Gopal, Tel, 1993)
Mechhida Madumaga (C. Palraj, K, 1992)
Medicinal Drugs (**Pradeep Krishen**, E, 1977)
Meech Tujhi Priya (**Datta Keshav**, Mar, 1970)
Meen (**I.V. Sasi**, Mal, 1980)
Meena (*aka* Vanarani: **Phani Majumdar**, H, 1944)
Meena (**Vijayanirmala**, Tel, 1973)
Meena Bazaar (**Ravindra Dave**, H, 1950)
Meena Bazaar (P. Chandrakumar, H, 1991)
Meenakshi (**Modhu Bose**, B/H, 1942)
Meenakshi (Ramanarayanan/D. Kandaswamy, Tam, 1980)
Meenakshi Kalyanam (**R. Padmanabhan**, Tam, 1940)
Meenakshi Kumkumam (K. Narayanan, Tam, 1978)
Meenakshi Thiruvilayadal (K. Shankar, Tam, 1989)
Meena Kumari Ki Amar Kahani (**Sohrab Modi**, H, 1979)
Meenamasathile Sooryan (**Lenin Rajendran**, Mal, 1985)

Meenar (**Hemen Gupta**, H, 1954)
Meenavan (K.S. Ramadas, Tam, 1969)
Meenava Nanban (**C.V. Sridhar**, Tam, 1977)
Meenda Sorgam (**C.V. Sridhar**, Tam, 1960)
Meendum Kokila (G.N. Rangarajan, Tam, 1981)
Meendum Mahan (Uthaman, Tam, 1987)
Meendum Oru Kadhal Kadai (**Prathap Pothan**, Tam, 1984)
Meendum Pallavi (A.P. Jagadish, Tam, 1985)
Meendum Parasakthi (A. Jagannathan, Tam, 1985)
Meendum Sandhippam (M.A. Raja, Tam, 1981)
Meendum Vazhvan (T.N. Balu, Tam, 1971)
Meera (**Ellis Duncan**, Tam/H, 1945)
Meera (**S.S. Gulzar**, H, 1979)
Meerabai *see* Matwali Meera
Meerabai (**Kanjibhai Rathod**, St, 1921)
Meerabai (Ramnik Desai, H, 1932)
Meerabai/Rajrani Meera (**Debaki Bose**, B/H, 1933)
Meerabai (**A. Narayanan**/T.C. Vadivelu Naicker, Tam, 1936)
Meerabai (**Bhimavarapu Narasimha Rao**, Tel, 1940)
Meerabai (**Nanabhai Bhatt**, G, 1947)
Meerabai (W.Z. Ahmed, H, 1947)
Meera Ka Chitra (**Kidar Sharma**, H, 1960)
Meera Ka Mohan (K. Ravishankar, H, 1992)
Meera Ke Girdhar (Vijay Deep, H, 1993)
Meera Shyam (Satish Kumar, H, 1976)
Meetha Zaher (*aka* She-wolf: A.P. Kapur, St, 1930)
Meetha Zaher (**Sohrab Modi**, H, 1938)
Meetha Zaher (Mohinder, H, 1985)
Meeth Bhakar (**Bhalji Pendharkar**, Mar, 1949)
Meethi Churi (*aka* Eye for an Eye: Madanrai Vakil, St, 1931)
Meethi Meethi Baatein (**K. Balachander**, H, 1977)
Meethi Nazar (**Harshadrai Mehta**, H, 1935)
Meet Mere Man Ke (**Mehul Kumar**, H, 1991)
Megathukum Daagham Undu (S. Jagadeeshan, Tam, 1980)
Megh (**Utpal Dutt**, B, 1961)
Megh (**Atul Bordoloi**, A, 1979)
Megha Mandhra (K. Vojayaram, K, 1992)
Megham Karuthiukku (Ramanarayanan, Tam, 1987)
Meghamukti (Bandhu, A, 1979)
Meghamukti (Binu Bardhan, O, 1980)
Megha Sandesam (**Dasari Narayana Rao**, Tel, 1982)
Meghdoot (**Debaki Bose**, H, 1945)
Meghe Dhaka Tara (**Ritwik Ghatak**, B, 1960)
Megher Pare Megh (Ajit Bandyopadhyay, B, 1973)
Megh Kalo (Sushil Mukherjee, B, 1970)
Meghla Bhanga Rodh (Tilak Dutta, B, 1983)
Megh Malhar (Pinaki Mukherjee, B, 1958)
Meghmukti (Chitta Bose, B, 1952)
Meghmukti (**Tarun Majumdar**, B, 1981)
Megh-o-Roudra (**Arundhati Devi**, B, 1969)
Mehak (Chander Behl, H, 1985)
Meharbaan (**A. Bhimsingh**, H, 1967)
Meharbaan (K. Ravi Shankar, H, 1993)
Meharbani (**K. Amarnath**, H, 1950)
Meharbani (Ajit Singh Deol/A. Nairang, H, 1982)
Mehbooba (**K. Amarnath**, H, 1954)
Mehbooba (A. Karim, H, 1965)
Mehbooba (**Shakti Samanta**, H, 1976)
Mehboob Ki Mehndi (**H.S. Rawail**, H, 1971)
Mehboob Mere Mehboob (Raman Jit Juneja, H, 1992)
Mehfil (A. Karim, H, 1957)
Mehfil (Amar Kumar, H, 1978)
Mehlon Ke Khwab (Hyder, H, 1960)
Mehmaan (*aka* The Guest: **Chaturbhuj Doshi**, H, 1942)
Mehmaan (**Ramanand Sagar**, H, 1953)
Mehmaan (**K.P. Atma**, H, 1973)
Mehmil (Bibhuti Mitra, H, 1972)
Mehndi (S. Fazli, H, 1947)
Mehndi (S.M. Yusuf, H, 1958)
Mehndi (**Asit Sen**, H, 1983)
Mehndi Ban Gayi Khoon (R.S. Ghelani, H, 1991)
Mehndi Lagi Mere Haath (Suraj Prakash, H, 1962)
Mehndino Rang (Kishore Vyas, G, 1981)
Mehndi Rang Lagyo (**Manhar Raskapur**, G, 1960)
Mehndi Rang Layegi (**Dasari Narayana Rao**, H, 1982)
Mehulo Luhar (Jasubhai Trivedi, G, 1981)
Meja Jamai (Shri Bhaskar, B, 1958)
Mejdidi (Sabhyasachi, B, 1950)
Mejo Bou (Debnarayan Gupta, B, 1955)
Mela (S.U. Sunny, H, 1948)
Mela (**Prakash Mehra**, H, 1971)
Mela (*aka* Festival: **K.G. George**, Mal, 1980)
Melam Kootu Thalli Kattu (Deenadayal, Tam, 1988)
Melathalangal (R. Pattabhiraman/Swarnam, Tam, 1978)
Mele Mitran De (J. Samra/S. Bhakri, P, 1972)
Meleprambil Aan Veedu (Rajasenan, Mal, 1993)
Mellappesungal (Bharativasu, Tam, 1983)
Mella Thirandathu Kathavu (A. Sundarrajan, Tam, 1986)
Mel Maruvathur Adi Parasakthi (S. Jagadeeshan, Tam, 1985)
Mel Maruvathur Arputhangal (S. Jagadeeshan, Tam, 1986)
Melnattu Marumagal (**A.P. Nagarajan**, Tam, 1975)
Melukolupu (**K.S. Prakash Rao**, Tel, 1956)
Melukolupu (B.V. Prasad, Tel, 1978)
Memdidi (**Hrishikesh Mukherjee**, H, 1961)
Memory Episodes *see* **Smritichitre**
Memsaab (**Atma Ram**, H, 1971)
Mem Sahib (R.C. Talwar, H, 1956)
Mem Sahib (Pinaki Mukherjee, B, 1972)
Memu Manushulame (**K. Bapaiah**, Tel, 1973)
Memu Meelanti Manushulame (Jessie S. Barnabbas, Tel, 1984)
Mena Gurjari (Dinesh Rawal, G, 1975)
Menaka (**Raja Sandow**, Tam, 1935)
Menaka (V.C. Subbaraman, Tam, 1955)
Menakodalu (B.S. Narayana, Tel, 1972)
Mena Kumari (**M. Bhavnani**, St, 1926)
Menamama (Rajasekhara Reddy, Tel, 1987)
Menarikam (Jampana, Tel, 1954)
Menechippu Thurannapol (**Balachandra Menon**, Mal, 1985)
Mera Bhai Mera Dushman (Mohammed Hussain, H, 1967)
Mera Desh Mera Dharam (**Dara Singh**, H, 1973)
Mera Dharam (**Bapu**, H, 1986)
Mera Dharam Meri Maa (**Bhupen Hazarika**, H, 1976)
Mera Dil Tere Liye (S.A. Chandrasekharan, H, 1991)
Mera Dost (Roshanlal Malhotra, H, 1969)
Mera Dost Mera Dushman (**Raj Khosla**, H, 1984)
Mera Faisla (**S.V. Rajendra Singh**, H, 1984)
Mera Farz (R.P. Swamy, H, 1989)
Mera Gaon (*aka* My Village: Prafulla Roy, H, 1942)
Mera Gaon Mera Desh (**Raj Khosla**, H, 1971)
Mera Geet (Shantikumar, H, 1946)
Mera Ghar Mere Bachche (**Sohrab Modi**, H, 1960)
Mera Ghar Mere Bachche (Chander Vora, H, 1985)
Mera Haq *see* Sukhacha Shodh
Mera Haq (Ajay Kashyap, H, 1986)
Mera Imaan (**Nagendra Majumdar**, H, 1934)
Mera Inteqam (S.P.M. Raman, H, 1985)
Mera Jawab (Raj Bharath, H, 1985)
Mera Jeevan (Bindu Shukla, H, 1976)
Mera Karam Mera Dharam (Dulal Guha, H, 1987)
Mera Kasoor Kya Hai (**Krishnan-Panju**, H, 1964)
Mera Khwab (*aka* My Dream: Hansraj Patel/Nizam, H, 1943)
Mera Ladka *see* **Mazha Mulga**
Mera Lahu (Veerendra, H, 1987)
Mera Mahi (Shankar Mehta, P, 1941)
Mera Munna (**Vishram Bedekar**, H, 1948)
Mera Munna (Madhusudhan, H, 1967)
Mera Muqaddar (K. Pappu, H, 1989)
Mera Naam Johar (Sarankant, H, 1967)
Mera Naam Joker (**Raj Kapoor**, H, 1970)
Mera Naseeb (S. Karnan, H, 1990)
Mera Pati Sirf Mera Hai (Manobala, H, 1990)
Mera Punjab (Krishnadev Mehra?, P/H, 1940)
Mera Pyar *see* My Love
Mera Pyara (*aka* My Beloved: **Ezra Mir**, H, 1935)
Mera Rakshak (R. Thyagaraj, H, 1978)
Mera Saathi (**K. Raghavendra Rao**, H, 1985)
Mera Saaya (**Raj Khosla**, H, 1966)
Mera Salaam (Harbans, H, 1957)
Mera Salaam (G. Ishwar, H, 1980)
Mera Shikar (Kamran, H, 1973)
Mera Shikar (Keshu **Ramsay**, H, 1988)
Mera Suhaag (**Amiya Chakravarty**, H, 1947)
Mera Suhaag (**Hunsur Krishnamurthy**, H, 1961)
Mera Suhaag (Ajay Sharma, H, 1987)
Mera Vachan Geeta Ki Kasam (Vinod Kumar, H, 1974)
Mera Watan (*aka* My Country: My Kingdom: Inamdar, H, 1939)
Mera Yaar Mera Dushman (Anil Ganguly, H, 1987)
Merchant of Arabia *see* Char Darvesh
Merchant of Venice (*aka* Zalim Saudagar: **J.J. Madan**, H, 1941)
Mere Apne (**S.S. Gulzar**, H, 1971)
Mere Arman Mere Sapne (Aravind Sen, H, 1963)
Mere Baad (Vishwamitra, H, 1988)
Mere Bhagwan (Mohan Sinha, H, 1947)
Mere Bhaiya (**Satyen Bose**, H, 1972)
Mere Garib Nawaz (G. Ishwar, H, 1973)
Mere Humdum Mere Dost (Amar Kumar, H, 1968)
Mere Humsafar (Dulal Guha, H, 1970)
Mere Huzoor (Vinod Kumar, H, 1968)
Mere Jeevan Saathi (Ravi Nagaich, H, 1972)
Mere Lal (Dada Gunjal, H, 1937)
Mere Lal (Bal Gajbar, H, 1948)
Mere Lal (**Satyen Bose**, H, 1966)
Mere Mehboob (**H.S. Rawail**, U, 1963)
Mere Raja (T.M. Mani, H, 1941)
Mere Raja (Ram Narayan Dave, H, 1949)
Mere Sajan (*aka* Midnight Angel: A.H. Essa, H, 1941)
Mere Sajna (Kewal Kumar, H, 1975)
Mere Sajna Saath Nibhana (Rajesh Vakil, H, 1992)
Mere Sanam (Amar Kumar, H, 1965)
Mere Sartaj (**A.R. Kardar**, H, 1975)
Meri Aan (Roopesh Kumar, H, 1993)
Meri Aankhen (*aka* My Eyes: Dwarka Khosla, H, 1939)
Meri Adalat (A.T. Raghu, H, 1984)
Meri Amanat (P. Gupte/S. Sutar, H, 1947)
Meri Asha (Dr Alam, H, 1950)
Meri Awaaz Suno (**S.V. Rajendra Singh**, Hind, 1981)
Meri Bahen (**Hemchandra Chunder**, H, 1944)
Meri Bahen (**A.S.A. Sami**, H, 1962)
Meri Bhabhi (?, Jubilee Pics, H, 1948)
Meri Bhabhi (Khalid Akhtar, H, 1969)
Meri Bhool (*aka* Kunwari Patni, Repentance: Shaily Ghosh, H, 1937)
Meri Biwi Ki Shaadi (Rajat Rakshit, H, 1979)
Meri Dosti Mera Pyar (A. Brij, H, 1977)
Meri Duniya (*aka* Umar Marvi: Mazhar Khan, H, 1942)
Meri Izzat Bachao (?, Devi Films, H, 1984)
Meri Jaan (*aka* Romantic Prince: Prafulla Ghosh, H, 1931)
Meri Jaaneman (Chander Sharma, H, 1992)
Meri Jung (**Subhash Ghai**, H, 1982)
Meri Kahani (Keki Mistry, H, 1948)
Meri Kahani (Asha Dutta, H, 1984)
Meri Khwaish (*aka* Khwaish, Desire: Harbanslal, R.D. Rajput, H, 1941)
Meri Lalkaar (Yash Chouhan, H, 1990)
Meri Maa (*aka* My Mother: K.P. Bhave, St, 1931)
Meri Mashuq (*aka* Divine Lady: Prafulla Ghosh, St, 1931)
Meri Soorat Teri Aankhen (R.K. Rakhan, H, 1963)
Meri Zabaan (Shibu Mitra, H, 1988)
Merry-go-round *see* Dorangi Duniya
Meru Malan (**Mehul Kumar**, G, 1985)
Meru Mulande (**Krishnakant**, G, 1980)
Merupu Dadi (N. Ramchandra Rao, Tel, 1984)
Message *see* Paigham
Methavigal (K. Vembu, Tam, 1955)
Metric Measures (**Govind Saraiya**, E, 1962)
Metric System, The (**Govind Saraiya**, E, 1958)
Metti (**J. Mahendran**, Tam, 1982)
Mewad No Mawali (*aka* Rogue of Rajasthan: Madanrai Vakil, St, 1930)
Mewad Nu Moti (*aka* Jewel of Rajputana: **B.P. Mishra**, St, 1929)
Mewadpati Bappa Rawal (?, Eastern Film, Baroda, St, 1925)
MGR Nagaril (Ashraf, Tam, 1991)
Mhari Pyari Chanana (Jatin Kumar, R, 1983)
Michael Madana Kamarajan (**Singeetham Srinivasa Rao**, Tam, 1990)
Michael Madhusudhan (**Modhu Bose**, B, 1950)
Michael Raj (V.C. Guhanathan, Tam, 1987)
Michcha Maya Sansar/Sansar (Uday Shankar Pani, O/B, 1989)
Michke Patash (Anim: Bhakta Ram Mitra, B, 1951)
Mi Daru Sodli (**Bhalji Pendharkar**, Mar, 1950)
Middle Fail (*aka* Ganwaar: Kishore Sharma, H, 1948)
Middleman, The *see* **Jana Aranya**
Midhunam (**Priyadarshan**, Mal, 1993)
Midida Hridayagalu (A.T. Raghu, K, 1993)
Midida Shruthi (M.S. Rajasekhar, K, 1992)
Midnight Angel *see* Mere Sajan
Midnight Girl *see* Nisha Sundari
Midnight Mail (**K. Amarnath**, H, 1939)
Midnight Man *see* Madh Raat Ka Mehmaan
Midnight Rider *see* Pahadi Pindharo
Midnight Romance *see* Raat Ki Rani
Midnight Tale *see* Raat Ki Baat
Midsummer Sun *see* **Meenamasathile Sooryan**
Midukki Ponnamma (A.B. Raj, Mal, 1978)
Midumidukki (Mani, Mal, 1968)
Mihi Manoosach Aahe (**Dinkar D. Patil**, Mar, 1971)
Milan *see* **Nauka Dubi**
Milan (**Jyotish Bannerjee**, B, 1942)
Milan (Kedar Kapoor, H, 1958)
Milan (**Adurthi Subba Rao**, H, 1967)
Milan Dinar (Fatma Begum, St, 1929)
Milan Ki Aag (K.R. Ranjan, H, 1992)
Milan Ki Raat (R. Bhattacharya, H, 1967)
Milan-Tithi (Sukhen Das, B, 1985)
Milap (**A.R. Kardar**, H, 1937)
Milap (**Raj Khosla**, H, 1955)
Milap (**B.R. Ishara**, H, 1972)
Mil Gayi Manzil Mujhe (Moeen Ahmed, H, 1988)
Mili (**Hrishikesh Mukherjee**, H, 1975)
Milk Maid *see* Gwalan
Mill, The *see* **Mazdoor**
Millionaire *see* Karodpati
Mill Thozhilali (A. Jagannathan, Tam, 1991)
Milne Ka Din (?, Ruby Films, H, 1952)
Minal Devi (*aka* The Sin Redeemed: **Kanjibhai Rathod**, St, 1923)
Minchina Belakalli (K.S. Satyanarayana, K, 1981)
Minchina Ota (**Shankar Nag**, K, 1980)
Mindapennu (**K.S. Sethumadhavan**, Mal, 1970)
Mind of Clay *see* **Mati Manas**
Minimol (**Sasikumar**, Mal, 1977)
Minimol Vathikanil (**I.V. Sasi**, Mal, 1984)
Minister (Ramanlal Desai, H, 1959)
Minister's Daughter, The *see* **Manthiri Kumari**
Minmini (T.V. Ramnath/Krishnaswamy, Tam, 1953)
Minmini Poochigal (Raghu Vyas, Tam, 1993)
Minnalkodi (**K. Amarnath**, Tam, 1937)
Minnal Padayali (G. Vishwanathan, Mal, 1959)
Minnal Veeran (Jampana, Tam, 1959)
Minnaminungu (**Ramu Kariat**, Mal, 1957)
Minnolveerakul (P.C. Reddy, Mal, 1985)

Minnunnathellan Ponnalla (R. Velappan, Mal, 1957)
Minoo (Pushp Raj, H, 1977)
Minor Babu (**T. Prakash Rao**, Tel, 1973)
Minorin Kadal (K.S. Mani, Tam, 1941)
Minor Raja (?, Rakesh Prod., Tel, 1991)
Minor Rajamani (**Raja Sandow**, Tam, 1937)
Minoti (Binoy Bannerjee, B, 1951)
Mint, The *see* **Taksaal**
Mirabai *see* Meerabai
Mirage, The *see* **Maya Miriga** *or* Mrigajaal
Mirch Masala (**Ketan Mehta**, H, 1985)
Mirror, The *see* Aaina
Mirror of Illusion *see* **Maya Darpan**
Mirza Ghalib (**Sohrab Modi**, U, 1954)
Mirza Ghalib (TV: **S.S. Gulzar**, H, 1988)
Mirza Jatt (Ravinder Ravi, P, 1992)
Mirza Sahiban *see* Ishq-e-Punjab
Mirza Sahiban (**B.P. Mishra**, St, 1929)
Mirza Sahiban (**Nagendra Majumdar**, H, 1933)
Mirza Sahiban (D.N. Madhok, P, 1939)
Mirza Sahiban (**K. Amarnath**, H, 1947)
Mirza Sahiban (Ravi Kapoor, H, 1957)
Misaal (Mirza Bros, H, 1985)
Misar Ka Khazana (Rajhans, H, 1935)
Misar Ka Sitara (*aka* Son of Desert: Minoo Katrak, H, 1935)
Misar Nu Moti (*aka* Pearl of Egypt: **Homi Master**, St, 1933)
Misbegotten, The *see* **Aakriet**
Miser *see* **Kanjan**
Mishar Rani (**Jyotish Bannerjee**, St, 1924)
Mi SM (**Jabbar Patel**, Mar, 1987)
Missamma/Missiamma (**L.V. Prasad**, Tel/Tam, 1955)
Miss Bangalore (P.S. Murthy, K, 1967)
Miss Beatty's Children (Pamela Rooks, E, 1992)
Miss Bombay (Kedar Kapoor, H, 1957)
Miss Calcutta *see* Nariraj
Miss Chaalbaaz (Pyarelal, H, 1961)
Miss Coca Cola (Kedar Kapoor, H, 1955)
Miss Devi (C.M. Trivedi, H, 1944)
Miss Dolly (**Harshadrai Mehta**, St, 1929)
Miss Frontier Mail (**Homi Wadia**, H, 1936)
Miss Goodnight (Jugal Kishore, H, 1960)
Miss Hunterwali (?, New Angel Films, H, 1959)
Missi (**Thoppil Bhasi**, Mal, 1976)
Missiamma *see* **Missamma**
Miss India (I.S. Johar, H, 1957)
Missing Bracelet *see* Indrajal
Mission Girl, The (*aka* Christian Kumari: **Homi Master**, St, 1927)
Mississippi Masala (**Mira Nair**, E, 1991))
Miss Kamala (**T.P. Rajalakshmi**, Tam, 1936)
Miss Leelavathi (M.R. Vittal, K, 1965)
Miss Lightning *see* Bijli
Miss Mala (**Jayant Desai**, H, 1954)
Miss Malini (Kothamangalam Subbu, Tam, 1947)
Miss Manorama (Faredoon R. Irani, H, 1935)
Miss Mary (**L.V. Prasad**, H, 1957)
Miss Mary (Jambu, Mal, 1972)
Miss 1933 (**Chandulal Shah**, H, 1933)
Miss 1949 *see* Galat Faimi
Miss 1958 (Kuldip Kumar, H, 1958)
Miss Priyambada (Rabi Basu/Dushyanta Choudhury, B, 1967)
Miss Punjab Mail (**Nanubhai Vakil**, H, 1958)
Miss Stella (**I.V. Sasi**, Mal, 1991)
Miss Sundari (**S. Soundararajan**, Tam, 1937)
Miss Toofan Mail (B.J. Patel, H, 1958)
Mr & Mrs (Sajan, Mal, 1992)
Mr & Mrs Bombay (**Nanubhai Vakil**, H, 1936)
Mr & Mrs Choudhury (Ashim Pal, B, 1961)
Mr and Mrs '55 (**Guru Dutt**, H, 1955)
Mr & Mrs Peacock (**Kantilal Rathod**, E, 1956)
Mr Ammanji (**K. Subramanyam**/C.S.V. Iyer. Tam, 1937)
Mr Bharat (Rajachandra, Tel, 1986)
Mr Bharat (S.P. Muthuraman, Tam, 1986)
Mr Bond (Raj Sippy, H, 1992)
Mr Chakram (**S.P. Bakshi**, H, 1955)
Mr Dynamite (M. Havewala, H, 1947)
Mr 420 *see* **Shri 420**
Mr 420 (Sorabji Kerawala, H, 1937)
Mr Hero (Satya Reddy, Tel, 1988)
Mr India (**G.P. Sippy**, H, 1961)
Mr India (**Shekhar Kapur**, H, 1987)
Mr Jhatpat (Harbans, H, 1943)
Mr John (Inder, H, 1959)
Mr Karthick (Kalaivannan, Tam, 1990)
Mr Kerala (?, Prathana Pics, Mal, 1969)
Mr Lambu (N.A. Ansari, H, 1956)
Mr Miehael (Williams, Mal, 1980)
Mr Murder (N.A. Ansari, H, 1969)
Mr Natwarlal (Rakesh Kumar, H, 1979)
Mr Pellam (**Bapu**, Tel, 1993)
Mr Prasad (P.S. Dharan, Tam, 1992)
Mr Q (K. Pervez, H, 1958)
Mr Qartoon M.A. (Ved-Madan, H, 1958)
Mr Raja (V. Somashekhar, K, 1987)
Mr Rajanikant (K.S.R. Doss, Tel, 1980)
Mr Rajkumar (**B.S. Ranga**, K, 1970)
Mr Romeo (Subhash Mukherjee, H, 1973)
Mr Sampat (**S.S. Vasan**, H, 1952)
Mr Sampath (Cho, Tam, 1972)
Mr Sundari (Dr Vasan, Mal, 1974)
Mr Superman Ki Wapasi *see* Return of Mr Superman
Mr Tight and Mr Loose (?, Sundaram Talkies, Tam, 1937)
Mr Toofan (Sheikh, H, 1943)
Mr Vijay (A. Kodandarami Reddy, Tel, 1984)
Mr X (Dwarka Khosla, H, 1938)
Mr X (**Nanabhai Bhatt**, H, 1957)
Mr X (*aka* Ek Aadmi: **K.A. Abbas**, H, 1984)
Mr X in Bombay (Shantilal Soni, H, 1964)
Mr Yogi (TV: **Ketan Mehta**, H, 1989)
Mithileya Seetheyaru (Ravi, K, 1988)
Mithuna (Mavinakare Ranganath, K, 1980)
Mithun Lagna (Shiva Bhattacharya, B, 1961)
Mittai Mummy (Avinashi Mani, Tam, 1976)
Mittar Pyare Noon (B.S. Shaad, P, 1975)
Mitti (Ravindra Jayakar, H, 1947)
Mitti Aur Sona (Shiv Kumar, H, 1989)
Mitti Ka Putla (*aka* Dolls of Clay: **Jayant Desai**, H, 1937)
Mitti Ke Khilone (Prahlad Dutt, H, 1948)
Mitti Mein Sona (Chandar Saigal, H, 1960)
Mi Tulas Tujhya Angani (**Raja Thakur**, Mar, 1955)
Mi Tuzha Pati Nahi (**Anant Mane**, Mar, 1973)
Mitwa (Govind Moonis, Bh, 1966)
Miya Bibi (*aka* Always Tell Your Wife: **Franz Osten**, H, 1936)
Miya Bibi Razi (Jyoti Swaroop, H, 1960)
Miya Fuski 007 (**Manhar Raskapur**, G, 1978)
Mizhigal (Suresh Menon, Mal, 1991)
Mizhineer Poovukkal (?, Shri Sai Prod, Mal, 1986)
Mizhiyithalil Kanneerumai (?, Mal, 1988)
Mizoram (**Harisadhan Dasgupta**, E, 1982)
MLA (K.B. Tilak, Tel, 1957)
MLA Yedukondalu (**Dasari Narayana Rao**, Tel, 1983)
Mochanam (**Thoppil Bhasi**, Mal, 1979)
Mock Marriage, The *see* **Gejje Pooje**
Modada Mareyalli (M.S. Rajashekhar, K, 1991)
Modala Rathri (Vijay, K, 1970)
Modalatedi/Mudhal Thedi (**P. Neelakantan**, K/Tam, 1955)
Modathi Rathri (**K.S. Prakash Rao**, Tel, 1950)
Modati Anubhavam (P. Chandrakumar, Tel, 1988)
Modern Girl *see* Pistolwali
Modern Girl (*aka* Chandra: B.S. Rajhans, H, 1935)
Modern Girl (R. Bhattacharya, H, 1961)
Modern Hero *see* Jawahir-e-Hind
Modern Lady (Jyotish Mukherjee, H, 1937)
Modern Wife *see* **Dr Madhurika**
Modern Youth *see* Navayuvan
Modern Youth (*aka* Jung-e-Jawani: D.T. Shivdasani/C.N. Lala, H, 1937)
Moguda Pellamma (B.A. Subba Rao, Tel, 1975)
Mogudugaru (A. Mohan Gandhi, Tel, 1993)
Mogudu Kavali (K. Subba Rao, Tel, 1980)
Mogudu Pellalu (Jandhyala, Tel, 1985)
Mohabbat (**Phani Majumdar**, H, 1943)
Mohabbat (**Bapu**, H, 1985)
Mohabbat Aur Jung (*aka* Love and War: ?, Uppal Prod, H, 1967)
Mohabbat Isko Kehte Hain (Akhtar Mirza, H, 1965)
Mohabbat Ka Paigam (Padmini?, P.K. Prod, H, 1989)
Mohabbat Ka Toofan (*aka* Nigah-e-Ulfat: Fram Sethna, H, 1936)
Mohabbat Ke Aansoo (*aka* Tears of Love: **Premankur Atorthy**, U, 1932)
Mohabbat Ke Dushman (**Prakash Mehra**, H, 1988)
Mohabbat Ki Duniya (**Nanubhai Vakil**/A. Shareef, H, 1946)
Mohabbat Ki Jeet (Ramanlal Desai, H, 1943)
Mohabbat Ki Jeet (**B.S. Ranga**, H, 1960)
Mohabbat Ki Kasam (K. Pappu, H, 1986)
Mohabbat Ki Kasauti *see* Rooplekha
Mohabbat Ki Maar *see* Inteqam
Mohabbat Ke Musibat (*aka* Love and Romance: ?, **Saurashtra Film**, St, 1927)
Mohabbat Ki Putli (Shinde, St, 1931)
Mohabbat Nu Phool (*aka* Love Triumphant: ?, Royal Art Studio, St, 1930)
Mohabbat Zindabad (B. Choksi, H, 1962)
Mohabbat Zindagi Hai (*aka* Love Is Life: Jagdish Nirula, H, 1966)
Moham (Randor Guy, Mal, 1974)
Mohammed-bin-Tughlaq (Cho Ramaswamy, Tam, 1971)
Mohammed-bin-Tughlaq (B.V. Prasad, Tel, 1972)
Mohammed Mustafa (Rehman, Mal, 1978)
Moham Muppathu Varusham (S.P. Muthuraman, Tam, 1976)
Mohamum Mukthiyum (**Sasikumar**, Mal, 1977)
Mohan (Anadinath Bannerjee, H, 1947)
Mohana Ponnagai (**C.V. Sridhar**, Tam, 1981)
Mohana Ragam (Y.R. Babu, Tel, 1980)
Mohana Rani (*aka* Chhelbatao: Jhaveri?, Royal Art Studio, St, 1927)
Mohanasundaram (A.T. Krishnaswamy, Tam, 1951)
Mohan Baganer Meye (Manu Sen, B, 1975)
Mohaney Dike (Biresh Chatterjee, B, 1983)
Mohan Joshi Haazir Ho! (**Saeed Mirza**, H, 1983)
Mohar (P. Jairaj, H, 1959)
Mohini (*aka* Ekadashi, Triumph of Fate: **Sisir Bhaduri**, St, 1921)
Mohini (Annasaheb Rajopadhye/Madhukar Bavdekar, Mar, 1940)
Mohini (Mahendra Gill/Niranjan, H, 1947)
Mohini (Lanka Sathyam, Tam, 1948)
Mohini (Raman B. Desai, H, 1957)
Mohini Attam (Shrikumaran Thampi, Mal, 1976)
Mohini Attam (**M.T. Vasudevan Nair**, E, 1977)
Mohini Avatar (**R.S. Prakash**, St, 1926)
Mohini Bhasmasur (**Dadasaheb Phalke**, St, 1914)
Mohini Bhasmasura (**C. Pullaiah**, Tel, 1938)
Mohini Bhasmasura (B.A. Subba Rao, Tel, 1966)
Mohini Bhasmasura (N.S. Varma, K, 1966)

Bina Rai in *Vallah Kya Baat Hai* (1962)

Mohini Rugmangada (**S. Soundararajan**, Tam, 1935)
Mohini Rugmangada (**Ch. Narasimha Rao**, Tel, 1937)
Mohini Rugmangada (**K.S. Prakash Rao**, Tel, 1962)
Mohini Sapatham (**B. Vittalacharya**, Tel, 1986)
Mohityanchi Manjula (**Bhalji Pendharkar**, Mar, 1963)
Moh-jaal (*aka* Lure of the Lust: Nirbhoy Thakkar, St, 1928)
Mohor (**Gautam Ghosh**, H, 1990)
Mohre (Raghuvir Kul, H, 1987)
Mohtaj Mashuq (*aka* Belle of Baluchistan: ?, Indore Pics., St, 1932)
Mojili Mashuq (*aka* Desert Damsel: **Nanubhai Vakil**, St, 1931)
Mojili Mumbai (**Manilal Joshi**, St, 1925)
Mojina Madhuve (V. Narayanaswamy, K, 1993)
Moksha (*aka* Salvation: Pankaj Butalia, H, 1993)
Molkarin (Yeshwant Pethkar, Mar, 1963)
Mom Batti (Yatrik, B, 1976)
Momer Alo (Salil Dutta, B, 1964)
Mom Ki Gudiya (Mohan Kumar, H, 1972)
Monagadosthunnadu Jagratha (K.V.S. Kutumbarao, Tel, 1972)
Monagadu (T. Krishna, Tel, 1976)
Monagadu (N.B. Chakraborty, Tel, 1987)
Monagadu Mosagadu (A.S. Prakasham, Tel, 1985)
Monagalluku Monagadu (S.D. Lall, H, 1966)
Monchor (Salil Sen, B, 1983)
Monday the Good Day *see* **Thinkalazhcha Nalla Divasam**
Mondighatam (Rajachandra, Tel, 1982)
Mon Dilona Bandhu (Santosh Mukherjee, B, 1962)
Mone Chhilo Asha (Binoy Bannerjee, B, 1948)
Mone Mone (Partha Prathim Choudhury, B, 1989)
Moner Mayur (**Sushil Majumdar**, B, 1954)
Money *see* Daulat Ka Nasha
Money (Sivanageshwara Rao, Tel, 1993)
Money Makes What Not *see* Takay Ki Na Hay
Money Order (TV: **P.N. Menon**, Mal, 1990)
Monihara *see* **Teen Kanya**
Mon Jare Chai (Niranjan Dey, B, 1975)
Mon Mandir (Siva Prasad Thakur, A, 1985)
Mon-Niye (Salil Sen, B, 1969)
Monologue *see* **Anantaram**
Mon Prajapati (**Bhupen Hazarika**, A, 1979)
Monsoon Day, A *see* **Ashad Ka Ek Din**
Montu (Durga Bhattacharya, B, 1978)
Monument of Tears *see* Anarkali
Moodalamanju (Sudhin Menon, Mal, 1970)
Moodillu Muchata (Kodi Ramakrishna, Tel, 1984)
Moodu Mandiram (Manobala, Tam, 1989)
Moodu Mulla Bandhan (Mutyala Subbaiah, Tel, 1980)
Moodu Mullu (Jandhyala, Tel, 1983)
Moodupadam (**Ramu Kariat**, Mal, 1963)
Moodupani (**Balu Mahendra**, Tam, 1980)
Moodu Puvvulu Aaru Kayalu (**Vijayanirmala**, Tel, 1978)
Moogajeevulu (**G. Varalakshmi**, Tel, 1968)
Moogaku Matta Vastha (V. Madhusudhana Rao, Tel, 1980)
Moogamanushulu (**Adurthi Subba Rao**, Tel, 1963)
Moogamudra (Ali Akbar, Mal, 1992)
Mooganomu (**Yoganand**, Tel, 1969)
Mooga Prema (G. Ramineedu, Tel, 1971)
Moogavani Paga (B.A. Subba Rao, Tel, 1983)
Mooguru Kodukalu *see* Moonru Pillaigal
Mooguthi Poomele (Sangaman, Tam, 1991)
Mookkanna Kayiru (S. Subbaiah, Tam, 1985)
Mookkilla Rajathu (Ashokan-Thaha, Mal, 1991)
Mooladanam (**P. Bhaskaran**, Mal, 1969)
Moon Cursed By Ganapati *see* Chaturthicha Chandra
Moondram Padi (Karvannan, Tam, 1992)
Moondram Pirai (**Balu Mahendra**, Tam, 1982)
Moondravadhu Kann (Manivannan, Tam, 1993)
Moondru Daivangal (Dada Mirasi, Tam, 1971)
Moondru Mudichu (**K. Balachander**, Tam, 1976)
Moondru Mugam (A. Jagannathan, Tam, 1983)
Moondru Penngal (**R.S. Prakash**, Tam, 1956)
Moonnam Mura (K. Madhu, Mal, 1988)
Moonnam Pakkam (**P. Padmarajan**, Mal, 1988)
Moonnu Masangalkku Mumpu (?, Mannil Prod, Mal, 1986)
Moonnupukkal (**P. Bhaskaran**, Mal, 1971)
Moonrezuthu (Ramanna, Tam, 1968)
Moonru Pillaigal/Mooguru Kodukalu (**R. Nagendra Rao**, Tel/Tam, 1952)
Moorkhan (Joshi, Mal, 1980)
Mooru Darigalu (**Girish Kasaravalli**, K, 1981)
Mooru Janma (Bhargava, K, 1984)
Mooru Muttugalu (Aruru Pattabhi, K, 1970)
Morals Sugar-coated *see* Neki Aur Badi
Moram *see* Maram
Morcha (Ravi Nagaich, H, 1980)
Mordhwaj (**Balwant Bhatt**, H, 1952)
More Man Mitwa (Girish Ranjan, Magadhi, 1965)
Morni (Jugal Kishore, P, 1975)
Moromi (Dwijendra Narayan Deb, A, 1977)
Moroo (?, Indian Pics., St., 1930)
Morotudu (C.K. Nagesh, Tel, 1977)
Mortuary (Baby, Mal, 1983)
Moruchi Mavshi (**P.K. Atre**, Mar, 1948)
Mosagalluku Mosagadu (**B. Vittalacharya**, Tel, 1971)
Mosambi Narangi (**Datta Keshav**, Mar, 1981)
Mota Gharni Vahu (G.K. Mehta, G, 1967)
Mota Gharni Vahu (Arun Bhatt, G, 1978)
Mother *see* Amma *or* Mamata *or* Mata
Mother (Narayan Chakraborty, B, 1979)
Mother (Vishukumar, K, 1980)
Mother/Child/Community (**Fali Bilimoria/Paul Zils**, E, 1948)
Mother India (*aka* Old Vimala: ?, International Pics., St, 1929)
Mother India (Dada Gunjal, H, 1938)
Mother India (**Mehboob**, H, 1957)
Mother India (T.V. Ramana Reddy, Tel, 1992)
Motherland *see* **Mathru Bhoomi** *or* **Desher Mati** *or* **Maabhoomi** *or* **Janmabhoomi**
Mother Love *see* Maa Ki Mamta
Mother's Devotion, A *see* Matri Sneh
Mothi Manse (Vamanrao Kulkarni/Vishnupant Chavan, Mar, 1949)
Moti (Chandrasekhar Bose, H, 1947)
Moti Baa (Yeshwant Pethkar, G, 1966)
Moti Ka Haar (*aka* Pearl Necklace: **Jaddanbai**, H, 1937)
Moti Mahal (**Ravindra Dave**, H, 1952)
Moti Verana Chokhma (Abbas-Mastan, G, 1987)
Motor Sundaram Pillai (Balu, Tam, 1966)
Motorwali (A.M. Khan, H, 1942)
Mouchak (Aravind Mukherjee, B, 1974)
Mouchake Dhil (Manujendra Bhanja, B, 1946)
Mouna Geethangal (**K. Bhagyaraj**, Tam, 1981)
Mounam Kalaigirathu (?, H.M.C. Prod, Tam, 1986)
Mounam Sammadham (**Madhu**, Tam, 1990)
Mouna Mozhi (Kasthuriraja, Tam, 1992)
Mouna Mukhar (Sarit Bannerjee, B, 1987)
Mouna Nombaram (**Sasikumar**, Mal, 1985)
Mouna Poratam (A. Mohan Gandhi, Tel, 1989)
Mouna Ragam (Ambili, Mal, 1983)
Mouna Ragam (**Mani Rathnam**, Tam, 1986)
Mouna Yuddham (N. Sambandam, Tam, 1981)
Mounto (Jambu, H, 1975)
Moving Perspective (**Mrinal Sen**, E, 1967)
Moving Pictures of Natural Scenes and Religious Rituals (**Hiralal Sen**, St, 1899)
Moyla Kagaj (**Premendra Mitra**, B, 1954)
Moyna (Ashim Bannerjee, B, 1978)
Moyna Tadanta (**Utpalendu Chakraborty**, B, 1980)
Mrichhakatik *see* Vasantsena
Mrichhakatik (**Suchet Singh**, St, 1920)
Mridanga Chakravarthi (K. Shankar, Tam, 1983)
Mridula (?, Mal, 1988)
Mrigajaal (*aka* The Mirage: ?, **Sharda Film**, St, 1932)
Mrigalaya (V. Somashekhar, K, 1986)
Mriga Trishna (P. Sambhasiva Rao, Tel, 1991)
Mrigaya (**Mrinal Sen**, H, 1976)
Mrignayani (*aka* Divine Dowry: **Nanubhai Vakil**, St, 1929)
Mrignayani (TV: **Amol Palekar**, H, 1991)
Mrig Trishna (*aka* Mirage: Rajendranath Shukla, H, 1975)
Mrinalini (**Jyotish Bannerjee**, St, 1930)
Mriter Martye Agaman (**Pashupati Chatterjee**, B, 1959)
Mrityunjavan (?, Mal, 1988)
Mrityu Panjaradalli Goodarachari 555 (Sunand, K, 1970)
Mubarak (Barkat Mehra, P, 1941)
Muchataga Mugguru (Relangi Narasimha Rao, Tel, 1985)
Mucheettu Kalikarante Magal (**Thoppil Bhasi**, Mal, 1975)
Mud *see* **Apni Nagariya**
Mudalali (Muktha V. Srinivasan, Tam, 1957)
Mudalili Amma (V.C. Guhanathan, Tam, 1990)
Muddabanthi Puvvu (**Dasari Narayana Rao**, Tel, 1976)
Mudda Mandaram (Jandhyala, Tel, 1981)
Muddat (**K. Bapaiah**, H, 1986)
Muddayi (K.S.R. Doss, Tel, 1987)
Muddina Mava (Saiprakash, K, 1993)
Muddubidda (K.B. Tilak, Tel, 1956)
Muddubidda (P. Chandrasekhara Reddy, Tel, 1987)
Muddula Chellelu (Imandi Rama Rao, Tel, 1985)
Muddula Koduku (V.B. Rajendra Prasad, Tel, 1979)
Muddula Krishnaiah (Kodi Ramakrishna, Tel, 1986)
Muddula Mamaiah (Kodi Ramakrishna, Tel, 1989)
Muddula Manavaralu (Jandhyala, Tel, 1985)
Muddula Mogadu (**K.S. Prakash Rao**, Tel, 1983)
Muddu Meena (Y.R. Swamy, K, 1967)
Mudhal *see* Muthal
Mudhalai (*aka* Dost Magarmach: Romulus Whittaker, Tam, 1988)
Mudhal Iravu (A. Jagannathan, Tam, 1979)
Mudhal Padal (Arul Krishnan, Tam, 1993)
Mudhal Papam (P. Chandrakumar, Tam, 1988)
Mudhal Seethanam (Erode Sundar, Tam, 1992)
Mudhal Thedi *see* **Modalatedi**
Mudhal Vasantham (Manivannan, Tam, 1986)
Mudichooda Mannan (R. Vittal, Tam, 1978)
Mudivalla Arambham (N. Mohideen, Tam, 1984)
Mudiyanaya Puthran (**Ramu Kariat**, Mal, 1961)
Mud Mud Ke Na Dekh (R. Tiwari, H, 1960)
Mudra (**Sibi Malayil**, Mal, 1988)
Mudra Mothiram (**Sasikumar**, Mal, 1978)
Mududida Tavare Aralitu (K.V. Jayaram, K, 1983)
Muflis Ashiq (**J.J. Madan**, H, 1932)
Mugana Sedu (B. Subba Rao, K, 1980)
Mugathil Mugam Parkalam (A. Jagannathan, Tam, 1979)
Mugdha Manava (K.S.L. Swamy, K, 1977)
Mugguramayula Mogadu (Relangi Narasimha Rao, Tel, 1983)
Mugguru Ammayilu (**K. Pratyagatma**, Tel, 1974)
Mugguru Attalu Muddula Alludu (Sunil Varma, Tel, 1991)
Mugguru Kodukulu (**Ghantamneni Krishna**, Tel, 1988)
Mugguru Maratilu (**G. Balaramaiah**, Tel, 1946)
Mugguru Mithrulu (Rajachandra, Tel, 1985)
Mugguru Monagallu (**T. Rama Rao**, Tel, 1983)
Mugguru Moorkhuralu (Mahesh, Tel, 1978)
Mugguru Muggure (S.D. Lall, Tel, 1978)
Mugguru Murkhulu (K. Hemambharadhara Rao, Tel, 1976)
Mugguru Veeralu (Joseph Taliath, Tel, 1960)
Mughal-e-Azam (**K. Asif**, U, 1960)
Mughal Gardens Pinjore (**Santi P. Choudhury**, E, 1972)
Mughal Prince, The *see* Julia Dalia
Mughlani Begum (Surjit Singh Sethi, P, 1979)
Mugila Mallige (**K. Balachander**, K, 1985)
Mugiyada Kathe (**Durai**, K, 1976)
Muhafiz *see* In Custody
Muharassi (M.A. Thirumugham, Tam, 1966)
Muharattu Kalai (S.P. Muthuraman, Tam, 1980)
Muhurta Naal (P. Madhavan, Tam, 1967)
Muhurtabalam (M. Mallikarjuna Rao, Tel, 1969)
Muhurtam at 11.30 (Joshi, Mal, 1985)
Muhurthangal (P.M. Benny, Mal, 1977)
Mujhe Insaaf Chahiye (**T. Rama Rao**, H, 1983)
Mujhe Jeene Do (*aka* Cry for Life: Moni Bhattachaya, H, 1963)
Mujhe Kasam Hai (Subhash Sharma, H, 1985)
Mujhe Seene Se Laga Lo (**Datta Dharmadhikari**, H, 1969)
Mujhe Shakti Do (Sharad Choudhury, H, 1984)
Mujhe Vachan Do (Shibu Mitra, H, 1983)
Mujhse Dosti Karoge (Gopi Desai, H, 1992)
Mujrim (**Nitin Bose**, H, 1944)
Mujrim (O.P. Ralhan, H, 1958)
Mujrim (Kewal Mishra, H, 1970)
Mujrim (Umesh Mehra, H, 1989)
Mujrim Hazir (TV: ?, H, 1985)
Mujrim Kaun (K.K. Reddy, H, 1966)
Mujrim Kaun Khooni Kaun (Ramnik Vaidya, H, 1965)
Muka Ghya Muka (**Dada Kondke**, Mar, 1987)
Muka Lekru (Bal Gajbar, Mar, 1953)
Mukha Mukham (**Adoor Gopalakrishnan**, Mal, 1984)
Mukhangal (P. Chandrakumar, Mal, 1982)
Mukhda (**Roop K. Shorey**, H, 1951)
Mukhda Chan Warga (Joginder Samra, P, 1969)
Mukhujey Paribar (Ajit Ganguly, B, 1965)
Mukhya Manthri (Alleppey Ashraf, Mal, 1985)
Mukhya Mantri (**Vijayanirmala**, Tel, 1984)
Mukhya Mantri Zindabad (?. Shri Simhapuri Art Creations, Tel, 1987)
Mukkam Post Dhebevadig (Madhukar Pathak, Mar, 1969)
Mukkopi (**Vijayanirmala**, Tel, 1984)
Mukku Pudaka (Kodi Ramakrishna, Tel, 1983)
Mukkuvane Snehicha Bhootham (**Sasikumar**, Mal, 1978)
Muklawa (Majnu, P, 1957)
Mukta Pran (Samir Ghosh, B, 1984)
Mukti (**P.C. Barua**, B/H, 1937)
Mukti (N. Buli, H, 1960)
Mukti (**N. Lakshminarayan**, K, 1970)
Mukti (Byomkesh Tripathi, O, 1977)
Mukti (Raj Tilak, H, 1977)
Mukti (**I.V. Sasi**, Mal, 1988)
Mukti Chai (**Utpalendu Chakraborty**, B, 1977)
Muktir Bandhan (Akhil Neogy, B, 1947)
Muktir Din (Jayanta Purkayastha, B, 1983)
Mukti Sangram (*aka* Vagabond Lover: **Jayant Desai**, St, 1931)
Muktisnan (**Sushil Majumdar**, B, 1937)
Muktisnan (Ajit Ganguly, B, 1970)
Mukto Pran (Samir Ghosh, B, 1986)
Mukunda Chandra (S.K. Ananthachari, K, 1969)
Mukunthetta Sumitra Vilikkunnu (**Priyadarshan**, Mal, 1988)
Mukuta (**Brojen Barua**, A, 1970)
Mukutamleni Maharaju *see* Makutamleni Maharaju
Mulamoottil Adima (P.K. Joseph, Mal, 1985)
Mulaqat (Munshi Dil, H, 1947)
Mulga (Namdev Vhatkar, Mar, 1956)
Mulgi Jhali Ho (Sushil Gajwani, Mar, 1985)
Mul Illatha Roja (K. Rangaraj, Tam, 1982)
Mulkireedam (N.N. Pishareddy, Mal, 1967)
Mullaivanam (V. Krishnan, Tam, 1955)
Mullina Gulabi (Vijay, K, 1982)
Mullum Malarum (**J. Mahendran**, Tam, 1978)
Mulraj Solanki (K.P. Bhave, St, 1925)
Mulu Manek (**Manhar Raskapur**, G, 1955)
Mulu Manek (Manibhai Vyas, G, 1977)
Mulzim (N.A. Ansari, H, 1963)
Mulzim (K.S.R. Doss, H, 1988)
Mumbaicha Fauzdar (**Rajdutt**, Mar, 1984)
Mumbaicha Javai (**Raja Thakur**, Mar, 1970)
Mumbaigara (Nautam Trivedi, G, 1950)
Mumbai Ni Mohini (**Nanubhai Desai**, St, 1925)

Mumbai Ni Sethani (*aka* Call of Satan: **Ardeshir Irani/Naval Gandhi**, St, 1924)
Mumbaino Mawali (*aka* The Blackguard: Saqi, St, 1929)
Mumbaino Satodio (*aka* Speculator: **N.G. Devare**/Vaidya, St, 1929)
Mummy Daddy (Narendra Dev, H, 1963)
Mumtaz *see* Mumtaz Mahal
Mumtaz Begum (Akhtar Nawaz, H, 1934)
Mumtaz Mahal (**Homi Master**, St, 1926)
Mumtaz Mahal (*aka* Mumtaz: **Kidar Sharma**, H, 1944)
Mumtaz Mahal (Ram Daryani, H, 1957)
Mun Arivippu (R.S. Bhuvan, Tam, 1993)
Mundadugu (Krishnarao, Tel, 1958)
Mundadugu (**K. Bapaiah**, Tel, 1983)
Munda Naram Te Kudi Garam (**S.P. Bakshi**, P, 1986)
Mundhanai Mudichu (**K. Bhagyaraj**, Tam, 1983)
Mundhanai Sabatham (M.R. Yogaraj, Tam, 1989)
Mundu (Ajit Gupta, H, 1983)
Mungerilal Ke Haseen Sapne (TV: **Prakash Jha**, H, 1990)
Municipal Elections (**Dadasaheb Phalke**, St, 1924)
Municipality/Sthanik Swarajya (Baburao Apte, Mar, 1941)
Munimji (**Subodh Mukherjee**, H, 1955)
Munimji (Jugal Kishore, H, 1972)
Muniyana Madari (Dorairaj-Bhagavan, K, 1981)
Munna (**K.A. Abbas**, H, 1954)
Munna (**Phani Majumdar**, H, 1969)
Munnettam (Shrikumaran Thampi, Mal, 1981)
Munnooru Naal (S.S. Devadas, Tam, 1977)
Munshiji (R.N. Goswami, H, 1973)
Mupperum Theviyar (K. Shankar, Tam, 1987)
Muqabala (**Nanabhai Bhatt/Babubhai Mistri**, H, 1942)
Muqabala (?, M.G.A. Films, H, 1970)
Muqabala (Rajkumar Kohli, H, 1979)
Muqabala (**T. Rama Rao**, H, 1992)
Muqaddar (Aravind Sen, H, 1950)
Muqaddar (Ravi Tandon, H, 1978)
Muqaddar Ka Badshah (**T. Rama Rao**, H, 1990)
Muqaddar Ka Faisla (**Prakash Mehra**, H, 1987)
Muqaddar Ka Sikandar (**Prakash Mehra**, H, 1978)
Murad (Saqi, H, 1939)
Murad (Nari Ghadiali, H, 1961)
Muradhan Muthu *see* Chinnada Gombe
Murai Ponnu (R. Krishnamurthy, Tam, 1982)
Murali Krishna (**P. Pullaiah**, Tel, 1964)
Murali Krishnudu (Kodi Ramakrishna, Tel, 1988)
Murali Malhari Rayachi (Govind Kulkarni, Mar, 1969)
Muraliwala *see* Kaliya Mardan
Muraliwala (**Baburao Painter**, St, 1927)
Muraliwala (Vasant Painter, H, 1951)
Murappennu (**A. Vincent**, Mal, 1965)
Murattu Kalai (S.P. Muthuraman, Tam, 1980)
Murattu Karangal (Rajasekhar, Tam, 1985)
Murde *see* Corpses
Murde Ki Jaan Khatre Mein (Navin Kumar, H, 1984)
Murderer *see* Sulagto Sansar
Murder in Circus (A. Salaam, H, 1971)
Murder of Narayanrao Peshwa *see* Dha Cha Ma
Muriyada Mane (Y.R. Swamy, K, 1964)
Murti (**Chaturbhuj Doshi**, H, 1945)
Murugan Adimai (R. Thyagarajan, Tam, 1977)
Murugane Thunai (?, Murugalayam Films, Tam, 1990)
Murugan Kattiya Vazhi (P. Madhavan, Tam, 1974)
Muruvare Vajragalu (Y.R. Swamy, K, 1973)
Musafir (**Chaturbhuj Doshi**, H, 1940)
Musafir (**Hrishikesh Mukherjee**, H, 1957)
Musafir (A.K. Soni, H, 1984)
Musafir (**Jabbar Patel**, H, 1986)
Musafirkhana (M. Sadiq, H, 1955)
Mushkil Ashan (Soumyen Mukherjee, B, 1953)
Music of Satyajit Ray (**Utpalendu Chakraborty**, E, 1984)
Music Room, The *see* **Jalsaghar**
Muskurahat (Dwarka Khosla/Vedi/Ram Kamlani, H, 1943)
Muskurahat (**Priyadarshan**, H, 1992)
Muslim Ka Lal (A.M. Khan, H, 1941)
Musugu Donga (B. Subba Rao, Tel, 1985)
Muthalaly (M.A.V. Rajendran, Mal, 1965)
Muthal Kural (V.C. Guhanathan, Tam, 1992)
Muthal Mappillai (**H.L.N. Simha**, Tam, 1938)
Muthal Mariyathai (**Bharathirajaa**, Tam, 1985)
Muthana Muthallava (R. Vittal, Tam, 1976)
Mutharamkunnu P.O. (**Sibi Malayil**, Mal, 1985)
Muthassi (**P. Bhaskaran**, Mal, 1971)
Muthbhar Chane (**Dinkar D. Patil**, Mar, 1955)
Muthichippikal (**T. Hariharan**, Mal, 1980)
Muthina Hara (**S.V. Rajendra Singh**, K, 1990)
Muthinantha Attige (Banduru Giribabu, K, 1982)
Muthinantha Manushya (Saiprakash, K, 1989)
Muthodu Muthu (M. Mani, Mal, 1984)
Muthrugai (Manobala, Tam, 1992)
Muthu (N.N. Pishareddy, Mal, 1976)
Muthu Chippi (M. Krishnan, Tam, 1968)
Muthu Engal Sotthu (G.N. Rangarajan, Tam, 1983)
Muthu Mandapam (**A.S.A. Sami**, Tam, 1962)
Muthyala Jallu (Mano Bala, Tel, 1985)
Muthyala Muggu (**Bapu**, Tel, 1975)
Muthyala Pallaki (B.V. Prasad, Tel, 1976)
Mutiyar (Jaggi Rampal, P, 1950)
Mutiyar (**Surinder Singh**, P, 1979)
Muttaide (Renuka Sharma, K, 1988)
Muttaide Bhagya (**B. Vittalacharya**, K, 1956)
Muttaide Bhagya (K.N. Chandrasekhar Sharma, K, 1983)
Mutta Mestri (A. Kodandarami Reddy, Tel, 1992)
Muttathe Mulla (**Sasikumar**, Mal, 1977)
Mutthaiduva (A.C. Trilogchandar, Tel, 1979)
Mutthi Bhar Chawal (Surendra Sailaj, H, 1975)
Muttidella Chinna (D. Shankar Singh, K, 1954)
Muttinantha Attige (Bandaru Giribabu, K, 1982)
Muttu Ondu Muttu (R.N. Jayagopal, K, 1991)
Mutukkal Moonru (A. Jagannathan, Tam, 1987)
Mu Tume O Se (Kumar Anand, O, 1984)
Mutyamanta Muddu (Raviraja Pinisetty, Tel, 1989)
Muvva Gopaludu (Kodi Ramakrishna, Tel, 1987)
Muyalukku Moonu Kaal (V.C.Guhanathan, Tam, 1980)
Muyarchi (Joseph Pallippad, Tam, 1953)
Muyyi (**N. Lakshminarayan**, K, 1979)
Muyyige Muyyi (Y.R. Swamy, K, 1978)
Muzhu Nilavu (Udumalai Chandran, Tam, 1980)
My Beloved *see* Mera Pyara
My Country *see* Mera Watan *or* Swadesh Seva
My Darling *see* Diwani Dilbar *or* Pardesi Saiyan
My Dear Kuttichathan/Chhota Chetan (Jijo, Mal/H, 1984)
My Dear Lisa (Baby, Tam, 1987)
My Dear Marthandan (Prathap, Tam, 1990)
My Dear Muthachan (Sathyan Andhikkad, Mal, 1992)
My Dream *see* Mera Khwab
My Dreams (**Ismat Chughtai**, H, 1975)
My Eyes *see* Meri Aankhen
My Friend (Rehman, H, 1974)
My Hero *see* Matrubhoomi
My Husband *see* En Kanavar
My Kingdom *see* Mera Watan
My Love (*aka* Mera Pyar: **S. Sukhdev**, H, 1970)
My Man *see* **Piya Pyare**
My Mother *see* Meri Maa
My Own *see* Swaham
My Queen *see* Rani Saheba
My Sister *see* **Bahen** *or* **Meri Bahen**
My Son *see* **Mazha Mulga**
My Son, My Precious *see* Imagi Ningthem
Mysore Bandit, The *see* Naveena Nirupama
Mysore: Gem City of India (**M. Bhavnani**, St, 1929)
Mysore Jana (A.T. Raghu, K, 1992)
Mysore Mallige (**T.S. Nagabharana**, K, 1991)
Mysore Tonga (**G.V. Iyer**/T.V. Singh Thakore, K, 1968)
Mysterious Bandit (?, United Players, St, 1931)
Mysterious Eagle *see* Husn Ka Daku
Mysterious Man *see* Farebi Duniya
Mysterious Prince *see* Bhedi Rajkumar *or* Prince Thaksen
Mysterious Sage, The *see* **Marmayogi**
Mysterious Shadow *see* Chhupa Rustom
Mystery Man *see* Mayabee
Myth, The (**Adoor Gopalakrishnan**, E, 1977)
My Village *see* Mera Gaon
My Village My People (**Shantaram Athavale**, E, 1971)
My Wife *see* En Manaivi *or* Mari Dhaniyani
My Wise Daddy (**Govind Saraiya**, E, 1965)

N

Naa (Shri Tara Shankar, B, 1954)
Naach (**Ravindra Dave**, H, 1949)
Naa Chellelu (**Ch. Narayanamurthy**, Tel, 1953)
Naache Mayuri (**T. Rama Rao**, H, 1986)
Naache Nagin Baaje Been (Tara Harish, H, 1960)
Naache Nagin Gali Gali (Mohanji Prasad, H, 1990)
Naach Ghar (R.S. Tara, H, 1959)
Naach Govinda Naach (?, H, 1991)
Naachnewale Ganewale (B. Subhash, H, 1991)
Naach Utha Sansar (Yakub Hasan Rizvi, H, 1976)
Naachwali (*aka* Dancing Girl: Ramnik Desai, H, 1934)
Naa Desam (**K. Bapaiah**, Tel, 1982)
Naad-o-Nadi (Chitta Bose, B, 1954)
Naag Champa (Vinod Desai, H, 1958)
Naag Champa (S.N. Tripathi, H, 1976)
Naagdand *see* Phantom Foe
Naag Devata (**V.M. Vyas**, G, 1955)
Naag Devata (Shantilal Soni, H/Tel, 1962)
Naag Jyoti (Shantilal Soni, H, 1963)
Naag Lok (**Babubhai Mistri**, H, 1957)
Naag Lok (**Babubhai Mistri**, H, 1970)
Naag Mandir (Shantilal Soni, H, 1966)
Naag Mani (Raman B. Desai, H, 1957)
Naag Mani (V. Menon, H, 1991)
Naag Mere Saathi (Shantilal Soni, H, 1973)
Naag Mohini (Shantilal Soni, H, 1963)
Naag Nagin (Ramkumar Bohra, H, 1989)
Naag Padmini (*aka* The Shepherd King: **N.G. Devare**, St, 1928)
Naag Padmini (Lekhraj Bhakri, H, 1957)
Naag Panchami (Raman B. Desai, H, 1953)
Naag Panchami (Shantilal Soni, Bh, 1964)
Naag Panchami (**Babubhai Mistri**, H, 1972)
Naag Panchami (Shantilal Soni, G, 1981)
Naagphani (?, Rich Arts, H, 1987)
Naag Pooja (Shantilal soni, H, 1971)
Naag Rani *see* Cobra Girl
Naagu (T. Prasad, Tel, 1984)
Naa Ille Naa Swargam (Rushyendra Reddy, Tel, 1991)
Naa Illu *see* En Veedu
Naa Illu Naa Vellu (Rajachandra, Tel, 1979)
Naa-Insaafi *see* Na-Insaafi
Naaku Pellam Kavali (Vijaya Bapineedu, Tel, 1987)
Naaku Swatantram Vachindi (Laxmi Deepak, Tel, 1975)
Naalugu Sthambalata (Jandhyala, Tel, 1982)
Naalum Therinthavan (Jambulingam, Tam, 1968)
Naalu Veli Neelam (Muktha V. Srinivasan, Tam, 1959)
Naam (A. Kasilingam, Tam, 1953)
Naam (R.C. Sakthi, Tam, 1985)
Naam (**Mahesh Bhatt**, H, 1986)
Naamcheen (Ajit Dewani, H, 1991)
Naa Mechida Huduga (R.N. Jayagopal, K, 1972)
Naa Mela Thatiya (K. Hemambharadhara Rao, Tel, 1979)
Naami Chor (Kamal Mehra, H, 1977)
Naam Moovar (Jambulingam, Tam, 1966)
Naa Mogadu Brahmachari (M.S. Kota Reddy, Tel, 1981)
Naa Mogadu Nanke Sontham (**Dasari Narayana Rao**, Tel, 1989)
Naam-o-Nishan (Ajay Kashyap, H, 1987)
Naam Pirandha Maan (**A. Vincent**, Tam, 1977)
Naan (Ramanna, Tam, 1967)
Naan Adimai Illai (Dwarkeesh, Tam, 1986)
Naanal (**K. Balachander**, Tam, 1965)
Naan Anaittal (**Tapi Chanakya**, Tam, 1966)
Naan Avanillai (**K. Balachander**, Tam, 1974)
Naan En Pirandein (M. Krishnan, Tam, 1972)
Naan Kanda Sorgam (**P. Pullaiah**, Tam, 1960)
Naan Kudithu Konde Irupen (Kadalur Purshottaman, Tam, 1982)
Naanku Killadikal (L. Babu, Tam, 1969)
Naan Mahaan Alla (S.P. Muthuraman, Tam, 1984)
Naan Nandri Solven (Panasai Maniyan, Tam, 1979)
Naan Naneythan (P. Madhavan, Tam, 1980)
Naan Oru Kayi Parkiren (K. Sornam, Tam, 1979)
Naan Padum Padal (R. Sundarrajan, Tam, 1984)
Naan Pesa Ninaipathelam (Vikraman, Tam, 1993)
Naan Petra Selvam (K. Somu, Tam, 1956)
Naan Pogum Padhai (Vetrivendhan, Tam, 1991)
Naan Potta Saval (Puratchidasan, Tam, 1980)
Naan Pudicha Mappillai (V. Sekhar, Tam, 1991)
Naan Sigappu Manithan (S.A. Chandrasekharan, Tam, 1985)
Naan Sollum Rahasiyam (P. Sridhar Rao, Tam, 1959)
Naan Sonnadhe Sattam (Rameshraj, Tam, 1988)
Naan Sootiya Malar (C.S. Govindarajan, Tam, 1983)
Naanum Oru Penn/Nadi Aada Janma (A.C. Trilogchandar, Tam/Tel, 1963)
Naan Ungal Rasigan (Manobala, Tam, 1985)
Naan Unnai Ninachen (G.V. Saravanan, Tam, 1983)
Naan Valartha Poove (Rakeshkhanna, Tam, 1991)
Naan Valartha Thangai (**Ch. Narayanamurthy**, Tam, 1958)
Naan Vanangum Daivam (K. Somu, Tam, 1963)
Naan Vazhavippen (**D. Yoganand**, Tam, 1979)
Naan Yaar Theriyuma (V.N. Raman, Tam, 1967)
Naa Pelli Naa Ishtam (Anand Babu, Tel, 1991)
Naa Pere Bhagwan (S.D. Lall, Tel, 1976)
Naa Pilupe Prabhanjanam (**Ghantamneni Krishna**, Tel, 1986)
Naar Nirmite Nara (**Anant Mane**, Mar, 1963)
Naata (D.N Madhok, H, 1955)
Naa Thammudu (**K.S. Prakash Rao**, Tel, 1971)
Naav Motha Lakshan Khota (Murlidhar Kapdi, Mar, 1977)
Naaz (S.K. Ojha, H, 1954)
Nababidhan (Haridas Bhattacharya, B, 1954)
Nabadiganta (**Agradoot**, B, 1962)
Nabadiganta (Palash Bannerjee, B, 1979)
Nabajanma (**Debaki Bose**, B, 1956)
Nabajanma (Sachin Mukherjee, O, 1964)
Nabaraag (Bijoy Bose, B, 1971)
Nabegebaboa Hennu (**B. Vittalacharya**, K, 1958)
Na Bhule Hain Na Bhulenge (?, P.K. Arts, H, 1988)
Nabin Yatra/Naya Safar (Subodh Mitra, B/H, 1953)
Nachdi Jawani (Som Haksar, P, 1977)
Nadaan (**Zia Sarhadi**, H, 1943)
Nadaan (Hira Singh, H, 1951)
Nadaan (Deven Verma, H, 1971)
Nadaaniyan (Ved Rahi, H, 1984)
Nadagame Ulagam (**Krishnan-Panju**, Tam, 1979)
Nadamadum Silaigal (Malleeshwar, Tam, 1982)
Nada Manne Nada Koolu (S.R. Rajan, Coorgi, 1972)
Nadan Pennu (**K.S. Sethumadhavan**, Mal, 1967)
Nadan Premam (Mani, Mal, 1972)
Nader Nimai (Bimal Roy Jr., B, 1960)
Nadham (Lawrence Gaulbert, Mal, 1983)
Nadhi (**A. Vincent**, Mal, 1969)
Nadhi Muthal Nadhi Vare (Vijayanand, Mal, 1983)
Nadhi Nadanmare Avasiamundu (Mani, Mal, 1974)
Nadhi Ondru Karai Moondru (S. Iski Pandyan/S. Muthaiyad Deval, Tam, 1981)
Nadhiyai Thedi Vandha Kadal (B. Lenin, Tam, 1980)

Nadi Aada Janma *see* Naanum Oru Penn
Nadigan (P. Vasu, Tam, 1990)
Nadi Kinare (*aka* On the River: Manibhai Vyas, H, 1939)
Nadimantrapu Siri (**T. Rama Rao**, Tel, 1968)
Nadina Bhagya (**R. Nagendra Rao**, K, 1970)
Nadira (**Jayant Desai**, H, 1934)
Nadira (?, Bhagwant Singh Issar, H, 1962)
Nadira (**Naval Gandhi**, St, 1931)
Nadir Shah (S.N. Tripathi, H, 1968)
Nadi Theke Sagare (Aurobindo Mukherjee, B, 1978)
Nadiya Ke Paar (**Kishore Sahu**, H, 1948)
Nadiya Ke Paar (Govind Moonis, H, 1982)
Nadiya Nagar (Sushil Mukherjee, B, 1987)
Nadodi (**B.R. Panthulu**, Tam, 1966)
Nadodi (Thambi Kannathanam, Mal, 1992)
Nadodikal (S. Ramanathan, Mal, 1959)
Nadodikattu (Sathyan Andhikkad, Mal, 1987)
Nadodi Mannan (**M.G. Ramachandran**, Tam, 1958)
Nadodi Pattukaran (N.K. Vishwanathan, Tam, 1992)
Nadodi Raja (I.N. Murthy, Tam, 1982)
Nadodi Thendral (**Bharathirajaa**, Tam, 1992)
Nadu Athai Nadu (Rama Thilakarajan, Tam, 1991)
Nadu Iravil (**S. Balachander**, Tam, 1970)
Nadu Nedu (P. Shekhar, Tel, 1976)
Nadurathri (Rajan, K, 1980)
Naduvazhigal (Joshi, Mal, 1989)
Nafrat (Shyam Ralhan, H, 1973)
Nafrat (Anoop Kumar, H, 1986)
Nafrat (Anup Malik, H, 1987)
Nafrat Ki Aandhi (**Mehul Kumar**, H, 1989)
Naga Bairava (K.S. Rami Reddy, Tel, 1984)
Nagabala (Ramanarayanan, Tel, 1992)
Nagabekamma Nagabeku (B. Subba Rao, K, 1983)
Naga Devata (Ramanarayan, Tel, 1986)
Nagad Narayan *see* **Paise Bolto Aahe**
Naga Kala Bhairava (Tiptur Raghu, K, 1981)
Nagakannika (G. Vishwanathan, K, 1949)
Naga Kanya (Chozha Rajan, Tel, 1991)
Naga Kanye (**S.V. Rajendra Singh**, K, 1975)
Nagalu Stambalata (Jandhyala, Tel, 1982)
Nagam (Chozhan Raja, Tam, 1985)
Nagamadhathu Thampuratti (?, Mal, 1981)
Nagamalai Azhgai (G. Vishwanathan, Tam, 1962)
Naga Malli (Devadas Kanakala, Tel, 1980)
Nagan (*aka* Haseen Qatil: **Jyotish Bannerjee**, H, 1934)
Naganand (**Y.V. Rao**, H/Mar, 1935)
Naga Nandini (**T.R. Raghunath**, Tam, 1961)
Nagan Ki Ragini *see* **Karma**
Naga Panchami (**Ch. Narayanamurthy**, Tam, 1956)
Naga Panchami (**Kadaru Nagabhushanam**, Tel, 1956)
Naga Phasha (Basant Naik, O, 1977)
Naga Pooja (Rajagopal, K, 1965)
Nagara Haavu (**Puttanna Kanagal**, K, 1972)
Nagara Mahime (Kallesh, K, 1984)
Nagarame Nandi (**A. Vincent**, Mal, 1967)
Nagaram Sagaram (K.R. Pillai, Mal, 1974)
Nagarangalil Chennu Raparkkam (Viji Thampi, Mal, 1989)
Nagarathil Samsara Vizhiyam (Prashanth, Mal, 1991)
Nagar Darpane (Yatrik, B, 1975)
Nagardola (Amalendu Basu, B, 1956)
Nagarhole (**S.V. Rajendra Singh**, K, 1977)
Nagarik (**Ritwik Ghatak**, B, 1952)
Nagarjuna (**Y.V. Rao**, K/Tel, 1961)
Nagar Vadhu Jo Bani Kulavadhu *see* Bankelal
Nagastharam (**Ghantamneni Krishna**, Tel, 1991)
Nagin (**Nandlal Jaswantlal**, H, 1954)
Nagin (Rajkumar Kohli, H, 1976)
Nagin (Ramakant Kavthekar/Vivek Vasant, Mar, 1981)
Nagina (**Ravindra Dave**, H, 1951)
Nagina (Harmesh Malhotra, H, 1986)
Nagina-II *see* Nigahen
Nagin Aur Lutere (Mohan T. Gehani, H, 1992)
Nagin Aur Sapera (**Balwant Bhatt**, H, 1966)
Nagin Aur Suhagan (Shantilal Soni, H, 1979)
Nagini (Sripriya, K, 1991)
Nagini Kanyar Kahini (Salil Sen, B, 1958)
Nagma (Nakshab, H, 1953)
Nagma-e-Sahra (*aka* Song of the Desert: **Master Bhagwan**, H, 1945)
Nagmati (Gautam Chattopadhyay, B, 1983)
Nagmati Nagvalo (**Ravindra Dave**, G, 1984)
Nagpash (**Rajen Tarafdar**, B, 1981)
Nagula Chaviti/Adarshasati (**Ch. Narayanamurthy**, Tel/K, 1956)
Nagunagutha Nali (Bhargava, K, 1991)
Naguva Hoovu (R.N. Krishnaprasad, K, 1971)
Naharsinh Daku (**B.P. Mishra**, St, 1925)
Nahi Amhi Vanar Bannar (*aka* We Are Not Your Monkeys: **Anand Patwardhan**, Mar, 1993)
Na Honewali Baat (*aka* Impossible: R.N. Vaidya, H, 1938)
Nai Baat (M.S. Choudhury/D. Bhalchandra, H, 1947)
Nai Bhabhi (S.D. Narang, H, 1950)
Naidu Bava (P. Chandrasekhara Reddy, Tel, 1978)
Nai Duniya (*aka* Sacred Scandal: **Balwant Bhatt**, H, 1934)
Nai Duniya (**A.R. Kardar**, H, 1942)
Nai Duniya Naye Log (*aka* Nisha: **B.R. Ishara**, H, 1973)
Naihar Chhutal Jaye (Devendra, Bh, 1964)
Naihar Ki Chunari (Hasmukh Rajput, Bh, 1985)
Nai Imarat (Ram Pahwa, H, 1981)
Nai Kahani (D.D. Kashyap, H, 1943)
Naikinichi Sajja (**Bhalji Pendharkar**, Mar, 1957)
Nai Maa (Kant J. Parmar, H, 1946)
Nai Maa (P.L. Santoshi, H, 1960)
Naina (**Ravindra Dave**, H, 1953)
Naina (Kanak Mishra, H, 1973)
Nain Mile Chain Kahan (Shankar Vyas, H, 1985)
Na Insaafi (**Mehul Kumar**, H, 1989)
Nai Raahein (Brij Sadanah, H, 1959)
Nai Reet (S.K. Ojha, H, 1948)
Nai Roshni *see* Vishnu Bhakti
Nai Roshni (*aka* Royal Rivals: **B.P. Mishra**, St, 1930)
Nai Roshni (C. Gandhi/L. Mehta, H, 1941)
Nai Roshni (**C.V. Sridhar**, H, 1967)
Nair Pidicha Pulivalu (**P. Bhaskaran**, Mal, 1958)
Nair Saab (Joshi, Mal, 1989)
Nai Taleem (*aka* The Country Teacher: ?, Diamond Pics, H, 1949)
Nai Umar Ki Nai Fasal (*aka* New Crop of the New Age: R. Chandra, H, 1965)
Naiya (Aslam Noori, H, 1947)
Naiya (**Prashanta Nanda**, H, 1979)
Nai Zindagi (*aka* Gharonda: S. Khalil, H, 1943)
Nai Zindagi (Mohan Sinha, H, 1951)
Nai Zindagi (Dada Pathare, H, 1969)
Naizraat (Jaggi Rampal, Kashmiri, 1964)
Najaria (Murtaza Chenghezi, H, 1952)
Najma (**Mehboob**, H, 1943)
Nakabandi (Shibu Mitra, H, 1990)
Nakal Sona (Aravind Mukherjee, B, 1973)
Naked Truth *see* Jhoothi Sharm
Nakhangal (**A. Vincent**, Mal, 1973)
Nakhre (Surya Kumar, H, 1951)
Nakhreli Nar (*aka* Naughty Maid: **Nanubhai Vakil**, St, 1932)
Nakhrewali (?, Cine Arts Pics, H, 1960)
Nakhuda (Dilip Naik, H, 1981)
Nakili Manishi (S.D. Lall, Tel, 1980)
Nakkala Rajkumari (**Prema Karanth**, K, 1989)
Nakkare Ade Swarga (M.R. Vittal, K, 1967)
Nakoga Bai Lagna (*aka* Goodbye Marriage: **N.D. Sarpotdar**, St, 1931)
Nakshatra Koodaram (Joshi Mathew, Mal, 1992)
Nakshatra Nayakan (Senthilnathan, Tam, 1992)
Nakshatrangal (**T. Hariharan**, Mal, 1986)
Nakshatrangale Kaval (**K.S. Sethumadhavan**, Mal, 1978)
Nakshatrangale Sakshi (Babu Radhakrishnan, Mal, 1979)
Nakuli Shaan (Tulsi/Shyam **Ramsay**, Sindhi, 1971)
Nala Damayanti (Eugenio De Liguoro, St, 1920)
Nala Damayanti (**Dadasaheb Phalke**, St, 1927)
Nala Damayanti (?, East India Film, H, 1933)
Nala Damayanti (Fram Sethna, Tam, 1935)
Nala Damayanti (Kumarsen Samarth, H, 1945)
Nala Damayanti (**Kemparaj Urs**, K/Tel/Tam, 1957)
Nala Damayanti (Gopal Krishna Roy, B, 1970)
Nala Damayanti (Jasubhai Trivedi, G, 1982)
Nala Damayanti (Bibhutibhushan Mishra, O, 1985)
Nalaga Endaro (Eranki Sharma, Tel, 1978)
Nalai Namadhe (**K.S. Sethumadhavan**, Tam, 1975)
Nalai Onadu Naal (A. Jagannathan, Tam, 1984)
Nalam Nalamariya Aval (P. Jayadevi, Tam, 1984)
Nalanthana (**Durai**, Tam, 1982)
Nalayak (Padmanabh, H, 1978)
Nalaya Manithan (V. Prabhakar, Tam, 1989)
Nalaya Seithi (G.B. Vijay, Tam, 1992)
Nalaya Theerpu (S.S. Chandrasekharan, Tam, 1992)
Nalayini (**R. Padmanabhan**, Tam, 1936)
Nalayini (**R.S. Prakash**, Tam, 1936)
Nalegalannu Maduvavaru (**G.V. Iyer**, K, 1976)
Nale Gnangalude Vivaham (Sajan, Mal, 1986)
Naleyallam Pournami (Uthaman, Tam, 1986)
Nalkawala (**I.V. Sasi**, Mal, 1987)
Nalladhai Nadu Ketkum (Jeppiar, Tam, 1991)
Nalla Idathu Sambandham (K. Somu, Tam, 1958)
Nallakalam (K. Vembu/Jyotish Sinha, Tam, 1954)
Nallakalam Porandachu (T.P. Gajendran, Tam, 1990)
Nalla Marumagal (**A. Vincent**, Tam, 1975)
Nalla Mudivu (C.N. Shanmugham, Tam, 1973)
Nalla Naal (R. Thyagarajan, Tam, 1984)
Nalla Neram (M.A. Thirumugham, Tam, 1972)
Nalla Pambu (Ramanarayanan, Tam, 1987)
Nalla Penmani (?, Srinivas Pics, Tam, 1955)
Nalla Penmani (A. Jagannathan, Tam, 1976)
Nallathambi (**Krishnan-Panju**, Tam, 1949)
Nallathambi (S.P. Muthuraman, Tam, 1985)
Nalla Thangai (P.V. Krishna Iyer, Tam, 1955)
Nalla Thangai (S.A. Nataraj, Tam, 1955)
Nalla Thangal (**R. Padmanabhan**, Tam, 1935)
Nallathanka (P.V. Krishna Iyer, Mal, 1950)
Nalla Theerpu (**T. Prakash Rao**, Tam, 1959)
Nallathe Nadakkum (K. Shankar, Tam, 1993)
Nallathoru Kudumbam (K. Vijayan, Tam, 1979)
Nalla Thrachu (Nandakumar, Tel, 1988)
Nallathukku Kalamillai (T.N. Balu, Tam, 1977)
Nallathu Nadanthe Theerum (Karaikudi Narayanan, Tam, 1981)
Nallavan (M. Thiruvengadam, Tam, 1955)
Nallavan (S.P. Muthuraman, Tam, 1988)
Nallavanukku Nallavan (S.P. Muthuraman, Tam, 1984)
Nallavan Vazhvan (**P. Neelakantan**, Tam, 1961)
Nalla Veedu (Jyotish Sinha, Tam, 1956)
Nalumani Pookkal (K.S. Gopalakrishnan, Mal, 1977)
Nalu Perukku Nandri (M.R. Rajamani/M.R. Somasundar, Tam, 1983)
Nalvar (V. Krishnan, Tam, 1953)
Nal Varavu (Charlie/Manian, Tam, 1964)
Namacha Mahima (*aka* Sant Namdev: Baburao Apte, Mar, 1937)
Namadhu Daivam (?, Apple Creations, Tam, 1990)
Namak (Balwant Dave, H, 1947)
Namak Halal (**Prakash Mehra**, H, 1982)
Namak Haram (*aka* Traitor, Maratha War Cry: **N.D. Sarpotdar**, St, 1928)
Namak Haram (**Hrishikesh Mukherjee**, H, 1973)
Namak Haram Kon (*aka* Bid for the Throne: Madanrai Vakil, St, 1931)
Namaskar (P.A. Prabhu, H, 1978)
Namaste (M. Sadiq/S.U. Sunny, H, 1943)
Namaste Ji (Daljit Krishna, H, 1965)
Nambiakka *see* Shivasharane Nambekka
Nambikkai Natchathram (Thirumalai-Mahalingam, Tam, 1975)
Nambinal Nambugal (M.S. Gopinath, Tam, 1982)
Nam Iruvar (**A.V. Meiyappan**, Tam, 1947)
Nam Iruvar (R. Krishnamurthy, Tam, 1985)
Namkeen (**S.S. Gulzar**, H, 1982)
Nam Kuzhandai (K.S. Gopalakrishnan, Tam, 1955)
Namma Baduku (M.N. Aradhya, K, 1971)
Namma Bhoomi (R. Thyagarajan, K, 1985)
Nammaka Drohulu (K.V.S. Kutumba Rao, Tel, 1971)
Namma Kuzhandiagal (Srikanth Poovannan, Tam, 1970)
Namma Makkalu (**R. Nagendra Rao**, K, 1969)
Namma Mane (Bhangararaj, K, 1970)
Namma Mane Sose (Vadiraj-Jawahar, K, 1980)
Nammana Mali (TV: **T.S. Nagabharana**, K, 1986)
Namma Ooru (C.V. Shivashankar, K, 1968)
Namma Ooru Mariamma (K. Rajan, Tam, 1991)
Namma Oru Nayakan (Kannan, Tam, 1988)
Namma Samsara (Siddalingaiah, K, 1971)
Namma Ura Devaru (N.T. Jayaram Reddy, K, 1974)
Namma Uru Poovatha (Manivasagam, Tam, 1990)
Nammaveeti Lakshmi (**B.R. Panthulu**, Tam, 1966)
Namma Veetu Daivam (G.N. Velumani, Tam, 1970)
Namminabantu/Pattayilin Vetri (**Adurthi Subba Rao**, Tel/Tam, 1960)
Namminabantu (?, Shri Jayabheri Art Prod, Tel, 1987)
Nammina Thayi Annamma (C. Chandrasekhar, K, 1981)
Nammoora Basvi (Ugranarasimha, K, 1983)
Nammoora Hemmira (Perala?, K, 1990)
Nammoora Raja (Bhargava, K, 1988)
Nam Naadu *see* Apna Desh
Nam Naadu (Jambulingam, Tam, 1969)
Namni Nagarvel (Radhakant, G, 1980)
Nam Ooru Nalla Ooru (V. Azhagappan, Tam, 1986)
Nampalli Nagu (M.S. Kota Reddy, Tel, 1984)
Namukku Parkkan Munthiri Thoppukal (**P. Padmarajan**, Mal, 1986)
Namumkin (*aka* Impossible: Nari Ghadiali, H, 1946)
Namumkin (**Hrishikesh Mukherjee**, H, 1983)
Namuna (Hira Singh, H, 1949)
Nanabhai Ko Mayero (Kamal Dadhicha, R, 1963)
Nanagu Hendthi Beku (B. Ramamurthy, K, 1991)
Nanak Dukhiya Sab Sansar (**Dara Singh**, P, 1970)
Nanak Naam Jahaz Hai (Ram Maheshwari, P, 1969)
Nanand Bhavjai (Kamalakar Torne, Mar, 1981)
Nanand Bhojai (**Manilal Joshi**, St, 1927)
Nanand Bhojai (**Nanubhai Vakil**, H, 1934)
Nanand Bhojai (**Ratibhai Punatar**, G/H, 1948)
Nanand Bhojai (Prabhakar Mandloi, R, 1985)
Nana Ranger Dinguli (Kanak Mukherjee, B, 1976)
Nana Vagarno Nathiyo (S.J. Talukdar, G, 1982)
Nanayam (**I.V. Sasi**, Mal, 1983)
Nanayam Illatha Nanayam (Visu, Tam, 1984)
Nanban (P.S. Srinivasa Rao, Tam, 1954)
Nanbargal (Shobha, Tam, 1991)
Nandadeep (Krishnarao Chonkar, Mar, 1962)
Nanda Deepa (M.R. Vittal, K, 1963)
Nanda En Nilla (A. Jagannathan, Tam, 1977)
Nanda Gokula (Y.R. Swamy, K, 1972)
Nandaila Jato (Yeshwant Pethkar, Mar, 1969)
Nandakumar (**Keshavrao Dhaiber**, Mar/H, 1938)
Nandakumar (**N.D. Sarpotdar**, Tam, 1938)
Nandan (Aravind Mukherjee, B, 1979)
Nandanar *see* Bhakta Nandan
Nandanar (*aka* The Elevation of the Downtrodden: **Raja Sandow**?/**A. Narayanan**?, St, 1929)
Nandanar (P.V. Rao, Tam, 1933)
Nandanar (M.L. Tandon, Tam, 1935)
Nandanar (**Murugadasa**, Tam, 1942)

Nandanvan (Ganpatrao Bhatt, G, 1961)
Nandaranir Sansar (Surendraranjan Sarkar, B, 1948)
Nand Batrisi (?, Majestic Film, St, 1924)
Nandi (**N. Lakshminarayan**, K, 1964)
Nandini *see* Kamavalli
Nandini (**Sailajananda Mukherjee**, B, 1941)
Nandini (Madhukar Pathak, Mar, 1969)
Nandita (**Sukumar Dasgupta**, B, 1945)
Nandita (Swadesh Sarkar, B, 1976)
Nandi Veedum Varukka (?, S.S. Movie Prod, Mal, 1986)
Nand Ke Lala *see* Radha Mohan
Nand Ke Lala (?, Asiatic Film, St, 1931)
Nand Kishore (*aka* Krishna Janma: ?, Hind Vijay Film, St, 1931)
Nand Kishore (Vasant Joglekar, Mar/H, 1951)
Nand Kumar (V.H. Palnitkar, St, 1930)
Nandri (Ramanarayanan, Tam, 1984)
Nandri Kalangal (**K.S. Gopalakrishnan**, Tam, 1980)
Nandri Meendum Varuga (Mouli, Tam, 1982)
Nandu (**J. Mahendran**, Tam, 1981)
Nane Bhagyavati (**G.V. Iyer**/T.V. Singh Thakore, K, 1968)
Nanendu Nimmavane (Phani Ramchandra, K, 1993)
Nane Raja (**A. Bhimsingh**, Tam, 1956)
Nane Raja (C.V. Rajendran, K, 1984)
Nane Raja Nane Mandiri (Balu Anand, Tam, 1985)
Nane Varuven (Sripriya, Tam, 1992)
Nanga Fakir (TV: **K.A. Abbas**, H, 1984)
Nangal (Hasan, Tam, 1992)
Nangal Pudhiavargal (?, Moovendar Movies, Tam, 1990)
Nangalude Kochu Doctor (Harikumar, Mal, 1989)
Nanghu Suvarkal (**K. Balachander**, Tam, 1971)
Nangooram (T. Veeratna, Tam, 1979)
Nanibai Ko Maryo (*aka* Narsi Bhagat: Kamal Dadhich, R, 1963)
Nanibai Ko Maryo (Ramnesh Puri, R, 1988)
Nani Gopaler Biye (Sudhir Mukherjee, B, 1973)
Nani Maa (*aka* The Grandma: Parvati Menon, H, 1980)
Nani Vahu (Bhupen Desai, G, 1982)
Nanjunda (S. Narayanan, K, 1992)
Nanjunda Nakkaga (Basavaraj Kestur, K, 1975)
Nanjundi Kalyana (M.S. Rajashekhar, K, 1989)
Na Ninna Bedenu (M.A. Raja Ram, K, 1979)
Na Ninna Bidalare (Vijay, K, 1979)
Na Ninna Mareyalare (Vijay, K, 1976)
Na Ninna Preetisuve (V. Somasekhar, K, 1986)
Na Niruvude Ninagangi (A.V. Sheshgiri Rao, K, 1979)
Nanna Devaru (B. Mallesh, K, 1982)
Nanna Kartavya (**Vedantam Raghavaiah**, K, 1965)
Nannambikkai (K. Vembu/Charlie, Tam, 1956)
Nanna Prathigne (K.S.R. Doss, K, 1985)
Nanna Prayashchitta (Ugranarasimha, K, 1978)
Nanna Rosha Nooru Varusha (Joe Simon, K, 1980)
Nanna Thamma (K. Babu Rao, K, 1970)
Nannha Farishta (**T. Prakash Rao**, H, 1969)
Nannha Shikari (Shomu Mukherjee, H, 1973)
Nannhe Munne *see* **Chimni Pakhare**
Nannhi Kaliyan (?, Raja Films, H, 1971)
Nanobba Kalla (Dorairaj-Bhagavan, K, 1979)
Nanu Baalabeku (K.S. Satyanara, K, 1974)
Nanum Inda Ooruthan (?, Sudalaya Prod, Tam, 1990)
Nanum Manidanthan (A. Sheshgiri Rao, Tam, 1964)
Nanum Neeyum (?, Tam, 1987)
Nanum Oru Penn (A.C. Trilogchander, Tam, 1963)
Nanum Oru Thozhilali (**C.V. Sridhar**, Tam, 1986)
Nanu Nanna Hendthi (D. Rajendra Babu, K, 1985)
Nao (D.N. Madhok, H, 1948)
Naqab (TV: **Amol Palekar**, H, 1988)
Naqab (Lekhraj Bhakri, H, 1955)
Naqab (**Raj Khosla**, H, 1988)
Naqab Posh (Ram Pawa, H, 1956)
Naqli Baap (Ahmed Gazi, H, 1949)
Naqli Doctor (**J.J. Madan**, H, 1933)
Naqli Heera (Ramanlal B. Desai, H, 1948)
Naqli Nawab (Tara Harish, H, 1962)
Naqli Rani (*aka* Sham Queen: **Harshadrai Mehta**?, St, 1927)
Naqsh-e-Sulemani (*aka* Tilasmi Taveez: A.P. Kapur, H, 1933)
Narada Naradi (Dev/**C. Pullaiah**, Tel, 1946)
Naradan Keralathil (?, Vidya Movietone, Mal, 1987)
Naradar (**S. Soundararajan**, Tam, 1942)
Narada's Worldly Life *see* Narad Sansar
Narada Vijaya (Siddalingaiah, K, 1980)
Naradhar Kalyanam (**C.S. Rao**, Tam, 1959)
Narad Leela (**Dhirubhai Desai**, H, 1972)
Narad Muni (Raman B. Desai, H/G, 1949)
Narad Naradi (**R.G. Torney**, Mar, 1941)
Narad Sansar (*aka* Narada's Worldly Life: Shinde, St, 1928)
Narakasur (**Nip Barua**, A, 1961)
Nara Kesari (*aka* Lion of Maharashtra: K.P. Bhave, St, 1928)
Nara Ki Narayan (*aka* Valmiki: ?, Sarosh Film, St, 1933)
Naramedh Yagna (Bijon Kumar Sen, B, 1954)
Naram Garam (**Hrishikesh Mukherjee**, H, 1981)
Nara Narayan (**Jyotish Bannerjee**, B, 1939)
Nara Narayan (Raja Yagnik, H, 1949)
Nara Narayana (**R.S. Prakash**/Jiten Bannerjee, St, 1931)
Nara Narayana (K. Rangarao, Tel, 1937)
Narasaiyani Hundi (**V.M. Vyas**, G, 1961)
Narasimha (Saiprakash, K, 1989)
Narasimha (**N. Chandra**, H, 1991)
Narasinh Avatar *see* Bhakta Prahlad
Narasinh Avatar (**S.N. Patankar**, St, 1920)
Narasinh Avatar (**Sohrab Modi**, H, 1949)
Narasinh Mehta (*aka* Great Devotee of Shri Krishna: **Suchet Singh**/Shukle, St, 1920)
Narasinh Mehta (G.S. Devare, St, 1924)
Narasinh Mehta (**Nanubhai Vakil**, G, 1932)
Nargis (D.D. Kashyap, H, 1946)
Nari (Prafulla Roy, B, 1942)
Nari (Raja Yagnik, H, 1942)
Nari (Trilochan, O, 1963)
Nari (S.K. Chand, H, 1981)
Nari Jaat (*aka* Oh Thou Woman: Haribhai Desai, St, 1931)
Nari Ke Nagan (*aka* Soul of a Snake: K.P. Bhave, St, 1927)
Nari Munidare Mari (Geethapriya, K, 1972)
Nari Nari Naduma Murari (A. Kodandarami Reddy, Tel, 1989)
Nariraj (*aka* Miss Calcutta: **Nanubhai Vakil**, H, 1936)
Narir Rup (Satish Dadgupta, B, 1948)
Nari Swargakke Dari (Siddalingaiah, K, 1981)
Nari Tu Narayani (**Manhar Raskapur**, G, 1978)
Narrow Footpaths, The *see* **Ottayadi Paathakal**
Narsi Bhagat *see* Nanibai Ko Maryo
Narsi Bhagat (**Vijay Bhatt**, H, 1940)
Narsi Bhagat (*aka* Ram Dhun: Devendra Goel, H, 1957)
Narsi Bhagat (Vijay B. Chauhan, H, 1985)
Nartaki (**Debaki Bose**, B/H, 1940)
Nartaki (**Nitin Bose**, H, 1963)
Nartaki Tara (*aka* Tara the Dancer: **Jyotish Bannerjee**?, St, 1922)
Nartanasala (**K. Kameshwara Rao**, Tel, 1963)
Narveer Tanaji (Ram Gabale, Mar, 1952)
Nasamajh (Virendra Sharma, H, 1986)
Nasbandi (I.S. Johar, H, 1978)
Naseeb (*aka* Can't Help It: Vedi, H, 1945)
Naseeb (**Manmohan Desai**, H, 1981)
Naseeb Apna Apna (**T. Rama Rao**, H, 1986)
Naseebdar (Maganlal Thakar, G, 1950)
Naseebdar (Kishore Vyas, G, 1981)
Naseeb Ka Chakkar (*aka* Wheels of Destiny: Pesi Karani, H, 1936)
Naseeb Ni Balihari (*aka* Troubles Never Come Alone: **Niranjan Pal**, St, 1930)
Naseeb Ni Balihari (Nimesh Desai, G, 1982)
Naseeb Ni Devi (*aka* Goddess of Luck: Fatma Begum, St, 1929)
Naseeb Ni Lili (*aka* Kicks of Kismet: **M. Bhavnani**, St, 1927)
Naseeb Ni Nakhara (*aka* Shattered Hopes: Vithaldas Panchotia, St, 1929)
Naseeb Ni Nauka (*aka* Winds of Fate: ?, New Kohinoor Film, St, 1930)
Naseeb No Khel (**Mehul Kumar**, G, 1982)
Naseebwala (Kalpataru, H, 1992)
Naseema (A. Sharief, Mal, 1983)
Nashibvaan (N.S. Vaidya, Mar, 1988)
Nashikcha Panjarpol (**Dadasaheb Phalke**, St, 1926)
Nasihat (Om Patwar, H, 1967)
Nasihat (Aravind Sen, H, 1986)
Nasoor (Ashok Chopra, H, 1985)
Nastaneer (**Pashupati Chatterjee**, B, 1951)
Nastik (I.S. Johar, H, 1954)
Nastik (Pramod Chakraborty, H, 1983)
Nastik Prem *see* Zan Mureed
Nasti Uthathev (**Datta Dharmadhikari**, Mar, 1973)
Natak (S.U. Sunny, H, 1947)
Natak (Sohanlal Kanwar, H, 1975)
Natakalarayudu (A. Sanjivi, Tel, 1969)
Natasarva Bhowma (Aruru Pattabhi, K, 1968)
Natashekhara (C.V. Raju, K, 1954)
Natchatiram (**Dasari Narayana Rao**, Tam, 1980)
Nate Jadle Don Jivache (Gurubal, Mar, 1971)
Nathayil Muthu (**K.S. Gopalakrishnan**, Tam, 1973)
Nathoon (K. Narayanan, Mal, 1974)
Natija (Najam Naqvi, H, 1947)
Natija (Rajesh Nanda, H, 1969)
Natir Puja (Rabindranath Tagore, B, 1932)
Natpu (Ameerjan, Tam, 1986)
Nattai Thirudathe (Senthilnathan, Tam, 1991)
Nattarangu (**P. Bhaskaran**, Mal, 1987)
Nattuchakkiruttu (Ravigupthan, Mal, 1980)
Nattukoru Nallaval (K. Dasharatha Ramaiah, Tam, 1959)
Nattukoru Nallavan (V. Ravichandran, Tam, 1991)
Nattu Vishesham (Paul Garakkal, Mal, 1991)
Natun Asha (Prabin Mitra, A, 1977)
Natun Bou (Surendraranjan Sarkar, B, 1946)
Natun Diner Alo (Ajit Ganguly, B, 1972)
Natun Fasal (**Hemchandra Chunder**, B, 1960)
Natun Khabar (**Premendra Mitra**, B, 1947)
Natun Pata (**Dinen Gupta**, B, 1969)
Natun Pathshala (Biren Das, B, 1952)
Natun Prabhat (Bikash Roy, B, 1957)
Natun Prithibi (**Anwar Hussain**, A, 1958)
Natun Surya (Jagdish Bhattacharya, B, 1974)
Natun Surya (Sachin Adhikari, B, 1989)
Natun Tirtha (Sudhir Mukherjee, B, 1964)
Natun Yahudi (Salil Sen, B, 1953)
Nature Symphony (**Shyam Benegal**, E, 1990)
Natya Rani (**Balkrishna Narayan Rao**, Tam, 1949)
Naubahar (Anand Kumar, H, 1952)
Nau Do Gyarah (**Vijay Anand**, H, 1957)
Naughty Boy (**Shakti Samanta**, H, 1962)
Naughty Girl *see* Toofani Taruni
Naughty Maid *see* Nakhreli Nar
Naujawan (Aspi, H, 1937)
Naujawan (**Mahesh Kaul**, H, 1951)
Naujawan (Chand, H, 1966)
Nauka Bilash (Sudhir Mukherjee, B, 1959)
Nauka Dubi (**Naresh Mitra**, St, 1932)
Nauka Dubi/Milan (**Nitin Bose**, B/H, 1946)
Nauka Dubi (**Ajoy Kar**, B, 1979)
Naukar (Shaukat Hussain Rizvi, H, 1943)
Naukar (Ismail Memon, H, 1979)
Naukar Biwi Da (H.S. Kanwal, P, 1976)
Naukar Biwi Ka (Rajkumar Kohli, H, 1983)
Naukri (**Bimal Roy**, H, 1954)
Naukri (**Hrishikesh Mukherjee**, H, 1978)
Naulakha Haar (B. Shukla/H. Bhatt, H, 1953)
Naunihal (Raj Marbros, H, 1967)
Nausherwan-e-Adil (*aka* Farz Aur Mohabbat: **Sohrab Modi**, H, 1957)
Navabharata (K.V. Raju, K, 1988)
Navabharatam (Mutyala Subbaiah, Tel, 1988)
Navadakku Paniyedukku (A.R. Rajan, Mal, 1985)
Navagraham (**K. Balachander**, Tam, 1970)
Navagraha Nayaki (K. Shankar, Tam, 1985)
Navagraha Pooja Mahima (**B. Vittalacharya**, Tel, 1964)
Navajeevan/Navajeevanam (**Kadaru Nagabhushanam**, Tel/Tam, 1949)
Navajeevana (P.S. Murthy, K, 1964)
Navakoti Narayana (S.K. Ananthachari, K, 1964)
Navalakh Haar *see* Kanak Kanta
Navalkatha (Sushil Gajwani, Mar, 1985)
Navalokam (V. Krishnan, Mal, 1951)
Navalsha Hirji (**Ardeshir Irani**, St, 1925)
Nava Mohini (**B. Vittalacharya**, Tel, 1984)
Navara Baiko (Bal Gajbar, Mar, 1950)
Navara Baiko (N.S. Vaidya, Mar, 1989)
Navara Mazha Brahmachari (**Datta Keshav**, Mar, 1977)
Navara Mhanu Naye Aapla (**Dinkar D. Patil**, Mar, 1957)
Navarathnam (**A.P. Nagarajan**, Tam, 1977)
Navarathri (**A.P. Nagarajan**, Tam, 1964)
Navarathri (**T. Rama Rao**, Tel, 1966)
Navardev (**R.G. Torney**, Mar, 1941)
Navare Sagle Gadhav (Kamalakar Torne, Mar, 1982)
Navari Mile Navaryala (Sachin, Mar, 1984)
Navaryana Sodli (G.G. Bhonsle, Mar, 1987)
Nava Tare (Nanjunde Gowda, K, 1991)
Navavadhu (**P. Bhaskaran**, Mal, 1971)
Navayuvan (*aka* Geetha Saram, Modern Youth: Michael Ormalov, Tam, 1937)
Navbharat (Chunilal Parekh, St, 1933)
Navbharat (*aka* Jawan Mard: Chunilal Parekh, H, 1934)
Navchetan (G.R. Sethi, H, 1932)
Nav Durga (**Babubhai Mistri**, H, 1953)
Naveena Markandeya (A.T. Krishnaswamy, Tam, 1941)
Naveena Nirupama (*aka* The Mysore Bandit: V. Thimmaiah, Tam, 1937)
Naveena Sadarame (**K. Subramanyam**, Tam, 1935)
Naveena Sarangadhara (**K. Subramanyam**, Tam, 1935)
Naveena Stree Sahasam (T.C. Vadivelu Naicker, Tam, 1937)
Naveena Tenali Raman (C.V. Raman, Tam, 1940)
Naveena Valli (T. Balaji Singh, Tam, 1948)
Naveena Vikramadithan (K.S. Mani, Tam, 1940)
Navin Bharat (**Jyotish Bannerjee**/Kashinath Chatterjee, St, 1924)
Navi Sethani *see* Kanya Vikraya Ni Kahani
Navjatak (Biren Das, H, 1976)
Navjeevam *see* Navajeevanam
Navjeevan (**M. Bhavnani**, H, 1935)
Navjeevan (**Franz Osten**, H, 1939)
Navodayam (P. Purushottam Rao, Tel, 1978)
Navodayam (P. Chandrasekhara Reddy, Tel, 1982)
Navrang (**V. Shantaram**, H, 1959)
Navrang Chundadi (Kishore Vyas, G, 1979)
Navratri (Raman B. Desai, H, 1955)
Navratri (Ashish Kumar, H, 1983)
Navu Yarigenu Kadime (Rajachandra, K, 1983)
Navvitte Navarathrulu (**S. Soundararajan**, Tel, 1951)
Nawab Narkali (C.V. Rajendran, Tam, 1972)
Nawab Sahib (**Rajinder Singh Bedi**, H, 1978)
Nawab Siraj-ud-Dowla (**Ramchandra Thakur**, H, 1967)
Nawabzadi *see* Payame Ulfat
Naxalites, The (**K.A. Abbas**, H, 1979)
Naya Admi *see* Santosham
Naya Andaz (**K. Amarnath**, H, 1956)
Naya Bakra (K. Babuji, H, 1979)
Naya Daur (**B.R. Chopra**, H, 1957)
Naya Daur (**Mahesh Bhatt**, H, 1978)
Naya Din Nayi Raat (**A. Bhimsingh**, H, 1974)
Nayadugarabbai (B.V. Prasad, Tel, 1981)
Naya Ghar (D.D. Kashyap, H, 1953)

Nayak (**Satyajit Ray**, B, 1966)
Nayaka (V. Chandrahasa, K, 1991)
Naya Kadam (S.P. Kalla, H, 1958)
Naya Kadam (**K. Raghavendra Rao**, H, 1984)
Nayakan (Balu Kiriyath, Mal, 1984)
Nayakan (**Mani Rathnam**, Tam, 1987)
Naya Kanoon (R.C. Talwar, H, 1965)
Nayakarin Magal (**K.S. Gopalakrishnan**, Tam, 1982)
Naya Khoon (Rajat Rakshit, H, 1990)
Nayakudu Vinayakudu (**K. Pratyagatma**, Tel, 1980)
Nayakulaku Saval (K.S.R. Doss, Tel, 1984)
Nayakuralu (Sathya Reddy, Tel, 1991)
Naya Michhil (Piyush Kanti Ganguly, B, 1972)
Nayam Vethamakkunnu (**Balachandra Menon**, Mal, 1991)
Nayan (Sukhen Das, B, 1976)
Naya Nasha (Hari Dutt, H, 1973)
Nayanmoni (**Suprabha Debi**, A, 1983)
Nayanmoni (Sachin Adhikari, B, 1989)
Nayan Shyama (Nitish Mukherjee, B, 1983)
Naya Paisa (Aspi, H, 1958)
Naya Raasta (**Jayant Desai**, H, 1953)
Naya Raasta (**Nabyendu Chatterjee**, H, 1967)
Naya Raasta (Khalid Akhtar, H, 1970)
Naya Safar *see* Nabin Yatra
Naya Safar (Pawan Kumar, H, 1985)
Naya Sansar (**N.R. Acharya**, H, 1941)
Naya Sansar (**Nanabhai Bhatt**, H, 1959)
Naya Tarana (Najam Naqvi, H, 1943)
Nayattu (Shrikumaran Thampi, Mal, 1980)
Naya Zamana (**Homi Master**, H, 1935)
Naya Zamana (**Nanubhai Vakil**, H, 1943)
Naya Zamana (Lekhraj Bhakri, H, 1957)
Naya Zamana (Pramod Chakraborty, H, 1971)
Naya Zamana Nai Kranti (Chandresh Chaitnya, H, 1990)
Nayikar Bhumikay (Aravind Mukherjee, B, 1972)
Nayika Sangbad (**Agradoot**, B, 1967)
Nazar (**Mani Kaul**, H, 1989)
Nazare (Prahlad Dutt, H, 1949)
Nazar Ka Shikar (A.P. Kapur, H, 1936)
Nazhikakallu (Sudhin Menon, Mal, 1970)
Nazneen (N.K. Ziree, H, 1951)
Nazrana (G.P. Kapoor, Marwari/H, 1942)
Nazrana (**C.V. Sridhar**, H, 1961)
Nazrana (Ravi Tandon, H, 1987)
Nazrana Pyar Ka (S.M. Sagar, H, 1980)
Necklace *see* Chandramani
Necklace (Dilip Nag, B, 1961)
Nee (?, Shri Vinay*aka* Pics, Tam, 1965)
Nee Allenkil Gnan (?, Mal, 1987)
Nee Bareda Kadambari (Dwarkeesh, K, 1985)
Neecha Nagar (**Chetan Anand**, H, 1946)
Needa (**Dasari Narayana Rao**, Tel, 1979)
Needaleni Adhadi (B.V. Prasad, Tel, 1974)
Needhi Peedham (Mani, Mal, 1977)
Needhikku Mun Neeya Nana (**Durai**, Tam, 1979)
Needhikkupin Pasam (M.A. Thirumugham, Tam, 1963)
Needhikku Thalai Vanangu (**P. Neelakantan**, Tam, 1976)
Needhikku Thandanai (S.A. Chandrasekharan, Tam, 1987)
Needle's Eye *see* Sui Ka Naka
Nee Ente Lahari (P.G. Vishwambaran, Mal, 1976)
Nee Indri Nanillai (A.C. Trilogchander, Tam, 1976)
Neeku Naaku Pellanta (Jandhyala, Tel, 1988)
Neela (Baburao Khandekar, Mar/H, 1935)
Neela Akash (Rajendra Bhatia, H, 1965)
Neelachaley Mahaprabhu (**Kartick Chattopadhyay**, B, 1957)
Neelagiri (**I.V. Sasi**, Mal, 1991)
Neelakadalin Orathile (K. Shankar, Tam, 1979)
Neela Kannukal (**Madhu**, Mal, 1974)
Neel Akasher Neechey (**Mrinal Sen**, B, 1958)
Neelakuyil (**P. Bhaskaran/Ramu Kariat**, Mal, 1954)
Neelam (*aka* Dilruba: Essa, H, 1945)
Neela Madhab (J.P. Bhagat, O, 1979)
Neelamalai Kaidhi (**Homi Master**/D.V. Sami, Tam, 1940)
Neelamalai Thirudan (M.A. Thirumugham, Tam, 1957)
Neela Malargal (**Krishnan-Panju**, Tam, 1979)
Neelam Manek (**Kanjibhai Rathod**, St, 1928)
Neelam Pari (**Dhirubhai Desai**, H, 1952)
Neela Ponman (**Kunchako**, Mal, 1975)
Neelasari (M. Krishnan Nair, Mal, 1976)
Neelavanam (Pattu Films, Tam, 1965)
Neelavukku Niranja Manasu (K. Somu, Tam, 1958)
Neeli Aankhen (Ved-Madan, H, 1962)
Neelima (Pushpraj, H, 1975)
Neelisally (**Kunchako**, Mal, 1960)
Neel Kamal (**Kidar Sharma**, H, 1947)
Neel Kamal (Ram Maheshwari, H, 1968)
Neelkantha (Dilip Roy, B, 1985)
Neel Mani (Kundan Kumar, H, 1957)
Neem Annapurna (**Buddhadev Dasgupta**, B, 1979)
Neem Hakim (B.S. Glaad, P, 1967)
Nee Nakkaga (C.S. Manju, K, 1985)
Nee Nanna Gellalare (Vijay, K, 1981)
Neend Hamari Khwab Tumhare (Shiv Sahni, H, 1966)
Neengal Kettavai (**Balu Mahendra**, Tam, 1984)
Neengalum Herothan (V. Shekhar, Tam, 1990)
Neenga Nalla Erukkanum (Visu, Tam, 1992)
Neenkada Ninaivu (**Adurthi Subba Rao**, Tam, 1963)
Neenu Nakkare Haalu Sakkare (Dorairaj-Bhagavan, K, 1991)
Nee Oru Maharani (K. Swarnam, Tam, 1976)
Neepathi Naan Pathi (Vasanth, Tam, 1991)
Neera (**R.S. Choudhury/R.G. Torney**, St, 1926)
Neera Aur Nanda (R.S. Junnarkar, H, 1946)
Neerab Jhada (**Manmohan Mahapatra**, O, 1984)
Neerajanam (Ashok Kumar, Tel, 1989)
Neera Neela (?, O, 1988?)
Neer Kumizhi (**K. Balachander**, Tam, 1965)
Neer Nilam Neruppu (**K.S. Gopalakrishnan**, Tam, 1980)
Neerottam (Jaidurai, Tam, 1980)
Neerum Neruppum (**P. Neelakantan**, Tam, 1971)
Neeru Poothatha Neruppu (K. Vijayan, Tam, 1983)
Neer Vazhi (M.M.A. Chinappa Devar, Tam, 1968)
Nee Sirithal Deepavali (Malaysia Vasu, Tam, 1990)
Nee Sirithal Naan Sirippen (V. Rajagopal, Tam, 1979)
Neethana Anda Kuyil (R. Selvaraj, Tam, 1986)
Nee Thanda Kanike (Dwarkeesh, K, 1985)
Neethi (A.B. Raj, Mal, 1971)
Neethi (C.V. Rajendran, Tam, 1972)
Neethi Devan (R. Devarajan, Tam, 1971)
Neethi Devan Mayakam (**Bapu**, Tam, 1982)
Neethikku Oru Penn (Kalaignanam, Panassai Mani, Tam, 1984)
Neethi Nijayathi (**Singeetham Srinivasa Rao**, Tel, 1972)
Neethipathi (**A.S.A. Sami**, Tam, 1955)
Neethipathi (K. Krishnamurthy, Tam, 1983)
Neethi Pizhanthathu (?, Tam, 1981)
Neethiyin Marupakkam (S.A. Chandrasekharan, Tam, 1985)
Neethiyin Nizhal (Bharathi Vasu, Tam, 1985)
Nee Thodum Pothu (V.C. Guhanathan, Tam, 1984)
Nee Ulla Varai (C.V. Ramana, Tam, 1973)
Nee Vanthal Vasantham (A. Radhakrishnan, Tam, 1989)
Nee Vazhavendum (**A. Bhimsingh**, Tam, 1977)
Neeya (**Durai**, Tam, 1979)
Neeya Nanna *see* Nuvva Nena
Neeyat (Anil Ganguly, H, 1980)
Neeyethra Dhanya (?, Chitrakaumudi Films, Mal, 1987)
Neeyo Jnano (Chandrakumar, Mal, 1979)
Neeyum Nanum (Ramanna, Tam, 1968)
Neezhal Kolam (Ramanna, Tam, 1979)
Neglected Wife *see* Matlabi Duniya
Nehle Pe Dehla (Hansraj Patel, H, 1946)
Nehle Pe Dehla (**Raj Khosla**, H, 1976)
Nehru (**Shyam Benegal**/Yuri Aldokin, E/Russian, 1983)
Nek Abla (*aka* Scented Devil: Rustom Poonawala, H, 1932)
Nek Dil (?, Lighthouse Prod, H, 1948)
Nek Dost (*aka* Royal Friend: G.P. Pawar, St, 1933)
Neki Aur Badi (*aka* Morals Sugar-coated: **Kidar Sharma**, H, 1949)
Neki Ka Taj (**N.G. Devare**, H, 1934)
Nek Khatoon (Pyarelal, H, 1959)
Nek Perveen (S.M. Yusuf, H, 1946)
Nek Perveen (K. Shareef, H, 1982)
Nelavanka (Jandhyala, Tel, 1983)
Nellikani (Kalaignanam, Tam, 1981)
Nellu (**Ramu Kariat**, Mal, 1974)
Nemesis of Lust *see* Aseer-e-Hirs
Nenaivellam Nithya (**C.V. Sridhar**, Tam, 1982)
Nenante Nene (V. Ramchandra Rao, Tel, 1968)
Nenapina Doni (**T.S. Nagabharana**, K, 1986)
Nenara Police (Anilkumar, Tel, 1991)
Nene Maa Avide (Relangi Narasimha Rao, Tel, 1981)
Nene Monaganni (S.D. Lall, Tel, 1968)
Nene Raju Nene Manthri (**Dasari Narayana Rao**, Tel, 1987)
Nenjamellam Neeye (K. Rangaraj, Tam, 1983)
Nenjam Marappathillai (**C.V. Sridhar**, Tam, 1963)
Nenjangal (Major Sundarrajan, Tam, 1982)
Nenjathai Allitha (Ameerjan, Tam, 1984)
Nenjathai Killathey (*aka* Don't Pinch the Heart: **J. Mahendran**, Tam, 1980)
Nenja Thottu Chollu (T.N. Kanna, Tam, 1992)
Nenjile Thunivirundhal (S.A. Chandrasekharan, Tam, 1981)
Nenjil Ore Alayam (**C.V. Sridhar**, Tam, 1962)
Nenjil Oru Mul (Mathiali Shanmugham, Tam, 1981)
Nenjil Oru Ragam (**T. Rajendar**, Tam, 1982)
Nenjirukumvarai (**C.V. Sridhar**, Tam, 1967)
Nenjukku Needhi (?, Sivaleela Cine Arts, Tam, 1979)
Nentaro Gantu Kallaro (A.V. Sheshgiri Rao, K, 1979)
Nenu Manishine (G.V.R. Sheshgiri Rao, Tel, 1971)
Nenu Naa Desam (M.S. Gopinath, Tel, 1973)
Neram Nadhikadhu (A. Kodandarami Reddy, Tel, 1989)
Neram Nadhikadu Akalidi (S.D.Lall, Tel, 1976)
Neram Nalla Irukku (**Manoj Kumar**, Tam, 1987)
Neram Nalla Neram (N. Sambandan, Tam, 1984)
Neram Pularumbol (**K.P. Kumaran**, Mal, 1985)
Neramu Siksha (**K. Vishwanath**, Tel, 1973)
Neram Vadatchu (M. Vellaisami, Tam, 1982)
Nerariyum Nerathu (Salam Chembazhanthi, Mal, 1985)
Nerasthudu (K.S.R. Doss, Tel, 1985)
Nermai (R. Krishnamurthy, Tam, 1985)
Nerupil Pootha Malar (Kowshik, Tam, 1981)
Neruppukkul Eeram (R. Krishnamurthy, Tam, 1984)
Nest, The *see* Gharonda
Nestmates (**Pradeep Krishen**, E, 1978)
Nest of Rhythm, The *see* **Chhandaneer**
Netaji Palkar (**V. Shantaram/Keshavrao Dhaiber**, St, 1927)
Netaji Palkar (**Bhalji Pendharkar**, Mar, 1939)
Netaji Palkar (Kamalakar Torne, Mar, 1978)
Netaji Subhash (*aka* Jai Hind: Chhotubhai Desai, H, 1947)
Netaji Subhashchandra Bose (**Hemen Gupta**, H, 1966)
Nethavu (Hassan, Mal, 1984)
Nethiadi (R. Pandiarajan, Tam, 1989)
Neti Bharatham (T. Krishna, Tel, 1983)
Neti Charitra (Muthyala Subbaiah, Tel, 1990)
Neti Sudhantaram (T. Gopalakrishna, Tel, 1989)
Neti Yugadharmam (G. Rammohan Rao, Tel, 1986)
Netraheen Sakshi (Nabendu Ghosh, H, 1991)
Netra Pallavi (**T.S. Nagabharana**, K, 1985)
Netrikkan (S.P. Muthuraman, Tam, 1981)
Netru Indru Nalai (**P. Neelakantan**, Tam, 1974)
New Crop of the New Age *see* Nai Umar Ki Nai Fasal
New Day, The *see* Prabhat
New Delhi (**Mohan Segal**, H, 1956)
New Delhi (Joshi, Mal/H, 1987)
New Delhi Times (**Ramesh Sharma**, H, 1985)
New Earth (**Gautam Ghosh**, E, 1973)
New Horizons in Steel (**Shyam Benegal**, E, 1981)
New Leaf, The *see* **Natun Pata**
New Life of a Displaced Person (**Paul Zils**, E, 1957)
New Marketplace (**Fali Bilimoria**, E, 1961)
New Moulds, The *see* **Puthiya Varpugal**
New Searchlight (**Homi Master**, H, 1937)
Newspaper Boy (P. Ramadas, Mal, 1955)
New Vedas *see* **Vedham Pudithu**
New World *see* **Navalokam**
New World of Power (**S. Sukhdev**, E, 1977)
New Year (Viji Thampi, Mal, 1989)
Next to God *see* Pyar
NGO (S.S. Rajan, Mal, 1967)
Ngak-E-Ko-Nangse (S.N. Chand `Sajatia', Manipuri, 1974)
NH 47 (Baby, Mal, 1984)
Nichayam (S. Venkat, Tam, 1984)
Nidhi Ram Sardar (**Robi Ghosh**, B, 1976)
Nidra (**B.G. Bharathan**, Mal, 1981)
Nidrit Bhagwan (*aka* Sleeping God: ?, Indian Film, St, 1931)
Nigah-e-Kaamil (*aka* Perfect Man: Rukesh?, H, 1938)
Nigahen (*aka* Nagina-II: Harmesh Malhotra, H, 1989)
Nigah-e-Nafrat *see* **Vilasi Ishwar**
Nigah-e-Ulfat *see* Mohabbat Ka Toofan
Nighooda Rahasya (Perala, K, 1990)
Night Bird (*aka* Raat Ka Raja, Nishachar: **Dhiren Ganguly**, H, 1934)
Night Bird (A.R. Zamindar, H, 1961)
Night Club (Naresh Saigal, H, 1958)
Night Duty (**Sasikumar**, Mal, 1974)
Night in Calcutta *see* Calcutta After Midnight
Nightingale *see* Ban Ki Chidiya
Night in London (Brij Sadanah, H, 1967)
Night in the City, A *see* **Jagte Raho**
Night of Love *see* Prem Raatri
Night of Terror *see* Dushman Ki Raat
Night's End *see* **Nishant** *or* Raat Bhore
Night Side of Bombay *see* **Mumbai Ni Mohini**
Nijam (Devadas Kanakala, Tel, 1980)
Nijam Cheppithe Nammaru (Rajesh, Tel, 1973)
Nijam Cheppithe Nerama (M. Baliah, Tel, 1983)
Nijam Nidra Podu (Rajashri, Tel, 1976)
Nijam Nirupistha (Janakiram, Tel, 1972)
Nijangal (**K.S. Sethumadhavan**, Tam, 1982)
Nija Roopalu (K.V. Nandan Rao, Tel, 1973)
Nijhum Ratir Sathi (Biswajit Das, O, 1979)
Nikaah (**B.R. Chopra**, H, 1982)
Nikhare (Dr. Devdutt Mhatre, Mar, 1985)
Nikhettoo (Hyder Shah: Union Pics, Lahore, P, 1943)
Nikki (?, Indrapuri Studio, P, 1958)
Nilagiri Express (Mahalingam, Tam, 1968)
Nilakatha Chalanangal (K. Sukumaran, Mal, 1970)
Nilakurinhi Poothappol (**B.G. Bharathan**, Mal, 1986)
Nilanguriya (Gunamaya Bannerjee, B, 1943)
Nilapennay (Thamizazhagan, Tam, 1990)
Nilathamara (Yusuf Ali Kacheri, Mal, 1979)
Nilavai Kail Pudichen (Ramanarayanan, Tam, 1987)
Nilave Malare (S.A. Chandrasekharan, Tam, 1986)
Nilave Nee Satchi (?, S.P. Pics, Tam, 1970)
Nilavinte Nattil (Vijay Menon, Mal, 1986)
Nilavu Suduvathillai (K. Rangaraj, Tam, 1984)
Nildarpan (Bimal Roy Jr., B, 1952)
Nili (**Ratibhai Punatar**, H, 1950)
Nil Kavani Kadhali (C.V. Rajendran, Tam, 1969)
Niloufer (P.N. Arora, H, 1957)
Nilshari (Sudhir Bandhu, B, 1954)
Niluvu Dopidi (**C.S. Rao**, Tel, 1968)

Nimaijanam (B.S. Narayana, Tel, 1984)
Nimai Sanyasi (**Phani Burma**, B, 1940)
Nimila Anka (Lakhyadhar Choudhury, A, 1955)
Nimantran (**Tarun Majumdar**, B, 1971)
Nimirnthu Nil (Devan, Tam, 1968)
Nimishangal (?, Mal, 1986)
Nimmo (Veerendra, P, 1984)
Ninad (J.H. Sattar, O, 1984)
Ninagagi Nanu (**C.V. Sridhar**, K, 1975)
Ninaikka Therindha Maname (D.F.T. Suresh, Tam, 1987)
Ninaipadarku Neramillai (K.C.K., Tam, 1963)
Ninaippathu Niraiverum (S.T. Dandapani, Tam, 1975)
Ninaithale Inikkum (**K. Balachander**, Tam, 1979)
Ninaithathai Mudippavan (**P. Neelakantan**, Tam, 1975)
Ninaivel Nidraval (V. Srinivasan, Tam, 1967)
Ninaive Oru Sangeetham (K. Rangaraj, Tam, 1987)
Ninaivu Chinnam (Anumohan, Tam, 1989)
Ninaivugal (M. Vellaisamy, Tam, 1984)
Ninaivugal Marappathillai (?, T.M. Pics., Tam, 1993)
Ninakku Gnanam Enikku Neeyum (**Sasikumar**, Mal, 1978)
Ninamanninnya Kalapadakal (N.N. Pishareddy, Mal, 1963)
Nindu Dampatulu (**K. Vishwanath**, Tel, 1971)
Nindu Hridayalu (**K. Vishwanath**, Tel, 1969)
Nindu Kutumbam (P. Sambhasiva Rao, Tel, 1973)
Nindu Manishi (S.D. Lall, Tel, 1978)
Nindu Manushulu (S.D. Lall, Tel, 1967)
Nindu Noorellu (**K. Raghavendra Rao**, Tel, 1979)
Nindu Samsaram (**C.S. Rao**, Tel, 1968)
Nine Months to Freedom: The Story of Bangladesh (**S. Sukhdev**, E, 1972)
1921 *see* **Ayarthi Thollayirathi Irupathonnu**
1990 Kaliyuga Vishwamitra (Pradeep Shakthi, Tel, 1989)
Ningalenne Communistaki (**Thoppil Bhasi**, Mal, 1970)
Ningalil Oru Stree (A.B. Raj, Mal, 1984)
Ninne Pelladuta (**B. Vittalacharya**, Tel, 1968)
Ninnishtam Ennishtam (**Priyadarshan**, Mal, 1986)
Nippulanti Manishi (S.D. Lall, Tel, 1974)
Nippulanti Manishi (N.B. Chakraborty, Tel, 1986)
Nippulanti Nijam (**K. Raghavendra Rao**, Tel, 1980)
Nippuravva (A. Kodandarami Reddy, Tel, 1993)
Nipputho Chelagatam (Kommineni, Tel, 1982)
Nirabhedangal (Sajan, Mal, 1987)
Niradhar *see* Aarti
Niradhar Nira (*aka* Deity in Distress: Chunilal Parekh, St, 1931)
Nirai Kudam (V. Srinivasan, Tam, 1969)
Nirakkootte (Joshi, Mal, 1985)
Nirakshar (Gunamaya Bannerjee, B, 1952)
Nirakudam (**A. Bhimsingh**, Mal, 1977)
Nirala (Devendra Mukherjee, H, 1950)
Nirala Hindustan (*aka* Industrial India: Mohan Sinha, H, 1938)
Nirali Duniya (*aka* Trust Your Wife: **V.M. Vyas**, H, 1940)
Niram Maratha Pookal/Niram Maradha Pushpangal (**Bharathirajaa**, Tam/Tel, 1979)
Niram Marunna Nimishangal (?, Mal, 1982)
Niramulla Ravukal (N. Shankaran Nair, Mal, 1986)
Nirantharam (R.K. Murthy, Tam, 1982)
Niraparadhi *see* **Nirdoshi**
Niraparadhi (B. Vallinayagam, K, 1969)
Niraparadhi (K. Vijayan, Tam/Mal, 1984)
Niraparayum Nilavilakkum (**Singeetham Srinivasa Rao**, Mal, 1977)
Nirbhagi Nirmala (*aka* Woman in the Wilderness: **Kanjibhai Rathod**, St, 1930)
Nirdharita Silpir Anupastithi Tey (**Nirmal Dey**, B, 1959)
Nirdosh (Virendra M. Desai, Mar/H, 1941)
Nirdosh (Najam Naqvi, H, 1950)
Nirdosh (S.M. Sagar, H, 1973)
Nirdosh Abla (**N.G. Devare**, St, 1929)
Nirdosh Abla (*aka* Asmat Ki Devi, Broken Hearts: Vijay Ghaswala, H, 1935)
Nirdosh Abla (S. Srivastava, H, 1949)
Nirdoshi/Niraparadhi (**H.M. Reddy**, Tel/Tam, 1951)
Nirdoshi (Dada Mirasi, Tel, 1967)
Nirdoshi (Rajachandra, Tel, 1984)
Nirdosh Nritika *see* Pak Daman Raqasa
Nireekshana (**Balu Mahendra**, Tel, 1982)
Nireekshe (Kovi Manisekaran, K, 1975)
Nirjan Saikate (**Tapan Sinha**, B, 1963)
Nirmaan (Ravi Tandon, H, 1974)
Nirmaan (Arun Jaitly, H, 1987)
Nirmal (S. Upendra, H, 1952)
Nirmala (**Franz Osten**, H, 1938)
Nirmala (P.V. Krishna Iyer, Mal, 1948)
Nirmala (P. Ramadas, Mal, 1975)
Nirmalayam (**M.T. Vasudevan Nair**, Mal, 1973)
Nirmohi (Baij Sharma, H, 1952)
Nirnayam (**Priyadarshan**, Tel, 1991)
Niruddesh (**Niren Lahiri**, B, 1949)
Nirupama Ani Parirani (Vinay Kale, Mar, 1961)
Nirupedalu (**T. Prakash Rao**, Tel, 1954)
Nirvana (Jalal Agha, H, 1983)
Nisbat (S. Shamsuddin, H, 1949)
Nisha *see* Nai Duniya Naye Log
Nishachar *see* Night Bird
Nishachar (Bhupen Roy, B, 1971)
Nishagandhi (A.N. Thambi, Mal, 1970)
Nishan *see* **Apoorva Sahodarargal**
Nishan (Aspi Irani, H, 1965)
Nishan (S.S. Balan, B, 1978)
Nishan (Surendra Mohan, H, 1983)
Nishana (K.L. Kahan, H, 1946)
Nishana (Wajahat Mirza, H, 1950)
Nishana (**K. Raghavendra Rao**, H, 1980)
Nishan Danka (*aka* Flag of Honour: **Dhirubhai Desai**, St, 1929)
Nishan Danka (**Jayant Desai**, H, 1952)
Nishanebaazi (V.N. Menon, H, 1989)
Nishan-e-Jung (A.R. Kabuli, H, 1937)
Nishani (**Roop K. Shorey**, H, 1942)
Nishant (**Shyam Benegal**, H, 1975)
Nishantay (Narayan Chakraborty, B, 1985)
Nishar Chakulu (Deb Kumar Barua, A, 1979)
Nisha Sundari (*aka* Midnight Girl: **Moti Gidwani**, St, 1929)
Nishchay (Esmayeel Shroff, H, 1992)
Nishchaya Thambulam *see* Pelli Thambulam
Nishedhi (K.S. Gopalakrishnan, Mal, 1984)
Nishi Badhu (Robi Bose, B, 1989)
Nishi Basar (Niranjan Dey, B, 1987)
Nishi Bhor (Rashbehari Sinha, B, 1983)
Nishiddha Phal (*aka* Forbidden Fruit: **Kaliprasad Ghosh**, St, 1928)
Nishiddha Phal (**Pashupati Chatterjee**, B, 1955)
Nishi Kanya (Ashutosh Bandyopadhyay, B, 1973)
Nishi Mrigaya (**Dinen Gupta**, B, 1975)
Nishipadma (Aravind Mukherjee, B, 1970)
Nishir Dak *see* Abhinav
Nishir Dak (**Debaki Bose**, St, 1932)
Nishir Dak (Ashwini Mitra, B, 1949)
Nishitrishna (Parimal Bhattacharya, B, 1989)
Nisithe (Agragami, B, 1963)
Niskriti (**Pashupati Chatterjee**, B, 1953)
Niskriti (Sunil Basu Mullick, B, 1978)
Nithya Kanyaka (**K.S. Sethumadhavan**, Mal, 1963)
Nithiyavasatham (**Sasikumar**, Mal, 1979)
Niti Vijay *see* Payame Haq
Niti Vijay (*aka* Nurani Moti: **Moti Gidwani**, H, 1932)
Nityakalayanam Pachathoranam (Raviraja Pinisetty, Tel, 1960)
Nitya Sumangali (**Balkrishna Narayan Rao**, Tel, 1974)
Nivadung (Mahesh Satoskar, Mar, 1989)
Nivedita (Pratibha Sasmal, B, 1946)
Nivedyam (**Sasikumar**, Mal, 1978)
Nivurigappina Nippu (P. Chandrasekhara Reddy, Tel, 1982)
Niyantha (**Dasari Narayan Rao**, Tel, 1991)
Niyati (Jogesh Choudhury, St, 1934)
Niyati (**Naresh Mitra**, B, 1951)
Niyati (Indukalpa Hazarika, A, 1978)
Niyaz Aur Namaaz (A. Shamsheer, H, 1977)
Nizhalattam (**A. Vincent**, Mal, 1970)
Nizhalgal (*aka* The Shadows: **Bharathirajaa**, Tam, 1980)
Nizhal Moodiya Nirangal (Jesey, Mal, 1983)
Nizhal Nijamkirathu (**K. Balachander**, Tam, 1978)
Nizhal Suduvathillai (?, Tam, 1982)
Nizhal Thedum Nenjangal (Nivas, Tam, 1982)
Nizhal Yuddham (?, Evershine Prod, Mal, 1981)
Njattadi (*aka* Transplant: **Gopi**, Mal, 1979)
Noble Scamp, The *see* Khandani Khavis
Noblesse Oblige *see* Sorathi Shamsher
Nodi Swamy Navirodu Hige (**Shankar Nag**, K, 1983)
Nokketha Dhoorathu Kannum Nattu (**Fazil**, Mal, 1984)
Nokkukuthi (Ravi Varma, Mal, 1983)
Nomad Puppeteers, The (**Mani Kaul**, H, 1974)
Nombarathi Poovu (**P. Padmarajan**, Mal, 1987)
Nomu (S. Pattu, Tel, 1974)
Nool Veli (**K. Balachander**, Tam, 1979)
Noopur (TV: **Hema Malini**, H, 1990)
Noorandu Kalam Vazhka (R. Sampath, Tam, 1970)
Noorani Moti *see* Niti Vijay
Noorava Roju (Manivannan, Tel, 1984)
Nooravathunaal (Manivannan, Tam, 1984)
Noor-e-Alam (*aka* Queen of Love: **Nanubhai Vakil**, St, 1931)
Noor-e-Arab (*aka* Tilasmi Heer: A.M. Khan, H, 1946)
Noor-e-Deccan (*aka* Light of the Deccan: **B.P. Mishra**, St, 1925)
Noor-e-Ilahi (Sheikh Nissar, H, 1976)
Noor-e-Imaan (Madanrai Vakil, H, 1933)
Noor-e-Ishq (*aka* Light of Love: Maneklal Thakkar, St, 1931)
Noor-e-Islam (?, Trilok Cinetone, H, 1934)
Noor-e-Wahadat (G.R. Sethi, H, 1936)
Noor-e-Watan (*aka* Glory of India: **Jayant Desai**, St, 1930)
Noor-e-Watan (**Jayant Desai**, H, 1935)
Noor-e-Yaman (**J.B.H. Wadia**, H, 1935)
Noor-e-Yaman (*aka* Hatimtai Ka Beta: Aakkoo, H, 1956)
Noorie (?, Durge, H, 1934)
Noorie (Manmohan Krishna, H, 1979)
Noorjehan (*aka* Light of the World: **J.J. Madan**, St, 1923)
Noorjehan (**Ezra Mir**, H, 1931)
Noorjehan (M. Sadiq, H, 1967)
Noor Mahal (*aka* Kamar-al-Zaman: **Moti Gidwani**, H, 1934)
Noor Mahal (**Nanubhai Vakil**, H, 1954)
Noor Mahal (Naushir Engineer, H, 1965)
Nootrukku Nooru (**K. Balachander**, Tam, 1971)
Northern Ballad, A *see* **Oru Vadakkan Veeragatha**
No Sad Tomorrow *see* Kal Udaas Na Hogi
Notes on the Green Revolution (**Shyam Benegal**, E, 1972)
Notes that Matter (**Govind Saraiya**, E, 1959)
Not Guilty *see* Khooni Kon?
No Tree Grows (**Rabindra Dharmaraj**, E, 1974)
Novemberinte Nashtam (**P. Padmarajan**, Mal, 1982)
Nrithyasala (A.B. Raj, Mal, 1972)
Nrityer Tale Tale (Sudhirbandhu Bannerjee, B, 1959)
Nua Bou (Prabhat Mukherjee, O, 1962)
Nukkad (TV: **Kundan Shah/Saeed Mirza** et al., H, 1987)
Nulli Novikkathe (Mohan Roop, Mal, 1985)
Number Aidu Uyekka (Shivakumar, K, 1981)
Numbri Admi (Swaroop Kumar, H, 1991)
Nupur *see* Noopur
Nupur (Dilip Nag, B, 1958)
Nurayum Pathayum (J.D. Thottan, Mal, 1976)
Nurjehan *see* Noorjehan
Nurse *see* Chhoti Maa *or* Daya Ni Devi
Nurse (**Thikkurisi Sukumaran Nair**, Mal, 1969)
Nurse Sisi (Subodh Mitra, B, 1947)
Nutan Jiban (Aravind Mukherjee, B, 1966)
Nuvva Nena/Neeya Nanna (A. Sheshgiri Rao, Tel/Tam, 1962)
Nuvva Nena (Jagannath, Tel, 1984)
Nyay *see* Insaaf
Nyaya Chakra *see* Jaa Devi Sarva Bhuteshu
Nyayada Kannu (K. Sridhar Raj, K, 1985)
Nyayadanda (Mangal Chakraborty, B, 1963)
Nyayadansh (?, Vivek Films, H, 1989)
Nyay Adhikar (Anjan Mukherjee, B, 1987)
Nyaya Gedditu (Joe Simon, K, 1983)
Nyayakini Siksha (**T. Rama Rao**, Tel, 1988)
Nyayam (R. Krishnamurthy, Tam, 1984)
Nyayam Kavali (A. Kodandarami Reddy, Tel, 1981)
Nyayam Ketkiram C.V. Rajendran, Tam, 1973)
Nyayam Ketkirane (S. Muthusamy, Tam, 1984)
Nyayam Kosam (Raviraja Pinisetty, Tel, 1988)
Nyayam Meere Cheppali (G. Ram Mohan Rao, Tel, 1985)
Nyayangal Jeyikattum (*aka* Gnanangal Jeikattum: Lakshmi, Tam, 1990)
Nyayaniku Samkellu (A. Mohan Gandhi, Tel, 1987)
Nyaya Neethi Dharma (A.T. Raghu, K, 1980)
Nyay Anyay (Sukhen Das, B, 1981)
Nyay Anyay (Lawrence D'Souza, H, 1990)
Nyaya Thrasu (K. Rajeshwar, Tam, 1989)
Nyayave Devaru (Siddalingaiah, K, 1971)
Nyayavidhi (?, Jubilee Prod, Mal, 1986)
Nyaya Yellide? (S.V. Chandrasekhar, K, 1982)
Nyayi *see* Adl-e-Jehangir
Nymph Celestial *see* Urvashi

O

O Adadi O Magadu (**Dasari Narayana Rao**, Tel, 1982)
O Amar Desher Mati (Pathikrit, B, 1958)
O Amma Katha (Vasanta Sen, Tel, 1981)
Oath *see* Kasam
Obbarigintha Obbaru (A.M. Samiullah, K, 1992)
O Bewafa (Sawan Kumar, H, 1980)
O Bharya Katha (Mouli, Tel, 1988)
Object (**Kumar Shahani**, Wordless, 1971)
Obsession, The *see* **Junoon**
Occupation, The *see* **Dakhal**
Odahuttidavaru (B.N. Haridas, K, 1969)
Odakkuzhal (**P.N. Menon**, Mal, 1975)
Odangai (Amirjan, Tam, 1986)
Ode to the Child (**Prakash Jha**, E, 1979)
Odeyil Ninnu (**K.S. Sethumadhavan**, Mal, 1965)
Odhun To Odhun Tari Chundadi (Arun Bhatt, G, 1985)
Odi Vilayadu Thatha (T.N. Balu, Tam, 1977)
Odukkam Thudakkam (Malayathur Ramakrishna, Mal, 1982)
Odum Nadhi (Dada Mirasi, Tam, 1969)
Oduvil Kittiya Vartha (Yatheendradas, Mal, 1985)
Offering, The *see* **Nirmalayam**
Ogo Bodhu Sundari (Salil Dutta, B, 1981)
Ogo Sunchho (Kamal Ganguly, B, 1957)
Ohileshwara (T.V. Singh Thakore, K, 1956)
Oh Manju (**C.V. Sridhar**, Tam, 1976)
Oh Thou Woman *see* Nari Jaat
O Inti Bagothan (Devadas Kankala, Tel, 1980)
O Janewale (S. Sardesai, H, 1948)
Oka Challani Rathri (K. Vasu, Tel, 1979)
Oka Deepam Veligindhi (**Singeetham Srinivasa Rao**, Tel, 1976)
Oka Nari Vandha Thupakulu (K.V.S. Kutumba Rao, Tel, 1973)
Oka Oorie Katha (**Mrinal Sen**, Tel, 1977)
Oka Radha Idduru Krishnulu (A. Kodandarami Reddy, Tel, 1986)
Okaroju Raju (Jyotish Sinha, Tel, 1944)
Oka Talli Katha (**K. Balachander**, Tel, 1977)

Oka Talli Pillalu (V.S.V. Swamy/P. Srinivasa Rao, Tel, 1953)
O'Kay? (Dilip Bose, B, 1965)
Oke Kutumbam (**A. Bhimsingh**, Tel, 1970)
Oke Naate Rathri (**P. Bhanumathi**, Tel, 1980)
Oke Raktham (P. Chandrasekhara Reddy, Tel, 1977)
Okha Haran (Yusuf Mulji, G, 1948)
Okha Haran (Navneet Bham, G, 1975)
Olangal (**Balu Mahendra**, Mal, 1982)
Olangthagee Wangmadasoo (**Aribam Syam Sharma**, Manipuri, 1979)
Olave Bedaku (K.V. Jayaram, K, 1984)
Olavina Asare (K.V. Jayaram, K, 1988)
Olavina Kanike (Boodal Krishnamurthy, K, 1993)
Olavina Udugore (D. Rajendra Babu, K, 1987)
Olavu Moodidaga (B. Mallesh, K, 1984)
Olavum Theeravum (**P.N. Menon**, Mal, 1969)
Old Vimala *see* Mother India
Olimayamana Ethirkalam (K. Krishnamurthy, Tam, 1977)
Oli Pirandathu (**Durai**, Tam, 1980)
Oli Vilakku (**Tapi Chanakya**, Tam, 1968)
Oliyambugal (**T. Hariharan**, Mal, 1990)
Ollathu Mathi (**K.S. Sethumadhavan**, Mal, 1967)
Omana (J.D. Thottan, Mal, 1972)
Omana Kunju (A.B. Raj, Mal, 1975)
Omanakuttan (**K.S. Sethumadhavan**, Mal, 1964)
Omana Swapnangal (P.K. Radhakishnan, Mal, 1991)
Omana Thingal (Yatindra Das, Mal, 1983)
Omanikkan Ormavaikkan (A.B. Roy, Mal, 1985)
O Mani Mane (A. Jagannathan, Tam, 1984)
O Manishi Thirigi Chudu (**Dasari Narayana Rao**, Tel, 1976)
Omar Khayyam (Mohan Sinha, H, 1946)
Om Dar-b-dar (Kamal Swaroop, H, 1988)
Om Jai Jagdish Hare (?, H, 1982)
Omnipotent, The *see* Rajadhi Raja
Omniscient, The *see* **Sarvasakshi**
Om Shakti (S.A. Chandrasekharan, Tam, 1982)
Onam Manam Poomanam (?, Lilly Films, Mal, 1987)
Onam Prathi Olivil (Baby, Mal, 1985)
Onappudava (**K.G. George**, Mal, 1978)
Onathumbikorunjai (Suresh, Mal, 1985)
Once Again *see* Ek Baar Phir
Once Upon a Time *see* **Ondanondu Kaladalli**
Once Upon a Time in a Village *see* **Ore Oru Gramathile**
Ondagi Baalu (K.S.R. Doss, K, 1989)
Ondanondu Kaladalli (**Girish Karnad**, K, 1978)
Ondebaliya Hoogalu (M.S. Nayak, K, 1967)
Onde Guri (Bhargava, K, 1983)
Ondekula Ondedaiva (D. Shankar Singh, K, 1971)
Onde Raktha (Shrikumaran Thampi, K, 1984)
Onderupa Eradu Guna (A.M. Samiulla, K, 1975)
Ondrey Kulam (N. Krishnaswamy, Tam, 1956)
Ondrupattal Undu Vazhvu (Ramanna, Tam, 1960)
Ondu Cinema Kathe (Phani Ramchandra, K, 1992)
Ondu Hennina Kathe (**B.R. Panthulu**, K, 1972)
Ondu Hennu Aaru Kannu (V. Madhusudhana Rao, K, 1980)
Ondu Muthina Kathe (**Shankar Nag**, K, 1987)
Ondu Oorina Kathe (Baraguru Ramchandrappa, K, 1978)
Ondu Premada Kathe (Joe Simon, K, 1977)
One Day, Every Day *see* **Ek Din Pratidin**
One Fatal Night *see* Bala Ki Raat
One Hundred and Eighty Days of SITE (**Jahnu Barua**, E, 1976)
100 Days (Partho Ghosh, H, 1991)
100 Lashes *see* Ishrat Ki Maut
One's Own Choice *see* **Swayamvaram**
1000 Thalaivangi Apoorva Chintamani (**T.R. Sundaram**, Tam, 1947)
Onkarer Joy Jatra (**Phani Burma**, B, 1957)
Only the Lonely *see* **Yaadein**
Only Way, The *see* Shesh Path *or* **Ek Hi Raasta**
Onnaiappol Oruvan (?, Tam, 1965)

Shashikala in *Naag Devata* (1963)

Onnanam Kunnil Oradi Kunnil (**Priyadarshan**, Mal, 1985)
Onnanu Nammal (P.G. Vishwambaran, Mal, 1984)
Onne Onnu Kanne Kannu (Ra. Shankaran, Tam, 1974)
Onningu Vannengil (Joshi, Mal, 1985)
Onninu Pinne Mattonnu (M.G. Tulasidas, Mal, 1988)
Onnu Chirikku (P.G. Vishwambaran, Mal, 1983)
Onnum Mindatha Bharya (Balu Kiriyeth, Mal, 1984)
Onnum Theriatha Pappa (S.S. Vikram, Tam, 1983)
Onnum Theriatha Pappa G.B. Thambidurai, Tam, 1991)
Onnu Muthal Poojyam Vare (?, Navodaya 3-D, Mal, 1986)
Onnu Rendu Mooru (Rajasenan, Mal, 1986)
Onru Engal Jadhiye (S. Jagadeeshan, Tam, 1987)
On Stamps and Stamping (**Govind Saraiya**, E, 1959)
On the River *see* Nadi Kinare
On the Seashore *see* **Kadal Theerathu**
On the Way *see* Chalte Chalte
Onti Dhwani (**T.S. Nagabharana**, K, 1983)
Onti Salaga (V. Somasekhar, K, 1989)
Onum Onum Pathinonnu (?, Mal, 1988)
Oodarathuammava Alariyum (**Priyadarshan**, Mal, 1984)
Oohakachavadam (K. Madhu, Mal, 1988)
Oomai Janangal (Jayabharati, Tam, 1984)
Oomai Kanavu Kandaal (Vijayaraja, Tam, 1980)
Oomaithurai (K.G. Rajasekharan, Tam, 1988)
Oomai Vizhigal (R. Aravindraj, Tam, 1986)
Oomakuyil (**Balu Mahendra**, Mal, 1983)
Oomakuyil (M.R. Yogaraj, Tam, 1988)
Oonche Log (**Phani Majumdar**, H, 1965)
Oonche Log (Brij Sadanah, H, 1985)
Oonchi Haveli (**Dhirubhai Desai**, H, 1955)
Oonch Neech *see* Pratibad
Oonch Neech Beech (Wasi Khan, H, 1989)
Oonjal (**I.V. Sasi**, Mal, 1977)
Oon Paoos (**Raja Paranjpe**, Mar, 1954)

Oont (Amit Khanna, H, 1986)
Ooparwala Jaane (Naresh Saigal, H, 1977)
Oorai Therinchikitten (G. Sekharan, Tam, 1988)
Oorigenpu *see* Urigenpu
Oorigittakolli (Kallesh, K, 1988)
Oor Kavalan (Mano Bala, Tam, 1987)
Oor Kuruvi (O.S. Sivakumar, Tam, 1987)
Oor Mariyadhai (K.S. Ravikumar, Tam, 1992)
Oor Panjayathu (**J. Mahendran**, Tam, 1992)
Oorukku Manushyan (Crossbelt Mani, Mal, 1986)
Oorukku Mushtikal (?, Mal, 1981)
Oorukku Nallavan (S.D. Lall, Tam, 1977)
Oorukku Oru Pillai (**Yoganand**, Tam, 1982)
Oorukku Oru Raja (S.T. Dhandapani, Tam, 1978)
Oorukku Upadesham (S.P. Muthuraman, Tam, 1984)
Oorukku Uzhaippavan (M. Krishnan, Tam, 1976)
Oorum Uravum (Major Sundarrajan, Tam, 1982)
Ooruvam G.M. Kumar, Tam, 1991)
Ooru Vittu Oru Vandhu (Gangai Amaran, Tam, 1990)
Ootappandhayam (S. Navaraj, Tam, 1993)
Oothikachiya Ponnu (P.K. Joshi/R. Gopi, Mal, 1981)
Ootivarai Uravu (**C.V. Sridhar**, Tam, 1967)
Ootpatang (**Chandulal Shah**, H, 1955)
Oozham (Hari Kumar, Mal, 1988)
Opaja Sonor Mati (**Brojen Barua**, A, 1972)
O Panchhi (Zahur Raja, H, 1944)
Opar Mahala (Jiten Sarma, A, 1971)
Opening and Closing of Howrah Bridge (Jyotish Sarkar?, Elphinstone
Bioscope, St, 1905)
Opera House (P.L. Santoshi, H, 1961)
Operation Diamond Rocket (Dorairaj-Bhagavan, K, 1978)
Operation Jackpot (Dorairaj-Bhagavan, K, 1969)
Operation Khedda (**M. Bhavnani**, E, 1956)
Operation Sky (**Govind Saraiya**, E, 1957)
Oppantham (Vijayaganesh, Tam, 1983)
Oppol (**K.S. Sethumadhavan**, Mal, 1980)
Oppom Oppathinoppam (Soman, Mal, 1986)

Ora Charjon (Samit Bhanja, B, 1988)
Oralkoodi Kalanayi (P.A. Thomas, Mal, 1964)
Oraons of Bihar ((**Paul Zils**, E, 1958)
Ora Thake Odhare (**Sukumar Dasgupta**, B, 1954)
Ordeal *see* **Agnisnan**
Ore Eratham (K. Sornam, Tam, 1987)
Ore Iravu (**P. Neelakantan**, Tam, 1951)
Ore Jatri (Rajen Choudhury, B, 1951)
Ore Mutham (C.A. Mugilan, Tam, 1980)
Ore Oru Gramathile (Jyothi Pandian, Tam, 1987)
Ore Satchi (K. Vijayam, Tam, 1974)
Ore Thanthai (M. Karnan, Tam, 1976)
Ore Thayi Ore Kulam (S. Jagadeeshan, Tam, 1989)
Ore Thooval Pakshikal (Raveendran, Mal, 1988)
Ore Vanam Ore Bhoomi (**I.V. Sasi**, Tam, 1979)
Ore Vazhi (K. Shankar/Vasudeva Menon, Tam, 1959)
Ore Velaiyadu Papa (Mukta V. Srinivasan, Tam, 1959)
Oridathoru Phayalwan (**P. Padmarajan**, Mal, 1981)
Oridathu (**G. Aravindan**, Mal, 1986)
Orikkalkoodi (**I.V. Sasi**, Mal, 1981)
Orikkal Oridathu (Jesey, Mal, 1985)
Orkapurathu (Kamal, Mal, 1988)
Orkkuka Vallappozhum (S. Babu, Mal, 1978)
Ormakale Vida Tharu (Raviguptan, Mal, 1980)
Ormakal Marikkumo (**K.S. Sethumadhavan**, Mal, 1977)
Ormakkayi (**B.G. Bharathan**, Mal, 1982)
Ormayil Ennum (T.V. Mohan, Mal, 1988)
Ormayil Nee Mathram (**Sasikumar**, Mal, 1979)
Orphan Girl *see* Anadhai Penn *or* Abala
Orphan's Daughter *see* Anadhai Penn
Orphans of the Storm *see* **Vilasi Ishwar**
Oru CBI Diary Kuruppu (K. Madhu, Mal, 1988)
Oru Indhiya Kanavu (**Komal Swaminathan**, Tam, 1983)
Oru Iniya Udhayam (?, Pondu Cine Arts, Tam, 1986)

Oru Iravu Oru Paravai (P.C. Reddy, Tam, 1980)
Oru Kadangadhapol (Joshi Mathew, Mal, 1993)
Oru Kaithiyin Diary (**Bharathirajaa**, Tam, 1984)
Oru Katha Oru Nunakkatha (Mohan, Mal, 1986)
Oru Kayi Osai (**K. Bhagyaraj**, Tam, 1980)
Oru Kayi Paapam (S.P. Muthuraman, Tam, 1983)
Oru Kochu Bhoomi Kulukkam (Chandrasekharan, Mal, 1992)
Oru Kochu Katha Arum Parayatha Katha (P.G. Vishwambaran, Mal, 1984)
Oru Kochu Swapnam (Vipin Das, Mal, 1984)
Oru Kodiyil Iru Malargal (S.P. Muthuraman, Tam, 1976)
Oru Koyil Eru Deepangal (S.P. Muthuraman, Tam, 1979)
Oru Kudakkezhil (Joshi, Mal, 1985)
Oru Kudumbathin Kathai (**Durai**, Tam, 1975)
Oru Kunji Janikkunnu Mathurka Kutumbam (P.R.S. Pillai/M. Krishnan Nair,
Mal, 1982)
Oru Madaupravinte Katha (Alleppey Ashraf, Mal, 1983)
Oru Malarin Payanam (Muktha V. Srinivasan, Tam, 1985)
Oru Manithan Oru Manaivi (**Durai**, Tam, 1986)
Oru Marathu Paravaigal (Ra. Shankaran, Tam, 1980)
Oru Maymasappularayil (V.R. Gopinath, Mal, 1987)
Oru Minnaminuginte Nurungu Vettam (*aka* Glimpse of Light of a Flying
Fireball: **B.G. Bharathan**, Mal, 1987)
Oru Mugham Pala Mugham (P.K. Joseph, Mal, 1983)
Oru Muthassi Katha (**Priyadarshan**, Mal, 1988)
Oru Nadigai Nadagam Parkiral (**A. Bhimsingh**, Tam, 1978)
Orunal Innorunal (Reji, Mal, 1985)
Oru Nidhiyude Katha (?, Mal, 1987)
Oru Nokku Kannan (Sajan, Mal, 1985)
Oru Odai Nadhiyagiradhu (**C.V. Sridhar**, Tam, 1983)
Oru Oomayin Ragam (G. Gurushankar, Tam, 1991)
Oru Painkilli Katha (**Balachandra Menon**, Mal, 1984)
Oru Penninte Katha (**K.S. Sethumadhavan**, Mal, 1971)
Oru Pidi Ari (**P. Bhaskaran**, Mal, 1974)
Oru Ponnu Nenacha (K. Chozharajan, Tam, 1989)
Oru Pudhiya Kadhai (?, Kumar Movies, Tam, 1990)
Oru Pullanghuzhal Adupputhukirathu (Mouli, Tam, 1983)
Oru Ragam Pala Thalam (M. Krishnan Nair, Mal, 1979)
Oru Sandesha Koodi (Haneef, Mal, 1985)
Oru Sayahnathinte Swapnam (**B.G. Bharathan**, Mal, 1988)
Oru Sindoorappottinte Ormakku (?, Mannil Prod, Mal, 1987)
Oru Sumangaliyuda Katha (Baby, Mal, 1984)
Oru Sundariyude Katha (**Thoppil Bhasi**, Mal, 1972)
Oru Swakariam (Hari Kumar, Mal, 1983)
Oru Thai Makkal (**P. Neelakantan**, Tam, 1971)
Oru Thalai Ragam (E.M. Ibrahim, Tam, 1980)
Oru Thayin Sabatham (**T. Rajendar**, Tam, 1987)
Oru Thettinde Katha (P.K. Joseph, Mal, 1984)
Oruthi Mattam Karaiyinile (J. Ramu, Tam, 1981)
Oru Thira Pinneyum Thira (P.G. Vishwambaran, Mal, 1982)
Oru Thottil Sabatham (Bharati Mohan, Tam, 1989)
Oru Udhappu Kann Simittukirathu (S.P. Muthuraman, Tam, 1976)
Oru Vadakkan Veeragatha (**T. Hariharan**, Mal, 1989)
Oruvanukku Oruthi (Ra. Shankaran, Tam, 1977)
Oru Varisu Uruvagirathu (Mouli, Tam, 1982)
Oru Varsham Oru Masam (**Sasikumar**, Mal, 1980)
Oruvar Vazhum Alayam (Shanmugha Pillai, Tam, 1988)
Oru Veedu Iru Vasal (**K. Balachander**, Tam, 1990)
Oru Veedukathai Oru Thodarkathai (M.A. Kaja, Tam, 1979)
Oru Veedu Oru Ulagam (**Durai**, Tam, 1978)
Oru Velladu Vengai Agirathu (Devaraj-Mohan, Tam, 1980)
Oru Vilippadakale (Jesey, Mal, 1982)
Oru Viral (C.M.V. Raman, Tam, 1965)
Oru Vivadha Vishayam (P.G. Vishwambaran, Mal, 1988)
Oru Yuga Sandhya (**Madhu**, Mal, 1986)
Osai (K. Vijayan, Tam, 1984)
O Seeta Katha (**K. Vishwanath**, Tel, 1974)
O Tera Kya Kehana (K. Pervez, H, 1959)
Othaidi Pathaile (A.S. Prakasham, Tam, 1980)
O Thandri Teerpu (Rajachandra, Tel, 1985)
Othenente Makan (**Kunchako**, Mal, 1970)
Other Calcutta, The (**Santi P. Choudhury**, E, 1971)
Other Shore, The *see* **Akkare**
Other Side, The (**Anand Patwardhan**, E, 1993)
Ottapettavar (V.K. Krishnan, Mal, 1979)
Ottayadi Paathakal (C. Radhakrishnan, Mal, 1990)
Ottayal Pattalam (Rajeev Kumar, Mal, 1991)
Ottayan (Cherri, Mal, 1985)
Our Children Will Know Each Other Better (**Harisadhan Dasgupta**, E, 1960)
Our Daily Bread *see* **Uski Roti**
Our Darling *see* **Engal Thangam**
Our Darling Daughters *see* **Hamari Betiyan**
Our Hindustan *see* Amru Hindustan
Our India *see* Amru Hindustan *or* **Hindustan Hamara**
Our Indian Empire (?, St, 1897)
Our Land *see* **Maabhoomi**
Our Struggle *see* Andolan
Our Universe (**Kumar Shahani**, E, 1976)
Outcast Girl, The *see* **Malapilla**
Outlaw *see* Farari *or* Lutera
Outlaw of Sorath *see* Sorathi Baharvatiyo
Outsiders, The *see* **Oka Oorie Katha**
Ovalani (**Anant Mane**, Mar, 1954)
Ovalite Bhauraya (**Datta Keshav**, Mar, 1975)
Over Again *see* **Punashcha**
Oyilattam (R. Sundarrajan, Tam, 1991)
Ozhivukalam (**B.G. Bharathan**, Mal, 1985)
Ozhukkinethire (P.G. Vishwambaran, Mal, 1976)

P

Paach Nazuk Bote (Vasant Painter, Mar, 1972)
Paach Rangachi Paach Pakhare (**Anant Mane**, Mar, 1975)
Paaku Vethalai (Ra. S. Vairavan, Tam, 1981)
Paalam (M. Krishnan Nair, Mal, 1983)
Paala Manushulu (S.S.R. Sharma, Tel, 1968)
Paal Kudam (Pattu, Tam, 1969)
Paal Manam (**K.S. Sethumadhavan**, Tam, 1968)
Paalu Neelu (**Dasari Narayana Rao**, Tel, 1980)
Paanch Dost (Vijay, H, 1974)
Paanch Dushman (Bimal S. Rawal, H, 1973)
Paanch Fauladi (Mohan Bhakri, H, 1988)
Paanch Khiladi (Waqatullah, H, 1985)
Paanch Mahabhoot (**S.N. Patankar**, St, 1926)
Paanch Paapi (Shibu Mitra, H, 1989)
Paanch Qaidi (Shibu Mitra, H, 1981)
Paanchvi Manzil (Jagdish Sidana, H, 1982)
Paan Khaye Saiyan Hamaar (Sujeet Kumar, Bh, 1984)
Paap Aru Prayashchitta (**Anwar Hussain**, A, 1977)
Paap Aur Punya (Prayag Raj, H, 1974)
Paapi (Majnu, H, 1943)
Paapi (**Chandulal Shah**, H, 1953)
Paapi (O.P. Ralhan, H, 1977)
Paapi Pet Ka Sawaal Hai (Sohanlal Kanwar, H, 1984)
Paapi Sansar (Pravin Kumar/G. Vohra, H, 1984)
Paap Ka Ant (Vijay Reddy, H, 1989)
Paap Ki Aandhi (**Mehul Kumar**, H, 1990)
Paap Ki Duniya (Shibu Mitra, H, 1988)
Paap Ki Kamaai (Kawal Sharma, H, 1990)
Paap Ki Nagari (?, Ravi Talkies, Punjab, H, 1939)
Paap Ki Sazaa (K. Thyagarajan, H, 1989)
Paap Ko Jalakar Raakh Kar Doonga (K.R. Reddy, H, 1988)
Paap No Fej (**Ardeshir Irani/Naval Gandhi**, St, 1924)
Paap No Pashchatap (*aka* Repentance: **Naval Gandhi**, St, 1924)
Paap-o-Paapi (Bijon Sen, B, 1956)
Paap Punya (Rajat Das, B, 1987)
Paap Punya (Surya Mishra, O, 1988)
Paar (**Gautam Ghosh**, H, 1984)
Paara (Aleppey Ashraf, Mal, 1985)
Paari Poyina Kaidilu (Vallabhaneni Janardhan, Tel, 1985)
Paar Magale Paar (**A. Bhimsingh**, Tam, 1963)
Pachaikodi (?, Tam, 1990)
Pachai Malai Kurathi (**K. Kameshwara Rao**, Tam, 1959)
Pachai Vilakku (**A. Bhimsingh**, Tam, 1964)
Pachani Kapuram (**T. Rama Rao**, Tel, 1985)
Pachani Samsaram (**P. Pullaiah**, Tel, 1961)
Pachani Samsaram (Laxmi Deepak, Tel, 1970)
Pachani Samsaram (Bharatwaja, Tel, 1992)
Pacha Nottukal (A.B. Raj, Mal, 1973)
Pachavelicham (M. Mani, Mal, 1985)
Padada (**Shantaram Athavale**, Mar, 1958)
Padaharalli Ammayi (P.S. Krishnamohana Reddy, Tel, 1986)
Padaharella Vayasu (B. Satyanarayana Reddy, Tel, 1978)
Padakkudhira (P.G. Vasudevan, Mal, 1978)
Padakottai (**T. Prakash Rao**, Tam, 1964)
Padamudra (R. Sukumaran, Mal, 1988)
Padandi Munduku (Uma Maheshwara Rao, Tel, 1985)
Padandi Munduku (V. Madhusudhana Rao, Tel, 1962)
Padarachya Savleet (**Prabhakar Nayak**, Mar, 1977)
Padasaram (A.N. Thampi, Mal, 1978)
Padatha Paingili (**P. Subramanyam**, Mal, 1957)
Padatha Thenikkal (V.M.C. Hanifa, Tam, 1988)
Padatik (**Mrinal Sen**, B, 1973)
Padavidhara (C.V. Shivashankar, K, 1967)
Padavoyi Bharatheeyuda (**Dasari Narayana Rao**, Tel, 1976)
Padayani (T.S. Mohan, Mal, 1986)
Padayottam (Appachan, Mal, 1982)
Padchaya (**Raja Paranjpe**, Mar, 1965)
Padhai *see* Pathai
Padhai Maria Payanam (A. Balakrishnan, Tam, 1991)
Padhai Theriyudu Paar (**Nemai Ghosh**/V. Ramamurthy, Tam, 1960)
Padhayam (**B.G. Bharathan**, Mal, 1993)
Padhimoonam Number Veedu (Baby, Tam, 1990)
Padhukappu (S.A. Chandramohan, Tam, 1993)
Padhyam (A. Kasilingam, Tam, 1967)
Padicha Kallan (M. Krishnan Nair, Mal, 1969)
Padicha Pullai (Senthilnathan, Tam, 1989)
Padikkadhavan (Rajasekhar, Tam, 1985)
Padikkatha Methai (**A. Bhimsingh**, Tam, 1960)
Padikkatha Padam (Bharat, Tam, 1986)
Padikkatha Panayar (**K.S. Gopalakrishnan**, Tam, 1985)
Padi Panthulu (P. Chandrasekhara Reddy, Tel, 1975)
Padi Pishir Barmi Baksha (**Arundhati Devi**, B, 1972)
Padippura (**P.N. Menon**, Mal, 1988)
Padithal Mattu Pothuma (**A. Bhimsingh**, Tam, 1962)
Paditha Manaivi (Krishnaswamy, Tam, 1965)
Paditha Penn (A.L. Narayanan?, Shyamala Pics, Tam, 1956)
Padmagolap (Ajit Lahiri, B, 1970)
Padma Jyothi (**T.R. Sundaram**, Tam, 1937)
Padmalata (*aka* Kantakma Gulab, Lily in the Mud: D.A. Dandekar, St, 1928)
Padma Nadir Majhi (**Gautam Ghosh**, B, 1992)
Padma Parmatti Nadi (Ardhendu Mukherjee, B, 1948)
Padmaragam (**Sasikumar**, Mal, 1975)
Padmatheeratham (K.G. Rajashekharan, Mal, 1978)
Padmati Sandhyaragam (Jandhyala, Tel, 1987)
Padmavyuham (P. Chinappa Reddy, Tel, 1973)
Padmavyuham (**Sasikumar**, Mal, 1973)
Padmavyuham (G.C. Shekhar, Tel, 1984)
Padmini (Walli, H, 1948)
Padosan (Jyoti Swaroop, H, 1968)
Padosi *see* **Shejari**
Padosi (Jagdish Raj, H, 1971)
Padosi Ki Biwi (?, Gordia Films, H, 1988)
Paduka Pattabhishekham (**Sarvottam Badami**, Tel, 1932)
Paduka Pattabhishekham (**Murugadasa/K. Ramnoth**, Tam, 1936)
Paduka Pattabhishekham (**Kadaru Nagabhushanam**, Tel, 1945)
Paduka Pattabhishekham (Amravati Technical Unit, Tel, 1966)
Padum Vanambadi (M. Jayakumar, Tam, 1985)
Padu Nilave (K. Rangaraj, Tam, 1987)
Padunna Puzha (M. Krishnan Nair, Mal, 1968)
Paduvarahalli Pandavaru (**Puttanna Kanagal**, K, 1978)
Pagabattina Paduchu (Ramchandra Rao, Tel, 1971)
Pagabattina Puli (Ram Narayan, Tel, 1984)
Pagabattina Simham (P. Chandrasekhara Reddy, Tel, 1982)
Pagadai Pannirendu (N. Damodaran, Tam, 1982)
Pagal (**A.R. Kardar**, H, 1940)
Pagalil Oru Iravu (**I.V. Sasi**, Tam, 1979)
Pagal Kinavu (S.S. Rajan, Mal, 1966)
Pagal Nilavu (**Mani Rathnam**, Tam, 1985)
Pagal Premi (*aka* Girl Mad: **M. Bhavnani**, St, 1926)
Pagal Thakur (Hiranmoy Sen, B, 1966)
Pagasadhishta (K. Kutumbarao, Tel, 1970)
Pagasadhishta (**Vijayanirmala**, Tel, 1987)
Pagati Donga (P. Jaya, Tel, 1985)
Pagdandi (Ram Narayan Dave, H, 1947)
Pagdi (Anant Thakur, H, 1948)
Pagdi Samhal Jatta (Majnu, P, 1960)
Pagdi Samhal Jatta (Iqbal Channa, P, 1992)
Pagetha Puge (*aka* Taking Revenge: Aruru Pattabhi, Tulu, 1972)
Pagla Kahin Ka (**Shakti Samanta**, H, 1970)
Pagle (**Protima Dasgupta**, H, 1950)
Pagli (Shankar Mehta, H, 1943)
Pagli (C.P. Dixit, H, 1974)
Pagli Duniya (Aspi, H, 1944)
Pahadi Jawan (?, Nayampali Films, H, 1964)
Pahadi Kanya (*aka* The Wild Flower: **Nandlal Jaswantlal**, St, 1930)
Pahadi Kanya (*aka* Maid of the Mountains: **Harshadrai Mehta**, H, 1936)
Pahadi Kanya (**Munin Barua**, A, 1991)
Pahadi Nagin (S. Azeem, H, 1964)
Pahadi Noor (*aka* Rose of Baluchistan: ?, **Sharda Film**, St, 1931)
Pahadi Phool (Sridip Ghosh, B, 1981)
Pahadi Pindharo (*aka* Midnight Rider: **B.P. Mishra**, St, 1926)
Pahadi Sawar (*aka* Wild Cavalier: Chunilal Parekh, St, 1933)
Pahala Adhyay *see* **Pehla Adhyay**
Pahalil Pournami (V.M.C. Haniffa, Tam, 1990)
Pahar Theke Shahar (**Santi P. Choudhury**, B, 1980)
Pahechan *see* Pehchan
Paheli (**Prashanta Nanda**, H, 1977)
Paheli Nazar *see* Pehli Nazar
Paheli Tareekh *see* **Pehli Tareekh**
Pahila Palna (**Vishram Bedekar**, Mar, 1942)
Pahila Prem (**Raja Nene**, Mar, 1957)
Pahili Mangalagaur (R.S. Junnarkar, Mar, 1942)
Pahunche Huye Log (Johnny Walker, H, 1985)
Pahuni (**Anant Mane**, Mar, 1976)
Pahure Kiti Vaat! (**Raja Thakur**, Mar, 1963)
Paidali Padleli Phule (**Anant Mane**, Mar, 1956)
Paigham (*aka* Message: Gyan Dutt, H, 1943)
Paigham (**S.S. Vasan**, H, 1959)
Paigham (?, Five Star Movies, H, 1988)
Paigoon (Arun Karnataki, Mar, 1983)
Paij (Babasaheb S. Fattelal, Mar, 1980)

Paijaniyan (Aslam Sheikh, Bh, 1986)
Paijecha Vida (Kamalakar Torne, Mar, 1979)
Paila Pacheesu (Mouli, Tel, 1989)
Paimarakappal (K. Radha, Tam, 1988)
Painted Angel *see* Ghunghatwali
Painted Sin *see* Stree Dharma
Painter Babu (Ashok, H, 1983)
Painter of Our Times, A (**Santi P. Choudhury**, E, 1974)
Paisa (G.P. Pawar, H/Mar, 1941)
Paisa (**Prithviraj Kapoor**, H, 1957)
Paisa Bolto Aahe/Nagad Narayan (**Vishram Bedekar**, Mar/H, 1943)
Paisa Hi Paisa (Mehrish, H, 1956)
Paisa Na Gulam (*aka* All for Money: Prafulla Ghosh, St, 1929)
Paisa Ni Khumari (**B.P. Mishra**, St, 1925)
Paisa Ya Pyar (Jawar Seetarama, H, 1969)
Paisa Yeh Paisa (Sohanlal Kanwar, H, 1985)
Paise Ki Gudiya (*aka* Ghunghat Aur Ghunghroo: Brij Sadanah, H, 1974)
Paishyacha Paoos (**Anant Mane**, Mar, 1960)
Paiso Bole Chhe (**Ravindra Dave**, G, 1977)
Paithiakaran (*aka* Mad Man: **Krishnan-Panju**, Tam, 1947)
Paithrukam (Jayaraj, Mal, 1993)
Paka Dekha (Aravind Mukherjee, B, 1980)
Pakal Kambal Pot Chhota (**Prashanta Nanda**, O, 1986)
Pakavaruthiya Vina (P.C. Reddy, Mal, 1985)
Pak Daman (*aka* The Love, Bolto Kagal: **Kanjibhai Rathod**, H, 1931)
Pak Daman (*aka* Shaheed-e-Naaz: Rustom Modi, H, 1940)
Pak Daman (S.M. Yusuf, H, 1957)
Pak Daman Raqasa (*aka* Innocent Raqasa, Innocent Dancer, Nirdosh Nritika: B.R. Oberoi, H, 1932)
Pakeezah (**Kamal Amrohi**, H, 1971)
Pakhandi (Samir Ganguly, H, 1984)
Pakka Kalla (Y.R. Swamy, K, 1979)
Pakkalo Bellem (**Puttanna Kanagal**, Tel, 1965)
Pakkathu Veetu Roja (M. Bhaskar, Tam, 1982)
Pakke Badmash (*aka* Secret Five: A.H. Essa, H, 1939)
Pakkinti Ammayi (**C. Pullaiah**, Tel, 1953)
Pakshiraj (S.N. Tripathi, H, 1959)
Palabhisekham (**K.S. Gopalakrishnan**, Tam, 1977)
Paladai (**A. Bhimsingh**, Tam, 1967)
Palaivanaparavaigal (Senthilnathan, Tam, 1990)
Palaivana Ragangal (senthilnathan, Tam, 1992)
Palaivana Rojakkal (Manivannan, Tam, 1986)
Palaivana Solai (Robert Rajasekhar, Tam, 1981)
Palaivanathil Pattampoochi (**Durai**, Tam, 1988)
Palam (Karvannan, Tam, 1990)
Palangal (**B.G. Bharathan**, Mal, 1981)
Palanka (**Rajen Tarafdar**, B, 1975)
Pala Parikshai (Muktha V. Srinivasan, Tam, 1977)
Palasor Rong (Jibon Bora, A, 1976)
Palatak (Kalidas Batabyal, B, 1951)
Palatak (Yatrik, B, 1963)
Palatak (Natya Rashmi/Prafulla Rath, O, 1985)
Palattukoman (**Kunchako**, Mal, 1962)
Palattu Kunjikannan (Pappan Kunchako, Mal, 1980)
Palavade Bandhi Preet (**Ravindra Dave**, G, 1983)
Palay Khan (Ashim Samanta, H, 1986)
Palazhi Madhanam (**Sasikumar**, Mal, 1975)
Pal Do Pal Ka Saath (**B.R. Ishara**, H, 1978)
Paligebandadde Pamchamrutha (M.B. Ganesh, K, 1963)
Paliyano Padkar (Rajendra Vyas, G, 1985)
Palkadal (T.K. Prasad, Mal, 1975)
Palki (S.U. Sunny/**Mahesh Kaul**, H, 1967)
Palkon Ki Chhaon Mein (Meraj, H, 1977)
Pallandhu Vazhga (K. Shankar, Tam, 1975)
Pallava Sevangal *see* Kanchukota
Pallavi (Balakrishnan Pottekkad, Mal, 1976)
Pallavi (**P. Lankesh**, K, 1976)
Pallavi Anupallavi (**Mani Rathnam**, K, 1983)
Palle Paduchu (B.A. Subba Rao, Tel, 1954)
Palle Paduchu (K. Satyam, Tel, 1974)
Palle Seema (P. Chandrasekhara Reddy, Tel, 1976)
Palletoori Bhava (**K. Pratyagatma**, Tel, 1973)
Palletoori Chinnodu (**B. Vittalacharya**, Tel, 1973)
Palletoori Monagadu *see* Palletooru Monagallu
Palletoori Pellam (K. Vasu, Tel, 1991)
Palletoori Pidugu (B.A. Subba Rao, Tel, 1983)
Palletoori Pilla (*aka* Village Girl: B.A. Subba Rao, Tel, 1950)
Palletooru (**T. Prakash Rao**, Tel, 1952)
Palletooru Monagallu (S.A. Chandrasekharan, Tel, 1983)
Palli Natakam (**T.R. Sundaram**, Tam, 1944)
Palli Samaj (**Sisir Bhaduri**, B, 1932)
Palli Samaj (**Niren Lahiri**, B, 1952)
Pallum Pazhamum (**A. Bhimsingh**, Tam, 1961)
Palnati Puli (T. Prasad, Tel, 1984)
Palnati Rudrayya (B.L.V. Prasad, Tel, 1989)
Palnati Simham (A. Kodandarami Reddy, Tel, 1985)
Palnati Yuddham (**Gudavalli Ramabrahmam/L.V. Prasad**, Tel, 1947)
Palnati Yuddham (G. Ramineedu, Tel, 1966)
Palunku Pathram (**Thikkurisi Sukumaran Nair**, Mal, 1970)
Paluti Valartha Kili (Devaraj-Mohan, Tam, 1976)
Palva Palvi (**Dada Kondke**, Mar, 1990)
Pampa (Pradeep Bhattacharya, B, 1979)
Pamparam (Baby, Mal, 1979)
Pampered Youth *see* Adooray Chheley
Pamposh (*aka* Lotus of Kashmir: **Ezra Mir**, H, 1954)
Panaah (Krishnakant Pandya, H, 1992)
Panakara Kudumbam (Ramanna, Tam, 1964)
Panakara Penn (U. Rajendran, Tam, 1976)
Panakara Pillai (Jambulingam, Tam, 1968)
Panakkaran (P. Vasu, Tam, 1990)
Panakkari (K.S. Gopalakrishnan, Tam, 1953)
Panam (N.S. Krishnan, Tam, 1952)
Panama Pasama (**K.S. Gopalakrishnan**, Tam, 1968)
Panam Padaithavan (Ramanna, Tam, 1965)
Panam Paduthu Padu (Y.R. Swamy, Tam, 1954)
Panam Panthiyile (?, M.A.V. Pics, Tam, 1961)
Panam Patheyum Seyum (G. Subramaniya Reddiar, Tam, 1975)
Panam Pathum Seivam (T. Vijayasingham, Tam, 1985)
Panam Penn Pasam (M.A. Kaja, Tam, 1980)
Panam Tharum Parisu (M. Krishnaswamy, Tam, 1965)
Panathottam (K. Shankar, Tam, 1963)
Panathukkaga (M.S. Senthil, Tam, 1974)
Pancha Bhoothalu (P. Chandrasekhara Reddy, Tel, 1979)
Panchabhutham (Satyam, Tam, 1979)
Panchagni (*aka* Five Fires: **T. Hariharan**, Mal, 1986)
Panchajanyam (Rajasekharan, Mal, 1982)
Pancha Kalyani Dongala Rani (G. Suryam, Tel, 1969)
Pancha Kalyani (N. Sambandam, Tam, 1979)
Panchali (V. Srinivasan, Tam, 1959)
Panchami (**T. Hariharan**, Mal, 1976)
Panchamirutham (Jiten Bannerjee, Tam, 1942)
Panchamurtham/Panchamirutham (**Sasikumar**, Mal/Tam, 1976/8)
Pancharathna (K. Vembu, K, 1956)
Pancharati (Datta Mane, Mar, 1960)
Panchasar (*aka* The Blind God: **Debaki Bose**, St, 1930)
Panchasar (Arup Guha-Thakurta, B, 1968)
Panchatanthram (**Sasikumar**, Mal, 1974)
Panchatapa (**Asit Sen**, B, 1957)
Panchavadippalam (**K.G. George**, Mal, 1984)
Panchavan Kadu (**Kunchako**, Mal, 1971)
Panchavarna Kili (?, Saravana Films, Tam, 1965)
Panchavarnam (Manimaran?, Tam, 1982)
Panchavati (**Sasikumar**, Mal, 1973)
Panchavati (**Basu Bhattacharya**, H, 1986)
Panchayat (Sudhish Ghatak, B, 1950)
Panchayat (Lekhraj Bhakri, H, 1958)
Panchayathi (**Vijayanirmala**, Tel, 1977)
Panchdanda (*aka* Five Divine Wands: **Chandulal Shah**, St, 1925)
Panchhi (Barkat Mehra, H, 1944)
Panch Kalyani (*aka* Parijatak, Flying Horse: **Harshadrai Mehta**, St, 1926)
Panch Ratan (Kamran, H, 1965)
Panchthupi: A Village in West Bengal (**Harisadhan Dasgupta**, E, 1955)
Pandanti Jeevitham (**Bapu**, Tel, 1980)
Pandanti Kapuram (Laxmi Deepak, Tel, 1972)
Pandanti Kapuraniki 12 Suthralu (Rajachandra, Tel, 1983)
Pandanti Samsaram (P. Chandrasekhara Reddy, Tel, 1975)
Pandarimancham (Omkar, Tel, 1991)
Pandava Agyathavas (*aka* Pandava Nirvana: **Y.V. Rao**, St, 1930)
Pandava Nirvana *see* Pandava Agyathavas
Pandavapuram (G.S. Panicker, Mal, 1986)
Pandava Vanavasam (**K. Kameshwara Rao**, Tel/Tam, 1965)
Pandav Kaurav (*aka* Mahabharat: **Nanubhai Vakil**, H, 1933)
Pandav Patrani (*aka* Celestial Lotus: **M. Bhavnani**, St, 1928)
Pandav Rajasuya Yagam (?, Exhibitors Film Service, St, 1927)
Pandav Shodh (G.V. Sane, St, 1925)
Pandav Vanavas (G.V. Sane, St, 1922)
Pandharicha Patil (Raja Pandit, Mar, 1949)
Pandharichi Vari (Ramakant Kavthekar, Mar, 1988)
Pandhattam (M.A. Laxmanan, Tam, 1974)
Pandhiri Mancham (Omkar, Tel, 1991)
Pandian (S.P. Muthuraman, Tam, 1992)
Pandidurai (Manoj Kumar, Tam, 1991)
Pandinattu Thangam (T.P. Gajendran, Tam, 1989)
Pandit Aur Pathan (Joginder, H, 1977)
Pandit Bhimsen Joshi (**S.S. Gulzar**, H, 1992)
Pandithevan (**K. Subramanyam**, Tam, 1959)
Panditji (G.R. Durrani, H, 1946)
Pandit Moshai (**Satu Sen**, B, 1936)
Pandit Moshai (**Naresh Mitra**, B, 1951)
Pandoba Porgi Phasli (**Prabhakar Nayak**, Mar, 1975)
Pandu Havaldar (**Dada Kondke**, Mar, 1975)
Panduranga Mahatyam (**K. Kameshwara Rao**, Tel, 1957)
Panduranga Mahima *see* **Chakradhari**
Pandurangan (D.C. Gune, Tam, 1939)
Panduranga Vithal (K. Ramachandra Rao, Tel, 1939)
Panetar (F.R. Irani, G, 1965)
Panetar (Mohan Thakkar, G, 1987)
Pangali (K. Subhash, Tam, 1992)
Panghat (K.J. Parmar/Maheshchandra, H, 1943)
Panghat (V. Shafi, Haryanvi, 1985)
Pangs of Love, The *see* Dard-e-Ulfat
Panhalgad (?, South Indian Film, St, 1928)
Panic in Baghdad *see* Arabian Nights
Panic in Goa *see* Spy in Goa
Panihari (*aka* Bade Log: Dada Gunjal, H, 1946)
Panima Aag (*aka* Sweet Adversity: **Nagendra Majumdar**, St, 1926)
Panimalar (Hemachandran, Tam, 1981)
Panimudakku (**P.N. Menon**, Mal, 1972)
Pani Teertha Veedu (**K.S. Sethumadhavan**, Mal, 1972)
Panithirai (V. Srinivasan, Tam, 1961)
Panjaramlo Pasipapa (Giduthri Satyam, Tel, 1973)
Panjarathnam (Mani, Mal, 1979)
Pankaj (D.D. Chavan, G, 1949)
Pankajavalli (**Krishnan-Panju**, Tam, 1946)
Pankalikal (G. Ramakrishna, Tam, 1961)
Pankatilak (Mangal Chakraborty, B, 1961)
Pankhiraj (Piyush Bose, B, 1980)
Panna (Najam Naqvi, H, 1944)
Panna (Mohan Sinha, H, 1956)
Panna (Amit Moitra, B, 1967)
Pannadai (Ram Daryani, H, 1945)
Panna Hirey Chunni (Amal Dutta, B, 1969)
Pannaipurathu Pandavargal (B. Lenin, Tam, 1982)
Pannaiyar Magan (Jampana, Tam, 1963)
Panna Ratna (*aka* Jewel of Mewar: **Harshadrai Mehta**, St, 1926)
Panneer Nadhigal (M. Bhaskar, Tam, 1986)
Panneer Pushpangal (Bharathi Vasu, Tam, 1981)
Panorama of Calcutta (?, Warwick Trading, St, 1898)
Panorama of Indian Scenes and Procession, A (Prof. Stevenson, St, 1898)
Panorama of West Bengal (**Harisadhan Dasgupta**, E, 1961)
Pan-Raksha (Binoy Bannerjee, B, 1954)
Pantalu Pattimpulu (K.B. Tilak, Tel, 1968)
Panthulamma (**Gudavalli Ramabrahmam**, Tel, 1943)
Panthulamma (**Singeetham Srinivasa Rao**, Tel, 1977)
Paokhum Ama (**Aribam Syam Sharma**, Manipuri, 1982)
Paoolkhuna (TV: **Amol Palekar**, Mar, 1993)
Papakosam (G.V.R. Sheshgiri Rao, Tel, 1968)
Papa Miyan of Aligarh (**K.A. Abbas**, H, 1975)
Papam Pasivadu (V. Ramchandra Rao, Tel, 1972)
Papa Pariharam (**A. Bhimsingh**, Tel, 1966)
Papa Punya (M.V. Krishnaswamy, K, 1971)
Papa's Wife *see* Babanchi Bayko
Papayude Sontham Appoose (**Fazil**, Mal, 1992)
Papeeha (**Sai Paranjpye**, H, 1993)
Pape Maa Pranam (V. Madhusudhana Rao, Tel, 1989)
Paper Flowers *see* **Kaagaz Ke Phool**
Paper Parinam (*aka* Crime and Punishment: ?, **Madan** Theatres, St, 1924)
Paper Pathey (Prafulla Roy, B, 1943)
Papiha Re (Dawood Chand, H, 1948)
Papikondalu (Gavini Krishna, Tel, 1984)
Papi Tarey Anek (Dharam Kumar, P, 1976)
Papori (**Jahnu Barua**, A, 1986)
Pappan Priyapetta Pappan (Sathyan Andhikkad, Mal, 1986)
Pappathi (R.K. Shanmugham, Tam, 1979)
Pappu (Baby, Mal, 1980)
Parabat Priya (Dipranjan Bose, B, 1984)
Parabhritika (Bidhayak Bhattacharya, B, 1947)
Paradh (Kishore Miskine, Mar, 1977)
Paradhin (**Modhu Bose**, B, 1956)
Parai Aag (Najam Naqvi, H, 1948)
Parajay *see* **Jawani Ki Reet**
Para Jhia Ghara Bhangena (Ramesh Chandra, O, 1985)
Parakh (*aka* Prem Kasauti: Bapurao Apte, H, 1937)
Parakh (**Sohrab Modi**, H, 1944)
Parakh (**Bimal Roy**, H, 1960)
Parakh (?, Dinanath Obhan, H, 1987)
Parakkum Pavai (Ramanna, Tam, 1966)
Paral Ko Aago (Pratap Subha, Nepali, 1978)
Parallel *see* **Samandaram**
Parallel College (Tulsidas, Mal, 1991)
Parama *see* **Paroma**
Paramanandayya Sishyulu Katha (**C. Pullaiah**, Tel, 1966)
Paramanandayya Sishyulu Katha (K. Sivarao, Tel, 1950)
Paramashivudu (**Ghantamneni Krishna**, Tel, 1991)
Param Dharam (Swaroop Kumar, H, 1987)
Parameshi Prema Prasanga (Ramesh Bhatt, K, 1985)
Parampara (TV: **Gautam Ghosh**, H, 1985)
Parampara (**Sibi Malayil**, Mal, 1990)
Parampara (**Yash Chopra**, H, 1992)
Paramparyam (Manobala, Tam, 1993)
Param Veer Chakra (TV: **Chetan Anand**, H, 1988)
Paranjoti (**T.R. Raghunath**, Tam, 1945)
Parankimala (**B.G. Bharathan**, Mal, 1981)
Parannu Parannu Parannu (**P. Padmarajan**, Mal, 1984)
Paran Pandit (Tulsi Lahiri, B, 1939)
Paraparey (Jatin Das, B, 1936)
Paras (Anant Thakur, H, 1949)
Paras (C.P. Dixit, H, 1971)
Parasakthi (**Krishnan-Panju**, Tam, 1952)
Parasakthi (Raji Koti, Tel, 1987)
Parasangada Gendethimma (Maruti Shivram, K, 1978)
Parash Pathar (Surendraranjan Sarkar, B, 1949)

Parash Pathar (**Satyajit Ray**, B, 1957)
Parashuram (**Kanjibhai Rathod**, St, 1922)
Parashuram (**Dadasaheb Phalke**, St, 1928)
Parashuram (Ramnik Desai, H, 1947)
Parashuram (**Mrinal Sen**, B, 1978)
Parashurama (V. Somasekhar, K, 1989)
Parashuramer Kuthar (**Nabyendu Chatterjee**, B, 1989)
Parasmani *see* Bhakta Puran
Parasmani (Prafulla Roy, B, 1939)
Parasmani (**Babubhai Mistri**, H, 1963)
Parasmani (Mohan T. Gehani, H, 1992)
Parasmoni (**Tarun Majumdar**, B, 1988)
Paras Padamani (Arun Bhatt, G, 1987)
Parasparam (Shajiyem, Mal, 1983)
Parasuraman (**C.S. Rao**, Mal, 1978)
Parasuramar (**Harshadrai Mehta**, Tam, 1940)
Parasuramudu (**Vijayanirmala**, Tel, 1986)
Paravaigal Palavidham (Robert-Rajasekharan, Tam, 1988)
Paravum-18 (Thilakam-Balraj, Tam, 1985)
Paraya Dhan *see* Bichar
Paraya Dhan (Rajendra Bhatia, H, 1971)
Paraya Ghar *see* Chingari
Paraya Ghar (Kalpataru, H, 1989)
Parayana To Pyara Ladi (**Chandrakant Sangani**, G, 1980)
Parayanumvayya Parayathirikkanumvayya (**Priyadarshan**, Mal, 1985)
Paraye Bas Mein (Dawood Chand, H, 1946)
Parbat (O.P. Dutta, H, 1952)
Parbatiya Banal Panditayan (Ramnath Ray, Bh, 1986)
Parbat Ke Us Paar (Raman Kumar, H, 1988)
Parbat Ki Rani (A. Karim, H, 1948)
Parbat Pe Apna Dera (**V. Shantaram**, H, 1944)
Parbhavni Preet (Bimal Mangalia, G, 1975)
Parchain (**V. Shantaram**, H, 1952)
Parchain (Narayan Tomar, H, 1980)
Parchaiyan (Sharan Kumar Chand, H, 1972)
Parda (A.G. Soorma, H, 1949)
Parda Hai Parda (**K. Bapaiah**, H, 1992)
Pardanasheen (I.A. Hafizji, H, 1942)
Parde Ke Peeche (K. Shankar, H, 1971)
Pardes (M. Sadiq, H, 1950)
Pardesan (Khawai Zaman, P, 1969)
Pardesi *see* **Poongothai**
Pardesi (**Chaturbhuj Doshi**, H, 1941)
Pardesi (**K.A. Abbas**/Vassili M. Pronin, H, 1957)
Pardesi (Kundan Kumar, H, 1970)
Pardesi (Raj Sippy, H, 1993)
Pardesia (*aka* Gypsy: **Niranjan Pal**, St, 1931)
Pardesi Dhola (R.C. Talwar, P, 1941)
Pardesi Dhola (**S.P. Bakshi**, P, 1962)
Pardesi Mehmaan (Aspi, H, 1948)
Pardesi Pankhi (*aka* Flower Bird: **Chandulal Shah**, H, 1937)
Pardesi Preetam (*aka* Street Angels: **Nandlal Jaswantlal**, H, 1933)
Pardesi Saiyan *see* Sudhaar
Pardesi Saiyan (*aka* Lovers: **Nandlal Jaswantlal**, St, 1929)
Pardesi Saiyan (*aka* My Darling, Chand Ka Tukda: Baburaj Patel, H, 1935)
Pardes Ni Preet (*aka* Warrior from the Wild: **Harshadrai Mehta**, St, 1931)
Pardhudu (K.S.R. Doss, Tel, 1989)
Pareeksha (**Yoganand**, H, 1963)
Pareeksha (**P. Bhaskaran**, Mal, 1967)
Parer Chheley (Ardhendu Sen, B, 1957)
Paresh (**Ajoy Kar**, B, 1955)
Pare Solla Oru Pillai (**Krishnan-Panju**, Tam, 1978)
Parghat (Prabin Phukan, A, 1948)
Pari (Jagannath Chatterjee, B, 1966)
Paribartan (**Satyen Bose**, B, 1949)
Paribesh (Kalpataru, B, 1980)
Parichay/Lagan (**Nitin Bose**, B/H, 1941)
Parichay (**Satyen Bose**, H, 1954)
Parichay (**S.S. Gulzar**, H, 1972)
Parichay (Nirmal Mitra, B, 1978)
Parichay (Amar Bhattacharya, B, 1983)
Pariharam (?, Tam, 1990)
Parijata (Siddalingaiah, K, 1982)
Parijatak *see* Panch Kalyani
Parijatak (*aka* The Flower of Heaven: **N.D. Sarpotdar**, St, 1929)
Parijatak/Shri Krishna Satyabhama (**Raja Paranjpe**, Mar/H, 1951)
Parijata Pushpaharanam (**Raja Sandow**, Tam, 1932)
Parijatha (Tatineni Prasad, Tel, 1986)
Parijatham (K.S. Gopalakrishnan, Tam, 1950)
Parijatham (Manzoor, Mal, 1976)
Parijatham (T. Madhava Rao, Tel, 1986)
Parikshit (?, **Madan Theatres**, St, 1922)
Parinam (Vishwanath Naik, O, 1961)
Parinam (Probin Bora, A, 1973)
Parinati (Palash Bannerjee, B, 1986)
Parinati (**Prakash Jha**, H, 1987)
Parinay (**Kantilal Rathod**, H, 1974)
Parinda (Vidhu Vinod Chopra, H, 1989)
Parinde (**P.K. Atre**, H, 1945)
Parineeta (**Pashupati Chatterjee**, B, 1942)
Parineeta (**Bimal Roy**, H, 1953)
Parineeta (**Ajoy Kar**, B, 1969)
Parisam Pottachu (Chozharajan, Tam, 1987)
Paris By Night (**P.V. Pathy**, E, 1934)
Parishkaram (Dharani, Tel, 1991)
Parishodh (**Sukumar Dasgupta**, B, 1955)
Parishodh (Ardhendu Sen, B, 1968)
Paris Ki Ek Shyam *see* An Evening in Paris
Paris Paris (Rajan, Tam, 1988)
Paristan (**Mahesh Kaul**, H, 1944)
Paristan (*aka* Gul-e-Bakavali: **Dhirubhai Desai**, H, 1957)
Parisu (**Yoganand**, Tam, 1963)
Paritchaikku Neramchu (Muktha V. Srinivasan, Tam, 1982)
Paritran (Bholanath Mitra, B, 1951)
Parivar (**Asit Sen**, H, 1956)
Parivar (K.P. Kashyap, H, 1967)
Parivar (K.H.D. Rao, O, 1978)
Parivar (Shashilal Nair, H, 1987)
Parivartan *see* Graduate
Parivartan (*aka* Revolution in Life: Prafulla Ghosh, St, 1929)
Parivartan (*aka* Regeneration: **Ezra Mir**, H, 1936)
Parivartan (**N.R. Acharya**, H, 1949)
Parivartan (D.S. Sultania, H, 1972)
Parivartan (Prabhakar Gokhale, Mar, 1980)
Parivarthana (**T. Prakash Rao**, Tel, 1954)
Parivarthana (K. Hemambharadhara Rao, Tel, 1975)
Parivarthanam (**Sasikumar**, Mal, 1977)
Parka Potana (Ramkumar Bohra, G, 1982)
Parkhino Melo (Arun Bhatt, G, 1981)
Parki Thapan (Arun Bhatt, G, 1979)
Parmatma (Chand, H, 1978)
Parnetar (Manibhai Vyas, G, 1951)
Parnetar (Devraj, G, 1984)
Paro (**Roop K. Shorey**, H, 1947)
Paroma/Parama (**Aparna Sen**, B/H, 1985)
Paropakaram (Kamal Ghosh, Tel/Tam, 1953)
Paropakari (Y.R. Swamy, K, 1970)
Parrot that Never Sings, The *see* **Padatha Paingili**
Parsa Eblis (*aka* Pavitra Satan: **Manilal Joshi**, St, 1927)
Partha Gnabagam Illayo (Nagesh, Tam, 1985)
Parthakumar (**Bhalji Pendharkar**, Mar/H, 1934)
Parthal Pasi Theerum (**A. Bhimsingh**, Tam, 1962)
Parthal Pasu (**K.S. Gopalakrishnan**, Tam, 1988)
Parthiban Kanavu (**Yoganand**, Tam, 1960)
Parthudu (K.S.R. Doss, Tel, 1989)
Partner (Anil Tejani, H, 1982)
Parts that Built the Auto, The (**Kantilal Rathod**, E, 1966)
Party (Govind Nihalani, H, 1984)
Paru Paru Pattinam Paru (Manobala, Tam, 1986)
Parutha Pournami (Narayan Kutty Vallam, Mal, 1968)
Paruvakalam (Jos A.N. Fernando, Tam, 1974)
Paruvamazhai (N. Shankaran Nair, Tam, 1978)
Paruva Ragam (V. Ravichandran, Tam, 1987)
Paruvathu Vasalile (Krupa Shankar, Tam, 1980)
Paruvu Pratishtha (V.C. Guhanathan, Tel, 1993)
Paruvu Pratishthalu (Manapuram Apparao, Tel, 1963)
Parvarish (S. Bannerjee, H, 1958)
Parvarish (**Manmohan Desai**, H, 1977)
Parvathalu Pangallu (Muthyala Subbaiah, Tel, 1992)
Parvathi (**B.G. Bharathan**, Mal, 1981)
Parvathi (**Balachandra Menon**, Mal, 1985)
Parvathi Ennai Paradi V. shekhar, Tam, 1993)
Parvathi Kalyanam (**B.S. Ranga**, K, 1967)
Parvati (**Santi P. Choudhury**, B, 1977)
Parvati Kalyanam (**P.Y. Altekar**, Tam, 1936)
Parvati Kalyanam (**G. Balaramaiah**, Tel, 1941)
Parvati Kalyanam (**M.V. Raman**, Tam, 1945)
Parvati Kalyanam (B. Bhaskara Rao, Tel, 1958)
Parvati Parameshwarulu (M.S. Kota Reddy, Tel, 1981)
Parvayin Marupakkam (K.M. Balakrishnan, Tam, 1982)
Parvin (**Nanubhai Vakil**, H, 1957)
Parviz *see* Watan Parast
Parviz Parizad *see* **Lal-e-Yaman**
Parwana (*aka* Butterfly: H.E. Khatib, St, 1933)
Parwana (S. Usman, H, 1941)
Parwana (J.K. Nanda, H, 1947)
Parwana (Jyoti Swaroop, H, 1971)
Parwane (Ashok Gaikwad, H, 1993)
Pasa Deepam (Pattu, Tam, 1973)
Pasam (Ramanna, Tam, 1962)
Pasamalar (**A. Bhimsingh**, Tam, 1961)
Pasamalar/Raktha Sambandham (V. Madhusudhana Rao, Tam/Tel, 1961)
Pasa Mazhai (V.M.C. Hanifa, Tam, 1989)
Pasam Oru Vesam (Jayadevi, Tam, 1987)
Pasamum Nesamum (**Yoganand**, Tam, 1964)
Pasand Apni Apni (Brij Katyal, H, 1972)
Pasand Apni Apni (**Basu Chatterjee**, H, 1983)
Pasant Aahe Mulgi (**Raja Paranjpe**, Mar, 1956)
Pasaparaivaigal (V.M.C. Hanifa, Tam, 1988)
Pasavalai (A.S. Nagarajan, Tam, 1956)
Paschatap (Yeshwant Singh, H, 1980)
Pas De Deux (**Prakash Jha**, E, 1981)
Pashan Devata (**Sukumar Dasgupta**, B, 1942)
Pasher Bari (Sudhir Mukherjee, B, 1952)
Pashu Palan (**Shyam Benegal**, H, 1979)
Pasi (**Durai**, Tam, 1979)
Pasidi Manushulu (V. Subramanyam, Tel, 1970)
Pasidi Mogalu (Durga Nageshwara Rao, Tel, 1980)
Pasi Hridayalu (M. Mallikarjuna Rao, Tel, 1973)
Pasivadi Pranam (A. Kodandarami Reddy, Tel, 1987)
Pasivani Paga (K.V.S. Kutumba Rao, Tel, 1973)
Pasiyin Kodumai (K.J. Mohan Rao, Tam, 1952)
Passing Show *see* Chalta Purza
Passing Show (Dwarka Khosla, H, 1936)
Passing Show (**Master Bhagwan**, H, 1956)
Passion *see* Asuri Lalsa *or* Husn Ka Gulam
Passionate Prince *see* Rangilo Rajavi
Pass Mark (V. Balakrishnan, Tam, 1993)
Passport (Pramod Chakraborty, H, 1961)
Passport (Thampi Kannomthanam, Mal, 1983)
Past in Perspective (**Adoor Gopalakrishnan**, E, 1975)
Past, Present and Future *see* **Trikaal**
Pasupatastrama (K. Rangarao, Tel, 1939)
Pasupu Kumkuma (G.D. Joshi, Tel, 1955)
Pasupu Thada Vuri Thada (Shrirangam Sridhar, Tel, 1983)
Pasuputhadu (M. Baliah, Tel, 1986)
Pataal Bhairavi *see* **Patala Bhairavi**
Pataal Bhairavi (**K. Bapaiah**, H, 1985)
Pataal Ketu (K.P. Bhave, St, 1928)
Pataal Nagari (Ramkumar Bohra, H, 1963)
Pataal Padmini (*aka*: The Beauty from Hell: **Harshadrai Mehta**, St, 1929)
Pataal Pari (**S.P. Bakshi**, H, 1957)
Pataal Puri (**Priyanath Ganguly**, B, 1935)
Patala Bhairavi/Pataal Bhairavi (**K.V. Reddy**, Tel/Tam/H, 1951)
Patala Mohini (S.N. Singh, K, 1965)
Patalam Pandu (S.D. Lall, Tel, 1981)
Patala Nagu (P.S. Prakash, Tel, 1985)
Patali Parmar (**Ravindra Dave**, G, 1978)
Patang (Hargovind/Suraj Prakash, H, 1960)
Patang (*aka* The Kite: **Gautam Ghosh**, H, 1993)
Patanga (**H.S. Rawail**, H, 1949)
Patanga (Kedar Kapoor, H, 1971)
Patan Ni Paniari (*aka* Damsel of Patan: **Homi Master**, St, 1930)
Patched-up Coat, The *see* **Kandam Bacha Coat**
Pathai Marinal (**Durai**, Tam, 1979)
Patha Kannikkai (K. Shankar, Tam, 1962)
Pathamudayam (**Sasikumar**, Mal, 1985)
Pathan (Ataullah Khan, H, 1962)
Patha Nirdesh (Sarathi, B, 1953)
Patha Poojai (**A. Bhimsingh**, Tam, 1974)
Path Bendhe Dilo (**Premendra Mitra**, B, 1945)
Pathbhola (**Tarun Majumdar**, B, 1986)
Path Bhoole (**Dhiren Ganguly**, B, 1940)
Pathcha Bhau (Datta Mane, Mar, 1967)
Pathe Holo Dekha (Sachin Adhikari, B, 1968)
Pathe Holo Deri (**Agradoot**, B, 1957)
Pathe Jetey Jetey (Umanath Bannerjee, B, 1988)
Pather Daabi *see* Sabhyasachi
Pather Daabi (Satish Dasgupta/Digambar Chatterjee, B, 1947)
Pather Panchali (**Satyajit Ray**, B, 1955)
Pather Sathi (**Naresh Mitra**, B, 1946)
Pather Sheshey (Jyotish Mukherjee, B, 1936)
Pather Sheshey (Ardhendu Chatterjee, B, 1955)
Pathetic Fallacy, *see* **Ajantrik**
Pathik (**Charu Roy**, B, 1939)
Pathik (**Debaki Bose**, B, 1953)
Pathik (Jabbar Patel, E, 1988)
Pathinalam Ravu (Shrini, Mal, 1979)
Pathinaru Vayathinile (**Bharathirajaa**, Tam, 1977)
Pathini Penn (R.C. Sakthi, Tam, 1993)
Pathirai Matru Thangam (K.S. Mani, Tam, 1959)
Pathirapattu (N. Prakash, Mal, 1967)
Pathiravum Pakalvelichavum (M. Azad, Mal, 1974)
Pathivratha (M.S. Chakraborty, Mal, 1979)
Pathiya Suryan (K.P. Pillai, Mal, 1981)
Pathiye Daiva (**R. Nagendra Rao**, K, 1964)
Pathlaag (**Raja Paranjpe**, Mar, 1964)
Pathni Daivam (**Ch. Narayanamurthy**, Tam, 1957)
Path of Glory *see* Vijay Marg
Path-o-Prasad (**Tarun Majumdar**, B, 1991)
Pathrakhin (**Prabhakar Nayak**, Mar, 1972)
Pathukappu (**A. Bhimsingh**, Tam, 1970)
Pathumatha Bandham (**Krishnan-Panju**, Tam, 1974)
Pati Bhakti (**J.J. Madan**, St, 1922)
Pati Bhakti (*aka* Pavitra Leelavati: ?, **Madan**/Bharatlaxmi Pics, H, 1932)
Pati Bhakti (**P.Y. Altekar**, Tam, 1936)
Pati Bhakti (P.N. Srinivasa Rao, Tel, 1943)
Pati Bhakti (**A. Bhimsingh**, Tam, 1958)
Patighatini Sati *see* Gunial Gulab
Pati Hach Parmeshwar (?, Ram Davri, Mar, 1967)
Patindalla Bangaram (G.V.R. Sheshgiri Rao, Tel, 1971)
Pati Parmeshwar (Manu Desai, H, 1958)
Pati Parmeshwar (**Babubhai Mistri**, G, 1979)
Pati Parmeshwar (Madan Joshi, H, 1989)
Pati Patni *see* Pati Pooja
Pati Patni (*aka* Husband and Wife: **Chandulal Shah**, St, 1929)
Pati Patni (Dada Gunjal, H, 1939)
Pati Patni (S.A. Akbar, H, 1966)
Pati Patni (M.S.K. Reddy, O, 1978)
Pati Patni Aur Tawaif (Raj Kumar Kohli, H, 1990)
Pati Patni Aur Woh (**B.R. Chopra**, H, 1978)
Pati Pooja (*aka* Pati Patni: ?, Bharatlaxmi Pics, H, 1943)
Pati Sansodhini Samiti (Bishu Dasgupta, B, 1965)
Pati Seva (*aka* Aurat Ka Dil: S.M. Yusuf, H, 1947)
Patita (**Amiya Chakravarty**, H, 1953)
Patita (**I.V. Sasi**, H, 1980)
Patitoddhar *see* Aurat Ka Dil
Patitoddhar (*aka* Reclamation: **N.D. Sarpotdar**, St, 1928)

Patit Pawan (*aka* Ahilyoddhar: **Nagendra Majumdar**, H, 1933)
Patit Pawan (Vasant Painter, H, 1955)
Pativrata *see* **Dharmapatni**
Pativrata (Jagadish Chakraborty, B, 1942)
Pativrata (**Datta Dharmadhikari**, Mar, 1959)
Pativrata (**Ch. Narayanamurthy**, Tel, 1964)
Pativrata (P.S. Murthy, K, 1965)
Patjhad (**Ravindra Dave**, H, 1948)
Patlacha Por (**Dinkar D. Patil**, Mar, 1951)
Patlachi Soon (Datta Mane, Mar, 1966)
Patla Tar Vhay Mhana (**Prabhakar Nayak**, Mar, 1973)
Patleen (Chandrakant Shinde, Mar, 1981)
Patnam Pilla Palletoori (Mouli, Tel, 1986)
Patnam Vachina Pativrathalu (Mouli, Tel, 1982)
Patnavasam (P. Chandrasekhara Reddy, Tel, 1978)
Patni (**Gudavalli Ramabrahmam**, Tel, 1942)
Patni (V.R. Naidu, H, 1970)
Patni Pratap (**J.J. Madan**, St, 1923)
Patondru Ketten (S. Krishnamurthy/S. Raghavan, Tam, 1971)
Pat Paintings of Orissa (**Nirad Mahapatra**, E, 1987)
Patrani (**Vijay Bhatt**, H, 1956)
Patri Chai (Sunil Majumdar, B, 1952)
Patriot *see* Banke Sipahi *or* Desh Bhakt *or* Desh Deepak
Pattabhishekham (Mallikarjuna Rao, Mal, 1974)
Pattabhishekham (**K. Raghavendra Rao**, Tel, 1985)
Pattakathi Bhairavan (V.B. Rajendra Prasad, Tam, 1979)
Pattalam Janaki (Mani, Mal, 1977)
Pattalimagan (?, Anbulakshmi Films, Tam, 1990)
Pattam Bharathamum (P. Madhavan, Tam, 1975)
Pattam Pathavi (R. Kalaivanan, Tam, 1981)
Pattam Pazhali (**K. Balachander**, Tam, 1970)
Pattam Poochi (A.S. Prakasham, Tam, 1975)
Pattanakke Banda Patniyaru (A.V. Sheshgiri Rao, K, 1980)
Pattanamthan Pogalamadi (?, Anitha Cine Creations, Tam, 1990)
Pattana Praveshanam (Sathyan Andhikkad, Mal, 1988)
Pattanathil Bhootam (**M.V. Raman**, Tam, 1967)
Pattanathil Naradan (Siddalingaiah, Mal, 1984)
Pattanathil Petti (?, Mother Cine Prod, Tam, 1990)
Pattathu Rajakkal (S.A. Chandrasekharan, Tam, 1982)
Pattathu Rani (S. Ramanathan, Tam, 1967)
Pattathu Rani (Manivasagam, Tam, 1992)
Pattayilin Vetri *see* Namminabantu
Pattaylin Vetri *see* Namminabantu
Patthar (Deepak Bahry, H, 1985)
Pattharar Kahini (Debnarayan Gupta, B, 1950)
Patthar Aur Payal (Harmesh Malhotra, H, 1974)
Patthar Dil (Surender Mohan, H, 1985)
Patthar Ke Insaan (Shomu Mukherjee, H, 1990)
Patthar Ke Khwab (Pal Premi, H, 1969)
Patthar Ke Log (Daljit, H, 1984)
Patthar Ke Phool (Anant Balani, H, 1990)
Patthar Ke Sanam (Raja Nawathe, H, 1967)
Patthar Ki Lakeer (Din Dayal Sharma, H, 1982)
Pattharon Ka Saudagar (Shourie Daulatavi, H, 1944)
Patthar Se Takkar (Gulab Mehta, H, 1980)
Patthe Bapurao (**Raja Nene**, Mar, 1950)
Pattikada Pattanama (P. Madhavan, Tam, 1972)
Pattikattan (Krishnakumar, Tam, 1990)
Pattikattu Thambi (Senthilanathan, Tam, 1988)
Pattikatu Ponnaiah (**B.S. Ranga**, Tam, 1973)
Pattikatu Raja (K. Shanmugham, Tam, 1975)
Pattina Pravesham (**K. Balachander**, Tam, 1977)
Pattinathar (V.S.K. Patham, Tam, 1935)
Pattinathar (**Murugadasa**, Tam, 1936)
Pattinathar (K. Somu, Tam, 1962)
Patti Sollai Thattathe (Rajasekhar, Tam, 1988)
Patti Sona Kathai (G. Suryam, Tam, 1969)
Pattola (L. Yakub/M.H. Kasim, P, 1942)
Pattola (Raj Oberai, P, 1973)
Pattola (Jagjeet, P, 1987)
Patton Ki Baazi (Ram Govind, H, 1986)
Pattuchelai (M.S. Raja Annadurai, Tam, 1985)
Pattukku Naan Adimai (Ramadas E., Tam, 1990)
Pattukoru Thalaivan (Liaqat Ali Khan, Tam, 1989)
Pattu Kunte Laksha (B. Harinarayana, Tel, 1971)
Pattu Kunte Padivelu (M. Mallikarjuna Rao, Tel, 1967)
Pattundru Kettin (V.C. Guhanathan, Tam, 1991)
Pattuthala (G.B. Sekhar, Tel, 1992)
Pattu Thoovala (**P. Subramanyam**, Mal, 1965)
Patwardhan's Royal Circus (**Dadasaheb Phalke**, St, 1922)
Patwari (B.S. Rajhans, P, 1942)
Patwari (S.S. Arora, P, 1983)
Paun Baran (Rajendra Sharma, P, 1969)
Pauper Princess (Ramakant-Gharekhan, St, 1928)
Pavadakkari (Alex, Mal, 1978)
Pavai Vilakku (K. Somu, Tam, 1960)
Pavalakkodi (**R.S. Prakash**, St, 1931)
Pavalakkodi (*aka* Coral Queen: **K. Subramanyam**, Tam, 1934)
Pavalakkodi (S.M. Sreeramulu Naidu, Tam, 1949)
Pavamanippu (**A. Bhimsingh**, Tam, 1961)
Pavam Krooran (Rajasenan, Mal, 1984)
Pavam Poornima (Balu Kiriyath, Mal, 1984)
Pavanaganga (Y.R. Swamy, K, 1977)
Pavanakathcha Dhondi (Anant Thakur, Mar, 1966)
Pavangal Pennungal (**Kunchako**, Mal, 1973)
Pavankhind (**Bhalji Pendharkar**, Mar, 1956)
Pavapettaval (P.A. Thomas, Mal, 1967)
Pavathin Sambalam (**Durai**, Tam, 1978)
Pavitra (Vinay, Tel, 1986)
Pavitra Bandham (V. Madhusudhana Rao, Tel, 1971)
Pavitra Ganga (*aka* Sacred Ganges: J.K. Nanda, H, 1932)
Pavitra Ganga (H.N. Reddy, H, 1984)
Pavitra Hridayalu (A.C. Trilogchander, Tel, 1971)
Pavitra Leelavati *see* Pati Bhakti
Pavitra Papi (Rajendra Bhatia, H, 1970)
Pavitra Prema (**A. Bhimsingh**, Tel, 1962)
Pavitra Prema (A.V. Sheshgiri Rao, K, 1984)
Pavitra Satan *see* Parsa Eblis
Pavizha Muthu (Jesey, Mal, 1980)
Pavunnu Pavanuthan (**K. Bhagyaraj**, Tam, 1991)
Pavurnami Nilavil (M.A. Kaja, Tam, 1980)
Pawan Basanti (?, Shankar's International Movies, H, 1980)
Pawan Putra Hanuman (**Babubhai Mistri**, H, 1957)
Payachi Dasi/Charnon Ki Dasi (**Gajanan Jagirdar**, Mar/H, 1941)
Payal (A. Shakoor, H, 1948)
Payal (Joseph Taliath, H, 1957)
Payal (Mahendra Shah, H, 1992)
Payal Ki Jhankaar (**M.V. Raman**, H, 1968)
Payal Ki Jhankaar (**Satyen Bose**, H, 1980)
Payame Haq (*aka* Niti Vijay: **Dhirubhai Desai**, H, 1939)
Payame Ulfat (*aka* Nawabzadi, Lal-o-Gauhar: Soni/Kabuli, H, 1935)
Payanam (Vietnam Veedu Sundaram, Tam, 1976)
Payanangal Mudivathillai (R. Sundarrajan, Tam, 1982)
Payer Dhulo (Jyotish Mukherjee, B, 1935)
Paying Guest (**Subodh Mukherjee**, H, 1957)
Payum Puli (S.P. Muthuraman, Tam, 1983)
Pazhani (**A. Bhimsingh**, Tam, 1965)
Pazhassi Raja (**Kunchako**, Mal, 1964)
PC 369 (?, Maryland Movies, Mal, 1987)
Peaceful Revolution, The (**Atma Ram**, E, 1961)
Peace Maker *see* Raj Bhakt
Peace Time Armada (**Kantilal Rathod**, 1967)
Pear Brothers (**Rai Chand Boral**, B, 1934)
Pearl, The *see* **Swati** *or* Mahasagar Nu Moti
Pearl Necklace *see* Moti Ka Haar
Pearl of Egypt *see* Misar Nu Moti
Pearl View (**Kunchako**, Mal, 1970)
Pedaraitu (**Kadaru Nagabhushanam**, Tel, 1952)
Pedarasi Pedamma Katha (G. Surya, Tel, 1968)
Pedda Gedda (Bhargava, K, 1982)
Peddakayya (B.A. Subba Rao, Tel, 1967)
Pedda Koduku (**K.S. Prakash Rao**, Tel, 1972)
Peddalu Marali (P. Chandrasekhara Reddy, Tel, 1974)
Pedda Manushulu (**K.V. Reddy**, Tel, 1954)
Peddanayya (P.D. Prasad, Tel, 1976)
Peddarikalu (**Tapi Chanakya**, Tel, 1957)
Peddarikam (A.M. Rathnam, Tel, 1992)
Peddillu Chinnillu (**Dasari Narayana Rao**, Tel, 1979)
Peddinti Alludu (Sarath, Tel, 1991)
Peddinti Kodalu (Srinivasa Reddy, Tel, 1975)
Pedgaonche Shahane (**Raja Paranjpe**, Mar, 1952)
Pedro (Aakkoo, H, 1960)
Peecha Karo (Pankaj Parashar, H, 1988)
Peenai Vazha Vidungal (Devarajan, Tam, 1969)
Peetalameeda Pelli (G. Krishnamurthy, Tel, 1964)
Pehchan (**P.C. Barua**, H, 1946)
Pehchan (Sohanlal Kanwar, H, 1970)
Pehchan (Deepak Shivdasani, H, 1993)
Pehla Adhyay (**Vishnu Mathur**, H, 1981)
Pehla Admi (**Bimal Roy**, H, 1950)
Pehla Kadam (*aka* The First Step: **Kidar Sharma**, H, 1981)
Pehla Kadam (**Ketan Mehta**, H, 1988)
Pehla Nasha (Ashutosh Gowarikar, H, 1993)
Pehla Pehla Pyar (**Nanubhai Vakil**, H, 1958)
Pehla Pyar *see* Sansar Chakra
Pehla Pyar (A.P. Kapur, H, 1947)
Pehle Aap (*aka* Prestige: **A.R. Kardar**, H, 1944)
Pehli Aurat Pehla Mard (P. Chandrakumar, H, 1988)
Pehli Jhalak (**M.V. Raman**, H, 1954)
Pehli Mulaqat (?, Manmohan Films, H, 1957)
Pehli Nazar (Mazhar Khan, H, 1945)
Pehli Pehchaan (Raman B. Desai, H, 1947)
Pehli Raat (P.L. Santoshi, H, 1959)
Pehli Shaadi (Ram Daryani, H, 1953)
Pehli Tareekh (**Raja Nene**, H, 1954)
Pei Veedu (Ramanarayanan, Tam, 1984)
Pellade Bomma (Chakraborty, Tel, 1976)
Pellama Majaka (Relangi Narasimha Rao, Tel, 1993)
Pellam Chattu Mogudu (Relangi Narasimha Rao, Tel, 1992)
Pellam Cheppathe Vinali (Kodi Ramakrishna, Tel, 1992)
Pellaniki Premalekha Priyuraliki Subhalekha (Relangi Narasimha Rao, Tel, 1992)
Pellante Bhayam (K. Shankar, Tel, 1978)
Pellante Noorella Panta (Mutyalla Subbaiah, Tel, 1992)
Pelli Chesi Choodu/Kalyanam Panni Paar (**L.V. Prasad**, Tel/Tam, 1952)
Pelli Chesi Choodu (Relangi Narasimha Rao, Tel, 1988)
Pelli Chesi Choodupishthanam (N.A. Pendyala, Tel, 1983)
Pelli Chuputlu (P. Sambhasiva Rao, Tel, 1982)
Pellidu Pillalu (**Bapu**, Tel, 1982)
Pelli Gola (K. Subba Rao, Tel, 1980)
Pelli Gola (Mutyala Subbaiah, Tel, 1993)
Pellikani Pelli (Adiraju Anand Mohan, Tel, 1976)
Pellikani Pillalu (**C.S. Rao**, Tel, 1961)
Pellikani Thandri (Padmanabham, Tel, 1975)
Pelli Kanuka (**C.V. Sridhar**, Tel, 1960)
Pelli Kodukulosthunnaru (Relangi Narasimha Rao, Tel, 1988)
Pelli Koothuru *see* Manamagal
Pelli Koothuru (V. Ramachandra Rao, Tel, 1970)
Pellila Perayya (Kommineni, Tel, 1982)
Pelli Meeda Pelli (**B. Vittalacharya**, Tel, 1959)
Pelli Meeku Akshintalu Naaku (**Dasari Narayana Rao**, Tel, 1985)
Pellinati Pramanulu (**K.V. Reddy**, Tel, 1958)
Pelli Neeku Sobhanam Neeku (V. Ramachandra Rao, Tel, 1992)
Pelli Pilupu (A. Sheshgiri Rao, Tel, 1961)
Pelli Pustakam (**Bapu**, Tel, 1990)
Pelliroju (M. Apparao, Tel, 1968)
Pelli Sambandham (K. Varaprasadarao, Tel, 1970)
Pelli Sandadi/Kalyana Penn (**Yoganand**, Tel/Tam, 1959)
Pelli Thambulam/Nishchaya Thambulam (**B.S. Ranga**, Tel/Tam, 1961)
Pempudu Koduku (**L.V. Prasad**, Tel, 1953)
Pempudu Koothuru *see* Saaku Magalu
Penalty *see* Jurmana
Penbuthi Munbuthi (Senthilnathan, Tam, 1989)
Penchina Prema *see* Annai
Penchu Pandav (Sisir Mohan Pati, O, 1989)
Pengal (A.K. Sahadevan, Mal, 1968)
Pengal Veettin Kangal (T.P. Gajendran, Tam, 1990)
Penki Pellam (**K. Kameshwara Rao**, Tel, 1956)
Penkipilla (B.V. Ramanandam, Tel, 1951)
Penmanamum Pesugirathu (A. Jagannathan, Tam, 1981)
Penmani Aval Kanmani (Visu, Tam, 1988)
Penn/Ladki (**M.V. Raman**, Tam/H, 1953)
Pennai Nambungal (B.V. Srinivasan, Tam, 1973)
Pennai Solli Kutramillai (S.P. Muthuraman, Tam, 1977)
Pennarasi (K. Somu, Tam, 1955)
Penn Daivam (M.A. Thirumugham, Tam, 1970)
Penne Nee Vazhgai (P. Madhavan, Tam, 1967)
Penn Entral Penn (Arurdas, Tam, 1967)
Penning Saval (K.S.R. Doss, Tam, 1972)
Pennin Perumai *see* **Ardhangi**
Pennin Vazhkai (K. Vijayan, Tam, 1981)
Penn Janmam (A.C. Trilogchander, Tam, 1977)
Pennmakkal (**Sasikumar**, Mal, 1966)
Penn Manam *see* Manchi Manushulu
Penn Manam (**S. Soundararajan**, Tam, 1952)
Penn Manam (?, Mokeshwar Chitra, Tam, 1963)
Pennmayin Unnai (Charles Selva, Tam, 1983)
Penn Ondru Kanden (Gopu, Tam, 1974)
Pennoruppetal (P.K. Joseph, Mal, 1979)
Pennpada (Mani, Mal, 1975)
Pennpuli (Mani, Mal, 1977)
Pennsimham (?, Mal, 1987)
Pennukku Yar Kaval (**Durai**, Tam, 1980)
Pennu Pidichirukku (K. Rangaraj, Tam, 1984)
Pensioner (Jagdish Sethi, H, 1934)
Pen to People (**P.V. Pathy**, E, 1960)
People, The *see* **Ganadevata**
People of India: The Anglo Indians (**Fali Bilimoria**, E, 1982)
Peoples' Encounter (A. Mohan Gandhi, Tel, 1990)
Perantalu (**T. Gopichand**, Tel, 1951)
Perchance *see* Ram Bharose
Percy (Pervez Mehrwanji, G, 1989)
Perfect Day, A (**Harisadhan Dasgupta**, E, 1948)
Perfect Man *see* Nigah-e-Kaamil
Perfect Murder, The (Zafar Hai, E, 1988)
Perfect Murder, The (Ashwini Kumar, Tel, 1989)
Performing Beasts *see* **Valarthu Mrugangal**
Periakovil (A.K. Velan, Tam, 1958)
Periamma (**P. Bhanumathi**, Tam, 1992)
Periaveetu Pannaikaran (N.K. Vishwanathan, Tam, 1990)
Periya Gounder Ponnu (Manivasagam, Tam, 1992)
Periya Idathu Penn (Ramanna, Tam, 1963)
Periya Idathu Pillai (Raja, Tam, 1990)
Periya Manithan (?, Saraswathi Pics, Tam, 1966)
Periyar (**P.J. Anthony**, Mal, 1973)
Persollum Pillai (S.P. Muthuraman, Tam, 1987)
Personal Assistant (Chitrakar, B, 1959)
Perumai (C.V. Rajendran, Tam, 1985)
Perumaikuriyaval (Ra. Shankaran, Tam, 1977)
Perum Puli (Vikraman, Tam, 1991)
Perum Pukazhum (Muktha V. Srinivasan, Tam, 1976)
Perumthachan (*aka* The Master Carpenter: Ajayan, Mal, 1990)
Peruvannapurathe Visheshangal (Kamal, Mal, 1989)
Peruvazhiyampalam (**P. Padmarajan**, Mal, 1979)
Pestonjee (**Vijaya Mehta**, H, 1987)
Pesum Daivam (**K.S. Gopalakrishnan**, Tam, 1967)
Pesum Padum (**Singeetham Srinivasa Rao**, Tam, 1987)
Petha Manam Pithu (S.P. Muthuraman, Tam, 1973)
Petit Brigand *see* Chhota Chor
Pet Pyar Aur Paap (**Durai**, H, 1984)

Petral Than Pillayya (**Krishnan-Panju**, Tam, 1966)
Petramaganai Vitra Annai (V. Ramanathan, Tam, 1958)
Petra Manam (**A. Bhimsingh**, Tam, 1960)
Petrathai *see* **Kanna Talli**
Petraval Kanda Peru Vazhvu (**P. Subramanyam**, Tam, 1960)
Petredutha Pillai (Poornachandran, Tam, 1993)
Pettandarulu (**C.S. Rao**, Tel, 1970)
Peyum Pennum (*aka* Devil and the Damsel: **Raja Sandow**, St, 1930)
Phaansi (Harmesh Malhotra, H, 1978)
Phaansi Ka Phanda (Madhusudhan Kalelkar, H, 1986)
Phaansi Ka Phanda (**Rajdutt**, H, 1990)
Phaansi Ke Baad (Harmesh Malhotra, H, 1984)
Phagun (Bibhuti Mitra, H, 1958)
Phagun (**Rajinder Singh Bedi**, H, 1973)
Phaguni (Siva Prasad Thakur, A, 1978)
Phalithamsha (**Puttanna Kanagal**, K, 1976)
Phanda (Somesh Joshi/Vijay Mhatre, H, 1975)
Phandebaaz (Samir Ganguly, H, 1978)
Phaniyamma (**Prema Karanth**, K, 1982)
Phantom, The *see* Abad Chor
Phantom Foe *see* Jadui Jung
Phantom of Calcutta (Andymoore Roy, B, 1935)
Phantom of the Hills *see* Farzande Hind
Phase of Life, A *see* Sansar
Phatakadi (**Datta Keshav**, Mar, 1980)
Phatikchand (Sandip Ray, B, 1983)
Phera (**Buddhadev Dasgupta**, B, 1986)
Pherey (?, Anis Pics, Lahore: P, 1950)
Philosopher, The *see* **Adi Shankaracharya**
Philosopher's Stone, The *see* **Parash Pathar**
Phir Aayi Barsaat (Jaiprakash K. Vinayak, H, 1985)
Phir Aya Toofan (B.J. Patel, H, 1973)
Phir Bhi (Shivendra Sinha, H, 1971)
Phir Bhi Apna Hai (*aka* Bhai Ka Pyar: **Raja Nene**, H, 1946)
Phir Bolo Aaye Sant Kabir (**K.A. Abbas**, H, 1976)
Phir Janam Lenge Hum *see* Janam Janamma Saathi
Phir Kab Milogi (**Hrishikesh Mukherjee**, H, 1974)
Phir Milenge (**Sohrab Modi**, H, 1942)
Phir Subah Hogi (Ramesh Saigal, H, 1958)
Phir Teri Kahani Yaad Aayi (**Mahesh Bhatt**, H, 1993)
Phir Wohi Dil Laya Hoon (**Nasir Hussain**, H, 1963)
Phir Wohi Raat (Danny, H, 1980)
Phoenix (Ugranarasimha, K, 1976)
Phool (**K. Asif**, H, 1944)
Phool (**Singeetham Srinivasa Rao**, H, 1993)
Phoolan Devi (Ashok Roy, B, 1984)
Phoolan Hasina Ramkali (Kanti Shah, H, 1993)
Phool Aur Angaar (Ashok Gaikwad, H, 1993)
Phool Aur Insaan (Kartar Singh, H, 1976)
Phool Aur Kaanta *see* Do Behnen
Phool Aur Kaante (*aka* Flowers and Thorns: Achyut Ranade, H, 1948)
Phool Aur Kaante (Kuku Kohli, H, 1992)
Phool Aur Kaliyan (Ram Gabale, H, 1960)
Phool Aur Patthar (O.P. Ralhan, H, 1966)
Phool Bane Angarey (Suraj Prakash, H, 1963)
Phool Bane Angarey (K.C. Bokadia, H, 1991)
Phool Khile Hain Gulshan Gulshan (Sikandar Khanna, H, 1978)
Phoolon Ke Haar (G.P. Pawar, H, 1951)
Phoolon Ki Sej (**Inder Raj Anand**, H, 1964)
Phool Sajya (Sarathi, B, 1975)
Phoolwati (Mohanji Prasad, H, 1992)
Phooman (Rajpal, P, 1951)
Phukat Chambu Baburao (G.G. Bhonsle, Mar, 1985)
Phula Chandana (Mohammed Mohsin, O, 1982)
Phuleshwari (**Tarun Majumdar**, B, 1974)
Phulu Thakurma (Sadhan Sarkar, B, 1974)
Phulwari (**Chaturbhuj Doshi**, H, 1946)
Phulwari (Prafulla Roy, H, 1951)
Phulwari (Mukul Dutt, Bh, 1983)
Pichaikari *see* **Jeevitha Nauka**
Pichathikkuttappan (Venu, Mal, 1979)
Pichhipanthulu (Rajachandra, Tel, 1983)
Pichhipullaiah (**T. Prakash Rao**, Tel, 1953)
Pichimaraju (V.B. Rajendra Prasad, Tel, 1975)
Pichippoo (P. Gopikumar, Mal, 1978)
Pichodi Pelli (K.S. Rami Reddy, Tel, 1975)
Pickpocket *see* Jeb Katra
Pickpocket (Rajesh Nanda, H, 1962)
Pickpocket (**Sasikumar**, Mal, 1976)
Pickpocket (G.M. Kumar, Tam, 1989)
Picnic (Shaheed Latif, H, 1966)
Picnic (Inder Sen, B, 1972)
Picnic (**Sasikumar**, Mal, 1975)
Picnic (TV: **Aparna Sen**, H, 1990)
Pidikedu Akasam (S.D. Lall, Tel, 1983)
Pidikkitapuli (K.S. Gopalakrishnan, Mal, 1986)
Piduguramudu (**B. Vittalacharya**, Tel, 1966)
Piece of Land, A *see* Kaani Nilam
Pighalta Aasmaan (?, Shammi, H, 1985)
Pikoo (**Satyajit Ray**, B, 1980)
Pilgrimage to Prison *see* Jail Yatra
Pilgrims of Love *see* Prem Yatra
Pilgrims of Love (*aka* Soul of a Slave: ?, Photoplay Syndicate of India, St, 1929)
Pilipili Saheb (H.S. Kwatra, H, 1954)
Pillai Nila (Manobala, Tam, 1985)
Pillaikaniamudhu (M.A. Thirumugham, Tam, 1958)
Pillaikkaga (P. Vasu, Tam, 1989)
Pillai Selvam (V. Ramchandra Rao, Tam, 1973)
Pillaiyar (V.T.Arasu, Tam, 1984)
Pillaiyo Pillai (**Krishnan-Panju**, Tam, 1972)
Pillalu Diddina Kapuram (Perala, Tel, 1993)
Pillalu Techina Chalana Rajyam *see* Makkala Rajya
Pilla? Piduga? (**B. Vittalacharya**, Tel, 1972)
Pilla Zamindar (**Singeetham Srinivasa Rao**, Tel, 1980)
Pilot Premnath (A.C. Trilogchander, Tam, 1978)
Pinchu Hridayam (M. Krishnan Nair, Mal, 1966)
Pind Di Kudi *see* Sheila
Pind Di Kudi (Baldev R. Jhingan, P, 1963)
Pingala *see* Sati Pingala
Pingan (S. Naseem/Aran Malik, P, 1957)
Pingan (?, Popular Prod, P, 1979)
Pingan Pyar Diyan (S. Jasbir, P, 1986)
Pinjarvat (Himmat Dave, G, 1978)
Pinjhu Manam (A.K. Subramanyam, Tam, 1975)
Pinjra (**Kantilal Rathod**, 1968)**Pinjra** (**V. Shantaram**, Mar/H, 1972)
Pinjra Preeticha (Sarfaraz Khan, Mar, 1987)
Pinjre Ke Panchhi (**Salil Choudhury**, H, 1966)
Pinneyum Pookunna Kadu (Shrini, Mal, 1981)
Pinni (B.A. Subba Rao, Tel, 1967)
Pinni (**Vijayanirmala**, Tel, 1989)
Pinninvalu (P.G. Vishwambaran, Mal, 1983)
Pioli Phukan (**Phani Sarma**, A, 1955)
Piparsod (**Saeed Mirza**, E, 1982)
Pipasa (Basudev, O, 1978)
Pipasa (Inder Sen, B, 1982)
Pirandanal (K. Narayanan/J.P. Raj, Tam, 1962)
Piranden Valardhen (Vijayasingham, Tam, 1986)
Piravi (**Shaji N. Karun**, Mal, 1988)
Pirayachitham (R.Sundaram, Tam, 1974)
Piritiya Ke Khel (Jagdish Sinha, Bh, 1987)
Piriya Vidhai (Srikanth, Tam, 1975)
Piriyilla Naam (Joshi, Mal, 1984)
Pistolwali (*aka* Modern Girl: Nari Ghadiali, H, 1943)
Pistolwali (K.S.R. Doss, H, 1972)
Pita (**Govind Nihalani**, H, 1991)
Pita Ke Parmeshwar (*aka* Father o'Mine: **R.S. Choudhury**, St, 1928)
Pitamah (Ravi, K, 1985)
Pitambar (Imran, H, 1992)
Pita Pooja (?, **Madan Theatres**, St, 1927)
Pita Putra (Aravind Mukherjee, B, 1969)
Pita Putra (**Munin Barua**, A, 1987)
Pithache Panje (**Dadasaheb Phalke**, St, 1914)
Pithino Rang (Dinesh Rawal, G, 1979)
Pithi Pithino Rang Rato (Chandravadan Sheth, G, 1981)
Pitroddhar (*aka* Ganga the Redeemer: ?, Star Film, St, 1922)
Pitru Prem (Harilal M. Bhatt, St, 1929)
Piya Bina Nahin Chain (?, Bh, 1991)
Piya Ghar Aaja (Prahlad Dutt, H, 1947)
Piya Ka Ghar (**Basu Chatterjee**, H, 1971)
Piya Ka Sagar (Devendra Goel, H, 1961)
Piya Ke Gaon (Dilip Bose, Bh, 1985)
Piya Ki Jogan (*aka* Purchased Bride: Hiren Bose, H, 1936)
Piya Ki Pyari (Prem Singh, Bh, 1987)
Piya Milan (S.M. Yusuf, H, 1945)
Piya Milan (K.P. Singh, H, 1985)
Piya Milan (**T.R. Raghunath**, H, 1958)
Piya Milan Ki Aas (Kanwar Jagdish, R, 1983)
Piya Milan Ki Aas (S.N. Tripathi, H, 1961)
Piya Nirmohiya (Prem Singh, Bh, 1983)
Piya Pyare (**R.S. Choudhury**, H, 1934)
Piya Rakheena Senurwa Ke Laaj (B.P. Vishwakarma, Bh, 1987)
Piya Toote Na Piritiya Hamaar (?, Bh, 1989)
Pizhaikkum Vazhi (Mithradas, Tam, 1948)
Planes of Hindustan, The (**P.V. Pathy**, E, 1940)
Platform (Deepak Pawar, H, 1993)
Playboy (*aka* Rangila Mastana: T. Janakiram, H, 1975)
Pleasure Mad *see* Be Ghadi Mouj
Pledge, The *see* Saugandh
Plight of the Poor *see* **Ezhai Padum Padu**
Plot No. 5 (Yogesh Saxena, H, 1981)
Pocketmaar (**H.S. Rawail**, H, 1956)
Pocketmaar (Ramesh Lakhanpal, H, 1974)
Pocketmaar (Sushil Vyas, G, 1982)
Poem in Stone, A *see* Geet Gaya Pattharone
Pogarubottu (**T. Prakash Rao**, Tel, 1976)
Poikkal Kuthirai (**K. Balachander**, Tam, 1983)
Point Parimala (V. Somasekhar, K, 1980)
Poison Tree, The *see* Bishabriksha
Pokkattadikkari (P.G. Vishwambaran, Mal, 1978)
Pokkiri Thambi (Senthilnathan, Tam, 1992)
Pokkuveyil (**G. Aravindan**, Mal, 1981)
Poladi *see* Fauladi
Police (Kalidas, H, 1958)
Police Ariyaruthu (M.S. Senthilkumar, Mal, 1973)
Police Aur Mujrim (K.C. Bokadia, H, 1992)
Police Detective (**Nanabhai Bhatt**, H, 1960)
Police Diary (Devan, Mal, 1992)
Police File (G.K. Mudduraj, K, 1992)
Policekaran Magal (**C.V. Sridhar**, Tam, 1962)
Police Lockup (K.V. Raju, K, 1992)
Police Mattu Dada *see* Inspector Dhanush
Police Officer (Vijaya Bapineedu, Tel, 1986)
Police Officer (Ashok Gaikwad, H, 1992)
Police Papanna (**Dasari Narayana Rao**, K, 1984)
Police Police (Y.V. Gopikrishna, Tam, 1983)
Police Public (Esmayeel Shroff, H, 1990)
Police Report (Hari Anmulu, Tel, 1989)
Police Station (K. Kant, H, 1959)
Police Station (TV: **Kundan Shah**, H, 1987)
Police Venkataswamy (**Dasari Narayana Rao**, Tel, 1983)
Policewala (Sikandar Bharti, H, 1993)

Nishi (right) in *Chaubis Ghante* (1958)

Policewali (A.M. Khan, H, 1949)
Poli Huduga (S.S. Ravichandra, K, 1989)
Poli Panchali (A.T. Krishnaswamy, Tam, 1940)
Polladhavan (Muktha V. Srinivasan, Tam, 1980)
Ponakan (**Abdul Majid**, A, 1981)
Pona Vachan Thirumbi Vandhan (**C.S. Rao**, Tam, 1954)
Pondatti Pondatithan (Manian Sivabalam, Tam, 1991)
Pondatti Rajyam (K.S. Ravikumar, Tam, 1992)
Pondatti Thevai (Parthiban, Tam, 1990)
Ponga Pandit (Prayag Raj, H, 1975)
Pongivarum Kaveri (T.K. Bose, Tam, 1989)
Ponimudakku *see* Panimudakku
Ponkathir (E.R. Cooper, Mal, 1953)
Pon Magal Vanthal (Vijaya Narayanan, Tam, 1972)
Ponmana Selvan (P. Vasu, Tam, 1989)
Ponmudi (*aka* Ethirparatha Mutham: **Ellis Duncan**, Tam, 1949)
Ponmudi (N. Shankaran Nair, Mal, 1982)
Ponn (**Thoppil Bhasi**, Mal, 1976)
Ponnagaram (Mathangan, Tam, 1980)
Ponnana Vazhvu (R. Devarajan, Tam, 1967)
Ponnapuram Kotta (**Kunchako**, Mal, 1973)
Ponnaram Thottathe Rajavu (?, Rajaputhra Films, Mal, 1992)
Ponnavayal/Bangaru Bhoomi (A.T. Krishnaswamy, Tam/Tel, 1954)
Ponnazhagi (O. Muthu, Tam, 1981)
Ponni (**A.S.A. Sami**/**C.S. Rao**, Tam, 1953)
Ponnil Kulicha Rathri (Alex, Mal, 1979)
Ponni Thirunal (A.K. Velan, Tam, 1960)
Ponnmuttayidunna Tharavu (Sathyan Andhikkad, Mal, 1988)
Ponnu (P.G. Vishwambaran, Mal, 1987)
Ponnukketha Purushan (Gangai Amaran, Tam, 1992)
Ponnukku Thanga Manasu (Devaraj-Mohan, Tam, 1973)
Ponnumani (R.V. Udayakumar, Tam, 1993)
Ponnu Mappillai (Ramanathan, Tam, 1969)
Ponnum Kudathinum Pottu (?, Sunitha Prod, Mal, 1986)
Ponnunjal (C.V. Rajendran, Tam, 1973)
Ponnu Parka Poren (M. Thiagarajan, Tam, 1989)
Ponnu Poovum (**A. Vincent**, Mal, 1982)
Ponnnurukkum Pakshi (Adoor Nairhogam, Mal, 1992)
Ponnuruvi (C.V. Raman, Tam, 1946)
Ponnu Urukku Puthusu (R. Selvaraj, Tam, 1979)
Ponnu Vilayum Bhoomi (**A. Bhimsingh**, Tam, 1959)
Pon Thooval (J. Williams, Mal, 1983)
Pon Vandu (N.S. Maniam, Tam, 1973)
Ponvayal (A.T. Krishnaswamy, Tam, 1954)
Ponvilangu (K.S. Rajkumar, Tam, 1993)
Poochaikku Yar Manikattum (Tulsidas, Mal, 1992)
Pooja (**A.R. Kardar**, H, 1940)
Pooja (Bhagwandas Varma, H, 1954)
Pooja (P. Karmachandran, Mal, 1967)
Pooja (Murugan-Kumaran, Tel, 1975)
Pooja (**Prashanta Nanda**, O, 1981)
Pooja (Dara Ahmed, A, 1985)
Pooja (?, RICA Films, H, 1988)
Pooja Aur Payal *see* Jai Jwala
Poojaiku Vanthamalar (V. Srinivasan, Tam, 1965)
Pooja Ke Phool (**A. Bhimsingh**, H, 1964)
Poojakkedukatha Pookkal (N. Shankaran Nair, Mal, 1977)
Poojaku Panikirani Puvva (A. Mohan Gandhi, Tel, 1988)
Poojana Phool (Arun Bhatt, G, 1983)
Poojapalam (**B.N. Reddi**, Tel, 1964)
Poojaphala (N.S. Dhananjaya, K, 1984)
Pooja Phula (J.H. Sattar, O, 1985)
Poojapushpam (**Thikkurisi Sukumaran Nair**, Mal, 1969)
Pookalai Parikkatheerkal (V. Azhappan, Tam, 1986)
Pookkalam Varavai (Kamal, Mal, 1991)
Pookkal Vidum Thoothu (Sridhar Rajan, Tam, 1987)
Pookkari (**Krishnan-Panju**, Tam, 1973)
Pookkari Raja (S.P. Muthuraman, Tam, 1982)
Poola Mala (P. Vasanthakumara Reddy, Tel, 1973)
Poolapallaki (Uma Maheshwara Rao, Tel, 1982)
Poolarangudu (**Adurthi Subba Rao**, Tel, 1967)
Poolarangudu (Relangi Narasimha Rao, Tel, 1989)
Poomadathu Pennu (**T. Hariharan**, Mal, 1984)
Poomalai (**P. Neelakantan**, Tam, 1965)
Poomalai Pozhugirathu (V. Azhagappan, Tam, 1987)
Poomanam (S. Rajasekharan, Tam, 1989)
Poombatta (B.K. Pottekkad, Mal, 1971)
Poompavai (Balaji Singh/**Krishnan-Panju**, Tam, 1944)
Poompuhar (**P. Neelakantan**, Tam, 1964)
Poomugappadiyil Ninneyum Kathu (Bhadran, Mal, 1986)
Poonam (M. Sadiq, H, 1952)
Poonam (Harmesh Malhotra, H, 1981)
Poonam Ka Chand (Suresh Tripathi, H, 1967)
Poonam Ki Raat (**Kishore Sahu**, H, 1965)
Poonam No Chand (*aka* Jewelled Arrow: **B.P. Mishra**, St, 1927)
Poona Par Hallo *see* **Poona Raided**
Poona Races '98 (?, Andersonoscopograph, St, 1898)
Poona Raided (Mama Warerkar, St, 1924)
Poongothai/Pardesi (**L.V. Prasad**, Tam/Tel, 1953)
Poonji (*aka* Wealth: Vishnu Pancholi/**Ravindra Dave**, H, 1943)
Poonthalir (Devaraj-Mohan, Tam, 1979)
Poonthenaruvi (**Sasikumar**, Mal, 1974)
Poonthota Kavalkaran (Senthilnathan, Tam, 1988)
Poonuswamy (Ali Akbar, Mal, 1993)
Poo Pootha Nandavanam (B.V. Balaguru, Tam, 1988)
Poo Poova Poothu Irukku (V.Azhagappan, Tam, 1987)
Pooram (Nedumudi Venu, Mal, 1989)
Poornachandra (D.R. Das, Tam, 1935)
Poornachandra (C.V. Rajendran, K, 1987)
Poorna Satya (Bhaskar Jadhav, Mar, 1987)
Poor Sweethearts *see* Bhole Bhale
Poothali (**P. Subramanyam**, Mal, 1960)
Poottadha Poothukkal *see* Puttadha Poothukkal
Poovanam (**Shyam Benegal**, E, 1968)
Poova Thalaiya (**K. Balachander**, Tam, 1969)
Poove Illam Poove (Chiramughai Ravi, Tam, 1987)
Poove Poo Chooda Va (**Fazil**, Tam, 1985)
Poovilangu (Amirjan, Tam, 1984)
Poovinnu Puthiya Poonthennal (**Fazil**, Mal, 1986)
Pooviriyum Pulari (G. Premkumar, Mal, 1982)
Poovizhi Raja (Santhana Bharati, Tam, 1988)
Poovizhi Vasalile (**Fazil**, Tam, 1987)
Poovukkul Pookambalam (D.R. Thyagarajan, Tam, 1988)
Poovum Pottum (Dada Mirasi, Tam, 1968)
Poovum Puyalum (S.A. Chandrasekharan, Tam, 1988)
Poradha Veeda Puguntha Veeda (V. Sekhar, Tam, 1993)
Poraki (K. Borasadi/P. Gokhale, Mar, 1970)
Porandhalum Ambalay Porakka Koothadu (N.K. Vishwanathan, Tam, 1993)
Poratham (Kodi Ramakrishna, Tel, 1983)
Poratham (Kaladharan, Mal, 1993)
Porichi Dhamal Bapachi Kamal (**Datta Keshav**, Mar, 1987)
Pori Jara Japoon (**Anant Mane**, Mar, 1981)
Porkalam (**Durai**, Tam, 1980)
Porsilai (A.V. Francis, Tam, 1969)
Porter Kandhan (K. Vembu, Tam, 1955)
Porter Kunjali (P.A. Thomas/**Sasikumar**, Mal, 1964)
Porter Ponnusami (Adiyar, Tam, 1979)
Port of Calcutta (**Harisadhan Dasgupta**, E, 1971)
Portrait of a City (**Chidananda Das Gupta**, E, 1961)
Portrait of a Postman (**Govind Saraiya**, E, 1961)
Poruginti Pulla Koora (V. Madhusudhana Rao, Tel, 1976)
Poruthanthu Potham (P. Kalaimani, Tam, 1989)
Poruttam (Mouli, Tam, 1984)
Porveeran Manaivi (**R.S. Prakash**, Tam, 1938)
Poshya Putra (Satish Dasgupta, B, 1943)
Possessed *see* **Junoon**
Postatil Mulgi (Ram Gabale, Mar, 1954)
Post Box 999 (**Ravindra Dave**, H, 1958)
Post Box No. 27 (P. Anil, Mal, 1991)
Poster (R.S. Vinod, H, 1984)
Posters-Neons (**Kundan Shah**, H, 1976)
Posti (Krishnadev Mehra, P, 1950)
Postman *see* **Abhilasha**
Postman (P.A. Thomas, Mal, 1967)
Postmane Kananilla (**Kunchako**, Mal, 1972)
Postmaster *see* **Teen Kanya**
Post Master (**G.V. Iyer**, K, 1964)
Post Mortem (**Sasikumar**, Mal, 1982)
Potharillu (M.S. Kotareddy, Tel, 1980)
Potohu Bitiya (Aslam Sheikh, Bh, 1989)
Pottelu Punnamma (R. Thyagarajan, Tel, 1978)
Potti Pleader (K. Hemambharadhara Rao, Tel, 1966)
Pournami Alaigal (M. Bhaskar, Tam, 1985)
Pournami Rathriyil (Viji Shrikumar, Mal, 1985)
Pournami Ravil (**A. Vincent**, Mal, 1985)
Power to the People (**Shyam Benegal**, E, 1972)
Poyi Mukhangal (B.N. Prakash, Mal, 1973)
Poyi Mukhangal (C.V. Rajendran, Tam, 1986)
Poyi Satchi (**K. Bhagyaraj**, Tam, 1982)
Poyi Sollathe (B. Lenin, Tam, 1971)
Pozhudu Vidinachu (Gangai Amaran, Tam, 1984)
Prabas Milan (**Phani Burma**, B, 1936)
Prabesh Nishedh (Sushil Ghosh, B, 1960)
Prabhat (*aka* The New Day: **V.M. Vyas**, H, 1941)
Prabhat (Sikandar Khanna, H, 1973)
Prabhata Sandhya (Chandrakumar, Mal, 1979)
Prabhater Rang (**Ajoy Kar**, B, 1964)
Prabhat Priya (Dipranjan Basu, B, 1984)
Prabhavati (**N.D. Sarpotdar**, St, 1925)
Prabhavati (G.V. Sane, St, 1929)
Prabhavati (**T.R. Raghunath**, Tam, 1944)
Prabhu (Baby, Mal, 1979)
Prabhu Ka Ghar (Wajahat Mirza, H, 1945)
Prabhu Ka Pyara (**Chandulal Shah**, H, 1936)
Prabhu Ki Maya (Vithaldas Panchotia, H, 1955)
Prabhu Na Chor (*aka* Four Devils: **Homi Master**, St, 1932)
Prachanda Bhairavi (**C.S. Rao**, Tel, 1965)
Prachanda Bhairavi (B.V. Srinivas, Tel, 1985)
Prachanda Kulla (P.S. Prakash, K, 1984)
Prachanda Putanigalu (Geethapriya, K, 1981)
Pradeshika Varthagal (Kamal, Mal, 1989)
Pradyumna (*aka* Krishna Kumar: Vishnupant Divekar, St, 1921)
Prafulla (**Jyotish Bannerjee**, St, 1926)
Prafulla (Tinkari Chakraborty, B, 1935)
Prafulla (Chitta Bose, B, 1954)
Prafulla (Sujoy Datta, B, 1982)
Pragoitibashik (Jochon Dastidar, B, 1984)
Prahaar (Nana Patekar, H, 1991)
Prahari (Batra Mohinder, B, 1982)
Prahlad (**Priyanath Ganguly**, B/H, 1931)
Prahlad (**Phani Burma**, B, 1952)
Prahlada (P.V. Rao, Tam, 1933)
Prahlada (**Balkrishna Narayan Rao**, Tam, 1939)
Prahladan (**K. Subramanyam**, Mal, 1941)
Prahlad Charitra (Elphinstone Bioscope, St, 1917)
Prajala Manishi (**Ghantamneni Krishna**, Tel, 1989)
Prajanayakudu (V. Madhusudhana Rao, Tel, 1972)
Praja Poratam (Sirimugam Ravi, Tel, 1985)
Praja Pratinidhi (**Dasari Narayana Rao**, Tel, 1988)
Praja Rajyam (Kasalingam, Tel, 1950)
Praja Rajyam (M. Mallikarjuna Rao, Tel, 1983)
Praja Ramudu (R. Vittal, Tel, 1984)
Prajaseva (K. Prabhakar, Tel, 1952)
Praja Shakti (Navatharam, Tel, 1983)
Prajaswamyam (Parachuri Bros., Tel, 1988)
Praja Theerpu (Dothuneedi Krishna, Tel, 1989)
Prajegalu Prabhugalu (Bhima-Nagaraj, K, 1992)
Prakatanam (**Sasikumar**, Mal, 1980)
Pralaya Garjanai (P. Chandrasekhara Reddy, Tel, 1983)
Pralaya Rudrulu (A. Kodandarami Reddy, Tel, 1982)
Pralayam (Chandrakumar, Mal, 1980)
Pralayam Simham (P. Chandrasekhara Reddy, Tel, 1984)
Pramanigal (Augustin Prakash, Mal, 1992)
Prameela Arjuna (S. Gopal?, **General Pics.**, St, 1930)
Prameelarjuneyam (D.V. Subbarao, Tel, 1936)
Prameelarjuneyam (M. Mallikarjuna Rao, Tel, 1965)
Pranadata (A. Mohan Gandhi, Tel, 1991)
Pranamam (**B.G. Bharathan**, Mal, 1986)
Pranamithrulu (**P. Pullaiah**, Tel, 1967)
Pranam Khareedu (K. Vasu, Tel, 1978)
Prana Snehitha (Bhargava, K, 1993)
Pranasnehitulu (V. Madhusudhana Rao, Tel, 1988)
Pranaya Geetham (P. Sambhasiva Rao, Tel, 1981)
Pranaya Pakshigalu (Mahendra, K, 1992)
Pranayapasha (Mangal Chakraborty, B, 1978)
Pranay Geet *see* Sundari
Pranay Milan *see* Ra Kawat
Praner Thakur Ramkrishna (Niranjan Dey, B, 1977)
Pran Ganga (Rabin Chetia, A, 1976)
Pran Jaye Par Vachan Na Jaye (Ali Raza, H, 1973)
Pranta Rekha (**Dinen Gupta**, B, 1973)
Prapancha (Madhukar Pathak, Mar, 1961)
Prapancham (L.S. Ramachandran, Tel, 1953)
Prapancham (Sudhin Menon, Mal, 1971)
Prapancha Pash (**Franz Osten**, St, 1929)
Praptham (**K. Savitri**, Tam, 1971)
Prarthana (**Sarvottam Badami**, H, 1943)
Prarthana (Pranab Roy, B, 1952)
Prarthana (*aka* Garibi Hatao: Vasant Joglekar, H, 1969)
Prarthana (A.B. Raj, Mal, 1978)
Prarthana (**Asit Sen**, B, 1984)
Prarthana (K. Vijay Bhaskar, Tel, 1991)
Prarthanai (Kaushikan, Tam, 1973)
Prasadam (A.B. Raj, Mal, 1976)
Prasanna (S.M. Sreeramulu Naidu, Mal, 1950)
Prashna (Chandrasekhar Bose, B, 1955)
Prashnam Orutharam (**Balachandra Menon**, Mal, 1983)
Prastar *see* Trikon Ka Chautha Kon
Prastar Swakshar (Salil Dutta, B, 1967)
Pratap (V. Somasekhar, K, 1990)
Pratap (Arjun, Tam, 1993)
Pratapgad (Balkrishna, Mar, 1952)
Prateeksha (Lawrence D'Souza, H, 1993)
Prathama Usha Kirana (**Suresh Heblikar**, K, 1990)
Pratham Basanta (Nirmal Mitra, B, 1971)
Pratham Kadam Phool (Inder Sen, B, 1970)
Pratham Pratisruti (**Dinen Gupta**, B, 1971)
Pratham Prem (Ajoy Biswas, B, 1965)
Prathan Ragini (?, Dhiru Bhuyan, A, 1987)
Prathistha (Chandrahasan, Mal, 1979)
Prathyekam Sradhikkuka (P.G. Vishwambaran, Mal, 1986)
Pratibad/Oonch Neech (**Hemchandra Chunder**, B/H, 1948)
Pratibad (Tapeshwar Prasad, B, 1971)
Pratibandh (Ravi Raja, H, 1990)
Pratibha (**Baburao Painter**, Mar/H, 1937)
Pratibha (Chiranjeet Dhawan, H, 1983)
Pratibha (Hiren Nag, B, 1987)
Pratibhavanthudu (M. Prabhakara Reddy, Tel, 1986)
Pratibimba (Sharan Dey, B, 1974)
Pratibimbalu (?, Tel, 1980)
Pratidan (Dara Ahmed, A, 1987)
Pratidhwani (Kalipada Ghosal, B, 1951)
Pratidhwani/Ka Swariti (**Bhupen Hazarika**, A/Khasi, 1964)
Pratidhwani (Dorairaj-Bhagavan, K, 1971)
Pratidhwani (B. Gopal, Tel, 1986)
Pratidhwani (Pee Cee Das, O, 1984)
Pratidwandi (**Satyajit Ray**, B, 1970)
Pratighaat (**N. Chandra**, H, 1987)
Pratighatana (T. Krishna, Tel, 1985)
Pratigna (Y.R. Swamy, Tel, 1953)
Pratigna (B. Subba Rao, Tel, 1982)
Pratigna (P.N. Sundaram, Mal, 1983)

Pratignapalana (**C.S. Rao**, Tel, 1965)
Pratigne (**B.S. Ranga**, K, 1964)
Pratigya (**Nandlal Jaswantlal**, H, 1943)
Pratigya (Dulal Guha, H, 1975)
Pratigya (**Asit Sen**, B, 1985)
Pratigyabadh (Ravi Chopra, H, 1991)
Pratik (Prabhat Roy, B, 1988)
Pratikar (**Chhabi Biswas**, B, 1944)
Pratikar (Prabhat Roy, B, 1987)
Pratikar (**T. Rama Rao**, H, 1991)
Pratikara (M.S. Gopinath, K, 1970)
Pratikaram (M. Nageshwara Rao, Tel, 1969)
Pratikaram (S. Kumar, Mal, 1972)
Pratikaram (G. Ramineedu, Tel, 1982)
Pratiksha (Bhaskar Acharya, B, 1955)
Pratiksha (Chandra?, Mal, 1979)
Pratima (*aka* Prem Murti: Ram Daryani, H, 1936)
Pratima (Jairaj, H, 1945)
Pratima (Khagen Roy, B, 1946)
Pratima (Palash Bannerjee, B, 1977)
Pratima (Sudhin Menon, K, 1978)
Pratima (**Munin Barua**, A, 1987)
Pratima Aur Payal (Sharan Agarwal, H, 1977)
Pratinidhi (*aka* Two Plus One: **Mrinal Sen**, B, 1964)
Prati Paksha (Rathish De Sarkar, B, 1988)
Pratiphala (N. Shankaran Nair, K, 1993)
Pratirodh (Khagen Roy, B, 1949)
Pratishodh (**Sushil Majumdar**, B, 1941)
Pratishodh (*aka* Retaliation: **I.V. Sasi**, H, 1980)
Pratishodh (Sukhen Das, B, 1981)
Pratishodh (R.N. Dhir, H, 1982)
Pratishodh Aparadh Nuhen (Binoy Nanda, O, 1989)
Pratispandhana (Anil Kumar, Tel, 1987)
Pratisruti (**Hemchandra Chunder**, B, 1941)
Pratisruti (Pinaki Mukherjee, B, 1976)
Pratyabartan (**Sukumar Dasgupta**, B, 1951)
Pratyusha (Jatla Venkataswamy Naidu, Tel, 1979)
Pravaham (**Sasikumar**, Mal, 1975)
Pravajagan (P.G. Vishambaran, Mal, 1993)
Pravasi Mandira (**Kalyana Kumar**, K, 1968)
Prayanam (**B.G. Bharathan**, Mal, 1975)
Prayanamlo Padanisalu (M.S. Kotareddy, Tel, 1977)
Praya Praya Praya (**T.S. Nagabharana**, K, 1982)
Prayashchit *see* Chimni Ka Dhuan
Prayashchit (Kamal Majumdar, H, 1977)
Prayashchitta (Aravind Mukherjee, B, 1983)
Prayatnam (Parachuri Bros., Tel, 1991)
Precious Tears *see* Keemti Ansoo
Precious Time *see* **Anmol Ghadi**
Preet (Ram Daryani, H, 1945)
Preetam (Mohan Sinha, H, 1942)
Preetam (Bhappi Sonie, H, 1971)
Preetam More Ganga Teere (Rajkumar Pardesi, Bh/H, 1985)
Preetghelan Manavi (S.J. Rajdev, G, 1987)
Preethi (William Thomas, Mal, 1972)
Preethiya Nanna Daiva (J. Amjad, K, 1991)
Preeti (A.T. Raghu, K, 1986)
Preeti (Sawan Kumar, H, 1986)
Preeti Madu Tamashe Nodu (C.V. Rajendran, K, 1979)
Preetisangam (**Anant Mane**, Mar, 1957)
Preetisi Nodu (Geethapriya, K, 1981)
Preeti Vatsalya (Bhargava, K, 1984)
Preeti Vivah (**Anant Mane**, Mar, 1962)
Preet Ka Geet (Girish Trivedi, H, 1950)
Preet Khandani Dhar (**Ravindra Dave**, G, 1979)
Preet Ki Dori (Satish Kumar, H, 1971)
Preet Ki Reet (*aka* Love Path, Raah-e-Mohabbat: Bapurao Apte, H, 1935)
Preet Na Jane Reet (S. Bannerjee, H, 1966)
Preet Na Jane Reet (Shama Kakkar/Lalit Kohli, H, 1982)
Preet Na Karsho Koi (**Mehul Kumar**, G, 1985)
Preet Piyu Ne Panetar (Vasant Dalal, G, 1978)
Preet Shikva Mala (Bal Korade, Mar, 1968)
Preet Tujhi Majhi (Dinesh, Mar, 1975)
Prema/Kathal (**P.S. Ramakrishna Rao**, Tel/Tam, 1952)

Prema (Suresh Krishna, Tel, 1989)
Premabandhan (**P. Pullaiah**, Tam, 1941)
Premabandham (**K. Vishwanath**, Tel, 1976)
Premabhishekham (**Dasari Narayana Rao**, Tel, 1980)
Premabhishekham (R. Krishnamurthy, Mal, 1982)
Prema Brindavanam (Ameerjan, Tel, 1985)
Prema Chesina Pelli (**Vijayanirmala**, Tel, 1978)
Prema Chitra Pelli Vichitra (K. Vasu, Tel, 1991)
Premada Kanike (V. Somasekhar, K, 1976)
Premada Putri/Preme Daivam/Anbe Daivam (**R. Nagendra Rao**, K/Tel/Tam, 1957)
Premada Yuvale (?, sathyashree Chitra, K, 1992)
Prema Deepalu (C.S. Bose, Tel, 1987)
Prema Drohi (Kondaveeti Sathyam, Tel, 1992)
Prema Entha Maduram (Jandhyala, Tel, 1991)
Prema Gange (Gururaja, K, 1986)
Prema Geethangal (**Balachandra Menon**, Mal, 1981)
Premagni (**T.S. Nagabharana**, K, 1989)
Premagola (M. Lakshminarayana, Tel, 1984)
Prema Jeevalu (K.S.R. Doss, Tel, 1971)
Prema Jwala (P.V. Raju, Tel, 1983)
Premajwale (Geethapriya, K, 1980)
Prema Jyoti (Joe Simon, K, 1984)
Prema Kaidi (E.V.V. Satyanarayana, Tel, 1990)
Prema Kama (V.R.K. Prasad, K, 1979)
Prema Kanuka (Shobhandirao, Tel, 1969)
Prema Kanuka (**K. Raghavendra Rao**, Tel, 1980)
Prema Kireetalu (Sripriya, Tel, 1984)
Prema Kiritam (G. Rammohan Rao, Tel, 1988)
Premakku Permitte (**R. Nagendra Rao**, K, 1967)
Premalekha (M.K. Mani, Mal, 1952)
Premalekhalu (**K. Raghavendra Rao**, Tel, 1977)
Prema Lekhanam (**P.A. Backer**, Mal, 1985)
Premaloka (Ravichandran, K, 1987)
Premalopramadam (J. Taliath, Tel, 1967)
Premalu Pellilu (V. Madhusudhana Rao, Tel, 1974)
Prema Mandira (Vijayakala, K, 1984)
Prema Mandiram (**Dasari Narayana Rao**, Tel, 1981)
Prema Matsara (C.V. Rajendran, K, 1982)
Prema Mayi (M.R. Vittal, K, 1966)
Prema Moorthalu (A. Kodandarami Reddy, Tel, 1982)
Prema Nakshatram (P. Sambhasiva Rao, Tel, 1982)
Prema Natakam (K. Subba Rao, Tel, 1981)
Prem Andhala Asta (**Dinkar D. Patil**, Mar, 1962)
Prem Ane Vaasna (*aka* Wife and the Vampire: **Saurashtra Film**/British India Films, St, 1928)
Premanjali (*aka* Homage of Love: **Jyotish Bannerjee**, St, 1924)
Premanu Bandha (R. Ramamurthy, K, 1981)
Prema Paga (B.V. Prasad, Tel, 1978)
Prema Pallavi (Venugopal, K, 1981)
Prema Panjaram (B.V. Ramana Reddy, Tel, 1991)
Prema Pariksha (Mouli, Tel, 1983)
Prema Parva (Siddalingaiah, K, 1983)
Prema Pasam (K. Vijayan, Tam, 1985)
Premapasha (Aruru Pattabhi, K, 1973)
Prema Pasham *see* Bhale Ramudu
Prema Pichhi (C.V. Rajendran, Tel, 1981)
Prema Pichollu (A. Kodandarami Reddy, Tel, 1983)
Prema Poratam (M. Subbaiah Naidu, Tel, 1988)
Prema Prema Prema (**T. Rajendar**, Tel, 1984)
Prema Pustakam (Gollapudi Srinivas, Tel, 1993)
Prema Saathi Vatelte (**Datta Keshav**, Mar, 1987)
Premasakshi (B. Mallesh, K, 1984)
Prema Samrat (A. Mohan Gandhi, Tel, 1987)
Prema Sangama (Bhargava, K, 1992)
Prema Sangamam (**C.V. Sridhar**, Tel, 1984)
Prema Sankellu (**Vijayanirmala**, Tel, 1982)
Prema Shikharam (Sathya, Tel, 1992)
Prema Shilpi (V.T. Thyagarajan, Mal, 1978)
Prema Simhasanam (**Dasari Narayana Rao**, Tel, 1981)
Prema Tapasu (N. Sivaprasad, Tel, 1991)
Prema Tapaswi (H. Ramesh, K, 1988)

Prema Tarangalu (S.P. Chittibabu, Tel, 1980)
Premave Balina Belaku (A.V. Sheshgiri Rao, K, 1983)
Premavijayam (K. Nageshwara Rao, Tel, 1936)
Prema Vijeta (K. Sadasiva Rao, Tel, 1992)
Premayana (Geethapriya, K, 1978)
Premayanam (Naganjaneyulu, Tel, 1976)
Premayanam (**C.V. Sridhar**, Tel, 1988)
Prema Yuddham *see* Prem Yuddham
Prema Yuddha (**T.S. Nagabharana**, K, 1983)
Prem Bandhan (*aka* Victim of Love: C.N. Lala/Ramnik Desai, H, 1936)
Prem Bandhan (**Ramanand Sagar**, H, 1978)
Prem Bandhan (Rathish De Sarkar, B, 1986)
Prem Diwani (*aka* Devotee: A.P. Kapur, St, 1930)
Prem Diwani (**Chandrakant Sangani**, G, 1982)
Prem Diwani (Sachin, H, 1992)
Preme Daivam *see* Premada Putri
Preme Naa Pranam (?, Shiva Art, Tel, 1993)
Premer Phande (Chitradoot, B, 1974)
Prem Geet (Sudesh Issar, H, 1981)
Premigala Saval (V. Somasekhar, K, 1984)
Premi Gangaram (Jagdish Nirula, P/H, 1977)
Premika (Brij Katyal, H, 1977)
Preminchi Choodu (**P. Pullaiah**, Tel, 1965)
Preminchi Choodu (Relangi Narasimha Rao, Tel, 1991)
Preminchi Pelli Chesuko (K. Hemambharadhara Rao, Tel, 1977)
Preminchu Pelladu (**Vamsy**, Tel, 1985)
Premi Pagal (*aka* Madcap: **Ezra Mir**, H, 1933)
Premi Pankhida (*aka* Love Birds: **Nagendra Majumdar**, St, 1931)
Premi Ramphal (Satyapal Saini, Haryanvi, 1985)
Prem Jeevan (*aka* Love Life: ?, Sarda Rajoo, St, 1933)
Prem Jogan (**Nandlal Jaswantlal**, St, 1931)
Prem Kahani (**Franz Osten**, H, 1937)
Prem Kahani (**Raj Khosla**, H, 1975)
Prem Ka Nasha (?, **Madan** Theatres, H, 1933)
Prem Karuya Khullam Khulla (Girish Ghanekar, Mar, 1987)
Prem Kasauti *see* Parakh
Prem Ki Aag (M.L. Kapoor, H, 1936)
Prem Ki Devi (Sorabji Kerawala, H, 1936)
Prem Ki Duniya (**Jyotish Bannerjee**, H, 1946)
Prem Ki Ganga (Prahlad Sharma, H, 1971)
Prem Ki Jyot (*aka* Do Dost: Dada Gunjal, H, 1939)
Prem Ki Kahani *see* Jeevan Saathi
Prem Ki Ragini (?, **Madan** Theatres, H, 1935)
Prem Lagna (**Krishnakant**, G, 1982)
Prem Laksh (*aka* Arrow of Destiny, Taqdeer Ka Teer: Fram Sethna, H, 1936)
Prem Masaa (*aka* Heart Thief: ?, Sharda Film, St, 1931)
Prem Murti *see* Pratima
Prem Nagar (**M. Bhavnani**, H, 1940)
Prem Nagar (**K.S. Prakash Rao**, Tel, 1971)
Prem Nagar (**K.S. Prakash Rao**, H, 1974)
Premna Pichhi (C.V. Rajendran, Tel, 1981)
Prem Nazirine Kanmanilla (**Lenin Rajendran**, Mal, 1983)
Prem Ni Pratima (*aka* Lovers: **Manilal Joshi**, St, 1927)
Prem Nirasha (*aka* Forsaken Love: Pesi Karani, St, 1925)
Prem-o-Paap (Umanath Bannerjee, B, 1985)
Premotsavam (Umesh, Mal, 1991)
Prem Paigham (?, Raj Lakshmi Films, H, 1989)
Prem Parbat (Ved Rahi, H, 1973)
Prem Pareeksha (G.R. Sethi, H, 1934)
Prem Pash (*aka* Law of Love: Bidkar, St, 1929)
Prem Patra (**Bimal Roy**, H, 1962)
Prem Pooja (?, Reema Rakesh Nath, H, 1993)
Prem Pratigya (**Bapu**, H, 1989)
Prem Pujari (*aka* Mareez-e-Ishq: Rafique Ghaznavi, H, 1935)
Prem Pujari (**Dev Anand**, H, 1970)
Prem Purnima *see* Jaan-e-Alam Anjuman Ara
Prem Qaidi (K. Muralimohana Rao, H, 1991)
Prem Raatri (*aka* Night of Love: Dwarka Khosla, H, 1936)
Prem Rog (**Raj Kapoor**, H, 1982)
Prem Sagar (Narottam Vyas, H, 1939)

Prem Samadhi (*aka* Justice: G.K. Mehta, H, 1938)
Prem Samadhi (*aka* Khemro Lodan: Chandravadan Bhatt, G, 1955)
Prem Sandesh (?, Kapur Entertainers, H, 1988)
Prem Sangam (*aka* When Lovers Unite: **Baburao Painter**, St, 1932)
Prem Sangeet (W.Z. Ahmed, H, 1943)
Prem Sanyas (**Franz Osten**, St, 1925)
Prem Shastra (**B.R. Ishara**, H, 1974)
Prem Tapasya (**Dasari Narayana Rao**, H, 1983)
Premveer (**Master Vinayak**, Mar/H, 1937)
Prem Vijay (*aka* Triumphant Love: ?, Oriental Pics., St, 1931)
Prem Vivah (**Basu Chatterjee**, H, 1979)
Prem Yatra (*aka* Pilgrims of Love: Ramakant-Gharekhan/Vaidya, St, 1929)
Prem Yatra (Prafulla Roy, H, 1937)
Prem Yuddham/Prem Yudh (**S.V. Rajendra Singh**, Tel/H, 1985)
Prerana (Moti Sagar, H, 1984)
Preservation of Ancient Monuments (**Harisadhan Dasgupta**, E, 1976)
President *see* **Didi**
Presidentgari Abbayi (**T. Rama Rao**, Tel, 1987)
Presidentgari Pellam (A. Kodandarami Reddy, Tel, 1992)
President Nyrere's Visit to India (**Vishnu Mathur**, E, 1973)
President Panchatcharam (**A. Bhimsingh**, Tam, 1959)
President Peramma (**K. Vishwanath**, Tel, 1979)
Prestige *see* Pehle Aap
Pretender, The *see* Totayache Bund
Prethangalude Thazhvara (Venu, Mal, 1973)
Preyasi (Shrikanta Guha-Thakurta, B, 1982)
Price of a Woman *see* Balidan
Pride of Hindustan *see* Taranhaar
Pride of India *see* Shaan-e-Hind
Pride of Islam *see* Fakhr-e-Islam
Pride of Satyabhama *see* Garuda Garvabhangam
Prime Honour *see* **Muthal Mariyathai**
Prince (Lekh Tandon, H, 1969)
Prince Ascetic *see* Raj Yogi
Prince Charming *see* Banke Savaria
Prince Indeed, A *see* Veer Bhushan
Prince of Paupers *see* Garib Ka Lal
Prince of the People *see* Raj Dharma
Prince of Thieves *see* Shahu Chor
Princess *see* Raj Nandini *or* Rajkumari
Princess Budur (*aka* Kamar-al-Zaman: **J.J. Madan**, St, 1922)
Princess Rajba (*aka* Rajba, *aka* Daughters of India: **N.G. Devare**, St, 1928)
Princess Saba (R.K. Rehman, H, 1958)
Prince Thaksen (*aka* Mysterious Prince: G.P. Pawar, St, 1929)
Prince Vijaykumar *see* Vijaykumar
Principal Olivil (L. Gopi Krishnan, Mal, 1985)
Prison Bars *see* Salaakhen
Prisoner *see* Qaidi
Prisoner of Golconda (*aka* Golconda Ka Qaidi: Premnath, H, 1954)
Prisoner of the Andamans *see* **Andaman Kaithi**
Prisoners of Conscience (**Anand Patwardhan**, E/H, 1978)
Prisoners of Love *see* Raj Tarang
Prisoner's Wife, The *see* Usne Kya Socha
Prithibi Amar Chai (**Niren Lahiri**, B, 1957)
Prithvi Putra *see* Bhasmasur Vadh
Prithvi Putra (G.S. Devare, St, 1926)
Prithvi Putra (Potina Srinivasa Rao, Tel, 1933)
Prithvi Putra (**Jayant Desai**, H, 1938)
Prithviraj (Vaidya, St, 1931)
Prithviraj (Perala, Tel, 1988)
Prithviraj (Renuka Sharma, Tel, 1992)
Prithviraj Chouhan (?, Eastern Film, St, 1924)
Prithviraj Samyukta (Najam Naqvi, H, 1946)
Prithviraj Samyukta (Vijay B. Chauhan, G, 1988)
Prithviraj Sanyogita (**N.D. Sarpotdar**, St, 1929)
Prithviraj Sanyogita (**N.D. Sarpotdar**, H, 1933)
Prithvirajan (B. Sampathkumar, Tam, 1942)
Prithvi Vallabh *see* Malavpati Munj
Prithvi Vallabh (**Manilal Joshi**, St, 1924)
Prithvi Vallabh (**Sohrab Modi**, H, 1943)

Private Detective (*aka* CID Inspector: A. Shamsheer, H, 1962)
Private Life (B.K. Adarsh, H, 1983)
Private Life of a Silk Worm, The (**M. Bhavnani**, E, 1950)
Private Master (**K. Vishwanath**, Tel, 1967)
Private Secretary (Chander, H, 1962)
Priya (Salil Sen, B, 1958)
Priya (**John Abraham**, H, 1969)
Priya (**Govind Saraiya**, H, 1970)
Priya (**Madhu**, Mal, 1970)
Priya (S.P. Muthuraman, Tam/Tel/K, 1978)
Priya Bandhabi (Soumyen Mukherjee, B, 1943)
Priya Bandhabi (Hiren Nag, B, 1975)
Priya Bandhavi (**Durai**, Tel, 1979)
Priyadarshini (Peruvarum Chandrasekhar, Mal, 1978)
Priyamudan Prabhu (Gangai Kondan, Tam, 1984)
Priyamulla Sophia (**A. Vincent**, Mal, 1975)
Priyamvadha (**K.S. Sethumadhavan**, Mal, 1976)
Priyasakhi *see* Atmasakhi
Priyasakhi Radha (K.P. Pillai, Mal, 1982)
Priyatama (*aka* Redemption: **Harshadrai Mehta**, St, 1931)
Priyatama (**Pashupati Chatterjee**, B, 1948)
Priyatama (**P. Subramanyam**, Mal, 1966)
Priyatama (**Basu Chatterjee**, H, 1977)
Priyatama (Biswajit Das, O, 1978)
Priyatama (**Dinen Gupta**, B, 1980)
Priyatama (Geethakrishna, Tel, 1992)
Priyatame (Jayaprakash, K, 1981)
Priye Nikkadu Vendi (M. Mallikarjuna Rao, Mal, 1975)
Priyuralu (**T. Gopichand**, Tel, 1952)
Prize, The *see* Safed Hathi
Problem of Urban Housing, The (**Saeed Mirza**, E, 1977)
Procession of Memories *see* **Yaadon Ki Baraat**
Proclamation *see* Shahi Firman
Prodigal Son, The *see* **Mudiyanaya Puthran**
Professor (Lekh Tandon, H, 1962)
Professor (**P. Subramanyam**, Mal, 1972)
Professor and Jadugar (Sultan, H, 1966)
Professor Huchuraya (M.R. Vittal, K, 1974)
Professor Janaki (R.C. Shakthi, Mal, 1983)
Professor Kelpha's Magic (**Dadasaheb Phalke**, St, 1916)
Professor Pyarelal (Brij Sadanah, H, 1981)
Professor Waman M. Sc (Manibhai Vyas, H, 1938)
Professor X (Rajesh Nanda, H, 1966)
Promise *see* Wayada
Pronami Tomai (Prabhat Roy, B, 1989)
Pronoy Pasha (Mangal Chakraborty, B, 1978)
Proposal, A (Ashok Ahuja, H, 1976)
Protector, The *see* Ajit Yoddho
Protidan (Ajit Ganguly, B, 1969)
Protidan (Prabhat Roy, B, 1983)
Proxy (**Dinen Gupta**, B, 1977)
Pua Mor Kala Thakur (Raju Mishra, O, 1988)
Puberun (Prabhat Mukherjee, A, 1958)
Public Rowdy (Sagar, Tel, 1992)
Pucca Rowdy (**K. Amarnath**, Tam, 1937)
Puchakanni (**Puttanna Kanagal**, Mal, 1966)
Puchakkoru Mookuthi (**Priyadarshan**, Mal, 1984)
Pucha Sanyasi (**T. Hariharan**, Mal, 1981)
Pudhari (Keshav Toro, Mar, 1972)
Pudhcha Paool (**Raja Paranjpe**, Mar, 1950)
Pudhcha Paool (**Rajdutt**, Mar, 1986)
Pudhiavan (Amirjan, Tam, 1984)
Pudhir (Siddalingaiah, Tam, 1985)
Pudhisalikal (T.P.Arun, Tam, 1968)
Pudhiya *see* Puthiya
Pudhiya Athiyayam (**Durai**, Mal, 1990)
Pudhiya Bhoomi (**Tapi Chanakya**, Tam, 1968)
Pudhiya Katru (Karvannan, Tam, 1990)
Pudhiya Paravai (Dada Mirasi, Tam, 1964)
Pudhiya Pathai (**Tapi Chanakya**, Tam, 1960)
Pudhiya Pathai (R. Parthiban, Tam, 1989)
Pudhiya Poovithu (?, Golden Moon Creations, Tam, 1986)
Pudhiya Ragam (Jayachitra, Tam, 1991)
Pudhiya Sangamam (Charuhasan, Tam, 1983)
Pudhiya Sapatham (Visu, Tam, 1985)
Pudhiya Sarithiram (Robert C. Rajasekhar, Tam, 1990)
Pudhiya Theerpu (C.V. Rajendran, Tam, 1985)
Pudhiya Thendral (Prabhakar, Tam, 1993)
Pudhiya Thoranangal (M. Karnan, Tam, 1980)
Pudhiya Vanam (R.V. Udayakumar, Tam, 1988)
Pudhiya Varavu (T.R.R. Natakamaran, Tam, 1983)
Pudhiya Vazhkai (C.V. Rajendran, Tam, 1971)
Pudhu Manithan (Manivannan, Tam, 1991)
Pudhu Mappillai (Gangai Amaran, Tam, 1989)
Pudhu Nellu Pudhu Nathu (**Bharathirajaa**, Tam, 1991)
Pudhu Padagan (S. Thanu, Tam, 1990)
Pudhu Pattu (?, Ilaiyaraja Creations, Tam, 1990)
Pudhupiravi (Prem, Tam, 1993)
Pudhu Pudhu Arthangal (**K. Balachander**, Tam, 1989)
Pudhu Pudhu Ragangal (?, Deivanai Movies, Tam, 1990)
Pudhusa Padikkiren Pattu (Vetriselvan?, Tam, 1992)
Pudhu Varisu (Rajasekhar, Tam, 1990)
Pudhu Vasantham (Vikraman, Tam, 1990)
Pudhuvayal (**Krishnan-Panju**, Tam, 1957)
Pudhuvayal (Nanjil Kennedy, Tam, 1993)
Pudhu Vazhvu (**M.K. Thyagaraja Bhagavathar**, Tam, 1957)
Pudhu Yugam (Gopu/Sundar, Tam, 1954)
Pudhu Yugam (S.A. Chandrasekharan, Tam, 1985)
Pudumaipithan (Ramanna, Tam, 1957)
Pugunda Veedu (A.S. Prakasham, Tam, 1972)
Puiyal (G. Vishwanathan, Tam, 1952)
Pujari (**Niranjan Pal**, St, 1931)
Pujari (Aspi, H, 1946)
Pujarin (Prafulla Roy, H, 1936)
Pujarin (**Dhirubhai Desai**, H, 1969)
Pujarini (*aka* Dancer of the Temple: **Nandlal Jaswantlal**, H, 1935)
Pujarini (Partha Prathim Choudhury, B, 1984)
Pukar (**Sohrab Modi**, U/Persian, 1939)
Pukar (Ramesh Behl, H, 1983)
Pul (*aka* Bridge: Sudhir Sen, H, 1947)
Pulan Visaranai (R.K. Selvamani, Tam, 1990)
Puli (M.S. Rajbharath, Tel, 1985)
Puli Bebbuli (K.S.R. Doss, Tel, 1983)
Puli Bidda (V. Madhusudhana Rao, Tel, 1981)
Puli Debba (K.S.R. Doss, Tel, 1983)
Pulijudam (P. Chandrasekhara Reddy, Tel, 1984)
Puli Panja (K. Hemambharadhara Rao, Tel, 1985)
Pulival (**Sasikumar**, Mal, 1975)
Puli Valartha Pillai (Ma. Lakshmanan, Tam, 1985)
Puli Varunne Puli (Hari Kumar, Mal, 1985)
Pulliman (E.N. Balakrishnan, Mal, 1972)
Pulsating Giant (**Shyam Benegal**, E, 1971)
Punadhirallu (Rajkumar, Tel, 1978)
Punaradatta (**C.S. Rao**, K, 1976)
Punarjanma (*aka* Incarnation: Jaigopal Pillai, St, 1927)
Punarjanma (**Premankur Atorthy**, B, 1932)
Punarjanma (*aka* Life Divine: ?, Mahalakshmi Cinetone, St, 1933)
Punarjanma (*aka* Reunion: Ramnik Desai, H, 1938)
Punarjanma (**Prabhakar Nayak**, Mar, 1958)
Punarjanma (**K. Pratyagatma**, Tel, 1963)
Punarjanma (Pekati Shivram, K, 1969)
Punarjanmam (**C.V. Sridhar**, Tam, 1961)
Punarjanmam (**K.S. Sethumadhavan**, Mal, 1972)
Punarlagnani Patni (*aka* Second Wife: **Nagendra Majumdar**, St, 1928)
Punar Milan (Najam Naqvi, H, 1940)
Punar Milan (Manu Sen, B, 1957)
Punar Milan (**Ravindra Dave**, H, 1964)
Punar Milan (K.H.D. Rao, O, 1977)
Punar Milan (Jayanta Basu, B, 1988)
Punarmilana (M.R. Vittal, K, 1976)
Punashcha (**Mrinal Sen**, B, 1961)
Punashcha Parba (Siddhartha Datta, B, 1983)
Punavechi Raat (**Anant Mane**, Mar, 1955)
Pundalik (P.R. Tipnis/N.G. Chitre, St, 1912)
Pundalik (Shinde, St, 1921)
Pundalik (**Kanjibhai Rathod**, St, 1921)
Pundalik (**Vishram Bedekar**/V. Bhatt, Mar, 1936)
Pundalik (R.S. Junnarkar, Mar, 1944)
Punda Prachanda (Sudhira Kallol, K, 1991)
Pundara Ganda (P. Raju, K, 1990)
Pundenaruvi Chuvannu (Balu, Mal, 1991)
Punitha Anthoniar (Nanjil Dorai, Tam, 1977)
Punithavathi (?, Sri Shankar Films, Tam, 1962)
Punjabi Munda (S. Upendra, P, 1968)
Punjab Ka Sinh (*aka* Veer: **Kanjibhai Rathod**, H, 1936)
Punjab Kesari (*aka* Lion of Punjab: **Homi Master**, St, 1929)
Punjab Kesari (Fram Sethna, Tam, 1938)
Punjab Ki Padmini *see* Bulbul-e-Punjab
Punjab Lancers (**Homi Master/N.G. Devare**, H, 1937)
Punjab Mail (**R.S. Choudhury**, St, 1929)
Punjab Mail (**Homi Wadia**, H, 1939)
Punnagai (**K. Balachander**, Tam, 1971)
Punnagai Mannan (**K. Balachander**, Tam, 1986)
Punnami Chandrulu (Vijaya Bapineedu, Tel, 1987)
Punnami Rathri (P. Chandrasekhara Reddy, Tel, 1985)
Punnapra Vyalar (**Kunchako**, Mal, 1968)
Punnaram Cholli Cholli (**Priyadarshan**, Mal, 1985)
Punniyam Seithaval (**K.S. Gopalakrishnan**, Tam, 1977)
Punya Bhoomi (K. Vijayan, Tam, 1978)
Punya Dampathulu (Anil Kumar, Tel, 1987)
Punyam Kodi Purushudu (Katta Subbarao, Tel, 1984)
Punya Prabhav (**Homi Master**, St, 1929)
Punya Purusha (Janakiram, K, 1969)
Punya Stree (Raviraja Pinisetty, Tel, 1986)
Punyavati (Dada Mirasi, Tel, 1967)
Purab Aur Paschim (**Manoj Kumar**, H, 1970)
Purabi (Chitta Bose, Ben, 1948)
Purana Mandir (Tulsi **Ramsay**, H, 1984)
Purana Purush (G.K. Murthy, H, 1978)
Puran Bhagat (Pesi Karani, St, 1928)
Puran Bhagat (**R.L. Shorey**, P, 1939)
Puran Bhakt (**Debaki Bose**, H, 1933)
Purandaradasa *see* Bhakta Purandaradasa
Purandaradasar (R. Ramamurthy, Tam, 1981)
Purani Haveli (Tulsi/Shyam **Ramsay**, H, 1989)
Purani Pehchan (Kewal Mishra, H, 1971)
Purappad (Rajeev Nath, Mal, 1983)
Puraskaar *see* Safed Hathi
Puraskaar (*aka* CID Agent: Ram Kumar Bohra, H, 1970)
Puratchi Veeran Pulithevan (A. Raja Raman, Tam, 1963)
Puravrutham (**Lenin Rajendran**, Mal, 1988)
Purbaraag (Ardhendu Mukherjee, B, 1947)
Purchased Bride *see* Piya Ki Jogan
Pure Heart *see* **Pakeezah**
Purge *see* **Purusharthamm**
Purir Mandir (Moni Ghosh, B, 1958)
Puriyatha Pudhir (K.S. Ravikumar, Tam, 1990)
Purnandayya Shishyulu Katha (Bhargava, Tel, 1984)
Purnima (**Balwant Bhatt**, H, 1938)
Purnima (Narendra Suri, H, 1965)
Purnima (R. Dayanandsagar, K, 1971)
Purshachi Jaat (Madhav Kambli, Mar, 1954)
Puruliar Chhou Nritya (**Ritwik Ghatak**, B, 1970)
Pururava Chakravarthi *see* **Jayapradha**
Purush (Rajan Kothari, H, 1992)
Purushan Enakku Arasan (Ramanarayanan, Tam, 1992)
Purushartham (**K.R. Mohanan**, Mal, 1987)
Purushottama (M.S. Rajasekhar, K, 1992)
Pushpadhanu (**Sushil Majumdar**, B, 1959)
Pushpak/Pushpaka Vimana (**Singeetham Srinivasa Rao**, Wordless, 1987)
Pushpaka Vimana *see* **Pushpak**
Pushpanjali (**Kishore Sahu**, H, 1970)
Pushpanjali (**Sasikumar**, Mal, 1972)
Pushpa Sarem (**Sasikumar**, Mal, 1976)
Pushyaragam (C. Radhakrishnan, Mal, 1979)
Putalaghar (Samarendra Narayan Deb, A, 1976)
Putani Agents 1-2-3/Agent 1-2-3 (Geethapriya, K/H, 1979)
Putani Pattu Chera (B. Subbarao, Tel, 1990)
Puthadi Bomma (Jandhyala, Tel, 1984)
Puthanveedu (K. Sukumaran, Mal, 1971)
Puthariangam (P.G. Vishwambaran, Mal, 1978)
Puthiya *see* Pudhiya
Puthiya Aksham Puthiya Bhoomi (M.S. Mani, Mal, 1962)
Puthiya Chakravalangal (**P. Bhaskaran**, Mal, 1989)
Puthiya Karukkal (S.P. Venkatesh, Mal, 1989)
Puthiya Manithan (Thirumalai Mahalingam, Tam, 1974)
Puthiya Mukham (Suresh Menon, Tam, 1993)
Puthiya Varpugal (**Bharathirajaa**, Tam, 1979)
Puthiya Velicham (Shrikumaran Thampi, Mal, 1979)
Puthradharmam (Vimal Kumar, Mal, 1954)
Puthri (**P. Subramanyam**, Mal, 1966)
Puthu Kavithai (S.P. Muthuraman, Tam, 1982)
Puthumai Penn (M. Thiruvengadam, Tam, 1959)
Puthu Vellam (K. Vijayan, Tam, 1975)
Putli (Walli, H, 1950)
Putli Bai (Ashok Roy, H, 1972)
Putrabadhu (Chitta Bose, B, 1956)
Putrakameshti (Mani, Mal, 1972)
Putravadhu (Jasubhai Trivedi, G, 1982)
Putra Vhava Aisa (**Raja Thakur**, Mar, 1961)
Puttadha Poothukkal (*aka* Unlocked Doors: **J. Mahendran**, Tam, 1979)
Putthisali Paithiyangal (Raghu, Tam, 1983)
Puttillu (Dr Rajarao, Tel, 1953)
Puttinillu Mettinillu (Pattu, Tel, 1973)
Puttinti Gauravam (P. Chandrasekhara Reddy, Tel, 1975)
Putt Jattan De (Jagjeet, P, 1983)
Putulghar (Amit Sarkar, B, 1985)
Putul Nacher Itikatha (Ashit Bannerjee, B, 1949)
Puwati Nishar Sapon (**Phani Sarma**, A, 1959)
Puyal Kadantha Bhoomi (Visu, Tam, 1984)
Puyal Padum Pattu (Manivannan, Tam, 1987)
Puzha (Jesey, Mal, 1980)
Puzhayozhukum Vazhi (M. Krishnan Nair, Mal, 1985)
Pyaas *see* Apna Ghar Apni Kahani
Pyaas (Ram Daryani, H, 1941)
Pyaas (O.P. Ralhan, H, 1982)
Pyaasa (**Guru Dutt**, H, 1957)
Pyaasa Sawan (**Dasari Narayana Rao**, H, 1981)
Pyaase Dil (Charandas Shokh, H, 1974)
Pyaase Nain (S. Ram, H, 1955)
Pyaase Nain (?, Show People, H, 1989)
Pyaase Panchhi (Harsukh Bhatt, H, 1961)
Pyaasi Aankhen (Ram Kelkar, H, 1983)
Pyaasi Atma (A.K. Mishra/Ismail Inamdar?, H, 1988)
Pyaasi Nadi (Shankar Kinnagi, H, 1973)
Pyaasi Nigahen (Kesar, H, 1990)
Pyaasi Shyam (Amar Kumar, H, 1969)
Pyar (*aka* Next to God: **Dhirubhai Desai**, H, 1940)
Pyar (**V.M. Vyas**, H, 1950)
Pyar (Prahlad Sharma, H, 1969)
Pyara Dost (Imtiaz Khan, H, 1982)
Pyara Dushman (**R.G. Torney**/Amir Ali, H, 1935)
Pyara Dushman (**Master Bhagwan**, H, 1955)
Pyara Dushman (*aka* A Loveable Enemy: Anand Sagar, H, 1980)
Pyara Tarana (**K. Balachander**, H, 1982)
Pyara Watan (M. Udwadia, H, 1942)
Pyar Bhara Dil (Chandra Barot, H, 1991)
Pyar Bina Jag Soona (Surendra Sinha, H, 1985)
Pyar Diwana (Samar Chatterjee, H, 1972)
Pyar Diwana Hota Hai (Anand S. Vardhan, H, 1992)
Pyar Hi Pyar (Bhappi Sonie, H, 1969)
Pyar Ho Gaya (Rakesh Wadhawan, H, 1986)
Pyar Hua Chori Chori (**K. Bapaiah**, H, 1991)
Pyari (Bimal Pal, St, 1929)
Pyari Behna (**Basu Chatterjee**, H, 1985)
Pyari Bhabhi (K.C. Agarwal, H, 1985)

Pyari Dulhania (Ramnath Shukla, Bh, 1988)
Pyari Katar (*aka* Beloved Blade: G.P. Pawar, St, 1933)
Pyari Mamta (*aka* Bird of Prey: **B.P. Mishra**, St, 1926)
Pyar Jhuka Nahin (Vijay Sadanah, H, 1984)
Pyar Ka Bandhan (Naresh Saigal, H, 1963)
Pyar Ka Devata (**K. Bapaiah**, H, 1990)
Pyar Ka Karz (**K. Bapaiah**, H, 1990)
Pyar Ka Mandir (**K. Bapaiah**, H, 1988)
Pyar Ka Mausam (**Nasir Hussain**, H, 1969)
Pyar Ka Pehla Sawan (?, Zulfikar Pics, H, 1988)
Pyar Ka Rishta (Sultan Ahmed, H, 1973)
Pyar Karke Dekho (D. Rajendra Babu, H, 1987)
Pyar Ka Saaya (Vinod Verma, H, 1991)
Pyar Ka Sagar (Devendra Goel, H, 1961)
Pyar Ka Sapna (**Hrishikesh Mukherjee**, H, 1969)
Pyar Ka Sawan (Kanak Mishra, H, 1989)
Pyar Ka Sindoor (**Bapu**, H, 1985)
Pyar Ka Tarana (**Dev Anand**, H, 1992)
Pyar Ka Toofan (S.M. Iqbal, H, 1990)
Pyar Ke Do Char Din (Jagdish Gautam, H, 1984)
Pyar Ke Do Pal (Rajiv Mehra, H, 1986)
Pyar Ke Kabil (Anil Ganguly, H, 1987)
Pyar Ke Naam Qurban (B. Subhash, H, 1990)
Pyar Ke Rahi (**Atma Ram**, H, 1982)
Pyar Ki Baatein *see* Sneh Lagna
Pyar Ki Baatein (Akhtar Hussain, H, 1951)
Pyar Ki Baazi (K. Mullik/Shaukat, H, 1967)
Pyar Ki Dastaan (P.L. Santoshi, H, 1961)
Pyar Ki Jeet (O.P. Dutta, H, 1948)
Pyar Ki Jeet (Vasant Painter, H, 1962)
Pyar Ki Jeet (Sawan Kumar, H, 1986)
Pyar Ki Kahani (Ravi Nagaich, H, 1971)
Pyar Ki Maar (*aka* Devi Ya Danvi, Queen's Wrath: A.P. Kapur, H, 1935)
Pyar Ki Manzil (Keki Mistry, H, 1950)
Pyar Ki Pyaas (**Mahesh Kaul**, H, 1961)
Pyar Ki Raahein (Lekhraj Bhakri, H, 1959)
Pyar Ki Raat (A.R. Zamindar, H, 1949)
Pyar Kiya Hai Pyar Karenge (Vijay Reddy, H, 1986)
Pyar Kiya To Darna Kya (**B.S. Ranga**, H, 1963)
Pyar Kiye Jaa (**C.V. Sridhar**, H, 1966)
Pyar Mein Sauda Nahin (Santosh Saroj, H, 1981)
Pyar Mohabbat (Shankar Mukherjee, H, 1966)
Pyar Mohabbat (Ajay Kashyap, H, 1988)

Q

Qaid (**Atma Ram**, H, 1975)
Qaidi (*aka* Prisoner: S.F. Hasnain, H, 1940)
Qaidi (Mohammed Hussain, H, 1957)
Qaidi (S.S. Ravichandra, H, 1984)
Qaidi No 911 (Aspi, H, 1959)
Qaid Mein Hai Bulbul (Ravindra Peepat, H, 1992)
Qasoor Kiska (?, Pushpa International, H, 1988)
Qatil (Shanti Kumar, H, 1944)
Qatil (Mohammed Hussain, H, 1960)
Qatil (K. Mullick, H, 1970)
Qatil (Ashok Gaikwad, H, 1988)
Qatil Aur Ashiq (Swaroop Kumar, H, 1986)
Qatil Katar (G.P. Pawar, H, 1935)
Qatil Katari (*aka* The Knife: **Jayant Desai**, St, 1931)
Qatil Kathiyani (*aka* La Belle: **Nagendra Majumdar**, St, 1928)
Qatil Kaun (Amit Bose, H, 1980)
Qatilon Ke Qatil (Arjun Hingorani, H, 1981)
Qatl (R.K. Nayyar, H, 1986)
Qatl-e-Aam (Rele/Arolkar, H, 1935)
Qaumi Diler *see* Taranhaar
Qawali Ki Raat (Durgesh Kumar/Santoshi, H, 1964)
Qayamat (Raj N. Sippy, H, 1983)
Qayamat Ki Raat (Harvey-Pappu, H, 1990)
Qayamat Se Qayamat Tak (Mansoor Khan, U, 1988)
Quarrel Game of Narad *see* Kalicha Narad
Queen of Ahmednagar *see* Chandbibi
Queen of Fairies *see* Husn Pari
Queen of Hearts *see* Jaanbaaz Mallika
Queen of Love *see* Noor-e-Alam
Queen of Seven Seas *see* Saat Samundaron Ki Mallika
Queen of Women's Land *see* Swapna Sundari
Queen's Wrath *see* Pyar Ki Maar
Queen that Would Not Speak, The *see* Abola Rani
Quest for a Nation (**Shyam Benegal**, E, 1970)
Quest for Health (**Harisadhan Dasgupta**, E, 1965)
Question, The *see* Yeh Kyun?
Quickfire Plan (**Govind Saraiya**, E, 1963)
Quiet Revolution, The-1/2 (**Shyam Benegal**, E, 1975/9)
Quilt of Many Cultures, A: South India (**Shyam Benegal**, 1990)
Qurban (Deepak Bahry, H, 1991)
Qurbani (*aka* Martyr: Baburao/**Sundarrao Nadkarni**, St, 1931)
Qurbani (Ram Daryani, H, 1943)
Qurbani (Feroz Khan, H, 1980)
Qurbani Jatt Di (Priti Sapru, P, 1990)

R

Raag Anuraag (**Dinen Gupta**, B, 1975)
Raag Darbari (TV: Krishna Raghav, H, 1986)
Raag Rang (Digvijay, H, 1952)
Raah-e-Mohabbat *see* Preet Ki Reet
Raaka (Kedar Kapoor, H, 1965)
Raakasi Nagu (D. Rajendra Babu, Tel, 1984)
Raakh (Aditya Bhattacharya, H, 1988)
Raakh Aur Chingari (S.U. Syed, H, 1981)
Raakhi (Shanti Kumar, H, 1949)
Raakhi (**Modhu Bose**, B, 1953)
Raakhi (**A. Bhimsingh**, H, 1962)
Raakhi Aur Hathkadi (S.M. Sagar, H, 1972)
Raakhi Aur Rifle (Radhakant Sharma, H, 1976)
Raakhi Ki Saugand (Shibu Mitra, H, 1979)
Raakhi Raakhi (**Mahesh Kaul**, H, 1969)
Raakhna Ramakada (**Chandrakant Sangani**, G, 1983)
Raakuvil (P. Vijayan, Mal, 1973)
Raaraju (G. Rammohan Rao, Tel, 1984)
Raasta (Harprasad, H, 1947)
Raaste Aur Manzil (C. Vishwanath, H, 1968)
Raaste Aur Rishte (M. Hanif, H, 1983)
Raaste Ka Patthar (Mukul Dutt, H, 1972)
Raaste Pyar Ke (V.B. Rajendra Prasad, H, 1981)
Raas Vilas (**Nagendra Majumdar**, H, 1932)
Raat *see* Ratri
Raat Andheri Thi (Shiv Kumar, H, 1967)
Raat Aur Din (**Satyen Bose**, H, 1967)
Raat Bhore (**Mrinal Sen**, B, 1956)
Raat Dastay (**Niren Lahiri**, B, 1983)
Raat Ekta (Kalipada Das, B, 1957)
Raat Ka Raja *see* Night Bird
Raat Ke Andhere Mein (Devraj, H, 1969)
Raat Ke Andhere Mein (Vinod Talwar, H, 1987)
Raat Ke Rahi (Naseem, H, 1959)
Raat Ki Baat (*aka* Secrets of the Night: K.P. Bhave, St, 1930)
Raat Ki Baat (*aka* Midnight Tale: Dada Gunjal, H, 1935)
Raat Ki Rani (*aka* Midnight Romance: **Raja Sandow**, H, 1935)
Raat Ki Rani (Jagdish Sethi, H, 1949)
Raaton Ka Raja (Rajesh Nahata, H, 1970)
Raaz (Immanuel, H, 1949)
Raaz (**Ravindra Dave**, H, 1967)
Raaz (Harmesh Malhotra, H, 1981)
Rabindranather Chitrakala (**Santi P. Choudhury**, B, 1962)
Rabindranath's Shantiniketan (**Santi P. Chourhury**, E, 1960)
Rabindranath Tagore (**Satyajit Ray**, E/B, 1961)
Race Boat, The *see* **Kavalam Chundan**
Rachana (Satish, H, 1982)
Rachana (Mohan, Mal, 1983)
Racing in India (**Santi P. Choudhury**, E, 1982)
Radha (A.C. Trilogchander, Tam, 1973)
Radha (J.H. Sattar, O, 1984)
Radha Aur Seeta (Vijay Kapoor, H, 1979)
Radha Chakram (V.C. Sasi, Mal, 1992)
Radha Enna Pennkutti (**Balachandra Menon**, Mal, 1979)
Radhai Ketra Kannan (R. Krishnamurthy, Tam, 1978)
Radha Kalyanam (C.K. Sachi, Tam, 1935)
Radha Kalyanam (**Bapu**, Tel, 1981)
Radha Ka Sangam (Kirti Kumar, H, 1992)
Radha Kathal Varatha (K. Dhennadayalam, Tam, 1989)
Radha Krishna *see* Amar Prem *or* Jamuna Puliney
Radha Krishna (?, Laxmi Cinetone, Tel, 1939)
Radha Krishna (**Raja Nene**, H, 1954)
Radha Krishna (Ardhendu Mukherjee, B, 1964)
Radha Krishna (**K. Raghavendra Rao**, Tel, 1978)
Radha Krishna Prem *see* Krishna Leela
Radha Madhav (K.P. Bhave, St, 1926)
Radha Madhavan (**Sibi Malayil**, Mal, 1990)
Radhamma Mogadu (**C.S. Rao**, Tel, 1982)
Radhamma Pelli (**Dasari Narayana Rao**, Tel, 1974)
Radha Mohan/Nand Ke Lala (**Nanubhai Vakil**, Mar/H, 1934)
Radha My Darling (B. Bhaskara Rao, Tel, 1982)
Radha Ramana (Jyotish Sinha, K, 1943)
Radha Rani (**Jyotish Bannerjee**, St, 1930)
Radha Rani (**Chandulal Shah**, H, 1932)
Radha Rani (Sudhish Ghatak, B, 1950)
Radha Rani (Ajit Bannerjee, B, 1987)
Radhasarathi (Sarat, Tel, 1993)
Radha Vilas (Vishnupant Divekar, St, 1922)
Radhayude Kamukan (Hassan, Mal, 1984)
Radhe Shyam (Madhusudan Smart/Chauhan, St, 1930)
Radhe Shyam (*aka* Zulmi Kansa: **R.L. Shorey**/A.P. Kapur, H, 1932)
Radhe Shyam (Raman B. Desai, G, 1948)
Radhika (Virendra Desai, H, 1941)
Radhika (K. Sadasiva Rao, Tel, 1947)
Radio Girl (B. Roy, St, 1929)
Radio Singer *see* Lajwanti
Raees (Kaiser Sabai, H, 1948)
Raees (Vishnu Raje, H, 1976)
Raeeszada (**Raja Thakur**, H, 1976)
Raeeszada (Bharat Kapoor, H, 1990)
Raffoo Chakkar (**Narendra Bedi**, H, 1975)
Raftaar (Nakshab, H, 1955)
Raftaar (Dinesh-Ramanesh, H, 1975)
Raga and Melody (**Shyam Benegal**, E, 1972)
Raga Deepam (**Dasari Narayana Rao**, Tel, 1982)
Raga Leela (Jandhyala, Tel, 1987)
Ragam (**A. Bhimsingh**, Mal, 1975)
Ragam Thanam Pallavi (A.T. Abu, Mal, 1980)
Ragam Thedum Pallavi (**T. Rajendar**, Tam, 1982)
Ragangal Maruvathillai (Sirimughai Ravi, Tam, 1983)
Ragasangamam (Subhash, Mal, 1985)
Raga Tala (H.M. Krishnamurthy, K, 1982)
Raghir (A. Rashid, H, 1943)
Raghu Dakat (Girin Choudhury, B, 1952)
Raghumaina (**Rajdutt**, Mar, 1983)
Raghunathrao and Sharayubala (Madanrai Vakil, St, 1927)
Raghupati Raghava Rajaram (**Durai**, Tam, 1977)
Raghu Ramudu (Kommineni, Tel, 1983)
Raghuvamsam (**Adoor Bhasi**, Mal, 1978)
Ragile Gundelu (P. Chandrasekhara Reddy, Tel, 1985)
Ragile Hrudayalu (M. Mallikarjuna Rao, Tel, 1980)
Ragile Jwala (**K. Raghavendra Rao**, Tel, 1980)
Ragini (Shankar Mehta, H, 1945)
Ragini (Rakhan, H, 1958)
Ragini (P.B. Unni, Mal, 1968)
Ragulatunna Bharatamu (Allani Sridhar, Tel, 1991)
Rahasiya Police 115 (**B.R. Panthulu**, Tam, 1968)
Rahasya Hanthakudu (A. Jagannath, Tel, 1985)
Rahasyam (**Sasikumar**, Mal, 1969)
Rahasyam (**Vedantam Raghavaiah**, Tel, 1967)
Rahasyam (Ramanarayanan, Tam, 1985)
Rahasya Penn 117 (P.A. Krishnan, Tam, 1972)
Rahasya Rathri (A.B. Raj, Mal, 1974)
Rahasya Rathri (M.S. Kumar, K, 1980)
Rahat (Ramniklal Desai, H, 1945)
Rahemdil Jallad (Qamar Narvi, H, 1985)
Rahgir (**Tarun Majumdar**, H, 1969)
Rahi/Two Leaves and a Bud (**K.A. Abbas**, H/E, 1952)
Rahi (Raman Kumar, H, 1986)
Rahi Badal Gaye (Ravi Tandon, H, 1985)
Rahnuma (Habib Sarhadi, H, 1948)
Rahu Ketu (**B.R. Ishara**, H, 1978)
Rahul (Ram Gabale, H, 1964)
Raibahadur (Ardhendu Mukherjee, B, 1961)
Rai Daich (J.B. Lulla, Sindhi, 1958)
Raiders of the Railroad (*aka* Captain Virendra: H.S. Thakur, H, 1936)
Raigad (**N.G. Devare**/G.S. Devare, Mar, 1940)
Raigadacha Rajbandi (**Raja Thakur**, Mar, 1965)
Raikamal (Subodh Mitra, B, 1955)
Rail Ka Dibba (P.N. Arora, H, 1953)
Rail Payanangalil (**T. Rajendar**, Tam, 1981)
Rails for the World (**Kumar Shahani**, E, 1970)
Railu Dopidi (K.S. Rami Reddy, Tel, 1984)
Railukku Neramachu (Bharati Mohan, Tam, 1988)
Railway Cross (?, Mal, 1986)
Railway Platform (Ramesh Saigal, H, 1955)
Rain *see* **Barsaat**
Rain Basera (*aka* Kabeela: ?, Asha Pics, H, 1947)
Rainbow *see* Vanavil
Raisaheb (S.M. Yusuf, H, 1942)
Raitana Makkalu (Chindodi Bangaresh, Tel/K, 1981)
Raithe Raju (B.S. Srinivas, Tel, 1970)
Raitu Bidda (B.A. Subba Rao, Tel, 1971)
Raitu Bidda (**Gudavalli Ramabrahmam**, Tel, 1939)
Raitu Kutumbam (**T. Rama Rao**, Tel, 1971)
Raja (**Kishore Sahu**, H, 1943)
Raja (Radhakant, H, 1963)
Raja (M. Karnan, Tam/Tel, 1972)
Raja (C.V. Rajendran, Tam, 1972)
Raja (**Tapan Sinha**, B, 1974)
Raja (K. Shankar, H, 1975)
Raja (**K. Raghavendra Rao**, Tel, 1976) Raja (?, A, 1982)
Raja Aur Rana (Shibu Mitra, H, 1983)
Raja Aur Runk (**K.P. Atma**, H, 1968)
Raja Bhakti (*aka* Rakshasi Mahatvakanksha: **Sundarrao Nadkarni**, Tam, 1936)
Raja Bhakti (?, P. Rajamanikam, Tam, 1960)
Raja Bhartrahari (Ramnik Vaidya, G, 1949)
Raja Bhartrahari (**Ravindra Dave**, G, 1973)
Raja Bhartrahari *see* Bhartrahari
Raja Bhoj (?, **Madan Theatres**, St, 1922)
Raja Bhoj (*aka* Man and his Destiny, Trial of Destiny: D.J. Jhaveri, St, 1926)
Raja Bhoja (P.V. Rao, Tam, 1935)
Raja Chinna Roja (S.P. Muthuraman, Tam, 1989)
Raja Desingu (**Raja Chandrasekhar**, Tam, 1936)
Raja Desingu (**T.R. Raghunath**, Tam, 1960)
Rajadhi Raja (*aka* The Omnipotent: Haribhai Desai, St, 1932)
Rajadhi Raja (R. Sundarrajan, Tam, 1989)
Rajadhi Raja (Bhargava, K, 1992)
Rajadhi Raja (Balu Anand, Tam, 1993)
Rajadhi Raju (**Bapu**, Tel, 1979)
Rajadrohi (**S. Soundararajan**, Tam, 1938)
Rajadurai (S.A. Chandrasekharan, Tam, 1993)
Rajadurgada Rahasya (A.C. Narasimhamurthy/S.K. Bhagavan, K, 1967)
Raja Gopichand *see* Alakh Niranjan
Raja Gopichand (B.M. Shukla, H, 1933)
Raja Gopichand (**Bhalji Pendharkar**, Mar/H, 1938)
Raja Gopichand (**Master Bhagwan**, Tam, 1941)
Raja Gopichand (Bhupen Desai, G, 1979)
Raja Gopuram (P.G. Pandian, Tam, 1985)
Raja Gosavichi Goshta (Baburao Gokhale/Raja Katre, Mar, 1958)
Raja Hamsam (**T. Hariharan**, Mal, 1974)
Raja Harishchandra *see* Satya Harishchandra
Raja Harishchandra (**Dadasaheb Phalke**, St, 1913)

Raja Harishchandra (**Homi Master**, St, 1924)
Raja Harishchandra (Y.D. Sarpotdar, St, 1928)
Raja Harishchandra (Raman B. Desai, H, 1952)
Raja Harishchandra (Ashish Kumar, H, 1979)
Raja Harishchandra (Bibhan Barua, A, 1980)
Raja Harishchandra (Uma Prasad Moitra, B, 1984)
Rajahmundhry Romeo (K.V.S. Prasad Reddy, Tel, 1984)
Raja Jani (**Mohan Segal**, H, 1972)
Raja Jogi (Daljit, H, 1983)
Raja Kaiye Vacha (Suresh Krishna, Tam, 1990)
Raja Kaka (Chhotu Bihari, H, 1973)
Rajakiya (Sivamani, K, 1992)
Rajakiya Chadurangam (P. Chandrasekhara Reddy, Tel, 1989)
Rajakota Rahasyam (**B. Vittalacharya**, Tel, 1971)
Raja Krishna Chandra (Sudhir Bandhu, B, 1953)
Rajakumar (G. Ramineedu, Tel, 1983)
Rajakumari (**A.S.A. Sami**, Tam, 1947)
Rajalakshmi (**B. Vittalacharya**, K, 1954)
Rajalakshmi-o-Shrikanta (Haridas Bhattacharya, B, 1958)
Raja Maharaja (Manimurughan, K, 1982)
Raja Malaya Simhan (**B.S. Ranga**, Tam/Tel, 1959)
Rajamalli (R.S. Prabhu, Mal, 1965)
Raja Mariyadhai (Kartick Raghunathan, Tam, 1987)
Raja Mayurdhwaja (?, Star Film, St, 1923)
Rajambal (**A. Narayanan**, Tam, 1935)
Rajambal (R.M. Krishnaswamy, Tam, 1951)
Rajamohan (Fram Sethna, Tam, 1937)
Raja Mordhwaj *see* Bhakta Ke Bhagwan
Raja Mukthi (**Raja Chandrasekhar**, Tam, 1948)
Raja Mukutam (**B.N. Reddi**, Tel/Tam, 1959)
Rajana Bajavala Baja (Girish Ghanekar, Mar, 1989)
Rajanadai (S.A. Chandrasekharan, Tam, 1989)
Raja Nagam (N.S. Maniam, Tam, 1974)
Raja Nandini (**Vedantam Raghavaiah**, Tel, 1958)
Raja Nanna Raja (A.V. Sheshgiri Rao, K, 1976)
Rajanarthakiya Rahasya (B. Harinarayana, K, 1976)
Raja Nee Vazhga (C.V. Rajendran, Tam, 1986)
Raja Ne Gami Te Rani (*aka* Love Is Blind: **Kanjibhai Rathod**, St, 1926)
Rajangam (R.C. Sakthi, Tam, 1981)
Rajani (**Jyotish Bannerjee**, St, 1929)
Rajani (**Jyotish Bannerjee**, B, 1936)
Rajani (**Dinen Gupta**, B, 1977)
Rajani (Rajamohanan, Mal, 1977)
Rajani (TV: **Basu Chatterjee**, H, 1985)
Rajani Bala (?, Kohinoor Film, St, 1928)
Rajani Chandra (*aka* The Blind Girl: ?, Paramount Film, St, 1933)
Rajanigandha (**Basu Chatterjee**, H, 1974)
Rajanigandhi (M. Krishnan Nair, Mal, 1980)
Rajanigandha (Profulla Bora, A, 1981)
Rajankanam (Jesey, Mal, 1976)
Rajan Paranja Katha (Mani Swami, Mal, 1978)
Raja Parambara (E.N. Balakrishnan, Mal, 1976)
Raja Parikshit (*aka* Janmejaya's Serpent Sacrifice: **Manilal Joshi**, St, 1922)
Raja Part Rangadurai (P. Madhavan, Tam, 1973)
Raja Parvai (**Singeetham Srinivasa Rao**, Tam, 1981)
Rajaputra Rahasyam (S.D. Lall, Tel, 1978)
Raja Raja Chozhan (**A.P. Nagarajan**, Tam, 1973)
Rajarajan (T.V. Sundaram, Tam, 1957)
Raja Rajathan (Ramadas E., Tam, 1989)
Raja Rajeshwari (M.L. Tandon, Tam, 1944)
Raja Rajeshwari (N. Sambandam, Tam, 1979)
Raja Ramesh (V. Madhusudhana Rao, Tel, 1977)
Raja Rammohun (Bijoy Basu, B, 1965)
Raja Rani (Najam Naqvi, H, 1942)
Raja Rani (**A. Bhimsingh**, Tam, 1956)
Raja Rani (Sachin Bhowmick, H, 1973)
Raja Rani Ko Chahiye Pasina (Sulabha Deshpande, H, 1978)
Raja Ravi Varma (J. Sasikumar, E, 1990)
Raja Rishi (K. Shankar, Tam, 1985)
Raja Saab (Suraj Prakash, H, 1969)
Raja Saheb (Palash Bannerjee, B, 1980)
Raja-Saja (Bikash Roy, B, 1960)
Raja Satya Vrata (D. Shankar Singh, K, 1961)
Rajasekharan (**A. Narayanan/R.S. Prakash**?, Tam, 1937)
Raja Sevai (**K. Kameshwara Rao**, Tam, 1959)Rajashekhara (**G.V. Iyer**, K, 1967)
Rajashilpi (*aka* The Royal Sculptor: R. Sukumaran, Mal, 1991)
Raja Shivachhatrapati (Chandravadan, Mar, 1974)
Raja Shriyal *see* Bhakta Ke Bhagwan
Raja Shriyal (G.P. Pawar, Mar, 1939)
Rajasimha (K.S.R. Doss, Tel, 1969)
Rajasimha (Joe Simon, K, 1989)
Rajasuyam (Sama-Ramu, Tam, 1942)
Rajasuya Yaga (T. Dwarkanath, K, 1937)
Rajathanthiram (Visu, Tam, 1984)
Rajathi (M. Lakshmanan, Tam, 1967)
Rajathi Rojakili (S. Devaraj, Tam, 1985)
Rajat Jayanti (**P.C. Barua**, B, 1939)
Raja Veetu Kannukutti (C.V. Rajendran, Tam, 1984)
Raja Veetu Pillai (Dada Mirasi, Tam, 1967)
Raja Vempala (K.S. Gopalakrishnan, Mal, 1984)
Rajavidhi (Senan, Mal, 1979)
Raja Vikram (**Dhirubhai Desai**, H, 1957)
Raja Vikrama (**Kemparaj Urs**, Tam/K, 1950)
Raja Vikramarka (Raviraja Pinisetty, Tel, 1990)
Rajavinte Makan (?, Sharon Pics, Mal, 1986)
Rajavukku Etha Rani (L. Balu, Tam, 1978)
Rajayogam (**T.R. Sundaram**, Tam, 1940)
Rajayogam (K.S.R. Doss, Tel, 1968)
Rajayogam (**T. Hariharan**, Mal, 1976)
Raja Yogi *see* Bhakta Kumanan
Raja Yuvaraja (Soma Sundaram, Tam, 1985)
Rajbansha (Piyush Bose, B, 1976)
Raj Bhakta (*aka* Peace Maker: **Harshadrai Mehta**, St, 1931)
Raj Bodhu (Partha Prathim Choudhury, B, 1982)
Rajdanda (*aka* King's Justice: ?, Gopal Cinetone, St, 1934)
Rajdhani (Naresh Saigal, H, 1956)
Rajdhani (Kodi Ramakrishna, Tel, 1993)
Rajdhani Express (B.J. Patel, H, 1972)
Rajdhani Theke (Nirmal Mitra, B, 1958)
Raj Dharma (*aka* Prince of the People: Harilal M. Bhatt, St, 1929)
Rajdoot (*aka* Beggar Meets Beggar: Haribhai Desai, St, 1930)
Rajdrohi (**Niren Lahiri**, B, 1966)
Raj Dulara (Khayal Nohvi?, H, 1987)
Rajdulari (?, Tollywood Studio/**Madan** Theatres, H, 1936)
Raj Durbar (?, Deepak Pictures, H, 1955)
Rajendrudu Gajendrudu (S.V. Krishna Reddy, Tel, 1993)
Rajeshwari (**Raja Sandow**, St, 1930)
Rajeshwari (**R. Padmanabhan**, Tel, 1952)
Rajeshwari (H.M.K. Murthy, K, 1981)
Rajeshwari (Salil Dutta, B, 1983)
Rajeshwari Kalyanam (Kranthi Kumar, Tel, 1992)
Rajgee (**Sukumar Dasgupta**, B, 1937)
Rajguru (S.A.V. Samy, Tel, 1954)
Rajhaath (**Sohrab Modi**, H, 1956)
Raj Hansa (**Kanjibhai Rathod**, St, 1929)
Raj Hriday (*aka* Heart of a King: Haribhai Desai?, **Sharda Film**, St, 1929)
Raji En Kanmani/Raji Naa Pranam (K.J. Mahadevan, Tam/Tel, 1954)
Raji Naa Pranam *see* Raji En Kanmani
Raj Kanya (Vinod Desai, H, 1955)
Raj Kanya (Sunil Mukherjee, B, 1965)
Rajkumar (*aka* Rajkunwar: ?, New India Film, St, 1928)
Rajkumar (K. Shankar, H, 1964)
Rajkumarer Nirbashan (**Sukumar Dasgupta**, B, 1940)
Rajkumari (*aka* Princess: Ramakant-Gharekhan, St, 1930)
Rajkumari (Dwarka Khosla, H, 1938)
Rajkumari (**T.R. Raghunath**, H, 1955)
Rajkumari (Salil Sen, B, 1970)
Rajkumari (Sultan, H, 1979)
Rajkumari Budur *see* Princess Budur
Rajkumari Ni Ranagarjana (*aka* Valiant Princess: **Kanjibhai Rathod**, St, 1930)
Rajkumar Thagsen *see* Vikram Charitra
Rajkunwar *see* Rajkumar
Rajkunwar (Subhash Shah, G, 1986)
Raj Lakshmi (**Chandulal Shah**, St, 1930)
Raj Lakshmi (?, Surya Film Co., St, 1932)
Raj Lakshmi (**Premendra Mitra**, H, 1945)
Raj Lakshmi (?, Neo Films, H, 1987)
Raj Mahal (**Nanubhai Vakil**, H, 1953)
Raj Mahal (**P. Neelakantan**, H, 1963)
Raj Mahal (B. Harinarayana, Tel, 1972)
Raj Mahal (K. Parvez, H, 1982)
Rajmanya Rajashri (**Raja Thakur**, Mar, 1959)
Rajmata (*aka* Tapasya: ?, Unity Prod, H, 1947)
Rajmohaner Bou (Hiranmaya Sen, B, 1951)
Raj Mukut (*aka* Royal Crown: Behram Vasania, St, 1930)
Raj Mukut (*aka* Betaaj Badshah: Govindrao Tembe, H, 1935)
Raj Mukut (**Nanubhai Vakil**, H, 1950)
Raj Nandini (*aka* Johar-e-Shamsheer, Princess: Dinkar Bidkar, St, 1931)
Raj Nandini (Ramchandra Pal, H, 1962)
Raj Nandini (Sukhen Das, B, 1980)
Raj Nartaki/Court Dancer (**Modhu Bose**, B/H/E, 1941)
Rajnati Basantsena (**Charu Roy**, B, 1934)
Rajnigandha (Bijoy Mishra, O, 1989)
Rajpath (Gunamaya Bannerjee, B, 1956)
Raj Prapanch (Keshavlal Joshi, St, 1930)
Raj Pratigya (Jaswant Jhaveri, H, 1958)
Raj Purush (Iman Kalyan Chatterjee, B, 1987)
Rajput (Lekhraj Bhakri, H, 1951)
Rajput (**Vijay Anand**, H, 1982)
Rajputani (**Chandulal Shah**, St, 1929)
Rajputani (Aspi, H, 1946)
Rajputani (**Mehul Kumar**, G, 1979)
Rajput Cavalier *see* Rajput Sawar
Rajput Ramani *see* Jigarme Gha
Rajput Ramani (**Keshavrao Dhaiber**, H, 1936)
Rajputra Thagsen *see* Bhedi Rajkumar
Rajput Sawar (*aka* Rajput Cavalier: Ramakant-Gharekhan, St, 1929)
Raj Ramani (*aka* Vanishing Hopes: **B.P. Mishra**, St, 1929)
Raj Ramani (**Jayant Desai**, H, 1936)
Rajrang (*aka* Vengeance: **B.P. Mishra**, St, 1928)
Rajrani (Satish Nigam, H, 1950)
Rajrani Damayanti (**Raja Nene**, H, 1952) Rajrani Meera *see* **Meerabai**
Rajrani Meera (G.P. Pawar, H, 1956)
Raj Ratan (Indu Kumar, H, 1953)
Rajrishi Ambarish (*aka* Bhakta Shiromani: **Dadasaheb Phalke**, St, 1922)
Rajrishi Vishwamitra (Sheshaiah?, **General Pics**., St, 1931)
Raj Sanyas (?, United Pics. Syndicate, St, 1929)
Rajsingha (**Jyotish Bannerjee**, St, 1930)
Raj Singhasan (Kundan Kumar, H, 1958)
Raj Tarang (*aka* Prisoners of Love: **Harshadrai Mehta**, St, 1928)
Raj Tarang (*aka* Prisoners of Love: M.R. Kapoor, H, 1935)
Raj Tilak (Madanrai Vakil, St, 1931)
Raj Tilak (**S.S. Vasan**, H, 1958)
Raj Tilak (Rajkumar Kohli, H, 1984)
Raju (Om Bedi, H, 1967)
Raju Aur Gangaram (*aka* The Boy and the Parrot: **Ezra Mir**, H, 1964)
Raju Ban Gaya Gentleman (Aziz Mirza, H, 1992)
Raju Dada (?, Suri Art International, H, 1992)
Raju Peda (B.A. Subba Rao, Tel, 1954)
Raju Rahim (A.B. Raj, Mal, 1978)
Raju Rani Jackie (**Singeetham Srinivasa Rao**, Tel, 1983)
Raju Vedale (**T. Rama Rao**, Tel, 1976)
Rajwadana Ranga (*aka* Female Feet: Krishna Kumar, St, 1928)
Rajyamlo Rabandulu (K.S. Prasad, Tel, 1975)
Raj Yogi (*aka* Prince Ascetic: **Manilal Joshi**, St, 1925)
Rajyogi Bhartrahari (Raman B. Desai, H, 1954)
Ra Kawat (*aka* Pranay Milan: **M. Bhavnani**, St, 1926)
Rake, The *see* Takht-e-Toofan
Rakhandar (Sushil Gajwani, Mar, 1982)
Rakhi (*aka* Rocky: R. Chandrasekhara Reddy, Tel, 1988)
Rakhna Ramakada *see* Raakhna Ramakada
Rakhwala (**Adurthi Subba Rao**, H, 1971)
Rakhwala (K. Muralimohana Rao, H, 1989)
Rakhwala Mare Ghanshyamna (Vallabh Choksi, G, 1976)
Rakkayi Koyil (Manivasagam, Tam, 1993)
Rakkuyil (**P. Bhaskaran**, Mal, 1973)
Rakkuyilin Rajassadasil (**Priyadarshan**, Mal, 1986)
Raksha (Ravi Nagaich, H, 1981)
Raksha Bandhan (Shantilal Soni, H, 1976)
Rakshana (K. Narayana Rao, Tel, 1993)
Raksharekha (**R. Padmanabhan**, Tel, 1949)
Rakshas (Hassan, Mal, 1984)
Rakshasa Samharam (Raghav, Tel, 1988)
Rakshasi Loya (V. Vidyasagar, Tel, 1983)
Rakshasi Mahatvakanksha *see* Raja Bhakti
Rakshasudu (A. Kodandarami Reddy, Tel, 1986)
Rakta Bandhan (Rajat Rakshit, H, 1984)
Raktacha Rajmukut *see* Khooni Taj
Raktacha Sood (*aka* Lohini Vasulat, Blood for Blood: P.S. Talegiri, St, 1929)
Rakta Golap (Bhimeshwar Rao/Bibhuti Mishra, O, 1977)
Rakta Palash (Pinaki Mukherjee, B, 1962)
Rakta Pushpam (**Sasikumar**, Mal, 1970)
Rakta Rekha (Umaprasad Maitra, B, 1968)
Rakta Tilak (Biswajit, B, 1974)
Rakta Tilaka (Joe Simon, K, 1983)
Rakta Tilakam *see* Rakhta Tilakam
Rakter Tan (Kamal Chatterjee, B, 1950)
Raktha Bandham (Velswami Kavi, Mal, 1951)
Raktha Bandham (Alluri Ravi, Tel, 1980)
Rakthabhisekham (A. Kodandarami Reddy, Tel, 1988)
Raktha Kanneeru (G. Ram Mohana Rao, Tel, 1989)
Raktham (Joshi, Mal, 1981)
Raktha Sakshi (P. Chandrakumar, Mal, 1982)
Raktha Sambandhalu (M. Mallikarjuna Rao, Tel, 1975)
Raktha Sambandham *see* Pasamalar
Raktha Sambandham (**Vijayanirmala**, Tel, 1980)
Raktha Sindooram (C. Seetaram, Tel, 1967)
Raktha Sindooram (A. Kodandarami Reddy, Tel, 1985)
Raktha Tilakam (Dada Mirasi, Tam, 1963)
Raktha Tilakam (Maniram, Tel/Tam, 1964)
Raktha Tilakam (B. Gopal, Tel, 1988)
Raktorin (Sushil Mukherjee, B, 1990)
Ramabanam (Y. Eswara Reddy, Tel, 1979)
Ramachari (D. Rajendra Babu, K, 1991)
Ramachilaka (**Singeetham Srinivasa Rao**, Tel, 1978)
Ramadas (**Y.V. Rao**, Tam, 1948)
Ramadasu (?, East India Film, Tel, 1933)
Ramadasu (**Chittor V. Nagaiah**, Tel, 1964)
Rama Dhandru (N.S. Maniam, Tel, 1981)
Ramaiah Thandri (B.V. Prasad, Tel, 1974)
Ramakrishnamanulu (R. Thyagarajan, Tel, 1981)
Ramakrishnulu (V.B. Rajendra Prasad, Tel, 1978)
Rama Lakshman (R. Thyagarajan, Tam, 1981)
Rama Lakshmana (Ravi Shankar, K, 1980)
Ramalayam (K. Babu Rao, Tel, 1971)
Ramalinga Swamigal (*aka* Jyothi Ramalingaswamy: **T.R. Raghunath**, Tam, 1939)
Raman (Hiren Bose, H, 1954)
Ramanama Mahimai (A.N. Kalyanasundaram, Tam, 1939)
Ramanan (D.M. Pottakad, Mal, 1967)
Ra Mandlik (**Homi Master**, St, 1924)
Ra Mandlik (Ramnik Acharya, G, 1961)
Ra Mandlik (Himmat Dave, G, 1975)
Raman Ethanai Ramanadi (P. Madhavan, Tam, 1970)
Ramani Ki Rakshasi *see* Khubsoorat Bala
Ramanna Shamanna (B. Subba Rao, K, 1988)
Raman Parashuraman (M.S. Gopinath, Tam, 1980)
Raman Shri Raman (T.K. Prasad, Tam, 1985)
Raman Thediya Seethai (**P. Neelakantan**, Tam,

1972)
Rama-o-Rama (Mirza Bros, H, 1988)
Rama Or Maya (**Suchet Singh**/Shukle, St, 1920)
Rama Paduka Pattabhishekham *see* **Paduka Pattabhishekham**
Rama Parashurama (Vijay, K, 1980)
Ramapir (Dinesh Rawal, G, 1988)
Rama Rajyamlo Bheemaraju (A. Kodandarami Reddy, Tel, 1983)
Rama Rajyamlo Raktha Pasam (P. Sambasiva Rao, Tel, 1976)
Ramasundari *see* Ashasundari
Ramat Ramade Ram (Dinesh Rawal, G, 1964)
Ram Aur Shyam (**Tapi Chanakya**, H, 1967)Ram Avatar (Sunil Hingorani, H, 1988)
Ramayan (Serial: Eugenio De Liguoro, St, 1922)
Ramayan (?, **Madan** Theatres, H, 1933)
Ramayan (Sudarshan/Prafulla Roy, H, 1934)
Ramayan (**Vijay Bhatt**, H, 1954)
Ramayan (K. Somu, H, 1960)
Ramayan (Govind Tej, O/B, 1980)
Ramayan (Girish Manukant, G, 1981)
Ramayan (TV: **Ramanand Sagar**, H, 1986-8)
Ramayana (Girish, Haryanvi, 1985)
Ramayanam (?, East India Film, Tam, 1932)
Ramayanamlo Bhagavatham (T.L.V. Prasad, Tel, 1984)
Ramayanamlo Pidakala Veta (Rajachandra, Tel, 1982)
Ramayani (**Sarvottam Badami**, H, 1945)
Ramayi Vayasukku Vandhutta (Vedhanpatti Azhagapan, Tam, 1980)
Rambaan (**Vijay Bhatt**, H, 1948)
Ram Balram (**Vijay Anand**, H, 1980)
Ram Balram (A. Sanjivi, O, 1980)
Rambayin Kadhal (*aka* Yathbavishyam, Rambha's Love: **Balkrishna Narayan Rao**, Tam, 1939)
Rambayin Kadhali (R.R. Chandran, Tam, 1956)
Ram Bhakta Hanuman (Shantilal Soni, H, 1969)
Ram Bhakta Vibhishan (Samar Chatterjee, H, 1958)
Ram Bhakti (?, Shri Nityananda Chitra, H, 1958)
Rambhalosthunnaru Jagratha (G.G. Dhar, Tel, 1992)
Rambha of Rajnagar (**Homi Master**, St, 1925)
Rambha Rani (*aka* Stree Charitra: **Harshadrai Mehta**, H, 1933)
Ram Bharose (*aka* Perchance: **Harshadrai Mehta**, St, 1926)
Ram Bharose (Ismail Abbasi, H, 1951)
Ram Bharose (*aka* God's Own Man: Anand Sagar, H, 1977)
Rambha's Love *see* Rambayin Kadhal
Rambha Urvashi Men*aka* (P. Sambasiva Rao, Tel, 1977)
Ram Darshan (Ramesh Gupta, H, 1950)
Ramdas (?, Peninsular Film Service, St, 1929)
Ramdev *see* **Baba Ramdev**
Ramdev Pirno Vivah (Vinod Parmar, G, 1988)
Ramdhakka (Taru Mukherjee, B, 1966)
Ram Dhun *see* Narsi Bhagat
Ram Doota *see* Lanka Dahana
Ram Duhai (Dinesh Rawal, G, 1984)
Ramer Sumati/Chhota Bhai (**Kartick Chattopadhyay**, B/H, 1947)
Ramer Sumati (**Gurudas Bagchi**, B, 1977)
Ramgarh Ke Sholay (Ajit Dewani, H, 1991)
Ram Hanuman Yuddha (S.N. Tripathi, H, 1957)
Ramhari of Champapara (Samiran Dutta, O, 1985)
Rami Chandidas (Debnarayan Gupta, B, 1953)
Rami Dhoban (Hiren Bose, H/B, 1953)
Ram Jaisan Bhaiya Hamaar (Adarsh Jain, Bh, 1986)
Ram Janma (G.V. Sane, St, 1920)
Ram Janma (**Nanabhai Bhatt**, H, 1951)
Ramji Rao Speaking (Siddique, Mal, 1989)
Ramjoshi *see* **Lokshahir Ramjoshi**
Ramkali (Shyam Ralhan, H, 1985)
Ram Kasam (Chand, H, 1978)
Ram Ke Naam (**Anand Patwardhan**, H, 1992)
Ram Ki Ganga (Sharan K. Chand, H, 1984)
Ramkinker (**Ritwik Ghatak**, B, 1975: Incomplete)
Ramkudi Jhamkudi (Mohansingh Rathod, R, 1989)
Ram Lakhan (**Subhash Ghai**, H, 1989)
Ram Lakshman (Mohan Sinha, H, 1957)
Ram Lakshman (R. Thyagarajan, Tam, 1981)
Ramlal Shyamlal (TV: **Atma Ram**, H, 1978)
Ramleela (**Chandrakant**, H, 1961)
Ram Maruti Yuddha *see* Kalicha Narad
Ram Milai Jodi (H.S.Kanwal, H, 1986)
Ramnagari (**Kantilal Rathod**, H, 1982)
Ram Navami (Raman B. Desai, H, 1956)
Ramprasad (Debnarayan Gupta, B, 1947)
Ram Pratigya (*aka* Seeta Haran: Amar Varma, H, 1949)
Rampurada Ravana (Rajachandra, K, 1984)
Rampur Ka Lakshman (**Manmohan Desai**, H, 1972)
Ram Rahim (K.P. Bhave, St, 1930)
Ram Rahim (C.V. Raman, Tam, 1946)
Ram Rahim (B.A. Subba Rao, Tel, 1974)
Ram Rahim (Sushil Mukherjee, O, 1983)
Ramrajya (**Vijay Bhatt**, H/Mar, 1943)
Ramrajya (**Vijay Bhatt**, H, 1967)
Ramrajyadalli Rakshasaru (D. Rajendra Babu, K, 1990)
Ramrajyam (K. Babu Rao, Tel, 1973)
Ramrajya Vijay (G.V. Sane, St, 1926)
Ram Rakhe Ene Kon Chakhe (S.J. Talukdar, G, 1982)
Ram Ram Amtharam (Arunkumar, G, 1981)
Ram Ram Gangaram (**Dada Kondke**, Mar, 1977)
Ram Ram Pahuna (**Dinkar D. Patil**, Mar, 1950)
Ram Ravan Yuddha (*aka* Seeta Shuddhi: G.V. Sane, St, 1924)
Ram Robert Rahim (**Vijayanirmala**, Tel, 1980)
Ramshastri (**Gajanan Jagirdar**, Mar/H, 1944)
Ramshastri Ka Nyay (**Vishram Bedekar**, Mar, 1956)
Ramtaram (**Chaturbhuj Doshi**, G, 1950)
Ram Tera Desh (Swaroop Kumar, H, 1984)
Ram Tere Kitne Naam (P. Madhavan, H, 1985)
Ram Teri Ganga Maili (**Raj Kapoor**, H, 1985)
Ramu (A.C. Trilogchander, Tam/Tel, 1966)
Ramu (D. Rama Naidu, Tel, 1987)
Ramu Chanana (Purshottam Saraf, R, 1984)
Ramu Dada (Adarsh, H, 1961)
Ramude Devudu (B.V. Prasad, Tel, 1973)
Ramudu Bheemudu (**Tapi Chanakya**, Tel, 1964)
Ramudu Bheemudu (K. Muralimohana Rao, Tel, 1988)
Ramudu Kadu Krishnudu (**Dasari Narayana Rao**, Tel, 1983)
Ramudu Kadu Rakshasudu (**Dasari Narayana Rao**, Tel, 1991)
Ramudu Parashuramudu (M.S. Gopinath, Tel, 1980)
Ramudu Rangadu (P. Chandrasekhara Reddy, Tel, 1978)
Ramu Nenapena Nagarhole *see* **Nagarhole**
Ramuni Minchina Ramudu (M.S. Gopinath, Tel, 1975)
Ramu Ustad (Mohammed Hussain, H, 1971)
Ram Vanvas (*aka* Exile of Shri Rama: **S.N. Patankar**, St, 1918)
Ram Vivah (Prem Adib, H, 1949) Ranabheri (*aka* The Drums of War: R.N. Vaidya, St, 1933)
Ranabheri (G. Suryam, Tel, 1968)
Ranabheri (V. Somasekhar, K, 1990)
Ranabhoomi (Deepak Sarin, H, 1991)
Ranadevata (*aka* God of War: **Homi Master**, St, 1932)
Ranadheera (Ravichandran, K, 1988)
Ranadheera Kanteerava (N.C. Rajan, K, 1960)
Ranagarjana (*aka* What Price Loyalty: **Harshadrai Mehta**, St, 1929)
Rana Hamir (*aka* Samrat Hamir: **Baburao Painter**, St, 1925)
Ranakdevi (**S.N. Patankar**, St, 1923)
Ranakdevi (**Nanubhai Vakil**, St, 1930)
Ranakdevi (**V.M. Vyas**, G, 1946)
Ranakdevi (**Babubhai Mistri**, G, 1973)
Rana Pratap (**B.P. Mishra**, St, 1925)
Ranaranga (V. Somashekhar, K, 1988)
Ranarangam (Giribabu, Tel, 1985)
Rana Sangram (A.M. Khan, H, 1939)
Ra Navghan (*aka* Vir Pasali: **Nagendra Majumdar**, St, 1925)
Ra Navghan (W. Garcher, G, 1948)
Ra Navghan (Dinesh Rawal, G, 1976)
Ranchandi (*aka* Goddess of War: **Homi Master**, St, 1930)
Ranchandi (Babubhai Jani, H, 1934)
Ranchandi (**Mehul Kumar**, G, 1981)
Ranchayithri (**P. Bhanumathi**, Tel, 1980)
Randhali (Dwijendra Narayan Deb, A, 1979)
Randhir (*aka* Dauntless: **Sundarrao Nadkarni**, St, 1930)
Randidangazhi (**P. Subramanyam**, Mal, 1958)
Randu Mukhangal (?, Mal, 1981)
Randu Penkuttikal (Mohan, Mal, 1978)
Rang (TV: **Utpalendu Chakraborty**, B, 1986)
Rang (Talat Jani, H, 1993)
Ranga (R. Krishnamurthy, Tam, 1982)
Ranga Aur Raja (Virendra Sonik, H, 1977)
Ranga Bou (**Jyotish Bannerjee**, B, 1937)
Ranga Khush (Joginder Singh, H, 1975)
Rangalya Ratri Asha (**Raja Thakur**, Mar, 1962)
Rangam (**I.V. Sasi**, Mal, 1985)
Rangamahal Rahasya (Vijay, K, 1970)
Rangamati (Pranab Roy, B, 1949)
Ranganayaki (**Puttanna Kanagal**, K, 1981)
Ranganna Sabatham (S. Ramanathan, Tel, 1972)
Rangapanchami (**Anant Mane**, Mar, 1961)
Ranga Police (**Nip Barua**, A, 1958)
Ranga Rathnam (**Krishnan-Panju**, Tam, 1971)
Rangat Sangat (Girish Ghanekar, Mar, 1988)
Rang Berang (**Sailajananda Mukherjee**, B, 1948)
Rang Bhoomi (*aka* Diwani Duniya: **N.G. Devare**, H, 1935)
Rang Bhoomi (**M. Bhavnani**, H, 1946)
Rang Birangi (**Hrishikesh Mukherjee**, H, 1983)
Rangeen Gunah *see* Stree Dharma
Rangeen Kahani (Anjum Husaini, H, 1947)
Rangeen Raatein (**Kidar Sharma**, H, 1956)
Rangeen Zamana *see* **Ajit**
Rangeli Raja (**C.S. Rao**, Tel, 1971)
Ranger Golam *see* Raunger Gholam
Ranger Kuheli (Prahlad Sharma, B, 1988)
Ranger Saheb (Ramaprasad Chakraborty, B, 1978)
Rangi Chunariya Rane Mein Tohar (?, Bh, 1986)
Rangila (**Master Bhagwan**, H, 1953)
Rangila Jawan (S.M. Yusuf, H, 1940)
Rangila Mastana *see* Playboy
Rangila Mazdoor (S.M. Yusuf, H, 1938)
Rangila Nawab (*aka* Fighting Cavalier, Khandana Khel: **Nagendra Majumdar**, H, 1935)
Rangila Raja (*aka* Gay Prince: **Jayant Desai**, H, 1936)
Rangila Raja (Esmail, H, 1960)
Rangila Rajasthan (Bharat Vyas, H, 1949)
Rangila Rajput (*aka* The Gay Cavalier: **M. Bhavnani**, H, 1933)
Rangila Ratan (S. Ramanathan, H, 1976)
Rangile Dost (Ramanlal Desai, H, 1944)
Rangile Musafir (A. Karim, H, 1950)
Rangili (Najam Naqvi, H, 1952)
Rangili Gujaratan (S.J. Talukdar, G, 1979)
Rangilo Rajavi (*aka* Passionate Prince: ?, Kohinoor U.A., St, 1929)
Rangilo Rajput (*aka* Warrior: A.P. Kapur, St, 1929)
Rangilo Rajput (*aka* Village Warrior: **Nagendra Majumdar**, St, 1932)
Rang Mahal (Anand Kumar, H, 1948)
Rangmahal Ni Ramani (*aka* Fairy of Delhi: **Homi Master**, St, 1927)
Rangoli (*aka* A Colourful Pattern of Life: Amar Kumar, H, 1962)
Rangoon Radha (A. Kasilingam, Tam, 1956)
Rangoon Rowdy (**Dasari Narayana Rao**, Tel, 1979)
Rang Rakhya Chhe (Vithaldas Panchotia, St, 1926)
Rang Raliyan (?, Achche Sahib, H, 1947)
Rang Rasiya (Ramkumar Bohra, G, 1979)
Rangu Bajarla Jate (Shivkant Pawar, Mar, 1969)
Rangula Kala (*aka* Colourful Dreams: **B. Narasinga Rao**, Tel, 1983)
Rangula Puli (Kodi Ramakrishna, Tel, 1983)
Rangula Ratnam (**B.N. Reddi**, Tel, 1966)
Ran Haq (*aka* His Highness: Saqi, St, 1931)
Rani *see* Chandar Kalanka
Rani (**L.V. Prasad**, Tam/H, 1952)
Rani (**B.G. Bharathan**, Tam, 1981)
Rani Aur Jani (K.S.R. Doss, H, 1973)
Rani Aur Lalpari (Ravi Nagaich, H, 1975)
Rani Aur Maharani (Kanti Shah, H, 1993)
Rani Bhabani (Ratan Chatterjee, B, 1952)
Rani Chanamma *see* Kittur Chanamma
Rani Dongala Rani (**B. Vittalacharya**, Tel, 1969)
Rani Honamma (K.R. Seetarama Sastry, K, 1960)
Rani Kasularangamma (T.L.V. Prasad, Tel, 1981)
Rani Lalithangi (**T.R. Raghunath**, Tam, 1957)
Ranima (Abanish Bandyopadhyay, B, 1987)
Rani Maharani (B. Ramamurthy, K, 1990)
Rani Mera Naam (K.S.R. Doss, H, 1972)
Rani Mohana *see* Mohana Rani
Ranine Daav Jinkla (**Datta Keshav**, Mar, 1983)
Rani Rangamma (**T.R. Sundaram**?, Tel, 1956)
Rani Rashmoni (**Kaliprasad Ghosh**, B, 1955)
Rani Ratnaprabha (B.A. Subba Rao, Tel, 1960)
Rani Ṙikshawali (Radhakant, G, 1982)
Rani Rupmati (*aka* Baaz Bahadur, Love Immortal: **Bhalji Pendharkar**, St, 1931)
Rani Rupmati (S.N. Tripathi, H, 1959)
Rani Saheba (*aka* My Queen *aka* Bazarbattu: **V. Shantaram**//**Keshavrao Dhaiber**, St, 1930)
Rani Saheba (*aka* Her Highness: Chunilal Parekh/D. Desai, H, 1940)
Rani Samyuktha (**Yoganand**, Tam, 1962)
Rani Ṭheni (G.N. Rangarajan, Tam, 1982)
Rani Yar Kulandai? (**D. Yoganand**, Tam, 1972)
Ranjhan Mera Yar (Jagjit Singh Sidhu, P, 1984)
Ranjit (?, Jayadurga Combines, K, 1993)
Rank and File, The *see* **Padatik**
Rank Nu Ratan (*aka* Savior, A.P. Kapur, St, 1929)
Rank Ramani (*aka* Sitamgarh Samaj, Cruelties of Society: ?, Union Stars Film, St, 1929)
Rano (Satish Bhakri, P, 1982)
Rano Kunwar (Honey Chhaya, G, 1981)
Ranpakhare (Bhai Bhagat, Mar, 1956)
Ranpakhare (Arun Karnataki, Mar, 1980)
Rantu Janmam (Nagavalli, Mal, 1978)
Ranujana Raja Ramdev (Vallabh Choksi, G, 1974)
Ranur Pratham Bhaag (**Nabyendu Chatterjee**, B, 1972)
Ranuva Veeran (S.P. Muthuraman, Tam, 1981)
Rao Saheb (*aka* Battalion of the Blunder: **Homi Master**, St, 1931)
Rao Saheb (**Vijaya Mehta**, H, 1986)
Rape *see* Aurat Ka Inteqam
Rape of Burma *see* Ghulami
Rappadigalude Gatha (**K.G. George**, Mal, 1978)
Ra Ra Krishnaiah (Yogi, Tel, 1979)
Rareeram (?, Jagan Pics, Mal, 1986)
Rarichan Enna Pauran (**P. Bhaskaran**, Mal, 1956)
Rasakutty (**K. Bhagyaraj**, Tel, 1992)
Rasaleela (N. Shankaran Nair, Mal, 1975)
Rasathi Kalyanam (V.P. Sundar, Tam, 1989)
Rasathi Varum Naal (Rafi, Tam, 1991)
Rasave Unnai Nambi (T.K. Bose, Tam, 1988)
Rascal *see* Badmash
Rashida (*aka* Turki Hoor: **Ezra Mir**, H, 1935)
Rashifal (**Dinen Gupta**, B, 1984)
Rashk-e-Laila (**Nanubhai Vakil**, H, 1934)
Rashmi Rekha (Prafulla Barua, A, 1973)
Rashpurnima (**Niranjan Pal**, B, 1941)
Rashtraveer Shivaji (Talwar, H, 1962)
Rasikan Oru Rasikai (Balu Anand, Tam, 1986)
Rasili (Hanuman Prasad, H, 1946)
Rasili Radha (*aka* Romances of Radha: **Nanubhai Vakil**, St, 1930)
Rasili Rani (*aka* Triumph of Love: **Nagendra Majumdar**, St, 1930)
Rasi Nalla Rasi (Gopu, Tam, 1977)
Rasiya *see* Bankelal

Rastano Raja (Iqbal Sheikh, G, 1983)
Rastar Chhele (Chitta Bose, B, 1957)
Raste Raja (Prasad Rao, K, 1986)
Rasukutty *see* Rasakutty
Ratan *see* **Rattan**
Ratanlal (Nalin Duara, A, 1975)
Ratan Manjari (**Manilal Joshi**, St, 1926)
Ratan Manjari (*aka* Udta Mahal: J. Arastani, H, 1935)
Ratan Manjari (**Nanubhai Vakil**, H, 1948)
Ratan Manjari (G.P. Pawar, H, 1955)
Rater Andhakare (Agrani, B, 1959)
Rater Kuheli (Prahlad Sharma, B, 1984)
Rater Rajanigandha (Ajit Ganguly, B, 1973)
Ratha Dhanam (Sivachandran, Tam, 1988)
Ratha Kanneer (**Krishnan-Panju**, Tam, 1954)
Rathammillatha Manushyan (Jesey, Mal, 1979)
Ratha Pasam (R.S. Mani, Tam, 1954)
Ratha Pasam (K. Vijayan, Tam, 1980)
Rathilayalu (Kommineni, Tam, 1990)
Rathi Layam (P. Chandrakumar, Mal, 1983)
Rathi Manmathan (**Sasikumar**, Mal, 1977)
Rathinapuri Ilavarasi (Ramanna, Tam, 1960)
Rathi Nirvedham (**B.G. Bharathan**, Mal, 1978)
Rath Jagannathacha (Shrikant Sutar, Mar, 1984)
Rathod Kumari (Bhende, St, 1931)
Rathrikal Ninakuvedi (Alex, Mal, 1979)
Rathri Vandi (Vijayanarayanan, Mal, 1971)
Rathriyile Yatrakar (Venu, Mal, 1976)
Ratkana (Jatin Das, B, 1935)
Ratnadeep/Ratnadeepam (**Debaki Bose**, H/B/Tam, 1951)
Ratnadeep (**Basu Chatterjee**, H, 1979)
Ratnaghar (Yeshwant Pethkar, H, 1955)
Ratnagiri Rahasya/Tangamalai Rahasyam (**B.R. Panthulu**, K/Tam, 1957)
Ratnakar (*aka* Valmiki: Surendra Narayan Roy, St, 1921)
Ratnakumar (**Krishnan-Panju**, Tam, 1949)
Ratna Lutari (*aka* The Lady Cavalier: W. Garcher, St, 1933)
Ratna Lutari (*aka* The Lady Cavalier: A.M. Khan, H, 1939)
Ratnamala (**P.S. Ramakrishna Rao**, Tel, 1947)
Ratnamanjari *see* Ratan Manjari
Ratnamanjari (**Hunsur Krishnamurthy**, K/Tam, 1962)
Ratnavali (*aka* Lady from Lanka: **Manilal Joshi**, St, 1922)
Ratnavali (*aka* Sea Nymph of Ceylon: C. Legrand, St, 1922)
Ratnavali (Prafulla Ghosh, Tam, 1935)
Ratnavali (Surendra Desai, H, 1945)
Ratra Vadali Kalokhachi (Devdutt, Mar, 1969)
Ratri (Manu Sen, B, 1947)
Ratri (Tony, B, 1989)
Ratri/Raat (Ramgopal Varma, Tel/H, 1991)
Ratrir Tapasya (**Sushil Majumdar**, B, 1952)
Ratri Sheshey (Santosh Guha Roy, B, 1957)
Rattalu Rambabu (Giribabu, Tel, 1976)
Rattan (M. Sadiq, H, 1944)
Rattha Katteriyin Marma Maligai (A.M. Rajaram, Tam, 1983)
Rattha Poyi (?, Tam, 1969)
Ratthathin Ratthamey (Joe Devanand, Tam, 1981)
Rat Trap, The *see* **Elippathayam**
Raunaq (Dwarka Khosla, H, 1944)
Raunger Gholam (Incomplete: **Ritwik Ghatak**, B, 1968)
Ravan (Johnny Bakshi, H, 1984)
Ravana Brahma (**K. Raghavendra Rao**, Tel, 1986)
Ravana Rajya (**T.S. Nagabharana**, K, 1987)
Ravana Vijayam (?, Ganga Films, Tam, 1941)
Ravanude Ramudaithe (**Dasari Narayana Rao**, Tel, 1979)
Ravichandra (A.V. Sheshgiri Rao, K, 1980)
Ravi Paar (?, Maheshwari Pics, P, 1942)
Ravi Varma (Joe Simon, K, 1992)
Ravugarillu (Tharani, Tel, 1988)
Ravu Gopal Rao (Jandhyala, Tel, 1984)
Rayara Bandharu Mavana Manege (Sri Anupama Prod., K, 1993)
Rayara Sose (R. Ramamurthy/K.S. Murthy, K, 1957)
Ray of Light *see* **Dhare Aalua**
Razia (?, Malti Arts, H, 1988)
Razia Begum (**Nanubhai Desai/B.P. Mishra**, St, 1924)
Razia Sultan (**Kamal Amrohi**, H, 1983)
Razia Sultana (Devendra, H, 1961)
Reaching out to People (**Shyam Benegal**, E, 1979)
Reading the Moon Rocks (**Pradeep Krishen**, E, 1977)
Readymade Ganda (Saiprakash, K, 1991)
Reason, Debate and a Story *see* **Jukti Takko Aar Gappo**
Rebecca (**Kunchako**, Mal, 1963)
Rebellion, The *see* Baghavat
Rechukka (**P. Pullaiah**, Tel, 1954)
Rechukka (Ravindra Babu, Tel, 1985)
Rechukka Pragatichukka (**K. Kameshwara Rao**, Tel, 1959)
Reckless Rogues *see* Toofani Toli
Reclamation *see* Patitodhar
Red Archer *see* Teer-e-Qatil
Redemption *see* Priyatama
Red Letter *see* Lal Chitthi
Red Light *see* Lal Batti
Red Lion *see* Vanraj Kesari
Red Panther *see* Lal Chitta
Red Rider *see* Lal Swar
Red Rose (**Bharathirajaa**, H, 1980)
Red Seedling *see* **Chuvanna Vithukal**
Red Signal (K.P. Bhave, St, 1929)
Red Signal (Nari Ghadiali, H, 1941)
Reen Mukti (Tinkari Chakraborty, B, 1934)
Refugee (*aka* Sharanarthi: Harish, H, 1948)
Refugee (Shantipriya Mukherjee, B, 1954)
Regeneration *see* Parivartan
Region of Harmony (**Santi P. Choudhury**, E, 1980)
Registan Ki Rani (*aka* Desert Queen: A.P. Kapur, H, 1935)
Rehana (*aka* Beggar Girl: Harbans, H, 1946)
Rehearsal of Calcutta's Pageant and Viceroy's Cup (Excelsior Cinematograph, St, 1911)
Reinventing the Wheel (**Pradeep Krishen**, E, 1977)
Rekha (Mahendra Thakore, H, 1943)
Rekha (?, Ashapriya Prod, Tam, 1987)
Renaissance of Hinduism *see* Shankaracharya
Rendezvous (Rajendra Nath Shukla/**Ritwik Ghatak**, H, 1965)
Rendilla Poojari (T. Prabhakar, Tel, 1993)
Rendu Jella Seeta (Jandhyala, Tel, 1983)
Rendu Kutumbala Katha (**C.S. Rao**, Tel, 1970)
Rendu Lokam (**Sasikumar**, Mal, 1977)
Rendum Rendum Anju (Jayabharati, Tam, 1988)
Rendu Pondatti Policekaran (Relangi Narasimha Rao, Tam, 1992)
Rendurellu Aaru (B. Subba Rao, Tel, 1986)
Rendu Thokala Titta (**Balu Mahendra**, Tel, 1987)
Renuka (Ramesh Saigal, H, 1947)
Renukadevi Mahatyam (**K.S. Prakash Rao**, Tel, 1960)
Renuka Mahatme (Y.R. Swamy, K, 1956)
Repati Koduku (Muthyala Subbaiah, Tel, 1992)
Repati Pourulu (T. Krishna, Tel, 1986)
Repati Swarajyam (Parchuri Bros., Tel, 1987)
Repentance *see* Meri Bhool *or* Paap No Pashchatap
Reporter (M.R. Kapoor, H, 1946)
Reporter Raju (Dwarka Khosla, H, 1962)
Report to Mother *see* **Amma Ariyan**
Republic Day 1955 (**M. Bhavnani**, E, 1955)
Republic Day Record (**M. Bhavnani**, E, 1953)
Repu Neede (B. Bhaskara Rao, Tel, 1957)
Resham (Lekhraj Bhakri, H, 1952)
Resham Ki Dori (**Atma Ram**, H, 1973)
Reshim Gaathi (Ravi Nemade, Mar, 1988)
Reshma (**Surinder Singh**, P, 1982)
Reshma Aur Shera (Sunil Dutt, H, 1971)
Reshmachya Gaathi (**Raja Thakur**, Mar, 1954)
Reshmi Rumal (Tinkari Chakraborty, B, 1938)
Reshmi Rumal (Harsukh Bhatt, H, 1961)
Reshmi Sari (*aka* Follies of the Rich: **Nanubhai Desai**, St, 1927)
Reshmi Sari (G.P. Pawar, H, 1940)
Rest House (**Sasikumar**, Mal, 1969)
Restless Corpse, The *see* **Chithegu Chinthe**
Resurrection *see* **Duniya Kya Hai**
Retaliation *see* Pratishodh
Retina Ratan (Shridhar Prasad, G, 1982)
Ret Mahal (B.N. Chauhan, H, 1949)
Rettai Kuzhal Thuppakki (M. Karnan, Tam, 1989)
Return, The *see* **Phera**
Returning Soldier (**Ellis Duncan**, Tam/Tel, 1945)
Return of Kala Naag (*aka* Kalapani No Kaidi: **Homi Master**, St, 1927)
Return of Mr Superman (*aka* Mr Superman Ki Wapasi: Manmohan Sabir, H, 1960)
Return of Toofan Mail (Aspi, H, 1942)
Return of Wrangler Paranjpye *see* Sir Wrangler Mr R.P. Paranjpye
Reunion *see* Punarjanma *or* Gandharva Kanya
Revathi (?, Diamond Films, Tam, 1960)
Revathi (Sundar K. Vijayan, Tam, 1986)
Revathikkoru Pavakkutty (Sathyan Andhikkad, Mal, 1986)
Revenge *see* Azad Veer *or* Inteqam
Revenge (Crossbelt Mani, Mal, 1985)
Revolutionary, The *see* **Biplabi**
Revolution in Life *see* Parivartan
Revolver Raja (Karnan, Tel, 1983)
Revolver Rani (K.V.S. Kutumba Rao, Tel/H, 1971)
Rewards of Blind Passion *see* Veer Garjana
Rhino (Shashank Shankar, H, 1987)
Rhythm of Steel (**Buddhadev Dasgupta**, E, 1981)
Rhythms of a Land and its People (**Prakash Jha**, E, 1976)
Rickshawala (*aka* Bhola Raja: **Ezra Mir**, H, 1938)
Rickshawala (**Satyen Bose**, B, 1955)
Rickshawala (Shankar Mehta, H, 1960)
Rickshawala (K. Shankar, H, 1973)
Rickshawala (**Ghantamneni Krishna**, Tel, 1989)
Rickshawkaran (M. Krishnan, Tam, 1971)
Rickshaw Pullers of Jabalpur (**Saeed Mirza**, E, 1984)
Rickshaw Raji (D.S. Prakash Rao, Tel, 1978)
Ricky (Ashok Bhushan, H, 1985)
Riding Hero (**Chandrakant**, H, 1951)
Rifle Girl (**R.S. Choudhury**, H, 1938)
Rifle Girl (B.J. Patel, H, 1958)
Rihaee (**K. Ramnoth**, H, 1954)
Rihaee (**Aruna Raje**, H, 1988)
Riki Tiki Tavi (A. Zagredi, **CFS**, H, 1979)
Rikta (**Sushil Majumdar**, B, 1939)
Rimjhim (Ramesh Gupta/Sushil Sahu, H, 1949)
Rimjhim Geeton Ki (?, Rashmi Prod, H, 1986)
Ripening Seed, The (**Paul Zils**, E, 1956)
Rise, The *see* Tumhari Jeet
Rishi Moolam (S.P. Muthuraman, Tam, 1980)
Rishir Prem (**Jyotish Bannerjee**, B, 1931)
Rishta (Aslam, H, 1954)
Rishta Kaagaz Ka (Ajay Goel, H, 1983)
Rishte Naate (**K.S. Gopalakrishnan**, H, 1965)
Rishyashringar *see* **Rushya Shringa**
Rishyashringar (**S. Soundararajan**, Tam, 1941)
Rising Sun *see* Arunodaya

Pataal Nagari (1963)

Rithuganga (Vijayakumar, K, 1977)
Ritimata Prahasan (Kumar Mitra, B, 1939)
Ritual, The *see* **Ghattashraddha**
Rivaaj (Ishwarlal, H, 1947)
Rivaaj (**T. Prakash Rao**, H, 1972)
River, The *see* **Ganga**
River Named Titash, A *see* **Titash Ekti Nadir Naam**
Rivers of Life/Jeevan Ki Nadiyan (**Fali Bilimoria**, E/H, 1961)
Riyasat (Jaswant Jhaveri, H, 1955)
Road No. 303 (Dharam Kumar, H, 1960)
Road to Sikkim (**Ravindra Dave**, H, 1969)
Road to Victory (**Ezra Mir**, E, 1939)
Roaring Lion *see* Sinh Ka Bachha Sinh
Robes and the Rags *see* Dorangi Duniya
Robin Master (**Jyotish Bannerjee**, B, 1949)
Robi Shom (Bhaskar Choudhury, B, 1983)
Rocket Girl (**Nanabhai Bhatt**, H, 1962)
Rocket Rani (T. Janakiram, Tam, 1972)
Rocket Tarzan (B.J. Patel, H, 1963)
Rocky *see* Rakhi
Rocky (**Sunil Dutt**, H, 1981)
Rocky Mera Naam (Satram Rohra, H, 1973)
Rodon Bhora Basanta (Sushil Mukherjee, B, 1973)
Rogue of Rajasthan *see* Mewad No Mawali
Rohi Bhini Chundadi (Vijay B. Chauhan, G, 1986)
Rohini (Kamal Ghosh, Tel/Tam, 1953)
Roja (**Mani Rathnam**, Tam, 1992)
Roja Malare (Y. Prabhu, Tam, 1985)
Rojavin Raja (K. Vijayan, Tam, 1976)
Rojulu Marayi (Vejalla Satyanarayana, Tel, 1983)
Rojulu Marayi/Kalam Maripochu (**Tapi Chanakya**, Tel/Tam, 1955)
Role, The *see* **Bhumika**
Rollcall Ramakrishna (B. Ramamurthy, K, 1991)
Rolls-28 (Kalyan Gupta, O, 1951)
Romance *see* Dard-e-Dil *or* Dil Ki Baat *or* **Romantic India**
Romance (**Ramanand Sagar**, H, 1983)
Romance of a Youth *see* Bachha-i-Sakka
Romance of the Indian Coin (**Govind Saraiya**, E, 1961)
Romances of Radha *see* Rasili Radha
Romantic India (*aka* Romance: Mohan Sinha, H, 1936)
Romantic Lovers (Charu Ghosh, St, 1931)
Romantic Prince *see* Meri Jaan
Romeo (S.S. Nair, Mal, 1976)
Romeo and Juliet (Akhtar Hussain, H, 1947)
Romeo in Sikkim (Harikishen Kaul, H, 1975)
Ronak Mahal (**Harshadrai Mehta**, St, 1931)
Roof over the Head (**Sarvottam Badami**, E, 1952)
Room Number Nine (*aka* Kamra Number Nau: Vedi, H, 1946)
Room No. 17 (R.D. Rajput, H, 1961)
Room No. 203 (D.S. Azad, H, 1980)
Roopa (?, N.R. Desai Prod, H, 1944)
Roopavati (K. Prabhakara Rao, Tel, 1951)
Roop Basant (*aka* Madan Mohana: Haribhai Desai, St, 1928)
Roop Basant (A.P. Kapur, H, 1933)
Roop Basant (Amulakh Desai, H, 1949)
Roop Basant (A.M. Khan, H, 1955)
Roop Kahani *see* Roopkatha *or* Rooplekha
Roopkatha/Roop Kahani (Souren Sen, B/H, 1950)
Roop Ki Rani Choron Ka Raja (**H.S. Rawail**, H, 1961)
Roop Ki Rani Choron Ka Raja (Satish Kaushik, H, 1992)
Roop Kumari (**J.J. Madan**, H, 1934)
Roop Kumari (Manibhai Vyas, H, 1956)
Rooplekha/Mohabbat Ki Kasauti (**P.C. Barua**, B/H, 1934)
Roop Lekha (Mohammed Hussain, H, 1949)
Roop Lekha (Mohammed Hussain, H, 1962)
Roopli Daatanwali (S.J. Rajdev, G, 1979)
Roop Nagar (**K. Amarnath**, H, 1947)
Roop Rekha (Samar Ghosh, H, 1948)
Roop Rupaiya (Pyarelal Santoshi, H, 1949)
Roop Sanatan (Sunil Baran, B, 1965)
Roop Shoukeenan Da (Kawal Viala, P, 1983)
Roop Sundari (*aka* Ideal Womanhood *aka* Adarsha Veerangana: **Harshadrai Mehta**, St, 1927)
Roop Sundari (*aka* Wages of Sin: ?, Mysore Pics Corp, St, 1931)
Roop Sundari (Narayan Patel/Ambalal Dave, H, 1949)
Roop Sundari (**Chandrakant**, H, 1964)
Roop Tera Mastana (Khalid Akhtar, H, 1972)
Roos Gailen Saiyan Hamaar (**Nasir Hussain**, Bh, 1980)
Rootha Na Karo (Sundar Dar, H, 1970)
Rosappu Ravikkaikari (Devaraj-Mohan, Tam, 1979)
Rose of Baluchistan *see* Pahadi Noor
Rose of Kashmir *see* Kashmir Nu Gulab
Rose of Komalner *see* Komalner Ni Kusum
Rose of Rajasthan (**R.S. Prakash**, St, 1931)
Rosha Gadu (K.S.R. Doss, Tel, 1983)
Roshagara (Saiprakash, K, 1992)
Roshakkari (Madurai Thirumaran, Tam, 1974)
Roshan Ara *see* Hoor-e-Roshan
Roshanara (G.R. Sethi, H, 1932)
Roshanara (Bimal Roy Jr., B, 1953)
Roshni (Ramanlal Desai, H, 1949)
Rosy (**P.N. Menon**, Mal, 1965)
Rotation Chakravarthi (Relangi Narasimha Rao, Tel, 1987)
Roti (**Mehboob**, H, 1942)
Roti (**Manmohan Desai**, H, 1974)
Roti Kapda Aur Makaan (**Manoj Kumar**, H, 1974)
Roti Ki Keemat (Ramesh Ahuja, H, 1990)
Roudra Chhaya (Sachin Adhikari, B, 1973)
Rowdicaku Saval (**C.V. Sridhar**, Tel, 1984)
Rowdigari Pellam (**K.S. Prakash**, Tel, 1991)
Rowdilaki Rowdeelu (K.S.R. Doss, Tel, 1971)
Rowdy (**K.S. Sethumadhavan**, Mal, 1966)
Rowdy (A. Mohan Gandhi, Tel, 1984)
Rowdy Alludu (**K. Raghavendra Rao**, Tel, 1991)
Rowdy and MLA (Saiprakash, K, 1991)
Rowdygari Pellam (K.S. Prakash, Tel, 1991)
Rowdygari Teacher (Omkar, Tel, 1993)
Rowdy Inspector (P. Gopal, Tel, 1992)
Rowdyism Nasinchali (A. Kodandarami Reddy, Tel, 1990)
Rowdy No. 1 (S.S. Ravichandra, Tel, 1988)
Rowdy Police (Mouli, Tam, 1987)
Rowdy Raja (Joe Simon, K, 1984)
Rowdy Rajamma (**P. Subramanyam**, Mal, 1977)
Rowdy Rakkamma (**K.S. Gopalakrishnan**, Tam, 1977)
Rowdy Ramu (M. Krishnan Nair, Mal, 1978)
Rowdy Ramudu Konte Krishnudu (**K. Raghavendra Rao**, Tel, 1980)
Rowdy Rangadu (K.V. Nandana Rao, Tel, 1971)
Rowdy Rangamma (**Vijayanirmala**, Tel, 1978)
Rowdy Ranganna (R. Ramamurthy, K, 1968)
Rowdy Rani (K.S.R. Doss, Tel, 1970)
Royal Commander (M. Udwadia, H, 1938)
Royal Crown *see* Raj Mukut
Royal Friend *see* Nek Dost
Royal Gambler *see* Jugari Dharma
Royal Hunt, The *see* **Mrigaya**
Royal Mail (Nari Ghadiali, H, 1946)
Royal Mail (B.J. Patel, H, 1963)
Royal Musician, The *see* Vasavadatta
Royal Rivals *see* Nai Roshni
Royal Romance *see* Vijay Lakshmi *or* Shahi Ishq
Royal Savage *see* Kalika No Kop
Royal Visit to Calcutta (?, Elphinstone Bioscope, St, 1906)
Roy Choudhury (**Sailajananda Mukherjee**, B, 1947)
Ruby My Darling (**Durai**, Mal, 1982)
Rudaali (**Kalpana Lajmi**, H, 1992)
Rudo Rabari (B.J. Patel, G, 1980)
Rudra (K.S.R. Doss, K, 1989)
Rudrabina (Pinaki Mukherjee, B, 1987)
Rudrakali (**Dasari Narayana Rao**, Tel, 1983)
Rudranaga (K. Manimurughan, K, 1984)
Rudra Neta (**K. Raghavendra Rao**, Tel, 1989)
Rudra Thandavam (K. Vijayan, Tam, 1978)
Rudraveena (**K. Balachander**, Tel, 1988)
Rudri (Chi. Dattaraj, K, 1982)
Rugmangad Mohini (**Dadasaheb Phalke**, St, 1927)
Rugmangathan (P.S.V. Iyer, Tam, 1946)
Ruhi (S.U. Syed, H, 1981)
Ruins, The *see* **Khandhar**
Rukhsana (R.C. Talwar, H, 1955)
Rukhsat (Simi Garewal, H, 1988)
Rukma (P.G. Vishwambaran, Mal, 1983)
Rukmavati Ki Haveli (**Govind Nihalani**, H, 1991)
Rukmini (Bhola Addi, H, 1939)
Rukmini (**Jyotish Bannerjee**, B, 1939)
Rukmini (**K.P. Kumaran**, Mal, 1988)
Rukmini Haran (*aka* Triumph of Love: **Kanjibhai Rathod**, St, 1921)
Rukmini Haran (**Dadasaheb Phalke**, St, 1927)
Rukmini Haran (?, **Krishna Film**, St, 1929)
Rukmini Haran (**N.D. Sarpotdar**, Mar/H, 1933)
Rukmini Kalyanam (*aka* Rukmini Satyabhama: **R. Nataraja Mudaliar**, St, 1921)
Rukmini Kalyanam (**Bhalji Pendharkar**, Tam, 1936)
Rukmini Kalyanam (Vibhuti Das, Tel, 1937)
Rukmini Satyabhama *see* Rukmini Kalyanam
Rukmini Swayamvar (**Baburao Painter**, Mar/H, 1946)
Rumal (**Ramchandra Thakur**, H, 1949)
Rumbling *see* **Marmaram**
Rumtek: A Monastery Wreathed in a 1000 Rainbows (**Ramesh Sharma**, E, 1979)
Runamukthalu (**Puttanna Kanagal**, K, 1984)
Runanubandham (**Vedantam Raghavaiah**, Tel, 1960)
Runaway, The *see* Bari Theke Paliye
Rundil Onnu (A.S. Prakasham, Mal, 1978)
Runumi (Suresh Goswami, A, 1953)
Rupahi (Parbati Prasad Barua, A, 1941)
Rupaiya (G.P. Pawar, H, 1950)
Rupande Malde (Mohan Thakkar, G, 1977)
Rupantar (Ardhendu Mukherjee, B, 1951)
Rupasi (Ajit Ganguly, B, 1970)
Rupaye Dus Karod (Sikandar Bharati, H, 1991)
Rupiye Ki Kahani (Kumarsen Samarth, H, 1948)
Rupkonwar Jyotiprasad Aru Joymati (**Bhupen Hazarika**, A, 1976)
Rupor Jhumko (**Jyotish Bannerjee**, B, 1938)
Rushya Shringa (V.R.K. Prasad, K, 1976)
Rushyashrunga/Rishyashringar (**K. Mukkamala**, Tel/Tam, 1961)
Rusi (Manamohan, Tam, 1984)
Rusi Kanda Poonai (G.N. Rangarajan, Tam, 1980)
Rustom (*aka* Champion: **Dara Singh**, H, 1982)
Rustom (A. Kodandarami Reddy, Tel, 1984)
Rustom-e-Baghdad (B.J. Patel, H, 1963)
Rustom-e-Hind (Kedar Kapoor, H, 1965)
Rustom-e-Rome (Radhakant, H, 1964)
Rustom Jodi (K. Vijayan, K, 1980)
Rustom Kaun (Dharam Kumar, H, 1966)
Rustom Sohrab (**Vishram Bedekar**, H, 1963)
Rusvai (Rajat Rakshit, H, 1985)
Ruthubhedam (**Prathap Pothan**, Mal, 1987)
Rut Rangili Aayi (M.M. Pushkarna, H, 1972)

S

Saagar *see* Sagar
Saajan (**Kishore Sahu**, H, 1947)
Saajan (**Mohan Segal**, H, 1969)
Saajan (Lawrence D'Souza, H, 1991)
Saajan Bina Suhagan (Sawan Kumar, H, 1978)
Saajan Ka Ghar (Shorey Daulatavi, H, 1948)
Saajan Ki Saheli (Sawan Kumar, H, 1980)
Saajan Mere Main Saajan Ki (Hiren Nag, H, 1980)
Saakshi (**Bapu**, Tel, 1967)
Saakshi Gopal (Bhalchandra Shukla/Ramnik Vaidya, H, 1957)
Saaku Magalu/Pempudu Koothuru (**B.R. Panthulu**, K/Tel, 1963)
Saal Solvan Chadiya (**Surinder Singh**, P, 1977)
Saamna (**Jabbar Patel**, Mar, 1975)
Saamri (Tulsi/Shyam **Ramsay**, H, 1985)
Saanch Ko Aanch Nahin (**Satyen Bose**, H, 1979)
Saaphabee (G. Joykumar Sharma, Manipuri, 1976)
Saapni (Baldev R. Jhingan, P, 1965)
Saaransh (**Mahesh Bhatt**, H, 1984)
Saas Bhi Kabhi Bahu Thi (V. Madhusudhana Rao, H, 1970)
Saat Bijliyan (*aka* 7 Bijliyan: Raju Saigal, H, 1988)
Saatchi (S.A. Chandrasekharan, Tam, 1983)
Saath Saath (Raman Kumar, H, 1982)
Saathi *see* Savangadi *or* **Street Singer**
Saathi (M. Sadiq, H, 1946)
Saathi (**C.V. Sridhar**, H, 1968)
Saathi (**Mahesh Bhatt**, H, 1991)
Saat Hindustani (**K.A. Abbas**, H, 1969)
Saat Kedi (Asrani, G, 1986)
Saat Ladkiyan (?, R.S. Pics, H, 1989)
Saat Pake Bandha (**Ajoy Kar**, B, 1963)
Saat Phere (?, Filmkar Productions, H, 1970)
Saat Saal Baad (S.U. Sayed, H, 1987)
Saat Samandar Paar (Mohammed Hussain, H, 1965)
Saat Samundaron Ki Mallika (*aka* Queen of Seven Seas: **Dhirubhai Desai**, H, 1947)
Saat Sawaal (*aka* Hatimtai: **Babubhai Mistri**, H, 1971)
Saatwan Asmaan (**Mahesh Bhatt**, H, 1992)
Saaya (Shriram, H, 1961)
Saaya (Keshu **Ramsay**, H, 1989)
Saaz Aur Awaz (**Subodh Mukherjee**, H, 1966)
Saaz Aur Sanam (**J.B.H. Wadia**, H, 1971)
Saazish (Suryakumar, H, 1959)
Saazish (Kalidas, H, 1975)
Saazish (Rajkumar Kohli, H, 1988)
Sabak (M. Sadiq, H, 1950)
Sabak (Jugal Kishore, H, 1973)
Sabari (Ashok Das, B, 1972)
Sabarimalai Shri Ayyappan (S.M. Sreeramulu Naidu, Tam, 1962)
Sabarimala Shri Dharmasastha (M. Krishnan Nair, Mal, 1970)
Sabarmati (Hiren Nag, B, 1969)
Sabar Uparey (**Agradoot**, B, 1955)
Sabatham (P. Madhavan, Tam, 1971)
Sabhapati (**A.V. Meiyappan**/A.T. Krishnaswamy, Tam, 1941)
Sabhyasachi/Pather Daabi (**Agradoot**, H/B, 1948)
Sabhyasachi (Piyush Bose, B, 1975)
Sabitri (Jyotish Mukherjee, B, 1933)
Sabitri (**Naresh Mitra**, B, 1933)
Sabitri Satyavan (Dilip Mukherjee, B, 1952)
Saboot (Tulsi/Shyam **Ramsay**, H, 1980)
Sabse *see* Subse
Sabuj Dwiper Raja (**Tapan Sinha**, B, 1979)
Sabuj Pahar (Apurba Mitra, B, 1953)
Sabur Shah *see* Kamala Kumari
Sabz Bagh (Aziz Kashmiri, H, 1951)
Sabz Pari *see* Indra Sabha
Sach (**Vinod Pande**, H, 1989)
Sachaai (K. Shankar, H, 1969)
Sachaai Ibadat (?, Lokdhwani Films, H, 1987)
Sachaai Ki Taaqat (**T. Rama Rao**, H, 1989)
Sach Bhaile Sapanawa Hamaar (Amar Gupta, Bh, 1988)
Sachcha Jhutha (**Manmohan Desai**, H, 1970)
Sachcha Mera Roop Hai (*aka* Khalsa Mera Roop He: B.S. Shaad/**Surinder Singh**, P, 1976)
Sachcha Pyar (*aka* Aanchal: Niranjan, H, 1950)
Sachcha Sapna (Madhav Kale, H, 1942)
Sachche Ka Bol Bala (**Master Bhagwan**, H, 1958)
Sachche Ka Bol Bala (**Dev Anand**, H, 1989)
Sachche Moti (Om Bedi, H, 1962)
Sachchi Mohabbat *see* Wamaq Azra
Sach Hai (*aka* It's True: **R.S. Choudhury**, H, 1939)
Sachidulal (Prafulla Roy, B, 1934)
Sachimar Sansar (Bhupen Roy, B, 1971)
Sacho Haqdaar *see* Krishna Kumar
Sachun Sagapan (Anand Bhatt, G, 1980)
Sachun Sukh Sasaryiaman (Dahyabhai Bhakta, G, 1980)
Sacred Cow *see* Gomata

Sacred Ganges *see* Pavitra Ganga
Sacred Scandal *see* Nai Duniya
Sacrifice *see* **Balidan** *or* Yashodevi
Sacrifice of Babulal Bhuiya, The (Manjira Dutta, O/H, 1987)
Sadak (**Mahesh Bhatt**, H, 1991)
Sada-Kalo (Amal Kumar Basu, B, 1954)
Sadak Chhaap (Anil Ganguly, H, 1987)
Sadananda (Ananth Hiregowder, K, 1979)
Sadanander Mela (**Sukumar Dasgupta**, B, 1954)
Sadaram (V.C. Subburaman, Tam, 1956)
Sadarame (**Raja Chandrasekhar**, K, 1935)
Sadarame/Sadarama (K.R. Seetarama Sastry, K/Tel, 1956)
Sadarangam (B. Bhaskara Rao, Tel, 1984)
Sada Suhagan (**T. Rama Rao**, H, 1986)
Sadavant Savlinga (?, Kohinoor Film, St, 1924)
Sadavant Savlinga (Mahesh Chunawala, G, 1949)
Sadavant Savlinga (Sushil Vyas, G, 1977)
Sadayam (**Sibi Malayil**, Mal, 1992)
Sadgati (**Satyajit Ray**, H, 1981)
Sadguni Sushila (**Kanjibhai Rathod**?, St, 1924)
Sadhak Bama Kshyapa (Narayan Ghosh, B, 1958)
Sadhak Kamalakanta (Apurba Mitra, B, 1961)
Sadhak Ramprosad (Bangsi Ash, B, 1956)
Sadhana (V.C. Desai/M. Thakore, H, 1939)
Sadhana (Mohini Choudhury, B, 1956)
Sadhana (**B.R. Chopra**, H, 1958)
Sadhana (Prabhat Mukherjee, O, 1964)
Sadhanai (A.S. Prakasham, Tam, 1986)
Sadharan Meye (**Niren Lahiri**, B, 1948)
Sadhi Manse (**Bhalji Pendharkar**, Mar, 1965)
Sadhu Aur Shaitan (N.C. Laharry, St, 1922)
Sadhu Aur Shaitan (**A. Bhimsingh**, H, 1968)
Sadhu Judhishthirer Karcha [Ekalavya(**Robi Ghosh**), B, 1974]
Sadhu Mirandal (Mahalingam-Thirumalai, Tam, 1966)
Sadhu Ya Shaitan (*aka* The Scoundrel: M.D. Shah, H, 1939)
Sadhvi Meerabai (**Baburao Painter**, Mar, 1937)
Sadma (?, Asiatic Prod, H, 1954)
Sadma (**Balu Mahendra**, H, 1983)
Saeed-e-Havas (**Sohrab Modi**, H/Urdu, 1936)
Safar (B. Mitra, H, 1946)
Safar (**Asit Sen**, H, 1970)
Safdar Jung (**A.R. Kardar**, St, 1930)
Safed Daku *see* White Face
Safed Ghoda Kala Sawar *see* Black Rider
Safed Hathi (*aka* White Elephant, Puraskaar, The Prize: **Tapan Sinha**, H, 1977)
Safed Jhooth (**Basu Chatterjee**, H, 1977)
Safed Sawar (*aka* White Horseman, White Rider: Fram Sethna, St, 1930)
Safed Sawar (*aka* White Rider: Nari Ghadiali, H, 1941)
Sagaai (**H.S. Rawail**, H, 1951)
Sagaai (S.D. Narang, H, 1966)
Sagalikade Bomba Bomb (Avinash Thakur, Mar, 1988)
Sagan Sahu Swarthana (Bhagwan Sarang, G, 1985)
Sagar (Jairaj, H, 1951)
Sagar (Kranthi Kumar, Tel, 1985)
Sagar (**Ramesh Sippy**, H, 1985)
Sagar (Rajusingh, O, 1989)
Sagaram Shantham (P.G. Vishwambaran, Mal, 1983)
Sagara Sangamam (**K. Vishwanath**, Tel, 1983)
Sagar Balaka (**Dinen Gupta**, B, 1983)
Sagarika (Agragami, B, 1956)
Sagar Kanya (*aka* Daughter of the Sea: Henry Dargewitz, H, 1936)
Sagar Ka Sher (*aka* Lion of Sagar: Yakub, H, 1937)
Sagar Sangam (Dulal Guha, H, 1988)
Sagar Sangamey (**Debaki Bose**, B, 1959)
Sagattu Manushi (Mutyala Subbaiah, Tel, 1988)
Sage from the Sea *see* **Kondura**
Sage Soyre (Murlidhar Kapdi, Mar, 1984)
Saghakkale Munottu (**Sasikumar**, Mal, 1977)
Sagina (**Tapan Sinha**, H, 1974)
Sagina Mahato (**Tapan Sinha**, B, 1970)
Sagol Sanabi (**Aribam Syam Sharma**, Manipuri, 1983)
Saguna Sarasa (**N.G. Devare**, Tam, 1939)
Sahacharayam (C.V. Rajendran, Mal, 1984)
Sahadevan Mahadevan (Ramanarayanan, Tam, 1988)
Sahadharmini (Anupam Bannerjee, St, 1931)
Sahadharmini (**Niren Lahiri**, B, 1943)
Sahadharmini (P.A. Thomas, Mal, 1967)
Sahadharmini (K.S. Satyanarayana, K, 1973)
Sahadharmini (Ramprasad Chakraborty, B, 1987)
Sahaja (*aka* Becoming: **G. Aravindan**, Wordless, 1988)
Sahajatri (**Agradoot**, B, 1951)
Sahakar Samrat (Dattaram Tawde, Mar, 1980)
Sahalakala Sambandhi (Visu, Tam, 1989)
Sahalakala Vallavan (S.P. Muthuraman, Tam, 1982)
Sahara (**J.P. Advani**, H, 1943)
Sahara (Sunil Majumdar, B, 1948)
Sahara (Lekhraj Bhakri, H, 1958)
Sahari Bhaga (Mohammed Mohsin, O, 1985)
Sahas (Ravi Nagaich, H, 1981)
Sahasa (Soumyen Mukherjee, B, 1952)
Sahasam (Rajasekharan, Mal, 1981)
Sahasam (Suresh Krishna, Tel, 1992)
Sahasame Jeevitham (Bharati Vasu, Tel, 1984)
Sahasame Naa Upiri (**Vijayanirmala**, Tel, 1989)
Sahasam Seyara Dimbaka (Relangi Narasimha Rao, Tel, 1988)
Sahasa Samrat (**K. Raghavendra Rao**, Tel, 1987)
Sahasa Simha (Joe Simon, K, 1982)
Sahasa Simham (Damodaran, Tel, 1984)
Sahasavanthudu (**K. Bapaiah**, Tel, 1978)
Sahasi (?, Sai Arts, K, 1992)
Sahasrachirasedha Chintamani (S.D. Lala, Tel, 1960)
Saheb (Bijoy Bose, B, 1981)
Saheb (Anil Ganguly, H, 1985)
Saheb Bahadur (**Chetan Anand**, H, 1977)
Saheb Bibi Golam (**Kartick Chattopadhyay**, B, 1956)
Sahebzade (Ajay Kashyap, H, 1989)
Saheli (S.M. Yusuf, H, 1942)
Saheli (Arjun Hingorani, H, 1965)
Sahiban (Ramesh Talwar, H, 1993)
Sahib Bibi Aur Ghulam (Abrar Alvi, H, 1962)
Sahil (?, Filmnagar Studio, H, 1959)
Sahira (**S. Sukhdev/S.S. Gulzar**, H, 1980)
Sahodar (Chitta Bose, B, 1950)
Sahodarara Saval (K.S.R. Doss, K, 1977)
Sahodari (**A. Bhimsingh**/B.A. Subba Rao, Tam, 1959)
Saibaba (Aruru Pattabhi, Tel, 1950)
Saidan Jogan (B.S. Shaad, P, 1979)
Saif-e-Sulemani *see* Tilasmi Talwar
Sailaab (**Guru Dutt**, H, 1956)
Sailaab (Deepak Balraj Vij, H, 1990)
Sainik (Anjan Das, B, 1975)
Sainik (Sikandar Bharti, H, 1993)
Saint and the Peasant, The (**S. Sukhdev**, E, 1960)
Saint Arunagiri *see* Bhakta Arunagiri
Sainted Devil *see* Ek Abla
Sainthadamma Sainthadu (Devaraj-Mohan, Tam, 1977)
Saint of Paithan *see* Sant Eknath
Sairandhri *see* Keechaka Vadha
Sairandhri (**Baburao Painter**, St, 1919)
Sairandhri (*aka* Keechaka Vadha: ?, United Pics., St, 1928)
Sairandhri (**V. Shantaram**, Mar/H, 1933)
Sairandhri (*aka* Keechaka Vadham: **Kanjibhai Rathod**, Tam, 1939)
Sair-e-Paristan (*aka* Shaan-e-Khuda: **M. Bhavnani**, H, 1934)
Sair-e-Paristan (A.M. Khan, H, 1958)
Saiyan (M. Sadiq, H, 1951)
Saiyan Bina Ghar Soona (Lalji Yadav, Bh, 1987)
Saiyan Ke Gaon Mein (**Govind Saraiya**, H, 1991)
Saiyan Magan Pahalwani Mein (Radhakant, Bh, 1984)
Saiyan Se Bhaile Milanava (P.L. Santoshi, Bh, 1964)
Saiyan Se Neha Lagaibe (S.M. Abbas, Bh, 1965)
Saiyan Tore Karan (Radhakant, Bh, 1981)
Sajai Di Maang (Rati Kumar, Bh, 1983)
Sajan *see* Saajan
Sajani (*aka* Beloved: B.R. Mudnaney, H, 1947)
Sajani (**Sarvottam Badami**, H, 1940)
Sajani (Vasant Painter, H, 1956)
Sajani Go Sajani (**Tarun Majumdar**, B, 1991)
Sajan Sonalde (Subhash Shah, G, 1984)
Sajan Tara Sambharna (Abbas-Mastan, G, 1985)
Sajanwa Bairi Bhaile Hamar (Dilip Bose, Bh, 1987)
Sajarur Kanta (Manju Dey, B, 1973)
Sajeeva Murthulu (D. Mohanji, Tel, 1985)
Sajeev Murti (*aka* This Is Life: S.F. Hasnain, H, 1935)
Sajghar (**Ajoy Kar**, B, 1955)
Sajjan (Dwarka Khosla, H, 1941)
Sajjo Rani (**Govind Saraiya**, H, 1976)
Sajre Phool (*aka* Khilte Suman: **Sukhdev Ahluwalia**, P, 1981)
Sakalakala Vandugal (Jupiter Senthilkumar, Tam, 1992)
Sakarai Thevan (J. Panner, Tam, 1993)
Sakata Yogam (**R. Padmanabhan**, Tam, 1946)
Sakharpuda (Vasant Joglekar, Mar, 1949)
Sakhavu (K.S. Gopalakrishnan, Mal, 1986)
Sakher Chor (Prafulla Chakraborty, B, 1960)
Sakher Sramik (Nirmal Goswami, B, 1938)
Sakhi Gopinath (Ganesh Mahapatra, O, 1978)
Sakhi Hatim (**Nanubhai Vakil**, H, 1955)
Sakhi Lutera (S. Kerawala, H, 1934)
Sakhi Lutera (Mohammed Hussain, H, 1955)
Sakhi Lutera (Rustom Irani, H, 1969)
Sakhi Robin (B.J. Patel, H, 1962)
Sakhya Sajana (Govind Kulkarni, Mar, 1972)
Sakhya Savara Mala (Keshav Toro, Mar, 1960)
Sakida Sarpa (V. Krishnan Raju, K, 1984)
Sakkalathi (Devaraj-Mohan, Tam, 1979)
Sakkanodu (B. Bhaskara Rao, Tel, 1986)
Sakka Podu Podu Raja (S.P. Muthuraman, Tam, 1978)
Sakkubai (**Sundarrao Nadkarni**, Tam, 1934)
Sakkubai (?, Bharatlakshmi/Aurora, Tel, 1935)
Sakshatkara (**Puttanna Kanagal**, K, 1971)
Sakshigopal (Gour See/Chitta Mukherjee, B, 1949)
Salaakhen (*aka* Prison Bars: A. Salaam, H, 1975)
Salaam Aleikum (?, Oriental Film, St, 1921)
Salaam Bombay (**Mira Nair**, E/H, 1988)
Salaam-e-Mohabbat, (A. Shamsheer, H, 1983)
Salaam Memsaab (K. Parvez, H, 1961)
Salaam Memsaab (Mrinal Guha-Thakurta, B, 1975)
Salaam Memsaab (Asrani, H, 1979)
Salami (C. Vishwanath, Mar, 1960)
Salem Vishnu (?, Tam, 1990)
Salgirah (K.S. Daryani, H, 1946)
Salim Langde Pe Mat Ro (**Saeed Mirza**, H, 1989)
Salini Ente Kuttukari (Mohan, Mal, 1980)
Salivahan (A.P. Kapur, St, 1931)
Salivahanan (**Balkrishna Narayan Rao**, Tam, 1944)
Salma (Nazir, H, 1943)
Salma (**Ramanand Sagar**, H, 1985)
Saloni (**J.P. Advani**, H, 1952)
Salt *see* **Uppu**
Samadhan (**Premendra Mitra**, B, 1943)
Samadhan (Jayanta Basu, B, 1979)
Samadhan (?, Y.K. Mehra, H, 1980)
Samadhi (Ramesh Saigal, H, 1950)
Samadhi (**Prakash Mehra**, H, 1972)
Samadhi Kaduthunnan Sandhalvandi (Guna Nagendra Prasad, Tel, 1980)
Samagamam (George Kittu, Mal, 1993)
Samaj (Hemanta Gupta, B, 1944)
Samaj (Vasant Joglekar, H, 1954)
Samajam (A. Narayanarao, Tel, 1960)
Samajamlo Sthree (Mukkamala Ramakrishna, Tel, 1986)
Samajaniki Saval (S.P. Raja Rao, Tel, 1979)
Samaj Ka Shikar (?, **Madan** Theatres, H, 1931)
Samaj Ki Bhool (**Homi Master**, H, 1934)
Samaj Ko Badal Dalo (**Vijay Bhatt**, H, 1947)
Samaj Ko Badal Dalo (V. Madhusudhana Rao, H, 1970)
Samaj Na Vanked (*aka* Yug Darshan: Dakubhai Mehta, G, 1940)
Samaj Patan (*aka* Zalim Zamana: Prafulla Roy, H, 1937)
Samanaral (**Gurudas Bagchi**, B, 1970)
Samanata (**Nitin Bose**, H, 1972)
Samandaram (John Shankaramangalam, Mal, 1985)
Samandhi Poo (R.K. selvamani, Tel, 1992)
Samantak Mani *see* Krishna Satyabhama
Samanthi Poo (Mathangan, Tam, 1980)
Samapika (**Agradoot**, B, 1948)
Samapti (**Amar Mullick**, H, 1949)
Samapti *see* **Teen Kanya**
Samapti (Bijoy Basu, B, 1983)
Samar *see* **Mashaal**
Samara Simha (Joe Simon, K, 1992)
Samarpan (Nirmal Talukdar, B, 1949)
Samarpana (Profulla Kumar Rath/N. Gopal, O, 1978)
Samarpana (Lochander, Tel, 1992)
Samarpanam (Thillai Raghavan, Tam, 1974)
Samarpane (H.R. Bhargava, K, 1983)
Samarpita (**Gurudas Bagchi**, B, 1983)
Samar Saleem Simon (Sailajanand, O, 1979)
Samasya (Dayabhai Bhakt, H, 1975)
Samasya (K. Thankappan, Mal, 1976)
Samaya (Ganesh Mahapatra, O, 1975)
Samaya Bada Balabaan (**Sisir Mishra**, O, 1982)
Samayada Gombe (Dorairaj-Bhagavan, K, 1984)
Samayalkaran (Thirumalai-Mahalingam, Tam, 1974)
Samayamayilla Polum (U.P. Tomy, Mal, 1978)
Samayapurathale Satchi (Om Shakti Shri Jagadeeshan, Tam, 1985)
Samaya Sanjeevi (V.S. Raghavan, Tam, 1957)
Samay Bada Balwan (**Sohrab Modi**, H, 1969)
Samayer Kache (**Buddhadev Dasgupta**, B, 1968)
Samay Ki Dhara (**Sisir Mishra**, H, 1986)
Samayni Santakukdi (Hemant Desai, G, 1989)
Samayvarte Savdhan (B.J. Patel, G, 1967)
Sambandh (Ajoy Biswas, H, 1969)
Sambandh (Shibu Mitra, H, 1982)
Sambarala Rambabu (G.V.R. Sheshgiri Rao, Tel, 1970)
Sambhavam (P. Chandrakumar, Mal, 1981)
Sambhavame Yuge Yuge (Siddalingaiah, K, 1988)
Sambhavami Yuge Yuge (A.B. Raj, Mal, 1972)
Sambhavi (Ramanarayanan, Tel, 1993)
Sameera (Vinay Shukla, H, 1981)
Sami Potta Mudichu (R. Sundarrajan, Tam, 1991)
Samjhauta (Ajoy Biswas, H, 1973)
Sammanam (**Sasikumar**, Mal, 1975)
Sammelanam (C.P. Vijaykumar, Mal, 1985)
Samna *see* **Saamna**
Samoogam (Venu B. Nair, Mal, 1993)
Sampad (Ardhendu Mukherjee, B, 1951)
Sampark (Inder Sen, H, 1983)
Sampathige Saval (A.V. Sheshgiri Rao, K, 1974)
Sampoorna Devi Darshan (Shantilal soni, H, 1971)
Sampoorna Mahabharat (**Babubhai Mistri**, G, 1983)
Sampoorna Premayanam (N.B. Chakraborty, Tel, 1984)
Sampoorna Ramayan (**Babubhai Mistri**, H, 1961)
Sampoorna Ramayanam (E. Nagabhushanam/S.B. Narayana, Tel, 1936)
Sampoorna Ramayanam (K. Somu, Tam, 1958)
Sampoorna Ramayanam (**Bapu**, Tel, 1971)
Sampoorna Sant Darshan (Adarsh, H, 1978)
Sampoorna Santoshi Maa Ki Mahima (Hiralal R. Jain, H, 1981)
Sampoorna Teerthachi Yatra (Rajpati, Mar, 1985)
Sampoorna Teerth Yatra (**Dhirubhai Desai**, H, 1970)
Sampoorna Teerth Yatra (Rajpati, Bh/G, 1983)
Samp Tyan Jamp (Kishore Vyas, G, 1982)
Samrambham (Baby, Mal, 1983)
Samrat (Najam Naqvi, H, 1954)

Samrat (Ajit Lahiri, B, 1976)
Samrat (**Mohan Segal**, H, 1982)
Samrat (V. Madhusudhan Rao, Tel, 1987)
Samrat Ashok (*aka* Emperor Ashok: **B.P. Mishra**, St, 1928)
Samrat Ashok (K.B. Lall, H, 1947)
Samrat Ashok (**N.T. Rama Rao**, Tel, 1992)
Samrat Ashoka *see* Ashoka
Samrat Chandragupta (**Jayant Desai**, H, 1945)
Samrat Chandragupta (**Babubhai Mistri**, H, 1958)
Samrat Hamir *see* Rana Hamir
Samrat-o-Sundari (Bimal Roy Jr, B, 1987)
Samrat Prithviraj Chouhan (Harsukh Bhatt, H, 1959)
Samrat Shiladitya (*aka* The Greatest Sacrifice: **M. Bhavnani**, St, 1926)
Samsarada Guttu (Usha Raghavan, K, 1986)
Samsarada Simha (Joe Simon, K, 1992)
Samsarala Mechanic (Relangi Narasimha Rao, Tel, 1992)
Samsaram (Baburao Chavan/Vimal Kumar, Tam, 1948)
Samsaram (**L.V. Prasad**, Tel, 1950)
Samsaram (Chandru, Tam, 1951)
Samsaram (**T. Prakash Rao**, Tel, 1975)
Samsaram (Relangi Narasimha Rao, Tel, 1988)
Samsaram Athu Minsaram (Visu, Tam, 1986)
Samsaram Enbathu Veenai (S.A. Chandrasekharan, Tam, 1983)
Samsarame Saranam (M.R. Yogaraj, Tam, 1989)
Samsaramlo Sarigamalu (M.S. Kotareddy, Tel, 1976)
Samsaram Oka Chadarangam (S.P. Muthuraman, Tel, 1987)
Samsaram O Sagaram (Relangi Narasimha Rao, Tel, 1986)
Samsaram O Sangeetham (Relangi Narasimha Rao, Tel, 1985)
Samsaram Sagaram (**Dasari Narayana Rao**, Tel, 1973)
Samsaram Santhanam (V. Madhusudhana Rao, Tel, 1981)
Samsara Naradi (Barodakar/**Ch. Narayanamurthy**, Tel, 1944)
Samsara Nauka (**H.L.N. Simha**, K, 1936)
Samsara Nauka (**H.L.N. Simha**, Tam, 1948)
Samsara Nauka (D. Rajendra Babu, K, 1989)
Samsara Sangeetham (**T. Rajendar**, Tam, 1989)
Samsara Vandham (B. Subba Rao, Tel, 1980)
Samsara Veena (Mutyala Subbaiah, Tel, 1991)
Samsari (M. Krishnaratnam, Tam, 1942)
Samshayaphala (A.M. Samiulla, K, 1971)
Samskara (**Pattabhi Rama Reddy**, K, 1970)
Samson (**Nanabhai Bhatt**, H, 1964)
Samudhaya Chandhiyile (Thennavan, Tam, 1985)
Samudram (K. Sukumaran, Mal, 1977)
Samudra Madanam (**R.S. Prakash**, St, 1924)
Samudra Manthan (*aka* Ahankar Vijay, The Churning of the ocean, the Churning of the Sea: V.K. Pattani, St, 1924)
Samundar (Premnath, H, 1957)
Samundar (**Rahul Rawail**, H, 1986)
Samundari Daku (A.R. Zamindar, H, 1956)
Samvalsarangal (?, Mal, 1988)
Samyukta (K.N. Chandrasekhar Sharma, K, 1988)
Sanadhi Appanna (Vijay, K, 1977)
Sanai (**Dinen Gupta**, B, 1977)
Sanakeithel (**M.A. Singh**, Manipuri, 1983)
Sanam (**Nandlal Jaswantlal**, H, 1951)
Sanam Aap Ki Khatir (Kaka Sharma, H, 1992)
Sanamani Shodhma (Vaidya, St, 1925)
Sanam Bewafa (Sawan Kumar, H, 1990)
Sanam Tere Hain Hum (V. Menon, H, 1992)
Sanam Teri Kasam (**Narendra Bedi**, H, 1982)
Sanchalanam (K. Purnachandra Rao, Tel, 1985)
Sanchali (Abhijit, B, 1950)
Sanchari (Pappan Kunchako, Mal, 1981)
Sancharini (**Sushil Majumdar**, B, 1962)
Sanchar Suraksha *see* Communication Security
Sandarbha (Gauri Sunder, K, 1978)
Sandehi (F. Nagoor, Mal, 1953)
Sandesh (Bal Gajbar, H, 1952)
Sandesha (Nazir, H, 1940)
Sandhan (Chitta Sen, B, 1957)
Sandhana Katru (Manivannan, Tam, 1990)
Sandhi *see* Sondhi
Sandhippu (C.V. Rajendran, Tam, 1983)
Sandhya (Moni Ghosh, B, 1944)
Sandhya (Dr Vasan, Mal, 1969)
Sandhya (Mirza Masoom Baig/Sunil Kumar, H, 1975)
Sandhya (A. Kodandarami Reddy, Tel, 1980)
Sandhya-Belar Rupkatha (**Sailajananda Mukherjee**, B, 1950)
Sandhya Deeper Sikha (Haridas Bhattacharya, B, 1964)
Sandhyakenthinu Sindhuram (P.G. Vishwambaran, Mal, 1984)
Sandhyakku Virinja Poovu (P.G. Vishwambaran, Mal, 1983)
Sandhya Mayungam Neram (**B.G. Bharathan**, Mal, 1983)
Sandhya Pradeep (Anjan Mukhopadhyay, B, 1985)
Sandhya Raag (Jiban Ganguly, B, 1961)
Sandhya Raag (**Bhabendranath Saikia**, A, 1977)
Sandhya Raga (A.C. Narasimhamurthy/S.K. Bhagavan, K, 1966)
Sandhya Ragam (Govindan, Mal, 1979)
Sandhya Ragam (A.S. Ramchandra Rao, Tel, 1981)
Sandhya Ragam (**Balu Mahendra**, Tam, 1989)
Sandhya Surya (Amitava Mitra, B, 1976)
Sandhya Vandanam (**Sasikumar**, Mal, 1983)
Sandigdha (*aka* Suspicion: Prafulla Roy, St, 1932)
Sandipan Pathshala (Ardhendu Mukherjee, B, 1949)
Sangaili Thevan (**B.R. Panthulu**, Tam, 1960)
Sangai Dancing Deer of Manipur (**Aribam Syam Sharma**, E, 1988)
Sangam (R.S. Junnarkar, Mar/H, 1941)
Sangam (Kiran Kumar, H, 1954)
Sangam (**Raj Kapoor**, H, 1964)
Sangamam (Dada Mirasi, Tam, 1970)
Sangamam (**T. Hariharan**, Mal, 1977)
Sangam Chekkina Silpalu (**Vijayanirmala**, Tel, 1979)
Sanganatham (G. Ramineedu, Tam, 1984)
Sangat (**Basu Bhattacharya**, H, 1975)
Sangathan (**Shyam Benegal**, H, 1983)
Sangat Jadli Tujhi An Majhi (**Prabhakar Nayak**, Mar, 1960)
Sangdil (R.C. Talwar, H, 1952)
Sangdil (Dharam Kohli, H, 1967)
Sangdil Samaj (Ram Daryani, H, 1936)
Sangeet (**K. Vishwanath**, H, 1992)
Sangeeta (Ramanlal Desai, H, 1950)
Sangeetalakshmi (G. Surya, Tel, 1966)
Sangeetha (**Chandrasekhar Kambhar**, K, 1981)
Sangeetha Samrat (**Singeetham Srinivasa Rao**, Tel, 1984)
Sangeet Samrat Tansen (S.N. Tripathi, H, 1962)
Sange Meel Se Mulaqat (**Gautam Ghosh**, H, 1989)
Sangey Muzhangu (**P. Neelakantan**, Tam, 1972)
Sanghaganam (**P.A. Backer**, Mal, 1979)
Sangham (**M.V. Raman**, Tel, 1954)
Sangham (Joshi, Mal, 1988)
Sangharsh (**H.S. Rawail**, H, 1968)
Sangharsha (Basavaraja Kestur, K, 1976)
Sangharsha (Sunil Kumar Desai, K, 1993)
Sangharsham (P.G. Vishwamnaran, Mal, 1981)
Sangharshana (K. Muralimohana Rao, Tel, 1983)
Sanghya Balya (Sundarkrishna Urs, K, 1992)
Sangili (C.V. Rajendran, Tam, 1982)
Sangini (**Dinen Gupta**, B, 1974)
Sangram (Ardhendu Mukherjee, B, 1946)
Sangram (**Gyan Mukherjee**, H, 1950)
Sangram (**Babubhai Mistri**, H, 1965)
Sangram (Amar Pathak, A, 1968)
Sangram (Harmesh Malhotra, H, 1976)
Sangram (Lawrence D'Souza, H, 1993)
Sangrama (K.V. Raju, K, 1987)
Sangtye Aika (**Anant Mane**, Mar, 1959)
Sangu Kashi Mi (**Anant Mane**, Mar, 1967)
Sangu Pushpangal (Anbukkani, Tam, 1989)
Sanjeeva Murthalu (D. Mohanji, Tel, 1985)
Sanjh Aur Savera (**Hrishikesh Mukherjee**, H, 1964)
Sanjher Pidim (Tinkari Chakraborty, B, 1935)
Sanjher Pradeep (Sudhangshu Mukherjee, B, 1955)
Sanjhi (Pradeep Hooda, H, 1984)
Sanjh Ki Bela (Madhusudhan, H, 1980)
Sanjibani (**Sukumar Dasgupta**, B, 1952)
Sanjog (**A.R. Kardar**, H, 1943)
Sanjog (Pramod Chakraborty, H, 1961)
Sanjog (S.S. Balan, H, 1971)
Sanjog (**K. Vishwanath**, H, 1985)
Sankalp (*aka* Determination: Ramesh Saigal, H, 1974)
Sankalpa (**Agradoot**, B, 1949)
Sankalpa (P.V. Nanjaraje Urs, K, 1972)
Sankalpa (Sujit Guha, B, 1982)
Sankalpa (Hem Bora, A, 1986)
Sankalpam (Ranganath Das, Tel, 1957)
Sankat Main Swasthya Aur Safai (**Shantaram Athavale**, H, 1968)
Sankeerthana (Geetha Krishna, Tel, 1987)
Sankellu (P. Sambhasiva Rao, Tel, 1988)
Sanket (Ardhendu Mukherjee, B, 1951)
Sankhabani (Jyotirmoy Roy, B, 1951)
Sankha Bela (Agragami, B, 1966)
Sankhabish (Rathish De Sarkar, B, 1976)
Sankhachur (Jahar Biswas, B, 1988)
Sankha Mahuri (Akshay Mohanty/R.G. Gope, O, 1978)
Sankharavam (**Vijayanirmala**, Tel, 1987)
Sankha Sindoor (Manujendra Bhanja, B, 1948)
Sankha Sindoora (?, P.K. Mohanty, O, 1985)
Sankhupushpam (Baby, Mal, 1977)
Sankhu Teertham (**Vijayanirmala**, Tel, 1979)
Sankoch (Anil Ganguly, H, 1976)
Sankranti (**C. Pullaiah**, Tel, 1952)
Sanlagna Ras (**Dadasaheb Phalke**, St, 1916)
Sanmanassu Illavakkaru Samadhanam (?, Kokers Films, Mal, 1986)
Sanmitra Ki Shaitan (*aka* Friend Or Fiend: Bhaidas Kewalram, St, 1929)
Sannaham (Jose, Mal, 1985)
Sannarbham (Joshi, Mal, 1984)
Sannata (M. Sabharwal, H, 1966)
Sannata (Tulsi/Shyam **Ramsay**, H, 1981)
Sannayi Appanna (Laxmi Deepak, Tel, 1980)
Sansani (Irshad, H, 1983)
Sansar *see* **Grihalakshmi** *or* Michcha Maya Sansar
Sansar (*aka* A Phase of Life: V.K. Pattani, St, 1927)
Sansar (**S.S. Vasan**, H, 1951)
Sansar (Dilip Bose, H, 1971)
Sansar (Gouru Ghosh/**Parbati Ghosh**, O, 1971)
Sansar (Salil Sen, B, 1971)
Sansar (Madhav Shinde, Mar, 1980)
Sansar (**T. Rama Rao**, H, 1987)
Sansar Chakra (*aka* Pehla Pyar: ?, **Madan**, St, 1925)
Sansar Chakra (Ramanlal Desai, G, 1978)
Sansar Chhe Chalya Kare (Chandrima Bhaduri, G, 1983)
Sansarer Itikatha (Aravind Mukherjee, B, 1983)
Sansari (?, Savera Films, H, 1949)
Sansar Karaychay Mala (**Shantaram Athavale**, Mar, 1954)
Sansar Leela (**Balwant Bhatt**, G, 1935)
Sansar Leela (**Babubhai Mistri**, G, 1969)
Sansar Naiya (**Nanubhai Vakil**, H, 1939)
Sansar Pakharancha (**Anant Mane**, Mar, 1983)
Sansar Sagar (Bapurao Apte, H, 1939)
Sansar Simantey (**Tarun Majumdar**, B, 1975)
Sansar Swapna (*aka* Dream of Life: **Homi Master**, St, 1925)
Sanskar (*aka* Chhoti Bahu: Virendra C. Desai, H, 1940)
Sanskar (**V.M. Vyas**, H, 1952)
Sanskar (**Chaturbhuj Doshi**, H, 1958)
Sanskar (Harbans, G, 1970)
Sanskar (Udaya Shankar Das, O, 1985)
Santan (Ram Prakash/B. Damania, H, 1946)
Santan (Jyoti Swaroop, H, 1959)
Santan (Amar Pathak, A, 1974)
Santan (**Mohan Segal**, H, 1976)
Santan (**Dasari Narayana Rao**, H, 1993)
Sant Bahinabai (R.S. Junnarkar, Mar, 1953)
Sant Bhanudas (G.P. Pawar, Mar, 1953)
Sant Changdev (Gangadhar Raut, Mar, 1958)
Sant Chokhamela *see* Johar Maibaap
Sant Dnyaneshwar (**V. Damle/S. Fattelal**, Mar/H, 1940)
Sant Dnyaneshwar (Manibhai Vyas, H, 1964)
Sant Dnyaneshwar (S.N. Tripathi, H, 1981)
Sant Eknath (*aka* Saint of Paithan: **Dadasaheb Phalke**, St, 1926)
Sant Gajanan Shegavicha (**Datta Keshav**, Mar, 1987)
Sant Gora Kumbhar (**Raja Thakur**, Mar, 1967)
Santham Bheekaram (Rajasenan, Mal, 1985)
Santhanadevam (S. Nottani, Tam, 1939)
Santhanam (C.V. Ranganatha Das, Tel, 1955)
Santhanam (T. Varaprasad, Tel, 1984)
Santhanam Saubhagyam (D.S. Prakash Rao, Tel, 1975)
Santha Oru Devatha (M. Krishnan Nair, Mal, 1977)
Santha Shishunala Shareefa (**T.S. Nagabharana**, K, 1990)
Santhathi (Kaushikan, Tam, 1976)
Santha Vahate Krishnamai (Madhukar Pathak, Mar, 1967)
Santhosha Kanavugal (R.C. Sakthi, Tam, 1985)
Santi (Binoy Bannerjee, B, 1946)
Sant Janabai (G.V. Sane, St, 1925)
Sant Janabai (**N.G. Devare/N.D. Sarpotdar**, Mar, 1938)
Sant Janabai (Govind Ghanekar, Mar/H, 1949)
Sant Kanhopatra (D.S. Ambapkar, Mar, 1950)
Sant Meerabai (**Dadasaheb Phalke**, St, 1929)
Sant Namdev *see* Namacha Mahima
Sant Namdev (**Dadasaheb Phalke**, St, 1922)
Sant Namdev (Keshav Talpade, Mar, 1949)
Sant Nivrutti-Dnyandev (Madhukar Pathak, Mar, 1964)
Santo (?, P, 1979)
Santo Banto (Ajit Singh Deol, P, 1977)
Santosh (Balbir Wadhawan, H, 1989)
Santosham/Naya Admi (C.P. Dixit, Tel/H, 1955)
Santoshi Mata Vratha Mahatyam (**K. Kameshwara Rao**, Tel, 1983)
Sant Raghu (**Chandrakant**, H, 1957)
Sant Ramdas (**Raja Nene**, Mar, 1949)
Sant Ravidas Ki Amar Kahani (**Babubhai Mistri**, H, 1983)
Sant Rohidas (Dinesh Rawal, G, 1982)
Sant Sakhu (**V. Damle/S. Fattelal/Raja Nene**, Mar/H, 1941)
Sant Sakhu (**Krishnan-Panju**, K, 1955)
Sant Sakhubai (G.V. Sane, St, 1922)
Sant Sakhubai (Yeshwant S. Kothare, Mar, 1932)
Sant Sakhubai (D. Datta, Mar, 1987)
Sant Sakkubai (**Sundarrao Nadkarni**, Tam, 1939)
Sant Shiromani (Ganpatrao Bhrambhatt, G, 1965)
Sant Surdas (**Ravindra Dave**, G, 1975)
Sant Tukaram *see* Jai Vithal *or* Tukaram
Sant Tukaram (?, Kalanidhi Pics., St, 1921)
Sant Tukaram (*aka* Jai Hari Vithal: Babajirao Rane, Mar, 1932)
Sant Tukaram (K.B. Athavale, Mar, 1932)
Sant Tukaram (**V. Damle/S. Fattelal**, Mar, 1936)
Sant Tukaram (**Sundarrao Nadkarni**, K, 1963)
Sant Tukaram (Rajesh Nanda, H, 1965)
Sant Tulsidas (**N.G. Devare**, H, 1934)
Sant Tulsidas (**Jayant Desai**, H/Mar, 1939)
Sant Tulsidas (P. Bhalchandra, Mar/H, 1972)
Sant Tulsidas (Dilip Bhatt, G, 1984)
Santu Jamadar *see* Chandu Jamadar
Santu Rangili (**Manhar Raskapur**, G, 1976)
Sanwaria (*aka* Sawaria: Nasrat A. Mansoori, H, 1949)
Sanyasi (**Naval Gandhi**, St, 1924)
Sanyasi (M. Krishnaratnam, Tam, 1942)
Sanyasi (**A.R. Kardar**, H, 1945)
Sanyasi (Sohanlal Kanwar, H, 1975)
Sanyasi Raja (Piyush Bose, B, 1975)

Sapala (Devdutt, Mar, 1976)
Sapana Banika (P.D. Shenoy, O, 1985)
Sapan Suhane (Kedar Kapoor, H, 1961)
Sapath Nilam (Sachin Adhikari, B, 1972)
Sapera *see* **Sapurey**
Sapera (B.J. Patel, H, 1961)
Saphabee (**Aribam Syam Sharma**, Manipuri, 1976)
Sapna (**Kidar Sharma**, H, 1952)
Sapna (R. Kaushik, H, 1969)
Sapne Huye Sakaar (**Prema Karanth**, H, 1990)
Sapne Sajan Ke (Lawrence D'Souza, H, 1992)
Sapne Suhane (A.K. Chalukya, H, 1974)
Sapnon Ka Mandir (Pradeep Jain, H, 1991)
Sapnon Ka Saudagar (**Mahesh Kaul**, H, 1968)
Saptapadi (**Ajoy Kar**, B, 1961)
Saptapadi (**Datta Dharmadhikari**, Mar, 1962)
Saptapadi (**K. Vishwanath**, Tel, 1981)
Saptarshi (Uma Prasad Moitra, B, 1964)
Saptasajya (Kalyan Gupta, O, 1950)
Sapta Swarangal (Baby, Mal, 1974)
Saptaswarulu (**Vedantam Raghavaiah**, Tel, 1969)
Sapurey/Sapera (**Debaki Bose**, B/H, 1939)
Saqi (**J.P. Advani**, H, 1937)
Saqi (**H.S. Rawail**, H, 1952)
Sara Akash (**Basu Chatterjee**, H, 1969)
Sarai Ke Bahar (*aka* Inquilab: **Krishan Chander**, H, 1947)
Sara Jahan Hamara (Prakash Chhabra, H, 1961)
Sarala (*aka* Swarnalata: Priyanath Ganuly, St, 1928)
Sarala (**Charu Roy**, B, 1936)
Sarala (**Premankur Atorthy**, H, 1936)
Saral Biswas (**Phani Majumdar**, H, 1959)
Saram (Joshi, Mal, 1982)
Saranam Ayyappa (Dasarathan, Tam, 1980)
Saranga (**Dhirubhai Desai**, H, 1960)
Sarangadhara (**Y.V. Rao**, St, 1930)
Sarangadhara (**Homi Wadia**/S.K. Patham, Tam, 1935)
Sarangadhara (**P. Pullaiah**, Tel/Tam, 1937)
Sarangadhara (V.S. Raghavan, Tel/Tam, 1957)
Sarapat (**Anwar Hussain**, A, 1955)
Sarasa B.A. (?, Ganesh Films, Tam, 1965)
Sarasayya (**Thoppil Bhasi**, Mal, 1971)
Saraswathi (**Thikkurisi Sukumaran Nair**, Mal, 1970)
Saraswathi Sabatham (**A.P. Nagarajan**, Tam, 1966)
Saraswathiyamam (Mohankumar, Mal, 1980)
Saraswatichandra (**Govind Saraiya**, H, 1968)
Saratchandra (**Buddhadev Dasgupta**, B, 1974)
Saravarsham (Baby, Mal, 1982)
Sarbahara (**Sushil Majumdar**, B, 1948)
Sarbajan (**Suprabha Debi**/Hiren Choudhury, A, 1985)
Sarbajanin Bibahotsab (**Satu Sen**, B, 1938)
Sardar (A. Salaam, H, 1983)
Sardar (**Babubhai Mistri**, H, 1967)
Sardar (Dwarka Khosla, H, 1940)
Sardar (**Gyan Mukherjee**, H, 1955)
Sardar (**Ketan Mehta**, H, 1993)
Sardar (N. Harishchandra Rao, Tel, 1984)
Sardara Kartara (Harbux Latta, P, 1983)
Sardar-e-Awwal *see* Hero No. 1
Sardar-e-Azam (Satish Bhakri, P, 1979)
Sardar Krishnama Nayudu (A. Kodandarami Reddy, Tel, 1987)
Sardar Paparayudu (**Dasari Narayana Rao**, Tel, 1980)
Sardar Ramudu (Bhargava, Tel, 1984)
Sardar Vallabhbhai Patel (**Kantilal Rathod**, E, 1976)
Sa Re Ga Ma Pa (**Satyen Bose**, H, 1972)
Sarfarosh *see* Baghi
Sarfarosh (*aka* Brave Hearts: **A.R. Kardar**, St, 1930)
Sarfarosh (Dharam Kumar, H, 1964)
Sarfarosh (**Dasari Narayana Rao**, H, 1985)
Sargam (P.L. Santoshi, H, 1950)
Sargam (**K. Vishwanath**, H, 1979)
Sargam (**Dinen Gupta**, B, 1987)
Sargam (**T. Hariharan**, Mal, 1992)
Sarhad (Shankar Mukherjee, H, 1960)
Sarhad (**J.P. Dutta**, H, 1990)
Sarhadi Lutera (S.M. Sagar, H, 1966)
Sarigamalu (Kranthi Kumar, Tel, 1993)
Sario Thetto (**Thikkurisi Sukumaran Nair**/V.A. Reynold, Mal, 1953)
Sarisreep (**Nabyendu Chatterjee**, B, 1987)
Saritha (Govindan, Mal, 1977)
Sariyana Jodi (V. Prabhakaran, Tam, 1989)
Sarja (**Rajdutt**, Mar, 1987)
Sarkar (**K. Amarnath**, H, 1951)
Sarkarai Pandal (Gangai Amaran, Tam, 1988)
Sarkarakke Saval (V. Somasekhar, K, 1993)
Sarkari Mehmaan (N.B. Kothari, H, 1978)
Sarkari Pahune (**Master Vinayak**, Mar, 1942)
Sarnalayam (**R. Sundararajan**, Tam, 1983)
Sarojini *see* Ghor Pratigna
Sarojini (?, Kohinoor Film, St, 1928)
Sarojini (T.G. Lalwani, H, 1937)
Sarojini (A.L. Ramesh, H, 1949)
Sarothi (**Bhabendranath Saikia**, A, 1991)
Sarovaram (Jesey, Mal, 1993)
Sarovar Ki Sundari (*aka* Lady of the Lake: **R.S. Choudhury**, St, 1928)
Sarovar Ki Sundari (*aka* Lady of the Lake: A.M. Khan, H, 1942)
Sarpakadu (J.D. Thottan, Mal, 1965)
Sarpa Kavalu (S.N. Singh, K, 1975)
Sarpam (Baby, Mal, 1979)
Sarpanch (Veerendra, P, 1981)
Sarpayagam (Parachuri Bros., Tel, 1991)
Sarphira (Ashok Gaikwad, H, 1992)
Sarsaperila of W. Major Company (**Hiralal Sen**, St, 1905)
Sartaj (S. Khalil, H, 1950)
Sarvabhowmudu (S.S. Ravichandra, Tel, 1989)
Sarvadhikari (**T.R. Sundaram**, Tam, 1951)
Sarvagna Murthy (Aruru Pattabhi, K, 1965)
Sarvakalasala (Venu Nagavalli, Mal, 1987)
Sarvamangala (Chaduranga, K, 1968)
Sarvan Shaktimayam (P.R. Somasundar, Tam, 1986)
Sarvasakshi (Ramdas Phutane, Mar, 1978)
Sarvasreshtha (Dr. Shreeram Mali, Mar, 1988)
Sarvekkalu (**Thoppil Bhasi**, Mal, 1976)
Sasar Maher (D.S. Ambapkar, Mar, 1954)
Sasidharan (T. Janakiram, Mal, 1950)
Sasirekha Parinayam *see* Maya Bazaar
Sasirekha Sabatham (U.V. Babu, Tel, 1991)
Sassi Punnu *see* Bulbul-e-Punjab
Sassi Punnu (**Harshadrai Mehta**, St, 1928)
Sassi Punnu (**Chimanlal Luhar**/S.R. Apte, H, 1932)
Sassi Punnu (?, Indra Movietone, P, 1939)
Sassi Punnu (**J.P. Advani**, H/P, 1946)
Sassi Punnu (**S.P. Bakshi**, P, 1965)
Sassi Punnu (Satish Bhakri, P, 1983)
Sasta Khoon Mehnga Pyar (?, Sharda Films, H, 1970)
Sasthi Ki Shanti (**Jyotish Bannerjee**, St, 1928)
Sasthi Viratam (R. Thyagarajan, Tam, 1983)
Sasti (Brindaban Jena, O, 1989)
Sasti Dulhan Mehnga Dulha (Bhappi Sonie, H, 1985)
Sastram Jayichu Manushyan Thottu (A.B. Raj, Mal, 1973)
Sasural (**Chaturbhuj Doshi**, H, 1941)
Sasural (**T. Prakash Rao**, H, 1961)
Sasural (Govind Moonis, H, 1984)
Sasurvas (**Bhalji Pendharkar**, Mar, 1946)
Sasurvasheen (Babasaheb S. Fattelal, Mar, 1978)
Sasu Varchad Javai (**Rajdutt**, Mar, 1983)
Satah Se Uthata Admi (**Mani Kaul**, H, 1980)
Satajanmacha Sobti (**Anant Mane**, Mar, 1959)
Satan's Victim *see* Shaitani Chakkar
Satan Weeps *see* Maya Jaal
Sat Bhai (Taru Mukherjee, B, 1963)
Sat Bhai Champa (Chitrasarathi, B, 1978)
Satero Bachhar Pare (Girin Choudhury/Biren Das, B, 1949)
Sat Guru Teri Oat (Kaka Sharma, P, 1974)
Sathan Sollai Thattathe (Ramanarayanan, Tam, 1990)
Sathe Satyam (**Dinen Gupta**, B, 1982)
Sathi (**Madhu**, Mal, 1972)
Sathi Hara (**Sukumar Dasgupta**, B, 1961)
Sathya (Suresh Krishna, Tam, 1988)
Sathyam (S.A. Kannan, Tam, 1976)
Sathyam (M. Krishnan Nair, Mal, 1980)
Sathyam Adhu Nichyam (T. Dorairaj, Tam, 1992)
Sathyam Sundaram (K.S. Rao, Tam, 1981)
Sathyam Thavarathe (Pondy Selvaraj, Tam, 1968)
Sathya Prajhinja (Suresh Unnithan, Mal, 1992)
Sathya Shodhanai *see* Gunasagari
Sathyathinde Nizhalil (Babu Nathencode, Mal, 1975)
Sathya Vakku (Aravindaraj, Tam, 1990)
Sati *see* Daksha Yagna
Sati (*aka* Daksha Yagna: ?, **Madan** Theatres, St, 1922)
Sati (**Amar Mullick**, B, 1954)
Sati (**Aparna Sen**, B, 1989)
Sati Ahalya (?, Chandra Bharati Cinetone, Tam, 1935)
Sati Ahalya (**T.R. Sundaram**, Tam, 1937)
Sati Ahalya (Vasant Painter, H, 1949)
Sati Ahalya (Lal Mohan Ghosh, B, 1956)
Sati Ahilya *see* Jai Ambe Ma
Sati Analde *see* Shetalne Kanthe
Sati Analde (Ramnik Acharya, G, 1956)
Sati Anjani *see* Hanuman Janma
Sati Anjani (*aka* The Birth of Hanuman: **S.N. Patankar**, St, 1922)
Sati Anjani (*aka* Hanuman Janma: ?, British-India Film, St, 1932)
Sati Anjani (*aka* Hanuman Janma: **Kanjibhai Rathod**, H, 1934)
Sati Annapurna *see* Janam Janam Ke Phere
Sati Ansuya *see* Mahasati Ansuya *or* Datta Janma
Sati Ansuya (Madanrai Vakil, H, 1933)
Sati Ansuya (Fram Sethna, Tam, 1937)
Sati Ansuya (**Dhirubhai Desai**, H, 1956)
Sati Ansuya (**Kadaru Nagabhushanam**, Tel, 1957)
Sati Ansuya (B.A. Subba Rao, Tel, 1971)
Sati Ansuya (A. Sanjiva Rao, O, 1978)
Sati Ansuya (S.J. Rajdev, G, 1978)
Sati Arundhati (K.V. Nandana Rao, Tel, 1968)
Sati Aur Bhagwan (Shantilal Soni, H, 1982)
Sati Behula (Sunil Ganguly, A/B, 1953)
Saticha Vaan (**Datta Dharmadhikari**, Mar, 1969)
Satichi Punyayi (**Datta Dharmadhikari**, Mar, 1980)
Sati Jasma (**Homi Master**, St, 1926)
Sati Jasma (**V.M. Vyas**, G, 1947)
Sati Jasma Odan (**Chandrakant Sangani**, G, 1976)
Sati Ka Shaap *see* Sati No Sraap
Sati Kausalya (?, Associated Films, St, 1931)
Sati Lakshmi (**Jyotish Bannerjee**, St, 1925)
Sati Leelavathi (**Ellis Duncan**, Tam, 1936)
Sati Madalasa (**S.N. Patankar**, St, 1920)
Sati Madalasa (**B.P. Mishra**, H, 1932)
Sati Madalasa (**Jayant Desai**, H, 1955)
Sati Madalasa (Girish Manukant, G, 1984)
Sati Madri (**Chandulal Shah/N.G. Devare**, St, 1927)
Sati Mahananda (*aka* Song of Celestial: Baburao Patel, H, 1933)
Sati Mahananda (Baburao Chavan, Tam, 1940)
Sati Mandodhari (Jethalal Joshi, St, 1931)
Sati Menadevi (*aka* Bolto Lekh, Costly Couplet: P.J. Jhaveri, St, 1926)
Sati Murali (**Balkrishna Narayan Rao**, Tam, 1940)
Sati Naagkanya (**Babubhai Mistri**, H, 1956)
Sati Naagkanya (**Babubhai Mistri**, H, 1982)
Sati Nalayini (T.R.S. Gopu, K, 1957)
Sati Nari (Pankaj, H, 1963)
Sati Narmada (**Kanjibhai Rathod**, St, 1923)
Sati Narmada (*aka* Har Har Gange: Ishwarlal, H, 1950)
Sati No Sraap (*aka* Sati Ka Shaap, Silent Curse: **Manilal Joshi**, St, 1923)
Sati Padmini (**Baburao Painter**, St, 1924)
Sati Pariksha (**Nanubhai Vakil**, H, 1957)
Sati Parvati *see* Daksha Yagna
Sati Parvati (*aka* Daksha Yagna: Vishnupant Divekar, St, 1920)
Sati Pingala (G.V. Sane, St, 1928)
Sati Pingala (*aka* Pingala: D.K. Kale, H, 1937)
Satir Dehatyaag (Manu Sen, B, 1954)
Sati Sakkubai (**Kadaru Nagabhushanam**, Tel, 1954)
Sati Sakkubai (**Vedantam Raghavaiah**, Tel, 1965)
Sati Sakkubai (N.S. Dhananjaya, K, 1985)
Sati Sarala (Abhaycharan Lahiri, St, 1930)
Sati Sardarba (**Nanubhai Desai**, St, 1924)
Sati Saroj (*aka* Shiyal Ni Kasoti: ?, Saraswati Film, St, 1926)
Sati Savitri (**Baburao Painter**, St, 1927)
Sati Savitri (*aka* Savitri Satyavan: Pandurang Talegiri, St, 1927)
Sati Savitri (Dinkar Bidkar, St, 1931)
Sati Savitri (**Chandulal Shah**, H/G, 1932)
Sati Savitri (**Kadaru Nagabhushanam**, Tel/Tam, 1957)
Sati Savitri (Shantilal Soni, H, 1964)
Sati Savitri (P.R. Kaundinya, K, 1965)
Sati Savitri (B.A. Subba Rao, Tel, 1977)
Sati Seeta (?, Kohinoor Film, St, 1924)
Sati Seeta (**H.M. Reddy**, H, 1946)
Sati Seeta Lav Kush (Jagdish?, H, 1981)
Sati Shakthi (Kanagal Prabhakara Sastry, K, 1963)
Sati Simantini (**Dhiren Ganguly**, St, 1924)
Sati Simantini (**Manilal Joshi**, St, 1925)
Sati Simantini (Gunamaya Bannerjee, B, 1950)
Sati Sone *see* Halaman Jethvo
Sati Sone (*aka* Halaman Jethvo: **Homi Master**, St, 1924)
Sati Sone (Madanrai Vakil, H, 1932)
Sati Sone (*aka* Halaman Jethvo: **Chaturbhuj Doshi**, G, 1948)
Sati Sorath (B.J. Patel, G, 1978)
Sati Sukanya (**T.R. Sundaram**/D.V. Chari, Tam, 1942)
Sati Sukanya (Raman B. Desai, G, 1949)
Sati Sukanya (**Chandramohan**, Tel, 1959)
Sati Sukanya (Y.R. Swamy, K, 1967)
Sati Sulochana (G.V. Sane, St, 1921)
Sati Sulochana (**Y.V. Rao**, K, 1934)
Sati Sulochana (**P. Sambandam Mudaliar**, Tam, 1934)
Sati Sulochana (Mamasaheb Shinde, H, 1935)
Sati Sulochana (Rajanikanth, Tel, 1961)
Sati Sulochana (S.N. Tripathi, H, 1969)
Sati Sumati (**Vedantam Raghavaiah**, Tel, 1967)
Sati Tara (*aka* Vali Sugriva Yudh, War between Vali and Sugriva: Shinde, St, 1925)
Sati Toral (**Kanjibhai Rathod**, St, 1922)
Sati Toral (*aka* Zulmi Jesal: Chunilal Parekh, H, 1935)
Sati Toral (**Nandlal Jaswantlal**, H, 1947)
Sati Toral (Vinod Parmar, G, 1989)
Sati Tulasi (**Ch. Narasimha Rao**, Tel, 1936)
Sati Tulasi (M.A.N. Iyengar, K, 1949)
Sati Tulasi (V. Madhusudhana Rao, Tel, 1959)
Sati Usha Sundari (**Raja Sandow**, St, 1930)
Sati Vaishalini (*aka* Janam Janam Ka Naata: Sadhu Singh, H, 1959)
Sati Veermati (*aka* Jagdev Parmar: **S.N. Patankar**, St, 1923)
Sati Vijaya *see* Bhakta Vijaya
Sati Vijaya (?, British India Film, St, 1930)
Sati Vijaya (K.J. Parmar, H, 1948)
Sati Vimala *see* Swarg Ki Sidhi
Satma (Sachin Adhikari, B, 1981)
Satna Parkha (G.K. Mehta, G, 1976)
Sat Number Bari (**Sukumar Dasgupta**, B, 1946)
Sat Number Kayedi (**Sukumar Dasgupta**, B, 1953)
Satrathil Oru Rathri (N. Shankaran Nair, Mal, 1978)
Satruvu *see* Shatruvu
Sat Saliyan (Karunesh Thakur, P, 1964)
Satsang (?, Aurora Cinema, St, 1927)
Sat Shri Akal (Chaman Nillay, P, 1977)
Satta Bazaar (**Ravindra Dave**, H, 1959)
Sattai Illatha Pambaram (Erode N. Murugesh, Tam, 1983)

Sattai Rani (K.S. Rami Reddy, Tam, 1972)
Sattam Oru Iruttarai (S.A. Chandrasekharan, Tam, 1981)
Sattam Oru Vilayattu (S.A. Chandrasekharan, Tam, 1987)
Sattam Sirikkirathu (Ramanna, Tam, 1982)
Satta No Mad (*aka* Wages of Virtue: **Harshadrai Mehta**, St, 1929)
Sattathai Thiruthungal (Ramanarayanan, Tam, 1984)
Sattathin Thirappu Vizha (Shankar Ganesh, Tam, 1989)
Sattawis Down *see* **27 Down**
Satteche Prayog (V.N. Bhatt/**Vishram Bedekar**, Mar, 1935)
Sattekalapu Sattaiah (**K. Balachander**, Tel, 1969)
Satte Pe Satta (Raj N. Sippy, H, 1981)
Satwadi Raja Harishchandra *see* Satyavadi Raja Harishchandra
Satya (Suresh Krishna, Tel, 1988)
Satyabhama (**Dadasaheb Phalke**, St, 1925)
Satyabhama (**Y.V. Rao**, Tel, 1942)
Satyabhama (M.S. Mani, Mal, 1963)
Satyabhama (**K. Raghavendra Rao**, Tel, 1981)
Satyagraham (Jandhyala, Tel, 1988)
Satya Harishchandra (**R. Nagendra Rao**, K, 1943)
Satya Harishchandra (**Hunsur Krishnamurthy**, K/**K.V. Reddy**, Tel, 1965)
Satya Harishchandra/Raja Harishchandra (**C.S. Rao**, Tel/O, 1984)
Satyajit Ray (**Shyam Benegal**, E, 1984)
Satyajit Ray: An Introspection (K. Bikram Singh, E, 1990)
Satya Jyothi (K. Rangaraju, K, 1986)
Satyakam (**Hrishikesh Mukherjee**, H, 1969)
Satyame Jayam *see* **Gharana Donga**
Satyame Jayam (P.V. Ramarao, Tel, 1967)
Satyameva Jayate *see* Unmayin Veetri
Satyamev Jayate (Raj N. Sippy, H, 1987)
Satyam Neeye (P. Madhavan, Tam, 1984)
Satyam Shivam (**K. Raghavendra Rao**, Tel, 1981)
Satyam Shivam Sundaram (**Raj Kapoor**, H, 1978)
Satyam Shivam Sundaram (K. Subba Rao, Tel, 1985)
Satyam Shivam Sundaram (V.S.R. Das, K, 1987)
Satyam Shivam Sundaram (?, Azhagar Films, Tam, 1990)
Satyanarayan *see* Bhikari
Satyanarayan (V.S. Nirantar, St, 1922)
Satyanarayana Mahatyam (Rajanikanth, Tel, 1964)
Satyanarayana Vratam (**C. Pullaiah**, Tel, 1938)
Satyanathayam (?, Arunodaya Kalamandir, Tam, 1950)
Satyaniki Sankellu (**K.S. Prakash Rao**, Tel, 1974)
Satya Pareekshe (Srinivas, K, 1987)
Satya Pathe (Amar Choudhury, B, 1935)
Satya Sandesha (K.M. Khelendar, K, 1991)
Satya Seelan (B. Sampathkumar, Tam, 1936)
Satya Shodhanai *see* **Gunasagari**
Satyavadi Harishchandra (**Dhirubhai Desai**, G, 1948)
Satyavadi Raja Harishchandra (**Dadasaheb Phalke**, St, 1917)
Satyavadi Raja Harishchandra (?, **J.F. Madan**, St, 1917)
Satyavadi Raja Harishchandra (**J.J. Madan**, H, 1931)
Satyavadi Raja Harishchandra (Shantilal Soni, R/G, 1989)
Satyavani (S. Nottani, Tam, 1939)
Satyavan Savithri (P.G. Vishwambaran, Mal, 1977)
Satyavan Savitri *see* Sati Savitri
Satyavan Savitri (**Dadasaheb Phalke**, St, 1914)
Satyavan Savitri (Manibhai Vyas, G/H, 1948)
Satyavan Savitri (Dinesh Rawal, G, 1963)
Satyavanthudu (P.G. Vishwambaran, Tel, 1980)
Satyavatharam (?, Arunoday Kalamandir, Tam, 1951)
Satyavijaya (**S.N. Patankar**, St, 1926)
Saubhagya (**Chimanlal Luhar**, H, 1940)
Saubhagya (**Datta Dharmadhikari**, Mar, 1953)
Saubhagya Kankshini (Bal Saraf, Mar, 1974)
Saubhagya Lakshmi (**V.M. Vyas**, H, 1934)
Saubhagya Lakshmi (**B. Vittalacharya**, K, 1953)
Saubhagya Lakshmi (Bhargava, K, 1987)
Saubhagya Lene (**Datta Keshav**, Mar, 1985)
Saubhagya Sindoor (**Chandrakant Sangani**, G, 1977)
Saubhagya Sundari (**Homi Master**, H, 1933)
Saubhagyavan (V. Ravindra, Mar, 1980)
Saubhagyavati (Fram Sethna, Tam, 1939)
Saubhagyavati (Jampana, Tam/Tel, 1957)
Saubhagyavati (P. Chandrasekhara Reddy, Tel, 1975)
Saubhagyavati Bhava (Prem Manik, Mar/H, 1958)
Sauda (Sudesh Issar, H, 1974)
Sauda (TV: **B.R. Chopra**, H, 1992)
Saudagar (M.I. Dharamsey, H, 1951)
Saudagar (*aka* Trader: Sudhendu Roy, H, 1973)
Saudagar (**Subhash Ghai**, H, 1991)
Saudamini (P.C. Joshi, H, 1950)
Saudamini (**Kadaru Nagabhushanam**, Tel/Tam, 1951)
Sau Din Saas Ke (Vijay Sadanah, H, 1980)
Saugandh (*aka* The Pledge: **Hemchandra Chunder**, H, 1942)
Saugandh (G.K. Ramu, H, 1961)
Saugandh (Ravi Nagaich, H, 1982)
Saugandh (Raj Sippy, H, 1991)
Sau Ka Note (Yeshwant Pethkar, H, 1955)
Sau Karod (**Dev Anand**, H, 1991)
Saundamevide? Bandamevide? (**Sasikumar**, Mal, 1984)
Saundarya Jwala *see* Falak Numa
Saundarya Pooja (B.K. Pottekkat, Mal, 1973)
Saundarya Sura (*aka* Wine of Youth: **Harshadrai Mehta**, St, 1928)
Saurashtra Veer (**Nanubhai Desai**, St, 1925)
Saurashtrano Sinh-Chhelbhai (**Manhar Raskapur**, G, 1980)
Sau Saal Baad (B.K. Dubey, H, 1966)
Sau Saal Baad (Mohan Bhakri, H, 1989)
Sau Saal Beet Gaye (?, Natraj Prod, H, 1970)
Sautela Bhai (**Mahesh Kaul**, H, 1962)
Sautela Pati (**B.R. Ishara**, H, 1985)
Sauteli Maa *see* Step Mother
Sautuni (Akshay Mohanty, O, 1979)
Savage Princess, The *see* **Aan**
Savaj (**Anant Mane**, Mar, 1980)
Saval (Niranjan, H, 1943)
Saval (R. Krishnamurthy, Tam, 1981)
Saval (B. Subba Rao, Tel, 1982)
Saval (Ramesh Talwar, H, 1982)
Savale Samali (Mallaiyam Rajagopal, Tam, 1971)
Savalige Saval (Ramesh-Shivram, K, 1978)
Saval Mazha Aika (**Anant Mane**, Mar, 1964)
Savalukku Saval (H.S. Venu, Tam/Tel, 1972)
Savalya Tandel (Dr. Deshmukh?, South Indian Film of Sholapur, St, 1927)
Savalya Tandel (Madhukar Bavdekar, Mar, 1942)
Savangadi/Saathi (*aka* Companion: **P.Y. Altekar**, Mar/H, 1938)
Savasagallu (B. Subba Rao, Tel, 1977)
Savasam (Raja of Mirzapur, Tel, 1952)
Sava Ser Gehnu (?, Gol Behar Singh, B, 1989)
Savat (**Dinkar D. Patil**, Mar, 1980)
Savathiya Neralu (Y.R. Swamy, K, 1979)
Savati Koduku (Y. Rangarao, Tel, 1963)
Savati Matsar (Shinde, St, 1930)
Savdhan (Tulsi Lahiri, B, 1940)
Savdhan (**Datta Dharmadhikari**, H, 1954)
Savdhan (Sudhir Ghosh, B, 1956)
Save Energy Through Efficient Motors (**Kantilal Rathod**, E, 1989)
Savera (*aka* The Dawn: Virendra Desai, H, 1942)
Savera (**Satyen Bose**, H, 1958)
Savera (V.K. Sharma, H, 1972)
Savere Wali Gadi (**Bharathirajaa**, H, 1985)
Saviour, The *see* Rank Nu Ratan *or* Apath Bhandavulu
Savithri (**C. Pullaiah**, Tel, 1933)
Savithri (?, **Madan** Theatres, Tam, 1933)
Savithri (Ramanandam, Tel, 1933)
Savithri (**Y.V. Rao**, Tam, 1941)
Savithri (**B.G. Bharathan**, Tam, 1980)
Savithri (T.S. Ranga, K, 1980)
Savithri Poru (**T.R. Sundaram**?, Tel, 1952)
Savitri (**S.N. Patankar**/A.P. Karandikar/V.P. Divekar, St, 1912)
Savitri (*aka* Savitri Satyavan: Giorgio Mannini, St, 1923)
Savitri (**H.M. Reddy**, H, 1933)
Savitri (**Bhalji Pendharkar**, Mar, 1936)
Savitri (**Franz Osten**, H, 1937)
Savitri (**Phani Majumdar**, H, 1961)
Savitri (Murlidhar Kapdi, Mar, 1983)
Savitri Satyavan *see* **Savitri** *or* Sati Savitri
Savkari Pash (**Baburao Painter**, St, 1925)
Savkari Pash (**Baburao Painter**, Mar, 1936)
Savkharavam (**Ghantamneni Krishna**, Tel, 1987)
Savki Maa (Raja Yagnik, G, 1948)
Savli Premachi (**Datta Keshav**, Mar, 1980)
Savvasher (Sachin, Mar, 1984)
Sawaal *see* Saval
Sawa Lakh Se Ek Ladaun (**Dara Singh**, P, 1976)
Sawan (Dwarka Khosla, H, 1945)
Sawan (Ramesh Tiwari, H, 1959)
Sawan Aya Re (**Kishore Sahu**, H, 1949)
Sawan Bhadon (**Ravindra Dave**, H, 1949)
Sawan Bhadon (**Mohan Segal**, H, 1970)
Sawan Ka Mahina (Kalpataru, H, 1989)
Sawan Ke Geet (R. Bhattacharya, H, 1978)
Sawan Ki Ghata (**Shakti Samanta**, H, 1966)
Sawan Ko Aane Do (Kanak Mishra, H, 1979)
Sawan Ri Teej (Naval Mathur, R, 1984)
Sawaria *see* Sanwaria
Sayaji-di-Maang Hamaar (Ratikumar, Bh, 1983)
Sayam Sandhya (?, Mal, 1986)
Sayba Mora (**Mehul Kumar**, G, 1986)
Sayujiyam (Premkumar, Mal, 1979)
Sayyad Waris Shah (Sewak/R.K. Sharma, H, 1980)
Sazaa (Fali Mistry, H, 1951)
Sazaa (Chand, H, 1972)
Sazaaye Maut (Vidhu Vinod Chopra, H, 1981)
Scale, The *see* Thrasam
Scales of Justice, The *see* **Insaaf Ka Tarazu**
Scattered Flowers *see* Udhiri Pookal
Scene No. 7 (Ambili, Mal, 1985)
Scenes from Alibaba (**Hiralal Sen**, St, 1901)
Scenes from Bhramar (**Hiralal Sen**, St, 1901)
Scenes from Buddhadev (**Hiralal Sen**, St, 1901)
Scenes from Dol Leela (**Hiralal Sen**, St, 1901)
Scenes from Hariraj (**Hiralal Sen**, St, 1901)
Scenes from Maner Matan (**Hiralal Sen**, St, 1903)
Scenes from Sarala (**Hiralal Sen**, St, 1901)
Scenes from Seetaram (**Hiralal Sen**, St, 1901)
Scenes from Sonar Swapan (**Hiralal Sen**, St, 1903)
Scenes of the River Godavari (**Dadasaheb Phalke**, St, 1914)
Scented Devil *see* Nek Abla
School, The (**Paul Zils**, E, 1956)
School Master (**Chimanlal Luhar**, H, 1943)
School Master/Badi Panthulu (**B.R. Panthulu**, K/H/Tel, 1958)
School Master (**Puttanna Kanagal**, Mal, 1964)
School Master (**B.R. Panthulu**, Tam, 1973)
School Master (Govind Tej, O, 1985)
Science for Children (**Santi P. Choudhury**, E, 1963)
Science-4 (**S. Sukhdev**, E, 1973)
Science India (**Basu Bhattacharya**, E, 1982)
Scientists of Tomorrow (**Ritwik Ghatak**, E, 1967)
Scissors (**Ritwik Ghatak**, B, 1962)
Scoundrel, The *see* Sadhu Ya Shaitan
Scout Camp (**Kidar Sharma**, H, 1958)
Sea Forts (**Jabbar Patel**, E, 1990)
Sea Goddess *see* Dariyai Devangana
Sea Nymph of Ceylon *see* Ratnavali
Search, The *see* Shodh
Search for Self-Reliance (**Santi P. Choudhury**, E, 1975)
Search for Truth *see* Talash-e-Haq
Search of Alice, The *see* **Alicinte Anveshanam**
Season *see* Innale
Seba (Bhola Auddy, B, 1967)
Second Wife *see* Punarlagnani Patni
Secretary (**Chaturbhuj Doshi**, H, 1938)
Secretary (**K.S. Prakash Rao**, Tel, 1976)
Secret Five *see* Pakke Badmash
Secrets of the Night *see* Raat Ki Baat
Secularism (**Santi P. Choudhury**, E, 1969)
Sedige Sedu (A.V. Sheshgiri Rao, K, 1970)
Sedina Hakki (Dorairaj-Bhagavan, K, 1985)
Sedina Kidi (B. Krishan, K, 1971)
Sedina Sanchu (**T.S. Nagabharana**, K, 1984)
Sedin Du-janay (**Agradoot**, B, 1974)
Seedha Raasta (Dawood Baig, H, 1941)
Seedha Raasta (Vasant Painter, H, 1947)
Seedling, The *see* **Ankur**
Seeds of the Green Revolution (**Santi P. Choudhury**, E, 1971)
Seelaniki Shiksha (D.S. Prakash Rao, Tel, 1976)
Seelu Nakshatra (?, Bhavani Art Creations, K, 1986)
Seema (**Amiya Chakravarty**, H, 1955)
Seema (Surendra Mohan, H, 1971)
Seemabaddha (**Satyajit Ray**, B, 1971)
Seemandini (P.G. Vishwambaran, Mal, 1978)
Seemantha Puthran (A.B. Raj, Mal, 1976)
Seerum Singangal (Ramanarayanan, Tam, 1983)
Seervarisai (Sornam, Tam, 1976)
Seer Who Walks Alone, The (**G. Aravindan**, E, 1986)
Seeta (**Sisir Bhaduri**, B, 1933)
Seeta (**Debaki Bose**, H, 1934)
Seeta (**Kunchako**, Mal, 1960)
Seeta (**A.P. Nagarajan**, Tam, 1967)
Seeta (Vadiraj, K, 1970)
Seeta (Govindan, Mal, 1980)
Seeta (Ardhendu Chatterjee, B, 1980)
Seeta (S.A. Chandrasekharan, Tam, 1990)
Seeta Anjaneya (Boodal Krishnamurthy, K, 1993)
Seeta Aur Geeta (**Ramesh Sippy**, H, 1972)
Seeta Bibaha (Mohan Sunder Dev Goswami, O, 1934)
Seeta Devi (Mehana Sharma, Tel, 1982)
Seeta Geeta Datithe (**C.V. Sridhar**, Tel, 1977)
Seeta Haran *see* Ram Pratigya
Seeta Haran (?, Asian Film, Indore, St, 1930)
Seeta Haran (?, Tollywood Studio/**Madan** Theatres, H, 1936)
Seeta Janaman *see* Vedavathi
Seeta Kalyanam (Baburao Pendharkar, Tam, 1933)
Seeta Kalyanam (**Ch. Narasimha Rao**, Tel, 1934)
Seeta Kalyanam (**Bapu**, Tel, 1976)
Seeta Labakusha (Jagadishchandra, O, 1980)
Seetalu (Durga Nageshwara Rao, Tel, 1984)
Seeta Maiya (S.N. Tripathi, Bh, 1964)
Seetamalakshmi (**K. Vishwanath**, Tel, 1978)
Seetamma Pelli (**Bapu**, Tel, 1984)
Seetamma Santhanam (K.S. Rami Reddy, Tel, 1976)
Seetapaharanam (M.P. Sundarrajan, Tam, 1939)
Seetapati Chalo Tirupati (Vijaya Bapineedu, Tel, 1992)
Seetapatni Samsaram (M.S. Kota Reddy, Tel, 1978)
Seetapur Ki Geeta (Shibu Mitra, H, 1987)
Seeta Raati (*aka* Winter Night: **Manmohan Mahapatra**, O, 1982)
Seeta Ramaigari Manavarulu (Kranthi Kumar, Tel, 1991)
Seeta Rama Jananam (**G. Balaramaiah**, Tel, 1942)
Seeta Rama Kalyanam (**N.T. Rama Rao**, Tel, 1961)
Seeta Rama Kalyanam (Jandhyala, Tel, 1986)
Seeta Rama Vanavasu (**K. Kameshwara Rao**, Tel, 1977)
Seetaram Radheshyam (Himmat Dave, H, 1973)
Seeta Ramu (V. Somasekhar, K, 1979)
Seeta Ramudaithe (B. Subba Rao, Tel, 1979)
Seeta Ramulu (**Dasari Narayana Rao**, Tel, 1980)
Seetarathammagari Ammayi (E.V.V. Satyanarayana, Tel, 1992)

Seeta Shuddhi *see* Ram Ravan Yuddha
Seeta Swayamvar *see* Kodandhari Ram
Seeta Swayamvar (**Baburao Painter**, St, 1918)
Seeta Swayamvar (**S.N. Patankar**, St, 1920)
Seeta Swayamvar (**H.M. Reddy**, H, 1933)
Seeta Swayamvar (R.A. Sheikh, Mar/H, 1948)
Seeta Swayamvar (**Bapu**, H, 1976)
Seeta's Wedding *see* **Seeta Kalyanam**
Seeta Vanavas (*aka* Uttar Ramcharitra: V.S. Nirantar, St, 1924)
Seeta Vanavasam (?, East India Film, Tam, 1934)
Seeta Vanvas (Pranbhai Jani, G, 1949)
Seethakoka Chilaka (**Bharathirajaa**, Tel, 1981)
Seetheyalla Savithri (Vadiraj, K, 1973)
Sehra (D.B. Joshi/R. Bali, H, 1948)
Sehra (**V. Shantaram**, H, 1963)
Sehti Murad (Barkat Mehra, P, 1941)
Sehti Murad (Kailash Bhandari, P, 1979)
Sei Chokh (Salil Dutta, B, 1975)
Sei Sur (Niranjan Dey, B, 1981)
Sejal Sumro (Sharad Palekar, G, 1985)
Selima (**Modhu Bose**, H, 1935)
Sellakutti (K. Nataraj, Tam, 1987)
Selvakku (M.A. Kaja, Tam, 1986)
Selvam (**K.S. Gopalakrishnan**, Tam, 1966)
Selva Maghal (K.V. Srinivasan, Tam, 1967)
Selvi (K. Nataraj, Tam, 1985)
Selviyin Selvan (Mohan Gandhiram, Tam, 1968)
Semal Ki Darakht (**Muzaffar Ali**, H, 1986)
Senapati (Kedar Kapoor, H, 1961)
Sendhooradevi (Ramanarayanan, Tam, 1991)
Sendhoora Poove (P.R. Devaraj, Tam, 1988)
Sendur (Pulak Gogoi, A, 1984)
Sengamala Theevu (Rajendran, Tam, 1962)
Sengottai Singam (V.N. Reddy, Tam, 1958)
Senthamarai (**A. Bhimsingh**, Tam, 1962)
Senthamizh Pattu (P. Vasu, Tam, 1992)
Senthil Kumar (G. Vishwanathan, Tam, 1967)
Senur (Amar Gupta, Bh, 1983)
Senurwa Bhayeel Mohal (Gyan Kumar, Bh, 1986)
Sepoy Chinnaiah (G.V.R. Sheshgiri Rao, Tel, 1969)
Seragu (M. Rajagopal, K, 1992)
Serne Mathe Savaser (Ramkumar Bohra, G, 1982)
Server Somanna (K. Vasu, K, 1993)
Server Sundaram (**Krishnan-Panju**, Tam/Tel, 1964)
Service Limited *see* **Seva Samaj**
Sesham Kazhchayil (**Balachandra Menon**, Mal, 1983)
Seshpath *see* Shesh Path
Seth *see* Sheth
Seth Jagadusha (**Ravindra Dave**, G, 1981)
Seth Sagalsha (*aka* Wealth and the World: **M. Bhavnani**, St, 1925)
Seth Sagalsha (**Balwant Bhatt**, G, 1947)
Seth Sagalsha (Girish Manukant, G, 1975)
Setu (**Premendra Mitra**, B, 1951)
Setu Bandhan (*aka* Bridging of Ocean: **Dadasaheb Phalke**, St, 1932)
Setu Bandhanam (**R. Padmanabhan**, Tam, 1937)
Setu Bandhanam (**R. Padmanabhan**, Tel, 1946)
Setu Bandhanam (**Sasikumar**, Mal, 1974)
Seva (**Dhirubhai Desai**, H, 1942)
Sevagan (Arjun, Tam, 1992)
Sevagram (Narottam Vyas, H, 1947)
Seva Sadan (*aka* Bazaar-e-Husn: **Nanubhai Vakil**, H, 1934)
Seva Sadan (**K. Subramanyam**, Tam, 1938)
Seva Samaj (**Chimanlal Luhar**, H, 1939)
Seven (**Santi P. Choudhury** E, 1980)
Seventh Horse of the Sun, The *see* **Suraj Ka Satwan Ghoda**
Seventh Man, The *see* **Ezhavathu Manithan**
Sewak (S.M. Abbas, H, 1975)
Sewali (?, A, 1989)
Sex *see* Stree Shakti
Sexilla Stuntilla (B.N. Prakash, Mal, 1976)
Sey Nilo Bidaya (Jyotsnamoy Bhattacharya, B, 1951)
Shaaka (Shyam Ralhan, H, 1981)
Shaan (**Jayant Desai**, H, 1950)
Shaan (**Ramesh Sippy**, H, 1980)
Shaandaar *see* Shandaar
Shaan-e-Hatim (**Nanubhai Vakil**, H, 1958)
Shaan-e-Hind (*aka* Pride of India: **R.S. Choudhury**, H, 1936)
Shaan-e-Hind (Mohan Sinha, H, 1960)
Shaan-e-Hindustan (*aka* India in Glory: Navayug Film, St, 1932)
Shaan-e-Islam *see* Baag-e-Misar
Shaan-e-Khuda *see* Sair-e-Paristan
Shaan-e-Khuda (**Nanubhai Vakil**, H, 1971)
Shaan-e-Subhaan (*aka* Will of Allah: F.R. Irani, H, 1933)
Shabab (M. Sadiq, H, 1954)
Shabari (R.C. Deepak, H, 1947)
Shabash (?, Cartoonistan, Calcutta, H, 1949)
Shabash (**Paul Zils**, H, 1952)
Shabash (Ramanarayanan, Tam, 1984)
Shabash Babu (Haribabu, Tel, 1993)
Shabash Babu (Sasi Mohan, Tam, 1993)
Shabash Baby (N. Prasad, Tel, 1972)
Shabash Daddy (**Kishore Kumar**, H, 1978)
Shabash Gopi (M. Madhusudhana Rao, Tel, 1978)
Shabash Mappillai (S. Raghavan, Tam, 1961)
Shabash Maruti (K. Narayanan, Tel, 1980)
Shabash Meena (**B.R. Panthulu**, Tam, 1958)
Shabash Papanna (Shahidlal, Tel, 1972)
Shabash Pilla (**B.R. Panthulu**, Tel, 1959)
Shabash Raja (**P.S. Ramakrishna Rao**, Tel, 1961)
Shabash Ramudu/Shabash Ramu (**C.S. Rao**, Tel/Tam, 1959)
Shabash Satyam (G. Vishwanathan, Tel, 1969)
Shabash Soori (I.S. Murthy, Tel, 1964)
Shabash Thambi (Jambulingam, Tam, 1967)
Shabash Vadina (M. Mallikarjuna Rao, Tel, 1972)
Shabash Vikrama (Renuka Sharma, K, 1985)
Shabas Sunbai (Prabhakar Pendharkar, Mar, 1986)
Shabdagalu (M. Suresh Davangere, K, 1985)
Shabistan (B. Mitra, H, 1951)
Shabnam (B. Mitra, H, 1949)
Shabnam (Aspi, H, 1964)
Shadayantra (Rajan Johri, H, 1990)
Shadi (**Jayant Desai**, H, 1941)
Shadi (**Krishnan-Panju**, H, 1962)
Shadi Ka Mamla *see* Vijayachi Lagne
Shadi Ke Baad (Prem Mehra/Billoo Mehra, H, 1949)
Shadi Ke Baad (**L.V. Prasad**, H, 1972)
Shadi Ki Raat (*aka* Bridegrooms Wanted, Swapna Swayamvar: **M. Bhavnani**, H, 1935)
Shadi Ki Raat (Yeshwant Pethkar, H, 1950)
Shadi Se Pehle (Karunesh Thakur, H, 1980)
Shadi Se Pehle (*aka* Jue Ka Nateeja: **Raja Nene/Datta Dharmadhikari**, H, 1947)
Shadi Ya... (TV: **Aruna Raje**, H, 1993)
Shadow *see* Abad Veer
Shadows, The *see* Nizhalgal
Shadows of the Dead (**Debaki Bose**, St, 1931)
Shadyantra (Ratan Johri, H, 1989)
Shagird (Samir Ganguly, H, 1967)
Shagufa (**H.S. Rawail**, H, 1953)
Shagun (S. Arora, H, 1951)
Shagun (Nazar, H, 1964)
Shagun (?, Raba Films, H, 1989)
Shahala Shah (*aka* Check to the King: **Baburao Painter**, St, 1925)
Shaharer Itikatha (Bishu Dasgupta, B, 1960)
Shahar Theke Dooray (**Sailajananda Mukherjee**, B, 1943)
Shahar Theke Dooray (**Tarun Majumdar**, B, 1981)
Shah Behram (**J.P. Advani**, H, 1935)
Shah Behram (**Nanubhai Vakil**, H, 1955)
Shaheed (Ramesh Saigal, H, 1948)
Shaheed (S. Ram Sharma, H, 1965)
Shaheed Bhagat Singh (K.N. Bansal, H, 1963)
Shaheed-e-Azam Bhagat Singh (Jagdish Gautam, H, 1954)
Shaheed-e-Azam Sardar Bhagat Singh (Om Bedi, P, 1974)
Shaheed-e-Mohabbat (Homi Bode, H, 1936)
Shaheed-e-Naaz *see* Pak Daman
Shaheed Kartar Singh (Pratap Sagar, P, 1979)
Shaheed Udham Singh (Brij Mohan, P, 1977)
Shaheen (Khalid Siddiq, H, 1984)
Shah-e-Iran (*aka* Sher-e-Shapur, Shapur the Great, Iran Ka Shah: ?, Central Movietone, H, 1934)
Shah-e-Jigar (*aka* King of Hearts: Dr Alvao?, Surya Prakash Film, St, 1931)
Shah-e-Jungle (*aka* King of Forest: K.P. Bhave, St, 1926)
Shah-e-Misar (*aka* Firaun: G.R. Sethi, H, 1946)
Shahenshah (**Amiya Chakravarty**, H, 1953)
Shahenshah (Tinnu Anand, H, 1988)
Shahenshah Akbar (G.R. Sethi/R. Rai, H, 1943)
Shahenshah Babar (Wajahat Mirza, H, 1944)
Shaher Aur Sapna (**K.A. Abbas**, H, 1963)
Shaher Di Kudi (J.D. Bhambri, P, 1968)
Shaher-e-Khamosha *see* Khooni Jadugar
Shaher Ka Jadoo (**Kaliprasad Ghosh**, H, 1934)
Shaher Ki Jhalak (**Harisadhan Dasgupta**, E, 1953)
Shaher Se Door (Barkat Mehra, H, 1946)
Shahi Bazaar (Balwant Dave/Padmakant Phatak, H, 1957)
Shahi Chor (*aka* Wonderful Prince: Fatma Begum/Janibabu, St, 1929)
Shahi Chor (Naseem Siddiqui, H, 1955)
Shahi Fakir *see* Bolti Bulbul
Shahi Firman (*aka* Proclamation: **Homi Master**, St, 1931)
Shahi Firman (Ketan Anand, H, 1961)
Shahi Gawaiya *see* Vasavadatta
Shahi Ishq (*aka* Royal Romance: Chunilal Parekh, St, 1930)
Shahi Khazana (S. Usman, H, 1946)
Shahi Lakkadhara (*aka* Veenaveli: Chunilal Parekh, H, 1934)
Shahi Lutera (A.R. Kabuli, H, 1935)
Shahi Lutera (Aakkoo, H, 1965)
Shahi Lutera (Mohammed Hussain, H, 1976)
Shahi Mehmaan (**Balwant Bhatt**, H, 1955)
Shahi Raqasa (?, Vidya Movietone, H, 1965)
Shahir Parashuram (**Anant Mane**, Mar, 1961)
Shahjehan (**Ardeshir Irani/Naval Gandhi**, St, 1924)
Shahjehan (**A.R. Kardar**, H, 1946)
Shahji (S. Arora, P, 1954)
Shahkar (*aka* The Masterpiece: S. Khalil, H, 1947)
Shahnaz (Sheikh, H, 1948)
Shahu Chor (*aka* Prince of Thieves: M. Udwadia, H, 1936)
Shaila Sasanam (Kodi Ramakrishna, Tel, 1990)
Shaitan (Feroz Chinoy, H, 1974)
Shaitani Chakkar (*aka* Satan's Victim: Ata Mohammed, St, 1933)
Shaitani Ilaaka (Kiran **Ramsay**, H, 1990)
Shaitan Ka Pash (*aka* Kamala CID, Devil's Dice: **Ezra Mir**, H, 1936)
Shaitan Ki Shikar (*aka* Daivache Bhaksha: Shinde, St, 1931)
Shaitan Mujrim (Nazar Khan?, H, 1980)
Shaitan Pujari (?, Punjab Film, St, 1923)
Shake Hands (**Master Bhagwan**, H, 1947)
Shakespeare Wallah (James Ivory, E, 1965)
Shakha Proshakha (**Satyajit Ray**, B, 1990)
Shakti (S.I. Hasan, H, 1948)
Shakti (Mani, Mal, 1972)
Shakti (Vijayanand, Mal, 1980)
Shakti (**Ramesh Sippy**, H, 1982)
Shakti (**K. Raghavendra Rao**, Tel, 1983)
Shakti (Prabhakar, K, 1988)
Shakti (P.N. Ramachandra Rao, Tel, 1989)
Shakti Leela (Ramanna, Tam, 1972)
Shaktiman (K.C. Bokadia, H, 1993)
Shakti Maya (**Harshadrai Mehta**, Tam, 1939)
Shakti Parasakthi (?, Tirupathi Movies, Tam, 1990)
Shakti Pooja (Santosh Bannerjee, St, 1932)
Shaktiya Yuktiya (G.C. Sekhar, Tam, 1979)
Shakti Yukti (B. Ramamurthy, K, 1992)
Shakuntala (**Suchet Singh**, St, 1920)
Shakuntala (*aka* The Fateful Ring, The Lost Ring: **S.N. Patankar**, St, 1920)
Shakuntala (Fatma Begum, St, 1929)
Shakuntala (?, Cine Film Agency, St, 1931)
Shakuntala (**J.J. Madan**, H, 1931)
Shakuntala (**M. Bhavnani**, H, 1931)
Shakuntala (**Sarvottam Badami**, Tel, 1932)
Shakuntala (**Jyotish Bannerjee**, B, 1941)
Shakuntala (**V. Shantaram**, H, 1943)
Shakuntala (**Bhupen Hazarika**, A, 1961)
Shakuntala (**Kunchako**, Mal, 1965)
Shakuntala (**K. Kameshwara Rao**, Tel, 1966)
Shakuntala (TV: **Vijaya Mehta**, H, 1986)
Shakuntala Aru Shankar Joseph Ali (**Nip Barua**, A, 1984)
Shakuntalai (**Ellis Duncan**, Tam, 1940)
Shalimar (**Roop K. Shorey**, H, 1946)
Shalimar (Krishna Shah, E/H, 1978)
Shalivahan *see* Salivahan
Sham *see* Shyam
Shama (Adi Keeka/Abdul Majid/R. Khambatta, H, 1946)
Shama (Lekhraj Bhakri, H, 1961)
Shama (Naseem Basit, H, 1981)
Shamalshano Vivah (**V.M. Vyas**, G, 1948)
Shamalshano Vivah (Jasubhai Trivedi, G, 1976)
Shama Parwana (*aka* Flame of Love: D.N. Madhok, H, 1937)
Shama Parwana (D.D. Kashyap, H, 1954)
Shambhavi (Ramanarayanan, K, 1992)
Shame of the Nation *see* Dalit Kusum
Shaminchu Ennoruvakku (Joshi, Mal, 1986)
Sham Queen *see* Naqli Rani
Shamsheer (**Gyan Mukherjee**, H, 1953)
Shamsheer (**Babubhai Mistri**, H, 1967)
Shamsheerbaaz (*aka* Swordsman: Saqi, St, 1930)
Shamsheerbaaz (*aka* Handsome Prisoners, Swordsmen: **Balwant Bhatt**, H, 1940)
Shamsheerbaaz (Noshir Engineer, H, 1953)
Shamsheer-e-Arab (Niranjan P. Bhardwaj, H, 1935)
Shamsher Bahadur (*aka* Sword Champion: Y.D. Sarpotdar, St, 1930)
Shamsher-e-Jung *see* Amar Shaheed
Shamsher Pratigna (R.N. Vaidya/Subedar, St, 1928)
Shamsher Shankar (K.S.R. Doss, Tel, 1982)
Shanbagavalli (Lanka Sathyam, Tam, 1947)
Shandaar (**Krishnan-Panju**, H, 1974)
Shandaar (Vinod Dewan, H, 1990)
Shani Mahatmya *see* Ishwar Bhakti
Shani Prabhav (G.V. Sane, St, 1921)
Shani Prabhava (Ratnakar-Madhu, K, 1977)
Shankara (Sudarshan Nag, H, 1991)
Shankarabharanam (*aka* The Jewel of Shiva: **K. Vishwanath**, Tel, 1979)
Shankaracharyar (J. Chakraborty, Tam, 1939)
Shankaracharya (*aka* Renaissance of Hinduism: **Kaliprasad Ghosh**, St, 1927)
Shankar Dada (Shibu Mitra, H, 1976)
Shankar Guru (V. Somasekhar, K, 1978)
Shankar Guru (Raja, Tam, 1987)
Shankar Hussain (Yusuf Naqvi, H, 1977)
Shankari (T.R. Ramanna, Tam, 1984)
Shankar Khan (**Nanabhai Bhatt**, H, 1966)
Shankarlal (T.N. Balu, Tam, 1981)
Shankar Narayan Bank (**Niren Lahiri**, B, 1956)
Shankar Parvati (**Chaturbhuj Doshi**, H, 1943)
Shankar Parvati (**Chandrakant**, G, 1979)
Shankar Saleem Simon (P. Madhavan, Tam, 1978)
Shankar Seeta Ansuya (Manibhai Vyas, H, 1965)
Shankar Shambhu (Chand, H, 1976)
Shankar Sundar (A.T. Raghu, K, 1982)
Shankhanadam (Suresh Babu, Mal, 1988)
Shanmughapriya (K. Krishnamurthy, Tam, 1973)
Shanta (?, **Madan Theatres**, St, 1925)
Shanta (P.S. Srinivasa Rao, Tam, 1941)
Shanta (Manapuram, Tel, 1961)
Shantabalanagamma (M.V.S. Rama Rao, Tel, 1942)
Shantata! Court Chalu Aahe (Satyadev Dubey, Mar, 1971)
Shantata! Khoon Jhala Aahe (Devdutt, Mar, 1975)
Shanti (S.U. Sunny, H, 1947)

Shanti (**Vedantam Raghavaiah**, Tel, 1952)
Shanti (Raviraja Pinisetty, Tel, 1991)
Shanti (?, A.L.S. Prod, Tam, 1965)
Shanti Enathu Shanti (**T. Rajendar**, Tam, 1991)
Shanti Kranti (Ravichandran, K/Tam/Tel/H, 1991)
Shantimuhurtam (Sripriya, Tam, 1984)
Shanti Nilayam (G.S. Mani, Tam, 1969)
Shanti Nilayam (C. Vaikuntarama Sastry, Tel, 1972)
Shanti Nivasa (Bhargava, K, 1988)
Shantinivasam (**C.S. Rao**, Tel, 1960)
Shantinivasam (**Vijayanirmala**, Tel, 1986)
Shapamoksham (Jesey, Mal, 1974)
Shapath (Ravi Nagaich, H, 1984)
Shapatha (Amrutham, K, 1984)
Shapatham (M.R. Joseph, Mal, 1984)
Shapit (**Rajdutt**/Arvind Deshpande, Mar, 1982)
Shap Mochan (Sudhir Mukherjee, B, 1955)
Shapmukti (**P.C. Barua**, B, 1940)
Shapmukti (Ajit Ganguly, B, 1985)
Shap Sambhram *see* Mahashweta Kadambari
Shapur the Great *see* Shah-e-Iran
Shaque (*aka* Doubt: **Aruna Raje**/Vikas Desai, H, 1976)
Sharabi (Raj Rishi, H, 1964)
Sharapanjaram (**T. Hariharan**, Mal, 1979)
Sharara (**S.V. Rajendra Singh**, H, 1984)
Shararat (**Kishore Sahu**, H, 1944)
Shararat (**H.S. Rawail**, H, 1959)
Shararat (**Manmohan Desai**, H, 1972)
Sharbati Aankhen (**Ramchandra Thakur**, H, 1945)
Shareef Badmash *see* Guru Ghantal
Shareef Badmash (*aka* Society Scoundrel: **Kanjibhai Rathod**, St, 1924)
Shareef Badmash (?, **Madan Theatres**, St, 1930)
Shareef Badmash (*aka* Invention: ?, Ganesh Film, St, 1934)
Shareef Badmash (**Raj Khosla**, H, 1973)
Shareef Daku (G.R. Sethi, H, 1938)
Shareef Daku (S. Joshi, H, 1960)
Sharey Chuattar (**Nirmal Dey**, B, 1953)
Sharing Experience (**Vishnu Mathur**, E, 1976)
Sharmila (Sunil Ghosh, B, 1974)
Sharmilee (Samir Ganguly, H, 1971)
Sharmistha (*aka* Sharmistha Devayani: Vishnupant Divekar, St, 1922)
Sharmistha (**Naresh Mitra**, B, 1939)
Sharmistha Devayani *see* Sharmistha
Shart (B. Mitra, H, 1954)
Shart (Kewal Mishra, H, 1969)
Shart (Ketan Anand, H, 1985)

Nazima in *Nishan* (1965)

Sharabi (**Prakash Mehra**, H, 1984)
Sharabi Ki Ladki (?, R.A. Prod, H, 1960)
Sharada *see* Kanya Vikraya
Sharada (**A.R. Kardar**, H, 1942)
Sharada (**Dinkar D. Patil**, Mar, 1951)
Sharada (**L.V. Prasad**, H, 1957)
Sharada (**K.S. Gopalakrishnan**, Tam, 1962)
Sharada (**K. Vishwanath**, Tel, 1973)
Sharada (Lekh Tandon, H, 1981)
Sharadamba (Kranthi Kumar, Tel, 1987)
Sharada Ramudu (Vasu, Tel, 1980)
Sharadasandhya *see* Manju
Sharad Poonam (Ramnik Acharya, G, 1950)
Sharad Purnima (**Harshadrai Mehta**, St, 1927)
Sharafat (C.M. Trivedi, H, 1943)
Sharafat (**Asit Sen**, H, 1970)
Sharafat Chhod Di Maine (Jagdev Bhambhri, H, 1976)
Sharafi Loot (*aka* Lure of Gold: D.N. Madhok, H, 1937)
Sharanarthi *see* Refugee
Sharan Tula Bhagavanta (Shashikant Nalavade, Mar, 1980)
Sharapanjara (**Puttanna Kanagal**, K, 1971)
Shashi (R.S. Junnarkar, Mar, 1954)
Shashi Babur Sansar (Sudhir Mukherjee, B, 1959)
Shashikala (?, Lokmanya Film, St, 1928)
Shasti (Daya Bhai, B, 1962)
Shasti (Swadesh Sarkar, B, 1970)
Shatakarta Shivaji (**Nagendra Majumdar**, Mar, 1934)
Shatamukh Ravan Vadh (*aka* Kalikecha Janma, Birth of Kalika: Kashinath
Bharadi, St, 1925)
Shatarupa (Anjan Choudhury, B, 1989)
Shathru Samharam (**Sasikumar**, Mal, 1978)
Shatranj (Vaju Kotak/G.S. Potdar, H, 1946)
Shatranj (**Gyan Mukherjee**, H, 1956)
Shatranj (**S.S. Vasan**, H, 1969)
Shatranj (Aziz Sejawal, H, 1993)
Shatranj Ke Khiladi (**Satyajit Ray**, Urdu, 1977)
Shatranj Ke Mohre (Shibu Mitra, H, 1974)
Shatru (H.S.G. Mekman, K, 1979)
Shatru (Anjan Choudhury, B, 1984)
Shatru (T.S. Mohan, Mal, 1985)
Shatru (Pramod Chakraborty, H, 1986)
Shatrupaksha (Nripen Saha, B, 1989)
Shatruvu (Kodi Ramakrishna, Tel, 1990)
Shattered Experience *see* **Anubhavangal Palichakal**
Shattered Hopes *see* Naseeb Ni Nakhara
Shauhar (Veena Kumari, H, 1948)
Shaukeen (**Nanabhai Bhatt**, H, 1949)
Shaukeen (**Basu Chatterjee**, H, 1981)
Shavukaru (**L.V. Prasad**, Tel, 1950)
Shayad (Madan Bawaria, H, 1979)
Shayar (Chawla, H, 1949)
Shayar-e-Kashmir Mahjoor (Prabhat Mukherjee, H, 1972)
She *see* **Aval** *or* Bahadur Beti
Sheba and Hercules (B.S. Choudhury, H, 1967)
Sheela (Aravind Mukherjee, B, 1970)
Sheela (Deepak Balraj, H, 1987)
Sheelavati (P.B. Unni, Mal, 1967)
Sheel Prabhav (*aka* Glory of Virtue: Vishnupant Aundhkar?, United Pics., St,
1927)
Sheesha (Shaheed Latif, H, 1952)
Sheesha (**Basu Chatterjee**, H, 1986)
Sheeshe Ka Ghar (Amit Khanna, H, 1984)
Sheeshe Ki Deewar (Manmohan Sabir, H, 1954)
Sheesh Mahal (**B.P. Mishra**, St, 1926)
Sheesh Mahal (**Sohrab Modi**, H, 1950)
Sheeshon Ka Masiha (**Muzaffar Ali**, H, 1985)
Sheet Grishmer Smriti (TV: **Buddhadev Dasgupta**, B, 1982)
Shehar *see* Shaher
Shehnai (P.L. Santoshi, H, 1947)
Shehnai (S.D. Narang, H, 1964)
Shehzada (Mohan Sinha, H, 1955)
Shehzada (K. Shankar, H, 1972)
Shehzade (Raj Sippy, H, 1989)
Shehzadi (**J.P. Advani**, H, 1941)
Shehzadi (?, Shalimar Pics, H, 1947)
Shehzadi (A. Habib, H, 1992)
Sheikh Chilli (*aka* Castles in the Air: **Nanubhai Vakil**, St, 1930)
Sheikh Chilli (*aka* Ghanchakkar: Kikubhai Desai, H, 1942)
Sheikh Chilli (**Ramchandra Thakur**, H, 1956)
Sheila (*aka* Pind Di Kudi: Krishnadev Mehra, P, 1935)
Sheila (Deepak Balraj Vij, H, 1987)
Sheilbala (**Chandulal Shah**, H, 1932)
She Is Like That *see* **Aval Appadithan**
Shejari/Padosi (**V. Shantaram**, Mar/H, 1941)
Shelter (Uma Segal, E, 1982)
Shelter *see* Abhayam
Shenbagame Shenbagame (Gangai Amaran, Tam, 1988)
Shenbaga Thottam (Manobala, Tam, 1992)
Sheni Vijanand (Yusuf Mulji, G, 1948)
Shepherd *see* Farebi Shahzada
Shepherd King, The *see* Naag Padmini
Shera Daku (Radhakant, H, 1966)
Sher Afghan (B.R. Jhingan, H, 1966)
Sheran De Putt Sher (Anil Pandit, P, 1990)
Shera Shamshera (S.R. Pratap, H, 1990)
Sheras Savasher (Datta Mane, Mar, 1966)
Sher Dil *see* Gypsy Girl
Sher Dil (*aka* Dashing Devil: Haribhai Desai, St, 1931)
Sher Dil (Boman Shroff, H, 1954)
Sher Dil (Chand, H, 1965)
Sher Dil (Jagdish Sidana, H, 1990)
Sher Dil Aurat (*aka* Free Souls, Veer Nari, Azadi Ke Deewane: A.P. Kapur, H,
1935)
Sher-e-Arab (*aka* The Arabian Knight: **B.P. Mishra**, St, 1930)
Sher-e-Baghdad (*aka* Lion of Baghdad: **Homi Wadia**, H, 1946)
Sher-e-Baghdad (Om Sonik, H, 1957)
Sher-e-Bengal (Ramjibhai Arya/Mohammed Hussain, H, 1947)
Sher-e-Hind *see* Veer Bharat
Sher-e-Jawan (*aka* Dashing Youth: Ramakant-Gharekhan, St, 1930)
Sher-e-Jung (*aka* Suleman the Tiger: ?, International Pics., St, 1930)
Sher-e-Jungle *see* Mala the Mighty *or* Zambo the Ape Man
Sher-e-Kabul (?, Pioneer Films, H, 1936)
Sher-e-Shapur *see* Shah-e-Iran
Sher-e-Watan (Harbans, H, 1971)
Sher Ka Bachcha (*aka* Happy Warrior: R.N. Vaidya, St, 1933)
Sher Ka Panja (Dwarka Khosla, H, 1936)
Sher Khan (Radhakant, H, 1962)
Sher Ki Garaj *see* Bhishma
Sherne Mathe Savasher (Ramkumar Bohra, G, 1982)
Sherni (Chaman Nillay, P, 1973)
Sherni (Harmesh Malhotra, H, 1988)
Sherni Ki Garaj *see* Khubsoorat Bala
Sheroo (**Shakti Samanta**, H, 1957)
Sher Puttar (Subhash Bhakri, P, 1977)
Sher Shivaji (Ram Gabale, H, 1987)
Shesh (?, Mediacorp, H, 1988)
Sheshakriya (Ravi Algmmoid?, Mal, 1982)
Shesh-Anka (Haridas Bhattacharya, B, 1963)
Shesha Pratiksha (Pranab Das, O, 1985)
Shesha Shrabana (**Prashanta Nanda**, O, 1976)
Sheshbesh (**Jyotish Bannerjee**, B, 1950)
Shesh Bichar (Bimal Roy Jr, B, 1980)
Shesh Bishar (Deb Kumar Basu, A, 1971)
Shesh Chinha (Bibhuti Chakraborty, B, 1962)
Shesher Kabita (**Modhu Bose**, B, 1953)
Shesh Kothai (?, B, 1952)
Shesh Naag (**Chaturbhuj Doshi**, H, 1957)
Shesh Naag (K.R. Reddy, H, 1990)
Shesh Nibedan (**Dhiren Ganguly**, B, 1948)
Shesh Parba (Chitta Bose, B, 1972)
Shesh Parichaya (**Sushil Majumdar**, B, 1957)
Shesh Paryanta (Sudhir Mukherjee, B, 1960)
Shesh Path (*aka* The Only Way: **Phani Burma**, St, 1930)
Shesh Prahar (Prantik, B, 1963)
Shesh Pristhay Dekhun (Salil Dutta, B, 1973)
Shesh Raksha (**Pashupati Chatterjee**, B, 1944)
Shesh Raksha (Shankar Bhattacharya, B, 1977)
Shesh Theke Shuru (Chitrasathi, B, 1969)
Shesh Tin Din (Prafulla Chakraborty, B, 1966)
Shesh Uttar/Jawab (**P.C. Barua**, B/H, 1942)
Shetalne Kanthe (*aka* Sati Analde: **Ravindra Dave**, G, 1975)
Shetal Tara Unda Pani (Arun Bhatt, G, 1986)
Shethno Salo (**Homi Master/Kanjibhai Rathod**, G, 1949)
She Too is a Woman *see* **Avalum Penn Thane**
Shevatcha Malusara (Vasant Joglekar, Mar, 1965)
Shevgyachya Shenga (**Shantaram Athavale**, Mar, 1955)
She-wolf *see* Meetha Zaher
Shield Against the Evil Eye *see* **Chashme Buddoor**
Shikamani (Sudarshan, Tam, 1948)
Shikar (**Ravindra Dave**, H, 1955)
Shikar (Mangal Chakraborty, B, 1958)
Shikar (Mohammed Hussain, H, 1963)
Shikar (**Atma Ram**, H, 1968)
Shikarangal (Sheela, Mal, 1979)
Shikari (*aka* Gulshan-e-Havas: **Naval Gandhi**, H, 1932)
Shikari (Savak Vacha, H, 1946)
Shikari (C.R. Simha, K, 1981)
Shikari (Umesh Mehra, H, 1991)
Shikarpuri (A. Shah Aziz, H, 1947)
Shikast (Ramesh Saigal, H, 1953)
Shikayat (Shaheed Latif, H, 1948)
Shikharam (Ananthu, Tam, 1991)
Shikleli Baiko (Madhav Shinde, Mar, 1959)
Shiksha (N. Prakash, Mal, 1971)
Shiksha (S. Ramanathan, H, 1979)
Shiksha (Relangi Narasimha Rao, Tel, 1985)
Shikwa (Ramchandra, H, 1974)
Shilalipi (Palash Bannerjee, B, 1983)
Shilanganache Sone (**Bhalji Pendharkar**, Mar, 1949)
Shilpi (Agragami, B, 1956)
Shilpi (**Nabyendu Chatterjee**, B, 1993)
Shin Shinaki Boobla Boo (P.L. Santoshi, H, 1952)
Ship Aground, A (**Kumar Shahani**, E, 1989)
Shipyards to Seaways (**P.V. Pathy**, E, 1957)

Shiraz (**Franz Osten**, St, 1928)
Shiraz-ud-Dowla (*aka* By Sheer Valour: A.P. Kapur, St, 1927)
Shiraz-ud-Dowla (?, Int. Pics, St, 1929)
Shirdiche Shri Saibaba (Kumarsen Samarth, Mar, 1955)
Shirdi Ke Sai Baba (Ashok Bhushan, H, 1977)
Shirin Farhad (*aka* At the Altar of Love: **Homi Master**, St, 1926)
Shirin Farhad (**J.J. Madan**, H, 1931)
Shirin Farhad (Prahlad Dutt, H, 1945)
Shirin Farhad (Aspi, H, 1956)
Shirin Khushrau (**R.S. Choudhury**, St, 1929)
Shisham (Kishore Sharma, H, 1952)
Shishupalan (K.K. Sampathkumar, Tam, 1974)
Shishupala Vadh (G.V. Sane, St, 1922)
Shitala Mata (Rajpati, H, 1981)
Shiulibari (Piyush Basu, B, 1962)
Shiva (Ameerjan, Tam, 1989)
Shiva (Ram Gopal Varma, Tel/H, 1989)
Shiva Bhakta (K.V. Srinivas, K, 1969)
Shiva Bhakta Naga Shakti (Kallesh, Tel, 1985)
Shivagange Mahatme (Govindaiah, K, 1964)
Shivaji Alive *see* Shivaji Nu Janma
Shivajichi Agryahun Sutaka (*aka* Shivaji's Escape from Agra: **Dadasaheb Phalke**, St, 1924)
Shivaji Nu Janma (*aka* Shivaji Alive, Birth of Shivaji: Pandurang Talegiri, St, 1931)
Shiva Ka Insaaf (Raj N. Sippy, H, 1985)
Shivakanya/Shivakanye (**Hunsur Krishnamurthy**, Tel/K, 1984)
Shiva Kavi (S.M. Sreeramulu Naidu, Tam, 1943)
Shiva Kotta Saubhagya (**Hunsur Krishnamurthy**, K, 1985)
Shivalinga Sakshi (**Chandramohan**, K, 1960)
Shivalinga Satchi *see* Sivalinga Satchi
Shiva Mahima *see* Shri Markandeya Avatar
Shiva Mahima (**Hunsur Krishnamurthy**, Mal, 1981)
Shiva Mechhida Kannappa (Vijay, K, 1988)
Shivamettina Satyam (Madhusudhana Rao, Tel, 1979)
Shivanaga (K.S.R. Doss, K, 1992)
Shiva Parvati (T. Janakiram, K, 1950)
Shiva Ramoshi (K.P. Bhave, Mar, 1951)
Shivarathri (Ramanarayanan, Tam/Tel, 1993)
Shivarathri Mahatme (P.R. Kaundinya, K, 1964)
Shivaratri (Prafulla Kumar Mitra, B, 1936)
Shivarayachi Soon Tararani (**Dinkar D. Patil**, Mar, 1993)
Shivashakti *see* Shiv Shakti
Shivashakti (**Jayant Desai**, H, 1952)
Shivashakti (Ardhendu Chatterjee, B, 1954)
Shiva Shankar (Bhargava, K, 1990)
Shivashankari (Ramanarayanan, Tam, 1992)
Shivasharane Nambekka (**P. Neelakantan**, K, 1955)
Shivasharane Nambiyakka (D. Shankar Singh, K, 1955)
Shivayogi Akkamahadevi (Chandrahas Alva, K, 1991)
Shiv Bhakta (**H.L.N. Simha**, H, 1955)
Shiv Bhakt Baba Balak Nath (Avtar, H, 1972)
Shiv Charan (Anil Kumar, H, 1982)
Shiv Ganga (Satish Kumar, H, 1988)
Shiv Kanya (**Dhirubhai Desai**, H, 1954)
Shiv Leela *see* Markandeya
Shiv Leela (Govind Ghanekar, Mar/H, 1951)
Shiv Mahima (Shantilal Soni, H, 1992)
Shiv Parvati (S.N. Tripathi, H, 1962)
Shiv-Ram (Jagdish A. Sharma, H, 1991)
Shiv Ramoshi (K.P. Bhave, Mar, 1951)
Shiv Ratri (*aka* Lore of Faith: C. Legrand, St, 1921)
Shiv Ratri (**Jayant Desai**, H, 1954)
Shiv Shakti *see* Shivashakti
Shiv Shakti (Satish Kumar, H, 1980)
Shiv Shakti (Anand, H, 1988)
Shiv Teri Mahima Nyari (Suresh Sinh Gohil, H, 1993)
Shiyal Ni Kasoti *see* Sati Saroj
Shobha (Kumarsen Samarth, H, 1942)
Shobha (**Niren Lahiri**, H, 1954)
Shobha (**K. Kameshwara Rao**, Tel, 1958)
Shodh (*aka* The Search: Biplab Roy Choudhury, H, 1980)
Shodha Mhanje Sapdel (Sharad Niphadkar, Mar, 1966)
Shodhbodh (Soumyen Mukherjee, B, 1942)
Shohrat (**K. Amarnath/N.R. Acharya**, H, 1949)
Shokan Mele Di (Kewal Mishra, P, 1965)
Shokh Dilruba (**J.P. Advani**, H, 1936)
Shokhiyan (**Kidar Sharma**, H, 1951)
Shokila Rayudu (S.D. Lall, Tel, 1979)
Shola Aur Shabnam (Ramesh Saigal, H, 1961)
Shola Aur Shabnam (David Dhawan, H, 1992)
Shola Jo Bhadke (**Master Bhagwan**, H, 1961)
Sholay (*aka* Shole: **B.R. Chopra**, H, 1953)
Sholay (**Ramesh Sippy**, H, 1975)
Shoora Mi Vandile (Ramkrishna Ullal, Mar, 1975)
Shoorana Sangram (*aka* Benevolent Bravery: Mohanlal Shah, St, 1930)
Shoor Killedarin (*aka* A Fair Warrior: Vishnupant Aundhkar, St, 1927)
Shooro Sainik (*aka* Brave Warrior: Mohanlal Shah, St, 1931)
Shoorveer (Shyam Ralhan, H, 1988)
Shoorveer Sharada (*aka* Gallant Girl: **Homi Master**, St, 1930)
Shor (**Manoj Kumar**, H, 1972)
Shorgol (Biswajit, B, 1984)
Shoroshi (**Pashupati Chatterjee**, B, 1954)
Short Cut (**Kantilal Rathod**, E, 1973)
Shraddha (Himmat Dave, G, 1978)
Shraddhanjali (Anil Sharma, H, 1981)
Shrant (G.G. Bannerjee, H, 1982)
Shravana Bantu (**Singeetham Srinivasa Rao**, K, 1984)
Shravana Sandhya (A. Kodandarami Reddy, Tel, 1986)
Shravani Satam (Babubhai Thakkar, G, 1977)
Shravan Kumar (A.R. Kabuli, H, 1932)
Shravan Kumar (Ram Daryani, H, 1946)
Shravan Kumar (Sharad Desai, H, 1960)
Shravan Kumar (**Chandrakant**, H/G, 1984)
Shravan Sandhya (Bireshwar Basu, B, 1973)
Shravanti (Kranthi Kumar, Tel, 1986)
Shreyasi (Shyam Chakraborty, B, 1963)
Shri Andal (S. Velsami Kavi, Tam, 1948)
Shri Aurobindo: Glimpses of his Life (**Phani Majumdar**, E, 1975)
Shri Ayyappanum Vavarum (Suresh, Mal, 1982)
Shri Balaji (Sane Mama, St, 1929)
Shribatsa Chinta (**Phani Burma**, B, 1955)
Shri Chaitanya Mahaprabhu (**Vijay Bhatt**, H, 1953)
Shri Chaitanya Mahaprabhu (Harindra Joshi, G, 1987)
Shri Chottanikkara Bhagavathi (Vijayakumar, Mal, 1977)
Shri Datta Darshanam (**K. Kameshwara Rao**, Tel, 1985)
Shri Dharmasthala Mahatme (D. Shankar Singh, K, 1962)
Shri Dnyaneshwar (**S.N. Patankar**, St, 1923)
Shri Dwarkadheesh (Ramakant-Gharekhan, St, 1928)
Shri 420 (**Raj Kapoor**, H, 1955)
Shri Ganesh (S.S. Dharwadkar, H, 1962)
Shri Ganesh Janma (**Jayant Desai**, H, 1951)
Shri Ganesh Mahima (*aka* Shri Krishna Vivah: **Homi Wadia**, H, 1950)
Shri Ganesh Vivah (Jaswant Jhaveri, H, 1955)
Shri Gauri Mahatyam (**Yoganand**, Tel, 1956)
Shri Gouranga *see* Char Darvesh
Shri Gouranga Leela *see* Hari Bhakti
Shri Gurudev Dutt (R.V. Rane, Mar, 1952)
Shri Guruvayoorappan (S. Ramanathan, Mal, 1964)
Shri Guruvayoorappan (S. Ramanathan, Tam, 1967)
Shri Guruvayoorappan (**P. Subramanyam**, Mal, 1972)
Shri Jagannath (Chiraranjan Mitra, O, 1950)
Shri Jagannath (Bijoy Bhaskar, O, 1979)
Shri Jagannath (Jyoti Prakash Roy, B, 1985)
Shri Kanakadurga Mahima (Surati Durga Rao, Tel, 1973)
Shri Kanakamahalakshmi Recording Dance Troupe (Ramesh Reddy, Tel, 1988)
Shri Kanchi Kamakshi (**K.S. Gopalakrishnan**, Tam, 1978)
Shri Kanda Leela (**Harshadrai Mehta**, Tam, 1938)
Shri Kannika Parameshwari (**R.S. Prakash**, St, 1929)
Shri Kannika Parameshwari Kathe (**Hunsur Krishnamurthy**, K, 1966)
Shri Katna Leelalu (Parchuri Bros., Tel., 1985)
Shri Krishna (C.V. Raju, K, 1953)
Shri Krishna *see* Krishna
Shri Krishna Arjun Yudh (**Babubhai Mistri**, H, 1971)
Shri Krishna Avatar (**Baburao Painter**, St, 1923)
Shri Krishna Bhakta Peepaji (**S.N. Patankar**, St, 1923)
Shri Krishna Bhakti (**Babubhai Mistri**, H, 1955)
Shri Krishna Bhakti (Manibhai Vyas, H, 1973)
Shri Krishna Darshan (A.R. Sheikh, Mar/H, 1950)
Shri Krishnadevaraya (**B.R. Panthulu**, K, 1970)
Shri Krishna Garudi (**Hunsur Krishnamurthy**, K, 1958)
Shri Krishna Garudi (**Y.V. Rao**, Tel, 1958)
Shri Krishna Janma (**Dadasaheb Phalke**, St, 1917)
Shri Krishna Janma (?, Indore Pics., St, 1932)
Shri Krishna Leela (G.V. Sane, St, 1920)
Shri Krishna Leela (Bijon Sen/Arun Choudhury, B, 1953)
Shri Krishna Leela (**Homi Wadia**, H, 1970)
Shri Krishna Leela (**A.P. Nagarajan**, Tam, 1977)
Shri Krishna Leelalu (**Ch. Narasimha Rao**, Tel, 1935)
Shri Krishna Leelalu (Parachuri Bros, Tel, 1985)
Shri Krishna Maya (Sane Mama, St, 1931)
Shri Krishna Maya (**C.S. Rao**, Tel, 1958)
Shri Krishna Naradi *see* Krishna Naradi
Shri Krishnanjaneya Yuddham (**C.S. Rao**, Tel, 1972)
Shri Krishna Pandiviyam (**N.T. Rama Rao**, Tel, 1966)
Shri Krishnaparunthu (**A. Vincent**, Mal, 1984)
Shri Krishna Raas Leela (Kamallochan Mohanty, O, 1979)
Shri Krishnarjuna Yuddham (**K.V. Reddy**, Tel/Tam, 1962)
Shri Krishnarjun Yuddha (Mohan Sinha, H, 1945)
Shri Krishna Rukmini (**Dhirubhai Desai**, G, 1949)
Shri Krishna Rukmini Satyabhama (Ravi, K, 1971)
Shri Krishna Satya (**K.V. Reddy**, Tel, 1971)
Shri Krishna Satyabhama *see* Parijatak *or* Krishna Satyabhama
Shri Krishna's Devotee *see* Chandidas
Shri Krishna Sharanam Mama (**Chandrakant**, G, 1977)
Shri Krishna Shishtai (**Dadasaheb Phalke**, St, 1928)
Shri Krishna Sudama (Vishnupant Divekar, St, 1920)
Shri Krishna Sudama (Shyam Chakraborty, B, 1955)
Shri Krishna Tulabharam (**C. Pullaiah**, Tel, 1935)
Shri Krishna Tulabharam (A.A. Somayajalu, Tam, 1948)
Shri Krishna Tulabharam (**Kadaru Nagabhushanam**, Tel, 1955)
Shri Krishna Tulabharam (**C.S. Rao**, Tel, 1955)
Shri Krishna Tulabharam (**K. Kameshwara Rao**, Tel/Tam, 1966)
Shri Krishnavataram (**K. Kameshwara Rao**, Tel/Tam, 1967)
Shri Krishna Vijayam (**K. Kameshwara Rao**, Tel, 1970)
Shri Krishna Vivah *see* Shri Ganesh Mahima
Shri Lakshmamma Katha (**G. Balaramaiah**, Tel, 1950)
Shri Loknath (Prafulla Sengupta, O, 1960)
Shrimad Virata Parvam (**N.T. Rama Rao**, Tel, 1979)
Shrimad Virat Veerabrahmendra Swamy Charitra (**N.T. Rama Rao**, Tel, 1984)
Shriman (Geethapriya, K, 1981)
Shriman Ashiq (Deepak Anand, H, 1993)
Shriman Balasaheb (Datta Chavan, Mar, 1964)
Shriman Funtoosh (Shantilal Soni, H, 1965)
Shrimanji (Ram Dayal, H, 1968)
Shriman Petra Selvangal (R.R. Chandran, Tam, 1962)
Shriman Prithviraj (**Tarun Majumdar**, B, 1972)
Shriman Satyavadi (S.M. Abbas, H, 1960)
Shriman Shrimanya (TV: **T.S. Nagabharana**, K, 1986)
Shriman Shrimati (?, Chitrakala Sagar, Mal, 1981)
Shriman Shrimati (Vijay Reddy, H, 1982)
Shrimant Mehuna Pahije (A. Shamsheer, Mar, 1967)
Shrimanthudu (**K. Pratyagatma**, Tel, 1971)
Shri Markandeya Avatar (*aka* Shiva Mahima, Devotion's Reward: **S.N. Patankar**, St, 1922)
Shrimati (Vijayareddy, Tel, 1966)
Shrimati 420 (**G.P. Sippy**, H, 1956)
Shrimati Garu (Rajachandra, Tel, 1985)
Shrimati Hansraj (Ajit Ganguly, B, 1989)
Shrimatiji (I.S. Johar, H, 1952)
Shrimati Kavali (Janardan, Tel, 1984)
Shrimati Mohinamoyee (Puluk Gogoi, A, 1979)
Shrimati Nalini (**Manilal Joshi**, St, 1927)
Shrimati Oka Vegumathai (Visu, Tel, 1987)
Shrimati Parinayam Mannarsami (T.P. Kalyana Sastry, Tam, 1936)
Shrimatir Sansar (Benu Das, B, 1957)
Shrimp, The *see* **Chemmeen**
Shri Murugan (V.S. Narayanan, Tam, 1946)
Shri Murugan (**P. Subramanyam**, Mal, 1977)
Shri Naqad Narayan (I.S. Johar, H, 1955)
Shri Narayana Guru (**P.A. Backer**, Mal, 1985)
Shrinatha Kavi Sarvabhowma (**Bapu**, Tel, 1993)
Shringara Ramudu (K. Shankar, Tel, 1979)
Shri Purandaradasaru (C.V. Raju, K, 1967)
Shri Radha (**Jyotish Bannerjee**, B, 1941)
Shri Radha (Surendra Ranjan Sarkar, B, 1959)
Shri Radha Krishna (*aka* Yashoda Nandan: N.C. Laharry/**Dhiren Ganguly**, St, 1921)
Shri Radhar Maanbhanjan (Sona Mukherjee, B, 1983)
Shri Raghavendrar (S.P. Muthuraman, Tam, 1985)
Shri Raghavendra Vaibhava (Babu Krishnamurthy, K, 1981)
Shri Raghavendra Vaibhavam (**B. Vittalacharya**, Tel, 1981)
Shri Rajeshwari Vilas Coffee Club (Chakrapani/**Bapu**, Tel, 1976)
Shri Rama Bantu (I.N. Murthy, Tel, 1979)
Shri Ramachandra (D. Rajendra Babu, K, 1992)
Shri Ramajayam (V. Srinivasan, Tam, 1979)
Shri Rama Katha (B. Padmanabham, Tel, 1969)
Shri Ramanjaneya Yuddha (M.S. Nayak, K, 1963)
Shri Ramanjaneya Yuddham (Acharya, Tel, 1958)
Shri Ramanjaneya Yuddham (**Bapu**, Tel, 1974)
Shri Ramanuja (**Debaki Bose**, H, 1943)
Shri Ramanujacharya (**G.V. Iyer**, Tam, 1989)
Shri Ramanujar (N. Ramarathnam, Tam, 1938)
Shri Rama Pattabhishekham (**P. Subramanyam**/G.K. Raman, Mal, 1962)
Shri Rama Pattabhishekham (**N.T. Rama Rao**, Tel, 1978)
Shrirama Pooja (B.R. Krishnamurthy, K, 1955)
Shri Rama Raksha (**T. Rama Rao**, Tel, 1978)
Shri Ram Avatar (W. Garcher, H, 1950)
Shri Rambhakta Hanuman (**Homi Wadia**, H, 1948)
Shri Ram Bharat Milap (Manibhai Vyas, H, 1965)
Shri Ramchandrudu (B. Bhaskara Rao, Tel, 1989)
Shri Ranchhodrai *see* Bhakta Bodana
Shri Ranganeethulu (A. Kodandarami Reddy, Tel, 1983)
Shri Renukadevi Mahatme (**C.S. Rao**, K, 1977)
Shri Sabarimalai Shri Ayyappan (S.M. Sreeramulu Naidu, Mal, 1961)
Shri Saila Bhamarambika Katakasham (**B.

Vittalacharya, Tel, 1991)
Shri Satyanarayan (**Kanjibhai Rathod**, St, 1922)
Shri Satyanarayan (Dhrupad Rai, H, 1935)
Shri Satyanarayan Ki Mahapooja (D. Raman, H, 1975)
Shri Seeta Rama Hanuman (**K. Kameshwara Rao**, Tam, 1969)
Shrishaila Mahatme (Aruru Pattabhi, K, 1961)
Shrishaila Bhamarambika Katakshyam (**B. Vittalacharya**, Tel, 1991)
Shri Shirdi Saibaba Mahatyam (K. Vasu, Tel, 1985)
Shri Shri Maa (**Kaliprasad Ghosh**, B, 1958)
Shri Shri Maa Kamakhya (**Anwar Hussain**, A, 1983)
Shri Shri Ma Lakshmi (Prabhat Chakraborty, B, 1976)
Shri Shri Nityananda Prabhu (Ashim Pal, B, 1959)
Shri Shri Patita Pawan (Sukumar Ganguly, O, 1962)
Shri Shri Ramakrishna Kathamrita (Bikash Goswami, B, 1982)
Shri Shri Satyanarayan (Hari Bhanja, B, 1953)
Shri Shri Tarakeshwar (Bangsi Ash, B, 1958)
Shri Srinivasa Kalyana (**B. Vittalacharya**/D. Shankar Singh, K, 1952)
Shri Srinivasa Kalyana (Vijay, K, 1974)
Shri Subramanyam (*aka* Valli Kumariche Lagna, Valli's Wedding: Rao, St, 1930)
Shri Tatavatharam (B. Bhaskara Rao, Tel, 1988)
Shri Thyagaraja (Virendra Desai, Tam, 1937)
Shri Tirupati Venkateshwara Kalyanam (**N.T. Rama Rao**, Tel, 1979)
Shri Tulsidas (Hiren Bose, B, 1950)
Shri Valli (**A.V. Meiyappan**/A.T. Krishnaswamy, Tam, 1945)
Shri Valli (T.R. Ramanna, Tam, 1961)
Shri Vamanavatharam (**Sasikumar**, Tel, 1985)
Shri Vari Pelli (Rangaraja, Tel, 1984)
Shri Vasavi Kannika Parameshwari Mahatyam (**K. Kameshwara Rao**, Tel, 1980)
Shri Vatsa (**Prakash Jha**, H, 1983)
Shrivatsa Chinta (?, Indian Pics., St, 1925)
Shri Vemana Charitra (Vijayachander, Tel, 1986)
Shrivenella (**K. Vishwanath**, Tel, 1986)
Shri Venkateshwara Mahatyam (*aka* Balaji: **P. Pullaiah**, Tel, 1939)
Shri Venkateshwara Mahatyam (*aka* Bhagwan Balaji: **P. Pullaiah**, Tel, 1960)
Shri Venkateshwara Mahime (Anil Baindoor, K, 1988)
Shri Venkateshwara Vaibhavam (C.D. Prasad, Tel, 1971)
Shri Venkateshwara Vrata Mahatyam (K.S.R. Doss, Tel, 1980)
Shri Vinayaka Vijayam (**K. Kameshwara Rao**, Tel, 1980)
Shri Vishnu Bhagwan (**Raja Nene**, H, 1951)
Shruti Seridaga (B. Dattaraj, K, 1987)
Shubha Bibaha (**Sombhu Mitra**/Amit Moitra, B, 1959)
Shubhadinam (Srikanth, Tam, 1969)
Shubha Drishti (Chitta Bose, B, 1962)
Shubhajatra (Chitta Bose, B, 1954)
Shubha Lagna (**Modhu Bose**, B, 1956)
Shubhalekha (**K. Vishwanath**, Tel, 1982)
Shubhamangal (**Anant Mane**, Mar, 1954)
Shubhamangala (**Puttanna Kanagal**, K, 1975)
Shubha Milana (Bhargava, K, 1987)
Shubha Muhurta (Geethapriya, K, 1984)
Shubha Muhurtam (Raghu, Tam, 1983)
Shubha Muhurtam (T. Prasad, Tel, 1983)
Shubharatri (**Sushil Majumdar**, B, 1956)
Shubh Din (P. Thyagarajan, H, 1974)
Shubh Kaamna (**K. Vishwanath**, H, 1983)
Shuk Deo *see* Shuk Rambha
Shukradeshe (Aruru Pattabhi, K, 1957)
Shuk Rambha (*aka* Shuk Deo: **Kanjibhai Rathod**?, St, 1923)
Shuk Rambha (**Dhirubhai Desai**, H, 1953)
Shukravaram Mahalakshmi (?, Sri Charanu Chitra, Tel, 1992)
Shukriya (**H.S. Rawail**, H, 1944)
Shukriya (A.C. Trilogchander, H, 1989)
Shuk Sari (**Sushil Majumdar**, B, 1969)
Shuparna (Parimal Ghosh, B, 1983)
Shura Mi Vandile *see* Shoora Mi Vandile
Shuri Sinha (*aka* Lioness: Prafulla Ghosh, St, 1931)
Shwetagni (B. Ramamurthy, K, 1991)
Shweta Gulabi (K.V. Jayaram, K, 1985)
Shyama (?, Omkar Lalit Prod, H, 1937)
Shyama (Joshi, Mal, 1986)
Shyamala (B.A. Subba Rao, Tam, 1952)
Shyamala (Joginder Shaily, H, 1979)
Shyamalachechi (**P. Bhaskaran**, Mal, 1965)
Shyamali (**Ajoy Kar**, B, 1956)
Shyamalir Swapna (Ratan Chatterjee, B, 1948)
Shyamchi Aai (**P.K. Atre**, Mar, 1953)
Shyam Ki Jogan (S.P. Kalla, H, 1957)
Shyamoli (Binoy Bannerjee, B, 1952)
Shyam Saheb (Salil Dutta, B, 1986)
Shyam Savera (M. Sadiq, H, 1946)
Shyam Sundar (**Bhalji Pendharkar**, Mar/H, 1932)
Shyam Sundar (Hemanta Gupta, B, 1936)
Shyam Sundar (?, Lakshmi Cinetone, Tam, 1940)
Shyam Tere Kitne Naam (Shantilal Soni, H, 1977)
Shylock (Sama-Ramu, Tam, 1940)
Siddhalingeshwar Mahima *see* Edeyuru Siddhalingeshwara
Siddhartha (Conrad Rooks, E, 1978)
Siddhartha (Kranthi Kumar, Tel, 1990)
Siddhartha and the City *see* **Pratidwandi**
Siddheshwari (**Mani Kaul**, H, 1989)
Sididedda Gandu (S. Umesh, K, 1990)
Sididedda Sahodara (Joe Simon, K, 1983)
Sidila Mari (**B.S. Ranga**, K, 1971)
Sidilu (B. Subba Rao, K, 1984)
Sidukabeda Singari (Guruprasad, K, 1993)
Siege of Chittor *see* **Sati Padmini**
Sigappu *see* Sivappu
Sigappukkal Mookuthi (Valampuri Somanathan, Tam, 1979)
Sigappu Malargal (S.A. Chandrasekharan, Tam, 1986)
Sigappu Nila (Ramanarayanan, Tam, 1985)
Sigappu Rojakkal (**Bharathirajaa**, Tam, 1978)
Sigappu Suryan (Muktha V. Srinivasan, Tam, 1983)
Sigappu Thali (D.R. Thyagarajan, Tam, 1988)
Sigasanam (Shrikumaran Thampi, Mal, 1979)
Signalman Siddappa (Tekkatte Nagaraj, K, 1971)
Signet Ring (**Raja Sandow**, St, 1931)
Sikandar (**Sohrab Modi**, U/Persian, 1941)
Sikandar (**Sai Paranjpye**, H, 1976)
Sikandar-e-Azam (Kedar Kapoor, H, 1965)
Sikappukili (Ramanarayanan, Tam, 1985)
Sikka (Dilip Bose, H, 1976)
Sikka (**K. Bapaiah**, H, 1989)
Sikkim (**Satyajit Ray**, E, 1971)
Sila (Augustine Prakash?, Mal, 1982)
Sila (**B.R. Ishara**, H, 1987)
Silambu (Netaji, Tam, 1990)
Sila Nerangalil Sila Manithargal (**A. Bhimsingh**, Tam, 1976)
Silence! The Court is in Session *see* **Shantata! Court Chalu Aahe**
Silent Curse *see* Sati No Sraap
Silent Raga *see* **Mouna Ragam**
Silent Service (**Santi P. Choudhury**, E, 1974)
Silent Storm, The *see* **Neerab Jhada**
Silicone Chip, The (**Pradeep Krishen**, E, 1978)
Silk Silk Silk (Y.G. Gopikrishnan, Tam, 1983)
Silpi *see* Shilpi
Silsila (**Yash Chopra**, H, 1981)
Silver Cloud *see* Varachat Vidhwa
Silver King (**Chimanlal Luhar**, H, 1935)
Silver King (B.J. Patel, H, 1957)
Silver Queen (Raja Yagnik, H, 1946)
Simantak Mani (*aka* Krishna Under Charge of Theft: **Dadasaheb Phalke**, St, 1925)
Simanta Raag (Pradeep Bhattacharya, B, 1982)
Simantik (Ardhendu Mukherjee, B, 1950)
Simantini (**Ellis Duncan**, Tam, 1936)
Simba (Mohammed Hussain, H, 1951)
Simha Baladu (**K. Raghavendra Rao**, Tel, 1978)
Simhachala Kshetram (B.V. Prasad, Tel, 1965)
Simhachanam (Shrikumaran Thampi, Mal, 1979)
Simhada Mari Sainya (**S.V. Rajendra Singh**, K, 1981)
Simha Garjana (K. Sheshgiri Rao, Tel, 1978)
Simha Garjane (S.A. Chandrasekharan, K, 1983)
Simha Jodi (Joe Simon, K, 1980)
Simham Navindi (**Yoganand**, Tel, 1983)
Simhapuri Simham (Kodi Ramakrishna, Tel, 1983)
Simhasana (C.R. Simha, K, 1983)
Simhasanam *see* Sinhasan
Simha Soppanam (S.S. Karuppuswamy, Tam, 1984)
Simha Swapna (W.R. Subba Rao, K, 1968)
Simha Swapnam (V.B. Rajendra Prasad, Tel, 1989)
Simla Road (Jugal Kishore, H, 1969)
Simla Special (Muktha V. Srinivasan, Tam, 1982)
Simon Peter Ninakku Vendi (P.G. Vishwambaran, Mal, 1988)
Sim Sim Marjina (Naren Dave, H, 1958)
Sinbad Alibaba and Alladdin (P.N. Arora, H, 1965)
Sinbad Jahazi *see* Sinbad the Sailor
Sinbad Khalashi (*aka* Sinbad the Sailor: **R.G. Torney**, St, 1930)
Sinbad Ki Beti (*aka* Daughter of Sinbad: Ratilal, H, 1958)
Sinbad the Sailor (*aka* Sinbad Jahazi: **Nanubhai Vakil**/Amulakh Desai, H, 1946)
Sinbad the Sailor (*aka* Sinbad Jahazi: **Nanabhai Bhatt**, H, 1952)
Sindabad Khalashi *see* Sinbad Khalashi
Sindh Ni Sumari (*aka* Sumari of Sind: **Chandulal Shah**, St, 1927)
Sindhu (**Sasikumar**, Mal, 1975)
Sindhu Bhairavi (**K. Balachander**, Tam, 1985)
Sindoor (**Kishore Sahu**, H, 1947)
Sindoor (Sudhir Mukherjee, B, 1957)
Sindoor (K. Ravi Shankar, H, 1987)
Sindooracheppu (**Madhu**, Mal, 1971)
Sindooram (Jesey, Mal, 1976)
Sindoora Sandhyakku Mounam (**I.V. Sasi**, Mal, 1982)
Sindoor Aur Bandook (Vinod Talwar, H, 1989)
Sindoor Bane Jwala (**K. Bapaiah**, H, 1981)
Sindoor Box *see* **Sindooracheppu**
Sindoore Megh (Sushil Ghosh, B, 1964)
Sindoor Ka Daan (O.P. Agarwal, H, 1984)
Sindoor Ki Awaaz (P. Chandrasekhar, H, 1990)
Sindoorthapa (Dinesh Rawal, G, 1984)
Sindura Bindu (**Sisir Mishra**, O, 1976)
Sinhastha Parvani (*aka* Sinhastha Mela: **Dadasaheb Phalke**, St, 1919)
Sinehithi (G. Ramakrishnan, Tam, 1970)
Singaar (J.K. Nanda, H, 1949)
Singapore (**Shakti Samanta**, H, 1960)
Singaporenalli Raja Kulla (C.V. Rajendran, K, 1978)
Singapore Seeman (M.A.V. Rajendran, Tam, 1969)
Singaravelan (R.V. Udayakumar, Tam, 1991)
Singari (**T.R. Raghunath**, Tam, 1951)
Singari Bangari (Chandrahas Alva, K, 1989)
Singhasan *see* Sinhasan
Singhdwar (**Niren Lahiri**, B, 1949)
Singhdwar (Sukhen Das, B, 1978)
Sinhagad (**Baburao Painter**, St, 1923)
Sinhagad (**V. Shantaram**, Mar, 1933)
Sinhaldweep Ki Sundari (Kikubhai Desai, H, 1937)
Sinhaldweep Ki Sundari (Shantilal Soni, H, 1960)
Sinhaldweep Ki Sundari (*aka* Fairy of Sinhaldwip: **Nanubhai Vakil**, St, 1929)
Sinhasan (**Gajanan Jagirdar**, H, 1934)
Sinhasan (**Jabbar Patel**, Mar, 1979)
Sinhasan/Simhasanam (**Ghantamneni Krishna**, H/Tel, 1986)
Sinhasta: Path to Immortality (**Shyam Benegal**, E, 1968)
Sinh Garjana (*aka* Lion Man: **J.B.H. Wadia**, St, 1932)
Sinh Ka Bachha Sinh (*aka* Roaring Lion: **Homi Master**, St, 1929)
Sinh Ki Pyaas (*aka* Brave Lion: ?, Daphtary Bros., St, 1934)
Sinh No Panja (*aka* Lion's Claw: Pesi Karani, St, 1930)
Sinh Santaan (*aka* Lion's Cub: **Dhirubhai Desai**, St, 1932)
Sinner, The *see* Gunehgaar
Sinning Souls *see* Vilasi Atma
Sin Redeemed, The *see* Minal Devi
Sinthir Sindoor (Ardhendu Sen, B, 1956)
Sinyor (**Atul Bordoloi**, A, 1991)
Sipahi *see* Jai Hind
Sipahi (Dawood, H, 1941)
Sipahi Ka Sapna *see* Soldier's Dream
Sipahi Ki Sajni/Sipahini Sajni (**Chandulal Shah**, H/G, 1936)
Sipahiya (Aspi, H, 1949)
Sipahsalaar (*aka* Captain: **Jayant Desai**, St, 1932)
Sipahsalaar (**J.P. Advani**, H, 1936)
Sipahsalaar (Mohammed Hussain, H, 1956)
Sipayi Kooturu (Chengaiah, Tel, 1959)
Sipayi Ramu (Y.R. Swamy, K, 1971)
Sir (**Mahesh Bhatt**, H, 1993)
Sirai *see* **Chirai**
Sirai Paravai (Manobala, Tam, 1987)
Siraj (Bishnu Rabha/**Phani Sarma**, A, 1948)
Siraj (**Bhupen Hazarika**, A, 1988)
Siraj-ud-Dowla (Amar Dutta, B, 1952)
Sirayil Pootha Chinnamalar (Amirtham, Tam, 1990)
Sirayil Sila Ragangal (Rajendra Kumar, Tam, 1990)
Sircar Express (Krishnan, Tel, 1968)
Siren of Baghdad *see* Baghdad Nu Bulbul
Sirikathe (**R.S. Prakash** et al, Tam, 1939)
Sir I Love You (C.N. Rangarajan, Tam, 1991)
Sirimalle Navvindi (**Vijayanirmala**, Tel, 1980)
Sirimuvvala Simhanadamu (**K. Vishwanath**, Tel, 1990)
Siripuram Chinnodu (Raviraja Pinisetty, Tel, 1988)
Siripuram Monagadu (K.S.R. Doss, Tel, 1983)
Sirirasthu Subhamasthu (Kotta Subba Rao, Tel, 1981)
Siri Sampadalu (**P. Pullaiah**, Tel, 1962)
Siri Siri Mama (**Karunanidhi**, Tam, 1979)
Siri Siri Muvva (**K. Vishwanath**, Tel, 1976)
Siritanakke Saval (T.R. Ramanna, K, 1978)
Siritha Mugham (V.V. Raman, Tam, 1968)
Sirithu Vazha Vendum (S.S. Balan, Tam, 1974)
Sirivenella *see* Shrivenella
Sir Shankarnath (**Debaki Bose**, B, 1948)
Siruthonda Nayanar (C.V. Raman, Tam, 1935)
Sir Wrangler R.P. Paranjpye (**H.S. Bhatavdekar**, St, 1902)
Sisindri Chittibabu (A. Sanjivi, Tel, 1971)
Sisirathil Oru Vasantham (?, Yogadweep Creations, Mal, 1980)
Sister *see* **Bahen**
Sister (Piyush Bose, B, 1977)
Sister (Rajdeep, H, 1980)
Sisters *see* Alakh Kishori
Sita *see* Seeta
Sitam (**Aruna Raje**/Vikas Desai, H, 1982)
Sitamgarh (*aka* Tyrant: Haribhai Desai, St, 1930)
Sitamgarh (**Jayant Desai**, H, 1934)
Sitamgarh (*aka* Khubsoorat Taapoo: Aakkoo, H, 1954)
Sitamgarh (**T. Prakash Rao**, H, 1958)
Sitamgarh (Raj N. Sippy, H, 1985)
Sitamgarh Samaj *see* Rank Ramani
Sitara (**Ezra Mir**, H, 1939)
Sitara (S.K. Ojha, H, 1955)
Sitara (Meraj, H, 1980)
Sitara (**Vamsy**, Tel, 1984)
Sitaramayyagari Manamralu (Kranthi Kumar, Tel, 1991)
Sitar Patal Prabesh (Dilip Mukherjee, B, 1953)
Sitaron Se Aage (**Satyen Bose**, H, 1958)
Sivagami (Mithradas, Tam, 1960)
Sivagangai Seemai (K. Shankar, Tam, 1959)
Sivakamyin Selvan (C.V. Rajendran, Tam, 1974)
Sivakavi (?, Central Studios, Tam, 1943)

Sivalinga Satchi (S. Nottani, Tam, 1942)
Sivamettina Satyam (**Dasari Narayana Rao**, Tel, 1982)
Sivantha Kangal (Ramanarayanan, Tam, 1982)
Sivantha Malar (Sasi Mohan, Tam, 1992)
Sivantha Mann (**C.V. Sridhar**, Tam, 1969)
Sivappu Malli (Ramanarayanan, Tam, 1981)
Sivappu Nirathil Chinnapu (?, Rajeshwari Films, Tam, 1990)
Sivappu Parvai (L. Selva, Tam, 1992)
Sivaranjani (**Dasari Narayana Rao**, Tel, 1978)
Sivaranjani (K. Rangaraj, Tam, 1991)
Sivathandavam (N. Shankaran Nair, Mal, 1976)
Sivude Shankaradu (Surendra Babu, Tel, 1988)
Sivudu Sivudu Sivudu (A. Kodandarami Reddy, Tel, 1983)
6.40 p.m. (**Mani Kaul**, H, 1967)
16 Vayathinile *see* **Pathinaru Vayathinile**
Sixth International Film Festival of India (**Vishnu Mathur**, E, 1976)
Siyasat (Sukhwant Dhadda, H, 1992)
Sizzling Bodies *see* Jalte Badan
Slave *see* Gulam
Slave Girl of Agra *see* Madhabi Kankan
Slaves *see* **Adimagal**
Slaves of Custom (**B.P. Mishra**, St, 1926)
Slaves of Luxury, The *see* **Mojili Mumbai**
Sleeping God *see* Nidrit Bhagwan
Slum Eviction (**Saeed Mirza**, E, 1978)
Small Family, A (**Fali Bilimoria**, H, 1976)
Small Scale Industries of India (**Vishnu Mathur**, E, 1973)
SM Joshi *see* Mi SM
Smoking Tuna (**Suresh Heblikar**, E, 1984)
Smritichitre (**Vijaya Mehta**, Mar, 1983)
Smritir Parash (**Nip Barua**, A, 1955)
Smriti Tuku Thak (Yatrik, B, 1960)
Smuggler (Aspi Irani, H, 1936)
Snake Charmer, The *see* **Sapurey**
Snapaka Yohannan (**P. Subramanyam**, Mal, 1963)
Snehabandham (P. Chandrasekhara Reddy, Tel, 1973)
Snehabandham (K. Vijayan, Mal, 1983)
Snehabhishekham (Mukta V. Srinivasan, Tel, 1983)
Snehada Kadalalli (Joe Simon, K, 1992)
Snehada Sankole (A. Kashilingam, K, 1982)
Sneha Deepam (**P. Subramanyam**, Mal, 1962)
Snehadeepame Mizhi Thurakku (**P. Bhaskaran**, Mal, 1972)
Sneham (**A. Bhimsingh**, Mal, 1977)
Sneham (**Bapu**, Tel, 1977)
Sneham Oru Pravaham (Dr Shah Jehan, Mal, 1981)
Snehamulla Simham (?, Vijaya Movies Prod, Mal, 1986)
Snehapoorvam Meera (Harikumar, Mal, 1982)
Sneha Sagaram (Sathyan Andhikkad, Mal, 1992)
Sneha Sambandha (Rajachandra, K, 1985)
Sneha Sedu (V. Madhusudhana Rao, K, 1978)
Snehaseema (S.S. Rajan, Mal, 1954)
Snehathinte Mukhangal (**T. Hariharan**, Mal, 1978)
Sneha Yamuna (Raghu, Mal, 1977)
Sneh Bandhan (*aka* Intezaar: **J.P. Advani**, H, 1940)
Snehicha Kuttathinu (P.K. Joseph, Mal, 1985)
Snehikkan Oru Pennu (K. Sukumaran, Mal, 1978)
Snehikkan Samayamilla (Vijayanand, Mal, 1978)
Snehitara Saval (K.S.R. Doss, K, 1981)
Sneh Jyoti (*aka* Love Flame: **Raja Sandow**/Vaidya, St, 1928)
Sneh Lagna (Love Marriage, Pyar Ki Baatein: Chandrarao Kadam, H, 1938)
Snehlata (*aka* Bharat Ki Devi: **Balwant Bhatt**, H/G, 1936)
Sneh Samadhi (*aka* Martyrs of Love: Ramakant-Gharekhan, St, 1929)
Sneh Vina (*aka* Song of my Heart: A.P. Kapur, St, 1932)
Sobhraj (?, Shirdi-Sai Creations, Mal, 1986)
Sobti (M.S. Rajan, Mar, 1980)
Socha Na Tha (Hassan Sharif, H, 1989)
Social Life of the Honey Bee, The (**Pradeep Krishen**, E, 1977)
Social Pirates *see* Mumbai Ni Mohini
Society (S. Nazir, H, 1942)
Society (Shaheed Latif, H, 1955)
Society (?, Johnny Whisky, H, 1987)
Society Butterfly *see* Khubsoorat Bala
Society Lady (A.B. Raj, Mal, 1978)
Society Scoundrel *see* Shareef Badmash
So Dahada Sasuna To Ek Dahado Vahuno (Kishore Vyas, G, 1980)
Sodari (T.V. Singh Thakore, K, 1955)
So Far from India (**Mira Nair**, E, 1982)
Sofia (G.S. Devare, H, 1946)
Sogandh Tari Rakhdina (Himmat Dave, G, 1984)
Soggadu (**K. Bapaiah**, Tel, 1975)
Sohni Kumharan (Raj Hans, P, 1939)
Sohni Mahiwal (K.P. Bhave, St, 1928)
Sohni Mahiwal (A.P. Kapur, St, 1928)
Sohni Mahiwal (**Harshadrai Mehta**, H, 1933)
Sohni Mahiwal (**R.L. Shorey**?, Kamala Movietone, P, 1939)
Sohni Mahiwal (Ishwarlal/Ravindra Jayakar, H, 1946)
Sohni Mahiwal (Raja Nawathe, H, 1958)
Sohni Mahiwal (Kanwal Viola, P, 1984)
Sohni Mahiwal (Umesh Mehra, H, 1984)
Soil, The *see* **Mannu**
Solaho Singaar Kare Dulhania (Romani De, Bh, 1965)
Solah Satra (Munna Rizvi, H, 1990)
Solah Shukrawar (Ashish Kumar, H, 1977)
Solai Kuyil (Rajan, Tam, 1989)
Solaimalai Rani (A. Rajaram, Tam, 1960)
Solaiyamma (Kasthuriraja, Tam, 1992)
Solanki Shamsher (*aka* The Combat: **Harshadrai Mehta**, St, 1931)
Solar Energy (**Basu Bhattacharya**, E, 1986)
Soldier (*aka* Thakur Diler Singh: Shyam, H, 1969)
Soldier of Madurai *see* **Madurai Veeran**
Soldier's Dream (*aka* Sipahi Ka Sapna: **Sushil Majumdar**, H, 1948)
Soldier's Sweetheart *see* **Sipahi Ki Sajni**
Soldier's Wife (**R.S. Prakash**, Tam, 1937)
Sole Sajya Singar (Ramanlal Desai, G, 1977)
Sole Somwar (Radhakant, G, 1988)
Solillada Saradada (Saiprakash, K, 1992)
Soli Pushpangale (A. Ramarajan, Tam, 1986)
Sollathen Ninaikiran (**K. Balachander**, Tam, 1973)
Sollathey Yarum Kettal (Rajbharath, Tam, 1981)
Solla Thudikuthu Manasu (B. Lenin, Tam, 1988)
Sollu Thambi Sollu (T.V. Sundaram, Tam, 1959)
Solva Saal (**Raj Khosla**, H, 1958)
Solva Sawan (**Bharathirajaa**, H, 1978)
Solvathellam Unmai (Nethaji, Tam, 1987)
Somari Pothu (V. Ramchandra Rao, Tel, 1972)
Somavara Vratham (R.M. Krishnaswamy, Tel, 1963)
Someone Unknown *see* **Yaro Oral**
Some People Sometimes *see* **Sila Nerangalil Sila Manithargal**
Something Like a War (Deepa Dhanraj, E, 1991)
Somewhere *see* **Oridathu**
Som Mangal Shani (Sayyad Abrar, H, 1988)
Sommokadidhi Sokokadidhi (**Singeetham Srinivasa Rao**, Tel, 1978)
Somnambulism *see* **Swapnadanam**
Sona (*aka* Gold: Mazhar Khan, H, 1948)
Sona Ani Mona (**Dinkar D. Patil**, Mar, 1992)
Sona Boudi (Piyush Kanti Ganguli, B, 1971)
Sona Chandi (*aka* Bhai Bhai: R.D. Parineeja, H, 1946)
Sona Indhoni Roopa Bedlun (Jasubhai Trivedi, G, 1979)
Sonal (Prabhat Mukherjee, H, 1973)
Sonal Sundari (Sushama Shiromani, G, 1985)
Sonamurar Kiron Kishore (Nana Bose, B, 1983)
Sonani Jaal (Arun Bhatt, G, 1984)
Sonano Suraj *see* Vasavadatta
Sonano Suraj (Girish Manukant, G, 1978)
Sonaran Tochla Kaan (Anant Marathe, Mar, 1973)
Sonar Chheye Dami (TV: **Utpalendu Chakraborty**, B, 1989)
Sonar Harin (Mangal Chakraborty, B, 1959)
Sonar Harin (Samarendra Narayan Deb, A, 1979)
Sonar Kathi (**Debaki Bose**, B, 1958)
Sonar Kella (**Satyajit Ray**, B, 1974)
Sonar Khancha (**Agradoot**, B, 1973)
Sonar Sansar/Sunehra Sansar (**Debaki Bose**, B/H, 1936)
Sonar Sansar (Rathish De Sarkar, B, 1984)
Sonava Ka Pinjra (Lalji Yadav, Bh, 1983)
Sonay Suhaga (Ranjan Majumdar, B, 1981)
Sonba Ane Rupba (**Krishnakant**, G, 1979)
Sonbaini Chundadi (Girish Manukant, G, 1976)
Sondangal Vazhka (Madurai Thirumaran, Tam, 1975)
Sondhadu Needana (C.N.Muthu, Tam, 1978)
Sondhakkaran (Raja, Tam, 1989)
Sondham (A.C. Trilogchander, Tam, 1973)
Sondham Padinaru (T.S. Krishnakumar, Tam, 1989)
Sondhi/Sandhi (*aka* Suleh: Apurba Mitra, B/H, 1944)
Sondhi (Amal Dutta, B, 1980)
Sone Ka Dil Lohe Ke Haath (Naresh Kumar, H, 1978)
Sone Ka Shaher (*aka* Golden City: A.P. Kapur, H, 1935)
Sone Ke Haath (P.D. Shenoy, H, 1973)
Sone Ki Chidiya (*aka* Biswi Sadi: G.R. Sethi, H, 1934)
Sone Ki Chidiya (E. Bilimoria, H, 1948)
Sone Ki Chidiya (Shaheed Latif, H, 1958)
Sone Ki Lanka (Ajay Kashyap, H, 1992)
Sone Ki Zanjeer (Shiv Kumar, H, 1992)
Sone Pe Suhaaga (**K. Bapaiah**, H, 1988)
Sone Rani *see* **Sati Sone**
Soneri Jaal (*aka* Ex-husband: Gordhanbhai Patel, St, 1927)
Soneri Khanjar (*aka* Kindred of the Dust: **Harshadrai Mehta**, St, 1930)
Soneri Savli (C. Raghuvir, Mar, 1953)
Soneri Toli *see* Golden Gang
Sonetara (**Nip Barua**, A, 1973)
Song, The *see* Geet
Songadya (Govind Kulkarni, Mar, 1971)
Song of Baghdad (?, Solar Films, H, 1947)
Song of Celestial *see* Sati Mahananda
Song of Life *see* **Bhikharan**
Song of Life (G.P. Pawar, St, 1930)
Song of Love *see* Sundari
Song of my Heart *see* Sneh Vina
Song of Punjab (**Santi P. Choudhury**, E, 1965)
Song of the Desert *see* Nagma-e-Sahara
Song of the Little Road *see* **Pather Panchali**
Song of the Parrot *see* **Kilippattu**
Song of the Road *see* **Pather Panchali**
Song of the Serpent *see* **Karma**
Song of the Wilds *see* India in Africa
Songs of Bengal (**Santi P. Choudhury**, E, 1957)
Songs of Sorrow *see* Dard-e-Jigar
Son Kansari (**Ravindra Dave**, G, 1977)
Son Kunwar (Bhogilal Pattani, G, 1983)
Sonmai (**Nip Barua**, A, 1977)
Son Moina (Siva Prasad Thakur, A, 1984)
Sonna Nambamattenga (S. Jaichander, Tam, 1985)
Sonnathai Seivan (**Krishnan-Panju**, Tam, 1977)
Son of Alibaba (Majnu, H, 1955)
Son of Alladdin (*aka* Alladdin Ka Beta: **Nanubhai Vakil**, H, 1939)
Son of Alladdin (*aka* Alladdin Ka Beta: R. Rizvi, H, 1955)
Son of a Shepherd *see* Bhagyavaan Bharwad
Son of Ashoka *see* Veer Kunal
Son of Hatimtai *see* Hatimtai Ka Beta
Son of Hatimtai (Dharam Kumar, H, 1965)
Son of Hercules (Sultan, H, 1964)
Son of India (**Mehboob**, H, 1962)
Son of Sinbad (**Nanabhai Bhatt**, H, 1958)
Son of the Desert *see* Misar Ka Sitara
Son of Toofan Mail (?, Super Pics, H, 1947)
Son of Zambo *see* Zambo Ka Beta
Sons of the Rich *see* Vasant Leela
Sontavooru (I.S.S. Murthy, Tel, 1956)
Sonthamadi Nee Yenakku (S.P. Muthuraman, Tam, 1977)
Sonyachi Lanka (Shrikant Sutar, Mar, 1950)
Sonyachi Paoole (**Raja Paranjpe**, Mar, 1962)
Sood *see* Badla
Sood (*aka* Vengeance: ?, Shri Narendra Film, St, 1930)
Sookha *see* Bara
Soolam (M. Bhaskar, Tam, 1980)
Soon Ladki Hya Gharchi (Yeshwant Pethkar, Mar, 1972)
Soon Majhi Lakshmi (Datta Gorle, Mar, 1981)
Soon Majhi Savitri (Krishna Patil, Mar, 1974)
Soorakottai Singhakutty (Ramanarayanan, Tam, 1983)
Soora Puli (**T.R. Sundaram**, Tam, 1944)
Soora Samharam (Chitra Lakshmanan, Tam, 1988)
Soorat (Nasrat A. Mansoori, H, 1947)
Soorat Aur Seerat (Bahl, H, 1963)
Sooravalli (**Nemai Ghosh**, Tam, 1981)
Soori Gadu (**Dasari Narayana Rao**, Tel, 1992)
Soorma Bhopali (Jagdeep, H, 1988)
Sooryan (**Sasikumar**, Mal, 1982)
Sooryan (Pavithran, Tam, 1992)
Sooryan Chandran (K.S. Ravikumar, Tam, 1993)
Sooryante Maranam (Rajeev Nath, Mal, 1978)
Soppu Seeppu Kannadi (Thirumalai-Mahalingam, Tam, 1968)
Sorathi Baharvatiyo (*aka* Outlaw of Sorath: **Nanubhai Vakil**, St, 1930)
Sorathi Shamsher (*aka* Noblesse Oblige: ?, **Indulal Yagnik**, St, 1929)
Sorathi Sinh (Ramnik Acharya, G, 1976)
Sorathiyani Son (Dinesh Rawal, G, 1977)
Sorathi Yoddho (*aka* Valiant Warrior: Fram Sethna, St, 1931)
Sorathni Padmini (Vijay Datt, G, 1980)
Sorathno Savaj (**Chandrakant Sangani**, G, 1985)
Sorgam (T.R. Ramanna, Tam, 1970)
Sorgathil Thirumanam (Ramanna, Tam, 1974)
Sorgathin Thirappu Vizha (A. Jagannathan, Tam, 1981)
Sorgavasal (A. Kasilingam, Tam, 1954)
Sorrow of a Moor *see* Aansuon Ki Duniya
Sorry Madam (Dilip Bose, B, 1962)
Sose Thanda Saubhagya (A.V. Sheshgiri Rao, K, 1977)
SOS Jasoos 007 (*aka* Jasoos 007: Sultan, H, 1969)
Sosur Bari (Arun Choudhury, B, 1953)
Sothu Geddavalu (S.K. Ananthachari, K, 1971)
Sought but Didn't Find *see* **Anveshichu Kandatiyilla**
Soul of a Slave *see* Lohika Lilam *or* Pilgrims Of Love
Soul of a Slave (Hemchandra Mukherjee, St, 1922)
Soul of a Snake *see* Nari Ke Nagan
Soul of Darkness, The *see* **Irutinte Atmavu**
Soundaryame Varuga Varuga *see* Sundarime Varuga Varuga
Soundarya Pooja (B.K. Pottekkat, Mal, 1973)
Soundaryappinakkam (Rajasenan, Mal, 1985)
Sounh Meno Punjab Di (**Sukhdev Ahluwalia**, P, 1990)
Souridham (?, Sunitha Prod., Mal, 1991)
Souten (Sawan Kumar, H, 1983)
Souten Ki Beti (Sawan Kumar, H, 1989)
Soyreek (Subhash Bhurke, Mar, 1977)
Spandana (P.N. Srinivas, K, 1979)
Sparisam (R.C. Sakthi, Tam, 1982)
Sparkling Youth *see* Jagmagti Jawani
Sparsh (**Sai Paranjpye**, H, 1979)
Sparshamani (Sudhin Majumdar, B, 1951)
SP Bhargavi (V. Somashekhar, K, 1991)
SP Bhayankar (V.B. Rajendra Prasad, Tel, 1984)
Speculator *see* Mumbaino Satodia
Speed Queen (Nari Ghadiali, H, 1947)
Speed Spider *see* Toofan Queen
Sphotanam (?, Mal, 1981)
Spices *see* **Mirch Masala**
Spinning Wheel *see* Anath Abala
Splendid New Views of Bombay (F.B. Thanawala,

St, 1900)
SP Sangliana (P. Nanjundappa, K, 1988)
SP Sangliana II (P. Nanjundappa, K, 1990)
Spy in Goa (*aka* Panic In Goa: Dharam Kumar, H, 1966)
Spy in Rome (Adarsh, H, 1968)
Sreedharante Onam Thirumurivu (?, Mal, 1987)
Sreekovil (S. Ramanathan/P.A. Thomas, Mal, 1962)
Sreevari Chindulu (Relangi Narasimha Rao, Tel, 1991)
Sreevari Muchatlu (**Dasari Narayana Rao**, Tel, 1980)
Sreevari Shobhanam (Jandhyala, Tel, 1985)
Sreevariki Premalekha (Jandhyala, Tel, 1984)
Sreevaru (B. Bhaskara Rao, Tel, 1985)
Sreevaru Maavaru (B.S. Narayan, Tel, 1973)
Sridevi (B.S. Narayana, Tel, 1970)
Sridevi (N. Shankaran Nair, Mal, 1977)
Sridevi (Balaji, Tam, 1980)
Sridevi Kamakshi Kataksham (**B. Vittalacharya**, Tel, 1988)
Srikakula Andhra Mahavishnu Katha (A.K. Sekhar, Tel, 1966)
Srikanta (Tara Kumar Bhadury, St, 1930)
Srikanter Will (**Dinen Gupta**, B, 1979)
Srikkathe *see* Sirikathe
Srimadh Bhagavad Geeta (**P. Bhaskaran**, Mal, 1976)
Srimanthana Magalu (A.V. Sheshgiri Rao, K, 1977)
Sringara Kavya (S. Narayan, K, 1993)
Sringara Masa (**Pattabhi Rama Reddy**, K, 1984)
Sringara Rasa (Anand, K, 1993)
Sringuru Yatra (A. Raghurami Reddy, Tel, 1990)
Srinivasa Kalyanam (**A. Narayanan**, Tam, 1934)
Srinivasa Kalyanam (Kodi Ramakrishna, Tel, 1987)
Srinkhal (**Dhiren Ganguly**, B, 1947)
Srinkhal (Abir Basu, B, 1983)
Srirasthu Subamasthu (K. Subba Rao, Tel, 1981)
Srishti (K.T. Mohammed, Mal, 1975)
Srishtichhara (**Gurudas Bagchi**, B, 1975)
Srishti Rahasyulu (Tatineni Prasad, Tel, 1980)
Sruthi (Mohan, Mal, 1987)
Sruti and Graces in Indian Music (**Shyam Benegal**, E, 1972)
Srutilayalu (**K. Vishwanath**, Tel, 1987)
SS Jaldevi *see* Toofani Khazana
Stage (Vijay Mhatre, H, 1951)
Stage Girl (**R.S. Prakash**, St, 1929)
Stage Girl (S.H. Tharani, H, 1947)
Stain, The *see* **Daag**
Staircases *see* **Enippadikal**
Star, A *see* **Sitara**
Star (**Vinod Pande**, H, 1982)
Star of Asia *see* Asiai Sitara
Stars of the East *see* Hind Ke Tare
State Express (**Vijay Bhatt**, H, 1938)
State Express (Babubhai, H, 1961)
State Guests *see* **Sarkari Pahune**
State Rowdy (B. Gopal, Tel, 1989)
Station Master (**Chimanlal Luhar**, H, 1942)
Station Master (P.A. Thomas, Mal, 1966)
Station Master (Kodi Ramakrishna, Tel, 1988)
Stay Awake *see* **Jagte Raho**
Steel: A Whole New Way of Life (**Shyam Benegal**, E, 1971)
Stephen *see* **Estheppan**
Step Mother *see* Bimata
Step Mother (*aka* Sauteli Maa: S.D. Kerawala, H, 1935)
Sterilisation of the Female (**Govind Saraiya**, E, 1964)
Sthalathe Pradhana Payyans (Shaji Kailash, Mal, 1992)
Sthanarthi Saramma (**K.G. Sethumadhavan**, Mal, 1966)
Sthanik Swarajya *see* Municipality
Stigma *see* **Daag**
Stinger Stung, The *see* Katorabhar Khoon
Stolen Bride *see* Zulm
Stone Boy (TV: **T.S. Nagabharana**, H, 1991)
Storm, The *see* Alochhaya *or* **Jhor**
Storm of Death *see* Atashi Toofan *or* Maut Ka Toofan
Story of a Village *see* **Oka Oorie Katha**
Story of a Woman *see* **Oru Penninte Katha**
Story of Cement, The (**Nirad Mahapatra**, E, 1978)
Story of Glass (**Buddhadev Dasgupta**, E, 1985)
Story of Steel, The (*aka* Indian Iron and Steel: **Harisadhan Dasgupta**, E, 1956)
Strange Brothers *see* **Apoorva Sahodarargal**
Strange Fate of Arvind Desai *see* **Arvind Desai Ki Ajeeb Dastaan**
Stranger, The *see* **Agantuk**
Stree (*aka* Jawani Ka Rang: Saqi, H, 1938)
Stree (R. Velappan Nair, Mal, 1950)
Stree (**V. Shantaram**, H, 1961)
Stree (Siddharth, O, 1966)
Stree (**P. Bhaskaran**, Mal, 1970)
Stree (Salil Dutta, B, 1972)
Stree (**K. Pratyagatma**, Tel, 1973)
Stree Charitra *see* Rambha Rani *or* Vikram Shashikala
Streedhan (Babasaheb Fattelal, Mar, 1985)
Streedhanam (Anil Babu, Mal, 1993)
Stree Dharma (*aka* Rangeen Gunah, Painted Sin: C.M. Rafi, H, 1935)
Stree Durga (**Sailajananda Mukherjee**, B, 1945)
Stree Gauravam (S.S. Devadas, Tel, 1973)
Stree Hrudayan (J.D. Thottan, Mal, 1960)
Stree Janma Hi Tujhi Kahani (**Datta Dharmadhikari**, Mar, 1952)
Stree Janmam (**K.S. Prakash Rao**, Tel, 1967)
Stree Janma Tujhi Kahani (Bhaskar Jadhav, Mar, 1987)
Stree Oru Dukham (A.G. Baby, Mal, 1978)
Stree Purush (Rajkumar, H, 1975)
Stree Ratna (**K. Subramanyam**, K, 1955)
Streer Patra (Purnendu Pattrea, B, 1972)
Stree Shakti (*aka* Sex, The Super Sex: Haribhai Desai, St, 1932)
Street Angels *see* Pardesi Preetam
Street Girl *see* Dukhiari
Street Singer/Saathi (**Phani Majumdar**, H/B, 1938)
Street Singer (Chandrasekhar, H, 1966)
Streeyaraj *see* Guru Machhindranath
Strife to Stability (**Kantilal Rathod**, E, 1969)
Striker (Archan Chakraborty, B, 1978)
Strisahasam (**Vedantam Raghavaiah**, Tel/Tam, 1951)
Struggle *see* Jeevan Sangram
Students Today *see* **Vidyarthikale Ithile Ithile**
Stuff of Steel, The (**Chidananda Das Gupta**, E, 1969)
Stunt King *see* Dil-e-Dilar
Stunt King (Keshav Talpade, H, 1944)
Stunt Queen (Ramnik Vyas, H, 1947)
Stuvartpuram Dongalu (Sagar, Tel, 1991)
Stuvartpuram Police Station (Yandamuri Virendranath, Tel, 1991)
Subah *see* **Umbartha**
Subah Hone Tak (?, Chhabra Films, H, 1988)
Subah Ka Sitara (**Premankur Atorthy**, Urdu, 1932)
Subah Ka Tara (**V. Shantaram**, H, 1954)
Subah-o-Debatargrash (Partha Prathim Choudhury, B, 1964)
Subah-o-Shyam (**Tapi Chanakya**, H, 1972)
Subah Shyam (**P.C. Barua**, H, 1944)
Subah Zaroor Ayegi (Mahendra Pran/Datta Chouhan, H, 1977)
Subaida (M.S. Mani, Mal, 1965)
Subarna Golak (Manu Sen, B, 1981)
Subarnalata (Bijoy Bose, B, 1981)
Subarnarekha (**Ritwik Ghatak**, B, 1962)
Subarna Seeta (**Sisir Mishra**, O, 1983)
Subbaravuki Kopam Vachindi (Dhavala Satyam, Tel, 1982)
Subba Sastry (M.V. Krishnaswamy, K, 1966)
Subbi Subakka Suvvalali (N.S. Dhananjaya, K, 1980)
Subhadra (**C. Pullaiah**, K, 1941)
Subhadra (**T.R. Sundaram**, Tam, 1945)
Subhadra (**Master Vinayak**, H, 1946)
Subhadra (**Niren Lahiri**, B, 1952)
Subhadra Arjuna (Sama-Ramu, Tam, 1941)
Subhadra Haran (**Datta Dharmadhikari**, Mar/H, 1963)
Subhadra Haran (**Kanjibhai Rathod**, St, 1921)
Subhadra Haran (**N.D. Sarpotdar**, St, 1929)
Subhadra Haran (Prafulla Ghosh, H, 1932)
Subhadra Haran (**R. Padmanabhan**, Tam, 1935)
Subhadra Kalyanam (Kanagal Prabhakar Sastry, K, 1972)
Subhashaya (V.T. Thyagarajan, K, 1977)
Subhashchandra (Piyush Bose, B, 1966)
Subha Tryaha Sparsha (Manmatha Ray, B, 1934)
Subhodayam (**K. Vishwanath**, Tel, 1980)
Subho Tagore (**Santi P. Choudhury**, E, 1981)
Sub Ka Saathi (**A. Bhimsingh**, H, 1972)
Sub Ka Ustad (R. Thakur, H, 1967)
Subrahmanyam (Y.D. Sarpotdar, St, 1930)
Subramanyam *see* Valli Kalyanam
Subse Bada Rupaiya (P.L.Santoshi, H, 1955)
Subse Bada Rupaiya (S. Ramanathan, H, 1976)
Subse Bada Sukh (**Hrishikesh Mukherjee**, H, 1972)
Sudamyache Pohe (**Keshavrao Dhaiber**, Mar, 1958)
Sudarshan (G.V. Sane, St, 1928)
Sudarshan (**Sundarrao Nadkarni/A.S.A. Sami**, Tam, 1951)
Sudarshan (Datta Mane, Mar, 1967)
Sudarshan Chakra (**Datta Dharmadhikari**, H, 1956)
Suddenly One Day *see* **Ek Din Achanak**
Sudhaar (*aka* Pardesi Saiyan: Batuk Bhatt, H, 1949)
Sudha Binduvulu (Sai Raojee, Tel, 1978)
Sudhandhira Nattu Adimagal (S.A. Chandrasekharan, Tam, 1988)
Sudharlelya Baika (**Prabhakar Nayak**, Mar, 1965)
Sudhar Prem (**Premankur Atorthy**, B, 1950)
Sudhatham (Mathurai Thirumaran, Tam, 1971)
Sudheral Shaitan (*aka* Cultured Criminal: ?, **Saurashtra Film**, St, 1927)
Sudhikalasham (Chandrakumar, Mal, 1979)
Sudhu Ekti Bachhar (**Uttam Kumar**, B, 1966)
Sudhu Tomari (Prabir Mitra, B, 1988)
Sudigundalu (**Adurthi Subba Rao**, Tel, 1967)
Sudur Niharika (Sushil Mukherjee, B, 1975)
Sudurum Sudavalliyum (**Puttanna Kanagal**, Tam, 1971)
Sugamana Sumaigal (R. Parthiban, Tam, 1992)
Sugam Engay (**K. Ramnoth**, Tam, 1954)
Sugandh (Raveekant Nagaich, H, 1982)
Sugandhi Katta (Vasant Painter, Mar, 1974)
Suguna Sundari Katha (H.S. Venu, Tel, 1970)
Suhaag (**Balwant Bhatt**, H, 1940)
Suhaag (**B.R. Panthulu**, H, 1958)
Suhaag (**Manmohan Desai**, H, 1979)
Suhaag Bindiya (P.S. Sangma, Bh, 1985)
Suhaag Ka Balidan (?, Vision International, H, 1987)
Suhaag Ka Daan (?, Taj Prod, H, 1936)
Suhaag Ki Raat *see* Dharam Ki Devi
Suhaag Raat (**Kidar Sharma**, H, 1948)
Suhaag Raat (R. Bhattacharya, H, 1968)
Suhaag Ri Aas (Shrigopal Yogesh, R, 1990)
Suhaag Sindoor (Colin Pal, H, 1953)
Suhaag Sindoor (**Krishnan-Panju**, H, 1961)
Suhagan (**J.P. Advani**, H, 1942)
Suhagan (Anant Mane, H, 1954)
Suhagan (**K.S. Gopalakrishnan**, H, 1964)
Suhagan (S.J. Talukdar, G, 1981)
Suhagan (**K. Raghavendra Rao**, H, 1986)
Suhagan Ro Singar (Gajanan Manav, R, 1983)
Suhag Chuda (?, Amit Films, P, 1988)
Suhagi (A. Shakoor, H, 1948)
Suhana Geet (*aka* Toote Dil: M.A. Mirza, H, 1941)
Suhana Safar (Vijay, H, 1970)
Suhani Raat (Vijay Mohan Gupta, H, 1974)
Suhani Sadak (**Shyam Benegal**, H, 1973)
Suhruthu (Joseph Palliputtu, Mal, 1952)
Sui Ka Naka (*aka* Needle's Eye: **Niranjan Pal**, St, 1931)
Sujata (**Bimal Roy**, H, 1959)
Sujata (Pinaki Mukherjee, B, 1974)
Sujatha (**T. Hariharan**, Mal, 1977)
Sujatha (Mohan, Tam, 1980)
Sukamana Ragangal (R. Sundarrajan, Tam, 1985)
Sukanya Savitri (**Kanjibhai Rathod**, St, 1922)
Sukhacha Shodh/Mera Haq (*aka* In Search of Happiness: **P.Y. Altekar**, Mar/H, 1939)
Sukhache Sobti (Raja Bargir, Mar, 1958)
Sukhachi Savli (**Gajanan Jagirdar**, Mar, 1963)
Sukha Dukhalu (I.S. Murthy, Tel, 1968)
Sukh Ale Majhya Daari (Datta Mane, Mar, 1962)
Sukhamo Devi (?, Gandhimati Films, Mal, 1986)
Sukha Samsara (Vijaya Satyam, K, 1970)
Sukha Samsarakke Hanneradu Sutragalu (Rajachandra, K, 1984)
Sukhathinte Pinnale (P.K. Joseph, Mal, 1979)
Sukhi Jeevan (Harishchandra/**Master Bhagwan**, H, 1942)
Sukhi Parivar (Dharam Kumar, P, 1979)
Sukhi Sansar (Shrikant Sutar, Mar, 1967)
Sukhma Sau Dukhma Vahu (Anand Brahmbhatt, G, 1980)
Sukradasa (Anthikad Mani, Mal, 1977)
Sukradasai (T.K. Mohan, Tam, 1984)
Suktara (**Niranjan Pal**, B, 1940)
Sukumar Ray (**Satyajit Ray**, B, 1987)
Sulagte Arman (Himmat Dave, H, 1984)
Sulagto Sansar (*aka* Murderer: G.R. Sethi, H, 1935)
Sulakshana (**Dinkar D. Patil**, Mar, 1985)
Sulavarchi Poli (**Dinkar D. Patil**, Mar, 1980)
Suleh *see* Sondhi
Sulemani Setranji *see* Baghdad Ka Chor
Suleman the Tiger *see* Sher-e-Jung
Suli (**B.S. Ranga**, K, 1978)
Sulochana (*aka* Temple Bells: **R.S. Choudhury**, H, 1933)
Sulochana (K. Sadasiva Rao, Tel, 1936)
Sulochana (**T.R. Sundaram**, Tam, 1946)
Sultana (**A.R. Kardar**, H, 1934)
Sultana Chandbibi *see* Chandbibi
Sultana Chandbibi (A.R. Kabuli, H, 1936)
Sultana Daku (Mohan Sinha, H, 1956)
Sultana Daku (Mohammed Hussain, H, 1972)
Sultanat (Dwarka Khosla, H, 1954)
Sultanat (**Mukul S. Anand**, H, 1986)
Sultan-e-Alam (?, Sharda Films, H, 1956)
Sultan-e-Deccan (*aka* Banda Nawaz: Mallik Anwar, H, 1982)
Sultan-e-Hind (K. Sharif, H, 1978)
Sumai (Ramanarayanan, Tam, 1981)
Sumaithangal (**C.V. Sridhar**, Tam, 1962)
Sumangali (**B.N. Reddi**, Tel, 1940)
Sumangali (M.K.R. Nambiar, Tam, 1959)
Sumangali (**Adurthi Subba Rao**, Tel, 1965)
Sumangali (M.K. Raman, Mal, 1971)
Sumangali (T.V. Singh Thakore, K, 1978)
Sumangali (**D. Yoganand**, Tam, 1983)
Sumangali Kolam (**Vijayanirmala**, Tam, 1984)
Sumari of Sind *see* Sindh Ni Sumari
Sumathi En Sundari (C.V. Rajendran, Tam, 1971)
Sumati (**Kadaru Nagabhushanam**, Tel, 1942)
Sumitra (Basant Kumar, H, 1949)
Summer *see* **Greeshamam**
Summons for Mohan Joshi, A *see* **Mohan Joshi Hazir Ho!**
Suna Chadhei (Ravi Kinnagi, O, 1988)
Sunandar Biye (Sudhir Sarkar, B, 1951)
Sun and Showers *see* **Megh-o-Roudra**
Suna Sansar (**Sisir Mishra**, O, 1978)
Sunayana (Hiren Nag, H, 1979)
Sunayani (Sukhen Das, B, 1979)
Sunbai (**Bhalji Pendharkar**, Mar, 1942)
Sunbai (Madhav Shinde, Mar, 1962)
Sunbai Oti Bharun Ja (**Dinkar D. Patil**, Mar, 1979)
Sundara Kanda (K.V. Raju, K, 1991)
Sundara Kanda (**K. Raghavendra Rao**, Tel, 1992)
Sundara Kandam (**K. Bhagyaraj**, Tam, 1990)
Sundara Manamadhye Bharli (Devdutt, Mar, 1964)
Sundaramurthy Nayanar (**Murugadasa**, Tam, 1937)

Sundaramurthy Nayanar (K. Somu, Tam, 1967)
Sundara Satarkar (Prabhakar Nilkanth, Mar, 1981)
Sundara Swapnagalu (**K. Balachander**, K, 1986)
Sundari (*aka* Pranay Geet, Song of Love: Aspi, H, 1936)
Sundarikaka (Mahesh Soman, Mal, 1991)
Sundari Marudde Swapnangal (K. Shankar, Mal, 1978)
Sundarime Varuga Varuga (**C.V. Sridhar**, Tam, 1980)
Sundari Subbarao (Relangi Narasimha Rao, Tel, 1984)
Sundar Kamdar *see* Atma Bal
Sundopasund (G.V. Sane, St, 1924)
Sunehra Baal (*aka* Golden Hair: Narottam Vyas, H, 1938)
Sunehra Jaal (Kedar Kapoor, H, 1966)
Sunehra Sansar *see* Sonar Sansar
Sunehra Sansar (**Adurthi Subba Rao**, H, 1975)
Sunehre Din (Satish Nigam, H, 1949)
Sunehre Kadam (Satish Nigam, H, 1966)
Sunehre Sapne (**Muzaffar Ali**, H, 1983)
Sunehri Nagin (**Babubhai Mistri**, H, 1963)
Sunehri Raatein (*aka* Honeymoon: Lekhraj Bhakri, H, 1960)
Sunehri Toli (*aka* Golden Gang: Kikubhai Desai, H, 1939)
Sunehri Yaadein (Sandeep Mehta, H, 1980)
Sunehri Zamana *see* Vijayachi Lagne
Sunil Vayasu 20 (**K.S. Sethumadhavan**, Mal, 1986)
Suniye/Aika (**S.S. Gulzar**, H/Mar, 1984)
Sun Meri Laila (Chander Behl, H, 1983)
Sunmica (**Nirad Mahapatra**, E, 1971)
Sunny (**Raj Khosla**, H, 1984)
Suno Baro Nari (**Ajoy Kar**, B, 1960)
Suno Sunata Hoon (Raj Kumar, H, 1944)
Sun Sajna (Chander Behl, H, 1982)
Sun To Le Hasina (**S.P. Bakshi**, H, 1958)
Supattar Binani (Satyen/Mahendra Pujari, R, 1981)
Superman (Mohammed Hussain/Anant Thakur, H, 1960)
Superman (V. Madhusudhana Rao, Tel, 1980)
Superman (?, Ramayana Chitra Association, H, 1987)
Superman (?, Fine Art Pics., H, 1993)
Super Nanna Maga (G.K. Muddu Raju, K, 1992)
Super Sex, The *see* Stree Shakti
Suprabhata (Dinesh Babu, K, 1988)
Suprabhatam (M. Krishnan Nair, Mal, 1974)
Suprabhatam (**K.S. Prakash Rao**, Tel, 1976)
Suprabhatam (K. Shankar, Tam, 1979)
Supreme Test *see* Kasauti
Suputhrudu (**T. Rama Rao**, Tel, 1971)
Suraag (*aka* The Clue: Jagmohan Mundhra, H, 1982)
Surabhiyamangal (P. Ashok Kumar, Mal, 1986)
Suraj (**T. Prakash Rao**, H, 1966)
Suraj (?, S.S. Films, H, 1987)
Suraj Aur Chanda (T. Madhava Rao, H, 1973)
Suraj Chandra Ni Sakhe (**Ravindra Dave**, G, 1979)
Suraj Ka Satwan Ghoda (**Shyam Benegal**, H, 1992)
Surajmukhi (O.P. Dutta, H, 1950)
Suraksha (Ravi Nagaich, H, 1979)
Surang (**V. Shantaram**, H, 1953)
Suranga Mhantyat Mala (**Dinkar D. Patil**, Mar, 1967)
Surangani (K. Babuji, Tam, 1984)
Surappuli (?, Modern Theatres, Tam, 1943)
Surappuli (Venkat, Tam, 1983)
Sura Sundaranga (**T.S. Nagabharana**, K, 1989)
Surat No Sahukar (*aka* Why Sons Go Astray: **Homi Master**, St, 1927)
Surdas (Krishnadev Mehra?, Moti Mahal Theatres, P, 1939)
Surdas (**Vishnu Mathur**, H, 1978)
Surekha Abhimanyu *see* Surekha Haran
Surekha Haran *see* Maya Bazaar *or* Veer Ghatotkach
Surekha Haran (*aka* Surekha Abhimanyu: **Baburao Painter**, St, 1921)
Surer Agun (Bolai Sen, B, 1965)
Surer Akashe (Biresh Chatterjee, B, 1988)
Surer Parashey (Chitta Bose, B, 1957)
Surer Pyasi (Bishu Dasgupta, B, 1960)
Surer Sathi (**Tapan Saha**, B, 1988)
Suri (L. Raja, K, 1992)
Suringudu (A. Mohan Gandhi, Tel, 1992)
Surjo Kanya (Alamgir Kabir, B, 1976)
Surkhiyaan (Ashok Tyagi, H, 1985)
Surooj (Pulak Gogoi, A, 1985)
Sur Sangam (**K. Vishwanath**, H, 1985)
Suruma Yitta Kannugal (S. Konnattu, Mal, 1983)
Surya (Baraguru Ramchandrappa, K, 1987)
Suryaa (Esmayeel Shroff, H, 1989)
Surya Chandra (**Vijayanirmala**, Tel, 1985)
Surya Chandrulu (V.C. Kuganathan, Tel, 1977)
Suryadaham (Mohan, Mal, 1980)
Surya Devata (Sharad Desai, H, 1969)
Surya IPS (A. Kodandarami Reddy, Tel, 1991)
Suryakanthi (V. Srinivasan, Tam, 1973)
Suryakanthi (Baby, Mal, 1977)
Surya Kumari (**Kanjibhai Rathod**, St, 1922)
Surya Kumari (**Dhirubhai Desai**, H, 1933)
Suryamanasam (Viji Thambi, Mal, 1992)
Suryamukhi (Bikash Roy, B, 1956)
Suryamukhi (Prafulla Sengupta, O, 1963)
Surya Nethram (L.P.C. Mohan, Tel, 1987)
Surya Prabha (Keshavlal Joshi, St, 1930)
Suryaputri (**Ellis Duncan**, Tam, 1940)
Surya Sakhi (**Agradoot**, B, 1981)
Surya Sikha (Salil Dutta, B, 1963)
Suryasnan (Ajay Kumar, B, 1962)
Surya Tapa (**Agradoot**, B, 1965)
Surya Toran (**Agradoot**, B, 1958)
Surya Trishna (Ashutosh Bannerjee, B, 1984)
Surya Vamsam (A.B. Raj, Mal, 1975)
Suryavanshi (Rakesh Kumar, H, 1992)
Suryodaya (A.T. Raghu, K, 1993)
Susan (Ajit Simha, Konkani, 1982)
Susan (Ajit Simha, H, 1983)
Susanta Sha (Ardhendu Sen, B, 1966)
Sushila (**K.S. Sethumadhavan**, Mal, 1963)
Sushila (Mahendra Pran, H, 1966)
Sushila (**Anant Mane**, Mar, 1978)
Sushila the Virtuous *see* **Sadguni Sushila**
Susie (**Kunchako**, Mal, 1969)
Susman (**Shyam Benegal**, H, 1986)
Suspicion *see* Sandigdha
Suthrakkari (Alex, Mal, 2978)
Sutlej De Kande (Padam Maheshwari, P, 1964)
Sutrada Bombe (Pekati Shivram, K, 1976)
Sutradhar (Chandrakant Joshi, H, 1986)
Sutradharulu (**K. Vishwanath**, Tel, 1989)
Sutrapat (Mridul Gupta, A, 1987)
Sutti Poonai (Manobala, Tam, 1988)
Suvar Illatha Chitrangal (**K. Bhagyaraj**, Tam, 1979)
Suvarna (**Manilal Joshi**, St, 1925)
Suvarnabhoomi (A.M. Samiulla, K, 1969)
Suvarna Kamal (K.P. Bhave, St, 1926)
Suvarnamala (M.D. Shah, St, 1930)
Suvarnamala (K. Sadasiva Rao, Tel, 1948)
Suvarna Mandir (M.G. Rangnekar, Mar, 1934)
Suvarnamanjari *see* Swarnamanjari
Suvarna Sethuve (Geethappriya, K, 1982)
Suvarna Sundari/Manalane Mangayin Bhagyam (**Vedantam Raghavaiah**, H/Tel/Tam, 1957)
Suvarna Sundari (Beeram Mastan Rao, Tel, 1984)
Suva Sangbad (Jagannath Chatterjee, B, 1978)
Suvasini (**Raja Paranjpe**, Mar, 1961)
Suyamariyadhai (R. Vijay Ganesh, Tam, 1992)
Suzanne *see* Susan
Swabhimana (D. Rajendra Babu, K, 1985)
Swadesh Seva (*aka* My Country: **Harshadrai Mehta**, St, 1927)
Swadesh Seva (*aka* My Country: **Nagendra Majumdar**, H, 1946)
Swagatham (Venu Nagavalli, Mal, 1989)
Swaham (*aka* My Own *aka* Destiny: **Shaji N. Karun**, Mal, 1994)
Swami (**Charu Roy**, St, 1931)
Swami (**A.R. Kardar**, H, 1941)
Swami (**Pashupati Chatterjee**, B, 1949)
Swami (**Amar Mullick**, B, 1949)
Swami (**Basu Chatterjee**, H, 1977)
Swami (TV: **Shankar Nag**, H, 1987)
Swami (TV: **Gajanan Jagirdar**, Mar, 1988)
Swami Ayyappan (**P. Subramanyam**, Mal/Tam, 1975)
Swami Bhakti (?, **Madan** Theatres, H, 1932)
Swami Dada (**Dev Anand**, H, 1982)
Swami Drohulu (Giduthuri Satyam, Tel, 1976)
Swamiji (Basavaraj Kestur, K, 1980)
Swaminath (Wajahat Mirza, H, 1942)
Swamir Ghar (Birendra Krishna Bhadra, B, 1943)
Swami Shri Narayana Guru (G. Krishnaswamy, Mal, 1985)
Swami Stri (**Satu Sen**, B, 1940)
Swami Stri (**Gurudas Bagchi**, B, 1981)
Swami Vivekananda (**Amar Mullick**, H, 1955)
Swan Song, The *see* **Hamsa Geethe**
Swantham Enna Padam (Shrikumaran Thampi, Mal, 1980)
Swantham Sarika (Ambili, Mal, 1984)
Swapna (**Zia Sarhadi**, H, 1942)
Swapna (**Dasari Narayana Rao**, Tel/K, 1980)
Swapnabhoomi (**Puttanna Kanagal**, Mal, 1967)
Swapnadanam (**K.G. George**, Mal, 1975)
Swapnalokam (John Peters, Mal, 1983)
Swapnam (Babu Nathencode, Mal, 1973)
Swapnangal (**P. Subramanyam**, Mal, 1970)
Swapnaniye (Purnendu Pattrea, B, 1966)
Swapna-o-Sadhana (**Agradoot**, B, 1947)
Swapna-o-Samadhi (Debnarayan Gupta, B, 1952)
Swapna Puri (Kumar Sarkar, B, 1959)
Swapna Sagara (**Prashanta Nanda**, O, 1983)
Swapna Sundari (*aka* Dream Damsel, Queen of Women's Land: **Harshadrai Mehta/Kanjibhai Rathod**, St, 1925)
Swapna Sundari (**G. Balaramaiah**, Tel/Tam, 1950)
Swapna Swayamvar *see* Shadi Ki Raat
Swapna Tech Lochani (Chandravadan, Mar, 1967)
Swapna Vihar (**Dadasaheb Phalke**, St, 1916)
Swaraj Ke Sipahi (Mohan Sinha, H, 1937)
Swarajyacha Shiledar (**Master Vithal**, Mar, 1951)
Swarajyam (Navatharam, Tel, 1983)
Swarajya Seemevar (Dadasaheb Nimbalkar, Mar, 1937)
Swara Kalpana (Vamsi, Tel, 1989)
Swaralipi (**Asit Sen**, B, 1961)
Swarangal Swapnangal (A.N. Thampi, Mal, 1981)
Swarg (David Dhawan, H, 1990)
Swargadalli Madhuve (Manimurugan, K, 1983)
Swarga Devata (Charles/Ayampalli, Mal, 1980)
Swarga Hotey Biday (Manju Day, B, 1964)
Swargam (Durga Nageshwara Rao, Tel, 1981)
Swargam (?, Divya Movies, Mal, 1987)
Swarga Martya (Asim Pal, B, 1958)
Swargam Narakam (**Dasari Narayana Rao**, Tel, 1975)
Swargam Narakam (R. Thyagarajan, Tam, 1977)
Swarganiki Nitchenalu (N. Gopalakrishna, Tel, 1977)
Swargaputhri (**P. Subramanyam**, Mal, 1973)
Swargarajyam (P.B. Unni, Mal, 1962)
Swargaseema (**B.N. Reddi**, Tel, 1945)
Swargaseema (P. Chandrasekhara Reddy, Tel, 1978)
Swarga Sukh (Bablu Samaddar, B, 1986)
Swarga Vihar (*aka* Dreamland: **Kanjibhai Rathod**, St, 1928)
Swarg Jaisa Ghar (Swaroop Kumar, H, 1991)
Swarg Ki Sidhi (*aka* Sati Vimala: **A.R. Kardar**, H, 1935)
Swarg Narak (**Dasari Narayana Rao**, H, 1978)
Swarg Se Sundar (**K. Bapaiah**, H, 1986)
Swarg Se Sundar Desh Hamara (*aka* Call of the Motherland: **Debaki Bose**, H, 1945)
Swarg Se Sundar Desh Hamara (Praveen Kumar, H, 1959)
Swarg Yahan Narak Yahan (Vimal Kumar, H, 1991)
Swarna Bhoomi (**Bhalji Pendharkar**, H, 1944)
Swarna Gauri (Y.R. Swamy, K/Tel, 1962)
Swarna Gopuram (A.B. Ayyappan Nair, Mal, 1984)
Swarna Kamal *see* **Suvarna Kamal**
Swarna Kamalam (**K. Vishwanath**, Tel, 1988)
Swarnalata *see* Sarala
Swarnalatha (**Y.V. Rao**, Tam, 1938)
Swarna Mahal (Sukhen Das, B, 1982)
Swarnamahal Rahasya (Tiptur Raghu, K, 1982)
Swarna Malsiyam (B.K. Pottekkad, Mal, 1974)
Swarna Mandir (?, Men*aka* Pics, H, 1934)
Swarnamanjari/Mangayir Ullam Mangada Selvam (**Vedantam Raghavaiah**, Tel/Tam, 1962)
Swarnamoir Thikana (Sushil Mukherjee, B, 1987)
Swarna Pakshigal (P.N. Nair, Mal, 1981)
Swarna Samsara (?, Shreedevi Pics, K, 1990)
Swarnaseeta (Ajit Ghosh, B, 1948)
Swarna Sikhar Pranganey (Piyush Basu, B, 1970)
Swarna Trishna (Mangal Chakraborty, B/H, 1989)
Swarna Vigraham (Mohan Gandhiraman, Mal, 1974)
Swaroopam (**K.R. Mohanan**, Mal, 1992)
Swarthi (Radhakant, H, 1986)
Swastik (Mohan Sinha, H, 1939)
Swatantraniki Oopari Poyandi (U. Venkatababu/Chinna, Tel, 1987)
Swatantrata Ke Path Par *see* Azadi Ki Raah Par
Swathi Nakshatram (**K.S. Gopalakrishnan**, Tam, 1974)
Swathi Thirunal (**Lenin Rajendran**, Mal, 1987)
Swathu (Shankaran Nair, Mal, 1980)
Swati (Agragami, B, 1977)
Swati (Kranthi Kumar, Tel/H, 1984/86)
Swati Chinukulu (Chakraborty, Tel, 1989)
Swati Kiranam (**K. Vishwanath**, Tel, 1991)
Swati Muthyam (**K. Vishwanath**, Tel, 1985)
Swayam (**Mahesh Bhatt**, H, 1991)
Swayambara (K. Bhushan, B, 1935)
Swayambara (**Asit Sen**, B, 1961)
Swayamkrushi (**K. Vishwanath**, Tel, 1987)
Swayamprabha (Shobhandirao, Tel, 1957)
Swayamsiddha (**Naresh Mitra**, B, 1947)
Swayamsiddha (Shyam Dass, H, 1949)
Swayamsiddha (Sushil Mukherjee, B, 1975)
Swayamvar (P. Sambasiva Rao, H, 1980)
Swayamvara (Y.R. Swamy, K, 1973)
Swayamvaram (**Adoor Gopalakrishnan**, Mal, 1972)
Swayamvaram (**Dasari Narayana Rao**, Tel, 1982)
Swayamvar Jhale Seeteche (Madhukar Pathak, Mar, 1964)
Sweekar (Sudhendu Roy, H, 1973)
Sweekar Kiya Maine (Zaheer D. Lari, H, 1983)
Sweet Adversity *see* Panima Aag
Sweet Angel *see* Mastikhor Mashuq
Sweetheart *see* Khubsoorat Khawasan
Sweetie (Eesh Nanda?, H, 1980)
Sweet Lie *see* Chhed Chhaad
Sweet Revenge *see* Verni Vasulat
Sweet 16 *see* **Pathinaru Vayathinile**
Swikarokti (Gnanesh Mukherjee, B, 1974)
Swikarokti (**Bhupen Hazarika**, A, 1986)
Swimming Pool (**Sasikumar**, Mal, 1976)
Swing, The *see* **Uyyale**
Sword Champion *see* Shamsher Bahadur
Sword of Allah *see* Gurjoki Maar
Sword of Victory *see* Bhawani Talwar
Swordsman/Swordsmen *see* Shamsheerbaaz
Sword to Sword *see* Talwar Ka Dhani
Symbolesque, The (**Ezra Mir**, St, 1929)
Symphony *see* Bharatham

T

Taakra (**Sukhdev Ahluwalia**, P, 1976)
Taapoi (Sarat Pujari, O, 1978)
Taaqat (**Narendra Bedi**, H, 1982)
Taaqatwar (David Dhawan, H, 1989)
Tabarana Kathe (**Girish Kasaravalli**, K, 1986)
Tabbaliyu Neenade Magane/Godhuli (**Girish Karnad/B.V. Karanth**, Kan/H, 1977)

Taboot Procession at Kalbadevi (F.B. Thanawala, St, 1900)
Tadbir (**Jayant Desai**, H, 1945)
Tadipaar (**Mahesh Bhatt**, H, 1992)
Tagori (Ajit Ganguly, B, 1985)
Tahader Katha (**Buddhadev Dasgupta**, B, 1992)
Tahalka (Anil Sharma, H, 1992)
Tahkhana (Tulsi/Shyam **Ramsay**, H, 1986)
Ta Holey (**Gurudas Bagchi**, B, 1964)
Tahqiqaat (A. Jagannath, H, 1993)
Tailangaswami (Chitra Sarathi, B, 1960)
Tainted Heart *see* Dagabaaz Bhai
Tainted Virtue *see* Karmayili Kali
Tai Teleen (**N.D. Sarpotdar**, St, 1926)
Tai Teleen (K.P. Bhave/Anto Narahari, Mar, 1953)
Taj (**Nandlal Jaswantlal**, H, 1956)
Taj Aur Talwar (Dwarka Khosla, H, 1956)
Tajayali Taruni (*aka* Forsaken Wife: **N.G. Devare**, St, 1928)
Taj Ke Talwar (*aka* Jawbreakers: Baburao/**Sundarrao Nadkarni**, St, 1931)
Taj Mahal (**Nanubhai Vakil**, H, 1941)
Taj Mahal (M. Sadiq, H, 1963)
Taj Poshi (Dwarka Khosla, H, 1957)
Taj-ul-Mulk *see* Bakavali
Tajurba (Nikhil Saini, H, 1981)
Taka-Ana-Pai (Jyotirmoy Roy, B, 1956)
Takay Ki Na Hay (*aka* Money Makes What Not: **Dhiren Ganguly**, St, 1931)
Takht Aur Talwar (?, Kanchenjunga Films, H, 1970)
Takht-e-Toofan (*aka* The Rake: Ramakant-Gharekhan, St, 1931)
Taking Revenge *see* Pagetha Puge
Takka! Bitre Sikka!! (A.M. Samiulla, K, 1970)
Takkar (**K. Bapaiah**, H, 1980)
Takkaridonga (S.P. Muthuraman, Tel, 1984)
Takkaridonga Chakkanichukka (K.S.R. Doss, Tel, 1969)
Takraar (*aka* All for a Son, Taqraar: **Hemen Gupta**, H, 1944)
Takraar (**Sukhdev Ahluwalia**, P, 1985)
Taksaal (**Hemen Gupta**, H, 1956)
Tala and Rhythm (**Shyam Benegal**, E, 1972)
Talaaq (**Sohrab Modi**, H, 1938)
Talaaq (**Mahesh Kaul**, H, 1958)
Talabandi (Sunil Chhadha, H, 1983)
Talambaralu (Kodi Ramakrishna, Tel, 1986)
Talash (A. Karim, H, 1943)
Talash (**Vishram Bedekar**, H, 1957)
Talash (O.P. Ralhan, H, 1969)
Talash (TV: **Hrishikesh Mukherjee**, H, 1992)
Talash-e-Haq (*aka* Search for Truth: **Chimanlal Luhar**, H, 1935)
Tala Vanchani Veerudu *see* Vanangamudi
Tal Bhairav (?, Omkar Films, St, 1929)
Tale, The *see* **Katha**
Tale of Four Cities, A *see* **Char Shaher Ek Kahani**
Tale of Toddy, A *see* Kallinde Katha
Tale of Two Leaves and a Bud, The (**Harisadhan Dasgupta**, E, 1971)
Tale of Yesterday, A *see* Kal Ki Baat
Tales of Courage (**Aribam Syam Sharma**, E, 1986)
Talismi Talwar *see* Tilasmi Talwar
Talkie of Talkies (**Sisir Bhaduri**, B, 1937)
Talking Pot *see* Bolki Tapeli
Talla Pellama (**N.T. Rama Rao**, Tel, 1970)
Talle Challani Daivam (M.S. Gopinath, Tel, 1977)
Tallibiddalu (P.N. Srinivasa Rao, Tel, 1963)
Talli Bottu (Madhavarao, Tel, 1970)
Tallichina Ajna (**Ch. Narayanamurthy**, Tel, 1961)
Talli Deevina (Gona Vijayarathnam, Tel, 1980)
Talli Kodakala Anubandham (K.S.R. Doss, Tel, 1981)
Talli Kodakulu (P. Chandrasekhara Reddy, Tel, 1973)
Talli Kuthulu (G. Ramineedu, Tel, 1971)
Talliprema (Jyotish Sinha, Tel, 1941)
Talliprema (Srikanth, Tel, 1968)
Talli Tandrulu (K. Baburao, Tel, 1970)
Talli Tandrulu (**T. Rama Rao**, Tel, 1991)
Talwar Ka Dhani (*aka* Sword to Sword: **R.S. Choudhury**, St, 1929)
Talwar Ka Dhani (**Dhirubhai Desai**, H, 1938)
Talwar Ka Dhani (Dwarka Khosla, H, 1956)
Talwar Ka Pati (*aka* Ace of Sword: **Harshadrai Mehta**, St, 1930)
Talwarwala (**Nagendra Majumdar**, H, 1946)
Tamacha (Ramesh Ahuja, H, 1988)
Tamanna (**Phani Majumdar**, H, 1942)
Tamanna (**K.P. Atma**, H, 1969)
Tamas (TV: **Govind Nihalani**, H, 1987)
Tamasa Teere (TV: Panchajanya, O, 1989)
Tamasgeer (Govind Kulkarni, Mar, 1981)
Tamasha (Dwarka Khosla, H, 1942)
Tamasha (**Phani Majumdar**, H, 1952)
Tamasha (Bangsi Ash, B, 1957)
Tambdi Mati (**Bhalji Pendharkar**, Mar, 1969)
Tamere Champone Ame Kel (**Chandrakant Sangani**, G, 1978)
Tamil Thayi (*aka* Mathru Dharma: ?, Saraswati Pics, Tam, 1939)
Tamil Who Launched a Ship, The *see* **Kappalotiya Thamizhan**
Taming of the Shrew *see* Hathili Dulhan
Tamizh Ponnu (K. Muthu Vijayan, Tam, 1992)
Tanariri (**Chandrakant Sangani**, G, 1975)
Tanaya (Narayan Chakraborty, B, 1983)
Tan Badan (Anand, H, 1986)
Tandava Krishnudu (P. Chandrasekhara Reddy, Tel, 1984)
Tandra Paparayudu (**Dasari Narayana Rao**, Tel, 1986)
Tandri (M.R.S. Mani, Tel, 1953)
Tandri Kodukula Challenge (M. Mallikarjuna Rao, Tel, 1987)
Tandrulu Kodukulu (K. Hemabharadara Rao, Tel, 1961)
Tangamalai Rahasyam *see* Ratnagiri Rahasya
Tangewala (Naresh Kumar, H, 1972)
Tangewali (Lekhraj Bhakri, H, 1955)
Tanhaai (Ram Gabale, H, 1961)
Tanhaai (Jagdish Nirula, H, 1972)
Tania (Ramprasad Chakraborty, B, 1987)
Tankha (M. Changhezi, H, 1956)
Tan Ki Haar *see* Man Ki Jeet
Tansen (**Jayant Desai**, H, 1943)
Tansen (**Niren Lahiri**, B, 1958)
Tapalkaran Thangai (**K.S. Gopalakrishnan**, Tam, 1970)
Tapasi *see* Diwani
Tapasi (Chitta Bose, B, 1957)
Tapasi (**Agradoot**, B, 1965)
Tapaswini (M. Krishnan Nair, Mal, 1971)
Tapasya *see* Rajmata
Tapasya (Anil Ganguly, H, 1975)
Tapasya (Nagen Ray, O, 1980)
Tapobhanga (Bibhuti Das, B, 1947)
Taqdeer (**Mehboob**, H, 1943)
Taqdeer (Babubhai Jani, H, 1945)
Taqdeer (*aka* Apna Khoon: A.S. Arora, H, 1958)
Taqdeer (A. Salaam, H, 1967)
Taqdeer (Brij Sadanah, H, 1983)
Taqdeer Ka Badshah (B. Subhash, H, 1982)
Taqdeer Ka Tamasha (Anand, H, 1990)
Taqdeer Ka Teer *see* Prem Laksh
Taqdeer Ki Tope (Vithaldas Panchotia, H, 1939)
Taqdeerwale (*aka* Lucky Friends: S.H. Tharani, H, 1948)
Taqraar *see* Takraar
Tara (R.D. Parineeja, H, 1949)
Tara (M. Krishnan Nair, Mal, 1970)
Taraka (**Dinkar D. Patil**, Mar, 1954)
Tarakki (?, Army Film Centre: Pushtu, 1943)
Taramati (**Raja Nene**, H, 1945)
Tarana (Ram Daryani, H, 1951)
Tarana (Deepak Bahry, H, 1979)
Tarang (I.C. Kapoor, H, 1952)
Tarang (**Kumar Shahani**, H, 1984)
Tarangalu (Kodi Ramakrishna, Tel, 1991)
Tarangini (Kodi Ramakrishna, Tel, 1982)
Taranhaar (*aka* Pride of Hindustan: **Raja Sandow**, St, 1931)
Taranhaar (*aka* Qaumi Diler: Kikubhai Desai, H, 1937)
Tarani Sen Badh (Chitra Sarathi, B, 1962)
Tara Sasankam (**A. Narayanan**, Tam, 1936)
Tara Sasankam (**R.S. Prakash**, Tel, 1941)
Tara Sasankam (M. Apparao, Tel, 1969)
Tara Sundari (**Chandulal Shah**, H, 1934)
Tara the Dancer *see* Nartaki Tara
Tarka (Sunilkumar Desai, K, 1989)
Tarkeeb (Ravi Nagaich, H, 1984)
Tarnetar Fair *see* Folk Fair at Tarnetar
Tarubala (**Sushil Majumdar**, B, 1936)
Tarumaru (S. Jagannath, Tel, 1941)
Taruner Swapna (Akhilesh Chatterjee, B, 1948)
Taruni (**Priyanath Ganguly**, B, 1934)
Tarunina Tarang (*aka* Brother to Brother: Prafulla Ghosh, St, 1928)
Tarun Tapaswini (*aka* Young Ascetic: Prafulla Ghosh, St, 1929)
Tarzan (*aka* Adventures of Tarzan: B. Subhash, H, 1985)
Tarzan and Captain Kishore (Jal, H, 1964)
Tarzan and Cobra (Bhagwant Choudhury, H, 1987)
Tarzan and Delilah (A. Shamsheer, H, 1964)
Tarzan and Gorilla (Pyarelal, H, 1963)
Tarzan and Hercules (Mehmood, H, 1966)
Tarzan and King Kong (A. Shamsheer, H, 1965)
Tarzan and the Circus (Shiv Kumar, H, 1965)
Tarzan Aur Jadugar (Radhakant, H, 1963)
Tarzan Aur Jadui Chirag (*aka* Alladdin and the Wonderful Lamp: Babubhai Bhanji, H, 1966)
Tarzan Aur Jalpari (*aka* Jalpari: Radhakant, H, 1964)
Tarzan Comes to Delhi (*aka* Tarzan Delhi Mein: Kedar Kapoor, H, 1965)
Tarzan Delhi Mein *see* Tarzan Comes to Delhi
Tarzan in Fairyland (*aka* Tarzan Paristan Mein: Sushil Gupta, H, 1968)
Tarzan Ki Beti (**Roop K. Shorey**, H, 1938)
Tarzan Ki Mehbooba (Ram Rasila, H, 1966)
Tarzan Mera Saathi (*aka* Tarzan Goes to India: John Guillermin, H, 1962)
Tarzan Paristan Mein *see* Tarzan in Fairyland
Tarzan 303 (**Chandrakant**, H, 1970)
Taser Ghar (Mangal Chakraborty, B, 1957)
Tasveer (Najam Naqvi, H, 1943)
Tasveer (**J.B.H. Wadia**, H, 1966)
Tasveer Apni Apni (TV: **Mrinal Sen**, H, 1984)
Tasveer-e-Wafaa *see* Fida-e-Watan
Tatamma Kala (**N.T. Rama Rao**, Tel, 1974)
Tata Manuvudu (**Dasari Narayana Rao**, Tel, 1972)
Tatar Ka Chor (*aka* Thief of Tatar: **K. Amarnath**, H, 1940)
Tatar Ka Chor (Majnu, H, 1955)
Tatar Ki Hasina (Aslam Allahabadi, H, 1968)
Tata Steel (**Shyam Benegal**, E, 1983)
Tathaiah Prema Leelalu (B.V. Prasad, Tel, 1980)
Tathapi (Manoj Bhattacharya, B, 1950)
Tathapio Nadi (Hemanta Das, A, 1990)
Tathiah Pelli Manavadi Sobhanam (Sahili, Tel, 1989)
Tatinir Bichar (**Sushil Majumdar**, B, 1940)
Tati Talwar (*aka* Glittering Sword: **Kanjibhai Rathod**, St, 1930)
Tauheen (Madan Joshi, H, 1989)
Tawaif (**B.R. Chopra**, H, 1985)
Tawaif Ki Beti (K.S. Thaliya, H, 1988)
Tawangarni Talwar (M. Udvadia, St, 1929)
Taxi Car (Venu, Mal, 1972)
Taxi Chor (Sushil Vyas, H, 1980)
Taxi Driver (S.M. Raza, H, 1944)
Taxi Driver (**Chetan Anand**, H, 1954)
Taxi Driver (Mohammed Hussain, H, 1973)
Taxi Driver (**P.N. Menon**, Mal, 1977)
Taxi Driver (N.S. Maniam, Tam, 1978)
Taxi 555 (Lekhraj Bhakri, H, 1958)
Taxi Ramudu (V. Madhusudhana Rao, Tel, 1961)
Taxi Stand (**Gajanan Jagirdar**, H, 1958)
Taxi Taxi (Irshad, H, 1977)
Teacheramma (**Puttanna Kanagal**, Tam, 1968)
Tears of Love *see* Mohabbat Ke Aansoo
Teen Adhyay (Mangal Chakraborty, B, 1968)
Teenage Love (K. Krishnachandra, Mal, 1990)
Teen Bahuraniyan (**S.S. Vasan**/S.S. Balan, H, 1968)
Teen Batti Char Raasta (**V. Shantaram**, H, 1953)
Teen Bhai (**Hemchandra Chunder**, H, 1955)
Teen Bhubhaner Parey (Ajitesh Bannerjee, B, 1969)
Teen Chehre (Y.N. Kapoor, H, 1979)
Teen Chor (V. Dada Mirasi, H, 1973)
Teen Deviyan (Amarjeet, H, 1965)
Teen Dost (Joseph Taliath, H, 1964)
Teen Gharaney (**K.A. Abbas**, H, 1963)
Teen Ikke (Joginder, H, 1979)
Teen Kanya (**Satyajit Ray**, B, 1961)
Teen Mule (Baburao Gokhale/Bal Saraf, Mar, 1954)
Teen Murti *see* Jagir
Teen Sardar (Dossani/S. Joshi, H, 1955)
Teen Sardar (Radhakant, H, 1965)
Teen Sau Din Ke Baad *see* **Three Hundred Days and After**
Teen Tasveerein (S.S. Solanki, H, 1954)
Teen Ustad (**Nanabhai Bhatt**, H, 1961)
Teeratha Vilayattu Pillai (Ramanarayanan, Tam, 1982)
Teer Aur Talwar (Mohammed Hussain, H, 1960)
Teer Bhanga Dheu (Arun Choudhury, B, 1976)
Teer Bhoomi (**Gurudas Bagchi**, B, 1969)
Teer-e-Qatil (*aka* Red Archer: **Sundarrao Nadkarni**, St, 1931)
Teertha Bandhangal (Joshna?, Mal, 1982)
Teertha Karayanile (Manivannan, Tam, 1987)
Teerthayatra (*aka* Holy India: Adarsh, H, 1958)
Teerthayatra (**A. Vincent**, Mal, 1972)
Teesmar Khan (H.S. Kwatra, H, 1955)
Teesra Kaun (Mohammed Hussain, H, 1965)
Teesra Kinara (**Krishnakant**, H, 1986)
Teesri Aankh (**Subodh Mukherjee**, H, 1982)
Teesri Gali (Kundan Kumar, H, 1958)
Teesri Kasam (**Basu Bhattacharya**, H, 1966)
Teesri Manzil (**Vijay Anand**, H, 1966)
Teevra Madhyam (Arun Khopkar, H, 1974)
Teewin Rakh Neewin *see* Tera Jawab Nahin
Tehmuras & Tehmuljee (?, **Madan Theatres**, St, 1921)
Tehsildar (**Y.V. Rao**, Tel, 1944)
Tehsildarugari Ammayi (**K.S. Prakash Rao**, Tel, 1971)
Teja (Ramnesh Puri, H, 1990)
Teja (N. Haribabu, Tel, 1992)
Tejal Garasni (Kishore Vyas, G, 1984)
Tejaswini (**H.L.N. Simha**, K, 1962)
Tejimola (**Anwar Hussain**, A, 1963)
Telephone (Tulsi/Shyam **Ramsay**, H, 1985)
Telephone Girl, The (**Homi Master**, St, 1926)
Tella Gulabeelu (Relangi Narasimha Rao, Tel, 1984)
Tel Malish Boot Polish (Romney Dey, H, 1961)
Telugu Nadu (Laxmi Deepak, Tel, 1982)
Te Mazhe Ghar (**Dinkar D. Patil**, Mar, 1963)
Tempest, The *see* Alochhaya
Temple Bells *see* Sulochana
Temple of Tortures *see* Bhawani No Bhog
Temptress *see* Vishwamohini
Tenali Ramakrishna (**H.M. Reddy**, Tel, 1941)
Tenali Ramakrishna/Tenali Raman (**B.S. Ranga**, Tel/Tam/K, 1956)
Tenali Raman (**A. Narayanan**, Tam, 1938)
Tenali Raman (TV: **T.S. Nagabharana**, K, 1990)
Tenateega (M. Nandakumar, Tel, 1991)
10 O'Clock *see* **Daha Wajta**
Ten O'Clock (Jugal Kishore, H, 1958)
Tera Jawab Nahin (*aka* Teewin Rakh Neewin: Shanti S. Kalra, P, 1978)
Tera Karam Mera Dharam (K.K. Reddy, H, 1987)
Tera Naam Mera Naam (Ramesh Talwar, H, 1987)
Tera Sahara (?, Dreamland Pics, H, 1949)
Tere Bina Kya Jeena (P.P. Ghosh, H, 1989)
Tere Dwar Khada Bhagwan (*aka* Jisne Tera Naam Liya: **Ravindra Dave**, H, 1964)
Tere Ghar Ke Saamne (**Vijay Anand**, H, 1963)
Tere Mere Beech Mein (**Dada Kondke**, H, 1984)
Tere Mere Sapne (**Vijay Anand**, H, 1971)

Tere Pyar Mein (Subhash Sharma, H, 1978)
Tere Rang Nyare (Pushp Raj, P, 1973)
Tere Shaher Mein (Sagar Sarhadi, H, 1985)
Teri Baahon Mein (Umesh Mehra, H, 1984)
Teri Kasam (A.C. Trilogchander, H, 1982)
Teri Maang Sitaron Se Bhar Doon (**Raj Khosla**, H, 1982)
Teri Maherbaniyan (Vijay Reddy, H, 1985)
Teri Meri Ik Jindri (Dharam Kumar, P, 1975)
Teri Payal Mere Geet (Rehman Naushad, H, 1993)
Teri Pooja Kare Sansar (Thakur Tapasvi, H, 1984)
Teri Talash Mein (Kewal Mishra, H, 1968)
Teri Talash Mein (Vinod Talwar, H, 1990)
Tero Nadir Parey (Barin Saha, B, 1961)
Tero Sandhyar Galpo (TV: **Dinen Gupta**, B, 1990)
Terracotta *see* **Mati Manas**
Terracotta Temples (**Harisadhan Dasgupta**, E, 1970)
Terrible Hyderabad Floods, The (?, Excelsior Cinematograph, St, 1908)
Terrific Ordeal, The *see* King Shriyal
Terror, The *see* Krusinka
Terror *see* Khabardar
Terror (A. Mohan Gandhi, Tel, 1985)
Terror of the Hills *see* Bahadur Baharvatiyo
Tested Berries (**Kantilal Rathod**, E, 1973)
Test of Chastity *see* Bhadra Bhamini
Tevdha Sodun Bola (**Prabhakar Nayak**, Mar, 1974)
Textiles (**Fali Bilimoria**, E, 1956)
Tezaab (**N. Chandra**, H, 1988)
Thacholi Ambu (Appachan, Mal, 1978)
Thacholi Marumagan Chandu (**P. Bhaskaran**, Mal, 1974)
Thacholi Othenan (S.S. Rajan, Mal, 1964)
Thacholi Thankappan (P. Venu, Mal, 1984)
Thadagam (**I.V. Sasi**, Mal, 1982)
Thadavara (P. Chandrakumar, Mal, 1981)
Thagini (**Tarun Majumdar**, B, 1974)
Thaikku Oru Pillai (Pattu, Tam, 1972)
Thaikku Oru Thalattu (**Balachandra Menon**, Tam, 1986)
Thaikku Pinn Tharam (M.A. Thirumugham, Tam, 1956)
Thaikku Thalaimagan (M.A. Thirumugham, Tam, 1967)
Thaimel Anai (Raja, Tam, 1988)
Thaipasam (R. Krishnamurthy, Tam, 1988)
Thakara (**B.G. Bharathan**, Mal, 1979)
Thakas Mahathak (Raja Bargir, Mar, 1984)
Thakicha Lagna (V.N. Bhatt/**Vishram Bedekar**, Mar, 1935)
Thakilukottampuram (?, Mal, 1981)
Thaksen Rajputra *see* Bhedi Rajkumar
Thakurain (Mini Thakur, Bh, 1984)
Thakur Diler Singh *see* Soldier
Thakur Haridas (Govinda Roy, B, 1959)
Thakur Jarnail Singh (Mohammed Hussain, H, 1966)
Thala (Babu Radhakrishnan, Mal, 1988)
Thalai Koduthan Thambi (**T.R. Sundaram**, Tam, 1959)
Thalai Magan (M.R. Vijayachander, Tam, 1983)
Thalai Pravasam (M. Krishnan, Tam, 1973)
Thalaivan (P.A. Thomas/Singamuthu, Tam, 1970)
Thalaivanukkor Thalaivi (Vittal T. Gnanam, Tam, 1989)
Thalaivasal (Selva, Tam, 1992)
Thalaiyana Mandiram (N. Venkatesh, Tam, 1984)
Thalam Manasinte Thalam (A.T.Abu, Mal, 1981)
Thalam Thettiya Tharattu (A.B. Raj, Mal, 1983)
Thalappoli (M. Krishnan Nair, Mal, 1977)
Thalasthanam (Shaji Kailash, Mal, 1992)
Thalattu (Vipur Dass, Tam, 1969)
Thalattu (T.K. Rajendran, Tam, 1993)
Thalattu Padava (R. Sundarrajan, Tam, 1990)
Thalavattam (**Priyadarshan**, Mal, 1986)
Thalayatti Bommaigal K. Nataraj, Tam, 1986)
Thali Bhagyam (**Kadaru Nagabhushanam**, Tam, 1966)
Thali Dhanam (R.C. Sakthi, Tam, 1987)
Thaligagi (A.V. Sheshgiri Rao, K, 1989)
Thali Kattiya Rasa (Vijayakhanna, Tam, 1992)

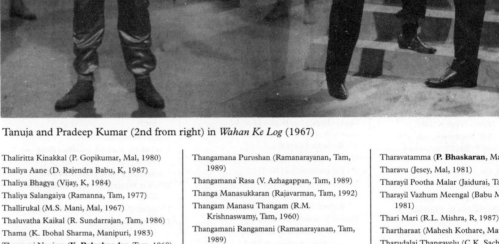

Tanuja and Pradeep Kumar (2nd from right) in *Wahan Ke Log* (1967)

Thaliritta Kinakkal (P. Gopikumar, Mal, 1980)
Thaliya Aane (D. Rajendra Babu, K, 1987)
Thaliya Bhagya (Vijay, K, 1984)
Thaliya Salangaiya (Ramanna, Tam, 1977)
Thallirukal (M.S. Mani, Mal, 1967)
Thaluvatha Kaikal (R. Sundarrajan, Tam, 1986)
Thama (K. Ibohal Sharma, Manipuri, 1983)
Thamarai Nenjam (**K. Balachander**, Tam, 1968)
Thamaraikulam (Muktha V. Srinivasan, Tam, 1959)
Thamarathoni (Mani, Mal, 1975)
Thambathigal (M.S. Rajendra, Tam, 1983)
Thambathiyam (K. Vijayan, Tam, 1987)
Thambikku Entha Ooru (Rajasekhar, Tam, 1984)
Thambikku Ooru Pattu (Ashok Kumar, Tam, 1991)
Thambi Oorukku Pudhusu (R. Umashankar, Tam, 1991)
Thambi Thanga Kambi (K. Shankar, Tam, 1988)
Thambi Varuvanam (F.S. Maniar, Tam, 1991)
Thamb Lakshmi Kunku Lavte (**Datta Dharmadhikari**, Mar, 1967)
Thamizhariyum Perumal (**T.R. Raghunath**, Tam, 1942)
Thammil Thammil (Sajan, Mal, 1985)
Thampi Pondatti (Panchu Arunachalam, Tam, 1992)
Thampu (**G. Aravindan**, Mal, 1978)
Thampuratti (M. Shankaran Nair, Mal, 1978)
Thanal (T. Rajeevnath, Mal, 1976)
Thana Theke Aschhi (Hiren Nag, B, 1965)
Thande Makkalu (Srikanth, K, 1971)
Thandikapatha Nyayangal (M. Bhaskar, Tam, 1983)
Thandoora (R. Narayanamurthy, Tel, 1993)
Thanduvitten Ennai (**C.V. Sridhar**, Tam, 1991)
Thanedar (Raj Sippy, H, 1990)
Thangachi (R. Krishnamurthy, Tam, 1987)
Thangachi Kalyanam (Prem, Tam, 1989)
Thanga Gopuram (M.S.Solaimalai, Tam, 1971)
Thangai (A.C. Trilogchander, Tam, 1967)
Thangaikkaga (**Yoganand**, Tam, 1971)
Thangaikku Oru Thalattu (?, Shri Raghavendralaya Cine Creations, Tam, 1990)
Thangaikoppai (R.C. Sakthi, Tam, 1984)
Thangaikor Geetham (**T. Rajendar**, Tam, 1983)
Thanga Kalasam (London Gopal, Tam, 1988)
Thangakili (Rajavarman, Tam, 1993)
Thanga Magan (A. Jagannathan, Tam, 1983)
Thanga Malar (D.S. Rajagopal, Tam, 1969)
Thanga Mana (K. Simon, Tam, 1985)
Thangamana Purushan (Ramanarayanan, Tam, 1989)
Thangamana Rasa (V. Azhagappan, Tam, 1989)
Thanga Manasukkaran (Rajavarman, Tam, 1992)
Thangam Manasu Thangam (R.M. Krishnaswamy, Tam, 1960)
Thangamani Rangamani (Ramanarayanan, Tam, 1989)
Thangamdi Thangam (Ramanarayanan, Tam, 1984)
Thanga Padakkam (P. Madhavan, Tam, 1974)
Thangapapa (R. Aravindraj, Tam, 1993)
Thangapathumai (**A.S.A. Sami**, Tam, 1959)
Thanga Rangan (S.R. Dakshinamurthy, Tam, 1978)
Thangarasu (K. Alexander, Tam, 1992)
Thangarathinam (M.A. Thirumugham, Tam, 1960)
Thanga Surangam (T.R. Ramanna, Tam, 1969)
Thanga Thambi (Ramanath/Francis, Tam, 1967)
Thangathile Vairam (K. Swarnam, Tam, 1975)
Thangathin Thangam (?, Anbalaya Films, Tam, 1990)
Thanga Thurai (A. Kasilingam, Tam, 1972)
Thangavu Palithamma (S. Ramanathan, Tam, 1965)
Thanikatu Raja (V.C. Guhanathan, Tam, 1982)
Thani Kudithanam (S.A. Kannan, Tam, 1977)
Thani Maram (**Durai**, Tam, 1980)
Thani Niram (**Sasikumar**, Mal, 1973)
Thanipiravi (M.A. Thirumugham, Tam, 1966)
Thaniyatha Dagam (E.M. Abraham, Tam, 1982)
Thaniyavartanam (**Sibi Malayil**, Mal, 1987)
Thankakudam (S.S. Rajan, Mal, 1965)
Thank You *see* Adab Arz
Thanneer Thanneer (**K. Balachander**, Tam, 1981)
Thanthaikupin Thamayan (G.R. Rao, Tam, 1960)
Thanthram (Joshi, Mal, 1988)
Thanthulli (**K.P. Kumaran**, Mal, 1979)
Thapadya (**Prabhakar Nayak**, Mar, 1973)
Thappida Tala/Thappu Thalangal (**K. Balachander**, K/Tam, 1978)
Thappu Kanaku (Jeevabalan, Tam, 1988)
Thappu Thalangal *see* Thappida Tala
Tharale Nanna Maga (Upendra, K, 1992)
Tharam Marindi (**Singeetham Srinivasa Rao**, Tel, 1977)
Tharangam (Baby, Mal, 1979)
Tharasu (Raja Ganapathy, Tam, 1984)
Tharattu (**Balachandra Menon**, Mal, 1981)
Tharavatamma (**P. Bhaskaran**, Mal, 1966)
Tharavu (Jesey, Mal, 1981)
Tharayil Pootha Malar (Jaidurai, Tam, 1980)
Tharayil Vazhum Meengal (Babu Maharaja, Tam, 1981)
Thari Mari (R.L. Mishra, R, 1987)
Thartharaat (Mahesh Kothare, Mar, 1989)
Tharudalai Thangavelu (C.K. Sachi, Tam, 1940)
Tharu Oru Janmam Koodi (N. Shankaran Nair, Mal, 1978)
Thasippen (*aka* Jyoti Malar: **T.R. Raghunath**, Tam, 1942)
Thaskara Veeran (S.M. Sreeramulu Naidu, Mal, 1958)
That Girl *see* Woh Chokri
Thathamme Poocha Poocha (Balu Kiriyeth, Mal, 1984)
Thattungal Thirakapadam (Chandrababu, Tam, 1966)
Thavalam (Thambi Kannathanam, MAl, 1983)
Thavam (R.C. Sakthi, Tam, 1985)
Thavani Kanavukal (**K. Bhagyaraj**, Tam, 1983)
Thavaputhalvan (V. Srinivasan, Tam, 1972)
Thavaru Mane (Vijay, K, 1986)
Thayai Katha Thanayan (M.A. Thirumugham, Tam, 1962)
Thayalkaran (S.P. Muthuraman, Tam, 1991)
Thayamma (Gopi Bhimsingh, Tam, 1991)
Thayam Onnu (Selvakumar, Tam, 1988)
Thayapol Pillai Noolaipol Pillai (K. Somu, Tam, 1959)
Thayaramma Bangaraiah (Kommineni, Tel, 1978)
Thayaramma Tandavakrishna (Kommineni, Tel, 1987)
Thaya Tharamma (T.P. Gajendran, Tam, 1989)
Thaye Unakkaga (**P. Pullaiah**, Tam, 1966)
Thayi (**D. Yoganand**, Tam, 1974)
Thayi (Perala, K, 1987)
Thayi Devaru (Siddalingaiah, K, 1971)
Thayige Takka Maga (V. Somasekhar, K, 1978)
Thayiginte Devarilla (Y.R. Swamy, K, 1977)
Thayigobba Karna (Raj Kishore, K, 1988)
Thayi Kanasu (Vijay, K, 1985)
Thayi Karulu (N.S. Dhananjaya, K, 1988)
Thayi Karulu/Thayin Karunai (**G.V. Iyer**, K/Tam, 1962)
Thayikotta Thali (Ravindranath, K, 1987)
Thayilla Kuzhandhai (R. Thyagarajan, Tam, 1976)
Thayillamal Nannilai (R. Thyagarajan, Tam, 1979)
Thayilla Pillai (**L.V. Prasad**, Tam, 1961)

Thayi Magalukku Kattiya Thali (R.R. Chandran, Tam, 1959)
Thayi Mamathe (B. Subba Rao, K, 1985)
Thayi Masam Poovasam (Amirjan, Tam, 1990)
Thayi Meethu Sathyam (R. Thyagarajan, Tam, 1978)
Thayi Moogambikai (K. Shankar, Tam, 1982)
Thayi Mozhi (Ilavarasan, Tam, 1992)
Thayi Nadu (Battling Mani, Tam, 1947)
Thayi Nadu (Vijay, K, 1984)
Thayi Nadu (Aravindraj, Tam, 1989)
Thayin Karunai *see* Thayi Karulu
Thayin Madiyil (**Adurthi Subba Rao**, Tam, 1964)
Thayinmel Aanai (G.R. Nathan, Tam, 1966)
Thayi Pasam (B.V. Srinivasan, Tam, 1974)
Thayi Pirandhal (A.K. Subramanyam, Tam, 1974)
Thayi Pirandal Vazhi Pirakkum (A.K. Velan, Tam, 1958)
Thayi Pongal (?, Anjaneya Combines, Tam, 1980)
Thayi Poosam (Ramanarayanan, Tam, 1991)
Thayi Sollai Thatthathe (M.A. Thirumugham, Tam, 1961)
Thayi Thande (V. Satyanarayana, K, 1985)
Thayi Ullam (**K. Ramnoth**, Tam, 1952)
Thayi Veedu (R. Thyagarajan, Tam, 1983)
Thayi Veetu Seetanam (Madurai Thirumaran, Tam, 1975)
Thayiya Aase (Raj Kishore, K, 1988)
Thayiya Madilalli (B. Subba Rao, K, 1981)
Thayiya Nudi (B. Subba Rao, K, 1983)
Thayiye Nanna Devaru (Vijay, K, 1985)
Thayumanavar (**T.R. Sundaram**, Tam, 1938)
Thayum Maghalum (?, Dhandayuthapani Films, Tam, 1965)
Thazampoo (M.S. Ramadas, Tam, 1965)
Thazhvaram (**B.G. Bharathan**, Mal, 1989)
Thedi Vantha Lakshmi (G.R. Nathan, Tam, 1973)
Thedi Vantha Mappillai (**B.R. Panthulu**, Tam, 1970)
Thedi Vantha Selvam (**P. Neelakantan**, Tam, 1958)
Thedivantha Thirumagal (Sathyam, Tam, 1966)
Thee (R. Krishnamurthy, Tam, 1981)
Theechatti Govindan (Sasi Mohan, Tam, 1991)
Theekadal (Appachan, Mal, 1980)
Theekali (**Sasikumar**, Mal, 1981)
Theekkanal (**Madhu**, Mal, 1976)
Theekkattu (?, Aji Arts, Mal, 1987)
Theenalagal (**Sasikumar**, Mal, 1980)
Theeram Thedunna Thira (**A. Vincent**, Mal, 1983)
Theeram Thedunnavar (Chandrakumar, Mal, 1980)
Theerangal (Rajeevnath, Mal, 1978)
Theere Pratikshikathe (Chandrakumar, Mal, 1984)
Theerpu (U. Vishweshwara Rao, Tel, 1974)
Theerpu (R. Krishnaswamy, Tam, 1982)
Theerpu En Kayil (V.P. Sundar, Tam, 1984)
Theerpugal Thirutha Padalam (**Durai**, Tam, 1982)
Theerumanam (U. Vishweshwara Rao, Mal, 1984)
Their Imperial Majesties in Delhi (**Bourne & Shepherd**, St, 1911)
Their Majesties in Bombay (Advanced Bioscope, St, 1911)
Their Majesties in Calcutta (Globetrotter Bioscope, St, 1912)
Their New Roots (**Santi P. Choudhury**, E, 1959)
Their Own Faces *see* **Tasveer Apni Apni**
Thekkan Kattu (**Sasikumar**, Mal, 1973)
Themmadi Velappan (**T. Hariharan**, Mal, 1976)
Thenaruvi (**Kunchako**, Mal, 1973)
Thendrale Ennai Thodu (**C.V. Sridhar**, Tam, 1985)
Thendral Thodatha Malar (G.P. Balan, Tam, 1985)
Thendral Veesum (**B.S. Ranga**, Tam, 1962)
Thene Kinnam (K.K.R. Murthy, Tam, 1971)
Thene Manushulu (**Adurthi Subba Rao**, Tel, 1965)
Thene Manushulu (**S.V. Rajendra Singh**, Tel, 1987)
Thene Mazhai (V. Srinivasan, Tam, 1966)
Then Koodu (Satyanarayanan, Tam, 1984)
Thennal Thedunna Poovu (Pugazh Mani, Mal, 1984)
Thennankeetru (Kovi Manisekharan, Tam, 1975)
Thennilavu (**C.V. Sridhar**, Tam, 1961)
Then Pandi Seemayile (C.P. Kollapan, Tam, 1988)
Thenral Sudum (Manobala, Tam, 1989)
Then Sindhuthe Vanam (Ra. Shankaran, Tam, 1975)
Then Sittukkal (N. Damodaran, Tam, 1984)
Thenum Palum (P. Madhavan, Tam, 1971)
Thenum Vayampum (?, Mal, 1981)
There Is Another Way (**Fali Bilimoria**, E, 1976)
There Lived a Wrestler *see* **Oridathoru Phayalwan**
There Thiruvizha (M.A. Thirumugham, Tam, 1968)
Therkkithi Kallan (Kalaimani, Tam, 1988)
Therotham (V.T.Arasu, Tam, 1971)
Therukku Theru Machan (Manivannan, Tam, 1992)
Theru Vilakku (M.A. Kaja, Tam, 1980)
Theruyu Nartaki (?, Mal, 1988)
Thes (**Kidar Sharma**, H, 1949)
Thettu (**K.S. Sethumadhavan**, Mal, 1971)
Thevar Magan (**B.G. Bharathan**, Tam, 1992)
Theviagal (N.S. Ravishankar, Tam, 1979)
Theye Neeye Thunai (P.R. Somu, Tam, 1987)
They Met the Challenge (**Santi P. Choudhury**, E, 1963)
Thief of Baghdad *see* Baghdad Ka Chor
Thief of Baghdad (*aka* Baghdad Ka Chor: Shreeram, H, 1968)
Thief of Baghdad (Ravi Nagaich, H, 1977)
Thief of Delhi *see* Delhi No Thug
Thief of Iraq *see* Iraq Ka Chor
Thief of Iraq (*aka* Iraq Ka Chor: **Kanjibhai Rathod**, H, 1934)
Thief of Tatar *see* Tatar Ka Chor
Thikadar (Prafulla Roy, B, 1940)
Thikana (**Mahesh Bhatt**, H, 1987)
Thikkutheriyatha Kattil (N.C. Chakraborty, Tam, 1972)
Thilakam (**Krishnan-Panju**, Tam, 1960)
Thilakam (Raghuvasan, Tam, 1992)
Thili Jhai Heli Bahu (Bijoy Bhaskar, O, 1988)
Thillana Mohanambal (**A.P. Nagarajan**, Tam, 1968)
Thillu Mullu (**K. Balachander**, Tam, 1981)
Thimingalam (Crossbelt Mani, Mal, 1983)
Thingi (G.G. Bhonsle, Mar, 1983)
Thinkalazhcha Nalla Divasam (**P. Padmarajan**, Mal, 1985)
Thirakal (K. Vijayan, Mal, 1984)
Thirakkil Alpa Samayam (P.G. Vishwambaran, Mal, 1984)
Thiramai (Vijay Krishnaraj, Tam, 1985)
Thiramala (Vimal Kumar/P.R.S. Pillai, Mal, 1953)
Thirayum Thiravum (Rajashekharan, Mal, 1979)
Third Vow, The *see* **Teesri Kasam**
Third Wife (?, **Madan** Theatres, H, 1931)
Thirichadi (**Kunchako**, Mal, 1968)
Thiripura Sundari (Vijaya Ganesan, Tam, 1978)
Thirisoolam (**K. Raghavendra Rao**, Tel, 1982)
Thirisulam (K. Vijayan, Tam, 1979)
Thirst *see* **Dhakam**
Thirsty One, The *see* **Pyaasa**
Thirtham (Mohan, Mal, 1987)
Thirty-Seventh Gaya Congress, The (**Dadasaheb Phalke**, St, 1923)
36 Chowringhee Lane (**Aparna Sen**, E, 1981)
36 Ghante *see* Chhattis Ghante
Thirudan (A.C. Trilogchander, Tam, 1969)
Thirudanukku Thirudan (T.M. Thirumalai Sami Nadar, Tam, 1974)
Thirudargal Jagrathi *see* Dongalunnaru Jagratha
Thirudatha Thirudan (?, Sangham Prod, Tam, 1970)
Thirudathe (**P. Neelakantan**, Tam, 1961)
Thiruda Thiruda (**Mani Rathnam**, Tam, 1993)
Thirudi (Madurai Thirumanam, Tam, 1974)
Thirugubana (TV: **T.S. Nagabharana**, K, 1992)
Thirugubatu (**Dasari Narayana Rao**, Tel, 1985)
Thirugubatu (**P. Pullaiah**, Tel, 1950)
Thirukalyanam (K. Chandra Bose, Tam, 1978)
Thirumagal (**A.S.A. Sami**, Tam, 1971)
Thirumalai Daivam (**A.P. Nagarajan**, Tam, 1973)
Thirumalai Thenkumari (**A.P. Nagarajan**, Tam, 1970)
Thirumal Perumai (**A.P. Nagarajan**, Tam, 1968)
Thirumanam (**A. Bhimsingh**, Tam, 1958)
Thirumangai Alwar (**S. Soundararajan**, Tam, 1940)
Thirumangalyam (**A. Vincent**, Tam, 1974)
Thirumathi Oru Vegumathi (Visu, Tam, 1987)
Thirumathi Pazhanichami (R. Sundarrajan, Tam, 1992)
Thirumazhissai Alwar (B.S. Kotnis/P.S. Chettiar, Tam, 1948)
Thirumbi Paar (**T.R. Sundaram**, Tam, 1953)
Thiruneelakantar (**Raja Sandow**, Tam, 1939)
Thiruneelakantar (Jambulingam, Tam, 1972)
Thiruppam (R. Krishnamurthy, Tam, 1984)
Thiruppumunai (Kalaivannan Ksan, Tam, 1989)
Thiruttu Rajakkal (Ramanarayanan, Tam, 1984)
Thiruvabharanam (**Sasikumar**, Mal, 1973)
Thiruvalluvar (?, Pragati Pics, Tam, 1941)
Thiruvarul (R. Thyagarajan, Tam, 1975)
Thiruvarut Selvar (**A.P. Nagarajan**, Tam, 1967)
Thiruvazhathan (Jiten Bannerjee, Tam, 1942)
Thiruvillaiyadal (**A.P. Nagarajan**, Tam, 1965)
Thiruvonam (Shrikumaran Thampi, Mal, 1975)
Thisai Mariya Paravaigal (S. Jagadeeshan, Tam, 1979)
This Is Life *see* Sajeev Murti
This Land Is Mine (**Harisadhan Dasgupta**, E, 1982)
This Our Only Earth (**Vishnu Mathur**, E, 1973)
This Way Students *see* **Vidyarthikale Ithile Ithile**
Thobuttuvulu (Ranganath Das, Tel, 1963)
Thodasa Rumani Ho Jaye (**Amol Palekar**, H, 1990)
Thodi Kodallu (**Adurthi Subba Rao**, Tel, 1957)
Thodi Ragam (Ramki, Tam, 1983)
Thodisi Bewafayi (Esmayeel Shroff, H, 1980)
Thokar (*aka* The Kick: **A.R. Kardar**, H, 1939)
Thokar (Lekhraj Bhakri, H, 1953)
Thokar (Dilip Bose, H, 1974)
Thokkukal Katha Parayunnu (**K.S. Sethumadhavan**, Mal, 1968)
Tholikodi Koosindhi (**K. Balachander**, Tel, 1981)
Tholireyi Gadichindi (K.S. Rami Reddy, Tel, 1977)
Tholkkan Enikku Manassilla (**T. Hariharan**, Mal, 1977)
Thomasleeha (P.A. Thomas, Mal, 1975)
Thommente Makkal (**Sasikumar**, Mal, 1965)
Thoodu Po Sellakiliye (Kasturiraja, Tam, 1991)
Thoogu Deepa (K.S.L. Swamy, K, 1966)
Thooku Medai (Amirtham, Tam, 1982)
Thooku Thooki (**R.S. Prakash**, Tam, 1935)
Thooku Thooki (R.M. Krishnaswamy, Tam, 1954)
Thoondil Meen (Ra. Shankaran, Tam, 1976)
Thoongathe Thambi Thoongathe (S.P. Muthuram, Tam, 1983)
Thooral Ninnu Pochu (**K. Bhagyaraj**, Tam, 1982)
Thoorathu Pachai (Manobala, Tam, 1987)
Thoorathu Sontham (K.S. Adhiyaman, Tam, 1992)
Thoorpu Padamara (**Dasari Narayana Rao**, Tel, 1976)
Thoorpu Velle Rayulu (**Bapu**, Tel, 1979)
Thoovana Thumbigal (**P. Padmarajan**, Mal, 1987)
Thooya Ullam *see* Velugu Needulu
Thoranam (Joseph Madapally, Mal, 1987)
Thoratanchi Kamala (**N.D. Sarpotdar**, St, 1927)
Thoratanchi Kamala (**Bhalji Pendharkar**, Mar, 1941)
Thoratanchi Kamala (Madhav Shinde, Mar, 1963)
Thorli Jau (Kamalakar Torne, Mar, 1983)
Thorn and a Flower, A *see* **Mullum Malarum**
Thoshaas Thosa (Dattaram Tawade, Mar, 1989)
Thotalopilla Kotalo Rani (G. Vishwanathan, Tel, 1964)
Thota Ramudu (B.V. Prasad, Tel, 1975)
Thottalsudum (Rajbharath, Tam, 1982)
Thottathellam Ponnagum (R. Vittal, Tam, 1975)
Thottavadi (M. Krishnan Nair, Mal, 1973)
Thottilla (Karamachandran, Mal, 1972)
Thoughts in a Museum (**S. Sukhdev**, E, 1968)
Thozhan (K. Vembu, Tam, 1960)
Thozhilali (M.A. Thirumugham, Tam, 1964)
Thozhil Aliengil Jail (?, K.G. Rajasekharan/V.R.Redappa, Mal, 1985)
Thrasam (*aka* The Scale: Padiyan, Mal, 1978)
Three Daggers *see* Bhedi Khanjar
Three Daughters *see* **Teen Kanya**
Three Hundred Days and After (*aka* Teen Sau Din Ke Baad: **Sarvottam Badami**, H, 1938)
Three Warriors *see* Dilfarosh
Threshhold *see* **Umbartha**
Throne, The *see* **Sinhasan**
Throne of Capricorn *see* **Uttarayanam**
Throne of Delhi *see* Afghan Abla
Through Melody and Rhythm (**Bhupen Hazarika**, E, 1977)
Through the Looking Glass (**Vishnu Mathur**, E, 1985)
Throw of Dice, A *see* **Prapancha Pash**
Thudarkatha (Dennis Joseph, Mal, 1991)
Thudikkum Karangal (**C.V. Sridhar**, Tam, 1983)
Thulabharam (**A. Vincent**, Mal/Tam, 1968)
Thulabharam (Pendyala Naganjaneyulu, Tel, 1974)
Thulavarsham (N. Shankaran Nair, Mal, 1976)
Thuli Visham (**A.S.A. Sami**, Tam, 1954)
Thulli Odum Pullimann (?, Natarajan Pics, Tam, 1971)
Thumbolarcha (**Kunchako**, Mal, 1974)
Thunai (**Durai**, Tam, 1982)
Thunai Eruppal Meenakshi (Valampuri Somanathan, Tam, 1977)
Thunaivan (M.A. Thirumugham, Tam, 1969)
Thunaive Thozhan (R. Sundaram, Tam, 1980)
Thunaivi (Valampuri Somanathan, Tam, 1982)
Thunder *see* Dharti Kaamp
Thunder (A.H. Essa, H, 1939)
Thunderbolt *see* Diler Daku *or* Kadakti Bijli
Thunder of Freedom (**S. Sukhdev**, E, 1976)
Thunder of the Hills *see* **Udaykal**
Thungatha Kanniru Onru (R. Sundarrajan, Tam, 1983)
Thunive Thunai (S.P. Muthuraman, Tam, 1976)
Thurakatha Vathil (**P. Bhaskaran**, Mal, 1970)
Thuramukham (Jesey, Mal, 1979)
Thuranna Jail (**Sasikumar**, Mal, 1982)
Thuruppu Gulam (**Sasikumar**, Mal, 1976)
Thusharam (M. Krishnan Nair, Mal, 1981)
Thyagabhoomi (**K. Subramanyam**, Tam, 1939)
Thyagam (K. Vijayan, Tam, 1978)
Thyaga Ullam (R. Pattabhiraman, Tam, 1985)
Thyagayya (**Chittor V. Nagaiah**, Tel, 1946)
Thyagayya (**Bapu**, Tel/Mal, 1981)
Thyagi (C.V. Rajendran, Tam, 1982)
Thyagi (Ramjibai Arya/S.R. Krishna Iyer, Tam, 1947)
Thyagu (S.P. Muthuraman, Tam, 1990)
Ti Ani Te (Nandu Khote, Mar, 1948)
Tibet Ka Jadoo *see* Yangrilla
Ticket Master *see* Ji Haan
Tiger *see* Bewafa Qatil
Tiger (N. Ramesh, Tel, 1979)
Tiger and the Flame, The *see* **Jhansi Ki Rani**
Tiger Dancer, The se **Bagh Bahadur**
Tiger Gangu (K. Sundarnath Suvarna, K, 1990)
Tiger Man (Ramanlal Desai, H, 1947)
Tiger of Rajputana *see* Mallaraj
Tiger Queen (A.M. Khan, H, 1947)
Tiger Rajani (S.P. Muthuraman, Tel, 1984)
Tiger Ramudu (**C.S. Rao**, Tel, 1962)
Tiger Salim (Joshi, Mal, 1978)
Tiger Tatachari (V.T. Arasu, Tam, 1974)
Tigress, The *see* Vifreli Waghan
Tigress (K. Talpade, H, 1948)

Tikadambaaz (Shivram, H, 1959)
Tike Hasa Tike Luha (Sushil Mukherjee, O, 1981)
Tikhat Mirchi Ghatavarchi (Arun Karnataki, Mar, 1979)
Tikka Shankaraiah (**Yoganand**, Tel, 1968)
Tik Tik Tik (**Bharathirajaa**, Tam, 1981)
Tikuli Ke Laaj (?, Bh, 1988)
Tilak (Yash Chauhan, H, 1992)
Tilak Bathing at the Ganges (**Hiralal Sen**, St, 1906)
Tila Lavite Mi Raktacha (Vasant Painter, Mar, 1969)
Tilasmi Chirag *see* Alladdin and the Wonderful Lamp
Tilasmi Duniya (A.M. Khan, H, 1946)
Tilasmi Duniya (A.M. Khan, H, 1962)
Tilasmi Heer *see* Noor-e-Arab
Tilasmi Heera (H.R. Soni, H, 1934)
Tilasmi Khanjar (K.R. Khan, H, 1949)
Tilasmi Talwar (*aka* Saif-e-Sulemani: **J.P. Advani**, H, 1934)
Tilasmi Taveez *see* Naqsh-e-Sulemani
Till Theke Tal (Shantimoy Bannerjee, B, 1985)
Tilottama (**H.L.N. Simha**, Tam, 1940)
Tilottama (Sanjib Chatterjee, B, 1949)
Tilottama/Mayamalai (Raja of Mirzapur, Tel/Tam, 1951)
Tilottama (**Babubhai Mistri**, H, 1954)
Tilottama (**Kunchako**, Mal, 1966)
Tilottama (**Dinen Gupta**, B, 1978)
Tilottame (R.M. Veerabhadraiah, K, 1951)
Til Til Da Lekha (**Sukhdev Ahluwalia**, P, 1979)
Time Addiction *see* **Kaal Abhirati**
Time to Rise, A (**Anand Patwardhan**, E et al, 1981)
Ti Mi Navhech (Madhukar Bavdekar, Mar, 1970)
Tin Pari Chhoy Premik (Dilip Bannerjee, B, 1975)
Tin Purush (Umanath Bhattacharya, B, 1986)
Tinguranga (B.A. Subba Rao, Tel, 1952)
Tingu Rangudu (T.L.V. Prasad, Tel, 1982)
Tinku (K. Parvez, H, 1977)
Tin Tin Tin (Shivram, H, 1959)
Tiny Thing Brings Death, A (**Paul Zils/Fali Bilimoria**, E, 1949)
Tipu Sultan (Jagdish Gautam, H, 1969)
Tirada Bayake (Raju, K, 1981)
Tiraga Bidda Telugu Bidda (A. Kodandarami Reddy, Tel, 1988)
Tirandaz (*aka* The Archer: **Harshadrai Mehta**, St, 1931)
Tirandaz (**H.S. Rawail**, H, 1955)
Tiranga (**Mehul Kumar**, H, 1992)
Tirapathi (**Dasari Narayana Rao**, Tel, 1974)
Tir Bhanga Dheu (Arun Choudhury, B, 1977)
Tired Afternoon *see* **Klanta Aparanha**
Tirughu Bhana (K.S.R. Doss, K, 1983)
Tiruguleni Manishi (**K. Raghavendra Rao**, Tel, 1981)
Tirupathamma Katha (B.S. Narayana, Tel, 1963)
Tirupati Kanyakumari Yatra (**A.P. Nagarajan**, Tel, 1972)
Tiruppangal (Joseph Anandan, Tam, 1981)
Titali *see* For Ladies Only
Titash Ekti Nadir Naam (**Ritwik Ghatak**, B, 1973)
Tit for Tat (**Nanubhai Vakil**, St, 1929)
Tithe Nandate Lakshmi (Bal Korade, Mar, 1971)
Tochi Sadhu Olakhava (Datta Mane, Mar, 1966)
Tocsin of Death *see* Vichitra Ver
Todallu (Relangi Narasimha Rao, Tel, 1988)
Today or Tomorrow *see* Aaj Aur Kal *or* Aaj Kal
Todu Dongalu (**Yoganand**, Tel, 1954)
Todu Dongalu (Vasu, Tel, 1981)
Todu Needa (**Adurthi Subba Rao**, Tel, 1965)
Todu Needa (V. Janardan, Tel, 1983)
Together Forever (**Muzaffar Ali**, E, 1984)
Tohfa (Aga Jani Kashmiri, H, 1969)
Tohfa (**K. Raghavendra Rao**, H, 1984)
Tohfa Mohabbat Ka (Ram S. Govind, H, 1988)
To Light a Candle (**Santi P. Choudhury**, E, 1964)
Tolling of the Bell *see* **Manimuzhakkum**
Toll of Destiny *see* Karmano Kaher
Toll of Love (*aka* Ulfat-e-Bayan: ?, Hindmata Cinetone, Lahore, H, 1935)
Tomorrow Begins Today (**Shyam Benegal**, E, 1976)
Tomorrow May Be too Late (**S. Sukhdev**, E, 1970)
Tomorrow Shall Be Better (**K.A. Abbas**, E, 1965)
Tonsil (**Tapan Sinha**, B, 1956)
Tony (Bhargava, K, 1982)
Toofan (*aka* Children of the Storm: **B.P. Mishra**, St, 1931)
Toofan (Chaturbhai Patel, H, 1940)
Toofan (Ram Prakash, H, 1954)
Toofan (Radhakant, H, 1969)
Toofan (Kedar Kapoor, H, 1975)
Toofan (Biresh Chatterjee, B, 1989)
Toofan (Ketan Desai, H, 1989)
Toofan Aur Bijli (**Homi Wadia**, H, 1976)
Toofan Aur Diya (Prabhat Kumar, H, 1956)
Toofan Express (Chunilal Parekh, H, 1938)
Toofani *see* Chevrolet 1936
Toofani Khazana (*aka* S.S. Jaldevi: Gopal Krishna Mehta, H, 1937)
Toofani Sawar (N.C. Pandey, H, 1947)
Toofani Takkar (A.M. Khan, H, 1947)
Toofani Takkar (Ram Rasila, H, 1978)
Toofani Tamancha (*aka* Hands Up: R.N. Vaidya, H, 1935)
Toofani Taruni (*aka* Cyclone Girl: **B.P. Mishra**, St, 1931)
Toofani Taruni (*aka* Naughty Girl: **Chandulal Shah**, H, 1934)
Toofani Tarzan (**Homi Wadia**, H, 1937)
Toofani Tarzan (A.R. Zamindar, H, 1962)
Toofani Tirandaz (Boman Shroff, H, 1947)
Toofani Tirandaz (A.R. Zamindar, H, 1959)
Toofani Toli (*aka* Reckless Rogues: **Jayant Desai**, H, 1937)
Toofan Mail (**J.B.H. Wadia**, St, 1932)
Toofan Mail (**Jayant Desai**, H, 1934)
Toofan Mail (K.S. Rami Reddy, Tel, 1978)
Toofan Mein Pyar Kahan (**Phani Majumdar**, H, 1966)
Toofan Queen (Dave?, Prakash Lakshmi Prod, Tam, 1938)
Toofan Queen (*aka* Speed Spider: Ramnik Vaidya, H, 1946)
Toorpu Velle Railu *see* Thoorpu Velle Rayulu
Toote Dil *see* Suhana Geet
Toote Khilone (**Nanabhai Bhatt**, H, 1954)
Toote Khilone (Ketan Anand, H, 1978)
Toote Naa Piritiya Ke Dor (Akbar Alam, Bh, 1990)
Toote Tare (Harish, H, 1948)
Topaye Sindoora Deepata Sankha (J.H. Sattar, O, 1989)
Tope Ka Gola (**Balwant Bhatt**, H, 1936)
Toramai (**Nip Barua**, A, 1975)
Torpedo (N.A. Mansoori, H, 1941)
To Share and to Learn (**Santi P. Choudhury**, E, 1967)
Totaya Amdaar (**Anant Mane**, Mar, 1981)
Totayache Bund (*aka* The Pretender: **N.D. Sarpotdar**, St, 1926)
Tottadellam Ponnagum *see* Thottathellam Ponnagum
Touch, The *see* **Sparsh**
Touch Wood *see* **Chashme Buddoor**
Tourist Bungalow (A.B. Raj, Mal, 1975)
Towards National STD (**Adoor Gopalakrishnan**, E, 1969)
Towards Zero Population Growth in Kerala (**Vishnu Mathur**, E, 1983)
Tower House (N.A. Ansari, H, 1962)
Town Bus (K. Somu, Tam, 1955)
Toy, The *see* Khilona
Toy Cart, The *see* Vasantsena
TP Balagopalan MA (?, Ajay Arts, Mal, 1986)
Trader *see* Saudagar
Train, The (Ravi Nagaich, H, 1970)
Train Arriving at Bombay Station (?, Andersonoscopograph, St, 1898)
Train to Benares, The *see* **27 Down**
Traitor *see* **Namak Haram** *or* Dharmapuri Rahasyam
Tramp, The *see* **Awara**
Transplant *see* **Njattadi**
Tran Treniya Chha Chhabila Baharvatiya/Bachche Teen Aur Daku Chhe (**Govind Saraiya**, G/H, 1982)
Trapped *see* Farebi Jaal
Traveller *see* **Musafir**
Treasure, The *see* Khazana
Treasures of Kalyan, The *see* **Kalyan Khajina**
Tree *see* **Maram**
Trial of Destiny *see* Raja Bhoj
Tribal Festival (**Prakash Jha**, E, 1990)
Tribute to Odissi, A (**Gautam Ghosh**, E, 1986)
Tridandi Sanyas (Vishnupant Divekar, St, 1921)
Tridev (Rajiv Rai, H, 1989)
Tridhara (Sudhir Mukherjee, B, 1963)
Trijama (**Agradoot**, B, 1956)
Trikaal (**Shyam Benegal**, H, 1985)
Trikon Ka Chautha Kon (*aka* Prastar: Madhusudhan, H, 1983)
Triloka Sundari/Trilok Sundari (**Singeetham Srinivasa Rao**, Tel/Tam/H, 1980)
Trimurthi (C.V. Rajendran, K, 1975)
Trimurti (Rajendra Bhatia, H, 1974)
Trimurtulu (K. Muralimohana Rao, Tel, 1987)
Trinath Mela (Krishnachandra Rath, O, 1980)
Trinayani Maa (Birendra Krishna Bhadra, B, 1971)
Trinetra (Raj Kishore, K, 1990)
Trinetra (Harry Baweja, H, 1991)
Trinetrudu (A. Kodandarami Reddy, Tel, 1988)
Trip to the Moon (*aka* Chand Par Chadhai: T.P. Sundaram, H, 1967)
Trisandhya (Raj Marbros, H, 1972)
Trisandhya (**Manmohan Mahapatra**, O, 1986)
Trishagni (Nabyendu Ghosh, H, 1988)
Trishna (**Asit Sen**, B, 1965)
Trishna (Anil Ganguly, H, 1978)
Trishna (**I.V. Sasi**, Mal, 1981)
Trishul (**Yash Chopra**, H, 1978)
Tritiya Paksha (Amar Choudhury, B, 1931)
Triumph, The *see* Veer Haq
Triumphant Love *see* Prem Vijay
Triumph of Devotion *see* **Dhruva Charitra**
Triumph of Fate *see* Mohini
Triumph of Justice *see* **Kala Naag**
Triumph of Love *see* Rukmini Haran *or* Falak Numa *or* Rasili Rani
Triumph of Truth *see* **Sadguni Sushila**
Triveni (**A. Vincent**, Mal, 1970)
Triveni (M.N. Prasad, K, 1973)
Triveni (Rajan Thakur, H, 1985)
Triveni Sangamam (Komineni, Tel, 1983)
Triya Charitra (S.F. Hasnain, H, 1935)
Triya Rajya *see* **Maya Machhindra**
Triyatri (Parvati Menon, H, 1990)
Trolley Driver (**Gajanan Jagirdar**, H, 1958)
Troubles Never Come Alone *see* Naseeb Ni Balihari
Truck Driver (Dharam Kumar, H, 1970)
True Warrior *see* Karmaveer
Trunk Call (Balraj Mehta, H, 1960)
Trust Your Wife *see* Nirali Duniya
Trust Your Wife (**M. Bhavnani**, St, 1927)
Tube Rose *see* **Rajanigandha**
Tuch Majhi Rani (R. Tipnis, Mar, 1976)
Tuch Majhi Vahini (Yeshwant Pethkar, Mar, 1966)
Tu Hi Meri Zindagi (Ronodeb Mukherjee, H, 1965)
Tujhe Nahin Chhodunga (Iqbal Khan, H, 1989)
Tujhi Majhi Jamli Jodi (Raja Bargir, Mar, 1990)
Tujhyavachun Karamena (Damu Kenkre, Mar, 1986)
Tuka Jhalase Kalasa (**Raja Nene**, Mar, 1964)
Tukaram (*aka* Sant Tukaram, Shinde, St, 1921)
Tukaram (M.L. Tandon, Tel, 1937)
Tukaram (**Balkrishna Narayan Rao**, Tam, 1938)
Tukaram (Shinde, St, 1921)
Tulabharam *see* Thulabharam
Tulasi (Dada Gunjal, H, 1941)
Tulasi (K. Babu Rao, Tel, 1974)
Tulasi (K.S.L. Swamy, K, 1976)
Tulasi (Virendra, H, 1985)
Tulasi (Amirjan, Tam, 1987)
Tulasi Brinda (**A. Narayanan**, Tam, 1938)
Tulasi Dala (Vemagal Jagannatha Rao, K, 1985)
Tulasi Jalandhar (**Kadaru Nagabhushanam**, Tam, 1947)
Tulasi Maadam (K.B. Srinivasan, Tam, 1963)
Tulasi Vivah (**Chandrakant**, H, 1971)
Tulasi Vivah (Radhakant, G, 1984)
Tulsidas (Jyotish Mukherjee, B, 1934)
Tulsidas (Bhalchandra/Harsukh Bhatt, H, 1954)
Tulsidas (**Atma Ram**, H, 1992)
Tulsi Soye Hamar Angana (Rakesh Pandey, Bh, 1986)
Tum Aur Main *see* Tumi Aar Ami
Tumbidakoda (N.C. Rajan, K, 1964)
Tumcha Amcha Jamla (**Dada Kondke**, Mar, 1976)
Tumchi Khushi Haach Mazha Sauda (Anand Dhumal, Mar, 1977)
Tu Meri Main Tera (Kewal Mishra, H, 1980)
Tumhara Kalloo (**Basu Bhattacharya**, H, 1975)
Tumhare Bina (**Satyen Bose**, H, 1982)
Tumhare Liye (**Basu Chatterjee**, H, 1978)
Tumhari Jeet (*aka* The Rise: Ranjeet Sen, H, 1939)
Tumhari Kasam (G.P. Pawar, H, 1948)
Tumhari Kasam (Ravi Chopra, H, 1978)
Tum Haseen Main Jawan (Bhappi Sonie, H, 1970)
Tumi Aar Ami/Tum Aur Main (Apurba Mitra, B/H, 1946)
Tumi Koto Sundar (Manoj Ghosh, B, 1988)
Tum Karo Vaada (Robin Khosla, H, 1993)
Tum Laut Aao (Bhimsain, H, 1983)
Tum Mere Ho (Tahir Hussain, H, 1990)
Tum Par Hum Qurban (Tabassum, H, 1985)
Tumsa Nahin Dekha (**Nasir Hussain**, H, 1957)
Tumse Achha Kaun Hai (Pramod Chakraborty, H, 1969)
Tu Nagin Main Sapera (Anwar Usman/V. Menon?, H, 1989)
Tu Nahin Aur Sahi (Brij Sadanah, H, 1960)
Tunda Baida (Govind Tej, O, 1987)
Tunibou (Hiren Nag, B, 1987)
Tunka Pyar Da (Anil Pandit, P, 1989)
Turki Hoor *see* Rashida
Turki Hoor (**J.J. Madan**, St, 1924)
Turki Sher (**J.J. Madan**, H, 1933)
Turmoil, The *see* **Kolahal**
Tu Saubhagyavati Ho (Murlidhar Kapdi, Mar, 1986)
Tushar Tirtha Amarnath (Prabhat Mukherjee, B, 1978)
Tusi (**Gurudas Bagchi**, B, 1978)
Tu Sukhi Raha (Datta Mane, Mar, 1963)
Tuzhach (R.S. Junnarkar, Mar, 1942)
Twelve o'Clock (Pramod Chakraborty, H, 1958)
Twentieth Century *see* **Bismi Sadi**
25th July (?, Benimadhav Prod., Calcutta, H, 1951)
24 Ghante *see* Chaubis Ghante
24 Mani Neram/24 Hours (Manivannan, Tam/Tel, 1984)
27 Down (Avtar Kaul, H, 1973)
26 January (*aka* Bharati: Ramesh Saigal, H, 1956)
22 June 1897 (**Jayoo/Nachiket Patwardhan**, Mar, 1979)
Twilight *see* **Pokkuveyil**
Two (**Satyajit Ray**, B, 1964)
Two Acres of Land *see* **Do Bigha Zameen**
Two Brothers *see* **Iru Sahodarargal** *or* **Matir Manisha**
Two Daughters *see* **Teen Kanya**
Two Eyes Twelve Hands *see* **Do Aankhen Barah Haath**
Two Impostors *see* Do Badmash
Two Leaves and a Bud *see* **Rahi**
Two Little Untouchables *see* **Maharachi Por**
Two Measures of Paddy *see* **Randidangazhi**
Two Plus One *see* Pratinidhi
Two Roads *see* **Duvidha**
Two Town Rowdy (**Dasari Narayana Rao**, Tel, 1989)
Two Women *see* Do Auratein
Two Worlds (**Paul Zils**, E, 1949)

Two Worlds (**Phani Majumdar**, E, 1954)
Tyaag *see* Iqraar
Tyaag (Din Dayal Sharma, H, 1976)
Tyaagi (C.V. Rajendran, Tam, 1982)
Tyaagi (K.C. Bokadia, H, 1992)
Tyaagpatra (Ramesh Gupta, H, 1978)
Typist Girl (*aka* Why I Became a Christian: **Chandulal Shah**, St, 1926)
Typist Girl (A.R. Kabuli, H, 1935)
Tyrant *see* Sitamgarh

U

Uchakattam (Rajbharath, Tam, 1980)
Uchcha Da Baba Nanak Da (K. Pappu, P, 1987)
Uchi Veyil (Jayabharati, Tam, 1989)
Udan Khatola (S.U. Sunny, H, 1955)
Udanpirappu (P. vasu, Tam, 1993)
Udantappu (*aka* Vagabond: **N.D. Sarpotdar**, St, 1928)
Udanthudu (P. Sambasiva Rao, Tel, 1984)
Udaya Geetham (K. Rangaraj, Tam, 1985)
Udayam (**P. Bhaskaran**, Mal, 1973)
Udayam (Kodi Ramakrishna, Tel, 1987)
Udayam Agirathu (Ranjeth, Tam, 1981)
Udayam Padinjaru (**Madhu**?, Mal, 1986)
Udayanan Vasavadattha (**T.R. Raghunath**, Tam, 1946)
Udayer Pathey/Hamrahi (**Bimal Roy**, B/H, 1944)
Udaykal (**V. Shantaram**, St, 1930)
Udbhava (Koodulu Ramakrishna, K, 1990)
Udeekan (Hari Datta, P, 1978)
Udhaar (S.S. Kulkarni, H, 1949)
Udhaar Ka Sindoor (Chandar Vora, H, 1976)
Udhayam Kizhakku Thanne (**P.N. Menon**, Mal, 1976)
Udhiri Pookal (*aka* Scattered Flowers: **J. Mahendran**, Tam, 1979)
Udikan Saun Diyan (**Surinder Singh**, P, 1992)
Udta Ghoda *see* Flying Horse
Udta Mahal *see* Ratan Manjari
Udugore (Mahesh Swami, K, 1977)
Udyanalakshmi (K.S. Gopalakrishnan, Mal, 1976)
Udyogastha (Venu, Mal, 1967)
Ugranarasimham (**Dasari Narayana Rao**, Tel, 1986)
Ugranethrudu (B.L.V. Prasad, Tel, 1988)
Ugra Roopam (M. Rosi Raju, Tel, 1984)
Ujala (K.M. Multani, H, 1942)
Ujala (**Paul Zils/Fali Bilimoria**, H, 1954)
Ujala (Naresh Saigal, H, 1959)
Ujala Hi Ujala (S.M. Sagar, H, 1974)
Ujali Meraman (**Mehul Kumar**, G, 1986)
Ukkumanishi (N.S. Rajbharath, Tel, 1985)
Ukkupidugu (K.S.R. Doss, Tel, 1969)
Ukku Sankellu (P. Chandrasekhara Reddy, Tel, 1986)
Ulagam (L.S. Ramachandran, Tam, 1953)
Ulagam Ivvalavuthan (**Vedantam Raghavaiah**, Tam, 1969)
Ulagam Palavitham (S.A. Murugesh, Tam, 1955)
Ulagam Piranthathi Enakkaga (S.P. Muthuraman, Tam, 1990)
Ulagam Sirikkirathu (K. Ramamurthy, Tam, 1959)
Ulagam Sudurum Valiban (**M.G. Ramachandran**, Tam, 1973)
Ulfat-e-Bayan *see* Toll of Love
Ulfat-e-Mohammed (*aka* Loves of Prince Mohammed: **N.G. Devare**, St, 1929)
Ulhasa Payanam (Sathyam, Tam, 1964)
Ulhasa Yathra (A.B. Raj, Mal, 1975)
Uljhan (**N.R. Acharya**, H, 1942)
Uljhan (Raghunath Jhalani, H, 1975)
Ulka (**Naresh Mitra**, B, 1957)
Ulka (Surya Mishra, O, 1981)
Ulkadal (**K.G. George**, Mal, 1979)
Ulladakkam (Kamal, Mal, 1991)
Ullam Kavarntha Kalvan (Ashok Kumar, Tam, 1987)
Ullam Uruguthadi (Erode N. Murugesh, Tam, 1984)
Ullasa Jodi (Babu, Mal, 1979)
Ullasa Paravaigal (C.V. Rajendran, Tam, 1980)
Ullasa Yathra (A.B. Raj, Mal, 1979)
Ullathil Kuzhanthayadi (**K.S. Gopalakrishnan**, Tam, 1978)
Ullathil Nalla Ullam (Manivannan, Tam, 1988)
Ulle Veliye (Parthiban, Tam, 1993)
Ulsavam (**I.V. Sasi**, Mal, 1975)
Ulsavapittennu (**Gopi**, Mal, 1989)
Ulta Seedha (**Subodh Mukherjee**, H, 1984)
Ulti Ganga (**Keshavrao Dhaiber**, H, 1942)
Ultimatum *see* Elaan-e-Jung
Ultorath (Amal Kumar Bose, B, 1949)
Umachandi Gauri Shankarula Katha (**K.V. Reddy**, Tel, 1968)
Umaji Naik (**N.D. Sarpotdar**, St, 1926)
Umaji Naik (**Gajanan Jagirdar**, Mar, 1938)
Umaji Naik (**Gajanan Jagirdar**, Mar, 1960)
Umaj Padel Tar (**Dinkar D. Patil**, Mar, 1960)
Umang (**Atma Ram**, H, 1970)
Umang (K.M. Multani, H, 1944)
Uma Nilayam (Joshi, Mal, 1984)
Umar Marvi *see* Meri Duniya
Umar Pachpan Ki Dil Bachpan Ka (Ajay Mehra, H, 1992)
Umar Prem (Khagen Roy, B, 1948)
Umar Qaid (Sikandar Khanna, H, 1975)
Umasundari (**P. Pullaiah**, Tel, 1956)
Umasundari (Anil Kumar, Tel, 1983)
Umbartha/Subah (**Jabbar Patel**, Mar/H, 1981)
Umma (**Kunchako**, Mal, 1960)
Ummachu (**P. Bhaskaran**, Mal, 1971)
Ummadi Kutumbam (**Yoganand**, Tel, 1967)
Ummadi Mogudu (B. Bhaskara Rao, Tel, 1987)
Ummeed (Manibhai Vyas, H, 1941)
Ummeed (**Nitin Bose**, H, 1962)
Umminithanka (G. Vishwanath, Mal, 1961)
Umno-o-Jhumno (Trayee, B, 1974)
Umrao Jaan (**Muzaffar Ali**, U, 1981)
Unaad Maina (Meenal Bhatia, Mar, 1988)
Unakkaga Naan (C.V. Rajendran, Tam, 1976)
Unakkaga Oru Roja (C.V. Rajendran, Tam, 1985)
Unakkaga Piranthen (Balu Anand, Tam, 1992)
Unakkagave Vazhkiran (K. Rangaraj, Tam, 1986)
Unakkum Enakkum (N.S. Maniam, Tam, 1972)
Unakkum Vazhvu Varum (G. Srinivasan, Tam, 1978)
Unarchikal (R.C. Sakthi, Tam, 1976)
Unaroo (**Mani Rathnam**, Mal, 1984)
Unarthupattu (*aka* Awakening Song: **P.A. Backer**, Mal, 1979)
Uncle (Surajit Choudhury, B, 1984)
Unda Mitterandi Yaad Pyari (**Anand Patwardhan**, P/E, 1989)
Undamma Bottupeduta (**K. Vishwanath**, Tel, 1968)
Undaunted, The *see* Laparwah
Under Cover of Night *see* **Jagte Raho**
Under the Blue Sky *see* **Neel Akasher Neechey**
Underworld *see* Diwani Duniya
Undu Roda Konda Hoda (Nagathahalli Chandrasekhar, K, 1992)
Unees Bees (Swaroop Kumar, H, 1980)
Unending Flow, The *see* Anandi Dhara
Unexpected, The *see* **Kunku**
Unfinished Story, An *see* **Ek Adhuri Kahani**
Unfinished Tale *see* **Adhuri Kahani**
Ungalil Oruthi (Devaraj-Mohan, Tam, 1976)
Ungal Virupam (K. Krishnamurthy, Tam, 1974)
Unga Veetu Kalyanam (K. Krishnamurthy, Tam, 1975)
Unga Veetu Pillai (C.V. Rajendran, Tam, 1984)
Ungrateful, The *see* **Namak Haram**
Union Leader (K. Bhaskara Raja, Tel, 1993)
Unjaladum Uravugal (**B.G. Bharathan**, Tam, 1985)
Un Kannil Neer Vazhindal (**Balu Mahendra**, Tam, 1985)
Unkhili Muttiar (**Dara Singh**, P, 1983)
Unlocked Doors *see* Puttadha Poothukkal
Unmaikal (R.C. Sakthi, Tam, 1983)
Unmaikke Vetri (Thellur M. Dharmarajan, Tam, 1983)
Unmaiye Un Vilai Enna (Cho, Tam, 1976)
Unmayin Veetri (*aka* Satyameva Jayate: Haribhai Desai, Tam, 1950)
Unmechanical, The *see* **Ajantrik**
Unnai Chutrumugalam (G. Subramaniya Reddiar, Tam, 1977)
Unnaidathil Naan (Arun Verappan, Tam, 1986)
Unnai Naan Santhithan (K. Rangaraj, Tam, 1984)
Unnai Ninaichen Pattu Padichan (Guru Dhanapal, Tam, 1992)
Unnai Ontru Ketpam (Kannan, Tam, 1986)
Unnai Sollai Kutramillai (?, Kavithalaya Prod, Tam, 1990)
Unnaithan Thambi (R. Vittal, Tam, 1974)
Unnai Thedi Varuven (**C.V. Sridhar**, Tam, 1985)
Unnai Vazhthi Padukiren (Sridev, Tam, 1992)
Unnai Vidamatten (Netaji, Tam, 1985)
Unnal Mudiyum Thambi (**K. Balachander**, Tam, 1988)
Unni (**G. Aravindan**, Mal, 1989)
Unnikale Oru Katha Parayam (Kamal, Mal, 1987)
Unnikrishnante Adyathe Christmas (**Madhu**, Mal, 1988)
Unni Vanna Divasam (Rajan Balakrishnan, Mal, 1984)
Unniyarcha (**Kunchako**, Mal, 1961)
Unnodunaan Varuven (E.R. Shivaraj, Tam, 1984)
Unopened Door, The *see* **Thurakatha Vathil**
Unpractical *see* Vadia Dhor
Unprotected Woman *see* Anath Abala
Unspoken, The *see* **Ankahee**
Untouchable, The *see* **Achhut** *or* Harijan
Untouchable Girl, The *see* **Achhut Kanya**
Untouchables, The *see* **Maharachi Por**
Untrodden Road, The *see* **Amada Bata**
Unusual Scenes from Bodhgaya (**Dadasaheb Phalke**?, St, 1923)
Unvanquished, The *see* **Aparajito**
Unwritten Story *see* **Ezhuthatha Katha**
Up in the Clouds *see* **Akash Kusum**
Upaasna (Mohan, H, 1971)
Upagraha (Bhaben Das, A, 1972)
Upahar (**Tapan Sinha**, B, 1955)
Upaharam (Sajan, Mal, 1985)
Upalabdhi (Tapan Saha, B, 1981)
Upalabdhi (Shyamal Ghosh, B, 1983)
Upapath (Hemanta Dutta, A, 1980)
Upar Gagan Vishal (**Manhar Raskapur**, G, 1971)
Upasane (**Puttanna Kanagal**, K, 1974)
Upayamlo Apayam (T. Krishna, Tel, 1967)
Upendra Bhanja *see* Kabi Samrat Upendra Bhanja
Uphaar (Sudhendu Roy, H, 1971)
Upkaar (**Manoj Kumar**, H, 1967)
Uppu (**V.K. Pavithran**, Mal, 1986)
Uppukundam Brothers (T.S. Suresh Babu, Mal, 1993)
Uprant (Ashok Sood, H, 1987)
Uprooted, The *see* **Chinnamul**
Uprooted Ones, The *see* **Disha**
Uranchoo (Shivendra Sinha, H, 1976)
Urangadha Kangal (A.K. Velan, Tam, 1979)
Urangatha Ninaivugal (R. Bhaskaran, Tam, 1983)
Urangatha Sundari (**P. Subramanyam**, Mal, 1969)
Urantha Golanta (Manishankar, Tel, 1989)
Urantha Sankranthi (**Dasari Narayana Rao**, Tel, 1983)
Uravadum Nenjam (Devaraj-Mohan, Tam, 1976)
Uravai Katha Kili (**T. Rajendar**, Tam, 1984)
Uravugal (A.V. Babu, Tam, 1984)
Uravugal Endrum Vazhga (H.S. Venu, Tam, 1978)
Uravukku Kayi Koduppam (Y.G. Mahendra, Tam, 1975)
Uravu Solla Oruvan (Devaraj-Mohan, Tam, 1975)
Urbashe (Salil Dutta, B, 1986)
Urigenpu (P.L. Narayana, Tel, 1988)
Urige Upakari (Joe Simon, K, 1982)
Urikichina Mata (T.S. Baliah, Tel, 1981)
Uriki Soggadu (B.V. Prasad, Tel, 1985)
Uriki Upakari (K.S.R. Doss, Tel, 1972)
Urimai (Ramanarayanan, Tam, 1985)
Urimai Geetham (Udayakumar, Tam, 1988)
Urimai Kural (**C.V. Sridhar**, Tam, 1974)
Urimai Oonchaladugirathu (Visu, Tam, 1992)
Urimai Thedum Uravu (Sakthi Das, Tam, 1984)
Urinki Monagadu (**K. Raghavendra Rao**, Tel, 1981)
Urudhimozhi (R.V. Udayakumar, Tam, 1990)
Urumulu Merupulu (K.S. Satyanarayana, Tel, 1983)
Uruvavugal Maralam (S.V. Ramanan, Tam, 1983)
Urvashi (*aka* Nymph Celestial: Vishnupant Divekar, St, 1921)
Urvashi (Babubhai Jani, H, 1946)
Urvashi (**K. Bapaiah**, Tel, 1974)
Urvashi (Tiptur Raghu, K, 1974)
Urvashi Bharathi (**Thikkurisi Sukumaran Nair**, Mal, 1973)
Urvashi Kalyana (?, shri Chowdeshwari Art, K, 1993)
Urvashi Neenu Nanna Preyasi/Urvashi Nive Naa Preyasi (**C.V. Sridhar**, K/Tel, 1979)
Urvashi Sahasam (**Murugadasa**/G. Ramaseshan, Tam, 1940)
Usha (**Baburao Painter**, Mar/H, 1935)
Usha (Bhargava, K, 1986)
Usha Haran (Varma, H, 1940)
Usha Haran (Shanti Kumar, H, 1949)
Usha Kalyanam (**K. Subramanyam**, Tam, 1936)
Usha Kalyanam (**Kadaru Nagabhushanam**, Tam, 1966)
Usha Kiron (Jawad Hussain, H, 1952)
Usha Parinayam (G. Venkateshwara Rao, Tel, 1939)
Usha Parinayam (**Kadaru Nagabhushanam**, Tel, 1961)
Usha Swayamvara (C.V. Rajendran, K, 1980)
Usha Swapna (G.V. Sane, St, 1919)
Usha Swapna (**R.S. Prakash**, St, 1924)
Uske Baad (Dayanand, H, 1985)
Uski Kahani (**Basu Bhattacharya**, H, 1966)
Uski Roti (**Mani Kaul**, H, 1969)
Uski Tamanna (*aka* Her Last Desire: Yakub, H, 1939)
Usne Kaha Tha (Moni Bhattacharya, H, 1960)
Usne Kya Socha (*aka* The Prisoner's Wife: I.A. Hafizji, H, 1937)
Us Paar (**Chimanlal Luhar**, H, 1944)
Us Paar (**Basu Chatterjee**, H, 1974)
Us Raat Ke Baad (?, Cine Corporation, H, 1970)
Ustad (*aka* Master Man: G.K. Mehta, H, 1938)
Ustad (**Nanabhai Bhatt**, H, 1957)
Ustad (Kawal Sharma, H, 1989)
Ustad Allauddin Khan (**Ritwik Ghatak**, B, 1963: Uncredited)
Ustad Amjad Ali Khan (**S.S. Gulzar**, H, 1990)
Ustad 420 (Chand, H, 1969)
Ustadi Ustad Se (?, Gautam Bhatia/Mohan T. Gehani, H, 1981)
Ustadonke Ustad (Brij Sadanah, H, 1963)
Ustad Pedro (Harish, H, 1951)
Ustad Pedro (Chand, H, 1971)
US Vice President Humphrey Visits India (**Fali Bilimoria**, E, 1966)
Uthaman (V.B. Rajendra Prasad, Tam, 1976)
Uthama Pethra Rathinam (M.A. Thirumugham, Tam, 1959)
Uthama Purushan (K. Subbaiah, Tam, 1989)
Uthama Puthran (**T.R. Sundaram**, Tam, 1940)
Uthama Puthran (**T. Prakash Rao**, Tam, 1958)
Uthamarasa (Rajkapoor, Tam, 1993)
Uthami (?, Shyamala Pics, Tam, 1943)
Uthami (M. Vellaichami, Tam, 1985)
Uthavala Narad (**Raja Thakur**, Mar, 1957)
Uthavgar (*aka* Master Villain, Bhedi Khavis: Behram Vasunia, St, 1931)
Uthiravinri Ulle Vaa (N.C. Chakraborty, Tam, 1971)
Utho Jaago (Pramod Chandra, H, 1947)
Uthradha Rathri (**Balachandra Menon**, Mal, 1978)
Utsarga (Tapan Saha, B, 1983)
Utsav (**Girish Karnad**, H, 1984)
Utsavamelam (Suresh Unnithan, Mal, 1991)
Uttama Illalu (P. Sambhasiva Rao, Tel, 1974)
Uttami Petra Rathinam (M.A. Thirumugham, Tam, 1960)
Uttamuralu (Srinivasa Reddy, Tel, 1976)
Uttara Abhimanyu (**Sarvottam Badami**, H, 1946)

Uttara Dakshina (Vijaya Satyam, K, 1972)
Uttaradhikar (Amar Bhattacharya, B, 1985)
Uttaram (**V.K. Pavithran**, Mal, 1989)
Uttaran (Monoranjan Sur, A, 1973)
Uttarayan (**P.C. Barua**, B, 1941)
Uttarayan (**Agradoot**, B, 1963)
Uttarayan (Lekh Tandon, B, 1985)
Uttarayanam (**G. Aravindan**, Mal, 1974)
Uttar Dakshin (Prabhat Khanna, H, 1987)
Uttar Falguni (**Asit Sen**, B, 1963)
Uttarkaal (**Abdul Majid**, A, 1990)
Uttar Lipi (Bijoy Basu, B, 1986)
Uttar Megh (Jiban Ganguly, B, 1960)
Uttar Meleni (Uday Bhattacharya, B, 1982)
Uttar Purush (Chitrakar, B, 1966)
Uttar Ramcharitra *see* Seeta Vanavas
Uttar Sunya (?, A, 1981)
Uttoran (*aka* The Broken Journey: Sandip Ray, B, 1993)
Uyaram Gnan Nadake (P. Chandrakumar, Mal, 1985)
Uyaran Onnikkan (Vayanar Vallaban, Mal, 1988)
Uyarntha Manithan (**Krishnan-Panju**, Tam, 1968)
Uyarntha Ullam (S.P. Muthuraman, Tam, 1985)
Uyarnthavargal (T.N. Balu, Tam, 1977)
Uyir (B.R. Somu, Tam, 1971)
Uyira Manama (**K.S. Gopalakrishnan**, Tam, 1968)
Uyire Unakkaga (K. Rangaraj, Tam, 1986)
Uyiril Oru Ragam (A. Sivaprakash, Tam, 1992)
Uyirmel Asai (Jambulingam, Tam, 1967)
Uyirthezhunnelppu (Suresh K. Baby, Mal, 1985)
Uyir Ulla Varai Usha (**T. Rajendar**, Tam, 1983)
Uyyala Jampala (K.B. Tilak, Tel, 1965)
Uyyale (**N. Lakshminarayan**, K, 1969)
Uyyarangalil (**I.V. Sasi**, Mal, 1984)
Uzhaikum Karangal (K. Shankar, Tam, 1976)
Uzhaippali (P. Vasu, Tam, 1993)
Uzhaithu Vazhavendum (Ameerjan, Tam, 1988)
Uzhavan (S. Kadir, Tam, 1993)
Uzhavan Magan (Aravindaraj, Tam, 1987)
Uzhavukkum Thozhilukkum Vandhanai Seivom (M.A. Thirumugham, Tam, 1959)

V

Vaa Arugil Vaa (**Kannadasan**, Tam, 1991)
Vaada Tera Vaada (Batra Mohinder, H, 1974)
Vaade Veedu (**Yoganand**, Tel, 1973)
Vaa Intha Pakkam (Mouli, Tam, 1981)
Vaa Kanna Vaa (**Yoganand**, Tam, 1982)
Vaa Raja Vaa (**A.P. Nagarajan**, Tam, 1969)
Vaasi (M.R. Joseph, Mal, 1983)
Vaasna (Rameshwar Sharma, H, 1952)
Vaasna (**T. Prakash Rao**, H, 1968)
Vaasna (R. Thakur, H, 1991)
Vaasna Ki Aag (Madan Sinha, H, 1988)
Vaat Chuklele Navre (Datta Mane, Mar, 1964)
Vachan (**Franz Osten**, H, 1938)
Vachan (Raj Rishi, H, 1955)
Vachan (Suraj Prakash, H, 1974)
Vachanam (**Lenin Rajendran**, Mal, 1989)
Vachanbhang (**Dadasaheb Phalke**, St, 1925)
Vachda Dadani Dikri (Himmat Dave, G, 1983)
Vachina Kodulu Nachindi (**Yoganand**, Tel, 1959)
Vadagaikku Oru Hridayam (**I.V. Sasi**, Mal, 1978)
Vadagai Veedu (**Durai**, Tam, 1981)
Vadai Malai (Maruthi-Vali, Tam, 1982)
Vadakath: A Thervad in Kerala (**Muzaffar Ali**, E, 1984)
Vadakaveedu (Mohan, Mal, 1979)
Vadakkunokki Yanthram (Srinivasan, Mal, 1989)
Vadal (Madhav Shinde, Mar, 1953)
Vaddante Dabbu (Y.R. Swamy, Tel, 1954)
Vaddante Pelli (**B. Vittalacharya**, Tel, 1957)
Vaddante Pelli (**K. Bhagyaraj**, Tel, 1988)
Vadhiyar Veetu Pillai (P. Vasu, Tam, 1989)
Vadhu Varulu (N.D. Vijaya Babu, Tel, 1976)
Vadia Dhor (*aka* Unpractical: **Harshadrai Mehta**, St, 1927)
Vadilona Vanke (**Ramchandra Thakur**, G, 1948)
Vadilono Varso (Mahendra Thakore, G, 1951)

Vadina (**M.V. Raman**, Tel, 1955)
Vadinagari Gajalu (Rajanikanth, Tel, 1955)
Vadinagari Gajalu (S.P. Rajaram, Tel, 1992)
Vadina Mata (**Vijayanirmala**, Tel, 1991)
Vadivangal (Madukkor Kannan, Tam, 1982)
Vadivukku Valai Kappu (**A.P. Nagarajan**, Tam, 1962)
Vagabond *see* Udantappu *or* **Awara**
Vagabond Lover *see* Banke Savaria *or* Mukti Sangram
Vagabond Prince *see* Awara Shehzada
Vagdanam (**Acharya Athreya**, Tel, 1961)
Vagdhana (Shankar V. Giri, K, 1970)
Vaghya Murali (Krishna Patil, Mar, 1964)
Vaheta Ansu Vahuna (Anant Brahmbhatt, G, 1981)
Vahinichya Bangdya (**Shantaram Athavale**, Mar, 1953)
Vahini Saheb (Raju Phirke, Mar, 1987)
Vahue Vagovya Mota Khorda (Ramkumar Bohra, G, 1979)
Vaibhav (Kamalakar Torne, Mar, 1963)
Vaidehi Kalyanam (Manivasagam, Tam, 1991)
Vaidehi Kathirunthal (R. Sundarrajan, Tam, 1984)
Vaijayanti (**Gajanan Jagirdar**, Mar, 1961)
Vaikasi Poranthachu (Radha Bharati, Tam, 1990)
Vaiki Odunna Varathi (P.K. Radhakrishnan, Mal, 1986)
Vaiki Vanna Vasantham (**Balachandra Menon**, Mal, 1980)
Vaikozhuppu (Muktha V. Srinivasan, Tam, 1989)
Vaikunthapali (**K. Bapaiah**, Tel, 1975)
Vai Pandhal (Ramanarayanan, Tam, 1984)
Vairagyam (A. Kasilingam, Tam, 1970)
Vairagyam (Sundar K. Vijayan, Tam, 1987)
Vairam (Ramanna, Tam, 1974)
Vaira Malai (N. Jagannath, Tam, 1954)
Vaira Nenjam (**C.V. Sridhar**, Tam, 1975)
Vairi Jat (V.K. Sobti, P, 1985)
Vair Ka Badla *see* Vengeance Is Mine
Vaisakhi *see* Baisakhi
Vaishakada Dinagalu (Katte Ramchandra, K, 1993)
Vaishakh Vanava (**Datta Dharmadhikari**, Mar, 1964)
Vaishali (**B.G. Bharathan**, Mal, 1988)
Vai Sollil Veeranadi (Visu, Tam, 1984)
Vajrada Jalapata (Bhandaru Giribabu, K, 1980)
Vajra Mushti (Bhargava, K, 1985)
Vajrayudha (?, K, 1992)
Vajrayudham (**K. Raghavendra Rao**, Tel, 1985)
Vakda Paool (Shrikant Sutar, Mar, 1956)
Vakil Babu (**Asit Sen**, H, 1981)
Vakil Saheb (Mohan Sinha, H, 1943)
Vakkumoolam (K. Subhash, Tam, 1991)
Vakkuruthi (Mohan Gandhiram, Tam, 1973)
Valadhu Kalai Vaithu Vaa (K. Raghunathan, Tam, 1989)
Valaduthavan Valal (Rajasekharan, Mal, 1979)
Valaikappu (A. Jayaraman, Tam, 1988)
Valakkaran (E.R. Cooper, Mal, 1953)
Valar Pirai (?, Padma Films, Tam, 1962)
Valartha Kada (Kandaswamy Singaram, Tam, 1983)
Valarthu Mrugangal (**T. Hariharan**, Mal, 1981)
Vala Taro Deshma Danko (**Manhar Raskapur**, G, 1973)
Valayal Santham (Jeevabalan, Tam, 1987)
Valayam (**Sibi Malayil**, Mal, 1992)
Valayapathi (**T.R. Sundaram**/Masthan, Tam, 1952)
Vale of Kashmir (**M. Bhavnani**, E, 1949)
Valiant *see* Mard Ka Bachcha
Valiant Angel *see* Chittor Ni Veerangana
Valiant Princess *see* Rajkumari Ni Ranagarjana
Valiant Warrior *see* Sorathi Yoddho
Valibame Vaa (**Bharathirajaa**, Tam, 1982)
Valibar Sangham (A.N. Kalyanasundaram, Tam, 1938)
Valiba Vilayattu (?, Tam, 1990)
Vali Bharawadan (Ashwini Kumar, G, 1985)
Vali-e-Azam (M.A. Syed, H, 1985)
Valipa Virunthu (Murasoli Maran, Tam, 1967)

Vali Sugriv (?, Star Film, St, 1923)
Vali Sugriva (Jampana, Tel, 1950)
Vali Sugriva Yudh *see* Sati Tara
Vallah Kya Baat Hai (Hari Valia, H, 1962)
Vallal Maharaja (*aka* King Vallalah: C.S.U. Shankar, Tam, 1937)
Vallavan Oruvan (R. Sundaram, Tam, 1966)
Vallavanukku Vallavan (R. Sundaram, Tam, 1965)
Vallavan Varugiran (R. Sundaram, Tam, 1979)
Valley, The *see* **Thazhvaram**
Valley of the Immortals *see* Baji Prabhu Deshpande
Valli (K. Nataraj, Tam, 1993)
Valli Daivanai (Thillai Raghavan, Tam, 1973)
Valli Kalyanam (*aka* Subramanyam: ?, United Pics., St, 1930)
Valli Kumariche Lagna *see* Shri Subramanyam
Valli Mayil (M.A. Kaja, Tam, 1980)
Valli's Wedding *see* Shri Subramanyam
Valli Thirumanam (*aka* Valli's Wedding: Whittaker, St, 1921)
Valli Thirumanam (*aka* Valli's Wedding: P.V. Rao, Tam, 1933)
Valliyin Selvam (Kothamangalam Subbu, Tam, 1955)
Valmiki *see* Ratnakar *or* Nara Ki Narayan
Valmiki (G.V. Sane, St, 1921)
Valmiki (**Ellis Duncan**/M.L.Tandon, Tel, 1945)
Valmiki (**Sundarrao Nadkarni**, Tam, 1946)
Valmiki (**Bhalji Pendharkar**, H, 1946)
Valmiki (**C.S. Rao**, Tel/K, 1963)
Valo Nameri Urfe Vala Taro Deshma Danko (**Manhar Raskapur**, G, 1973)
Valujada Thodu Belt (Vijaya Bapineedu, Tel, 1992)
Vamana Avataram (Fram Sethna, Tam, 1939)
Vaman Avatar *see* Mahabali
Vaman Avatar (*aka* Bali Raja: **S.N. Patankar**, St, 1923)
Vaman Avatar (?, **Madan** Theatres, St, 1930)
Vaman Avatar (*aka* Dani Samrat: **J.B.H. Wadia**, H, 1934)
Vaman Avatar (Hari Bhanja, B, 1939)
Vaman Avatar (Raman B. Desai, H, 1955)
Vamp, The *see* Yauvan Chakra
Vampan (?, Mal, 1987)
Vamsagauravam (N. Ravindra Reddy, Tel, 1982)
Vamsa Jyothi (**A. Bhimsingh**, K, 1978)
Vamsa Vilakku (R. Krishnamurthy, Tam, 1984)
Vamsha Vriksha (**Girish Karnad**/**B.V. Karanth**, K, 1971)
Vamsha Vriksham (**Bapu**, Tel, 1980)
Vamsodharakudu (P. Sambasiva Rao, Tel, 1972)
Vanadevatha (Yusuf Ali Kacheri, Mal, 1976)
Vanadevi (Ramakant-Gharekhan, St, 1931)
Vanaja Girija (Gowtham, Tel, 1975)
Vanakathukuria Kathaliye (A.C. Trilogchander, Tam, 1978)
Vanakesari (Vishwanath Kamat, Mar, 1960)
Vanakkam Vadiyare (Amirjan, Tam, 1991)
Vanamala (Mohan Sinha, H, 1941)
Vanamala (G. Vishwanathan, Mal, 1950)
Vanambadi (G.R. Nathan, Tam, 1963)
Vaname Ellai (**K. Balachander**, Tam, 1992)
Vanamohini (**Master Bhagwan**, Tam, 1941)
Vanangamudi/Tala Vanchani Veerudu (**P. Pullaiah**, Tam/Tel, 1957)
Vanaraja Tarzan (Nari Ghadiali, Tam, 1938)
Vanarani *see* Meena
Vanarani (A. Surya, Tel, 1946)
Vanarsena (*aka* Jai Bajrang: **Homi Master**, St, 1932)
Vanasundari *see* Daughter of the Jungle
Vanasundari (**T.R. Raghunath**, Tam, 1951)
Vanavil (*aka* Rainbow: K.R. Sanjeevi/Bal G. Gaddar, Tam, 1948)
Vanchit (Surendra Jain, H, 1989)
Vandana (Narendra Suri, H, 1975)
Vandanam (**Priyadarshan**, Mal, 1989)
Vande Mataram (**B.N. Reddi**, Tel, 1939)
Vande Mataram (Sudhirbandhu Bannerjee, B, 1946)
Vande Mataram (Ram Gabale, Mar, 1948)
Vande Mataram (**Ghantamneni Krishna**, Tel, 1985)

Vande Mataram Ashram (**Bhalji Pendharkar**, St, 1926)
Vandhale Magarasi (**K.S. Gopalakrishnan**, Tam, 1973)
Vandi Chakram (K. Vijayan, Tam, 1980)
Vandikaran Mahan (Amirtham, Tam, 1978)
Vandikkari (**P. Subramanyam**, Mal, 1974)
Vangaar (Prof. Nirula, P, 1977)
Vanga Mappillai Vanga (Sivashankar, Tam, 1984)
Vanga Sambandhi Vanga (**P. Bhanumathi**, Tam, 1976)
Vani (K. Hirannaiah/Gopal, K, 1943)
Vani Dongala Rani (A.V. Sheshgiri Rao, Tel, 1974)
Vani Rani (C.V. Rajendran, Tam, 1974)
Vanishing Hopes *see* Raj Ramani
Vanishing Tribe, The (**Paul Zils**/**Fali Bilimoria**, E, 1958)
Vanitha Police (Alleppey Ashrej, Mal, 1984)
Vanity Fair *see* Bahuroopi Bazaar
Vanjam (Y.R. Swamy, Tam, 1953)
Vanjara (Majnu, P, 1954)
Vanjari Vav (**Chandrakant Sangani**, G, 1977)
Vanjikottai Valiban (**S.S. Vasan**, Tam, 1958)
Vanna Kanavugal (Amirjan, Tam, 1987)
Vannakkili (**T.R. Raghunath**, Tam, 1959)
Vanna Vanna Pookkal (**Balu Mahendra**, Tam, 1991)
Vannu Kandu Keezhadakki (Joshi, Mal, 1985)
Vanraj (*aka* King of the Jungle: **Nanubhai Vakil**, St, 1930)
Vanraj (Mohammed Hussain, H, 1952)
Vanraj Chavdo (**S.N. Patankar**, St, 1923)
Vanraj Chavdo (Navneet Bham, G, 1963)
Vanraj Kesari (*aka* Red Lion: **Harshadrai Mehta**, St, 1932)
Vanraj Kesari (**Dhirubhai Desai**, H, 1937)
Vansdi Vagi Valamni (**Chandrakant Sangani**, G, 1981)
Vansh (Pappu Verma, H, 1992)
Vanshacha Diva (Govind Ghanekar, Mar, 1950)
Vanthel Veshya (K.P. Bhave, St, 1926)
Vantolio (*aka* Whirlwind: **J.B.H. Wadia**, St, 1933)
Varaat (R.H. Meherkar, Mar, 1955)
Varaat (**Prabhakar Nayak**, Mar, 1975)
Varachat Vidhwa (*aka* Silver Cloud: ?, Excelsior Film, St, 1928)
Varachhada Dada *see* Bhathiji Maharaj
Varadakshina (**Dinkar D. Patil**, Mar, 1962)
Varadakshina (**Sasikumar**, Mal, 1977)
Varadakshine (**Chandramohan**, K, 1957)
Varadakshine (M.R. Vittal, K, 1980)
Varagala Bete (Renuka Sharma, K, 1991)
Varakatnam (**N.T. Rama Rao**, Tel, 1968)
Varalakshmi Vratam (**B. Vittalacharya**, Tel, 1961)
Varam (R.C. Sakthi, Tam, 1989)
Varam (Haridas, Mal, 1993)
Varanecha Vagh (Vasant Painter, Mar, 1970)
Varanmare Avashyamundu (**T. Hariharan**, Mal, 1983)
Varaprasadam (K. Narayanan, Tam, 1976)
Varasatwam (**Tapi Chanakya**, Tel, 1964)
Varasdar (Maganlal Thakar, G, 1948)
Varasoduchadu (A. Mohan Gandhi, Tel, 1988)
Varasudu (E.V.V. Satyanarayana, Tel, 1993)
Varasuralu (B. Harinarayana, Tel, 1973)
Varavelpu (Sathyan Andhikkad, Mal, 1989)
Varaverpu (I.N. Murthy, Tam, 1972)
Varavikrayam (**C. Pullaiah**, Tel, 1939)
Varavu Nalla Uravu (Visu, Tam, 1990)
Vardan (Arun Bhatt, H, 1974)
Vardan (**Shyam Benegal**, E, 1983)
Vardi (Umesh Mehra, H, 1988)
Vargheli (Bapuji Vikaji, G, 1949)
Varhadi Ani Vajantri (**Rajdutt**, Mar, 1973)
Varhadi Jhatka Puneri Phatka (Anantrao Tale, Mar, 1983)
Vari Jaoon Balaji (Ramesh Puri, R, 1990)
Varikkuzhi (**M.T. Vasudevan Nair**, Mal, 1982)
Varna Chakra (K.V. Jayaram, K, 1988)
Varnam (Ashokan, Mal, 1989)
Varno Baap (Babubhai Jani, G, 1950)
Var Pahije (Achyut Ranade, Mar, 1950)

Varshangal Poyathariyathe (Mohan Roop, Mal, 1987)
Vartha (**I.V. Sasi**, Mal, 1986)
Vartmaan (Pradeep Maini, H, 1992)
Varudini (B.V. Ramanandam, Tel, 1946)
Varudukavali/Manamagal Thevai (**P.S. Ramakrishna Rao**, Tel/Tam, 1957)
Varumayin Niram Sigappu (**K. Balachander**, Tam, 1980)
Varusham 16 (**Fazil**, Tam, 1989)
Varuvan Vadivelan (K. Shankar, Tam, 1978)
Var Var Vari (**Kumar Shahani**, H, 1987)
Vasalile Oru Vennila (V.M.C. Hanifa, Tam, 1991)
Vasal Ni Raat (*aka* Vasal Ki Raat, Wedding Night: **P.Y. Altekar**, St, 1929)
Vasant Aala Partun (Manohem Mistrial, Mar, 1986)
Vasanta Nilaya (K. Kutumba Rao, K, 1982)
Vasant Bala (**Nanubhai Desai**, St, 1926)
Vasant Bengali (*aka* The Bomb, The Bengali Bomb: Pesi Karani, St, 1930)
Vasant Bengali (Aspi, H, 1938)
Vasantha Azhaippukkal (**T. Rajendar**, Tam, 1980)
Vasantha Geetam (**Singeetham Srinivasa Rao**, Tel, 1984)
Vasantha Geethe (Dorairaj-Bhagavan, K, 1980)
Vasantha Kalam (M.A. Kaja, Tam, 1981)
Vasanthakala Parvai (Pavithran, Tam, 1991)
Vasanthalakshmi (A.V. Sheshgiri Rao, K, 1978)
Vasantha Malargal (A.R. Ramesh, Tam, 1992)
Vasantha Maligai (**K.S. Prakash Rao**, Tam, 1972)
Vasantha Purnima (Bhargava, K, 1993)
Vasantha Ragam (S.A. Chandrasekharan, Tam, 1986)
Vasanthathil Oru Naal (A.C. Trilogchander, Tam, 1982)
Vasanthi (Gopu, Tam, 1988)
Vasanti (K.M. Multani, H, 1938)
Vasant Leela (*aka* Sons of the Rich: G.S. Devare/Dandekar, St, 1928)
Vasant Padmini (?, South Indian Films of Sholapur, St, 1929)
Vasant Prabha (*aka* Basanta Prabha: ?, **Madan Theatres**, St, 1924)
Vasant Prabha (Mohammed Hussain/Abbas Ali, H, 1935)
Vasantsena (**Dadasaheb Phalke**, St, 1929)
Vasantsena (*aka* Mrichhakatik, The Toy Cart: **M. Bhavnani**, St, 1930)
Vasantsena (*aka* Mrichhakatik, **J.P. Advani**, H, 1934)
Vasantsena (**Raja Sandow**, Tam, 1936)
Vasantsena (Ramayyar Sirur, K, 1941)
Vasantsena (**Gajanan Jagirdar**, Mar/H, 1942)
Vasantsena (**B.S. Ranga**, Tel, 1967)
Vasantsena (K. Vijayan, Mal, 1985)
Vasavadatta (*aka* Sonano Suraj: **Nagendra Majumdar**, St, 1928)
Vasavadatta (*aka* The Royal Musician, Shahi Gawaiya: **P.Y. Altekar**, H, 1934)
Vasiquedars: Pensioners of Avadh (**Muzaffar Ali**, H, 1982)
Vasiyat (*aka* The Will: K.M. Multani, H, 1940)
Vasiyatnama (Soumyen Mukherjee, H, 1945)
Vasthaad (N. Ramchandra Rao, Tel, 1985)
Vasthade Maa Bava (T. Gopalakrishna, Tel, 1977)
Vasthavam (Valmiki, Tel, 1993)
Vasthuhara (**G. Aravindan**, Mal, 1990)
Vastraharan *see* Bastraharan
Vasudha (Y. Babu, Mal, 1992)
Vasundhara (Shekhar Chatterjee, B, 1984)
Vatsala Haran *see* Maya Bazaar
Vatsala Kalyanam *see* Maya Bazaar
Vatsalya (Y.R. Swamy, K, 1965)
Vatsalyam (Cochin Haniffa, Mal, 1993)
Vatsalya Patha (A.S.R. Rao, K, 1980)
Vattathukkul Chaduram (S.P. Muthuraman, Tam, 1978)
Vat Vachanne Ver (Subhash Shah, G, 1982)
Va Va Vasanthame (Pazha Karuppaiah, Tam, 1992)
Vavazodun (Raaj Jalandhari, G, 1984)
Vavtal (**Shantaram Athavale**, Mar, 1965)
Vayadi (Kannan, Tam, 1940)
Vayadi (Maruthai Thirumanam, Tam, 1973)
Vayal (Anthony Eastman, Mal, 1981)
Vayanadan Thampan (**A. Vincent**, Mal, 1978)
Vayasochina Pilla (Laxmi Deepak, Tel, 1975)
Vayasu Pilichindi (**C.V. Sridhar**, Tel, 1978)
Vayasu Ponnu (K. Shankar, Tam, 1978)
Vaya Viramgam (Arun Bhatt, G, 1980)
Vayilla Poochi (**K.S. Gopalakrishnan**, Tam, 1976)
Vayyari Bhama (P. Subba Rao, Tel, 1953)
Vayyari Bhamulu Vagalamari Bharthulu (K. Subba Rao, Tel, 1982)
Vazhai Yadi Vazhai (**K.S. Gopalakrishnan**, Tam, 1972)
Vazha Ninaithal Vazhalam (Devaraj-Mohan, Tam, 1978)
Vazhanthu Kattukiran (**Krishnan-Panju**, Tam, 1975)
Vazha Pirandhaval (Ramanna, Tam, 1953)
Vazha Vaitha Daivam (M.A. Thirumugham, Tam, 1959)
Vazhgai Valarga (Vijaya Krishnaraj, Tam, 1987)
Vazhikal Yathrakar (A.B. Raj, Mal, 1981)
Vazhikatti (?, Kanaga Movies, Tam, 1965)
Vazhi Piranthudu (**A.S.A. Sami**, Tam, 1964)
Vazhipizhacha Santhathi (O. Ramadas, Mal, 1968)
Vazhi Vilakku (**P. Bhaskaran**, Mal, 1976)
Vazhiyora Kazhchagal (Thambi Knam, Mal, 1987)
Vazhkai/Jeevitham (*aka* Life: **M.V. Raman**, Tam/Tel, 1949)
Vazhkai (C.V. Rajendran, Tam, 1984)
Vazhkai Alaigal (G.C. Sekhar, Tam, 1978)
Vazhkai Chakram (Manivannan, Tam, 1990)
Vazhkai Oppantham (**K.V. Reddy**, Tam, 1959)
Vazhkai Padakku (?, **Gemini** Studios, Tam, 1965)
Vazhkai Vazhvadarke (**Krishnan-Panju**, Tam, 1964)
Vazhndu Kattuvom (?, Vivekananda Pics, Tam, 1990)
Vazhthungal (C.V. Rajendran, Tam, 1978)
Vazhve Mayam (**K.S. Sethumadhavan**, Mal, 1970)
Vazhve Mayam (R. Krishnamurthy, Tam, 1982)
Vazhvile Oru Naal (A. Kasilingam, Tam, 1956)
Vazhvu En Pakkam (**Krishnan-Panju**, Tam, 1976)
Vazir-e-Azam (R.S. Rahi, H, 1961)
Vedanai Thediya Maan (Avinashi Mani, Tam, 1980)
Vedantha (K.C. Panduk, K, 1977)
Vedavathi (*aka* Seeta Jananam: **T.R. Raghunath**, Tam, 1941)
Vedhalapuram (?, Bhaskar Pics, Tam, 1946)
Vedham Pudithu (**Bharathirajaa**, Tam, 1987)
Vedhan (Suresh Krishna, Tam, 1993)
Vedikkai Mainthargal (B.V. Balaguru, Tam, 1982)
Vedikkai Porandachu (Radha Bharati, Tam, 1990)
Vedikkettu (K.A. Sivadas, Mal, 1980)
Veediyum Varai Kathiru (**K. Bhagyaraj**, Tam, 1981)
Veedu (Rashid Karappuzha, Mal, 1982)
Veedu (**Balu Mahendra**, Tam, 1987)
Veedu Manaivi Makkal (T.P. Gajendran, Tam, 1988)
Veedu Oru Swargam (Jesey, Mal, 1977)
Veedu Varai Uravu (S.K.A. John, Tam, 1976)
Veelunama (K. Hemambharadhara Rao, Tel, 1965)
Veena (**J.P. Advani**, H, 1948)
Veenaiyum Nadamum (Mugavai Mahizhan, Tam, 1984)
Veena Poovu (Ambili, Mal, 1982)
Veenaveli *see* Shahi Lakkadhara
Veenaveli (**V.M. Vyas**, G, 1949)
Veenaveli (Honey Chhaya, G, 1978)
Veendum (?, Vijaya Films Circuit, Mal, 1986)
Veendum Chalikunna Chakram (P.G. Vishwambaran, Mal, 1984)
Veendum Lisa (?, Asha Creations, Mal, 1987)
Veendum Prabhatam (**P. Bhaskaran**, Mal, 1973)
Veer *see* Punjab Ka Sinh
Veera (Amrit Rana, P, 1984)
Veerabhadran (Shankaran Nair, Mal, 1979)
Veerabhadrulu (Raviraja Pinisetty, Tel, 1984)
Veer Abhimanyu (**Manilal Joshi**, St, 1922)
Veer Abhimanyu (Prafulla Ghosh, H, 1931)
Veer Abhimanyu (V.D. Amin, Tel, 1936)
Veer Abhimanyu (Prafulla Ghosh, Tam, 1936)
Veer Abhimanyu (?, Rajalakshmi Prod, Tam, 1965)
Veer Abhimanyu (V. Madhusudhana Rao, Tel, 1965)
Veera Dalapathi Veluthambi (G. Vishwanathan, Tam, 1963)
Veera Deera (Mudduraju, K, 1991)
Veeradhi Veera (Vijay, K, 1985)
Veer Ahir (**Homi Master**, St, 1924)
Veerakanal (G.K. Ramu, Tam, 1960)
Veera Kankanam (G.R. Rao, Tel, 1957)
Veera Kesari/Bandhipotu (**B. Vittalacharya**, K/Tam, 1963)
Veer Amarsinh Rathod (Radhakant, H, 1972)
Veeran (Ramanarayanan, Tam, 1985)
Veerana (Tulsi/Shyam **Ramsay**, H, 1985)
Veerangana *see* Aflatoon Aurat
Veerangana (**Homi Master**, St, 1928)
Veerangana (**Nandlal Jaswantlal**, H, 1947)
Veeranganai (?, Oriental Movies, Tam, 1964)
Veerangana Panna (**Harshadrai Mehta**, H, 1934)
Veeranjaneya (**K. Kameshwara Rao**, Tel, 1968)
Veeran Veluthambi (Ramanarayanan, Tam, 1987)
Veera Pandian (**B. Vittalacharya**, Tam, 1964)
Veera Pandian (**Durai**, Tam, 1987)
Veerapandiya Kattaboman/Amar Shaheed (**B.R. Panthulu**, Tam/H, 1959)
Veerapooja (A. Sheshgiri Rao, Tel, 1968)
Veer Arjun (**Ramchandra Thakur**, H, 1952)
Veera Sankalpa (**Hunsur Krishnamurthy**, K, 1964)
Veera Sindhoora Lakshmana (**Hunsur Krishnamurthy**, K, 1977)
Veeraval (G. Vishwanathan, Tam, 1969)
Veeraviharam (Mani, Tel, 1987)
Veera Vikrama (S.R. Rajan, K, 1965)
Veer Babruwahan (**Jayant Desai**, H, 1934)
Veer Babruwahan (**Nanabhai Bhatt**, H, 1950)
Veer Bahadur (**V.M. Vyas**, St, 1931)
Veer Baji (?, Omkar Films, St, 1929)
Veer Bajrang (Manibhai Vyas, H, 1966)
Veer Bala (**M. Bhavnani**, St, 1925)
Veer Bala (A.R. Kabuli, H, 1938)
Veer Bharat (**Jyotish Bannerjee**, St, 1924)
Veer Bharat (*aka* Sher-e-Hind: **Homi Wadia**, H, 1934)
Veer Bhaskaradu (**Kadaru Nagabhushanam**, Tel, 1959)
Veer Bhimsen (**Kanjibhai Rathod**, St, 1923)
Veer Bhimsen (*aka* Bhimsen: **Jayant Desai**, H, 1950)
Veer Bhimsen (**Chandrakant**, H, 1964)
Veer Bhimsen (Sushil Vyas, G/H, 1985)
Veer Bhushan (*aka* A Prince Indeed: Keshavlal Joshi, St, 1930)
Veer Champrajvalo (Radhakant, G, 1975)
Veer Chhatrasal (Harsukh Bhatt, H, 1971)
Veer Durgadas (**B.P. Mishra**, St, 1924)
Veer Durgadas (**Ramchandra Thakur**, H, 1960)
Veer Ebhalvalo (Jasubhai Trivedi, G, 1976)
Veer Garjana (*aka* Rewards of Blind Passion: **Nanubhai Desai**, St, 1927)
Veer Garjanai (?, Imperial Films, Tam, 1939)
Veer Ghatotkach (*aka* Surekha Haran: **Nanabhai Bhatt**, H, 1949)
Veer Ghatotkach (Shantilal Soni, H, 1970)
Veer Ghatotkajan (**Babubhai Mistri**, Tam, 1959)
Veer Haq (*aka* The Triumph: A.P. Kapur, St, 1929)
Veer Jagdish (?, V.S. Talkies, Tam, 1938)
Veer Kesari (**Kanjibhai Rathod**, St, 1926)
Veer Kesari (Dawood, H, 1938)
Veer Kumari (**Balkrishna Narayan Rao**, H, 1935)
Veer Kunal (**Manilal Joshi**, St, 1925)
Veer Kunal (*aka* Son of Ashoka: **M. Bhavnani**/G.S. Devare, H, 1932)
Veer Kunal (**Kishore Sahu**, H, 1945)
Veer Mangdavalo (**Babubhai Mistri**, G, 1976)
Veer Na Ver (*aka* The Conqueror: **Moti Gidwani**, St, 1930)
Veer Nari *see* Sher Dil Aurat
Veer Pasali (S.J. Rajdev, G, 1979)
Veer Pujan (*aka* Hero Worship: **Nanubhai Vakil**, St, 1929)
Veer Pujan (*aka* Jung-e-Azadi: G.R. Sethi, H, 1934)
Veer Purush (**Phani Majumdar**, H/E, 1960)
Veer Rajput (**Naval Gandhi**, St, 1930)
Veer Rajputani (**J.B.H. Wadia**, H, 1955)
Veer Ramani (?, Alexandra Film, St, 1928)
Veer Ramani (**K. Amarnath**, Tam, 1938)
Veer Ramwalo (Sharad Desai, G, 1961)
Veer Ramwalo (Ganpatrao Brahmbhatt, G, 1976)
Veer Rathod (*aka* Daring Rathod: **Kanjibhai Rathod**, St, 1929)
Veerta (Shibu Mitra, H, 1993)
Veer Tejaji (Naval Mathur, P, 1982)
Veer Thirumagan (A.C. Trilogchander, Tam, 1962)
Veeru Dada (K.R. Reddy, H, 1990)
Veeru Ustad (Jagdish Nirula, H, 1977)
Veer Vairagi (?, Venus Film, St, 1930)
Veer Vijaysingh (**V.M. Vyas**, St, 1930)
Veetile Eli Velile Puli (Venkat, Tam, 1991)
Veetile Raman Veliyele Krishnan (Manivannan, Tam, 1983)
Veetukkari (**P. Pullaiah**, Tel, 1950)
Veetukkari (Ramanarayanan, Tam, 1985)
Veetukku Oru Pillai (Kanaka Subramanyam, Tam, 1971)
Veetukku Vandha Marumagal (R. Vithal, Tam, 1973)
Veetukku Veedu (C.V. Rajendran, Tam, 1970)
Veetukku Veedu Vasappadi (P. Madhavan, Tam, 1979)
Veetuku Oru Kannagi (S.A. Chandrasekharan, Tam, 1984)
Veetu Mappillai (A.K. Subramanyam, Tam, 1973)
Veetu Mrugham (Venu, Mal, 1969)
Veguchukka Pagattaichukka (Satya Reddy, Tel, 1988)
Veguli Penn (S.S. Devadas, Tam, 1971)
Veham *see* Weham
Vehami Duniya (Anant Desai, H, 1934)
Vehra Lambran Da (Pavan Dev, P, 1982)
Veil, The *see* Ghunghat
Veiled Enemy *see* Burkhawali
Velai Kidaichiruchu (P. Vasu, Tam, 1990)
Velaikkaran (P.V. Krishnan, Tam, 1952)
Velaikkaran (E.R. Cooper, Mal, 1953)
Velaikkaran (S.P. Muthuraman, Tam, 1987)
Velaikkari (*aka* Maid Servant: **A.S.A. Sami**, Tam, 1949)
Velaikkari Magal (C.V. Ranganatha Das, Tam, 1953)
Velaikkari Vijaya (V.K. Pratap, Tam, 1984)
Veli (**Durai**, Tam, 1985)
Velicham (K. Vijayan, Tam, 1987)
Velicham Akale (Mani, Mal, 1975)
Velicham Illatha Veedi (J. Kallan, Mal, 1983)
Velicham Vitharunna Penkutty (**Durai**, Mal, 1982)
Velichathukku Vanga (Vijayasarathi, Tam, 1981)
Veli Ne Avya Phool (Manukant Patel, G, 1970)
Veli Thandiya Velladu (M.A. Kaja, Tam, 1980)
Veliyettam (?, Mal, 1981)
Vellai Manasu (Chitralaya Gopu, Tam, 1985)
Vellai Pura Ondru (Gangai Amaran, Tam, 1984)
Vellai Roja (A. Jagannathan, Tam, 1983)
Vellankalude Naatil (?, Mal, 1988)
Vellayanni Paramu (**Sasikumar**, Mal, 1979)
Vellaya Thevan (**Manoj Kumar**, Tam, 1990)
Vellikizhamai Veeratham (R. Thyagarajan, Tam, 1974)
Vellinakshatram (Felix J.H. Beyis?: Mal, 1949)
Velli Ratham (**Krishnan-Panju**, Tam, 1979)
Velli Vizha (**K. Balachander**, Tam, 1972)
Velliyazhcha (M.M. Nesan, Mal, 1969)
Vellom (**T. Hariharan**, Mal, 1984)
Vellu Vili (K.G. Rajashekharan, Mal, 1978)
Velugu Needulu/Thooya Ullam (**Adurthi Subba Rao**, Tel, 1961)
Velum Mailum Thunai (Ra. Shankaran, Tam, 1979)

Velundu Vinayilli (K. Shankar, Tam, 1987)
Velutha Kathrina (**Sasikumar**, Mal, 1968)
Veluthampi Dalava (Vishwanathan/S.S. Rajan, Mal, 1962)
Vembanad (Sivaprasad, Mal, 1990)
Vemulavada Bhimakavi (**Yoganand**, Tel, 1975)
Venal (**Lenin Rajendran**, Mal, 1981)
Venalil Oru Mazha (Shrikumaran Thampi, Mal, 1979)
Venalkala Vasathi (?, Mal, 1988)
Venal Kinavukal (**K.S. Sethumadhavan**, Mal, 1991)
Venella (S.P. Raja, Tel, 1991)
Vengai Nattu Veeran (?, Rajalakshmi Prod., Tam, 1964)
Vengalam (**B.G. Bharathan**, Mal, 1992)
Vengayan (D.A. Babu, Tam, 1985)
Vengayin Maindhan (Ramanarayanan, Tam, 1984)
Vengeance *see* Rajrang *or* Sood
Vengeance Is Mine (*aka* Ver Ni Vasulat, Vair Ka Badla: **Sarvottam Badami**, H, 1935)
Veni Bandhan *see* Draupadi Veni Bandhan
Venkanna Babu (**Dasari Narayana Rao**, Tel, 1992)
Vennira Adai (**C.V. Sridhar**, Tam, 1965)
Venue India (**Muzaffar Ali**, E, 1982)
Venuganam (**Murugadasa**, Tam, 1941)
Venukumar *see* Gayatri Mahatmya
Vepralam (Menon Suresh, Mal, 1984)
Ver Na Aansoo (*aka* Avenging Tears: Fram Sethna, St, 1931)
Verna Valamana (Bhupen Desai, G, 1983)
Ver Ni Aag (S.J. Talukdar, G, 1982)
Ver Ni Vasulat *see* Vengeance Is Mine
Ver Ni Vasulat (*aka* Sweet Revenge: **Harshadrai Mehta**, St, 1925)
Ver Ni Vasulat (S.S. Balan, G, 1978)
Verno Varas (Arun Bhatt, G, 1976)
Verum Pechalla (Joseph Taliath, Tam, 1956)
Veruthe Oru Pinakkam (Sathyan Andhikkad, Mal, 1984)
Vesham (Ramanarayanan, Tam, 1985)
Veta (A. Kodandarami Reddy, Tel, 1986)
Vetagadu (**K. Raghavendra Rao**, Tel, 1979)
Vethala Ulagam (*aka* Demon Land: **A.V. Meiyappan**, Tam, 1948)
Vetri (S.A. Chandrasekharan, Tam, 1984)
Vetrikani (Ramanarayanan, Tam, 1985)
Vetri Karangal (R. Krishnamurthy, Tam, 1991)
Vetrikku Oruvan (S.P. Muthuraman, Tam, 1979)
Vetri Malai (?, Tam, 1990)
Vetrimel Vetri (M. Thyagarajan, Tam, 1989)
Vetri Namathey (R. Sundaram, Tam, 1982)
Vetri Padigal (Manobala, Tam, 1991)
Vetri Thirumagal (H.V. Babu, Tam, 1977)
Vetri Vizha (*aka* Victory Celebration: **Prathap Pothan**, Tam, 1989)
Vettah (Mohan Roop, Mal, 1984)
Vettaikaran (M.A. Thirumugham, Tam, 1964)
Vettai Puli (?, Seetalakshmi Films, Tam, 1986)
Vettayadu Vilayadu (Raja, Tam, 1989)
Vevishal (**Chaturbhuj Doshi**, G, 1949)
Vezhambal (Stanley Jose, Mal, 1977)
Vice Chancellor (Chellappan, Mal, 1988)
Vicharana (**Sibi Malayil**, Mal, 1988)
Vichitra Bandham (**Adurthi Subba Rao**, Tel, 1972)
Vichitra Dampathyam (P. Chandrasekhara Reddy, Tel, 1971)
Vichitra Gutika (*aka* The Enchanted Pills: **S.N. Patankar**, St, 1920)
Vichitra Jeevitham (V. Madhusudhana Rao, Tel, 1978)
Vichitra Kutumbam (**K.S. Prakash Rao**, Tel, 1969)
Vichitra Prapancha (Bal Gajbar, K, 1955)
Vichitra Prema (Jandhyala, Tel, 1992)
Vichitra Shilpa (**Dadasaheb Phalke**, St, 1925)
Vichitra Vanitha (**K. Subramanyam**, Tam, 1947)
Vichitra Ver (*aka* Tocsin of Death, Vijay Dhwani: Haribhai Desai, St, 1931)
Vichitra Vivaham (**P. Bhanumathi**, Tel, 1973)
Vicious Circle *see* **Chakra**
Vicky Dada (A. Kodandarami Reddy, Tel, 1989)
Victim, The *see* Bhool No Bhog
Victim of Love *see* Prem Bandhan
Victim of Society, The *see* **Nanand Bhojai**
Victims *see* **Irakal**
Victims of Fate *see* Kismet Ka Shikar
Victor *see* Vijeta
Victoria No. 203 (Brij Sadanah, H, 1972)
Victory Celebration *see* Vetri Vizha
Vida Parayan Mathram (P.K. Joseph, Mal, 1988)
Vida Parayum Munpe (*aka* Before Taking Leave: Mohan, Mal, 1981)
Vidarunna Mottugal (**P. Subramanyam**, Mal, 1977)
Videhi Janak (**S.N. Patankar**, St, 1923)
Videsh (Avtar Bhogal, H, 1984)
Vidhan (?, Riddhi Siddhi Films, H, 1989)
Vidhana Naach Nachawe (?, Bh, 1968)
Vidhata (Jal K.C. Baliwala, G, 1956)
Vidhata (**Subhash Ghai**, H, 1982)
Vidheyan (**Adoor Gopalakrishnan**, Mal/K, 1993)
Vidhi (A. Salaam, Tan, 1968)
Vidhi (K. Vijayan, Tam, 1984)
Vidhichathum Kothichathum (T.S. Mohan, Mal, 1982)
Vidhilikhit (Padmanabh, Mar, 1989)
Vidhina Lekh (Himmat Dave, G, 1969)
Vidhithanna Vilakku (S.S. Rajan, Mal, 1962)
Vidhi Vilasa (S.V. Mahesh, K, 1962)
Vidhi Vilasam (**Tapi Chanakya**, Tel, 1970)
Vidhiyin Vilayadal (P.S. Prakash, Tam, 1985)
Vidiveli (**C.V. Sridhar**, Tam, 1960)
Vidrohi (Harmesh Malhotra, H, 1989)
Vidunja Kalyanam (Manivannan, Tam, 1986)
Viduthalai (**K. Ramnoth**, Tam, 1954)
Viduthalai (K. Vijayan, Tam, 1986)
Vidya (Girish Trivedi, H, 1948)
Vidya Haran *see* Kacha Devayani
Vidyapati *see* **Bidyapati**
Vidyapati (A.T. Krishnaswamy, Tam, 1946)
Vidyapati (Prahlad Sharma, Bh, 1964)
Vidyarambham (Jayaraj, Mal, 1991)
Vidyarthi (Talib Hussaini, H, 1966)
Vidyarthi (**Sasikumar**, Mal, 1968)
Vidyarthikale Ithile Ithile (**John Abraham**, Mal, 1971)
Vidyasagar (**Kaliprasad Ghosh**, B/H, 1950)
Vietnam Colony (Sidiolal Kanaka, Mal, 1992)
Vietnam Veedu (*aka* Vietnam House: P. Madhavan, Tam, 1970)
View of Bombay, A (?, Excelsior Cinematograph, St, 1909)
Vifreli Waghan (*aka* The Tigress: **Nanubhai Vakil**, St, 1930)
Vifreli Waghan (S.J. Talukdar, G, 1981)
Vigathakumaran (J.C. Daniel, St, 1928)
Vignan O Tar Avishkar (**Buddhadev Dasgupta**, B, 1980)
Vigneshwara (R. Raghu, Tam, 1991)
Vigneshwara Vahana (P.S. Prakash, K, 1984)
Vijay (Mohan Sinha, H, 1942)
Vijay (**Yash Chopra**, H, 1988)
Vijay (B. Gopal, Tel, 1989)
Vijaya (**B.P. Mishra**?, Star Film, St, 1924)
Vijaya (Vietnam Veedu Sundaram, Tam, 1973)
Vijayachi Lagne/Shadi Ka Mamla (*aka* Sunehri Zamana: Mama Warerkar, Mar/H, 1936)
Vijayadashami (D.G. Gune, Tel, 1937)
Vijayagauri (**Yoganand**, Tel, 1955)
Vijaya Khadga (V. Somasekhar, K, 1988)
Vijaya Kranthi (Rajendrakumar Arya, K, 1993)
Vijaykumar (**H.M. Reddy**, St, 1930)
Vijayakumari (**A.S.A. Sami**, Tam, 1950)
Vijayalakshmi (?, Star Combines, Tam, 1946)
Vijayam Manade (**B. Vittalacharya**, Tel, 1970)
Vijayam Nammude Senani (Rajasekharan, Mal, 1979)
Vijayanagarada Veeraputra (**R. Nagendra Rao**, K, 1961)
Vijay and Basanta *see* Bimata
Vijayanum Veeranum (Venkitasamy, Mal, 1979)
Vijayapuri Veerathan (Joseph Taliath Jr., Tam, 1960)
Vijaya Ramudu (G. Vishwanadham, Tel, 1974)
Vijayasankalam (K.V. Nandanarao, Tel, 1966)
Vijayasimha (**B. Vittalacharya**, Tel, 1965)
Vijayavani (N. Venkatesh, K, 1976)
Vijaya Veeran (G. Vishwanathan, Tam, 1964)
Vijaya Vikram (V. Somasekhar, K, 1979)
Vijay Danka (*aka* Laurels of Loyalty: Radha Kishore, St, 1933)
Vijay Danka (Bapurao Apte, H, 1938)
Vijay Dhwani *see* Vichitra Ver
Vijaygarh (Y.A. Sheikh, H, 1940)
Vijay Kumar (Aspi/Raja Yagnik, H, 1940)
Vijay Lakshmi (*aka* Royal Romance: **Jayant Desai**, St, 1931)
Vijay Lakshmi (G.S. Casshyap, H, 1943)
Vijay Marg (*aka* Path of Glory: Niranjan Bhardwaj, H, 1938)
Vijay Yatra *see* Jayjatra
Vijeta (*aka* Victor: Dada Gunjal, St, 1930)
Vijeta (Govind Nihalani, H, 1982)
Vijeta (A. Kodandarami Reddy, Tel, 1985)
Vijetha Vikram (S.S. Ravichandra, Tel, 1987)
Vikasikkunna Chirakukal (**P. Bhaskaran**, Mal, 1989)
Vikatakavi (*aka* Vikatayogi: **K. Subramanyam**, Tam, 1946)
Vikatakavi (**T. Hariharan**, Mal, 1984)
Vikatayogi *see* Vikatakavi
Vikral Varu (*aka* Wild Wolf: ? Surya Film, St, 1931)
Vikram (Rajasekhar, Tam, 1986)
Vikram (V. Madhusudhana Rao, Tel, 1986)
Vikram (Srikant Kulkarni, K, 1992)
Vikramadithan (**T.R. Raghunath**/M.S. Ramadass, Tam, 1962)
Vikramaditya (**Vijay Bhatt**, H, 1945)
Vikramarka Vijayam (G. Suryam, Tel, 1971)
Vikrama Stree Sahasam (T.V. Vadivelu Naicker, Tam, 1937)
Vikrama Urvashi (**T.R. Sundaram**, Tam, 1940)
Vikram Betaal *see* Jai Mahakali
Vikram Charitra (*aka* Buddhibal: **Nanubhai Desai**/Dorabsha Kohla, St, 1924)
Vikram Charitra (*aka* Rajkumar Thagsen: **Harshadrai Mehta**, H, 1933)
Vikram Satvapariksha (G.V. Sane, St, 1921)
Vikram Shashikala (*aka* Kalank Shobha, Stree Charitra: D.K. Kane, H, 1949)
Vikram Urvashi (**Kanjibhai Rathod**, St, 1920)
Vikram Urvashi (**Modhu Bose**, B, 1954)
Vikram Vetal (Shantilal Soni, G/H, 1985)
Vilakatriaval (Joseph Taliath, Tam, 1965)
Vilakkapetta Bandhangal (M.S. Mani, Mal, 1969)
Vilakkum Velichavum (**P. Bhaskaran**, Mal, 1978)
Vilakku Vangiya Veena (**P. Bhaskaran**, Mal, 1971)
Vila Kuranja Manushyar (M.A. Rajendran, Mal, 1969)
Vilambaram (**Balachandra Menon**, Mal, 1987)
Vilangu (P. Jayadevi, Tam, 1987)
Vilangu Meen (P. Jayadevi, Tam, 1985)
Vilasi Atma (*aka* Sinning Souls: **Jayant Desai**, St, 1931)
Vilasi Ishwar/Nigah-e-Nafrat (**Master Vinayak**, Mar/H, 1935)
Vilasi Kanta (*aka* Flirting Wife: ?, Social Pics., St, 1927)
Vilayati Babu (Dharam Kumar, P, 1981)
Vilayat Pass (Ved-Madan, P, 1961)
Vilayattu Bommai (**T.R. Raghunath**, Tam, 1954)
Vilayattu Pillai (**A.P. Nagarajan**, Tam, 1970)
Vile Woman *see* Kal Ratrinu Khuni Khanjar
Vilichu Vilikettu (Shrikumaran Thampi, Mal, 1985)
Vilkannudu Swapnangal (Azad, Mal, 1980)
Village Girl *see* **Gamdani Gori** *or* **Grama Kanya** *or* Palletoori Pilla
Village Girl (*aka* Gaon Ki Gori: **K. Amarnath**, H, 1945)
Village in Travancore, A (**Fali Bilimoria**, E, 1956)
Villager *see* Dehati
Village Smiles, A (**S. Sukhdev**, E, 1971)
Village Warrior *see* Rangilo Rajput
Villainpur Matha (K. Thangappan Master, Tam, 1983)
Vimala (**Chandulal Shah**/D.D. Dabke, St, 1925)
Vimala (S.M. Sreeramulu Naidu, Tel, 1960)
Vimochanam (A.N. Kalyanarayan, Tam, 1939)
Vimochana Samaram (Mohan Gandhiraman, Mal, 1971)
Vimukti Kosam (Udayakumar, Tel, 1983)
Vinayaka Chaviti (**Samudrala Raghavacharya**, Tel, 1957)
Vinayaka Vijayam *see* Shri Vinayaka Vijayam
Vinchavacha Dansh (**Dadasaheb Phalke**, St, 1924)
Vindesher Meye (Indumadhab Bhattacharya, B, 1952)
Vindhyarani (**C. Pullaiah**, Tel, 1948)
Vinoba Bhave (**Sarvottam Badami**, E, 1951)
Vinoba Bhave: The Man (**Vishram Bedekar**, E, 1963)
Vinodini (Ramjibhai Arya, Tam, 1949)
Vintha Dampathulu (K. Hemambharadhara Rao, Tel, 1972)
Vintha Dongalu (Kodi Ramakrishna, Tel, 1989)
Vintha Illu Santha Gola (Laxmi Deepak, Tel, 1976)
Vintha Kapuram (V.V. Subba Rao, Tel, 1968)
Vintha Katha (V.S. Bose, Tel, 1973)
Vintha Kodalu (K. Subhash, Tel, 1992)
Vintha Samsaram (**K. Savitri**, Tel, 1971)
Violence: What Price? Who Pays?: No 4 (**S. Sukhdev**, E, 1974)
Violence: What Price? Who Pays?: No 5 (**Shyam Benegal**, E, 1974)
VIP (Asha Khan, Mal, 1989)
Viplavakarikal (Mahesh, Mal, 1968)
Viplava Sankham (Beeram Mastan Rao, Tel, 1982)
Viplava Vanithe (Chakraborty, K, 1975)
Vipranarayana (?, Peninsular Film, St, 1930)
Vipranarayana (**A. Narayanan**, Tam, 1937)
Vipranarayana (**Ahindra Choudhury**, Tel, 1937)
Vipranarayana (**P.S. Ramakrishna Rao**, Tel, 1954)
Virangana Nathibai (**Ravindra Dave**, G, 1980)
Virata Parvam (**A. Narayanan**, Tam, 1937)
Virat Parva (Vishnupant Divekar, St, 1922)
Virat Swarup *see* **Veer Abhimanyu**
Virginia (K.M. Multani, H, 1940)
Virni Vibhuti (*aka* Goodbye Kingship: ?, Sharda Film, St, 1931)
Virodhi (Rajkumar Kohli, H, 1992)
Vir Pasali *see* Ra Navghan
Vir Ram Walo (Sharad Desai, G, 1961)
Virsa and the Magic Doll (**Santi P. Choudhury**, E/H/B, 1958)
Virtuous Sinner (?, Pioneer Film, St, 1922)
Virunnukari (Venu, Mal, 1969)
Viruthan Sanku (Venu, Mal, 1968)
Visa (Balu Kiriyeth, Mal, 1983)
Visamo (**Krishnakant**, G, 1978)
Visappinte Vili (Mohan Rao, Mal, 1952)
Vishakanya (**Hunsur Krishnamurthy**, K, 1971)
Vishal (Dinesh, H, 1985)
Vishala Hridayalu (B.S. Narayana, Tel, 1965)
Vishali (A. Sanjeevi, Tel, 1973)
Visham (?, Mal, 1981)
Vish Kanya (**Kidar Sharma**, H, 1943)
Vish Kanya (Vijaya Bapineedu, Tel, 1985)
Vishkanya (Jagmohan Mundhra, H, 1991)
Vishnu Avatar (C. Legrand, St, 1921)
Vishnu Bhakti (*aka* Nai Roshni: G.R. Sethi, H, 1934)
Vishnu-Devaa (K. Pappu, H, 1991)
Vishnu Leela (**R.S. Prakash**, St, 1932)
Vishnu Leela (**Raja Sandow**, Tam, 1938)
Vishnulokam (Kamal, Mal, 1991)
Vishnu Maya (**Jyotish Bannerjee**, B/H, 1932)
Vishnu Maya (Nammalvar, Tel, 1963)
Vishnu Puran (Shridhar Prasad, H, 1973)
Vishnu Vijaya (Keshu **Ramsay**?, Vishnupriya Combines, K, 1993)
Vishnu Vijayam (N. Shankaran Nair, Mal, 1974)
Vishukkani (**Sasikumar**, Mal, 1977)
Vish Vaman (?, Educational Cinetone, H, 1936)
Vishwamitra (**A. Narayanan**, Tam, 1936)
Vishwamitra (**Baburao Painter**, H, 1952)
Vishwamitra (**Phani Burma**, B, 1952)

Vishwamitra Menaka (**Kanjibhai Rathod**, St, 1921)
Vishwamohini (**Chandulal Shah**, St, 1928)
Vishwamohini (*aka* Temptress: **Chandulal Shah**, H, 1933)
Vishwamohini (**Y.V. Rao**, Tel, 1940)
Vishwanath (**Subhash Ghai**, H, 1978)
Vishwanatha Nayakudu (**Dasari Narayana Rao**, Tel, 1987)
Vishwanathan Velai Venum (K.S. Raghuram, Tam, 1985)
Vishwa Roopam (P.V. Narayanan/T.K. Vasudevan, Mal, 1978)
Vishwa Roopam (A.C. Trilogchander, Tam, 1980)
Vishwa Roopam (**Dasari Narayana Rao**, Tel, 1981)
Vishwas (**Homi Wadia**, H, 1943)
Vishwas (Kewal P. Kashyap, H, 1969)
Vishwas (**Datta Keshav**, Mar, 1982)
Vishwasachalum Illenkilum (?, AKG Creations, Mal, 1986)
Vishwasghaat (**Mahesh Bhatt**, H, 1976)
Vishwatma (Rajiv Rai, H, 1992)
Vision *see* **Drishti**
Vision of the Blind (**Kundan Shah**, E, 1981)
Vithal Payi (A.R. Sheikh, Mar, 1953)
Vithal Rakhumai (Yeshwant Pethkar, Mar, 1951)
Vithukal (**P. Bhaskaran**, Mal, 1971)
Vithu Mazha Lekurvala (**Datta Dharmadhikari**, Mar, 1962)
Viti (**G. Aravindan**, Mal, 1985)
Vivahabandham (**P.S. Ramakrishna Rao**, Tel, 1964)
Vivahabandham (G. Rammohan Rao, Tel, 1986)
Vivaha Bojanambu (Jandhyala, Tel, 1988)
Vivaham Swargathil (J.D. Thottan, Mal, 1970)
Vivahasammanam (J.D. Thottan, Mal, 1971)
Vivahitare Itihile (**Balachandra Menon**, Mal, 1986)
Vivahitha (M. Krishnan Nair, Mal, 1970)
Vivasayee (M.A. Thirumugham, Tam, 1967)
Vividha (TV: **Atma Ram**, H, 1993)
Viyalavari Kayalu (K. Subba Rao, Tel, 1979)
Viyarppinte Vila (M. Krishnan Nair, Mal, 1962)
Vizhiyora Kavithai (T.S. Chandrasekhar, Tam, 1989)
Vohti Haath Sohti (Mohan Bhakri, P, 1983)
Voice of Satan (**Ezra Mir**, E, 1941)
Voice of the People (**S. Sukhdev**, E, 1974)
Voices of Silence (**Manmohan Mahapatra**, E, 1982)
Vokkamayi Bathukulu (B.S. Narayana, Tel, 1976)
Volunteer *see* Bahadur Ramesh
Vontari Poratham (**K. Raghavendra Rao**, Tel, 1989)
Vooriki Upakari (K.S.R. Doss, Tel, 1972)
Voorummadi Brathukulu (B.S. Narayana, Tel, 1976)
Vote Bhondool (Jyotish Mukherjee, B, 1936)
Votuku Viluvivandi (Vejalla Satyanarayana, Tel, 1985)
Voyage Beyond, The *see* **Antarjali Jatra**
Vratrasur Vadha (*aka* Indra the Victorious: **Kanjibhai Rathod**, St, 1923)
Vrindavanam (K.P. Pillai, Mal, 1974)
Vrutham (**I.V. Sasi**, Mal, 1987)
Vyamoham (**K.G. George**, Mal, 1977)

W

Wafaa (**J.P. Advani**, H, 1950)
Wafaa (Ramanna, H, 1972)
Wafaa (S.M. Abbas, H, 1990)
Wafadaar (Harikrishna Kaul, H, 1976)
Wafadaar (**Dasari Narayana Rao**, H, 1985)
Wafadaar Aurat *see* Rajnati
Wafadari (*aka* Fidelity: Haribhai Desai, St, 1931)
Wager in Love, A *see* Bar Ke Pobar
Wages and Profit *see* **Tarang**
Wages of Sin *see* Roop Sundari
Wages of Sin (?, **Madan Theatres**, St, 1924)
Wages of Virtue *see* Satta No Mad
Wagle Ki Duniya (TV: **Kundan Shah**, H, 1989)
Wahan (**K. Narayan Kale**, H, 1937)
Wahan Ke Log (N.A. Ansari, H, 1967)
Wahem (Desh Gautam, H, 1986)
Wah! Maan Gaye Ustad (**Muzaffar Ali**, H, 1983)
Wah Ri Duniya (Dada Gunjal, H, 1937)
Wailings of the Oppressed *see* Aah-e-Mazluman
Wall, The *see* **Deewar**
Wall Poster (**G.V. Iyer**, K, 1989)
Walls *see* **Mathilukal**
Walter Vetrivel (P. Vasu, Tam, 1992)
Wamaq Azra (*aka* Sachchi Mohabbat: Tarit Bose, H, 1935)
Wamaq Azra (Nazir, H, 1946)
Wandering Dancer *see* Bhatakta Joban
Wandering Phantom *see* Bhamto Bhoot
Wandering Soul *see* **Ashwathama**
Wangama Wangama (Banka, Manipuri, 1981)
Wanted (N.A. Ansari, H, 1961)
Wanted (Ambarish Sangal, H, 1983)
Wanted (Joe Simpn, K, 1993)
Wanted Thangaraj (K. Hariharan, Tam, 1980)
Wapas (**Hemchandra Chunder**, H, 1943)
Wapas (**Satyen Bose**, H, 1969)
Wapas Chalo (TV: **Muzaffar Ali**, H, 1984)
Waqt (**Yash Chopra**, H, 1965)
Waqt Hamara Hai (Bharat Rangachary, H, 1993)
Waqt Ka Badshah (Manmohan K. Sabir, H, 1992)
Waqt Ke Shehzade (*Kaka* Kapoor, H, 1982)
Waqt Ki Awaaz (**K. Bapaiah**, H, 1988)
Waqt Ki Deewar (Ravi Tandon, H, 1980)
Waqt Ki Pukar (Desh Gautam, H, 1984)
Waqt Ki Zanjeer (?, Roshni Films, H, 1989)
Waqt Se Pehle (**Govind Saraiya**, H, 1984)
Waqt Waqt Ki Baat (Santosh Saroj, H, 1982)
War Between Vali and Sugriva *see* Sati Tara
Wardat (Ravi Nagaich, H, 1981)
Ward No. 7 (Venu, Mal, 1979)
Wardrobe (**Vishnu Mathur**, H, 1969)
Warehouse *see* **Godam**
Waris (**Nitin Bose**, H, 1954)
Waris (Ramanna, H, 1969)
Waris (Ravindra Peepat, H, 1988)
Warisdaar *see* Chhote Sarkar
Warning Signal (**Fali Bilimoria**, E, 1980)
Warrant (Kedar Kapoor, H, 1961)
Warrant (Pramod Chakraborty, H, 1975)
Warrior *see* Rangilo Rajput
Warrior from the Wild *see* Pardes Ni Preet
Wasta (Nasir Ahmed, H, 1989)
Wat Tamari (TV: **Ketan Mehta**, G, 1977-78)
Watan (**Mehboob**, H, 1938)
Watan (**Nanabhai Bhatt**, H, 1954)
Watan Farosh (*aka* Zigomar: Raja Yagnik, H, 1943)
Watan Ke Liye (M. Udwadia, H, 1939)
Watan Ke Rakhwale (**T. Rama Rao**, H, 1987)
Watan Ki Pukar (*aka* Country Calls: Chandrarao Kadam, H, 1943)
Watan Parast (*aka* Desh Bhakt, Parviz: D.N. Madhok, H, 1934)
Watan Se Door (Kamran, H, 1968)
Water (**Fali Bilimoria**, E, 1968)
Water Water *see* **Thaneer Thaneer**
Wat Tamari (TV: **Kehtan Mehta**, H, 1976)
Wave, The *see* **Kallol** *or* **Tarang**
Waves and Shore *see* **Olavum Theeravum**
Waves of Revolution (**Anand Patwardhan**, E, 1975)
Wayada (*aka* Promise: Rafiq Rizvi, H, 1940)
Way of the World *see* Dagabaaz Duniya
Wayside Inn *see* **Peruvazhiyampalam**
Wazir the Kazhgi (**S. Sukhev**, E, 1958)
Wealth *see* Poonji
Wealth and the World *see* Seth Sagalsha
We Are Not Your Monkeys *see* Nahi Amhi Vanar Bannar
Weavers, The (**Fali Bilimoria**, E, 1965)
Weavers of Maindargi (**Harisadhan Dasgupta**, E, 1953)
Web, The *see* Dav Pech
Wedding Day, The *see* **Baishey Shravan**
Wedding Gift, The *see* **Kalyana Parisu**
Wedding Night *see* Vasal Ki Raat
We're Building an IOL Pipeline for You (**Santi P. Choudhury**, E, 1976)
We Shall Overcome (**Saeed Mirza**, E, 1988)
We Three *see* **Hum Tum Aur Woh**
We Two *see* **Hum Dono** *or* **Nam Iruvar**
What is Your Choice? *see* Choice is Yours, The
What Makes Albert Pinto Angry *see* **Albert Pinto Ko Gussa Kyon Aata Hai**
What Price Loyalty *see* Ranagarjana
Wheel of Fate *see* **Bhagya Chakra**
Wheel of Fortune *see* Bharater Pher
Wheels of Destiny *see* Naseeb Ka Chakkar
When Dreams Come True (**Govind Saraiya**, E, 1960)
When Love Blazes *see* Flame Of Love
When Love Calls *see* **Maine Pyar Kiya**
When Lovers Unite *see* Prem Sangam
When the Kabani River Turned Red *see* **Kabani Nadi Chuvannappol**
Where is the Nest? *see* **Koodevide?**
Whipman, The *see* Chabuk Sawar
Whirlwind *see* Vantolio
Whispering Legend (**Ezra Mir**, E, 1942)
White Devil *see* Burkhewala *or* Delhi Ka Thug
White Elephant *see* Safed Hathi
White Face (*aka* Safed Daku: Balwant Dave, H, 1948)
White Horseman *see* Safed Sawar
White Magic (**Paul Zils/Fali Bilimoria**, E, 1949)
White Rider *see* Safed Sawar
Who? *see* E Kon?
Who is He *see* Woh Kaun
Whole Sky, The *see* **Sara Akash**
Who Pays the Piper *see* **Jaane Bhi Do Yaaron**
Whose Darling *see* Kiski Pyari
Whose Fault *see* **Kono Vak?**
Who Was She? *see* **Woh Kaun Thi**
Why Birds Sing (**Pradeep Krishen**, E, 1979)
Why Export? (**Shyam Benegal**, E, 1970)
Why Husbands Go Astray *see* **Gunsundari**
Why I Became a Christian *see* Typist Girl
Why Sons Go Astray *see* Surat No Sahukar
Wicked Deeds of Cherian *see* **Cheriachente Kroora Krithyangal**
Wife, The *see* Ghar Ki Lakshmi
Wife and the Vampire *see* Prem Ane Vaasna
Wife's Destiny *see* Bhagya Lakshmi
Wildcat *see* **Bambai Ki Billi**
Wildcat of Bombay (**M. Bhavnani**, St, 1927)
Wild Cavalier *see* Pahadi Sawar
Wild Flower, The *see* Pahadi Kanya
Wild Horse, The *see* **Kaadu Kudure**
Wild Life Sanctuaries of India (**S. Sukhdev**, E, 1974)
Wild Rose *see* Mastana Mehboob
Wild Tigress *see* Kali Waghan
Wild Wolf *see* Vikral Varu

Hanuman Chalisa (1969)(B)

Will, The *see* Vasiyat
Will of Allah *see* Shaan-e-Subhaan
Wily Heroine *see* Chatur Sundari
Window *see* Jalakam
Winds of Fate *see* Naseeb Ni Nauka
Wine and Woman *see* Amrit Ki Zaher
Wine of Youth *see* Saundarya Sura
Winter Night *see* **Seeta Raati**
Wise Fool *see* Madan Manjari
Wish Fulfilment *see* Ichhapuran
Withering Flowers (**Kantilal Rathod**, E, 1960)
Within the Law *see* Khoon-e-Jigar
Witness (Viji Thampi, Mal, 1988)
Woh Chokri (*aka* That Girl: Subhankar Ghosh, H, 1993)
Woh Din Aayega (**Satyen Bose**, H, 1986)
Woh Din Yaad Karo (**K. Amarnath**, H, 1971)
Woh Dono (?, Deluxe Pics, H, 1947)
Woh Ghar (TV: **Girish Karnad**, H, 1984)
Wohi Bhayanak Raat (Vinod Talwar, H, 1989)
Wohi Ladki (Prahlad Sharma, H, 1967)
Wohi Raat Wohi Awaaz (Dev Kishen, H, 1973)
Woh Jo Haseena (Deepak Bahry, H, 1983)
Woh Kata *see* Kite Fight
Woh Kaun (*aka* Who is He: A.M. Khan, H, 1935)
Woh Kaun Thi (**Raj Khosla**, H, 1964)
Woh Koi Aur Hoga (A. Shamsheer, H, 1967)
Woh Main Nahin (**Mohan Segal**, H, 1974)
Woh Mili Thi (?, Lokesh Movies, H, 1988)
Woh Phir Aayegi (**B.R. Ishara**, H, 1988)
Woh Phir Nahin Aayi (Joginger Shaily, H, 1981)
Woh Saat Din (**Bapu**, H, 1983)
Woh Zamana (Manibhai Vyas, H, 1947)
Woman *see* **Aurat**
Woman in the Wilderness *see* Nirbhagi Nirmala
Woman's Faithfulness *see* Balidan
Woman's Vengeance, A *see* Hridaya Jwala
Women of India (**Fali Bilimoria**, E, 1975)
Women's Challenge *see* Hind Mahila
Wonderful Prince *see* Shahi Chor
Woodcraft of Sahranpur (**Muzaffar Ali**, E, 1982)
Wooing Nightingale *see* Bolti Bulbul
Wooing Tactics *see* Kalabaaz Ashaq
Working Together (**Santi P. Choudhury**, E/H, 1971)
Work Study in Tea Planting, A (**Kalpana Lajmi**, E, 1979)
World of Apu, The *see* **Apur Sansar**
World of Illusion *see* **Vazhve Mayam**
World Teacher, The *see* Jagadguru Shrimad Shankaracharya
World Within, World Without *see* **Mahaprithibi**
Wosobipo (Gautam Bora, Karbi, 1990)
Wounded Hearts *see* Zakhmi Jigar
Wrath *see* **Khuda Ki Shaan**
Wrath of the Sea *see* **Chemmeen**
Wrestlers, The (**H.S. Bhatavdekar**, St, 1899)
Wrestling (**M. Bhavnani**, E, 1936)
Write it Right (**Shantaram Athavale**, E, 1960)
Writing *see* **Rachana**
Wronged Wife *see* Jigarme Gha
Wrong Number (S.K. Sham, H, 1959)

Y

Yaad (Mazhar Khan, H, 1942)
Yaadein (**Sunil Dutt**, H, 1964)
Yaadgaar (?, Hind Pics, H, 1947)
Yaadgaar (S. Ram Sharma, H, 1970)
Yaadgaar (**Dasari Narayana Rao**, H, 1984)
Yaadon Ka Bazaar (?, New Nidhi Prod, H, 1988)
Yaadon Ka Mausam (Salahuddin Pervez, H, 1990)
Yaadon Ki Baraat (**Nasir Hussain**, H, 1973)
Yaadon Ki Kasam (Vinod Dewan, H, 1985)
Yaadon Ki Zanjeer (Shibu Mitra, H, 1984)
Yaad Rahe (*aka* Young India: N. Bulchandani, H, 1940)
Yaad Rekhegi Duniya (Deepak Anand, H, 1992)
Yaar (Sakthi-Kannan, Tam, 1985)
Yaara Dildara (Mirza Brothers, H, 1991)
Yaarana (Rakesh Kumar, H, 1981)
Yaar Gariban Da (Uttam Tulsi, P, 1986)
Yaar Kasam (K. Prasad, H, 1985)
Yaar Mere (**Atma Ram**, H, 1971)
Yaaron Ka Yaar (**A. Bhimsingh**, H, 1977)
Yaatana (Rakesh Saraiya, H, 1986)
Yachakan (R. Velappan Nair, Mal, 1951)
Yadav Vinas (*aka* Doom of the Yadavas: ?, Star Film, St, 1922)
Yadhavam (Joemon, Mal, 1993)
Yagagni (?, Jay Arts, Mal, 1987)
Yagam (Sivan, Mal, 1980)
Yagasalai (Kovai Manisekharan, Tam, 1980)
Yagaswam (**T. Hariharan**, Mal, 1978)
Yagnam (G. Ramineedu, Tel, 1991)
Yahan Se Shaher Ko Dekho (R.K. Munir, H, 1983)
Yahan Wahan (Rajat Rakshit, H, 1984)
Yahi Hai Zindagi (**K.S. Sethumadhavan**, H, 1977)
Yahudi (**Bimal Roy**, H, 1958)
Yahudi Ki Beti (**Nanubhai Vakil**, H, 1956)
Yahudi Ki Ladki (**Premankur Atorthy**, H-Urdu, 1933)
Yahudi Ki Ladki (S.D. Narang, H, 1957)
Yairipok Thambalnu (Banka, Manipuri, 1984)
Yajaman (R.V. Udayakumar, Tam, 1993)
Yakeen (Brij Sadanah, H, 1969)
Yakshagana (**Adoor Gopalakrishnan**, E, 1979)
Yakshaganam (Sheela, Mal, 1976)
Yakshi (**K.S. Sethumadhavan**, Mal, 1968)
Yala Jeevan Aise Nav (**Raja Nene**, Mar, 1959)
Yalgaar (Feroze Khan, H, 1992)
Yamadharma Raju (Relangi Narasimha Rao, Tel, 1990)
Yamadhoothalu (P. Chandrasekhara Reddy, Tel, 1984)
Yama Gola (**T. Rama Rao**, Tel, 1977)
Yamakinkarudu (Raj Bharat, Tel, 1982)
Ya Malak (Nandu Khote, Mar, 1964)
Yamalaya Jibanta Manush (Prafulla Chakraborty, B, 1958)
Yamalokapu Goodachari (P. Srinivas, Tel, 1970)
Yamanam (**Gopi**, Mal, 1991)
Yamanukku Yaman (**D. Yoganand**, Tam, 1980)
Yamapasam (Raviraja Pinisetty, Tel, 1989)
Yamini (M. Krishnan Nair, Mal, 1973)
Yamirukka Bayamen (K. Shankar, Tam, 1983)
Yamla Jat (**Moti Gidwani**, P, 1940)
Yamla Jat (A.S. Arora, P, 1960)
Yamla Jat (Om Bedi, P, 1977)
Yamudanaki Mogudu (Dasineni Kanakasayana, Tel, 1992)
Yamudiki Mogadu (Raviraja Pinisetty, Tel, 1988)
Yamudu (N. Ramchandra Rao, Tel, 1985)
Yanai Pagan (M.A. Thirumugham, Tam, 1960)
Yanai Valartha Vanampadi (**P. Subramanyam**, Tam, 1959)
Yanai Valartha Vanampadi Magan (**P. Subramanyam**, Tam, 1971)
Yanda Kartavya Aahe (Mangesh Shirodkar, Mar, 1958)
Yangana Nee Marakkum (M. Mani, Mal, 1983)
Yangrilla (*aka* Tibet Ka Jadoo: **M. Bhavnani**, H, 1938)
Yarakku Yaar Kaval (Malliyam Rajagopal, Tam, 1979)
Yara Sakshi (M.R. Vittal, K, 1972)
Yar Gulabi (**Bharathirajaa**, Tel, 1979)
Yari Dosti (?, Film Man, H, 1989)
Yari Dushmani (Sikandar Khanna, H, 1980)
Yari Jat Di (Veerendra, P, 1987)
Yari Umran Di (S.P. Puri, P, 1987)
Yarivanu? (Dorairaj-Bhagavan, K, 1984)
Yari Zindabad (Joginder, H, 1976)
Yar Jambulingam (M.S. Gopinath, Tam, 1972)
Yar Manamagam (**P. Subramanyam**, Tam, 1961)
Yar Nee (Sathyam, Tam, 1966)
Yaro Azhaikirargal (Rajan Sharma, Tam, 1985)
Yaro Ezhuthai Kavithai (**C.V. Sridhar**, Tam, 1986)
Yaro Oral (**V.K. Pavithran**, Mal, 1978)
Yar Paiyan (**T.R. Raghunath**, Tam, 1957)
Yaru Hithavaru (P. Satyamurthy, K, 1976)
Yarukaka Azhudan (Jayakantam, Tam, 1966)
Yarukku Mappillai Yaro (S.P. Muthuraman, Tam, 1975)
Yarukkum Vetkamillai (Cho, Tam, 1975)
Yarukku Sontham (K.V. Srinivasan, Tam, 1963)
Yar Vallavan (**B. Vittalacharya**, Tam, 1967)
Yashipparu (Rajashekharan, Mal, 1979)
Yashoda (Bhai Bhagat, Mar, 1974)
Yashoda Krishna (**C.S. Rao**, Tel, 1975)
Yashoda Nandan *see* Shri Radha Krishna
Yashodevi (*aka* Sacrifice: **Nagendra Majumdar**, St, 1925)
Yasmin (H.K. Shivdasani, H, 1935)
Yasmin (**A.R. Kardar**, H, 1955)
Yasmina (Prafulla Ghosh, St, 1930)
Ya Sukhano Ya (**Rajdutt**, Mar, 1975)
Yateem (**Zia Sarhadi**, H, 1945)
Yateem (**J.P. Dutta**, H, 1988)
Yathbavishyam *see* Rambayin Kadhal
Yatheem (M. Krishnan Nair, Mal, 1977)
Yathra (**Balu Mahendra**, Mal, 1985)
Yathrayude Anthyam (TV: **K.G. George**, Mal, 1988)
Yatra (Rajendra Sharma, H, 1959)
Yatra (TV: **Shyam Benegal**, H, 1986-87)
Yatra Holo Suru (Santosh Ganguly, B, 1957)
Yatri (Sachidananda Sen, B, 1960)
Yatrik *see* Mahaprasthaner Pathe
Yatrik (**Mani Kaul**, H, 1967)
Yauvan (Ranjan Bose, H, 1973)
Yauvanada Anubhava (Venkata Rao Naidu, K, 1993)
Yauvanada Suliyalli (T. Janardhan, K, 1985)
Yauvanam (Babu Nathencode, Mal, 1974)
Yauvanam Daham (Mani, Mal, 1980)
Yauvan Chakra (*aka* The Vamp: **Naval Gandhi**, St, 1926)
Yava Hoovu Yara Mudigo (Babu Venkata Rao, K, 1981)
Yavajanmada Maitri (Geethapriya, K, 1972)
Yavanam Katesindi (**Dasari Narayana Rao**, Tel, 1976)
Yavanika (**K.G. George**, Mal, 1982)
Yayati (**Dhiren Ganguly**, St, 1923)
Yayati (M.L. Tandon, Tam, 1938)
Yazhu Nirangal (Jesey, Mal, 1979)
Yeda Ki Khula (**Datta Keshav**, Mar, 1991)
Yeduru Mane Meena (V. Balakrishna, K, 1990)
Yeetta (**I.V. Sasi**, Mal, 1978)
Yeh Aag Kab Bujhegi (**Sunil Dutt**, H, 1991)
Yeh Bambai Hai *see* Kya Yeh Bambai Hai
Yeh Chor Yeh Lutere (I.N. Murthy, H, 1974)
Yeh Desh (**T. Rama Rao**, H, 1984)
Yeh Dharti Punjab Di (Satyajit Pal, P, 1966)
Yeh Dil Kisko Doon (K. Mishra, H, 1963)
Yeh Gulistan Hamara (**Atma Ram**, H, 1972)
Yeh Hai Duniya (Aspi Azad, H, 1948)
Yeh Hai Zindagi (S.D. Narang, H, 1947)
Yeh Ishq Nahin Asaan (Tinnu Anand, H, 1983)
Yeh Jo Hai Zindagi (TV: **Kundan Shah**, H, 1985)
Yeh Kahani Nahin (Biplab Roy Choudhury, H, 1985)
Yeh Kaisa Farz (Madan Sinha, H, 1984)
Yeh Kaisa Insaaf (**Dasari Narayana Rao**, H, 1980)
Yeh Kaisa Nasha Hai (D.S. Sultania, H, 1981)
Yeh Khoon Rang Layega (Roshan Bhardwaj, H, 1970)
Yeh Kyun? (*aka* The Question: **Ritwik Ghatak**, H, 1970)
Yeh Nazdeekiyan (**Vinod Pande**, H, 1982)
Yeh Preet Na Hogi Kam (Sheetal, H, 1986)
Yeh Pyar Nahin (Loveleen Merck, H, 1988)
Yeh Raaste Hain Pyar Ke (R.K. Nayyar, H, 1963)
Yeh Raat Phir Na Aayegi (Brij Sadanah, H, 1966)
Yeh Raat Phir Na Aayegi (Nusrat Saeed, H, 1992)
Yeh Rishta Na Toote (K. Vijayan, H, 1981)
Yeh Sach Hai (?, Nitin Films, H, 1975)
Yeh Sach Hai (**Atma Ram**, H, 1988)
Yeh To Kamaal Ho Gaya (**T. Rama Rao**, H, 1982)
Yeh Vaada Raha (Kapil Kapoor, H, 1982)
Yeh Woh Manzil To Nahin (Sudhir Mishra, H, 1986)
Yeh Zindagi Kitni Haseen Hai (R.K. Nayyar, H, 1966)
Yematrathe Yemarathe (V.C. Guhanathan, Tam, 1985)
Yemudiki Mogudu (Raviraja Pinisetty, Tel, 1988)
Yengal Kural (A. Mohan Gandhi, Tam, 1985)
Ye Re Majhya Maglya (**Bhalji Pendharkar**, Mar, 1955)
Yes Please *see* Ji Haan
Yethe Shahane Rahataat (**Datta Keshav**, Mar, 1968)
Yevu Ka Gharat (**Dada Kondke**, Mar, 1992)
Yoddha (Sangeeth Sivan, Mal, 1992)
Yodha (**Rahul Rawail**, H, 1991)
Yogam Raja Yogam (T.S. Krishnakumar, Tam, 1989)
Yogamullaval (Shankar, Mal, 1971)
Yogi Vemana (**K.V. Reddy**, Tel, 1947)
Yogi Vemana (**C.S. Rao**, Tel, 1988)
You and the Railways: Footboard Travel (**Govind Saraiya**, E, 1958)
You Can Prevent Burns (**Shyam Benegal**, E, 1974)
You Made Me a Communist *see* **Ningalenne Communistaki**
You Must Be Your Own Policemen (**S. Sukhdev**, E, 1973)
Young Ascetic *see* Tarun Tapaswini
Young India *see* Jai Bharati *or* Yaad Rahe
Your Enemy: TB (**M.S. Sathyu**, E, 1981)
Your Home Defence: Home Guards (**Santi P. Choudhury**, E, 1963)
Youth, The *see* **Zalim Jawani**
Yuddha Bhoomi (Mani, Mal, 1976)
Yuddha Bhoomi (**K. Raghavendra Rao**, Tel, 1983)
Yuddhakanda (K.V. Raju, K, 1989)
Yuddha Kandam (**Thoppil Bhasi**, Mal, 1977)
Yuddha Kandam (**Komal Swaminathan**, Tam, 1983)
Yuddham (**Sasikumar**, Mal, 1983)
Yuddham (**Dasari Narayana Rao**, Tel, 1984)
Yuddhaparva (Madhu, K, 1991)
Yudh (Rajiv Rai, H, 1985)
Yudhpath (Ravi Ravan, H, 1992)
Yuga Dharmam (**K.S. Gopalakrishnan**, Tam, 1983)
Yuga Karthulu (Aditya?, Pratap Art Pics, Tel, 1987)
Yugala Geetham (Phani Sridhar, Tel, 1992)
Yugandhar (K.S.R. Doss, Tel, 1979)
Yugandhar (N. Chandra, H, 1993)
Yugantam (Raviteja Katragadda, Tel, 1991)
Yuga Purusha (D. Rajendra Babu, K, 1989)
Yuga Purushudu (**K. Bapaiah**, Tel, 1978)
Yug Darshan *see* Samaj Na Vanked
Yugo Manab Kabir (Dipankar, B, 1976)
Yugo Yugo Mi Vaat Pahili (C. Vishwanath, Mar, 1965)
Yuvadharam Bilisindi (**Bharathirajaa**, Tam, 1985)
Yuvajanolsavam (?, Mal, 1986)
Yuvaraju (**Dasari Narayana Rao**, Tel, 1982)
Yuvatharam Kadhilindi (D. Sathyam, Tel, 1980)
Yuvraaj (T.R. Ramanna, H, 1979)

Z

Zaat-e-Sharif (*aka* Jat-e-Sharif: **Homi Master**, H, 1936)
Zabaan (**Jayant Desai**, H, 1943)
Zabak (**Homi Wadia**, H, 1961)
Zabardast (**Nasir Hussain**, H, 1985)
Zadpat Karu De Khatpat (Shreeram Gojamgunde, Mar, 1982)
Zahare Ishq *see* Zehar-e-Ishq
Zakhm (Irfan Khan, H, 1989)
Zakhmi (**Raja Thakur**, H, 1975)
Zakhmi Aurat (Avtar Bhogal, H, 1988)
Zakhmi Dil (B.S. Shaad, H, 1982)
Zakhmi Insaan (Deepak Balraj Vij, H, 1982)
Zakhmi Jigar (*aka* Wounded Hearts, Broken Hearts: **N.G. Devare**, St, 1929)
Zakhmi Rooh (Pawan Kumar, H, 1993)
Zakhmi Sher (**Dasari Narayana Rao**, H, 1984)
Zakhmi Zameen (Mahendra Shah, H, 1990)
Zakhmon Ka Hisab (Talukdar, H, 1993)
Zakhmon Ke Nishan (Diljeet Bassi, H, 1979)
Zalim (Behram Mukadam, H, 1947)

Zalim (B. Subhash, H, 1979)
Zalim Jadugarin (*aka* The Enchantress: A.P. Kapoor, St, 1930)
Zalim Jawani (**B.P. Mishra**, H, 1932)
Zalim Saudagar *see* Merchant of Venice
Zalim Tera Jawab Nahin (Ramanlal Desai, H, 1960)
Zalim Zamana *see* Samaj Patan
Zalim Zulekha (Dr Alvaro, St, 1930)
Zalzala (Sorabji Kerawala, H, 1936)
Zalzala (**Paul Zils**, H, 1952)
Zalzala (Harish Shah, H, 1988)
Zamana (Ram Daryani, H, 1938)
Zamana (Aravind Sen, H, 1957)
Zamana (Ramesh Talwar, H, 1985)
Zamana Badal Gaya (**Jayant Desai**, H, 1961)
Zamanat (A. Salaam, H, 1977)
Zamane Ki Hawa (Walli, H, 1952)
Zamane Ko Dikhana Hai (**Nasir Hussain**, H, 1981)
Zamane Se Poocho (Abrar, H, 1976)
Zambo Ka Beta (*aka* Son of Zambo: **M. Bhavnani**, H, 1939)
Zambo the Ape Man (*aka* Sher-e-Jungle: **M. Bhavnani**, H, 1937)
Zameen (Anand Kumar, H, 1943)
Zameen (**Mahesh Bhatt**, H, 1989)
Zameen Aasmaan (Dwarka Khosla, H, 1946)
Zameen Aasmaan (A. Veerappan, H, 1972)
Zameen Aasmaan (Bharat Rangachary, H, 1984)
Zameen Ka Chand (*aka* Love of a Slave: **Jayant Desai**, H, 1937)
Zameen Ke Tare (**Chandulal Shah**, H, 1960)
Zameer (Ravi Chopra, H, 1975)
Zamindar *see* Zamindar Ka Prem
Zamindar (**Moti Gidwani**, H, 1942)
Zamindar (P.V. Krishnan, Tam, 1952)
Zamindar (V. Madhusudhana Rao, Tel, 1966)
Zamindar Ka Prem (*aka* Zamindar: ?, National Pics, H, 1937)
Zamindarugari Ammayi (**Singeetham Srinivasa Rao**, Tel, 1975)
Zangbo and the Zing Zing Bar (**Kantilal Rathod**, H, 1977)
Zanjeer (Kishore Sharma, H, 1947)
Zanjeer (**Prakash Mehra**, H, 1973)
Zan Mureed (*aka* Kafir-e-Ishq, Nastik Prem: Shanti Kumar, H, 1936)
Zanzibar *see* Anokha Jungle
Zara Bachke (N.A. Ansari, H, 1959)
Zarak Khan (Harbans, H, 1963)
Zara Palat Ke Dekh *see* Kismat Palat Ke Dekh
Zara Si Zindagi (**K. Balachander**, H, 1983)
Zarina (**Ezra Mir**, H, 1932)
Zaroorat (**B.R. Ishara**, H, 1972)
Zaroorat Ki Purti (**Chidananda Das Gupta**, H, 1979)
Zee Horror Show, The (TV: Tulsi/Shyam **Ramsay**, H, 1993)
Zeenat *see* Ziarat Gahe Hind
Zeenat (Shaukat Hussain Rizvi, H, 1945)
Zehar-e-Ishq (**J.P. Advani**, H, 1933)
Zehari Saap (K.B. Athavale, St, 1929)
Zehari Saap (**J.J. Madan**, H, 1933)
Zehreela Insaan (**Puttanna Kanagal**, H, 1974)
Zehreelay (Jyotin Goel, H, 1990)
Zehreeli (V.N. Reddy, H, 1977)
Zer To Pidhan Jani Jani (**Upendra Trivedi**, G, 1972)
Zevar (**K. Amarnath**, H, 1942)
Zevar (**Basu Chatterjee**, H, 1987)
Zevaraat (Habib Sarhadi, H, 1949)
Ziarat Gahe Hind (*aka* Zeenat: A. Shamsheer, H, 1970)
Zid (**H.S. Rawail**, H, 1945)
Zid (Vijay, H, 1976)
Ziddi (Shaheed Latif, H, 1948)
Ziddi (Pramod Chakraborty, H, 1964)
Zigomar *see* Watan Farosh
Zilla Parishad *see* ZP (**Anant Mane**, Mar, 1991)
Zimbo (**Homi Wadia**, H, 1958)
Zimbo comes to Town (*aka* Zimbo Shaher Mein: **Nanabhai Bhatt**, H, 1960)
Zimbo finds a Son (*aka* Zimbo Ka Beta: John Cawas, H, 1966)
Zimmedar (Santosh Kumar Chauhan, H, 1990)
Zinda Bhoot (?, **Madan** Theatres, H, 1937)
Zinda Dil (S.M. Raza, H, 1947)
Zinda Dil (Sikandar Khanna, H, 1975)
Zindagani (Prabhat Roy, H, 1986)
Zindagi (**P.C. Barua**, H, 1940)
Zindagi (C.L. Dheer, H, 1956)
Zindagi (**Ramanand Sagar**, H, 1964)
Zindagi (Ravi Tandon, H, 1976)
Zindagi (TV: ?, H, 1987)
Zindagi Aur Hum (Anand Kumar, H, 1962)
Zindagi Aur Khwab (S. Bannerjee, H, 1961)
Zindagi Aur Maut (N.A. Ansari, H, 1965)
Zindagi Aur Toofan (Umesh Mathur, H, 1975)
Zindagi Ek Jua (**Prakash Mehra**, H, 1992)
Zindagi Jeene Ke Liye (**K.S. Sethumadhavan**, H, 1984)
Zindagi Ke Mele (K.B. Lall, H, 1956)
Zindagi Nu Jugar (*aka* Gamble of Life: Baburao/**Sundarrao Nadkarni**, St, 1931)
Zindagi Ya Maut *see* Do *or* Die
Zindagi Ya Toofan (Nakshab, H, 1958)
Zindagi Zindagi (**Tapan Sinha**, H, 1972)
Zinda Lash (*aka* A Living Corpse: **Premankur Atorthy**, Urdu, 1932)
Zinda Lash (Manmohan Sabir, H, 1985)
Zingaro (S.N. Bhende, H, 1935)
Zingaro (**Chandrakant**, H, 1963)
Zoo, The *see* **Chidiakhana**
Zorro (Shibu Mitra, H, 1975)
ZP (*aka* Zilla Parishad: **Anant Mane**, Mar, 1991)
Zulf Ke Saye Saye (Sagar, H, 1983)
Zulm (*aka* Stolen Bride: **Keshavrao Dhaiber**, St, 1931)
Zulmi Jesai *see* Sati Toral
Zulmi Kansa *see* Radhe Shyam
Zulm Ka Badla (K. Prasad, H, 1985)
Zulm Ki Hukumat (Bharat Rangachary, H, 1992)
Zulm Ki Pukar (Dinesh-Ramanesh, H, 1979)
Zulm Ki Zanjeer (S.P. Muthuraman, H, 1984)
Zulm Ko Jala Doonga (Mahendra Shah, H, 1988)
Zunz (Kiran Shantaram, Mar, 1975)(B

Mahipal in *Parasmani*